Contents

ON THE ROAD

GRAND CANYON NATIONAL PARK P845

WWW.FISCHERFOTOGRAFIE.NL/GETTY IMAGES ©

lonely planet

USA

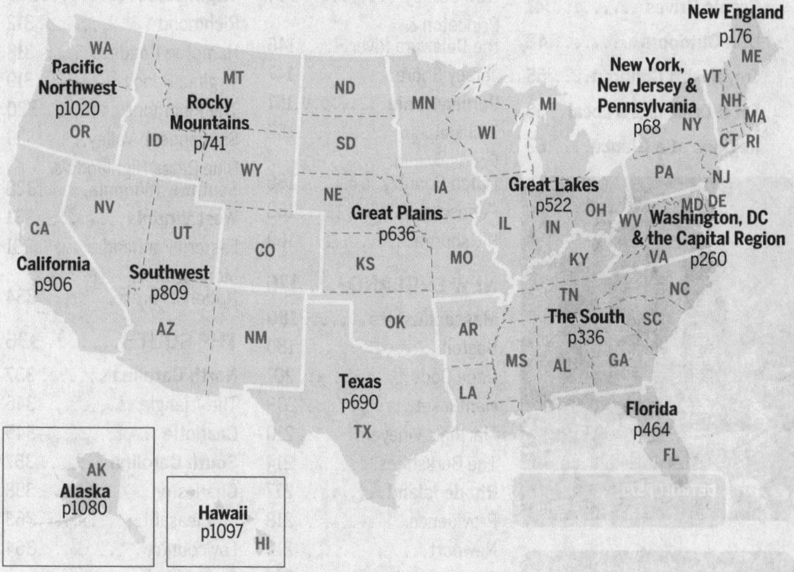

THIS EDITION WRITTEN AND RESEARCHED BY

Regis St Louis,

Amy Balfour, Sandra Bao, Sara Benson, Adam Karlin, Becky Ohlsen,

Zo ... er Berkmoes,

... an

PLAN YOUR TRIP

DETROIT P575

GRAND TETON NATIONAL PARK P792

ON THE ROAD

Contents

UNDERSTAND

SURVIVAL GUIDE

TLINGIT TOTEM POLE (ALAKSA) P1080

SPECIAL FEATURES

Welcome to the USA

The great American experience is about so many things: bluegrass and beaches, snow-covered peaks and redwood forests, restaurant-loving cities and big open skies.

Bright Lights, Big Cities

America is the birthplace of LA, Las Vegas, Chicago, Miami, Boston and New York City – each a brimming metropolis whose name alone conjures a million different notions of culture, cuisine and entertainment. Look more closely, and the American quilt unfurls in all its surprising variety: the eclectic music scene of Austin, the easygoing charms of antebellum Savannah, the eco-consciousness of free-spirited Portland, the magnificent waterfront of San Francisco and the captivating French Quarter of jazz-loving New Orleans.

On the Road Again

This is a country of road trips and great open skies, where 4 million miles of highways lead past red-rock deserts, below towering mountain peaks, and across fertile wheat fields that roll off toward the horizon. The sun-bleached hillsides of the Great Plains, the lush rainforests of the Pacific Northwest and the scenic country lanes of New England are a few fine starting points for the great American road trip.

Food-Loving Nation

On one evening in the US, thick barbecue ribs and smoked brisket come piping hot at a Texas roadhouse, while talented chefs blend organic produce with Asian accents at award-winning West Coast restaurants. Locals get their fix of bagels and lox at a century-old deli in Manhattan's Upper West Side, and several states away, plump pancakes and fried eggs disappear under the clatter of cutlery at a 1950s-style diner. Steaming plates of fresh lobster served off a Maine pier, oysters and champagne in a fashion-forward wine bar in California, Korean tacos out of a Portland food truck – these are just a few ways to dine à la Americana.

Cultural Behemoth

The USA has made tremendous contributions to the arts. Georgia O'Keeffe's wild landscapes, Robert Rauschenberg's surreal collages, Alexander Calder's elegant mobiles and Jackson Pollock's drip paintings have entered the vernacular of 20th-century art. Chicago and New York have become veritable drawing boards for the great architects of the modern era. And America has invented sounds integral to modern music, from the soulful blues born in the Mississippi Delta to the bluegrass of Appalachia and Detroit's Motown sound – plus jazz, funk, hip-hop, country, and rock and roll.

Why I Love the USA

By Regis St Louis, Writer

When it comes to travel, America has always floored me with its staggering range of possibilities. Not many other countries have so much natural beauty – mountains, beaches, rainforests, deserts, canyons, glaciers – coupled with fascinating cities to explore, an unrivaled music scene and all the things that make travel so rewarding (friendly locals, great restaurants and farmers markets, and plenty of quirky surprises). I love walking and pedaling around cities, but there's nothing quite like hitting the open road for the unsung wonders and hidden corners of this inspiring country.

For more about our writers, see page 1216

Above: New York City (p69)

USA

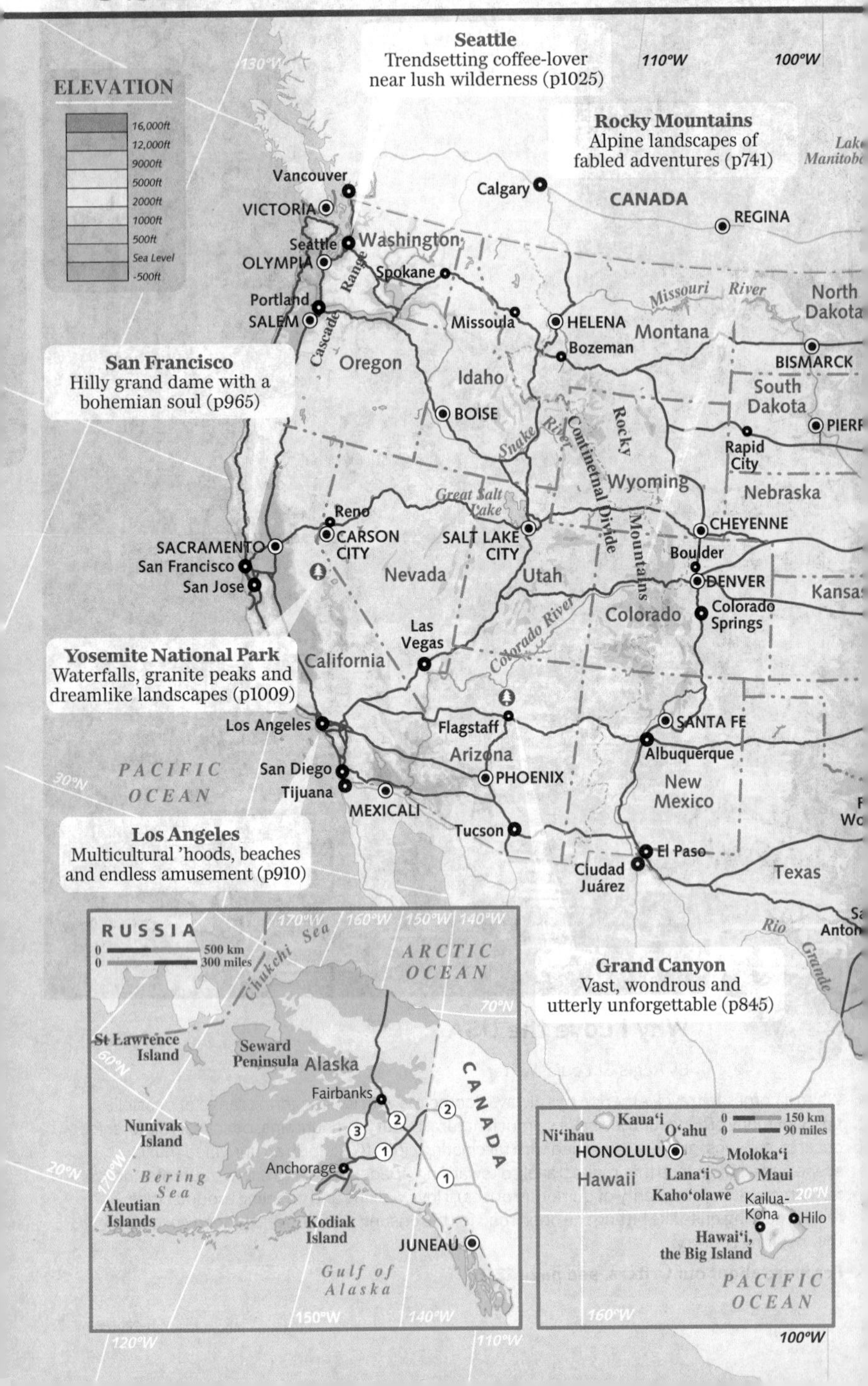

Seattle
Trendsetting coffee-lover near lush wilderness (p1025)
Rocky Mountains
Alpine landscapes of fabled adventures (p741)
San Francisco
Hilly grand dame with a bohemian soul (p965)
Yosemite National Park
Waterfalls, granite peaks and dreamlike landscapes (p1009)
Los Angeles
Multicultural 'hoods, beaches and endless amusement (p910)
Grand Canyon
Vast, wondrous and utterly unforgettable (p845)
ELEVATION
16,000ft
12,000ft
9000ft
5000ft
2000ft
1000ft
500ft
Sea Level
-500ft
130°W
110°W
100°W
120°W
30°N
CANADA
Vancouver
VICTORIA
Seattle
OLYMPIA
Washington
Cascade Range
Portland
SALEM
Oregon
Spokane
Missoula
HELENA
Bozeman
Montana
Calgary
REGINA
Missouri River
North Dakota
BISMARCK
South Dakota
PIERRE
Rapid City
Idaho
BOISE
Snake River
Continental Divide
Rocky Mountains
Wyoming
Nebraska
CHEYENNE
Great Salt Lake
SALT LAKE CITY
Utah
Reno
CARSON CITY
Nevada
SACRAMENTO
San Francisco
San Jose
Boulder
DENVER
Colorado
Colorado Springs
Kansas
Colorado River
Las Vegas
California
Los Angeles
Flagstaff
Arizona
SANTA FE
Albuquerque
New Mexico
San Diego
Tijuana
MEXICALI
PHOENIX
Tucson
El Paso
Ciudad Juárez
Texas
San Antonio
Rio Grande
PACIFIC OCEAN
RUSSIA
0 500 km
0 300 miles
Chukchi Sea
ARCTIC OCEAN
170°W
160°W
150°W
140°W
70°N
60°N
St Lawrence Island
Seward Peninsula
Alaska
CANADA
Fairbanks
Nunivak Island
Anchorage
Bering Sea
Aleutian Islands
Kodiak Island
JUNEAU
Gulf of Alaska
20°N
170°W
150°W
140°W
110°W
Kaua'i
Ni'ihau
O'ahu
0 150 km
0 90 miles
HONOLULU
Moloka'i
Hawaii
Lana'i
Maui
Kaho'olawe
Kailua-Kona
Hilo
20°N
Hawai'i, the Big Island
PACIFIC OCEAN
160°W
100°W

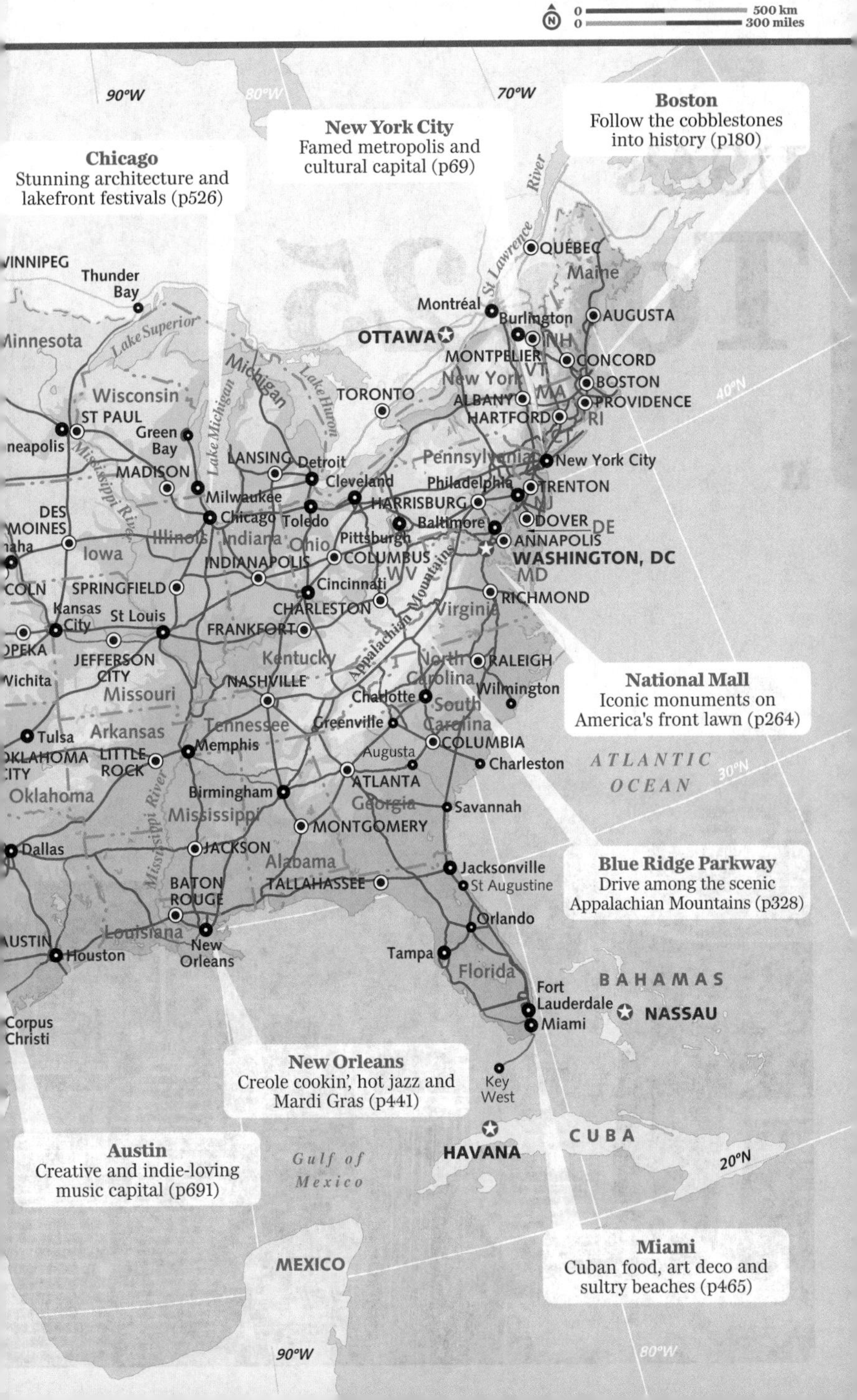

0 500 km
0 300 miles
Chicago
Stunning architecture and lakefront festivals (p526)
New York City
Famed metropolis and cultural capital (p69)
Boston
Follow the cobblestones into history (p180)
National Mall
Iconic monuments on America's front lawn (p264)
Blue Ridge Parkway
Drive among the scenic Appalachian Mountains (p328)
New Orleans
Creole cookin', hot jazz and Mardi Gras (p441)
Austin
Creative and indie-loving music capital (p691)
Miami
Cuban food, art deco and sultry beaches (p465)
90°W
80°W
70°W
40°N
30°N
20°N
Thunder Bay
Lake Superior
Minnesota
Wisconsin
ST PAUL
Green Bay
MADISON
Milwaukee
Chicago
Lake Michigan
Michigan
Lake Huron
LANSING
Detroit
Cleveland
Toledo
TORONTO
OTTAWA
Montréal
QUÉBEC
St Lawrence River
Maine
AUGUSTA
Burlington
NH
MONTPELIER
VT
CONCORD
BOSTON
PROVIDENCE
MA
RI
CT
New York
ALBANY
HARTFORD
New York City
Pennsylvania
Philadelphia
TRENTON
NJ
HARRISBURG
Baltimore
DOVER
DE
ANNAPOLIS
WASHINGTON, DC
MD
Pittsburgh
Ohio
COLUMBUS
WV
Appalachian Mountains
RICHMOND
Virginia
Cincinnati
CHARLESTON
Mississippi River
DES MOINES
Iowa
Illinois
Indiana
INDIANAPOLIS
SPRINGFIELD
Kansas City
St Louis
FRANKFORT
Kentucky
JEFFERSON CITY
Missouri
NASHVILLE
Tennessee
North Carolina
RALEIGH
Wilmington
Charlotte
South Carolina
Greenville
COLUMBIA
Charleston
Tulsa
Arkansas
Memphis
LITTLE ROCK
Augusta
ATLANTA
Georgia
Savannah
Oklahoma
Birmingham
Mississippi
MONTGOMERY
Dallas
JACKSON
Alabama
Jacksonville
St Augustine
TALLAHASSEE
BATON ROUGE
Louisiana
New Orleans
Houston
Orlando
Tampa
Florida
Fort Lauderdale
Miami
Corpus Christi
Key West
ATLANTIC OCEAN
BAHAMAS
NASSAU
HAVANA
CUBA
Gulf of Mexico
MEXICO

USA's Top 25

1

New York City

1 Home to striving artists, hedge-fund moguls and immigrants from every corner of the globe, New York City (p69) is constantly reinventing itself. It remains one of the world centers of fashion, theater, food, music, publishing, advertising and finance. A staggering number of museums, parks and ethnic neighborhoods are scattered through the five boroughs. Do as every New Yorker does: hit the streets. Every block reflects the character and history of this dizzying kaleidoscope, and on even a short walk you can cross continents.

Grand Canyon

2 You've seen it on film, heard about it from all and sundry who've made the trip. Is it worth the hype? The answer is a resounding yes. The Grand Canyon (p845) is vast and nearly incomprehensible in age – it took six million years for the canyon to form and some rocks exposed along its walls are two billion years old. Peer over the edge and you'll confront the great power and mystery of this earth we live on. Once you see it, no other natural phenomenon quite compares.

2

3

4

Route 66

3 This ribbon of concrete was the USA's original road trip, connecting Chicago with Los Angeles in 1926. You'll find neon signs, motor courts, pie-filled diners and drive-in theaters along the way. The route was bypassed by I-40 in 1984, but many original sites remain and tracing Route 66 (p41) today is a journey through small-town America. Whether you do the whole length or just a stretch, you'll come face to face with classic, nostalgic Americana.

New Orleans

4 Reborn after devastating Hurricane Katrina in 2005, New Orleans (p441) is back. Caribbean-colonial architecture, Creole cuisine and a riotous air of celebration seem more alluring than ever in the Big Easy. Nights out are spent catching Dixieland jazz, blues and rock amid bouncing live-music joints, and the city's riotous annual fests (Mardi Gras, Jazz Fest) are famous the world over. Feast on jambalaya, soft-shelled crab and Louisiana *cochon* (pulled pork) before hitting the bar scene on Frenchmen St in food-loving Nola. Dixieland musicians

Yellowstone National Park

5 Stunning natural beauty, amazing geology and some of the best wildlife-watching in North America: these are just a few reasons why Yellowstone (p785) has such star power among the world's national parks. Divided into five distinct regions, this place is huge – almost 3500 sq miles – and you could spend many days exploring the park's wonders. Highlights include massive geysers, waterfalls, fossil forests, rugged mountains, scenic overlooks and gurgling mud pools – with some 1100 miles of hiking trails providing the best way to take it all in.

New England in Fall

6 It's a major event, one approaching epic proportions in New England (p176): watching the leaves change color. You can do it just about anywhere – all you need is one brilliant tree. But if you're most people, you'll want lots of trees. From the Litchfield Hills in Connecticut and the Berkshires in Massachusetts to the Green Mountains in Vermont, entire hillsides blaze in brilliant crimsons, oranges and yellows. Covered bridges and white-steeple churches with abundant maple trees put Vermont and New Hampshire at the forefront of leaf-peeping heaven.

7

MITCHELL FUNK / GETTY IMAGES ©

8

9

San Francisco & Wine Country

7 Amid the clatter of old-fashioned trams and thick fog that sweeps in by night, the diverse hill and valley neighborhoods of San Francisco (p965) invite long days of wandering, with colorful Victorian architecture, great indie shops and world-class restaurants. Round a corner to waterfront views and you'll be hooked. If you can tear yourself away, the lush vineyards of Napa, Sonoma and the Russian River Valley lie just north. Touring vineyards, drinking great wine and lingering over farm-to-table meals – it's all part of the wine-country experience.

Chicago

8 The Windy City will blow you away with its cloud-scraping architecture, lakefront beaches and world-class museums. But its true mojo is its blend of high culture and earthy pleasures. Is there another city that dresses its Picasso sculpture in local sports-team gear? Where residents queue for hot dogs in equal measure to some of North America's top restaurants? Winters are brutal, but come summer, Chicago (p526) fetes the warm days with food and music festivals.

Walt Disney World

9 Want to set the bar high? Call yourself 'the happiest place on earth.' Walt Disney World (p514) does, and then pulls out all the stops to deliver the exhilarating sensation that you are the most important character in the show. Despite all the frantic rides, entertainment and nostalgia, the magic is watching your own child swell with belief after they have made Goofy laugh, been curtsied to by Cinderella, guarded the galaxy with Buzz Lightyear and battled Darth Maul like your very own Jedi knight.

The Deep South

10 Steeped in history and complex regional pride, the Deep South (p336) is America at its weirdest and most fascinating. From the moss-draped South Carolina swamps to the cinder-block juke joints of the steamy Mississippi Delta, and the isolated French-speaking enclaves of the Louisiana bayou. Famous for its slow pace, the Deep South is all about enjoying life's small pleasures: sucking down fresh Gulf oysters at an Alabama seafood shack, strolling Savannah's antebellum alleys or sipping sweet tea on the porch with new friends. Louisiana swampland

Las Vegas

11 Sin City (p814) is a neon-fueled ride through the nerve center of American strike-it-rich fantasies. See billionaires' names gleam from the marquees of luxury hotels. Hear a raucous soundscape of slot machines, clinking martini glasses and the hypnotic beats of DJs spinning till dawn. Sip cocktails under palm trees and play blackjack by the pool. Visit Paris, the Wild West and a tropical island, in one night. It's all here and it's open 24 hours, for the mere price of a poker chip (and a little luck).

10

11

Yosemite National Park

12 The iconic glacier-carved valley of Yosemite (p1009) never fails to get the heart racing, even when it's loved bumper-to-bumper in summer. In springtime, get drenched by the spray of its thundering snowmelt waterfalls, and twirl singing to the *Sound of Music* in high-country meadows awash with wildflowers. The scenery of Yosemite is intoxicating, with dizzying rock walls and formations, and ancient giant sequoia trees. If you look for it, you'll find solitude and space in the 1169 sq miles of development-free wilderness.

Miami

13 How does one city get so lucky? Most content themselves with one or two attributes, but Miami (p465) seems to have it all. Beyond the stunning beaches and Art Deco Historic District, there's culture at every turn. In cigar-filled dance halls, Havana expats dance to *son* and boleros, in exclusive nightclubs stiletto-heeled, fiery-eyed Brazilian models shake to Latin hip-hop, and in the park old men clack dominoes. To top it off, street vendors and restaurants dish out flavors from the Caribbean, Cuba, Argentina and Spain.

12

KENRINGER / GETTY IMAGES ©

13

14

15

Pacific Coast Highways

14 Stunning coastal highways (p43) wind their way down the US West Coast from Canada all the way to the Mexican border and offer dramatic scenery that's hard to match anywhere in the world: cliff-top views over crashing waves, sunlit rolling hills, fragrant eucalyptus forests and lush redwoods. There are wild and remote beaches, idyllic towns and fishing villages, and primeval rainforest. Amid the remote natural beauty you can mix things up with big-city adventures, dipping into Seattle, Portland, San Francisco and Los Angeles.

National Mall

15 Nearly 2 miles long and lined with iconic monuments and hallowed marble buildings, the National Mall (p264) is the epicenter of Washington, DC's political and cultural life. In the summer massive festivals are staged here, while year-round visitors wander the halls of America's finest museums lining the green. For exploring American history, there's no better place to ruminate, whether tracing your hand along the Vietnam War Memorial or ascending the steps of Lincoln Memorial, where Martin Luther King Jr gave his famous speech.

Rocky Mountains

16 The Rockies (p741) are home to the highest peaks in the lower 48 states. Craggy peaks, raging rivers, age-old canyons and national parks set the scene. Go skiing and snowboarding down pristine, powdery slopes in the winter, hike and mountain bike amid spring wildflowers or feel the rush of white water on sun-drenched summer afternoons. After a good dose of the fine fresh air, recharge at microbreweries, farm-to-table restaurants and invigorating hot springs.

Boston & Cape Cod

17 You can hardly walk a step of the cobblestone streets in Boston (p180) without running into some historic site. The Freedom Trail winds its way around the city, connecting sites from the city's revolutionary history; there are also centuries-old pubs, the esteemed Harvard University and America's oldest baseball park. After all that history, Cape Cod is the perfect place to cool off on dune-backed beaches and slurp down raw oysters.

Harvard University (p187)

16

17

ROBBIE GEORGE / GETTY IMAGES ©

ERNESTO BURCIAGA / GETTY IMAGES ©

Blue Ridge Parkway

18 In the southern Appalachian Mountains of Virginia and North Carolina, you can take in sublime sunsets, watch for wildlife and lose all sense of the present while staring off at the vast wilderness surrounding this 469-mile roadway (p44). Dozens of great hikes take you deeper into nature, from easy trails along lakes and streams to challenging scrambles up to eagles' nest heights. Camp or spend the night at forest lodges and don't miss the great bluegrass and mountain-music scene of nearby towns such as Asheville in North Carolina, and Floyd and Galax in Virginia.

Austin & San Antonio

19 One of Texas' brightest stars, Austin (p691) is a great dining, drinking and shopping city, with a creative, bohemian vibe courtesy of its university and renegade subculture. Austin is one of America's music capitals, with a variety of sounds playing out on stages nightly. Two major music fests showcase the best of the best. Southwest of Austin, San Antonio beguiles visitors with its pretty Riverwalk, lively festivals (including the 10-day San Antonio fest) and rich history (from serene Spanish missions to the battle-scarred Alamo).

Riverwalk (p705)

Native American Sites

20 The Southwest (p809) is Native American country, with a fantastic array of sites covering both the distant past and the present. In Colorado and Arizona, you can visit the ancient cliff-top homes of Puebloan peoples who lived among this dramatic and rocky landscape before mysteriously abandoning it. For living cultures, pay a visit to the Navajo Nation. Amid spectacular scenery, you can hire a guide and trek to the bottom of the Canyon de Chelly, overnight on the reservation land and purchase handicrafts directly from the artisans.

Mesa Verde National Park (p775)

BRUCE YUANYUE BI / GETTY IMAGES ©

Seattle

21 A cutting-edge Pacific Rim city with an uncanny habit of turning locally hatched ideas into global brands, Seattle has earned its place in the pantheon of 'great' US metropolises, with a world-renowned music scene, a mercurial coffee culture, and a penchant for internet-driven innovation. But, while Seattle's trendsetters rush to unearth the next big thing, city traditionalists guard its soul with distinct urban neighborhoods, a homegrown food culture and what is arguably the nation's finest public market, Pike Place (p1025).
Pike Place Market

Middle Americana

22 Endless open roads, stunning parks like the Badlands and great food in Kansas City are just some of the myriad allures of the Great Plains (p636). Surprises abound, some much more surprising than you'd expect: Nebraska's *Carhenge*, South Dakota's Corn Palace (just down the road from the huckster mecca of Wall Drug) and Kansas' fantabulous space museum plus its wild art in Lucas are but a few. Start down iconic old roads like US50 and you'll find so many diversions that the journey is the point of the trip. *Carhenge* by Jim Reinders (p679)

Great Lakes

23 This watery region (p522) is prime for off-the-beaten-path touring. Intrepid outdoors folk can wet a paddle in Minnesota's Boundary Waters, where nighttime brings a blanket of stars and the lullaby of wolf howls. Or trek to Michigan's Upper Peninsula, a remote landscape of rugged forests and wave-bashed cliffs. If that seems too far flung, there's always dairy-farm-hopping in Wisconsin to test the cheeses. And unsung but rockin' towns such as Minneapolis, Milwaukee and Detroit offer groovy neighborhoods where local beers and bands thrive. Detroit

Los Angeles

24 Although it's the entertainment capital of the world, Los Angeles (p910) is more than two-dimensional silver-screen stars. This is the city of quirky Venice Beach, art galleries and dining in Santa Monica, indie neighborhoods such as Los Feliz and Silverlake, surfer beaches like Malibu, and rugged and wild Griffith Park. And this is just the beginning. Dig deeper and you'll find an assortment of museums displaying every kind of ephemera, a cultural renaissance happening downtown and vibrant multiethnic 'hoods where great food lies just around the corner. Venice Beach (p919)

Columbia River Gorge

25 Carved out by the mighty Columbia as the Cascades uplifted, the Columbia River Gorge (p1065) is a geologic marvel. With Washington State on its north side and Oregon at its south, the state-dividing gorge offers countless waterfalls and spectacular hikes, as well as agricultural bounties of apples, pears and cherries. And if you're into windsurfing or kiteboarding, head straight to the sporty town of Hood River, ground zero for these extreme sports. Whether you're a hiker, fruit-lover or adrenaline junkie, the gorge delivers.

Need to Know

For more information, see Survival Guide (p1165)

Currency
US dollar ($)

Language
English

Visas
Visitors from Canada, the UK, Australia, New Zealand, Japan and many EU countries don't need visas for less than 90-day stays. Other nations see http://travel.state.gov.

Money
ATMs widely available. Credit cards accepted at most hotels, restaurants and shops.

Cell Phones
Foreign phones that operate on tri- or quad-band frequencies will work in the USA. Or purchase inexpensive cell phones with a pay-as-you-go plan here.

Driving
Drive on the right; steering wheel is on the left side of the car.

When to Go

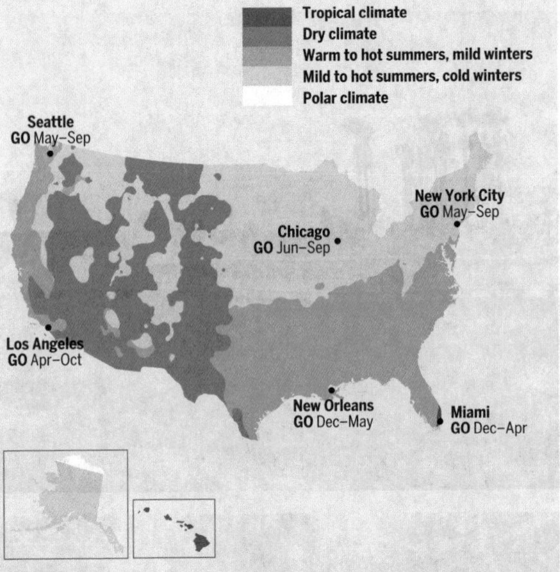

High Season
(Jun–Aug)

➡ Warm days across the country, with generally high temperatures.

➡ Busiest season, with big crowds and higher prices.

➡ In ski resort areas, January to March is high season.

Shoulder Season
(Oct & Apr–May)

➡ Milder temps, fewer crowds.

➡ Spring flowers (April); fiery autumn colors (October) in many parts.

Low Season
(Nov–Mar)

➡ Wintery days, with snowfall in the north, and heavier rains in some regions.

➡ Lowest prices for accommodations (aside from ski resorts and warmer getaway destinations).

Useful Websites

Lonely Planet (www.lonelyplanet.com/usa) Destination information, hotel bookings, travel forum and photos.

National Park Service (NPS; www.nps.gov) Gateway to America's greatest natural treasures, its national parks.

Eater (www.eater.com) Foodie insight into two dozen American cities.

New York Times Travel (http://travel.nytimes.com) Travel news, practical advice and engaging features.

Roadside America (www.roadsideamerica.com) For all things weird and wacky.

Important Numbers

Emergency	☎911
USA country code	☎1
Directory assistance	☎411
International directory assistance	☎00
International access code from the USA	☎011

Exchange Rates

Australia	A$0.72
Canada	C$0.76
Europe	€1.11
Japan	¥0.82
New Zealand	NZ$0.68
UK	UK£1.54

For current exchange rates see www.xe.com

Daily Costs

Budget: Less than $100

- Dorm beds: $25–40; campgrounds: $15–30; budget motels: $60–80
- Travel on buses, subways and other mass transit: $2–3
- Lunch from a cafe or food truck: $5–9

Midrange: $150–250

- Double room in midrange hotel: $100–250
- Popular restaurant dinner: $50–80 for two
- Car hire: from $30 per day

Top End: More than $250

- Lodging in a resort: from $250
- Dining in top restaurants: $60–100 per person
- Big nights out (plays, concerts, nightclubs): $60–200

Opening Hours

Bars 5pm–midnight Sunday to Thursday, to 2am Friday & Saturday

Banks 8:30am–4:30pm Monday to Friday

Nightclubs 10pm–4am Thursday to Saturday

Post offices 9am–5pm Monday to Friday

Shopping malls 9am–9pm

Stores 9am–6pm Monday to Saturday, noon to 5pm Sunday

Supermarkets 8am–8pm, some open 24 hours

Arriving in the USA

John F Kennedy International Airport (New York; p1183)
From JFK take the AirTrain to Jamaica Station and then LIRR to Penn Station, which costs $12 to $15 (45 minutes). A taxi to Manhattan costs $52, plus toll and tip (45 to 90 minutes).

Los Angeles International Airport (p1183)
LAX Flyaway Bus to Union Station costs $8 (30 to 50 minutes); door-to-door Prime Time & SuperShuttle costs $16 to $30 (35 to 90 minutes); and a taxi to Downtown costs $51 (25 to 50 minutes).

Miami International Airport (p481)
SuperShuttle to South Beach for $21 (50 to 90 minutes); taxi to Miami Beach for $35 (40 to 60 minutes); or take the Metrorail to downtown (Government Center) for $2.25 (15 minutes).

Time Zones in the USA

There are four time zones in the continental USA:

EST Eastern (GMT -5 hours): NYC, New England and Atlanta

CST Central (GMT -6 hours): Chicago, New Orleans and Houston

MST Mountain (GMT -7 hours): Denver, Santa Fe and Phoenix

PST Pacific (GMT -8 hours): Seattle, San Francisco and Las Vegas

Most of Alaska is one hour behind Pacific time (GMT -9 hours), while Hawaii is two hours behind Pacific time.

Daylight saving time runs from March to November. A few places (such as Hawaii and Arizona) don't observe daylight saving time.

For much more on **getting around**, see p1183.

First Time USA

For more information, see Survival Guide (p1165)

Checklist

- Check visa requirements for entering the US (p1175).
- To get the best deal, be sure to check all airlines before booking a flight.
- Find out if you can use your phone in the US and ask about roaming charges (p1173).
- At the very least, book your first few nights of accommodations to ensure an easy start to your stay.
- Check the calendar to figure out which festivals to attend or avoid.
- Organize travel insurance.
- Inform bank and credit-card company of upcoming travel.
- Reserve a car if needed (and make sure it includes unlimited miles).

What to Pack

- Passport
- Driver's license
- Cell phone (and charger)
- Good walking shoes
- A rain jacket or umbrella
- Electrical adapter
- Clothing with a stretchable waistband

Top Tips for Your Trip

- Make the effort to meet the locals. Americans are generally quite friendly, and often happy to share insight into their neighborhood or city.
- If you're driving, get off the interstates and take the back roads. Some of the best scenery lies on winding country lanes.
- Plan carefully to avoid the worst of the crowds; visit resort areas, popular restaurants and sights etc on weekdays.
- Take photographic ID out to bars; many establishments have a policy to check ID for anyone buying alcohol, even if you are obviously over 21, or even 30.
- If renting a car, note that most vehicles in the US are automatic. You might want to familiarize yourself with automatic controls if used to a gear shift.
- US immigration officers can seem intimidating on arrival at border control. To ease a swift process, answer all questions fully, politely and calmly.
- Keep in mind that laws and attitudes vary considerably from state to state. What's legal in Colorado and Washington state, for example (smoking marijuana), is illegal in Texas and South Carolina.

What to Wear

In America just about anything goes, and you'll rarely feel uncomfortable because of what you're wearing. That said, it's worth bringing along dressier attire (smart casual) for dining at nice restaurants, or going to upscale bars or clubs.

Sleeping

If you're visiting during high season (June to August for summer resort areas and January to February for wintery ski destinations), you should try to book at least three months ahead. For lodging options in popular national parks, you'll need to book much further ahead – up to a year in advance in places like the Grand Canyon, Yosemite and Yellowstone. See p1166 for more accommodations information.

➡ **Hotels** Options range from boxy and bland chain hotels, to beautifully designed boutique and luxury hotels, with an equally varied price range.

➡ **B&Bs** These small guesthouses offer a more homey stay (sometimes in heritage houses). If traveling with children, keep in mind that many B&Bs don't allow kids under a certain age (usually 12 years).

➡ **Motels** Cheaper and simpler than most hotels, these cluster along interstates, and often have inexpensive rooms.

➡ **Hostels** A growing network in the US, though still mostly limited to urban areas.

➡ **Camping** Many campsites, including some national and state parks, can be booked online (and it's wise to do so if coming in peak season).

Money-Saving Strategies

While the US can be a pricey place to visit, there are many ways frugal travelers can save some dollars.

➡ You can save by eating your bigger meals at lunchtime, when many restaurants offer lunch specials, and main courses are much better value for money.

➡ Many museums have one or more free periods in which to visit (Thursday evening or Sunday morning for instance).

➡ Cheaper rental cars often lie just outside of major city centers (Oakland and Jersey City, we're looking at you).

➡ Booking online and well ahead of time for buses and trains will get you much lower prices than buying tickets on the spot.

Bargaining

Gentle haggling is common in flea markets; in all other instances you're expected to pay the stated price.

Tipping

Tipping is not optional; only withhold tips in cases of outrageously bad service.

➡ **Airport & Hotel Porters** Tip $2 per bag, minimum per cart $5.

➡ **Bartenders** Add a tip of 15% to 20% per round; minimum per drink is $1.

➡ **Hotel Maids** Leave $2 to $4 per night, under the card provided.

➡ **Restaurant Servers** Tip servers 20%, unless a gratuity is already charged on the bill. Anything below 15% implies dissatisfaction.

➡ **Taxi Drivers** Tip 10% to 15%, rounded up to the next dollar.

➡ **Valet Parking Attendants** Tip at least $2 when handed back the keys.

Etiquette

➡ **Greeting** Don't be overly physical if you greet someone. Some Americans will hug, urbanites may exchange cheek kisses, but most – especially men – shake hands.

➡ **Smoking** Don't assume you can smoke – even if you're outside. Most Americans have little tolerance for smokers and have even banned smoking from many parks, boardwalks and beaches.

➡ **Punctuality** Do be on time. Many folks in the US consider it rude to be kept waiting.

➡ **Politeness** It's common practice to greet the staff when entering and leaving a shop ('hello' and 'have a nice day' will do). Also, Americans smile a lot (often a symbol of politeness, nothing more).

Eating

Some restaurants (typically the most popular places) don't take reservations. For those that do, it's wise to book ahead, especially on weekends. If you don't have reservations (or can't make them), plan to dine early. You can avoid lengthy waits by dining at 5pm or 6pm. See p1140 for more information

➡ **Restaurants** American restaurants cover all prices and foods: diners, burger joints, crab and lobster shacks, Michelin-starred dining rooms, and every cuisine you can imagine.

➡ **Cafes** Open during daytime (sometimes at night), cafes are good for a casual breakfast or lunch, or simply a cup of coffee.

➡ **Informal Eateries** Look for food trucks, farmers markets and other casual options (some bars also serve great food).

What's New

National Museum of African American History & Culture

The Smithsonian's newest and most architecturally striking museum, opening in 2016 on the Mall, has everything from Louis Armstrong's trumpet to Nat Turner's bible. (p268)

Queens on the Rise

New York's largest and most ethnically diverse borough is taking the stage. The draw: creative microbreweries, new boutique hotels, a reinvented seaside at Rockaway, art galleries and a truly global food culture. (p99)

Microbreweries

The brew scene has exploded across the US, which is now home to nearly 2000 craft breweries. No matter where you roam, you won't be far from refreshment. (p1144)

The 606

In 2015 Chicago saw the opening of the 606, a once tumbledown rail line converted into an urban-cool elevated path running for 2.7 miles across several northwest-side Chicago neighborhoods. (p534)

Center for Civil & Human Rights

This new 42,000-sq-ft museum in Atlanta delves deeply into the Civil Rights Movement, its hometown hero Martin Luther King Jr and present-day Civil Rights struggles around the globe. (p401)

SFJAZZ Center

Jazz lovers who are passing through San Francisco shouldn't miss the striking new $64-million performance space in the Hayes Valley. There are loads of great concerts throughout the year. (p986)

Eat in Philly

Philadelphia's dining scene continues to heat up thanks to celebrated restaurateur Michael Solomonov. His latest openings – Dizengoff and Abe Fisher – add to his other hit restaurants (Zahav and Federal Donuts). (p161)

Harvard Art Museum

The university's expanded and renovated art museum – designed by architect Renzo Piano – brings three distinct collections to coexist under one exquisite roof. (p187)

International Tennis Hall of Fame

After a complete overhaul, the all-new museum in Rhode Island features loads of multimedia exhibits, including a Roger Federer hologram and a chance to play broadcaster and 'call the match.' (p220)

One World Trade Center

The tallest building in America has opened at last. Soaring high above Lower Manhattan, this 104-story tower offers magnificent views from its multilevel observation deck. (p74)

For more recommendations and reviews, see lonelyplanet.com/usa

If You Like...

Beaches

Coastlines on two oceans and the Gulf of Mexico make tough choices for beach lovers, from the rugged and wild shores of Maine to the surf-loving beauties of Southern California.

Point Reyes National Seashore The water is cold but the scenery is magical along this beautiful stretch of untamed coastline in Northern California. (p991)

South Beach This world-famous strand is less about wave frolicking than taking in the parade of passing people on Miami's favorite playground. (p468)

Cape Cod National Seashore Massive sand dunes, picturesque lighthouses and cool forests invite endless exploring on the Massachusetts cape. (p205)

Outer Banks Runs for 100 miles along North Carolina, with breezy beaches, lighthouses and wild horses at Corolla. (p337)

Montauk At the eastern tip of Long Island, windswept Montauk has a pretty shoreline, beach camping and a still-functioning 18th-century lighthouse. (p129)

Santa Monica Hit the shore, then go celeb-spotting at edgy art galleries and high-end LA bistros. (p919)

Grayton Beach State Park This pristine coastal park on the Florida panhandle has beautiful beaches. (p520)

Theme Parks

America's theme parks come in many varieties – from old-fashioned cotton candy and roller-coaster fun to multiday immersions in pure Peter Pan–style make-believe.

Disney With theme parks on either coast, Disney makes things easy when you're ready to delve into this enchanting fairy-tale world. (p514 & p932)

Dollywood A paean to the much-loved country singer Dolly Parton, with Appalachian-themed rides and attractions in the hills of Tennessee. (p392)

Legoland Everyone's favorite building block gets its due in this creative hands-on park for the younger set outside of San Diego. (p946)

Cedar Point Amusement Park Home to several of the globe's tallest and fastest roller coasters, like the 120mph Top Thrill Dragster. (p566)

Universal Orlando Resort Famed Florida home of Universal Studios and the Wizarding World of Harry Potter. (p510)

Wine

Visiting wineries isn't just about tasting first-rate drops but drinking in the pretty countryside and sampling the enticing farm stands and delectable bistros that often sprout alongside vineyards.

Napa Valley Home to more than 200 vineyards, Napa is synonymous with world-class winemaking. You'll find superb varietals, gourmet bites and beautiful scenery. (p993)

Willamette Valley Outside of Portland, OR, this fertile region produces some of the tastiest Pinot Noir on the planet. (p1062)

Finger Lakes Upstate New York is a prime growing region. After a few quaffs, you can walk it off at nearby state parks. (p134)

Virginia Wine Country There's much history in this up-and-coming wine district. You can even sample the wines grown on Thomas Jefferson's old estate. (p320)

Verde Valley If you think Arizona is all desert, guess again. Take a winery tour in this lush setting near Sedona. (p840)

Yakima Valley Sample velvety reds in Washington state's biggest and oldest wine region. (p1050)

Great Food

The classic American dining experience: making a mess at a Maine lobster shack; plowing through BBQ in Texas Hill Country; and feasting at world-famous restaurants in New York, Los Angeles and beyond.

New York City Whatever you crave, the world's great dining capital has you covered. (p106)

New England Lobsters, clambakes, oysters and fresh fish galore – the Northeast is a paradise for seafood lovers. (p192)

Chicago The city that earns rave reviews for its Greek, Vietnamese and Mexican cuisine; molecular gastronomy; famously deep-dish pizzas and much more. (p541)

San Francisco Real-deal taquerias and trattorias, magnificent farmers markets and acclaimed chefs all fire up world-class California cuisine. (p982)

Lockhart Texas smokes them all – at least when it comes to barbecue. Carnivores shouldn't miss the legendary capital of mouth-watering brisket. (p703)

Portland, OR Boasts a cutting-edge food scene; its food trucks serve imaginative dishes from every corner of the globe. (p1057)

New Orleans French, Spanish, Filipinos, Haitians and other nationalities have contributed to the gastro-amalgamation, making Nola one of America's most food-centric cities. (p451)

Hiking

The stage is set: soaring mountains, mist-covered rainforests, red-rock canyons and craggy clifftops overlooking wild, windswept seas. These are just a few places

Top: Surf boards on Montauk beach
Bottom: Tule elk, Point Reyes National Seashore

where you can hike the great American wilderness.

Appalachian Trail Even if you chose not to walk all 2178 miles, the AT is well worth visiting. Fourteen states provide access. (p332)

Yosemite National Park Hike amid thundering waterfalls, wildflower-strewn meadows and granite peaks in the Sierra Nevada. (p1009)

North Cascades Glaciers, jagged peaks and alpine lakes are all part of the scenery at this wild and remote Washington state wilderness. (p1044)

Acadia National Park Hiking trails through Maine's dramatic park pass along sea cliffs, through forests and near boulder-strewn peaks. (p255)

Rocky Mountain National Park This Colorado stunner has snowcapped peaks, wildflower-filled valleys and picturesque mountain lakes. (p757)

Presidential Range In the stunning White Mountains of New Hampshire, you'll find challenging trails, lofty peaks, forests and an excellent hut-to-hut system. (p241)

Big Bend National Park Dry mountainous scenery amid some 200 miles of trails in a massive Texas park. (p732)

Off-Beat America

When you tire of traipsing through museums and ticking off well-known sights, unbuckle your safety belt and throw yourself into the strange world of American kitsch.

Carhenge A cheeky homage to Stonehenge made of old cars assembled in a Nebraska field. (p679)

NashTrash Tours Nashville's tall-haired 'Jugg Sisters' take visitors on a deliciously tacky journey through Nashville's spicier side. (p379)

Key West Cemetery Gothic labyrinth full of colorful epitaphs, such as 'I told you I was sick.' (p493)

American Visionary Art Museum See outsider art (including pieces created by the clinically insane) at this Baltimore gem. (p293)

Loneliest Road Take the empty highway through Nevada, and don't forget to stop at the Shoe Tree. (p829)

Mini Time Machine Museum of Miniatures This whimsical new museum in Tucson is devoted to tiny things. (p856)

Marfa Lights Sit at dusk in west Texas looking for the ghostly lights, which many visitors see playing on the horizon. (p735)

Architecture

Whether you're a devotee of Frank Lloyd Wright or simply enjoy gazing at beautifully designed buildings, the US has a treasure chest of architectural wonders.

Chicago Birthplace of the skyscraper, Chicago has magnificent works by many of the great 20th-century architects. (p526)

Fallingwater This Frank Lloyd Wright masterpiece blends into the forested Pennsylvania landscape and the waterfall over which the house is built. (p171)

New York City Much-photographed classics include the art-deco Chrysler Building, the spiraling Guggenheim and the majestic Brooklyn Bridge. (p69)

Miami Miami's art-deco Historic District is a Technicolor dream come to life. (p469)

San Francisco See elegant Victorians and cutting-edge 21st-century masterpieces in perhaps America's most European city. (p965)

Savannah This Southern belle never fails to turn heads with her striking antebellum architecture. (p414)

New Orleans A gorgeous French colonial center, plus grand antebellum mansions reached via a historic streetcar. (p441)

Native American Culture

The continent's first peoples have a connection to the land and its animals that stretches back many generations and is most evident in sites of the Southwest.

National Museum of the American Indian Appropriately, the capital holds America's finest museum dedicated to native peoples. (p272)

Mesa Verde Carved into the mountains of Southern Colorado, this fascinating site was mysteriously abandoned by Ancestral Puebloans. (p775)

Pine Ridge Indian Reservation Visit the tragic South Dakota site where Lakotas were massacred by US Cavalry, then visit nearby Red Cloud to learn more about the Lakota. (p669)

Navajo Nation Take in the stunning scenery and learn more about this proud people in Arizona. (p853)

Zuni Pueblo Purchase beautifully wrought silver jewelry and overnight at a tribally licensed New Mexico inn. (p885)

Carlsbad Caverns National Park

Museum of the Cherokee Indian Learn about the native tribes that once lived in North Carolina and the heartbreaking Trail of Tears. (p356)

Historical Sights

The East Coast is where you'll find the original 13 colonies. To delve into the past, head south and west, where Spanish explorers and indigenous peoples left their mark.

Philadelphia The nation's first capital is where the idea of America as an independent nation coalesced. Excellent museums tell the story. (p152)

Boston Visit Paul Revere's former home, an 18th-century graveyard and the decks of the 1797 USS *Constitution*. (p180)

Williamsburg Step back into the 1700s in the preserved town of Williamsburg, VA, the largest living-history museum on the planet. (p97)

Washington, DC Visit the sites where Lincoln was assassinated, Martin Luther King Jr gave his most famous speech and Nixon's presidency was undone. (p261)

Harpers Ferry A fascinating open-air museum of 19th-century village life beautifully framed by the mountains and rivers of West Virginia. (p332)

St Augustine Cobblestone streets, 300-year-old forts and a youthful fountain at this Spanish Colonial town founded in the 1500s. (p498)

Beer & Microbreweries

Microbreweries have exploded in popularity, and you'll never be far from a finely crafted pint. Colorado, Washington and Oregon are particularly famed for their breweries.

Magic Hat Brewery Vermont, one of America's microbrewery capitals, deserves special mention – and Magic Hat makes for a refreshing and entertaining beer outing. (p236)

Mountain Sun Pub & Brewery Boulder's favorite microbrewery serves an array of excellent drafts, plus good food and regular music jams. (p756) (p756)

Portland, OR Valhalla for beer lovers, Portland has more than

70 microbreweries within city limits. (p1060)

Mammoth Brewing Company Head to this laid-back California mountain town for a dazzling tasting. (p1017)

Asheville Home to more than 20 microbreweries and brewpubs, Asheville is leading North Carolina's beer renaissance. (p352)

Geologic Wonders

With red-rock deserts, petrified forests, blasting geysers and one massive hole in the ground, you might feel like you've stepped onto another planet.

Grand Canyon Needing little introduction, this mile-deep, 10-mile-wide hole was carved over six million years. Take your time when you go. (p845)

Yellowstone National Park Massive geysers, rainbow-colored thermal pools and the supervolcano it all sits on: this Northwestern national park certainly puts on a show. (p785)

Hawai'i Volcanoes National Park Glimpse lava deserts, smoldering craters and the ongoing process of volcanism – going strong for 70 million years. (p1109)

Carlsbad Caverns National Park Take a 2-mile walk along a subterranean passage to arrive in the great room – a veritable underground cathedral in New Mexico. (p904)

Southern Utah National Parks See 3000ft-tall slot canyons, eroding pinnacles and spires in the seven national parks and monuments of Utah's red-rock country. (p876)

Live Music

Americans know where to catch a good live band – whether they're after Memphis blues, Appalachian bluegrass, New Orleans jazz, fist-pumping rock, sultry salsa, country crooning or much, much more.

Austin Home to more than 200 venues and the country's biggest music fest, Austin proudly wears the music crown. (p700)

New Orleans The Big Easy has a soundtrack as intoxicating as the city itself – from room-filling big-band jazz to indie rock. (p454)

Nashville This river city is a showcase for country, bluegrass, blues, folk and plenty of rough-and-tumble honky-tonks. (p386)

Los Angeles LA is a magnet for aspiring stars and draws serious talent. Don't miss the legendary Sunset Strip for A-list artists. (p928)

Memphis Juke joints and dive bars host blazing live bands. (p376)

Kansas City This barbecue-loving Missouri city has a venerable live-music scene, especially when it comes to jazz. (p654)

Month by Month

> **TOP EVENTS**
>
> **Mardi Gras**, February or March
>
> **South by Southwest**, March
>
> **National Cherry Blossom Festival**, March
>
> **Chicago Blues Festival**, June
>
> **Independence Day**, July

January

The New Year starts off with a shiver, as snowfall blankets large swaths of the country. Ski resorts kick into high gear, while sun lovers seek refuge in warmer climes (especially Florida).

Mummers Parade

Philadelphia's biggest event is this brilliant parade (www.mummers.com), where local clubs spend months creating costumes and mobile scenery in order to win top honors on New Year's Day. String bands and clowns add to the general good cheer at this long-running fest.

Chinese New Year

In late January or early February, you'll find colorful celebrations and feasting anywhere there's a Chinatown. NYC throws a festive parade, though San Francisco's is the best, with floats, firecrackers, bands and plenty of merriment.

☆ Sundance Film Festival

The legendary Sundance Film Festival (www.sundance.org) brings Hollywood stars, indie directors and avid film-goers to Park City, UT, for a 10-day indie extravaganza in late January. Plan well in advance, as passes sell out fast.

February

Aside from mountain getaways, many Americans dread February with its long dark nights and frozen days. For foreign visitors, this can be the cheapest time to travel, with ultradiscount rates for flights and hotels.

Mardi Gras

Held in late February or early March, on the day before Ash Wednesday, Mardi Gras (Fat Tuesday) is the finale of Carnival. New Orleans' celebrations (www.mardigrasneworleans.com) are legendary as colorful parades, masquerade balls, feasting and plenty of hedonism rule the day.

March

The first blossoms of spring arrive (at least in the south – the north still shivers in the chill). In the mountains, it's still high season for skiing. Meanwhile, drunken spring-breakers descend on Florida.

St Patrick's Day

On the 17th, the patron saint of Ireland is honored with brass bands and ever-flowing pints of Guinness; huge parades occur in New York, Boston and Chicago (which goes all out by dyeing the Chicago River green).

National Cherry Blossom Festival

The brilliant blooms of Japanese cherry blossoms around DC's Tidal Basin are celebrated with concerts, parades, *taiko* drumming, kite-flying and 90 other events during the five-week fest (www.nationalcherryblossomfestival.org). More than one million go each year, so don't forget to book ahead.

South by Southwest

Each year Austin, TX, becomes ground zero for one of the biggest music fests in North America. More than 2000 performers play at nearly 100 venues. SXSW is also a major film festival and interactive fest – a platform for ground-breaking ideas. (p695)

April

The weather is warming up, but April can still be unpredictable, with chilly weather mixed with a few teasingly warm days up north. Down south, it's a fine time to travel.

Fiesta San Antonio

Mid-April is the liveliest time to visit this pretty river town in Texas, as you'll find 10 days of fiesta (www.fiesta-sa.org) with carnivals, parades, dancing and lots of great eating options.

Jazz Fest

On the last weekend in April, New Orleans hosts the country's best jazz jam (www.nojazzfest.com), with top-notch acts (local resident Harry Connick Jr sometimes plays) and plenty of good cheer. In addition to world-class jazz, there's also great food and crafts.

Juke Joint Festival

In mid-April, Clarksdale, MS, stages a memorable blues fest. The feel is very authentic, as you roam among a dozen stages, with plenty of great food and the odd amusement (pig racing!) to boot.

Patriot's Day

Massachusetts' big day out falls on the third Monday in April and features Revolutionary War re-enactments and parades in Lexington and Concord, plus the running of the Boston Marathon and a much-watched Red Sox game at home.

Gathering of Nations

For an immersion in indigenous culture, head to Albuquerque for the Gathering of Nations (www.gatheringofnations.com), the largest Native American powwow in the world. You'll find traditional dance, music, food, crafts and the crowning of Miss Indian World.

May

May is true spring and one of the loveliest times to travel, with blooming wildflowers and generally mild sunny weather. Summer crowds and high prices have yet to arrive.

Beale Street Music Festival

Blues lovers descend on Memphis for this venerable music fest held over three days in early May. (p373)

Cinco de Mayo

Celebrate Mexico's victory over the French with salsa music and pitchers of margaritas across the country. LA, San Francisco and Denver all throw some of the biggest bashes.

June

Summer is here. Americans spend more time at outdoor cafes and restaurants, and head to the shore or to national parks. School is out; vacationers fill the highways and resorts, bringing higher prices.

Bonnaroo Music & Arts Festival

In the heartland of Tennessee, this sprawling music fest showcases big-name rock, soul, country and more over four days in mid-June.

Gay Pride

In some cities, gay pride celebrations last a week, but in San Francisco, it's a month-long party, where the last weekend in June sees giant parades. You'll find other great pride events at major cities across the country.

Chicago Blues Festival

It's the globe's biggest free blues fest (www.chicagobluesfestival.us), with three days of the music that made Chicago famous. More than 500,000 people unfurl blankets by the multiple stages that take over Grant Park in early June.

Mermaid Parade

In Brooklyn, NYC, Coney Island celebrates summer's steamy arrival with a kitsch-loving parade (www.coneyisland.com), complete with skimpily attired mermaids and horn-blowing mermen.

☆ CMA Music Festival

This legendary country-music fest (www.cmaworld.com) has more than 400 artists performing at stages on Riverfront Park and LP Field.

☆ Telluride Bluegrass Festival

The banjo gets its due at this festive, boot-stomping music jam (www.planet-bluegrass.com) in Colorado mountain country. You'll find nonstop performances, excellent regional food stalls and great locally crafted microbrews. It's good all-comers entertainment and many folks even camp.

☆ Tanglewood Musical Festival

Open-air concerts run all summer long (late June to early September) in an enchanting setting in western Massachusetts.

July

With summer in full swing, Americans break out the backyard barbecues or head for the beach. The prices are high and the crowds can be fierce, but it's one of the liveliest times to visit.

Independence Day

The nation celebrates its birthday with a bang, as nearly every town and city stages a massive fireworks show. Washington, DC, New York, Philadelphia and Boston are all great spots.

Oregon Brewers Festival

The beer-loving city of Portland pulls out the stops and pours a heady array of handcrafted perfection (www.oregonbrewfest.com). Featuring 90 different beers from around the country (and a dozen or so international brewers), there are plenty of choices; and it's nicely set along the banks of the Willamette River.

☆ Pageant of the Masters

This eight-week arts fest (www.lagunafestivalofarts.org) brings a touch of the surreal to Laguna Beach, CA. On stage, meticulously costumed actors create living pictures – imitations of famous works of art – which are accompanied by narration and an orchestra.

☆ Newport Folk Festival

Newport, RI, a summer haunt of the well-heeled, hosts a world-class music fest (www.newportfolkfest.com) in late July. Top folk artists take to the stage at this fun, all-welcoming event.

August

Expect blasting heat in August, with temperatures and humidity less bearable the further south you go. You'll find people-packed beaches, high prices and empty cities on weekends, when residents escape to the nearest waterfront.

☆ Lollapalooza

This mondo rock fest (www.lollapalooza.com) sees more than 100 bands spilling off eight stages in Grant Park on the first Friday-to-Sunday in August.

Iowa State Fair

If you've never been to a state fair, now's your chance. This event (www.iowastatefair.org) is where you'll find country crooning, wondrous carvings (in butter), livestock shows, sprawling food stalls and a down-home good time in America's heartland.

September

With the end of summer, cooler days arrive, making for pleasant outings nationwide. The kids are back in school, and concert halls, gallery spaces and performing-arts venues kick off a new season.

Santa Fe Fiesta

Santa Fe hosts the nation's longest-running festival (www.santafefiesta.org), a spirited two-week-long event with parades, concerts and the burning of Old Man Gloom.

Burning Man Festival

Over one week, some 50,000 revelers, artists and assorted free spirits descend on Nevada's Black Rock Desert to create a temporary metropolis of art installations, theme camps and environmental curiosities. It culminates in the burning of a giant stick figure (www.burningman.com).

New York Film Festival

Just one of many big film fests (www.filmlinc.com) in NYC (Tribeca Film Fest in late April is another goodie); this one features world premieres from across the globe.

October

Temperatures are falling as autumn brings fiery colors to northern climes. It's high season where the leaves are most brilliant (New England); elsewhere expect lower prices and fewer crowds.

Fantasy Fest

Key West's answer to Mardi Gras brings more than 100,000 revelers to the subtropical enclave in the week leading up to Halloween. Expect parades, colorful floats, costume parties, the selecting of a conch king and queen, and plenty of alcohol-fueled merriment (www.fantasyfest.net).

Halloween

In NYC, you can don a costume and join the Halloween parade up Sixth Ave. West Hollywood in Los Angeles and San Francisco's Castro district are great places to see outrageous outfits. Salem, MA, also hosts spirited events throughout October.

November

No matter where you go, this is generally low season, with cold winds discouraging visitors despite lower prices (although airfares skyrocket around Thanksgiving). There's much happening culturally in the cities.

Thanksgiving

On the fourth Thursday of November, Americans gather with family and friends over day-long feasts – roast turkey, sweet potatoes, cranberry sauce, wine, pumpkin pie and loads of other dishes. NYC hosts a huge parade, and there's pro football on TV.

December

Winter arrives as ski season kicks off in the Rockies (out east conditions aren't usually ideal until January). Aside from winter sports, December means heading inside and curling up by the fire.

Art Basel

This massive arts fest (www.artbaselmiamibeach.com) is four days of cutting-edge art, film, architecture and design. More than 250 major galleries from across the globe come to the event, with works by some 2000 artists; plus much hobnobbing with a glitterati crowd in Miami Beach.

New Year's Eve

Americans are of two minds when it comes to ringing in the New Year. Some join festive crowds to celebrate; others plot a getaway to escape the mayhem. Whichever you choose, plan well in advance. Expect high prices (especially in NYC).

Itineraries

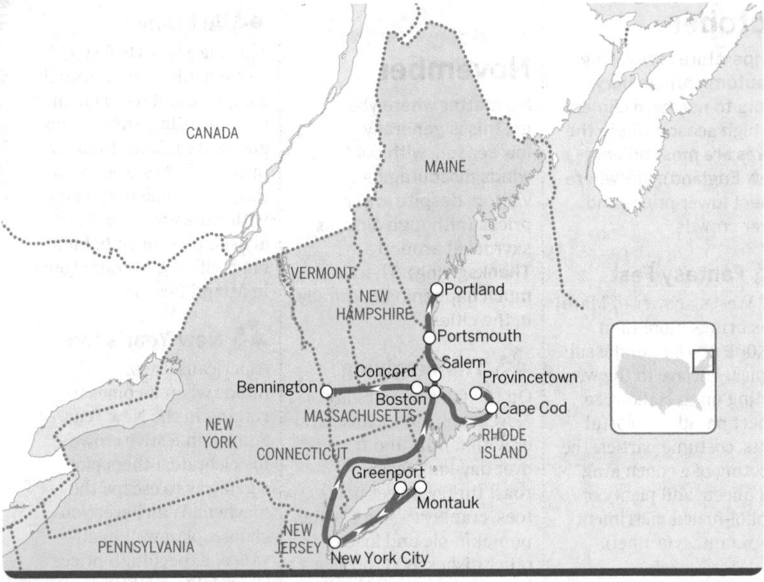

2–3 WEEKS

East Coasting

The great dynamo of art, fashion and culture, **New York City** is America at her most urbane. Spend four days exploring the metropolis, visiting memorable people-watching 'hoods such as the West and East Villages, the Lower East Side, Soho, Nolita and the Upper West Side, with a museum-hop down the Upper East Side. Have a ramble in Central Park, stroll the High Line and take detours to Brooklyn and Queens. After big-city culture, catch your breath at the pretty beaches and seaside eateries of **Greenport** and **Montauk** on Long Island. Back in NYC, catch the train to **Boston** for two days visiting historic sights, dining in the North End and pub-hopping in Cambridge. Strike out for **Cape Cod**, with its idyllic dunes, forests and pretty shores. Leave time for **Provincetown**, the Cape's liveliest settlement. Back in Boston, hire a car and take a three-day jaunt taking in New England's back roads, covered bridges, picturesque towns and beautiful scenery, staying at heritage B&Bs en route. Highlights include **Salem** and **Concord** in Massachusetts; **Bennington**, VT; and **Portsmouth**, NH. If time allows, head all the way up to **Maine** for lobster feasts amid beautifully rugged coastline. **Portland** is a great place to start.

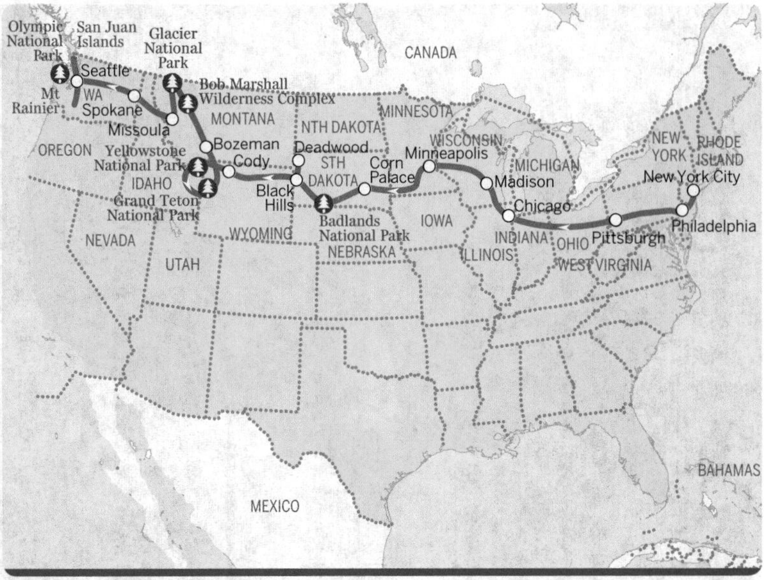

3 WEEKS Northern Exposure

For a different take on the transcontinental journey, plan a route through the north. From **New York City**, head southwest to historic **Philadelphia**, then continue west to the idyllic backroads of Pennsylvania Dutch Country. Next is **Pittsburgh**, a surprising town of picturesque bridges and green spaces, cutting-edge museums and lively neighborhoods. Enter Ohio by interstate, but quickly step back in time on a drive through old-fashioned Amish Country. Big-hearted **Chicago** is the Midwest's greatest metropolis. Stroll or bike the lakefront, marvel at famous artwork and grand architecture, and check out the celebrated restaurant scene. Head north to **Madison**, a youthful green-loving university town.

Detour north to the land of 10,000 lakes (aka Minnesota) for a stop in friendly, arty **Minneapolis**, followed by a visit to its quieter historic twin, St Paul, across the river. Return to I-90 and activate cruise control, admiring the corn (and the **Corn Palace**) and the flat, flat South Dakota plains. Hit the brakes for the **Badlands National Park** and plunge into the Wild West. In the **Black Hills**, contemplate the nation's complex history at the massive monuments of Mt Rushmore and Crazy Horse, then make a northern detour to watch mythic gunfights in **Deadwood**.

Halfway across Wyoming, cruise into **Cody** to catch a summer rodeo. Then take in the wonders of **Yellowstone National Park**. Next, detour south for hikes past jewel-like lakes and soaring peaks in **Grand Teton National Park**. Drive back up north, and continue west through rural Montana. The outdoorsy towns of **Bozeman** and **Missoula** make fun stops either side of exploring the alpine beauty of **Glacier National Park** and trekking through the **Bob Marshall Wilderness Complex**.

After a few days out in the wild, surprising **Spokane** is a great place to recharge, with a pleasant riverfront and historic district sprinkled with enticing eating and drinking spots. For more cosmopolitan flavor, keep heading west to **Seattle**, a forward-thinking, ecominded city with cafe culture, abundant nightlife and speedy island escapes on Puget Sound. If you still have time, the region has some great places to explore, including **Mt Rainier**, **Olympic National Park** and the **San Juan Islands**.

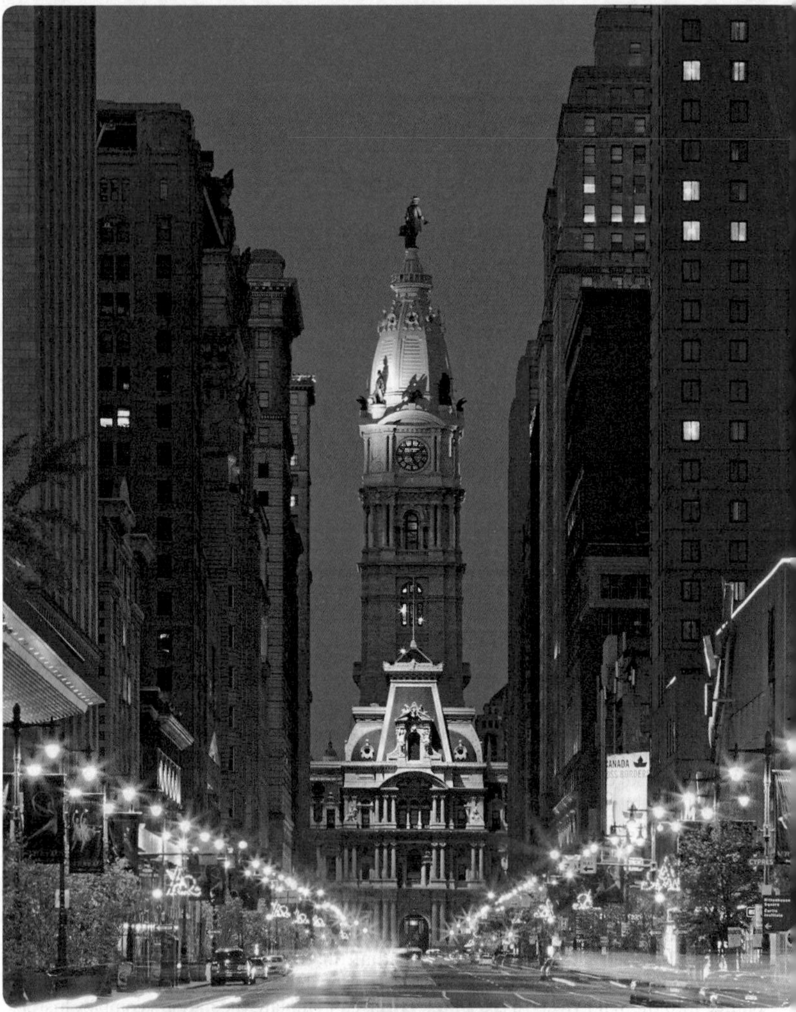

Above: Philadelphia

Left: Motown Museum, Detroit

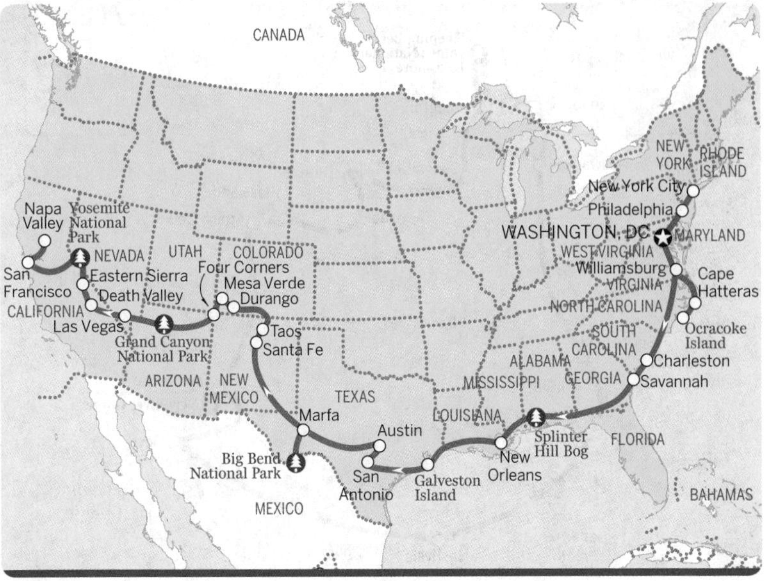

4 WEEKS Coast to Coast

The Great American road trip: it's been mythologized hundreds of ways. Now live the dream, driving the length and breadth of the USA. Start in **New York City** (but hire a car in cheaper New Jersey) and hit the road. First stop: **Philadelphia**, a historic city with a burgeoning food, art and music scene. Continue on to **Washington, DC**. The nation's capital has a dizzying array of sights, plus great dining and revelry after the museums close. Continue south through Virginia, taking a detour to visit the historic settlement of colonial **Williamsburg**. Stick to the coast as you drive south, visiting **Cape Hatteras** with its pristine dunes, marshes and woodlands. Catch the ferry to remote **Ocracoke Island**, where the wild ponies run. Further down, take in the antebellum allure of **Charleston** and **Savannah**. Afterward stop in **Splinter Hill Bog** in Alabama, a fantastic site for exploring the biodiversity of the coast. Next, it's on to jazz-loving **New Orleans**, with a soundtrack of smokin' hot funk brass bands, and succulent Cajun and Creole food.

The big open skies of Texas are next. Hit the beach at **Galveston** outside Houston. Follow the Mission Trail and stroll the tree-lined riverwalk in thriving **San Antonio**, then revel in the great music and drinking scene in **Austin**. Afterward, eat your way through scenic Hill Country, stop for art and star-filled nights at **Marfa**, and then hike through jaw-dropping **Big Bend National Park**. Head north to New Mexico, following the Turquoise Trail up to artsy **Santa Fe** and far-out **Taos**. Roll up through Colorado and into mountain-beauty **Durango**, continuing to the Amerindian cliff-top marvel of **Mesa Verde** and the curious four-state intersection of the **Four Corners**. The awe-inspiring **Grand Canyon** is next. Stay in the area to maximize time near this great wonder. Try your luck amid the bright lights of (luck be a lady tonight?) **Las Vegas**, then take in the stunning desert landscapes at **Death Valley** on your ride into California. From there, head up into the majestic forests of the **Eastern Sierra**, followed by hiking and wildlife-watching in **Yosemite**, California's most revered national park. The last stop is in hilly **San Francisco**, an enchanting city spread between ocean and bay with beautiful vistas, fascinating neighborhoods to explore and seemingly endless cultural attractions. If there's time, tack on a grand finale, enjoying the vineyards and gourmet produce of **Napa Valley**.

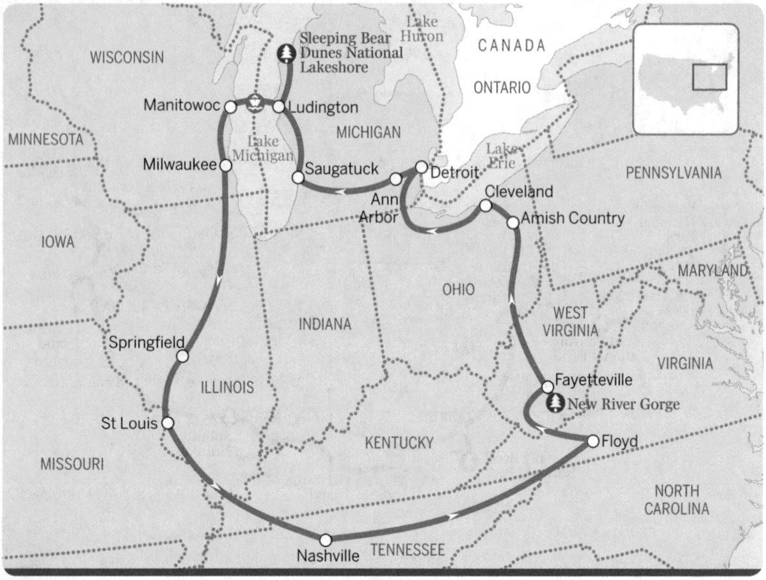

2 WEEKS

Off the Beaten Path

Underdog cities, lakeside islands and boot-scootin' mountain music are just a few of the things you'll encounter on this off-the-beaten-path ramble around the central US. Start off in **Detroit**, which isn't quite the apocalyptic landscape it's sometimes made it out to be. Stroll the riverwalk, explore recent history (Motown, automobiles) and take in the River City's underground nightlife scene. Next head to nearby **Ann Arbor**, with its easy-going college-town charm (coffee shops, farmers markets, pubby bars), before continuing west to Lake Michigan. Drive up through waterfront towns (stopping perhaps in **Saugatuck** for gallery-hopping) and continue all the way to **Sleeping Bear Dunes National Lakeshore**, with its dramatic sandscapes, scenic drives and wilderness-covered islands.

From there backtrack to **Ludington** and take the ferry across Lake Michigan to **Manitowoc** in Wisconsin. Continue south to **Milwaukee**, one of the best little cities in America, with great art and architecture, abundant microbreweries, summer festivals and memorable riverfront cycling. From there, it's a 4½-hour drive south to **Springfield**, where you can delve into the fascinating past of hometown hero (and America's favorite president) Abraham Lincoln. Two hours' drive south is **St Louis**, with walkable neighborhoods and green spaces (including a park that dwarfs Central Park), plus blues, barbecue and bumping music joints. Speaking of music, up next is **Nashville**, a mecca for lovers of country and blues. Head toward Appalachia (start in **Floyd**, VA) for an authentic music scene – a frenzy of fiddles, banjos and boot-stompin' – amid the rolling hills of southeastern Virginia. Continue north to **Fayetteville** in West Virginia, gateway to the breathtaking **New River Gorge**, which has superb hiking, climbing, mountain biking and whitewater rafting.

A five-hour drive takes you to the epicenter of America's largest Amish community in **Amish Country** near Kidron in Ohio. Step back in time at antique shops, old-fashioned farms and bakeries, and quaint 19th-century inns. Afterwards, fast-forward into **Cleveland**, a city on the cusp of reinvention with up-and-coming gastropubs, newly expanded art museums, green markets and the massive Rock and Roll Hall of Fame. It's less than three hours back to Detroit.

Plan Your Trip

Road Trips & Scenic Drives

Fill up the gas tank and buckle up. Everyone knows road-tripping is the ultimate way to see America. You can drive up, down, across, around or straight through every state on the continental US. Revel in yesteryear along Route 66, marvel at spectacular sunsets on the Pacific Coast Hwy, or take in sublime scenery in the Appalachian Mountains or along the mighty Mississippi.

Road-Tripping Tips

Best Experiences

Dazzling coastal scenery on the Pacific Coast Hwy; the charming, rarely visited destinations on Route 66; dramatic sunsets over the Appalachian Mountains on the Blue Ridge Pkwy; listening to Memphis blues at a jumping music joint off the Great River Rd.

Key Starting Points

Chicago or Los Angeles for Route 66; Seattle or San Diego for the Pacific Coast Hwy; Waynesboro, VA, or Cherokee, NC, for Blue Ridge Pkwy; Itasca State Park, MN, or Venice, LA, for Great River Road.

Major Sights

Grand Canyon on Route 66; Point Reyes National Seashore on the Pacific Coast Hwy; Peaks of Otter on Blue Ridge Pkwy; Shawnee National Park on Great River Rd.

Route 66

For a classic American road trip, nothing beats good ol' Route 66. Nicknamed the nation's 'Mother Road' by novelist John Steinbeck, this string of small-town main streets and country byways first connected big-shouldered Chicago with the waving palm trees of Los Angeles in 1926.

Why Go?

Whether you seek to explore retro Americana or simply want to experience big horizons and captivating scenery far from the maddening crowd, Route 66 will take you there. The winding journey passes some of the USA's greatest outdoor attractions – not just the Grand Canyon, but also the Mississippi River, Arizona's Painted Desert and Petrified Forest National Park, and, at road's end, the Pacific beaches of sun-kissed Southern California.

Other highlights along the way: old-fashioned museums stocked with strange and wondrous objects from the past, Norman Rockwell-ish soda fountains, classic mom-and-pop diners, working gas stations that seem to have fallen right out of an old James Dean film clip and ghost towns (or soon-to-be ghost towns) hunkering on the edge of the desert.

Culturally speaking, Route 66 can be an eye-opener. Discard your preconceptions of small-town American life and unearth the joys of what bicoastal types dismissively term 'flyover' states. Mingle with farmers in Illinois and country-and-western stars in Missouri. Hear the legends of cowboys and Indians in Oklahoma. Visit Native American tribal nations and contemporary pueblos across the Southwest, all the while discovering the traditions of the USA's indigenous peoples. Then follow the trails of miners and desperados deep into the Old West.

When to Go

The best time to travel Route 66 is May to September, when the weather is warm and you can take advantage of open-air activities. Take care if you travel in the height of summer (July and August) as the heat can be unbearable – particularly in desert areas. Avoid traveling in the winter (December to March), when snow can lead to perilous driving conditions or outright road closures.

The Route

The journey starts in Chicago, just west of Michigan Ave, and runs for some 2400 miles across eight states before terminating in Los Angeles near the Santa Monica pier. The road remains a never-ending work in progress as old sections get resurrected or disappear owing to the rerouting of other major roads.

History of the Mother Road

Route 66 didn't really hit its stride until the Great Depression, when migrant farmers followed it as they fled the Dust Bowl across the Great Plains. Later, during the post-WWII baby boom, newfound prosperity encouraged many Americans to hit the road and 'get their kicks' on Route 66.

Almost as soon as it came of age, however, Route 66 began to lose steam. The shiny blacktop of an ambitious new interstate system started systematically paving over Route 66, bypassing its mom-and-pop diners, drugstore soda fountains and once-stylish motor courts. Railway towns were forgotten and way stations for travelers became dusty. Even entire towns began to disappear.

By the time Route 66 was officially decommissioned in 1984, preservation associations of Mother Road fans had sprung up. Today you can still get your kicks on Route 66, following gravel frontage roads and blue-line highways across the belly of America. It's like a time warp – connecting places where the 1950s seem to have stopped just yesterday.

Getting Lost

You need to be an amateur sleuth to follow Route 66 these days. Historical realignments of the route, dead-ends in farm fields and tumbleweed-filled desert patches, and rough, rutted driving conditions are par for the course. Remember that getting lost every now and then is inevitable. But never mind; the road offers a leap back through time to see what America once was, and still sometimes is. Nostalgia never tasted so sweet.

ROADSIDE ODDITIES: ROUTE 66

Kitschy, time-warped and just plain weird roadside attractions? Route 66 has got 'em in spades. Here are a few beloved Mother Road landmarks to make your own scavenger hunt:

- A massive statue of legendary lumberjack Paul Bunyan clutching a hotdog in Illinois.
- Pacific's Black Madonna Shrine and Red Oak II outside Carthage in Missouri.
- The 80ft-long Blue Whale in Catoosa, OK.
- Devil's Rope Museum, Cadillac Ranch and Bug Ranch in Texas.
- Seligman's Snow Cap Drive-In and Holbrook's WigWam Motel and Meteor Crater in Arizona.
- Roy's Motel & Cafe in Amboy, in the middle of California's Mojave Desert.

Scenic Drives

Resources

Before you hit the road, arm yourself with useful maps and key insider tips to help you make the most of your trip.

Here It Is: Route 66 Maps with directions (traveling both east-to-west and west-to-east) that you'll definitely want to take along for the ride; available from booksellers.

Historic Route 66 (www.historic66.com) Excellent website, with turn-by-turn directions for each state.

Route 66: EZ66 Guide for Travelers By Jerry McClanahan; earns high marks for its glossy easy-to-follow maps.

Route 66: The Mother Road This book by Michael Wallis is a fascinating look at the history and lore of the great road with old photographs bringing it all to life.

Pacific Coast Highway

The classic West Coast journey through California, Oregon and Washington takes in cosmopolitan cities, surf towns and charming coastal enclaves ripe for exploration. For many travelers, the real appeal of the Pacific Coast Hwy (PCH) is the magnificent scenery – wild and remote beaches, cliff-top views overlooking crashing waves, rolling hills and lush forests (redwoods, eucalyptus trees) – that sometimes lies just beyond a city's outskirts.

Why Go?

The PCH is an epic adventure for water babies, surfers, kayakers, scuba divers and every other kind of outdoor enthusiast, including landlubbers. Or if you're a more laid-back road-tripper, who just dreams of cruising alongside the ocean in a cherry-red convertible, drifting from sunrise to sunset, the insanely scenic PCH can deliver that, too.

The PCH is a road trip for lovers, nomadic ramblers, bohemians, beatniks and curiosity seekers keen to search out every nook and cranny of forgotten beachside hamlets and pastoral farm towns along the way.

The Route

The PCH is one of several coastal highways, including Hwy 101, stretching nearly 2000 miles from Tijuana, Mexico, to British Columbia, Canada. The route connects the dots between some of the West Coast's most striking cities, starting from surf-style San Diego, through hedonistic Los Angeles and offbeat San Francisco in California, then moving north to equally alternative-minded and arty Seattle, WA.

When the urban streets start to make you feel claustrophobic, just head out back on the open road and hit the coast again, heading north or south. The direction doesn't really matter – the views and hidden places you find along the way make for rewarding exploring.

You could bypass metro areas and just stick to the places in between, like the almost too-perfect beaches of California's Orange County ('the OC') and Santa Barbara (the 'American Riviera'); wacky Santa Cruz, a university town and surfers' paradise; redwood forests along the Big Sur coast and north of Mendocino; the sand dunes, seaside resorts and fishing villages of coastal Oregon; and finally, the wild lands of Washington's Olympic Peninsula, with its primeval rainforest, and bucolic San Juan Islands, served by coastal ferries.

When to Go

There's no very bad time of year to drive the PCH, although northern climes will be rainier and snowier during winter. Peak travel season is June through August, which isn't always the best time to see the road – as thick fog blankets many stretches of the coast during early summer (locals call it 'June Gloom'). The shoulder seasons before Memorial Day (ie April and May) and after Labor Day (ie September and October) can be ideal, with sunny days, crisply cool nights and fewer crowds.

Blue Ridge Parkway

Snaking for some 469 miles through the southern Appalachian Mountains, the Blue Ridge Pkwy is the land of great hiking and wildlife-watching, old-fashioned music and captivating mountainous scenery – all of which make for a memorable and easily accessible road trip.

Construction on the parkway began in 1935 under President Franklin D Roosevelt and it was one of the great New Deal projects that helped put people back to work. It was a huge effort that took over 52 years to complete, with the final section laid in 1987.

Why Go?

Watch the sunset over this wilderness of forest, mountain and tranquil streams in blissful silence; you might feel like you've gone back a few centuries. Although it skirts dozens of towns and a few metropolitan areas, the Blue Ridge Pkwy feels far removed from modern-day America. Here, rustic log cabins with rocking chairs on the front porch still dot the rolling hillsides, while signs for folk-art shops and

BEFORE YOU HIT THE ROAD

A few things to remember to ensure your road trip is as happy-go-lucky as possible:

- Join an automobile club that provides members with 24-hour emergency roadside assistance and discounts on lodging and attractions; some international clubs have reciprocal agreements with US automobile associations, so check first and bring your member card from home.
- Check the spare tire, tool kit (eg jack, jumper cables, ice scraper, tire pressure gauge) and emergency equipment (eg flashers) in your car; if you're renting a vehicle and these essential safety items are not provided, consider buying them.
- Bring good maps, especially if you're touring off-road or away from highways; don't rely on a GPS unit – they can malfunction, and in remote areas such as deep canyons or thick forests they may not even work.
- Always carry your driver's license and proof of insurance.
- If you're an international traveler, review the USA's road rules and common road hazards.
- Fill up the tank often, because gas stations can be few and far between on the USA's scenic byways.

Blue Ridge Parkway

live bluegrass music joints entice travelers onto side roads. History seems to permeate the air of these rolling backwoods – once home to Cherokee tribal people and later early colonial homesteads and Civil War battlefields.

There are great places to sleep and eat. Early 20th-century mountain and lakeside resorts still welcome families like old friends, while log-cabin diners dish up heaping piles of buckwheat pancakes with blackberry preserves and a side of country ham.

When you need to work off all that good Southern cooking, over 100 hiking trails can be accessed along the Blue Ridge Pkwy, from gentle nature walks and easily summited peaks to rough-and-ready tramps along the legendary Appalachian Trail. Or clamber on a horse and ride off into the refreshingly shady forests. Then go canoeing, kayaking or inner-tubing along rushing rivers, or dangle a fishing line over the side of a rowboat on petite lakes. And who says you even have to drive? The parkway makes an epic trip for long-distance cyclists, too.

The Route

This rolling, scenic byway still connects Virginia's Shenandoah National Park with Great Smoky Mountains National Park, straddling the North Carolina–Tennessee border. Towns include Boone and Asheville in North Carolina, and Galax and Roanoke in Virginia, with Charlottesville, VA, also within a short drive of the park. Cities within range of the parkway are Washington, DC (140 miles) and Richmond, VA (95 miles).

Detour: Skyline Drive

If you want to extend your journey through this scenic region, you can do so by hooking up with Skyline Dr. The northern terminus of the Blue Ridge Pkwy meets up with this 105-mile road (which continues northeast) around Rockfish Gap.

Travel along the road is slow (speed limit 35mph), but that forces you to take in the amazing scenery (wildflowers on the hillsides in spring, blazing colors in autumn and gorgeous blue skies in summer). Shenandoah National Park surrounds Skyline Dr, and has an excellent range of hikes, some of which scramble up mountain peaks and offer panoramic views. There are campgrounds in the park as well as nicely set lodges – all of which add up to worthwhile reasons not to rush through the area. Nearby attractions include the lively mountain town of Staunton (with its Shakespearean theater and farm-to-table restaurants), and an elaborate cave system at Luray Caverns.

OTHER GREAT ROAD TRIPS

ROUTE	STATE(S)	START/END	SIGHTS & ACTIVITIES	BEST TIME
Rte 28	NY	Stony Hollow/Arkville	Catskills mountains, lakes, rivers, hiking, leaf-peeping, tubing	May-Sep
Old Kings Hwy	MA	Sagamore/Provincetown	historic districts, period homes, coastal scenery	Apr-Oct
Natchez Trace Hwy	AL/MS/TN	Nashville/Natchezs	'Old South' history, archaeological sites, scenic waterways, cycling, camping, hiking,	Mar-Nov
Beartooth Hwy	MT	Red Lodge/Yellowstone	wildflowers, mountains, alpine scenery, camping	Jun-Sep
Alpine Loop Backcountry Byway	CO	Ouray/Lake City	mountains, views, valleys, abandoned mines	Jun-Sep
Maui's Rd to Hana	HI	Paia/Hana	jungle waterfalls, beaches, hiking, swimming, surfing	year-round
Great River Road	IA	Effigy Mounds National Monument/Keokuk	scenic views, riverside beauty, little-visited towns & villages	May-Sep
Hwy 61	MN	Duluth/Canadian Border	state parks, waterfalls, quaint towns, hiking	May-Sep
Hwy 2	NE	I-80/Alliance	grass-covered sand dunes, open vistas	May-Sep
El Camino Real	TX	Lajitas/Presidio	vast desert & mountain landscapes, hot springs, hiking, horseback riding	Feb-Apr & Oct-Nov
Sawtooth Scenic Byway	ID	Ketchum/Stanley	jagged mountains, verdant forests, backpacking, hiking, wildlife-watching	May-Sep
Turquoise Trail	NM	Albuquerque/Santa Fe	mining towns, quirky museums & folk art, cycling, hiking	Mar-May & Sep-Nov
US 50	NV	Fernley/Baker	'Loneliest Road in America,' epic wilderness, cycling, hiking, spelunking	May-Sep
Historic Columbia River Hwy	OR	Portland/Portland	scenery, waterfalls, wildflowers, cycling, hiking	Apr-Sep
Monument Valley	UT	Monument Valley	iconic buttes, movie-set locations, 4WD tours, horseback riding	year-round
VT 100	VT	Stamford/Newport	rolling pastures, green mountains, hiking, skiing	Jun-Sep
Kancamagus Hwy	NH	Conway/Lincoln	craggy mountains, streams & waterfalls, camping, hiking, swimming	May-Sep

One caveat: you will have to pay to travel along Skyline Dr ($10 for a seven-day pass in winter, $15 in summer). This is not a toll, but rather an admission charge for visiting Shenandoah National Park. Expect heavy traffic on weekends.

When to Go

Keep in mind that the weather can vary greatly, depending on your elevation. While mountain peaks are snowed in during winter, the valleys can still be invitingly warm. Most visitor services along the parkway are only open from April through October. May is best for wildflowers, although most people come for leaf-peeping during autumn. Spring and autumn are good times for bird-watching, with nearly 160 species having been spotted in the skies over the parkway. Expect big crowds if you go during the summer or early autumn.

Resources

Blue Ridge Parkway (www.blueridgeparkway.org) Maps, activities and places to stay along the way. You can also download the free *Blue Ridge Parkway Travel Planner.*

Hiking the Blue Ridge Parkway By Randy Johnson; has in-depth trail descriptions, topographic trail maps and other essential info for hikes both short and long (including overnight treks).

Recreation.gov (www.recreation.gov) You can reserve some campsites through this site.

Skyline Drive (www.visitskylinedrive.org) Lodging, hiking, wildlife and more: the complete overview of the national park surrounding this picturesque drive.

Great River Road

Established in the late 1930s, the Great River Road is an epic journey from the Mississippi's headwaters in the northern lakes of Minnesota, floating downstream all the way to the river's mouth on the Gulf of Mexico near New Orleans. For a look at America across cultural divides – north-south, urban-rural, Baptist-bohemian – this is the road trip to make.

Why Go?

You'll be awed by the sweeping scenery as you meander alongside North America's second-longest river, from the rolling plains of Iowa down to the sunbaked cotton fields of the Mississippi Delta. Limestone cliffs, dense forests, flower-filled meadows and steamy swamps are all part of the backdrop – along with smokestacks, riverboat casinos and urban sprawl: this is the good, the bad and the ugly of life on the Mississippi. The portrait isn't complete without mentioning the great music, lip-smacking food and down-home welcome at towns well off the beaten path on this waterfront itinerary.

Small towns provide a glimpse into American culture: there's Hibbing, MN, where folk rocker Bob Dylan grew up; Brainerd, MN, as seen in the Coen Brothers' film *Fargo;* Spring Green, WI, where architect Frank Lloyd Wright cut his teeth; pastoral Hannibal, MO, boyhood home of Mark Twain; and Metropolis, IL, where you'll find Superman's quick-change phone booth.

The southern section of this route traces American musical history, from rock and roll in St Louis to Memphis blues and New Orleans jazz. And you won't go hungry either, with retro Midwestern diners, Southern barbecue joints and smokehouses, and Cajun taverns and dance halls in Louisiana.

The Route

The Great River Road is not really one road at all, but a collection of roads that follow the 2300-mile-long Mississippi River, and takes travelers through 10 different states. Major urban areas that provide easy access to the road include New Orleans, Memphis, St Louis and Minneapolis.

When to Go

The best time to travel is from May to October, when the weather is warmest. Avoid going in the winter (or else stick to the deep south) when you'll have to contend with snowstorms.

Resources

Mississippi River Travel (www.experiencemississippiriver.com) 'Ten states, one river' is the slogan for this official site, which is a great resource for history, outdoor recreation, live music and more.

Plan Your Trip
USA Outdoors

Towering redwoods, red-rock canyons, snow-covered peaks and a dramatic coastline of unrivaled beauty: the USA has no shortage of spectacular settings for a bit of adventure. No matter your weakness – hiking, cycling, kayaking, rafting, surfing, horseback riding, rock climbing – you'll find world-class places to commune with the great outdoors.

Best Outdoor Adventures

Best Wildlife-Watching

Bears in Glacier National Park, MT; elk, bison and gray wolves in Yellowstone National Park, WY; alligators, manatees and sea turtles in the Florida Everglades; whales and dolphins on Monterey Bay, CA.

Top Aquatic Activities

White-water rafting on the New River, WV; surfing perfect waves in Oahu, HI; diving and snorkeling off the Florida Keys; kayaking pristine Penobscot Bay, ME.

Best Multiday Adventures

Hiking the Appalachian Trail; mountain-biking Kokopelli's Trail, UT; climbing 13,770ft Grand Teton in Grand Teton National Park, WY; canoeing, portaging and camping in the vast Boundary Waters, MN.

Best Winter Activities

Downhill skiing in Vail, CO; snowboarding in Stowe, VT; cross-country skiing off Lake Placid, NY.

Hiking & Trekking

Fitness-focused Americans take great pride in their formidable network of trails – literally tens of thousands of miles – and there's no better way to experience the countryside up close and at your own pace.

The wilderness is amazingly accessible, making for easy exploration. National parks are ideal for short and long hikes, and if you're hankering for nights in the wilderness beneath star-filled skies, plan on securing a backcountry permit in advance, especially in places like the Grand Canyon – spaces are limited, particularly during summer.

Beyond the parks, you'll find troves of trails in every state. There's no limit to the places you can explore, from sun-blasted hoodoos and red spires in Arizona's Chiricahua Mountains to dripping trees and mossy nooks in Washington's Hoh River Rainforest; from dogwood-choked Wild Azalea Trail in Louisiana to the tropical paradise of Kaua'i's Na Pali Coast. Almost anywhere you go, great hiking and backpacking is within easy striking distance. All you need is a sturdy pair of shoes (sneakers or hiking boots) and a water bottle.

Hiking Resources

➡ **Survive Outdoors** (www.surviveoutdoors.com) Dispenses safety and first-aid tips, plus helpful photos of dangerous critters.

TOP HIKING TRAILS IN THE USA

Ask 10 people for their top trail recommendations and it's possible that no two answers will be alike. The country is varied and distances enormous, so there's little consensus. That said, you can't go wrong with the following all-star sampler.

➡ **Appalachian Trail** (www.appalachiantrail.org) Completed in 1937, the country's longest footpath is more than 2100 miles, crossing six national parks, traversing eight national forests and hitting 14 states from Georgia to Maine.

➡ **Pacific Crest Trail** (PCT; www.pcta.org) Follows the spines of the Cascades and Sierra Nevada, traipsing 2650 miles from Canada to Mexico, passing through six of North America's seven ecozones.

➡ **John Muir Trail in Yosemite National Park, CA** (http://johnmuirtrail.org) Find 222 miles of scenic bliss, from Yosemite Valley up to Mt Whitney.

➡ **Enchanted Valley Trail, Olympic National Park, WA** Magnificent mountain views, roaming wildlife and lush rainforests – all on a 13-mile out-and-back trail.

➡ **Great Northern Traverse, Glacier National Park, MT** A 58-mile haul that cuts through the heart of grizzly country and crosses the Continental Divide; check out the Lonely Planet *Banff, Jasper & Glacier National Parks* guide for more information.

➡ **Kalalau Trail, Na Pali Coast, Kaua'i, HI** Wild Hawaii at its finest – 11 miles of lush waterfalls, hidden beaches, verdant valleys and crashing surf.

➡ **Mount Katahdin, Baxter State Park, ME** A 9.5-mile hike over the 5267ft summit, with panoramic views of the park's 46 peaks.

➡ **South Kaibab/North Kaibab Trail, Grand Canyon, AZ** A multiday cross-canyon tramp down to the Colorado River and back up to the opposite rim.

➡ **South Rim, Big Bend National Park, TX** A 13-mile loop through the ruddy 7000ft Chisos Mountains, with views into Mexico.

➡ **Tahoe Rim Trail, Lake Tahoe, CA** (www.tahorimtrail.org) A 165-mile all-purpose trail that circumnavigates the lake from high above, affording glistening Sierra views.

➡ **Wilderness Survival** Gregory Davenport has written what is easily the best book on surviving nearly every contingency.

➡ **American Hiking Society** (www.americanhiking.org) Links to 'volunteer vacations' building trails.

➡ **Backpacker** (www.backpacker.com) Premier national magazine for backpackers, from novices to experts.

➡ **Rails-to-Trails Conservancy** (www.railstotrails.org) Converts abandoned railroad corridors into hiking and cycling trails; publishes free trail reviews at www.traillink.com.

Cycling

Cycling's popularity increases by the day, with numerous cities (including New York) adding more cycle lanes and becoming more bike-friendly, and a growing number of greenways dotting the countryside. You'll find die-hards in every town, and outfitters offering guided trips for all levels and durations. For the best advice on rides and rentals, stop by a local bike shop or do an internet search of the area you plan to visit.

Many states offer social multiday rides, such as **Ride the Rockies** (www.ridetherockies.com) in Colorado. For a modest fee, you can join the peloton on a scenic, well-supported route; your gear is ferried ahead to that night's camping spot. Other standout rides include Arizona's Mt Lemmon, a thigh-zinging 28-mile climb from the Sonoran Desert floor to the 9157ft summit, and Tennessee's Cherohala Skyway, 51 glorious miles of undulating road and Great Smoky Mountain views.

Top Cycling Towns

➡ **Portland, OR** One of America's most bike-friendly cities has a trove of great cycling routes.

➡ **San Francisco, CA** A pedal over the Golden Gate Bridge lands you in the stunningly beautiful, and stunningly hilly, Marin Headlands.

MAD FOR MOUNTAIN BIKING

Mountain-biking enthusiasts will find trail nirvana in Boulder, CO; Moab, UT; Bend, OR; Ketchum, ID; and Marin, CA, where Gary Fisher and Co bunny-hopped the sport forward by careening down the rocky flanks of Mt Tamalpais on home-rigged bikes. There are many other great destinations. For info on trails, tips and gear, check out **Bicycling magazine** (www.bicycling.com/mountainbike) or **IMBA** (www.imba.com/destinations).

➡ **Kokopelli's Trail, UT** One of the premier mountain-biking trails in the Southwest stretches 140 miles on mountainous terrain between Loma, CO, and Moab, UT. Other nearby options include the 206-mile, hut-to-hut ride between Telluride, CO, and Moab, UT, and the shorter but very challenging 38-mile ride from Aspen to Crested Butte – an equally stunning ride.

➡ **Maah Daah Hey Trail, ND** A 96-mile jaunt over rolling buttes along the Little Missouri River.

➡ **Sun Top Loop, WA** A 22-mile ride with challenging climbs that rewards with superb views of Mt Rainier and surrounding peaks on the western slopes of Washington's Cascade Mountains.

➡ **Flume Trail, CA** A moderately challenging trail with stunning views along Lake Tahoe. This 14-mile trail runs one way at 7000ft to 8000ft elevation, with about 4.5 miles of singletrack.

➡ **Finger Lakes Trail, Letchworth State Park, NY** A little-known treasure, 35 miles south of Rochester in upstate New York, featuring more than 20 miles of singletrack along the rim of the 'Grand Canyon of the East.'

➡ **McKenzie River Trail, Willamette National Forest, OR** (www.mckenzierivertrail.com) Twenty-two miles of blissful singletrack winding through deep forests and volcanic formations. The town of McKenzie is located about 50 miles east of Eugene.

➡ **Porcupine Rim, Moab, UT** A 30-mile loop from town, this venerable high-desert romp features stunning views and hairy downhills.

➡ **Madison, WI** More than 120 miles of cycle paths, taking in the city's pretty lakes, parks and university campus.

➡ **Boulder, CO** Outdoors-loving town with loads of great cycling paths, including the 16-mile Boulder Creek Trail.

➡ **Austin, TX** Indie-rock-loving town with nearly 200 miles of trails and great year-round weather.

➡ **Burlington, VT** Bike haven in the Northeast, with great rides, the best-known along Lake Champlain.

Surfing

Hawaii

Blessed is the state that started it all, where the best swells generally arrive between November and March.

➡ **Waikiki (South Shore of Oahu)** Hawaii's ancient kings rode waves on wooden boards well before 19th-century missionaries deemed the sport a godless activity. With warm water and gentle rolling waves, Waikiki is perfect for novices, offering long and sudsy rides.

➡ **Pipeline & Sunset Beach (North Shore of Oahu)** Home to the classic tubing wave, which form as deep-water swells break over reefs into shallows; these are expert-only spots but well worth an ogle.

West Coast/California

➡ **Huntington Beach, CA (aka Surf City, USA)** The quintessential surf capital, with perpetual sun and a 'perfect' break, particularly during winter when the winds are calm.

➡ **Black's Beach, San Diego, CA** This 2-mile sandy strip at the base of 300ft cliffs in La Jolla is known as one of the most powerful beach breaks in SoCal, thanks to an underwater canyon just offshore.

➡ **Oceanside Beach, Oceanside, CA** One of SoCal's prettiest beaches boasts one of the world's most consistent surf breaks come summer. It's a family-friendly spot.

➡ **Rincon, Santa Barbara, CA** Arguably one of the planet's top surfing spots; nearly every major surf champion on the globe has taken Rincon for a ride.

➡ **Steamer Lane & Pleasure Point, Santa Cruz, CA** There are 11 world-class breaks, including the point breaks over rock bottoms at these two sweet spots.

➡ **Swami's, Encinitas, CA** Located below Seacliff Roadside Park, this popular surfing beach has multiple breaks guaranteeing you some fantastic waves.

East Coast

The Atlantic seaboard states harbor some terrific and unexpected surfing spots – especially if you're after more moderate swells. You'll find the warmest waters off Florida's Gulf Coast.

➡ **Cocoa Beach, Melbourne Beach, FL** Small crowds and mellow waves make it a paradise for beginners and longboarders. Just south is the Inlet, known for consistent surf and crowds to match.

➡ **Reef Rd, Palm Beach, FL** This stellar spot features exposed beach and reef breaks with consistent surf, especially at low tide; winter is best.

➡ **Cape Hatteras Lighthouse, NC** This very popular area has several quality spots and infinitely rideable breaks that gracefully handle swells of all sizes and winds from any direction.

➡ **Long Island, Montauk, NY** More than a dozen surfing areas dot the length of Long Island from Montauk's oft-packed Ditch Plains to Nassau County's Long Beach, with its 3-mile stretch of curling waves.

➡ **Casino Pier, Seaside Heights, NJ** Largely restored after Hurricane Sandy in 2012, this area is one of the best pier breaks in New Jersey. It's packed with locals who are glad to have it back.

➡ **Point Judith, Narragansett, RI** Rhode Island has premier surfing, with 40 miles of coastline and more than 30 surf spots, including this rocky point break offering long rollers as well as hollow barrels. Not for beginners.

➡ **Coast Guard Beach, Eastham, MA** Part of the Cape Cod National Seashore, this family-friendly beach is known for its consistent shortboard/longboard swell all summer long.

White-Water Rafting

East of the Mississippi, West Virginia has an arsenal of legendary white water. First, there's the New River Gorge National River, which, despite its name, is one of the oldest rivers in the world. Slicing from North Carolina into West Virginia, it cuts a deep gorge, known as the Grand Canyon of the East, producing frothy rapids in its wake. Then there's the Gauley, arguably among the world's finest white water. Revered for its ultrasteep and turbulent chutes, this venerable Appalachian river is a watery roller coaster, dropping more than 668ft and churning up 100-plus rapids in a mere 28 miles. Six more rivers, all in the same neighborhood, offer training grounds for less-experienced river rats. North Carolina has two choice places for paddlers: the US National Whitewater Center outside Charlotte, and the Nantahela Outdoor Center in Bryson City.

Out west there's no shortage of scenic and spectacular rafting, from Utah's Cataract Canyon, a thrilling romp through the red rocks of Canyonlands National Park, to the Rio Grande in Texas, a lazy run through limestone canyons. The North Fork of the Owyhee – which snakes from the high plateau of southwest Oregon to the rangelands of Idaho – is rightfully popular and features towering hoodoos. In California, both the Tuolumne and American Rivers surge with moderate-to-extreme rapids, while in Idaho the Middle Fork of the Salmon River has it all: abundant wildlife, thrilling rapids, a rich homesteader history, waterfalls and hot springs. If you're organized enough to plan a few years in advance, book a spot on the Colorado River, the quintessential river trip. And if you're not after white-knuckle rapids, fret not – many rivers have sections suitable for peaceful float trips or inner-tube drifts that you can traverse with a cold beer in hand.

Kayaking & Canoeing

For exploring flat water (no rapids or surf), opt for a kayak or canoe. While kayaks are seaworthy, they are not always suited for carrying bulky gear. For big lakes and the seacoast (including the San Juan Islands), use a sea kayak. For month-long wilderness trips – including the 12,000 miles of watery routes in Minnesota's Boundary Waters or Alabama's Bartram Canoe Trail, with 300,000 acres of marshy delta bayous, lakes and rivers – use a canoe.

You can kayak or canoe almost anywhere in the USA. Rentals and instruction are yours for the asking, from Wisconsin's Apostle Islands National Seashore and Utah's celebrated Green River to Hawaii's Na Pali Coast. Hire kayaks in Maine's Penobscot Bay to poke around the briny waters and spruce-fringed islets, or join a full-moon paddle in Sausalito's Richardson Bay, CA.

Skiing & Winter Sports

You can hit the slopes in 40 states, making for tremendous variety in terrain and ski-town vibe. Colorado has some of the best skiing in the nation, though California, Vermont and Utah are also top-notch destinations. Ski season typically runs from mid-December to April, though some resorts run longer. In summer, many resorts are great for mountain biking and hiking, courtesy of chairlifts. Ski packages (including airfare, hotel and lift tickets) are easy to find through resorts, travel agencies and online travel booking sites and can be a good deal.

Wherever you ski, though, it won't come cheap. Find the best deals by going midweek, purchasing multiday tickets, heading to lesser-known 'sibling' resorts (like Alpine Meadows near Lake Tahoe) or checking out mountains that cater to locals, including Vermont's Mad River Glen, Santa Fe Ski Area and Colorado's Wolf Grade.

Top Ski & Snowboard Resorts

Vermont's first-rate Stowe draws seasoned souls – freeze your tail off on the lifts, but thaw out nicely après-ski in timbered bars with local brews. Find more snow, altitude and attitude out west at Vail, CO, Squaw Valley, CA, and high-glitz Aspen, CO. For an unfussy scene and steep vertical chutes, try Alta, UT, Telluride, CO, Jackson, WY, and Taos, NM. In Alaska, slopes slice through spectacular terrain outside Juneau, Anchorage and Fairbanks. Mt Aurora SkiLand has the most northerly chairlift in North America and, from spring to summer, the shimmering green-blue aurora borealis.

Rock Climbing

Scads of climbers flock to Joshua Tree National Park, an otherworldly shrine in southern California's sun-scorched desert. There, amid craggy monoliths and the country's oldest trees, they make the pilgrimage on more than 8000 routes, tackling sheer verticals, sharp edges and bountiful cracks. A top-notch climbing school offers classes for all levels. In Zion National Park, UT, multiday canyoneering classes teach the fine art of going *down:* rappelling off sheer sandstone cliffs into glorious, red-rock canyons filled with trees. Some of the sportier pitches are made in dry suits, down the flanks of roaring waterfalls into ice-cold pools. Other great spots abound.

➡ **Grand Teton National Park, WY** A great spot for climbers of all levels. Beginners can take basic climbing courses; the more experienced can join two-day expeditions up to the top of Grand Teton itself: a 13,770ft peak with majestic views.

➡ **City of Rocks National Reserve, ID** Home to more than 500 routes up wind-scoured granite and pinnacles 60 stories tall.

➡ **Yosemite National Park, CA** A hallowed shrine for rock climbers, this park offers superb climbing courses (p1011) for first timers as well as for those craving a night in a hammock 1000ft above terra firma.

➡ **Bishop, CA** South of the Yosemite National Park and favored by many top climbers, this sleepy town in the Eastern Sierra is the gateway to excellent climbing in nearby Owens River Gorge and Buttermilk Hills.

➡ **Red Rock Canyon, NV** Ten miles west of Las Vegas is some of the world's finest sandstone climbing.

➡ **Enchanted Rock State Natural Area, TX** Located 70 miles west of Austin, this national park with its huge pink granite dome has hundreds of routes and stellar views of the Texas Hill Country.

➡ **Rocky Mountain National Park, CO** Offers alpine climbing near Boulder.

➡ **Flatirons, CO** Near Boulder, the Flatirons have fine multipitch ascents.

➡ **Chatanooga, TN** This world-class climbing destination has many nearby sites, including the Tennessee Wall, with over 400 established routes.

➡ **Red River Gorge, KY** With over 100 cliffs and some 2000 different routes, this is a climber's paradise – all the more so given its location inside lush forested parkland.

➡ **Shawangunk Ridge, NY** Located within a two-hour drive north of NYC, this ridge stretches some 50 miles, and the 'Gunks' are where many East Coast climbers tied their first billets.

➡ **Hueco Tanks, TX** From October to early April, Hueco Tanks ranks among the world's top rock-climbing destinations, when other prime climbs become inaccessible (although in summer, the desert sun generally makes the rocks too hot to handle).

Climbing & Canyoneering Resources

➡ **American Canyoneering Association** (www.canyoneering.net) An online canyons database and links to courses, local climbing groups and more.

➡ **Climbing** (www.climbing.com) Cutting-edge rock-climbing news and information since 1970.

➡ **SuperTopo** (www.supertopo.com) One-stop shop for rock-climbing guidebooks, free topo maps and route descriptions.

Scuba Diving & Snorkeling

The most exotic underwater destination in the USA is Hawaii. There, in shimmering aquamarine waters that stay warm year-round, you'll be treated to a psychedelic display of surreal colors and shapes. Swim alongside sea turtles, octopuses and fiesta-colored parrot-fish – not to mention lava tubes and black coral. Back on shore, cap off the reverie with *poke* made from just-caught 'ahi tuna.

The best diving is off the coast or between the islands, so liveaboards are the way to go for scuba buffs. From the green turtles and WWII wrecks off the shores of Oahu to the undersea lava sculptures near little Lana'i, the Aloha State offers endless underwater bliss – but plan ahead, as dive sites change with the seasons.

On the continental USA, Florida has the lion's share of great diving, with more than 1000 miles of coastline subdivided into 20 unique undersea areas. There are hundreds of sites and countless dive shops offering equipment and guided excursions. South of West Palm Beach, you'll find clear waters and fantastic year-round diving with ample reefs. In the Panhandle, or northern part of the state, you can scuba in the calm and balmy waters of the Gulf of Mexico; off Pensacola and Destin, there are fabulous wreck dives; and you can dive with manatees near Crystal River.

The Florida Keys, a curving string of 31 islets, are the crown jewels; expect a brilliant mix of marine habitats, North America's only living coral garden and the occasional shipwreck. Key Largo is home to the John Pennekamp Coral Reef State Park and more than 200 miles of underwater idyll.

There's terrific diving and snorkeling (and much warmer water) beyond the mangrove swamps of the Florida Keys, FL, boasting the world's third-largest coral system. Look for manatees off Islamorada or take an expedition to Dry Tortugas, where the expansive reef swarms with barracuda, sea turtles and a couple of hundred sunken ships.

Other Underwater Destinations

For the latest on diving destinations in the US and abroad, visit **Scuba Diving** (www.scubadiving.com), or check out the USA overview on **DT Mag** (www.dtmag.com/dive-usa/divingusa.html).

➡ **Hanauma Bay Nature Preserve, Oahu, HI** Despite the crowds, this is still one of the world's great spots for snorkeling, with more than 450 resident species of reef fish.

➡ **San Diego-La Jolla Underwater Park** Offers excellent shore-diving amid four different habitats in a 6000-acre reserve. There are two roofs and seven caves, and with 30ft visibility you have the chance to spot a wide range of sealife, including eels, Garibaldi and leopard sharks.

➡ **The Channel Islands, CA** Lying between Santa Barbara and Los Angeles, these harbor spiny lobsters, angel sharks and numerous dive sites best accessed by liveaboard charter.

HONE YOUR SKILLS (OR LEARN SOME NEW ONES)

Whether you're eager to catch a wave or dangle from a cliff, learn some new outdoor tricks in these high-thrill programs.

➡ **Chicks with Picks** (www.chickswithpicks.net) Based in Ridgway, CO, this group gives women's workshops across the country in mountaineering, climbing and ice-climbing.

➡ **Club Ed Surf Camp** (www.club-ed.com) Learn to ride the waves from Manresa Beach to Santa Cruz, CA, with field trips to the surfing museum and surfboard companies included.

➡ **Craftsbury Outdoor Center** (www.craftsbury.com) Come here for sculling, cross-country skiing and running amid the forests and hills of Vermont.

➡ **Joshua Tree Rock Climbing School** (www.joshuatreerockclimbing.com) Local guides lead beginners to experts on 7000 different climbs in Joshua Tree National Park, CA.

➡ **LL Bean Discovery Schools** (www.llbean.com) The famous Maine retailer offers instruction in kayaking, snowshoeing, cross-country skiing, wilderness first-aid, fly-fishing and more.

➡ **Nantahala Outdoor Center** (www.noc.com) Learn to paddle like a pro at this North Carolina–based school, which offers world-class instruction in canoeing and kayaking in the Great Smoky Mountains.

➡ **Otter Bar Lodge Kayak School** (www.otterbar.com) Top-notch white-water kayaking instruction is complemented by saunas, hot tubs, salmon dinners and a woodsy lodge on California's north coast.

➡ **Steep & Deep Ski Camp** (www.jacksonhole.com/steep-ski-camp.html) Finesse skiing extreme terrain (and snagging first tracks), then wind down over dinner parties. You can also ski with Olympian Tommy Moe.

➡ **Jade Cove, CA** About 10 miles south of Lucia on Hwy 1, this aptly named spot has the world's only underwater concentration of jade, making for an unforgettable dive.

➡ **Cape Hatteras National Seashore, NC** Along the northern coast of North Carolina, divers can explore historical wrecks from the Civil War (and encounter tiger sand sharks); there are also numerous options for dive charters within the Outer Banks and the Cape Lookout areas.

➡ **Great Lakes, MI** The USA's most unexpected dive spot? Michigan's Lakes Superior and Huron, with thousands of shipwrecks lying strewn on the sandy bottoms – just don't expect to see any angelfish!

Horseback Riding

Cowboy wannabes will be happy to learn that horseback riding of every style, from Western to bareback, is available across the USA. Out west, you'll find truly memorable experiences – everything from week-long expeditions through the canyons of southern Utah and cattle wrangling in Wyoming, to pony rides along the Oregon coast. Finding horses is easy; rental stables and riding schools are located around and in many of the national parks. Experienced equestrians can explore alone or in the company of guides familiar with local flora, fauna and history. Half- and full-day group trail rides are popular and plentiful.

California is terrific for riding, with fog-swept trails leading along the cliffs of Point Reyes National Seashore, longer excursions through the high-altitude lakes of the Ansel Adams Wilderness, and multiday pack trips in Yosemite and Kings Canyon. Utah's Capitol Reef and Canyonlands also provide spectacular four-hoofed outings, as do the mountains, arroyos and plains of Colorado, Arizona, New Mexico, Montana and Texas.

Dude ranches come in all varieties, from down-duvet luxurious to barn-duty authentic on working cattle ranches. They're found in most of the western states, and even some eastern ones (such as Tennessee and North Carolina). Real-life cowboys are included.

Plan Your Trip

Travel with Children

From coast to coast, you'll find superb attractions for all ages: bucket-and-spade fun at the beach, amusement parks, zoos, eye-popping aquariums and natural history exhibits, hands-on science museums, camping adventures, battlefields, hikes in wilderness reserves, leisurely bike rides through countryside, and plenty of other activities likely to wow young ones.

The USA for Kids

Traveling with children can bring a whole new dimension to the American experience. You may make deeper connections, as locals (especially those with their own children) brighten and coo and embrace your family like long-lost cousins. From the city to the country, most facilities are ready to accommodate a child's needs.

To find family-oriented sights and activities, accommodations, restaurants and entertainment, just look for the child-friendly icon 👪.

Dining with Children

The US restaurant industry seems built on family-style service: children are not just accepted almost everywhere, but usually are encouraged by special children's menus with smaller portions and lower prices. In some restaurants children under a certain age even eat for free. Restaurants usually provide high chairs and booster seats. Some restaurants may also offer children crayons and puzzles, and occasionally live performances by cartoon-like characters.

Restaurants without children's menus don't necessarily discourage kids, though higher-end restaurants might; however, even at the nicer places, if you show up

Best Regions for Kids

New York City

The Big Apple has many kid-friendly museums, plus carriage rides and row-boating in Central Park, cruises on the Hudson and theme restaurants in Times Square.

California

Get behind the movie magic at Universal Studios, hit the beaches then head south to Disneyland and the San Diego Zoo Safari Park. In Northern California, see redwoods and the Golden Gate Bridge.

Washington, DC

Washington has unrivaled allure for families with free museums, a panda-loving zoo and boundless green spaces. Nearby, Virginia's Williamsburg is a slice of 18th-century America with costumed interpreters and fanciful activities.

Florida

Orlando's Walt Disney World is well worth planning a vacation around. Then hit the beautiful beaches.

Colorado

Ski resorts go full throttle in summer with camps, mountain biking, slides and zip lines.

DISCOUNTS FOR CHILDREN

Child concessions often apply for tours, admission fees and transport, with some discounts as high as 50% off the adult rate. However, the definition of 'child' can vary from under 12 to under 16 years. Unlike in Europe, very few popular sights have discount rates for families; those that do will help you save a few dollars compared to buying individual tickets. Most sights give free admission to children under two years.

early enough (right on dinner-time opening hours, often 5pm or 6pm), you can usually eat without too much stress – and you'll likely be joined by other foodies with kids. You can ask if the kitchen will make a smaller order of a dish (also ask how much it will cost), or if they will split a normal-size main dish between two plates for the kids. Chinese, Mexican and Italian restaurants seem to be the best bet for finicky young eaters.

Farmers markets are growing in popularity in the USA, and every sizable town has at least one a week. This is a good place to assemble a first-rate picnic, sample local specialties and support independent growers in the process. After getting your stash, head to the nearest park or waterfront.

Accommodations

Motels and hotels typically have rooms with two beds, which are ideal for families. Some also have rollaway beds or cribs that can be brought into the room for an extra charge – but keep in mind these are usually Pack 'n' Plays (portable cots), which not all children sleep well in. Some hotels offer 'kids stay free' programs for children up to 12 or sometimes 18 years old. Be wary of B&Bs, as most don't allow children; inquire before reserving.

Babysitting

Resort hotels may have on-call babysitting services; otherwise, ask the front-desk staff or concierge to help you make arrangements. Always ask if babysitters are licenced and bonded (ie they are qualified and insured), what they charge per hour per child, whether there's a minimum fee, and if they charge extra for transportation or meals. Most tourist bureaus list local resources for childcare and recreation facilities, medical services and so on.

Necessities, Driving & Flying

Many public toilets have a baby-changing table (sometimes in men's toilets too), and gender-neutral 'family' facilities appear in airports.

Medical services and facilities in America are of a high standard, and items such as baby food, formula and disposable diapers (nappies) are widely available – including organic options – in supermarkets across the country.

Every car-rental agency should be able to provide an appropriate child seat, since these are required in every state, but you need to request it when booking and expect to pay around $13 more per day.

Domestic airlines don't charge for children under two years. Those aged two and up must have a seat, and discounts are unlikely. Rarely, some resorts (eg Disneyland) offer a 'kids fly free' promotion. Amtrak and other train operators run similar deals (with kids up to age 15 riding free) on various routes.

Children's Highlights

Outdoor Adventure

All national parks have Junior Ranger programs that include activity booklets and badges upon completion.

➡ **Florida Everglades, FL** (p485) Kayak, canoe or take guided walks.

➡ **Yellowstone National Park, WY** (p785) Watch powerful geysers, spy on wildlife and take magnificent hikes.

➡ **Grand Canyon National Park, AZ** (p845) Gaze across one of earth's great wonders.

➡ **Black Hills, South Dakota and Wyoming** (p673) State and national parks – like Mt Rushmore – are filled with kid-friendly natural sights and adventures; and the buffalo do indeed roam free.

➡ **New River Gorge National River, West Virginia** (p334) Go white-water rafting.

➡ **Zion National Park, UT** (p878) Wade in the Virgin River and hike to the Emerald Pools beneath the crimson canyon walls.

Theme Parks & Zoos

➡ **Bronx Wildlife Conservation Park, NY** (p99) One of the nation's biggest and best zoos is just a subway ride from Manhattan.

➡ **Walt Disney World, FL** (p514) With four action-packed parks spread across 20,000 acres, this is a place your children will long remember.

➡ **Disneyland, CA** (p932) Kids aged four and up appreciate the original Disneyland, while teenagers go nuts next door at **California Adventure**.

➡ **San Diego Zoo Safari Park, CA** (p945) A fantastic place to see creatures great and small, it has more than 4000 animals (880 species).

➡ **Six Flags** (www.sixflags.com) One of America's favourite amusement parks, with 16 locations across the country.

➡ **Cedar Point, Northern Ohio** (p566) Has some of the planet's most terrifying roller coasters, plus a mile-long beachfront, a waterpark and live entertainment.

Traveling in Time

➡ **Plimoth Plantation** (p201), **Williamsburg** (p316), **Yorktown** (p317) and **Jamestown** (p317) Don 18th-century garb and mingle with costumed interpreters in these history-rich settings.

➡ **Fort Mackinac, MI** (p589) Plug your ears as soldiers in 19th-century garb fire muskets and cannons.

➡ **Freedom Trail, Boston** (p187) Go on a walking tour with Ben Franklin (or at least his 21st-century lookalike).

➡ **Lincoln Presidential Library & Museum, IL** (p552) Fun, interactive galleries where you can learn about one of America's greatest presidents.

➡ **St Augustine, FL** (p498) Rattle along in a horse-drawn carriage through the historic streets.

Rainy-Day Activities

➡ **National Air & Space Museum, Washington, DC** (p265) Rockets, spacecraft, old-fashioned biplanes and ride simulators to inspire any budding aviator.

➡ **American Museum of Natural History, NYC** (p89) Kids of all ages will enjoy a massive planetarium, immense dinosaur skeletons and 30 million other artifacts.

➡ **City Museum, St Louis** (p641) There's a packed funhouse of unusual exhibits here, plus a Ferris wheel on the roof.

➡ **Port Discovery, Baltimore** (p297) Three stories of adventure and (cleverly disguised) learning, including an Egyptian tomb, farmers market, train, art studio and physics stations.

➡ **Pacific Science Center, Seattle** (p1033) Fascinating, hands-on exhibits, plus an IMAX theater, planetarium and laser shows.

➡ **Children's Museum of Indianapolis, IN** (p555) The world's largest kids museum with five floors of fun stuff (including dinosaur displays).

➡ **Montshire Museum of Science, Norwich, VT** (p232) Interactive science museum that kids love (despite the strong educational component!)

Planning

Weather and crowds are all-important considerations when planning a US family getaway. The peak travel season across the country is from June to August, when schools are out and the weather is warmest. Expect high prices and abundant crowds – meaning long lines at amusement and water parks, fully booked resort areas and heavy traffic on the roads; you'll need to reserve well in advance for popular destinations. The same holds true for winter resorts (in the Rockies, Tahoe and the Catskills) during their high season of January to March.

For all-around information and advice, check out Lonely Planet's *Travel with Children*. To get the kids excited, check out *Not for Parents: USA* (also by Lonely Planet).

Useful Websites

Baby's Away (www.babysaway.com) Rents cribs, high chairs, car seats, strollers and even toys at locations across the country.

Family Travel Files (www.thefamilytravelfiles.com) Ready-made vacation ideas, destination profiles and travel tips.

Kids.gov (www.kids.usa.gov) Eclectic, enormous national resource; download songs and activities, or even link to the CIA Kids' Page.

Travel Babees (www.travelbabees.com) A reputable baby-gear rental outfit, with locations nationwide.

Plan Your Trip

Eat & Drink Like a Local

Americans have rich variety in their cuisine, based on the bounty of the continent: drawing on the seafood of the North Atlantic, Gulf of Mexico and Pacific Ocean; the fertility of Midwest farmlands; and vast western ranchlands.

The Year in Food

In a country as large as the US, you'll find food festivals and local specialties all year long. For more details on food events, see p1140.

Spring (Mar–May)

One of the best times to hit local markets that sell bounty from farm and field (ramps, strawberries, rhubarb, spring lamb), plus Easter treats. Across the country major festivals showcase crawfish, barbecue, oysters and more.

Summer (Jun–Aug)

A great time for seafood feasting by the shore, outdoor barbecue and county fairs. Don't miss fresh berries, peaches, corn on the cob and much more.

Autumn (Sep–Nov)

Crisp days bring apple picking, pumpkin pies, harvest wine festivals and some major food-focused events, including Thanksgiving.

Winter (Dec–Feb)

Hearty stews, roasted late-harvest vegetables, plus decadent holiday treats are the order of the day. Get toasty by the fire, with a hot toddy or other warming drink in hand.

Food Experiences

Meals of a Lifetime

➡ **Alinea** (p542) You'll have to be very lucky to score a ticket to this pillar of molecular gastronomy in Chicago.

➡ **Black's Barbecue** (p703) Serves up some of America's best brisket, from an atmospheric location in Lockhart, Texas.

➡ **Lobster Dock** (p254) It's worth making a pilgrimage to Maine to sample fresh-caught succulent lobster from casual, waterside places like this one in Boothbay Harbor.

➡ **Crab Claw** (p300) Feasting on steamed crabs at a picnic table overlooking the Chesapeake.

➡ **Café Sole** (p495) Serves amazingly fresh seafood in Key West.

➡ **Rolf and Daughters** (p383) Serves superb new Italian cooking in a buzzing space in Nashville.

➡ **French Laundry** (p995) It may cost you a month's wages, but this northern California icon never fails to dazzle.

➡ **Salt** (p756) Local, seasonal, organic and delicious dishes in Boulder.

➡ **Andina** (p1058) New Peruvian cuisine with brilliantly creative tapas plates in Portland's Pearl District.

➡ **Grey Plume** (p677) In Omaha, works seasonal magic with the produce and meats of the region.

➡ **Eataly** (p112) Eat your way into a stupor on myriad Italian delicacies at this sprawling NYC food hall.

➡ **Water Table** (p116) A moveable feast that happens inside a former WWII patrol boat that sails from Brooklyn.

Cheap Treats

➡ **Food trucks** The variety of offerings is staggering in towns like Portland, San Francisco, LA and Austin.

➡ **Tacos** A handheld favorite all across the US. Some of the best are served off street carts and food trucks.

➡ **Green chili** A Rockies classic, best when served atop a burger.

➡ **Doughnuts** Not just for police officers, seemingly everyone loves doughnuts these days. Look for gourmet varieties (pistachio, hibiscus, lemon ginger).

➡ **Fried chicken** Famed spots in the South include Prince's Hot Chicken in Nashville (p384) and Willie Mae's in New Orleans (p451).

➡ **Frozen custard** Nothing else quite hits the spot on a hot day, especially if it's from Ted Drewes (p646) in St Louis.

➡ **Fried clams** A cheap and filling snack available all along the eastern seaboard.

➡ **Beignets** Fried dough topped with powdered sugar is a must-have when visiting New Orleans.

➡ **Half smokes** A bigger spicier version of the hot dog, this is a DC specialty.

Dare to Try

➡ **Bison short ribs** Sometimes spotted in the Rockies; Yellowstone is a reliable place to find them.

➡ **Alligator** A roadhouse special in some parts of the south. Try some at Joannie's Blue Crab Café (p488) in the Everglades.

➡ **Poke** A Hawaiian specialty of cubed raw fish cube (often 'ahi tuna); it's spectacularly good.

➡ **Foraged food** At The Curious Kumquat (p901) ingredients are foraged in the nearby Gila Mountains, including crayfish from streams and wild nuts and seeds.

➡ **Lobster ice cream** You'll never go back to strawberry after trying this popular crustacean flavor at Ben & Bill's Chocolate Emporium (p201) out on Cape Cod.

➡ **A steak** Not just any steak, but a 72oz steak for one served at Big Texan Steak Ranch (p732). If you eat it and all the sides in under an hour, it's free!

➡ **Triple bypass burger** At the Vortex (p408) in Atlanta you can try a stack of three half-pound burgers with 14 slices of American cheese, 10 bacon strips and three fried eggs served between grilled cheese sandwiches for buns.

➡ **Pork ear sandwich** Served with panache since the 1930s at the Big Apple Inn (p430) in Jackson, MS.

➡ **Dirty water dog** It takes a special appetite to crave a hot dog that's been sitting in murky water all day in a NYC food cart.

Local Specialties

NYC: Foodie Capital

They say that you could eat at a different restaurant every night of your life in New York City, and not exhaust the possibilities. Considering that there are more than 20,000 restaurants in the five boroughs, with scores of new ones opening each year, it's true. Owing to its huge immigrant population and an influx of over 50 million tourists annually, New York captures the title of America's greatest restaurant city, hands down. Its diverse neighborhoods serve up authentic Italian food and thin-crust pizza, all manner of Asian food, French haute cuisine and classic Jewish deli food, from bagels to piled-high pastrami on rye. More exotic cuisines are found here as well, from Ethiopian to Scandinavian.

HAPPY HOUR

Gastropubs, microbreweries that serve meals and even traditional restaurants with bar seating often host great-value happy hours. Sometime before the dinner rush (usually 3pm to 5pm or 4pm to 6pm), you can score great deals on fresh oysters, appetizers and other light fare. Add to this the drink specials (along the lines of half-priced cocktails), and you have the makings for a great start to the night.

Check out *Eater New York* (www.ny.eater.com), *New York* magazine (www.nymag.com) or *Time Out* (www.timeout.com/newyork) for the latest restaurant openings, reviews and insight into famed and up-and-coming chefs. Finally, don't let NYC's image as expensive get to you: you can eat well here without breaking the bank, especially if you limit your cocktail intake. There may be no free lunch in New York but, compared to other world cities, eating here can be a bargain.

New England: Clambakes & Lobster Boils

New England's claim to have the nation's best seafood is hard to beat, because the North Atlantic offers up clams, mussels, oysters and huge lobsters, along with shad, bluefish and cod. New Englanders love a good chowder (seafood stew) and a good clambake, an almost ritual meal where the shellfish are buried in a pit fire with corn, chicken, potatoes and sausages. Fried clam fritters and lobster rolls (lobster meat with mayonnaise served in a bread bun) are served throughout the region. There are excellent cheeses made in Vermont, cranberries (a Thanksgiving staple) harvested in Massachusetts and maple syrup tapped from New England's forests. Maine's coast is lined with lobster shacks; baked beans and brown bread are Boston specialties; and Rhode Islanders pour coffee syrup into milk and embrace traditional cornmeal johnnycakes.

Mid-Atlantic: Cheesesteaks & Crabcakes

From New York down through Maryland and Virginia, the mid-Atlantic states share a long coastline and a cornucopia of apple, pear and berry farms. New Jersey and New York's Long Island are famous for their spuds (potatoes). Chesapeake Bay's blue crabs are the finest anywhere and Virginia salt-cured 'country-style' hams are served with biscuits. In Philadelphia, you can gorge on 'Philly' cheesesteaks, made with thin sautéed beef and onions and melted cheese on a bun. And in Pennsylvania Dutch Country, stop by a farm restaurant for chicken pot pie, noodles and meatloaf-like scrapple.

Clambake

The South: BBQ, Biscuits & Gumbo

No region is prouder of its food culture than the South, which has a long history of mingling Anglo, French, African, Spanish and Native American foods in dishes such as slow-cooked barbecue, which has as many meaty and saucy variations as there are towns in the South. Southern fried chicken is crisp outside and moist inside. In Florida, dishes made with alligator, shrimp and conch incorporate hot chili peppers and tropical spices. Breakfasts are as big as can be, and treasured dessert recipes tend to produce big layer cakes or pies made with pecans, bananas and citrus. Light, fluffy hot biscuits are served well buttered, and grits (ground corn cooked to a porridge-like consistency) are a passion among Southerners, as are cool mint-julep cocktails.

Louisiana's legendary cuisine is influenced by colonial French and Spanish cultures, Afro Caribbean cooking and Choctaw traditions. Cajun food is found in the bayou country and marries native spices such as sassafras and chili peppers with provincial French cooking. Famous dishes include

Burger, fries and beer

gumbo, a roux-based stew of chicken and shellfish, or sausage and often okra; jambalaya, a rice-based dish with tomatoes, sausage and shrimp; and blackened catfish. Creole food is more urban, and centered in New Orleans, where dishes such as shrimp rémoulade, crabmeat ravigote, crawfish étouffée and beignets are ubiquitous.

Midwest: Burgers, Bacon & Beer

Midwesterners eat big and with plenty of gusto. Portions are huge – this is farm country, where people need sustenance to get their day's work done. So you might start off the day with eggs, bacon and toast; have a double cheeseburger and potato salad for lunch; and fork into steak and baked potatoes for dinner – all washed down with a cold brew, often one of the growing numbers of microbrews. Barbecue is very popular here, especially in Kansas City, St Louis and Chicago. Chicago is also an ethnically diverse culinary center, with some of the country's top restaurants. One of the best places to sample Midwestern foods is at a county fair, which offers everything from bratwurst to fried dough to grilled corn on the cob. Elsewhere at diners and family restaurants, you'll taste the varied influences of Eastern European, Scandinavian, Latino and Asian immigrants, especially in the cities.

The Southwest: Chili, Steak & Salsa

Two ethnic groups define Southwestern food culture: the Spanish and Mexicans, who controlled territories from Texas to California until well into the 19th century. While there is little actual Spanish food today, the Spanish brought cattle to Mexico, which the Mexicans adapted to their own corn-and-chili-based gastronomy to make tacos, tortillas, enchiladas, burritos, chimichangas and other dishes made of corn or flour pancakes filled with everything from chopped meat and poultry to beans. Don't leave New Mexico without trying a bowl of spicy green chili stew. Steaks and barbecue are always favorites on Southwestern menus, and beer is the drink of choice for dinner and a night out. Don't miss the forearm-sized burritos in San Francisco's Mission District and fish tacos in San Diego.

TOP VEGETARIAN RESTAURANTS

In many American cities, you'll find a wealth of restaurants that cater to vegetarians and vegans. Once you head out into rural areas and away from the coast, the options are slimmer. We note eateries that are cater well to vegetarians or vegans by using the symbol. To find more vegetarian and vegan restaurants, browse the online directory at www.happycow.net. Here are a few of our go-to faves across the country:

- **Greens** (p983), San Francisco, CA
- **Native Foods Cafe** (p541), Chicago, IL
- **Clover Food Lab** (p194), Boston, MA
- **Green Elephant** (p252), Portland, ME
- **Moosewood Restaurant** (p173), Ithaca, NY
- **Bouldin Creek Coffee House** (p698), Austin, TX
- **Sweet Melissa's** (p781), Laramie, WY
- **Zenith** (p173), Pittsburgh, PA
- **High Noon Cafe** (p431), Jackson, MS
- **Angelica Kitchen** (p110), NYC

California: Farm-to-Table Restaurants & Taquerias

Owing to its vastness and variety of microclimates, California is truly America's cornucopia for fruits and vegetables, and a gateway to myriad Asian markets. The state's natural resources are overwhelming, with wild salmon, Dungeness crab and oysters from the ocean; robust produce year-round; and artisanal products such as cheese, bread, olive oil, wine and chocolate. Starting in the 1970s and '80s, star chefs such as Alice Waters and Wolfgang Puck pioneered 'California cuisine' by incorporating the best local ingredients into simple, yet delectable, preparations. The influx of Asian immigrants, especially after the Vietnam War, enriched the state's urban food cultures with Chinatowns, Koreatowns and Japantowns, along with huge enclaves of Mexican Americans who maintain their own culinary traditions across the state. Global fusion restaurants are another hallmark of California's cuisine.

Pacific Northwest: Salmon & Cafe Culture

The cuisine of the Pacific Northwest region draws on the traditions of the local tribes of Native Americans, whose diets traditionally centered on game, seafood – especially salmon – and foraged mushrooms, fruits and berries. Seattle spawned the modern international coffeehouse craze with Starbucks – though these days Portland gets more attention for its excellent coffee scene, with some of the country's best roasters.

Hawaii: Island Style

In the middle of the Pacific Ocean, Hawaii is rooted in a Polynesian food culture that takes full advantage of locally caught fish such as mahimahi, 'opakapaka, *'ono* and 'ahi. Traditional luau celebrations include cooking kalua pig in an underground pit layered with hot stones and ti leaves. Hawaii's contemporary cuisine incorporates fresh, island-grown produce and borrows liberally from the islands' many Asian and European immigrant groups. This also happens to be the only state to grow coffee commercially; 100% Kona beans from the Big Island have the most gourmet cachet.

Regions at a Glance

Deciding where to go can be daunting in the massive USA. The East Coast has big-city allure, picturesque towns (especially New England), historic attractions, bountiful feasts (Maine lobsters, Maryland crabs) and outdoor beauty (beaches, islands, mountains).

The West Coast has memorable urban exploring (San Francisco, LA, Seattle), stunning scenery (dramatic coastline, redwoods, high Sierra) and feasting aplenty (wineries, award-winning restaurants).

In between, there's much more: soulful music and belly-pleasing fare in the South; big skies and Native American culture in the Rockies, Southwest and Great Plains; live music and barbecue in Texas; and off-the-beaten path adventures in the Great Lakes.

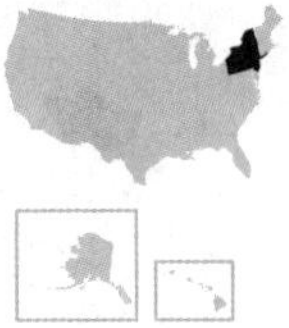

New York, New Jersey & Pennsylvania

Arts
History
Outdoors

Culture Spot

Home to the Met, MOMA and Broadway – and that's just NYC. Buffalo, Philadelphia and Pittsburgh also have a share of world-renowned cultural institutions.

A Living Past

From preserved Gilded Age mansions in the Hudson Valley to Independence National Historic Park in Philadelphia and sites dedicated to formative moments in the nation's founding, the region gives an interactive education.

Wild Outdoors

The outdoors lurks beyond the city's gaze, with hiking in the Adirondack wilderness and Catskills, rafting down the Delaware River and Atlantic Ocean, and frolics along the Jersey Shore and the Hamptons.

p68

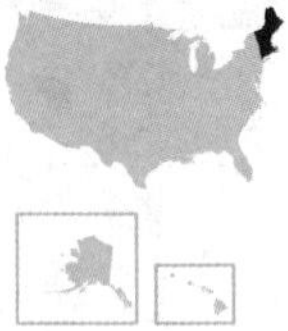

New England

Seafood
History
Beaches

Land of Lobsters

New England is justifiably famous for its fresh seafood. The coast is peppered with seaside eateries where you can feast on fresh oysters, lobster and fish as you watch the day-boats haul in their catch.

Legends of the Past

From the Pilgrims landing in Plymouth and the witch hysteria in Salem to Paul Revere's revolutionary ride, New England has shaped American history.

Fall Foliage

The brilliance of fall in these parts is legendary. Changing leaves put on a fiery display all around New England, from the Litchfield Hills in Connecticut all the way up to the White Mountains in New Hampshire and Maine.

p176

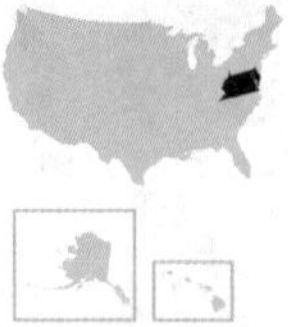

Washington, DC & the Capital Region

Arts
History
Food

Top-Notch Arts

Washington has a superb collection of museums and galleries. You'll also find down-home mountain music on Virginia's Crooked Road, famous theaters and edgy art in Baltimore.

Early America

For historical lore, Jamestown, Williamsburg and Yorktown offer windows into Colonial America, while Civil War battlefields litter the Virginia countryside. There are fascinating presidential estates such as Mount Vernon and Monticello.

Culinary Feasts

Maryland blue crabs, oysters and seafood platters; international restaurants in DC; and farm-to-table dining rooms in Baltimore, Charlottesville, Staunton and Rehoboth.

p260

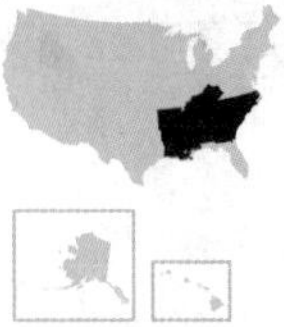

The South

Food
Music
Charm

Southern Cookin'

From Memphis BBQ to Mississippi soul food to the Cajun-Creole smorgasbord in Louisiana, the South is a diverse and magnificent place to eat.

Country, Jazz & Blues

Nowhere on earth has a soundtrack as influential as the South. Head to music meccas for the authentic experience: country in Nashville, blues in Memphis and big-band jazz in New Orleans.

Southern Belles

Picture-book towns such as Charleston and Savannah, among others, have captivated visitors with their historic tree-lined streets, antebellum architecture and down-home welcome.

p336

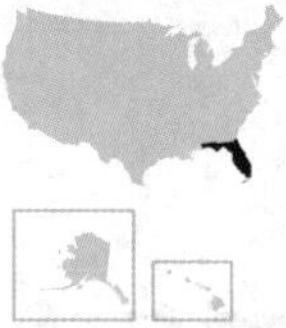

Florida

Fun
Wildlife
Beaches

Good Times

Florida has a complicated soul: it's the home of Miami's art-deco district and Little Havana, plus historical attractions in St Augustine, theme parks in Orlando, and museums and island heritage in Key West.

Whales, Birds & Gators

Immerse yourself in aquatic life on a snorkeling or diving trip. For bigger beasts, head off on a whale-watching cruise, or spy alligators – along with egrets, eagles, manatees and other wildlife – on the Everglades.

Head in the Sand

You'll find an array of sandy shores from steamy South Beach to upscale Palm Beach, seashell-lined Sanibel and Captiva, and panhandle rowdiness in Pensacola.

p464

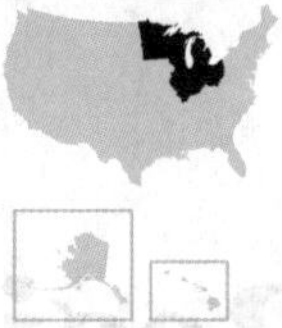

Great Lakes

Food
Music
Attractions

Heartland Cuisine

From James Beard Award–winning restaurants in Chicago and Minneapolis to fresh-from-the-dairy milkshakes, the Midwest's farms, orchards and breweries satisfy the palate.

Rock & Roll

Home to the Rock and Roll Hall of Fame, blowout fests like Lollapalooza and thrashing clubs in all the cities, the Midwest rocks, baby.

Quirky Sights

A big ball of twine, a mustard museum, a cow-doo throwing contest: the quirks rise from the Midwest's backyards and back roads, wherever there are folks with a passion, imagination and maybe a little too much time on their hands.

p522

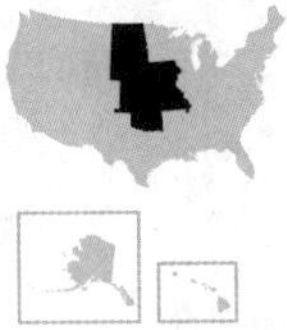

Great Plains

Scenery
Geology
Nightlife

The Open Road

Beneath big open skies, a two-lane highway passes sunlit fields, rolling river valleys and dramatic peaks on its journey to the horizon – all par for the course (along with oddball museums and cozy cafes) on the great American road trip.

Nature Unbound

The Badlands are b-a-a-a-d in every good sense. These geological wonders are matched by the wildlife-filled beauty of the Black Hills and Theodore Roosevelt National Park.

Big-City Soundtrack

Out in the wilds, streets roll up at sunset but in St Louis and Kansas City that's when the fun begins. Legendary jazz, blues and rock are played in clubs and bars, big and small.

p636

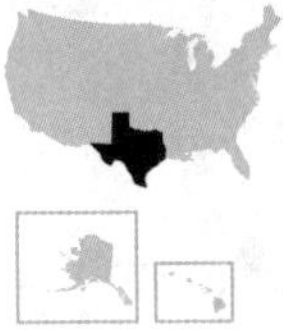

Texas

Barbecue
Live Music
Outdoors

BBQ Delight

Meat lovers, you've died and gone to heaven (vegetarians, you're somewhere else). Some of the best barbecue on earth is served up in Lockhart near Austin, although you can dig in to brisket, ribs and sausage all across the state.

Tap to the Beat

Austin has proclaimed itself (and no one's arguing) the 'Live Music Capital of the World.' Two-step to live bands on worn wooden floors at honky-tonks and dance halls all around the state.

Big-Sky Scenery

Canyons, mountains and hot springs set the scene for memorable outings in Texas. Go rafting on the Big Bend River or get a beach fix along the pretty Southern Gulf Coast.

p690

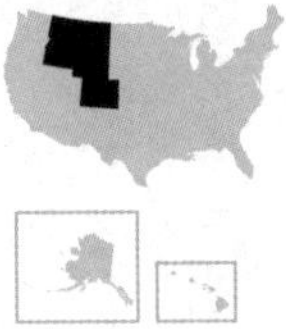

Rocky Mountains

Outdoors
Culture
Landscapes

Mountain High

Skiing, hiking and boating make the Rockies a playground for adrenaline junkies, with hundreds of races and group rides, and an incredible infrastructure of parks, trails and cabins.

Old Meets New

Once a people of Stetsons and prairie dresses, today's Rocky folk are more often spotted in lycra, mountain bike nearby, sipping a microbrew or latte at a cafe. Hard playing and slow living still rule.

Perfect Views

The snow-covered Rocky Mountains are pure majesty. With chiseled peaks, clear rivers and red-rock contours, the Rockies contain some of the world's most famous parks and bucketloads of clean mountain air.

p741

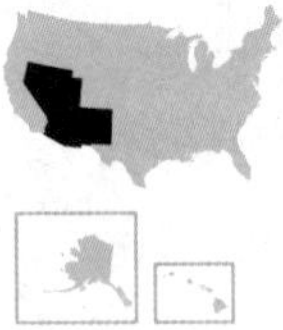

Southwest

Scenery
Outdoors
Cultures

Natural Beauty

Home to spectacular national parks, the Southwest is famous for the jaw-dropping Grand Canyon, the dramatic red buttes of Monument Valley and the vast Carlsbad Caverns.

Hiking & Skiing

Ski powdery slopes at Park City, splash and frolic in Slide Rock State Park, skitter down dunes at White Sands, and hike to your heart's content at Bryce, Zion and countless other spots.

Indigenous Peoples

This is Native American country, and visiting the Hopi and Navajo Nations provides a fine introduction to America's first peoples. For a journey back in time, explore clifftop dwellings abandoned by ancient Puebloans.

p809

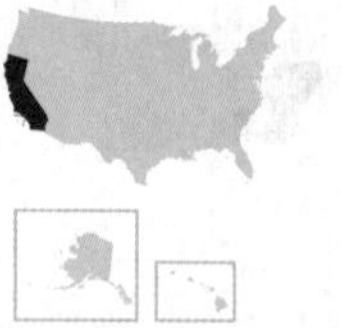

California

Beaches
Outdoors
Eating

Sunny Shores

With more than 1100 miles of coast, California rules the sands: rugged, pristine beaches in the north and people-packed beauties in the south, with great surfing, sea kayaking and beach walking all along the coast.

Captivating Vistas

Snow-covered mountains, glittering sea and old-growth forests set the stage for skiing, hiking, cycling, wave frolicking, wildlife-watching and more.

California Cooking

Fertile fields, talented chefs and an insatiable appetite for the new make California a major culinary destination. Browse food markets, sample the produce at lush vineyards and eat well in many celebrated dining rooms.

p906

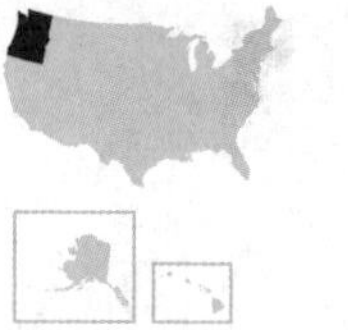

Pacific Northwest

Food & Wine
Skiing
Parks

Culinary Bounty

Portland and Seattle have celebrated food scenes with wild-caught fish, superb wines and locally sourced vegetables among the Northwest bounty.

Powdery Allure

Year-round ski areas, rustic cross-country and snow-boarding heaven at Mt Baker: the region with the highest snowfalls in North America delivers unparalleled winter sports. Cross-country skiing in the Methow Valley is world renowned.

Vast Nature

The Northwest has four national parks: three Teddy Roosevelt–era classics – Olympic, Mt Rainier and Crater Lake – each bequeathed with historic lodges; and a wilder addition – the North Cascades.

p1020

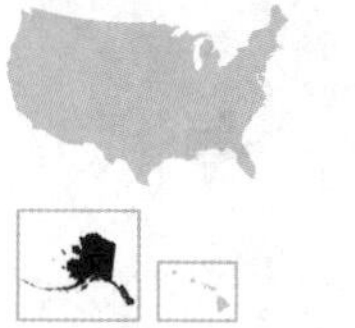

Alaska

Wildlife
Glaciers
Outdoor Adventure

Creatures Great & (Not So) Small

Alaska offers some of the best wildlife-viewing opportunities in the country. The sight of breaching whales and foraging bears in Southeast Alaska is unforgettable. Denali National Park is home to caribou, dall sheep, moose and yet more bears.

Cinematic Landscapes

If you want to explore glaciers in the USA, Alaska is the place. Glacier Bay National Park is the crown jewel for the cruise ships and a favorite for kayakers.

Hiking

Alaska offers some of the rawest hiking experiences in North America, from the Chilkoot trail to Denali National Park.

p1080

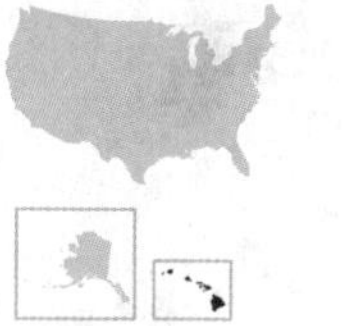

Hawaii

Beaches
Adventure
Scenery

Tropical Shores

There's great sunning and people-watching on Waikiki (among dozens of other spots); stunning black-sand beaches on the Kona Coast, and world-class surfing all over Hawaii.

Outdoor Highs

You can trek through rainforest, kayak the Na Pali Coast, go zip-lining on the four biggest islands and go eye-to-eye with aquatic life in marvelous Hanauma Bay.

Unrivaled Landscapes

Hawaii has its share of head-turners: volcanoes, ancient rainforests, picturesque waterfalls, clifftop vistas and jungle-lined valleys – and sparkling seas surrounding the islands.

p1097

On the Road

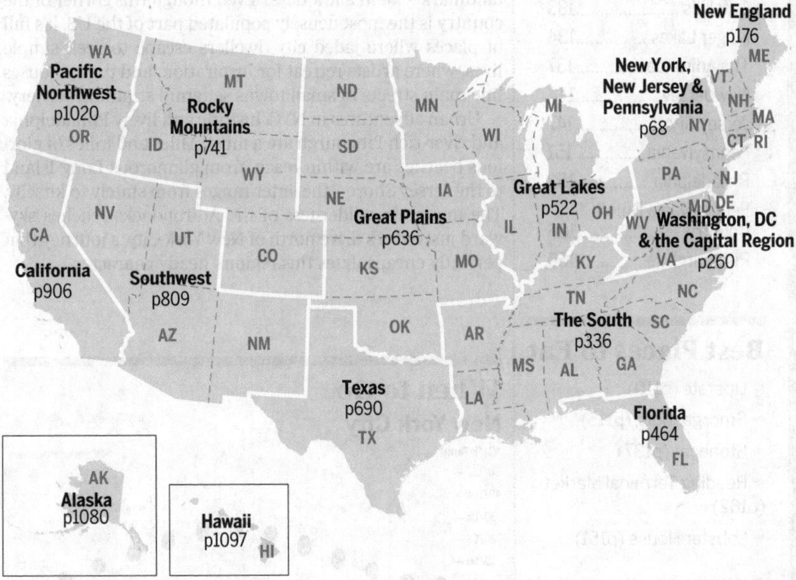
New England
p176
ME
VT
NH
MA
CT
RI
New York, New Jersey & Pennsylvania
p68
NY
PA
NJ
MD
DE
Washington, DC & the Capital Region
p260
WV
VA
NC
SC
The South
p336
TN
KY
MS
AL
GA
AR
LA
Florida
p464
FL
Great Lakes
p522
MI
WI
IL
IN
OH
MN
Great Plains
p636
ND
SD
NE
IA
KS
MO
OK
Texas
p690
TX
Rocky Mountains
p741
MT
ID
WY
CO
UT
Southwest
p809
AZ
NM
NV
California
p906
CA
Pacific Northwest
p1020
WA
OR
AK
Alaska
p1080
Hawaii
p1097
HI

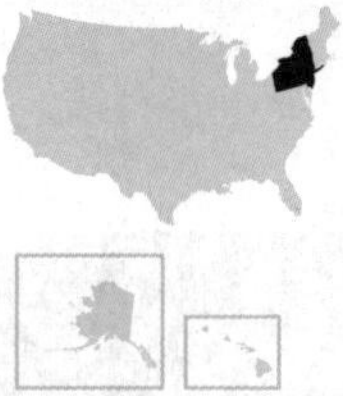

New York, New Jersey & Pennsylvania

Includes ➡

Best Places to Eat

- Upstate (p110)
- Smorgasburg (p115)
- Stonecat (p137)
- Reading Terminal Market (p162)
- Lobster House (p151)

Best Places to Stay

- Wythe Hotel (p106)
- Roxbury Motel (p133)
- White Pine Camp (p139)
- Starlux (p151)
- General Sutter Inn (p167)

Why Go?

Where else could you visit an Amish family's farm, camp on a mountaintop, read the Declaration of Independence and view New York, New York from the 86th floor of an art-deco landmark – all in a few days? Even though this corner of the country is the most densely populated part of the US, it's full of places where jaded city dwellers escape to seek simple lives, where artists retreat for inspiration, and pretty houses line main streets in small towns set amid stunning scenery.

Urban adventures in NYC, historic and lively Philadelphia and river-rich Pittsburgh are a must. Miles and miles of glorious beaches are within reach, from glamorous Long Island to the Jersey Shore – the latter ranges from stately to kitschy. The mountain wilderness of the Adirondacks reaches skyward just a day's drive north of New York City, a journey that perfectly encapsulates this region's heady character.

When to Go

New York City

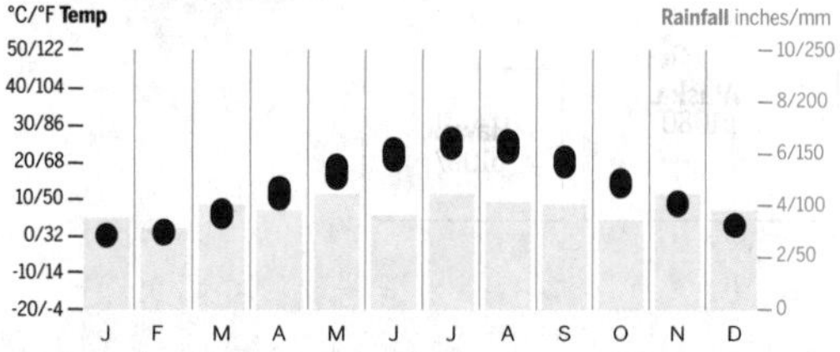

Oct–Nov Autumn in NYC brings cool temps, festivals, the marathon and gearing up for holiday season.

Feb Winter-sports buffs head to the mountains of the Adirondacks, Catskills and Poconos.

31 May–5 Sep Memorial Day through Labor Day is for beaches from Montauk to Cape May.

NEW YORK CITY

Loud and fast and pulsing with energy, New York City is symphonic, exhausting and always evolving. Maybe only a Walt Whitman poem cataloguing typical city scenes, from the humblest hole-in-the-wall to grand buildings, could begin to do the city justice. It remains one of the world centers of fashion, theater, food, music, publishing, advertising and finance.

Coming here for the first time from anywhere else is like stepping into a movie, one you've probably been unknowingly writing, one that contains all imagined possibilities. From the middle of Times Square to the most obscure corner of the Bronx, you'll find extremes. From Brooklyn's Russian enclave in Brighton Beach to the mini South America in Queens, virtually every country in the world has a bustling proxy community in the city. You can experience a little bit of everything on a visit here, as long as you take care to travel with a loose itinerary and an open mind.

History

After Henry Hudson first claimed this land in 1609 for his Dutch East India Company sponsors, he reported it to be 'as beautiful a land as one can hope to tread upon.' Soon after it was named 'Manhattan,' derived from local Munsee Native American words and meaning 'Island of Hills.'

By 1625 a colony, soon called New Amsterdam, was established, and the island was bought from the Munsee Indians by Peter Minuit. George Washington was sworn in here as the republic's first president in 1789, and when the Civil War broke out in 1861, New York City, which supplied a significant contingent of volunteers to defend the Union, became an organizing center for the movement to emancipate slaves.

Throughout the 19th century successive waves of immigrants – Irish, German, English, Scandinavian, Slavic, Italian, Greek and central European Jewish – led to a swift population increase, followed by the building of empires in industry and finance, and a golden age of skyscrapers.

After WWII New York City was the premier city in the world, but it suffered from a new phenomenon: 'white flight' to the suburbs. By the 1970s the graffiti-ridden subway system had become a symbol of New York's civic and economic decline. But NYC regained much of its swagger in the 1980s, led by colorful three-term mayor Ed Koch. The city elected its first African American mayor, David Dinkins, in 1989, but ousted him after a single term in favor of Republican Rudolph Giuliani (a 2008 primary candidate for US president). It was during Giuliani's reign that catastrophe struck on September 11, 2001, when the 110-story Twin Towers of the World Trade Center were struck

NEW YORK, NEW JERSEY & PENNSYLVANIA IN...

One Week

Start off with a gentle introduction in **Philadelphia**, birthplace of American independence. After a day touring the historic sites and a night sampling the great restaurants and bars, head into New Jersey for a bucolic night in **Cape May**. Stop off at another beach town like **Wildwood** or **Asbury Park** further north along the Jersey Shore, landing in **New York City** the following day. Spend the rest of your visit here, blending touristy must-dos – such as the **Top of the Rock** and **Central Park** – with vibrant nightlife and eclectic dining adventures, perhaps in the city's bustling East Village.

Two Weeks

Begin with several days in **New York City**, then a night or two somewhere in the **Hudson Valley**, before reaching the **Catskills**. After touring this bucolic region, head further north to **Lake Placid** and the **High Peaks** area of the **Adirondacks** where the outdoor-minded will have trouble leaving. Then loop back south through the **Finger Lakes** region with stops in wineries and waterfall-laden parks along the way, and a night in college-town **Ithaca**. From here you can head to **Buffalo** and **Niagara Falls** or southwest to **Pittsburgh**. Work your way back east via the **Pennsylvania Wilds**, then rest up in **Lancaster County**, where you can stay on a working Amish farm. From here it's a short jaunt to **Philadelphia**, which deserves at least a couple of nights. Follow it up with a stay at a quaint B&B in **Cape May**, then a day of boardwalk amusements in **Wildwood**.

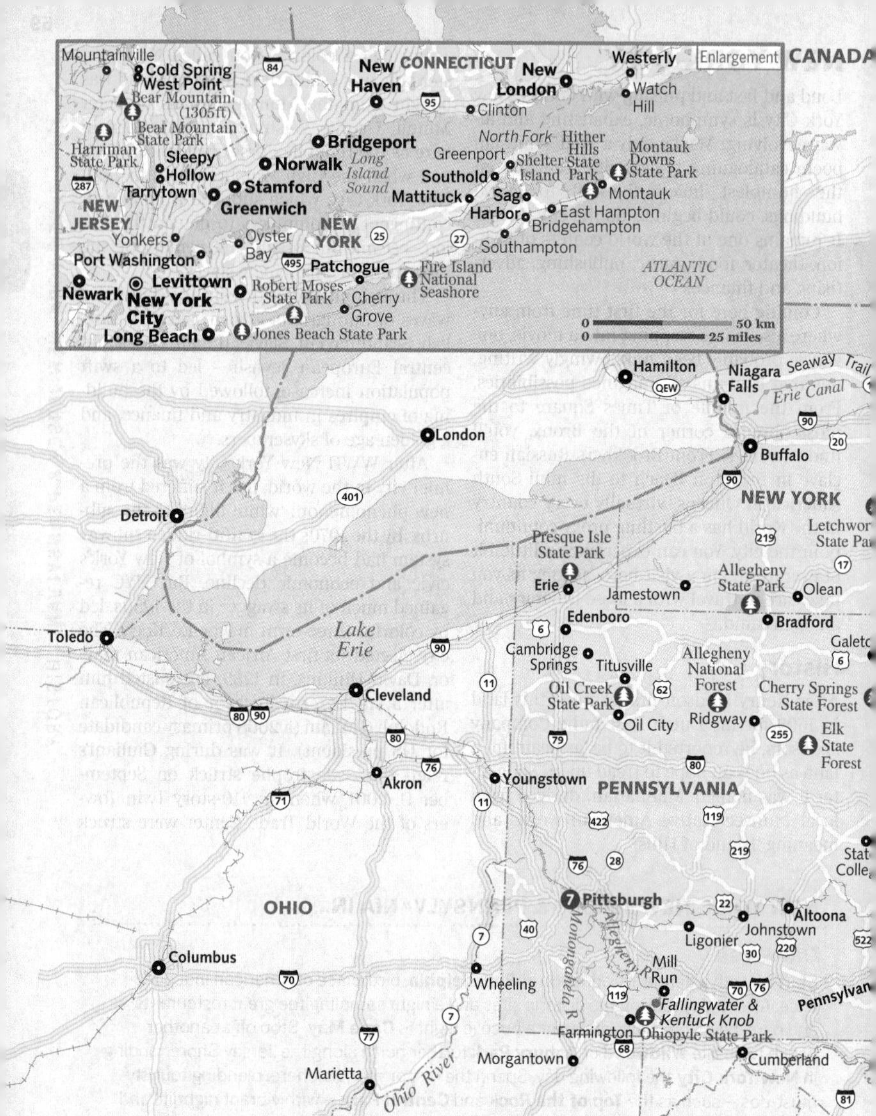

New York, New Jersey & Pennsylvania Highlights

1. Traveling round the world without ever leaving the kaleidoscope of neighborhoods and cultures that is **New York City** (p69).
2. Enjoying the kitsch and calm of the **Jersey Shore** (p147).
3. Absorbing the story of the birth of the nation in Philadelphia's **Independence National Historic Park** (p153).
4. Walking the densely forested paths of the **Catskills** (p133).
5. Exploring the wild beauty of the **Adirondacks** (p137).

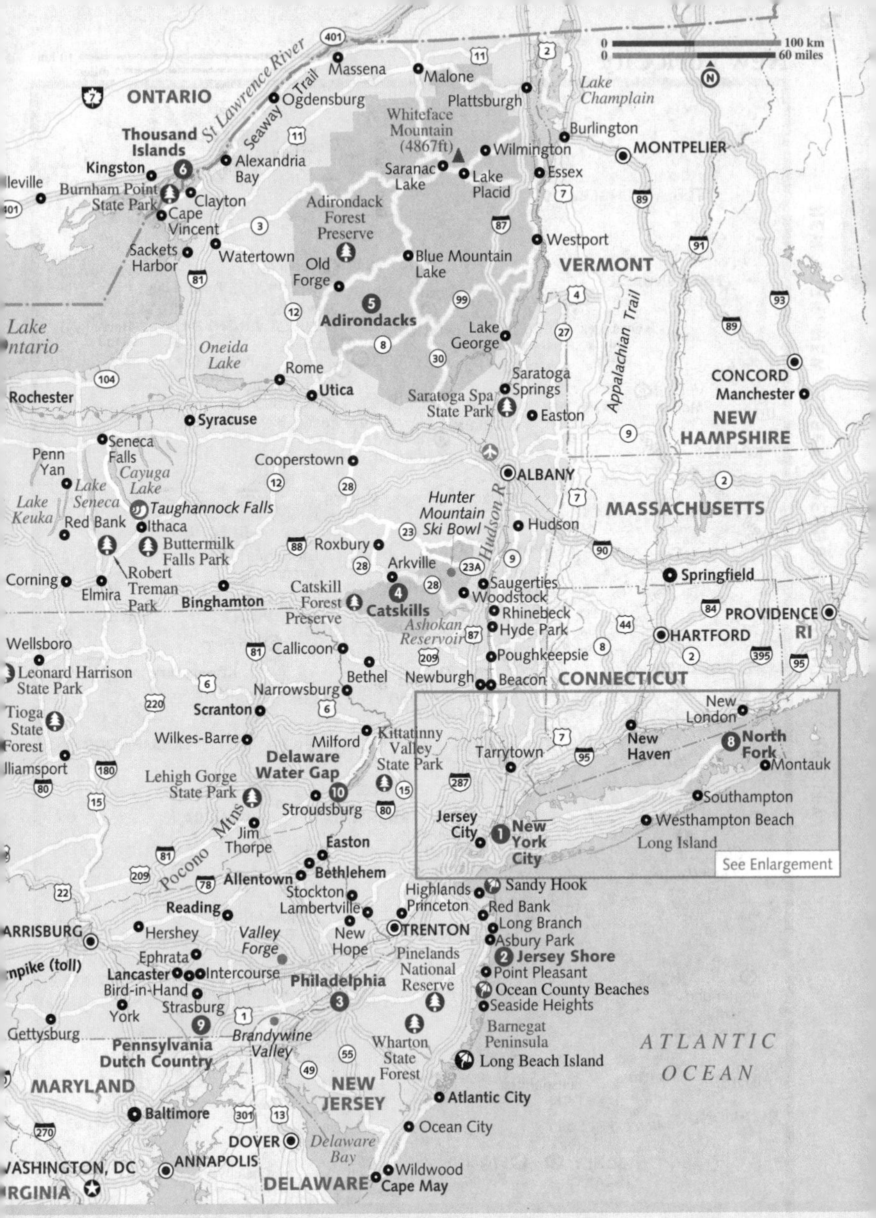

6 Camping along the shores of the St Lawrence River in the **Thousand Islands** (p139).

7 Admiring great modern art and old industry in **Pittsburgh** (p169).

8 Wine tasting on Long Island's **North Fork** (p129).

9 Touring the back roads of **Pennsylvania Dutch Country** (p166).

10 Floating past bucolic scenery in the **Delaware Water Gap** (p145).

New York City

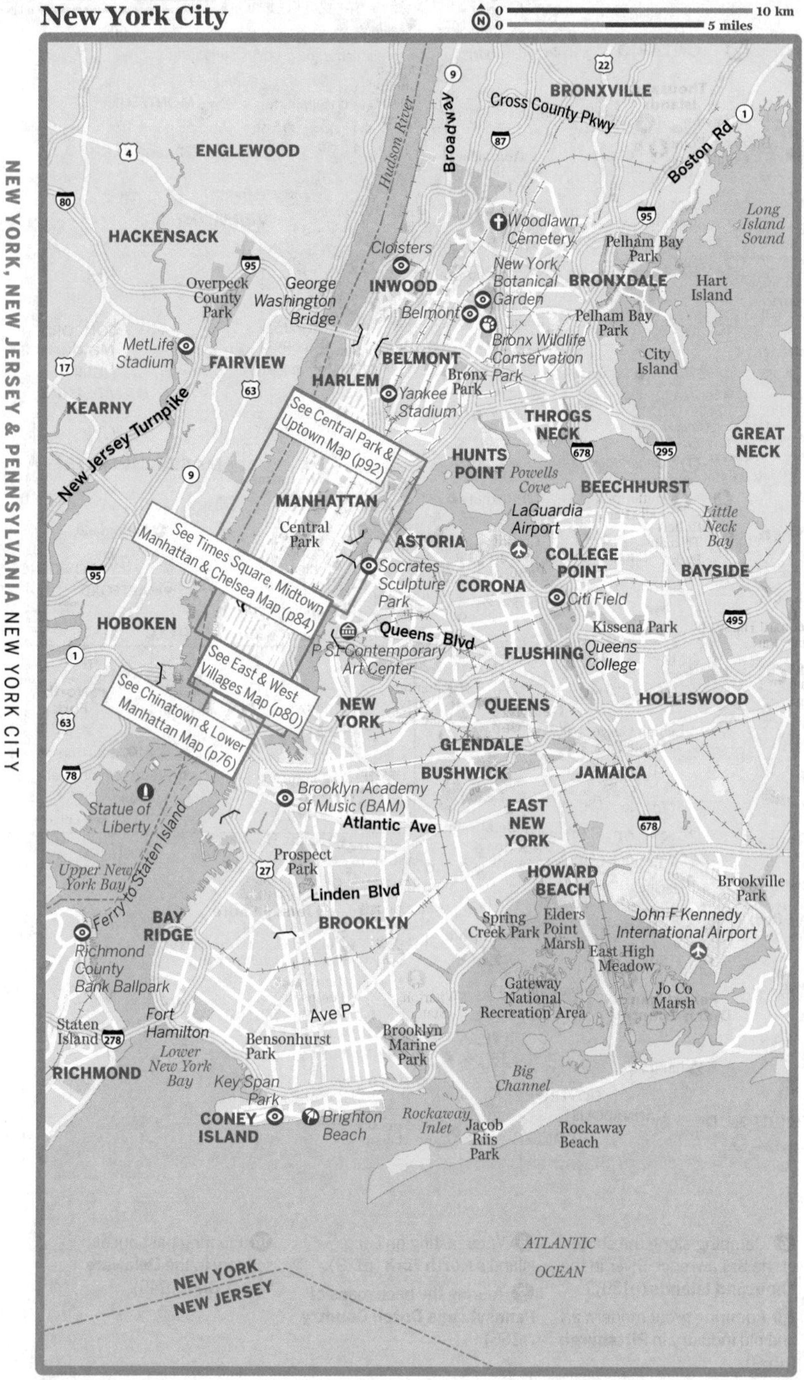

by hijacked commercial airliners, became engulfed in balls of fire and then collapsed, killing 3000 people, the result of a now infamous terrorist attack.

The billionaire Republican Mayor Michael Bloomberg, first elected in an atmosphere of turmoil and grief, served as mayor for a controversial three terms. Considered an independent political pragmatist, he earned raves and criticism for his dual pursuit of environmental and development goals through a challenging period that has included the Global Financial Crisis and Hurricane Sandy.

Brooklyn-based Democrat Bill de Blasio became mayor in 2014, riding a wave of popular support for his proposals to address the social and economic inequalities of the city. He oversaw the creation of free pre-kindergarten education for all, greenlighted the creation of more affordable housing and tried to heal the divide between African Americans and a sometimes divisive police force.

Sights

Lower Manhattan

★Brooklyn Bridge BRIDGE

(Map p76; Ⓢ4/5/6 to Brooklyn Bridge-City Hall, J to Chambers St) Inspiration to artists and writers throughout the years, the Brooklyn Bridge is one of New York's best-loved monuments. Walking across it is a rite of passage for New Yorkers and visitors alike – with this in mind, walk no more than two abreast or you'll be in danger of colliding with runners and speeding cyclists.

With a span of 1596ft, it remains a compelling symbol of US achievement and a superbly graceful structure, despite the fact that its construction was plagued by budget overruns and the death of 20 workers. Among the casualties was designer John Roebling, who was knocked off a pier in 1869 while scouting a site for the western bridge tower and later died of tetanus poisoning. The bridge and the smooth pedestrian/cyclist path, beginning just east of City Hall, affords wonderful views of Lower Manhattan and Brooklyn. On the Brooklyn side, the ever-expanding Brooklyn Bridge Park is a great place to continue your stroll.

Statue of Liberty MONUMENT

(☎877-523-9849; www.nps.gov/stli; Liberty Island; adult/child incl Ellis Island $18/9, incl crown $21/12; ⏲8:30am-5:30pm, check website for seasonal changes; Ⓢ1 to South Ferry, 4/5 to Bowling Green) In a city full of American icons, the Statue of Liberty is perhaps the most famous. Conceived as early as 1865 by French intellectual Edouard Laboulaye as a monument to the republican principles shared by France and the USA, it's still generally recognized as a symbol for the ideals of opportunity and freedom to many.

French sculptor Frédéric Auguste Bartholdi traveled to New York in 1871 to select the site, then spent more than 10 years in Paris designing and making the 151ft-tall figure of Liberty Enlightening the World. It was then shipped to New York, erected on a small island in the harbor and unveiled in 1886.

Access to the crown is limited, so reservations are required: book as far in advance as possible. Pedestal access is also limited, so reserve in advance. Keep in mind there's no elevator and the climb from the base is equal to a 22-story building. Otherwise, a visit means you can wander the grounds, take in the small museum and enjoy the view from the 16-story observation deck in the pedestal. Make the most of your visit by picking up a free audio guide when you reach the island (there's even a kid's version).

The trip to Liberty island, via ferry, is usually made in conjunction with nearby Ellis Island. Ferries leave from Battery Park and tickets include admission to both sights. Reserve in advance to cut down on long wait times.

Ellis Island LANDMARK, MUSEUM

(☎212-363-3200; www.nps.gov/elis; admission free, ferry incl Statue of Liberty adult/child $18/9; ⏲8:30am-5:30pm, check website for seasonal changes; Ⓢ1 to South Ferry, 4/5 to Bowling Green) An icon of mythical proportions for the descendants of those who passed through here, this island and its hulking building served as New York's main immigration station from 1892 until 1954, processing an astounding 12 million arrivals – who came from far-flung corners of the globe. The process involved getting the once-over by doctors, being assigned new names if their own were deemed too difficult to spell or pronounce, and basically getting the green light to start new lives in America.

Now anybody who visits the island can get an understanding of the experience, thanks to an interactive Immigration Museum that's housed in the red-brick structure. You can peruse fascinating exhibits and watch a film that delves into the immigrant experience, explaining and how the influx changed the USA.

★National September 11 Memorial MONUMENT
(Map p76; www.911memorial.org; 180 Greenwich St; 7:30am-9pm; S E to World Trade Center, N/R to Cortlandt St, 2/3 to Park Pl) FREE One of New York's most solemn spaces is the National September 11 Memorial. Titled 'Reflecting Absence', the memorial's two massive reflecting pools are as much a symbol of hope and renewal as they are a tribute to the thousands who lost their lives on September 11, 2001.

National September 11 Memorial Museum MUSEUM
(Map p76; www.911memorial.org/museum; 180 Greenwich St, near Fulton St; adult/child $24/15; 9am-8pm Sun-Thu, to 9pm Fri & Sat; S E to World Trade Center, N/R to Cortlandt St, 2/3 to Park Pl) Just beyond the reflecting pools of the September 11 Memorial, you'll see an entrance pavilion that subtly, yet eerily, evokes a toppled tower. Inside, a gently sloping ramp leads to the subterranean exhibition galleries that recall that horrific summer day on 2001.

One World Observatory VIEWPOINT
(Map p76; 844-696-1776; www.oneworldobservatory.com; cnr West & Vesey Sts; adult/child $32/26; 9am-8pm; S E to World Trade Center, N/R to Cortlandt St, 2/3 to Park Pl) Atop the highest building in the Western Hemisphere, One World Observatory, which opened in 2015, offers dazzling views from its 102-story perch. No other building in town rivals the jaw-dropping panorama of New York's urban landscape and its surrounding geography spread before you.

Aside from the sky-high spectacle, the experience also includes a video called 'Voices' about those who built the One World Trade Center; there's also a virtual time-lapse that shows the evolution of the city skyline from the 1600s to the present. Visitors are whisked up to the top in under 60 seconds in so-called 'skypods' – a surprisingly smooth ride, considering these are among the fastest elevators on the planet.

Not unexpectedly, this is a hugely popular site. Purchase tickets online: you'll need to choose the date and time of your visit.

Governors Island PARK
(www.govisland.com; 10am-6pm Mon-Fri, to 7pm Sat & Sun from late May-late Sep; S 1 to South Ferry, then ferry from Battery Marine Terminal) FREE Off-limits to the public for 200 years, former military outpost Governors Island is now one of New York's most popular summer playgrounds. From late May through September, ferries make the seven-minute trip from Lower Manhattan (or Brooklyn Bridge Park's pier 6) to the 172-acre oasis. Highlights include 19th-century fortifications, open lawns, massive shade trees, a hammock grove and unsurpassed city views. There are art installations, concerts and food trucks throughout the summer. You can hire bikes when you arrive.

The **ferry** (Map p76; www.govisland.com; one-way $2; 10am-4pm Mon-Fri, 10am-5:30pm Sat & Sun; S 1 to South Ferry) leaves every 30 to 60 minutes from the Battery Marine Terminal next to the Staten Island Ferry Whitehall Terminal in Lower Manhattan.

South Street Seaport NEIGHBORHOOD
(Map p76; www.southstreetseaport.com; S A/C, J/Z, 2/3, 4/5 to Fulton St) This 11-block enclave of shops, piers and sights combines the best and worst in historic preservation. It's not on the radar for most New Yorkers, but tourists are drawn to the sea air, the nautical feel, the frequent street performers and the mobbed restaurants.

The pedestrian malls, historic tall ships and riverside locale of this neighborhood create a lovely backdrop if you happen to be standing in line for discounted Broadway tickets at the downtown TKTS booth.

Bowling Green Park PARK
(Map p76; cnr State & Whitehall Sts; S 4/5 to Bowling Green) At Bowling Green Park, British residents relaxed with quiet games in the late 17th century. The large **Bronze Bull** here is a tourist photo stop.

National Museum of the American Indian MUSEUM
(Map p76; www.nmai.si.edu; 1 Bowling Green; 10am-5pm Fri-Wed, to 8pm Thu; S 4/5 to Bowling Green, R to Whitehall St) FREE Set in Cass Gilbert's spectacular 1907 Custom House, this Smithsonian affiliate has exhibitions documenting Native American art, textiles, culture, life and beliefs.

Wall Street & the Financial District

The etymological origin of **Wall Street**, both an actual street and the metaphorical home of US commerce, is the wooden barrier built by Dutch settlers in 1653 to protect Nieuw Amsterdam from Native Americans and the British.

Battery Park & Around NEIGHBORHOOD

The southwestern tip of Manhattan Island has been extended with landfill over the years to form **Battery Park** (Map p76; www.nycgovparks.org; Broadway at Battery Pl; ⏲ sunrise-1am; S 1 to South Ferry, 4/5 to Bowling Green), so named for the gun batteries that used to be housed at the bulkheads. **Castle Clinton** (Map p76; www.nps.gov/cacl; ⏲ 8:30am-5pm; S 1 to South Ferry, 4/5 to Bowling Green), a fortification built in 1811 to protect Manhattan from the British, was originally 900ft offshore but is now at the edge of Battery Park, with only its walls remaining.

Hudson River Park PARK

(Map p76; www.hudsonriverpark.org; S 1 to Franklin St, 1 to Canal St) Stretching for five miles from Battery Park to Hell's Kitchen (59th St), 550-acre Hudson River Park runs along the lower western side of Manhattan. Diversions include a bike/run/skate path that snakes along its entire length, community gardens, playgrounds, sculpture exhibitions, and renovated piers reinvented as riverfront esplanades, miniature golf courses, alfresco summertime movie theaters and concert venues.

Skyscraper Museum MUSEUM

(Map p76; www.skyscraper.org; 39 Battery Pl; admission $5; ⏲ noon-6pm Wed-Sun; S 4/5 to Bowling Green) Housed in a ground-floor space of the Ritz-Carlton Hotel, the Skyscraper Museum features rotating exhibits plus a permanent study of high-rise history.

★ **Museum of Jewish Heritage** MUSEUM

(Map p76; www.mjhnyc.org; 36 Battery Pl; adult/child $12/free, 4-8pm Wed free; ⏲ 10am-5:45pm Sun-Tue & Thu, to 8pm Wed, to 5pm Fri Apr-Sep, to 3pm Fri Oct-Mar; S 4/5 to Bowling Green) This evocative waterfront museum explores all aspects of modern Jewish identity, with often poignant personal artifacts, photographs and documentary films. Outside it stands a Holocaust memorial.

Museum of American Finance MUSEUM

(Map p76; www.moaf.org; 48 Wall St, btwn Pearl & William Sts; adult/child $8/free; ⏲ 10am-4pm Tue-Sat; S 2/3, 4/5 to Wall St) Money makes this museum go round; its focus is on historic moments in American financial history.

Federal Reserve Bank of New York NOTABLE BUILDING

(Map p76; ☎ 212-720-6130; www.newyorkfed.org; 33 Liberty St, at Nassau St, entry via 44 Maiden Lane; reservation required; ⏲ guided tours 11:15am, noon, 12:45pm, 1:30pm, 2:15pm & 3pm Mon-Fri, museum 10am-3pm; S A/C, J/Z, 2/3, 4/5 to Fulton St) FREE The best reason to visit the Federal Reserve Bank is the chance to (briefly) ogle its high-security vault – more than 10,000 tons of gold reserves reside here, 80ft below ground. You'll only see a small part of that fortune, but signing on to a free tour (the only way down; book several months ahead) is worth the effort.

Tribeca & SoHo

The 'TRIangle BElow CAnal St,' bordered roughly by Broadway to the east and Chambers St to the south, is the more downtown of these two sister 'hoods. It has old warehouses, very expensive loft apartments and chichi restaurants.

SoHo takes its name from its geographical placement: SOuth of HOuston St. SoHo is filled with block upon block of cast-iron industrial buildings that date to the period just after the Civil War, when this was the city's leading commercial district. It had a Bohemian/artsy heyday that had ended by the 1980s, and now this super-gentrified area is a major shopping destination, home to chain stores and boutiques alike and to hordes of consumers, especially on weekends.

SoHo's cup overfloweth to the northern side of Houston St and the east side of Lafayette St, where two small areas, **NoHo** ('north of Houston') and **NoLita** ('north of Little Italy'), respectively, are known for small, independent boutiques and charming restaurants. Add them to SoHo and Tribeca for a great experience of strolling, window-shopping and cafe-hopping, and you'll have quite a packed afternoon.

Chinatown & Little Italy

Endless exotic moments await in Chinatown, one of New York City's most colorful neighborhoods. Catch the whiff of fresh fish and ripe persimmons, hear the clacking of mah-jongg tiles on makeshift tables, drool over dangling duck roasts swinging in store windows, and shop for mementos from the Far East, from rice-paper lanterns to loose oolong tea.

Little Italy, once an authentic enclave of Italian people, culture and eateries, is constantly shrinking (Chinatown keeps encroaching). Still, loyal Italian Americans, mostly from the suburbs, flock here to gather around red-and-white-checked tablecloths

Chinatown & Lower Manhattan

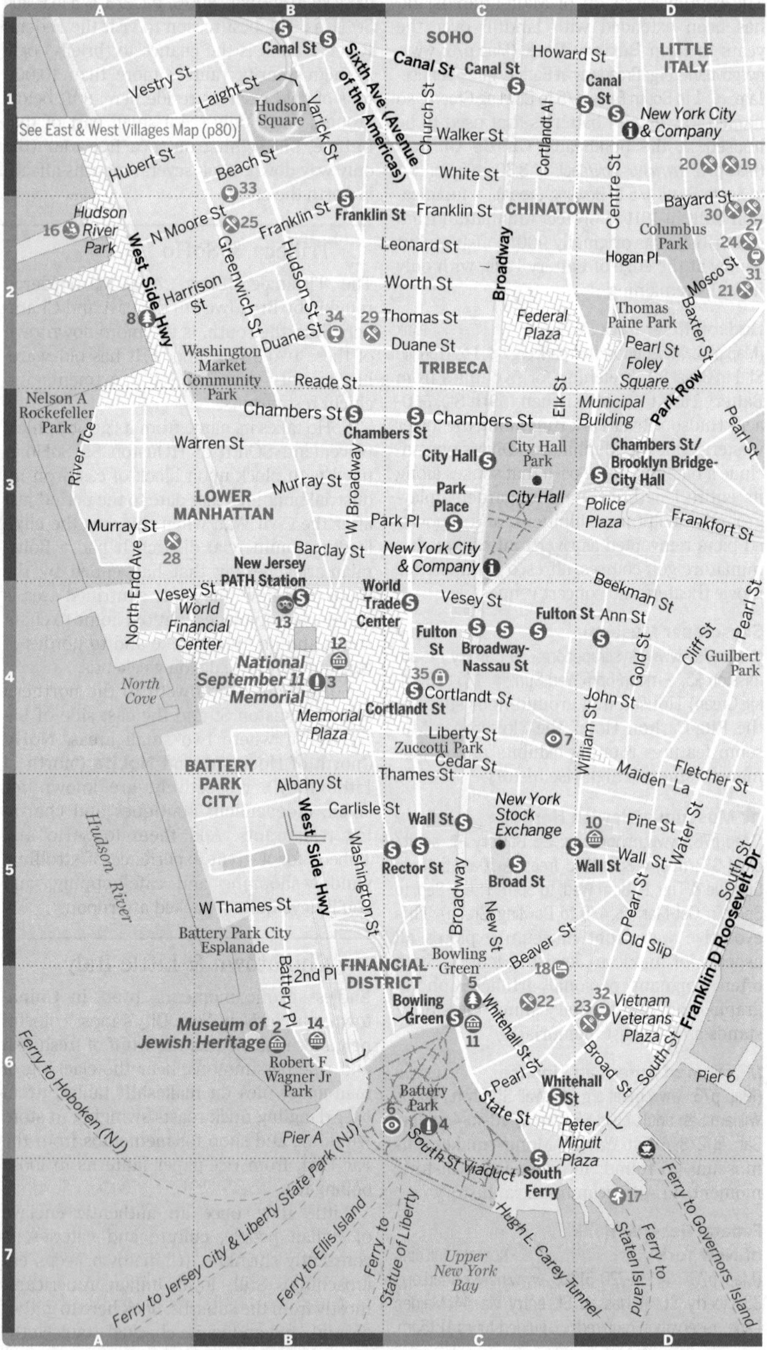

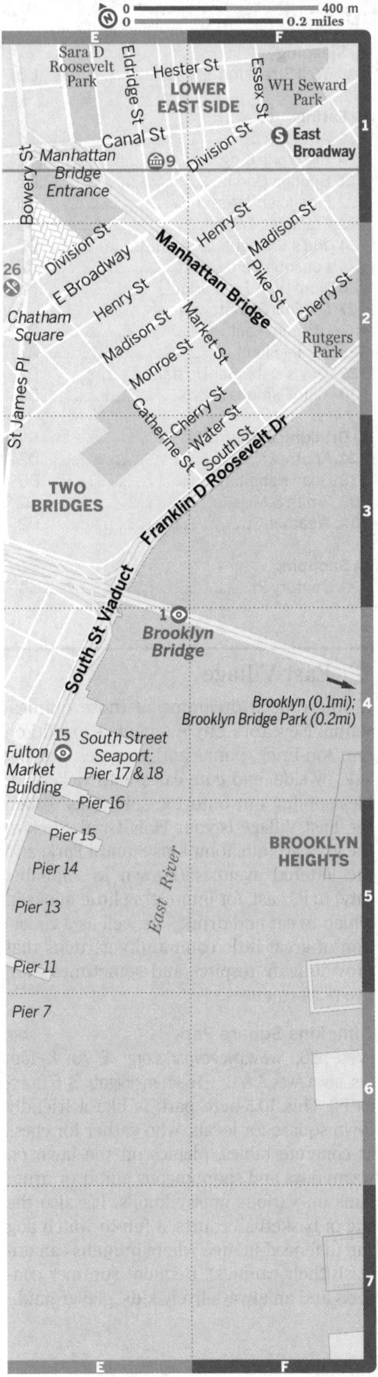

at one of a handful of longtime red-sauce restaurants along Mulberry St.

Museum of Chinese in America MUSEUM
(Map p80; ☎212-619-4785; www.mocanyc.org; 215 Centre St, btwn Grand & Howard Sts; adult/child $10/free, Thu free; ⏰11am-6pm Tue, Wed, Fri-Sun, to 9pm Thu; Ⓢ N/Q/R, J/Z, 6 to Canal St) Strikingly designed and cutting-edge interactive exhibits trace the history and cultural impact of Chinese communities in the US. Also offers lectures, film series and walking tours.

St Patrick's Old Cathedral CHURCH
(Map p80; www.oldsaintpatricks.com; 263 Mulberry St, entrance on Mott St; ⏰8am-6pm; Ⓢ N/R to Prince St) Though St Patrick's Cathedral is now famously located on Fifth Ave in Midtown, its first congregation was housed here, in this 1809–15 Gothic Revival church designed by Joseph-François Mangin.

Lower East Side

First came the Jews, then the Latinos, followed by the hipsters and accompanying posers and frat boy bro contingents. Today, this neighborhood, once the densest in the world, is focused on being cool – offering low-lit lounges, live-music clubs and trendy bistros.

Lower East Side Tenement Museum MUSEUM
(Map p80; ☎212-982-8420; www.tenement.org; 103 Orchard St, btwn Broome & Delancey Sts; admission $25; ⏰10am-6:30pm Fri-Wed, to 8:30pm Thu; Ⓢ B/D to Grand St, J/M/Z to Essex St, F to Delancey St) This museum puts the neighborhood's heartbreaking but inspiring heritage on full display in three re-creations of turn-of-the-20th-century tenements, including the late 19th-century home and garment shop of the Levine family from Poland, and two immigrant dwellings from the Great Depressions of 1873 and 1929. Visits are by tour only, with knowledgeable guides bringing the past to life. Check the website for the full range of tours that operate throughout the day. Reserve ahead (tours fill up).

New Museum of Contemporary Art MUSEUM
(Map p80; ☎212-219-1222; www.newmuseum.org; 235 Bowery, btwn Stanton & Rivington Sts; adult/child $16/free, by donation 7-9pm Thu; ⏰11am-6pm Tue-Sun, to 9pm Thu; Ⓢ N/R to Prince St, F to 2nd Ave, J/Z to Bowery, 6 to Spring St) Housed in an architecturally ambitious building on Bowery, this is the city's sole museum dedicated to contemporary art – with often excellent

Chinatown & Lower Manhattan

Top Sights
1 Brooklyn Bridge ... E4
2 Museum of Jewish Heritage ... B6
3 National September 11 Memorial ... B4

Sights
4 Battery Park ... C6
5 Bowling Green Park ... C6
6 Castle Clinton ... C6
7 Federal Reserve Bank of New York ... C4
8 Hudson River Park ... A2
9 Museum at Eldridge Street Synagogue ... E1
10 Museum of American Finance ... D5
11 National Museum of the American Indian ... C6
12 National September 11 Memorial Museum ... B4
13 One World Observatory ... B4
14 Skyscraper Museum ... B6
15 South Street Seaport ... E4

Activities, Courses & Tours
16 Downtown Boathouse ... A2
17 Staten Island Ferry ... D7

Sleeping
18 Wall Street Inn ... C6

Eating
19 Amazing 66 ... D1
20 Big Wong King ... D1
21 Buddha Bodai ... D2
22 Financier Patisserie ... C6
23 Fraunces Tavern ... D6
24 Joe's Shanghai ... D2
25 Locanda Verde ... B2
26 Nom Wah Tea Parlor ... E2
27 Original Chinatown Ice Cream Factory ... D2
28 Shake Shack ... A3
29 Tiny's & the Bar Upstairs ... B2
30 Xi'an Famous Foods ... D2

Drinking & Nightlife
31 Apothéke ... D2
32 Dead Rabbit ... D6
33 Smith & Mills ... B1
34 Weather Up ... B2

Shopping
35 Century 21 ... C4

shows (there's no permanent collection). To save cash, stop by on Thursday evenings between 7pm and 9pm, when admission is pay what you wish.

International Center of Photography GALLERY
(ICP; Map p80; www.icp.org; 250 Bowery, btwn Houston & Prince Sts ; adult/child $14/free, Fri 5-8pm by donation; 10am-6pm Tue-Thu, Sat & Sun, to 8pm Fri; S F to 2nd Ave, J/Z to Bowery) The city's most important showcase for major photographers, both past and present. Previous exhibitions have included work by Sebastião Salgado, Henri Cartier-Bresson and Matthew Brady. It recently moved from Midtown to this high-design space downtown.

Museum at Eldridge Street Synagogue MUSEUM
(Map p76; 212-219-0302; www.eldridgestreet.org; 12 Eldridge St, btwn Canal & Division Sts; adult/child $12/8, Mon free; 10am-5pm Sun-Thu, 10am-3pm Fri; S F to East Broadway) This landmarked house of worship, built in 1887, was once the center of Jewish life before falling into squalor in the 1920s. Left to rot, it has only recently been reclaimed, and now shines with its original splendor. The on-site museum gives tours every half hour, with the last one departing at 4pm.

East Village

If you've been dreaming of those quintessential New York City moments – graffiti on crimson brick, punks and grannies walking side by side, and cute cafes with rickety tables spilling out onto the sidewalks – then the East Village is your Holy Grail. Stick to the area around Tompkins Square Park, and the lettered avenues (known as Alphabet City) to its east, for interesting little nooks in which to eat and drink – as well as a collection of great little community gardens that provide leafy respites and sometimes even live performances.

Tompkins Square Park PARK
(Map p80; www.nycgovparks.org; E 7th & 10th Sts, btwn Aves A & B; 6am-midnight; S 6 to Astor Pl) This 10.5-acre park is like a friendly town square for locals, who gather for chess at concrete tables, picnics on the lawn on warm days and spontaneous guitar or drum jams on various grassy knolls. It's also the site of basketball courts, a fun-to-watch dog run (a fenced-in area where humans can unleash their canines), frequent summer concerts and an always-lively kids' playground.

Astor Place SQUARE

(Map p80; 8th St btwn Third & Fourth Aves; S N/R to 8th St-NYU, 6 to Astor Pl) This square is named after the Astor family, who built an early New York fortune on beaver pelts (check out the tiles in the wall of the Astor Place subway platform) and lived on Colonnade Row, just south of the square; four of the original nine marble-faced Greek Revival residences on Lafayette St still exist.

The large, brownstone Cooper Union, the public college founded in 1859 by glue millionaire Peter Cooper, dominates the square – you can't miss the new academic building, a wildly futuristic nine-story sculpture of glazed glass wrapped in perforated stainless steel (and LEED-certified, too) by architect Thom Mayne of Morphosis.

Russian & Turkish Baths BATHHOUSE

(Map p80; 212-674-9250; www.russianturkishbaths.com; 268 E 10th St, btwn First Ave & Ave A; per visit $35; noon-10pm Mon-Tue & Thu-Fri, from 10am Wed, from 9am Sat, from 8am Sun; S L to First Ave, 6 to Astor Pl) The historic bathhouse is a great place to work out your stress in one of the four hot rooms; traditional massages are also offered. It's authentic and somewhat grungy, and you're as likely to share a sauna with a downtown couple on a date, a well-known actor looking for a time-out or an actual Russian.

West Village & Greenwich Village

Once a symbol for all things artistic, outlandish and Bohemian, this storied and popular neighborhood – the birthplace of the gay-rights movement as well as former home of Beat poets and important artists – feels worlds away from busy Broadway, and in fact almost European. Known by most visitors as 'Greenwich Village,' although that term is not used by locals (West Village encompasses Greenwich Village, which is the area immediately around Washington Square Park), it has narrow, tree-lined streets lined with eye-catching stores and lovely brownstones, as well as cafes and restaurants, making it an ideal place to wander.

Washington Square Park PARK

(Map p80; Fifth Ave at Washington Sq N; S A/C/E, B/D/F/M to W 4th St-Washington Sq, N/R to 8th St-NYU) This park began as a 'potter's field' – a burial ground for the penniless – and its status as a cemetery protected it from development. It is now a completely renovated and incredibly well-used park, especially on the weekend. Children use the playground, NYU students catch some rays and friends meet 'under the arch,' the renovated landmark on the park's northern edge, designed in 1889 by society architect Stanford White.

Dominating a huge swath of property in the middle of the Village, New York University, one of the largest in the country, defines the area around the park and beyond architecturally and demographically.

Christopher Street Piers/ Hudson River Park PIER, PARK

(Map p80; Christopher St & West Side Hwy; S 1 to Christopher St-Sheridan Sq) Like so many places in the Village, the extreme west side was once a derelict eyesore used mostly as a cruising ground. Now it's a pretty waterside hangout, bisected by the Hudson River Park's slender bike and jogging paths. It's still a place to cruise, just much less dangerous.

Sheridan Square & Around NEIGHBORHOOD

The western edge of the Village is home to **Sheridan Square** (Map p80; Christopher St & Seventh Ave; S 1 to Christopher St-Sheridan Sq), a small, triangular park where life-sized white statues by George Segal honor the gay community and gay pride movement that began in the nearby renovated **Stonewall Inn** sitting just across the street from the square.

A block further east, an appropriately bent street is officially named Gay St. Although gay social scenes have in many ways moved further uptown to Chelsea, **Christopher Street** is still the center of gay life in the Village.

Meatpacking District

Nestled between the far West Village and the southern border of Chelsea is the gentrified and now inappropriately named Meatpacking District. The neighborhood was once home to 250 slaughterhouses and was best known for its groups of tranny hookers, racy S&M sex clubs and, of course, its sides of beef. These days the hugely popular High Line park has only intensified an ever-increasing proliferation of trendy wine bars, eateries, nightclubs, high-end designer clothing stores, chic hotels and high-rent condos.

★**The High Line** OUTDOORS

(Map p80; 212-500-6035; www.thehighline.org; Gansevoort St; 7am-7pm Oct-Mar, to 10pm Apr-May, to 11pm Jun-Sep; M11 to Washington St, M11,

East & West Villages

M14 to 9th Ave, M23, M34 to 10th Ave; S L, A/C/E to 14th St-8th Ave; C/E to 23rd St-8th Ave) FREE With the completion of the High Line, a 30ft-high abandoned stretch of elevated railroad track transformed into a long ribbon of parkland (from Gansevoort St to W 34th St; entrances are at Gansevoort, 14th, 16th, 18th, 20th, 30th and 34th Sts with elevator access at all but 18th St), there's finally some greenery amid the asphalt jungle.

Only three stories above the streetscape, this thoughtfully and carefully designed mix of contemporary, industrial and natural elements is nevertheless a refuge and escape from the ordinary. A glass-front amphitheater with bleacher-like seating sits just above 10th Ave – bring some food and join local workers on their lunch break.

Whitney Museum of American Art MUSEUM (Map p80; ☎212-570-3600; www.whitney.org; 99 Gansevoort St; adult/child $22/free; ⊙10:30am-6pm Mon, Wed & Sun, to 10pm Thu-Sat; S L to 8th Ave) After years of construction, the Whitney's new downtown location opened to much fanfare in 2015. Perched near the foot of the High Line, this architecturally stunning building – designed by Renzo Piano – makes a suitable introduction to the museum's superb collection. Inside the spacious, light-filled galleries, you'll find works by all the great American artists, including Edward Hopper, Jasper Johns, Georgia O'Keeffe and Mark Rothko.

In addition to rotating exhibits, there is a biennial on even-numbered years, an ambitious survey of contemporary art that rarely fails to generate controversy.

Chelsea

This 'hood is popular for two main reasons: one, the parade of gorgeous gay men (known affectionately as 'Chelsea boys') who roam Eighth Ave, darting from gyms to

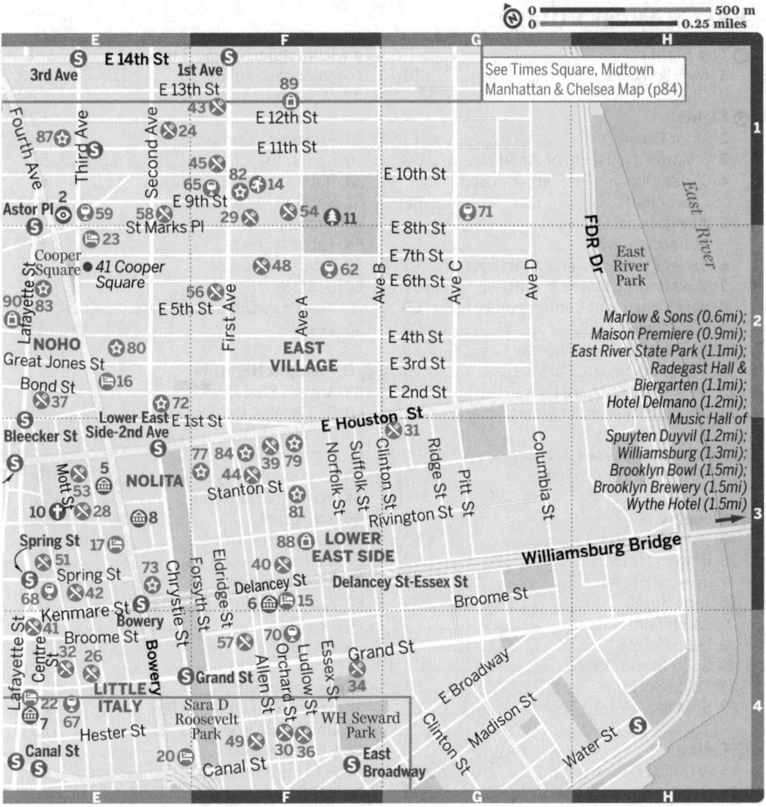

trendy happy hours; and two, as the hubs of the city's art-gallery scene, it's currently home to nearly 200 modern-art exhibition spaces, most of which are clustered west of Tenth Ave. For a handy list of specific galleries and upcoming shows, check out www.chelseagallerymap.com.

Rubin Museum of Art MUSEUM

(Map p84; ☎212-620-5000; www.rmanyc.org; 150 W 17th St at Seventh Ave; adult/child $15/free, 6-10pm Fri free; ⏲11am-5pm Mon & Thu, to 9pm Wed, to 10pm Fri, to 6pm Sat & Sun; S1 to 18th St) Dedicated to the art of the Himalayas and surrounding regions, this museum's impressive collection includes embroidered textiles from China, metal sculptures from Tibet, intricate Bhutanese paintings, and ritual objects and dance masks from various Tibetan regions, spanning from the 2nd to 19th centuries.

On Friday nights, museum admission is free and the cafe transforms into the K2 Lounge, where you can nibble on pan-Asian tapas, sip cocktails and enjoy a mix of DJs, films and other programs.

Chelsea Piers Complex SPORTS

(Map p84; ☎212-336-6666; www.chelseapiers.com; Hudson River at end of W 23rd St; SC/E to 23rd St) A waterfront sports center that caters to the athlete in everyone. It's got a four-level driving range, an indoor ice rink, a jazzy bowling alley, Hoop City for basketball, a sailing school for kids, batting cages, a huge gym, indoor rock-climbing walls – the works.

Flatiron District

The famous 1902 **Flatiron Building** (Map p84; Broadway, cnr Fifth Ave & 23rd St; SN/R, F/M, 6 to 23rd St) has a distinctive triangular shape to match its site. It was New York's first iron-frame high-rise, and the world's tallest building until 1909. The surrounding

East & West Villages

Top Sights
1 The High Line ... B1

Sights
2 Astor Place ... E1
3 Children's Museum of the Arts ... C3
4 Christopher Street Piers/Hudson River Park ... B2
5 International Center of Photography ... E3
6 Lower East Side Tenement Museum ... F3
7 Museum of Chinese in America ... E4
8 New Museum of Contemporary Art ... E3
9 Sheridan Square ... C2
10 St Patrick's Old Cathedral ... E3
11 Tompkins Square Park ... F1
12 Washington Square Park ... D2
13 Whitney Museum of American Art ... A1

Activities, Courses & Tours
14 Russian & Turkish Baths ... F1

Sleeping
15 Blue Moon Hotel ... F3
16 Bowery Hotel ... E2
17 Bowery House ... E3
18 Jane Hotel ... A1
19 Larchmont Hotel ... D1
20 Leon Hotel ... E4
21 Soho Grand Hotel ... D4
22 Solita SoHo ... E4
23 St Mark's Hotel ... E2

Eating
24 Angelica Kitchen ... E1
25 Balthazar ... D3
26 Bánh Mì Saigon Bakery ... E4
27 Boqueria Soho ... D3
28 Café Gitane ... E3
29 Cafe Mogador ... F1
30 Cheeky Sandwiches ... F4
31 Clinton Street Baking Company ... G3
32 Da Nico ... E4
33 Dominique Ansel Bakery ... D3
34 Doughnut Plant ... F4
35 Dutch ... D3
36 Fung Tu ... F4
37 Il Buco ... E2
38 Joe's Pizza ... C2
39 Katz's Delicatessen ... F3
40 Kuma Inn ... F3
41 La Esquina ... E4
42 Lombardi's ... E3
43 Luzzo's ... F1
44 Meatball Shop ... F3
45 Momofuku Noodle Bar ... F1
46 Mooncake Foods ... D4
47 Moustache ... C2
48 Porchetta ... F2
49 Prosperity Dumpling ... F4
50 RedFarm ... B2
51 Ruby's ... E3
52 Spotted Pig ... B2
53 Tacombi ... E3
54 Tacos Morelos ... F1
55 Taïm ... C1
56 Upstate ... F2
57 Vanessa's Dumpling House ... F4
58 Veselka ... E1

Drinking & Nightlife
59 Angel's Share ... E1
60 Bell Book & Candle ... C1
61 Buvette ... C2
62 Eastern Bloc ... F2
63 Employees Only ... B2
64 Henrietta Hudson ... C2
65 Immigrant ... F1
66 Marie's Crisis ... C2
67 Mulberry Project ... E4
68 Spring Lounge ... E3
69 Stonewall Inn ... C2
70 Ten Bells ... F4
71 Wayland ... G1

Entertainment
72 Anthology Film Archives ... E2
73 Bowery Ballroom ... E3
74 Comedy Cellar ... C2
75 Film Forum ... C3
76 IFC Center ... C2
Joe's Pub ... (see 83)
77 Landmark Sunshine Cinema ... F3
78 Le Poisson Rouge ... D2
79 Mercury Lounge ... F3
80 New York Theater Workshop ... E2
81 Pianos ... F3
82 PS 122 ... F1
83 Public Theater ... E2
84 Rockwood Music Hall ... F3
85 Smalls ... C2
86 Village Vanguard ... C1
87 Webster Hall ... E1

Shopping
88 Economy Candy ... F3
89 Obscura Antiques ... F1
90 Other Music ... E2
91 Strand Book Store ... D1

district is a fashionable area of boutiques, loft apartments and a burgeoning high-tech corridor, the city's answer to Silicon Valley. Peaceful **Madison Square Park**, bordered by 23rd and 26th Sts, and Fifth and Madison Aves, has an active dog run, rotating outdoor sculptures, shaded park benches and a popular burger joint.

Museum of Sex MUSEUM
(Map p84; www.museumofsex.com; 233 Fifth Ave, at 27th St; adult $17.50; ⏱10am-8pm Sun-Thu, to 9pm Fri & Sat; S N/R to 23rd St) Get the lowdown on anything from online fetishes to homosexual necrophilia in the mallard duck at this slick, smallish ode to all things hot and sweaty.

Union Square

Like the Noah's Ark of New York, **Union Square** (Map p84; www.unionsquarenyc.org; 17th St btwn Broadway & Park Ave S; S L, N/Q/R, 4/5/6 to 14th St-Union Sq) rescues at least two of every kind from the curling seas of concrete. Here, amid the tapestry of stone steps and fenced-in foliage, it's not uncommon to find denizens of every ilk: suited businessfolk gulping fresh air during their lunch breaks, dreadlocked loiterers tapping beats on their tabla, skateboarding punks flipping tricks on the southeastern stairs, rowdy college kids guzzling student-priced eats, and throngs of protesting masses chanting fervently for various causes.

Gramercy Park PARK
(Map p84; E 20th St btwn Park & Third Aves; S N/R, F/M, 6 to 23rd St) Gramercy Park, a few blocks northeast of Union Square, is named after one of New York's loveliest parks; for residents only, though, and you need a key to get in!

★ **Greenmarket Farmers Market** MARKET
(Map p84; ☎212-788-7476; www.grownyc.org; 17th St btwn Broadway & Park Ave S; ⏱8am-6pm Mon, Wed, Fri & Sat) On most days, Union Square's north end hosts the most popular of the nearly 50 greenmarkets throughout the five boroughs, where even celebrity chefs come for just-picked rarities including fiddlehead ferns, heirloom tomatoes and fresh curry leaves.

Midtown

The classic NYC fantasy – shiny skyscrapers, teeming mobs of worker bees, Fifth Ave store windows, taxi traffic – and some of the city's most popular attractions can be found here.

★ **Museum of Modern Art** MUSEUM
(MoMA; Map p84; www.moma.org; 11 W 53rd St, btwn Fifth & Sixth Aves; adult/child $25/free, 4-8pm Fri free; ⏱10:30am-5:30pm Sat-Thu, to 8pm Fri, to 8pm Thu Jul-Aug; S E, M to 5th Ave-53rd St) Superstar of the modern art scene, MoMA's booty makes many other collections look, well, endearing. You'll find more A-listers here than at an Oscars after-party: Van Gogh, Matisse, Picasso, Warhol, Lichtenstein, Rothko, Pollock and Bourgeois. Since its founding in 1929, the museum has amassed over 150,000 artworks, documenting the emerging creative ideas and movements of the late 19th century through to those that dominate today.

For art buffs, it's Valhalla. For the uninitiated, it's a thrilling crash course in all that is beautiful and addictive about art.

Times Square LANDMARK
(Map p84; www.timessquare.com; Broadway at Seventh Ave; S N/Q/R, S, 1/2/3, 7 to Times Sq-42nd St) Love it or hate it, the intersection of Broadway and Seventh Ave (better known as Times Square) is New York City's hyperactive heart; a restless, hypnotic torrent of glittering lights, bombastic billboards and raw urban energy. It's not hip, fashionable or in-the-know, and it couldn't care less. It's too busy pumping out iconic, mass-marketed NYC – yellow cabs, golden arches, soaring skyscrapers and razzle-dazzle Broadway marquees.

Theater District NEIGHBORHOOD
(S N/Q/R, S, 1/2/3, 7 to Times Sq-42nd St) The Times Square area is at least as famous as New York's official Theater District, with dozens of Broadway and off-Broadway theaters located in an area that stretches from 41st to 54th Sts, between Sixth and Ninth Aves. The Times Square branch of tourist information center New York City & Company (p125) sits smack in the middle of this famous crossroads. Broadway, the road, once ran all the way to the state capital in Albany.

Rockefeller Center NOTABLE BUILDING
(Map p84; www.rockefellercenter.com; Fifth to Sixth Aves & 48th to 51st Sts; S B/D/F/M to 47th-50th Sts-Rockefeller Center) During the height of the Great Depression in the 1930s, construction of the 22-acre Rockefeller Center (including the landmark art-deco skyscraper) gave jobs to 70,000 workers over nine years. It was the first project to combine retail, entertainment and office space in what is often referred to as a 'city within a city.'

In winter the ground floor outdoor space is abuzz with ice-skaters and Christmas-tree gawkers.

NBC Studio Tours GUIDED TOUR
(Map p84; ☎212-664-3700; www.thetouratnbcstudios.com; 30 Rockefeller Plaza, at 49th St;

Times Square, Midtown Manhattan & Chelsea

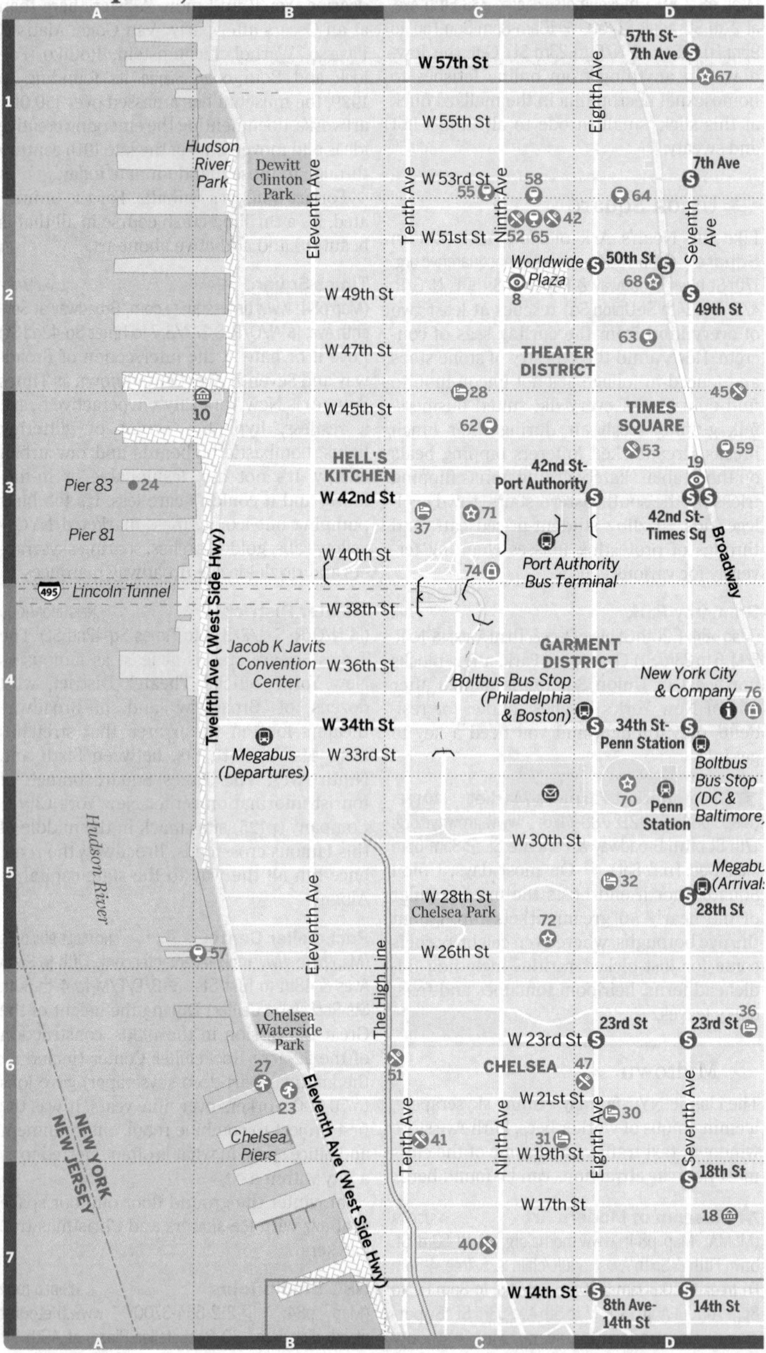

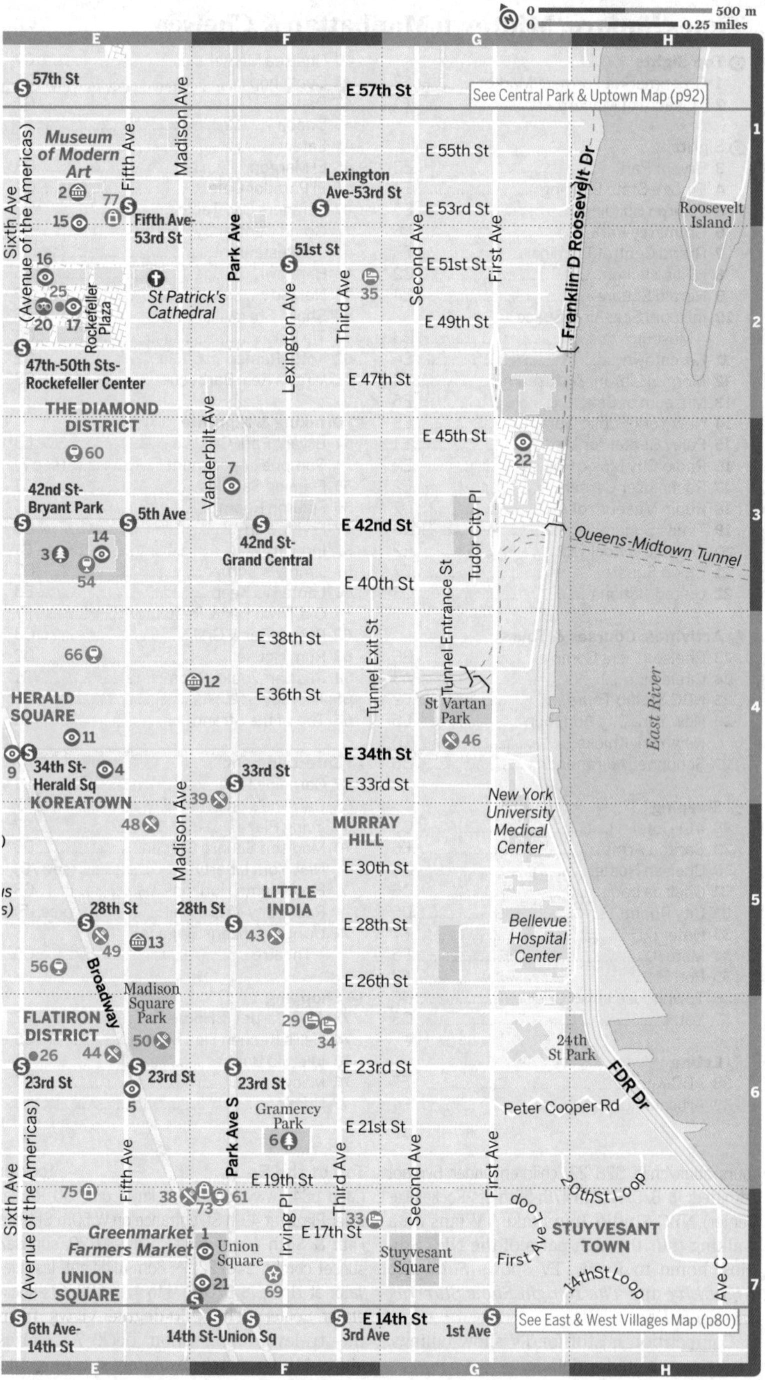
0 500 m
0 0.25 miles
E
F
G
H
1
2
3
4
5
6
7
See Central Park & Uptown Map (p92)
See East & West Villages Map (p80)
57th St
E 57th St
Madison Ave
Fifth Ave
Sixth Ave (Avenue of the Americas)
Museum of Modern Art
2
77
15
Fifth Ave-53rd St
Lexington Ave-53rd St
E 55th St
E 53rd St
Park Ave
51st St
E 51st St
35
Second Ave
First Ave
Franklin D Roosevelt Dr
Roosevelt Island
16
25
20
17
Rockefeller Plaza
St Patrick's Cathedral
Lexington Ave
Third Ave
E 49th St
47th-50th Sts-Rockefeller Center
E 47th St
THE DIAMOND DISTRICT
Vanderbilt Ave
E 45th St
22
60
7
42nd St-Bryant Park
5th Ave
42nd St-Grand Central
E 42nd St
Tudor City Pl
Queens-Midtown Tunnel
3
14
54
E 40th St
Tunnel Entrance St
E 38th St
66
12
E 36th St
Tunnel Exit St
St Vartan Park
46
HERALD SQUARE
11
East River
9
34th St-Herald Sq
4
E 34th St
33rd St
E 33rd St
KOREATOWN
39
48
New York University Medical Center
MURRAY HILL
E 30th St
LITTLE INDIA
28th St
28th St
E 28th St
43
Bellevue Hospital Center
49
13
56
Broadway
E 26th St
Madison Square Park
FLATIRON DISTRICT
29
34
50
24th St Park
26
44
23rd St
23rd St
23rd St
E 23rd St
FDR Dr
5
Park Ave S
Gramercy Park
6
E 21st St
Peter Cooper Rd
E 19th St
20th St Loop
75
38
73
61
Irving Pl
33
E 17th St
STUYVESANT TOWN
First Ave Loop
Greenmarket Farmers Market
1
Union Square
Stuyvesant Square
14th St Loop
UNION SQUARE
21
69
Ave C
6th Ave-14th St
14th St-Union Sq
E 14th St
3rd Ave
1st Ave

Times Square, Midtown Manhattan & Chelsea

Top Sights
1 Greenmarket Farmers Market ... F7
2 Museum of Modern Art ... E1

Sights
3 Bryant Park ... E3
4 Empire State Building ... E4
5 Flatiron Building ... E6
6 Gramercy Park ... F6
7 Grand Central Terminal ... F3
8 Hell's Kitchen ... C2
9 Herald Square ... E4
10 Intrepid Sea, Air & Space Museum ... B3
11 Koreatown ... E4
12 Morgan Library & Museum ... F4
13 Museum of Sex ... E5
14 New York Public Library ... E3
15 Paley Center for Media ... E1
16 Radio City Music Hall ... E2
17 Rockefeller Center ... E2
18 Rubin Museum of Art ... D7
19 Times Square ... D3
20 Top of the Rock ... E2
21 Union Square ... F7
22 United Nations ... G3

Activities, Courses & Tours
23 Chelsea Piers Complex ... B6
24 Circle Line ... A3
25 NBC Studio Tours ... E2
26 New York City Audubon ... E6
New York Knicks ... (see 70)
27 Schooner Adirondack ... B6

Sleeping
28 414 Hotel ... C3
29 Carlton Arms ... F6
30 Chelsea Hostel ... D6
31 Chelsea Lodge ... C6
32 City Rooms ... D5
33 Hotel 17 ... F7
34 Marcel ... F6
35 Pod 51 ... F2
36 Townhouse Inn of Chelsea ... D6
37 Yotel ... C3

Eating
38 ABC Kitchen ... E7
39 Artisanal ... F4
40 Chelsea Market ... C7
41 Cookshop ... C6
42 Danji ... C2
43 Dhaba ... F5
44 Eataly ... E6
45 El Margon ... D3
46 El Parador Cafe ... G4
47 Foragers City Table ... D6
Grand Central Oyster Bar & Restaurant ... (see 7)
48 Hangawi ... E5
49 NoMad ... E5
50 Shake Shack ... E6
51 Tía Pol ... C6
52 Totto Ramen ... C2
53 Virgil's Real Barbecue ... D3

Drinking & Nightlife
54 Bryant Park Grill ... E3
Campbell Apartment ... (see 7)
55 Flaming Saddles ... C1
56 Flatiron Room ... E5
57 Frying Pan ... B5
58 Industry ... C1
59 Jimmy's Corner ... D3
60 Lantern's Keep ... E3
61 Old Town Bar & Restaurant ... F7
62 Rudy's Bar & Grill ... C3
63 Rum House ... D2
64 Russian Vodka Room ... D1
65 Therapy ... C2
66 Top of the Strand ... E4

Entertainment
67 Carnegie Hall ... D1
68 Caroline's on Broadway ... D2
69 Irving Plaza ... F7
70 Madison Square Garden ... D5
New York Liberty ... (see 70)
71 Playwrights Horizons ... C3
Radio City Music Hall ... (see 16)
72 Upright Citizens Brigade Theatre ... C5

Shopping
73 ABC Carpet & Home ... F7
74 Hell's Kitchen Flea Market ... C3
75 Idlewild Books ... E7
76 Macy's ... D4
77 Uniqlo ... E1

tours adult/child $28/22, children under 6yr not admitted; S B/D/F/M to 47th-50th Sts-Rockefeller Center) NBC Studio Tours take TV fans on a walking tour through parts of the NBC Studios, home to iconic TV shows *Saturday Night Live* and *The Tonight Show Starring Jimmy Fallon*.

Competition is stiff for TV show tapings. Visit the website for details.

Top of the Rock LOOKOUT

(Map p84; www.topoftherocknyc.com; 30 Rockefeller Plaza, at 49th St, entrance on W 50th St btwn Fifth & Sixth Aves; adult/child $30/20, sunrise/sunset combo $40/22; 8am-midnight, last elevator at 11pm; S B/D/F/M to 47th-50th Sts-Rockefeller Center) The 360-degree views from the tri-level observation deck 70 stories above Midtown are absolutely stunning and should not be missed. You get an excellent view of the Empire State Building, as well as Central Park's perfect patch of green.

Radio City Music Hall NOTABLE BUILDING

(Map p84; www.radiocity.com; 1260 Sixth Ave, at 51st St; tours adult/child $27/18; ⏲tours 10am-5pm; Ⓢ B/D/F/M to 47th-50th Sts-Rockefeller Center) Within the Rockefeller complex is the 6000-seat Radio City Music Hall from 1932. To get an inside look at this former movie palace and protected landmark, which has been gorgeously restored in all its art-deco grandeur, join one of the frequent guided tours that leave the lobby.

New York Public Library BUILDING

(Stephen A Schwarzman Bldg; Map p84; ☎917-275-6975; www.nypl.org; Fifth Ave at 42nd St; ⏲10am-6pm Mon & Thu-Sat, to 8pm Tue & Wed, 1-5pm Sun, guided tours 11am & 2pm Mon-Sat, 2pm Sun; Ⓢ B/D/F/M to 42nd St-Bryant Park, 7 to 5th Ave) FREE Flanked by two huge marble lions, the massive, superb beaux-arts library stands as testament to the value of learning and culture in the city, as well as to the wealth of the philanthropists who made its founding possible.

A magnificent 3rd-floor reading room has a painted ceiling and bountiful natural light – rows of long wooden tables are occupied by studious folk working away at laptops. This, the main branch of the entire city library system, has galleries of manuscripts on display, as well as fascinating temporary exhibits.

Bryant Park PARK

(Map p84; www.bryantpark.org; 42nd St btwn Fifth & Sixth Aves; ⏲7am-midnight Mon-Fri, to 11pm Sat & Sun Jun-Sep, shorter hours rest of year; Ⓢ B/D/F/M to 42nd St-Bryant Park, 7 to Fifth Ave) Nestled behind the grand New York Public Library building, Bryant Park is a whimsical spot for a little time-out from the Midtown madness. You'll find European coffee kiosks, alfresco chess games, summer film screenings and winter ice-skating.

Empire State Building NOTABLE BUILDING

(Map p84; www.esbnyc.com; 350 Fifth Ave, at 34th St; 86th-fl observation deck adult/child $32/26, incl 102nd-fl observation deck $52/46; ⏲8am-2am, last elevators up 1:15am; Ⓢ B/D/F/M, N/Q/R to 34th St-Herald Sq) Catapulted to Hollywood stardom both as the planned meeting spot for Cary Grant and Deborah Kerr in *An Affair to Remember,* and the vertical perch that helped to topple King Kong, the towering Empire State Building is one of the most famous members of New York's skyline. It's a limestone classic built in just 410 days, or seven million man-hours, during the depths of the Depression, at a cost of $41 million.

On the site of the original Waldorf-Astoria Hotel, the 102-story, 1472ft (to the top of the antenna) Empire State Building opened in 1931 after 10 million bricks were laid, 6400 windows installed and 328,000 sq ft of marble laid. Today you can ride the elevator to observatories on the 86th and 102nd floors, but be prepared for crowds; try to come very early or very late (and purchase your tickets ahead of time, online or pony up for $55 'express passes') for an optimal experience.

Grand Central Terminal NOTABLE BUILDING

(Map p84; www.grandcentralterminal.com; 42nd St at Park Ave, Midtown East; ⏲5:30am-2am; Ⓢ S, 4/5/6, 7 to Grand Central-42nd St) Completed in 1913, Grand Central is another of New York's stunning beaux-arts buildings, boasting 75ft-high glass-encased catwalks and a vaulted ceiling bearing a mural of the constellations streaming across it. The balconies overlooking the main concourse afford an expansive view.

There's a high-end food market and the lower level houses an excellent array of eateries.

Fifth Avenue & Around NEIGHBORHOOD

(725 Fifth Ave, at 56th St) Immortalized in both film and song, Fifth Ave first developed its high-class reputation in the early 20th century, when it was considered desirable for its 'country' air and open spaces. A series of mansions called **Millionaire's Row** extended right up to 130th St, though most of the heirs to the millionaire mansions on Fifth Ave above 59th St sold them for demolition or converted them to the cultural institutions that now make up Museum Mile.

The avenue's Midtown stretch still boasts upmarket shops and hotels, including Trump Tower and the Plaza (corner Fifth Ave and Central Park South). While a number of the more exclusive boutiques have migrated to Madison Ave – leaving outposts of Gap and H&M in their wake – several superstars still reign over Fifth Ave above 50th St, including the famous Tiffany & Co.

Morgan Library & Museum MUSEUM

(Map p84; www.morganlibrary.org; 29 E 36th St, at Madison Ave, Midtown East; adult/child $18/12; ⏲10:30am-5pm Tue-Thu, to 9pm Fri, 10am-6pm Sat, 11am-6pm Sun; Ⓢ 6 to 33rd St) The beautifully renovated library is part of the 45-room mansion once owned by steel magnate JP Morgan. His collection features a phenomenal array of manuscripts, tapestries and books, a study filled with Italian Renaissance artwork, a marble rotunda and the three-tiered East Room main library. Temporary exhibitions delve into the lives of literary greats (Cervantes, Poe, Proust).

United Nations NOTABLE BUILDING

(UN; Map p84; ☎212-963-4475; http://visit.un.org; visitors' gate First Ave at 46th St, Midtown East; guided tours adult/child $20/11, children under 5yr not admitted, grounds access Sat & Sun free; ⏲tours 9:30am-4:15pm Mon-Fri, visitor center also open 10am-4:30pm Sat & Sun; S S, 4/5/6, 7 to Grand Central-42nd St) The UN is technically on a section of international territory overlooking the East River. Take a guided 45-minute tour (English-language tours are frequent; limited tours in several other languages) of the facility and you'll get to see (when official meetings are not in session) the General Assembly, where the annual fall convocation of member nations takes place, the Security Council Chamber, the Trusteeship Council Chamber and also the Economic & Social Council Chamber.

There is a park to the south of the complex which is home to several sculptures with a peace theme.

Paley Center for Media BUILDING

(Map p84; www.paleycenter.org; 25 W 52nd St, btwn Fifth & Sixth Aves; adult/child $10/5; ⏲noon-6pm Wed & Fri-Sun, to 8pm Thu; S E, M to 5th Ave-53rd St) TV fanatics who spent their childhood glued to the tube and proudly claim instant recall of all of Fonzi's *Happy Days* exploits can hold their heads high. This is the 'museum' for them. Search through a catalog of more than 100,000 US TV and radio programs and advertisements and a click of the mouse will play your selection on one of the library's computer screens. A comfy theater shows some great specials on broadcasting history, and there are frequent events and screenings.

Intrepid Sea, Air & Space Museum MUSEUM

(Map p84; www.intrepidmuseum.org; Pier 86, Twelfth Ave at 46th St, Midtown West; Intrepid & Growler submarine adult/child $24/19, incl Space Shuttle Pavilion $31/24; ⏲10am-5pm Mon-Fri, to 6pm Sat & Sun Apr-Oct, 10am-5pm Mon-Sun Nov-Mar; 🚌M42, M50 westbound, S A/C/E to 42nd St-Port Authority Bus Terminal) The USS *Intrepid*, a hulking aircraft carrier that survived both a WWII bomb and kamikaze attacks has been transformed into a military museum with high-tech exhibits and fighter planes and helicopters for view on the outdoor flight deck. The pier area contains the guided-missile submarine *Growler*, a decommissioned Concorde and the *Enterprise* space shuttle.

Herald Square SQUARE

(Map p84; cnr Broadway, Sixth Ave & 34th St; S B/D/F/M, N/Q/R to 34th St-Herald Sq) This crowded convergence of Broadway, Sixth Ave and 34th St is best known as the home of Macy's (p124) department store, where you can still ride some of the remaining original wooden elevators to floors ranging from home furnishings to lingerie. But the busy square gets its name from a long-defunct newspaper, the *Herald*, and the small, leafy park here bustles during business hours.

Koreatown NEIGHBORHOOD

(Map p84; 31st to 36th Sts & Broadway to Fifth Ave; S B/D/F/M, N/Q/R to 34th St-Herald Sq) For kimchi and karaoke, it's hard to beat Koreatown (Little Korea). Mainly concentrated on 32nd St, with some spillover into the surrounding streets both south and north of this strip, it's a Seoul-ful jumble of Korean-owned restaurants, shops, salons and spas.

Hell's Kitchen NEIGHBORHOOD

(Clinton; Map p84) For years, the far west side of Midtown was a working-class district of tenements and food warehouses known as Hell's Kitchen – supposedly its name was muttered by a cop in reaction to a riot in the neighborhood in 1881. A 1990s economic boom seriously altered the character and developers reverted to using the cleaned-up name, Clinton, a moniker originating from the 1950s; locals are split on usage.

New, primarily inexpensive ethnic restaurants have exploded along Ninth and Tenth Aves between about 37th and 55th Sts. Antique hunters should visit the **Hell's Kitchen Flea Market** (☎212-243-5343; 39th St btwn Ninth & Tenth Aves; ⏲9am-5pm Sat & Sun; S A/C/E to 42nd St), boasting 170 vendors of vintage clothing, antique jewelry, period furniture and more.

Museum of Arts & Design MUSEUM

(MAD; Map p92; www.madmuseum.org; 2 Columbus Circle, btwn Eighth Ave & Broadway; adult/child $16/free, by donation 6-9pm Thu; ⏲10am-6pm Tue, Wed, Sat & Sun, to 9pm Thu & Fri; S A/C, B/D, 1 to 59th St-Columbus Circle) On the southern side of the circle, exhibiting a diverse international collection of modern, folk, craft and fine-art pieces. The plush and trippy design of **Robert**, the 9th-floor restaurant, complements fantastic views of Central Park.

Upper West Side

Shorthand for liberal, progressive and intellectual New York – think Woody Allen movies (although he lives on the Upper East Side) and Seinfeld – this neighborhood comprises the west side of Manhattan from Central Park to the Hudson River, and from Columbus Circle to 110th St. You'll find massive, ornate apartments, a diverse mix of stable, upwardly mobile folks (with many actors and classical musicians sprinkled throughout), and some lovely green spaces, including scenic Riverside Park.

★Central Park PARK

(Map p92; www.centralparknyc.org; 59th & 110th Sts, btwn Central Park West & Fifth Ave; 6am-1am;) One of the world's most renowned green spaces, Central Park checks in with 843 acres of rolling meadows, boulder-studded outcroppings, elm-lined walkways, manicured European-style gardens, a lake and a reservoir — not to mention an outdoor theater, a memorial to John Lennon, an idyllic waterside eatery (the **Loeb Boathouse**) and one very famous statue of Alice in Wonderland. The big challenge? Figuring out where to begin.

Highlights include **Sheep Meadow** (mid-park from 66th to 69th Sts), where tens of thousands of people lounge and play on warm weather weekends; **Central Park Zoo** (212-439-6500; www.centralparkzoo.com; 64th St, at Fifth Ave; adult/child $12/7; 10am-5:30pm Apr-Oct, to 4:30pm Nov-Mar; ; S N/Q/R to 5th Ave-59th St); and the **Ramble**, a rest stop for nearly 250 migratory species of birdlife – early morning is best for sightings. A favorite tourist activity is to rent a horse-drawn carriage or hop in a **pedicab** (one hour tours from $45); the latter congregate at Central Park West and 72nd St.

★Lincoln Center CULTURAL CENTER

(Map p92; 212-875-5456; lc.lincolncenter.org; Columbus Ave btwn 62nd & 66th Sts; public plazas free, tours adult/student $18/15; ; S 1 to 66th St-Lincoln Center) The billion-dollar-plus redevelopment of the world's largest performing-arts center includes the dramatically redesigned **Alice Tully Hall** and other stunning venues surrounding a massive fountain; public spaces, including the roof lawn of the North Plaza (an upscale restaurant is underneath), have been upgraded. The lavishly designed **Metropolitan Opera House** (MET), the largest opera house in the world, seats 3900 people.

Fascinating one-hour tours of the complex leave from the lobby of Avery Fisher Hall from 10:30am to 4:30pm daily; these vary from architectural to backstage tours. Free wi-fi is available on the property as well as at the **David Rubenstein Atrium** (Broadway, btwn 62nd & 63rd Sts; S 1 to 66th St-Lincoln Center), a modern public space featuring a lounge area, cafe, information desk, and ticket center offering day-of discounts to Lincoln Center performances.

★American Museum of Natural History MUSEUM

(Map p92; 212-769-5100; www.amnh.org; Central Park West, at 79th St; suggested donation adult/child $22/12.50; 10am-5:45pm, Rose Center to 8:45pm Fri, Butterfly Conservatory Oct-May; ; S B, C to 81st St-Museum of Natural History, 1 to 79th St) Founded in 1869, this museum includes more than 30 million artifacts, interactive exhibits and loads of taxidermy. It's most famous for its three large dinosaur halls, an enormous (fake) blue whale that hangs from the ceiling above the Hall of Ocean Life and the elaborate **Rose Center for Earth & Space** – home to space-show theaters and the planetarium.

Riverside Park OUTDOORS

(Map p92; 212-870-3070; www.riversideparknyc.org; Riverside Dr, btwn 68th & 155th Sts; 6am-1am; ; S 1/2/3 to any stop btwn 66th & 157th Sts) This waterside spot, running north on the Upper West Side and banked by the Hudson River from 59th to 158th Sts, is lusciously leafy. Plenty of bike paths and playgrounds make it a family favorite.

New-York Historical Society MUSEUM

(Map p92; www.nyhistory.org; 2 W 77th St, at Central Park West; adult/child $19/6, by donation 6-8pm Fri, library free; 10am-6pm Tue-Thu & Sat, to 8pm Fri, 11am-5pm Sun; S B, C to 81st St-Museum of Natural History) This museum, founded in 1804, is widely credited with being the city's oldest. The quirky and wide-ranging permanent collection, including a leg brace worn by President Franklin D. Roosevelt and a 19th-century mechanical bank in which a political figure slips coins into his pocket, is now housed in a spruced-up contemporary exhibition space.

Central Park

THE LUNGS OF NEW YORK

The rectangular patch of green that occupies Manhattan's heart began life in the mid-19th century as a swampy piece of land that was carefully bulldozed into the idyllic nature-scape you see today. Since officially becoming Central Park, it has brought New Yorkers of all stripes together in interesting and unexpected ways. The park has served as a place for the rich to show off their fancy carriages (1860s), for the poor to enjoy free Sunday concerts (1880s) and for activists to hold be-ins against the Vietnam War (1960s).

Since then, legions of locals – not to mention travelers from all kinds of faraway places – have poured in to stroll, picnic, sunbathe, play ball and catch free concerts and performances of works by Shakespeare.

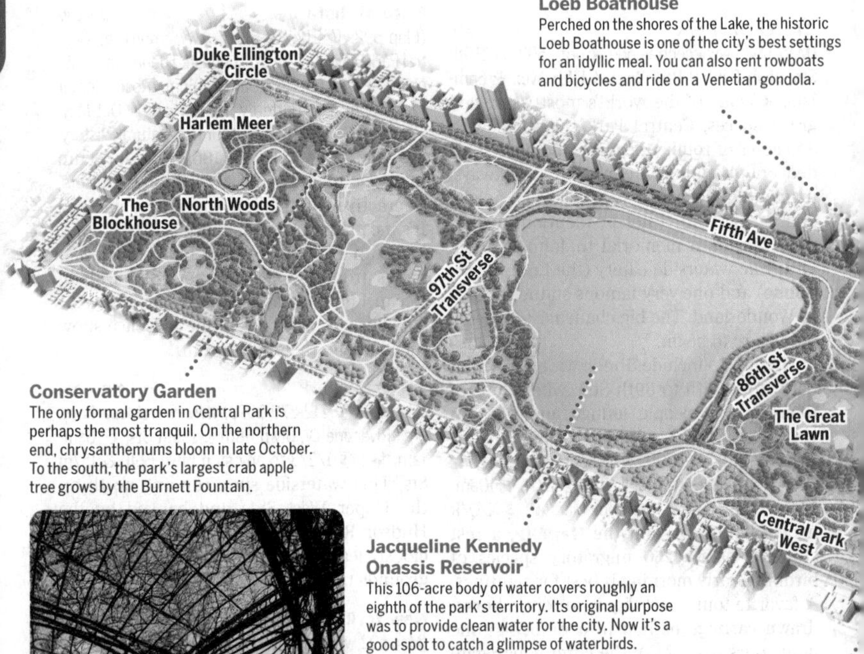

Loeb Boathouse

Perched on the shores of the Lake, the historic Loeb Boathouse is one of the city's best settings for an idyllic meal. You can also rent rowboats and bicycles and ride on a Venetian gondola.

Conservatory Garden

The only formal garden in Central Park is perhaps the most tranquil. On the northern end, chrysanthemums bloom in late October. To the south, the park's largest crab apple tree grows by the Burnett Fountain.

STEVEN GREAVES / GETTY IMAGES ©

Jacqueline Kennedy Onassis Reservoir

This 106-acre body of water covers roughly an eighth of the park's territory. Its original purpose was to provide clean water for the city. Now it's a good spot to catch a glimpse of waterbirds.

ANGUS OSBORN / GETTY IMAGES ©

Belvedere Castle

A so-called 'Victorian folly,' this Gothic-Romanesque castle serves no other purpose than to be a very dramatic lookout point. It was built by Central Park co-designer Calvert Vaux in 1869.

The park's varied terrain offers a wonderland of experiences. There are quiet, woodsy knolls in the north. To the south is the reservoir, crowded with joggers. There are European gardens, a zoo and various bodies of water. For maximum flamboyance, hit the Sheep Meadow on a sunny day, when all of New York shows up to lounge.

Central Park is more than just a green space. It is New York City's backyard.

FACTS & FIGURES

» **Landscape architects** Frederick Law Olmsted and Calvert Vaux

» **Year that construction began** 1858

» **Acres** 843

» **On film** Hundreds of movies have been shot on location, from Depression-era blockbusters such as *Gold Diggers* (1933) to the monster-attack flick *Cloverfield* (2008).

DENNIS JOHNSON / GETTY IMAGES ©

Conservatory Water

This pond is popular in the warmer months, when children sail their model boats across its surface. Conservatory Water was inspired by 19th-century Parisian model-boat ponds and figured prominently in EB White's classic book, *Stuart Little*.

CHRISTOPHER GROENHOUT / GETTY IMAGES ©

Bethesda Fountain

This neoclassical fountain is one of New York's largest. It's capped by the *Angel of the Waters*, which is supported by four cherubim. The fountain was created by bohemian-feminist sculptor Emma Stebbins in 1868.

Strawberry Fields

A simple mosaic memorial pays tribute to musician John Lennon, who was killed across the street outside the Dakota Building. Funded by Yoko Ono, its name is inspired by the Beatles song 'Strawberry Fields Forever.'

The Mall/Literary Walk

A Parisian-style promenade – the only straight line in the park – is flanked by statues of literati on the southern end, including Robert Burns and Shakespeare. It is lined with rare North American elms.

Central Park & Uptown

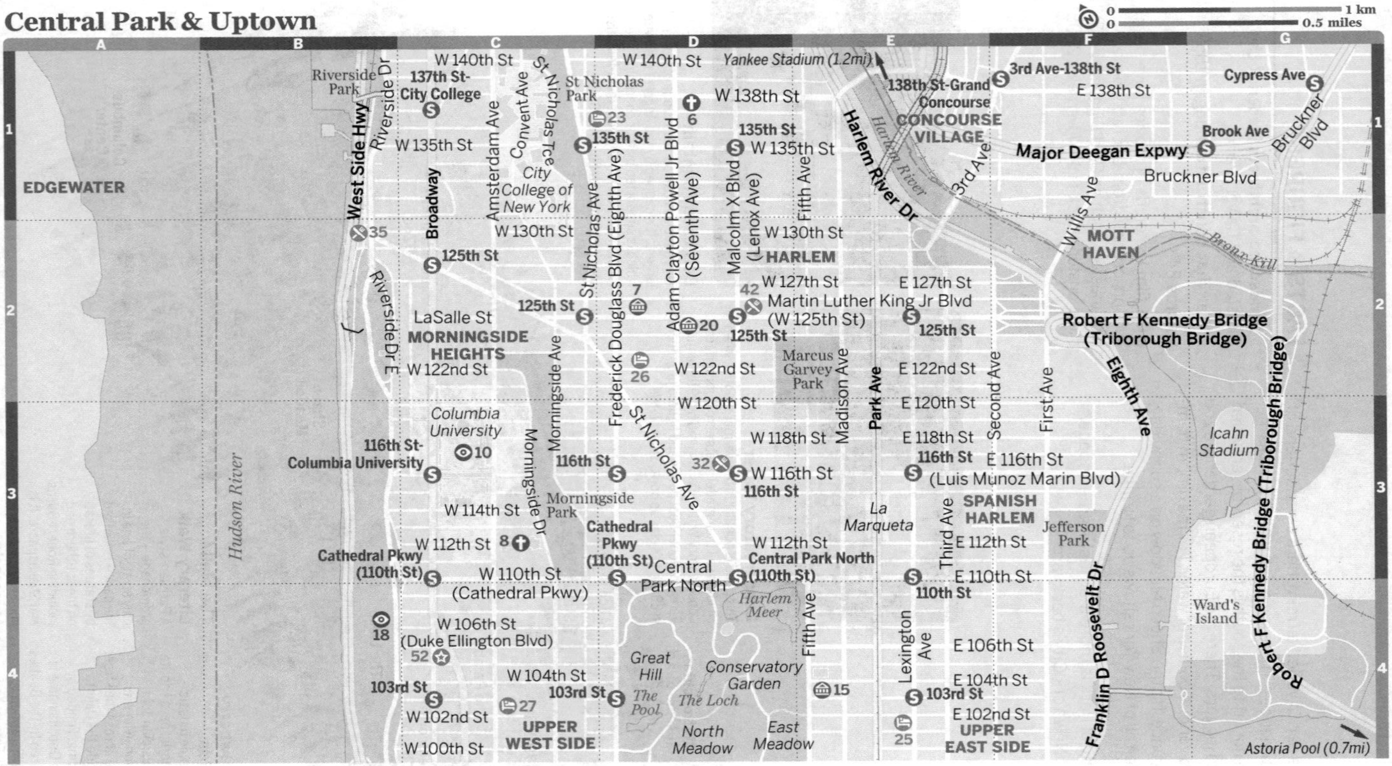
0 1 km
0 0.5 miles
A
B
C
D
E
F
G
1
2
3
4
EDGEWATER
Hudson River
Riverside Park
West Side Hwy
Riverside Dr
Riverside Dr E
W 140th St
137th St-City College
W 135th St
Broadway
Amsterdam Ave
Convent Ave
St Nicholas Tce
St Nicholas Park
City College of New York
23
135th St
W 130th St
35
125th St
LaSalle St
MORNINGSIDE HEIGHTS
W 122nd St
Morningside Ave
St Nicholas Ave
Frederick Douglass Blvd (Eighth Ave)
7
26
Columbia University
10
116th St-Columbia University
116th St
Morningside Dr
Morningside Park
W 114th St
W 112th St
8
Cathedral Pkwy (110th St)
W 110th St (Cathedral Pkwy)
18
W 106th St (Duke Ellington Blvd)
52
103rd St
W 104th St
W 102nd St
27
W 100th St
UPPER WEST SIDE
W 140th St
Yankee Stadium (1.2mi)
W 138th St
6
Adam Clayton Powell Jr Blvd (Seventh Ave)
Malcolm X Blvd (Lenox Ave)
W 135th St
Fifth Ave
HARLEM
42
W 127th St
Martin Luther King Jr Blvd (W 125th St)
20
W 122nd St
W 120th St
Marcus Garvey Park
Madison Ave
Park Ave
W 118th St
32
W 116th St
La Marqueta
W 112th St
Central Park North (110th St)
Central Park North
Harlem Meer
Great Hill
The Pool
The Loch
Conservatory Garden
North Meadow
East Meadow
15
25
Harlem River Dr
Harlem River
138th St-Grand Concourse
CONCOURSE VILLAGE
3rd Ave-138th St
3rd Ave
E 138th St
Major Deegan Expwy
Brook Ave
Bruckner Blvd
Cypress Ave
Willis Ave
MOTT HAVEN
Bronx Kill
E 127th St
E 122nd St
E 120th St
E 118th St
E 116th St (Luis Munoz Marin Blvd)
Second Ave
First Ave
Third Ave
SPANISH HARLEM
E 112th St
E 110th St
110th St
Lexington Ave
E 106th St
E 104th St
103rd St
E 102nd St
UPPER EAST SIDE
Jefferson Park
Robert F Kennedy Bridge (Triborough Bridge)
Eighth Ave
Franklin D Roosevelt Dr
Icahn Stadium
Ward's Island
Astoria Pool (0.7mi)

ASTORIA
LONG ISLAND CITY
UNION CITY
NEW JERSEY
NEW YORK
East River
East Channel
Mill Rock Island
Mill Rock Light Park
Carl Schurz Park
Rainey Park
Vernon Blvd
Roosevelt Island Bridge
Main St
Roosevelt Island
The Local NYC (0.7mi); PS 1 Contemporary Art Center (1.2mi); Paper Factory Hotel (1.2mi); Museum of the Moving Image (1.5mi); Jackson Heights Historic District (3.6mi)
Ed Koch Queensboro Bridge
FDR Dr
East End Ave
York Ave
First Ave
Second Ave
Third Ave
Lexington Ave
Park Ave
Madison Ave
Fifth Ave
Rockefeller University
Hunter College
E 99th St
E 97th St
E 96th St
E 94th St
E 92nd St
E 90th St
E 88th St
E 86th St
E 84th St
E 82nd St
E 80th St
E 79th St
E 77th St
E 75th St
E 72nd St
E 70th St
E 68th St
E 65th St
E 62nd St
E 59th St
E 57th St
96th St
86th St
77th St
68th St-Hunter College
Lexington Ave-63rd St
Lexington Ave-59th St
5th Ave-59th St
Roosevelt Island
Metropolitan Museum of Art
Frick Collection
Conservatory Water
Central Park
Jacqueline Kennedy Onassis Reservoir
Great Lawn
Turtle Pond
The Ramble
The Lake
Bethesda Fountain
Strawberry Fields
Naumburg Bandshell
The Mall
Literary Walk
The Pond
East Dr
West Dr
Central Park West
81st St-Museum of Natural History
72nd St
59th St-Columbus Circle
66th St-Lincoln Center
79th St
Amsterdam Ave
Broadway
West End Ave
Ninth Ave
Riverside Dr
West Side Hwy
W 97th St
W 96th St
W 94th St
W 92nd St
W 90th St
W 88th St
W 85th St
W 83rd St
W 81st St
W 77th St
W 75th St
W 72nd St
W 70th St
W 66th St
W 62nd St
W 60th St
W 57th St
American Museum of Natural History
Dakota Building
Lincoln Center
See Times Square, Midtown Manhattan & Chelsea Map (p84)
1
2
3
4
5
9
11
12
13
14
16
17
19
21
22
24
28
29
30
31
33
34
36
37
38
39
40
41
43
44
45
46
47
48
49
50
51
53
54
A
B
C
D
E
F
G
5
6
7
8

Central Park & Uptown

Top Sights
1 American Museum of Natural History ... C6
2 Central Park ... D6
3 Frick Collection ... E7
4 Lincoln Center ... C8
5 Metropolitan Museum of Art ... D6

Sights
6 Abyssinian Baptist Church ... D1
7 Apollo Theater ... D2
8 Cathedral Church of St John the Divine ... C3
9 Central Park Zoo ... D8
10 Columbia University ... C3
11 David Rubenstein Atrium ... C8
12 Guggenheim Museum ... E5
13 Jewish Museum ... E5
14 Museum of Arts & Design ... D8
15 Museum of the City of New York ... E4
16 Neue Galerie ... E6
17 New-York Historical Society ... D7
18 Riverside Park ... B4
19 Socrates Sculpture Park ... G6
20 Studio Museum in Harlem ... D2

Activities, Courses & Tours
21 Loeb Boathouse ... D7
22 Municipal Art Society ... D8

Sleeping
23 Allie's Inn ... D1
24 Bentley ... F8
25 Bubba & Bean Lodges ... E4
26 Harlem Flophouse ... D2
27 Hostelling International New York ... C4
28 Jazz on Amsterdam Ave ... C6
29 Lucerne ... C6
30 Park Savoy ... D8
31 YMCA ... D8

Eating
32 Amy Ruth's Restaurant ... D3
33 Barney Greengrass ... C6
34 Candle Cafe ... E7
35 Dinosaur Bar-B-Que ... B2
36 Earl's Beer & Cheese ... E5
37 Jacob's Pickles ... C6
38 JG Melon ... E7
39 Jones Wood Foundry ... F7
40 Peacefood Cafe ... C6
41 PJ Clarke's ... C8
42 Red Rooster ... D2
43 Tanoshi ... F7

Drinking & Nightlife
44 79th Street Boat Basin ... B6
45 Auction House ... F5
46 Barcibo Enoteca ... C7
47 Dead Poet ... C6
48 Manhattan Cricket Club ... C6
49 Penrose ... F6

Entertainment
50 Beacon Theatre ... C7
51 Jazz at Lincoln Center ... C8
52 Smoke Jazz & Supper Club-Lounge ... C4
53 Symphony Space ... C5

Shopping
54 Bloomingdale's ... E8

Upper East Side

The Upper East Side (UES) is home to New York's greatest concentration of cultural centers, including the grande dame that is the Metropolitan Museum of Art, and many refer to Fifth Ave above 57th St as Museum Mile. The real estate, at least along Fifth, Madison and Park Aves, is some of the most expensive in the world. Home to ladies who lunch as well as frat boys who drink, the neighborhood becomes decidedly less chichi the further east you go.

★Metropolitan Museum of Art MUSEUM
(Map p92; ☎212-535-7710; www.metmuseum.org; 1000 Fifth Ave, at 82nd St; suggested donation adult/child $25/free; ⊙10am-5.30pm Sun-Thu, to 9pm Fri & Sat; 👪; S 4/5/6 to 86th St) With more than two million objects in its collections, the Met is simply dazzling. Its great works span the world, from the chiseled sculptures of ancient Greece to the evocative tribal carvings of Papua New Guinea. The renaissance galleries are packed with Old World masters, while the relics of ancient Egypt fire the imagination – particularly the reconstructed Temple of Dendur, complete with papyrus pond and 2000-year-old stone walls covered in hieroglyphics.

After you think you've seen enough, head to the rooftop (open early May through October) for drinks (coffee, martinis) with a sweeping view over Central Park. Note that the suggested donation (which is, truly, a *suggestion* – the rule is you simply must pay something, even if only a penny) includes same-day admission to the Cloisters (p97).

★Frick Collection GALLERY
(Map p92; ☎212-288-0700; www.frick.org; 1 E 70th St, at Fifth Ave; admission $20, by donation 11am-1pm Sun, children under 10yr not admitted; ⊙10am-6pm Tue-Sat, 11am-5pm Sun; S 6 to 68th

St-Hunter College) This spectacular art collection sits in a mansion built by Henry Clay Frick in 1914. The 12 richly furnished rooms on the ground floor display paintings by Titian, Vermeer, El Greco, Goya and other masters. Perhaps the best asset here is that it's rarely crowded, providing a welcome break from the swarms of gawkers at larger museums, especially on weekends.

Guggenheim Museum MUSEUM
(Map p92; ☎212-423-3500; www.guggenheim.org; 1071 Fifth Ave, at 89th St; adult/child $25/free, by donation 5:45-7:45pm Sat; ⏰10am-5:45pm Sun-Wed & Fri, to 7:45pm Sat; 👪; Ⓢ4/5/6 to 86th St) A sculpture in its own right, architect Frank Lloyd Wright's building almost overshadows the collection of 20th-century art that it houses. Completed in 1959, the inverted ziggurat structure was derided by some critics, but it was hailed by others as an architectural icon. Stroll its sweeping spiral staircase to view masterpieces by Picasso, Pollock, Chagall, Kandinsky and others.

Neue Galerie MUSEUM
(Map p92; ☎212-628-6200; www.neuegalerie.org; 1048 Fifth Ave, cnr E 86th St; admission $20, free 6-8pm 1st Fri of every month, children under 12yr not admitted; ⏰11am-6pm Thu-Mon; Ⓢ4/5/6 to 86th St) This restored Carrère and Hastings mansion from 1914 is a resplendent showcase for German and Austrian art, featuring works by Gustav Klimt, Paul Klee and Egon Schiele. It also boasts the lovely, street-level eatery, Café Sabarsky.

Jewish Museum MUSEUM
(Map p92; ☎212-423-3200; www.jewishmuseum.org; 1109 Fifth Ave, at 92nd St; adult/child $15/free, Sat free, by donation 5-8pm Thu; ⏰11am-6pm Fri-Tue, to 8pm Thu; 👪; Ⓢ6 to 96th St) This New York City gem is tucked into a French-Gothic mansion from 1908, which houses 30,000 items of Judaica, as well as sculpture, painting and decorative arts. It hosts excellent temporary exhibits, featuring retrospectives on influential figures such as Art Spiegelman, as well as world-class shows on the likes of Chagall, Édouard Vuillard and Man Ray among other past luminaries.

Museum of the City of New York MUSEUM
(Map p92; ☎212-534-1672; www.mcny.org; 1220 Fifth Ave, btwn 103rd & 104th Sts; suggested admission adult/child $14/free; ⏰10am-6pm; Ⓢ6 to 103rd St) Situated in a colonial Georgian-style mansion, this local museum focuses solely on New York City's past, present and future. Don't miss the 22-minute film *Timescapes* (on the 2nd floor), which charts NYC's growth from tiny native trading post to burgeoning metropolis. Temporary exhibits cover everything from 19th-century activism to 1970s hip-hop.

Morningside Heights

The Upper West Side's northern neighbor comprises the area of Broadway and west up to about 125th St. Dominating the neighborhood is Columbia University, the highly regarded Ivy League college.

Cathedral Church of St John the Divine CHURCH
(Map p92; ☎tours 212-932-7347; www.stjohndivine.org; 1047 Amsterdam Ave at W 112th St; suggested donation $10, highlights tour $6, vertical tour $15; ⏰7:30am-6pm; ⓈB, C, 1 to 110th St-Cathedral Pkwy) This storied Episcopal cathedral, the largest place of worship in the United States, commands attention with its ornate Byzantine-style facade, booming vintage organ and extravagantly scaled nave – twice as wide as Westminster Abbey in London. High Mass, held at 11am Sunday, often comes with sermons by well-known intellectuals.

Columbia University UNIVERSITY
(Map p92; www.columbia.edu; Broadway at 116th St; Ⓢ1 to 116th St-Columbia University) Founded in 1754 as King's College, the oldest university in New York is now one of the world's premier research institutions. The principal point of interest is the main courtyard (located on College Walk at the level of 116th St), which is surrounded by various Italian Renaissance-style structures.

Harlem

The heart of African American culture has been beating in Harlem since its emergence as a black enclave in the 1920s. This neighborhood north of Central Park has been the setting for extraordinary accomplishments in art, music, dance, education and letters from the likes of Frederick Douglass, Paul Robeson, James Baldwin, Alvin Ailey, Billie Holiday and many other African American luminaries. After steady decline from the 1960s to early '90s, Harlem is booming again in the form of million-dollar brownstones and condos for sale next door to neglected tenement buildings and chain stores along 125th St.

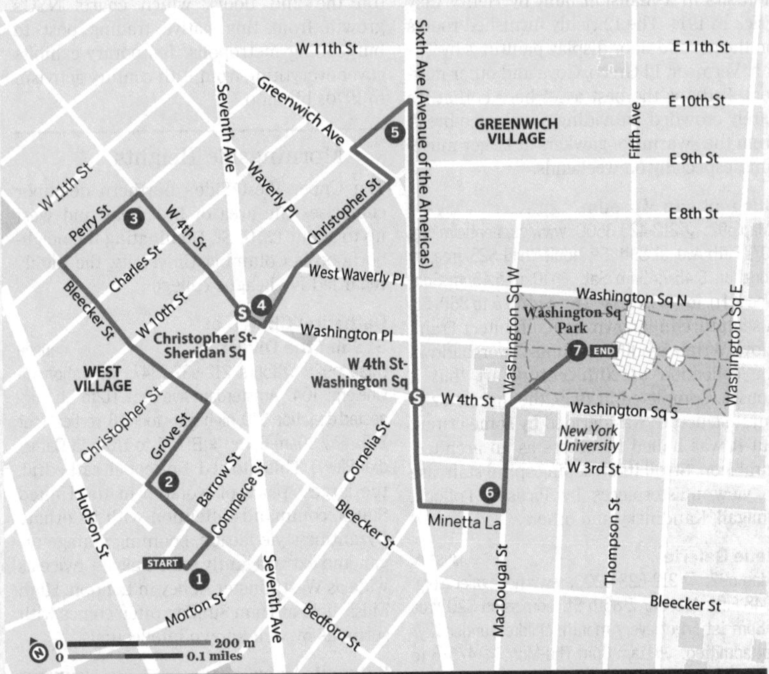

City Walk
A Village Stroll

START COMMERCE ST
END WASHINGTON SQUARE PARK
LENGTH 1 MILE; ONE HOUR

Of all the neighborhoods in New York City, Greenwich Village is the most pedestrian-friendly, with its cobbled corners that stray from the signature gridiron that unfurls across the rest of the island. Start your walkabout at the 1 **Cherry Lane Theatre**. Established in 1924, the small theater is the city's longest continuously running off-Broadway establishment, and was the center of creative activity during the 1940s. Make a left on Bedford and you'll find 2 **90 Bedford** on the right-hand side at the corner of Grove St. You might recognize the apartment block as the fictitious home of the cast of Friends. For another iconic TV landmark, wander up Bleecker St and make a right on Perry St, stopping at 3 **66 Perry St**, which was used as the facade and stoop of the city's 'It Girl', Carrie Bradshaw, in Sex and the City. Make a right on W 4th St until you reach 4 **Christopher Park**, where two white, life-sized statues of same-sex couples stand guard. On the north side of the greenspace is the legendary Stonewall Inn, where a clutch of fed-up drag queens rioted for their civil rights in 1969, signaling the start of what would become the gay revolution. Follow Christopher St to Sixth Ave to find the 5 **Jefferson Market Library** straddling a triangular plot of land. The 'Ruskinian Gothic' spire was once a fire lookout tower. Today the structure houses a branch of the public library; in the 1870s it was used as a courthouse. Stroll down Sixth Ave taking in the flurry of passersby, then make a left on Minetta Lane to swing by 6 **Café Wha?**, the notorious institution where many young musicians and comedians – like Bob Dylan and Richard Pryor – got their start. End your wandering further along MacDougal St in 7 **Washington Square Park**, the Village's unofficial town square, which plays host to loitering NYU students, buskers and a regular crowd of protestors.

For a traditional view of Harlem, visit on Sunday morning, when well-dressed locals flock to neighborhood churches. Just be respectful of the fact that these people are attending a religious service (rather than being on display for tourists). Unless you're invited by a member of a small congregation, stick to the bigger churches.

Apollo Theater HISTORIC BUILDING
(Map p92; 212-531-5300, tours 212-531-5337; www.apollotheater.org; 253 W 125th St at Frederick Douglass Blvd; admission from $20; S A/C, B/D to 125th St) Not just a mythical legend but a living theater. Head here for high-profile concerts and its famous long-running amateur night, 'where stars are born and legends are made,' which takes place every Wednesday night.

Abyssinian Baptist Church CHURCH
(Map p92; www.abyssinian.org; 132 W 138th St btwn Adam Clayton Powell Jr & Malcolm X Blvds; S 2/3 to 135th St) Has a superb choir and a charismatic pastor, Calvin O Butts, who welcomes tourists and prays for them. Sunday services start at 9am and 11am – the later one is *very* well attended.

Studio Museum in Harlem MUSEUM
(Map p92; 212-864-4500; www.studiomuseum.org; 144 W 125th St at Adam Clayton Powell Jr Blvd, Harlem; suggested donation $7, free Sun; noon-9pm Thu & Fri, 10am-6pm Sat, noon-6pm Sun; S 2/3 to 125th St) One of the premier showcases for African American artists; look for rotating exhibits from painters, sculptors, illustrators and other installation artists.

Washington Heights

Near the northern tip of Manhattan (above 155th St), Washington Heights takes its name from the first US president, who set up a Continental Army fort here during the Revolutionary War. An isolated spot until the end of the 19th century, it attracted lots of new blood as New Yorkers sniffed out affordable rents. Still, this neighborhood manages to retain its Latino – mainly Dominican – flavor, and is an interesting mix of blocks that alternate between former downtowners and longtime residents who operate within a tight, warm community.

★Cloisters MUSEUM
(Map p72; 212-923-3700; www.metmuseum.org/cloisters; Fort Tryon Park, at 190th St; suggested donation adult/child $25/free; 10am-5:15pm; S A to 190th St) Constructed in the 1930s using stones and fragments from several French and Spanish medieval monasteries, the romantic, castle-like creation houses medieval frescoes, tapestries, courtyards, gardens and paintings, and has commanding views of the Hudson. The walk from the subway stop to the museum through Fort Tryon Park offers fine views of the river; rock climbers head here for practice.

Brooklyn

Brooklyn is a world in and of itself; residents sometimes don't go into Manhattan for days or even weeks at a time. With 2.6 million people and growing, from well-to-do new parents seeking stately brownstones in Carroll Gardens to young band members wanting cheap rents near gigs in Bushwick, this outer borough has long surpassed Manhattan in the cool and livability factors in many people's minds. From sandy beaches and breezy boardwalks at one end to foodie destinations at the other, and with a massive range of ethnic enclaves, world-class entertainment, stately architecture and endless shopping strips in between, Brooklyn is a rival to Manhattan's attractions.

Coney Island NEIGHBORHOOD
About one hour by subway from Midtown, the wide sandy beach of Coney Island has retained its nostalgic and kitschy wood-plank boardwalk (partly destroyed and replaced after Hurricane Sandy) and famous 1927 Cyclone roller coaster, despite a sanitized makeover of the amusement park area including a handful of new adrenaline-pumping thrill rides. For better or worse, its slightly sleazy charm is a thing of the past and developers plan to transform the area into a sleek residential city complete with high-rise hotels.

Brighton Beach NEIGHBORHOOD
Walking about 1 mile east of Coney Island along the boardwalk leads to Brighton Beach ('Little Odessa'), where old-timers play chess and locals enjoy pierogies (boiled dumplings filled with meat or vegetables) and vodka shots in the sun at several boardwalk eateries. The heart of the 'hood is busy Brighton Beach Ave, with its many Russian shops, bakeries and restaurants.

Williamsburg, Greenpoint & Bushwick NEIGHBORHOOD
There is a definite Williamsburg look: skinny jeans, tattoos, a discreet body piercing, a

bushy beard for men, maybe some kind of retro head covering for a woman. Denizens of this raggedy and rowdy neighborhood across the East River on the L train seem to have the time and money to slouch in cafes and party all night in bars; a fair share of older – early 30s – transplants from Manhattan and Europe qualify as elders.

The main artery is Bedford Ave between N 10th St and Metropolitan Ave, where there are boutiques, cafes, bars and cheap eateries. But the hipster scene roams everywhere (lately Berry St is where the action is). The uber-hip even consider Williamsburg over and have long-since moved on to colonizing next door Greenpoint, a traditionally Polish neighborhood as well as the former warehouse buildings further out in Bushwick.

Brooklyn Brewery BREWERY, PUB
(☎718-486-7422; www.brooklynbrewery.com; 79 N 11th St, btwn Berry St & Wythe Ave; tours free Sat & Sun, $10 Mon-Thu; ⏲tours 5pm Mon-Thu, 1-5pm Sat, 1-4pm Sun, tasting room 6-11pm Fri, noon-8pm Sat, noon-6pm Sun; S L to Bedford Ave) Harking back to a time when this area of New York was a beer-brewing center, the Brooklyn Brewery not only brews and serves tasty local suds, but offers tours of its facilities. Reserve ahead for weekday (small-batch) tours.

Park Slope NEIGHBORHOOD
The Park Slope neighborhood is known for its classic brownstones, tons of great eateries and boutiques and liberal-minded stroller-pushing couples who resemble those on the Upper West Side (but have a backyard attached to their apartment).

Prospect Park OUTDOORS
(☎718-965-8951; www.prospectpark.org; Grand Army Plaza; ⏲5am-1am; S 2/3 to Grand Army Plaza, F to 15th St-Prospect Park) Created in 1866, Prospect Park is a showcase of resplendent greenery. A long meadow runs along the western half (where soccer, football, cricket and baseball is the order of the day). Dotted across the rest of the park you'll find hilly forests, a serene canal and a wide lake.

The **Lakeside** (www.lakesideprospectpark.com; near Ocean & Parkside Aves; ⏲11am-6pm Mon-Thu, 9am-10pm Fri & Sat, to 8pm Sun; 👪; S B, Q to Prospect Park) complex features two winter ice rinks (one indoor, one outdoor); in summer it becomes a roller rink and a giant wading pool with sprinklers for kiddies.

There are also free summer concerts at the Prospect Park Bandshell (near the 9th St and Prospect Park West entrance). Visit www.bricartsmedia.org for the lineup.

Brooklyn Botanic Garden GARDENS
(www.bbg.org; 1000 Washington Ave, at Crown St; adult/child $10/free, free Tue & 10am-noon Sat; ⏲8am-6pm Tue-Fri, 10am-6pm Sat & Sun; 👪; S 2/3 to Eastern Pkwy-Brooklyn Museum) One of Brooklyn's most picturesque attractions, this 52-acre garden is home to thousands of plants and trees, as well as a Japanese garden where river turtles swim alongside a Shinto shrine. The best time to visit is late April or early May, when the blooming cherry trees (a gift from Japan) are celebrated in Sakura Matsuri, the Cherry Blossom Festival.

Brooklyn Museum MUSEUM
(☎718-638-5000; www.brooklynmuseum.org; 200 Eastern Pkwy; suggested donation $12; ⏲11am-6pm Wed & Fri-Sun, to 10pm Thu; S 2/3 to Eastern Pkwy-Brooklyn Museum) This encyclopedic museum is housed in a five-story, 560,000-sq-ft beaux-arts building that houses more than 1.5 million objects, including ancient artifacts, 19th-century period rooms, and sculptures and painting from across several centuries. Admission is free on the first Saturday of every month after 5pm.

Brooklyn Heights & Downtown Brooklyn NEIGHBORHOOD
When Robert Fulton's steam ferries started regular services across the East River in the early 19th century, well-to-do Manhattanites began building stellar houses – Victorian Gothic, Romanesque, neo-Greco, Italianate and others – in Brooklyn Heights. Strolling along the tree-lined streets to gaze at them now is a lovely afternoon activity.

Follow **Montague St**, the Heights' main commercial avenue, down to the waterfront until you hit the **Brooklyn Heights Promenade**, which juts out over the Brooklyn-Queens Expwy to offer stunning views of Lower Manhattan.

★**Brooklyn Bridge Park** PARK
(☎718-222-9939; www.brooklynbridgepark.org; East River Waterfront, btwn Atlantic Ave & Adams St; ⏲6am-1am; 👪; S A/C to High St, 2/3 to Clark St, F to York St) FREE This 85-acre park is one of Brooklyn's best-loved new attractions. Wrapping around a bend on the East River, it runs for 1.3 miles from the edge of the Brooklyn Bridge in Dumbo to the west end of Atlantic Ave in Cobble Hill. It has revitalized a once barren stretch of shoreline, turning a series of abandoned piers into beautifully land-

scaped park land with jaw-dropping views of Manhattan.

There's lots to see and do here, with playgrounds, walkways and lawns. You'll find free open-air summertime events like film screenings (Pier 1); courts for basketball, handball and bocce, plus a skating rink (Pier 2); kayak and stand-up-paddleboard hire (Pier 4 beach). Summertime ferries to Governors Island depart from Pier 6. Pier 5 has sand volleyball courts and good food options. Empire Fulton Ferry, just past the Brooklyn Bridge, has the lovingly restored 1922 Jane's Carousel and the best views of the bridge framed against the towering skyscrapers of Lower Manhattan.

Boerum Hill, Cobble Hill & Carroll Gardens NEIGHBORHOOD

These neighborhoods, home to a mix of families, most with Italian roots who have lived here for generations, alongside former Manhattanites looking for a real life after the city, are full of tree-lined streets with rows of attractively restored brownstones. Smith St and Court St are the two main arteries connecting to the most southerly area of the three, Carroll Gardens. The former is known as 'restaurant row,' while the latter has more of the old-school groceries, bakeries and red-sauce restaurants.

Red Hook NEIGHBORHOOD

Red Hook is a waterfront area with cobblestone streets and hulking industrial buildings. Though it's a bit of a hike from the subway line, the formerly gritty area is now home to a handful of bars and eateries, as well as a massive waterfront branch of Fairway, a beloved gourmet grocery with breathtaking views of NY harbor. A daily water taxi (www.nywatertaxi.com/tours/ikea) goes to Red Hook (near Ikea) from Lower Manhattan.

Dumbo NEIGHBORHOOD

Dumbo's nickname is an acronym for its location: 'Down Under the Manhattan-Brooklyn Bridge Overpass,' and while this north Brooklyn slice of waterfront used to be strictly for industry, it's now the domain of high-end condos, furniture shops and art galleries. The Empire-Fulton Ferry State Park hugs the waterfront and offers picture postcard Manhattan views.

The Bronx

This 42-sq-mile borough to the north of Manhattan has several claims to fame: the Yankees, fondly known as the Bronx Bombers, who can be seen in all their pinstriped glory at the **Yankee Stadium** (Map p72; ☎718-293-4300, tours 646-977-8687; www.yankees.com; E 161st St at River Ave; tours $20; S B/D, 4 to 161st St-Yankee Stadium) in spring and summer; the 'real' Little Italy, namely **Belmont** (Map p72; www.arthuravenuebronx.com), where bustling stretches of Arthur and Belmont Aves burst with Italian gourmet markets and eateries; and a super-sized attitude that's been mythologized in Hollywood movies from *The Godfather* to *Rumble in the Bronx*. But it also has some cool surprises up its sleeve: a quarter of the Bronx is parkland, including the city beach of Pelham Bay Park. Also up in these parts is the magical City Island, a little slice of New England in the Bronx.

★ New York Botanical Garden GARDENS

(Map p72; www.nybg.org; Bronx River Pkwy & Fordham Rd; grounds only adult/child $13/3, all-garden pass $20/8, Wed & 9-10am Sat free; 10am-6pm Tue-Sun; ; Metro-North to Botanical Garden) There are 250 acres, with old-growth forest, a wetlands trail, nearly 3000 roses and tens of thousands of azalea plants. Springtime is fabulous.

Bronx Wildlife Conservation Park ZOO

(Map p72; ☎718-220-5100; www.bronxzoo.com; Bronx River Pkwy, at Fordham Rd; adult/child from $20/13, Wed free; 10am-5pm; BxM11, S 2 to Pelham Pkwy) Otherwise known as the Bronx Zoo, this is one of the biggest, best and most progressive zoos anywhere.

Woodlawn Cemetery CEMETERY

(Map p72; ☎718-920-0500; www.thewoodlawncemetery.org; Webster Ave at E 233rd St; 8:30am-4:30pm; S 4 to Woodlawn) Famous, historic and fascinating, this 400-acre burial ground is the resting place of many notable Americans, including Miles Davis and Herman Melville.

Queens

The biggest borough by size, Queens is home to over two million people. It's also the city's most ethnically diverse borough, with more than 100 nationalities speaking some 160 different languages. There are few of the tree-lined brownstone streets you find in Brooklyn, and the majority of the neighborhoods, architecturally speaking at least, do not befit this borough's royal name. However, because close to half its residents were born abroad, parts of Queens are endlessly reconstituting themselves, creating a vibrant and heady alternative universe to Manhattan. It's also home to two major airports, the Mets, a hip modern-art scene, miles of excellent beaches in the **Rockaways** and walking trails in the **Gateway National Recreation Area** (www.nps.gov/gate), a wildlife refuge in Jamaica Bay only minutes from JFK airport. The **Queens Historical Society** (☎718-939-0647; www.queenshistoricalsociety.org) offers tours through many areas of the massive borough.

Long Island City NEIGHBORHOOD
(admission $15; ⏰2-9pm; Ⓢ G to 21st St) Neighboring Long Island City has several high-rise condominiums lining the riverfront with fantastic views of Manhattan. The area has also become a hub of art museums.

PS 1 Contemporary Art Center ARTS CENTER
(Map p72; ☎718-784-2084; www.momaps1.org; 22-25 Jackson Ave, at 46th Ave; suggested donation $10; ⏰noon-6pm Thu-Mon) PS 1 Contemporary Art Center is dedicated solely to new, cutting-edge works. On Saturdays from late June to early September, the center's outdoor courtyard is transformed into an installation art space with DJs spinning for young crowds during the Warm Up series. Sunday sessions (May through October) feature live performances and other events.

Socrates Sculpture Park ART
(Map p92; www.socratessculpturepark.org; Broadway, at Vernon Blvd, Long Island City; ⏰10am-dusk; Ⓢ N/Q to Broadway) FREE Whimsical sculptures dot this 4.5-acre open-air space, right on the East River. Try to time a visit around free events – like yoga and tai chi on weekends from mid-May to late September, and movie screenings on Wednesday from early July to late August.

Astoria NEIGHBORHOOD
Home to the largest Greek community outside of Greece, this is obviously the place to find amazing Greek bakeries, restaurants and gourmet shops, mainly along **Broadway**. An influx of Eastern European, Middle Eastern (Steinway Ave, known as 'Little Egypt,' is the place for falafel, kebabs and hookah pipes) and Latino immigrants have created a rich and diverse mix. Young Bohemian types have also migrated here, making the area Queens' answer to Williamsburg.

In summer, cool off at the **Astoria Pool** (www.nycgovparks.org/parks/astoriapark; Astoria Park, cnr 19th St & 23rd Dr; ⏰11am-7pm late Jun-early Sep; Ⓢ N/Q to Astoria Blvd), the city's largest and oldest.

★ **Museum of the Moving Image** MUSEUM
(www.movingimage.us; 36-01 35th Ave, at 37th St, Astoria; adult/child $12/6, admission free 4-8pm Fri; ⏰10:30am-5pm Wed & Thu, to 8pm Fri, 11:30am-7pm Sat & Sun; Ⓢ M/R to Steinway St) This super-cool complex is now one of the world's top film, television and video museums. State-of-the-art galleries show off the museum's collection of 130,000-plus TV and movie artifacts.

NYC FOR CHILDREN

Contrary to popular belief, New York can be a pretty child-friendly city. Cutting-edge playgrounds have proliferated from Union Square to Battery Park and of course the city's major parks, including **Central Park** (p89; check out Heckscher, Adventure and Ancient playgrounds), have them in abundance. The best playgrounds in Brooklyn are at Pier 6 in **Brooklyn Bridge Park** (p98; there's even a small summertime water park, so bring bathing suits and towels).

For hands-on activities check out the **Children's Museum of the Arts** (Map p80; ☎212-274-0986; www.cmany.org; 103 Charlton St, btwn Greenwich & Hudson Sts; admission $11, by donation 4-6pm Thu; ⏰noon-5pm Mon & Wed, noon-6pm Thu & Fri, 10am-5pm Sat & Sun; 👪; Ⓢ 1 to Houston St, C/E to Spring St) and the **Brooklyn Children's Museum** (www.brooklynkids.org; 145 Brooklyn Ave, at St Marks Ave, Crown Heights; admission $9, free 3-5pm Thu; ⏰10am-5pm Tue-Sun; 👪; Ⓢ C to Kingston-Throop Aves, 3 to Kingston Ave). Kids can have close encounters with wildlife at the Central Park and Bronx zoos and the Coney Island aquarium. The boat rides to Lady Liberty, a Circle Line cruise or the cheaper ferries (Staten Island or East River ferries) offer the opportunity to chug around New York Harbor. Vintage carousels can be found in Bryant Park, Central Park and Brooklyn Bridge Park. Governors Island is a great place for a picnic, free play and biking (with big four-wheel bikes for hire).

For dining, nearly any place is fair game if you go early enough – at 5pm you'll probably be eating with other young families. Check out the weekend Arts section of the *New York Times* for kid-themed events and performances.

Flushing & Corona NEIGHBORHOOD
The intersection of Main St and Roosevelt Ave, downtown Flushing, can feel like the Times Square of a city a world away from NYC. Immigrants from all over Asia, primarily Chinese and Korean, make up this neighborhood bursting at the seams with markets and restaurants filled with delicious and cheap delicacies.

Flushing Meadows Corona Park, meanwhile, is the home of Citi Field, the **USTA National Tennis Center** (the US Open is held here every August) and many lakes, ball fields, bike paths and grassy expanses, and was used for the 1939 and 1964 World's Fairs, of which there are quite a few faded leftovers. Kids can learn about science and technology through fun hands-on exhibits at the **New York Hall of Science** (☎718-699-0005; www.nysci.org; 47-01 111th St; adult/child $15/12; free 2-5pm Fri & 10-11am Sun; ⏲9:30am-5pm Mon-Fri, 10am-6pm Sat & Sun; S 7 to 111th St). Also within this massive park is the **Queens Museum** (QMA; www.queensmuseum.org; suggested donation adult/child $8/free; ⏲noon-6pm Wed-Sun; S 7 to 111th St), which faces a massive and very photogenic globe.

Jackson Heights Historic District NEIGHBORHOOD
(btwn Roosevelt & 34th Aves, from 70th to 90th Sts; S E, F/V, R to Jackson Heights-Roosevelt Ave) A fascinating mix of Indian and South American (Roosevelt Ave) cultures, this is the place to purchase saris and 22-karat gold, dine on South Indian *masala dosas* – huge, paper-thin rice crepes folded around flavorful mixtures of masala potatoes, peas, cilantro and other earthy treats – and continue on with a plate of Colombian arepas (corn pancakes) and a bite of Argentine empanadas.

Staten Island

While many New Yorkers will say that Staten Island has more in common with its neighbor, New Jersey, because of its suburban house and car cultures, there are compelling reasons to include this borough in your urban explorations. First and foremost is the **Staten Island Ferry** (Map p76; www.siferry.com; Whitehall Terminal at Whitehall & South Sts; ⏲24hr; S 1 to South Ferry) FREE, which shuttles blasé commuters to work while offering breathtaking views of the Statue of Liberty and the Manhattan skyline (the world's largest Ferris wheel is to be built amid a large shopping and retail complex near the ferry terminal). Not far from the ferry station on the Staten Island side is the Richmond County Bank Ballpark (p124), home to the minor-league Staten Island Yankees, as well as the hip neighborhood of St George.

Activities

Cycling

New York has hundreds of miles of designated bike lanes, making the city a surprisingly bicycle-friendly destination. For quick jaunts across town (under 30 minutes), hop on a **Citi Bike** (www.citibikenyc.com; 24hr/7 days $11/27), the Big Apple's bike-sharing program. Hundreds of kiosks in Manhattan and parts of Brooklyn house the bright blue bicycles and checking one out is as easy as swiping your credit card. However, unless you're an experienced urban cyclist, pedaling through the streets can be a risky activity, as bike lanes are often blocked by trucks, taxis and double-parked cars. More than 28-miles, mostly riverfront, have been integrated into the **Manhattan Waterfront Greenway**, a patchwork of park pathways, overpasses and a few city streets that circle the entire island of Manhattan. The mostly uninterrupted 10-mile stretch from the GW Bridge to Battery Park, including **Hudson River Park**, is perhaps the most spectacular. Of course **Central Park** and Brooklyn's **Prospect Park** have lovely cycling paths.

For bike rentals (other than Citi Bike), visit one of many locations of **Bike and Roll** (www.bikenewyorkcity.com; bikes from $10/30 per hour/half day). It has a quick-rent branch outside Central Park on 59th St and Central Park West.

Water Sports

This is an island, after all, and as such there are plenty of opportunities for boating and kayaking. The **Downtown Boathouse** (Map p76; www.downtownboathouse.org; Pier 26 near N Moore St; ⏲9am-5:30pm Sat & Sun mid-May–mid-Oct, & 5-6:30pm Mon-Fri Jul & Aug; S 1 to Houston St) offers free 20-minute kayaking (including equipment) in the protected embayment of the Hudson River. Other locations include 56th St, 72nd St and Governors Island.

In Central Park, **Loeb Boathouse** (Map p92; ☎212-517-2233; www.thecentralparkboathouse.com; btwn 74th & 75th Sts; boating per hour $12, bike rental per hour $9-15; ⏲10am-6pm Apr-Nov; 👪; S B, C to 72nd St, 6 to 77th St) rents rowboats for romantic trysts, and even fills Venice-style gondolas in summer. For a sailing adventure, hop aboard the **Schooner Adirondack** (Map p84; 212-913-9991; www.sail-nyc.com; Chelsea Piers, Pier 62 at W 22th St; tours $48-78; S C, E to 23rd St) at **Chelsea Piers**.

Surfers may be surprised to find a tight group of wave worshippers within city limits, at Queens' **Rockaway Beach** at 90th St, where you can hang ten after only a 75-minute ride on the A train from Midtown.

Tours

The following is a small sample of available tours.

Big Onion Walking Tours WALKING TOUR
(888-606-9255; www.bigonion.com; tours $20) Popular and quirky guided tours specializing in ethnic and neighborhood tours.

Circle Line BOAT TOUR
(Map p84; 212-563-3200; www.circleline42.com; Pier 83, W 42nd St; tickets from $29; S A/C/E to 42nd St-Port Authority Bus Terminal) Ferry boat tours, from semicircle to a full island cruise with guided commentary, as well as powerful speedboat trips on the *Beast*.

Municipal Art Society WALKING TOUR
(Map p92; 212-935-3960; www.mas.org; 111 W 57th St; tours adult/child $20/15; S F to 57th St) Various scheduled tours focusing on architecture and history, including daily 12:30pm tours of Grand Central Terminal.

New York City Audubon WALKING TOUR
(Map p84; 212-691-7483; www.nycaudubon.org; 71 W 23rd St, Ste 1523; tours free-$100; S F/M to 23rd St) Expert instructors and guides lead trips including birding in Central Park and the Bronx and ecology cruises of the Jamaica Bay Wildlife Refuge.

NYC Gangster Tours WALKING TOUR
(www.nycgangstertours.com; tours $25-40) Sure, it's a little schticky, but colorful and knowledgeable guides make these walking tours focusing on NYC's Italian, Chinese and Jewish mafia interesting and fun.

On Location Tours BUS TOUR
(212-683-2027; www.onlocationtours.com; tours $33-59) *Gossip Girl* and *How I Met Your Mother* are on the list of tours as well as long-running ones that allow you to flesh out your Carrie Bradshaw or Tony Soprano fantasies.

Festivals & Events

From cultural street fairs to foodie events, you are bound to find something that will excite you, no matter the time of year, but there's almost too much to digest in summer when outdoor celebrations proliferate.

Restaurant Week FOOD
(212-484-1222; www.nycgo.com; Feb & July) Dine at top restaurants with three-course dinner specials for $38 (and $25 at lunchtime).

Armory Show CULTURAL
(212-645-6440; www.thearmoryshow.com; Piers 92 & 94, West Side Hwy at 52nd & 54th Sts; Mar) New York's biggest contemporary art fair sweeps the city, showcasing the new work of thousands of artists from around the world.

Tribeca Film Festival FILM
(212-941-2400; www.tribecafilm.com; late Apr & early May) Robert De Niro co-organizes this local downtown film fest, which is quickly rising in prestige.

Fleet Week NAVAL
(212-245-0072; www.fleetweeknewyork.com; May) Dressed in their formal whites, an annual convocation of sailors and their naval ships and air rescue teams descend on the city.

NYC Pride GAY & LESBIAN
(212-807-7433; www.nycpride.org; Jun) Pride month, with a packed calendar of parties and events, culminates with a major march down Fifth Ave on the last Sunday of June.

Mermaid Parade PARADE
(www.coneyisland.com; late Jun) Something of Mardi Gras on the boardwalk, this parade turns Surf Ave on Coney Island in Brooklyn into a free-expression zone that's fun, crazy and artistic.

Village Halloween Parade PARADE
(www.halloween-nyc.com; Sixth Ave from Spring St to 16th St; 7-11pm Oct 31) This fabulous parade features wildly costume-clad marchers and cheering onlookers. Anyone can join.

Sleeping

Tax adds an additional 14.75% plus $3.50 per night. A cluster of national chains, including Sheraton, Ramada and Holiday Inn, have affordably priced rooms in hotels within a few blocks of one another around 39th Ave in Long Island City, Queens, a quick N, Q or R train from midtown Manhattan directly across the East River.

Lower Manhattan & Tribeca

Wall Street Inn LUXURY HOTEL $$
(Map p76; ☎212-747-1500; www.thewallstreetinn.com; 9 S William St; r from $240; ❄📶; S 2/3 to Wall St) Lehman Brothers once occupied this classic limestone building and, while the mood of the hotel is very early American banker, there's little risk in a stay here. Old-fashioned and warm rather than stuffy, the rooms, with luxurious marble baths, are slightly over-furnished for their size.

SoHo

Leon Hotel HOTEL $$
(Map p80; ☎212-390-8833; www.leonhotelnyc.com; 125 Canal St, btwn Bowery & Christie; r from $240; ❄📶; S B/D to Grand St) At the entrance to the Manhattan Bridge, this boxy space offers clean, no-frills accommodation that is a decent value for pricey NYC. Rooms are comfortable if minimally furnished, and some have quite nice views of Lower Manhattan, with One World Trade Center in plain sight. Friendly staff.

Solita SoHo HOTEL $$
(Map p80; ☎212-925-3600; www.solitasohohotel.com; 159 Grand St, at Lafayette St; r from $220; ❄📶; S N/Q/R, J/Z, 6 to Canal St) The Solita is a clean, functional alternative with boutique-style furnishings close to Chinatown, NoLita, Soho and the Lower East Side. Lower winter rates.

Soho Grand Hotel BOUTIQUE HOTEL $$
(Map p80; ☎212-965-3000; www.sohogrand.com; 310 W Broadway; d from $290; ❄@📶🐾; S 6, N/Q/R, J to Canal St) The original boutique hotel of the 'hood still reigns, with its striking glass-and-cast-iron lobby stairway, and 353 rooms with cool, clean lines plus Frette linens, plasma flat-screen TVs and CO Bigelow grooming products. The lobby's Grand Lounge buzzes with action.

Lower East Side, East Village & NoLita

Bowery House HOSTEL $$
(Map p80; ☎212-837-2373; www.theboweryhouse.com; 220 Bowery btwn Prince & Spring Sts; s/d with shared bath from $90/160; ❄📶; S J/Z to Bowery) Across the street from the New Museum, this former 1920s-era flophouse has been resurrected as an upmarket hostel, its cubicle-sized rooms decked out with Bowery-themed film posters and custom-made mattresses (ie shorter and narrower), while communal bathrooms feature rain showers and heated floors. There's also a lounge with Chesterfield sofas and chandeliers, a bar and a roof terrace.

St Mark's Hotel HOTEL $$
(Map p80; ☎212-674-0100; www.stmarkshotel.net; 2 St Marks Pl at Third Ave; d from $140; ❄📶; S 6 to Astor Pl) This East Village budget option draws a young, nightlife-loving crowd, who enjoy being within strolling distance of the city's best concentration of bars and cocktail lounges. Not surprisingly, the rooms are tiny, but clean and adequately equipped, with flat-screen TVs and private bathrooms in each. Wi-fi costs extra.

Blue Moon Hotel BOUTIQUE HOTEL $$
(Map p80; ☎212-533-9080; www.bluemoon-nyc.com; 100 Orchard St, btwn Broome & Delancey Sts; r incl breakfast from $250; ❄📶; S F to Delancey St, J/M to Essex St) You'd never guess that this quaint, welcoming brick guesthouse – full of festive colors – was once a foul tenement back in the day (the day being in 1879). Except for a few ornate touches, like wrought-iron bed frames and detailed molding, Blue Moon's clean, spare rooms are entirely modern and comfortable.

Bowery Hotel BOUTIQUE HOTEL $$$
(Map p80; ☎212-505-9100; www.theboweryhotel.com; 335 Bowery, btwn 2nd & 3rd Sts; r from $375; ❄@📶; S F/V to Lower East Side-Second Ave, 6 to Bleecker St) Perhaps as far as you can get from the Bowery's gritty flophouse history, this stylish hotel is all 19th-century elegance. Rooms come equipped with lots of light and sleek furnishings mixed with antiques. The baroque-style lobby bar attracts the young and chic and on-site restaurant Gemma serves upscale Italian.

Chelsea, Meatpacking District & West (Greenwich) Village

Chelsea Hostel HOSTEL $
(Map p84; ☎212-647-0010; www.chelseahostel.com; 251 W 20th St btwn Seventh & Eighth Aves; dm $40-80, s $75-100, d from $130; ❄@📶; S A/C/E, 1/2 to 23rd St, 1/2 to 18th St) Walkable to the Village and Midtown, Chelsea Hostel capitalizes on its convenient location with somewhat steep prices, but it's kept clean and there's access to common rooms and kitchens where other budget travelers often meet and hang.

Jane Hotel HOTEL $
(Map p80; ☎212-924-6700; www.thejanenyc.com; 113 Jane St, btwn Washington St & West Side Hwy; r with shared/private bath from $105/250; P ❄ 📶; S L to Eighth Ave, A/C/E to 14th St, 1/2 to Christopher St-Sheridan Sq) Originally built for sailors (obvious after one look at the cabin-sized rooms), the Jane became a temporary refuge for survivors of the *Titanic*, then a YMCA and a rock-and-roll venue. The single-bunk rooms feature flat-screen TVs and the communal showers are more than adequate.

Chelsea Lodge HOTEL $
(Map p84; ☎212-243-4499; www.chelsealodge.com; 318 W 20th St btwn Eighth & Ninth Aves; s/d from $130/140; ❄ 📶; S A/C/E to 14th St, 1 to 18th St) Housed in a landmark brownstone in Chelsea, the European-style, 20-room Chelsea Lodge is a super deal. Space is tight, so you won't get more than a bed, with a TV plopped on an old wooden cabinet. There are showers and sinks in rooms, but toilets are down the hall. Six suite rooms have private bathrooms, and two come with private garden access.

Larchmont Hotel HOTEL $
(Map p80; ☎212-989-9333; www.larchmonthotel.com; 27 W 11th St, btwn Fifth & Sixth Aves; s/d with shared bath from $110/120; ❄ 📶; S 4/5/6, N/Q/R to 14th St-Union Sq) Housed in a prewar building that blends in with the other fine brownstones on the block, a stay at the Larchmont is about location. The carpeted rooms are basic and in need of updating, as are the communal baths, but it's not a bad deal for the price.

Townhouse Inn of Chelsea B&B $$
(Map p84; ☎212-414-2323; www.townhouseinnchelsea.com; 131 W 23rd St, btwn Sixth & Seventh Aves; r incl breakfast from $150; ❄ 📶; S F/V, 1 to 23rd St) Housed in a lone 19th-century, five-story townhouse on busy 23rd St, this 14-room B&B is a Chelsea gem. The rooms are big and welcoming, with exposed brick walls, fine linens and attractive furnishings. There's also an elegant all-Victorian library that adds to the charm. Friendly hosts have a wealth of info on the neighborhood.

Union Square, Flatiron District & Gramercy Park

Carlton Arms HOTEL $
(Map p84; ☎212-679-0680; www.carltonarms.com; 160 E 25th St btwn Lexington & Third Aves; s/d $142/176, s/d with shared bath $96/142; S 6 to 23rd St or 28th St) Though it has a sordid past (speakeasy, drugs, prostitution), these days, the Carlton Arms feels equal parts art gallery and budget hotel. Murals cover the walls up five flights of stairs, and snake into each of the tiny guest rooms and shared bathrooms (there is a small sink in each guestroom). It draws an eclectic mix of bohemian travelers.

Hotel 17 BUDGET HOTEL $
(Map p84; ☎212-475-2845; www.hotel17ny.com; 225 E 17th St, btwn Second & Third Aves; d with shared bath from $113; ❄ 📶; S N/Q/R, 4/5/6 to 14th St-Union Sq, L to Third Ave) Right off Stuyvesant Sq on a leafy residential block, this no-frills, eight-floor townhouse has relatively affordable prices. Rooms are small, with traditional, basic furnishings (gray carpet, chintzy bedspreads, burgundy blinds) and lack much natural light.

The Marcel at Gramercy BOUTIQUE HOTEL $$
(Map p84; ☎212-696-3800; www.themarcelatgramercy.com; 201 E 24th St, at Third Ave; d from $180-410; ❄ @ 📶; S 6 to 23rd St) Minimalist with earth-tone touches, this 97-room inn is a poor-man's chic boutique and that's not a bad thing. Modernist rooms on the avenue have great views, and the sleek lounge is a great place to unwind after a day of exploring.

Midtown

Pod 51 HOTEL $
(Map p84; ☎212-355-0300; www.thepodhotel.com; 230 E 51st St, btwn Second & Third Aves, Midtown East; r from $147; ❄ 📶; S 6 to 51st St, E/M to Lexington Ave-53rd St) A dream come true for folks who'd like to live inside their iPod – or at least curl up and sleep with it – this affordable hot spot has a range of room types, most barely big enough for the bed. 'Pods' have bright bedding, tight workspaces, flat-screen TVs, iPod docking stations and 'rain' showerheads.

Park Savoy HOTEL $
(Map p92; ☎212-245-5755; www.parksavoyny.com; 158 W 58th St btwn Seventh & Sixth Aves; d from $145; ❄ 📶; S N/Q/R to 57th St-7th Ave) The best thing about the Park Savoy is its low price and great location near Central Park. The trade-off: worn carpets, cheap bedspreads and showers with trickling water pressure, to say nothing of the unhelpful staff.

★**Yotel** HOTEL $$
(Map p84; ☎646-449-7700; www.yotel.com; 570 Tenth Ave, at 41st St, Midtown West; r from $190;

; S A/C/E to 42nd St-Port Authority Bus Terminal, 1/2/3, N/Q/R, S, 7 to Times Sq-42nd St) Part futuristic spaceport, part Austin Powers set, this uber-cool 669-room option bases its rooms on airplane classes. Small but cleverly configured Premium cabins include automated adjustable beds, while all cabins feature floor-to-ceiling windows with killer views, slick bathrooms and iPod connectivity.

City Rooms HOTEL **$$**
(Map p84; 917-475-1285; www.cityroomsnyc.com; 368 Eighth Ave btwn 28th & 29th Sts; r with shared bath from $150; ; S C/E to 23rd St, 1 to 28th St) If you spurn luxury and don't suffer from claustrophobia, this friendly 13-room hotel is a decent option. The rooms are clean and basic, with comfortable mattresses, but extremely short on space. NYC-themed stencils add a dash of character to the otherwise white walls. Note that all rooms share bathrooms (which are also a tight fit).

414 Hotel HOTEL **$$**
(Map p84; 212-399-0006; www.414hotel.com; 414 W 46th St, btwn Ninth & Tenth Aves, Midtown West; r from $285; ; S C/E to 50th St) Set up like a guesthouse, this affordable, friendly option offers 22 tidy and tastefully decorated rooms a couple of blocks west of Times Square. Rooms facing the leafy inner courtyard, which is a perfect spot to enjoy your complimentary breakfast, are the quietest.

Upper West Side

Hostelling International New York HOSTEL **$**
(HI; Map p92; 212-932-2300; www.hinewyork.org; 891 Amsterdam Ave, at 103rd St; dm $50-75; ; S 1 to 103rd St) This red-brick mansion from the 1880s houses HI's 672 well-scrubbed bunks. It's rather 19th-century industrial, but benefits include good public areas, a backyard, a communal kitchen and a cafe.

Jazz on Amsterdam Ave HOSTEL **$**
(Map p92; 646-490-7348; www.jazzhostels.com; 201 W 87th St at Amsterdam Ave; dm $50, r $130; ; S 1 to 86th St) Only a short walk to Central Park, this hostel chain's Upper West Side branch has clean rooms, both private rooms and two- to six-bed dorms. Free wi-fi in the lobby. There are other branches in Harlem and Chelsea.

YMCA HOSTEL **$$**
(Map p92; 212-912-2625; www.ymcanyc.org; 5 W 63rd St at Central Park West; d $210, s/d with shared bath from $114/160; @; S A/B/C/D to 59th St-Columbus Circle) Just steps from Central Park, this grand art-deco building has several floors – 8th to the 13th – of basic, but clean, rooms. Guests have access to an extensive but old-school gym, racquet ball courts, pool and sauna. There's also a lounge and a cafe. Other locations on the Upper East Side and Harlem.

Lucerne HOTEL **$$**
(Map p92; 212-875-1000; www.thelucernehotel.com; 201 W 79th St, cnr Amsterdam Ave; d from $186; ; S B, C to 81st St) This unusual 1903 structure breaks away from beaux arts in favor of the baroque, with an ornately carved terracotta-colored facade. Inside is a stately 197-room hotel with nine types of guest rooms evoking a contemporary Victorian look. Think: flowered bedspreads, scrolled headboards and plush pillows with fringe.

Upper East Side

Bubba & Bean Lodges B&B **$$**
(Map p92; 917-345-7914; www.bblodges.com; 1598 Lexington Ave, btwn 101st & 102nd Sts; r $130-260; ; S 6 to 103rd St) Owners Jonathan and Clement have turned a charming Manhattan townhouse into an excellent home away from home. The five guest rooms are simply furnished, with crisp, white walls, hardwood floors and navy linens, providing the place with a modern, youthful feel. All units are equipped with private bathrooms as well as kitchenettes with cookware.

Bentley Hotel BOUTIQUE HOTEL **$$**
(Map p92; 212-247-5000; www.bentleyhotelnyc.com; 500 E 62nd St, at York Ave; r from $220; ; S N/Q/R to Lexington Ave/59th St) Featuring great East River views, the Bentley overlooks FDR Dr, as far east as you can go. Formerly an office building, the hotel has shed its utilitarian past in the form of chic boutique-hotel styling, a swanky lobby and sleek rooms.

Harlem

Harlem Flophouse GUESTHOUSE **$**
(Map p92; 212-662-0678; www.harlemflophouse.com; 242 W 123rd St, btwn Adam Clayton Powell Jr & Frederick Douglass Blvds; r with shared bath $125-150; ; S A/B/C/D, 2/3 to 124th St) The four attractive bedrooms have antique light fixtures, glossed-wood floors and big beds, plus classic tin ceilings and wooden shutters. Cat on the premises.

Allie's Inn B&B $$
(Map p92; ☎212-690-3813; www.alliesinn.com; 313 W 136th St btwn Frederick Douglass Blvd & Edgecombe Ave; r $175-325; ; S A/C, B to 135th St) This Harlem charmer has just three guest rooms, which are clean and comfortable, with oak floors, simple modern furnishings and small kitchen units. There are a growing number of appealing eating and drinking options in the neighborhood, and the subway station is just around the corner.

Brooklyn

★**New York Loft Hostel** HOSTEL $
(☎718-366-1351; www.nylofthostel.com; 249 Varet St, btwn Bogart & White Sts, Bushwick; dm $40-80, d $140; ; S L to Morgan Ave) Live like a Williamsburg – or more accurately Bushwick – hipster in this renovated loft building. Brick walls, high ceilings, a beautiful kitchen, a back garden and a rooftop sundeck make Manhattan hostels seem like tenements.

Wythe Hotel BOUTIQUE HOTEL $$
(☎718-460-8000; wythehotel.com; 80 Wythe Ave, at N 11th St, Williamsburg; r $205-600;) In the heart of nightlife-loving Williamsburg, the red-brick Wythe Hotel makes for a stylish getaway. The industrial-chic rooms have custom-made wallpaper (from Brooklyn's own Flavor Paper), exposed brick, polished concrete floors and original 13ft timber ceilings. There's a lovely brasserie on the ground floor and a rooftop bar with fine views of Manhattan.

Nu Hotel HOTEL $$
(☎718-852-8585; www.nuhotelbrooklyn.com; 85 Smith St; d incl breakfast $170-300; ; S F, G to Bergen St) This location, only blocks from Brooklyn Heights and a nexus of attractive brownstone neighborhoods, is absolutely ideal – except for the fact that it's across the street from the Brooklyn House of Detention. It has a chic minimalist vibe and the clean all-white rooms are comfortable.

Queens

The Local NYC HOSTEL $$
(☎347-738-5251; www.thelocalny.com; 1302 44th Ave btwn 12th & 13th Sts; dm/d from $45/160; ; S E, M to Court Sq) This stylish hostel has clean and small, simply designed rooms, with comfy mattresses and plenty of natural light. The airy cafe-bar is a fine place to meet other travelers, with good coffees by day, and wine and beer by night. Throughout the week, there's a regular line-up of events (movie nights, live music, pub quizzes).

Paper Factory Hotel HOTEL $$
(☎718-392-7200; www.thepaperfactoryhotel.com; 37-06 36th St, Long Island City; d from $180; ; S M/R to 36th St) This former paper factory and warehouse has 123 rooms that evoke industrial chic. Reclaimed lumber and polished concrete feature prominently, and the artfully designed common areas are great spots to unwind.

Eating

In a city with over 20,000 restaurants, and new ones opening every single day, where are you supposed to begin? From Little Albania to Little Uzbekistan, your choice of ethnic eats is only a short subway ride away. A hotbed of buzz-worthy culinary invention and trends like artisanal doughnuts, farm-to-table pork sandwiches and *haute cuisine* reinterpretations of fried chicken, pizza and good ol' burgers and fries, NYC's restaurant scene, like the city, is constantly reinventing itself.

Lower Manhattan & Tribeca

Financier Patisserie BAKERY, SANDWICHES $
(Map p76; ☎212-334-5600; www.financierpastries.com; 62 Stone St at Mill Lane; pastries $3-4, sandwiches $8-10; ⏰7am-7pm Mon-Fri, 9am-5pm Sat & Sun; ; S 2/3, 4/5 to Wall St, J/Z to Broad St) There are now three Patisserie outposts in Lower Manhattan because nobody can get enough of the buttery croissants, berry tarts or chocolate éclairs. Savory items include homemade soups, flavorful sandwiches and creamy quiches.

Shake Shack BURGERS $
(Map p76; ☎646-545-4600; www.shakeshack.com; 215 Murray St btwn West St & North End Ave; burgers $5-10; ⏰11am-11pm; S A/C, 1/2/3 to Chambers St) Danny Meyer's cult burger chain is fast food at its finest: cotton-soft burgers made with prime, freshly ground mince; Chicago-style hot dogs in poppy-seed potato buns; and seriously good cheesy fries. Drink local with a beer from Brooklyn brewery Sixpoint.

Fraunces Tavern AMERICAN $$
(Map p76; ☎212-968-1776; www.frauncestavern.com; 54 Pearl St; mains lunch $15-26, dinner $20-38; ⏰11am-10pm; S N/R to Whitehall) Can you really pass up a chance to eat where George Washington supped in 1762? Expect heaped portions of beer-battered fish and chips,

slow-roasted chicken pot pie and braised short ribs. Fraunces Tavern has great atmosphere – particularly on Sundays when there's traditional Irish music (3:30pm to 6:30pm).

★ Locanda Verde ITALIAN **$$$**
(Map p76; ☎212-925-3797; www.locandaverdenyc.com; 377 Greenwich St at Moore St; lunch $19-29, mains dinner $22-37; ⏰7am-11pm Mon-Fri, from 8am Sat & Sun; Ⓢ A/C/E to Canal St, 1 to Franklin St) Step through the velvet curtains into a scene of loosened button-downs, black dresses and slick bartenders behind a long, crowded bar. This celebrated brasserie showcases modern Italian fare like pappardelle with lamb bolognese and steamed black bass with green garlic puree. Weekend brunch features no less creative fare: try scampi and grits or lemon ricotta pancakes with blueberries.

Tiny's & the Bar Upstairs AMERICAN **$$$**
(Map p76; ☎212-374-1135; www.tinysnyc.com; 135 W Broadway btwn Duane & Thomas Sts; mains lunch $16-20, dinner $22-30; ⏰8am-midnight Mon-Fri, from 9am Sat & Sun; Ⓢ A/C, 1/2/3 to Chambers St) Snug and adorable (book ahead!), Tiny's comes with a crackling fire in the back room and an intimate bar upstairs. Served on vintage porcelain, dishes are soulful, subtly retweaked delights; think kale salad with maple mustard and shredded Gouda, marinated shrimp with squid ink cavatelli or grilled skirt steak with pickled ramps.

Chinatown, Little Italy & NoLita

Tacombi MEXICAN **$**
(Map p80; www.tacombi.com; 267 Elizabeth St, btwn E Houston & Prince Sts; tacos $4-6; ⏰11am-midnight; Ⓢ B/D/F/M to Broadway-Lafayette St, 6 to Bleecker St) Festively strung lights, foldaway chairs and Mexican men flipping tortillas in an old VW Kombie: if you can't make it to the Yucatán shore, here's your Plan B. Casual, convivial and ever-popular, Tacombi serves up delicious tacos, tender ceviche and creamy guacamole. Wash it all down with a pitcher of sangria, a glass of horchata or a mezcal margarita.

Ruby's CAFE **$**
(Map p80; ☎212-925-5755; www.rubyscafe.com; 219 Mulberry St, btwn Spring & Prince Sts; mains $10-15; ⏰9:30am-11pm; Ⓢ 6 to Spring St, N/R to Prince St) All bases are covered at this inviting Aussie-inspired cafe. You'll find breakie-friendly avo toast (mashed avocado and fresh tomato on seven grain toast) and pancakes with caramelized apples and pears, and lunch-pleasers like pumpkin salad, pastas and juicy burgers (best ordered with truffle fries). Flat-white coffees and bottles of Boags complete your antipodean experience.

> **A, B, C**
>
> Those letter grades you see posted in the windows of every NYC restaurant aren't the report cards of the owner's kids. They're issued by the NYC health department after an inspection of each establishment's hygiene standards. A is best and C worst – anything lower, well, you probably wouldn't want to eat there anyway.

Café Gitane MEDITERRANEAN **$**
(Map p80; ☎212-334-9552; www.cafegitanenyc.com; 242 Mott St, at Prince St; mains $14-17; ⏰8:30am-midnight; 📶; Ⓢ N/R to Prince St, 6 to Spring St) Clear the Gauloises smoke from your eyes and blink twice if you think you're in Paris. Label-conscious shoppers love this authentic bistro, with its dark, aromatic coffee and well-executed dishes, such as blueberry and almond *friands* (small French cake), smoked trout salad or Moroccan couscous with organic chicken.

La Esquina MEXICAN **$$**
(Map p80; ☎646-613-7100; www.esquinanyc.com; 114 Kenmare St, at Petrosino Sq; tacos from $3.50, mains cafe $15-25, brasserie $18-34; ⏰noon-late; Ⓢ 6 to Spring St) This mega-popular and quirky little spot is three places really: a stand-while-you-eat taco window (open till 2am), a casual Mexican cafe (entrance on Lafayette St) and, downstairs, a dim, slinky, cavernous brasserie requiring reservations. Standouts include grilled pulled pork tacos and mango and jicama salad, among other authentic and delicious options.

Lombardi's PIZZA **$$**
(Map p80; ☎212-941-7994; www.firstpizza.com; 32 Spring St btwn Mulberry & Mott Sts; small/large pizza from $17/21; ⏰11:30am-11pm; Ⓢ 6 to Spring St) Lombardi's was the very first pizzeria in America, opening here in 1905. It's justifiably proud of its New York style: thin crust and an even thinner layer of sauce.

Da Nico ITALIAN **$$**
(Map p80; ☎212-343-1212; www.danicoristorante.com; 164 Mulberry St; mains $18-40; ⏰noon-11pm

EATING NYC: CHINATOWN

With hundreds of restaurants, from holes-in-the-wall to banquet-sized dining rooms, Chinatown is wonderful for exploring cheap eats on an empty stomach.

Xi'an Famous Foods (Map p76; 67 Bayard St; mains $6-9; S J/Z, N/Q, 6 to Canal St) Take-out counter serving delicious hand-pulled noodles and spicy cumin lamb 'burgers'; eat them in nearby Columbus Park.

Amazing 66 (Map p76; ☎212-334-0099; www.amazing66.com; 66 Mott St, at Canal St; mains $9-16; ⊙11am-11pm; S 6, J, N/Q to Canal St) Terrific Cantonese lunches.

Prosperity Dumpling (Map p80; ☎212-343-0683; www.prosperitydumpling.com; 46 Eldridge St btwn Hester & Canal Sts; dumplings $1-3; ⊙7:30am-10pm; S B/D to Grand St; F to East Broadway; J to Bowery) Among the best dumpling joints.

Vanessa's Dumpling House (Map p80; ☎212-625-8008; www.vanessasdumplinghouse.com; 118 Eldridge St, btwn Grand & Broome Sts; dumplings $1.25-5; ⊙11am-10pm; S B/D to Grand St, J to Bowery, F to Delancey St) Great dumplings and sesame pancakes (get one with Peking duck).

Bánh Mì Saigon Bakery (Map p80; ☎212-941-1541; www.banhmisaigonnyc.com; 198 Grand St, btwn Mulberry & Mott Sts; sandwiches $5-6; ⊙8am-6pm; S N/Q/R, J/Z, 6 to Canal St) Some of the best Vietnamese sandwiches in town.

Joe's Shanghai (Map p76; ☎212-233-8888; www.joeshanghairestaurants.com; 9 Pell St btwn Bowery & Doyers St; mains $11-18; ⊙11am-11pm; S N/Q/R, J/Z, 6 to Canal St, B/D to Grand St) Always busy and tourist-friendly. Does good noodle and soup dishes.

Buddha Bodai (Map p76; ☎212-566-8388; 5 Mott St; mains $8-15; ⊙10am-10pm; S) Serves exquisite vegetarian cuisine.

Big Wong King (Map p76; ☎212-964-0540; www.bigwongking.com; 67 Mott St, at Canal; mains $10-14; ⊙8:30am-9pm; S 6, J, N/Q to Canal St) Perennial favorite. Look for the roast ducks hanging in the window.

Nom Wah Tea Parlor (Map p76; ☎212-962-6047; www.nowah.com; 13 Doyers St; dim sum $4-11; ⊙10:30am-9pm; S 6, J, N/Q to Canal St) Looks like an old-school American diner, but is the oldest dim sum place in the city.

Original Chinatown Ice Cream Factory (Map p76; ☎212-608-4170; www.chinatownicecreamfactory.com; 65 Bayard St; ice cream $4.50-8.25; ⊙11am-10pm; S N/Q/R, J/Z, 6 to Canal St) Refreshing scoops of green tea, ginger, durian and lychee flavored sorbets.

Sun-Thu, to midnight Fri & Sat; S J/M/Z N/Q/R/W, 6 to Canal St) If you're hell-bent on having a Little Italy dinner, Da Nico is a classic. It's family-run and traditional in feel and the extensive menu highlights both northern and southern Italian cuisine that's red-sauce predictable but delicious.

Lower East Side

Cheeky Sandwiches SANDWICHES $
(Map p80; ☎646-504-8131; www.cheeky-sandwiches.com; 35 Orchard St; mains $7-9; ⊙7am-9pm Mon-Thu, 8am-midnight Fri & Sat, 8am-9pm Sun; S F to East Broadway) This ramshackle little eatery looks like it's been airlifted in from New Orleans. The biscuit sandwiches are outstanding – try one topped with fried chicken, coleslaw and gravy. Add on chicory coffee and bread pudding and you have a great cheap meal.

Meatball Shop ITALIAN $
(Map p80; ☎212-982-8895; www.themeatballshop.com; 84 Stanton St, btwn Allen & Orchard Sts; mains from $11; ⊙noon-2am Sun-Thu, to 4am Fri-Sat; S 2nd Ave; F to Delancey St; J/M/Z to Essex St) Masterfully executed meatball sandwiches have suddenly spiked in popularity, and the Meatball Shop is riding the wave of success with moist incarnations of the traditional hero. Three other branches in the city.

Doughnut Plant DESSERT $
(Map p80; ☎212-505-3700; www.doughnutplant.com; 379 Grand St, at Norfolk; doughnuts $4; ⊙6:30am-8pm; S J/M/Z to Essex St, F to Delancey St) A New York legend, Doughnut Plant whips up sweet decadence, in inven-

tive flavors (pistachio, tres leches, cashew and orange blossom) made from all-natural ingredients.

Clinton Street Baking Company AMERICAN $$
(Map p80; ☎646-602-6263; www.clintonstreetbaking.com; 4 Clinton St, btwn Stanton & Houston Sts; mains $12-20; ⏱8am-4pm & 6-11pm Mon-Sat, 9am-6pm Sun; Ⓢ J/M/Z to Essex St, F to Delancey St, F to Second Ave) Mom-and-pop shop extraordinaire Clinton Street Baking Company gets the blue ribbon in so many categories – stellar blueberry pancakes, buttermilk biscuit sandwiches, fish tacos, fried chicken – that you're pretty much guaranteed a memorable meal no matter what time you stop by.

Katz's Delicatessen DELI $$
(Map p80; ☎212-254-2246; www.katzsdelicatessen.com; 205 E Houston St, at Ludlow St; sandwiches $13-21; ⏱8am-10:45pm Mon-Wed & Sun, to 2:45am Thu, open all night Fri & Sat; Ⓢ F to 2nd Ave) One of the few remaining Jewish delicatessens in the city, Katz's attracts locals, tourists and celebrities whose photos line the walls. Massive pastrami, corned beef, brisket and tongue sandwiches are throwbacks, as is the payment system: hold on to the ticket you're handed when you walk in and pay cash only.

Fung Tu FUSION $$
(Map p80; www.fungtu.com; 22 Orchard St btwn Hester & Canal Sts; small plates $13-18, mains $24-32; ⏱6pm-midnight Tue-Sat, 4pm-10pm Sun; Ⓢ F to East Broadway) Celebrated chef Jonathan Wu brilliantly blends Chinese cooking with global accents at this elegant little eatery on the edge of Chinatown. The complex sharing plates are superb (try scallion pancakes with cashew salad and smoked chicken or crepe roll stuffed with braised beef, pickled cucumbers and watercress) and pair nicely with creative cocktails like the Fung Tu Gibson.

Kuma Inn PAN-ASIAN $$
(Map p80; ☎212-353-8866; www.kumainn.com; 113 Ludlow St, btwn Delancey & Rivington Sts; small dishes $9-15; ⏱6-11pm Sun-Thu, to midnight Fri & Sat; Ⓢ F, J/M/Z to Delancey-Essex Sts) Reservations are a must at this spot in a secretive 2nd-floor location (look for a small red door with 'Kuma Inn' painted on the concrete side). The Filipino- and Thai-inspired tapas runs the gamut, from vegetarian summer rolls (with jicama) to spicy drunken shrimp, and pan-roasted scallops with bacon and sake. Bring your own beer, wine or sake (corkage fee applies).

SoHo & NoHo

Dominique Ansel Bakery DESSERTS $
(Map p80; 189 Spring St; desserts $6-7; ⏱8am-7pm Mon-Sat, 9am-7pm Sun; Ⓢ C/E to Spring St) The most famous patisserie in NYC has much more up its sleeve than just cronuts (the half-doughnut half-croissant it invented back in 2013). Buttery *kouign-amman* (a Breton cake), salted caramel éclairs and photogenic berry tarts are among the many hits. FYI: if you want a cronut before they sell out each day, arrive by 7:30am on weekdays (earlier on weekends).

Mooncake Foods ASIAN, SANDWICHES $
(Map p80; ☎212-219-8888; www.mooncakefoods.com; 28 Watts St , btwn Sullivan & Thompson Sts; mains from $11; ⏱11am-10pm; Ⓢ 1 to Canal St) This unpretentious family-run restaurant serves some of the best sandwiches in the neighborhood. Try the smoked white-fish salad sandwich or Vietnamese pork meatball hero. Other locations in the Financial District, Chelsea and uptown in Hell's Kitchen.

Boqueria Soho TAPAS $$
(Map p80; ☎212-343-4255; 171 Spring St, btwn West Broadway & Thompson St; tapas $7-19; ⏱noon-11pm; Ⓢ C/E to Spring St) This expansive, welcoming tapas joint features delectable classics, including *pulpo a la gallega* (Galician octopus), *gambas al ajillo* (garlic marinated shrimp) and creamy tortilla (Spanish omelet). You can watch the chefs in action as you sip a pink grapefruit sangria and peer into the open kitchen.

★**Il Buco** ITALIAN $$$
(Map p80; ☎212-533-1932; www.ilbuco.com; 47 Bond St btwn Bowery & Lafayette St; mains lunch $17-30, dinner $24-36; ⏱noon-midnight Tue-Sat, 6pm-midnight Sun & Mon; Ⓢ B/D/F/V to Broadway-Lafayette St; 6 to Bleecker St) This charmingly rustic nook boasts hanging copper pots, kerosene lamps and antique furniture, plus a stunning menu and wine list. Sink your teeth into seasonal and ever-changing highlights like pan-roasted black bass with celery root puree or risotto with wild nettles, melted leeks and fresh goat's cheese.

Dutch MODERN AMERICAN $$$
(Map p80; ☎212-677-6200; www.thedutchnyc.com; 131 Sullivan St, btwn Prince & Houston Sts; mains lunch $18-33, dinner $30-58; ⏱11:30am-3pm & 5:30-11pm daily, from 10am Sat & Sun; Ⓢ C/E to Spring St, N/R to Prince St, 1 to Houston St) Oysters on ice and freshly baked homemade

pies are the notable bookends of a meal – in the middle is delectable fresh-from-the-farm comfort fare. Artisanal cocktails add to the festive cheer.

Balthazar FRENCH $$$
(Map p80; ☎212-965-1414; www.balthazarny.com; 80 Spring St, btwn Broadway & Crosby St; mains lunch $18-29, dinner $21-45; ⏰8am-midnight; Ⓢ6 to Spring St; N/R to Prince St) Still the king of bistros, bustling Balthazar is never short of a discriminating mob. That's all thanks to its uplifting Paris-meets-NYC ambience and its stellar something-for-everyone menu. Highlights include the outstanding raw bar, rich onion soup, steak frites and salade Niçoise. Weekend brunch here is a very crowded (and delicious) production.

For a decadent treat to go, grab a pastry from the Balthazar bakery next door.

East Village

Every cuisine and style is represented in the East Village, though even the very best places are certainly more casual than stuffy. St Marks Place and around, from Third to Second Ave, has turned into a little Tokyo with loads of Japanese sushi and grill restaurants. Cookie-cutter Indian restaurants line Sixth St between First and Second Ave.

Tacos Morelos MEXICAN $
(Map p80; ☎347-772-5216; 438 E 9th St, btwn First Ave & Ave A; tacos from $3; ⏰noon-midnight Sun-Thu, to 2am Fri & Sat; ⓈL to 1st Ave) This famed food truck put down roots in a no-frills East Village storefront in 2013, quickly becoming one of Manhattan's favorite taco joints. Order yours with chicken, steak, roast pork, beef tongue or vegetarian. Tip: pay the $0.50 extra for the homemade tortilla.

Porchetta SANDWICHES $
(Map p80; ☎212-777-2151; www.porchetta.com; 110 E 7th St; sandwiches $10-12; ⏰11:30am-10pm Sun-Thu, to 11pm Fri & Sat; Ⓢ6 to Astor Pl) This tiny white-tiled storefront serves tender boneless roasted pork that's been wrapped in a pork belly and seasoned with fennel pollen, rosemary, sage, thyme and garlic, available in sandwich or platter-with-sides versions.

Veselka UKRAINIAN $
(Map p80; ☎212-228-9682; www.veselka.com; 144 Second Ave, at 9th St; mains $10-19; ⏰24hr; ⓈL to 3rd Ave, 6 to Astor Pl) Generations of East Villagers have been coming to this bustling institution for blintzes and breakfast regardless of the hour.

Cafe Mogador MOROCCAN $$
(Map p80; ☎212-677-2226; www.cafemogador.com; 101 St Marks Pl; mains lunch $8-14, dinner $17-21; ⏰9am-midnight; Ⓢ6 to Astor Pl) Family-run Mogador is a long-standing NYC classic, serving fluffy piles of couscous, char-grilled lamb and merguez sausage over basmati rice and its famous tangines – traditionally spiced, long-simmered chicken or lamb dishes served up five different ways. A garrulous young crowd packs the space, spilling out onto the small cafe tables on warm days. Brunch is also first-rate.

Luzzo's PIZZA $$
(Map p80; ☎212-473-7447; www.luzzosgroup.com; 211 First Ave, btwn 12th & 13th Sts; pizzas $18-26; ⏰noon-11pm Sun-Thu, to midnight Fri & Sat; ⓈL to 1st Ave) Fan-favorite Luzzo's occupies a thin sliver of real estate, which gets stuffed to the gills each evening as discerning diners feast on thin-crust pies, kissed with ripe tomatoes and cooked in a coal-fired oven. Cash only.

Angelica Kitchen VEGETARIAN $$
(Map p80; ☎212-228-2909; www.angelicakitchen.com; 300 E 12th St, btwn First & Second Aves; mains $17-21; ⏰11:30am-10:30pm; 🖉; ⓈL to 1st Ave) This enduring herbivore classic has a calming vibe and enough creative options to make your head spin. Some dishes get too-cute names, but all do wonders with tofu, seitan, spices and soy products, and sometimes an array of raw ingredients. Cash only.

★Momofuku Noodle Bar NOODLES $$
(Map p80; ☎212-777-7773; www.momofuku.com; 171 First Ave btwn 10th & 11th Sts; mains $17-28; ⏰noon-11pm Sun-Thu, to 1am Fri & Sat; ⓈL to 1st Ave, 6 to Astor Pl) Ramen and steamed buns are the name of the game at this infinitely creative Japanese eatery, part of the growing David Chang empire. Seating is on stools at a long bar or at communal tables. Momofuku's famous steamed chicken and pork buns are recommended.

★Upstate SEAFOOD $$
(Map p80; ☎917-408-3395; www.upstatenyc.com; 95 First Ave, btwn 5th & 6th Sts; mains $15-30; ⏰5-11pm; ⓈF to 2nd Ave) Tiny Upstate serves outstanding seafood dishes and craft beers. The small always-changing menu features the likes of beer-steamed mussels, seafood stew, scallops over mushroom risotto, softshell crab and wondrous oyster selections. There's no freezer – seafood comes from the market each day, so you know you'll be getting only the freshest ingredients.

Chelsea, Meatpacking District & West (Greenwich) Village

Chelsea Market MARKET $

(Map p84; www.chelseamarket.com; 75 9th Ave; ⏲7am-9pm Mon-Sat, 8am-8pm Sun; S A/C/E to 14th St) This former cookie factory has been turned into an 800ft-long shopping concourse that caters to foodies with boutique bakeries, gelato shops, ethnic eats and a food court for gourmands.

★**Moustache** MIDDLE EASTERN $

(Map p80; ☎212-229-2220; www.moustachepitza.com; 90 Bedford St btwn Grove & Barrow Sts; mains $8-17; ⏲noon-midnight; S 1 to Christopher St-Sheridan Sq) Small and delightful Moustache serves up rich, flavorful sandwiches (leg of lamb, merguez sausage, falafel), thin-crust pizzas, tangy salads and hearty specialties like *ouzi* (filo stuffed with chicken, rice and spices). Start with a platter of creamy hummus or baba ghanoush, served with fluffy, piping hot pitas.

Taïm ISRAELI $

(Map p80; ☎212-691-1287; www.taimfalafel.com; 222 Waverly Pl btwn Perry & W 11th Sts; sandwiches $7-8; ⏲11am-10pm; S 1/2/3 to 14th St) This tiny joint whips up some of the best falafels in the city. There are also mixed platters, zesty salads and delicious smoothies (try the date, lime and banana). There's also a NoLita location.

Joe's Pizza PIZZA $

(Map p80; ☎212-366-1182; www.joespizzanyc.com; 7 Carmine St btwn Sixth Ave & Bleecker St; slices from $3; ⏲10am-4am; S A/C/E, B/D/F/M to W 4th St; 1 to Christopher St-Sheridan Sq or Houston St) Joe's is the Meryl Streep of pizza parlors, collecting dozens of awards and accolades over the last four decades. No-frills slices are served up indiscriminately to students, tourists and celebrities alike.

★**Foragers City Table** MODERN AMERICAN $$

(Map p84; ☎212-243-8888; www.foragerscitygrocer.com; 300 W 22nd St, cnr Eighth Ave; mains $23-36; ⏲5:30-10pm daily & 10:30am-2:30pm Sat & Sun; 🍷; S C/E, 1 to 23rd St) Owners of this excellent restaurant in Chelsea run a 28-acre farm in the Hudson Valley, from which much of their menu is sourced. Recent temptations include squash soup with Jerusalem artichokes and black truffles; roasted chicken with polenta; heritage pork loin; and the season's harvest featuring toasted quinoa and a flavorful mix of vegetables.

Spotted Pig PUB FOOD $$

(Map p80; ☎212-620-0393; www.thespottedpig.com; 314 W 11th St at Greenwich St; mains lunch $15-26, dinner $21-35; ⏲noon-2am Mon-Fri, from 11am Sat & Sun; 🍷 👪; S A/C/E to 14th St; L to 8th Ave) This Michelin-starred gastro-pub is a favorite of Villagers, serving an upscale blend of hearty Italian and British dishes. Its two floors are bedecked with old-timey trinkets that give the whole place an air of relaxed elegance. It doesn't take reservations, so there is often a wait for a table. Lunch on weekdays is less crowded.

Cookshop MODERN AMERICAN $$

(Map p84; ☎212-924-4440; www.cookshopny.com; 156 Tenth Ave btwn 19th & 20th Sts; mains $18-36; ⏲8am-11:30pm Mon-Fri, from 10am Sat & Sun; S L to 8th Ave; A/C/E to 23rd St) A brilliant brunching pit stop before (or after) tackling the verdant High Line across the street, Cookshop is a lively spot for eye-opening cocktails, a perfectly baked breadbasket and a selection of inventive egg mains. Dinner is a sure-fire win as well. Ample outdoor seating on warm days.

Tía Pol TAPAS $$

(Map p84; ☎212-675-8805; www.tiapol.com; 205 Tenth Ave btwn 22nd & 23rd Sts; small plates $4-16; ⏲noon-11pm Tue-Sun, from 5:30pm Mon; S C/E to 23rd St) Wielding Spanish tapas amid closet-sized surrounds, Tia Pol is the real deal, as the hordes of locals swarming the entrance can attest. There's a great wine list and a tantalizing array of small plates: fried chickpeas, squid and ink with rice, cockles in white wine and garlic, Navarran-style trout with *serrano* ham, and fried chickpeas.

★**RedFarm** FUSION $$$

(Map p80; ☎212-792-9700; www.redfarmnyc.com; 529 Hudson St btwn 10th & Charles Sts; mains $22-46; ⏲5pm-11pm daily & 11am-2:30pm Sat & Sun; S A/C/E, B/D/F/M to W 4th St; 1 to Christopher St-Sheridan Sq) RedFarm transforms Chinese cooking into pure, delectable artistry at this small, buzzing space on Hudson St. Crispy duck and crab dumplings, sauteed black cod with black bean and Thai basil, and pastrami egg rolls are among the many creative dishes that brilliantly blend East with West. Waits can be long, so arrive early (no reservations).

Union Square, Flatiron District & Gramercy Park

Shake Shack BURGERS $
(Map p84; ☎212-989-6600; www.shakeshack.com; Madison Square Park, cnr 23rd St & Madison Ave; burgers $5-10; ⏰11am-11pm; Ⓢ N/R, F/M, 6 to 23rd St) Tourists line up in droves for the hamburgers and shakes at this Madison Square Park counter-window-serving institution.

★**Eataly** ITALIAN
(Map p84; www.eatalyny.com; 200 Fifth Ave, at 23rd St; ⏰8am-11pm; Ⓢ F/M, N/R, 6 to 23rd St) The promised land for lovers of Italian food, this 50,000-sq-ft emporium has a countless array of tempting food counters, doling out brick-oven pizza, fresh-made pastas, pecorino-covered salads, oysters, creamy gelato, perfectly pulled espresso and much more. It's all set amid a gourmet market, with plenty of picnic ideas. The pièce de résistance is a rooftop beer garden called **Birreria**.

ABC Kitchen MODERN AMERICAN $$$
(Map p84; ☎212-475-5829; www.abckitchennyc.com; 35 E 18th St, at Broadway; pizzas $16-24, dinner mains $24-40; ⏰noon-3pm & 5:30-10:30pm Mon-Fri, from 11am Sat & Sun; ✎; Ⓢ L, N/Q/R, 4/5/6 to Union Sq) Looking part gallery, part rustic farmhouse, sustainable ABC Kitchen is the culinary avatar of the chi-chi home goods department store ABC Carpet & Home. Organic gets haute in dishes like tuna sashimi with ginger and mint, or crispy pork confit with grilled ramps. For a more casual bite, try the scrumptious wholewheat pizzas.

Midtown

★**Totto Ramen** JAPANESE $
(Map p84; ☎212-582-0052; www.tottoramen.com; 366 W 52nd St, btwn Eighth & Ninth Aves, Midtown West; ramen $10-16; ⏰noon-midnight Mon-Fri, noon-11pm Sat, 5-11pm Sun; Ⓢ C/E to 50th St) Write your name and number of guests on the clipboard by the door and wait for your (cash-only) ramen revelation. Skip the chicken and go for the pork, which sings in dishes like miso ramen (with fermented soybean paste, egg, scallion, bean sprouts, onion and homemade chili paste).

El Margon CUBAN $
(Map p84; ☎212-354-5013; www.margonnyc.com; 136 W 46th St, btwn Sixth & Seventh Aves, Midtown West; sandwiches $4-8, mains $10-15; ⏰7am-5pm Mon-Fri, to 3pm Sat; Ⓢ B/D/F/M to 47-50th Sts-Rockefeller Center) It's still 1973 at this ever-packed Cuban lunch counter, where orange Laminex and greasy goodness never went out of style. Go for gold with the legendary cubano sandwich (a pressed panino jammed with rich roast pork, salami, cheese, pickles, mojo and mayo).

★**Danji** KOREAN $$
(Map p84; ☎212-586-2880; www.danjinyc.com; 346 W 52nd St, btwn Eighth & Ninth Aves, Midtown West; sharing plates $13-20; ⏰noon-2:30pm & 5pm-11pm Mon-Thu, noon-2:30pm & 5pm-midnight Fri, 5pm-midnight Sat; Ⓢ C/E to 50th St) Young-gun chef Hooni Kim has captured tastebuds with his Michelin-starred Korean 'tapas' served in a snug and slinky contemporary space. The celebrity dish on the menu (divided into 'traditional' and 'modern' options) are the sliders, a duo of *bulgogi* beef and spiced pork belly served on butter-grilled buns.

Hangawi KOREAN $$
(Map p84; ☎212-213-0077; www.hangawirestaurant.com; 12 E 32nd St, btwn Fifth & Madison Aves; mains lunch $11-24, dinner $19-30; ⏰noon-2:45pm & 5-10:15pm Mon-Thu, to 10:30pm Fri, 1-10:30pm Sat, 5-9:30pm Sun; ✎; Ⓢ B/D/F/M, N/Q/R to 34th St-Herald Sq) Sublime, flesh-free Korean is the draw at high-achieving Hangawi. Leave your shoes at the entrance and slip into a soothing, zenlike space of meditative music, soft low seating and clean, complexly flavored dishes. Show-stoppers include the leek pancakes and a seductively smooth tofu claypot in ginger sauce.

Virgil's Real Barbecue AMERICAN BBQ $$
(Map p84; ☎212-921-9494; www.virgilsbbq.com; 152 W 44th St btwn Broadway & Eighth Ave; mains $14-25; ⏰11:30am-midnight; Ⓢ N/R, S, W, 1/2/3, 7 to Times Sq-42nd St) Menu items cover the entire BBQ map, with Oklahoma State Fair corndogs, pulled Carolina pork and smoked Maryland ham sandwiches, and platters of sliced Texas beef brisket and Georgia chicken-fried steak.

Dhaba INDIAN $$
(Map p84; ☎212-679-1284; www.dhabanyc.com; 108 Lexington Ave btwn 27th & 28th Sts; mains $12-24; ⏰noon-midnight Mon-Sat, to 10pm Sun; Ⓢ 6 to 28th St) Murray Hill (aka Curry Hill) has no shortage of subcontinental bites, but funky Dhaba packs one serious flavor punch. Mouthwatering standouts include the crunchy, tangy *lasoni gobi* (fried cauliflower with tomato and spices), and the

insanely flavorful *murgh bharta* (minced chicken cooked with smoked eggplant).

There's also a good-value lunch buffet ($11 Monday to Saturday, $13 Sunday).

El Parador Cafe MEXICAN **$$**

(Map p84; ☎212-679-6812; www.elparadorcafe.com; 325 E 34th St, btwn First & Second Aves, Midtown East; mains $20-32; ⏲noon-11pm Mon-Sat, 2-10pm Sun; Ⓢ6 to 33rd St) Well off the beaten path, this far-flung Mexican stalwart has abundant old-school charm, from the beveled candleholders and dapper Latino waiters to the satisfying south-of-the-border standbys. House classics include the mussels in red wine, cilantro and garlic, served with green chili corn bread, and the signature mole poblano (chicken stewed in a rich chili-and-chocolate-spiked sauce).

Artisanal FRENCH **$$$**

(Map p84; ☎212-725-8585; www.artisanalbistro.com; 2 Park Ave S at 32nd St; mains $24-38; ⏲10am-1am Mon-Fri, from 8:30am Sat & Sun; ✍; Ⓢ6 to 33rd St) For those who live, love and dream *fromage,* Artisanal is a must-eat. More than 250 varieties of cheese, from stinky to sweet, are found at this classic Parisian-style bistro. Creamy goodness aside, other favorite items include mussels, braised lamb shank and onion soup gratinée (with a three-cheese blend of course).

NoMad NEW AMERICAN **$$$**

(Map p84; ☎212-796-1500; www.thenomadhotel.com; NoMad Hotel, 1170 Broadway, at 28th St; mains $30-45; ⏲noon-2pm & 5:30-10:30pm Mon-Thu, to 11pm Fri, 11am-2pm & 5:30-11pm Sat, 11am-3pm & 5:30-10pm Sun; ⓈN/R, 6 to 28th St; F/M to 23rd St) Sharing the same name as the 'It kid' hotel it inhabits, NoMad has become one of Manhattan's culinary highlights. Carved up into a series of distinctly different spaces – including a see-and-be-seen Atrium, an elegant Parlour and a snacks-only Library – the restaurant serves delicacies like roasted quail with morels, suckling pig with ramps, and foie gras marinated with rhubarb.

Grand Central Oyster Bar & Restaurant SEAFOOD **$$$**

(Map p84; ☎212-490-6650; www.oysterbarny.com; Grand Central Terminal, 42nd St at Park Ave; mains $23-38; ⏲11:30am-9:30pm Mon-Sat; Ⓢ4/5/6 to 42nd St) This buzzing bar and restaurant within Grand Central is hugely atmostpheric, with a vaulted tiled ceiling by Catalan-born engineer Rafael Guastavino. The two dozen oyster varieties present some dizzying choices, along with clam chowder, seafood stews, pan-fried softshell crab and an overabundance of fresh fish.

Upper West Side

Jacob's Pickles AMERICAN **$$**

(Map p92; ☎212-470-5566; www.jacobspickles.com; 509 Amsterdam Ave, btwn 84th & 85th Sts; mains $15-24; ⏲10am-2am Mon-Thu, to 4am Fri, 9am-4am Sat, to 2am Sun; Ⓢ1 to 86th St) On a restaurant-lined stretch of Amsterdam Ave, this inviting and warmly lit eatery serves upscale comfort food, like catfish tacos, wine-braised turkey leg dinner, and St Louis ribs slathered with coffee molasses barbecue sauce. The biscuits and pickles are top-notch, and you'll find two dozen or so craft beers on tap from New York, Maine and beyond.

PJ Clarke's AMERICAN **$$**

(Map p92; ☎212-957-9700; www.pjclarkes.com; 44 W 63rd St, cnr Broadway; burgers $14-19, mains $19-42; ⏲11:30am-2am; Ⓢ1 to 66th St-Lincoln Center) Across the street from Lincoln Center, this red-checked-tablecloth spot has a buttoned-down crowd, friendly bartenders and a solid menu. If you're in a rush, belly up to the bar for a Black Angus burger and a Brooklyn Lager. A raw bar offers fresh Long Island Little Neck and Cherry Stone clams, as well as jumbo shrimp cocktails.

Barney Greengrass DELI **$$**

(Map p92; ☎212-724-4707; www.barneygreengrass.com; 541 Amsterdam Ave, at 86th St; mains $10-21; ⏲8:30am-4pm Tue-Sun; Ⓢ1 to 86th St) Old-school Upper Westsiders and pilgrims from other neighborhoods crowd this century-old 'sturgeon king' on weekends. It serves a long list of traditional if pricey Jewish delicacies, from bagels and lox to sturgeon scrambled with eggs and onions.

Peacefood Cafe VEGAN **$$**

(Map p92; ☎212-362-2266; www.peacefoodcafe.com; 460 Amsterdam Ave, at 82nd St; mains $10-18; ⏲10am-10pm; ✍; Ⓢ1 to 79th St) This bright and airy vegan haven dishes up a popular fried seitan panino (served on homemade focaccia and topped with cashew, arugula, tomatoes and pesto), as well as pizzas, roasted vegetable plates and an excellent quinoa salad. There are daily raw specials, organic coffees and rich desserts. Healthy and good.

Upper East Side

JG Melon PUB FOOD $

(Map p92; 212-744-0585; 1291 Third Ave, at 74th St; mains $11-18; 11:30am-4am; S 6 to 77th St) JG's is a loud, old-school pub that has been serving juicy burgers on tea plates since 1972. It's a local favorite for both eating and drinking (the Bloody Marys are excellent) and it gets crowded in the after-work hours.

Earl's Beer & Cheese AMERICAN $

(Map p92; 212-289-1581; www.earlsny.com; 1259 Park Ave, btwn 97th & 98th Sts; grilled cheese $8; 4pm-midnight Mon & Tue, 11am-midnight Wed-Thu & Sun, to 2am Fri & Sat; S 6 to 96th St) Chef Corey Cova's comfort-food outpost channels a hipster hunting vibe. The NY state cheddar grilled cheese is a paradigm shifter, served with pork belly, fried egg and kimchi. Other popular dishes: mac 'n' cheese, a braised pork shoulder taco, and a Sriracha tomato soup. Earl's also has an excellent craft beer selection.

Candle Cafe VEGAN $$

(Map p92; 212-472-0970; www.candlecafe.com; 1307 Third Ave, btwn 74th & 75th Sts; mains $15-22; 11:30am-10:30pm Mon-Sat, to 9:30pm Sun; ; S 6 to 77th St) The moneyed yoga set piles into this attractive vegan cafe serving a long list of sandwiches, salads, comfort food and market-driven specials. The specialty here is the house-made seitan.

Jones Wood Foundry BRITISH $$

(Map p92; 212-249-2700; www.joneswood-foundry.com; 401 E 76th St, btwn First & York Aves; mains lunch $12-24, dinner $19-26; 11am-11pm; ; S 6 to 77th St) Inside a narrow brick building that once housed an ironworks, the Jones Wood Foundry is a British-inspired gastropub serving first-rate beer-battered fish and chips, bangers and mash, lamb and rosemary pie and other hearty temptations. On warm days, grab a table on the enclosed courtyard patio.

Tanoshi SUSHI $$$

(Map p92; 646-727-9056; www.tanoshisushinyc.com; 1372 York Ave, btwn 73rd & 74th Sts; chef's sushi selection around $80; 6-10:30pm Mon-Sat; S 6 to 77th St) The setting may be humble, but the flavors are simply magnificent at this small, wildly popular sushi spot: think Hokkaido scallops, Atlantic shad, seared salmon belly or mouthwatering uni (sea urchin). Only sushi is on offer and only *omakase* – the chef's selection of whatever is particularly outstanding that day. It's BYO beer, sake or what-not. Reserve well in advance.

Harlem

★ **Red Rooster** MODERN AMERICAN $$

(Map p92; 212-792-9001; www.redroosterharlem.com; 310 Malcolm X Blvd btwn 125th & 126th Sts, Harlem; mains $18-30; 11:30am-10:30pm Mon-Fri, 10am-11pm Sat & Sun; S 2/3 to 125th St) Transatlantic super-chef Marcus Samuelsson laces upscale comfort food with a world of flavors at his effortlessly cool, swinging brasserie. Try blackened catfish with curried peas and pickled mango, meatballs with lingonberries and buttermilk mashed potatoes, or mac 'n' cheese with lobster.

Amy Ruth's Restaurant SOUTHERN $$

(Map p92; 212-280-8779; www.amyruthsharlem.com; 113 W 116th St near Malcolm X Blvd; mains $12-24; 11am-11pm Mon, 8:30am-11pm Tue-Thu, 8:30am-5am Fri, 7.30am-5am Sat, 7:30am-11pm Sun; S B, C, 2/3 to 116th St) This perennially crowded restaurant is *the* place to go for classic soul food, serving up fried catfish, mac 'n' cheese and fluffy biscuits. But it's the waffles that are most famous – dished up 14 different ways, including with shrimp. Our favorite is the 'Rev Al Sharpton': waffles topped with succulent fried chicken.

Dinosaur Bar-B-Que STEAK $$

(Map p92; 212-694-1777; www.dinosaurbar-bque.com; 700 W 125th St at Twelfth Ave; mains $13-25; 11:30am-11pm Mon-Thu, to midnight Fri & Sat, noon-10pm Sun; ; S 1 to 125th St) Get messy with dry-rubbed, slow-pit-smoked ribs, slabs of juicy steak, and succulent burgers. The very few vegetarian options include a fantastic version of Creole-spiced deviled eggs. There's live music weekend nights (from 10:30pm).

Brooklyn

Of course it's impossible to begin to do justice to Brooklyn's eating options – it's as much a foodie's paradise as Manhattan. Virtually every ethnic cuisine has a significant presence somewhere in this borough. As far as neighborhoods close to Manhattan go: Williamsburg is chockablock with eateries, as are Fifth and Seventh Aves in Park Slope. Smith St is 'Restaurant Row' in the Carroll Gardens and Cobble Hill neighborhoods. Atlantic Ave, near Court St, has a number of excellent Middle Eastern restaurants and groceries.

Mile End DELI $
(☎718-852-7510; www.mileendbrooklyn.com; 97A Hoyt St, Boerum Hill; sandwiches $9-15; ⏰8am-10pm Mon-Fri, from 10am Sat & Sun; Ⓢ A/C/G to Hoyt Schermerhorn Sts) Mile End is small, like its portions, but big on flavors. Try a smoked beef brisket on rye with mustard – the bread is sticky soft and the meat will melt in your mouth.

Tom's Restaurant DINER $
(☎718-636-9738; 782 Washington Ave, at Sterling Pl, Prospect Heights; mains $8-12; ⏰7am-4pm Mon-Sat, from 8am Sun; Ⓢ 2/3 to Eastern Pkwy-Brooklyn Museum) Inspiration for the eponymously named Suzanne Vega song, this old-school soda fountain diner's specialty is its variety of pancakes (eg pumpkin walnut). Coffee and cookies are served to those waiting in the line that invariably snakes out the door on weekend mornings.

Chuko JAPANESE $
(☎718-576-6701; www.barchuko.com; 552 Vanderbilt Ave, cnr Dean St, Prospect Heights; ramen $13; ⏰noon-3pm & 5:30-10pm Sun-Thu, to 11pm Fri & Sat; 🌱; Ⓢ B/Q to 7th Ave, 2/3 to Bergen St) This cozy wood-lined ramen shop brings a top-notch noodle game to Prospect Heights. Steaming bowls of al dente ramen are paired with silky broths, including an excellent roasted pork and a full-bodied vegetarian. Don't overlook the appetizers, particularly the fragrant salt-and-pepper chicken wings.

★Pok Pok THAI $$
(☎718-923-9322; www.pokpokny.com; 117 Columbia St, cnr Kane St; sharing plates $12-18; ⏰5:30-10:30pm Mon-Fri, from 10am Sat & Sun; Ⓢ F to Bergen St) Andy Ricker's NYC outpost is a smashing success, wowing diners with a rich and complex menu inspired by Northern Thailand street food. Fiery fish-sauce-slathered chicken wings, spicy green papaya salad with salted black crab, smoky grilled eggplant salad and sweet pork belly with ginger, turmeric and tamarind are among the many unique dishes.

The setting is fun and ramshackle, with a small backyard festooned with fairy lights. Waits can be long; thankfully there's a great little bar (**Whiskey Soda Lounge**) across the street, which serves imaginative concoctions (tamarind whiskey sours, Vietnamese coffee spiked with brandy) as well as bar nibbles from Pok Pok's menu.

SMORGASBURG!

On weekends, it's well worth planning a day around Brooklyn's **Smorgasburg** (www.smorgasburg.com; ⏰11am-6pm Sat & Sun Apr-Nov). At this sprawling food market you can nibble your way around the globe with over 100 food vendors on hand. Among the countless temptations you'll find chocolate salted caramel doughnuts (**Dough**), pork and crackling sandwiches (**Porchetta**), Japanese-inspired tacos (**Takumi**), sweet potato masala (**Dosa Royale**), Mexican street food (**Cemita's**), cold brew coffee (**Grady's**), strawberry rhubarb popsicles (**People's Pops**) and much more.

On Saturdays you'll find it at **East River State Park** (www.nysparks.com/parks/155; Kent Ave, btwn 8th & 9th Sts; ⏰9am-dusk; 👪; Ⓢ L to Bedford Ave) and Sundays at Pier 5 in **Brooklyn Bridge Park** (p98). Check the website for more details.

Battersby MODERN AMERICAN $$
(☎718-852-8321; www.battersbybrooklyn.com; 255 Smith St, btwn Douglass & Degraw Sts; mains $17-32, tasting menu $75-95; ⏰5:30-11pm Mon-Sat, to 10pm Sun; Ⓢ F, G to Bergen St) A top choice in Brooklyn, Battersby serves magnificent seasonal dishes. The small menu changes regularly, but be on the lookout for veal sweetbreads, pappardelle with duck ragu, chatham cod with braised fennel and delightfully tender lamb. The space is Brooklyn-style quaint (plank floors, brick walls, tin ceiling), but tiny and cramped.

To get in without a long wait, plan ahead: arrive at opening time or make a reservation – accepted only for folks partaking of the tasting menu.

Juliana's PIZZA $$
(☎718-596-6700; www.julianaspizza.com; 19 Old Fulton St, btwn Water & Front Sts; pizza $16-32; ⏰11:30am-11pm; Ⓢ A/C to High St) Legendary pizza maestro Patsy Grimaldi has returned to Brooklyn, with delicious thin-crust perfection in both classic and creative combos (like the No 5, with smoked salmon, goat's cheese and capers). It's in Dumbo and the Brooklyn waterfront.

Marlow & Sons MODERN AMERICAN $$
(718-384-1441; www.marlowandsons.com; 81 Broadway, btwn Berry St & Wythe Ave; mains lunch $14-18, dinner $24-28; 8am-midnight; S J/M/Z to Marcy Ave, L to Bedford Ave) The dimly lit, wood-lined space feels like an old farmhouse cafe, which hosts a buzzing nighttime scene as diners and drinkers crowd in for oysters, tip-top cocktails and a changing menu of locavore specialties (smoked pork loin, crunchy crust pizzas, carmelized turnips, fluffy Spanish-style tortillas). Brunch is also a big draw, though prepare for lines.

Roberta's PIZZA $$
(718-417-1118; www.robertaspizza.com; 261 Moore St, near Bogart St, Bushwick; pizzas $14-18; 11am-midnight; ; S L to Morgan Ave) This hipster-saturated warehouse restaurant in Bushwick consistently produces some of the best pizza in New York. Service can be lackadaisical and the waits long, but the brick-oven pies are the right combination of chewy and fresh.

Water Table MODERN AMERICAN $$$
(917-499-5727; www.thewatertablenyc.com; Skyport Marina, 23rd St & FDR Drive, Greenpoint; prix fixe $75; 7:30-10pm Thu-Sat, 6-8pm Sun; S) Scoring high on novelty, the Water Table is set inside a rustically converted WWII navy patrol boat. The three-course dinner (smoked scallop lobster bisque, kale salad, New England dry rub chicken, and seafood stew were recent selections) would seem a bit pricey if not for the memorable experience of sailing past soaring skyscrapers and the Statue of Liberty by night. Reserve a spot online.

Drinking & Nightlife

Watering holes come in many forms in this city: sleek lounges, pumping clubs, cozy pubs and booze-soaked dives – no smoke, though, thanks to city law. The majority are open to 4am, though closing (and opening) times do vary; most nightclubs are open from 10pm. Here's a highly selective sampling.

Lower Manhattan

★**Dead Rabbit** COCKTAIL BAR
(Map p76; 646-422-7906; www.deadrabbitnyc.com; 30 Water St; 11am-4am; S R to Whitehall St, 1 to South Ferry) Far from dead, this rabbit has won a warren full of awards for its magnificent cocktails. During the day, hit the sawdust-sprinkled taproom for specialty beers, historic punches and pop-inns (lightly hopped ale spiked with different flavors). Come evening, scurry upstairs to the cozy Parlour for 72 meticulously researched cocktails.

Smith & Mills COCKTAIL BAR
(Map p76; 212-226-2515; www.smithandmills.com; 71 N Moore St btwn Hudson & Greenwich Sts; 11am-2am Sun-Wed, to 3am Thu-Sat; S 1 to Franklin St) Petite Smith & Mills ticks all the cool boxes: unmarked exterior, kooky industrial interior and expertly crafted cocktails. Space is limited so head in early if you fancy kicking back on a plush banquette. A seasonal menu spans light snacks to a particularly notable burger.

Weather Up COCKTAIL BAR
(Map p76; 212-766-3202; www.weatherupnyc.com; 159 Duane St btwn Hudson St & W Broadway; 5pm-midnight Mon-Wed, to 2am Thu-Sun; S 1/2/3 to Chambers St) Softly lit subway tiles, amiable barkeeps and seductive cocktails set the stage for a fine night out. Try a Whizz Bang (Scotch whiskey, dry vermouth, house-made grenadine, orange bitters and absinthe) while munching fine snacks, including oysters slapped with gin-martini granita.

Chinatown, SoHo & NoLita

Mulberry Project COCKTAIL BAR
(Map p80; 646-448-4536; www.mulberryproject.com; 149 Mulberry St, btwn Hester & Grand Sts; 5pm-2am Sun-Thu, to 4am Fri & Sat; S N/Q/R, J/Z, 6 to Canal St) Lurking behind an unmarked door is this intimate, cavernous cocktail den, with its festive, 'garden-party' backyard one of the best spots to imbibe in the 'hood.

Apothéke COCKTAIL BAR
(Map p76; 212-406-0400; www.apothekenyc.com; 9 Doyers St; 6:30pm-2am Mon-Sat, 8pm-2am Sun; S J to Chambers St, 4/5/6 to Brooklyn Bridge-City Hall) It takes a little effort to track down this former opium den turned apothecary bar on Doyers St. Inside, skilled barkeeps work like careful chemists, using local and organic produce from greenmarkets or the rooftop herb garden to produce intense, flavorful 'prescriptions.' Toast to your health with the invigorating Harvest of Mexico (roasted corn, Herba Sainte, mezcal, agave, lime and habanero-infused bitters).

Spring Lounge DIVE BAR
(Map p80; 212-965-1774; www.thespringlounge.com; 48 Spring St, at Mulberry St; 8am-4am Mon-Sat, from noon Sun; S 6 to Spring St, N/R

to Prince St) This neon-red rebel has never let anything get in the way of a good time. These days, this pretension-free drinking den is best known for its kooky stuffed sharks, early-start regulars and come-one-come-all late-night revelry. Fueling the fun are cheap drinks and free grub (hot dogs on Wednesdays from 5pm, bagels on Sundays from noon, while they last).

East Village & the Lower East Side

Ten Bells TAPAS BAR

(Map p80; ☎212-228-4450; www.tenbellsnyc.com; 247 Broome St, btwn Ludlow & Orchard Sts; ⏰5pm-2am Mon-Fri, from 3pm Sat & Sun; Ⓢ F to Delancey St, J/M/Z to Essex St) This charmingly tucked-away tapas bar has a grotto-like design, with flickering candles, dark tin ceilings, brick walls and a U-shaped bar that's an ideal setting for conversation with a new friend. The chalkboard menu features excellent wines by the glass, which go nicely with *boquerones* (marinated anchovies) and other Iberian hits. The entrance is unsigned.

Wayland BAR

(Map p80; ☎212-777-7022; www.thewaylandnyc.com; 700 E 9th St, cnr Ave C; ⏰5pm-4am; Ⓢ L to 1st Ave) Whitewashed walls, weathered floorboards and salvaged lamps give this urban outpost a Mississippi flair, which goes just right with the live music (bluegrass, jazz, folk) from Sunday through Wednesday. Decent drink specials and $1 oysters from 5pm to 7pm on weekdays.

Angel's Share BAR

(Map p80; ☎212-777-5415; 2nd fl, 8 Stuyvesant St, near Third Ave & E 9th St; ⏰6pm-1:30am Sun-Thu, until 2:30am Fri & Sat; Ⓢ 6 to Astor Pl) Show up early and snag a seat at this hidden gem, behind a Japanese restaurant on the same floor. It's quiet and elegant with creative cocktails, but you can't stay if you don't have a table or a seat at the bar, and they tend to go fast.

Immigrant WINE & BEER

(Map p80; ☎646-308-1724; www.theimmigrantnyc.com; 341 E 9th St, btwn First & Second Aves; ⏰5pm-1am Sun-Wed, to 2am Thu-Sat; Ⓢ L to 1st Ave, 4/6 to Astor Pl) Wholly unpretentious, these twin boxcar-sized bars could easily become your neighborhood local if you decide to stick around town. Enter the right side for the wine bar. The left entrance takes you into the taproom, where the focus is on unique microbrews. Both have a similar design – chandeliers, exposed brick, vintage charm.

West Village & Chelsea

Bell Book & Candle BAR

(Map p80; ☎212-414-2355; www.bbandcnyc.com; 141 W 10th St btwn Waverley & Greenwich Ave; ⏰5:30pm-2am Sun-Wed, to 4am Thu-Sat; Ⓢ A/B/C, B/D/F/M to W 4th St; 1 to Christopher St-Sheridan Sq) Step down into this candelit gastropub for strong, inventive libations and hearty pub grub. A twenty-something crowd gathers around the small, packed bar (for $1 oysters and happy-hour drink specials early in the night), though there's a lot more seating hidden in the back, with big booths ideal for larger groups.

Employees Only BAR

(Map p80; ☎212-242-3021; www.employeesonlynyc.com; 510 Hudson St near Christopher St; ⏰6pm-4am; Ⓢ 1 to Christopher St-Sheridan Sq) Duck behind the neon 'Psychic' sign to find this hidden hangout. The bar gets busier as the night wears on. Bartenders are ace mixologists, fizzing up crazy, addictive libations like the Ginger Smash and the Mata Hari. Great for late-night drinking, and eating, courtesy of the on-site restaurant that serves till 3:30am.

Buvette WINE BAR

(Map p80; ☎212-255-3590; www.ilovebuvette.com; 42 Grove St btwn Bedford & Bleecker Sts; ⏰9am-2am; Ⓢ 1 to Christopher St-Sheridan Sq; A/C/E, B/D/F/M to W 4th St) The rustic-chic decor here (think delicate tin tiles and a swooshing marble countertop) make it the perfect place for a glass of wine – no matter the time of day. For the full experience at this self-proclaimed *gastrotèque*, grab a seat at one of the surrounding tables, and nibble on small plates while enjoying the Old-World wines (mostly from France and Italy).

Frying Pan BAR

(Map p84; ☎212-989-6363; www.fryingpan.com; Pier 66 at W 26th St; ⏰noon-midnight May-Oct; Ⓢ C/E to 23rd St) The lightship *Frying Pan* and the two-tiered dockside bar where it's parked are fine go-to spots for a sundowner. On warm days, the rustic open-air space brings in the crowds, who come to laze on deck chairs, eat burgers off the sizzling grill, drink ice-cold beers and admire the waterside views.

Union Square, Flatiron District & Gramercy Park

Old Town Bar & Restaurant BAR

(Map p84; ☎212-529-6732; www.oldtownbar.com; 45 E 18th St, btwn Broadway & Park Ave S; ⏰11:30am-1:30am Mon-Sat, 1pm-midnight Sun; Ⓢ L, N/Q/R, 4/5/6 to 14th St-Union Sq) It still looks like 1892 in here, with the original tile floors and tin ceilings – the Old Town is an 'old world' drinking-man's classic (and woman's: Madonna lit up at the bar here, when lighting up was still legal, in her 'Bad Girl' video). There are cocktails around, but most come for beers and a burger (from $12).

Flatiron Room COCKTAIL BAR

(Map p84; ☎212-725-3860; www.theflatironroom.com; 37 W 26th St btwn Sixth Ave & Broadway; ⏰5pm-2am Mon-Sat, to midnight Sun; Ⓢ N/R to 28th St) This beautifully designed drinking den has vintage wallpaper, a glittering chandelier, hand-painted coffer ceilings and artfully lit cabinets filled with rare whiskeys. The fine cocktails pair nicely with high-end sharing plates (sweet potato tacos, wild mushroom flatbread, roasted bone marrow). There's also live music (jazz, bluegrass) most nights. Reservations essential.

Midtown

★Rum House COCKTAIL BAR

(Map p84; ☎646-490-6924; www.therumhousenyc.com; 228 W 47th St, btwn Broadway & Eighth Ave, Midtown West; ⏰1pm-4am; Ⓢ N/Q/R to 49th St) Inside this beautifully polished drinking parlor, you'll find well-crafted drinks, red leather banquettes and a classy old-timey vibe. There's live music daily – sometimes just a lone pianist, other times a jaunty jazz trio or sentimental torch singer.

Campbell Apartment COCKTAIL BAR

(Map p84; ☎212-953-0409; www.hospitalityholdings.com; Grand Central Terminal, 15 Vanderbilt Ave, at 43rd St; ⏰noon-midnight Sun-Thu, to 2am Fri & Sat; Ⓢ S, 4/5/6, 7 to Grand Central-42nd St) This sublime, deliciously buttoned-up gem in Grand Central was once the office of a '20s railroad magnate fond of Euro eccentricities: think Florentine-style carpets, decorative wooden ceiling beams and a soaring lead-glass window. Suitably tucked away from the hordes, reach it from the lift beside the Oyster Bar or the stairs to the West Balcony.

Russian Vodka Room BAR

(Map p84; ☎212-307-5835; www.russianvodkaroom.com; 265 W 52nd St, btwn Eighth Ave & Broadway; ⏰4pm-2am Mon-Thu, to 4am Fri & Sat; Ⓢ C/E to 50th St) Actual Russians aren't uncommon at this swanky and welcoming bar. The lighting is dark and the corner booths intimate, but more importantly the dozens of infused vodkas, from cranberry to horseradish, are fun to experiment with.

Lantern's Keep COCKTAIL BAR

(Map p84; ☎212-453-4287; www.thelanternskeep.com; Iroquois Hotel, 49 W 44th St, btwn Fifth & Sixth Aves; ⏰5pm-midnight Mon-Fri, 6pm-1am Sat; Ⓢ B/D/F/M to 42nd St-Bryant Park) Cross the lobby of the Iroquois Hotel and slip into this dark, intimate cocktail salon. Its specialty is pre-Prohibition libations, shaken and stirred by passionate, personable mixologists. Reservations recommended.

Top of the Strand COCKTAIL BAR

(Map p84; www.topofthestrand.com; Strand Hotel, 33 W 37th St, btwn Fifth & Sixth Aves; ⏰5pm-midnight Mon & Sun, to 1am Tue-Sat; Ⓢ B/D/F/M to 34th St) For that 'Oh my God, I'm in New York' feeling, head to the Strand Hotel's rooftop bar, order a martini and admire the jaw-dropping view of the Empire State Building.

Rudy's Bar & Grill DIVE BAR

(Map p84; ☎646-707-0890; www.rudysbarnyc.com; 627 Ninth Ave, at 44th St, Midtown West; ⏰8am-4am Mon-Sat, noon-4am Sun; Ⓢ A/C/E to 42nd St-Port Authority Bus Terminal) The big pantless pig in a red jacket out front marks Hell's Kitchen's best divey mingler, with cheap pitchers of Rudy's two beers, half-circle booths covered in red duct tape, and free hot dogs. A mix of folks come to flirt or watch muted Knicks games as classic rock plays.

Bryant Park Grill BAR, RESTAURANT

(Map p84; ☎212-840-6500; www.arkrestaurants.com/bryant_park.html; 25 W 40th St btwn Fifth & Sixth Aves; ⏰11:30am-11pm; Ⓢ B/D/F/M to 42nd St-Bryant Park, 7 to Fifth Ave) When the weather is warm, head to this lovely restaurant and bar situated at the eastern end of Bryant Park. The patio bar is a perfect spot for a twilight cocktail or three.

Jimmy's Corner DIVE BAR

(Map p84; ☎212-221-9510; 140 W 44th St, btwn Sixth & Seventh Aves, Midtown West; ⏰10am-4am; Ⓢ N/Q/R, 1/2/3, 7 to 42nd St-Times Sq; B/D/F/M to

42nd St-Bryant Park) This skinny, welcoming, completely unpretentious dive off Times Square is owned by an old boxing trainer – as if you wouldn't guess by all the framed photos of boxing greats. The jukebox covers Stax to Miles Davis.

Upper West Side

79th Street Boat Basin BAR
(Map p92; ☎212-496-5542; www.boatbasincafe.com; W 79th St, in Riverside Park; ⏰noon-11pm Apr-Oct; Ⓢ1 to 79th St) A covered, open-sided party spot under the ancient arches of a park overpass, this is an Upper West Side favorite once spring hits. Order a pitcher, some snacks and enjoy the sunset view over the Hudson River.

Manhattan Cricket Club COCKTAIL LOUNGE
(Map p92; ☎646-823-9252; www.mccnewyork.com; 226 W 79th St, btwn Amsterdam Ave & Broadway; ⏰6pm-2am Tue-Sat; Ⓢ1 to 79th St) Above an Australian bistro, this elegant drinking lounge is modeled on the classy Anglo-Aussie cricket clubs of the early 1900s. Sepia-toned photos of batsmen adorn the gold brocaded walls, while mahogany bookshelves and Chesterfield sofas create a fine setting for quaffing well-made but pricey cocktails.

Dead Poet BAR
(Map p92; ☎212-595-5670; www.thedeadpoet.com; 450 Amsterdam Ave, btwn 81st & 82nd Sts; ⏰noon-4am; Ⓢ1 to 79th St) This skinny, mahogany-paneled pub has been a neighborhood favorite for over a decade, with a mix of locals and students nursing pints of Guinness and cocktails named after dead poets.

Barcibo Enoteca WINE BAR
(Map p92; ☎212-595-2805; www.barciboenoteca.com; 2020 Broadway, cnr 69th St; ⏰4:30pm-11:30am Tue-Fri, from 3:30pm Sat-Mon; Ⓢ1/2/3 to 72nd St) Just north of Lincoln Center, this casual chic marble-table spot is ideal for sipping, with a long list of vintages from all over Italy, including 40 different varieties sold by the glass.

Upper East Side

Auction House BAR
(Map p92; ☎212-427-4458; 300 E 89th St; ⏰7:30pm-4am; Ⓢ4/5/6 to 86th St) Dark maroon doors lead into a candlelit hangout that's perfect for a relaxing drink. Victorian-style couches and overstuffed chairs are strewn about the wood-floored rooms, while oil paintings of nudes adorn the exposed brick walls.

Penrose BAR
(Map p92; ☎212-203-2751; www.penrosebar.com; 1590 Second Ave, btwn 82nd & 83rd Sts; ⏰3pm-4am Mon-Thu, noon-4am Fri, 10:30am-4am Sat & Sun; Ⓢ4/5/6 to 86th St) The Penrose brings a dose of style to the Upper East Side, with craft beers, vintage mirrors, floral wallpaper and friendly bartenders setting the stage for fine evening among friends.

Brooklyn

★ **Maison Premiere** COCKTAIL BAR
(☎347-335-0446; www.maisonpremiere.com; 298 Bedford Ave, btwn 1st & Grand Sts, Williamsburg; ⏰4pm-2am Mon-Fri, from 11am Sat & Sun; ⓈL to Bedford Ave) This old-timey place features a chemistry-lab-style bar full of syrups and essences and suspendered bartenders to mix them all up. The epic cocktail list includes more than 20 absinthe drinks and a raw bar provides a long list of snacks on the half shell.

Radegast Hall & Biergarten BEER HALL
(☎718-963-3973; www.radegasthall.com; 113 N 3rd St, at Berry St, Williamsburg; ⏰noon-2am; ⓈL to Bedford Ave) This lively Austro-Hungarian beer hall in Williamsburg offers up a huge selection of Bavarian brews as well as a kitchen full of munchable meats.

Spuyten Duyvil BAR
(☎718-963-4140; www.spuytenduyvilnyc.com; 359 Metropolitan Ave, btwn Havemayer & Roebling, Williamsburg; ⏰5pm-late Mon-Fri, from noon Sat & Sun; ⓈL to Lorimer St, G to Metropolitan Ave) Red ceilings, vintage maps on the walls and tattered furniture recede into the background when perusing the staggering beer selection of this hallowed brew parlor. A leafy patio opens in good weather.

Hotel Delmano COCKTAIL BAR
(☎718-387-1945; www.hoteldelmano.com; 82 Berry St, at N 9th St; ⏰5pm-late Mon-Fri, frm 2pm Sat & Sun; ⓈL to Bedford Ave) This low-lit cocktail bar aims for the speakeasy vibe, with old mirrors, unpolished floorboards and vintage chandeliers.

Pine Box Rock Shop BAR
(☎718-366-6311; www.pineboxrockshop.com; 12 Grattan St, btwn Morgan Ave & Bogart St, Bushwick; ⏰4pm-4am Mon-Fri, from 2pm Sat & Sun; ⓈL to Morgan Ave) The cavernous Pine Box is

GAY & LESBIAN NYC

Few cities make being queer so utterly fabulous. New York's vibrant gay scene is spread across Hell's Kitchen, Chelsea and the West Village, with an ever-expanding choice of gay and gay-friendly eateries, bars, clubs and shops. For nightlife, here are a few highlights:

Eastern Bloc (Map p80; ☎212-777-2555; www.easternblocnyc.com; 505 E 6th St, btwn Aves A & B, East Village; ⏰7pm-4am; Ⓢ F to 2nd Ave) Though the theme may be 'Iron Curtain,' the drapery is most definitely velvet and taffeta at this East Village gay bar. Spring forth into the crowded sea of boys – some flirting with the topless barkeeps, others pretending not to stare at the retro '70s porno playing on the TVs.

Industry (Map p84; ☎646-476-2747; www.industry-bar.com; 355 W 52nd St, btwn Eighth & Ninth Aves, Midtown West; ⏰4pm-4am; Ⓢ C/E, 1 to 50th St) One of the hottest gay bars in Hell's Kitchen, this slick 4000-sq-ft watering hole has handsome lounge areas, a pool table, and a stage for top-notch drag divas.

Therapy (Map p84; ☎212-397-1700; www.therapy-nyc.com; 348 W 52nd St, btwn Eighth & Ninth Aves, Midtown West; ⏰5pm-2am Sun-Thu, to 4am Fri & Sat; Ⓢ C/E, 1 to 50th St) This long-running multilevel space still draws throngs to Hell's Kitchen with its nightly shows (from music to boylesque).

Flaming Saddles (Map p84; ☎212-713-0481; www.flamingsaddles.com; 793 Ninth Ave, btwn 52nd & 53rd Sts, Midtown West; ⏰3pm-4am Mon-Fri, noon-4am Sat & Sun; Ⓢ C/E to 50th St) *Coyote Ugly* meets *Calamity Jane* at this Hell's Kitchen hangout, complete with studly bar-dancing barmen, aspiring urban cowboys and a rough 'n' ready vibe.

Marie's Crisis (Map p80; ☎212-243-9323; www.manhattan-monster.com; 59 Grove St, btwn Seventh Ave & Bleecker St, West Village; ⏰4pm-4am; Ⓢ 1 to Christopher St-Sheridan Sq) One-time hooker hangout turned showtune piano bar. It's old-school fun, no matter how jaded you were when you went in.

Stonewall Inn (Map p80; ☎212-488-2705; www.thestonewallinnnyc.com; 53 Christopher St, West Village; ⏰2pm-4am; Ⓢ 1 to Christopher St-Sheridan Sq) Site of the Stonewall riots in 1969, this historic bar draws varied crowds nightly for parties that cater to everyone under the rainbow flag.

Henrietta Hudson (Map p80; ☎212-924-3347; www.henriettahudson.com; 438 Hudson St, West Village; ⏰ 5pm-2am Mon & Tue, 4pm-4am Wed-Fri, 2pm-4am Sat & Sun; Ⓢ 1 to Houston St) All sorts of cute young dykes, many from neighboring New Jersey and Long Island, storm this sleek 'bar & girl'. Varying theme nights bring in spirited DJs, who spin a mix of hip-hop, house and Latin beats.

a former Bushwick casket factory that has 16 drafts to choose from, as well as spicy, pint-sized Bloody Marys. Run by a friendly musician couple, the walls are filled with local artwork and a performance space in the back hosts regular gigs.

61 Local BAR

(☎718-875-1150; www.61local.com; 61 Bergen St, btwn Smith St & Boerum Pl, Cobble Hill; ⏰7am-late Mon-Fri, from 9am Sat & Sun; 📶; Ⓢ F, G to Bergen) A roomy brick-and-wood hall in Cobble Hill manages to be both chic and warm, with large communal tables, a mellow vibe and a good selection of craft beers. There's a simple menu of charcuterie and other snacks.

Sunny's BAR

(☎718-625-8211; www.sunnysredhook.com; 253 Conover St, btwn Beard & Reed Sts, Red Hook; ⏰6pm-late Tue-Fri, from 2pm Sat, 4-11pm Sun; 🚌 B61 to Coffey & Conover Sts, Ⓢ F, G to Carroll St) Way out in Red Hook, this super-inviting longshoreman bar – the sign says 'bar' – is straight out of *On the Waterfront*. Every Saturday at 10pm it hosts a foot-stomping bluegrass jam.

☆ Entertainment

Those with unlimited fuel and appetites can gorge themselves on a seemingly infinite number of entertainments – from Broadway shows to performance art in someone's Brooklyn living room, and everything in between. *New York* magazine and the weekend editions of the *New York Times* are great guides for what's on once you arrive.

Live Music

Joe's Pub LIVE MUSIC
(Map p80; ☎212-539-8778; www.joespub.com; Public Theater, 425 Lafayette St, btwn Astor Pl & 4th St; Ⓢ R/W to 8th St-NYU, 6 to Astor Pl) Part cabaret theater, part rock and new-indie venue, this small and lovely supper club hosts a wonderful variety of styles, voices and talent.

Rockwood Music Hall LIVE MUSIC
(Map p80; ☎212-477-4155; www.rockwoodmusichall.com; 196 Allen St, btwn Houston & Stanton Sts; Ⓢ F/V to Lower East Side-Second Ave) This bread-box-sized concert space features a rapid-fire flow of bands and singer/songwriters on three different stages. Many shows are free.

Pianos LIVE MUSIC
(Map p80; ☎212-505-3733; www.pianosnyc.com; 158 Ludlow St, at Stanton St; cover $8-10; ⊙noon-4am; Ⓢ F to 2nd Ave) A Lower East Side stalwart, two-story Pianos stages a mix of genres and styles, leaning more toward pop, punk and new wave, but throwing in some hip-hop and indie for good measure.

Bowery Ballroom LIVE MUSIC
(Map p80; ☎212-533-2111; www.boweryballroom.com; 6 Delancey St, at Bowery St; Ⓢ J/Z to Bowery) This terrific, medium-sized venue has the perfect sound and feel for more blown-up indie-rock acts (Interpol, Belle & Sebastian, Morrissey).

Le Poisson Rouge LIVE MUSIC
(Map p80; ☎212-505-3474; www.lepoissonrouge.com; 158 Bleecker St; Ⓢ A/C/E, B/D/F/M to W 4th St-Washington Sq) This Bleecker St basement club is one of the premier venues for experimental contemporary, from classical to indie rock to electro-acoustic.

Mercury Lounge LIVE MUSIC
(Map p80; ☎212-260-4700; www.mercuryloungenyc.com; 217 E Houston St btwn Essex & Ludlow Sts; cover charge $10-15; ⊙4pm-4am; Ⓢ F/V to Lower East Side-2nd Ave) The Mercury dependably pulls in a new or comeback band that draws the downtown crowds.

Beacon Theatre LIVE MUSIC
(Map p92; www.beacontheatre.com; 2124 Broadway, btwn 74th & 75th Sts; Ⓢ 1/2/3 to 72nd St) This Upper West Side venue hosts big acts in an environment that's more intimate than a big concert arena.

Radio City Music Hall CONCERT VENUE
(Map p84; ☎212-247-4777; www.radiocity.com; Sixth Ave, at W 50th St; Ⓢ B/D, F, M to 47-50th Sts) The architecturally grand concert hall in Midtown hosts the likes of Tony Bennett, Kelly Clarkson and the famous Christmas spectacular.

Irving Plaza LIVE MUSIC
(Map p84; www.irvingplaza.com; 17 Irving Pl at 15th St; Ⓢ L, N/Q/R/W, 4/5/6 to 14th St-Union Sq) A great 1000-seat setting for quirky mainstream acts.

Webster Hall CLUB
(Map p80; ☎212-353-1600; www.websterhall.com; 125 E 11th St, near Third Ave; ⊙10pm-4am Thu-Sat; Ⓢ L, N/Q/R/W, 4/5/6 to 14th St-Union Sq) The granddaddy of dancehalls.

★ **Brooklyn Bowl** LIVE MUSIC
(☎718-963-3369; www.brooklynbowl.com; 61 Wythe Ave, btwn 11th & 12th Sts; ⊙6pm-2am Mon-Thu, to 4am Fri, noon-4am Sat, noon-2am Sun; Ⓢ L to Bedford Ave, G to Nassau Ave) This 23,000-sq-ft venue inside the former Hecla Iron Works Company combines bowling, microbrews, food and groovy live music.

Bell House LIVE MUSIC
(www.thebellhouseny.com; 149 7th St, Gowanus; ⊙5pm-4am; 📶; Ⓢ F, G, R to 4th Ave-9th St) A converted warehouse in the industrial neighborhood of Gowanus, the Bell House features live performances, indie rockers, DJ nights, comedy shows and burlesque parties.

Jalopy LIVE MUSIC
(www.jalopy.biz; 315 Columbia St, at Woodhull St, Red Hook; Ⓢ F, G to Carroll St) This fringe Carroll Gardens/Red Hook banjo shop and bar features bluegrass, country and ukulele shows, including a feel-good Roots 'n' Ruckus show on Wednesday nights.

Music Hall of Williamsburg LIVE MUSIC
(www.musichallofwilliamsburg.com; 66 N 6th St, btwn Wythe & Kent Aves, Williamsburg; show $15-35; Ⓢ L to Bedford Ave) This popular Williamsburg music venue is *the* place to see indie bands in Brooklyn. (For many groups traveling through New York, this is their one and only spot.)

Theater

In general, 'Broadway' productions are staged in the lavish, early 20th-century theaters surrounding Times Square.

Choose from current shows by checking print publications, or a website such as **Theater Mania** (☎212-352-3101; www.

theatermania.com). You can purchase tickets through **Telecharge** (212-239-6200; www.telecharge.com) and **Ticketmaster** (800-448-7849, 800-745-3000; www.ticketmaster.com) for standard ticket sales, or **TKTS ticket booths** (www.tdf.org/tkts; cnr Front & John Sts; 11am-6pm Mon-Sat, to 4pm Sun; S A/C to Broadway-Nassau; 2/3, 4/5, J/Z to Fulton St) for same-day tickets to a selection of Broadway and off-Broadway musicals at up to 50% off regular prices.

Some distinguished theaters:

★Public Theater THEATER
(Map p80; 212-539-8500; www.publictheater.org; 425 Lafayette St, btwn Astor Pl & E 4th St; S R/N to 8th St, 6 to Astor Pl) Excellent downtown venue that stages works by some of the best contemporary and classic playwrights.

★St Ann's Warehouse THEATER
(718-254-8779; www.stannswarehouse.org; 45 Water St, Dumbo; S A/C to High St) This avant-garde performance company hosts innovative theater and dance happenings that attract the Brooklyn literati.

PS 122 THEATER
(Map p80; 212-477-5288; www.ps122.org; 150 First Ave, at E 9th St) Catch dance shows, film screenings and various festivals for up-and-coming talents.

Playwrights Horizons THEATER
(Map p84; 212-279-4200; www.playwrightshorizons.org; 416 W 42nd St, btwn Ninth & Tenth Aves, Midtown West; S A/C/E to 42nd St-Port Authority Bus Terminal) An excellent place to catch what could be the next big thing.

New York Theater Workshop THEATER
(Map p80; 212-460-5475; www.nytw.org; 79 E 4th St, btwn Second & Third Aves; S F to 2nd Ave) A treasure to those seeking cutting-edge, contemporary plays with purpose.

Comedy

Comedy Cellar COMEDY
(Map p80; 212-254-3480; www.comedycellar.com; 117 MacDougal St btwn W 3rd & Minetta Ln; cover $12-24; S A/C/E, B/D/F/M to W 4th St-Washington Sq) This long-established basement club in Greenwich Village is one of New York's best comedy venues.

Caroline's on Broadway COMEDY
(Map p84; 212-757-4100; www.carolines.com; 1626 Broadway, at 50th St; S N/Q/R to 49th St, 1 to 50th St) A top spot to catch US comedy big guns and sitcom stars.

★Upright Citizens Brigade Theatre COMEDY
(Map p84; 212-366-9176; www.ucbtheatre.com; 307 W 26th St btwn Eighth & Ninth Aves; cover $5-10; S C/E to 23rd St) Improv venue featuring well-known, emerging and probably-won't-emerge comedians in a small basement theater nightly.

Cinemas

★Film Forum CINEMA
(Map p80; 212-727-8110; www.filmforum.com; 209 W Houston St btwn Varick St & Sixth Ave; S 1 to Houston St) The long and narrow theaters can't dent cineastes' love for this institution showing revivals, classics and documentaries.

JAZZ

From bebop to free improvisation, in classic art-deco clubs and at intimate jam sessions, New York remains one of the great capitals of jazz.

Smalls (Map p80; 212-252-5091; www.smallsjazzclub.com; 183 W 4th St; 7:30pm-12:30am cover $20, after $10; 4pm-4am; S 1 to Christopher St-Sheridan Sq) is a subterranean jazz dungeon that rivals the world-famous **Village Vanguard** (Map p80; 212-255-4037; www.villagevanguard.com; 178 Seventh Ave at 11th St; cover around $30; 7:30pm-12:30am; S 1/2/3 to 14th St) in terms of sheer talent. Of course, the latter has hosted every major star of the past 50 years; there's a one-drink minimum and a serious no-talking policy.

Heading uptown, **Dizzy's Club Coca-Cola: Jazz at the Lincoln Center** (Map p92; tickets to Dizzy's Club Coca-Cola 212-258-9595, tickets to Rose Theater & Allen Room 212-721-6500; www.jazz.org; Time Warner Center, Broadway at 60th St; S A/C, B/D, 1 to 59th St-Columbus Circle), one of Lincoln Center's three jazz venues, has stunning views overlooking Central Park and nightly shows featuring top lineups. Further north on the Upper West Side, check out the **Smoke Jazz & Supper Club-Lounge** (Map p92; 212-864-6662; www.smokejazz.com; 2751 Broadway, btwn W 105th & 106th Sts; 5:30pm-3am Mon-Sat, 11am-3am Sun; S 1 to 103rd St), which gets crowded on weekends.

IFC Center CINEMA
(Map p80; ☎212-924-7771; www.ifccenter.com; 323 Sixth Ave at 3rd St; tickets $14; Ⓢ A/C/E, B/D/F/M to W 4th St-Washington Sq) This three-screen art-house cinema shows new indies, cult classics and foreign films.

Landmark Sunshine Cinema CINEMA
(Map p80; ☎212-260-7289; www.landmarktheatres.com; 143 E Houston St, btwn Forsyth & Eldridge Sts; Ⓢ F/V to Lower East Side-Second Ave) Housed in a former Yiddish theater; shows first-run indies.

Anthology Film Archives CINEMA
(Map p80; ☎212-505-5181; www.anthologyfilmarchives.org; 32 Second Ave, at 2nd St; Ⓢ F to 2nd Ave) Film studies majors head to this schoolhouse-like building for independent and avant-garde cinema.

Performing Arts

★Carnegie Hall LIVE MUSIC
(Map p84; ☎212-247-7800; www.carnegiehall.org; W 57th St at Seventh Ave, Midtown West; ⏲tours 11:30am, 12:30pm, 2pm & 3pm Mon-Fri, 11:30am & 12:30pm Sat, 12:30pm Sun Oct-May; Ⓢ N/Q/R to 57th St-7th Ave) Since 1891, the historic Carnegie Hall has hosted performances by the likes of Tchaikovsky, Mahler and Prokofiev, as well as Stevie Wonder, Sting and João Gilberto. It's mostly closed in July and August.

★Brooklyn Academy of Music PERFORMING ARTS
(BAM; Map p72; www.bam.org; 30 Lafayette Ave, at Ashland Pl, Fort Greene; 📶; Ⓢ D, N/R to Pacific St, B, Q, 2/3, 4/5 to Atlantic Ave) Sort of a Brooklyn version of the Lincoln Center – in its all-inclusiveness rather than its vibe, which is much edgier – the spectacular academy also hosts everything from modern dance to opera, cutting-edge theater and music concerts.

Symphony Space LIVE MUSIC
(Map p92; ☎212-864-5400; www.symphonyspace.org; 2537 Broadway, btwn 94th & 95th Sts; Ⓢ 1/2/3 to 96th St) A multigenre space with several facilities in one. This Upper West Side gem is home to many performance series as well as theater, cabaret, comedy, dance and world-music concerts throughout the week.

Shopping

Home to myriad fashion boutiques, flea markets, booksellers, record stores, antique shops and gourmet grocers – New York City is quite simply one of the best shopping destinations on the planet.

Downtown

Downtown's coolest offerings are in NoLita (just east of SoHo), the East Village and the Lower East Side. SoHo has more expensive and equally fashionable stores, while Broadway from Union Sq to Canal St is lined with big retailers like H&M and Urban Outfitters, as well as dozens of jeans and shoe stores.

ABC Carpet & Home HOMEWARES, GIFTS
(Map p84; ☎212-473-3000; www.abchome.com; 888 Broadway, at 19th St; ⏲10am-7pm Mon-Wed, Fri & Sat, to 8pm Thu, noon-6pm Sun; Ⓢ L, N/Q/R, 4/5/6 to 14th St-Union Sq) A mecca for home designers, this beautifully curated, six-level store heaves with housewares, designer jewelry and global gifts.

★Strand Book Store BOOKS
(Map p80; ☎212-473-1452; www.strandbooks.com; 828 Broadway at 12th St; ⏲9:30am-10:30pm Mon-Sat, from 11am Sun; Ⓢ L, N/Q/R, 4/5/6 to 14th St-Union Sq) The city's preeminent bibliophile warehouse, selling new and used books.

★Century 21 FASHION
(Map p76; www.c21stores.com; 22 Cortlandt St btwn Church St & Broadway; ⏲7:45am-9pm Mon-Fri, 10am-9pm Sat, 11am-8pm Sun; Ⓢ A/C, J/Z, 2/3, 4/5 to Fulton St, N/R to Cortlandt St) A four-level department store loved by New Yorkers of every income. It's shorthand for designer bargains.

Other Music MUSIC
(Map p80; ☎212-477-8150; www.othermusic.com; 15 E 4th St, btwn Lafayette St & Broadway; ⏲11am-9pm Mon-Fri, noon-8pm Sat, noon-7pm Sun; Ⓢ 6 to Bleecker St) This indie-run CD store feeds its loyal fan base with a clued-in selection of offbeat lounge, psychedelic, electronica, indie rock etc, available new and used. There's also vinyl.

Obscura Antiques ANTIQUES
(Map p80; ☎212-505-9251; 207 Ave A, btwn 12th & 13th Sts; ⏲noon-8pm Mon-Sat, to 7pm Sun; Ⓢ L to 1st Ave) Browsing here is like stepping into a small cabinet of curiosities with taxidermy, tiny (dental?) instruments, old poison bottles, glass eyes, cane toad purses, anatomical drawings and other great gift ideas for that special someone (your mother-in-law?).

Idlewild Books BOOKS
(Map p84; ☎212-414-8888; www.idlewildbooks.com; 12 W 19th St, btwn Fifth & Sixth Aves; ⏲noon-7.30pm Mon-Thu, to 6pm Fri & Sat, to 5pm Sun; Ⓢ L, N/Q/R, 4/5/6 to 14th St-Union Sq) This wondrous

WATCHING SPORTS IN NYC

The uber-successful **New York Yankees** (☎718-293-6000, tickets 877-469-9849; www.yankees.com; tickets $20-300) play at **Yankee Stadium** (Map p72; ☎718-293-4300, tickets 212-926-5337; E 161st St at River Ave, the Bronx; tours $20; **S** B/D, 4 to 161st St-Yankee Stadium), while the more historically beleaguered **New York Mets** (☎718-507-8499; www.mets.com; tickets $19-130) play at **Citi Field** (Map p72; 126th St, at Roosevelt Ave, Flushing, Queens; **S** 7 to Mets-Willets Pt). For less-grand settings but no-less-pleasant outings, check out the minor-league **Staten Island Yankees** (☎718-720-9265; www.siyanks.com; tickets $12) at **Richmond County Bank Ballpark** (75 Richmond Tce, Staten Island ⛴ Staten Island Ferry) or the **Brooklyn Cyclones** (☎718-372-5596; www.brooklyncyclones.com; tickets from $15, $10 on Wed) at **MCU Park** (Map p72; 1904 Surf Ave & W 17th St, Coney Island; **S** D/F, N/Q to Coney Island-Stillwell Ave).

For basketball, you can get courtside with the NBA's **New York Knicks** (www.nyknicks.com; tickets from $109) at **Madison Square Garden** (Map p84; www.thegarden.com; Seventh Ave btwn 31st & 33rd Sts, Midtown West; **S** 1/2/3 to 34th St-Penn Station), called the 'mecca of basketball,' and the **Brooklyn Nets** (www.nba.com/nets; tickets from $15), who play at the **Barclays Center** (www.barclayscenter.com; cnr Flatbush & Atlantic Aves, Prospect Heights; **S** B/D, N/Q/R, 2/3, 4/5 to Atlantic Ave) near downtown Brooklyn. Also playing at Madison Square Garden, the women's WNBA league team **New York Liberty** (☎212-564-9622, tickets 212-465-6073; www.nyliberty.com; tickets $10-85) provides a more laid-back time.

New York City's NFL (pro-football) teams, the **Giants** (☎201-935-8222; www.giants.com) and **Jets** (☎800-469-5387; www.newyorkjets.com), share **MetLife Stadium** (Map p72; www.metlifestadium.com; 1 MetLife Stadium Dr; 🚌351 from Port Authority, 🚆NJ Transit from Penn Station to Meadowlands) in East Rutherford, NJ.

travel bookshop stocks fiction, travelogues, history, cookbooks, foreign-language titles and other stimulating fare.

Economy Candy CANDY
(Map p80; ☎212-254-1531; www.economycandy.com; 108 Rivington St at Essex St; ⏲9am-6pm Tue-Fri, 10am-6pm Sat-Mon; **S** F, J/M/Z to Delancey St-Essex St) Bringing sweetness to the 'hood since 1937, this candy shop is stocked with floor-to-ceiling goods in package and bulk.

Midtown & Uptown

Midtown's Fifth Ave and the Upper East Side's Madison Ave have the famous high-end fashion and clothing by international designers.

Uniqlo FASHION
(Map p84; www.uniqlo.com; 666 Fifth Ave, at 53rd St; ⏲10am-9pm Mon-Sat, 11am-8pm Sun; **S** E, M to Fifth Ave-53rd St) Uniqlo is Japan's answer to H&M and this is its showstopping 89,000-sq-ft flagship megastore. The forte here is affordable, fashionable, quality basics, from tees and undergarments, to Japanese denim, cashmere sweaters and high-tech parkas.

Macy's DEPARTMENT STORE
(Map p84; www.macys.com; 151 W 34th St, at Broadway; ⏲9am-9.30pm Mon-Fri, 10am-9:30pm Sat, 11am-8:30pm Sun; **S** B/D/F/M, N/Q/R to 34th St-Herald Sq) The grande dame of Midtown department stores sells everything from jeans to kitchen appliances.

Bloomingdale's DEPARTMENT STORE
(Map p92; www.bloomingdales.com; 1000 Third Ave, at E 59th St, Midtown East; ⏲10am-8:30pm Mon-Sat, 11am-7pm Sun; 📶; **S** 4/5/6 to 59th St, N/Q/R to Lexington Ave-59th St) Uptown, the sprawling, overwhelming Bloomingdale's is akin to the Metropolitan Museum of Art for shoppers.

Information

INTERNET ACCESS

Free wi-fi hot spots include Bryant Park, Battery Park, Tompkins Square Park, Union Square Park, Lincoln Center and many cafes in the city.

New York Public Library (Map p84; ☎212-930-0800; www.nypl.org; E 42nd St, at Fifth Ave; **S** B, D, F or M to 42nd St-Bryant Park) Free wi-fi and internet terminals.

MEDIA

WFUV-90.7FM The area's best alternative-music radio station.

WNYC 820AM or 93.9FM National Public Radio's local affiliate.

Daily News (www.nydailynews.com) A daily tabloid, leaning toward the sensational.

New York (www.newyorkmagazine.com) Weekly featuring NYC-centric news and listings for the arts and culture-oriented reader.

New York Post (www.nypost.com) Famous for spicy headlines, celebrity scandal-laden Page Six and good sports coverage.

New York Times (www.nytimes.com) The 'Gray Lady' is the newspaper of record for readers throughout the US.

NY1 (www.ny1.com) This is the city's all-day news station on Time Warner Cable's Channel 1.

Village Voice (www.villagevoice.com) The weekly tabloid is still a good resource for events, clubs and music listings.

MEDICAL SERVICES

New York County Medical Society (☎212-684-4670; www.nycms.org) Makes doctor referrals by phone, based on type of problem and language spoken.

Tisch Hospital (New York University Langone Medical Center; ☎212-263-7300; 550 First Ave; ⏰24hr) Medical care downtown.

Travel MD (☎212-737-1212; www.travelmd.com) A 24-hour house-call service for travelers and residents.

TOURIST INFORMATION

New York City & Company (Map p84; ☎212-484-1222; www.nycgo.com; 151 W 34th St btwn Seventh Ave & Broadway, at 53rd St; ⏰9am-7pm Mon-Fri, 10am-7pm Sat, 11am-7pm Sun; Ⓢ1/2/3, A/C/E to 34th St-Herald Sq) The official information service of the Convention & Visitors Bureau, it has helpful multilingual staff. Other branches include Chinatown (Map p76; cnr Canal, Walker & Baxter Sts; ⏰10am-6pm; Ⓢ6/J/N/Q to Canal St) and Lower Manhattan (Map p76; City Hall Park at Broadway; ⏰9am-6pm Mon-Fri, 10am-5pm Sat & Sun; Ⓢ4/5/A/C to Fulton St).

ℹ Getting There & Away

AIR

Three major airports serve New York City. The biggest is **John F Kennedy International Airport** (JFK; ☎718-244-4444; www.panynj.gov), in the borough of Queens, which is also home to **La Guardia Airport** (LGA; www.panynj.gov/aviation/lgaframe). **Newark Liberty International Airport** (EWR; ☎973-961-6000; www.panynj.gov), across the Hudson River in Newark, NJ, is another option.

BUS

The massive and confusing **Port Authority Bus Terminal** (Map p84; ☎212-564-8484; www.panynj.gov; 41st St at Eighth Ave; ⓈA, C, E, N, Q, R, 1, 2, 3, & 7) is the gateway for buses into and out of Manhattan.

A number of comfortable and reliably safe bus companies depart from curbside locations, including **BoltBus** (☎877-265-8287; www.boltbus.com) and **Megabus** (☎877-462-6342; us.megabus.com), linking NYC to Philadelphia ($9-15, two hours), Boston ($17-36, 4¼ hours) and Washington, DC ($16-36, 4½ hours); there's free wi-fi on board.

CAR & MOTORCYCLE

Note that renting a car in the city is expensive, starting at about $80 a day including tax for a compact car.

FERRY

Seastreak (www.seastreak.com) goes to Sandy Hook (return $45) in New Jersey from Pier 11 near Wall St and from E 35th St. There's also a weekend, summer-only ferry to Martha's Vineyard (one-way/round-trip $165/240, five hours) in Massachusetts from E 35th St.

TRAIN

Penn Station (33rd St, btwn Seventh & Eighth Aves; Ⓢ1/2/3/A/C/E to 34th St-Penn Station) is the departure point for all **Amtrak** (☎800-872-7245; www.amtrak.com) trains, including service to Boston (3¾ hours) and Washington, DC (3 hours). Also arriving into Penn Station (NYC), as well as points in Brooklyn and Queens, is the **Long Island Rail Road** (LIRR; ☎718-217-5477; www.mta.info/lirr; furthest zone one-way off-peak/peak $27/34), which serves several hundred-thousand commuters each day. New Jersey Transit (p145) also operates trains from Penn Station (NYC), with services to the suburbs and the Jersey Shore. Another option for getting into New Jersey, but strictly to points north of the city such as Hoboken and Newark, is the **New Jersey PATH** (☎800-234-7284; www.panynj.gov/path), which runs trains on a separate-fare system ($2.75) along the length of Sixth Ave, with stops at 34th, 23rd, 14th, 9th and Christopher Sts and the World Trade Center station.

The only train line that departs from Grand Central Terminal, Park Ave at 42nd St, is the **Metro-North Railroad** (☎511; www.mta.info/mnr), which serves the northern city suburbs, Connecticut and locations throughout the Hudson Valley.

ℹ Getting Around

TO/FROM THE AIRPORT

Taxis from JFK to Midtown cost a $52 flat rate (plus toll and tip). You'll have to pay the metered fare from LaGuardia (around $30) and Newark Airport (around $55, not including toll and tip).

A cheaper but slow option to/from JFK is the AirTrain ($5 one way), which connects to subway lines into the city ($2.75; coming from the city, take the Far Rockaway–bound A train). A faster route to Penn Station is to take the AirTrain to Jamaica

Station ($5 one way) and hopping aboard the LIRR ($10, one way) train, which only makes a few stops before arriving at Penn Station in the city.

To/from Newark, the AirTrain links all terminals to a New Jersey Transit train station, which connects to Penn Station in NYC ($13 one way combined NJ Transit/AirTrain ticket).

For LaGuardia, you can take the M60 bus, which goes to/from Manhattan across 125th St in Harlem and makes stops along Broadway on the Upper West Side.

All three airports are also served by express buses ($16) and shuttle vans (from $20); such companies include the **NYC Airporter** (www.nycairporter.com), which leaves every 30 or so minutes for Grand Central Terminal, Port Authority Terminal and Penn Station; and **Super Shuttle Manhattan** (www.supershuttle.com), which picks you (and others) up anywhere, on demand, with a reservation.

BICYCLE

NYC has a bike-sharing program, called Citi Bike (p101).

CAR & MOTORCYCLE

Traffic and parking are always problematic and anxiety-provoking. If you do drive, be aware of local laws: you can't make a right on red (like you can in the rest of the state), and every other street is one way.

FERRY

The **East River Ferry** (www.eastriverferry.com) service (one way $4, every 20 minutes) connects spots in Brooklyn (Greenpoint, North and South Williamsburg and Dumbo) and Queens (Long Island City) with Manhattan (Pier 11 at Wall St and E 35th St). And **New York Water Taxi** (☎212-742-1969; www.nywatertaxi.com; hop-on-hop-off service 1-day $31) has a fleet of zippy yellow boats that run along several different routes, including a hop-on, hop-off weekend service around Manhattan and Brooklyn.

METROCARDS

All buses and subways use the yellow-and-blue MetroCard, which you can purchase or add value to at an easy-to-use automated machine at any station. You can use cash or an ATM or credit card. Just select 'Get new card' and follow the prompts. The card itself costs $1. You then select one of two types of MetroCard. The 'pay-per-ride' is $2.75 per ride, though the MTA tacks on an 11% bonus on MetroCards over $5.50. Tip: if you're not from the US, when the machine asks for your zipcode, enter 99999.

PUBLIC TRANSPORTATION

The New York subway system, run by the **Metropolitan Transport Authority** (MTA; ☎718-330-1234; www.mta.info), is iconic, cheap ($2.75 per ride, regardless of the distance traveled), round-the-clock and often the fastest and most reliable way to get around the city. It's also safer and (a bit) cleaner than it used to be.

TAXI

Current taxi fares are $2.50 for the initial charge (first one-fifth mile), 50¢ each additional one-fifth mile, as well as per 60 seconds of being stopped in traffic, $1 peak surcharge (weekdays 4pm to 8pm), and 50¢ night surcharge (8pm to 6am daily). Tips are expected to be 10% to 15%; minivan cabs can hold five passengers. You can only hail a cab that has a lit light on its roof.

NEW YORK STATE

Upstate New York – anywhere outside the city, essentially – and downstate share virtually nothing but a governor and dysfunctional legislature in the capital, Albany. This incongruity produces political gridlock, but it's a blessing for those who cherish a hike up a mountaintop as much as a bar crawl around the Lower East Side. Upstate is defined largely by its inland waterways. The Hudson River heads straight north from NYC, like an escape route. From Albany, the 524-mile Erie Canal cuts due west to Lake Erie, by the world-famous Niagara Falls and Buffalo, a lively city despite its epic winters. And the St Lawrence River forms the border with Canada in the under-the-radar Thousand Islands area. Another patch of water is the Finger Lakes region, and the college town of Ithaca, known for its wines. Add in the rugged backcountry of the Adirondack mountains and the lush farms of the Catskills, plus miles and miles of sandy beaches along Long Island, and it's easy to understand why people leave the city, never to return.

Information

511 NY (☎ in NY 511, elsewhere 800-465-1169; www.511ny.org) Statewide traffic and transit info, with weather advisories and more.

I Love NY (☎800-225-5697; www.iloveny.com) Comprehensive state tourism bureau.

New York State Office of Parks, Recreation and Historic Preservation (☎518-474-0456; www.nysparks.com) Camping, lodging and general info on all state parks. Reservations can be made up to nine months in advance.

NEW YORK FACTS

Nicknames Empire State, Excelsior State, Knickerbocker State

Population 19.8 million

Area 54,5226 sq miles, including water

Capital city Albany (population 98,400)

Other cities New York City (population 8.4 million)

Sales tax 4%, plus additional municipal taxes (total usually around 8%)

Birthplace of Poet Walt Whitman (1819–92), President Theodore Roosevelt (1858–1919), President Franklin D Roosevelt (1882–1945), first lady Eleanor Roosevelt (1884–1962), painter Edward Hopper (1882–1967), movie star Humphrey Bogart (1899–1957), comic Lucille Ball (1911–89), filmmaker Woody Allen (b 1935), actor Tom Cruise (b 1962), athlete Michael Jordan (b 1963), pop star Jennifer Lopez (b 1969)

Home of Six Nations of the Iroquois Confederacy, first US cattle ranch (1747, in Montauk, Long Island), US women's suffrage movement (1848), Erie Canal (1825)

Politics Democratic governor Andrew Cuomo, NYC overwhelmingly Democratic, upstate more conservative

Famous for Niagara Falls (half of it), the Hamptons, wineries, Hudson River

Unusual river Genesee River is one of the few rivers in the world that flows south–north, from south-central New York into Lake Ontario at Rochester

Driving distances NYC to Albany 150 miles, NYC to Buffalo 375 miles

Long Island

Technically, the 118 miles of Long Island includes the boroughs of Brooklyn and Queens on the west edge, but in the popular imagination, 'Long Island' begins only where the city ends, in a mass of traffic-clogged expressways and suburbs that every teenager aspires to leave. (Levittown, the first planned 1950s subdivision, is in central Nassau County.) But there's plenty more out on 'Lawn-guy-land' (per the local accent). Push past the central belt of 'burbs to windswept dunes, glitzy summer resorts, fresh farms and wineries, and whaling and fishing ports established in the 17th century. Then you'll see why loyalists prefer the nickname 'Strong Island.'

Getting There & Around

Thanks to the Long Island Rail Road (p125), which runs three lines from NYC's Penn Station to the furthest east ends of the island, it's possible to visit without a car. Additionally, the **Hampton Jitney** (☎212-362-8400; www.hamptonjitney.com; one way $30) and **Hampton Luxury Liner** (☎631-537-5800; www.hamptonluxuryliner.com; one way $45) buses connect Manhattan to various Hamptons' villages and Montauk; the former also picks up in Brooklyn, and runs to the North Fork. With a car, however, it is easier to visit several spots on the island in one go. I-495, aka the Long Island Expwy (LIE), runs down the middle of the island – but avoid rush hour, when it's commuter hell.

North Shore

Relatively close to NYC, the so-called 'Gold Coast' is where the Vanderbilts, Chryslers and Guggenheims, not to mention Gatsby, summered in the roaring '20s. Now it's mostly suburban, but a few remnants of the age survive, along with some pretty wild spots. Near the town of Port Washington, **Sands Point Preserve** (☎516-571-7901; www.sandspointpreserve.org; 127 Middle Neck Rd, Sands Point; parking $10, Falaise tours $10; ⏲8am-5pm, to 7pm Jul-Aug, Falaise tours hourly noon-3pm Thu-Sun mid-May–Nov), formerly the Guggenheim estate, covers forest and a beautiful bayfront beach; the visitor center is in Castle Gould, built in the 19th century by railroad heir Howard Gould. Visitors can also tour the 1923 mansion **Falaise**, one of the few intact and furnished mansions from that era. Further east, beyond the town of Oyster Bay, **Sagamore Hill** (☎516-922-4788; www.nps.gov/sahi; 12 Sagamore Hill Rd, Oyster Bay; museum & grounds free, house tours adult/child $10/free; ⏲9am-5pm Wed-Sun) is where president

Theodore Roosevelt and his wife raised six children. A nature trail from behind the museum ends at a picturesque beach. The 23-room Victorian home was rehabilitated in 2015; it's accessible by guided tour, but can get very crowded in summer.

South Shore

Easily accessible by public transit, these beaches can get crowded, but they're a fun day out. The train runs directly to **Long Beach**, just over the border from NYC, and its main town strip is busy with ice-cream shops, bars and eateries. Just east, **Jones Beach State Park** (516-785-1600; www.nysparks.com; 1 Ocean Pkwy; parking $10, lounge chairs $10, pools adult/child $3/1, mini-golf $5; 10am-7pm, though hours vary by area) is a 6-mile microcosm of beach culture, with surfers, old-timers, local teens and gay men each claiming patches of sand. Access is by train to Freeport, then a bus; in July and August, LIRR sells a combo ticket (round-trip $20.50).

The next barrier island east is **Fire Island National Seashore** (631-687-4750; www.nps.gov/fiis; dune camping permit $20) FREE. Except for the west end, where a bridge crosses the bay to **Robert Moses State Park**, the island is accessible only by **ferry** (631-665-3600; www.fireislandferries.com; 99 Maple Ave, Bay Shore; one-way adult/child $10/5) and is free of cars – regulars haul their belongings on little wagons instead. The island is edged with a dozen or so tiny hamlets, mostly residential. Party center Ocean Beach Village and quieter Ocean Bay Park (take ferries from the Bayshore LIRR stop) have a few hotels; Cherry Grove and the Pines (ferries from Sayville) are gay enclaves, also with hotels. Lodging is not cheap; **Seashore Condo Motel** (631-583-5860; www.seashorecondomotel.com; Bayview Ave, Ocean Bay Park; r from $219;) is a typical no-frills option. At the east end (ferry from Patchogue), there is camping with services at **Watch Hill** (631-567-6664; www.watchhillfi.com; tent sites $25; early May-late Oct) and backcountry camping in the dunes beyond. Bring plenty of cash to the island.

The Hamptons

This string of villages is a summer escape for Manhattan's wealthiest, who zip to mansions by helicopter. Mere mortals take the Hampton Jitney and chip in on rowdy rental houses. Behind the glitz is a long cultural history, as noted artists and writers have lived here.

The area is small, connected by often traffic-clogged Montauk Hwy. **Southampton**, to the west, has many of the nightclubs, as well as good museums. Its sweeping beaches are gorgeous; in summer nonresidents can park only at Coopers Beach (per day $40) and Road D (free). **Bridgehampton** has its share of boutiques and fine restaurants; it's where you turn north to **Sag Harbor**, a one-time whaling town with pretty, narrow old streets. **East Hampton** is where the highest-profile celebrities party – and sometimes act, in plays at **Guild Hall** (631-324-0806; www.guildhall.org; 158 Main St; museum 11am-5pm Jul-Aug, Fri-Mon only Sep-Jun) FREE.

Sights

Parrish Art Museum MUSEUM
(631-283-2118; www.parrishart.org; 279 Montauk Hwy, Water Mill; adult/child $10/free, Wed free; 10am-5pm Wed-Mon, to 8pm Fri) In a sleek long barn designed by Herzog & de Meuron, this institution spotlights local artists such as Jackson Pollock, Willem de Kooning and Chuck Close.

For more Pollock, make reservations to see his nearby paint-drizzled **studio and home** (631-324-4929; 830 Springs-Fireplace Rd, East Hampton; adult/child $10/5; tours hourly 11am-4pm Thu-Sat May-Oct).

Shinnecock Nation Cultural Center & Museum MUSEUM
(631-287-4923; www.shinnecockmuseum.com; 100 Montauk Hwy, Southampton; adult/child $15/8.50; 11am-5pm Thu-Sun;) The 1300-member Shinnecock tribe runs this museum and living-history village, one of the few reminders of Native American life on Long Island.

Southampton Historical Museum MUSEUM
(631-283-2494; www.southamptonhistoricalmuseum.org; 17 Meeting House Ln, Southampton; adult/child $4/free; 11am-4pm Wed-Sun Mar-Dec) Before the Hamptons was the Hamptons, there was this clutch of nicely maintained old buildings, including a whaling captain's mansion.

Sleeping & Eating

Bridge Inn MOTEL $$
(631-537-2900; www.hamptonsbridgeinn.com; 2668 Montauk Hwy, Bridgehampton; r from $209;) Get your foot in the Hamptons door at this clean and sleek motel, tucked behind hedges like all the neighboring mansions.

Provisions CAFE $
(cnr Bay & Division Sts, Sag Harbor; sandwiches $9-16; 8am-6pm;) Find gourmet sustenance at this natural foods market with take-out sandwiches.

Candy Kitchen DINER $
(2391 Montauk Hwy, Bridgehampton; mains $5-12; 7am-7:30pm;) An antidote to glitz, this corner diner has been serving good soups, ice cream and other staples since 1925.

Nick & Toni's MEDITERRANEAN $$$
(631-324-3550; 136 North Main St, East Hampton; pizzas $17, mains $24-42; 6-10pm Wed-Mon, to 11pm Fri & Sat, also 11:30am-2:30pm Sun) A good bet for celebrity sightings, this institution serves Italian food with ingredients from nearby farms.

Montauk

Toward the east-pointing tip of Long Island's South Fork, you'll find the mellow town of Montauk, aka 'The End,' and the famous surfing beach **Ditch Plains**. With the surfers have come affluent hipsters and boho-chic hotels like Surf Lodge and Ruschmeyer's. But the area is still far less of a scene than the Hamptons, with proudly blue-collar residents and casual seafood restaurants.

The road divides after **Napeague State Park**, with Montauk Hwy going direct; Old Montauk Hwy bears right to hug the water. The roads converge at the edge of central Montauk and Fort Pond, a small lake. Two miles east is a large inlet called Lake Montauk, with marinas strung along its shore. Another 3 miles is **Montauk Point State Park**, with the wind-whipped **Montauk Point Lighthouse** (631-668-2544; www.montauklighthouse.com; 2000 Montauk Hwy; adult/child $10/4; 10:30am-5:30pm in summer, reduced hours rest of year), active since 1796.

Sleeping

Hither Hills State Park CAMPGROUND $
(631-668-2554; www.nysparks.com; 164 Old Montauk Hwy; tent & RV sites weekday/weekend $56/64, reservation fee $9) These wooded dunes have 168 sites for tents and RVs; online reservations are a must.

Ocean Resort Inn HOTEL $$
(631-668-2300; www.oceanresortinn.com; 95 S Emerson Ave; r/ste from $135/185;) All rooms at this small, L-shaped hotel open onto a large porch or balcony. It's walking distance to the beach and the main town.

Sunrise Guesthouse GUESTHOUSE $$
(631-668-7286; www.sunrisebnb.com; 681 Old Montauk Hwy; r $130, ste $195;) A good old-school option a few miles west of town, just across the road from the beach.

Eating & Drinking

Lobster Roll SEAFOOD $$
(1980 Montauk Hwy, Amagansett; mains $14-28; 11:30am-10pm summer) 'Lunch' is the sign to look for on the roadside west of Montauk, marking the clam-and-lobster shack that's been in operation since 1965.

Cyril's Fish House SEAFOOD $$
(2167 Montauk Hwy, Amagansett; mains $15-22; 11am-7pm summer) As much an outdoor party as a seafood shack, this place puts the islands in Long Island with its signature Bailey's banana coladas (aka BBCs).

★ **Westlake Fish House** SEAFOOD $$
(631-668-3474; 352 W Lake Dr; mains $21-36; noon-9pm Thu-Sun, to 10pm Fri & Sat;) In the marina of the same name, this is a great place for seafood, all caught the same day.

Montauket BAR
(88 Firestone Rd; from noon Thu-Sun) Experts agree: this is the best place to watch the sun go down on Long Island.

North Fork & Shelter Island

The North Fork of Long Island is known for its farmland and vineyards – bucolic, though weekends can draw rowdy limo-loads on winery crawls. Still, Rte 25, the main road through the towns of **Jamesport**, **Cutchogue** and **Southold**, is pretty and edged with farm stands.

The largest town on the North Fork is **Greenport**, a laid-back place with working fishing boats, a history in whaling and an old carousel in its Harbor Front Park. It's compact and easily walkable from the LIRR station. If you're driving, you can carry on to **Orient**, with its sandy point, and **Orient Beach State Park** (631-323-2440; 40000 Main Rd, Orient; per car $8; from 8am year-round, swimming only Jul-Aug), a slip of a peninsula with clean beaches and a calm bay for kayaking.

Like a little pearl in Long Island's claw, **Shelter Island** rests between the North and South Forks. **North Ferry** (631-749-0139; www.northferry.com; on foot $2, with bicycle $3, with car one-way/same-day return $11/16; every 10-20min 6am-midnight) connects to Greenport; **South Ferry** (631-749-1200; www.

southferry.com; on foot $1, with bicycle $4, vehicle & driver one-way/same-day round-trip $14/17; ⌚ every 15min 6am-1:30am Jul-Aug, to midnight Sep-Jun) runs to North Haven, near Sag Harbor. The island is a smaller, lower-key version of the Hamptons, with a touch of maritime New England. Parking is limited; long **Crescent Beach**, for instance, has spots only by permit. If you don't mind a few hills, it's a nice place to visit by bike. On the southern part of the island, 2000-acre **Mashomack Nature Preserve** (☎631-749-1001; www.nature.org; Rte 114; ⌚9am-5pm Mar-Sep, to 4pm Oct-Feb) is great for kayaking.

Sleeping & Eating

Greenporter Hotel BOUTIQUE HOTEL **$$**
(☎631-477-0066; www.greenporterhotel.com; 326 Front St, Greenport; r from $199;) An older motel redone with white walls and Ikea furniture, this place is good value for the area. Its on-site restaurant, Cuvée, is very good.

North Fork Table & Inn INN **$$$**
(☎631-765-0177; www.nofoti.com; 57225 Main Rd, Southold; r from $250) A favorite foodies' escape, this four-room inn has an excellent farm-to-table restaurant (three-course prix-fixe $75), run by alums of the esteemed Manhattan restaurant Gramercy Tavern.

Four & Twenty Blackbirds DESSERTS **$**
(☎347-940-6717; 1010 Village Ln, Orient; pie slice $5; ⌚8am-6pm Wed-Mon mid-May–Sep) An outpost of the Brooklyn pie experts, with delectable fruit and chocolate varieties.

Love Lane Kitchen MODERN AMERICAN **$$**
(☎631-298-8989; 240 Love Ln, Mattituck; mains lunch $12-15, dinner $16-30; ⌚8am-9:30pm Thu-Mon, 7am-4pm Tue & Wed) At this popular place on a cute street, local meat and vegetables drive the global-diner menu: burgers, of course, plus spicy chickpeas and duck tagine.

Claudio's SEAFOOD **$$$**
(☎631-477-0627; 111 Main St, Greenport; mains $25-36; ⌚11:30am-9pm Sun-Thu, to 10pm Fri & Sat) A Greenport legend, owned by the Portuguese Claudio family since 1870. For a casual meal, hit Claudio's Clam Bar, on the nearby pier.

Hudson Valley

Just north of New York City, the vistas of the Hudson River inspired the 19th-century Hudson River School of landscape painting as well as scores of wealthy families, who built grand estates here. Today it's dotted with farms and parks, and populated by longtime nature-lovers and more recent city escapees. The towns closer to NYC are more populated and suburban but easy to reach by Metro-North train; the further north you go, the more rural (and sometimes desolate) the towns can be.

Getting There & Away

Metro-North Railroad (p125) runs as far north as Poughkeepsie out of NYC's Grand Central; another line runs through New Jersey and gives access to Harriman. **Amtrak** (www.amtrak.com) also stops in Rhinecliff (for Rhinebeck), Poughkeepsie and Hudson. For New Paltz, you'll need the bus: **Short Line** (☎212-736-4700; www.shortlinebus.com), which also does a day trip to Storm King.

Lower Hudson Valley

Several magnificent homes can be found near **Tarrytown** and **Sleepy Hollow**, east of the Hudson. For arts, beeline north to formerly industrial **Beacon**, revived as an outpost of the avant-garde. For a taste of the outdoors, the village of **Cold Spring** offers good hiking on Bull Hill and other trails not far from the train station. If you have a car, cross to the Hudson's west bank to explore **Harriman State Park** (☎845-947-2444; www.nysparks.com; Seven Lakes Dr, Ramapo; parking per car $8) and adjacent **Bear Mountain State Park** (☎845-786-2701; www.nysparks.com; Palisades Pkwy, Bear Mountain; parking per car $8 summer; ⌚8am-dusk), with views down to Manhattan from its 1303ft peak.

Sights

Sunnyside HISTORIC BUILDING
(☎914-591-8763, Mon-Fri 914-631-8200; www.hudsonvalley.org; 3 W Sunnyside Ln, Sleepy Hollow; adult/child $12/6; ⌚tours 10:30am-3:30pm Wed-Sun May-Oct;) Washington Irving, famous for tales such as *The Legend of Sleepy Hollow,* built this imaginative home. Tour guides in 19th-century costume tell good stories.

Kykuit HISTORIC SITE
(☎914-366-6900; www.hudsonvalley.org; 381 N Broadway, Sleepy Hollow; tours adult/child $25/23; ⌚tour hours vary May-early Nov, closed Tue) This onetime Rockefeller summer home has a remarkable collection of modern art.

West Point HISTORIC SITE
(US Military Academy Visitors Center; ☎845-938-2638; www.usma.edu; 2107 N South Post Rd, West Point; 1hr tours adult/child $14/11; ⊙9am-4:45pm) A bus tours the scenic grounds of this US Army academy, which has been training officers since 1802. The museum (free) is a must for military buffs.

Storm King Art Center GALLERY
(☎845-534-3115; www.stormking.org; 1 Museum Rd, New Windsor; adult/child $15/8; ⊙10am-5:30pm Wed-Sun Apr-Oct, to 4:30pm Nov) This 500-acre sculpture park, established in 1960, has works by Mark di Suvero, Andy Goldsworthy and others, all carefully placed in nooks formed by the land's natural breaks and curves.

★**Dia Beacon** GALLERY
(Beacon; ☎845-440-0100; www.diaart.org; 3 Beekman St, Beacon; adult/child $12/free; ⊙11am-6pm Thu-Mon Apr-Oct, 11am-4pm Fri-Mon Nov-Mar) This former factory houses monumental contemporary sculpture by the likes of Richard Serra and Dan Flavin, plus ever-changing, always surprising installations.

Eating

The Hop MODERN AMERICAN $$
(☎845-440-8676; 554 Main St, Beacon; sandwiches $15, mains $24-36; ⊙noon-10pm Wed-Mon, to midnight Fri & Sat) Craft beer and cider is this casual spot's raison d'être, and it goes perfectly with local cheeses and hearty creations like the Huff-n-Puff, a pork burger with ham and bacon.

Blue Hill at Stone Barns MODERN AMERICAN $$$
(☎914-366-9600; www.bluehillfarm.com; 630 Bedford Rd, Pocantico Hills; prix fixe $218; ⊙cafe & farm 10am-4:30pm Wed-Sun, restaurant 5-10pm Wed-Sat, from 1pm Sun) Go maximum locavore at chef Dan Barber's farm (it also supplies his Manhattan restaurant). By day, visitors are welcome to tour the fields and pastures, and there's a very basic cafe.

New Paltz

On the west bank of the Hudson is New Paltz, a conclave of hippies old and young. You'll find a campus of the State University of New York here, as well as historic **Huguenot St**, a strip of early 18th-century stone houses. It's also the gateway to Shawangunk Ridge (aka 'The Gunks'), for hiking and some of the best rock climbing in the eastern US, particularly in the **Mohonk Preserve** (☎845-255-0919; www.mohonkpreserve.org; 3197 Rte 55, Gardiner; day pass hikers/climbers & cyclists $12/17; ⊙9am-5pm) and nearby **Minnewaska State Park Preserve** (☎845-255-0752; www.nysparks.com; 5281 Rte 44-55, Kerhonkson; per vehicle $10). For climbing instruction and equipment, contact **Alpine Endeavors** (☎877-486-5769; www.alpineendeavors.com; Rosendale).

To stay in style in the area, visit the landmark Victorian-era castle that is the **Mohonk Mountain House** (☎845-255-1000; www.mohonk.com; 1000 Mountain Rest Rd; d all-inclusive from $558;); its all-inclusive rates cover a huge range of activities. Day guests are welcome for hiking for the price of a meal (reserve ahead) or an entrance fee ($26/21 per adult/child per day, less on weekdays). At the other end of the spectrum is the excellent **New Paltz Hostel** (☎845-255-6676; www.newpaltzhostel.com; 145 Main St; dm $30, r from $70).

Poughkeepsie & Hyde Park

The largest town in the Hudson Valley, **Poughkeepsie** (puh-*kip*-see) is home to Vassar, a college that was women-only until 1969, as well as an IBM office – once the 'Main Plant' where notable early computers were built. Most visitors head north to pastoral **Hyde Park** for Roosevelt lore or to visit the 'other CIA' – the Culinary Institute of America, the country's most prestigious cooking school. It also has an old **drive-in movie theater** (☎845-229-4738; www.hydeparkdrivein.com; 4114 Albany Post Rd, Hyde Park; adult/child $9/6; ⊙mid-Apr–mid-Sep) and

APPALACHIAN TRAIL ACCESS

The Appalachian Trail covers a total of 390 miles in New York, New Jersey and Pennsylvania. One of the most accessible stretches is through **Harriman and Bear Mountain State Parks**, on nicely varied but not too strenuous terrain. The trail passes close to Metro-North's Harriman Station (though no other services there). In New Jersey, the trail runs along the east side of the **Delaware Water Gap**, and the town of the same name, actually in Pennsylvania, is very hiker-friendly. The majority of the route (230 miles) is in Pennsylvania, where it reaches the Appalachian Mountains for which it's named. The trail runs north of Pennsylvania Dutch Country, and about 20 miles west of **Gettysburg**.

Roller Magic (☎845-229-6666; www.hydeparkrollermagic.com; 4178 Albany Post Rd, Hyde Park; admission $7, skate rental $2; ⊙7:30-10:30pm Fri, also 1-4:30pm Sat & Sun) skating rink, home of the local roller derby team.

Sights

Walkway Over the Hudson PARK
(☎845-454-9649; www.walkway.org; 61 Parker Ave, Poughkeepsie; ⊙7am-sunset) Once a railroad bridge crossing the Hudson, this is now the world's longest pedestrian bridge – 1.28 miles – and a state park.

Franklin D Roosevelt Home HISTORIC BUILDING
(☎845-486-7770; www.nps.gov/hofr; 4097 Albany Post Rd, Hyde Park; adult/child $18/free, museum only $9/free; ⊙9am-5pm) FDR served three terms as president and instituted lasting progressive programs; he also made the decision to drop the A-bomb on Japan to end WWII. A tour of his home, relatively modest considering his family wealth, is interesting, but it can be unpleasantly crowded in summer.

In this case, better to focus on the excellent museum, built around FDR's own library, where he recorded his groundbreaking radio program of 'fireside chats.' You can also visit **Val-Kill** (☎845-229-9422; www.nps.gov/elro; 54 Valkill Park Rd, Hyde Park; adult/child $10/free; ⊙9am-5pm daily May-Oct, Thu-Mon Nov-Apr), Eleanor Roosevelt's cottage hideaway.

Vanderbilt Mansion HISTORIC SITE
(☎877-444-6777; www.nps.gov/vama; 119 Vanderbilt Park Rd, Hyde Park; grounds free, tours adult/child $10/free; ⊙9am-5pm) The railroad-wealthy Vanderbilt family's summer 'cottage' is a beaux arts spectacle, with most of the original furnishings.

Sleeping & Eating

★**Roosevelt Inn** MOTEL $
(☎845-229-2443; www.rooseveltinnofhydepark.com; 4360 Albany Post Rd, Hyde Park; r $85-115; ⊙closed Jan & Feb) A fantastically clean roadside motel; its pine-paneled 'rustic' rooms are a bargain.

Journey Inn INN $$
(☎845-229-8972; www.journeyinn.com; 1 Sherwood Pl, Hyde Park; r $160-215) Across the road from the Vanderbilt Mansion, this country home has tastefully designed theme rooms (Kyoto, Tuscany, Roosevelt) and better-than-average breakfast.

Bocuse MODERN FRENCH $$$
(☎845-451-1012; www.ciarestaurantgroup.com; 1946 Campus Dr, Hyde Park; mains $26-31; ⊙11:30am-1pm & 6-8:30pm Tue-Sat) One of several excellent student-run restaurants at the Culinary Institute of America, this place does traditional truffles and modern tableside tricks like liquid-nitrogen ice cream. Lunch is good value. For a snack, head for **Apple Pie Cafe** (☎845-905-4500; sandwiches $10-15; ⊙7:30am-5pm Mon-Fri).

Rhinebeck & Hudson

Midway up the east side of the Hudson, Rhinebeck has a charming main street. The surrounding land is farms and wineries, as well as the holistic **Omega Institute** (☎877-944-2002; www.eomega.org; 150 Lake Dr), for every kind of healing and yoga, and super-liberal Bard College. As a result, Rhinebeck cafes tend to host interesting conversations. The northernmost town in the river valley, Hudson is still a bit ragged but has been partially remade by a small community of ex-NYC artists and writers. Warren St is lined with antiques shops, design stores, galleries and cafes.

Sights

Old Rhinebeck Aerodrome MUSEUM
(☎845-752-3200; www.oldrhinebeck.org; 9 Norton Rd, Red Hook; adult/child Mon-Fri $10/3, airshows adult/child $20/5, flights $75; ⊙10am-5pm May-Oct, airshows from 2pm Sat & Sun) This museum has a collection of vintage planes that date back as far as 1909. On weekends you can watch an airshow or take a ride in an old biplane.

★**Olana** HISTORIC SITE
(☎518-828-0135; www.olana.org; 5720 Rte 9G, Hudson; tours adult/child $12/free, grounds per vehicle $5; ⊙grounds 8am-sunset daily, tours 10am-4pm Tue-Sun May-Oct, self-guided tour only 2-5pm Sat) In pure aesthetic terms, this is finest of the Hudson Valley mansions, as landscape painter Frederic Church designed every detail, inspired by his travels in the Middle East and his appreciation of the river view.

Sleeping & Eating

Wm Farmer and Sons GUESTHOUSE $$
(☎518-828-1635; www.wmfarmerandsons.com; 20 S Front St, Hudson; r from $149; ❄📶) This rustic-chic former boarding house, steps from the train station and a short walk to Warren St, has rough-hewn furniture and claw-foot tubs. Its restaurant gets high marks.

Helsinki MODERN AMERICAN $$
(☎ 518-828-4800; www.helsinkihudson.com; 405 Columbia St, Hudson; mains $13-25; ⏲ 5-10pm Thu-Tue) This restored carriage house is a sort of clubhouse for the valley's working artists. A music venue showcases rock, jazz and even global touring acts, while the restaurant does locally sourced cuisine like garlicky kale salads.

Catskills

This mountainous region west of the Hudson Valley hosts a mix of cultures, both manmade and natural. The romantic image of mossy gorges and rounded peaks, as popularized by Hudson Valley School painters, encouraged a preservation movement; in 1894 the state constitution was amended so that thousands of acres are 'forever kept as wild forest lands.'

In the 20th century, the Catskills became synonymous with so-called 'borscht belt' hotels, summer escapes for middle-class NYC Jews. Those hotels have all closed, but Jewish communities still thrive in many towns – as does a back-to-the-land, hippie ethos on numerous small farms. In the past decade, more sophisticated places have opened, catering to nostalgic NYC hipsters in search of weekends away. In the fall, this is the closest place to NYC with really dramatic colors in the trees.

Getting There & Around

Having a car is near essential; be sure you have a paper map, as the 'forever wild' ethos of the forest preserve means mobile-phone service is often nonexistent.

There is some bus service: the most useful is **Trailways** (☎ 800-858-8555; www.trailwaysny.com), from NYC through Kingston to Woodstock ($28, three hours) and Phoenicia ($32.25, 3½ hours).

Route 28 & Around

Starting off I-87, this road cuts through the heart of the Catskills and past some of the best places to eat and sleep in the area. Before the road narrows, it passes glittering **Ashokan Reservoir**, one source for NYC's drinking water. In denser forest is **Phoenicia**, a one-street town that's a pleasant place for a meal and a splash in the creek.

In **Arkville**, you can turn north on Rte 30 through **Roxbury**. Then head back east on Rte 23, which passes through colorfully painted **Tannersville**, an only-in-the-Catskills collision of skiers from nearby Hunter Mountain and Orthodox Jewish vacationers. A few miles east is the mile-long trail to New York's tallest waterfalls, **Kaaterskill Falls**; the trail starts near a horseshoe curve in Rte 23A.

Activities

Town Tinker Tube Rental WATER SPORTS
(☎ 845-688-5553; www.towntinker.com; 10 Bridge St, Phoenicia; tubes per day $15, package incl transportation $25; 👪) Visit this outfitter for everything you need to ride an inner tube down wet and wild (and cold!) Esopus Creek.

Belleayre Beach SWIMMING
(☎ 845-254-5202; 33 Friendship Manor Rd, Pine Hill; per person/car $3/10; ⏲ 10am-6pm mid-Jun–Labor Day, to 7pm Sat & Sun) At the base of Belleayre ski area, this lake is a popular and refreshing swimming spot.

Sleeping

Phoenicia Lodge MOTEL $
(☎ 845-688-7772; www.phoenicialodge.com; 5987 Rte 28, Phoenicia; r from $90, cottage from $110; ❄ 📶 🐾) This classic roadside motel has cozy, wood-paneled rooms and a touch of mid-century modern decor. Groups can opt for a cottage or suite.

★ **Roxbury Motel** BOUTIQUE HOTEL $$
(☎ 607-326-7200; www.theroxburymotel.com; 2258 County Rd 41, Roxbury; r $158-550; ❄ 📶) Every room is a work of art: sleep in a glam version of a Flintstones cave, Oz' Emerald City or even a dreamy cream pie. (A couple of more subdued rooms are available for $100.) Breakfast is continental but generous, and there's a full spa.

Eating

★ **Phoenicia Diner** AMERICAN $
(5681 Rte 28, Phoenicia; mains $9-12; ⏲ 7am-5pm Thu-Mon; 🌿) Farm-fresh and fabulous, this roadside place is a must for all-day breakfast and nourishing versions of club sandwiches and burgers.

Last Chance Cheese AMERICAN $$
(☎ 518-589-6424; 6009 Main St, Tannersville; mains $9-20; ⏲ 11am-midnight Fri & Sat, to 9pm Sun, to 4pm Mon) This four-decade-old institution is part roadhouse with live bands, part candy store and part restaurant, serving hearty meals.

WORTH A TRIP

THE OTHER WOODSTOCK

Bethel Woods Center for the Arts
(☎866-781-2922; www.bethelwoodscenter.org; 200 Hurd Rd; museum adult/child $15/6; ⏲museum 10am-7pm daily May-Sep, 10am-5pm Thu-Sun Oct-Apr) The site of the Woodstock Music & Art Fair, on Max Yasgur's farm outside Bethel, is 70 miles from the town of Woodstock. It's now home to an amphitheater with great summer concerts and an evocative museum dedicated to the hippie movement and the 1960s.

Peekamoose MODERN AMERICAN $$$
(☎845-254-6500; 8373 Rte 28, Big Indian; mains $20-36; ⏲4-10pm Thu-Mon) The finest restaurant in the Catskills, this renovated farmhouse has been promoting local products for more than a decade. The main dining room can feel a bit austere; some regulars prefer the cozier bar.

Woodstock & Saugerties

A minor technicality: the 1969 music *festival* was actually held in Bethel, an hour away. Nonetheless, the *town* of Woodstock still cultivates the free spirit of that era, with rainbow tie-dye style and local grassroots everything, from radio to movies to a farmers market (Wednesdays in summer; fittingly billed as a 'farm festival'). Just 7 miles east, Saugerties is not nearly as quaint and feels by comparison like the big city, but the lighthouse on the point in the Hudson is well worth a visit.

For a very rural drive, head to **West Saugerties** (FYI, rock aficionados: site of Big Pink, the house made famous by Bob Dylan and the Band) and take Platte Clove Rd (Cty Rd 16) northwest. The seven winding miles are some of the most scenic in the Catskills. The road eventually emerges around Tannersville.

Sights

Opus 40 SCULPTURE PARK
(☎845-246-3400; www.opus40.org; 50 Fite Rd, Saugerties; adult/child $10/3; ⏲11am-5:30pm Thu-Sun May-Sep) Beginning in 1938, artist Harvey Fite worked for nearly four decades to coax an abandoned quarry into an immense work of land art, all sinuous walls, canyons and pools.

Saugerties Lighthouse LIGHTHOUSE
(☎845-247-0656; www.saugertieslighthouse.com; 168 Lighthouse Dr, Saugerties; tours suggested donation adult/child $5/3; ⏲sunrise-sunset, tours noon-3pm Sun summer) FREE A half-mile nature trail leads to this 1869 landmark on the point where Esopus Creek joins the Hudson. You can also stay the night in the lighthouse's two-room B&B ($225), but you must book at least six months ahead.

Sleeping & Eating

White Dove Rockotel INN $$
(☎845-306-5419; www.thewhitedoverockotel.com; 148 Tinker St, Woodstock; r $135-169, ste $255-325; 📶) A couple of Phish fans run this purple-painted Victorian. The four party-ready rooms are decorated with psychedelic concert posters, record players and vintage vinyl.

Cucina ITALIAN $$
(☎845-679-9800; 109 Mill Hill Rd, Woodstock; mains $16-26; ⏲5am-late, from 11am Sat & Sun) Sophisticated seasonal Italian fare, including thin-crust pizzas, in a farmhouse with a large communal table.

Finger Lakes

Stretching across west-central New York, the rolling hills are cut through with 11 long narrow lakes – the eponymous fingers. The Finger Lakes region is an outdoor paradise, as well as the state's premier wine-growing region, with more than 80 vineyards.

Getting There & Around

Ithaca is the region's major hub: **Short Line** (www.coachusa.com; 710 W State St) has eight daily departures from NYC ($53.50, five hours). **Ithaca Tompkins Regional Airport** (ITH; ☎607-257-0456; www.flyithaca.com; 1 Culligan Dr) has direct flights to Detroit, Newark and Philadelphia. For renting a car in the area, however, you may find cheaper in Rochester or Syracuse.

Ithaca & Cayuga Lake

An idyllic home for college students and first-wave hippies, Ithaca, on the southern tip of Cayuga Lake, is the largest town around the Finger Lakes. With art-house cinemas, good eats and great hiking ('Ithaca is gorges' goes the slogan, for all the surrounding canyons and waterfalls), it's both a destination in itself and a convenient halfway point between NYC and Niagara Falls.

The center of Ithaca is a pedestrian street called the Commons. On a steep hill above is Ivy League Cornell University, founded in 1865, with a small business strip at the campus's front gates, called Collegetown. The drive from Ithaca up scenic Rte 89 to Seneca Falls, at the north end of Cayuga Lake, takes about an hour.

For maps and other info, head to the **Visit Ithaca Information Center** (☎607-272-1313; www.visitithaca.com; 904 E Shore Dr).

Sights & Activities

Exploring Ithaca's gorges can start in town, at **Cascadilla Gorge**, where the trail starts a few blocks from the Commons and climbs to campus. Or head north to **Taughannock Falls State Park** (☎607-387-6739; www.nysparks.com; 1740 Taughannock Blvd, Trumansburg; per car $7), where you can rent a canoe on the lake, or **Buttermilk Falls State Park** (☎607-273-5761; www.nysparks.com; 112 E Buttermilk Falls Rd; per car $7) and **Robert H Treman State Park** (☎607-273-3440; www.nysparks.com; 105 Enfield Falls Rd; per car $7), both south of town. All have stunning waterfalls, camping space and swimming holes, open in high summer; the one at Robert H Treman is especially large and popular. Birders shouldn't miss **Sapsucker Woods** (☎800-843-2473; www.birds.cornell.edu; 159 Sapsucker Woods Rd; visitor center 8am-5pm Mon-Thu, to 4pm Fri, 9:30am-4pm Sat, 11am-4pm Sun Apr-Dec only) FREE, managed by Cornell's world-renowned ornithology department.

Herbert F Johnson Museum of Art MUSEUM
(☎607-255-6464; www.museum.cornell.edu; 114 Central Ave; 10am-5pm Tue- Sun) FREE Inside the brutal IM Pei building is an eclectic collection, pleasantly crowded on the walls and ranging from medieval wood carvings to modern masters. There's a nice view from the veranda, and just down the hill behind is Fall Creek, with a scenic bridge across it.

Sciencenter MUSEUM
(☎607-272-0600; www.sciencenter.org; 601 1st St; adult/child $8/6; 10am-5pm Tue-Sat, from noon Sun;) The local children's museum, where the definition of science includes both compost and mini-golf.

Women's Rights National Historical Park MUSEUM
(☎315-568-0024; www.nps.gov/wori; 136 Fall St, Seneca Falls; 9am-5pm Wed-Sun) FREE In the quiet, post-industrial town of Seneca Falls is the chapel where Elizabeth Cady Stanton and friends declared in 1848 that 'all men and women are created equal,' the first step toward suffrage. The adjacent museum tells the story, including the complicated relationship with abolition.

LOCAL KNOWLEDGE

FINGER LAKES WINERIES

With its cool climate and short growing season, the Finger Lakes region is similar to Germany's Rhine valley, and is similarly strong in off-dry whites such as Riesling. More than 80 wineries make it easy to spend a day sipping. It pays to pack a picnic lunch; food options at wineries are limited. A few to try:

Cayuga & Seneca Lakes

Lucas Vineyards (www.lucasvineyards.com; 3862 Cty Rd 150, Interlaken; 10:30am-6pm Jun-Aug, to 5:30pm Mon-Sat Sep-May) One of the pioneer wineries in the region.

Sheldrake Point Winery (www.sheldrakepoint.com; 7448 Cty Rd 153, Ovid; 10am-5:30pm Apr-Oct, 11am-5pm Fri-Mon Nov-Mar) Lake views and award-winning Chardonnays.

Hazlitt 1852 Vineyards (5712 Rte 414, Hector; 11am-5pm) Long-established, with a solid Pinot Noir.

Keuka Lake

Keuka Spring Vineyards (www.keukaspringwinery.com; 243 E Lake Rd, Penn Yan; 10am-5pm Apr-Nov, Sat & Sun only Dec-Mar) Just south of Penn Yan, a local favorite in a pastoral setting.

Dr Konstantin Frank (www.drfrankwines.com; 9749 Middle Rd, Hammondsport; 9am-5pm Mon-Sat, from noon Sun) Don't miss the rkatsiteli, an acidic and floral white.

Keuka Lake Vineyards (www.klvineyards.com; 8882 Cty Rd 76, Hammondsport; 10am-5pm May-Nov, Fri-Sun only Dec-Apr) Try the vignoles.

WORTH A TRIP

CORNING

An hour's drive southwest of Ithaca is the town of Corning, put on the map by Corning Glass Works, a company most Americans associate with sturdy Corningware plates but which now excels in industrial materials of all kinds. Here, the massive **Corning Museum of Glass** (☎800-732-6845; www.cmog.org; 1 Museum Way; adult/child $18/free; ⏲9am-5pm, to 8pm Memorial Day-Labor Day; 👪) presents the substance as both art and science, illustrated through live glass-blowing demonstrations and workshops to make your own glass crafts. Just over the river, in the former city hall, is the **Rockwell Museum of Western Art** (☎607-937-5386; www.rockwellmuseum.org; 111 Cedar St; adult/child $10/free; ⏲9am-5pm, to 8pm summer; 👪), a varied collection from beautiful pottery to contemporary Native American work. It's a manageable size, and a combination ticket with the glass museum ($25) makes it an easy add-on.

Corning is a pretty town, still energetic thanks to the corporate headquarters here. Stroll Market St, around the corner from the Rockwell Museum, for coffee, snacks and a bit of shopping.

Sleeping

Perhaps due to Cornell's prestigious hotel school, local lodging is generally excellent, but, with one exception, not cheap. Budget travelers might also consider Keuka Lake.

Hillside Inn HOTEL $
(☎607-272-9507; www.hillsideinnithaca.com; 518 Stewart Ave; r from $69; ❄📶) A bit ramshackle, with rooms in odd corners, but homey. Plus, very close to campus (though a steep walk up from the Commons).

Frog's Way B&B GUESTHOUSE $
(☎607-592-8402; www.frogsway-bnb.com; 211 Rachel Carson Way; r $100; 📶) 🍃 Get the full green Ithaca experience at this house in EcoVillage, a planned community just west of town. Two rooms share a bathroom; breakfast is organic and local, of course.

★ **William Henry Miller Inn** B&B $$
(☎607-256-4553; www.millerinn.com; 303 N Aurora St; r from $195; ❄📶) Gracious and grand, and only a few steps from the Commons, this is a historic home with luxurious rooms – three have Jacuzzis – and a gourmet breakfast.

Buttonwood Grove Winery CABIN $$
(☎607-869-9760; www.buttonwoodgrove.com; 5986 Rte 89, Romulus; r $140; ⏲Apr-Nov; 🐾) The winery rents out four comfortably furnished log cabins, all with lake views. Slightly rustic and remote – you can see the stars at night.

Inn on Columbia INN $$
(☎607-272-0204; www.columbiabb.com; 228 Columbia St; r from $195; ❄📶🐾) Several homes clustered in a quiet residential area, with a refreshing modern style.

Eating & Drinking

Restaurants with outdoor seats line North Aurora St south of Seneca St, around the corner from the Commons. Ithaca's **Farmers Market** (☎607-273-7109; www.ithacamarket.com; 545 3rd St; ⏲Apr-Dec) is the region's standout; check the website for hours. Ithaca excels in natural elixirs – local mini-chain Gimme! Coffee for standard caffeine, **Mate Factor** (143 E State St; mains $8; ⏲9am-9pm Mon-Thu, to 3pm Fri, from noon Sun) for the South American upper and even **Sacred Root Kava Lounge** (☎607-272-5282; 139 W State St; ⏲4pm-midnight Mon-Sat) to chill in the Polynesian style.

Ithaca Bakery DELI $
(☎607-273-7110; 400 N Meadow St; sandwiches $9; ⏲6am-8pm) An epic selection of pastries, smoothies, sandwiches and prepared food, serving Ithacans of every stripe. Ideal for picnic goods.

Glenwood Pines BURGERS $
(☎607-273-3709; 1213 Taughannock Blvd; burgers $6; ⏲11am-10pm) If you work up an appetite hiking at Taughannock Falls, stop by this roadside restaurant for good burgers.

★ **Moosewood Restaurant** VEGETARIAN $$
(☎607-273-9610; www.moosewoodcooks.com; 215 N Cayuga St; mains $8-18; ⏲11:30am-9pm; 🌿) Established in 1973, this near-legendary restaurant is run by a collective. It has a slightly upscale feel, with a full bar and global menu.

Felicia's Atomic Lounge & Cupcakery COCKTAIL BAR
(☎607-273-2219; 508 W State St; ⏲noon-midnight Tue-Thu, to 1am Fri, 10:30am-1am Sat, to 11pm

Sun) Felicia's does a super-creative and locally sourced brunch on weekends, then serves up cocktails, snacks and live bands at night.

Seneca & Keuka Lakes

Pretty Geneva, at the northern tip of Seneca Lake, is a lively little town, thanks to the student population at Hobart & William Smith Colleges. South Main St is lined with impressive turn-of-the-century homes, and the restored 1894 Smith Opera House (☑315-781-5483; www.thesmith.org; 82 Seneca St) is a vibrant center for performing arts.

To the west, Y-shaped Keuka Lake is edged by two small state parks that keep it relatively pristine; it's a favorite for trout fishing. The nicest town for visitors is sweet little Hammondsport, on the southwest end. An old canal on the north end has a rustic bike trail to Seneca Lake.

🛏 Sleeping

Keuka Lakeside Inn　　　　MOTEL $$
(☑607-569-2600; www.keukalakesideinn.com; 24 Water St, Hammondsport; r $120; ❇ 🕸) What this place lacks in historic charm (it's a simple motel block), it more than makes up for in location, right on the edge of the water. The 17 rooms have all been redone since 2010, with a crisp style.

Belhurst Castle　　　　INN $$
(☑315-781-0201; www.belhurst.com; 4069 West Lake Rd, Geneva; r $160-295; ❇ 🕸) This 1880s lakefront folly is worth a stop just to see its ornate interior (its casual Stonecutter's restaurant has live music on weekends) and the gorgeous view. The best rooms in the main mansion have stained glass, heavy antique furniture and fireplaces. It's a popular wedding locale, so book ahead.

🍴 Eating & Drinking

★Stonecat　　　　AMERICAN $$$
(☑607-546-5000; 5315 Rte 414, Hector; mains $23-31; ⊙noon-3pm & 5-9pm Wed-Sat, from 10:30am Sun May-Oct) This foodie haven on the southeast side of Seneca Lake is mostly casual but serious where it counts: smart service, impeccable local ingredients, and excellent wine and cocktails. Sunday brunch, with mellow live music and dishes like duck-confit eggs benedict, is popular, as is Wednesday for the snacky bar menu.

Microclimate　　　　WINE BAR
(☑315-787-0077; 38 Linden St, Geneva; ⊙5-10pm Sun & Mon, 4:30pm-midnight Wed & Thu, to 1am Fri & Sat) This cool little wine bar serves tasting flights that compare locally produced varietals with their international counterparts.

The Adirondacks

The Adirondack Mountains may not compare in drama and height with mountains in the western US, but they make up for it in size, covering 9375 sq miles, from the center of the state up to the Canada border. And with 46 peaks over 4000ft high, this area is some of the most wild-feeling terrain in the east. Like the Catskills to the south, much of the Adirondacks' dense forest is protected by the state constitution, and it's a great place to see the color show of autumn leaves. Hiking, canoeing and backcountry camping are the most popular activities, and there's good fishing, along with power-boating on the bigger lakes.

ℹ Getting There & Around

Both **Greyhound** (☑800-231-2222; www.greyhound.com) and **Trailways** (☑800-858-8555; www.trailwaysny.com) serve various towns in the Adirondacks, though a car is essential for exploring widely. **Amtrak** (www.amtrak.com) runs once a day to Ticonderoga ($68, five hours) and Westport ($68, six hours), on Lake Champlain, with a bus connection to Lake Placid ($93, seven hours); once there, you can take the town shuttle to activities.

Lake George

The gateway to the Adirondacks is a tourist town with arcades and paddle-wheel boat rides on the crystalline, 32-mile-long lake. Small motels and mini-resorts line Rte 9 all the way to the village of Bolton Landing; a nice older one on the lakefront in town is Lake Crest Inn (☑518-668-3374; www.lakecrestinn.com; 376 Canada St; r from $119; ❇🕸🌊); its clean rooms have, shall we say, vintage style. For perfectly fried seafood and massive lobster rolls, visit Saltwater Cowboy (☑518-685-3116; 164 Canada St; mains $11-28; ⊙11am-9pm).

A major draw in the area: the wonderfully secluded state-maintained campgrounds (☑800-456-2267; www.dec.ny.gov/outdoor; tent sites $28) on the lake's numerous islands. You'll need to reserve ahead and rent your own power boat or canoe. If canoeing, focus on sites in the southern end of the Narrows

DON'T MISS

LOCAL MUSEUMS

Adirondack Museum (518-352-7311; www.adkmuseum.org; 9097 Rte 30, Blue Mountain Lake; adult/child $18/6; 10am-5pm late May–mid-Oct;) Set on 30 acres, this museum has creative exhibits on the mountains' human-centered stories, from mining and logging industries to quirky hermits and Victorian tourists. You can easily spend half a day here.

Wild Center (518-359-7800; www.wildcenter.org; 45 Museum Dr, Tupper Lake; adult/child $20/13; 10am-6pm late May-early Sep, to 5pm Sep–mid-Oct, to 5pm Fri-Sun May;) Dedicated to local ecosystems, this hands-on museum has everything from rare frogs to live river otters. Outdoors is a trail to the river and, new in 2015, the Wild Walk, connected platforms and bridges in the treetops, with amazing views. Ticket prices are lower off-season; if you've also visited the Adirondack Museum, show your receipt for $2 discount.

Great Camp Sagamore (Sagamore Institute; 315-354-5311; www.greatcampsagamore.org; Sagamore Rd, Raquette Lake; tours adult/child $16/8; hours vary late May–mid-Oct) 'Great camps,' big compounds of log cabins built by wealthy families, were a popular way of vacationing in the Adirondacks. Many have been turned into kids' summer camps, but this one, a former Vanderbilt vacation estate on the west side of the Adirondacks, is open for tours, workshops and overnight stays on occasional history-oriented weekends.

area, a one- or two-hour paddle from Bolton Landing, and go on a weekday, when powerboat traffic is much lighter.

Lake Placid

The tiny resort town of Lake Placid is synonymous with snow sports – it hosted the Winter Olympics in 1932 and 1980. Elite athletes still train here; the rest of us can ride real bobsleds, speed-skate and more. Mirror Lake (the main lake in town) freezes thick enough for ice-skating, tobogganing and dogsledding. The town is also pleasant in summer, as the unofficial center of the High Peaks region of the Adirondacks. There are good hiking trails around, for instance on Rte 73 toward **Keene** – look for the pullout in Cascade Pass for a 2.2-mile hike to Cascade Peak.

Sights & Activities

Olympic Center STADIUM
(Olympic Museum; box office 518-523-3330, museum 518-302-5326; www.whiteface.com; 2634 Main St; museum adult/child $7/5, skating shows adult/child $10/8; 10am-5pm, skating shows 4:30pm Fri, 7:30pm Sat;) This hockey stadium hosted the 1980 'Miracle on Ice', when the upstart US team trumped the unstoppable Soviets. This and more Olympic triumphs are covered in the museum. Year-round, there are usually figure-skating shows on Fridays and Saturdays.

Whiteface Mountain Toll Road MOUNTAIN
(Veterans Memorial Hwy; www.whiteface.com; Cty Rd 18; car with driver $11, passenger $8; 8:45am-5:30pm Jul–mid-Oct, Sat & Sun only May-Jun) Whiteface is the only peak in the Adirondacks accessible by car, with a neat castle-style lookout and cafe at the top. It can be socked in with clouds, making for an unnerving drive up, but when the fog clears, the 360-degree view is awe-inspiring.

Olympic Sports

One major draw at Lake Placid is the opportunity to play like an Olympian (or just watch athletes train). Most activities are managed by **Whiteface Mountain** (518-946-222; www.whiteface.com; 5021 Rte 86, Wilmington; full-day lift ticket adult/child $89/57) ski area (where the Olympic ski races were held) but located in other spots around the area. Among other activities, you can do a half-mile on the **bobsled** track ($90) or a modified **biathlon** (cross-country skiing and shooting; $55). A private group organizes **speed-skating** rental and tutorials ($20) at the Olympic Center. Many sports are modified for summer – bobsledding on wheels, for instance. For the very energetic, Whiteface's Olympic Sites Passport ticket ($35) can be a good deal, covering admission at sites (such as the tower at the **ski-jump** complex) and offering discounts on some activities.

Sleeping & Eating

★**Adirondack Loj** LODGE $

(☎518-523-3441; www.adk.org; 1002 Adirondack Loj Rd; dm/r $60/169) The Adirondack Mountain Club runs this rustic retreat on the shore of Heart Lake. Lean-tos and cabins are also available, and trails take off in all directions.

Hotel North Woods HISTORIC HOTEL $$

(☎518-523-1818; www.hotelnorthwoods.com; 2520 Main St; r from $140;) Lake Placid's oldest hotel got a total rehab in 2015. Its stylish modern-rustic rooms have either lake views or balconies facing the forest.

ADK Corner Store SANDWICHES $

(☎518-523-1689; 188 Newman Rd; sandwiches from $4; 5:30am-9pm) This general store caters to the early-start hiker with great breakfast sandwiches.

★**Chair 6** MODERN AMERICAN $$$

(☎518-523-3630; 5993 Sentinel Rd; breakfasts $12, dinner mains $26-34, five-course menu $60; 8am-9pm Wed-Mon) So much flavor in such a tiny house: try venison dumplings for dinner, or sweet potato pancakes for breakfast.

Saranac Lake

A short drive from Lake Placid, this town is not so tourist-oriented, and gives a better idea of regular Adirondacks life. **St Regis Canoe Outfitters** (☎518-891-1838; www.canoeoutfitters.com; 73 Dorsey St) can provide gear, maps and tips for exploring the gemlike lakes to the north; you can even do a combo canoe-train trip with the **Adirondack Scenic Railroad** (☎800-819-2291; www.adirondackrr.com; 42 Depot St; round-trip to Lake Placid adult/child $19/11). The town built up in the early 20th century as a retreat for tuberculosis patients, and it still has a sturdy, if slightly scruffy, main street. Check on the grand old **Hotel Saranac** (www.hotelsaranac.com; 100 Main St) – it was being renovated in 2015. If you prefer the wilderness, book at the excellent **White Pine Camp** (☎518-327-3030; www.whitepinecamp.com; 432 White Pine Rd, Paul Smiths; r from $165, cabins from $315), 14 miles north on Osgood Pond, one of the best places to stay in the Adirondacks.

Lake Champlain

This 125-mile lake divides New York from Vermont. The road along its eastern shore is exceptionally scenic – you may want to drive this way when going to or coming from Lake George.

Sights & Activities

Fort Ticonderoga FORT

(☎518-585-2821; www.fortticonderoga.org; 100 Fort Ti Rd; adult/child $19.50/8; 9:30am-5pm mid-May–mid-Oct) In a major victory in the American Revolution, the Green Mountain Boys took this fort from the British in 1775. With costumed guides, reenactments, a museum and hiking trails, it's possible to spend a full day here.

Crown Point State Historic Site FORT

(☎518-597-4666; www.nysparks.com; 21 Grandview Dr, Crown Point; museum adult/child $4/free; grounds 9am-6pm, museum 9:30am-5pm Thu-Mon May–mid-Oct) The remains of two major 18th-century forts occupy a dramatic promontory where Lake Champlain narrows.

Ausable Chasm OUTDOORS

(☎518-834-7454; www.ausablechasm.com; 2144 Rte 9, Ausable; adult/child hiking $18/10, rafting $12/10; 9am-4pm, to 5pm summer, to 3pm Dec-Mar;) This 2-mile-long fissure can be explored on foot or by raft – good to do with kids, for managed adventure. Incongruously, across the parking lot, there's also a free museum about the Underground Railroad.

Sleeping & Eating

Essex Inn INN $$$

(☎518-963-4400; www.essexinnessex.com; 2297 Main St, Essex; r from $250;) A 200-year-old charmer, with rooms decorated with period furnishings, plus a wide veranda and back garden. Its restaurant, Room 12, serves excellent fresh food.

Wind-Chill Factory ICE CREAM $

(☎518-585-3044; 794 Rte 9N, Ticonderoga; burgers from $5, ice cream from $3; 11am-8pm in season) This humble ice-cream stand has fresh flavors, and its burgers use locally raised beef.

Thousand Islands

To downstate New Yorkers, this region is the mythical source of a salad dressing made of ketchup, mayonnaise and relish. In fact, it's a scenic wonderland along the St Lawrence River, with more than 1800 islands of all sizes. The area was a Gilded Age playground; now it's more populist. Pros: beautiful sunsets, good-value lodging and the exotic sound of Canadian radio. Cons: very large mosquitoes; bring ample repellent.

Where the river meets Lake Ontario is the French-heritage village of **Cape Vincent**, marked by the 1854 **Tibbetts Point Lighthouse**. Fifteen miles east along the Seaway Trail (Rte 12), **Clayton** has a pretty old main strip and a few good eating options. Further east, **Alexandria Bay** (Alex Bay) is the center of tourism in the area. Clayton is the most attractive place to spend the night, but if you're traveling with kids, Alex Bay is preferable, as there's entertainment such as mini-golf and a **drive-in movie theater** (☎315-482-3874; www.baydrivein.com; Rte 26; adult/child $6/2; ⏲Fri-Sun; 👪). Both towns have boat-tour operators with similar offerings – **Clayton Island Tours** (☎315-686-4820; www.claytonislandtours.com; 39621 Chateau Ln, Clayton; 2hr tour adult/child $22/12) and **Uncle Sam Boat Tours** (☎315-482-2611; www.usboattours.com; 45 James St, Alexandria Bay; 2hr tours adult/child $22/11), respectively.

Getting There & Around

JetBlue (☎1-800-538-2583; www.jetblue.com) has flights from NYC to Hancock International Airport (SYR) in Syracuse, where you can rent a car.

Sights & Activities

★Boldt Castle CASTLE
(☎800-847-5263; www.boldtcastle.com; Heart Island; adult/child $8.50/6; ⏲10am-6:30pm mid-May–mid-Oct) This Gothic gem was (partly) built by George C Boldt, a Prussian immigrant who rose to the uppermost class by managing Manhattan's Waldorf-Astoria hotel in the late 19th century. Midway through construction, Boldt's wife died suddenly, and the project was abandoned. One floor has been finished the way Boldt intended; the rest is a ghostly monument.

Access to the castle is by boat (additional fee) from Clayton or Alexandria Bay.

Singer Castle CASTLE
(☎877-327-5475; www.singercastle.com; Dark Island; adult/child $14.25/6.25; ⏲10am-4pm mid-May–mid-Oct) This castle, full of secret passages and hidden doors, is less visited – a plus in summer, when Boldt Castle can be very busy. Romantics should check the option of staying overnight in the main bedroom ($700!). Uncle Sam (p140) runs boats from Alex Bay; **Schermerhorn Harbor** (☎315-324-5966; www.schermerhornharbor.com; 71 Schermerhorn Landing, Hammond) also visits.

Antique Boat Museum MUSEUM
(☎315-686-4104; www.abm.org; 750 Mary St, Clayton; adult/child $14/free; ⏲9am-5pm mid-May–mid-Oct; 👪) This museum lets you row old skiffs as you learn about them. You can also tour George Boldt's glam 1903 houseboat; reserve a tour time in advance.

Wellesley Island State Park OUTDOORS
(☎315-482-2722; www.nysparks.com; 44927 Cross Island Rd, Fineview; beach $7; ⏲year-round; swimming 11am-7pm Jul-Aug) FREE This is essentially a 2600-acre floating village attached to the mainland by the Thousand Islands International Bridge (toll $2.75). The park is full of wildlife and has a nature center and a beautiful swimming beach. Camping options here are excellent, with riverfront tent sites, cabins and family cottages.

Sleeping & Eating

★Wooden Boat Inn MOTEL $
(☎315-686-5004; www.woodenboatinn.com; 606 Alexandria St, Clayton; r from $89, boat $175; ❄📶) The six motel rooms are great value, but anyone with a nautical bent should book the 36ft trawler moored on the riverfront.

HI Tibbetts Point Lighthouse HOSTEL $
(☎315-654-3450; www.hihostels.com; 33439 Cty Rte 6, Cape Vincent; dm $30, r from $65; ⏲Jul–mid-Sep) The lighthouse keepers' house is now this well-kept hostel. Book ahead – there are only 18 beds.

Otter Creek Inn MOTEL $
(☎315-482-5248; www.ottercreekinnabay.com; 2 Crossmon St Extension, Alexandria Bay; r from $95; ❄📶) This motel sits next to a quiet bay, away from the sometimes rowdy town center (easy walking distance, though).

Lyric Coffee House CAFE $$
(☎315-686-4700; 246 James St, Clayton; mains $7-20; ⏲8am-5pm, to 8pm Fri & Sat summer, Sat-Mon only winter; 📶) A nice break from the burgers-and-BBQ menus in these parts, this cafe has great cakes, sandwiches and daily specials such as duck terrine; there's live music some Fridays and Saturdays.

Western New York

Much activity in this region revolves around Buffalo, New York State's (very distant) second-largest city, with about 250,000 people.

The area first developed thanks to the hydroelectric power of Niagara Falls and the Erie Canal, which linked the Great Lakes to the Atlantic Ocean. The falls are now better known as a tourist destination, with 12 million visitors annually.

Buffalo

The winters are long and cold, and abandoned industrial buildings dot the skyline, but Buffalo stays warm with a vibrant creative community and strong local pride. Settled by the French in 1758, the city is believed to derive its name from *beau fleuve* (beautiful river). With power from nearby Niagara Falls, it boomed in the early 1900s; Pierce-Arrow cars were made here, and it was the first American city to have electric streetlights. Its strong bones include art-deco masterpieces and a gracious park system laid out by Frederick Law Olmsted, of NYC's Central Park fame. It's about an eight-hour trip from NYC through the Finger Lakes region and only half an hour south of Niagara Falls.

Sights

Architecture buffs will enjoy a stroll around downtown, marked by the towering art-deco **City Hall** (716-852-3300; www.preservationbuffaloniagara.org; 65 Niagara Sq; tours noon Mon-Fri) FREE and the **Theatre District**, a string of beautiful late 19th-century buildings along Main St. For more detail, join a tour with **Explore Buffalo** (716-245-3032; www.explorebuffalo.org; 1 Symphony Circle). **Elmwood Ave** is a lively thoroughfare, leading north to the State Univeristy of New York's Buffalo campus and Olmsted's **Delaware Park**.

This is a hard-core sports town: the **Buffalo Bills** (www.buffalobills.com) play pro football in a stadium in the suburb of Orchard Park; the **Buffalo Sabres** (www.sabres.com) rule ice hockey at HarborCenter downtown; and the minor-league baseball team, **Buffalo Bisons** (www.bisons.com), play in a trendy-traditional downtown ballpark.

★ **Martin House** ARCHITECTURE
(716-856-3858; www.darwinmartinhouse.org; 125 Jewett Pkwy; tours basic/extended $17/35; tours hourly 10am-3pm, closed Tue & some Thu) An early work of Frank Lloyd Wright's, in his horizontal Prairie style, the 15,000-sq-ft Martin House has been meticulously restored and even rebuilt. A guided tour reveals the exacting details; the very worthwhile longer tour visits three neighboring buildings. Buy tickets online; Wright fans may want the combo ticket to Graycliff, a vacation home outside Buffalo.

Albright-Knox Art Gallery MUSEUM
(716-882-8700; www.albrightknox.org; 1285 Elmwood Ave; adult/child $12/5; 10am-5pm, closed Mon) Renowned for its collection of Ruscha, Rauschenberg and other abstract expressionists, this sizable museum occupies a neoclassical building from Buffalo's 1901 Pan-American Exposition. Its temporary exhibits are particularly creative and compelling.

Burchfield Penney Art Center MUSEUM
(716-878-6011; www.burchfieldpenney.org; 1300 Elmwood Ave; adult/child $10/free; 10am-5pm Tue, Wed, Fri & Sat, to 9pm Thu, 1-5pm Sun) Dedicated to artists of Western New York, past and present, this museum shows great range. Namesake Charles Burchfield's paintings and prints reflect the local landscape.

Theodore Roosevelt Inaugural National Historic Site MUSEUM
(716-884-0095; www.nps.gov/thri; 641 Delaware Ave; adult/child $10/5; tours hourly 9:30am-3:30pm Mon-Fri, from 12:30pm Sat & Sun) Guided tours of the Ansley-Wilcox house tell the dramatic tale of Teddy's emergency swearing-in here in 1901, after President William McKinley was assassinated while attending Buffalo's Pan-American Exposition.

Canalside PARK
(716-574-1537; www.canalsidebuffalo.com; 44 Prime St) Buffalo's once derelict waterfront now offers summer parkland and winter ice skating. The area includes the **Buffalo & Erie County Naval & Military Park** (716-847-1773; www.buffalonavalpark.org; 1 Naval Park Cove; adult/child $10/6; 10am-5pm Apr-Oct, Sat & Sun Nov), with two WWII-era ships and a submarine, and **BFLO Harbor Kayak** (716-288-5309; www.bfloharborkayak.com; 1 Naval Park Cove; tours from $25; Memorial Day-Labor Day).

Sleeping

★ **Hostel Buffalo Niagara** HOSTEL $
(716-852-5222; www.hostelbuffalo.com; 667 Main St; dm/r $25/65;) Conveniently located in Buffalo's downtown Theatre District, this hostel occupies three floors of a former school, with a basement rec room, plenty of kitchen and lounge space, and spotless if insitutional bathrooms. Services include laundry facilities, bikes, and lots of info on local music, food and arts happenings.

Hotel @ The Lafayette BOUTIQUE HOTEL $$
(716-853-1505; www.thehotellafayette.com; 391 Washington St; r $169, ste from $199; P) This seven-story early 1900s building has been restored with stylish furnishings in its rooms. The location is handy, with a very good brewpub, Pan-American Grill, set in some of the fantastically ornate public spaces. Also recommended: the same owners' **Lofts on Pearl** (716-856-0098; www.loftsonpearl.com; 92 Pearl St; ste from $169), a few blocks away.

Mansion on Delaware Avenue HOTEL $$$
(716-886-3300; www.mansionondelaware.com; 414 Delaware Ave; r/ste from $195/390; P@) For truly special accommodations and flawless service, head to this hotel in a grand and regal home c 1862. Room 200 has a fireplace and floor-to-ceiling windows. Amenities include daily self-serve drinks in the lounge, and car service around central Buffalo.

Eating

The neighborhood of Allentown is a strong destination for dining (and nightlife), and food trucks rally around Larkin Sq, east of downtown. Also keep an eye out for branches of Mighty Taco, Buffalo's answer to Taco Bell, as famed for its weird ads as its satisfying burritos, as well as extra-savory Ted's Hot Dogs, in the northeast suburb of Williamsville and other spots around western New York.

★ **Anchor Bar** AMERICAN $
(716-886-8920; 1047 Main St; 10/20 wings $13/20; 11am-11pm) Admirably, the place that invented that ultimate bar snack, Buffalo wings (here, of course, they're just called 'wings'), is not a massive tourist trap, but a functioning neighborhood hangout, with a broad menu beyond the spicy, deep-fried chicken. There's live music, often jazz, Thursday, Friday and Saturday nights.

Sweetness 7 CAFÉ $
(301 Parkside Ave; crepes $10; 8am-6pm;) A comfy, somewhat hippie-feeling cafe with sweet and savory crepes, good coffee and fresh baked goods. It can get packed, but Delaware Park is just across the road. There's another branch on Buffalo's **west side** (220 Grant St; 7am-6pm, from 8am Sat & Sun;).

Cantina Loco MEXICAN $
(716-551-0160; 191 Allen St; mains $7; 4-10pm Mon-Thu, to 11pm Fri & Sat, 4-8pm Sun) Hip and always packed, this Allentown restaurant with a backyard patio serves up tacos, burritos and quesadillas. Some come with a twist like the Koreatown (short ribs and kimchi). The desserts are excellent and superefficient bartenders know their mescals.

Parkside Candy SWEETS $
(3208 Main St; 11am-6pm Mon-Thu, to 9pm Fri & Sat, noon-8pm Sun) A landmark sweet shop, with decor as beautiful as the lollipops and bonbons. Sponge candy (aka honeycomb toffee) is a Buffalo favorite.

Ulrich's 1868 Tavern GERMAN $$
(716-989-1868; 674 Ellicott St; mains $15; 11am-9pm Mon & Tue, to 10pm Wed & Thu, to 11pm Fri, 3-10pm Sat) Buffalo's oldest bar has been partially modernized and now draws a slightly younger clientele. Traditional German schnitzel is on the menu alongside western New York pub food such as beef on weck, a roast-beef sandwich on a caraway-flecked roll.

Betty's AMERICAN $$
(716-362-0633; 370 Virginia St; mains $9-22; 8am-9pm Tue-Thu, to 10pm Fri, 9am-10pm Sat, 9am-2pm Sun;) On a quiet Allentown corner, bohemian Betty's does flavorful, fresh interpretations of American comfort food like meatloaf. Brunch is deservedly popular.

Drinking & Entertainment

With a young populace and most bars open till 4am, Buffalo can keep you out late. The bars along Chippewa St (aka the Chip Strip) cater primarily to a mainstream college crowd, while nearby Allentown has a more eclectic scene. For events listings, pick up the excellent free weeklies *Artvoice* (www.artvoice.com) and *The Public* (www.dailypublic.com).

Founding Fathers BAR
(716-855-8944; 75 Edward St; 11:30am-2am Mon-Fri, 4pm-4am Sat, 4-10pm Sun) Any questions about American history? Ask the knowledgeable owner of this laid-back neighborhood bar with a presidential theme. You'll also find free popcorn and nachos and good sandwiches ($9).

Allen Street Hardware Cafe BAR
(716-882-8843; 245 Allen St; 5pm-4am, music from 9pm) One of the more sophisticated options in Allentown, with a good restaurant (mains $14 to $25) and eclectic local music.

Nietzsche's LIVE MUSIC
(716-886-8539; www.nietzsches.com; 248 Allen St; 1pm-2am Mon & Tue, from noon Sun & Wed, to 4am Thu & Fri, 3pm-4am Sat) One of the original Allentown dives, with live music every night.

Information

Visit Buffalo Niagara (☎800-283-3256; www.visitbuffaloniagara.com; 403 Main St; ⊙9am-5pm Mon-Fri) The helpful tourism board has a great website, good walking-tour pamphlets and a small gift shop.

Getting There & Around

Buffalo Niagara International Airport (BUF; ☎716-630-6000; www.buffaloairport.com; 4200 Genesee St), about 10 miles east of downtown, is a regional hub. JetBlue Airways offers affordable round-trip fares from New York City. **NFTA** (☎716-855-7300; www.nfta.com), the local transit service, runs express bus 204 to the **Buffalo Metropolitan Transportation Center** (☎716-855-7300; www.nfta.com; 181 Ellicott St) downtown. (Greyhound buses also pull in here.) NFTA local bus 40 goes to the American side of Niagara Falls ($2, one hour); express bus 60 also goes to the area, but requires a transfer. From Amtrak's downtown **Exchange Street Station** (☎716-856-2075; www.amtrak.com; 75 Exchange St), you can catch trains to NYC ($63, eight hours), Niagara Falls ($14, one hour), Albany ($50, six hours) and Toronto ($45, four hours). It's desolate late at night; you may prefer to use the **Buffalo-Depew Station** (www.amtrak.com; 55 Dick Rd), 8 miles east.

Niagara Falls

It's a tale of two cities: Niagara Falls, New York (USA), and Niagara Falls, Ontario (Canada). Both overlook a natural wonder – 150,000 gallons of water per second, plunging more than 1000ft – and both provide a load of tourist kitsch surrounding it. The Canadian side, with its somewhat better views and much larger town, is where almost everyone visits. The view from the New York side is still impressive, though the town is much quieter, even a bit derelict. It's easy to walk across the Rainbow Bridge between the two – be sure to bring your passport.

Sights & Activities

The area around the falls is New York's first state park, pleasantly landscaped by Frederick Law Olmsted in the 1880s. (Unfortunately, this came at the expense of the town of Niagara Falls, as many central blocks were razed in the process.) From the walking paths, you can see the **American Falls** and their western portion, the **Bridal Veil Falls**. Walk out on the deck of the **Prospect Point Observation Tower** (☎716-278-1796; admission $1, free from 5pm and off-season; ⊙9:30am-7pm) for a better view, or midway across the windy Rainbow Bridge, where you can also see the Horseshoe Falls on the Canadian side.

Upstream from the main falls, cross the small bridge to **Goat Island**, which forms the barrier between the American Falls and Horseshoe Falls. From Terrapin Point, on the southwest corner, there's a fine view of Horseshoe Falls. Additional pedestrian bridges lead further to the **Three Sisters Islands** in the upper rapids.

Cave of the Winds VIEWPOINT
(☎716-278-1730; Goat Island Rd; adult/child $14/11; ⊙9am-7:30pm mid-May–Oct) On the north corner of Goat Island, don a rain poncho (provided) and take an elevator down to walkways just 25ft from the crashing water at the base of Bridal Veil Falls. (Despite the name, the platforms run in front of the falls, not into a cave.)

Wax Museum at Niagara MUSEUM
(☎716-285-1271; Prospect & Old Falls Sts; adult/child $7/5; ⊙10am-9pm) Not the most state-of-the-art museum, but huge, entertaining and packed with interesting stories: massacres, stunt-jumpers and that time the water stopped flowing. Pose for a photo in an actual barrel someone rode over the falls.

★**Maid of the Mist** BOAT TRIP
(☎716-284-8897; www.maidofthemist.com; 1 Prospect Pt; adult/child $17/9.90; ⊙9am-7pm summer; check website for other times) The traditional way to see Niagara Falls is on this boat cruise, which has ferried soaking visitors into the rapids right below the falls since 1846. It typically runs from mid-May through October, with departures from the bank below Prospect Point.

Sleeping & Eating

Many national hotel chains are represented, but the quality is poor compared with the Canadian side. The majority of restaurants near the falls are Indian, catering to the high number of Indian tourists, and their buffets are decent value.

Giacomo BOUTIQUE HOTEL $$$
(☎716-299-0200; www.thegiacomo.com; 220 1st St; r from $250; P ❄ ☎) A rare bit of style on either the US or Canadian sides, the luxe Giacomo occupies part of a gorgeous art-deco office tower, with spacious, ornately decorated rooms. Even if you're not staying here, have a drink in the 19th-floor lounge (from 5pm) for spectacular views and music on Thursday and Friday.

BORDER CROSSING: CANADIAN NIAGARA FALLS

The Canadian side of the falls is naturally blessed with superior views. **Horseshoe Falls**, on the west half of the river, are wider than Bridal Veil Falls on the eastern, American side, and they're especially photogenic from Queen Victoria Park. The **Journey Behind the Falls** (905-354-1551; 6650 Niagara Pkwy; adult/child Apr-Dec $16.75/10.95, Jan-Mar $11.25/7.30; 9am-10pm) gives access to a spray-soaked viewing area (similar to Cave of the Winds).

The Canadian town is also livelier, in an over-the-top touristy way. Chain hotels and restaurants dominate, but there is a HI hostel, and some older motels have the classic honeymooners' heart-shaped tubs. For more local info, visit the **Niagara Falls Tourism office** (905-356-6061; www.niagarafallstourism.com; 5400 Robinson St; 9am-5pm), near the base of the Skylon Tower observation deck.

Crossing the Rainbow Bridge and returning costs US$3.25/1 per car/pedestrian. Walking takes about 10 minutes; car traffic can grind to a standstill in summer. US citizens and overseas visitors must show a passport or an enhanced driver's license at immigration at either end. Driving a rental car from the US over the border should not be a problem, but check with your rental company.

Zaika INDIAN $
(421 3rd St; buffet $14; 11:30am-9pm Sun-Thu, to 10pm Fri & Sat;) Zaika is a cut above the Indian joints immediately adjacent to the falls. À la carte items are available when it's not too crowded, but the buffet is fresh and varied.

Buzzy's PIZZA $
(7617 Niagara Falls Blvd; mains $7-15; 11am-11pm Sun-Thu, to midnight Fri & Sat) Enjoy excellent NYC-style pizza and other bar food at this long-established place a good drive east of the falls.

Information

Niagara Tourism (716-282-8992; www.niagara-usa.com; 10 Rainbow Blvd; 9am-7pm Jun-Sep, to 5pm Oct-May) At the bridge crossing to Goat Island, this office is stocked with very good maps and information for all of western New York. The combo pass it sells is not great value, though, as the museum and aquarium it gives admission to are quite small.

Getting There & Around

NFTA (p143) bus 40 connects downtown Buffalo and Niagara Falls ($2, one hour); the stop in Niagara Falls is at 1st St and Rainbow Blvd. Express bus 60 goes to a terminal east of the town center; you'll have to transfer to bus 55 to reach the river. The **Amtrak train station** (716-285-4224; 2701 Willard Ave) is about 2 miles northeast of downtown; the station on the Canadian side is more central, but coming from NYC, you have to wait for Canadian customs. From Niagara Falls, daily trains go to Buffalo ($14, 35 minutes), Toronto ($34, three hours) and NYC ($63, nine hours).

Greyhound (www.greyhound.com; 240 1st St) buses stop at the Quality Inn.

Parking costs $8 to $10 a day on either side of the falls. Most midrange hotels offer complimentary parking to guests, while upscale hotels on the Canadian side tend to charge $15 to $20 a day. To avoid traffic mayhem in summer, you can park along Niagara Falls Blvd and ride the NFTA bus 55 west to the river. At the falls, the Niagara Scenic Trolley runs a loop around the American side.

NEW JERSEY

Everything you've seen on TV, from the McMansions of *Real Housewives of New Jersey* to the thick accents of *The Sopranos*, is at least partially true. But Jersey (natives lose the 'New') is at least as well defined by its high-tech and banking headquarters, and a quarter of it is lush farmland (hence the 'Garden State' nickname). And on the 127 miles of beautiful beaches, you'll find, yes, the guidos and guidettes of *Jersey Shore*, but also many other oceanfront towns, each with a distinct character.

Information

Edible Jersey (www.ediblejersey.com) Where to enjoy the bounty of the Garden State; also a free print quarterly.

New Jersey Monthly (www.njmonthly.com) Monthly glossy for residents and visitors.

NJ.com (www.nj.com) Statewide news from all the major dailies including the *Newark Star-Ledger* and Hudson County's *Jersey Journal*.

Getting There & Around

Though many New Jersey folks do love their cars, there are other transportation options.

PATH Train (www.panynj.gov/path) Connects lower Manhattan to Hoboken, Jersey City and Newark.

NJ Transit (☎973-275-5555; www.njtransit.com) Operates buses and trains around the state, including bus service to NYC's Port Authority and downtown Philadelphia, and trains to Penn Station, NYC.

New York Waterway (☎800-533-3779; www.nywaterway.com) Its ferries run up the Hudson River and from the NJ Transit train station in Hoboken to the World Financial Center in Lower Manhattan.

Northern New Jersey

Stay east and you'll experience the Jersey (sub)urban jungle. Go west to find its opposite: the peaceful, refreshing landscape of the Delaware Water Gap.

Hoboken & Jersey City

A sort of TV-land version of a cityscape, Hoboken is a cute little urban pocket just across the Hudson River from NYC. On weekends the bars come alive, and loads of restaurants line commercial Washington St. Gritty *On the Waterfront* was filmed here, but today the riverside is leafy and revitalized – and has dazzling views of Manhattan.

High-rise condominiums and financial towers have transformed the Jersey City waterfront from a primarily blue-collar zone into an upwardly mobile address. The 1200-acre **Liberty State Park** (☎201-915-3440; www.libertystatepark.org; Morris Pesin Dr; ⏱6am-10pm) hosts outdoor concerts with the Manhattan skyline as a backdrop; the expansive **Liberty Science Center** (☎201-200-1000; www.lsc.org; 222 Jersey City Blvd; adult/child $19.75/15.75, extra for IMAX & special exhibits; ⏱9am-4pm Mon-Fri, to 5:30pm Sat & Sun; 👪) is at one end. Ellis Island and the Statue of Liberty are not far; **ferries** (☎877-523-9849; www.statuecruises.com; adult/child from $18/9; ⏱from 9am mid-Feb–Labor Day) leave from here. Movie buffs can head inland to the **Landmark Loew's Jersey Theatre** (☎201-798-6055; www.loewsjersey.org; 54 Journal Sq; ⏱10am-6pm Mon-Fri, plus movie screenings), a classic cinema, half-restored, with a working pipe organ.

Delaware Water Gap

The beautiful spot where the Delaware River makes a tight S-curve through the ridge of the Kittatinny Mountains, was, in the pre-air-conditioning days, a popular resort destination. In 1965 the **Delaware Water Gap National Recreation Area** (☎570-426-2452; www.nps.gov/dewa) was established, covering land in both New Jersey and Pennsylvania, and it's still an unspoiled recreational spot – just 70 miles east of New York City. The 30-mile road on the Pennsylvania side has several worthwhile stops including the small but pretty **Raymondskill Falls**, the **Pocono Environmental Education Center** (☎570-828-2319; www.peec.org; 538 Emery Rd, Dingmans Ferry; ⏱9am-5pm; 👪) 🍃 and the developed but stunning **Bushkill Falls** (☎570-588-6682; www.visitbushkillfalls.com; Bushkill Falls Rd, off Rte 209; adult/child $13.50/8; ⏱opens 9am, closing times vary, closed Dec-Mar).

On the New Jersey side, bump along unpaved Old Mine Rd, one of the oldest continually operating commercial roads in the US, to trailheads for day hikes such as the one to the top of 1574ft Mt Tammany in **Worthington State Forest** (☎908-841-9575; www.njparksandforests.org; Old Mine Rd; ⏱sunrise-sunset).

For river fun, contact **Adventure Sports** (☎570-223-0505; www.adventuresport.com; Rte 209, Marshalls Creek; canoe/kayak $43/47 per day; ⏱9am-6pm Mon-Fri, from 8am Sat & Sun May-Oct) for everything you need for a day or, better, multiday trip on the water. Camping along the way, at sites accessible only by canoe or kayak, is a great way to see the area.

Northeast of here, **High Point State Park** (☎973-875-4800; www.njparksandforests.org; 1480 Rte 23, Sussex; per vehicle $10; ⏱8am-8pm Apr-Oct, to 4:30pm Nov-Mar) has a monument that, at 1803ft above sea level, affords wonderful views of surrounding lakes, hills and farmland.

For food and lodging, visit charming **Milford**, PA, on the north end of the gap; it has several good restaurants, as well as **Grey Towers** (☎570-296-9630; www.greytowers.org; 122 Old Owego Turnpike; tours adult/child $8/free; ⏱grounds dawn-dusk), the gorgeous chateau-style home of Gifford Pinchot, former governor of Pennsylvania and founder of the US Forest Service. On the south end, the somewhat groovier town of Delaware Water Gap, PA, has the **Deer Head Inn** (☎570-424-2000; www.deerheadinn.com; 5 Main St, Delaware Water Gap; r from $90; ❄📶), with Victorian rooms and great live jazz on weekends.

Princeton & the Delaware River

Settled by an English Quaker missionary, the tiny town of Princeton is filled with lovely architecture and several noteworthy sites, number one of which is its Ivy League **Princeton University** (☎609-258-3000; www.princeton.edu), which was built in the mid-1700s and soon became one of the largest structures in the early colonies. You can rove around on your own or join a free student-led tour. The town is more upper-crust than collegiate, with preppie boutiques edging central **Palmer Sq**.

About 20 miles west, on the banks of the Delaware River, is **Lambertville** and its sister town across the water, **New Hope**, PA. New Hope has a faintly hippie-meets-goth sensibility (Doc Martens sold here!) while Lambertville is preppier. Together they're good for an afternoon stop if you're road-tripping. Browse the stalls at **Golden Nugget Antique & Flea Market** (☎609-397-0811; www.gnmarket.com; 1850 River Rd, Lambertville; 6am-4pm Wed, Sat & Sun), and stroll along the peaceful towpaths that edge the river. A few miles south is where George Washington crossed the Delaware in December 1776 (as depicted in Emanuel Leutze's iconic painting).

As for **Trenton**, the state capital just south along the river, it's small and fairly scruffy. Its motto – 'Trenton makes, the world takes' – strikes another downbeat note, considering the riverside city no longer manufactures anything. But travelers with an affection for urban underdogs may appreciate its several historic sites, museum and farmers market.

Sights & Activities

★Princeton University Art Museum MUSEUM
(☎609-258-3788; www.princetonartmuseum.org; McCormick Hall; 10am-5pm Tue-Sat, to 10pm Thu, 1-5pm Sun) FREE This wide-ranging collection is particularly strong on antiquities, Asian art and photography.

Bucks County River Country BOATING
(☎215-297-5000; www.rivercountry.net; 2 Walters Lane, Point Pleasant; tube $22-26, canoe $70; rental 9am-3pm, return by 5pm) North of Lambertville, on the Pennsylvania side, this outfitter rents rafts, tubes and canoes for floating down the serene Delaware River, plus transportation back to base.

Sleeping & Eating

Accommodations are expensive and hard to find during reunions and graduation, from Memorial Day to the end of the month.

Inn at Glencairn B&B $$
(☎609-497-1737; www.innatglencairn.com; 3301 Lawrenceville Rd; r from $199;) The best val-

NEW JERSEY FACTS

Nickname Garden State

Population 8.9 million

Area 8722 sq miles

Capital city Trenton (population 84,000)

Other cities Newark (population 278,000)

Sales tax 7%

Birthplace of Musician Count Basie (1904–84), singer Frank Sinatra (1915–98), actress Meryl Streep (b 1949), musician Bruce Springsteen (b 1949), actor John Travolta (b 1954), musician Jon Bon Jovi (b 1962), rapper Queen Latifah (b 1970)

Home of The first movie (1889), first official baseball game (1846), first drive-in theater (1933)

Politics Republican governor Chris Christie, though strong traditionally Democratic legislature

Famous for *Jersey Shore* (the real thing and the reality show), 'Joisey' accent, turnpikes, roadside diners, tomatoes and sweet corn, full-service (not pump-your-own) gas stations

Number of wineries 36

Driving distances Princeton to NYC 52 miles, Atlantic City to NYC 130 miles

ue in the Princeton area: five serene rooms in a renovated Georgian manor, 10 minutes' drive from campus.

Nassau Inn INN $$$
(☎609-921-7500; www.nassauinn.com; 10 Palmer Sq; r from $259;) Pricey, due to its prime location, and the history-soaked rooms can feel a little frumpy (some may prefer the new wing). Visit the classic bar even if you don't stay the night.

Olives BAKERY, DELI $
(22 Witherspoon St; sandwiches $7; ⊙7am-8pm Mon-Fri, from 8am Sat, 9am-6pm Sun) Reasonably priced, Greek-inspired food, mainly for takeout.

Swan AMERICAN $
(☎609-397-1960; 43 S Main St, Lambertville; burgers $11; ⊙5-10pm Mon-Fri, from 1pm Sat, 1-9pm Sun) This late 19th-century building – once the village hotel – is a scenic place for a burger. The same owners also have the bar, **Boat House** (8 Coryell St, Lambertville; ⊙4:30-11pm), on the towpath, which oozes even more historic atmosphere.

Mistral MEDITERRANEAN $$$
(☎609-688-8808; 66 Witherspoon St; sharing plates $17-28; ⊙5-9pm Mon-Wed, 11:30am-9pm Thu & Sun, 11.30am-10pm Fri & Sat) Princeton's most creative restaurant, largely Mediterranean, with an occasional dash of Asian. The BYOB policy offsets the menu prices.

Jersey Shore

Perhaps the most famous and revered feature of New Jersey is its sparkling shore – and heading 'down the shore' (in local parlance, never 'to the beach') is an essential summer ritual. Stretching from Sandy Hook to Cape May, the coastline is dotted with resort towns both tacky and tony. In 2012 much of the shore was devastated by Hurricane Sandy – the roller coaster at Seaside Heights was even knocked into the ocean. Repairs are ongoing, but the area has largely returned to its vibrant state. It's mobbed on summer weekends (traffic is especially bad on the bridges to the barrier islands), and finding good-value accommodation is nearly as difficult as locating un-tattooed skin; campgrounds can be low-cost alternatives. But by early fall, you could find yourself blissfully alone on the sand.

Sandy Hook

The northernmost tip of the Jersey Shore is the **Sandy Hook Gateway National Recreation Area** (☎718-354-4606; www.nps.gov/gate; parking $15 summer) FREE, a 7-mile barrier island at the entrance to New York Harbor. From your beach blanket, you can see the NYC skyline. The wide beaches, including New Jersey's only legal nude beach (Gunnison), are edged by a system of bike trails, while the bay side is great for fishing or bird-watching. The **Sandy Hook Lighthouse** (☎732-872-5970; ⊙visitor center 9am-5pm, tours 1-4:30pm) FREE is the oldest in the country. Bug spray is recommended as biting flies can be a nuisance at dusk.

A fast ferry service, **Seastreak** (☎800-262-8743; www.seastreak.com; 2 First Ave, Atlantic Highlands; one way/return $26/45, bicycle $5), runs between Sandy Hook (and the Highlands) and Pier 11 in Lower Manhattan.

Asbury Park & Ocean Grove

During decades of economic stagnation, the town of Asbury Park had nothing more to its name than the fact that state troubadour Bruce Springsteen got his start at the **Stone Pony** (☎732-502-0600; www.stoneponyonline.com; 913 Ocean Ave) nightclub here in the mid-1970s. But since 2000, blocks of previously abandoned Victorian homes have seen such a revival that Asbury is sometimes called the Brooklyn of New Jersey. The downtown, several blocks of Cookman and Bangs Aves, has antiques shops, hip restaurants (from vegan to French bistro) and bars, and an art-house cinema. On the boardwalk, pinball fans shouldn't miss the **Silver Ball Museum** (☎732-774-4994; www.silverballmuseum.com; 1000 Ocean Ave; per hour/half-day $10/15; ⊙11am-9pm Mon-Thu, to 1am Fri & Sat, 10am-10pm Sun;), dozens of mint-condition games, all ready to play.

Immediately south of Asbury Park, Ocean Grove is a kind of time and culture warp. 'God's square mile at the Jersey Shore,' as it's still known, was founded by Methodists in the 19th century as a revival camp, and it's still a 'dry' town – no liquor sold here – and the beach is closed Sunday mornings. Its Victorian architecture is so covered in gingerbread trim you want to eat it. At the center, around a 6500-seat wooden auditorium with a huge pipe organ, the former revival camp is now **Tent City** – a historic site with more than a hundred quaint canvas tents used as summer homes. Among the many beautiful B&Bs, **Quaker Inn** (☎732-775-7525; www.quakerinn.com;

BEACH FEES

Many communities on the Jersey Shore charge $5 or so for access, issuing a badge (also called a tag) for the day. From Long Beach Island north to near Sandy Hook, all beaches have a fee; the southern shore is mostly but not entirely free.

39 Main St, Ocean Grove; r $90-200;) is a good deal, and don't miss **Nagle's Fountain** (732-776-9797; 43 Main Ave; ice cream $3; 8:30am-9pm Wed-Mon;) for an ice-cream sundae.

Barnegat Peninsula

Locals call this 22-mile stretch 'the barrier island,' though it is technically a peninsula, connected to the mainland on the north end at **Point Pleasant Beach**. Surfers should seek out **Inlet Beach** in Manasquan, immediately north (not on the peninsula), for the shore's most reliable year-round waves.

South of **Mantoloking** and **Lavallette**, midway down the island, a bridge from the mainland (at Toms River) deposits the hordes in **Seaside Heights**, notorious location of the MTV reality show *Jersey Shore*. As campy as the show was, it did capture the deliciously tacky essence of a certain shore culture. It's still a sticky pleasure to lick a Kohr's orange-vanilla twist cone and stroll through the boardwalk's raucous, deeply tanned, scantily clad crowds. You can refuel at an above-average number of bars. Also look out for the 1932 wooden carousel, still undergoing post-Sandy restoration in 2015.

For a bit of quiet, escape south to residential **Seaside Park** and the wilderness of Island Beach State Park beyond.

Sights & Activities

Island Beach State Park PARK
(732-793-0506; www.njparksandforests.org; Seaside Park; summer weekday/weekend $12/20; dawn-dusk) Of the 10 miles of relatively untouched beach, one is open for swimming; the rest makes a nice bike ride. On the bay side, the lush tidal marshes are good for kayaking.

Jenkinson's AMUSEMENT PARK
(732-295-4334; www.jenkinsons.com; 300 Ocean Ave, Point Pleasant Beach; aquarium adult/child $11/7; rides noon-11pm, aquarium 10am-10pm Ju-Aug, hours vary off-season;) The focus is on kids at this boardwalk in Point Pleasant Beach: small-scale rides, mini-golf, an aquarium and plenty of candy.

Casino Pier AMUSEMENT PARK
(732-793-6488; www.casinopiernj.com; 800 Ocean Terrace, Seaside Heights; rides from $5, water park adult/child $35/29; noon-late Jun-Aug, hours vary rest of year;) The amusement pier at the north end of the Seaside boardwalk has a few kiddie rides and more extreme thrills for the 48in-and-taller set, plus a chairlift that runs above the boardwalk. Nearby is Breakwater Beach, a water park with tall slides.

Sleeping & Eating

Staying in Seaside Heights proper is too noisy to recommend in summer, but can be a good deal off-season.

Surf & Stream Campground CAMPGROUND $
(732-349-8919; www.surfnstream.com; 1801 Ridgeway Rd, Toms River; campsites from $45;) A well-tended alternative to the crash-pad motels in Seaside Heights.

Luna-Mar Motel MOTEL $
(732-793-7955; www.lunamarmotel.com; 1201 N Ocean Ave, Seaside Park; r from $129;) Directly across the road from the beach, this tidy motel has tile floors (no sandy carpets). Rates include beach badges.

★ **Klee's** PUB FOOD $
(www.kleesbarandgrill.com; 101 Blvd, Seaside Heights; pizza from $8, mains $9-20; 10:30am-11pm Mon-Thu, to midnight Fri & Sat) Don't ask why an Irish bar has the best thin-crust pizza on the shore – just enjoy. The rest of the menu is solid, if standard, and comes in mammoth portions.

Music Man ICE CREAM $
(www.njmusicman.com; 2305 Grand Central Ave, Lavallette; ice cream $3-8; 11am-midnight, shows from 5:30pm;) Have a little razzle-dazzle with your ice-cream sundae – the waitstaff belt out Broadway show tunes all night. Cash only.

Long Beach Island

Accessible only by a bridge (Rte 72) across Manahawkin Bay, Long Beach Island is an 18-mile-long barrier island at the dead center of the Jersey Shore. LBI, as it's known, is a string of townships, all with beautiful beaches and strong surf culture (Ron Jon started here). South of the bridge, **Long Beach** and

Beach Haven are where the action is, and quieter, more affluent **Surf City**, **Harvey Cedars** and **Barnegat Light** are to the north.

The landmark **Barnegat Lighthouse** (☎609-494-2016; www.njparksandforests.org; off Long Beach Blvd; lighthouse adult/child summer $3/1; ⏲park 8am-6pm, lighthouse 10am-4:30pm), in the small state park at the northern tip of the island, offers panoramic views at the top. On the southern end, the **Jolly Roger** (☎609-492-6931; www.jollyrogerlbi.com; 5416 S Long Beach Blvd, Beach Haven; r $150-180; ⏲Apr-Oct; ❄📶) is an excellent little motel. Tucked down a residential street is **Hudson House** (☎609-492-9616; 19-E 13th St, Beach Haven; ⏲5pm-1am summer), a friendly dive bar with pinball, shuffleboard and lots of lore. And there are seven – count 'em, *seven* – mini-golf courses on the island.

Atlantic City

Atlantic City (AC) may be the largest city on the shore, but that currently doesn't mean much, as the vision of Vegas on the East Coast has foundered, and casinos gone bankrupt. But the hotels can be a bargain and the lovely beach is free and often empty because most visitors are indoors playing the slots. And in contrast with many homogenous beach enclaves, the population here is more diverse.

As for the Prohibition-era glamour depicted in the HBO series *Boardwalk Empire*, there's little trace – though you can still ride along the boardwalk on a nifty wicker rolling chair. As you do, consider that the first boardwalk was built here, and if Baltic Ave rings a bell, it's because the game Monopoly uses AC's street names. A later contribution: the Miss America pageant, though it's now held in Vegas; the Miss'd America drag pageant fills the gap.

Sights

Atlantic City Historical Museum MUSEUM
(☎609-347-5839; www.atlanticcityexperience.org; Garden Pier, S New Jersey Ave at the boardwalk; ⏲10am-5pm Sat-Wed) FREE Small but informative – you'll learn all about AC's quirkiest details, such as the high-diving horses that once leapt off a 40ft tower at Steel Pier.

Lucy the Elephant MONUMENT
(☎609-823-6473; www.lucytheelephant.org; 9200 Atlantic Ave, Margate; adult/child $8/4; ⏲10am-8pm Mon-Sat, 10am-5pm Sun, check for winter hours) This six-story wooden pachyderm was constructed in 1881 as a land developer's weird scheme to attract customers. It's in Margate (just south of AC), and you can now climb up inside on a guided tour (on the half-hour).

Sleeping & Eating

The casinos often have very low midweek room rates. A handful of motor inns and cheap motels are on Pacific Ave, a block inland from the boardwalk.

Chelsea BOUTIQUE HOTEL $
(☎800-548-3030; www.thechelsea-ac.com; 111 S Chelsea Ave; r from $99; P❄@📶🏊) This stylish place looks a little better in the photos than in real life (maintenance can be patchy). But it's reasonably priced, either in the quieter Luxe section or slightly groovier (and cheaper) style in the Annex.

Kelsey & Kim's Café BARBECUE $
(☎609-350-6800; 201 Melrose Ave; mains $9-12; ⏲7am-10pm) In the pretty residential Uptown area, this friendly cafe does excellent Southern comfort food, from morning grits and waffles to fried whiting and barbecue brisket. BYOB makes it a deal.

White House Subs SANDWICHES $
(☎609-345-8599; 2301 Arctic Ave; sandwiches $7-16; ⏲10am-8pm Mon-Thu, to 9pm Fri-Sun; 👪) Legendary, giant and delicious sub sandwiches. A half is plenty for two.

Knife and Fork Inn AMERICAN $$$
(☎609-344-1133; www.knifeandforkinn.com; 3600 Atlantic Ave; mains $26-45; ⏲4-10pm, from 11:30am Fri) This vestige of Prohibition style was restored in 2005. Happy hour, 4pm to 6:30pm, is a good way to see the interior murals and mahogany trim.

Information

Atlantic City Weekly (www.acweekly.com) The free paper has listings for events, clubs and food.

DO AC (www.atlanticcitynj.com) The local tourism organization has a main branch on the Boardwalk (☎609-348-7100; Boardwalk at Mississippi Ave; ⏲9:30am-5:30pm) and another on the AC Expwy (☎609-449-7130; Atlantic City Expwy; ⏲9am-5pm).

Getting There & Around

Small **Atlantic City International Airport** (ACY; ☎609-645-7895; www.acairport.com) is a 20-minute drive from the town center. If you happen to be coming from Florida (where most of the flights come from), it's a great option for South Jersey or Philadelphia.

OFF THE BEATEN TRACK

PINE BARRENS

New Jersey is America's most densely populated state, but you'd never know it in the million or so acres of state parks and wildlife refuges that make up **Pinelands National Reserve** (☎609-894-7300; www.nj.gov/pinelands). That's the official name, but to Jersey natives, the area will always be the Pine Barrens, an apt adjective for the flat, sandy-soil forest and eerie cedar bogs. And never mind its rare conifers and orchids – this is foremost the home of the sinister 'Jersey Devil.' Ask any local you meet about it – or read John McPhee's 1968 classic, *The Pine Barrens*.

The 50-mile **Batona Trail** cuts through east–west, rewarding hikers with wild blueberries in midsummer. The route passes the **Apple Pie Hill Fire Tower**, giving a view over a veritable sea of forest. (You can drive to the tower too; turn on paved Ringler Rd, rather than sand roads suggested by some GPS.)

Batsto Village (☎609-561-0024; www.batstovillage.org; 31 Batsto Rd, Hammonton; mansion tours $3; ⏰9am-4pm, mansion Fri-Sun only; 👪) This 18th-century village is an open-air museum about the bog-iron industry, as well as a nature center. Guided tours of the central Batsto Mansion are available on weekends.

Whitesbog Village (☎609-893-4646; www.whitesbog.org; 120-34 Whitesbog Rd, Browns Mills; ⏰dawn-dusk; 👪) Visit one of New Jersey's first cranberry bogs, and the place where the highbush blueberry was cultivated. Nature trails wind through the property. Check the website for organized tours & events.

Micks Pine Barrens Canoe Rental (☎609-726-1380; www.mickscanoerental.com; 3107 Rte 563; per day kayak/canoe $45/55; ⏰9am-5pm Mon-Fri, from 8:30am Sat & Sun) This outfitter has maps and other details for water trips in the area.

Atsion Campground (☎609-268-0444; www.njparksandforests.org; 744 Hwy 206, Shamong; campsites $25; ⏰Apr-Oct) Try to reserve a lakeside spot.

Penza's at the Red Barn (☎609-567-3412; 51 Myrtle St, Hammonton; pie slice $5, mains $9-12; ⏰8am-5pm) This rather grandmotherly place serves fruit pies and omelets with farm-fresh vegetables.

The only train service is NJ Transit (p145) from Philadelphia (one way $10, 1½ hours), arriving at the **train station** (☎973-491-9400; 1 Atlantic City Expwy) next to the convention center. AC's **bus station** (☎609-345-5403; 1901 Atlantic Ave) receives NJ Transit and Greyhound service from NYC ($25 to $36, 2½ hours) and Philadelphia (1½ hours). A casino will often refund much of the fare (in chips, coins or coupons) if you get a bus, such as Greyhound's Lucky Streak service, directly to its door. When leaving AC, buses first stop at various casinos and only stop at the bus station if not already full.

Ocean City, Strathmere & Sea Isle

South of Atlantic City are several smaller beach communities. Ocean City is an old-fashioned family spot, maintaining its wholesome reputation with a no-alcohol policy. It has child-centric arcades, a small waterpark, mini-golf courses and themed playlands along its lively boardwalk. Motels are plentiful, relatively cheap and old-fashioned, as are the myriad crab shacks and seafood joints. On the next barrier island down, Sea Isle City and Strathmere are both low-key – the closest you'll get to 'secret' shore spots. Strathmere's beach is free, and **DiGenni's Centennial Guest House** (☎609-263-6945; centennialguesthouse@gmail.com; 127 39th St, Sea Isle City; r from $75; ❄) in Sea Isle is a homey treat, with shared bathrooms, outdoor showers and ceiling fans.

Wildwoods

The three towns of **North Wildwood**, **Wildwood** and **Wildwood Crest** are a virtual outdoor museum of 1950s motel architecture and neon signs. The vintage style has been self-consciously preserved – visit the **Doo Wop Experience** (☎609-523-1958; www.doowopusa.org; 4500 Ocean Ave, Wildwood; ⏰4-9pm Tue & Thu, to 8pm Wed & Fri, 9am-9pm Sat & Sun Jun-Aug, trolley tours 8pm Tue & Thu Jun-Aug) FREE for the whole story, loads of old neon and even a trolley tour around the best landmarks.

The community has a relaxed atmosphere, somewhere between wild party and clean-cut fun. The beach is the widest in

New Jersey, and there's no admission fee. Along the 2-mile boardwalk, several massive piers have roller coasters and rides best suited to aspiring astronauts. A miniature rubber-tired **tram** (one way $3; ⏲11am-1am) runs the length of the boardwalk, intermittently chirping 'Watch the tram car, *please*.'

With some 250 small motels – no corporate chains here – in the area, and rooms from $50 to $250, you're spoiled for choice. A typical option is the **Starlux** (☎609-522-7412; www.thestarlux.com; 305 E Rio Grande Ave, Wildwood; r from $157, trailers $240;), decked out with lava lamps and boomerang-print bedspreads; it even rents two chrome Airstream trailers. For breakfast, **Key West Cafe** (☎609-522-5006; 4701 Pacific Ave, Wildwood; mains $8-10; ⏲7am-2pm) does the best pancakes and eggs.

Cape May

Established in 1620, Cape May is a town with deep history and some 600 gorgeous Victorian buildings. Its sweeping beaches are a draw in summer, but its year-round population of more than 4000 makes it a lively off-season destination, unlike most of the rest of the Jersey Shore. Whales can be spotted off the coast May to December, and migratory birds are plentiful in spring and fall. And thanks to the location on New Jersey's southern tip (it's Exit 0 from the turnpike), you can watch the sun both rise and set over the water.

Sights & Activities

Cape May Lighthouse LIGHTHOUSE
(☎609-884-5404; 215 Lighthouse Ave; adult/child $8/3; ⏲9am-8pm summer, hours vary rest of year) In the lush wetlands of Cape May Point State Park, this 1869 lighthouse gives a fine view. It's also open full-moon nights April through September. At the base are exhibits on wildlife in the area.

Cape May Bird Observatory BIRD-WATCHING
(☎609-884-2736; www.birdcapemay.org; 701 East Lake Dr; ⏲9am-4:30pm Apr-Oct, closed Tue Nov-Mar) FREE Cape May is one of the country's top birding spots, with more than 400 species during migration season. The mile-long loop trail here is a good introduction.

Aqua Trails KAYAKING
(☎609-884-5600; www.aquatrails.com; 1600 Delaware Ave; per hour single/double $25/35, tours single/double from $45/75) Based at Cape May's nature center, this outfitter rents gear and leads tours through the wetlands at sundown and during the full moon.

Sleeping & Eating

★**Congress Hall** HOTEL $$$
(☎609-884-8421; www.caperesorts.com; 200 Congress Pl; r from $259;) Opened in 1816, the enormous Congress Hall is a local landmark, now suitably modernized without wringing out all the history. The same company manages several other excellent hotels in the area.

★**Lobster House** SEAFOOD $$
(☎609-884-8296; 906 Schellengers Landing Rd; mains $14-30; ⏲11:30am-3pm & 4:30-10pm Apr-Dec, to 9pm rest of year) This clubby-feeling classic on the wharf serves local oysters and scallops. No reservations means very long waits – go early or late.

Mad Batter AMERICAN $$
(19 Jackson St; breakfast $8-11, dinner mains $32; ⏲8am-9pm summer, hours vary rest of year) Tucked in a white Victorian, this restaurant is locally beloved for brunch – including fluffy oat pancakes and rich clam chowder. (Dinner is fine, but pricier.)

Getting There & Away

NJ Transit (p145) buses serve Cape May, direct from NYC ($45, three hours) and connecting from Philadelphia. For onward car travel, the **Cape May-Lewes Ferry** (☎800-643-3779; www.cmlf.com; 1200 Lincoln Blvd; car/passenger $45/10; ⏲hourly in summer 7am-7pm, check website rest of year) crosses the bay in 1½ hours to Lewes, DE, near Rehoboth Beach.

PENNSYLVANIA

More than 300 miles across, stretching from the East Coast to the edge of the Midwest, Pennsylvania contains multitudes. Philadelphia, once the heart of the British colonial empire, is very much a part of the east, a link on the Boston–Washington metro corridor. Outside the city, though, the terrain turns pastoral, emphasized by the Pennsylvania Dutch – that is, Mennonite, Amish and others – who tend their farms by hand, as if it were still the 18th century. West of here, the Appalachian mountains begin, as do the so-called Pennsylvania Wilds, a barely inhabited patch of deep forest. In the far west edge of the state, Pittsburgh, the state's only other large city and once a staggeringly wealthy steel manufacturing center, is fascinating in its combination of rust-belt decay and new energy.

Philadelphia

With giant NYC less than 100 miles north and Washington, DC, due south, Philadelphia often gets knocked down the must-visit list. In many ways, though, the City of Brotherly Love can be as rewarding as its bigger neighbors. It has its own distinct traditions, and outsize food, music and art scenes – unfettered by crushing real-estate prices. Because the city's oldest buildings are so well preserved, America's early history and its role in building democracy is sometimes more accessible here than in the capital. Moreover, it's a beautiful place that is easy and rewarding to explore, its streets dotted with gracious squares and linked with cobbled alleys.

For a time in its early years, Philadelphia was the second-largest city in the British empire, after London, then, along with Boston, the Empire's undoing. From the start of the Revolutionary War until 1790 (when Washington, DC, was founded), it was the new nation's capital. Eventually, NYC rose as a cultural, commercial and industrial center, and Philly slipped into a decline, enhanced by the loss of industrial jobs. Some areas of the city are still blighted, but its core, from the manicured campuses of the University of Pennsylvania to the redbrick buildings of Old City, is solid.

Sights & Activities

Most visitors will spend time in central Philadelphia, an area between the Delaware and Schuylkill (*skoo*-kill) Rivers. It's easy to navigate and distances are walkable, or a short bus ride at most. If you head west of the Schuylkill, you hit the area known as University City, with several campuses; for this trip, the nifty underground trolley comes in handy.

Old City

The area along the Delaware River bounded by Walnut, Vine and 6th Sts has been dubbed 'America's most historic square mile,' thanks to its role in the American Revolution and the earliest years of American democracy. A large, L-shaped chunk of the neighborhood is designated **Independence National Historic Park**, with many of the buildings managed by the National Park Service.

Front St used to mark the edge of the river port (now a freeway separates it from the wharves at **Penn's Landing**), and the blocks adjacent are lined with centuries-old homes and warehouses, now converted to lofts, galleries and shops. The mix of modern use and history makes this a fascinating place to stroll, even at the height of the summer tourist crush.

Liberty Bell Center HISTORIC SITE
(Map p158; www.nps.gov/inde; 526 Market St; 9am-5pm, to 7pm late May-early Sep) FREE A glass-walled building protects this icon of Philadelphia history from the elements. You can peek from outside, or join the line to file past, reading about the 2080lb object's history along the way. The queue starts on the building's north end, where the foundations of George Washington's house are marked.

The gist of the story: the bell was made in 1751 to commemorate the 50th anniversary of Pennsylvania's constitution. Mounted in Independence Hall, it tolled on the first public reading of the Declaration of Independence. The crack developed in the 19th century, and it was retired in 1846.

★**Independence Hall** HISTORIC BUILDING
(Map p158; 877-444-6777; www.nps.gov/inde; 520 Chestnut St; 9am-5pm, to 7pm late May-early Sep) FREE The 'birthplace of American government,' a modest Quaker building, is where delegates from the 13 colonies met to approve the Declaration of Independence on July 4, 1776. Entrance is at the corner of Chestnut and 5th Sts. Even without a ticket, you can pass through to see **Congress Hall** (215-965-2305; cnr S 6th & Chestnut Sts; 9am-5pm, tours every 20-30min) FREE, where the congress met when Philly was the nation's capital.

★**Benjamin Franklin Museum** MUSEUM
(Map p158; www.nps.gov/inde; Market St, btwn 3rd & 4th Sts; adult/child $5/2; 9am-5pm, to 7pm late May-early Sep) In the courtyard south of Market St, underground, is a museum dedicated to Benjamin Franklin's storied life as a printer (he started the nation's first newspaper), inventor (bifocals! lightning rods!) and statesman who signed the Declaration of Independence.

In the same courtyard, don't miss the newspaper office where Franklin worked – park rangers demonstrate the printing press.

National Constitution Center MUSEUM
(Map p158; ☎215-409-6600; www.constitutioncenter.org; 525 Arch St; adult/child $14.50/8; ⊙9:30am-5pm Mon-Fri, to 6pm Sat, noon-5pm Sun;) This whiz-bang museum makes the US Constitution jump off the page, starting with a dramatic theater-in-the-round presentation. This exits into a dizzying array of interactive exhibits, from voting booths to trivia games. You can also see an original version of the Bill of Rights. Go early, both for lighter crowds and a fresher brain – this place is hard to skim through.

Elfreth's Alley HISTORIC SITE
(Map p158; ☎215-627-8680; www.elfrethsalley.org; off 2nd St, btwn Arch & Race Sts; tours $5; ⊙museum noon-5pm Fri-Sun) This tiny, cobblestone lane has been occupied since the 1720s. One home is a museum that leads a tour inside and down the alley. The 32 well-preserved brick row houses are inhabited by regular Philadelphians, so be considerate in the narrow space.

National Museum of American Jewish History MUSEUM
(Map p158; ☎215-923-3811; www.nmajh.org; 101 S Independence Mall E; adult/child $12/free; ⊙10am-5pm Tue-Fri, to 5:30pm Sat & Sun) With lots of multimedia displays, this museum is a solid introduction to the role of Jewish culture in the US in everything from entertainment to the civil rights movement.

United States Mint HISTORIC BUILDING
(Map p158; ☎215-408-0112; www.usmint.gov; 151 N Independence Mall E; ⊙9am-4:30pm Mon-Fri, incl Sat summer) FREE Take the 45-minute self-guided tour to see coins being made, and to admire the Tiffany mosaics inside this stately building.

Dream Garden HISTORIC BUILDING
(Map p158; ☎215-238-6450; 601 Walnut St; ⊙8am-6pm Mon-Fri, 10am-1pm Sat) FREE In the east lobby of the Curtis Center is a masterpiece of American craft: a luminous wall-size Tiffany mosaic of more than 100,000 pieces of glass, depicting a lush landscape by Maxfield Parrish.

Independence Seaport Museum MUSEUM
(Map p154; ☎215-413-8655; www.phillyseaport.org; 211 S Columbus Blvd; adult/child $15/10; ⊙10am-5pm, to 7pm Thu-Sat summer; ; 21, 25, 76) Worth the trek to Penn's Landing, this well-done museum honors Philadelphia's shipyards, which operated until 1995. You can walk through an 1892 steel warship and a WWII submarine.

VISITING INDEPENDENCE NATIONAL HISTORIC PARK

This national park includes old buildings, museums, landmarks such as the Liberty Bell, and even a restaurant, **City Tavern** (Map p158; ☎215-413-1443; www.citytavern.com; 138 S 2nd St; mains $22-30; ⊙11:30am-9pm), with waiters in 18th-century costume. With some exceptions, most sites are open 9am to 5pm every day and entrance is free. Independence Hall requires a timed ticket; reserve online (fee $1.50) or go in the morning to the Independence Visitor Center (p165) for same-day tickets (and good maps).

In peak summer, the central park of Independence Mall and surrounding major sights can be an epic tourist scene. You can still find quiet in lesser-known park buildings. Just pick a dot on the map and head for it – there are cool historical details in every corner.

Society Hill

Architecture from the 18th and 19th centuries defines this lovely residential neighborhood, bounded by Front, Walnut, Lombard and 8th Sts. Come here just to ramble past brick row homes and down some of the city's prettiest alleys. (The anachronistic Society Hill Towers, designed by IM Pei, overshadow a bit on the north side.) Two 18th-century mansions are open for tours: **Physick House** (Map p158; ☎215-925-7866; www.philalandmarks.org; 321 S 4th St; admission $8; ⊙noon-4pm Thu-Sat, 1-4pm Sun, by appt Jan & Feb), home of an influential surgeon, and **Powel House** (Map p158; ☎215-627-0364; www.philalandmarks.org; 244 S 3rd St; adult/child $5/free; ⊙noon-4pm Thu-Sat, 1-4pm Sun, by appt Jan & Feb), the original interior of which is installed in the Philadelphia Museum of Art. At the south edge is Headhouse Shambles, a market hall built in the early 1800s and now the site of the city's largest **farmers market** (Map p154; www.thefoodtrust.org; 2nd St, south of Lombard St; ⊙10am-2pm Sun May-Oct).

Chinatown & Around

The fourth-largest Chinatown in the USA, Philly's version has existed since the 1860s, thanks to Chinese immigrants who built

Philadelphia

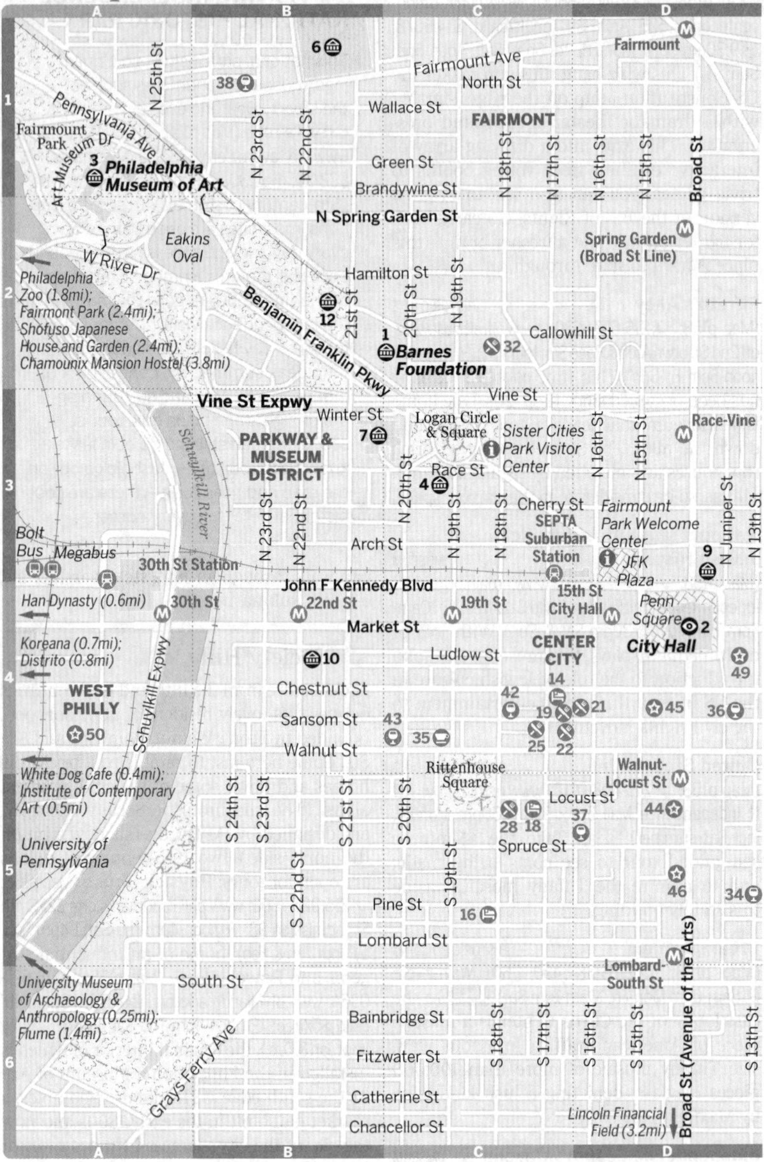

America's transcontinental railroads. Now many residents come from Malaysia, Thailand and Vietnam in addition to every province in China. The multicolored, four-story **Chinese Friendship Gate** (Map p154; N 10th St, btwn Cherry & Arch Sts) is the neighborhood's most conspicuous landmark.

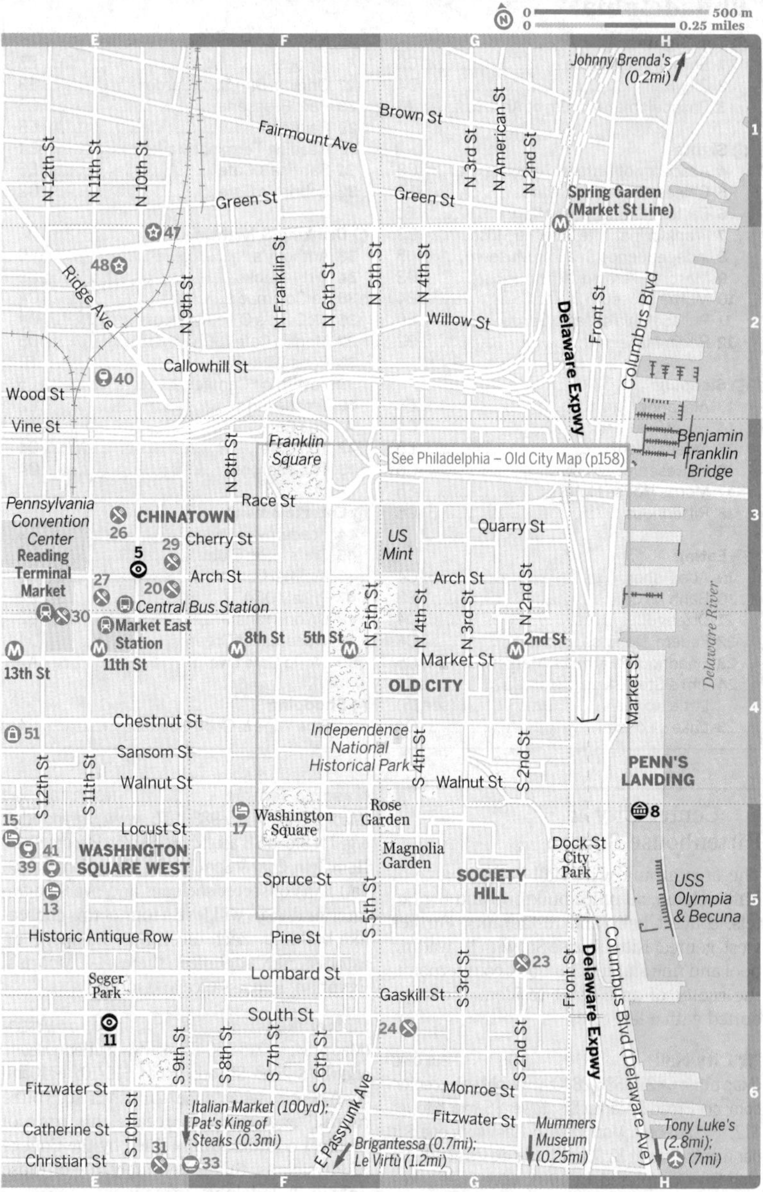

African American Museum in Philadelphia MUSEUM

(Map p158; ☎215-574-0380; www.aampmuseum.org; 701 Arch St; adult/child $14/10; ⊙10am-5pm Thu-Sat, from noon Sun; 🚸) The ground floor has exhibits on notable African American Philadelphians – a bit kid-oriented, but these stories aren't commonly told elsewhere in the city.

Philadelphia

Top Sights

1 Barnes Foundation ... C2
2 City Hall ... D4
3 Philadelphia Museum of Art ... A1

Sights

4 Academy of Natural Sciences ... C3
5 Chinese Friendship Gate ... E3
6 Eastern State Penitentiary ... B1
7 Franklin Institute Science Museum ... B3
8 Independence Seaport Museum ... H5
9 Masonic Temple ... D3
10 Mütter Museum ... B4
11 Philadelphia's Magic Gardens ... E6
12 Rodin Museum ... B2

Sleeping

13 Alexander Inn ... E5
14 Hotel Palomar ... C4
15 Independent ... E5
16 La Reserve ... C5
17 Morris House Hotel ... F5
18 Rittenhouse 1715 ... C5

Eating

19 Abe Fisher ... C4
20 Banh Mi Cali ... E3
21 Dizengoff ... D4
22 Federal Donuts ... C4
23 Headhouse Farmers' Market ... G5
24 Jim's Steaks ... G6
Little Nonna's ... (see 15)
25 Luke's Lobster ... C4
26 Nan Zhou Hand Drawn Noodle House ... E3
27 Original Dim Sum Garden ... E3
28 Parc Brasserie ... C5
29 Rangoon ... E3
30 Reading Terminal Market ... E4
31 Sabrina's Cafe ... E6
32 Sabrina's Cafe ... C2

Drinking & Nightlife

33 Anthony's ... F6
34 Dirty Franks ... D5
35 La Colombe ... C4
36 McGillin's Olde Ale House ... D4
37 Monk's Cafe ... D5
38 Paris Wine Bar ... B1
39 Tavern on Camac ... E5
40 Trestle Inn ... E2
41 Tria Cafe ... E5
42 Tria Cafe ... C4
43 Tria Taproom ... C4

Entertainment

44 Academy of Music ... D5
45 Chris' Jazz Club ... D4
46 Kimmel Center ... D5
47 PhilaMOCA ... E2
48 Union Transfer ... E2
49 Wanamaker Organ ... D4
50 World Cafe Live ... A4

Shopping

51 Fine Wine & Good Spirits ... E4

Center City & Rittenhouse Square

The area around City Hall is the engine of Philadelphia, all office buildings and big hotels, concert halls and restaurants. Further west, genteel Rittenhouse Sq, with its wading pool and fine statues, is a quiet counterpoint, the center of an elegant residential district dotted with a few cafés.

★City Hall BUILDING

(Map p154; ☎215-686-2840; www.phlvisitorcenter.com; cnr Broad & Market Sts; tower $6, tour & tower $12; ⏰9am-5pm Mon-Fri, also 11am-4pm one Sat per month, tour at 12:30pm, tower closes at 4:15pm Mon-Fri) Completed in 1901, City Hall takes up a whole block, and, at 548ft, not counting the 27-ton bronze statue of William Penn, it's the world's tallest structure without a steel frame. The view from the observation deck near the top of the tower takes in most of the city (reserve tickets ahead). The daily interior tour is a treat too. In winter, there's ice skating on the west-side plaza.

Masonic Temple HISTORIC BUILDING

(Map p154; ☎215-988-1917; www.pagrandlodge.org; 1 N Broad St; adult/child $13/5; ⏰tours 10am, 11pm, 1pm, 2pm & 3pm Tue-Fri, 10am, 11am & noon Sat) Fans of secret societies and over-the-top interior design will love a tour of this church-like building. Each meeting room sports an astonishingly detailed theme – Moorish, Egyptian, Renaissance and more.

Mütter Museum MUSEUM

(Map p154; ☎215-560-8564; www.muttermuseum.org; 19 S 22nd St; adult/child $15/10; ⏰10am-5pm) Know what a bezoar is? If so, you're morbid enough to appreciate this trove of medical oddities. Maintained by the College of Physicians, this is definitely one of those only-in-Philadelphia attractions.

Fairmount

Starting at JFK Plaza (where the iconic red-and-blue *Love* statue, by sculptor Robert Indiana, stands), the Benjamin Franklin Pkwy is lined with museums and other civic landmarks. It runs northwest, ending at the Philadelphia Museum of Art and Fairmount Park.

★ **Philadelphia Museum of Art** MUSEUM
(Map p154; ☎215-763-8100; www.philamuseum.org; 2600 Benjamin Franklin Pkwy; adult/child $20/free; ⏰10am-5pm Tue, Thu, Sat & Sun, to 8:45pm Wed & Fri) To many, this building is simply the steps Sylvester Stallone ran up in the 1976 flick *Rocky*. But well beyond that, this is one of the nation's finest treasure troves, featuring excellent collections of Asian art, Renaissance masterpieces, post-impressionist works and modern pieces by Picasso, Duchamp and Matisse. Especially neat are the complete rooms: a medieval cloister, a Chinese temple, an Austrian country house.

There's so much to see that a ticket gives admission for two days, here and at the separate Perelman Building, two nearby historic homes and the **Rodin Museum** (Map p154; www.rodinmuseum.org; 2151 Benjamin Franklin Pkwy; admission suggested $10; ⏰10am-5pm Wed-Mon). Wednesday and Friday nights are pay-what-you-wish (but note the Perelman is closed).

★ **Barnes Foundation** MUSEUM
(Map p154; ☎215-278-7200; www.barnesfoundation.org; 2025 Benjamin Franklin Pkwy; adult/child $25/10; ⏰10am-5pm Wed-Mon) In the first half of the 20th century, collector and educator Albert C Barnes amassed a remarkable trove of artwork by Cézanne, Degas, Matisse, Renoir, Van Gogh and other European stars. Alongside, he set beautiful pieces of folk art from Africa and the Americas – an artistic desegregation that was shocking at the time. Today's Barnes Foundation is a modern shell, inside which is a faithful reproduction of Barnes' original mansion (still in the Philadelphia suburbs).

The art is hung according to his vision, a careful juxtaposition of colors, themes and materials. In one room, all the portraits appear to be staring at a central point. Even more remarkable: you've likely never seen any of these works before, because Barnes' will limits reproduction and lending.

Franklin Institute Science Museum MUSEUM
(Map p154; ☎215-448-1200; www.fi.edu; 222 N 20th St; adult/child $19.95/15.95; ⏰9:30am-5pm; 👪; 🚌33, 38, 48) Blockbuster science displays, such as under-the-skin Bodies series, plus a planetarium and a Ben Franklin memorial and show.

Academy of Natural Sciences MUSEUM
(Map p154; ☎215-299-1000; www.ansp.org; 1900 Benjamin Franklin Pkwy; adult/child $15.95/13.95; ⏰10am-4:30pm Mon-Fri, to 5pm Sat & Sun; 👪; 🚌32, 33, 38) Kid-pleasing exhibits such as a butterfly room and a terrific dinosaur exhibition where you can dig for fossils and bones.

Eastern State Penitentiary MUSEUM
(Map p154; ☎215-236-3300; www.easternstate.org; 2027 Fairmount Ave; adult/child $14/10; ⏰10am-5pm) The modern prison didn't just happen – it was invented, and Eastern State Penitentiary was the first one, opened in 1829 and finally closed in 1971. An excellent audioguide leads you through the eerie, echoing halls. There's also broader information on America's current prison system, and fascinating art installations throughout.

From mid-September through Halloween, the prison hosts a truly terrifying haunted house.

Fairmount Park OUTDOORS
(www.phila.gov/parksandrecreation) FREE The snaking Schuylkill River bisects this 9200-acre green space, the largest city park in the US. On the east bank, admire the Victorian-era rowing clubs at Boathouse Row; there's a fine view from in front of the art museum. On either side of the river are playing fields and lawns, public art, historic houses and a very large **zoo** (☎215-243-1100; www.philadelphiazoo.org; 3400 W Girard Ave; adult/child $20/18; ⏰9:30am-5pm Mar-Oct, to 4pm Nov-Feb; 👪; 🚌38, trolley15). In cherry-blossom season especially, don't miss the 16th-century-style **Shofuso Japanese House and Garden** (☎215-878-5097; www.shofuso.com; Horticultural Dr; adult/child $7/5; ⏰10am-4pm Wed-Fri, 11am-5pm Sat & Sun Apr-Oct).

South Philadelphia

South St, dotted with slightly grungy, youth-oriented bars and music venues, marks the approximate border of South Philadelphia, generally held up as the stronghold of old-style, working-class Philly culture, of the Italian, Irish and German variety. In practice, it's a lot more mixed than that, with distinct enclaves of Mexicans, Vietnamese, African Americans and even that other burgeoning 'ethnic' group, Hipster Coffee Shop Owners.

Philadelphia – Old City

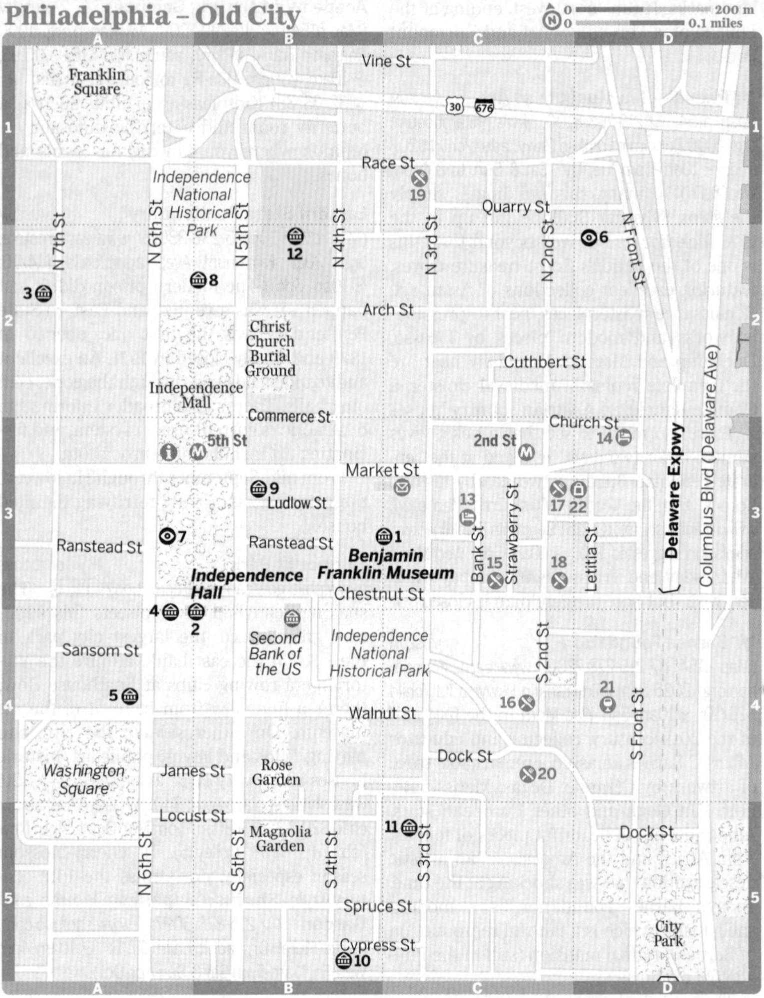

Philadelphia's Magic Gardens GARDENS

(Map p154; ☎215-733-0390; www.phillymagicgardens.org; 1020 South St; adult/child $7/3; ⊙11am-6pm Sun-Thu, to 8pm Fri & Sat Apr-Oct, to 5pm Nov-Mar; 👪) The ongoing life's work of Isaiah Zagar, this is a folk-art wonderland of mirror mosaics, bottle walls and quirky sculpture. Zagar has done work around the city – visit here first, and you'll know what to look for.

Italian Market MARKET

(☎215-278-2903; www.italianmarketphilly.org; S 9th St, btwn Fitzwater & Wharton Sts; ⊙9am-5pm Tue-Sat, to 2pm Sun) A vibrant part of South Philadelphia, this long commercial strip is lined with produce stalls, while the stores are butchers, fishmongers and delis. The northern end is still predominantly Italian; south of Washington St skews Mexican, so you can pick up tortillas and tortellini in the same trip.

Mummers Museum MUSEUM

(☎215-336-3050; www.mummersmuseum.com; 1100 S 2nd St; admission by donation; ⊙9:30am-4pm Wed-Sat; 🚌4, 57) The Mummers Parade, a dazzling display of homegrown costumes, is a local New Year's ritual with roots in South

Philadelphia – Old City

Top Sights
1 Benjamin Franklin Museum........C3
2 Independence Hall........B4

Sights
3 African American Museum in Philadelphia........A2
4 Congress Hall........A4
5 Dream Garden........A4
6 Elfreth's Alley........D2
7 Liberty Bell Center........A3
8 National Constitution Center........B2
9 National Museum of American Jewish History........B3
10 Physick House........B5
11 Powel House........C5
12 United States Mint........B2

Sleeping
13 Apple Hostels........C3
14 Penn's View Hotel........D3

Eating
15 Amada........C3
16 City Tavern........C4
17 Franklin Fountain........C3
18 Han Dynasty........C3
19 Wedge + Fig........C1
20 Zahav........C4

Drinking & Nightlife
21 Olde Bar........D4

Shopping
22 Shane Confectionery........D3

Philly and, before that, Germany and Switzerland. Learn to tell your Fancy Brigades from your String Bands at this museum – and even try on a costume or two.

University City

This neighborhood, separated from downtown Philly by the Schuylkill River, feels like one big college town. That's because it's home to both Drexel University and the Ivy League University of Pennsylvania ('U Penn'), founded in 1740. The leafy, bustling campus makes for a pleasant afternoon stroll; you might also visit two museums.

University Museum of Archaeology & Anthropology MUSEUM
(215-898-4000; www.penn.museum; 3260 South St; adult/child $15/10; 10am-5pm Tue & Thu-Sun, to 8pm Wed; 21, 30, 40, 36th St Station) Penn's magical museum contains archaeological treasures from ancient Egypt, Mesopotamia, the Mayan world and more.

Institute of Contemporary Art GALLERY
(215-898-7108; www.icaphila.org; 118 S 36th St; 11am-8pm Wed, to 6pm Thu & Fri, to 5pm Sat & Sun) FREE Worth a stop if you're in the area; usually two exhibits up at a time, from retrospectives to themed group shows.

Tours

Mural Tours TROLLEY TOUR
(215-925-3633; www.muralarts.org/tours; tours free-$30) FREE Guided trolley, train and walking tours of the city's numerous outdoor murals. A free self-guided tour and map is available online.

Taste of Philly Food Tour TOUR
(800-838-3006; www.tasteofphillyfoodtour.com; adult/chid $17/10; 10am Wed & Sat) Snack and learn Philly food lore at the Reading Terminal Market, with a local writer. Reservations required.

Festivals & Events

Mummers Parade CARNIVAL
(www.mummers.com; Jan 1) Uniquely Philly: the closest parallel may be New Orleans' Mardi Gras krewes, with their elaborate costumes, music and deep lore – but in the bracing cold of winter. It often stretches more than a mile through the city center.

Fringe Festival PERFORMING ARTS
(www.fringearts.com; Sep) Philly's performance fest has been running since 1996. Also on: Feastival, featuring local chefs.

Sleeping

Because central Philadelphia is so compact, your hotel, no matter the neighborhood, will never be too far from your day's activities. Busy, businessy Center City is where most hotels are located, while B&Bs provide quieter alternatives in the residential blocks around Rittenhouse Sq. There is no shortage of rooms, especially with the national chains (the Loews, Sofitel and Westin can all be recommended). For parking, plan on paying $20 to $45 per day for space in a hotel lot; on-street parking is difficult in the center.

★ **Apple Hostels** HOSTEL $
(Map p158; 215-922-0222; www.applehostels.com; 32 Bank St; dm $38, r from $80;) This gem of a hostel is hidden down an Old

City alley. The apple-green color scheme is a bit intense, but the HI-affiliated place is strong on details: power outlets in lockers, USB ports and reading lights at every bed, free coffee and earplugs. The huge kitchen is spotless; so are the laundry machines.

There are male, female and coed dorms, plus two private rooms. The friendly staff run nightly activities such as walking tours, pasta nights and a bar crawl.

Chamounix Mansion Hostel HOSTEL $

(☎215-878-3676; www.philahostel.org; 3250 Chamounix Dr, West Fairmount Park; dm $25; ⊙closed mid-Dec–mid-Jan; P @; 38) In a lovely wooded area on the north side of the city, this HI hostel is best for guests with a car. In its public areas, set with 19th-century furnishings, the place looks more like a B&B than a hostel; the dorms themselves are basic but clean.

★**Alexander Inn** BOUTIQUE HOTEL $$

(Map p154; ☎215-923-3535; www.alexanderinn.com; cnr 12th & Spruce Sts; s/d from $119/129; ❄@ 📶) Online photos undersell this place. The impeccably kept rooms have a subdued, slightly vintage style; some have old-fashioned half-size tubs. The continental breakfast is a bit generic – but you're in a good area for something more interesting.

Morris House Hotel BOUTIQUE HOTEL $$

(Map p154; ☎215-922-2446; www.morrishousehotel.com; 225 S 8th St; r from $179; ❄📶) In a landmark building near Washington Sq, Morris House conjures colonial elegance without too much formality or frilliness. Beyond the 15 rooms, its finest asset is the courtyard garden (with a locally loved dinner restaurant), a true respite from the city. In winter, cozy up by the fireplace.

Hotel Palomar DESIGN HOTEL $$

(Map p154; ☎215-563-5006; www.hotelpalomar-philadelphia.com; 117 S 17th St; r from $229; P❄📶🐾) One of Philadelphia's two hotels in the excellent Kimpton chain (the other is the more central Monaco), the Palomar is preferable for its lower rates and its quieter location, a few blocks from Rittenhouse Sq. The rooms have a dark but not serious elegance (leopard-spot bathrobes).

Independent BOUTIQUE HOTEL $$

(Map p154; ☎215-772-1440; www.theindependenthotel.com; 1234 Locust St; r from $145; ❄📶) A good Center City option housed in a handsome brick Georgian-Revival building with a four-story atrium. The 24 wood-floored rooms are uncluttered and sunny, and the complimentary off-site gym pass and wine and cheese every evening sweeten the deal.

Penn's View Hotel HISTORIC HOTEL $$

(Map p158; ☎215-922-7600; www.pennsviewhotel.com; cnr Front & Market Sts; r from $149; ❄📶) Penn's View shows its age – mostly in a good way. The rooms, some with fireplace or balcony, have a quaint style, with orien-

PENNSYLVANIA FACTS

Nicknames Keystone State, Quaker State

Population 12.8 million

Area 46,055 sq miles

Capital city Harrisburg (population 49,500)

Other cities Philadelphia (population 1.55 million), Pittsburgh (population 306,000), Erie (population 101,000)

Sales tax 6%

Birthplace of Writer Louisa May Alcott (1832–88), dancer Martha Graham (1894–1991), anthropologist Margaret Mead (1901–78), artist Andy Warhol (1928–87), movie star Grace Kelly (1929–82)

Home of US Constitution, the Liberty Bell, first daily newspaper (1784), first auto service station (1913), first computer (1946)

Politics 'Swing state,' Democrat governor, majority Republican state house and senate

Famous for Soft pretzels, Amish people, Philadelphia cheesesteak, Pittsburgh steel mills

Wildlife Home of the largest herd of wild elk east of the Mississippi

Driving distances Philadelphia to NYC 95 miles, Philadelphia to Pittsburgh 306 miles

tal rugs. Maintenance is an occasional issue, and while river views are nice, the nearby freeway is noisy if windows are open. Still, it's great value for its location on the edge of Old City.

La Reserve B&B **$$**
(Map p154; ☎215-735-1137; www.lareservebandb.com; 1804 Pine St; r $155, without bathroom $120; ❄📶) This 1850s row house sits on a quiet street south of Rittenhouse Sq. The 12 rooms have well-worn charm, with faded oriental rugs, plush drapes, high ceilings and (it seems) the fragile furniture of a minor 19th-century French aristocrat. Some may find the style fussy, but the price is right.

Rittenhouse 1715 BOUTIQUE HOTEL **$$$**
(Map p154; ☎215-546-6500; www.rittenhouse1715.com; 1715 Rittenhouse Square St; r from $289; ❄📶) Around the corner from Rittenhouse Sq, this 1911 mansion is a top-notch choice for those who prefer their luxury small and local. The place oozes old-world sophistication, the 23 rooms are more than comfortable, and the staff is friendly and efficient. But this is a B&B in its bones; some may prefer the amenities of a larger hotel.

Eating

Philly is a great food town, full of variety and mostly reasonably priced – though you can splash out if you want to. The liveliest new restaurant areas are East Passyunk in the south and Northern Liberties and Fishtown north of Old City, along the river. Stephen Starr and Jose Garces are two rival restaurateurs who together account for some two dozen on-trend operations – you'll almost certainly wind up in one of their places during your visit. Wherever you go, it's a good idea to make reservations; most restaurants are on OpenTable (OpenTable.com). For cheap eats, including the legendary Philly cheesesteak, South St is a go-to spot. Finally, don't miss local gelato chain Capogiro, with branches all over the city.

Old City

★Franklin Fountain ICE CREAM **$**
(Map p158; ☎215-627-1899; 116 Market St; sundaes $10; ⏲11am-midnight Sun-Thu, to 1am Fri & Sat; 👪) A fantastic yet kitsch-free throwback, from the phosphates and vintage ice-cream flavors (try the teaberry) right down to the ancient telephone and the carton cups (cash only). Also check out the owners' equally old-school **Shane Confectionery** (Map p158; ☎215-922-1048; 10 Market St; ⏲11am-10pm, to 11pm Fri & Sat) down the block, with historic hot chocolate in the back.

> **LOCAL KNOWLEDGE**
>
> **BYOB**
>
> One nice feature of Philly's restaurant scene is that many restaurants have a BYOB – bring your own bottle of wine – policy, which means a cheaper night out. As a bonus, the majority of the clientele is usually local, as people who live in the area are more likely to take the extra step of first going to a wine shop (not very common, due to Pennsylvania liquor laws). Look out for a branch of the state-run liquor store, **Fine Wine & Good Spirits** (Map p154; ☎215-560-4380; 1218 Chestnut St; ⏲9am-9pm Mon-Sat, noon-5pm Sun), in Center City; there's another at Reading Terminal Market (p162).

Wedge + Fig SANDWICHES **$**
(Map p158; 160 N 3rd St; sandwiches $10; ⏲11am-8pm Tue-Sat, 10:30am-3:30pm Sun) Grilled-cheese fans will be bowled over by the options at this 'cheese bistro,' which also has big fresh salads and heartier mains. Two bonuses: BYOB policy and a cute garden.

★Zahav MIDDLE EASTERN **$$**
(Map p158; ☎215-625-8800; 237 St James Pl, off Dock St; mains $14; ⏲5-10pm Sun-Thu, to 11pm Fri & Sat) Sophisticated 'modern Israeli' cuisine, drawing primarily from North African, Persian and Levantine kitchens. Pick your own meze and grills, or go for the $54 Mesibah (Party Time) set menu. In a slightly incongruous building on Society Hill Towers grounds.

Han Dynasty CHINESE **$$**
(Map p158; ☎215-922-1888; 123 Chestnut St; mains $13-21; ⏲11:30am-10pm Sun-Tue & Thu, to midnight Wed, to 10:30pm Fri & Sat) Part of a local mini-empire of sizzling Szechuan goodness. This location has the bonus of a glam dining room in an old bank building. There's another branch in **University City** (☎215-222-3711; 3711 Market St; ⏲11:30am-10pm Sun-Tue & Thu, to midnight Wed, to 10:30pm Fri & Sat).

Amada SPANISH **$$**
(Map p158; ☎215-625-2450; 217 Chestnut St; tapas $6-20; ⏲11:30am-2:30pm & 5-10pm Mon-Fri, from 10:30am Sat & Sun) See why Jose Garces was an Iron Chef – his traditional Spanish tapas are

fresh and garlicky, and the atmosphere is bustling and loud at the long communal tables.

Chinatown

Banh Mi Cali VIETNAMESE $
(Map p154; 900 Arch St; sandwiches $5; ⊙9:30am-7:30pm) For cheap, fast eats after Old City sightseeing, nothing beats one of these 'Vietnamese hoagies,' as locals call *banh mi*.

Nan Zhou Hand Drawn Noodle House CHINESE $
(Map p154; 1022 Race St; mains $6-10; ⊙11am-10pm, to 10:30pm Fri & Sat) Delicious and inexpensive meat soups (skip the skimpy seafood options) with perfectly chewy noodles, plus standard stir-fries and less common treats like pig ears. Cash only.

Rangoon BURMESE $
(Map p154; 112 N 9th St; mains $9-17; ⊙11:30am-9pm Sun-Thu, to 10pm Fri & Sat) This Burmese spot offers a huge array of tantalizing specialties from spicy red-bean shrimp and curried chicken with egg noodles to coconut tofu.

Original Dim Sum Garden CHINESE $
(Map p154; 59 N 11th St; mains $6; ⊙11am-10:30pm Sun-Fri, to 11pm Sat) Not the most salubrious looking hole-in-the-wall near the bus station, but some of the tastiest buns and soup dumplings in the city.

Center City & Around

★**Reading Terminal Market** MARKET $
(Map p154; ☎215-922-2317; www.readingterminalmarket.org; 51 N 12th St; ⊙8am-6pm Mon-Sat, 9am-5pm Sun) Among the many highlights at this massive, multiethnic food market: Beiler's doughnuts, Miller's Twist buttery pretzels, Tommy Dinic's roast pork and Amish meals at Dutch Eating Place. On weekends, due to crowds, think twice about visiting with small children or large groups (at least with the latter, you can fan out to join different lines).

Luke's Lobster SEAFOOD $
(Map p154; 130 S 17th St; sandwiches $8-15; ⊙11am-9pm Sun-Thu, to 10pm Fri & Sat) Part of an East Coast mini-chain serving authentic tastes of Maine, from sustainably sourced seafood. Wash down your buttered-bun lobster roll with a wild-blueberry soda.

Federal Donuts FAST FOOD $
(Map p154; ☎215-665-1101; 1632 Sansom St; doughnuts $1.50, chicken $9; ⊙7am-7pm) All fried, all day: in the morning, the menu is cake doughnuts and quality coffee. After 11am comes the super-crispy Korean-style fried chicken. There's a branch in **University City** (3428 Sansom St; ⊙7am-7pm), next to White Dog Cafe.

Abe Fisher JEWISH $$
(Map p154; ☎215-867-0088; 1623 Sansom St; small plates $10-14, 4-course prix fixe $39; ⊙5-10pm Sun-Thu, to 11pm Fri & Sat) 'Foods of the Jewish diaspora,' taken to a higher, slightly whimsical level. Seltzer flows freely; beets abound. Next door, under the same ownership, is equally hot snack bar **Dizengoff** (1625 Sansom St; hummus from $9; ⊙10:30am-7pm; ✎), for hummus straight out of Tel Aviv.

LOCAL KNOWLEDGE

CLASSIC PHILLY FLAVOR

Philadelphians argue over the nuances of cheesesteaks – hot sandwiches of thin-sliced, griddle-cooked beef on a chewy roll – like biblical scholars parsing Deuteronomy. What a visitor most needs to know is how to order. Say first the kind of cheese – **prov** (provolone), **American** (melty yellow) or **whiz** (molten orange Cheez Whiz!) then **wit** (with) or **widdout** (without), referring to fried onions: 'Prov wit,' for instance, or 'whiz widdout.'

Pat's King of Steaks (1237 E Passyunk Ave; sandwiches $8; ⊙24hr) Pat's invented the cheesesteak, way back in 1930.

Jim's Steaks (Map p154; 400 South St; sandwiches $8; ⊙10am-1am Mon-Thu, to 3am Fri & Sat, from 11am Sun) 'Pizza steak' – topped with tomato sauce – is an option, as are cold hoagies. More comfortable than most, with indoor seats and beer.

Tony Luke's (39 E Oregon Ave; sandwiches $7; ⊙6am-midnight Mon-Thu, to 2am Fri & Sat, 11am-8pm Sun) Famous for its roast pork sandwich with broccoli rabe and provolone. A veggie-only version is great too.

Little Nonna's ITALIAN $$
(Map p154; ☎215-546-2100; 1234 Locust St; mains $20-24; ⌚11:45am-2:45pm & 5-10pm Mon-Sat, 5-10pm Sun) 'Sunday gravy,' that delectable tomato-meat sauce that's a staple of Italian-American tables, is served every night at this homey BYOB.

Parc Brasserie FRENCH $$$
(Map p154; ☎215-545-2262; 227 S 18th St; mains from $23; ⌚7:30am-11pm Sun-Thu, to midnight Fri & Sat) Soak up the elegant Rittenhouse vibe at this enormous, polished bistro right on the park. Dinner is a little steep, but brunch and lunch are good value, and prime people-watching time.

South Philadelphia

The area around the corner of Washington and 11th Sts is chockablock with Vietnamese restaurants, not to mention the Italian Market (p158). There are classic cheesesteak places here too – in sharp contrast with the everything-artisanal restaurant scene further south on E Passyunk Ave.

Sabrina's Cafe BREAKFAST $
(Map p154; 910 Christian St; breakfast $10-14; ⌚8am-5pm; ✎) Sabrina's made its name with brunch: stuffed French toast, gooey pork sandwiches – in short, what you need to ease into the day, in a pretty atmosphere. There's also a branch in **Fairmount** (Map p154; 1804 Callowhill St; ⌚8am-10pm Tue-Sat, to 4pm Sun & Mon), near the art museum.

★**Le Virtù** ITALIAN $$$
(☎215-271-5626; 1927 E Passyunk Ave; mains $24-28; ⌚5-10pm Mon-Sat, 4-9:30pm Sun) The owner of this restaurant is dedicated, obsessively so, to the cuisine of Abruzzo, the region east of Rome, where he long studied with home cooks. He also runs more casual **Brigantessa** (☎267-318-7341; 1520 E Passyunk Ave; pizzas $16, mains $26; ⌚5pm-midnight) up the street, with a slightly broader menu that includes pizzas. Tuesday is BYOB.

University City

Koreana KOREAN $
(3801 Chestnut St; mains $9; ⌚11am-10pm) Satisfying students and others interested in good, inexpensive Korean fare; enter from the parking lot in the back of the shopping plaza.

★**White Dog Cafe** ORGANIC $$
(☎215-386-9224; 3420 Sansom St; dinner mains $18-29; ⌚11:30am-9:30pm Mon-Fri, 10am-10pm Sat, 10am-9pm Sun) If the atmosphere and food here seems more refined than your average farm-to-table restaurant, it's because it has been serving since 1983. Come here for your spring ramps and morels, peak summer tomatoes and plenty more.

Distrito MEXICAN $$
(☎215-222-1657; 3945 Chestnut St; mains $9-30; ⌚11:30am-10pm; 👪) Vibrant pink and lime decor is a fitting backdrop for modern Mexican-ish street snacks. Kids will be delighted to sit in the old VW Bug.

Drinking & Nightlife

As one might expect in a city with strong working-class pride, dive bars are well represented, but so are chic cocktail lounges, wine bars and gastropubs intensely focused on local brews. In fact, Old City boasts the highest concentration of liquor licenses in the US after New Orleans, most on S 2nd and S 3rd Sts. Another party strip is on South St, particularly the east end. The whole craft-beer-and-indie-rock scene can be found in Northern Liberties and Fishtown. Impromptu parties happen the first Friday night of the month in Old City, particularly along N 3rd St, when galleries and shops are open late and serving wine. For gay and lesbian bars, look no further than 'The Gayborhood,' roughly bounded by Chestnut, Pine, Juniper and 11th Sts; it's so established that the street signs are trimmed with rainbows.

Cafes

La Colombe COFFEE
(Map p154; 130 S 19th St; ⌚7am-7pm Mon-Fri, from 8am Sat & Sun) Many cafes now carry the beans from these excellent local coffee roasters (since 1994), but this is the original, in a pleasant spot near Rittenhouse Sq.

Anthony's CAFE
(Map p154; 903 S 9th St; gelato $3.50; ⌚7am-7pm, to 8pm Sat, to 5pm Sun) Classic Italian Market spot for espresso, cannoli and panini.

Bars

★**Monk's Cafe** BAR
(Map p154; www.monkscafe.com; 264 S 16th St; ⌚11:30am-2am, kitchen to 1am) Hop fans crowd this mellow, wood-paneled place for Belgian and American craft beers on tap. There's also

a reasonably priced menu, with typical mussels-and-fries as well as a daily vegan special.

★**Trestle Inn** BAR
(Map p154; ☎267-239-0290; 339 N 11th St; ⏰5pm-2am Wed-Sat) On a dark corner in the so-called 'Eraserhood' (the semi-industrial zone where director David Lynch found inspiration for his film *Eraserhead*), this classed-up old dive has craft cocktails and go-go dancers.

Olde Bar COCKTAIL BAR
(Map p158; ☎215-253-3777; 125 Walnut St; cocktails $10-15; ⏰5pm-midnight, from 4pm Sat, bar 11am-2am) This Jose Garces remake of a classic Philly oyster house (formerly Bookbinders) kept the stately, nostalgic vibe while improving the cocktails as well as the solid regional dishes ($15 to $20), such as snapper soup and pepper pot.

Tria Cafe WINE BAR
(Map p154; 1137 Spruce St; glass wine $9-12; ⏰noon-late) An elegant but informal wine bar with an excellent menu of small plates and sandwiches (snacks $4 to $10). There's also one near **Rittenhouse Sq** (Map p154; 123 S 18th St; ⏰noon-late), and a new-in-2015 **taproom** (Map p154; 2005 Walnut St; ⏰noon-late) that applies the same thoughtfulness to beer.

Dirty Franks BAR
(Map p154; 347 S 13th St; ⏰11am-2am) The regulars at this place call it an 'institution' with some irony. Like many Philly dives, it offers the 'citywide special,' a shot of Jim Beam and a can of PBR for $3.

Fiume BAR
(229 S 45th St; ⏰6pm-2am) To find this unmarked dive in University City, enter next to Abyssinia restaurant). Live rock and bluegrass and good craft beers.

McGillin's Olde Ale House IRISH PUB
(Map p154; www.mcgillins.com; 1310 Drury St; ⏰11am-2am) Philadelphia's oldest continually operating tavern (since 1860) – it remained open as a speakeasy in the Prohibition years – is a chummy Irish-style pub, with karaoke on Wednesdays and Sundays.

Tavern on Camac GAY & LESBIAN
(Map p154; www.tavernoncamac.com; 243 S Camac St; ⏰piano bar 4pm-2am, club 9pm-2am Tue-Sun) One of the longest-established gay bars in Philly, with a piano bar and restaurant downstairs. Upstairs is a small club, called Ascend; Wednesday is ladies' night, Friday and Saturday have DJs.

Paris Wine Bar WINE BAR
(Map p154; 2301 Fairmount Ave; glass wine $8-11; ⏰5pm-midnight Thu-Sat) Handy for a post-museum glass of wine, this French-ish place (with an English-ish pub adjacent) serves PA vintages on tap and light meals ($11 to $15) and has occasional live jazz.

☆ Entertainment

Philadelphia's culture scene hums, both with home-grown talent and great touring acts. For classical music and ballet, ticket prices are low compared with NYC; likewise, you could see a great rock show for $10. And totally free are the daily classical and pop concerts on the lavish 1909 **Wanamaker Organ** (Map p154; www.wanamakerorgan.com; 1300 Market St; ⏰concerts noon Mon-Sat, also 5:30pm Mon, Tue, Thu & Sat, 7pm Wed) FREE, inside Macy's.

In sports, the **Philadelphia Eagles** (www.philadelphiaeagles.com) are legendary, not entirely for the team's (unreliable) performance but for the fervid fans, who party pre-game outside **Lincoln Financial Field** (www.lincolnfinancialfield.com; 1 Lincoln Financial Field Way) in South Philly (pro baseball and basketball stadiums are in the same area). The season runs August through January.

Johnny Brenda's LIVE MUSIC
(☎215-739-9684; www.johnnybrendas.com; 1201 N Frankford Ave; tickets $10-15; ⏰kitchen 11am-1am, showtimes vary; Ⓜ Girard) The hub of Fishtown/Northern Liberties' indie-rock scene, this is a great small venue with a balcony, plus a solid restaurant and bar with equally indie-minded beers.

Kimmel Center PERFORMING ARTS
(Map p154; ☎215-790-5800; www.kimmelcenter.org; 300 S Broad St) The city's most active and prestigious arts institution, this modern concert hall hosts the Philadelphia Orchestra, the Pennyslvania Ballet and more. It also manages the gorgeous old baroque **Academy of Music** (Map p154; 240 S Broad St) – it's a real treat to see a show here.

PhilaMOCA PERFORMING ARTS
(Philadelphia Mausoleum of Contemporary Art; Map p154; ☎267-519-9651; www.philamoca.org; 531 N 12th St) A former tombstone store, then producer Diplo's studios, this eclectic space now hosts movies, live shows, art, comedy and more.

Union Transfer CONCERT VENUE
(Map p154; ☎215-232-2100; www.utphilly.com; 1026 Spring Garden St; tickets $15-40) Opened in 2011, this music hall is one of the best spaces for bigger-name bands, with eclectic booking and good bar service.

Chris' Jazz Club JAZZ
(Map p154; ☎215-568-3131; www.chrisjazzcafe.com; 1421 Sansom St; cover $10-20) Showcasing local talent along with national greats, this intimate space features a 4pm piano happy hour Tuesday through Friday and good bands Monday through Saturday nights.

World Cafe Live LIVE MUSIC
(Map p154; ☎215-222-1400; www.worldcafelive.com; 3025 Walnut St; cover $10-40; ⏰from 11am Mon-Fri, from 5pm Sat & Sun) Home to U Penn's radio station, WXPN, this former factory has upstairs and downstairs performance spaces for jazz, folk and global acts, plus good food.

ℹ Information

Hospital of the University of Pennsylvania (☎800-789-7366; www.pennmedicine.org; 800 Spruce St; ⏰24hr) Philadelphia's largest medical facility.

Independence Visitor Center (Map p158; ☎800-537-7676; www.phlvisitorcenter.com; 599 Market St; ⏰8:30am-6pm Sep-May, 8:30am-7pm Jun-Aug) Run by the city and the National Park Service, the center covers the national park and all of the sights in Philadelphia.

Philadelphia Magazine (www.phillymag.com) Monthly glossy, with excellent food writing by Jason Sheehan.

Philadelphia Visitor Center (www.phlvisitorcenter.com) The city tourism service has convenient branches at Logan Sq (Map p154; ☎267-514-4761; www.phlvisitorcenter.com; 200 N 18th St; ⏰11am-4pm May-Sep) and JFK Plaza (Map p154; ☎215-683-0246; 1599 JFK Blvd; ⏰10am-5pm Mon-Sat).

Philadelphia Weekly (www.philadelphiaweekly.com) Free alternative rag available at street boxes around town.

ℹ Getting There & Away

AIR

Philadelphia International Airport (PHL; ☎215-937-6937; www.phl.org; 8000 Essington Ave; 🚊Airport Line), 7 miles southwest of Center City, is a hub for American Airlines, and served by direct international flights.

BUS

Greyhound (☎215-931-4075; www.greyhound.com), **Peter Pan Bus Lines** (www.peterpanbus.com) and **NJ Transit** (☎973-275-5555; www.njtransit.com) all depart from the **central bus station** (Map p154; 1001 Filbert St) downtown, near the convention center; Greyhound goes nationwide, Peter Pan focuses on the northeast and NJ Transit gets you to New Jersey. The former two offer cheaper online fares; Greyhound to Washington, DC, for example, can be $14.50 (3½ hours).

From near 30th St Station, **Megabus** (Map p154; www.us.megabus.com; JFK Blvd & N 30th St) serves major cities in the northeast, and Toronto. For NYC and Boston, Greyhound subsidiary **Bolt Bus** (Map p154; ☎877-265-8287; www.boltbus.com; JFK Blvd & N 30th St) has the roomiest buses; fares to NYC (2½ hours) can be as low as $7 when booked online.

CAR & MOTORCYCLE

From the north and south, I-95 (Delaware Expwy) follows the east edge of the city along the Delaware River, with several exits for Center City. In the north of the city, I-276 (Pennsylvania Turnpike) runs east over the river to connect with the New Jersey Turnpike.

TRAIN

Just west of downtown across the Schuylkill, beautiful neoclassical **30th St Station** (www.amtrak.com; 30th & Market Sts) is a major hub. From here, Amtrak provides service on its Northeast Corridor line to New York City ($54 to $196, one to 1½ hours) and Boston ($96 to $386, five to 5¾ hours), and Washington, DC ($53 to $242, two hours), as well as to Lancaster (from $16, one hour) and Pittsburgh (from $55, 7½ hours).

A slower but cheaper way to get to NYC is on regional **Septa** (☎215-580-7800; www.septa.org) to Trenton ($9, 50 minutes), then NJ Transit to NYC's Penn Station ($15.50, 1½ hours).

ℹ Getting Around

Septa (☎215-580-7800; www.septa.org) operates Philadelphia's transit system, including the Airport Line train ($8.75, 25 minutes, every 30 minutes), which stops in University City and Center City. A taxi to the center costs a flat fare of $28.50.

Downtown, it's barely 2 miles between the Delaware and the Schuylkill, so you can walk most places. To rest your feet or travel further afield, choose from a web of Septa buses, two subway lines and a trolley (fare $2.25). Purchase multiple tokens (phasing out in 2016) or the stored-value Key card (phasing in) for discounted fares. Market St is the main artery – hop on buses here to cross the center, or go underground to take the trolley to University City. In high tourist seasons, the purple **Phlash** (www.ridephillyphlash.com; ride/day pass $2/5; ⏰10am-6pm daily May-Aug & Dec, Fri-Sun only Sep-Nov) bus makes a loop around major tourist sites; pay on board with exact change.

Philly's bike-share system is **Indego** (☎844-446-3346; www.rideindego.com). Walk-up rates are $4 for 30 minutes; a 30-day membership is a steal at $15, but you must order the key ahead of time.

Cabs, especially around City Center, are easy to hail. The flag drop or fare upon entry is $2.70, then $2.30 per mile or portion thereof. All licensed taxis have GPS and most accept credit cards.

Pennsylvania Dutch Country

Lancaster County and the broader area roughly between Reading and the Susquehanna River is the center of the so-called Pennyslvania Dutch community (now often corrected to Pennsylvania German). These are myriad religious orders and cultures, of Germanic roots and established here since the 18th century. Amish, Mennonites and German Baptist (Brethren) are the best known. One common cultural thread: all are devoted to various degrees of low-tech, plain living.

Somewhat paradoxically, this simple life, with its picturesque horse-drawn buggies and ox teams tilling fields, attracts busloads of visitors and is spawning an astoundingly kitschy tourist industry that can be off-putting. But if you get onto the back roads, you can appreciate the quiet these religious orders have preserved. And some of that kitsch is undeniably fun.

The city of **Lancaster**, population 60,000, has a nice old downtown and some good restaurants that use the fruits of the surrounding farmland; its First Friday party on Prince St draws a good local crowd. The main PA Dutch tourist zone is east of here: along Rte 30 and Old Philadelphia Pike (Rte 340), between **Ronks**, **Bird-in-Hand**, **Intercourse** and **Paradise**. The stretch is essentially farmland interrupted by strip malls and attractions such as kiddie theme park Dutch Wonderland, and souvenir shop Dutch Haven, shaped like a windmill (which does nevertheless make a killer shoo-fly pie and some serious birch beer).

South of Lancaster, **Strasburg** and **Christiana** are pleasant tiny towns, as are, to the north, **Ephrata** and **Lititz**. Lititz is home to Wilbur Chocolates, what locals prefer to giant Hershey's (based north of here), and America's first pretzel factory, Sturgis. Ephrata is the headquarters of Ten Thousand Villages, a massive Mennonite-run fair-trade imports store with branches all over.

Sights

★Strasburg Railroad TRAIN

(☎866-725-9666; www.strasburgrailroad.com; 301 Gap Rd, Ronks; coach class adult/child $14/8; ⏲multiple trips daily, times vary by season; 👪) It's only a 45-minute ride to Paradise and back, but this steam train is a treat, with grand old carriages (wood-stove-heated in winter) running on a line laid down in 1832. Package tickets are available for the **Railroad Museum of Pennsylvania** (☎717-687-8628; www.rrmuseumpa.org; 300 Gap Rd, Ronks; adult/child $10/8; ⏲9am-5pm Mon-Sat, from noon Sun, closed Sun & Mon winter; 👪) across the road, which has scores of mechanical marvels to admire.

For a fully rail-themed trip, book a night in a train car motel room at the **Red Caboose** (☎717-687-5000; www.redcaboosemotel.com; 312 Paradise Ln, Ronks; s/d from $95/129; ❄📶👪), or just visit its **restaurant** (☎717-687-7759; breakfasts $8, dinners $14; ⏲7:30am-3pm Tue & Wed, to 8pm Thu-Sat, to 4pm Sun).

Landis Valley Museum MUSEUM

(☎717-569-0401; www.landisvalleymuseum.org; 2451 Kissel Hill Rd, Lancaster; adult/child $12/8; ⏲9am-5pm, from noon Sun, closed Mon & Tue Jan-Feb) Based on an 18th-century village, this open-air museum is the best way to get an overview of the early PA Dutch culture and Mennonites in particular. Costumed staff are on hand to demonstrate tinsmithing, for instance, and there's a beautiful crafts exhibit.

Ephrata Cloister MUSEUM

(☎717-733-6600; www.ephratacloister.org; 632 W Main St, Ephrata; adult/child $10/6; ⏲9am-5pm, from noon Sun, closed Mon & Tue Jan-Feb, tours hourly 10am-3pm) One of the area's myriad breakaway religious sects established this community in 1732; despite celibacy vows and infighting, it lasted until 1934. Now it has an almost ghost-town feel. You can walk around alone, but ideally join a tour, to see inside all the buildings.

Lancaster Mennonite Historical Society MUSEUM

(☎717-393-9745; www.lmhs.org; 2215 Millstream Rd, Lancaster; museum $5; ⏲8:30am-4:30pm Tue-Sat) The small museum here displays beautiful glass and woodwork along with the story

WORTH A TRIP

GETTYSBURG

This town 145 miles west of Philadelphia, now quite tranquil and pretty, is synonymous with one of the bloodiest battles of the Civil War. Over three days in July 1863, some 8000 people were killed. Later that year, President Abraham Lincoln delivered his Gettysburg Address ('Four score and seven years ago...'), reinforcing the war's mission of equality.

Gettysburg National Military Park (☑717-334-1124; www.nps.gov/gett; 1195 Baltimore Pike; museum adult/child $12.50/8.50, ranger tours per vehicle $65, bus tours adult/child $30/18; ⊗museum 8am-6pm Apr-Oct, to 5pm Nov-Mar, grounds 6am-10pm Apr-Oct, to 7pm Nov-Mar) covers 8 sq miles of land marked with monuments and trails. The museum at the visitor center is a must-see, for the awe-inspiring cyclorama – a life-size, 360-degree painting – of Pickett's Charge, the especially disastrous battle on the last day. Originally made in 1884, the painting was restored and reinstalled in 2008, with a dramatic light show and narration. Out in the park, you can explore on your own, or on a bus tour or – most recommended – on a two-hour ranger-led tour in your own car.

Gettysburg itself is a pretty town, worth spending the night in, but plan ahead in summer, especially in July, when the town is mobbed with battle reenactors. For accommodations, try **Brickhouse Inn** (☑717-338-9337; www.brickhouseinn.com; 452 Baltimore St; r from $149; P❋ 🛜), two adjacent old buildings with a lovely back garden; the owners take breakfast so seriously there's even a pie course. **Dobbin House** (☑717-334-2100; 89 Steinwehr Ave; sandwiches $10, mains $25; ⊗tavern 11:30am-9pm, main restaurant from 5pm), built in 1776, is an inn and restaurant. The food is average, but the setting, all candlelit and creaky, is great. The tavern in the basement has a cheaper bar menu, with burgers and soups.

---

of how Mennonites established themselves in this area. There's a well-stocked shop and bookstore too.

👉 Tours

Aaron & Jessica's Buggy Rides   TOUR
(☑717-768-8828; www.amishbuggyrides.com; 3121 Old Philadelphia Pike, Bird-in-Hand; adult/child tours from $10/6; ⊗9am-5pm Mon-Sat; 🚼) Hop in one of those black horse-drawn buggies, for a 30-minute cruise through the country or an hour-long farm tour. Drivers are Amish, Mennonite or Brethren and open to questions.

🛏 Sleeping

★Quiet Haven   MOTEL $
(☑717-397-6231; www.quiethavenmotel.com; 2556 Siegrist Rd, Ronks; r from $76) If your vision of a PA Dutch getaway is sitting in a rocking chair and gazing out over farmland, book in at this family-owned motel, surrounded by green fields. Most of the 15 rooms still have a hint of 1960s flair.

A Farm Stay   ACCOMMODATION SERVICE $
(www.afarmstay.com; r from $80; 🚼) This website is a network of 20 or so lodging options on area farmland – some more typical B&Bs and others full working farms where guests are welcome to pet goats and milk cows.

★General Sutter Inn   INN $$
(☑717-626-2115; www.generalsutterinn.com; 14 East Main St, Lititz; s/d/ste from $70/110/185; ❋🛜) At this 18th-century inn, 10 rooms are furnished with tasteful antiques, and on the incongruous top floor, six suites have a loose rock-and-roll theme. Downstairs is the popular Bulls Head Pub, for Scotch eggs and cask ales.

Fulton Steamboat Inn   HOTEL $$
(☑717-299-9999; www.fultonsteamboatinn.com; 1 Hartman Bridge Rd, Lancaster; r from $140; ❋🛜🏊) Even if you know the inventor of the steamboat was born in this area, this nautical-themed hotel is a bit gimmicky. But the brass fixtures and flowery wallpaper are all well kept, the rooms are comfortable, and there's even an indoor pool.

Cork Factory   BOUTIQUE HOTEL $$
(☑717-735-2075; www.corkfactoryhotel.com; 480 New Holland Ave, Lancaster; r from $159; ❋🛜) An abandoned brick behemoth now houses this stylish hotel. It's a short drive from downtown.

🍴 Eating

Local aficionados agree, the best PA Dutch cooking is done for church suppers. Keep an eye out for special events.

★**Katie's Kitchen** AMERICAN $
(200 Hartman Bridge Rd, Ronks; mains $8; 7:30am-7:30pm) This typical PA Dutch diner serves locals and tourists alike with dishes such as creamed chipped beef and 'egg-in-the-nest.' Food is freshly cooked, and fortunately available in half-portions.

★**Tomato Pie Cafe** SANDWICHES $
(717-627-1762; 23 N Broad St, Lititz; mains $8; 7am-9pm Mon-Sat;) The creative, fresh food and the complex coffee drinks wouldn't be out of place in a city, but the atmosphere is pure friendly small town.

Central Market MARKET $
(717-735-6890; www.centralmarketlancaster.com; 23 N Market St, Lancaster; snacks from $2; 6am-4pm Tue & Fri, to 2pm Sat) The produce and food stalls at this indoor market represent a great cross-section of Lancaster. You can pick up fresh PA Dutch sausages or horseradish, as well as Thai noodles and Lebanese salads.

Bird-in-Hand Farmers Market MARKET $
(717-393-9674; 2710 Old Philadelphia Pike; pretzels $2, lunches $8; 8:30am-5:30pm Fri & Sat, also Wed Apr-Nov, Thu Jul-Oct) A one-stop shop of Dutch Country highlights, both genuine and tourist-friendly. Load up on tasty homemade jams, pastries, pretzels, beef jerky and more. Two lunch counters serve meals.

Dienner's BUFFET $
(2855 Lincoln Hwy, Ronks; dinner $11-15; 7am-6pm Mon-Thu, to 8pm Fri & Sat) Pace yourself at this all-you-can-eat PA Dutch extravaganza: one of the three buffet lines is dedicated to sweets. The food tends toward bland, but everyone will find something to like; daily specials like chicken pot pie are generally good.

★**Lancaster Brewing Co** PUB FOOD $$
(302 N Plum St; mains $16-24; 11:30am-10pm;) This brewery, established in 1995, is a local favorite. The restaurant serves hearty but sophisticated food – lamb chops with tzatziki, say, and housemade sausage. But you can't beat specials like $5 all-you-can-eat wings.

Maison EUROPEAN $$$
(717-293-5060; 230 N Prince St, Lancaster; mains $26-30; 5-11pm Wed-Sat;) A husband-and-wife team run this homey but meticulous place downtown, giving local farm products a rustic Italian-French treatment: pork braised in milk, fried squash blossoms, handmade gnocchi, depending on the season.

Information

Discover Lancaster Visitors Center (800-723-8824; www.padutchcountry.com; 501 Greenfield Rd; 10am-4pm, to 5pm summer) Just off Rte 30, with info on all of Pennsylvania, good area maps and free coffee, which goes with cinnamon rolls sold in the parking lot.

Getting There & Around

A car is the most practical way; get a good map (mobile service is poor) and take smaller roads. If you have time, you could go Amish-style: Amtrak serves the **Lancaster train station** (800-872-7245; www.amtrak.com; 53 McGovern Ave, Lancaster) with frequent trains from Philadelphia ($16, 1¼ hours), but only once-daily service to Pittsburgh ($51, 6¼ hours). Lancaster's bus system, **RRTA** (Red Rose Transit Authority; 717-393-3315; www.redrosetransit.com; 225 North Queen St, Lancaster; fare from $1.70, transfer from $.05), covers the greater county. Bike rental is a possibility, though the terrain is hilly and road shoulders thin or nonexistent; **Intercourse Bike Works** (717-929-0327; www.intercourse-bikeworks.com; 3614 Old Philadelphia Pike, Intercourse; 10am-5pm Mon-Sat) rents bikes and leads tours many summer Saturdays.

Pennsylvania Wilds

North-central Pennsylvania, called 'the Wilds,' is largely deep forest, with an occasional regal building or grand mansion, remnants of a time when lumber, coal and oil brought wealth to this now little-visited patch of the state. Several museums (in **Titusville**, **Bradford** and **Galeton**) tell the boom and bust story. Since the bust, this swath of 12 counties has reverted to its wild state; much of the area is national forest or state park land.

Scenic **Rte 6** cuts through east–west, with the tiny college town of **Mansfield** as an eastern gateway. Just west of here, **Pine Creek Gorge** cuts south; its deeper end (1450ft) is down near Waterville, but it's more accessible, with good views and trails along the rim and down into the canyon, on the north end at **Colton Point State Park** (570-724-3061; www.visitpaparks.com; 4797 Rte 660, Wellsboro) FREE. Follow signs outside the pretty, gas-lamp-lit town of **Wellsboro**.

Further west, stop at **Kinzua Bridge Skywalk** (814-965-2646; www.visitanf.com; 1721 Lindholm Rd, Mt Jewett; dawn-dusk) FREE, a

300ft-high train viaduct, partially destroyed in 2003 by a tornado and now an observation point with an unnerving glass floor and views of the ruined steel piers in the valley below.

Deeper in the Wilds is **Cherry Springs State Park** (☎814-435-5010; www.visitpaparks.com; 4639 Cherry Springs Rd, Coudersport; campsites from $17). Due its position on a mountaintop, it is one of the best places for stargazing east of the Mississippi, and people book the campsites well ahead in July and August, when the Milky Way is almost directly overhead.

Sleeping & Eating

Mansfield Inn MOTEL $
(☎570-662-2136; www.mansfieldinn.com; 26 S Main St, Mansfield; r from $60; ❄📶) There may be more charming B&Bs deeper in the PA Wilds, but this well-maintained motel is hard to beat for straight-ahead value.

Lodge at Glendorn LODGE $$$
(☎800-843-8568; www.glendorn.com; 1000 Glendorn Dr, Bradford; r from $550) Legacy of the Wilds' former industrial wealth, this 1200-acre estate was developed by an early 20th-century oil baron. Its 'big house' and log cabins (all with wood-burning fireplaces) are now the state's finest resort. The restaurant is excellent, and the nightly fee includes activities from skeet shooting to curling.

Yorkholo Brewing AMERICAN $
(☎570-662-0241; 19 N Main St, Mansfield; mains $11-14; ⏲4-10pm Mon & Tue, 11am-10pm Wed-Sat, to 9pm Sun; 🖉) A welcome alternative to standard diner food in this area, this brick-walled brewpub has fresh salads, creative pizzas and some excellent Belgian-style beers.

Pittsburgh

For decades in the second half of the 20th century, Pittsburgh looked like it would be another notch in America's rust belt, a desolate city where the once-churning steel mills and blast furnaces had all shuttered. But thanks to latent wealth and some creative thinking, it has earned a reputation for being one of the more livable small cities in the country. It has a distinct topography, a mass of green hills (the climate is very rainy) rising straight up from the Monongahela and Allegheny Rivers, which converge here and join the Ohio, all connected by picturesque bridges – Istanbul in western Pennyslvania, if you squint hard enough. It's a far more cultured city than a population of 300,000 would suggest, with top-notch museums and universities, abundant greenery and several bustling neighborhoods with lively restaurant and bar scenes.

Carnegie is the biggest name in Pittsburgh – Scottish-born Andrew modernized steel production, and his legacy is still synonymous with the city and its many cultural and educational institutions. Second-biggest: Heinz, of ketchup fame, a company established here in 1869.

Sights & Activities

Points of interest in Pittsburgh are scattered in every neighborhood, and because of the hills, it's a bit difficult to walk between them. You could drive, but the bus goes everywhere and gives you a chance to enjoy the views.

Downtown & the Strip District

The so-called Golden Triangle where the Monongahela and Allegheny converge is Pittsburgh's center of finance, business and high culture. Every Friday from May to October, there's a farmers market in **Market Sq**, a slick modern piazza surrounded by restaurants. Just south is PPG Place, a clutch of dazzling 1980s glass office towers, with **ice skating** (www.ppgplace.com; adult/child $8/7, skate rental $3; ⏲mid-Nov–Feb) in winter. Northeast of downtown, along the Allegheny, are the warehouses of the **Strip District**, a longtime hub for wholesalers and now a lively stretch of ethnic food stores and cafes; it's even livelier on Saturdays, when street vendors add to the mix.

Fort Pitt Museum MUSEUM
(☎412-281-9284; www.heinzhistorycenter.org; 601 Commonwealth Pl; adult/child $6/3; ⏲10am-5pm) This museum tells the story of the French and Indian War of the mid-18th century, which brought Pittsburgh into being. The surrounding waterfront, a state park, is lovely on a summer day.

Heinz History Center MUSEUM
(☎412-454-6000; www.heinzhistorycenter.org; 1212 Smallman St; adult/child incl Sports Museum $15/6; ⏲10am-5pm) Local history and lore is shared with verve and color – there's even an exhibit dedicated to children's TV host and native son Fred Rogers. It also contains

the **Western Pennsylvania Sports Museum**, focusing on Pittsburgh's many beloved champs.

North Side

This part of town across the Allegheny River is mobbed when the Steelers (football, at **Heinz Field**) or Pirates (baseball, at **PNC Park**) are playing; bridges from downtown close to cars at this time. But this is also where the city's best art museums are, and the pretty **Mexican War Streets** neighborhood (streets are named for battles) is a pleasant place to stroll among the restored row houses – look for colorful **Randyland** on Arch St.

★Andy Warhol Museum MUSEUM

(☎412-237-8300; www.warhol.org; 117 Sandusky St; adult/child $20/10, 5-10pm Fri $10/5; ⏲10am-5pm Tue-Sun, to 10pm Fri) This six-story museum celebrates Pittsburgh's coolest native son, who moved to NYC, got a nose job and made himself famous with pop art. The exhibits start with Warhol's earliest drawings and commercial illustrations and include a simulated Velvet Underground happening, a DIY 'screen test,' and pieces of Warhol's extensive knickknack collection.

★Mattress Factory ARTS CENTER

(☎412-231-3169; www.mattress.org; 500 Sampsonia Way; adult $20; ⏲10am-5pm Tue-Sat, 1-5pm Sun, café 11:30am-3pm Tue-Sat) Since 1977, this art space has hosted the absolute avant-garde. It now occupies several neighborhood buildings, and always has something surprising on. Note the good café here too, as there's a shortage of food in the area.

National Aviary ZOO

(☎412-323-7235; www.aviary.org; 700 Arch St; adult/child $14/12; ⏲10am-5pm; 👪) Often overlooked due to its proximity to the excellent science center and children's museum, this is nonetheless a fantastic opportunity to see all kinds of birds up close and very personal, in big open habitats.

Carnegie Science Center MUSEUM

(☎412-237-3400; www.carnegiesciencecenter.org; 1 Allegheny Ave; adult/child $19/12, IMAX & special exhibits extra; ⏲10am-5pm, to 7pm Sat; 👪) A cut above the average science museum, with exhibits on everything from outer space to candy, this is a favorite with Pittsburgh parents.

South Side & Mt Washington

Across the Monongahela River is the South Side, which rises steeply to a ridge called Mt Washington. The neighborhood called the **South Side Slopes** is a fascinating community of houses on the incline, accessible via steep, winding roads and hundreds of stairs. Most visitors come for the dozens of bars in the flatland along E Carson St.

★Monongahela & Duquesne Inclines TRAM

(www.duquesneincline.org; one-way adult/child $2.50/1.25; ⏲5:30am-12:45am Mon-Sat, from 7am Sun) These two funiculars, built in the late 19th century, are Pittsburgh icons, zipping up the steep slope of Mt Washington every five to 10 minutes. They provide commuters a quick connection and they give visitors great city views, especially at night. You can make a loop, going up one, walking along aptly named Grandview Ave (about 1 mile, or take bus 40) and coming down the other.

If you ride just one, make it the Duquesne (du-*kane*). At the top, you can pay 50¢ to see the gears and cables at work. Outside the station, **Altius** (☎412-904-4442; 1230 Grandview Ave; mains $28-44, bar snacks $8-18; ⏲5-10pm Mon-Thu, to 11pm Fri & Sat, to 9pm Sun) restaurant is a good place to enjoy the view over a drink.

Oakland & Around

The University of Pittsburgh and Carnegie Mellon University are here, and the surrounding streets are packed with cheap eateries, cafes, shops and student homes.

Carnegie Museums MUSEUM

(☎412-622-3131; www.carnegiemuseums.org; 4400 Forbes Ave; adult/child both museums $20/12; ⏲10am-5pm Tue-Sat, from noon Sun; 👪) Founded in 1895, these neighboring institutions are both tremendous troves of knowledge. The **Carnegie Museum of Art** has European treasures and an excellent architectural collection, while the **Carnegie Museum of Natural History** features a complete *Tyrannosaurus rex* skeleton and beautiful old dioramas.

Cathedral of Learning TOWER

(☎412-624-6001; 4200 Fifth Ave; audio tour adult/child weekends only $4/2; ⏲9am-4pm Mon-Sat, from 11am Sun) FREE Soaring 42 stories, this Gothic tower at the center of University of Pittsburgh is a city landmark. Visit to see

DON'T MISS

FALLINGWATER

A Frank Lloyd Wright masterpiece, **Fallingwater** (724-329-8501; www.fallingwater.org; 1491 Mill Run Rd, Mill Run; adult/child $25/18, grounds only $8; tours Thu-Tue mid-Mar–Nov, weekends only Dec, closed Jan & Feb) is south of Pittsburgh, and a visit here makes a good day out in the pretty area known as the Laurel Highlands. Completed in 1939 as a weekend retreat for the Kaufmanns, owners of a Pittsburgh department store, Fallingwater melds elegantly with the natural setting, including the stream that runs through. It is furnished largely as the Kaufmanns left it. Access is by guided tour only; reservations are recommended. The attractive forested grounds open at 8:30am, and there's a good cafe (it closes before the last tour ends).

A 20-minute drive away – crossing the pretty Youghiogheny River, where you can go rafting – is a smaller Wright home, **Kentuck Knob** (724-329-1901; www.kentuckknob.com; 723 Kentuck Rd, Chalk Hill; adult/child $22/16; tours daily Mar-Nov, weekends in Dec, closed Jan & Feb), which he designed when he was in his 80s. Nowhere near as extravagant, as it adheres more closely to his austere Usonian principles, it is nonetheless interesting for its use of hexagons – and it is seldom crowded. Tours last about an hour and include a jaunt through the current owners' sculpture garden.

You can even spend a night nearby at **Polymath Park** (877-833-7829; www.franklloydwrightovernight.net; 187 Evergreen Ln, Acme; house from $199 ;), a kind of mini-resort with one Wright home and three others designed by his apprentices. Don't expect loads of Wright flair – these are all Usonia-style homes, and the furniture is not Wright's designs. Still, it's a pretty area and a rare opportunity for architecture buffs. The homes are open for tours, and there's a restaurant here too – though you could also stop for an exceptionally good fish sandwich en route at **Johnny L's Sandwich Works** (1240 S Main St, Greensburg; sandwiches $7; 11am-11pm Mon-Sat).

the delightful Nationality Rooms, themed classrooms ranging from Russian to Syrian to African.

Frick Art & Historical Center MUSEUM
(412-371-0600; www.thefrickpittsburgh.org; 7227 Reynolds St; tours adult/child $12/6; 10am-5pm Tue-Sun; P1, 71C) FREE Henry Clay Frick, of Manhattan's Frick Museum fame, built his steel fortune in Pittsburgh. This Frick shows a small art collection (beautiful medieval icons), plus his cars. For more art and general splendor, join a tour of Clayton, the family mansion. The cafe here is excellent; reserve.

Phipps Conservatory GARDENS
(412-622-6914; www.phipps.conservatory.org; 1 Schenley Park; adult/child $15/11; 9:30am-5pm, to 10pm Fri;) An impressive steel-and-glass greenhouse with beautifully designed and curated gardens, at the northwest corner of Schenley Park.

Squirrel Hill & Shadyside

These long-established wealthier neighborhoods have an almost village-like atmosphere, each with a central business street lined with boutiques and cafés. **Squirrel Hill** is home to Pittsburgh's large Jewish community, the city's best kosher eateries, butchers and Judaica shops. In **Shadyside**, Walnut St is the bustling main strip. The leafy campus of **Chatham University**, located between the two neighborhoods, is a nice place to stroll.

Lawrenceville, Bloomfield & East Liberty

Formerly gritty Lawrenceville, along the Allegheny northeast of the Strip District, has become one of the city's coolest neighborhoods. Butler St from around 34th St all the way up to 54th St is a spotty strip of shops, galleries, studios, bars and eateries on every hipster's radar. East of Allegheny Cemetery (a trove of history itself) are the slightly gentrifying Garfield and Bloomfield neighborhoods, still both strong Polish and Italian enclaves. Due east is the intensely overhauled East Liberty area, now home to a Google office.

Center for PostNatural History MUSEUM
(412-223-7698; www.postnatural.org; 4913 Penn Ave; admission by donation; 6-8pm 1st Fri of month, noon-4pm Sun & by appointment) FREE 'Postnatural history,' according to the artist founder of this quirky museum, is the field

of plants and animals manipulated by humankind. Learn all about spider-silk-making goats, selective breeding and more.

Tours

Rivers of Steel TOUR
(412-464-4020; www.riversofsteel.com; 623 E 8th Ave, Homestead; tours adult/child $20/12.50; museum 10am-4pm Mon-Fri, Carrie Furnace tours 10am & 11am Sat May-Oct, also 10am Fri Jun-Aug) This organization leads tours of Carrie Blast Furnace, a huge and derelict structure on the riverfront. At the group's offices in Homestead, there's a neat free museum about the area's industrial labor history. Great info online too.

Alan Irvine Storyteller Tours TOUR
(412-508-2077; www.alanirvine.com; tours $15) This historian brings the city's past to life in a journey through several neighborhoods.

'Burgh Bits & Bites TOUR
(412-901-7150; www.burghfoodtour.com; tours $39) These food tours through various neighborhoods are a fun way to discover the city's unique ethnic eats.

Pittsburgh History & Landmarks Foundation TOUR
(412-471-5808; www.phlf.org; 100 W Station Sq Dr; some tours free, others from $5) This group runs a free walking tour from Market Sq on Fridays at noon, among other excursions.

Sleeping

Many hotels cater to business travelers, so rates are significantly lower on weekends. Pittsburgh has no real hostel, although there seem to be eternal plans for one. An Ace Hotel was set to open in East Liberty in 2016.

★ **Priory** INN $$
(412-231-3338; www.thepriory.com; 614 Pressley St; s/d/ste from $105/170/235; P ❄ ☎) The monks had it good when this was still a Catholic monastery: spacious rooms, high ceilings, a fireplace in the parlor. Breakfast, with its pastries and cold cuts, is reminiscent of a European hostel. It's on the North Side, in the historic-but-scruffy Deutschtown area.

Friendship Suites APARTMENT $$
(412-392-1935; www.friendshipsuites.com; 301 Stratford Ave; r/ste/apt $129/145/175; ❄ ☎) In several neighboring buildings, these fully furnished small apartments on the edge of East Liberty are not bursting with style, but they're good value and close to transportation.

Morning Glory Inn B&B $$
(412-721-9174; www.gloryinn.com; 2119 Sarah St; r/ste from $155/190; P ❄ ☎) An Italianate-style Victorian brick town house, the Morning Glory is in the heart of the lively South Side. The overall decor (white wicker, floral patterns) might strike some as too frilly, but there's a charming backyard patio and delicious breakfasts.

Parador Inn B&B $$
(412-231-4800; www.theparadorinn.com; 939 Western Ave; r $160; P ❄ ☎) A Victorian mansion renovated with a Caribbean color sensibility, this North Side inn delights the eyes in each of the nine rooms.

Mansions on Fifth B&B $$
(412-381-5105; www.mansionsonfifth.com; 5105 Fifth Ave; r from $225; P ❄ ☎) These two early 20th-century homes are convenient to the University of Pittsburgh and the Carnegie Museums. Rooms are spacious and plush, but it's the stained glass, intricate tile and other details that set it apart.

Monaco DESIGN HOTEL $$$
(412-471-1170; www.monaco-pittsburgh.com; 620 William Penn Pl; r from $279; P ❄ ☎) The cool Kimpton chain opened this place in 2015, done up in eye-popping colors. Enthusiastic staff and a good restaurant make it the best value downtown.

Omni William Penn Hotel HOTEL $$$
(412-281-7100; www.omnihotels.com; 530 William Penn Pl; r from $299; P ❄ ☎) Pittsburgh's stateliest old hotel, built by Henry Frick, has great public spaces, but the rooms feel a bit stuck in the '90s. Worth booking if you can find it at a discount.

Eating

E Carson St on the South Side has the highest concentration of restaurants, but the Strip District comes a close second. As in many categories, Lawrenceville has the most up-and-coming activity. Catering to a large Catholic population, many Pittsburgh restaurants serve fish on Fridays, and fried-fish sandwiches are especially popular.

Downtown & the Strip District

Grazing is easy in the Strip, with all kind of food vendors and one-of-a-kind markets such as mega-grocery Wholey, Greek Stamoolis Brothers and the epic cheese counter at Pennsylvania Macaroni (though note many businesses are closed Sunday).

Original Oyster House SEAFOOD $
(20 Market Sq; mains $9; 10am-10pm Mon-Sat, 11am-7pm Sun) Operating in one form or another since 1870, this place often has a line out the door for its fish sandwiches. It is not quite the best in the area, but the bar side is a historical gem. Cash only.

Enrico Biscotti Cafe ITALIAN $
(2022 Penn Ave; mains $10; 11am-3pm Mon-Fri, from 7am Sat) Bread, pizza and torta rustica round out the menu alongside the biscotti. Charismatic owner Larry Laguttata offers a bread-baking class ($85) every Sunday.

Prantl's BAKERY $
(438 Market St; cake slice $3; 7am-6pm Mon-Fri, 9am-4pm Sat, 10am-3pm Sun) Don't leave Pittsburgh without tasting burnt almond torte, Prantl's signature. Also in **Shadyside** (5525 Walnut St; 7:30am-6pm Tue-Sat, 9am-4pm Sun & Mon).

Primanti Bros FAST FOOD $
(412-263-2142; www.primantibros.com; 46 18th St; sandwiches $6; 24hr) The sandwiches Pittsburghers miss when they move away: hot, greasy and always stuffed with french fries and coleslaw. Other outlets are in **Oakland** (3803 Forbes Ave; 10am-midnight, to 3am Thu-Sat), **Market Sq downtown** (2 S Market Sq; 10am-midniight, to 2am Fri & Sat) and **South Side** (1832 E Carson St; 11am-2am, from 10am Sat & Sun).

Pamela's DINER $
(60 21st St; mains $6-9; 7am-3pm Mon-Sat, from 8am Sun) Unpretentious Pamela's has a few branches around the city, all with a classic chrome diner look and its signature lacy-thin pancakes. Cash only.

★ **Bar Marco** ITALIAN $$
(412-471-1900; 2216 Penn Ave; mains $18-26, tasting menu $75; 5-11pm Wed-Sun, to 10pm Mon, also 10am-3pm Sat & Sun;) One of the city's more sophisticated kitchens, with an excellent brunch too. Snack in the bar or reserve in the Wine Room, for the chef's great-value tasting menu. Refreshing no-tipping policy.

North Side

Wilson's Bar-B-Q BARBECUE $
(700 N Taylor Ave; mains $8.50; noon-8pm Mon-Sat) Your clothes will smell like a campfire after a plastic-plate meal in this zero-frills place, but the ribs can't be beat.

South Side

Zenith VEGAN $
(412-481-4833; 86 S 26th St; mains $7-10; 11:30am-8:30pm Thu-Sat, 11am-2:30pm Sun;) A meal here is like eating in an antique shop, as everything, including the Formica tables, is for sale. The buffet Sunday brunch ($11.50) draws a great community of regulars.

Dish Osteria Bar ITALIAN $$
(412-390-2012; www.dishosteria.com; 128 S 17th St; mains $20-26; 5pm-2am Mon-Sat, kitchen till midnight) An intimate locals' fave, with sometimes extravagant Mediterranean dishes such as fettuccine with lamb ragù.

Oakland

★ **Conflict Kitchen** FAST FOOD $
(412-802-8417; 221 Schenley Dr; mains $8-12; 11am-6pm) This takeout stand near the Cathedral of Learning reinvents itself periodically, cooking food from another country the US has issues with. It has so far been Afghani, Palestinian and Cuban, among other cuisines.

Original Hot Dog Shop FAST FOOD $
(412-621-7388; 3901 Forbes Ave; sandwiches $4-7; 10am-1:30am Tue-Sat, to 9pm Sun & Mon) Affectionately nicknamed 'The Dirty O,' this neon-lit shop is a late-night favorite. With good chili dogs and mountains of twice-fried fries, inebriation isn't necessary – just very common.

Lawrenceville & East Liberty

★ **Smoke BBQ Taqueria** MEXICAN $
(412-224-2070; 4115 Butler St; tacos $6; 11am-11pm;) Two Austin, TX, natives combine barbecue skills with Mexican flour-tortilla tech for super-savory food and even good veg options. BYOB; there's a great beer store adjacent.

Coca Cafe CAFE $
(3811 Butler St; mains $10-14, dinner small plates $10-15; ⏲8am-3pm Mon-Wed, to 5pm Thu, to 9pm Fri, 9am-9pm Sat, to 2pm Sun;) Creative and fresh breakfasts (eggplant benedict, say) are a big draw here, but this two-room cafe is pleasant any time. Good coffee too.

Franktuary FAST FOOD $
(3810 Butler St; hot dogs from $3.50; ⏲11:30am-11:30pm Tue-Thu, to 1am Fri & Sat, to 3pm Sun) Giving dignity to the simple frankfurter, with quality meat and toppings ('vestments,' per the menu) such as blue cheese to kimchi. Good salads and a full cocktail list make it a meal.

Cure MODERN AMERICAN $$$
(☎412-252-2595; 5336 Butler St; mains $28-34; ⏲5-10pm) This gold-lit temple to the pig is so devoted it even serves garlic-and-caper-studded lard with the bread. Its 'charcroute' plate presents all its lovely housemade preserved meats.

Drinking & Nightlife

E Carson St on the South Side is the biggest party strip in town, while Lawrenceville has many of the cooler bars. Most gay bars are in a short stretch of Liberty Ave downtown. Drinks are a steal but bring cash. Also, many places still allow smoking.

★ **Allegheny Wine Mixer** WINE BAR
(5326 Butler St; ⏲5pm-midnight Tue-Thu, to 1am Fri-Sun) All the perks of a high-end wine bar – great list, smart staff, tasty nibbles – in the comfort of a neighborhood dive.

Gooski's BAR
(3117 Brereton St; beers $3; ⏲11am-2am) Pierogi, punk rock and a near-legendary bartender have made this a consistently great dive bar in Polish Hill for decades.

Park House BAR
(403 E Ohio St; ⏲5pm-2am Mon-Sat) A friendly bar in Deutschtown on the North Side, with free peanuts, popcorn and music. A menu of hummus and falafel balances out the beer. Wednesday is bluegrass night.

Bloomfield Bridge Tavern BAR
(☎412-682-8611; 4412 Liberty Ave; ⏲5pm-2am Tue-Sat) 'The Polish Party Place' is a pub with an '80s-rec-room look, excellent pierogi and sauerkraut, and indie-rock bands on the weekends.

Kelly's COCKTAIL BAR
(6012 Penn Circle S; drinks from $6; ⏲11:30am-2am Mon-Sat) This old bar has weathered the East Liberty neighborhood's shift to upwardly mobile style with class, developing great Prohibition-era cocktails while keeping the crackly vinyl booths.

Brillobox Bar BAR
(www.brillobox.net; 4104 Penn Ave; ⏲5pm-2am Tue-Sun) Live music and DJs (upstairs, with a cover), veg-friendly food and 'starving artist Sunday' $7 dinner make this a popular spot just up the hill from the Lawrenceville strip.

Nied's Hotel BAR
(5438 Butler St; beers $2; ⏲7am-midnight or later, closed Sun) An anchor in Upper Lawrenceville since 1941, this great community restaurant-bar serves one of the city's better fish sandwiches ($2), and its house band is a crowd-pleaser. In summer, bands play in the 'amphitheater' (empty lot) next door.

Wigle Whiskey Garden at the Barrelhouse BAR
(☎412-224-2827; www.wiglewhiskey.com; 1055 Spring Garden Ave; ⏲5-9pm Wed-Fri, from 3pm Sat, 11am-4pm Sun) This craft whiskey maker's barreling facility on the North Side hosts bands and bingo in a pretty outdoor space. Its **distillery** (2401 Smallman St; ⏲10am-6pm Tue-Sat, to 4pm Sun), in the Strip District, is open for tours and tastings too.

Entertainment

★ **Elks Lodge** LIVE MUSIC
(☎412-321-1834; 400 Cedar Ave; cover $5; ⏲bluegrass 8pm Wed, big band 7pm 1st & 3rd Thu) Find out why Pittsburgh is known as the Paris of Appalachia at the Elks' Banjo Night, when the stage is packed with players and the audience sings along to all the bluegrass classics. Also hosts big-band night twice a month, with dance classes first. On the North Side in Deutschtown.

Pittsburgh Cultural Trust PERFORMING ARTS
(☎412-471-6070; www.pgharts.org; 803 Liberty Ave) An umbrella group for all the arts in downtown's Cultural District, from Pittsburgh Opera to global-minded Pittsburgh Dance Council to creative theater from Bricolage. Check the website for an events calendar and tickets.

Rex Theater LIVE MUSIC

(☎412-381-6811; www.rextheatre.com; 1602 E Carson St) A favorite South Side venue, a converted movie theater, for touring jazz, rock and indie bands.

MCG Jazz LIVE MUSIC

(☎412-322-0800; www.mcgjazz.org; 1815 Metropolitan St; ⊙Oct-Apr) Part of a community arts-and-crafts school on the North Side, this 350-seat venue hosts top jazz musicians.

Row House Cinema CINEMA

(☎412-904-3225; www.rowhousecinema.com; 4115 Butler St; ticket $9) This art-house and repertory cinema in Lawrenceville has theme weeks and gives a discount for wearing a costume.

Information

Greater Pittsburgh Convention & Visitors Bureau Main Branch (☎412-281-7711; www.visitpittsburgh.com; 120 Fifth Ave, Suite 2800; ⊙10am-6pm Mon-Fri, to 4pm Sat, to 3pm Sun) Publishes the *Official Visitors Guide* and provides maps and tourist advice.

Pittsburgh City Paper (www.pghcitypaper.com) Independent local alt-weekly with good arts listings.

Pittsburgh Post-Gazette (www.post-gazette.com) A major daily.

Pop City (www.popcitymedia.com) Weekly e-magazine with a focus on arts and community.

University of Pittsburgh Medical Center (☎412-647-2345; www.upmc.com; 200 Lothrop St; ⊙24hr) Pittsburgh's top hospital.

Getting There & Away

AIR

Pittsburgh International Airport (☎412-472-3525; www.pitairport.com; 1000 Airport Blvd), 18 miles west of downtown, has direct connections to Europe, Canada and major US cities via a slew of airlines.

BUS

The **Greyhound bus station** (Grant Street Transportation Center; ☎412-392-6514; www.greyhound.com; 55 11th St) has frequent buses to Philadelphia (from $33, six to seven hours), New York (from $31, 8½ to 11 hours) and Chicago ($68, 11 to 14 hours).

CAR & MOTORCYCLE

Pittsburgh is accessible via I-76 or I-79 from the west and from the east on I-70. It's about a six-hour drive from NYC and about three hours from Buffalo.

TRAIN

Pittsburgh has a magnificent old train station – and **Amtrak** (☎800-872-7245; www.amtrak.com; 1100 Liberty Ave) drops you off in a dismal modern building behind it. Service runs to Philadelphia (from $55, 7½ hours) and NYC (from $73, 9½ hours). One also runs to Chicago ($107, 10 hours) and Washington, DC ($50, eight hours).

Getting Around

PortAuthority (www.portauthority.org) provides public transportation around Pittsburgh, including the 28X Airport Flyer ($3.75, 40 minutes, every 30 minutes 5:30am to midnight) from the airport to downtown and Oakland. Taxis cost about $40 (not including tip) to downtown. Various shuttles also make downtown runs for $25 or so per person one way.

Driving in Pittsburgh can be frustrating – roads end with no warning or deposit you suddenly on bridges. Parking is scarce downtown. Where possible, use the extensive bus network, which includes a fast express busway (routes beginning with P). There is also a limited light-rail system, the T, useful for the South Side. Rides on the T downtown are free; other in-city fares are $2.50, and $1 for a transfer.

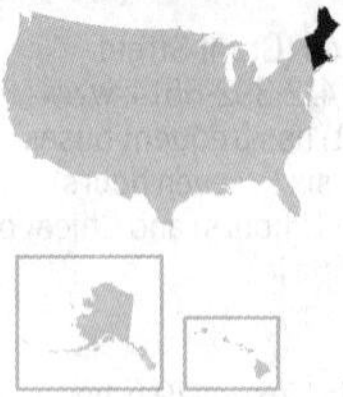

New England

Includes ➡

Best Places to Eat

➡ Row 34 (p192)

➡ Chatham Fish Pier Market (p205)

➡ Fore Street (p252)

➡ Nudel (p215)

➡ Art Cliff Diner (p211)

Best Places to Stay

➡ Verb Hotel (p191)

➡ Carpe Diem (p208)

➡ Inn at Shelburne Farms (p237)

➡ The Attwater (p221)

Why Go?

The history of New England is the history of America. It's the Pilgrims who came ashore at Plymouth Rock and the minutemen who fought for American independence. It's hundreds of years of progressive thinkers who dared to dream and dared to do. Nowadays, New England is still at the cutting edge of culture, with top-notch art museums and music festivals.

For outdoor adventure, the region undulates with the rolling hills and rocky peaks of the ancient Appalachian Mountains. Plus, nearly 5000 miles of coastline make for unlimited opportunities for fishing, swimming, surfing and sailing. Those are surefire ways to work up an appetite. Fortunately, New England is a bounty of epicurean delights: pancakes drenched in maple syrup; just-picked fruit and sharp cheddar cheese; and – most importantly – sublimely fresh seafood that is the hallmark of this region.

When to Go

Boston

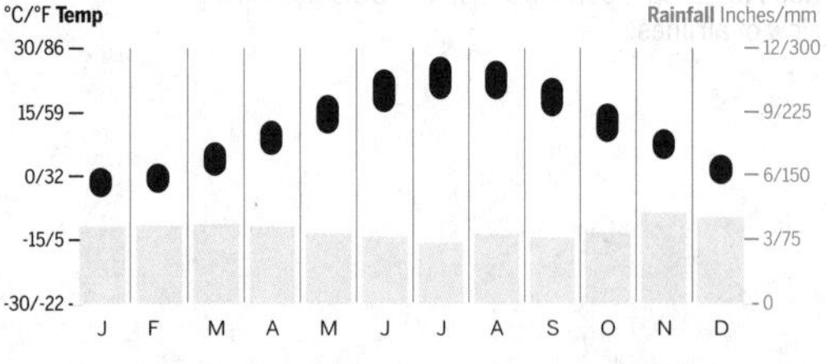

May–Jun
Uncrowded sights and lightly trodden trails. Whale-watching begins.

Jul–Aug
Top tourist season with summer festivals and warmer ocean water.

Sep–Oct
New England's blazing foliage peaks from mid-September to mid-October.

History

When the first European settlers arrived, New England was inhabited by native Algonquians who lived in small tribes, raising corn and beans, hunting game and harvesting the rich coastal waters.

In 1602 English captain Bartholomew Gosnold landed at Cape Cod and sailed north to Maine; but it wasn't until 1614 that Captain John Smith, who charted the region's coastline for King James I, christened the land 'New England.' With the arrival of the Pilgrims at Plymouth in 1620, European settlement began in earnest. Over the next century the colonies expanded, often at the expense of the indigenous people.

Although subjects of the British Crown, New Englanders governed themselves with their own legislative councils and they came to view their affairs as separate from those of England. In the 1770s King George III imposed a series of taxes to pay for England's involvement in costly wars. The colonists, unrepresented in the British parliament, protested under the slogan 'no taxation without representation.' Attempts to squash the protests eventually led to battles at Lexington and Concord, setting off the War for Independence. The historic result was the birth of the USA in 1776.

Following independence, New England became an economic powerhouse, its harbors booming centers for shipbuilding, fishing and trade. New England's famed Yankee Clippers plied ports from China to South America. A thriving whaling industry brought unprecedented wealth to Nantucket and New Bedford. The USA's first water-powered cotton-spinning mill was established in Rhode Island in 1793.

No boom lasts forever. By the early 20th century many of the mills had moved south. Today education, finance, biotechnology and tourism are linchpins of the regional economy.

Local Culture

New Englanders tend to be reserved by nature, with the Yankee brusqueness standing in marked contrast to the casual outgoing nature of some other American regions. This taciturn quality shouldn't be confused with unfriendliness, as it's simply a more formal regional style.

Particularly in rural areas, folks take pride in their ingenuity and self-sufficient character. These New Englanders remain fiercely independent, from the fishing boat crews who brave Atlantic storms to the small Vermont farmers who fight to keep operating independently within America's agribusiness economy. Fortunately for the farmers and fishers, buy-local and go-organic movements have grown by leaps and bounds throughout New England. From bistros in Boston to small towns in the far north the menus are greening.

One place you won't find that ol' Yankee reserve is at the ball field. New Englanders are fanatical about sports. Attending a Red Sox game is as close as you'll come to a modern-day gladiators-at-the-coliseum scene – wild cheers and nasty jeers galore.

Generally regarded as a liberal enclave, New England is at the forefront on progressive political issues from gay rights to health-care reform. Indeed the universal health-insurance program in Massachusetts became the model for President Obama's national plan.

NEW ENGLAND IN...

One Week

Start in **Boston**, following the **Freedom Trail**, dining at a cozy **North End bistro** and exploring the city's highlights. Spend a day ogling the mansions in **Newport**. Then hit the beaches on **Cape Cod** or hop a ferry to **Nantucket** or **Martha's Vineyard**. End the week with a jaunt north to New Hampshire's **White Mountains** or the **Maine coast**.

Two Weeks

On your second week, take a leisurely drive through the **Litchfield Hills** and the **Berkshires.** Bookend the week with visits to the lively burgs of **Providence** and **Burlington**. Alternatively, plan an extended stay on the Maine coast, with time to explore **Bar Harbor** and kayak along the shores of **Acadia National Park**. Wrap it up in Maine's vast wilderness, where you can work up a sweat on a hike up the northernmost peak of the **Appalachian Trail** or take an adrenaline-pumping ride down the **Kennebec River**.

New England Highlights

1 Following in the footsteps of Colonial rabble-rousers along **Boston's Freedom Trail** (p187).

2 Romping across the dunes at **Cape Cod National Seashore** (p205).

3 Wandering the cobbled streets and windswept beaches of **Nantucket** (p209).

4 Listening to world-class music under the stars at **Tanglewood Music Festival** (p215) in Lenox.

5 Taking a fall drive past colorful foliage on the **Kancamagus Highway** (p242) in the White Mountains.

6 Anticipating a black-diamond run from the last single chairlift in the Lower

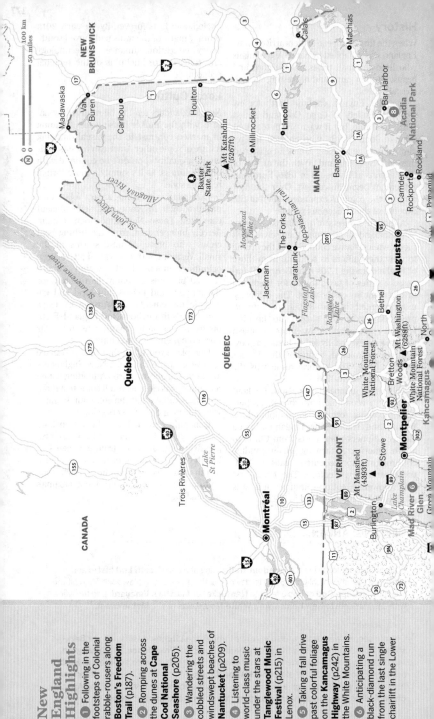

48 at **Mad River Glen** (p233).

7 Catching your breath as raptors swoop past at **VINS Nature Center** (p232).

8 Enjoying lofty views from a ladder trail at **Acadia National Park** (p255).

9 Cracking open a steamed lobster at the **Lobster Dock** (p254) in Boothbay Harbor.

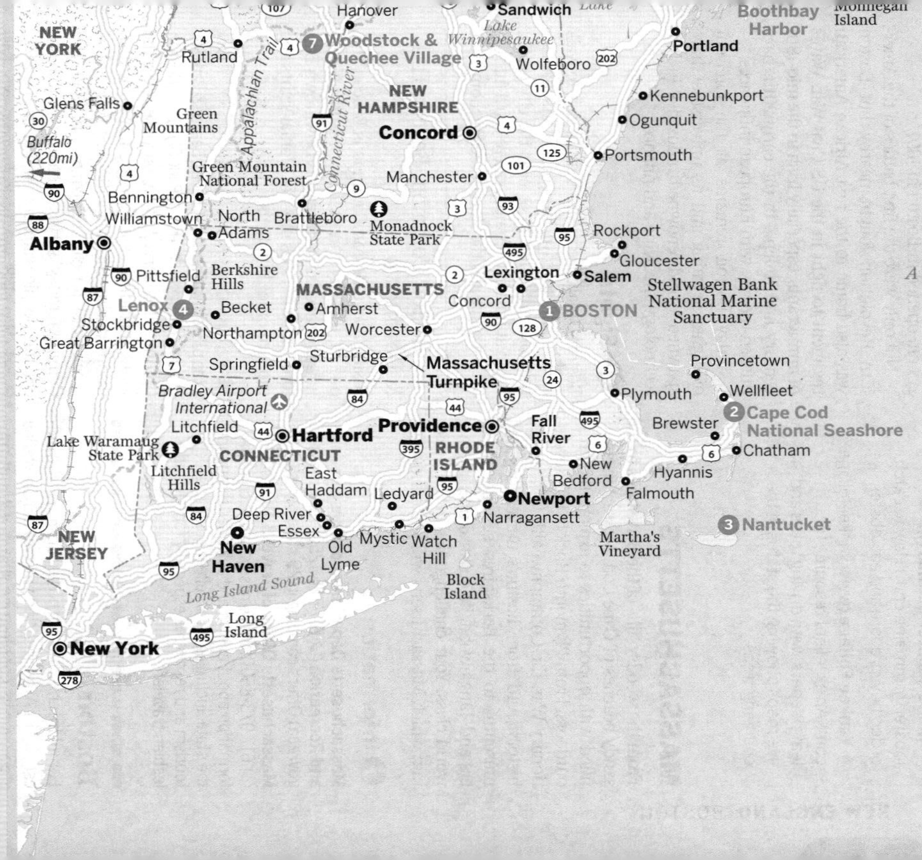

RESOURCES

➡ **Yankee Magazine** (www.yankeemagazine.com) Great destination profiles, recipes and events.

➡ **Appalachain Mountain Club** (www.outdoors.org) The ultimate resource for outdoor adventures in the New England hills.

➡ **Maine Lobster Council** (www.lobsterfrommaine.com) How to catch, order, buy, prepare and eat lobster.

➡ **Yankee Foliage** (www.yankeefoliage.com) An excellent resource for leaf-peepers, with driving tours and live maps showing the status of the changing trees.

MASSACHUSETTS

From the woodsy hills of the Berkshires to the sandy beaches of Cape Cod, Massachusetts is filled with opportunities to explore the great outdoors. From Plymouth Rock to the Revolutionary War, the Commonwealth is rich with history. And from Boston's universities and museums to the Berkshires' summer theaters and Tanglewood, its cultural offerings are world class. Your challenge lies in the deciding: which Massachusetts will you discover?

Information

Massachusetts Department of Conservation and Recreation (☎617-626-1250; www.mass.gov/eea) Offers camping in 29 state parks.

Massachusetts Office of Travel & Tourism (☎617-973-8500; www.massvacation.com) Information about events and activities throughout the state, including an excellent guide to green tourism and resources especially for gay and lesbian travelers.

Boston

For all intents and purposes, Boston is the oldest city in America. And you can hardly walk a step over its cobblestone streets without running into some historic site. But Boston has not been relegated to the past. The city's art and music scenes continue to charm and challenge contemporary audiences; cutting-edge urban planning projects are reshaping the city; and scores of universities guarantee an infusion of cultural energy year after year.

History

When the Massachusetts Bay Colony was established by England in 1630, Boston became its capital. It's a city of firsts: Boston Latin School, the first public school in the USA, was founded in 1635, followed a year later by Harvard, the nation's first university. The first newspaper in the colonies was printed here in 1704, America's first labor union organized here in 1795 and the country's first subway system opened in Boston in 1897.

Not only were the first battles of the American Revolution fought nearby, but Boston was also home to the first African American regiment to fight in the US Civil War. Waves of immigrants, especially Irish in the mid-18th century and Italians in the early 20th, have infused the city with European influences.

Today Boston remains at the forefront of higher learning and its universities have spawned world-renowned industries in biotechnology, medicine and finance.

Sights

Boston's small size means that it's easy to walk and difficult to drive. Most of Boston's main attractions are found in or near the city center. Begin at Boston Common, where you'll find the tourist office and the start of the Freedom Trail.

Boston Common, Beacon Hill & Downtown

Rising above Boston Common is Beacon Hill, one of the city's most historic and affluent neighborhoods. To the east is Downtown Boston, with a curious mix of Colonial sights and modern office buildings.

★ **Boston Common** PARK
(Map p188; btwn Tremont, Charles, Beacon & Park Sts; 6am-midnight; P 🚻; T Park St) The Boston Common has served many purposes over the years, including as a campground for British troops during the Revolutionary War and as green grass for cattle grazing until 1830. The Common today serves picnickers, sunbathers and people-watchers. In winter, the **Frog Pond** (Map p188; www.bostonfrogpond.com; Boston Common; admission adult/child $5/free, rental $10/5; 10am-4pm Mon, to 9pm Tue-Sun mid-Nov–mid-Mar; 🚻; T Park St) attracts ice-skaters, while summer draws theater lovers for **Shakespeare on the Common** (Map p188; www.commshakes.org; Boston Common; 8pm Tue-Sat, 7pm Sun Jul & Aug; T Park St). This is also the starting point for the Freedom Trail.

Massachusetts State House NOTABLE BUILDING
(Map p188; www.sec.state.ma.us; cnr Beacon & Bowdoin Sts; ⌚9am-5pm, tours 10am-3:30pm Mon-Fri; T Park St) FREE High atop Beacon Hill, Massachusetts' leaders and legislators attempt to turn their ideas into concrete policies and practices within the State House. John Hancock provided the land (previously part of his cow pasture); Charles Bulfinch designed the commanding state capitol; but it was Oliver Wendell Holmes who called it 'the hub of the solar system' (thus earning Boston the nickname 'the Hub'). Free 40-minute tours cover the history, artwork, architecture and political personalities of the State House.

Granary Burying Ground CEMETERY
(Map p188; Tremont St; ⌚9am-5pm; T Park St) Dating to 1660, this atmospheric spot is crammed with historic headstones, many with evocative (and creepy) carvings. This is the final resting place of all your favorite revolutionary heroes including Paul Revere, Samuel Adams, John Hancock and James Otis. Benjamin Franklin is buried in Philadelphia, but the Franklin family plot contains his parents.

Old South Meeting House HISTORIC BUILDING
(Map p188; www.osmh.org; 310 Washington St; adult/child $6/1; ⌚9:30am-5pm Apr-Oct, 10am-4pm Nov-Mar; T Downtown Crossing or State) 'No tax on tea!' That was the decision on December 16, 1773, when 5000 angry colonists gathered here to protest British taxes, leading to the Boston Tea Party. Visit the graceful meeting house to check out an exhibit about the history of the building and listen to an audio of the historic pre–Tea Party meeting.

Old State House HISTORIC BUILDING
(Map p188; www.revolutionaryboston.org; 206 Washington St; adult/child $10/free; ⌚9am-6pm Jun-Aug, to 5pm Sep-May; T State) Dating to 1713, the Old State House is Boston's oldest surviving public building, where the Massachusetts Assembly used to debate the issues of the day before the revolution. The building is best known for its balcony, where the Declaration of Independence was first read to Bostonians in 1776. Inside, the Old State House contains a small museum of revolutionary memorabilia, with videos and multimedia presentations about the Boston Massacre, which took place out front.

Faneuil Hall HISTORIC BUILDING
(Map p188; www.nps.gov/bost; Congress St; ⌚9am-5pm; T Haymarket or Government Center) FREE 'Those who cannot bear free speech had best go home,' said Wendell Phillips. 'Faneuil Hall is no place for slavish hearts.' Indeed, this public meeting place was the site of so much rabble-rousing that it earned the nickname the 'Cradle of Liberty'. After the revolution, Faneuil Hall was a forum for meetings about abolition, women's suffrage and war. The historic hall is normally open to the public, who can hear about the building's history from National Park Service (NPS) rangers.

★ **New England Aquarium** AQUARIUM
(Map p188; www.neaq.org; Central Wharf; adult/child $25/18; ⌚9am-5pm Mon-Fri, to 6pm Sat & Sun, 1hr later Jul & Aug; P 🚸; T Aquarium) Teeming with sea creatures of all sizes, shapes and colors, this giant fishbowl is the centerpiece of downtown Boston's waterfront. The main attraction is the newly renovated three-story Giant Ocean Tank, which swirls with thousands of creatures great and small, including turtles, sharks and eels. Countless side exhibits explore the lives and habitats of other underwater oddities, as well as penguins and marine mammals.

MASSACHUSETTS FACTS

Nickname Bay State

Population 6.7 million

Area 7840 sq miles

Capital city Boston (population 646,000)

Other cities Worcester (population 182,500), Springfield (population 153,700)

Sales tax 6.25%

Birthplace of Inventor Benjamin Franklin (1706–90), John F Kennedy (1917–63), authors Jack Kerouac (1922–69) and Henry David Thoreau (1817–62)

Home of Harvard University, Boston Marathon, Plymouth Rock

Politics Democratic

Famous for Boston Tea Party, first state to legalize gay marriage

Driving distances Boston to Provincetown 115 miles, Boston to Northampton 104 miles, Boston to Acadia National Park 280 miles

State Sweets Boston Cream Pie, Dunkin' Donuts, Fig Newtons

Boston

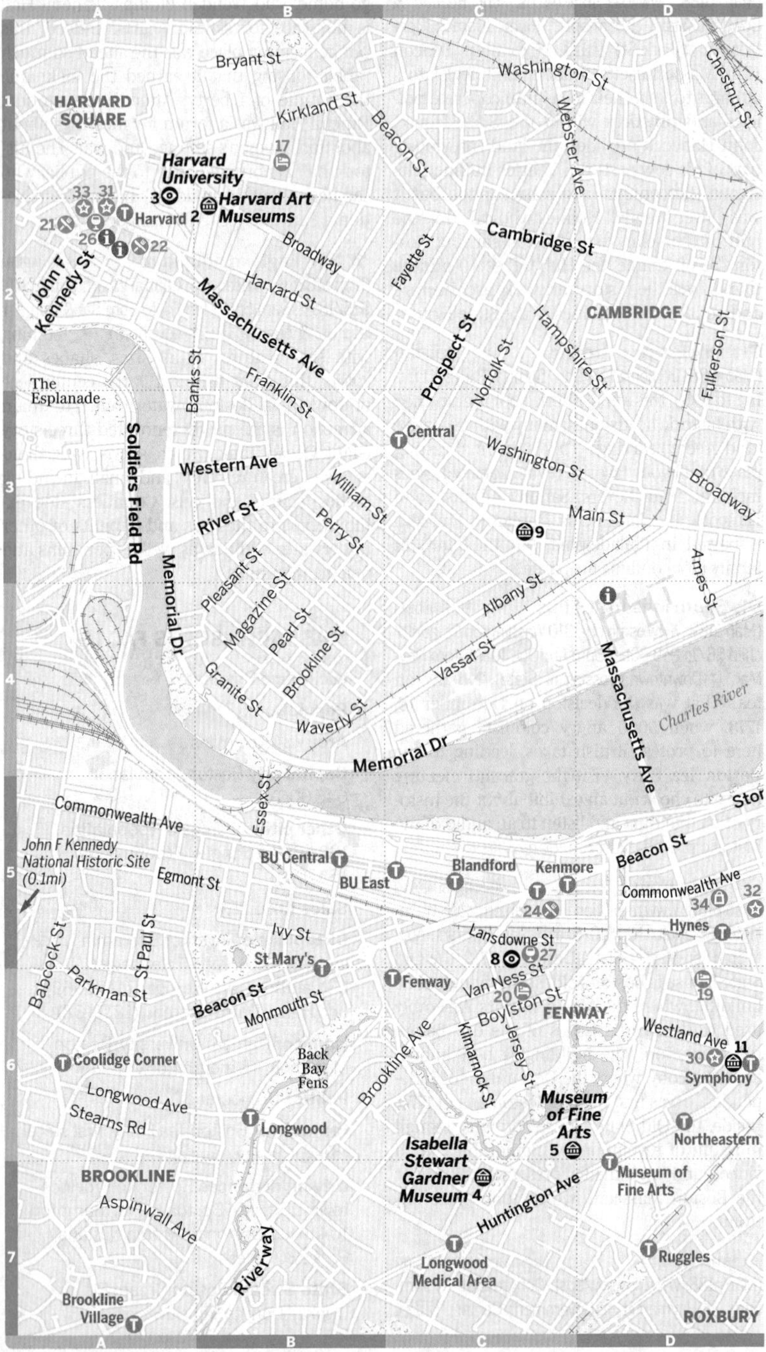

A
B
C
D
1
2
3
4
5
6
7
HARVARD SQUARE
Bryant St
Kirkland St
Washington St
Chestnut St
Beacon St
Webster Ave
17
Harvard University
3
Harvard Art Museums
2
33
31
Harvard
21
26
22
John F Kennedy St
Broadway
Cambridge St
Fayette St
Harvard St
Massachusetts Ave
CAMBRIDGE
Hampshire St
Fulkerson St
Prospect St
Norfolk St
The Esplanade
Banks St
Franklin St
Central
Soldiers Field Rd
Western Ave
Washington St
Broadway
William St
River St
Perry St
Main St
9
Memorial Dr
Pleasant St
Magazine St
Albany St
Ames St
Pearl St
Brookline St
Vassar St
Massachusetts Ave
Granite St
Charles River
Waverly St
Memorial Dr
Essex St
Commonwealth Ave
Stor
John F Kennedy National Historic Site (0.1mi)
Egmont St
BU Central
BU East
Blandford
Kenmore
Beacon St
Commonwealth Ave
32
34
24
Babcock St
St Paul St
Ivy St
Lansdowne St
Hynes
8
27
St Mary's
Parkman St
Fenway
Van Ness St
20
19
Beacon St
Monmouth St
Boylston St
FENWAY
Westland Ave
11
30
Symphony
Coolidge Corner
Back Bay Fens
Brookline Ave
Kilmarnock St
Jersey St
Museum of Fine Arts
Longwood Ave
Stearns Rd
Longwood
Northeastern
5
Isabella Stewart Gardner Museum
4
Museum of Fine Arts
BROOKLINE
Aspinwall Ave
Huntington Ave
Riverway
Longwood Medical Area
Ruggles
Brookline Village
ROXBURY

NEW ENGLAND

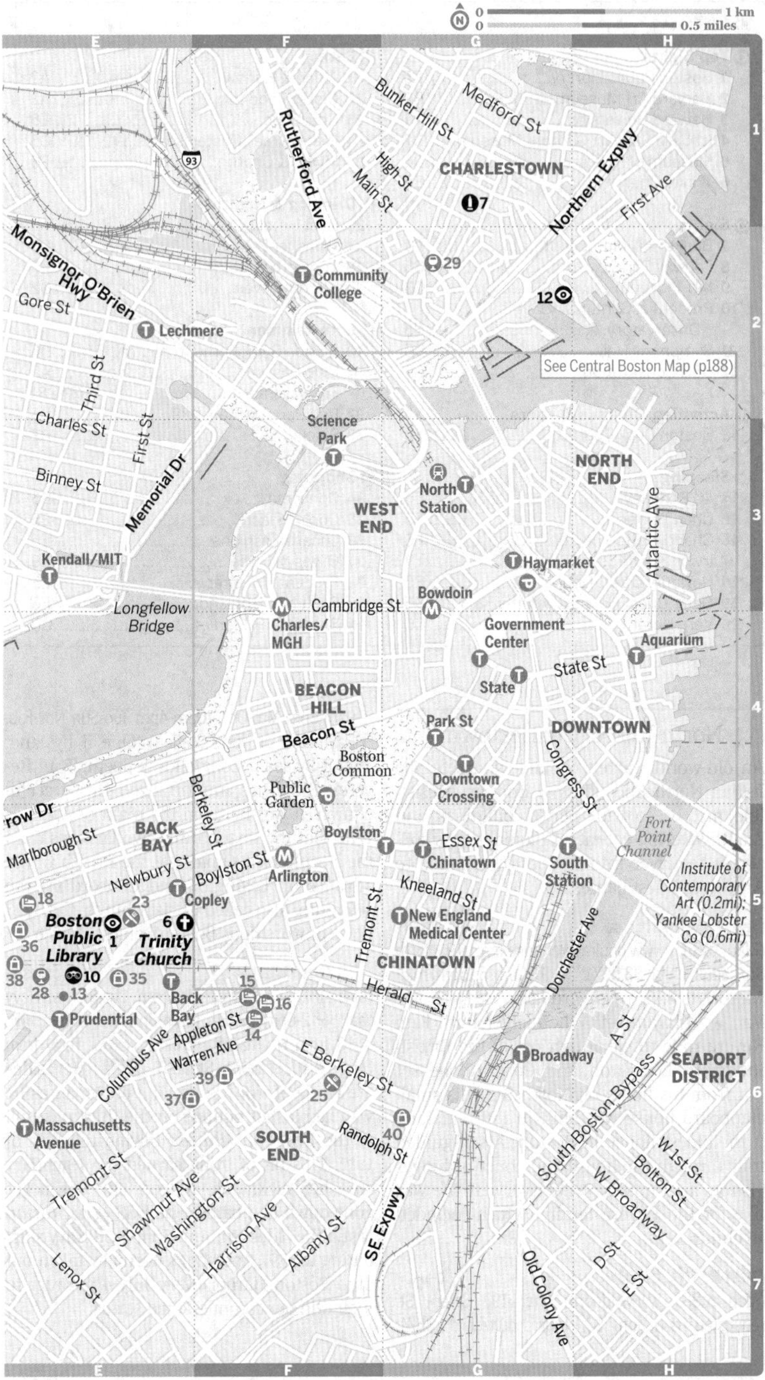
0 1 km
0 0.5 miles
E
F
G
H
1
2
3
4
5
6
7
Bunker Hill St
Medford St
Rutherford Ave
93
High St
Main St
CHARLESTOWN
7
Northern Expwy
First Ave
Monsignor O'Brien Hwy
Community College
29
12
Gore St
Lechmere
See Central Boston Map (p188)
Third St
Charles St
First St
Memorial Dr
Science Park
Binney St
North Station
WEST END
NORTH END
Atlantic Ave
Kendall/MIT
Haymarket
Bowdoin
Longfellow Bridge
Cambridge St
Charles/MGH
Government Center
Aquarium
State St
State
BEACON HILL
Beacon St
Park St
DOWNTOWN
Congress St
Boston Common
Downtown Crossing
Public Garden
Berkeley St
rrow Dr
BACK BAY
Marlborough St
Boylston
Essex St
Fort Point Channel
Newbury St
Boylston St
Arlington
Chinatown
South Station
Institute of Contemporary Art (0.2mi); Yankee Lobster Co (0.6mi)
18
23
Copley
Kneeland St
Tremont St
Boston Public Library
1
6
Trinity Church
New England Medical Center
Dorchester Ave
36
38
10
35
CHINATOWN
28
13
15
16
Herald St
Back Bay
Prudential
Appleton St
14
Columbus Ave
Warren Ave
E Berkeley St
Broadway
A St
SEAPORT DISTRICT
39
37
25
South Boston Bypass
40
Massachusetts Avenue
SOUTH END
Randolph St
W 1st St
Bolton St
Tremont St
Shawmut Ave
Washington St
Harrison Ave
Albany St
SE Expwy
W Broadway
D St
E St
Lenox St
Old Colony Ave

Boston

North End & Charlestown

An old-world warren of narrow streets, the Italian North End offers visitors an irresistible mix of colorful period buildings and mouthwatering eateries. Colonial sights spill across the river into Charlestown, home to America's oldest battleship.

Paul Revere House HISTORIC SITE

(Map p188; www.paulreverehouse.org; 19 North Sq; adult/child $3.50/1; 9:30am-5:15pm mid-Apr–Oct, to 4:15pm Nov–mid-Apr, closed Mon Jan-Mar; ; Haymarket) When silversmith Paul Revere rode to warn patriots of the British march to Lexington and Concord, he set out from his home on North Sq. This small clapboard house was built in 1680, making it the oldest house in Boston. A self-guided tour through the house and courtyard gives visitors a glimpse of what everyday life was like for the Revere family (which included 16 children!).

Old North Church CHURCH

(Map p188; www.oldnorth.com; 193 Salem St; requested donation $3, tour adult/child $6/4; 9am-5pm Mar-Oct, 10am-4pm Tue-Sun Nov-Feb; Haymarket or North Station) 'One if by land, Two if by sea...' Longfellow's poem, 'Paul Revere's Ride,' has immortalized this graceful church. It was here, on the night of April 18, 1775, that the sexton hung two lanterns from the steeple, as a signal that the British would advance on Lexington and Concord via the sea route. Also called Christ Church, this 1723 place of worship is Boston's oldest church.

USS Constitution HISTORIC SITE

(Map p182; www.oldironsides.com; Charlestown Navy Yard; 2-6pm Tue-Fri, 10am-6pm Sat & Sun; ; 93 from Haymarket, Inner Harbor Ferry from Long Wharf, North Station) FREE 'Her sides are made of iron!' So cried a crewman as he watched a shot bounce off the thick oak hull of the USS *Constitution* during the War of 1812. This bit of irony earned the legendary ship her nickname. Indeed, she has never gone down in a battle. The USS *Constitution* is still the oldest commissioned US Navy ship, dating to 1797, and she is normally taken out onto Boston Harbor every July 4 in order to maintain her commissioned status.

Bunker Hill Monument MONUMENT

(Map p182; www.nps.gov/bost; Monument Sq; 9am-5:30pm Jul & Aug, to 4:15pm Sep-Jun; ; 93 from Haymarket, T Community College) FREE This 220ft granite obelisk monument commemorates the turning-point battle that was fought on the surrounding hillside on June 17, 1775. Ultimately, the Redcoats prevailed, but the victory was bittersweet, as they lost more than one-third of their deployed forces, while the colonists suffered relatively few casualties. Climb the 294 steps to the top of the monument to enjoy the panorama of the city, the harbor and the North Shore.

Seaport District

Following the HarborWalk, it's a pleasant stroll into the up-and-coming Seaport District.

★ **Boston Tea Party Ships & Museum** MUSEUM

(Map p188; www.bostonteapartyship.com; Congress St Bridge; adult/child $25/15; 10am-5pm, last tour 4pm; ; T South Station) 'Boston Harbor a teapot tonight!' To protest unfair taxes, a gang of rebellious colonists dumped 342 chests of tea into the water. The 1773 protest – the Boston Tea Party – set into motion the events leading to the Revolutionary War. Nowadays, replica Tea Party Ships are moored at the reconstructed Griffin's Wharf, alongside an excellent experiential museum dedicated to the revolution's most catalytic event.

Institute of Contemporary Art MUSEUM

(ICA; www.icaboston.org; 100 Northern Ave; adult/child $15/free; 10am-5pm Tue, Wed, Sat & Sun, to 9pm Thu & Fri; ; SL1 or SL2, T South Station) Boston is fast becoming a focal point for contemporary art in the 21st century, with the Institute of Contemporary Arts leading the way. The building is a work of art in itself: a glass structure cantilevered over a waterside plaza. The vast light-filled interior allows for multimedia presentations, educational programs and studio space. More importantly, it allows for the development of the ICA's permanent collection.

Chinatown, Theater District & South End

Compact Chinatown offers enticing Asian eateries, while the overlapping Theater District is clustered with performing-arts venues. To the west, the sprawling South End boasts one of America's largest concentrations of Victorian row houses, a burgeoning art community and a terrific restaurant scene.

Back Bay

Extending west from Boston Common this well-groomed neighborhood boasts graceful brownstone residences, grand edifices and tony shopping on Newbury St.

★ **Public Garden** GARDENS

(Map p188; www.friendsofthepublicgarden.org; Arlington St; 6am-midnight; ; T Arlington) Adjoining Boston Common, the Public Garden is a 24-acre botanical oasis of Victorian flower beds, verdant grass and weeping willow trees shading a tranquil lagoon. The old-fashioned pedal-powered **Swan Boats** (Map p188; www.swanboats.com; Public Garden; adult/child $3/1.50; 10am-5pm Jun-Aug, to 4pm mid-Apr–May, noon-4pm Sep; T Arlington) have been delighting children for generations. The most endearing

BOSTON IN...

Two Days

Spend one day reliving revolutionary history by following the **Freedom Trail**. Take time to lounge on the **Boston Common**, peek in the **Old State House** and imbibe a little history at the **Union Oyster House**. Afterwards, stroll into the **North End** for an Italian dinner. On your second day, rent a bike and ride along the Charles River. Go as far as **Harvard Sq** to cruise the campus and browse the bookstores.

Four Days

On your third day, peruse the impressive American collection at the **Museum of Fine Arts**. In the evening, catch a performance of the world-famous **Boston Symphony Orchestra** or watch the Red Sox play at **Fenway Park**.

Spend your last day discovering Back Bay. Window-shop and gallery-hop on **Newbury St**, go to the top of the **Prudential Center** and browse the **Boston Public Library**.

WORTH A TRIP

JFK SITES

John F Kennedy Library & Museum (www.jfklibrary.org; Columbia Point; adult/child $14/10; ⊙9am-5pm; Ⓣ JFK/UMass) The legacy of JFK is ubiquitous in Boston, but the official memorial to the 35th president is the presidential library and museum – a striking modern marble building designed by IM Pei. The architectural centerpiece is the glass pavilion, with soaring 115ft ceilings and floor-to-ceiling windows overlooking Boston Harbor. The museum is a fitting tribute to JFK's life and legacy. The effective use of video recreates history for visitors who may or may not remember the early 1960s.

John F Kennedy National Historic Site (www.nps.gov/jofi; 83 Beals St; ⊙9:30am-5pm Wed-Sun May-Oct; Ⓣ Coolidge Corner) Four of the nine Kennedy children were born and raised in this modest house, including Jack, who was born in the master bedroom in 1917. Matriarch Rose Kennedy oversaw the restoration of the house in the late 1960s; today her narrative sheds light on the Kennedys' family life. Guided tours allow visitors to see furnishings, photographs and mementos that have been preserved from the time the family lived here.

statue in the Public Garden is *Make Way for Ducklings,* depicting Mrs Mallard and her eight ducklings, the main characters in the beloved book by Robert McCloskey.

★Boston Public Library LIBRARY
(Map p182; www.bpl.org; 700 Boylston St; ⊙9am-9pm Mon-Thu, to 5pm Fri & Sat year-round, also 1-5pm Sun Oct-May; Ⓣ Copley) Dating from 1852, the esteemed Boston Public Library lends credence to Boston's reputation as the 'Athens of America.' The old McKim building is notable for its magnificent facade and exquisite interior art. Pick up a free brochure and take a self-guided tour; alternatively, free guided tours depart from the entrance hall (times vary).

★Trinity Church CHURCH
(Map p182; www.trinitychurchboston.org; 206 Clarendon St; adult/child $7/free; ⊙9am-4:30pm Mon, Fri & Sat, to 5:30pm Tue-Thu, 1-5pm Sun; Ⓣ Copley) A masterpiece of American architecture, Trinity Church is the country's ultimate example of Richardsonian Romanesque. The granite exterior, with a massive portico and side cloister, uses sandstone in colorful patterns. The interior is an awe-striking array of vibrant murals and stained glass, most by artist John LaFarge, who cooperated closely with architect Henry Hobson Richardson to create an integrated composition of shapes, colors and textures. Free architectural tours are offered following Sunday service at 11:15am.

Prudential Center Skywalk Observatory LOOKOUT
(Map p182; www.skywalkboston.com; 800 Boylston St; adult/child $16/11; ⊙10am-10pm Mar-Oct, to 8pm Nov-Feb; Ⓟ 👪; Ⓣ Prudential) Technically called the Shops at Prudential Center, this landmark Boston building is not much more than a fancy shopping mall. But it does provide a bird's-eye view of Boston from its 50th-floor skywalk. Completely enclosed by glass, the skywalk offers spectacular 360-degree views of Boston and Cambridge, accompanied by an entertaining audio tour (with a special version catering to kids). Alternatively, enjoy the same view from **Top of the Hub** (Map p182; ☎617-536-1775; www.topofthehub.net; 800 Boylston St; ⊙11:30am-1am; 📶; Ⓣ Prudential) for the price of a drink.

Fenway & Kenmore Square

Kenmore Sq is best for baseball and beer, while the southern part of the Fenway is dedicated to higher-minded cultural pursuits.

★Museum of Fine Arts MUSEUM
(MFA; Map p182; www.mfa.org; 465 Huntington Ave; adult/child $25/10; ⊙10am-5pm Sat-Tue, to 10pm Wed-Fri; 👪; Ⓣ Museum or Ruggles) Since 1876, the Museum of Fine Arts has been Boston's premier venue for showcasing art by local, national and international artists. Nowadays, the museum's holdings encompass all eras, from the ancient world to contemporary times, and all areas of the globe, making it truly encyclopedic in scope. Most recently, the museum has added gorgeous new wings dedicated to the Art of the Americas and to contemporary art, contributing to Boston's emergence as an art center in the 21st century.

★ Isabella Stewart Gardner Museum MUSEUM

(Map p182; www.gardnermuseum.org; 280 The Fenway; adult/child $15/free; 11am-5pm Mon, Wed & Fri-Sun, to 9pm Thu; ; T Museum) The magnificent Venetian-style palazzo that houses this museum was home to 'Mrs Jack' Gardner herself until her death in 1924. A monument to one woman's taste for acquiring exquisite art, the Gardner is filled with almost 2000 priceless objects, primarily European, including outstanding tapestries and Italian Renaissance and 17th-century Dutch paintings. The four-story greenhouse courtyard is a masterpiece and a tranquil oasis that alone is worth the price of admission.

Cambridge

On the north side of the Charles River lies politically progressive Cambridge, home to academic heavyweights Harvard University and Massachusetts Institute of Technology (MIT). **Harvard Square** overflows with cafes, bookstores and street performers.

★ Harvard University UNIVERSITY

(Map p182; www.harvard.edu; Massachusetts Ave; tours free; tours hourly 10am-3pm Mon-Sat; T Harvard) Founded in 1636 to educate men for the ministry, Harvard is America's oldest college. The original Ivy League school has eight graduates who went on to be US presidents, not to mention dozens of Nobel laureates and Pulitzer Prize winners. It educates 6500 undergraduates and about 12,000 graduates yearly in 10 professional schools. The geographic heart of Harvard University – where red-brick buildings and leaf-covered paths exude academia – is Harvard Yard.

★ Harvard Art Museums MUSEUM

(Map p182; www.harvardartmuseums.org; 32 Quincy St; adult/child $15/free; 10am-5pm; T Harvard) Architect extraordinaire Renzo Piano has overseen a renovation and expansion of Harvard's art museums, allowing the university's massive 250,000-piece collection to come together under one very stylish roof. Harvard's art spans the globe, with separate collections devoted to Asian and Islamic cultures (formerly the Arthur M Sackler Museum), Northern European and Germanic cultures (formerly the Busch-Reisinger Museum) and other Western art, especially European modernism (formerly the Fogg).

Tours

★ Urban AdvenTours BICYCLE TOUR

(Map p188; 617-379-3590; www.urbanadventours.com; 103 Atlantic Ave; tours $55; ; T Aquarium) Founded by avid cyclists who believe the best views of Boston are from a bicycle. The City View Ride provides a great overview of how to get around by bike, but there are other specialty tours such as Bikes at Night and the Emerald Necklace tour.

Boston by Foot WALKING TOUR

(www.bostonbyfoot.com; adult/child $15/10;) This fantastic nonprofit offers 90-minute walking tours, with neighborhood-specific walks and specialty theme tours such as Literary Landmarks, the Dark Side of Boston and Boston for Little Feet – a kid-friendly version of the Freedom Trail.

NPS Freedom Trail Tour WALKING TOUR

(Map p188; www.nps.gov/bost; Faneuil Hall; 10am & 2pm Apr-Oct; T State) FREE Show up at least 30 minutes early to snag a spot on one of the free, ranger-led Freedom Trail tours provided by the NPS. Tours depart from the visitor center in Faneuil Hall, and follow a portion of the Freedom Trail (not including Charlestown), for a total of 90 minutes. Each tour is limited to 30 people.

Boston Duck Tours BOAT TOUR

(Map p182; 617-267-3825; www.bostonducktours.com; adult/child $36/25; ; T Aquarium, Science Park or Prudential) These ridiculously popular tours use WWII amphibious vehicles that cruise the downtown streets before splashing into the Charles River. The 80-minute tours depart from the Museum

DON'T MISS

BOSTON GOES GREEN

The gateway to the newly revitalized waterfront is the **Rose Kennedy Greenway** (Map p188; www.rosekennedygreenway.org; ; T Aquarium or Haymarket). Where once was a hulking overhead highway, now winds a 27-acre strip of landscaped gardens and fountain-lined greens, with an artist market for Saturday shoppers, and food trucks for weekday lunchers. Cool off in the whimsical Rings Fountain, walk the calming labyrinth, or take a ride on the custom-designed Greenway carousel.

Central Boston

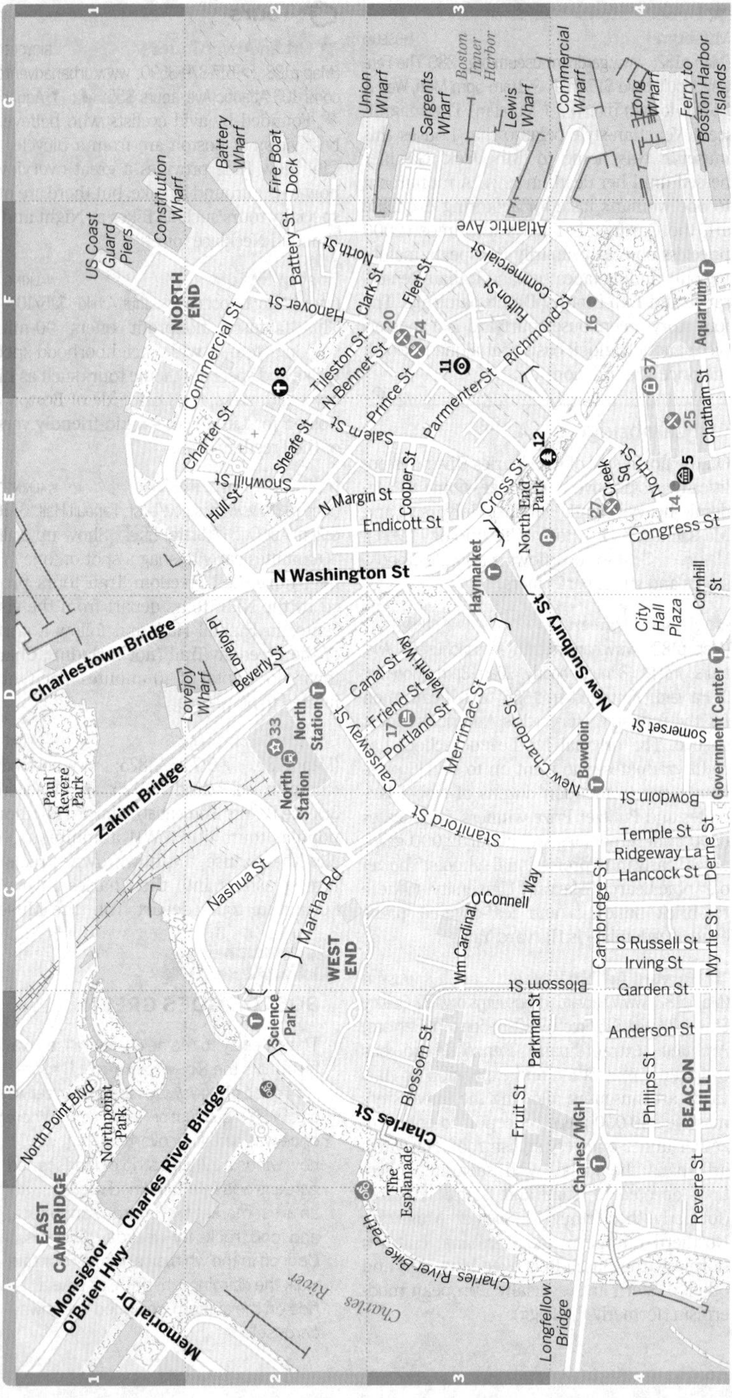

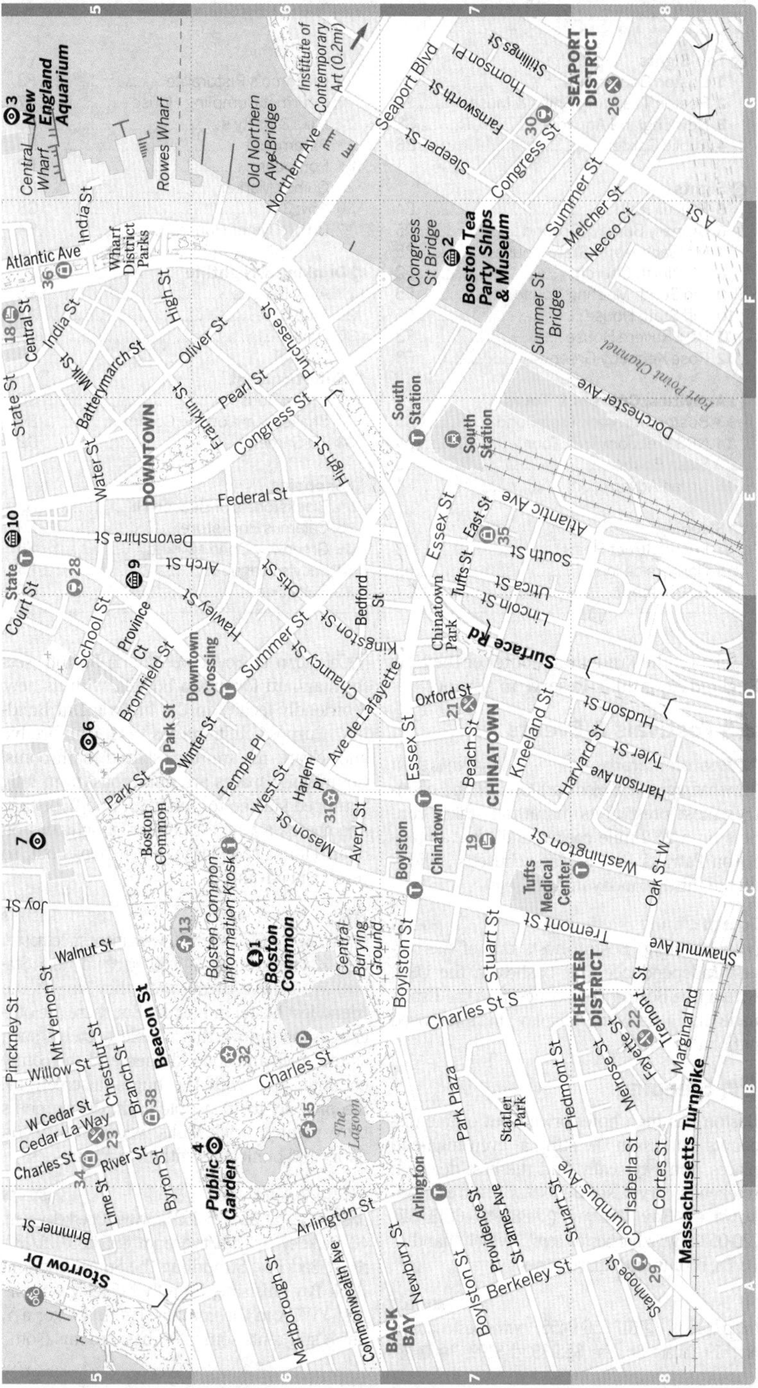
New England Aquarium
Central Wharf
Rowes Wharf
Institute of Contemporary Art (0.2mi)
Old Northern Ave Bridge
Northern Ave
Seaport Blvd
Thomson Pl
Stillings St
Farnsworth St
Sleeper St
Congress St
SEAPORT DISTRICT
Summer St
Melcher St
Necco Ct
A St
Congress St Bridge
Boston Tea Party Ships & Museum
Summer St Bridge
Fort Point Channel
Dorchester Ave
South Station
Atlantic Ave
Wharf District Parks
India St
Central St
State St
Milk St
Batterymarch St
High St
Oliver St
Purchase St
Pearl St
Franklin St
Water St
DOWNTOWN
Federal St
Devonshire St
Arch St
Otis St
Bedford St
Essex St
East St
South St
Tufts St
Utica St
Lincoln St
Chinatown Park
Surface Rd
Court St
School St
Province Ct
Hawley St
Summer St
Kingston St
Chauncy St
Ave de Lafayette
Downtown Crossing
Bromfield St
Park St
Winter St
Temple Pl
West St
Harlem Pl
Oxford St
Beach St
CHINATOWN
Kneeland St
Hudson St
Harvard St
Tyler St
Harrison Ave
Park St
Boston Common
Mason St
Avery St
Boylston
Chinatown
Washington St
Tufts Medical Center
Oak St W
Joy St
Walnut St
Beacon St
Boston Common Information Kiosk
Boston Common
Central Burying Ground
Boylston St
Stuart St
Tremont St
Shawmut Ave
THEATER DISTRICT
Charles St S
Pinckney St
Mt Vernon St
Willow St
Chestnut St
Branch St
Charles St
Melrose St
Fayette St
Tremont St
Marginal Rd
W Cedar St
Cedar La Way
Charles St
River St
Byron St
Lime St
Public Garden
The Lagoon
Park Plaza
Statler Park
Piedmont St
Isabella St
Cortes St
Massachusetts Turnpike
Brimmer St
Storrow Dr
Arlington St
Arlington
Stuart St
Columbus Ave
Marlborough St
Commonwealth Ave
Newbury St
Boylston St
Providence St
St James Ave
Berkeley St
Stanhope St
BACK BAY

Central Boston

Top Sights
1 Boston Common....C6
2 Boston Tea Party Ships & Museum....F7
3 New England Aquarium....G5
4 Public Garden....B6

Sights
5 Faneuil Hall....E4
6 Granary Burying Ground....D5
7 Massachusetts State House....C5
8 Old North Church....F2
9 Old South Meeting House....E5
10 Old State House....E5
11 Paul Revere House....F3
12 Rose Kennedy Greenway....E3

Activities, Courses & Tours
13 Boston Common Frog Pond....C5
14 NPS Freedom Trail Tour....E4
15 Swan Boats....B6
16 Urban AdvenTours....F4

Sleeping
17 Friend Street Hostel....D3
18 Harborside Inn....F5
19 HI-Boston....C7

Eating
20 Giacomo's Ristorante....F3
21 Gourmet Dumpling House....D7
22 Mike & Patty's....B8
23 Paramount....B5
24 Pomodoro....F3
25 Quincy Market....E4
26 Row 34....G8
27 Union Oyster House....E4

Drinking & Nightlife
28 Alley Bar....E5
29 Club Café....A8
30 Drink....G7

Entertainment
31 Opera House....C6
32 Shakespeare on the Common....B6
33 TD Garden....D2

Shopping
34 Blackstone's of Beacon Hill....B5
35 Calamus Bookstore....E7
36 Greenway Open Market....F5
37 Lucy's League....F4
38 Ruby Door....B5

of Science, the Prudential Center or the New England Aquarium. Reserve in advance.

Festivals & Events

★ Boston Marathon SPORTING EVENT
(www.baa.org; 3rd Mon Apr) One of the country's most prestigious marathons takes runners on a 26.2-mile course ending at Copley Sq on Patriots Day, a Massachusetts holiday on the third Monday in April.

Fourth of July HOLIDAY
(www.july4th.org) Boston hosts one of the biggest Independence Day bashes in the USA, with a free Boston Pops concert on the Esplanade and a fireworks display that's televised nationally.

Sleeping

Boston has high hotel prices, but online discounts can lessen the sting at even high-end places. You'll typically find the best deals on weekends. Try also **Bed & Breakfast Associates Bay Colony** (888-486-6018, 617-720-0522; www.bnbboston.com), which handles B&Bs, rooms and apartments.

HI-Boston HOSTEL $
(Map p188; 617-536-9455; www.bostonhostel.org; 19 Stuart St; dm $55-65, d $199; T Chinatown or Boylston) HI-Boston sets the standard for urban hostels, with its new, ecofriendly facility in the historic Dill Building. Purpose-built rooms are comfortable and clean, as are the shared bathrooms. Community spaces are numerous, from fully equipped kitchen to trendy ground-floor cafe, and there's a whole calendar of activities on offer. The place is large, but it books out, so reserve in advance.

Friend Street Hostel HOSTEL $
(Map p188; 617-248-8971; www.friendstreethostel.com; 234 Friend St; dm $45-50; T North Station) We believe them when they say it's the friendliest hostel in Boston. But there are other reasons to love this affable hostelry, such as the spick-and-span kitchen and the comfy common area with the huge flatscreen TV. Sleeping six to 10 people each, dorm rooms have painted brick walls, wide-plank wood floors and bunk beds with thin mattresses.

40 Berkeley HOSTEL $$
(Map p182; 617-375-2524; www.40berkeley.com; 40 Berkeley St; s/d/tr/q from $95/103/121/130; T Back Bay) Straddling the South End and Back Bay, this safe, friendly hostelry was the first YWCA in the country. It's no longer a Y, but it still rents some 200 basic rooms (some

overlooking the lovely garden) to guests on a nightly and long-term basis. Bathrooms are shared, as are other useful facilities including the telephone, library, TV room and laundry.

★Newbury Guest House GUESTHOUSE $$
(Map p182; ☎617-437-7666, 617-437-7668; www.newburyguesthouse.com; 261 Newbury St; d from $209; P ❄ 📶; T Hynes or Copley) Dating to 1882, these three interconnected brick and brownstone buildings offer a prime location in the heart of Newbury St. A recent renovation has preserved the charming features such as ceiling medallions and in-room fireplaces, but now the rooms feature clean lines, luxurious linens and modern amenities. Each morning, a complimentary continental breakfast is laid out next to the marble fireplace in the salon.

★Oasis Guest House & Adams B&B GUESTHOUSE $$
(Map p182; ☎617-230-0105, 617-267-2262; www.oasisguesthouse.com; 22 Edgerly Rd; s/d without bathroom $109/149, r with bathroom from $189; P ❄ 📶; T Hynes or Symphony) These homey side-by-side (jointly managed) guesthouses offer a peaceful, pleasant oasis in the midst of Boston's chaotic city streets. Thirty-odd guest rooms occupy four attractive brick, bow-front town houses on this tree-lined lane. The modest, light-filled rooms are tastefully and traditionally decorated, most with queen beds, floral quilts and nondescript prints.

Irving House GUESTHOUSE $$
(Map p182; ☎617-547-4600; www.irvinghouse.com; 24 Irving St; s/d without bathroom $135/165, r with bathroom from $185; P ❄ @ 📶; T Harvard) 🍃 Call it a big inn or a homey hotel, this property welcomes the world-weariest of travelers. The 44 rooms range in size, but every bed is covered with a quilt and big windows let in plenty of light. There is a bistro-style atmosphere in the brick-lined basement, where you can browse the books on hand, plan your travels or munch on free continental breakfast.

Chandler Inn HOTEL $$
(Map p182; ☎617-482-3450; www.chandlerinn.com; 26 Chandler St; r from $179; ❄ 📶; T Back Bay) Small but sleek rooms show off a designer's touch, giving them a sophisticated, urban glow. Travelers appreciate the plasma TVs and iPod docks, all of which come at relatively affordable prices. As a bonus, congenial staff provide super service. Across the street, the inn rents out 11 newly renovated, modern apartments of various sizes, under the moniker **Chandler Studios** (Map p182; www.chandlerstudiosboston.com; 54 Berkeley St; ste from $269; ❄ 📶; T Back Bay).

BOSTON STRONG

On Patriot's Day 2013, the nation (and the world) turned their eyes to Boston when two bombs exploded near the finish line of the Boston Marathon, killing three and injuring hundreds. Several days later, an MIT police officer was shot dead and the entire city was locked down, as Boston became a battleground for the War on Terror. The tragedy was devastating, but Boston can claim countless heroes, especially the many victims who have inspired others with their courage and fortitude throughout their recoveries.

★Verb Hotel BOUTIQUE HOTEL $$$
(Map p182; ☎855-695-6678; www.theverbhotel.com; 1271 Boylston St; r from $250; P ❄ 📶 🏊 🐾; T Kenmore) The Verb Hotel took a down-and-out HoJo property and turned it into Boston's most radical, retro, rock and roll hotel. The style is mid-century modern; the theme is music. Memorabilia is on display throughout the joint, with a jukebox cranking out tunes in the lobby. Classy, clean-lined rooms face the swimming pool or Fenway Park. A+ for service and style.

★Harborside Inn BOUTIQUE HOTEL $$$
(Map p188; ☎617-723-7500; www.harborsideinnboston.com; 185 State St; r from $269; P ❄ @ 📶; T Aquarium) Steps from Faneuil Hall and the waterfront, this boutique hotel inhabits a respectfully renovated 19th-century mercantile warehouse. The 116 rooms are on the small side, but comfortable and appropriately nautically themed. Note that Atrium Rooms face the atrium (ahem) and Cabin Rooms have no windows at all. Add $20 for a city view (worth it).

✕ Eating

New England cuisine is known for summertime clambakes and Thanksgiving turkey. But the Boston dining scene changes it up with wide-ranging international influences and contemporary interpretations. Indulge in affordable Asian fare in Chinatown and Italian feasts in the North End; or head to the South End for the city's trendiest foodie scene.

SEAFOOD SPECIALTIES

Lobster The mighty crustacean, steamed, and usually served in its shell

Lobster roll The succulent meat of the tail and claws, mixed with a touch of mayo and served on a grilled hotdog bun

Clam chowder Or, as Bostonians say, *chow-dah*, combines chopped clams, potatoes and clam juice in a milk base

Oysters Usually served raw on the half-shell, with lemon and cocktail sauce

Steamers Soft-shelled clams, steamed and served in a bucket of briny broth

Beacon Hill & Downtown

Quincy Market FOOD COURT $

(Map p188; www.faneuilhallmarketplace.com; Congress St; 10am-9pm Mon-Sat, noon-6pm Sun; ; Haymarket) Behind Faneuil Hall, this food court offers a variety of places under one roof: the place is packed with about 20 restaurants and 40 food stalls. Choose from chowder, bagels, Indian, Greek, baked goods and ice cream, and take a seat at one of the tables in the central rotunda.

★Paramount CAFETERIA $$

(Map p188; www.paramountboston.com; 44 Charles St; mains breakfast & lunch $6-12, dinner $15-23; 7am-10pm Mon-Thu, to 11pm Fri, 8am-11pm Sat, to 10pm Sun; ; Charles/MGH) This old-fashioned cafeteria is a neighborhood favorite. A-plus diner fare includes pancakes, home fries, burgers and sandwiches, and big, hearty salads. Banana and caramel French toast is an obvious go-to for the brunch crowd. Don't sit down until you get your food! At dinner, add table service and candlelight, and the place goes upscale without losing its down-home charm.

Union Oyster House SEAFOOD $$$

(Map p188; www.unionoysterhouse.com; 41 Union St; mains lunch $15-20, dinner $22-32; 11am-9:30pm; Haymarket) The oldest restaurant in Boston, ye olde Union Oyster House has been serving seafood in this historic red-brick building since 1826. Countless history-makers have propped themselves up at this bar, including Daniel Webster and John F Kennedy. (Apparently JFK used to order the lobster bisque.) Overpriced but atmospheric.

North End

★Pomodoro ITALIAN $$

(Map p188; 617-367-4348; 351 Hanover St; mains brunch $12, dinner $23-24; 5-11pm Mon-Fri, noon-11pm Sat & Sun; Haymarket) Pomodoro has a new (only slightly larger) location, but it's still one of the North End's most romantic settings for delectable Italian. The food is simple but perfectly prepared: fresh pasta, spicy tomato sauce, grilled fish and meats, and wine by the glass. If you're lucky, you might be on the receiving end of a complimentary tiramisu for dessert. Cash only.

Giacomo's Ristorante ITALIAN $$

(Map p188; www.giacomosblog-boston.blogspot.com; 355 Hanover St; mains $14-19; 4:30-10:30pm Mon-Sat, 4-9:30pm Sun; ; Haymarket) Customers line up before the doors open so they can guarantee themselves a spot in the first round of seating at this North End favorite. Enthusiastic and entertaining waiters plus cramped quarters ensure that you get to know your neighbors. The cuisine is no-frills southern Italian fare, served in unbelievable portions. Cash only.

Seaport District

Yankee Lobster Co SEAFOOD $

(www.yankeelobstercompany.com; 300 Northern Ave; mains $11-20; 10am-9pm Mon-Sat, 11am-6pm Sun; SL1 or SL2, South Station) The Zanti family has been fishing for three generations, so they definitely know their stuff. A relatively recent addition is this retail fish market, scattered with a few tables in case you want to dine in. And you do. Order something simple like clam chowder or a lobster roll, accompany it with a cold beer, and you will not be disappointed.

★Row 34 SEAFOOD $$

(Map p188; 617-553-5900; www.row34.com; 383 Congress St; oysters $2-3, mains lunch $13-18, dinner $21-28; 11:30am-10pm Mon-Fri, 5-10pm Sat & Sun; South Station) In the heart of the new Seaport District, this is a 'workingman's oyster bar' (by working man, they mean yuppie). Set in a sharp, post-industrial space, the place offers a dozen types of raw oysters and clams, alongside an amazing selection of craft beers. There's also a full menu of cooked seafood, ranging from the traditional to the trendy.

City Walk
Freedom Trail

START BOSTON COMMON
FINISH BUNKER HILL MONUMENT
LENGTH 2.5 MILES; THREE HOURS

Trace America's earliest history along the Freedom Trail, which covers Boston's key revolutionary sites. The well-trodden route is marked by a double row of red bricks, starting at the 1 **Boston Common** (p180), America's oldest public park. Follow the trail north to the gold-domed 2 **State House** (p181), designed by Charles Bulfinch, America's first homegrown architect. Rounding Park St takes you past the Colonial-era 3 **Park Street Church**; the 4 **Granary Burying Ground** (p181), where victims of the Boston Massacre lie buried; and 5 **King's Chapel**, topped with one of Paul Revere's bells. Continue down School St, past the site of 6 **Boston's first public school** and the 7 **Old Corner Bookstore**, a haunt of 19th-century literati.

Nearby, the 8 **Old South Meeting House** (p181) tells the backstory of the Boston Tea Party. There are more Revolutionary exhibits at the 9 **Old State House** (p181). Outside, a ring of cobblestones at the intersection marks the 10 **Boston Massacre Site**, the first violent conflict of the American Revolution. Next up is 11 **Faneuil Hall** (p181), a public market since Colonial times.

Cross the Greenway to Hanover St, the main artery of the North End. Treat yourself to lunch before continuing to North Sq, where you can tour the 12 **Paul Revere House** (p184), the Revolutionary hero's former home. Follow the trail to the 13 **Old North Church** (p184), where a lookout in the steeple signaled to Revere that the British were coming, setting off his famous midnight gallop.

Walk northwest on Hull St, where you'll find more Colonial graves at 14 **Copp's Hill Burying Ground**. Then cross the Charlestown Bridge to reach the 15 **USS Constitution** (p184), the world's oldest commissioned warship. To the north lies 16 **Bunker Hill Monument** (p185), the site of the first battle fought in the American Revolution.

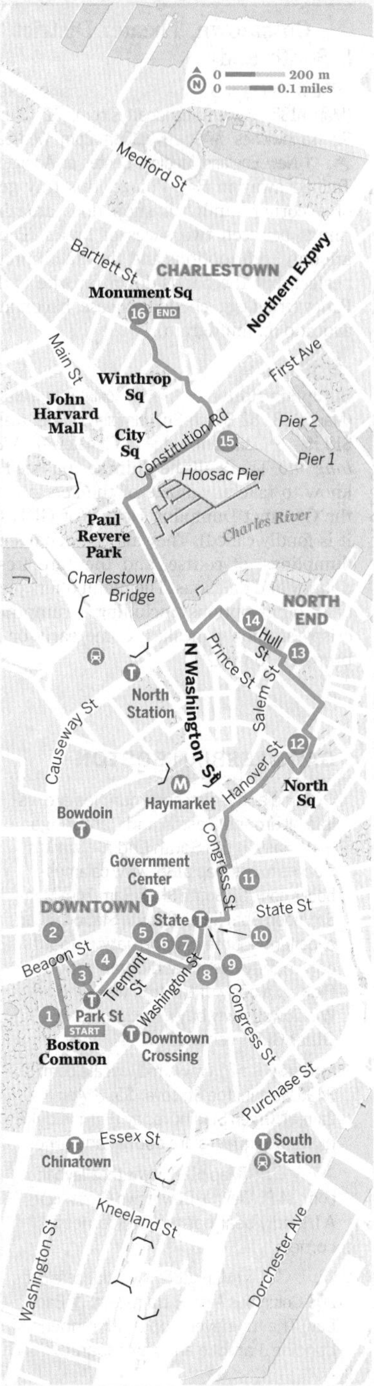

Chinatown, Theater District & South End

Mike & Patty's SANDWICHES $

(Map p188; www.mikeandpattys.com; 12 Church St; sandwiches $7-9; 7:30am-2pm Wed-Sun; ; New England Medical Center or Arlington) Tucked away in Bay Village, this tiny gem of a corner sandwich shop does amazing things between two slices of bread. There are only eight options and they're all pretty perfect, but the hands-down favorite is the Fancy (fried egg, cheddar cheese, bacon and avocado on multigrain).

★**Gourmet Dumpling House** CHINESE, TAIWANESE $

(Map p188; 52 Beach St; dumplings $2-8, mains $10-15; 11am-1am; ; Chinatown) *Xiao long bao*. That's all the Chinese you need to know to take advantage of the specialty at the Gourmet Dumpling House (or GDH, as it is fondly called). They are Shanghai soup dumplings, of course, and they are fresh, doughy and delicious. The menu offers plenty of other options, including scrumptious crispy scallion pancakes. Come early or be prepared to wait.

GAY & LESBIAN BOSTON

Out and active gay communities are visible all around Boston and Cambridge, especially in the South End. **Calamus Bookstore** (Map p188; www.calamus-books.com; 92 South St; 9am-7pm Mon-Sat, noon-6pm Sun; South Station) is an excellent source of information about community events and organizations. Pick up a copy of the free weekly *Bay Windows* (www.baywindows.com). Other GLBT venues:

Midway Café (www.midwaycafe.com; 3496 Washington St; cover $5; 4pm-2am; Green St) Thursday night is dyke night, but queers are cool at any time.

Alley Bar (Map p188; www.thealleybar.com; 14 Pi Alley; Downtown Crossing) A friendly bear bar that welcomes all comers.

Club Café (Map p188; www.clubcafe.com; 209 Columbus Ave; 11am-2am; Back Bay) The fun never stops with dinner, dancing, karaoke and gay cabaret.

Myers & Chang ASIAN $$

(Map p182; 617-542-5200; www.myersandchang.com; 1145 Washington St; small plates $10-18; 11:30am-10pm Sun-Thu, to 11pm Fri & Sat; ; SL4 or SL5, New England Medical Center) This super-hip Asian spot blends Thai, Chinese and Vietnamese cuisines, which means delicious dumplings, spicy stir-fries and oodles of noodles. The kitchen staff does amazing things with a wok, and the menu of small plates allows you to sample a wide selection of dishes. The vibe is casual but cool, international and original.

Back Bay & Fenway

★**Courtyard** MODERN AMERICAN $$

(Map p182; www.thecateredaffair.com; 700 Boylston St; mains $17-22; 11:30am-4pm Mon-Fri; ; Copley) The perfect destination for an elegant luncheon with artfully prepared food is – believe it or not – the Boston Public Library. Overlooking the beautiful Italianate courtyard, this grown-up restaurant serves seasonal, innovative and exotic dishes (along with a few standards). After 2pm, the Courtyard serves a delightful afternoon tea ($32), with a selection of sandwiches, scones and sweets.

★**Island Creek Oyster Bar** SEAFOOD $$$

(Map p182; 617-532-5300; www.islandcreekoysterbar.com; 500 Commonwealth Ave; oysters $2.50-4, mains lunch $18-21, dinner $25-35; 4pm-1am; Kenmore) Island Creek has united 'farmer, chef and diner in one space' – and what a space it is. ICOB serves up the region's finest oysters, along with other local seafood, in an ethereal new-age setting. The specialty – lobster roe noodles topped with braised short ribs and grilled lobster – lives up to the hype.

Cambridge

★**Clover Food Lab** VEGETARIAN $

(Map p182; www.cloverfoodlab.com; 7 Holyoke St; mains $6-7; 7am-midnight Mon-Sat, to 7pm Sun; ; Harvard) Clover is on the cutting edge. It's all high-tech with its 'live' menu updates and electronic ordering system. But it's really about the food – local, seasonal, vegetarian food – that is cheap, delicious and fast. How fast? Check the menu. Interesting tidbit: Clover started as a food truck (and still has a few trucks making the rounds).

★**Alden & Harlow** MODERN AMERICAN $

(Map p182; 617-864-2100; www.aldenharlow.com; 40 Brattle St; small plates $9-17; 5pm-1am Sun-

Wed, to 2am Thu-Sat; ; Harvard) This spanking-new place in a cozy subterranean space is offering a brand-new take on American cooking. The small plates are made for sharing, so everyone in your party gets to sample. And you will want to sample, because these local ingredients are prepared in ways you've never seen before. By the way, it's no secret that the 'Secret Burger' is amazing.

Drinking & Nightlife

★Bleacher Bar SPORTS BAR
(Map p182; www.bleacherbarboston.com; 82a Lansdowne St; 11am-1am Sun-Wed, to 2am Thu-Sat; Kenmore) Tucked under the bleachers at Fenway Park, this classy bar offers a view onto center field. It's not the best place to watch the game, as the place gets packed, but it's a fun way to experience America's oldest ballpark, even when the Sox are not playing. Gentlemen: enjoy the view from the loo!

If you want a seat in front of the window, get your name on the waiting list an hour or two before game time; once seated, diners have 45 minutes in the hot seat.

★Drink COCKTAIL BAR
(Map p188; www.drinkfortpoint.com; 348 Congress St; 4pm-1am; SL1 or SL2, South Station) There is no cocktail menu at Drink. Instead you have a little chat with the bartender, and he or she will whip something up according to your specifications. The bar takes seriously the art of drink mixology – and you will too, after you sample one of its concoctions. The subterranean space creates a dark, sexy atmosphere, which makes for a great date destination.

Beat Hotel BAR
(Map p182; www.beathotel.com; 13 Brattle St; 4pm-midnight Mon-Wed, to 2am Thu & Fri, 10am-2am Sat, to midnight Sun; Harvard) A great addition to Harvard Sq, this vast, underground bistro packs in good-looking patrons for international food, classy cocktails and live jazz and blues. It's inspired by the Beat Generation writers – and named for a rundown Parisian motel where they hung out – but there's nothing down-and-out about this hot spot.

Warren Tavern PUB
(Map p182; www.warrentavern.com; 2 Pleasant St; 11am-1am Mon-Fri, 10am-1am Sat & Sun; Community College) One of the oldest pubs in Boston, the Warren Tavern has been pouring pints for its customers since George Washington and Paul Revere drank here. It is named for General Joseph Warren, a fallen hero of the Battle of Bunker Hill (shortly after which – in 1780 – this pub was opened). Also recommended as a lunch stop.

> **CHEAP SEATS**
>
> **BosTix kiosks** (www.bostix.org; 10am-6pm Tue-Sat, 11am-4pm Sun) Offers discounted tickets to theater productions citywide (up to 25% off for advance purchases online). Discounts up to 50% are available for same-day purchase: check the website to see what's available. Purchases must be made in person, in cash, at outlets on Copley Sq or at Quincy Market.

Entertainment

For up-to-the-minute listings, grab a copy of the free *Boston Phoenix*.

Live Music

★Club Passim LIVE MUSIC
(Map p182; 617-492-7679; www.clubpassim.org; 47 Palmer St; tickets $15-30; Harvard) Folk music in Boston seems to be endangered outside of Irish bars, but the legendary Club Passim does such a great job booking top-notch acts that it practically fills in the vacuum by itself. The colorful, intimate room is hidden off a side street in Harvard Sq, just as it has been since 1969.

★Red Room @ Café 939 LIVE MUSIC
(Map p182; www.cafe939.com; 939 Boylston St; 8-11pm Wed-Sun; Hynes) Run by Berklee students, the Red Room @ 939 has emerged as one of Boston's least predictable and most enjoyable music venues. The place has an excellent sound system and a baby grand piano; most importantly, it books interesting, eclectic up-and-coming musicians. Check out wicked local Wednesdays to sample the local sound. Buy tickets in advance at the Berklee Performance Center.

Sinclair LIVE MUSIC
(Map p182; www.sinclaircambridge.com; 52 Church St; tickets $15-18; 5pm-1am Mon, 11am-1am Tue-Sun; Harvard) This is a great small venue to hear live music. The acoustics are excellent and the mezzanine level allows you to escape the crowds on the floor. The club attracts a good range of local and regional bands and DJs.

Classical Music & Theater

★Boston Symphony Orchestra CLASSICAL MUSIC
(BSO; Map p182; ☎617-266-1200; www.bso.org; 301 Massachusetts Ave; tickets $30-115; Ⓣ Symphony) Flawless acoustics match the ambitious programs of the world-renowned Boston Symphony Orchestra. From September to April, the BSO performs in the beauteous **Symphony Hall** (Map p182; www.bso.org; 301 Massachusetts Ave; ⏰tours 4pm Wed & 2pm Sat, reservation required), featuring an ornamental high-relief ceiling and attracting a fancy-dress crowd. In summer months, the BSO retreats to Tanglewood in Western Massachusetts.

Opera House LIVE PERFORMANCE
(Map p188; www.bostonoperahouse.com; 539 Washington St; Ⓣ Downtown Crossing) This lavish theater has been restored to its 1928 glory, complete with mural-painted ceiling, gilded molding and plush velvet curtains. The glitzy venue regularly hosts productions from the Broadway Across America series, and is also the main performance space for the Boston Ballet.

Sports

★Fenway Park BASEBALL
(Map p182; www.redsox.com; 4 Yawkey Way; bleachers $12-40, grandstand $29-78, box $50-75; Ⓣ Kenmore) From April to September you can watch the Red Sox play at **Fenway Park** (Map p182; www.redsox.com; 4 Yawkey Way; tours adult/child $18/12; ⏰10am-5pm; 👪; Ⓣ Kenmore), the nation's oldest and most storied ballpark. Unfortunately, it is also the most expensive – not that this stops the Fenway faithful from scooping up the tickets. There are sometimes game-day tickets on sale starting 90 minutes before the opening pitch.

TD Garden BASKETBALL, ICE HOCKEY
(Map p188; ☎information 617-523-3030, tickets 617-931-2000; www.tdgarden.com; 150 Causeway St; Ⓣ North Station) The TD Garden is home to the Bruins, who play hockey here from September to June, and the Celtics, who play basketball from October to April. It's the city's largest venue, so big-name musicians perform here, too.

Shopping

Newbury St in the Back Bay and Charles St on Beacon Hill are Boston's best shopping destinations for the biggest selection of shops, both traditional and trendy. Harvard Sq is famous for bookstores and the South End is the city's up-and-coming art district. **Copley Place** (Map p182; www.simon.com; 100 Huntington Ave; ⏰10am-8pm Mon-Sat, noon-6pm Sun; Ⓣ Back Bay) and the **Prudential Center** (Map p182; www.prudentialcenter.com; 800 Boylston St; ⏰10am-9pm Mon-Sat, 11am-8pm Sun; 📶; Ⓣ Prudential), both in Back Bay, are big indoor malls.

★Ruby Door JEWELRY
(Map p188; www.therubydoor.com; 15 Charles St; ⏰11am-6pm Mon-Sat; Ⓣ Charles/MGH) What will you find behind the ruby door? Gorgeous, hand-crafted jewelry, much of it featuring intriguing gemstones and unique vintage

BOSTON FOR CHILDREN

Boston is one giant history museum, the setting for many educational and lively field trips. Cobblestone streets and costume-clad tour guides can bring to life events from American history. Hands-on experimentation and interactive exhibits fuse education and entertainment.

Changing stations are ubiquitous in public restrooms and many restaurants offer children's menus and high chairs. You'll have no trouble taking your kid's stroller on the T.

A good place to start your family's exploration is the **Public Garden** (p185), where Swan Boats ply the lagoon and tiny tots climb on the bronze ducklings. Across the street at the **Boston Common** (p180), kids can cool their toes in the Frog Pond, ride the carousel and romp at the playground. At the **New England Aquarium** (p181), kids of all ages will enjoy face-to-face encounters with underwater creatures.

Great tours for kids:

Boston for Little Feet (p187) The only Freedom Trail walking tour designed especially for children aged six to 12

Urban AdvenTours (p187) Rents kids' bikes and helmets, as well as bike trailers for toddlers

Boston Duck Tours (p187) Quirky quackiness is always a hit

elements. Designer and owner Tracy Chareas reworks antique and vintage jewels into thoroughly modern pieces of art. There is also plenty of more affordable jewelry for bauble lovers. Great for browsing, with no pressure to buy.

Blackstone's of Beacon Hill GIFTS, ACCESSORIES
(Map p188; www.blackstonesbeaconhill.com; 46 Charles St; ⏲10am-6:30pm Mon-Sat, 11am-5pm Sun; Ⓣ Charles/MGH) Here's a guarantee: you will find the perfect gift for that certain someone at Blackstone's. This little place is crammed with classy, clever and otherwise unusual items. Highlights include the custom-designed stationery, locally made handicrafts and quirky Boston-themed souvenirs like clocks and coasters. Otherwise, you can't go wrong with a solar-powered rotating globe – everyone needs one!

Lucy's League CLOTHING
(Map p188; www.rosterstores.com/lucysleague; North Market, Faneuil Hall; ⏲10am-9pm Mon-Sat, to 6pm Sun; Ⓣ Government Center) We're not advocating those pink Red Sox caps, but sometimes a girl wants to look good while she's supporting the team. At Lucy's League, fashionable sports fans will find shirts, jackets and other gear sporting the local teams' logos in super-cute styles designed to flatter the female figure.

Converse SHOES, CLOTHING
(Map p182; www.converse.com; 348 Newbury St; ⏲10am-7pm Mon-Fri, to 8pm Sat, 11am-6pm Sun; Ⓣ Hynes) Converse started making shoes right up the road in Malden, Massachusetts way back in 1908. Chuck Taylor joined the 'team' in the 1920s and the rest is history. This retail store (one of three in the country) carries sneakers, denim and other gear. The iconic shoes come in all colors and patterns; make them uniquely your own at the in-store customization area.

Sault New England CLOTHING, GIFTS
(Map p182; www.saultne.com; 577 Tremont St; ⏲11am-7pm Tue-Sun; Ⓣ Back Bay) Blending prepster and hipster, rustic and chic, this little basement boutique packs in a lot of intriguing stuff. The eclectic mix of merchandise runs the gamut from new and vintage clothing to coffee-table books and homemade terrariums. A New England theme runs through the store, with nods to the Kennedys, *Jaws* and LL Bean.

DON'T MISS

OPEN MARKETS

Part flea market and part artists' market, this weekly outdoor event is a fabulous opportunity for strolling, shopping and people-watching. More than 100 vendors set up shop under white tents. It's never the same two weeks in a row, but there's always plenty of arts and crafts, as well as edgier art, vintage clothing, jewelry, local farm produce and homemade sweets. In summer months, catch it on Saturday on the **Rose Kennedy Greenway** (Map p188; www.newenglandopenmarkets.com; Rose Kennedy Greenway; ⏲11am-5pm Sat May-Oct; 📶; Ⓣ Aquarium) and Sunday in the **South End** (Map p182; www.newenglandopenmarkets.com; Thayer St; ⏲10am-4pm Sun May-Oct; 🚌 SL4 or SL5, Ⓣ New England Medical Center).

Olives & Grace GIFTS
(Map p182; www.olivesandgrace.com; 623 Tremont St; ⏲10am-7pm; Ⓣ Back Bay) This little shoebox of a store offers an eclectic array of gift items – many from New England – all of them made with love and thoughtfulness by artisans. The most enticing items are the foodstuffs, including chocolate bars, hot sauces, raw honey, saltwater taffy and, um, beef jerky.

Lunarik Fashions ACCESSORIES
(Map p182; 279 Newbury St; ⏲11am-7pm Mon-Fri, 10am-8pm Sat, noon-6pm Sun; Ⓣ Hynes) Like a modern woman's handbag, Lunarik is packed with useful stuff, much of it by local designers. Look for whimsical collage-covered pieces by Jenn Sherr, beautiful hand-crafted jewelry by Dasken Designs, and the best-selling richly colored leather handbags by Saya Cullinan. Who wouldn't want to pack their stuff into that!

ℹ Information

INTERNET ACCESS

Aside from hotels, wireless access is common at cafes, on buses and even in public spaces like Faneuil Hall and the Greenway. Many cafes charge a fee, though they may offer the first hour free of charge.

Boston Public Library (www.bpl.org; 700 Boylston St; ⏲9am-9pm Mon-Thu, to 5pm Fri & Sat year-round, 1-5pm Sun Oct-May; 📶; Ⓣ Copley) Internet access free for 15-minute intervals. Or get a visitor courtesy card at the circulation

GETTING TO NYC

The cheapest travel between Boston and NYC is by bus, including **Lucky Star Bus** (www.luckystarbus.com; South Station; one way $20; wi-fi) and **Megabus** (www.megabus.com; South Station; one-way $10-30; wi-fi), both departing from South Station. **Go Bus** (www.gobuses.com; Alewife Brook Pkwy; one way $18-34; wi-fi; T Alewife) departs from Alewife station in Cambridge.

desk and sign up for one hour of free terminal time. Arrive first thing in the morning to avoid long waits.

Wired Puppy (www.wiredpuppy.com; 250 Newbury St; 6:30am-7:30pm; wi-fi; T Hynes) Free wireless access and free computer use in case you don't have your own. This is also a comfortable, cozy place to just come and drink coffee.

MEDIA

Boston Globe (www.boston.com) One of two major daily newspapers, the *Globe* publishes an extensive Calendar section every Thursday and the daily Sidekick, both of which include entertainment options.

Improper Bostonian (www.improper.com) A sassy biweekly distributed free from sidewalk dispenser boxes.

TOURIST INFORMATION

Cambridge Visitor Information Kiosk (Map p182; www.cambridge-usa.org; Harvard Sq; 9am-5pm Mon-Fri, 1-5pm Sat & Sun; T Harvard) Detailed information on current Cambridge happenings and self-guided walking tours.

Boston Common Information Kiosk (GBCVB Visitors Center; Map p188; www.bostonusa.com; Boston Common; 8:30am-5pm; T Park St) Starting point for the Freedom Trail and many other walking tours.

USEFUL WEBSITES

My Secret Boston (www.mysecretboston.com) Not-that-secret restaurants, nightlife, cultural and family events.

Universal Hub (www.universalhub.com) Round-up of local news, with rich local commentary.

City of Boston (www.cityofboston.gov) Official website of Boston city government with links to visitor services.

Getting There & Away

Getting in and out of Boston is easy. The train and bus stations are conveniently side by side, and the airport is a short subway ride away.

AIR

Logan International Airport (800-235-6426; www.massport.com/logan), just across Boston Harbor from the city center, is served by major US and foreign airlines and has full services.

BUS

South Station is the terminal for an extensive network of long-distance buses operated by Greyhound and regional bus companies.

TRAIN

MBTA Commuter Rail (800-392-6100, 617-222-3200; www.mbta.com) trains connect Boston's North Station with Concord and Salem and Boston's South Station with Plymouth and Providence.

The **Amtrak** (800-872-7245; www.amtrak.com; South Station) terminal is at South Station; trains to New York cost $75 to $125 for the Northeast Regional (4¼ hours) or $130 to $170 on the speedier *Acela Express* (3½ hours).

Getting Around

TO/FROM THE AIRPORT

Logan International Airport is just a few miles from downtown Boston: take the blue-line subway or the silver-line bus.

CAR

Driving in Boston is not for the faint of heart. It's easier to get around the city on public transportation.

SUBWAY

The **MBTA** (617-222-3200; www.mbta.com; per ride $2.10-2.65; 5:30am-12:30am Sun-Thu, to 2am Fri & Sat) operates the USA's oldest subway (known as the 'T'), built in 1897. Five color-coded lines – red, blue, green and orange – radiate from the downtown stations of Park St, Downtown Crossing and Government Center. 'Inbound' trains are headed for one of these stations, 'outbound' trains away from them. Note that the silver line is actually a 'bus rapid transit service' that is useful for Logan airport and some other destinations.

TAXI

Taxis are plentiful; expect to pay between $15 and $25 between two points within the city limits. Flag taxis on the street or find them at major hotels. For airport transfers, call **Cabbie's Cab** (617-547-2222; www.cabbiescab.com; airport $35).

Around Boston

Boston may be the state capital, but it's not the only town in Massachusetts with traveler appeal. Up and down the coast, destinations with rich histories, vibrant cultural scenes and unique events merit a venture outside the city. Easily accessible from Boston by car or train, these are ideal day-trip destinations.

Lexington & Concord

Students of history and lovers of liberty can trace the events of the fateful day that started a revolution – April 19, 1775. Follow in the footsteps of British soldiers and colonial minutemen, who tromped out to Lexington to face off on the town green, then continued on to Concord for the battle at the Old North Bridge.

A century later, Concord harbored a vibrant literary community, including the likes of Nathaniel Hawthorne, Ralph Waldo Emerson, Henry David Thoreau and Louisa May Alcott, whose homes are now open for visitors. The **Concord Chamber of Commerce** (www.concordchamberofcommerce.org; 58 Main St; ⏲10am-4pm Mar-Oct) has full details on the sites, as well as walking tours of Concord.

★Old North Bridge HISTORIC SITE

(www.nps.gov/mima; Monument St; ⏲dawn-dusk) A half-mile north of Memorial Sq in Concord center, the wooden span of Old North Bridge is the site of the 'shot heard around the world' (as Emerson wrote in his poem 'Concord Hymn'). This is where enraged minutemen fired on British troops, forcing them to retreat to Boston. Daniel Chester French's first statue, *Minute Man*, presides over the park from the opposite side of the bridge.

Battle Green HISTORIC SITE

(Massachusetts Ave) The historic Battle Green is where the skirmish between patriots and British troops jump-started the War for Independence. The **Lexington Minuteman Statue** (crafted by Henry Hudson Kitson in 1900) stands guard at the southeast end of Battle Green, honoring the bravery of the 77 minutemen who met the British here in 1775, and the eight who died.

Minute Man National Historic Park PARK

(www.nps.gov/mima; 250 North Great Rd, Lincoln; ⏲9am-5pm Apr-Oct; 👪) FREE Two miles west of Lexington center, the route that British troops followed to Concord has been designated the Minute Man National Historic Park. The **visitors center** at the eastern end of the park shows an informative multimedia presentation depicting Paul Revere's ride and the ensuing battles.

Walden Pond STATE PARK

(www.mass.gov/dcr/parks/walden; 915 Walden St; parking $5; ⏲dawn-dusk) FREE Thoreau took the naturalist beliefs of Transcendentalism out of the realm of theory and into practice when he left the comforts of town and built a rustic cabin at Walden Pond. Now a state park, the glacial pond is surrounded by acres of forest preserved by the nonprofit Walden Woods project. The site of Thoreau's cabin is on the northeast side, marked by a cairn and signs.

ℹ Getting There & Away

MBTA buses 62 and 76 run from Alewife T-station (Cambridge) to Lexington center, though they don't run on Sunday. For Concord, take the **MBTA**

GRAB A BIKE

Note that the Hubway pricing is designed so a bike ride can substitute for a cab ride (eg to make a one-way trip or run an errand). For leisurely riding or long trips, go for a longer-term rental.

Hubway (www.thehubway.com; 24/72hr membership $6/12, 30/60/90 minutes free/$2/4; ⏲24hr) Boston's bike-share program is the Hubway. There are 140 Hubway stations around Boston, Cambridge, Brookline and Somerville, stocked with 1300 bikes that are available for short-term loan. Purchase a temporary membership at any bicycle kiosk, then pay by the half-hour for the use of the bikes (free under 30 minutes). Return the bike to any station in the vicinity of your destination.

Urban AdvenTours (www.urbanadventours.com; 103 Atlantic Ave; per day $35; ⏲9am-6pm Mon-Sat; T Aquarium) Bikes available for rental include road bikes and mountain bikes, in addition to the standard hybrids. For an extra fee these guys will bring your bike to your doorstep in a BioBus powered by vegetable oil.

commuter rail (☎617-222-3200, 800-392-6100; www.mbta.com; Concord Depot, 90 Thoreau St) from North Station to Concord Depot ($8.50, 40 minutes, 12 daily).

Salem

A lot of history is packed into this gritty city. The town's very name conjures up images of diabolical witchcraft and women being burned at the stake. The famous Salem witch trials of 1692 are engrained in the national memory, and the town embraces its role as 'Witch City', with witchy museums, spooky tours and Halloween madness.

These incidents obscure Salem's true claim to fame: its glory days as a center for clipper-ship trade with the Far East. The **NPS Regional Visitor Center** (www.nps.gov/sama; 2 New Liberty St; ⌚9am-5pm) has complete information about the National Historic Site and environs.

★ **Salem Maritime National Historic Site** HISTORIC SITE
(www.nps.gov/sama; 193 Derby St; ⌚9am-5pm) FREE This National Historic Site comprises the Custom House, the wharves and the other buildings that are remnants of the shipping industry that once thrived here. Of the 50 wharves that once lined Salem Harbor, only three remain, the longest of which is **Derby Wharf**. Visitors can stroll out to the end and peek inside the 1871 lighthouse or climb aboard the tall ship *Friendship*.

★ **Peabody Essex Museum** ART MUSEUM
(www.pem.org; 161 Essex St; adult/child $18/free; ⌚10am-5pm Tue-Sun; 👪) All of the art, artifacts and curiosities that Salem merchants brought back from the Far East were the foundation for this museum. Founded in 1799, it is the country's oldest museum in continuous operation. The building itself is impressive, with a light-filled atrium, and is a wonderful setting for the vast collections, which focus on New England decorative arts and maritime history. Predictably, PEM is also strong in Asian art, especially the collection from pre-industrial Japan.

ℹ Getting There & Away

The **MBTA commuter rail** (www.mbta.com) runs from Boston's North Station to Salem depot ($7, 30 minutes). **Boston Harbor Cruises** (Salem Ferry; www.bostonharborcruises.com; 10 Blaney St; round-trip adult/child $27/22; ⌚May-Oct) operates the ferry from Long Wharf to Salem (1 way adult/child $25/20, 50 minutes).

Plymouth

Plymouth calls itself 'America's Home Town.' It was here that the Pilgrims first settled in the winter of 1620, seeking a place where they could practice their religion without interference from government. An innocuous, weathered ball of granite – the famous **Plymouth Rock** – marks the spot where where they supposedly first stepped ashore in this foreign land, and many museums and historic houses in the surrounding streets recall their struggles, sacrifices and triumphs.

★ **Mayflower II** HISTORIC SITE
(www.plimoth.org; State Pier, Water St; adult/child $12/8; ⌚9am-5pm Apr-Nov; 👪) If Plymouth Rock tells us little about the Pilgrims, *Mayflower II* speaks volumes. It is a replica of the small ship in which they made the fateful voyage. Actors in period costume are often on board, recounting harrowing tales from the journey.

WITCH CITY

The city of Salem embraces its witchy past with a healthy dose of whimsy. But the history offers a valuable lesson about what can happen when fear and frenzy are allowed to trump common sense and compassion.

By the time the witch hysteria of 1692 had finally died down, a total of 156 people had been accused, 55 people had pleaded guilty and implicated others to save their own lives, and 14 women and five men had been hanged. Stop by at the **Witch Trials Memorial** (Charter St), a simple but dramatic monument that honors the innocent victims.

The most authentic of more than a score of witchy museums, the **Witch House** (Jonathan Corwin House; www.witchhouse.info; 310 Essex St; adult/child $8.25/4.25, tour extra $2; ⌚10am-5pm Mar-Nov) was once the home of Jonathan Corwin, a local magistrate who investigated witchcraft claims.

For an informative, accurate overview of Salem's sordid past, sign up with **Hocus Pocus Tours** (www.hocuspocustours.com; adult/child $16/8), which is neither hokey nor pokey.

★**Plimoth Plantation**   MUSEUM
(www.plimoth.org; 137 Warren Ave; adult/child
$26/15; ⊙9am-5pm Apr-Nov; 🚻) Three miles
south of Plymouth center, Plimoth Plantation authentically recreates the Pilgrims' settlement, in its primary exhibit entitled 1627
English Village. Everything in the village –
costumes, implements, vocabulary, artistry,
recipes and crops – has been painstakingly researched and remade. Costumed interpreters,
acting in character, explain the details of daily
life and answer your questions as you watch
them work and play.

❶ Getting There & Away

Plymouth & Brockton (P&B; www.p-b.com)
buses travel hourly from Boston South Station
(adult/child $15/8, one hour). Alternatively, take
the **MBTA commuter rail** (☑617-222-3200, 800-
392-6100; www.mbta.com) ($10.50, 90 minutes),
also from South Station.

Cape Cod

Fringed with 400 miles of sparkling shoreline,
the Cape offers a beach for every mood. Besides sun, surf and sand, there are lighthouses to climb, oysters to eat, art to admire, and
trails to hike or bike. Find all the info you
need at the Cape Cod Chamber of Commerce (☑508-362-3225; www.capecodchamber.
org; MA 132 at US 6, Hyannis; ⊙9am-5pm Mon-Sat,
10am-2pm Sun).

Sandwich

Cape Cod's oldest town (founded in 1637)
makes a perfect first impression as you cross
over the canal from the mainland. In the village center, white-steepled churches, period
homes and a working grist mill surround
a picturesque swan pond. Before you leave
town, take a stroll across the Sandwich
boardwalk, which extends 1350 scenic feet
across an expansive marsh to Town Neck
Beach.

◉ Sights

Heritage Museums & Gardens   MUSEUM
(www.heritagemuseumsandgardens.org; 67 Grove
St; adult/child $18/8; ⊙10am-5pm; 🚻) Fun for
kids and adults alike, this 76-acre site sports
a superb vintage automobile collection in a
Shaker-style round barn, a working 1912 carousel, folk art collections and an outdoor play
area for kids. The grounds also contain one

LOBSTER ICE CREAM

Lobster mania takes a new twist at
Ben & Bill's Chocolate Emporium
(☑508-548-7878; 209 Main St; cones $5;
⊙9am-11pm) where the crustacean has
crawled onto the ice-cream menu. Forget plain vanilla. Step up to the counter
and order a scoop of lobster ice cream.
Now there's one you won't find with the
old 31 flavors folks.

of the country's finest rhododendron gardens,
which is ablaze with color in early June.

If museums and gardens sound sedate,
think again. The on-site Adventure Center
(www.heritageadventurepark.org; 67 Grove St; adult/
child $43/38; ⊙9am-6pm daily Jun-Oct, 9am-6pm
Sat & Sun only May & Nov) has five 'aerial trails'
that offer a whole new perspective on the forest and gardens.

Sandwich Glass Museum   MUSEUM
(www.sandwichglassmuseum.org; 129 Main St;
adult/child $9/2; ⊙9:30am-5pm Apr-Dec, to 4pm
Wed-Sun Feb-Mar) Artfully displayed here is
the town's 19th-century glass-making heritage. Glass-blowing demonstrations are given
hourly throughout the day.

Cape Cod Canal   CANAL
(www.capecodcanal.us; 🚻🐕) **FREE** The Cape
Cod Canal was dug in 1914 to save ships the
treacherous 135-mile sail around the tip of the
Cape. The 7-mile canal is bordered on both
sides by paved bike paths, also ideal for ideal for walking, in-line skating and fishing. In
Sandwich, get more info at the Cape Cod Canal Visitors Center (www.capecodcanal.us; 60
Ed Moffitt Dr; ⊙10am-5pm May-Oct) **FREE**, near
the marina.

🛏 Sleeping & Eating

Shawme-Crowell State Forest CAMPGROUND **$**
(☑508-888-0351; www.reserveamerica.com; MA
130; tent sites $17; 🐕) You'll find 285 shady
campsites in this 760-acre woodland near
MA 6A.

Belfry Inn & Bistro   B&B **$$$**
(☑508-888-8550; www.belfryinn.com; 8 Jarves St;
r incl breakfast $179-299; 🅿🛜) Ever fall asleep
in church? Then you'll love the rooms, some
with stained-glass windows, in this creative-
ly restored former church. If you're uneasy
about the angel Gabriel watching over you
in bed, Belfry has two other nearby inns with

LOCAL KNOWLEDGE

SCENIC DRIVE: CAPE COD BAY

The best way to explore the Cape is on the **Old King's Highway (MA 6A)**, which snakes along Cape Cod Bay from Sandwich to Orleans. The longest continuous stretch of historic district in the USA, it's lined with gracious period homes, antique shops and art galleries, all of which make for good browsing en route.

conventional rooms. There's also a lovely high-ceiling, stained-glass restaurant.

Seafood Sam's SEAFOOD $$
(508-888-4629; www.seafoodsams.com; 6 Coast Guard Rd; mains $8-20; 11am-9pm;) Sam's is a good family choice for fish and chips, fried clams and lobster rolls. Dine at outdoor picnic tables overlooking Cape Cod Canal and watch the fishing boats sail by.

Falmouth

Crowd-pleasing beaches, a terrific bike trail and the quaint seaside village of Woods Hole are the highlights of the Cape's second-largest town.

Sights & Activities

Old Silver Beach BEACH
(off MA 28A;) Deeply indented Falmouth has 70 miles of coastline, none of it finer than this long, sandy stretch of beach. A rock jetty, sandbars and tidal pools provide fun diversions for kids. Parking costs $20.

★**Shining Sea Bikeway** CYCLING
A bright star among the Cape's stellar bike trails, this 10.7-mile beaut runs along the entire west coast of Falmouth, offering unspoiled views of salt ponds, marsh and seascapes. Bike rentals are available at the north end of the trail.

Sleeping

Falmouth Heights Motor Lodge MOTEL $$
(508-548-3623; www.falmouthheightsresort.com; 146 Falmouth Heights Rd; r incl breakfast $129-259;) Don't be fooled by the name. This tidy operation is no drive-up motor lodge – it's not even on the highway. All 28 rooms are a cut above the competition. The beach and Vineyard ferry are minutes away.

Tides Motel of Falmouth MOTEL $$
(508-548-3126; www.tidesmotelcapecod.com; 267 Clinton Ave; r $180) It's all about the water. This place is smack on its own private beach, and you could spit into the ocean from your deck. Frankly, the same rooms elsewhere would be a yawn. But you came to the Cape for the water, right?

Eating

Maison Villatte CAFE $
(774-255-1855; 267 Main St; snacks $3-10; 7am-7pm Wed-Sat, to 5pm Sun) A pair of French bakers crowned in toques work the ovens, creating crusty artisan breads, flaky croissants and sinful pastries at this bakery-cafe. Hearty sandwiches and robust coffee make it an ideal lunch spot.

Pickle Jar Kitchen MODERN AMERICAN $
(508-540-6760; www.picklejarkitchen.com; 170 Main St; mains $7-14; 7am-3pm Wed-Mon;) Hearty, healthy comfort food, prepared with seasonal ingredients and lots of love. Look for satisfying hash for breakfast, delicious sammies for lunch, and lots of fresh fruit and veggies all around. And of course, don't miss the housemade pickles.

Clam Shack SEAFOOD $
(508-540-7758; 227 Clinton Ave; mains $6-15; 11:30am-7:30pm) A classic of the genre, right on Falmouth Harbor. It's tiny, with picnic tables on the back deck and lots of fried seafood.

Hyannis

Ferries, buses and planes all converge on the Cape's commercial hub. Hyannis is a launching point for boats to Nantucket and Martha's Vineyard. It was also the summer home of the Kennedys – and the site where Teddy passed away in 2009.

Sights

Hyannis is blessed with a couple of wide, warm-water beaches that are ideal for swimming. **Kalmus Beach** (Ocean St, Hyannis) is popular for windsurfing, while **Craigville Beach** (Craigville Beach Rd, Centerville) is where the college set goes; parking at either costs $15 to $20.

Cape Cod, Martha's Vineyard & Nantucket

0 10 km
0 5 miles

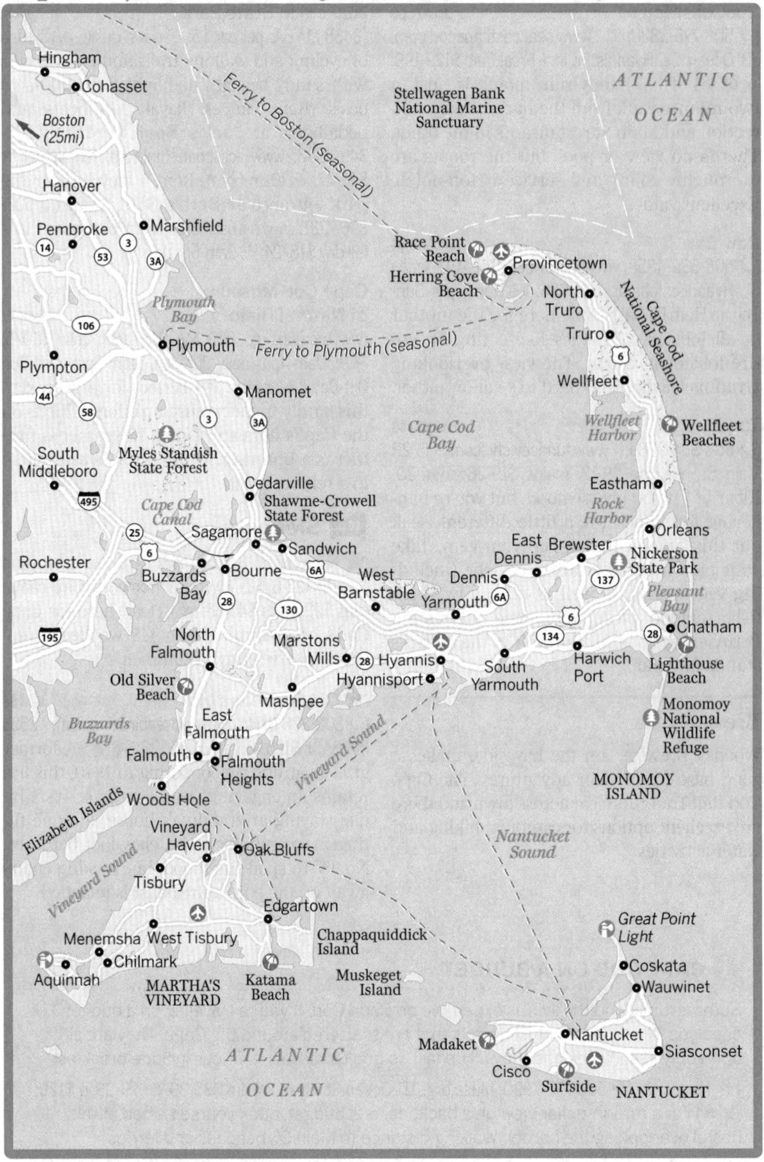

John F Kennedy Hyannis Museum MUSEUM (www.jfkhyannismuseum.org; 397 Main St, Hyannis; adult/child $10/5; ⏲9am-5pm Mon-Sat, noon-5pm Sun) Celebrates America's 35th president with photographs, videos and mementos.

For more Kennedy nostalgia, pick up a map of the **Hyannis Kennedy Legacy Trail** (www.kennedylegacytrail.org) FREE. The museum also holds the **Cape Cod Baseball League Hall of Fame**.

Sleeping & Eating

SeaCoast Inn MOTEL $$
(508-775-3828; www.seacoastcapecod.com; 33 Ocean St, Hyannis; r incl breakfast $129-199;) This family-run motel is just a two-minute walk from the harbor in one direction and Main St restaurants in the other. There's no view or pool, but the rooms are thoroughly comfy and service is top-notch. Excellent value.

Raw Bar SEAFOOD $$
(508-539-4858; www.therawbar.com; 230 Ocean St, Hyannis; lobster rolls $26; 11am-8pm Sun-Thu, to 11pm Fri-Sat) Come here for the mother of all lobster rolls – it's like eating an entire lobster in a bun. The view overlooking Hyannis Harbor isn't hard to swallow either.

Tumi SEAFOOD $$
(508-534-9289; www.tumiceviche.com; 592R Main St; ceviche $9-12, mains $19-28; 4:30-10pm;) If you love seafood, but you're hankering for something a little different, seek out this hidden Italian-Peruvian gem. Take your pick from 10 kinds of ceviche (including vegetarian), as well as other raw shellfish, seafood pasta and some interesting Peruvian options. Hint: the R in the address stands for 'rear'.

Brewster

Woodsy Brewster, on the bay side, makes a good base for outdoor adventures. The Cape Cod Rail Trail cuts clear across town and there are excellent options for camping, hiking and water activities.

Sights & Activities

Nickerson State Park PARK
(3488 MA 6A; per car $5; dawn-dusk;) Miles of cycling and walking trails and eight ponds with sandy beaches highlight this 2000-acre oasis. Rent canoes, kayaks, sailboats and pedalboats at **Jack's Boat Rental** (508-349-9808; www.jacksboatrental.com; rentals per hr $32-47; 10am-6pm). Rent a bicycle near the park entrance at **Barb's Bike Shop** (508-896-7231; www.barbsbikeshop.com; bicycles per half/full day $18/24; 9am-6pm).

Cape Cod Museum of Natural History MUSEUM
(www.ccmnh.org; 869 MA 6A; adult/child $10/5; 9:30am-4pm daily Jun-Sep, 11am-3pm Wed-Sun Oct-Dec & Mar-May;) Perfect for a rainy day, this family-friendly museum offers exhibits on the Cape's flora and fauna. If weather is fine, there's a **boardwalk trail** across a salt marsh to a remote beach.

Sleeping

★ **Nickerson State Park** CAMPGROUND $
(877-422-6762; www.reserveamerica.com; campsites $22; yurts $45-55;) Head here for Cape Cod's best camping with 418 wooded campsites. Reserve early in summer.

★ **Old Sea Pines Inn** B&B $$
(508-896-6114; www.oldseapinesinn.com; 2553 MA 6A; r $120-165, ste $155-190;) A former girls' boarding school dating to 1840, this inn retains an engaging yesteryear look. It's a bit like staying at grandma's house: antique fittings, sepia photographs, claw-foot bathtubs. No TV to spoil the mood, but rocking chairs await on the porch. Breakfast is included.

CAPE COD ON A BUDGET

Summertime, and the livin' is expensive on Cape Cod. If you're traveling on a budget, check out these excellent HI hostels that are scattered around the Cape. They are all open only in summer, and they fill up fast so book in advance. Prices include breakfast.

HI-Hyannis (508-775-7990; hiusa.org; 111 Ocean St, Hyannis; dm $35-39, d $79-99, q $129;) For a million-dollar view on a backpacker's budget, book yourself a bed at this hostel overlooking the harbor. Walking distance to Main St, beaches and ferries.

Hostelling International Eastham (508-255-2785; hiusa.org; 75 Goody Hallett Dr; dm $33-36;) This hostel is close to the beach and the bike trail, but surrounded by quiet woods. Basic cabins serve as dormitories, sleeping five to eight people each.

Hostelling International Truro (508-349-3889; hiusa.org; N Pamet Rd; dm incl breakfast $45;) Budget digs don't get more atmospheric than this former coast-guard station perched amid undulating dunes and a short stroll to the beach. It's so remote that wild turkeys are the only traffic along the road.

Eating

★ Brewster Fish House SEAFOOD $$
(☎508-896-7867; www.brewsterfish.com; 2208 MA 6A; lunch mains $12-18, dinner $25-32; ⏲11:30am-3pm & 5-9:30pm) Once a retail fish market, this tiny, unassuming bistro has earned fiercely loyal patrons, thanks to artful presentations of classic seafood dishes. Just 11 tables, and no reservations.

Cobie's SEAFOOD $$
(☎508-896-7021; www.cobies.com; 3260 MA 6A; mains $9-23; ⏲11am-9pm; 👪) Conveniently located near Nickerson State Park, this roadside clam shack dishes out fried seafood that you can crunch and munch at outdoor picnic tables.

Chatham

Main St Chatham is lined with upscale inns and shops – a hallmark of this genteel town; but there's something for everyone here. At **Chatham Fish Pier** (Shore Rd), fishers unload their catch and seals bask on nearby shoals. A mile south on Shore Rd, **Chatham Light** (⏲20min tours 1-3:30pm Wed May-Oct) FREE overlooks picturesque **Lighthouse Beach**, an endless expanse of sea and sandbars.

The two uninhabited islands off the elbow comprise the 7600-acre **Monomoy National Wildlife Refuge** (www.fws.gov/northeast/monomoy) 🍃. Take a boat tour with the **Beachcomber** (☎508-945-5265; www.sealwatch.com; Crowell Rd; North Beach water taxi adult/child $20/10; seal-watching trips adult/child $29/25; ⏲10am-5pm) or **Monomoy Island Excursions** (☎508-430-7772; www.monomoysealcruise.com; 702 MA 28, Harwich Port; 1½hr tours adult/child $36/30) to get a good look at hundreds of gray seals, harbor seals and shorebirds.

Sleeping

Chatham Highlander MOTEL $$
(☎508-945-9038; www.chathamhighlander.com; 946 Main St; r $119-209; ❄📶🏊) The rooms here, about 1 mile from the town center, are straightforward but large and clean. Unlike some stodgier resorts in town that cater to an older set, this motel welcomes families; kids will love the pair of heated pools.

Hawthorne Motel MOTEL $$$
(www.thehawthorne.com; 196 Shore Rd; d $225-330; ⏲May-Oct; ❄📶🏊) Here's your chance to wake up to a fabulous sunrise over the sandbars. It's pricey for a motel, but the rooms are tasteful, service is charming and the view is unbeatable. If you can drag yourself away from the private beach, it's a short walk into town.

> **SNACK ATTACK**
>
> On your way into Hyannis, stop at the **Cape Cod Potato Chip Factory** (☎508-775-3358; www.capecodchips.com; 100 Breeds Hill Rd, Hyannis; ⏲9am-5pm Mon-Fri) FREE for a free tour and a free sample. From MA 132 (just west of the airport), take Independence Rd a half-mile north to the factory.

Eating

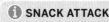

Chatham Cookware Café CAFE $
(☎508-954-1250; www.chathamcookware.com; 524 Main St; sandwiches $8; ⏲6:30am-4pm) No, it's not a place to buy pots and pans, but rather *the* downtown spot for a coffee fix, homemade muffins and sandwiches.

★ Chatham Fish Pier Market SEAFOOD $$
(☎508-945-3474; www.chathamfishpiermarket.com; 45 Barcliff Ave; mains $12-25; ⏲10am-6pm Wed-Sun) If you like it fresh and local to the core, this salt-sprayed fish shack, with its own sushi chef and day boats, is for you. The chowder's incredible, the fish so fresh it was swimming earlier in the day. It's all takeout, but there are shady picnic tables and a harbor full of sights.

Cape Cod National Seashore

Cape Cod National Seashore PARK
(www.nps.gov/caco; beach pass pedestrian/car $3/20) Cape Cod National Seashore extends some 40 miles around the curve of the Outer Cape and encompasses most of the shoreline from Eastham to Provincetown. It's a treasure trove of unspoiled beaches, dunes, salt marshes and forests. Thanks to President John F Kennedy, this vast area was set aside for preservation in the 1960s, just before a building boom hit the rest of his native Cape Cod.

The **Salt Pond Visitor Center** (☎508-255-3421; 50 Doane Rd, cnr US 6 & Nauset Rd, Eastham; ⏲9am-5pm) FREE is the place to start. Here you will find exhibits and films about the area's ecology, as well as information on the park's numerous cycling and hiking trails, some of which begin right at the center.

Coast Guard Beach BEACH

Just down the beach from the Salt Pond Visitor Center, Coast Guard Beach is a stunner that attracts everyone from surfers to beachcombers. The view of untouched Nauset Marsh from the dunes above the beach is nothing short of spectacular.

Nauset Light LIGHTHOUSE

(www.nausetlight.org; 1-4pm or 4:30-7:30pm Sun May-Oct, 4:30-7:30pm Wed Jul & Aug) Photogenic Nauset Light has been shining over Cape Cod since 1877. It stands proudly over Nauset Light Beach, which stretches north from Coast Guard Beach.

Wellfleet

Wellfleet is one of Cape Cod's unsung gems, offering some unspoiled beaches, dozens of art galleries, and plenty of opportunities to slurp those glorious oysters.

Sights

Wellfleet Beaches BEACHES

Ocean-side Wellfleet is part of the Cape Cod National Seashore, so the pristine beaches backed by undulating dunes. **Marconi Beach** has a monument to Guglielmo Marconi, who sent the first wireless transmission across the Atlantic from this site. The adjacent **White Crest Beach** and **Cahoon Hollow Beach** offer high-octane surfing. Rent your gear at **SickDay Surf Shop** (508-214-4158; www.sickdaysurf.com; 361 Main St; surfboards per day $30; 9:30am-5pm Mon-Fri).

Wellfleet Bay Wildlife Sanctuary NATURE RESERVE

(www.massaudubon.org; West Rd, off US 6; adult/child $5/3; 8:30am-dusk) Birders flock to Mass Audubon's 1100-acre sanctuary, where trails cross tidal creeks, salt marshes and beaches.

Festivals & Events

Wellfleet OysterFest FOOD

(www.wellfleetoysterfest.org; mid-Oct) The town becomes a food fair for a weekend, with a beer garden, an oyster-shucking contest and, of course, belly-busters of the blessed bivalves.

Sleeping & Eating

Even'Tide Motel MOTEL $$

(508-349-3410; www.eventidemotel.com; 650 US 6; r $89-187, cottages per week $1400-2800; May-Oct) This 31-room motel, set back from the highway in a grove of pine trees, also has nine cottages. It's a simple, friendly place with a large indoor pool, picnic facilities and a small playground.

PB Boulangerie & Bistro BAKERY $

(508-349-1600; www.pbboulangeriebistro.com; 15 Lecount Hollow Rd; pastries from $3; 7am-7pm Tue-Sun) When you walk through the door and scan the glass cases full of flaky fruit tarts and chocolate croissants, you'll think you've died and gone to Paris. Cape Cod's only Michelin-starred chef is behind this gem.

Mac's Seafood Market SEAFOOD $$

(508-349-9611; www.macsseafood.com; 265 Commercial St, Wellfleet Town Pier; mains $7-20; 11am-3pm Mon-Thu, to 8pm Fri-Sun) Head here for market-fresh seafood at bargain prices. Fried fish standards are paired with snappy-fresh oysters harvested from nearby flats. Order at a window and chow down at picnic tables overlooking Wellfleet Harbor. **Mac's Shack** (508-349-6333; 91 Commercial St; mains $15-30; 4:30-9:45pm) is a proper full-service restaurant up the street.

Entertainment

★Beachcomber LIVE MUSIC

(508-349-6055; www.thebeachcomber.com; 1120 Cahoon Hollow Rd; 5pm-1am Jun-Aug) It's a bar. It's a restaurant. It's a dance club. It's the coolest summertime hangout on the entire Cape,

DON'T MISS

CAPE COD RAIL TRAIL

One of the finest cycling trails in New England, the **Cape Cod Rail Trail** follows a former railroad track for 22 glorious miles past cranberry bogs, through quaint villages, and along sandy ponds ideal for a dip. The path begins in Dennis on MA 134 and continues all the way to Wellfleet. If you have time to do only part of the trail, begin at Nickerson State Park in Brewster and head for the Cape Cod National Seashore in Eastham. Bicycle rentals are available at the trailhead in Dennis, at Nickerson State Park and opposite the National Seashore's **Salt Pond Visitor Center** (p205).

set in a former lifesaving station right on Cahoon Hollow Beach. You can watch the surf action till the sun goes down, and after dark some really hot bands take the stage.

Wellfleet Drive-In CINEMA
(☎508-349-7176; www.wellfleetcinemas.com; US 6; adult/child $9/6;) Park your car at this 1950s-era drive-in, where everything except the feature flick is true to the era. Grab a bite to eat at the old-fashioned snack bar, hook the mono speaker over the car window and settle in for a double feature.

Provincetown

Provincetown is as far as you can go on the Cape, and more than just geographically. Fringe writers and artists began making a summer haven in Provincetown a century ago. Today this sandy outpost has morphed into the hottest gay and lesbian destination in the Northeast. Flamboyant street scenes, brilliant art galleries and unbridled nightlife paint the town center. Away from Commercial St, Provincetown's untamed coastline and vast beaches beg exploring. Sail off on a whale-watch, cruise the night away, get lost in the dunes – but whatever you do, don't miss this unique corner of New England.

Sights & Activities

Provincetown is a perfect gateway to the Cape Cod National Seashore (p205). On the wild tip of the Cape, **Race Point Beach** is a breathtaking stretch of sand with crashing surf and undulating dunes as far as the eye can see. The west-facing **Herring Cove Beach** is popular for swimming and sunset-watching. Eight exhilarating miles of **paved bike trails** crisscross the forest and dunes, providing access to both beaches. Get more information or sign up for a tour at **Province Lands Visitor Center** (www.nps.gov/caco; Race Point Rd; car/bike/pedestrian $15/3/3; 9am-5pm; P) .

★ **Provincetown Art Association & Museum** MUSEUM
(PAAM; www.paam.org; 460 Commercial St; adult/child $10/free; 11am-8pm Mon-Thu, to 10pm Fri, to 5pm Sat & Sun) Founded in 1914 to celebrate the town's thriving art community, this vibrant museum showcases the works of artists who have found their inspiration in Provincetown. Chief among them is Edward Hopper, who had a home and gallery in the Truro dunes.

DON'T MISS

FIRST PORT OF CALL

Erected in 1860 as a church, **Provincetown Public Library** (www.provincetownlibrary.org; 356 Commercial St; 10am-5pm Mon & Fri, to 8pm Tue-Thu, 1-5pm Sat & Sun;) was turned into a museum a century later, complete with a half-size replica of Provincetown's race-winning schooner *Rose Dorothea*. When the museum went bust, the town converted the building to a library. One catch: the boat was too big to remove. So it's still there, with bookshelves built around it. Pop upstairs and take a look.

Pilgrim Monument & Provincetown Museum MUSEUM
(www.pilgrim-monument.org; High Pole Rd; adult/child $12/4; 9am-5pm Apr-Nov, to 7pm Jul & Aug) Climb to the top of the USA's tallest all-granite structure (253ft) for a sweeping view of town and coast. At the base of the c 1910 tower an evocative museum depicts the landing of the *Mayflower* Pilgrims and other Provincetown history.

Whydah Pirate Museum MUSEUM
(www.whydah.com; MacMillan Wharf; adult/child $10/8; 10am-5pm May-Oct) See the salvaged booty from a pirate ship that sank off Cape Cod in 1717.

East End Gallery District GALLERIES
(Commercial St) With the many artists who have worked here, it's no surprise that Provincetown hosts some of the finest art galleries in the region. Most of them are packed into the East End of Commercial St: begin at PAAM and start walking southwest for the town's finest browsing.

★ **Dolphin Fleet Whale Watch** WHALE-WATCHING
(☎800-826-9300; www.whalewatch.com; MacMillan Wharf; adult/child $46/31; Apr-Oct;) Provincetown is the perfect launch point for whale-watching, since it's the closest port to Stellwagen Bank National Marine Sanctuary, a summer feeding ground for humpback whales. Dolphin offers as many as 12 whale-watch tours daily. Humpback whales have a flair for acrobatic breaching and come surprisingly close to the boats, offering great photo ops.

GAY & LESBIAN PROVINCETOWN

Provincetown is awash with gay clubs, drag shows and cabarets. And don't be shy if you're straight – everyone's welcome.

A-House (Atlantic House; www.ahouse.com; 4 Masonic Pl; ⌚ pub noon-1am, club 10pm-1am) P-town's gay scene got its start here and it's still one of the leading bars in town. Includes an intimate 1st-floor pub with fireplace, as well as a dance club and cabaret through a separate entrance.

Boatslip Resort (www.boatslipresort.com; 161 Commercial St; ⌚ 4-7pm) Hosts wildly popular afternoon tea dances.

Crown & Anchor (www.onlyatthecrown.com; 247 Commercial St; ⌚ hours vary) The queen of the gay scene, this multiwing complex has a nightclub, a video bar, a leather bar and a steamy cabaret that takes it to the limit.

Pied Bar (www.piedbar.com; 193 Commercial St; ⌚ noon-1am May-Oct) This woman-owned waterfront lounge is a popular dance spot for all genders. The main event is the 'After Tea T-Dance,' so folks head here after the Boatslip. Also hosts 'Women's Week' in October.

Festivals & Events

Provincetown Carnival CARNIVAL
(www.ptown.org/carnival; ⌚ 3rd week of August) Mardi Gras, drag queens, flowery floats – this is the ultimate gay party event in this gay party town, attracting tens of thousands of revelers.

Sleeping

Provincetown offers nearly 100 guesthouses, without a single chain hotel to mar the view. In summer it's wise to book ahead, doubly so on weekends. If you do arrive without a booking, the chamber of commerce keeps tabs on available rooms.

Dunes' Edge Campground CAMPGROUND $
(☎ 508-487-9815; www.dunesedge.com; 386 US 6; tent/RV sites $49/61; ⌚ mid-May–mid-Oct) Camp amid the dunes at this family-friendly campground.

Moffett House GUESTHOUSE $$
(☎ 508-487-6615; www.moffetthouse.com; 296a Commercial St; d without bathroom $75-164, d with bathroom $115-185; ❄ 📶 🐾) Set back in a quiet alleyway, this guesthouse has a bonus: free bicycles. Rooms are basic – feels sort of like crashing with a friend – but you get kitchen privileges and lots of ops to meet fellow travelers.

Captain's House B&B $$
(☎ 508-487-9353; www.captainshouseptown.com; 350A Commercial St; r without bathroom $100-175, r with bathroom $210; P ❄ 📶) Occupying an actual former sea captain's house, this small B&B is a charming affordable option in the heart of P-town. Rooms are small, but cozy and comfortable. Your hosts Peter and Mauricio are equally charming. Breakfast features Mauricio's delicious homemade granola.

★ **Carpe Diem** BOUTIQUE HOTEL $$$
(☎ 508-487-4242; www.carpediemguesthouse.com; 12 Johnson St; r incl breakfast $279-469; ❄ @ 📶) Sophisticated yet relaxed, this boutique inn blends a soothing mix of smiling Buddhas, orchid sprays and artistic decor. Each guest room is inspired by a different gay literary genius; the room themed on poet Raj Rao, for example, has sumptuous embroidered fabrics and hand-carved Indian furniture. The onsite spa includes a Finnish sauna, hot tub and massage therapy.

Revere Guesthouse B&B $$$
(☎ 508-487-2292; www.reverehouse.com; 14 Court St; r incl breakfast $169-359; ❄ 📶) Tasteful rooms, fresh-baked breakfast goodies and welcoming little touches will make you feel right at home here. The setting is peaceful, yet just minutes from all the action.

Eating

Cafe Heaven CAFE $
(☎ 508-487-9639; 199 Commercial St; mains $7-12; ⌚ 8am-10pm; 🖉) Light and airy but small and crowded, this art-filled storefront is an easy-on-the-wallet eating place. The menu ranges from sinful croissant French toast to healthy salads. Don't be deterred by the wait – the tables turn over quickly.

★Mews Restaurant & Cafe
MODERN AMERICAN $$$

(☎508-487-1500; www.mews.com; 429 Commercial St; mains bistro $13-22, restaurant $27-31; ⏰5:30-10pm) Want affordable gourmet? Skip the excellent but pricey restaurant and go upstairs to the bar for a fab view, great martinis and scrumptious bistro fare.

Lobster Pot
SEAFOOD $$$

(☎508-487-0842; www.ptownlobsterpot.com; 321 Commercial St; mains $22-37; ⏰11:30am-9pm) True to its name, this bustling fish house is *the* place for lobster. Service can be s-l-o-w. Best way to beat the crowd is to come mid-afternoon.

Drinking

Aqua Bar
BAR

(207 Commercial St; ⏰10am-1am) Imagine a food court where the options include a raw bar, sushi, gelato and other international delights. Add a fully stocked bar with generous tenders pouring the drinks. Now put the whole place in a gorgeous seaside setting, overlooking a little beach and beautiful harbor. Now, imagine this whole scene at sunset. That's no fantasy, that's Aqua Bar.

Ross' Grill
BAR

(www.rossgrille.com; 237 Commercial St; ⏰11:30am-10pm) For an romantic place to have a drink with a water view, head to the bar at this smart bistro. The food also gets rave reviews.

Harbor Lounge
COCKTAIL BAR

(www.theharborlounge.com; 359 Commercial St; ⏰noon-10pm) The Harbor Lounge takes full advantage of its seaside setting, with floor-to-ceiling windows and a boardwalk stretching out into the bay. Candlelit tables and black leather sofas constitute the decor – nothing else is needed. The cocktails are surprisingly affordable, with many martini concoctions to sample.

Information

Provincetown Business Guild (www.ptown.org) Oriented to the gay community.

Provincetown Chamber of Commerce (www.ptownchamber.com; 307 Commercial St; ⏰9am-6pm) The town's helpful tourist office is at MacMillan Wharf, where the ferries dock.

Provincetown on the Web (www.provincetown.com) Online guide with the entertainment scoop.

Wired Puppy (www.wiredpuppy.com; 379 Commercial St; ⏰6:30am-10pm; 📶) Free online computers for the price of an espresso.

Getting There & Away

Plymouth & Brockton buses (www.p-b.com) connect Provincetown to Boston ($31, 3½ hours) and other towns on the Cape. From mid-May to mid-October, **Bay State Cruise Company** (☎877-783-3779; www.boston-ptown.com; 200 Seaport Blvd, Boston; ⏰mid-May–mid-Oct) runs a ferry (round-trip $88, 1½ hours) between Boston's World Trade Center Pier and MacMillan Wharf. From late June to early September, the **Plymouth-to-Provincetown Express Ferry** (www.p-townferry.com; State Pier, 77 Water St) plies that route twice a day (round-trip $45, 1½ hours).

Nantucket

Nantucket is New England at her most rose-covered, cobblestoned, picture-postcard perfect. the island's only population center, Nantucket Town, was once home port to the world's largest whaling fleet. Now a national Historic Landmark, the town boasts leafy streets lined with gracious period homes and public buildings. Walk up cobbled Main St, where the grandest whaling-era mansions are lined up in a row. Get your questions answered at the **Visitors Services kiosk** (☎508-228-0925; www.nantucket-ma.gov; 25 Federal St; ⏰9am-5pm), near the ferry dock.

Sights & Activities

★Nantucket Whaling Museum
MUSEUM

(13 Broad St; adult/child $20/5; ⏰10am-5pm mid-May–Oct, 11am-4pm Nov–mid-May) Occupies a former spermaceti (whale-oil) candle factory. The evocative exhibits relive Nantucket's 19th-century heyday as the whaling center of the world. A 46ft-long sperm-whale skeleton, a rigged whaleboat and assorted whaling implements recount the history.

Beaches

Right in town, **Children's Beach** has calm water and a playground. For wilder, less frequented strands, pedal a bike or hop on a bus to **Surfside Beach**, 2 miles to the south. The best place to catch the sunset is **Madaket Beach**, 5.5 miles west of town.

Cycling

Cycling around Nantucket is an unbeatable way to explore the island. Dedicated bike paths connect the town with the main beaches and the villages of Madaket and 'Sconset – no place is more than 8 miles away. Rent bikes near Steamboat Wharf.

DON'T MISS

NANTUCKET BREW

Enjoy a hoppy pint of Whale's Tale Pale at **Cisco Brewers** (☎508-325-5929; www.ciscobrewers.com; 5 Bartlett Farm Rd; tours $20; ⊙10am-7pm Mon-Sat & noon-6pm Sun, tours 1pm & 4pm daily), the friendliest brewery you'll likely ever see. In addition to brewery tours, there are a few bars where you can hear spirited live music played on the mountain banjo in the late afternoons. Bonus: in season, Cisco operates a free shuttle bus from the Visitor Services kiosk.

Sleeping

HI Nantucket HOSTEL $

(Star of the Sea; ☎508-228-0433; hiusa.org; 31 Western Ave; dm $42-45; ⊙mid-May–mid-Sep; @) Occupying an 1873 lifesaving station, this atmospheric hostel has a million-dollar spot near Surfside Beach. Prices include breakfast.

Barnacle Inn B&B $$

(☎508-228-0332; www.thebarnacleinn.com; 11 Fair St; r without/with bathroom from $115/125; ❄📶) This is what old Nantucket is all about: folksy owners and simple, quaint accommodations that hearken to earlier times. Rooms in this turn-of-the-19th-century inn offer excellent value. Breakfast included.

Eating

Downyflake DINER, BAKERY $

(☎508-228-4533; www.thedownyflake.com; 18 Sparks Ave; mains $5-10; ⊙6am-2pm Mon-Sat, to 1pm Sun) First and foremost, the doughnuts are tried-and-true, old-fashioned goodness, in three varieties only (plain, sugar and chocolate). That should be enough. But there's also a full-service diner, with delicious blueberry pancakes for breakfast and burgers, reubens and tuna melts for lunch.

Black-Eyed Susan's CAFE $$

(☎508-325-0308; www.black-eyedsusans.com; 10 India St; breakfast mains $8-12, dinner $24-26; ⊙7am-1pm daily, 6-10pm Mon-Sat; 🖉) No reservations, no credit cards and no alcohol (unless you bring it yourself). Yet islanders line up out the door to get one of a dozen tables at this understated gem. This is New American at its finest: you've eaten these ingredients, but never before in these creative, decidedly delicious combinations.

Club Car AMERICAN, SEAFOOD $$

(☎508-228-1101; www.theclubcar.com; 1 Main St; mains $12-30; ⊙11:30am-1am) This converted railroad car is a vestige of the actual railroad that sank in the sands of Nantucket. The lively place dishes up sing-along piano music and consistently good food, including an excellent lobster roll.

Getting There & Around

AIR

Cape Air (www.flycapeair.com) flies from Boston, Hyannis and Martha's Vineyard to Nantucket Memorial Airport (ACK).

BOAT

The **Steamship Authority** (☎508-477-8600; www.steamshipauthority.com) runs ferries throughout the day between Hyannis and Nantucket. The fast ferry (round-trip adult/child $69/35) takes an hour; the slow ferry (round-trip adult/child $37/19) takes 2¼ hours. Also from Hyannis, **Hy-Line Cruises** (☎508-778-2600, 888-492-8082; www.hylinecruises.com; Ocean St Dock) has a high-speed ferry (adult/child $77/51, one hour, five or six daily) and a slow ferry ($45/free, two hours, two daily).

BUS

Getting around Nantucket is a snap. The **NRTA Wave** (www.nrtawave.com; rides $1-2, day pass $7; ⊙late May-Sep) operates buses around town and to 'Sconset, Madaket and the beaches. Buses have bike racks, so cyclists can bus one way and pedal back.

Martha's Vineyard

Bathed in scenic beauty, Martha's Vineyard attracts wide-eyed day-trippers, celebrity second-home owners, and urbanites seeking a restful getaway. The Vineyard remains untouched by the kind of rampant commercialism found on the mainland. Instead you'll find cozy inns, chef-driven restaurants and a bounty of green farms and grand beaches.

Vineyard Haven is the island's commercial center. Most ferries arrive in Oak Bluffs, which is the center of all summer fun on the Vineyard. Edgartown has a rich maritime history and more of a patrician air.

Sights & Activities

Campgrounds & Tabernacle HISTORIC SITE

(Oak Bluffs) Oak Bluffs started out in the mid-19th century as a summer retreat for a revivalist church, whose members enjoyed a day at the beach as much as a gospel service. They built some 300 cottages, each adorned with whimsical gingerbread trim. These brightly painted cottages – known today as the Campgrounds – surround Trinity Park and its open-air Tabernacle (1879), a venue for festival and concerts.

For a peek inside one, visit the **Cottage Museum** (www.mvcma.org; 1 Trinity Park; adult/child $2/50¢; ⏲10am-4pm Mon-Sat & 1-4pm Sun May-Sep), which contains exhibits on CMA history.

Flying Horses Carousel HISTORIC SITE
(www.mvpreservation.org; 15 Lake Ave, Oak Bluffs; rides $2.50; ⏲10am-10pm; 👪) Take a nostalgic ride on the USA's oldest merry-go-round, which has been captivating kids of all ages since 1876. The antique horses have manes of real horse hair and, if you stare into their glass eyes, you'll see neat little silver animals inside.

Katama Beach BEACH
(Katama Rd; 👪) The Vineyard's best beach lies 4 miles south of Edgartown center. Also called South Beach, Katama stretches for three magnificent miles. Rugged surf will please surfers on the ocean side, while some swimmers may prefer the protected salt ponds on the inland side.

Cycling

A scenic bike trail runs along the coast connecting Oak Bluffs, Vineyard Haven and Edgartown – it's largely flat so makes a good pedal for families. Rent bicycles at **Anderson's Bike Rental** (☎508-693-9346; www.andersonsbikerentals.com; 1 Circuit Ave Extension; bicycles per day adult/child $20/15; ⏲9am-6pm) near the ferry terminal.

Sleeping

HI Martha's Vineyard HOSTEL $
(☎508-693-2665; http://hiusa.org; 525 Edgartown–West Tisbury Rd; dm $35-39, d/q $99/135; ⏲mid-May–mid-Oct; @📶) Reserve early for a bed at this popular purpose-built hostel in the center of the island. It has everything you'd expect of a top-notch hostel: a solid kitchen, bike delivery and no curfew. The hostel is 1 mile east of the village of West Tisbury; take bus 3 from Vineyard Haven.

Nashua House INN $$
(☎508-693-0043; www.nashuahouse.com; 30 Kennebec Ave, Oak Bluffs; r without/with bathroom from $99/129; ❄📶) Despite the (mostly) shared bathrooms, these accommodations are spotlessly clean, cozily comfortable and quite lovely. There's no breakfast, but there are coffee and snacks all day. Staff is eager to please.

Down the road, the **Madison Inn** (☎508-693-2760; www.madisoninnmv.com; 18 Kennebec Ave; r incl breakfast from $169; ❄📶) is the slightly more upscale sister property.

Narragansett House B&B $$
(☎508-693-3627; www.narragansetthouse.com; 46 Narragansett Ave, Oak Bluffs; d $150-235; ❄📶) On a quiet residential street, this B&B occupies two nearby Victorian gingerbread-trimmed houses, just a stroll from the town center. The wide porch and blooming gardens are both delightful places to enjoy your complimentary breakfast.

Edgartown Inn GUESTHOUSE $$$
(☎508-627-4794; www.edgartowninn.com; 56 N Water St, Edgartown; r $200-325; ❄📶) This stately inn was built in 1798 as a sea captain's home, but later was converted into an inn, welcoming such distinguished guests as Nathaniel Hawthorne and Daniel Webster. Nowadays, it is a lovely, relatively affordable inn with period furnishings and old-fashioned charm.

Eating

★**Art Cliff Diner** CAFE $
(☎508-693-1224; 39 Beach Rd, Vineyard Haven; mains $8-16; ⏲7am-2pm Thu-Tue) *The* place for breakfast and lunch. Chef-owner Gina Stanley adds flair to everything she touches, from the almond-encrusted French toast to the fresh-fish tacos. The food is thoroughly modern, but the diner itself is charmingly retro.

MV Bakery BAKERY $
(☎508-693-3688; www.mvbakery.com; 5 Post Office Sq, Oak Bluffs; baked goods $1-3; ⏲7am-5pm) Inexpensive coffee, apple fritters and cannoli are served all day, but the best time to swing by is from 9pm to midnight, when folks line up at the back door to buy hot doughnuts straight from the baker.

Among the Flowers Café CAFE $$
(☎508-627-3233; www.amongtheflowersmv.com; 17 Mayhew Lane, Edgartown; mains $8-20; ⏲8am-10pm; 🖉) This is a sweet spot, hidden among the flowers on a garden patio off the main drag. It's a darling setting for delicious food, even if it is served on paper plates. In-the-know folks line up at breakfast time for decadent cinnamon rolls, waffles and omelets. But you won't be disappointed at lunch, especially if you order the lobster roll.

Slice of Life CAFE $$
(508-693-3838; www.sliceoflifemv.com; 50 Circuit Ave, Oak Bluffs; mains $8-24; 8am-9pm;) The look is casual; the fare is gourmet. At breakfast, there's kick-ass coffee, portobello omelets and fab potato pancakes. At dinner the roasted cod with sun-dried tomatoes is a savory favorite. And the desserts – decadent crème brûlée and luscious lemon tarts – are as good as you'll find anywhere.

Drinking & Nightlife

Offshore Ale Co BREWPUB
(www.offshoreale.com; 30 Kennebec Ave, Oak Bluffs; 11:30am-10pm) This popular microbrewery offers about a half-dozen different ales, including the award-winning Beach Road Nut Brown Ale. Seasonal favorites feature the bounty of the island, such as blueberries or sugar pumpkins.

Lampost NIGHTCLUB
(www.lampostmv.com; 6 Circuit Ave, Oak Bluffs; 4pm-1am) Head to this combo bar and nightclub for the island's hottest dance scene. Downstairs, you'll find some 100 brands of beer on offer at the **Dive Bar** (www.divebarmv.com; 6 Circuit Ave; noon-1:30am Jun-Sep).

Entertainment

★**Flatbread Company** LIVE MUSIC
(www.flatbreadcompany.com; 17 Airport Rd; 4pm-late May-Sep) Formerly the home of Carly Simon's legendary Hot Tin Roof, Flatbread continues the tradition, staging the best bands on the island. And it makes damn good organic pizzas too. It's adjacent to Martha's Vineyard Airport.

Getting There & Around

BOAT

Frequent ferries operated by the Steamship Authority (p210) link Woods Hole to both Vineyard Haven and Oak Bluffs (round-trip $17, 45 minutes). If you're bringing a car, book well in advance.

From Falmouth Harbor, the passenger-only ferry **Island Queen** (508-548-4800; www.islandqueen.com; 75 Falmouth Heights Rd) sails to Oak Bluffs several times daily in summer (round-trip $20, 40 minutes).

From Hyannis, **Hy-Line Cruises** (508-778-2600; www.hylinecruises.com; Ocean St Dock) operates a slow ferry ($45, 1½ hours, daily) and a high-speed ferry ($72, 55 minutes, several daily) to Oak Bluffs.

BUS

Martha's Vineyard Regional Transit Authority (www.vineyardtransit.com; per ride $2.50, day pass $7) operates a bus network around the island. Bus 13 travels frequently between the three main towns, while other buses go to more out-of-the-way destinations.

Central Massachusetts

Poking around this central swath of Massachusetts, between big-city Boston and the fashionable Berkshires, provides a taste of the less-touristed stretch of the state. But it's no sleeper, thanks largely to a score of colleges that infuse a youthful spirit to the region.

The **Central Massachusetts Convention & Visitors Bureau** (508-755-7400; www.centralmass.org; 91 Prescott St, Worcester; 9am-5pm Mon-Fri) and the **Greater Springfield Convention & Visitors Bureau** (413-787-1548;

OFF THE BEATEN TRACK

UP-ISLAND

Known as **Up-Island**, the rural western half of Martha's Vineyard is a patchwork of rolling hills, small farms and open fields frequented by wild turkeys and deer. Feast your eyes and your belly at the picturesque fishing village of **Menemsha**, where you'll find seafood shacks where the boats unload their catch at the back door. Watch oysters being shucked and lobsters steamed while you dine al fresco on a harborside bench.

The coastal **Aquinnah Cliffs**, also known as the Gay Head Cliffs, are a National Natural Landmark. These 150ft-high cliffs glow with an amazing array of colors in the late-afternoon light. You can hang out at **Aquinnah Public Beach** (parking $15), just below the multihued cliffs, or walk a mile north along the shore to an area that's popular with nude sunbathers.

Much of this area is protected in one form or another. **Cedar Tree Neck Sanctuary** (www.sheriffsmeadow.org; Indian Hill Rd, off State Rd; 8:30am-5:30pm) FREE has an inviting 2.5-mile hike across native bogs and forest to a coastal bluff with views of Cape Cod. **Felix Neck Wildlife Sanctuary** (www.massaudubon.org; Edgartown–Vineyard Haven Rd; adult/child $4/3; dawn-dusk;) is a birder's paradise with 4 miles of trails skirting marshes and ponds.

www.valleyvisitor.com; 1441 Main St, Springfield; 8:30am-5pm Mon-Fri) provide regional visitor information.

Springfield

Workaday Springfield gave birth to two American cultural icons, both of which are memorialized here.

★Naismith Memorial Basketball Hall of Fame MUSEUM
(www.hoophall.com; 1000 W Columbus Ave; adult/child $22/15; 10am-5pm; P) Basketball devotees will be thrilled to shoot baskets, feel the center-court excitement and learn about the sport's history and great players.

Dr Seuss National Memorial Sculpture Garden PARK
(www.catinthehat.org; 21 Edwards St; dawn-dusk;) FREE Life-size bronze sculptures of the Cat in the Hat and other wonky characters look beseechingly at passers-by. Oh me, oh my. Welcome to the world of Theodor Seuss Geisel, Springfield's favorite native son.

Northampton

The region's best dining, hottest nightlife and most interesting street scenes all await in this uber-hip burg known for its liberal politics and outspoken lesbian community. Easy to explore on foot, the eclectic town center is chockablock with cafes, funky shops and art galleries. **Greater Northampton Chamber of Commerce** (413-584-1900; www.explorenorthampton.com; 99 Pleasant St; 9am-5pm Mon-Fri year-round, 10am-2pm Sat & Sun May-Oct) is information central.

Sights

Smith College COLLEGE CAMPUS
(www.smith.edu; Elm St; P) Founded 'for the education of the intelligent gentlewoman' in 1875, Smith College is one of the largest women's colleges in the country, with 2600 students. The verdant 125-acre campus holds an eclectic architectural mix of nearly 100 buildings as well as a pretty pond.

Smith College Museum of Art MUSEUM
(www.smith.edu/artmuseum; Elm St at Bedford Tce; adult/child $5/2; 10am-4pm Tue-Sat, noon-4pm Sun; P) This impressive campus museum boasts a 25,000-piece collection which is particularly strong in 17th-century Dutch and 19th- and 20th-century European and North American paintings, including works by Degas, Winslow Homer, Picasso and James Abbott McNeill Whistler.

DON'T MISS

WORCESTER DINERS

The state's second-largest city nurtured a great American icon: the diner. Here, in this rustbelt city, you'll find a dozen of them tucked behind warehouses, underneath old train trestles, or steps from dicey bars. **Miss Worcester Diner** (508-753-5600; 300 Southbridge St; mains $6-10; 5am-2pm Mon-Fri, 6am-2pm Sat & Sun) is a classic of the genre. Built in 1948, it was a showroom diner of the Worcester Lunch Car Company, which produced 650 diners at its factory right across the street. Harleys parked on the sidewalk and Red Sox paraphernalia on the walls set the tone. Enticing selections such as banana-bread French toast compete with the usual greasy-spoon menu of chili dogs and biscuits with gravy. It's one tasty slice of Americana.

Sleeping

Autumn Inn MOTEL $$
(413-584-7660; www.hampshirehospitality.com; 259 Elm St/MA 9; r incl breakfast $119-179; P@) Despite the motel layout, this two-story place near Smith campus has an agreeable ambience and large, comfy rooms.

Hotel Northampton HISTORIC HOTEL $$
(413-584-3100; www.hotelnorthampton.com; 36 King St; r $185-275; P) Northampton's finest sleep since 1927, the 100-room hotel in the town center features period decor and well-appointed rooms.

Eating

Haymarket Café CAFE $
(413-586-9969; www.haymarketcafe.com; 185 Main St; items $5-10; 7am-10pm;) Northampton's coolest (and perhaps longest-standing) hangout for bohemians and caffeine addicts, the Haymarket serves up heady espresso, fresh juices and an extensive vegetarian menu.

Paul & Elizabeth's SEAFOOD $$
(413-584-4832; www.paulandelizabeths.com; 150 Main St; mains $13-17; 11:30am-9:15pm;) This airy, plant-adorned restaurant, known locally as P&E's, sits on the top floor

of Thornes Marketplace and is the town's premier natural-foods restaurant. It serves delectable vegetarian and seafood, often with an Asian bend.

Bela VEGETARIAN $$
(☎413-586-8011; www.belaveg.com; 68 Masonic St; mains $9-13; ⊙noon-8:30pm Tue-Sat;) This cozy vegetarian restaurant puts such an emphasis on fresh ingredients that the chalkboard menu changes daily depending on what local farmers are harvesting. Cash only.

Drinking & Entertainment

For a smallish town, Northampton sees a great line-up of indie bands, folk artists and jazz musicians, who play at the restored **Calvin Theatre** (☎413-586-8686; www.iheg.com; 19 King St) or other smaller venues around town.

Northampton Brewery BREWPUB
(www.northamptonbrewery.com; 11 Brewster Ct; ⊙11:30am-1am;) The oldest operating brewpub in New England enjoys a loyal summertime following thanks to its generously sized outdoor deck and delicious libations.

Diva's LESBIAN
(www.divasofnoho.com; 492 Pleasant St; ⊙10pm-2am Tue-Sat) The city's main gay-centric club hosts dance nights, drag shows, Latin nights and other high-energy weekly events. Located about a mile south of the main intersection on Rte 5.

Amherst

This college town, a short drive from Northampton, is built around the mega **University of Massachusetts** (UMass; www.umass.edu) and two small colleges, the liberal **Hampshire College** (www.hampshire.edu) and the prestigious **Amherst College** (www.amherst.edu). Contact the admissions offices for campus tours and event information. Amherst is also something of a literary center, thanks to two noteworthy museums.

Emily Dickinson Museum MUSEUM
(www.emilydickinsonmuseum.org; 280 Main St; adult/child $10/5; ⊙11am-4pm Wed-Mon Mar-Dec) The lifelong home of poet Emily Dickinson (1830–86), also known as the 'belle of Amherst.' Her verses on love, nature and immortality have made her one of the most important poets in the US. Tours depart every half-hour.

Eric Carle Museum of Picture Book Art MUSEUM
(www.carlemuseum.org; 125 W Bay Rd; adult/child $9/6; ⊙10am-4pm Tue-Fri, to 5pm Sat, noon-5pm Sun;) Co-founded by the author and illustrator of *The Very Hungry Caterpillar*, this superb museum celebrates book illustrations from around the world. All visitors (grown-ups included) are encouraged to express their own artistic sentiments in the **hands-on art studio**.

The Berkshires

Tranquil towns and a wealth of cultural attractions are nestled in these cool green hills. For more than a century the Berkshires have been a favored retreat for wealthy Bostonians and New Yorkers. And we're not just talking Rockefellers – the entire Boston symphony summers here as well. The **Berkshire Visitors Bureau** (☎413-743-4500; www.berkshires.org; 66 Allen St, Pittsfield; ⊙10am-5pm) provides information on the whole region.

Great Barrington

Woolworths, diners and hardware stores have given way to art galleries, urbane boutiques and locavore restaurants on Main St, Great Barrington. The picturesque Housatonic River flows through the center of town, with the **River Walk** (www.gbriverwalk.org) offering a perfect perch from which to admire it. Access the walking path from Main St (behind Rite-Aid) or from Bridge St. At the intersection of Main and Railroad Sts, you'll find an artful mix of galleries and eateries.

Gypsy Joynt CAFE $$
(☎413-644-8811; www.gypsyjoyntcafe.net; 293 Main St; mains $10-15; ⊙11am-midnight Wed-Sat, to 9pm Sun, to 4pm Mon;) This is a family affair, with three generations pitching in to serve innovative pizzas, beefy sandwiches and bountiful salads. Most everything is organic and locally sourced. The Gypsy Joynt also throws in great coffee, live music and a super boho atmosphere.

Baba Louie's PIZZA $$
(☎413-528-8100; www.babalouiespizza.com; 286 Main St; pizzas $12-18; ⊙11:30am-9:30pm;) Baba's is known for its wood-fired pizza with organic sourdough crust, and guys with dreadlocks. There's a pizza for every taste, including vegan and gluten-free options.

Barrington Brewery BREWPUB
(www.barringtonbrewery.net; 420 Stockbridge Rd; mains $8-20; ⏲11:30am-9:30pm; 📶) Solar-powered microbrews – you know you're in Great Barrington! Outdoor seating is divine on a balmy summer night. Located 2 miles north of the town center on the road to Stockbridge.

Stockbridge

This timeless New England town, with not even a single traffic light, looks like something straight out of a Norman Rockwell painting. No coincidence! Rockwell (1894–1978), the most popular illustrator in US history, lived on Main St and used the town and its residents as subjects. See his slice-of-life artwork up close, as well has his studio, at the evocative **Norman Rockwell Museum** (☎413-298-4100; www.nrm.org; 9 Glendale Rd/MA 183; adult/child $18/6; ⏲10am-5pm).

Lenox

The refined village of Lenox is the cultural heart of the Berkshires, thanks to the open-air **Tanglewood Music Festival** (☎888-266-1200; www.tanglewood.org; 297 West St/MA 183, Lenox; ⏲late Jun-early Sep). One of the country's premier music series, Tanglewood hosts the Boston Symphony Orchestra and guest artists like James Taylor and Yo-Yo Ma. Buy a lawn ticket, spread a blanket, uncork a bottle of wine and enjoy the quintessential Berkshires experience. Other excellent summertime cultural fare includes **Shakespeare & Company** (☎413-637-1199; www.shakespeare.org; 70 Kemble St; ⏲late Jun-early Sep) and the renowned **Jacob's Pillow Dance Festival** (☎413-243-0745; www.jacobspillow.org; 358 George Carter Rd, Becket; ⏲mid-Jun–Aug).

Sleeping

Cornell in Lenox B&B $$
(☎413-637-4800; www.cornellbb.com; 203 Main St; r incl breakfast from $149; @📶) With three historic houses on 4 acres, Cornell offers a variety of comfortable room layouts and friendly, accommodating service.

Birchwood Inn INN $$$
(☎413-637-2600; www.birchwood-inn.com; 7 Hubbard St; r incl breakfast $249-379; ❄📶🐾) The oldest house in Lenox (1767), the Birchwood Inn offers gorgeous period rooms, scrumptious breakfast and warm hospitality.

OFF THE BEATEN TRACK

HANCOCK SHAKER VILLAGE

Just west of the town of Pittsfield, **Hancock Shaker Village** (www.hancockshakervillage.org; US 20; adult/youth/child $20/8/free; ⏲10am-5pm mid-Apr–Oct; 👪) is a fascinating museum illustrating the lives of the Shakers, the religious sect that founded the village in 1783. The Shakers believed in communal ownership, the sanctity of work and celibacy, the latter of which proved to be their demise. Their handiwork – graceful in its simplicity – includes wooden furnishings and 20 buildings, the most famous of which is the round stone barn.

Eating

Haven Cafe & Bakery CAFE $
(☎413-637-8948; www.havencafebakery.com; 8 Franklin St; mains $8-15; ⏲7:30am-3pm; 📶✍) It looks like a cafe, but the sophisticated food evokes a more upscale experience. Try inventive egg dishes for breakfast or fancy salads and sandwiches for lunch – all highlighting local organic ingredients.

★**Nudel** AMERICAN $$$
(☎413-551-7183; www.nudelrestaurant.com; 37 Church St; mains $22-26; ⏲5:30-9:30pm Tue-Sun) A driving force in the area's sustainable-food movement, just about everything on Nudel's menu is seasonally inspired and locally sourced. Incredible flavors. Nudel doesn't take reservations, so arrive early to avoid a long wait.

Williamstown

Cradled by the Berkshire's rolling hills, Williamstown is a picture-perfect New England college town revolving around the leafy campus of **Williams College** (www.williams.edu). It's a mini cultural capital, with two stellar art museums holding down opposite ends of the town. In summer months, the **Williamstown Theatre Festival** (☎413-597-3400; www.wtfestival.org; 👪) mounts a mix of classics and contemporary works by up-and-coming playwrights, attracting plenty of well-known thespians to the stage.

WORTH A TRIP

SCENIC DRIVE

For the finest fall foliage drive in Massachusetts, head west on MA 2 from Greenfield to Williamstown on the 63-mile route known as the **Mohawk Trail** (www.mohawktrail.com). The lively Deerfield River slides alongside, with roaring, bucking stretches of white water that turn leaf-peeping into an adrenaline sport for kayakers.

Sights

★Clark Art Institute MUSEUM
(www.clarkart.edu; 225 South St, Williamstown; adult/child $20/free; ⏲10am-5pm Tue-Sun) Set on a gorgeous 140-acre campus, the Sterling & Francine Clark Art Institute is a gem among small art museums. The collections are particularly strong in the Impressionists, but the highlight is the rich collection of paintings by Winslow Homer, George Innes and John Singer Sargent.

Williams College Museum of Art MUSEUM
(www.wcma.org; 15 Lawrence Hall Dr, Williamstown; ⏲10am-5pm, closed Wed Sep-May) FREE Gracing the center of town, this is the sister museum of the Clark Art Institute. Around half of its 13,000 pieces comprise the American Collection, with substantial works by notables such as Edward Hopper *(Morning in a City)*, Winslow Homer and Grant Wood, to name a few.

Sleeping

River Bend Farm B&B B&B $$
(☎413-458-3121; www.riverbendfarmbb.com; 643 Simonds Rd/US 7, Williamstown; r incl breakfast $120; ⏲Apr-Oct; ❄📶) Step back to the 18th century in this Georgian Colonial B&B, furnished with real-deal antiques and boasting five fireplaces. Four doubles share two bathrooms. Located one mile north of town. Credit cards are not accepted.

Maple Terrace Motel MOTEL $$
(☎413-458-9677; www.mapleterrace.com; 555 Main St, Williamstown; d incl breakfast $128-188; 📶🏊) The Maple Terrace is a simple, yet cozy 15-room place on the eastern outskirts of town. The Swedish innkeepers have snazzed up the grounds with gardens that make you want to linger.

Eating & Drinking

Pappa Charlie's Deli DELI $
(☎413-458-5969; 28 Spring St; mains $5-9; ⏲7:30am-8pm) The stars themselves created the lunch sandwiches that bear their names. (Order a Politician and get anything you want on it.)

★Mezze Bistro & Bar FUSION $$
(☎413-458-0123; www.mezzerestaurant.com; 777 Cold Spring Rd/US 7, Williamstown; mains $16-28; ⏲5-9pm) Situated on 3 acres, Mezze's farm-to-table approach begins with an edible garden right on site. Much of the rest of the seasonal menu, from small-batch microbrews to organic meats, is locally sourced as well.

Hops & Vines BEER GARDEN
(www.hopsandvinesma.com; ⏲noon-10pm Tue-Sat, to 8pm Sun; 📶) This two-sided bar and restaurant offers an experience for every mood. The quirky, casual ambiance and excellent beer selection make 'Hops' the hands-down favorite, but some occasions call for a classy dining room like 'Vines'.

North Adams

Gritty North Adams is a former manufacturing center that was long dominated by the vast campus of the Sprague Electric Company. When Sprague closed in the 1980s, the site was converted into the USA's largest contemporary museum. North Adams is also a jumping-off point for Mt Greylock, the highest mountain in Massachusetts.

Sights

MASS MoCA MUSEUM
(www.massmoca.org; 87 Marshall St, North Adams; adult/child $18/8; ⏲10am-6pm Jul & Aug, 11am-5pm Wed-Mon Sep-Jun; 👪) The museum encompasses 222,000 sq ft and over 25 buildings, including art construction areas, performance centers and 19 galleries. One gallery is the size of a football field, giving installation artists the opportunity to take things into a whole new dimension. Bring your walking shoes!

Mt Greylock State Reservation PARK
(☎413-499-4262; www.mass.gov/dcr; parking $5-6; ⏲visitor center 9am-5pm) FREE At 3491ft, the state's highest peak may seem modest, but the summit rewards you with a panorama stretching across three mountain ranges and five states. The reservation has 45 miles of

hiking trails, including several routes to the top. Alternatively, you can drive up the auto road (open May to October). There's also a rustic, seasonal summit lodge.

Sleeping & Eating

Porches BOUTIQUE HOTEL $$

(413-664-0400; www.porches.com; 231 River St, North Adams; r incl breakfast $135-225;) Across the street from MASS MoCA, the artsy rooms here offer soothing color palettes, tasteful furnishings and – appropriately – private porches.

Public Eat & Drink PUB FOOD $$

(413-664-4444; www.publiceatanddrink.com; 34 Holden St, North Adams; mains $10-22; 4-10pm Mon-Wed, 11:30am-10pm Thu-Sun;) Come to this cozy North Adams pub for an excellent selection of craft beers and gourmet pub fare, such as brie burgers, flatbread pizzas and bistro steak.

RHODE ISLAND

America's smallest state makes up for its lack of land with 400 miles of craggy coastline, deeply indented bays and enticing beaches. The state capital, Providence, is home to stellar artistic and academic institutions, cutting-edge galleries and top-notch dining, all with a dash of urban grit. Down the coast, Newport shines with opulent mansions, pretty yachts and world-class music festivals. Don't forget that this is the Ocean State, so there's no shortage of beaches, boats and other ways to appreciate the deep blue.

History

Ever since it was founded in 1636 by Roger Williams, a religious outcast from Boston, Providence has enjoyed an independent frame of mind. Williams' guiding principle, the one that got him ostracized from Massachusetts, was that all people should have freedom of conscience. He put his liberal beliefs into practice when settling Providence, purchasing the land from the local Narragansett Native Americans and remaining on friendly terms with them – a bold experiment in tolerance and peaceful coexistence.

As Providence and Newport grew and merged into a single colony, competition and conflict with area tribes sparked several wars, leading to the decimation of the Wampanoag, Pequot, Narragansett, and Nipmuck peoples. Rhode Island was also a prolific slave trader and its merchants would control much of that trade in the years after the Revolutionary War.

The city of Pawtucket was an early player in the American industrial revolution, with the 1790 establishment of the water-powered Slater Mill. Industrialism impacted the character of Providence and surrounds, particularly along the Blackstone River, creating urban density. As with many small East-Coast cities, these urban areas went into a precipitous decline in the 1940s and '50s as manufacturing industries (textiles and costume jewelry) faltered. In the 1960s, preservation efforts salvaged the historic architectural framework of Providence and Newport. The former has emerged as a lively place with a dynamic economy and the latter, equally lively, survives as a museum city.

Information

Providence Journal (www.providencejournal.com) The state's largest daily newspaper.

Rhode Island Parks (www.riparks.com) Offers camping in five state parks.

Rhode Island Tourism Division (800-556-2484; www.visitrhodeisland.com) Distributes visitor information on the whole state.

RHODE ISLAND FACTS

Nicknames Ocean State, Little Rhody

Population 1.05 million

Area 1034 sq miles

Capital city Providence (population 178,400)

Other city Newport (population 24,000)

Sales tax 7%

Birthplace of Broadway composer George M Cohan (1878–1942) and toy icon Mr Potato Head (b 1952)

Home of The first US tennis championships

Politics Majority vote Democrat

Famous for Being the smallest state

Official state bird A chicken? Why not? The Rhode Island Red revolutionized the poultry industry

Driving distances Providence to Newport 37 miles, Providence to Boston 50 miles

Providence

Rhode Island's capital city, Providence offers some fine urban strolling, whether in the crisp autumn afternoons or balmy summer mornings. Wander through Brown University's leafy campus on 18th-century College Hill; follow the Riverwalk into Downcity for eating, drinking and browsing. Get your questions answered at the **Providence Visitor Information Center** (☎401-751-1177; www.goprovidence.com; Rhode Island Convention Center, 1 Sabin St; ⏲9am-5pm Mon-Sat).

Sights

Exit 22 off I-95 deposits you Downcity, while the university area is on the East Side of the Providence River.

★Brown University ACADEMIC INSTITUTION
(www.brown.edu) Covering much of College Hill, the campus of Brown University exudes Ivy League charm. The centerpiece is **University Hall**, a 1770 brick edifice that was used as a barracks during the Revolutionary War. To explore the campus, start at the wrought-iron gates at the top of College St and make your way across the green toward Thayer St.

College Hill NEIGHBORHOOD
East of the Providence River, College Hill contains over 100 Colonial, Federal and Revival houses dating from the 18th century. Stroll down **Benefit Street** for a sampling. Don't miss the Greek Revival **Providence Athenaeum** (www.providenceathenaeum.org; 251 Benefit St; ⏲9am-7pm Mon-Thu, to 5pm Fri & Sat, 1-5pm Sun) FREE, designed by William Strickland and completed in 1838. Inside, plaster busts of Greek gods and philosophers preside over the collection.

RISD Museum of Art MUSEUM
(www.risdmuseum.org; 224 Benefit St; adult/child $12/3; ⏲10am-5pm Tue-Sun, to 9pm Thu; 👪) Wonderfully eclectic, the Rhode Island School of Design's art museum showcases everything from ancient Greek art to 20th-century American paintings and decorative arts. Free admission on Sundays.

State House HISTORIC BUILDING
(www.sos.ri.gov; 82 Smith St; ⏲8:30am-4:30pm Mon-Fri, hourly tours 9am-2pm) FREE The focal point of Providence, the State House was designed by McKim, Mead and White. It is crowned with one of the world's largest self-supporting marble domes. Go inside to see a replica of the Liberty Bell, as well as Gilbert Stuart's famous portrait of George Washington (which you might also see on the $1 bill in your wallet).

Roger Williams Park PARK
(1000 Elmwood Ave) FREE The parkland was donated in 1871 by a descendent of Roger Williams himself. Today this 430-acre expanse of greenery includes lakes and ponds, forest copses and broad lawns, picnic grounds and a planetarium, not to mention the excellent **zoo** (www.rwpzoo.org; adult/child $15/10; ⏲10am-4pm Oct-Mar, to 5pm Apr-Sep; P 👪). The park is about 4 miles south of downtown Providence; take exit 17 off I-95.

Sleeping

Old Court B&B HISTORIC INN $$
(☎401-751-2002; www.oldcourt.com; 144 Benefit St; r weekday $135-185, weekend $165-215) Well positioned among the historic buildings of College Hill, this three-story, 1863 Italianate home has stacks of charm. Enjoy eccentric wallpaper, good jam at breakfast and occasional winter discounts.

Christopher Dodge House B&B $$
(☎401-351-6111; www.providence-hotel.com; 11 W Park St; r incl breakfast $149-189; P) This 1858 Federal-style house is furnished with early American reproduction furniture and marble fireplaces. Austere on the outside, it has elegant proportions, large, shuttered windows and wooden floors on the inside.

DON'T MISS

BONFIRES AFTER DARK

Occasionally and throughout the summer, much of central Providence takes on a carnival atmosphere, as 100 flaming braziers illuminate the water at the convergence of the Providence, Moshassuck and Woonasquatucket rivers. Pedestrians can witness the spectacle of **WaterFire** (www.waterfire.org) from the bridges and riverside, while also enjoying live music, outdoor theater and ballroom dancing. WaterFire occurs about a dozen times a year from May to October and begins at sunset.

Providence Biltmore HISTORIC HOTEL $$$
(☎401-421-0700; www.providencebiltmore.com; 11 Dorrance St; r Mon-Fri/Sat & Sun from $169/229; P 📶) The granddaddy of Providence's hotels, the Biltmore dates to the 1920s. The lobby, both intimate and regal, nicely combines dark wood, twisting staircases and chandeliers, while well-appointed rooms stretch many stories above the old city. Lovely views from the upper floors.

Eating

Both the Rhode Island School of Design and Johnson & Wales University have top-notch culinary programs that annually turn out creative new chefs. The large student population on the East Side ensures that there are plenty of affordable places along Thayer St in College Hill. For Italian eats, head to Federal Hill, just west of Downcity.

East Side Pocket MEDITERRANEAN $
(☎401-453-1100; www.eastsidepocket.com; 278 Thayer St; mains $4-7; ⏰10am-1am Mon-Sat, to 10pm Sun; 🖉) Fabulous falafels and wraps at student-friendly prices.

Haven Brothers Diner DINER $
(Washington St; meals $5-10; ⏰5pm-3am) Legend has it that the Haven Brothers started as a horse-drawn lunch wagon in 1893. Climb up a rickety ladder to get basic diner fare alongside everyone from prominent politicians to college kids pulling an all-nighter, to drunks.

Aspire MODERN AMERICAN $$
(☎401-521-3333; www.aspirerestaurant.com; 311 Westminster St; mains $10-20; ⏰6:30am-9pm Mon-Thu, to 11pm Fri-Sat, to 3pm Sun; 🖉) Aspire has a swanky, chandelier-lit interior, but the reason to come here is the delightful patio seating, known as A-Garden. It's a perfect place to sample the seasonal small-plate menu. The place seems to be understaffed; but if you have to wait for your food, this is a fine setting to do it in.

★ **birch** MODERN AMERICAN $$$
(☎401-272-3105; www.birchrestaurant.com; 200 Washington St; 4-course dinner $49, beverage pairings $35; ⏰5-10pm Thu-Mon) Eighteen chairs surround a U-shaped bar at this innovative kitchen. The intimate size and style of the place means attention to detail is exacting in both the decor and the food, which focuses on small-batch and hyper-seasonal produce. Reservations are essential.

Drinking & Nightlife

Trinity Brewhouse MICROBREWERY
(www.trinitybrewhouse.com; 186 Fountain St; ⏰11:30am-1am Sun-Thu, to 2am Fri-Sat) This microbrewery in the Downcity entertainment district brews terrific British-style beers.

AS220 CLUB
(www.as220.org; 115 Empire St; ⏰food noon-10pm, bar 5pm-1am) A longstanding outlet for all forms of Rhode Island art, AS220 (say 'A-S-two-twenty') books experimental bands, hosts readings and provides gallery space for a very active artistic community.

The Salon BAR, CLUB
(www.thesalonpvd.com; 57 Eddy St; ⏰5pm-1am Tue-Thu, to 2am Fri-Sat) The Salon mixes ping-pong tables and pinball machines with '80s pop and pickleback shots (whiskey with a pickle juice chaser). Downstairs, you'll find live music, DJs and dance parties.

Getting There & Away

TF Green Airport (PVD; www.pvdairport.com; I-95, exit 13, Warwick), 20 minutes south of downtown Providence, is served by major US airlines and car-rental companies.

Peter Pan Bus Lines (www.peterpanbus.com) connects Providence with Boston ($8, one hour) and New York ($30, 3¾ hours). **Amtrak** (www.amtrak.com; 100 Gaspee St) trains also link cities in the Northeast with Providence.

Rhode Island Public Transit Authority (RIPTA; www.ripta.com; one way $2, day pass $6) bus 60 links Providence with Newport.

Newport

Established by religious moderates fleeing persecution from Massachusetts Puritans, this 'new port' flourished to become the fourth richest city in the newly independent colony. Downtown, the Colonial-era architecture is beautifully preserved.

In later years, bolstered by the boom in shipping, wealthy industrialists made Newport their summer vacation spot and built opulent country 'cottages' down lantern-lined Bellevue Ave. Modelled on Italianate palazzos, French chateaux and Elizabethan manor houses, and decorated with priceless furnishings and artwork, they remain the town's premier attraction, alongside a series of top-notch summer music festivals. Get the scoop at the **Newport Visitor Center** (☎401-845-9123; www.discovernewport.com; 23 America's Cup Ave; ⏰9am-5pm).

Sights

Several of the city's grandest mansions are managed by the **Preservation Society of Newport County** (☎401-847-1000; www.newportmansions.org; 424 Bellevue Ave; 5-site ticket adult/child $33/11). Each mansion takes about 90 minutes to tour. Or gawk at them from the 3.5-mile **Cliff Walk**, which hugs the coast behind the mansions. Start the walk at Ruggles Ave near the Breakers.

★Breakers MANSION
(www.newportmansions.org; 44 Ochre Point Ave; adult/child $21/7; ⏲9am-5pm Apr-mid-Oct, hours vary mid-Oct–Mar; P) If you have time for only one Newport mansion, make it this extravagant 70-room, 1895 Italian Renaissance mega-palace built for Cornelius Vanderbilt II, patriarch of America's then-richest family.

★The Elms MANSION
(www.newportmansions.org; 367 Bellevue Ave; adult/child $16/7, servant life tour adult/child $15/5; ⏲9am-5pm Apr–mid-Oct, hours vary mid-Oct–Mar; P 👪) Built in 1901, the Elms is a replica of Château d'Asnières, built near Paris in 1750. Here you can take a 'behind-the-scenes' tour which will have you snaking through the servants' quarters and up onto the roof.

★Rough Point MANSION
(www.newportrestoration.com; 680 Bellevue Ave; adult/child $25/free; ⏲10am-2pm Thu-Sat mid-Apr–mid-May, 10am-3:45pm Tue-Sun mid-May–mid-Nov; P) Once called the 'richest little girl in the world,' Doris Duke (1912–93) was just 13 years old when she inherited this English manor estate from her father. Duke had a passion for travel and art collecting; Rough Point houses many of her holdings, from Ming dynasty ceramics to Renoir paintings.

★Fort Adams State Park PARK
(www.fortadams.org; Harrison Ave; fort tours adult guided/self-guided $12/6, child $6/3; ⏲sunrise-sunset) Fort Adams is America's largest coastal fortification and is the centerpiece of this gorgeous state park, which juts out into Narragansett Bay. It's the venue for the Newport Jazz and Folk Festivals.

Rosecliff MANSION
(548 Bellevue Ave; adult/child $16/7; ⏲9am-4pm Apr–mid-Oct, hours vary mid-Oct–Mar; P) A 1902 masterpiece of architect Stanford White, Rosecliff resembles the Grand Trianon at Versailles. Its immense ballroom had a starring role in Robert Redford's *The Great Gatsby*.

International Tennis Hall of Fame MUSEUM
(www.tennisfame.com; 194 Bellevue Ave; adult/child $15/free; ⏲10am-5pm) The historic Newport Casino building (1880) served as a summer club for Newport's wealthiest residents. Now it houses this newly revamped museum, with plenty of interactive and high-tech exhibits about the game.

Touro Synagogue National Historic Site SYNAGOGUE
(www.tourosynagogue.org; 85 Touro St; adult/child $12/free; ⏲noon-1.30pm Sun-Fri May-Jun, 10am-4pm Sun-Fri Jul & Aug, to 1:30pm Sun-Fri Sep-Oct, noon-1.30pm Sun Nov-Apr) Tour the oldest synagogue (c 1763) in the USA, an architectural gem that treads the line between austere and lavish.

Activities

★America's Cup Charters YACHT TOURS
(☎401-846-9886; www.americacupcharters.com; 49 America's Cup Ave, Newport Harbor Hotel Marina; sunset tour adult/child $75/40; ⏲May-Sep; 👪) Take the ultimate waterborne tour aboard a 12m America's Cup racing yacht. Ticketed two-hour sunset sails and private charters are available daily in season and offer a thrilling experience.

★Sail Newport SAILING
(☎401-846-1983; www.sailnewport.org; 60 Fort Adams Dr; 6hr instruction $150-179, sailboat rental per 3hr $73-138; ⏲9am-7pm; 👪) As you'd expect in the hometown of the prestigious America's Cup, the sailing in breezy Newport is phenomenal.

Festivals & Events

Newport Folk Festival MUSIC
(www.newportfolk.org; Fort Adams State Park; 1-/3-day pass $49/120, parking $18; ⏲late Jul) Big-name stars and up-and-coming groups perform at Fort Adams State Park. Bring sunscreen.

Newport Jazz Festival MUSIC
(www.newportjazzfest.org; Fort Adams State Park; tickets $40-85, 3-day $155; ⏲early Aug) The roster reads like a who's who of jazz, with the likes of Dave Brubeck and Wynton Marsalis.

Newport Music Festival MUSIC
(www.newportmusic.org; tickets $30-45; ⏲mid-Jul) This internationally regarded festival offers classical music concerts in many of the great mansions.

Sleeping

★Newport International Hostel HOSTEL $
(William Gyles Guesthouse; 401-369-0243; www.newporthostel.com; 16 Howard St; dm $35-65; Apr-Dec;) Welcome to Rhode Island's only hostel, run by an informal and knowledgeable host. The tiny guesthouse offers spare, clean digs in a dormitory room, as well as a simple breakfast and laundry facilities. Private rooms are also available.

Sea Whale Motel MOTEL $$
(888-257-4096; www.seawhale.com; 150 Aquidneck Ave, Middletown; d $109-229; P) This owner-occupied motel is a lovely place to stay with rooms facing Easton's Pond and flowers hung about the place. Rooms have little pizzazz, but they are comfortable and neat with fridges and microwaves. The motel is about 2 miles from town and 400 yards from the beach.

★The Attwater BOUTIQUE HOTEL $$$
(401-846-7444; www.theattwater.com; 22 Liberty St; r from $259; P) This newish hotel has the bold attire of a midsummer beach party with turquoise, lime green and coral prints, ikat headboards and snazzily patterned geometric rugs. Picture windows and porches capture the summer light and rooms come furnished with thoughtful luxuries such as iPads, Apple TV and beach bags.

Eating

★Rosemary & Thyme Cafe BAKERY, CAFE $
(401-619-3338; www.rosemaryandthymecafe.com; 382 Spring St; baked goods $2-5, sandwiches & pizza $6-8; 7:30am-3pm Tue-Sat, to 11:30am Sun;) With a German baker in the kitchen it's hardly surprising that the counter here is piled high with buttery croissants, apple and cherry tarts and plump muffins. At lunch time there are gourmet salads and sandwiches, including an award-winning grilled cheese.

Salvation Café CAFE $$
(401-847-2620; www.salvationcafe.com; 140 Broadway; mains $12-25; 5pm-midnight daily, plus 11am-3pm Sun) A funky, eclectic decor and brilliant food are in store at this bohemian cafe. The multi-ethnic menu ranges far and wide, from pad Thai to Moroccan spiced lamb, but seldom misses the mark.

The Mooring SEAFOOD $$$
(401-846-2260; www.mooringrestaurant.com; Sayer's Wharf; sandwiches $12-16, mains $19-38; 11:30am-10pm) A harborfront setting and a menu brimming with fresh seafood make this an unbeatable combination for seaside dining. Tip: if it's packed, take the side entrance to the bar, grab a stool and order the meaty clam chowder and a 'bag of doughnuts' (tangy lobster fritters).

Drinking & Entertainment

Coffee Grinders COFFEEHOUSE
(www.coffeegrindernewport.com; 33 Bannister's Wharf; 8am-5pm, longer hours in summer) Enjoy espresso and a pastry on some benches at this small shingled shack at the end of Bannister's Wharf. You'll be surrounded by water, with great views over yacht activity and crustaceans being unloaded at the Aquidneck Lobster Company.

Newport Blues Café CLUB
(www.newportblues.com; 286 Thames St; 7pm-1am Tue-Sat, shows 10pm) This popular rhythm-and-blues bar and restaurant draws top acts to an old brownstone. It's an intimate space with many enjoying quahogs, house-smoked ribs or pork loins at tables adjoining the small stage.

Getting There & Away

Peter Pan (www.peterpanbus.com) has several daily buses to Boston ($22, two hours), while **RIPTA** (www.ripta.com) operates frequent buses (one way $2, day pass $6) from the visitor center to the mansions and beaches, and as far as Providence.

Rhode Island Beaches

If you're wondering why it's called the Ocean State, drive down Rte 1A to check out the **South County Beaches** (800-548-4662; www.southcountyri.com). Surfers, head to the mile-long **Narragansett Town Beach** in Narragansett. The nearby **Scarborough State Beach** is among Rhode Island's finest, with a wide sandy shore, a classic pavilion and inviting boardwalks. At the state's southwestern tip, **Watch Hill** is a wonderful place to turn back the clock, with its Flying Horse Carousel and Victorian mansions.

CONNECTICUT

Sandwiched between sexy New York City and quainter quarters in northern New England, Connecticut often gets short shrift from travelers. But the Constitution State has long

OFF THE BEATEN TRACK

BLOCK ISLAND

Separated from the rest of Rhode Island by 12 miles of open ocean, this unspoiled island offers simple pleasures: rolling farms, uncrowded beaches and miles of quiet hiking and cycling trails.

Ferries dock at **Old Harbor**, the main town, which has changed little since its gingerbread houses were built in the late 19th century. A lovely beach stretches several miles to the north. About 2 miles away, the **Clay Head Nature Trail** (off Corn Neck Rd) follows high clay bluffs above the beach, offering good bird-watching along the way.

A mere 7 miles long, Block Island is perfect for exploration by bicycle; rent them near the ferry dock. The **Block Island Chamber of Commerce** (800-383-2474; www.blockislandchamber.com), at the ferry dock, can help with accommodations, but be aware the island's inns typically book out in summer and many require minimum stays.

The **Block Island Ferry** (401-783-4613; www.blockislandferry.com) offers several options for getting to the island. From Point Judith in Narragansett, there is a high-speed ferry (round-trip adult/child $36/20, 30 minutes) and a traditional ferry (adult/child $28/14, one hour). The latter is the only car ferry, for which reservations are essential. There is an additional fast ferry from Newport (adult/child $50/26, one hour).

been luring artists, celebrities and moneyed Manhattanites, who appreciate the rural landscape sprinkled with small vineyards and genteel Colonial towns.

History

The name 'Connecticut' comes from the Mohegan name for the great river that bisects the state. A number of Native American tribes (including the Mohegan, as well as the Pequot and others) were here when the first European explorers, primarily Dutch, appeared in the early 17th century. The first English settlement was at Old Saybrook in 1635, followed a year later by the Connecticut Colony, built by Massachusetts Puritans under Thomas Hooker. A third colony was founded in 1638 in New Haven. After the Pequot War (1637), the Native Americans were no longer a check to colonial expansion in New England, and Connecticut's English population grew. In 1686 Connecticut was brought into the Dominion of New England.

The American Revolution swept through Connecticut, leaving scars with major battles at Stonington (1775), Danbury (1777), New Haven (1779) and Groton (1781). Connecticut became the fifth state in 1788. It embarked on a period of prosperity, propelled by its whaling, shipbuilding, farming and manufacturing industries (from firearms to bicycles to household tools), which lasted well into the 19th century.

The 20th century brought world wars and the depression but, thanks in no small part to Connecticut's munitions industries, the state was able to fight back. Everything from planes to submarines was made in the state, and when the defense industry began to decline in the 1990s, the growth of other businesses (such as insurance) helped pick up the slack.

Information

There are welcome centers at the Hartford airport and on I-95 and I-84 when entering the state by car.

Connecticut Tourism Division (www.ctvisit.com) Distributes visitor information for the entire state.

Hartford Courant (www.courant.com) The state's largest newspaper.

Hartford

Connecticut's capital city, Hartford has been lovingly dubbed the 'filing cabinet of America.' But this underappreciated city – one of the oldest in New England – harbors a rich cultural heritage. Besides being the former 'insurance capital' of America, it is also a former publishing center, which means that Hartford was home to some of the country's most celebrated writers. The **Greater Hartford Welcome Center** (860-244-0253; www.letsgoarts.org/welcomecenter; 100 Pearl St; 9am-5pm Mon-Fri) distributes tourist information.

Options for sleeping in Hartford are limited to national chain hotels.

Sights

★Mark Twain House & Museum MUSEUM

(www.marktwainhouse.org; 351 Farmington Ave; adult/child $19/11; 9:30am-5:30pm, closed Tue in Mar) It was at this former home of Samuel Langhorne Clemens, aka Mark Twain, that the legendary author penned many of his greatest works, including *The Adventures of Huckleberry Finn* and *Tom Sawyer*. The house itself, a Victorian Gothic with fanciful turrets and gables, reflects Twain's quirky character.

★Wadsworth Atheneum MUSEUM

(www.thewadsworth.org; 600 Main St; adult/child $10/5; 11am-5pm Wed-Fri, 10am-5pm Sat & Sun) The nation's oldest public-art museum, the Wadsworth Atheneum houses nearly 50,000 pieces. On display are paintings by members of the Hudson River School, European Old Masters, 19th-century Impressionist works, sculptures by Connecticut artist Alexander Calder; and a small yet outstanding array of surrealist works.

Harriet Beecher Stowe House MUSEUM

(www.harrietbeecherstowe.org; 77 Forest St; adult/child $10/7; 9:30am-5pm Tue-Sat, noon-5pm Sun) Next door to the Twain house is the house of the woman who wrote the anti-slavery book *Uncle Tom's Cabin*. It rallied so many Americans against slavery that Abraham Lincoln once credited Stowe with starting the US Civil War.

Old State House HISTORIC BUILDING

(www.ctoldstatehouse.org; 800 Main St; adult/child $6/3; 10am-5pm Tue-Sat Jul–mid-Oct, Mon-Fri mid-Oct–Jul;) Connecticut's original capitol building, designed by Charles Bulfinch, was the site of the trial of the *Amistad* prisoners. Gilbert Stuart's famous 1801 portrait of George Washington hangs in the senate chamber. Dedicated museum space houses interactive exhibits aimed at kids, as well as a **Museum of Curiosities** that features a two-headed calf, a narwhal's horn and a variety of mechanical devices.

Eating & Drinking

Salute ITALIAN $$

(860-899-1350; www.salutect.com; 100 Trumbull St; lunch mains $9-13, dinner $12-20; 11:30am-11pm Mon-Thu, to midnight Fri-Sat, 3-10pm Sun;) Charming service is the hallmark of this urban gem, which offers a contemporary take on Italian flavors. Regulars rave about the cheesy garlic bread, but other offerings are a tad more sophisticated. The pleasant patio overlooks Bushnell Park.

Bin 228 WINE BAR $$

(860-244-9463; www.bin228winebar.com; 228 Pearl St; paninis & small plates $8-15; 11:30am-10pm Mon-Thu, to midnight Fri, 4pm-midnight Sat) This wine bar serves Italian fare – paninis, cheese platters, salads – alongside its expansive all-Italian wine list. On weekends, the kitchen stays open until midnight (later for drinks).

City Steam Brewery Café BREWPUB

(citysteam.biz; 942 Main St; 11:30am-1am Mon-Sat, 4-10pm Sun) This big and boisterous place has housemade beers on tap. The Naughty Nurse Pale Ale is a bestseller, but the seasonals are also worth a try. The brewery's basement is home to the **Brew Ha Ha Comedy Club** (tickets $10-15; Fri & Sat), where you can yuk it up with visiting comedians from New York and Boston.

CONNECTICUT FACTS

Nicknames Constitution State, Nutmeg State

Population 3.6 million

Area 4845 sq miles

Capital city Hartford (population 124,700)

Other cities New Haven (population 130,280)

Sales tax 6.35%

Birthplace of Abolitionist John Brown (1800–59), circus man PT Barnum (1810–91), actress Katharine Hepburn (1907–2003)

Home of The first written constitution in the US; the first lollipop, Frisbee and helicopter

Politics Democrat-leaning

Famous for Starting the US insurance biz and building the first nuclear submarine

Quirkiest state song lyrics 'Yankee Doodle', which entwines patriotism with doodles, feathers and macaroni

Driving distances Hartford to New Haven 40 miles, Hartford to Providence 75 miles

Getting There & Away

Central **Union Station** (www.amtrak.com; 1 Union Pl) links Hartford to cities throughout the Northeast, including New Haven (from $14, one hour) and New York City ($42 to $60, three hours).

Litchfield Hills

The rolling hills in the northwestern corner of Connecticut are sprinkled with lakes and carpeted with forests. Historic Litchfield is the hub of the region, but lesser-known villages such as Bethlehem, Kent, Lakeville and Norfolk are just as photogenic. The **Western Connecticut Convention & Visitors Bureau** (☎800-663-1273; www.litchfieldhills.com) has information on the region.

Litchfield

Founded in 1719, Litchfield prospered from the commerce brought by stagecoaches en route between Hartford and Albany, and its many handsome period buildings are a testimony to that era. A row of shops, restaurants and historic buildings overlooks the picturesque green. Stroll along North and South Sts to see the finest homes, including the 1773 **Tapping Reeve House & Law School** (www.litchfieldhistoricalsociety.org; 82 South St; adult/child $5/free; ⏰11am-5pm Tue-Sat, 1-5pm Sun mid-Apr–Nov), the country's first law school.

Connecticut's largest wildlife preserve, the **White Memorial Conservation Center** (www.whitememorialcc.org; US 202; park free, museum adult/child $6/3; ⏰park dawn-dusk, museum 9am-5pm Mon-Sat & noon-5pm Sun), 2 miles west of town, has 35 miles of walking trails and good bird-watching.

Lake Waramaug

The most beautiful of the dozens of lakes and ponds in the Litchfield Hills is Lake Waramaug. As you make your way around North Shore Rd, stop at **Hopkins Vineyard** (☎860-868-7954; www.hopkinsvineyard.com; 25 Hopkins Rd; ⏰10am-5pm Mon-Sat & 11am-5pm Sun Mar-Dec, 10am-5pm Fri-Sun only Jan-Mar) for wine tastings. The view from the bar is worth the trip, particularly when the foliage changes in the fall. Across the street, the 19th-century **Hopkins Inn** (☎860-868-7295; www.thehopkinsinn.com; 22 Hopkins Rd, Warren; r without/with bathroom from $125/135, apt $150; P ❄ 🐾) has lake-view accommodation and a recommended restaurant.

Connecticut Coast

Connecticut has a surprisingly delightful and diverse strip of coastline. At the eastern end of the state, Mystic houses a magnificent recreated 19th-century whaling town, spread across 17 acres. Well-preserved historic towns grace the banks of the mighty Connecticut River. The western end of the state's coastline is largely a bedroom community connected by commuter rail to New York City; but the artsier (and more academic) elements are on display in New Haven.

Mystic

From simple beginnings in the 17th century, the village of Mystic grew to become a prosperous whaling center and one of the great shipbuilding ports of the East Coast. In the mid-19th century, Mystic's shipyards launched clipper ships, gunboats and naval transport vessels, many from the George Greenman & Co Shipyard, now the site of the state's largest tourist attraction. The charming town center – complete with sailboats bobbing and drawbridge clanging – makes Mystic a popular summertime destination. The **Greater Mystic Chamber of Commerce** (☎860-572-9578; www.mysticchamber.org; 12 Roosevelt Ave; ⏰9am-4:30pm), next to the train station, has visitor information.

Sights & Activities

There's no shortage of outfits in Mystic ready to whisk you away on a watery adventure. Sail away on the schooner **Argia** (☎860-536-0416; www.argiamystic.com; 15 Holmes St; adult/child $44/35) or take a historic harbor tour on the **Mystic Express** (1 Holmes St; adult/child $20/10; ⏰11am Sat-Sun May-Jun, daily Jun-Oct). There are also cruises and boat rentals at the Seaport Museum.

★ **Mystic Seaport Museum** MUSEUM
(www.mysticseaport.org; 75 Greenmanville Ave/CT 27; adult/child $25/16; ⏰9am-5pm mid-Feb–Oct, to 4pm Nov-Dec; P 👪) America's maritime history springs to life as costumed interpreters ply their trades at this sprawling re-created 19th-century seaport village. You can explore several historic sailing vessels, including the *Charles W Morgan* (built in 1841), the last surviving wooden whaling ship in the world.

Mystic Aquarium & Institute for Exploration AQUARIUM
(www.mysticaquarium.org; 55 Coogan Blvd; adult/child $35/25; ⌚9am-4pm Mar-Nov, to 5pm Apr-Aug, from 10am Dec-Feb; 👪) This state-of-the-art aquarium boasts more than 6000 species of sea creatures, as well as an outdoor viewing area for watching seals and sea lions below the waterline and a penguin pavilion. The aquarium's most famous (and controversial) residents are the three beluga whales, who reside in the Arctic Coast exhibit.

Sleeping

★ **Steamboat Inn** INN $$$
(☎860-536-8300; www.steamboatinnmystic.com; 73 Steamboat Wharf; d incl breakfast $160-280; P❄📶) Located right in the heart of downtown Mystic, the 11 rooms of this historic inn have wraparound water views and luxurious amenities, including two-person whirlpool tubs. Antiques lend the interior a romantic atmosphere. Bonus: complimentary bikes.

Eating & Drinking

★ **Captain Daniel Packer Inne** AMERICAN $$
(☎860-536-3555; www.danielpacker.com; 32 Water St; mains $14-24; ⌚11am-10pm) This 1754 historic house has a low-beam ceiling, creaky floorboards and a casual (and loud) pub downstairs. Upstairs, the dining room has river views and an imaginative American menu.

Engine Room BURGERS $$
(860-415-8117; 14 Holmes St; mains $12-20; ⌚noon-10pm Thu-Mon, 4-10pm Tue-Wed ; 🌿👪) Promising beer, bourbon and burgers, this place delivers, with dozens of enticing beers on tap and perfectly cooked, damn tasty burgers coming off the grill. (We didn't try the bourbon.) Evocatively set in the old Lathrup Marine Engine building, it's an excellent place to eat and drink, even for vegetarians.

Oyster Club SEAFOOD $$$
(☎860-415-9266; www.oysterclubct.com; 13 Water St; oysters $2, lunch mains $12-18, dinner $18-34; ⌚4-9pm Mon-Thu, noon-10pm Fri-Sun) A little off the main drag, this is the place locals come for oysters served grilled or raw. The deck out back, also known as the Treehouse, is the best perch in town.

Lower Connecticut River Valley

Several lovely Colonial-era towns grace the banks of the Connecticut River, offering up their rural charm at an unhurried pace. The

WORTH A TRIP

GILLETTE CASTLE

Looming on the hilltop above East Haddam is **Gillette Castle** (☎860-526-2336; www.ct.gov/dep/gillettecastle; 67 River Rd; adult/child $6/2; ⌚castle 10am-4:30pm late May–mid-Oct, grounds 8am-dusk year-round; P), a turreted mansion built in 1919. The eccentric actor William Gillette made his fortune in the role of Sherlock Holmes. His fascinating home is modeled on the medieval castles of Germany. The surrounding 125 acres are a designated state park with loads of walking trails and picnic areas.

In summer, you can cross the Connecticut River on the **Chester-Hadlyme Ferry** (car/pedestrian $5/2; ⌚7am-6:45pm Mon-Fri, 10:30am-5pm Sat & Sun Apr-Nov). It's a short, five-minute river crossing on the *Selden III*, the second-oldest ferry in America (since 1769). The ferry affords great views of the river and the castle, and deposits passengers at the foot of the castle in East Haddam.

River Valley Tourism District (☎860-787-9640; www.visitctriver.com) provides information on the region.

OLD LYME

Set near the mouth of the Connecticut River, Old Lyme is the picturesque setting for the Lyme Art Colony, which cultivated the American Impressionist movement in the early 20th century. It all started when art patron Florence Griswold opened her estate to visiting artists, many of whom offered paintings in lieu of rent. Her Georgian mansion, now the **Florence Griswold Museum** (www.flogris.org; 96 Lyme St; adult/child $10/free; ⌚10am-5pm Tue-Sat, 1-5pm Sun; P) contains a fine selection of both Impressionist and Barbizon paintings.

ESSEX

The main town along the lower Connecticut River is tree-lined Essex, established in 1635. The well-preserved Federal-period houses along Main St are legacies of rum and tobacco fortunes made in the 19th century. The landmark **Griswold Inn** (☎860-767-1776; www.griswoldinn.com; 36 Main St; r incl breakfast $115-205, ste $190-324; P📶) has been Essex's physical and social centerpiece since 1776.

Connecticut River Museum MUSEUM
(www.ctrivermuseum.org; 67 Main St; adult/child $9/6; ⌚10am-5pm Tue-Sun; P 👪) Next to the steamboat dock, the Connecticut River Museum meticulously recounts the history of the region. Exhibits include a reproduction of the world's first submarine, *Turtle*, a hand-propelled vessel built by a Yale student in 1776.

The museum runs summer **schooner cruises** (adult/child $30/18; ⌚1:30pm & 3:30pm daily, Jun-Oct) and weekend **eagle-watch tours** (per person $40, h 11am & 1pm Fri-Sun, Jan-Mar).

Essex Steam Train & Riverboat Ride STEAM TRAIN
(☎860-767-0103; www.essexsteamtrain.com; 1 Railroad Ave; adult/child $19/10, with cruise $29/19; 👪) The old-fashioned way to see the river valley is to hop aboard this antique steam locomotive that runs six scenic miles to the town of Deep River. There you can connect with a cruise on a Mississippi-style riverboat, before returning by train. There's also an excursion to Gillette Castle.

New Haven

Head straight to New Haven Green, graced by old Colonial churches and the ivy-covered walls of Yale University. The oldest planned city in America (1638), New Haven is laid out in orderly blocks spreading out from the Green, making it a cinch to get around. Opposite the green, **INFO New Haven** (☎203-773-9494; www.infonewhaven.com; 1000 Chapel St; ⌚10am-9pm Mon-Sat, noon-5pm Sun) is the city's helpful tourist office.

Sights

★Yale University UNIVERSITY
(www.yale.edu) Each year, thousands of high-school students make pilgrimages to Yale, nursing dreams of attending the country's third-oldest university, which boasts such notable alums as Noah Webster, Eli Whitney, Samuel Morse, and Presidents William H Taft, George HW Bush, Bill Clinton and George W Bush. You don't need to share the students' ambitions in order to take a stroll around the campus, just pick up a map at the **Visitors Center** (☎203-432-2300; www.yale.edu/visitor; 149 Elm St; walking tours free; ⌚9am-4:30pm Mon-Fri, 11am-4pm Sat & Sun, walking tours 10:30am & 2pm Mon-Fri, 1:30pm Sat) or join a free, one-hour guided tour.

★Yale University Art Gallery MUSEUM
(artgallery.yale.edu; 1111 Chapel St; ⌚10am-5pm Tue-Fri, to 8pm Thu, 11am-5pm Sat & Sun) FREE America's oldest university art museum boasts American masterworks by Edward Hopper and Jackson Pollock, as well as a superb European collection that includes Vincent van Gogh's *The Night Café*.

Peabody Museum of Natural History MUSEUM
(www.peabody.yale.edu; 170 Whitney Ave; adult/child $9/5; ⌚10am-5pm Mon-Sat, noon-5pm Sun; P 👪) Wannabe paleontologists will be thrilled by the dinosaurs here. There are also excellent anthropology exhibits, including a replica of an Egyptian tomb.

Yale Center for British Art MUSEUM
(www.ycba.yale.edu; 1080 Chapel St; ⌚10am-5pm Tue-Sat, noon-5pm Sun) FREE The most comprehensive British art collection outside the UK. Closed for conservation at the time of research, the museum is expected to reopen in 2016.

Sleeping

Hotel Duncan HISTORIC HOTEL $
(☎203-787-1273; www.hotelduncan.net; 1151 Chapel St; s/d $65/85; ❄ 📶) Though the shine has rubbed off this New Haven gem it's the enduring features that still make it worth a stay, like the handsome lobby and the hand-operated elevator.

Study at Yale HOTEL $$$
(☎203-503-3900; www.studyatyale.com; 1157 Chapel St; r $199-259; P 📶) The Study at Yale manages to evoke a mid-century modern sense of sophistication without being over-the-top or intimidating. Ultra-contemporary touches include in-room iPod docking stations and cardio machines with built-in televisions.

Eating

★Frank Pepe PIZZA $
(☎203-865-5762; www.pepespizzeria.com; 157 Wooster St; pizza $10-20; ⌚11:30am-10pm; 🍷 👪) Pepe's serves delectable, crispy, thin-crust pizza, fired in a coal oven, just as it has since 1925. Go for 'Frank Pepe's original tomato pie' or try a New Haven specialty white-clam pizza. No credit cards.

Booktrader Cafe CAFE $

(203-787-8147; www.booktraderatyale.com; 1140 Chapel St; sandwiches $7-10; 7:30am-9pm Mon-Fri, 9am-9pm Sat, to 7pm Sun;) This light-filled, book-filled atrium is a delightful place to devour scrumptious sandwiches and spell-binding literature. In nice weather, there's a shady patio.

Caseus Fromagerie Bistro CHEESE SHOP $$

(203-624-3373; www.caseusnewhaven.com; 93 Whitney Ave; mains $12-25; 11:30am-2:30pm Mon-Sat & 5:30-9pm Wed-Sat;) With a boutique cheese counter piled with locally sourced labels and a concept menu devoted to *le grand fromage*, Caseus has hit upon a winning combination. After all, what's not to like about a perfectly executed mac 'n' cheese or the dangerously delicious poutine (pommes frites, cheese curds and velouté).

☆ Entertainment

New Haven has a first-rate theater scene. The free weekly *New Haven Advocate* (www.ct-now.com) has current entertainment listings.

Toad's Place MUSIC

(203-624-8623; www.toadsplace.com; 300 York St) Toad's is one of New England's premier music halls, having earned its rep hosting the likes of the Rolling Stones, U2 and Bob Dylan.

Shubert Theater THEATER

(203-562-5666; www.shubert.com; 247 College St) Dubbed 'Birthplace of the Nation's Greatest Hits,' since 1914 the Shubert has been hosting ballet and Broadway musicals on their trial runs before heading off to New York City.

Yale Repertory Theatre THEATER

(203-432-1234; www.yalerep.org; 1120 Chapel St) Performing classics and new works in a converted church.

Getting There & Away

By train from New York City skip Amtrak and take **Metro North** (www.mta.info; one way $10-16), which has near-hourly services and the lowest fares. Heading north, you can take Amtrak to Hartford ($14, one hour) or Boston (from $54, 2½ hours). **Greyhound Bus Lines** (www.greyhound.com) also connects New Haven to scores of cities including Hartford ($15, one hour) and Boston ($23 to $27, four hours).

VERMONT

Vermont, we like your crunchy soul. Green, upbeat and a little bit quirky, it's a pretty place that embraces its natural beauty with a respectful *joie de vivre*. And the eating is darn good too, from the artisanal cheeses to Ben & Jerry's ice cream to the buckets of maple syrup. Fortunately, there are plenty of ways to work it off: hike the trails of the Green Mountains, paddle a kayak on Lake Champlain or hit the snowy slopes.

Vermont gives true meaning to the word rural. Its capital would barely rate as a small town in other states and even its largest city, Burlington, has just 42,200 contented souls. The countryside is a blanket of rolling green, with 80% of the state forested and most of the rest given over to some of the prettiest farms you'll ever see. The Green Mountain State is also home to more than 100 covered bridges. So take your time, meander down quiet side roads, stop in those picturesque villages, and sample a taste of the good life.

History

Frenchman Samuel de Champlain explored Vermont in 1609, becoming the first European to visit these lands long inhabited by the native Abenaki.

Vermont played a key role in the American Revolution in 1775 when Ethan Allen led a local militia, the Green Mountain Boys, to Fort Ticonderoga, capturing it from the British. In 1777 Vermont declared independence as the Vermont Republic, adopting the first New World constitution to abolish slavery and establish a public school system. In 1791, Vermont was admitted to the USA as the 14th state.

The state's independent streak is as long and deep as a vein of Vermont marble. Long a land of dairy farmers, Vermont is still largely agricultural and has the lowest population of any New England state.

Information

Vermont Dept of Tourism (www.vermontvacation.com) Online information by region, season and other user-friendly categories.

Vermont Public Radio (VPR; www.vpr.net) Vermont's excellent statewide public radio station. The radio frequency varies across the state, but the following selection covers most areas: Burlington (northwestern Vermont – 107.9); Brattleboro (southeastern Vermont – 88.9); Manchester

VERMONT FACTS

Nickname Green Mountain State

Population 626,500

Area 9217 sq miles

Capital city Montpelier (population 7755)

Other city Burlington (population 42,200)

Sales tax 6%

Birthplace of Mormon leader Brigham Young (1801–77), President Calvin Coolidge (1872–1933)

Home of More than 100 covered bridges

Politics Independent streak, leaning Democrat

Famous for Ben & Jerry's ice cream

Sudsiest state Most microbreweries per capita in the USA

Driving distances Burlington to Brattleboro 151 miles, Burlington to Boston 216 miles

(southwestern Vermont – 106.9); and St Johnsbury (northeastern Vermont – 88.5).

Vermont State Parks (☎888-409-7579; www.vtstateparks.com) Complete camping and parks information.

Southern Vermont

The southern swath of Vermont holds the state's oldest towns and plenty of scenic back roads.

Brattleboro

Ever wonder where the 1960s counter-culture went? It's alive and well in this riverside burg overflowing with artsy types and more tie-dye per capita than any other place in New England.

Sights

Paralleling the Connecticut River, Main St is lined with period buildings, including the handsome art-deco **Latchis Building**. The surrounding area boasts several **covered bridges**; pick up a map at the Bennington Chamber of Commerce.

Brattleboro Museum & Art Center MUSEUM
(www.brattleboromuseum.org; 10 Vernon St; adult/student/child under 18yr $8/4/free; ⏰11am-5pm Wed-Mon) Located in a 1915 railway station, this museum hosts rotating exhibitions of contemporary art, including multimedia works by local artists.

Sleeping

If all you're after is a cheap sleep, there are plenty of motels on Putney Rd north of town; take Exit 3 off I-91.

Latchis Hotel HOTEL **$$**
(☎802-254-6300, 800-798-6301; www.latchis.com; 50 Main St; r incl breakfast $115-170, ste $185; 📶) The decor is retro and your view from an interior room may be a red-brick wall, but this art-deco hotel has charm. And you can't beat the prime downtown location and the attached historic theater.

Forty Putney Road B&B B&B **$$$**
(☎800-941-2413, 802-254-6268; www.fortyputneyroad.com; 192 Putney Rd; r incl breakfast $159-329; @📶) In a sweet riverside location just north of town, this 1930 B&B has a cheery pub, pool table, hot tub, a glorious backyard, four rooms and a separate self-contained cottage. Easy access to river trails from the property.

Eating

Brattleboro Food Co-op DELI **$**
(☎802-257-0236; www.brattleborofoodcoop.com; 2 Main St; sandwiches $7-9; ⏰7am-9pm Mon-Sat, 9am-9pm Sun) 🍃 At this thriving downtown community market, load up your basket with wholefood groceries, organic produce, and local cheeses, or visit the juice bar and deli for healthy takeaway treats.

Whetstone Station PUB FOOD **$$**
(☎802-490-2354; www.whetstonestation.com; 36 Bridge St; mains $10-22; ⏰11:30am-10pm Sun-Thu, to 11pm Fri & Sat) At sunset, dine on the deck overlooking the Connecticut River for one of the finest views in town. This busy brewery and eatery has 20 or so craft beers on tap – with house and guest brewery selections – plus a wide range of craft bottles and cans. For a light but filling meal, try the grilled sirloin tips with a dipping sauce. Fantastic! Welcoming service, too.

TJ Buckley's AMERICAN **$$$**
(☎802-257-4922; www.tjbuckleys.com; 132 Elliot St; mains $40; ⏰5:30-9pm Thu-Sun) 🍃 Chef-owner Michael Fuller founded this

exceptional, upscale 18-seat eatery in an authentic 1927 diner over 30 years ago. The oral menu of four nightly changing items is sourced largely from local organic farms. Reserve ahead.

Information

Brattleboro Chamber of Commerce (877-254-4565, 802-254-4565; www.brattleboro-chamber.org; 180 Main St; 9am-5pm Mon-Fri) Stop by for a free historical society walking-tour map.

Bennington

Southern Vermont is rural, and cozy Bennington, with about 15,000 inhabitants, ranks as the region's largest town. An interesting mix of cafes and shops downtown line Main St, while the adjacent Old Bennington historic district boasts Colonial homes, the early 19th-century **Old First Church**, where poet Robert Frost is buried, and a trio of covered bridges. A hilltop granite obelisk commemorating the 1777 Battle of Bennington towers above it all.

Sights

Bennington Battle Monument HISTORIC SITE
(www.benningtonbattlemonument.com; 15 Monument Circle; adult/child 6-14yr $5/1; 9am-5pm mid-Apr–Oct) This striking structure, which rises more than 300ft, offers an unbeatable 360-degree view of the surrounding countryside. An elevator whisks you painlessly to the top.

Bennington Museum MUSEUM
(802-447-1571; www.benningtonmuseum.org; 75 Main St; adult/child under 18yr $10/free; 10am-5pm daily, closed Jan, closed Wed Nov-Jun) Between downtown and Old Bennington, this museum's houses an outstanding early Americana collection which includes Bennington pottery and the Bennington Flag, one of the oldest surviving American Revolutionary flags, and works by American folk artist 'Grandma Moses.'

Sleeping & Eating

Greenwood Lodge & Campsites HOSTEL, CAMPGROUND $
(802-442-2547; www.campvermont.com/greenwood; VT 9, Prospect Mountain; 2-person tent/RV site $29/35, dm $30-36, private room 1/2 people $72/75; mid-May–late Oct;) Nestled in the Green Mountains 8 miles east of town, this 120-acre space with three ponds holds one of Vermont's best-sited hostels and campgrounds.

Henry House B&B $$
(802-442-7045; www.thehenryhouseinn.com; 1338 Murphy Rd, North Bennington; r incl breakfast $100-155;) Sit on the rocking chair and watch the traffic trickle across a covered bridge at this Colonial home on 25 peaceful acres, built in 1769 by American Revolution hero William Henry.

Blue Benn Diner DINER $
(802-442-5140; 314 North St; mains $7-16; 6am-4:45pm Mon-Fri, 7am-3:45pm Sat & Sun;) This classic 1950s-era diner serves breakfast all day and a healthy mix of American and international fare. Enhancing the retro experience are little tabletop jukeboxes where you can play Willie Nelson's 'Moonlight in Vermont' till your neighbors scream for mercy. Cash only.

Pangaea INTERNATIONAL $$$
(802-442-7171; www.vermontfinedining.com; 1 Prospect St, North Bennington; lounge mains from $10-23, restaurant mains $30; lounge from 5pm daily, restaurant 5-9pm Tue-Sat) Offering fine

WORTH A TRIP

SCENIC DRIVE: COVERED BRIDGES OF BENNINGTON

North of Bennington, a 30-minute detour takes you across three picture-perfect covered bridges spanning the Wallomsac River. To get started, turn west onto VT 67A just north of Bennington's tourist office and continue 3.5 miles, bearing left on Murphy Rd at the 117ft-long **Burt Henry Covered Bridge** (1840). Exhale, slow down: you're back in horse-and-buggy days. After curving to the left, Murphy Rd next loops through the **Paper Mill Bridge**, which takes its name from the 1790 mill whose gear works are still visible along the river below. Next turn right onto VT 67A, go half a mile and turn right onto Silk Rd where you'll soon cross the **Silk Road Bridge** (c 1840). Continue southeast for two more miles, bearing left at two T-intersections, to reach the **Bennington Battle Monument** (p229).

Vermont & New Hampshire

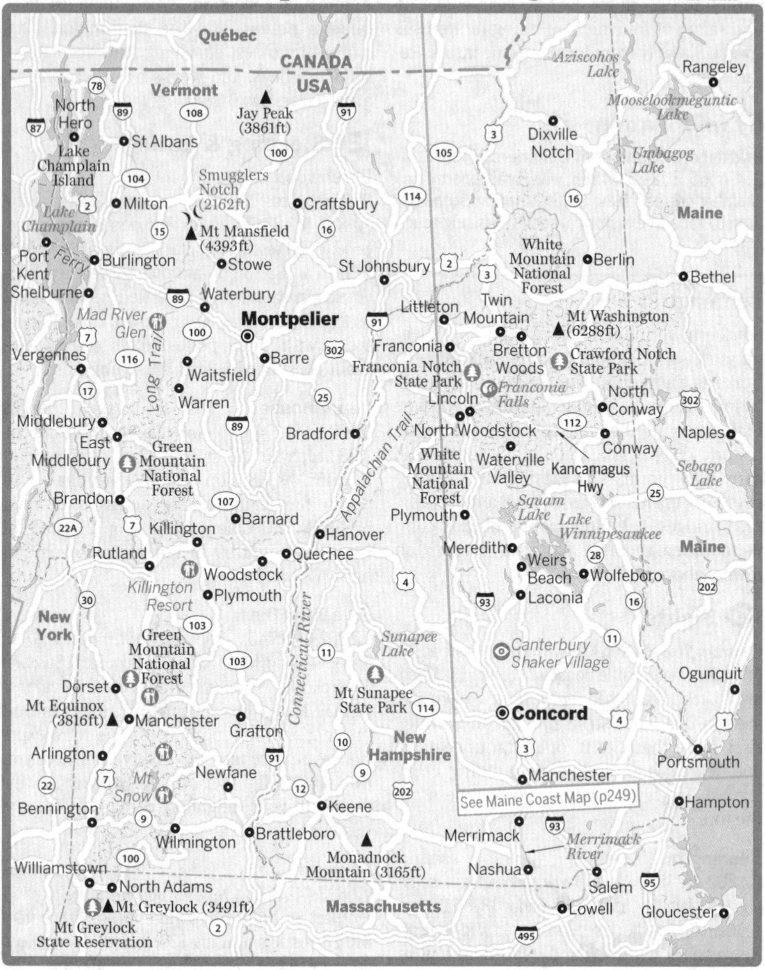

dining for every budget, this top-end North Bennington restaurant sits side-by-side with a more casual, intimate lounge. Opt for gourmet burgers served on the riverside terrace out back, or head to the tastefully decorated dining room next door for international specialties like *filet mignon* on risotto and topped with pancetta and taleggio.

Information

Bennington Area Chamber of Commerce (☎802-447-331; www.bennington.com; 100 Veterans Memorial Dr; ⊙10am-5pm Mon-Fri) One mile north of downtown. The chamber also runs the Bennington Welcome Center (100 Route 279, 7am to 9pm), near the Rte 279 and US 7 interchange, which is open daily .

Manchester

Sitting in the shadow of Mt Equinox, Manchester's been a fashionable summer retreat since the 19th century. The mountain scenery, the agreeable climate and the Batten Kill River – Vermont's best trout stream – continue to draw vacationers today.

Manchester Center, at the town's north end, sports cafes and upscale outlet stores. Further south lies dignified Manchester Village, lined with marble sidewalks, stately homes and the posh Equinox hotel.

Sights & Activities

The **Appalachian Trail**, which overlaps the **Long Trail** in southern Vermont, passes just east of Manchester. For trail maps and details on shorter day hikes, stop by the **Green Mountain National Forest office** (802-362-2307; www.fs.usda.gov/greenmountain; 2538 Depot St, Manchester Center; 8am-4:30pm Mon-Fri).

★Hildene HISTORIC SITE

(802-362-1788, 800-578-1788; www.hildene.org; 1005 Hildene Rd/VT 7A; adult/child 6-14yr $16/5, guided tours $5/2; 9:30am-4:30pm) This stately 24-room Georgian Revival mansion was home to members of Abraham Lincoln's family from the 1800s until 1975, when it was converted into a museum. The collection of family heirlooms includes the hat Lincoln probably wore while delivering the Gettysburg Address – one of the three surviving Lincoln top hats. The gorgeous grounds offer 12 miles of walking and cross-country ski trails.

American Museum of Fly Fishing & Orvis MUSEUM

(www.amff.com; 4070 Main St; adult/child 5-14yr $5/3; 10am-4pm Tue-Sun Jun-Oct, Tue-Sat Nov-May) In this small museum, check out fly-fishing gear once owned by America's manliest men, including Ernest Hemingway, Babe Ruth, Zane Grey and former president George Bush. Another exhibit traces the history of trout fishing and fly fishing.

BattenKill Canoe BOATING

(802-362-2800; www.battenkill.com; 6328 VT 7A, Arlington; canoe/kayak rental $73/45; 9:30am-5:30pm May-Oct) These outfitters 6 miles south of Manchester rent paddling equipment and organize trips on the lovely Battenkill River.

Skyline Drive SCENIC DRIVE

(802-362-1114; www.equinixmountain.com; car & driver $15, extra passenger $5; 9am-5pm late May-Oct, cars admitted until 4pm) For spectacular views, drive to the summit of **Mt Equinox** (3816ft) via Skyline Drive, a private 5-mile toll road off VT 7A.

Sleeping & Eating

Aspen Motel MOTEL $

(802-362-2450; www.theaspenatmanchester.com; 5669 Main St/VT 7A; r $85-150;) Rhododendrons and bright flowers set a pretty stage at this family-run motel set back serenely from the road. The 24-room motel is within walking distance of Manchester Center.

Inn at Manchester INN $$

(802-362-1793, 800-273-1793; www.innatmanchester.com; 3967 Main St/VT 7A; r/ste incl breakfast from $165/255;) The hospitality is what you notice first at this delightful inn and carriage house in the heart of downtown. Relax in comfy rooms with quilts and country furnishings or step out your door for the big front porch, afternoon teas, an expansive backyard and a wee pub. The new Celebration Barn works well for weddings and meetings.

Spiral Press Café CAFE $

(802-362-9944; cnr VT 11 & VT 7A; mains $8-10; 7:30am-7pm Mon-Sat, 8:30-7pm Sun;) Attached to the fabulous Northshire Bookstore, Manchester Center's favorite cafe draws locals and tourists alike with good coffee, tasty cookies, flaky croissants and delicious sandwiches.

Ye Olde Tavern AMERICAN $$$

(802-362-0611; www.yeoldetavern.net; 5183 Main St; mains $18-35; 5-9pm) At this gracious roadside 1790s inn, hearthside dining at candlelit tables enhances the wide-ranging menu of 'Yankee favorites' such as traditional pot roast (cooked in the tavern's own ale) or local venison (a Friday evening special).

Information

Manchester and the Mountains Regional Chamber of Commerce (802-362-6313; www.visitmanchestervt.com; 39 Bonnet St, Manchester Center; 9am-5pm Mon-Fri, 10am-3pm Sat, 11am-3pm Sun;) Spiffy office has free wi-fi.

Central Vermont

Nestled in the Green Mountains, central Vermont is classic small-town, big-countryside New England. Its picturesque villages and venerable ski resorts have been luring travelers for generations.

Woodstock & Quechee

The archetypal Vermont town, Woodstock has streets lined with graceful Federal- and Georgian-style houses. The Ottauquechee River, spanned by a covered bridge, meanders right through the heart of town. Quechee (*kwee-chee*), 7 miles to the northeast, is famous for

WORTH A TRIP

MONTSHIRE MUSEUM OF SCIENCE

Play a musical fence. Study leaf cutter ants in action. Wander a riverside trail. And view current images from the Hubble telescope. Yep, the hands-on exhibits at the family-friendly **Montshire** (802-649-2200; www.montshire.org; 1 Montshire Rd; adult/child 2-12yr $14/11; 10am-5pm;) are pretty darn cool and tend to be more thoughtful and engaging than those at other children's museums. Here, the focus is on the science, with exhibits tackling questions in ecology, technology and the physical and natural sciences. Adults will learn something too.

The museum sits on a scenic 110-acre perch beside the Connecticut River, 20 miles east of Woodstock. The Montshire is also easy to reach if you're in downtown Hanover, NH – just drive across the river.

its dramatic gorge, dubbed 'Vermont's Little Grand Canyon.'

Sights

★Quechee Gorge CANYON
(visitor center 9am-5pm) FREE Quechee Gorge, an impressive 170ft-deep, 3000ft-long chasm cut by the Ottauquechee River, can be viewed from above or explored via nearby walking trails. The adjacent **visitor center** (5966 Woodstock Rd; 9am-5pm) has trail maps and local information

★VINS Nature Center RAPTOR CENTER
(802-359-5000; www.vinsweb.org; 6565 Woodstock Rd; adult/child 4-17yr $13.50/11.50; 10am-5pm mid-Apr–Oct, to 4pm Nov–mid-Apr ;) You may feel like ducking during the live raptor show when several magnificent raptors show off their mad flight skills. Visit this nature center, a mile west of Quechee Gorge, for a close-up look at bald eagles, snow owls, and red-tailed hawks. More than 40 raptors are rehabilitated here.

Marsh-Billings-Rockefeller National Historical Park PARK
(802-457-3368; www.nps.gov/mabi; 53 Elm St, Woodstock; mansion tours adult/child under 16yr $8/free, trails free; visitor center 10am-5pm late May-Oct, tours 10am-4pm) Encompassing the historic home and estate of early American conservationist George Perkins Marsh, Vermont's only national park offers mansion tours on the hour, plus 20 miles of trails and carriage roads for walkers, cross-country skiers and snowshoers. Advance reservations are recommended for tours. Specialty tours may be substituted for the mansion tour on certain days, so call ahead to confirm which tour is being offered.

Billings Farm & Museum FARM
(802-457-2355; www.billingsfarm.org; 69 Old River Rd, Woodstock; adult/child 5-15yr/child 3-4yr $14/8/4; 10am-5pm daily May-Oct, to 4pm Sat & Sun Nov-Feb;) A mile north of the village green, this historic farm delights children with its pretty Jersey cows and hands-on demonstrations of traditional farm life. Family-friendly seasonal events include wagon and sleigh rides, a pumpkin and apple festival and old-fashioned Halloween, Thanksgiving and Christmas celebrations.

Sleeping

Quechee State Park CAMPGROUND $
(802-295-2990; www.vtstateparks.com/htm/quechee.htm; 5800 Woodstocck Rd/US 4, Quechee; tent & RV sites/lean-tos from $20/25; mid-May–mid-Oct) Perched on the edge of Quechee Gorge, this 611-acre spot has 45 pine-shaded campsites and seven lean-tos.

Ardmore Inn B&B $$
(802-457-3887; www.ardmoreinn.com; 23 Pleasant St, Woodstock; r incl breakfast $219-259;) Congenial owners and lavish breakfasts enhance the considerable appeal of this stately, centrally located 1867 Victorian-Greek Revival inn with five antique-laden rooms.

Shire Riverview Motel MOTEL $$
(802-457-2211; www.shiremotel.com; 46 Pleasant St/US 4, Woodstock; r $149-209;) Spring the extra few dollars for a river view at this 42-room motel, which features a wraparound porch overlooking the Ottauquechee River. Expect classic, not-too-fancy decor and a few country prints.

Eating

Mon Vert Cafe CAFE $

(☎802-457-7143; www.monvertcafe.com; 67 Central St; breakfast $6-13, lunch $9-11; ⏲7:30am-5pm Mon-Thu, to 6pm Fri & Sat) Pop into this bright and airy cafe for croissants, scones, and egg sandwiches in the morning or settle in on the patio for salads and paninis at lunch. Enjoy the maple latte anytime. Ingredients are sourced locally, and farms and food purveyors are listed on the wall.

Melaza Caribbean Bistro PUERTO RICAN $$

(☎802-457-7110; www.melazabistro.com; 71 Central St; small plates $5-12, mains $16-25; ⏲5:30-8:30 Sun, Wed & Thu, to 9pm Fri & Sat) Service was a little too casual on our visit, but all was forgiven after the first bite of the perfectly seasoned rice and chicken *sofrito,* served with avocados and brava sauce. Unwind here after day of exploring, with a glass of wine and an enticing mix of Puerto Rican and tropically inspired tapas and entrees.

★ **Simon Pearce Restaurant** NEW AMERICAN $$$

(☎802-295-1470; www.simonpearce.com; 1760 Main St, Quechee; lunch $13-19, dinner $22-38; ⏲11:30am-2:45pm & 5:30-9pm Mon-Sat, 10:30am-2:45 & 5:30-9pm Sun) Reserve ahead for a window table suspended over the river in this converted brick mill, where fresh-from-the-farm local ingredients are used to inventive effect. The restaurant's beautiful stemware is blown by hand in the Simon Pearce Glass workshops next door. The Vermont cheddar soup is always a good choice.

Information

Woodstock Area Chamber of Commerce Welcome Center (☎802-432-1100; www.woodstockvt.com; Mechanic St, Woodstock; ⏲9am-5pm) On a riverside backstreet, two blocks from the village green.

Killington

A half-hour's drive west of Woodstock, **Killington Resort** (☎802-422-6200; www.killington.com; adult/senior/child 7-18yr lift ticket weekend $92/78/71, midweek $84/71/65) is New England's answer to Vail, boasting more than 200 runs on seven mountains, a vertical drop of 3150ft and 29 lifts. Thanks to the world's most extensive snowmaking system, Killington has one of the East's longest ski seasons. Come summer, mountain bikers and hikers claim the slopes.

Killington is jam-packed with accommodations, from cozy ski lodges to chain hotels. Most are along Killington Rd, the 6-mile road that heads up the mountain from US 4. The **Killington Chamber of Commerce** (☎802-773-4181; www.killingtonchamber.com; 2319 US 4, Killington; ⏲10am-5pm Mon-Fri, to 2pm Sat) has all the nitty-gritty.

Mad River Valley

The Mad River Valley, centered around the towns of Warren and Waitsfield, boasts two significant ski areas: **Sugarbush** (☎802-583-6300, 800-537-8427; www.sugarbush.com; 1840 Sugarbush Access Rd, Warren; adult lift ticket weekend/midweek $91/84; discount if purchased online) and **Mad River Glen** (☎802-496-3551; www.madriverglen.com; VT 17; adult lift ticket weekend/midweek $75/60), in the mountains west of VT 100. Opportunities abound for cycling, canoeing, horseback riding, kayaking, gliding and other activities. Stop at the **Mad River Valley Chamber of Commerce** (☎802-496-3409, 800-828-4748; www.madrivervalley.com; 4061 Main St, Waitsfield; ⏲9am-5pm Mon-Fri) for a mountain of information.

Northern Vermont

Boasting some of New England's lushest and prettiest landscapes, northern Vermont cradles the fetching state capital of Montpelier, the ski mecca of Stowe, the vibrant college town of Burlington and the state's highest mountains.

Montpelier

America's smallest capital, Montpelier is a thoroughly likable town of period buildings backed by verdant hills and crowned by the gold-domed 19th-century **State House** (www.vtstatehouse.org; 115 State St; ⏲tours 10am-3:30pm Mon-Fri, 11am-2:30pm Sat Jul-Oct) FREE. Tours of the capitol building run on the hour and the half hour. Right across the street, the **Capitol Region Visitors Center** (☎802-828-5981; 134 State St; ⏲6am-5pm Mon-Fri, 9am-5pm Sat & Sun) has tourist information.

Bookstores, boutiques and restaurants throng the town's twin thoroughfares, State and Main Sts. Forget about junk food – Montpelier prides itself on being the only state capital in the USA without a McDonald's! The bakery-cafe **La Brioche** (www.neci.edu/labrioche; 89 Main St; pastries $1-5, sandwiches $5-8; ⏲7am-6pm Mon-Fri, to 3pm Sat), run by students from Montpelier's New England Culinary Institute, gets an A-plus for its innovative sandwiches and flaky French pastries.

Stowe & Around

With Vermont's highest peak, **Mt Mansfield** (4393ft), as its backdrop, Stowe ranks as Vermont's classiest ski destination. It packs all the alpine thrills you could ask for – both cross-country and downhill skiing, with gentle runs for novices and challenging drops for pros. Cycling, hiking and kayaking take center stage in the summer. Lodgings and eateries are thick along VT 108 (Mountain Rd), which continues northwest from Stowe village to the ski resorts.

Sights & Activities

In warm weather, don't miss the drive through dramatic **Smugglers Notch**, northwest of Stowe on VT 108 (closed by heavy snows in winter). This narrow pass slices through mountains with 1000ft cliffs on either side. Roadside trails lead into the surrounding high country.

★Ben & Jerry's Ice Cream Factory FACTORY
(☎802-882-1240; www.benjerrys.com; 1281 VT 100, Waterbury; adult/child under 13yr $4/free; ⏲9am-9pm Jul–mid-Aug, to 7pm mid-Aug–Oct, 10am-6pm Nov-Jun; 👪) A far cry from the abandoned Burlington gas station where ice cream pioneers Ben Cohen and Jerry Greenfield first set up shop in 1978, this legendary factory, just north of I-89 in Waterbury, draws crowds for tours that include a campy moo-vie and a taste tease of the latest flavor.

Behind the factory, a mock cemetery holds 'graves' of Holy Cannoli and other long-forgotten flavors.

Long Trail HIKING
Vermont's 300-mile Long Trail, which passes west of Stowe, follows the crest of the Green Mountains and runs the entire length of Vermont, with rustic cabins, lean-tos and campsites along the way. Its caretaker, the **Green Mountain Club** (☎802-244-7037; www.greenmountainclub.org; 4711 Waterbury-Stowe Rd/VT 100) 🍃, has full details on the Long Trail and shorter day hikes around Stowe.

★Stowe Recreation Path OUTDOORS
(www.stowerec.org/paths; 👪🐾) 🍃 This flat to gently rolling 5.3-mile path offers a fabulous four-season escape for all ages, as it rambles through woods, meadows and outdoor sculpture gardens along the West Branch of the Little River, with sweeping views of Mt Mansfield in the distance. Bike, walk, skate, ski and/or swim in one of the swimming holes along the way. If you're traveling with your dog, veer onto the 1.8-mile **Quiet Path** extension, open only to joggers and walkers, and their dogs.

Stowe Mountain Resort SKIING
(☎888-253-4849, 802-253-3000; www.stowe.com; 5781 Mountain Rd) This venerable resort encompasses two major mountains, Mt Mansfield (vertical drop 2360ft) and Spruce Peak (1550ft). It offers 48 beautiful trails: 16% beginner, 55% intermediate and 29% for hardcore backcountry skiers.

Umiak Outdoor Outfitters OUTDOORS
(☎802-253-2317; www.umiak.com; 849 S Main St; ⏲9am-6pm) Rents kayaks, snowshoes and telemark skis, offers boating lessons and leads river and moonlight snowshoe tours.

AJ's Ski & Sports EQUIPMENT RENTAL
(☎802-253-4593, 800-226-6257; www.stowesports.com; 350 Mountain Rd; ⏲9am-6pm) Rents bikes, ski and snowboard equipment in the village center.

Sleeping

Smugglers Notch State Park CAMPGROUND $
(☎888-409-7579, 802-253-4014; www.vtstateparks.com/htm/smugglers.htm; 6443 Mountain Rd; tent & RV sites/lean-tos from $20/$27; ⏲mid-May–mid-Oct) This 35-acre park, 8 miles northwest of Stowe, is perched on the mountainside, with 20 tent and trailer sites and 14 lean-tos.

Stowe Motel & Snowdrift MOTEL, APARTMENT $$
(☎802-253-7629, 800-829-7629; www.stowemotel.com; 2043 Mountain Rd; r $108-188, ste $192-208, apt $172-240; @📶🏊) Active guests will do just fine at this motel, set on 16 acres and home to a tennis court, hot tubs, lawn games and free bicycles or snowshoes for use on the adjacent Stowe Recreation Path. Units range from simple to deluxe.

Trapp Family Lodge LODGE $$$
(☎802-253-8511, 800-826-7000; www.trappfamily.com; 700 Trapp Hill Rd; r from $295; @📶🏊🐾) The setting is appropriately breathtaking, and you'd surely be forgiven if you broke into

song. Surrounded by wide-open fields and mountain vistas, this Austrian-style chalet, built by Maria von Trapp of *Sound of Music* fame, boasts Stowe's best setting. Traditional lodge rooms are complemented by guesthouses scattered across the 2700-acre property. A network of trails offers stupendous hiking, snowshoeing and cross-country skiing. Pet fee is $50 per night.

Eating

Harvest Market MARKET $

(☎802-253-3800; www.harvestatstowe.com; 1031 Mountain Rd; ⏲7am-5:30pm) Before heading for the hills, stop here for coffee, pastries, Vermont cheeses, sandwiches, gourmet deli items, wines and local microbrews.

Pie-casso PIZZA $$

(☎802-253-4411; www.piecasso.com; 1899 Mountain Rd; sandwiches $9-13, pizza $11-22; ⏲11am-10pm Sun-Thu, to 11pm Fri & Sat) Organic arugula chicken salad and portobello panini supplement the menu of excellent hand-tossed pizzas. There's a bar and live music too.

Gracie's Restaurant BURGERS $$

(☎802-253-8741; www.gracies.com; 18 Edson Hill Rd; mains $12-44; ⏲5pm until close) Halfway between the village and the mountain, this animated, dog-themed eatery serves big burgers, hand-cut steaks, Waldorf salad and garlic-laden shrimp scampi.

★Hen of the Wood AMERICAN $$$

(☎802-244-7300; www.henofthewood.com; 92 Stowe St, Waterbury; mains $22-29; ⏲5-9pm Tue-Sat) Arguably the finest dining in northern Vermont, this chef-driven restaurant in Waterbury gets rave reviews for its innovative farm-to-table cuisine. The setting in a historic grist mill rivals the extraordinary food, which features densely flavored dishes, like ham-wrapped rabbit loin and sheep's-milk gnocchi.

Information

Stowe Area Association (☎802-253-7321; www.gostowe.com; 51 Main St; ⏲9am-5pm Mon-Sat, to 8pm Jun-Oct & Jan-Mar) In the heart of the village.

Burlington

This hip college town on the shores of scenic Lake Champlain is one of those places that makes you think, wouldn't it be great to live here? The cafe and club scene is on par with a much bigger city, while the slow, friendly pace is pure small town. And where else can you walk to the end of Main St and paddle off in a kayak?

WORTH A TRIP

SCENIC DRIVE: VERMONT'S GREEN MOUNTAIN BYWAY

Following Vermont's Green Mountain spine through the state's rural heart, the **VT 100** rambles past rolling pastures speckled with cows, tiny villages with country stores and white-steepled churches, and verdant mountains crisscrossed with hiking trails and ski slopes. It's the quintessential side trip for those who want to slow down and experience Vermont's bucolic essence. The road runs north to south all the way from Massachusetts to Canada. Even if your time is limited, don't miss the scenic 45-mile stretch between Waterbury and Stockbridge, an easy detour off I-89. For details about attractions along the way, visit www.vermont-byways.us.

Sights

Burlington's shops, cafes and pubs are concentrated around Church St Marketplace, a bustling brick-lined pedestrian mall midway between the University of Vermont and Lake Champlain.

★Shelburne Museum MUSEUM

(☎802-985-3346; www.shelburnemuseum.org; 6300 Shelburne Rd/US 7, Shelburne; adult/youth 13-17yr/child 5-12yr $24/14/12; ⏲10am-5pm mid-May–Oct;) Wear your walking shoes for this extraordinary 45-acre museum, which showcases a Smithsonian-caliber collection of Americana – 150,000 objects in all. The mix of folk art, decorative arts and more is housed in 39 historic buildings, most of them relocated here from other parts of New England to ensure their preservation. Located 9 miles south of Burlington.

Shelburne Farms FARM

(☎802-985-8686; www.shelburnefarms.org; 1611 Harbor Rd, Shelburne; adult/child 3-17yr $8/5; ⏲9am-5:30pm mid-May–mid-Oct, 10am-5pm mid-Oct–mid-May;) This 1400-acre estate, designed by landscape architect Frederick Law Olmsted (who also designed New York's Central Park), was both a country house for the aristocratic Webb family and a working farm, with stunning lakefront perspectives. Still a working farm, the property today welcomes visitors. Guests can milk a cow in the farmyard (11am, 2pm), sample the farm's superb cheddar cheese, tour the magnificent barns and walk the network of trails. Enjoy afternoon tea while a guest at the award-winning inn (p237), or stop by for farm-sourced produce and local meats at its restaurant.

Echo Lake Aquarium & Science Center SCIENCE CENTER
(☎802-864-1848; www.echovermont.org; 1 College St; adult/child 3-17yr $13.50/10.50; ⏲10am-5pm; 👪) Examining the colorful past, present and future of Lake Champlain, this lakeside museum features a multitude of small aquariums and rotating science exhibits with plenty of hands-on, kid-friendly activities. Don't miss the Into the Lake exhibit which spotlights Champ, a local 'sea monster' allegedly dwelling in the lake.

Magic Hat Brewery BREWERY
(☎802-658-2739; www.magichat.net; 5 Bartlett Bay Rd, South Burlington; ⏲10am-7pm Mon-Sat Jun–mid-Oct, to 6pm Mon-Thu, to 7pm Fri & Sat mid-Oct-May, noon-5pm Sun year-round) Drink in the history of one of Vermont's most dynamic microbreweries on the fun, free, self-guided tour. Afterwards, sample a few of the eight brews on tap in the on-site Growler Bar. Recent samples included the Peppercorn Pilsner, made with pink peppercorns, and the Electric Peel, a grapefruit IPA.

Activities

Ready for outdoor adventures? Head to the waterfront, where options include boating on **Lake Champlain** and cycling, in-line skating and walking on the 7.5-mile shorefront **Burlington Bike Path**. Jump-off points and equipment rentals for all these activities are within a block of each other near the waterfront end of Main St.

Local Motion BICYCLE RENTAL
(☎802-652-2453; www.localmotion.org; 1 Steele St; bicycles per day $32; ⏲9am-6pm July & Aug, 10am-6pm May & Jun, Sept & Oct; 👪) Rents quality bikes beside the Burlington Bike Path between Main St and King St.

Whistling Man Schooner Company SAILING
(☎802-598-6504; www.whistlingman.com; Boathouse, 1 College St, at Lake Champlain; 2hr cruises adult/child under 13yr $40/25; ⏲3 trips daily, late May–early Oct) Explore Lake Champlain on the *Friend Ship*, a 17-passenger, 43-foot sailboat.

LOCAL KNOWLEDGE

BURLINGTON'S SECRET GARDEN

Hidden away less than 2 miles from Burlington's city center is one of Vermont's most idyllic green spaces. Tucked among the lazy curves of the Winooski River, the **Intervale Center** (www.intervale.org; 180 Intervale Rd) FREE encompasses a dozen organic farms and a delightful trail network, open to the public 365 days a year for hiking, biking, skiing, berry picking and more; check the website for details.

Sleeping

Burlington's budget and midrange motels are on the outskirts of town, clustered along Shelburne Rd (US 7) in South Burlington, Williston Rd (US 2) east of I-89 exit 14, and US 7 north of Burlington in Colchester (I-89 exit 16).

North Beach Campground CAMPGROUND $
(☎802-862-0942; www.enjoyburlington.com; 60 Institute Rd; tent/RV site $36/41; ⏲May–mid-Oct; 📶) Two miles north of downtown, this wonderful spot on Lake Champlain offers 137 campsites on 45 wooded acres, with picnic tables, fire rings, hot showers, a playground, beach and bike path.

Burlington Hostel HOSTEL $
(☎802-540-3043; www.theburlingtonhostel.com; 53 Main St; dm incl breakfast $40; ❄@📶) Just minutes from Church St and Lake Champlain, Burlington's hostel offers both mixed and single sex dorms, with eight beds per room.

Lang House B&B $$
(☎802-652-2500; www.langhouse.com; 360 Main St; r incl breakfast $199-259; ❄@📶) The Lang House may be Burlington's most elegant B&B, but you can still kick back and relax like the proletariat - this is Burlington, after all. This tastefully restored 19th-century Victorian home and carriage house occupies a centrally located spot not far from downtown. Reserve ahead for one of the 3rd-floor rooms with lake views.

Hilton Garden Inn Burlington Downtown HOTEL $$
(☎802-951-0099; www.hiltongardeninn3.hilton.com; 101 Main St; r from $229; P❄@📶🏊) Hip *and* historic? Yep, and the combination works seamlessly at this Hilton Garden, which opened in 2015. Housed in a former

armory, the hotel is within walking distance of Church St Marketplace and Lake Champlain. The airy pavilion lobby pops with bright colors and crisp decor. Rooms are a bit less exuberant but come with Serta beds, mini-fridges, and microwaves. Note that weekends book up far in advance. Parking is $16 per night and valet only.

★Inn at Shelburne Farms INN $$$
(☎802-985-8498; www.shelburnefarms.org/stay-dine; 1611 Harbor Rd, Shelburne; r with private/shared bath from $210/165, cottage from $320, guesthouse from $450; ⊙May-Oct;) At this historic 1400-acre estate (p235) on the shore of Lake Champlain, 7 miles south of Burlington, guests stay in a gracious, welcoming country manor house, or in four independent, kitchen-equipped cottages and guest houses scattered across the property. The attached farm-to-table restaurant is superb. And those lake sunsets? Ahhhh.

Eating

On Saturday mornings, City Hall Park hosts Burlington's thriving **farmers market** (www.burlingtonfarmersmarket.org) in downtown.

Penny Cluse Cafe CAFE $
(☎802-651-8834; www.pennycluse.com; 169 Cherry St; mains $6-12.25; ⊙6:45am-3pm Mon-Fri, 8am-3pm Sat & Sun) Did somebody say bucket-o-spuds? Oh yes, they did. And that's just the first thing listed on the enticing menu at Penny Cluse, one of Burlington's most popular downtown eateries. The kitchen also whips up pancakes, biscuits and gravy, omelets and tofu scrambles along with sandwiches, fish tacos, salads and excellent *chile relleno*. Expect long lines on weekends. One quibble? Weak coffee on our visit. Sad face.

City Market MARKET $
(☎802-861-9700; www.citymarket.coop; 82 S Winooski Ave; sandwiches $8-10; ⊙7am-11pm) If there's a natural-foods heaven, it must look something like this downtown co-op: chock-full of local produce and products (with more than 1000 Vermont-based producers represented) and a huge takeout deli.

Stone Soup VEGETARIAN $
(☎802-862-7616; www.stonesoupvt.com; 211 College St; buffet per lb $10.75, sandwiches under $10; ⊙7am-9pm Mon-Fri, 9am-9pm Sat;) Squeeze in at lunchtime for the small but excellent vegetarian- and vegan-friendly buffet at this longtime local favorite. Also good: homemade soups, sandwiches on home-baked bread, a salad bar and pastries.

★Pizzeria Verita PIZZA $$
(☎802-489-5644; www.pizzeriaverita.com; 156 Paul St; pizza $8-18; ⊙5-10pm Sun-Thu, to 11pm Fri & Sat) You can't walk two steps in Burlington without somebody recommending new-on-the-scene Pizzeria Verita. And their recommendation is spot-on. It's heaven on a thin crust. Step into this modernly rustic trattoria (you know what we mean – wine casks for bar tables, etc) for the *quatro formaggi*, the *funghi rustico* or the Ring of Fire with hot cherry peppers.

At the bar, sip interesting seasonal cocktails and Vermont craft beers.

Daily Planet INTERNATIONAL $$
(☎802-862-9647; www.dailyplanet15.com; 15 Center St; mains $11-24; ⊙4-9pm Sun-Thu, to 9:30pm Fri & Sat;) This stylish downtown haunt serves everything from confit duck poutine to burgers with tasty trimmings to pan-roasted lamb lollipops to caramelized sea scallops. The bar stays open until 2am nightly.

Leunig's Bistro FRENCH $$$
(☎802-863-3759; www.leunigsbistro.com; 115 Church St; lunch $12-22, dinner $18-34; ⊙11am-10pm Mon-Thu, to 11pm Fri, 9am-11pm Sat , to 10pm Sun) With sidewalk seating and an elegant, tin-ceilinged dining room, this convivial Parisian-style brasserie is a longstanding Burlington staple. It's as much fun for the people-watching (windows face busy Church St Marketplace) as for the excellent wine list and food.

Drinking & Nightlife

The free weekly *Seven Days* (www.7dvt.com) has event and entertainment listings.

Radio Bean BAR
(www.radiobean.com; 8 N Winooski Ave; ⊙8am-2am Mon-Sat, 10am-2am Sun;) This funky cafe-bar features its own low-power FM radio station, a trendy attached eatery serving international street food, and live performances nightly that include jazz, acoustic music and poetry readings.

Vermont Pub & Brewery MICROBREWERY
(www.vermontbrewery.com; 144 College St; mains $5-18; ⊙11:30am-1am Sun-Wed, to 2am Thu-Sat) Specialty and seasonal brews, including weekly limited releases, are made on the premises, accompanied by British-style pub fare.

Splash at the Boathouse BAR
(☎802-658-2244; www.splashattheboathouse.com; 0 College St; ⏰10am-2am mid-May–Sep) Perched atop Burlington's floating boathouse, this restaurant-bar with stellar views over Lake Champlain is perfect for kicking back with an evening cocktail or microbrew at sunset.

☆ Entertainment

Nectar's LIVE MUSIC
(www.liveatnectars.com; 188 Main St; ⏰7pm-2am Sun-Tue, 5pm-2am Wed-Sat) Nectar's celebrated its 40th birthday in 2015, and the joint still rocks out with a mix of theme nights and live acts. Indie darlings Phish got their start here.

Shopping

You'll find boutiques and smart craft shops along Church St Marketplace. Don't miss the **Frog Hollow Craft Center** (www.froghollow.org; 85 Church St; ⏰10am-6pm Mon-Wed, to 8pm Thu-Sat, 11am-7pm Sun mid-Apr–Nov, reduced hours rest of the year) FREE, a collective featuring some of the finest work in Burlington.

ℹ Information

University of Vermont Medical Center (☎802-847-0000; www.uvmhealth.org; 111 Colchester Ave; ⏰24hr) Vermont's largest hospital. Has a 24hr level 1 trauma center.

Lake Champlain Regional Chamber of Commerce (☎802-863-3489, 877-686-5253; www.vermont.org; 60 Main St; ⏰8am-5pm Mon-Fri) Downtown tourist office.

ℹ Getting There & Away

Greyhound (☎800-231-2222, 802-864-6811; www.greyhound.com; 1200 Airport Dr) offers bus service between Burlington International Airport and Boston and Montreal. **Megabus** (☎877-462-6342; www.megabus.com; 116 University Pl) runs from the University of Vermont campus in Burlington to Amherst, MA and New York City. **Amtrak's Vermonter train** (☎800-872-7245; www.amtrak.com/vermonter-train) runs south daily to Brattleboro, New York City and Washington, DC. **Lake Champlain Ferries** (☎802-864-9804; www.ferries.com; King St Dock; adult/child 6-12yr/car $8/3.10/30) runs ferries mid-June through September across the lake to Port Kent, NY (one hour 20 minutes).

NEW HAMPSHIRE

New Hampshire needs to work on its marketing: The Granite State? Live Free or Die? Do they want anyone to visit? In truth, this state has the scale of things just right for residents and travelers: the towns are small and personable, the mountains majestic and rugged. The heart of New Hampshire is unquestionably the granite peaks of the White Mountain National Forest. Outdoor enthusiasts of all stripes flock to New England's highest range (6288ft at Mt Washington) for cold-weather skiing, summer hiking and brilliant fall foliage scenery. And don't be fooled by that politically conservative label that people stick on the state. The aforementioned state mantra, 'Live Free or Die,' indeed rings from every automobile license plate, but residents here pride themselves on their independent spirit more than right-wing politics.

History

Named in 1629 after the English county of Hampshire, New Hampshire was one of the first American colonies to declare its independence from England in 1776. During the 19th-century industrialization boom, the state's leading city, Manchester, became such a powerhouse that its textile mills were the world's largest.

New Hampshire played a high-profile role in 1944 when president Franklin D Roosevelt gathered leaders from 44 Allied nations to remote Bretton Woods for a conference to rebuild global capitalism. It was at the Bretton Woods Conference that the World Bank and the International Monetary Fund emerged.

In 1963 New Hampshire, long famed for its anti-tax sentiments, found another way to raise revenue – by becoming the first state in the USA to have a legal lottery.

ℹ Information

Welcome centers are situated at major state border crossings.

New Hampshire Division of Parks & Recreation (☎603-271-3556; www.nhstateparks.org) Offers information on hiking, biking, camping and other outdoor activities.

New Hampshire Division of Travel & Tourism Development (☎603-271-2665; www.visitnh.gov) Order a visitor's guide and check out the adventure itineraries.

Portsmouth

America's third-oldest city (1623), Portsmouth wears its history on its sleeve. Its roots are in shipbuilding, but New Hampshire's sole coastal city also has a hip, youthful energy. The old maritime warehouses along the harbor now house cafes and boutiques. Elegant period homes built by shipbuilding tycoons have been converted into B&Bs.

Sights & Activities

Strawbery Banke Museum MUSEUM

(☎603-433-1100; www.strawberybanke.org; cnr Hancock & Marcy Sts; adult/child 5-17yr $20/10; ⏲10am-5pm May-Oct) Spread across a 10-acre site, the Strawbery Banke Museum is an eclectic blend of period homes that date back to the 1690s. Costumed guides recount tales that took place among the 40 buildings (10 furnished). Strawbery Banke includes **Pitt Tavern** (1766), a hotbed of American revolutionary sentiment, **Goodwin Mansion** (a grand 19th-century house from Portsmouth's most prosperous time) and **Abbott's Little Corner Store** (1943). The admission ticket is good for two consecutive days.

USS Albacore MUSEUM

(☎603-436-3680; http://ussalbacore.org; 600 Market St; adult/child 7-13yr $7/3; ⏲9:30am-5pm Jun–mid-Oct, to 4pm Thu-Mon mid-Oct–May) Audio recollections add context as you squeeze through the narrow compartments packed inside the USS *Albacore* – which was home to 55 officers and crew in its heyday. Like a fish out of water, this 205ft-long submarine is now a beached museum on a grassy lawn. Launched from Portsmouth Naval Shipyard in 1953, the *Albacore* was once the world's fastest submarine.

Isles of Shoals Steamship Co CRUISE

(☎603-431-5500; www.islesofshoals.com; 315 Market St; adult/child 4-12yr $28/18; 👪) From mid-June through September the company runs an excellent tour of the harbor and the historic Isles of Shoals aboard a replica 1900s ferry. Also offers sunset, country music, reggae and dinner cruises.

Sleeping

Ale House Inn INN $$

(☎603-431-7760; www.alehouseinn.com; 121 Bow St; r $209-359; P 📶) Thank you for the two Smuttynose beers, Ale House Inn. We like it here already. Portsmouth's snazziest boutique, this brick warehouse for the Portsmouth Brewing Company fuses contemporary design with comfort. Rooms are modern with clean lines of white and flatscreen TVs, plush tan sofas fill the suites. Deluxe rooms feature an in-room iPad. Rates include use of vintage cruising bikes.

Port Inn MOTEL $$

(☎603-436-4378; www.choicehotels.com; 505 Rte 1 Bypass; r/ste incl breakfast $127/178 ; ❄@📶🏊🐾) Wrapped neatly around a small courtyard, this welcoming motel is conveniently located off I-95, about a mile and a half southwest of downtown. In the rooms, monochromatic pillows and throws add a dash of color to classic furnishings. Pets are $20 per night.

Eating & Drinking

Head to the intersection of Market and Congress Sts, where restaurants and cafes are thick on the ground.

NEW HAMPSHIRE FACTS

Nicknames Granite State, White Mountain State

Population 1.3 million

Area 8968 sq miles

Capital city Concord (population 42,400)

Other cities Manchester (population 110,300), Portsmouth (21,400)

Sales tax None

Birthplace of America's first astronaut Alan Shepard (1923–98), *The Da Vinci Code* author Dan Brown (b 1964)

Home of The highest mountains in northeastern USA

Politics New England's most Republican state

Famous for Being the first to vote in US presidential primaries, which gives the state enormous political influence for its size

Most extreme state motto Live Free or Die

Driving distances Boston to Portsmouth 60 miles, Portsmouth to Hanover 118 miles

Friendly Toast DINER $

(☎603-430-2154; www.thefriendlytoast.com; 113 Congress St; breakfast $8-14, lunch $11-19; ⏰7am-9pm Sun-Thu, to 10pm Thu, 2am Fri & Sat;) Fun, whimsical furnishings set the scene for filling sandwiches, omelets, Tex-Mex and vegetarian fare at this retro diner. The breakfast menu is huge and is served around the clock – good thing since weekend morning waits can be long.

Surf SEAFOOD $$

(☎603-334-9855; www.surfseafood.com; 99 Bow St; lunch $9-18, dinner $12-38; ⏰4-9pm Sun-Thu, to 10pm Fri & Sat) We're not sure if the view of the Pisquataqua River complements the food or the food complements the view, especially at sunset at this airy restaurant. Either way, both are a satisfying way to close out the day. The seafood offerings have some global flair, with shrimp and avocado quesadillas, haddock crepes, and shrimp vindaloo with curry sauce.

Black Trumpet Bistro INTERNATIONAL $$$

(☎603-431-0887; www.blacktrumpetbistro.com; 29 Ceres St; mains $19-31; ⏰5:30-9pm) With brick walls and sophisticated ambience, this bistro serves unique combinations (anything from pork sirloin with collard greens to quail with sausage stuffing). The full menu is also available at its wine bar upstairs, which whips up equally inventive cocktails.

Thirsty Moose Taphouse PUB

(www.thirstymoosetaphouse.com; 21 Congress St; bar snacks $5-13, mains $10-14; ⏰11am-1pm) From Abita to Widmer Bros, with Clown Shoes in between, this convivial spot pours more than 100 beers on tap, leaning heavily on New England brews (and a staff that can walk you through most – it's impressive). A fine spot to kick back and relax. Bites include *poutine* (fries drenched in cheese and gravy), sandwiches and burgers.

Information

Greater Portsmouth Chamber of Commerce
(☎603-436-3988; www.portsmouthchamber.org; 500 Market St; ⏰8:30am-5pm Mon-Thu, to 7pm Fri, 10am-5pm Sat & Sun Jun–mid-Oct, 8:30am-5pm Mon-Fri mid-Oct–May) Also operates an information kiosk in the city center at Market Sq.

Monadnock State Park & Around

The climb to the 3165ft summit of **Mt Monadnock** (www.nhstateparks.org; 116 Poole Rd, Jaffrey, NH 124; adult/child 6-11yr $4/2) is rocky and steep, but the view from the boulder-capped summit is oh-so-worth-the-burn. Mt Monandnock, in the southwestern corner of the state, is the most hiked summit in New England. 'Mountain That Stands Alone' in Algonquian, Monadnock is relatively isolated from other peaks, which means hikers who make the 5-mile round-trip to the summit are rewarded with unspoiled views of three states. Best bet for first-timers? Hike up on the White Dot Trail and return via the White Cross Trail.

The best post-hike reward? Everyone knows it's a heaping scoop of ice cream from **Kimball Farm** (www.kimballfarm.com; 158 Turnpike Rd; small scoop $5; ⏰ice cream 10am-10pm) just up the road. Choose from more than 50 flavors, including chocolate raspberry, maple walnut, and coffee Oreo. For a drink or an overnight stay near the mountain, try the quirky charms of the **Monadnock Inn** (☎603-532-7800; www.monadnockinn.com; 379 Main St; r $110-190), where the tavern is cozy and your room may include a wire birdcage.

Lake Winnipesaukee

A popular summer retreat for families looking for a break from the city, New Hampshire's largest lake stretches 28 miles in length, contains 274 islands and offers abundant opportunities for swimming, boating and fishing.

Weirs Beach

This lakeside town dishes up a curious slice of honky-tonk Americana with its celebrated video arcades, mini-golf courses and go-cart tracks. The **Lakes Region Chamber of Commerce** (☎603-524-5531; www.lakesregionchamber.org; 383 S Main St, Laconia ; ⏰9am-3pm Mon-Fri, 10am-5pm Sat) supplies information about the area.

Mount Washington Cruises (☎603-366-5531; www.cruisenh.com; 211 Lakeside Ave; cruises $30-47) operates scenic lake cruises, the pricier ones with champagne brunch and live music, from Weirs Beach aboard the old-fashioned MS *Mount Washington*.

Winnipesaukee Scenic Railroad (603-745-2135; www.hoborr.com; 211 Lakeside Ave, Weirs Beach; adult/child 3-11yr 1hr $12/14, 2hr $14/18) offers train rides along the shore of Lake Winnipesaukee.

Wolfeboro

On the opposite side of Lake Winnipesaukee, and a world away from the ticky-tacky commercialism of Weirs Beach, sits genteel Wolfeboro. Anointing itself 'the oldest summer resort in America,' the town is awash with graceful period buildings, including several that are open to the public. The **Wolfeboro Chamber of Commerce** (603-569-2200; www.wolfeborochamber.com; 32 Central Ave; 10am-3pm Mon-Fri, to noon Sat), in the old train station, has the scoop on everything from boat rentals to lakeside beaches.

Wolfeboro is home to the **Great Waters Music Festival** (603-569-7710; www.greatwaters.org; Jun-Aug), featuring folk, jazz and blues artists at different venues throughout town.

Off NH 28, about 4 miles north of town, is lakeside **Wolfeboro Campground** (603-569-9881; www.wolfeborocampground.com; 61 Haines Hill Rd; tent & RV sites $32; mid-May–mid-Oct) with 50 wooded campsites.

For breakfast, lunch or coffee with a Lake Winnipesaukee view, stop by the **Downtown Grille Cafe** (www.downtowngrillecafe.com; 33 S Main St; breakfast $3.25-7, lunch $8-12; 7am-3pm), which serves a tasty array of omelets, sandwiches, wraps and burgers. The cozy bar at **Wolfe's Tavern** (www.wolfestavern.com; Wolfeboro Inn, 90 N Main St; bar menu appetizers $5-12, sandiwches $11-13; 8am-10pm) offers numerous regional beers and a bar menu with pork belly tacos, calamari and sandwiches. Ice cream from **Bailey's Bubble** (603-569-3612; www.baileysbubble.com; 5 Railroad Ave; small scoop $2.75; 11am-10pm May–mid-Oct, shorter hours spring and fall) is always a good idea.

White Mountains

What the Rockies are to Colorado the White Mountains are to New Hampshire. New England's loftiest mountain range is a magnet for adventurers, with boundless opportunities for everything from hiking and kayaking to skiing. Those who prefer to take it in from the comfort of a car seat won't be disappointed either, as scenic drives wind over rugged mountains ripping with waterfalls, sheer rock faces and sharply cut gorges.

You'll find information on the White Mountains at ranger stations throughout the **White Mountain National Forest** (www.fs.usda.gov/whitemountain) and chambers of commerce in the towns along the way.

Mount Washington Valley

Stretching north from the eastern terminus of the Kancamagus Hwy, Mt Washington Valley includes the towns of Conway, North Conway, Intervale, Glen, Jackson and Bartlett. Every conceivable outdoor activity is available. The area's hub and biggest town, North Conway, is also a center for outlet shopping, including some earthy stores like LL Bean.

Sights & Activities

★**Conway Scenic Railroad** TRAIN
(603-356-5251; www.conwayscenic.com; 38 Norcross Circle; Notch Train adult/child 4-12yr/child 1-3yr from $55/39/11, Valley Train from $16.50/11.50; mid-Jun–Oct;) The **Notch Train**, built in 1874 and restored in 1974, offers New England's most scenic journey. The spectacular five- to 5½-hour trip passes through Crawford Notch. Accompanying live commentary recounts the railroad's history and folklore. Reservations required.

Alternatively, the same company operates the antique steam **Valley Train**, which makes a shorter journey south through the Mt Washington Valley, stopping in Conway and Bartlett. Look for seasonal excursions like the Pumpkin Patch Express in October and the Polar Bear Express in November and December.

★**Mount Washington Observatory Weather Discovery Center** MUSEUM
(603-356-2137; www.mountwashington.org; 2779 White Mountain Hwy; adult/child 7-17yr $2/1; 10am-5pm) If you don't have time to drive to the summit of Mt Washington but you think wild weather is cool, take an hour to explore this small but fascinating weather museum instead. Shoot an air cannon, interrupt a mini-tornado and learn why temperatures are so extremely cold atop Mount Washington. What happens when you push the red button inside the mock observatory shack? All we'll say is, hold on tight.

WORTH A TRIP

SCENIC DRIVE: WHITE MOUNTAIN NATIONAL FOREST

One of New England's finest, the 35-mile **Kancamagus Hwy (NH 112)** is a beauty of a road cutting through the **White Mountain National Forest** (p241) between Conway and Lincoln. Laced with excellent hiking trails, scenic lookouts and swimmable streams, this is as natural as it gets. There's absolutely no development along the entire highway, which reaches its highest point at **Kancamagus Pass** (2868ft).

Pick up brochures and hiking maps at the **Saco Ranger District Office** (☎603-447-5448; 33 Kancamagus Hwy; ⏰8am-4:30pm) at the eastern end of the highway near Conway. On the western end, stop by the National Forest desk at the **White Mountains Visitor Center** in North Woodstock.

Coming from Conway, 6.5 miles west of the Saco ranger station, you'll see **Lower Falls** on the north side of the road – stop here for the view and a swim. No trip along this highway is complete without taking the 20-minute hike to the breathtaking cascade of **Sabbaday Falls**; the trail begins at Mile 15 on the south side of the road. The best place to spot moose is along the shores of **Lily Pond**; stop at the roadside overview at Mile 18. At the Lincoln Woods ranger station, which is near the Mile 29 marker, cross the suspension footbridge over the river and hike 3 miles to **Franconia Falls**, the finest swimming hole in the entire national forest, complete with a natural rock slide. Parking anywhere along the highway costs $3 per day (honor system) or $5 per week; just fill out an envelope at any of the parking areas.

The White Mountain National Forest is ideal for campers, and you'll find several campgrounds run by the forest service accessible from the Kancamagus Hwy. Most are on a first-come, first-served basis; pick up a list at the Saco ranger station.

Echo Lake State Park PARK

(www.nhstateparks.org; River Rd; adult/child 6-11yr $4/2) Two miles west of North Conway via River Rd, this placid mountain lake lies at the foot of **White Horse Ledge**, a sheer rock wall. A scenic trail circles the lake, which has a small beach. There is also a mile-long auto road and hiking trail leading to the 700ft-high **Cathedral Ledge**, with panoramic White Mountains views. Both Cathedral Ledge and White Horse Ledge are excellent for rock climbing. This is also a fine spot for swimming and picknicing.

Saco Bound CANOEING

(☎603-447-2177; www.sacobound.com; 2561 E Main/US 302, Conway; rentals per day $26-45; ⏰late Apr–mid-Oct) Saco Bound Inc organizes canoe trips with shuttle service ($12 TO $15 per canoe/kayak), including the introductory trip to Weston's Bridge. Also runs overnight camping trips. Inner tubes (adult/child under 12 $20/10) available for rent, too.

Sleeping

North Conway in particular is thick with sleeping options from resort hotels to cozy inns.

White Mountains Hostel HOSTEL $

(☎603-447-1001; www.whitemountainshostel.com; 36 Washington St, Conway; dm/r $20/20-30; Wi-Fi) Set in an early-1900s farmhouse, this cheery place in Conway is now under new ownership. The environmentally conscientious hostel has dorm bedrooms with bunk beds and five private rooms, and a communal lounge and kitchen. Excellent hiking, bicycling and kayaking opportunities are all found nearby. Our only gripe is the location, which is 5 miles south of the action in North Conway.

Not a party hostel, but a great choice if you want to explore the outdoors.

Saco River Camping Area CAMPGROUND $

(☎603-356-3360; www.sacorivercampingarea.com; 1550 White Mountain Hwy/NH 16; tent/RV sites from $33/43, huts $47; ⏰May–mid-Oct; Wi-Fi, pool) A riverside campground, away from the highway, with 140 wooded and open sites as well as rustic huts (literally walls and a roof; no electricity or kitchen). Canoe and kayak rental available.

Cranmore Inn B&B $$

(☎603-356-5502; www.cranmoreinn.com; 80 Kearsarge St; r incl breakfast $149-369; Wi-Fi, pool) Under new ownership and recently renovated, the Cranmore has lost the country frills. Rooms now sport a fresh, more contemporary style. In addition to standard rooms, there are several two-room suites and one apartment with a kitchen. The inn has been operating as a country inn since 1863. There's a year-round hot tub on-site, perfect for post-hike sore muscles.

Hampton Inn North Conway HOTEL $$$
(☎603-356-7736; www.hamptoninn3.hilton.com; 1788 White Mountain Hwy; r from $279;) Traveling with high-energy kids? Let them loose in the 5000-sq-ft indoor water park, with two slides, at this super welcoming location of the national chain.

Eating

Peach's CAFE $
(☎603-356-5860; www.peachesnorthconway.com; 2506 White Mountain Hwy; breakfast $6-10, lunch $8-9; 7am-2:30pm) Away from the in-town bustle, this perennially popular little house is an excellent option for soups, sandwiches and breakfast. Who can resist fruit-smothered waffles and pancakes and fresh-brewed coffee, served in somebody's cozy living room?

Moat Mountain Smoke House & Brewing Co PUB FOOD $$
(☎603-356-6381; www.moatmountain.com; 3378 White Mountain Hwy; mains $10-23; 11:30am-midnight) With its great food, on-point service and tasty homemade beers, Moat Mountain wins best all around for New Hampshire brewpubs. Come here for a wide array of American fare, with a nod to the South: BBQ sandwiches, beefy chili, juicy burgers, wood-grilled pizzas and a delicious curried crab and corn bisque. Wash it down with one of the numerous brews made on-site.

The friendly bar is also a popular local hangout.

Information

Mt Washington Valley Chamber of Commerce (☎603-356-5701; www.mtwashingtonvalley.org; 2617 White Mountain Hwy; 9am-5pm) Tourist information just south of the town center. Hours are notoriously unreliable.

North Woodstock & Lincoln

The twin towns of Lincoln and North Woodstock break up the drive between the Kancamagus Hwy and Franconia Notch State Park, so they are a handy place to stop for a bite or a bed. The towns straddle the Pemigewasset River at the intersection of NH 112 and US 3. Ratchet up the adrenaline by zipping 2000ft down a hillside while strapped to just a cable with the treetop zip line at **Alpine Adventure** (☎603-745-9911; www.alpinezipline.com; 41 Main St, Lincoln; zips from $64; 11am-4pm).

Sleeping & Eating

Woodstock Inn INN $$
(☎603-745-3951; www.woodstockinnnh.com; US 3; r incl breakfast with shared/private bath from $147/178;) Anchoring downtown North Woodstock, this Victorian country inn features 34 individually appointed rooms across five separate buildings (three in a cluster, two across the street), each with modern amenities but old-fashioned style. For dinner, you have your choice of the on-site upscale restaurant and microbrewery (Woodstock Station & Microbrewery).

Woodstock Inn Station & Brewery PUB FOOD $$
(☎603-745-3951; www.woodstockinnnh.com; US 3; mains $12-24; 11:30am-10pm) On warm days, the sunny front patio is a nice place to eat, drink and watch the world go by. Formerly a railroad station, this eatery tries to be everything to everyone, with more than 150 items on the menu. Pasta, sandwiches and burgers are the most interesting. The beer-sodden rear tavern is one of the most happening places in this neck of the woods.

Information

Lincoln/Woodstock Chamber of Commerce (☎603-745-6621; www.lincolnwoodstock.com; 126 Main St/NH 112, Lincoln; 9am-5pm Mon-Fri) Offers area information.

White Mountains Visitor Center (☎603-745-8720, National Forest 603-745-3816; www.visitwhitemountains.com; 200 Kancamagus Hwy; visitor info 8:30am-5pm, National Forest desk 9am-3pm daily mid-May–Oct, Fri, Sat & Sun only Nov–mid-May) A life-size stuffed moose (not real) sets a mood for adventure while brochures and trail maps provide the details. You can also buy a White Mountain National Forest Pass here ($3/5 per day/week), which is required for extended stops at national forest trailheads.

Franconia Notch State Park

Franconia Notch is the most celebrated mountain pass in New England, a narrow gorge shaped over the eons by a rushing stream slicing through the craggy granite. I-93, in places feeling more like a country road than a highway, runs straight through the state park. The **Franconia Notch State Park visitor center** (☎603-745-8391; www.nhstateparks.org; I-93, exit 34A; 9am-5pm mid-May–Oct), 4 miles north of North Woodstock, can give you details on hikes in the park, which range from short nature walks to day-long treks.

Take a walk or a bike ride on the 8.8-mile **bike path** that tracks the Pemigewasset River and links Flume Gorge and Cannon Mountain. Bike rentals available at the tramway (half/full day $25/40).

Sights & Activities

Cannon Mountain Aerial Tramway CABLE CAR
(603-823-8800; www.cannonmt.com; I-93, exit 34B; round-trip adult/child 6-12yr $17/14; 9am-5pm late May–mid-Oct;) This tramway shoots up the side of Cannon Mountain, offering a breathtaking view of Franconia Notch. In 1938 the first passenger aerial tramway in North America was installed on this slope. It was replaced in 1980 by the current, larger cable car, capable of carrying 80 passengers up to the summit in five minutes – a 2022ft, 1-mile ride. Or, visitors can hike up the mountain and take the tramway down.

Flume Gorge HIKING
(www.nhstateparks.org; adult/child 6-12yr $16/13; 9am-5pm May-Oct) To see this natural wonder, take the 2-mile self-guided nature walk that includes the 800ft boardwalk through the Flume, a natural cleft (12ft to 20ft wide) in the granite bedrock. The granite walls tower 70ft to 90ft above you, with moss and plants growing from precarious niches and crevices. Signs explain how nature formed this natural phenomenon. A nearby covered bridge is thought to be one of the oldest in the state, perhaps erected as early as the 1820s.

Echo Lake BEACH
(603-823-8800; I-93, exit 34C; adult/child 6-11yr $4/2; 10am-5pm mid-Jun–Aug) Despite its proximity to the highway, this little lake at the foot of Cannon Mountain is a pleasant place to pass an afternoon swimming, kayaking or canoeing (rentals $20 per hour) in the crystal-clear waters. And many people do. The small beach gets packed, especially on weekends.

Sleeping

Lafayette Place Campground CAMPGROUND $
(877-647-2757; www.reserveamerica.com; campsites $25; mid-May–early Oct) This popular campground has 97 wooded tent sites that are in heavy demand in summer. Reservations are accepted for 89 of the sites. For the others, arrive early in the day and hope for the best. Many of the state park's hiking trails start here.

Bretton Woods & Crawford Notch

Before 1944, Bretton Woods was known primarily as a low-key retreat for wealthy visitors who patronized the majestic Mt Washington Hotel. After President Roosevelt chose the hotel for the historic conference that established a new post-WWII economic order, the town's name took on worldwide recognition. The countryside, with Mt Washington looming above it, is as magnificent today as it was back then. The **Twin Mountain-Bretton Woods Chamber of Commerce** (800-245-8946; www.twinmountain.org; cnr US 302 & US 3; 9am-5pm Jul & Aug, 9am-5pm Fri-Sun foliage season, closed rest of yr) information booth details about the area.

The state's largest ski area, **Bretton Woods** (603-278-3320; www.brettonwoods.com; US 302; Sat, Sun & holidays lift ticket adult/child 13-17/child 6-12 & seniors $85/65/49, Mon-Fri $75/58/43) offers downhill and cross-country skiing, and a zipline in warmer months (May-Sep).

US 302 heads south from Bretton Woods to Crawford Notch (1773ft) through stunning mountain scenery ripe with towering cascades. **Crawford Notch State Park** (603-374-2272; www.nhstateparks.org; 1464 US Route 302; adult/child 6-11yr $4/2) maintains an extensive system of hiking trails, including short hikes around a pond and to a waterfall, and a longer trek up Mt Washington.

Sleeping

AMC Highland Center LODGE $$
(information 603-278-4453, reservations 603-466-2727; www.outdoors.org/lodging/whitemountains/highland; NH 302, Bretton Woods; dm incl breakfast & dinner adult/child $106/55, s/d incl breakfast & dinner $153/89) This cozy Appalachian Mountain Club (AMC) lodge is set amid the splendor of Crawford Notch, an ideal base for hiking the many trails criss-crossing the Presidential Range. The grounds are beautiful, rooms are basic but comfortable, meals are hearty and guests are outdoor enthusiasts. Discounts are available for AMC members. The information center, open to the public, has loads of information about regional hiking.

★**Omni Mt Washington Hotel & Resort** HOTEL $$$
(603-278-1000; www.omnihotels.com; 310 Mt Washington Hotel Rd, Bretton Woods; r from $339, ste $869;) Open since 1902, this grand hotel maintains a sense of fun – note the

moose's head overlooking the lobby and the framed images of local wildflowers in many of the guest rooms. It also offers 27 holes of golf, red-clay tennis courts, an equestrian center and a spa. A sunset cocktail on the back porch, with the mountains before you, is perfection. There's a $27.25 daily resort fee.

Mount Washington

From Pinkham Notch (2032ft), on NH 16 about 11 miles north of North Conway, a system of hiking trails provides access to the natural beauties of the Presidential Range, including lofty Mt Washington (6288ft), the highest mountain east of the Mississippi and north of the Smoky Mountains.

Hikers need to be prepared: Mt Washington's weather is notoriously severe and can turn on a dime. Dress warmly – not only does the mountain register New England's coldest temperatures (in summer, the average at the summit is 45°F/7°C) but unrelenting winds make it feel colder than the thermometer reading. In fact, Mt Washington holds the record for the USA's strongest wind gust – 231mph!

The **Pinkham Notch Visitor Center** (603-278-4453; www.outdoors.org; NH 16; 6:30am-10pm May-Oct, to 9pm Nov-Apr), run by the Appalachian Mountain Club (AMC), is the area's informational nexus for like-minded adventurers and a good place to buy hiking necessities, including topographic trail maps and the handy *AMC White Mountain Guide*.

One of the most popular trails up Mt Washington begins at the Visitor Center and runs 4.2 strenuous miles to the summit, taking four to five hours to reach the top and a bit less on the way down.

If your quads aren't up for a workout, the **Mt Washington Auto Road** (603-466-3988; www.mountwashingtonautoroad.com; 1 Mt Washington Auto Rd, off NH 16; car & driver $28, extra adult/child 5-12yr $8/6; 7:30-6pm early Jun-Aug, shorter hr mid-May–early Jun, Sep-mid-Oct), 2.5 miles north of Pinkham Notch Camp, offers easier summit access, weather permitting.

While purists walk, and the out-of-shape drive, the quaintest way to reach the summit is to take the **Mt Washington Cog Railway** (603-278-5404; www.thecog.com; 3168 Bass Station Rd; adult/child 4-12yr $68/39; May-Oct). Since 1869, coal-fired steam-powered locomotives have followed a 3.5-mile track up a steep mountainside trestle for a jaw-dropping excursion.

OFF THE BEATEN TRACK

AMC WHITE MOUNTAIN HUTS

The Appalachian Mountain Club manages eight overnight huts along the Appalachian Trail in the Presidential Range. In summer and early fall a small 'croo' at each hut welcomes hikers, prepares meals and shares information about conservation and natural sciences. The hut system here has been in operation for more than 125 years. If you're a hiker but not sure about backpacking, an overnight hut trip is a great way to test the waters. Just pack overnight clothes, toiletries, trail snacks, water, and a headlamp. The croo will take care of the rest. It ain't fancy – hikers sleep in bunks in co-ed dorms with rustic bathrooms – but the views and the community? Awesome. Reservations are key. (www.outdoors.org/lodging/huts).

Dolly Copp Campground (603-466-2713, reservations 877-444-6777; www.fs.usda.gov; NH 16; tent & RV sites $22; mid-May–mid-Oct), a USFS campground 6 miles north of the AMC's Pinkham Notch facilities, has 176 simple campsites.

Hanover

The archetypal New England college town, Hanover has a town green that is bordered on all four sides by the handsome brick edifices of Dartmouth College. Virtually the whole town is given over to this Ivy League school; chartered in 1769, Dartmouth is the nation's ninth-oldest college.

Main St, rolling down from the green, is surrounded by perky pubs, shops and cafes that cater to the collegian crowd. The Appalachian Trail runs along Main St right through downtown.

Sights

Dartmouth College COLLEGE
(603-646-1110; www.dartmouth.edu) Hanover is all about Dartmouth College, so hit the campus. Join a free student-guided **campus walking tour** (603-646-2875; https://admissions.dartmouth.edu; 6016 McNutt Hall), or grab a map at the admissions office across from the green in McNutt Hall. Maps are also available online. Don't miss the **Baker-Berry Library**, splashed with the grand *Epic of American*

Civilization, painted by the outspoken Mexican muralist José Clemente Orozco (1883–1949), who taught at Dartmouth in the 1930s.

Hood Museum of Art MUSEUM
(☎603-646-2808; http://hoodmuseum.dartmouth.edu/; E Wheelock St; ⏰10am-5pm Tue, Thu-Sat, to 9pm Wed, noon-5pm Sun) FREE Shortly after the university's founding in 1769 Dartmouth began to acquire artifacts of artistic or historical interest. Since then the collection has expanded to include nearly 65,000 items, which are housed at the Hood Museum of Art. The collection is particularly strong in American pieces, including Native American art. One of the highlights is a set of Assyrian reliefs from the Palace of Ashurnasirpal that date to the 9th century BC. Special exhibits often feature contemporary artists.

Sleeping & Eating

Storrs Pond Recreation Area CAMPGROUND $
(☎603-643-2134; www.storrspond.com; 59 Oak Hill DR/NH 10; tent/RV sites $32/40; ⏰Jun–early Oct; 📶) As well as woodsy sites next to a 15-acre pond, this private campground has tennis courts and two sandy beaches for swimming. 18 RV sites available and 12 tent sites. From I-89 exit 13, take NH 10 north and look for signs.

Hanover Inn INN $$$
(☎603-643-4300, 800-443-7024; www.hanoverinn.com; 2 E Wheelock St, cnr W Wheelock & S Main Sts; r from $249; @📶🐾) A 2800lb handmade granite table now anchors the lobby at the recently revamped Hanover Inn, the city's loveliest guesthouse. Owned by Dartmouth College, the inn has nicely appointed rooms with custom art work, collegiate-style throws, and elegant wood furnishings. It has a farm-to-table restaurant on site. Pets are $50 per night.

Lou's DINER $
(☎603-643-3321; www.lousrestaurant.net; 30 S Main St; breakfast $8-12, lunch $9-12; ⏰6am-3pm Mon-Fri, 7am-3pm Sat & Sun) A Dartmouth institution since 1947, this is Hanover's oldest establishment, always packed with students meeting for a coffee or perusing their books. From the retro tables or the Formica-topped counter, order typical diner food like eggs, sandwiches and burgers. The bakery items – I'm talking about you ginger molasses cookie – are also highly recommended.

Canoe Club Bistro CAFE $$
(☎603-643-9660; www.canoeclub.us; 27 S Main St; lunch $12-24, dinner $10-23; ⏰11:30am-11:30pm) 🌿 This smart cafe does a fine job with grilled food – not just burgers and steaks, but also a range of farm-to-table fare with global accents including a crispy pork schnitzel and malay curry shrimp. There's also live entertainment nightly, anything from acoustic to jazz to a Monday night magic show.

Drinking & Entertainment

Murphy's on the Green PUB
(☎603-643-4075; wwwmurphysonthegreen.com; 11 S Main St; mains $12-24; ⏰4pm-12:30am Mon-Thu, 11-12:30am Fri-Sun) This classic collegiate tavern is where students and faculty meet over pints (it carries over 10 beers on tap, including local microbrews like Long Trail Ale) and satisfying pub fare (mains $12 to $24). Stained-glass windows, church-pew seating and book-lined shelves enhance the cozy atmosphere.

Hopkins Center for the Arts PERFORMING ARTS
(☎603-646-2422; www.hop.dartmouth.edu; 4 E Wheelock St) A long way from the big-city lights of New York and Boston, Dartmouth hosts its own entertainment at this outstanding performing-arts venue. The season brings everything from movies to live performances by international companies.

Information

Hanover Area Chamber of Commerce
(☎603-643-3115; www.hanoverchamber.org; 53 S Main St, Suite 208; ⏰9am-4pm Mon-Fri) For tourist information. It's inside the Nugget Building and also maintains an **information booth** (⏰9:30am-3pm Mon-Wed, to 6pm Thu & Fri, 10am-3pm Sat & Sun) on the village green, staffed daily from late June to early September.

MAINE

Maine is New England's frontier – a land so vast it could swallow the region's five other states with scarcely a gulp. The sea looms large with mile after mile of sandy beaches, craggy sea cliffs and quiet harbors. While time-honored fishing villages and seaside lobster joints are the fame of Maine, inland travel also offers ample reward. Maine's rugged interior is given over to rushing rivers, dense forests and lofty mountains just aching to be explored.

As a traveler in the Pine Tree State, your choices are as spectacularly varied as the landscape. You can opt to sail serenely along the coast on a graceful schooner or rip through white-water rapids on a river raft, spend the night in an old sea captain's home-turned-B&B, or camp among the moose on a backwoods lake.

History

It's estimated that 20,000 Native Americans from tribes known collectively as Wabanaki ('People of the Dawn') inhabited Maine when the first Europeans arrived. The French and English vied to establish colonies in Maine during the 1600s but, deterred by the harsh winters, these settlements failed.

In 1652 Massachusetts annexed the territory of Maine to provide a front line of defense against potential attacks during the French and Indian Wars. And indeed Maine at times did become a battlefield between English colonists in New England and French forces in Canada. In the early 19th century, in an attempt to settle sparsely populated Maine, 100-acre homesteads were offered free to settlers willing to farm the land. In 1820 Maine broke from Massachusetts and entered the Union as a state.

In 1851 Maine became the first state to ban the sale of alcoholic beverages, the start of a temperance movement that eventually took hold throughout the United States. It wasn't until 1934 that Prohibition was finally lifted.

MAINE FACTS

Nickname Pine Tree State

Population 1.3 million

Area 35,387 sq miles

Capital city Augusta (population 18,700)

Other cities Portland (population 66,300)

Sales tax 5.5%

Birthplace of Poet Henry Wadsworth Longfellow (1807–82)

Home of Horror novelist Stephen King

Politics Split between Democrats and Republicans

Famous for Lobster, moose, blueberries, LL Bean

State drink Maine gave the world Moxie, America's first (1884) and spunkiest soft drink

Driving distances Portland to Acadia National Park 160 miles, Portland to Boston 150 miles

Information

If you're entering the state on I-95 heading north, stop at the well-stocked visitor information center on the highway.

Maine Bureau of Parks and Land (☎800-332-1501; www.campwithme.com) Offers camping in 12 state parks.

Maine Office of Tourism (☎888-624-6345; www.visitmaine.com; 59 State House Station, Augusta) These folks maintain information centers on the principal routes into the state – Calais, Fryeburg, Hampden, Houlton, Kittery and Yarmouth. Each facility is open 9am to 5:30pm, with extended hours in summer. Many offer wi-fi.

Southern Maine Coast

Maine's most touristed quarter, this seaside region lures visitors with its sandy beaches, resort towns and outlet shopping. The best place to stop for the latter is the southernmost town of Kittery, which is chockablock with outlet stores.

Ogunquit

Aptly named, Ogunquit means 'Beautiful Place by the Sea' in the native Abenaki tongue, and its 3-mile beach has long been a magnet for summer visitors. Ogunquit Beach, a sandy barrier beach, separates the Ogunquit River from the Atlantic Ocean, offering beachgoers the appealing option to swim in cool ocean surf or in the warmer, calmer cove.

As a New England beach destination, Ogunquit is second only to Provincetown for the number of gay travelers who vacation here. Most of the town lies along Main St (US 1), lined with restaurants, shops and motels. For waterfront dining and boating activities head to Perkins Cove at the south end of town.

Sights & Activities

A highlight is walking the scenic 1.5-mile **Marginal Way**, the coastal footpath that skirts the 'margin' of the sea from Shore Rd, near the center of town, to Perkins Cove. A sublime stretch of family-friendly coastline, **Ogunquit Beach**, also called Main Beach by locals, begins right in the town center at

Maine Coast

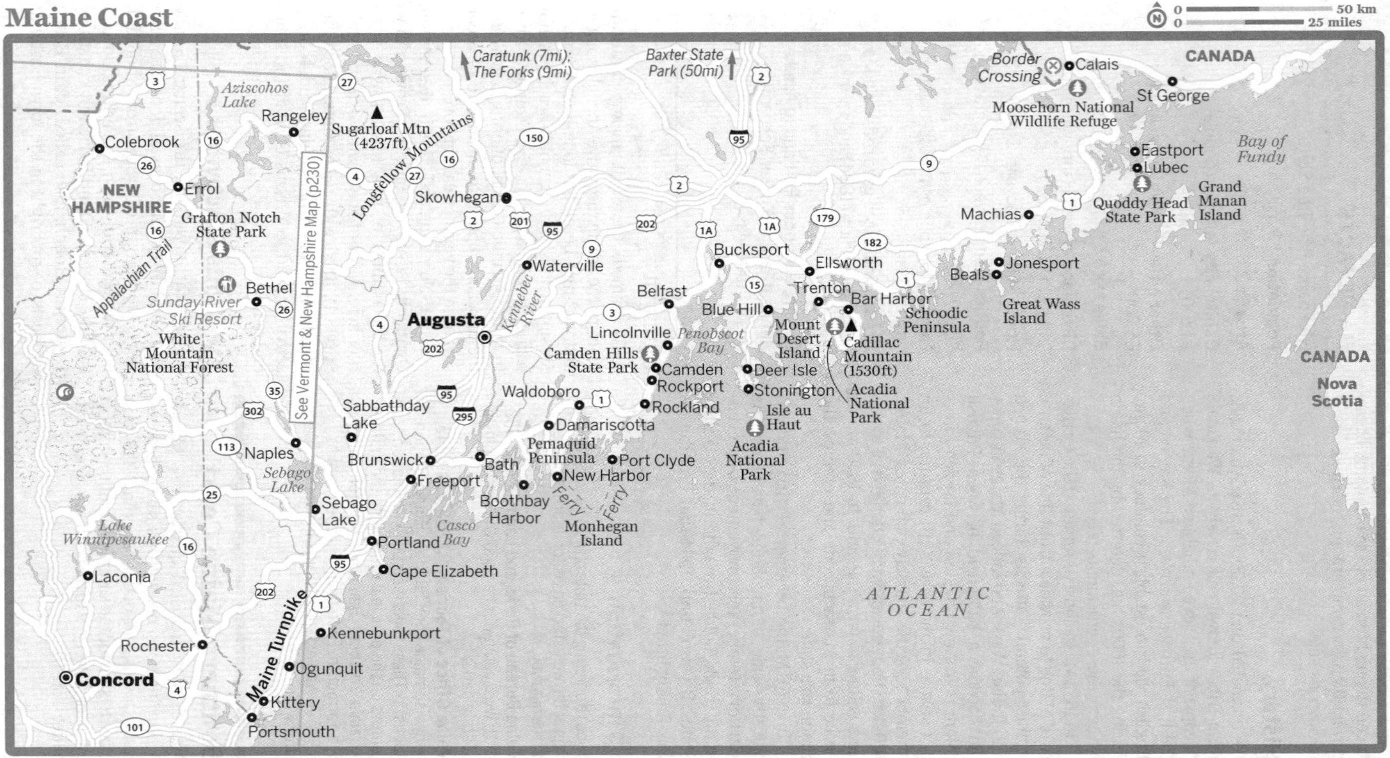
0 50 km
0 25 miles
Caratunk (7mi):
The Forks (9mi)
Baxter State
Park (50mi)
Border
Crossing
Calais
CANADA
St George
Moosehorn National
Wildlife Refuge
Eastport
Lubec
Bay of
Fundy
Quoddy Head
State Park
Grand
Manan
Island
Machias
Jonesport
Beals
Great Wass
Island
Schoodic
Peninsula
Bar Harbor
Cadillac
Mountain
(1530ft)
Acadia
National
Park
Trenton
Ellsworth
Mount
Desert
Island
Bucksport
Blue Hill
Deer Isle
Stonington
Isle au
Haut
Acadia
National
Park
Belfast
Lincolnville
Penobscot
Bay
Camden Hills
State Park
Camden
Rockport
Rockland
Waldoboro
Damariscotta
Pemaquid
Peninsula
Port Clyde
New Harbor
Ferry
Ferry
Monhegan
Island
Boothbay
Harbor
Bath
Brunswick
Freeport
Casco
Bay
Portland
Cape Elizabeth
Sabbathday
Lake
Augusta
Kennebec
River
Waterville
Skowhegan
Longfellow Mountains
Sugarloaf Mtn
(4237ft)
Rangeley
Aziscohos
Lake
Colebrook
Errol
NEW
HAMPSHIRE
Grafton Notch
State Park
Appalachian Trail
Bethel
Sunday River
Ski Resort
White
Mountain
National Forest
See Vermont & New Hampshire Map (p230)
Naples
Sebago
Lake
Sebago
Lake
Lake
Winnipesaukee
Laconia
Rochester
Concord
Maine Turnpike
Kennebunkport
Ogunquit
Kittery
Portsmouth
ATLANTIC
OCEAN
CANADA
Nova
Scotia

the end of Beach St. Want to escape town? Park at **Footbridge Beach** just north at the end of Ocean St.

Finestkind Scenic Cruises CRUISES
(207-646-5227; www.finestkindcruises.com; Perkins Cove; adult/child 4-11yr from $18/9) Offers many popular trips, including a 50-minute lobstering trip, a sunset cocktail cruise and a two-hour cruise aboard the twin-sailed *Cricket*.

Sleeping

Pinederosa Camping CAMPGROUND $
(207-646-2492; www.pinederosa.com; 128 North Village Rd, Wells; campsites from $35; mid-Jun–early Sep;) This wholesome, wooded campground has 85 well-tended sites, some of which overlook the Ogunquit River. Amenities include a lovely in-ground heated pool and camp store. Ogunquit Beach is about 3 miles away.

Gazebo Inn B&B $$
(207-646-3733; www.gazeboinnogt.com; 572 Main St; r/ste incl breakfast $239-269/299-599;) This stately 1847 farmhouse features 14 rooms that feel more like a private boutique hotel. Rustic-chic touches include heated wood floors, stone fireplaces in the bathrooms, and a media room with beamed ceilings and a wall-size TV.

Ogunquit Beach Inn B&B $$
(207-646-1112; www.ogunquitbeachinn.com; 67 School St; r incl breakfast $179-209; @) In a tidy little Craftsman-style bungalow, this gay-and-lesbian-friendly B&B has colorful, homey rooms and chatty owners who know all about the best new bistros and bars in town. The central location makes walking to dinner a breeze.

Eating

You'll find Ogunquit's restaurants on the south side of town at Perkins Cove and in the town center along Main St.

Bread & Roses BAKERY $
(www.breadandrosesbakery.com; 246 Main St; snacks $3-10; 7am-9pm Sun-Thu, to 11pm Sat & Sun Jun-Aug, shorter hours rest of the year;) Get your coffee and blueberry-scone fix at this teeny slip of a bakery, in the heart of downtown Ogunquit. The cafe fare, like veggie burritos and organic egg-salad sandwiches, is good for a quick lunch. No seating.

★ **Lobster Shack** SEAFOOD $$
(www.lobster-shack.com; 110 Perkins Cove Rd; mains $5-29; 11am-8pm) If it's available, the homemade chowder and lobster roll special ($19) is the way to go. Lobster Shack is a great choice if you're craving good seafood and aren't particular about the view. This reliable joint serves lobster in all its various incarnations.

Barnacle Billy's SEAFOOD $$$
(207-646-5575; www.barnbilly.com; 183 Shore Rd; mains $3-21; 11am-9pm Apr-Oct) This big, noisy barn of a restaurant overlooking Perkins Cove is a longtime favorite for casual seafood – steamers, crab rolls, clam chowder and, of course, whole lobsters.

Entertainment

Ogunquit Playhouse THEATER
(207-646-5511; www.ogunquitplayhouse.org; 10 Main St;) First opened in 1933, presents both showy Broadway musicals and children's theater each summer.

Information

Ogunquit Chamber of Commerce (207-646-2939; www.ogunquit.org; 36 Main St; 9am-5pm Mon-Sat, 11am-4pm Sun) Located on US 1, near the Ogunquit Playhouse and just south of the town's center.

Kennebunkport

On the Kennebunk River, Kennebunkport fills with tourists in summer who come to stroll the streets, admire the century-old mansions and get their fill of sea views. Be sure to take a drive along **Ocean Ave**, which runs along the east side of the Kennebunk River and then follows a scenic stretch of the Atlantic that holds some of Kennebunkport's finest estates, including the summer home of former president George Bush Snr. To view the Bush compound, drive almost 2 miles from US 9 downtown then look for a small pullover and marker.

Three public beaches extend along the west side of the Kennebunk River and are known collectively as **Kennebunk Beach**. The center of town spreads out from Dock Sq, which is along ME 9 (Western Ave) at the east side of the Kennebunk River bridge.

Sleeping

Franciscan Guest House GUESTHOUSE $$
(207-967-4865; www.franciscanguesthouse.com; 26 Beach Ave; r/ste $119-209/200-259;) You can almost smell the blackboard chalk inside this high school–turned-guesthouse, on the peaceful grounds of the St Anthony Monastery. Guest rooms, once classrooms, are basic and unstylish – acoustic tile, faux-wood paneling, motel beds. If you don't mind getting your own sheets out of the supply closet (there's no daily maid service), staying here's a great value and a unique experience.

Kennebunkport Inn INN $$$
(207-967-2621; www.kennebunkportinn.com; 1 Dock Sq; r from $199;) Crisp blues and whites evoke a breezy, nautical mood at this finger-popping inn on Dock Square, Get comfortable in the stylish rooms, beside the sundeck firepit or at the in-house bar and restaurant. Complimentary bikes are available for your riding pleasure. Ocean Ave – and its scenic estates – are short ride away.

Eating

Clam Shack SEAFOOD $$
(207-967-3321; www.theclamshack.net; 2 Western Ave; mains $4-30; 11am to close May–mid-Oct) Standing in line at this teeny gray hut, perched on stilts above the river, is a time-honored Kennebunkport summer tradition. Order a box of succulent fried whole-belly clams or a one-pound lobster roll, which is served with your choice of mayo or melted butter. Outdoor seating only. In June, you might catch former first lady Barbara Bush here celebrating her birthday. Cash only.

Closing time is based on the crowd, anytime between 6 and 9:30pm.

★Bandaloop BISTRO $$
(207-967-4994; www.bandaloop.biz; 2 Ocean Ave; small plates $8-12, mains $18-31; 5-9:30pm;) The Casco Bay garlic mussels? Hands down the tastiest bowl of mussels we've ever had. We recommend washing them down with a Peak's organic ale. And the rest of the menu? Local, organic and deliciously innovative, running the gamut from a rosemary grilled sirloin to Vermont cheddar mac-and-cheese to a massaged kale salad with hemp seeds, beets and pecans.

Portland

The 18th-century poet Henry Wadsworth Longfellow referred to his childhood city as the 'jewel by the sea,' and, thanks to a hefty revitalization effort, Portland once again sparkles. Its lively waterfront, burgeoning gallery scene and manageable size add up to great exploring. Foodies, rev up your taste buds: cutting-edge cafes and chef-driven restaurants have turned Portland into the hottest dining scene north of Boston.

Portland sits on a hilly peninsula surrounded on three sides by water: Back Cove, Casco Bay and the Fore River. It's easy to find your way around. Commercial St (US 1A) runs along the waterfront through the Old Port, while the parallel Congress St is the main thoroughfare through downtown.

Sights

Old Port NEIGHBORHOOD
Handsome 19th-century brick buildings line the streets of the Old Port, with Portland's most enticing shops, pubs and restaurants located within this five-square-block district. By night, flickering gas lanterns add to the atmosphere. What to do here? Eat some wicked fresh seafood, down a local microbrew, buy a nautical-themed T-shirt from an up-and-coming designer, peruse the many tiny local art galleries. Don't forget to wander the authentically stinky wharfs, ducking into a fishmongers to order some lobsters.

Portland Museum of Art MUSEUM
(207-775-6148; www.portlandmuseum.org; 7 Congress Sq; adult/child $12/6, 5-9pm Fri free; 10am-5pm Sat-Thu, to 9pm Fri, closed Mon mid-Oct–May) Founded in 1882, this well-respected museum houses an outstanding collection of American artists. Maine artists, including Winslow Homer, Edward Hopper, Louise Nevelson and Andrew Wyeth, are well represented. You'll also find a few works by European masters, including Degas, Picasso and Renoir. The majority of works are found in the postmodern Charles Shipman Payson building, designed by the firm of famed architect IM Pei.

Fort Williams Park LIGHTHOUSE
(sunrise-sunset) FREE Four miles southeast of Portland on Cape Elizabeth, 90-acre Fort Williams Park is worth visiting simply for the panoramas and picnic possibilities. Stroll around the ruins of the fort, a late-19th-century artillery base, checking out the WWII bunkers and gun emplacements (a German

U-boat was spotted in Casco Bay in 1942) that still dot the rolling lawns. Strange as it may seem, the fort actively guarded the entrance to Casco Bay until 1964.

Adjacent to the fort stands the **Portland Head Light**, the oldest of Maine's 52 functioning lighthouses. It was commissioned by George Washington in 1791 and staffed until 1989, when machines took over. The keeper's house has been passed into service as the **Museum at Portland Head Light** (207-799-2661; www.portlandheadlight.com; 1000 Shore Rd; lighthouse museum adult/child 6-18yr $2/1; 10am-4pm Jun-Oct), which traces the maritime and military history of the region.

Longfellow House HISTORIC BUILDING
(207-879-0427; www.mainehistory.org; 489 Congress St; guided tour adult/child 7-17yr $15/3; 10am-5pm Mon-Sat, noon-5pm Sun May-Oct, closed Sun & Mon Nov-Apr) Visitors have been checking out dusty artifacts in the home of revered American poet Henry Wadsworth Longfellow for more than 110 years. A thought that can creep you out if you think about it too much while squinting at the framed needlepoint displays – just like the thousands who have squinted before you. Most now dead. But whatever. Longfellow grew up in this Federal-style house, built in 1788 by his Revolutionary War hero grandfather. The house has been impeccably restored to look like it did in the 1800s, complete with original furniture and artifacts. Tours last one hour.

Activities

For a whole different angle on Portland and Casco Bay, hop one of the boats offering narrated scenic cruises out of Portland Harbor.

Casco Bay Lines CRUISE
(207-774-7871; www.cascobaylines.com; 56 Commercial St; adult $13-24, child $7-11) This outfit cruises the Casco Bay islands delivering mail, freight and visitors looking to bike or explore. It also offers cruises to Bailey Island (adult/child 5-9yr $26/12).

Maine Island Kayak Company KAYAKING
(207-766-2373; www.maineislandkayak.com; 70 Luther St, Peak Island; tour $65; May-Nov) On Peak Island, a 15-minute cruise from downtown on the Casco Bay Lines, this well-run outfitter offers fun day and overnight trips exploring the islands of Casco Bay.

Maine Brew Bus TOUR
(207-200-9111; www.themainebrewbus.com; tour $50-75; tour times vary) Hop aboard the green bus for tours and tastings at some of Portland's most beloved breweries and brewpubs, from Allagash to Sebago. Lunch at a brewpub is included on the Casco Fiasco tour.

Portland Schooner Company CRUISE
(207-766-2500; www.portlandschooner.com; 56 Commercial St; adult/child under 13yr $42/21; May-Oct) Offers tours aboard an elegant, early-20th-century schooner. In addition to two-hour sails, you can book overnight tours ($250 per person, including dinner and breakfast).

Sleeping

Portland has a healthy selection of midrange and upscale B&Bs, though very little at the budget end. The most idyllic accommodations are in the old town houses and grand Victorians in the West End.

Inn at St John INN $$
(207-773-6481; www.innatstjohn.com; 939 Congress St; r incl breakfast $125-275; P) On the western fringe of downtown, this turn-of-the-century hotel has a stuck-in-time feel, from the old-fashioned pigeonhole mailboxes behind the lobby desk to the narrow, sweetly floral rooms. Ask for a room away from noisy Congress St. The value rooms come with a private hall bath or shared hall bath. Book early for big weekends.

Morrill Mansion B&B $$
(207-774-6900; www.morrillmansion.com; 249 Vaughan St; r incl breakfast $169-239;) Charles Morrill, the original owner of this 19th-century West End town house, made his fortune by founding B&M baked beans, still a staple of Maine pantries. His home has been transformed into a handsome B&B, with eight guest rooms furnished in a trim, classic style. Think hardwood floors, lots of tasteful khaki and taupe shades.

Some rooms are a bit cramped; if you need lots of space, try the two-room Morrill Suite.

Portland Harbor Hotel HOTEL $$$
(207-775-9090; www.portlandharborhotel.com; 468 Fore St; r from $339; P) This independent hotel has a classically coiffed lobby, where guests relax on upholstered leather chairs surrounding the glowing fireplace. The rooms carry on the classicism, with sunny gold walls and pert blue toile bedspreads. The windows face Casco Bay, the interior garden or the street; garden rooms are quieter. Parking is $18 (valet only). Pets are $25 per night.

Eating

Two Fat Cats Bakery BAKERY $
(207-347-5144; www.twofatcatsbakery.com; 47 India St; treats $3-7; 8am-6pm Mon-Fri, to 5pm Sat, to 4pm Sun, closed Mon Jan & Feb) Tiny bakery serving pastries, pies, melt-in-your-mouth chocolate-chip cookies and fabulous Whoopie Pies.

DuckFat SANDWICHES $
(207-774-8080; www.duckfat.com; 43 Middle St; small fries $5, sandwiches $10-14; 11am-10pm) DuckFat has the best fries we've tasted in our many decades of fry-eating. No lie. Fried in – yes – duck fat, they're shatteringly crisp, with melt-in-your-mouth fluffy centers. Dipping sauces, like truffle ketchup, are good, but unnecessary. Panini are also excellent. But again, it's about the fries. Decor is 'hipster fast-food joint,' with a blackboard menu and a handful of bistro tables.

★**Green Elephant** VEGETARIAN $$
(207-347-3111; www.greenelephantmaine.com; 608 Congress St; mains $10-15; 11:30am-2:30pm, 5-9:30pm Mon-Sat, to 9pm Sun;) They'll spice it as hot as you like it at this Zen-chic, Thai-inspired cafe, which serves brilliant vegetarian fare in an airy and spare nook downtown. Start with the crispy spinach wontons, then move on to one of the exotic soy creations like garlic and ginger tofu or a flavorful curry like the panang coconut curry with vegetables.

Susan's Fish & Chips SEAFOOD $$
(207-878-3240; www.susansfishnchips.com; 1135 Forest Ave/US 302; mains $9-22; 11am-8pm) Pop in for chowder and fish and chips at this no-fuss but welcoming eatery on US 302, where the tartar sauce comes in mason jars. Located in a former garage.

J's Oyster SEAFOOD $$
(207-772-4828; www.jsoyster.com; 5 Portland Pier; sandwiches $5-18, mains $25-31; 11:30am-11pm) Maybe not the friendliest place on the planet, but this well-loved dive has the cheapest raw oysters in town. Eat 'em on the deck overlooking the pier. The oyster-averse have plenty of sandwiches and seafood mains to choose from.

★**Fore Street** NEW AMERICAN $$$
(207-775-2717; www.forestreet.biz; 288 Fore St; small plates $13-22, mains $28-40; 5:30-10pm Sun-Thu, to 10:30 Fri & Sat) Roasting is a high art at Fore Street, one of Maine's most lauded restaurants. Chickens turn on spits in the open kitchen as chefs slide iron kettles of mussels into the wood-burning oven. Local, seasonal eating is taken very seriously, and the menu changes daily to offer what's freshest. The large, noisy dining room nods towards its warehouse past with exposed brick and pine paneling.

Offerings may include a fresh pea salad, periwinkles (a local shellfish) in herbed cream, and roast bluefish with pancetta. The chilled and smoked seafood platter, offered daily, is a palate pleaser. Reservations needed, but you may be able to snag a bar seat between 5:30 and 6pm.

Drinking & Entertainment

Gritty McDuff's Brew Pub BREWPUB
(www.grittys.com; 396 Fore St; 11am-1am) Gritty is an apt description for this party-happy Old Port pub. You'll find a generally raucous crowd drinking excellent beers – Gritty brews its own award-winning ales downstairs.

Port City Music Hall CONCERT HALL
(207-956-6000; www.portcitymusichall.com; 504 Congress St) This three-story performance space hosts big-name and smaller-name bands.

Shopping

For boutiques, galleries and craft shops, head downtown to Exchange and Fore Sts in Old Port.

Portland Farmers Market FARMERS MARKET
(http://portlandmainefarmersmarket.org; 7am-noon Sat, to 1pm Mon & Wed May-Nov) Vendors hawk everything from Maine blueberries to homemade pickles on Saturdays in summer and fall in Deering Oaks Park downtown (Park Ave at Forest Ave). On Monday and Wednesday the market is in Monument Sq on Congress St. Saturdays only in winter at 200 Anderson St.

Harbor Fish Market FISHMONGER
(207-775-0251; www.harborfish.com; 9 Custom House Wharf; 8:30am-5:30pm Mon-Sat, 9am-noon Sun) On Custom House Wharf, this iconic fishmonger packs lobsters and seafood for roadtrips, island trips, flights, and ships to anywhere in the US.

Maine Potters Market POTTERY
(www.mainepottersmarket.com; 376 Fore St; 10am-9pm daily) A cooperatively owned gallery featuring the work of a dozen or so different Maine ceramists.

Information

Greater Portland Convention & Visitors Bureau (www.visitportland.com; Ocean Gateway Bldg, 14 Ocean Gateway Pier; 9am-5pm Mon-Fri, to 4pm Sat & Sun Jun-Oct, hours vary rest of year) Stop by for brochures and maps.

Getting There & Around

Portland International Jetport (PWM; 207-874-8877; www.portlandjetport.org) has non-stop flights to cities in the eastern US.

Greyhound (www.greyhound.com; 950 Congress St) buses and **Amtrak** (800-872-7245; www.amtrak.com; 100 Thompson's Point Rd) trains connect Portland and Boston; both take about 2½ hours and charge $14 to $34 one way.

The local bus **Metro** (www.gpmetrobus.com; fares $1.50), which runs throughout the city, has its main terminus at Monument Sq, the intersection of Elm and Congress Sts.

Central Maine Coast

Midcoast Maine is where the mountains meet the sea. You'll find craggy peninsulas jutting deep into the Atlantic, alluring seaside villages and endless opportunities for hiking, sailing and kayaking.

Freeport & Around

The fame and fortune of Freeport, 16 miles northeast of Portland, began a century ago when Leon Leonwood Bean opened a shop to sell equipment to hunters and fishers heading north into the Maine wilderness. Bean's good value earned him loyal customers, and over the years the LL Bean Store has expanded.

Sights

LL Bean Flagship Store OUTDOOR EQUIPMENT
(www.llbean.com; 95 Main St; 24hr) A 10ft-tall model of the Bean Boot marks the entrance to the LL Bean store, which has expanded to add sportswear to its outdoor gear. Although a hundred other stores have joined the pack in Freeport, the wildly popular LL Bean is still the epicenter of town and one of the most popular tourist attractions in Maine. It's part store, part outdoor-themed amusement park, with an archery range, an indoor trout pond and a coffee shop.

DeLorme Mapping Company BUILDING
(207-846-7100; www.delorme.com; 2 DeLorme Dr; 9:30am-6pm Mon-Sat, to 5pm Sun) Don't miss a visit to this office, with its giant 5300-sq-ft rotating globe, Eartha, in nearby Yarmouth at exit 17 off I-95. Maker of the essential *Maine Atlas and Gazetteer,* DeLorme also creates maps and software for every destination in the United States. You'll find regional hiking guides and trail maps here, too.

WHOOPIE!

Looking like steroid-pumped Oreos, these marshmallow-cream-filled chocolate snack cakes are a staple of bakeries and seafood-shack dessert menus across the state. Popular both in Maine and in Pennsylvania's Amish country, whoopie pies are said to be so named because Amish farmers would shout 'whoopie!' when they discovered one in their lunch pail. Don't leave the state without trying at least one. For our money, Portland's **Two Fat Cats Bakery** has the best.

Eating & Drinking

★**Harraseeket Lunch & Lobster Co** SEAFOOD $$
(207-865-4888; www.harraseeketlunchandlobster.com; 36 Main St, South Freeport; mains $5-29; 11am-7:45pm, to 8:45pm Jul & Aug;) Head down to the marina to feast on lobster at this iconic red-painted seafood shack. If it's nice out, grab a picnic table – or just do like the locals and sit on the roof of your car. Come early to beat the crowds. Finish with a slice of blueberry pie. BYOB. Cash or check only.

Gritty McDuff's Brew Pub PUB FOOD $$
(www.grittys.com; 187 Lower Main St; mains $10-14) Kids getting cranky, and momma needs a beer? Let the young ones run wild on the back lawn while you sip an IPA and savor a cheeseburger on the deck. This offshoot of the popular Gritty's in Portland is 2 miles south of LL Bean.

Bath

Bath has been renowned for shipbuilding since Colonial times and that remains the raison d'être for the town today. **Bath Iron Works**, one of the largest shipyards in the USA, builds steel frigates and other ships for the US Navy. The substantial **Maine Maritime Museum** (207-443-1316; www.mainemaritimemuseum.org; 243 Washington St; adult/child under 17yr $15/10; 9:30am-5pm), south of the ironworks on the Kennebec River,

OFF THE BEATEN TRACK

PEMAQUID PENINSULA

Adorning the southernmost tip of the Pemaquid Peninsula, **Pemaquid Point** is one of the most wildly beautiful places in Maine, with its tortured igneous rock formations pounded by treacherous seas. Perched atop the rocks in the 7-acre **Lighthouse Park** (☎207-677-2494; www.bristolparks.org; Pemaquid Point; adult/child under 12yr $2/free; ⏰sunrise-sunset daily, facilities early May-Oct, lighthouse 10:30am-5pm) is the 11,000 candle power Pemaquid Light, built in 1827. A climb to the top will reward you with a fine coastal view. A star of the 61 surviving lighthouses along the Maine coast, you may well be carrying an image of Pemaquid Light in your pocket without knowing it – it's the beauty featured on the back of the Maine state quarter. The keeper's house now serves as the **Fishermen's Museum** (⏰9am-5pm early-May–Oct) displaying period photos, old fishing gear and lighthouse paraphernalia. Admission is included in the park fee. Pemaquid Peninsula is 15 miles south of US 1 via ME 130.

showcases the town's centuries-old maritime history, which included construction of the six-mast schooner *Wyoming*, the largest wooden vessel ever built in the USA.

Boothbay Harbor

On a fjord-like harbor, this picturesque fishing village with narrow, winding streets is thick with tourists in the summer. Other than eating lobster, the main activity here is hopping on boats. **Balmy Days Cruises** (☎207-633-2284; www.balmydayscruises.com; Pier 8; harbor tour adult/child 3--11yr $18/9 (Mar-Nov), day-trip cruise to Monhegan adult/child 3-11yr $39/19 (Jun-early Oct), sailing tour adult/child under 12yr $26/18 (mid-Jun-mid-Sep)) runs one-hour harbor tour cruises, day trips to Monhegan Island and 1.5 hour sailing trips around the scenic islands near Boothbay. The **Boothbay Harbor Region Chamber of Commerce** (☎207-633-2353; www.boothbayharbor.com; 192 Townsend Ave; ⏰8am-5pm Mon-Fri, 10am-4pm Sat & Sun Jun-mid-Oct, closed wknds mid-Oct-May) provides visitor information.

Sleeping & Eating

Topside Inn B&B $$
(☎207-633-5404; www.topsideinn.com; 60 McKown St; r incl breakfast $199-360; 📶) Under new ownership, this grand gray mansion atop McKown Hill has Boothbay's best harbor views. Rooms are elegantly turned out in crisp nautical prints and beachy shades of sage, sea grass and khaki. Main-house rooms have more historic charm, but rooms in the two adjacent modern guesthouses are sunny and lovely, too. Enjoy the sunset from an Adirondack chair on the inn's sloping, manicured lawn.

Lobster Dock SEAFOOD $$
(www.thelobsterdock.com; 49 Atlantic Ave; mains $6-25; ⏰11:30am-8:30pm) Of all the lobster joints in Boothbay Harbor, this sprawling wooden waterfront shack is one of the best. It's also a little different. You don't order at the counter but a server stops by your table. Take your pick of traditional fried seafood platters, sandwiches and steamers, plus a couple of seafood pastas, but whole butter-dripping lobster is definitely the main event.

Rockland, Camden & Around

The pretty towns of Rockland, Rockport and Camden hug the coast. Rockland is a thriving commercial port with an inviting downtown lined with eateries and independently owned shops. With rolling hills as a backdrop and a harbor full of sailboats, Camden is a gem. Both towns are home to Maine's famed fleet of windjammers, which attract nautical-minded souls. Rockport sits prettily between the two towns.

Lobster fanatics (and who isn't!) won't want to miss the **Maine Lobster Festival** (www.mainelobsterfestival.com; ⏰early Aug), New England's ultimate homage to the crusty crustacean, held in Rockland.

The **Camden-Rockport-Lincolnville Chamber of Commerce** (☎207-236-4404; www.camdenme.org; 2 Public Landing; ⏰9am-5pm), near the harbor, provides visitor information on the region.

Sights & Activities

★**Rockland Breakwater Lighthouse** LIGHTHOUSE
(www.rocklandharborlights.org) Stroll down the 4300ft granite breakwater (nearly one mile long) to gape at the sweet white light sitting atop the brick-and white house with a sweep-

ing view of town. The breakwater took 18 years to build.

Camden Hills State Park PARK
(☎207-236-3109; wwwmmaine.gov; 280 Belfast Rd/US 1; adult/child 3-11yr $4.50/1; ⏰9am-sunset) A favorite hike in this densely forest park is the 45-minute (half mile) climb up Mt Battie, which offers exquisite views of Penobscot Bay. Simple trail maps are available at the park entrance, just over 1.5 miles northeast of Camden center on US 1. The picnic area has short trails down to the shore. Feeling lazy? You can also drive to the summit.

Maine Media Workshops ART CLASSES
(www.mainemedia.edu; 70 Camden St, Rockport) One of the world's leading instructional centers in photography, film and digital media, this institute offers more than 450 beginner- through professional-level workshops throughout the year. Intensive one-week workshops are taught by leaders in their fields. Changing exhibitions of student and faculty work are displayed in a gallery (18 Central St) in Rockport.

Sleeping & Eating

Island View Inn MOTEL $$
(☎207-596-0040; www.islandviewinnmaine.com; 908 Commercial St, Rockport; r/ste $119/189-259; ❄📶🏊) Each room comes with a pair of binoculars at this inviting motel, where scanning Penobscot Bay for wildlife from your balcony is a nice way to start the day. Rooms are bright, crisp and spacious with modern but comfy decor. On Route 1 between Rockland and Rockport. A fantastic low-price option.

Boynton-McKay Food Co BREAKFAST; COFFEE $
(☎207-236-2465; www.boynton-mckay.com; mains $6.25-10; ⏰7am-3pm Tue-Sat, 8am-3pm Sun) Watch the world go by while you sip coffee and dig into a skillet breakfast of eggs, chorizo and Monterey Jack cheese. In a former apothecary shop in downtown Camden, this snug but sunny cafe and coffee shop fills quickly, so get here early. Fresh lunch fare includes salads and sandwiches.

Clan MacLaren SANDWICHES $
(☎207-593-7778; www.clanmaclaren.net; 395 Main St, Rockland; mains $7-10; ⏰10am-4:30pm Mon-Sat) Fresh, simple and oh-so-tasty subs and paninis are the draw at Clan MacClaren, a welcoming lunch spot in downtown Rockland. Per the website, the owners descend from the Scottish MacLaren clan. Ordering the Erin MacLaren (a not-so-Scottish combo of salami and provolone) will get your brogue rolling.

Cappy's SEAFOOD $$
(☎207-236-2254; www.cappyschowder.com; 1 Main St, Camden; mains $10-26; ⏰11am-11pm; 📶) Renovated in 2015, this friendly longtime favorite is popular with locals and tourists alike. Known best for its bar and its convivial atmosphere, it does serve an excellent bowl of chowder and other casual New England fare.

Acadia National Park

The only national park in New England, **Acadia** (www.nps.gov/acad) encompasses an unspoiled wilderness of undulating coastal mountains, towering sea cliffs, surf-pounded beaches and quiet ponds. The dramatic landscape offers a plethora of activities for both leisurely hikers and adrenaline junkies.

The park, which celebrates its centennial in 2016 (www.acadiacentennial2016.org), was established on land that John D Rockefeller donated to the national parks system to save from encroaching lumber interests. Today you can hike and bike along the same carriage roads that Rockefeller once rode his horse and buggy on. The park covers over 62 sq miles, including most of mountainous Mt Desert Island and tracts of land on the Schoodic Peninsula and Isle au Haut, and holds a wide diversity of wildlife including moose, puffins and bald eagles.

Sights & Activities

Park Loop Road

Unfurling for 27 gorgeous miles, Park Loop Rd, is the main sightseeing jaunt through the park (mid-April to November). If you're up for a bracing swim or just want to stroll Acadia's longest beach, stop at **Sand Beach**. About a mile beyond Sand Beach you'll come to **Thunder Hole**, where wild Atlantic waves crash into a deep, narrow chasm with such force that it creates a thundering boom, loudest during incoming tides. Look to the south to see **Otter Cliffs**, a favorite rock-climbing spot that rises vertically from the sea. At **Jordan Pond** choose from a 1-mile nature trail loop around the south side of the pond or a 3.2-mile trail that skirts the entire pond perimeter. After you've worked up an appetite, reward yourself with a relaxing afternoon tea on the lawn of Jordan Pond House (p256). Near the end of Park Loop Rd a side road leads up to Cadillac Mountain.

Cadillac Mountain

The majestic centerpiece of Acadia National Park is Cadillac Mountain (1530ft), the highest coastal peak in the eastern US, reached by a 3.5-mile spur road off Park Loop Rd. Four **trails** lead to the summit from four directions should you prefer hiking boots to rubber tires. The panoramic 360-degree view of ocean, islands and mountains is a winner any time of the day, but it's truly magical at dawn when hardy souls flock to the top to watch the sun rise over Frenchman Bay.

Other Activities

Some 125 miles of **hiking trails** crisscross Acadia National Park, from easy half-mile nature walks and level rambles to mountain treks up steep and rocky terrain. A standout is the 3-mile round-trip **Ocean Trail**, which runs between Sand Beach and Otter Cliffs and takes in the most interesting coastal scenery in the park. Look for a trail summary on the park website. The helpful *A Walk in the Park: Acadia's Hiking Guide* by Tom St Germain ($14) is for sale in the Hull Visitor Center.

The park's 45 miles of carriage roads are the prime attraction for **cycling**. You can rent quality mountain bikes, replaced new at the start of each season, at **Acadia Bike** (☎207-288-9605; www.acadiabike.com; 48 Cottage St; per day $23; ⏰8am-6pm Jul & Aug, 9am-6pm May & Jun, Sep & Oct).

Rock climbing on the park's sea cliffs and mountains is breathtaking. Gear up with **Acadia Mountain Guides** (☎207-288-8186; www.acadiamountainguides.com; 228 Main St, Bar Harbor; half-day outing $75-140; ⏰May-Oct); rates include a guide, instruction and equipment.

Scores of **ranger-led programs**, including nature walks, birding talks and kids' field trips, are available in the park. Check out the stars fom the sand during the Stars over Sand Beach program. Check the schedule online or at the Hulls Cove Visitor Center.

Sleeping & Eating

The park has two campgrounds, both wooded and with running water, showers and barbecue pits. A third is set to open in the fall of 2015.

There are scores of restaurants, inns and hotels in Bar Harbor, just a mile beyond the park.

Acadia National Park Campgrounds CAMPGROUND $
(☎877-444-6777; www.nps.gov/acad; campsites $22-30) Four miles south of Southwest Harbor, **Seawall** has both by-reservation and walk-up sites. Five miles south of Bar Harbor on ME 3, year-round **Blackwoods** fills quickly in summer, when reservations are strangely recommended. Both sites have restrooms and pay showers. Both are also densely wooded but only a few minutes' walk to the ocean. A third campground with 92 campsites, **Schoodic Woods**, was scheduled to open in September 2015 on the Schoodic Peninsula.

Jordan Pond House AMERICAN $$
(☎207-276-3316; www.thejordanpondhouse.com; afternoon tea $10.50, mains $9-24; ⏰11am-8pm mid-May–Oct) Afternoon tea at this lodge-like teahouse has been an Acadia tradition since the late 1800s. Steaming pots of Earl Grey come with hot popovers (hollow rolls made with egg batter) and strawberry jam. Eat outside on the broad lawn overlooking the lake. The park's only restaurant, Jordan Pond also does fancy but often mediocre lunches and dinners.

Information

Granite mountains and coastal vistas greet you upon entering Acadia National Park. The park is open year-round, though Park Loop Rd and most facilities are closed in winter. An admission fee is charged from May 1 to October 31. The fee, which is valid for seven consecutive days, is $25 per vehicle, $20 per motorcyle and $12 on bike or foot between mid-June and early October (no fee rest of the year).

Start your exploration at **Hulls Cove Visitor Center** (☎207-288-3338; ME 3; 7-day park admission per vehicle $25, motorcycle $20, walkers & cyclists $12; ⏰8:30am-4:30pm mid-Apr–Jun, Sep & Oct, 8am-6pm Jul & Aug), from where the 27-mile Park Loop Rd circumnavigates the eastern portion of the park.

Getting There & Around

The convenient **Island Explorer** (www.exploreacadia.com; ⏰late Jun-early Oct) runs eight shuttle bus routes throughout Acadia National Park and to adjacent Bar Harbor, linking trailheads, campgrounds and accommodations.

Bar Harbor

Set on the doorstep of Acadia National Park, this alluring coastal town once rivaled Newport, RI as a trendy summer destination for

WORTH A TRIP

HOIST THE SAILS

Feel the wind in your hair and history at your side aboard the gracious, multimasted sailing ships known as windjammers. The sailing ships, both historic and replicas, gather in the harbors at Camden and neighboring Rockland to take passengers out on day trips and overnight sails.

Day sails cruise for two hours in Penobscot Bay from June to October for around $40 and you can usually book your place on the day. On the Camden waterfront, look for the 86ft wooden tall ship **Appledore** (207-236-8353; www.appledore2.com) and the two-masted schooner **Olad** (207-236-2323; www.maineschooners.com).

Other schooners make two- to six-day cruises, offer memorable wildlife viewing (seals, whales and puffins) and typically include stops at Acadia National Park, small coastal towns and offshore islands for a lobster picnic.

You can get full details on several glorious options in one fell swoop through the **Maine Windjammer Association** (800-807-9463; www.sailmainecoast.com), which represents eight traditional tall ships, several of which have been designated National Historic Landmarks. Among them is the granddaddy of the schooner trade, the *Lewis R French*, America's oldest (1871) windjammer. Rates range from $400 for a two-day cruise to $1100 for a six-day voyage and are a bargain when you consider they include meals and accommodations. Reservations for the overnight sails are a must. Prices are highest in midsummer.

wealthy Americans. Today many of the old mansions have been turned into inviting inns and the town has become a magnet for outdoor enthusiasts. The **Bar Harbor Chamber of Commerce** (207-288-5103; www.barharborinfo.com; 1201 Bar Harbor Rd/ME 3, Trenton; 9am-5pm Mon-Fri May-Aug, hours vary fall, closed Nov-Apr) has a convenient welcome center just before the bridge onto Mt Desert Island.

Activities

Bar Harbor Whale Watch Co CRUISE
(207-288-2386; www.barharborwhales.com; 1 West St; adult $29-63, child 6-14 yr $18-35, child under 6yr free-$9; mid-May–Oct) Operates four-hour whale-watching and puffin-watching cruises, among other options.

Downeast Windjammer Cruises CRUISE
(207-288-4585; www.downeastwindjammer.com; 19 Cottage St; adult/child 6-11yr/2-5yr $38/30/5) Offers two-hour cruises on the majestic 151ft, four-masted schooner *Margaret Todd*.

Acadian Nature Cruises CRUISE
(207-801-2300; www.acadiannaturecruises.com; 119 Eden St; adult/child 6-14yr/under 6yr $30/18/5; mid-May–Oct) See whales, porpoises, bald eagles, seals and more on these narrated two-hour nature cruises.

Sleeping

There's no shortage of sleeping options in Bar Harbor in summer, ranging from period B&Bs to the usual chain hotels. Note that many inns and B&B's close from late fall to early spring.

Holland Inn B&B $$
(207-288-4804; www.hollandinn.com; 35 Holland Ave; r incl breakfast $145-185; late Apr-Oct;) In a quiet residential neighborhood within walking distance of downtown, this restored 1895 house with two adjacent buildings has 13 inviting, unfrilly rooms. Ambience is low-key – you'll feel like you're staying in a friend's private home – and the breakfasts are gourmet. Innkeeper Evin Carson will tell you everything you need to know for a great time in Bar Harbor.

Bar Harbor Grand Hotel HOTEL $$
(207-288-5226; 207-288-5226; 269 Main St; r incl breakfast $239; Apr-early Nov;) A replica of Bar Harbor's 19th-century Rodick House Hotel, this four-story property offers a lofty view of the town. Decor is classic, if a bit uninspired, but the staff is accommodating and the hotel is open a bit longer in the season than other local properties.

Eating

Cafe This Way AMERICAN $$
(207-288-4483; www.cafethisway.com; 14½ Mount Desert St; mains breakfast $6-17, dinner $18-28; 7-11:30am Mon-Sat, 8am-1pm Sun, 5:30-9pm nightly May-Oct;) In a sprawling white cottage, this quirky eatery is *the* place for breakfast, with plump Maine blueberry pancakes and eggs Benedict with smoked salmon. It also serves

eclectic, sophisticated dinners, like roasted duck with blueberries, Moroccan-style squash and tuna tempura. Sit in the garden.

2 Cats CAFE **$$**
(207-288-2808; www.2catsbarharbor.com; 130 Cottage St; mains $7-20; 7am-1pm;) On weekends crowds line up for smoked-trout omelets and homemade muffins at this sunny, arty little cafe. Lunch offerings include slightly heartier fare, such as burritos and seafood dishes.

Mâche Bistro FRENCH **$$$**
(207-288-0447; www.machebistro.com; 321 Main Street; mains $18-29; 5:30 until close Mon-Sat early May-Oct) Almost certainly Bar Harbor's best midrange restaurant, Mâche serves contemporary French-inflected fare in a stylishly renovated cottage. The changing menu highlights the local riches – think pumpkin-seed-dusted scallops, lobster-and-brie flatbread, and wild blueberry trifle. Specialty cocktails add to the appeal. Reservations are crucial.

Downeast Maine

The 900-plus miles of coastline running northeast from Bar Harbor are sparsely populated, slower-paced and foggier than southern and western Maine. Highlights include the **Schoodic Peninsula**, whose tip is a noncontiguous part of Acadia National Park; the lobster fishing villages of **Jonesport** and **Beals**; and **Great Wass Island**, a nature preserve with walking paths and good bird-watching, including the chance to see puffins.

Machias, with a branch of the University of Maine, is the center of commerce along this stretch of coast. **Lubec** is about as far east as you can go and still be in the USA; folks like to watch the sun rise at nearby **Quoddy Head State Park** so they can say they were the first in the country to catch the sun's rays.

Interior Maine

Sparsely populated northern and western Maine is rugged outdoor country. River rafting, hiking trails up Maine's highest mountain and the ski town of Bethel make the region a magnet for adventurers.

Sabbathday Lake

The nation's only active Shaker community is at Sabbathday Lake, 25 miles north of Portland. Founded in the early 18th century, a handful of devotees keep the Shaker tradition of simple living, hard work and fine artistry alive. You can tour several of their buildings on a visit to the **Shaker Museum** (207-926-4597; www.maineshakers.com; adult/child 6-12yr $10/2; 10am-4:30pm Mon-Sat late May–mid-Oct). To get there, take exit 63 off the Maine Turnpike and continue north for 8 miles on ME 26.

Bethel

The rural community of Bethel, nestled in the rolling Maine woods 12 miles east of New Hampshire on ME 26, offers an engaging combination of mountain scenery, outdoor escapades and good-value accommodations. **Bethel Area Chamber of Commerce** (207-824-2282; www.bethelmaine.com; 8 Station Pl; 9am-5pm Jun–mid-Oct, closed Sat & Sun mid-Oct-May) provides information for visitors.

Activities

Bethel Outdoor Adventure KAYAKING
(207-824-4224; www.betheloutdooradventure.com; 121 Mayville Rd/US 2; per day kayak/canoe $46/67; 8am-6pm mid-May-mid-Oct) This downtown outfitter rents canoes, kayaks and bicycles, and it arranges lessons, guided trips and shuttles to and from the Androscoggin River.

Grafton Notch State Park HIKING
(207-824-2912; www.maine.gov; ME 26; adult/child 5-11yr $3/1; 9am-sunset May 15-Oct 15) If you're ready for a hike, head to this park north of Bethel for pretty mountain scenery, waterfalls and lots of trails of varying lengths. Walking in for the trails is okay in the off-season.

Sunday River Ski Resort SKIING
(800-543-2754; www.sundayriver.com; ME 26; full-day lift ticket adult/child 13-18yr/6-12yr & seniors $89/69/57;) Six miles north of Bethel along ME 5/26, Sunday River has eight mountain peaks and 135 trails, with 15 lifts. It's regarded as one of the region's best family ski destinations. They've also got summer activities, including chairlift rides, ziplines, hiking trails, disc golf and a mountain-bike park. Two huge lodges have more than 400 rooms.

Sleeping

Chapman Inn B&B $

(207-824-2657; www.chapmaninn.com; 2 Church St; dm/rm/ste incl breakfast $35/$89-129/139;) This roomy downtown guesthouse has character in spades. The nine private rooms are done up in florals and antiques, with slightly sloping floors attesting to the home's age. In winter, skiers bunk down in the snug dorm, complete with a wood-paneled game room presided over by a massive mounted moose head. Breakfast is a lavish spread of homemade pastries and made-to-order omelets.

Sudbury Inn & Suds Pub INN $$

(207-824-2174; www.sudburyinn.com; 151 Main St; r/ste incl breakfast $119-139/189-199; pub from 11:30am daily, restaurant 5:30-9pm Thu-Sat;) The choice place to stay in downtown Bethel, this historic inn has 17 rooms, a pub with 29 beers on tap, pizza and live weekend entertainment. It also has an excellent dinner restaurant serving Maine-centric fare (mains $20 to $34).

Caratunk & The Forks

For white-water rafting at its best, head to the **Kennebec River**, below the Harris Dam, where the water shoots through a dramatic 12-mile gorge. With rapid names like Whitewasher and Magic Falls, you know you're in for an adrenaline rush.

The adjoining villages of Caratunk and The Forks, on US 201 south of Jackman, are at the center of the Kennebec River rafting operations. The options range from rolling rapids and heart-stopping drops to calmer waters where children as young as seven can join in. Rates range from $99 to $120 per person for a day-long outing. Multiday packages, with camping or cabin accommodations, can also be arranged.

Reliable operators include **Crab Apple Whitewater** (800-553-7238; www.crabapplewhitewater.com) and **Three Rivers Whitewater** (877-846-7238; www.threeriverswhitewater.com).

Baxter State Park

Set in the remote forests of northern Maine, **Baxter State Park** (207-723-5140; www.baxterstateparkauthority.com; per car $14) centers on Mt Katahdin (5267ft), Maine's tallest mountain and the northern terminus of the 2175-mile **Appalachian Trail** (www.nps.gov/appa). This vast 209,500-acre park is maintained in a wilderness state – no electricity and no running water (bring your own or plan on purifying stream water) – and there's a good chance you'll see moose, deer and black bear. Baxter has extensive hiking trails, several leading to the top of Mt Katahdin, which can be hiked round-trip in a day as long as you're in good shape and get an early start.

At **Millinocket**, south of Baxter State Park, there are motels, campgrounds, restaurants and outfitters that specialize in white-water rafting and kayaking on the Penobscot River. Get information from the **Katahdin Area Chamber of Commerce** (207-723-4443; www.katahdinmaine.com; 1029 Central St, Millinocket; 9am-2pm Mon-Fri).

Washington, DC & the Capital Region

Includes ➡

Best Places to Eat

- Rose's Luxury (p282)
- Woodberry Kitchen (p296)
- Mama J's (p314)
- Blue Pete's (p320)
- Oakhart Social (p321)

Best Places to Stay

- Hotel Lombardy (p280)
- The Georges (p327)
- Peaks of Otter (p328)
- HI Richmond (p313)
- Colonial Williamsburg Historic Lodging (p316)

Why Go?

No matter your politics, it's hard not to fall for the nation's capital. Iconic monuments, vast (and free) museums and venerable restaurants serving global cuisines are just the beginning of the great DC experience. There's much to discover: cobblestoned neighborhoods, sprawling markets, heady multicultural nightspots and verdant parks – not to mention the corridors of power, where visionaries and demagogues alike still roam.

Beyond the Beltway, the diverse landscapes of Maryland, Virginia, West Virginia and Delaware offer potent enticement to travel beyond the marble city. Craggy mountains, rushing rivers, vast nature reserves (including islands where wild horses run), sparkling beaches, historic villages and the magnificent Chesapeake Bay form the backdrop to memorable adventures: sailing, hiking, rafting, camping or just sitting on a pretty stretch of shoreline, planning the next seafood feast. It's a place where traditions run deep, from the nation's birthplace to Virginia's still-thriving bluegrass scene.

When to Go

Washington, DC

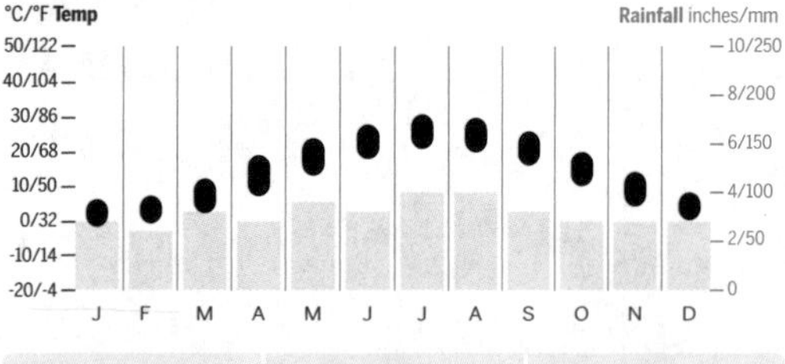

May–Apr Cherry blossoms bring crowds to the city during DC's most popular festival.

Jun–Aug Beaches and resorts heave; prices are high and accommodations scarce.

Sep–Oct Fewer crowds and lower prices, but with pleasant temperatures and fiery fall scenery.

History

Native Americans populated this region long before European settlers arrived. Many of the area's geographic landmarks are still known by their Native American names, such as Chesapeake, Shenandoah, Appalachian and Potomac. In 1607 a group of 108 English colonists established the first permanent European settlement in the New World: Jamestown. During the early years, colonists battled harsh winters, starvation, disease and, occasionally, hostile Native Americans.

Jamestown survived, and the Royal Colony of Virginia came into being in 1624. Ten years later, fleeing the English Civil War, Lord Baltimore established the Catholic colony of Maryland at St Mary's City, where a Spanish Jewish doctor treated a town council that included a black Portuguese sailor and Margaret Brent, the first woman to vote in North American politics. Delaware was settled as a Dutch whaling colony in 1631, practically wiped out by Native Americans, and later resettled by the British. Celts displaced from Britain filtered into the Appalachians, where their fiercely independent culture persists today. Border disputes between Maryland, Delaware and Pennsylvania led to the creation of the Mason–Dixon line, which eventually separated the industrial North from the agrarian, slave-holding South.

The fighting part of the Revolutionary War finished here with the British surrender at Yorktown in 1781. To diffuse regional tension, central, swampy Washington, District of Columbia (DC), was made the new nation's capital. But divisions of class, race and economy were strong, and this area in particular split along its seams during the Civil War (1861–65): Virginia seceded from the Union, while its impoverished western farmers, long resentful of genteel plantation owners, seceded from Virginia. Maryland stayed in the Union, but its white slave-owners rioted against Northern troops, while thousands of black Marylanders joined the Union Army.

Local Culture

The North–South tension long defined this area, but the region has also swung between the cultures of Virginia aristocrats, miners, waterfolk, immigrants and the ever-changing rulers of Washington, DC. Since the Civil War, local economies have made the shift from agriculture and manufacturing to high technology and the servicing and staffing of the federal government.

Many African Americans settled this border region, either as slaves or escapees running for Northern freedom. Today African Americans still form the visible underclass of its major cities, but in the rough arena of the disadvantaged they compete with Latino immigrants, mainly from Central America.

At the other end of the spectrum, ivory towers – in the form of world-class universities and research centers such as the National Institute of Health – attract intelligentsia from around the world. The local high schools are often packed with the children of scientists and consultants who staff some of the world's most prestigious think tanks.

All of this has spawned a culture that is, in turns, as sophisticated as a journalists' book club, as linked to the land as bluegrass festivals in Virginia and as hooked into the main vein of African American culture as Tupac Shakur, go-go, Baltimore Club and DC Hardcore. And, of course, there's always politics, a subject continually simmering under the surface here.

WASHINGTON, DC

The USA's capital teems with iconic monuments, vast museums and the corridors of power where visionaries and demagogues roam. But it's more than that. It's also home to tree-lined neighborhoods and groovy markets, with ethnically diverse restaurants, large numbers of immigrants and a dynamism percolating just beneath the surface. There's always a buzz here – no surprise, as DC gathers more overachieving and talented types than any city of this size deserves.

Plan on jam-packed days sightseeing in the countless museums (most of them free). At night, join the locals sipping DC-made brews and chowing in cozy restaurants in buzzy quarters such as U St and Logan Circle.

History

Following the Revolutionary War, a balance was struck between Northern and Southern politicians, who wanted to plant a federal city somewhere between their power bases. Potential capitals such as Boston, Philadelphia and Baltimore were rejected by Southern plantation owners, as too urban-industrial so it was decided a new city would be carved at midway point of the 13 colonies, along the banks of the Potomac River. Maryland and Virginia donated the land.

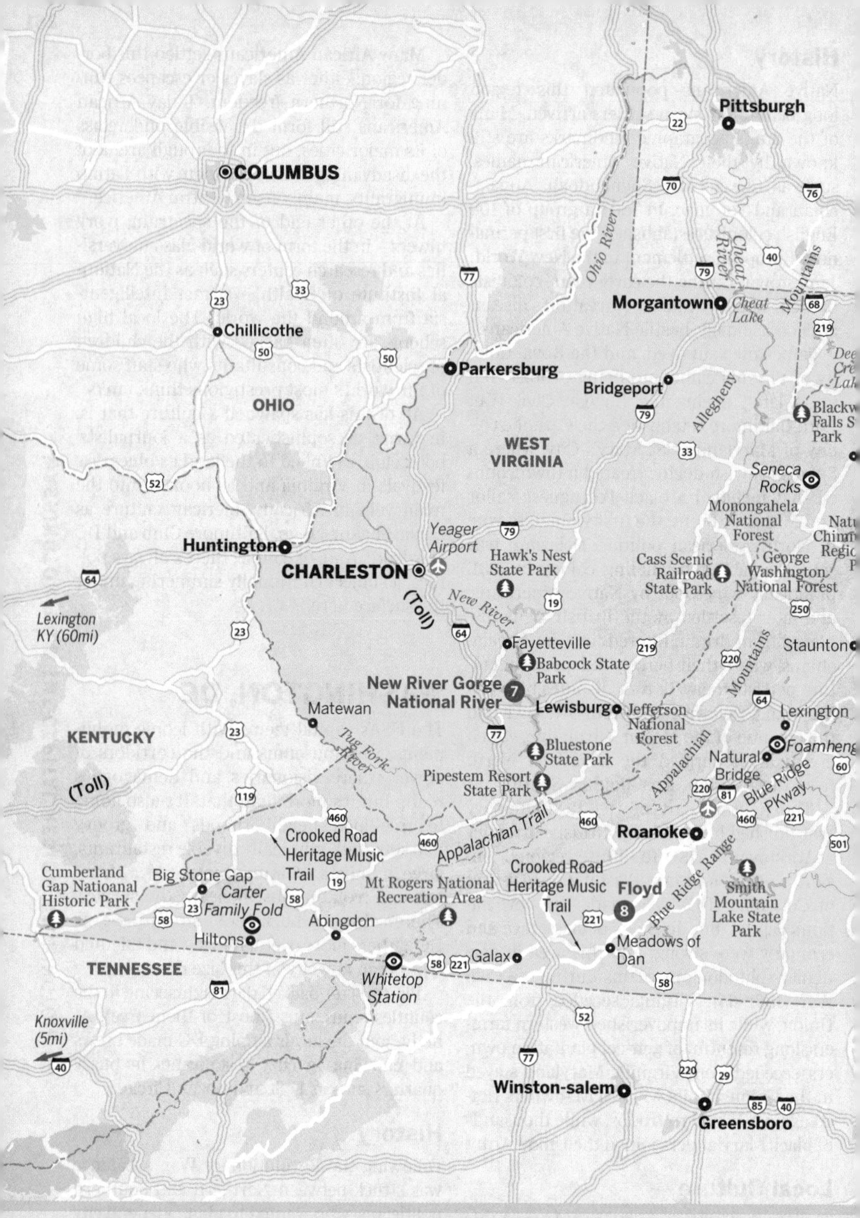

Washington, DC & the Capital Region Highlights

1. Visiting Washington's **Smithsonian Institution museums** (p273), then watching the sun set over **Lincoln Memorial** (p264).
2. Tracing America's roots at the living-history museum of **Colonial Williamsburg** (p316).
3. Exploring the region's nautical past with a pub crawl through Baltimore's cobblestoned port-town neighborhood of **Fell's Point** (p296).
4. Taking a Sunday drive along **Skyline Drive** (p325), followed by hiking and camping

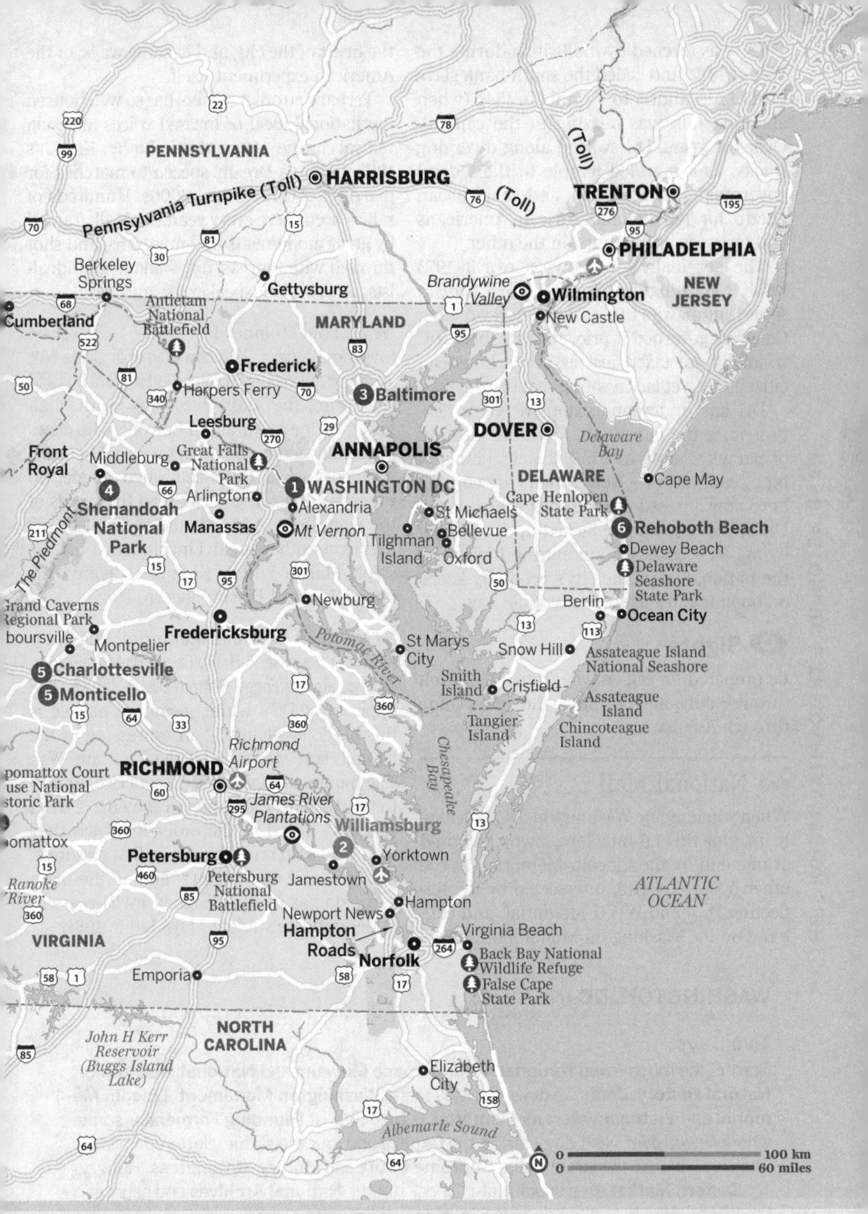

under the stars in **Shenandoah National Park** (p323).

5 Marveling at Thomas Jefferson's masterpieces of **Monticello** (p323) and the **University of Virginia** (p321) in historic Charlottesville.

6 Strolling the boardwalk in the family- and gay-friendly resort of **Rehoboth Beach** (p305).

7 Tackling the rapids of **New River Gorge National River** (p334) in Fayetteville.

8 Feeling the beat of the clog dancers at a jamboree in **Floyd** (p330).

DC was torched by the British during the War of 1812, and ceded the south-bank slave port of Alexandria to Virginia in 1846 (when abolition talk was buzzing in the capital). Over the years, DC evolved along diverging tracks: as a marbled temple to the federal government on one hand, and as an urban ghetto for northbound African Americans and overseas immigrants on the other.

The city finally got its own mayor in 1973 (Walter Washington, among the first African American mayors of a major American city); Congress governed it prior to that. Today DC residents are taxed just as other American citizens are, yet lack a voting seat in Congress.

DC has undergone extensive gentrification since the late 1990s. With the election of Barack Obama in 2008, the city gained a bit of cool cachet – New Yorkers are coming here now, instead of the other way around. Unfortunately, they've jacked up the cost of living. DC's costs are among the highest in the nation, and as the city's economy keeps on booming, it's likely to stay that way.

Sights

Be prepared for big crowds from late March through July, and for sticky-hot days June through August.

National Mall

When you imagine Washington, DC, you likely imagine this 1.9-mile-long lawn: anchored at one end by the Lincoln Memorial; at the other by Capitol Hill; intersected by the Reflecting Pool and WWII Memorial; and centered on the Washington Monument. This is the heart of the city, and in some ways, of the American experiment itself.

Perhaps no other symbol has so well housed the national ideal of massed voices affecting radical change – from Martin Luther King Jr's 1963 'I Have a Dream' speech to marches for marriage equality in the 2000s. Hundreds of rallies occur here every year: the Mall, framed by great monuments and museums, and shot through with tourists, dog walkers and idealists, acts as a loudspeaker for any cause.

★Lincoln Memorial MONUMENT

(www.nps.gov/linc; 2 Lincoln Memorial Circle NW; 24hr; Circulator, M Foggy Bottom-GWU) FREE Anchoring the Mall's west end is the hallowed shrine to Abraham Lincoln, who gazes peacefully across the reflecting pool beneath his neoclassical Doric-columned abode. To the left of Lincoln you can read the words of the Gettysburg Address, and the hall below highlights other great Lincoln-isms; on the steps, Martin Luther King Jr delivered his famed 'I Have a Dream' speech.

★Vietnam Veterans Memorial MONUMENT

(www.nps.gov/vive; 5 Henry Bacon Dr NW; 24hr; Circulator, M Foggy Bottom-GWU) FREE The opposite of DC's white, gleaming marble is this black, low-lying 'V,' an expression of the psychic scar wrought by the Vietnam War. The monument follows a descent deeper into the earth, with the names of the 58,272 dead soldiers – listed in the order in which they died – chiseled into the dark wall. It's a subtle, but profound monument – and all the more surprising as it was designed by 21-year-old undergraduate student Maya Lin in 1981.

WASHINGTON, DC IN...

Two Days

Start at the much-loved **National Air and Space Museum** and **National Museum of Natural History**. Continue down the Mall to the **Washington Monument**, **Lincoln Memorial** and **Vietnam Veterans Memorial**. Have dinner at **Founding Farmers** or somewhere **Downtown**. Next day, start at the **Capitol** and tour the statue-cluttered halls. Then walk across the street to the **Supreme Court** and **Library of Congress**. Hungry? Try **Eastern Market** for a snack. Later, check out the **National Archives** and saunter by the **White House**. At night go to **U Street** for jazz, rock and clubs.

Four Days

On day three, go to **Georgetown** for a stroll along the Potomac, followed by window-shopping and lunch at **Martin's Tavern**. Afterward, visit the lovely gardens of **Dumbarton Oaks**. In the evening, catch a show at the **Kennedy Center**. On day four, start at **Dupont Circle** and gape at the enormous mansions along **Embassy Row**. Swing into the **Phillips Collection**, **National Gallery of Art**, **Newseum** or any other top museums you might have missed. For dinner, browse 14th St in **Logan Circle**.

★**Washington Monument** MONUMENT
(www.nps.gov/wamo; 2 15th St NW; ⏲9am-5pm, to 10pm Jun-Aug; 🚌Circulator, Ⓜ Smithsonian) FREE Just peaking at 555ft (and 5in), the Washington Monument is the tallest building in the district. It took two phases of construction to complete; note the different hues of the stone. A 70-second elevator ride whisks you to the observation deck for the city's best views. Same-day tickets for a timed entrance are available at the **kiosk** (15th St, btwn Madison Dr NW & Jefferson Dr SW; ⏲from 8:30am) by the monument. Arrive early.

★**National Air & Space Museum** MUSEUM
(☎202-633-1000; www.airandspace.si.edu; cnr 6th St & Independence Ave SW; ⏲10am-5:30pm, to 7:30pm mid-Mar–early Sep; 👪; 🚌Circulator, Ⓜ L'Enfant Plaza) FREE The Air and Space Museum is one of the most popular Smithsonian museums. Everyone flocks to see the Wright brothers' flyer, Chuck Yeager's Bell X-1, Charles Lindbergh's *Spirit of St Louis,* Amelia Earhart's natty red plane and the Apollo Lunar Module. An IMAX theater, planetarium and flight simulators are all here ($7 to $9 each). More avionic pieces reside in Virginia at the Steven F Udvar-Hazy Center, an annex to hold this museum's leftovers.

★**United States Holocaust Memorial Museum** MUSEUM
(☎202-488-0400; www.ushmm.org; 100 Raoul Wallenberg Pl SW; ⏲10am-5:20pm, to 6:20pm Mon-Fri Apr & May; Ⓜ Smithsonian) FREE For a deep understanding of the Holocaust – its victims, perpetrators and bystanders – this harrowing museum is a must-see. The main exhibit gives visitors the identity card of a single Holocaust victim, whose story is revealed as you take a winding route into a hellish past marked by ghettos, rail cars and death camps. It also shows the flip side of human nature, documenting the risks many citizens took to help the persecuted.

National Gallery of Art MUSEUM
(☎202-737-4215; www.nga.gov; Constitution Ave NW, btwn 3rd & 7th Sts; ⏲10am-5pm Mon-Sat, 11am-6pm Sun; 🚌Circulator, Ⓜ Archives) FREE The staggering collection spans the Middle Ages to the present. The neoclassical west building showcases European art through the early 1900s; highlights include a da Vinci painting and a slew of impressionist and postimpressionist works. The IM Pei-designed east building displays modern art, with works by Picasso, Matisse, Pollock and a massive Calder mobile over the entrance lobby. Alas, it's closed (except for the lobby) until 2016 for renovations. A trippy underground walkway connects the two wings.

WASHINGTON, DC FACTS

Nickname DC, the District, Chocolate City

Population 659,000

Area 68.3 sq miles

Capital city Exactly!

Sales tax 5.75%

Birthplace of Duke Ellington (1899–1974), Marvin Gaye (1939–84), Dave Chappelle (b 1973)

Home of The Redskins, cherry blossoms, all three branches of American government

Politics Overwhelmingly Democrat

Famous for National symbols, crime, partying interns, struggle for Congressional recognition

Unofficial motto and license-plate slogan Taxation Without Representation

Driving distances Washington, DC, to Baltimore: 40 miles; Washington, DC, to Virginia Beach: 210 miles

National Sculpture Garden GARDENS
(cnr Constitution Ave NW & 7th St NW; ⏲10am-7pm Mon-Thu & Sat, 10am-9:30pm Fri, 11am-7pm Sun; 🚌Circulator, Ⓜ Archives) FREE The National Gallery of Art's 6-acre garden is studded with whimsical sculptures such as Roy Lichtenstein's *House,* a giant Claes Oldenburg typewriter eraser and Louise Bourgeois' leggy *Spider.* They are scattered around a fountain – a great place to dip your feet in summer. From November to March the fountain becomes a festive **ice rink** (adult/child $8/7, skate rental $3).

In summer, the garden hosts free evening jazz concerts on Fridays from 5pm to 8:30pm.

National Museum of Natural History MUSEUM
(www.mnh.si.edu; cnr 10th St & Constitution Ave NW; ⏲10am-5:30pm, to 7:30pm Jun-Aug; 👪; 🚌Circulator, Ⓜ Smithsonian) FREE Smithsonian museums don't get more popular than this

Washington, DC

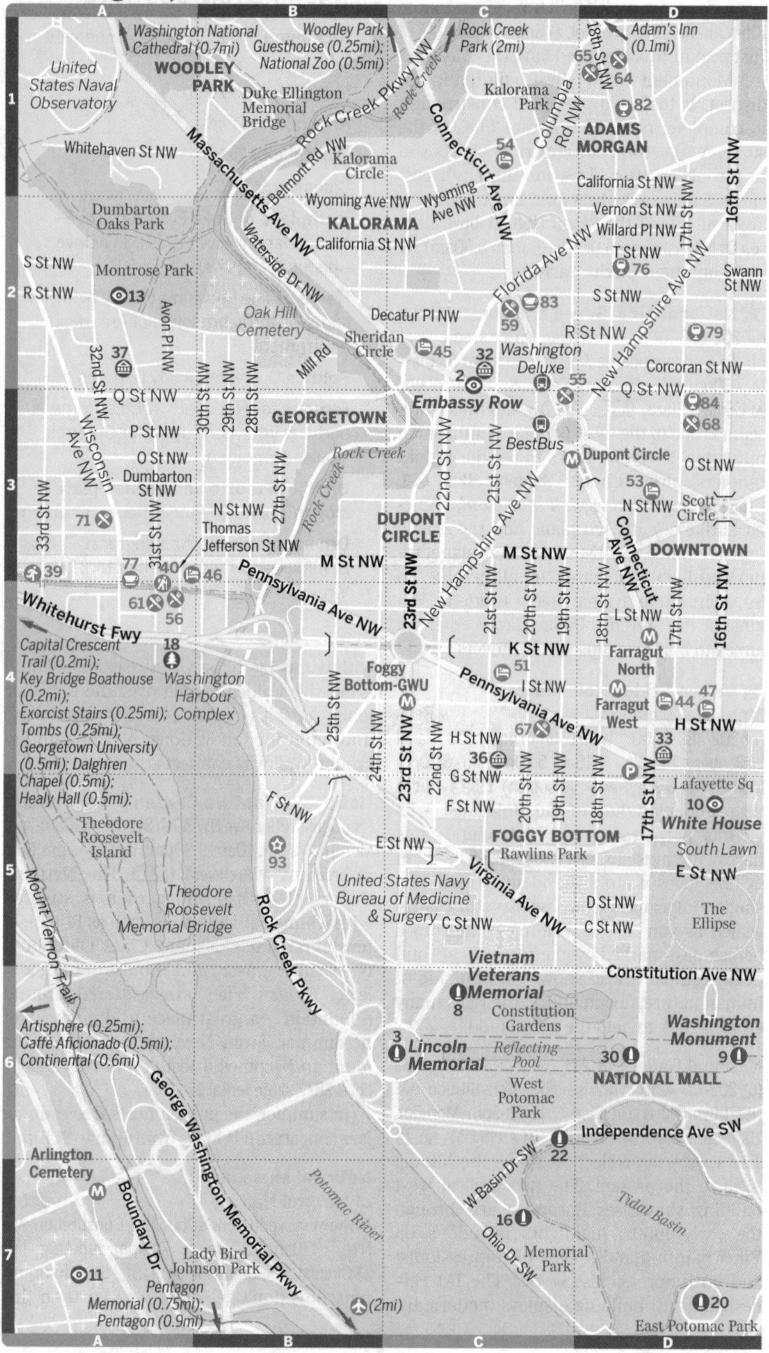

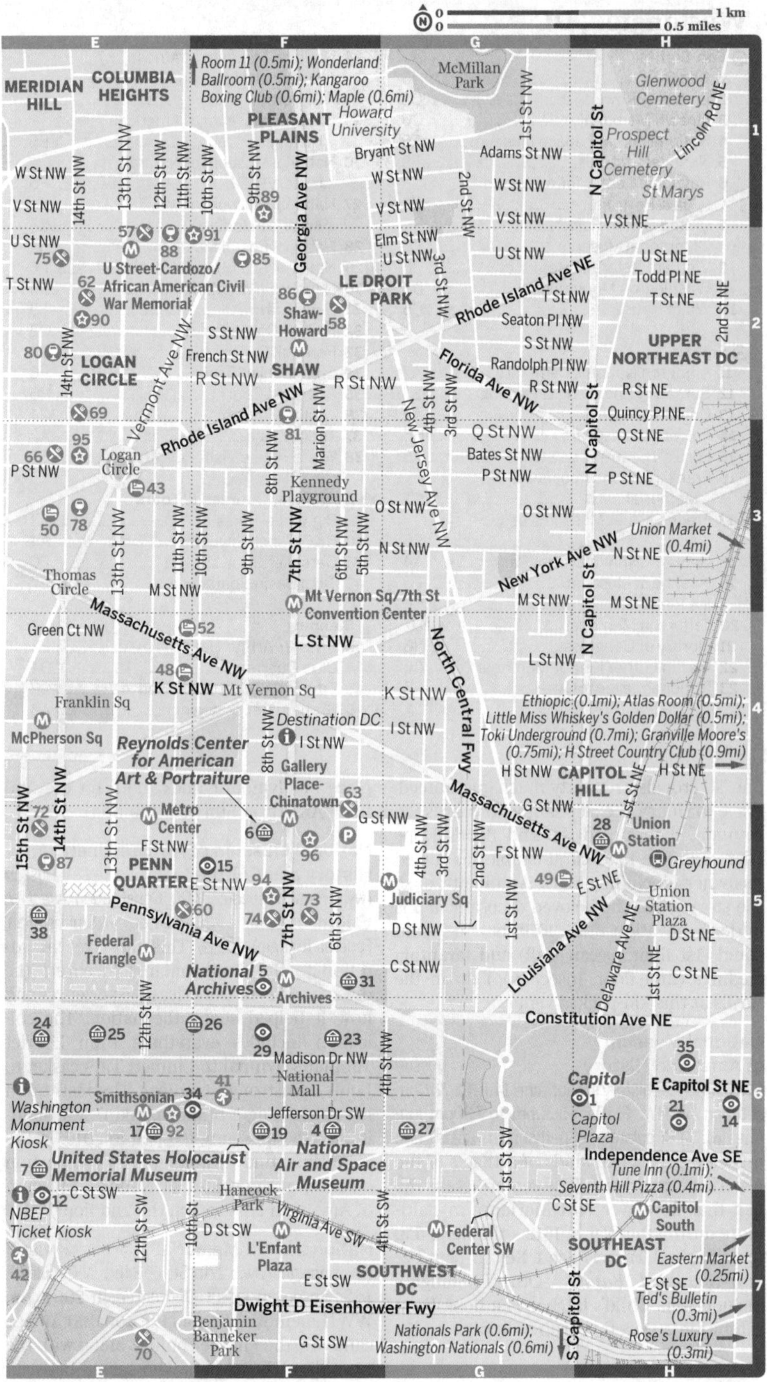
0 1 km
0 0.5 miles
E
F
G
H
1
2
3
4
5
6
7
MERIDIAN HILL
COLUMBIA HEIGHTS
Room 11 (0.5mi); Wonderland Ballroom (0.5mi); Kangaroo Boxing Club (0.6mi); Maple (0.6mi)
McMillan Park
Glenwood Cemetery
Lincoln Rd NE
PLEASANT PLAINS
Howard University
Prospect Hill Cemetery
St Marys
1st St NW
N Capitol St
Bryant St NW
Adams St NW
W St NW
14th St NW
13th St NW
12th St NW
11th St NW
10th St NW
9th St NW
Georgia Ave NW
2nd St NW
V St NW
V St NE
U St NW
Elm St NW
U St NE
U Street-Cardozo/ African American Civil War Memorial
LE DROIT PARK
3rd St NW
Rhode Island Ave NE
Todd Pl NE
T St NW
T St NE
2nd St NE
Shaw-Howard
Seaton Pl NW
S St NW
French St NW
UPPER NORTHEAST DC
LOGAN CIRCLE
Vermont Ave NW
SHAW
Randolph Pl NW
Florida Ave NW
R St NW
R St NE
Rhode Island Ave NW
Marion St NW
New Jersey Ave NW
4th St NW
Quincy Pl NE
Q St NW
Q St NE
Logan Circle
Bates St NW
8th St NW
P St NW
P St NE
Kennedy Playground
O St NW
Union Market (0.4mi)
7th St NW
6th St NW
5th St NW
N St NW
N St NE
New York Ave NW
Thomas Circle
M St NW
M St NE
Mt Vernon Sq/7th St Convention Center
Massachusetts Ave NW
Green Ct NW
L St NW
North Central Fwy
K St NW
Mt Vernon Sq
Franklin Sq
Destination DC
I St NW
Ethiopic (0.1mi); Atlas Room (0.5mi); Little Miss Whiskey's Golden Dollar (0.5mi); Toki Underground (0.7mi); Granville Moore's (0.75mi); H Street Country Club (0.9mi)
McPherson Sq
Reynolds Center for American Art & Portraiture
Gallery Place-Chinatown
H St NW
CAPITOL HILL
H St NE
1st St NE
15th St NW
Metro Center
G St NW
Union Station
F St NW
Greyhound
PENN QUARTER
E St NW
Judiciary Sq
E St NE
Pennsylvania Ave NW
Union Station Plaza
Federal Triangle
D St NW
Louisiana Ave NW
Delaware Ave NE
D St NE
National Archives
Archives
C St NW
C St NE
Constitution Ave NE
Madison Dr NW
National Mall
Capitol
E Capitol St NE
Smithsonian
Washington Monument Kiosk
Jefferson Dr SW
Capitol Plaza
1st St SW
United States Holocaust Memorial Museum
National Air and Space Museum
Independence Ave SE
Tune Inn (0.1mi); Seventh Hill Pizza (0.4mi)
C St SW
NBEP Ticket Kiosk
Hancock Park
C St SE
Capitol South
12th St SW
10th St
D St SW
Virginia Ave SW
4th St SW
L'Enfant Plaza
Federal Center SW
SOUTHEAST DC
Eastern Market (0.25mi)
E St SW
SOUTHWEST DC
E St SE
Ted's Bulletin (0.3mi)
Dwight D Eisenhower Fwy
Benjamin Banneker Park
G St SW
Nationals Park (0.6mi); Washington Nationals (0.6mi)
S Capitol St
Rose's Luxury (0.3mi)
1
4
5
6
7
12
14
15
17
19
21
23
24
25
26
27
28
29
31
34
35
38
41
42
43
48
49
50
52
57
58
60
62
63
66
69
70
72
73
74
75
78
80
81
85
86
87
88
89
90
91
92
94
95
96

Washington, DC

Top Sights

1	Capitol	H6
2	Embassy Row	C2
3	Lincoln Memorial	C6
4	National Air and Space Museum	F6
5	National Archives	F5
6	Reynolds Center for American Art & Portraiture	F5
7	United States Holocaust Memorial Museum	E6
8	Vietnam Veterans Memorial	C6
9	Washington Monument	D6
10	White House	D5

Sights

11	Arlington National Cemetery	A7
12	Bureau of Engraving & Printing	E7
13	Dumbarton Oaks	A2
14	Folger Shakespeare Library	H6
15	Ford's Theatre	F5
16	Franklin Delano Roosevelt Memorial	C7
17	Freer-Sackler Museums of Asian Art	E6
18	Georgetown Waterfront Park	A4
19	Hirshhorn Museum	F6
	Ice Rink	(see 29)
20	Jefferson Memorial	D7
21	Library of Congress	H6
22	Martin Luther King Jr Memorial	C6
23	National Gallery of Art	F6
24	National Museum of African American History and Culture	E6
25	National Museum of American History	E6
26	National Museum of Natural History	F6
27	National Museum of the American Indian	G6
28	National Postal Museum	H5
29	National Sculpture Garden	F6
30	National WWII Memorial	D6
31	Newseum	F5
32	Phillips Collection	C2
33	Renwick Gallery	D4
34	Smithsonian Castle	E6
35	Supreme Court	H6
36	Textile Museum	C4
37	Tudor Place	A2
38	White House Visitor Center	E5

Activities, Courses & Tours

39	Big Wheel Bikes	A3
40	C&O Canal Towpath	A4
41	Carousel	F6
42	Tidal Basin Boathouse	E7

Sleeping

43	Chester Arthur House	E3
44	Club Quarters	D4
45	Embassy Circle Guest House	C2
46	Graham Georgetown	A3

one, so crowds are pretty much guaranteed. Wave to Henry, the elephant who guards the rotunda, then zip to the 2nd floor's Hope Diamond. The 45.52-carat bauble has cursed its owners, including Marie Antoinette, or so the story goes. The beloved dinosaur hall is under renovation until 2019, but the giant squid (1st floor, Ocean Hall) and tarantula feedings (2nd floor, Insect Zoo) fill in the thrills at this kid-packed venue.

National Museum of American History MUSEUM

(www.americanhistory.si.edu; cnr 14th St & Constitution Ave NW; 10am-5:30pm, to 7:30pm Jun-Aug; ; Circulator, Smithsonian) FREE The museum collects all kinds of artifacts of the American experience. The centerpiece is the flag that flew over Fort McHenry in Baltimore during the War of 1812 – the same flag that inspired Francis Scott Key to pen *The Star-Spangled Banner*. Other highlights include Julia Child's kitchen (1st floor, Food exhibition), Dorothy's ruby slippers and a piece of Plymouth Rock (both on the 2nd floor, American Stories exhibition).

National Museum of African American History and Culture MUSEUM

(www.nmaahc.si.edu; 1400 Constitution Ave NW; 10am-5:30pm; Circulator, Smithsonian, Federal Triangle) FREE This most recent addition to the Smithsonian fold covers the diverse African American experience and how it helped shape the nation. The collection includes everything from Harriet Tubman's hymnal to Emmett Till's casket to Louis Armstrong's trumpet. The institution is constructing a brand-spankin' new building for the museum, to open in 2016. In the meantime, find exhibits from the collection on show at the next-door National Museum of American History (on the 2nd floor).

National WWII Memorial MONUMENT

(www.nps.gov/wwii; 17th St; 24hr; Circulator, Smithsonian) FREE Dedicated in 2004, the WWII memorial honors the 400,000 Americans who died in the conflict, along with the 16 million US soldiers who served between

47 Hay-Adams Hotel	D4
48 Hostelling International – Washington DC	E4
49 Hotel George	G5
50 Hotel Helix	E3
51 Hotel Lombardy	C4
52 Morrison-Clark Inn	E4
53 Tabard Inn	D3
54 Taft Bridge Inn	C1

Eating

55 Afterwords Cafe	C3
56 Baked & Wired	A4
57 Ben's Chili Bowl	E2
58 Bistro Bohem	F2
59 Bistrot du Coin	C2
60 Central Michel Richard	E5
61 Chez Billy Sud	A4
62 Compass Rose	E2
63 Daikaya	F5
64 Diner	D1
65 Donburi	D1
Duke's Grocery	(see 68)
66 Estadio	E3
67 Founding Farmers	C4
68 Komi	D3
69 Le Diplomate	E2
Little Serow	(see 68)
70 Maine Avenue Fish Market	E7
71 Martin's Tavern	A3
Mitsitam Native Foods Cafe	(see 27)
72 Old Ebbitt Grill	E5
73 Rasika	F5
74 Red Apron Butchery	F5
75 Tico	E2

Drinking & Nightlife

76 Bar Charley	D2
77 Ching Ching Cha	A3
78 Churchkey	E3
79 Cobalt	D2
80 Cork Wine Bar	E2
81 Dacha Beer Garden	F2
82 Dan's Cafe	D1
83 Filter	C2
84 JR's	D3
85 Nellie's	F2
86 Right Proper Brewing Co	F2
87 Round Robin	E5
Tabard Inn Bar	(see 53)
88 U Street Music Hall	E2

Entertainment

89 9:30 Club	F1
90 Black Cat	E2
91 Bohemian Caverns	F2
92 Discovery Theater	E6
93 Kennedy Center	B5
94 Shakespeare Theatre Company	F5
95 Studio Theatre	E3
96 Washington Capitals	F5
Washington Wizards	(see 96)

1941 and 1945. The plaza's dual arches symbolize victory in the Atlantic and Pacific theaters. The 56 surrounding pillars represent each US state and territory. Stirring quotes speckle the monument. You'll often see groups of veterans paying their respects.

Hirshhorn Museum MUSEUM
(www.hirshhorn.si.edu; cnr 7th St & Independence Ave SW; 10am-5:30pm; ; Circulator, M L'Enfant Plaza) FREE The Smithsonian's cylindrical modern art museum stockpiles sculptures and canvases from modernism's early days to pop art to contemporary art. Special exhibits ring the 2nd floor. Rotating pieces from the permanent collection circle the 3rd floor, where there's also a swell sitting area with couches, floor-to-ceiling windows and a balcony offering Mall views.

Smithsonian Castle NOTABLE BUILDING
(202-633-1000; www.si.edu; 1000 Jefferson Dr SW; 8:30am-5:30pm; Circulator, M Smithsonian) James Renwick designed this turreted red-sandstone fairytale in 1855. Today the castle houses the **Smithsonian Visitors Center**, which makes a good first stop on the Mall. Inside you'll find history exhibits, multilingual touch-screen displays, a staffed information desk, free maps, a cafe – and the tomb of James Smithson, the institution's founder. His crypt lies inside a little room by the main entrance off the Mall.

Freer-Sackler Museums of Asian Art MUSEUM
(www.asia.si.edu; cnr Independence Ave & 12th St SW; 10am-5:30pm; Circulator, M Smithsonian) FREE This is a lovely spot in which to while away a Washington afternoon. Japanese silk scrolls, smiling Buddhas, rare Islamic manuscripts and Chinese jades spread through cool, quiet galleries. The Freer and Sackler are actually separate venues, connected by an underground tunnel. The Sackler focuses more on changing exhibits, while the Freer, rather incongruously, also houses works by American painter James Whistler. Don't miss the blue-and-gold, ceramics-crammed Peacock Room.

National Mall

Folks often call the Mall 'America's Front Yard,' and that's a pretty good analogy. It is indeed a lawn, unfurling scrubby green grass from the Capitol west to the Lincoln Memorial. It's also America's great public space, where citizens come to protest their government, go for scenic runs and connect with the nation's most cherished ideals writ large in stone, landscaping, monuments and memorials.

You can sample quite a bit in a day, though it'll be a full one that requires roughly 4 miles of walking. Start at the **Vietnam Veterans Memorial** ❶, then head counterclockwise around the Mall, swooping in on the **Lincoln Memorial** ❷, **Martin Luther King Jr Memorial** ❸ and **Washington Monument** ❹. You can also pause for the cause of the Korean War and WWII, among other monuments that dot the Mall's western portion.

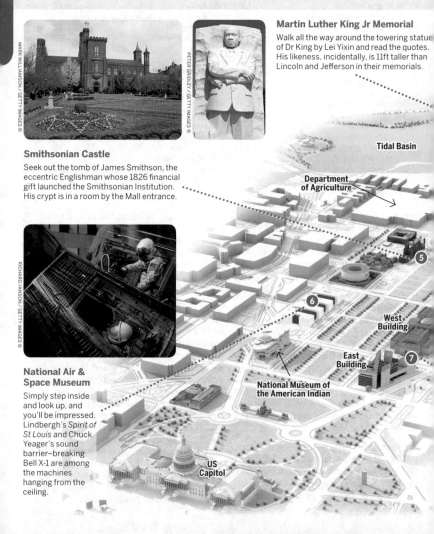

MARK WILLIAMSON / GETTY IMAGES ©

PETER GRIDLEY / GETTY IMAGES ©

Martin Luther King Jr Memorial

Walk all the way around the towering statue of Dr King by Lei Yixin and read the quotes. His likeness, incidentally, is 11ft taller than Lincoln and Jefferson in their memorials.

Smithsonian Castle

Seek out the tomb of James Smithson, the eccentric Englishman whose 1826 financial gift launched the Smithsonian Institution. His crypt is in a room by the Mall entrance.

RICHARD I'ANSON / GETTY IMAGES ©

National Air & Space Museum

Simply step inside and look up, and you'll be impressed. Lindbergh's *Spirit of St Louis* and Chuck Yeager's sound barrier–breaking Bell X-1 are among the machines hanging from the ceiling.

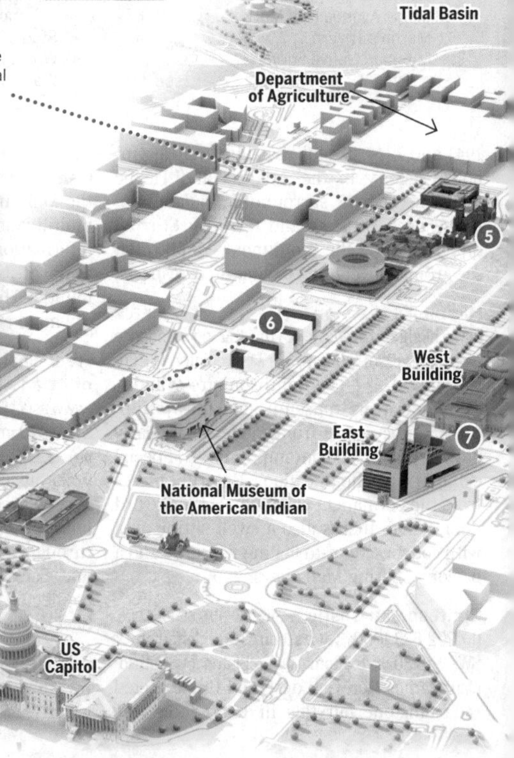

Then it's onward to the museums, all fabulous and all free. Begin at the **Smithsonian Castle** ❺ to get your bearings – and to say thanks to the guy making all this awesomeness possible – and commence browsing through the **National Air & Space Museum** ❻, **National Gallery of Art & National Sculpture Garden** ❼ and **National Museum of Natural History** ❽.

TOP TIPS

Start early, especially in summer. You'll avoid the crowds, but more importantly you'll avoid the blazing heat. Try to finish with the monuments and be in the air-conditioned museums by 10:30am. Also, consider bringing snacks, since the only food available is from scattered cart vendors and museum cafes.

Lincoln Memorial

Commune with Abe in his chair, then head down the steps to the marker where Martin Luther King Jr gave his 'Dream' speech. The view of the Reflecting Pool and Washington Monument is one of DC's best.

STEVEN GREAVES /GETTY IMAGES ©

Vietnam Veterans Memorial

Check the symbol that's beside each name. A diamond indicates 'killed, body recovered.' A plus sign indicates 'missing and unaccounted for.' There are approximately 1200 of the latter.

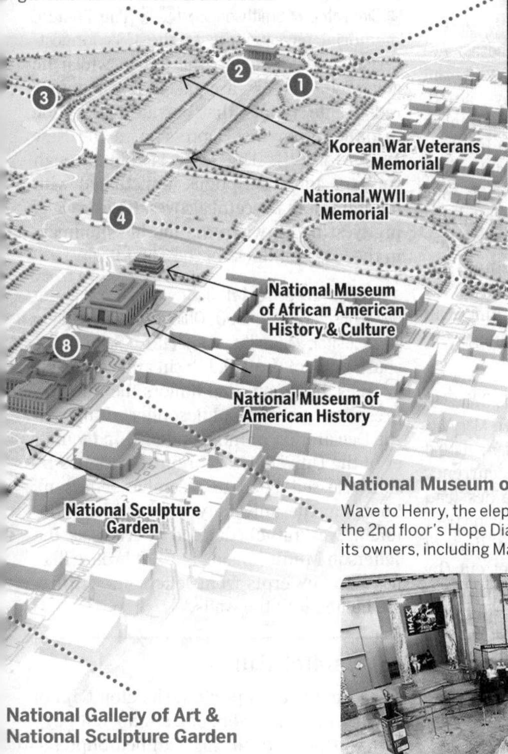

Washington Monument

As you approach the obelisk, look a third of the way up. See how it's slightly lighter in color at the bottom? Builders had to use different marble after the first source dried up.

National Museum of Natural History

Wave to Henry, the elephant who guards the rotunda, then zip to the 2nd floor's Hope Diamond. The 45.52-carat bauble has cursed its owners, including Marie Antoinette, or so the story goes.

EDDIE BRADY / GETTY IMAGES ©

National Gallery of Art & National Sculpture Garden

Beeline to Gallery 6 (West Building) and ogle the Western Hemisphere's only Leonardo da Vinci painting. Outdoors, amble amid whimsical sculptures by Miró, Calder and Lichtenstein. Also check out IM Pei's design of the East Building.

EATING ON THE MALL

Stock up on snacks before visiting the Mall, since there are few good dining options. One exception: the unique **Mitsitam Native Foods Cafe** (www.mitsitamcafe.com; cnr 4th St & Independence Ave SW, National Museum of the American Indian; mains $10-18; 11am-5pm; Circulator, M L'Enfant Plaza) in the American Indian Museum.

Like all Smithsonian institutions, the venues host free lectures, concerts and film screenings, though the ones here typically have an Asian bent; the website has the schedule. Alas, the Freer is closed for structural renovations from January 1, 2016 until summer of 2017. The Sackler will stay open throughhout the period.

National Museum of the American Indian MUSEUM
(www.nmai.si.edu; cnr 4th St & Independence Ave SW; 10am-5:30pm; ; Circulator, M L'Enfant Plaza) FREE Ensconced in honey-colored, undulating limestone, this museum makes a striking architectural impression. Inside it offers cultural artifacts, costumes, video and audio recordings related to the indigenous people of the Americas. Exhibits are largely organized and presented by individual tribes, which provides an intimate, if sometimes disjointed, overall narrative. The 'Our Universes' gallery (on Level 4) about Native American beliefs and creation stories is intriguing.

Bureau of Engraving & Printing LANDMARK
(www.moneyfactory.gov; cnr 14th & C Sts SW; 9-10:45am, 12:30-3:45pm & 5-6pm Mon-Fri Mar-Aug, reduced hours Sep-Feb; M Smithsonian) FREE Cha-ching! The nation's paper currency is designed and printed here. Guides lead 40-minute tours during which you peer down onto the work floor where millions of dollars roll off the presses and get cut (by guillotine!). In peak season (March to August), timed entry tickets are required. Get in line early at the **ticket kiosk** (Raoul Wallenberg Pl, aka 15th St). It opens at 8am.

Tidal Basin

It's magnificent to stroll around this constructed inlet and watch the monument lights wink across the Potomac River. The blooms here are loveliest during the Cherry Blossom Festival, the city's annual spring rejuvenation, when the basin bursts into a pink-and-white floral collage. The original trees, a gift from the city of Tokyo, were planted in 1912.

Martin Luther King Jr Memorial MONUMENT
(www.nps.gov/mlkm; 1850 W Basin Dr SW; 24hr; Circulator, M Smithsonian) FREE Opened in 2011, this is the Mall's first memorial dedicated to a nonpresident, as well as to an African American. Sculptor Lei Yixin carved the piece. Besides Dr King's image, known as the *Stone of Hope*, there are two blocks behind him that represent the Mountain of Despair. A wall inscribed with King's stirring quotes flanks the statues. It sits in a lovely spot on the banks of the Tidal Basin.

Franklin Delano Roosevelt Memorial MONUMENT
(www.nps.gov/frde; 400 W Basin Dr SW; 24hr; Circulator, M Smithsonian) FREE The 7.5-acre memorial pays tribute to the US's longest-serving president and the era in which he governed. Visitors are taken through four red-granite 'rooms' that narrate FDR's time in office, from the Depression to the New Deal to WWII. The story is told through statuary and inscriptions, punctuated with fountains and peaceful alcoves. It's especially pretty at night, when the marble shimmers in the glossy stillness of the Tidal Basin.

Jefferson Memorial MONUMENT
(www.nps.gov/thje; 900 Ohio Dr SW; 24hr; Circulator, M Smithsonian) FREE Set on the south bank of the Tidal Basin amid the cherry trees, this memorial honors the third US president, political philosopher, drafter of the Declaration of Independence and founder of the University of Virginia. Designed by John Russell Pope to resemble Jefferson's library at the university, the rounded monument was initially derided by critics as 'the Jefferson Muffin.' Inside is a 19ft bronze likeness, and excerpts from Jefferson's writings are etched into the walls.

Capitol Hill

The Capitol, appropriately, sits atop Capitol Hill (we'd say it's more of a stump, but hey), across a plaza from the dignified Supreme Court and Library of Congress. Congressional office buildings surround the plaza. A pleasant brownstone residential district stretches from E Capitol St to Lincoln Park.

DON'T MISS

SMITHSONIAN INSTITUTION MUSEUMS

It's not a single place, as commonly thought: rather, the **Smithsonian Institution** (www.si.edu) consists of 19 museums, the National Zoo and nine research facilities. Most are in DC, but others are further flung in the US and abroad. Together they comprise the world's largest museum and research complex – and it's all free to visitors. You could spend weeks wandering endless corridors taking in the great treasures, artifacts and ephemera from America and beyond; massive dinosaur skeletons, lunar modules and artworks from every corner of the globe are all part of the largesse. For perspective, consider this: of the approximately 140 million objects in the Smithsonian's collection, only 1% are on display at any given time. Thanks go to the curious Englishman James Smithson (1765–1829): he never visited the USA but in his will bequeathed the fledgling nation $508,318 to found an 'establishment for the increase and diffusion of knowledge.'

Most Smithsonian museums are open daily (except Christmas Day). Some have extended hours in summer. Be prepared for lines and bag checks.

★Capitol LANDMARK
(www.visitthecapitol.gov; First St NE & E Capitol St; 8:30am-4:30pm Mon-Sat; M Capitol South) FREE Since 1800, this is where the legislative branch of American government – ie Congress – has met to write the country's laws. The lower House of Representatives (435 members) and upper Senate (100) meet respectively in the south and north wings of the building. Enter via the underground visitor center below the East Plaza. Guided tours of the building are free, but you need a ticket. Get one at the information desk, or reserve online in advance (there's no fee).

Library of Congress LIBRARY
(www.loc.gov; 1st St SE; 8:30am-4:30pm Mon-Sat; M Capitol South) FREE The world's largest library – 29 million books and counting – awes in both scope and design. The centerpiece is the 1897 Jefferson Building. Gawk at the Great Hall, done up in stained glass, marble and mosaics of mythical characters, the Gutenberg Bible (c 1455), Thomas Jefferson's round library and the reading-room viewing area. Free tours of the building take place between 10:30am and 3:30pm on the half-hour.

Supreme Court LANDMARK
(202-479-3030; www.supremecourt.gov; 1 1st St NE; 9am-4:30pm Mon-Fri; M Capitol South) FREE The highest court in the USA sits in a pseudo-Greek temple that you enter through 13,000lb bronze doors. Arrive early to watch arguments (periodic Monday through Wednesday, October to April). You can visit the permanent exhibits and the building's five-story marble-and-bronze spiral staircase year-round. On days when court is not in session you can also hear lectures (every hour on the half-hour) in the courtroom.

Folger Shakespeare Library LIBRARY
(www.folger.edu; 201 E Capitol St SE; 10am-5pm Mon-Sat, noon-5pm Sun; M Capitol South) FREE Bard-o-philes will be all of a passion here, as the library holds the largest collection of old Billy's works in the world. Stroll through the Great Hall to see Elizabethan artifacts, paintings, etchings and manuscripts. The highlight is a rare First Folio that you can leaf through digitally. The evocative theater on site stages Shakespearean plays.

National Postal Museum MUSEUM
(www.postalmuseum.si.edu; 2 Massachusetts Ave NE; 10am-5:30pm; ; M Union Station) FREE The Smithsonian-run Postal Museum is way cooler than you might think. Level 1 has exhibits on postal history from the Pony Express to modern times, where you'll see antique mail planes and touching old letters from soldiers and pioneers. Level 2 holds the world's largest stamp collection. Join the stamp geeks pulling out drawers and snapping photos of the world's rarest stamps (the Ben Franklin Z Grill!), or start your own collection by choosing from thousands of free international stamps (Guyana, Congo, Cambodia...).

White House Area & Foggy Bottom

An expansive park called the Ellipse borders the Mall; on the east side is the power-broker block of Pennsylvania Ave. Foggy Bottom was named for the mists that belched out of a local gasworks; now home to the State Department and George Washington University, it's an upscale (if not terribly lively) neighborhood crawling with students and professionals.

★White House LANDMARK
(☎tours 202-456-7041; www.whitehouse.gov; ⏲tours 7:30-11:30am Tue-Thu, to 1:30pm Fri & Sat; Ⓜ Federal Triangle, McPherson Sq, Metro Center) FREE The White House has survived both fire (the Brits torched it in 1814) and insults (Jefferson groused that it was 'big enough for two emperors, one Pope and the grand Lama'). Tours must be arranged in advance. Americans must apply via one of their state's members of Congress, and non-Americans must apply through either the US consulate in their home country or their country's consulate in DC. Applications are taken from 21 days to six months in advance; three months ahead is the recommended sweet spot.

White House Visitor Center MUSEUM
(www.nps.gov/whho; 1450 Pennsylvania Ave NW; ⏲7:30am-4pm; Ⓜ Federal Triangle) FREE Getting inside the White House can be tough, so here is your backup plan. Browse artifacts such as Roosevelt's desk for his fireside chats and Lincoln's cabinet chair. Multimedia exhibits give a 360-degree view into the White House's rooms. It's not the same as seeing the real deal first-hand, but the center does do its job very well, giving good history sprinkled with great anecdotes on presidential spouses, kids, pets and dinner preferences.

STEVEN F UDVAR-HAZY CENTER

The National Air and Space Museum on the Mall is so awesome they made an attic for it: the **Steven F Udvar-Hazy Center** (www.airandspace.si.edu/visit/udvar-hazy-center; 14390 Air & Space Museum Pkwy; ⏲10am-5:30pm, to 6:30pm late May-early Sep; 👪; Ⓜ Wiehle-Reston East for bus 983) FREE, in Chantilly, VA. It's three times the size of the DC museum and sprawls through two massive hangars near Dulles Airport. Highlights include the SR-71 Blackbird (the fastest jet in the world), the space shuttle *Discovery* (which was retired in 2011) and the *Enola Gay* (the B-29 that dropped the atomic bomb on Hiroshima).

Though the museum is free, parking costs $15. To get here on public transportation, take the metro silver line to Wiehle-Reston East station. Then transfer to the Fairfax Connector bus 983 and take it one stop to the museum.

Textile Museum MUSEUM
(www.museum.gwu.edu; 701 21st St NW; admission $8; ⏲11:30am-6:30pm Mon & Wed-Fri, 10am-5pm Sat, 1-5pm Sun, closed Tue; Ⓜ Foggy Bottom-GWU) This gem is the country's only textile museum. Galleries hold exquisite fabrics and carpets. Exhibits revolve around a theme, say Asian textiles depicting dragons or Kuba cloth from the Democratic Republic of Congo, and rotate a few times a year. Bonus: the museum shares space with George Washington University's Washingtonia trove of historic maps, drawings and ephemera.

Renwick Gallery MUSEUM
(www.americanart.si.edu/renwick; 1661 Pennsylvania Ave NW; ⏲10am-5:30pm; 👪; Ⓜ Farragut West) FREE Part of the Smithsonian empire, the Renwick Gallery is set in a stately 1859 mansion and exhibits a superb collection of American crafts and decorative-art pieces. Closed until early 2016 for infrastructure upgrades.

Downtown

This neighborhood bustles day and night, and several major sights are located here. It's also DC's shiny theater district and convention hub.

★National Archives LANDMARK
(☎866-272-6272; www.archives.gov/museum; 700 Pennsylvania Ave NW; ⏲10am-5:30pm Sep–mid-Mar, to 7pm mid-Mar–Aug; Ⓜ Archives) FREE It's hard not to feel a little in awe of the big three documents in the National Archives: the Declaration of Independence, the Constitution and the Bill of Rights, plus one of four copies of the Magna Carta. Taken together, it becomes clear just how radical the American experiment was for its time. The Public Vaults, a bare scratching of archival bric-a-brac, make a flashy rejoinder to the main exhibit.

★Reynolds Center for American Art & Portraiture MUSEUM
(☎202-633-1000; www.americanart.si.edu; cnr 8th & F Sts NW; ⏲11:30am-7pm; Ⓜ Gallery Pl) FREE If you only visit one art museum in DC, make it the Reynolds Center, which combines the National Portrait Gallery and the American Art Museum. There is, simply put, no better collection of American art in the world than at these two Smithsonian museums. Famed works by Edward Hopper, Georgia O'Keeffe, Andy Warhol, Winslow Homer and loads more celebrated artists fill the galleries.

Ford's Theatre HISTORIC SITE

(☎202-426-6924; www.fords.org; 511 10th St NW; ⏲9am-4:30pm; Ⓜ Metro Center) FREE On April 14, 1865, John Wilkes Booth assassinated Abraham Lincoln in his box seat here. Timed-entry tickets let you see the flag-draped site. They also provide entry to the basement museum (displaying Booth's .44-caliber pistol, his muddy boot etc) and to Petersen House (across the street), where Lincoln died. Arrive early because tickets do run out. Reserve online ($6.25 fee) to ensure admittance.

Newseum MUSEUM

(www.newseum.org; 555 Pennsylvania Ave NW; adult/child $23/14; ⏲9am-5pm; 👪; Ⓜ Archives, Judiciary Sq) This six-story, highly interactive news museum is worth the admission price. You can delve into the major events of recent years (the fall of the Berlin Wall, September 11, Hurricane Katrina), and spend hours watching moving film footage and perusing Pulitzer Prize–winning photographs. The concourse level displays FBI artifacts from news stories, such as the Unabomber's cabin and John Dillinger's death mask.

U Street, Shaw & Logan Circle

These neighborhoods have changed in recent years more than almost anywhere else in DC. The U Street Corridor, DC's richest nightlife zone, has quite a history: it was once the 'Black Broadway,' where Duke Ellington and Ella Fitzgerald hit their notes in the early 1900s, and later the smoldering epicenter of the 1968 race riots. The area's history is acknowledged by the African American Civil War Memorial at the U Street metro station. After a troubled descent, it's had a vibrant rebirth in recent years; a stroll around this neighborhood is a must.

U Street becomes part of the larger Shaw district, which is DC's current 'it' neighborhood. But it's not annoyingly trendy – the breweries, bars and cafes that seem to pop up weekly are true local places. Logan Circle, next door, is also booming: walk down 14th St NW and hot-chef wine bars, gastropubs, tapas places and oyster bars flash by. The side streets hold stately old manors that give the area its class.

Dupont Circle

A well-heeled splice of the gay community and the DC diplomatic scene, this is city life at its best. Great restaurants, bars, bookstores and cafes, captivating architecture and the electric energy of a lived-in, happening neighborhood make Dupont worth a linger. Most of the area's historic mansions have been converted into embassies.

★ **Embassy Row** ARCHITECTURE

(www.embassy.org; Massachusetts Ave NW btwn Observatory & Dupont Circles NW; Ⓜ Dupont Circle) How quickly can you leave the country? It takes about five minutes; just stroll north along Massachusetts Ave from Dupont Circle (the actual traffic circle) and you pass more than 40 embassies housed in mansions that range from elegant to imposing to discreet. Technically they're on foreign soil, as embassy grounds are the embassy nation's territory.

Phillips Collection MUSEUM

(www.phillipscollection.org; 1600 21st St NW; Sat & Sun $10, Tue-Fri free, ticketed exhibitions per day $12; ⏲10am-5pm Tue, Wed, Fri & Sat, to 8:30pm Thu, 11am-6pm Sun, chamber-music series 4pm Sun Oct-May; Ⓜ Dupont Circle) The first modern-art museum in the country (opened in 1921) houses a small but exquisite collection of European and American works. Renoir's *Luncheon of the Boating Party* is a highlight, along with pieces by Gauguin, Van Gogh, Matisse, Picasso and many other greats. The intimate rooms, set in a restored mansion, put you unusually close to the artworks. The permanent collection is free on weekdays.

Georgetown

Thousands of the bright and beautiful, from Georgetown students to ivory-tower academics and diplomats, call this leafy, aristocratic neighborhood home. At night, chockablock M St becomes congested with traffic, a weird mix of high-school cruising and high-street boutique.

Dumbarton Oaks GARDENS, MUSEUM

(www.doaks.org; 1703 32nd St NW; museum free, gardens adult/child $8/5; ⏲museum 11:30am-5:30pm Tue-Sun, gardens 2-6pm) The mansion's 10 acres of enchanting formal gardens are straight out of a storybook. In springtime, the blooms – including heaps of cherry blossoms – are stunning. The mansion itself is worth a walk-through to see exquisite Byzantine and pre-Columbian art (including El Greco's *The Visitation*) and the fascinating library of rare books.

Georgetown Waterfront Park PARK

(Water St NW, btwn 30th St & Key Bridge;) The park is a favorite with couples on first dates, families on an evening stroll and power players showing off their big yachts. Benches dot the way, where you can sit and watch the rowing teams out on the Potomac River. Alfresco restaurants cluster near the harbor at 31st St NW. They ring a terraced plaza filled with fountains (which become an ice rink in winter). The docks are also here for sightseeing boats that ply the Potomac to Alexandria, VA.

Georgetown University UNIVERSITY

(www.georgetown.edu; cnr 37th & O Sts NW) Georgetown is one of the nation's top universities, with a student body that's equally hardworking and hard-partying. Founded in 1789, it was America's first Roman Catholic university. Notable Hoya (derived from the Latin *hoya saxa,* 'what rocks') alumni include Bill Clinton, as well many international royals and heads of state. Near the campus' east gate, medieval-looking **Healy Hall** impresses with its tall, Hogwarts-esque clock tower. Pretty **Dalghren Chapel** and its quiet courtyard hide behind it.

Exorcist Stairs FILM LOCATION

(3600 Prospect St NW) The steep set of stairs dropping down to M St is a popular track for joggers, but more famously it's the spot where demonically possessed Father Karras tumbles to his death in 1973 horror classic *The Exorcist.* Come on foggy nights, when the stone steps really are creepy as hell.

Tudor Place MUSEUM

(www.tudorplace.org; 1644 31st St NW; 1hr house tour adult/child $10/3, self-guided garden tour $3; 10am-4pm Tue-Sat, from noon Sun, closed Jan) This 1816 neoclassical mansion was owned by Thomas Peter and Martha Custis Peter, the granddaughter of Martha Washington. Today the mansion functions as a small museum, and features furnishings and artwork from Mt Vernon, which give a nice insight into American decorative arts. The grand, 5-acre gardens bloom with roses, lilies, poplar trees and exotic palms.

Upper Northwest DC

The far reaches of northwest DC are primarily made up of leafy residential neighborhoods.

National Zoo ZOO

(www.nationalzoo.si.edu; 3001 Connecticut Ave NW; 10am-6pm Apr-Oct, to 4:30pm Nov-Mar, grounds 6am-8pm daily, to 6pm Nov-Mar; M Cleveland Park, Woodley Park-Zoo/Adams Morgan) FREE Home to over 2000 individual animals (400 different species) in natural habitats, the National Zoo is famed for its giant pandas Mei Xiang and Tian Tian, along with their cub Bao Bao (born to Mei Xiang in 2013). Other highlights include the African lion pride, Asian elephants, and dangling orangutans swinging 50ft overhead from steel cables and interconnected towers (aka the 'O Line').

Washington National Cathedral CHURCH

(202-537-6200; www.nationalcathedral.org; 3101 Wisconsin Ave NW; adult/child $10/$6, admission free Sun; 10am-5:30pm Mon-Fri, to 8pm some days May-Sep, 10am-4:30pm Sat, 8am-4pm Sun; M Tenleytown-AU to southbound bus 31, 32, 36, 37) This Gothic cathedral, as dramatic as its European counterparts, blends both the spiritual and the profane in its architectural treasures. The stained-glass windows are stunning (check out the 'Space Window' with an imbedded lunar rock); you'll need binoculars to spy the Darth Vader gargoyle on the exterior. Specialized tours delve deeper into the esoteric; call or go online for the schedule. There's also an excellent cafe here.

Anacostia

The drive from Georgetown eastbound to Anacostia takes about 30 minutes – and the patience to endure a world of income disparity. The neighborhood's poverty in contrast to the Mall, sitting mere miles away, forms one of DC's (and America's) great contradictory panoramas. Some high-end condos have sprung up around Nationals Park, the baseball stadium for the Washington Nationals.

Yards Park PARK

(www.yardspark.org; 355 Water St SE; 7am-2hr past sunset; M Navy Yard) The riverside green space is just down the road from the Nationals' stadium. There are shaded tables by the water, a wooden boardwalk, fountains and a funky modernist bridge that looks like a giant, open-faced plastic straw. Look left

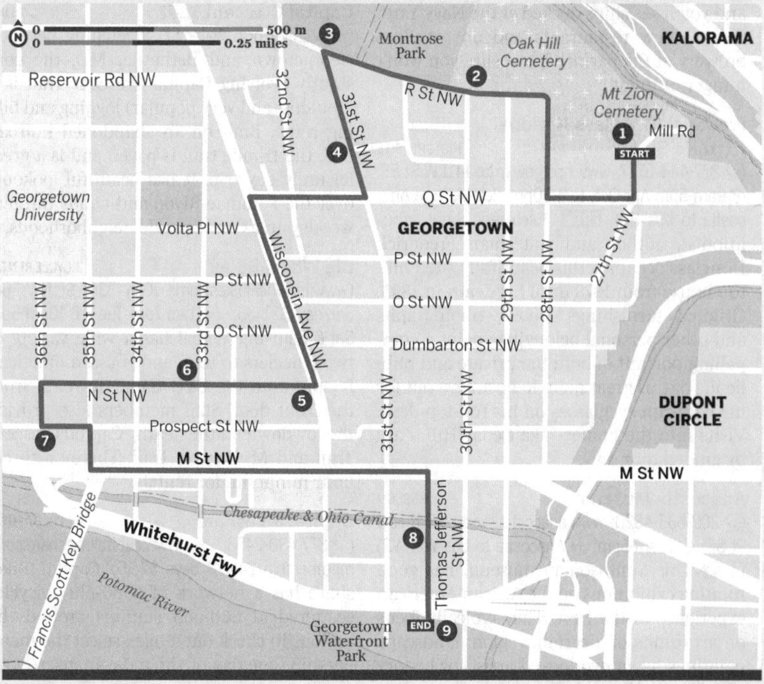

City Walk
Genteel Georgetown

START MT ZION CEMETERY
END GEORGETOWN WATERFRONT PARK
LENGTH 3 MILES; THREE HOURS

Georgetown, in all its leafy, filigreed-manor glory, is a prime neighborhood for ambling.

African American **1 Mt Zion Cemetery**, near the intersection of 27th and Q Sts, dates from the early 1800s. The nearby Mt Zion church (1334 29th St) was a stop on the Underground Railroad; escaping slaves hid in a vault in the cemetery.

The entrance to **2 Oak Hill Cemetery** is a few blocks away at 30th and R Sts NW. Stroll the obelisk-studded grounds and look for graves of prominent Washingtonians such as Edwin Stanton (Lincoln's war secretary). Up the road, **3 Dumbarton Oaks** offers exquisite Byzantine art and sprawling, fountain-dotted gardens: the blooms in springtime are stunning.

George Washington's step-granddaughter Martha Custis Peter owned **4 Tudor Place**, the neoclassical mansion at 1644 31st St. It features some of George's furnishings from Mount Vernon and pretty, landscaped grounds.

Head over to Wisconsin Ave NW and stop in at **5 Martin's Tavern**, where John F Kennedy proposed to Jackie Bouvier. Walk along N St and you'll pass several Federal-style townhouses in the 3300 block. The Kennedys lived at **6 3307 N St** from 1958 to 1961, before they left for the White House.

At the corner of 36th St and Prospect Ave, stare down the **7 Exorcist Stairs**, where demonically possessed Regan of *The Exorcist* sent victims to their screaming deaths. Joggers use the stairs by day; at night the steps are legitimately creepy as hell.

Go down to M St NW, popping in to whatever boutiques and high-end chain stores your wallet permits. At Jefferson St turn right and sniff your way to **8 Baked & Wired** to replenish with a monster cupcake and cappuccino. From there you can stroll down to **9 Georgetown Waterfront Park** to watch boats along the Potomac River.

and you'll see ships docked at the Navy Yard. Several new restaurants and an excellent brewery at the park's edge ensure you won't hunger or thirst.

Frederick Douglass National Historic Site HISTORIC SITE
(☎877-444-6777; www.nps.gov/frdo; 1411 W St SE; ⏰9am-5pm Apr-Oct, to 4:30pm Nov-Mar; Ⓜ Anacostia to bus B2) FREE Escaped slave, abolitionist, author and statesman Frederick Douglass occupied this beautifully sited hilltop house from 1878 until his death in 1895. Original furnishings, books, photographs and other personal belongings paint a compelling portrait of both the private and public life of this great man. Keep an eye out for his wire-rim eyeglasses on his roll-top desk. Visits into the home – aka Cedar Hill – are by guided tour only.

Anacostia Museum MUSEUM
(☎202-633-4820; www.anacostia.si.edu; 1901 Fort Pl SE; ⏰10am-5pm; Ⓜ Anacostia to bus W2, W3) FREE This Smithsonian museum has good rotating exhibitions on the African American experience in the USA. They typically focus on art (quilts of a certain region; landscape paintings by an overlooked artist) or history (the first black baseball teams in the area; a slave family's story). The museum also serves as a community hall for the surrounding neighborhood of Anacostia. Call ahead, as it often closes between installations.

Activities

Hiking & Cycling

C&O Canal Towpath WALKING, CYCLING
(www.nps.gov/choh; 1057 Thomas Jefferson St NW) The shaded hiking-cycling path – part of a larger national historic park – runs alongside a waterway constructed in the mid-1800s to transport goods all the way to West Virginia. Step on at Jefferson St for a lovely green escape from the crowd.

In its entirety, the gravel path runs for 185 miles from Georgetown to Cumberland, MD. Lots of cyclists do the 14-mile ride from Georgetown to Great Falls, MD. The tree-lined route goes over atmospheric wooden bridges and past waterwheels and old lock houses. It's mostly flat, punctuated by occasional small hills. The park's website and **Bike Washington** (www.bikewashington.org/canal) have trail maps.

Capital Crescent Trail CYCLING
(www.cctrail.org; Water St) Stretching between Georgetown and Bethesda, MD, the constantly evolving Capital Crescent Trail is a fabulous (and very popular) jogging and biking route. Built on an abandoned railroad bed, the 11-mile trail is paved and is a great leisurely day trip. It has beautiful lookouts over the Potomac River, and winds through woodsy areas and upscale neighborhoods.

Big Wheel Bikes BICYCLE RENTAL
(www.bigwheelbikes.com; 1034 33rd St NW; per 3hr/day $21/35; ⏰11am-7pm Tue-Fri, 10am-6pm Sat & Sun) Big Wheel has a wide variety of two-wheelers to rent, and you can practically spin onto the C&O Canal Towpath from the front door. Staff members also provide the lowdown on the nearby Capital Crescent Trail and Mt Vernon Trail. There's a three-hour minimum for rentals.

Capital Bikeshare BICYCLE RENTAL
(☎877-430-2453; www.capitalbikeshare.com; membership 24hr/3 days $7/15) Capital Bikeshare has a network of 2500-plus bicycles scattered at 300-odd stations around the region. To check out a bike, select the membership (one day or three days), insert your credit card, and off you go. The first 30 minutes are free; after that, rates rise fast ($2/6/14 per extra 30/60/90 minutes). Call or go online for complete details.

Boating

Tidal Basin Boathouse BOATING
(www.tidalbasinpaddleboats.com; 1501 Maine Ave SW; 2-/4-person boat rental $14/22; ⏰10am-6pm mid-Mar–Aug, Wed-Sun only Sep–mid-Oct, closed mid-Oct–mid-Mar; 🚌Circulator, Ⓜ Smithsonian) It rents paddleboats to take out on the Tidal Basin. Make sure you bring a camera. There are great views, of the Jefferson Memorial in particular, from the water.

Key Bridge Boathouse KAYAKING
(www.boatingindc.com; 3500 Water St NW; ⏰hours vary Mar-Oct) Located beneath the Key Bridge, the boathouse rents canoes, kayaks and stand-up paddleboards (prices start at $15 per hour). It also offers guided, 90-minute kayak trips ($45 per person) in summer that glide past the Lincoln Memorial as the sun sets. If you have a bike, the boathouse is a mere few steps from the Capital Crescent Trail.

Tours

DC by Foot WALKING TOUR
(www.dcbyfoot.com) Guides for this pay-what-you-want walking tour offer engaging stories and historical details on different jaunts covering the National Mall, Lincoln's assassination, Georgetown's ghosts, U Street's food and many more. Most takers pay around $10 per person.

Bike & Roll BICYCLE TOUR
(www.bikeandrolldc.com; adult/child from $40/30; ⌚ mid-Mar–Nov) Offers day and evening bike tours around the Mall and Capitol Hill. The 'Monuments at Night' tour is especially atmospheric. The company also arranges combo boat-bike trips to Mt Vernon.

DC Brew Tours BUS TOUR
(☎202-759-8687; www.dcbrewtours.com; tours $85; ⌚ noon & 5pm Thu & Fri, 11am & 5pm Sat & Sun) DC Brew Tours offers five-hour jaunts by van that take in four breweries. Routes vary, but could include DC Brau, Right Proper Brewing, Chocolate City, 3 Stars and Atlas Brew Works, among others. Tastings of 15-plus beers and a beer-focused meal are part of the package. Departure is from downtown at 710 12th St NW, by the Metro Center station.

Festivals & Events

National Cherry Blossom Festival CULTURAL
(www.nationalcherryblossomfestival.org; ⌚ late Mar–early Apr) DC at her prettiest.

Smithsonian Folklife Festival CULTURAL
(www.festival.si.edu; ⌚ Jun & Jul) This fun family event, held over two weekends in June and July, features distinctive regional folk art, crafts, food and music.

Independence Day CULTURAL
(⌚ Jul 4) Not surprisingly, a big deal here, celebrated on July 4 with a parade, an open-air concert and fireworks over the Mall.

WASHINGTON, DC FOR CHILDREN

The top destination for families is undoubtedly the (free!) **National Zoo** (p276). Other museums around the city will also entertain and educate children of all ages. Institutions with especially good programming include:

National Air and Space Museum (p265)

National Museum of Natural History (p265)

Newseum (p275)

National Gallery of Art (p265)

Some other family hot spots:

Carousel (tickets $3.50; ⌚ 10am-6pm; 🚌 Circulator, Ⓜ Smithsonian) Take a spin on the old-fashioned merry-go-round on the Mall, then romp around the wide-open lawn.

Discovery Theater (www.discoverytheater.org; 1100 Jefferson Dr SW; tickets $6-12; 👪; 🚌 Circulator, Ⓜ Smithsonian) The Smithsonian's kids' theater focuses on cultural plays and storytelling.

Yards Park (p276) Play and splash in this enticing green space.

Six Flags America (☎301-249-1500; www.sixflags.com/america; 13710 Central Ave, Upper Marlboro, MD; adult/child $60/40; ⌚ May-Oct, hours vary) The park offers a full array of roller coasters and tamer kiddie rides. It's located about 15 miles east of downtown DC in Maryland.

Good resources for parents:

DC Cool Kids features activity guides, insider tips from local youngsters on things to do, and museum info.

Smithsonian Kids has educational games and projects, plus the lowdown on pint-sized activities at the museums.

Our Kids has loads of listings for kid-centric shows and events, family-friendly restaurants and activity ideas.

Sleeping

Lodging is expensive in DC. The high-season apex is mid-March through April (cherry-blossom season). Crowds and rates also peak in May, June, September and October. Hotel tax adds 14.5% to rates. If you have a car, figure on $35 to $55 per day for in-and-out privileges.

Airbnb can also be a good option in the city. For B&Bs and private apartments citywide, contact **Bed & Breakfast DC** (www.bedandbreakfastdc.com).

Capitol Hill

Hotel George BOUTIQUE HOTEL $$
(☎202-347-4200; www.hotelgeorge.com; 15 E St NW; r from $300; Ⓟ; Ⓜ Union Station) DC's first chic boutique hotel is still one of its best. Chrome-and-glass furniture and modern art frame the bold interior. Rooms exude a cool, creamy-white Zen. The pop-art presidential accents (paintings of American currency, artfully rearranged and diced up) are a little overdone, but that's a minor complaint about what is otherwise the hippest lodging on the Hill.

Downtown & White House Area

Hostelling International – Washington DC HOSTEL $
(☎202-737-2333; www.hiwashingtondc.org; 1009 11th St NW; dm $33-55, r $110-150; Ⓜ Metro Center) Top of the budget picks, this large, friendly hostel attracts a laid-back international crowd and has loads of amenities: lounge rooms, a pool table, a 60in TV for movie nights, free tours, free continental breakfast and free wi-fi.

★ **Hotel Lombardy** BOUTIQUE HOTEL $$
(☎202-828-2600; www.hotellombardy.com; 2019 Pennsylvania Ave NW; r $180-330; Ⓟ; Ⓜ Foggy Bottom-GWU) Done up in Venetian decor (shuttered doors, warm gold walls), and beloved by World Bank and State Department types, this European boutique hotel has multilingual staff and an international vibe – you hear French and Spanish as often as English in its halls. The attitude carries into rooms decorated with original artwork and Chinese and European antiques.

Morrison-Clark Inn HISTORIC HOTEL $$
(☎202-898-1200; www.morrisonclark.com; 1015 L St NW; r $150-250; Ⓟ; Ⓜ Mt Vernon Sq) Listed on the Register of Historic Places and helmed by a doting staff, the elegant Morrison-Clark comprises two 1864 Victorian residences filled with fine antiques, chandeliers, richly hued drapes and other features evocative of the pre–Civil War South. Some rooms are on the small side, but more options are coming: the inn is expanding into a church next door.

Club Quarters HOTEL $$
(☎202-463-6400; www.clubquarters.com/washington-dc; 839 17th St NW; r $125-205; Ⓟ; Ⓜ Farragut West) Club Quarters is a no-muss, no-fuss kind of place often used by business travelers on the go. Room are small and without views, they lack charm or quirk, but the bed is restful, the desk workable, the wi-fi fast enough and the coffee maker well stocked. Oh, and the prices are reasonable in an area where they're usually sky-high.

★ **Hay-Adams Hotel** HERITAGE HOTEL $$$
(☎202-638-6600; www.hayadams.com; 800 16th St NW; r from $350; Ⓟ; Ⓜ McPherson Sq) One of the city's great heritage hotels, the Hay is a beautiful old building where 'nothing is overlooked but the White House.' The property has a palazzo-style lobby and probably the best rooms of the old-school, luxury genre in the city, all puffy mattresses like clouds shaded by four-poster canopies and gold-braid tassels.

U Street, Shaw & Logan Circle

Hotel Helix BOUTIQUE HOTEL $$
(☎202-462-9001; www.hotelhelix.com; 1430 Rhode Island Ave NW; r $200-300; Ⓟ; Ⓜ McPherson Sq) Modish and highlighter bright, the Helix is playfully hip – the perfect hotel for the bouncy international set that makes up the surrounding neighborhood. Little touches suggest a youthful energy (Pez dispensers in the minibar) balanced with worldly cool (like the pop-punk decor). All rooms have comfy, crisp-sheet beds and 37in flat-screen TVs.

Chester Arthur House B&B $$
(☎877-893-3233; www.chesterarthurhouse.com; 23 Logan Circle NW; r $175-215; Ⓜ U St) Snooze in one of four rooms in this beautiful Logan Circle row house, located a stumble from the restaurant boom along P and 14th Sts. The 1883 abode is stuffed with crystal chandeliers, antique oil paintings and a ma-

hogany-paneled staircase, plus ephemera from the hosts' global expeditions.

Adams Morgan

Adam's Inn B&B $

(☎202-745-3600; www.adamsinn.com; 1746 Lanier Pl NW; r $109-179, without bathroom $79-100; P ⊖ ❄ @ ☜; M Woodley Park) Tucked on a shady residential street, the 26-room inn is known for its personalized service, fluffy linens and handy location just a few blocks from 18th St's global smorgasbord. Inviting, homey rooms sprawl through two adjacent townhouses and a carriage house. The common areas have a nice garden patio, and there's a general sense of sherry-scented chintz.

Taft Bridge Inn B&B $$

(☎202-387-2007; www.taftbridgeinn.com; 2007 Wyoming Ave NW; r $179-205, without bathroom $100-140; P ⊖ ❄ ☜; M Dupont Circle) Named for the bridge that leaps over Rock Creek Park just north, this beautiful 19th-century Georgian mansion is an easy walk to 18th St or Dupont Circle. The inn has a paneled drawing room, classy antiques, six fireplaces and a garden. Some of the 12 rooms have a Colonial Americana theme, accentuated by Amish quilts; others are more tweedy, exuding a Euro-renaissance vibe.

Dupont Circle

★ **Tabard Inn** BOUTIQUE HOTEL $$

(☎202-785-1277; www.tabardinn.com; 1739 N St NW; r $195-250, without bathroom $135-155; ⊖ ❄ @ ☜; M Dupont Circle) Named for the inn in *The Canterbury Tales*, the Tabard spreads through a trio of Victorian-era row houses. The 40 rooms are hard to generalize: all come with vintage quirks such as iron bed frames and wing-backed chairs, though little accents distinguish – a Matisse-like painted headboard here, Amish-looking quilts there. There are no TVs, and wi-fi can be dodgy, but the of-yore atmospherics prevail.

Continental breakfast is included. Downstairs the parlor, beautiful restaurant and bar have low ceilings and old furniture, highly conducive to curling up with a vintage port and the Sunday *Post*.

Embassy Circle Guest House B&B $$

(☎202-232-7744; www.dcinns.com; 2224 R St NW; r $180-300; ⊖ ❄ ☜; M Dupont Circle) Embassies surround this 1902 French country-style home, which sits a few blocks from Dupont's nightlife hubbub. The 11 big-windowed rooms are decked out with Persian carpets and original art on the walls; they don't have TVs or radios, though they do each have wi-fi. Staff feeds you well throughout the day, with a hot organic breakfast, afternoon cookies, and an evening wine and beer soiree.

Embassy Circle's sister property – the **Woodley Park Guest House** (☎202-667-0218; www.dcinns.com; 2647 Woodley Rd NW; r $180-250, without bathroom $135-165; P ❄ @ ☜; M Woodley Park-Zoo, Adams Morgan) in farther-flung northwest DC – is a hot spot.

Georgetown

Graham Georgetown BOUTIQUE HOTEL $$

(☎202-337-0900; www.thegrahamgeorgetown.com; 1075 Thomas Jefferson St NW; r $270-350; P ⊖ ❄ @ ☜; M Foggy Bottom-GWU to DC Circulator) Set smack in the heart of Georgetown, the Graham occupies the intersection between stately tradition and modernist hip. Rooms have tasteful floral prints and duochrome furnishings with geometric accents. Even the most basic rooms have linens by Liddell Ireland and L'Occitane bath amenities, which means you'll be as fresh, clean and beautiful as the surrounding Georgetown glitterati.

Eating

Washington's dining scene is booming. The number of restaurants has doubled over the past decade, with small, independent spots helmed by local chefs leading the way. There's also a delicious glut of global cuisines (Salvadoran, Ethiopian, Vietnamese, French) and traditional Southern fare (fried chicken, grits, biscuits and sweet iced tea).

Capitol Hill

This hood has two particularly rich veins for eating and drinking. You'll find 8th St SE (near Eastern Market) – also known as Barracks Row – packed with venues. So is H St NE, an edgy corridor a mile east of Union Station; catch bus X2 or a taxi (about $8). The District's long-awaited streetcars might be rolling there soon, as well.

Toki Underground ASIAN $

(☎202-388-3086; www.tokiunderground.com; 1234 H St NE; mains $10-12; ⏲11:30am-2:30pm & 5-10pm Mon-Thu, to midnight Fri & Sat; 🚌X2 from Union Station) Spicy ramen noodles and dumplings sum up wee Toki's menu. Steaming pots obscure the busy chefs, while diners slurp and sigh contentedly. The eatery doesn't take reservations and there's typically a wait. Take the opportunity to explore surrounding bars; Toki will text when your table is ready. The restaurant isn't signposted; look for the Pug bar, and Toki is above it.

Maine Avenue Fish Market SEAFOOD $

(1100 Maine Ave SW; mains $7-13; 8am-9pm; M L'Enfant Plaza) The pungent, open-air Maine Avenue Fish Market is a local landmark. No-nonsense vendors sell fish, crabs, oysters and other seafood so fresh it's almost still flopping. They'll kill, strip, shell, gut, fry or broil your desire, which you can take to the waterfront benches and eat blissfully (mind the seagulls!).

Atlas Room AMERICAN $$

(202-388-4020; www.theatlasroom.com; 1015 H St NE; mains $21-25; 5:30-9:30pm Tue-Thu, 5:30-10pm Fri & Sat, 5-9pm Sun; X2 from Union Station) Set in a snug, candle-shimmering room, Atlas is a neighborhood favorite on edgy H St. The bistro takes cues from classical French and Italian gastronomy but blends them in approachable American ways using seasonal ingredients. In summer you might enjoy crab fritters, while in winter a braised daube of beef will melt your tongue (in a good way!).

Ted's Bulletin AMERICAN $$

(202-544-8337; www.tedsbulletincapitolhill.com; 505 8th St SE; mains $10-19; 7am-10pm Sun-Thu, to 11pm Fri & Sat; ; M Eastern Market) Plop into a booth in the art-deco-meets-diner ambience, and loosen the belt. Beer biscuits and sausage gravy for breakfast, meatloaf with ketchup glaze for dinner and other hipster spins on comfort foods hit the table. You've got to admire a place that lets you substitute pop tarts for toast. Breakfast is available all day.

Ethiopic ETHIOPIAN $$

(202-675-2066; www.ethiopicrestaurant.com; 401 H St NE; mains $12-18; 5-10pm Tue-Thu, from noon Fri-Sun; ; M Union Station) In a city with no shortage of Ethiopian joints, Ethiopic stands above the rest. Top marks go to the various *wats* (stews) and the signature *tibs* (sauteed meat and veg), derived from tender lamb that has sat in a bath of herbs and hot spices. Vegans get lots of love here.

★ Rose's Luxury MODERN AMERICAN $$$

(202-580-8889; www.rosesluxury.com; 717 8th St SE; small plates $12-14, family-style plates $28-33; 5:30-10pm Mon-Thu, to 11pm Fri & Sat; M Eastern Market) Rose's is DC's most buzzed-about eatery – and that was before *Bon Appetit* named it the nation's best new restaurant in 2014. Crowds fork into worldly Southern comfort food as twinkling lights glow overhead and candles flicker around the industrial, half-finished room. Rose's doesn't take reservations, but ordering your meal at the upstairs bar can save time (and the cocktails are delicious).

Downtown & White House Area

★ Red Apron Butchery DELI $

(202-524-5244; www.redapronbutchery.com; 709 D St NW; mains $5-10; 7:30am-8pm Mon-Fri, 9am-8pm Sat, 9am-5pm Sun; M Archives) Red Apron makes a helluva breakfast sandwich. Plop into one of the comfy booths and wrap your lips around the ricotta, honey and pine-nut 'aristocrat' or the egg and chorizo 'buenos dias.' They're all heaped onto tigelle rolls, a sort of Italian flatbread. But you have to order before 10:30am (2:30pm on weekends).

Daikaya JAPANESE $

(202-589-1600; www.daikaya.com; 705 6th St NW; mains $12-14; 11:30am-10pm Sun & Mon, to 11pm Tue-Thu, to midnight Fri & Sat; M Gallery Pl) Daikaya offers two options. Downstairs it's a casual ramen-noodle shop, where locals swarm in and slurp with friends in the slick wooden booths. Upstairs it's a sake-pouring Japanese izakaya (tavern), with rice-bowl lunches and fishy small plates for dinner. Note the upstairs closes between lunch and dinner (ie between 2pm and 5pm).

★ Founding Farmers MODERN AMERICAN $$

(202-822-8783; www.wearefoundingfarmers.com; 1924 Pennsylvania Ave NW; mains $14-26; 11am-10pm Mon, 11am-11pm Tue-Thu, 11am-midnight Fri, 9am-midnight Sat, 9am-10pm Sun; ; M Foggy Bottom-GWU, Farragut West) A frosty decor of pickled goods in jars adorns this buzzy dining space. The look is a combination of rustic-cool and modern art that reflects the nature of the food: locally sourced, New American fare. Buttermilk fried chicken and waffles and zesty pork and lentil stew are a few of the favorites. The restaurant is located in the IMF building.

Rasika INDIAN $$

(202-637-1222; www.rasikarestaurant.com; 633 D St NW; mains $14-28; 11:30am-2:30pm

DON'T MISS

MARKET FARE

A couple of groovy markets offer good eats:

Union Market (www.unionmarketdc.com; 1309 5th St NE; ⏲11am-8pm Tue-Sun; Ⓜ NoMa) The cool crowd hobnobs here as foodie entrepreneurs sell their banana-ginger chocolates, herbed goat cheeses and smoked meats; pop-up restaurants use the space to try out concepts for everything from Taiwanese ramen to Indian dosas. Craft beers and coffee drinks help wash it all down. Tables dot the sunlit warehouse, and many locals make an afternoon of it, nibbling and reading. The market is about a half-mile walk from the NoMa Metro station in Northeast DC.

Eastern Market (www.easternmarket-dc.org; 225 7th St SE; ⏲7am-7pm Tue-Fri, to 6pm Sat, 9am-5pm Sun; Ⓜ Eastern Market) One of the icons of Capitol Hill, Eastern Market sprawls with delectable chow and good cheer. The covered arcade holds a bakery, dairy, butcher, blue-crab-and-shrimp company, and vendors of fresh produce. It's not that large…until the weekend, when artisans and farmers join the fun and the market spills out onto the street.

Mon-Fri, 5:30-10:30pm Mon-Thu, 5-11pm Fri & Sat; ✎; Ⓜ Archives) Rasika is as cutting edge as Indian food gets. The room resembles a Jaipur palace decorated by a flock of modernist art-gallery curators. Narangi duck is juicy, almost unctuous, and pleasantly nutty thanks to the addition of cashews; the deceptively simple *dal* (lentils) has the right kiss of sharp fenugreek. Vegans and vegetarians will feel a lot of love here.

Old Ebbitt Grill AMERICAN $$

(☎202-347-4800; www.ebbitt.com; 675 15th St NW; mains $12-22; ⏲7:30am-1am Mon-Fri, from 8:30am Sat & Sun; Ⓜ Metro Center) The Grill has occupied its prime, by the White House, real estate since 1846. Political players (and lots of tourists) pack into the brass and wood interior, the sound of their conversation rumbling across a dining room where thick burgers, crab cakes and fish-and-chip type fare are rotated out almost as quickly as the clientele. Pop in for a drink and oysters during happy hour.

★Central Michel Richard MODERN AMERICAN $$$

(☎202-626-0015; www.centralmichelrichard.com; 1001 Pennsylvania Ave NW; mains $19-34; ⏲11:30am-2:30pm Mon-Fri, 5-10:30pm Mon-Thu, 5-11pm Fri & Sat; Ⓜ Federal Triangle) Michel Richard is known for his high-end eating establishments in the District, but Central stands out as a special experience. It's aimed at hitting a comfort-food sweet spot. You're dining in a four-star bistro where the food is old-school favorites with a twist: lobster burgers, a sinfully complex meatloaf and fried chicken that redefines what fried chicken can be.

U Street, Shaw & Logan Circle

★Ben's Chili Bowl AMERICAN $

(www.benschilibowl.com; 1213 U St; mains $5-10; ⏲6am-2am Mon-Thu, 6am-4am Fri, 7am-4am Sat, 11am-midnight Sun; Ⓜ U St) Ben's is a DC institution. The main stock in trade is half-smokes, DC's meatier, smokier version of the hot dog, usually slathered in mustard, onions and the namesake chili. For nearly 60 years presidents, rock stars and Supreme Court justices have come in to indulge in the humble diner; but, despite the hype, Ben's remains a true neighborhood establishment. Cash only.

★Compass Rose INTERNATIONAL $$

(☎202-506-4765; www.compassrosedc.com; 1346 T St NW; small plates $10-15; ⏲5pm-2am Sun-Thu, to 3am Fri & Sat; Ⓜ U St) Compass Rose feels like a secret garden, set in a discreet townhouse a whisker from 14th St's buzz. The exposed brick walls, rustic wood decor and sky-blue ceiling give it a casually romantic air. The menu is a mash-up of global comfort foods, so dinner might entail, say, a Chilean *lomito* (pork sandwich), Lebanese *kefta* (ground lamb and spices) and Georgian *khachapuri* (buttery, cheese-filled bread).

Estadio SPANISH $$

(☎202-319-1404; www.estadio-dc.com; 1520 14th St NW; tapas $5-15; ⏲11:30am-2pm Fri-Sun; 5-10pm Mon-Thu, to 11pm Fri & Sat, to 9pm Sun; Ⓜ U St) Estadio buzzes with a low-lit, date-night vibe. The tapas menu (which is the focus) is as deep as an ocean trench. There are three variations of *Iberico* ham and a delicious foie gras, scrambled egg and truffle open-faced sandwich. Wash it down with some traditional *calimocho* (red wine and Coke). No reservations after 6pm, which usually means a wait at the bar.

Bistro Bohem EASTERN EUROPEAN $$

(202-735-5895; www.bistrobohem.com; 600 Florida Ave NW; mains $12-21; 5-11pm Mon-Thu, 5pm-2am Fri, 10am-2am Sat, 10am-11pm Sun; ; M Shaw-Howard U) Cozy Bistro Bohem is a community favorite for its rib-sticking Czech schnitzels, goulash and pilsners, served with a side of local art on the walls and occasional live jazz. By day the action shifts to adjoining Kafe Bohem, which opens at 7am (8am weekends) for espresso, pastries and flat sandwiches. The warm, bohemian environs make you swear you're in Prague.

Tico LATIN AMERICAN $$

(202-319-1400; www.ticodc.com; 1926 14th St NW; small plates $9-14; 4pm-midnight Sun-Thu, from 10am Fri & Sat; ; M U St) Loud, fun and clattering, Tico draws a young and artsy crowd for its nouveau tacos, small plates and 140 tequilas. Top honors go to the scallop ceviche with crispy rice, the Manchego cheese fritters and hibiscus margaritas. Vegetarians get some love from the edamame tacos, roasted cauliflower and other dishes. The bright-hued, mural-splashed eatery is mega popular, so make reservations.

★ **Le Diplomate** FRENCH $$$

(202-332-3333; www.lediplomatedc.com; 1601 14th St NW; mains $22-31; 5-10pm Mon & Tue, 5-11pm Wed & Thu, 5pm-midnight Fri, 9:30am-midnight Sat, 9:30am-10pm Sun; M U St) This charming French bistro is a relative newcomer, but it has skyrocketed to one of the hottest tables in town. DC celebrities galore cozy up in the leather banquettes and at the sidewalk tables. They come for an authentic slice of Paris, from the *coq au vin* (wine-braised chicken) and aromatic baguettes to the vintage curios and nudie photos decorating the bathrooms. Make reservations.

Adams Morgan

The area around 18th St and Columbia Rd NW is loaded with ethnic eateries and funky diners.

Diner AMERICAN $

(www.dinerdc.com; 2453 18th St NW; mains $9-17; 24hr; ; M Woodley Park-Zoo/Adams Morgan) The Diner serves hearty comfort food, any time of the day or night. It's ideal for wee-hour breakfast scarf-downs, weekend bloody-Mary brunches (if you don't mind crowds) or any time you want unfussy, well-prepared American fare. Omelets, fat pancakes, mac 'n' cheese, grilled Portobello sandwiches and burgers hit the tables with aplomb. It's a good spot for kids, too.

★ **Donburi** JAPANESE $

(202-629-1047; www.facebook.com/donburidc; 2438 18th St NW; mains $9-12; 11am-10pm; M Woodley Park-Zoo/Adams Morgan) Hole-in-the-wall Donburi has 15 seats at a wooden counter where you get a front-row view of the slicing, dicing chefs. *Donburi* means 'bowl' in Japanese, and that's what arrives steaming hot and filled with, say, panko-coated shrimp atop rice and blended with the house's sweet-and-savory sauce. It's a simple, authentic meal. There's often a line, but it moves quickly. No reservations.

It's located in the same building as the DC Arts Center.

Dupont Circle

★ **Afterwords Cafe** AMERICAN $$

(202-387-3825; www.kramers.com; 1517 Connecticut Ave; mains $15-21; 7:30am-1am Sun-Thu, 24hr Fri & Sat; M Dupont Circle) Attached to Kramerbooks, this buzzing spot is not your average bookstore cafe. The packed indoor tables, wee bar and outdoor patio overflow with good cheer. The menu features tasty bistro fare and an ample beer selection, making it a prime spot for happy hour, for brunch and at all hours on weekends (open 24 hours, baby!).

Duke's Grocery CAFE $$

(202-733-5623; www.dukesgrocery.com; 1513 17th St NW; mains $11-16; 5:30-10pm Mon, 8am-10pm Tue & Wed, to 1am Thu & Fri, 11am-1am Sat, to 10pm Sun; ; M Dupont Circle) 'The taste of East London in East Dupont' is the Duke's tagline, and that means black pudding and baked beans in the morning, spiced-lentil rotis in the afternoon and Brick Lane salt-beef sandwiches late night. Couples on low-maintenance dates and groups of chit-chatty friends angle for tables by the bay windows to people-watch. The genial vibe invites all-day lingering.

Bistrot du Coin FRENCH $$

(202-234-6969; www.bistrotducoin.com; 1738 Connecticut Ave NW; mains $14-24; 11:30am-11pm Sun-Wed, to 1am Thu-Sat; M Dupont Circle) The lively and much-loved Bistrot du Coin is a neighborhood favorite for roll-up-your-

TOP CAFES

Baked & Wired (☎202-333-2500; www.bakedandwired.com; 1052 Thomas Jefferson St NW; baked goods $3-6; ⏰7am-8pm Mon-Thu, to 9pm Fri, 8am-9pm Sat, 9am-8pm Sun; wi-fi) This cheery little Georgetown cafe whips up beautifully made coffees and delectable desserts; it's a fine spot to join students in both real and virtual chatter (free wi-fi, of course).

Ching Ching Cha (1063 Wisconsin Ave NW; teas $6-12; ⏰11am-9pm) An airy, Zen-like teahouse that feels a world away from the shopping mayhem of Georgetown's M Street. Stop in for a pot of rare tea (more than 70 varieties), or try the steamed dumplings, sweets and other little snacks.

Filter (www.filtercoffeehouse.com; 1726 20th St NW; ⏰7am-7pm Mon-Fri, 8am-7pm Sat & Sun; wi-fi; M Dupont Circle) On a quiet street in Dupont, Filter is a jewel-box-sized cafe with a tiny front patio, a hipsterish, laptop-toting crowd and, most importantly, great coffee. Those who seek caffeinated perfection can get a decent flat white here.

sleeves, working-class French fare. The kitchen sends out consistently good onion soup, classic *steak-frites* (grilled steak and French fries), cassoulet, open-face sandwiches and nine varieties of its famous *moules* (mussels). Regional wines from around the motherland accompany the food by the glass, carafe and bottle.

★Little Serow THAI $$$

(www.littleserow.com; 1511 17th St NW; fixed menu per person $45; ⏰5:30-10pm Tue-Thu, to 10:30pm Fri & Sat; M Dupont Circle) Little Serow has no phone, no reservations and no sign on the door. It only seats groups of four or fewer (larger parties will be separated) but, despite all this, people line up around the block. And what for? Superlative northern Thai cuisine. The single-option menu – which consists of six or so hot-spiced courses – changes by the week.

Komi FUSION $$$

(☎202-332-9200; www.komirestaurant.com; 1509 17th St NW; set menu $135; ⏰5-9:30pm Tue-Thu, to 10pm Fri & Sat; M Dupont Circle) There is an admirable simplicity to Komi's changing menu, which is rooted in Greece and influenced by everything – primarily genius. Suckling pig for two; scallops and truffles; roasted baby goat. Komi's fairytale of a dining space doesn't take groups larger than four, and you need to reserve way in advance – like, now.

Georgetown

★Chez Billy Sud FRENCH $$

(☎202-965-2606; www.chezbillysud.com; 1039 31st St NW; mains $17-29; ⏰11:30am-2pm Tue-Fri, 11am-2pm Sat & Sun, 5-10pm Tue-Thu & Sun, 5-11pm Fri & Sat; wine list) An endearing little bistro tucked away on a residential block, Billy's mint-green walls, gilt mirrors and wee marble bar exude laid-back elegance. Mustachioed servers bring baskets of warm bread to the white-linen–clothed tables, along with crackling pork and pistachio sausage, golden trout, tuna nicoise salad and plump cream puffs.

Martin's Tavern AMERICAN $$

(☎202-333-7370; www.martins-tavern.com; 1264 Wisconsin Ave NW; mains $17-32; ⏰11am-1:30am Mon-Thu, 11am-2:30am Fri, 9am-2:30am Sat, 8am-1:30am Sun) John F Kennedy proposed to Jackie in booth three at Georgetown's oldest saloon, and if you're thinking of popping the question there today, the attentive waitstaff keep the champagne chilled for that very reason. With an old-English country scene, including the requisite fox-and-hound hunting prints on the wall, this DC institution serves unfussy classics such thick burgers, crab cakes and icy-cold beers.

Upper Northwest DC

★Comet Ping Pong PIZZA $

(www.cometpingpong.com; 5037 Connecticut Ave NW; pizzas $12-15; ⏰5-10pm Mon-Thu, 11:30am-11pm Fri & Sat, to 10pm Sun; family-friendly; M Van Ness-UDC) Proving that DC is more than a city of suits and corporate offices, Comet Ping Pong offers a fun and festive counterpoint to the marble city, with its ping-pong tables, industrial chic interior and delicious thin-crust pizzas cooked up in a wood-burning oven.

★Macon FUSION $$

(☎202-248-7807; www.maconbistro.com; 5520 Connecticut Ave NW; mains $22-28; ⏰5-10pm Tue-Thu, to 11pm Fri & Sat, 10am-2pm & 5-10pm Sun; M Friendship Heights then bus E2) Macon,

LOCAL KNOWLEDGE

EAT STREETS

14th St NW (Logan Circle) DC's most happening road: an explosion of hot-chef bites and bars.

18th St NW (Adams Morgan) Korean, West African, Japanese and Latin mash-up, plus late-night snacks.

11th St NW (Columbia Heights) Ever-growing scene of hipster cafes and edgy gastropubs.

8th St SE (Capitol Hill) Known as Barracks Row, it's the locals' favorite for welcoming comfort-food-type spots.

H St NE (Capitol Hill) Hip strip of pie cafes, noodle shops and foodie pubs.

9th St NW (Shaw) Aka 'Little Ethiopia', it has all the wats and injera you can handle.

Georgia, meets Mâcon, France, in this wild mash-up of delectable southern cooking with creative European accents. The space is always buzzing, as a local, well-dressed crowd comes to feast on fried catfish with smoked aioli, seared chicken breast with almondine sauce, and piping hot biscuits served with pepper jelly. Creative cocktails, refreshing microbrews and an appealing all-French wine list round out the menu.

Columbia Heights

Hipsters and Latino immigrants share the sidewalks in this unassuming neighborhood, set a short distance from U St.

Maple ITALIAN **$$**
(202-588-7442; www.dc-maple.com; 3418 11th St NW; mains $14-22; 5:30pm-midnight Mon-Thu, 5pm-1am Fri & Sat, 11am-11pm Sun; M Columbia Heights) At snug Maple, ladies in thrifty dresses and black tights fork into rich pasta dishes next to guys clad in T-shirts and tattoo sleeves on a reclaimed wood bar. House-made limoncello, Italian craft beers and unusual wine varietals also move across the lengthy slab (the wood type, incidentally, is what gives the venue its name).

Kangaroo Boxing Club AMERICAN **$$**
(KBC; 202-505-4522; www.kangaroodc.com; 3410 11th St NW; mains $13-18; 5-11pm Mon-Thu, 5pm-1:30am Fri, 10am-1:30am Sat, 10am-10pm Sun; M Columbia Heights) The gastropub concept – but a hip, laid-back, Brooklyn-esque gastropub – is all the rage among DC's hip young things and the restaurateurs who cater to them. Enter the KBC: it has a quirky theme (vintage boxing), a delicious menu (burgers, barbecue, sweet spoon bread and loaded mac 'n' cheese and the like) and a deep beer menu.

Drinking & Nightlife

See the free alternative weekly *Washington City Paper* (www.washingtoncitypaper.com) for comprehensive listings. DC is a big happy-hour town – practically all bars have some sort of drink special for a few hours between 4pm and 7pm.

Capitol Hill

Little Miss Whiskey's Golden Dollar BAR
(www.littlemisswhiskeys.com; 1104 H St NE; 5pm-2am; X2 from Union Station) If Alice had returned from Wonderland so traumatized by her near-beheading that she needed a stiff drink, we imagine she'd pop down to Little Miss Whiskey's. She'd love the whimsical-meets-dark-nightmares decor. And she'd probably have fun with the club kids partying on the upstairs dance floor on weekends. She'd also adore the weirdly fantastic back patio.

★ **Bluejacket Brewery** BREWERY
(202-524-4862; www.bluejacketdc.com; 300 Tingey St SE; 11am-1am Sun-Thu, to 2am Fri & Sat; M Navy Yard) Beer lovers' heads will explode in Bluejacket. Pull up a stool at the mod-industrial bar, gaze at the silvery tanks bubbling up the ambitious brews, then make the hard decision about which of the 25 tap beers you want to try. A dry-hopped kolsch? Sweet-spiced stout? A cask-aged farmhouse ale? Four-ounce tasting pours help with decision-making.

H Street Country Club BAR
(www.thehstreetcountryclub.com; 1335 H St NE; 5pm-1am Mon-Thu, 4pm-3am Fri, 11am-3am Sat, 11am-1am Sun; X2 from Union Station) The Country Club is two levels of great. The bottom floor is packed with pool tables, skeeball and shuffleboard, while the top contains its own mini-golf course ($7 to play) done up to resemble a tour of the city on a small scale. You putt-putt past a trio of Lego lobbyists, through Beltway traffic snarls and past a King Kong–clad Washington Monument.

Granville Moore's PUB
(www.granvillemoores.com; 1238 H St NE; ⏲5pm-midnight Mon-Thu, 5pm-3am Fri, 11am-3am Sat, 11am-midnight Sun; X2 from Union Station) Besides being one of DC's best places to grab frites and a steak sandwich, Granville Moore's has an extensive Belgian beer menu that should satisfy any fan of low-country boozing. With raw, wooden fixtures and walls that look as if they were made from daub and mud, the interior resembles a medieval barracks. The fireside setting is ideal on a winter's eve.

Tune Inn BAR
(331 Pennsylvania Ave SE; mains $7-14; ⏲8am-2am Sun-Fri, to 3am Sat; Ⓜ Capitol South, Eastern Market) Dive bar Tune Inn has been around for decades and is where the neighborhood's older residents come to knock back Budweisers. The mounted deer heads and antler chandelier set the mood, as greasy-spoon grub and all-day breakfasts get scarfed in the vinyl-backed booths.

U Street, Shaw & Logan Circle

★ **Right Proper Brewing Co** BREWERY
(www.rightproperbrewery.com; 624 T St NW; ⏲5-11pm Tue-Thu, to midnight Fri & Sat, to 10pm Sun; Ⓜ Shaw-Howard U) As if the artwork – a chalked mural of the National Zoo's giant pandas with laser eyes destroying downtown DC – wasn't enough, Right Proper Brewing Co makes sublime ales in a building where Duke Ellington used to play pool. It's the Shaw district's neighborhood clubhouse, a big, sunny space filled with folks gabbing at reclaimed wood tables.

Churchkey BAR
(www.churchkeydc.com; 1337 14th St NW; ⏲4pm-1am Mon-Thu, 4pm-2am Fri, noon-2am Sat, noon-1am Sun; Ⓜ McPherson Sq) Coppery, mod-industrial Churchkey glows with hipness. Fifty beers flow from the taps, including five brain-walloping, cask-aged ales. If none of those please you, another 500 types of brew are available by the bottle (including gluten-free suds). Churchkey is the upstairs counterpart to Birch & Barley, a popular nouveau comfort-food restaurant, and you can order much of its menu at the bar.

Cork Wine Bar WINE BAR
(www.corkdc.com; 1720 14th St NW; ⏲5pm-midnight Tue & Wed, 5pm-1am Thu-Sat, 11am-3pm & 5-10pm Sun; Ⓜ U St) This dark 'n' cozy wine bar manages to come off as foodie magnet and friendly neighborhood hangout all at once, which is a feat. Around 50 smart wines are available by the glass and 160 types by the bottle. Accompanying nibbles include cheese and charcuterie platters, as well as small plates such as chicken livers on marmalade-dolloped rosemary bruschetta.

Dacha Beer Garden BEER GARDEN
(www.dachadc.com; 1600 7th St NW; ⏲4-10:30pm Mon-Thu, 4pm-midnight Fri, noon-midnight Sat, noon-10:30pm Sun; Ⓜ Shaw-Howard U) Happiness reigns in Dacha's freewheeling beer garden. Kids and dogs bound around the picnic tables, while adults hoist glass boots filled with German brews. When the weather gets nippy, staff bring heaters and blankets and stoke the fire pit. And it all takes place under the sultry gaze of Elizabeth Taylor (or a mural of her, which sprawls across the back wall).

U Street Music Hall CLUB
(www.ustreetmusichall.com; 1115 U St NW; ⏲hours vary; Ⓜ U St) FREE This is the spot to get your groove on sans the VIP/bottle-service crowd. Two local DJs own and operate the basement club. It looks like a no-frills rock bar, but it has a pro sound system, cork-cushioned dance floor and other accoutrements of a serious dance club. Alternative bands also thrash a couple of nights per week to keep it fresh.

Dupont Circle & Adams Morgan

★ **Dan's Cafe** BAR
(2315 18th St NW; ⏲7pm-2am Tue-Thu, to 3am Fri & Sat; Ⓜ Woodley Park-Zoo/Adams Morgan) This is one of DC's great dive bars. The interior looks sort of like an evil Elks Club, all unironically old-school 'art,' cheap paneling and dim lights barely illuminating the unapologetic slumminess. It's famed for its

LOCAL KNOWLEDGE

BEER TOWN

Washington is serious about beer, and even brews much its own delicious stuff. That trend started in 2009, when DC Brau became the District's first brewery to launch in more than 50 years (several more beer makers followed). As you drink around town, keep an eye out for local concoctions from Chocolate City, 3 Stars, Atlas Brew Works, Hellbender and Lost Rhino (from northern Virginia).

GAY & LESBIAN WASHINGTON, DC

The community concentrates in Dupont Circle, but U St, Shaw, Capitol Hill and Logan Circle also have lots of gay-friendly businesses. The free weeklies *Washington Blade* and *Metro Weekly* have the nightlife lowdown.

Cobalt (www.cobaltdc.com; 1639 R St NW; 5pm-2am; Dupont Circle) Featuring lots of hair product and faux-tanned gym bodies, Cobalt tends to gather a better-dressed late-20s-to-30-something crowd who come for fun (and loud!) dance parties throughout the week.

Nellie's (www.nelliessportsbar.com; 900 U St NW; 5pm-1am Mon-Thu, from 3pm Fri, from 11am Sat & Sun; Shaw-Howard U) The vibe here is low-key; Nellie's is a good place to hunker down among a friendly crowd for tasty bar bites, event nights (including karaoke Tuesdays) and early-evening drink specials.

JR's (www.jrsbar-dc.com; 1519 17th St NW; 4pm-2am Mon-Thu, 4pm-3am Fri, 1pm-3am Sat, 1pm-2am Sun; Dupont Circle) This popular gay hangout is a great spot for happy hour and is packed more often than not. Embarrassing show-tunes karaoke is great fun on Monday nights.

whopping, mix-it-yourself drinks, where you get a ketchup-type squirt bottle of booze, a can of soda and bucket of ice for barely $20. Cash only.

Bar Charley BAR

(www.barcharley.com; 1825 18th St NW; 5pm-12:30am Mon-Thu, 4pm-1:30am Fri, 10am-1:30am Sat, 10am-12:30am Sun; Dupont Circle) Bar Charley draws a mixed crowd from the neighborhood – young, old, gay and straight. They come for groovy cocktails sloshing in vintage glassware and ceramic tiki mugs, served at very reasonable prices by DC standards. Try the gin and gingery Suffering Bastard. The beer list isn't huge, but it is thoughtfully chosen with some wild ales. Around 60 wines are available, too.

Tabard Inn Bar BAR

(www.tabardinn.com; 1739 N St NW; 11:30am-1:30am Mon-Fri, from 10:30am Sat & Sun; Dupont Circle) The Tabard Inn Bar is in a hotel, but plenty of locals come to swirl an Old Fashioned or gin and tonic in the wood-beamed, lodge-like lounge. On warm nights, maneuver for an outdoor table on the ivy-clad patio.

Georgetown & White House Area

Tombs PUB

(www.tombs.com; 1226 36th St NW; 11:30am-1:30am Mon-Thu, to 2:30am Fri & Sat, 9:30am-1:30am Sun) Every college of a certain pedigree has 'that' bar – the one where faculty and students alike sip pints under athletic regalia of the old school. The Tombs is Georgetown's contribution to the genre. If it looks familiar, think back to the '80s: the subterranean pub was one of the settings for the film *St Elmo's Fire*.

Round Robin BAR

(1401 Pennsylvania Ave NW, Willard InterContinental Hotel; noon-1am Mon-Sat, to midnight Sun; Metro Center) Dispensing drinks since 1850, the bar at the Willard hotel is one of DC's most storied watering holes. The small, circular space is done up in Gilded Age accents, all dark wood and velvet-green walls, and while it's touristy, you'll still see officials here likely determining your latest tax hike over a mint julep or single-malt Scotch.

Columbia Heights

★Room 11 CAFE

(www.room11dc.com; 3234 11th St NW; 8am-1am Sun-Thu, to 2am Fri & Sat; Columbia Heights) Room 11 isn't much bigger than an ambitious living room, and as such it can get pretty jammed. On the plus side, everyone is friendly, the intimacy is warmly inviting on chilly winter nights and there's a spacious outdoor area for when it gets too hot inside. The low-key crowd sips excellent wines hand-selected by the management and whiz-bang cocktails.

Wonderland Ballroom BAR

(www.thewonderlandballroom.com; 1101 Kenyon St NW; 5pm-2am Mon-Thu, 4pm-3am Fri, 11am-3pm Sat, 10am-2am Sun; ; Columbia Heights) Wonderland embodies the edgy, eccentric Columbia Heights vibe to perfection. The interior is decked out in vintage signs and found objects to the point it could be a folk-art museum, the outdoor patio is a good spot for meeting strangers, and the upstairs dance floor is a good place to take said strangers for a bit of bump and grind.

☆ Entertainment

Live Music

Black Cat LIVE MUSIC

(www.blackcatdc.com; 1811 14th St NW; M U St) A pillar of DC's rock and indie scene since the 1990s, the battered Black Cat has hosted all the greats of years past (White Stripes, the Strokes, Arcade Fire and others). If you don't want to pony up for $20-a-ticket bands on the upstairs main stage (or the smaller Backstage below), head to the Red Room for jukebox, pool and strong cocktails.

9:30 Club LIVE MUSIC

(www.930.com; 815 V St NW; admission from $10; M U St) This place, which can pack 1200 people into a surprisingly compact venue, is the granddaddy of the live music scene in DC. Pretty much every big name that comes through town ends up on this stage, and a concert here is the first-gig memory of many a DC-area teenager. Headliners usually take the stage between 10:30pm and 11:30pm.

Bohemian Caverns JAZZ

(www.bohemiancaverns.com; 2001 11th St NW; admission $7-22; ⏲7pm-midnight Mon-Thu, 7:30pm-2am Fri & Sat, 6pm-midnight Sun; M U St) Back in the day, Bohemian Caverns hosted the likes of Miles Davis, John Coltrane and Duke Ellington. Today you'll find a mix of youthful renegades and soulful legends. Monday night's swingin' house band draws an all-ages crowd.

Performing Arts

Kennedy Center PERFORMING ARTS

(☎202-467-4600; www.kennedy-center.org; 2700 F St NW; M Foggy Bottom-GWU) Sprawled on 17 acres along the Potomac River, the magnificent Kennedy Center hosts a staggering array of performances – more than 2000 each year among its multiple venues, including the Concert Hall (home to the National Symphony) and Opera House (home to the National Opera). A free shuttle bus runs to and from the Metro station every 15 minutes from 9:45am (noon on Sunday) to midnight.

Shakespeare Theatre Company THEATER

(☎202-547-1122; www.shakespearetheatre.org; 450 7th St NW; M Archives) The nation's foremost Shakespeare company presents masterful works by the bard, as well as plays by George Bernard Shaw, Oscar Wilde, Ibsen, Eugene O'Neill and other greats. The season spans about a half-dozen productions annually, plus a free summer Shakespeare series on-site for two weeks in late August.

Studio Theatre THEATER

(www.studiotheatre.org; 1501 14th St NW; M Dupont Circle) The contemporary four-theater complex has been staging Pulitzer Prize-winning and premiere plays for more than 35 years. It cultivates a lot of local actors.

Sports

★ **Washington Nationals** BASEBALL

(www.nationals.com; 1500 S Capitol St SE; 📶; M Navy Yard) The major-league Nats play baseball at **Nationals Park** (www.nationals.com; 1500 S Capitol St SE; M Navy Yard) beside the Anacostia River. Don't miss the mid-fourth-inning 'Racing Presidents' – an odd foot race between giant-headed caricatures of George Washington, Abraham Lincoln, Thomas Jefferson, Teddy Roosevelt and William Taft. The stadium itself is spiffy, and hip eateries and mod Yards Park have cropped up around it as the area gentrifies.

Washington Redskins FOOTBALL

(☎301-276-6800; www.redskins.com; 1600 Fedex Way, Landover, MD; M Morgan Blvd) Washington's NFL team, the Redskins, plays September through January at FedEx Field. The team has experienced a lot of controversy recently, and not only because of its woeful play. Many groups have criticized the Redskins' name and logo as insulting to Native Americans. The US Patent and Trademark Office agreed, and revoked the team's trademark.

Washington Capitals HOCKEY

(http://capitals.nhl.com; 601 F St NW; M Gallery Pl) Washington's rough-and-tumble pro hockey team skates at the Verizon Center from October to April. Tickets start from around $40.

ℹ KENNEDY CENTER FREEBIES

Don't have the dough for a big-ticket show? No worries. Each evening the Kennedy Center's **Millennium Stage** (www.kennedy-center.org/millennium; Kennedy Center; M Foggy Bottom-GWU) puts on a first-rate music or dance performance at 6pm in the Grand Foyer. The cost is absolutely nada. Check the website to see who's playing.

Washington Wizards BASKETBALL
(www.nba.com/wizards; 601 F St NW; Ⓜ Gallery Pl) Washington's winning pro basketball team plays at the Verizon Center from October through April. The lowest-price tickets are around $30 for the nosebleed section, and the cost goes way up from there.

Orientation

Remember: lettered streets go east–west, and numbered streets, north–south. On top of that the city is divided into four quadrants with identical addresses in different divisions – F and 14th NW puts you near the White House, while F and 14th NE puts you near Rosedale Playground.

Information

Cultural Tourism DC (www.culturaltourismdc.org) Offers a large range of DIY neighborhood walking tours.

Destination DC (☎202-789-7000; www.washington.org) DC's official tourism site, with the mother lode of online information.

George Washington University Hospital (☎202-715-4000; 900 23rd St NW; Ⓜ Foggy Bottom-GWU)

Washington City Paper (www.washingtoncitypaper.com) Free edgy weekly with entertainment and dining listings.

Washington Post (www.washingtonpost.com) Respected daily city (and national) paper. Its tabloid-format daily *Express* is free.

Getting There & Away

AIR

Ronald Reagan Washington National Airport (DCA; www.metwashairports.com) DC's smaller airport, located 4.5 miles south of DC in Arlington, VA.

Dulles International Airport (IAD; www.metwashairports.com) Found 26 miles west of DC, in Virginia. It's the larger airport, and handles most international flights.

Baltimore/Washington International Thurgood Marshall Airport (BWI; ☎410-859-7111; www.bwiairport.com) Set 30 miles northeast, in Maryland. It's a Southwest Airlines hub, and often has cheaper flights.

BUS

Cheap bus services to and from Washington abound. Most charge around $25 for a one-way trip to NYC, which takes four to five hours. Tickets usually need to be bought online.

BoltBus (☎877-265-8287; www.boltbus.com; 50 Massachusetts Ave NE; 📶) The best of the budget options for NYC trips; it uses Union Station as its terminal.

BestBus (☎202-332-2691; www.bestbus.com; 20th St & Massachusetts Ave NW; 📶) Several trips to/from NYC daily. The main bus stop is by Dupont Circle; there's another at Union Station.

Greyhound (☎202-589-5141; www.greyhound.com; 50 Massachusetts Ave NE) Provides nationwide service. The terminal is at Union Station.

Megabus (☎877-462-6342; http://us.megabus.com; 50 Massachusetts Ave NE; 📶) Offers the most trips to NYC (more than 20 per day), as well as other east-coast cities; arrives at/departs from Union Station.

Washington Deluxe (☎866-287-6932; www.washny.com; 1610 Connecticut St NW; 📶) Good express service to/from NYC. It has stops at both Dupont Circle and Union Station.

TRAIN

The magnificent beaux-arts Union Station is the city's rail hub. Trains depart at least once per hour for major east coast cities, including New York City (3½ hours) and Boston (six to eight hours).

Amtrak (☎800-872-7245; www.amtrak.com) Trains depart for nationwide destinations, including New York City (3½ hours), Chicago (18 hours), Miami (24 hours) and Richmond, VA (three hours).

MARC (Maryland Rail Commuter; www.mta.maryland.gov) This regional rail service for the Washington, DC–Baltimore metro area runs trains frequently to Baltimore and other Maryland towns; also goes to Harpers Ferry, WV.

Getting Around

TO/FROM THE AIRPORT

Ronald Reagan Washington National Airport Has its own Metro station. Trains (around $2.50) depart every 10 minutes or so between 5am and midnight (to 3am Friday and Saturday) and reach downtown in 20 minutes. Taxis cost $13 to $22 and take 10 to 30 minutes.

Baltimore/Washington International Thurgood Marshall Airport Both local MARC trains and Amtrak travel from the airport to DC's Union Station. Trains leave once or twice per hour, but there's no service after 9:30pm (and limited service on weekends). It takes 30 to 40 minutes; fares start at $6. Or consider the B30 bus, which runs to the Greenbelt Metro station (75 minutes, $10.50 for total bus/Metro fare).

Washington Dulles International Airport The Metro Silver Line is slated to reach Dulles in 2018. In the meantime, options include taxis (30 to 60 minutes, $62 to $73), the Metrobus 5A and the Washington Flyer.

Metrobus 5A (www.wmata.com) Runs every 30 to 40 minutes from Dulles to the Rosslyn Metro station (Blue, Orange and Silver Lines) and on to central DC (L'Enfant Plaza) between 5:50am (6:30am weekends) and 11:35pm. Total time to the center is about an hour; total bus/Metro fare is about $9.

Washington Flyer (☎888-927-4359; www.washfly.com) The company's Silver Line Express bus runs every 15 to 20 minutes from Dulles airport (main terminal, arrivals level door 4) to the Wiehle-Reston East Metro station between 6am and 10:40pm (from 7:45am weekends). Total time to DC's center is 60 to 75 minutes, total bus-Metro cost around $11.

PUBLIC TRANSPORTATION

The system is a mix of Metro trains (subway) and buses, but the Metro is the main way to go. Buy a rechargeable SmarTrip card at any station. It costs $10, with $8 of that stored for fares. You can add value as needed. Without a SmarTrip card, each ride is subject to a $1 surcharge for using a disposable fare card. Use the card to enter *and* exit station turnstiles. The card is also usable on buses. Another option: buy an unlimited-ride day pass for $14.50.

Metrorail (☎202-637-7000; www.wmata.com) The Metro will get you to most sights, hotels and business districts, and to the Maryland and Virginia suburbs. Trains start running at 5am Monday through Friday (from 7am on weekends); the last service is around midnight Sunday through Thursday and 3am on Friday and Saturday. Machines inside stations sell computerized fare cards; fares are based on distance traveled.

DC Circulator (www.dccirculator.com; fare $1) Red Circulator buses run along handy local routes, including Union Station to/from the Mall (looping by all major museums and memorials), Union Station to/from Georgetown (via K St), Dupont Circle to/from Georgetown (via M St), and the White House area to/from Adams Morgan (via 14th St). Buses operate from roughly 7am to 9pm weekdays (to midnight or so on weekends).

Metrobus (www.wmata.com; fare $1.75) Operates clean, efficient buses throughout the city and suburbs, typically from early morning until late evening.

TAXI

Taxis are relatively easy to find (less so at night), but costly. **DC Yellow Cab** (☎202-544-1212) is reliable. The rideshare company Uber is used more in the District.

MARYLAND

Maryland is often described as 'America in Miniature,' and for good reason: this small state possesses all of the best bits of the country, from the Appalachian Mountains in the west to sandy white beaches in the east. A blend of Northern streetwise and Southern down-home gives this most osmotic of border states an appealing identity crisis. Its main city, Baltimore, is a sharp, demanding port town; the Eastern Shore jumbles art-and-antique-minded city refugees and working fisherfolk; while the DC suburbs are packed with government and office workers seeking green space, and the poor seeking lower rents. Yet it all somehow works – scrumptious blue crabs, Natty Boh beer and lovely Chesapeake country being the glue that binds all. This is also an extremely diverse and progressive state, and was one of the first in the country to legalize gay marriage.

History

George Calvert established Maryland as a refuge for persecuted English Catholics in 1634 when he purchased St Mary's City from the local Piscataway tribespeople, with whom he initially tried to coexist. Puritan refugees drove both Piscataway and Catholics from control and shifted power to Annapolis; their harassment of Catholics produced the Tolerance Act, a flawed but progressive law that allowed freedom of any (Christian) worship in Maryland – a North American first.

That commitment to diversity has always characterized this state, despite a mixed record on slavery. Although state loyalties were split during the Civil War, a Confederate invasion was halted here in 1862 at Antietam. Following the war, Maryland harnessed its black, white and immigrant work force, splitting the economy between Baltimore's industry and shipping, and the later need for services in Washington, DC. Today the answer to 'What makes a Marylander?' is 'all of the above': the state mixes rich, poor, the foreign-born, urban sophisticates and rural villages like few other states do.

Baltimore

Once among the most important port towns in America, Baltimore – or 'Bawlmer' to locals – is a city of contradictions. On one hand it remains something of an ugly duckling – a defiant, working-class, gritty city still tied to its nautical past. But in recent years Baltimore has begun to grow into a swan – or, more accurately, gotten better at showing the world the swan that was always there, in the form of world-class museums, trendy shops, ethnic restaurants, boutique hotels, culture and sports. 'B'more' (another nickname) does this all with a twinkle in the eye and a wisecrack on the lips; this quirky city spawned Billie Holiday and John Waters. Yet it remains intrinsically tied to the water, from the Disney-fied Inner Harbor and cobblestoned streets of portside Fell's Point to the shores of Fort McHenry, birthplace of America's national anthem, 'The Star-Spangled Banner.' There's an intense, sincere friendliness to this burg, which is why Baltimore lives up to its final, most accurate nickname: 'Charm City.'

Sights & Activities

Harborplace & Inner Harbor

This is where most tourists start and, unfortunately, end their Baltimore sightseeing. The Inner Harbor is a big, gleaming waterfront-renewal project of shiny glass, air-conditioned malls and flashy bars that manages to capture the maritime heart of this city, albeit in a safe-for-the-family kinda way. But it's also just the tip of Baltimore's iceberg.

National Aquarium AQUARIUM
(☎410-576-3833; www.aqua.org; 501 E Pratt St, Piers 3 & 4; adult/child $35/22; ⏰9am-5pm Sun-Thu, to 8pm Fri, to 6pm Sat) Standing seven stories high and capped by a glass pyramid, this is widely considered to be the best aquarium in America, with 17,000 creatures (over 750 species), a rooftop rainforest, a central ray pool and a multistory shark tank. There's also a reconstruction of the Umbrawarra Gorge in Australia's Northern Territory, complete with 35ft waterfall, rocky cliffs and free-roaming birds and lizards.

The largest exhibit contains eight bottlenose dolphins kept in captivity, though at press time the aquarium was exploring the possibility of retiring them to an oceanside sanctuary (freeing them in the wild is not an option, since they lack survival skills). Kids will love the 4-D Immersion Theater (admission costs an additional $5). There are loads of unique, behind-the-scenes tours, as well as dolphin and shark sleepovers. Go on weekdays (right at opening time) to beat the crowds.

Baltimore Maritime Museum MUSEUM
(☎410-539-1797; www.historicships.org; 301 E Pratt St, Piers 3 & 5; adult 1/2/4 ships $11/14/18, child $5/6/7; ⏰10am-4:30pm) Ship-lovers can take a tour through four historic ships: a Coast Guard cutter that saw action in Pearl Harbor, a 1930 lightship, a submarine active in WWII and the **USS Constellation** – one of the last sail-powered warships built (in 1797) by the US Navy. Admission to the 1856 Seven Foot Knoll Lighthouse, on Pier 5, is free.

Downtown & Little Italy

You can easily walk from downtown Baltimore to Little Italy, but follow the delineated path: there's a rough housing project along the way.

National Great Blacks in Wax Museum MUSEUM
(☎410-563-3404; www.greatblacksinwax.org; 1601 E North Ave; adult/child $13/11; ⏰9am-6pm Mon-Sat, noon-6pm Sun Feb & Jul-Aug, closed Mon rest of year) This excellent African American history museum has exhibits on Frederick Douglass, Jackie Robinson, Martin Luther King Jr and Barack Obama, as well as lesser-known figures, such as explorer Matthew Henson. The

MARYLAND FACTS

Nickname The Old Line State, the Free State

Population 5.8 million

Area 12,407 sq miles

Capital city Annapolis (population 39,000)

Other cities Baltimore (621,000), Frederick (66,000), Hagerstown (40,000), Salisbury (30,500)

Sales tax 6%

Birthplace of Abolitionist Frederick Douglass (1818–95), baseball great Babe Ruth (1895–1948), actor David Hasselhoff (b 1952), author Tom Clancy (b 1947), swimmer Michael Phelps (b 1985)

Home of 'The Star-Spangled Banner,' Baltimore Orioles, TV crime shows *The Wire* and *Homicide: Life on the Street*

Politics Staunch Democrats

Famous for Blue crabs, lacrosse, Chesapeake Bay

State sport Jousting

Driving distances Baltimore to Annapolis 29 miles; Baltimore to Ocean City 147 miles

museum also covers slavery, the Jim Crow era and African leaders – all told in surreal fashion through Madame Tussaud–style wax figures.

Star-Spangled Banner Flag House & 1812 Museum MUSEUM
(410-837-1793; www.flaghouse.org; 844 E Pratt St; adult/child $8/6; 10am-4pm Tue-Sat;) This historic home, built in 1793, is where Mary Pickersgill sewed the gigantic flag that inspired America's national anthem. Costumed interpreters and 19th-century artifacts transport visitors back in time to dark days during the War of 1812; there's also a hands-on discovery gallery for kids.

Jewish Museum of Maryland MUSEUM
(410-732-6400; www.jewishmuseummd.org; 15 Lloyd St; adult/student/child $8/4/3; 10am-5pm Sun-Thu) Maryland has traditionally been home to one of the largest, most active Jewish communities in the country, and this is a fine place to explore their experience in America. It also houses two wonderfully preserved historical synagogues. Call or go online for the scheduled times of synagogue tours.

Edgar Allan Poe House & Museum MUSEUM
(410-396-7932; www.poeinbaltimore.org; 203 N Amity St; adult/student/child $5/4/free; 11am-4pm Sat & Sun late May-Dec) Home to Baltimore's most famous adopted son from 1832 to 1835, it was here that the macabre poet and writer first found fame after winning a $50 short-story contest. After moving around, Poe later returned to Baltimore in 1849, where he died under mysterious circumstances. His grave can be found in nearby Westminster Cemetery.

Mt Vernon

★Walters Art Museum MUSEUM
(410-547-9000; www.thewalters.org; 600 N Charles St; 10am-5pm Wed-Sun, to 9pm Thu) FREE Don't pass up this excellent, eclectic gallery: it spans more than 55 centuries, from ancient to contemporary, with excellent displays of Asian treasures, rare and ornate manuscripts and books, and a comprehensive French paintings collection.

Washington Monument MONUMENT
(mvpconservancy.org; 699 Washington Pl; suggested donation $5; 4-9pm Thu, noon-5pm Fri-Sun) For the best views of Baltimore, climb the 228 steps of the 178ft-tall Doric column dedicated to America's Founding Father, George Washington. It was designed by Robert Mills, who also created DC's Washington Monument, and is looking better than ever after a $6 million restoration project. The ground floor contains a museum about Washington's life. To climb the monument, call or email ahead.

Maryland Historical Society MUSEUM
(www.mdhs.org; 201 W Monument St; adult/child $9/6; 10am-5pm Wed-Sat, noon-5pm Sun) With more than 350,000 objects and seven million books and documents, this is one of the largest collections of Americana in the world. Highlights include one of three surviving Revolutionary War officer's uniforms, photographs from the 1930s Civil Rights movement in Baltimore and Francis Scott Key's original manuscript of 'the Star-Spangled Banner.' There are often excellent temporary exhibits that explore the role of Baltimore residents in historic events.

Federal Hill & Around

On a bluff overlooking the harbor, **Federal Hill Park** lends its name to the comfortable neighborhood that's set around Cross St Market and comes alive after sundown.

★American Visionary Art Museum MUSEUM
(AVAM; 410-244-1900; www.avam.org; 800 Key Hwy; adult/child $16/10; 10am-6pm Tue-Sun) Housing a jaw-dropping collection of self-taught (or 'outsider' art), AVAM is a celebration of unbridled creativity utterly free of arts-scene pretension. You'll find broken-mirror collages, homemade robots and flying apparatuses, elaborately sculptural works made of needlepoint, and gigantic model ships painstakingly created from matchsticks.

Fort McHenry National Monument & Historic Shrine HISTORIC SITE
(410-962-4290; 2400 E Fort Ave; adult/child $7/free; 9am-5pm) On September 13 and 14, 1814, this star-shaped fort successfully repelled a British Navy attack during the Battle of Baltimore. After a long night of bombs bursting in the air, prisoner Francis Scott Key saw, 'by dawn's early light,' the tattered flag still waving, inspiring him to pen 'The Star-Spangled Banner,' which was set to the tune of a popular drinking song.

WORTH A TRIP

SCENIC DRIVE: MARITIME MARYLAND

Maryland and Chesapeake Bay have always been inextricable, but there are some places where the old-fashioned way of life on the bay seems to have changed little over the passing centuries.

About 150 miles south of Baltimore, at the edge of the Eastern Shore, is **Crisfield**, the top working water town in Maryland. Get visiting details at the **J Millard Tawes Historical Museum** (☎410-968-2501; www.crisfieldheritagefoundation.org/museum; 3 Ninth St; adult/child $3/1; ⏲10am-4pm Mon-Sat), which doubles as a visitor center. Any seafood you eat will be first-rate, but for a true Shore experience, **Watermen's Inn** (☎410-968-2119; 901 W Main St; mains $12-25; ⏲11am-8pm Thu & Sun, to 9pm Fri & Sat, closed Mon-Wed) is legendary; in an unpretentious setting you can feast on local catch from an ever-changing menu. You can find local waterfolk at their favorite hangout – **Gordon's Confectionery** (831 W Main St) – having 4am coffee before shipping off to check and set traps.

From here you can leave your car and take a boat to **Smith Island** (www.visitsmithisland.com), the only offshore settlement in the state. Settled by fisherfolk from the English West Country some 400 years ago, the island's tiny population still speak with what linguists reckon is the closest thing to a 17th-century Cornish accent.

We'll be frank: this is more of a dying fishing town than charming tourist attraction, although there are B&Bs and restaurants (check the website for details). But it's also a last link to the state's past, so if you approach Smith Island as such, you may appreciate the limited amenities on offer. These notably include paddling through miles of some of the most pristine marshland on the eastern seaboard. Ferries will take you back to the mainland (and the present day) at 3:45pm.

Fell's Point & Canton

Once the center of Baltimore's shipbuilding industry, the historic cobblestoned neighborhood of Fell's Point is now a gentrified mix of 18th-century homes and restaurants, bars and shops. The neighborhood has been the setting for several films and TV series, most notably *Homicide: Life on the Street*. Further east, the slightly more sophisticated streets of Canton fan out, with its grassy square surrounded by great restaurants and bars.

North Baltimore

The 'Hon' expression of affection – an oft-imitated, never-quite-duplicated 'Bawl-merese' peculiarity – originated in **Hampden**, an area straddling the line between working class and hipster-creative class. Spend a lazy afternoon browsing kitsch, antiques and vintage clothing along the **Avenue** (aka W 36th St). To get to Hampden, take the I-83 N, merge onto Falls Rd (northbound) and take a right onto the Avenue. The prestigious **Johns Hopkins University** (3400 N Charles St) is nearby.

★**Evergreen Museum** MUSEUM
(☎410-516-0341; http://museums.jhu.edu; 4545 N Charles St; adult/child $8/5; ⏲11am-4pm Tue-Fri, noon-4pm Sat & Sun) Well worth the drive, this grand 19th-century mansion provides a fascinating glimpse into upper-class Baltimore life of the 1800s. The house is packed with fine art and masterpieces of the decorative arts – including paintings by Modigliani, glass by Louis Comfort Tiffany and exquisite Asian porcelain – not to mention the astounding rare-book collection, numbering some 32,000 volumes.

More impressive than the collection, however, is the compelling story of the Garrett family, who were world travellers (John W was an active diplomat for some years) and astute philanthropists, as well as lovers of the arts, if not always successful performers in their own right – though that didn't stop Alice from taking to the stage (her own, which you'll see in the intimate theater below the house).

☞ Tours

Baltimore Ghost Tours WALKING TOUR
(☎410-357-1186; www.baltimoreghosttours.com; adult/child $15/10; ⏲7pm Fri & Sat Mar-Nov) Offers several walking tours exploring the spooky and bizarre side of Baltimore. The popular Fell's Point ghost walk departs from Max's on Broadway (731 S Broadway). Book online to save $2 per ticket.

Festivals & Events

Honfest CULTURAL
(www.honfest.net; Jun) Put on your best 'Bawlmerese' accent and head to Hampden for this celebration of kitsch, beehive hairdos, rhinestone glasses and other Baltimore eccentricities.

Artscape CULTURAL
(www.artscape.org; mid-July) America's largest free arts festival features art displays, live music, theater and dance performances.

Sleeping

Stylish and affordable B&Bs are mostly found in the downtown burbs of Canton, Fell's Point and Federal Hill.

HI-Baltimore Hostel HOSTEL $
(410-576-8880; www.hiusa.org/baltimore; 17 W Mulberry St, Mt Vernon; dm $31;) Located in a beautifully restored 1857 mansion, the HI-Baltimore has four-, eight- and 12-bed dorms. Helpful management, nice location and a filigreed classical chic look make this one of the region's best hostels. Breakfast included.

★**Inn at 2920** B&B $$
(410-342-4450; www.theinnat2920.com; 2920 Elliott St, Canton; r $185-272;) Housed in a former bordello, this boutique B&B offers five individual rooms; high-thread-count sheets; sleek, avant-garde decor; and the nightlife-charged neighborhood of Canton right outside your door. The Jacuzzi bathtubs and green sensibility of the owners add a nice touch.

Hotel Brexton HOTEL $$
(443-478-2100; www.brextonhotel.com; 868 Park Ave, Mt Vernon; r $130-240;) This red-brick 19th-century landmark building has recently been reborn as an appealing, if not overly lavish, hotel. Rooms offer a mix of wood floors or carpeting, comfy mattresses, mirrored armoires and framed art prints on the walls. Curious historical footnote: Wallis Simpson, the woman for whom Britain's King Edward VIII abdicated the throne, lived in this building as a young girl.

It's in a good location, just a short walk to the heart of Mt Vernon.

Eating

Baltimore is an ethnically rich town that sits on top of the greatest seafood repository in the world, not to mention the fault line between the down-home South and cutting-edge innovation of the Northeast.

Dooby's Coffee CAFE $
(www.doobyscoffee.com; 802 N Charles St, Mt Vernon; mains lunch $8-11, dinner $13-18; 7am-11pm Mon-Fri, 8am-midnight Sat, 8am-5pm Sun;) A short stroll from the Washington Monument, this hip but unpretentious place is equal parts sunny cafe and creative eating and drinking spot. Come in the morning for tasty pastries and egg-and-Gruyère sandwiches, or at lunchtime for Korean-style rice bowls and toasted sandwiches. At night, there are bourbon-braised sticky ribs, steaming bowls of mushroom-and-leek ramen and other Asian infusions.

Papermoon Diner DINER $
(www.papermoondiner24.com; 227 W 29th St, Harwood; mains $9-17; 7am-midnight Sun-Thu, to 2am Fri & Sat) This brightly colored, quintessential Baltimore diner is decorated with thousands of old toys, creepy mannequins and other quirky knickknacks. The real draw here is the anytime breakfast – fluffy buttermilk pancakes, crispy bacon and crab-and-artichoke-heart omelets. Wash it down with a caramel-and-sea-salt milkshake.

Artifact CAFE $
(www.artifactcoffee.com; 1500 Union Ave, Woodberry; mains $7-13; 7am-5pm Mon-Tue, to 7pm Wed-Fri, 8am-7pm Sat & Sun;) Artifact serves the city's best coffee, along with tasty light meals such as egg muffins, spinach salad, vegetarian *banh mi* and pastrami sandwiches. It's inside a former mill space, handsomely repurposed from its industrial past. It's a two-minute stroll from the Woodberry light-rail station.

Vaccaro's Pastry ITALIAN $
(www.vaccarospastry.com; 222 Albemarle St, Little Italy; desserts around $7; 9am-10pm Sun-Thu, to midnight Fri & Sat) Vaccaro's serves some of the best desserts and coffee in town. The cannolis are legendary.

Lexington Market FAST FOOD $
(www.lexingtonmarket.com; 400 W Lexington St, Mt Vernon; 8:30am-6pm Mon-Sat) Around since 1782, Mt Vernon's Lexington Market is one of Baltimore's true old-school food markets. It's a bit shabby on the outside, but the food is great. Don't miss the crab cakes at **Faidley's** (410-727-4898; www.faidleyscrabcakes.com; mains $10-20; 9:30am-5pm Mon-Sat) seafood stall, because my goodness, they are amazing.

★Thames St Oyster House SEAFOOD $$
(☎443-449-7726; www.thamesstreetoysterhouse.com; 1728 Thames St, Fell's Point; mains $14-29; ⏲11:30am-2:30pm Wed-Sun, 5-10pm daily) An icon of Fell's Point, this vintage dining and drinking hall serves some of Baltimore's best seafood. Dine in the polished upstairs dining room with views of the waterfront, take a seat in the backyard, or plunk down at the bar in front (which stays open till midnight) and watch the drink-makers and oyster-shuckers in action.

Birroteca PIZZA $$
(☎443-708-1935; www.bmorebirroteca.com; 1520 Clipper Rd, Roosevelt Park; pizzas $17-19; ⏲5-11pm Mon-Fri, noon-midnight Sat, to 10pm Sun) Amid stone walls and indie rock, Birroteca fires up delicious thin-crust pizzas in imaginative combos (like duck confit with fig-onion jam). There's craft beer, good wines, fancy cocktails and impressively bearded bartenders. It's about a half-mile from either Hampden's 36th St or the Woodberry light-rail station.

Helmand AFGHAN $$
(☎410-752-0311; 806 N Charles St, Mt Vernon; mains $14-17; ⏲5-10pm Sun-Thu, to 11pm Fri & Sat) The Helmand is a longtime favorite for its *kaddo borawni* (pumpkin in yogurt-garlic sauce), vegetable platters and flavorful beef-and-lamb meatballs followed by cardamom ice cream. If you've never tried Afghan cuisine, this is a great place to do so.

LP Steamers SEAFOOD $$
(☎410-576-9294; 1100 E Fort Ave, South Baltimore; mains $10-28; ⏲11:30am-9:30pm) LP is the best in Baltimore's seafood stakes: working class, teasing smiles and the freshest crabs on the southside.

★Woodberry Kitchen AMERICAN $$$
(☎410-464-8000; www.woodberrykitchen.com; 2010 Clipper Park Rd, Woodberry; mains $24-39; ⏲dinner 5-10pm Mon-Thu, to 11pm Fri & Sat, to 9pm Sun, brunch 10am-2pm Sat & Sun) The Woodberry takes everything the Chesapeake region has to offer, plops it into an industrial barn and creates culinary magic. The entire menu is like a playful romp through the best of local produce, seafood and meats, from Maryland rockfish with Carolina Gold grits to Shenandoah Valley lamb with collard greens, and hearty vegetable dishes plucked from nearby farms. Reserve ahead.

Food Market MODERN AMERICAN $$$
(☎410-366-0606; www.thefoodmarketbaltimore.com; 1017 W 36th St, Hampden; mains $20-34; ⏲5-11pm daily plus 9am-3pm Fri-Sun) On Hampden's lively restaurant- and shop-lined main drag, the Food Market was an instant success when it opened back in 2012. Award-winning local chef Chad Gauss elevates American comfort fare to high art in dishes like bread-and-butter-crusted sea bass with black-truffle vinaigrette, and crab cakes with lobster mac 'n' cheese.

🍷 Drinking & Nightlife

On weekends, Fell's Point and Canton turn into temples of alcoholic excess that would make a Roman emperor blush. Mt Vernon and North Baltimore are a little more civilized, but any one of Baltimore's neighborhoods houses a cozy local pub. Closing time is generally 2am.

Brewer's Art PUB
(☎410-547-6925; 1106 N Charles St, Mt Vernon; ⏲4pm-2am) In a vintage early-20th-century mansion, Brewer's Art serves well-crafted Belgian-style microbrews to a laid-back Mt Vernon crowd. There's tasty pub fare (mac 'n' cheese, portobello wraps) in the bar, and upscale American cuisine in the elegant back dining room. Head to the subterranean drinking den downstairs for a more raucous crowd. During happy hour (4pm to 7pm) drafts are just $3.75.

Club Charles BAR
(☎410-727-8815; 1724 N Charles St, Mt Vernon; ⏲6pm-2am) Hipsters adorned in the usual skinny jeans and vintage T-shirt uniform, as well as characters from other walks of life, flock to this 1940s art-deco cocktail lounge to enjoy good tunes and cheap drinks.

Ale Mary's BAR
(☎410-276-2044; 1939 Fleet St, Fell's Point; ⏲4pm-2am Mon-Fri, from 10am Sat & Sun) Its name and decor pay homage to Maryland's Catholic roots, with crosses and rosaries scattered about. It draws a buzzing neighborhood crowd that comes for strong drinks and good, greasy bar food (tater tots, cheesesteak subs) as well as mussels and Sunday brunch.

Little Havana BAR
(☎410-837-9903; 1325 Key Hwy, Federal Hill; ⏲4pm-2am Mon-Thu, from 11:30am Fri-Sun) A good after-work spot and a great place to sip mojitos on the waterfront deck, this converted brick warehouse is a major draw on

BALTIMORE FOR CHILDREN

Most attractions are centered on the Inner Harbor, including the **National Aquarium** (p292), perfect for pint-sized visitors. Kids can run wild o'er the ramparts of historic **Fort McHenry National Monument & Historic Shrine** (p293), too.

Maryland Science Center (☎410-685-2370; www.mdsci.org; 601 Light St; adult/child $19/16; ⏲10am-5pm Mon-Fri, to 6pm Sat, 11am-5pm Sun, longer hours in summer) is an awesome center featuring a three-story atrium, tons of interactive exhibits on dinosaurs, outer space and the human body, and the requisite IMAX theater ($4 extra).

Two blocks north is the converted fish market of **Port Discovery** (☎410-727-8120; www.portdiscovery.org; 35 Market Pl; admission $15; ⏲10am-5pm Mon-Sat, noon-5pm Sun, reduced hours in winter), which has a playhouse, a laboratory, a TV studio and even a pharaoh's tomb. Wear your kids out here.

At **Maryland Zoo in Baltimore** (www.marylandzoo.org; Druid Hill Park; adult/child $18/13; ⏲10am-4pm daily Mar-Dec, 10am-4pm Fri-Mon Jan & Feb), lily-pad hopping, adventures with Billy the Bog Turtle and grooming live animals are all in a day's play here.

warm, sunny days (especially around weekend brunch time).

☆ Entertainment

Baltimoreans *love* sports. The town plays hard and parties even harder, with tailgating parties in parking lots and games showing on numerous televisions.

Baltimore Orioles BASEBALL
(☎888-848-2473; www.orioles.com) The Orioles play at **Oriole Park at Camden Yards** (333 W Camden St, Downtown), arguably the best ballpark in America. Daily tours (adult/child $9/6) of the stadium are offered during the regular season (April to October).

Baltimore Ravens FOOTBALL
(☎410-261-7283; www.baltimoreravens.com) The Ravens play at **M&T Bank Stadium** (1101 Russell St, Downtown) from September to January.

ℹ Information

Baltimore Area Visitor Center (☎877-225-8466; www.baltimore.org; 401 Light St, Inner Harbor; ⏲9am-6pm May-Sep, 10am-5pm Oct-Apr) Located on the Inner Harbor. Sells the **Harbor Pass** (adult/child $50/40), which gives admission to five major area attractions.

Baltimore Sun (www.baltimoresun.com) Daily city newspaper.

City Paper (www.citypaper.com) Free alt-weekly.

Enoch Pratt Free Library (400 Cathedral St, Mt Vernon; ⏲10am-7pm Mon-Wed, to 5pm Thu-Sat, 1-5pm Sun; wi-fi) There's free wi-fi and some public access computers (also free).

University of Maryland Medical Center (☎410-328-9400; 22 S Greene St, University of Maryland-Baltimore) Has a 24-hour emergency room.

ℹ Getting There & Away

The Baltimore/Washington International Thurgood Marshall Airport (p290) is 10 miles south of downtown via I-295.

Departing from a terminal 2 miles southwest of Inner Harbor, **Greyhound** (www.greyhound.com) and **Peter Pan Bus Lines** (☎410-752-7682; 2110 Haines St, Carroll-Camden) have numerous buses from Washington, DC ($10 to $14, roughly every 45 minutes, one hour), and from New York ($14 to $50, 12 to 15 per day, 4½ hours). The **BoltBus** (☎877-265-8287; www.boltbus.com; 1610 St Paul St, Carroll-Camden; wi-fi) has six to nine buses a day to/from NYC ($15 to $33); it departs from a streetside location outside of Baltimore's Penn Station.

Penn Station (1500 N Charles St, Charles North) is in north Baltimore. MARC operates weekday commuter trains to/from Washington, DC ($7, 71 minutes). **Amtrak** (☎800-872-7245; www.amtrak.com) trains serve the East Coast and beyond.

ℹ Getting Around

Light-Rail (☎866-743-3682; mta.maryland.gov/light-rail; one way/day pass $1.60/3.50; ⏲6am-midnight Mon-Sat, 7am-11pm Sun) runs from BWI airport to Lexington Market and Penn Station. Train frequency is every five to 10 minutes. MARC trains run hourly on weekdays (and six to nine times daily on weekends) between Penn Station and BWI airport for $4. Check **Maryland Transit Administration** (MTA; www.mtamaryland.com) for all local transportation schedules and fares.

Supershuttle (☎800-258-3826; www.supershuttle.com; ⏲5:30am-12:30am) provides a BWI-van service to the Inner Harbor for $16.

Baltimore Water Taxi (☎410-563-3900; www.baltimorewatertaxi.com; Inner Harbor; daily pass adult/child $12/6; ⏲10am-11pm Mon-Sat, to 9pm Sun) docks at all harborside attractions and neighborhoods.

Annapolis

Annapolis is as charming as state capitals get. The Colonial architecture, cobblestones, flickering lamps and brick row houses are worthy of Dickens, but the effect isn't artificial: this city has preserved, rather than created, its heritage.

Perched on Chesapeake Bay, Annapolis revolves around the city's rich maritime traditions. It's home to the US Naval Academy, whose 'middies' (midshipmen students) stroll through town in their starched white uniforms. Sailing is not just a hobby here, but a way of life, and the city docks are crammed with vessels of all shapes and sizes.

Sights & Activities

Annapolis has more 18th-century buildings than any other city in America, including the homes of all four Marylanders who signed the Declaration of Independence.

Think of the State House as a wheel hub from which most attractions fan out, leading to the City Dock and historic waterfront.

US Naval Academy UNIVERSITY
(visitor center 410-293-8687; www.usnabsd.com/for-visitors; Randall St btwn Prince George and King George Sts) The undergraduate college of the US Navy is one of the most selective universities in America. The **Armel-Leftwich visitor center** (410-293-8687; tourinfo@usna.edu; Gate 1, City Dock entrance; tours adult/child $10.50/8.50; 9am-5pm) is the place to book tours and immerse yourself in all things Academy-related. Come for the formation weekdays at 12:05pm sharp, when the 4000 midshipmen and -women conduct a 20-minute military marching display in the yard. Photo ID is required for entry. If you've got a thing for American naval history, revel in the **Naval Academy Museum** (410-293-2108; www.usna.edu/museum; 118 Maryland Ave; 9am-5pm Mon-Sat, 11am-5pm Sun) FREE.

Maryland State House HISTORIC BUILDING
(410-946-5400; 91 State Circle; 9am-5pm) FREE The country's oldest state capitol in continuous legislative use, the grand 1772 State House also served as national capital from 1733 to 1734. The Maryland Senate is in action here from January to April. The upside-down giant acorn atop the dome stands for wisdom.

Banneker-Douglass Museum MUSEUM
(http://bdmuseum.maryland.gov; 84 Franklin St; 10am-4pm Tue-Sat) FREE A short stroll from the State House, this small but worthwhile museum highlights great achievements of Marylanders of African American ancestry. There are permanent exhibits on the likes of US Supreme Court justice Thurgood Marshall, explorer Matthew Henson and public intellectual Frederick Douglass, as well as temporary exhibitions that often run the gamut from historical forays into the Civil Rights era to today's crop of great African American artists, musicians and writers.

Hammond Harwood House MUSEUM
(410-263-4683; www.hammondharwoodhouse.org; 19 Maryland Ave; adult/child $10/5; noon-5pm Tue-Sun Apr-Dec) Of the many historical homes in town, the 1774 HHH is the one to visit. It has a superb collection of decorative arts, including furniture, paintings and ephemera dating to the 18th century, and is one of the finest existing British Colonial homes in America. Knowledgeable guides help bring the past to life on 50-minute house tours (held at the top of the hour).

William Paca House & Garden HISTORIC BUILDING
(410-990-4543; www.annapolis.org; 186 Prince George St; adult/child $10/6; 10am-5pm Mon-Sat, noon-5pm Sun) Take a tour (offered hourly on the half-hour) through this Georgian mansion for an insight into 18th-century life for the upper class in Maryland. Don't miss the blooming garden in spring.

Kunta Kinte–Alex Haley Memorial MONUMENT
At the City Dock, the Kunta Kinte–Alex Haley Memorial marks the spot where Kunta Kinte – ancestor of *Roots* author Alex Haley – was brought in chains from Africa.

Tours

Four Centuries Walking Tour WALKING TOUR
(www.annapolistours.com; adult/child $18/10) A costumed docent will lead you on this great introduction to all things Annapolis. The 10:30am tour leaves from the visitor center and the 1:30pm tour leaves from the information booth at the City Dock; there's a slight variation in sights visited by each, but both cover the country's largest concentration of 18th-century buildings, influential African Americans and colonial spirits who don't want to leave.

The associated one-hour **Pirates of the Chesapeake Cruise** (☎410-263-0002; www.chesapeakepirates.com; admission $20; ⊙mid-Apr–Sep; 👪) is good 'yar'-worthy fun, especially for the kids.

Woodwind CRUISE
(☎410-263-7837; www.schoonerwoodwind.com; 80 Compromise St; sunset cruise adult/child $44/27; ⊙mid-Apr–Oct) This beautiful 74ft schooner offers two-hour day and sunset cruises. Or splurge for the *Woodwind* 'boat & breakfast' package (rooms $305, including breakfast), one of the more unique lodging options in town.

Sleeping

ScotLaur Inn GUESTHOUSE **$$**
(☎410-268-5665; www.scotlaurinn.com; 165 Main St; r $95-140; P❄📶) The folks from Chick & Ruth's Delly offer 10 rooms, each with wrought-iron beds, floral wallpaper and private bath. The quarters are small but have a familial atmosphere (the guesthouse is named after the owners' children Scott and Lauren, whose photos adorn the hallways).

O'Callaghan Hotel HOTEL **$$**
(☎410-263-7700; www.ocallaghanhotels-us.com; 174 West St; r $99-180; ❄📶) This Irish chain offers attractively furnished rooms that are nicely equipped, with big windows, a writing desk, brass fixtures and comfy mattresses. It's on West St, just a short stroll to a good selection of bars and restaurants, and about a 12-minute walk to the old quarter.

Historic Inns of Annapolis HOTEL **$$**
(☎410-263-2641; www.historicinnsofannapolis.com; 58 State Circle; r $140-200; ❄📶) The Historic Inns comprise three different boutique guesthouses, each set in a heritage building in the heart of old Annapolis: the Maryland Inn, the Governor Calvert House and the Robert Johnson House. Common areas are packed with period details, and the best rooms boast antiques, a fireplace and attractive views (while the cheapest are small and cramped and could use a good cleaning).

Eating & Drinking

With the Chesapeake at its doorstep, Annapolis has superb seafood.

49 West CAFE **$**
(☎410-626-9796; 49 West St; mains $7-15; ⊙7:30am-midnight; 📶) This comfy, art-filled coffeehouse is a good spot for coffee and light bites during the day (sandwiches, soups, salads) and heartier bistro fare by night, along with wines and cocktails. There's live music some nights.

Chick & Ruth's Delly DINER **$**
(☎410-269-6737; www.chickandruths.com; 165 Main St; mains $7-14; ⊙6:30am-11:30pm; 👪) A cornerstone of Annapolis, the Delly is bursting with affable quirkiness and a big menu, heavy on sandwiches and breakfast fare. Patriots can relive grade-school days reciting the Pledge of Allegiance, weekdays at 8:30am (and 9:30am on weekends).

★**Vin 909** AMERICAN **$$**
(☎410-990-1846; 909 Bay Ridge Ave; small plates $13-16; ⊙5:30-10pm Tue-Sun & noon-3pm Wed-Fri) Perched on a little wooded hill and boasting intimate but enjoyably casual ambience, Vin is the best thing happening in Annapolis for food. Farm-sourced goodness features in the form of duck confit, BBQ sliders and homemade pizzas with toppings that include wild

MARYLAND BLUE CRABS

Eating at a crab shack, where the dress code stops at shorts and flip-flops, is the quintessential Chesapeake Bay experience. Folks in these parts take their crabs seriously, and can spend hours debating the intricacies of how to crack a crab, the proper way to prepare crabs and where to find the best ones. There is one thing Marylanders can agree on: they must be blue crabs (scientific name: *Callinectes sapidus*, 'beautiful swimmers'). Sadly, blue crab numbers have suffered with the continuing pollution of the Chesapeake Bay, and many crabs you eat here are imported from elsewhere.

Steamed crabs are prepared very simply, using beer and Old Bay seasoning. One of the best crab shacks in the state is near Annapolis at **Jimmy Cantler's Riverside Inn** (www.cantlers.com; 458 Forest Beach Rd, Annapolis; mains $17-32; ⊙11am-11pm Sun-Thu, to midnight Fri & Sat), located 4 miles northeast of the Maryland State House, across the Severn River Bridge; here, eating a steamed crab has been elevated to an art form – a hands-on, messy endeavor, normally accompanied by corn on the cob and ice-cold beer. Another fine spot is across the bay at the **Crab Claw** (p300).

mushrooms, foie gras and Spanish chorizo. There's a great wine selection, including over three-dozen wines by the glass.

No reservations are accepted, so go early to beat the often lengthy waits.

Boatyard Bar & Grill SEAFOOD $$
(☑ 410-216-6206; www.boatyardbarandgrill.com; 400 4th St ; mains $14-27; ⊙ 8am-midnight; 🖐) This bright, nautically themed restaurant is an inviting spot for crab cakes, fish and chips, fish tacos and other seafood. Happy hour (3pm to 7pm) draws in the crowds with 99¢ oysters and $3 drafts. It's a short drive (or 10-minute walk) from the City Dock, across the Spa Creek Bridge.

Rams Head Tavern PUB FOOD $$$
(☑ 410-268-4545; www.ramsheadtavern.com; 33 West St; mains $12-32; ⊙ 11am-2am Mon-Sat, from 10am Sun) Serves pub fare and refreshing microbrews in an attractive exposed-brick and oak-paneled setting. Well-known bands perform next door at the Rams Head On Stage (tickets $22 to $80).

❶ Information

There's a **visitor center** (☑ 410-280-0445; www. visitannapolis.org; 26 West St; ⊙ 9am-5pm) and a seasonal information booth at City Dock.

❶ Getting There & Away

Greyhound (www.greyhound.com) runs buses to Washington, DC (once daily). **Dillon's Bus** (www.dillonbus.com; tickets $4.25) has 26 weekday-only commuter buses between Annapolis and Washington, DC, connecting with various DC Metro lines.

Eastern Shore

Just across the Chesapeake Bay Bridge, nondescript suburbs give way to unbroken miles of bird-dotted wetlands, serene waterscapes, endless cornfields, sandy beaches and friendly little villages. The Eastern Shore retains its charm despite the growing influx of city-dwelling yuppies and day-trippers. This area revolves around the water: working waterfront communities still survive off Chesapeake Bay and its tributaries, and boating, fishing, crabbing and hunting are integral to local life.

St Michaels & Tilghman Island

The prettiest little village on the Eastern Shore, **St Michaels** lives up to its motto as the 'Heart and Soul of Chesapeake Bay.' It's a mix of old Victorian homes, quaint B&Bs, boutique shops and working docks, where escape artists from Washington mix with salty-dog watermen. During the War of 1812, inhabitants rigged up lanterns in a nearby forest and blacked out the town. British naval gunners shelled the trees, allowing St Michaels to escape destruction. The building now known as the **Cannonball House** (Mulberry St) was the only structure to have been hit.

At the end of the road over the Hwy 33 drawbridge, tiny **Tilghman Island** still runs a working waterfront, where local captains take visitors out on graceful sailing vessels.

◉ Sights & Activities

**Chesapeake Bay
Maritime Museum** MUSEUM
(☑ 410-745-2916; www.cbmm.org; 213 N Talbot St, St Michaels; adult/child $13/6; ⊙ 9am-5pm May-Oct, 10am-4pm Nov-Apr; 🖐) At the lighthouse, the Chesapeake Bay Maritime Museum delves into the deep ties between shore folk and America's largest estuary.

Lady Patty Classic Yacht Charters SAILING
(☑ 410-886-1127; www.ladypatty.com; 6176 Tilghman Island Rd, Tilghman Island; cruise adult/child from $27/42; ⊙ May-Oct) Lady Patty Yacht Charters runs memorable two-hour sails on the Chesapeake.

🛏 Sleeping & Eating

Parsonage Inn INN $$
(☑ 410-745-8383; www.parsonage-inn.com; 210 N Talbot St; r $160-225; 🅿 ❄) Laura Ashley's most lurid fantasies probably resemble the rooms in the red-brick Parsonage Inn, which is run by a very hospitable innkeeper (and her canine companion). Off-season prices drop as low as $90 per night.

Crab Claw SEAFOOD $$
(☑ 410-745-2900; www.thecrabclaw.com; 304 Burns St, St Michaels; mains $16-30; ⊙ 11am-9pm mid-Mar–Oct) Next door to the Chesapeake Bay Maritime Museum, the Crab Claw serves up tasty Maryland blue crabs to splendid views over the harbor. Avoid the seafood sampler, unless you're a fan of deep-fried seafood.

Oxford

Oxford is a small village with a history dating back to the 1600s and a fine spread of leafy streets and waterfront homes. Although you can drive there via US 333, it's well worth taking the old-fashioned **ferry** (☎410-745-9023; www.oxfordbellevueferry.com; Bellevue Rd near Bellevue Park; one way car/additional passenger/pedestrian $12/1/3; ⏲9am-sunset mid-Apr–mid-Nov) from Bellevue. Try to go around sunset for memorable views.

Once in Oxford, don't miss the chance to dine at the celebrated **Robert Morris Inn** (☎410-226-5111; www.robertmorrisinn.com; 314 N Morris St; mains $17-29; ⏲7:30-10am, noon-2:30pm & 5:30-9:30pm), near the ferry dock. Award-winning crab cakes, grilled local rockfish and medallions of spring lamb are nicely matched by wines and best followed by pavlova with berries and other desserts. You can also overnight in one of the inn's heritage-style rooms (from $145).

Berlin & Snow Hill

Imagine a typical small-town-America Main St, cute that vision up by a few points, and you've come close to these Eastern Shore villages. Most buildings here are handsomely preserved, and antique shops litter the area.

In **Berlin**, the **Globe Theater** (☎410-641-0784; www.globetheater.com; 12 Broad St; mains $10-26; ⏲11am-10pm; 📶) is a lovingly restored main stage that serves as a restaurant, bar, art gallery and theater for nightly live music; the kitchen serves eclectic American fare with global accents.

There are B&Bs galore, but we prefer the **Atlantic Hotel** (☎410-641-3589; www.atlantichotel.com; 2 N Main St; r $125-275; P❄📶), a Gilded Era lodger that gives guests the time-warp experience with all the modern amenities.

A few miles from Berlin, **Snow Hill** has a splendid location along the idyllic Pocomoke River. Get on the water with the **Pocomoke River Canoe Company** (☎410-632-3971; www.pocomokerivercanoe.com; 2 River St; canoe hire per hr/day $15/50). They'll even take you upriver so you can have a leisurely paddle downstream. Nearby **Furnace Town** (☎410-632-2032; www.furnacetown.com; Old Furnace Rd; adult/child $7/4; ⏲10am-5pm Mon-Sat Apr-Oct, from noon Sun; P👪), off Rte 12, is a living-history museum that marks the old location of a 19th-century iron-smelting town. In Snow Hill itself, while away an odd, rewarding half-hour in the **Julia A Purnell Museum** (☎410-632-0515; 208 W Market St; adult/child $2/; ⏲10am-4pm Tue-Sat, from 1pm Sun Apr-Oct), a tiny structure that feels like an attic for the entire Eastern Shore.

Staying in town? Check out Snow Hill's **River House Inn** (☎410-632-2722; www.riverhouseinn.com; 201 E Market St; r $160-210, cottage $275-350; P❄📶🐾), with a lush backyard that overlooks a scenic bend of the river. The **Blue Dog Cafe** (☎410-251-7193; www.bluedogsnowhill.com; 300 N Washington St; mains $10-21) serves up tasty crab cakes, burgers and Cajun-style shrimp. There's live music some nights – from old-fashioned brass bands to fiddle players and singing waitstaff.

Ocean City

'The OC' is where you'll experience the American seaside resort at its tackiest. Here you can take a spin on nausea-inducing thrill rides, buy a T-shirt with obscene slogans and drink to excess at cheesy theme bars. The center of action is the 2.5-mile-long boardwalk, which stretches from the inlet to 27th St. The beach is attractive, but you'll have to contend with horny teenagers, heavy traffic and noisy crowds; the beaches north of the boardwalk are much quieter.

Sleeping

The **visitor center** (☎800-626-2326; www.oc-ocean.com; Coastal Hwy at 40th St; ⏲9am-5pm), in the convention center on Coastal Hwy, can help you find lodgings.

King Charles Hotel GUESTHOUSE **$$**
(☎410-289-6141; www.kingcharleshotel.com; cnr N Baltimore Ave & 12th St; r $115-190; P❄📶) This place could be a quaint summer cottage, except it happens to be a short stroll to the heart of the boardwalk action. It has aging but clean rooms with small porches attached, and it's quiet.

Eating & Drinking

Surf 'n' turf and all-you-can-eat deals are the order of the day.

Liquid Assets MODERN AMERICAN **$$**
(☎410-524-7037; cnr 94th St & Coastal Hwy; mains $13-34; ⏲11:30am-11pm) Like a diamond in the rough, this bistro and wine shop is hidden in a strip mall in north OC. The menu is a refreshing mix of innovative seafood, grilled meats and regional classics.

Seacrets BAR
(www.seacrets.com; cnr W 49th St & the Bay; ⏲8am-2am) A Jamaican-themed, rum-soaked bar straight out of MTV's *Spring Break*. You can drift around in an inner tube while sipping a drink and people-watching at OC's most famous meat market.

WORTH A TRIP

ASSATEAGUE ISLAND

Just 8 miles south but a world away from Ocean City is Assateague Island seashore, a perfectly barren landscape of sand dunes and beautiful secluded beaches. This undeveloped barrier island is populated by the only herd of wild horses on the East Coast, made famous in the book *Misty of Chincoteague*.

The island is divided into three sections. In Maryland there's **Assateague State Park** (☎410-641-2918; Rte 611; admission/campsites $6/28; ⏰campground late Apr–Oct) and federally administered **Assateague Island National Seashore** (☎410-641-1441; www.nps.gov/asis; Rte 611; admission pedestrian/vehicle/campsite per week $3/15/25; ⏰visitor center 9am-5pm). **Chincoteague National Wildlife Refuge** (www.fws.gov/refuge/chincoteague; 8231 Beach Road, Chincoteague Island; daily/weekly pass $8/15 ; ⏰5am-10pm May-Sep, 6am-6pm Nov-Feb, to 8pm Mar, Apr & Oct; P 👪) is in Virginia.

As well as swimming and sunbathing, recreational activities include birding, kayaking, canoeing, crabbing and fishing. There are no services on the Maryland side of the island, so you must bring all your own food and drink. Don't forget insect repellent: the mosquitoes and biting horseflies can be ferocious!

Getting There & Around

Greyhound (☎410-289-9307; www.greyhound.com; 12848 Ocean Gateway) buses run daily to and from Washington, DC (four hours), and Baltimore (3½ hours).

Ocean City Coastal Highway Bus (day pass $3) runs up and down the length of the beach, from 6am to 3am. There's also a tram ($3) that runs along the boardwalk.

Western Maryland

The western spine of Maryland is mountain country. The Appalachian peaks soar to 3000ft above sea level, and the surrounding valleys are packed with rugged scenery and Civil War battlefields. This is Maryland's playground, where hiking, skiing, rock climbing and white-water rafting draw the outdoors-loving crowd.

Frederick

Halfway between the battlefields of Gettysburg, PA and Antietam is Frederick; its handsome 50-square-block historic district resembles an almost perfect cliche of a mid-sized city.

Sights

National Museum of Civil War Medicine MUSEUM
(www.civilwarmed.org; 48 E Patrick St; adult/student/child $9.50/7/free; ⏰10am-5pm Mon-Sat, from 11am Sun) This museum provides a fascinating, and sometimes gruesome, look at the health conditions soldiers and doctors faced during the war, as well as important medical advances that resulted from the conflict.

Sleeping & Eating

Hollerstown Hill B&B B&B $$
(☎301-228-3630; www.hollerstownhill.com; 4 Clarke Pl; r $145-175; P ❄ 📶) The elegant, friendly Hollerstown has four pattern-heavy rooms, two resident terriers and an elegant billiards room. This lovely Victorian sits right in the middle of the historic downtown area of Frederick, so you're within easy walking distance of all the goodness. No children under 16.

Brewer's Alley GASTROPUB $$
(☎301-631-0089; 124 N Market St; mains $10-26; ⏰noon-11:30pm; 📶) This bouncy brewpub is one of our favorite places in Frederick for several reasons. First, the beer: house-brewed, plenty of variety, delicious. Second, the burgers: enormous, half-pound monstrosities of staggeringly yummy proportions. Third, the rest of the menu: excellent Chesapeake seafood (including a wood-fired pizza topped with crab) and Frederick county farm produce and meats.

Getting There & Away

Frederick is accessible via **Greyhound** (☎301-663-3311; www.greyhound.com) and **MARC** (☎301-682-9716) trains, located across from the visitor center at 100 S East St.

Antietam National Battlefield

The site of the bloodiest day in American history is now, ironically, supremely peaceful, quiet and haunting – uncluttered save for plaques and statues. On September 17, 1862, General Robert E Lee's first invasion of the North was stalled here in a tactical stalemate that left more than 23,000 dead, wounded or missing – more casualties than America had suffered in all her previous wars combined. Poignantly, many of the battlefield graves are inscribed with German and Irish names, a roll call of immigrants who died fighting for their new homeland. The **visitor center** (☎301-432-5124; State Rd 65; 3-day pass per person/family $4/6; ⏰9am-5pm) shows a short film (playing on the hour and half-hour) about the events that transpired here. It also sells books and materials, including self-guided driving and walking tours of the battlefield.

Cumberland

At the Potomac River, the frontier outpost of Fort Cumberland (not to be confused with the Cumberland Gap between Virginia and Kentucky) was the pioneer gateway across the Alleghenies to Pittsburgh and the Ohio River. Today Cumberland has expanded into the outdoor recreation trade to guide visitors to the region's rivers, forests and mountains. Sights are a short stroll from the pedestrian-friendly streets of downtown Cumberland.

Sights & Activities

C&O Canal National Historic Park NATIONAL PARK
(www.nps.gov/choh) FREE A marvel of engineering, the C&O Canal was designed to stretch alongside the Potomac River from Chesapeake Bay to the Ohio River. Construction on the canal began in 1828 but halted here in 1850 by the Appalachian Mountains. The park's protected 185-mile corridor includes a 12ft-wide towpath, hiking and bicycling trail, which goes all the way from here to Georgetown in DC. The **Cumberland Visitor Center** (☎301-722-8226; 13 Canal St; ⏰9am-5pm; P) has displays chronicling the importance of river trade in eastern seaboard history.

Allegany Museum MUSEUM
(www.alleganymuseum.org; 3 Pershing St; ⏰10am-4pm Tue-Sat, from 1pm Sun) FREE Set in the old courthouse, this is an intriguing place to delve into Cumberland's past, with exhibits by local folk artist and woodcarver Claude Yoder; a model of the old shanty town that sprang up along the canal; 1920s firefighting gear; beautifully garbed mechanized puppets and other curiosities.

Western Maryland Scenic Railroad TOUR
(☎800-872-4650; www.wmsr.com; 13 Canal St; adult/child $35/18; ⏰11:30am Fri-Sun May-Dec) Outside the Cumberland visitor center, near the start of the C&O Canal, passengers can catch steam-locomotive rides, traversing forests and steep ravines to Frostburg, a 3½-hour round-trip.

Cumberland Trail Connection CYCLING
(☎301-777-8724; www.ctcbikes.com; 14 Howard St, Canal Pl; half-day/day/week from $20/30/120; ⏰8am-7pm) Conveniently located near the start of the C&O Canal, this outfit rents out bicycles (cruisers, touring bikes and mountain bikes), and also arranges shuttle service anywhere from Pittsburgh to DC.

Sleeping & Eating

Inn on Decatur GUESTHOUSE $$
(☎301-722-4887; www.theinnondecatur.net; 108 Decatur St; d $125-136;) Offers comfy guestrooms just a short stroll to pedestrianized Baltimore St in downtown Cumberland. The friendly owners have a wealth of knowledge on the area, and also lead bike tours (rentals available).

Queen City Creamery & Deli DINER $
(☎240-979-4125; 108 Harrison St; mains $6-9; ⏰7am-9pm) This retro soda fountain is like a 1940s time warp, with creamy shakes and homemade frozen custard, thick sandwiches and belly-filling breakfasts.

DELAWARE

Wee Delaware, the nation's second-smallest state (96 miles long and less than 35 miles across at its widest point) is overshadowed by its neighbors – and often overlooked by visitors to the Capital Region. And that's too bad, because Delaware has a lot more on offer than just tax-free shopping and chicken farms.

Long white sandy beaches, cute Colonial villages, a cozy countryside and small-town charm characterize the state that happily calls itself the 'Small Wonder.'

WORTH A TRIP

DEEP CREEK LAKE

In the extreme west of the panhandle, Maryland's largest freshwater lake is an all-seasons playground. The crimson and copper glow of the Alleghenies attracts thousands during the annual **Autumn Glory Festival** (www.visitdeepcreek.com; ⏲ early Oct), rivaling New England's leaf-turning backdrops.

History

In Colonial days Delaware was the subject of an aggressive land feud between Dutch, Swedish and British settlers. The former two imported classically northern European middle-class concepts, the latter a plantation-based aristocracy – which is partly why Delaware remains a typically mid-Atlantic cultural hybrid today.

The little state's big moment came on December 7, 1787, when Delaware became the first colony to ratify the US Constitution, thus becoming the first state in the Union. It remained in that union throughout the Civil War, despite supporting slavery. During this period, as throughout much of the state's history, the economy drew on its chemical industry. DuPont, the world's second-largest chemical company, was founded here in 1802 as a gunpowder factory by French immigrant Eleuthère Irénée du Pont. Low taxes drew other firms (particularly credit card companies) in the 20th century, boosting the state's prosperity.

Delaware Beaches

Delaware's 28 miles of sandy Atlantic beaches are the best reason to linger. Most businesses and services are open year-round. Off-season (outside of June to August), bargains abound.

Lewes

In 1631 the Dutch gave this whaling settlement the pretty name of Zwaanendael, or Valley of the Swans, before promptly getting massacred by local Nanticokes. The name was changed to Lewes (*loo*-iss) when William Penn gained control of the area. Today it's an attractive seaside gem with a mix of English and Dutch architecture.

The **visitor center** (www.leweschamber.com; 120 Kings Hwy; ⏲ 10am-4pm Mon-Fri, 9am-3pm Sat, 10am-2pm Sun) provides useful insight into attractions and outings in the surrounding area.

Sights & Activities

Zwaanendael Museum MUSEUM
(102 Kings Hwy; ⏲ 10am-4:30pm Tue-Sat, 1:30-4:30pm Sun) FREE This small, appealing museum is a good place to learn about the Dutch roots of Lewes.

Quest Fitness Kayak KAYAKING
(☎ 302-745-2925; www.questfitnesskayak.com; 514 E Savannah Rd; kayak hire per 2/8hr $25/50) For aquatic action, Quest Fitness Kayak operates a kayak rental stand next to the Beacon Motel. It also runs scenic paddle tours around the Cape (adult/child $65/35).

Sleeping & Eating

Hotel Rodney HOTEL $$
(☎ 302-645-6466; www.hotelrodneydelaware.com; 142 2nd St; r $150-260; P ❄ ☎ ≋) This charming boutique hotel features exquisite bedding and antique furniture, and also has some modern touches.

Wharf SEAFOOD $$
(☎ 302-645-7846; 7 Anglers Rd; mains $13-29; ⏲ 11:30am-1am; P 👪) Across the drawbridge, the Wharf has a relaxing waterfront location and serves a big selection of seafood and pub grub. Live music on weekends.

Getting There & Away

Cape May–Lewes Ferry (☎ 800-643-3779; www.capemaylewesferry.com; 43 Cape Henlopen Dr; per motorcycle/car $37/45, per adult/child $10/5) Runs daily 90-minute ferries across Delaware Bay to New Jersey from the terminal, 1 mile from downtown Lewes. For foot passengers, a seasonal shuttle bus ($4) operates between the ferry terminal and Lewes. Reservations recommended.

Cape Henlopen State Park

One mile east of Lewes, more than 4000 acres of dune bluffs, pine forests and wetlands are preserved at this lovely **state park** (☎ 302-645-8983; www.destateparks.com/park/cape-henlopen/; 15099 Cape Henlopen Dr; admission per car out-of-state/in-state $10/5; ⏲ 8am-sunset) that's popular with bird-watchers, beachgoers and campers. You can see clear to Cape May from the observation tower. **North Shores beach** draws many gay and lesbian couples.

Rehoboth Beach & Dewey Beach

As the closest stretch of sand to Washington, DC (121 miles), **Rehoboth Beach** is often dubbed 'the Nation's Summer Capital.' It is both a family-friendly and gay-friendly destination. To escape the chaos of busy Rehoboth Ave (and the heavily built-up outskirts), wander into the side streets downtown. There you'll find a mix of gingerbread houses, posh restaurants and kiddie amusements, plus a wide beach fronted by a mile-long boardwalk.

Less than 2 miles south on Hwy 1 is the tiny hamlet of **Dewey Beach**. Unapologetically known as 'Do Me' Beach for its (heterosexual) hook-up scene and hedonistic nightlife, Dewey is a major party beach. Another 3 miles past Dewey is **Delaware Seashore State Park** (☎302-227-2800; www.destateparks.com/park/delaware-seashore/; 39415 Inlet Rd; per vehicle $10; ⏲8am-sunset), a windswept slice of preserved dunes and salty breezes possessed of a wild, lonely beauty.

Sleeping

As elsewhere on the coast, prices skyrocket in high season (June to August). Cheaper lodging options are located on Rte 1.

Crosswinds Motel MOTEL $$
(☎302-227-7997; www.crosswindsmotel.com; 312 Rehoboth Ave; r $110-220; P❄☜) In the heart of Rehoboth Ave, this simple but nicely designed motel is great value for money, with welcome amenities (minirefridgerator, coffeemaker, flat-screen TV). Walk to the beach in 12 minutes.

Eating & Drinking

Cheap eats are available on the boardwalk. For classier dining, browse the inviting restaurants sprinkled along Wilmington Ave.

Henlopen City Oyster House SEAFOOD $$$
(50 Wilmington Ave; mains $14-34; ⏲from 3pm) Seafood lovers won't want to miss this spot, where an enticing raw bar and mouthwatering seafood dishes draw crowds (arrive early; no reservations). Good microbrews, cocktails and wine selection.

★**Dogfish Head** MICROBREWERY
(www.dogfish.com; 320 Rehoboth Ave; mains $9-25; ⏲noon-late) This iconic brewery serves up tasty pizzas, burgers, crab cakes and other pub fare, which go perfectly with the award-winning IPAs.

Getting There & Around

BestBus (www.bestbus.com) Offers bus service from Rehoboth to DC ($40, 2½ hours) and NYC ($46, 4½ hours). Runs summertime only (late May through early September).

Jolly Trolley (one way/round-trip $3/5; ⏲8am-2am Jun-Aug) Connects Rehoboth and Dewey Beaches, and makes frequent stops along the way.

Northern & Central Delaware

The grit of Wilmington is balanced by the rolling hills and palatial residences of the Brandywine Valley, particularly the soaring estate of Winterthur. Dover is cute, friendly and gets a little lively after hours.

Wilmington

A unique cultural milieu (African Americans, Jews and Caribbeans) and an energetic arts scene make this town worth a visit. The **visitor center** (☎800-489-6664; www.visitwilmingtonde.com; 100 W 10th St; ⏲9am-4:30pm Mon-Fri) is downtown.

DELAWARE FACTS

Nickname The First State, Small Wonder

Population 917,000

Area 1982 sq miles

Capital city Dover (population 36,000)

Sales tax None

Birthplace of Rock musician George Thorogood (b 1952), actress Valerie Bertinelli (b 1960), actor Ryan Phillippe (b 1974)

Home of Vice President Joe Biden, the Du Pont family, DuPont chemicals, credit card companies, lots of chickens

Politics Democrat

Famous for Tax-free shopping, attractive beaches

State bird Delaware Blue Hen chicken

Driving distances Wilmington to Dover 52 miles; Dover to Rehoboth Beach 43 miles

DON'T MISS

CYCLING THE JUNCTION & BREAKWATER TRAIL

For a scenic ride between Rehoboth and Lewes, rent a bicycle and hit the 6-mile **Junction & Breakwater Trail**. Named after the former rail line that operated here in the 1800s, this smooth, graded greenway travels through wooded and open terrain, over coastal marshes and past farmland. Pick up a map from the Rehoboth visitor center or from **Atlantic Cycles** (☑ 302-226-2543; www.atlanticcycles.net; 18 Wilmington Ave; half-/full day from $16/24), also in Rehoboth, which offers inexpensive rentals. In Lewes, try **Ocean Cycles** (☑ 302-537-1522; www.oceancycles.com; 526 E Savannah Rd) at the Beacon Motel.

◉ Sights & Activities

Delaware Art Museum   MUSEUM
(☑ 302-571-9590; www.delart.org; 2301 Kentmere Pkwy; adult/child $12/6, Sun free; ◷ 10am-4pm Wed-Sun) The Delaware Art Museum exhibits work of the local Brandywine School, including Edward Hopper, John Sloan and three generations of Wyeths.

Wilmington Riverfront   WATERFRONT
The Wilmington Riverfront consists of several blocks of redeveloped waterfront shops, restaurants and cafes; the most striking building is the **Delaware Center for the Contemporary Arts** (☑ 302-656-6466; www.thedcca.org; 200 S Madison St; ◷ 10am-5pm Tue & Thu-Sat, noon-5pm Wed & Sun) **FREE**, which consistently displays innovative exhibitions.

🛏 Sleeping & Eating

Inn at Wilmington   HOTEL $$
(☑ 855-532-2216; www.innatwilmington.com; 300 Rocky Run Pkwy; r from $120; P❉ ⧉) This is a charming, good-value option 5 miles north of downtown.

Iron Hill Brewery   BREWERY $$
(☑ 302-472-2739; www.ironhillbrewery.com; 620 Justison St; mains $11-27; ◷ 11:30am-11pm) The spacious and airy multilevel Iron Hill Brewery is set in a converted brick warehouse on the riverfront. Satisfying microbrews go nicely with hearty pub grub.

ℹ Getting There & Away

Wilmington is accessible by Greyhound bus from the **Wilmington Transportation Center** (100 S French St). **Amtrak** (www.amtrak.com; 100 S French St) trains connect with DC (1½ hours), Baltimore (45 minutes) and New York (1¾ hours).

Brandywine Valley

After making their fortune, the French-descended Du Ponts turned the Brandywine Valley into a sort of American Loire Valley. It remains a nesting ground for the wealthy and ostentatious to this day.

◉ Sights & Activities

Winterthur   HISTORIC SITE
(☑ 302-888-4600; www.winterthur.org; 5105 Kennett Pike, Rte 52; adult/child $20/5; ◷ 10am-5pm Tue-Sun) Six miles northwest of Wilmington is the 175-room estate of industrialist Henry Francis du Pont and his collection of antiques and American arts, one of the world's largest.

Brandywine Creek State Park   PARK
(☑ 302-577-3534; www.destateparks.com/park/brandywine-creek/; 41 Adams Dam Rd; per vehicle $8; ◷ 8am-sunset) Brandywine Creek State Park is the gem of the area. This green space would be impressive anywhere, but is doubly so considering how close it is to prodigious urban development. Nature trails and shallow streams wend through the park.

Wilderness Canoe Trips   CANOEING
(☑ 302-654-2227; www.wildernesscanoetrips.com; 2111 Concord Pike; kayak/canoe trip from $47/57, per tube $19) Call this outfit for for information on paddling or tubing down Brandywine Creek.

New Castle

As cute as a colonial kitten, New Castle is a web of cobblestoned streets and beautifully preserved 18th-century buildings lying near a riverfront (that said, however, the surrounding area is unfortunately a bit of an urban wasteland). Sights include the **Old Court House** (☑ 302-323-4453; 211 Delaware St, New Castle; ◷ 10am-3:30pm Wed-Sat, 1:30-4:30pm Sun) **FREE**, the arsenal on the Green, churches and cemeteries dating back to the 17th century.

The five-room **Terry House B&B** (☑ 302-322-2505; www.terryhouse.com; 130 Delaware St, New Castle; r $90-110; P⧉) is idyllically set in the historic district.

A few doors down, **Jessop's Tavern** (☎302-322-6111; 114 Delaware St, New Castle; mains $14-24; ⏰11:30am-10pm Mon-Sat, to 9pm Sun) serves up Dutch pot roast, 'Pilgrim's Feast' (oven-roasted turkey with all the fixings) and Belgian beers in a Colonial atmosphere.

Dover

Dover's city center is quite attractive; the row-house-lined streets are peppered with restaurants and shops, while broadleaf trees spread their branches over pretty little lanes.

Sights & Activities

First State Heritage Park Welcome Center & Galleries MUSEUM
(☎302-739-9194; www.destateparks.com/park/first-state-heritage/; 121 Martin Luther King Blvd N; ⏰9am-4:30pm Mon-Sat, 1:30-4:30pm Sun) FREE Delve into the history of Delaware at the First State Heritage Park, which serves as a welcome center for the city of Dover, the state of Delaware and the adjacent state house. This so-called park without boundaries includes some two dozen historic sites within a few blocks of one another. Start out at the Welcome Center & Galleries, which has exhibitions exploring Delaware's history. You can also pick up more info here on other key sites nearby.

Old State House MUSEUM
(☎302-744-5055; http://history.delaware.gov/museums/; 25 The Green; ⏰9am-4:30pm Mon-Sat, from 1:30pm Sun) FREE Built in 1791 and since restored, the Old State House contains art galleries and in-depth exhibits on the First State's history and politics.

Sleeping & Eating

State Street Inn B&B $$
(☎302-734-2294; www.statestreetinn.com; 228 N State St; r $125-135; ❄) Although it's a bit over the top in its cuteness and flower-patterned wallpapers and sheets, the State Street remains a solid accommodation choice, with friendly, knowledgeable service and an unbeatable central location.

Golden Fleece PUB FOOD $
(☎302-674-1776; 132 W Lockerman St; mains $4-10; ⏰4pm-midnight) The best bar in Dover also serves up some good food. First priority is maintaining the atmosphere of an old English pub, which meshes well with the surrounding red-brick Dover historical center. Has an outdoor patio for summer nights.

Bombay Hook National Wildlife Refuge

Bombay Hook National Wildlife Refuge PARK
(☎302-653-9345; www.fws.gov/refuge/Bombay_Hook; 2591 Whitehall Neck Rd, Smyrna; per vehicle/pedestrian $4/2; ⏰sunrise-sunset) Hundreds of thousands of waterfowl use this protected wetland as a stopping point along their migration routes. A 12-mile wildlife driving trail, running through 16,251 acres of saltwater marsh, cordgrass and tidal mud flats, manages to encapsulate all of the soft beauty of the DelMarVa peninsula in one perfectly preserved ecosystem. There are also short walking trails and observation towers.

VIRGINIA

Beautiful Virginia is a state steeped in history. It's the birthplace of America, where English settlers established the first permanent colony in the New World in 1607. From then on, the Commonwealth of Virginia has played a lead role in nearly every major American drama, from the Revolutionary and Civil Wars to the Civil Rights movement and the attacks of September 11, 2001.

Virginia's natural beauty is as diverse as its history and people. Chesapeake Bay and the wide sandy beaches kiss the Atlantic Ocean. Pine forests, marshes and rolling green hills form the soft curves of the central Piedmont region, while the rugged Appalachian Mountains and stunning Shenandoah Valley line its back.

History

Humans have occupied Virginia for at least 5000 years. Several thousand Native Americans were already here in May 1607, when Captain James Smith and his crew sailed up Chesapeake Bay and founded Jamestown, the first permanent English colony in the New World. Named for Queen Elizabeth I – aka the 'Virgin Queen' – the territory originally occupied most of America's eastern seaboard. By 1610 most of the colonists had died from starvation in their quest for gold, until colonist John Rolfe (husband of Pocahontas) discovered Virginia's real riches: tobacco.

A feudal aristocracy grew out of tobacco farming, and many gentry scions became Founding Fathers, including native son George Washington. In the 19th century the slave-based plantation system grew both in size and incompatibility with the industrializing North; Virginia seceded in 1861 and became the epicenter of the Civil War. Following its defeat the state walked a tense cultural tightrope, accruing a layered identity that included older aristocrats, a rural and urban working class, waves of immigrants and, today, the burgeoning tech-heavy suburbs of DC. The state revels in its history, yet still wants to pioneer the American experiment; thus, while Virginia only reluctantly desegregated in the 1960s, today it houses one of the most ethnically diverse populations of the New South.

Northern Virginia

Hidden within its suburban sprawl, Northern Virginia (NoVa) mixes small-town charm with metropolitan chic. Colonial villages and battlefields bump up against skyscrapers, shopping malls and world-class arts venues.

Arlington

Green-conscious and well trimmed, Arlington sits just across the Potomac River from DC. It has a couple of crucial capital sites, along with tempting dining and nightlife options. Most are easy-peasy to reach via the Metro.

Sights

Arlington National Cemetery HISTORIC SITE
(☎877-907-8585; www.arlingtoncemetery.mil; 8am-7pm Apr-Sep, to 5pm Oct-Mar; M Arlington Cemetery) FREE The county's best-known attraction is the somber final resting place for more than 400,000 military personnel and their dependents, with veterans of every US war from the Revolution to Iraq. The cemetery is spread over 612 hilly acres. Departing from the visitor center, bus tours are a handy way to visit the cemetery's memorials.

Highlights include the Tomb of the Unknowns, with its elaborate Changing of the Guard ceremony, and the gravesite of John F and Jacqueline Kennedy, marked by an eternal flame.

Pentagon BUILDING
(☎703-697-1776; pentagontours.osd.mil; Arlington, VA; memorial 24hr, tours by appointment; M Pentagon) South of Arlington Cemetery is the Pentagon, the largest office building in the world. Outside you may visit the **Pentagon Memorial** (www.pentagonmemorial.org; M Pentagon) FREE; 184 illuminated benches honor each person killed in the September 11, 2001, terrorist attack on the Pentagon. To get inside the building, you'll have to book a free guided tour on the website. Make reservations 14 to 90 days in advance.

Artisphere ARTS CENTER
(☎703-875-1100; www.artisphere.com; 1101 Wilson Blvd; 4-11pm Wed-Fri, noon-11pm Sat, noon-5pm Sun; ; M Rosslyn) For something completely different from memorials and museums, check out the excellent exhibits at this sleek, modern arts complex, which opened in 2011. Its several theaters host live performances (many free), including world music, film and experimental theater. There's also a cafe, restaurant and bar.

Eating & Drinking

In addition to hotels, there are dozens of chic restaurants and bars located along Clarendon and Wilson Blvds, clustered near the Rosslyn and Clarendon Metro stations.

★ Myanmar BURMESE $
(☎703-289-0013; 7810 Lee Hwy, Falls Church; mains $10-14; noon-10pm; M Dunn Loring Merrifield, then bus 2A) Myanmar's decor is bare bones; the service is slow; the portions are small; and the food is delicious. This is home-cooked Burmese: curries prepared with lots of garlic, turmeric and oil, chili fish, mango salads and chicken swimming in rich gravies.

Caffé Aficionado CAFE $
(1919 N Lynn St; sandwiches around $8; 7am-6pm Mon-Fri, 8am-3pm Sat; M Rosslyn) This friendly cafe whips up excellent lattes, pastries, waffles and thick baguette-style sandwiches. The space is tiny though, so you may have to get it to go (and enjoy it at the Freedom Park or on the Mt Vernon Trail).

Eden Center VIETNAMESE $$
(www.edencenter.com; 6571 Wilson Blvd, Falls Church; mains $9-15; 9am-11pm; ; M East Falls Church then bus 26A) One of Washington's most fascinating ethnic enclaves isn't technically in Washington. Instead, drive west past Arlington to Falls Church, VA and the Eden Center, which is, basically, a bit of Saigon that got lost in America. And we mean 'Saigon' – this is a shopping center/strip mall entirely occupied and operated by South Vietnamese refugees and their descendants.

Continental LOUNGE
(www.continentalpoollounge.com; 1911 N Fort Myer Dr; ⏲11:30am-2am Mon-Fri, 6pm-2am Sat & Sun; Ⓜ Rosslyn) A stone's throw from many Rosslyn hotels, this buzzing pool lounge evokes a trippy, tropical vibe with its murals of palm trees, oversized tiki heads and color-saturated bar stools. All of which sets the stage for an alternative night of shooting pool, playing ping-pong or trying your hand at shuffleboard.

☆ Entertainment

★ Iota LIVE MUSIC
(www.iotaclubandcafe.com; 2832 Wilson Blvd; tickets $10-15; ⏲4pm-2am Mon-Thu, from 10am Fri-Sun; 📶; Ⓜ Clarendon) With shows almost every night of the week, Iota is the best venue for live music in Clarendon's music strip. Bands span genres: folk, reggae, traditional Irish and Southern rock are all distinct possibilities. Tickets are available at the door only (no advance sales) and this place packs 'em in (the seating is first come, first served).

Alexandria

The charming Colonial village of Alexandria is just 5 miles – and 250 years – away from Washington. Once a salty port town, today it is a posh collection of red-brick Colonial homes, cobblestone streets, flickering gas lamps and a waterfront promenade. King St, the main thoroughfare, is packed with boutiques, outdoor cafes and neighborhood bars and restaurants.

Sights

★ Carlyle House HISTORIC BUILDING
(☎703-549-2997; www.nvrpa.org/park/carlyle_house_historic_park; 121 N Fairfax St; admission $5; ⏲10am-4pm Tue-Sat, noon-4pm Sun; Ⓜ King St then trolley) If you have time for just one historic house tour in Alexandria, make it this one. It dates from 1753 when merchant and city founder John Carlyle built the most lavish mansion in town (which in those days was little more than log cabins and muddy lanes). The Georgian Palladian-style house is packed with paintings, historic relics and period furnishings that help bring the past to life.

Freedom House Museum MUSEUM
(☎708-836-2858; www.nvul.org/freedomhouse; 1315 Duke St; ⏲10am-4pm Mon-Thu, to 3pm Fri; Ⓜ King St then trolley) FREE For a look at one of the darkest eras of American history, pay a visit to this small museum on Duke St. In the 1830s, this nondescript brick building housed the headquarters of the largest domestic slave-trading company in the country. Among the shackles, iron bars and low ceilings in the basement, multimedia exhibits give a glimpse of what life was like for the enslaved people held here.

George Washington Masonic National Memorial MONUMENT, LOOKOUT
(www.gwmemorial.org; 101 Callahan Dr at King St; admission $7, incl guided tour $10; ⏲9am-5pm; Ⓜ King St) Alexandria's most prominent landmark features a fine view from its 333ft tower, where you can see the Capitol, Mt Vernon and the Potomac River. It is modeled after Egypt's Lighthouse of Alexandria, and honors the first president (who was initiated into the shadowy Masons in Fredericksburg in 1752 and later became Worshipful Master of Alexandria Lodge No 22).

Torpedo Factory Art Center ARTS CENTER
(www.torpedofactory.org; 105 N Union St; ⏲10am-6pm, to 9pm Thu; Ⓜ King St then trolley) FREE

VIRGINIA FACTS

Nickname Old Dominion

Population 8.4 million

Area 42,774 sq miles

Capital city Richmond (population 205,000)

Other cities Virginia Beach (450,000), Norfolk (247,000), Chesapeake (231,000), Richmond (215,000), Newport News (183,000)

Sales tax 5.3 to 6%

Birthplace of George Washington (1732–99) and seven other US presidents, Confederate General Robert E Lee (1807–70), tennis ace Arthur Ashe (1943–93), author Tom Wolfe (b 1931), actor Sandra Bullock (b 1964)

Home of The Pentagon, the CIA, more technology workers than any other state

Politics Republican

Famous for American history, tobacco, apples, Shenandoah National Park

State beverage milk

Driving distances Arlington to Shenandoah 113 miles; Richmond to Virginia Beach 108 miles

What do you do with a former munitions dump and arms factory? How about turn it into one of the best art spaces in the region? Three floors of artist studios and free creativity are on offer in Old Town Alexandria, as well as the opportunity to buy paintings, sculptures, glassworks, textiles and jewelry direct from creators. The Torpedo Factory anchors Alexandria's revamped waterfront with a marina, parks, walkways, residences and restaurants.

Eating & Drinking

Eamonn's Dublin Chipper PUB FOOD $

(www.eamonnsdublinchipper.com; 728 King St; mains $7-10; ⏰11:30am-11pm, to 1am Fri & Sat; Ⓜ King St then trolley) You'll find no better execution of the fish and chips genre than at this upscale temple to classic pub fare. How authentic is it? It imports Batchelors baked beans from Ireland, and also serves deep-fried Mars Bars, Milky Way and Snickers. Like many resto-pubs in this part of Old Town, Eamonn's is a good place for a drink on weekend nights.

Brabo Tasting Room BELGIAN $$

(☎703-894-5252; www.braborestaurant.com; 1600 King St; mains $16-20; ⏰7:30-10:30am & 11:30am-11pm; Ⓜ King St then trolley) The inviting and sunlit Brabo Tasting Room serves its signature mussels, tasty wood-fired tarts and gourmet sandwiches, with a good beer and wine selection. In the morning, stop by for brioche French toast and Bloody Marys. Brabo restaurant, next door, is the high-end counterpart serving seasonal fare.

Restaurant Eve AMERICAN $$$

(☎703-706-0450; www.restauranteve.com; 110 S Pitt St; mains $36-45, 6-course tasting menu $135; ⏰11:30am-2:30pm Mon-Fri, 5:30-10:30pm Mon-Sat; 🖉; Ⓜ King St then trolley) One of Alexandria's best (and priciest) dining rooms, Eve blends great American ingredients, precise French technique and first-rate service. Splurge here on the tasting menus, which are simply on another level of gastronomic experience.

PX BAR

(www.barpx; 728 King St, entrance on S Columbus St; ⏰6pm-midnight Wed-Thu, to 1:30am Fri & Sat; Ⓜ King St then trolley) This elegant, low-lit drinking den is a magical spot to linger over a cocktail or two. Jauntily attired bartenders shake up beautifully hued elixirs to a well-dressed crowd, perfectly in keeping with the speakeasy theme. True to form, there's no sign, just a blue light and a red door to mark the entrance. It's best to reserve ahead.

As expected, cocktails are in the $14 to $18 range, so sip sloooowly.

Entertainment

Basin Street Lounge JAZZ

(☎703-549-1141; www.219restaurant.com; 219 King St; admission Fri & Sat $5; ⏰shows 9pm Tue-Sat; Ⓜ King St then trolley) Tortoise-shell glasses and black turtlenecks ought to be the uniform of choice at this low-key jazz venue and cigar bar, located above the 219 Restaurant. The extensive whiskey selection, amber lighting and long wooden bar make a fine backdrop to bluesy jazz performances.

Information

The **visitor center** (☎703-838-5005; www.visitalexandriava.com; 221 King St; ⏰10am-5pm) issues parking permits and discount tickets to historic sites.

Getting There & Away

To get to Alexandria from downtown DC, take the Metro to the King St station. A free trolley makes the 1-mile journey between the Metro station and the waterfront (every 15 minutes, from 10am to 10:15pm Sunday to Wednesday, and until midnight Thursday to Saturday).

Mount Vernon

One of the most visited historic shrines in the nation, **Mt Vernon** (☎703-780-2000, 800-429-1520; www.mountvernon.org; 3200 Mount Vernon Memorial Hwy; adult/child $17/9; ⏰8am-5pm Apr-Aug, 9am-4pm Nov-Feb, to 5pm Mar, Sep & Oct, gristmill & distillery 10am-5pm Apr-Oct) was the beloved home of George and Martha Washington, who lived here from the time of their marriage in 1759 until George's death in 1799. Now owned and operated by the Mt Vernon Ladies Association, the estate offers glimpses of 18th-century farm life and the first president's life as a country planter. Mt Vernon does not gloss over the Founding Father's slave ownership: visitors can tour the slave quarters and burial ground. Other sights include Washington's **distillery and gristmill** (5513 Mount Vernon Memorial Hwy; ⏰10am-5pm Apr-Oct), 3 miles south of the estate.

Mt Vernon is 16 miles south of DC off the Mt Vernon Memorial Hwy. By public transportation, take the Metro to Huntington, then switch to Fairfax Connector bus

101. **Grayline** (202-289-1999; www.grayline.com; adult/child incl Mt Vernon admission $90/30) and **OnBoard Tours** (301-839-5261; www.onboardtours.com; adult/child incl Mt Vernon admission from $80/70) run bus tours from DC, stopping at Arlington and Mt Vernon.

Several companies offer seasonal boat trips from DC and Alexandria; the cheapest is **Potomac Riverboat Company** (703-684-0580; www.potomacriverboatco.com; adult/child incl Mt Vernon admission $42/22). A healthy alternative is to take a lovely bike ride along the Potomac River from DC (18 miles from Roosevelt Island). You can even bike one way from the Alexandria waterfront and return by boat with **Bike and Roll DC** (202-842-2453; www.bikeandrolldc.com; adult/child $63/40).

Manassas

On July 21, 1861, Union and Confederate soldiers clashed in the first major land battle of the Civil War. Expecting a quick victory, DC residents flocked here to picnic and watch the First Battle of Bull Run (known in the South as First Manassas). The surprise Southern victory erased any hopes of a quick end to the war. Union and Confederate soldiers again met on the same ground for the larger Second Battle of Manassas in August 1862; again the South was victorious. Today, **Manassas National Battlefield Park** is a curving green hillscape, sectioned into fuzzy fields of tall grass and wildflowers by split-rail wood fences. Start your tour at the **Henry Hill Visitor Center** (703-361-1339; www.nps.gov/mana; adult/child $3/free; 8:30am-5pm) to watch the orientation film and pick up park and trail maps.

Daily **Amtrak** (www.amtrak.com; one way $16-28) and **Virginia Railway Express** (VRE; www.vre.org; one way $9.10; Mon-Fri) trains make the 50-minute journey between DC's Union Station and the historic **Old Town Manassas Railroad Station** (9451 West St); from there it's a 6-mile taxi ride to the park. There are several restaurants and bars around the Manassas train station, but the rest of the city is a mess of strip malls and suburban sprawl.

Fredericksburg

Fredericksburg is a pretty town with a historical district that's almost a cliché of small-town Americana. George Washington grew up here, and the Civil War exploded in the streets and surrounding fields. Today the main street is a pleasant amble of bookstores, gastropubs and cafes.

Sights

Fredericksburg & Spotsylvania National Military Park HISTORIC SITE
(www.nps.gov/frsp) FREE More than 13,000 Americans were killed during the Civil War in four battles fought in a 17-mile radius covered by this park, today maintained by the NPS (National Park Service). Don't miss the burial site of Stonewall Jackson's amputated arm near the **Fredericksburg Battlefield visitor center** (540-373-6122; www.nps.gov/frsp; 1013 Lafayette Blvd; film $2; 9am-5pm) FREE.

James Monroe Museum & Memorial Library HISTORIC SITE
(540-654-1043; http://jamesmonroemuseum.umw.edu; 908 Charles St; adult/child $6/2; 10am-5pm Mon-Sat, from 1pm Sun) The museum's namesake was the nation's fifth president. US history nerds will delight in the small curious collection of Monroe memorabilia, including the desk on which he wrote the famous Monroe Doctrine.

Mary Washington House HISTORIC BUILDING
(540-373-5630; 1200 Charles St; adult/child $5/2; 11am-5pm Mon-Sat, noon-4pm Sun) At the 18th-century home of George Washington's mother, knowledgeable tour guides in period costume shed light on Mary and what life was like in her time. The lovely garden is an excellent recreation from the era.

Sleeping & Eating

You'll find dozens of restaurants and cafes along historic Caroline and William Sts.

Richard Johnston Inn B&B $$
(540-899-7606; www.therichardjohnstoninn.com; 711 Caroline St; r $125-250; P) In an 18th-century brick mansion, this cozy B&B scores points for location, comfort and friendliness.

Foode AMERICAN $$
(540-479-1370; www.foodeonline.com; 1006C/D Caroline St; mains lunch $9-11, dinner $15-25; 11am–3pm & 4:30pm–8pm Tue-Sat, 10am-2pm Sun) Foode serves up tasty farm-to-table fare in a rustic but artsy setting.

Getting There & Away

Virginia Railway Express ($11.55, 1½ hours) and **Amtrak** ($26 to $50, 1¼ hours) trains depart from the **Fredericksburg train station** (200 Lafayette Blvd) with service to DC.

Greyhound has buses to/from DC ($15 to $24, five per day, 1½ hours) and Richmond ($15 to $27, three per day, one hour). The **Greyhound station** (540-373-2103; 1400 Jefferson Davis Hwy) is roughly 1.5 miles west of the historic district.

Richmond

Richmond has been the capital of the Commonwealth of Virginia since 1780. It's an old-fashioned Southern city that's grounded in tradition on one hand, but full of income disparities and social tensions on the other. Yet it's an undeniably handsome town, with red-brick row houses, a rushing river and leafy parks.

Its history is ubiquitous and, sometimes, uncomfortable; this was where patriot Patrick Henry gave his famous 'Give me Liberty, or give me Death!' speech, and where the slave-holding Southern Confederate States placed their capital. Today the 'River City' is a surprisingly dynamic place, with a buzzing food-and-drink scene, fascinating neighborhoods and a wide range of attractions.

Sights

American Civil War Center at Historic Tredegar MUSEUM
(www.tredegar.org; 500 Tredegar St; adult/child $8/4; 9am-5pm) Located in an 1861 gun foundry, this fascinating site explores the causes and course of the Civil War from the perspectives of Union, Confederate and African American experiences. Next door is a free site run by the National Park Service that delves into Richmond's role during the war. This is one of 13 protected area sites that make up **Richmond National Battlefield Park** (www.nps.gov/rich).

Canal Walk WATERFRONT
(www.rvariverfront.com; btwn 5th and 17th Sts) The 1.25-mile waterfront Canal Walk between the James River and the Kanawha (ka-*naw*) and Haxall Canals is a lovely way of seeing a dozen highlights of Richmond history in one go. There's also a pedestrian bridge across to Belle Isle, a scruffy but intriguing island in the James.

Belle Isle PARK
(www.jamesriverpark.org) A long pedestrian bridge leads from Tredegar St (just past the national park site) out to this car-free island. Once a quarry, power plant and POW camp during the Civil War (though never all at once), today this is one of Richmond's finest city parks. The big flat rocks are lovely for sunbathing, and hiking and biking trails abound – but don't swim in the James River. It's polluted and the currents are treacherous.

White House of the Confederacy HISTORIC SITE
(www.moc.org; cnr 12th & Clay Sts; adult/child $10/6; 10am-5pm) While this was once a shrine to the Southern 'Lost Cause,' the Confederate White House is recommended for its quirky insights (did you know the second-most powerful man in the Confederacy may have been a gay Jew?).

Virginia State Capitol BUILDING
(www.virginiacapitol.gov; cnr 9th & Grace Sts, Capitol Sq; 8am-5pm Mon-Sat, 1-5pm Sun) FREE Designed by Thomas Jefferson, the capitol building was completed in 1788 and houses the oldest legislative body in the Western Hemisphere – the Virginia General Assembly, established in 1619. Free tours available.

Virginia Historical Society MUSEUM
(www.vahistorical.org; 428 North Blvd; adult/student $6/4; 10am-5pm Mon-Sat, from 1pm Sun) The VHS is looking grander than ever following a multi-million-dollar renovation. Changing and permanent exhibits trace the history of the Commonwealth from prehistoric to present times.

St John's Episcopal Church CHURCH
(www.historicstjohnschurch.org; 2401 E Broad St; tours adult/child $7/5; 10am-4pm Mon-Sat, from 1pm Sun) It was here that firebrand Patrick Henry uttered his famous battle cry – 'Give me Liberty, or give me Death!' – during the rebellious 1775 Second Virginia Convention. His speech is re-enacted from 1pm to 3pm on Sundays in summer.

Virginia Museum of Fine Arts MUSEUM
(VMFA; 804-340-1400; www.vmfa.museum; 200 North Blvd; 10am-5pm Sun-Wed, to 9pm Thu & Fri) FREE Has a remarkable collection of European works, sacred Himalayan art and one of the largest Fabergé egg collections on display outside Russia. Also hosts excellent temporary exhibitions (admission ranges from free to $20).

WORTH A TRIP

VINEYARDS OF VIRGINIA

Home to some 230 vineyards, Virginia has a rising presence in the wine world. Good places to begin the foray lie just outside of DC in Loudon County. For maps, wine routes and loads of other viticultural info, visit www.virginiawine.org.

King Family Vineyards (☑ 434-823-7800; www.kingfamilyvineyards.com; 6550 Roseland Farm, Crozet; tastings $8; ⊙ 10am-5:30pm) Consistently ranks as one of Virginia's best wineries. Bring a picnic (the winery also sells gourmet goodies) and enjoy the expansive scenery. At 1pm on summer Sundays (late May to mid-October), you can also catch a free polo match. It's 18 miles east of Charlottesville.

Jefferson Vineyards (☑ 434-977-3042; www.jeffersonvineyards.com; 1353 Thomas Jefferson Pkwy, Charlottesville; tastings $10; ⊙ 10am-6pm) Near Charlottesville, this winery harvests from its namesake's original 1774 vineyard site. It also hosts twice-monthly free outdoor concerts in summer.

Bluemont Vineyard (☑ 540-554-8439; www.bluemontvineyard.com; 18755 Foggy Bottom Rd, Bluemont; tastings $5; ⊙ 11am-6pm Wed-Mon) Bluemont produces ruby-red Nortons and crisp Viogniers, though it's equally famous for its spectacular location – at a 950ft elevation with sweeping views over the countryside.

Chrysalis Vineyards (☑ 540-687-8222; www.chrysaliswine.com; 23876 Champe Ford Rd, Middleburg; tastings $7-10; ⊙ 10am-6pm) Proudly using the native Norton grape (which dates back to 1820), Chrysalis produces highly drinkable reds and whites – including a refreshing Viognier. The pretty estate hosts a bluegrass fest in October.

Tarara Vineyard (☑ 703-771-7100; www.tarara.com; 13648 Tarara Lane, Leesburg; tastings $10; ⊙ 11am-5pm) On a bluff overlooking the Potomac, this 475-acre estate provides guided tours showing the grape's journey from vine to glass. The winery has a 6000-sq-ft cave/cellar, and visitors can pick fruit in the orchard or hike the 6 miles of trails through rolling countryside. Tarara also hosts summertime Saturday-evening concerts and three major wine festivals.

Poe Museum MUSEUM
(☑ 804-648-5523; www.poemuseum.org; 1914-16 E Main St; adult/student $6/5; ⊙ 10am-5pm Tue-Sat, from 11am Sun) Contains the world's largest collection of manuscripts and memorabilia of poet Edgar Allan Poe, who lived and worked in Richmond.

Hollywood Cemetery CEMETERY
(☑ 804-649-0711; www.hollywoodcemetery.org; entrance cnr Albemarle & Cherry Sts; ⊙ 8am-5pm, to 6pm summer) FREE This tranquil cemetery, perched above the James River rapids, contains the gravesites of two US presidents (James Monroe and John Tyler), the only Confederate president (Jefferson Davis) and 18,000 Confederate soldiers. Free walking tours are given at 10am Monday through Saturday and 2pm on Sunday.

Monument Avenue Statues STATUE
(btwn N Lombardy St & Roseneath Rd) Monument Ave, a tree-lined boulevard in northeast Richmond, holds statues of such revered Southern heroes as JEB Stuart, Robert E Lee, Matthew Fontaine Maury, Jefferson Davis, Stonewall Jackson and – in a nod to diversity – African American tennis champion Arthur Ashe.

🛏 Sleeping

★ **HI Richmond** HOSTEL $
(www.hiusa.org; 7 N 2nd St; dm around $30; ❄ 🅐) Inside a historic 1924 building, this new, eco-friendly hostel has a great central location and bright rooms (both dorms and private rooms), with high ceilings and loads of original details. There's a kitchen for guests, inviting common areas, and it's also completely accessible for travelers with disabilities.

Linden Row Inn BOUTIQUE HOTEL $$
(☑ 804-783-7000; www.lindenrowinn.com; 100 E Franklin St; r $100-190; 🅟 ❄ @ 🅐) This antebellum gem has 70 attractive rooms (with period Victorian furnishings) spread among neighboring Greek Revival town houses in an excellent downtown location. Friendly southern hospitality and thoughtful extras (free passes to the YMCA, free around-town shuttle service) sweeten the deal.

Museum District B&B B&B $$
(804-359-2332; www.museumdistrictbb.com; 2811 Grove Ave; r from $150; P ❄) In a fine location near the dining and drinking of Carytown, this stately 1920s brick B&B has earned many admirers for its warm welcome. Rooms are comfortably set and guests can enjoy the wide front porch, cozy parlor with fireplace, and excellent cooked breakfasts – plus wine and cheese in the evenings.

Jefferson Hotel LUXURY HOTEL $$$
(804-649-4750; www.jeffersonhotel.com; 101 W Franklin St; r $365; P ❄) The Jefferson is Richmond's grandest hotel and one of the finest in America. The vision of tobacco tycoon and Confederate major Lewis Ginter, the beaux-arts-style hotel was completed in 1895. According to rumor, the magnificent grand staircase in the lobby served as the model for the famed stairs in *Gone with the Wind*.

Even if you don't stay here, it's worth having a peek inside. If you have time, try the hotel's afternoon tea, served beneath Tiffany stained glass in the Palm Court lobby (from 3pm Friday to Sunday), or have a drink at the grand Lemaire Bar.

Eating

You'll find dozens of restaurants along the cobbled streets of Shockoe Slip and Shockoe Bottom. Further west in Carytown (W Cary St between S Blvd and N Thompson St) are even more dining options.

★ **Mama J's** AMERICAN $
(415 N 1st St; mains $7-10; 11am-9pm Sun-Thu, to 10pm Fri & Sat) Set in the historic African American neighborhood of Jackson Ward, Mama J's serves up delicious fried chicken and legendary fried catfish, along with collard greens, mac 'n' cheese, candied yams and other fixings. The service is friendly and the lines are long – go early to beat the crowds.

17th Street Farmers Market MARKET $
(cnr 17th & E Main Sts; 8:30am-4pm Sat & Sun) For cheap eats and fresh produce, check out this bustling market, which runs from late April through early October. On Sundays, the market sells antiques.

Sub Rosa BAKERY $
(620 N 25th St; pastries $3-5; 7am-6pm Tue-Fri, 8:30am-5pm Sat & Sun) In the historic Church Hill neighborhood, Sub Rosa is a wood-fired bakery serving some of the best baked goods in the south.

Kuba Kuba CUBAN $
(1601 Park Ave; mains $7-17; 9am-9:30pm Mon-Sat to 8pm Sun) In the Fan district, this tiny hole in the wall feels like a bodega straight out of Old Havana, with mouth-watering roast pork dishes, Spanish-style omelets and panini at rock-bottom prices.

Sidewalk Cafe AMERICAN $
(2101 W Main St; mains $9-18; 11:30am-2am Mon-Fri, from 9am Sat & Sun) A much-loved local haunt, Sidewalk Cafe feels like a dive bar (year-round Christmas lights, wood-paneled walls, kitschy artwork), but the food is first rate. There's outdoor seating on the sidewalk, daily specials (eg Taco Tuesdays) and legendary weekend brunches.

The Daily MODERN AMERICAN $$
(804-342-8990; 2934 W Cary St; mains $10-25; 7am-10pm Sun-Thu, to midnight Fri & Sat;) In the heart of Carytown, the Daily is a great dining and drinking choice no matter the time of day. Stop by for lump crab omelets at breakfast, blackened mahimahi BLT at lunch and seared scallops by night. Extensive vegan options, first-rate cocktails and a buzzing, artfully designed space (complete with dramatically lit trees) seal the deal.

Millie's Diner MODERN AMERICAN $$
(804-643-5512; 2603 E Main St; lunch $9-12, dinner $22-26; 11am-2:30pm & 5:30-10:30pm Tue-Fri, 9am-3pm & 5:30-10:30pm Sat & Sun) Lunch, dinner or weekend brunch – Richmond icon Millie's does it all, and does it well. It's a small but handsomely designed space, with creative seasonal fare. The Devil's Mess – an open-faced omelet with spicy sausage, curry, veg, cheese and avocado – is legendary.

Boathouse at Rocketts Landing SEAFOOD $$$
(804-622-2628; 4708 E Old Main St; mains $14-32; 5pm-midnight Mon-Thu, from 3pm Fri, from noon Sat & Sun) The Boathouse serves good seafood plates (crispy calamari, Chapel Creek oysters, sesame-seared tuna) and pub fare in a fabulous setting overlooking the James River. The breezy deck is also a fine spot for a sundowner. It's located about 1 mile south of Shockoe Bottom.

Drinking & Entertainment

Legend Brewing Company MICROBREWERY
(804-232-3446; www.legendbrewing.com; 321 W 7th St; 11:30am-11pm Mon-Sat, to 10pm Sun) On the south side of the James River, this place has excellent microbrews, tasty pub grub and fine views of the city from its popular out-

door deck. There's live bluegrass on Sundays (6:30pm), rock and other music on Fridays (8pm), and free brewery tours on Saturdays (1pm).

From downtown, it's a short hop across the bike- and pedestrian-friendly Manchester (S 9th St) Bridge.

Saison COCKTAIL BAR
(23 W Marshall St; ⏲5pm-2am) This classy drinking den attracts serious cocktail lovers, who clink glasses over creative libations, craft beer and farm-to-table fare. It's in Jackson Ward, near downtown.

Capital Ale House BAR
(623 E Main St; ⏲11am-1:30am) Popular with political wonks from the nearby state capitol, this downtown pub has a superb beer selection (more than 50 on tap and 250 bottled) and decent pub grub.

Cary Street Cafe LIVE MUSIC
(☎804-353-7445; www.carystreetcafe.com; 2631 W Cary St; ⏲8am-2am Mon-Fri, from 11am Sat & Sun) Live music (plus the odd karaoke crooner) emanates from this excellent bar just about every night of the week. This spot is proudly pro-hippie, but doesn't just bust hippie tunes; the gigs juke from reggae and folk to alt-country and gypsy rock.

Byrd Theater CINEMA
(☎804-353-9911; www.byrdtheatre.com; 2908 W Cary St; tickets from $2) You can't beat the price at this classic 1928 cinema, which shows second-run films. Wurlitzer-organ concerts precede the Saturday-night shows.

Information

Johnston-Willis Hospital (☎804-330-2000; 1401 Johnston-Willis Dr)

Post Office (700 E Main St; ⏲7:30am-5pm Mon-Fri)

Richmond-Times Dispatch (www.richmond.com) Daily newspaper.

Richmond Visitor Center (☎804-783-7450; www.visitrichmondva.com; 405 N 3rd St; ⏲9am-5pm)

Style Weekly (www.styleweekly.com) Alternative weekly with listings of events, restaurants, nightlife and the arts.

Getting There & Around

The cab fare from **Richmond International Airport** (RIC; ☎804-226-3000; www.flyrichmond.com), 10 miles east of town, costs about $30.

Amtrak (☎800-872-7245; www.amtrak.com) trains stop at the **main station** (7519 Staples Mill Rd), 7 miles north of town (accessible to downtown via bus 27). More-convenient but less-frequent trains stop downtown at the **Main St Station** (1500 E Main St).

A new **Bikeshare** program is slated to launch by 2016.

Greater Richmond Transit Company (GRTC; ☎804-358-4782; www.ridegrtc.com; fares from $2) Runs local buses. Takes exact change only.

Greyhound/Trailways Bus Station (☎804-254-5910; www.greyhound.com; 2910 North Blvd)

Petersburg

About 25 miles south of Richmond, the little town of Petersburg played a big role in the Civil War as a major railway junction, transporting Confederate troops and supplies. Union troops laid a 10-month siege of Petersburg in 1864–65, the longest on American soil. The **Siege Museum** (☎804-733-2404; 15 W Bank St; adult/child $5/4, incl Old Blandford Church $11/9; ⏲10am-5pm) relates the plight of civilians during the siege. Several miles east of town, **Petersburg National Battlefield** (nps.gov/pete; per vehicle/pedestrian $5/3; ⏲9am-5pm) is where Union soldiers planted explosives underneath a Confederate breastwork, leading to the Battle of the Crater (novelized and cinematized in *Cold Mountain*). West of downtown in Pamplin Historical Park, the excellent **National Museum of the Civil War Soldier** (☎804-861-2408; www.pamplinpark.org; 6125 Boydton Plank Rd; adult/child $13/8; ⏲9am-5pm) illustrates the hardships faced by soldiers on both sides of the conflict.

Historic Triangle

This is America's birthplace. Nowhere else in the country has such a small area played such a pivotal role in the nation's history. The nation's roots were planted in Jamestown, the first permanent English settlement in the New World; the flames of the American Revolution were fanned at the Colonial capital of Williamsburg; and America finally won its independence from Britain at Yorktown.

You'll need at least two days to do the Triangle any justice. A daily free shuttle travels between the Williamsburg visitor center, Yorktown and Jamestown.

Williamsburg

If you visit only one historical town in Virginia, make it Williamsburg – home to Colonial Williamsburg, one of the largest, most comprehensive living-history museums in the world. If any place is going to get kids into history, this is it, but it's plenty of fun for adults, too.

The actual town of Williamsburg, Virginia's capital from 1699 to 1780, is a stately place. The prestigious campus of the College of William & Mary adds a decent dash of youth culture, with coffee shops, cheap pubs and fashion boutiques.

Sights

Colonial Williamsburg HISTORIC SITE
(www.colonialwilliamsburg.org; adult/child 1-day $41/21, multi-day $51/26; 9am-5pm) The restored capital of England's largest colony in the New World is a must-see attraction for visitors of all ages. This is not some phony, fenced-in theme park: Colonial Williamsburg is a living, breathing, working history museum with a painstakingly researched environment that brilliantly captures America of the 1700s.

➡ The Site

The 301-acre historic area contains 88 original 18th-century buildings and several hundred faithful reproductions. Costumed townsfolk and 'interpreters' in period dress go about their colonial jobs as blacksmiths, apothecaries, printers, barmaids, soldiers and patriots, breaking character only long enough to pose for a snapshot.

Costumed patriots including Patrick Henry and Thomas Jefferson still deliver impassioned speeches for freedom, but the park doesn't gloss over America's less glorious moments. Today's re-enactors debate and question slavery, women's suffrage, the rights of indigenous Americans and whether or not it is even moral to engage in revolution.

➡ Entrance

Walking around the historic district and patronizing the shops and taverns is free, but entry to building tours and most exhibits is restricted to ticketholders. Expect crowds, lines and petulant children, especially in summer.

To park and to purchase tickets, follow signs to the **visitor center** (757-220-7645; 101 Visitor Center Dr; 8:45am-5pm), found north of the historic district between Hwy 132 and Colonial Pkwy; kids can also hire period costumes here for $25 per day. Start off with a 30-minute film about Williamsburg, and ask about the day's programs and events.

Parking is free; shuttle buses run frequently to and from the historic district, or you can walk along the tree-lined footpath. You can also buy tickets at the **Merchants Square information booth** (W Duke of Gloucester St; 9am-5pm).

College of William & Mary HISTORIC BUILDING
(www.wm.edu; 200 Stadium Dr) Chartered in 1693, the College of William & Mary is the second-oldest college in the country and retains the oldest academic building in continued use in the USA, the **Sir Christopher Wren Building**. The school's alumni include Thomas Jefferson, James Monroe and comedian Jon Stewart.

Sleeping

The visitor center can help find and book accommodations at no cost. If you stay in Colonial Williamsburg, guesthouses can provide discount admission tickets (adult/child $30/15).

Governor's Inn HOTEL $
(757-220-7940; www.colonialwilliamsburg.com; 506 N Henry St; r $70-93; P 📶 🏊) Williamsburg's official 'economy' choice is a big box by any other name, but rooms are clean, and guests can use the pool and facilities of the Woodlands Hotel. It's in a great location near the visitor center, three blocks from the historic district.

Williamsburg Woodlands Hotel & Suites HOTEL $$
(757-220-7960; www.colonialwilliamsburg.com; 105 Visitor Center Dr; r from $165; P ❄ 📶 🏊) This good-value option has comfy, carpeted rooms (some of which go a bit heavy on the patterned wallpaper) near the main visitor center in Colonial Williamsburg. The splash park, games (mini-golf, volleyball court) and complimentary breakfast make it a hit with families.

★ Colonial Williamsburg Historic Lodging GUESTHOUSE $$$
(888-965-7254, 757-220-7978; www.colonialwilliamsburg.com; 136 E Francis St; r $220) For true 18th-century immersion, guests can stay in one of 26 original Colonial houses inside the historic district. Accommodations range in

size and style, though the best have period furnishings, canopy beds and wood-burning fireplaces.

✖ Eating

You'll find many restaurants, cafes and pubs in Merchants Sq, adjacent to Colonial Williamsburg.

Cheese Shop   DELI $
(410 W Duke of Gloucester St, Merchants Sq; mains $6-8; ⊘10am-8pm Mon-Sat, 11am-6pm Sun) This gourmet deli showcases some flavorful sandwiches and antipasti, plus baguettes, pastries, wine, beer and wonderful cheeses.

Aromas   CAFE $
(www.aromasworld.com; 431 Prince George St; mains $6-15; ⊘7am-10pm Mon-Sat, 8am-8pm Sun; 🛜) One block north of Merchants Sq, Aromas is an inviting coffeehouse serving a wide range of fare, plus wine and beer. It has outdoor seating and live music (jazz on Tuesdays; wide-ranging sounds on weekends).

King's Arms Tavern   MODERN AMERICAN $$$
(☑888-965-7254; 416 E Duke of Gloucester St; lunch mains $14-16, dinner $32-37; ⊘11:30am-2:30pm & 5-9pm) Of the four restaurants within Colonial Williamsburg, this is the most elegant, serving early-American cuisine, such as game pie – venison, rabbit and duck braised in port-wine sauce.

ℹ Getting There & Around

Williamsburg Transportation Center (☑757-229-8750; cnr Boundary & Lafayette Sts) **Amtrak** (www.amtrak.com) trains run from here twice a day to Washington, DC ($44, four hours), and Richmond ($21, one hour).

Jamestown

On May 14, 1607, a group of 104 English men and boys settled on this swampy island, bearing a charter from the Virginia Company of London to search for gold and other riches. Instead, they found starvation and disease. By January of 1608, only about 40 colonists were still alive, and these had resorted to cannibalism to survive. The colony survived the 'Starving Time' with the leadership of Captain James Smith and help from Powhatan, a local Native American leader. In 1619 the elected House of Burgesses convened, forming the first democratic government in the Americas.

◉ Sights & Activities

Historic Jamestowne   HISTORIC SITE
(☑757-856-1250; www.historicjamestowne. org; 1368 Colonial Pkwy; adult/child $14/free; ⊘8:30am-4:30pm) Run by the NPS, this is the original Jamestown site. Start your visit at the on-site museum and check out the statues of John Smith and Pocahontas. The original Jamestown ruins were rediscovered in 1994; visitors can watch the ongoing archaeological work at the site.

Jamestown Settlement   HISTORIC SITE
(☑757-253-4838; www.historyisfun.org; 2110 Jamestown Rd; adult/child $17/8, incl Yorktown Victory Center $21/11; ⊘9am-5pm; P🚸) Popular with kids, the state-run Jamestown Settlement reconstructs the 1607 **James Fort**; a **Native American village**; and full-scale replicas of the first ships that brought the settlers to Jamestown, along with living-history fun. Multimedia exhibits and costumed interpreters bring the 17th century to life.

Yorktown

On October 19, 1781, British General Cornwallis surrendered to George Washington here, effectively ending the American Revolution. Overpowered by massive American guns on land and cut off from the sea by the French, the British were in a hopeless position. Although Washington anticipated a much longer siege, the devastating barrage quickly overwhelmed Cornwallis, who surrendered within days.

Yorktown itself is a pleasant waterfront village overlooking the York River, with a nice range of shops, restaurants and pubs.

◉ Sights & Activities

Yorktown Battlefield   HISTORIC SITE
(☑757-898-3400; www.nps.gov/york; 1000 Colonial Pkwy; incl Historic Jamestowne adult/child $7/free; ⊘9am-5pm; P🚸) 🚲 Yorktown Battlefield, run by the NPS, is the site of the last major battle of the American Revolution. Start your tour at the visitor center and check out the orientation film and the display of Washington's original tent. The 7-mile Battlefield Rd Tour takes you past the major highlights. Don't miss a walk through the last British defensive sites, Redoubts 9 and 10.

Yorktown Victory Center   MUSEUM
(☑757-887-1776; www.historyisfun.org; 200 Water St; adult/child $10/6; ⊘9am-5pm; P🚸) 🚲 The

state-run Yorktown Victory Center is an interactive, living-history museum that focuses on reconstruction, re-enactment and the Revolution's impact on the people who lived through it. At the re-created encampment, costumed Continental soldiers fire cannons and discuss food preparation and field medicine of the day.

Eating

Carrot Tree CAFE $
(☎757-988-1999; 323 Water St; mains $7-9; ⌚11am-4pm; ✎) On the waterfront, Carrot Tree is a good, affordable spot serving wraps, salads and veggie burgers.

James River Plantations

The grand homes of Virginia's slave-holding aristocracy were a clear sign of the era's class divisions. A string of them line scenic Hwy 5 on the north side of the river, though only a few are open to the public.

Sights & Activities

Sherwood Forest HISTORIC SITE
(☎804-829-5377; www.sherwoodforest.org; 14501 John Tyler Memorial Hwy, Charles City; self-guided tours adult/child $10/free; ⌚grounds 9am-5pm) The longest frame house in the country, this was the home of 10th US president John Tyler. Full tours are available by advance appointment only ($35 per person), though the grounds are open to self-guided tours.

Berkeley Plantation HISTORIC SITE
(☎804-829-6018; www.berkeleyplantation.com; 12602 Harrison Landing Rd, Charles City; adult/child $11/7.50; ⌚9:30am-4:30pm) Berkeley was the site of the first official Thanksgiving in 1619. It was the birthplace and home of Benjamin Harrison V, a signatory to of the Declaration of Independence, and his son William Henry Harrison, the 9th US president.

Shirley Plantation HISTORIC SITE
(☎800-829-5121; www.shirleyplantation.com; 501 Shirley Plantation Rd, Charles City; adult/child $11/7.50; ⌚9:30am-4:30pm) Shirley, situated picturesquely on the river, is Virginia's oldest plantation (1613) and is perhaps the best example of how a British-model plantation actually appeared, with its tidy row of brick service and trade houses – tool barn, ice house, laundry, etc – leading up to the big house.

Hampton Roads

The Hampton Roads (named not for asphalt, but the confluence of the James, Nansemond and Elizabeth Rivers and Chesapeake Bay) have always been prime real estate. The Powhatan Confederacy fished these waters and hunted the fingerlike protrusions of the Virginia coast for thousands of years before John Smith arrived in 1607. Today Hampton Roads is known for congestion and a cultural mishmash of history, the military and the arts.

Norfolk

As home to the world's largest naval base, it's not surprising that Norfolk has had a reputation as a rowdy port town filled with drunken sailors. In recent years the city has worked hard to clean up its image through development, gentrification and focusing on its burgeoning arts scene.

Sights

Naval Station Norfolk MILITARY SITE
(☎757-444-7955; www.cnic.navy.mil/norfolksta; 9079 Hampton Blvd; adult/child $10/5) The world's largest navy base, and one of the busiest airfields in the country, this is a must-see. The 45-minute bus tours are conducted by naval personnel and must be booked in advance (hours vary). Photo ID is required for adults.

Nauticus MUSEUM
(☎757-664-1000; www.nauticus.org; 1 Waterside Dr; adult/child $16/11.50; ⌚10am-5pm Tue-Sat, noon-5pm Sun) This massive, interactive, maritime-themed museum has exhibits on undersea exploration, the aquatic life of the Chesapeake Bay and US Naval lore. The highlight for visitors is clambering around the decks and inner corridors of the **USS Wisconsin**. Built in 1943, it was the largest (887ft long) and last battleship built by the US Navy.

Chrysler Museum of Art MUSEUM
(☎757-664-6200; www.chrysler.org; 245 W Olney Rd; ⌚10am-5pm Tue-Sat, noon-5pm Sun) FREE A glorious setting for an eclectic collection of artifacts from ancient Egypt to the present day, including works by Monet, Matisse, Renoir, Warhol and a world-class collection of Tiffany blown glass.

Sleeping

For waterfront digs, there are tons of budget to midrange options lining Ocean View Ave (which actually borders the bay).

Tazewell Hotel HOTEL $
(757-623-6200; www.thetazewell.com; 245 Granby St; r from $89;) Set in a heritage 1906 building, the Tazewell has a great location in the heart of the Granby St dining and drinking district. The carpeted rooms have aging wooden furnishings, and the place could use an update, but it's still a good value. There's a low-lit wine bar and Italian restaurant on the 1st floor.

Page House Inn B&B $$
(757-625-5033; www.pagehouseinn.com; 323 Fairfax Ave; r $160-245; P) Opposite the Chrysler Museum of Art, this luxurious B&B is a cornerstone of Norfolk elegance.

Eating

Two of the best dining strips are downtown's Granby St and Ghent's Colley Ave.

Cure CAFE $
(www.curenorfolk.com; 503 Botetourt St; mains $6-9; 8am-10pm Mon-Sat, 9am-8pm Sun;) The Cure is a picture-perfect neighborhood cafe on the edge of the historic district, with tasty and creative sandwiches, great coffee (from Counter Culture), and microbrews and charcuterie later in the day.

Field Guide MODERN AMERICAN $
(429 Granby St; mains $8-10; 11am-10pm Tue-Thu, to 1am Fri & Sat) On restaurant-lined Granby St, Field Guide is a standout for its market-fresh fare: zingy salads, flavor-rich rice bowls and decadent sandwiches, plus fun cocktails (try a margarita slushie). It's a casual but hip affair, with communal tables and a sliding garage door that opens wide on sunny days.

Press 626 Cafe & Wine Bar MODERN AMERICAN $$
(757-282-6234; 626 W Olney Rd; mains lunch $8-13, dinner $16-26; 11am-11pm Mon-Fri, from 5pm Sat, 10:30am-2:30pm Sun;) Embracing the Slow Food movement, the very charming Press 626 has a wide-ranging menu, with pressed gourmet sandwiches (at lunch), seared scallops, bouillabaisse and a great wine selection.

Drinking & Entertainment

Elliot's Fair Grounds CAFE
(806 Baldwin Ave; 7am-10pm Mon-Sat, from 8am Sun;) This tiny, funky coffeehouse attracts everyone from students to sailors. Aside from good caffeinated drinks, Elliot's serves sandwiches and desserts.

Taphouse Grill at Ghent PUB
(931 W 21st St; 11am-2am) Good microbrews are served and good local bands jam at this warm little pub.

Getting There & Around

The region is served by **Norfolk International Airport** (NIA; 757-857-3351), 7 miles northeast of downtown Norfolk. **Greyhound** (757-625-7500; www.greyhound.com; 701 Monticello Ave) runs buses to Virginia Beach ($16, 35 minutes), Richmond ($32, 2¾ hours) and Washington, DC ($50, 6½ hours).

Hampton Roads Transit (757-222-6100; www.gohrt.com) serves the entire Hampton Roads region. Buses ($1.75) run from downtown throughout the city and to Newport News and Virginia Beach.

Newport News

The city of Newport News comes off as a giant example of suburban sprawl, but there are several attractions here, notably the amazing **Mariners' Museum** (757-596-2222; www.marinersmuseum.org; 100 Museum Dr; adult/child $14/9; 9am-5pm Mon-Sat, from 11am Sun), one of the biggest, most comprehensive maritime museums in the world. The on-site **USS Monitor Center** houses the dredged carcass of the Civil War–era *Monitor,* one of the world's first ironclad warships, as well as a life-size replica of the real deal.

The **Virginia Living Museum** (757-595-1900; www.thevlm.org; 524 J Clyde Morris Blvd; adult/child $17/13; 9am-5pm, from noon Sun; P) is a fine introduction to Virginia's terrestrial and aquatic life, set in naturalistic ecosystems. The complex comprises open-air animal enclosures, an aviary, gardens and a planetarium.

Virginia Beach

With 35 miles of sandy beaches, a 3-mile concrete oceanfront boardwalk and nearby outdoor activities, it's no surprise that Virginia Beach is a prime tourist destination. The city has worked hard to shed its reputation as a rowdy 'Redneck Riviera,' and hey, the beach *is* wider and cleaner now and there are fewer louts. Beach aside, you'll find some lovely parks and nature sites beyond the crowded high-rises lining the shore. Expect thick crowds and heavy traffic if visiting in the summer.

Sights

Virginia Aquarium & Marine Science Center AQUARIUM
(757-385-3474; www.virginiaaquarium.com; 717 General Booth Blvd; adult/child $22/15; 9am-5pm) If you want to see an aquarium done right, come here. In various habitats, you can see a great array of aquatic life, including sea turtles, river otters and Komodo dragons.

First Landing State Park NATURE RESERVE
(2500 Shore Dr; admission per vehicle $6-7) This 2888-acre woodland has 20 miles of **hiking trails**, plus opportunities for camping, cycling, fishing, kayaking and swimming.

Virginia Museum of Contemporary Art MUSEUM
(www.virginiamoca.org; 2200 Parks Ave; adult/child $7.70/5.50; 10am-9pm Tue, to 5pm Wed-Fri, to 4pm Sat & Sun) Has excellent rotating exhibitions housed in a fresh, ultramodern building.

Back Bay National Wildlife Refuge NATURE RESERVE
(www.fws.gov/backbay; per vehicle/pedestrian Apr-Oct $5/2, Nov-Mar free; sunrise-sunset) This 9250-acre wildlife and migratory-bird marshland habitat is most stunning during the December migration season.

Great Dismal Swamp National Wildlife Refuge NATURE RESERVE
(757-986-3705; www.fws.gov/refuge/great_dismal_swamp; 3100 Desert Rd, Suffolk; sunrise-sunset;) FREE Some 30 miles southwest of Virginia Beach, this 112,000-acre refuge, which straddles the North Carolina border, is rich in flora and fauna, including black bears, bobcats and more than 200 bird species.

Sleeping

Angie's Guest Cottage & Hostel GUESTHOUSE $
(757-491-1830; www.angiescottage.com; 302 24th St; dm $32, d $70-110;) Located just one block from the beach, Angie's offers dormitories and private rooms with kitchenettes. It's a good value for the area.

First Landing State Park CAMPGROUND $
(800-933-7275; http://dcr.virginia.gov; Cape Henry; campsites $28, cabins from $75;) You couldn't ask for a prettier campground than the one at this bayfront state park, though the cabins have no water view.

Eating

★Blue Pete's SEAFOOD $$
(757-426-2278; www.bluepetespungo.com; 1400 N Muddy Creek Rd; mains $10-25; 5-10pm Wed-Fri, noon-10pm Sat & Sun) Perched over a peaceful creek near Back Bay, Blue Pete's has an enchanting woodland setting and a wide-ranging menu: crab cakes, brisket sandwiches, pastas and coconut-breaded shrimp.

Mahi Mah's SEAFOOD $$$
(757-437-8030; www.mahimahs.com; 615 Atlantic Ave; mains $10-36; 7am-midnight Sun-Thu, to 2am Fri & Sat;) This oceanfront local is the go-to for scrumptious seafood. From happy hour (when oysters are 50¢) onwards, it's a buzzing spot for a drink.

Information

The I-264 runs straight to the **visitor center** (800-822-3224; www.visitvirginiabeach.com; 2100 Parks Ave; 9am-5pm) and the beach.

Getting There & Around

Greyhound (757-422-2998; www.greyhound.com; 971 Virginia Beach Blvd) has five buses a day to Richmond ($15.50, 3½ hours), which also stop in Norfolk and Newport News; transfer in Richmond for services to Washington, DC; Wilmington; NYC and beyond. Buses depart from Circle D Food Mart, 1 mile west of the boardwalk.

Hampton Roads Transit runs the Virginia Beach Wave trolley (tickets $2), which plies Atlantic Ave in summer.

The Piedmont

Central Virginia's rolling central hills and plateaus separate the coastal lowlands from the mountainous frontier. The fertile valley gives way to dozens of wineries, country villages and grand colonial estates.

Charlottesville

Set in the shadow of the Blue Ridge Mountains, Charlottesville is regularly ranked as one of the country's best places to live. This culturally rich town of 45,000 is home to the University of Virginia (UVA), which attracts Southern aristocracy and artsy lefties in equal proportion. With the UVA grounds and pedestrian downtown area overflowing with students, couples, professors and the occasional celebrity under a blanket of blue skies, 'C-ville' is practically perfect.

Charlottesville Visitor Center (☎877-386-1103; www.visitcharlottesville.org; 610 E Main St; ⏲9am-5pm) is a helpful office in the heart of downtown.

Sights

University of Virginia UNIVERSITY
(☎434-924-0311; www.uvaguides.org; 400 Ray C Hunt Dr, Charlottesville) Thomas Jefferson founded the University of Virginia, whose classically designed buildings and grounds embody the spirit of communal living and learning that Jefferson envisioned. Free, student-led guided tours of the campus depart daily from the Harrison Institute at 10am, 11am and 2pm during the school year. The Jefferson-designed **Rotunda** (☎434-924-7969; rotunda.virginia.edu; 1826 University Ave), a scale replica of Rome's Pantheon, reopens in 2016 following restoration. UVA's **Fralin Art Museum** (☎434-924-3592; 155 Rugby Rd; ⏲noon-5pm Tue-Sun) FREE has an eclectic, interesting collection of American, European and Asian arts.

Sleeping

There's a good selection of budget and midrange chain motels lining Emmet St/US 29 north of town. If you're after a reservation service, try **Guesthouses** (☎434-979-7264; www.va-guesthouses.com; r from $150), which provides cottages and B&B rooms in private homes. Two-night minimum stays are commonly required on weekends.

Fairhaven GUESTHOUSE $
(☎434-933-2471; www.fairhavencville.com; 413 Fairway Ave; r $65-75; P ❄ 📶) This friendly and welcoming guesthouse is a great deal if you don't mind sharing facilities (there's just one bathroom for the three rooms). Each room has wood floors, with comfy beds and a cheerful color scheme, and guests can use the kitchen, living room or backyard. It's about a 1-mile walk to the pedestrian mall.

English Inn HOTEL $$
(☎434-971-9900; www.englishinncharlottesville.com; 2000 Morton Dr; r $120-160; P ❄ 📶 🏊) British hospitality and furnishings and a Tudor facade accent this unique hotel. It's 1.5 miles north of UVA. Cheaper rates on weekdays.

South Street Inn B&B $$
(☎434-979-0200; www.southstreetinn.com; 200 South St; r $150-190, ste $230-275; P ❄ 📶) In the heart of downtown Charlottesville, this elegant 1856 building has gone through previous incarnations as a girls' finishing school, a boarding house and a brothel. Now it houses heritage-style rooms – a total of two dozen, which gives this place more depth and diversity than your average B&B. Includes breakfast.

Eating & Drinking

The Downtown Mall, a pedestrian zone lined with dozens of shops and restaurants, is great for people-watching and outdoor dining on warm days. Follow Main St west for another good selection of restaurants. The Belmont area (about a half-mile southeast of the Downtown Mall) has a handful of local eating and drinking options. At night the bars along University Ave attract students and 20-somethings.

Feast! AMERICAN $
(416 W Main St; mains $8-10; ⏲10am-7pm Mon-Fri, 9am-6pm Sat) Inside the Main St Market, Feast! is a fine spot to load up on picnic fare, with wines, cheeses, fruits and other temptations, plus fresh sandwiches (made to order from 11am to 3pm), soups and salads.

Citizen Burger AMERICAN $
(212 E Main St; mains $12-15; ⏲noon-midnight Sun-Thu, to 2am Fri & Sat) On the pedestrian mall, Citizen Burger serves up delicious burgers and microbrews in a buzzing brick-lined dining room. The ethos is local and sustainable (organically raised, grass-fed cows, Virginia-made cheeses and beers). Don't miss the truffle fries.

Blue Moon Diner AMERICAN $
(www.bluemoondiner.net; 512 W Main St; mains $8-12; ⏲8am-10pm Mon-Fri, 9am-3pm Sat & Sun) Serving breakfast all day, the Blue Moon is a festive retro-style diner that also has Virginia beers on tap and live music (Wednesday through Friday nights). Pancakes come decorated with unusual portraits.

★**Oakhart Social** MODERN AMERICAN $$
(☎434-995-5449; 511 W Main St; small plates $7-15; ⏲5pm-2am Tue-Sun) The stylish new kid on the block serves creative, seasonally inspired small plates (grilled octopus with garbanzo

puree, sweet and crispy pork-belly salad) as well as wood-fired pizzas, in a handsomely laid-back setting. The front patio is a festive spot to sit and sip a refreshing 'Corpse Reviver #2,' and other well-made cocktails.

Whiskey Jar SOUTHERN **$$**
(☎434-202-1549; 227 West Main St; mains lunch $10-15, dinner $12-32; ⊙11am-midnight Mon-Thu, to 2am Fri & Sat, 10am-2:30pm Sun; 🍸) The Whiskey Jar does neo-Southern comfort food in a rustic setting of wooden furniture, where waitstaff wear plaid and drinks are served out of Mason jars. There's great barbecue and a huge (125 varieties!) whiskey selection.

The Local MODERN AMERICAN **$$**
(☎434-984-9749; 824 Hinton Ave; mains $13-25; ⊙5:30-10pm Sun-Thu, to 11pm Fri & Sat) The Local has earned many fans for its locavore-loving menu (try roast squash with goat cheese or roast duck with blood-orange gastrique) and the elegant, warmly lit interior (exposed brick trimmed with colorful oil paintings). It offers sidewalk and rooftop dining in warmer months, plus great cocktails.

ℹ Getting There & Around

Amtrak (www.amtrak.com; 810 W Main St) Two daily trains to Washington, DC (from $33, three hours).

Charlottesville Albemarle Airport (CHO; ☎434-973-8342; www.gocho.com) Ten miles north of downtown; offers regional flights.

Greyhound/Trailways Terminal (☎434-295-5131; 310 W Main St) Runs three daily buses to both Richmond (from $21, 1¼ hours) and Washington, DC (from $28, three hours).

Trolley (⊙6:40am-11:30pm Mon-Sat, 8am-5pm Sun) A free trolley connects W Main St with UVA.

Barboursville & Around

BARBOURSVILLE

Take Hwy 20 north of Charlottesville for a scenic drive amid rolling hills, past forested strands and picturesque farms. About a half-hour from Charlottesville (18 miles), you'll reach the tiny settlement of Barboursville, home to one of the oldest and best vineyards in the region. Spread across 900 acres, the **Barboursville Vineyards** (☎540-832-3824; www.bbv.wine.com; 17655 Winery Rd; tastings $7; ⊙tasting room 10am-5pm Mon-Sat, from 11am Sun) has earned high praise for its fine Cabernet Francs, and you can plan an afternoon of wine-tasting (a great value, considering the many wines you can sample), strolling the grounds, having a picnic (a shop sells goodies to go with the wine), or indulging in a decadent meal at the **Palladio** (☎540-832-7848; Barboursville Winery; 2-/4-course lunch $41/55, four-course dinner $80; ⊙noon-2:30pm Wed-Sun & 6:30-9:30pm Fri & Sat) restaurant. On the grounds, you'll find the ruins of the estate of James Barbour, the former governor of Virginia and friend of Thomas Jefferson, who designed the building. You can overnight at the Vineyard's lavish **1804 Inn** (Barboursville Winery; r $240-450; P❄📶).

MONTPELIER

Thomas Jefferson gets all the attention in these parts, but it's well worth branching out and visiting James Madison's **Montpelier** (www.montpelier.org; 11350 Constitution Hwy; adult/child $18/7; ⊙9am-5pm Apr-Oct, 10am-4pm Nov-Mar), a spectacular estate 25 miles northeast of Charlottesville (off Hwy 20). Madison was a brilliant but shy man who devoted himself to his books; he's almost singlehandedly responsible for developing and writing the US Constitution. **Guided tours** shed a light on the life and times of James as well as his gifted and charismatic wife Dolley, plus other residents of the estate: carefully reconstructed cabins show what life was like for Madison's slaves. There's an archaeology lab, where on-site archaeologists can explain recent findings. **Hiking trails** lead through the forests beyond the estate; the ambitious can even walk 4 miles to the **Market at Grelen** (www.themarketatgrelen.com; 15091 Yager Rd, Somerset; sandwiches $7; ⊙cafe 11:30am-2pm Tue-Sun, shop 10am-4pm Tue-Sat), a charming lunch spot and garden center, where you can pick your own berries on the rolling 600-acre grounds.

Appomattox Court House & Around

At the McLean House in the town of Appomattox Court House, General Robert E Lee surrendered the Army of Northern Virginia to General Ulysses S Grant, in effect ending the Civil War. Instead of coming straight here, follow **Lee's retreat** (☎800-673-8732; www.varetreat.com) on a winding, 25-stop tour that starts in **Petersburg** at Southside Railroad Station (River St and Cockade Alley) and cuts through some of the most attractive countryside in Virginia. Best take a detailed road map, as the trail is not always clearly marked.

DON'T MISS

MONTICELLO & AROUND

Monticello (☎ 434-984-9800; www.monticello.org; 931 Thomas Jefferson Pkwy; adult/child $25/8; ⏲ 9am-6pm Mar-Oct, 10am-5pm Nov-Feb) is an architectural masterpiece designed and inhabited by Thomas Jefferson, Founding Father and third US president. 'I am as happy nowhere else and in no other society, and all my wishes end, where I hope my days will end, at Monticello,' wrote Jefferson, who spent 40 years building his dream home, finally completed in 1809. Today it is the only home in America designated a UN World Heritage site. Built in Roman neoclassical style, the house was the centerpiece of a 5000-acre plantation tended by 150 slaves. Monticello today does not gloss over the complicated past of the man who declared that 'all men are created equal' in the Declaration of Independence, while owning slaves and likely fathering children with slave Sally Hemings. Jefferson and his family are buried in a small wooded plot near the home.

Visits to the house are conducted by guided tours only; you can take self-guided tours of the plantation grounds, gardens and cemetery. A high-tech exhibition center delves deeper into Jefferson's world – including exhibits on architecture, enlightenment through education, and the complicated idea of liberty. Frequent shuttles run from the visitor center to the hilltop house, or you can take the wooded footpath.

It's well worth planning a trip around the nearby 1784 **Michie Tavern** (☎ 434-977-1234; www.michietavern.com; 683 Thomas Jefferson Pkwy; buffet adult/child $18/11; ⏲ 11:15am-3:30pm), which spreads a filling Southern-style lunch buffet. Another excellent attraction is James Monroe's estate **Ash Lawn-Highland** (☎ 434-293-8000; www.ashlawnhighland.org; 2050 James Monroe Pkwy; adult/child $14/8; ⏲ 9am-6pm Apr-Oct, 11am-5pm Nov-Mar), 2.5 miles east of Monticello.

Monticello is about 4.5 miles northwest of downtown Charlottesville.

You'll finish at the 1700-acre **Appomattox Court House National Historic Park** (☎ 434-352-8987; www.nps.gov/apco; admission Jun-Aug $4, Sep-May $3; ⏲ 8:30am-5pm). The park comprises over two dozen restored buildings. A number of buildings are open to visitors, and set with original and period furnishings from 1865. Highlights include the parlor of the **McLean House**, where Lee and Grant met; the **Clover Hill Tavern**, used by Union soldiers to print 30,000 parole passes for Confederate soldiers; and the dry-goods-filled **Meeks General Store**.

The town of **Appomatox** (3 miles southwest of the national park) is small but charming, with a main street dotted with antique shops (a gold mine for hunters of Civil War memorabilia). Stop in **Baine's Books and Coffee** (www.bainesbooks.com; 205 Main St; snacks $3-6; ⏲ 8:30am-8pm Mon-Sat, 9am-5pm Sun) for sandwiches, quiche and scones (plus live bluegrass several nights a week). If you need a place to stay, nearby **Longacre** (☎ 800-758-7730; www.longacreva.com; 1670 Church St; r from $90; P ❄) looks as if it got lost somewhere in the English countryside and decided to set up shop in Virginia. Its elegant rooms are set with antiques, and lush grounds surround the sprawling Tudor house.

Shenandoah Valley

Local lore says Shenandoah was named for a Native American word meaning 'Daughter of the Stars.' True or not, there's no question this is God's country, one of the most beautiful places in America. The 200-mile-long valley and its Blue Ridge Mountains are packed with picturesque small towns, wineries, preserved battlefields and caverns. This was once the western border of Colonial America, settled by Scotch-Irish frontiersmen who were Highland Clearance refugees. Outdoor activities – hiking, camping, fishing, horseback riding and canoeing – abound.

Shenandoah National Park

One of the most spectacular national parks in the country, **Shenandoah** (☎ 540-999-3500; www.nps.gov/shen; 1-week pass per car $20) is like a new smile from nature: in spring and summer the wildflowers explode; in fall the leaves burn bright red and orange; and in winter a cold, starkly beautiful hibernation period sets in. White-tailed deer are a common sight and, if you're lucky, you might spot a black bear, bobcat or wild turkey. The park lies just 75 miles west of Washington, DC.

🏃 **Activities**

There are two visitor centers in the park, **Dickey Ridge** (☑540-635-3566; Skyline Dr, Mile 4.6; ⊙9am-5pm Apr-Nov) in the north and **Harry F Byrd** (☑540-999-3283; Skyline Dr, Mile 50; ⊙9am-5pm Apr-Nov) in the south. Both have maps and backcountry permits, as well as information on horseback riding, hang gliding, cycling (only on public roads) and other outdoors activities. Shenandoah has more than 500 miles of hiking trails, including 101 miles of the Appalachian Trail.

Old Rag Mountain   HIKING
This is a tough, 8-mile circuit trail that culminates in a rocky scramble that's suitable only for the physically fit. Your reward is the summit of Old Rag Mountain and, along the way, some of the best views in Virginia.

Big Meadows   HIKING
A very popular area, with four easy-to-medium-difficulty hikes. The **Lewis Falls** and **Rose River** trails run by the park's most spectacular waterfalls; the former accesses the Appalachian Trail.

Bearfence Mountain   HIKING
A short trail leads to a spectacular 360-degree viewpoint. The circuit hike is only 1.2 miles, but it involves a strenuous scramble over rocks.

Riprap Trail   HIKING
Three trails of varying difficulty. **Blackrock Trail** is an easy 1-mile loop that yields fantastic views. You can either hike the moderate 3.4-mile Riprap Trail to **Chimney Rock**, or detour and make a fairly strenuous 9.8-mile circuit that connects with the Appalachian Trail.

🛏 **Sleeping & Eating**

Camping is at four **NPS campgrounds** (☑877-444-6777; www.recreation.gov): **Mathews Arm** (Mile 22.1; campsite $15; ⊙May-Oct), **Big Meadows** (Mile 51.3; campsite $20; ⊙late Mar–Nov), **Lewis Mountain** (Mile 57.5; campsite $15, no reservations; ⊙mid-Apr–Oct) and **Loft Mountain** (Mile 79.5; campsite $15; ⊙mid-May–Oct). Camping elsewhere requires a backcountry permit, available for free from any visitor center.

For not-so-rough lodging, stay at **Skyland Resort** (☑540-999-2212; Skyline Dr, Mile 41.7; r $115-210, cabins $97-235; ⊙Apr-Oct; 🅿🏧🛜🐾), **Big Meadows Lodge** (☑540-999-2221; Skyline Dr, Mile 51.2; r $94-210; ⊙mid-May–Oct; 🛜)

or **Lewis Mountain Cabins** (☑540-999-2255; Skyline Dr, Mile 57.6; cabins $117; ⊙Apr-Oct; 🅿🐾); booking is available online at www.goshenandoah.com.

Skyland and Big Meadows both have restaurants and taverns with occasional live music. Big Meadows offers the most services, including gas, laundry and camp store. It's best to bring your own food into the park if you're going camping or on extended hikes.

ℹ **Getting There & Around**

Amtrak (www.amtrak.com) trains run to Staunton, in the Shenandoah Valley, once a day from Washington, DC (from $34, four hours). You'll really need your own wheels to explore the length and breadth of the park, which can be easily accessed from several exits off I-81.

Front Royal & Around

The northernmost tip of Skyline Dr looks like a drab strip of gas stations, but a friendly main street and some cool caverns nearby. Stop at the **visitor center** (☑800-338-2576; 414 E Main St; ⊙9am-5pm) before heading 'up' the valley. Kids may enjoy mini-train rides ($5) and the mirror maze ($6).

⊙ **Sights & Activities**

Skyline Caverns   CAVE
(☑800-296-4545; www.skylinecaverns.com; entrance to Skyline Dr, Front Royal; adult/child $20/10; ⊙9am-5pm) Front Royal's claim to fame is Skyline Caverns, which boasts rare white-spiked anthodites – mineral formations that look like sea urchins.

Museum of the Shenandoah Valley MUSEUM
(☑888-556-5799, 540-662-1473; www.themsv.org; 901 Amherst St, Winchester; adult/student/child $10/8/free, admission Wed free; ⊙10am-4pm Tue-Sun) Located in the town of Winchester, some 25 miles north of Front Royal, the Museum of the Shenandoah Valley comprises an 18th-century house museum filled with period furnishings, a 6-acre garden and a multimedia museum that delves into the valley's history.

Luray Caverns   CAVE
(☑540-743-6551; www.luraycaverns.com; Rte 211, Luray; adult/child $26/14; ⊙9am-7pm daily Jun-Aug, to 6pm Sep-Nov, Apr & May, to 4pm Mon-Fri Dec-Mar) If you can only fit one cavern into your itinerary, head 25 miles south from Front Royal to the world-class Luray Cav-

erns and hear the 'Stalacpipe Organ' – hyped as the largest musical instrument on Earth.

Sleeping & Eating

Woodward House on Manor Grade B&B **$$**
(☎540-635-7010, 800-635-7011; www.acountry-home.com; 413 S Royal Ave/US 320, Front Royal; r $110-155, cottage $225; P 📶) Offers seven cheerful rooms and a separate cottage (with wood-burning fireplaces). Sip your coffee on the deck and don't let the busy street below distract from the Blue Ridge Mountain vista.

Element FUSION **$$**
(☎540-636-9293; www.jsgourmet.com; 206 S Royal Ave, Front Royal; mains lunch $8-14, dinner $14-22; ⏲11am-3pm & 5-10pm Tue-Sat; ✍) Element is a foodie favorite for quality bistro fare. The small dinner menu features changing specials such as roasted quail with Mexican corn salad and sweet potatoes; at lunch, come for gourmet sandwiches, soups and salads.

Apartment 2G FUSION **$$$**
(☎540-636-9293; www.jsgourmet.com; 206 S Royal Ave, Front Royal; 5-course meal $50; ⏲from 6:30pm Sat) The best restaurant in Front Royal is open just once a week. Owned and operated by a husband-and-wife team – two chefs from the acclaimed Inn at Little Washington – the Apartment's culinary philosophy is simple: uncompromisingly fresh ingredients fashioned into ever-changing five-course fixed menus.

Staunton & Around

This small-town beauty has much going for it, including a historic and walkable town center, a great foodie scene, several microbreweries, some intriguing museums and a first-rate theater. Add to this an abundance of outdoor activities nearby and you may find yourself looking into local real estate when you get here.

Sights

The pedestrian-friendly, handsome center boasts more than 200 buildings designed by noted Victorian architect TJ Collins. There's an artsy yet unpretentious bohemian vibe thanks to the presence of Mary Baldwin, a small, women's liberal arts college.

Blackfriars Playhouse THEATER
(☎540-851-1733; www.americanshakespeare-center.com; 10 S Market St; tickets $24-37) Don't leave Staunton without catching a show at the Blackfriars Playhouse, where the American Shakespeare Center company performs in the world's only re-creation of Shakespeare's original indoor theater.

DON'T MISS

SCENIC DRIVE: SKYLINE DRIVE

A 105-mile-long road running down the spine of the Blue Ridge Mountains, Shenandoah National Park's **Skyline Drive** redefines the definition of 'Scenic Route.' You're constantly treated to an impressive view, but keep in mind the road is bendy, slow-going (35mph limit) and is congested in peak season. It's best to start this drive just south of Front Royal, VA; from here you'll snake over Virginia wine and hill country. Numbered mileposts mark the way; there are lots of pull-offs. Our favorite is around Mile 51.2, where you can take a moderately difficult 3.6-mile-loop hike to **Lewis Spring Falls**.

Woodrow Wilson Presidential Library HISTORIC SITE
(www.woodrowwilson.org; 20 N Coalter St; adult/student/child $14/7/5; ⏲9am-5pm Mon-Sat, from noon Sun) History buffs should check out the Woodrow Wilson Presidential Library across town. Stop by and tour the hilltop Greek Revival house where Wilson grew up, which has been faithfully restored to its original 1856 appearance.

Frontier Culture Museum MUSEUM
(☎540-332-7850; www.frontiermuseum.org; 1290 Richmond Rd; adult/student/child $10/9/6; ⏲9am-5pm mid-Mar–Nov, 10am-4pm Dec–mid-Mar) The excellent Frontier Culture Museum has authentic historic buildings from Germany, Ireland and England, plus re-created West African dwellings and a separate area of American frontier dwellings on the site's 100-plus acres. Costumed interpreters (aided by bleating livestock) do an excellent job showing what life was like for the disparate ancestors of today's Virginians. It's 2 miles southeast of the center.

Sleeping

Frederick House B&B **$$**
(☎540-885-4220; www.frederickhouse.com; 28 N New St; r $120-185; P ❄ 📶) Stay right downtown in the thoroughly mauve and immensely welcoming Frederick House, which

consists of five historical residences with 25 varied rooms and suites – all with private bathrooms and some with antique furnishings and decks.

Anne Hathaway's Cottage B&B $$
(540-885-8885; www.anne-hathaways-cottage.com; 950 W Beverley St; r $130-160; P ✱) Head out of town to Anne Hathaway's Cottage, named for Shakespeare's wife, who would have thoroughly enjoyed a night in one of the three rooms in this ridiculously romantic Tudor-style, thatched-roof cottage.

Eating & Drinking

West Beverley St is sprinkled with restaurants and cafes.

Split Banana ICE CREAM $
(7 W Beverley St; ice cream $2.60-5.20; noon-11pm;) This locals' favorite ice cream parlor has delicious flavors, served up in a charmingly old-fashioned setting.

Byers Street Bistro MODERN AMERICAN $$
(540-887-6100; www.byersstreetbistro.com; 18 Byers St; mains lunch $9-14, dinner $16-26; 11am-midnight) By the train station, Byers Street Bistro cooks up high-end pub grub (applewood bacon and carmelized onion pizzas, mahimahi tacos, Angus burgers, slow-roasted babyback ribs) that's best enjoyed at the outdoor tables on warm days. Come on Friday and Saturday nights for live bands (bluegrass, blues and folk).

Zynodoa SOUTHERN $$$
(540-885-7775; 115 E Beverley St; mains $22-29; 5-9:30pm Sun-Tue, to 10:30pm Wed-Sat;) Classy Zynodoa puts together some fine dishes in the vein of Virginia artisan cheeses, Shenandoah-sourced roasted chick-

SCENIC DRIVE: VIRGINIA'S HORSE COUNTRY

About 40 miles west of Washington, DC, suburban sprawl gives way to endless green farms, vineyards, quaint villages and palatial estates and ponies. This is 'Horse Country,' where wealthy Washingtonians pursue their equestrian pastimes.

The following route is the most scenic drive to Shenandoah National Park. From DC, take Rte 50 West to **Middleburg**, a too-cute-for-words town of B&Bs, taverns, wine shops and boutiques. The **National Sporting Library** (540-687-6542; www.nsl.org; 102 The Plains Rd, Middlesburg; museum admission $10, library free; 10am-5pm Wed-Sat, from 1pm Sun) is a museum and research center devoted to horse and field sports such as foxhunting, dressage, steeplechase and polo. About 20 miles northeast of Middleburg is **Leesburg**, another town with colonial charm and historic sites. Stop in **Morven Park** (703-777-2414; www.morvenpark.org; 17263 Southern Planter Lane, Leesburg; grounds admission free, mansion tours adult/child $10/5; grounds dawn-dusk daily, tours hourly noon-4pm Mon, Fri & Sat, 1-4pm Sun) for a tour of a staggering Virginia home on 1000 acres. For more Greek Revival grandeur, visit **Oatlands Plantation** (703-777-3174; www.oatlands.org; 20850 Oatlands Plantation Lane, Leesburg; adult/child $12/8, grounds only $8; 10am-5pm Mon-Sat, 1-5pm Sun Apr-Dec), outside of town.

The area has a wealth of appealing dining options. Stop in the **Shoes Cup & Cork** (703-771-7463; www.shoescupandcork.com; 17 N King St, Leesburg; mains lunch $8-16, dinner $15-25; 7am-5pm Mon-Wed, to 9pm Thu & Fri, 9am-9pm Sat & Sun) in Leesburg for creative American fare or **Chimole** (703-777-7011; 10 S King St, Leesburg; tapas $8-18; 5-9pm Sun & Wed, to 11pm Thu-Sat) for wine and Latin American tapas. In Middleburg, the **Red Fox Inn & Tavern** (540-687-6301; www.redfox.com; 2 E Washington St, Middlesburg; mains lunch $11-18, dinner $26-42; 8am-10am, 11:30am-2:30pm & 5-8:30pm Mon-Sat, 10am-2:30pm & 5-7:30pm Sun) has first-rate American cooking served in a beautifully preserved 1728 dining room.

Located 6 miles west of Middleburg, the **Welbourne B&B** (540-687-3201; www.welbourneinn.com; 22314 Welbourne Farm Lane, Middleburg; r $143; ✱) has five heritage rooms set in a historic landmark house (c 1770) surrounded by 520 acres. The **Leesburg Colonial Inn** (703-777-5000; www.theleesburgcolonialinn.com; 19 S King St; d $70-150) has a great central location and unbeatable prices.

Further down the road at the foothills of the Blue Ridge Mountains is **Sperryville.** Its many galleries and shops are a must-stop for antique-lovers. Continue 9 miles west to reach the Thornton Gap entrance of Skyline Dr in Shenandoah National Park.

en and and rainbow trout from Casta Line (raised nearby). Local farms and wineries are the backbone of Zynodoa's larder (and, by extension, your table).

Redbeard Brewery MICROBREWERY
(www.redbeardbrews.com; 102 S Lewis St; ⊙4-11pm Thu & Fri, 1-11pm Sat & Sun) A small-batch brewery that serves up tasty IPAs, saison, ambers and other seasonal selections. There's often a barbecue food truck parked out back on weekends. Occasional live music, too.

Lexington & Around

This is the place to see Southern gentry at their stately best, as cadets from the Virginia Military Institute jog past the prestigious academics of Washington & Lee University. The **visitor center** (☎540-463-3777; 106 E Washington St; ⊙9am-5pm) has handy maps with self-guided walking tours.

Sights & Activities

Founded in 1749, colonnaded **Washington & Lee University** is one of the top small colleges in America. The **Lee Chapel & Museum** (☎540-458-8768; http://leechapel.wlu.edu; ⊙9am-4pm Mon-Sat, 1pm-4pm Sun Nov-Mar, to 5pm Apr-Oct) inters Robert E Lee, while his horse Traveller is buried outside. One of the four Confederate banners surrounding Lee's tomb is set in an original flagpole, a branch a rebel soldier turned into a makeshift standard.

Virginia Military Institute UNIVERSITY
(VMI; www.vmi.edu; Letcher Ave) You'll either be impressed or put off by the extreme discipline of the cadets at Virginia Military Institute, the only university to have sent its entire graduating class into combat (plaques to student war dead are touching and ubiquitous). The **VMI Museum** (☎540-464-7334; ⊙9am-5pm) FREE houses the stuffed carcass of Stonewall Jackson's horse, a homemade American flag made by an alumnus prisoner of war in Vietnam, and a tribute to VMI students killed in the War on Terror.

Contact the museum for a free guided tour of the campus, offered at noon. A full-dress parade takes place most Fridays at 4:30pm during the school year. The school's **George C Marshall Museum** (☎540-463-2083; www.marshallfoundation.org/museum/; adult/student $5/2; ⊙11am-4pm Tue-Sat) honors the creator of the Marshall Plan for post-WWII European reconstruction.

Stonewall Jackson House HISTORIC BUILDING
(www.stonewalljackson.org; 8 E Washington St; adult/child $8/6; ⊙9am-5pm Mon-Sat, from 1pm Sun) One of the most revered generals of the south, Thomas Jonathon 'Stonewall' Jackson lived in this handsome brick two-story house from 1851 to 1861, while he taught at nearby VMI. The house is remarkably preserved, with guided tours providing fascinating insight into Jackson's life and times. His body (all but his left arm, anyway) is buried in the cemetery a few blocks away.

Natural Bridge & Foamhenge LANDMARK
Yes, it's a kitschy tourist trap, and yes, vocal creationists who insist it was made by the hand of God are dominating the site, but the 215ft-high **Natural Bridge** (www.naturalbridgeva.com; bridge adult/child $20/12, bridge & caverns $28/18; ⊙9am-dusk), 15 miles from Lexington, is still pretty cool. It was surveyed by a 16-year-old George Washington, who supposedly carved his initials into the wall, and was once owned by Thomas Jefferson. You can also take a tour of some exceptionally deep caverns here.

Just up the road, check out **Foamhenge** (www.thefoamhenge.com; Hwy 11) FREE, a marvelous full-sized replica of Stonehenge made entirely of Styrofoam. There are fine views – and even an on-site wizard. It's 1 mile north of Natural Bridge.

Sleeping

★**The Georges** BOUTIQUE HOTEL $$
(☎540-463-2500; thegeorges.com; 11 N Main St; r from $165; P❄️📶) Set in two historic buildings on opposite sides of Main St, the Georges has beautifully set rooms, each custom-designed with high-end furnishings. The great location, friendly service and on-site eateries (with locally focused cuisine) add to the appeal.

Applewood Inn & Llama Trekking INN $$
(☎800-463-1902; www.applewoodbb.com; 242 Tarn Beck Lane; r $164-172; P❄️) The charming, eco-minded Applewood Inn & Llama Trekking offers accommdations and a slew of outdoorsy activities (including, yes, llama trekking) on a farm in a bucolic valley just a 10-minute drive away from downtown Lexington.

Eating & Drinking

Pure Eats AMERICAN $
(107 N Main St; mains $7-9; ⊙8am-2:30pm & 5-8pm Tue-Thu, 8am-8pm Fri-Sun) In a former gas station, Pure Eats whips up delicious

doughnuts and egg-and-cheese biscuits in the morning, and burgers and milkshakes later in the day.

Blue Sky Bakery SANDWICHES $
(125 W Nelson St; mains $7-10; ⏲10:30am-4pm Mon-Fri) This local favorite has tasty focaccia sandwiches, hearty soups and fresh salads.

Red Hen SOUTHERN $$$
(☎540-464-4401; 11 E Washington St; mains $24-30; ⏲5-9:30pm Tue-Sat; 🍷) 🌿 Reserve well ahead for a memorable meal at Red Hen, which features a creative menu showcasing the fine local produce.

Haywood's COCKTAIL BAR
(11 N Main St; ⏲5-10pm Wed-Sun) For a kitschy good time, stop by this small, cozy piano bar, where you can sometimes catch a lounge singer lighting up the crowd alongside a piano-playing colleague.

☆ Entertainment

Hull's Drive-in CINEMA
(☎540-463-2621; www.hullsdrivein.com; 2367 N Lee Hwy/US 11; adult/child $7/3; ⏲7pm Fri-Sun May-Oct) For old-fashioned amusement, catch a movie at this drive-in movie theater, set 5.5 miles north of Lexington.

Blue Ridge Highlands & Southwest Virginia

The southwestern tip of Virginia is the most rugged part of the state. Turn onto the Blue Ridge Pkwy or any side road and you'll immediately plunge into dark strands of dogwood and fir, fast streams and white waterfalls. You're bound to see Confederate flags in the small towns, but there's a proud hospitality behind the fierce veneer of independence.

Blue Ridge Parkway

Where Skyline Dr ends, the **Blue Ridge Parkway** (www.blueridgeparkway.org) picks up. The road is just as pretty and runs from the southern Appalachian ridge in Shenandoah National Park (at Mile 0) to North Carolina's Great Smoky Mountains National Park (at Mile 469). Wildflowers bloom in spring, and fall colors are spectacular, but watch out for foggy days; the lack of guardrails can make for hairy driving. There are a dozen visitor centers scattered over the Pkwy, and any of them make a good kick-off point to start your trip.

Sights & Activities

There are all kinds of sights running along the parkway.

Mabry Mill HISTORIC SITE
(Mile 176) One of the most-photographed buildings in the state, the mill nestles in such a fuzzy green vale you'll think you've entered the opening chapter of a Tolkien novel.

Humpback Rocks HIKING
(Mile 5.8) Tour 19th-century farm buildings or take the steep trail to Humpback Rocks, offering spectacular 360-degree views.

Sherando Lake Recreation Area SWIMMING
(☎540-291-2188; off Mile 16) In George Washington National Forest, you'll find two pretty lakes (one for swimming, one for fishing), with hiking trails and campsites. To get there, take Rte 664 W.

Peaks of Otter HIKING
(Mile 86) There are trails to the tops of these mountains: Sharp Top, Flat Top and Harkening Hill. Shuttles run to the top of Sharp Top, or you can try a fairly challenging hike (3 miles return) to the summit.

Sleeping

There are nine local **campgrounds** (☎877-444-6777; www.recreation.gov; campsites $19; ⏲May-Oct), four in Virginia. Sites are generally open from April to November.

★ **Peaks of Otter** LODGE $$
(☎540-586-1081; www.peaksofotter.com; 85554 Blue Ridge Pkwy, Mile 86; r $97-145; ❄📶) A pretty, split-rail-surrounded lodge on a small lake that's nestled between two of its namesake mountains. It has a restaurant and wi-fi, but no public phones and no cellphone reception.

Roanoke & Around

Illuminated by the giant star atop Mill Mountain, Roanoke is the largest city in the valley and is the self-proclaimed 'Capital of the Blue Ridge.'

There are good eating and drinking options downtown (near Market and Campbell Sts), and appealing options 3 miles west along Grandin Rd.

Sights & Activities

Mill Mountain Park PARK
Mill Mountain Park has walking trails, a discovery center, a zoo and grand views of Ro-

anoke. You can drive up (via Walnut Ave SE) or hike up (take the Monument Trail just off Sylvan Ave SE or the Star Trail near Riverland Rd SE)

Taubman Museum of Art MUSEUM
(www.taubmanmuseum.org; 110 Salem Ave SE; 10am-5pm Tue-Sat, to 9pm Thu & 1st Fri of month; P) FREE The striking Taubman Museum of Art is set in a sculptural steel-and-glass edifice that's reminiscent of the Guggenheim Bilbao. Inside, you'll find a superb collection of artworks spanning 3500 years; it's particularly strong in 19th- and 20th-century American works.

National D-Day Memorial MONUMENT
(540-587-3619; www.dday.org; US 460 & Hwy 122; adult/child $10/6; 10am-5pm) About 30 miles east of Roanoke, the tiny town of Bedford suffered the most casualties per capita in the US during WWII, and hence was chosen to host the moving National D-Day Memorial. Among its towering arch and flower garden is a cast of bronze figures re-enacting the storming of the beach, complete with bursts of water symbolizing the hail of bullets the soldiers faced.

Sleeping & Eating

Rose Hill B&B $$
(540-400-7785; www.bandbrosehill.com; 521 Washington Ave; r $100-125) Rose Hill is a charming and welcoming three-room B&B in Roanoke's historic district.

Texas Tavern DINER $
(114 Church Ave SW; burgers $1.30-2.45; 24hr) The legendary Texas Tavern is a boxcar-sized diner serving juicy burgers.

Local Roots MODERN AMERICAN $$
(540-206-2610; www.localrootsrestaurant.com; 1314 Grandin Rd; mains lunch $11-13, dinner $21-33; 11:30am-2pm & 5-10pm Tue-Sun) Local Roots serves up catfish and chips, black bass, bison steak and other delectable fare.

Lucky's MODERN AMERICAN $$
(540-982-1249; www.eatatlucky.com; 18 Kirk Ave SW; mains $17-25; 5-9pm Mon-Wed, to 10pm Thu-Sat) Lucky's has excellent cocktails (try 'The Cube') and a seasonally inspired menu of small plates (hickory-smoked porchetta, roasted oysters) and heartier mains (buttermilk fried chicken, morel and asparagus gnocchi).

Mt Rogers National Recreation Area

This seriously beautiful district is well worth a visit from outdoor enthusiasts. Hike, fish or cross-country ski among ancient hardwood trees and the state's tallest peak. The **park headquarters** (276-783-5196, 800-628-7202; www.fs.usda.gov/gwj; 3714 Hwy 16, Marion) offers maps and recreation directories. The NPS operates five campgrounds in the area; contact park headquarters for details.

Abingdon

One of the most photogenic towns in Virginia, Abingdon retains fine Federal and Victorian architecture in its historic district, and hosts the bluegrass **Virginia Highlands Festival** over the first half of August. The **visitor center** (800-435-3440; www.visitabingdonvirginia.com; 335 Cummings St; 9am-5pm) has exhibits on local history.

Sights & Activities

Barter Theatre THEATER
(276-628-3991; www.bartertheatre.com; 133 W Main St; performances from $25) Founded during the Depression, Barter Theatre earned its name from audiences trading food for performances. Actors Gregory Peck and Ernest Borgnine cut their teeth on Barter's stage.

Heartwood ARTS CENTER
(276-492-2400; www.myswva.org/heartwood; One Heartwood Circle; 9am-5pm Mon-Wed & Fri-Sat, to 9pm Thu, 10am-3pm Sun) Heartwood is a showcase of regional crafts, cuisine (sandwiches, salads, Virginia wines) and traditional music. Don't miss Thursday nights, when bluegrass bands and barbecue draw a festive local crowd. It's about 3 miles east of town (off Hwy 11).

Virginia Creeper Trail TRAIL
(www.vacreepertrail.org) Named for the railroad that once ran this route, the Virginia Creeper Trail travels 33 miles between Whitetop Station (near the North Carolina border) and downtown Abingdon. Several outfitters rent bicycles, organize outings and run shuttles, including **Virginia Creeper Trail Bike Shop** (276-676-2552; www.vacreepertrailbikeshop.com; 201 Pecan St; per 2hr/day $10/20; 9am-6pm Sun-Fri, from 8am Sat), near the trailhead.

🛏 Sleeping

Alpine Motel
MOTEL $

(☑ 276-628-3178; www.alpinemotelabingdon.com; 882 E Main St; s/d from $59/69; P ✳ 🕏) The Alpine Motel is a simple but good-value option, with carpeted rooms, old TVs, and chirping birds across the way; it's located about 2 miles west of downtown.

Martha Washington Inn
HOTEL $$$

(☑ 276-628-3161; www.marthawashingtoninn.com; 150 W Main St; r from $225; P ✳ @ 🕏 ⛱) Opposite the Barter, this is the region's premier historic hotel, a Victorian sprawl of historical classiness and wrought-iron style.

🍴 Eating & Drinking

128 Pecan
MODERN AMERICAN $$

(☑ 276-698-3159; 128 Pecan St; mains $9-22; ⊙ 11am-9pm Tue-Sat; 🕏) This local favorite serves up excellent sandwiches, tacos and heartier meat or seafood dishes, with seating on a front veranda. It's a short stroll to the Virginia Creeper Trail.

The Tavern
MODERN AMERICAN $$$

(☑ 276-628-1118; 222 E Main St; mains $28-42; ⊙ 5-9pm Mon-Sat) Inside the oldest building in town (built in 1779) you'll find tasty crab cakes, French onion soup and oysters served in a cozy setting, with low ceilings and brick floors.

Wolf Hills Brewery
MICROBREWERY

(350 Park St; ⊙ 5-8pm Mon-Fri, from 1pm Sat, 1-5pm Sun) For satisfying microbrews and the occasional live music session, head to Wolf Hills Brewery.

The Crooked Road

When Scotch–Irish fiddle-and-reel married African American banjo-and-percussion, American mountain or 'old-time' music was born, spawning such genres as country and bluegrass. The latter genre still dominates the Blue Ridge, and Virginia's Heritage Music Trail, the 250-mile-long Crooked Road (www.myswva.org/tcr), takes you through nine sites associated with that history, along with some eye-stretching mountain scenery. It's well worth taking a detour and joining the music-loving fans of all ages who kick up their heels (many arrive with tap shoes) at these festive jamborees. During a live show you'll witness elders connecting to deep cultural roots and a new generation of musicians keeping that heritage alive and evolving.

FLOYD

Tiny, cute-as-a-postcard Floyd is nothing more than an intersection between Hwy 8 and 221, but life explodes on Friday nights at the Floyd Country Store (☑ 540-745-4563; www.floydcountrystore.com; 206 S Locust St; ⊙ 11am-5pm Tue-Thu, to 11pm Fri, to 5pm Sat, noon-5pm Sun). Every Friday starting at 6:30pm, $5 gets you four bluegrass bands in four hours and the chance to watch happy crowds jam along to regional heritage. No smokin', no drinkin', but there's plenty of dancin' (of the jig-and-tap style) and good cheer. On weekends, there's lots of live music happening nearby.

🛏 Sleeping

Oak Haven Lodge
INN $

(☑ 540-745-5716; www.oakhavenlodge.com; 323 Webb's Mill Rd, Route 8; r $75-90; P ✳ 🕏) Just a mile north of Floyd, this good-value place has spacious rooms (some with Jacuzzi tubs) that open onto a shared balcony with rocking chairs.

Hotel Floyd
HOTEL $$

(☑ 540-745-6080; www.hotelfloyd.com; 120 Wilson St; r $119-169; P ✳ 🕏 ⛱) 🌿 Built with eco-friendly materials and furnishings, Hotel Floyd is a model of sustainability. Works by local artisans adorn its attractive rooms.

🍴 Eating & Drinking

Harvest Moon
MARKET $

(227 N Locust St; ⊙ 9am-6:30pm Mon-Sat, noon-6pm Sun) A great place to stock up on picnic fare.

Oddfella's
FUSION $$

(☑ 540-745-3463; 110 N Locust St; lunch mains $8-10, dinner $13-26; ⊙ 11am-2:30pm Tue-Sat, 4-10pm Thu-Sat, 10am-3pm Sun; P 🍴) 🌿 When you're all jigged out, head for Oddfella's, a comfy spot for Tex-Mex fare (plus tapas) – and tasty microbrews.

Dogtown Roadhouse
PIZZA $$

(302 S Locust St; mains $10-18; ⊙ 5-10pm Thu, to midnight Fri, noon-midnight Sat, noon-10pm Sun) The lively Dogtown Roadhouse is the go-to for pizzas (fired up in a wood-burning oven) and microbrews, with live rock on Friday and Saturday nights.

GALAX

Galax claims to be the world capital of mountain music, although it feels like anywhere-else-ville outside of the immediate downtown area, which is on the National Register of Historic Places. The main attraction is the **Rex Theater** (☎276-236-0329; www.rextheatergalax.com; 113 E Grayson St), a musty, red-curtained belle of yore. Frequent bluegrass acts cross its stage, but the easiest one to catch is the Friday-night live WBRF 98.1 show (admission $5), which pulls in crowds from across the mountains.

Tom Barr of **Barr's Fiddle Shop** (☎276-236-2411; www.barrsfiddleshop.com; 105 S Main St; ⏲9am-5pm Mon-Sat) is the Stradivarius of the mountains, a master craftsman sought out by fiddle and mandolin aficionados from across the world. The **Old Fiddler's Convention** (www.oldfiddlersconvention.com), held over five days in August in Galax is one of the premier mountain-music festivals in the world.

Doctor's Inn (☎276-238-9998; www.thedoctorsinnvirginia.com; 406 W Stuart Dr; r $140-150; P❄📶) is a welcoming guesthouse with antique-filled chambers and excellent breakfasts.

Creek Bottom Brews (☎276-236-2337; 307 Meadow St; mains $7-16; ⏲11am-9pm Tue-Sat, 1-6pm Sun) has a changing lineup of craft brews, which go nicely with the brick-oven pizza and smoked chicken wings fired up on site.

WORTH A TRIP

CARTER FAMILY FOLD

In a tiny hamlet of southwest Virginia, formerly known as Maces Spring (today part of Hiltons), you'll find one of the hallowed birthplaces of mountain music. The **Carter Family Fold** (☎276-386-6054; www.carterfamilyfold.org; 3449 AP Carter Hwy, Hiltons; $10/1 adult/child; ⏲7:30pm Sat) continues the musical legacy begun by the talented Carter family back in 1927. Every Saturday night, the 900-person arena hosts first-rate bluegrass and gospel bands; there's also a museum with family memorabilia and the original mid-1800s log cabin where AP Carter was born. With no nearby lodging, your best bet is to stay in Abingdon (30 miles east); Kingsport, TN (12 miles southwest); or Bristol, TN (25 miles southeast).

WEST VIRGINIA

Wild and wonderful West Virginia is often overlooked by both American and foreign travelers. It doesn't help that the state can't seem to shake its negative stereotypes. That's too bad, because West Virginia is one of the prettiest states in the Union. With its line of unbroken green mountains, raging white-water rivers and snowcapped ski resorts, this is an outdoor-lovers' paradise.

Created by secessionists from secession, the people here still think of themselves as hardscrabble sons of miners, and that perception isn't entirely off. But the Mountain State is also gentrifying and, occasionally, that's a good thing: the arts are flourishing in the valleys, where some towns offer a welcome break from the state's constantly evolving outdoor activities.

History

Virginia was once the biggest state in America, divided between the plantation aristocracy of the Tidewater and the mountains of what is now West Virginia. The latter were settled by tough farmers who staked out independent freeholds across the Appalachians. Always resentful of their Eastern brethren and their reliance on cheap (ie slave) labor, the mountaineers of West Virginia declared their independence from Virginia when the latter tried to break off from America during the Civil War.

Yet the scrappy, independent-at-all-costs stereotype was challenged in the late 19th and early 20th centuries, when miners here formed cooperative unions and fought employers in some of the bloodiest battles in American labor history. That mix of chip-on-the-shoulder resentment toward authority and look-out-for-your-neighbor community values continues to characterize West Virginia today.

ℹ Information

West Virginia Division of Tourism (☎800-225-5982; www.wvtourism.com) operates welcome centers at interstate borders and in **Harpers Ferry** (☎866-435-5698; www.wveasterngateway.com; 37 Washington Ct). Check the Division of Tourism's website for info on the state's myriad adventure-tourism opportunities.

Eastern Panhandle

The most accessible part of the state has always been a mountain getaway for DC types.

Harpers Ferry

History lives on in this attractive town, set with steep cobblestoned streets, framed by the Shenandoah Mountains and the confluence of the rushing Potomac and Shenandoah Rivers. The lower town functions as an open-air museum, with more than a dozen buildings that you can wander through to get a taste of 19th-century small-town life. Exhibits narrate the town's role at the forefront of westward expansion, American industry and, most famously, the slavery debate – in 1859 old John Brown tried to spark a slave uprising here and was hanged for his efforts; the incident rubbed friction between North and South into the fires of Civil War.

Pick up a pass to visit the historic buildings at the **Harpers Ferry National Historic Park Visitor Center** (☎304-535-6029; www.nps.gov/hafe; 171 Shoreline Dr; per person/vehicle $5/10; ⏲9am-5pm; 🚻) off Hwy 340. You can also park and take a free shuttle from here. Parking is extremely limited in Harpers Ferry proper.

Sights

You can freely enter over a dozen buildings that are part of the **Harpers Ferry National Historic Park**. Start your exploring at the information center on Shenandoah St, near the riverfront. From there, you can pick up a map and stroll into nearby buildings, all of which offer a unique perspective on life in the past.

Black Voices MUSEUM
(High St; ⏲9am-5pm) FREE This worthwhile, interactive exhibit has narrated stories of hardships and hard-won victories by African Americans from the times of enslavement through the Civil Rights era. Across the street is the Storer College exhibit, which gives an overview of the groundbreaking educational center and Niagara movement that formed in its wake.

John Brown Museum MUSEUM
(Shenandoah St; ⏲9am-5pm) FREE Across from Arsenal Sq, this three-room gallery gives a fine overview (through videos and period relics) of the events surrounding John Brown's famous raid.

Master Armorer's House HISTORIC SITE
(☎304-535-6029; www.nps.gov/hafe; Shenandoah St; ⏲9am-5pm) FREE One of the free sites in the historic district, this 1858 house explains how rifle technology developed here went on to revolutionize the firearms industry.

Storer College Campus HISTORIC SITE
(www.nps.gov/hafe; Fillmore St) Founded immediately after the Civil War, Storer College grew from a one-room schoolhouse for freed slaves to a respected college open to all races and creeds. It closed in 1955. You can freely wander the historic campus, reachable by taking the path to upper town, past St Peter's church, Jefferson Rock and Harper Cemetery.

John Brown Wax Museum MUSEUM
(☎304-535-6342; www.johnbrownwaxmuseum.com; 168 High St; adult/child $7/5; ⏲9am-4:30pm Apr-May & Sep-Nov, 10am-5:30pm Jun-Aug, 9am-4:30pm Sat & Sun only Mar & Dec, closed Jan-Feb) Not to be confused with the National Park–run museum, this private wax museum is a kitschy (and rather overpriced) attraction that pays tribute to the man who led an ill-conceived slave rebellion here. The exhibits are laughably old-school; nothing says historical accuracy like scratchy vocals, jerky animatronics and dusty old dioramas.

Activities

There are great hikes in the area, from three-hour scrambles to the scenic overlook from the Maryland Heights Trail, past Civil War fortifications on the Loudoun Heights Trail or along the Appalachian Trail. You can also cycle or walk along the C&O Canal towpath.

Appalachian Trail Conservancy HIKING
(☎304-535-6331; www.appalachiantrail.org; cnr Washington & Jackson Sts; ⏲9am-5pm) The 2160-mile Appalachian Trail is headquartered here at this tremendous resource for hikers.

River Riders ADVENTURE SPORTS
(☎800-326-7238; www.riverriders.com; 408 Alstadts Hill Rd) The go-to place for rafting, canoeing, tubing, kayaking and multiday cycling trips, plus cycle rental. There's even a new 1200ft zip line that opened in 2014.

O Be Joyfull WALKING TOUR
(☎732-801-0381; www.obejoyfull.com; 175 High St; day/night tours $22/14) Offers eye-opening historical daytime walking tours (lasting three to four hours) around Harpers Ferry, as well as a spooky 90-minute evening tour.

Sleeping

Teahorse Hostel HOSTEL $
(☎304-535-6848; www.teahorsehostel.com; 1312 Washington St; dm/ste $33/150; P ❄ @ 📶) Popular with cyclists on the C&O Canal towpath and hikers on the Appalachian Trail, Teahorse is a welcoming place with comfy rooms and common areas (including an outdoor patio). It's located 1 mile (uphill) from the historic lower town of Harpers Ferry.

HI-Harpers Ferry Hostel HOSTEL $
(☎301-834-7652; www.hiusa.org; 19123 Sandy Hook Rd, Knoxville, MD; dm/d $25/61; ⊙May–mid-Nov; P ❄ @ 📶) Located 2 miles from downtown on the Maryland side of the Potomac River, this friendly hostel has plenty of amenities, including a kitchen, laundry and lounge area with games and books.

Jackson Rose B&B $$
(☎304-535-1528; www.thejacksonrose.com; 1167 W Washington St; r Mon-Fri/Sat & Sun $135/150; ❄ 📶) This marvelous 18th-century brick residence with stately gardens has three attractive guest rooms, including a room where Stonewall Jackson lodged briefly during the Civil War. Antique furnishings and vintage curios are sprinkled about the house, and the cooked breakfast is excellent. It's a 600m walk downhill to the historic district. No children under 12.

Town's Inn INN $$
(☎304-932-0677; www.thetownsinn.com; 179 High St; r $120-140; ❄) Spread between two neighboring pre–Civil War residences, the Town's Inn has rooms ranging from small and minimalist to charming heritage-style quarters. It's set in the middle of the historic district and has an indoor-outdoor restaurant as well.

Eating

Potomac Grille AMERICAN $
(186 High St; mains $10-16; ⊙noon-9pm) Serves good pub food (fish and chips, crab cakes, huge burgers) and local brews in an old-fashioned tavern atmosphere in the historic district. The outdoor patio has fine views over the train station and Maryland Heights.

Beans in the Belfry AMERICAN $
(☎301-834-7178; 122 W Potomac St, Brunswick, MD; sandwiches around $7; ⊙9am-9pm Mon-Sat, 8am-7pm Sun; 📶 👪) Across the river in Brunswick, MD (roughly 10 miles east), you'll find this converted red-brick church sheltering mismatched couches and kitsch-laden walls, featuring light fare (chili, sandwiches, quiche) and a tiny stage where live folk, blues and bluegrass bands strike up several nights a week. Sunday jazz brunch ($18) is a hit.

Canal House AMERICAN $$
(1226 Washington St; mains $11-24; ⊙noon-8pm Mon, to 9pm Fri & Sat, to 6pm Sun; 👪) Roughly 1 mile west (and uphill) from the historic district, Canal House is a perennial favorite for delicious sandwiches, locally sourced seasonal fare and friendly service in a flower-trimmed stone house. Outdoor seating. You can bring your own beer or wine.

Getting There & Around

Amtrak (www.amtrak.com; one way $13-16) trains run to Washington's Union Station (once daily, 71 minutes). **MARC trains** (http://mta.maryland.gov; one way $11) run three times daily during the week (Monday to Friday).

WEST VIRGINIA FACTS

Nickname Mountain State

Population 1.85 million

Area 24,230 sq miles

Capital city Charleston (population 52,000)

Other cities Huntington (49,000), Parkersburg (31,500), Morgantown (29,500), Wheeling (28,500)

Sales tax 6%

Birthplace of Olympic gymnast Mary Lou Retton (b 1968), writer Pearl S Buck (1892–1973), pioneer aviator Chuck Yeager (b 1923), actor Don Knotts (1924–2006)

Home of the National Radio Astronomy Observatory, much of the American coal industry

Politics Republican

Famous for Mountains, John Denver's 'Take Me Home, Country Roads,' the Hatfield–McCoy feud

State slogan 'Wild and Wonderful'

Driving distances Harpers Ferry to Fayetteville 280 miles; Fayetteville to Morgantown 148 miles

Berkeley Springs

America's first spa town (George Washington relaxed here) is an odd jumble of spiritualism, artistic expression and pampering spa centers. Farmers in pickups sporting Confederate flags and acupuncturists in tie-dye smocks regard each other with bemusement on the roads of Bath (still the official name).

Sights & Activities

The Berkeley Springs State Park's **Roman Baths** (☎304-258-2711; www.berkeleyspringssp.com; 2 S Washington St; 30min bath $22, 1hr massage $85-95; ⏱9am-4:30pm mon-Fri, 10am-3pm Sat) are uninspiring soaks in dimly lit, individual tile-lined rooms, but it's the cheapest spa deal in town, and you can also book a massage there. (Fill your water bottle with some of the magic stuff at the fountain outside the door.) In the summer, kids will enjoy the spring-fed (but chlorinated) outdoor **swimming pool** (adult/child $3/2; ⏱10am-6pm) in the middle of the green.

Eating & Drinking

Cacapon State Park CABIN $
(☎304-258-1022; 818 Cacapon Lodge Dr; lodge/cabins from $89/91) Cacapon State Park has simple lodge accommodations plus modern and rustic cabins (some with fireplaces) in a peaceful wooded setting, 9 miles south of Berkeley Springs (off US 522). The park has hiking, lake swimming, horseback riding and a golf course.

Country Inn of Berkeley Springs HOTEL $$
(☎304-258-1200; www.thecountryinnwv.com; 110 S Washington St; d from $120; P ❄ ᯤ) The Country Inn, right next to the park, offers luxurious treatment plus lodging package deals. There's a good restaurant on hand.

Tari's FUSION $$
(☎304-258-1196; 33 N Washington St; lunch $9-12, dinner $19-29; ⏱11am-9pm; ✎) Tari's is a very Berkeley Springs sort of spot, with fresh local food and good vegetarian options served in a laid-back atmosphere with all the right hints of good karma abounding. The Caribbean-spiced mahimahi tacos are a delicious way to satisfy one's lunch cravings.

Monongahela National Forest

Almost the entire eastern half of West Virginia is marked as green parkland on the map, and all that goodness falls under the auspices of this stunning national forest. Within its 1400 sq miles are wild rivers, caves and the highest peak in the state, **Spruce Knob**. More than 850 miles of trails include the 124-mile **Allegheny Trail**, for hiking and backpacking, and the 75-mile rails-to-trails **Greenbrier River Trail**, popular with cyclists.

Elkins, at the forest's western boundary, is a good base of operations. The **National Forest Service Headquarters** (☎304-636-1800; www.fs.usda.gov/mnf/; 200 Sycamore St; campsites $5-37, primitive camping free) distributes recreation directories for hiking, cycling and camping. After the hike, enjoy wood-fired pizzas, almond-crusted trout and wine at **Vintage** (304-636-0808; 25 Randolph Ave, Elkins; mains $12-29; ⏱11am-10pm).

In the southern end of the forest, **Cranberry Mountain Nature Center** (☎304-653-4826; cnr Hwys 150 & 39/55; ⏱9am-4:30pm Thu-Mon mid-Apr–Oct) FREE has scientific information on the forest and the surrounding 750-acre bog ecosystem, the largest of its kind in the state.

The surreal landscapes at **Seneca Rocks**, 35 miles southeast of Elkins, attract rock climbers up the 900ft-tall sandstone strata. **Seneca Shadows Campground** (☎877-444-6777; www.recreation.gov; campsites $15-40; ⏱Apr-Oct) lies 1 mile east.

Southern West Virginia

This part of the state has carved out a viable stake as adventure-sports capital of the eastern seaboard.

New River Gorge National River

The New River is actually one of the oldest in the world, and the primeval forest gorge it runs through is one of the most breathtaking in the Appalachians. The NPS protects a stretch of the New River that falls 750ft over 50 miles, with a compact set of rapids up to Class V concentrated at the northernmost end.

Canyon Rim visitor center (☎304-574-2115; www.nps.gov/neri; 162 Visitor Center Rd Lansing, WV , GPS 38.07003 N, 81.07583 W; ⏲9am-5pm;) , just north of the impressive gorge bridge, is only one of five NPS visitor centers along the river. It has information on scenic drives (including a memorable outing to the abandoned mining town of **Nuttallburg**), river outfitters, gorge climbing, hiking and mountain biking, as well as white-water rafting to the north on the **Gauley River**. Rim and gorge trails offer beautiful views. There are several free basic camping areas.

For a hair-raising stroll over the gorge, sign up for a tour with **Bridgewalk** (☎304-574-1300; www.bridgewalk.com; per person $69; ⏲10am-3pm), which takes visitors out across the catwalk below the bridge.

Hawks Nest State Park offers views from its rim-top **lodge** (☎304-658-5212; www.hawksnestsp.com; 49 Hawks Nest Park Rd; r $91-98, ste $111-134;). It has short hiking trails and an aerial tram (open May to October) to the river, where you can sign up for a jet-boat ride.

Babcock State Park (☎304-438-3004; www.babcocksp.com; 486 Babcock Rd; cabins $76-121, campsites $21-24) has hiking, canoeing, horseback riding, camping and cabin accommodations. The park's highlight is its very photogenic **Glade Creek Grist Mill**.

The reputable **Adventures on the Gorge** (☎855-379-8738; www.adventuresonthegorge.com; 219 Chestnutburg Rd, Lansing; cabin from $150) offers a wide range of activities, including white-water rafting ($94 to $144 per person), zip-lining, rappelling and more. It has camping, a range of cabins and several popular restaurants.

Fayetteville & Around

Pint-sized Fayetteville acts as jumping-off point for New River thrill-seekers and is an artsy mountain enclave besides. On the third Saturday in October, hundreds of BASE jumpers parachute from the 876ft-high New River Gorge Bridge during the massive **Bridge Day Festival**.

WORTH A TRIP

ROADSIDE MYSTERIES

See gravity and the known limits of tackiness defied at the **Mystery Hole** (☎304-658-9101; www.mysteryhole.com; 16724 Midland Trail, Ansted; adult/child $7/6; ⏲10:30am-6pm), one of the great attractions of roadside America. Everything inside this madhouse *tilts at an angle!* It's located 1 mile west of Hawks Nest State Park. Call ahead to check open days.

Among the many state-licenced rafting outfitters in the area, **Cantrell Ultimate Rafting** (☎304-877-8235; www.cantrellultimaterafting.com; 49 Cantrell Dr; half-/full-day rafting from $89/109) stands out for its white-water rafting trips. **Hard Rock** (☎304-574-0735; www.hardrockclimbing.com; 131 South Court St; half-/full day from $80/150) offers trips and training courses for rock climbers. Mountain biking is superb in the area, on the graded loops of the **Arrowhead Trails**. Hire wheels at **New River Bikes** (☎304-574-2453; www.newriverbikes.com; 221 N Court St; bike hire per day $35, tours $59-110; ⏲10am-6pm Mon-Sat).

The **Beckley Exhibition Coal Mine** (☎304-256-1747; www.beckley.org/exhibition_coal_mine; adult/child $20/12; ⏲10am-6pm Apr-Oct) in nearby Beckley is a museum for the region's coal heritage. Visitors can descend 1500ft to a former coal mine. Bring a jacket, as it's cold underground!

River Rock Retreat Hostel (☎304-574-0394; www.riverrockretreatandhostel.com; Lansing-Edmond Rd; dm $26;), located less than 1 mile north of the New River Gorge Bridge, has basic, clean rooms and plenty of common space. Owner Joy Marr is a wealth of local information.

Start the day with breakfast and coffee under stained-glass windows at **Cathedral Café** (☎304-574-0202; 134 S Court St; mains $6-10; ⏲7:30am-4pm Sun-Thu, to 9pm Fri & Sat;) . The **Secret Sandwich Society** (103 Keller Ave; mains $9-12; ⏲11am-10pm Wed-Mon) has delicious burgers, hearty salads and a changing lineup of local microbrews.

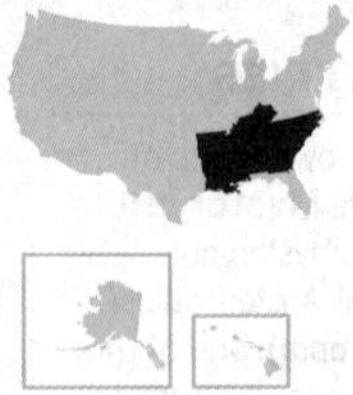

The South

Includes ➡

Best Places to Eat

- ➡ The Optimist (p407)
- ➡ Decca (p395)
- ➡ Cúrate (p355)
- ➡ Boucherie (p453)
- ➡ Octopus Bar (p408)

Best Places to Stay

- ➡ Crash Pad (p389)
- ➡ La Belle Esplanade (p449)
- ➡ 21c Museum Hotel (p394)
- ➡ Lodge on Little St Simons (p419)
- ➡ Capital Hotel (p434)

Why Go?

Beneath its hospitable exterior, the South has a feisty streak. It's a unique combination of 'Hey y'all' and 'Don't tell me what to do.' This dissonance makes the region a bit of a conundrum to outsiders, as well as a compelling place to visit. Well, that and the lyrical dialect, complicated political history and exuberant food. Nurtured by deep roots yet shaped by hardship, the South has a rich legacy in politics and culture. Icons like Martin Luther King Jr, Rosa Parks and Bill Clinton, and novelists like William Faulkner, Eudora Welty and Flannery O'Connor are all Southern-born. So are barbecue and grits, bourbon and Coca-Cola, and bluegrass and the blues.

The cities are some of the country's most fascinating, from antebellum beauties like New Orleans and Savannah to New South powerhouses like Atlanta and Nashville. Natural treasures include golden beaches and forested mountain ranges. Tying it all together? That Southern hospitality.

When to Go

New Orleans

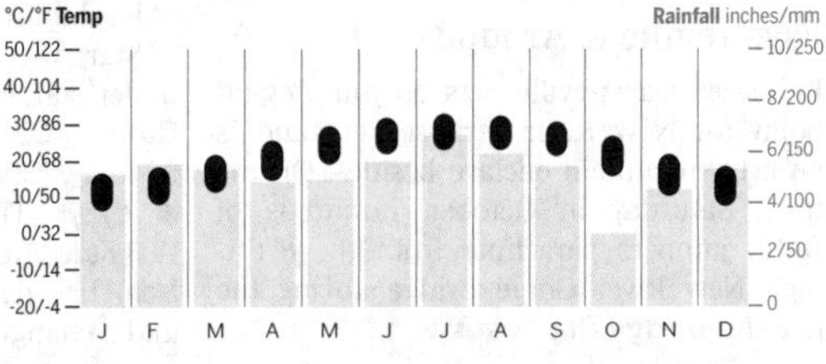

Nov–Feb Winter is generally mild here, and Christmas is a capital-E Event.

Apr–Jun Spring is lush and warm, abloom with fragrant jasmine, gardenia and tuberose.

Jul–Sep Summer is steamy, often unpleasantly so, and locals hit the beaches.

NORTH CAROLINA

The conservative Old South and the liberal New South are jostling for political dominance in the fast-growing Tar Heel State, home to hipsters, hog farmers, hi-tech wunderkinds and an increasing number of craft brewers. For the most part, though, from the ancient mountains in the west to the sandy barrier islands of the Atlantic, the various cultures and communities here coexist.

Agriculture is an important economic force, and there are 52,200 farms across the state. North Carolina leads the nation in tobacco production and is the second-largest producer of pigs. But new technologies also drive the economy, and more than 190 businesses operate in Research Triangle Park alone. Other important industries include finance, nanotechnology and Christmas trees. Craft brewers have contributed nearly $800 million to the economy.

Though the bulk of North Carolinians live in the business-oriented urban centers of the central Piedmont region, most travelers stick to the scenic routes along the coast and through the Appalachian Mountains.

So come on down, grab a platter of barbecue and watch the Duke Blue Devils battle the Carolina Tar Heels on the basketball court. College hoops rival Jesus for Carolinians' souls.

History

Native Americans have inhabited North Carolina for more than 10,000 years. Major tribes included the Cherokee in the mountains, the Catawba in the Piedmont and the Waccamaw in the Coastal Plain.

North Carolina was the second territory to be colonized by the British, named in memory of King Charles I (Carolus in Latin), but the first colony to vote for independence from the Crown. Several important Revolutionary War battles were fought here.

The state was a sleepy agricultural backwater through the 19th century, earning it the nickname the 'Rip Van Winkle State.' Divided on slavery (most residents were too poor to own slaves), North Carolina was the last state to secede during the Civil War, but went on to provide more Confederate soldiers than any other state.

North Carolina was a civil rights hotbed in the mid-20th century, with highly publicized lunch-counter sit-ins in Greensboro and the formation of the influential Student Nonviolent Coordinating Committee (SNCC) in Raleigh. The latter part of the century brought finance to Charlotte, and technology and medicine to the Raleigh-Durham area, driving a huge population boom and widening cultural diversity.

Information

North Carolina Division of Tourism (☎ 919-733-8372; www.visitnc.com; 301 N Wilmington St, Raleigh; ⏲ 8am-5pm Mon-Fri) Sends out good maps and information, including its annual *Official Travel Guide*.

North Carolina State Parks (www.ncparks.gov) Offers info on North Carolina's 41 state parks and recreation areas, many of which have camping (campsite fees range from $10 to $45).

North Carolina Coast

The coastline of North Carolina stretches just over 300 miles. Remarkably, it remains underdeveloped and the beach is often visible from coastal roads. Yes, the wall of cottages stretching south from Corolla to Kitty Hawk can seem endless, but for the most part the state's shores remain free of flashy, highly commercialized resort areas. Instead you'll find rugged, windswept barrier islands, Colonial villages once frequented by pirates and laid-back beach towns full of locally owned ice-cream shops and mom-and-pop motels. Even the most touristy beaches have a small-town vibe.

For solitude, head to the isolated Outer Banks (OBX), where fishermen still make their living hauling in shrimp and the older locals speak in an archaic British-tinged brogue. The Hwy 158 bypass from Kitty Hawk to Nags Head gets congested in summer, but the beaches themselves still feel uncrowded. Further south, Wilmington is known as a center of film and TV production, and its surrounding beaches are popular with local spring breakers and tourists.

Outer Banks

These fragile ribbons of sand trace the coastline for 100 miles, cut off from the mainland by various sounds and waterways. From north to south, the barrier islands of Bodie (pronounced 'Body'), Roanoke, Hatteras and Ocracoke, essentially large sandbars, are linked by bridges and ferries. The far-northern communities of **Corolla** (pronounced kur-*all*-ah, not like the car), **Duck** and **Southern Shores** are former duck-hunting

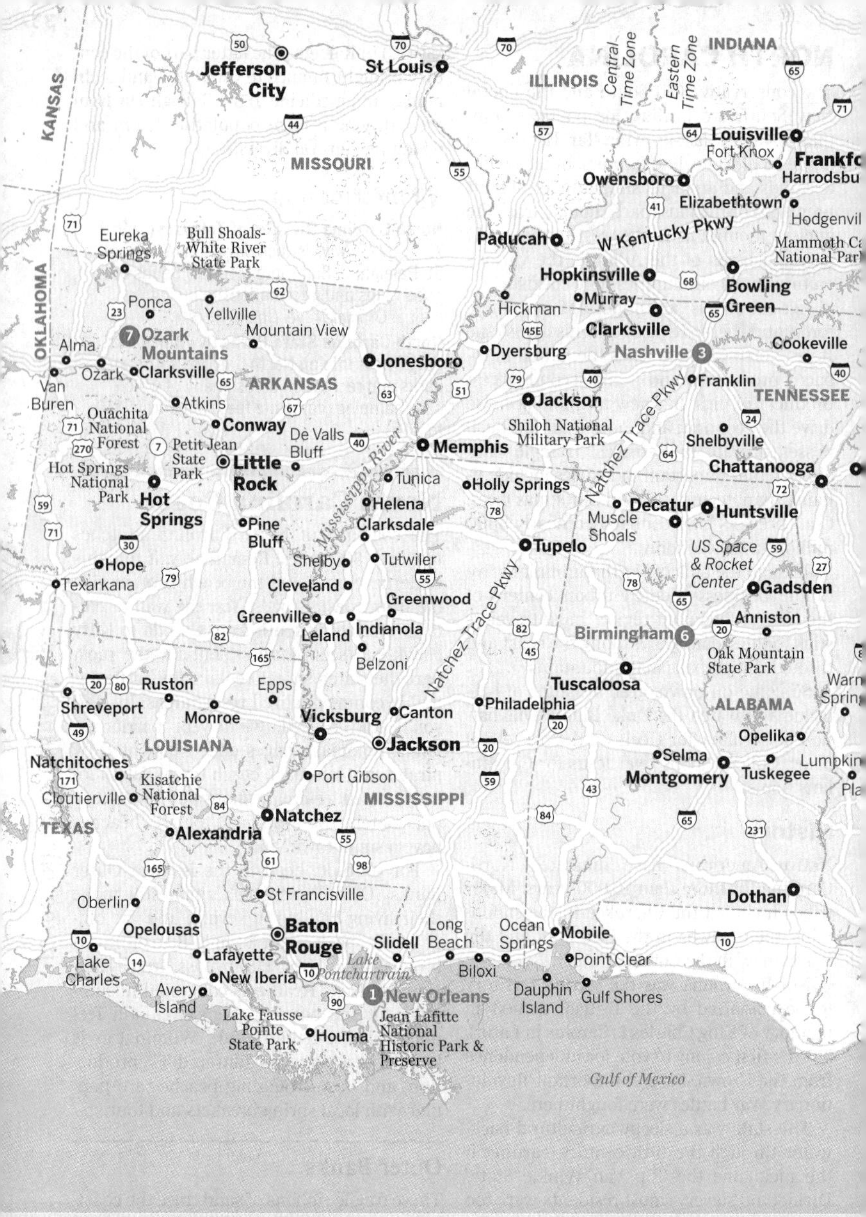

The South Highlights

1 Donning a costume and joining the crowds during Mardi Gras in **New Orleans** (p441).

2 Hiking and camping in the magnificent **Great Smoky Mountains National Park** (p356).

3 Stomping your boots in honky-tonks along Lower Broadway in **Nashville** (p378).

4 Driving windswept Hwy 12 the length of North Carolina's **Outer Banks** (p337) and riding the ferry to Ocracoke Island.

5 Touring the grand antebellum homes and

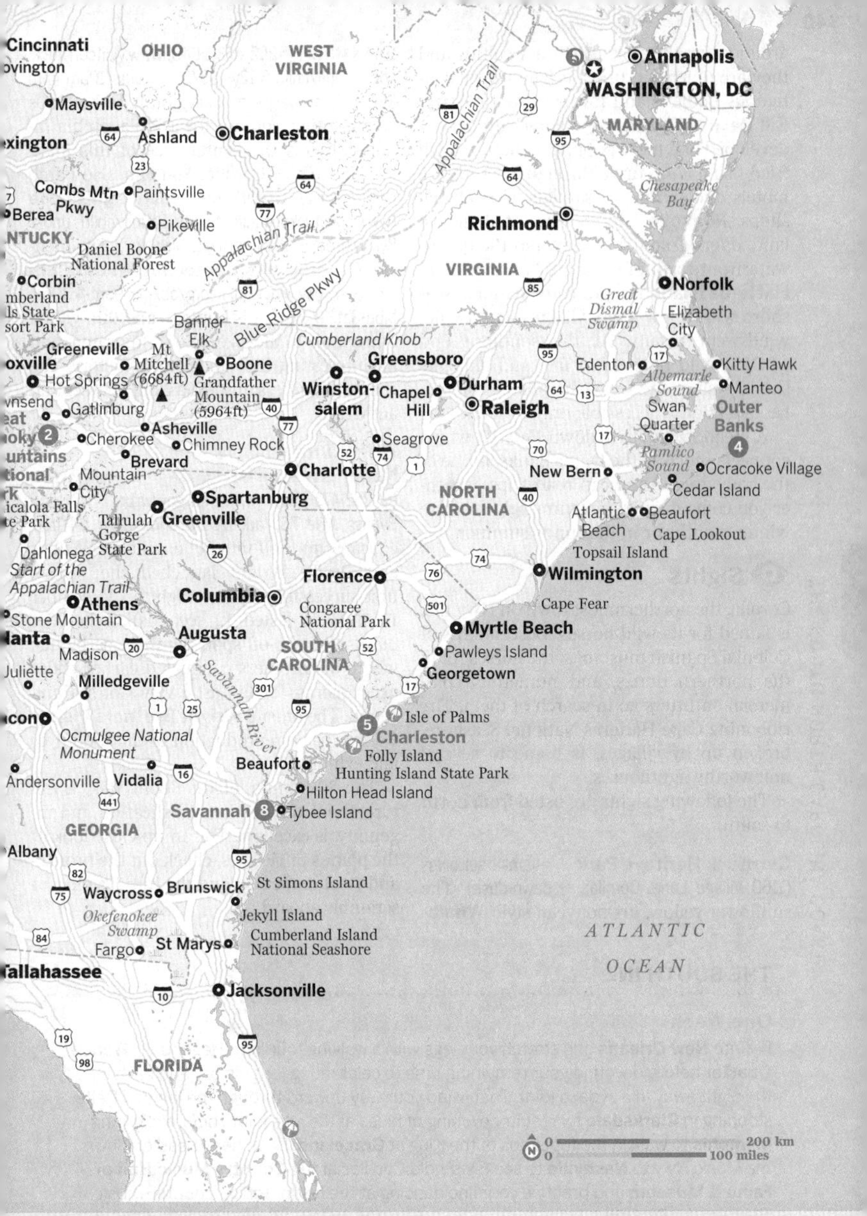

dining on Lowcountry fare in **Charleston** (p358).

6 Learning the story of segregation and the Civil Rights movement at the **Birmingham Civil Rights Institute** (p421).

7 Exploring Arkansas' **Ozark Mountains** (p437), where folk music reigns.

8 Falling for the hauntings, murderous tales and Southern hospitality in Georgia's living romance novel, the architecturally pristine **Savannah** (p414).

grounds for the northeastern wealthy, and they are quiet and upscale. The nearly contiguous Bodie Island towns of **Kitty Hawk**, **Kill Devil Hills** and **Nags Head** are heavily developed and more populist in nature, with fried-fish joints, drive-through beer shops, motels and dozens of sandals 'n' sunblock shops. **Roanoke Island**, west of Bodie Island, offers Colonial history and the quaint waterfront town of **Manteo**. Further south, **Hatteras Island** is a protected national seashore with a few teeny villages and a wild, windswept beauty. At the southern end of OBX, wild ponies run free and old salts shuck oysters and weave hammocks on **Ocracoke Island**, accessible only by ferry.

A meandering drive down Hwy 12, which connects much of the Outer Banks, is one of the truly great American road trips, whether you come during the stunningly desolate winter months or in the sunny summer.

Sights

Corolla, the northernmost town on Hwy 158, is famed for its wild horses. Descendants of Colonial Spanish mustangs, the horses roam the northern dunes, and numerous commercial outfitters go in search of them. The ribboning Cape Hatteras National Seashore, broken up by villages, is home to several noteworthy lighthouses.

The following sights are listed from north to south.

Currituck Heritage Park HISTORIC BUILDINGS

(1160 Village Lane, Corolla; dawn-dusk) The sunflower-yellow, art-nouveau-style **Whalehead Club** (252-453-9040; www.visitcurrituck.com; adult/child 6-12yr $5/3; tours 10am-4pm Mon-Sat, may vary seasonally), built in the 1920s as a hunting 'cottage' for a Philadelphia industrialist, is the centerpiece of this manicured park in Corolla. You can also climb the redbrick **Currituck Beach Lighthouse** (www.currituckbeachlight.com; adult/child under 8yr $7/free; 9am-5pm late Mar-Nov). The modern **Outer Banks Center for Wildlife Education** (www.ncwildlife.org/obx; 9am-4:30pm Mon-Sat;) FREE is home to an 8000-gallon aquarium, a life-size marsh diorama and an interesting film about area history. The center also offers numerous kids' classes and activities.

Wright Brothers National Memorial PARK, MUSEUM

(252-473-2111; www.nps.gov/wrbr; US 158 Bypass, Mile 7.5; adult/child under 16yr $4/free; 9am-5pm) Self-taught engineers Wilbur and Orville Wright launched the world's first successful airplane flight on December 17, 1903 (it lasted 12 seconds). A boulder marks the take-off spot. Climb a nearby hill, where the brothers conducted earlier glider experiments, for fantastic views of sea and sound. The on-site **Wright Brothers Visitor Center** has a reproduction of the 1903 flyer and exhibits.

The 30-minute 'Flight Room Talk,' a lecture about the brothers' dedication and ingenuity, is excellent. For an up-close look at the plane's intricacies, check out the bronze-and-steel replica behind the hill; it's okay to scramble aboard.

THE SOUTH IN...

One Week

Fly into **New Orleans** and stretch your legs with a walking tour in the legendary **French Quarter** before devoting your remaining time to celebrating jazz history and partying the night away in a zydeco joint. Then wind your way upward through the languid Delta, stopping in **Clarksdale** for a sultry evening of blues at the juke joints before alighting in **Memphis** to walk in the footsteps of the King at **Graceland**. From here, head on down the Music Hwy to **Nashville** to see Elvis' gold Cadillac at the **Country Music Hall of Fame & Museum** and practice your line dancing at the honky-tonks (country-music clubs) of the **District**.

Two to Three Weeks

From Nashville, head east to hike amid the craggy peaks and waterfalls of **Great Smoky Mountains National Park** before a revitalizing overnight in the arty mountain town of **Asheville** and a tour of the scandalously opulent **Biltmore Estate**, America's largest private home. Plow straight through to the coast to loll on the sandy barrier islands of the isolated **Outer Banks**, then head down the coast to finish up in **Charleston**, with decadent food and postcard-pretty architecture.

Fort Raleigh National Historic Site — HISTORIC BUILDING

In the late 1580s, three decades before the Pilgrims landed at Plymouth Rock, a group of 116 British colonists disappeared without a trace from their Roanoke Island settlement. Were they killed off by drought? Did they run away with a Native American tribe? The fate of the 'Lost Colony' remains one of America's greatest mysteries. Explore their story in the **visitor center** (www.nps.gov/fora; 1401 National Park Dr, Manteo; ⏲grounds dawn-dusk, visitor center 9am-5pm) FREE. One of the site's star attractions is the beloved musical the **Lost Colony Outdoor Drama** (www.thelostcolony.org; 1409 National Park Dr; adult/child 6-12yr $30/10; ⏲7:30pm Mon-Sat late May-late Aug).

The play, from Pulitzer Prize-winning North Carolina playwright Paul Green, dramatizes the fate of the colonists and will celebrate its 80th anniversary in 2017. It plays at the Waterside Theater throughout summer.

Other attractions include exhibits, artifacts, maps and a free film to fuel the imagination, hosted at the visitor center. The 16th-century-style **Elizabethan Gardens** (www.elizabethangardens.org; 1411 National Park Dr; adult/child 6-17yr $9/6; ⏲9am-7pm Jun-Aug, shorter hours Sep-May) include a Shakespearian herb garden and rows of beautifully manicured flower beds. A commanding statue of Queen Elizabeth I stands guard at the entrance.

Cape Hatteras National Seashore — ISLANDS

(www.nps.gov/caha) Extending some 70 miles from south of Nags Head to the south end of Ocracoke Island, this fragile necklace of islands remains blissfully free from overdevelopment. Natural attractions include local and migratory water birds, marshes, woodlands, dunes and miles of empty beaches.

Bodie Island Lighthouse — LIGHTHOUSE

(☎255-473-2111; Bodie Island Lighthouse Rd, Bodie Island; museum free, tours adult/child under 11yr $8/4; ⏲visitor center 9am-5pm, lighthouse 9am-4:30pm late Apr-early Oct; 👪) Built in 1872, this photogenic lighthouse opened its doors to visitors in 2013. The 156ft-high structure still has its original Fresnel lens – a rarity. It's just over 200 steps to the top. The lighthouse keeper's former home is now the visitor center.

Pea Island National Wildlife Refuge — PRESERVE

(☎252-987-2394; www.fws.gov/refuge/peaisland; Hwy 12; ⏲visitor center 9am-4pm, trails dawn-dusk) At the northern end of Hatteras Island, this 5834-acre preserve is a bird-watcher's heaven, with two nature trails (both are fully accessible to people with disabilities) and 13 miles of unspoiled beach. Viewer scopes inside the visitor center overlook an adjacent pond. Check the online calendar for details about guided bird walks, turtle talks and canoe tours.

Cape Hatteras Lighthouse — LIGHTHOUSE

(www.nps.gov/caha; climbing tours adult/child under 12yr $8/4; ⏲visitor center 9am-5pm Sep-May, to 6pm Jun-Aug, lighthouse 9am-5:30pm Jun-Aug, until 4:30pm spring & fall) At 208ft, this striking black-and-white-striped edifice is the tallest brick lighthouse in the US and is one of North Carolina's most iconic images. Climb the 248 steps then check out the interesting exhibits about local history in the Museum of the Sea, located in the lighthouse keeper's former home.

NORTH CAROLINA FACTS

Nickname Tar Heel State

Population 9.9 million

Area 48,711 sq miles

Capital city Raleigh (population 431,000)

Other cities Charlotte (population 792,000)

Sales tax 4.75% plus municipality taxes, plus an additional hotel-occupancy tax of up to 8%

Birthplace of President James K Polk (1795–1849), jazzman John Coltrane (1926–67), Nascar driver Richard Petty (b 1937), singer-songwriter Tori Amos (b 1963)

Home of America's first state university, the Biltmore Estate, Krispy Kreme doughnuts

Politics Conservative in rural areas, increasingly liberal in urban ones

Famous for *The Andy Griffith Show*, first airplane flight, college basketball

Pet name Natives are called 'tar heels,' a nickname of uncertain origin but said to be related to their pine-tar production and their legendary stubbornness

Driving distances Asheville to Raleigh 247 miles, Raleigh to Wilmington 131 miles

Graveyard of the Atlantic Museum MUSEUM
(☎252-986-2995; www.graveyardoftheatlantic.com; 59200 Museum Dr; ⏲10am-4pm) FREE Exhibits about shipwrecks, piracy and salvaged cargo are highlights at this maritime museum at the end of the road. There have been more than 2000 shipwrecks off the coast of the Outer Banks. According to one exhibit, in 2006 a container washed ashore near Frisco, releasing thousands of Doritos bags. One local told us that residents were enjoying Doritos casseroles for months! Donations appreciated.

Activities

The same strong wind that helped the Wright brothers launch their biplane today propels windsurfers, sailors and hang gliders. Other popular activities include kayaking, fishing, cycling, horse tours, stand-up paddleboarding and scuba diving. The coastal waters kick up between August and October, creating perfect conditions for bodysurfing.

Kitty Hawk Kites ADVENTURE SPORTS
(☎252-449-2210; www.kittyhawk.com; 3925 S Croatan Hwy, Mile 12.5; electric bike rental per day $50, kayaks $39-49, stand-up paddleboards $59) In business more than 30 years, Kitty Hawk Kites has several locations along the OBX coast. They offer beginners' kiteboarding lessons (five hours, $400) in Kitty Hawk and Rodanthe and hang-gliding lessons at Jockey's Ridge State Park (from $109). Also rents kayaks, sailboats, stand-up paddleboards, bikes and inline skates and offers a variety of tours and courses.

Corolla Outback Adventures DRIVING TOUR
(☎252-453-4484; www.corollaoutback.com; 1150 Ocean Trail, Corolla; 2hr tour adult/child under 13yr $50/25) Tour operator Jay Bender, whose family started Corolla's first guide service, knows his local history and his local horses. Tours bounce you down the beach and through the dunes to see the wild mustangs that roam the northern Outer Banks.

Sleeping

Crowds swarm the Outer Banks in summer, so reserve in advance. The area has few massive chain hotels, but hundreds of small motels, rental cottages and B&Bs; the visitor centers offer referrals. Also check www.outer-banks.com. For cottage rentals, try www.sunrealtync.com or www.southernshores.com.

Campgrounds CAMPGROUND $
(☎252-473-2111; www.nps.gov/caha; tent sites $20-23; ⏲late spring-early fall) The National Park Service runs four campgrounds on the islands which feature cold-water showers and flush toilets. They are located at Oregon Inlet (near Bodie Island Lighthouse), Cape Point and Frisco (near Cape Hatteras Lighthouse) and **Ocracoke** (☎800-365-2267; www.recreation.gov). Sites at Oregon Inlet, Frisco and Ocracoke can be reserved; Cape Point is first-come, first-served. You'll enjoy close proximity to the coast at these campsites, but you won't find many trees for shade.

Breakwater Inn MOTEL $$
(☎252-986-2565; www.breakwaterhatteras.com; 57896 Hwy 12; r/ste $159/189, motel $104/134; P❄📶🏊) The end of the road doesn't look so bad at this three-story inn. Rooms come with kitchenettes and private decks that have views of the sound. On a budget? Try one of the older 'Fisherman's Quarters' rooms, with microwave and refrigerator. The inn is near the Hatteras–Ocracoke ferry landing.

Shutters on the Banks HOTEL $$
(☎252-441-5581; www.shuttersonthebanks.com; 405 S Virginia Dare Trail; r $159-284, ste $229-725; P❄📶🏊) Centrally located in Kill Devil Hills, this welcoming beachfront hotel exudes a snappy, colorful style. The inviting rooms come with plantation windows and colorful bedspreads as well as a flat-screen TV, refrigerator and microwave. Some rooms come with a full kitchen.

Sanderling Resort & Spa RESORT $$$
(☎252-261-4111; www.sanderling-resort.com; 1461 Duck Rd; r $399-539; P❄📶🏊) Two dozen revamped rooms opened their doors in 2015, giving this posh place a stylish kick in the pants. Or should we say the Lululemons? Because yes, the resort does offer sunrise yoga on the beach. Decor is impeccably tasteful, and the attached balconies are an inviting place to enjoy the ocean sounds and breezes.

The property includes several restaurants and bars, and a spa offering luxe massage. Daily resort fee is $25 from mid-May to October, $15 from November to mid-May.

Eating & Drinking

The main tourist strip on Bodie Island has the most restaurants and nightlife options. Many places are only open Memorial Day (last Monday in May) through early fall, or have reduced hours in the off-season.

WORTH A TRIP

OCRACOKE ISLAND

Crowded in summer and desolate in winter, **Ocracoke Village** (www.ocracokevillage.com) is a funky little community that moves at a slower pace. The village is at the southern end of 14-mile-long Ocracoke Island and is accessed from Hatteras via the free Hatteras–Ocracoke **ferry** (p344). The ferry lands at the northeastern end of the island. With the exception of the village, the National Park Service owns the island.

The older residents still speak in the 17th-century British dialect known as 'Hoi Toide' (their pronunciation of 'high tide') and refer to non-islanders as 'dingbatters.' Edward Teach, aka Blackbeard the pirate, used to hide out in the area and was killed here in 1718. You can camp by the beach where wild ponies run, have a fish sandwich in a local pub, bike around the village's narrow streets or visit the 1823 **Ocracoke Lighthouse**, the oldest one still operating in North Carolina.

The island makes a terrific day trip from Hatteras Island, or you can stay the night. There are a handful of B&Bs, a park service campground near the beach and rental cottages.

Locals and tourists converge at **Ocracoke Coffee** (www.ocracokecoffee.com; 226 Back Rd; ⏲7am-6pm Mon-Sat, to 1pm Sun), home of the Grasshopper latte (chocolate mint and toffee), and friendly **Howard's Pub** (1175 Irvin Garrish Hwy; mains $9-25; ⏲11am-10pm early Mar-late Nov, may stay open later Fri & Sat), a big old wooden pub that's been an island tradition for beer and fried seafood since the 1850s.

Want to get on the water? Take a kayaking tour with **Ride the Wind** (☎252-928-6311; www.surfocracoke.com; 486 Irvin Garrish Hwy; 2-2½ hr tours adult $39-45, child under 13yr $18; ⏲9am-9pm Mon-Sat, to 8pm Sun). The sunset tours are easy on the arms, and the guides (we hear) are easy on the eyes.

John's Drive-In SEAFOOD, ICE CREAM **$**
(www.johnsdrivein.com; 3716 N Virginia Dare Trail; mains $2-16; ⏲11am-5pm Thu-Tue) A Kitty Hawk institution for perfectly fried baskets of mahi-mahi, to be eaten at outdoor picnic tables and washed down with one of hundreds of possible milkshake combinations. Some folks just come for the soft-serve.

★Blue Moon Beach Grill SEAFOOD, SANDWICHES **$$**
(☎252-261-2583; www.bluemoonbeachgrill.com; 4104 S Virginia Dare Trail, Mile 13; mains $10-29) Would it be wrong to write an ode to a side of french fries? Because Lord almighty, the lightly spiced fries at this casual hot spot are the stuff of sonnets and monologues. And we haven't even mentioned the BLT with seared mahi-mahi, Applewood bacon, local Currituck tomatoes and a jalapeño rémoulade for slathering. Other choices include seafood sandwiches, burgers and voodoo pasta.

The strip mall view won't inspire poetry, but the friendly staff, come-as-you-are atmosphere and upbeat play list – Elvis' 'Jailhouse Rock' – will invigorate your spirit for sure.

Trio WINE BAR
(www.obxtrio.com; 3708 N Croatan Hwy, Mile 4.5; cheese plates $7-21, tapas $7-11, panini $9-10; ⏲11am-11pm Mon-Sat, noon-11pm Sun) This simple but stylish wine bar is a welcome – and welcoming – addition to OBX. Select from two-dozen wines in the self-service tasting bar then complement your choice with housemade hummus, a cheese plate or one of seven different panini. The retail store sells a wide selection of craft beer, wine and artisanal cheese.

ℹ Orientation

Hwy 12, also called Virginia Dare Trail or 'the coast road,' runs close to the Atlantic for the length of the Outer Banks. US 158/Croatan Hwy, usually called 'the Bypass,' begins just north of Kitty Hawk and merges with US 64 as it crosses onto Roanoke Island. Locations are usually given in terms of 'mile posts' (Mile or MP), beginning with Mile 0 at the foot of the Wright Memorial Bridge at Kitty Hawk.

ℹ Information

The best sources of information are at the main visitor centers. Many smaller centers are open seasonally. Also useful is www.outerbanks.org. The entire Manteo waterfront has free wi-fi.

Aycock Brown Visitor Center (☎252-261-4644; www.outerbanks.org; US 158, Mile 1, Kitty Hawk; ⏲9am-5:30pm Mar-Oct, to 5pm Nov-Feb) On the bypass in Kitty Hawk; has maps and information.

Hatteras Island Visitor Center (☎252-473-2111; www.nps.gov/caha; ⏲9am-6pm Jun-Aug, to 5pm Sep-May) Beside Cape Hatteras Lighthouse.

Ocracoke Island Visitor Center (☎252-928-4531; www.nps.gov/caha; ⏲9am-5pm) Near the southern ferry dock.

Outer Banks Welcome Center on Roanoke Island (☎252-473-2138; www.outerbanks.org; 1 Visitors Center Circle, Manteo; ⏲9am-5:30pm Mar-Oct, to 5pm Nov-Feb) Just east of Virginia Dare Memorial Bridge on the US 64 Bypass.

Getting There & Around

No public transportation exists to or on the Outer Banks. However, the **North Carolina Ferry System** (☎800-293-3779; www.ncdot.gov/ferry) operates several routes, including the free one-hour Hatteras–Ocracoke car ferry, which runs at least hourly from 5am to midnight from Hatteras in high season; reservations aren't accepted. North Carolina ferries also run between Ocracoke and Cedar Island (one-way car/motorcycle $15/10, 2¼ hours) and Ocracoke and Swan Quarter on the mainland ($15/10, 2¾ hours) every three hours or so; reservations are recommended in summer for these two routes.

Crystal Coast

The southern Outer Banks are collectively called the 'Crystal Coast,' at least for tourist offices' promotional purposes. Less rugged than the northern beaches, they include several historic coastal towns, sparsely populated islands, and vacation-friendly beaches.

An industrial and commercial stretch of US 70 goes through **Morehead City**, with plenty of chain hotels and restaurants. The **Bogue Banks**, across the sound from Morehead City via the Atlantic Beach Causeway, have several well-trafficked beach communities – try Atlantic Beach if you like the smell of coconut suntan oil and doughnuts.

Just north, postcard-pretty **Beaufort** (bow-fort), the third-oldest town in the state, has a charming boardwalk and lots of B&Bs. Blackbeard himself is said to have lived in the Hammock House off Front St. You can't go inside, but some claim you can still hear the screams of the pirate's murdered wife at night.

Sights

North Carolina Maritime Museum MUSEUM
(http://ncmaritimemuseums.com/beaufort; 315 Front St, Beaufort; ⏲9am-5pm Mon-Fri, 10am-5pm Sat, 1-5pm Sun) FREE The pirate Blackbeard was a frequent visitor to the Beaufort area in the early 1700s. In 1996 the wreckage of his flagship, the *Queen Anne's Revenge*, was discovered at the bottom of Beaufort Inlet. You'll see plates, bottles and other artifacts from the ship in this small but engaging museum, which also spotlights the seafood industry as well as maritime rescue operations.

North Carolina Aquarium AQUARIUM
(www.ncaquariums.com; 1 Roosevelt Blvd, Pine Knoll Shores; adult/child 3-12yr $11/9; ⏲9am-5pm; 👪) Aquatic life from the North Carolina mountains to the sea is covered in this small but engaging aquarium. The fast-moving river otters are mesmerizing, and there's a cool exhibit re-creating the local shipwreck of a U-352 German submarine.

Fort Macon State Park FORT
(www.ncparks.gov; 2303 E Fort Macon Rd, Atlantic Beach; ⏲8am-9pm Jun-Aug, shorter hours Sep-May) FREE This sturdy, five-sided fort, with 26 vaulted rooms, was completed in 1834. Exhibits in rooms near the entrance spotlight the fort's construction as well as the daily lives of soldiers stationed there. The fort, built from brick and stone, changed hands twice during the Civil War.

Sleeping & Eating

Hampton Inn Morehead City HOTEL $$$
(☎252-240-2300; www.hamptoninn3.hilton.com; 4035 Arendell St, Morehead City; r from $209; ❄@📶🏊) Yep, it's part of a national chain, but the helpful staff and the views of Bogue Sound make this Hampton Inn a nice choice, plus it's convenient to US 70 for those driving the coast. Rates drop significantly on weeknights in summer.

El's Drive-In SEAFOOD $
(3706 Arendell St, Morehead City; mains $2-14; ⏲10:30am-10pm Sun-Thu, to 10:30pm Fri & Sat) The food is brought to you by carhop at this legendary seafood spot, open since 1959. Our recommendation? The fried shrimp burger with ketchup and slaw plus a side of fries. Cash only.

Front Street Grill at Stillwater RESTAURANT $$
(www.frontstreetgrillatstillwater.com; 300 Front St, Beaufort; brunch & lunch $11-17, dinner $17-30; ⏲11:30am-9pm Tue-Thu & Sun, to 10pm Fri & Sat) The view reigns supreme at this inviting seafood spot overlooking Taylor's Creek. Nibble chili-lime shrimp tacos at lunch or seared

backfin crabcakes at dinnertime. Enjoy people-watching at the small Rhum Bar.

Wilmington

Wilmington is pretty darn fun, and it's worth carving out a day or two for a visit if you're driving the coast. This seaside charmer may not have the name recognition of Charleston and Savannah, but eastern North Carolina's largest city has historic neighborhoods, azalea-choked gardens and cute cafes aplenty. All that plus reasonable hotel prices. At night the historic riverfront downtown becomes the playground for local college students, craft beer enthusiasts, tourists and the occasional Hollywood type – there are so many movie studios here the town has earned the nickname 'Wilmywood'.

Sights

Wilmington sits at the mouth of the Cape Fear River, about 8 miles from the beach. The historic **riverfront** is perhaps the city's most important sight, abounding with boutiques and boardwalks. Nearby **Wrightsville Beach** bustles with fried-fish joints, shops selling sunglasses and summer crowds.

A free **trolley** (www.wavetransit.com) runs through the historic district from morning through evening.

Cape Fear Serpentarium ZOO
(☎910-762-1669; www.capefearserpentarium.com; 20 Orange St; admission $9; ⊙11am-5pm Mon-Fri, to 6pm Sat & Sun) Herpetologist Dean Ripa's museum is a fun and informative place to spend an hour or two – if you don't mind standing in a building slithering with venomous snakes, giant constrictors and big-teethed crocodiles. They're all behind glass but…sssssss. Just hope there's not an earthquake. One sign explains the effects of a bite from a bushmaster: 'It is better to just lie down under a tree and rest, for you will soon be dead.' Enjoy! Cash only.

The Serpentarium may close on Monday and Tuesday in the off-season. Live feedings are held at 3pm on Saturday and Sunday, but call ahead to confirm.

Battleship North Carolina HISTORIC SITE
(www.battleshipnc.com; 1 Battleship Rd; adult/child 6-11yr $14/6; ⊙8am-5pm Sep-May, to 8pm Jun-Aug) Self-guided tours take you through the decks of this 45,000-ton megaship, which earned 15 battle stars in the Pacific theater in WWII before it was decommissioned in 1947. Sights include the bake shop and galley, the print shop, the engine room, the powder magazine and the communications center. Note that there are several steep stairways leading to lower decks. Take the Cape Fear Bridge from downtown to get here.

Airlie Gardens GARDENS
(www.airliegardens.org; 300 Airlie Rd; adult/child 4-12yr $9/3; ⊙9am-5pm, closed Mon in winter) In spring, wander past thousands of bright azaleas at this 67-acre wonderland, also home to bewitching formal flower beds, seasonal gardens, pine trees, lakes and trails. The Airlie Oak dates to 1545.

Sleeping & Eating

There are numerous budget hotels on Market St, just north of downtown. Restaurants directly on the waterfront can be crowded and mediocre; head a block or two inland for the best eats and nightlife.

★CW Worth House B&B $$
(☎910-762-8562; www.worthhouse.com; 412 S 3rd St; r $154-194; ❄@📶) One of our favorite B&Bs in North Carolina, this turreted 1893 home is dotted with antiques and Victorian touches, but still manages to feel kick-back and cozy. Breakfasts are top-notch. The B&B is within a few blocks of downtown.

Best Western Plus Coastline Inn HOTEL $$
(☎910-763-2800; www.bestwestern.com; 503 Nutt St; r/ste $209/239; ❄@📶🐾) We're not sure what we like best: the gorgeous views of the Cape Fear River, the wooden boardwalk or the short walk to downtown fun. Standard rooms aren't huge, but they do pop with a bit of modern style. Every room has a river view. Pet fee is $20 per day.

Fork & Cork BURGERS, SANDWICHES $
(www.theforkncork.com; 122 Market St; ⊙11am-11pm Mon-Thu, 11am-midnight Sat, noon-10pm Sun) The kitchen's not afraid of kicky flavors at new-on-the-scene Fork & Cork, a former food truck that has cleaned up nice – just look at those exposed brick walls. Juicy burgers like the Hot Mess – with bacon, jalapeños, grilled onions, and blue and cheddar cheese – draw raves, as do the poutine, duck wings and the day's mac 'n' cheese.

Flaming Amy's Burrito Barn MEXICAN $
(☎910-799-2919; www.flamingamys.com; 4002 Oleander Dr; mains $5-9; ⊙11am-10pm) The burritos are big and tasty at Flaming Amy's, a scrappy barn filled with kitschy decor from

Elvis to Route 66. Burritos include the Philly Phatboy, the Thai Mee Up and the jalapeño-and-pepper-loaded Flaming Amy itself. Everyone in town is here or on the way.

Drinking & Nightlife

Flytrap Brewing MICROBREWERY
(www.flytrapbrewing.com; 319 Walnut St; ⌚3-10pm Mon-Thu, noon-midnight Fri & Sat, noon-10pm Sun) Half-a-dozen new microbreweries have opened in Wilmington in the last few years, and the one consistently recommended is Flytrap. Located in a bright space in the Brooklyn Arts District just a short walk from Front St, the brewery specializes in American and Belgian-style ales. Look for food-truck fare and live music on weekend nights.

The brewery is named for the Venus flytrap, the carnivorous plant whose only native habitat is within 60 miles of Wilmington.

Entertainment

Dead Crow Comedy Room COMEDY
(☎910-399-1492; www.deadcrowcomedy.com; 265 N Front St; tickets $13-16) Dark, cramped, underground and in the heart of downtown, just like a comedy club should be. Before heading out, stop in for improv, open-mike nights and touring comedians. Bar service and full menu available.

Information

Visitor Center (☎877-406-2356, 910-341-4030; www.wilmingtonandbeaches.com; 505 Nutt St; ⌚8:30am-5pm Mon-Fri, 9am-4pm Sat, 1-4pm Sun) The visitor center, in an 1800s freight warehouse, has a walking-tour map of downtown.

The Triangle

The cities of Raleigh, Durham and Chapel Hill form a rough triangle in the central Piedmont region. Three top research universities – Duke, University of North Carolina and North Carolina State – are located here, as is the 7000-acre computer and biotech-office campus known as Research Triangle Park. Swarming with egghead computer programmers, bearded peace activists and hip young families, each town has its own unique personality, despite being only a few miles apart. In March, everyone – we mean *everyone* – goes crazy for college basketball.

Getting There & Around

Raleigh-Durham International Airport (RDU; ☎919-840-2123; www.rdu.com), a significant hub, is a 25-minute (15 mile) drive northwest of downtown Raleigh.

In 2014 **Greyhound** (☎919-834-8275; 2210 Capital Blvd) moved from downtown Raleigh to a location 3 miles northeast and not easy to reach for pedestrians and connections. For a better downtown stop, try Durham (515 W Pettrigrew St), near the Amtrak station in the Durham Station Transportation Center. The **Triangle Transit Authority** (☎919-549-9999; www.triangletransit.org; adult $2.25) operates buses linking Raleigh, Durham and Chapel Hill to each other and the airport. Rte 100 runs from downtown Raleigh to the airport, and the Regional Transit Center near Research Triangle Park where there are connections to Durham and Chapel Hill.

Raleigh

Founded in 1792 specifically to serve as the state capital, Raleigh remains a rather staid government town with major sprawl issues. Still, the handsome downtown has some neat (and free!) museums and galleries, and the food and music scene is on the upswing. The handsome 1840 **state capitol** is a fine example of Greek Revival architecture.

Sights

★**North Carolina Museum of Art** MUSEUM
(www.ncartmuseum.org; 2110 Blue Ridge Rd; ⌚10am-5pm Tue-Thu, Sat & Sun, 10am-9pm Fri, park dawn-dusk) FREE The light-filled glass-and-anodized-steel West Building won praise from architecture critics nationwide when it opened in 2010. The fine and wide-ranging collection, with everything from ancient Greek sculptures to commanding American landscape paintings to elaborate African masks, is worthy as well. Short on time? Then stretch your legs on the winding outdoor sculpture trail. It's a few miles west of downtown.

North Carolina Museum of Natural Sciences MUSEUM
(www.naturalsciences.org; 11 W Jones St; ⌚9am-5pm Mon-Sat, noon-5pm Sun, to 9pm 1st Fri of month) FREE Whale skeletons hang from the ceiling. Butterflies flutter past your shoulder. Emerald tree boas make you shiver. And swarms of unleashed elementary school children rampage all over the place if you arrive after 10am on a school day. Be warned. The glossy new **Nature Research Center**, fronted by a three-story multimedia globe, spot-

lights scientists and their projects. Visitors can watch them at work. Skywalks lead to the main museum building, which also holds habitat dioramas and well-done taxidermy.

Don't miss the exhibit about the Acrocanthosaurus dinosaur, a three-ton carnivore known as the Terror of the South. Its toothy skull is the stuff of nightmares.

North Carolina Museum of History MUSEUM
(www.ncmuseumofhistory.org; 5 E Edenton St; 9am-5pm Mon-Sat, noon-5pm Sun) FREE This engaging museum is low on tech but high on straightforward information. Artifacts in the *Story of North Carolina* exhibit include a 3000-year-old canoe; the state's oldest house, dating from 1742; a restored slave cabin; and a 1960s sit-in lunch counter. The special exhibits typically shine too.

Sleeping & Eating

Downtown is pretty quiet at nights and on weekends, except for the City Market area at E Martin and S Person Sts. Just to the northwest, the Glenwood South neighborhood hops with cafes, bars and clubs. Raleigh claims to have the most live music in the state. Check www.themostnc.for upcoming shows.

You'll find plenty of moderately priced chain hotels around exit 10 off I-440 and off I-40 near the airport.

Umstead Hotel & Spa HOTEL $$$
(919-447-4000; www.theumstead.com; 100 Woodland Pond Dr; r $329-389, s $409-599;) In a wooded suburban office park, the Umstead caters to visiting biotech CEOs with simple, sumptuous rooms and a Zen-like spa. A 3-acre lake sits behind the property complete with a quarter-mile walking trail. The pet fee is $200 per stay, and the hotel has a new fenced playground for Fido, DogWoods.

Raleigh Times PUB FOOD $
(www.raleightimesbar.com; 14 E Hargett St; mains $8-14; 11am-2am) Chase plates of BBQ nachos and PBR-battered fish and chips with pints of North Carolina craft brews at this popular downtown pub.

Beasley's Chicken + Honey SOUTHERN $
(www.ac-restaurants.com; 237 Wilmington St; mains $7-13; 11:30am-10pm Mon-Wed, 11:30am-midnight Thu & Fri, 11am-midnight Sat, 11am-10pm Sun) You'll need to loosen your belt after a meal at this crispy venture from James Beard Award winner and local restaurant maven Ashley Christensen. Inside this airy downtown eatery, fried chicken is the star – on a biscuit, with waffles, in a pot pie. The sides are decadent too.

If you've ever wanted to try collard greens, the creamed ones here are a good place to start.

Cowfish Sushi Burger Bar BURGERS, SUSHI $$
(919-784-0400; www.thecowfish.com; 4208 Six Forks Rd; burgers $11-16, sushi $12-29) The name doesn't lie at this busy eatery in North Hills. Popular with families as well as stylish after-work crowds, this burger-and-sushi joint serves great food in a fun atmosphere. And yes, the sushi and burger menus do overlap – on the 'burgushi' menu – but it all seems to work. Portions are generous too. The amusing pop art on the walls is worth a closer look.

Information

Raleigh Visitor Information Center (919-834-5900; www.visitraleigh.com; 500 Fayetteville St; 8:30am-5pm Mon-Fri, 9am-5pm Sat) Hands out maps and other info. Office is closed on Sundays, but the city visitor guide and map are available on the counter.

Durham & Chapel Hill

Ten miles apart, these two university towns are twinned by their rival basketball teams and left-leaning attitudes. Chapel Hill is a pretty Southern college town whose culture revolves around the nearly 30,000 students at the prestigious University of North Carolina, founded in 1789 as the nation's first state university. A funky, forward-thinking place, Chapel Hill is renowned for its indie rock scene and loud 'n' proud hippie culture. Down the road, Durham is a once-gritty tobacco-and-railroad town whose fortunes collapsed in the 1960s and have only recently begun to revive. Though still fundamentally a working-class Southern city, the presence of top-ranking Duke University has long drawn progressive types to the area and Durham is now making its name as a hot spot for gourmands, artists and gays and lesbians.

The hip former mill town of **Carrboro** is just west of downtown Chapel Hill. Here, the big lawn at **Weaver Street Market** (www.weaverstreetmarket.com) grocery co-op serves as an informal town square, with live music and free wi-fi.

In Durham, activity revolves around the renovated brick tobacco warehouses of the handsome downtown: check out Brightleaf

Sq and the American Tobacco Campus for shopping and outdoor dining.

Sights

★Duke Lemur Center ZOO
(☎919-489-3364; www.lemur.duke.edu; 3705 Erwin Rd, Durham; adult/child $10/7;) The secret is out: the Lemur Center is the coolest attraction in Durham. Located about 2 miles from the main campus, this research and conservation center is home to the largest collection of endangered prosimian primates outside their native Madagascar. Only a robot could fail to melt at the sight of these big-eyed fuzzy-wuzzies. Visits are by guided tour only. To guarantee a tour spot, make your reservation well ahead of your visit. Call at least three weeks in advance for weekdays, and one to two months ahead for weekends.

Duke University UNIVERSITY, GALLERY
(www.duke.edu; Campus Dr) Endowed by the Duke family's cigarette fortune, the university has a Georgian-style East Campus and a neo-Gothic West Campus notable for the towering 1930s **Duke Chapel** (https://chapel.duke.edu; 401 Chapel Dr). This breathtaking place, with its 210ft tower and colorful, Bible-themed glass windows, is impressive. The **Nasher Museum of Art** (http://nasher.duke.edu; 2001 Campus Dr; adult/child under 16yr $5/free; ⏲10am-5pm Tue, Wed, Fri & Sat, to 9pm Thu, noon-5pm Sun) is also worth a gander, as is the heavenly 55-acre **Sarah P Duke Gardens** (www.gardens.duke.edu; 420 Anderson St; ⏲8am to dusk) FREE. Metered parking on campus is $2 per hour.

University of North Carolina UNIVERSITY
(www.unc.edu) America's oldest public university has a classic quad lined with flowering pear trees and gracious antebellum buildings. Don't miss the Old Well, said to give good luck to students who drink from it. Pick up a map of the school at the **visitor center** (☎919-962-1630; 250 E Franklin St; ⏲9am-5pm Mon-Fri) inside the Morehead Planetarium and Science Center or the Chapel Hill Visitor Center (p349).

Durham Bulls Athletic Park STADIUM
(www.dbulls.com; 409 Blackwell St, Durham; tickets $7-10;) Have a quintessentially American afternoon of beer and baseball watching the minor-league Durham Bulls (of 1988 Kevin Costner film *Bull Durham* fame), who play from April to early September.

Sleeping

There are plenty of cheap chain motels off I-85 in north Durham.

Duke Tower HOTEL $
(☎866-385-3869, 919-687-4444; www.duketower.com; 807 W Trinity Ave, Durham; ste $88-103; P) For less than most local hotel rooms you can enjoy a condo with hardwood floors, full kitchen and a Tempur-Pedic mattress. The decor is nothing fancy, but a central pool, picnic tables and grills add a community feel. Located in Durham's historic downtown tobacco-mill district. Pet fee is $5 per night.

★Carolina Inn HOTEL $$$
(☎919-933-2001; www.carolinainn.com; 211 Pittsboro St, Chapel Hill; r from $259; P) Even if you're not a Tar Heel, this lovely on-campus inn will win you over with its hospitality and historic touches. The charm starts in the snappy lobby then continues through the hallways, lined with photos of alums and championship teams. Classic decor – inspired by Southern antiques – feels fresh in the bright rooms, where silhouettes of famous graduates join the party.

Spring through fall, stop by on Friday afternoon for Fridays on the Front Porch, with food trucks and live music.

Eating

The region abounds with top-notch restaurants. Downtown Durham has scads of great eateries, coffee shops and bars in close proximity. Most of Chapel Hill's better restaurants are found along Franklin St.

Neal's Deli BREAKFAST, DELI $
(www.nealsdeli.com; 100 E Main St, Carrboro; breakfast $3-6, lunch $5-10; ⏲7:30am-4pmTue-Fri, 8am-4pm Sat & Sun) Before starting your day, dig into a delicious buttermilk breakfast biscuit at this tiny deli in downtown Carrboro. The egg, cheese and bacon is some kind of good. For lunch, Neal's serves sandwiches and subs, from chicken salad to pastrami to a three-cheese pimiento with a splash of bourbon. A good coffee shop, Open Eye Cafe, is next door.

Toast SANDWICHES $
(www.toast-fivepoints.com; 345 W Main St, Durham; sandwiches $8; ⏲11am-3pm Mon, to 8pm Tue-Sat) Families, couples, solos and the downtown lunch crowd – everybody loves this tiny Italian sandwich shop, one of the eateries at the

forefront of downtown Durham's revitalization. Order your panini (hot and grilled), tramezzini (cold) or crostini (bundle of joy) at the counter then grab a table by the window – if you can – for people-watching.

Guglhupf Bakery & Cafe BAKERY, CAFE **$$**
(www.guglhupf.com; 2706 Durham-Chapel Hill Blvd, Durham; breakfast $7-9, lunch $8-10, dinner $15-23; ⏲bakery 7am-6pm Tue-Fri, to 5pm Sat, 8:30am-2pm Sun, cafe till 10pm Tue-Sun) We like Guglhupf for lunch, when skirt steak sandwiches with blue cheese, housemade bratwurst on sub rolls and grilled pear salads bring an upbeat crowd to the sunny patio at this superior German-style bakery and cafe. Add a German pilsner and a chocolate mousse tart – with salted caramel – and call it a day. Check website for full opening hours.

★**Lantern** ASIAN **$$$**
(☎919-969-8846; www.lanternrestaurant.com; 423 W Franklin St, Chapel Hill; mains $23-32; ⏲5:30-10pm Mon-Sat) If you only have time for one dinner in the Triangle, dine here. This modern Asian spot, sourced with North Carolina ingredients, has earned a slew of accolades and chef Andrea Reusing is a James Beard Award winner. The current menu includes NC crabcakes with Japanese mustard, tea-smoked chicken and coconut-braised pork shank. For dessert? Warm brown buttercake with strawberries and peppercorn ice cream.

For special occasions, the stylish front rooms are just right, but for a more casual, convivial atmosphere try the bar and lounge in back.

Drinking & Nightlife

Chapel Hill has an excellent music scene. For entertainment listings, pick up the free weekly *Independent* (www.indyweek.com). A good cluster of brew providers – both coffee and beer – are within walking distance along Geer St and Rigbee Ave.

★**Cocoa Cinnamon** COFFEE
(www.cocoacinnamon.com; 420 W Geer St, Durham; ⏲7:30am-10pm Mon-Thu, 7:30am-midnight Fri & Sat, 9am-9pm Sun; 📶) If someone tells you that you *must* order a hot chocolate at Cocoa Cinnamon, ask them to be more specific. This talk-of-the town coffee shop offers several cocoas, and newbies may be paralyzed by the plethora of chocolatey awesomeness. Come to this one-time service station to enjoy cocoa, teas, single-source coffee, and the energetic vibe.

The wi-fi is strong and the Mac count high. Indoor and outdoor seating.

Fullsteam Brewery BREWERY
(www.fullsteam.ag; 726 Rigsbee Ave, Durham; ⏲4pm-midnight Mon-Thu, 2pm-2am Fri, noon-2am Sat, noon-midnight Sun) Calling itself a 'plow-to-pint' brewery, Fullsteam has gained national attention for pushing the boundaries of beer with wild, super-Southern concoctions like the Summer Basil Farmhouse Ale and the Carver Sweet Potato Lager. Mixed-age crowds.

Top of the Hill PUB
(www.thetopofthehill.com; 100 E Franklin St, Chapel Hill; ⏲11am-2am) The 3rd-story patio of this downtown restaurant and microbrewery, nicknamed TOPO, is *the* place for the Chapel Hill preppy set to see and be seen after football games. Now serving organic spirits from its own distillery.

Entertainment

Cat's Cradle MUSIC
(☎919-967-9053; www.catscradle.com; 300 E Main St, Carrboro) Everyone from Nirvana to Arcade Fire has played the Cradle, hosting the cream of the indie-music world for three decades. Most shows are all-ages.

Information

Chapel Hill Visitor Center (☎919-245-4320; www.visitchapelhill.org; 501 W Franklin St, Chapel Hill; ⏲8:30am-5pm Mon-Fri, 10am-2pm Sat) Lots of helpful information including a UNC campus map.

Durham Visitor Center (☎919-687-0288; www.durham-nc.com; 101 E Morgan St, Durham; ⏲8:30am-5pm Mon-Fri, 10am-2pm Sat) Has information and maps.

Charlotte

The largest city in North Carolina and the biggest US banking center after New York, Charlotte has the sprawling, sometimes faceless look of many New South suburban megalopolises. But though the Queen City, as it's known, is primarily a business town, it's got a few good museums, stately old neighborhoods and lots of fine food.

Busy Tryon St cuts through skyscraper-filled 'uptown' Charlotte, home to banks, hotels, museums and restaurants. The renovated textile mills of the NoDa neighborhood (named for its location on N Davidson St) and the funky mix of boutiques and restaurants

LOCAL KNOWLEDGE

THE BARBECUE TRAIL

North Carolina pulled-pork BBQ is practically a religion in these parts, and the rivalry between Eastern Style (with a thin vinegar sauce) and Western Style (with a sweeter, tomato-based sauce) occasionally comes to blows. The North Carolina Barbecue Society has an interactive **Barbecue Trail Map** (www.ncbbqsociety.com), directing pilgrims to the best spots. So try both styles, then take sides (hint: Eastern style is better. Just kidding! Sort of).

in the Plaza-Midwood area, just northeast of uptown, have a hipper vibe. Uptown's new **Romare Bearden Park** (300 S Church St) is a pretty place to watch the sunset.

For more information about the city's greenways and new bike-share program visit https://charlotte.bcycle.com.

Sights & Activities

Billy Graham Library RELIGIOUS SITE
(www.billygrahamlibrary.org; 4330 Westmont Dr; 9:30am-5pm Mon-Sat) FREE This multimedia 'library' is a tribute to the life of superstar evangelist and 'pastor to the presidents' Billy Graham, a Charlotte native. The 90-minute tour, 'The Journey of Faith', starts with a gospel-preaching animatronic cow then spotlights key moments in Graham's life, including his transformative 1949 tent revival in Los Angeles (where he first inspired *Unbroken* hero, Louis Zamperini). The tour is engaging and informative, especially if you're curious about Graham's journey and the roots of modern evangelicalism.

Levine Museum of the New South MUSEUM
(www.museumofthenewsouth.org; 200 E 7th St; adult/child 6-18yr $8/5; 10am-5pm Mon-Sat, noon-5pm Sun) Interested in the South's complicated post–Civil War history? Then set aside an hour or two for the comprehensive *From Cotton Fields to Skyscrapers* exhibit at this slick museum, which spotlights the cotton industry, Jim Crow laws, sit-ins, women's advancement and recent immigration trends.

NASCAR Hall of Fame MUSEUM
(www.nascarhall.com; 400 E Martin Luther King Blvd; adult/child 5-12yr $20/13; 10am-6pm) The race car simulator at this rip-roaring museum hurtles you onto the track and into an eight-car race that feels surprisingly real. Elsewhere, learn the history of this American-born sport (which traces back to moonshine running), check out six generations of race cars and test your pit crew skills. NASCAR, if you're wondering, is short for National Association for Stock Car Auto Racing.

One quibble? Exhibits are geared toward visitors who have some knowledge of cars and racing, so casual fans be warned!

★**US National Whitewater Center** ADVENTURE SPORTS
(www.usnwc.org; 5000 Whitewater Center Pkwy; all-sport day pass adult/child under 10yr $54/44, individual activities $20-25, 3hr canopy tours $89; dawn-dusk) A beyond-awesome hybrid of nature center and waterpark, this 400-acre facility is home to the largest artificial white-water river in the world, whose rapids serve as training grounds for Olympic canoe and kayak teams. Paddle it yourself as part of a guided rafting trip, or try one of the center's other adventurous activities: multiple ropes courses, an outdoor rock-climbing wall, paddleboarding, zip lines and miles of wooded hiking and mountain-biking trails. Parking is $5.

Sip a craft brew and watch the kayaks in action from the Pump House Biergarten.

Sleeping & Eating

Because so many uptown hotels cater to the business traveler, rates are often lower on weekends. Cheaper chains cluster off I-85 and I-77.

Uptown eating and drinking options draw the preppy young banker set; you'll see more tattoos at the laid-back bars and bistros of NoDa. Numerous breweries have opened across the city in the last few years. Several of the best line N Davidson St. See www.charlottesgotalot.com/breweries for a full list.

Dunhill Hotel BOUTIQUE HOTEL $$
(704-332-4141; www.dunhillhotel.com; 237 N Tryon St; r from $219; P) The staff shines at this heart-of-uptown hotel, and the property has been welcoming guests since 1929. Classic decor gives a nod to the 1920s, but large flat-screen TVs and Keurig coffeemakers keep the rooms firmly in the 21st century. Parking is $18 per night.

Hyatt Place Charlotte Downtown HOTEL $$
(704-227-0500; www.charlottedowntown.place.hyatt.com; 222 S Caldwell St, GPS: 459 E 3rd St; r

from $229; P ❄ 📶) The breakfast spread is impressive at this mod hotel perched on the edge of uptown. Rooms are spare and contemporary, and big windows offer sweeping views of the city. Get tipsy in style at Fahrenheit, the sultry rooftop bar. The hotel lobby is on the 10th floor.

Valet parking is $20 per night, but a cheaper, machine-pay city lot is behind the hotel.

Price's Chicken Coop SOUTHERN $
(www.priceschickencoop.com; 1614 Camden Rd; mains $2-12; ⏲10am-6pm Tue-Sat) A Charlotte institution, scruffy Price's regularly makes 'Best Fried Chicken in America' lists. Line up to order your 'dark quarter' or 'white half' from the army of white-jacketed cooks, then take your bounty outside – there's no seating. Latta Park is a few blocks east on E Park Ave if you want to spread out. Cash only but an ATM on-site.

Amelie's French Bakery & Cafe CAFE $
(www.ameliesfrenchbakery.com; 2424 N Davidson St; pastries $2-6, sandwiches $6; ⏲24hr; 📶) Stop by for fancy coffees, cheesy sandwiches on croissants and baguettes, and a decadent line-up of cookies, tarts, petits fours and slices of cake. It's an inviting place to plan your day or spend some time online. And it's open all the time.

★ **Soul Gastrolounge Tapas** SUSHI, SANDWICHES $$
(☎704-348-1848; www.soulgastrolounge.com; 1500 Central Ave; small plates $8-20, sushi $5-24, sandwiches $6-15; ⏲5pm-2am Mon-Sat, 11am-3pm & 5pm-2am Sun) In Plaza Midtown, this sultry but welcoming speakeasy serves a globally inspired selection of small plates. Choices are wide-ranging, from skewers to sushi rolls to Cuban and Vietnamese sandwiches, but the kitchen takes care to infuse each little snowflake with unique, satisfying flavors. The dancing tuna rolls with jalapeños and two spicy mayos is highly recommended if you like heat.

Information

Check out the alt-weekly *Creative Loafing* (www.clclt.com) for entertainment listings.

Main Library (www.cmlibrary.org; 310 N Tryon ST; ⏲10am-8pm Mon-Thu, until 5pm Fri & Sat; 📶 👪) The public library has internet terminals and wi-fi.

Visitor Center (☎704-331-2700; www.charlottesgotalot.com; 330 S Tryon St; ⏲9am-5pm Mon-Sat) The downtown visitor center publishes maps and a visitors' guide.

Getting There & Around

Charlotte Douglas International Airport (CLT; ☎704-359-4027; www.charmeck.org/departments/airport; 5501 Josh Birmingham Pkwy) is a US Airways hub with direct flights from Europe and the UK. Both the **Greyhound station** (601 W Trade St) and **Amtrak** (1914 N Tryon St) are handy to uptown. **Charlotte Area Transit** (www.charmeck.org; one-way fare $2.20) runs local bus and light-rail services. The Charlotte Transit Center in uptown is on Brevard St between 4th and Trade St.

North Carolina Mountains

The Cherokee came to these ancient mountains to hunt, followed by 18th-century Scots-Irish immigrants looking for a better life. Lofty towns like Blowing Rock drew the sickly, who came for the fresh air. Today, scenic drives, leafy trails and roaring rivers draw outdoor adventurers.

The Appalachians in the western part of the state include the Great Smoky, Blue Ridge, Pisgah and Black Mountain subranges. Carpeted in blue-green hemlock, pine and oak trees, these cool hills are home to cougars, deer, black bears, wild turkeys and great horned owls. Hiking, camping, climbing and rafting adventures abound,

BIKE-SHARING IN THE CAROLINAS

If you like exploring cities by bicycle, consider buying a 24-hour pass under the B-cycle bike-share programs in Charlotte, NC ($8; https://charlotte.bcycle.com) and Greenville, SC ($5; https://greenville.bcycle.com). In Charlotte, 24 bike stations dot uptown and nearby greenways, with 200 bikes available. In Greenville, there are 10 stations, many along popular Main St and near the Swamp Rabbit Trail, with 35 bikes in service. Note that these are bike *sharing* programs, not rentals. To encourage turnover, the 24-hour pass includes rides taken in 30 to 60 minute increments within the 24-hour time period. You must check the bikes in and out to avoid additional fees. Pay by credit card at the station kiosk.

and there's another jaw-dropping photo opportunity around every bend.

High Country

The northwestern corner of the state is known as 'High Country.' Its main towns are Boone, Blowing Rock and Banner Elk, all short drives from the Blue Ridge Pkwy. **Boone** is a lively college town, home to Appalachian State University (ASU). **Blowing Rock** and **Banner Elk** are quaint tourist centers near the winter ski areas.

Sights & Activities

Hwy 321 from Blowing Rock to Boone is studded with **gem-panning mines** and other tourist traps. In Boone, check out the shops on King St and keep an eye out for the bronze **statue** of local bluegrass legend Doc Watson. He's strumming his guitar on the corner of King and Depot Sts.

Grandfather Mountain HIKING
(☎828-733-4337; www.grandfather.com; Blue Ridge Pkwy, Mile 305; adult/child 4-12yr $20/9; ⏰8am-7pm Jun-Aug, closes earlier Sep-May) Hold up. Is the Mile High Suspension Bridge really swinging 1 mile above the ground? Not exactly, so don't fret if you don't love heights. The park's star attraction is 1-mile *above sea level*, but the chasm beneath? It's 80ft deep. Nothing to sneeze at, but the distance is a bit less horrifying. Lose the crowds on one of 11 hiking trails; the most difficult include steep hands-and-knees scrambles. A small museum and wildlife reserve spotlights local plants and animals.

In 2008 the family that owns the mountain sold the backcountry to the state park system, which opened the adjacent **Grandfather Mountain State Park** (www.ncparks.gov) the following year.

River and Earth Adventures OUTDOORS
(☎828-963-5491; www.raftcavehike.com; 1655 Hwy 105; half-/full-day rafting from $60/100; 👪) Offers everything from family-friendly caving trips to rafting Class V rapids at Watauga Gorge. Eco-conscious guides even pack organic lunches. Canoe ($60), kayak ($35 to $60) and tube ($20) rentals.

Sleeping & Eating

Chain motels abound in Boone. You'll find private campgrounds and B&Bs scattered throughout the hills.

Mast Farm Inn B&B $$
(☎828-963-5857; www.themastfarminn.com; 2543 Broadstone Rd, Valle Crucis; r/cottages from $189/319; P ❄ 📶) In the beautiful hamlet of Valle Crucis, this restored farmhouse defines rustic chic with worn hardwood floors, clawfoot tubs and handmade toffees on your bedside table. Eight cabins and cottages also available. The upscale mountain cuisine at the inn's restaurant, Simplicity, is worth a trip in itself. The Over Yonder, focusing on simpler Appalachian fare, opened in 2014.

Six Pence Pub PUB FOOD $$
(www.sixpencepub.com; 1121 Main St, Blowing Rock; mains $6-14; ⏰restaurant 11:30am-10:30pm Sun-Thu, to midnight Fri & Sat, bar to 2am) The bartenders keep a sharp but friendly eye on things at this lively British pub, where the shepherd's pie comes neat, not messy.

Hob Nob Farm Cafe CAFE $$
(www.hobnobfarmcafe.com; 506 West King St, Boone; breakfast & lunch $3-11, dinner $9-14; ⏰10am-10pm Wed-Sun; 🌶) Gobble up avocado-tempeh melts, Thai curry bowls and sloppy burgers made from local beef at a wildly painted cottage near ASU. Brunch is served until 5pm.

Information

Visitor Center (☎828-264-1299; www.highcountryhost.com; 1700 Blowing Rock Rd, Boone; ⏰9am-5pm Mon-Sat, to 3pm Sun) The High Country visitor center has info on accommodations and outdoors outfitters.

Asheville

With its homegrown microbreweries, decadent chocolate shops and stylish New Southern eateries, Asheville is one of the trendiest small cities in the East. Glossy magazines swoon for the place. But don't be put off by all the flash. At heart, Asheville is still an overgrown mountain town, and it holds tight to its traditional roots. Just look around. There's a busker fiddling a high lonesome tune on Biltmore Ave. Over there, hikers chow down after climbing Mt Pisgah. Cars swoop on and off the Blue Ridge Pkwy, which swings around the city. A huge artist population and a visible contingent of hardcore hippies also keep things real.

Sights & Activities

Downtown is compact and easy to negotiate on foot. The art-deco buildings remain

DON'T MISS

SCENIC DRIVE: BLUE RIDGE PARKWAY

You won't find one stoplight on the entire Blue Ridge Pkwy, which traverses the southern Appalachians from Virginia's Shenandoah National Park at Mile 0 to North Carolina's Great Smoky Mountains National Park at Mile 469.

Commissioned by President Franklin D Roosevelt as a Depression-era public-works project, it's one of America's classic drives. North Carolina's piece of the parkway twists and turns for 262 miles of killer mountain vistas.

The **National Park Service** (NPS; www.nps.gov/blri; ⌚May-Oct) runs campgrounds and visitor centers. Note that restrooms and gas stations are few and far between. For more details about stops, visit www.blueridgeparkway.org.

Parkway highlights and campgrounds include the following, from the Virginia border south:

Cumberland Knob (Mile 217.5) NPS visitor center; easy walk to the knob.

Doughton Park (Mile 241.1) Trails and camping.

Blowing Rock (Mile 291.8) Small town named for a craggy, commercialized cliff that offers great views, occasional updrafts and a Native American love story.

Moses H Cone Memorial Park (Mile 294.1) A lovely old estate with carriage trails and a craft shop.

Julian Price Memorial Park (Mile 296.9) Camping.

Grandfather Mountain (Mile 305.1) Hugely popular for its mile-high pedestrian 'swinging bridge.' Also has a nature center and a small wildlife reserve.

Linville Falls (Mile 316.4) Short hiking trails to the falls; campsites.

Little Switzerland (Mile 334) Old-style mountain resort.

Mt Mitchell State Park (Mile 355.5) Highest peak east of the Mississippi (6684ft); hiking and camping.

Craggy Gardens (Mile 364) Hiking trails explode with rhododendron blossoms in summer.

Folk Art Center (Mile 382) High-end Appalachian crafts for sale.

Blue Ridge Pkwy Visitor Center (Mile 384) Inspiring film, interactive map, trail information.

Mt Pisgah (Mile 408.8) Hiking, camping, restaurant, inn.

Graveyard Fields (Mile 418) Short hiking trails to waterfalls.

much as they were in 1930. The shopping's fantastic, with everything from hippie-dippy candle shops to vintage shops to trendy boutiques and high-end local art. Start your shopping on Lexington Ave. West Asheville is an up-and-coming area, still gritty but very cool. On Friday nights, look for the drum circle on Pack Square in the heart of downtown.

★Biltmore Estate HOUSE, GARDENS

(☎800-411-3812; www.biltmore.com; 1 Approach Rd; adult/child 10-16yr $60/30; ⌚house 9am-4:30pm) The country's largest privately owned home, and Asheville's number-one tourist attraction, the Biltmore was built in 1895 for shipping and railroad heir George Washington Vanderbilt II. He modeled it after the grand chateaux he'd seen on his various European jaunts. Viewing the estate and its 250 acres of gorgeously manicured grounds and gardens takes several hours.

Tours of the house are self-guided. To get the most out of your visit, pay an extra $10 for the informative audio tour. Also available is a behind-the-scenes guided tour ($17) covering the servants, guest rooms and parties. In summer, children visiting with an adult are free.

Beyond the house, there are numerous cafes, a gift shop the size of a small supermarket, a hoity-toity hotel and an award-winning winery with free tastings. In Antler Village, the new Biltmore Legacy exhibit *The Vanderbilts at Home and Abroad* provides a more personal look at the family.

Chimney Rock Park PARK
(www.chimneyrockpark.com; Hwy 64/74A; adult/child 5-15yr $15/7; ⊙8:30am-5:30pm mid-Mar-Oct, hours vary Nov-mid-Mar) Views of the Broad River and Lake Lure are superb from atop the namesake chimney – a 315ft granite monolith. An elevator takes visitors up to the chimney, but the real draw is the exciting hike around the cliffs to a 404ft waterfall. The park, once privately owned, is now part of the state park system; access to the rock is still managed commercially. The park is a 20-mile drive southeast of Asheville.

Thomas Wolfe Memorial HOUSE
(www.wolfememorial.com; 52 N Market St; museum free, house tours adult/child 7-17yr $5/2; ⊙9am-5pm Tue-Sat) This downtown memorial, with a small museum and a separate house tour, honors *Look Homeward Angel* author Thomas Wolfe. The author grew up in Asheville, which was the inspiration for the novel's setting.

Tours

Brews Cruise MICROBREWERIES
(828-545-5181; www.ashevillebrewscruise.com; per person $57) Tour several of Asheville's microbreweries, with samples.

Lazoom Comedy Tour COMEDY
(828-225-6932; www.lazoomtours.com; per person $21-29) For a hysterically historical tour of the city, hop on the purple bus – and bring your own booze.

Sleeping

The **Asheville Bed & Breakfast Association** (877-262-6867; www.ashevillebba.com) handles bookings for numerous area B&Bs, from gingerbread cottages to alpine cabins.

Sweet Peas HOSTEL $
(828-285-8488; www.sweetpeashostel.com; 23 Rankin Ave; dm/pod/r $28/35/60; P❄@☕) This spick-and-span hostel gleams with IKEA-like style, with shipshape steel bunk beds and blond-wood sleeping 'pods.' The loftlike space is very open and can be noisy (a downstairs pub adds to the ruckus) – what you lose in privacy and quiet, you gain in style, cleanliness, sociability and an unbeatable downtown location.

Campfire Lodgings CAMPGROUND $$
(828-658-8012; www.campfirelodgings.com; 116 Appalachian Village Rd; tent sites $35-38, RV sites $45-65, yurts $115-135, cabins $160; P❄☕) All yurts should have flat-screen TVs, don't you think? Sleep like the world's most stylish Mongolian nomad in one of these furnished multiroom tents, on the side of a wooded hill. Cabins and tent sites are also available. Wi-fi access at RV sites, which have stunning valley views.

Omni Grove Park Inn RESORT $$$
(828-252-2711; www.omnihotels.com; 290 Macon Ave; r from $349; P❄@☕≋🐾) This titanic arts-and-crafts-style stone lodge has a hale-and-hearty look that sets a tone for adventure. But no worries modern mavens, the well-appointed rooms sport 21st-century amenities. The spa is an underground grotto with stone pools and an indoor waterfall. Feeling sporty? The property offers a golf course and tennis courts, and the Nantahala Outdoor Center (p357) has a 'basecamp' here.

The hotel turned 100 in 2013. The resort fee is $25 per day. The pet fee is $150 per stay.

Aloft Asheville HOTEL $$$
(828-232-2838; www.aloftasheville.com; 51 Biltmore Ave; r from $320; P❄@☕≋🐾) With a giant chalkboard in the lobby, a groovy young staff and an outdoor clothing store on the 1st floor, this place looks like the seventh circle of hipster. The only thing missing is a wool-cap-wearing bearded guy drinking a hoppy microwbr– oh, wait, over there. We jest. Once settled, you'll find the staff knowledgeable, the rooms spacious and the vibe convivial.

The hotel is close to several downtown hot spots, including Wicked Weed Brewery and the Orange Peel.

Eating

Asheville is a great foodie town – many visitors come here just to eat!

★ **White Duck Taco Shop** MEXICAN $
(www.whiteducktacoshop.com; 12 Biltmore Ave; tacos under $7; ⊙11:30am-9pm) The chalkboard menu at this downtown taco shop will give you fits – every taco sounds like a must-have flavor bomb: spicy buffalo chicken with blue cheese sauce, crispy pork belly, mole-roasted duck. Even better? These soft tacos are hefty. The chips and salsa appetizer comes with three salsas, and it works well for a group. The margaritas are mighty fine too.

In the River Arts District? Stop by the original location at 1 Roberts St.

12 Bones BARBECUE $
(www.12bones.com; 5 Riverside Dr; dishes $6-21; 11am-4pm Mon-Fri) How good is the BBQ? Well, President Obama and wife Michelle stopped by a few years ago for a meal. The slow-cooked meats are smoky tender, and the sides, from the jalapeño cheese grits to the buttery green beans, will have you kissing your mama and blessing the day you were born. Order at the counter and grab a picnic table.

French Broad Chocolate Lounge BAKERY, DESSERTS $
(www.frenchbroadchocolates.com; 10 S Pack Sq; desserts under $7; 11am-11pm Sun-Thu, to midnight Fri & Sat) This beloved downtown chocolate shop may have moved to larger, glossier digs beside Pack Square Park, but she hasn't lost her chocolate heart. Small-batch organic chocolates, chunky chocolate brownies, chocolate-dipped ginger cookies, a sippable 'liquid truffle'...hey, where'd you go?

★**Cúrate** SPANISH, TAPAS $$
(828-239-2946; www.curatetapasbar.com; 11 Biltmore Ave; small plates $4-20) This convivial place celebrates the simple charms and sensual flavors of traditional Spanish tapas, with a few Southern twists here and there: tender lamb skewers with Moorish spices; spicy chorizo wrapped in potato chips; sauteed shrimp with sliced garlic. This is a place to savor the flavors, order another glass of garnacha and converse with your dinner companions, not your phone.

Reservations are a must, especially on weekends, but you can probably snag a bar seat fairly quickly after 9pm. And calling it Karate is only funny once.

Drinking & Nightlife

Downtown Asheville has a range of bars and cafes, from frat-boy beer halls to hippie holes-in-the-wall to spare new microbreweries. West Asheville has a more laid-back townie vibe. Stop by the visitor center or ask your hotel for a copy of the free *Field Guide to Breweries*, which provides key details and maps for the breweries (currently 27), taprooms and beer pubs on the **Asheville Ale Trail** (www.ashevillealetrail.com).

Wicked Weed MICROBREWERY
(www.wickedweedbrewing.com; 91 Biltmore Ave; 11:30-11pm Mon & Tue, to midnight Wed & Thu, to 1am Fri & Sat, noon-11pm Sun) Henry VIII called hops 'a wicked and pernicious weed' that ruined the taste of beer. His subjects kept quaffing it anyway – just like the hordes at this restaurant and microbrewery, which overflows with hoppy brews and lively crowds. In a former gas station with a wide front patio, it's a big and breezy spot to chill.

The downstairs taproom can get elbow-to-elbow on weekend nights.

Hi-Wire Brewing Co MICROBREWERY
(www.hiwirebrewing.com; 197 Hilliard Ave; 4-11pm Mon-Thu, 2pm-2am Fri, noon-2am Sat, 1-10pm Sun) Beers are named for old-school circus acts at this swift-growing downtown brewery. The brews are easy drinking, and the taproom is a chilled place to hang with friends on a Saturday afternoon.

Thirsty Monk BEER HALL
(www.monkpub.com; 92 Patton Ave; 4pm-midnight Mon-Thu, noon-2am Fri & Sat, noon-10pm Sun) Try a variety of North Carolina craft beers and plenty of Belgian ales at this scruffy but lovable beer bar.

☆ Entertainment

Orange Peel LIVE MUSIC
(www.theorangepeel.net; 101 Biltmore Ave; tickets $10-35) For live music, try this warehouse-sized place showcasing big-name indie and punk.

Information

Pack Memorial Library (67 Haywood Ave; 10am-8pm Mon-Thu, to 6pm Fri, to 5pm Sat;) Free wi-fi, and computers with free internet.
Visitor Center (828-258-6129; www.exploreasheville.com; 36 Montford Ave; 8:30am-5:30pm Mon-Fri, 9am-5pm Sat & Sun) The shiny visitor center is at I-240 exit 4C. You can buy Biltmore admission tickets here, with a reduced rate for the audio tour. Downtown, there is a satellite visitor center, with restrooms, beside Pack Square Park.

Getting There & Around

Asheville Transit (www.ashevilletransit.com; tickets $1) has 17 local bus routes that run from about 5:30am to 10:30pm Monday through Saturday, with reduced hours Sunday. There are free bike racks on the front of buses. **Greyhound** (2 Tunnel Rd) is about 1 mile northeast of downtown.

Twenty minutes south of town, **Asheville Regional Airport** (AVL; 828-684-2226; www.flyavl.com) has a handful of nonstop flights, including to/from Atlanta, Charlotte, Chicago and New York.

Great Smoky Mountains National Park

This moody and magical place sprawls across 521,000 acres in both North Carolina and Tennessee. It is one of the world's most diverse areas; landscapes range from deep, dim spruce forest to sunny meadows carpeted with daisies and Queen Anne's lace to wide, coffee-brown rivers. There's ample hiking and camping, and opportunities for horseback riding, bike rental and fly-fishing. Unfortunately, with more than 10 million annual visitors – which is the highest of any national park in the US – the place can get annoyingly crowded. The North Carolina side has less traffic than the Tennessee side, however, so even at the height of summer tourist season you'll still have room to roam.

Newfound Gap Rd/Hwy 441 is the only thoroughfare that crosses Great Smoky Mountains National Park, winding through the mountains from Gatlinburg, TN, to the town of Cherokee and the busy **Oconaluftee Visitor Center** (☎828-497-1904; www.nps.gov/grsm; 1194 Newfound Gap Rd, North Cherokee, NC; ⏰8am-7:30pm Jun-Aug, hours vary Sep-May), in the southeast. Pick up your backcountry camping permits here. The **Oconaluftee River Trail**, one of only two in the park that allows leashed pets and bicycles, leaves from the visitor center and follows the river for 1.5 miles.

SMOKY MOUNTAINS DAY HIKES

These are a few of our favorite short hikes on, or bordering, the North Carolina side of the park.

Charlie's Bunion Follow the Appalachian Trail 4 miles from the Newfound Gap overlook to a rocky outcrop for sweeping mountain-and-valley views.

Big Creek Trail Hike an easy 2 miles to Mouse Creek Falls or go another 3 miles to a backcountry campground; the trailhead is near I-40 on the park's northeastern edge.

Boogerman Trail Moderate 7-mile loop passing old farmsteads; accessible via Cove Creek Rd.

Chasteen Creek Falls From Smokemont campground, this 4-mile round-trip passes a small waterfall.

The on-site **Mountain Farm Museum** (☎865-436-1200; www.nps.gov/grsm; ⏰dusk-dawn) FREE is a restored 19th-century farmstead, complete with barn, blacksmith shop and smokehouse (with real pig heads!), assembled from original buildings from different parts of the park. Just north is the 1886 **Mingus Mill** (⏰9am-5pm daily mid-Mar–mid-Nov, plus Thanksgiving weekend) FREE, a turbine-powered mill that still grinds wheat and corn much as it always has. A few miles away the **Smokemont Campground** (www.nps.gov/grsm; tent & RV sites $20) is the only North Carolina campground open year-round.

To the east, remote **Cataloochee Valley** has several historic buildings to wander through and is a prime location for elk and black bears.

Around Great Smoky Mountains National Park

The state's westernmost tip is blanketed in parkland and sprinkled with tiny mountain towns. The area has a rich but sad Native American history – many of the original Cherokee inhabitants were forced off their lands during the 1830s and marched to Oklahoma on the Trail of Tears. Descendants of those who escaped are known as the Eastern Band of the Cherokee and many still live on the 56,000-acre Qualla Boundary territory at the edge of Great Smoky Mountains National Park.

The town of **Cherokee** anchors the Qualla Boundary with ersatz Native American souvenir shops, fast-food joints and **Harrah's Cherokee Casino** (www.caesars.com/harrahs-cherokee; 777 Casino Dr; ⏰24hr), which has an impressive water and video display, the Rotunda, in the lobby. The best sight is the modern and engaging **Museum of the Cherokee Indian** (☎828-497-3481; www.cherokeemuseum.org; 589 Tsali Blvd/Hwy 441, at Drama Rd; adult/child 6-12yr $11/7; ⏰9am-5pm daily, to 7pm Mon-Sat Jun-Aug), with an informative exhibit about the Trail of Tears.

South of Cherokee, the contiguous Pisgah and Nantahala National Forests have more than a million acres of dense hardwood trees, windswept mountain balds and some of the country's best white water. Both contain portions of the Appalachian Trail. **Pisgah National Forest** highlights include the bubbling baths in the village of **Hot Springs** (www.hotspringsnc.org), the natural waterslide at **Sliding Rock**, and the 3.2-mile round-trip hike to the summit of 5721ft **Mt Pisgah**, which has a view of Cold Mountain (of book and movie fame). **Nantahala National Forest** has several recreational lakes and dozens of roaring waterfalls.

Just north of Nantahala is quaint **Bryson City**, an ideal jumping-off point for outdoor adventures. It's home to the huge and highly recommended **Nantahala Outdoor Center** (NOC; 828-366-7502, 888-905-7238; www.noc.com; 13077 Hwy 19/74; kayak/canoe rental per day $30/50, guided trips $30-189), which specializes in wet and wild rafting trips down the Nantahala River. The 500-acre site also offers zip-lining and mountain biking. It even has its own lodge, a hostel, a year-round restaurant and one seasonal BBQ and beer joint (May through September). The Appalachian Trail rolls across the property too.

From the Bryson City depot, the **Great Smoky Mountains Railroad** (800-872-4681; www.gsmr.com; 226 Everett St; Nantahala Gorge trip adult/child 2-12yr from $55/31) runs scenic train excursions through the dramatic river valley.

For lodging and dining try the lofty **Fryemont Inn** (828-488-2159; www.fryemontinn.com; 245 Fryemont St; lodge/ste/cabins from $110/180/245; nonguests breakfast $5-9, dinner $21-31; restaurant 8am-10am & 6-8pm Sun-Tue, 6-9pm Fri & Sat mid-Apr–late Nov; P), a family-owned lodge and restaurant. The bark-covered inn has a front-porch view of the Smokies and downtown Bryson City.

SOUTH CAROLINA

Moss-draped oaks. Stately mansions. Wide beaches. Rolling mountains. And an ornery streak as old as the state itself. Ah yes, South Carolina, where the accents are thicker and the traditions more dear. From its Revolutionary War patriots to its 1860s secessionist government to its current crop of outspoken legislators, the Palmetto State has never shied away from a fight.

From the silvery sands of the Atlantic Coast, the state climbs westward from the Coastal Plain across the Piedmont and up into the Blue Ridge Mountains. Most travelers stick to the coast, with its splendid antebellum cities and palm-tree-studded beaches. But the interior has a wealth of sleepy old towns, wild and undeveloped state parks and spooky black-water swamps. Along the sea islands you hear the sweet songs of the Gullah, a culture and language created by former slaves who held onto many West African traditions through the ravages of time.

From well-bred, gardenia-scented Charleston to bright, tacky Myrtle Beach, South Carolina is always a fascinating destination.

History

More than 28 separate tribes of Native Americans have lived in what is now South Carolina, many of them Cherokee who were later forcibly removed during the Trail of Tears era.

The English founded the Carolina colony in 1670, with settlers pouring in from the royal outpost of Barbados, giving the port city known as Charles Towne a Caribbean flavor. West African slaves were brought over to turn the thick coastal swamps into rice paddies and by the mid-1700s the area was deeply divided between the slave-owning aristocrats of the Lowcountry and the poor Scots-Irish and German farmers of the rural backcountry.

South Carolina was the first state to secede from the Union, and the first battle of the Civil War occurred at Fort Sumter in Charleston Harbor. The end of the war left much of the state in ruins.

South Carolina traded in cotton and textiles for most of the 20th century. It remains a relatively poor agricultural state, though with a thriving coastal tourism business.

In recent years the Palmetto State has garnered headlines because of its politicians, from Nikki Haley, the state's first woman and first Native American governor, to Congressman Joe Wilson, who yelled 'You lie!' during a speech by President Obama to Congress. Congressman Mark Sanford, while serving as governor, famously claimed that he was hiking the Appalachian Trail when he was in fact visiting his Argentinian girlfriend.

In 2015, following the shooting of nine members of a historically black church for what appeared to be racially motivated reasons, the state legislature voted to remove the Confederate flag from the grounds of the state capitol, where it had flown since 1962.

Information

South Carolina Department of Parks, Recreation & Tourism (803-734-1700; www.discoversouthcarolina.com; 1205 Pendleton St, Columbia;) Sends out the state's official vacation guide. The state's nine highway

SOUTH CAROLINA FACTS

Nickname Palmetto State

Population 4.8 million

Area 30,109 sq miles

Capital city Columbia (population 133,300)

Other cities Charleston (population 127,900)

Sales tax 6%, plus up to 8.5% extra tax on accommodations

Birthplace of Jazzman Dizzy Gillespie (1917–93), political activist Jesse Jackson (b 1941), boxer Joe Frazier (b 1944), *Wheel of Fortune* hostess Vanna White (b 1957)

Home of The first US public library (1698), museum (1773) and steam railroad (1833)

Politics Leans Republican

Famous for Firing the first shot of the Civil War, from Charleston's Fort Sumter

State dance The shag

Driving distances Columbia to Charleston 115 miles, Charleston to Myrtle Beach 97 miles

welcome centers offer free wi-fi. Ask inside for password.

South Carolina State Parks (camping reservations 866-345-7275, 803-734-0156; www.southcarolinaparks.com) The helpful website lists activities and hiking trails, and allows online reservations for campsites ($6 to $40 per night).

Charleston

This lovely city will embrace you with the warmth and hospitality of an old and dear friend – who died in the 18th century. We jest, but the cannons, cemeteries and carriage rides do conjure an earlier era. And that historic romanticism, along with the food and Southern graciousness, is what makes Charleston one of the most popular tourist destinations in the South, drawing more than 4.8 million visitors every year.

How best to enjoy its charms? Charleston is a city for savoring – stroll past the historic buildings, admire the antebellum architecture, stop to smell the blooming jasmine and enjoy long dinners on the verandah. It's also a place for romance; everywhere you turn another blushing bride is standing on the steps of yet another charming church.

In the high season the scent of gardenia and honeysuckle mixes with the tang of horses from the aforementioned carriage tours that clip-clop down the cobblestones. In winter the weather is milder and the crowds thinner, making Charleston a great bet for off-season travel.

History

Well before the Revolutionary War, Charles Towne (named for Charles II) was one of the busiest ports on the eastern seaboard, the center of a prosperous rice-growing and trading colony. With influences from the West Indies and Africa, France and other European countries, it became a cosmopolitan city, often compared to New Orleans.

A tragic but important component of the city's history? Slavery. Charleston was a key port and trade center for the slave industry, and bustling slave auction houses clustered near the Cooper River. The first shots of the Civil War rang out at Fort Sumter, in Charleston's harbor. After the war, as the labor-intensive rice plantations became uneconomical without slave labor, the city's importance declined.

A mass shooting in the historically black Emanuel African Methodist Episcopal (AME) Church in 2015 reopened questions about the city's racially fraught past and its effects on the present.

Sights

Historic District

The quarter south of Beaufain and Hasell Sts has the bulk of the antebellum mansions, shops, bars and cafes. At the southernmost tip of the peninsula are the antebellum mansions of the Battery. A loose path, the **Gateway Walk**, winds through several church grounds and graveyards between **St John's Lutheran Church** (5 Clifford St) and **St Philip's Church** (146 Church St).

Old Exchange & Provost Dungeon HISTORIC BUILDING
(www.oldexchange.org; 122 E Bay St; adult/child 7-12yr $10/5; 9am-5pm) Kids love the creepy dungeon, used as a prison for pirates and for American patriots held by the British during the Revolutionary War. The

cramped space sits beneath a stately Georgian Palladian customs house completed in 1771. Costumed guides lead the dungeon tours. Exhibits about the city are displayed on the upper floors.

Combination ticket with the Old Slave Mart Museum is adult/child $15/8.

Old Slave Mart Museum MUSEUM
(www.nps.gov/nr/travel/charleston/osm.htm; 6 Chalmers St; adult/child 5-17yr $7/5; ⏲9am-5pm Mon-Sat) Ryan's Mart was an open-air market that auctioned African men, women and children in the mid-1800s. It's now a museum about South Carolina's shameful past. Text-heavy exhibits illuminate the slave experience; the few artifacts, such as leg shackles, are especially chilling. For first-hand stories, listen to the oral recollections of former slave Elijah Green and others.

Combination ticket with the Old Exchange is adult/child $15/8.

Gibbes Museum of Art GALLERY
(www.gibbesmuseum.org; 135 Meeting St; adult/child $9/7; ⏲10am-5pm Tue-Sat, 1-5pm Sun) Houses a decent collection of American and Southern works. The contemporary collection includes works by local artists, with Lowcountry life as a highlight. The museum was closed for renovations in 2015 but is scheduled to reopen in the spring of 2016.

Battery & White Point Gardens GARDENS
The Battery is the southern tip of the Charleston Peninsula, buffered by a seawall. Stroll past cannons and statues of military heroes in the gardens then walk the promenade and look for Fort Sumter.

Kahal Kadosh Beth Elohim SYNAGOGUE
(www.kkbe.org; 90 Hasell St; ⏲tours 10am-noon & 1:30-3:30pm Mon-Thu, 10am-noon & 1-3pm Fri, 1-3:30pm Sun) The oldest continuously used synagogue in the country. There are free docent-led tours; check website for times.

Rainbow Row AREA
With its candy-colored houses, this stretch of lower E Bay St is one of the most photographed areas of town. The houses are around the corner from White Point Garden.

Historic Homes

About half a dozen majestic historic homes are open to visitors. Discounted combination tickets may tempt you to see more, but one or two will be enough for most people. Guided tours run every half-hour and start before the closing times noted in our reviews.

Aiken-Rhett House HISTORIC BUILDING
(www.historiccharleston.org; 48 Elizabeth St; adult/child 6-16yr $12/5; ⏲10am-5pm Mon-Sat, 2-5pm Sun) The only surviving urban plantation, this house gives a fascinating glimpse into antebellum life. The role of slaves is also presented, and you can wander into their dorm-style quarters behind the main house. The Historic Charleston Foundation manages the house with a goal of preserving and conserving, but not restoring, the property, meaning there have been few alterations.

Joseph Manigault House HISTORIC BUILDING
(www.charlestonmuseum.org; 350 Meeting St; adult/child 13-17yr/child 3-12yr $12/10/5; ⏲9am-5pm Mon-Sat, noon-5pm Sun) The three-story Federal-style house was once the showpiece of a French Huguenot rice planter. Don't miss the tiny neoclassical temple in the garden.

Nathaniel Russell House HISTORIC BUILDING
(www.historiccharleston.org; 51 Meeting St; adult/child 6-16yr $12/5; ⏲10am-5pm Mon-Sat, 2-5pm Sun) A spectacular, self-supporting spiral staircase is the highlight at this 1808 Federal-style house, built by a Rhode Islander, known in Charleston as 'the king of the Yankees.' The small but lush English garden is also notable as is the square-circle-rectangle footprint of the home.

Marion Square

Formerly home to the state weapons arsenal, this 10-acre park is Charleston's living room, with various monuments and an excellent Saturday farmers market.

Charleston Museum MUSEUM
(www.charlestonmuseum.org; 360 Meeting St; adult/child 13-17yr/child 3-12yr $12/10/5; ⏲9am-5pm Mon-Sat, noon-5pm Sun) Founded in 1773, this claims to be the country's oldest museum. It's helpful and informative if you're looking for historic background before strolling through the historic district. Exhibits spotlight various periods of Charleston's long and storied history.

Artifacts include a whale skeleton, slave tags and the 'secession table' used for the signing of the state's secession documents. And don't miss Charleston's polar bear.

Aquarium Wharf

Aquarium Wharf surrounds pretty Liberty Sq and is a great place to stroll and watch the tugboats guiding ships into the fourth-

GULLAH CULTURE

African slaves were transported from the region known as the Rice Coast (Sierra Leone, Senegal, Gambia and Angola) to a landscape of remote islands that was shockingly similar – swampy coastlines, tropical vegetation and hot, humid summers.

These new African Americans were able to retain many of their homeland traditions, even after the fall of slavery and well into the 20th century. The resulting Gullah (also known as Geechee) culture has its own language, an English-based Creole with many African words and sentence structures, and many traditions, including fantastic storytelling, art, music and crafts. The Gullah culture is celebrated annually with the energetic **Gullah Festival** (www.theoriginalgullahfestival.org; late May) in Beaufort.

largest container port in the US. The wharf is one of two embarkation points for tours to Fort Sumter; the other is at Patriot's Point.

Fort Sumter HISTORIC SITE
The first shots of the Civil War rang out at Fort Sumter, on a pentagon-shaped island in the harbor. A Confederate stronghold, the fort was shelled to bits by Union forces from 1863 to 1865. A few original guns and fortifications give a feel for the momentous history. The only way to get here is by **boat tour** (boat tour 843-722-2628, park 843-883-3123; www.nps.gov/fosu; adult/child 4-11yr $19/12), which depart from 340 Concord St at 9:30am, noon and 2:30pm in summer (less frequently in winter) and from Patriot's Point in Mt Pleasant, across the river, at 10:45am, 1:30pm and 4pm from mid-March to late August (less frequently the rest of the year).

Tours

Listing all of Charleston's walking, horse-drawn carriage, bus and boat tours could take up this entire book. Ask at the visitor center for the gamut.

Culinary Tours of Charleston CULINARY
(843-722-8687; www.culinarytoursofcharleston.com; 2½hr tour $50) You'll likely sample grits, pralines and BBQ on the Savor the Flavors of Charleston walking tour of restaurants and markets.

Adventure Harbor Tours BOAT
(843-442-9455; www.adventureharbortours.com; adult/child 3-12yr $55/30) Runs fun trips to uninhabited Morris Island – great for shelling.

Charleston Footprints WALKING
(843-478-4718; www.charlestonfootprints.com; 2hr tour $20) A highly rated walking tour of historical Charleston sights.

Festivals & Events

Lowcountry Oyster Festival FOOD
(www.charlestonrestaurantassociation.com/low-country-oyster-festival; Jan) Oyster-lovers in Mt Pleasant feast on 80,000lb of the salty bivalves in January.

Spoleto USA PERFORMING ARTS
(www.spoletousa.org; May) This 17-day performing-arts festival is Charleston's biggest event, with operas, dramas and concerts staged across the city.

MOJA Arts Festival PERFORMING ARTS
(www.mojafestival.com; Sep) Spirited poetry readings and gospel concerts mark this two-week celebration of African American and Caribbean culture.

Sleeping

Staying in the historic downtown is the most attractive option, but it's also the most expensive, especially on weekends and in high season. The rates below are for high season (spring and early summer). The chain hotels on the highways and near the airport offer significantly lower rates. Hotel parking in central downtown is usually between $12 and $20 a night; accommodations on the fringes of downtown often have free parking.

The city is bursting with charming B&Bs serving Southern breakfasts and Southern hospitality. They fill up fast, so try using an agency such as **Historic Charleston B&B** (843-722-6606; www.historiccharlestonbedandbreakfast.com; 57 Broad St; 9am-5pm Mon-Fri).

James Island County Park CAMPGROUND $
(843-795-4386; www.ccprc.com; 871 Riverland Dr; tent sites from $25, 8-person cottages $169;) A great budget option, this 643-acre park southwest of downtown has meadows, a marsh and a dog park. Rent bikes and kayaks or play the disc golf course. The park

offers shuttle services to downtown and Folly Beach ($10). Reservations are highly recommended. There are 124 campsites and 10 marsh-adjacent rental cottages. Cottages require a one-week rental June to August.

1837 Bed & Breakfast B&B **$$**
(☎877-723-1837, 843-723-7166; www.1837bb.com; 126 Wentworth St; r $135-189; P ❄ ᯤ) Close to the College of Charleston, this B&B may bring to mind the home of your eccentric, antique-loving aunt. The 1837 has nine charmingly overdecorated rooms, including three in the old brick carriage house.

Indigo Inn BOUTIQUE HOTEL **$$**
(☎843-577-5900; www.indigoinn.com; 1 Maiden Lane; r $249; P ❄ ᯤ 🐾) Our favorite part? The tasty ham biscuits at breakfast. Other perks include a prime location in the middle of the historic district and an oasis-like private courtyard, where guests can enjoy free wine and cheese by the fountain. Decor gives a nod to the 18th century, and the beds are quite comfy. Pets are $40 per night.

Town & Country Inn & Suites HOTEL **$$**
(☎843-571-1000; www.thetownandcountryinn.com; 2008 Savannah Hwy; r/ste from $169/189; P ❄ @ ᯤ ≋) About six miles from downtown, Town & Country offers modern and stylish rooms at a reasonable price. The inn is a good launch pad if you want to get a jump on traffic for a morning visit to the Ashley River plantations.

★ **Ansonborough Inn** HOTEL **$$$**
(☎800-522-2073; www.ansonboroughinn.com; 21 Hasell St; r from $299; P ❄ @ ᯤ) Droll neo-Victorian touches like the Persian-carpeted glass elevator, the closet-sized British pub and the formal portraits of dogs add a sense of fun to this intimate historic district hotel, which also manages to feel like an antique sailing ship. Huge guest rooms mix old and new, with worn leather couches, high ceilings and flat-screen TVs.

Complimentary wine and cheese social, with great pimiento cheese, runs from 5pm to 6pm.

Vendue Inn INN **$$$**
(☎843-577-7970; www.vendueinn.com; 19 Vendue Range; r/ste $265/435; P ❄ ᯤ) Fresh off a $4.8 million revamp and expansion, this boutique inn exudes a smart modern style that is also very inviting. Reimagined as an art hotel, it displays artwork property-wide, and the inn itself unfurls like a masterpiece of architecture and design. Simplicity and comfort blend seamlessly in rooms in the main building, while eye-catching art adds oomph to classically styled rooms across the street.

The popular Rooftop Bar is worth a stop even if you're not staying here. Parking is $16 per night.

Eating

Charleston is one of America's finest eating cities, and there are enough fabulous restaurants here for a town three times its size. The 'classic' Charleston establishments stick to fancy seafood with a French flair, while many of the trendy up-and-comers are reinventing Southern cuisine with a focus on the area's copious local bounty, from oysters to heirloom rice to heritage pork. On Saturday, stop by the terrific **farmers market** (Marion Sq; ⏲8am-1pm Sat Apr-Oct).

Sugar Bakeshop BAKERY **$**
(www.sugarbake.com; 59 1/2 Cannon St; pastries under $4; ⏲10am-6pm Mon-Fri, 11am-5pm Sat) The staff is as sweet as the cupcakes at Sugar, a teensy space north of downtown. If available, try the Lady Baltimore cupcake, a retro Southern specialty with dried fruit and white frosting.

Artisan Meat Share SANDWICHES **$**
(www.artisanmeatsharecharleston.com; 33 Spring St; sandwiches $7-12; ⏲11am-7pm Mon-Fri, 10am-7pm Sat & Sun) Meat, man, meat. Stuffed in a biscuit. Piled high on potato bread. Or lurching across your charcuterie board – damn that's fresh. Order at the counter, find a seat if you can, then give a nod to artisan hipsters, bless their hearts. You know the drill: fresh, local, delicious and the condiments are housemade. The pea and peanut salad is superb.

Gaulart & Maliclet FRENCH **$**
(www.fastandfrenchcharleston.com; 98 Broad St; breakfast under $7, lunch $5-9, dinner $5-18; ⏲8am-4pm Mon, to 10pm Tue-Thu, to 10:30pm Fri & Sat) Oooh la la. Locals crowd around the shared tables at this tiny spot, known as 'Fast & French,' to nibble on Gallic cheeses and sausages or nightly specials ($16) that include bread, soup, a main dish and wine.

Fleet Landing SEAFOOD **$$**
(☎843-722-8100; www.fleetlanding.net; 186 Concord St; lunch $9-23, dinner $10-26; ⏲11am-4pm daily, 5-10pm Sun-Thu, to 11pm Fri & Sat) Come here for the perfect Charleston lunch: a river

view, a cup of she-crab soup with a splash of sherry, and a big bowl of shrimp and grits. Housed in an old naval building on a pier, Fleet Landing is a convenient and scenic spot to enjoy fresh fish, a fried seafood platter or a burger after a morning of downtown exploring.

Smothered in tasso ham gravy, the shrimp and grits here look dirty, not high-falutin', and they're our favorite version in the city.

Poe's Tavern PUB FOOD **$$**
(www.poestavern.com; 2210 Middle St, Sullivan's Island; mains $9-13; ⏲11am-2am) On a sunny day the front porch of Poe's on Sullivan's Island is the place to be. The tavern's namesake, master of the macabre Edgar Allan Poe, was once stationed at nearby Fort Moultrie. The burgers are superb, and the Amontillado comes with guacamole, jalapeño jack, pico de gallo and chipotle sour cream. Quoth the raven: 'Gimme more.'

Xiao Bao Biscuit ASIAN **$$**
(www.xiaobaobiscuit.com; 224 Rutledge Ave, cnr of Spring St; lunch $10, dinner small plates $8-10, mains $12-17; ⏲11:30am-2pm & 5:30-10pm Mon-Sat) Exposed brick walls, concrete floor and housed in a former gas station – this casual but stylish eatery hits the hipster high marks. But the food? Now we're talking. The short but palate-kicking menu spotlights simple pan-Asian fare enhanced by local ingredients and spicy flavors. For something different and memorable, try the *okonomiyaki* – a cabbage pancake – with egg and bacon.

Hominy Grill NEW SOUTHERN **$$**
(www.hominygrill.com; 207 Rutledge Ave; breakfast $8-16, lunch & dinner mains $9-19; ⏲7:30am-9pm Mon-Fri, 9am-9pm Sat, to 3pm Sun; 🖉) Slightly off the beaten path, this neighborhood cafe serves modern, vegetarian-friendly Lowcountry cuisine in an old barbershop. The shaded patio is tops for brunch.

★ **FIG** NEW SOUTHERN **$$$**
(☎843-805-5900; www.eatatfig.com; 232 Meeting St; mains $29-31; ⏲5:30-10:30pm Mon-Thu, to 11pm Fri & Sat) FIG has been a long-time foodie favorite, and it's easy to see why. Welcoming staff, efficient but unrushed service, and top-notch nouvelle Southern fare from James Beard Award winner Mike Lata. The six nightly dishes embrace what's fresh and local from the sea and local farms and mills. FIG stands for Food is Good. And the gourmands agree.

Reservations highly recommended, but rogue solos might be able to snag a seat quickly at the communal table or bar.

Drinking & Nightlife

Balmy Charleston evenings are perfect for lifting a cool cocktail or dancing to live blues. Check out the weekly *Charleston City Paper* and the 'Preview' section of Friday's *Post & Courier*.

Husk Bar BAR
(www.huskrestaurant.com; 76 Queen St; ⏲from 4pm) Adjacent to Husk restaurant, this intimate brick-and-worn-wood spot recalls a speakeasy, with historic cocktails such as the Monkey Gland (gin, OJ, raspberry syrup).

Rooftop at Vendue Inn BAR
(www.vendueinn.com; 23 Vendue Range; ⏲11:30am-10pm Sun-Thu, to midnight Fri & Sat) This rooftop bar has the best views of downtown, and the crowds to prove it. Enjoy crafts, cocktails and live music on Sundays (6pm to 9pm).

Blind Tiger PUB
(www.blindtigercharleston.com; 36-38 Broad St; ⏲11am-2am) A cozy and atmospheric dive, with stamped-tin ceilings, a worn wood bar and good pub grub.

Closed for Business PUB
(www.closed4business.com; 453 King St; ⏲11am-2am Mon-Sat, 10am-2pm Sun) A wide beer selection and raucous neighborhood pub vibe.

Shopping

The historic district is clogged with overpriced souvenir shops and junk markets. Head instead to King St: hit lower King for antiques, middle King for cool boutiques, and upper King for trendy design and gift shops. The main stretch of Broad St is known as 'Gallery Row' for its many art galleries.

Shops of Historic Charleston Foundation GIFTS
(www.historiccharleston.org; 108 Meeting St; ⏲9am-6pm Mon-Sat, noon-5pm Sun) This place showcases jewelry, home furnishings and furniture inspired by the city's historic homes.

Charleston Crafts Cooperative CRAFTS
(www.charlestoncrafts.org; 161 Church St; ⏲10am-6pm) A pricey, well-edited selection of contemporary South Carolina–made crafts such as sweetgrass baskets, hand-dyed silks and wood carvings.

Blue Bicycle Books BOOKS
(www.bluebicyclebooks.com; 420 King St; ⏲10am-7:30pm Mon-Sat, 1-6pm Sun) Excellent new-and-used bookshop with a great selection of Southern history and culture.

Information

The City of Charleston maintains free public internet (wi-fi) access throughout the downtown area.

Charleston City Paper (www.charlestoncity-paper.com) Published each Wednesday, this alt-weekly has good entertainment and restaurant listings.

Police Station (☎non-emergencies 843-577-7434; 180 Lockwood Blvd) The police station is just northwest of downtown.

Post & Courier (www.postandcourier.com) Charleston's daily newspaper.

Post Office (www.usps.com; 83 Broad St; ⏲11:30am-3:30pm) At the corner of Broad St and Meeting St.

University Hospital (Medical University of South Carolina; ☎843-792-1414; www.musc health.org; 171 Ashley Ave; ⏲24hr) Emergency room.

Visitor Center (☎843-853-8000; www.charlestoncvb.com; 375 Meeting St; ⏲8:30am-5pm Apr-Oct, to 5pm Nov-Mar) Find help with accommodations and tours or watch a half-hour video on Charleston history in this spacious renovated warehouse.

Getting There & Around

Charleston International Airport (CHS; ☎843-767-7000; www.chs-airport.com; 5500 International Blvd) is 12 miles outside of town in North Charleston, with nonstop flights to 18 destinations.

The **Greyhound station** (3610 Dorchester Rd) and the **Amtrak train station** (4565 Gaynor Ave) are both in North Charleston.

CARTA (www.ridecarta.com; one-way fare $1.75) runs city-wide buses; the free DASH streetcars do three loop routes from the visitor center.

Mt Pleasant

Across the Cooper River from Charleston is the residential and vacation community of Mt Pleasant, originally a summer retreat for early Charlestonians, along with the slim barrier resort islands of **Isle of Palms** and **Sullivan's Island**. Though increasingly glutted with traffic and strip malls, the area still has some charm, especially in the historic downtown, called the **Old Village**. Some good seafood restaurants overlook the water at **Shem Creek**, where it's fun to dine creekside at sunset and watch the incoming fishing-boat crews unload their catch. This is also a good place to rent kayaks to tour the estuary.

MEXICAN HAT DANCE

Yes, that's a giant sombrero rising above I-95 on the North Carolina–South Carolina state line. *Bienvenidos* to **South of the Border** (www.thesouthoftheborder.com; 3346 Hwy 301 N Hamer), a Mexican-flavored monument to American kitsch. Begun in the 1950s as a fireworks stand – pyrotechnics are illegal in North Carolina – it's morphed into a combo rest stop, souvenir mall, motel and (mostly defunct) amusement park, promoted on hundreds of billboards by a wildly stereotypical Mexican cartoon character named Pedro. The place has been looking tired, but it's still worth a quick stop for a photo and some taffy.

Sights

Patriot's Point Naval & Maritime Museum MUSEUM
(☎866-831-1720; www.patriotspoint.org; 40 Patriots Point Rd; adult/child 6-11yr $20/12; ⏲9am-6:30pm) Patriot's Point Naval & Maritime Museum is home to the USS *Yorktown*, a giant aircraft carrier used extensively in WWII. You can tour the ship's flight deck, bridge and ready rooms and get a glimpse of what life was like for its sailors. Also on-site is a submarine, a naval destroyer, the Medal of Honor Museum and a re-created 'fire base' from Vietnam. You can also catch the Fort Sumter boat tour (p360). Parking is $5.

Boone Hall Plantation HISTORIC BUILDING
(☎843-884-4371; www.boonehallplantation.com; 1235 Long Point Rd; adult/child 6-12yr $20/10; ⏲8:30am-6:30pm Mon-Sat, noon-5pm Sun early Mar-Aug, shorter hours Sep-Jan, closed Feb) Just 11 miles from downtown Charleston on Hwy 17N, Boone Hall Plantation is famous for its magical Avenue of Oaks, planted by Thomas Boone in 1743. Boone Hall is still a working plantation, though strawberries, tomatoes and Christmas trees long ago replaced cotton as the primary crop. The main house, built in 1936, is the fourth house on the site. The most compelling buildings are the Slave Street cabins, built between 1790 and 1810 and now lined with exhibits.

Ashley River Plantations

Three spectacular plantations line the Ashley River about a 20-minute drive from downtown Charleston. You'll be hard-pressed for time to visit all three in one outing, but you could squeeze in two (allow at least a couple of hours for each). Ashley River Rd is also known as SC 61, which can be reached from downtown Charleston via Hwy 17.

Sights

★ **Middleton Place** HISTORIC BUILDING, GARDENS
(☎843-556-6020; www.middletonplace.org; 4300 Ashley River Rd; gardens adult/child 6-13yr $28/10, house museum tour adult & child extra $15; ⏰9am-5pm) Designed in 1741, this plantation's vast gardens are the oldest in the US. One hundred slaves spent a decade terracing the land and digging the precise geometric canals for the owner, wealthy South Carolina politician Henry Middleton. The bewitching grounds are a mix of classic formal French gardens and romantic woodland, bounded by flooded rice paddies and rare-breed farm animals. Union soldiers burned the main house in 1865; a 1755 guest wing, now housing the **house museum**, still stands.

The on-site **inn** is a series of ecofriendly modernist glass boxes overlooking the Ashley River. Enjoy a traditional Lowcountry plantation lunch of she-crab soup and hoppin' john at the highly regarded **cafe**.

Magnolia Plantation HOUSE, GARDENS
(www.magnoliaplantation.com; 3550 Ashley River Rd; adult/child 6-10yr $15/10, tours $8; ⏰8am-5:30pm Mar-Oct, to 4:30pm Nov-Feb) Up for a spooky stroll? Then follow the boardwalk through the trees and bog on the Swamp Garden tour – it's a unique experience. The 500-acre plantation, which has been owned by the Drayton family since 1676, is a veritable theme park. Enjoy a tram tour, a petting zoo and a guided house tour. At the reconstructed slave cabins, the Slavery to Freedom Tour traces the African American experience at the plantation.

Drayton Hall HOUSE
(☎843-769-2600; www.draytonhall.org; 3380 Ashley River Rd; adult/child $18/8; ⏰9am-5pm Mon-Sat, 11am-5pm Sun, last tour 3:30pm) This 1738 Palladian brick mansion was the only plantation house on the Ashley River to survive the Revolutionary and Civil Wars and the great earthquake of 1886. Guided tours explore the unfurnished house, which has been preserved, but not restored. Walking trails wander along the river and a marsh.

Lowcountry

From just north of Charleston, the southern half of the South Carolina coast is a tangle of islands cut off from the mainland by inlets and tidal marshes. Here, descendants of West African slaves known as the Gullah maintain small communities in the face of resort and golf-course development. The landscape ranges from tidy stretches of shimmery, oyster-gray sand to wild, moss-shrouded maritime forests.

Charleston County Sea Islands

Several islands are within an hour's drive of Charleston. About 8 miles south of Charleston, **Folly Beach** is good for a day of sun and sand. **Folly Beach County Park** (☎843-588-2426; www.ccprc.com; 1100 W Ashley Ave, Folly Beach; parking per vehicle $7-10, walk-in/bicycle free; ⏰9am-7pm May-Aug, 10am-6pm Mar, Apr, Sep & Oct, 10am-5pm Nov-Feb), on the west side, has public changing areas and beach-chair rentals. The other end of the island is popular with surfers.

Upscale rental homes, golf courses and the swanky **Sanctuary Resort** mark **Kiawah Island**, just southeast of Charleston, while nearby **Edisto Island** (*ed*-is-tow) is a homespun family vacation spot without a single traffic light. At its southern tip, **Edisto Beach State Park** (☎843-869-2156; www.southcarolinaparks.com; adult/child 6-15yr $5/3; tent/RV sites from $20/26, cabins from $110) has a gorgeous, uncrowded beach and oak-shaded hiking trails and campgrounds.

Sleeping

The Sanctuary at Kiawah Island Golf Resort RESORT $$$
(☎843-768-2121; www.kiawahresort.com; 1 Sanctuary Beach Dr; r/ste from $570/1675, villa from $275, house from $8,100 per week; ❄@📶🏊) Ready to swank it up? Consider an idyll at the Sanctuary, sitting prettily by the sea 21 miles south of downtown Charleston. Hotel rooms glow with freshly classic decor – think soft greens, four-poster beds, Italian linens, custom-made mattresses and marble showers. Villas and houses also available. Amenities include two tennis complexes, 90 holes of golf, a spa and Kamp Kiawah for the kids.

Beaufort & Hilton Head

The southernmost stretch of South Carolina's coast is popular with a mostly upscale set of golfers and B&B aficionados, but the area's got quirky charms aplenty for everyone.

On Port Royal Island, the darling colonial town of **Beaufort** (byoo-furt) is often used as a set for Hollywood films about the South. The streets of the historic district are lined with antebellum homes and magnolias dripping with Spanish moss. The riverfront downtown has gobs of linger-worthy cafes and galleries.

South of Beaufort, some 20,000 young men and women go through boot camp each year at the **Marine Corps Recruit Depot** on Parris Island, made notorious by Stanley Kubrick's *Full Metal Jacket*. The facility has been 'welcoming' recruits for 100 years. Come for Friday graduations to see newly minted marines parade proudly for family and friends. You may be asked to show ID and car registration before driving onto the base.

East of Beaufort, the Sea Island Pkwy/Hwy 21 connects a series of marshy, rural islands, including **St Helena Island**, considered the heart of Gullah country and the site of a coastal state park.

Across Port Royal Sound, tiny **Hilton Head Island** is South Carolina's largest barrier island and one of America's top golf spots. There are dozens of courses, many enclosed in posh private residential communities called 'plantations.' The overall set-up is a bit unwelcoming. Summer traffic and miles of stoplights also make it hard to appreciate the beauty of the island, but there are some lush nature preserves and wide, white beaches hard enough for bike riding. Stop by the **visitor center** (800-523-3373; www.hiltonheadisland.org; 1 Chamber of Commerce Dr; 8:30am-5:30pm Mon-Fri), on the island, for information and brochures.

Sights

Parris Island Museum MUSEUM
(843-228-2951; www.mcrdpi.marines.mil; 111 Panama St; 10am-4:30pm) FREE This fascinating museum has antique uniforms and weaponry, and covers marine corps history. There are also a few rooms dedicated to local history. Don't miss the introductory movie.

DON'T MISS

BOWEN'S ISLAND RESTAURANT

Down a long dirt road through Lowcountry marshland near Folly Beach, this unpainted wooden **shack** (1870 Bowen's Island Rd; 5-10pm Tue-Sat) is one of the South's most venerable seafood dives – grab an oyster knife and start shucking! Cool beer and friendly locals give the place its soul.

Penn Center MUSEUM
(843-838-2474; www.penncenter.com/museum; 16 Penn Center Circle W; adult/child 6-16yr $5/3; 9am-4pm Mon-Sat) Once the home of one of the nation's first schools for freed slaves, the Penn Center on St Helena Island has a small museum that covers Gullah culture and traces the history of Penn School.

Hunting Island State Park PARK
(843-838-2011; www.southcarolinaparks.com; 2555 Sea Island Pkwy; adult/child 6-15yr $5/3; visitor center 9am-5pm Mon-Fri, 11am-5pm Sat & Sun) Lush and inviting, Hunting Island State Park impresses visitors with acres of spooky maritime forest, tidal lagoons and empty, bone-white beach. The Vietnam War scenes from *Forrest Gump* were filmed in the marsh, a nature-lover's dream. Campgrounds fill up quickly in summer. Climb the **lighthouse** ($2) for sweeping coastal views.

Sleeping & Eating

Hunting Island State Park Campground CAMPGROUND $
(reservations 866-345-7275, office 843-838-2011; www.southcarolinaparks.com; 2555 Sea Island Pkwy; tent sites $18.50-29, RV sites $23-32, cabin $23-201; 6am-6pm, to 9pm early Mar-early Nov) At South Carolina's most visited park, you can camp under pine trees or palm trees. Several campsites are just steps from the beach. All sites are available by walk-up or reservation, but reservations are advisable in summer.

City Loft Hotel HOTEL $$
(843-379-5638; www.cityloft hotel.com; 301 Carteret St, Beaufort; r/ste $209/229;) The chic City Loft Hotel adds a refreshing dash of modern style to a town heavy on historic homes and stately oak trees. Enjoy flat-screen

DON'T MISS

MUST-EAT SOUTHERN FOODS

Barbecue – region-wide, especially in North Carolina and Tennessee

Fried chicken – region-wide

Cornbread – region-wide

Shrimp and grits – South Carolina and Georgia coasts

Lowcountry boil/Frogmore stew – crabs, shrimp, oysters and other local seafood boiled in a pot with corn and potatoes; South Carolina and Georgia coasts

Boudin – Cajun pork and rice sausage; Southern Louisiana

Gumbo/jambalaya/étouffée – rice and seafood or meat stew or a mixture; Southern Louisiana

Po'boy – sandwich, traditionally with fried seafood or meat; Southern Louisiana

Collards – a leafy green, often cooked with ham; region-wide

Pecan pie, coconut cake, red velvet cake, sweet-potato pie – region-wide

Bourbon – Kentucky

TVs in the bedroom and bathroom, artisan-tile showers and Memory Foam–topped beds. Other perks include a gym, complimentary bicycle use and an on-site coffee shop.

Sgt White's SOUTHERN, BARBECUE $
(1908 Boundary St, Beaufort; meat & three platter $9; ⏲11am-3pm Mon-Fri) A retired Marine sergeant serves up classic meat and three platters. At the counter, order your juicy BBQ ribs or meat dish, then choose three sides, which can include collards, okra stew and cornbread.

North Coast

Stretching from the North Carolina border south to the city of Georgetown, the coastal region known as the Grand Strand bustles with some 60 miles of fast-food joints, beach resorts and three-story souvenir shops. What was once a laid-back summer destination for working-class people from across the Southeast has become some of the most overdeveloped real estate in the country. Whether you're ensconced in a behemoth resort or sleeping in a tent at a state park, all you need to enjoy your stay is a pair of flip-flops, a margarita and some quarters for the pinball machine.

Myrtle Beach

The towering Sky Wheel spins fantastically beside the coast in downtown Myrtle Beach, anchoring a 60-mile swath of sun-bleached excess. Love it or hate it, Myrtle Beach means summer vacation, American-style.

Bikers take advantage of the lack of helmet laws to let their graying ponytails fly in the wind, bikini-clad teenagers play video games and eat hot dogs in smoky arcades, and whole families roast like chickens on the white sand.

North Myrtle Beach, actually a separate town, is slightly lower-key, with a thriving culture based on the 'shag' (no, not that kind of shag) – a jitterbug-like dance invented here in the 1940s.

It ain't for nature-lovers, but with enormous outlet malls and innumerable mini-golf courses, water parks, daiquiri bars and T-shirt shops, it's a rowdy good time.

Sights & Activities

The beach itself is pleasant enough – wide, hot and crowded with umbrellas. Beachfront Ocean Blvd has the bulk of the hamburger stands and seedy gift shops. Hwy 17 is choked with over-the-top mini-golf courses. Several amusement park and shopping mall hybrids teem with people at all hours.

Brookgreen Gardens GARDENS
(www.brookgreen.org; adult/child 4-12yr $15/7; ⏲9:30am-5pm, to 8pm Apr) These magical gardens, 16 miles south of town on Hwy 17S, are home to the largest collection of American sculpture in the country, set amid more than 9000 acres of rice plantation turned subtropical garden paradise. Seasonal blooms are listed on the website.

SkyWheel AMUSEMENT PARK
(www.myrtlebeachskywheel.com; 1110 N Ocean Blvd; adult/child 3-11yr $13/9; ⏲11am-midnight) The 187ft high SkyWheel overlooks the 1.2-mile coastal boardwalk. One ticket includes three revolutions in an enclosed gondola. At night the wheel is bewitching, with more than a million dazzling colored lights.

Broadway at the Beach MALL
(www.broadwayatthebeach.com; 1325 Celebrity Circle; ⏲10am-11pm May-Jun, shorter hours rest of year) With shops, restaurants, nightclubs, rides, an aquarium and a giant-screen digital movie theater, this is Myrtle Beach's nerve center.

Family Kingdom AMUSEMENT PARK
(www.family-kingdom.com; combo pass $38; 👪) An old-fashioned amusement-and-water-park combo overlooking the ocean. Hours vary seasonally. Closed in winter.

Sleeping

Hundreds of hotels, ranging from retro family-run motor inns to vast resort complexes, have prices that vary widely by season; a room might cost $30 in January and more than $150 in July. The following are high-season rates.

Myrtle Beach State Park CAMPGROUND $
(☎843-238-5325; www.southcarolinaparks.com; 4401 S Kings Hwy; rustic tents May-Jun $30, tent/RV sites from $38/42, cabins from $149; P 📶 🏊) Sleep beneath the pines or rent a cabin, all just steps from the shore. The park is 3 miles south of central Myrtle Beach.

Best Western Plus Grand Stand Inn & Suites HOTEL $$
(☎843-448-1461; www.myrtlebeachbestwestern.com; 1804 S Ocean Blvd; r/ste from $157/177; ❄ @ 📶 🏊) Yes, it's part of a large national chain, but rates are reasonable, the beach is steps away and the complimentary breakfast is filling. The hotel sprawls across two buildings, one of them oceanfront and one just across Ocean Blvd. Rooms sport a bit of modern style. The boardwalk is 1 mile north.

Hampton Inn Broadway at the Beach HOTEL $$$
(☎843-916-0600; www.hamptoninn3.hilton.com; 1140 Celebrity Circle; r/ste from $249/389; ❄ @ 📶 🏊) The bright rooms overlooking the lake and Broadway at the Beach are a great choice at this hotel, which feels less hectic than properties along Ocean Blvd. If you're traveling with pre-teens, you may feel more comfortable letting them roam the adjacent shops and attractions rather than the boardwalk.

Eating

The hundreds of restaurants are mostly high-volume and middlebrow – think buffets longer than bowling alleys and 24-hour doughnut shops. Ironically, good seafood is hard to come by; locals go to the nearby fishing village of **Murrells Inlet**.

Prosser's BBQ SOUTHERN $$
(www.prossersbbq.com; 3750 Business Hwy 17, Murrells Inlet; buffet breakfast/lunch/dinner $6.50/9/12-14; ⏲6:30-10:30am Mon-Sat, 11am-2pm Mon-Sat, 11am-2:30pm Sun, 4-8:30pm Tue-Sat; 👪) The gut-busting lunch buffet is down-home delicious. It includes fried fish and chicken, sweet potato soufflé, mac 'n' cheese, green beans and vinegary pulled pork. Your best bet on Murrells Inlet's 'restaurant row.' Worth the drive.

Aspen Grille SOUTHERN $$$
(☎843-449-9191; www.aspen-grille.com; 5101 N Kings Hwy; mains $20-55) Impress your palate, escape the madness and shake off the fried seafood baskets that bind you at Aspen Grille. Sophisticated yet inviting, it seems worlds away from the roar of the Kings Hwy. Chef Curry Martin serves fresh and locally sourced fare with style and Southern sensibilities. Think shrimp and cheese grits with pan gravy and andouille sausage.

If triggerfish is the catch of the day, don't miss it. Live music and half off wines on Wednesday nights.

Entertainment

★ **Fat Harold's Beach Club** DANCE
(www.fatharolds.com; 212 Main St; ⏲from 4pm Mon & Tue, from 11am Wed-Sun) Folks groove to doo-wop and old-time rock and roll at this North Myrtle institution, which calls itself 'Home of the Shag.' The dance, that is. Free shag lessons are offered at 7pm every Tuesday.

Information

Visitor Center (☎843-626-7444; www.visitmyrtlebeach.com; 1200 N Oak St; ⏲8:30am-5pm Mon-Fri, 9am-5pm Sat, 10am-2pm Sun May-Aug, 9am-2pm Sat and closed Sun Sep-May) Has maps and brochures.

WORTH A TRIP

EXPLORING THE SWAMP AT CONGAREE NATIONAL PARK

Inky-black water, dyed with tannic acid leached from decaying plant matter. Bone-white cypress stumps like the femurs of long-dead giants. Spanish moss as dry and gray as witches' hair. There's nothing like hiking or canoeing through one of South Carolina's unearthly swamps to make you feel like a character in a Southern Gothic novel.

Near Columbia, the 22,000-acre **Congaree National Park** (☎803-776-4396; www.nps.gov/cong; 100 National Park Rd, Hopkins; ⏲visitor center 9am-5pm Tue-Sat), America's largest contiguous, old-growth floodplain forest, has camping and free ranger-led canoe trips (reserve in advance). Casual day-trippers can wander the 2.4-mile elevated boardwalk. Look carefully at the Blue Sky mural in the visitor center – the scene seems to change as you move.

Between Charleston and Myrtle Beach, **Francis Marion National Forest** has 259,000 acres of black-water creeks, camping, and hiking trails, including the 42-mile Palmetto Trail, which runs along old logging routes. Charleston-based Nature Adventures Outfitters leads kayak and canoe trips.

Getting There & Around

The traffic coming and going on Hwy 17 Business/Kings Hwy can be infuriating. To avoid 'the Strand' altogether, stay on the Hwy 17 bypass, or take Hwy 31/Carolina Bays Pkwy, which parallels Hwy 17 between Hwy 501 and Hwy 9.

Myrtle Beach International Airport (MYR; ☎843-448-1589; www.flymyrtlebeach.com; 1100 Jetport Rd) is located within the city limits, as is the **Greyhound** (☎843-448-2472; 511 7th Ave N) station.

Greenville & the Upcountry

Cherokee once roamed the state's mountain foothills, which they called 'The Great Blue Hills of God.' The region today is known as the Upcountry. Geographically, it's the spot where the Blue Ridge Mountains drop dramatically to meet the Piedmont.

The region is anchored by Greenville, home to one of the most photogenic downtowns in the South. The Reedy River twists through the city center, and its dramatic falls tumble beneath Main St at **Falls Park** (www.fallspark.com). Pedal along the river on the **Swamp Rabbit Trail** on one of the new bike-share bikes (https://greenville.bcycle.com). Dowtown Main St rolls past a lively array of indie shops, good restaurants and craft-beer pubs. Whimsical quotes, called 'Thoughts on a Walk' dot the sidewalk. Kids will get a kick out of **Mice on Main**, a find-the-bronze-mouse scavenger hunt inspired by the book *Goodnight Moon*.

The region's marquee natural attraction is Table Rock Mountain, a 3124ft-high mountain with a striking granite face. The 7.2-mile round-trip hike to its summit at **Table Rock State Park** (☎864-878-9813; www.southcarolinaparks.com; 158 Ellison Lane, Pickens; adult/child 6-15yr $5/3 Jun-Nov, adult/child under 16yr $2/free Dec-May; ⏲7am-7pm Sun-Thu, to 9pm Fri & Sat, extended hours mid-May–early Nov) is a popular local challenge. For overnight stays, camping is available (campsites $16 to $21) as are cabins built by the Civilian Conservation Corps ($52 to $181).

Sleeping & Eating

Drury Inn & Suites HOTEL **$$**
(☎864-288-4401; www.druryhotels.com; 10 Carolina Point Pkwy; r/ste from $107/166; P ❄ @ ☎) It's not downtown and it's part of a cookie-cutter chain, but the price includes a nightly happy hour with a hearty array of appetizers as well as a filling breakfast. The hotel is on I-85, 7 miles from downtown.

Lazy Goat MEDITERRANEAN **$$**
(☎864-679-5299; www.thelazygoat.com; 170 River Pl; lunch $5-15, dinner small plates $5-10, dinner mains $12-25; ⏲11:30am-9pm Mon-Wed, to 10pm Thu-Sat) Nibble pimiento cheese and ciabbata bread and sip wine beside the river at this stylish spot, known for its Mediterranean small plates.

TENNESSEE

Most states have one official state song. Tennessee has seven. And that's not just a random fact – Tennessee has music deep within its soul. Here, the folk music of the Scots-Irish in the eastern mountains combined with the bluesy rhythms of the African Americans in the western Delta to give birth to the modern country music that makes Nashville famous.

These three geographic regions, represented by the three stars on the Tennessee flag, have their own unique beauty: the heather-colored peaks of the Great Smoky Mountains; the lush green valleys of the central plateau around Nashville; and the hot, sultry lowlands near Memphis.

In Tennessee you can hike shady mountain trails in the morning, and by evening whoop it up in a Nashville honky-tonk or walk the streets of Memphis with Elvis' ghost.

Information

Department of Environment & Conservation (☎888-867-2757; www.state.tn.us/environment/parks) Check out the well-organized website for camping, hiking and fishing info for Tennessee's more than 50 state parks.

Department of Tourist Development (☎615-741-2159; www.tnvacation.com; 312 8th Ave N, Nashville) Has welcome centers at the state borders.

Memphis

Memphis doesn't just attract tourists. It draws pilgrims. Music-lovers lose themselves to the throb of blues guitar on Beale St. Barbecue connoisseurs descend to stuff themselves silly on smoky pulled pork and dry-rubbed ribs. Elvis fanatics fly in to worship at the altar of the King at Graceland. You could spend days hopping from one museum or historic site to another, stopping only for barbecue, and leave happy.

But once you get away from the lights and the tourist buses, Memphis is a different place entirely. Named after the capital of ancient Egypt, it has a certain baroque ruined quality that's both sad and beguiling. Though poverty is rampant – Victorian mansions sit beside tumbledown shotgun shacks (a narrow style of house popular in the South) and college campuses lie in the shadow of eerie abandoned factories – whiffs of a renaissance are in the air. Neighborhoods once downtrodden, abandoned and/or otherwise reclaimed by kudzu – South Main, Binghampton, Crosstown and others – are being reinvented with kitschy boutiques, hipster lofts and daring restaurants, all dripping with Memphis' wild river-town spirit.

Sights

Downtown

The pedestrian-only stretch of Beale St is a 24-hour carnival zone, where you'll find deep-fried funnel cakes, to-go beer counters, and music, music, music. Although locals don't hang out here much, visitors tend to get a kick out of it. Look out for the Memphis Music Hall of Fame and the Blues Hall of Fame, both of which opened in 2015.

★**National Civil Rights Museum** MUSEUM
(Map p372; www.civilrightsmuseum.org; 450 Mulberry St; adult $15, student & senior $14, child $12; 9am-5pm Mon & Wed-Sat, 1-5pm Sun Sep-May, to 6pm Jun-Aug) Housed across the street from the Lorraine Motel, where the Rev Dr Martin Luther King Jr was fatally shot on April 4, 1968, is the gut-wrenching National Civil Rights Museum. Five blocks south of Beale St, this museum's extensive exhibits and detailed timeline chronicle the struggle for African American freedom and equality.

TENNESSEE FACTS

Nickname Volunteer State

Population 6.54 million

Area 42,146 sq miles

Capital city Nashville (population 634,000)

Other cities Memphis (population 653,000)

Sales tax 7%, plus local taxes of up to about 15%

Birthplace of Frontiersman Davy Crockett (1786–1836), soul diva Aretha Franklin (b 1942), singer Dolly Parton (b 1946)

Home of Graceland, Grand Ole Opry, Jack Daniel's distillery

Politics Pretty darn conservative, with liberal hot spots in urban areas

Famous for 'Tennessee Waltz,' country music, Tennessee walking horses, soul music

Odd law In Tennessee, it's illegal to fire a gun at any wild game, other than whales, from a moving vehicle

Driving distances Memphis to Nashville 213 miles, Nashville to Great Smoky Mountains National Park 223 miles

Greater Memphis

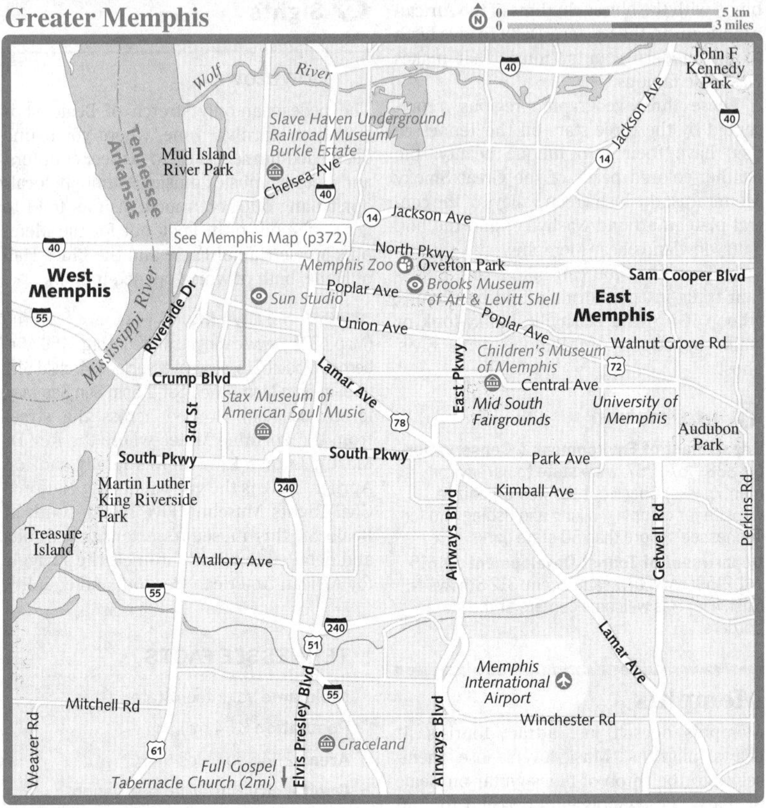

Both Dr King's cultural contribution and his assassination serve as prisms for looking at the Civil Rights movement, its precursors and its continuing impact on American life.

The turquoise exterior of the 1950s motel and two preserved interior rooms remain much as they were at the time of King's death.

Memphis Rock 'n' Soul Museum MUSEUM
(Map p372; www.memphisrocknsoul.org; 191 Beale St; adult/child $12/9; ⏲10am-7pm) The Smithsonian's museum, next to FedEx Forum, examines how African American and white music mingled in the Mississippi Delta to create the modern rock and soul sound.

Gibson Beale Street Showcase FACTORY TOUR
(Map p372; www2.gibson.com; 145 Lt George W Lee Ave; admission $10, no children under 5yr; ⏲hourly tours 11am-4pm Mon-Sat, noon-4pm Sun) Take the fascinating 45-minute tours, which vary throughout the day by worker presence and noise level, of this enormous place to see master craftspeople transform solid blocks of wood into Les Pauls.

WC Handy House Museum MUSEUM
(Map p372; www.wchandymemphis.org; 352 Beale St; adult/child $6/4; ⏲11am-4pm Tue-Sat winter, to 5pm summer) On the corner of 4th St, this shotgun shack once belonged to the composer called the 'father of the blues.' He was the first to transpose the 12 bars and later wrote 'Beale Street Blues' in 1916.

Peabody Ducks MARCHING DUCKS
(Map p372; www.peabodymemphis.com; 149 Union Ave; ⏲11am & 5pm; 👪) FREE A tradition dating to the 1930s begins every day at 11am sharp when five ducks file from the Peabody Hotel's gilded elevator, waddle across the red-carpeted lobby, and decamp in the marble lobby fountain for a day of happy splashing. The ducks make the reverse march at 5pm, when they retire to their penthouse accompanied by their red-coated Duckmaster.

Get here early to secure your spot among the heavy crowds (the mezzanine has the best views).

North of Downtown

Mud Island PARK

(Map p372; www.mudisland.com; 125 N Front St; 10am-5pm Tue-Sun mid-Apr-Oct;) FREE A small peninsula jutting into the Mississippi, Mud Island is downtown Memphis' best-loved green space. Hop the monorail ($4, or free with Mississippi River Museum admission) or walk across the bridge to the park, where you can jog and rent bikes.

Slave Haven Underground Railroad Museum/Burkle Estate MUSEUM

(www.slavehavenundergroundrailroadmuseum.org; 826 N 2nd St; adult/child $10/8; 10am-4pm Mon-Sat, to 5pm Jun-Aug) This unimposing clapboard house is thought to have been a way station for runaway slaves on the Underground Railroad, complete with trapdoors, cellar entry and cubby-holes.

East of Downtown

★ **Sun Studio** STUDIO TOUR

(800-441-6249; www.sunstudio.com; 706 Union Ave; adult/child $12/free; 10am-6:15pm) This dusty storefront is ground zero for American rock and roll music. Starting in the early 1950s, Sun's Sam Phillips recorded blues artists such as Howlin' Wolf, BB King and Ike Turner, followed by the rockabilly dynasty of Jerry Lee Lewis, Johnny Cash, Roy Orbison and, of course, the King himself (who started here in 1953).

Packed 40-minute guided tours (no children under five allowed; hourly from 10:30am to 5:30pm) through the tiny studio offer a chance to hear original tapes of historic recording sessions. Guides are full of anecdotes; you can pose for photos on the 'X' where Elvis once stood, or buy a CD of the 'Million Dollar Quartet,' Sun's spontaneous 1956 jam session between Elvis, Johnny Cash, Carl Perkins and Jerry Lee Lewis. From here, hop on the studio's free shuttle (hourly, starting at 11:15am), which does a loop between Sun Studio, Beale St and Graceland.

Children's Museum of Memphis MUSEUM

(www.cmom.com; 2525 Central Ave; admission $12; 9am-5pm, to 6pm summer;) Gives the kids a chance to let loose and play in, on and with exhibits such as an airplane cockpit or tornado generator.

Overton Park

Stately homes surround this 342-acre rolling green oasis – home to the Memphis Zoo – off Poplar Ave in the middle of this often gritty city. If Beale St is Memphis' heart, then Overton Park is its lungs.

Brooks Museum of Art GALLERY

(www.brooksmuseum.org; 1934 Poplar Ave; adult/child $7/3; 10am-4pm Wed & Fri, to 8pm Thu, to 5pm Sat, from 11am Sun) At this well-regarded art museum on the park's western fringe, the excellent permanent collection encompasses everything from Renaissance sculpture to Impressionists to abstract expressionists.

Levitt Shell ARCHITECTURE, CONCERT VENUE

(www.levittshell.org; 1928 Poplar Ave) A historic band shell and the site of Elvis' first concert in 1954. Today the mod-looking white shell hosts free concerts all summer.

South of Downtown

★ **Graceland** HISTORIC BUILDING

(901-332-3322; www.graceland.com; Elvis Presley Blvd/US 51; tours house only adult/child $36/16, expanded tours from $40/19; 9am-5pm Mon-Sat, to 4pm Sun, shorter hours & closed Tue Dec; P) If you only make one stop in Memphis, it should be here: the sublimely kitschy, gloriously bizarre home of the King of Rock and Roll. Though born in Mississippi, Elvis Presley was a true son of Memphis, raised in the Lauderdale Courts public housing projects, inspired by blues clubs on Beale St, and discovered at Sun Studio. In the spring of 1957, the already-famous 22-year-old spent $100,000 on a Colonial-style mansion, named Graceland by its previous owners.

The King himself had the place, ahem, redecorated in 1974. With a 15ft couch, fake waterfall, yellow vinyl walls and green shag-carpet ceiling – it's a virtual textbook of ostentatious '70s style. You'll begin your tour at the visitor plaza on the other side of Elvis Presley Blvd. Book ahead in the busy season (June to August and important Elvis dates) to ensure a prompt tour time. The basic self-guided mansion tour comes with an engaging multimedia iPad narration. Pay just $4 extra to see the car museum, and $9 extra to tack on the two custom planes (check out the blue-and-gold private bathroom on the *Lisa Marie*, a Convair 880 Jet).

Priscilla Presley (who divorced Elvis in 1973) opened Graceland to tours in 1982,

Memphis

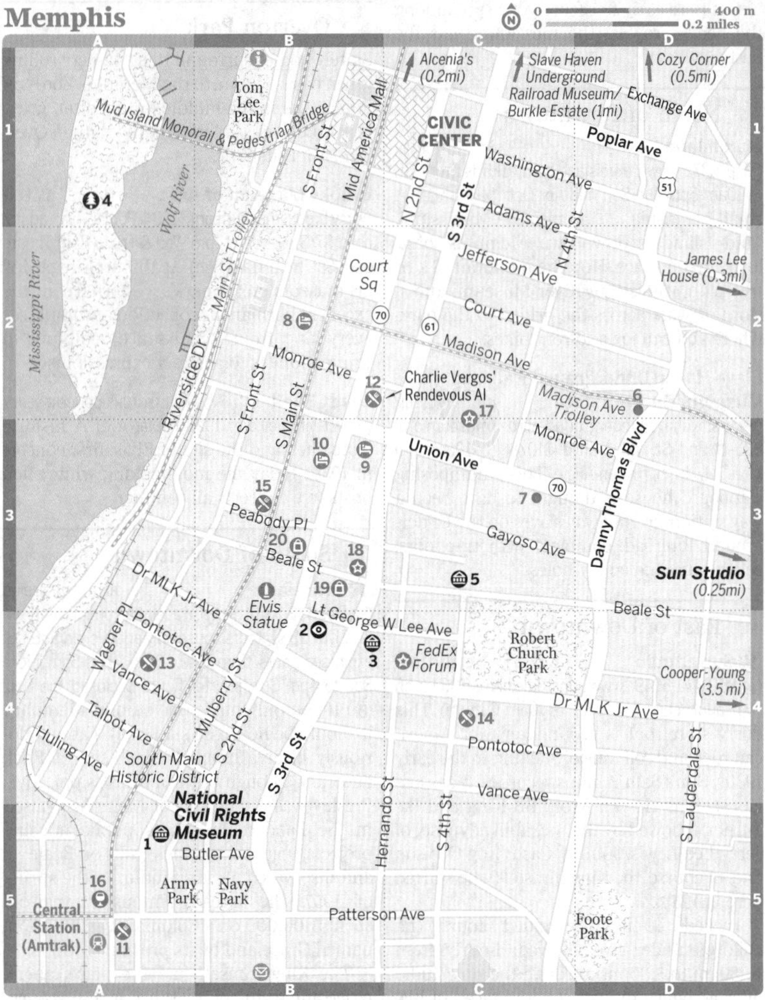

and now millions come to pay homage to the King who died here (in the upstairs bathroom) from heart failure in 1977. Throngs of fans still weep at his grave, next to the swimming pool out back. Graceland is 9 miles south of downtown on US 51, also called 'Elvis Presley Blvd.' A free shuttle runs from Sun Studio (p371). Parking costs $10.

★ Stax Museum of American Soul Music MUSEUM

(☎901-942-7685; www.staxmuseum.com; 926 E McLemore Ave; adult/child $13/10; ⏰10am-5pm Tue-Sat, 1-5pm Sun) Wanna get funky? Head directly to Soulsville USA, where this 17,000-sq-ft museum sits on the site of the old Stax recording studio. This venerable spot was soul music's epicenter in the 1960s, when Otis Redding, Booker T and the MGs and Wilson Pickett recorded here.

Dive into soul music history with photos, displays of '60s and '70s stage clothing and, above all, Isaac Hayes' 1972 Superfly Cadillac outfitted with shag-fur and 24-carat-gold exterior trim.

Memphis

◉ Top Sights
  1 National Civil Rights Museum A5

◉ Sights
  2 Gibson Beale Street Showcase............ B4
  3 Memphis Rock 'n' Soul Museum B4
  4 Mud Island A1
    Peabody Ducks ....(see 9)
  5 WC Handy House Museum C3

◉ Activities, Courses & Tours
  6 American Dream Safari D2
  7 Blues City Tours.................................. C3

◉ Sleeping
  8 Madison Hotel B2
  9 Peabody Hotel..................................... B3
  10 Talbot Heirs B3

◉ Eating
  11 Arcade... A5
  12 Charlie Vergos' Rendezvous................ B2
  13 Gus's World Famous Fried Chicken...... A4
  14 LUNCHBOXeats C4
  15 Majestic Grille B3

◉ Drinking & Nightlife
  16 Earnestine & Hazel's........................... A5

◉ Entertainment
  17 AutoZone Park.................................... C2
  18 Rum Boogie.. B3

◉ Shopping
  19 A Schwab's... B3
  20 Lanksy Brothers................................. B3

Full Gospel Tabernacle Church   CHURCH
(787 Hale Rd; ⊙ services 11am) On Sunday, put on your smell goods and head to services in South Memphis, where soul music legend turned reverend Al Green presides over a powerful choir. Visitors are welcome; it's a fascinating cultural experience.

Tours

American Dream Safari   CULTURAL
(Map p372; ☑ 901-428-3602; www.american-dreamsafari.com; 343 Madison Ave; walking tours per person $15, driving tours per vehicle from $200) Southern culture junkie Tad Pierson shows you the quirky, personal side of Memphis – juke joints, gospel churches, decaying buildings – on foot or in his pink Cadillac (if you can get ahold of him, that is).

Blues City Tours   BUS TOUR
(Map p372; ☑ 901-522-9229; www.bluescitytours. com; adult/child from $24/19) A variety of themed bus tours, including an Elvis tour and a Memphis Music Tour.

Festivals & Events

Trolley Night   ART
(www.gosouthmain.com/trolley-night.html; S Main St; ⊙ 6-9pm last Fri of month) FREE On Trolley Night galleries on South Main stay open late and pour wine for the people.

Beale Street Music Festival   MUSIC
(www.memphisinmay.org; Tom Lee Park; 3-day passes $95; ⊙ 1st weekend in May) You've heard of Coachella, New Orleans Jazz Fest and Bonnaroo, but Memphis' Beale Street Music Festival gets very little attention, consider-

ing it offers one of the country's best lineups of old-school blues masters, up-and-coming rockers and gloriously past their prime pop and hip-hop artists.

Sleeping

Chain motels lie off I-40, exit 279, across the river in West Memphis, AR. Look out for the new Guest House at Graceland, a 450-room luxury hotel steps from Graceland due to open in 2016.

Downtown

Talbot Heirs   GUESTHOUSE $$
(Map p372; ☑ 901-527-9772; www.talbothouse. com; 99 S 2nd St; ste $130-195; ❄ @ 🛜) Inconspicuously located on the 2nd floor of a busy downtown street, this cheerful guesthouse is one of Memphis' best kept and most unique secrets. Spacious suites are more like hip studio apartments than hotel rooms, with Asian rugs, funky local artwork and kitchens stocked with (included!) snacks.

Big stars like Harvey Keitel, Matt Damon and John Grisham have nested here as well as Bobby Whitlock of Derek and the Dominos fame, who signed a piano.

Peabody Hotel   HOTEL $$
(Map p372; ☑ 901-529-4000; www.peabodymemphis.com; 149 Union Ave; r from $219; ❄ 🛜 🏊) Memphis' most storied hotel has been catering to a who's who of Southern gentry since the 1860s. The current incarnation, a 13-story Italian Renaissance Revival–style building, dates to the 1920s and remains a social center, with a spa, shops, restaurants,

an atmospheric lobby bar and 464 guest rooms in soothing turquoise tones.

Madison Hotel BOUTIQUE HOTEL **$$$**
(Map p372; ☎901-333-1200; www.madisonhotelmemphis.com; 79 Madison Ave; r from $259; P ❄ @ 📶 🏊) If you're looking for a sleek treat, check into these swanky, music-themed boutique sleeps. The rooftop Sky Terrace ($10 for nonguests) is one of the best places in town to watch a sunset, and stylish rooms have nice touches like hardwood entryways, high ceilings and Italian linens.

★ **James Lee House** B&B **$$$**
(☎901-359-6750; www.jamesleehouse.com; 690 Adams Ave; r $245-450; P ❄ @ 📶) This exquisite Victorian mansion sat abandoned for 56 years in the city's historic Victorian Village on the edge of downtown; $2 million later and the owner's keen eye for detail and design, and it's one of Memphis' most refined sleeps.

Dating in parts to 1848 and 1872, a glorious renovation preserved crown moldings, mirrors, cornices, 14 fireplaces and some hardwood flooring. The five spacious suites are impeccably furnished, and there's a peaceful garden with original fountain.

East of Downtown

Pilgrim House Hostel HOSTEL **$**
(☎901-273-8341; www.pilgrimhouse.org; 1000 S Cooper St; dm/r $25/55; P ❄ @ 📶) Yes, it's in a church. No, no one will try to convert you. Dorms and private rooms are clean and spare. An international crowd plays cards and chats (no alcohol) in open common areas flush with secondhand furniture, and all guests must do a brief daily chore.

South of Downtown

Graceland RV Park & Campground CAMPGROUND **$**
(☎901-396-7125; www.graceland.com/visit/graceland_campground.aspx; 3691 Elvis Presley Blvd; tent sites/cabins from $25/47; P 📶 🏊) Keep Lisa Marie in business when you camp out or sleep in the no-frills log cabins (with shared bathrooms) next to Graceland.

Heartbreak Hotel HOTEL **$$**
(☎901-332-1000; www.graceland.com/visit/heartbreakhotel.aspx; 3677 Elvis Presley Blvd; d from $115; P ❄ @ 📶 🏊) At the end of Lonely St (seriously) across from Graceland, this basic hotel is tarted up with all things Elvis. Ramp up the already-palpable kitsch with one of the themed suites, such as the red-velvet Burnin' Love room. Good value.

Days Inn Graceland MOTEL **$$**
(☎901-346-5500; www.daysinn.com; 3839 Elvis Presley Blvd; r from $100; P ❄ 📶 🏊) With a guitar-shaped pool, gold records and Elvis memorabilia in the lobby and neon Cadillacs on the roof, the Days Inn manages to out-Elvis the neighboring Heartbreak Hotel. Guest rooms themselves are clean but nothing special.

Eating

Locals come to blows over which of the city's chopped-pork sandwiches or dry-rubbed ribs are the best. Barbecue joints are scattered across the city; the ugliest exteriors often yield the tastiest goods. Hip young locals head to the South Main Arts District, Midtown's Cooper-Young or Overton Square neighborhoods, all fashionable evening enclaves.

Downtown

Gus's World Famous Fried Chicken FRIED CHICKEN **$**
(Map p372; 310 S Front St; plates $5.65-9.95; ⏲11am-9pm Sun-Thu, to 10pm Fri & Sat) Fried-chicken connoisseurs across the globe twitch in their sleep at night, dreaming about the gossamer-light fried chicken at this downtown concrete bunker with the fun, neon-lit interior and vintage jukebox. On busy nights, waits can top an hour.

LUNCHBOXeats SOUTHERN **$**
(Map p372; www.lunchboxeats.com; 288 S 4th St; sandwiches $8-11; ⏲10:30am-3pm; 📶) Classic soul food gets a seriously tasty makeover at this creative sandwich shop, resulting in such ridiculousness as chicken and waffle sandwiches (Belgian waffles serve as the slices of 'bread'); crawfish étouffée sloppy Joes; a pork butt, onion and mac 'n' cheese club sandwich and more, served on traditional school lunch trays.

Alcenia's SOUTHERN **$**
(www.alcenias.com; 317 N Main St; mains $9.55-11; ⏲11am-5pm Tue-Fri, 9am-3pm Sat) The only thing sweeter than Alcenia's famous 'Ghetto-Aid' (a diabetes-inducing fruit drink) is owner Betty-Joyce 'BJ' Chester-Tamayo – don't be surprised to receive a kiss on the top of the head as soon as you sit down.

The lunch menu at this funky little gold- and purple-painted cafe rotates daily – look for killer fried chicken and catfish, melt-in-the-mouth spiced cabbage and an exquisite eggy custard pie.

Arcade DINER $

(Map p372; www.arcaderestaurant.com; 540 S Main St; mains $7-10; 7am-3pm Sun-Wed, to 11pm Thu-Sat) Step inside this ultra-retro diner, Memphis' oldest, and wander to the Elvis booth, strategically located near the rear exit. The King used to sit here and eat griddle-fried peanut butter and banana sandwiches and would bolt out the door if fan-instigated pandemonium ensued. Crowds still pack in for sublime sweet-potato pancakes – as fluffy, buttery and addictive as advertised.

The rest of the dishes are standard greasy-spoon fare (don't tell Elvis).

Charlie Vergos' Rendezvous BARBECUE $$

(Map p372; 901-523-2746; www.hogsfly.com; 52 S 2nd St; mains $8-20; 4:30-10:30pm Tue-Thu, 11am-11pm Fri, from 11:30am Sat) Tucked in its own namesake alleyway off Monroe Ave, this subterranean institution sells an astonishing 5 tons of its exquisite dry-rubbed ribs weekly. The ribs don't come with any sauce, but the pork shoulder does, so try a combo and you'll have plenty of sauce to enjoy. The beef brisket is also tremendous. Expect a wait.

Majestic Grille EUROPEAN $$$

(Map p372; 901-522-8555; www.majesticgrille.com; 145 S Main St; mains $16-47; 11am-10pm Mon-Thu, to 11pm Fri & Sat, to 9pm Sun;) Set in an old silent-movie theater near Beale St, with pre-talkie black and whites strobing in the handsome dark-wood dining room, the Majestic serves classic continental fare, from roasted half chicken, to seared tuna and grilled pork tenderloin, and four varieties of hand-cut filet mignon.

East of Downtown

★Payne's Bar-B-Q BARBECUE $

(1762 Lamar Ave; sandwiches $4.50-8.50, plates $7.50-10.50; 11am-5:30pm Tue-Sat) We'd say this converted gas station has the best chopped-pork sandwich in town, but we don't want to have to fight anyone.

Bar DKDC GASTROPUB $

(www.bardkdc.com; 964 S Cooper St; dishes $5-14; 5pm-3am Tue-Sat) Cheap and flavorful global street food is the calling at this ever-evolving Cooper-Young staple. South American *arepas*, Vietnamese *banh-mi* sandwiches, Caribbean jerked fish, Greek *souvlaki* – you get the idea. The space sports an eclectic decor, chalkboard wine list and friendly bartenders.

WORTH A TRIP

JACK DANIEL'S DISTILLERY

The irony of the recently revamped **Jack Daniel's Distillery** (www.jackdaniels.com; 182 Lynchburg Hwy; 9am-4:30pm) FREE being in a 'dry county' is lost on no one – local liquor laws dictate that no hard stuff can be sold within county lines, but they do give out small samples on their free hour-long tours. For $10 you can take a two-hour Distillery Tour (book in advance), where you'll get a more generous sample and a scenic tour of the countryside. This is the oldest registered distillery in the US; the folks at Jack Daniel's have been dripping whiskey through layers of charcoal then aging it in oak barrels since 1866. It's located off Hwy 55 in tiny Lynchburg.

Cozy Corner BARBECUE $

(www.cozycornerbbq.com; 745 N Pkwy; mains $4.95-12.75; 11am-6pm Tue-Sat) Slouch in a torn vinyl booth and devour an entire barbecued Cornish game hen ($11.75), the house specialty at this pug-ugly cult favorite. Ribs and wings are spectacular too, and the fluffy, silken sweet-potato pie is an A-plus specimen of the classic Southern dessert. (Note: during renovations Cozy Corner will be serving across the street at 726 N Pkwy.)

Brother Juniper's BREAKFAST $

(www.brotherjunipers.com; dishes $3.50-13; 6:30am-1pm Tue-Fri, 7am-12:30pm Sat, 8am-1pm Sun) This humble breakfast spot started as a chain out of San Francisco's Haight-Ashbury district to feed the homeless; today, the Memphis location is the last man standing and it's pretty much unanimously voted the best breakfast in town. Think huge portions of omelets, pancakes, breakfast burritos, waffles, biscuits and home fries. A must.

Hog & Hominy SOUTHERN, ITALIAN $$

(901-207-7396; www.hogandhominy.com; 707 W Brookhaven Circle; pizza $14-17; 11am-2pm & 5-10pm Tue-Thu, to late Fri-Sat, 10:30am-10pm Sun;) The chef-driven, Southern-rooted Italian at this Brookhaven Circle hot spot has grabbed the nation's attention, winning best-new-this and best-new-that from everyone from *GQ* to *Food & Wine* magazines. Small plates (often with adventurous ingredients like frog legs, pig ears and beef hearts) and perfect brick-oven pizza are the mainstays; along with seasonal cocktails, craft beers and bocce.

Soul Fish Cafe SEAFOOD **$$**
(www.soulfishcafe.com; 862 S Cooper St; mains $9.50-16; ⏲11am-10pm Mon-Sat, to 9pm Sun) A cute cinderblock cafe in the Cooper-Young neighborhood, known for delectable po'boys, fried fish plates and some rather indulgent cakes.

★**Restaurant Iris** NEW SOUTHERN **$$$**
(☎901-590-2828; www.restaurantiris.com; 2146 Monroe Ave; mains $27-39; ⏲5-10pm Mon-Sat) Chef Kelly English crafts special, avant-garde Southern fusion dishes that delight foodies, hence the James Beard noms. He's got a fried-oyster-stuffed steak, a sublime shrimp and grits, and some scrumptious Brussels sprouts dressed up with smoky bacon and sherry, all served in a refined residential home. Next door he has opened Second Line, a more affordable New Orleans bistro.

Sweet Grass SOUTHERN **$$$**
(☎901-278-0278; www.sweetgrassmemphis.com; 937 S Cooper St; mains $23-32; ⏲5:30pm-late Tue-Sun, 11am-2pm Sun) Contemporary Low-country cuisine (the seafood-heavy cooking of the South Carolina and Georgia coasts) wins raves at this casual Midtown restaurant, split between a more rambunctious bar side and a more refined bistro side (different menus). The shrimp and grits is one of the best you'll try.

Drinking & Nightlife

The East Memphis neighborhoods of Cooper-Young and Overton Square offer the best concentration of hip bars and restaurants. Both are about 4 miles east of downtown. Last call is 3am.

★**Wiseacre Brewing Co** MICROBREWERY
(www.wiseacrebrew.com; 2783 Broad Ave; beers $5, tours $10; ⏲4-9pm Wed-Fri, 1-9pm Sat) Our favorite Memphis taproom is in the warehouse district of Binghampton, 5 miles east of downtown. Sample year-round and seasonal craft brews on the outside deck, which features a wraparound porch hugging two enormous, near 100-year-old cement wheat silos.

Earnestine & Hazel's BAR
(Map p372; www.earnestineandhazelsjukejoint.com; 531 S Main St; ⏲5pm-3am Sun-Fri, from 11am Sat) One of the great dive bars in Memphis has a 2nd floor full of rusty bedsprings and claw-foot tubs, remnants of its brothel past. Its Soul Burger is the stuff of legend. Things heat up after midnight.

Hammer & Ale BEER HALL
(www.hammerandale.com; 921 S Cooper; beers $5; ⏲2-9pm Tue-Thu, 11am-10pm Fri-Sat, noon-3pm Sun; 📶) Hopheads descend on this barn-like Cooper-Young craft beer bar decked out in light cypress woods throughout. Memphis breweries Wiseacre, High Cotton, Memphis Made and Ghost River are represented among the 24 taps of mostly Southern microbrews. Cash *not* accepted!

Entertainment

Beale St is the obvious spot for live blues, rock and jazz. There's no cover at most clubs, or it's only a few bucks, and the bars are open all day, while neighborhood clubs tend to start filling up around 10pm. Check the *Memphis Flyer* (www.memphisflyer.com) online calendar for listings.

Wild Bill's BLUES
(1580 Vollintine Ave; cover Fri-Sat $10; ⏲Wed-Thu noon-9pm, noon-3am Fri-Sat) Don't even think of showing up at this gritty hole-in-the-wall before midnight. Order a 40oz beer and a basket of wings then sit back to watch some of the greatest blues acts in Memphis from 11pm Friday and Saturday only. Expect some stares from the locals; it's worth it for the kick-ass, ultra-authentic jams.

Lafayette's Music Room LIVE MUSIC
(☎901-207-5097; www.lafayettes.com/memphis; 2119 Madison Ave; cover Fri-Sat $5; ⏲11am-10pm Mon-Wed, to midnight Tue & Sun, to 2am Fri-Sat) This newly reopened historic Overton Square music venue once hosted Kiss and Billy Joel in its '70s heyday. The lights were out for 38 years, but it's now one of the most intimate music venues in town.

Hi-Tone Cafe LIVE MUSIC
(www.hitonememphis.com; 412-414 N Cleveland St; cover $5-20) In new digs in Crosstown, this unassuming little dive is one of the city's best places to hear live local bands and touring indie acts.

Young Avenue Deli LIVE MUSIC
(www.youngavenuedeli.com; 2119 Young Ave; ⏲11am-3pm Mon-Sat, from 11:30am Sun) This Midtown favorite has food, pool, occasional live music and a laid-back young crowd.

Rum Boogie BLUES
(Map p372; www.rumboogie.com; 182 Beale St) Huge, popular and loud, this Cajun-themed Beale St club hops every night to the tunes of a tight house blues band.

Shopping

Beale St abounds with cheesy souvenir shops, while Cooper-Young is the place for boutiques and bookshops. The streets around South Main have been branded an arts district.

City & State FOOD & DRINK, ACCESSORIES
(www.cityandstate.us; 2625 Broad Ave; coffee $2.50-4.75; ⏲7am-6pm Mon-Sat, 8am-2pm Sun; 📶) This fabulous new artisan-centric store and coffeehouse in Binghampton stocks exquisitely curated everyday coolness (handcrafted soaps, boutique camping items, waxed canvas lunch bags, ceramic pour-over coffee mugs) and is the only place in Memphis for a barista-level coffee experience.

A Schwab's GIFTS
(Map p372; www.a-schwab.com; 163 Beale St; ⏲noon-7pm Mon-Wed, to 7pm Thu, to 10pm Fri & Sat, 11am-6pm Sun) It has everything from denim shirts to flasks to rubber duckies to fine hats to overalls. But the real attractions are the antiques upstairs. Think vintage scales and irons, hat stretchers and a cast-iron anchor of a cash register.

Lanksy Brothers CLOTHING
(Map p372; ☎901-425-3960; www.lanskybros.com; 126 Beale St; ⏲9am-6pm Sun-Wed, to 9pm Thu-Sat) The 'Clothier to the King,' this mid-century men's shop once outfitted Elvis with his two-tone shirts. Today it has a retro line of menswear (including blue suede shoes!) plus gifts and women's clothes. It has relocated in its original location on Beale St (in addition to its store in the Peabody Hotel).

Information

Commercial Appeal (www.commercialappeal.com) Daily newspaper with local entertainment listings.

Main Post Office (Map p372; www.usps.com; 555 S 3rd St; ⏲9:30am-6pm Mon-Fri) Downtown postal services.

Memphis Flyer (www.memphisflyer.com) Free weekly distributed on Wednesday; has entertainment listings.

Memphis Visitor's Center (☎888-633-9099; www.memphistravel.com; 3205 Elvis Presley Blvd; ⏲9am-6pm Apr-Sep, to 5pm Oct-Mar, to 4pm Sun Nov-Feb) City information center near exit for Graceland.

Police Station (☎901-636-4099; www.memphispolice.org; 545 S Main St) Terribly hard to find. It's above Amtrak's Central Station.

Regional Medical Center at Memphis (☎901-545-7100; www.the-med.org; 877 Jefferson Ave) Has the only level-one trauma center in the region.

Tennessee State Visitor Center (☎901-543-6757; www.tnvacation.com; 119 N Riverside Dr; ⏲7am-11pm) Brochures for the whole state.

Getting There & Around

Memphis International Airport (MEM; ☎901-922-8000; www.memphisairport.org; 2491 Winchester Rd) is 12 miles southeast of downtown via I-55; taxis to Downtown cost about $30. **Memphis Area Transit Authority** (MATA; www.matatransit.com; 444 N Main St; fares $1.75) operates local buses; buses 2 and 20 go to the airport.

MATA's vintage trolleys ($1, every 12 minutes) ply Main St and Front St downtown. **Greyhound** (☎901-395-8770; www.greyhound.com; 3033 Airways Blvd) is located at the MATA's Airways Transit Center near Memphis International Airport. Amtrak's **Central Station** (www.amtrak.com; 545 S Main St) is right downtown.

Shiloh National Military Park

'No soldier who took part in the two day Battle at Shiloh ever spoiled for a fight again,' said one veteran of the bloody 1862 clash, which took place among these lovely fields and forests. Ulysses S Grant, then a major general, led the Army of Tennessee. After a vicious Confederate assault on the first day that took Grant by surprise, his creative maneuver on the second day held Pittsburgh Landing, and turned the Confederates back. During the fight over 3500 soldiers died and nearly 24,000 were wounded. A relative unknown at the beginning of the war, Grant went on to lead the Union to victory and eventually became the 18th president of the United States.

Vast **Shiloh National Military Park** (☎731-689-5696; www.nps.gov/shil; 1055 Pittsburg Landing Rd; ⏲park dawn-dusk, visitor center 8am-5pm) FREE is located just north of the Mississippi border near the town of Crump, TN, and can only be seen by car. Sights include the Shiloh National Cemetery, and an overlook of the Cumberland River where Union reinforcement troops arrived by ship. The visitor center offers maps, shows a video about the battle, and sells an audio driving tour.

Nashville

Imagine you're an aspiring country singer arriving in downtown Nashville after days of hitchhiking, with nothing but your battered guitar on your back. Gaze up at the neon lights of Lower Broadway, take a deep breath of smoky, beer-perfumed air, feel the boot-stompin' rumble from deep inside the crowded honky-tonks, and say to yourself: 'I've made it.'

For country-music fans and wannabe songwriters all over the world, a trip to Nashville is the ultimate pilgrimage. Since the 1920s the city has been attracting musicians who have taken the country genre from the 'hillbilly music' of the early 20th century to the slick 'Nashville sound' of the 1960s to the punk-tinged alt-country of the 1990s.

Its many musical attractions range from the Country Music Hall of Fame to the revered Grand Ole Opry to Jack White's niche of a record label. It also has a lively university community, some excellent down-home grub and some seriously kitschy souvenirs.

Sights

Downtown

The historic **2nd Ave N** business area was the center of the cotton trade in the 1870s and 1880s, when most of the Victorian warehouses were built; note the cast-iron and masonry facades. Today it's the heart of the **District**, with shops, restaurants, underground saloons and nightclubs. It's a bit like the French Quarter meets Hollywood Boulevard drenched in bourbon and country twang. South of Lower Broadway is the **SoBro** district, revitalized by the opening of the $635-million **Music City Center** (www.nashvillemusiccitycenter.com; Broadway St, btwn 5th & 8th Aves) convention center, restaurants, bars and hotels. Two blocks west of 2nd Ave N, **Printers Alley** is a narrow cobblestoned lane known for its nightlife since the 1940s. Along the Cumberland River, **Riverfront Park** is a landscaped promenade that's being redeveloped; **West Riverfront Park**, an 11-acre civic park will include over 1 mile of multi-use greenway trails, Nashville's first downtown dog park, ornamental gardens, a 1.5-acre event lawn called The Green and an amphitheater.

★Country Music Hall of Fame & Museum MUSEUM
(www.countrymusichalloffame.com; 222 5th Ave S; adult/child $25/15, with audio tour $27/18, with Studio B 1hr tour $40/30; ⏲9am-5pm) Following a $100 million expansion in 2014, this monumental museum, reflecting the near-biblical importance of country music to Nashville's soul, is a must-see, whether you're a country music fan or not. Gaze at Carl Perkins' blue suede shoes, Elvis' gold Cadillac (actually white) and gold piano (actually gold), and Hank Williams' western-cut suit with musical note appliqués.

Highlights of the ambitious 210,000-sq-ft expansion include the 800-seat CMA Theater, the Taylor Swift Education Center and the relocation of the legendary letterpress operation of Hatch Show Print (p000). Written exhibits trace country's roots, computer touch screens access recordings and photos from the enormous archives, and the fact- and music-filled audio tour is narrated by contemporary stars.

Ryman Auditorium HISTORIC BUILDING
(www.ryman.com; 116 5th Ave N; adult/child self-guided tours $15/10, backstage tours $20/15; ⏲9am-4pm) The so-called 'Mother Church of Country Music' has hosted a laundry list of performers, from Martha Graham to Elvis, and Katherine Hepburn to Bob Dylan. The soaring brick tabernacle (1892) was built by wealthy riverboat captain Thomas Ryman to house religious revivals, and watching a show from one of its 2000 seats can still be described as a spiritual experience.

The *Grand Ole Opry* (p000) took place here for 31 years until it moved out to the Opryland complex in Music Valley in 1974. Today the *Opry* returns to the Ryman during winter. In 2015 a $14 million visitor experience renovation installed a new event space, cafe and bars.

Johnny Cash Museum & Store MUSEUM
(www.johnnycashmuseum.com; 119 3rd Ave; adult/child $16/12; ⏲8am-7pm) The new museum dedicated to 'The Man in Black' is smallish but houses the most comprehensive collection of Johnny Cash artifacts and memorabilia in the world, officially endorsed by the Cash family.

Tennessee State Museum MUSEUM
(www.tnmuseum.org; 5th Ave, btwn Union & Deaderick Sts; 10am-5pm Tue-Sat, 1-5pm Sun;) FREE For history buffs, this engaging but not-flashy museum on the ground floor of a massive office tower provides a worthy look at the state's past, with Native American handicrafts, a life-size log cabin and quirky historical artifacts such as President Andrew Jackson's inaugural hat.

Frist Center for the Visual Arts GALLERY
(www.fristcenter.org; 919 Broadway; adult/child $12/free; 10am-5:30pm Mon-Wed & Sat, to 9pm Thu & Fri, 1-5pm Sun) A top-notch post office turned art museum and complex hosting traveling exhibitions of everything from American folk art to Picasso.

Tennessee State Capitol HISTORIC BUILDING
(www.capitol.tn.gov; Charlotte Ave; tours 9am-4pm Mon-Fri) FREE This 1845–59 Greek Revival building was built from local limestone and marble by slaves and prison inmates working alongside European artisans. Around back, steep stairs lead down to the **Tennessee Bicentennial Mall**, whose outdoor walls are covered with historical facts about Tennessee's history, and the wonderful daily **Farmers Market**.

Free tours leave from the Information Desk on the 1st floor of the Capitol every hour on the hour.

West End

Along West End Ave, starting at 21st Ave, sits prestigious **Vanderbilt University**, founded in 1883 by railway magnate Cornelius Vanderbilt. The 330-acre campus buzzes with some 12,000 students, and student culture influences much of Midtown's vibe.

Parthenon PARK, GALLERY
(www.parthenon.org; 2600 West End Ave; adult/child $6/4; 9am-4:30pm Tue-Sat, 12:30-4:30pm Sun) Yes, that is indeed a reproduction Athenian Parthenon sitting in **Centennial Park**. Originally built in 1897 for Tennessee's Centennial Exposition and rebuilt in 1930 due to popular demand, the full-scale plaster copy of the 438 BC original now houses an art museum with a collection of American paintings and a 42ft statue of the Greek goddess Athena.

Music Row AREA
(Music Sq West & Music Sq East) Just west of downtown, sections of 16th and 17th Aves, called Music Sq West and Music Sq East, are home to the production companies, record labels, agents, managers and promoters who run Nashville's country-music industry, including the famed RCA Studio B.

Historic RCA Studio B LANDMARK
(www.countrymusichalloffame.org; 1611 Roy Acuff Pl; tours adult/child $40/30) One of Music Row's most historic studios, this is where Elvis, the Everly Brothers and Dolly Parton all recorded numerous hits. It's marked by the Heartbreak Hotel guitar sculpture emblazoned with a pelvis-jutting image of the King. You can tour the studio via the Country Music Hall of Fame's Studio B Tour, included with their Platinum Package.

Music Valley

This suburban tourist zone is about 10 miles northeast of downtown at Hwy 155/Briley Pkwy, exits 11 and 12B, and reachable by bus.

Grand Ole Opry House MUSEUM
(615-871-6779; www.opry.com; 2802 Opryland Dr; tours adult/child $22/17; tours 9am-4pm) This unassuming modern brick building seats 4400 for the Grand Ole Opry (p386) on Tuesday, Friday and Saturday from March to November and Wednesday from June to August. Guided backstage tours are offered every 15 minutes daily from October to March.

Willie Nelson Museum MUSEUM
(www.willienelsongeneralstore.com; 2613 McGavock Pike; admission $8; 8:30am-9pm) 'Outlaw Country' star Willie Nelson sold all his worldly goods to pay off $16.7 million in tax debt in the early 1990s. You can see them at this quirky museum not far from the Grand Ole Opry.

Tours

★**NashTrash** BUS TOUR
(615-226-7300; www.nashtrash.com; 722 Harrison St; tours $32-35) The big-haired 'Jugg Sisters' lead a campy frolic through the risqué side of Nashville history while guests sip BYO booze on the big pink bus. Buy in advance: tours can sell out *months* in advance. Meet the bus at the south end of the Nashville Farmers Market.

Tommy's Tours BUS TOUR
(615-335-2863; www.tommystours.com; 2120 Lebanon Pike; tours $35) Wisecracking local Tommy Garmon leads highly entertaining three-hour tours of country-music sights.

Nashville

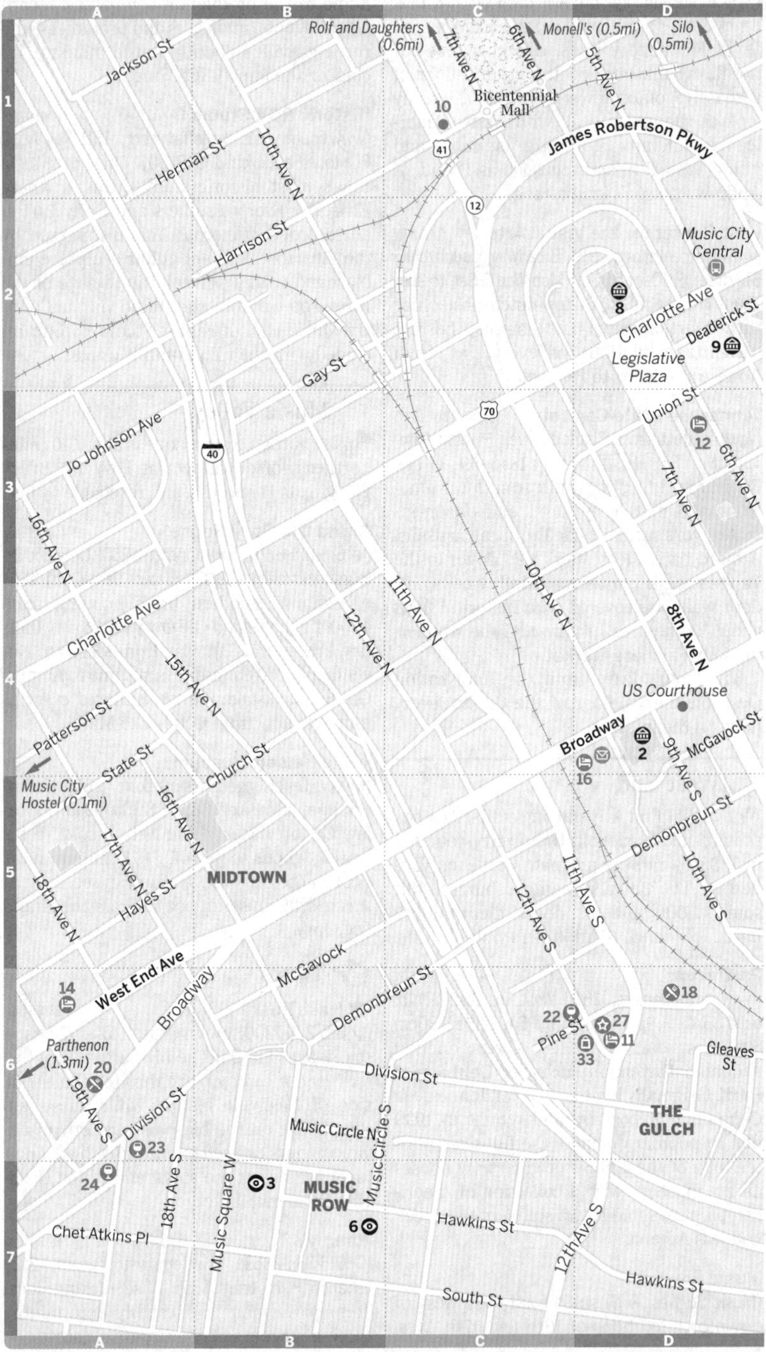

A
B
C
D
1
2
3
4
5
6
7
Rolf and Daughters (0.6mi)
Monell's (0.5mi)
Silo (0.5mi)
Jackson St
Herman St
10th Ave N
7th Ave N
6th Ave N
5th Ave N
Bicentennial Mall
10
41
James Robertson Pkwy
12
Harrison St
Music City Central
8
Charlotte Ave
Deaderick St
9
Legislative Plaza
Gay St
70
Union St
12
Jo Johnson Ave
40
6th Ave N
7th Ave N
16th Ave N
10th Ave N
11th Ave N
12th Ave N
8th Ave N
Charlotte Ave
15th Ave N
US Courthouse
Patterson St
Broadway
2
McGavock St
State St
Church St
16
9th Ave S
Music City Hostel (0.1mi)
16th Ave N
Demonbreun St
17th Ave N
MIDTOWN
10th Ave S
18th Ave N
Hayes St
12th Ave S
11th Ave S
West End Ave
McGavock
14
Broadway
Demonbreun St
18
22
27
Pine St
11
33
Parthenon (1.3mi)
20
Gleaves St
Division St
19th Ave S
Division St
THE GULCH
Music Circle N
Music Circle S
23
24
18th Ave S
Music Square W
3
MUSIC ROW
6
Hawkins St
12th Ave S
Chet Atkins Pl
Hawkins St
South St

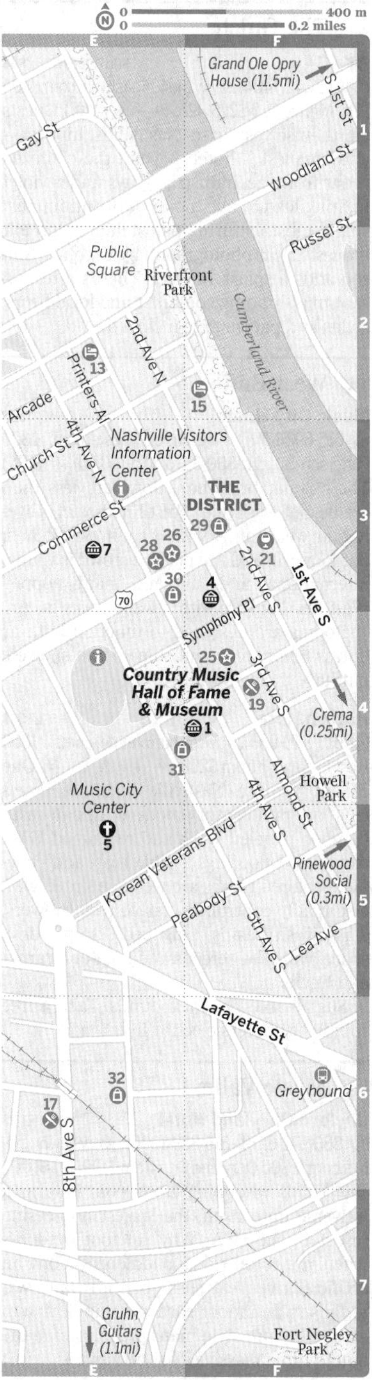

Nashville

Top Sights

1 Country Music Hall of Fame & Museum F4

Sights

2 Frist Center for the Visual Arts D4
3 Historic RCA Studio B B7
4 Johnny Cash Museum & Store F3
5 Music City Center E5
6 Music Row B7
7 Ryman Auditorium E3
8 Tennessee State Capitol D2
9 Tennessee State Museum D2

Activities, Courses & Tours

10 NashTrash C1

Sleeping

11 404 .... D6
12 Hermitage Hotel D3
13 Hotel Indigo E2
14 Hutton Hotel A6
15 Nashville Downtown Hostel F2
16 Union Station Hotel D4

Eating

17 Arnold's E6
18 Biscuit Love D6
19 Etch F4
20 Hattie B's A6

Drinking & Nightlife

21 Acme Feed & Seed F3
22 Hops + Craft C6
23 Patterson House A6
24 Soulshine A7

Entertainment

25 Nashville Symphony F4
26 Robert's Western World E3
Ryman Auditorium .... (see 7)
27 Station Inn D6
28 Tootsie's Orchid Lounge E3

Shopping

29 Boot Country F3
30 Ernest Tubb E3
31 Hatch Show Print E4
32 Third Man Records E6
33 Two Old Hippies D6

Festivals & Events

CMA Music Festival MUSIC
(www.cmafest.com; Jun) Draws tens of thousands of country-music fans to town.

Tennessee State Fair FAIR
(www.tnstatefair.org; Sep) Nine days of racing pigs, mule-pulls and cake bake-offs.

Sleeping

Bargain-bin chain motels cluster on all sides of downtown, along I-40 and I-65. Music Valley has a glut of family-friendly midrange chains.

Downtown

★Nashville Downtown Hostel HOSTEL $

(☎615-497-1208; www.nashvillehostel.com; 177 1st Ave N; dm $35-40, r $128-140; P) Well located and up-to-the-minute in style and function. The common space in the basement, with its rather regal exposed stone walls and beamed rafters, is your all-hours mingle den. Dorm rooms are on the 3rd and 4th floors, and have lovely wood floors, exposed timber columns, silver-beamed ceilings and four, six or eight bunks to a room.

Hotel Indigo BOUTIQUE HOTEL $$

(☎615-891-6000; www.hotelindigo.com; 301 Union St; r from $199; P ⊖ ❄ @ ☜) Part of a boutique international chain, the Indigo has a fun, pop-art look, with 160 rooms (30 of which are brand new). Avoid the original (but tacky) Terrazo floor rooms in favor of those spacious King Rooms, with brand-new hardwood floors, high ceilings, flat-screens, leather headboards and office chairs.

Union Station Hotel HOTEL $$$

(☎615-726-1001; www.unionstationhotelnashville.com; 1001 Broadway; r from $259; P ❄ ☜) This soaring Romanesque gray stone castle was Nashville's train station back in the days when rail travel was a grand affair; today it's downtown's most iconic hotel. The vaulted lobby is dressed in peach and gold with inlaid marble floors and a stained-glass ceiling.

Rooms are tastefully modern, with flat-screen TVs and deep soaking tubs, and are set for an upcoming renovation.

Hermitage Hotel HOTEL $$$

(☎888-888-9414, 615-244-3121; www.thehermitagehotel.com; 231 6th Ave N; r from $399; P ❄ ☜) Nashville's first million-dollar hotel was a hit with the socialites when it opened in 1910. The beaux-arts lobby feels like a czar's palace, every surface covered in rich tapestries and ornate carvings. The original art-deco men's room, dating to the 1930s, is worth a pop-in, as is the Capitol Grille restaurant, which sources from its own farm.

Rooms are upscale, with plush, four-poster beds, marble baths with soaking tubs, and mahogany furniture (ask for those ending in -08-14 for Capitol views).

The Gulch

★404 BOUTIQUE HOTEL $$$

(☎615-242-7404; www.the404nashville.com; 404 12th Avenue S; r $275-425; P ⊖ ❄ @ ☜) Guests let themselves in to Nashville's hippest – and smallest – hotel. Beyond the ebonized cedar frontage, industrial grays under violet lighting lead to five rooms in the minimalist space, most featuring painstakingly hip loft spaces. Local photography by Caroline Allison adds a splash of color. There's a restaurant in a shipping container and local beers, sodas and parking are included.

West End

Music City Hostel HOSTEL $

(☎615-692-1277; www.musiccityhostel.com; 1809 Patterson St; dm $30-35, d $85-100; P ❄ @ ☜) These squat brick bungalows are less than scenic, but Nashville's West End hostel is lively and welcoming, with a common kitchen, outdoor grill and fire pit. The crowd is young, international and fun, and many hoppin' West End bars are within walking distance.

Rooms are designed to function both as dorms or privates and some share showers but have their own toilet.

Hutton Hotel HOTEL $$$

(☎615-340-9333; www.huttonhotel.com; 1808 West End Ave; r from $259; P ⊖ ❄ @ ☜) One of our favorite Nashville boutique hotels riffs on mid-century-modern design with bamboo-paneled walls and reclaimed WWI barn wood flooring. Sizable rust- and chocolate-colored rooms are well appointed with electrically controlled marble rain showers, glass wash basins, king beds, ample desk space, wide flat-screens and high-end carpet and linens.

Sustainable luxury abounds. Take a free spin in the hotel's electric Tesla!

Music Valley

Gaylord Opryland Hotel RESORT $$

(☎866-972-6779, 615-889-1000; www.gaylordhotels.com; 2800 Opryland Dr; r from $199; P ❄ @ ☜ ≋) This whopping 2882-room hotel is a universe unto itself, the largest non-casino resort in the USA. Why set foot outdoors when you could ride a paddleboat along an artificial river, eat sushi beneath faux waterfalls in an indoor garden or sip Scotch in an antebellum-style mansion, all *inside* the hotel's three massive glass atriums.

Eating

The classic Nashville meal is the 'meat-and-three' – a heaping portion of meat, served with your choice of three home-style sides. Gentrifying Germantown offers a handful of cafes and restaurants, including two standouts. Five Points in East Nashville is the epicenter of Nashville's hipster scene and is covered with cafes, restaurants and shops, with most of the action in the area of Woodlawn St between 10th and 11th.

Downtown & Germantown

Arnold's SOUTHERN $

(www.arnoldscountrykitchen.com; 605 8th Ave S; meals $9-10; 10:30am-2:45pm Mon-Fri) Grab a tray and line up with college students, garbage collectors and country-music stars at Arnold's, king of the meat-and-three. Slabs of drippy roast beef are the house specialty, along with fried green tomatoes, cornbread two ways, and big gooey wedges of chocolate meringue pie.

★Rolf and Daughters MODERN EUROPEAN $$

(615-866-9897; www.rolfanddaughters.com; 700 Taylor St; mains $17-26; 5:30-10pm;) The epicenter of Germantown's foodie revival is this stunning kitchen run by Belgian chef Philip Krajeck, whose earthy pastas, rustic sauces and seasonal-changing 'modern peasant food' will stand your taste buds on end as if to say, 'What was *that*?'

Standouts of the European-inspired, locally sourced fare – it's a feeding frenzy here as the menu fluctuates with the arrival of the season's first crops – include *garganelli verde* (green from fresh spinach) and a devastatingly good pastured chicken with preserved lemon and garlic confit. Reservations? Certainly. But there's a communal table and bar for walk-ins as well.

Silo NEW SOUTHERN $$

(615-750-2912; www.silotn.com; 1222 4th Ave N; mains $17-26; 5-11pm Tue-Sun, bar from 4pm) This Southern-influenced farm-to-table bistro in Germantown is easy on the eyes: Amish-crafted carpentry and pendant lighting by artist John Beck. The food follows suit. Though the menu changes faster than your Twitter feed, dishes like braised rabbit in housemade pasta and pan-seared Gulf corvina pop with savory and rich deliciousness.

Monell's SOUTHERN $$

(615-248-4747; www.monellstn.com; 1235 6th Ave N; all you can eat $13-18; 10:30am-2pm Mon, 8:30am-4pm & 5-8:30pm Tue-Fri, 8:30am-8:30pm Sat, 8:30am-4pm Sun) In an old brick house just north of the District, Monell's is beloved for down-home Southern food served family style. This is not just a meal, it's an experience, as platter after platter of skillet-fried chicken, pulled pork, corn pudding, baked apples, mac and cheese and mashed potatoes keep coming...and coming. Clear your afternoon schedule!

★Etch MODERN AMERICAN $$$

(615-522-0685; www.etchrestaurant.com; 303 Demonbreun St; dinner mains $21-38; 11am-2pm & 5-10pm Mon-Thu, 11am-2pm & 5-10:30pm Fri, 5-10:30pm Sat;) Well-known Nashville chef Deb Paquette's Etch serves some of Nashville's most inventive cuisine – comfort food whose flavors and textures have been manipulated into tantalizing combinations that surpass expectations in every bite. Octopus and shrimp bruschetta, roasted cauliflower with truffled pea pesto, cocoa-chili-spiced venison, grilled filet with sourdough baked potato bread pudding – all masterpieces. Reservations essential.

The Gulch

★Biscuit Love BREAKFAST $

(www.biscuitlovebrunch.com; 316 11th Ave; biscuits $10-14; 7am-3pm;) Championing everything that is wrong about American breakfast, Biscuit Love started life as a food truck in 2012. Its gluttonous gourmet takes on the Southern biscuit and gravy experience took off, allowing it to graduate to this supremely cool brick-and-mortar location in the Gulch.

Look no further than the menu's first item, the East Nasty – a perfectly fluffy buttermilk biscuit smothered by an insanely good piece of fried chicken thigh, aged chedder and perfect sausage gravy. If that's wrong, we don't wanna be right!

West End & Midtown

★Hattie B's SOUTHERN $

(www.hattieb.com; 112 19th Ave S; quarter/half plates from $8.50/12; 11am-10pm Mon-Thu, to midnight Fri-Sat, to 4pm Sun) Hattie's may be the hipsterized, social-media savvy yin to Prince's Hot Chicken's off-the-grid yang, but if this isn't Nashville's best cayenne-rubbed 'hot' fried chicken, our name is mud. Perfectly moist, high-quality bird comes devilishly fried to levels that top out at 'Shut

WORTH A TRIP

PLANTATIONS NEAR NASHVILLE

Hermitage (☎615-889-2941; www.thehermitage.com; 4580 Rachel's Lane; adult/child $20/14, with multimedia player $28/18; ⏰8:30am-5pm mid-Mar–mid-Oct 15, 9am-4:30pm mid-Oct–mid-Mar) The former home of seventh president Andrew Jackson lies 15 miles east of downtown Nashville. The 1150-acre plantation is a peek into what life was like for a Mid-South gentleman farmer in the 19th century. Tour the Federal-style brick mansion, now a furnished house museum with costumed interpreters, and see Jackson's original 1804 log cabin and the old slave quarters (Jackson was a lifelong supporter of slavery, at times owning up to 100 slaves; a special exhibit tells their stories).

Belle Meade Plantation (☎615-356-0501; www.bellemeadeplantation.com; 5025 Harding Pike; adult/student 13-18yr/child under 13yr $18/12/10; ⏰9am-5pm) The Harding-Jackson family began raising thoroughbreds here (6 miles west of Nashville) in the early 1800s. Several Kentucky Derby winners have been descendants of Belle Meade's studly sire, Bonnie Scotland, who died in 1880. Yes, Bonnie can be a boy's name! The 1853 mansion is open to visitors, as are various interesting outbuildings, including a model slave cabin, and wine tasting is available on-site, too.

the Cluck Up!' hot and they mean business ('Damn Hot' was our limit). Get in line.

Fido CAFE $
(www.fidocafe.com; 1812 21st S; mains $5-11; ⏰7am-11pm; 📶) A Hillsboro institution, known for excellent coffees and breakfasts, as well as an affordable menu of salads and sandwiches. It's generally packed, yet spacious enough to accommodate the rather appealing crowd.

Pancake Pantry BREAKFAST $
(www.pancakepantry.com; 1796 21st Ave S; mains $6.50-10; ⏰6am-3pm Mon-Fri, to 4pm Sat-Sun) For 50-plus years, crowds have been lining up around the block for tall stacks of pancakes done up every which way at this iconic breakfast joint. Honestly, the pancakes underwhelmed us – until we doused them in that cinnamon cream syrup. Paradise found!

East Nashville

★The Pharmacy BURGERS, BEER GARDEN $
(www.thepharmacynashville.com; 731 Mcferrin Ave; burgers $8-11; ⏰11am-10pm Sun-Thu, to 11pm Fri-Sat; 📶) Prepare to go to war for a table at this burger bar, constantly voted Nashville's best, be it at the welcoming communal table, bar or spectacular backyard beer garden. Tattooed staff sling burgers, sausages and old-school sides (tater tots!) washed back with specialty beers and hand-mixed old fashioned sodas.

Pied Piper Creamery ICE CREAM $
(www.thepiedpipercreamery.com; 114 S 11th St; scoops $3.75; ⏰noon-9pm Sun-Thu, to 10pm Fri & Sat) Thicker, smoother and more packed with goodness than any other ice-cream shop in town. How to choose: Toffee Loaded Coffee? Chocolate with Cinnamon and Cayenne Pepper? Trailer Trash, with Oreo, Reese's Pieces, Snickers, Butterfinger, Twix *and* Nestlé's Crunch? It's in Five Points.

I Dream of Weenie HOT DOGS $
(www.facebook.com/IDreamofWeenie; 113 S 11th St; hot dogs $3-5; ⏰11am-4pm Mon-Thu, to 6pm Fri, 10:30am-6pm Sat, to 4pm Sun) Quick and easy, this VW bus turned hot-dog stand in Five Points slings beef, turkey or vegetarian tubular products drowned in indulgent toppings (hint: pimiento cheese with chili!).

Greater Nashville

Prince's Hot Chicken FRIED CHICKEN $
(123 Ewing Dr; quarter/half/whole chicken $6/11/22; ⏰11:30-10pm Tue-Thu, to 4am Fri-Sat; Ⓟ) Tiny, faded, family-owned Prince's serves Nashville's most legendary 'hot chicken.' It's set in a gritty, northside strip mall and attracts everyone from hipsters to frat boys to entire immigrant families to local heads to hillbillies.

Fried up mild (total lie), medium (what a joke), hot (verging on insanity), Xhot (extreme masochism) and XXXHot (suicide), its chicken will burn a hole in your stomach, and take root in your soul. Cash only.

King Market Cafe LAOTIAN, THAI $
(www.kingmarkettn.com; 300 Church St, Antioch Pike; dishes $6.50-11.50; ⏰9am-7:30pm) An authentic Southeast Asian cafe set inside

an Asian grocer in the Antioch Pike area – an east Nashville suburb where this city suddenly seems much less homogeneous. It does noodle dishes, soups, curries and stir-fries, a Thai-style country pork sausage, deep-fried mackerel, and adventurous eats like fried pork intestine. Worth a trip.

Drinking & Nightlife

Nashville has the nightlife of a city three times its size, and you'll be hard-pressed to find a place that doesn't have live music. College students, bachelor-party-goers, Danish backpackers and conventioneers all rock out downtown, where neon-lit Broadway looks like a country-fried Las Vegas. Bars and venues in neighborhoods such as East Nashville, Hillsboro Village, Germantown, the Gulch, 12 South and SoBro tend to attract more locals, with many places clustered near Vanderbilt University.

★Butchertown Hall BEER HALL

(www.butchertownhall.com; 1416 Fourth Ave N; beer $5-8; ⏲11am-late Mon-Fri, from 10am Sat-Sun; 📶) This hipster hangout in Germantown plays to the neighborhood's historical roots – it's the first beer hall in the neighborhood since 1909. The 2200-sq-ft space is gorgeous: vaulted ceilings, oversized subway tiles and stacked stone and chopped wood strategically used as earthy-accented space dividers. There are 31 taps specializing in local and rarer German options as well as cask-conditioned English ales.

The Latin-leaning, smoke-and-brimstone-heavy German-Southern comfort food is not to be missed, either.

Patterson House COCKTAIL BAR

(www.thepattersonnashville.com; 1711 Division St; cocktails $12-14; ⏲5pm-3am; 📶) Without a doubt Nashville's best spot for artisanal cocktails, so much so there is often a wait (yes, for a drink at a bar!). There is no service without a seat, either at the 30-stool bar or in the surrounding banquets. Meticulous Prohibition-era mixology is sipped amid vintage chandeliers and checks are delivered inside novels.

Acme Feed & Seed BAR, LIVE MUSIC

(www.theacmenashville.com; 101 Broadway; ⏲11am-late Mon-Fri, from 10am Sat-Sun; 📶) This ambitious, four-floor takeover of an old 1875 farm supply warehouse has finally given Nashvillians a reason to go downtown even when family is *not* visiting. The 1st floor is devoted to lightning-fast pub grub, craft beers and live music that's defiantly un-country most nights (Southern rock, indie, roots etc).

Head up a level for a casual cocktail lounge complete with rescued furniture, vintage pinball, walls made from old printing plates and a cornucopia of music memorabilia. And then there's the open-air rooftop, with unrivaled views over the Cumberland River and straight down the belly of Broadway.

Pinewood Social LOUNGE

(☎615-751-8111; www.pinewoodsocial.com; 33 Peabody St; ⏲7am-1am Mon-Fri, 9am-1am Sat-Sun) This all-in-one off-downtown hipster retreat aims to relieve you of your money from sunrise to sundown. Inside a stylish former trolley barn, there's a Crema coffeehouse, restaurant, bar and six vintage reclaimed wooden bowling lanes ($40 per hour). Outside is an artificial lawn and pool and bocce ball.

Hops + Craft BAR

(www.hopscrafts.com; 319 12th Ave S; beer $4.75-6.60; ⏲2-11pm Mon-Thu, noon-midnight Fri, from 11am Sat, noon-11pm Sun; 📶) You won't be raving about the ambiance on any postcards home, but this small (and devoted!) bar in the Gulch is Nashville's best for diving head-first into the local craft beer scene. Knowledgeable and friendly bartenders offer tastings on any number of their 36 draft offerings.

No 308 COCKTAIL BAR

(www.bar308.com; 407 Gallatan Ave; cocktails $11-14; ⏲5pm-3am) Cool kids gather at this unassuming East Nashville cocktail bar to knock back adult shots inspired by Beat novelists chosen from worn leather-bound menus. Pick your poison amid low coffee tables, taxidermy, black banquets and a long bar featuring lacquered pages of classic literature.

★Barista Parlor COFFEE

(www.baristaparlor.com; 519 Gallatin Ave; coffee $5-6; ⏲7am-8pm Mon-Fri, 8am-8pm Sat-Sun) Unrepentantly hipster coffee joint housed inside a huge former transmission shop in East Nashville. Some of America's best beans are put through methods all but fiendish coffee nerds will need defined (V60, Kone, Chemex etc). The lone turntable preserving vinyl is a mere afterthought. Prepare to wait – the art shall not be compromised.

The espresso comes courtesy of the famed, rare (and hand-built!) $18,000 Slayer machine.

Crema COFFEE
(www.crema-coffee.com; 15 Hermitage Ave; coffee $2.75-5; ⏲7am-7pm Mon-Fri, 8am-6pm Sat, 9am-4pm Sun; 📶) This hard-core, downtown-adjacent coffeehouse serves the best brew within relative walking distance of Broadway.

Soulshine PUB
(www.soulshinepizza.com; 1907 Division St; ⏲11am-10pm Sun-Wed, to midnight Thu-Sat) A two-story, concrete-floor, brickhouse pub and pizzeria in Midtown that attracts more jam-band-appreciating, middle-of-the-road types. Bands rock the wide rooftop patio most nights.

☆ Entertainment

Nashville's opportunities for hearing live music are unparalleled. As well as the big venues, many talented country, folk, bluegrass, Southern-rock and blues performers play smoky honky-tonks, college bars, coffee shops and organic cafes for tips. Cover charges are rare.

★Station Inn LIVE MUSIC
(☎615-255-3307; www.stationinn.com; 402 12th Ave S; ⏲open mike 7pm, live bands 9pm) Sit at one of the small cocktail tables, squeezed together on the worn-wood floor in this beer-only dive, illuminated with stage lights and neon signs, and behold the lightning fingers of bluegrass savants. We are talking stand-up bass, banjo, mandolin, fiddle and a modicum of yodeling.

Famed duo Doyle and Debbie, a cult-hit parody of a washed-up country-music duo, perform most Tuesdays ($20; reservations essential on ☎615-999-9244).

Bluebird Cafe CLUB
(☎615-383-1461; www.bluebirdcafe.com; 4104 Hillsboro Rd; cover free-$20; ⏲shows 6:30pm & 9:30pm) It's in a strip mall in suburban South Nashville, but don't let that fool you: some of the best original singer-songwriters in country music have graced this tiny stage. Steve Earle, Emmylou Harris and the Cowboy Junkies have all played the Bluebird, which is the setting for the popular television series, *Nashville*. Try your luck at Monday open-mike nights.

It's first-come, first-served seating, and it's best to show up at least an hour before the show begins. No talking during the show or you'll get bounced.

Tootsie's Orchid Lounge HONKY-TONK
(☎615-726-7937; www.tootsies.net; 422 Broadway; ⏲10am-late) FREE The most venerated of the downtown honky-tonks, Tootsie's is a blessed dive oozing boot-stomping, hillbilly, beer-soaked grace. In the 1960s club owner and den mother 'Tootsie' Bess nurtured Willie Nelson, Kris Kristofferson and Waylon Jennings on the come up. A new rooftop and stage, added in 2014, is one of Broadway's best parties-with-views.

Grand Ole Opry MUSICAL THEATER
(☎615-871-6779; www.opry.com; 2802 Opryland Dr; tickets $40-70) Though you'll find a variety of country shows throughout the week, the performance to see is the *Grand Ole Opry*, a lavish tribute to classic Nashville country music, every Tuesday, Friday and Saturday night. Shows return to the Ryman from November to June.

Robert's Western World HONKY-TONK
(www.robertswesternworld.com; 416 Broadway; ⏲11am-2am) FREE Buy a pair of boots, a beer or a burger at Robert's, a longtime favorite on the strip. Music starts at 11am and goes all night; Brazilbilly, the house band, rocks it after 10pm on weekends. All ages are welcome before 6pm, afterward it's strictly 21 and up.

Ryman Auditorium CONCERT VENUE
(☎615-889-3060; www.ryman.com; 116 5th Ave N) The Ryman's excellent acoustics, historic charm and large seating capacity have kept it the premier venue in town, with big names frequently passing through. The *Opry* returns for winter runs.

Nashville Symphony SYMPHONY
(☎615-687-6400; www.nashvillesymphony.org; 1 Symphony Pl) Hosts maestros, the local symphony and major pop stars from Randy Travis to Smokey Robinson, in the shiny new, yet beautifully antiquated, Schermerhorn Symphony Hall.

Shopping

Lower Broadway has tons of record shops, boot stores and souvenir stalls. The 12th Ave South neighborhood is the spot for ultra-trendy boutiques and vintage stores.

★Hatch Show Print ART, SOUVENIRS
(www.hatchshowprint.com; 224 5th Ave S; tours $15; ⏲9am-5pm Mon-Wed, to 8pm Thu-Sat) One of the oldest letterpress print shops in the US, Hatch has been using old-school, hand-cut blocks to print its bright, iconic posters

since Vaudeville. The company has produced graphic ads and posters for almost every country star since and have now graduated to newly expanded digs inside the revamped Country Music Hall of Fame (p000).

There are three daily tours (12:30pm, 2pm and 3:30pm); an expanded retail space; and a gallery, where you can purchase re-strikes made from original wood plates dating from the 1870s to 1960s and one-of-a-kind monoprints reinterpreted from original woodblocks by Nashville legend Jim Sherraden.

★Third Man Records MUSIC
(www.thirdmanrecords.com; 623 7th Ave S; ⌚10am-6pm Mon-Sat, 1-4pm Sun) In a still-industrial slice of downtown you'll find Jack White's boutique record label, shop and novelty lounge, complete with its own lathe and live venue. It sells only Third Man recordings on vinyl and CD, collectible T-shirts, stickers, headphones and Pro-Ject record players. You'll also find White's entire catalog of recordings; and you can record yourself on vinyl ($15).

Live shows go off in the studio's **Blue Room** once a month. They're typically open to the public (about $10), but are only announced a couple weeks in advance. Attendees receive an exclusive colored vinyl Black and Blue of the performance.

Two Old Hippies CLOTHING, LIVE MUSIC
(www.twooldhippies.com; 401 12th Ave S; ⌚10am-8pm Mon-Thu, to 9pm Fri-Sat, 11am-6pm Sun) Only in Nashville would an upscale retro-inspired clothing shop have a bandstand with regular live shows of high quality. And, yes, just like the threads, countrified hippie rock is the rule. The shop itself has special jewelry, fitted tees, excellent belts, made in Tennessee denim, a bounty of stage-worthy shirts and jackets and some incredible acoustic guitars.

There's live music four nights a week at 6pm and an open mike for kids on Sundays at 1pm.

Imogene + Willie CLOTHING
(www.imogeneandwillie.com; 2601 12th Ave S; ⌚10am-6pm Mon-Fri, 11am-6pm Sat, 1-5pm Sun) This independent purveyor of style in the hip neighborhood of 12 South does built-to-last, custom-tailored denim ($250) that ships to you within a week or two.

Ernest Tubb MUSIC
(www.etrecordshop.com; 417 Broadway; ⌚10am-10pm Sun-Thu, to midnight Fri-Sat) Marked by a giant neon guitar sign, this is the best place to shop for country and bluegrass records.

Boot Country BOOTS
(www.twofreeboots.com; 304 Broadway; ⌚10am-10:30pm Mon-Thu, to 11pm Fri & Sat, 11am-7:30pm Sun) If you're into leather, or worn rawhide, or anything close, they do all manner of boots here. Buy one pair, get two free. No joke!

Gruhn Guitars MUSIC
(www.gruhn.com; 2120 8th Ave S; ⌚9:30am-6pm Mon-Sat) This renowned vintage instrument store has expert staff, and at any minute some unassuming virtuoso may just walk in, grab a guitar, mandolin or banjo off the wall and jam.

Pangaea GIFTS
(www.pangaeanashville.com; 1721 21st Ave S; ⌚10am-6pm Mon-Thu, to 9pm Fri & Sat, noon-5pm Sun) There are no groovier shops in town. What with the beaded belts and silly scarves, funky hats and summery dresses, retro Portuguese soaps, Lionel Richie koozies, Day of the Dead figurines and literary-inspired jewelry.

WORTH A TRIP

FRANKLIN

About 20 miles south of Nashville off I-65, the historic town of **Franklin** (www.historicfranklin.com) has a charming downtown and beautiful B&Bs. It was also the site of one of the Civil War's bloodiest battlefields. On November 30, 1864, some 37,000 men (20,000 Confederates and 17,000 Union soldiers) fought over a 2-mile stretch of Franklin's outskirts. Nashville's sprawl has turned much of that battlefield into suburbs, but the **Carter House** (☎615-791-1861; www.boft.org; 1140 Columbia Ave, Franklin; adult/senior/child $15/12/8; ⌚9am-5pm Mon-Sat, 11-5pm Sun; 👪🐾) property preserves up to a 20-acre chunk of the Battle of Franklin. The house is one of the most bullet-ridden Civil War properties left in the USA (more than 1000 holes are estimated across its various buildings).

ℹ Information

Downtown Nashville and Centennial Park have free wi-fi, as do many hotels, restaurants and coffee shops.

Main Police Station (☎615-862-7611; 601 Korean Veterans Blvd) Nashville's Central Precinct.

Nashville Scene (www.nashvillescene.com) Free alternative weekly with entertainment listings.

Nashville Visitors Information Center (☎800-657-6910, 615-259-4747; www.visitmusiccity.com; 501 Broadway, Bridgestone Arena; ⏰8am-5:30pm Mon-Sat, 10am-5pm Sun) Pick up free city maps here at the glass tower. A second, smaller center (150 4th Ave N; ⏰8am-5pm Mon-Fri) is run out of the corporate offices in the Regions Bank Building lobby.

Out & About Nashville (www.outandaboutnashville.com) A monthly covering the local gay and lesbian scene.

Post Office (www.usps.com; 601 Broadway; ⏰6am-6pm Mon-Fri, to 12:30pm Sat) The most convenient downtown post office.

Tennessean (www.tennessean.com) Nashville's daily newspaper.

Vanderbilt University Medical Center (☎615-322-5000; www.mc.vanderbilt.edu; 1211 Medical Center Dr) Widely regarded as Tennessee's best hospital.

Getting There & Around

Nashville International Airport (BNS; ☎615-275-1675; www.nashintl.com; One Terminal Dr), 8 miles east of town, is not a major air hub. **Metropolitan Transit Authority** (MTA; www.nashvillemta.org; fares $1.70-2.25) bus 18 links the airport and downtown; **Jarmon Transportation** (www.jarmontransportation.com; fares $15) runs airport shuttles to major downtown and West End hotels. Taxis charge a flat rate of $25 to downtown or Opryland.

LOCAL KNOWLEDGE

SCENIC DRIVE: NASHVILLE'S COUNTRY TRACKS

About 25 miles southwest of Nashville off Hwy 100, drivers pick up the **Natchez Trace Parkway**, which leads 444 miles southwest to Natchez, MS. This northern section is one of its most attractive stretches, with broad-leafed trees leaning together to form an arch over the winding road. Near the parkway entrance, stop at the landmark **Loveless Cafe** (www.lovelesscafe.com; 8400 Hwy 100 , Nashville; breakfast $7.25-14.25; ⏰7am-9pm), a 1950s roadhouse famous for its biscuits with homemade preserves, country ham and ample portions of Southern fried chicken.

Greyhound (☎615-255-3556; www.greyhound.com; 709 5th Ave S) is downtown. The MTA operates city bus services, based downtown at **Music City Central** (400 Charlotte Ave), including the free Music City Circuit, whose three routes hit the majority of Nashville attractions. Express buses go to Music Valley.

Nashville B-Cycle (☎615-625-2153; www.nashville.bcycle.com), the city's public bike-share scheme, offers more than 30 stations throughout the city center. Your first hour is free; after that your credit card will be charged $1.50 per half-hour. Daily, weekly and monthly plans are also available.

Eastern Tennessee

Dolly Parton, Eastern Tennessee's most famous native, loves her home region so much she has made a successful career out of singing about girls who leave the honeysuckle-scented embrace of the Smoky Mountains for the false glitter of the city. They're always sorry. Largely a rural region of small towns, rolling hills and river valleys, the eastern third of the state has friendly folks, hearty country food and pastoral charm. The lush, heather-tinted Great Smoky Mountains are great for hiking, camping and rafting, while the region's two main urban areas, Knoxville and Chattanooga, are easygoing riverside cities with lively student populations.

Chattanooga

Named 'the dirtiest city in America' in the 1960s, today the city is recognized as being one of the country's greenest, with miles of well-used waterfront trails, electric buses and pedestrian bridges crossing the Tennessee River. With world-class rock-climbing, hiking, biking and water-sports opportunities, it's one of the South's best cities for outdoorsy types. And it's gorgeous now, too; just check out those views from the Bluff View Art District!

The city was once a major railway hub throughout the 19th and 20th centuries, hence the 'Chattanooga Choo-Choo,' which was originally a reference to the Cincinnati Southern Railway's passenger service from Cincinnati to Chattanooga and later the title of a 1941 Glen Miller tune. The eminently walkable downtown is an increasingly gentrified maze of historic stone and brick buildings and some tasty gourmet kitchens. There's a lot to love about the 'Noog.

Sights & Activities

Coolidge Park is a good place to start a riverfront stroll. There's a carousel, well-used playing fields and a 50ft climbing wall attached to one of the columns supporting the **Walnut Street Bridge**. Abutting that park, the city has installed gabions to restore the wetlands and attract more bird life. Check them out by strolling to the edge of the cool, floating decks that jut over the marsh. The much larger **Tennessee River Park** is an 8-mile, multi-use greenway that runs from downtown through Amincola Marsh and along South Chickamauga Creek. Plans are to expand its reach to a full 22 miles. **Chattanooga Nightfall** is a free concert series every Friday from May 1 to September 4 at Miller Plaza.

Hunter Museum of American Art GALLERY
(www.huntermuseum.org; 10 Bluff View; adult/child $10/5; ⏲10am-5pm Mon, Tue, Fri & Sat, to 8pm Thu, noon-5pm Wed & Sun) Set high on the river bluffs, this striking melted-steel and glass edifice is easily the most singular architectural achievement in Tennessee. Oh, and its 19th- and 20th-century art collection is fantastic. Permanent exhibits are free the first Sunday of the month (special exhibits cost $5).

Lookout Mountain OUTDOORS
(www.lookoutmountain.com; 827 East Brow Rd; adult/child $49/30; ⏲varies; 👪) Some of Chattanooga's oldest and best-loved attractions are 6 miles outside the city. Admission price includes: the **Incline Railway**, which chugs up a steep incline to the top of the mountain; the world's longest underground waterfall, **Ruby Falls**; and **Rock City**, a garden with a dramatic clifftop overlook.

Outdoor Chattanooga OUTDOORS
(☎423-643-6888; www.outdoorchattanooga.com; 200 River St) A city-run agency promoting active recreation; the website is a good resource for outdoor information, including river and trail suggestions, though walk-in visitors may be disappointed by the lack of spur-of-the-moment guidance.

BONNAROO

One of America's premier music festivals, **Bonnaroo** (www.bonnaroo.com; Manchester, TN; ⏲mid-Jun) is the only large-scale 24/7 event in the country. Set on a 700-acre farm in Mancester, 60 miles southeast of Nashville, Bonnaroo combines camping, comedy, cinema, food, beverage and arts components that lend a communal feel. But it's the music that rules. The 2015 iteration offered over 125 bands and 20 comedians on 12 stages, including sets from Billy Joel, Mumford & Sons, Kendrick Lamar, Florence & the Machine, Robert Plant & the Sensational Space Shifters, Slayer, Earth, Wind & Fire and so much more spread over four blissfully raging daze.

Sleeping & Eating

★**Crash Pad** HOSTEL $
(☎423-648-8393; www.crashpadchattanooga.com; 29 Johnson St; dm/d/tr $30/79/99; P❄@📶) 🍃 The South's best hostel, run by climbers, is a sustainable den of coolness in Southside, the 'Noog's hippest downtown neighborhood. Coed dorms overachieve: built-in lights, power outlets, fans and privacy curtains for each bed. Privates feature exposed concrete and bedside tables built into the bedframes. Access throughout is via hi-tech fobs; linens, padlocks and breakfast supplies are all included.

Up to 95% of the materials were reclaimed from the previous building and there's solar power to boot. It's the first LEED platinum-certified hostel *in the world*. Book ahead – it fills with outdoor enthusiasts of all ilk on the weekends.

Stone Fort Inn BOUTIQUE HOTEL $$
(☎423-267-7866; www.stonefortinn.com; 120 E 10th St; r $165-214; P❄📶) Ceilings are high, craft furnishings are vintage and service is mostly phenomenal at this 16-room historic downtown boutique hotel. Each room is unique but all are awash in exposed brick and we're partial to the ones with private terraces and outdoor Jacuzzi tubs. Its Appalachian-style, farm-to-table restaurant is one of city's best.

Chattanooga Choo-Choo HOTEL $$
(☎423-308-2440; www.choochoo.com; 1400 Market St; r/railcars from $155/189; P❄@📶🏊) Fresh off a centennial birthday and the wraps of an $8 million expansion at time of research, the city's grand old railway terminal is a bustling hotel, complete with 48 authentic Victorian railcar rooms, a retro Gilded Age bar and a stunning grand portico in the lobby. Standard rooms and suites, in separate buildings, are spacious but ordinary.

★ Public House NEW SOUTHERN $$
(☎423-266-3366; www.publichousechattanooga.com; 1110 Market St; mains $8.50-32; ⏰11am-2:30pm & 5-9pm Mon-Thu, to 10pm Fri, noon-3pm & 5-10pm Sat) A rather chic pub and restaurant in the refurbished warehouse district; the in-house bar, Social, is a dark welcoming brick house, the dining room is draped, bright and homey, and both rooms serve a tasty upscale menu (there's a divine pimiento cheese and bacon burger).

St John's Meeting Place AMERICAN $$$
(☎423-266-4571; www.stjohnsmeetingplace.com; 1274 Market St; mains $14-33; ⏰5-9:30pm Mon-Thu, to 10pm Fri & Sat) The culinary anchor of Chattanooga's Southside is widely considered the city's best night out. It's Johnny Cash black (black granite floor, black-glass chandeliers, black banquets) lending an unorthodox but mod elegance for a foodie habitat. The farm-to-table cuisine features bacon-wrapped quail, lamb tenderloin, pork belly/shoulder fried rice, local trout and so on. Live jazz Thursdays from 6pm to 9pm.

ℹ Information

Visitor Center (☎800-322-3344; www.chattanoogafun.com; 215 Broad St; ⏰10am-5pm) Easy to miss, located in an outdoor public breezeway.

ℹ Getting There & Around

Chattanooga's modest **airport** (CHA; ☎423-855-2202; www.chattairport.com; 1001 Airport Rd) is just east of the city. The **Greyhound station** (☎423-892-1277; www.greyhound.com; 960 Airport Rd) is just down the road. For access to most downtown sites, ride the free electric shuttle buses that ply the center and the North Shore. The visitor center has a route map.

Roadies should fill out an online application and take part in **Bike Chattanooga** (www.bikechattanooga.com), the city-sponsored bicycle-sharing program. Bikes are lined and locked up at 31 stations throughout the city. Rides under 60 minutes are free.

Knoxville

Once known as the 'underwear capital of the world' for its numerous textile mills, Knoxville is home to the University of Tennessee. Downtown's **Market Square** is full of ornate 19th-century buildings and lovely outdoor cafes shaded by pear trees, while **Old Town** and **Hundred Block** are arty, renovated warehouse districts centered on Gay St, where the best nightlife blooms.

◉ Sights & Activities

Sunsphere LANDMARK
(☎865-251-6860; World's Fair Park, 810 Clinch Ave; ⏰9am-10pm Apr-Oct, 11am-6pm Nov-Mar) The city's visual centerpiece is the Sunsphere, a golden orb (disco ball!) atop a tower that's the main remnant of the 1982 World Fair. You can take the elevator up to the 4th-floor viewing deck to see the skyline, an updated exhibit on the city or, one more floor up, a cocktail at Icon Ultra Lounge.

Women's Basketball Hall of Fame MUSEUM
(www.wbhof.com; 700 Hall of Fame Dr; adult/child $10/6; ⏰10am-5pm Mon-Sat summer, 11am-5pm Tue-Fri, 10am-5pm Sat winter; 👪) You can't miss the massive orange basketball that marks the Women's Basketball Hall of Fame, a nifty look at the sport from the time when women were forced to play in full-length dresses.

🛏 Sleeping & Eating

★ Oliver Hotel BOUTIQUE HOTEL $$
(☎865-521-0050; www.theoliverhotel.com; 700 Hall of Fame Dr; r $150-250; P ❄ @ 📶) Hipster receptionists man Knoxville's only boutique hotel, with 28 modern rooms with marble sink tops and rain-shower heads in the baths, plush linens and hand-crafted coffee tables. It has a suave, upmarket vibe and the Peter Kern Library bar draws craft cocktail enthusiasts.

★ Oli Bea BREAKFAST $
(www.olibea.net; mains $6-12; ⏰7am-1pm Mon-Sat; 📶) It's worth sleeping in Knoxville just to wake up to the Mexicanized Southern breakfast fare at this morning stop in the Old City. You'll find gussied up standards (country ham, sage sausage, organic chicken or duck eggs) but it's really about gourmet South of the Border fare: pork confit *carnitas* tostadas, *chilaquiles*, breakfast burritos – all full-stop fabulous!

Knox Mason NEW SOUTHERN $$
(www.knoxmason.com; 131 S Gay St; mains $16-24; ⏰4-11pm Tue-Thu, to midnight Fri-Sat, 10am-2pm Sun) In the historic 100 Block of Gay St, this is the go-to for seasonally focused, locally sourced creative New Southern fare.

ℹ Information

Visitor Center (☎800-727-8045; www.visitknoxville.com; 301 S Gay St; ⏰8:30am-5pm Mon-Sat, 9am-5pm Sun) Besides tourism info, the visitor center also welcomes bands across the Americana genre for WDVX's Blue Plate

Special, a free concert series at noon Monday to Saturday.

Great Smoky Mountains National Park

The Cherokee called this territory Shaconage (shah-*cone*-ah-jey), meaning roughly 'land of the blue smoke,' for the heather-colored mist that hangs over the ancient peaks. The Southern Appalachians are the world's oldest mountain range, with mile upon mile of cool, humid deciduous forest.

The 815-sq-mile **park** (www.nps.gov/grsm) FREE is the country's most visited (double that of the Grand Canyon!) and, while the main arteries and attractions can get crowded, 95% of visitors never venture further than 100yd from their cars, so it's easy to leave the teeming masses behind. There are sections of the park in Tennessee and North Carolina.

Unlike most national parks, Great Smoky charges no admission fee. Stop by a visitor center to pick up a park map and the free *Smokies Guide*. The remains of the 19th-century settlement at **Cades Cove** are some of the park's most popular sights, as evidenced by the teeth-grinding summer traffic jams on the loop road.

Mt LeConte offers terrific hiking, as well as the only non-camping accommodations, **LeConte Lodge** (☎865-429-5704; www.lecontelodge.com; cabins per person adult/child 4-12yr $136/85). Though the only way to get to the lodge's rustic, electricity-free cabins is via five uphill hiking trails varying in length from 5.5 miles (Alum Cave Trail) to 8 miles (Boulevard), it's so popular you need to reserve up to a year in advance. You can drive right up to the dizzying heights of **Clingmans Dome**, the third-highest peak east of the Mississippi, with a futuristic observation tower (though it's clouded over more often than not).

With nine operating campgrounds offering about 900 campsites, you'd think finding a place to pitch would be easy. Not so in the busy summer season, so plan ahead. You can make **reservations** (☎800-365-2267; www.recreation.gov; camping site per night $17-23) for some sites; others are first-come, first-served. Cades Cove and Smokemont campgrounds are open year-round; others are open March to October.

Backcountry camping (☎reservations 865-436-1231; www.nps.gov/grsm/planyourvisit/backcountry-camping.htm; per night $4) is an excellent option, which is only chargeable up to five nights (beyond that, it's free). A permit is required; you can make reservations and get permits at the ranger stations or visitor centers.

Information

The park's four interior visitor centers are **Sugarlands Visitor Center** (☎865-436-1291; www.nps.gov/grsm; 107 Park Headquarters Rd; ⊙8am-7:30pm Jun-Aug, hours vary Sep-May), at the park's northern entrance near Gatlinburg; **Cades Cove Visitor Center** (Cades Cove Loop Rd; ⊙9am-7pm Apr-Aug, earlier Sep-Mar), halfway up Cades Cove Loop Rd, 24 miles off Hwy 441 from the Gatlinburg entrance; the Oconaluftee Visitor Center (p356), at the park's southern entrance near Cherokee in North Carolina; and the new **Clingmans' Dome Visitor Center** (Clingmans Dome Rd; ⊙10am-6pm Apr-Oct, 9:30am-5pm Nov).

Gatlinburg

Wildly kitschy Gatlinburg hunkers at the entrance of the Great Smoky Mountains National Park, waiting to stun hikers with the scent of fudge, cotton candy and pancakes, and various oddity museums and campy attractions.

Sights & Activities

★Ole Smoky Moonshine Holler DISTILLERY
(www.olesmokymoonshine.com; 903 Parkway; ⊙10am-11pm) At first glance, this stone-and-wood moonshine distillery, Tennessee's first licensed moonshine maker, appears to have a Disney flair, but it's the real deal. Gathering around the hysterical bartenders, drinking the free hooch and taking in all of their colorful commentary, is Gatlinburg's best time.

Ober Gatlinburg Aerial Tramway SKI AREA
(www.obergatlinburg.com; 1001 Parkway; adult/child $12.50/9.50; ⊙9:30am-5:40pm Sun-Fri, to 6:30pm Sat) Ride the scenic 2-mile aerial tramway to the Bavarian-themed Ober Gatlinburg Ski Resort.

Sleeping & Eating

Bearskin Lodge LODGE $$
(☎877-795-7546; www.thebearskinlodge.com; 840 River Rd; r from $110; P ❄ 🛜 ≋) This shingled riverside lodge is blessed with timber accents and a bit more panache than other Gatlinburg comers. All of the spacious rooms have flat-screen TVs and some come

DOLLYWOOD

A self-created ode to the patron saint of East Tennessee, the big-haired, bigger-bosomed country singer Dolly Parton, **Dollywood** (☎865-428-9488; www.dollywood.com; 2700 Dollywood Parks Blvd; adult/child $59/47; ⊙Apr-Dec) features Appalachian-themed rides and attractions, a water park, the new DreamMore Resort and more. Find it looming above **Pigeon Forge** (www.mypigeonforge.com), a secondhand Vegas-like mess drunk on American kitsch 9 miles north of Gatlinburg.

with gas fireplaces and private balconies jutting over the river.

Three Jimmys AMERICAN $

(www.threejimmys.com; 1359 East Pkwy; mains $10-25; ⊙11am-10pm;) Escape the tourist hordes on the main drag and grab a bite at this locals' favorite with friendly waitresses ('Here's your menu, baby...') and a long list of everything: BBQ, turkey Reubens, burgers, champagne chicken, steaks, a great spinach salad and so on.

KENTUCKY

With an economy based on bourbon, horse racing and tobacco, you might think Kentucky would rival Las Vegas as Sin Central. Well, yes and no. For every whiskey-soaked Louisville bar there's a dry county where you can't get anything stronger than ginger ale. For every racetrack there's a church. Kentucky is made of such strange juxtapositions. A geographic and cultural crossroads, the state combines the friendliness of the South, the rural frontier history of the West, the industry of the North and the aristocratic charm of the East. Every corner is easy on the eye, but there are few sights more heartbreakingly beautiful than the rolling limestone hills of horse country, where thoroughbred breeding is a multimillion-dollar industry. In spring the pastures bloom with tiny azure buds, earning it the moniker 'Bluegrass State.'

Information

The boundary between Eastern and Central time goes through the middle of Kentucky.

Kentucky State Parks (☎800-255-7275; www.parks.ky.gov) Offers info on hiking, caving, fishing, camping and more in Kentucky's 52 state parks. So-called 'Resort Parks' have lodges. 'Recreation Parks' are for roughin' it.

Kentucky Travel (☎800-225-8747, 502-564-4930; www.kentuckytourism.com) Sends out a detailed booklet on the state's attractions.

Louisville

Best known as the home of the Kentucky Derby, Louisville (or Luhvul, as the locals say) is handsome, underrated and undeniably cool. A major Ohio River shipping center during the days of westward expansion, Kentucky's largest city is on the come up, with hip bars, superb farm-to-table restaurants, and an engaging, young and increasingly progressive population. It's a fun place to spend a few days, checking out the museums, wandering the old neighborhoods and sipping some bourbon.

Sights & Activities

The Victorian-era **Old Louisville** neighborhood, just south of downtown, is well worth a stroll. Don't miss **St James Court**, just off Magnolia Ave, with its utterly charming gas-lamp-lit park. There are several wonderful **historic homes** (☎502-899-5079; www.historichomes.org) in the area open for tours, including Thomas Edison's old shotgun cottage.

★**Churchill Downs** RACETRACK

(www.churchilldowns.com; 700 Central Ave) On the first Saturday in May, a who's who of upper-crust America puts on their seersucker suits and most flamboyant hats and descends for the 'greatest two minutes in sports': the Kentucky Derby, the longest-running consecutive sporting event in North America.

After the race, the crowd sings 'My Old Kentucky Home' and watches as the winning horse is covered in a blanket of roses. Then they party. Actually, they've been partying for a while. The **Kentucky Derby Festival** (www.kdf.org), which includes a balloon race, a marathon, and the largest fireworks display in North America, starts two weeks before the big event. Most seats at the derby are by invitation only or have been reserved years in advance. On Derby Day, $60 gets you into the infield, which is a debaucherous rave with no seats, as well as the classier Paddock Area, where you can see the horses getting ready for each race. It's crowded and it was previously hard to see races, but the newly installed 4K video board (the world's largest) has alleviated that minor detail. If you are a connoisseur of the thoroughbreds, warm-ups and other races take place from April to June and again in September and November, where it's possible to snag $3 seats.

Kentucky Derby Museum MUSEUM
(www.derbymuseum.org; Gate 1, Central Ave; adult/senior/child $14/13/6; ⏲8am-5pm Mon-Sat, 11am-5pm Sun mid-Mar–mid-Nov, from 9am Mon-Sat, 11am-5pm Sun Dec–mid-Mar) On the racetrack grounds, the museum has exhibits on derby history, including a peek into the life of jockeys and a roundup of the most illustrious horses. Highlights include a 360-degree HD film about the race, the 30-minute walking tour of the grandstands (which includes some engaging yarns) and mint juleps in the museum cafe.

The 90-minute 'Inside the Gates Tour' ($11) leads you through the jockey's quarters and posh VIP seating areas known as Millionaire's Row.

Muhammad Ali Center MUSEUM
(www.alicenter.org; 144 N 6th St; adult/senior/child $9/8/4; ⏲9:30am-5pm Tue-Sat, noon-5pm Sun) A love offering to the city from its most famous native, and an absolute must-see. For a black man from the South during his era, to rejoice in his own greatness and beauty was revolutionary and inspiring to behold – and this museum captures it all.

Louisville Slugger Museum & Factory MUSEUM
(www.sluggermuseum.org; 800 W Main St; adult/senior/child $12/11/7; ⏲9am-5pm Mon-Sat, 11am-5pm Sun;) Look for the 120ft baseball bat leaning against the museum. Hillerich & Bradsby Co have been making the famous Louisville Slugger here since 1884. Admission includes a plant tour and a hall of baseball memorabilia, including Babe Ruth's bat, and a free mini slugger.

Frazier History Museum MUSEUM
(www.fraziermuseum.org; 829 W Main St; adult/student/child $12/10/8; ⏲9am-5pm Mon-Sat, noon-5pm Sun) Surprisingly ambitious for a midsized city, this state-of-the-art museum covers 1000 years of history with grisly battle dioramas and costumed interpreters demonstrating swordplay and staging mock debates.

Kentucky Science Center MUSEUM
(502-561-6100; www.kysciencecenter.org; 727 W Main St; adult/child $13/11; ⏲9:30am-5:30pm Sun-Thu, to 9pm Fri & Sat;) Set in a historic building on Main St there are three floors of exhibits that illuminate biology, physiology, physics, computing and more for families (kids love it). For an extra $8 to $10 you can catch a film in the IMAX theater.

Big Four Bridge WALKING, CYCLING
(East River Rd) Built between 1888 and 1895, the Big Four Bridge, which spans the Ohio River and reaches the Indiana shores, has been closed to vehicular traffic since 1969 but was reopened in 2013 as a pedestrian and cycling path; excellent city and river views throughout.

KENTUCKY FACTS

Nickname Bluegrass State

Population 4.4 million

Area 39,728 sq miles

Capital city Frankfort (population 25,500)

Other cities Louisville (population 750,000), Lexington (population 310,000)

Sales tax 6%

Birthplace of 16th US president Abraham Lincoln (1809–65), 'gonzo' journalist Hunter S Thompson (1937–2005), boxer Muhammad Ali (b 1942), actresses Ashley Judd (b 1968) and Jennifer Lawrence (b 1990)

Home of Kentucky Derby, Louisville Slugger, bourbon

Politics From generally to extremely conservative in rural areas

Famous for Horses, bluegrass music, basketball, bourbon, caves

Ongoing internal conflict North vs South allegiance during the Civil War

Driving distances Louisville to Lexington 77 miles, Lexington to Mammoth Cave National Park 135 miles

Sleeping

Chain hotels cluster near the airport off I-264.

Rocking Horse B&B B&B $$
(502-583-0408; www.rockinghorse-bb.com; 1022 S 3rd St; r from $125;) On a stretch of 3rd St once known as Millionaire's Row, this 1888 Richardsonian Romanesque mansion is chock-full of astounding historic detail. The six guest rooms are decorated with Victorian antiques and splendid original stained glass. Guests can eat their two-course breakfast in the English country garden or sip complimentary port in the parlor.The cheapest room sacrifices space and a bathtub for a street-facing balcony.

★ **21c Museum Hotel** HOTEL $$$
(502-217-6300; www.21chotel.com; 700 W Main St; r from $239;) This contemporary art museum–hotel features edgy design details: video screens project your distorted image and falling language on the wall as you wait for the elevator; water-blurred, see-through glass urinal walls line the men's rooms. Rooms, though not as interesting as the five contemporary art galleries/common areas, have iPod docks and mint julep kits.

Brown Hotel HOTEL $$$
(502-583-1234; www.brownhotel.com; 335 West Broadway; r $179-399;) Opera stars, queens and prime ministers have trod the marble floors of this storied downtown hotel, now restored to all its 1920s glamor with 294 comfy rooms and an impressive lobby bourbon bar under original English Renaissance gilded ceilings.

THE HAUNTED HOSPITAL

Towering over Louisville like a mad king's castle, the abandoned **Waverly Hills Sanatorium** once housed victims of an early 20th-century tuberculosis epidemic. When patients died, workers dumped their bodies down a chute into the basement. No wonder the place is said to be one of America's most haunted buildings. Search for spooks with a nighttime ghost-hunting **tour** (502-933-2142; www.therealwaverlyhills.com; 4400 Paralee Lane; 2hr tours/2hr ghost hunt/overnight $22.50/50/100; Fri & Sat Mar-Aug); the genuinely fearless can even spend the night! Many claim it's the scariest place they've ever been.

In 1926, Louisville's signature dish, the Hot Brown (open-faced turkey sandwich with turkey, bacon, pimientos, and Mornay sauce) was invented here and is still served in all three in-house restaurants.

Eating

The number of incredible kitchens multiplies every year, especially in the engaging **NuLu** ('New Louisville') area, where there are numerous galleries and boutiques to explore. The **Highlands** area around Bardstown and Baxter Rds is another popular nightlife and dining spot.

Gralehaus MODERN AMERICAN $
(www.gralehaus.com; 1001 Baxter Ave; mains $6-13; 8am-4pm Sun-Tue, to 10pm Wed-Sat;) There's breakfast all day at this small eatery housed in a historic early 20th-century home and you should indeed indulge in their chef-centric takes on traditional Southern comforts at all hours (think locally sourced biscuits and duck gravy, lamb and grits). Serious signature coffee drinks excel as well.

Upstairs, three rustic-chic rooms feature craft-beer-stocked mini-bars, hardwood ceilings and edgy furnishings.

The Post DELI $
(www.thepostlouisville.com; 1045 Goss Ave; mains $3-13; 11am-2am Wed-Mon;) In gentrifying Germantown, New York–style pizza by the slice, sub sandwiches and great spaces (sunny patio out the front, comfy bar in the back) evoke a pricier atmosphere and cooler vibe than your bill suggests.

★ **Mayan Cafe** MEXICAN $$
(502-566-0651; www.themayancafe.com; 813 E Market St; mains $14-23; 11am-2:30pm & 5-10pm Mon-Thu, to 10:30pm Fri-Sat;) Check your visions of piñatas and mariachis at the door – Chef Bruce Ucán's subtle farm-to-table Mexican mainstay is a journey about flavor, not patriotic pomp and circumstance. Impossibly fresh, sustainably produced seasonal menus draw heavily from the Yucatán Peninsula and dishes nail that just-right wallop between taste and texture.

Garage Bar GASTROPUB $$
(www.garageonmarket.com; 700 E Market St; dishes $5-17;) The best thing to do on a warm afternoon in Louisville is to make your way to this uber-hip converted NuLu service station (accented by two kissing Camaros) and order a round of basil gimlets and the ham platter (a tasting of four regionally

cured hams, served with fresh bread and preserves; $21).

Then move onto the menu which ranges from the best brick-oven pizza in town to divine rolled oysters.

★Decca MODERN AMERICAN $$$
(☎502-749-8128; www.deccarestaurant.com; 812 E Market St; mains $24-31; ⊙5:30-10pm Mon-Thu, to 11pm Fri & Sat; ⓦ) A beautiful space with a cork-and-wood floor, fountain-strewn patio and gorgeous Laguiole cutlery opened by a chef from San Francisco (albeit a Southerner by birth). Kentuckians were skeptical, but Annie Pettry wooed and won. The emphasis of the delectable, seasonally changing menu is wood-fired roasts.

But they aren't afraid to give veggies the treatment, too – the wood-grilled broccoli with almonds and anchovy is an absolute knockout.

Proof NEW SOUTHERN $$$
(☎502-217-6360; www.proofonmain.com; 702 W Main St; mains $11-34; ⊙7-10am, 11am-2pm & 5:30-10pm Mon-Thu, to 11pm Fri, 7am-3pm & 5:30-11pm Sat, to 1pm Sun; ⓦ) Arguably Louisville's best restaurant. The cocktails ($8 to $15) are incredible, the wine and bourbon 'library' (they're known to pour from exclusive and rare barrels of Woodford Reserve and Van Winkle) is long and satisfying, and startling dishes range from country ham falafel to a deliciously messy bison burger or a high-minded take on 'hot' fried chicken.

Drinking & Nightlife

The free *Weekly Leo* (www.leoweekly.com) lists local gigs.

Holy Grale PUB
(www.holygralelouisville.com; 1034 Bardstown Rd; ⊙4pm-late; ⓦ) One of Bardstown's best bars is housed in an old church, with a menu of funked-up pub grub (blistered shishito peppers, red curry mussels) and a buzzworthy beer list dependent on rarer German, Danish, Belgian and Japanese brews on tap. The most intense beers (up to 13% alcohol) can be found in the choir loft. Hallelujah!

Crescent Hill Craft House BAR
(www.crafthousebrews.com; 2636 Frankfort Ave; beers $5-6.50; ⊙4pm-midnight Mon-Thu, to 2am Fri, noon-2am Sat-Sun; ⓦ) The new darling of the artsy-upscale Crescent Hill neighborhood, 6 miles east of downtown, this bar-restaurant devotes its taps to 40 great-value microbrews, all of which are from Kentuckiana and projected on a side wall complete with alcohol content and IBU units.

Knock them back behind the hoity-toity (and at times progressively vegetarian) bar food like poutine with short ribs, pork belly BLTs or smoked eggplant barley burgers.

Ei8ht Up BAR
(www.8uplouisville.com; 350 West Chestnut St; cocktails $8-14; ⊙4pm-midnight Sun-Thu, to 2am Fri-Sat; ⓦ) Louisville's newest and hottest drinking den, on the rooftop of a Hilton Garden Inn (don't hold that against it). It's all about the open-air terrace, a come-one, come-all cornucopia of all leanings and persuasions, and its expansive good-time bar surrounded by a variety of cozy, fire-lit lounge areas.

Please & Thank You CAFE
(www.pleaseandthankyoulouisville.com; 800 E Market St; drinks $2-4.75; ⊙7am-6pm Mon-Fri, 8am-6pm Sat, 8am-4pm Sun; ⓦ) The kind of indie cafe that makes a neighborhood. It does creamy espresso and home-baked bread pudding, creative scones and coffee cakes, zucchini bread and gooey chocolate-chip cookies. Oh, and it also sells vinyl records, which only adds to its anti-Starbucks mystique.

Shopping

★Joe Ley Antiques ANTIQUES
(www.joeley.com; 615 E Market St; ⊙10am-5pm Tue-Sat) Go down the rabbit hole into this massive, three-story brick-and-stained glass antique emporium crammed with collectibles from eight decades. Think homely dolls, freaky furniture and chunky jewelry – and everything else *including* the kitchen sink.

Butchertown Market BOUTIQUES
(www.thebutchertownmarket.com; 1201 Story Ave; ⊙10am-6pm Mon-Fri, to 5pm Sat) This converted slaughterhouse complex that's been turned into a grab bag of quirky, cute and artsy boutiques is a zoo of desirables. Whether it's funky jewelry, kooky gifts, exquisite Cellar Door chocolates, craftsman metal fixtures, bath and body products or baby clothes, someone is selling it here.

Taste WINE
(☎502-409-4646; www.tastefinewinesandbourbons.com; 634 E Market St; tastings $3-5.50; ⊙11am-8pm Tue-Wed, to late Thu & Fri, 10:30am-late Sat) A high-end wine shop that sells small-batch wines and bourbons, and offers sips of either (or both) to help you decide (or perhaps it muddles the whole process).

Come, sip, buy. The 10-option wine list turns over every Tuesday.

Information

Visitor Center (☎502-379-6109; www.gotolouisville.com; 301 S 4th St; ⏲10am-6pm Mon-Sat, noon-5pm Sun) Stuffed with brochures and helpful staff.

Getting There & Around

Louisville's International Airport (SDF; ☎502-367-4636; www.flylouisville.com; 600 Terminal Drive) is 5 miles south of town on I-65. Get there by cab for a flat rate of $20 or local bus 2. The **Greyhound station** (☎502-561-2805; www.greyhound.com; 720 W Muhammad Ali Blvd) is just west of downtown. **TARC** (www.ridetarc.org; 1000 W Broadway; fares $1.75) runs local buses from the Union Station depot, including its free ZeroBus, an electric bus fleet that circles Main, Market and 4th Sts, taking in most of the city's attractions and coolest restaurants. Buses do not require exact change, but there is no mechanism for giving change back.

Bluegrass Country

Drive through northeast Kentucky's Bluegrass Country on a sunny day and glimpse horses grazing in the brilliant-green hills dotted with ponds, poplar trees and handsome estate houses. These once-wild woodlands and meadows have been a center of horse breeding for almost 250 years. The region's natural limestone deposits – you'll see limestone bluffs rise majestic from out of nowhere – are said to produce especially nutritious grass. The area's principal city, Lexington, is called the 'Horse Capital of the World.'

Lexington

Even the prison looks like a country club in Lexington, home of million-dollar houses and multimillion-dollar horses. Once the wealthiest and most cultured city west of the Allegheny Mountains, it was called 'the Athens of the West.' It's home to the University of Kentucky and is the heart of the thoroughbred industry. The small downtown has some pretty Victorian neighborhoods, but most of the attractions are in the countryside.

Sights & Activities

It's well worth taking a drive into the countryside, where postcard-perfect horse farms dot the landscape like a farmland fairy-tale across pastureland peppered with picket fences and whinnying thoroughbreds.

Kentucky Horse Park MUSEUM, PARK
(www.kyhorsepark.com; 4089 Iron Works Pkwy; adult/child $16/8, horseback riding $25; ⏲9am-5pm daily mid-Mar–Oct, Wed-Sun Nov–mid-Mar; 👪) An educational theme park and equestrian sports center sits on 1200 acres just north of Lexington. Horses representing 50 different breeds live in the park and participate in special live shows.

Also included, the **International Museum of the Horse**, with its neat dioramas of the horse through history, from the tiny prehistoric 'eohippus' to Pony Express mail carriers, and the **American Saddlebred Museum**, devoted to America's favorite native horse. Guided 35-minute horseback rides are offered seasonally and closer-look farm tours can be arranged.

Thoroughbred Center FARM
(☎859-293-1853; www.thethoroughbredcenter.com; 3380 Paris Pike; adult/child $15/8; ⏲tours 9am Mon-Sat Apr-Oct) Most farms are closed to the public, but you can see working racehorses up close here, with tours of the stables, practice tracks and paddocks.

Ashland HISTORIC BUILDING
(www.henryclay.org; 120 Sycamore Rd; adult/child $10/5; ⏲10am-4pm Tue-Sat, 1-4pm Sun Mar-Dec) Just 1.5 miles east of downtown, part historic home of one of Kentucky's favorite sons, part public park, this was the Italianate estate of famed statesman and great compromisor Henry Clay (1777–1852).

A gorgeous property set in the midst of a tony historic neighborhood, it's well worth the admission to enter the home, but you can walk the property for free, peer into the carriage house where his coach is on display, and you can see the, ahem, privy (outhouse) too.

Mary Todd-Lincoln House HISTORIC BUILDING
(www.mtlhouse.org; 578 W Main St; adult/child $10/5; ⏲10am-4pm Mon-Sat mid-Mar–mid-Nov) This modest 1806 house has articles from the first lady's childhood and her years as Abe's wife, including original White House pieces. Tours hourly on the hour; last at 3pm.

Sleeping

Look for the Lexington opening of trendy 21C Museum Hotel downtown at the corner of Main and Upper in the historic First National Bank Building by mid-2016.

Kentucky Horse Park CAMPGROUND $

(☎859-259-4257; www.kyhorsepark.com; 4089 Iron Works Pkwy; sites $20, powered sites $26-35;) There are 260 paved sites, plus showers, laundry, grocery, playgrounds and more. Primitive camping is also available.

★**Lyndon House** B&B $$

(☎859-420-2683; www.lyndonhouse.com; 507 N Broadway; r from $179;) A detail-oriented ordained-minister-turned-foodie is your host at this discerning and spacious downtown B&B in a historic mansion dating to 1885. Anton takes hospitality seriously, as he does breakfast. The seven rooms feature period furnishings and all the mod-cons; and you're steps from a long list of restaurants and breweries.

WORTH A TRIP

BLUEGRASS BONANZA!

Kentuckian Bill Monroe is considered the founding father of bluegrass music; his band, the Blue Grass Boys, gave the genre its name. Bluegrass has its roots in the old-time mountain music, mixed with the fast tempo of African songs and spiced with lashings of jazz. Any banjo picker or fiddle fan will appreciate the historic exhibits at the **International Bluegrass Music Museum** (www.bluegrassmuseum.org; 107 Daviess St; adult/student $5/2; 10am-5pm Tue-Sat, 1-4pm Sun) in Owensboro, where you can stumble into a jam session on the first Thursday of the month. If you miss it, head to the city's free **Friday After 5** (www.fridayafter5.com) concert series throughout summer, which also features bluegrass at 7pm. The pretty Ohio River town, about 100 miles west of Louisville, also hosts the **ROMP Bluegrass Festival** (www.rompfest.com; tickets $15-50; late Jun).

Eating & Drinking

Lexington's vibiest concentration of cutting-edge bars and restaurants is along and around revitalized Jefferson Ave between W 6th and Main, which includes several craft breweries.

★**County Club** BARBECUE $

(www.countyclubrestaurant.com; 555 Jefferson St; mains $8-12; 5-10pm Tue-Thu, from 11am Fri-Sun;) This smoked-meat sanctuary occupies the former storage garage of a Sunbeam bread factory. Though the service is best described as hipster aloof, the wares – a burger, brisket on rye, Sriracha-lime smoked chicken wings, flank steak etc – are moist, tender and perfectly smoked. Douse it all in four housemade sauces (vinegar, sweet, smoked habenero and mustard – oh, that mustard!). The rotating list of daily specials and draft beers help you forget the metallic vibe.

Stella's Kentucky Deli DELI $

(www.stellaskentuckydeli.com; 143 Jefferson St; sandwiches $3.50-9; 10:30am-4pm Mon-Tue, to 9pm Wed-Thu, 9am-1pm Fri-Sat, 9am-9pm Sun;) This don't-miss deli has 30 years under its apron, but the latest owners refocused a few years back, upping the cool quotient and concentrating on invaluable provisions from local farmers. Great sandwiches, soups and salads, along with seasonal brews, are served in a colorful historic home with reclaimed tin roof and sociable bar.

Doodles CAFE $

(www.doodlesrestaurant.com; 262 N Limestone; mains $4-10; 8am-2pm Tue-Sun;) Breakfast fiends should head to this former gas station to fill up on scrumptious comfort food led by shrimp and grits (with green onion rémoulade and country ham), oatmeal brûleé and local egg casseroles; all organic and local where possible.

Natural Provisions FRENCH $$

(264 Walton Ave; mains $15-25; 11am-3pm & 4-10pm;) This industrial-chic culinary complex in a former bottling factory houses a French brasserie, a boulangerie/coffee shop and gourmet beer hall/market; together, they bear the weight of Lexington's new cradle of cool. It oozes hipness from its colorful button-tufted banquets to its long, stylish bar with deer-antler beer taps. *Voilà!* Meet Lexington, Version 2.0.

Coles 735 Main MODERN AMERICAN $$$

(☎859-266-9000; www.coles735main.com; 735 E Main St; mains $19-33; 5-10pm Mon-Thu, to 11pm Fri-Sat;) Original fox-and-hound murals line the walls of this long-standing restaurant location (eight have tried and failed over the course of decades) but Coles 735 Main has spruced up what looks like little more than a chiropractic office, thrown in a Provençal color scheme, a charming front patio and, most importantly, nailed the food and drink.

You'll find it packed as early as 7pm on a Monday – Lexingtonians have embraced the change, flocking here for bourbon cocktails and top-end local takes on both classic (killer grit fries with pecorino cheese) and more adventurous dishes.

Country Boy Brewing MICROBREWERY
(www.countryboybrewing.com; 436 Chair Ave) True to its name, Country Boy – all trucker hats, taxidermy and camo – delivers the best beer in the most authentically Kentuckian climate. Up to 16 taps are devoted to their own experimental concoctions, brewed with a rural Mikkeller-like approach (spruce-needle ales, crab-apple saisons, jalapeño smoked porters) and another eight for guests. There's no food, but a different food truck pulls round each night.

THE BOURBON TRAIL

Silky, caramel-colored bourbon whiskey was likely first distilled in Bourbon County, north of Lexington, around 1789. Today 90% of all bourbon that comes out of the US is produced in Kentucky, thanks to its pure, limestone-filtered water. Bourbon must contain at least 51% corn, and be stored in charred oak barrels for a minimum of two years. While connoisseurs drink it straight or with water, you must try a mint julep, the archetypal Southern drink made with bourbon, simple syrup and crushed mint.

The **Oscar Getz Museum of Whiskey History** (www.whiskeymuseum.com; 114 N 5th St; 10am-4pm Tue-Sat, noon-4pm Sun), in Bardstown, tells the bourbon story with old moonshine stills and other artifacts.

Most of Kentucky's distilleries, which are centered on Bardstown and Frankfort, offer tours. Check out Kentucky's official **Bourbon Trail website** (www.kybourbontrail.com). Note that it doesn't include every distillery.

To get around the dilemma of drinking and driving, sit back with your whiskey snifter on a tour with **Mint Julep Tours** (502-583-1433; www.mintjuleptours.com; 140 N Fourth St, Suite 326; tours from $99).

Distilleries near Bardstown:

Heaven Hill (www.bourbonheritagecenter.com; 1311 Gilkey Run Rd; tours $10-40; 10am-5pm Mon-Fri, noon-4pm Sun, closed Sun-Mon Jan-Feb) Distillery tours are offered, but you may also opt to explore the interactive Bourbon Heritage Center.

Jim Beam (502-543-9877; www.americanstillhouse.com; 149 Happy Hollow Rd; tours per person $10; 9am-5:30pm Mon-Sat, noon-4:30pm Sun) Watch a film about the Beam family and sample small-batch bourbons at the country's largest bourbon distillery. Beam makes Knob Creek (good), Knob Creek Single Barrel (better), Basil Hayden's (velvety) and the fabulous Booker's (high-proof enlightenment).

Maker's Mark (270-865-2099; www.makersmark.com; 3350 Burks Spring Rd; tours $9; 9:30am-3:30pm Mon-Sat, 11:30-3:30pm Sun, closed Sun Jan-Feb) This restored Victorian distillery is like a bourbon theme park, with an old gristmill and a gift shop where you can seal your own bottle in molten red wax.

Willet (502-348-0899; www.kentuckybourbonwhiskey.com; Loretto Rd; tours $7-12; 9am-5:30pm Mon-Fri, 10am-5:30pm Sat, noon-4:30 Sun Mar-Dec) A craftsman, family-owned distillery making small-batch bourbon in its own patented style. It's a gorgeous 120-acre property and one of our favorites. Tours run throughout the day.

Distilleries near Frankfort/Lawrenceburg:

Buffalo Trace (800-654-8471; www.buffalotracedistillery.com; 1001 Wilkinson Blvd; 9am-5:30pm Mon-Sat, noon-5:30pm Sun Apr-Oct) FREE The nation's oldest continuously operating distillery has highly regarded tours and free tastings.

Four Roses (502-839-3436; www.fourrosesbourbon.com; 1224 Bonds Mills Rd; tours $5; 9am-4pm Mon-Sat, noon-4pm Sun, closed summer) One of the most scenic distilleries, in a riverside Spanish Mission–style building. Free tastings.

Woodford Reserve (859-879-1812; www.woodfordreserve.com; 7855 McCracken Pike; tours $10-30; 10am-3pm Mon-Sat, 1-3pm Sun Mar-Dec) The historic site along a creek is restored to its 1800s glory; the distillery still uses old-fashioned copper pots. By far the most scenic of the lot.

Entertainment

Keeneland Association RACETRACK
(☎859-254-3412; www.keeneland.com; 4201 Versailles Rd; general admission $5; ⊙races Apr & Oct) Second only to Churchill Downs in terms of quality of competition, races run in April and October, when you can also glimpse champions train from sunrise to 10am. Frequent horse auctions lure sheiks, sultans, hedgefund princes and those who love (or serve) them.

Red Mile RACETRACK
(www.theredmile.com; 1200 Red Mile Rd; admission $2; ⊙races Aug–first week of Oct) Head here to see live harness racing in the covered grandstand or in the plush comfort of the clubhouse, where drivers on sulkies race champion standardbred pacers and trotters on the most historic mile-long harness track in the world. Live races are in the fall, but you can watch and wager on simulcast racing year-round.

Information

Visitor Center (☎859-233-7299; www.visitlex.com; 401 W Main St; ⊙9am-5pm Mon-Fri, from 10am Sat, noon-5pm Sun) Pick up maps and area information from the visitor center, located downtown in an upscale restaurant complex known as the Square.

Getting There & Around

Blue Grass Airport (LEX; ☎859-425-3100; www.bluegrassairport.com; 4000 Terminal Dr) is west of town, with about a dozen domestic nonstops. **Greyhound** (☎859-299-0428; www.greyhound.com; 477 W New Circle Rd) is two miles from downtown. **Lex-Tran** (www.lextran.com) runs local buses ($1; bus 6 goes to the Greyhound station, bus 21 goes to the airport and Keeneland weekdays from 6:30am to 8:50am and 1:30pm to 6:10pm only) as well as the free Colt trolley, a diesel/electric hybrid trolleybus that operates on two downtown routes, taking in most major points of interest and nightlife.

Central Kentucky

The Bluegrass Pkwy runs from I-65 in the west to Rte 60 in the east, passing through some of the most luscious pastureland in Kentucky.

About 40 miles south of Louisville is **Bardstown**, the 'Bourbon Capital of the World'. The historic downtown comes alive for the **Kentucky Bourbon Festival** (www.kybourbonfestival.com; Bardstown; ⊙Sep). Have a meal, some bourbon and a good night's sleep in the dim limestone environs of **Old Talbott Tavern** (☎502-348-3494; www.talbotts.com; 107 W Stephen Foster Ave; r from $69; mains $10-23; P ❄), which has been welcoming the likes of Abraham Lincoln and Daniel Boone since the late 1700s.

Follow Hwy 31 southwest to **Hodgenville** and the **Abraham Lincoln Birthplace** (www.nps.gov/abli; 2995 Lincoln Farm Road, Hodgenville; ⊙8am-4:45pm, to 6:45pm summer) FREE, a faux-Greek temple constructed around an old log cabin. Ten minutes away is Honest Abe's boyhood home at Knob Creek, with access to hiking trails.

About 25 miles (30 minutes) southwest of Lexington is **Shaker Village at Pleasant Hill** (www.shakervillageky.org; 3501 Lexington Rd; adult/child $10/5, riverboat rides $10/5; ⊙10am-5pm), home to a community of the Shaker religious sect until the early 1900s. Tour impeccably restored buildings, set amid buttercup meadows and winding stone paths. There's a charming **inn** (☎859-734-5611; www.shakervillageky.org; 3501 Lexington Rd; r $110-300; P 📶) and restaurant, a paddle-boat ride beneath the limestone bluffs along the Kentucky River, and a gift shop.

Daniel Boone National Forest

More than 700,000 acres of rugged ravines and gravity-defying sandstone arches cover much of the Appalachian foothills of eastern Kentucky. The main **ranger station** (☎859-745-3100; www.fs.fed.us/r8/boone; 1700 Bypass Rd) is in Winchester.

An hour southeast of Lexington is the **Red River Gorge**, whose cliffs and natural arches make for some of the best rock climbing in the country. **Red River Outdoors** (☎859-230-3567; www.redriveroutdoors.com; 415 Natural Bridge Rd; full-day guided climb for two from $100, cabins from $110) offers guided climbing trips, cabins on the ridge line and yoga. **Red River Climbing** (www.redriverclimbing.com) offers detailed route information on their website. Climbers and hikers (only) can also pay $2 to camp out behind **Miguel's Pizza** (www.miguelspizza.com; 1890 Natural Bridge Rd; pizza from $10; ⊙7am-8:45pm Mon-Thu, to 9:45pm Fri & Sat; 📶) in the hamlet of Slade, which also runs a climbing shop. Bordering Red River Gorge is the **Natural Bridge State Resort Park** (☎606-663-2214; www.parks.ky.gov; 2135 Natural Bridge Rd; r $109-154, cottages $149-239; P 📶 🏊), notable for its sandstone arch, it's a family-friendly park, with camping, rooms and cottages at its Hemlock Lodge and 20 miles of short hiking trails. If you don't want to leg it, you can ride the sky lift over the arch ($13 return).

Mammoth Cave National Park

With the longest cave system on earth, **Mammoth Cave National Park** (www.nps.gov/maca; 1 Mammoth Cave Pkwy, exit 53, off I-65; tours adult $5-55, child $3.50-20; ⏲8am-6pm, to 6:30pm summer) has some 400 miles of surveyed passageways. Mammoth is at least three times longer than any other known cave, with vast interior cathedrals, bottomless pits and strange, undulating rock formations. The caves have been used for prehistoric mineral-gathering, as a source of saltpeter for gunpowder and as a tuberculosis hospital. Guided tours have been offered since 1816. The area became a national park in 1941 and now attracts 600,000 visitors each year.

The only way to see the caves is on the excellent **ranger-guided tours** (☎800-967-2283) and it's wise to book ahead, especially in summer. Tours range from subterranean strolls to strenuous, day-long spelunking adventures (adults only). The Historic tour is particularly interesting.

In addition to the caves, the park contains 85 miles of trails – all for hiking, 60 miles designated for horseback riding and 25 miles for mountain biking. There are also three campgrounds with restrooms, though only a few sites have electricity or water hookups ($12 to $50), and 13 free backcountry campsites. Get your backcountry permit at the park visitor center.

GEORGIA

The largest state east of the Mississippi River is a labyrinth of geographic and cultural extremes: right-leaning Republican politics rub against liberal idealism; small, conservative towns merge with sprawling, progressive, financially flush cities; northern mountains rise to the clouds and produce roaring rivers, while coastal marshlands teem with fiddler crabs and swaying cordgrass. Georgia's southern beaches and islands are a treat. And so are its restaurant kitchens.

Information

Your own car is the most convenient way to move around Georgia. I-75 bisects the state running north–south; I-20 runs east–west.

Discover Georgia (☎800-847-4842; www.exploregeorgia.org) For statewide tourism information.

Georgia Department of Natural Resources (☎800-864-7275; www.gastateparks.org) For information on camping and activities in state parks.

Atlanta

With 5.5 million residents in the metro and outlying areas, the so-called capital of the South continues to experience explosive growth thanks to southbound Yankees and international immigrants alike. It's also booming as a tourist destination. Beyond the big-ticket downtown attractions you'll find a constellation of superlative restaurants, a palpable Hollywood influence (Atlanta has become a highly popular production center) and iconic African American history.

Without natural boundaries to control development, Atlanta keeps growing. Yet for all this suburbanization, Atlanta is a pretty city covered with trees and elegant homes. Distinct neighborhoods are like friendly small towns stitched together. The economy is robust, the population is young and creative, and racial tensions are minimal in 'the city too busy to hate.'

Sights & Activities

Downtown

Downtown Atlanta is undergoing yet another transformation, continuing the recent trend of developers and politicians focusing on making the urban core more vibrant and livable. Two new world-class museums and a new Atlanta Falcons football stadium (and subsequent demolition of the 23-year-old Georgia Dome) by the 2017 NFL season have once again given the capital of the South a new face.

World of Coca-Cola MUSEUM
(www.woccatlanta.com; 121 Baker St; adult/senior/child $16/14/12; ⏲10am-5pm Sun-Thu, 9am-5pm Fri-Sat) This self-congratulatory museum might prove entertaining to fizzy beverage and rash commercialization fans. The climactic moment comes when guests sample Coke products from around the world – a taste-bud-twisting good time! But there are also Andy Warhol pieces on view, a 4D film, company history and promotional materials aplenty.

Center for Civil and Human Rights MUSEUM
(www.civilandhumanrights.org; 100 Ivan Allen Jr Blvd; adult/senior/child $15/13/10; ⌚10am-5pm Mon-Sat, noon-5pm Sun) This striking 2014 addition to Atlanta's Centennial Park is a sobering $68 million memorial to the American Civil Rights and Global Human Rights Movements. Beautifully designed and thoughtfully executed, the indisputable highlight centers around an absolutely harrowing interactive mock Woolworth's lunch-counter sit-in simulation that will leave you speechless and drive some to tears.

College Football Hall of Fame MUSEUM
(www.cfbhall.com; 250 Marietta St; adult/senior/child $20/18/17; ⌚10am-5pm Sun-Fri, 9am-6pm Sat; 👪) It is impossible to overstate the importance of college football to American culture. This new museum, relocated from Indiana in 2014 and revamped into this three-story, 94,256-sq-ft gridiron sanctuary, is a supremely cool and suitable shrine.

Pledge your allegiance to your team of choice upon entry and your interactive experience is customized as you make your way past famous trophies like the coveted Heisman and hands-on experiences like Fight Song Karaoke or attempting to kick a 20-yard field goal. Needless to say, kids go nuts here.

CNN Center TV STUDIO
(☎404-827-2300; www.cnn.com/tour/atlanta; 1 CNN Center; tours adult/senior/child $16/15/13; ⌚9am-5pm) The 55-minute behind-the-scenes tour through the headquarters of the international, 24-hour news giant is a good time for fans. Although visitors don't get very close to Wolf Blitzer (or his cronies), the 9am and noon timeslots offer the best bets for seeing anchors live on-air.

Midtown

Midtown is like a hipper version of downtown, with plenty of great bars, restaurants and cultural venues.

★**High Museum of Art** GALLERY
(www.high.org; 1280 Peachtree St NE; adult/child $19.50/12; ⌚10am-5pm Tue-Thu & Sat, to 9pm Fri, noon-5pm Sun) Atlanta's modern High Museum was the first to exhibit art lent from Paris' Louvre, and is a destination as much for its architecture as its world-class exhibits. The striking whitewashed multilevel building houses a permanent collection of eye-catching late 19th-century furniture, early American modern canvases from the likes of George Morris and Albert Gallatin, and postwar work from Mark Rothko.

Atlanta Botanical Garden GARDENS
(☎404-876-5859; www.atlantabotanicalgarden.org; 1345 Piedmont Ave NE; adult/child $19/13; ⌚9am-7pm Tue, to 5pm Wed-Sun) In the northwest corner of Piedmont Park, the stunning 30-acre botanical garden has a Japanese garden, winding paths and the amazing Fuqua Orchid Center.

Margaret Mitchell House & Museum LANDMARK
(☎404-249-7015; www.margaretmitchellhouse.com; 990 Peachtree St, at 10th St; adult/student/child $13/10/8.50; ⌚10am-5pm Mon-Sat, noon-5:30pm Sun) A shrine to the author of *Gone With the Wind*. Mitchell wrote her epic in a small apartment in the basement of this historic house, though nothing inside it actually belonged to her.

GEORGIA FACTS

Nickname Peach State

Population 10 million

Area 59,425 sq miles

Capital city Atlanta (population 5.5 million)

Other cities Savannah (population 142,772)

Sales tax 7%, plus 6% extra on hotel accommodations

Birthplace of Baseball legend Ty Cobb (1886–1961), president Jimmy Carter (b 1924), civil rights leader Martin Luther King Jr (1929–68), singer Ray Charles (1930–2004)

Home of Coca-Cola, the world's busiest airport, *Gone with the Wind*

Politics Socially conservative as a whole; Atlanta has been known to swing both ways

Famous for Peaches

Odd law Donkeys may not be kept in bathtubs. Seriously, don't do it.

Driving distances Atlanta to St Marys 343 miles, Atlanta to Dahlonega 75 miles

Atlanta

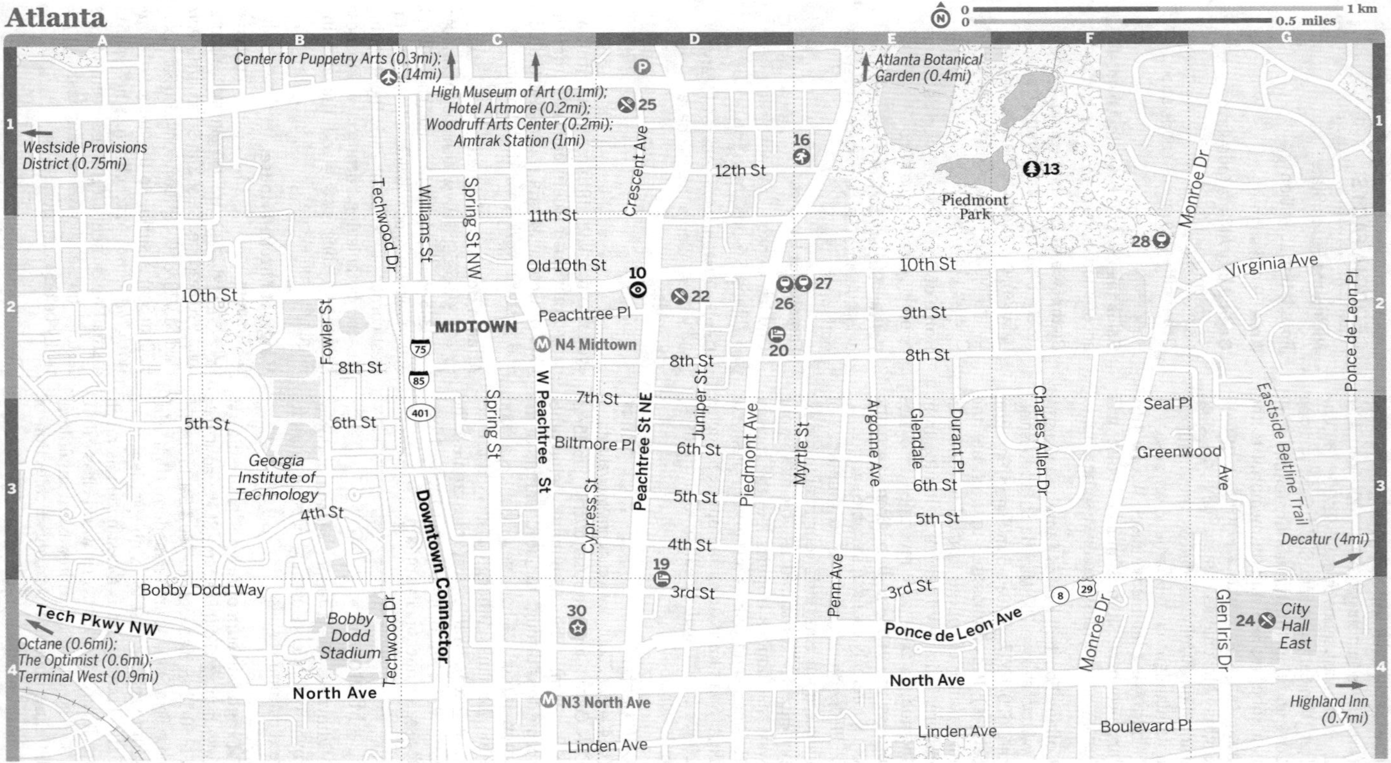
Center for Puppetry Arts (0.3mi); (14mi)
High Museum of Art (0.1mi); Hotel Artmore (0.2mi); Woodruff Arts Center (0.2mi); Amtrak Station (1mi)
Atlanta Botanical Garden (0.4mi)
Westside Provisions District (0.75mi)
Decatur (4mi)
Highland Inn (0.7mi)
Octane (0.6mi); The Optimist (0.6mi); Terminal West (0.9mi)
Piedmont Park
MIDTOWN
Georgia Institute of Technology
Bobby Dodd Stadium
City Hall East
Eastside Beltline Trail
Downtown Connector
Tech Pkwy NW
N4 Midtown
N3 North Ave
Ponce de Leon Pl
Ponce de Leon Ave
Virginia Ave
Monroe Dr
Seal Pl
Greenwood Ave
Glen Iris Dr
Boulevard Pl
Charles Allen Dr
Durant Pl
Glendale
Argonne Ave
Penn Ave
Myrtle St
Piedmont Ave
Juniper St
Peachtree St NE
Cypress St
Crescent Ave
Peachtree Pl
Biltmore Pl
W Peachtree St
Spring St
Spring St NW
Williams St
Techwood Dr
Fowler St
Bobby Dodd Way
North Ave
Linden Ave
12th St
11th St
10th St
Old 10th St
9th St
8th St
7th St
6th St
5th St
4th St
3rd St
75
85
401
29
8
1 km
0.5 miles
0
A
B
C
D
E
F
G
1
2
3
4
10
13
16
19
20
22
24
25
26
27
28
30

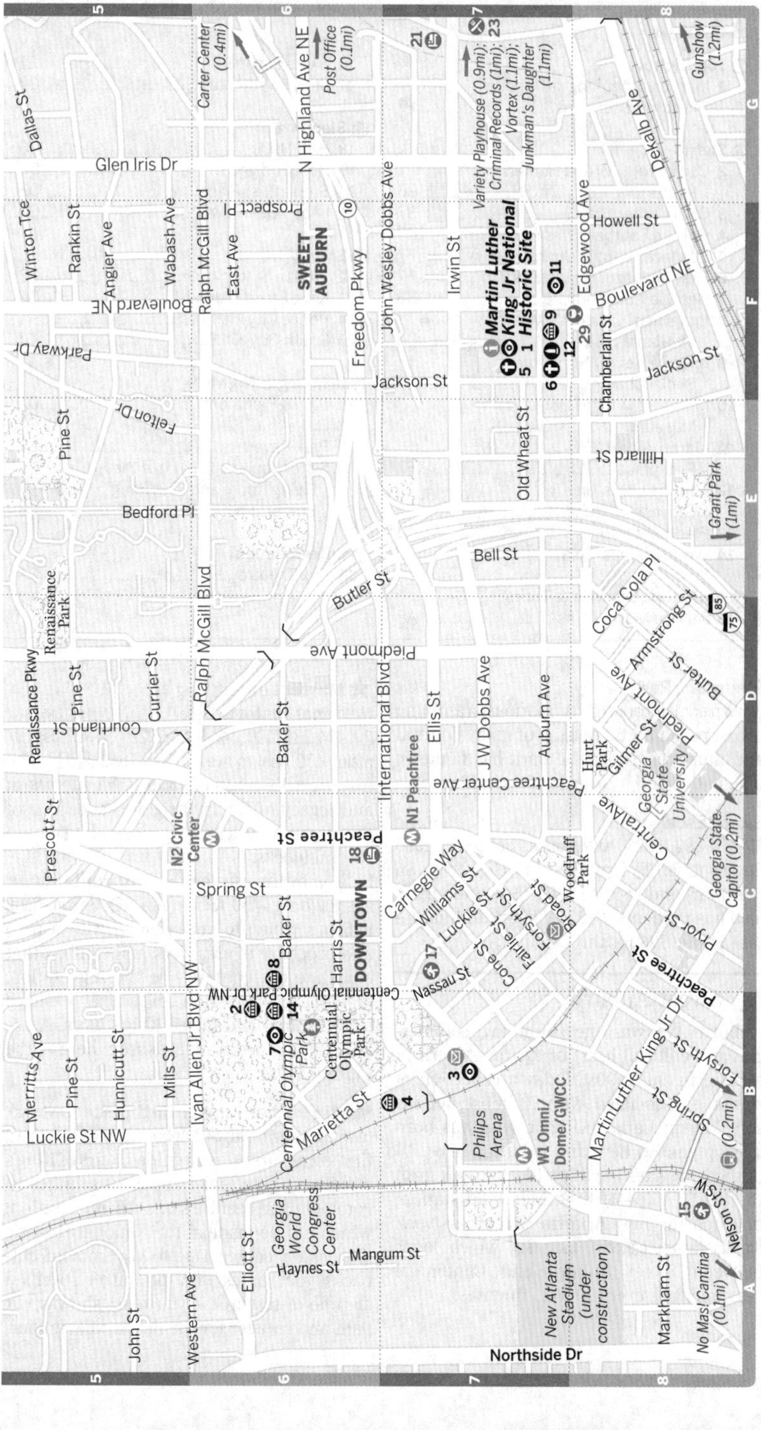
Dallas St
Glen Iris Dr
Winton Tce
Rankin St
Angier Ave
Wabash Ave
Ralph McGill Blvd
Carter Center (0.4mi)
N Highland Ave NE
Post Office (0.1mi)
Prospect Pl
East Ave
SWEET AUBURN
Freedom Pkwy
John Wesley Dobbs Ave
Irwin St
Variety Playhouse (0.9mi); Criminal Records (1mi); Vortex (1.1mi); Junkman's Daughter (1.1mi)
Martin Luther King Jr National Historic Site
Edgewood Ave
Howell St
Dekalb Ave
Gunshow (1.2mi)
Boulevard NE
Parkway Dr
Jackson St
Chamberlain St
Felton Dr
Pine St
Old Wheat St
Hilliard St
Bedford Pl
Grant Park (1mi)
Bell St
Renaissance Park
Butler St
Coca Cola Pl
Armstrong St
Renaissance Pkwy
Courtland St
Currier St
Piedmont Ave
Butler St
Baker St
International Blvd
Ellis St
J W Dobbs Ave
Auburn Ave
Hurt Park
Gilmer St
Georgia State University
Prescott St
N2 Civic Center
Peachtree St
N1 Peachtree
Peachtree Center Ave
Central Ave
Georgia State Capitol (0.2mi)
Spring St
DOWNTOWN
Harris St
Carnegie Way
Williams St
Luckie St
Forsyth St
Fairlie St
Cone St
Broad St
Woodruff Park
Pryor St
Centennial Olympic Park Dr NW
Nassau St
Centennial Olympic Park
Ivan Allen Jr Blvd NW
Merritts Ave
Hunnicutt St
Mills St
Luckie St NW
Marietta St
Philips Arena
W1 Omni/Dome/GWCC
Martin Luther King Jr Dr
Forsyth St
Spring St
Georgia World Congress Center
Mangum St
Haynes St
Elliott St
Western Ave
John St
New Atlanta Stadium (under construction)
Markham St
Nelson St
No Mas! Cantina (0.1mi)
Northside Dr

Atlanta

Piedmont Park PARK
(www.piedmontpark.org) A glorious, rambling urban park and the setting of many cultural and music festivals. The park has fantastic bike paths, and a Saturday **Green Market**.

Skate Escape CYCLING
(☎404-892-1292; www.skateescape.com; 1086 Piedmont Ave NE) Rents out bicycles (from $6 per hour) and in-line skates ($6 per hour). It also has tandems ($12 per hour) and mountain bikes ($25 for three hours).

Sweet Auburn

Auburn Ave was the thumping commercial and cultural heart of African American culture in the 1900s. Today a collection of sights is associated with its most famous son, Martin Luther King Jr, who was born here, preached here and is buried here. All of the King sites are a few blocks' walk from the MARTA (p411) King Memorial station; or catch the new **Atlanta Streetcar** (www.theatlantastreetcar.com; fares $1), which loops between Sweet Auburn and Centennial Olympic Park every 10 to 15 minutes.

★**Martin Luther King Jr National Historic Site** HISTORIC SITE
(☎404-331-5190, 404-331-6922; www.nps.gov/malu; 450 Auburn Ave; ⊙9am-5pm) FREE The historic site commemorates the life, work and legacy of the civil rights leader, one of the great Americans. The center takes up several blocks.

Stop by the excellent **visitor center** (www.nps.gov/malu; 450 Auburn Ave NE; ⊙9am-5pm, to 6pm summer) to get oriented with a map and brochure of area sites, and exhibits that elucidate the context – ie the segregation, systematic oppression and racial violence that inspired and fueled King's work. A 1.5-mile landscaped trail leads from here to the Carter Center.

Martin Luther King Jr Birthplace LANDMARK
(www.nps.gov/malu; 501 Auburn Ave) FREE Free, first-come, first-served guided tours of King's childhood home take about 30 minutes to complete and require same-day registration, which can be made at the National Historic Site visitor center. Due to government cutbacks, tour times were no longer specified at time of research – you must show up at 9am and register for the next available tour.

King Center for Non-Violent Social Change
MUSEUM

(www.thekingcenter.org; 449 Auburn Ave NE; ⊙9am-5pm, to 6pm summer) Across from the National Historic Site visitor center, this place has more information on King's life and work and a few of his personal effects, including his Nobel Peace Prize. His gravesite is surrounded by a long reflecting pool and can be viewed any time.

First Ebenezer Baptist Church
CHURCH

(www.historicebenezer.org; 407 Auburn Ave NE; ⊙tours 9am-5pm, to 6pm Summer) FREE Martin Luther King Jr, his father and grandfather were all pastors here, and King Jr's mother was the choir director. Sadly she was murdered here by a deranged gunman while she sat at the organ in 1974. A multimillion-dollar restoration, completed in 2011, brought the church back to the 1960–68 period when King Jr served as co-pastor with his father.

Sunday services are now held at a new Ebenezer across the street.

⊙ Virginia-Highland

Families enjoy the historic homes and quiet, leafy streets off North Highland Ave. The main focal point of the area is the triangular Virginia-Highland intersection turned commercial district, chockablock with restaurants, cafes and boutiques – corporate and indie.

Carter Center
LIBRARY, MUSEUM

(☑404-865-7100; www.jimmycarterlibrary.org; 441 Freedom Pkwy; adult/senior/child $8/6/free; ⊙9am-4:45pm Mon-Sat, noon-4:45pm Sun) Located on a hilltop overlooking downtown, it features exhibits highlighting Jimmy Carter's 1977–81 presidency, including a replica of the Oval Office and his Nobel Prize. Don't miss the tranquil Japanese garden and new butterfly garden out back. The 1.5-mile-long, landscaped, Freedom Park Trail leads from here to the Martin Luther King Jr National Historic Site through Freedom Park.

🎪 Festivals & Events

Atlanta Jazz Festival
MUSIC

(www.atlantafestivals.com; Piedmont Park; ⊙May) The month-long event culminates in live concerts in Piedmont Park on Memorial Day weekend.

Atlanta Pride Festival
GAY & LESBIAN

(www.atlantapride.org; ⊙Oct) Atlanta's annual GLBT festival.

ATLANTA BELTLINE

The **Atlanta BeltLine** (www.beltline.org) 🖉 is an enormous sustainable redevelopment project that is repurposing an existing 22-mile rail corridor encircling the city into 33 miles of connected multiuse trails. It is the most comprehensive transportation and economic development effort ever undertaken in Atlanta and among the largest, most wide-ranging urban redevelopment programs currently underway in the United States. At the time of research, four trails totaling 6.8 miles were complete. Of most interest to tourists is the 2.2-mile Eastside Trail, connecting the hip urban neighborhood of Inman Park with Piedmont Park in Midtown.

National Black Arts Festival
CULTURAL

(☑404-730-7315; www.nbaf.org; ⊙Jul) Artists from across the country converge to celebrate African American music, theater, literature and film.

🛏 Sleeping

Rates at downtown hotels tend to fluctuate wildly depending on whether there is a large convention in town. The least expensive option is to stay in one of the many chain hotels along the MARTA line outside downtown and take the train into the city for sightseeing.

★Urban Oasis B&B
B&B $$

(☑770-714-8618; www.urbanoasisbandb.com; 130A Krog St NE; r $125-195; P❄🛜) Hidden from view inside a gated and repurposed 1950s cotton sorting warehouse, this wonderful retro-modern loft B&B is urban dwelling at its best. Enter into a huge and funky common area stealing hordes of natural light through massive windows and make your way to one of three rooms, all discerningly appointed with Haywood Wakefield mid-Century Modern furnishings. It's on the doorstep of famed Atlanta chef Kevin Rathbun's culinary empire, the Krog Street Market, Edgewood, Inman Park MARTA *and* the Beltline. Two-night minimum.

Hotel Artmore
BOUTIQUE HOTEL $$

(☑404-876-6100; www.artmorehotel.com; 1302 W Peachtree St; r $139-399; P❄@🛜) This funky art-deco gem wins all sorts of accolades:

excellent service, a wonderful courtyard with fire pit and a superb location across the street from Arts Center MARTA station. The 1924 Spanish-Mediterranean architectural landmark has been completely revamped into an artistic boutique hotel that's become an urban sanctuary for those who appreciate their trendiness with a dollop of discretion.

Social Goat B&B B&B $$
(☎404-626-4830; www.thesocialgoatbandb.com; 548 Robinson Ave SE; r $155-245; P ❄ ☜) Skirting Grant Park, this wonderfully restored 1900 Queen Anne Victorian mansion has six rooms decorated in country French style and is loaded down with period antiques. More importantly, however, you'll share the real estate with goats, turkeys, chickens and cats!

Hotel Indigo BOUTIQUE HOTEL $$
(☎404-874-9200; www.hotelindigo.com; 683 Peachtree St; r $109-179; P ❄ @ ☜) A boutique-style chain hotel, the music-themed Indigo offers a whimsical personality and local in-room touches like custom-stitched domes on the bedspreads that echo the iconic Islamic-style domes of the Fox Theatre across the street. The outstanding Midtown location is within walking distance of bars, restaurants and MARTA.

A second location at **230 Peachtree St** (☎888-233-9450; www.hotelindigo.com; 230 Peachtree St NE; P ❄ @ ☜) near Centennial Park will open by 2016.

Highland Inn INN $$
(☎404-874-5756; www.thehighlandinn.com; 644 N Highland Ave; s/d from $73/103; P ❄ ☜) This European-style 65-room independent inn, built in 1927, has appealed to touring musicians over the years. Rooms aren't huge, but it's as affordably comfortable as in Atlanta city proper – to say nothing of its great location in the Virginia-Highland area. It's one of the few with single rooms.

★**Stonehurst Place** B&B $$$
(☎404-881-0722; www.stonehurstplace.com; 923 Piedmont Ave NE; r $199-429; P ❄ @ ☜) Built in 1896 by the Hinman family, this elegant B&B has all the modern amenities one could ask for, is fully updated with ecofriendly water treatment and heating systems, and has original Warhol illustrations on the wall. Well located, it's an exceptional choice if you have the budget.

Eating

After New Orleans, Atlanta is the best city in the South to eat and the food culture here is nothing short of obsessive. The **Westside Provisions District** (www.westsidepd.com; 100-1210 Howell Mill Rd; P), **Krog Street Market** (www.krogstreetmarket.com; 99 Krog St) and **Ponce City Market** (675 Ponce De Leon Ave NE) are all newish and hip mixed-use residential and restaurant complexes sprinkled among Atlanta's continually transitioning urban neighborhoods.

Downtown & Midtown

Empire State South NEW SOUTHERN $$
(www.empirestatesouth.com; 999 Peachtree St; mains $5-36; ⊙7am-10pm Mon-Wed, to 11pm Thu-Sat, 10:30am-2pm Sun; ☜) This rustic-hip Midtown bistro serves imaginative New Southern fare and does not disappoint, be it at breakfast (they make their own bagels, the attention to coffee detail approaches Pacific Northwest levels and they mix fried chicken, bacon *and* pimiento cheese!) or throughout the remains of the day.

No Mas! Cantina MEXICAN $$
(☎404-574-5678; www.nomascantina.com; 180 Walker St SW; mains $7-20; ⊙11am-10pm Sun-Thu, 11am-11pm Fri & Sat; ☜ 👪) Though the design overkill feels a bit like dining inside a hungover piñata, locals are sold on the festive Mexican at this downtown Castleberry Hill cantina. Despite its quiet location, it's walking distance from the New Atlanta Stadium, Phillips Arena, CNN Center and Centennial Park.

South City Kitchen SOUTHERN $$$
(☎404-873-7358; www.southcitykitchen.com; 1144 Crescent Ave; mains $18-36; ⊙11am-3:30pm & 5-10pm Sun-Thu, to 10:30pm Fri & Sat) An upscale Southern kitchen featuring tasty updated staples like buttermilk fried chicken served with sautéed collards and mash, and a Georgia trout, pan-fried with roasted heirloom carrots. Start with fried green tomatoes, a Southern specialty *before* the movie.

Westside

West Egg Cafe DINER $
(www.westeggcafe.com; 1100 Howell Mill Rd; mains $6.25-8; ⊙7am-3pm Mon & Tue, to 9pm Wed-Fri, 8am-9pm Sat, to 6pm Sun; P ☜ 👪) Belly up to the marble breakfast counter or grab a table and dive into black bean cakes and eggs, tur-

DON'T MISS

WALKER STALKERS: WELCOME TO WOODBURY!

The post-apocalyptic world of flesh-eating zombies on AMC's *The Walking Dead* has had much of the world paralyzed in front of their TVs and devices since its inaugural season in 2010, and the whole end-of-days showdown takes place right here in the Peach State. The city of Atlanta and the historic small town of Senoia and its surrounds, about an hour's drive south of Atlanta, are the setting for the fanatically popular show. **Atlanta Movie Tours** (855-255-3456; www.atlantamovietours.com; 327 Nelson St SW) offers two good-time Zombie tours to filming locations, one in Atlanta proper and another around Senoia (our favorite), narrated by extras from the show who are chomping at the bits to reveal all sorts of insidery tidbits about cast members and filming. Additionally, because its an active film set from May to November, the show's actors can often be seen around Senoia grabbing a morning coffee at **Senoia Coffee & Cafe** (www.senoiacoffeeandcafe.com; 1 Main St; mains $2.75-19; 7:30am-3pm Mon-Thu, to 9pm Fri, to 6pm Sat) or partying at Zac Brown's restaurant, **Southern Ground Social Club** (www.southerngroundsocialclub.com; 18 Main St; 11am-midnight Tue-Thu, to 2am Fri-Sat) – Norman Reedus drove himself right past our tour van on the way to the studio. The entire town, on the National Register of Historic Places, has been transformed into zombie central. Be sure to pop into the **Woodbury Shoppe** (www.woodburyshoppe.com; 48 Main St; 11am-5pm Mon-Sat, 1-5pm Sun), the official *Walking Dead* souvenir shop, which includes a *Walking Dead*–themed cafe downstairs and a small museum.

key sausage Benedict, pimento cheese and bacon omelet, or a fried green tomato BLT. It's all reimagined versions of old-school classics, served in a stylish and spare dining room.

Star Provisions SELF-CATERING $
(www.starprovisions.com; 1198 Howell Mill Rd; 10am-midnight Mon-Sat;) DIY gourmands will feel at home among the cheese shops and butcher cases, bakeries, organic cafe and kitchen hardware depots attached to the city's finest dining establishment, **Bacchanalia** (404-365-0410; www.starprovisions.com/bacchanalia; 1198 Howell Mill Rd; prix-fixe per person $85; from 6pm). Excellent picnic accoutrements.

★Cooks & Soldiers BASQUE $$
(404-996-2623; www.cooksandsoldiers.com; 691 14th St; dishes $8-32; 5-10pm Sun-Wed, to 11pm Thu, to 2am Fri-Sat;) A game-changing Westside newcomer, this Basque-inspired hot spot specializes in small plate *pintxos* (Basque tapas) and wood-fired *asadas* (grills) designed to share. Both the food and cocktails are outstanding. Highlights: blood orange gin and tonic, a black-truffled White American grilled cheese, a dehydrated tomato tartar and a perfectly charred Berkshire pork tenderloin with hazelnut romesco.

★The Optimist SEAFOOD $$$
(404-477-6260; www.theoptimistrestaurant.com; 914 Howell Mill Rd; mains $21-33; 11:30am-2:30pm & 5-10pm Mon-Thu, to 11pm Fri-Sat;) Guidebook space could never do this Westside sustainable-seafood mecca justice. In a word: astonishing! Start with the Spanish charred octopus, braised for four hours in red wine; move on to a duck-fat-poached swordfish or whole fish in garlicky ginger sauce and a side of corn-milk hushpuppies; finish with a scoop of housemade salted-caramel ice cream.

This is one of the South's most buzzed about hot spots, not a word of it heresy. If you cannot get a reservation, plop yourself down at the massive fresh-oyster bar. Alternatively, just practice your putting skills on their three-hole green and smell that miraculous food – a better option than actually eating at lesser establishments.

Virginia-Highland & Around

Little Five Points is Atlanta's bohemian home and has a fun vibe on weekends. Inman Park is a transitional neighborhood, set just east of downtown.

Sevananda SELF-CATERING $
(www.sevananda.coop; 467 Moreland Ave NE, Little Five Points; 8am-10pm) Voted Atlanta's best health-food store and a gold mine for self-caterers.

★Fox Brothers BARBECUE $$
(www.foxbrosbbq.com; 1238 DeKalb Ave NE; dishes $10-27; 11am-10pm Sun-Thu, to 11pm Fri & Sat;)

MARTIN LUTHER KING JR: A CIVIL RIGHTS GIANT

Martin Luther King Jr, the quintessential figure of the American Civil Rights movement and arguably America's greatest leader, was born in 1929, the son of an Atlanta preacher and choir leader. His lineage was significant not only because he followed his father to the pulpit of Ebenezer Baptist Church, but also because his political speeches rang out with a preacher's inflections.

In 1955 King led the year-long 'bus boycott' in Montgomery, AL, which resulted in the US Supreme Court removing laws that enforced segregated buses. From this successful beginning King emerged as an inspiring moral voice.

His nonviolent approach to racial equality and peace, which he borrowed from Gandhi and used as a potent weapon against hate, segregation and racially motivated violence – a Southern epidemic at the time – makes his death all the more tragic. He was assassinated on a Memphis hotel balcony in 1968, four years after receiving the Nobel Peace Prize and five years after giving his legendary 'I Have a Dream' speech in Washington, DC.

King remains one of the most recognized and respected figures of the 20th century. Over 10 years he led a movement that essentially ended a system of statutory discrimination in existence since the country's founding.

At this longtime Atlanta classic, set in Inman Park, ribs are scorched and smoked perfectly with a hint of charcoaled crust on the outside and tender on the inside. It's also known for its exceptional Texas-style brisket and Brunswick-stew-smothered tator tots. Always packed.

Vortex BURGERS $$

(www.thevortexbarandgrill.com; 438 Moreland Ave NE; burgers $8.25-16.25; 11am-midnight Sun-Thu, to 2am Fri & Sat) An NC-17 joint cluttered with Americana memorabilia, where alterna-hipsters mingle alongside Texas tourists and Morehouse College steppers at the Godfather of Atlanta burger joints, which veer from impressive to outlandish but are always some of the most heralded and heart-stopping in Atlanta. The 20ft-tall skull facade is a Little Five Points landmark of pre-Olympic Games outrageousness.

★**Octopus Bar** ASIAN FUSION $$

(www.octopusbaratl.com; 560 Gresham Ave SE, East Atlanta; dishes $9-15; 10:30pm-2:30am Mon-Sat) Do they keep odd hours? Is seating difficult to come by? Does it take so long to get your fusion grub because the chefs are too busy fielding industry complaints from a room full of sous chefs and servers? The answer, of course, is yes, to all of the above.

So leave your hang-ups at the hotel – this is punk-rock dining – and get to know what's good at this indoor-outdoor patio dive nuanced with graffed-up walls and ethereal electronica. No reservations, so line up early.

East Atlanta

★**Gunshow** NEW SOUTHERN $$$

(404-380-1886; www.gunshowatl.com; 924 Garrett St SE; dishes $12-20; 6-9pm Tue-Sat;) Celebrity chef Kevin Gillespie's latest lightbulb moment is an unorthodox evening out. Guests do not order at the three nightly seatings, but rather choose between 12 or so smallish dishes, dreamed up by five chefs in the open kitchen, who then hawk their blood, sweat and culinary tears dim-sum-style tableside.

It can be agonizing, turning your nose up at a smoked ham hock confit because you're holding out for the Saigon-style Kobe beef tartar, but it's a dining experience like no other and Atlanta's hottest table. Reservations open 30 days out.

Decatur

Independent Decatur, 6 miles east of downtown, is a countercultural enclave and a bona-fide foodie destination. Like most traditional Southern towns, the gazebo-crowned **Courthouse Square** is the center of the action, with a number of restaurants, cafes and shops surrounding it.

Victory SANDWICHES $

(www.vicsandwich.com; 340 Church St; sandwiches $4-5; 11am-2am;) This spare, converted Decatur brick house is a wonderful bargain gourmet sandwich counter where baguettes are stuffed with white anchovies and lemon mayo, or chicken and ghost pepper jack, among other intriguing options.

★Leon's Full Service FUSION **$$**

(☎404-687-0500; www.leonsfullservice.com; 131 E Ponce de Leon Ave; mains $12-24; ⏰5pm-1am Mon, 11:30am-1am Tue-Thu & Sun, to 2am Fri & Sat; 📶) Leon's can come across as a bit pretentious, but the gorgeous concrete bar and open floor-plan spilling out of a former service station and onto a groovy heated deck with floating beams remains cooler than thou and fully packed at all times.

Everything, from the beer, wine and cocktails (spirits are all craft, small-batch creations) to the menu, show love and attention to detail. No reservations.

Cakes & Ale MODERN AMERICAN **$$$**

(☎404-377-7994; www.cakesandalerestaurant.com; 155 Sycamore St; mains $9-32; ⏰11:30am-2:30pm & 6-10pm Tue-Thu, 11:30am-2:30pm & 5:30-10:30pm Fri-Sat) A Chez Panisse alum and pastry mastermind run this hip eatery. The bakery next door has life-affirming hot chocolate along with a case of delectable pastries, while the restaurant features spare but stunning selections that could mean perfectly grilled *framani soppresata* sandwiches with chard, preserved-lemon ricotta and Dijon (a lunch standout), and pork guinea hen or lamb at dinner.

🍷 Drinking & Nightlife

Edgewood, very near Sweet Auburn, is the latest edgy neighborhood to be flipped into the *en vogue* nightlife destination.

Brick Store Pub BAR

(www.brickstorepub.com; 125 E Court Sq; draft beers $5-12) Beer hounds geek out on Atlanta's best craft beer selection at this pub in Decatur, with some 30 meticulously chosen drafts (including those in the more intimate Belgian beer bar upstairs). It serves nearly 300 beers by the bottle from a 15,000-bottle vault and draws a fun, young crowd every night.

Argosy GASTROPUB

(www.argosy-east.com; 470 Flat Shoals Ave SE; ⏰5pm-2:30am Mon-Fri, from 11am Sat-Sun; 📶) This East Atlanta gastropub nails it with an extensive list of rare craft beers, perfect bar food (the Don-a-Tello pizza is insanely good) and a space that shocks and awes. The multi-angled bar snakes its way through the largely masculine space, a gorgeous specimen at which to socialize, and living-room-style lounge areas pepper the remaining real estate.

Kimball House COCKTAIL BAR

(www.kimball-house.com; 303 E Howard Ave; cocktails $8-12; ⏰5pm-1am Sun-Thu, to 2am Fri-Sat) Housed in an atmospheric restored train depot slightly off the grid in Decatur, Kimball House harbors a vaguely saloonlike feel and specializes in craft cocktails, absinthe service and a long list of flown-in-fresh oysters.

Sister Louisa's Church of the Living Room and Ping Pong Emporium BAR

(www.sisterlouisaschurch.com; 466 Edgewood Ave; ⏰5pm-3am Mon-Fri, 1pm-3am Sat, to midnight Sun; 📶) This cradle of Edgewood's bar revival fosters a church theme, but it's nothing like Westminster Abbey. Sacrilegious art peppers every patch of free wall space, the kind of offensive stuff that starts wars in some parts. Praise the resistance to fancy craft cocktails and join the congregation, chuckling at the artistry or staring at mesmerizing table-tennis matches.

GAY & LESBIAN ATLANTA

Atlanta – or 'Hotlanta' as some might call it – is one of the few places in Georgia with a noticeable and active gay and lesbian population. Midtown is the center of gay life; the epicenter is around Piedmont Park and the intersection of 10th St and Piedmont Ave, where you can check out **Blake's** (www.blakesontheparkatlanta.com; 227 10th St NE), Atlanta's classic gay bar, or the appropriately named hot spot of the moment, **10th & Piedmont** (www.communitashospitality.com/10th-and-piedmont; 991 Piedmont Ave NE; ⏰11:30am-4pm & 5-10pm Mon-Thu, 11:30am-4pm & 5-11pm Fri, 10am-4pm & 5-11pm Sat, 10am-4pm & 5-10pm Sun), good for both food and late-night shenanigans. The town of Decatur, east of downtown Atlanta, has a significant lesbian community. For news and information, grab a copy of *David Atlanta* (www.davidatlanta.com); also check out www.gayatlanta.com.

Atlanta Pride Festival (p405) is a massive annual celebration of the city's gay and lesbian community. Held in October in and around Piedmont Park.

Park Tavern BAR
(www.parktavern.com; 500 10th Street NE; 4:30pm-midnight Mon-Fri, from 11:30am Sat & Sun;) The outdoor patio of this staple microbrewery-restaurant on the edge of Piedmont Park is one of the most beautiful spots in Atlanta to sit back and drink away a weekend afternoon.

Octane CAFE
(www.octanecoffee.com; 1009-B Marietta St; coffee $2.50-5; 7am-11pm Mon-Thu, 7am-midnight Fri, 8am-11pm Sat-Sun;) This industrial-hip coffeehouse near Georgia Tech's campus, the original of three locations in the city, brews the joe of choice for severe caffeine junkies, following a 'direct trade' philosophy. It remains Atlanta's most serious coffeehouse.

Entertainment

Atlanta has big-city nightlife with lots of live music and cultural events. For listings, check out **Atlanta Coalition of Performing Arts** (www.atlantaperforms.com). The **Atlanta Music Guide** (www.atlantamusicguide.com) maintains a live-music schedule, plus a directory of local venues and links to online ticketing.

Theater

Woodruff Arts Center ARTS
(www.woodruffcenter.org; 1280 Peachtree St NE, at 15th St) An arts campus hosting the High Museum, the Atlanta Symphony Orchestra and the Alliance Theatre.

Fox Theatre THEATER
(855-285-8499; www.foxtheatre.org; 660 Peachtree St NE; box office 10am-6pm Mon-Fri, to 3pm Sat) A spectacular 1929 movie palace with fanciful Moorish and Egyptian designs. It hosts Broadway shows and concerts in an auditorium holding more than 4500 people. Tours are also available.

Live Music & Nightclubs

Cover charges at the following vary nightly. Check the respective websites for music calendars and ticket prices.

Terminal West LIVE MUSIC
(887 W Marietta St) Voted Atlanta's best live-music venue, it's inside a beautifully revamped 100-year-old iron and steel foundry on the Westside.

Eddie's Attic LIVE MUSIC
(404-377-4976; www.eddiesattic.com; 515b N McDonough St) In East Atlanta, this is one of the city's best venues for live folk and acoustic music, renowned for breaking local artists; nonsmoking atmosphere seven nights a week.

Variety Playhouse LIVE MUSIC
(www.variety-playhouse.com; 1099 Euclid Ave NE) A smartly booked and well-run concert venue featuring a variety of touring artists. It's the anchor that keeps Little Five Points relevant.

Shopping

Junkman's Daughter VINTAGE
(www.thejunkmansdaughter.com; 464 Moreland Ave NE; 11am-7pm Mon-Fri, from noon Sun) A defiant and fiercely independent cradle of counterculture since 1982, this 10,000-sq-ft alternative superstore stocks racks of vintage, ornery bumper stickers, kitschy toys and tchotchkes, *Star Wars* lunch boxes, incense, wigs, offensive coffee mugs and a whole lot more. It put Little Five Points on the map.

Criminal Records MUSIC
(www.criminalatl.com; 1154 Euclid Ave; 11am-9pm Mon-Sat, noon-7pm Sun) A throwback record store with used and new pop, soul, jazz and metal, on CD or vinyl. It has a fun music-related book section, and some decent comic books.

Information

EMERGENCY & MEDICAL SERVICES

Atlanta Medical Center (www.atlantamedcenter.com; 303 Pkwy Dr NE) A tertiary care hospital considered Atlanta's best since 1901.

Atlanta Police Department (404-614-6544; www.atlantapd.org) Atlanta's police department.

MEDIA

Atlanta (www.atlantamagazine.com) A monthly general-interest magazine covering local issues, arts and dining.

Atlanta Daily World (www.atlantadailyworld.com) The nation's oldest continuously running African American newspaper (since 1928).

Atlanta Journal-Constitution (www.ajc.com) Atlanta's major daily newspaper, with a good travel section on Sunday.

Creative Loafing (www.clatl.com) For hip tips on music, arts and theater, this free alternative weekly comes out every Wednesday.

POST

Post Office (800-275-8777; www.usps.com; 190 Marietta St NW, CNN Center; 11am-4pm Mon-Fri) Little Five Points (455 Moreland Ave NE; 9am-11am & noon-5pm Mon-Fri); North Highland (1190 N Highland Ave NE; 8:30am-6pm Mon-Fri, to noon Sat); Phoenix Station (41

ATLANTA FOR CHILDREN

Atlanta has plenty of activities to keep children entertained, delighted and educated.

Center for Puppetry Arts (tickets 404-873-3391; www.puppet.org; 1404 Spring St NW; museum $8.25, performances $16.50-20.59; 9am-3pm Tue-Fri, 10am-5pm Sat, noon-5pm Sun;) A wonderland for visitors of all ages and hands-down one of Atlanta's most unique attractions, the museum houses a treasury of puppets, some of which you get to operate yourself. A major addition is the Worlds of Puppetry Museum, housing the most comprehensive collection of Jim Henson puppets and artifacts in the world.

Imagine It! Children's Museum of Atlanta (www.childrensmuseumatlanta.org; 275 Centennial Olympic Park Dr NW; admission $12.75; 10am-4pm Mon-Fri, to 5pm Sat & Sun;) A hands-on museum geared towards kids aged eight and under. Adults aren't allowed in without a youngster in tow.

Georgia Aquarium (www.georgiaaquarium.com; 225 Baker St; adult/child $39/33; 10am-5pm Sun-Fri, 9am-6pm Sat; P) Whale sharks, beluga whales and more than 100,000 other animals representing 500 species swimming about in 8 million gallons of fresh and marine water make this the world's second-largest aquarium. It would be remiss not to note that holding whales and dolphins in captivity has fallen out of favor since the release of the 2013 documentary *Blackfish*.

Skyview Atlanta (www.skyviewatlanta.com; 168 Luckie St NW; adult/senior/child $13.50/12.15/8.50; noon-10pm Sun-Thu, to 11pm Fri, 10am-11pm Sat;) Soar 200ft above the Atlanta skyline in this 20-story, 42-gondola Ferris wheel installed in 2013.

Marietta St NW; 9am-5pm Mon-Fri) Postal services around town.

USEFUL WEBSITES

Scout Mob (www.scoutmob.com) Tips on what's new and hot in Atlanta.

Atlanta Travel Guide (www.atlanta.net) Official site of the Atlanta Convention & Visitors Bureau with excellent links to shops, restaurants, hotels and upcoming events. Its website also lets you buy a CityPass, a tremendous money saver that bundles admission to five of the city's attractions for a discounted price (see www.citypass.com/atlanta for more).

Getting There & Away

Atlanta's huge **Hartsfield-Jackson International Airport** (ATL; Atlanta; www.atlanta-airport.com), 12 miles north of downtown, is a major regional hub and an international gateway. The **Greyhound terminal** (www.greyhound.com; 232 Forsyth St) is next to the MARTA Garnett station. The **Amtrak station** (www.amtrak.com; 1688 Peachtree St NW, at Deering Rd) is just north of downtown.

Getting Around

The **Metropolitan Atlanta Rapid Transit Authority** (MARTA; 404-848-5000; www.itsmarta.com; fares $2.50) rail line travels to/from the airport to downtown, along with less useful commuter routes. Each customer must purchase a Breeze card ($1; www.breezecard.com), which can be loaded and reloaded as necessary. The shuttle and car-rental agencies have desks in the airport situated at baggage claim.

North Georgia

The southern end of the great Appalachian Range extends some 40 miles into Georgia's far north, providing superb mountain scenery, some decent wines, and frothing rivers. Fall colors emerge late here, peaking in October. A few days are warranted to see sites like the 1200ft-deep **Tallulah Gorge** (706-754-7981; www.gastateparks.org/tallulahgorge; entry per vehicle $5), and the mountain scenery and hiking trails at **Vogel State Park** (706-745-2628; www.gastateparks.org/vogel; entry per vehicle $5) and **Unicoi State Park** (706-878-4726; www.gastateparks.org/unicoi; entry per vehicle $5).

Dahlonega

In 1828 Dahlonega was the site of the first gold rush in the USA. The boom these days is in tourism, as it's an easy day excursion from Atlanta and is a fantastic mountain destination. Not only is it a hotbed of outdoor activities, but downtown Dahlonega around Courthouse Square is a delightful melange of tasting rooms, gourmet emporiums, great food, countrified shops and foothill charm.

Sights & Activities

Amicalola Falls State Park HIKING

(706-265-4703; www.gastateparks.org/amicalolafalls; 280 Amicalola Falls State Park Rd, Dawsonville; entry per vehicle $5; 7am-10pm) Amicalola Falls State Park, 18 miles west of Dahlonega on Hwy 52, features the 729ft Amicalola Falls, the tallest cascading waterfall in the Southeast. The park offers spectacular scenery, a lodge, and excellent hiking and mountain-biking trails.

★**Frogtown Cellars** WINERY

(706-865-0687; www.frogtownwine.com; 700 Ridge Point Dr; tastings $15; noon-5pm Mon-Fri, to 6pm Sat, 12:30-5pm Sun) Frogtown Cellars is a beautiful winery and has a killer deck on which to sip libations and nibble cheese. It bills itself as the most awarded North American winery *not* in California.

Sleeping & Eating

★**Hiker Hostel** HOSTEL $

(770-312-7342; www.hikerhostel.com; 7693 Hwy 19N; dm/r/cabin $18/42/55; P ❄ @) On Hwy 19N, 7 miles or so from town, this hostel is owned by an avid pair of cycling and outdoors enthusiasts. It caters to those looking to explore the Appalachian Trail. The hostel is a converted log cabin; each bunk room has its own bath and it is wonderfully neat and clean.

Two stylish new shipping-container cabins are built from reclaimed materials from throughout Georgia.

Spirits Tavern BURGERS $

(www.spirits-tavern.com; 19 E Main St; burgers $12; 11am-11pm Sun-Thu, to 1am Fri, to midnight Sat;) Dahlonega's only full bar dishes up surprisingly creative burgers, in Angus beef or free-range, hormone-free turkey versions, including crunchy mac 'n' cheese, Greek, Asian and Cajun versions.

Crimson Moon Café CAFE $

(www.thecrimsonmoon.com; 24 N Park St; mains $6.50-18; 11am-4pm Mon & Tue, to 9pm Wed & Thu, 10am-midnight Fri, 8:30am-midnight Sat, to 9pm Sun;) An organic coffeehouse offering great Southern comfort food and an intimate live-music venue.

Back Porch Oyster Bar SEAFOOD $$

(706-864-8623; www.backporchoysterbar.net; 19 N Chestatee St; mains $9-31; 11:30am-9pm Mon-Thu, to 10pm Fri-Sat, to 8pm Sun;) Oysters, ahi and clams are among the bounty flown in fresh daily to be shucked, seared and steamed at this neighborhood fish house, with a front porch overlooking the square that's perfect for taking it all down.

Information

Visitor Center (706-864-3513; www.dahlonega.org; 13 S Park St; 9am-5:30pm Mon-Fri, 10am-5pm Sat) The visitor center has plenty of information on area sites and activities, including hiking, canoeing, kayaking, rafting and mountain biking.

Athens

A beery, artsy and laid-back college town roughly 70 miles east of Atlanta, Athens has an extremely popular football team (the University of Georgia Bulldogs), a world-famous music scene (which has launched artists including the B-52s, R.E.M. and Widespread Panic) and a burgeoning restaurant culture. The university drives the culture of Athens and ensures an ever-replenishing supply of young bar-hoppers and concert-goers, some of whom stick around long after graduation and become 'townies.' The pleasant, walkable downtown offers a plethora of funky choices for eating, drinking and shopping.

Sights

★**Georgia Museum of Art** MUSEUM

(www.georgiamuseum.org; 90 Carlton St; 10am-5pm Tue-Wed, Fri & Sat, to 9pm Thu, 1-5pm Sun) FREE A smart, modern gallery open to the public where brainy, arty types set up in the wired lobby for personal study while art hounds gawk at modern sculpture in the courtyard garden and the tremendous collection from American realists of the 1930s.

State Botanical Garden of Georgia GARDENS

(www.botgarden.uga.edu; 2450 S Milledge Ave; 8am-6pm Oct-Mar, to 8pm Apr-Sep) Truly gorgeous, with winding outdoor paths and a socio-historical edge, Athens' gardens rival those in Atlanta. Signs provide smart context for its amazing collection of plants, which runs the gamut from rare and threatened species to nearly 5 miles of top-notch woodland walking trails.

Sleeping & Eating

Athens does not have a great selection of lodging. There are standard chains just out of town on W Broad St.

★Graduate Athens INN $$
(☎706-549-7020; www.graduateathens.com; 295 E Dougherty St; r $99-169, ste $159-229; P ❄ @ 📶 🏊) This newly revamped 122-room boutique hotel, the inaugural address of a new college-campus chain, is drowning in sexified retro hipness, from potted plants inside old-school Dewey Decimal card catalog filing cabinets in the lobby to the sweet Crosley turntables and classic video games in the suites.

Local accents, such as chalkboard-art of the chemical formula for sweet tea, fortify local allure. Also on-site is a great coffeehouse, bar and grill and live-music venue, all inside an old Confederate iron foundry.

Hotel Indigo BOUTIQUE HOTEL $$
(☎706-546-0430; www.indigoathens.com; 500 College Ave; r weekend/weekday from $169/139; P ❄ @ 📶 🏊) 🍃 Rooms are spacious, loft-like pods of cool at this eco-chic boutique hotel. Part of the Indigo chain, it's a Leadership in Energy and Environmental Design gold-certified sustainable standout. Green elements include regenerative elevators and priority parking for hybrid vehicles; 30% of the building was constructed from recycled content.

White Tiger BARBECUE $
(www.whitetigergourmet.com; 217 Hiawassee Ave; mains $6.50-10.50; ⏲11am-3pm Tue-Wed, 11am-3pm & 6-8pm Thu-Sat, 10am-2pm Sun) The 100-year-old structure doesn't invite confidence, but this off-the-beaten path local favorite does killer wood-smoked pulled pork sandwiches, burgers and even BBQ-smoked tofu for the vegetarians. Chef Ken Manring honed his skills in much higher-brow kitchens before settling in Athens.

Ike & Jane CAFE $
(www.ikeandjane.com; 1307 Prince Ave; mains $3.50-8; ⏲6:30am-5pm Mon-Fri, 8am-2pm Sat-Sun) This sunny little shingle in Normal Town serves decadent doughnuts bedazzled with crazy creative ingredients like red velvet, Cap'n Crunch cereal and peanut butter, banana and bacon. If that's all a bit much for you, the pimento cheese biscuit or roasted jalapeño and egg sandwich are both divine.

Ted's Most Best ITALIAN $
(www.tedsmostbest.com; 254 W Washington St; mains $7.50-9) This atmospheric budget eatery occupies a former Michelin tire shop (oh, the irony) and is a great spot for cheap eats. Pizzas and panini are what drives it, but the outdoor patio and sandbox/bocce court (when the little ones haven't commandeered it) is the real star of the show.

National NEW SOUTHERN $$
(☎706-549-3450; www.thenationalrestaurant.com; 232 W Hancock Ave; mains $12-29; ⏲11:30am-10pm Mon-Thu, to late Fri-Sat, 5-10pm Sun; 📶) An effortlessly cool bistro on the downtown outskirts, favored for its daily-changing, eclectic menu that jumps from roasted chicken breast with za'atar to lamb sandwiches with fennel-caper mayo. The bar is one where you may want to sit and sip a while. Outstanding vegetarian choices.

★Five & Ten AMERICAN $$$
(☎706-546-7300; www.fiveandten.com; 1653 S Lumpkin St; mains $24-36; ⏲5:30-10pm Sun-Thu, to 11pm Fri & Sat, 10:30am-2:30pm Sun) 🍃 Driven by sustainable ingredients, Five & Ten ranks among the South's best restaurants. Its menu is earthy and slightly gamey: sweatbreads, black-eyed-pea hummus and Frogmore stew (stewed corn, sausage and potato). In an about-face, Tuesday is *tonkotsu*-style ramen night. Reservations mandatory.

🍷 Drinking & Entertainment

Nearly 100 bars and restaurants dot Athens' compact downtown area, so it's not hard to find a good time. Pick up a free copy of **Flagpole** (www.flagpole.com) to find out what's on.

Trapeze Pub BEER HALL
(www.trappezepub.com; 269 N Hull St; beers $4.50-8; ⏲11am-2am Mon-Sat, to midnight Sun; 📶) Downtown's best craft beer bar installed itself well before the suds revolution. You'll find 33 taps, including loval fav Creature Comforts, and another 100 or so at any given time in bottles. Soak it all up with Belgian-style fries, the best in town.

World Famous COCKTAIL BAR
(www.facebook.com/theworldfamousathens; 351 N Hull; cocktails $4-9; ⏲11am-2m Mon-Sat, 11:30-midnight Sun; 📶) This trendy newcomer serves commendable craft cocktails in Mason jars amid retro French farmhouse decor. Also hosts intimate comedy and live-music events.

The Old Pal BAR
(www.theoldpal.com; 1320 Prince Ave; cocktails $7-9; ⏲4pm-2am Mon-Sat; 📶) Dark and taxidermied, the Old Pal is Normal Town's thinking man's bar, devoted to seasonal craft cocktails and a thoughtfully curated bourbon list. It's

a beautiful space that has been showered with local preservation awards.

Normal Bar BAR
(www.facebook.com/normal.bar.7; 1365 Prince Ave; 4pm-2am Mon-Thu, from 3pm Fri & Sat) This lovable dark storefront bar, a bit out of the way in Normal Town, is very unstudentlike but still very much Athens. The beer goes from PBR cheap to local craftsman IPA-sophisticati. There's a terrific wine list and the crowd is young, cute and doesn't care either way. It's the quintessential neighborhood bar.

Hendershots COFFEE
(www.hendershotscoffee.com; 237 Prince Ave; coffee $2.15-5.35; 6:30am-11pm Mon-Thu, to midnight Fri, 7:30am-midnight Sat, 7am-10pm Sun;) This is not Athens' best coffee, but it is its coolest coffeehouse, which pulls triple duty as a great bar and live-music venue. Pick your poison.

40 Watt Club LIVE MUSIC
(706-549-7871; www.40watt.com; 285 W Washington St; admission $5-25) Athens' most storied joint has lounges, a tiki bar and $2.50 PBRs, and has welcomed indie rock to its stage since R.E.M., the B-52s and Widespread Panic owned this town. It's still where the big hitters play when they visit and has recently embraced comedy as well.

Information

Athens Welcome Center (706-353-1820; www.athenswelcomecenter.com; 280 E Dougherty St; 10am-5pm Mon-Sat, noon-5pm Sun) The Athens Welcome Center, in a historic antebellum house at the corner of Thomas St, provides maps and information on local tours.

South Georgia

Once the unbounded urban sprawl of Atlanta meets the rear-view mirror, a more rustic and definitively genteel Georgia emerges, with swampy Savannah holding court as the state's irresistible Southern belle. But there's more to the region than antebellum architecture and Spanish moss: Georgia's wild and preserved barrier-island-riddled coast is an often overlooked stunner.

Savannah

Like a proper Southern belle with an electric-blue streak in her hair, this grand historic town revolves around formal antebellum architecture and the revelry of local students from Savannah College of Art and Design (SCAD). It sits alongside the Savannah River, about 18 miles from the coast, amid Lowcountry swamps and mammoth live oak trees dripping with Spanish moss. With its colonial mansions and beautiful squares, Savannah preserves its past with pride and grace. However, unlike its sister city of Charleston, SC, which retains its reputation as a dignified and refined cultural center, Savannah is a little gritty, lived-in, and real.

Sights & Activities

The Central Park of Savannah is a sprawling rectangular green space called **Forsyth Park**. The park's beautiful fountain is a quintessential photo op. Savannah's **riverfront** is mostly populated with forgettable shops and cafes, but it's worth a short stroll. As is **Jones Street**, among Savannah's prettiest thanks to the mossy oaks that hold hands from either side.

A $20 multivenue ticket gets you into the Jepson Center for the Arts, Telfair Academy and the Owens-Thomas House.

★Wormsloe Plantation Historic Site HISTORIC SITE
(www.gastateparks.org/Wormsloe; 7601 Skidaway Rd; adult/senior/child 6-17yr/child 1-5yr $10/9/4.50/2; 9am-5pm Tue-Sun) A short drive from downtown, on the beautiful **Isle of Hope**, this is one of the most photographed sites in town. The real draw is the dreamy entrance through a corridor of mossy, ancient oaks that runs for 1.5 miles, known as the **Avenue of the Oaks**.

But there are other draws, including an existing antebellum mansion still lived in by the descendants of the original owner, Noble Jones, some old colonial ruins, and a touristy site where you can see folks demonstrate blacksmithing and other bygone trades. There are two flat, wooded walking trails here too.

Owens-Thomas House HISTORIC BUILDING
(www.telfair.org; 124 Abercorn St; adult/senior/child $20/18/free; noon-4pm Sun-Mon, 10am-4:30pm Tue-Sat) Completed in 1819 by British architect William Jay, this gorgeous villa exemplifies English Regency-style architecture, which is known for its symmetry.

The guided tour is fussy, but it delivers interesting trivia about the spooky 'haint blue' ceiling paint in the slaves' quarters (made from crushed indigo, buttermilk and crushed oyster shells) and the number of years by which this mansion preceded the White House in getting running water (nearly 20).

Mercer-Williams House HISTORIC BUILDING
(www.mercerhouse.com; 429 Bull St; adult/student $12.50/8; ⌚10:30am-4:10pm Mon-Sat, noon-4pm Sun) Although Jim Williams, the Savannah art dealer portrayed by Kevin Spacey in the film version of *Midnight in the Garden of Good and Evil,* died back in 1990, his infamous mansion didn't become a museum until 2004. You're not allowed to see the upstairs, where Williams' family still lives, but the downstairs is an interior decorator's fantasy.

Telfair Academy of Arts & Sciences MUSEUM
(www.telfair.org; 121 Barnard St; adult/child $12/5; ⌚noon-5pm Sun-Mon, 10am-5pm Tue-Sat) Considered Savannah's top art museum, the historic Telfair family mansion is filled with 19th-century American art, silver from that era, and a smattering of European pieces.

SCAD Museum of Art ART MUSEUM
(www.scadmoa.org; 601 Turner Blvd; adult/child under 14yr $10/free; ⌚10am-5pm Tue-Wed, to 8pm Thu, to 5pm Fri, noon-5pm Sun) Brand new and architecturally striking, this brick, steel, concrete and glass longhouse delivers your modern art fix. With groovy, creative sitting areas inside and out, and fun rotating exhibitions.

Jepson Center for the Arts GALLERY
(JCA; www.telfair.org; 207 W York St; adult/child $12/5; ⌚noon-5pm Sun-Mon, 10am-5pm Tue-Sat; 👪) Looking pretty darn space-age by Savannah's standards, the JCA focuses on 20th- and 21st-century art.

Savannah Bike Tours BICYCLE TOUR
(☎912-704-4043; www.savannahbiketours.com; 41 Habersham St; tours $25) This outfit offers two-hour bike tours on its fleet of cruisers.

Sleeping

Luckily for travelers, it's become stylish for Savannah hotels and B&Bs to serve hors d'oeuvres and wine to guests in the evening. Cheap sleeps are difficult to find and all accommodations should be booked in advance.

Savannah Pensione GUESTHOUSE $
(☎912-236-7744; www.savannahpensione.com; 304 E Hall St; s/d/tr without bath from $48/57/77, d/tr from $71/82; P ❄ @) It was run as a hostel for some 15 years but the owner of this basic neighborhood crash-pad got tired of backpackers traipsing up and down the historic steps of the 1884 Italianate mansion. Fair enough. Now a bare-bones and vibeless pensione, it still offers the cheapest historic quarter rooms, though its potential is criminally unrealized.

Dorm beds can be had for $26, but only for groups of three or more who know each other.

Thunderbird Inn MOTEL $$
(☎912-232-2661; www.thethunderbirdinn.com; 611 W Oglethorpe Ave; r $109; P ❄ 📶) A 'tad Palm Springs, a touch Vegas' best describes this vintage-chic 1964 motel that wins its own popularity contest – a 'Hippest hotel in Savannah' proclamation greets guests in the '60s-soundtracked lobby. In a land of stuffy B&Bs, this groovy place is an oasis, made all the better by local Savannah College of Art and Design student art.

Krispy Kreme doughnuts for breakfast!

Azalea Inn INN $$
(☎912-236-2707; www.azaleainn.com; 217 E Huntingdon St; r/villa from $199/299; P ❄ 📶 🏊) A humble stunner on a quiet street, we love this sweet canary-yellow historic inn near Forsyth Park. The 10 house rooms aren't huge, but are well done with varnished dark-wood floors, crown moldings, four-poster beds and a small dipping pool out back. Three new villas offer more modern luxury for long-term stays.

Kehoe House B&B $$$
(☎912-232-1020; www.kehoehouse.com; 123 Habersham St; r from $239; ❄ 📶) This romantic, upscale Renaissance Revival B&B dates to 1892 and twins are said to have died in a chimney here, making it one of America's most haunted hotels. If you're skittish, steer clear of rooms 201 and 203! Ghosts aside, it's a beautifully appointed worthwhile splurge on picturesque Columbia Sq.

Mansion on Forsyth Park HOTEL $$$
(☎912-238-5158; www.mansiononforsythpark.com; 700 Drayton St; r weekend/weekday $299/199; P ❄ @ 📶 🏊) A choice location and chic design highlight the luxe accommodations on offer at the 18,000-sq-ft Mansion – the sexy bathrooms alone are practically worth the money. The best part of the hotel-spa is the amazing local and international art that crowds its walls and hallways – more than 400 pieces in all.

Savannah

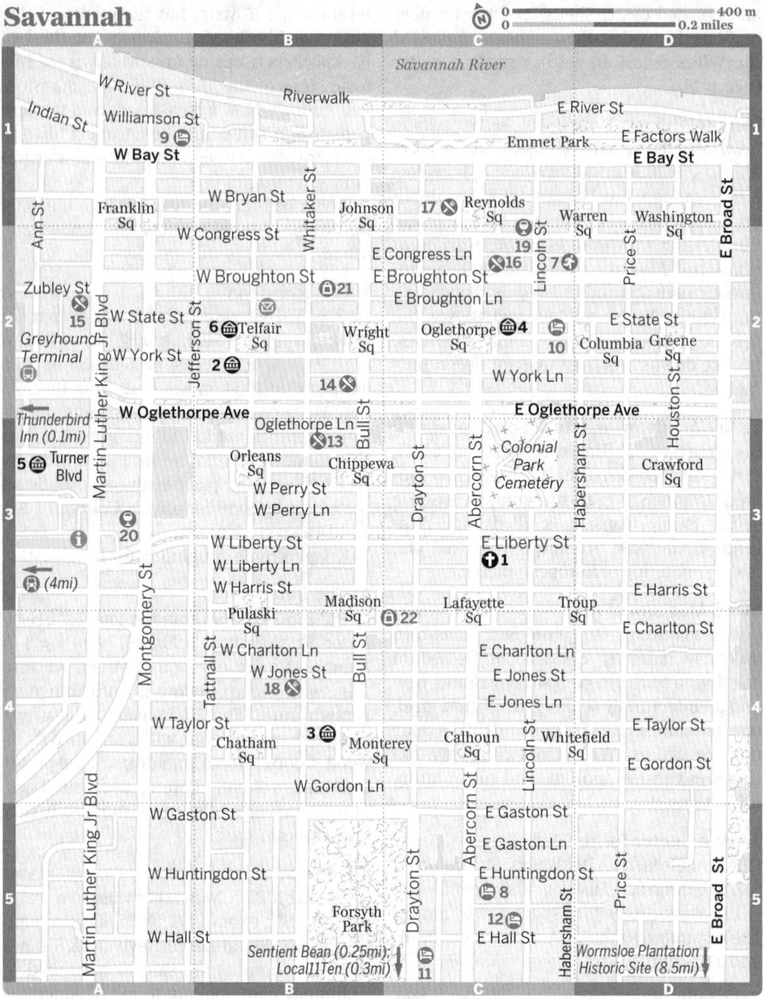

Bohemian Hotel BOUTIQUE HOTEL $$$
(☎912-721-3800; www.bohemianhotelsavannah.com; 102 West Bay St; r weekend/weekday $359/269; P ❄ @ 📶) Enjoy sleek, dark, Gothic hallways, a riverside perch and small touches like driftwood-and-oyster chandeliers. Rooms are stunning, though too low-lit for some. Personalized service makes it feel far more intimate than its 75 rooms indicate.

Eating

Angel's BBQ BARBECUE $
(www.angels-bbq.com; 21 W Oglethorpe Lane; sandwiches/plates $6.50/9; ⏲11:30am until sold out Wed-Sat) Utterly low-brow and hidden down an uneventful lane, Angel's pulled-pork sandwiches and sea-salted fries will leave you humbled and thoroughly satisfied – and that's before you tear through the impressive list of housemade sauces.

Leopold's Ice Cream ICE CREAM $
(www.leopoldsicecream.com; 212 E Broughton St; scoops $2.75-4.75; ⏲11am-11pm Sun-Thu, to midnight Fri-Sat; 📶) This classic American ice-cream parlor feels like the Last Man Standing, having been scooping up its creamy Greek recipes since 1919. Tutti Frutti was invented here, but we dig coffee, pistachio,

Savannah

Sights			
1	Cathedral of St John the Baptist	C3	
2	Jepson Center for the Arts	B2	
3	Mercer-Williams House	B4	
4	Owens-Thomas House	C2	
5	SCAD Museum of Art	A3	
6	Telfair Academy of Arts & Sciences	B2	
Activities, Courses & Tours			
7	Savannah Bike Tours	C2	
Sleeping			
8	Azalea Inn	C5	
9	Bohemian Hotel	A1	
10	Kehoe House	C2	
11	Mansion on Forsyth Park	C5	
12	Savannah Pensione	C5	
Eating			
13	Angel's BBQ	B3	
14	Collins Quarter	B2	
15	The Grey	A2	
16	Leopold's Ice Cream	C2	
17	Olde Pink House	C1	
18	Wilkes' House	B4	
Drinking & Nightlife			
19	Abe's on Lincoln	C2	
20	Distillery Ale House	A3	
	Rocks on the Roof	(see 9)	
Shopping			
21	Savannah Bee Company	B2	
22	ShopSCAD	C4	

honey almond and cream, and caramel swirl. Hurry up and wait.

★ Collins Quarter CAFE **$$**

(www.thecollinsquarter.com; 151 Bull St; mains $9-17; 6:30am-11pm;) If you have ever talked coffee with an Australian, you know they are particularly fussy about their java. This wildly popular newcomer is Australian-owned and turns Australian-roasted Brooklyn coffee into their beloved flat whites and long blacks. Beyond Savannah's best coffee, it serves excellent fusion fare, including a drool-inducing brisket burger. There's booze, too!

Wilkes' House SOUTHERN **$$**

(www.mrswilkes.com; 107 W Jones St; lunch adult/child $20/10; 11am-2pm Mon-Fri, closed Jan) The line outside can begin as early as 8am at this first-come, first-served, Southern comfort food institution. Once the lunch bell rings and you are seated family-style, the kitchen unloads on you: fried chicken, beef stew, meatloaf, cheese potatoes, collard greens, black-eyed peas, mac 'n' cheese, rutabaga, candied yams, squash casserole, creamed corn *and* biscuits.

It's like Thanksgiving and the Last Supper rolled into one massive feast, chased with sweet tea.

Olde Pink House NEW SOUTHERN **$$$**

(912-232-4286; 23 Abercorn St; mains $15-37; 11am-10:30pm, closed lunch Sun-Mon) Classic Southern food done upscale; our favorite appetizer is Southern sushi – shrimp and grits rolled in a coconut-crusted nori roll. Dine in the slender digs upstairs, or go underground to the fabulous tavern where the piano player rumbles and the room is cozy, funky and perfect. The building is a 1771 landmark and this is Savannah's most consistently great restaurant.

The Grey NEW SOUTHERN **$$$**

(912-662-5999; www.thegreyrestaurant.com; 109 Martin Luther King Jr Blvd; mains $25-44;) A wonderfully retro makeover of the 1960s Greyhound Bus Terminal gives us Savannah's latest culinary darling, where chef Mashama Bailey's 'Port City Southern' cuisine is a delightful immigrant-infused take on local grub. Bearded hipsters work the best seats in the house, around the U-shaped centerpiece bar, where scrumptious pork-belly country pasta and a gargantuan pork shank are standouts. Reservations essential.

Local11Ten MODERN AMERICAN **$$$**

(912-790-9000; www.local11ten.com; 1110 Bull St; mains $16-35; 6-10pm Mon-Sat) Upscale, sustainable, local, fresh: these elements help create an elegant, well-run restaurant that's easily one of Savannah's best. Start with a deconstructed rabbit ravioli, then move on to the fabulous seared sea scallops in mint beurre blanc or the harissa-marinated bison hanger steak and a salted caramel pot de crème for a happy ending. Wait. Scratch that. The menu already changed.

Drinking & Nightlife

River St, with its plastic cup open container laws, is the bar-hopping, spring-break-like nightlife corridor.

Rocks on the Roof BAR
(www.bohemianhotelsavannah.com/dining/lounge; 102 West Bay St; ⌚11am-midnight Sun-Wed, to 1am Thu-Sat; 📶) The expansive, viewriffic rooftop bar at the Bohemian Hotel is breezy, fun and best when the weather is fine and the fire pit is glowing.

Distillery Ale House BAR
(www.distilleryalehouse.com; 416 W Liberty St; ⌚11am-late Mon-Sat, from noon Sun) Formerly the Kentucky Distilling Co, opened in 1904 and closed at Prohibition, this is oddly *not* Savannah's local throat-burning swill house, but rather its go-to craft beer bar. Also popular with tourists and families for bar food.

Abe's on Lincoln BAR
(17 Lincoln St) Ditch the tourists – drink with the locals in dark, dank, all-wood environs.

Sentient Bean CAFE
(www.sentientbean.com; 13 E Park Ave; coffee $1.50-4.75; ⌚7am-10pm; 📶) 🍃 Everything you want from an indie coffeehouse: terrific brew, gourmet breakfasts, spacious boho interior and hipster clientele and baristas, all awash in sustainability. It's Savannah's favorite and just across from Forsyth Park.

Shopping

West Broughton St is Savannah's preeminent shopping district – with both corporate and indie entities shoulder to shoulder, and all of it punctuated with a distinctly SCAD flavor.

Savannah Bee Company FOOD
(www.savannahbee.com; 104 W Broughton St; ⌚10am-8pm Mon-Sat, 11am-5pm Sun) This internationally renowned honey dreamland is one of Savannah's must-stops. Expect artisanal honey of infinite variety and limitless free tastings.

ShopSCAD ARTS & CRAFTS
(www.shopscadonline.com; 340 Bull St; ⌚9am-5:30pm Mon-Fri, to 6pm Sat, noon-5pm Sun) All the wares at this funky, kitschy boutique were designed by students, faculty and alumni of Savannah's prestigious art college.

Information

Candler Hospital (www.sjchs.org; 5353 Reynolds St; ⌚24hr) Medical services.

Post Office (www.usps.com; 118 Barnard St; ⌚8am-5pm Mon-Fri) Historic district postal services.

Savannah Chatham Metropolitan Police (☎912-651-6675; www.scmpd.org; cnr E Oglethorpe Ave & Habersham St) Police headquarters.

Savannah Visitor Center (☎912-944-0455; www.savannahvisit.com; 301 Martin Luther King Jr Blvd; ⌚8:30am-5pm Mon-Fri, 9am-5pm Sat & Sun) Excellent resources and services are available in this center, based in a restored 1860s train station. Many privately operated city tours start here. There is also a small interactive tourist-info kiosk in the new visitor center at Forsyth Park.

Getting There & Around

The **Savannah/Hilton Head International Airport** (SAV; ☎912-966-3743; www.savannahairport.com; 400 Airways Ave) is about 5 miles west of downtown off I-16. Taxis from the airport to the historic district cost a standard $28. **Greyhound** (www.greyhound.com; 610 W Oglethorpe Ave) has connections to Atlanta (about five hours), Charleston, SC (about two hours) and Jacksonville, FL (2½ hours). The **Amtrak station** (www.amtrak.com; 2611 Seaboard Coastline Dr) is just a few miles west of the historic district.

Savannah is very foot-friendly. **Chatham Area Transit** (CAT; www.catchacat.org; per ride $1.50) operates local buses that run on bio-diesel, including a free shuttle (the Dot) that makes its way around the historic district and stops within a couple of blocks of nearly every major site.

CAT Bike (www.catbike.bcycle.com; ⌚per 30min $2) Convenient bike-hire scheme, run by Chatham Area Transit, with stations around town. It's free for the first hour.

Brunswick & the Golden Isles

Georgia has a coast? Oh yes, a righteously beautiful one, blessed with a string of picturesque islands ranging from rustic to kitschy to indulgent. With its large shrimp-boat fleet and downtown historic district shaded beneath lush live oaks, Brunswick dates from 1733 and has charms you might miss when sailing by on I-95 or the Golden Isle Pkwy (US Hwy 17). During WWII Brunswick shipyards constructed 99 Liberty transport ships for the navy. Today a 23ft scale model at **Mary Ross Waterfront Park** (Bay St) stands as a memorial to those ships and their builders.

Sleeping

Hostel in the Forest HOSTEL $
(☎912-264-9738; www.foresthostel.com; 3901 Hwy 82; per person $25; 🐾) The only budget base in the area is this set of bare-bones octagonal

WORTH A TRIP

CUMBERLAND ISLAND

An unspoiled paradise, a backpacker's fantasy, a site for day trips or extended stays – it's clear why the family of 19th-century industrialist and philanthropist Andrew Carnegie used Cumberland as a retreat long ago. Most of this southernmost barrier island is now occupied by the **Cumberland Island National Seashore** (www.nps.gov/cuis; admission $4). Almost half of its 36,415 acres consists of marsh, mudflats and tidal creeks. On the ocean side are 16 miles of wide, sandy beach that you might have all to yourself. The island's interior is characterized by maritime forest. Ruins from the Carnegie estate **Dungeness** are astounding, as are the wild turkeys, tiny fiddler crabs and beautiful butterflies. Feral horses roam the island and are a common sight.

The only public access to the island is via boat to/from the quirky, lazy town of **St Marys** (www.stmaryswelcome.com). Convenient and pleasant **ferries** (877-860-6787; www.nps.gov/cuis; round-trip adult/senior/child $25/23/15) leave from the mainland at the St Marys dock at 9am and 11:45am and return at 10:15am and 4:45pm (with an extra 2:45pm departure in spring and summer). Reservations are staunchly recommended well before you arrive, and visitors are required to check in at the **visitors center** (912-882-4336; www.nps.gov/cuis; 8am-4pm) at the dock at least 30 minutes prior to departure. December through February, the ferry does not operate on Tuesday or Wednesday.

On Cumberland Island, the only private accommodations (two-night minimum stay) are at the **Greyfield Inn** (904-261-6408; www.greyfieldinn.com; r incl meals $425-635), a mansion built in 1900. Camping is available at **Sea Camp Beach** (912-882-4335; www.nps.gov/cuis; tent sites per person $4), set among magnificent live oaks.

Note: there are no stores or waste bins on the island. Eat before arriving or bring lunch, and take your trash with you.

cedar huts and tree houses (sans air or heat) on an ecofriendly, sustainable campus. You must pay a member fee of $10 to stay and it's all very hippy-dippy with dinner included. It's tucked in the woods 10 miles outside Brunswick; phone reservations only.

St Simons Island

Famous for its golf courses, resorts and majestic live oaks, St Simons Island is the largest and most developed of the Golden Isles. It lies 75 miles south of Savannah and just 5 miles from Brunswick. The southern half of the island is a thickly settled residential and resort area.

Little St Simons is an all-natural jewel, accessible by boat only to guests at the exclusive **Lodge on Little St Simons** (888-733-5774; www.littlessi.com; 1000 Hampton Pt; all-inclusive d from $450) or to their **day trippers** (888-733-5774; www.littlestsimonsisland.com; Hampton Point Dr; per person $95; trips 10:30am).

Sights & Activities

Sea Island ISLAND

(www.seaisland.com) Sea Island offers tracts of coastal wilderness amid a tidewater estuary, but access is limited to guests of its three luxury hotels unless you make dining reservations at the Cloister's Georgian Room.

Massengale Park PARK, BEACH

(1350 Ocean Blvd) East Beach, the island's best, is accessible from Massengale Park.

Sleeping & Eating

St Simons Inn by the Lighthouse INN $$

(912-638-1101; www.saintsimonsinn.com; 609 Beachview Dr; r weekend/weekday from $159/139; P) Cute and comfortable good-value inn, accented with white wooden shutters. It's well located next to the downtown drag and a short pedal from East Beach. Continental breakfast included.

Southern Soul BBQ BARBECUE $

(www.southernsoulbbq.com; 2020 Demere Rd; mains $5-17; 11am-10pm) Succulent slow oak-smoked pulled pork, burnt-tipped brisket and daily specials like jerk chicken burritos. There are a number of wonderful house-made sauces and a great patio from which to take it all in. Packed always.

Halyards SEAFOOD $$$

(912-638-9100; www.halyardsrestaurant.com; 55 Cinema Lane; mains $14-42; 5-9pm Mon-Wed, to 10pm Thu-Sat;) Chef Dave Snyder's classy sustainable seafooder consistently hogs best-of-everything awards on St Simons, and for good reason. Go for the Chef's Highlights (our mahi-mahi over boursin grits, haricot verts and orange-vanilla butter was perfect).

Jekyll Island

An exclusive refuge for millionaires in the late 19th and early 20th centuries, Jekyll is a 4000-year-old barrier island with 10 miles of beaches. Today it's an unusual clash of wilderness, historically preserved buildings, modern hotels and a massive campground. It's an easily navigable place – you can get around by car, horse or bicycle, but there's a $6 parking fee per 24 hours.

Sights & Activities

Georgia Sea Turtle Center WILDLIFE
(☎912-635-4444; www.georgiaseaturtlecenter.org; 214 Stable Rd; adult/child $7/5; ⏱9am-5pm, closed Mon Nov-Mar; 👪) An endearing attraction is the Georgia Sea Turtle Center, a conservation center and turtle hospital where patients are on view for the public. Behind the Scenes tours ($22; 3pm) and Turtle Walks ($14; 8:30pm and 9:30pm; June 1 to July 31) are also available.

Sleeping & Eating

Villas by the Sea CONDOS $
(☎912-635-2521; www.villasbythesearesort.com; 1175 N Beachview Dr; r/condo from $99/129; P❄📶🏊) A nice choice on the north coast close to the best beaches. Rooms are spacious and the one-, two- and three-bedroom condos, set in a complex of lodge buildings sprinkled over a garden, are not fancy but plenty comfy.

★ **Jekyll Island Club Hotel** HISTORIC HOTEL $$
(☎912-635-2600; www.jekyllclub.com; 371 Riverview Dr; d/ste from $189/299, resort fee $15; P❄@📶🏊) A posh and storied historic hotel and the backbone of the island, featuring a rambling array of rooms spread out over five historic structures. Plans are in the works for 41 new beachfront suites.

Latitude 31 Restaurant & Rah Bar SEAFOOD $
(www.latitude31jekyllisland.com; 370 Riverview Dr; mains $6-36; ⏱11am-3pm & 5-10pm) This casual outdoor seafooder on the Jekyll Island wharf is a great spot for a sunset drink and fresh seafood.

ALABAMA

History suffuses Alabama, a description which could be true of many states. But there are few places where the perception of said history is so emotionally fraught. The Mississippian Native American culture built great mound cities here, and Mobile is dotted with Franco-Caribbean architecture. But for many, the word Alabama is synonymous with the American Civil Rights movement.

Perhaps such a struggle, and all of the nobility and desperation it entailed, was bound for a state like this, with its Gothic plantations, hardscrabble farmland and fiercely local sense of place. From the smallest hunting town to river-bound cities, Alabama is a place all its own, and its character is hard to forget. Some visitors have a hard time looking beyond the state's past, but the troubling elements of that narrative are tied up in a passion that constantly manifests in Alabama's arts, food and culture.

Information

Alabama Bureau of Tourism & Travel (www.alabama.travel) Sends out a vacation guide and has a website with extensive tourism options.

Alabama State Parks (☎800-252-7275; www.alapark.com) There are 23 parks statewide with camping facilities ranging from primitive ($16) to 15-person cabins ($200). Advance reservations are suggested for weekends and holidays.

Birmingham

Birmingham is a treasure of unexpected cool. This hilly, shady town, founded as an iron mine, is still a center for manufacturing – Mercedes-Benz USA is based out of nearby Tuscaloosa. In addition, universities and colleges pepper the town, and all of this comes together to create a city with an unreservedly excellent dining and drinking scene. The past also lurks in Birmingham, once named 'Bombingham,' and the history of the Civil Rights movement is very much at your fingers.

Sights & Activities

Art-deco buildings abound in trendy **Five Points South**, where you'll find shops, restaurants and nightspots. Once industrial **Avondale** is where the hipsters are congregating. Equally noteworthy is the upscale **Homewood** community's quaint commercial drag on 18th St S, close to the Vulcan which looms illuminated above the city and is visible from nearly all angles, day and night.

★ Birmingham Civil Rights Institute MUSEUM
(☎866-328-9696; www.bcri.org; 520 16th St N; adult/senior/child $12/5/3, Sun free; ⏲10am-5pm Tue-Sat, 1-5pm Sun) A maze of moving audio, video and photography exhibits tell the story of racial segregation in America, and the Civil Rights movement, with a focus on activities in and around Birmingham. There's an extensive exhibit on the 16th Street Baptist Church (located across the street), which was bombed in 1963; it's the beginning of the city's Civil Rights Memorial Trail.

Birmingham Museum of Art GALLERY
(www.artsbma.org; 2000 Rev Abraham Woods Jr Blvd; ⏲10am-5pm Tue-Sat, noon-5pm Sun) FREE This very fine museum collects works from Asia, Africa, Europe and the Americas. Don't miss the work of Rodin, Botero and Dalí in the sculpture garden.

Birmingham Civil Rights Memorial Trail WALKING TOUR
(www.bcri.org; 520 16th St N) Seven blocks long, this is a poignant walk perfect for the whole family. Installed in 2013 for the 50th anniversary of the Civil Rights campaign, the walk depicts 22 moving scenes with plaques, statues and photography, some of it quite conceptual and moving – to whit, a gauntlet of snapping, sculpted dog statues pedestrians must traverse. The experience peels back yet another layer of the sweat and blood behind a campaign that changed America.

Vulcan Park PARK
(☎205-933-1409; www.visitvulcan.com; 1701 Valley View Dr; observation tower & museum adult/child $6/4, 6-10pm $4; ⏲7am-10pm, observation tower 10am-10pm Mon-Sat, from noon Sun, museum 10am-6pm Mon-Sat, from noon Sun) Imagine Christ the Redeemer in Rio, but made of iron and depicting a beefcake Roman god of metalworking. Vulcan is visible from all over the city – this is actually the world's largest cast-iron statue – and the park he resides in offers fantastic views, along with an **observation tower**. A small on-site museum explores Birmingham history.

Sleeping

By the time you read this, the grand old **Redmont Hotel** (www.redmontbirmingham.com; 2101 5th Ave N), closed for renovation at the time of writing, will have reopened.

Hotel Highland HOTEL $$
(☎205-933-9555; www.thehotelhighland.com; 1023 20th St S; r from $129) Nuzzled right up next to the lively Five Points district, this colorful, slightly trippy but modern hotel is very comfortable and a good deal. The rooms are thankfully a bit less bright and funky than the lobby.

Eating

For such a small Southern city, student-oriented Birmingham has a wide variety of eateries and cafes, and plenty of free live music on weekends.

Saw's BBQ BARBECUE $
(☎205-879-1937; www.sawsbbq.com; 1008 Oxmoor Road; mains $9-16; ⏲11am-8pm Mon-Sat) Saw's has exploded onto the Birmingham barbecue scene with a vengeance, offering some of the most mouthwatering smoked meat in the city, served in a family-friendly atmosphere. Stuffed potatoes make a nice addition to your meal, and the

ALABAMA FACTS

Nickname The Heart of Dixie

Population 4.8 million

Area 52,419 sq miles

Capital city Montgomery (population 201,300)

Other cities Birmingham (population 212,113)

Sales tax 4%, but up to 11% with local taxes

Birthplace of Author Helen Keller (1880–1968), civil rights activist Rosa Parks (1913–2005), musician Hank Williams (1923–53)

Home of The University of Alabama Crimson Tide

Politics Republican stronghold – Alabama hasn't voted Democratic since 1976

Famous for Rosa Parks, the Civil Rights movement, and football

Bitter rivalry University of Alabama vs Auburn University

Driving distances Montgomery to Birmingham 91 miles, Mobile to Dauphin Island 38 miles, Mobile to Tuscaloosa 196 miles

smoked chicken with a tangy local white sauce is divine – although with that said, bring on the ribs!

Eagle's Restaurant AMERICAN $

(☎205-320-0099; www.eaglesrestaurant.com; 2610 16th St N; mains $5.50-15; ⊙10:30am-4pm Sun-Fri) Tucked away on a lonely strip is Eagle's, home of Birmingham's best soul food. Decidedly popular with the local African American population, Eagle's operates on a meat-and-two/three model: order a main, be it steak and gravy, neckbones and potatoes or chicken wings, then pick from a buffet tray of side options. It's delicious, cheap and local as anything.

Chez Fonfon FRENCH $$

(☎205-939-3221; www.fonfonbham.com; 2007 11th St S; mains $14.50-24; ⊙11am-10pm Tue-Thu, to 10:30pm Fri, 4:30-10:30pm Sat) The name of this place merits a slight snicker, but save your smiles for the food, because it's very good French bistro fare. Hanger steak comes with a fresh green salsa and crispy, warm frites, while trout sizzles next to some golden potatoes. Despite a 'no dress code' rule, folks tend to look nice, and reservations are recommended.

Drinking & Entertainment

There's a silly amount of good bars in Birmingham, many concentrated in Avondale and Five Points.

The Collins Bar BAR

(☎205-323-7995; 2125 2nd Ave N; ⊙4pm-midnight Tue-Thu, to 2am Fri & Sat, 6pm-midnight Sun) Birmingham's beautiful people pack into this cool space after work and on weekends, sipping handmade cocktails under giant paper planes and a Birmingham-centric Periodic Table of the Elements. There's no drink menu – tell the bartender what flavors you like and they'll mix something special for you.

Marty's BAR

(1813 10th Ct S; ⊙4pm-6am) Take note: Marty's is technically a drinking club; the first time you visit, you pay a $2 membership fee. That club status allows Marty's to stay open late, attracting an unapologetically geeky crowd to a friendly bar packed with comic book art, *Star Wars* memorabilia, role-playing game references and the occasional live-music gig.

Garage Café BAR

(☎205-322-3220; www.garagecafe.us; 2304 10th Terrace S; ⊙3pm-midnight Sun-Mon, 11am-2am Tue-Sat) A crowd of hipsters and older drinking pros knock back their brew while tapping their toes to live music in a courtyard full of junk, antiques, ceramic statues and quite literally, the kitchen sink.

41 Street Pub & Aircraft Sales BAR

(☎205-202-4187; 130 41st St S; ⊙4:30pm-midnight Mon-Thu, 4:30pm-2am Fri, 1pm-2am Sat, 1pm-noon Sun) A slick wooden bar fronts a large open space offset with some shuffleboard tables. Behind the bar, strong drinks (the Moscow Mule is a winner) are served to an attractive, hipster crowd in shiny copper mugs.

Getting There & Around

The **Birmingham International Airport** (BHM; www.flybirmingham.com) is about 5 miles northeast of downtown.

Greyhound (☎205-253-7190; www.greyhound.com; 618 19th St N), north of downtown, serves cities including Huntsville, Montgomery, Atlanta, GA, Jackson, MS, and New Orleans, LA (10 hours). **Amtrak** (☎205-324-3033; www.amtrak.com; 1819 Morris Ave), downtown, has trains daily to New York and New Orleans.

Birmingham Transit Authority (www.bjcta.org; adult $1.25) runs local buses.

Moundville

One of the largest and best preserved sites of the pre-Columbian Mississippian civilization sits outside of modern Moundville, about 17 miles south of Tuscaloosa. Here, on the dark forested banks of the Black Warrior River, you will find the grassy remains of the Mississippian mound city and an excellent museum, all managed by **Moundville Archaeological Park** (☎205-348-9826; www.moundville.ua.edu; 634 Mound Park; adult/senior/children $8/7/6; ⊙museum 9am-5pm, park 9am-dusk).

Within the complex you will find 26 mounds of varying sizes, arranged in a manner that suggests a highly stratified social structure. The museum is filled with pre-Columbian art, including pottery and disks inscribed with underwater panthers, feathered serpents and skulls. The highest mound at the site is topped by a small replica hut (closed to the public at the time of research).

ROLL TIDE!
....

Roll Tide! It's the call you'll hear pretty much everywhere in the town of Tuscaloosa, 60 miles southwest of Birmingham, but especially on Saturday afternoons in the fall. During football season, students and alumni gather in the **University of Alabama** (www.ua.edu) quad, hours before kickoff, for a pregame party like none other. White tents, wired with satellite TV, fill the expansive lawn. Barbecue is smoked and devoured, cornhole (drunken bean-bag toss) is played. At game time all migrate to **Bryant-Denny Stadium** (☑ 205-348-3600; www.rolltide.com; 920 Paul W Bryant Dr), a 102,000-capacity football stadium that looks out onto the rolling hills and is always packed with rabid fans, and with good reason. The Alabama Crimson Tide have won 19 national championships, including the last two, and three of the last four. Get a full dose of Crimson Tide football history at the **Paul W Bryant Museum** (☑ 205-348-4668; www.bryantmuseum.com; 300 Paul W Bryant Dr; adult/senior & child $2/1; ◷ 9am-4pm), named for the greatest coach of them all. Or so the legend goes...

Montgomery

In 1955 Rosa Parks refused to give up her seat to a white man on a city bus, launching a bus boycott and galvanizing the Civil Rights movement nationwide. The city has commemorated that incident with a museum, which along with a few other civil rights sights, is the main reason to visit. Alabama's capital, Montgomery is an otherwise charming but sleepy city.

◉ Sights

Montgomery's pleasant **Riverwalk** is accessed via a tunnel from downtown and is an extended plaza along a bend in the river with a natural amphitheater and a riverboat dock.

Rosa Parks Museum   MUSEUM
(☑ 334-241-8615; www.troy.edu/rosaparks; 251 Montgomery St; adult/child 4-12yr $7.50/5.50; ◷ 9am-5pm Mon-Fri, 9am-3pm Sat; ⊕) This museum, set in front of the bus stop where Rosa Parks took her stand, features a video re-creation of that pivotal moment that launched the 1955 boycott. The experience is very managed – you're given a small opportunity to explore on your own, but otherwise the museum feels something like an interactive movie. For the price of an additional full admission ticket, you can visit the children's wing, a kids-oriented time-travel exhibit to the Jim Crow South.

Civil Rights Memorial Center   MEMORIAL
(www.splcenter.org/civil-rights-memorial; 400 Washington Ave; adult/child $2/free; ◷ 9am-4:30pm Mon-Fri, 10am-4pm Sat) With its circular design crafted by Maya Lin, this haunting memorial focuses on 40 martyrs of the Civil Rights movement. Some cases remain unsolved. Martin Luther King Jr was the most famous, but there were many 'faceless' deaths along the way, both white and African American. The memorial is part of the Southern Poverty Law Center, a legal foundation committed to racial equality and equal opportunity for justice under the law.

Scott & Zelda Fitzgerald Museum   MUSEUM
(☑ 334-264-4222; www.fitzgeraldmuseum.net; 919 Felder Ave; adult/child donation $5/2; ◷ 10am-3pm Tue-Sat, noon-5pm Sun) ✿ The writers' home from 1931 to 1932 now houses first editions, translations and original artwork by Zelda from her sad last days when she was committed to a mental health facility. Unlike many 'homes of famous people,' there's a ramshackle charm to this museum – while the space is curated, you also feel as if you've stumbled into the Fitzgerald's attic, exemplified by loving handwritten letters from Zelda to Scott.

⌑ Sleeping & Eating

Montgomery isn't known for its restaurants and accommodations, and can be done on a day trip, but there are a couple of finds. **The Alley**, a dining and entertainment district, has helped perk up a dormant downtown.

Renaissance Hotel   HOTEL $$
(☑ 334-481-5000; www.marriott.com; 201 Tallapoosa St; r from $150; ⓟ ❊ @ ⎙ ☲) Yes, it's corporate and kind of faceless, but it is also well located and easily Montgomery's nicest address.

Central STEAK $$$
(☎334-517-1121; www.central129coosa.com; 129 Coosa St; mains $18-39; ⏰11am-2pm Mon-Fri, 5:30pm-late Mon-Sat; ✎) The gourmand's choice, this stunner has an airy interior with a reclaimed-wood bar. The booths are sumptuous and these guys were doing farm to table before it was 'A Thing'; The menu specializes in wood-fired fish, chicken, steaks and chops sourced from the region. Dishes like a pesto walnut pasta are nice for vegetarians.

ℹ Information

Montgomery Area Visitor Center (☎334-261-1100; www.visitingmontgomery.com; 300 Water St; ⏰8:30am-5pm Mon-Sat) Has tourist information and a helpful website.

ℹ Getting There & Around

Montgomery Regional Airport (MGM; ☎334-281-5040; www.montgomeryairport.org; 4445 Selma Hwy) is about 15 miles from downtown and is served by daily flights from Atlanta, GA, Charlotte, NC, and Dallas, TX. **Greyhound** (☎334-286-0658; www.greyhound.com; 950 W South Blvd) also serves the city. The **Montgomery Area Transit System** (www.montgomerytransit.com; tickets $2) operates city bus lines.

Selma

On Bloody Sunday, March 7, 1965, the media captured state troopers and deputies beating and gassing African Americans and white sympathizers near the **Edmund Pettus Bridge** (Broad St & Walter Ave). The crowd was marching to the state capital (Montgomery) to demonstrate against the murder of a local black activist by police during a demonstration for voting rights.

When the scene was broadcast on every network later that night, it marked one of the first times anyone outside the South had witnessed the horrifying images of the struggle, of booted policemen using night sticks and attack dogs on peaceful marchers while whites waving Confederate flags jeered from the sidelines. Shock and outrage was widespread, and support for the movement grew. Martin Luther King arrived swiftly in Selma and after another aborted attempt due to the threat of violence, helped lead what became 8000 people on a four-day, 54-mile march to Montgomery, culminating with a classic King speech on the capitol steps. Soon after, President Johnson signed the Voting Rights Act of 1965.

Selma's story is told at the **National Voting Rights Museum** (☎334-418-0800; www.nvrmi.com; 1012 Water Ave; adult/senior & student $6.50/4.50; ⏰10am-4pm Mon-Thu, by appt only Fri-Sun), near the Edmund Pettus Bridge, and at two interpretive sites run by the National Park Service: the **Selma Interpretive Center** (☎334-872-0509; www.nps.gov/semo; 2 Broad St; ⏰9am-4:30pm Mon-Sat) 🍃 and the **Lowndes County Interpretive Center** (☎334-877-1983; www.nps.gov/semo; 7002 US Hwy 80; ⏰9am-4:30pm) halfway between Selma and Montgomery. Both centers contain small, solid exhibitions that delve into the history of Jim Crow and the Civil Rights movement.

THE CARNIVOROUS BOG

The pitcher plant is the vegetarian's revenge: a carnivorous plant topped with a lovely, fluting champagne rim of petals. Insects are drawn into the plant's interior cavity, which is lined with a slippery surface; the bugs fall into a pocket of liquid at the flower's base and are digested into nutrients.

Blankets of white-topped pitcher plants can be found at the **Splinter Hill Bog** (www.nature.org; off Co Rd 47, Bay Minette, GPS N 31°02.638', W -87°68.500'; ⏰dawn-dusk), a 2100-acre plot of land owned and protected by the nonprofit Nature Conservancy. Walk into the pitcher plant bogs (almost immediately visible once you depart the parking area) and you may notice that the clouds of midges, mosquitoes and flies so common in Southern woodlands and wetlands are mysteriously absent. That's because many of these insects are busily being digested by a graceful field of wildflowers.

Besides pitcher plants, this is an area of startling diversity; in some spots scientists have found over 60 different species of plants in a square yard, which constitutes some of the highest concentrations of biodiversity in North America. For more information, check out *America's Amazon*, a documentary on this region, which forms part of the Mobile-Tensaw Delta.

Selma is a quiet, poor town located in the heart of the Alabama 'Black Belt,' so named for both its dark, high-quality soil and a large population of African Americans. A point of interest is the **Mishkan Israel** (503 Broad St), an enormous redbrick synagogue that once housed a thriving local Jewish community. Many of the members of said community have left the South, but occasionally, a service is held.

If you're hungry, swing into **Lannie's** (☎334-874-4478; 2115 Minter Ave; mains $5-11; ⊙9am-9pm Mon-Sat), which cranks out some of the finest barbecue around.

Mobile

Wedged between Mississippi and Florida, the only real Alabama coastal city is Mobile (mo-*beel*), a busy industrial seaport with a smattering of green space, shady boulevards and four historic districts. It's ablaze with azaleas in early spring, and festivities are held throughout February for **Mardi Gras** (www.mobilemardigras.com), which has been celebrated here for nearly 200 years (it actually predates Mardi Gras in New Orleans).

Sights

USS Alabama BATTLESHIP

(www.ussalabama.com; 2703 Battleship Pkwy; adult/child $15/6; ⊙8am-6pm Apr-Sep, to 5pm Oct-Mar) USS *Alabama* is a 690ft behemoth famous for escaping nine major WWII battles unscathed. It's a worthwhile self-guided tour for its awesome size and might. While there, you can also tour a submarine and get up close and personal with military aircraft. Parking's $2.

Sleeping & Eating

Battle House HOTEL $$

(☎251-338-2000; www.marriott.com; 26 N Royal St; r from $139; P ❄ @ 🛜 ≋) By far the best address in Mobile. Stay in the original historic wing with its ornate domed marble lobby, though the striking new tower is on the waterfront. Rooms are spacious, luxurious, four-star chic.

Callaghan's Irish Social Club PUB FOOD $

(☎251-433-9374; www.callaghansirishsocialclub.com; 916 Charleston St; burgers $7-9; ⊙11am-11pm Mon-Thu, to midnight Fri & Sat, 10am-11pm Sun) This ramshackle pub is located in a 1920s-era building that used to house a meat market. It serves a mean burger and a cold beer, and often feature live-music acts.

Drinking & Nightlife

OK Bicycle Shop BAR

(☎251-432-2453; 661 Dauphin St; ⊙11am-3am) This sweet bar carries a bicycle theme throughout; there's a fantastic outdoor space for humid Mobile nights.

MISSISSIPPI

The state named for the most vital waterway in North America encompasses, appropriately enough, a long river of identities. Mississippi features palatial mansions and rural poverty; haunted cotton flats and lush hill country; honey-dipped sand on the coast and serene farmland in the north. Oft mythologized and misunderstood, this is the womb of some of the rawest history – and music – in the country.

Getting There & Away

There are three routes most folks take when traveling through Mississippi. I-55 and US-61 both run north–south from the state's northern to southern borders. US-61 goes through the delta, and I-55 flows in and out of Jackson. The gorgeous Natchez Trace Pkwy runs diagonally across the state from Tupelo to Natchez.

Information

Mississippi Division of Tourism Development (☎866-733-6477, 601-359-3297; www.visitmississippi.org) Has a directory of visitor bureaus and thematic travel itineraries. Most are well thought-out and run quite deep.

Mississippi Wildlife, Fisheries, & Parks (☎800-467-2757; www.mississippistateparks.reserveamerica.com) Camping costs from $13 (tent only) to $35 (beachfront camping), depending on the facilities; some parks have cabins for rent.

Oxford

Oxford both confirms and explodes preconceptions you may have of Mississippi's most famous college town. Frat boys in Ford pickup trucks and debutante sorority sisters? Sure. But they're alongside doctoral candidates debating critical theory, and a lively arts scene. Local culture revolves around the Square, where you'll find bars, restaurants and decent shopping, and the regal **University of Mississippi** (www.olemiss.edu), aka

Ole Miss. All around are quiet residential streets, sprinkled with antebellum homes and shaded by majestic oaks.

Sights & Activities

The gorgeous, 0.6-mile-long and rather painless **Bailee's Woods Trail** connects two of the town's most popular sights: Rowan Oak and the University of Mississippi Museum. **The Grove**, the shady heart of Ole Miss (the university), is generally peaceful, except on football Saturdays, when it buzzes with one of the most unforgettable tailgating (pregame) parties in American university sports.

Rowan Oak HISTORIC BUILDING
(662-234-3284; www.rowanoak.com; Old Taylor Rd; adult/child $5/free; 10am-4pm Tue-Sat, 1-4pm Sun, to 6pm Jun-Aug) Literary pilgrims head directly here, to the graceful 1840s home of William Faulkner. He authored many brilliant and dense novels set in Mississippi, and his work is celebrated in Oxford with an annual conference in July. Tours of Rowan Oak – where Faulkner lived from 1930 until his death in 1962, and which may reasonably be dubbed, to use the author's own elegant words, his 'postage stamp of native soil' – are self-guided.

University of Mississippi Museum MUSEUM
(www.museum.olemiss.edu; University Ave at 5th St; admission $5; 10am-6pm Tue-Sat) This museum has fine and folk arts and a plethora of science-related marvels, including a microscope and electromagnet from the 19th century.

Sleeping & Eating

The cheapest accommodations are chains on the outskirts of town. A number of high-quality restaurants dot the Square.

5 Twelve B&B $$
(662-234-8043; www.the5twelve.com; 512 Van Buren Ave; r $140-200, studio $200-250; P ❄ 📶) This six-room B&B has an antebellum-style exterior and modern interior (think Tempur-Pedic beds and flat-screen TVs). Room rates include full Southern breakfast to order. It's an easy walk from shops and restaurants, and the hosts will make you feel like family.

Taylor Grocery SEAFOOD $$
(www.taylorgrocery.com; 4 County Rd 338A; dishes $9-15; 5-10pm Thu-Sat, to 9pm Sun) Be prepared to wait – and to tailgate in the parking lot – at this splendidly rusticated catfish haunt. Order fried or grilled (either way, it's amazing) and bring a marker to sign your name on the wall. It's about 7 miles from downtown Oxford, south on Old Taylor Rd.

Ravine AMERICAN $$$
(662-234-4555; www.oxfordravine.com; 53 County Rd 321; mains $19-32; 6-9pm Wed-Thu, to 10pm Fri & Sat, 10:30am-2pm & 6-9pm Sun; 📶) About 3 miles outside Oxford, this unpretentious, cozily elegant restaurant nuzzles up to the forest. Chef Joel Miller picks and pulls much of the produce and herbs from his garden and buys locally and organically whenever possible; he's been doing it long before locavore was a buzzword. The result is simply wonderful food and a delicious experience.

JAMES MEREDITH'S MARCH

On October 1, 1962, James Meredith, accompanied by his adviser, National Association for the Advancement of Colored People state chair Medgar Evers, marched through a violent mob of segregationists to become the first African American student to register for classes at Ole Miss (the University of Mississippi). He was supposed to have registered 10 days earlier, but riots ensued and the Kennedy administration had to call in 500 federal marshals and the National Guard to ensure his safety.

Evers was eventually assassinated, and Meredith later walked across the state to raise awareness about racial violence in Mississippi. Some of Meredith's correspondence is on display at the **Center for Southern Culture** (662-915-5855; 1 Library Loop, University of Mississippi, Oxford; 8am-9pm Mon-Thu, to 4pm Fri, to 5pm Sat, 1pm-5pm Sun;) FREE, at the campus library.

Meredith himself went on to a career in politics, but his views were never easy to categorize. He was an active Republican who distanced himself from the Civil Rights movement, and always claimed he fought for his rights as an individual, rather than as a torchbearer for a greater movement. Regardless, Ole Miss is one of the most iconic institutions in the state, and when it was desegregated by Meredith's actions, it was inevitable the rest of Mississippi – and in some ways, the South – would follow.

City Grocery AMERICAN $$$
(☎662-232-8080; www.citygroceryonline.com; 152 Courthouse Sq; mains $26-32; ⏲11:30am-2:30pm Mon-Sat, 6-10pm Mon-Wed, to 10:30pm Thu-Sat, 11am-3pm Sun) Chef John Currance won a James Beard award and quickly set about dominating the Oxford culinary scene. City Grocery is one of his finest restaurants, offering a menu of haute Southern goodness like rice grits risotto and lard-braised hanger steak. The upstairs bar, decked out with local folk art, is a treat. Reservations recommended.

Entertainment

On the last Tuesday of the month, an increasingly popular **Art Crawl** connects galleries across town with free buses carrying well-lubricated art lovers. Nibbles and wine aplenty.

Proud Larry's LIVE MUSIC
(☎662-236-0050; www.proudlarrys.com; 211 S Lamar Blvd; ⏲shows 9:30pm) On the Square, this iconic music venue hosts consistently good bands, and does a nice pub-grub business at lunch and dinner before the stage lights dim.

The Lyric LIVE MUSIC
(☎662-234-5333; www.thelyricoxford.com; 1006 Van Buren St) This old brickhouse, and rather intimate theater with concrete floors, exposed rafters and a mezzanine, is the place to see indie rockers and folksy crooners.

Shopping

Square Books BOOKS
(☎662-236-2262; www.squarebooks.com; 160 Courthouse Sq; ⏲9am-9pm Mon-Thu, to 10pm Fri & Sat, to 6pm Sun) Square Books, one of the South's great independent bookstores, is the epicenter of Oxford's lively literary scene and a frequent stop for traveling authors. There's a cafe and balcony upstairs, along with an immense section devoted to Faulkner. Nearby **Square Books Jr** stocks children's and young adult lit. **Off Square Books** (☎662-236-2828; 129 Courthouse Sq; ⏲9am-9pm Mon-Sat, noon-5pm Sun) trades in used books.

Mississippi Delta

A long, low land of silent cotton fields bending under a severe sky, the Delta is a place of surreal, Gothic extremes. Here, in a feudal society of great manors and enslaved servitude, songs of labor and love became American pop music. It traveled via Africa to sharecropping fields along Hwy 61, unfolding into the blues, the father of rock and roll. Tourism in this area, which still suffers some of the worst rural poverty rates in the country, largely revolves around discovering the sweat-soaked roots of this original, American art form.

> **THACKER MOUNTAIN RADIO**
>
> If you find yourself driving a lonely Mississippi back road or concrete strip of interstate on a Saturday evening at 7pm, turn your radio dial to the local NPR frequency (www.mpbonline.org/programs/radio for a listing). You'll be treated to **Thacker Mountain Radio**, a Mississippi variety show that showcases some of the region's finest authors and musicians. It's an enjoyable means of getting under the cultural skin of this state, and the music ain't half bad either. You can see the show being recorded at 6pm on Thursday nights at Off Square Books in Oxford (129 Courthouse Sq) during fall and spring.

Clarksdale

Clarksdale is the Delta's most useful base. It's within a couple of hours of all the blues sights, and big-name blues acts are regular weekend visitors. But this is still a poor Delta town, and it's jarring to see how many businesses find private security details a necessity after dark.

Sights

The **Crossroads** of Hwys 61 and 49 is supposedly the intersection where the great Robert Johnson made his mythical deal with the devil, immortalized in his tune 'Cross Road Blues.' Now all of the implied lonely fear and dark mysticism of the space is taken up by a tacky sculpture. For what it's worth, few historians agree where the actual crossroad is located.

Delta Blues Museum MUSEUM
(☎662-627-6820; www.deltabluesmuseum.org; 1 Blues Alley; adult/senior & student $7/5; ⏲9am-5pm Mon-Sat Mar-Oct, from 10am Nov-Feb) A small but well-presented collection of memorabilia is on display here. The shrine to

MISSISSIPPI FACTS

Nickname Magnolia State

Population 3 million

Area 48,430 sq miles

Capital city Jackson (population 175,437)

Sales tax 7%

Birthplace of Author Eudora Welty (1909–2001), musicians Robert Johnson (1911–38), Muddy Waters (1913–83), BB King (1925–2015) and Elvis Presley (1935–77), activist James Meredith (b 1933) and puppeteer Jim Henson (1936–90)

Home of The blues

Politics Conservative

Famous for Cotton fields

Kitschiest souvenir Elvis lunchbox in Tupelo

Driving distances Jackson to Clarksdale 187 miles, Jackson to Ocean Springs 176 miles

Delta legend Muddy Waters includes the actual cabin where he grew up. Local art exhibits and a gift shop round out the display. Occasionally hosts live-music shows on Friday nights.

Rock & Blues Heritage Museum MUSEUM
(☎901-605-8662; www.blues2rock.com; 113 E Second St; admission $5; ⏲11am-5pm Tue-Sat) A jovial Dutch transplant and blues fanatic has turned his immense personal collection of records, memorabilia and artifacts into a magic museum that traces the roots of blues and rock from the 1920s to the '70s.

Festivals & Events

Juke Joint Festival MUSIC
(www.jukejointfestival.com; tickets $15; ⏲Apr) There are more than 120 venues at this three-day festival held in joints sprinkled in and around Clarksdale.

Sunflower River Blues & Gospel Festival MUSIC
(www.sunflowerfest.org; ⏲Aug) Tends to draw bigger names than the Juke Joint Festival, and has a significant gospel component.

Sleeping & Eating

Riverside Hotel HISTORIC HOTEL $
(☎662-624-9163; ratfrankblues@yahoo.com; 615 Sunflower Ave; r with/without bath $75/65; ❄) Don't let a well-worn exterior put you off: this hotel, soaked in blues history – blues singer Bessie Smith died here when it was a hospital, and a festival's worth of blues artists, from Sonny Boy Williamson II to Robert Nighthawk have stayed here – offers clean and tidy rooms and sincere friendliness. It's been family-run since 1944, when it was 'the black hotel' in town. The original proprietor's son, Rat, will charm your socks off with history, hospitality and prices.

Shack Up Inn INN $
(☎662-624-8329; www.shackupinn.com; 001 Commisary Circle; Hwy 49; d $75-165; P❄📶) At the Hopson Plantation, this self-titled 'bed and beer' allows you to stay in refurbished sharecropper cabins or the creatively renovated cotton gin. The cabins have covered porches and are filled with old furniture and musical instruments. Years of being the most storied accommodation in Clarksdale have bred complacency, however, and service can be indifferent.

Larry's Hot Tamales AMERICAN $
(☎662-592-4245; 947 Sunflower Ave; mains $4-12; ⏲11am-11pm Mon-Sat) Friendly Larry's may have a small menu, but it's doing the Lord's work with what's on offer: sizzling hot Delta tamales and delicious rib tips. You'll bust your stomach way before you bust your wallet.

Yazoo Pass CAFE $$
(☎662-627-8686; www.yazoopass.com; 207 Yazoo Ave; lunch mains $6-10, dinner $13-26; ⏲7am-9pm Mon-Sat; 📶) A contemporary space where you can enjoy fresh scones and croissants in the mornings, salad bar, sandwiches and soups at lunch, and pan-seared ahi, filet mignon, burgers and pastas at dinner.

Entertainment

Red's BLUES
(☎662-627-3166; 395 Sunflower Ave; cover $7-10; ⏲live music 9pm Fri & Sat) Clarksdale's best juke joint, with its neon-red mood lighting, plastic-bag ceiling and general soulful disintegration, is the place to see bluesmen howl. Red runs the bar, knows the acts and slings a cold beer whenever you need one.

Ground Zero BLUES
(☎ 662-621-9009; www.groundzerobluesclub.com; 0 Blues Alley; ⏰ 11am-2pm Mon & Tue, to 11pm Wed & Thu, to 2am Fri & Sat) For blues in polished environs, Morgan Freeman's Ground Zero is a huge and friendly hall with a dancefloor surrounded by tables. Bands take to the stage Wednesday to Saturday, and there's good food available.

Shopping

Cat Head Delta Blues & Folk Art ARTS & CRAFTS
(☎ 662-624-5992; www.cathead.biz; 252 Delta Ave; ⏰ 10am-5pm Mon-Sat) Friendly St Louis carpetbagger and author Roger Stolle runs a colorful, all-purpose, blues emporium. The shelves are jammed with books, face jugs, local art and blues records. Stolle seems to be connected to everyone in the Delta, and knows when and where the bands will play.

Around Clarksdale

Down Hwy 49, **Tutwiler** is where the blues began its migration from oral tradition to popular art form. Here, WC Handy, known as the Father of the Blues, first heard a sharecropper moan his 12-bar prayer while the two waited for a train in 1903. That meeting is immortalized by a mural at the **Tutwiler Tracks** (off Hwy 49; 👪).

East of Greenville, Hwy 82 heads out of the Delta. The **Highway 61 Blues Museum** (☎ 662-686-7646; www.highway61blues.com; 307 N Broad St; ⏰ 10am-5pm Mon-Sat), at the start of the route known as the '**Blues Highway**,' packs a mighty wallop in a condensed, six-room space venerating local bluesmen from the Delta. Leland hosts the **Highway 61 Blues Festival** in late September or early October. **Highway 61** itself is a legendary road that traverses endless, eerie miles of flat fields, Gothic agricultural industrial facilities, one-room churches and moldering cemeteries.

Stopping in the tiny Delta town of **Indianola** is worthwhile to visit the modern **BB King Museum and Delta Interpretive Center** (☎ 662-887-9539; www.bbkingmuseum.org; 400 Second St; adult/student/child $15/5/free; ⏰ 10am-5pm Tue-Sat, noon-5pm Sun-Mon, closed Mon Nov-Mar). While the museum is dedicated to the legendary bluesman, it also tackles life in the Delta as a whole. This is the best museum in the region, filled with interactive displays, video exhibits and an amazing array of artifacts, effectively communicating the history and legacy of the blues while shedding light on the soul of the Delta.

Vicksburg

Lovely Vicksburg sits atop a high bluff overlooking the Mississippi River. During the Civil War, General Ulysses S Grant besieged the city for 47 days until its surrender on July 4, 1863, at which point the North gained dominance over North America's greatest river.

Sights

The major sights are readily accessible from I-20 exit 4B (Clay St). Charming historic downtown stretches along several cobblestoned blocks of Washington St. Down by the water is a block of murals depicting the history of the area, and a **Children's Art Park**.

Vicksburg National Military Park BATTLEFIELD
(☎ 601-636-0583; www.nps.gov/vick; Clay St; per car/individual $8/4; ⏰ 8am-5pm; 👪) Vicksburg controlled access to the Mississippi River, and its seizure was one of the turning points of the Civil War. A 16-mile driving tour passes historic markers explaining battle scenarios and key events from the city's long siege, when residents lived like moles in caverns to avoid Union shells. Plan on staying for at least 90 minutes. If you have your own bike, cycling is a fantastic way to tour the place. Locals use the scenic park for walking and running.

Lower Mississippi River Museum MUSEUM
(☎ 601-638-9900; www.lmrm.org; 910 Washington St; ⏰ 9am-4pm Wed-Sat; 👪) FREE Downtown Vicksburg's pride and joy is this surprisingly interesting museum which delves into such topics as the famed 1927 flood and the Army Corps of Engineers, who have managed the river since the 18th century. Kids will enjoy the aquarium and clambering around the dry-docked research vessel, the M/V *Mississippi IV*.

Sleeping & Eating

Corners Mansion B&B $$
(☎ 601-636-7421; www.thecorners.com; 601 Klein St; r $125-170; P ❄ 📶) The best part of this wedding-cake 1873 B&B is looking over the Yazoo and Mississippi Rivers from your porch swing. The gardens and Southern breakfast don't hurt either.

Walnut Hills SOUTHERN **$$**
(601-638-4910; www.walnuthillsms.net; 1214 Adams St; mains $8-25; 11am-9pm Mon-Sat, 11am-2pm Sun) For a dining experience that takes you back in time, head to this eatery where you can enjoy rib sticking, down-home Southern food elbow-to-elbow, family-style.

Drinking & Nightlife

★**Highway 61 Coffeehouse** CAFE
(601-638-9221; www.61coffee.blogspot.com; 1101 Washington St; 7am-5pm Mon-Fri, from 9am Sat;) This awesome coffee shop has occasional live music on Saturday afternoons, serves Fair Trade coffee and is an energetic epicenter of artsyness, poetry readings and the like.

Jackson

Mississippi's capital and largest city mixes up stately residential areas with large swaths of blight, peppered throughout with a surprisingly funky arts-cum-hipster scene in the Fondren District. There's a slew of decent bars, good restaurants and a lot of love for live music; it's easy to have a good time in Jackson.

Sights

Mississippi Museum of Art GALLERY
(601-960-1515; www.msmuseumart.org; 380 South Lamar St; special exhibitions $5-12; 10am-5pm Tue-Sat, noon-5pm Sun) FREE This is your must-stop sight when visiting Jackson. The collection of Mississippi art – and the permanent exhibit dubbed 'The Mississippi Story' – is superb, and the surrounding grounds are nicely landscaped into a bright and quirky garden area.

Old Capitol Museum MUSEUM
(www.mdah.state.ms.us/museum; 100 State St; 9am-5pm Tue-Sat, 1-5pm Sun) FREE The state's Greek Revival capitol building from 1839 to 1903 now houses a Mississippi history museum filled with films and exhibits. You'll learn that secession was far from unanimous, and how reconstruction brought some of the harshest, presegregation 'black codes' in the South.

Eudora Welty House HISTORIC BUILDING
(601-353-7762; www.eudorawelty.org; 1119 Pinehurst St; adult/student/child $5/3/free; tours 9am, 11am, 1pm & 3pm Tue-Fri) Literature buffs should make a reservation to tour the Pulitzer Prize–winning author's Tudor Revival house, where she lived for more than 75 years. It's now a true historical preservation down to the most minute details. It's free on the 13th day of any month, assuming that's a normal operating day.

Smith Robertson Museum MUSEUM
(601-960-1457; www.jacksonms.gov; 528 Bloom St; adult/child $4.50/1.50; 9am-5pm Mon-Fri, 10am-1pm Sat) Housed in Mississippi's first public school for African American kids is the alma mater of Richard Wright, author of *Black Boy*, among many other works. It offers insight and explanation into the pain and perseverance of the African American legacy in Mississippi, and into Wright's own searing race consciousness, which framed much of the literary record of the Civil Rights movement.

Museum of Natural Science MUSEUM
(601-576-6000; www.mdwfp.com/museum; 2148 Riverside Dr; adult/child $6/4; 8am-5pm Mon-Fri, from 9am Sat, from 1pm Sun;) Tucked way back in Lefleur's Bluff State Park is the Museum of Natural Science. It houses exhibits on the natural flora and fauna of Mississippi, and has aquariums inside, a replica swamp and 2.5 miles of trails traversing 300 acres of preserved prettiness.

Sleeping & Eating

The Fondren District is the budding artsy, boho area of town, with restaurants, art galleries and cafes dotting the happening commercial strip.

Old Capitol Inn BOUTIQUE HOTEL **$$**
(601-359-9000; www.oldcapitolinn.com; 226 N State St; r/ste from $99/145; P@) This 24-room boutique hotel, located near museums and restaurants, is terrific. The rooftop garden includes a hot tub. A full Southern breakfast (and early-evening wine and cheese) ia included, and the rooms are all comfortable and uniquely furnished.

Big Apple Inn AMERICAN **$**
(601-354-4549; 509 N Farish St; mains $2; 7:30am-9pm Tue-Fri, from 8am Sat) The Big Apple basically has two items on its menu: a hot sausage sandwich and a pig's ear sandwich. Both are small, served on soft rolls, and taste delicious. The interior is hot, cramped and dingy, and the surrounding neighborhood is fading fast, but this is a true Jackson original, and the pig's ear is worth a long drive.

High Noon Cafe VEGETARIAN **$**
(601-366-1513; www.rainbowcoop.org; 2807 Old Canton Rd; mains $7-10; 11:30am-2pm Mon-Fri;) Tired of fried, green, pulled-pork-covered catfish? This organic vegetarian grill, inside the Rainbow Co-op grocery store in the Fondren District, does beet burgers, portabello Reubens and other healthy delights. Stock up on organic groceries too.

Saltine SEAFOOD **$$**
(601-982-2899; www.saltinerestaurant.com; 622 Duling Ave; mains $12-19; 11am-10pm Mon-Thu, to 11pm Fri & Sat, to 9pm Sun) This playful spot takes on the delicious task of bringing oysters to the Jackson culinary world. The bivalves are served in several iterations: raw, woodfired, with Alabama white barbecue sauce and 'Nashville' *(very)* hot. Sop up some shellfish sauce with the excellent skillet cornbread, then give the grilled rainbow trout a whirl.

Walker's Drive-In SOUTHERN **$$$**
(601-982-2633; www.walkersdrivein.com; 3016 N State St; mains lunch $10-17, dinner $26-36; 11am-2pm Mon-Fri & from 5:30pm Tue-Sat) This retro masterpiece has been restored with love and infused with new Southern foodie ethos. Lunch is diner 2.0 fare with grilled redfish sandwiches, tender burgers and grilled oyster po'boys, as well as an exceptional seared, chili-crusted tuna salad, which comes with spiced calamari and seaweed.

Drinking & Entertainment

Martin's BAR
(601-354-9712; www.martinslounge.net; 214 S State St; 10am-1:30am Mon-Sat, to midnight Sun) This is a delightfully dirty dive, the kind of place where the bartenders know the phone numbers of their regulars in case said regulars pass out on their bar stools. Attracts a mix of old-timers, statehouse workers, slick lobbyists and lawyers plucked from a John Grisham novel. Live music and karaoke spice up weekends.

Sneaky Beans CAFE
(601-487-6349; www.sneakybeans.tumblr.com; 2914 N State St; 7am-9:30pm Mon-Fri, from 7:30am Sat) Every city deserves a great cafe with fast wi-fi, quirky art and an airy sense of space; Sneaky Beans, which also boasts a pretty great library, is Jackson's contribution to the genre.

The Apothecary at Brent's Drugs COCKTAIL BAR
(www.apothecaryjackson.com; 655 Duling Ave; 5pm-1am Tue-Thu, to 2am Fri & Sat) Tucked into the back of a '50s-style soda fountain shop is a distinctly early 21st-century craft cocktail bar, complete with bartenders sporting thick-framed glasses, customers with sleeve tattoos and a fine menu of expertly mixed libations.

F Jones Corner BLUES
(601-983-1148; www.fjonescorner.com; 303 N Farish St; 11am-2pm Tue-Fri, 10pm-late Thu-Sat) All shapes and sizes, colors and creeds descend on this down-home Farish St club when everywhere else closes. It hosts authentic Delta musicians who have been known to play until sunrise.

Hal & Mal's LIVE MUSIC
(601-948-0888; www.halandmals.com; 200 Commerce St) Hal & Mal's is simply an excellent mid-sized live-music venue. The sight lines are great, it feels neither too crowded nor annoyingly expansive, bar service is quick and whoever is doing the booking is killing it, bringing in a range of acts that speak to Jackson's under-appreciated capacity for funkiness.

Information

Convention & Visitors Bureau (601-960-1891; www.visitjackson.com; 111 E Capitol St, Suite 102; 8am-5pm Mon-Fri) Free information.

Getting There & Away

At the junction of I-20 and I-55, it's easy to get in and out of Jackson. Its international **airport** (JAN; 601-939-5631; www.jmaa.com; 100 International Dr) is 10 miles east of downtown. **Greyhound** (601-353-6342; www.greyhound.com; 300 W Capitol St) buses serve Birmingham, AL, Memphis, TN, and New Orleans, LA. Amtrak's *City of New Orleans* stops at the station.

Natchez

Some 668 antebellum homes pepper the oldest civilized settlement on the Mississippi River (beating New Orleans by two years). Natchez is also the end (or the beginning!) of the scenic 444-mile Natchez Trace Pkwy, the state's cycling and recreational jewel. Just

GRACE THE NATCHEZ TRACE

If you're driving through Mississippi, we highly recommend planning at least part of your trip around one of the oldest roads in North America: the Natchez Trace. This 444-mile trail follows a natural ridge line that was widely utilized by prehistoric animals as a grazing route; later, the area those animals trampled became a footpath and trading route utilized by Native American tribes. That route would go on to become the Natchez Trace, a major roadway into the early Western interior of the young United States, that was often plagued by roving bandits.

In 1938, 444 miles of the Trace, stretching from Pasquo, TN, southwest to Natchez, MS, was designated the federally protected **Natchez Trace Parkway** (662-680-4025, 800-305-7417; www.nps.gov/natr;), administered by the National Park Service. It's a lovely, scenic drive that traverses a wide panoply of Southern landscapes: thick, dark forests, soggy wetlands, gentle hill country and long swathes of farmland. There are more than 50 access points to the Parkway and a helpful **visitor center** (662-680-4027, 800-305-7417; www.nps.gov/natr; Mile 266, Natchez Trace Pkwy; 8am-5pm, closed Christmas;) outside of Tupelo.

outside of town, along the Trace, you'll find **Emerald Mound** (800-305-7417; www.nps.gov/natr; Mile 10.3, Natchez Trace Pkwy; dawn-dusk;), the grassy ruins of a Native American city that includes the second-largest pre-Columbian earthworks in the USA.

The **visitor and welcome center** (800-647-6724; www.visitnatchez.org; 640 S Canal St; tours adult/child $12/8; 8:30am-5pm Mon-Sat, 9am-4pm Sun;) is a large, well-organized tourist resource. Tours of the historic downtown and antebellum mansions leave from here. During the 'pilgrimage' seasons in spring and fall, local mansions are opened to visitors.

Sleeping & Eating

Mark Twain Guesthouse GUESTHOUSE $
(601-446-8023; www.underthehillsaloon.com; 33 Silver St; r without bath $65-85;) Mark Twain used to crash in room 1, above the bar at the current **Under the Hill Saloon** (601-446-8023; www.underthehillsaloon.com; 25 Silver St; 9am-late), when he was a riverboat pilot passing through town. There are three rooms in all. They share one bath and laundry facilities. Check-in for the guesthouse is at the saloon.

Historic Oak Hill Inn INN $$
(601-446-2500; www.historicoakhill.com; 409 S Rankin St; r incl breakfast from $135;) Staying at this classic Natchez B&B, you'll get a taste of antebellum aristocratic living, from period furniture to china. A charmingly high-strung staff makes for an immaculate experience.

Magnolia Grill AMERICAN $$
(601-446-7670; www.magnoliagrill.com; 49 Silver St; mains $13-20; 11am-9pm, to 10pm Fri & Sat;) Down by the riverside, this attractive wooden storefront grill with exposed rafters and outdoor patio is a good place for a pork tenderloin po'boy or a fried crawfish spinach salad.

Cotton Alley CAFE $$
(601-442-7452; www.cottonalleycafe.com; 208 Main St; mains $10-20; 11am-2pm & 5:30-9pm Mon-Sat) This cute whitewashed dining room is chocablock with knickknacks and artistic touches and the menu borrows from local tastes. Think: grilled chicken sandwich on Texas toast or jambalaya pasta, but it does a nice chicken Caesar and a tasty grilled salmon salad, too.

Gulf Coast

The Mississippi Gulf Coast is a long, low series of breeze-swept dunes, patches of sea oats, bayside art galleries and Vegas-style casinos clustered around Biloxi. This is a popular retreat for families and military members; several important bases pepper the coast from Florida to Texas.

Charming **Bay St Louis** attracts Federal employees, including many scientists, based out at Stennis Space Center near the Louisiana border; that presence gives the town a slightly more progressive cast than you'd expect from Mississippi. Yoga studios, antique stores and galleries cluster on **Main**

St. The **Starfish Cafe** (☎228-229-3503; www.starfishcafebsl.com; 211 Main St; mains $8-12; ⊙11am-2pm Tue-Sat, 5-8pm Mon & Tue;) provides job training for local youth, engages in sustainable sourcing of ingredients and serves up Southern fare (with a twist of cosmopolitanism), such as fish tacos, panko-crusted tofu and blackened Gulf shrimp.

Ocean Springs remains a peaceful getaway, with a lineup of shrimp boats in the harbor alongside recreational sailing yachts, a historic downtown core, and a powdery fringe of white sand on the Gulf. The highlight is the **Walter Anderson Museum** (☎228-872-3164; www.walterandersonmuseum.org; 510 Washington St; adult/child $10/5; ⊙9:30am-4:30pm Mon-Sat, from 12:30pm Sun;) . A consummate artist and lover of Gulf Coast nature, Anderson suffered from mental illness, which spurred his monastic existence and fueled his life's work: in his own words, being one of 'those who have brought nature and art together into one thing.' After he died, the beachside shack where he lived on **Horn Island** was discovered to be painted in mind-blowing murals, which you'll see here.

Hotels line the highway as you approach downtown. Nice camping (and a visitor center) can be found at **Gulf Islands National Seashore Park** (☎228-875-9057; www.nps.gov/guis; 3500 Park Rd, Ocean Springs, MS; per person entrance $3, camping $20-30) , just out of town. Here, you'll see lumps of sugary sand dunes grown hairy with tangles of weeds and sea oats, all lapped by the calm waters of the Gulf, one of the last undeveloped stretches of the coastal South.

ARKANSAS

Forming the mountainous joint between the Midwest and the Deep South, Arkansas (ar-kan-saw) is an often overlooked treasure of swift rushing rivers, dark leafy hollows, crenellated granite outcrops and the rugged spine of the Ozark and the Ouachita (wash-ee-tah) Mountains. The entire state is blessed with exceptionally well presented state parks and tiny, empty roads crisscrossing dense forests that let out onto breathtaking vistas and gentle pastures dotted with grazing horses. Mountain towns juke between Christian fundamentalism, hippie communes and biker bars, yet all of these divergent cultures share a love of their home state's stunning natural beauty.

Information

Arkansas State Parks (☎888-287-2757; www.arkansasstateparks.com) Arkansas' well-reputed park system has 52 state parks, 30 offering camping (tent and RV sites are $12 to $55, depending on amenities). A number of the parks offer lodge and cabin accommodations. Due to popularity, reservations on weekends and holidays often require multiday stays.

Little Rock

Little Rock lives up to its name; this charming state capital feels pretty petite. But this is center of urban life in Arkansas, and the angle of the urban experience this city embraces is quite cool: amid the leafy residential neighborhoods are hip bars, fresh restaurants, plenty of bike trails and a tolerant vibe. Small this town may be, but it's wonderfully situated on the Arkansas River, and as befits this state of natural wonders, you always feel as if you're within arm's reach of lush wooded river valleys.

Sights

The best stroll is in the **River Market district** (www.rivermarket.info; W Markham St & President Clinton Ave), an area of shops, galleries, restaurants and pubs along the riverbank. Keep an eye out for the **Butler Center** (☎501-320-5790; www.butlercenter.org; 401 President Clinton Ave; ⊙9am-6pm Mon-Sat) FREE. This research institute, dedicated to promoting an understanding of the state's arts and culture, boasts a series of lovely galleries stocked with local art works.

William J Clinton Presidential Center LIBRARY
(☎501-748-0419; www.clintonlibrary.gov; 1200 President Clinton Ave; adult/students & seniors/child $7/5/3, with audio $10/8/6; ⊙9am-5pm Mon-Sat, 1-5pm Sun) This library houses the largest archival collection in presidential history, including 80 million pages of documents and two million photographs (although there's not a lot related to a certain intern scandal). The entire experience feels like a time travel journey to the 1990s. Peruse the full-scale replica of the Oval Office, the exhibits on all stages of Clinton's life, or gifts from visiting dignitaries. The complex is built to environmentally friendly 'green' standards.

Little Rock Central High School HISTORIC SITE
(☎501-396-3001; www.nps.gov/chsc; 2125 Daisy Gatson Bates Dr; ⊙9:30am-4:30pm) Little Rock's most riveting attraction is the site of the 1957 desegregation crisis that changed the country forever. It was here that a group of African American students known as the Little Rock Nine were first denied entry inside the then all-white high school (despite a unanimous 1954 Supreme Court ruling forcing the integration of public schools).

Riverfront Park PARK
(☎501-371-6848; LaHarpe Blvd) Just northwest of downtown, Riverfront Park rolls pleasantly along the Arkansas River and both pedestrians and cyclists take advantage of this fantastic city park. It's a truly fine integration of a landscape feature (the river) into an urban setting. You can't miss the **Big Dam Bridge** (www.bigdambridge.com; 👪), a pedestrian- and cyclist-only span that connects 17 miles of multiuse trails which form a complete loop thanks to the renovation of the **Clinton Presidential Park Bridge**.

Arkansas Arts Center MUSEUM
(☎501-372-4000; www.arkansasartscenter.org; 9th & Commerce St; ⊙10am-5pm Tue-Sat, from 11am Sun) FREE Little Rock's art museum features excellent visiting exhibitions and a permanent collection that includes an impressive array of contemporary crafts, an engraving by naturalist John James Audubon and several works by pointillist Paul Signac.

Sleeping & Eating

At the time of writing, work was being done on the **Firehouse Hostel** (☎501-476-0294; www.firehousehostel.org; 1201 Commerce St). The planned location, in a gorgeous 1917 Craftsman-style building that once served as a city fire station, is fantastic.

★**Capital Hotel** BOUTIQUE HOTEL $$
(☎501-370-7062, 877-637-0037; www.capitalhotel.com; 111 W Markham St; r $190-220; P ❄ @ 📶) This 1872 former bank building with a cast-iron facade – a near-extinct architectural feature – is the top digs in Little Rock. There is a wonderful outdoor mezzanine for cocktails and a sense of suited, cigar-chomping posh throughout; if you want to feel like a wining, dining lobbyist, this is the place for you.

Rosemont B&B $$
(☎501-374-7456; www.rosemontoflittlerock.com; 515 W 15th St; r $105-145; P ❄ 📶) This 1880s restored farmhouse near the Governor's mansion oozes cozy Southern charm. The proprietors have also opened a bucolic historic cottage nearby (from $175).

Ottenheimer Market Hall MARKET $
(btwn S Commerce & S Rock Sts; ⊙7am-6pm Mon-Sat) Trawl the stalls for some good-value breakfast or lunch – you'll find everything from fresh fruits and pastries, to sushi, burgers and barbecue.

Big Orange AMERICAN $
(☎501-379-8715; www.bigorangeburger.com; 207 N University Ave; mains $9-13; ⊙Sun-Thu 11am-10pm, til 11pm Fri & Sat; 🌶 👪) Sometimes you need a burger, and not just a burger, but the sort of meat between two buttered buns that leaves you in a state of post-carnivore frenzy bliss. Enter Big Orange, which serves variations on the theme ranging from a classic with American cheese, topped with white truffle for the fancy, and falafel for the vegetarians.

ARKANSAS FACTS

Nickname Natural State

Population 2.9 million

Area 52,068 sq miles

Capital city Little Rock (population 193,357)

Other cities Fayetteville (population 78,690), Bentonville (population 40,167)

Sales tax 6.5%, plus 2% visitors tax and local taxes

Birthplace of General Douglas MacArthur (1880–1964), musician Johnny Cash (1932–2003), former president Bill Clinton (b 1946), author John Grisham (b 1955), actor Billy Bob Thornton (b 1955)

Home of Walmart

Politics Like most Southern states, opposition to civil rights turned the state Republican in the 1960s

Famous for Football fans 'calling the Hogs' – Woooooooooo, Pig! Sooie!

Official state instrument Fiddle

Driving distances Little Rock to Eureka Springs 182 miles, Eureka Springs to Mountain View 123 miles

★ South on Main AMERICAN $$

(☎501-244-9660; www.southonmain.com; 1304 S Main St; mains $16-24; ⏰11am-2:30pm Mon-Fri, 5-10pm Tue-Sat, 10am-2pm Sun) This wonderful spot is a gastronomic pet project of *The Oxford American*, the South's seminal quarterly literary magazine. It embraces the foodways of the region with a verve and dynamism that is creative and delicious; catfish comes with cornmeal pancakes, while rabbit leg is wrapped in country ham. A great bar and frequent live music round out the awesome.

Drinking & Entertainment

The fun-loving pubs in the River Market district buzz at night.

White Water Tavern LIVE MUSIC

(☎501-375-8400; www.whitewatertavern.com; 2500 W 7th St; ⏰noon-2am Mon-Fri, 6pm-1am Sat) The White Water manages to line up some excellent acts for its small stage, with bands ranging from straight-up rockers to alt country heroes to indie poppers to hip hop MCs. When the music isn't playing, this is an excellent, friendly corner pub.

Getting There & Around

Bill & Hillary Clinton National Airport (LIT; ☎501-372-3439; www.lrn-airport.com; 1 Airport Dr) lies just east of downtown. The **Greyhound station** (☎501-372-3007; www.greyhound.com; 118 E Washington St), in North Little Rock, serves Hot Springs (one to two hours), Memphis, TN (2½ hours), and New Orleans, LA (18 hours). Amtrak occupies **Union Station** (☎501-372-6841; 1400 W Markham St). **Central Arkansas Transit** (CAT; ☎501-375-6717; www.cat.org) runs local buses and the **River Rail Streetcar**, a trolley which makes a loop on W Markham and President Clinton Ave (adult/child $1/50¢).

Hot Springs

Hot Springs is a gem of a mountain town, and we're not the first to notice. The healing waters the town is named for have been attracting everyone from Native Americans to early 20th-century health nuts to a good chunk of the nation's organized crime leadership. When Hot Springs was at full throttle in the 1930s, it was a hotbed of gambling, bootlegging, prostitution and opulence. Elaborate restored bathhouses, where you can still get old-school spa treatments, line Bathhouse Row behind shady magnolias on the east side of Central Ave.

Sights & Activities

A promenade runs through the park around the hillside behind **Bathhouse Row**, where some springs survive intact, and a network of trails covers Hot Springs' mountains. Many of the old bathhouses have been converted into art galleries affiliated with the National Parks Service (NPS).

NPS Visitor Center MUSEUM

(Fordyce Bath House; ☎501-620-6715; www.nps.gov/hosp; 369 Central Ave; ⏰9am-5pm) On Bathhouse Row, set up in the 1915 Fordyce bathhouse, the NPS visitor center and museum has exhibits about the park's history, first as a Native American free-trade zone, and later as a turn-of-the-20th-century European spa. Most fascinating are the amenities and standards set forth by an early 20th-century spa; the stained glass work and Greek statues are opulent, but we could pass on the bare white walls, grout and electro-shock therapy.

Hot Springs Mountain Tower OUTDOORS

(401 Hot Springs Mountain Rd; adult/child $7/4; ⏰9am-5pm Nov-Feb, to 6pm Mar–mid-May & Labor Day-Oct, to 9pm mid-May–Labor Day) On top of Hot Springs Mountain, the 216ft tower has spectacular views of the surrounding mountains covered with dogwood, hickory, oak and pine – lovely in the spring and fall.

Gangster Museum of America MUSEUM

(☎501-318-1717; www.tgmoa.com; 510 Central Ave; adult/child $12/free; ⏰10am-5pm Sun-Thu, to 6pm Fri & Sat) Learn about the sinful glory days of Prohibition when this small town in the middle of nowhere turned into a hotbed of lavish wealth thanks to Chicago bootleggers like Capone, and his NYC counterparts. Highlights include original slots and a tommy gun. Entry is by guided tour, generally offered on the half-hour.

Galaxy Connection MUSEUM

(☎501-276-4432; www.thegalaxyconnection.com; 906 Hobson Ave; admission $10; ⏰10am-5pm Mon-Sat, from noon Sun) And now for something completely different: a museum dedicated to *Star Wars*. This fantastically geeky temple is the labor of love of one particularly obsessed Arkansan, and while it may feel a little on the amateur side, it's got enough paraphernalia from life-sized Boba Fett mannequins to a Jedi dress-up area to feel awesomely nostalgic to fans.

WORTH A TRIP

ARKANSAS DELTA

Roughly 120 miles east of Little Rock, and just 20 miles from Clarksdale, Hwy 49 crosses the Mississippi River into the Arkansas Delta. **Helena**, a formerly prosperous but currently depressed mill town with a blues tradition (Sonny Boy Williamson made his name here), awakens for its annual **Arkansas Blues & Heritage Festival** (www.kingbiscuitfestival.com; tickets $45; Oct) when blues musicians and their fans take over downtown for three days in early October. Year-round, blues fans and history buffs should visit the **Delta Cultural Center** (870-338-4350; www.deltaculturalcenter.com; 141 Cherry St; 9am-5pm Tue-Sat) FREE. The museum displays all manner of memorabilia such as Albert King's and Sister Rosetta Tharpe's guitars, and John Lee Hooker's signed handkerchief.

The world's longest-running blues radio program, *King Biscuit Time*, is broadcast here (12:15pm Monday to Friday), and *Delta Sounds* (1pm Monday to Friday) often hosts live musicians; both air on KFFA AM-1360. Before leaving town, make like Robert Plant and stop by the wonderfully cluttered **Bubba's Blues Corner** (870-338-3501; 105 Cherry St, Helena, AR; 9am-5pm Tue-Sat;) to pick up a blues record.

The hardscrabble railroad town of **McGehee** is the home of the touching **WWII Japanese American Internment Museum** (870-222-9168; 100 South Railroad St; admission $5; 10am-5pm Tue-Sat). During World War II, Japanese Americans were rounded up and evicted from their homes and businesses and sent to live in internment camps. One of these camps took root in the delta mud just outside McGehee, and this museum is dedicated to telling the story of its inmates via personal items, art and a small collection of intimate displays.

Buckstaff Bath House SPA
(501-623-2308; www.buckstaffbaths.com; 509 Central Ave; thermal bath $33, with massage $71; 8-11:45am & 1:30-3pm Mon-Sat Mar-Nov, closed Sat afternoon Dec-Feb) Spa service Hot Springs–style was never a 'foofy' experience. Buckstaff's no-nonsense staff whip you through the baths, treatments and massages, just as in the 1930s. Wonderful.

Sleeping & Eating

Restaurants congregate along the Central Ave tourist strip and offer ho-hum food.

★ **Alpine Inn** INN $
(501-624-9164; www.alpine-inn-hot-springs.com; 741 Park Ave/Hwy 7 N; r $65-95;) The friendly Scottish owners of this inn, less than a mile from Bathhouse Row, have spent a few years upgrading an old motel to remarkable ends. The impeccable rooms are comfortable and include new flat-screen TVs and sumptuous beds.

Arlington Resort Hotel & Spa HISTORIC HOTEL $
(501-623-7771; www.arlingtonhotel.com; 239 Central Ave; s/d/ste from $99/120/194;) This imposing historic hotel tops Bathhouse Row and constantly references its glory days, even if said days have passed. The grand lobby buzzes at night when there might be a live band. There's an in-house spa, and rooms are well-maintained, if aging. Corner rooms with a view are a steal.

Colonial Pancake House DINER $
(501-624-9273; 111 Central Ave; mains $6-10; 7am-3pm;) A Hot Springs classic, with turquoise booths and homey touches like quilts and doilies on the walls, this is almost like your grandma's kitchen. Except the pancakes, French toast (made with Texas toast) and malted or buckwheat waffles are better'n grandma's. Get yours with pecans inside. It does burgers and other diner grub at lunch.

McClard's BARBECUE $$
(501-623-9665; www.mcclards.com; 505 Albert Pike; mains $4-15; 11am-8pm Tue-Sat) Southwest of the center, Bill Clinton's favorite boyhood BBQ is still popular for ribs, slow-cooked beans, chili and tamales. It's on the outskirts of downtown.

Drinking & Nightlife

Maxine's BAR
(501-321-0909; www.maxineslive.com; 700 Central Ave; 3pm-3am Mon-Fri, to 2am Sat, noon-midnight Sun) If you're looking for some (loud) night music, head to this infamous cathouse turned live-music venue. It hosts bands out of Austin regularly.

Superior Bathhouse Brewery & Distillery BREWERY
(☎501-624-2337; www.superiorbathhouse.com; 329 Central Ave; ⏰11am-9pm, to 11pm Fri & Sat) It's surprising that an outdoorsy town with this many hikers and hipsters has lacked a craft brewery for so long, but as the sun rises in the east, so too does Hot Springs now have an indie brewery. The local suds are delicious – perfect for washing away any health benefits your body may have mistakenly acquired in Hot Springs.

Getting There & Away

Greyhound (☎501-623-5574; www.greyhound.com; 100 Broadway Tce) has buses heading to Little Rock (1½ hours, three daily).

Around Hot Springs

The wild, pretty **Ouachita National Forest** (☎501-321-5202; www.fs.usda.gov/ouachita; welcome center 100 Reserve St; ⏰8am-4:30pm) is studded with lakes and draws hunters, fisherfolk, mountain-bike riders and boaters. The small roads through the mountains unfailingly lead to hidden nooks and wonderful views. The Ouachita boasts two designated National Forest Scenic Byways: Arkansas Scenic Hwy 7 and Talimena Scenic Byway, navigating mountain ranges from Arkansas into Oklahoma.

Arkansas River Valley

The Arkansas River cuts a swath across the state from Oklahoma to Mississippi, where folks come to fish, canoe and camp along its banks and tributaries. The excellently maintained trails of **Petit Jean State Park** (☎501-727-5441; www.petitjeanstatepark.com; 1285 Petit Jean Mountain Rd, Morrilton, AR; 👪), west of Morrilton, wind past a lush 95ft waterfall, romantic grottoes, expansive vistas and dense forests. There's a rustic stone lodge, reasonable **cabins** (per night $85-185) and campgrounds.

Another stellar state park is **Mount Magazine** (☎479-963-8502; www.mountmagazinestatepark.com; 16878 Highway 309 S, Paris, AR; ⏰24hrs), which features 14 miles of trails around Arkansas' highest point. Outdoor enthusiasts enjoy great hang gliding and rock climbing here as well as hiking.

The spectacular **Highway 23/Pig Trail Byway**, lined with wild echinacea and lilies, climbs through **Ozark National Forest** and into the mountains; an excellent way to reach Eureka Springs.

Ozark Mountains

Stretching from northwest and central Arkansas into Missouri, the **Ozark Mountains** (☎870-404-2741; www.ozarkmountainregion.com) are an ancient range, once surrounded by sea and now well worn by time. Verdant mountains give way to misty fields and hard dirt farms, while dramatic karst formations line sparkling lakes, rivers and capillary thin back roads. The region derives a lot of pride from its independence and sense of place, a zeitgeist at least partially informed by multiple generations of familial roots and a long history of regional poverty. For literary company, pick up Daniel Woodrell's novel *Winter's Bone*, which was adapted into a critically acclaimed film of the same name.

Mountain View

Detour east of US 65 or along Hwy 5 to Mountain View, where an odd nexus of deeply spiritual Christianity and hippie folk-music culture yield a heartfelt mountain-town warmth. Creeping commercialism is taking its toll – the **Visitor Information Center** (☎870-269-8068; www.yourplaceinthemountains.com; 107 N Peabody Ave; ⏰9am-4:30pm Mon-Sat) promotes it as the 'Folk Music Capital of the World,' but cutesy sandstone architecture downtown, and impromptu folk, gospel and bluegrass hootenannies (jam sessions) by the Stone County **Court House Square** (Washington & Franklin St) – and on porches all around town anytime – make a visit here rather harmonious. The music goes till about 10pm most nights. Each spring the entire town becomes a main stage for the musical folkways of the Ozarks during the **Arkansas Folk Festival** (www.yourplaceinthemountains.com/calendar/arkansas-folk-festival; ⏰Apr).

Sights & Actitivies

Ozark Folk Center State Park STATE PARK
(☎870-269-3851; www.ozarkfolkcenter.com; 1032 Park Ave; auditorium adult/child $12/7; ⏰10am-5pm Tue-Sat Apr-Nov) The town's top cultural attraction, Ozark Folk Center State Park, just north of Mountain View, hosts ongoing craft demonstrations, a traditional herb garden,

and nightly live music that brings in an avid, older crowd.

LocoRopes OUTDOORS
(☎888-669-6717, 870-269-6566; www.locoropes.com; 1025 Park Ave; per zip line $7.50; ⊙10am-5pm Mar 1-Nov 30) LocoRopes offers a ropes course, slack lining, a freefall, a climbing wall and three zip lines.

Blanchard Springs Caverns OUTDOORS
(☎888-757-2246, 870-757-2211; www.blanchardsprings.org; NF 54, Forest Rd, off Hwy 14; Drip Stone Tour adult/child $10/5, Wild Cave Tour $75; ⊙10:30am-4:30pm; 👪) The spectacular Blanchard Springs Caverns, 15 miles northwest of Mountain View, were carved by an underground river and rival those at Carlsbad. It's another little-known, mind-blowing spot in Arkansas. Three Forest Service guided tours range from disabled-accessible to adventurous three- to four-hour spelunking sessions.

Sleeping & Eating

Wildflower B&B B&B $
(☎870-269-4383; www.wildflowerbb.com; 100 Washington; r $89-150; P❄📶) Set right on the Courtsquare with a rocking-chair-equipped wraparound porch and cool folk art on the walls. Ask for the front room upstairs; it's flooded with afternoon light, has a queen bed and a joint sitting room with TV. Booking online is best.

Tommy's Famous Pizza & BBQ PIZZA, BARBECUE $
(☎870-269-3278; www.tommysfamous.com; cnr Carpenter & W Main Sts; pizza $7-26, mains $7-13; ⊙from 3pm) Tommy's Famous Pizza & BBQ is run by the friendliest bunch of backwoods hippies you could hope to meet. The BBQ pizza marries Tommy's specialties indulgently. The affable owner, a former rocker from Memphis, plays great music, has a fun vibe, and asks just two things: no attitude and no loud kids.

Tommy's closes when the cash register hasn't opened for an hour.

Pj's Rainbow Cafe AMERICAN $
(☎870-269-8633; 216 W Main St; mains $5.50-16; ⊙7am-8pm Tue-Sat, to 2pm Sun; 🖉👪) This country fried cafe serves up some truly tasty diner food done with flair; think spinach-stuffed pork loin and fresh grilled rainbow trout caught in local rivers. Cash only.

Eureka Springs

Eureka Springs, near Arkansas' northwestern corner, perches in a steep valley filled with Victorian buildings, crooked streets and a crunchy, New Age–aligned local population that welcomes all – this is one of the most explicitly gay-friendly towns in the Ozarks, and mixes up an odd mash of liberal politics and rainbow flags with biker-friendly Harley bars. Hiking, cycling and horseback-riding opportunities abound. For information on LGBTQ travel in the area, log on to **Out In Eureka** (www.gayeurekasprings.com).

The **visitor center** (☎800-638-7352; www.eurekaspringschamber.com; 516 Village Circle, Hwy 62 E; ⊙9am-5pm) has information about lodging, activities, tours and local attractions, such as the rockin' **Blues Festival** (www.eurekaspringsblues.com; ⊙Jun).

Sights & Activities

1886 Crescent Hotel HISTORIC BUILDING
(☎855-725-5720; www.crescent-hotel.com; 75 Prospect Ave) Built in 1886, the Crescent is a gorgeous, functioning artifact of an older age. Step into the dark-wood lobby, with its roaring fireplace and carpets, all accented by little Jazz Age flourishes, and you'll feel the need to order a cognac and berate Daisy Buchanan for ever marrying Tom Buchanan, the *cad*. Er, sorry. The Crescent sits atop a hill, and is a great place to visit for a drink, the view from its rooftop, or both.

Thorncrown Chapel CHURCH
(☎479-253-7401; www.thorncrown.com; 12968 Hwy 62 W; ⊙9am-5pm Apr-Nov, 11am-4pm Mar & Dec) Thorncrown Chapel is a magnificent sanctuary made of glass, with its 48ft-tall wooden skeleton holding 425 windows. There's not much between your prayers and God's green earth here. It's just outside of town in the woods. Donation suggested.

Lake Leatherwood City Park PARK
(☎479-253-7921; www.lakeleatherwoodcitypark.com; 1303 Co Rd 204) This expansive park includes 21 miles of hiking and biking trails that crisscross the forested mountains and surround an 85-acre lake. Located about 3.5 miles from downtown, this is the closest managed wild space to Eureka Springs.

★**Historic Loop** WALKING TOUR
This 3.5-mile ring of history through downtown and surrounding residential neighborhoods, is simply gorgeous. The route is

dotted with more than 300 Victorian homes, all built before 1910, each a jaw-dropper and on par with any preserved historic district in the USA. You can access the loop via the Eureka Trolley, or just walk it – recommended if you're fit (the streets are steep!); pick up a map or buy trolley tickets at the visitor center.

Eureka Trolley   TROLLEY
(☑479-253-9572; www.eurekatrolley.org; 137 W Van Buren; day pass adult/child $6/2; ☉10am-6pm Sun-Fri, 9am-8pm Sat May-Oct, reduced hours Nov-Apr) This old-time hop-on, hop-off trolley service plies four routes through greater Eureka Springs. Each trip takes about 20 to 30 minutes, revealing a different angle on life in this mountain town. Check website or call ahead for running times.

🛏 Sleeping & Eating

★Treehouse Cottages   COTTAGE $$
(☑479-253-8667; www.treehousecottages.com; 165 W Van Buren St; cottages $149-169; ▣✲☎) Sprinkled amid 33 acres of pine forest, these cute, kitschy and spacious stilted wooden cottages are worth finding. There's lovely accent tile in the baths, a Jacuzzi overlooking the trees, a private balcony with grill at the ready, a flat-screen TV and a fireplace.

★FRESH   MODERN AMERICAN $
(☑479-253-9300; www.freshanddeliciousofeureka springs.com; 179 N Main St; mains $7-13; ☉11am-9pm Thu-Sat & Mon, to 7pm Sun; ☟) This beautiful cafe specializes in farm-to-table cuisine, brilliant baked goods and quirky service. The openface sandwiches with shaved ham served on fresh-baked French toast are stupidly decadent, and there are vegan options ranging from salads to pesto tossed pasta.

Oscar's   SANDWICHES $
(☑479-981-1436; www.oscarseureka.com; 17 White St; mains $3-7.50; ☉9am-3pm Tue-Fri, from 8am Sat, from 10am Sun; ☟) This little cafe has a small menu, but what a menu: chicken, walnut and cranberry salad, prosciutto sandwiches and fresh quiche. This is bright, breezy cuisine, the sort of food that fills you up without weighing you down (rare in the South), and served in the heart of Eureka Springs' cute historic district.

Mud Street Café   CAFE $$
(☑479-253-6732; www.mudstreetcafe.com; 22G S Main St; mains $9-13; ☉8am-3pm Thu-Mon) You'll find simple, tasty options such as gourmet sandwiches, wraps and salads. The

brilliant coffee drinks and breakfasts cultivate a devoted local following.

★Stone House   MODERN AMERICAN $$$
(☑479-363-6411; www.eurekastonehouse.com; 89 S Main St; cheese plates $25-47; ☉1-10pm Thu-Sun) The Stone House has all the ingredients for a pretty perfect evening: lots of wine; a menu that focuses on cheese, bread, olives, honey and charcuterie; live music; a cute courtyard; and did we mention lots of wine? It's open until 10pm, which constitutes late-night dining in this town.

🍷 Drinking & Entertainment

Chelsea's Corner Cafe & Bar   BAR
(☑479-253-8231; www.chelseascornercafe.com; 10 Mountain St; ☉noon-10pm Sun-Thu, to midnight Fri & Sat) Live music acts frequently take to the stage at this bar, which attracts a typically Eureka Springs blend of hippies and bikers. The kitchen is one of the few places in town open past 9pm, and even does pizza delivery.

Opera in the Ozarks   OPERA
(☑479-253-8595; www.opera.org; 16311 Hwy 62 West; tickets from $20) This much-acclaimed fine-arts program has kept opera alive and loud in the mountains. A packed performance schedule and a playhouse located just outside of town is the pride of Eureka Springs.

Buffalo National River

Yet another under-acknowledged Arkansas gem, and perhaps the best of them all, this 135-mile river flows beneath dramatic bluffs through unspoiled Ozark forest. The upriver section tends to have most of the white water, while the lower reaches ease lazily along – perfect for an easy paddle. The **Buffalo National River** (☑870-741-5443; www.nps.gov/buff) has 10 campgrounds and three designated wilderness areas; the most accessible is through the **Tyler Bend visitor center** (☑870-439-2502; www.nps.gov/buff; 170 Ranger Rd, St Joe, AR; ☉8:30am-4:30pm), 11 miles north of Marshall on Hwy 65, where you can also pick up a list of approved outfitters for self-guided rafting or canoe trips, the best way to tour the park and see the gargantuan limestone bluffs. Or seek out **Buffalo Outdoor Center** (BOC; ☑800-221-5514; www.buffaloriver.com; cnr Hwys 43 & 74; kayak/canoe per day $55/62, zip-line tour $89; ☉8am-6pm; ▣☎) in Ponca. They will point you in the right direction and rent out attractive cabins in the woods too.

WORTH A TRIP

WORTH A TRIP: BENTONVILLE, ARKANSAS

Bentonville was the site of Sam Walton's original five and dime corner store, which would go on to become Walmart, the world's largest company by revenue and largest private employer. Corporate headquarters is here and the distributors all maintain offices here, which means this once sleepy Arkansas town has rapidly evolved into a small city.

Bentonville includes plenty of sprawl and bland housing subdivisions, but it's anchored by a town center that is surprisingly pleasant, full of small businesses touting a locavore and 'shop local' ethos – a little ironic to say the least. But past that irony is some cool stuff.

Coolest, largest and most controversial is the **Crystal Bridges Museum of American Art** (479-418-5700; www.crystalbridges.org; 600 Museum Way; 11am-6pm Mon & Thu, to 9pm Wed & Fri, 10am-6pm Sat & Sun; P) FREE, sprawling across a series of creek ponds fed by mountain streams; the curved pavilions that house the extensive collections are connected by glass-encased tunnels, and the experience consistently filters sunlight through and across the grounds. The collections, which span the length and breadth of art in the USA, largely come from the Waltons – in particular, heiress Alice Walton – and the museum has been criticized as a tax write-off for the family's enormous wealth. Still, the space is impressive and the museum is free to the public, who seem to love the place.

The museum connects to downtown Bentonville via the **Crystal Bridges Trail** (www.crystalbridges.org/trails-and-grounds/trails), which winds past sculptures and through a series of shady woods. In Bentonville, skip the overhyped **Walmart Museum** in favor of some food; we recommend **Tusk & Trotter** (479-268-4494; www.tuskandtrotter.com; 110 SE A St; mains $13-28; 4-9:30pm Mon, 11am-9:30pm Tue-Thu, 11am-11pm Fri, 10am-11pm Sat, 10am-9pm Sun), which serves up some amazing tail-to-snout carnivore fare, including a sinful chicken and waffles. Crash at the **21c Museum Hotel** (200 NE A St; r $179-205), where every element, from the lobby and rooms to on-site galleries, feels like an extension of the Crystal Bridges experience.

LOUISIANA

Louisiana runs deep: a French colony turned Spanish protectorate turned reluctant American purchase; a southern fringe of swampland, bayou and alligators dissolving into the Gulf of Mexico; a northern patchwork prairie of heartland farm country; and everywhere, a population tied together by a deep, unshakable appreciation for the good things in life: food and music.

New Orleans, its first city, lives and dies by these qualities, and its restaurants and music halls are second to none. But everywhere, the state shares a love for this *joie de vivre*. We're not dropping French for fun, by the way; while the language is not a cultural component of North Louisiana, near I-10 and below it is a generation removed from the household – if it has been removed at all.

History

The lower Mississippi River area was dominated by the Mississippian mound-building culture until around 1592 when Europeans arrived and decimated the Native Americans with the usual combination of disease, unfavorable treaties and outright hostility.

The land was then passed back and forth between France, Spain and England. Under the French 'Code Noir,' slaves were kept, but retained a somewhat greater degree of freedom – and thus native culture – than their counterparts in British North America.

After the American Revolution the whole area passed to the USA in the 1803 Louisiana Purchase, and Louisiana became a state in 1812. The resulting blend of American and Franco-Spanish traditions, plus the influence of Afro-Caribbean communities, gave Louisiana the unique culture it retains to this day.

Following the Civil War, Louisiana was readmitted to the Union in 1868 and the next 30 years saw political wrangling, economic stagnation and renewed discrimination against African Americans.

Hurricane Katrina (2005) and the BP Gulf Coast oil spill (2010) significantly damaged the local economy and infrastructure. Louisiana remains a bottom-rung state in terms of per capita income and education levels, yet it ranks high in national happiness scales.

Information

Sixteen welcome centers dot freeways throughout the state, or contact the **Louisiana Office of Tourism** (☎225-342-8100; www.louisianatravel.com).

Louisiana State Parks (☎877-226-7652; www.crt.state.la.us/louisiana-state-parks) Louisiana has 22 state parks that offer camping (primitive/premium sites from $14/20). Some parks also offer lodge accommodations and cabins. Reservations can be made online, by phone or on a drop-in basis if there's availability. Camping fees rise slightly from April to September.

New Orleans

New Orleans is very much of America, but extraordinarily removed from it as well. Founded by the French and administered by the Spanish (and then the French again), New Orleans is – with its sidewalk cafes and iron balconies – the most European city in America. But, with the *vodoun* (voodoo), weekly second-line parades (essentially, neighborhood parades), Mardi Gras Indians, jazz and brass and gumbo, it's also the most African and Caribbean city in the country. New Orleans celebrates; while America is on deadline, this city is sipping a cocktail after a long lunch. But if you saw how people here rebuilt their homes after floods and storms, you'd be foolish to call the locals lazy.

Tolerating everything and learning from it is the soul of this city. When New Orleans' citizens aspire to that great Creole ideal – a mix of all influences into something better – we get: jazz; Nouveau Louisiana cuisine; storytellers from African *griots* (West African bards) to Seventh Ward rappers to Tennessee Williams; French townhouses a few blocks from Foghorn Leghorn mansions groaning under sweet myrtle and bougainvillea; Mardi Gras celebrations that mix pagan mysticism with Catholic pageantry. Just don't forget the indulgence and immersion, because that Creoleization gets watered down when folks don't live life to its intellectual and epicurean hilt.

New Orleans may take it easy, but it takes it. The whole hog. Stuffed with crawfish. Ya heard?

History

The town of Nouvelle Orléans was founded as a French outpost in 1718 by Jean-Baptiste Le Moyne de Bienville. Early settlers arrived from France, Canada and Germany, while the French imported thousands of African slaves. The city became a central port in the slave trade; due to local laws some slaves were allowed to earn their freedom and assume an established place in the Creole community as *les gens de couleur libres* (free people of color).

The Spanish were largely responsible for building the French Quarter as it still looks today after fires in 1788 and 1794 decimated the earlier French architecture. The influx of Anglo-Americans after the Louisiana Purchase led to an expansion of the city into the Central Business District (CBD), Garden District and Uptown.

New Orleans survived the Civil War intact after an early surrender to Union forces, but the economy languished with the end of the slavery-based plantations. In the early 1900s, New Orleans was the birthplace of jazz music. Many of the speakeasies and homes of the jazz originators have disappeared through neglect, but the cultural claim was canonized in 1994 when the National Park Service established the New

LOUISIANA FACTS

Nicknames Bayou State, Pelican State, Sportsman's Paradise

Population 4.6 million

Area 51,843 sq miles

Capital city Baton Rouge (population 229,426)

Other cities New Orleans (population 378,715)

Sales tax 4%, plus local city and county taxes

Birthplace of Jazz, naturalist John James Audubon (1785–1851), trumpeter Louis 'Satchmo' Armstrong (1901–71), author Truman Capote (1924–84), musician Antoine 'Fats' Domino (b 1928), pop star Britney Spears (b 1981)

Home of Tabasco sauce, chef Emeril Lagasse

Politics Republican stronghold with a very liberal large city (New Orleans)

Famous for Drive-thru margaritas

Official state reptile Alligator

Driving distances New Orleans to Lafayette 137 miles, New Orleans to St Francisville 112 miles

Orleans Jazz National Historical Park to celebrate the origins of America's most widely recognized indigenous music genre.

In 2005 Katrina, a relatively weak Category 3 hurricane, overwhelmed New Orleans' federal flood protection system in more than 50 places. Some 80% of the city was flooded, more than 1800 people lost their lives and the city was evacuated. A decade later, the population has largely returned, and the city is again one of the 50 most populous in the USA. This rebirth is not without its issues, though; gentrification has raised the cost of living, even as poverty and crime rates remain atrocious. Tourism is still the primary economic engine of the city.

◉ Sights

◉ French Quarter

Elegant, Caribbean-colonial architecture, lush gardens and wrought-iron accents are the visual norm in the French Quarter. But this is also the heart of New Orleans' tourism scene. Bourbon St generates a loutish membrane that sometimes makes the rest of the Quarter difficult to appreciate. Look past this. The Vieux Carré (Old Quarter; first laid out in 1722) is the focal point of much of this city's culture and in the quieter back lanes and alleyways there's a sense of faded time shaken and stirred with *joie de vivre*.

★ Cabildo   MUSEUM
(☑ 504-568-6968; http://louisianastatemuseum.org/museums/the-cabildo; 701 Chartres St; adult/child under 12yr/student $6/free/5; ⊙ 10am-4:30pm Tue-Sun, closed Mon; 🖼) 🖉 The former seat of government in colonial Louisiana now serves as the gateway to exploring the history of the state in general, and New Orleans in particular. It's also a magnificent building in its own right; the elegant Cabildo marries elements of Spanish colonial architecture and French urban design better than most buildings in the city. Exhibits range from Native American tools, to 'Wanted' posters for escaped slaves, to a gallery's worth of paintings of stone-faced old New Orleanians.

★ Presbytère   MUSEUM
(☑ 504-568-6968; http://louisianastatemuseum.org/museums/the-presbytere; 751 Chartres St; adult/student $6/5; ⊙ 10am-4:30pm Tue-Sun, closed Mon; 🖼) 🖉 The lovely Presbytère building, designed in 1791 as a rectory for the

St Louis Cathedral, serves as New Orleans' Mardi Gras museum. You'll find there's more to the city's most famous celebration than wanton debauchery – or, at least, discover the many levels of meaning behind the debauchery. There's an encyclopedia's worth of material on the krewes, secret societies, costumes and racial histories of the Mardi Gras tapestry, all intensely illuminating and easy to follow.

Jackson Square   SQUARE, PLAZA
(Decatur & St Peter Sts) Sprinkled with lazing loungers, surrounded by sketch artists, fortune-tellers and traveling performers, and watched over by cathedrals, offices and shops plucked from a Parisian fantasy, Jackson Sq is one of America's great town greens and the heart of the Quarter. The identical, block-long Pontalba Buildings overlook the scene, and the nearly identical Cabildo and Presbytère structures flank the impressive **St Louis Cathedral**, which fronts the square. In the middle of the park stands the Jackson monument – Clark Mills' bronze equestrian statue of the hero of the Battle of New Orleans, Andrew Jackson, which was unveiled in 1856.

The Historic New Orleans
Collection   MUSEUM
(THNOC; ☑ 504-523-4662; www.hnoc.org; 533 Royal St; admission free, tours $5; ⊙ 9:30am-4:30pm Tue-Sat, from 10:30am Sun) In several exquisitely restored buildings you'll find thoughtfully curated exhibits with an emphasis on archival materials, such as the original transfer documents of the Louisiana Purchase. Separate home, architecture/courtyard and history tours run at 10am, 11am, 2pm and 3pm, the home being the most interesting of them.

◉ The Tremé

The oldest African American neighborhood in the city is obviously steeped in a lot of history. Leafy **Esplanade Avenue**, which borders the neighborhood, is full of old-school Creole mansions, and is one of the prettiest streets in the city.

Backstreet Cultural Museum   MUSEUM
(☑ 504-522-4806; www.backstreetmuseum.org; 1116 Henriette Delille St/formerly St Claude Ave, per person $8; ⊙ 10am-5pm Tue-Sat) Mardi Gras Indian suits grab the spotlight with dazzling flair – and finely crafted detail – in this informative museum, which examines the dis-

NEW ORLEANS IN...

Two Days

On the first day, wander Jackson Sq and the French Quarter's museums. The **Cabildo** and **Presbytère** are adjacent to each other and give a good grounding in Louisiana culture, as does the nearby **Historic New Orleans Collection**. Afterwards, stroll along the mighty Mississippi.

Grab dinner at **Bayona**, locavore base of hometown legend Susan Spicer. Enjoy drinks at **Tonique** and go see some live music at **Preservation Hall**.

Next morning, stroll along Magazine St in a state of shopping nirvana. Then walk north, pop into **Lafayette Cemetery No 1**, consider having a drink at **Commander's Palace** (☎504-899-8221; www.commanderspalace.com; 1403 Washington Ave, Garden Distric) – it helps to be well-dressed – and hop onto the **St Charles Avenue Streetcar**. Have a haute Southern dinner at **Boucherie**.

Four Days

On day three, join the morning Creole Neighborhoods bike tour with **Confederacy of Cruisers**. This is exceptionally easy riding, and takes in all elements of the funky Marigny and Bywater, but if you don't fancy bikes, walk past Washington Sq Park and soak up the Marigny's vibe.

Have dinner at **Bacchanal** and enjoy great wine and cheese in this musical garden. If you're feeling edgy, head to St Claude Ave where the offerings range from punk to hip-hop to bounce to '60s mod. For more traditional Nola jazz and blues, head down Frenchmen St.

The next day drive, or consider renting a bicycle, and explore around the Tremé – don't miss the **Backstreet Cultural Museum** or **Willie Mae's** fried chicken. Head up Esplanade Ave and gawk at all the gorgeous Creole mansions sitting pretty under the big live oaks. Take Esplanade all the way to **City Park** and wander around the **New Orleans Museum of Art**.

tinctive elements of African American culture in New Orleans. The museum isn't terribly big – it's the former Blandin's Funeral Home – but if you have any interest in the suits and rituals of Mardi Gras Indians as well as Second Line parades and Social Aid & Pleasure Clubs (the local black community version of civic associations), you need to stop by.

Louis Armstrong Park PARK

(701 N Rampart St; ⏲8am-6pm) The entrance to this massive park has got to be one of the greatest gateways in the USA, a picturesque arch that ought rightfully be the final set piece in a period drama about Jazz Age New Orleans. The original Congo Sq is here, as well as a **Louis Armstrong statue** and a **bust of Sidney Bechet**. The **Mahalia Jackson Theater** (☎504-525-1052, box office 504-287-0350; www.mahaliajacksontheater.com; 1419 Basin St) hosts opera and Broadway productions.

St Louis Cemetery No 1 CEMETERY

(www.noladeadspace.com; 1300 St Louis St; admission by guided tour; ⏲9am-3pm Mon-Sat, to noon Sun; 👪) This cemetery received the remains of most early Creoles. The shallow water table necessitated above-ground burials, with bodies placed in the family tombs you see to this day. The supposed grave of voodoo queen Marie Laveau is here, scratched with 'XXX's from spellbound devotees. By request of the family that owns the tomb, do not add to this graffiti; to do so is also technically illegal. In 2015, in response to ongoing vandalism, cemetery visitation was limited to relatives of the interred and approved guided tours.

St Augustine's Church CHURCH

(☎504-525-5934; www.staugustinecatholic-church-neworleans.org; 1210 Governor Nicholls St) Open since 1841, 'St Aug's' is the second-oldest African American Catholic church in the country, a place where Creoles, émigrés from St-Domingue and free persons of color could worship shoulder to shoulder, even as separate pews were designated for slaves. The future of the church remains in question, so try to visit; more

New Orleans

0 — 480 m
0 — 0.25 miles

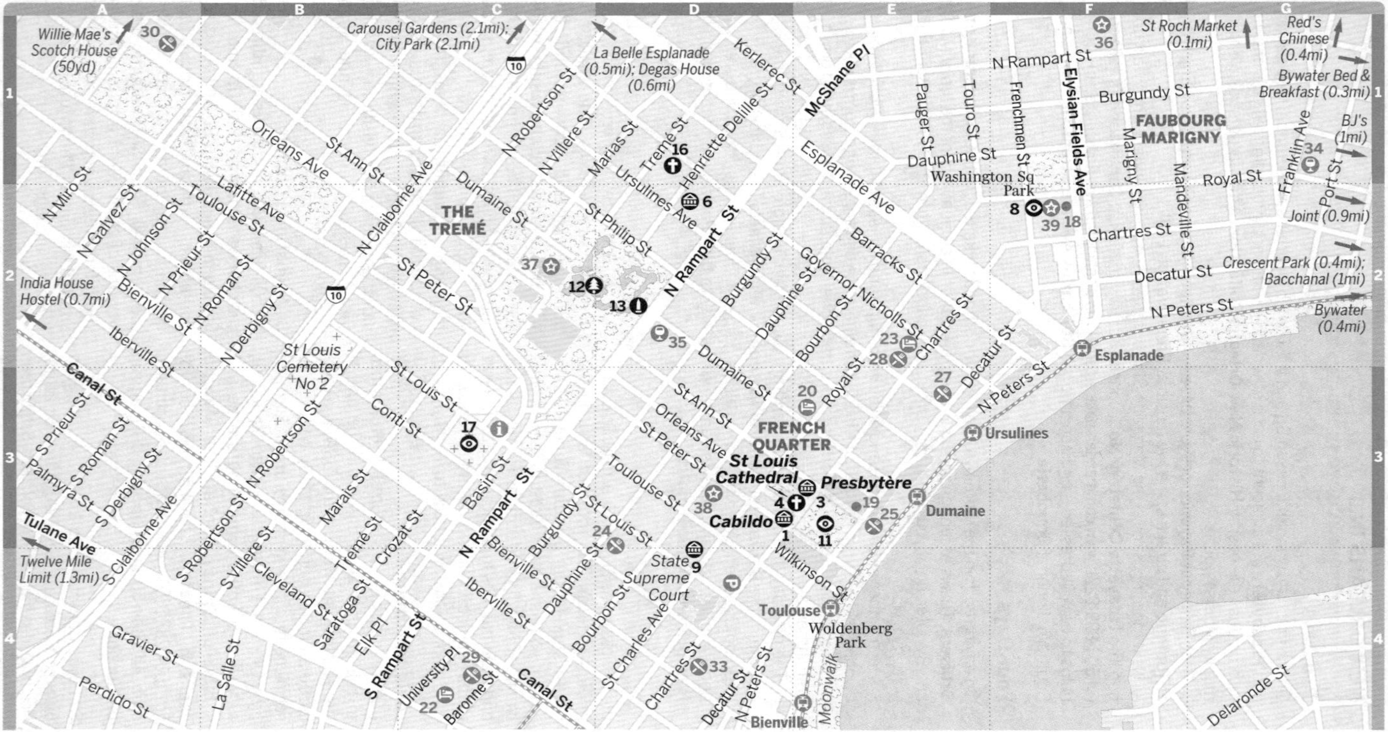

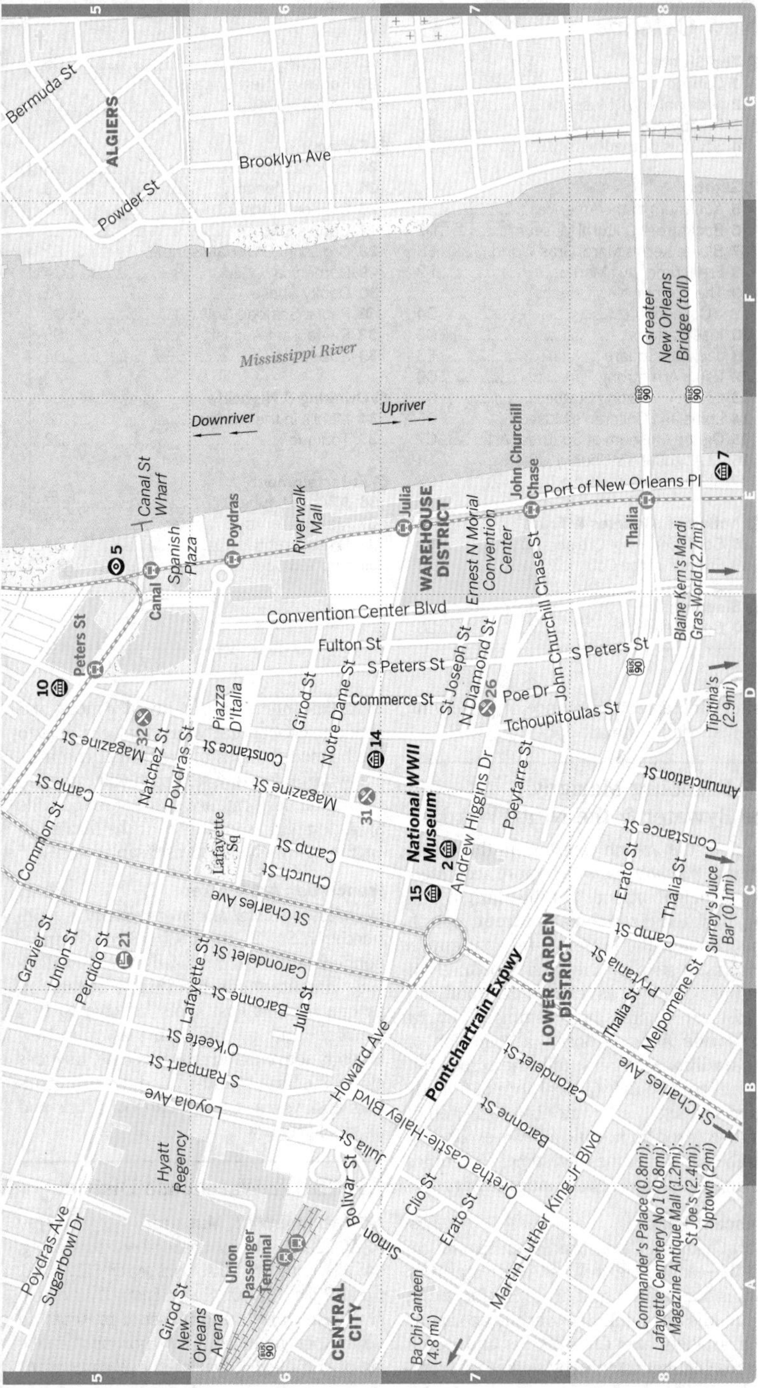
ALGIERS
Bermuda St
Powder St
Brooklyn Ave
Mississippi River
Downriver
Upriver
Canal St Wharf
Spanish Plaza
Canal
Poydras
Riverwalk Mall
Julia
WAREHOUSE DISTRICT
Ernest N Morial Convention Center
John Churchill Chase
Port of New Orleans Pl
Thalia
Greater New Orleans Bridge (toll)
Blaine Kern's Mardi Gras World (2.7mi)
Tipitina's (2.9mi)
Surrey's Juice Bar (0.1mi)
Commander's Palace (0.8mi); Lafayette Cemetery No 1 (0.8mi); Magazine Antique Mall (1.2mi); St Joe's (2.4mi); Uptown (2mi)
Ba Chi Canteen (4.8 mi)
Peters St
Convention Center Blvd
Fulton St
S Peters St
Commerce St
St Joseph St
N Diamond St
Poe Dr
John Churchill Chase St
Tchoupitoulas St
Piazza D'Italia
Girod St
Notre Dame St
Magazine St
Natchez St
Poydras St
Constance St
Camp St
Common St
National WWII Museum
Andrew Higgins Dr
Poeyfarre St
Annunciation St
Lafayette Sq
Church St
St Charles Ave
Gravier St
Union St
Perdido St
Lafayette St
Carondelet St
Baronne St
Julia St
O'Keefe St
S Rampart St
Loyola Ave
Howard Ave
Pontchartrain Expwy
LOWER GARDEN DISTRICT
Erato St
Thalia St
Prytania St
Melpomene St
Oretha Castle-Haley Blvd
Martin Luther King Jr Blvd
Hyatt Regency
Union Passenger Terminal
Bolivar St
Clio St
Simon
Poydras Ave
Sugarbowl Dr
Girod St
New Orleans Arena
CENTRAL CITY
5
10
32
26
14
31
2
15
21
7

THE SOUTH

New Orleans

Top Sights
1 Cabildo ... D3
2 National WWII Museum ... C7
3 Presbytère ... E3
4 St Louis Cathedral ... E3

Sights
5 Aquarium of the Americas ... E5
6 Backstreet Cultural Museum ... D2
7 Blaine Kern's Mardi Gras World ... E8
8 Frenchmen Art Market ... F2
9 The Historic New Orleans Collection ... D4
10 Insectarium ... D5
11 Jackson Square ... E3
12 Louis Armstrong Park ... C2
13 Louis Armstrong Statue ... D2
14 Louisiana Children's Museum ... D6
15 Ogden Museum of Southern Art ... C7
16 St Augustine's Church ... D1
17 St Louis Cemetery No 1 ... C3

Activities, Courses & Tours
18 Confederacy of Cruisers ... F2
19 Friends of the Cabildo ... E3

Sleeping
20 Cornstalk Hotel ... E3
21 Le Pavillon ... C5
22 Roosevelt New Orleans ... C4
23 Soniat House ... E2

Eating
24 Bayona ... D3
25 Café du Monde ... E3
26 Cochon Butcher ... D7
27 Coop's Place ... E3
28 Croissant D'Or Patisserie ... E2
29 Domenica ... C4
30 Dooky Chase ... A1
31 Peche Seafood Grill ... C6
32 Restaurant August ... D5
33 SoBou ... D4

Drinking & Nightlife
34 Mimi's in the Marigny ... G1
35 Tonique ... D2

Entertainment
36 AllWays Lounge ... F1
37 Mahalia Jackson Theater ... C2
38 Preservation Hall ... D3
39 Spotted Cat ... F2

visitors increases the chance of preserving this historic landmark.

Faubourg Marigny, the Bywater & the Ninth Ward

North of the French Quarter are the Creole suburbs (*faubourgs*, which more accurately means 'neighborhoods') of the Marigny and the Bywater. **Frenchmen Street**, which runs through the center of the Marigny, is a fantastic strip of live-music goodness. It used to be known as a locals' Bourbon, but tourists are increasingly common. Nearby **St Claude Avenue** boasts a collection of non-traditional venues; folks here rock out to punk and bounce (a local style of frenetic dance music). The Bywater is a collection of candy-colored homes and an ever-expanding number of sometimes awesome, sometimes cloyingly hip, new restaurants and bars.

Crescent Park PARK
(Piety, Chartres & Mazant Sts; 8am-6pm, to 7pm mid-Mar–early Nov; P) This waterfront park is our favorite spot in the city for taking in the Mississippi. Enter over the enormous arch at Piety and Chartres Sts and watch the fog blanket the nearby skyline. A promenade meanders past an angular metal and concrete conceptual 'wharf'' (placed next to the burned remains of the former commercial wharf); one day, said path will extend to a planned performance space at Mandeville St. A dog park is located near the Mazant St entrance, which also gives disabled access.

Frenchmen Art Market MARKET
(www.facebook.com/frenchmenartmarket; 619 Frenchmen St; 7pm-1am Thu-Sun) Independent artists and artisans line this alleyway market, which has built a reputation as one of the finest spots in town to find a unique gift to take home as your New Orleans souvenir. 'Art', in this case, includes clever T-shirts, hand-crafted jewelry, trinkets and, yes, a nice selection of prints and original artwork.

CBD & Warehouse District

★**National WWII Museum** MUSEUM
(504-528-1944; www.nationalww2museum.org; 945 Magazine St; adult/child/senior $23/14/20, plus 1/2 films $5/10; 9am-5pm) This extensive, heart-wrenching museum presents an admirably nuanced and thorough analysis of the biggest war of the 20th century.

And its exhibits, which are displayed in three grand pavilions, are amazing. Wall-sized photographs capture the confusion of D-Day. Riveting oral histories tell remarkable stories of survival. A stroll through the snowy woods of Ardennes feels eerily cold. The experience is personal, immersive and educational. Don't miss it.

Ogden Museum of Southern Art MUSEUM
(☎504-539-9650; www.ogdenmuseum.org; 925 Camp St; adult/child 5-17yr/student $10/5/8; ⏲10am-5pm Wed-Mon, plus 5:30-8pm Thu) One of our favorite museums in the city manages to be beautiful, educational and unpretentious all at once. New Orleans entrepreneur Roger Houston Ogden has assembled one of the finest collections of Southern art anywhere, which includes huge galleries ranging from impressionist landscapes to outsider folk-art quirkiness, to contemporary installation work.

On Thursday nights, pop in for Ogden After Hours, when you can listen to great Southern musicians and sip wine with a fun-loving, arts-obsessed crowd in the midst of the masterpieces.

Blaine Kern's Mardi Gras World MUSEUM
(☎504-361-7821; www.mardigrasworld.com; 1380 Port of New Orleans Pl; adult/child 2-11yr/senior $20/13/16; ⏲tours 9:30am-4:30pm; 👪) We dare say Mardi Gras World is one of the happiest places in New Orleans by day – but at night it must turn into one of the most terrifying funhouses this side of Hell. It's all those *faces,* man, the dragons, clowns, kings and fairies, leering and dead-eyed…

That said, by day we love touring Mardi Gras World – the studio warehouse of Blaine Kern (Mr Mardi Gras) and family, who have been making parade floats since 1947. Tours last 30 to 45 minutes.

Garden District & Uptown

The main architectural division in New Orleans is between the elegant townhouses of the Creole and French northeast and the magnificent mansions of the American district, which includes the Garden District and Uptown. Magnificent oak trees arch over St Charles Ave, which cuts through the heart of this sector and where the supremely picturesque **St Charles Avenue streetcar** (per ride $1.25; 👪) runs. The boutiques and galleries of **Magazine Street** form the best shopping strip in the city.

Lafayette Cemetery No 1 CEMETERY
(Washington Ave, at Prytania St; ⏲7am-2:30pm Mon-Fri, to noon Sat) FREE Shaded by groves of lush greenery, this cemetery exudes a strong sense of Southern subtropical gothic. Built in 1833, it is divided by two intersecting footpaths that form a cross. Look out for the crypts built by fraternal organizations such as the Jefferson Fire Company No 22, which took care of their members and their families in large shared tombs. Some of the wealthier family tombs were built of marble, with elaborate details, but most were constructed simply of inexpensive plastered brick.

Audubon Zoological Gardens ZOO
(☎504-581-4629; www.auduboninstitute.org; 6500 Magazine St; adult/child 2-12yr/senior $19/14/15; ⏲10am-4pm Tue-Fri, to 5pm Sat & Sun Sep-Feb, 10am-5pm Mon-Fri, to 6pm Sat & Sun Mar-Aug; 👪) This is among the country's best zoos. It contains the ultracool **Louisiana Swamp** exhibit, which is full of alligators, bobcats, foxes, bears and snapping turtles. Look for new and improved elephant and orangutan enclosures in late 2015, as well as a Lazy River water feature for kids. Open Mondays March through early September.

City Park & Mid-City

City Park PARK
(☎504-482-4888; www.neworleanscitypark.com; Esplanade Ave & City Park Ave) Live oaks, Spanish moss and lazy bayous frame this masterpiece of urban planning. Three miles long and 1 mile wide, dotted with gardens, waterways and bridges, and home to a captivating art museum, City Park is bigger than Central Park in NYC, and it's New Orleans' prettiest green space. It's also a perfect expression of a local 'park,' in the sense that it is an only slightly tamed expression of the forest and Louisiana wetlands that are the natural backdrop of the city.

New Orleans Museum of Art MUSEUM
(NOMA; ☎504-658-4100; www.noma.org; 1 Collins Diboll Circle; adult/child 7-17yr $10/6; ⏲10am-6pm Tue-Thu, to 9pm Fri, 11am-5pm Sat & Sun) Inside City Park, this elegant museum was opened in 1911 and is well worth a visit both for its special exhibitions and top-floor galleries of African, Asian, Native American and Oceanic art – don't miss the outstanding Qing dynasty snuff-bottle collection. Its **sculpture garden** (⏲10am-4:30pm Sat-Thu, to 8:45pm Fri)

FREE contains a cutting-edge collection in lush, meticulously planned grounds.

Tours

The Jean Lafitte National Historic Park and Preserve Visitor Center (p455) leads free walking tours of the French Quarter at 9:30am (get tickets at 9am).

Confederacy of Cruisers CYCLING
(504-400-5468; www.confederacyofcruisers.com; tours from $49) Our favorite bicycle tours in New Orleans set you up on cruiser bikes that come with fat tires and padded seats for Nola's flat, pot-holed roads. The main 'Creole New Orleans' tour takes in the best architecture of the Marigny, Bywater, Esplanade Ave and the Tremé. Confederacy also does a 'History of Drinking' tour ($49; you have to be 21 or over) and a tasty culinary tour ($89).

Friends of the Cabildo WALKING TOUR
(504-523-3939; www.friendsofthecabildo.org; 523 St Ann St; adult/student $20/15; 10am & 1:30pm Tue-Sun) These excellent walking tours are led by knowledgeable (and often funny) docents who will give you a great primer on the history of the French Quarter, the stories behind some of the most famous streets and details of the area's many architectural styles.

Festivals & Events

New Orleans never needs an excuse to party. Just a few listings are included here; check www.neworleansonline.com for a good events calendar.

Mardi Gras CULTURAL
(www.mardigrasneworleans.com; Feb or early Mar) Fat Tuesday marks the orgasmic finale of the Carnival season.

St Joseph's Day – Super Sunday CULTURAL
(Mar) March 19 and its nearest Sunday bring 'gangs' of Mardi Gras Indians out into the streets in all their feathered, drumming glory. The Super Sunday parade usually begins around noon at Bayou St John and Orleans Ave, but follows no fixed route.

French Quarter Festival MUSIC
(www.fqfi.org; 2nd weekend Apr) Free music on multiple stages.

Jazz Fest MUSIC
(www.nojazzfest.com; Apr-May) The last weekend of April and the first weekend of May; a world-renowned extravaganza of music, food, crafts and good living.

Sleeping

Rates peak during Mardi Gras and Jazz Fest, and fall in the hot summer months. Book early and call or check online for special deals. Parking in the Quarter costs $15 to $30 per day.

Bywater Bed & Breakfast B&B $
(504-944-8438; www.bywaterbnb.com; 1026 Clouet St; r without bath $100;) This is what happens when you fall through the rabbit hole and Wonderland is a B&B. This spot is popular with lesbians (it's owned by a lesbian couple), but welcomes everyone. It's about as homey and laid-back as it gets. Expect to stay in what amounts to a folk-art gallery with a bit of historical heritage and a hallucinogenic vibe.

India House Hostel HOSTEL $
(504-821-1904; www.indiahousehostel.com; 124 S Lopez St; dm/d $20/55;) This colorful place is larger than it looks. Half a block off Canal St in Mid-City, the hostel is a mini-complex of subtropically themed good times. The grounds include an above-ground pool, a cabana-like patio and three

SWAMP TOURS

We highly recommend visiting the **Barataria Preserve** (504-689-3690; www.nps.gov/jela/barataria-preserve.htm; 6588 Barataria Blvd, Crown Point; visitor center 9am-5pm) FREE. If you want a boat-bound swamp tour, these can be arranged in New Orleans; there are offices along Decatur St in the French Quarter. Or find some Lost Land, as it were...

Louisiana Lost Land Tours (504-400-5920; http://lostlandstours.org; tours from $90) runs wonderful tours that include kayak paddles into the wetlands and a motorboat tour of Barataria Bay. Excursions focus on land loss and wildlife threats, and are led by folks who genuinely love this land. Check out their blog on environmental issues in South Louisiana, http://lostlandstours.org/category/blog/, maintained by Pulitzer Prize–winning journalist Bob Marshall.

NEW ORLEANS FOR CHILDREN

Many of New Orleans' daytime attractions are well suited for kids, including the **Audubon Zoo** (p447), **Aquarium of the Americas** (☎504-581-4629; www.auduboninstitute.org; 1 Canal St; adult/child/senior $24/18/19, with IMAX $29/23/23; ⏱10am-5pm Tue-Sun; 👪) and **Insectarium** (☎504-581-4629; www.auduboninstitute.org; 423 Canal St; adult/child $16.50/12; ⏱10am-5pm; 👪). Other great options:

Carousel Gardens Amusement Park (☎504-483-9402; www.neworleanscitypark.com; 7 Victory Ave, City Park; admission adult/children 36in & under $4/free, each ride $4; ⏱10am-5pm Tue-Thu, 10am-10pm Fri, 11am-10pm Sat, 11am-6pm Sun Jun & July, Sat & Sun only spring & fall) The 1906 carousel is a gem of vintage carny-ride happiness. Other thrills include a Ferris wheel, bumper cars and a tilt-a-whirl. Buy an $18 pass for unlimited rides. Open nightly from Thanksgiving until the early new year for Celebration in the Oaks.

Louisiana Children's Museum (☎504-523-1357; www.lcm.org; 420 Julia St; admission $8.50; ⏱9:30am-4:30pm Tue-Sat, noon-4:30pm Sun mid-Aug–May, 9:30am-5pm Mon-Sat, noon-5pm Sun Jun–mid-Aug) This educational museum is like a high-tech kindergarten where the wee ones can play in interactive bliss till nap time. Lots of corporate sponsorship equals lots of hands-on exhibits. The Little Port of New Orleans gallery spotlights the five types of ships found in the local port. Kids can play in a galley kitchen, or they can load cargo. Elsewhere kids can check out optical illusions, shop in a pretend grocery store or get crafty in an art studio.

Milton Latter Memorial Library (☎504-596-2625; www.neworleanspubliclibrary.org; 5120 St Charles Ave; ⏱9am-8pm Mon & Wed, to 6pm Tue & Thu, 10am-5pm Sat, noon-5pm Sun) Poised elegantly above shady stands of palms, the Latter Memorial Library was once a private mansion. The Isaac family (owners 1907–12) – who installed Flemish-style carved woodwork, Dutch murals and French frescoed ceilings – passed the property to aviator Harry Williams and his silent-film-star wife, Marguerite Clark (1912–39). The couple was known for throwing grand parties. The next owner was local horse racer Robert S Eddy, followed by Mr and Mrs Harry Latter, who gave the building to the city in 1948.

well-worn old houses used for sleeping. And the ambience? India House has the sort of free-spirited party atmosphere that got you into backpacking in the first place.

★La Belle Esplanade B&B $$
(☎504-301-1424; www.labelleesplanade.com; 2216 Esplanade Ave; r incl breakfast $179-209; ❄📶) A little quirky, a little saucy, and the co-owner wears a jaunty fedora – a devil-may-care touch that ties the whole colorful shebang together. Furnishings in the five themed suites vary, but look for chunky headboards, plush chairs, Gibson Girl portraits and claw-foot tubs. Bright, monochromatic walls keep it all pretention-free. Savor crawfish pie and other tasty Southern fare for breakfast.

Le Pavillon HISTORIC HOTEL $$
(☎504-581-3111; www.lepavillon.com; 833 Poydras Ave; r $179-279, ste from $695; P❄📶🏊) Le Pavillon exudes an old-school *joie de vivre* that's easy to love. Fluted columns support the porte cochere off the alabaster facade, and the doorman wears white gloves and a top hat (and somehow doesn't look ridiculous). Both private and public spaces are redolent with historic portraits, magnificent chandeliers, marble floors and heavy drapery.

Degas House HISTORIC HOTEL $$
(☎504-821-5009; www.degashouse.com; 2306 Esplanade Ave; r/ste incl breakfast from $199/300; P❄📶) Edgar Degas, the famed French Impressionist, lived in this 1852 Italianate house when visiting his mother's family in the early 1870s. Rooms recall his time here through period furnishings and reproductions of his work. The suites have balconies and fireplaces, while the less expensive garret rooms are cramped top-floor quarters that once housed the Degas family's servants.

★Soniat House BOUTIQUE HOTEL $$$
(☎504-522-0570; www.soniathouse.com; 1133 Chartres St; r/ste from $245/425; ⊖❄📶) The three houses that make up this hotel in the Lower Quarter epitomize Creole elegance at its unassuming best. You enter via a cool loggia into a courtyard filled with ferns and

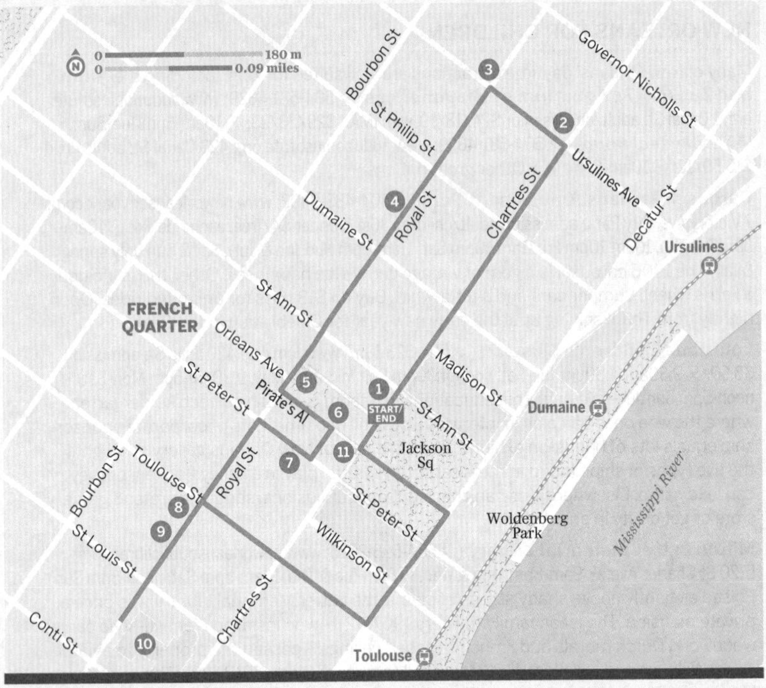

City Walk French Quarter

START JACKSON SQ
END JACKSON SQ
LENGTH 1.1 MILES; 1½ HOURS

Begin your walk at the **1 Presbytère** (p442) on Jackson Sq and head down Chartres St to the corner of Ursulines Ave. Directly across Chartres St, at No 1113, the 1826 **2 Beauregard-Keyes House** combines Creole and American styles of design. Walk along Ursulines Ave to Royal St – the soda fountain at the **3 Royal Pharmacy** is a preserved relic from halcyon malt-shop days.

When it comes to quintessential New Orleans postcard images, Royal St takes the prize. Cast-iron galleries grace the buildings and a profusion of flowers garland the facades.

At No 915 Royal, the **4 Cornstalk Hotel** stands behind one of the most frequently photographed fences anywhere. At Orleans Ave, stately magnolia trees and lush tropical plants fill **5 St Anthony's Garden**, behind **6 St Louis Cathedral** (p442).

Alongside the garden, take the inviting Pirate's Alley and turn right down Cabildo Alley and then right up St Peter St toward Royal St. Tennessee Williams shacked up at No 632 St Peter, the **7 Avart-Peretti House**, in 1946–47 while he wrote *A Streetcar Named Desire*.

Turn left on Royal St. At the corner of Royal and Toulouse Sts stands a pair of houses built by Jean François Merieult in the 1790s. The building known as the **8 Court of Two Lions**, at 541 Royal St, opens onto Toulouse St and next door is the **9 Historic New Orleans Collection** (p442).

On the next block, the massive 1909 **10 State Supreme Court Building** was the setting for many scenes in director Oliver Stone's movie *JFK*.

Turn around and head right on Toulouse St to Decatur St and turn left. Cut across the road and walk the last stretch of this tour along the river. As Jackson Sq comes into view, cross back over to the Presbytère's near-identical twin, the **11 Cabildo** (p442).

a trickling fountain. Some rooms open onto the courtyard, while winding stairways lead to elegant upstairs quarters. Singular attention has been paid to art and antiques throughout.

Roosevelt New Orleans HOTEL $$$
(☎504-648-1200; www.therooseveltneworleans.com; 123 Baronne St; r/ste from $269/329; P @ ☎ ≋) The majestic, block-long lobby harks back to the early 20th century, a golden age of opulent hotels and grand retreats. Swish rooms have classical details, but the spa, John Besh restaurant, storied Sazerac Bar and swanky new jazz lounge are at least half the reason to stay. The rooftop pool is pretty swell, too. It's an easy walk to the French Quarter.

Eating

Louisiana may have the greatest native culinary tradition in the USA – not necessarily by dint of the quality of food (although quality is very high) but from the long history that lies behind dishes that are older than most American states. While the rest of us eat to live, New Orleanians live to eat.

Just a heads up: if you're planning to head to **Cafe du Monde** (☎800-772-2927; www.cafedumonde.com; 800 Decatur St; beignets $2; ⏲24hr) for beignets (fried doughnuts), be warned the lines are obnoxious on weekends. Weekday nights are a good time to visit.

French Quarter

Croissant D'Or Patisserie BAKERY $
(☎504-524-4663; www.croissantdornola.com; 617 Ursulines Ave; meals $3-5; ⏲6am-3pm Wed-Mon) On the quieter side of the French Quarter, this spotlessly clean pastry shop is where many locals start their day. Bring a paper, order coffee and a croissant – or a tart, quiche or sandwich topped with béchamel sauce – and bliss out. Check out the tiled sign on the threshold that says 'ladies entrance' – a holdover from earlier days.

Coop's Place CAJUN $
(☎504-525-9053; www.coopsplace.net; 1109 Decatur St; mains $8-17.50; ⏲11am-3am) Coop's is an authentic Cajun dive, but more rocked out. Make no mistake: it's a grotty chaotic place, the servers have attitude and the layout is annoying. But it's worth it for the food: rabbit jambalaya, chicken with shrimp and *tasso* (smoked ham) in a cream sauce – there's no such thing as 'too heavy' here. No patrons under 21.

★ **Bayona** LOUISIANAN $$$
(☎504-525-4455; www.bayona.com; 430 Dauphine St; mains $29-38; ⏲11:30am-1:30pm Wed-Sun, 6-9:30pm Mon-Thu, 5:30-10pm Fri & Sat) Bayona is, for our money, the best splurge in the Quarter. It's rich but not overwhelming, classy but unpretentious, innovative without being precocious, and all around just a very fine spot for a meal. The menu changes regularly, but expect fresh fish, fowl and game prepared in a way that comes off as elegant and deeply cozy at the same time.

SoBou MODERN AMERICAN $$$
(☎504-552-4095; www.sobounola.com; 310 Chartres St; mains $24-38; ⏲7am-10pm) The name means 'South of Bourbon.' The food? Hard to pin, but uniformly excellent. The chefs play with a concept that mixes Louisiana indulgence with eccentricities: sweet-potato beignets slathered with duck gravy and chicory coffee glaze, and the infamous, decadent foie gras burger. The on-site bar mixes mean drinks, and there are tables with beer taps built in!

The Tremé

Willie Mae's Scotch House SOUTHERN $
(2401 St Ann St; fried chicken $11; ⏲10am-5pm Mon-Sat) Willie Mae's has been dubbed some of the best fried chicken in the world by the James Beard Foundation, the Food Network and other media. It thus sees a steady flow of tourist traffic. The chicken, served in a basket, is pretty damn good, as are the butter beans.

Dooky Chase SOUTHERN, CREOLE $$
(☎504-821-0600; 2301 Orleans Ave; buffet $20, mains $16-25; ⏲11am-3pm Tue-Thu, 11am-3pm & 5-9pm Fri) Ray Charles wrote 'Early in the Morning' about Dooky's; civil rights leaders used it as informal headquarters in the 1960s; and Barack Obama ate here after his inauguration. Leah Chase's labor of love is the backbone of the Tremé, and her buffets are the stuff of legend. Top-notch gumbo and excellent fried chicken are served in a white-linen dining room to office workers and ladies who lunch.

Bywater

★Bacchanal MODERN AMERICAN $

(☎504-948-9111; www.bacchanalwine.com; 600 Poland Ave; mains $8-16, cheese from $5; ⏰11am-midnight) From the outside, Bacchanal looks like a leaning Bywater shack; inside are racks of wine and stinky but sexy cheese. Musicians play in the garden, while cooks dispense delicious meals on paper plates from the kitchen in the back; on any given day you may try chorizo-stuffed dates or seared diver scallops that will blow your gastronomic mind.

★Red's Chinese CHINESE $

(☎504-304-6030; www.redschinese.com; 3048 St Claude Ave; mains $8-16; ⏰noon-3pm & 5-11pm) Red's has upped the Chinese cuisine game in New Orleans in a big way. The chefs aren't afraid to add lashings of Louisiana flavor, yet this isn't what we'd call 'fusion' cuisine. The food is grounded deeply in spicy Sichuan flavors, which pairs well with the occasional flash of cayenne. The General Lee's chicken is stupendously good.

St Roch Market MARKET $

(☎504-609-3813; www.strochmarket.com; 2381 St Claude Ave; mains $9-12; ⏰9am-11pm;) Once, the St Roch Market was the seafood and produce market for a working-class neighborhood. After it was nearly destroyed by Hurricane Katrina, it was renovated into a shiny food court. The airy interior space hosts 13 restaurants serving food ranging from New Orleans classics to coffee to Nigerian cuisine.

Joint BARBECUE $

(☎504-949-3232; http://alwayssmokin.com; 701 Mazant St; mains $7-17; ⏰11:30am-10pm Mon-Sat) The Joint's smoked meat has the olfactory effect of the Sirens' sweet song, pulling you, the proverbial traveling sailor, off course and into savory meat-induced blissful death (classical Greek analogies ending *now*). Knock back some ribs, pulled pork or brisket with some sweet tea in the backyard garden and learn to love life.

FROM THE MEKONG TO THE MISSISSIPPI

Following the Vietnam War, thousands of South Vietnamese fled to America, settling in Southern California, Boston, the Washington, DC area and New Orleans. If the last choice seems odd, remember that many of these refugees were Catholic and the New Orleans Catholic community – one of the largest in the country – was helping to direct refugee resettlement. In addition, the subtropical climate, rice fields and flat wetlands must have been geographically reassuring. For a Southeast Asian far from home, the Mississippi delta may have borne at least a superficial resemblance to the Mekong delta.

Probably the most pleasant way to experience local Vietnamese culture is by eating its delicious food and shopping in its markets. The following are all in the suburbs of Gretna or New Orleans East:

Dong Phuong Oriental Bakery (☎504-254-0296; www.dpbanhmi.com; 14207 Chef Menteur Hwy, New Orleans East; bakery $1.50-6, mains $7-13; ⏰8am-4pm Wed-Sun) For the best *banh mi* (Vietnamese bread rolls of sliced pork, cucumber, cilantro and other lovelies, locally called a 'Vietnamese po'boy') around and some very fine durian cake.

Tan Dinh (☎504-361-8008; 1705 Lafayette St, Gretna; mains $8-17; ⏰9:30am-9pm Mon, Wed-Fri, 9am-9pm Sat, to 8pm Sun) We'd happily contend that Tan Dinh is one of the best restaurants in greater New Orleans. The garlic butter chicken wings could be served in Heaven's pub, and the Korean short ribs are mouthwatering. Also a contender for high-quality pho (noodle soup).

Hong Kong Food Market (☎504-394-7075; 925 Behrman Hwy, Gretna; ⏰8am-8:30pm) Hong Kong Food Market is a general Asian grocery store that serves plenty of Chinese and Filipinos, but the main customer base is Vietnamese.

Vietnamese Farmers' Market (14401 Alcee Fortier Blvd, New Orleans East; ⏰6am-9am) The closest you'll come to witnessing Saigon on a Saturday morning (by the way, lots of local Vietnamese, being southern refugees, still call it 'Saigon') is the Vietnamese Farmers' Market, also known as the 'squat market' thanks to the ladies in *non la* (conical straw hats) squatting over their fresh, wonderful-smelling produce.

CBD & Warehouse District

★Cochon Butcher SANDWICHES $
(www.cochonbutcher.com; 930 Tchoupitoulas St; mains $10-12; ⏲10am-10pm Mon-Thu, to 11pm Fri & Sat, to 4pm Sun) Tucked behind the slightly more formal Cochon, this newly expanded sandwich and meat shop calls itself a 'swine bar & deli.' We call it our favorite sandwich shop in the city, if not the entire South. From the convivial lunch crowds to the savory sandwiches to the fun-loving cocktails, this welcoming place from local restaurant maestro Donald Link encapsulates the best of New Orleans.

★Peche Seafood Grill SEAFOOD $$
(☎504-522-1744; www.pecherestaurant.com; 800 Magazine St; small plates $9-14, mains $14-27; ⏲11am-10pm Mon-Thu, to 11pm Fri & Sat) We're not sure why, but there is a split opinion locally about this latest venture from Donald Link. Put us firmly in the lick-the-plate and order-more category. Coastal seafood dishes are prepared simply here, but unexpected flourishes – whether from salt, spices or magic – sear the deliciousness onto your taste buds. The vibe is convivial, with a happy, stylish crowd sipping and savoring among the exposed-brick walls and wooden beams.

Domenica ITALIAN $$
(☎504-648-6020; 123 Baronne St; mains $13-30; ⏲11am-11pm; 📝) With its wooden refectory tables, white lights and soaring ceiling, Domenica feels like a village trattoria gone posh. The 'rustic' pizza pies at this lively, often-recommended spot are loaded with nontraditional but enticing toppings – clams, prosciutto, smoked pork – and are big enough that solo diners should have a slice or two left over.

Restaurant August CREOLE $$$
(☎504-299-9777; www.restaurantaugust.com; 301 Tchoupitoulas St; lunch $23-36, dinner $33-42; ⏲5-10pm daily, 11am-2pm Fri & Sun; 📝) For a little romance, reserve a table at Restaurant August, the flagship of chef John Besh's nine-restaurant empire. This converted 19th-century tobacco warehouse, with its flickering candles and warm, soft shades, earns a nod for most aristocratic dining room in New Orleans, but somehow manages to be both intimate and lively. Delicious meals take you to another level of gastronomic perception.

Garden District & Uptown

★Surrey's Juice Bar AMERICAN $
(☎504-524-3828; 1418 Magazine St; breakfast & lunch $6-13; ⏲8am-3pm) Surrey's makes a simple bacon-and-egg sandwich taste – and look – like the most delicious breakfast you've ever been served. And you know what? It probably *is* the best. Boudin biscuits; eggs scrambled with salmon; biscuits swimming in salty sausage gravy; and a shrimp, grits and bacon dish that should be illegal. And the juice, as you might guess, is blessedly fresh. Cash only.

★Ba Chi Canteen VIETNAMESE $
(www.facebook.com/bachicanteenla; 7900 Maple St; mains $4-15; ⏲11am-2:30pm Mon-Fri,to 3:30pm Sat, 5:30-9pm Mon-Wed, 5:30-10pm Thu-Sat) Do not be skeptical of the bacos. These pillowy bundles of deliciousness – a *banh bao* crossed with a taco – successfully merge the subtle seasonings of Vietnamese fillings with the foldable convenience of a taco-shaped steamed flour bun. Pho and *banh mi* – dubbed po'boys here – round out the menu.

★Boucherie SOUTHERN $$
(☎504-862-5514; www.boucherie-nola.com; 1596 S Carrollton Ave; lunch $10-18, dinner $15-18; ⏲11am-3pm & 5:30-9:30pm Tue-Sat) The thick, glistening cuts of bacon on the BLT can only be the work of the devil – or chef Nathanial Zimet, whose house-cured meats and succulent Southern dishes are lauded citywide. Savor boudin balls with garlic aioli, blackened shrimp in bacon vinaigrette, and smoked Wagyu brisket with gloriously stinky garlic-Parmesan fries. The Krispy Kreme bread pudding with rum syrup is a wonder.

★Gautreau's MODERN AMERICAN $$$
(☎504-899-7397; www.gautreausrestaurant.com; 1728 Soniat St; mains $22-42; ⏲6-10pm Mon-Sat) There's no sign outside Gautreau's, just the number 1728 discreetly marking a nondescript house in a residential neighborhood. Cross the threshold to find a refined but welcoming dining room where savvy diners, many of them New Orleanian food aficionados, dine on fresh, modern American fare. Chef Sue Zemanick has won every award a rising young star can garner in American culinary circles.

Drinking & Nightlife

New Orleans is a drinking town. Bourbon St can be fun for a night, but you need to get into the neighborhoods to experience some of the best bars in America.

Most bars open every day, often by noon, get hopping around 10pm, and can stay open all night. There's no cover charge unless there's live music. It's illegal to have open glass liquor containers in the street, so all bars dispense plastic 'go cups' when you're ready to wander.

★Tonique BAR
(☎504-324-6045; http://bartonique.com; 820 N Rampart St; ⊙noon-2am) Tonique is a bartender's bar. Seriously: on a Sunday night, when the weekend rush is over, we've seen no less than three of the city's top bartenders arrive here to unwind. Why? Because this gem mixes some of the best drinks in the city, and it has a spirits menu as long as a Tolstoy novel to draw upon.

★Twelve Mile Limit BAR
(500 S Telemachus St; ⊙5pm-midnight Mon-Thu, to 2am Fri & Sat, to 11pm Sun) Twelve Mile is simply a great bar. It's staffed by people who have the skill, both behind the bar and in the kitchen, to work in four-star spots, but who chose to set up shop in a neighborhood, for a neighborhood. The mixed drinks are excellent, the match of any mixologist's cocktail in Manhattan, and the vibe is super accepting.

Mimi's in the Marigny BAR
(☎504-872-9868; 2601 Royal St; ⊙6pm-2am Sun-Thu, to 4am Fri & Sat) The name of this bar could justifiably change to 'Mimi's *is* the Marigny'; we can't imagine the neighborhood without this institution. Mimi's is as attractively disheveled as Brad Pitt on a good day, all comfy furniture, pool tables, an upstairs dance hall decorated like a Creole mansion gone punk, and dim, brown lighting like a fantasy in sepia.

St Joe's BAR
(www.stjoesbar.com; 5535 Magazine St; ⊙4pm-3am Mon-Fri, noon-3am Sat, to 1am Sun) The bartender might make a face when you order a blueberry mojito – mojitos are hard to make. But dang, dude, you make 'em so good. They've been voted the best in town by New Orleanians several times. Patrons at this dark-but-inviting place are in their 20s and 30s, and friendly and chatty, as is the staff.

BJ's BAR
(☎504-945-9256; 4301 Burgundy; ⊙5pm-late) This Bywater dive attracts a neighborhood crowd seeking cheap beers, chilled-out banter and occasional live music, especially the Monday blues-rock show by King James & the Special Men, which starts around 10pm. How great is this place? Robert Plant felt the need to put on an impromptu set here the last time he visited town.

☆ Entertainment

What's New Orleans without live local music? Almost any weekend night you can find something for every taste: jazz, blues, brass band, country, Dixieland, zydeco (Cajun dance music), rock or Cajun. Free shows in the daytime abound. Check *Gambit* (www.bestofneworleans.com), *Offbeat* (www.offbeat.com) or www.nolafunguide.com for schedules.

★Spotted Cat LIVE MUSIC
(www.spottedcatmusicclub.com; 623 Frenchmen St; ⊙4pm-2am Mon-Fri, from 3pm Sat & Sun) It's good the Spotted Cat is across the street from Snug Harbor. They're both great jazz clubs, but where the latter is a swish martini sorta spot, the former is a thumping sweatbox where drinks are served in plastic cups – an ideal execution of the tiny New Orleans music club.

★Mid-City Rock & Bowl LIVE MUSIC
(☎504-861-1700; www.rockandbowl.com; 3000 S Carrollton Ave; ⊙5pm-late) A night at the Rock & Bowl is a quintessential New Orleans experience. The venue is a strange, wonderful combination of bowling alley, deli and huge live-music and dance venue, where patrons get down to New Orleans roots music while trying to avoid that 7-10 split. The best time and place in the city to experience zydeco is the weekly Thursday-night dance party held here.

AllWays Lounge THEATER
(☎504-218-5778; http://theallwayslounge.net; 2240 St Claude Ave; ⊙6pm-midnight Sat-Wed, to 2am Thu & Fri) In a city full of funky music venues, the AllWays stands out as one of the funkiest. On any given night of the week you may see experimental guitar, local theater, thrashy rock, live comedy or a '60s-inspired shagadelic dance party. Also: the drinks are supercheap.

Tipitina's LIVE MUSIC
(☎504-895-8477; www.tipitinas.com; 501 Napoleon Ave) 'Tips,' as locals call it, is one of New Orleans' great musical meccas. The legendary Uptown nightclub, which takes its name

from Professor Longhair's 1953 hit single, is the site of some of the city's most memorable shows, particularly when big names such as Dr John come home to roost. Outstanding music from local talent packs 'em in year-round.

Preservation Hall JAZZ
(☎504-522-2841; www.preservationhall.com; 726 St Peter St; cover $15 Sun-Thu, $20 Fri & Sat; ⏲showtimes 8pm, 9pm & 10pm) Preservation Hall, housed in a former art gallery that dates back to 1803, is one of the most storied live-music venues in New Orleans. Barbara Reid and Grayson 'Ken' Mills formed the Society for the Preservation of New Orleans Jazz in 1961, at a time when Louis Armstrong's generation was already getting on in years. The resident performers, the Preservation Hall Jazz Band, are ludicrously talented, and regularly tour around the world. These white-haired musos and their tubas, trombones and cornets raise the roof every night.

Shopping

Magazine Antique Mall ANTIQUES
(☎504-896-9994; www.magazineantiquemall.com; 3017 Magazine St; ⏲10:30am-5:30pm, from noon Sun) Scary baby dolls. Hats. Chandeliers. Coca-Cola memorabilia. Inside this overstuffed emporium, rummagers are likely to score items of interest in the dozen or so stalls, where independent dealers peddle an intriguing and varied range of antique bric-a-brac. Bargain hunters aren't likely to have much luck, though.

Maple Street Book Shop BOOKS
(www.maplestreetbookshop.com; 7523 Maple St; ⏲10am-6pm Mon-Sat, 11am-5pm Sun) This beloved Uptown shop celebrated its 50th anniversary in 2014. Founded by sisters Mary Kellogg and Rhoda Norman, it is one of the most politically progressive, well-stocked bookshops in the city. The store sells new, used and rare books in an invitingly overstuffed setting.

Information

DANGERS & ANNOYANCES

New Orleans has a high violent-crime rate, and neighborhoods go from good to ghetto very quickly. Be careful walking too far north of Faubourg Marigny and the Bywater (St Claude Ave is a good place to stop), south of Magazine St (things get dodgier past Laurel St) and too far north of Rampart St (Lakeside) from the French Quarter into the Tremé without a specific destination in mind. Stick to places that are well peopled, particularly at night, and spring for a cab to avoid dark walks. In the Quarter, street hustlers frequently approach tourists – just walk away. With all that said, don't be paranoid. Crime here, as in most of America, tends to be between people who already know each other.

INTERNET ACCESS

There's pretty good wi-fi coverage in the CBD, French Quarter, Garden and Lower Garden Districts and Uptown. Almost every coffee shop in the city has wi-fi coverage. Libraries have free internet access for cardholders.

MEDIA

Gambit Weekly (www.bestofneworleans.com) Free weekly hot sheet of music, culture, politics and classifieds.

WWOZ 90.7 FM (www.wwoz.org) Tune in here for Louisiana music and more.

MEDICAL SERVICES

Tulane University Medical Center (☎504-988-5263; www.tulanehealthcare.com; 1415 Tulane Ave; ⏲24hr) Emergency room located in the CBD.

TOURIST INFORMATION

The city's official visitor website is www.neworleansonline.com.

Jean Lafitte National Historic Park and Preserve Visitor Center (☎504-589-2636; www.nps.gov/jela; 419 Decatur St, French Quarter; ⏲9am-4:30pm Tue-Sat) Operated by the NPS, with exhibits on local history, guided walks and daily live music. There's not much in the park office itself, but educational musical programs are held on most days of the week. Many of the park rangers are musicians and knowledgeable lecturers, and their presentations discuss musical developments, cultural changes, regional styles, myths, legends and musical techniques in relation to the broad subject of jazz.

Basin St Station (☎504-293-2600; www.basinststation.com; 501 Basin St; ⏲9am-5pm) Affiliated with the New Orleans CVB, this interactive tourist info center inside the former freight administration building of the Southern Railway has loads of helpful info and maps as well as an historical overview film and a small rail museum component. It's next door to St Louis Cemetery No 1.

Getting There & Away

Louis Armstrong New Orleans International Airport (MSY; ☎504-303-7500; www.flymsy.com; 900 Airline Hwy; 📶), 11 miles west of the city, handles primarily domestic flights.

The **Union Passenger Terminal** (☎504-299-1880; 1001 Loyola Ave) is home to **Greyhound**

(☎504-525-6075; www.greyhound.com; 1001 Loyola Ave; ⏲5:15am-10:30am, 11:30am-1pm & 2:30-9:25pm), which has regular buses to Baton Rouge (two hours), Memphis, TN (11 hours), and Atlanta, GA (12 hours). **Amtrak** (☎800-872-7245, 504-528-1610; ⏲ticketing 5:45am-10pm) trains also operate from the Union Passenger Terminal, running to Chicago, New York and Los Angeles and stops in-between.

Getting Around

TO/FROM THE AIRPORT

There's an information booth at the airport's A&B concourse. The **Airport Shuttle** (☎866-596-2699; www.airportshuttleneworleans.com; one way/round-trip $20/38) runs to downtown hotels. The **Jefferson Transit** (☎504-364-3450; www.jeffersontransit.org; adult $2) airport route E2 picks up outside entrance 7 on the airport's upper level; it stops along Airline Hwy (Hwy 61) on its way into town (final stop Tulane and Loyola Aves). After 7pm it only goes to Tulane and Carrollton Aves in Mid-City; a solid 5 miles to get to the CBD, and from here you must transfer to a Regional Transit Authority (RTA) bus – a haphazard transfer at best, especially with luggage.

Taxis downtown cost $33 for one or two people, $14 more for each additional passenger.

PUBLIC TRANSPORTATION

The **Regional Transit Authority** (RTA; ☎504-248-3900; www.norta.com) runs the local bus service. Bus and streetcar fares are $1.25, plus 25¢ for transfers; express buses cost $1.50. Exact change is required.

The RTA also operates three **streetcar** lines (one-way $1.25, one-day pass $3; exact change required). The historic St Charles streetcar is running only a short loop in the CBD due to hurricane damage to the Uptown tracks. The Canal streetcar makes a long journey up Canal St to City Park, with a spur on Carrollton Ave. The Riverfront line runs 2 miles along the levee from the Old US Mint, past Canal St, to the upriver convention center and back. A **Jazzy Pass** gives you unlimited rides (one/three days $3/9); they can be bought at local Walgreen's pharmacies, or order online, but if you go the latter route, you have to wait for them to be mailed to you.

For a taxi, call **United Cabs** (☎504-522-9771; www.unitedcabs.com; ⏲24hr).

Rent bicycles at **Bicycle Michael's** (☎504-945-9505; www.bicyclemichaels.com; 622 Frenchmen St; per day from $35; ⏲10am-7pm Mon, Tue & Thu-Sat, to 5pm Sun).

Around New Orleans

Leaving colorful New Orleans behind quickly catapults you into a world of swamps, bayous, antebellum plantation homes, laid-back small communities and miles of bedroom suburbs and strip malls.

Barataria Preserve

This section of the **Jean Lafitte National Historical Park & Preserve**, south of New Orleans near the town of Marrero, provides the easiest access to the dense swamplands that ring New Orleans. The 8 miles of boardwalk trails are a stunning way to tread lightly through the fecund, thriving swamp, home to alligators, nutrias (big invasive river rats), tree frogs and hundreds of species of birds.

Start at the **NPS Visitor Center** (☎504-689-3690; www.nps.gov/jela; Hwy 3134; ⏲9am-5pm, visitor center 9:30am-4:30pm Wed-Sun;) FREE, 1 mile west of Hwy 45 off the Barataria Blvd exit, where you can pick up a map or join a guided walk or canoe trip (most Saturday mornings and monthly on full-moon nights; call to reserve a spot). To rent canoes or kayaks for a tour or an independent paddle, go to **Bayou Barn** (☎504-689-2663; www.bayoubarn.com; 7145 Barataria Blvd; canoes per person $20, single kayak $25; ⏲10am-6pm Thu-Sun) about 3 miles from the park entrance.

The North Shore

Bedroom communities sprawl along **Lake Pontchartrain's** north shore, but head north of Mandeville and you'll reach the bucolic village of **Abita Springs**, which was popular in the late 19th century for its curative waters. Today the spring water still flows from a fountain in the center of the village, but the primary liquid attraction is the **Abita Brew Pub** (☎985-892-5837; www.abitabrewpub.com; 7201 Holly St; ⏲11am-9pm Tue-Thu & Sun, to 10pm Fri & Sat), where you can choose from the many tap beers brewed a mile west of town at the **Abita Brewery Tasing Room** (☎985-893-3143; www.abita.com; 166 Barbee Rd; tours free; ⏲tours 2pm Wed-Fri, 11am, noon, 1pm & 2pm Sat).

The 31-mile **Tammany Trace trail** (☎985-867-9490; www.tammanytrace.org;) connects north shore towns, beginning in Covington, passing through Abita Springs and pretty **Fontainebleau State Park**. In Lacombe, about 9 miles east of Mandeville, you can rent bicycles and kayaks at **Bayou Adventures** (985-882-9208; www.bayouadventure.com; 27725 Main St, Lacombe; bicycles per hr/day $8/25, single/double kayaks per day $35/50; 6am-5pm).

River Road

Elaborate plantation homes dot the east and west banks of the Mississippi River between New Orleans and Baton Rouge. First indigo, then cotton and sugarcane, brought great wealth to the plantation owners and many plantations are open to the public. Most tours focus on the lives of the owners, the restored architecture and the ornate gardens of antebellum Louisiana.

Sights

Whitney Plantation HISTORIC SITE
(225-265-3300; www.whitneyplantation.com; 5099 Highway 18, Wallace; adult/student $22/15, child under 12yr free; 9:30am-4:30pm Wed-Mon, tours 10am-3pm) The Whitney is the first plantation in the state to focus on the history and realities of slavery. Visitors are given a historical tour into the world of the German-American Haydel family and their slaves, but the visit emphasizes the lived experience of the latter group. Besides a tour that focuses on the appalling living conditions slaves toiled under, the property is speckled with memorials and monuments to the area's slave population.

Laura Plantation HISTORIC SITE
(225-265-7690; www.lauraplantation.com; 2247 Hwy 18, Vacherie; adult/child $20/6; 10am-4pm) This ever-evolving and popular plantation tour teases out the distinctions between Creole, Anglo, free and enslaved African Americans via meticulous research and the written records of the Creole women who ran the place for generations. Laura is also fascinating because it was a Creole mansion, founded and maintained by a continental European-descended elite, as opposed to Anglo-Americans; the cultural and architectural distinctions between this and other plantations is obvious and striking.

Oak Alley Plantation HISTORIC SITE
(225-265-2151; www.oakalleyplantation.com; 3645 Hwy 18, Vacherie; adult/child $20/7.50; 9am-5pm Mar-Oct, 9am-4:30pm Mon-Fri, to 5pm Sat & Sun Nov-Feb) The most impressive aspect of Oak Alley Plantation is its canopy of 28 majestic live oaks lining the entry to the grandiose Greek Revival–style home – even better with a fresh mint julep. The tour is relatively staid, but there are guest cottages ($145 to $200) and a restaurant on-site.

Baton Rouge

In 1699 French explorers named this area *baton rouge* (red stick) when they came upon a reddened cypress pole that Bayagoulas and Houma Native Americans had staked in the ground to mark the boundaries of their respective hunting territories. From one pole grew a lot of sprawl; Baton Rouge stretches out in an unplanned clutter in many directions. Visitors are mostly drawn to Baton Rouge for Louisiana State University (LSU) and Southern University; the latter is one of the largest historically African American universities in the country.

Sights & Activities

Louisiana State Capitol HISTORIC BUILDING
(225-342-7317; 900 N 3rd St; 8am-4:30pm Tue-Sat) FREE The art-deco skyscraper looming over town was built at the height of the Great Depression to the tune of $5 million. It's the most visible leftover legacy of populist governor 'Kingfish' Huey Long. The 27th-floor **observation deck** (closes 4pm) offers stunning views and the ornate lobby is equally impressive. The welcome desk offers free tours of the grounds.

LSU Museum of Art MUSEUM
(LSUMOA; 225-389-7200; www.lsumoa.com; 100 Lafayette St; adult/child $5/free; 10am-5pm Tue-Sat, to 8pm Thu, 1-5pm Sun) The physical space this museum inhabits – the clean, geometric lines of the Shaw Center – is as impressive as the on-site galleries, which include a permanent collection of over 5000 works and curated galleries exploring regional artistic heritage and contemporary trends.

Old State Capitol HISTORIC BUILDING
(225-342-0500; www.louisianaoldstatecapitol.org; 100 North Blvd; 9am-4pm Tue-Sat) FREE The Gothic Revival, pink fairytale castle is... well, it's a pink castle. Which should tell you something about how eccentric the government of its resident state can be. Today the structure houses exhibits about the colorful political history of Louisiana.

Rural Life Museum MUSEUM
(☎225-765-2437; http://sites01.lsu.edu/wp/rurallife; 4560 Essen Lane; adult/child $9/8; 8am-5pm; P) This outdoor museum promises a trip into the architecture, occupations and folkways of rural Louisiana. Numerous rough-hewn buildings are scattered over the bucolic campus, and exhibits are refreshingly honest and informative, lacking any rose-colored romanticization of the hard country legacy that built Louisiana.

Sleeping & Eating

Stockade Bed & Breakfast B&B $$
(☎225-769-7358; www.thestockade.com; 8860 Highland Rd; r $135-160, ste $215; P) Chain hotels line the sides of I-10. For a more intimate stay, try this wonderful B&B with five spacious, comfortable and elegant rooms just 3.5 miles southeast of LSU and within earshot of several standout neighborhood restaurants. Book ahead on weekends, especially during football season.

Schlittz & Giggles PIZZA $$
(☎225-218-4271; www.schlittzandgiggles.com; 301 3rd St; pizzas $10-22; 11am-midnight Sun-Wed, to 2am Thu-Sat;) The food stands up to this awesomely named downtown late-night bar and pizzeria. Bubbly coeds serve up thin-as-black-ice pizza slices ($3 to $3.50) and fabulous panini to a student crowd, while a gaggle of old-timer locals tend to belly up at the bar.

Louisiana Lagniappe CAJUN $$$
(☎225-767-9991; www.louisianalagniapperestaurant.com; 9900 Perkins Rd; mains $21-50; 5:30pm-9pm Mon-Thu, 5-10pm Fri & Sat; P) If you need a night out in Baton Rouge, and it requires the presence of delicious local cuisine, we'll direct you to Louisiana Lagniappe (lah-nyap). The second word means 'a little extra' in Louisiana French, and it's a misnomer, as you get a *lot* here: of fish topped with crab meat, rib-eye steaks and shrimp and sausage pasta.

Entertainment

Varsity Theatre LIVE MUSIC
(☎225-383-7018; www.varsitytheatre.com; 3353 Highland Rd; 8pm-2am) At the gates of LSU, there's live music here, often on weeknights. The attached restaurant boasts an extensive beer selection and a raucous college crowd.

Information

Visitor Center (☎225-383-1825; www.visitbatonrouge.com; 359 3rd St; 8am-5pm) The downtown city visitor center has maps, brochures of local attractions and festival schedules.

Capital Park (☎225-219-1200; www.louisianatravel.com; 702 River Rd N; 8am-4:30pm) Near the Baton Rouge visitor center, this is the extensive official gateway to Louisiana tourism.

Getting There & Around

Baton Rouge lies 80 miles west of New Orleans on I-10. **Baton Rouge Metropolitan Airport** (BTR; ☎225-355-0333; www.flybtr.com) is north of town off I-110; it's about 1½ hours from New Orleans, so it's a viable airport of entry if you're renting a car. **Greyhound** (☎225-383-3811; www.greyhound.com; 1253 Florida Blvd, at N 12th St) has regular buses to New Orleans, Lafayette and Atlanta, GA. **Capitol Area Transit System** (CATS; ☎225-389-8920; www.brcats.com; tickets $1.75) operates buses around town.

St Francisville

Lush St Francisville is the quintessential Southern artsy small town, a blend of historical homes, bohemian shops and outdoor activities courtesy of the nearby Tunica Hills (you read that right – hills in Louisiana). During the antebellum decade this was home to plantation millionaires, and much of the architecture these aristocrats built is still intact.

Sights & Activities

In town, stroll down historic **Royal St** to catch a glimpse of antebellum homes and buildings-turned-homes. The visitor center has self-guided tour brochures.

Myrtles Plantation HISTORIC BUILDING
(☎225-635-6277; www.myrtlesplantation.com; 7747 US Hwy 61 N; tours adult/child $10/7, night tours $12; 9am-5pm, tours 6pm, 7pm & 8pm Fri & Sat; P) Supposedly haunted, this plantation house has night mystery tours (by reservation) on weekends. We heard secondhand corroboration of the supernatural presence, so it might be fun to stay overnight in the B&B (rooms from $115) to commune with the other world.

Oakley Plantation & Audubon State Historic Site HISTORIC SITE
(☎225-635-3739; www.audubonstatehistoricsite.wordpress.com; 11788 Hwy 965; adult/student/

senior $8/4/6; ⌚9am-5pm Tue-Sat; P) Outside of St Francisville, Oakley Plantation & Audubon State Historic Site is where John James Audubon spent his tenure, arriving in 1821 to tutor the owner's daughter. Though his assignment lasted only four months (and his room was pretty spartan), he and his assistant finished 32 paintings of birds found in the plantation's surrounding forest.

The small West Indies–influenced house (1806) includes several original Audubon prints.

Mary Ann Brown Preserve NATURE RESERVE
(☎225-338-1040; www.nature.org; 13515 Hwy 965; ⌚sunrise-sunset) Operated by the Nature Conservancy, the 110-acre Mary Ann Brown Preserve takes in some of the beech woodlands, dark wetlands and low, clay-soil hill country of the Tunica uplands. A 2-mile series of trails and boardwalks crosses the woods – the same trees that John James Audubon tramped around when he began work on *Birds of America*.

Sleeping & Eating

★**Shadetree Inn** B&B $$
(☎225-635-6116; www.shadetreeinn.com; cnr Royal & Ferdinand Sts; r from $145; P❄📶) Sidled up against the historic district and a bird sanctuary, this super-cozy B&B has a gorgeous flower-strewn, hammock-hung courtyard and spacious but rustic upscale rooms. A deluxe continental breakfast can be served in your room and is included along with a bottle of wine or champagne. Rates plunge if you cut out breakfast and stay midweek.

3-V Tourist Court HISTORIC INN $$
(☎225-721-7003; www.themagnoliacafe.net/magnolia3vtouristcourts.html; 5687 Commerce St; 1-/2-bed cabins $75/125; P❄📶) One of the oldest motor inns in the United States (started in the 1930s and now on the National Register of Historic Places), the five units take you back to simpler times. Rooms have period decorations and fixtures, though a recent renovation upgraded the beds, hardwood floors and flat-screen TVs into borderline trendy territory.

Birdman Coffee & Books CAFE $
(☎225-635-3665; 5687 Commerce St; mains $5-6.50; ⌚7am-5pm Tue-Fri, 8am-2pm Sat & Sun; 📶) Birdman is *the* spot for a local breakfast (old-fashioned yellow grits, sweet-potato pancakes) and local art.

Magnolia Café CAFE $
(☎225-635-6528; www.themagnoliacafe.net; 5687 Commerce St; mains $7-13; ⌚10am-4pm daily, to 9pm Thu & Sat, to 10pm Fri) The nucleus of what's happening in St Francisville, the Magnolia Café was once a health-food store and VW bus repair shop. Now it's where people go to eat, socialize and, on Friday night, dance to live music. Try the cheesy shrimp po'boy.

Cajun Country

When people think of Louisiana, this (and New Orleans) is the image that comes to mind: miles of bayou, sawdust-strewn shacks, a unique take on French and lots of good food. Welcome to Cajun Country, also called Acadiana for the French settlers exiled from L'Acadie (now Nova Scotia, Canada) by the British in 1755.

Cajuns are the largest French-speaking minority in the US, and while you may not hear French spoken at the grocery store, it is still present in radio shows, church services and the sing-song lilt of local English accents. While Lafayette is the nexus of Acadiana, getting out among the waterways, villages and ramshackle roadside taverns really drops you into Cajun living. This is largely a socially conservative region, but the Cajuns also have a well-deserved reputation for hedonism. It's hard to find a bad meal here; jambalaya (a rice-based dish with tomatoes, sausage and shrimp) and crawfish étouffée (a thick Cajun stew) are prepared slowly with pride (and cayenne!), and if folks aren't fishing, they are probably dancing. Don't expect to sit on the sidelines...*allons danson* (let's dance).

LAFAYETTE

The term 'undiscovered gem' gets thrown around too much in travel writing, but Lafayette really fits the bill. First, the bad: this town is deader then a cemetery on Sundays. The rest: there's an entirely fantastic amount of good eating and lots of music venues here, plus one of the best free music festivals in the country. This is a university town so bands are rocking most any night. Heck, even those quiet Sundays have a saving grace: some famously delicious brunch options.

Sights

Vermilionville VILLAGE
(☎337-233-4077; www.vermilionville.org; 300 Fisher Rd; adult/student $10/6; ⌚10am-4pm Tue-Sun; 👪) This tranquil, re-created 19th-century

Cajun village wends along the bayou near the airport. Friendly, enthusiastic costumed docents explain Cajun, Creole and Native American history, and local bands perform on Sundays (1pm to 3pm). Guided **boat tours** (☎337-233-4077; adult/student $12/8; ⊙10:30am Tue-Sat Mar-May & Sep-Nov) of Bayou Vermilion are also offered.

Acadiana Center for the Arts GALLERY
(☎337-233-7060; www.acadianacenterforthearts.org; 101 W Vermilion St; adult/student/child $5/3/2; ⊙10am-5pm Mon-Sat) This arts center in the heart of downtown maintains three chic galleries and hosts dynamic theater, lectures and special events.

Acadian Cultural Center MUSEUM
(☎337-232-0789; www.nps.gov/jela; 501 Fisher Rd; ⊙9am-4:30pm Tue-Fri, 8:30am-noon Sat; P) This National Parks Service museum has extensive exhibits on Cajun culture.

Festivals & Events

Festival International de Louisiane MUSIC
(www.festivalinternational.com; ⊙last weekend Apr) At the fabulous Festival International de Louisiane, hundreds of local and international artists rock out for five days in the largest free music festival of its caliber in the US. Although 'Festival' avowedly celebrates Francophone music and culture, the event's remit has grown to accommodate world music in all its iterations and languages.

Sleeping & Eating

Chain hotels clump near exits 101 and 103, off I-10 (doubles from $65). Head to Jefferson St mid-downtown for a choice of bars and restaurants, from sushi to Mexican.

★**Blue Moon Guest House** GUESTHOUSE $
(☎337-234-2422; www.bluemoonpresents.com; 215 E Convent St; dm $18, r $70-90; P) This tidy home is one of Louisiana's travel gems: an upscale hostel-like hangout that's walking distance from downtown. Snag a bed and you're on the guest list for Lafayette's most popular down-home music venue, located in the backyard. The friendly owners, full kitchen and camaraderie among guests create a unique music-meets-migration environment catering to backpackers, flashpackers and those in transition (flashbackpackers?).

Prices skyrocket during festival time. Decidedly not a quiet spot.

Buchanan Lofts APARTMENTS $$
(☎337-534-4922; www.buchananlofts.com; 403 S Buchanan; r per night/week from $110/600; P) These uber-hip lofts could be in New York City if they weren't so big. Doused in contemporary-cool art and design – all fruits of the friendly owner's globetrotting – the extra-spacious units come with kitchenettes and are awash with exposed brick and hardwoods.

★**French Press** BREAKFAST $
(☎337-233-9449; www.thefrenchpresslafayette.com; 214 E Vermillion; mains $9-15; ⊙7am-2pm Mon-Fri, from 9am Sat & Sun;) This French-Cajun hybrid is the best culinary thing going in Lafayette. Breakfast is mind-blowing, with a sinful Cajun Benedict (*boudin* instead of ham), cheddar grits (that will kill you dead) and

CAJUNS, CREOLES AND...CREOLES

Tourists in Louisiana often use the terms 'Cajun' and 'Creole' interchangeably, but the two cultures are quite distinct. 'Creole' refers to descendants of the original European settlers of Louisiana, a blended mix of mainly French and Spanish ancestry. The Creoles tend to have urban connections to New Orleans and consider their own culture refined and urbanized.

The Cajuns can trace their lineage to the Acadians, colonists from rural France who settled Nova Scotia. After the British conquered Canada, the proud Acadians refused to kneel to the new crown and were exiled in the mid-18th century – an act known as the Grand Dérangement. Many exiles settled in South Louisiana; they knew the area was French, but the Acadians ('Cajun' is an English bastardization of the word) were often treated as country bumpkins by the Creoles. The Acadians-cum-Cajuns settled in the bayous and prairies, and to this day see themselves as a more rural, frontier-stye culture.

Adding confusion to this is the practice, standard in many post-colonial French societies, of referring to mixed-race individuals as 'Creoles.' This happens in Louisiana, but there is a cultural difference between Franco-Spanish Creoles and mixed-race Creoles, even though these two communities very likely share actual blood ancestry.

organic granola (offset the grits). Lunch ain't half bad either; the fried shrimp melt, doused in Sriracha mayo, is gorgeously decadent.

Johnson's Boucanière CAJUN $
(☎337-269-8878; www.johnsonsboucaniere.com; 1111 St John St; mains $3-7; ⊙7am-3pm Tue-Fri, to 5:30pm Sat) This resurrected 70-year-old family prairie smoker business turns out detour-worthy *boudin* (Cajun-style pork and rice sausage) and an unstoppable smoked pork-brisket sandwich topped with smoked sausage.

Dwyer's DINER $
(☎337-235-9364; 323 Jefferson St; mains $5-12; ⊙6am-2pm; 👪) This family-owned joint serves Cajun diner fare, finally bringing gumbo for lunch and pancakes for breakfast into one glorious culinary marriage. It's especially fun on Wednesday mornings when a French-speaking table is set up and local Cajuns shoot the breeze in their old-school dialect.

☆ Entertainment

To find out what's playing around town, pick up the free weekly *Times* (www.theadvertiser.com – check under Times of Acadiana) or *Independent* (www.theind.com).

Cajun restaurants such as **Randol's** (☎337-981-7080; www.randols.com; 2320 Kaliste Saloom Rd; ⊙5-10pm Sun-Thu, to 10:30pm Fri & Sat) and **Prejean's** (☎337-896-3247; www.prejeans.com; 3480 NE Evangeline Thruway/I-49; ⊙7am-10pm Sun-Thu, to 11pm Fri & Sat) feature live music on weekend nights.

Blue Moon Saloon LIVE MUSIC
(☎337-234-2422; www.bluemoonpresents.com; 215 E Convent St; cover $5-8; ⊙5pm-2am Tue-Sun) This intimate venue on the back porch of the accompanying guesthouse is what Louisiana is all about: good music, good people and good beer. What's not to love? Music tends to go off Wednesday to Saturday.

Artmosphere LIVE MUSIC
(☎337-233-3331; www.artmosphere.co; 902 Johnston St; ⊙10am-2am Mon-Sat, to midnight Sun) Graffiti, hookahs, hipsters and an edgy lineup of acts; it's more CBGBs then Cajun dancehall, but it's a lot of fun, and there's good Mexican food to boot.

ℹ Information

Visitor Center (☎337-232-3737; www.lafayettetravel.com; 1400 NW Evangeline Thruway; ⊙8:30am-5pm Mon-Fri, 9am-5pm Sat & Sun) Information on travel, lodging and events in Lafayette and greater Acadiana (Cajun Country).

ℹ Getting There & Away

From I-10, exit 103A, the Evangeline Thruway (Hwy 167) goes to the center of town. **Greyhound** (☎337-235-1541; www.greyhound.com; 100 Lee Ave) operates from a hub beside the central commercial district, making several runs daily to New Orleans (3½ hours) and Baton Rouge (one hour). The **Amtrak** (100 Lee Ave) train *Sunset Limited* goes to New Orleans three times a week.

CAJUN WETLANDS

In 1755, the Grand Dérangement, the British expulsion of rural French settlers from Acadiana (now Nova Scotia, Canada), created a homeless population of Acadians who searched for decades for a place to settle. In 1785, seven boatloads of exiles arrived in New Orleans. By the early 19th century, 3000 to 4000 Acadians occupied the swamplands southwest of New Orleans. Native American tribes such as the Attakapas helped them learn to eke out a living based on fishing and trapping, and the aquatic way of life is still the backdrop to modern living.

East and south of Lafayette, the **Atchafalaya Basin** is the preternatural heart of the Cajun wetlands. Stop in at the **Atchafalaya Welcome Center** (☎337-228-1094; www.dnr.louisiana.gov; I-10, exit 121; ⊙8:30am-5pm) to learn how to penetrate the dense jungle protecting these swamps, lakes and bayous from the casual visitor (incidentally, it also screens one of the most gloriously cheesy nature films in existence). They'll fill you in on camping in **Indian Bayou** and exploring the **Sherburne Wildlife Management Area**, as well as the exquisitely situated **Lake Fausse Pointe State Park**.

Eleven miles east of Lafayette in the compact, crawfish-lovin' town of **Breaux Bridge**, you'll find the utterly unexpected **Café des Amis** (☎337-332-5273; www.cafedesamis.com; 140 E Bridge St; mains $17-26; ⊙11am-9pm Tue-Thu, from 7:30am Fri & Sat, 8am-2pm Sun), where you can relax amid funky local art as waiters trot out sumptuous weekend breakfasts, all set to live zydeco music on Saturday mornings. Just 3.5 miles south of Breaux Bridge, **Lake Martin** (Lake Martin Rd) is a wonderful introduction to bayou landscapes. This bird sanctuary hosts thousands of great and cattle egrets, blue heron and more than a few gators.

WORTH A TRIP

THE TAO OF FRED'S

Deep in the heart of Cajun Country, Mamou is a typical South Louisiana small town six days of the week, worth a peek and a short stop before rolling on to Eunice. But on Saturday mornings, Mamou's hometown hangout, little **Fred's Lounge** (420 6th St, Mamou; ⏲8am-2pm Sat), becomes the apotheosis of a Cajun dancehall.

OK, to be fair: Fred's is more of a dance shack than hall. It's a small bar and it gets more than a little crowded from 8:30am to 2ish in the afternoon, when the staff host a Francophone-friendly music morning, with bands, beer, cigarettes and dancing (seriously, it gets smoky in here. Fair warning). Back in the day, owner Tante (Auntie, in Cajun French) Sue herself would take to the stage to dispense wisdom and songs in Cajun French, all while taking pulls from a bottle of brown liquor she kept in a pistol holster; she has since passed, but something of her amazing, anarchic energy has been imbued into the very bricks of this place.

Check out the friendly **Tourist Center** (☎337-332-8500; www.breauxbridgelive.com; 318 E Bridge St; ⏲8am-4pm Mon-Fri, to noon Sat), whose staff can hook you up with one of numerous B&Bs in town. The wonderful **Bayou Cabins** (☎337-332-6158; www.bayoucabins.com; 100 W Mills Ave; cabins $70-150) feature 14 completely individualized cabins situated on Bayou Teche, some with 1950s retro furnishings, others decked out in regional folk art. The included breakfast is delicious, but the smoked meats may shave a few years off your lifespan. If you're in town during the first week of May, don't miss the gluttony of music, dancing and Cajun food at the **Crawfish Festival** (www.bbcrawfest.com; ⏲May).

CAJUN PRAIRIE

Think dancing cowboys! Cajun and African American settlers in the higher, drier terrain north of Lafayette developed a culture based around animal husbandry and farming, and the 10-gallon hat still rules. It's also the hotbed of Cajun and zydeco music (and thus accordions) and crawfish farming.

Opelousas squats sleepily alongside Hwy 49, and its historic downtown is home to the **Museum & Interpretive Center** (☎337-948-2589; www.cityofopelousas.com; 315 N Main St; ⏲8am-4:30pm Mon-Fri, 10am-3pm Sat) FREE, a grandma's attic of exhibits, artifacts and esoterica related to the town. Hit up **Slim's Y-Ki-Ki** (☎337-942-6242; www.slimsykiki.com; cnr Main St & Park St, Opelousas; ⏲9pm-late), a few miles north, for some zydeco music, and bring your dancing shoes. Zydeco shoes also often go off at the **Yambilee Building** (1939 W Landry St), which is otherwise used throughout the year as a function hall.

Plaisance, northwest of Opelousas, hosts the grassroots, fun-for-the-family **Southwest Louisiana Zydeco Festival** (www.zydeco.org; ⏲late Aug or early Sep).

In **Eunice** there's the Saturday evening 'Rendez-Vous des Cajuns' at the **Liberty Theater** (☎337-457-6577; www.eunice-la.com/index.php/things-to-do/liberty-schedule; 200 Park Ave; admission $5; ⏲6-7:30pm), which is broadcast on local radio. Visitors are welcome all day at **KBON** (☎337-546-0007; www.kbon.com; 109 S 2nd St), 101.1FM. Browse the capacious Wall of Fame, signed by visiting musicians. Two blocks away, the **Cajun Music Hall of Fame & Museum** (☎337-457-6534; www.cajunfrenchmusic.org; 230 S CC Duson Dr; ⏲9am-5pm Tue-Sat) FREE is a dusty collection of instruments and cultural ephemera that caters to the die-hard music buff.

The NPS runs the **Prairie Acadian Cultural Center** (☎337-457-8499; www.nps.gov/jela; 250 West Park Ave; ⏲9:30am-4:30pm Wed-Fri, to 6pm Sat) FREE, which has exhibits on rural life and Cajun culture and shows a variety of documentaries explaining the history of the area. Want more music? The best time to visit Eunice is on a Saturday. From 9am to noon **Savoy Music Center** (☎337-457-9563; www.savoymusiccenter.com; Hwy 190; ⏲9am-5pm Tue-Fri, 9am-noon Sat), an accordion factory and shop, hosts a Cajun-music jam session. Musician Marc Savoy and his guitarist wife, Ann, often join in.

Ruby's Café (☎337-550-7665; 123 S 2nd St; mains $9-23; ⏲6am-2pm Mon-Fri, 5-9pm Wed & Thu, to 10pm Fri & Sat) does popular plate lunches in a 1950s diner setting and **Café Mosaic** (202 S 2nd St; meals $3-4.50; ⏲6am-10pm Mon-Fri, from 7am Sat, 7am-7pm Sun; 📶) is a smart coffeehouse with waffles and grilled sandwiches. **Le Village** (☎337-457-3573; www.levillagehouse.com; 121 Seale Lane; r $115-165, 3-bed cottage $375; P📶) is a lovely rural B&B.

Northern Louisiana

Make no mistake: the rural, oil-industry towns along the Baptist Bible-belt make Northern Louisiana as far removed from New Orleans as Paris, TX, is from Paris, France. There's a lot of optimistic tourism development, but at the end of the day, most folks come here from states like Texas and Arkansas to gamble.

Captain Henry Shreve cleared a 165-mile logjam on the Red River and founded the river-port town of **Shreveport** in 1839. The city boomed with oil discoveries in the early 1900s, but declined after WWII. Some revitalization came in the form of huge Vegas-sized casinos and a riverfront entertainment complex. The **visitor center** (☎888-458-4748; www.shreveport-bossier.org; 629 Spring St; ⊙8am-5pm Mon-Fri, 10am-2pm Sat) is downtown. If you're a rose-lover, it would be a shame to miss the **Gardens of the American Rose Center** (☎318-938-5402; www.rose.org; 8877 Jefferson Paige Rd; adult/child $5/2, tours $10; ⊙9am-5pm Mon-Sat, 1-5pm Sun), which contains more than 65 individual gardens designed to show how roses can be grown in a home garden – take exit 5 off I-20. If you're hungry, stop by **Strawn's Eat Shop** (☎318-868-0634; http://strawnseatshop.com; 125 E Kings Hwy; mains under $10; ⊙6am-8pm). This basic diner serves good, hearty Americana fare with a lot of Southern charm – think chicken-fried steak and mustard greens – but it's most notable for its delicious pies.

Shreveport boasts one of the finest, most underrated regional breweries in the nation: **Great Raft Brewing** (☎318-734-9881; www.greatraftbrewing.com; 1251 Dalzell St; ⊙4-9pm Thu & Fri, noon-9pm Sat). Drop by the tasting room and give the Schwarzbier a whirl – it's a dark lager the likes of which we've not had outside of Europe.

About 50 miles northeast of Monroe on Hwy 557, near the town of Epps, the **Poverty Point State Historic Site** (☎318-926-5492; www.nps.gov/popo; 6859 Highway 577, Pioneer; adult/child $4/free; ⊙9am-5pm) has a remarkable series of earthworks and mounds along what was once the Mississippi River. A two-story observation tower gives a view of the site's six concentric ridges, and a 2.6-mile hiking trail meanders through the grassy countryside. Around 1000 BC this was the hub of a civilization comprising hundreds of communities, with trading links as far north as the Great Lakes.

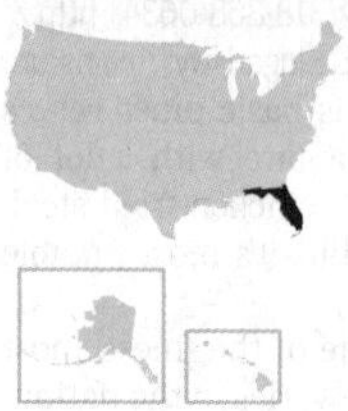

Florida

Includes ➡

Best Places to Eat

- NIU Kitchen (p479)
- Bern's Steak House (p504)
- Yellow Dog Eats (p511)
- Tap Tap (p478)
- Floridian (p500)

Best Places to Stay

- Gale South Beach (p478)
- Fairbanks House (p501)
- Pillars (p483)
- Pelican Hotel (p478)
- Everglades International Hostel (p488)

Why Go?

For countless visitors Florida is a place of promises: of eternal youth, sun, relaxation, clear skies, space, success, escape, prosperity and, for the kids, a chance to meet much-loved Disney characters in person.

No other state in America is as built on tourism, and tourism here comes in a thousand facets: cartoon mice, *Miami Vice,* country fried oysters, Spanish villas, gators kicking footballs, gators prowling golf courses, and of course, the beach. So. Much. Beach.

Don't think Florida is all marketing, though. This is one of the most genuinely fascinating states in the country. It's as if someone shook the nation and tipped it over, filling this sun-bleached peninsula with immigrants, country boys, Jews, Cubans, military bases, shopping malls and a subtropical wilderness laced with crystal ponds and sugary sand.

When to Go

Miami

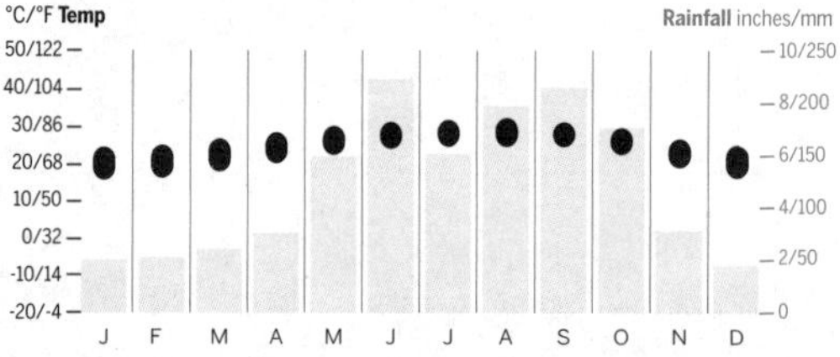

Feb–Apr Winter ends and high season begins, coinciding with spring break.

Jun–Aug The hot, humid wet months are peak season for northern Florida beaches and theme parks.

Sep–Oct The ideal shoulder season with fewer crowds, cooler temperatures and warm waters.

SOUTH FLORIDA

Once you head far enough south in Florida, you're no longer in 'the South' as a regional entity – you've slipped those bonds into South Florida, which is truly a hybrid of the USA, the Caribbean and Latin America. Miami is the area's beating urban heart, and one of the few truly international cities in the country. Wealthy oceanfront communities stretch from the Palm Beaches to Fort Lauderdale, while inland, the dreamscape of the Everglades, the state's most unique, dynamic wilderness, await. And when the state's peninsula ends, it doesn't truly end, but rather stretches into the Overseas Hwy, which leads across hundreds of mangrove islands to colorful Key West.

Miami

Miami moves to a different rhythm from anywhere else in the USA. Pastel-hued, subtropical beauty and Latin sexiness are everywhere: from the cigar-filled dance halls where Havana expats dance to *son* (a salsa-like dance that originated in Cuba) and *boleros* (a Spanish dance in triple meter) to the exclusive nightclubs where stiletto-heeled Brazilian models shake to Latin hip-hop. Whether you're meeting avant-garde gallery hipsters or passing the buffed, perfect bodies recumbent along South Beach, everyone can seem oh-so-artfully posed. Meanwhile, street vendors and restaurants dish out flavors of the Caribbean, Cuba, Argentina and Haiti. For travelers, the city can be as intoxicating as a sweaty-glassed *mojito*.

Miami is its own world, an international city whose tempos, concerns and inspirations often arrive from distant shores. Over half the population is Latino and more than 60% speak predominantly Spanish. In fact, many northern Floridians don't consider immigrant-rich Miami to be part of the state, and many Miamians, particularly Cubans, feel the same way.

FLORIDA FACTS

Nickname Sunshine State

Population 19.89 million

Area 53,927 sq miles

Capital city Tallahassee (population 186,411)

Other cities Jacksonville (842,583), Miami (417,650)

Sales tax 6% (some towns add 9.5% to 11.5% to accommodations and meals)

Birthplace of Author Zora Neale Hurston (1891–1960), actor Faye Dunaway (b 1941), musician Tom Petty (b 1950), author Carl Hiaasen (b 1953)

Home of Cuban Americans, manatees, Mickey Mouse, retirees, key lime pie

Politics Sharply divided between Republicans and Democrats

Famous for Theme parks, beaches, alligators, art deco

Notable local invention Frozen concentrated orange juice (1946)

History

Florida has the oldest recorded history of any US state, and also the most notorious and

MIAMI IN...

Two Days

Focus your first day on South Beach. Bookend an afternoon of sunning and swimming with a walking tour through the **Art Deco Historic District** and a visit to **Wolfsonian-FIU**, which explains it all. That evening, sample some Haitian cuisine at **Tap Tap** and have a low-key brew at **Room**. Next morning, shop for Cuban music along Calle Ocho in **Little Havana**, followed by classic Cuban cuisine at **El Exquisito**. Go for a stroll at **Vizcaya Museum & Gardens**, cool off with a dip at the **Venetian Pool**, then end the day with dinner and cocktails at **NIU Kitchen**.

Four Days

Follow the two-day itinerary, then head to the **Everglades** on day three and jump in a kayak. For your last day, immerse yourself in art and design in **Wynwood** and the **Design District**, followed by a visit to the **Miami Art Museum** or **Museum of Contemporary Art**. In the evening, party with the hipsters at **Wood Tavern**.

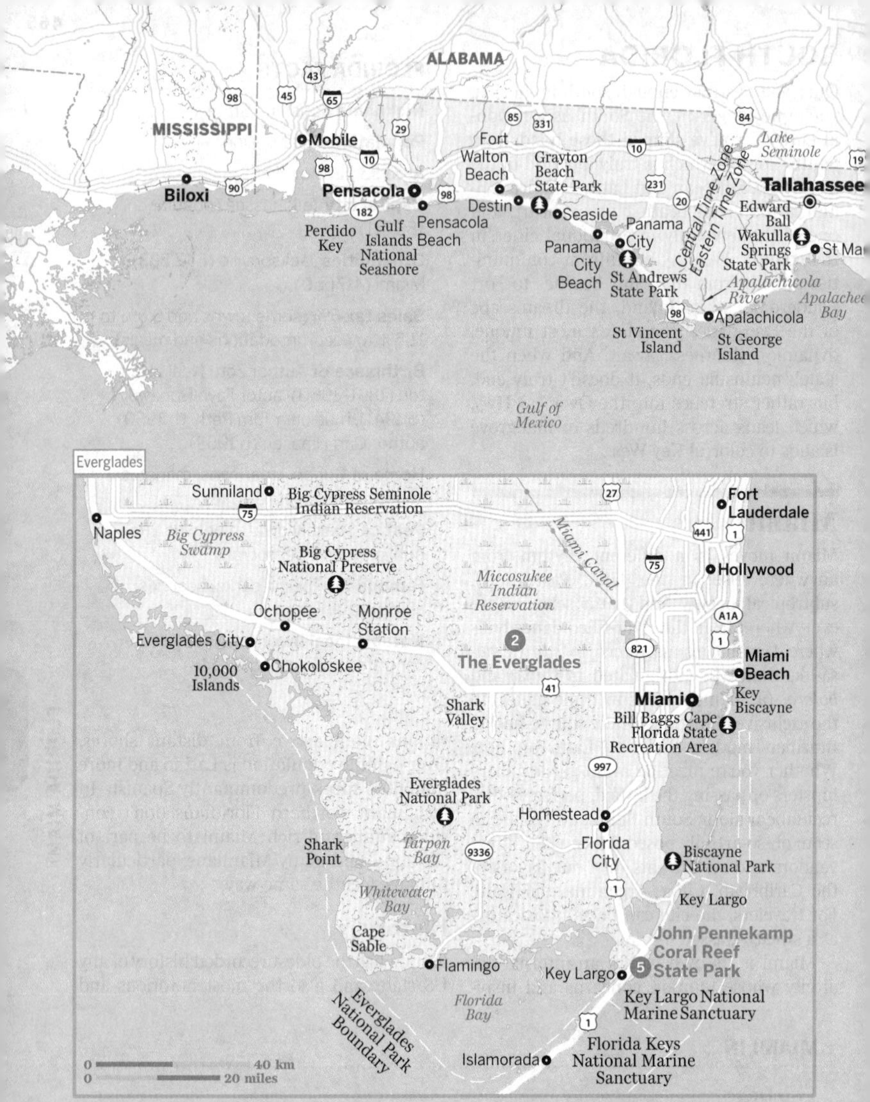

Florida Highlights

1. Joining the sunset bacchanal in Key West's **Mallory Square** (p492).
2. Paddling among alligators and sawgrass in **The Everglades** (p485).
3. Being swept up in nostalgia and thrill rides at **Walt Disney World** (p514).
4. Marveling at the murals all around **Wynwood** (p474) in Miami.
5. Snorkeling the continental USA's most extensive coral reef at **John Pennekamp Coral Reef Park** (p489).

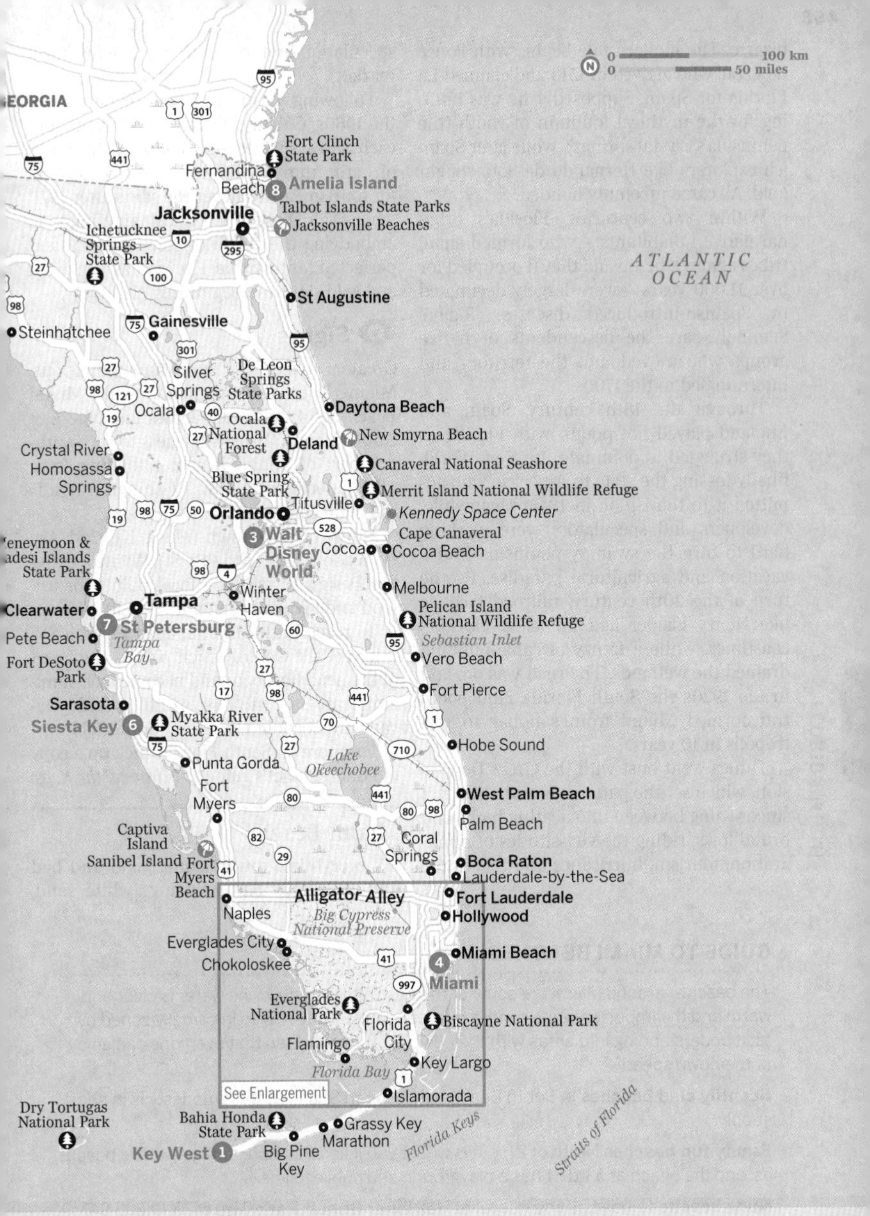

6 Relaxing on the sugar sand beaches of Sarasota's **Siesta Key** (p469).

7 Pondering the symbolism of the Hallucinogenic Toreador at the **Salvador Dalí Museum** in St Petersburg (p506).

8 Taking a bucolic breather amid the greenery on **Amelia Island** (p501).

bizarre. The modern tale begins with Ponce de León, who arrived in 1513 and claimed La Florida for Spain. Supposedly, he was hunting for the mythical fountain of youth (the peninsula's crystal springs), while later Spanish explorers like Hernando de Soto sought gold. All came up empty handed.

Within two centuries, Florida's original native inhabitants – who formed small tribes across a peninsula they'd occupied for over 11,000 years – were largely decimated by Spanish-introduced diseases. Today's Seminoles are the descendents of native groups who moved into the territory and intermingled in the 1700s.

Through the 18th century, Spain and England played hot potato with Florida as they struggled to dominate the New World, finally tossing the state to America, who admitted it to the Union in 1845. Meanwhile, developers and speculators were working hard to turn the swampy peninsula into a vacation and agricultural paradise. By the turn of the 20th century, railroad tycoons like Henry Flagler had unlocked Florida's coastlines, while a frenzy of canal-building drained the wetlands. The rush was on, and in the 1920s the South Florida land boom transformed Miami from sandbar to metropolis in 10 years.

Things went bust with the Great Depression, which set the pattern: Florida has ever since swung between intoxicating highs and brutal lows, riding the vicissitudes of immigration, tourism, hurricanes and real-estate speculation (not to mention a thriving black market).

Following Castro's Cuban revolution in the 1960s, Cuban exiles flooded Miami, and each successive decade has seen the ranks of Latin immigrants grow and diversify. As for tourism, it was never the same after 1971, when Walt Disney built his Magic Kingdom, embodying the vision of eternal youth and perfected fantasy that Florida has packaged and sold since the beginning.

Sights

Greater Miami is a sprawling metropolis. Miami is on the mainland, while Miami Beach lies 4 miles east across Biscayne Bay. **South Beach** (Map p472) refers to the southern part of Miami Beach, extending from 5th St north to 21st St. Washington Ave is the main commercial artery.

North of downtown (along NE 2nd Ave from about 17th St to 41st St), Wynwood and the Design District are focal points for art, food and nightlife. Just north is Little Haiti.

To reach Little Havana, head west on SW 8th St (Calle Ocho), which pierces the heart of the neighborhood (and becomes the Tamiami Trail/Hwy 41). Just south of Little Havana are Coconut Grove and Coral Gables.

For more on South Florida, pick up a copy of Lonely Planet's guide to *Miami & the Keys*.

Miami Beach

It's everything you imagine, good and bad and ridiculous and amazing: white sand,

GUIDE TO MIAMI BEACHES

The beaches around Miami are some of the best in the country. The water is clear and warm and the imported white sand is relatively white. They're also informally zoned by tacit understanding into areas with their own unique crowds so that everyone can enjoy at their own speed.

Scantily clad beaches In South Beach between 5th St and 21st St; modesty is in short supply.

Family-fun beaches North of 21st St is where you'll find the more family-friendly beaches, and the beach at 53rd St has a playground and public toilets.

Nude beaches Nude bathing is legal at **Haulover Beach Park** (Map p470; ☎305-947-3525; www.miamidade.gov/parks/parks/haulover_park.asp; 10800 Collins Ave; per car Mon-Fri $5, Sat & Sun $7; ⊙sunrise-sunset; P) in Sunny Isles. North of the lifeguard tower is predominantly gay; south is straight.

Gay beaches All of South Beach is gay-friendly, but a special concentration seems to hover around 12th St.

Windsurfing beaches Hobie Beach, along the Rickenbacker Causeway on the way to Key Biscayne, is actually known as 'Windsurfing Beach.'

deco design, preening models and shopaholic Europeans and Latin American royalty. That movie in your head of art-deco hotels, in-line-skating models, preening young studs and cruising cars? That's **Ocean Drive** (from 1st to 11th Sts), with the beach merely a backdrop for strutting peacocks. This confluence of waves, sunshine and exhibitionist beauty is what made South Beach (or 'SoBe') world-famous.

Just a few blocks north, **Lincoln Road** (between Alton Rd and Washington Ave) becomes a pedestrian mall, or outdoor fashion runway, so all may admire SoBe's fabulously gorgeous creatures. The excellent **Bass Museum of Art** (Map p470; ☎305-673-7530; www.bassmuseum.org; 2121 Park Ave; adult/child $8/6; ⌚noon-5pm Wed, Thu, Sat & Sun, to 9pm Fri) was closed for a major expansion during writing; it is scheduled to reopen in the fall of 2016.

★Art Deco Historic District AREA
(Map p472) South Beach's pastel heart is its Art Deco Historic District, which stretches from 18th St and south along Ocean Dr and Collins Ave. The smooth lines and pale color scheme of this designated historic district were ironically meant to, in the early 20th century, evoke the future and futuristic modes of transportation. Your first stop here should be the **Art Deco Welcome Center** (Map p472; ☎305-672-2014; www.mdpl.org; 1001 Ocean Dr, South Beach; ⌚9:30am-5pm Fri-Wed, to 7pm Thu), run by the Miami Design Preservation League (MDPL).

★Wolfsonian-FIU MUSEUM
(Map p472; ☎305-531-1001; www.wolfsonian.org; 1001 Washington Ave; adult/child 6-12yr $7/5, from 6-9pm Fri free; ⌚10am-6pm, to 9pm Thu & Fri) A fascinating collection that spans transportation, urbanism, industrial design, advertising and political propaganda from the late 19th to mid-20th century. Visit this excellent design museum early in your stay to put the aesthetics of Miami Beach into fascinating context. By chronicling the interior evolution of everyday life, the Wolfsonian reveals how these trends were architecturally manifested in SoBe's exterior deco.

Lincoln Road Mall ROAD
(Map p472; http://lincolnroadmall.com) This outdoor pedestrian thoroughfare between Alton Rd and Washington Ave is all about seeing and being seen; there are times when Lincoln feels less like a road and more like a runway. Carl Fisher, the father of Miami Beach, envisioned the road as a '5th Ave of the South.' Morris Lapidus, one of the founders of the loopy, neobaroque Miami Beach style, designed much of the mall, including shady overhangs, waterfall structures and traffic barriers that look like the marbles a giant might play with.

BEST BEACHES

You'll never want for shoreline in the Sunshine State. Here are a few of our favorites.

- Siesta Key (p506)
- South Beach (p468)
- Bahia Honda (p492)
- St George Island (p519)

New World Center BUILDING
(Map p472; ☎305-673-3330; www.newworldcenter.com; 500 17th St; tours $5; ⌚tours 4pm Tue & Thu, noon Fri & Sat) Designed by Frank Gehry, this performance hall rises majestically out of a manicured lawn just above Lincoln Rd, looking somewhat like a tissue box from the year 3000 with a glass facade; note the 'fluttering' stone waves that pop out of the exterior. The grounds form a 2.5-acre public park; performances inside the center are projected outside via a 7000-sq-ft projection wall (like you're in the classiest drive-in movie theater in the universe).

South Pointe Park PARK
(Map p472; ☎305-673-7779; 1 Washington Ave; ⌚sunrise-10pm; 👪🐾) The very southern tip of Miami Beach has been converted into a lovely park, replete with manicured grass for lounging; views over a remarkably teal and fresh ocean; a restaurant; a refreshment stand; warm, scrubbed-stone walkways; and lots of folks who want to enjoy the great weather and views sans the South Beach strutting. That said, we saw two model photo shoots here in under an hour, so it's not all casual relaxation.

Downtown Miami

Downtown Miami is rapidly evolving, as old bazaars of cheap luggage and electronics are gentrified and replaced by art galleries, publicly designated arts space, restaurants, bars and the real-estate projects that accompany such shifts. Want to watch the water? Head to pretty **Bayfront Park** (Map p470; ☎305-358-7550; www.bayfrontparkmiami.com; 301 N Biscayne Blvd).

Greater Miami

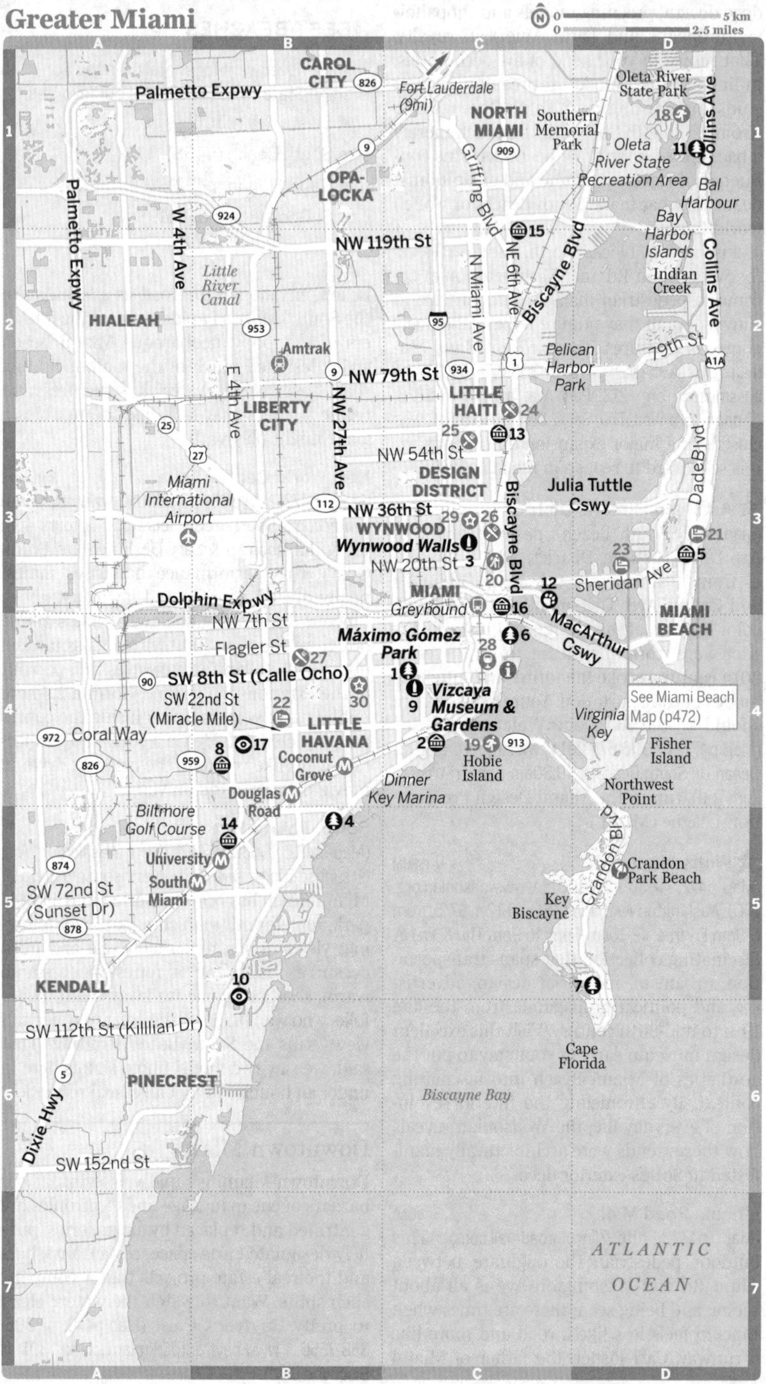

Greater Miami

Metromover MONORAIL
(☎305-891-3131; www.miamidade.gov/transit/metromover.asp; ⏰5am-midnight) This elevated, electric monorail is hardly big enough to serve the mass-transit needs of the city, and has become something of a tourist attraction. Whatever its virtues as a commuting tool, the Metromover is a really great (and free!) way to see central Miami from a height (which helps, given the skyscraper-canyon nature of downtown). Because it's gratis, Metromover has a reputation as a hangout for the homeless, but commuters use it as well.

Pérez Art Museum Miami MUSEUM
(PAMM; Map p470; ☎305-375-3000; www.pamm.org; 1103 Biscayne Blvd; adult/senior & student $16/12; ⏰10am-6pm Tue-Sun, to 9pm Thu, closed Mon; P) The Pérez can claim fine rotating exhibits that concentrate on post-WWII international art, but just as impressive are its location and exterior. This art institution inaugurated Museum Park, a patch of land that overseas the broad blue swath of Biscayne Bay. Swiss architects Herzog & de Meuron designed the structure, which integrates tropical foliage, glass and metal – a melding of tropical vitality and fresh modernism that is a nice architectural analogy for Miami itself.

★**Adrienne Arsht Center for the Performing Arts** BUILDING
(Map p470; ☎305-949-6722; www.arshtcenter.com; 1300 N Biscayne Blvd) This performing-arts center is Miami's beautiful, beloved baby. It is also a major component of downtown's urban equivalent of a face-lift and several regimens of Botox. Designed by Cesar Pelli (the man who brought you Kuala Lumpur's Petronas Towers), the center has two main components, connected by a thin pedestrian bridge. Inside the theaters there's a sense of ocean and land sculpted by wind; the rounded balconies rise up in spirals that resemble a sliced-open seashell

Little Havana

As SW 8th St heads away from downtown, it becomes **Calle Ocho** (pronounced *kah*-yeh *oh*-cho, Spanish for 'Eighth Street'). That's when you know you've arrived in Little Havana, the most prominent community of Cuban Americans in the US. Despite the cultural monuments, this is no Cuban theme

Miami Beach

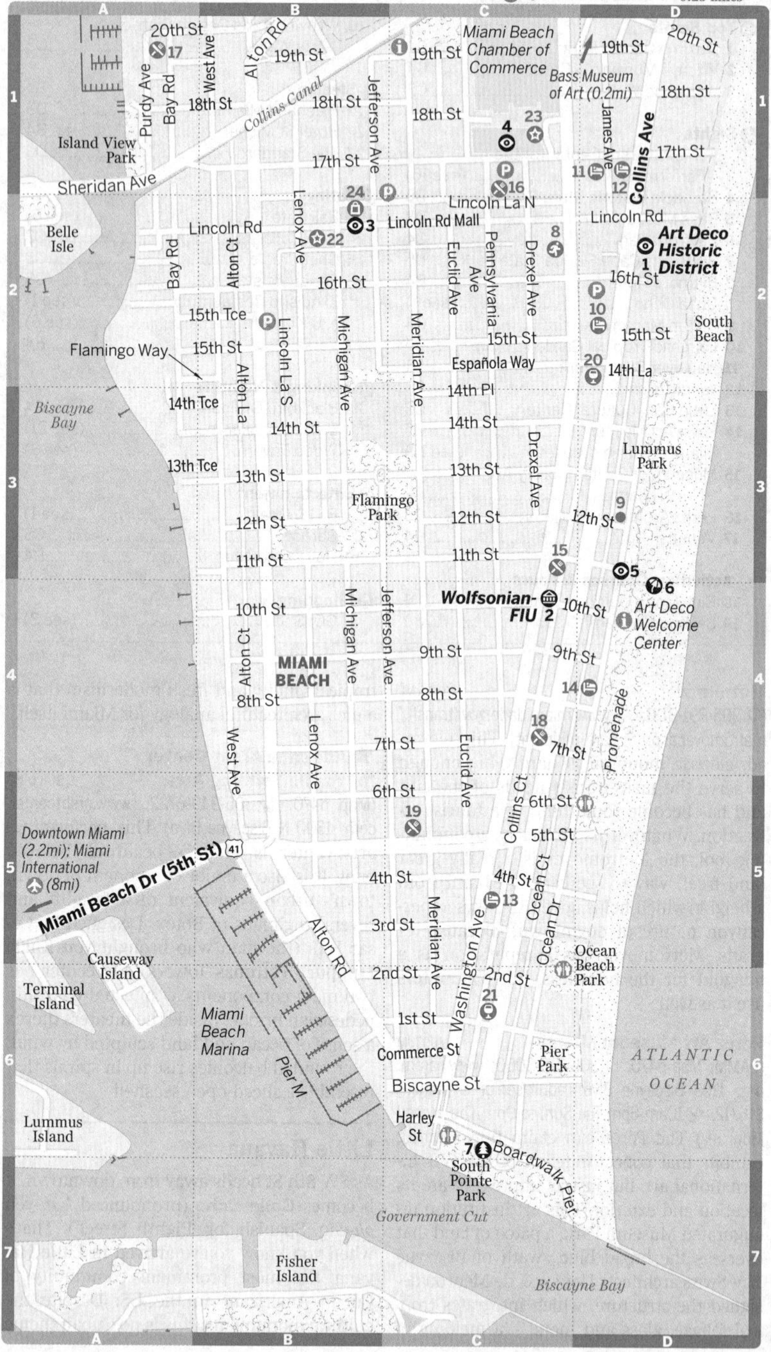

FLORIDA MIAMI

Miami Beach

Top Sights
1 Art Deco Historic District D2
2 Wolfsonian-FIU C4

Sights
3 Lincoln Road Mall B2
4 New World Center C1
5 Ocean Drive D3
6 South Beach D4
7 South Pointe Park C6

Activities, Courses & Tours
8 Fritz's Skate, Bike & Surf C2
9 Miami Design Preservation League D3
Miami Design Preservation League .... (see 9)

Sleeping
10 Aqua Hotel D2
11 Bed & Drinks D1
12 Gale South Beach D1
13 Hotel St Augustine C5
14 Pelican Hotel D4

Eating
15 11th St Diner C3
16 Oolite C1
17 Pubbelly A1
18 Puerto Sagua C4
19 Tap Tap C5

Drinking & Nightlife
20 Kill Your Idol D2
21 Room C6

Entertainment
22 Colony Theater B2
23 Fillmore Miami Beach C1

Shopping
24 Books & Books B2

park. The district remains a living, breathing immigrant enclave, though one whose residents have become, admittedly, more broadly Latin American than simply Cuban. One of the best times to come is the last Friday of the month during **Viernes Culturales** (www.viernesculturales.org; ⏲7-11pm), or 'Cultural Fridays,' a street fair showcasing Latino artists and musicians.

★ Máximo Gómez Park PARK
(Map p470; SW 8th St at SW 15th Ave; ⏲9am-6pm) Little Havana's most evocative reminder of Old Cuba is Máximo Gómez Park, or 'Domino Park,' where the sound of elderly men trash-talking over games of chess is harmonized by the quick clack-clack of slapping dominoes. The jarring backing track, plus the heavy smell of cigars and a sunrise-bright mural of the 1993 Summit of the Americas, combine to make Máximo Gómez one of the most sensory sites in Miami (although it's one of the most tourist-heavy as well).

Cuba Ocho GALLERY
(Map p470; ☎305-285-5880; www.cubaocho.com; 1465 SW 8th St; ⏲11am-3am Tue-Sat) The jewel of the Little Havana Art District, Cuba Ocho functions as a community center, art gallery and research outpost for all things Cuban. The interior resembles an old Havana cigar bar, yet the walls are decked out in artwork that references both the classical past of Cuban art and its avant-garde future. Frequent music, films, drama performances, readings and other events go off every week. The center opens during the evening for these events; check online for more information.

Cuban Memorials MONUMENT
(Map p470; SW 13th Ave & 8-10th St) Two blocks of SW 13th Ave contain a series of monuments to Cuban and Cuban American icons. The memorials include the **Eternal Torch in Honor of the 2506th Brigade**, for the exiles who died during the Bay of Pigs Invasion; a **José Martí memorial**; and a **Madonna statue**, supposedly illuminated by a shaft of holy light every afternoon. Bursting out of the island in the center of the boulevard is a massive ceiba tree, revered by followers of Santeria.

Design District, Wynwood & Little Haiti

Proving that SoBe doesn't hold the lease on hip, these two trendy areas north of downtown – all but deserted 25 years ago – have ensconced themselves as bastions of art and design. The Design District is a mecca for interior designers, home to dozens of galleries and contemporary furniture, fixture and design showrooms. Just south of the Design District, Wynwood is a notable arts district, with myriad galleries and art studios housed in abandoned factories and warehouses.

The home of Miami's Haitian refugees, Little Haiti is defined by brightly painted homes, markets and *botanicas* (voodoo shops).

DON'T MISS

WYNWOOD GALLERIES

In Wynwood, Miami's hip proving ground for avant-garde art, 'Wipsters' (Wynwood hipsters) stock dozens of galleries with 'guerrilla' installations, new murals, graffiti and other inscrutableness. The best way to experience the scene is to attend the **Wynwood and Design District Arts Walks** (Map p470; www.artcircuits.com; ⌚ 7-10pm 2nd Sat of the month) FREE, with music, food and wine.

★Wynwood Walls PUBLIC ART
(Map p470; www.thewynwoodwalls.com; NW 2nd Ave btwn 25th & 26th Sts) Wynwood Walls is a collection of murals and paintings laid out over an open courtyard that invariably bowls people over with its sheer color profile and unexpected location. What's on offer tends to change with the coming and going of major arts events such as Art Basel, but it's always interesting stuff.

Little Haiti Cultural Center GALLERY
(Map p470; ☎305-960-2969; http://littlehaiticulturalcenter.com; 212 NE 59th Tce; ⌚10am-9pm Tue-Fri, 9am-4pm Sat, 11am-7pm Sun) This cultural center hosts an art gallery, dance classes, drama productions and a Caribbean-themed market on weekends (9:30am to 8pm Thurday to Saturday, to 6pm Sunday). The best time to visit is for the **Big Night in Little Haiti** (www.rhythmfoundation.com/series/big-night-in-little-haiti), a street party held on the third Friday of every month from 6pm to 10pm. The celebration is rife with music, Caribbean food and beer, but was in need of external funding at the time of writing.

Coral Gables & Coconut Grove

For a slower pace and a more European feel, head inland. Designed as a 'model suburb' by George Merrick in the early 1920s, Coral Gables is a Mediterranean-style village that's centered around the shops and restaurants of the **Miracle Mile**, a four-block section of Coral Way between Douglas and LeJeune Rds. Coconut Grove is a trendy, student-oriented neighborhood filled with shopping, restaurants and jungly park space.

★Vizcaya Museum & Gardens HISTORIC BUILDING
(Map p470; ☎305-250-9133; www.vizcayamuseum.org; 3251 S Miami Ave; adult/6-12yr/student & senior $18/6/10; ⌚9:30am-4:30pm Wed-Mon; P) They call Miami the Magic City, and if it is, this Italian villa, the housing equivalent of a Fabergé egg, is its most fairy-tale residence. In 1916 industrialist James Deering started a Miami tradition by making a ton of money and building ridiculously grandiose digs. He employed 1000 people (then 10% of the local population) and stuffed his home with 15th- to 19th-century furniture, tapestries, paintings and decorative arts; today, the grounds are used for the display of rotating contemporary-art exhibitions.

Barnacle Historic State Park PARK
(Map p470; ☎305-442-6866; www.floridastateparks.org/thebarnacle; 3485 Main Hwy; admission $2, house tours adult/child $3/1; ⌚9am-5pm Wed-Mon; 👪) In the center of Coconut Grove is the 1891, 5-acre pioneer residence of Ralph Monroe, Miami's first honorable snowbird. The house is open for guided tours, and the park it's located on is a lovely, shady oasis for strolling. Barnacle hosts frequent (and lovely) moonlight concerts, from jazz to classical. A little way down Main Hwy, on the other side of the road, there's a small Buddhist temple shaded by large groves of banyan trees.

Biltmore Hotel HISTORIC BUILDING
(Map p470; ☎855-311-6903; www.biltmorehotel.com; 1200 Anastasia Ave; ⌚tours 1:30 & 2:30pm Sun; P) The crown jewel of Coral Gables is this magnificent edifice that once housed a speakeasy run by Al Capone. Back in the day, imported gondolas transported celebrity guests such as Judy Garland and the Vanderbilts around because, of course, there was a private canal system out the back. The largest hotel pool in the continental USA, which resembles a sultan's water garden from *One Thousand & One Nights*, is still here. Catch a free tour on Sunday afternoons.

Venetian Pool HISTORIC SITE
(Map p470; ☎305-460-5306; www.coralgablesvenetianpool.com; 2701 De Soto Blvd; adult/child $12/7; ⌚hours vary; 👪) One of the few pools listed on the National Register of Historic Places, this is a wonderland of coral rock caves, cascading waterfalls, a palm-fringed island and Venetian-style moorings. Take a swim and follow in the footsteps (fin-steps?) of stars like Esther Williams and Johnny 'Tarzan' Weissmuller. Opening hours vary depending on the season; call or check the website for details.

MIAMI FOR CHILDREN

The best beaches for kids are in Miami Beach north of 21st St, especially at 53rd St, which has a playground and public toilets, and the dune-packed beach around 73rd St. Also head south to Matheson Hammock Park, which has calm artificial lagoons.

Miami Children's Museum (Map p470; ☎305-373-5437; www.miamichildrensmuseum.org; 980 MacArthur Causeway; admission $18; ⏲10am-6pm; 👪) On Watson Island, between downtown Miami and Miami Beach, this hands-on museum has fun music and art studios, as well as some branded 'work' experiences that make it feel a tad corporate.

Jungle Island (Map p470; ☎305-400-7000; www.jungleisland.com; 1111 Parrot Jungle Trail, off MacArthur Causeway; adult/child/senior $40/32/38; ⏲10am-5pm; P 👪) Jungle Island is packed with tropical birds, alligators, orangutans, chimps and (to the delight of *Napoleon Dynamite* fans) a liger – a cross between a lion and a tiger.

Zoo Miami (Metrozoo; ☎305-251-0400; www.miamimetrozoo.com; 12400 SW 152nd St; adult/child $18/14; ⏲10am-5pm Mon-Fri, 9:30am-5:30pm Sat & Sun) Miami's tropical weather makes strolling around Zoo Miami almost feel like a day in the wild. For a quick overview (and because the zoo is so big and the sun is broiling), hop on the Safari Monorail; it departs every 20 minutes.

Monkey Jungle (☎305-235-1611; www.monkeyjungle.com; 14805 SW 216th St; adult/child/senior $30/24/28; ⏲9:30am-5pm, last entry 4pm; P 👪) The tagline, 'Where humans are caged and monkeys run free,' tells you all you need to know – except for the fact that it's in far south Miami.

Lowe Art Museum MUSEUM
(Map p470; ☎305-284-3535; www.lowemuseum.org; 1301 Stanford Dr; adult/student $10/5; ⏲10am-4pm Tue-Sat, noon-4pm Sun) The Lowe's tremendous collection satisfies a wide range of tastes, but it's particularly strong in Asian, African and South Pacific art and archaeology, and its pre-Columbian and Mesoamerican collection is stunning.

Greater Miami

Fairchild Tropical Garden GARDENS
(Map p470; ☎305-667-1651; www.fairchildgarden.org; 10901 Old Cutler Rd; adult/child/senior $25/12/18; ⏲7:30am-4:30pm; P 👪) If you need to escape Miami's madness, consider a green day in the country's largest tropical botanical garden. A butterfly grove, jungle biospheres, and marsh and keys habitats, plus art installations from folks like Roy Lichtenstein, are all stunning. In addition to easy-to-follow, self-guided walking tours, a free 40-minute tram tours the entire park on the hour from 10am to 3pm.

Museum of Contemporary Art North Miami MUSEUM
(MoCA; Map p470; ☎305-893-6211; www.mocanomi.org; 770 NE 125th St; adult/student & senior $5/3; ⏲11am-5pm Tue-Fri & Sun, 1-9pm Sat; P) North of downtown, MoCA has frequently changing exhibitions focusing on international, national and emerging artists.

Key Biscayne

Bill Baggs Cape Florida State Park PARK
(Map p470; ☎305-361-5811; www.floridastateparks.org/capeflorida; 1200 S Crandon Blvd; per car/person $8/2; ⏲8am-sunset; P 👪 🐾) If you don't make it to the Florida Keys, come to this park for a taste of their unique island ecosystems. The 494-acre space is a tangled clot of tropical fauna and dark mangroves, all interconnected by sandy trails and wooden boardwalks and surrounded by miles of pale ocean.

Activities

Cycling & In-Line Skating

Skating or cycling the strip along Ocean Dr in South Beach is pure Miami; also try the Rickenbacker Causeway to Key Biscayne.

DecoBike CYCLING
(☎305-532-9494; www.decobike.com; 30 min/1hr/2hr/4hr/1-day rental $4/6/10/18/24) Flat, architecturally rich Miami Beach and Miami are best accessed via bicycle, and the

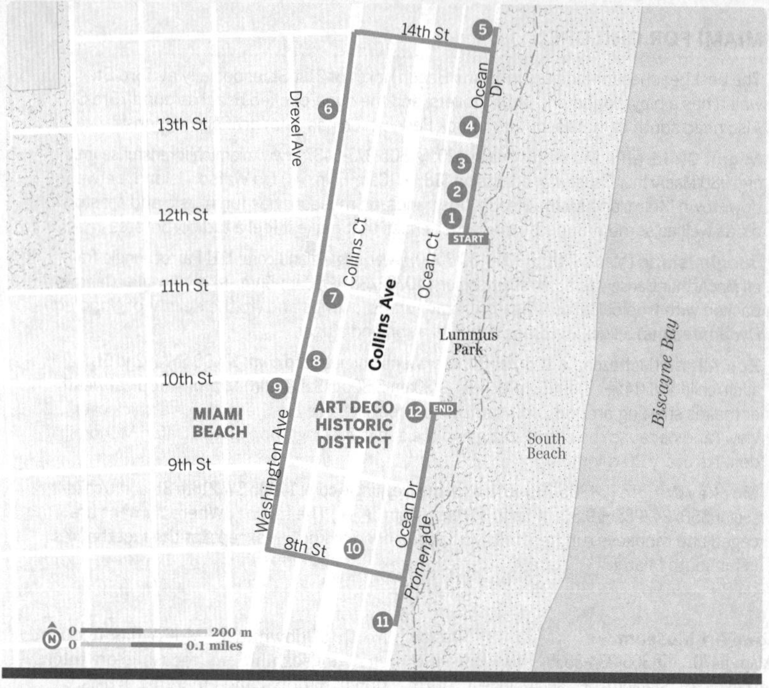

City Walk
Art-Deco Magic

START ART DECO WELCOME CENTER
END EDISON HOTEL
LENGTH 1-2 MILES; 30 MINUTES

There are excellent walking tours available for the Art Deco Historic District – both guided and self-guided – but if you just want to hit the highlights, follow this quick and easy path.

Start at the 1 **Art Deco Welcome Center** (p469) at the corner of Ocean Dr and 12th St, and head inside for a taste of deco style. Next, go north on Ocean Dr. Between 12th and 14th Sts, you'll see three classic examples of deco hotels: the 2 **Leslie**, with classic 'eyebrows' and a typically boxy shape; the 3 **Carlyle**, which was featured in the film *The Birdcage;* and the graceful 4 **Cardozo Hotel**, with sleek, rounded edges. At 14th St, peek inside 5 **Winter Haven** to see its fabulous terrazzo floors.

Turn left and head along 14th St to Washington Ave, and turn left again to find the 6 **US Post Office** at 13th St. Step inside to admire the domed ceiling and marble stamp tables, and try whispering into the domed ceiling. Two blocks down on your left is the 7 **11th St Diner** (p478), a gleaming aluminum deco-style Pullman car where you can also stop for lunch. At 10th St, you'll find the 8 **Wolfsonian-FIU** (p469), an excellent museum with many deco-era treasures, and across the street is the beautifully restored 9 **Hotel Astor**.

Turn left on 8th St and head east to Collins Ave. On the corner, you'll see 10 **The Hotel** – originally the Tiffany Hotel and still topped by a deco-style neon spire bearing that name. Continue to Ocean Dr and turn right to see the 11 **Colony Hotel** and its famous neon sign, then double back to find the 1935 12 **Edison Hotel**, a creation of deco legend Henry Hohauser, half a block past 9th St.

easiest way of finding a bicycle is this excellent bike-sharing program.

Fritz's Skate, Bike & Surf SKATING
(Map p472; ☎305-532-1954; www.fritzsmiamibeach.com; 1620 Washington Ave; bike & skate rentals per hour/day/week $10/24/69; ⏲10am-9pm Mon-Sat, to 8pm Sun) Sports equipment rentals and free in-line skate lessons (10:30am Sunday).

Water Sports

Blue Moon Outdoor Center WATER SPORTS
(Map p470; ☎305-957-3040; http://bluemoonoutdoor.com; 3400 NE 163rd St; kayaks per 90min/3hr $23/41; ⏲9am-7:30pm Mon-Fri, 8am-8pm Sat & Sun) The official concessionaire for outdoor rentals in Miami area state parks.

Sailboards Miami WATER SPORTS
(Map p470; ☎305-892-8992; www.sailboardsmiami.com; 1 Rickenbacker Causeway; ⏲10am-6pm Mon-Wed & Fri-Sun) The waters off Key Biscayne are perfect for windsurfing, kayaking and kiteboarding; get your gear and lessons here.

Tours

Miami Design Preservation League WALKING
(Map p472; ☎305-672-2014; www.mdpl.org; 1001 Ocean Dr; guided tours adult/student $25/20; ⏲10:30am daily & 6:30pm Thu) Learn about art deco and its icons on a 90-minute walking tour departing from the Art Deco Welcome Center.

History Miami Tours WALKING, CYCLING
(☎305-375-5792; www.historymiami.org/tours; tours $30-60) Historian extraordinaire Dr Paul George leads fascinating bike, boat, coach and walking tours, including those that focus on Stiltsville. Get the full menu online.

EcoAdventure Bike Tours CYCLING
(☎305-365-3018; www.miamidade.gov/ecoadventures; tours from $28) The Dade County parks system leads excellent bike tours through peaceful areas of Miami and Miami Beach, including along beaches, on Key Biscayne and into the Everglades.

Festivals & Events

Calle Ocho Festival CULTURAL
(Carnaval Miami; www.carnavalmiami.com; ⏲Mar) This massive street party in March is the culmination of Carnaval Miami, a 10-day celebration of Latin culture.

Winter Music Conference MUSIC
(http://wintermusicconference.com; ⏲Mar) This festival of dance music and electronica takes place every March.

Art Basel Miami Beach ART
(www.artbaselmiamibeach.com; ⏲Dec) An internationally known art show held each December.

Sleeping

Miami Beach is the well-hyped mecca for stylish boutique hotels in renovated art-deco buildings. For hotel parking, expect to pay $20 to $35 a night.

South Beach

Bed & Drinks HOSTEL $
(Map p472; ☎786-230-1234; http://bedsndrinks.com; 1676 James Ave; dm/d from $25/149, private 6-person dm $157) This hostel pretty shamelessly plays to the sex-appeal-seeking crowd – check the name – but hey, it's by Lincoln Rd, so the placement works. The rooms are functional and the vibe is young international folk down to party, while the staff seems a bit indifferent.

★**Hotel St Augustine** BOUTIQUE HOTEL $$
(Map p472; ☎305-532-0570; www.hotelstaugustine.com; 347 Washington Ave; r $152-289; P ❄ 📶) Wood that's blonder than Barbie and a crisp-and-clean deco theme combine to create one of South Beach's most elegant yet stunningly modern sleeps. The familiar, warm service is the cherry on top for this hip-and-homey standout, although the soothing lighting and glass showers – that turn into personal steam rooms at the flick of a switch – are pretty appealing too.

Aqua Hotel BOUTIQUE HOTEL $$
(Map p472; ☎305-538-4361; www.aquamiami.com; 1530 Collins Ave; r $133-180, ste from $200; P ❄ 📶 🏊) A front desk made of shiny surfboard sets the mellow tone at this former motel – the old, family kind where the rooms are set around a pool. That old-school vibe barely survives under the soft glare of aqua spotlights and an alfresco lounging area. The sleekness of the rooms is offset by quirky furniture and deep-blue-sea bathrooms.

★**The Standard** BOUTIQUE HOTEL $$$
(Map p470; ☎305-673-1717; www.standardhotels.com/miami; 40 Island Ave; r $180-300, ste $500-

965;) Look for the upside-down 'Standard' sign on the old Lido building on Belle Island (between South Beach and downtown Miami) and you'll find the Standard – which is anything but. This excellent boutique blends a bevy of spa services, hipster funk and South Beach sex, and the result is a '50s motel gone glam. There are organic wooden floors, raised white beds, and gossamer curtains, which open onto a courtyard of earthly delights, including a heated hammam (Turkish bath).

★Gale South Beach HOTEL **$$$**

(Map p472; 305-673-0199; http://galehotel.com; 1690 Collins Ave; r $160-300;) The Gale's exterior is an admirable re-creation of classic boxy deco aesthetic expanded to the grand dimensions of a modern SoBe super resort. This blend of classic and haute South Beach carries on indoors, where you'll find bright rooms with clean colors and sharp lines and a retro-chic vibe inspired by the mid-Century Modern movement.

★Pelican Hotel BOUTIQUE HOTEL **$$$**

(Map p472; 305-673-3373; www.pelicanhotel.com; 826 Ocean Dr; r $198-350, ste $400-850;) The owners of Diesel jeans are the minds behind this mad experiment: 30 themed rooms that come off like a fantasy-suite hotel dipped in hip. From the cowboy-hipster chic of 'High Corral, OK Chaparral' to the jungly electric tiger stripes of 'Me Tarzan, You Vain,' all the rooms are completely different fun and even come with their own 'suggested soundtrack'.

Northern Miami Beach

Freehand Miami BOUTIQUE HOTEL **$$**

(Map p470; 305-531-2727; http://thefreehand.com; 2727 Indian Creek Dr; dm $28-49, r $160-214;) The Freehand is the brilliant re-imagining of the old Indian Creek Hotel, a classic of the Miami Beach scene. Rooms are comfortably minimalist, with just the right amount of local artwork and wooden tones to strike a nice balance between warm funky and cool hip. Dorms serve the hostel crowd, and the on-site Broken Shaker (p480) is one of the best bars in town.

Coral Gables

Hotel St Michel HOTEL **$$**

(Map p470; 305-444-1666; www.hotelstmichel.com; 162 Alcazar Ave; r $124-225;) You could conceivably think you're in Europe in this vaulted place at Coral Gables, with inlaid floors, old-world charm and just 28 rooms.

Eating

Florida's most international city has an international-level food scene.

South Beach

Walking up Ocean Ave, you'll find a veritable gauntlet of restaurants taking over the patios and sidewalks of almost every hotel facing the beach, all hawking lunch specials and happy-hour deals. Competition is fierce, which means you can eat inexpensively. Stroll till you find something that suits, anywhere between 5th St and 14th Pl.

Puerto Sagua CUBAN **$**

(Map p472; 305-673-1115; 700 Collins Ave; mains $6-20; 7:30am-2am) Pull up to the counter for authentic, tasty and inexpensive *ropa vieja* (shredded beef), black beans and *arroz con pollo* (rice with chicken) – plus some of the best Cuban coffee in town – at this beloved Cuban diner.

11th St Diner DINER **$**

(Map p472; 305-534-6373; www.eleventhstreetdiner.com; 1065 Washington Ave; mains $9-18; 24hr except midnight-7am Wed) This deco diner housed inside a gleaming Pullman train car sees round-the-clock activity and is especially popular with people staggering home from clubs.

★Tap Tap HAITIAN **$$**

(Map p472; 305-672-2898; www.taptapmiamibeach.com; 819 5th St; mains $9-20; noon-9pm) In this tropi-psychedelic Haitian eatery, you dine under bright murals of Papa Legba, enjoying cuisine that's a happy marriage of West Africa, France and the Caribbean: try spicy pumpkin soup, curried goat and *mayi moulen*, a signature side of cornmeal.

★Pubbelly FUSION **$$**

(Map p472; 305-532-7555; www.pubbellyboys.com/miami/pubbelly; 1418 20th Street; mains $11-26; 6pm-midnight Tue-Thu & Sun, to 1am Fri & Sat) Pubbelly's dining genre is hard to pinpoint. It skews between Asian, North American and Latin American, gleaning the best from all cuisines. Examples? Try duck and scallion dumplings, or the mouth-watering udon 'carbonara' with pork belly, poached eggs and parmesan. Hand-crafted cocktails wash down the dishes a treat.

Oolite MODERN AMERICAN **$$$**
(Map p472; 305-907-5535; www.ooliterestaurant.com; 1661 Pennsylvania Ave; mains $20-49; 4-11pm Wed-Thu, to midnight Fri & Sat, 11am-11pm Sun) Oolite has all the elements of a trendy, twenty-teens Miami Beach hot spot: a James Beard–nominated chef; gluten-free menu that focuses on local sourcing and health-conscious ingredients; a weird name. But it's also very good; a tapenade of citrus, swordfish and peppers does a hot dance on the tongue, while guava curry goat is a revelation.

Downtown Miami

Bali Cafe INDONESIAN **$**
(Map p470; 305-358-5751; 109 NE 2nd Ave; mains $6-14; 11am-4pm daily, 6-10pm Mon-Fri;) It's odd to think of the clean flavors of sushi and the bright richness of Indonesian cuisine coming together in harmony, but they're happily married in this tropical hole-in-the-wall. Have some spicy tuna rolls for an appetizer, then follow up with *soto betawi* (beef soup cooked with coconut milk, ginger and shallots).

★**NIU Kitchen** SPANISH **$$**
(Map p470; 786-542-5070; http://niukitchen.com; 134 NE 2nd Ave; mains $14-22; noon-3:30pm Mon-Fri, 6-10pm Sun-Thu, to 11pm Fri & Sat, 1-4pm Sat & Sun;) NIU is a small living-room-sized restaurant consistently full of impossibly hip people eating impossibly good contemporary Catalan cuisine. Rarely have we had cuisine that's so compellingly different, from a poached egg with truffled potato foam to manchego and scallop pasta. Wash it all down with good wine and order multiple dishes to share.

Little Havana

★**Exquisito Restaurant** CUBAN **$**
(Map p470; 305-643-0227; www.elexquisitomiami.com; 1510 SW 8th St; mains $7-13; 7am-11pm) For great Cuban cuisine in the heart of Little Havana, this place is exquisite (ha ha). The roast pork has a tangy citrus kick and the *ropa vieja* is wonderfully rich and filling. Even standard sides like beans and rice and roasted plantains are executed with a little more care and tastiness. Prices are a steal.

Versailles CUBAN **$$**
(Map p470; 305-444-0240; www.versaillesrestaurant.com; 3555 SW 8th St; mains $5-26; 8am-1am Mon-Thu, to 2:30am Fri, to 3:30am Sat, 9am-1am Sun) Versailles (ver-sigh-yay) is an institution, one of the mainstays of Miami's Cuban gastronomic scene. Try the ground beef in a gratin sauce or chicken breast cooked in creamy garlic sauce. Older Cubans and Miami's Latin political elite still love coming here, so you've got a real chance to rub elbows with a who's who of Miami's most prominent Latin citizens.

Design District & Wynwood

Chef Creole HAITIAN **$**
(Map p470; 305-754-2223; http://chefcreole.com; 200 NW 54th St; mains $7-20; 11am-11pm Mon-Sat) When you need Caribbean food on the cheap, head to the edge of Little Haiti and this excellent take-out shack. Order up fried conch, oxtail or fish, ladle rice and beans on the side, and you'll be full for a week. Enjoy the food on nearby picnic benches while Haitian music blasts out of tinny speakers – as island an experience as they come.

LATIN AMERICAN SPICE IN MIAMI

Thanks to its immigrant heritage, Miami is legendary for its authentic Cuban, Haitian, Brazilian and other Latin American cuisines. Cuban food is a mix of Caribbean, African and Latin American influences, and the fertile cross-pollination of these traditions has given rise to endlessly creative, tasty gourmet fusions, sometimes dubbed 'nuevo Latino,' 'nouvelle Floridian' or 'Floribbean' cuisine.

For a good introduction to Cuban food, sidle up to a Cuban *loncheria* (snack bar) and order a *pan cubano:* a buttered, grilled baguette stuffed with ham, roast pork, cheese, mustard and pickles. For dinner, order the classic *ropa vieja:* shredded flank steak cooked in tomatoes and peppers, and accompanied by fried plantains, black beans and yellow rice.

Other treats to look for include Haitian *griots* (marinated fried pork), Jamaican jerk chicken, Brazilian BBQ, Central American *gallo pinto* (red beans and rice) and *batidos* (a milky, refreshing Latin American fruit smoothie).

Enriqueta's LATIN AMERICAN $

(Map p470; ☎305-573-4681; 186 NE 29th St; mains $5-8; ⏰6am-4pm Mon-Fri, to 2pm Sat) Back in the day, Puerto Ricans, not installation artists, ruled Wynwood. Have a taste of those times in this perpetually packed roadhouse, where the Latin-diner ambience is as strong as the steaming shots of *cortadito* (Cuban-style coffee) served at the counter. Balance the local gallery fluff with a steak-and-potato-stick sandwich.

★**Blue Collar** AMERICAN $$

(Map p470; ☎305-756-0366; www.bluecollarmiami.com; 6730 Biscayne Blvd; mains $15-24; ⏰11:30am-3:30pm Mon-Fri, 11am-3:30pm Sat & Sun, 6-10pm Sun-Thu, to 11pm Fri & Sat; P) It's not easy striking a balance between laid-back and delicious in a city like Miami, where even 'casual' eateries can feel like nightclubs, but Blue Collar has the formula nailed. Friendly staff serve all-American fare sexied the hell up, from crispy snapper to smoky ribs to a superlatively good cheeseburger. A well-curated veg board keeps non-carnivores happy.

Drinking & Nightlife

Miami truly comes alive at night. There is always something going on, and usually till the wee hours, with many bars staying open till 3am or 5am. For events calendars and gallery, bar and club reviews, check out www.cooljunkie.com and www.beachedmiami.com.

★**Wood Tavern** BAR

(Map p470; ☎305-748-2828; http://woodtavernmiami.com; 2531 NW 2nd Ave; ⏰5pm-3am Tue-Sat, to 11pm Sun) Wood is a lot of things: local Miami kids who don't want a dive, but don't want the long lines and attitude of South Beach. Ergo: a cozy front bar, an outdoor space that includes picnic benches, a wooden stage complete with bleachers and giant Jenga game, and an attached art gallery with rotating exhibits.

★**Room** BAR

(Map p472; ☎305-531-6061; www.theotheroom.com; 100 Collins Ave; ⏰7pm-5am) This dark, atmospheric boutique beer bar in SoBe is a gem: hip and sexy as hell but with a low-key attitude. Per the name, it's small and gets crowded.

★**Broken Shaker** BAR

(Map p470; ☎786-325-8974; 2727 Indian Creek Dr; ⏰6pm-3am Mon-Fri, 2pm-3am Sat & Sun) Craft cocktails are having their moment in Miami, and if mixology is in the spotlight, you can bet Broken Shaker is sharing the glare. Expert bartenders run this spot, located in the back of the Freehand Miami hotel (p478), which takes up one closet-sized indoor niche and a sprawling outdoor courtyard of excellent drinks and beautiful people.

★**Blackbird Ordinary** BAR

(Map p470; ☎305-671-3307; www.blackbirdordinary.com; 729 SW 1st Ave; ⏰3pm-5am Mon-Fri, 5pm-5am Sat & Sun) The Ordinary is almost that…well, no. It isn't ordinary at all – this is an excellent bar, with great cocktails (the London Sparrow, with gin, cayenne, lemon juice and passion fruit, goes down well) and an enormous courtyard. But it is 'ordinary' in the sense that it's a come-as-you-are joint that eschews judgment for easy camaraderie.

Kill Your Idol BAR

(Map p472; ☎305-672-1852; http://killyouridol.com; 222 Española Way; ⏰8pm-5am) This self-conscious dive aims snooty condescension at South Beach's celebrity scene with one hand (see: the name of the place) while sipping Pabst Blue Ribbon with the other. Precocious? But it does have sweet postmodern art, graffiti and undeniably cute hipsters.

Ball & Chain LIVE MUSIC

(Map p470; www.ballandchainmiami.com; 1513 SW 8th Street; ⏰noon-midnight, to 3am Thu-Sat, 2-10pm Sun) The Ball & Chain has survived several incarnations over the years. Back in 1935, when 8th St was more Jewish than Latino, it was the sort of jazz joint Billie Holiday would croon in. That iteration closed in 1957, but the new Ball & Chain is still dedicated to music and good times – specifically, Latin music and tropical cocktails.

Bardot CLUB

(Map p470; ☎305-576-5570; www.bardotmiami.com; 3456 N Miami Ave; ⏰8pm-3am Tue & Wed, to 5am Thu-Sat) You really should see the interior of Bardot before you leave the city. It's all sexy French vintage posters and furniture seemingly plucked from a private club that serves millionaires by day, and becomes a scene of decadent excess by night. The entrance looks to be on N Miami Ave, but it's actually in a parking lot behind the building.

Hoy Como Ayer LIVE MUSIC
(Map p470; ☎305-541-2631; www.hoycomoayer.us; 2212 SW 8th St; ⏲8:30pm-4am Thu-Sat) This Cuban hot spot – with authentic music, unstylish wood paneling and a small dance floor – is enhanced by cigar smoke and Havana transplants. Stop in nightly for *son*, *boleros* and modern Cuban beats.

☆ Entertainment

Cosmopolitan Miami attracts its fair share of creative types and wealthy patrons, and as such, has long been the seat of a thriving arts scene.

Colony Theater PERFORMING ARTS
(Map p472; ☎305-674-1040; www.colonytheatremiamibeach.com; 1040 Lincoln Rd) Everything – from off-Broadway productions to ballet and movies – plays in this renovated 1934 art-deco showpiece.

Fillmore Miami Beach PERFORMING ARTS
(Map p472; ☎305-673-7300; www.fillmoremb.com; 1700 Washington Ave) Miami Beach's premier showcase for Broadway shows and headliners.

Shopping

Browse for one-of-a-kind and designer items at the South Beach boutiques around Collins Ave between 6th and 9th Sts and along Lincoln Rd mall. For unique items, try Little Havana and the Design District.

Books & Books BOOKS
(Map p472; ☎305-532-3222; www.booksandbooks.com; 927 Lincoln Rd; ⏲10am-11pm Sun-Thu, to midnight Fri & Sat) Best indie bookstore in South Florida; the original location is in Coral Gables at 265 Aragon Ave.

GO! Shop ARTS, CRAFTS
(Map p470; ☎305-576-8205; http://thego-shop.com; 2516 NW 2nd Ave; ⏲noon-8pm Thu-Sat) If you fancy the art at the Wynwood Walls (p474), make sure to pop into the GO! shop, located within the street-art complex. Original artwork, prints and other arts accoutrements are presented on a rotating basis; the stuff for sale is either produced by or related to the works created by the current crop of Wynwood Walls artists.

ℹ Information

DANGERS & ANNOYANCES

Miami has a few areas considered dangerous at night: Little Haiti, stretches of the Miami riverfront and Biscayne Blvd, and areas below 5th St in South Beach. In Downtown, use caution near the Greyhound station and shantytowns around causeways, bridges and overpasses.

EMERGENCY

Beach Patrol (☎305-673-7714) Lifeguards and police provide life-saving services and security in Miami Beach.

INTERNET RESOURCES

Art Circuits (www.artcircuits.com) Insider info on art events; neighborhood-by-neighborhood gallery maps.

Miami Beach 411 (www.miamibeach411.com) A great general guide for Miami Beach visitors.

Short Order (http://blogs.miaminewtimes.com/shortorder) The best local food blog.

MEDIA

Miami Herald (www.miamiherald.com) The city's major English-language daily.

Miami New Times (www.miaminewtimes.com) Edgy, alternative weekly.

MEDICAL SERVICES

Mount Sinai Medical Center (☎305-674-2121, emergency room 305-674-2200; www.msmc.com; 4300 Alton Rd) The area's best emergency room.

TOURIST INFORMATION

Greater Miami & the Beaches Convention & Visitors Bureau (Map p470; ☎305-539-3000; www.miamiandbeaches.com; 701 Brickell Ave, 27th fl; ⏲8:30am-6pm Mon-Fri) Located in an oddly intimidating high-rise building.

Miami Beach Chamber of Commerce (Map p472; ☎305-674-1300; www.miamibeachchamber.com; 1920 Meridian Ave; ⏲9am-5pm Mon-Fri) Tourism and events information related to Miami Beach.

ℹ Getting There & Away

Miami International Airport (MIA; Map p470; ☎305-876-7000; www.miami-airport.com; 2100 NW 42nd Ave) is about 6 miles west of downtown and is accessible by **SuperShuttle** (☎305-871-8210; www.supershuttle.com), which costs about $21 to South Beach.

Greyhound (Map p470; ☎800-231-2222; www.greyhound.com) serves all the major cities in Florida with three stations in Miami; check its website to see which location is best for you.

Amtrak (☎305-835-1222, 800-872-7245; www.amtrak.com; 8303 NW 37th Ave) has a main Miami terminal. The **Tri-Rail** (☎800-874-7245; www.tri-rail.com) commuter system serves Miami (with a free transfer to Miami's transit system) and MIA, Fort Lauderdale and its airport, and West Palm Beach and its airport ($11.55 round-trip).

Getting Around

Metro-Dade Transit (☎305-891-3131; www.miamidade.gov/transit/routes.asp; tickets $2) runs the local Metrobus and Metrorail ($2), as well as the free Metromover monorail serving downtown.

Fort Lauderdale

Spring breakers grow into suit-clad executives who still want to party in a yacht, and that's an apt analogy for a sizable chunk of Fort Lauderdale, a town once known for spring-break bacchanals that is now more recognized as an enclave of wealth and pleasure boats. Much of the tropically broiled gentry live amid a wonderfully scenic series of canals and palm fronds, but it's not all money and outboard motors here. This is a popular LGBTIQ destination that boasts a thriving arts scene, good eating, and immigrants from across Latin America and the Caribbean. Plus the beach is lovely, as always.

Sights & Activities

Fort Lauderdale Beach & Promenade BEACH
(P) Fort Lauderdale's promenade – a wide, brick, palm-tree-dotted pathway swooping along the beach and A1A – is a magnet for runners, in-line skaters, walkers and cyclists. The white-sand beach is one of the nation's cleanest and best, stretching 7 miles to Lauderdale-by-the-Sea, and there are dedicated family-, gay- and dog-friendly sections. There are pay parking lots up and down the beach.

NSU Art Museum Fort Lauderdale MUSEUM
(http://nsuartmuseum.org; 1 E Las Olas Blvd; adult/child/student $12/free/8; 11am-5pm Tue-Sat, to 8pm Thu, noon-5pm Sun) A curvaceous Florida standout known for its William Glackens collection (among Glackens fans) and its exciting exhibitions (among everyone else).

Riverwalk & Las Olas Riverfront WATERFRONT
(www.goriverwalk.com) Curving along the New River, the meandering **Riverwalk** (www.goriverwalk.com) runs from Stranahan House to the Broward Center for the Performing Arts. Host to culinary tastings and other events, the walk connects a number of sights, restaurants and shops. **Las Olas Riverfront** (cnr SW 1st Ave & Las Olas Blvd) is basically a giant alfresco shopping mall with stores, restaurants and live entertainment nightly; it's also the place to catch many river cruises.

Hugh Taylor Birch State Recreation Area PARK
(☎954-564-4521; www.floridastateparks.org/park/Hugh-Taylor-Birch; 3109 E Sunrise Blvd; per vehicle/bike $6/2; 8am-sunset) This lusciously tropical park contains one of the last significant maritime hammocks in Broward County. There are mangroves and a freshwater lagoon system (great for birding) and several endangered plants and animals (including the golden leather fern and gopher tortoise). You can fish, picnic, stroll the short Coastal Hammock Trail or cycle the 1.9-mile park drive.

Museum of Discovery & Science MUSEUM
(☎954-467-6637; www.mods.org; 401 SW 2nd St; adult/child $14/12; 10am-5pm Mon-Sat, noon-6pm Sun) A 52ft kinetic-energy sculpture greets you, and fun exhibits include Gizmo City and Runways to Rockets – where it actually *is* rocket science. Plus there's an Everglades exhibit and IMAX theater.

Bonnet House HISTORIC BUILDING
(☎954-563-5393; www.bonnethouse.org; 900 N Birch Rd; adult/child $20/16, grounds only $10; 9am-4pm Tue-Sun) This pretty plantation-style property was once the home of artists and collectors Frederic and Evelyn Bartlett. Wandering the 35 acres of lush, subtropical gardens, you might just spot the resident Brazilian squirrel monkeys. The art-filled house is open to guided tours only.

Carrie B BOAT TOUR
(☎954-642-1601; www.carriebcruises.com; 440 N New River Dr E; tours adult/child $23/13; tours 11am, 1pm & 3pm, closed Tue & Wed May-Oct) Hop aboard this replica 19th-century riverboat for a narrated 90-minute 'lifestyles of the rich and famous' tour of the ginormous mansions along the Intracoastal and New River.

Water Taxi WATER TAXI
(954-467-6677; www.watertaxi.com; all-day pass adult/child $26/12) For a waterborne trolley experience, hop on the water taxi, the drivers of which offer a lively narration as they ply Fort Lauderdale's canals and waterways from Oakland Park Boulevard to the Riverwalk Arts District. Other routes head down the coast to Hollywood. Check online to buy tickets and for boarding locations.

Broward BCycle BICYCLE HIRE
(754-200-5672; https://broward.bcycle.com; first 30 min/additional 30 min $5/5) Flat Fort Lauderdale is an easy town to traverse via bicycle, or BCycle as the case may be. Broward County–operated bicycle-sharing stations can be found throughout town, and provide easy access to two -wheeled exploration. Maximum daily charge is $50.

Sleeping

The area from Rio Mar St in the south to Vistamar St in the north, and from Hwy A1A in the east to Bayshore Dr in the west, offers the highest concentration of accommodations in all price ranges. Check out the list of super-small lodgings at www.sunny.org/ssl.

★**Island Sands Inn** B&B $$
(954-990-6499; www.islandsandsinn.com; 2409 NE 7th Ave, Wilton Manors; r $129-209; P ❄ 📶 🏊) It's hard to say whether it's the ultrathick beach towels, the luxurious bed and bedding, the thoughtful attention to detail (tissues, bath products, minibar, microwave) or the utterly unpretentious *ease* of the place that makes Island Sands Inn so comfortable. Certainly your charming hosts, Mike and Jim, unobtrusively ensure that you get the best from your stay.

Sea Club Resort MOTEL $$
(954-564-3211; www.seaclubresort.com; 619 Fort Lauderdale Beach Blvd; r from $150; P ❄ 📶 🏊) After extensive remodeling this funky beachfront motel, which looks to all intents and purposes as if a spaceship has landed beachside, now sports fashion-forward rooms with plum-colored accents, new carpets and even plump pillowtop mattresses. With ocean views, free beach towels and chairs, and a resident parrot named Touki, it's unique.

★**Pillars** B&B $$$
(954-467-9639; www.pillarshotel.com; 111 N Birch Rd; r $205-569; P ❄ 📶 🏊) From the harp in the sitting area to the private balconies and the intimate prearranged dinners for two, this tiny boutique B&B radiates hushed good taste. It's a block from the beach, facing one of the best sunsets in town.

Eating

★**Gran Forno** ITALIAN $
(954-467-2244; http://gran-forno.com; 1235 E Las Olas Blvd; mains $6-12; 7am-6pm) The best lunch spot in downtown Fort Lauderdale is this delightfully old-school Milanese-style bakery and cafe: warm crusty pastries, bubbling pizzas, and fat golden loaves of ciabatta, sliced and stuffed with ham, roast peppers, pesto and other delicacies.

11th Street Annex AMERICAN $
(954-767-8306; www.twouglysisters.com; 14 SW 11th St; lunch $9; 11:30am-2pm Mon-Fri, to 3pm first Sat of the month;) In this off-the-beaten-path peach cottage, the 'two ugly sisters' serve whatever strikes their fancy: perhaps brie mac 'n' cheese, chicken confit and sour cream chocolate cake. Most of the vegetables are grown from the cottage's garden, and there's always a vegetarian option on the menu. It's located a mile south of E Las Olas Blvd, just off S Andrews Ave.

Lester's Diner DINER $
(954-525-5641; http://lestersdiner.com; 250 W State Rd 84; mains $4-17; 24hr;) Hailed endearingly as a greasy spoon, campy Lester's Diner has been keeping folks happy since the late 1960s. Everyone makes their way here at some point, from business types on cell phones, to clubbers and blue-haired ladies with third husbands, to travel writers needing pancakes at 4am.

★**Green Bar & Kitchen** VEGAN $$
(954-533-7507; www.greenbarkitchen.com; 1075 SE 17th St; mains $8-14; 11am-9pm Mon-Sat, to 3pm Sun;) Discover bright flavors and innovative dishes at this cult vegan eatery. Instead of pasta-layered lasagna, slithers of zucchini are layered with macadamia ricotta and sun-dried tomatoes. Almond milk replaces dairy in cold-pressed fruit smoothies, and the delectable cashew cup gives Reese's a run for its money.

Rustic Inn SEAFOOD $$
(954-584-1637; www.rusticinn.com; 4331 Ravenswood Rd; mains $9.50-30; 11:30am-10:45pm Mon-Sat, noon-9:30pm Sun) Hungry locals at this messy, noisy crab house use wooden mallets at long, newspaper-covered

GAY & LESBIAN FORT LAUDERDALE

Sure, Miami's South Beach is a mecca for gay travelers, but Fort Lauderdale has long been nipping at the high heels of its southern neighbor. For information on local gay life, visit www.gayftlauderdale.com. Other resources that cover South Florida include the glossy weekly *Hot Spots* (www.hotspotsmagazine.com), the insanely comprehensive www.jumponmarkslist.com, and www.sunny.org/glbt.

tables to get at the Dungeness crab, blue crab and golden crab drenched in garlic.

★**Casa D'Angelo** ITALIAN **$$$**
(☎954-564-1234; http://casa-d-angelo.com; 1201 N Federal Hwy; mains $25-50; ⏲5:30-10:30pm) Chef Angelo Elia presides over an impressive kitchen specializing in Tuscan and southern Italian dishes, many handed down by his mother. Seasonality and quality translate into intense flavors and delightful textures: the sunburst taste of just-ripe tomatoes, peppery arugula, silken sea bass and surprisingly spicy cinnamon gelato. The restaurant stocks one of the finest wine lists in the state.

Drinking & Entertainment

Bars generally stay open until 4am on weekends and 2am during the week. The Himmarshee area is the town's nightlife focus on weekends, when it resembles a scene from the Capital in *The Hunger Games*.

★**BREW Urban Cafe Next Door** CAFE
(☎954-357-3934; 537 NW 1st Ave; ⏲7am-7pm; 📶) Despite an awkward, unwieldy name, Brew is the coolest thing going in Fort Lauderdale: a kick-ass cafe located in a weird, semiabandoned studio space filled with bookshelves. It looks like a British lord's library that got lost in an '80s warehouse party. Bonus: the coffee is good too.

★**Stache** COCKTAIL BAR
(☎954-449-1044; http://stacheftl.com; 109 SW 2nd Ave; ⏲7am-4am Wed-Fri, 9am-6pm & 8pm-4am Sat, 9am-3pm Sun, 7am-6pm Mon & Tue) Stache is a sexy 1920s drinking den serving crafted cocktails and rocking a crossover classic rock/funk/soul/R&B blend. At weekends there's live music, dancing and burlesque. Dress up; this is where the cool cats come to play. Serves coffee during the day.

Laser Wolf BAR
(☎954-667-9373; www.laserwolf.com; 901 Progresso Dr, Suite 101; ⏲6pm-2am Mon-Thu, to 3am Fri, 8pm-3am Sat) We don't want to call Laser Wolf sophisticated, but its extensive booze menu and pop-art styling definitely attracts Fort Lauderdale's cerebral set. But they're a cerebral set that *loves* to party, so if this wolf is sophisticated, it knows how to let its hair down.

Information

For local information, head to the **visitor bureau** (☎954-765-4466; www.sunny.org; 101 NE 3rd Ave, Suite 100; ⏲8:30-5pm Mon-Fri).

Getting There & Around

The **Fort Lauderdale-Hollywood International Airport** (FLL; ☎954-359-1210; www.broward.org/airport; 320 Terminal Dr) is served by more than 35 airlines, some with nonstop flights from Europe. A taxi from the airport to downtown costs around $20.

The **Greyhound station** (☎954-764-6551; www.greyhound.com; 515 NE 3rd St) is four blocks from Broward Central Terminal, with multiple daily services. The **train station** (200 SW 21st Tce) serves **Amtrak** (☎800-872-7245; www.amtrak.com; 200 SW 21st Tce), and the **Tri-Rail** (☎954-783-6030; www.tri-rail.com; 6151 N Andrews Ave) has services to Miami and Palm Beach.

Hail a **Sun Trolley** (www.suntrolley.com; single fare/day pass $1/3) for rides between downtown, the beach, Las Olas and the Riverfront.

Palm Beach & Around

Palm Beach isn't all yachts and mansions – but just about. This is where railroad baron Henry Flagler built his winter retreat, and it's also home to Donald Trump's **Mar-a-Lago** (1100 S Ocean Blvd). In other words, if you're looking for middle-class tourism or Florida kitsch, keep driving. Contact the Palm Beach County **Convention & Visitor Bureau** (☎561-233-3000; www.palmbeachfl.com; 1555 Palm Beach Lakes Blvd; ⏲8:30am-5:30pm Mon-Fri) in West Palm Beach for area information and maps.

Palm Beach

About 30 miles north of Boca Raton are Palm Beach and West Palm Beach. The two towns have flip-flopped the traditional coastal hierarchy: Palm Beach, the beach town, is more upscale, while West Palm Beach on the mainland is younger and livelier.

Palm Beach is an enclave of the ultra-wealthy, especially during its winter 'social season,' so the main tourist activities involve gawking at oceanfront mansions and window-shopping the boutiques along the aptly named **Worth Avenue** (www.worth-avenue.com); to access the lives of the 1% on foot, trek the **Palm Beach Lake Trail** (Royal Palm Way, at the Intracoastal Waterway). You can also visit one of the country's most fascinating museums, the resplendent **Flagler Museum** (561-655-2833; www.flaglermuseum.us; 1 Whitehall Way; adult/child $18/10; 10am-5pm Tue-Sat, noon-5pm Sun), housed in the railroad magnate's 1902 winter estate, Whitehall Mansion. The elaborate 55-room palace is an evocative immersion in Gilded Age opulence.

Flagler's opulent oceanfront 1896 hotel, the **Breakers** (888-273-2537; www.thebreakers.com; 1 S County Rd; r $349-590, ste $650-2050; P ❄ @ 🛜 ≋ 🐾), is a superluxurious world unto itself, modeled after Rome's Villa Medici. It encompasses two golf courses, 10 tennis courts, a three-pool Mediterranean beach club and a trove of restaurants.

For a low-end treat, kick it Formica-style with an egg cream and a low-cal platter at the lunch counter in **Green's Pharmacy** (561-832-4443; 151 N County Rd; mains $4-11; 8am-6pm Mon-Fri, to 4pm Sat). If you fancy something, well, fancier, but reasonably priced, try the Modern American fare cooked by James Beard–nominee Clay Conley at **Būccan** (561-833-3450; www.buccanpalmbeach.com; 350 S County Rd; small plates $4.50-36; 4pm-midnight Mon-Thu, 5pm-1am Sat, to 10pm Sun).

West Palm Beach

Henry Flagler initially developed West Palm Beach as a working-class community to support Palm Beach, and indeed, West Palm today works harder, plays harder and is simply cooler and more relaxed. It's a groovy place to explore.

Florida's largest museum, the **Norton Museum of Art** (561-832-5196; www.norton.org; 1451 S Olive Ave; adult/child $12/5; 10am-5pm Tue-Sat, to 9pm Thu, 11am-5pm Sun) houses an enormous collection of American and European modern masters and Impressionists, along with a large Buddha head presiding over an impressive Asian art collection. If you like that, you'll love the outdoor **Ann Norton Sculpture Garden** (561-832-5328; www.ansg.org; 253 Barcelona Rd; adult/child $10/5; 10am-4pm Wed-Sun). This serene collection of sculptures sprinkled among verdant gardens is a real West Palm gem.

If you have children, take them to **Lion Country Safari** (561-793-1084; www.lioncountrysafari.com; 2003 Lion Country Safari Rd; adult/child $31.50/23; 9:30am-5:30pm; 👪), the country's first cageless drive-through safari, where around 900 creatures roam freely around 500 acres.

Book a room at **Grandview Gardens** (561-833-9023; www.grandview-gardens.com; 1608 Lake Ave; r $129-215; P ❄ 🛜 ≋) and you'll feel like a local in no time. Hidden in a tropical garden on Howard Park, the house is a period 1925 structure typical of the historic neighborhood and it sits opposite the Armory Art Center, so is perfect for longer stays for the arts-inclined.

Much of the action centers around **CityPlace** (561-366-1000; www.cityplace.com; 700 S Rosemary Ave; 10am-10pm Mon-Sat, noon-6pm Sun), a European-village-style outdoor mall with splashing fountains and a slew of dining and entertainment options. Clematis St also has several worthy bars, live-music clubs and restaurants, and every Thursday **Clematis by Night** (wpb.org/clematis-by-night; 6-9:30pm Thu) hosts friendly outdoor concerts. If you're hungry, **Curbside Gourmet** (561-371-6565; http://curbsidegourmet.com; 2000 S Dixie Hwy) is Palm Beach's first mobile food truck dedicated to bringing good, seasonal staples to resident gourmands; they tweet their location @curbsidegourmet (or give them a call).

The Everglades

South Florida is often conflated with beauty, but her most magnificent edges reside far away from models and lounges and white-sand beaches. The real glory of this region lays in the slow trickle of freshwater percolating over a sawgrass prairie, before winding its way into an alligator- and otterrich current that snakes over mudflats and sedge basins into the turquoise explosion of Florida Bay. This is the Everglades, and it is a wilderness like no other.

Contrary to what you may have heard, the Everglades isn't a swamp. Or at least, it's not *only* a swamp. It's most accurately characterized as a wet prairie – grasslands that happen to be flooded most of the year. Nor is it stagnant. In the wet season, a horizon-wide river creeps ever so slowly beneath the rustling saw grass and around the subtly raised cypress and hardwood hammocks toward the ocean.

The scenery here is slow and timeless, which is why we feel exploring the Everglades by foot, bicycle, canoe and kayak (or camping) is more satisfying than by noisy, vibrating airboat. There is an incredible variety of wonderful creatures to see within this unique subtropical wilderness, and there are accessible entrances that, at the cost of a few hours, get you easily into the Everglades' soft heart.

The Everglades has two seasons: the summer wet season and the winter dry season. Winter – from December to April – is the prime time to visit: the weather is mild and pleasant, and the wildlife is out in abundance. In summer – May through October – it's stiflingly hot, humid and buggy, with frequent afternoon thunderstorms. In addition, as water sources spread out, so the animals disperse.

Everglades National Park

While the Everglades have a history dating back to prehistoric times, the park wasn't founded until 1947. It's considered the most endangered national park in the USA, but the Comprehensive Everglades Restoration Plan (www.evergladesplan.org) has been enacted to undo some of the damage done by draining and development.

The park has three main entrances and areas: in the south along Rte 9336 through Homestead and Florida City to Ernest Coe Visitor Center and, at road's end, Flamingo; along the Tamiami Trail/Hwy 41 in the north to Shark Valley; and on the Gulf Coast near Everglades City.

The main park entry points have visitor centers where you can get maps, camping permits and ranger information. You only need to pay the entrance fee (per car/pedestrian $10/5 for seven days) once to access all points.

Even in winter it's almost impossible to avoid mosquitoes, but they're ferocious in summer: bring *strong* repellent. Alligators are also prevalent. As obvious as it sounds, never, ever feed them: it's illegal and a sure way to provoke attacks. Four types of poisonous snakes call the Everglades home; avoid all snakes, and wear long, thick socks and lace-up boots.

Activities

Based in Key Largo, Garl's Coastal Kayaking (p489) is an excellent outfitter that can arrange paddling tours of the Everglades backcountry.

Royal Palm Area WALKING
(☎305-242-7700; Hwy 9336) Two trails, the **Anhinga** and **Gumbo Limbo**, take all of an hour to walk and put you face to face with a panoply of Everglades wildlife. Gators sun on the shoreline, anhinga spear their prey and wading birds stalk haughtily through the reeds. Come at night for a ranger walk on the boardwalk and shine a flashlight into the water to see one of the coolest sights of your life: the glittering eyes of dozens of alligators prowling the waterways.

Shark Valley TOUR
(☎305-221-8776; www.nps.gov/ever/planyourvisit/svdirections.htm; 36000 SW 8th St, GPS N 25°45'27.60, W 80°46'01.01; car/cyclist $10/5; 9:15am-5:15pm; P) One of the best places to dip your toe into the Everglades (figuratively speaking) is Shark Valley, where you can take an excellent two-hour **tram tour** (☎305-221-8455; www.sharkvalleytramtours.com; adult/child under 12yr/senior $22/19/12.75; departures 9:30am, 11am, 2pm, 4pm May-Dec, 9am-4pm Jan-Apr every hour on the hour) along a 15-mile asphalt trail and see copious amounts of alligators in the winter months. Tours are narrated by knowledgeable park rangers who give a fascinating overview of the Everglades. Bicycles can be rented at the entrance for $7.50 per hour. Bring water.

Ernest Coe Visitor Center WALKING, CANOEING
(☎305-242-7700; www.nps.gov/ever; State Rd 9336; 9am-5pm, from 8am Dec-Apr) The main visitor center for the southern portion of the park has excellent, museum-quality exhibits and tons of activity info: the road accesses numerous short trails and lots of top-drawer canoeing opportunities. Call for a schedule of fun ranger-led programs, such as the two-hour 'slough slog.'

Flamingo Visitor Center HIKING, CANOEING
(☎239-695-3101; marina 7am-7pm, from 6am Sat & Sun) From Royal Palm, Hwy 9336 cuts through the belly of the park for 38 miles

A KINDER, GENTLER WILDERNESS ENCOUNTER

As you explore Florida's outdoors and encounter its wildlife, keep in mind the following guidelines.

Airboats and swamp buggies For exploring wetlands, airboats are better than big-wheeled buggies, but nonmotorized (and silent) canoes and kayaks are least damaging and disruptive.

Wild dolphins Captive dolphins are typically rescued animals already acclimated to humans. However, federal law makes it illegal to feed, pursue or touch wild dolphins in the ocean.

Manatee swims When swimming near manatees, a federally protected endangered species, look but don't touch. 'Passive observation' is the standard.

Feeding wild animals In a word, don't. Acclimating wild animals to humans usually leads to the animal's death, whether because of accidents or aggression.

Sea-turtle nesting sites It's a federal crime to approach nesting sea turtles or hatchling runs. Observe beach warning signs. If you encounter nesting turtles, keep your distance and no flash photos.

Coral-reef etiquette Never touch the coral reef. It's that simple. Coral polyps are living organisms. Touching or breaking coral creates openings for infection and disease.

until it reaches the isolated Flamingo Visitor Center, which has maps of canoeing and hiking trails. Call ahead about the status of facilities: the former Flamingo Lodge was wiped out by hurricanes in 2005. **Flamingo Marina** (☎239-695-3101; ⊙store 7am-5:30pm Mon-Fri, from 6am Sat & Sun) has reopened and offers backcountry boat tours and kayak/canoe rentals for self-guided trips along the coast.

Gulf Coast Visitor Center BOATING
(☎239-695-2591; http://evergladesnationalpark-boattoursgulfcoast.com; 815 Oyster Bar Lane, off Hwy 29; per day canoe/single kayak/tandem kayak $24/45/55; ⊙9am-4:30pm mid-Apr–mid-Nov, 8am-4:30pm mid-Nov–mid-Apr;) Those with more time should also consider visiting the northwestern edge of the Everglades, where the mangroves and waterways of the **10,000 Islands** offer incredible canoeing and kayaking opportunities, and great boat tours with a chance to spot dolphins. The visitor center is next to the marina, with rentals (from $13 per hour) and various guided boat trips (from $25). Everglades City also has other private tour operators who can get you camping in the 10,000 Islands.

Sleeping

Everglades National Park has two developed campgrounds, both of which have water, toilets and grills. The best are the first-come, first-served sites at **Long Pine Key** (☎305-242-7745; www.nps.gov/ever/planyourvisit/frontcamp; per campsite $16), just west of Royal Palm Visitor Center; reserve ahead for campsites at **Flamingo** (☎877-444-6777; www.nps.gov/ever/planyourvisit/frontcamp; per campsite $30), which have cold-water showers and electricity. **Backcountry camping** (☎239-695-2945, 239-695-3311; www.nps.gov/ever/planyourvisit/backcamp; permit $10, plus per person per night $2) is throughout the park and includes beach sites, ground sites and chickees (covered wooden platforms above the water). A permit from the visitor center is required.

Getting There & Around

The largest subtropical wilderness in the continental USA is easily accessible from Miami. The Glades, which comprise the 80 southernmost miles of Florida, are bound by the Atlantic Ocean to the east and the Gulf of Mexico to the west. The Tamiami Trail (US Hwy 41) goes east–west, parallel to the more northern (and less interesting) Alligator Alley (I-75).

You need a car to properly enter the Everglades and once you're in, wearing a good pair of walking boots is essential to penetrate the interior. Having a canoe or kayak helps as well; these can be rented from outfits inside and outside of the park, or else you can seek out guided canoe and kayak tours. Bicycles are well suited to the flat roads of Everglades National Park, particularly in the area between Ernest Coe and Flamingo Point, but they're useless off the highway. In addition, the road shoulders in the park are dangerously small.

Around the Everglades

Coming from Miami, the gateway town of Homestead on the east side of the park can make a good base, especially if you're headed for the Keys.

Biscayne National Park

Just south of Miami (and east of Homestead), this national park is only 5% land. The 95% that's water is **Biscayne National Underwater Park** (☎305-230-1100; www.nps.gov/bisc), containing a portion of the world's third-largest coral reef, where manatees, dolphins and sea turtles highlight a vibrant, diverse ecosystem. Get general park information from **Dante Fascell Visitor Center** (☎305-230-1144; www.nps.gov/bisc; 9700 SW 328th St; ⏲9am-5pm, from 10am May-Oct). The park offers canoe/kayak rentals, snorkel and dive trips, and popular three-hour glass-bottom boat tours; all require reservations.

Homestead & Florida City

Homestead and Florida City don't look like much, but they have some true Everglades highlights. Don't miss **Robert Is Here** (☎305-246-1592; www.robertishere.com; 19200 SW 344th St, Homestead; mains $3-8; ⏲8am-7pm) – a kitschy Old Florida institution with a petting zoo, live music and crazy-good milk shakes.

The Homestead–Florida City area has no shortage of chain motels along Krome Ave. If you don't mind hostel living, seriously consider the **Everglades International Hostel** (☎305-248-1122; www.evergladeshostel.com; 20 SW 2nd Ave, Florida City; camping $18, dm $28, d $61-75, ste $125-225; P❄📶🏊). Rooms are good value, the vibe is very friendly, but the back gardens – wow. It's a fantasia of natural delights, and the hostel conducts some of the best Everglades tours around, including 'wet walks' – slogs through the bog, as it were.

Tamiami Trail

The Tamiami Trail/Hwy 41 starts in Miami and beelines to Naples along the north edge of Everglades National Park. Just past the entrance to the Everglades' Shark Valley is **Miccosukee Village** (☎877-242-6464, 305-222-4600; www.miccosukee.com; Mile 70, Hwy 41; adult/child/5yr & under $12/6/free; ⏲9am-5pm; P👪), an informative, entertaining open-air museum showcasing Miccosukee culture.

About 20 miles west of Shark Valley, you reach the **Oasis Visitor Center** (☎941-695-1201; www.nps.gov/bicy; 52105 Tamiami Trail E; ⏲9am-4:30pm Mon-Fri; 👪) for 1139-sq-mile **Big Cypress National Preserve** (☎239-695-4758; www.nps.gov/bicy; 33000 Tamiami Trail E; ⏲8:30am-4:30pm; P👪) 🍃. Good exhibits and short trails bring the region's ecology to life, though the adventurous might consider tackling a portion of the **Florida National Scenic Trail** (☎850-523-8501; www.fs.usda.gov/fnst); 31 miles cut through Big Cypress.

Half a mile east of the visitor center, drop into the **Big Cypress Gallery** (☎239-695-2428; www.clydebutcher.com; Tamiami Trail; swamp walk 1½hr adult/child $50/35, 45min adult/child $35/25; ⏲10am-5pm; P) 🍃, displaying Clyde Butcher's work; his large-scale B&W landscape photographs spotlight the region's unusual beauty.

The tiny town of **Ochopee** is home to the country's smallest post office. If that's not enough to make you pull over, then stop into the eccentric **Skunk Ape Research Headquarters** (☎239-695-2275; www.skunkape.info; 40904 Tamiami Trail E; $5; ⏲7am-7pm, 'zoo' closes around 4pm; P), dedicated to tracking Bigfoot's legendary, if stinky, Everglades kin. It's goofy but sincere. Based out of Skunk Ape HQ, **Everglades Adventure Tours** (EAT; ☎800-504-6554; www.evergladesadventuretours.com; tours from $89) offers knowledgeable swamp hikes and trips being poled around in a canoe or skiff.

Finally, just east of Ochopee is the quintessential 1950s-style swamp shack, **Joannie's Blue Crab Cafe** (☎239-695-2682; 39395 Tamiami Trail E; mains $9-17; ⏲10:30am-5pm, closed seasonally, call to confirm), with open rafters, colorful shellacked picnic tables and a swamp dinner of gator nuggets and fritters.

Everglades City

This small town at the edge of the park makes a good base for exploring the **10,000 Islands** region. With large renovated rooms, **Everglades City Motel** (☎239-695-4224; www.evergladescitymotel.com; 310 Collier Ave; r from $89; P❄📶) is exceptionally good value, and the fantastically friendly staff can hook you up with any kind of tour. The same can be said for the **Ivey House Bed & Breakfast** (☎877-567-0679; www.iveyhouse.com; 107 Camellia St; inn r $99-179; P❄📶). Choose between basic lodge accommodations or somewhat sprucer inn rooms, then book nature trips with the on-site **Everglades Adventures** (NACT; ☎877-567-0679; www.evergladesadventures.com; Ivey House Bed & Breakfast, 107 Camellia St; tours from $89, rentals from $35; ⏲Nov–mid-Apr). Ask about room/tour packages. For dinner, the **Camellia Street Grill** (☎239-695-2003; 202 Camellia St; mains $10-20; ⏲noon-9pm) is as fancy as Everglades City gets, although the American Southern and Mediterranean food is down to earth.

Florida Keys

Laid out like a string of wacky green pearls on an asphalt string, the islands of the Florida Keys are where people go when they want to drop off the face of the earth and still have a good time doing so. Henry Flagler connected the Keys to the mainland in 1912; until then, this 126-mile-long series of islands was a pirate's den of smuggling, ship salvaging and fishing. These days there's still plenty of fishing, along with tourism, boozing, diving, snorkeling and living the most laid-back of lives.

The islands are typically divided into the Upper Keys (Key Largo to Islamorada), Middle Keys and Lower Keys (from Little Duck Key). Yet far from petering out, they crescendo at highway's end, reaching their grand finale in Key West – the Keys' gloriously unkempt, bawdy, freak-loving exclamation point.

Many addresses in the Keys are noted by their proximity to mile markers (indicated as MM), which start at MM 126 in Florida City and count down to MM 0 in Key West. They also might indicate whether they're 'oceanside' (the south side of the highway) or 'bayside' (which is north).

The **Florida Keys & Key West Visitors Bureau** (☎800-352-5397; www.fla-keys.com) has information; also check www.keysnews.com.

Key Largo

No, really, you're in the islands!

You'd be forgiven for not thinking so, though. As you drive south of Homestead, the land fringes into clumps of mangrove forest and you can't even see the water from the highway, then – bam – you're in Islamorada and water is everywhere.

Key Largo has long been romanticized in movies and song, so it can be a shock to arrive and find...no Bogart, no Bacall, no love-sick Sade. Yes, Key Largo is underwhelming, a sleepy island and town with middling views. That is, if all you do is stick to the highway and keep your head above water. On the side roads you can find some of those legendary island idiosyncracies, and dive underwater for the most amazing coral reef in the continental US.

For maps and brochures, visit the **chamber of commerce** (☎800-822-1088; www.keylargochamber.org; MM 106 bayside; ⏲9am-6pm), located in a yellow building just past Seashell World (not to be confused with the *other* yellow visitor center at 10624 that makes reservations and works on commission).

Activities

John Pennekamp Coral Reef State Park PARK

(☎305-451-6300; www.pennekamppark.com; MM 102.6 oceanside; car/motorcycle/cyclist or pedestrian $8/4/2; ⏲8am-sunset, aquarium to 5pm) The USA's first underwater park, Pennekamp contains the third-largest coral barrier reef in the world. Your options for seeing the reef are many: take a 2½-hour **glass-bottom boat tour** (☎305-451-6300; http://pennekamppark.com/glassbottom-boat; adult/child $24/17; ⏲9:15am, 12:15pm & 3:15pm) on a thoroughly modern 65ft catamaran. Dive in with a **snorkeling trip** (☎305-451-6300; http://pennekamppark.com/snorkeling-tours; adult/child $30/25; ⏲9am-4:30pm) or two-tank **diving trip** (☎305-451-6322; http://pennekamppark.com/scuba-tours; six-person charter $400); half-day trips leave twice daily, usually around 9am and 1pm. Or go DIY and rent a canoe, kayak (per hour single/double $12/17) or stand-up paddle board (per hour $25) and journey through a 3-mile network of water trails.

Garl's Coastal Kayaking ECOTOUR

(☎305-393-3223; www.garlscoastalkayaking.com; tours adult half-/full day $125/150, child $95/125, kayak single/double $30/45) Garl's is an excellent ecotour operator that gets customers into the Everglades backcountry and mangrove islets of Florida Bay via kayak and canoe. It also provides reasonable equipment rentals.

Sleeping

In addition to luxe resorts, Key Largo has loads of bright, cheery motels and camping.

**John Pennekamp
Coral Reef State Park**   CAMPGROUND $
(☑800-326-3521;   www.pennekamppark.com;
102601 Overseas Hwy; tent & RV sites $38.50; ℗)
Sleep with the – er, *near* the fishes at one of
the 47 coral-reef-adjacent sites here. Camping's popular; reserve well in advance.

Hilton Key Largo Resort   HOTEL $$
(☑888-871-3437, 305-852-5553; www.keylargore-
sort.com; MM 102 bayside; r/ste from $179/240;
℗🛜🏊) This Hilton has a ton of character.
Folks just seem to get all laid-back when
lounging in clean, designer rooms outfitted
in blues, greens and (why not?) blue-green.
The grounds are enormous and include an
artificial waterfall-fed pool and frontage to
a rather large stretch of private white-sand
beach. Book online for the best rates.

Largo Lodge   HOTEL $$$
(☑305-451-0424; www.largolodge.com; MM 102
bayside; cottages $375; ℗) These six lovely
cottages with their own private beach are
surrounded by palm trees, tropical flowers
and lots of roaming birds. They've been appointed with sleek, modern furnishings and
a Zen-esque sense of space and color design.

🍴 Eating & Drinking

Key Largo Conch House   FUSION $$
(☑305-453-4844; www.keylargoconchhouse.com;
MM 100.2 oceanside; lunch mains $8-16, dinner $13-
30; ⊙8am-10pm; ℗🛜🚻) Now *this* feels like
the islands: conch architecture, tropical fo-
liage, and crab and seafood dishes that ease
you off the mainland.

Mrs Mac's Kitchen   AMERICAN $$
(☑305-451-3722; www.mrsmacskitchen.com; MM
99.4 bayside; breakfast & lunch $8-16, dinner $10-
36; ⊙7am-9:30pm Mon-Sat; ℗🚻) This cute
roadside diner bedecked with rusty license
plates serves classic highway food such as
burgers and fish baskets. Look for a second
location just half a mile south on the opposite side of the road.

Islamorada

Islamorada is actually a string of several islands, the epicenter of which is Upper Mate-
cumbe Key. It's right around here that the
view starts to open up, allowing you to fully
appreciate the fact that you're surrounded
by water. Several little nooks of beach are
easily accessible, providing scenic rest stops.
Housed in an old red caboose, the **cham-**
ber of commerce (☑305-664-4503; www.isla
moradachamber.com; MM 87 bayside; ⊙9am-
5pm Mon-Fri, to 4pm Sat, to 3pm Sun) has area
information.

⊙ Sights & Activities

Billed as 'the Sportfishing Capital of the
World,' Islamorada is an angler's paradise.
Indeed, most of its highlights involve getting
on or in the sea.

★**Anne's Beach**   BEACH
(MM 73.5 oceanside) Anne's is one of the best
beaches in these parts. The small ribbon of
sand opens upon a sky-bright stretch of tidal flats and a green tunnel of hammock and
wetland. Nearby mudflats are a joy to get
stuck in, and will be much loved by the kids.

**Florida Keys
History of Diving Museum**   MUSEUM
(☑305-664-9737; www.divingmuseum.org; MM
83; adult/child $12/6; ⊙10am-5pm; ℗♿) Don't
miss this fantastically quirky collection
of diving paraphernalia from around the
world, including seemingly suicidal diving
'suits' and technology from the 19th century.

★**Robbie's Marina**   MARINA
(☑305-664-8070; www.robbies.com; MM 77.5 bayside; kayak & SUP rentals $40-75; ⊙9am-8pm; ♿)
This marina/roadside attraction offers the
buffet of boating options: fishing charters, Jet
Skiing, party boats, ecotours, snorkeling trips,
kayak rentals and more. Two historically significant offshore islands, **Indian Key** (☑305-
664-2540; www.floridastateparks.org/indiankey; MM
78.5 oceanside; admission $2.50; ⊙8am-sunset) and
Lignumvitae Key (☑305-664-2540; www.florida
stateparks.org/lignumvitaekey;   admission/tour
$2.50/2; ⊙9am-5pm, tours 10am & 2pm Fri-Sun),
are a paddle away for the moderately fit; access both via Robbie's. At a minimum, stop to
feed the freakishly large tarpon from the dock
($3 per bucket, $1 to watch), and sift the flea
market/tourist shop for tacky seaside trinkets.

🛌 Sleeping

Conch On Inn   MOTEL $
(☑305-852-9309; www.conchoninn.com; MM
89.5, 103 Caloosa St; apt $59-129; ℗) A simple
motel popular with yearly snowbirds, Conch
On Inn has basic rooms that are reliable,
clean and comfortable.

Ragged Edge Resort   RESORT $$
(☑305-852-5389; www.ragged-edge.com; 243
Treasure Harbor Rd; apt $69-259; ℗❄🛜🏊) This

low-key and popular efficiency and apartment complex, far from the maddening traffic jams, has 10 quiet units and friendly hosts. The larger studios have screened-in porches, and the entire vibe is happily comatose. There's no beach, but you can swim off the dock and at the pool.

Casa Morada HOTEL $$$
(☑ 305-664-0044; www.casamorada.com; 136 Madeira Rd, off MM 82.2; ste $359-659; P ❋ 🛜 🞄) Come for a dash of South Beach sophistication mixed with laid-back Keys style. The slick bar is a great oceanside sunset perch.

✖ Eating

★ **Midway Cafe** CAFE $
(☑ 305-664-2622; http://midwaycafecoffeebar.com; 80499 Overseas Hwy; dishes $2-11; ⊙ 7am-3pm, to 2pm Sun; P 🞄) Celebrate your Keys adventure with a friendly cup o' joe, a smoothie or a treat from the overflowing bakery case. The lovely folks who run this art-filled cafe roast their own beans and make destination-worthy baked goods.

The Beach Cafe at Morada Bay AMERICAN $$$
(☑ 305-664-0604; www.moradabay-restaurant.com; MM 81.6 bayside; mains $20-39; ⊙ 11:30am-10pm; P) Grab a table under a palm tree on the white-sand beach and sip a rum drink with your fresh seafood for a lovely, easygoing Caribbean experience. Don't miss the monthly full-moon party.

Marathon

Halfway between Key Largo and Key West, Marathon is the most sizable town; it's a good base and a hub for commercial fishing. Get local information at the **visitor center** (☑ 305-743-5417; www.floridakeysmarathon.com; MM 53.5 bayside; ⊙ 9am-5pm).

⊙ Sights & Activities

Crane Point Museum MUSEUM
(☑ 305-743-9100; www.cranepoint.net; MM 50.5 bayside; adult/child $12.50/8.50; ⊙ 9am-5pm Mon-Sat, from noon Sun; P 🞄) ∅ This is one of the nicest spots on the island to stop and smell the roses. And the pinelands. And the palm hammock – a sort of palm jungle (imagine walking under giant, organic Japanese fans) that only grows between MM 47 and MM 60. There's also Adderly House, a preserved example of a Bahamian immigrant

cabin (which must have baked in summer) and 63 acres of green goodness to stomp through.

Turtle Hospital WILDLIFE RESERVE
(☑ 305-743-2552; www.theturtlehospital.org; 2396 Overseas Hwy; adult/child $18/9; ⊙ 9am-6pm; P 🞄) ∅ Whether it is a victim of disease, boat-propeller strike, flipper entanglement with fishing lines or any other danger, an injured sea turtle in the Keys will hopefully end up in this motel-cum-sanctuary. We know we shouldn't anthropomorphize animals, but these turtles just seem so sweet. It's sad to see the injured and sick ones, but heartening to see them so well looked after. Tours are educational, fun and are offered on the hour from 9am until 4pm.

Pigeon Key National Historic District ISLAND
(☑ 305-743-5999; www.pigeonkey.net; MM 47 oceanside; adult/child/under 5yr $12/9/free; ⊙ tours 10am, noon & 2pm) On the Marathon side of Seven Mile Bridge, this tiny key served as a camp for the workers who toiled to build the Overseas Hwy in the 1930s. You can tour the historic structures or just sun and snorkel on the beach. Reach it by ferry, included in admission, or walk or bike your way there on the **Old Seven Mile Bridge**, which is closed to traffic but serves as the 'World's Longest Fishing Bridge.'

Sombrero Beach BEACH
(Sombrero Beach Rd, off MM 50 oceanside; P 🞄) This beautiful little white-sand beach has a playscape, shady picnic spots and big, clean bathrooms.

🛏 Sleeping & Eating

Siesta Motel MOTEL $
(☑ 305-743-5671; www.siestamotel.net; MM 51 oceanside; r $80-115; P 🛜) Head here for one of the cheapest, cleanest flops in the Keys, located in a friendly cluster of cute Marathon homes – with great service, to boot.

★ **Keys Fisheries** SEAFOOD $$
(☑ 305-743-4353; www.keysfisheries.com; 3502 Louisa St; mains $7-22; ⊙ 11am-9pm; P 🞄) Shoo the seagulls from your picnic table on the deck and dig in to fresh seafood in a down-and-dirty dockside atmosphere. The lobster Reuben is the stuff of legend.

Hurricane AMERICAN **$$**
(☎ 305-743-2200; www.hurricaneblues.com; 4650 Overseas Hwy; mains $9-19; ⏰ 11am-midnight; P ✎) As well as being a favorite Marathon bar, the Hurricane also serves an excellent menu of creative South Florida–inspired goodness, like snapper stuffed with crabmeat and conch sliders jerked in Caribbean seasoning.

Lower Keys

The Lower Keys (MM 46 to MM 0) are fierce bastions of conch culture in all its variety.

One of Florida's most acclaimed beaches – and certainly the best in the Keys for its shallow, warm water – is at **Bahia Honda State Park** (☎ 305-872-3210; www.bahiahondapark.com; MM 37; car/motorcycle/cyclist $5/4/2; ⏰ 8am-sunset; 👪), a 524-acre park with nature trails, ranger-led programs, water-sports rentals and some of the best coral reefs outside Key Largo.

Overnight camping at **Bahia Honda State Park** (☎ 800-326-3521; www.reserveamerica.com; MM 37, Bahia Honda Key; sites/cabins $38.50/122.50; P) 🍃 is sublime; it'd be perfect except for the sandflies. There are also six popular waterfront cabins. Reserve far ahead for all. For a completely different experience, book one of the four cozily scrumptious rooms at **Deer Run Bed & Breakfast** (☎ 305-872-2015; www.deerrunfloridabb.com; 1997 Long Beach Dr, Big Pine Key, off MM 33 oceanside; r $275-460; P 📶 🏊) 🍃. This state-certified green lodge and vegetarian B&B is a garden of quirky delights, and the owners are extremely helpful.

On Big Pine Key, stop in for a pizza, beer and ambience at **No Name Pub** (☎ 305-872-9115; www.nonamepub.com; N Watson Blvd, Big Pine Key, off MM 30.5 bayside; mains $7-18; ⏰ 11am-11pm; P), right before the causeway that gets you to **No Name Key**. While you're there, staple a dollar bill to the wall to contribute to the collection of approximately $60,000 wallpapering the room.

Key West

Key West's funky, laid-back vibe has long attracted artists, renegades and free spirits. Part of that independent streak is rooted in Key West's geography: it's barely connected to the USA, and it's closer to Cuba than to the rest of the States. There's only one road in, and it's not on the way to anywhere. In other words, it's an easy place to do your own thing, which here can mean anything from piracy to smuggling to fishing to drinking to opening an art gallery. Whatever said thing may be, Key West only requires you have fun doing it.

Sights

Key West has more than its fair share of historic homes, buildings and districts (like the colorful Bahama Village); it's a walkable town that rewards exploring. Naturally, you'll snap a pic at the USA's much ballyhooed **Southernmost Point Marker**, even though it's not technically the southernmost point in the USA. (That distinction goes to a point about half a mile down the beach, but since it's part of a naval air station, it's hardly tourist friendly.)

★ **Mallory Square** SQUARE
(👪) Sunset at Mallory Sq, at the end of Duval St, is a bizzaro attraction of the highest order. It takes all those energies, subcultures and oddities of Keys life – the hippies, the rednecks, the foreigners and the tourists – and focuses them into one torchlit, playfully edgy (but family-friendly) street party. Come for the jugglers, fire-eaters, sassy acrobats and tightrope-walking dogs, and stay for the after-dark madness.

Duval Street AREA
Key West locals have a love–hate relationship with their island's most famous road. Duval, Old Town Key West's main drag, is a miracle mile of booze, tacky everything and awful behavior that still manages, somehow, to be fun. At the end of the night, the 'Duval Crawl' is one of the best pub crawls in the country.

Hemingway House HOUSE
(☎ 305-294-1136; www.hemingwayhome.com; 907 Whitehead St; adult/child $13/6; ⏰ 9am-5pm) Ernest Hemingway lived in this Spanish Colonial house from 1931 to 1940 – to write, drink and fish, if not always in that order. Tours run every half-hour, and as you listen to docent-spun yarns of Papa, you'll see his studio, his unusual pool, and the descendants of his six-toed cats languishing in the sun, on furniture and pretty much wherever they feel like.

Florida Keys Eco-Discovery Center MUSEUM
(☎ 305-809-4750; http://eco-discovery.com/ecokw.html; 35 East Quay Rd; ⏰ 9am-4pm Tue-Sat; P 👪) 🍃 FREE This excellent nature center pulls together all the plants, animals and habitats that make up the Keys' unique ecosystem

and presents them in fresh, accessible ways. A great place for kids and the big picture.

Key West Cemetery CEMETERY
(www.friendsofthekeywestcemetery.com; cnr Margaret & Angela Sts; ⏲8:30am-4pm; 👪) This dark, alluring Gothic labyrinth is in the center of town. Livening up the mausoleums are famous epitaphs like 'I told you I was sick.'

Key West Butterfly & Nature Conservatory ANIMAL SANCTUARY
(☎305-296-2988; www.keywestbutterfly.com; 1316 Duval St; adult/4-12yr $12/8.50; ⏲9am-5pm; 👪) Even if you have only the faintest interest in butterflies, you'll find yourself entranced by the sheer quantity flittering around you here.

Activities

Seeing as how you're out in the middle of the ocean, getting out on or in the water is one of the top activities. Charters abound for everything from fishing to snorkeling to scuba diving, including dive trips to the **USS Vandenberg**, a 522ft transport ship sunk off the coast to create the world's second-largest artificial reef.

Fort Zachary Taylor BEACH
(☎305-292-6713; www.floridastateparks.org/forttaylor; 601 Howard England Way; per car/pedestrian $6/2; ⏲8am-sunset) Key West has three city beaches, but they aren't special; most people head to Bahia Honda. That said, Fort Zachary Taylor has the best beach on Key West, with white sand, decent swimming and some near-shore snorkeling; it's great for sunsets and picnics.

Dive Key West DIVING
(☎305-296-3823; www.divekeywest.com; 3128 N Roosevelt Blvd; snorkel/scuba from $60/75) Everything you need for wreck-diving trips, from equipment to charters.

Jolly Rover CRUISE
(☎305-304-2235; www.schoonerjollyrover.com; cnr Greene & Elizabeth Sts, Schooner Wharf; cruise adult/child $45/25) Set sail on a pirate-esque schooner offering daytime and sunset cruises.

Tours

Both the **Conch Tour Train** (☎888-916-8687; www.conchtourtrain.com; adult/child under 13yr/senior $30/free/27; ⏲tours 9am-4:30pm; 👪) and **Old Town Trolley** (☎855-623-8289; www.trolleytours.com/key-west; adult/child under 13yr/senior $30/free/27; ⏲tours 9am-4:30pm; 👪) offer tours leaving from Mallory Sq. The train offers a 90-minute narrated tour in a breezy, open car, while the hop-on/hop-off trolley makes 12 stops around town.

Original Ghost Tours TOUR
(☎305-294-9255; www.hauntedtours.com; adult/child $18/10; ⏲8pm & 9pm) Is your guesthouse haunted? Probably. Why should you fear Robert the Doll in East Martello? You're about to find out.

Festivals & Events

Key West hosts a party every sunset, but residents don't need an excuse to go crazy.

Conch Republic Independence Celebration CULTURAL
(www.conchrepublic.com; ⏲Aug) A 10-day tribute to Conch Independence, held every April; vie for (made-up) public offices and watch a drag queens footrace.

Fantasy Fest CULTURAL
(www.fantasyfest.net; ⏲late Oct) Room rates get hiked to the hilt for this raucous, 10-day Halloween-meets-Carnivale event in late October.

Sleeping

Key West lodging is generally pretty expensive – especially in the wintertime and even *more* especially during special events, when room rates can triple. Book ahead, or you may well end up joining the long traffic jam headed back to the mainland. Rates can be considerably reduced if booked online.

Caribbean House GUESTHOUSE $
(☎305-296-0999; www.caribbeanhousekw.com; 226 Petronia St; r from $95; P❄@) In the heart of Bahama Village, rooms are tiny, but they're clean, cozy and cheery. Add free breakfast and welcoming hosts and you get a rare find in Key West: a bargain.

★**Key West Bed & Breakfast** B&B $$
(☎305-296-7274; www.keywestbandb.com; 415 William St; r winter $89-265, summer $89-165; ❄📶) Sunny, airy and full of artistic touches: hand-painted pottery here, a working loom there – is that a ship's masthead in the corner? There is also a range of rooms to fit every budget.

Key Lime Inn HOTEL $$
(☎800-549-4430; www.historickeywestinns.com; 725 Truman Ave; r from $180; P📶🏊) These

GAY & LESBIAN KEY WEST

Gay and lesbian visitors can get information at the **Gay & Lesbian Community Center** (305-292-3223; www.glcckeywest.org; 513 Truman Ave). While you'll find the entire island extraordinarily welcoming, several bars and guesthouses cater specifically to a gay clientele. Toast your arrival in town at one of the following:

801 Bourbon Bar (305-294-4737; www.801bourbon.com; 801 Duval St; 9am-4am) Where boys will be boys.

Aqua (305-294-0555; www.aquakeywest.com; 711 Duval St; 3pm-2am) Caters to both gays and lesbians.

cozy cottages are scattered around a tropical hardwood backdrop. Inside, the blissfully cool rooms are greener than a jade mine, with wicker furniture and tiny flat-screen TVs to keep you from ever leaving.

★Tropical Inn BOUTIQUE HOTEL **$$$**
(888-651-6510; www.tropicalinn.com; 812 Duval St; r/ste from $230/375;) The Tropical Inn has excellent service and a host of individualized rooms spread out over a historic-home property. Each room comes decked out in bright pastels and shades of mango, lime and sea foam. A delicious breakfast is included and can be enjoyed in the jungly courtyard next to a lovely sunken pool. Two attached cottages offer romance and privacy for couples.

Mermaid & the Alligator GUESTHOUSE **$$$**
(305-294-1894; www.kwmermaid.com; 729 Truman Ave; r winter $298-468, summer $168-228; P @) Book way ahead: with only nine rooms, this place's charm exceeds its capacity. It's chock a block with treasures collected from the owners' travels, giving it a worldly flair that's simultaneously European and Zen.

Silver Palms Inn BOUTIQUE HOTEL **$$$**
(305-294-8700; www.silverpalmsinn.com; 830 Truman Ave; r from $220; P) Royal blues, sweet teals, bright limes and lemon-yellow color schemes douse the interior of this boutique property, which also boasts bicycle rentals, a saltwater swimming pool and a green certification from the Florida Department of Environmental Protection. Overall, the Silver Palms offers more of a modern, large-hotel vibe with a candy-colored dose of Keys tropics attitude.

Eating

You aren't technically allowed to leave the island without sampling the conch fritters – like hushpuppies, but made with conch – or the key lime pie, made with key limes, sweetened condensed milk, eggs and sugar on a Graham-cracker crust.

Café VEGETARIAN **$**
(305-296 5515; www.thecafekw.com; 509 Southard St; mains $7-17; 11am-10pm;) The Café is the only place in Key West that exclusively caters to herbivores (OK, it has one fish dish). By day, it's a cute, sunny, earthy-crunchy luncheonette; by night, with flickering votive candles and a classy main dish (grilled, blackened tofu and polenta cakes), it's a sultry-but-healthy dining destination.

Camille's FUSION **$$**
(305-296-4811; www.camilleskeywest.com; 1202 Simonton St; breakfast & lunch dishes $4-13, dinner mains $17-26; 8am-3pm & 6-10pm;) Ditch Duval St and dine with the locals at Camille's; this healthy and tasty neighborhood joint is where local families go for a casual meal. Its inventive menu ranges from French toast with Godiva liqueur to tasty chicken salad.

El Siboney CUBAN **$$**
(305-296-4184; www.elsiboneyrestaurant.com; 900 Catherine St; mains $8-17; 11am-9:30pm) Key West is only 90 miles from Cuba, so this awesome rough-and-ready corner establishment is quite literally the closest you can get to real Cuban food in the US. Cash only.

Mo's Restaurant CARIBBEAN **$$**
(305-296-8955; 1116 White St; mains $6-17; 11am-10pm Mon-Sat) If the phrase 'Caribbean home cooking' causes drool to form in the corners of your mouth, don't hesitate. The dishes are mainly Haitian, and they're delicious.

Blue Heaven AMERICAN **$$$**
(305-296-8666; http://blueheavenkw.homestead.com; 729 Thomas St; dinner mains $17-35; 8am-10:30pm;) One of the island's quirkiest venues (and it's a high bar), where you dine in an outdoor courtyard with a flock of chickens. Customers gladly wait, bemusedly, for Blue Heaven's well-executed, Southern-fried interpretation of Keys cuisine.

Café Solé FRENCH $$$
(☎305-294-0230; www.cafesole.com; 1029 Southard St; dinner $25-34; ⏲5:30-10pm) Conch carpaccio with capers? Yellowtail fillet and foie gras? Oh yes. This locally and critically acclaimed venue is known for its cozy back-porch ambience and innovative menus, the result of a French-trained chef exploring island ingredients.

Drinking & Entertainment

Hopping (or staggering) from one bar to the next – also known as the 'Duval Crawl' (p492) – is a favorite pastime here in the Conch Republic, and there are plenty of options for your drinking pleasure.

★**Green Parrot** BAR
(☎305-294-6133; www.greenparrot.com; 601 Whitehead St; ⏲10am-4am) This rogue's cantina has the longest tenure of any bar on the island (since 1890). It's a fabulous dive drawing a lively mix of locals and out-of-towners, with a century's worth of strange decor. Men, don't miss the urinal.

Captain Tony's Saloon BAR
(☎305-294-1838; www.capttonyssaloon.com; 428 Greene St; ⏲10am-2am) This former icehouse, morgue and Hemingway haunt is built around the town's old hanging tree. The eclectic decor includes emancipated bras and signed dollar bills.

Porch BAR
(☎305-517-6358; www.theporchkw.com; 429 Caroline St; ⏲11am-4am) Escape the Duval St frat-boy bars at the Porch, where knowledgeable bartenders dispense artisan beers. It sounds civilized, and almost is, by Key West standards.

Virgilio's JAZZ
(www.virgilioskeywest.com; 524 Duval St; ⏲7pm-3am, to 4am Thu-Sat) Thank God for a little variety. This town needs a dark, candlelit martini lounge where you can chill to jazz and salsa. Enter on Appelrouth Lane.

Information

A great trip-planning resource is www.fla-keys.com/keywest. In town, get maps and brochures at **Key West Chamber of Commerce** (☎305-294-2587; www.keywestchamber.org; 510 Greene St; ⏲8:30am-6:30pm Mon-Sat, to 6pm Sun).

Getting There & Around

The easiest way to travel around Key West and the Keys is by car, though traffic along the one major route, US 1, can be maddening during the winter high season. **Greyhound** (☎305-296-9072; www.greyhound.com; 3535 S Roosevelt Blvd) serves the Keys along US Hwy 1 from downtown Miami.

You can fly into **Key West International Airport** (EYW; ☎305-296-5439; www.keywestinternationalairport.com; 3491 S Roosevelt Blvd) with frequent flights from major cities, most going through Miami. Or, take a fast catamaran from Fort Myers or Miami; call the **Key West Express** (☎888-539-2628; www.seakeywestexpress.com; adult/child/junior/senior return $149/40/86/139, one way $89/20/60/89) for schedules and fares; discounts apply for advance booking.

Within Key West, bicycles are the preferred mode of travel (rentals along Duval St run $10 to $25 per day). **City Transit** (☎305-809-3700; www.kwtransit.com; tickets $2) runs color-coded buses through downtown and the Lower Keys.

ATLANTIC COAST

Florida's Atlantic Coast isn't all beach volleyball, surfing and lazing in the sun. It offers travelers a remarkably well-rounded experience, with something for everyone from history buffs to thrill seekers to art-lovers.

Space Coast

The Space Coast's main claim to fame (other than being the setting for the iconic 1960s TV series *I Dream of Jeannie*) is being the real-life home to the Kennedy Space Center and its massive visitor complex. Cocoa Beach is also a magnet for surfers, with Florida's best waves.

Sights

★**Merritt Island National Wildlife Refuge** WILDLIFE RESERVE
(☎321-861-5601; www.fws.gov/merrittisland; off FL-406; per vehicle Black Point Wildlife Dr $5; ⏲dawn-dusk) FREE This unspoiled 140,000-acre refuge is one of the country's best birding spots, especially from October to May. More endangered and threatened species of wildlife inhabit the swamps, marshes and hardwood hammocks here than at any other site in the continental US.

WORTH A TRIP

DRY TORTUGAS

Seventy miles west of the Keys in the middle of the Gulf, **Dry Tortugas National Park** (☎305-242-7700; www.nps.gov/drto; adult/15yr & under $5/free) is America's most inaccessible national park. Reachable only by boat or plane, it rewards your efforts to get there with amazing snorkeling, diving, bird-watching and stargazing.

Ponce de León christened the area Tortugas (tor-*too*-guzz) after the sea turtles he found here, and the 'Dry' part was added later to warn about the absence of fresh water on the island. But this is more than just a pretty cluster of islands with no drinking water. The never-completed Civil War–era **Fort Jefferson** provides a striking hexagonal centerpiece of red brick rising up from the emerald waters on **Garden Key**, meaning along with your bottled water, you should definitely bring your camera.

So how do you get there? **Yankee Freedom** (☎800-634-0939; www.drytortugas.com; Historic Seaport; adult/child $170/125) is a fast ferry that leaves from the north end of Grinnell St in Key West; the fare includes breakfast, a picnic lunch, snorkeling gear and tour of the fort. Or, you can hop on a **Key West Seaplane** (☎305-293-9300; www.keywestseaplanecharters.com; half-day trip adult/child 3-12yr $300/239) for a half-day or full-day trip. Whichever you choose, reserve at least a week ahead.

If you really want to enjoy the isolation, stay overnight at one of Garden Key's 13 campsites (per person $3). Reserve early through the park office, and bring everything you need, because once that boat leaves, you're on your own.

Kennedy Space Center Visitor Complex MUSEUM
(☎321-449-4444; www.kennedyspacecenter.com; adult/child $50/40, parking $10; ⏲9am-6pm) Once a working space-flight facility, Kennedy Space Center is shifting from a living museum to a historical one since the end of NASA's space-shuttle program in 2011. Devote most of your day to the **Space Shuttle Atlantis** attraction, IMAX theaters and **Rocket Garden**, featuring replicas of classic rockets towering over the complex.

Hungry space enthusiasts can add on **Lunch with an Astronaut;** (☎866-737-5235; adult/child $30/16) or the **Shuttle Launch Simulator**, which reaches a top 'speed' of 17,500mph and feels just like a space-shuttle takeoff, which you can also do alongside an astronaut; among other experiences. Book in advance!

Canaveral National Seashore PARK
(☎386-428-3384; www.nps.gov/cana; Merritt Island; car/bike $5/1; ⏲6am-6pm) This 24 miles of pristine, windswept beaches comprise the longest stretch of undeveloped beach on Florida's east coast.

Activities

Despite all the sunshine and shoreline, Florida is no *Endless Summer*. The water around Miami tends to stay flat, and much of the Gulf Coast is too protected to get much of a swell. But the 70 miles of beaches from New Smyrna to Sebastian Inlet are surfer central. Ten-time world-champion surfer Kelly Slater was born in Cocoa Beach, which remains the epicenter of the surf community. For the local scene and surf reports, visit **Florida Surfing** (www.floridasurfing.com) and **Surf Guru** (www.surfguru.com).

Ron Jon Surf Shop WATER SPORTS
(☎321-799-8888; www.ronjonsurfshop.com; 4151 N Atlantic Ave, Cocoa Beach; ⏲24hr) This massive, 24-hour surfing mecca rents just about anything water-related, from fat-tired beach bikes ($10 daily) to surfboards ($20 daily).

Ron Jon Surf School SURFING
(☎321-868-1980; www.cocoabeachsurfingschool.com; 160 E Cocoa Beach Causeway, Cocoa Beach; per hour $50-65; ⏲9am-5pm) The best surf school in Cocoa Beach for all ages and levels is the state's largest, run by ex-pro surfer and Kelly Slater coach Craig Carroll. Also offers kiteboarding lessons (intro package $375) and SUP river tours (from $65).

Sleeping

Charming Cocoa Beach has the most options, as well as the most chains.

Fawlty Towers MOTEL $
(☎321-784-3870; www.fawltytowersresort.com; 100 E Cocoa Beach Causeway, Cocoa Beach; r $99-109; P❄🛜🏊) After flirtations with being a

nudist resort went limp, this motel returned to its gloriously garish and extremely pink roots: straightforward rooms with an unbeatable beachside location; quiet pool and BYOB tiki hut.

★ **Beach Place Guesthouses** APARTMENT $$$
(321-783-4045; www.beachplaceguesthouses.com; 1445 S Atlantic Ave, Cocoa Beach; ste $199-399; P) A slice of heavenly relaxation in Cocoa Beach's partying beach scene, this laid-back collection of guesthouses in a residential neighborhood has roomy suites with hammocks and lovely hidden patios, all just steps from the dunes and beach.

Eating

Simply Delicious CAFE $
(321-783-2012; 125 N Orlando Ave, Cocoa Beach; mains $7-15; 8am-3pm Tue-Sat, to 2pm Sun) In a darling little yellow house on the southbound stretch of A1A, this homey Americana place packs in locals for a scrumptious menu with unusually delicious delights like mahi-mahi Reuben sandwiches and malted waffles.

★ **Fat Snook** SEAFOOD $$$
(321-784-1190; www.thefatsnook.com; 2464 S Atlantic Ave, Cocoa Beach; mains $22-33; 5:30-10pm) Hidden inside an uninspired building, yet sporting cool, minimalist decor, tiny Fat Snook stands out as an oasis of fine cooking. There's a distinct air of farm-to-table snobbery here; once the food arrives, you won't care.

Crush Eleven MODERN AMERICAN $$$
(321-634-1100; www.crusheleven.com/; 11 Riverside Drive, Cocoa Village; mains $18-49; 5.30-9pm Mon-Sat, 11am-8.30 Sun) This newcomer in noticeably charming Cocoa Village bills itself as 'rustic urban fare'; indeed, you'll see rarities like wild boar, rabbit and beef cheeks on the menu, chased with curated craft beer and cocktails.

Information

Space Coast Office of Tourism (321-433-4470; www.visitspacecoast.com; 430 Brevard Ave, Cocoa Village; 9am-5pm Mon-Fri) Next to Bank of America, one block south of the Village Playhouse.

Getting There & Away

From Orlando take Hwy 528 east, which connects with Hwy A1A. **Greyhound** (www.greyhound.com) has direct services from West Palm Beach to Titusville. **Vero Beach Shuttle** (772-834-1060; www.verobeachshuttle.com; Melbourne/Palm Beach/Orlando airport $95/130/175) provides shuttle service from area airports. **Space Coast Area Transit** (www.ridescat.com; fare $1.25) beach trolley (Route 9) combs up and down the beaches between Cocoa Beach and Port Canaveral.

Daytona Beach

With typical Floridian hype, Daytona Beach bills itself as 'The World's Most Famous Beach.' But its fame is less about quality than the size of the parties this expansive beach has witnessed during spring break, Speed-Weeks, and motorcycle events when half a million bikers roar into town. One Daytona title no one disputes is 'Birthplace of NASCAR,' which started here in 1947. Its origins go back as far as 1902 to drag races held on the beach's hard-packed sands.

Sights & Activities

★ **Daytona International Speedway** RACETRACK
(800-748-7467; www.daytonainternationalspeedway.com; 1801 W International Speedway Blvd; tours $16-50) Impressive and imposing, the Holy Grail of raceways is fresh off a $400-million face-lift. Ticket prices for its diverse race schedule accelerate rapidly the bigger the race, headlined by the **Daytona 500** in February.

Three first-come, first-served tram tours take in the track, pits and behind-the-scenes areas. Real fanatics can indulge in the **Richard Petty Driving Experience** (800-237-3889; www.drivepetty.com), where you can either ride shotgun ($69 to $135) around the track or take a day to become the driver ($549 to $2199); check schedule online.

Cici & Hyatt Brown Museum of Art MUSEUM
(www.moas.org; 352 S Nova Rd; adult/child $10.95/4.95; 10am-5pm Mon-Sat, from 11am Sun) Part of the **Museum of Arts & Sciences** (MOAS; 386-255-0285; www.moas.org; 352 S Nova Rd; adult/child $12.95/6.95; 10am-5pm Tue-Sat, from 11am Sun) complex, this striking must-see new museum, designed to look like a Florida Cracker house, tells the story of Florida via the largest collection of Florida-themed oil and watercolor paintings in the world.

★**Ponce de Leon Inlet Lighthouse & Museum** LIGHTHOUSE
(☎386-761-1821; www.ponceinlet.org; 4931 S Peninsula Dr, Ponce Inlet; adult/child $5/1.50; ⊙10am-6pm Sep-May, to 9pm Aug-Sep) It's 203 steps up to the top of Florida's tallest lighthouse.

Daytona Beach BEACH
(per car $10; ⊙beach driving 8am-7pm May-Oct, sunrise-sunset Nov-Apr) This perfectly planar stretch of sand was once the city's raceway. You can still drive sections at a strictly enforced top speed of 10mph.

Sleeping & Eating

Daytona lodging is plentiful and spans all budgets and styles. Prices soar during events; book well ahead.

Tropical Manor RESORT $
(☎386-252-4920; www.tropicalmanor.com; 2237 S Atlantic Ave, Daytona Beach Shores; r $88-135; P❄📶≋) This beachfront property is vintage Florida, with motel rooms, efficiencies and cottages all blanketed in a frenzy of murals and bright pastels.

Dancing Avocado Kitchen CAFE $
(☎386-947-2022; www.dancingavocadokitchen.com; 110 S Beach St; mains $7.51-13.15; ⊙8am-4:05pm Tue-Sat; 🌱) Fresh, healthful, eclectic sandwiches and wraps dominate the menu at this vegetarian-leaning cafe, but the signature Dancing Avocado Melt is tops.

Aunt Catfish's on the River SOUTHERN $$
(☎386-767-4768; www.auntcatfishontheriver.com; 4009 Halifax Dr, Port Orange; mains $8-27; ⊙11:30am-9pm Mon-Sat, from 9am Sun; P👪) Southern-style seafood lolling in butter and Cajun-spice catfish – paired with cinnamon rolls, no less! – make this place insanely popular.

Drinking

Daytona Taproom BEER HALL
(310 Seabreeze Blvd; burgers $4-13; ⊙noon-2am Sun-Tue, to 3am Wed-Sat; 📶) A bright spot among the biker and beach-bum status quo, this 'burger joint with a drinking problem' has 50 taps of regional and national microbrews and deliciously juicy, thick and creative burgers, hand-cut fries, gourmet hot dogs and waffles.

Information

Daytona Beach Area Convention & Visitors Bureau (☎386-255-0415; www.daytonabeach.com; 126 E Orange Ave; ⊙8:30am-5pm Mon-Fri) Reluctant tourist info; pickings are slim in the office.

Getting There & Around

Daytona Beach International Airport (☎386-248-8030; www.flydaytonafirst.com; 700 Catalina Dr) is just east of the Speedway, and the **Greyhound bus station** (☎386-255-7076; www.greyhound.com; 138 S Ridgewood Ave) is the starting point for services around Florida. **Votran** (☎386-756-7496; www.votran.org; adult/child under 7yr $1.75/free) runs buses and trolleys throughout the city.

St Augustine

The first this, the oldest that…St Augustine was founded by the Spanish in 1565, which means it's chock-full of age-related superlatives. Tourists flock here to stroll the ancient streets around the National Historic Landmark District, aka the oldest permanent settlement in the US.

At times St Augustine screams, 'Hey, everyone, look how quaint we are!' but it stops just short of feeling like a historic theme park because, well, the buildings and monuments are real – many of which were given a rejuvenating face-lift for the city's 450-year anniversary in 2015 – and the narrow, cafe-strewn lanes are genuinely charming. Walk the cobblestoned streets or stand where Juan Ponce de León landed in 1513, and the historical distance occasionally collapses into present-moment chills.

Sights & Activities

The town's two Henry Flagler buildings shouldn't be missed.

★**Lightner Museum** MUSEUM
(☎904-824-2874; www.lightnermuseum.org; 75 King St; adult/child $10/5; ⊙9am-5pm) Flagler's former Hotel Alcazar is now home to this wonderful museum, with a little bit of everything, from ornate Gilded Age furnishings to collections of marbles and cigar-box labels.

★**Hotel Ponce de León** HISTORIC BUILDING
(☎904-823-3378; http://legacy.flagler.edu/pages/tours; 74 King St; tours adult/child $10/1; ⊙tours hourly 10am-3pm summer, 10am & 2pm during school year) This gorgeous former hotel was built in the 1880s and is now the world's most gorgeous dormitory, belonging to Flagler College. Take a guided tour – or at least step inside to gawk at the lobby for free.

★Castillo de San Marcos National Monument FORT
(☎904-829-6506; www.nps.gov/casa; 1 S Castillo Dr; adult/child under 15yr $10/free; ⏲8:45am-5pm; 👪) The country's oldest masonry fort, completed by the Spanish in 1695. Park rangers lead programs hourly and shoot off cannons most weekends.

Colonial Quarter HISTORIC BUILDING
(☎904-342-2857; www.colonialquarter.com; 33 St George St; adult/child $13/7; ⏲10am-5pm) See how they did things back in the 18th century at this re-creation of Spanish Colonial St Augustine, complete with tour guides demonstrating blacksmithing and gunsmithing on the scheduled tours only (10:30am, noon, 1:30pm and 3pm). It's half price after 3pm.

Pirate & Treasure Museum MUSEUM
(☎1-877-467-5863; www.thepiratemuseum.com; 12 S Castillo Dr; adult/child $13/7; ⏲10am-7pm; 👪) A mash-up of theme park and museum, this celebration of all things pirate has real historical treasures (and genuine gold) as well as animatronic pirates, blasting cannons and a kid-friendly treasure hunt.

Fountain of Youth HISTORIC SITE
(☎904-829-3168; www.fountainofyouthflorida.com; 11 Magnolia Ave; adult/child $15/9; ⏲9am-6pm) As the story goes, Spanish explorer Juan Ponce de León came ashore here in 1513, and he considered this freshwater stream the possible legendary Fountain of Youth. Today, this archaeological theme park is part classic roadside attraction, part textbook history, newly madeover to include cannon-firing demonstrations and reconstructions of both the original settlement and the USA's first mission.

Anastasia State Recreation Area PARK
(☎904-461-2033; www.floridastateparks.org/anastasia; 1340 Hwy A1A; car/bike $8/2; ⏲8am-sunset) Locals escape the tourist hordes here, with a terrific beach, a campground (campsites $28) and rentals for all kinds of water sports.

Tours

St Augustine City Walks WALKING TOUR
(☎904-825-0087; www.staugcitywalks.com; 4 Granada St; tours $15-68; ⏲9am-8:30pm) Avoid the tourist trolleys and join extremely fun walking tours of all kinds.

Sleeping

St Augustine is a popular weekend escape; expect room rates to rise about 30% to 50% on Friday and Saturday. Inexpensive motels and chain hotels line San Marco Ave, near where it meets US Hwy 1, and around I-95 at SR-16. Two dozen atmospheric B&Bs can be found at www.staugustineinns.com.

Pirate Haus Inn HOSTEL $
(☎904-808-1999; www.piratehaus.com; 32 Treasury St; dm $25, r from $119; P❄📶) Yar, if ye don't be needing anything fancy, this family-friendly European-style guesthouse/hostel has an unbeatable location and includes a pirate pancake breakfast.

★At Journey's End B&B $$
(☎904-829-0076; www.atjourneysend.com; 89 Cedar St; r $166-279; P❄📶🐾) Free from the granny-ish decor that haunts many St Augustine B&Bs, this pet-friendly, kid-friendly and gay-friendly spot, run by affable hosts, is outfitted in a chic mix of antiques, modern furniture and new two-person steam showers.

Casa de Solana B&B $$
(☎904-824-3555; www.casadesolana.com; 21 Aviles St; r $179-249; P📶) Just off pedestrian-only Aviles St in the oldest part of town, this utterly charming little inn remains faithful to its early-1800s period decor. Rooms-smallish, but price and location equal great value.

Casa Monica HISTORIC HOTEL $$$
(☎904-827-1888; www.casamonica.com; 95 Cordova St; r $219-489, ste from $399; P❄📶🏊) 🍃 Built in 1888, this is *the* luxe hotel in town, with turrets and fountains adding to the Spanish-Moorish castle atmosphere. Rooms are richly appointed, with wrought-iron beds and velvet headboards, while the newly madeover restaurant and expanded lounge are equally regal.

Eating & Drinking

Kookaburra CAFE
(☎904-209-9391; www.kookaburrashop.com; 24 Cathedral Pl; coffee $2.40-4.40; ⏲7:30am-9pm Mon-Thu, to 10pm Fri & Sat, 8am-8pm Sun; 📶) 🍃 Ethically sourced Australian-American coffeehouse serving real Aussie meat pies and the best coffee in the historic quarter.

★**Floridian** MODERN AMERICAN $$
(☎904-829-0655; www.thefloridianstaug.com; 39 Cordova St; mains $11-24; ⏲11am-3pm Wed-Mon, 5-9pm Mon-Thu, to 10pm Fri & Sat) Oozing hipster-locavore earnestness, this vintage-fabulous farm-to-table restaurant serves whimsical neo-Southern creations in an oh-so-cool dining room.

★**Collage** INTERNATIONAL $$$
(☎904-829-0055; www.collagestaug.com; 60 Hypolita St; mains $28-43; ⏲5:30-9pm) Classy and upscale, with a world-class kitchen and service, this spot feels a world away from the bustling touristy downtown. The seafood-heavy menu wins raves for its subtle touch with global flavors.

★**Ice Plant** BAR
(☎904-829-6553; www.iceplantbar.com; 110 Riberia St; ⏲11:30am-2am Tue-Sat, to midnight Sun-Mon; 📶) The hottest spot in St Augustine flaunts exposed concrete, raw brickwork and soaring windows surrounding a vintage, dual-facing centerpiece bar all carved out of a former ice factory. Here coolsters imbibe in some of Florida's finest cocktails, coalesced by overall-clad mixologists wielding hand-cut ice; and excellent farm-to-table fare (mains from $15 to $29).

It's attached to the new St Augustine Distillery, which offers free tours and tastings.

Scarlett O'Hara's PUB
(www.scarlettoharas.net; 70 Hypolita St; ⏲11am-midnight Sun-Thu, to 2am Fri-Sat; 📶) Good luck grabbing a rocking chair: the porch of this pine building is packed all day, every day. Built in 1879, Scarlett's serves regulation pub grub, but it's got the magic ingredients – hopping happy hour, live entertainment nightly, hardworking staff, funky bar – that draw folks like spirits to a séance.

Information

Visitor Information Center (☎904-825-1000; www.FloridasHistoricCoast.com; 10 W Castillo Dr; ⏲8:30am-5:30pm) Hosts historical exhibits in addition a wealth of tourism information.

Getting There & Around

Northeast Florida Regional Airport (☎904-209-0090; www.flynf.com; 4900 US Highway 1), 5 miles north of town, began receiving limited commercial flights in 2014.

The **Greyhound bus station** (☎904-829-6401; www.greyhound.com; 52 San Marcos Ave) is just a few blocks north of the Visitor's Center.

Once you're in Old Town, you can get almost everywhere on foot.

Jacksonville

Are we there yet? Have we left yet? It's hard to tell, because Jacksonville sprawls out over a whopping 840 sq miles, making it the largest city by area in the continental US (eclipsed only by Anchorage, AK). Jacksonville Beach, known locally as 'Jax Beach,' is about 17 miles east of the city center and is where you'll find white sand and most of the action. For information, peruse www.visitjacksonville.com.

Sights & Activities

Atlantic and Neptune are the best beaches in the area, located 16 miles east of downtown. Don't miss the **Downtown Artwalk** (www.jacksonvilleartwalk.com), when artists, musicians, food trucks and pop-up galleries take over 16 downtown blocks on the first Wednesday of every month.

★**Cummer Museum of Art & Gardens** MUSEUM
(www.cummer.org; 829 Riverside Ave; adult/student $10/6; ⏲10am-9pm Tue, to 4pm Wed-Sat, noon-4pm Sun) Jacksonville's premier cultural space has a genuinely excellent collection of American and European paintings, Asian decorative art and antiquities.

Museum of Contemporary Art Jacksonville MUSEUM
(☎904-366-6911; www.mocajacksonville.org; 333 N Laura St; adult/child $8/2.50; ⏲11am-5pm Tue, Wed, Fri & Sat, to 9pm Thu, noon-5pm Sun) The focus of this ultramodern space extends beyond painting: get lost among contemporary sculpture, prints, photography and film; and refuel at the trendy Cafe Nola.

Sleeping & Eating

The cheapest rooms are along I-95 and I-10, where the lower-priced chains congregate. Beach lodging rates often rise in summer. You'll find most of the better bars and restaurants in Jax in the atmospheric neighborhoods of Riverside, 4 miles or so southwest of downtown, and San Marco, 3 miles southeast.

Riverdale Inn B&B $$
(☎904-354-5080; www.riverdaleinn.com; 1521 Riverside Ave; r $140-190, ste $220; P❄📶) In the early 1900s this was one of 50 or so

mansions lining Riverside. Now there are only two left. The good news is, this lovely 10-room stunner kept its full bar – the only inn in Duval County that boasts such a vital component to the traveling experience.

Clark's Fish Camp SOUTHERN **$$**
(☎904-268-3474; www.clarksfishcamp.com; 12903 Hood Landing Rd; mains $10-23; ⏲4:30-9:30pm Mon-Thu, to 10pm Fri, 11:30am-10pm Sat, 11:30am-9:30pm Sun) This unforgettable swamp shack will either disgust you or you'll lap up all of its ridiculousness. Dine on Florida's Southern 'Cracker' cuisine of gator, snake, camel, kangaroo or yak (often fried) or more mainstream seafood while surrounded by the surreal animal menagerie of 'America's largest private taxidermy collection.' It's a haul south of downtown.

★**Orsay** FRENCH, SOUTHERN **$$$**
(☎904-381-0909; www.restaurantorsay.com; 3630 Park St; mains $18-38; ⏲4-10pm Mon-Wed, to 11pm Thu, to midnight Fri, 11:30am-3:30pm & 4-10pm Sat & Sun;) This minimalist bistro in Riverside merges traditional French fare with Southern intuition leading to a menu chock-full of rich and vibrant dishes, most of which are locally sourced. We may or may not have delighted ourselves silly sopping up our incredible bouillabaisse gravy with black truffle mac 'n' cheese, chased with a few of those creative and boozy cocktails.

Drinking & Entertainment

Kickbacks Gastropub BAR
(www.kickbacksjacksonville.com; 910 King St; beers $3.45-10; ⏲7am-3am;) This sprawling copper-toned, penny-lined low-brow gastropub in Riverside has 204 craft beers on tap, including several of Jacksonville's finest. It's divided between the old bar and the new bar, the latter an industrial hodgepodge of massive ceiling fans and Edison-era light bulbs.

Freebird Live LIVE MUSIC
(☎904-246-2473; www.freebirdlive.com; 200 N 1st St, Jacksonville Beach; ⏲8pm-2am show nights) At the beach, a rocking music venue and home of the band Lynyrd Skynyrd.

Getting There & Around

North of the city, **Jacksonville International Airport** (JAX; ☎904-741-4902; www.flyjax.com; 2400 Yankee Clipper Dr) has rental cars. **Greyhound** (☎904-356-9976; www.greyhound.com; 10 N Pearl St) serves numerous cities, and **Amtrak** (☎904-766-5110; www.amtrak.com; 3570 Clifford Lane) has trains from the north and south.

The **Jacksonville Transportation Authority** (☎904-630-3100; www.jtafla.com) runs the free Skyway monorail and city buses (fare $1.50).

Amelia Island & Around

Residents are quick to tell you: Amelia Island is just as old as that braggart St Augustine – they just can't prove it. Unfortunately, no Ponce de León, no plaque, so they have to content themselves with being a pretty little island of moss-draped Southern charm and home to **Fernandina Beach**, a shrimping village with 40 blocks of historic buildings and romantic B&Bs.

Sights & Activities

Fort Clinch State Park PARK
(☎904-277-7274; www.floridastateparks.org/fortclinch; 2601 Atlantic Ave; park pedestrian/car $2/6; ⏲park 8am-sunset, fort 9am-5pm) Capping the north end of the island, the Spanish moss-draped Fort Clinch State Park has beaches, camping ($26), bike trails and a commanding Civil War–era fort, with reenactments taking place the first full weekend of every month.

Amelia Island Museum of History MUSEUM
(www.ameliamuseum.org; 233 S 3rd St; adult/student $7/4; ⏲10am-4pm Mon-Sat, 1-4pm Sun) Learn about Amelia Island's intricate history, which has seen it ruled under eight different flags starting with the French in 1562. Admission includes tours at 11am and 2pm; and additional ghost and pub-crawl tours originate here as well.

Talbot Islands State Parks PARK
(☎904-251-2320; ⏲8am-dusk) Amelia Island is part of the Talbot Islands State Parks, which includes the pristine shoreline at Little Talbot Island and the 'boneyard beach' at Big Talbot Island State Park, where silvered tree skeletons create a dramatic landscape.

Kelly Seahorse Ranch HORSEBACK RIDING
(☎904-491-5166; www.kellyranchinc.net; 7500 1st Coast Hwy; 1hr rides adult/child $70/80; ⏲10am, noon, 2pm & 4pm, closed Mon) Offers beachfront trail rides for riders aged 13 and over. Rents beach cruisers as well.

Sleeping

★**Fairbanks House** B&B **$$**
(☎904-277-0500; www.fairbankshouse.com; 227 S 7th St; r/ste/cottage from $185/265/230;

P ❄ 📶 🏊) This grand, Italianate mansion has undergone a green makeover, now featuring universal and Tesla electric car charging stations. Guest rooms are so large they feel like suites; we especially like the downstairs room carved out of the house's original 1800s kitchen.

Florida House Inn HISTORIC HOTEL **$$**
(☎904-491-3322; www.floridahouseinn.com; 22 S 3rd St; r $140-200) Florida's oldest hotel features an atmospheric structure dating to 1857 that is battling real estate with an ever-expanding 400-year-old oak tree.

Hoyt House B&B **$$$**
(☎904-277-4300; www.hoythouse.com; 804 Atlantic Ave; r from $199-349; P ❄ 📶 🏊) This tall 1905 Victorian boasts an enchanting gazebo that begs time with a cool drink. Ten rooms each have their own stylish mix of antiques and found treasures and three-course breakfasts are served.

Elizabeth Pointe Lodge B&B **$$$**
(☎904-277-4851; www.elizabethpointelodge.com; 98 S Fletcher Ave; r/ste from $299/375; P ❄ 📶) Located right on the ocean, this 25-room lodge looks like an old Nantucket-style sea-captain's house with wraparound porches, gracious service and beautifully appointed rooms.

Eating & Drinking

Gilbert's Underground Kitchen NEW SOUTHERN **$$**
(☎904-310-6374; www.undergroundkitchen.co; 510 S 8th Street; mains $13-23; ⏲6-10pm Mon & Wed-Thu, 11am-2pm & 6-10pm Fri, 10:30am-2pm & 6-10pm Sat & Sun) Celebrity *Top Chef* Kenny Gilbert's Underground Kitchen has sleepy Amelia Island abuzz with culinary glee. Feast on inventive Southern-soul hybrid dishes such as alligator BBQ ribs, noodles with collard green pesto or fried chicken with datil pepper hot sauce.

29 South SOUTHERN **$$**
(☎904-277-7919; www.29southrestaurant.com; 29 S 3rd St; mains $9-28; ⏲11:30am-2:30pm & 5:30-9:30pm Wed-Sat, 10am-2.30pm & 5:30-9:30pm Sun, 5:30-9:30pm Mon & Tue) Small plates and mains link arms happily at the tiny, stylish neo-Southern gourmet bistro.

Café Karibo & Karibrew FUSION **$$**
(☎904-277-5269; www.cafekaribo.com; 27 N 3rd St; mains $8-22; ⏲11am-3pm Mon, to 10pm Tue-Sat, to 8pm Sun; 📶) This funky side-street restaurant and brewery serves a large and eclectic menu in a sprawling two-story space. Live music on weekends.

★ **Palace Saloon** BAR
(www.thepalacesaloon.com; 113-117 Centre St; ⏲8pm-2am) One more superlative for Fernandina: Florida's oldest bar, sporting swinging doors, draped velvet and a deadly Pirate's Punch.

Information

Historic Downtown Visitor Center (☎904-277-0717; www.ameliaisland.com; 102 Centre St; ⏲10am-4pm) Reams of useful information and maps in the old railroad depot. A fun stop in itself.

WEST COAST

If Henry Flagler's railroad made the east coast of Florida what it is today, his lack of attention to the rest of the state similarly affected the west coast. Things are calmer here, with fewer tourist hordes and more room for nature to amuse us with shelling beaches, swamp lands and nature preserves. The west coast has front-row seats to flame-red sunsets emblazoned over the Gulf of Mexico, as well as adrenaline-pumping roller coasters, hand-rolled cigars and lip-synching mermaids.

Tampa

From the outside, Florida's third-largest city seems all business, even generically so. But Tampa surprises: its revitalized riverfront is a sparkling green swath dotted with intriguing cultural institutions, and its historic Ybor City district preserves the city's Cuban cigar-industry past while, at night, transforming into the Gulf Coast's hottest bar and nightclub scene. South Tampa, meanwhile, has a cutting-edge dining scene that's drawing food mavens from Orlando and Miami.

Sights

Downtown Tampa

Most of downtown's sights are in or along Tampa's newly completed 2.4-mile green space, **Riverwalk** (www.thetampariverwalk.com).

Tampa Museum of Art MUSEUM
(☎813-274-8130; www.tampamuseum.org; 120 W Gasparilla Plaza; adult/student $15/5; ⏲11am-7pm Mon-Thu, to 8pm Fri, to 5pm Sat & Sun) A modern, dramatically cantilevered museum with even galleries that balance Greek and Roman antiquities, contemporary photography and new media with major traveling exhibitions.

Henry B Plant Museum MUSEUM
(☎813-254-1891; www.plantmuseum.com; 401 W Kennedy Blvd; adult/child $10/5; ⏲10am-5pm Tue-Sat, from noon Sun) The silver minarets of Henry B Plant's 1891 Tampa Bay Hotel glint majestically. Now part of the University of Tampa, the audio tour re-creates the original hotel's luxurious, gilded late-Victorian world.

Tampa Bay History Center MUSEUM
(☎813-228-0097; www.tampabayhistorycenter.org; 801 Old Water St; adult/child $13/8; ⏲10am-5pm) This first-rate history museum presents the region's Seminole people, Cracker pioneers and Tampa's Cuban community and cigar industry. The on-again, off-again cartography collection dazzles.

Glazer Children's Museum MUSEUM
(☎813-443-3861; www.glazermuseum.org; 110 W Gasparilla Plaza; adult/child $15/9.50; ⏲10am-5pm Mon-Fri, to 6pm Sat, 1-6pm Sun; 👪) Creative play spaces for kids don't get any better than this crayon-bright, inventive museum. Eager staff and tons of fun; adjacent Curtis Hixon Park is picnic-and-playground friendly.

Ybor City

Like the illicit love child of Key West and Miami's Little Havana, Ybor City's cobblestoned 19th-century historic district is a redolent mix of wrought-iron balconies, globe streetlamps, immigrant history, ethnic cuisine, cigars and hip, happening nightlife. Diverse and youthful, Ybor (ee-bore) City oozes rakish, scruffy charm.

The main drag – along 7th Ave (La Septima) between 14th and 21st Sts – is packed with eats, drinks, shops and cigar stores.

Ybor City Museum State Park MUSEUM
(☎813-247-6323; www.ybormuseum.org; 1818 E 9th Ave; adult/child $4/free; ⏲9am-5pm) Join a **walking tour** (☎813-428-0854; online/audio tour $10/20) run by a cigar-maker with a PhD, check out the cool museum store, or delve into the old-school history museum that preserves a bygone era, with cigar-worker houses and wonderful photos.

Busch Gardens & Adventure Island

No, it's not as thematically immersive as Orlando's Disney World or Universal, but Tampa's big theme park, **Busch Gardens** (☎888-800-5447; http://seaworldparks.com/en/buschgardens-tampa; 10165 McKinley Dr; admission 3yr & up $95, discounts online; ⏲10am-7pm, hours vary), will satisfy your adrenaline craving with epic roller coasters and flume rides that weave through an African-theme wildlife park.

Adjacent **Adventure Island** (☎888-800-5447; www.adventureisland.com; 10001 McKinley Dr; admission 3yr & up $49; ⏲10am-5pm) is a massive water park with slides and rides galore. Discounts and combination tickets are available online.

Sleeping

Chains abound along Fowler Ave and Busch Blvd (Hwy 580), near Busch Gardens.

Gram's Place Hostel HOSTEL $
(☎813-221-0596; www.grams-inn-tampa.com; 3109 N Ola Ave; dm $23-26, r $50-60; ❄@📶) Gram's is a tiny, welcoming hostel for international travelers who prefer personality over perfect linens. Within a ramshackle two-home maze, it's like sleeping in a charismatic musical junkyard. Great-value private rooms.

★**Epicurean Hotel** BOUTIQUE HOTEL $$
(www.epicureanhotel.com; 1207 S Howard Ave; r $159-309; P❄@📶🏊) Foodies rejoice! Tampa's coolest hotel, opened in 2014, is a food- and drink-themed boutique Eden steeped in detailed design touches: vertical hydroponic lettuce and herb walls, a zinc bar, reclaimed woods from an 1820s railway station, oversized whiskers as test-kitchen door handles and so on.

Tahitian Inn HOTEL $$
(☎813-877-6721; www.tahitianinn.com; 601 S Dale Mabry Hwy; r $89-109, ste $119-139; P❄@📶🏊) The name is reminiscent of a tiki-theme motel, but this family-owned, full-service hotel offers fresh, boutique stylings on the cheap. Nice pool; and airport/cruise terminal transportation is included.

TAMPA BAY AREA BEACHES

The barrier islands of the Tampa Bay Area are graced with some of Florida's best beaches, whether you define 'best' as 'gorgeous untrammeled solitude' or 'family fun and thumping beach parties.' For more information, visit www.tampabaybeaches.com and www.visitstpeteclearwater.com. North to south, some highlights:

Honeymoon and Caladesi Islands Two of Florida's most beautiful beaches; unspoiled, lightly visited Caladesi Island is only reachable by ferry.

Clearwater Beach Idyllic soft white sand hosts raucous spring-break-style parties; huge resorts cater to the masses.

St Pete Beach Double-wide strand that's the epicenter of activities and all-ages fun; packed with hotels, bars and restaurants.

Pass-a-Grille Beach Most popular with city-based day-trippers; extremely long and backed by houses (not resorts); cute-as-a-button village for eats.

Fort Desoto Park and North Beach North Beach is one of Florida's finest white-sand beaches; ideal for families. Extensive park includes bike and kayak rentals, fishing piers and a cafe.

Eating

At mealtime, focus on Ybor City, South Tampa's SoHo area (South Howard Ave) and Seminole Heights.

Wright's Gourmet House SANDWICHES $

(www.wrightsgourmet.com; 1200 S Dale Mabry Hwy; sandwiches & salads $6.75-11; 7am-6pm Mon-Fri, 8am-4pm Sat) It doesn't look like much from outside (or in!) but it's been slinging sandwiches since 1963, and its unique combinations and hearty portions win it plenty of fans.

Refinery MODERN AMERICAN $$

(813-237-2000; www.thetamparefinery.com; 5137 N Florida Ave; mains $9-25; 11am-2pm & 5-10pm Mon-Thu, 11am-2pm & 5-11pm Fri, 11am-2:30pm & 5-11pm Sat, 11am-2:30pm Sun;) This blue-collar gourmet joint hawks playful, delicious hyperlocal cuisine that cleverly mixes a sustainability ethic with a punk attitude. Owners Michelle and Greg Baker are among a tiny number of Florida restaurateurs who are known outside the area, thanks no doubt to Greg's three James Beard nominations.

Ulele AMERICAN $$

(813-999-4952; www.ulele.com; 1810 North Highland Ave; mains $10-36; 11am-10pm Sun-Thu, to 11pm Fri-Sat;) This former water-pumping station has been transformed into an artsy-industrial restaurant and brewery with a menu that resurrects native Flordian recipes madeover for modern times. That means liberal use of datil peppers, sides like alligator beans and okra 'fries' (amazing!), mains such as local pompano fish and desserts including guava pie.

★Columbia Restaurant SPANISH $$$

(813-248-4961; www.columbiarestaurant.com; 2117 E 7th Ave; mains lunch $11-26, dinner $20-31; 11am-10pm Mon-Thu, to 11pm Fri & Sat, noon-9pm Sun) This Spanish Cuban restaurant is the oldest in Florida, dating to 1905. Occupying an entire block, it consists of 13 elegant dining rooms and romantic, fountain-centered courtyards. Many of the gloved waiters have been here a lifetime.

★Bern's Steak House STEAK $$$

(813-251-2421; www.bernssteakhouse.com; 1208 S Howard Ave; steaks for 1-2 people $32-105; 5-10pm Sun-Thu, to 11pm Fri & Sat) This legendary, nationally renowned steakhouse is an event as much as a meal. Dress up, agonize over your choice of incredibly extensive on-premises dry-aged beef, ask to tour the wine cellar and kitchens, and *don't* skip dessert.

Drinking & Entertainment

For nightlife, Ybor City is party central, while SoHo and Seminole Heights offer more cultured hipness. *Creative Loafing* (www.cltampa.com), Tampa Bay's alternative weekly, lists events and bars. Ybor City is also the center of Tampa's GLBT life; check out the **GaYBOR District Coalition** (www.gaybor.com) and **Tampa Bay Gay** (www.tampabaygay.com).

Cigar City Brewing BREWERY
(☎813-348-6363; www.cigarcitybrewing.com; 3924 West Spruce St; ⊙11am-11pm Sun-Thu, to 1am Fri & Sat) This is Tampa's premier craft brewery. It has dozens of crafted brews on tap, many exclusive to the brewery. Tours are $5 (with one beer included).

Information

Tampa Bay Convention & Visitors Bureau (☎813-223-1111; www.visittampabay.com; 615 Channelside Dr; ⊙10am-5:30pm Mon-Sat, 11am-5pm Sun) The visitor center has good free maps and lots of information. Book hotels directly through the website.

Ybor City Visitor Center (☎813-241-8838; www.ybor.org; 1600 E 8th Ave; ⊙10am-5pm Mon-Sat, from noon Sun) Get a great overview plus walking tour maps at the visitor center – itself an excellent small museum.

Getting There & Around

Tampa International Airport (TPA; ☎813-870-8700; www.tampaairport.com; 4100 George J Bean Pkwy) has car-rental agencies. **Greyhound** (☎813-229-2174; www.greyhound.com; 610 E Polk St, Tampa) has numerous services. Trains run south to Miami and north through Jacksonville from the **Amtrak station** (☎813-221-7600; www.amtrak.com; 601 N Nebraska Ave).

Hillsborough Area Regional Transit (HART; ☎813-254-4278; www.gohart.org; 1211 N Marion St; fares $2) connects downtown and Ybor City with buses, trolleys and old-style streetcars.

St Petersburg

In the bay area, St Petersburg is the more arty, youthful sibling. It also has a more compact and walkable tourist district along its attractive harbor. For a cultural city base within easy striking distance of the region's excellent beaches, St Pete is a great choice.

Sights

Most of the action is around and along Central Ave, from 8th Ave to Bayshore Dr, which fronts the harbor and tourist pier.

St Petersburg Museum of Fine Arts MUSEUM
(☎727-896-2667; www.fine-arts.org; 255 Beach Dr NE; adult/child $17/10; ⊙10am-5pm Mon-Sat, to 8pm Thu, from noon Sun) Boasts a broad collection traversing the world's antiquities and following art's progression through nearly every era.

Florida Holocaust Museum MUSEUM
(☎727-820-0100; www.flholocaustmuseum.org; 55 5th St S; adult/student $16/8; ⊙10am-5pm) The understated exhibits of this Holocaust museum, one of the country's largest, present these mid-20th-century events with moving directness.

Chihuly Collection GALLERY
(☎727-896-4527; www.moreanartscenter.org; 400 Beach Dr; adult/child $15/11; ⊙10am-5pm Mon-Sat, from noon Sun) A paean to Chihuly's glass artistry, with galleries designed to hold the dramatic installations.

Sleeping

★**Dickens House** B&B $$
(☎727-822-8622; www.dickenshouse.com; 335 8th Ave NE; r $135-245; P❄@📶) Five lushly designed rooms await in this passionately restored arts-and-crafts-style home. The gregarious, gay-friendly owner whips up a gourmet breakfast.

Ponce de Leon BOUTIQUE HOTEL $$
(☎727-550-9300; www.poncedeleonhotel.com; 95 Central Ave; r $99-149, ste $169; ❄@📶) A boutique hotel with Spanish flair in the heart of downtown. Splashy murals, designer-cool decor, and its hot restaurant and bar, are highlights; off-site parking is not.

Birchwood Inn BOUTIQUE HOTEL $$$
(☎727-896-1080; www.thebirchwood.com; 340 Beach Dr NE; r from $275; P❄📶) Rooms are simply gorgeous at this boutique gem: spacious, with claw-foot baths, king canopy beds and oozing vintage bordello elegance sexed up with a little South Beach sauciness. **Canopy**, the rooftop bar, is the hottest spot in town for cocktails.

Eating & Drinking

At night, focus anywhere on Central Ave and Beach Dr along the harborfront.

Taco Bus MEXICAN $
(www.taco-bus.com; 2324 Central Ave; mains $6-13; ⊙11am-10pm Sun-Thu, to 4am Fri & Sat; 📶) When this taco- and burrito-slinging food truck needed a bricks-and-mortar location, it just rolled right up next to a good-time patio and didn't skip a beat. *Cochinita pibil*, *carnitas* and *pollo chipotle* are highlights. A Tampa Bay institution.

Bella Brava ITALIAN $$
(☎727-895-5515; www.bellabrava.com; 204 Beach Dr NE; mains $9-27; ⊙11:30am-10pm, to 11pm Fri

DON'T MISS

SALVADOR DALÍ MUSEUM

Of course St Petersburg was the logical place to put a museum dedicated to Salvador Dalí, the eccentric Spanish artist who painted melting clocks, grew an exaggerated handlebar mustache to look like King Philip, and once filled a Rolls Royce with cauliflower. Right? In fact, **Salvador Dalí Museum** (727-823-3767; www.thedali.org; 1 Dali Blvd; adult/child 6-12yr $24/10, after 5pm Thu $10; 10am-5:30pm Mon-Wed, Fri & Sat, to 8pm Thu, noon-5:30pm Sun) is the largest Dalí collection outside of Spain. So how did that happen exactly?

In 1942 A Reynolds Morse and his wife Eleanor began what would become the largest private Dalí collection in the world. When it came time to find a permanent home for the collection, they had one stipulation: that the collection had to stay together. Only three cities could agree to the terms, and St Petersburg won out for its waterfront location.

The museum now has a brand-new building with a theatrical exterior that, when seen from the bay side, looks like a geodesic atrium oozing out of a shoebox. It doesn't have *the* melting clocks, but it does have *some* melting clocks, as well as an impressive collection of paintings with titles such as *The Ghost of Vermeer of Delft Which Can Be Used as a Table*.

& Sat, 1-9pm Sun;) Anchoring the prime waterfront intersection, Bella Brava continues to draw a noisy young, professional crowd with its contemporary Italian cooking, pizza menu and cocktail bar. There's also sidewalk seating on Beach Dr.

Ceviche TAPAS $$
(www.ceviche.com; 10 Beach Dr; tapas $4-15, mains $9-20; 5-11pm Mon-Fri, 8am-11pm Sat & Sun;) An upbeat Spanish atmosphere and flavorful, creative, generously portioned tapas. End the evening in the sexy, cavernlike Flamenco Room below.

3 Daughters Brewing BREWERY
(727-495-6002; www.3dbrewing.com; 222 22nd St S; 2-9pm Mon-Tue, to 10pm Wed & Thu, to midnight Fri & Sat, 1-9pm Sun) The best brewery experience we came across in four states: a 30-barrel brewhouse with drinking games and live music *in* the brewery itself!

Information

St Petersburg Area Chamber of Commerce (727-8388-0686; www.stpete.com; 100 2nd Ave N; 9am-5pm Mon-Fri, 10am-4pm Sat) Helpful, staffed chamber office has good maps and a driving guide.

Getting There & Around

St Petersburg-Clearwater International Airport (727-453-7800; www.fly2pie.com; Roosevelt Blvd & Hwy 686, Clearwater) is served by several major carriers. **Greyhound** (727-898-1496; www.greyhound.com; 180 Dr Martin Luther King Jr St N; 8:15-10am & 2:30-6:30pm Mon-Sun) services include Tampa.

Pinellas Suncoast Transit Authority (PSTA; www.psta.net; 340 2nd Ave N; adult/student $2/1.25) operates buses citywide, as well as the Suncoast Beach Trolley that links the beaches from Clearwater to Pass-a-Grille, and the Downtown Looper trolley, which is free within a defined zone around Beach Dr.

Sarasota

Artists, writers, musicians, entertainers – artsy types have flocked to Sarasota since the 1920s, with John Ringling leading the way. He set it on this course in 1911, when he made the town the winter home of his famous circus. Today the Ringling Museum Complex is a regional highlight, and Sarasota spills over with opera, theater and art.

Another considerable boost to Sarasota's popularity is its luscious white-sand beaches. **Lido Beach** is closest and has free parking, but 5 miles away **Siesta Key** has sand like confectioner's sugar and is one of Florida's best and most popular strands; Siesta Village is also a lively, family-friendly beach town.

Sights & Activities

Marie Selby Botanical Gardens GARDENS
(941-366-5731; www.selby.org; 811 S Palm Ave; adult/child 4-11yr $19/6; 10am-5pm) Boasts the world's largest scientific collection of orchids and bromeliads.

Myakka Outpost KAYAKING
(941-923-1120; www.myakkaoutpost.com; 13208 SR-72; canoes/bikes $20/15; 9:30am-5pm Mon-Fri, 8:30am-6pm Sat & Sun) Within the Myakka River State Park, this canoe outfitter can get you out on the Myakka River, a really cool

experience among hundreds of alligators about a half-hour from downtown.

🛏 Sleeping & Eating

In addition to downtown Sarasota and Siesta Village, **St Armands Circle** on Lido Key is an evening social hub, with a proliferation of stylish shops and restaurants.

The Capri at Siesta RESORT $$
(☑941-684-3244; www.capriinternational.com; 6782 SaraSea Circle; r $149-229, ste $189-329; P❄🐦📶🌊) As discerningly located – 200 steps from Siesta sands but tucked away from the hubbub – as it is well appointed, this 10-room boutique resort forgoes in-your-face tropicallia for more soothing, earth-toned decor and private refinement.

★Hotel Ranola BOUTIQUE HOTEL $$
(☑941-951-0111; www.hotelranola.com; 118 Indian Pl; r $109-179, ste $239-269; P❄📶) The nine rooms feel like a designer's brownstone apartment: free-spirited and effortlessly artful, but with real working kitchens. It's urban funk, walkable to downtown Sarasota.

Another Broken Egg Cafe BREAKFAST $
(www.anotherbrokenegg.com; 140 Avenida Messina, Siesta Key; mains $5-16; ⏰7:30am-2:30pm; 🪑) This chain, diner-style breakfast institution on Siesta Key is a social hub each morning. The menu is chock-full of scrumptious and creative breakfast fare (black bean Benedict with chipotle Hollandaise!).

Owen's Fish Camp SOUTHERN $$
(☑941-951-6936; www.owensfishcamp.com; 516 Burns Lane; mains $10-28; ⏰from 4pm) This ironically hip swamp shack downtown serves

upscale versions of Florida-style Southern cuisine with an emphasis on seafood.

ℹ Information

Sarasota Visitor Information Center (☑941-957-1877; www.sarasotafl.org; 14 Lemon Ave; ⏰10am-5pm Mon-Sat; 📶) Very friendly office with tons of info; sells good maps.

Sanibel & Captiva Islands

Shaped like a fish hook trying to lure Fort Myers, these two slivers of barrier island lie across a 2-mile causeway (toll $6). Upscale but unpretentious, with a carefully managed shoreline that feels remarkably lush and undeveloped, the islands are idyllic, cushy getaways, where bikes are the preferred mode of travel and the shelling is legendary and romantic.

⊙ Sights & Activities

JN 'Ding' Darling National Wildlife Refuge WILDLIFE RESERVE
(☑239-472-1100; www.fws.gov/dingdarling; 1 Wildlife Dr; car/cyclist $5/1; ⏰9am-5pm Jan-Apr, to 4pm May-Dec) In addition to its fabulous beaches, this splendid 6300-acre refuge that is home to an abundance of seabirds and wildlife. It has an excellent nature center, a 4-mile Wildlife Drive, narrated tram tours and easy kayaking in Tarpon Bay

Bailey-Matthews National Shell Museum MUSEUM
(☑239-395-2233; www.shellmuseum.org; 3075 Sanibel-Captiva Rd, Sanibel; adult/child 5-17yr $11/5; ⏰10am-5pm) Like a mermaid's jewel box, this fascinating museum offers a natural history

---

DON'T MISS

RINGLING COMPLEX

Who doesn't love the circus? Well, people who are afraid of clowns, perhaps, but a little coulrophobia isn't necessarily a deal-breaker at the **Ringling Museum Complex** (☑941-359-5700; www.ringling.org; 5401 Bay Shore Rd; adult/child 6-17yr $25/5; ⏰10am-5pm daily, to 8pm Thu; 🪑). On the grounds of the 66-acre complex are three separate museums, all included in your admission and each one a worthy attraction on its own. Railroad, real-estate and circus baron John Ringling and his wife Mabel put down roots here, building a Venetian Gothic waterfront mansion called **Ca d'Zan**. You can wander the ground floor at your own pace, or take a $5 or $20 guided tour add-on – totally worth it – which grants you access to the upstairs bedrooms and 'private places.'

Also on the grounds, the excellent **John & Mabel Museum of Art**; and the one-of-a-kind **Museum of the Circus**, with costumes, props, posters, antique circus wagons and a humongous (3800-sq-ft!), fantastical miniature model of the big-top era in its heyday.

DON'T MISS

THE ENLIGHTENED SNOWBIRDS OF FORT MYERS

Florida's snowbirds can be easy to mock, but not this pair. Famous inventor Thomas Edison built a winter home and lab here in Fort Myers in 1885, and automaker Henry Ford became his neighbor in 1916. The **Edison & Ford Winter Estates** (☎239-334-7419; www.edisonfordwinterestates.org; 2350 McGregor Blvd; tours adult $12-25, child $5-15; ⏰9am-5:30pm) is now the city's main claim to fame. The excellent museum focuses mainly on the overwhelming scope of Edison's genius, and their homes are genteel, landscaped delights.

If you're visiting the area, 15 miles south of Fort Myers, Fort Myers Beach is 7 miles of talcum-powder-fine sand along **Estero Island**, presided over by one of Florida's quintessential activity-and-party-fueled beach towns. Families often prefer Fort Myers Beach because it's more affordable than neighboring coastal towns, and coeds like it because its bars are louder and more raucous; the area is also the gateway for the far more-charming Sanibel & Captiva Islands. For town information, visit www.fortmyers-beachchamber.org.

of the sea, with covetous displays of shells from all over the world; and daily beach walks ($10).

Tarpon Bay Explorers KAYAKING
(☎239-472-8900; www.tarponbayexplorers.com; 900 Tarpon Bay Rd, Sanibel; ⏰8am-6pm) Within the Darling refuge, this outfitter rents canoes and kayaks ($25 for two hours) and SUP for easy, self-guided paddles in Tarpon Bay, a perfect place for young paddlers.

Billy's Rentals BICYCLE RENTAL
(☎239-472-5248; www.billysrentals.com; 1470 Periwinkle Way, Sanibel; bikes per 2hr/day $5/15; ⏰8:30am-5pm) Rents bikes or any other wheeled contrivance.

Sleeping & Eating

Tarpon Tale Inn COTTAGE $$
(☎239-472-0939; www.tarpontale.com; 367 Periwinkle Way, Sanibel; r $230-290; ❄@📶) For a more personal experience, this five-room inn hides its cottages away in jungly surrounds on peaceful, hammock-strung grounds. No breakfast, though.

Over Easy Cafe CAFE $
(www.overeasycafesanibel.com; 630 Tarpon Bay Rd, Sanibel; breakfast $4-12; ⏰7am-3pm; 📶👪) Despite Provence-style decor, the menu offers strictly top-quality diner fare, including healthy-dose scramblers, omelets, and various style of 'Benny's' (eggs Benedict).

★ **Sweet Melissa's Cafe** AMERICAN $$$
(☎239-472-1956; www.sweetmelissascafe.net; 1625 Periwinkle Way, Sanibel; tapas $9-16, mains $26-34; ⏰11:30am-2:30pm & 5-9pm Mon-Fri, 5-9pm Sat) From its menu to its atmosphere, Sweet Melissa's offers well-balanced, relaxed refinement.

Information

Sanibel & Captiva Islands Chamber of Commerce (☎239-472-1080; www.sanibel-captiva.org; 1159 Causeway Rd, Sanibel; ⏰9am-5pm; 📶) One of the more helpful visitor centers around; keeps an updated hotel-vacancy list with dedicated hotel hotline.

Naples

The Gulf Coast's answer to Palm Beach, Naples is a perfectly manicured, rich town with an adult sense of self and one of the most pristine, relaxed city beaches in the state. While it is certainly family friendly, it appeals most to romance-minded travelers seeking fine art and fine dining, trendy cocktails, fashion-conscious shopping and luscious sunsets.

Sights & Activities

★ **Baker Museum** MUSEUM
(☎239-597-1900; www.artisnaples.org; 5833 Pelican Bay Blvd; adult/child $10/free; ⏰10am-4pm Tue-Sat, noon-4pm Sun) The pride of Naples, this engaging, sophisticated art museum offers a rewarding collection with cleverly designed exhibits

Naples Nature Center NATURE RESERVE
(☎239-262-0304; www.conservancy.org/nature-center; 1450 Merrihue Dr; adult/child 3-12yr $13/9; ⏰9:30am-4:30pm Mon-Sat, open Sun Jun-Aug) One of Florida's best nature conservancies and rehabilitation centers, with a Leadership in Energy & Enivronmental design-certified campus and fantastic exhibits. The

21-acre park offers pleasant boardwalk trails and naturalist boat rides.

Sleeping & Eating

Lemon Tree Inn MOTEL $$
(239-262-1414; www.lemontreeinn.com; 250 9th St S; r $152-196;) You'll find 34 clean and brightly decorated rooms (some with passable kitchenettes and screened-in porches) forming a U around pretty, private gardens and a pool, where breakfast is served. Good value.

Inn on 5th HOTEL $$$
(239-403-8777; www.innonfifth.com; 699 5th Ave S; r $399, ste $599-999;) This well-polished, Mediterranean-style luxury hotel provides an unbeatable location in the midst of 5th Ave.

The Local MODERN AMERICAN $$
(www.thelocalnaples.com; 5323 Airport Pulling Rd N; mains $12-29; 11am-9pm Sun-Thu, to 10pm Fri & Sat;) The ethics of driving 6 miles from downtown to eat local aside, this strip-mall farm-to-table bistro is worth the carbon footprint for fab sustainable fare, from ceviche tacos to grass-fed beef. Escape tourists. Eat local.

IM Tapas SPANISH $$
(239-403-8272; www.imtapas.com; 965 4th Ave N; tapas $5.50-18; from 5:30pm Mon-Sat) A mother-and-daughter team serving Madrid-worthy Spanish tapas.

Information

Visitor Information Center (239-262-6141; www.napleschamber.org; 900 5th Ave S; 9am-5pm Mon-Sat, 10am-2pm Sun summer, 9am-5pm Mon-Fri, 9am-1pm Sun winter) Will help with accommodations; good maps, and acres of brochures.

CENTRAL FLORIDA

Before Disney – BD – most tourists came to Florida to see two things: the white-sand beaches and the alligator-infested Everglades. Walt Disney changed all that when he opened the Magic Kingdom in 1971. Today Orlando is the theme-park capital of the world, and Walt Disney World is Florida's number-one attraction.

Orlando

Like Las Vegas, Orlando is almost entirely given over to fantasy. It's a place to come when you want to imagine you're somewhere else: Hogwarts, perhaps, or Cinderella's Castle, or Dr Seuss' world, or an African safari. And like Vegas' casinos, Orlando's theme parks work hard to be constantly entertaining thrill rides where the only concern is your pleasure. Even outside the theme parks, Orlando can exhibit a hyper atmosphere of fiberglass-modeled, cartoon-costumed pop-culture amusement.

But if you're theme parked-out, there's a real city to explore, one with tree-shaded parks surrounding numerous lakes, art museums, orchestras, and dinners that don't involve high-fiving Goofy. And just outside the city, Florida's wilderness and wildlife, particularly its crystal springs, can be as memorably bizarre as anything Ripley ever dreamed up.

Sights & Activities

Downtown & Loch Haven Park

Fashionable Thornton Park is home to several good restaurants and bars, while Loch Haven Park is home to a cluster of cultural institutions.

★**Orlando Museum of Art** MUSEUM
(407-896-4231; www.omart.org; 2416 N Mills Ave; adult/child $8/5; 10am-4pm Tue-Fri, from noon Sat & Sun; ; Lynx 125, Florida Hospital Health Village) Spotlighting American and African art as well as unique traveling exhibits.

Mennello Museum of American Art MUSEUM
(407-246-4278; www.mennellomuseum.com; 900 E Princeton St, Loch Haven Park; adult/child 6-18yr $5/1; 10:30am-4:30pm Tue-Sat, from noon Sun; ; Lynx 125, Florida Hospital Health Village) Features the bright folk art of Earl Cunningham, plus traveling exhibitions.

Orlando Science Center MUSEUM
(407-514-2000; www.osc.org; 777 E Princeton St, Loch Haven Park; adult/child $19/13; 10am-5pm Thu-Tue; ; Lynx 125, Florida Hospital Health Village) Candy-coated hands-on science for the whole family.

International Drive

Like a theme park itself, International Dr (I-Dr) is shoulder to shoulder with high-energy amusements. Sprinkled among the major theme, wildlife and water parks, smaller attractions shout for attention: Ripley's Believe It or Not, the upside-down WonderWorks and the new Orlando Eye, a 400ft tall observation Ferris wheel. Chain restaurants and hotels also crowd the thoroughfare.

★Universal Orlando Resort THEME PARK
(☎407-363-8000; www.universalorlando.com; 1000 Universal Studios Plaza; single park 1 day/2 days $102/150, both parks $147/195, child $5-10 less; ⏲daily, hours vary; 🚌Lynx 21, 37, 40, 🚌Universal) Universal is giving Disney a run for its money with this megacomplex that features two theme parks, five hotels and Universal CityWalk, an entertainment district that connects the two parks. But where Disney World is all happy and magical, Universal Orlando gets your adrenaline pumping with revved-up rides and entertaining shows.

The first of the two parks, Universal Studios, has a Hollywood backlot feel and simulation-heavy rides dedicated to television and the silver screen, from *The Simpsons* and *Shrek* to *Revenge of the Mummy* and *Twister*. Universal's Islands of Adventure is tops with coaster-lovers but also has plenty for the little ones in Toon Lagoon and Seuss Landing.

But the absolute highlight – and the hottest thing to hit Orlando since Cinderella's Castle – is the expanded Wizarding World of Harry Potter, which features in both parks, connected by the Hogwarts Express. Together, Universal's Islands of Adventure Hogsmeade and the brand-new Universal Studios Diagon Alley are easily the most fantastically realized themed experience in Florida. Muggles are invited to poke along the cobbled streets and impossibly crooked buildings of Hogsmeade, sip frothy Butter Beer and mail a card via Owl Post, all in the shadow of Hogwarts Castle. Dine at the Leaky Cauldron, watch a wand choose a wizard at Ollivanders Wand Shop and be gobsmacked at the spectacular multidimensional 3D thrill ride at Gringotts Bank. The detail and authenticity tickle the fancy at every turn, from the screeches of the mandrakes in the shop windows to the groans of Moaning Myrtle in the bathroom.

Review multiple ticket options online, which can include add-ons such as Express Plus line skipping and a dining plan; resort hotel guests also get nice park perks. Parking is $17.

SeaWorld THEME PARK
(☎888-800-5447; www.seaworldparks.com; 7007 Sea World Dr; admission $95; ⏲9am-8pm; 👪; 🚌Lynx 8, 38, 50, 111, 🚌I-Ride Trolley Red Line Stop 33) One of Orlando's largest and most popular theme parks, SeaWorld is an aquatic-themed park filled with marine animal shows, roller coasters and up-close sea-life encounters. However, the park's biggest draw is now its most controversial: live shows featuring trained dolphins, sea lions and killer whales.

Since the release of the 2013 documentary *Blackfish*, SeaWorld's treatment of its captive orcas has come under intense scrutiny and the company has been hit by falling visitor numbers and a catalogue of negative PR.

Discounted tickets are available online; prices vary daily.

Discovery Cove THEME PARK
(☎877-434-7268; www.discoverycove.com; 6000 Discovery Cove Way; admission incl SeaWorld & Aquatica from $210, SeaVenture extra $59, prices vary daily; ⏲8am-5:30pm, all-day experience, advance reservations required; 👪; 🚌Lynx 8, 38, 50, 111) At Discovery Cove, guests spend the day snorkeling in a fish- and ray-filled reef, floating on a lazy river through an aviary, and simply relaxing in an intimate tropical sanctuary of white-sand beaches. For an added price beyond the Resort Only package, you can swim with dolphins and walk along the sea floor. It may seem like a fun idea, but since the early 1990s, there has been a growing controversy regarding the ethics of dolphin captivity for the purposes of public display and human interaction.

Winter Park

On the northern edge of Orlando, Winter Park is the gorgeous upscale anti-Orlando built around a chain of lakes with some outstanding museums, a relaxing downtown and great cafes and restaurants.

★Charles Hosmer Morse Museum of American Art MUSEUM
(☎407-645-5311; www.morsemuseum.org; 445 N Park Ave; adult/child $5/free; ⏲9:30am-4pm Tue-Sat, from 1pm Sun, to 8pm Fri Nov-Apr; 👪) Internationally famous, with the world's most comprehensive collection of Tiffany worldwide; the breathtaking centerpiece

is a chapel interior, but the stained glass throughout is stunning as well.

Scenic Boat Tour BOAT TOUR
(407-644-4056; www.scenicboattours.com; 312 E Morse Blvd; adult/child $12/6; hourly 10am-4pm;) This recommended one-hour boat ride floats through 12 coastal miles of tropical canals and lakes. The enthusiastic tour guide talks about the mansions, Rollins College and other sites along the way. Boats are small pontoons, holding about 18 people each.

Sleeping

In addition to the Walt Disney World resorts, Orlando has countless lodging options. Most are clustered around I-Dr, US 192 in Kissimmee and I-4. **Reserve Orlando** (www.reserveorlando.com) is a central booking agency.

Palm Lakefront Hostel HOSTEL $
(407-396-1759; www.orlandohostels.com; 4840 W Irlo Bronson/Hwy 192, Kissimmee; dm/d/q $19/36/60; ; Lynx 56, 55) If you can deal with the temperamental owner, this two-story roadside-motel-styed hostel is your budget bed, with a grassy lakeside picnic and BBQ area, a quiet fishing dock and a little pool. The public bus just outside connects directly to Disney's Transportation & Ticket Center.

Barefoot'n In The Keys MOTEL $
(407-589-2127; www.barefootn.com; 2754 Florida Plaza Blvd, Kissimmee; ste $76-130;) Clean, bright and spacious suites in yellow-and-blue Key West–style bungalows. Low-key, friendly and close to Disney, this makes an excellent alternative to generic chains.

EO Inn & Spa BOUTIQUE HOTEL $$
(407-481-8485; www.eoinn.com; 227 N Eola Dr, Thornton Park; r $140-250;) Sleek and understated, this downtown boutique inn overlooks Lake Eola near Thornton Park, with neutral-toned rooms that are elegant in their simplicity and were being done up with new bamboo flooring and all the fixins' when we came through.

Courtyard at Lake Lucerne B&B $$
(407-648-5188; www.orlandohistoricinn.com; 211 N Lucerne Circle E; r from $130;) This lovely 30-room historic inn, with enchanting gardens and genteel breakfast, has roomy art-deco suites and handsome antiques throughout. Complimentary cocktails help you forgive its location under two highway overpasses.

Eating

Orlando is no longer the culinary cesspool it once was. Though on and around I-Dr you'll find an explosion of chains, the city has learned to appreciate good food. A half-mile stretch of Sand Lake Rd has been dubbed 'restaurant row' for its upscale dining and there's a bona-fide foodie scene budding in Winter Park.

★**East End Market** MARKET $
(231-236-3316; www.eastendmkt.com; 3201 Corrine Dr, Audubon Park; 10am-7pm Tue-Sat, 11am-6pm Sun;) A revolving urban gourmet food court stocking delis, coffee, bars, bakeries and other locally sourced goodness.

Black Bean Deli CUBAN $
(www.blackbeandeli.com; 1835 E Colonial Dr; mains $6-9; 11am-9pm Mon-Thu, to 10pm Fri-Sat;) A former car dealership now wheels and deals exceptionally tasty *Cubano* specialties.

Pho 88 VIETNAMESE $
(www.pho88orlando.com; 730 N Mills Ave; mains $3.25-11; 10am-10pm) A flagship in Orlando's thriving Vietnamese district (known as ViMi) just northeast of downtown, this authentic, no-frills *pho* (Vietnamese noodle soup) specialist is always packed. Cheap and tasty!

★**Yellow Dog Eats** BARBECUE $$
(www.yellowdogeats.com; 1236 Hempel Ave, Windermere; mains $8-19; 11am-9pm;) Housed in an old, tin-roof general store, this quirky temple of dogs and barbeque is worth the haul for an incredible menu of delectable pulled-pork sandwiches in surrounds swarming with local color. Try the Fire Pig (with Gouda, pecan-smoke bacon, slaw, Sriracha and fried onions in a chipotle wrap).

★**Smiling Bison** AMERICAN $$
(407-898-8580; www.thesmilingbison.com; 745 Bennett Rd, Audubon Park; mains $12-36; 5pm-midnight Tue-Thu, to 2am Fri & Sat;) Dive exterior and empty-lot surrounds notwithstanding, this spunky little unaffected delight is justifiably famous for its bison burger, served on an English-muffin-like bun with homemade fries; and beers are carefully curated. Live jazz most nights.

Greater Orlando & Theme Parks

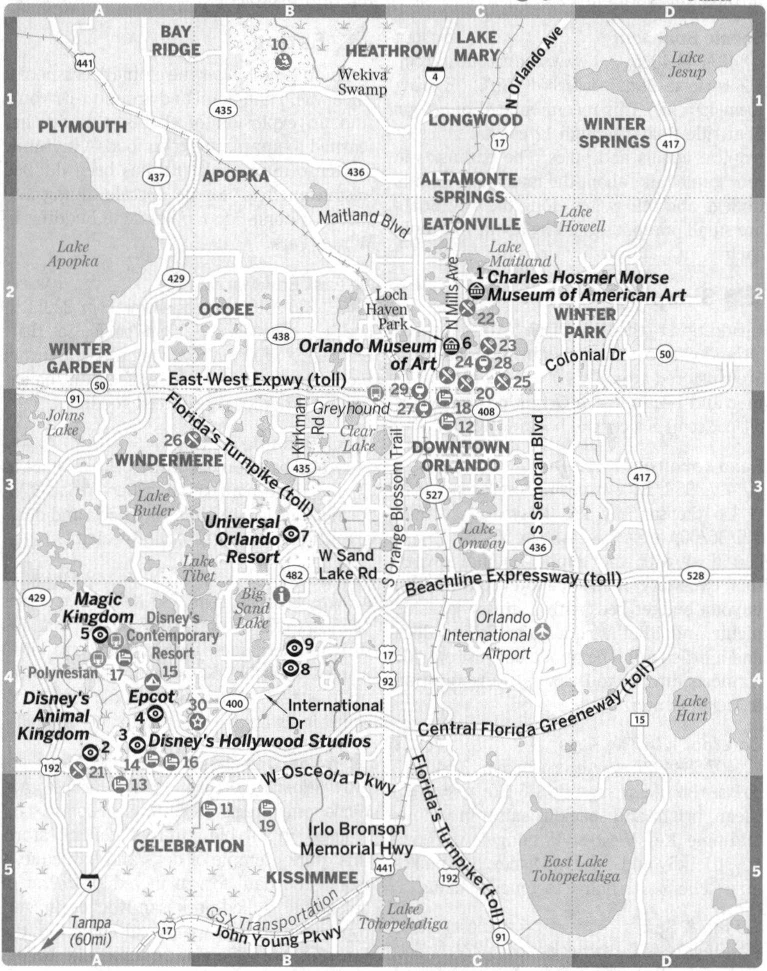

Cask & Larder AMERICAN $$$

(☎321-280-4200; www.caskandlarder.com; 565 W Fairbanks Ave, Winter Park; mains $24-46; ⏲5-10pm Mon-Sat, 10:30am-3pm Sun) From swampy taxidermy-meets-country-chic environs, the Cask & Larder serves an innovative menu of locally sourced Southern fare, including an extraordinary kale salad with bacon vinaigrette, charred okra and boar and dumplings. They brew their own craft beer here, and don't mess around when it comes to cocktails ($12).

Drinking & Entertainment

Orlando Weekly (www.orlandoweekly.com) is the best source for entertainment listings. There's plenty to do downtown, where there's a happening bar district around Orange Ave between Church St and Jefferson St.

Redlight, Redlight BAR

(www.redlightredlightbeerparlour.com; 2810 Corrine Dr, Audubon Park; beers $5-9; ⏲5pm-2am; 📶) Aficionados of the drink will love the 28 draft offerings of craft beers, cask-conditioned ales, meads and farmhouse

Greater Orlando & Theme Parks

Top Sights
1 Charles Hosmer Morse Museum of American Art C2
2 Disney's Animal Kingdom A4
3 Disney's Hollywood Studios A4
4 Epcot A4
5 Magic Kingdom A4
6 Orlando Museum of Art C2
7 Universal Orlando Resort B3

Sights
8 Discovery Cove B4
Mennello Museum of American Art .... (see 6)
Orlando Science Center .... (see 6)
9 SeaWorld B4

Activities, Courses & Tours
10 Nature Adventures B1
Scenic Boat Tour .... (see 1)

Sleeping
11 Barefoot'n In The Keys B5
12 Courtyard at Lake Lucerne C3
13 Disney's All-Star Movies Resort A5
Disney's All-Star Music Resort .... (see 13)
Disney's All-Star Sports Resort .... (see 13)
14 Disney's Art of Animation Resort A4
15 Disney's Fort Wilderness Resort A4
16 Disney's Pop Century Resort A4
17 Disney's Wilderness Lodge A4
18 EO Inn & Spa C3
19 Palm Lakefront Hostel B5

Eating
20 Black Bean Deli C2
21 Boma A4
California Grill .... (see 5)
22 Cask & Larder C2
Cinderella's Royal Table .... (see 5)
23 East End Market C2
24 Pho 88 .... C2
Sci-Fi Dine-In Theater .... (see 3)
25 Smiling Bison C2
Victoria & Albert's .... (see 5)
26 Yellow Dog Eats A3

Drinking & Nightlife
27 Hanson's Shoe Repair C3
28 Redlight, Redlight C2
29 Woods C3

Entertainment
30 Cirque du Soleil La Nouba B4

ciders at this unassuming strip-mall beer-geek hangout housed in a former air-conditioner repair shop.

Woods COCKTAIL BAR
(☎407-203-1114; www.thewoodsorlando.com; 49 N Orange Ave, 2nd fl, Historic Rose Bldg; cocktails $12; ⏰5pm-2am Mon-Fri, from 7pm Sat, 4pm-midnight Sun) It's been called Florida's best cocktail bar: a monthly changing menu of craft cocktails hidden in a cozy, smoke-free 2nd-floor setting, with exposed brick, a tree-trunk bar and not a smidgeon of mixology pretension.

Hanson's Shoe Repair COCKTAIL BAR
(☎407-476-9446; 27 E Pine St; cocktails $12; ⏰8pm-2am Tue-Thu & Sat, from 7pm Fri) This downtown Orlando Prohibition-era speakeasy, complete with historically accurate cocktails and secret passwords for entry, serves classic cocktails hidden away inside another bar (NV Art Bar). To get in, call in advance, they'll text you the password if they can accommodate you.

Information

Official Visitor Center (☎407-363-5872; www.visitorlando.com; 8723 International Dr; ⏰8:30am-6pm) Legitimate discount attraction tickets and best source for information on theme parks, accommodations, outdoor activities, performing arts and more.

Getting There & Around

Orlando International Airport (MCO; ☎407-825-8463; www.orlandoairports.net; 1 Jeff Fuqua Blvd) has buses and taxis to major tourist areas. **Mears Transportation** (☎customer service 407-423-5566, reservations 855-463-2776; www.mearstransportation.com) provides shuttles for $20 to $28 per person. **Greyhound** (☎407-292-3424; www.greyhound.com; 555 N John Young Pkwy) serves numerous cities. **Amtrak** (www.amtrak.com; 1400 Sligh Blvd) has daily trains south to Miami and north to New York City.

Orlando's bus network is operated by **Lynx** (☎route info 407-841-8240; www.golynx.com; per ride/day/week $2/4.50/16, transfers free). **I-Ride Trolley** (☎407-354-5656; www.iridetrolley.com; rides adult/child 3-9yr $2/1, passes 1/3/5/7/14 days $5/7/9/12/18; ⏰8am-10:30pm) buses run along I-Dr.

When driving, note that I-4 is the main north–south connector, though it's confusingly labeled east–west. To go north, take I-4 east (toward Daytona); to go south, get on I-4 west (toward Tampa). The main east–west roads are Hwy 50 and Hwy 528 (the Bee Line Expwy), which accesses Orlando International Airport.

Walt Disney World Resort

Covering 40 sq miles, Walt Disney World (WDW) is the largest theme-park resort in the world. It includes four separate theme parks, two water parks, a sports complex, three 18-hole golf courses, more than two dozen resort hotels, over 100 restaurants and dining options and two shopping, dining and entertainment districts – proving that it's not such a small world, after all. At times it feels ridiculously crowded and corporate, but with or without kids, you won't be able to inoculate yourself against Disney's highly infectious enthusiasm and warm-hearted nostalgia. Naturally, expectations run high, and even the self-proclaimed 'happiest place on earth' doesn't always live up to its billing. Still, it always happens: Cinderella curtsies to your little Belle, your own Jedi knight vanquishes Darth Maul, or you tear up on that corny ride about our tiny planet, and suddenly you're swept up in the magic.

Sights & Activities

★Magic Kingdom THEME PARK

(407-939-5277; www.disneyworld.disney.go.com; 1180 Seven Seas Dr; adult/child 3-10yr $105/99; 9am-11pm, hours vary; Disney, Disney, monorail Disney) When most people think of WDW – especially kids – it's really the Magic Kingdom they're picturing. This is where you'll find all the classic Disney experiences, such as the iconic Cinderella's Castle, rides like Space Mountain and the nighttime fireworks and light parade illuminating **Main Street, USA**. For Disney mythology, it doesn't get better.

Cinderella's Castle is at the center of the park, and from there paths lead to the different 'lands':

Tomorrowland is where Space Mountain hurtles you through the darkness of outer space. This indoor roller coaster is the most popular ride in the Magic Kingdom, so come first thing and if the line is already excruciating, get a FastPass+.

New Fantasyland is the highlight of any Disney trip for the eight-and-under crowd. This is the land of Mickey and Minnie, Goofy and Donald Duck, Snow White and the Seven Dwarves, and many more big names. Fresh off the largest expansion in Magic Kingdom history, new rides include the gentle Under the Sea – Journey of the Little Mermaid and the Seven Dwarfs Mine Train, a family-friendly steel roller coaster.

Adventureland features pirates and jungles, magic carpets and tree houses, whimsical and silly representations of the exotic locales from storybooks and imagination.

Liberty Square is the home of the the Haunted Mansion, a rambling, 19th-century mansion that's a Disney favorite, and **Frontierland** is Disney's answer to the Wild West.

★Epcot THEME PARK

(407-939-5277; www.disneyworld.disney.go.com; 200 Epcot Center Dr; adult/child 3-10yr $97/91; 11am-9pm, hours vary; Disney, Disney) An acronym for 'Experimental Prototype Community of Tomorrow,' Epcot was Disney's vision of a high-tech city when it opened in 1982. It's divided into two halves: **Future World**, with rides and corporate-sponsored interactive exhibits, and **World Showcase**, providing an interesting toe-dip into the cultures of 11 countries.

Epcot is much more soothingly low-key than other parks, and it has some of the best food, drinks and shopping.

★Disney's Animal Kingdom THEME PARK

(407-939-5277; www.disneyworld.disney.go.com; 2101 Osceola Pkwy; adult/child $97/91; 9am-7pm, hours vary; Disney) This sometimes-surreal blend of African safari, zoo, rides, costumed characters, shows and dinosaurs establishes its own distinct tone. It's best at animal encounters and shows, with the 110-acre **Kilimanjaro Safaris** as its centerpiece. The iconic **Tree of Life** houses the fun It's Tough to Be a Bug! show, and **Expedition Everest** and **Kali River Rapids** are top thrill rides.

★Disney's Hollywood Studios THEME PARK

(407-939-5277; www.disneyworld.disney.go.com; 351 S Studio Dr; adult/child 3-10yr $97/91; 9am-10pm, hours vary; Disney, Disney) The least charming of Disney's parks is set for a major transformation: a 14-acre *Star Wars* land and an 11-acre *Toy Story* area are planned for the next few years. Until then two of WDW's most exciting rides can be found here: the unpredictable elevator in the **Twi-**

TIPS & TRICKS

Tickets

Consider buying a ticket that covers more days in the parks than you think you'll need. It's less expensive per day, and it gives you the freedom to break up time at the theme parks with downtime in the pool or at low-key attractions beyond theme-park gates.

You can buy single or multiday tickets, and add a Park Hopper option ($64) that allows entrance to all four parks. Check online for packages, and buy in advance to avoid lines at the gate. If you want to pick up your prepurchased tickets ahead of the day you actually enter the parks, do so at Disney Spring's Guest Relations to avoid paying the $17 parking fee you'll have to pay to access other Guest Relations inside the four parks.

For discounts, check out www.mousesavers.com and www.undercovertourist.com.

When to Go

Anytime schools are out – during summer and holidays – Walt Disney Walt will be the most crowded. The least crowded times are January to February, mid-September through October and early December. Late fall tends to have the best weather; frequent downpours accompany the hot, humid summer months.

On the actual day you go, plan on arriving early so you can see as much of the park as possible before the midday peak. Consider going back to your hotel to recharge around 2pm or 3pm when it's the hottest and most crowded, then come back a few hours later and stay till close.

FastPass+ & My Disney Experience App

For the most popular attractions, Disney replaced the old FastPass paper system in 2014 with **FastPass+** (☎407-828-8739; www.disneyworld.disney.go.com), which is designed to allow guests to plan their days in advance and reduce time spent waiting in line. Visitors can reserve a specific time for up to three attractions per day through My Disney Experience accessible either at www.disneyworld.disney.go.com or by downloading the free mobile app. Once you link up your tickets, the latter is an invaluable tool for on-the-go planning and managing of your entire Disney experience.

light Zone Tower of Terror and the Aerosmith-themed **Rock 'n' Roller Coaster**.

Sleeping

While it's tempting to save money by staying elsewhere, the value of staying at a WDW resort lies in the conveniences they offer. WDW has more than 20 family-friendly sleeping options, from camping to deluxe resorts, and Disney guests receive great perks (extended park hours, discount dining plans, complimentary on-property transportation, airport transfers). Disney's thorough website outlines rates and amenities for every property. Don't expect the quality of the room and amenities to match the price: you're paying for WDW convenience, not for Ritz-like luxury.

Disney's Value Resorts, of which there are seven, are the least-expensive option (besides camping); quality is equivalent to basic chain hotels, and (fair warning) they are favored by school groups:

★ Disney's Fort Wilderness Resort CAMPGROUND, CABIN $
(☎407-939-5277, 407-824-2900; www.disneyworld.disney.go.com; 4510 N Fort Wilderness Trail; tent sites $75, RV sites $109-116, 6-person cabins $359; Disney, Disney) For wilderness on a budget, we love the Fort Wilderness Resort & Campground, located in a huge shaded natural preserve, with tent sites and cabins that sleep up to six people.

Disney's Art of Animation Resort HOTEL $$
(☎407-939-5277, 407-938-7000; www.disneyworld.disney.go.com; 1850 Animation Way; r $109-199, ste $269-457; P; Disney) Inspired by animated Disney classics including the *Lion King, Cars, Finding Nemo* and *The Little Mermaid.*

Disney's All-Star Movies Resort HOTEL $$
(☎407-939-7000, 407-939-5277; www.disneyworld.disney.go.com; 1901 W Buena Vista Dr; r $85-192; P; Disney) Icons from Disney movies including *Toy Story* and *101 Dalmatians.*

Disney's All-Star Music Resort HOTEL $$
(407-939-6000, 407-939-5277; www.disneyworld.disney.go.com; 1801 W Buena Vista Dr; r $85-192; ; Disney) Family suites and motel rooms surrounded by giant instruments.

Disney's All-Star Sports Resort HOTEL $$
(407-939-5000, 407-939-5277; www.disneyworld.disney.go.com; 1701 Buena Vista Dr; r $85-192; ; Disney) Five pairs of three-story buildings divided thematically by sport.

Disney's Pop Century Resort HOTEL $$
(407-939-5277, 407-938-4000; www.disneyworld.disney.go.com; 1050 Century Dr; r $95-210; ; Disney) Each section pays homage to a different decade of the late 20th century.

★ **Disney's Wilderness Lodge** RESORT $$$
(407-939-5277, 407-824-3200; www.disneyworld.disney.go.com; 901 Timberline Dr; r $289-998; ; Disney, Disney) One of our favorite deluxe resorts is the Yosemite-style Wilderness Lodge; the 'rustic opulence' theme includes erupting geysers, a lakelike swimming area and bunk beds for the kids.

Eating

Theme-park food ranges from OK to awful; the most interesting is served in Epcot's World Showcase. Sit-down meals are best, but *always* make reservations; seats can be impossible to get without one. For any dining, you can call central dining reservations (1-407-939-3463) up to 180 days in advance; or book online Open Table–style either on the website via the My Reservations section of My Disney Experience or using the app.

Disney has two dinner shows (a luau and country-style BBQ/vaudeville show) and 15 character meals, and these are insanely popular (see website for details). Book them the minute your 180-day window opens.

★ **Sci-Fi Dine-In Theater** AMERICAN $$
(407-939-3463; www.disneyworld.disney.go.com; Hollywood Studios; mains $14-32, theme park admission required; noon-4pm & 4-9pm; ; Disney, Disney) Dine in Cadillacs, drink craft beer and watch classic sci-fi flicks.

★ **Boma** BUFFET $$
(407-938-4744, 407-939-3463; www.disneyworld.disney.go.com; 2901 Osceola Pkwy, Disney's Animal Kingdom Lodge; adult/child breakfast $24.50/13, dinner $40.50/21; 7:30-11am & 4:30-9:30pm; ; Disney) African-inspired eatery with pleasant surroundings and a buffet several notches above the rest.

Cinderella's Royal Table AMERICAN $$$
(407-934-2927; www.disneyworld.disney.go.com; Cinderella's Castle, Magic Kingdom; adult $58-73, child $36-43; 8:05-10:40am, 11:45am-2:40pm & 3:50-9:40pm; ; Disney, Disney, Lynx 50, 56) The most sought-after meal at Disney is inside the Magic Kingdom's castle, where you dine with Disney princesses.

California Grill AMERICAN $$$
(407-939-3463; www.disneyworld.disney.go.com; 4600 World Dr, Disney's Contemporary Resort; mains $37-50; 5-10pm; ; Disney, Disney, monorail Disney) Contemporary California cuisine with two observation decks – great views of the Magic Kingdom fireworks!

Victoria & Albert's AMERICAN $$$
(407-939-3463; www.victoria-alberts.com; 4401 Floridian Way, Disney's Grand Floridian Resort; prix fixe from $159, wine pairing extra from $65; 5-9:20pm; ; Disney, Disney, monorail Disney) A true jacket-and-tie, crystal-goblet, romantic gourmet restaurant – no kidding, and no kids under 10.

Entertainment

In addition to theme-park events like Magic Kingdom parades and fireworks and Epcot's Illuminations, Disney has two entertainment districts – the newly revamped Disney Springs and Disney's Boardwalk – with eats, bars, music, movies, shops and shows.

★ **Cirque du Soleil La Nouba** PERFORMING ARTS
(407-939-7328, 407-939-7600; www.cirquedusoleil.com; Disney Springs; adult $59-139, child $48-115; 6pm & 9pm Tue-Sat; Disney, Disney, Lynx 50) This mind-blowing acrobatic extravaganza is one of the best shows at Disney.

Getting There & Around

Most hotels in Kissimmee and Orlando – and all Disney properties – offer free transportation to WDW. Disney-owned resorts also offer free transportation from the airport. Drivers can reach all four parks via I-4 and park for $17. The Magic Kingdom lot is huge; trams or ferries get you to the entrance.

Within WDW, a complex network of monorails, boats and buses gets you between the parks, resorts and entertainment districts.

Around Orlando

Just north of Orlando await some of Florida's best outdoor adventures, particularly swimming, snorkeling and kayaking in its crystal-clear, 72°F (22°C) natural springs. Closest is **Wekiwa Springs State Park** (☎407-884-2009; www.floridastateparks.org/wekiwasprings; 1800 Wekiwa Circle, Apopka; admission $6, campsites per person $5, hookups $24; ⏲7am-dusk), with 13 miles of hiking trails, a spring-fed swimming hole, nice campground and the tranquil 'Wild and Scenic' Wekiva River; rent kayaks from **Nature Adventures** (☎407-884-4311; www.canoewekiva.com; 1800 Wekiwa Circle, Wekiwa Springs State Park, Apopka; 2hr canoe/kayak $17, per additional hour $3; ⏲8am-8pm; 👪).

Blue Spring State Park (☎386-775-3663; www.floridastateparks.org/bluespring; 2100 W French Ave, Orange City; car/bike $6/2; ⏲8am-sunset) is a favorite of wintering manatees, and two-hour cruises ply the St John's River. Just north of Deland, **De Leon Springs State Park** (☎386-985-4212; www.floridastateparks.org/deleonsprings; 601 Ponce de Leon Blvd, De Leon Springs; car/bike $6/2; ⏲8am-sunset) has a huge swimming area, more kayaking and tours of the Ponce de León's alleged fountain of youth.

To really escape into raw wilderness, head for the **Ocala National Forest** (www.fs.usda.gov/ocala), which has dozens of campgrounds, hundreds of miles of trails and 600 lakes. The hiking, biking, canoeing and camping are some of the state's best. See the website for visitor centers and descriptions.

FLORIDA PANHANDLE

Take all the things that are great about the Deep South – friendly people, molasses-slow pace, oak-lined country roads, fried food galore – and then add several hundred miles of sugar-white beaches, dozens of gin-clear natural springs and all the fresh oysters you can suck down, and there you have it: the fantastic, highly underrated Florida Panhandle.

Tallahassee

Florida's capital, cradled between gently rising hills and beneath tree-canopied roadways, is a calm and gracious city. It's closer to Atlanta than it is to Miami – both geographically and culturally – and far more Southern than the majority of the state it administrates. Despite the city's two major universities (Florida State and Florida Agricultural and Mechanical University) and its status as a government center, there's not much to detain a visitor for more than a day or two.

Sights & Activities

Be sure to take a stroll through artsy **Railroad Square** (☎850-224-1308; www.railroadsquare.com; 567 Industrial Dr), a former lumber yard and industrial park between downtown and Florida State University full of funky boutiques, art galleries, cafes and microbreweries.

Mission San Luis HISTORIC SITE
(☎850-245-6406; www.missionsanluis.org; 2100 W Tennessee St; adult/child $5/2; ⏲10am-4pm Tue-Sun) The 60-acre site of a 17th-century Spanish and Apalachee mission that's been wonderfully reconstructed, especially the soaring Council House. Good tours included with admission provide a fascinating taste of 300 years ago.

Museum of Florida History MUSEUM
(☎850-245-6400; www.museumoffloridahistory.com; 500 S Bronough St; ⏲9am-4:30pm Mon-Fri, from 10am Sat, from noon Sun) FREE Here it is, Florida's history splayed out in fun, crisp exhibits: from mastodon skeletons to Florida's Paleo-Indians and Spanish shipwrecks, the Civil War to 'tin-can tourism.'

Florida Capitol Buildings HISTORIC BUILDING
Old and new, side by side. The current **Florida State Capitol** (www.myfloridacapitol.com; 402 South Monroe St; ⏲8am-5pm Mon-Fri) FREE is, in a word, ugly, but its top-floor observation deck gives you a bird's-eye view of the city. Next door, the **Historic Capitol** (www.flhistoriccapitol.gov; 400 S Monroe St; 👪) FREE is the more charming 1902 predecessor.

Inside, the **Historic Capitol Museum** (www.flhistoriccapitol.gov; 400 South Monroe St; ⏲9am-4:30pm Mon-Fri, from 10am Sat, from noon Sun) FREE has intriguing government and cultural exhibits, including one on the infamous 2000 US presidential election.

Sleeping

Chains are clumped at exits along I-10 and along Monroe St between I-10 and downtown.

Hotel Duval HOTEL $$
(☎850-224-6000; www.hotelduval.com; 415 N Monroe St; r $129-259; P❄📶) Tallahassee's

DON'T MISS

WAKULLA SPRINGS

Just 15 miles south of Tallahassee is the world's deepest freshwater spring at **Edward Ball Wakulla Springs State Park** (☎850-561-7276; www.floridastateparks.org/park/Wakulla-Springs; 465 Wakulla Park Dr; car/bike $6/2, boat tours adult/child $8/5; ⏰8am-dusk).The springs flow from massive underwater caves that are an archaeologist's dream, with fossilized bones including a mastodon that was discovered around 1850. These days you can swim in the icy springs or enjoy them from a glass-bottom boat chasing huge manatees. The wildlife-filled Wakulla River has been used as a movie set for several Tarzan movies, as well as *The Creature from the Black Lagoon*.

slickest digs. This 117-room hotel goes in for a neo-mod look while each floor is scented differently – the 3rd floor's Bourbon Vanilla smells like Dr Pepper! A rooftop bar and lounge is open until 2am most nights.

Governor's Inn HOTEL **$$**
(☎850-681-6855; www.thegovinn.com; 209 S Adams St; r $219-309; P ❄ 📶) In a stellar downtown location, this warm, inviting inn has everything from queen rooms to two-level loft suites, plus a daily cocktail hour.

Eating & Drinking

Many folks drive to quaint Thomasville, Georgia for top-end dining, but Tally's scene is evolving.

Paisley Cafe CAFE **$**
(www.thepaisleycafe.com; 1123 Thomasville Rd; mains $13.50-18; ⏰11am-2:30pm Mon-Thu, to 3pm Fri, 10am-3pm Sat & Sun; 📶) A wonderful Midtown cafe with delectable pressed sandwiches, salads and insane desserts (the slutty brownie will have your sweet tooth turning tricks in no time!).

Cypress NEW SOUTHERN **$$$**
(☎850-513-1100; www.cypressrestaurant.com; 320 E Tennessee St; mains $21-32; ⏰5-10pm Mon-Sat, 10:30am-2pm Sun) This unassuming spot is the domain of local chef David Gwynn, whose regional Southern dishes outshine expectations. Start with the roasted brussels sprout salad with poached egg and move on to souped-up classics like pork belly with pecan-fried quail or shrimp and grits with bourbon-orange-thyme jus.

Madison Social PUB
(www.madisonsocial.com; 705 South Woodward Ave; mains $9-20, beers $3-6; ⏰11:30am-2am Sun-Thu, from 10am Fri & Sat; 📶) Never mind the trend of flipping former transmission shops into hipster locales, this trendy hot spot was built to look that way from go! It swarms with a bold and beautiful mix of locals and FSU students, downing drinks at the stellar bar or aluminum picnic tables as the sun sets over Doak Campbell football stadium, the largest continuous brick structure in the USA.

Entertainment

Bradfordville Blues Club LIVE MUSIC
(☎850-906-0766; www.bradfordvilleblues.com; 7152 Moses Lane, off Bradfordville Rd; tickets $15-35; ⏰10pm Fri & Sat, 8:30pm some Thu, check online) Down the end of a dirt road lit by tiki torches, you'll find a bonfire raging under the live oaks at this hidden-away juke joint that hosts excellent national blues acts.

Information

Leon County Welcome Center (☎850-606-2305; www.visittallahassee.com; 106 E Jefferson St; ⏰8am-5pm Mon-Fri) An excellent visitor information center, with brochures on walking and driving tours.

Getting There & Around

The **Tallahassee Regional Airport** (☎850-891-7802; www.talgov.com/airport; 3300 Capital Circle SW) is about 5 miles southwest of downtown, off Hwy 263. The **Greyhound station** (☎850-222-4249; www.greyhound.com; 112 W Tennessee St) is right downtown.

Star Metro (☎850-891-5200; www.talgov.com/starmetro; single ride $1.25, daily unlimited $3) provides local bus service.

Apalachicola & Around

Slow, mellow and perfectly preserved, Apalachicola is one of the Panhandle's most irresistible, romantic villages. Perched on the edge of a broad bay famous for its oysters, the oak-shaded town is a hugely popular getaway, with a new wave of bistros, art galleries, eclectic boutiques and historic B&Bs.

Sights & Activities

St Vincent Island ISLAND
(☎850-653-8808; www.fws.gov/saintvincent) For nature, the pristine St Vincent Island holds pearly dunes, pine forests and wetlands teeming with wildlife.

St George Island State Park PARK
(☎850-927-2111; www.floridastateparks.org/stgeorgeisland; vehicle $6, tent & RV sites $24; ⏲8am-dusk) Offers 9 miles of glorious, undeveloped beaches. In town, seek out fishing charters and wildlife cruises.

Sleeping & Eating

Riverwood Suites BOUTIQUE INN $$
(☎850-653-3848; www.riverwoodsuites.com; 29 Ave F; r $139-169; P ❄ 📶) The four spacious rooms inside this formerly abandoned tin warehouse are the newest and best in town. Think hardwood floors, artsy headboards, modern fixins' and tuck-your-self-away romance.

Coombs House Inn B&B $$
(☎850-653-9199; www.coombshouseinn.com; 80 6th St; r $99-189; ❄ 📶) This stunning yellow Victorian inn was built in 1905 and features black-cypress wall paneling, nine fireplaces, a carved oak staircase, leaded glass windows and beadboard ceilings.

Owl Cafe & Tap Room MODERN AMERICAN $$
(☎850-653-9888; www.owlcafeflorida.com; 15 Ave D; mains $10-28; ⏲11am-3pm & 5:30-10pm Mon-Fri, from 11am Sat, 10:30am-3pm Sun; 📶) Everyone is catered to in this local favorite, with casual fine dining in the upstairs cafe and wine room and craft beers and tap-room-only offerings below.

Information

Apalachicola Bay Visitors Center (www.apalachicolabay.org; 122 Commerce Street) Pick up maps and info on walking tours.

Panama City Beach

There's no mistaking Panama City Beach for anything other than it is: a quintessentially Floridian, carnivalesqe beach town. Spring breakers and summer vacationers flock here for the beautiful white-sand beaches and the hurdy-gurdy of amusements, while mile after mile of high-rise condos insist on disrupting the view.

Sights & Activities

Shell Island has fantastic snorkeling, and **shuttles** (☎850-233-0504; www.shellislandshuttle.com; adult/child $16.95/8.95; ⏲9am-5pm) depart every 30 minutes in summer.

St Andrews State Park PARK
(☎850-233-5140; www.floridastateparks.org/standrews; 4607 State Park Lane, Panama City; vehicle/pedestrian $8/2; ⏲8am-sunset) A peaceful escape with nature trails, swimming beaches and wildlife.

Dive Locker DIVING
(☎850-230-8006; www.divelocker.net; 106 Thomas Dr, Panama City Beach; ⏲8am-6pm Mon-Fri, 7am-4pm Sat, to 5pm Sun) A renowned wreck-diving site, the area around Panama City Beach has dozens of natural, historic and artificial reefs. This well-respected outfitter and dive school knows all the local reefs. Basic supervised two-tank dives start at $142, gear included.

Sleeping

PCB Bed & Breakfast B&B $$
(☎850-867-0421; www.panamacitybeachbedandbreakfast.com; 127 Toledo Pl; r $149; P ❄ 📶) Steps from the development-free sun-toasted sands of pristine Laguna Beach, the only B&B in town is a three-room affair in a Key West–style cottage nicknamed 'Nostalgic 1950's Beach Cottage.' Luxury linens and big Vizio TVs ensure comfort; and there are plenty of porches and green space to while away the time.

Wisteria Inn MOTEL $$
(☎850-234-0557; www.wisteria-inn.com; 20404 Front Beach Rd; d from $119-159; P ❄ ≋ 🐾) Every room is different at this sweet little 14-room motel – we love the colorful Carribbean feel of No 8 – and there's poolside mimosa hours and an 'adults only' policy that discourages spring breakers.

Eating & Drinking

Gourmet by the Bay FAST FOOD $
(www.facebook.com/GourmetByTheBay; 284 Powell Adams Rd; mains $4-10; ⏲noon-7:30pm Mon-Fri & Sun, to 9:30pm Sat, to 11:30pm summer) Hidden away inside the small Miracle Strip Amusement Park is this wildly popular food stall that does tremendously good mahi-mahi or shrimp tacos on the cheap. No park admission charge if you're just eating.

DON'T MISS

SCENIC DRIVE: THE EMERALD COAST

Along the Panhandle coast between Panama City Beach and Destin, skip the main highway (Hwy 98) in favor of one of the most enchanting drives in Florida: **Scenic Highway 30A**. This 18-mile stretch of road hugs what's referred to as the Emerald Coast for its almost fluorescent, gem-colored waters lapping brilliant white beaches of ground-quartz crystal.

Leading off Scenic Hwy 30A are wild parklands like **Grayton Beach State Park** (☎850-267-8300; www.floridastateparks.org/graytonbeach; 357 Main Park Rd, Santa Rosa Beach; vehicle $5; ⏲8am-sunset), considered one of Florida's prettiest, most pristine strands. About 15 quaint communities hug the coast, some arty and funky, and some master-planned resorts with matchy-matchy architectural perfection. Of these, the most intriguing and surreal is the little village of **Seaside** (www.seasidefl.com), a Necco Wafer–colored town that was hailed as a model of New Urbanism in the 1980s.

Seaside is such an idealized vision that, unaltered, it formed the setting for the 1998 film *The Truman Show*, about a man whose 'perfect life' is nothing but a TV show. Good online resources are www.30a.com and www.visitsouthwalton.com.

The Craft Bar BAR
(www.thecraftbarfl.com; 15600 Panama City Beach Pkwy, Pier Park North; beers $4.50-12, mains $12-35; ⏲11am-11pm Mon-Thu, to midnight Fri & Sat, to 10pm Sun) Head to this anti-PCB choice to trade pirate-themed camp and beach blanket anarchy for 30 thoughtfully sourced microbrews on tap (Mikkeller!), craft cocktails and excellent pub grub.

ℹ Information

Visitors Information Center (☎850-233-5870; www.visitpanamacitybeach.com; 17001 Panama City Beach Pkwy; ⏲8am-5pm) Come for maps, brochures and the lowdown on what's up and coming in town.

ℹ Getting There & Around

The **Panama City International Airport** (PFN; ☎850-763-6751; www.iflybeaches.com; 6300 W Bay Pkwy, Panama City) is served by a few major airlines. The **Greyhound Station** (☎850-785-6111; www.greyhound.com; 917 Harrison Ave, Panama City) is in Panama City, and the limited **Bay Town Trolley** (www.baytowntrolley.org; fare $1.50) runs only weekdays from 6am to 8pm.

Pensacola & Pensacola Beach

Neighbors with Alabama, Pensacola and its adjacent beach town welcome visitors driving in from the west. Its gorgeous snow-white beaches and tolerance of the annual spring-break bacchanal ensure Pensacola's popularity, but the city has bounced back better than others from 2004's devastating Hurricane Ivan and the 2010 Deepwater Horizon oil spill in the Gulf of Mexico, resulting in a revitalized energy that has spawned a burgeoning foodie scene and hip cafes and bars to go with its already sultry Spanish-style downtown and wonderful preserved historic district.

Sights & Activities

★National Naval Aviation Museum MUSEUM
(☎850-452-3604; www.navalaviationmuseum.org; 1750 Radford Blvd; ⏲9am-5pm, guided tours 9:30am, 11am, 1pm & 2:30pm; 👪) FREE Home to a don't-miss collection of jaw-dropping military aircraft and the elite **Blue Angels** (www.blueangels.navy.mil) squadron. Shockingly, it's free, unless you sit down ($8.75 for IMAX movies, $20 for the Flight Simulators and dining). Bring ID – it's an active naval base.

Historic Pensacola Village HISTORIC BUILDING
(☎850-595-5985; www.historicpensacola.org; 205 E Zaragoza St; adult/child $6/3; ⏲10am-4pm Tue-Sat, tours 11am, 1pm & 2:30pm) Pensacola says 'take that, St Augustine!' with this village, a self-contained enclave of drop-dead-gorgeous historic homes and museums. Admission is good for one week and includes a guided tour and entrance to each building as well as admission to **TT Wentworth Florida State Museum** (www.historicpensacola.org; 330 S Jefferson St; adult/child $6/3; ⏲10am-4pm Tue-Sat) and **Pensacola Children's Museum** (☎850-595-1559; 115 E Zaragoza St; admission $3; ⏲10am-4pm Tue-Sat).

Pensacola Museum of Art MUSEUM
(☎850-432-6247; www.pensacolamuseum.org; 407 S Jefferson St; adult/student $10/8; ⏲10am-5pm Tue-Fri, from noon Sat) An impressive collection

of major 20th- and 21st-century artists, spanning cubism, realism, pop art and folk art, housed in the city's old jail (1908).

Gulf Islands National Seashore BEACH
(☎850-934-2600; www.nps.gov/guis; 7-day pass pedestrian/cyclist/car $3/3/8; ⊙sunrise-sunset) To enjoy the area's lovely white sands, head to the easy-access Pensacola Beach or the neighboring Gulf Islands National Seashore, part of a 160-mile (noncontinuous) stretch of undeveloped beach. The Pensacola portion was recently voted Florida's best beach by *USA Today*.

Sleeping

Paradise Inn MOTEL $
(☎850-932-2319; www.paradiseinn-pb.com; 21 Via de Luna Dr; r from $89; P ❄ 📶 🏊) Across from the beach, this '50s-era motel is a lively, cheery place thanks to its popular bar and grill. Rooms are small and clean, with tiled floors and brightly painted walls; and staff will cook up your fresh catches with all the fixins' for $13.

Noble Inn B&B $$
(☎850-434-9544; www.noblemanor.com; 110 W Strong St; r/ste $160/185; P ❄ 📶 🏊) This pretty 1905 mansion in the historic North Hill district is the most charming place to stay. The East Coast innkeeper, Bonnie, runs a one-woman show, from shining up those spick-and-span hardwood floors to whipping up praline French toast for breakfast.

New World Inn HOTEL $$
(☎850-432-4111; www.newworldlanding.com; 600 S Palafox St; r from $119; P ❄ 📶) Peek under the lid of this former box factory and you'll find surprisingly lovely rooms with luxe bedding and new hardwood flooring.

Eating & Drinking

For cheap eats, check out **Al Fresco** (www.eatalfresco.com; cnr Palafox & Main Sts), a collection of five Airstream trailer food trucks on the corner of Palafax and Main Sts. Downtown's South Palafax St is lined with drinking dens.

Blue Dot BURGERS $
(310 N De Villiers St; burgers $5.58-6.97; ⊙11:30am-3pm Tue-Fri, noon-3pm Sat) The line swells with locals-in-the-know before 11am for Pensacola's best burgers – a simple, greasy and perfectly seasoned affair. Know what you want before you get to the counter and dress appropriately. You're familiar with *Seinfeld*'s Soup Nazi? Meet the Burger Nazi. Get here early. Cash only.

Native Café BREAKFAST $
(www.thenativecafe.com; 45a Via de Luna Dr; mains $4.50-13; ⊙7:30am-3pm; 📶) Three words: crab cakes Benedict! Locals line up at this funky breakfast and lunch spot in a colorful strip mall at the beach. Adorable staff and great service to boot.

McGuire's Irish Pub IRISH $$
(www.mcguiresirishpub.com; 600 E Gregory St; mains $10-33; ⊙11am-2am) Promising 'feasting, imbibery and debauchery,' this barnlike spot delivers all three. Stick to steaks and burgers when you order, and don't mind the animal heads or dollar-bill-adorned walls.

★ **Iron** NEW SOUTHERN $$$
(☎850-476-7776; www.restaurantiron.com; 22 N Palafax St; mains $18-36; ⊙4:30-10pm Tue-Thu, to 1am Fri & Sat; 📶) Armed with New Orleans experience, chef Alex McPhail works his ever-changing-menu magic at downtown's Iron, the best of Pensacola's new line of vibrant, locally sourced, high-end culinary hotbeds. Extremely friendly mixologists know their craft; and McPhail's food – from beer-braised pork belly to creole-seasoned catch of the day – punches above the Emerald Coast's weight class.

★ **Seville Quarter** CLUB
(www.sevillequarter.com; 130 E Government St; cover $3-10; ⊙7am-2:30am) Taking up an entire city block, this multivenue complex always has something going on, from breakfast through last call, in its seven separate eating, drinking and music venues.

Information

Pensacola Visitors Information Center
(☎800-874-1234; www.visitpensacola.com; 1401 E Gregory St; ⊙8am-5pm Mon-Fri, 9am-4pm Sat, 10am-4pm Sun) Come to the foot of the Pensacola Bay Bridge for a bounty of tourist information and knowledgeable staff.

Getting There & Around

Five miles northeast of downtown, **Pensacola Regional Airport** (☎850-436-5000; www.flypensacola.com; 2430 Airport Blvd) is served by major airlines.

The **Greyhound station** (☎850-476-4800; www.greyhound.com; 505 W Burgess Rd) is 9 miles north of downtown.

A Downtown Pensacola–Pensacola Beach ferry is in the works for 2017; until then, bus 64 runs from Jefferson and Garden Sts downtown to the beach Friday to Sunday.

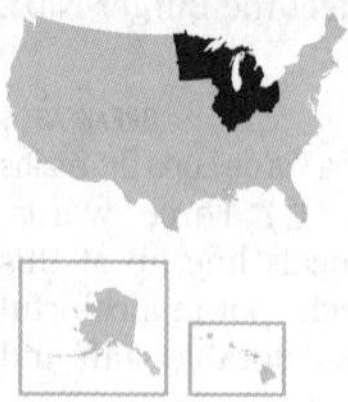

Great Lakes

Includes ➡

Best Places to Eat

- New Scenic Cafe (p616)
- Dove's Luncheonette (p543)
- Tucker's (p573)
- Slows Bar BQ (p579)
- The Old Fashioned (p598)

Best Places to Stay

- Freehand Chicago (p539)
- Hotel 340 (p613)
- Acme Hotel (p539)
- Brewhouse Inn & Suites (p595)
- Cleveland Hostel (p563)

Why Go?

Don't be fooled by all the corn. Behind it lurks surfing beaches and Tibetan temples, car-free islands and the green-draped night-lights of the aurora borealis. The Midwest takes its knocks for being middle-of-nowhere boring; so consider the moose-filled national parks, urban five-ways and Hemingway, Dylan and Vonnegut sites to be its little secret.

Roll call for the Midwest's cities starts with Chicago, which unfurls what is arguably the country's mightiest skyline. Milwaukee keeps the beer-and-Harley flame burning, while Minneapolis shines a hipster beacon out over the fields. Detroit rocks, plain and simple.

The Great Lakes are huge, offering beaches, dunes, resort towns and lighthouse-dotted scenery. Dairy farms and orchards blanket the region – fresh pie and ice cream await road-trippers. And when the Midwest flattens out? There's always a goofball roadside attraction, like the Spam Museum or world's largest ball of twine, to revive imaginations.

When to Go

Chicago

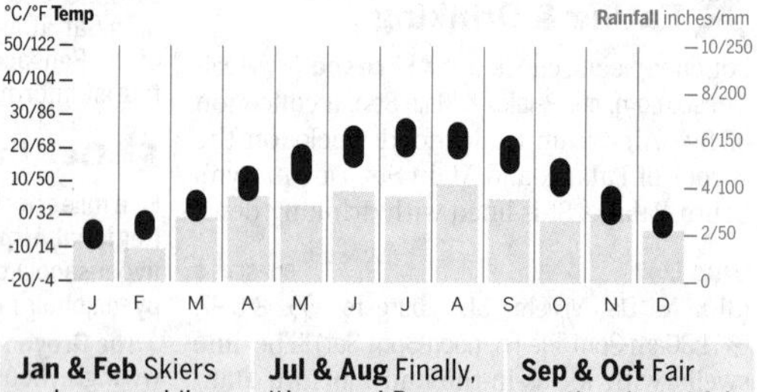

Jan & Feb Skiers and snowmobilers hit the trails.

Jul & Aug Finally, it's warm! Beer gardens hop, beaches splash, and festivals rock most weekends.

Sep & Oct Fair weather, bountiful farm and orchard harvests, and shoulder-season bargains.

History

The region's first residents included the Hopewell (around 200 BC) and Mississippi River mound builders (around AD 700). Both left behind mysterious piles of earth that were tombs for their leaders and possibly tributes to their deities. You can see remnants at Cahokia in southern Illinois, and Mound City in southeastern Ohio.

French voyageurs (fur traders) arrived in the early 17th century and established missions and forts. The British turned up soon after that, with the rivalry spilling over into the French and Indian War (Seven Years' War, 1754–61), after which Britain took control of all of the land east of the Mississippi. Following the Revolutionary War, the Great Lakes area became the new USA's Northwest Territory, which soon was divided into states and locked to the region after it developed its impressive canal and railroad network. But conflicts erupted between the newcomers and the Native Americans, including the 1811 Battle of Tippecanoe in Indiana; the bloody 1832 Black Hawk War in Wisconsin, Illinois and around, which forced indigenous people to move west of the Mississippi; and the 1862 Sioux uprising in Minnesota.

Throughout the late 19th and early 20th centuries, industries sprang up and grew quickly, fueled by resources of coal and iron, and cheap transportation on the lakes. The availability of work brought huge influxes of immigrants from Ireland, Germany, Scandinavia and southern and eastern Europe. For decades after the Civil War, a great number of African Americans also migrated to the region's urban centers from the South.

The area prospered during WWII and throughout the 1950s, but was followed by 20 years of social turmoil and economic stagnation. Manufacturing industries declined, which walloped Rust Belt cities such as Detroit and Cleveland with high unemployment and 'white flight' (white middle-class families who fled to the suburbs).

The 1980s and '90s brought urban revitalization. The region's population increased, notably with newcomers from Asia and Mexico. Growth in the service and high-tech sectors resulted in economic balance, although manufacturing industries such as car making and steel still played a big role, meaning that when the economic crisis hit in 2008, Great Lakes towns felt the pinch first and foremost.

ILLINOIS

Chicago dominates the state with its sky-high architecture and superlative museums, restaurants and music clubs. But venturing further afield reveals Hemingway's hometown of 'wide lawns and narrow minds,' scattered shrines to local hero Abe Lincoln, and a trail of corn dogs, pies and drive-in movie theaters down Route 66. A cypress swamp and a prehistoric World Heritage site make appearances in Illinois too.

Information

Illinois Office of Tourism (www.enjoyillinois.com)

Illinois Highway Conditions (www.gettingaroundillinois.com)

Illinois State Park Information (www.dnr.illinois.gov) State parks are free to visit. Campsites cost $6 to $35; some accept reservations (www.reserveamerica.com; $5).

GREAT LAKES IN...

Five Days

Spend the first two days in **Chicago**. On your third day, make the 1½-hour trip to **Milwaukee** for culture, both high- and lowbrow. Take the ferry over to Michigan and spend your fourth day beaching in **Saugatuck**. Circle back via **Indiana Dunes** or **Indiana's Amish Country**.

Ten Days

After two days in **Chicago**, on day three make for **Madison** and its surrounding quirky sights. Spend your fourth and fifth days at the **Apostle Islands**, and then head into the Upper Peninsula to visit **Marquette** and **Pictured Rocks** for a few days, followed by **Sleeping Bear Dunes** and the wineries around **Traverse City**. Return via the galleries, pies and beaches of **Saugatuck**.

Great Lakes Highlights

1. Absorbing the skyscrapers, museums, festivals and foodie bounty of **Chicago** (p526).
2. Beach lounging, berry eating and surfing on **Lake Michigan's western shore** (p585).
3. Slowing down for clip-clopping horses and buggies in **Ohio's Amish Country** (p567).
4. Polka dancing at a Friday-night fish fry in **Milwaukee** (p593).
5. Paddling the **Boundary Waters** (p618) and sleeping under a blanket of stars.
6. Cycling along the river against the urban backdrop of **Detroit** (p575).
7. Taking the slowpoke, pie-filled journey through Illinois on **Route 66** (p551).
8. Being surprised by the Tibetan temples, phenomenal architecture and green hills of **Central Indiana** (p557).

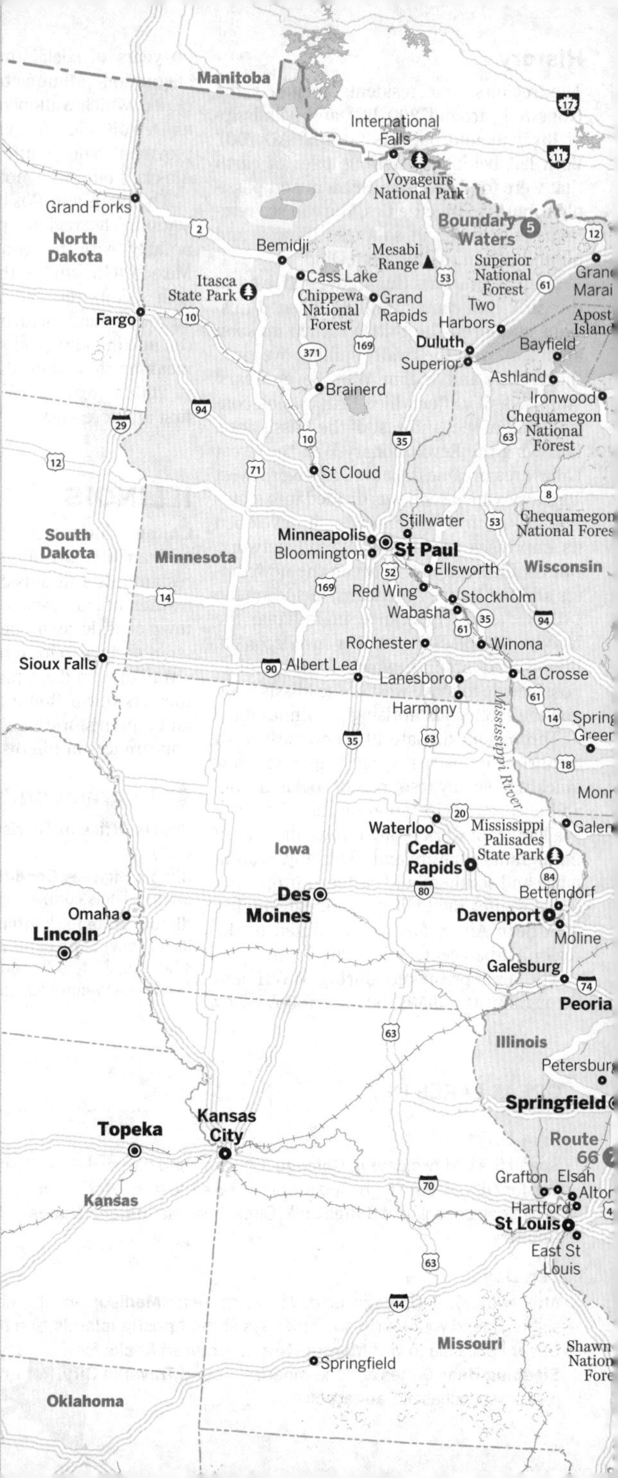

0 200 km
0 100 miles
N
11
hunder Bay
17
117
CANADA
Isle Royale National Park
Lake Superior
and
rtage
Copper Harbor
Keweenaw Peninsula
rcupine
ountains
ilderness
ate Park
41
Houghton
Pictured Rocks National Lakeshore
Tahquamenon Falls
Ontario
Ottawa National Forest
Marquette
41
123
Sault Ste Marie
17
Lake Nipissing
28
141
Naubinway
Iron Mountain
2
St Ignace
Manitoulin Island
Lake Michigan
Mackinaw City
Mackinac Island
Washington Island
Nicolet National Forest
41
Leelanau Peninsula
Petoskey
Boyne City
Georgian Bay
69
Wausau
Door Peninsula
Manitou Islands
Charlevoix
Lake Huron
Leland
Empire
Lake Simcoe
Traverse City
Huron National Forest
Green Bay
Frankfort
Sleeping Bear Dunes National Lakeshore
75
Saginaw Bay
400
Manitowoc
Central Time Zone
Eastern Time Zone
shkosh
Ludington
Toronto
43
Hamilton
31
131
Michigan
41
403
23
Port Huron
Muskegon
Grand Rapids
Milwaukee
Flint
94
69
402
London
4
Michigan's Western Shore
2
Lansing
adison
Holland
96
Detroit
New York
43
Lake Erie
Racine
Saugatuck/ Douglas
131
Dearborn
6
401
Erie
94
Kalamazoo
Ann Arbor
94
69
Madison
90
88
Chicago
1
31
Bass Islands
Pelee Island
Kelleys Island
Pennsylvania
Gary
Middlebury
79
East Chicago
South Bend
20
90
80
Toledo
Cleveland
80
Indiana Dunes State Park
Auburn
Akron
Indiana
Canton
55
57
75
23
71
Lexington
65
Marion
Ohio
Millersburg
3
Ohio's Amish Country
Bloomington
Fairmount
77
Atlanta
COLUMBUS
Champaign
70
465
68
Terre Haute
Indianapolis
Dayton
Yellow Springs
Lancaster
Logan
33
Marietta
70
46
37
9
50
Chillicothe
Athens
79
Bloomington
8
Columbus
Nashville
Cincinnati
Covington
23
West Virginia
Central Indiana
65
Madison
50
Vincennes
56
Ohio River
Huntington
Charleston
Louisville
Frankfort
64
New Harmony
Lexington
Harmonie State Park
77
Cypress Creek National Wildlife Refuge
75
Paducah
Kentucky
Virginia
airo

Chicago

Loving Chicago is 'like loving a woman with a broken nose: you may well find lovelier lovelies, but never a lovely so real.' Writer Nelson Algren summed it up well in *Chicago: City on the Make*. There's something about this cloud-scraping city that bewitches. Well, maybe not during the six-month winter, when the 'Windy City' gets slapped by snowy blasts; however, come May, when the weather warms and everyone dashes for the outdoor festivals, ballparks, lakefront beaches and beer gardens – ah, nowhere tops Chicago (literally: some of the world's tallest buildings are here).

Beyond its mighty architecture, Chicago is a city of Mexican, Polish, Vietnamese and other ethnic neighborhoods in which to wander. It's a city of blues, jazz and rock clubs any night of the week. And it's a chowhound's town, where the queues for hot dogs equal those at North America's top restaurants.

Forgive us, but it has to be said: the Windy City will blow you away with its low-key, cultured awesomeness.

History

In the late 17th century, the Potawatomi gave the name Checagou – meaning 'wild onions' – to the once-swampy environs. The new city's pivotal moment happened on October 8, 1871, when (so the story goes) Mrs O'Leary's cow kicked over the lantern that started the Great Chicago Fire. It torched the entire inner city and left 90,000 people homeless.

'Damn,' said the city planners. 'Guess we shouldn't have built everything from wood. It's flammable.' So they rebuilt with steel and created space for bold new structures, such as the world's first skyscraper, which popped up in 1885.

Al Capone's gang more or less ran things during the 1920s and corrupted the city's political system. Local government has had issues ever since, with 31 city council members going to jail over the last four decades.

Sights

Chicago's main attractions are found mostly in or near the city center, though visits to distant neighborhoods, like Pilsen and Hyde Park, can also be rewarding.

The Loop

The city center is named for the elevated train tracks that lasso its streets. It's busy all day, though not much happens at night other than in Millennium Park and the Theater District (near the intersection of N State and W Randolph Sts). Grant Park – where the city's mega-events like Blues Fest and Lollapalooza take place – forms a green buffer between the skyscrapers and Lake Michigan.

★Millennium Park PARK
(Map p530; ☎312-742-1168; www.millenniumpark.org; 201 E Randolph St; ⏰6am-11pm; 🚸; Ⓜ Brown, Orange, Green, Purple, Pink Line to Randolph) FREE
The city's showpiece is a trove of free and arty sights. It includes **Pritzker Pavilion**, Frank Gehry's swooping silver band shell, hosting free concerts nightly in summer

---

CHICAGO IN...

Two Days

On your first day, take an **architectural tour** and gaze up at the city's skyscrapers. Look down from the **Willis Tower**, the city's tallest building. See 'The Bean' reflect the skyline, and splash with Crown Fountain's human gargoyles at **Millennium Park**. Chow down on a deep-dish pizza at **Giordano's**.

Make the second day a cultural one: explore the **Art Institute of Chicago** or **Field Museum of Natural History** . Grab a stylish dinner in the **West Loop**. Or listen to blues at **Buddy Guy's Legends**.

Four Days

Follow the two-day itinerary. On your third day, dip your toes in Lake Michigan at **North Avenue Beach** and saunter through leafy **Lincoln Park**. If it's baseball season, head to **Wrigley Field** (p547) for a Cubs game. In the evening yuck it up at **Second City**.

Pick a neighborhood on your fourth day: vintage boutiques and rock and roll in **Wicker Park**, murals and mole sauce in **Pilsen** (p544), pagodas and Vietnamese sandwiches in **Uptown**, or Obama sights and the **Nuclear Energy sculpture** in Hyde Park.

(6:30pm; bring a picnic and bottle of wine); Anish Kapoor's beloved silvery sculpture **Cloud Gate** (aka 'The Bean'); and Jaume Plensa's **Crown Fountain**, a de facto water park that projects video images of locals spitting water, gargoyle style.

The **McCormick Tribune Ice Rink** fills with skaters in winter (and alfresco diners in summer). The hidden **Lurie Garden** blooms with prairie flowers and tranquillity. The Gehry-designed **BP Bridge** spans Columbus Dr and offers great skyline views. And the **Nichols Bridgeway** arches from the park up to the Art Institute's small, 3rd-floor sculpture garden (free to view).

Want more? Free yoga and Pilates classes take place Saturday mornings in summer on the Great Lawn, while the Family Fun Tent provides free kids' activities daily between 10am and 2pm.

★Art Institute of Chicago — MUSEUM

(Map p530; ☎312-443-3600; www.artic.edu; 111 S Michigan Ave; adult/child $25/free; ⏲10:30am-5pm, to 8pm Thu; 👪; Ⓜ Brown, Orange, Green, Purple, Pink Line to Adams) The second-largest art museum in the country, the Art Institute's collection of impressionist and post-impressionist paintings rivals those in France, and the number of surrealist works is tremendous. Download the free app for DIY tours. It offers 50 jaunts, everything from highlights (Grant Wood's *American Gothic*, Edward Hopper's *Nighthawks*) to a 'birthday-suit tour' of naked works.

Allow two hours to browse the museum's must-sees; art buffs should allocate much longer. The main entrance is on Michigan Ave, but you can also enter via the dazzling Modern Wing on Monroe St.

★Willis Tower — TOWER

(Map p530; ☎312-875-9696; www.theskydeck.com; 233 S Wacker Dr; adult/child $19.50/12.50; ⏲9am-10pm Apr-Sep, 10am-8pm Oct-Mar; Ⓜ Brown, Orange, Purple, Pink Line to Quincy) It's Chicago's tallest building, and the 103rd-floor Skydeck puts you 1353ft into the heavens. Take the ear-popping, 70-second elevator ride to the top, then step onto one of the glass-floored ledges jutting out in mid-air for a knee-buckling perspective straight down. The entrance is on Jackson Blvd.

Queues can be up to an hour on busy days (peak times are in summer, between 11am and 4pm Friday through Sunday). A bit of history: it was the Sears Tower until insurance broker Willis Group Holdings bought the naming rights in 2009.

ILLINOIS FACTS

Nicknames Prairie State, Land of Lincoln

Population 12.9 million

Area 57,900 sq miles

Capital city Springfield (population 117,000)

Other cities Chicago (population 2.7 million)

Sales tax 6.25%

Birthplace of Author Ernest Hemingway (1899–1961), animator Walt Disney (1901–66), jazz musician Miles Davis (1926–91), actor Bill Murray (b 1950)

Home of Cornfields, Route 66 starting point

Politics Democratic in Chicago, Republican downstate

Famous for Skyscrapers, corn dogs, Abe Lincoln sights

Official snack food Popcorn

Driving distances Chicago to Milwaukee 92 miles, Chicago to Springfield 200 miles

Chicago Cultural Center — BUILDING

(Map p530; ☎312-744-6630; www.chicagoculturalcenter.org; 78 E Washington St; ⏲9am-7pm Mon-Thu, to 6pm Fri & Sat, 10am-6pm Sun; Ⓜ Brown, Orange, Green, Purple, Pink Line to Randolph) FREE The block-long building houses ongoing art exhibitions and foreign films, as well as jazz, classical and electronic dance music concerts at lunchtime (12:15pm Monday to Friday). It also contains the world's largest Tiffany stained-glass dome and Chicago's main visitor center. Free building tours take place Wednesday, Friday and Saturday at 1:15pm; meet in the Randolph St lobby.

Maggie Daley Park — PARK

(Map p530; www.maggiedaleypark.com; 337 E Randolph St; ⏲6am-11pm; 👪; Ⓜ Brown, Orange, Green, Purple, Pink Line to Randolph) FREE Families love the park's fanciful free playgrounds in all their enchanted forest and pirate-themed glory. There's also a rock-climbing wall and 18-hole mini-golf course (which becomes an ice-skating ribbon in winter); these features have fees.

Metro Chicago Area

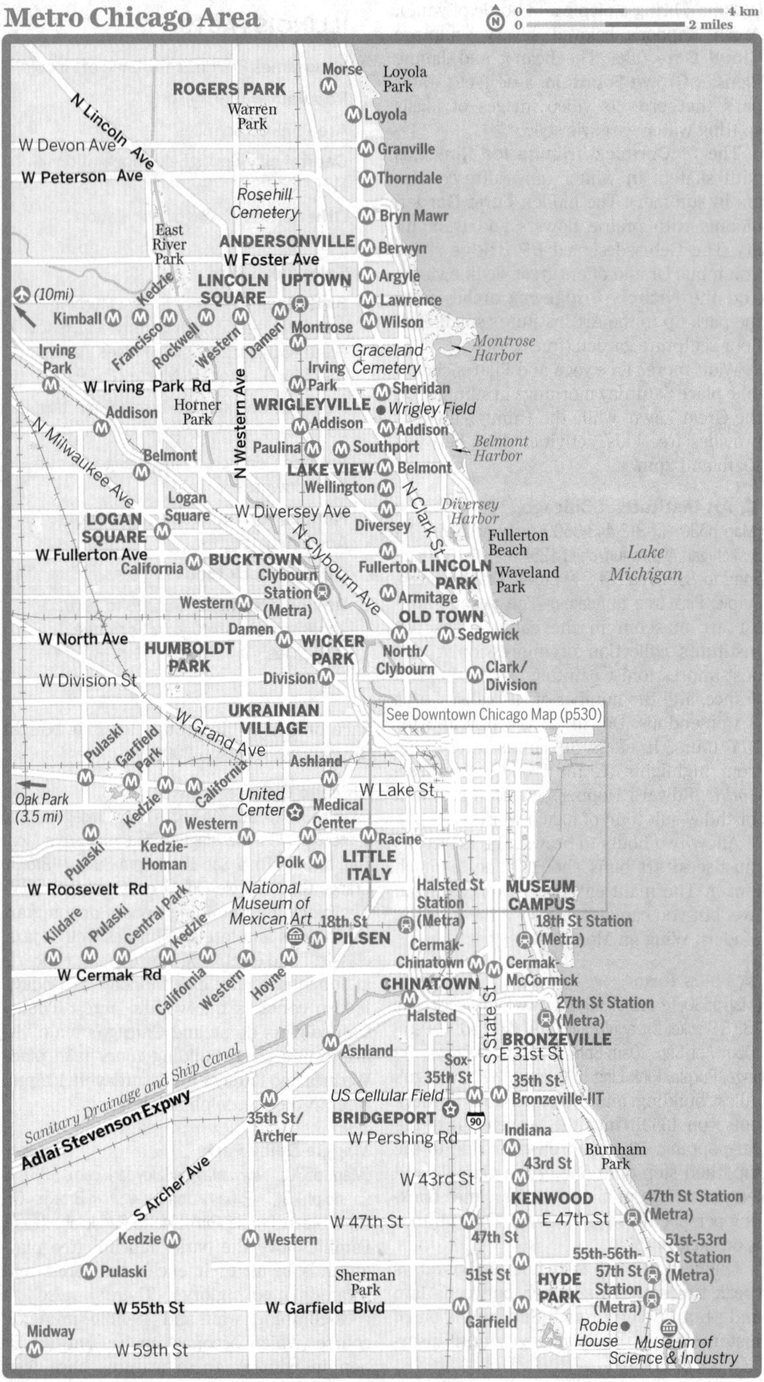
0 4 km
0 2 miles
ROGERS PARK
Warren Park
Morse
Loyola Park
Loyola
N Lincoln Ave
W Devon Ave
W Peterson Ave
Granville
Thorndale
Rosehill Cemetery
Bryn Mawr
East River Park
ANDERSONVILLE
W Foster Ave
Berwyn
LINCOLN SQUARE
UPTOWN
Argyle
Lawrence
Wilson
(10mi)
Kimball
Kedzie
Francisco
Rockwell
Western
Damen
Montrose
Montrose Harbor
Irving Park
Graceland Cemetery
Irving Park
W Irving Park Rd
Sheridan
Addison
Horner Park
WRIGLEYVILLE
Wrigley Field
N Western Ave
Addison
Addison
N Milwaukee Ave
Belmont
Paulina
Southport
Belmont Harbor
LAKE VIEW
Belmont
Wellington
N Clark St
Logan Square
LOGAN SQUARE
W Diversey Ave
Diversey
Diversey Harbor
N Clybourn Ave
W Fullerton Ave
Fullerton Beach
California
BUCKTOWN
Fullerton
LINCOLN PARK
Waveland Park
Lake Michigan
Clybourn Station (Metra)
Western
Armitage
OLD TOWN
Damen
Sedgwick
W North Ave
HUMBOLDT PARK
WICKER PARK
North/ Clybourn
Clark/ Division
W Division St
Division
UKRAINIAN VILLAGE
See Downtown Chicago Map (p530)
W Grand Ave
Pulaski
Garfield Park
Ashland
Kedzie
California
Oak Park (3.5 mi)
United Center
W Lake St
Medical Center
Western
Racine
Pulaski
Kedzie-Homan
LITTLE ITALY
Polk
W Roosevelt Rd
National Museum of Mexican Art
Halsted St Station (Metra)
MUSEUM CAMPUS
Kildare
Pulaski
Central Park
Kedzie
18th St
PILSEN
18th St Station (Metra)
Cermak-Chinatown
Cermak-McCormick
W Cermak Rd
California
Western
Hoyne
CHINATOWN
Halsted
27th St Station (Metra)
S State St
BRONZEVILLE
Ashland
E 31st St
Sanitary Drainage and Ship Canal
Sox-35th St
35th St-Bronzeville-IIT
Adlai Stevenson Expwy
US Cellular Field
35th St/ Archer
BRIDGEPORT
90
W Pershing Rd
Indiana
Burnham Park
43rd St
W 43rd St
S Archer Ave
KENWOOD
47th St Station (Metra)
W 47th St
E 47th St
47th St
Kedzie
Western
51st-53rd St Station (Metra)
55th-56th-57th St Station (Metra)
Pulaski
Sherman Park
51st St
HYDE PARK
W 55th St
W Garfield Blvd
Garfield
Robie House
Midway
Museum of Science & Industry
W 59th St

FAMOUS LOOP ARCHITECTURE

Ever since it presented the world with the first skyscraper, Chicago has thought big with its architecture and pushed the envelope of modern design. The Loop is a fantastic place to roam and gawk at these ambitious structures.

The **Chicago Architecture Foundation** (p537) runs tours that explain the following buildings and more:

Chicago Board of Trade (Map p530; 141 W Jackson Blvd; Ⓜ Brown, Orange, Purple, Pink Line to LaSalle) A 1930 art-deco gem. Inside, manic traders swap futures and options. Outside, check out the giant statue of Ceres, the goddess of agriculture, that tops the building.

Rookery (Map p530; www.flwright.org; 209 S LaSalle St; ⏲9:30am-5:30pm Mon-Fri; Ⓜ Brown, Orange, Purple, Pink Line to Quincy) The 1888 Rookery looks fortresslike outside, but the inside is light and airy thanks to Frank Lloyd Wright's atrium overhaul. Tours ($7 to $12) are available at noon weekdays. Pigeons used to roost here, hence the name.

Monadnock Building (Map p530; www.monadnockbuilding.com; 53 W Jackson Blvd; Ⓜ Blue Line to Jackson) Architectural pilgrims get weak-kneed when they see the Monadnock Building, which is two buildings in one. The north is the older, traditional design from 1891, while the south is the newer, mod half from 1893. See the difference? The Monadnock remains true to its original purpose as an office building.

Multiple picnic tables make the park an excellent spot to relax. It connects to Millennium Park via the pedestrian BP Bridge.

Buckingham Fountain FOUNTAIN

(Map p530; 301 S Columbus Dr; Ⓜ Red Line to Harrison) Grant Park's centerpiece is one of the world's largest squirters, with a 1.5-million-gallon capacity and a 15-story-high spray. It lets loose on the hour from 9am to 11pm mid-April to mid-October, accompanied at night by multicolored lights and music.

Route 66 Sign HISTORIC SITE

(Map p530; E Adams St btwn S Michigan & Wabash Aves; Ⓜ Brown, Orange, Green, Purple, Pink Line to Adams) Attention Route 66 buffs: the Mother Road's starting point is here. Look for the marker on Adams St's south side as you head west toward Wabash Ave.

South Loop

The South Loop, which includes the lower ends of downtown and Grant Park, bustles with the lakefront Museum Campus and gleaming residential high-rises.

★Field Museum of Natural History MUSEUM

(Map p530; ☎312-922-9410; www.fieldmuseum.org; 1400 S Lake Shore Dr; adult/child $18/13; ⏲9am-5pm; 👪; 🚌146, 130) The mammoth museum houses everything but the kitchen sink – beetles, mummies, gemstones, Bushman the stuffed ape. The collection's rock star is Sue, the largest *Tyrannosaurus rex* yet discovered. She even gets her own gift shop. Special exhibits, like the 3D movie, cost extra.

★Shedd Aquarium AQUARIUM

(Map p530; ☎312-939-2438; www.sheddaquarium.org; 1200 S Lake Shore Dr; adult/child $31/22; ⏲9am-5pm Mon-Fri, to 6pm Sat & Sun Sep-May, to 6pm daily Jun-Aug; 👪; 🚌146, 130) Top draws at the kiddie-mobbed Shedd Aquarium include the Wild Reef exhibit, where there's just 5in of Plexiglas between you and two dozen fierce-looking sharks, and the Oceanarium, with its rescued sea otters. Note the Oceanarium also keeps belugua whales and Pacific white-sided dolphins, a practice that has become increasingly controversial in recent years.

★Adler Planetarium MUSEUM

(Map p530; ☎312-922-7827; www.adlerplanetarium.org; 1300 S Lake Shore Dr; adult/child $12/8; ⏲9:30am-4pm Mon-Fri, to 4:30 Sat & Sun; 👪; 🚌146, 130) Space enthusiasts will get a big bang (pun!) out of the Adler. There are public telescopes to view the stars, 3D lectures to learn about supernovas and the *Planet Explorers* exhibit where kids can 'launch' a rocket. The immersive digital films cost $13 extra. The Adler's front steps offer Chicago's primo skyline view.

Downtown Chicago

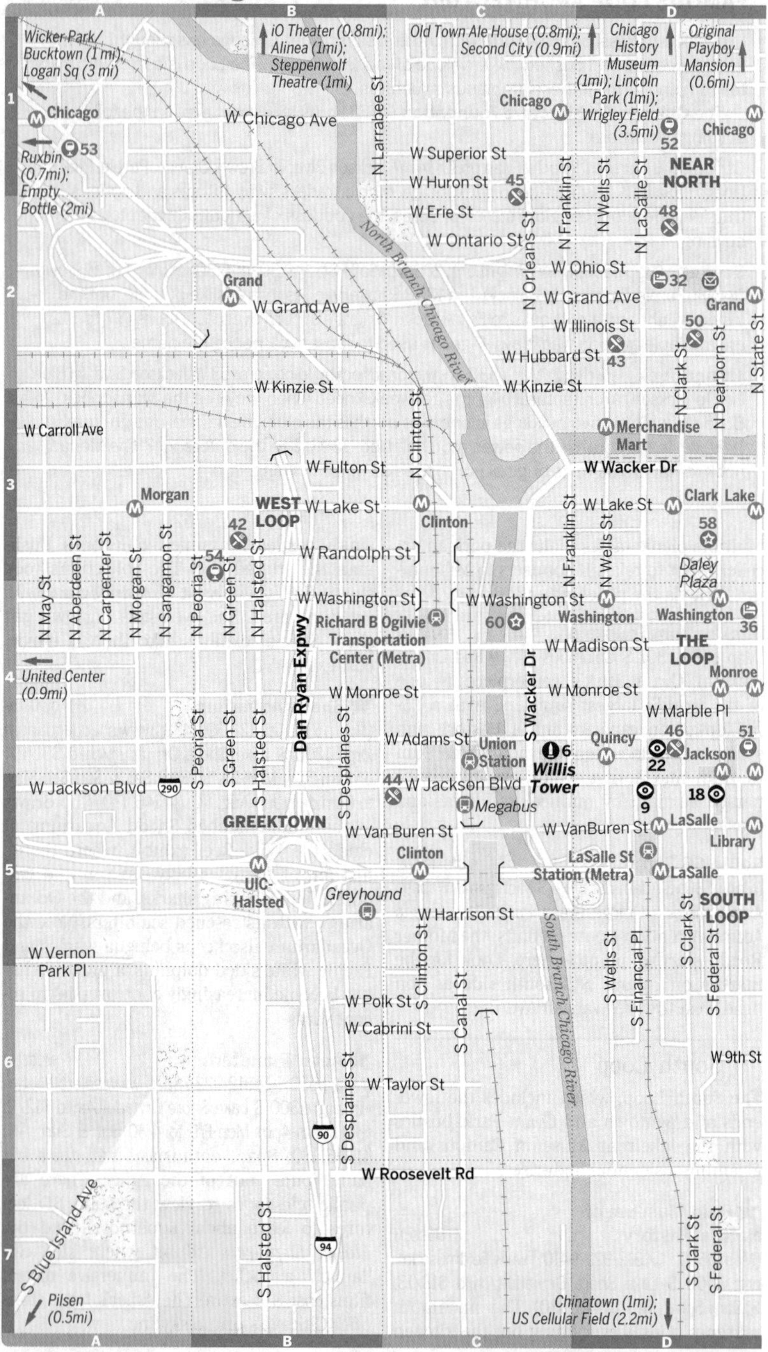
Wicker Park/ Bucktown (1 mi); Logan Sq (3 mi)
iO Theater (0.8mi); Alinea (1mi); Steppenwolf Theatre (1mi)
Old Town Ale House (0.8mi); Second City (0.9mi)
Chicago History Museum (1mi); Lincoln Park (1mi); Wrigley Field (3.5mi)
Original Playboy Mansion (0.6mi)
Ruxbin (0.7mi); Empty Bottle (2mi)
United Center (0.9mi)
Pilsen (0.5mi)
Chinatown (1mi); US Cellular Field (2.2mi)
NEAR NORTH
WEST LOOP
THE LOOP
GREEKTOWN
SOUTH LOOP
Willis Tower
Daley Plaza
Merchandise Mart
Union Station
Richard B Ogilvie Transportation Center (Metra)
LaSalle St Station (Metra)
Greyhound
Megabus
Chicago
Grand
Morgan
Clinton
Washington
Monroe
Quincy
Jackson
LaSalle
Library
Clark Lake
UIC-Halsted
North Branch Chicago River
South Branch Chicago River
W Chicago Ave
W Superior St
W Huron St
W Erie St
W Ontario St
W Ohio St
W Grand Ave
W Illinois St
W Hubbard St
W Kinzie St
W Carroll Ave
W Fulton St
W Wacker Dr
W Lake St
W Randolph St
W Washington St
W Madison St
W Monroe St
W Marble Pl
W Adams St
W Jackson Blvd
W Van Buren St
W VanBuren St
W Harrison St
W Vernon Park Pl
W Polk St
W Cabrini St
W Taylor St
W 9th St
W Roosevelt Rd
S Blue Island Ave
N Larrabee St
N Orleans St
N Franklin St
N Wells St
N LaSalle St
N Clark St
N Dearborn St
N State St
N Clinton St
N May St
N Aberdeen St
N Carpenter St
N Morgan St
N Sangamon St
N Peoria St
N Green St
N Halsted St
S Peoria St
S Green St
S Halsted St
Dan Ryan Expwy
S Desplaines St
S Wacker Dr
S Clinton St
S Canal St
S Wells St
S Financial Pl
S Clark St
S Federal St
290
90
94
6
9
18
22
32
36
42
43
44
45
46
48
50
51
52
53
54
58
60
A
B
C
D
1
2
3
4
5
6
7

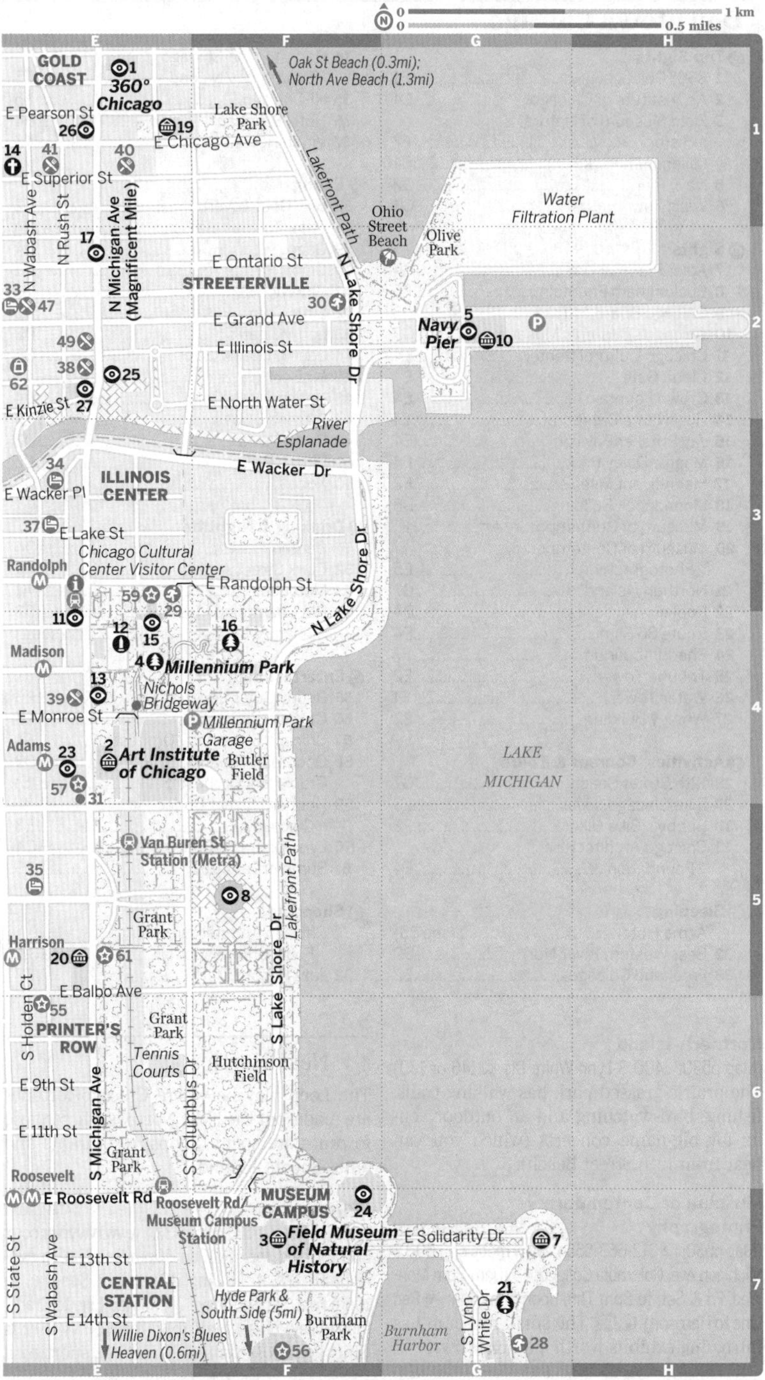
0 1 km
0 0.5 miles
E
F
G
H
1
2
3
4
5
6
7
GOLD COAST
1 360° Chicago
E Pearson St
26
19
Lake Shore Park
E Chicago Ave
Oak St Beach (0.3mi); North Ave Beach (1.3mi)
14
41
40
E Superior St
N Wabash Ave
N Rush St
N Michigan Ave (Magnificent Mile)
17
Lakefront Path
Ohio Street Beach
Olive Park
Water Filtration Plant
E Ontario St
STREETERVILLE
N Lake Shore Dr
33
47
30
E Grand Ave
5
Navy Pier
10
49
E Illinois St
62
38
25
27
E Kinzie St
E North Water St
River Esplanade
E Wacker Dr
34
E Wacker Pl
ILLINOIS CENTER
37
E Lake St
Randolph
Chicago Cultural Center Visitor Center
E Randolph St
59
29
11
12
15
16
Madison
4
Millennium Park
13
39
Nichols Bridgeway
E Monroe St
Millennium Park Garage
Adams
2
23
Art Institute of Chicago
Butler Field
57
31
LAKE MICHIGAN
Van Buren St Station (Metra)
35
8
Grant Park
Harrison
20
61
E Balbo Ave
S Holden Ct
55
PRINTER'S ROW
Grant Park
Tennis Courts
Hutchinson Field
S Lake Shore Dr
Lakefront Path
E 9th St
S Michigan Ave
S Columbus Dr
E 11th St
Grant Park
Roosevelt
E Roosevelt Rd
Roosevelt Rd/ Museum Campus Station
MUSEUM CAMPUS
24
3
Field Museum of Natural History
E Solidarity Dr
7
S State St
S Wabash Ave
E 13th St
CENTRAL STATION
21
E 14th St
Hyde Park & South Side (5mi)
Burnham Park
Burnham Harbor
S Lynn White Dr
Willie Dixon's Blues Heaven (0.6mi)
56
28

Downtown Chicago

Northerly Island PARK

(Map p530; 1400 S Lynn White Dr; 146 or 130) The prairie-grassed park has walking trails, fishing, bird-watching and an outdoor venue for big-name concerts (which you can hear from 12th Street Beach).

Museum of Contemporary Photography MUSEUM

(Map p530; 312-663-5554; www.mocp.org; 600 S Michigan Ave, Columbia College; 10am-5pm Mon-Wed, Fri & Sat, to 8pm Thu, noon-5pm Sun; M Red Line to Harrison) FREE The small museum has intriguing exhibits worth a quick browse.

Near North

The Loop may be where Chicago fortunes are made, but the Near North is where those fortunes are spent. Shops, restaurants and amusements abound.

★ **Navy Pier** WATERFRONT

(Map p530; 312-595-7437; www.navypier.com; 600 E Grand Ave; 10am-10pm Sun-Thu, to midnight Fri & Sat Jun-Aug, 10am-8pm Sun-Thu, to 10pm Fri & Sat Sep-May; ; M Red Line to Grand, then trolley) FREE Half-mile-long Navy Pier is Chicago's most-visited attraction, sporting a

196ft Ferris wheel and other carnival rides ($6 to $8 each), an IMAX theater, a beer garden and gimmicky chain restaurants. Locals groan over its commercialization, but its lakefront view and cool breezes can't be beat. The fireworks displays on summer Wednesdays (9:30pm) and Saturdays (10:15pm) are a treat too.

The Chicago Children's Museum (p539) is also on the pier, as are several boat-cruise operators. Try the Shoreline water taxi for a fun ride to the Museum Campus (adult/child $8/4). A renovation is bringing an ice rink and additional amusements by 2017.

Magnificent Mile STREET
(Map p530; www.themagnificentmile.com; N Michigan Ave; Ⓜ Red Line to Grand) Spanning Michigan Ave between the river and Oak St, the Mag Mile is the much-touted upscale shopping strip, where Bloomingdales, Neiman's and Saks will lighten your wallet.

Tribune Tower ARCHITECTURE
(Map p530; 435 N Michigan Ave; Ⓜ Red Line to Grand) Take a close look when passing by the Gothic tower to see chunks of the Taj Mahal, Parthenon and other famous structures embedded in the lower walls.

Wrigley Building ARCHITECTURE
(Map p530; 400 N Michigan Ave; Ⓜ Red Line to Grand) Built by the chewing-gum maker; the white exterior glows as white as the Doublemint Twins' teeth.

Gold Coast

The Gold Coast has been the address of Chicago's wealthiest for more than 125 years.

★360° Chicago OBSERVATORY
(Map p530; ☎888-875-8439; www.360chicago.com; 875 N Michigan Ave; adult/child $19/13; ⊙9am-11pm; Ⓜ Red Line to Chicago) This is the new name for the John Hancock Center Observatory. In many ways the view here surpasses the one at Willis Tower. The 94th-floor lookout has informative displays and the TILT feature (floor-to-ceiling windows that you stand in as they tip out over the ground; it costs $7 extra and is fairly cheesy). Not interested in such frivolities? Shoot straight up to the 96th-floor Signature Lounge, where the view is free if you buy a drink ($8 to $16).

Museum of Contemporary Art MUSEUM
(MCA; Map p530; ☎312-280-2660; www.mcachicago.org; 220 E Chicago Ave; adult/student $12/7; ⊙10am-8pm Tue, to 5pm Wed-Sun; Ⓜ Red Line to Chicago) Consider it the Art Institute's brash, rebellious sibling, with especially strong minimalist, surrealist and conceptual photography collections. Exhibits change regularly so you never know what you'll see.

Original Playboy Mansion BUILDING
(1340 N State Pkwy; Ⓜ Red Line to Clark/Division) Hugh Hefner began wearing his all-day jammies here, when the rigors of magazine production and heavy partying prevented him from getting dressed. The building contains

GANGSTER SITES

Chicago would rather not discuss its gangster past; consequently there are no brochures or exhibits about infamous sites. So you'll need to use your imagination when visiting the following places:

St Valentine's Day Massacre Site (2122 N Clark St; 🚌22) This is where Al Capone's goons, dressed as cops, lined up seven members of Bugs Moran's gang against the garage wall that used to be here and sprayed them with bullets. The garage was torn down in 1967; the site is now the parking lot of a retirement home.

Biograph Theater (2433 N Lincoln Ave; Ⓜ Brown, Purple, Red Line to Fullerton) In 1934, the 'lady in red' betrayed 'public enemy number one' John Dillinger at the Biograph. Dillinger was shot dead by the FBI in the alley beside the venue.

Holy Name Cathedral (Map p530; www.holynamecathedral.org; 735 N State St; Ⓜ Red Line to Chicago) Two murders took place near the church. In 1924 North Side boss Dion O'Banion was gunned down in his florist shop (738 N State St) after he crossed Al Capone. O'Banion's replacement, Hymie Weiss, fared no better. In 1926 he was killed on his way to church by bullets flying from a window at 740 N State St.

Green Mill (p546) The speakeasy in the basement of the glamorous jazz bar was a Capone favorite.

LOCAL KNOWLEDGE

THE 606

New York City has the High Line, and Chicago now has **The 606** (www.the606.org; 6am-11pm; M Blue Line to Damen). Opened in 2015, it converts a similar tumbledown train track into an urban-cool elevated path that runs for 2.7 miles between Wicker Park and Logan Square. Bike, run or stroll past factories, smokestacks, clattering El trains and locals' backyard affairs. It's a fascinating trek through the city's socioeconomic strata: moneyed at the east, becoming more industrial and immigrant to the west. The trail parallels Bloomingdale Ave, with access points every quarter mile. The entrance at Churchill Park (1825 N Damen Ave) is a handy place to ascend. And FYI: 606 is the zip code prefix all city neighborhoods share.

condos now, but a visit still allows you to boast that 'I've been to the Playboy Mansion.' Head east a block to Astor St and ogle more manors between the 1300 and 1500 blocks.

Water Tower LANDMARK

(Map p530; 108 N Michigan Ave; M Red Line to Chicago) The 154ft-tall, turreted tower is a defining city landmark: it was the sole downtown survivor of the 1871 Great Fire.

Lincoln Park & Old Town

Lincoln Park is Chicago's largest green space, an urban oasis spanning 1200 leafy acres along the lakefront. 'Lincoln Park' is also the name for the abutting neighborhood. Both are alive day and night with people jogging, walking dogs, pushing strollers and driving in circles looking for a place to park.

Old Town rests at the southwest foot of Lincoln Park. The intersection of North Ave and Wells St is the epicenter, with saucy bars, restaurants and the Second City improv club fanning out from here.

Lincoln Park Zoo ZOO

(312-742-2000; www.lpzoo.org; 2200 N Cannon Dr; 10am-4:30pm Nov-Mar, to 5pm Apr-Oct, to 6:30pm Sat & Sun Jun-Aug; ; 151) FREE A local family favorite, filled with gorillas, lions, tigers, snow monkeys and other exotic creatures in the shadow of downtown. Check out the Regenstein African Journey, Ape House and Nature Boardwalk for the cream of the crop.

Lincoln Park Conservatory GARDENS

(312-742-7736; www.lincolnparkconservancy.org; 2391 N Stockton Dr; 9am-5pm; 151) FREE Near the zoo's north entrance, the magnificent 1891 hothouse coaxes palms, ferns and orchids to flourish. In winter, it becomes a soothing, 75°F (24°C) escape from the icy winds raging outside.

Chicago History Museum MUSEUM

(312-642-4600; www.chicagohistory.org; 1601 N Clark St; adult/child $14/free; 9:30am-4:30pm Mon-Sat, noon-5pm Sun; ; 22) Multimedia displays cover it all, from the Great Fire to the 1968 Democratic Convention. President Lincoln's deathbed is here; so is the chance to 'become' a Chicago hot dog covered in condiments (in the kids' area, but adults are welcome for the photo op).

Lake View & Wrigleyville

North of Lincoln Park, these neighborhoods can be enjoyed by ambling along Halsted St, Clark St, Belmont Ave or Southport Ave, which are well supplied with restaurants, bars and shops. The only real sight is ivy-covered **Wrigley Field** (www.cubs.com; 1060 W Addison St; M Red Line to Addison), named after the chewing-gum guy and home to the much-loved but hard-luck Chicago Cubs. Ninety-minute tours ($25) of the iconic, century-old ballpark are available. The area around the facility is getting a makeover with spiffed-up amenities for visitors.

Andersonville & Uptown

These northern neighborhoods are good for a delicious browse. Andersonville is an old Swedish enclave centered on Clark St, where timeworn, European-tinged businesses mix with new foodie restaurants, funky boutiques, vintage shops and gay and lesbian bars. Take the CTA Red Line to the Berwyn stop, and walk west for six blocks.

A short distance south, Uptown is a whole different scene. Take the Red Line to the Argyle stop, and you're in the heart of 'Little Saigon' and its pho-serving storefronts.

Wicker Park, Bucktown & Ukrainian Village

West of Lincoln Park, these three neighborhoods – once havens for working-class, central European immigrants and Bohemian writers – are hot property. Heaps of fashion boutiques, hipster record stores, thrift shops and cocktail lounges have shot up, especially near the intersection of Milwaukee and N Damen Aves. Division St is also prime wandering territory. It used to be called 'Polish Broadway' for all the polka bars that lined it, but now the requisite cafes and crafty businesses have taken over. There aren't many actual sights here, aside from **Nelson Algren's House** (1958 W Evergreen Ave; Ⓜ Blue Line to Damen), where he wrote several gritty, Chicago-based novels. Alas, it's a private residence, so you can only admire it from the sidewalk.

Logan Square & Humboldt Park

When artists and hipsters got priced out of Wicker Park, they moved west to the Latino communities of Logan Sq and Humboldt Park. For visitors, these are places for small, cool-cat eateries, brewpubs and music clubs. Take the CTA Blue Line to Logan Sq or California.

Near West Side & Pilsen

Just west of the Loop is, well, the **West Loop**. It's akin to New York City's Meatpacking District, with chic restaurants, clubs and galleries poking out between meat-processing plants. W Randolph St and W Fulton Market are the main veins. Nearby **Greektown** runs along S Halsted St near W Jackson Blvd. The areas are about 1.25 miles west of the Loop and easily reached by taxi.

Southwest lies the enclave of Pilsen, a festive mix of art galleries, Mexican bakeries, hipster cafes and murals on the buildings. The CTA Pink Line to 18th St drops you in the midst.

National Museum of Mexican Art MUSEUM
(☎312-738-1503; www.nationalmuseumofmexicanart.org; 1852 W 19th St; ⏰10am-5pm Tue-Sun; Ⓜ Pink Line to 18th St) FREE It's the largest Latino arts institution in the US. The museum's vivid permanent collection includes classical paintings, shining gold altars, skeleton-rich folk art and colorful beadwork.

Chinatown

Chicago's small but busy Chinatown is an easy 10-minute train ride from the Loop. Take the Red Line to the Cermak-Chinatown stop, which puts you between the neighborhood's two distinct parts: Chinatown Sq (an enormous bilevel strip mall) unfurls to the north along Archer Ave, while Old Chinatown (the traditional retail area) stretches along Wentworth Ave to the south. Either zone allows you to graze through bakeries, dine on steaming bowls of noodles and shop for exotic wares.

Hyde Park & South Side

The South Side is the generic term applied to Chicago's myriad neighborhoods, including some of its most impoverished, that lie south of 25th St. Hyde Park and abutting Kenwood are the South Side's stars, catapulted into the spotlight by local boy Barack Obama. To get here, take the Metra Electric Line trains from Millennium Station downtown, or bus 6 from State St in the Loop. Several bicycle tours also cruise by the highlights.

University of Chicago UNIVERSITY
(www.uchicago.edu; 5801 S Ellis Ave; 🚌6, Ⓜ Metra to 55th-56th-57th) The campus is worth a stroll, offering grand Gothic architecture and free art and antiquities museums. It's also where the nuclear age began: Enrico Fermi and his Manhattan Project cronies built a reactor and carried out the world's first controlled atomic reaction on December 2, 1942. The **Nuclear Energy sculpture** (S Ellis Ave btwn E 56th & E 57th Sts), by Henry Moore, marks the spot where it blew its stack.

Museum of Science & Industry MUSEUM
(MSI; ☎773-684-1414; www.msichicago.org; 5700 S Lake Shore Dr; adult/child $18/11; ⏰9:30am-5:30pm Jun-Aug, reduced hours Sep-May; 👪; 🚌6 or 10, Ⓜ Metra to 55th-56th-57th) Geek out at the largest science museum in the western hemisphere. Highlights include a WWII German U-boat nestled in an underground display ($9 extra to tour it) and the *Science Storms* exhibit with a mock tornado and tsunami. Kids will love the 'experiments' staff conduct in various galleries, like dropping things off the balcony and creating mini explosions.

Robie House ARCHITECTURE
(☎312-994-4000; www.flwright.org; 5757 S Woodlawn Ave; adult/child $17/14; ⏰10:30am-3pm Thu-Mon; 🚌6, Ⓜ Metra to 55th-56th-57th) Of the numerous buildings that Frank Lloyd Wright designed around Chicago, none is more famous or influential than Robie House. The resemblance of its horizontal lines to the flat landscape of the Midwestern prairie became known as the Prairie style. Inside are

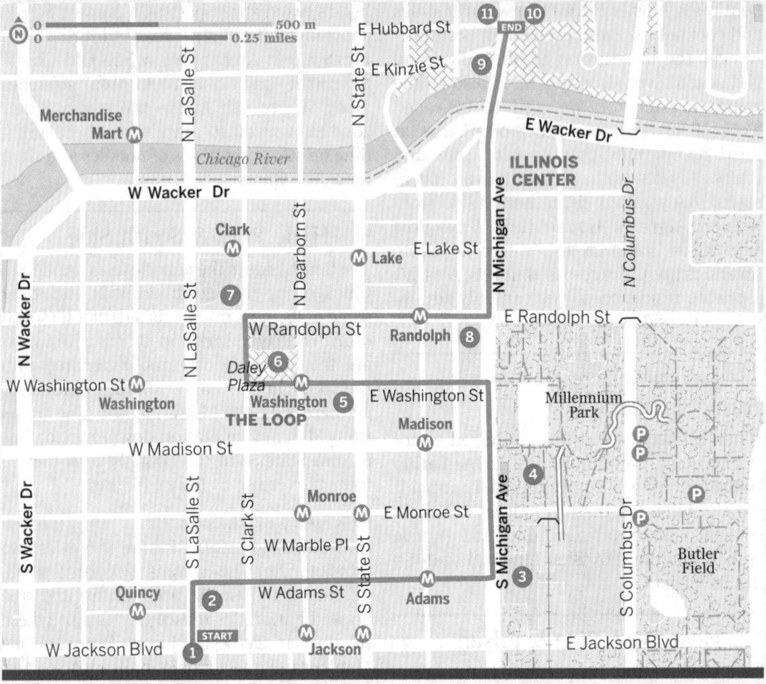

City Walk
The Loop

START CHICAGO BOARD OF TRADE
END BILLY GOAT TAVERN
LENGTH 3 MILES; ABOUT TWO HOURS

This tour swoops through the Loop, highlighting Chicago's revered art and architecture, with a visit to Al Capone's dentist thrown in for good measure.

Start at the 1 **Chicago Board of Trade** (p529), where guys in Technicolor coats swap corn (or something like that) inside a cool art-deco building. Step into the nearby 2 **Rookery** (p529) to see Frank Lloyd Wright's handiwork in the atrium.

Head east on Adams St to the 3 **Art Institute** (p527), one of the city's most-visited attractions. The lion statues out front make a classic photo. Walk a few blocks north to avant-garde 4 **Millennium Park** (p526).

Leave the park and head west on Washington St to 5 **Hotel Burnham** (p540). It's housed in the Reliance Building, which was the precursor to modern skyscraper design; Capone's dentist drilled teeth in what's now room 809. Just west, Picasso's abstract 6 **Untitled** sculpture is ensconced in Daley Plaza. Baboon, dog, woman? You decide. Then go north on Clark St to Jean Dubuffet's 7 **Monument with Standing Beast**, another head-scratching sculpture.

Walk east on Randolph St through the Theater District. Pop into the 8 **Chicago Cultural Center** (p527) to see what free art exhibits or concerts are on. Now go north on Michigan Ave and cross the Chicago River. Just north of the bridge you'll pass the 9 **Wrigley Building** (p533), shining bright and white, and the nearby Gothic, eye-popping 10 **Tribune Tower** (p533).

To finish your tour, visit 11 **Billy Goat Tavern** (p542), a vintage Chicago dive that spawned the Curse of the Cubs after the tavern's owner, Billy Sianis, tried to enter Wrigley Field with his pet goat. The smelly creature was denied entry, so Sianis called down a mighty curse on the baseball team in retaliation. They've pretty much stunk ever since.

LOCAL KNOWLEDGE

BLUES FANS' PILGRIMAGE

From 1957 to 1967, the humble building at 2120 S Michigan Ave was Chess Records, the seminal electric blues label. Muddy Waters, Howlin' Wolf and Bo Diddley cut tracks here, and paved the way for rock and roll with their sick licks and amped-up sound. Chuck Berry and the Rolling Stones arrived soon after. The studio is now called **Willie Dixon's Blues Heaven** (312-808-1286; www.bluesheaven.com; 2120 S Michigan Ave; tours $10; noon-4pm Mon-Fri, to 3pm Sat; M Green Line to Cermak-McCormick Pl), named for the bassist who wrote most of the Chess hits. Staff give hour-long tours of the premises. It's pretty ramshackle, with few original artifacts on display. Still, when Willie's grandson hauls out the bluesman's well-worn stand-up bass and lets you take a pluck, it's pretty cool. Free blues concerts rock the side garden on summer Thursdays at 6pm. The building is near Chinatown, and about a mile south of the Museum Campus.

174 stained-glass windows and doors, which you'll see on the hour-long tours (frequency varies by season).

Obama's House BUILDING
(5046 S Greenwood Ave) Hefty security means you can't get close to the president's abode, but you can stand across the street on Hyde Park Blvd and glimpse over the barricades at the redbrick Georgian-style manor.

Activities

Tucked away among Chicago's 580 parks are public golf courses, ice rinks, swimming pools and more. Activities are free or low cost, and the necessary equipment is usually available for rent. The **Chicago Park District** (www.chicagoparkdistrict.com) runs the show.

Cycling

Riding along the 18-mile lakefront path is a fantastic way to see the city. Bike rental companies listed here also offer two- to four-hour tours ($35 to $70, including bikes) that cover themes like the lakefront, beer and pizza munching, or gangster sites. Booking online saves money.

Bike Chicago CYCLING
(Map p530; 312-729-1000; www.bikechicago.com; 239 E Randolph St; per 1/4hr from $9/30; 6:30am-10pm Mon-Fri, from 8am Sat & Sun Jun-Aug, reduced hours Sep-May; M Brown, Orange, Green, Purple, Pink Line to Randolph) The company's main location – open year-round – is at Millennium Park. Other outposts include Navy Pier and the Riverwalk.

Bobby's Bike Hike CYCLING
(Map p530; 312-245-9300; www.bobbysbikehike.com; 540 N Lake Shore Dr; per 2/4hr from $20/25; 8:30am-8pm Mon-Fri, from 8am Sat & Sun Jun-Aug, 9am-7pm Sep-Nov & Mar-May; M Red Line to Grand) Bobby's earns raves from riders; enter through the covered driveway.

Water Sports

Visitors often don't realize Chicago is a beach town, thanks to mammoth Lake Michigan lapping its side. There are 26 official strands of sand patrolled by lifeguards in summer. Swimming is popular, though the water is pretty damn cold. Check www.cpdbeaches.com for water-quality advice before embarking.

North Avenue Beach BEACH
(www.cpdbeaches.com; 1600 N Lake Shore Dr; ; 151) Chicago's most popular and amenity-laden stretch of sand wafts a Southern California vibe. You can rent kayaks, jet skis, stand-up paddleboards (SUPs) and lounge chairs, as well as eat and drink at the party-orientated beach house. It's 2 miles north of the Loop.

Oak Street Beach BEACH
(www.cpdbeaches.com; 1000 N Lake Shore Dr; M Red Line to Chicago) Packs in bodies beautiful at the edge of downtown.

12th Street Beach BEACH
(Map p530; www.cpdbeaches.com; 1200 S Linn White Dr; 146, 130) A path runs from the Adler Planetarium to this secluded crescent of sand.

Tours

Many companies offer discounts if you book online. Outdoor-oriented tours operate from April to November only, unless otherwise specified.

Chicago Architecture Foundation BOAT TOUR
(CAF; Map p530; 312-922-3432; www.architecture.org; 224 S Michigan Ave; tours $15-50; M Brown, Orange, Green, Purple, Pink Line to Adams) The gold-standard boat tours ($40) sail

from Michigan Ave's river dock. The popular Evolution of the Skyscraper walking tours ($20) leave from the downtown Michigan Ave address. Weekday lunchtime tours ($15) explore individual landmark buildings. Buy tickets online or at CAF.

Chicago by Foot WALKING TOUR
(www.freetoursbyfoot.com/chicago) Guides for this pay-what-you-want walking tour offer engaging stories and historical details on different jaunts covering the Loop, Gold Coast, Lincoln Park's gangster sites and many more. Most takers pay around $10 per person.

Chicago Detours WALKING, BUS TOURS
(312-350-1131; www.chicagodetours.com; tours from $26) It offers engrossing, detail-rich tours (mostly walking, but also some by bus) that take in Chicago's architecture, history and culture. The Historic Pub Crawl Tour is a popular one.

InstaGreeter WALKING TOUR
(www.chicagogreeter.com/instagreeter; 77 E Randolph St; 10am-3pm Fri & Sat, 11am-2pm Sun; M Brown, Orange, Green, Purple, Pink Line to Randolph) FREE It provides one-hour Loop tours on the spot from the Chicago Cultural Center visitor center. In summer, free tours of Millennium Park also depart from here daily at 11:30am and 1pm.

Chicago History Museum TOUR
(312-642-4600; www.chicagohistory.org; tours $20-55) The museum counts El (elevated/subway system) jaunts, cycling routes and cemetery walks among its excellent tour arsenal. Departure points and times vary.

Chicago Food Planet Tours WALKING TOUR
(312-818-2170; www.chicagofoodplanet.com; 3hr tours $45-55) Go on a guided walkabout in Wicker Park, the Gold Coast or Chinatown, where you'll graze through five or more neighborhood eateries. Departure points and times vary.

Pilsen Mural Tours WALKING TOUR
(773-342-4191; per group 1½hr tour $125) Local artists lead the highly recommended tours, during which you can learn more about this traditional art form; call to arrange an excursion.

Festivals & Events

Chicago has a full events calendar all year, but the biggies take place in the summer. The following events are held downtown on a weekend, unless noted otherwise.

St Patrick's Day Parade CULTURAL
(www.chicagostpatsparade.com; mid-Mar) The local plumbers union dyes the Chicago River shamrock green; a big parade follows.

Blues Festival MUSIC
(www.chicagobluesfestival.us; mid-Jun) The biggest free blues fest in the world, with three days of the music that made Chicago famous.

Taste of Chicago FOOD
(www.tasteofchicago.us; mid-Jul) The free five-day bash in Grant Park includes bands and lots of food on a stick.

Pitchfork Music Festival MUSIC
(www.pitchforkmusicfestival.com; day pass $65; mid-Jul) Indie bands strum for three days in Union Park.

Lollapalooza MUSIC
(www.lollapalooza.com; day pass $110; early Aug) Around 130 bands spill off eight stages at Grant Park's three-day mega-gig.

Jazz Festival MUSIC
(www.chicagojazzfestival.us; early Sep) Top names on the national jazz scene play over Labor Day weekend.

Sleeping

Chicago lodging doesn't come cheap. In summer and when the frequent big conventions trample through town, your options become much slimmer, so plan ahead to avoid unpleasant surprises. The prices we've listed are for the summer peak season. Taxes add 16.4%.

Hotels in the Loop are convenient to the museums, festival grounds and business district, but the area is pretty dead come nightfall. Accommodations in the Near North and Gold Coast are most popular, given their proximity to eating, shopping and entertainment venues. Rooms in Lincoln Park, Lake View and Wicker Park are often cheaper than rooms downtown, plus they're near swingin' nightlife. In addition, Airbnb does big business in Chicago and offers bountiful, good-value listings.

Wi-fi is free unless noted otherwise. You pay dearly for parking in Chicago: $55 to $65 per night downtown, and around $25 in outlying neighborhoods.

CHICAGO FOR CHILDREN

Chicago is a kid's kind of town. *Chicago Parent* (www.chicagoparent.com) is a dandy resource. Top choices for toddlin' times include the following:

Chicago Children's Museum (Map p530; ☑312-527-1000; www.chicagochildrensmuseum. org; 700 E Grand Ave; admission $14; ☺10am-5pm Mon-Wed, to 8pm Thu, to 6pm Fri, to 7pm Sat & Sun; 👶; Ⓜ Red Line to Grand, then trolley) Climb, dig and splash in this educational playland on Navy Pier; follow with an expedition down the carnival-like wharf itself, including spins on the Ferris wheel and carousel.

Chicago Children's Theatre (☑773-227-0180; www.chicagochildrenstheatre.org) See a show by one of the best kids' theater troupes in the country. Performances take place at venues around town.

American Girl Place (www.americangirl.com; 835 N Michigan Ave; ☺10am-8pm Mon-Thu, 9am-9pm Fri & Sat, to 6pm Sun; 👶; Ⓜ Red Line to Chicago) Young ladies sip tea and get new hair-dos with their dolls at this multistory, girl-power palace.

Chic-A-Go-Go (www.facebook.com/chicagogo) Groove at a taping of this cable-access TV show that's like a kiddie version of *Soul Train*. Check the website for dates and locations.

Other kid-friendly offerings:

Maggie Daley Park (p527)

North Avenue Beach (p537)

Field Museum of Natural History (p529)

Shedd Aquarium (p529)

Lincoln Park Zoo (p534)

Museum of Science & Industry (p535)

🛏 The Loop & Near North

Freehand Chicago   HOSTEL, HOTEL $
(Map p530; ☑312-940-3699; www.thefreehand. com/chicago; 19 E Ohio St; dm $35-70, r $220-310; ❄️📶; Ⓜ Red Line to Grand) This is an outpost of Miami's super-hip hostel-hotel hybrid. Rooms are small but stylish, designed in warm woods, bright tiles and Central American-tinged fabrics. Travelers are split evenly between the private rooms and eight-person, bunk-bed dorms (way spiffier than most hostels, with privacy curtains around each bed). Everyone mingles in the shaggy, totem-pole-filled common area and in the on-site Broken Shaker bar.

HI-Chicago   HOSTEL $
(Map p530; ☑312-360-0300; www.hichicago. org; 24 E Congress Pkwy; dm $35-55; 🅿️❄️@📶; Ⓜ Brown, Orange, Purple, Pink Line to Library) Chicago's most stalwart hostel is immaculate, conveniently placed in the Loop, and offers bonuses like a staffed information desk, free volunteer-led tours, free breakfast and discount passes to museums and shows. The simple dorm rooms have eight or 10 beds, and most have attached baths.

★**Acme Hotel**   BOUTIQUE HOTEL $$
(Map p530; ☑312-894-0800; www.acmehotelcompany.com; 15 E Ohio St; r $179-289; 🅿️❄️@📶; Ⓜ Red Line to Grand) Urban bohemians are loving the Acme for its indie-cool style at (usually) affordable rates. The 130 rooms mix industrial fixtures with retro lamps, mid-century furniture and funky modern art. They're wired up with free wi-fi, good speakers, smart TVs and easy connections to stream your own music and movies. Graffiti, neon and lava lights decorate the common areas.

**Hampton Inn Chicago
Downtown/N Loop**   HOTEL $$
(Map p530; ☑312-419-9014; www.hamptonchicago.com; 68 E Wacker Pl; r $200-280; 🅿️❄️📶; Ⓜ Brown, Orange, Green, Purple, Pink Line to State/ Lake) Opened in spring 2015, this unique property makes you feel like a road-tripper of yore. Set in the 1928 art-deco Chicago Motor Club Building, the lobby sports a vintage Ford and cool USA mural map from the era. The

dark-wood-paneled rooms strike the right balance of retro vibe and modern amenities. Free wi-fi and hot breakfast are included.

Best Western River North HOTEL $$
(Map p530; ☎312-467-0800; www.rivernorthhotel.com; 125 W Ohio St; r $179-269; P ❄ @ ≋; M Red Line to Grand) Well-maintained rooms with maple veneer beds and desks, together with low-cost parking for the area (per night $25), an indoor pool and a sundeck overlooking the city make the Best Western good Near North value.

★ **Hotel Burnham** BOUTIQUE HOTEL $$$
(Map p530; ☎312-782-1111; www.burnhamhotel.com; 1 W Washington St; r $239-389; P ❄ @; M Blue Line to Washington) The proprietors brag that the Burnham has the highest guest return rates in Chicago; it's easy to see why. Housed in the landmark 1890s Reliance Building (precedent for the modern skyscraper), its super-slick decor woos architecture buffs. Big windows and pops of bright, whimsical art liven up the warm wood decor. A free wine happy hour takes place each evening.

Virgin Hotel HOTEL $$$
(Map p530; ☎312-940-4400; www.virginhotels.com; 203 N Wabash Ave; r $230-300; P ❄ @; M Brown, Orange, Green, Purple, Pink Line to State/Lake) Billionaire Richard Branson transformed the 27-story, art-deco Dearborn Bank Building into the first outpost of his cheeky new hotel chain. The airy, suite-like rooms have speedy free wi-fi and low-cost minibar items, plus a bed that can double as a work desk. An app controls the thermostat, TV and other electronics. Guests receive earplugs, handy for dulling noise from nearby El trains.

Lake View, Wicker Park & Bucktown

★ **Urban Holiday Lofts** HOSTEL $
(☎312-532-6949; www.urbanholidaylofts.com; 2014 W Wabansia Ave; dm $30-55, r from $80; ❄ @; M Blue Line to Damen) An international crowd fills the mix of dorms (with four to eight beds) and private rooms in this building of converted loft condos. Exposed-brick walls, hardwood floors and bunks with plump bedding are common to all 25 rooms. It's close to the El train station and in the

GAY & LESBIAN CHICAGO

Chicago has a flourishing gay and lesbian scene. The *Windy City Times* (www.windycitymediagroup.com) provides the local lowdown.

The biggest concentration of bars and clubs is in Wrigleyville on N Halsted St between Belmont Ave and Grace St, an area known as Boystown. Andersonville is the other main area for GLBT nightlife; it's a more relaxed, less party-oriented scene. Top picks:

Big Chicks (www.bigchicks.com; 5024 N Sheridan Rd; ⏲4pm-2am Mon-Fri, from 9am Sat, from 10am Sun; ; M Red Line to Argyle) Despite the name, both men and women frequent Big Chicks, with its weekend DJs, art displays and next-door organic restaurant **Tweet** (www.tweet.biz; 5020 N Sheridan Rd; mains $8-14; ⏲8:30am-3pm;), where weekend brunch packs 'em in. Cash only.

Sidetrack (www.sidetrackchicago.com; 3349 N Halsted St; ⏲3pm-2am Mon-Fri, from 1pm Sat & Sun; M Red, Brown, Purple Line to Belmont) Massive Sidetrack thumps dance music and show tunes and is prime for people-watching.

Hamburger Mary's (www.hamburgermarys.com/chicago; 5400 N Clark St; ⏲11:30am-midnight Sun-Wed, to 1:30am Thu & Fri, to 2:30am Sat; M Red Line to Berwyn) Cabaret, karaoke, burgers and a booze-soaked outdoor patio make for good times at this hot spot.

Chance's Dances (www.chancesdances.org) Organizes queer dance parties at clubs around town.

Pride Parade (http://chicagopride.gopride.com; ⏲late Jun) Pride winds through Boystown and attracts around 800,000 revelers.

Northalsted Market Days (www.northalsted.com; ⏲mid-Aug) Another raucous event on the Boystown calendar, featuring a street fair and wild costumes.

thick of Wicker Park's nightlife. Breakfast is included.

Longman & Eagle
INN **$$**

([✉]773-276-7110; www.longmanandeagle.com; 2657 N Kedzie Ave; r $95-200; [✿][☎]; [Ⓜ]Blue Line to Logan Sq) Check in at the Michelin-starred gastropub downstairs, then head to your wood-floored, vintage-stylish accommodations on the floor above. The six rooms aren't particularly soundproofed, but after using your whiskey tokens in the bar, you probably won't care. From the El stop, walk a block north on Kedzie Ave.

Wicker Park Inn
B&B **$$**

([✉]773-486-2743; www.wickerparkinn.com; 1329 N Wicker Park Ave; r $159-225; [✿][☎]; [Ⓜ]Blue Line to Damen) This brick row house is steps away from rockin' restaurants and nightlife. The sunny rooms aren't huge, but have hardwood floors, pastel colors and small desk spaces. Across the street, two apartments with kitchens provide a self-contained experience. The inn is about a half-mile southeast of the El stop.

Willows Hotel
BOUTIQUE HOTEL **$$**

([✉]773-528-8400; www.willowshotelchicago.com; 555 W Surf St; r $159-265; [Ⓟ][✿][☎]; [☐]22) Small and stylish, the Willows wins an architectural gold star. The chic little lobby provides a swell refuge of overstuffed chairs by the fireplace, while the 55 rooms, done up in shades of peach and soft green, evoke a 19th-century French countryside feel. Continental breakfast is included. It's a block north of the commercial hub where Broadway, Clark and Diversey Sts intersect.

Days Inn Lincoln Park North
HOTEL **$$**

([✉]773-525-7010; www.daysinnchicago.net; 644 W Diversey Pkwy; r $130-195; [Ⓟ][✿][@][☎]; [☐]22) This well-maintained chain hotel in Lincoln Park is a favorite of both families and touring indie bands, providing good service and perks like free breakfast and health club access. It's an easy amble to the lakefront's parks and beaches, and a 15-minute bus ride to downtown. It's right at the hustle-bustle intersection of Broadway, Clark and Diversey streets.

[✗] Eating

During the past decade, Chicago has become a gastronome's paradise. The beauty here is that even the buzziest restaurants are accessible: they're visionary yet traditional, pubby at the core and decently priced. You can also fork into a superb range of ethnic eats, especially if you break out of downtown and head for neighborhoods such as Pilsen or Uptown.

Need help deciding where to eat? **LTH Forum** (www.lthforum.com) is a great local resource.

[✗] The Loop

Most Loop eateries are geared to lunch crowds of office workers.

Cafecito
CUBAN **$**

(Map p530; [✆]312-922-2233; www.cafecitochicago.com; 26 E Congress Pkwy; mains $6-10; [◷]7am-9pm Mon-Fri, 10am-6pm Sat & Sun; [☎]; [Ⓜ]Brown, Orange, Purple, Pink Line to Library) Attached to the HI-Chicago hostel and perfect for the hungry, thrifty traveler, Cafecito serves killer Cuban sandwiches layered with citrus-garlic-marinated roast pork and ham. Strong coffee and hearty egg sandwiches make a fine breakfast.

Native Foods Cafe
VEGAN **$**

(Map p530; [✆]312-332-6332; www.nativefoods.com; 218 S Clark St; mains $9-11; [◷]10:30am-9pm Mon-Sat, 11am-7pm Sun; [✎]; [Ⓜ]Brown, Orange, Purple, Pink Line to Quincy) [✐] If you're looking for vegan fast-casual fare downtown, Native Foods is your spot. The meatball sandwich rocks the seitan, while the scorpion burger fires up hot-spiced tempeh. Local beers and organic wines accompany the wide-ranging menu.

Gage
MODERN AMERICAN **$$$**

(Map p530; [✆]312-372-4243; www.thegagechicago.com; 24 S Michigan Ave; mains $17-36; [◷]11am-10pm Mon, to 11pm Tue-Thu, to midnight Fri & Sat, 10am-10pm Sun; [Ⓜ]Brown, Orange, Green, Purple, Pink Line to Madison) This gastropub dishes up fanciful grub, from Gouda-topped venison burgers to mussels vindaloo to Guinness-battered fish and chips. The booze rocks, too, including a solid whiskey list and small-batch beers that pair with the food.

[✗] Near North

This is where you'll find Chicago's mother lode of restaurants.

Xoco
MEXICAN **$**

(Map p530; www.rickbayless.com; 449 N Clark St; mains $10-14; [◷]8am-9pm Tue-Thu, to 10pm Fri & Sat; [Ⓜ]Red Line to Grand) [✐] Crunch into warm *churros* (spiraled dough fritters) for breakfast,

CHICAGO'S HOLY TRINITY OF SPECIALTIES

Chicago cooks up three beloved specialties. Foremost is deep-dish pizza, a hulking mass of crust that rises two or three inches above the plate and cradles a molten pile of toppings. One gooey piece is practically a meal. Top spots:

Pizzeria Uno (Map p530; www.unos.com; 29 E Ohio St; small pizzas from $13; 11am-1am Mon-Fri, to 2am Sat, to 11pm Sun; M Red Line to Grand) The deep-dish concept supposedly originated here in 1943.

Lou Malnati's (Map p530; www.loumalnatis.com; 439 N Wells St; small pizzas from $12; 11am-11pm Sun-Thu, to midnight Fri & Sat; M Brown, Purple Line to Merchandise Mart) It also lays claim to inventing deep dish; famous for its butter crust.

Giordano's (Map p530; 312-951-0747; www.giordanos.com; 730 N Rush St; small pizzas from $15.50; 11am-11pm Sun-Thu, to midnight Fri & Sat; M Red Line to Chicago) It makes 'stuffed' pizza, a bigger, doughier version of deep dish.

Gino's East (Map p530; 312-266-3337; www.ginoseast.com; 162 E Superior St; small pizzas from $15; 11am-9:30pm; M Red Line to Chicago) Popular spot where you write on the walls while waiting for your pie.

No less iconic is the Chicago hot dog – a wiener that's been 'dragged through the garden' (ie topped with onions, tomatoes, shredded lettuce, bell peppers, pepperoncini and sweet relish, or variations thereof, but *never* ketchup), and then cushioned on a poppy-seed bun. Try it at **Portillo's** (Map p530; 312-587-8910; www.portillos.com; 100 W Ontario St; mains $4-7; 10am-11pm Sun-Thu, to midnight Fri & Sat; M Red Line to Grand).

The city is also revered for its spicy, drippy, only-in-Chicago Italian beef sandwiches. **Mr Beef** (Map p530; 312-337-8500; 666 N Orleans St; sandwiches $6-9; 9am-5pm Mon-Fri, 10am-3pm Sat, plus 10:30pm-4am Fri & Sat; M Brown, Purple Line to Chicago) serves the gold standard.

meaty *tortas* (sandwiches) for lunch and rich *caldos* (soups) for dinner at celeb chef Rick Bayless' Mexican street-food joint. His upscale restaurants Frontera Grill and Topolobampo are next door, but you'll need reservations or a whole lot of patience to get in.

★Billy Goat Tavern BURGERS $
(Map p530; 312-222-1525; www.billygoattavern.com; lower level, 430 N Michigan Ave; burgers $4-6; 6am-2am Mon-Fri, 10am-2am Sat & Sun; M Red Line to Grand) *Tribune* and *Sun-Times* reporters have guzzled in the subterranean Billy Goat for decades. Order a 'cheezborger' and Schlitz, then look around at the newspapered walls to get the scoop on infamous local stories, such as the Cubs Curse.

Purple Pig MEDITERRANEAN $$
(Map p530; 312-464-1744; www.thepurplepigchicago.com; 500 N Michigan Ave; small plates $9-19; 11:30am-midnight Sun-Thu, to 1am Fri & Sat; ; M Red Line to Grand) The Pig's Magnificent Mile location, wide-ranging meat and veggie menu, long list of affordable vinos and late-night serving hours make it a crowd pleaser. Milk-braised pork shoulder is the hamtastic specialty. No reservations.

Lincoln Park & Old Town

Halsted, Lincoln and Clark Sts are the main veins teeming with restaurants and bars.

Sultan's Market MIDDLE EASTERN $
(312-638-9151; www.chicagofalafel.com; 2521 N Clark St; mains $4-7; 10am-10pm Mon-Thu, to midnight Fri & Sat, to 9pm Sun; M Brown, Purple, Red Line to Fullerton) Neighborhood folks dig the falafel sandwiches, spinach pies and other quality Middle Eastern fare at family-run Sultan's Market. The small, homey space doesn't have many tables, but Lincoln Park is nearby for picnicking.

★Alinea MODERN AMERICAN $$$
(312-867-0110; www.alinearestaurant.com; 1723 N Halsted St; multicourse menu $210-265; 5-9:30pm Wed-Sun; M Red Line to North/Clybourn) Widely regarded as North America's best restaurant, Alinea brings on 20 courses of mind-bending molecular gastronomy. Dishes may emanate from a centrifuge or be pressed into a capsule, à la duck served

with a 'pillow of lavender air.' There are no reservations. Instead Alinea sells tickets two to three months in advance via its website. Check the Twitter feed (@Alinea) for last-minute seats.

Lake View & Wrigleyville

Clark, Halsted, Belmont and Southport are fertile grazing streets.

★Crisp ASIAN $

(www.crisponline.com; 2940 N Broadway; mains $9-13; 11:30am-9pm; Brown, Purple Line to Wellington) Music pours from the stereo, and cheap, delicious Korean fusions arrive from the kitchen at this cheerful cafe. The 'Bad Boy Buddha' bowl, a variation on *bi bim bop* (mixed vegetables with rice), is one of the best healthy lunches in town.

Mia Francesca ITALIAN $$

(773-281-3310; www.miafrancesca.com; 3311 N Clark St; mains $16-27; 5-10pm Mon-Thu, to 11pm Fri, 11:30am-11pm Sat, 10am-9pm Sun; Red, Brown, Purple Line to Belmont) Local chain Mia's buzzes with regulars who come for the trattoria's Italian standards, such as seafood linguine, spinach ravioli and mushroom-sauced veal medallions, all prepared with simple flair.

Andersonville & Uptown

For 'Little Saigon' take the CTA Red Line to Argyle. For the European cafes in Andersonville, go one stop further to Berwyn.

Nha Hang Viet Nam VIETNAMESE $

(773-878-8895; 1032 W Argyle St; mains $7-13; 7am-10pm Sun-Mon; Red Line to Argyle) Little Nha Hang may not look like much from the outside, but it offers a huge menu of authentic, well-made dishes from the homeland. It's terrific for slurping pho and claypot catfish.

★Hopleaf EUROPEAN $$

(773-334-9851; www.hopleaf.com; 5148 N Clark St; mains $12-27; noon-11pm Mon-Thu, to midnight Fri & Sat, to 10pm Sun; Red Line to Berwyn) A cozy, European-style tavern, Hopleaf draws crowds for its Montréal-style smoked brisket, cashew-butter-and-fig-jam sandwich and the house specialty – *frites* and ale-soaked mussels. It also pours 200 types of brew, heavy on the Belgian ales. No reservations.

Wicker Park, Bucktown & Ukrainian Village

Trendy restaurants open almost every day in these 'hoods.

Dove's Luncheonette TEX-MEX $

(773-645-4060; www.doveschicago.com; 1545 N Damen Ave; mains $12-15; 9am-10pm Sun-Thu, to 11pm Fri & Sat; Blue Line to Damen) Grab a seat at the retro diner counter for plates of pork shoulder *pozole* and shrimp-stuffed sweet-corn tamales. Dessert? It's pie, of course, maybe lemon cream or peach jalapeño, depending on what they've baked that day. Soul music spins on the record player, tequila flows from the 70 bottles rattling behind the bar, and suddenly all is right in the world.

★Ruxbin MODERN AMERICAN $$$

(312-624-8509; www.ruxbinchicago.com; 851 N Ashland Ave; mains $27-32; 6-10pm Tue-Fri, 5:30-10pm Sat, to 9pm Sun; Blue Line to Division) The passion of the brother-sister team who run Ruxbin is evident in everything from the warm decor made of found items to the artfully prepared flavors in dishes like the pork-belly salad with grapefruit, cornbread and blue cheese. It's a wee place of just 32 seats, and BYO.

Logan Square & Humboldt Park

Logan Sq has become a mecca for inventive, no-pretense chefs. Eats and drinks ring the intersection of Milwaukee, Logan and Kedzie Blvds.

Kuma's Corner BURGERS $

(773-604-8769; www.kumascorner.com; 2900 W Belmont Ave; mains $12-14; 11:30am-midnight Mon-Wed, to 1am Thu, to 2am Fri & Sat, noon-midnight Sun; 77) Ridiculously busy and head-bangingly loud, Kuma's attracts the tattooed set for its monster 10oz burgers, each named for a heavy-metal band and hefted onto a pretzel-roll bun. There's a mac 'n' cheese menu for vegetarians, and beer and bourbon for all. Expect to queue.

★Longman & Eagle AMERICAN $$

(773-276-7110; www.longmanandeagle.com; 2657 N Kedzie Ave; mains $15-30; 9am-2am Sun-Fri, to 3am Sat; Blue Line to Logan Sq) Hard to say whether this shabby-chic tavern is best for eating or drinking. Let's say eating, since it earned a Michelin star for its beautifully cooked comfort foods such as vanilla brioche French toast for breakfast, wild-boar sloppy joes for lunch and fried chicken and duck fat biscuits for dinner. There's a whole menu of juicy small plates and whiskeys, too. No reservations.

Near West Side & Pilsen

The West Loop booms with hot-chef restaurants. Stroll along Randolph and Fulton Market Sts and take your pick. Greektown extends along S Halsted St (take the Blue Line to UIC-Halsted). The Mexican Pilsen enclave has loads of eateries around W 18th St.

★ Lou Mitchell's BREAKFAST $

(Map p530; ☎312-939-3111; www.loumitchellsrestaurant.com; 565 W Jackson Blvd; mains $7-11; ⏲5:30am-3pm Mon-Fri, 7am-3pm Sat & Sun; 🚻; Ⓜ Blue Line to Clinton) Lou's is a relic of Route 66, where old-school waitresses deliver double-yoked eggs and thick-cut French toast just west of the Loop by Union Station. There's usually a queue, but free doughnut holes and Milk Duds help ease the wait.

Don Pedro Carnitas MEXICAN $

(1113 W 18th St; tacos $1.50-2; ⏲6am-6pm Mon-Fri, 5am-5pm Sat, to 3pm Sun; Ⓜ Pink Line to 18th) At this no-frills Pilsen meat hive, a man with a machete salutes you at the front counter. He awaits your command to hack off pork pieces, and then wraps the thick chunks with onion and cilantro in a fresh tortilla. Cash only.

★ Little Goat DINER $$

(Map p530; ☎312-888-3455; www.littlegoatchicago.com; 820 W Randolph St; mains $10-19; ⏲7am-10pm Sun-Thu, to midnight Fri & Sat; 📶 ✎; Ⓜ Green, Pink Line to Morgan) *Top Chef* winner Stephanie Izard opened this diner for the foodie masses across the street from her ever-booked main restaurant, Girl and the Goat. Sit on a vintage twirly stool and order off the all-day breakfast menu. Better yet, try lunchtime favorites such as the goat sloppy joe with mashed potato tempura or the pork belly on scallion pancakes.

Dusek's MODERN AMERICAN $$$

(☎312-526-3851; www.dusekschicago.com; 1227 W 18th St; mains $22-30; ⏲11am-1am Mon-Fri, from 9am Sat & Sun; Ⓜ Pink Line to 18th St) Pilsen's hipsters gather under the pressed tin ceiling of this gastropub to fork into an ever-changing menu of beer-inspired dishes, say beer-battered soft-shell crab or dark-lager-roasted duck. The eatery shares its historic building (modeled on Prague's opera house) with an indie band concert hall and basement cocktail bar.

DON'T MISS

MIDWESTERN BEERS

The Midwest is ready to pour you a cold one thanks to its German heritage. Yes, Budweiser and Miller are based here, but that's not what we're talking about. Far more exciting is the region's cache of craft brewers. Keep an eye on the taps for these slurpable suds-makers, available throughout the area:

- Bell's (Kalamazoo, MI)
- Capital (Middleton, WI)
- Founder's (Grand Rapids, MI)
- Great Lakes (Cleveland, OH)
- Lagunitas (Chicago, IL)
- Dark Horse (Marshall, MI)
- Summit (St Paul, MN)
- Surly (Minneapolis, MN)
- Three Floyds (Munster, IN)
- Two Brothers (Warrenville, IL)

Drinking & Nightlife

During the long winters, Chicagoans count on bars for warmth. The usual closing time is 2am, but some places stay open until 4am. In summer many bars boast beer gardens.

Clubs in the Near North and West Loop tend to be cavernous and luxurious (with dress codes). Clubs in Wicker Park are usually more casual.

The Loop & Near North

★ Signature Lounge LOUNGE

(Map p530; www.signatureroom.com; 875 N Michigan Ave; ⏲11am-12:30am Sun-Thu, to 1:30am Fri & Sat; Ⓜ Red Line to Chicago) Grab the elevator up to the 96th floor of the John Hancock Center (Chicago's fourth-tallest skyscraper) and order a beverage while looking out over the city. Ladies: don't miss the bathroom view.

Berghoff BAR

(Map p530; www.theberghoff.com; 17 W Adams St; ⏲11am-9pm Mon-Sat; Ⓜ Blue, Red Line to Jackson) The Berghoff was the first spot in town to serve a legal drink after Prohibition (ask to see the liquor license stamped '#1'). Little has changed around the antique wood bar since then. Belly up for frosty mugs of the house-brand beer and order sauerbraten from the adjoining German restaurant.

★**Clark Street Ale House** BAR
(Map p530; www.clarkstreetalehouse.com; 742 N Clark St; ⌚4pm-4am Mon-Fri, from 11am Sat & Sun; Ⓜ Red Line to Chicago) Do as the retro sign advises and 'Stop & Drink Liquor.' Midwestern microbrews are the main draw; order a three-beer sampler for $7. When the weather warms, a sweet beer garden beckons out back.

Old Town & Wrigleyville

★**Old Town Ale House** BAR
(www.theoldtownalehouse.com; 219 W North Ave; ⌚3pm-4am Mon-Fri, from noon Sat & Sun; Ⓜ Brown, Purple Line to Sedgwick) This venerated dive bar lets you mingle with beautiful people and grizzled regulars, seated pint by pint under the nude-politician paintings. It's across the street from Second City. Cash only.

★**Gingerman Tavern** BAR
(3740 N Clark St; ⌚3pm-2am Mon-Fri, from noon Sat & Sun; Ⓜ Red Line to Addison) The pool tables, good beer selection and pierced-and-tattooed patrons make Gingerman wonderfully different from the surrounding Wrigleyville sports bars.

Smart Bar CLUB
(www.smartbarchicago.com; 3730 N Clark St; ⌚10pm-4am Wed-Sun; Ⓜ Red Line to Addison) A long-standing, unpretentious favorite for dancing, attached to the Metro rock club.

Wicker Park, Bucktown & Ukrainian Village

Map Room BAR
(www.maproom.com; 1949 N Hoyne Ave; ⌚6:30am-2am Mon-Fri, from 7:30am Sat, from 11am Sun; 📶; Ⓜ Blue Line to Western) At this map-and-globe-filled 'traveler tavern' artsy types sip coffee by day and suds from the 200-strong beer list by night. Cash only.

Danny's BAR
(1951 W Dickens Ave; ⌚7pm-2am; Ⓜ Blue Line to Damen) Danny's comfortably dim and dog-eared ambience is perfect for conversations over a pint early on, then DJs arrive to stoke the dance party as the evening progresses. Cash only.

LOCAL KNOWLEDGE

HOW TO FIND A REAL CHICAGO BAR

Unfortunately, we can't list every watering hole in town, but we can give you the tools to go out and discover classic, character-filled bars on your own. Look for the following:

- an 'Old Style' beer sign swinging out front
- a well-worn dart board and/or pool table inside
- patrons wearing ballcaps with the logo of the Cubs, White Sox, Blackhawks or Bears
- bottles of brew served in buckets of ice
- sports on TV

Matchbox BAR
(Map p530; 770 N Milwaukee Ave; ⌚4pm-2am Mon-Fri, from 3pm Sat & Sun; Ⓜ Blue Line to Chicago) Lawyers, artists and bums all squeeze in for retro cocktails. It's small as – you got it – a matchbox, with about 10 barstools; everyone else stands against the back wall. Matchbox sits by its lonesome northwest of downtown.

Logan Square

Revolution Brewing BREWERY
(☎773-227-2739; www.revbrew.com; 2323 N Milwaukee Ave; ⌚11am-2am Mon-Fri, from 10am Sat & Sun; Ⓜ Blue Line to California) Raise your fist to Revolution, a big, industrial-chic brewpub that fills glasses with heady beers like the Eugene porter and hopped-up Anti-Hero IPA. The brewmaster here led the way for Chicago's huge craft beer scene, and his suds are top-notch.

West Loop

RM Champagne Salon BAR
(Map p530; ☎312-243-1199; www.rmchampagnesalon.com; 116 N Green St; ⌚5-11pm Mon-Wed, to 2am Thu & Fri, to 3am Sat, to 11pm Sun; Ⓜ Green, Pink Line to Morgan) This West Loop spot is a twinkling-light charmer for bubbles. Score a table in the cobblestoned courtyard and you'll feel transported to Paris.

DISCOUNT TICKETS

For same-week theater seats at half price, try **Hot Tix** (www.hottix.org). You can buy them online or in person at the three downtown booths. The selection is best early in the week.

☆ Entertainment

Check the *Chicago Reader* (www.chicagoreader.com) for listings.

Blues & Jazz

Blues and jazz have deep roots in Chicago.

★Green Mill JAZZ
(www.greenmilljazz.com; 4802 N Broadway; cover charge $5-15; ⏲noon-4am Mon-Sat, from 11am Sun; M Red Line to Lawrence) The timeless Green Mill earned its notoriety as Al Capone's favorite speakeasy. Sit in one of the leather booths and feel his ghost urging you on to another martini. Local and national jazz artists perform nightly; the venue also hosts the nationally acclaimed poetry slam on Sundays.

★Buddy Guy's Legends BLUES
(Map p530; www.buddyguy.com; 700 S Wabash Ave; ⏲5pm-2am Mon & Tue, 11am-2am Wed-Fri, noon-3am Sat, noon-2am Sun; M Red Line to Harrison) Top local and national acts wail on the stage of local icon Buddy Guy. Tickets cost $20 Friday and Saturday, $10 on other evenings. The man himself usually plugs in his axe for a series of shows in January. Free, all-ages acoustic performances take place from noon to 2pm Wednesday through Sunday.

Kingston Mines BLUES
(www.kingstonmines.com; 2548 N Halsted St; cover charge $12-15; ⏲8pm-4am Mon-Thu, from 7pm Fri & Sat, from 6pm Sun; M Brown, Purple, Red Line to Fullerton) Two stages, seven nights a week, ensure somebody's always on. It's noisy, hot, sweaty, crowded and conveniently located in Lincoln Park.

BLUES BLUES
(www.chicagobluesbar.com; 2519 N Halsted St; cover $7-10; ⏲8pm-2am Wed-Sun; M Brown, Purple, Red Line to Fullerton) This veteran club draws a slightly older crowd that soaks up every crackling, electrified moment.

Rock & World Music

★Hideout LIVE MUSIC
(www.hideoutchicago.com; 1354 W Wabansia Ave; ⏲7pm-2am Tue, 4pm-2am Wed-Fri, 7pm-3am Sat, varies Sun & Mon; 🚌72) Hidden behind a factory at Bucktown's edge, this two-room lodge of indie rock and alt-country is well worth seeking out. The owners have nursed an outsider, underground vibe, and the place feels like the downstairs of your grandma's rumpus room. Music and other events (bingo, literary readings etc) take place nightly.

SummerDance WORLD MUSIC
(Map p530; www.chicagosummerdance.org; 601 S Michigan Ave; ⏲6-9:30pm Fri & Sat, 4-7pm Sun late Jun–mid-Sep; M Red Line to Harrison) FREE Boogie at the Spirit of Music Garden in Grant Park with a multiethnic mash-up of locals. Bands play rumba, samba and other world beats preceded by fun dance lessons – all free.

Empty Bottle LIVE MUSIC
(www.emptybottle.com; 1035 N Western Ave; ⏲5pm-2am Mon-Thu, from 3pm Fri, from 11am Sat & Sun; 🚌49) The scruffy, go-to club for edgy indie rock and jazz; Monday's show is often free, with cheap beer to boot.

Whistler LIVE MUSIC
(☎773-227-3530; www.whistlerchicago.com; 2421 N Milwaukee Ave; ⏲6pm-2am Mon-Thu, from 5pm Fri-Sun; M Blue Line to California) FREE Indie bands and jazz trios brood at this artsy little club in Logan Sq. There's never a cover charge.

Theater

Chicago's reputation for stage drama is well deserved. Many productions export to Broadway. The Theater District is a cluster of big, neon-lit venues at State and Randolph Sts. **Broadway in Chicago** (☎800-775-2000; www.broadwayinchicago.com) handles tickets for most.

Steppenwolf Theatre THEATER
(☎312-335-1650; www.steppenwolf.org; 1650 N Halsted St; M Red Line to North/Clybourn) Drama club of John Malkovich, Gary Sinise and other stars; it's 2 miles north of the Loop in Lincoln Park.

Goodman Theatre THEATER
(Map p530; ☎312-443-3800; www.goodmantheatre.org; 170 N Dearborn St; M Brown, Orange, Green, Purple, Pink, Blue Line to Clark/Lake) The city's downtown powerhouse, known for new and classic American works.

Neo-Futurists THEATER
(☎773-275-5255; www.neofuturists.org; 5153 N Ashland Ave; M Red Line to Berwyn) Original works that make you ponder and laugh simultaneously; known for its manic, late-

night show of 30 plays in 60 minutes. It's located in Andersonville.

Comedy

Improv comedy began in Chicago, and the city still nurtures the best in the business.

Second City COMEDY
(312-337-3992; www.secondcity.com; 1616 N Wells St; M Brown, Purple Line to Sedgwick) Bill Murray, Stephen Colbert, Tina Fey and many more honed their wit at this slick venue. The Mainstage and ETC stage host sketch revues (with an improv scene thrown in); they're similar in price and quality. The UP stage hosts stand-up and experimental shows. Bargain: turn up around 10pm (Friday and Saturday excluded) and watch the comics improv a set for free.

iO Theater COMEDY
(312-929-2401; http://.ioimprov.com/chicago; 1501 N Kingsbury St; M Red Line to North/Clybourn) Chicago's other major improv house is a bit edgier than its competition, with four stages hosting bawdy shows nightly. Two bars and a beer garden add to the fun.

Sports

Chicago Cubs BASEBALL
(www.cubs.com; 1060 W Addison St; M Red Line to Addison) The Cubs last won the World Series in 1908, but that doesn't stop fans from coming out to see them. Part of the draw is atmospheric, ivy-walled Wrigley Field, which dates from 1914. The bleacher seats are the most popular place to sit. No tickets? Peep through the 'knothole,' a garage-door-sized opening on Sheffield Ave, to watch the action for free.

Chicago White Sox BASEBALL
(www.whitesox.com; 333 W 35th St; M Red Line to Sox-35th) The Sox are the Cubs' South Side rivals and play in the more modern 'Cell,' aka US Cellular Field. Tickets are usually cheaper and easier to get than at Wrigley Field; games on Sundays and Mondays offer the best deals.

Chicago Bears FOOTBALL
(Map p530; www.chicagobears.com; 1410 S Museum Campus Dr; 146, 128) Da Bears, Chicago's NFL team, tackle at Soldier Field, recognizable by its classical-meets-flying-saucer architecture. Expect beery tailgate parties, sleet and snow.

Chicago Bulls BASKETBALL
(www.nba.com/bulls; 1901 W Madison St; 19, 20) Who will be the new Michael Jordan? Find out at the United Center, where the Bulls shoot hoops. It's about 2 miles west of the Loop. CTA runs special buses (No 19) on game days; it's best not to walk here.

Chicago Blackhawks HOCKEY
(www.blackhawks.nhl.com; 1901 W Madison St; 19, 20) The Stanley Cup winners (in 2010, 2013 and 2015, most recently) skate in front of big crowds. They share the United Center with the Bulls.

Performing Arts

Grant Park Orchestra CLASSICAL MUSIC
(Map p530; 312-742-7638; www.grantparkmusicfestival.com; Pritzker Pavilion, Millennium Park; 6:30pm Wed & Fri, 7:30pm Sat mid-Jun–mid-Aug; M Brown, Orange, Green, Purple, Pink Line to Randolph) FREE The beloved group puts on free classical concerts in Millennium Park throughout the summer. Bring a picnic.

Chicago Symphony Orchestra CLASSICAL MUSIC
(CSO; Map p530; 312-294-3000; www.cso.org; 220 S Michigan Ave; M Brown, Orange, Green, Purple, Pink Line to Adams) The CSO is one of America's best symphonies; it plays in the Daniel Burnham–designed Orchestra Hall.

Lyric Opera Of Chicago OPERA
(Map p530; 312-332-2244; www.lyricopera.org; 20 N Wacker Dr; M Brown, Orange, Purple, Pink Line to Washington) The renowned Lyric Opera hits high Cs in a chandeliered venue a few blocks west of the Loop.

Hubbard Street Dance Chicago DANCE
(Map p530; 312-850-9744; www.hubbardstreetdance.com; 205 E Randolph St; M Brown, Orange, Green, Purple, Pink Line to Randolph) Chicago's pre-eminent dance company performs at the Harris Theater for Music and Dance.

Shopping

A siren song for shoppers emanates from N Michigan Ave, along the Magnificent Mile (p533). Moving onward, boutiques fill Wicker Park and Bucktown (indie and vintage), Lincoln Park (posh), Lake View (countercultural) and Andersonville (all of the above).

Chicago Architecture Foundation Shop SOUVENIRS
(Map p530; www.architecture.org/shop; 224 S Michigan Ave; 9am-6:30pm; M Brown, Orange, Green, Purple, Pink Line to Adams) Skyline posters, Frank Lloyd Wright note cards, skyscraper models and more for those with an edifice complex.

Strange Cargo CLOTHING
(www.strangecargo.com; 3448 N Clark St; ⌚11am-6:45pm Mon-Sat, to 5:30pm Sun; Ⓜ Red Line to Addison) This retro store in Wrigleyville stocks kitschy iron-on T-shirts featuring Ditka, Obama and other renowned Chicagoans.

Jazz Record Mart MUSIC
(Map p530; www.jazzmart.com; 27 E Illinois St; ⌚10am-7pm Mon-Sat, 11am-5pm Sun; Ⓜ Red Line to Grand) One-stop shop for Chicago jazz and blues CDs and vinyl.

Quimby's BOOKS
(www.quimbys.com; 1854 W North Ave; ⌚noon-9pm Mon-Thu, to 10pm Fri & Sat, to 7pm Sun; Ⓜ Blue Line to Damen) Ground Zero for comics, zines and underground culture; in Wicker Park.

ℹ Information

INTERNET ACCESS

Many bars and restaurants and even some beaches have free wi-fi, as does the Chicago Cultural Center.

Harold Washington Library Center (www.chipublib.org; 400 S State St; ⌚9am-9pm Mon-Thu, to 5pm Fri & Sat, 1-5pm Sun) A grand, art-filled building with free wi-fi throughout and 3rd-floor internet terminals (get a day pass at the counter).

MEDIA

Chicago Reader (www.chicagoreader.com) Free alternative newspaper with comprehensive arts and entertainment listings.

Chicago Sun-Times (www.suntimes.com) The daily, tabloid-style newspaper.

Chicago Tribune (www.chicagotribune.com) The stalwart daily newspaper; its younger, trimmed-down, freebie version is *RedEye*.

MEDICAL SERVICES

Northwestern Memorial Hospital (☎312-926-5188; www.nmh.org; 251 E Erie St; Ⓜ Red Line to Chicago) Well-respected hospital downtown.

Walgreens (☎312-664-8686; 757 N Michigan Ave; ⌚24hr; Ⓜ Red Line to Chicago) On the Magnificent Mile.

MONEY

ATMs are plentiful downtown, with many near Chicago and Michigan Aves. To change money, try Terminal 5 at O'Hare International Airport or the following places in the Loop:

Travelex (☎312-807-4941; www.travelex.com; 19 S LaSalle St; ⌚8am-5pm Mon-Fri; Ⓜ Blue Line to Monroe)

World's Money Exchange (☎312-641-2151; www.wmeinc.com; 203 N LaSalle St; ⌚8:45am-4:45pm Mon-Fri; Ⓜ Brown, Orange, Green, Purple, Pink, Blue Line to Clark/Lake)

POST

Post Office (Map p530; 540 N Dearborn St)

TOURIST INFORMATION

Chicago Cultural Center Visitor Center (Map p530; www.choosechicago.com; 77 E Randolph St; ⌚10am-5pm Mon-Sat, 11am-4pm Sun; 📶; Ⓜ Brown, Orange, Green, Purple, Pink Line to Randolph) It's sparse, but does offer a staffed information desk and sales of discount cards for attractions. InstaGreeter (Friday through Sunday year-round) and Millennium Park (daily in summer) tours also depart from here.

USEFUL WEBSITES

Chicagoist (www.chicagoist.com) Quirky take on food, arts and events.

Gapers Block (www.gapersblock.com) News and events site with Chicago attitude.

ONLINE TICKETS & DISCOUNT CARDS

Most major sights, including the Art Institute of Chicago and Willis Tower, allow you to buy tickets online. The advantage is that you're assured entry and you get to skip the regular ticket lines. The disadvantage is that you have to pay a service fee of $1.50 to $4 per ticket (sometimes it's just per order), and at times the prepay line is almost as long as the regular one. Our suggestion: consider buying online in summer and for big exhibits. Otherwise, there's no need.

Chicago offers a couple of discount cards that also let you skip the regular queues:

Go Chicago Card (www.smartdestinations.com/chicago) Allows you to visit an unlimited number of attractions for a flat fee; good for one, two, three or five consecutive days. The company also offers a three-choice or five-choice 'Explorer Pass' where you pick among 26 options; it's valid for 30 days.

CityPass (www.citypass.com/chicago) Gives access to five of the city's top draws, including the Art Institute, Shedd Aquarium and Willis Tower, over nine days. It's less flexible than the Go Chicago pass, but cheaper for those wanting a more leisurely sightseeing pace.

Getting There & Away

AIR

Chicago Midway Airport (MDW; www.flychicago.com) The smaller airport used mostly by domestic carriers, such as Southwest; often has cheaper flights than from O'Hare.

O'Hare International Airport (ORD; www.flychicago.com) Chicago's larger airport, and among the world's busiest. Headquarters for United Airlines and a hub for American. Most non-US airlines and international flights use Terminal 5 (except Lufthansa and flights from Canada).

BUS

Greyhound (Map p530; ☎312-408-5821; www.greyhound.com; 630 W Harrison St; Ⓜ Blue Line to Clinton) Buses run frequently to Cleveland (7½ hours), Detroit (seven hours) and Minneapolis (nine hours), as well as to small towns throughout the USA. Open 24 hours, the station is bit southwest of the Loop in a pretty desolate stretch of road.

Megabus (Map p530; www.megabus.com/us; Canal St & Jackson Blvd; 📶; Ⓜ Blue Line to Clinton) Travels only to major Midwestern cities. Prices are often less, and quality and efficiency are better than Greyhound on these routes. The bus stop is adjacent to Union Station.

TRAIN

Chicago's classic **Union Station** (www.chicagounionstation.com; 225 S Canal St; Ⓜ Blue Line to Clinton) is the hub for **Amtrak** (☎800-872-7245; www.amtrak.com) national and regional service. Routes include the following:

Detroit (5½ hours, three trains daily)

Milwaukee (1½ hours, seven trains daily)

Minneapolis-St Paul (eight hours, one train daily)

New York (20½ hours, one train daily)

San Francisco (Emeryville; 53 hours, one train daily)

St Louis (5½ hours, five trains daily)

Getting Around

TO/FROM THE AIRPORT

Chicago Midway Airport Eleven miles southwest of the Loop, connected via the CTA Orange Line ($3). Trains depart every 10 minutes or so; they reach downtown in 30 minutes. Shuttle vans cost $27, taxis cost $35 to $40.

O'Hare International Airport Seventeen miles northwest of the Loop. The CTA Blue Line train ($5) runs 24/7. Trains depart every 10 minutes or so; they reach downtown in 40 minutes. Airport Express shuttle vans cost $32, taxis around $50. Taxi queues can be lengthy, and the ride can take as long as the train, depending on traffic.

BICYCLE

Chicago is a cycling-savvy city with a well-used bike-share program. **Divvy** (www.divvybikes.com) has 3000 sky-blue bikes at 300 stations around town. Kiosks issue 24-hour passes ($10) on the spot. Insert a credit card, get your ride code, then unlock a bike. The first 30 minutes are free; after that, rates rise fast if you don't dock the bike. Note helmets and locks are not provided.

For traditional rentals (useful for longer rides), try Bike Chicago (p537) or Bobby's Bike Hike (p537) downtown.

CAR & MOTORCYCLE

Be warned: street and garage/lot parking is expensive. If you must, try **Millennium Park Garage** (www.millenniumgarages.com; 5 S Columbus Dr; per 3/24hr $25/33). Chicago's rush-hour traffic is abysmal.

PUBLIC TRANSPORTATION

The **Chicago Transit Authority** (CTA; www.transitchicago.com) operates the city's buses and the elevated/subway train system (aka the El).

- Two of the eight color-coded train lines – the Red Line, and the Blue Line to O'Hare airport – operate 24 hours a day. The other lines run from 4am to 1am daily. During the day, you shouldn't have to wait more than 15 minutes for a train. Get free maps at any station.
- CTA buses go everywhere from early morning until late evening.
- The standard fare per train is $3 (except from O'Hare, where it costs $5) and includes two transfers; per bus, it is $2.25.
- On the train, you must use a Ventra Ticket, which is sold from vending machines at train stations. You can also buy a Ventra Card, aka a rechargeable fare card, at stations. It has a one-time $5 fee that gets refunded once you register the card. It knocks 50 to 75 cents off the cost of each ride.
- On buses, you can use a Ventra Card or pay the driver with exact change.
- Unlimited ride passes (one-/three-day pass $10/20) are also available. Get them at rail stations and drug stores.

Metra commuter trains (www.metrarail.com; fares $3.25-10.25, all-weekend pass $8) have 12 routes serving the suburbs from four terminals ringing the Loop: LaSalle St Station, Millennium Station, Union Station and Richard B Ogilvie Transportation Center (a few blocks north of Union Station).

TAXI

Cabs are plentiful in the Loop, north to Andersonville and northwest to Wicker Park and Bucktown. Flagfall is $3.25, plus $1.80 per mile and $1 per extra passenger; a 15% tip is expected. The rideshare company Uber is also popular.

Flash Cab (☎773-561-4444; www.flashcab.com)

Yellow Cab (☎312-829-4222; www.yellowcabchicago.com)

Around Chicago

Oak Park

Located 10 miles west of the Loop and easily reached via CTA train, Oak Park has two famous sons: novelist Ernest Hemingway was born here, and architect Frank Lloyd Wright lived and worked here from 1889 to 1909.

During Wright's 20 years in Oak Park, he designed many houses. Chief among them is his own: the **Frank Lloyd Wright Home & Studio** (☎312-994-4000; www.flwright.org; 951 Chicago Ave; adult/child/camera $17/14/5; ⊙10am-4pm) offers a fascinating, hour-long walk-through that reveals his distinctive style. Tour frequency varies, from every 20 minutes on summer weekends to every hour in winter. The studio also offers guided neighborhood walking tours ($15), as well as a self-guided audio version (same price). Or you can explore on the cheap by buying an architectural site map ($4.25) from the studio shop, which gives the locations of other Wright-designed abodes. Ten of them cluster nearby along Forest and Chicago Aves; gawking must be from the sidewalk since they're privately owned.

Despite Hemingway allegedly calling Oak Park a 'village of wide lawns and narrow minds,' the town still pays homage to him at the **Ernest Hemingway Museum** (☎708-848-2222; www.ehfop.org; 200 N Oak Park Ave; adult/child $15/13; ⊙1-5pm Sun-Fri, from 10am Sat). Admission also includes entry to his birthplace home across the street.

From downtown Chicago, take the CTA Green Line to the Oak Park station, then walk north on Oak Park Ave. It's about a quarter mile to the Hemingway sights and a mile to the Wright home. The train traverses some bleak neighborhoods before emerging into Oak Park's wide-lawn splendor.

Evanston & North Shore

Evanston, 14 miles north of the Loop and reached via the CTA Purple Line, combines sprawling old houses with a compact downtown. It's home to Northwestern University.

Beyond are Chicago's northern lakeshore suburbs, which became popular with the wealthy in the late 19th century. A classic 30-mile drive follows Sheridan Rd through various well-off towns to the socioeconomic apex of Lake Forest. Attractions along the way include the **Baha'i House of Worship** (www.bahai.us/bahai-temple; 100 Linden Ave; ⊙6am-10pm) FREE, a glistening white architectural marvel, and the **Chicago Botanic Garden** (☎847-835-5440; www.chicagobotanic.org; 1000 Lake Cook Rd; per car weekday/weekend $25/30; ⊙8am-sunset), with hiking trails, 255 bird species and weekend cooking demos by well-known chefs.

Inland lies the **Illinois Holocaust Museum** (☎847-967-4800; www.ilholocaustmuseum.org; 9603 Woods Dr; adult/child $12/6; ⊙10am-5pm, to 8pm Thu). Besides its excellent videos of survivors' stories from WWII, the museum contains thought-provoking art about genocides in Armenia, Rwanda, Cambodia and elsewhere.

Galena & Northern Illinois

The highlight of this region is the hilly northwest, where cottonwood trees, grazing horses and scenic byways fill the pocket around Galena.

En route is Union, where the **Illinois Railway Museum** (☎815-923-4000; www.irm.org; US 20 to Union Rd; adult $10-14, child $7-10; ⊙May-Oct, hours vary) sends trainspotters into fits of ecstasy with 200 acres of locomotives.

Galena

While it sometimes gets chided as a place for the 'newly wed and nearly dead,' thanks to all the tourist-oriented B&Bs, and fudge and antique shops, there's no denying little Galena's beauty. It spreads across wooded hillsides near the Mississippi River, amid rolling, barn-dotted farmland. Redbrick mansions in Greek Revival, Gothic Revival and Queen Anne styles fill the streets, left over from the town's heyday in the mid-1800s, when local lead mines made it rich. Throw in cool kayak trips, horseback rides and winding back-road drives, and you've got a lovely, slowpoke getaway.

Sights & Activities

When entering town on US 20, turn on Park Ave, then Bouthillier St to reach the free parking lot beside the old train depot. Most sights, shops and restaurants are walkable from here.

Ulysses S Grant Home MUSEUM
(☎815-777-3310; www.granthome.com; 500 Bouthillier St; adult/child $5/3; ⊙9am-4:45pm Wed-Sun Apr-Oct, reduced hours Nov-Mar) The 1860 abode was a gift from local Republicans to the victorious general at the Civil War's end. Grant lived here until he became the country's 18th president.

Fever River Outfitters OUTDOORS
(☎815-776-9425; www.feverriveroutfitters.com; 525 S Main St; ⏲10am-5pm, closed Tue-Thu early Sep-late May) Outdoors enthusiasts should head to this shop, which rents canoes, kayaks, bicycles and snowshoes. It also offers guided tours, such as 9-mile kayak trips ($45 per person, equipment included) on the Mississippi River's backwaters.

Stagecoach Trail DRIVING TOUR
The Stagecoach Trail is a 26-mile ride on a narrow, twisty road en route to Warren. Pick it up by taking Main St northeast through downtown; at the second stop sign go right (you'll see a trail marker). And yes, it really was part of the old stagecoach route between Galena and Chicago.

Shenandoah Riding Center HORSEBACK RIDING
(☎815-777-9550; www.theshenandoahriding-center.com; 200 N Brodrecht Rd; 1hr ride $45) Saddle up at Shenandoah. It offers trail rides through the valley for all levels of riders. The stables are 8 miles east of Galena.

Sleeping

Galena brims with quilt-laden B&Bs. Most cost $100 to $200 nightly and fill up during weekends. Check www.galena.org for listings.

ROUTE 66: GET YOUR KICKS IN ILLINOIS

America's 'Mother Road' kicks off in Chicago on Adams St, just west of Michigan Ave. Before embarking, fuel up at Lou Mitchell's (p544) near Union Station. After all, it's 300 miles from here to the Missouri state line.

Sadly, most of the original Route 66 has been superseded by I-55 in Illinois, though the old road still exists in scattered sections often paralleling the interstate. Keep an eye out for brown 'Historic Route 66' signs, which pop up at crucial junctions to mark the way. Top stops include:

Gemini Giant (810 E Baltimore St) The first must-see rises from the cornfields 60 miles south of Chicago in Wilmington. Here the Gemini Giant – a 28ft fiberglass spaceman – stands guard outside the Launching Pad Drive In. The restaurant is now shuttered, but the green, rocket-holding statue remains a terrific photo op. To reach it, leave I-55 at exit 241, and follow Hwy 44 south a short distance to Hwy 53, which rolls into town.

Funk's Grove (☎309-874-3360; www.funksmaplesirup.com; ⏲9am-5pm Mon-Fri, from 10am Sat, from noon Sun) Drive 90 miles onward to see Funk's pretty, 19th-century maple-sirup farm (yes, that's sirup with an 'i'). It's in Shirley (exit 154 off I-55). Afterward, get on Old Route 66 – a frontage road that parallels the interstate here – and in 10 miles you'll reach...

Palms Grill Cafe (☎217-648-2233; www.thepalmsgrillcafe.com; 110 SW Arch St; mains $5-8; ⏲7am-7pm Tue-Sat) Pull up a chair at this diner in the throwback hamlet of Atlanta, where thick slabs of gooseberry, chocolate cream and other retro pies tempt from the glass case. Then walk across the street to snap a photo with Tall Paul, a sky-high statue of Paul Bunyan clutching a hot dog.

Cozy Dog Drive In (p553) Where the cornmeal-battered, fried hot dog on a stick was born. It's in Springfield, 50 miles down the road from Atlanta.

Ariston Cafe (☎217-324-2023; www.ariston-cafe.com; 413 N Old Rte 66; mains $7-20; ⏲11am-9pm Tue-Fri, 4-10pm Sat, 11am-8pm Sun) Further south, a good section of old Route 66 parallels I-55 through Litchfield, where you can fork into chicken fried steak and red velvet cake while chatting up locals at the 1924 restaurant.

Chain of Rocks Bridge (Old Chain of Rocks Rd; ⏲9am-sunset) Before driving into Missouri, detour off I-270 at exit 3. Follow Hwy 3 (aka Lewis and Clark Blvd) south, turn right at the first stoplight and drive west to the 1929 bridge. Open only to pedestrians and cyclists these days, the mile-long span over the Mississippi River has a 22-degree angled bend (the cause of many a crash, hence the ban on cars).

For more information, visit the **Route 66 Association of Illinois** (www.il66assoc.org) or **Illinois Route 66 Scenic Byway** (www.illinoisroute66.org). Detailed driving directions are at www.historic66.com/illinois.

Grant Hills Motel MOTEL $
(☎877-421-0924; www.granthills.com; 9372 US 20; r $80-100; ❄ 📶 🏊) The motel is a no-frills option 1.5 miles east of town, with countryside views and a horseshoe pitch.

DeSoto House Hotel HOTEL $$
(☎815-777-0090; www.desotohouse.com; 230 S Main St; r $155-205; ❄ 📶) 🍃 Grant and Lincoln stayed in the well-furnished rooms, and you can too. The hotel dates from 1855.

Eating & Drinking

Fritz and Frites FRENCH, GERMAN $$
(☎815-777-2004; www.fritzandfrites.com; 317 N Main St; mains $17-22; ⏰11:30am-8pm Tue-Sun) This romantic little bistro serves a compact menu of both German and French classics. Dig into mussels with champagne sauce or maybe a tender schnitzel.

111 Main AMERICAN $$
(☎815-777-8030; www.oneelevenmain.com; 111 N Main St; mains $17-26; ⏰4-9pm Mon & Thu, 11am-10pm Fri & Sat, to 9pm Sun) Pot roast, pork and beans and other Midwestern favorites, using ingredients sourced from local farms.

VFW Hall BAR
(100 S Main St; ⏰10am-11pm) The VFW Hall provides an opportunity to sip cheap beer and watch TV alongside veterans of long-ago wars. Don't be shy: as the sign out front says, the public is welcome.

Quad Cities

South of Galena along a pretty stretch of the **Great River Road** (www.greatriverroad-illinois.org) is scenic **Mississippi Palisades State Park** (☎815-273-2731), a popular rock-climbing, hiking and camping area; pick up trail maps at the north entrance park office.

Further downstream, the Quad Cities (www.visitquadcities.com) – Moline and Rock Island in Illinois, and Davenport and Bettendorf across the river in Iowa – make a surprisingly good stop. Rock Island has an appealing downtown (based at 2nd Ave and 18th St), with a couple of cafes and a lively pub and music scene. On the edge of town, **Black Hawk State Historic Site** (www.blackhawkpark.org; 1510 46th Ave; ⏰sunrise-10pm) is a huge park with trails by the Rock River. Its **Hauberg Indian Museum** (☎309-788-9536; Watch Tower Lodge; ⏰9am-noon & 1-5pm Wed-Sun) FREE outlines the sorry story of Sauk leader Black Hawk and his people.

Out in the Mississippi River, the actual island of **Rock Island** once held a Civil War–era arsenal and POW camp. It now maintains the impressive **Rock Island Arsenal Museum** (www.arsenalhistoricalsociety.org; ⏰noon-4pm Tue-Sat) FREE, Civil War cemetery, national cemetery and visitor center for barge viewing. Bring photo ID as the island is still an active army facility.

Moline is the home of John Deere, the international farm machinery manufacturer. Downtown holds the **John Deere Pavilion** (www.johndeerepavilion.com; 1400 River Dr; ⏰9am-5pm Mon-Fri, 10am-5pm Sat, noon-4pm Sun; 👪) FREE, a kiddie-beloved museum-showroom.

Springfield & Central Illinois

Abraham Lincoln and Route 66 sights are sprinkled liberally throughout central Illinois, which is otherwise farmland plain. East of Decatur, Arthur and Arcola are Amish centers.

Springfield

The small state capital has an obsession with Abraham Lincoln, who practiced law here from 1837 to 1861. Many of the attractions are walkable downtown and cost little or nothing.

Sights

Lincoln Home & Visitor Center HISTORIC SITE
(☎217-492-4150; www.nps.gov/liho; 426 S 7th St; ⏰8:30am-5pm) FREE Start at the National Park Service visitor center, where you must pick up a ticket to enter Lincoln's 12-room abode, located directly across the street. You can then walk through the house where Abe and Mary Lincoln lived from 1844 until they moved to the White House in 1861; rangers are stationed throughout to provide background information and answer questions.

Lincoln Presidential Library & Museum MUSEUM
(☎217-558-8844; www.illinois.gov/alplm; 212 N 6th St; adult/child $15/6; ⏰9am-5pm; 👪) This museum contains the most complete Lincoln collection in the world. Real-deal artifacts like Abe's shaving mirror and briefcase join whizbang exhibits and Disneyesque holograms that keep the kids agog.

Lincoln's Tomb TOMB
(www.lincolntomb.org; 1441 Monument Ave; ⏰9am-5pm Wed-Sat) FREE After his assassination, Lincoln's body was returned to

Springfield, where it lies in an impressive tomb in Oak Ridge Cemetery, 1.5 miles north of downtown. The gleam on the nose of Lincoln's bust, created by visitors' light touches, indicates the numbers of those who pay their respects here. On summer Tuesdays at 7pm, infantry re-enactors fire muskets and lower the flag outside the tomb.

Old State Capitol HISTORIC SITE
(217-785-7960; cnr 6th & Adams Sts; suggested donation $5; 9am-5pm Wed-Sat) Chatterbox docents will take you through the building and regale you with Lincoln stories, such as how he gave his famous 'House Divided' speech here in 1858.

Sleeping & Eating

State House Inn HOTEL $$
(217-528-5100; www.thestatehouseinn.com; 101 E Adams St; r $120-155; P ❄ @ ☜) It looks concrete-drab outside, but inside the State House shows its style. Comfy beds and large baths fill the rooms; a retro bar fills the lobby.

Inn at 835 B&B $$
(217-523-4466; www.innat835.com; 835 S 2nd St; r $135-205; P ❄ ☜) The historic arts-and-crafts-style manor offers 11 rooms of the four-post bed, claw-foot bathtub variety.

Cozy Dog Drive In AMERICAN $
(www.cozydogdrivein.com; 2935 S 6th St; mains $2-5; 8am-8pm Mon-Sat) This Route 66 legend – the reputed birthplace of the corn dog! – has memorabilia and souvenirs in addition to the deeply fried main course on a stick.

Norb Andy's Tabarin PUB FOOD $
(www.norbandys.com; 518 E Capitol Ave; mains $8-10; 4pm-1am Tue-Sat) A favorite with locals, Norb's is a dive bar-restaurant housed in the 1837 Hickox House downtown. It piles up Springfield's best 'horseshoe,' a local sandwich of fried meat on toasted bread, mounded with french fries and smothered in melted cheese.

Entertainment

Route 66 Drive In CINEMA
(217-698-0066; www.route66-drivein.com; 1700 Recreation Dr; adult/child $7.50/5; nightly Jun-Aug, weekends mid-Apr–May & Sep) Screens first-run flicks under the stars.

ADVANCE PLANNING

- Pre-book accommodations during summer, especially in resort-orientated places such as Mackinac Island in Michigan, and the North Shore in Minnesota. It's also advised for festival cities such as Milwaukee and Chicago.
- Pay attention to time zones: half of the Great Lakes region is on Eastern time (IN, OH, MI) and half on Central time (IL, WI, MN).
- Bring insect repellent, especially if you're heading to the Northwoods. The blackflies in spring and mosquitoes in summer can be brutal.
- Stock up on dollar bills and quarters for tollways.

Information

Springfield Convention & Visitors Bureau (www.visitspringfieldillinois.com) Produces a useful visitors' guide.

Getting There & Around

The downtown **Amtrak station** (217-753-2013; cnr 3rd & Washington Sts) has five trains daily to/from St Louis (two hours) and Chicago (3½ hours).

Petersburg

When Lincoln first arrived in Illinois in 1831, he worked variously as a clerk, storekeeper and postmaster in the frontier village of New Salem before studying law and moving to Springfield. In Petersburg, 20 miles northwest of Springfield, **Lincoln's New Salem State Historic Site** (217-632-4000; www.lincolnsnew-salem.com; Hwy 97; suggested donation adult/child $4/2; 9am-4pm Wed-Sun) reconstructs the village with building replicas, historical displays and costumed performances – a pretty informative and entertaining package.

Southern Illinois

A surprise awaits near Collinsville, 8 miles east of East St Louis: classified as a Unesco World Heritage site with the likes of Stonehenge and the Egyptian pyramids is **Cahokia Mounds State Historic Site** (618-346-5160; www.cahokiamounds.org; Collinsville Rd; suggested donation adult/child $7/2; grounds 8am-dusk, visitor center 9am-5pm Wed-Sun) Cahokia protects the remnants of North America's largest prehistoric city (20,000 people, with suburbs), dating from AD 1200. While the 65 earthen mounds, including the enormous Monk's Mound, are not overwhelmingly impressive in themselves, the whole site is worth seeing. If you're approaching from the north, take exit 24 off I-255 S; if approaching from St Louis, take exit 6 off I-55/70.

A short distance north in Hartford, the stellar **Lewis & Clark State Historic Site** (☎ 618-251-5811; www.campdubois.com; cnr Hwy 3 & Poag Rd; ⏰ 9am-5pm Wed-Sun) FREE marks the spot where the explorers departed on their journey. The 55ft boat replica (in the visitor center), reconstructed winter camp (out on the low-slung prairie) and Mississippi River bashing by give a real feel for the scene. The nearby **Lewis & Clark Confluence Tower** (www.confluencetower.com; 435 Confluence Tower Dr; adult/child $4/2; ⏰ 9:30am-5pm Mon-Sat, from noon Sun) provides sweeping views.

Continuing northwest along the water, Hwy 100 between **Alton** and **Grafton** is perhaps the most scenic 15 miles of the entire Great River Road. As you slip under windhewn bluffs, keep an eye out for the turnoff to itty-bitty **Elsah**, a hidden hamlet of 19th-century stone cottages, wood buggy shops and farmhouses.

An exception to the state's flat farmland is the green southernmost section, punctuated by rolling **Shawnee National Forest** (☎ 618-253-7114; www.fs.usda.gov/shawnee) and its rocky outcroppings. The area has numerous state parks and recreation areas good for hiking, climbing, swimming, fishing and canoeing, particularly around **Little Grassy Lake** and **Devil's Kitchen**. And who would think that Southern-style swampland, complete with moss-draped cypress trees and croaking bullfrogs, would be here? But it is, at **Cypress Creek National Wildlife Refuge** (☎ 618-634-2231; www.fws.gov/refuge/cypress_creek).

Union County, near the state's southern tip, has wineries and orchards. Sample the wares on the 35-mile **Shawnee Hills Wine Trail** (www.shawneewinetrail.com), which connects 12 vineyards.

INDIANA

The state revs up around the Indy 500 race, but otherwise it's about slow-paced pleasures in corn-stubbled Indiana: pie-eating in Amish Country, meditating in Bloomington's Tibetan temples and admiring the big architecture in small Columbus. For the record, folks have called Indianans 'Hoosiers' since the 1830s, but the word's origin is unknown. One theory is that early settlers knocking on a door were met with 'Who's here?' which soon became 'Hoosier.' It's certainly something to discuss with locals, perhaps over a traditional pork tenderloin sandwich.

ℹ Information

Indiana Highway Conditions (☎ 800-261-7623; http://indot.carsprogram.org)

Indiana State Park Information (☎ 800-622-4931; www.in.gov/dnr/parklake) Park entry costs $2 per day by foot or bicycle, $9 to $12 by vehicle. Campsites cost $12 to $44; reservations accepted (☎ 866-622-6746; www.camp.in.gov).

Indiana Tourism (☎ 800-677-9800; www.visitindiana.com)

Indianapolis

Clean-cut Indy is the state capital and a perfectly pleasant place to ogle racecars and take a spin around the renowned speedway. The art museum and White River State Park have their merits, as do the Mass Ave and Broad Ripple 'hoods for eating and drinking. And Kurt Vonnegut fans are in for a treat. A swell trail connects it all.

◉ Sights & Activities

Downtown's bull's-eye is Monument Circle. White River State Park and its many attractions lie about three-quarters of a mile west.

Indianapolis Motor Speedway MUSEUM
(☎ 317-492-6784; www.indianapolismotorspeedway.com; 4790 W 16th St; adult/child $8/5; ⏰ 9am-5pm Mar-Oct, 10am-4pm Nov-Feb) The Speedway, home of the Indianapolis 500 motor race, is Indy's supersight. The Hall of Fame Museum features 75 racing cars (including former winners), a 500lb Tiffany trophy and a track tour ($8 extra). OK, so you're on a bus for the latter and not even beginning to burn rubber at 37mph, but it's still fun to pretend.

The big race itself is held on the Sunday of Memorial Day weekend (late May) and attended by 450,000 crazed fans. **Tickets** (☎ 800-822-4639; www.imstix.com; $40-185) can be hard to come by. Try the pre-race trials and practices for easier access and cheaper prices. The track is about 6 miles northwest of downtown.

Dallara IndyCar Factory MUSEUM
(☎ 317-243-7171; www.indycarfactory.com; 1201 W Main St; adult/child $10/5; ⏰ 10am-6pm Mon-Sat)

The shiny factory is a short walk from the Speedway. It opened in 2012 and provides a peek at how the fast cars are made. The wind tunnel models raise hairs, as do driving simulators that let you feel what it's like to tear around the track at 200mph.

White River State Park STATE PARK
(http://inwhiteriver.wrsp.in.gov) The expansive park, located at downtown's edge, contains several worthwhile sights. The adobe **Eiteljorg Museum of American Indians & Western Art** (www.eiteljorg.org; 500 W Washington St; adult/child $12/6; ⏲10am-5pm Mon-Sat, from noon Sun) features Native American basketry, pots and masks, as well as several paintings by Frederic Remington and Georgia O'Keeffe. Other park highlights include an atmospheric **minor-league baseball stadium**, a **zoo**, a **canal walk**, **gardens**, a **science museum** and a **college sports museum**.

Indianapolis Museum of Art MUSEUM, GARDENS
(☎317-920-2660; www.imamuseum.org; 4000 Michigan Rd; adult/child $18/10; ⏲11am-5pm Tue-Sun, to 9pm Thu) The museum has a terrific collection of European art (especially Turner and post-Impressionists), African tribal art, South Pacific art and Chinese works. The complex also includes **Oldfields – Lilly House & Gardens**, where you can tour the 22-room mansion and flowery grounds of the Lilly pharmaceutical family, and **Fairbanks Art & Nature Park**, with eye-popping mod sculptures set amid 100 acres of woodlands. Fairbanks is free – perfect for those who need an art fix but without the steep admission price.

Kurt Vonnegut Memorial Library MUSEUM
(www.vonnegutlibrary.org; 340 N Senate Ave; ⏲11am-6pm Mon, Tue, Thu & Fri, noon-5pm Sat & Sun) FREE Author Kurt Vonnegut was born and raised in Indy, and this humble museum pays homage with displays including his Pall Mall cigarettes, droll drawings and rejection letters from publishers. The library also replicates his office, complete with checkerboard carpet, red rooster lamp and blue Coronamatic typewriter. You're welcome to sit at the desk and type Kurt a note; the library tweets the musings.

Rhythm! Discovery Center MUSEUM
(www.rhythmdiscoverycenter.org; 110 W Washington St; adult/child $10/6; ⏲10am-5pm Mon, Tue & Thu-Sat, noon-7pm Wed, noon-5pm Sun) Bang drums, gongs, xylophones and exotic percussive instruments from around the globe at this hidden gem downtown. Kids love the interactive whomping. Adults appreciate the exhibits of famous drummers' gear and the soundproof, drum-kitted studio where you can unleash (and record) your inner Neil Peart.

Indiana Medical History Museum MUSEUM
(☎317-635-7329; www.imhm.org; 3045 W Vermont St; adult/child $10/3; ⏲10am-3pm Thu-Sat) When you think 'horror movie insane asylum,' this century-old state psychiatric hospital is exactly what you envision. Guided tours roam the former pathology lab, from the cold-slabbed autopsy room to the eerie specimen room filled with brains in jars. Tours start on the hour. It's a few miles west of White River park.

Children's Museum of Indianapolis MUSEUM
(☎317-334-4000; www.childrensmuseum.org; 3000 N Meridian St; adult/child $21.50/18.50; ⏲10am-5pm, closed Mon mid-Sep–Feb) It's the world's largest kids' museum, sprawled over five floors holding dinosaurs aplenty and a 43ft sculpture by Dale Chihuly that teaches tykes to blow glass (virtually!).

Cultural Trail CYCLING, WALKING
(www.indyculturaltrail.org) The 8-mile bike and pedestrian path links cool sights and

INDIANA FACTS

Nickname Hoosier State

Population 6.6 million

Area 36,420 sq miles

Capital city Indianapolis (population 843,400)

Sales tax 7%

Birthplace of Author Kurt Vonnegut (1922–2007), actor James Dean (1931–55), TV host David Letterman (b 1947), rocker John Mellencamp (b 1951), King of Pop Michael Jackson (1958–2009)

Home of Farmers, corn

Politics Typically Republican

Famous for Indy 500 motor race, basketball fanaticism, pork tenderloin sandwich

Official pie Sugar cream

Driving distances Indianapolis to Chicago 185 miles, Indianapolis to Bloomington 53 miles

INDIANA FOODWAYS

Which restaurants serve the best pork tenderloin and sugar cream pie? Where are the local farmers markets and rib fests? What's the recipe for corn pudding? The **Indiana Foodways Alliance** (www.indianafoodways.com) is your one-stop shop for Hoosier cuisine information.

neighborhoods around Indy's center. Pacers Bikeshare stations dot the way and are handy for short jaunts.

Bicycle Garage Indy BICYCLE RENTAL
(www.bgindy.com; 222 E Market St; rental per 2hr/day $20/40; 7am-8pm Mon-Fri, 8am-4pm Sat) Rent bikes here for leisurely rides. Hop on the Cultural Trail in front of the shop; it eventually connects to the Monon Trail greenway. Rates include helmet, lock and map.

Sleeping

Hotels cost more and are usually full during race weeks in May, June, July and August. Add 17% tax to the prices listed here. Look for low-cost motels off I-465, the freeway that circles Indianapolis.

Indy Hostel HOSTEL $
(317-727-1696; www.indyhostel.us; 4903 Winthrop Ave; dm/r from $28/58;) This small, friendly hostel has a six-bed female dorm and 12-bed coed dorm. There are also four private rooms. Got a tent? Camp in the yard for $19. The Monon Trail hiking/cycling path runs beside the property, and the hostel rents bikes (per day $10). It's located by Broad Ripple, so a bit of a haul from downtown (on bus 17).

Hilton Garden Inn HOTEL $$
(317-955-9700; www.indianapolisdowntown.gardeninn.com; 10 E Market St; r $150-190;) The century-old, neoclassical architecture, plush beds and downtown location right by Monument Circle make this a fine chain-hotel choice. Valet parking is $27.

Stone Soup B&B $$
(866-639-9550; www.stonesoupinn.com; 1304 N Central Ave; r $90-150;) The nine rooms fill a rambling, antique-filled house. It's a bit ramshackle, but it has its charm. The less-expensive rooms share a bath.

The Alexander HOTEL $$
(317-624-8200; www.thealexander.com; 333 S Delaware St; r $170-270) The 209-room Alexander is all about art. Forty original works decorate the lobby; the Indianapolis Museum of Art curates the contemporary collection (the public is welcome to browse). The mod rooms have dark-wood floors and, of course, cool wall art. It's a block from the basketball arena, and it's where visiting teams sometimes stay. Valet parking is $29.

Eating

Massachusetts Ave (www.discovermassave.com), by downtown, is bounteous when the stomach growls. **Broad Ripple** (www.discoverbroadripplevillage.com), 7 miles north, has pubs, cafes and ethnic eateries.

Mug 'N' Bun AMERICAN $
(www.mug-n-bun.com; 5211 W 10th St; mains $4-8; 10am-9pm Sun-Thu, to 10pm Fri & Sat) The mugs are frosted and filled with a wonderful home-brewed root beer. The buns contain burgers, chili dogs and juicy pork tenderloins. And don't forget the fried mac 'n' cheese wedges. At this vintage drive-in near the Speedway, you are served – where else? – in your car.

Public Greens AMERICAN $
(www.publicgreensurbankitchen.com; 900 E 64th St; mains $7-14; 8am-9pm Sun-Thu, to 10pm Fri & Sat, reduced hours in winter) The on-site micro-farm raises kale, beets, eggs and other ingredients for the eatery's homey dishes; 100% of profits are then plowed back into the community to feed at-risk children. It's a cafeteria-style set up, where you order at the counter. Located in Broad Ripple, right by the Monon Trail.

Bazbeaux PIZZA $
(317-636-7662; www.bazbeaux.com; 329 Massachusetts Ave; mains $8-15; 11am-10pm Sun-Thu, to 11pm Fri & Sat) A local favorite, Bazbeaux offers an eclectic pizza selection, like the 'Tchoupitoulas,' topped with Cajun shrimp and andouille sausage. Muffaletta sandwiches, stromboli and Belgian beer are some of the other offerings.

City Market MARKET $
(www.indycm.com; 222 E Market St; 7am-9pm Mon-Fri, from 8am Sat;) A smattering of food stalls fill the city's old marketplace, which dates from 1886. The 2nd-floor bar pours 16 local brews; most other vendors close by 3pm.

Drinking & Entertainment

Downtown and Mass Ave have some good watering holes; Broad Ripple has several.

Bars

Sun King Brewing BREWERY
(www.sunkingbrewing.com; 135 N College Ave; 10am-7pm Mon-Wed, to 8pm Thu & Fri, 1-6pm Sat & Sun, reduced hours in winter) FREE You never know what'll be flowing at Sun King's unvarnished downtown taproom. Indy's young and hip pile in to find out, swilling brews from a cocoa-y Baltic porter to a popcorn-tinged pilsner (made with Indiana popcorn). Flights (six 3oz samples) cost $6. Friday, when the brewery offers free samples and cheap growlers, it's packed. The outdoor patio hops in summer.

Slippery Noodle Inn BAR
(www.slipperynoodle.com; 372 S Meridian St; 11am-3am Mon-Fri, noon-3am Sat, 4pm-12:30am Sun) Downtown's Noodle is the oldest bar in the state, and has seen action as a whorehouse, slaughterhouse, gangster hangout and Underground Railroad station; currently, it's one of the best blues clubs in the country. There's live music nightly, and it's cheap.

Rathskeller BEER HALL
(www.rathskeller.com; 401 E Michigan St; 2pm-late Mon-Fri, from 11am Sat & Sun) Quaff German and local brews at the outdoor beer garden's picnic tables in summer, or at the deer-head-lined indoor beer hall once winter strikes. It is located in the historic Athenaeum building near Mass Ave.

Sports

The motor races aren't the only coveted spectator events. The NFL's Colts win football games under a huge retractable roof at **Lucas Oil Stadium** (317-299-4946; www.colts.com; 500 S Capitol Ave). The NBA's Pacers shoot hoops at **Bankers Life Fieldhouse** (317-917-2500; www.nba.com/pacers; 125 S Pennsylvania St).

Shopping

You could buy a speedway flag or Colts jersey as your Indy souvenir. Or you could purchase a bottle of mead made by a couple of enthusiastic former beekeepers at **New Day** (www.newdaycraft.com; 1102 E Prospect St; 2-9pm Tue-Thu, to 10pm Fri, noon-10pm Sat, noon-6pm Sun). Sample the honeyed wares in the tasting room before making your selection. They also make cider.

Information

Indiana University Medical Center (317-274-4705; 550 N University Blvd)

Indianapolis Convention & Visitors Bureau (800-323-4639; www.visitindy.com) Download a free city app and print out coupons from the website.

Indianapolis Star (www.indystar.com) The city's daily newspaper.

Indy Rainbow Chamber (www.gayindynow.org) Provides info for gay and lesbian visitors.

Nuvo (www.nuvo.net) Free, weekly alternative paper with the arts and music low-down.

Getting There & Around

The fancy **Indianapolis International Airport** (IND; www.indianapolisairport.com; 7800 Col H Weir Cook Memorial Dr) is 16 miles southwest of town. The Washington bus (8) runs between the airport and downtown ($1.75, 50 minutes); the Go Green Airport van does it quicker ($10, 20 minutes). A cab to downtown costs about $35.

Greyhound (317-267-3074; www.greyhound.com) shares **Union Station** (350 S Illinois St) with Amtrak. Buses go frequently to Cincinnati (2½ hours) and Chicago (3½ hours). **Megabus** (www.megabus.com/us) stops at 200 E Washington St, and is often cheaper. Amtrak travels these routes but takes almost twice as long.

IndyGo (www.indygo.net; fares $1.75) runs the local buses. Bus 17 goes to Broad Ripple. Service is minimal during weekends.

Pacers Bikeshare (www.pacersbikeshare.org; 24hr pass $8) has 250 bikes at 25 stations along the Cultural Trail downtown. Additional charges apply for trips over 30 minutes.

For a taxi, call **Yellow Cab** (317-487-7777).

Bloomington & Central Indiana

Bluegrass music, architectural hot spots, Tibetan temples and James Dean all furrow into the farmland around here.

Fairmount

This small town, north on Hwy 9, is the birthplace of James Dean, one of the original icons of cool. Fans should head directly to the **Fairmount Historical Museum** (765-948-4555; www.jamesdeanartifacts.com; 203 E Washington St; 10am-5pm Mon-Fri, from noon Sat & Sun Apr-Oct) FREE to see Dean's bongo drums, among other artifacts. This is also the place to pick up a free map that will guide you to sites like the farmhouse where Jimmy grew up and his lipstick-kissed grave site.

WORTH A TRIP

GRAY BROTHERS CAFETERIA

Cafeterias are an Indiana tradition, but most have disappeared – except for **Gray Brothers** (www.graybroscafe.com; 555 S Indiana St; mains $4-8; ⌚11am-8:30pm). Enter the time-warped dining room, grab a blue tray and behold a corridor of food that seems to stretch the length of a football field. Stack on plates of pan-fried chicken, meatloaf, mac 'n' cheese and sugar cream pie, then fork in with abandon. It's located in Mooresville, about 18 miles south of downtown Indianapolis en route to Bloomington.

The museum sells Dean posters, Zippo lighters and other memorabilia, and sponsors the annual **James Dean Festival** (⌚late Sep), when thousands of fans pour in for four days of music and revelry. The privately owned **James Dean Gallery** (☎765-948-3326; www.jamesdeangallery.com; 425 N Main St; ⌚9am-6pm) FREE has more memorabilia a few blocks away.

Columbus

When you think of the USA's great architectural cities – Chicago, New York, Washington, DC – Columbus, Indiana, doesn't quite leap to mind, but it should. Located 40 miles south of Indianapolis on I-65, Columbus is a remarkable gallery of physical design. Since the 1940s the city and its leading corporations have commissioned some of the world's best architects, including Eero Saarinen, Richard Meier and IM Pei, to create both public and private buildings. Stop at the **visitor center** (☎812-378-2622; www.columbus.in.us; 506 5th St; ⌚9am-5pm Mon-Sat, noon-5pm Sun) to pick up a self-guided tour map ($3) or join a two-hour bus tour (adult/child $25/15); they depart at 10am Tuesday to Friday, 10am and 2pm Saturday, and 2pm Sunday. It's wise to reserve online in advance. Over 70 notable buildings and pieces of public art are spread over a wide area (car required), but about 15 diverse works can be seen on foot downtown.

Hotel Indigo (☎812-375-9100; www.hotelindigo.com; 400 Brown St; r $150-180; ❄📶🏊🐾), downtown, offers the chain's trademark mod, cheery rooms, plus a fluffy white dog who works as the lobby ambassador. A few blocks away you can grab a counter stool, chat up the servers, and let the sugar buzz begin at retro, stained-glass-packed **Zaharakos** (www.zaharakos.com; 329 Washington St; ⌚11am-8pm), a 1909 soda fountain.

Nashville

Gentrified and antique-filled, this 19th-century town west of Columbus on Hwy 46 is now a bustling tourist center, at its busiest in fall when leaf-peepers pour in. The **visitor center** (☎812-988-7303; www.browncounty.com; 10 N Van Buren St; ⌚9am-6pm Mon-Thu, 9am-7pm Fri & Sat, 10am-5pm Sun; 📶) provides maps and coupons.

Beyond gallery browsing, Nashville is the jump-off point to **Brown County State Park** (☎812-988-6406; tent & RV sites $16-33, cabins from $77), a 15,700-acre stand of oak, hickory and birch trees, where trails give hikers, mountain bikers and horseback riders access to the area's green hill country.

Among several B&Bs, central **Artists Colony Inn** (☎812-988-0600; www.artistscolonyinn.com; 105 S Van Buren St; r $125-180; ❄📶) stands out for its spiffy, Shaker-style rooms. The **dining room** (mains $10-19; ⌚7:30am-8pm Sun-Thu, to 9pm Fri & Sat) offers traditional Hoosier fare, such as catfish and pork tenderloins.

As with Nashville Tennessee, Nashville Indiana enjoys country music, and bands play regularly at several venues. To shake a leg, mosey into **Mike's Music & Dance Barn** (☎812-988-8636; www.mikesmusicbarn.com; 2277 Hwy 46; ⌚from 6:30pm Thu-Mon). The **Bill Monroe Museum** (☎812-988-6422; www.billmonroemusicpark.com; 5163 Rte 135 N; adult/child $4/free; ⌚9am-5pm Mon-Sat, noon-4pm Sun, closed Tue & Wed Nov-Apr), 5 miles north of town, hails the bluegrass hero; it hosts a popular, week-long bluegrass festival in mid-June.

Bloomington

Lively and lovely, limestone-clad and cycling mad, Bloomington – 53 miles south of Indianapolis via Hwy 37 – is the home of Indiana University. The town centers on Courthouse Sq, surrounded by restaurants, bars and bookshops. Nearly everything is walkable. The **Bloomington CVB** (www.visitbloomington.com) has a downloadable guide.

On the expansive university campus, the **Art Museum** (☎812-855-5445; https://artmuseum.indiana.edu; 1133 E 7th St; ⌚10am-5pm Tue-Sat, from noon Sun) FREE, designed by IM Pei, contains an excellent collection of African art and German expressionist paintings.

The colorful, prayer-flag-covered **Tibetan Mongolian Buddhist Cultural Center** (☎812-336-6807; www.tmbcc.org; 3655 Snoddy Rd; ⊙sunrise-sunset) FREE – founded by the Dalai Lama's brother – as well as the **Dagom Gaden Tensung Ling Monastery** (☎812-339-0857; www.dgtlmonastery.org; 102 Clubhouse Dr; ⊙9am-6pm) FREE, indicate Bloomington's significant Tibetan presence. Both have intriguing shops and offer free teachings and meditation sessions; check the websites for weekly schedules.

If you arrive in mid-April and wonder why an extra 20,000 people are hanging out in town, it's for the **Little 500** (www.iusf.indiana.edu; tickets $30). It's one of the coolest bike races you'll see, where amateurs ride one-speed Schwinns for 200 laps around a quarter-mile track.

Look for cheap lodgings along N Walnut St near Hwy 46. **Grant Street Inn** (☎800-328-4350; www.grantstinn.com; 310 N Grant St; r $159-239; @) has 24 rooms in a Victorian house and annex near campus.

For a town of its size, Bloomington offers a mind-blowing array of ethnic eats – everything from Burmese to Eritrean to Turkish. Browse Kirkwood Ave and E 4th St. **Anyetsang's Little Tibet** (☎812-331-0122; www.anyetsangs.com; 415 E 4th St; mains $13-14; ⊙11am-3pm & 5-9pm, closed Tue) offers specialties from the Himalayan homeland. Pubs on Kirkwood Ave, close to the university, cater to the student crowd. **Nick's English Hut** (www.nicksenglishhut.com; 423 E Kirkwood Ave; ⊙11am-2am Mon-Sat, to midnight Sat) pours not only for students and professors, but has filled the cups of Kurt Vonnegut and Dylan Thomas, as well. On the near north side, rustic **Upland Brewing Co** (www.uplandbeer.com; 350 W 11th St; ⊙11am-midnight Mon-Thu, to 1am Fri & Sat, noon-midnight Sun) makes creative suds like a seasonal persimmon lambic using local fruit.

Southern Indiana

The pretty hills, caves, rivers and utopian history of southern Indiana mark it as a completely different region from the flat and industrialized north.

Ohio River

The Indiana segment of the 981-mile Ohio River marks the state's southern border. From tiny Aurora, in the southeastern corner of the state, Hwys 56, 156, 62 and 66, known collectively as the **Ohio River Scenic Route**, wind through a varied landscape.

Coming from the east, a perfect place to stop is little **Madison**, a well-preserved river settlement from the mid-19th century where architectural beauties beckon genteelly from the streets. At the **visitor center** (☎812-265-2956; www.visitmadison.org; 601 W First St; ⊙9am-5pm Mon-Fri, to 4pm Sat, 11am-3pm Sun), pick up a walking-tour brochure, which will lead you by notable landmarks.

Madison has motels around its edges, as well as several B&Bs. Main St lines up numerous places for a bite, interspersed with antique stores. Large, wooded **Clifty Falls State Park** (☎812-273-8885; tent & RV sites $16-33), off Hwy 56 and a couple of miles west of town, has camping, hiking trails, views and waterfalls.

In Clarksville, **Falls of the Ohio State Park** (☎812-280-9970; www.fallsoftheohio.org; 201 W Riverside Dr) has only rapids, no falls, but is of interest for its 386-million-year-old fossil beds. The newly renovated **interpretive center** (adult/child $5/2; ⊙9am-5pm Mon-Sat, from 1pm Sun) explains it all. Quench your thirst in adjacent New Albany, home to the **New Albanian Brewing Company Public House** (www.newalbanian.com; 3312 Plaza Dr; ⊙11am-11pm Mon-Sat). Or cross the bridge to Louisville, KY, where the tonsil-singeing native bourbon awaits...

Scenic Hwy 62 heads west and leads to the Lincoln Hills and southern Indiana's limestone caves. A plunge into **Marengo Cave** (☎812-365-2705; www.marengocave.com; ⊙9am-6pm Jun-Aug, to 5pm Sep-May), north on Hwy 66, is highly recommended. It offers a 40-minute tour (adult/child $15/8.50), 60-minute tour ($18/10) or combination tour ($25/14) walking past stalagmites and other ancient formations. The same group operates **Cave Country Canoes** (www.cavecountrycanoes.com; 112 W Main St; ⊙May-Oct) in nearby Milltown, with half-day ($26), full-day ($30) or longer trips on the scenic Blue River; keep an eye out for river otters and rare hellbender salamanders.

Four miles south of Dale, off I-64, is the **Lincoln Boyhood National Memorial** (☎812-937-4541; www.nps.gov/libo; adult/child/family $5/free/$10; ⊙8am-5pm), where young Abe lived from age seven to 21. This isolated site also includes admission to a working **pioneer farm** (⊙8am-5pm May-Aug).

DON'T MISS

THE GREAT LAKES' BEST PIE

- **Village Inn** (p561) Mmm, rhubarb custard.
- **Crane's Pie Pantry** (p586) Apples and peaches picked from the surrounding orchard.
- **Palms Grill Cafe** (p551) Retro goodness on Route 66.
- **Boyd & Wurthmann Restaurant** (p568) Lots of flaky options in Amish Country.
- **Betty's Pies** (p617) Resistance is futile when the crunch-topping arrives.

New Harmony

In southwest Indiana, the Wabash River forms the border with Illinois. Beside it, south of I-64, captivating New Harmony is the site of two early communal-living experiments and is worth a visit. In the early 19th century a German Christian sect, the Harmonists, developed a sophisticated town here while awaiting the Second Coming. Later, the British utopian Robert Owen acquired the town. Learn more and pick up a walking-tour map at the angular **Atheneum Visitors Center** (☎812-682-4474; www.usi.edu/hnh; 401 N Arthur St; ⏲9:30am-5pm, closed Jan–mid-Mar).

Today New Harmony retains an air of contemplation, if not otherworldliness, which you can experience at its newer attractions, such as the templelike Roofless Church and the Labyrinth, a maze symbolizing the spirit's quest. The town has a couple of guesthouses and camping at **Harmonie State Park** (☎812-682-4821; campsites $23-33). Pop into **Main Cafe** (508 Main St; mains $4-7; ⏲5:30am-1pm Mon-Fri) for a ham, bean and cornbread lunch, but save room for the coconut cream pie.

Northern Indiana

The truck-laden I-80/I-90 tollways cut across Indiana's north. Parallel US 20 is slower and cheaper, but not much more attractive.

Indiana Dunes

Sunny beaches, rustling grasses and woodsy campgrounds are the claim to fame at **Indiana Dunes National Lakeshore** (☎219-926-7561; www.nps.gov/indu) FREE which stretches along 15 miles of Lake Michigan shoreline. Swimming is allowed anywhere along the expanse. A short walk away from the beaches, several hiking paths crisscross the sand and woodlands. The best are the **Bailly-Chellberg Trail** (2.5 miles) that winds by a still operating 1870s farm, and the **Heron Rookery Trail** (2 miles), where blue herons flock. Oddly, all this natural bounty lies smack-dab next to smoke-belching factories and steel mills, which you'll also see at various vantage points. Stop at the park **visitor center** (Hwy 49; ⏲8am-6pm Jun-Aug, to 4:30pm Sep-May) for beach details and to pick up hiking, biking and birding maps.

Indiana Dunes State Park (☎219-926-1952; www.dnr.in.gov/parklake; per car $12) is a 2100-acre shoreside pocket within the national lakeshore; it's located at the end of Hwy 49, near Chesterton. It has more amenities, but also more regulations and more crowds (plus the vehicle entry fee). Wintertime brings out the cross-country skiers; summertime brings out the hikers. Seven trails zigzag over the landscape; No 4 up Mt Tom rewards with Chicago skyline views.

Other than a couple of beachfront snack bars, you won't find much to eat in the parks, so stop at **Great Lakes Cafe** (201 Mississippi St; mains $6-9; ⏲5am-3pm Mon-Fri, 6am-1pm Sat; 👪), the steelworkers' hearty favorite, at the Dunes' western edge in Gary.

The Dunes are an easy day trip from Chicago. Driving takes one hour (though parking can be a hassle). The **South Shore Metra train** (www.nictd.com) makes the journey from Millennium Station downtown, and it's about 1¼ hours to the Dune Park or Beverly Shores stops (note both stations are a 1.5-mile walk from the beach). Those who want to make a night of it can camp (national lakeshore campsites $18, state park tent and RV sites $23 to $36).

Right by the Illinois border, the steel cities of **Gary** and **East Chicago** present some of the bleakest urban landscapes anywhere. Taking the train (Amtrak or South Shore line) through here will get you up close and personal with the industrial underbelly.

South Bend

South Bend is home to the **University of Notre Dame**. You know how people in certain towns say, 'football is a religion here'? They mean it at Notre Dame, where 'Touchdown Jesus' lords over the 80,000-capacity stadium (it's a mural of the resurrected Christ with arms raised, though the pose bears a striking resemblance to a referee signaling a touchdown).

Tours of the pretty campus, with its two lakes, Gothic-style architecture and iconic Golden Dome atop the main building, start at the **visitor center** (www.nd.edu/visitors; 111 Eck Center). Less visited but worth a stop is the **Studebaker National Museum** (☎574-235-9714; www.studebakermuseum.org; 201 S Chapin St; adult/child $8/5; ⏰10am-5pm Mon-Sat, from noon Sun) near downtown, where you can gaze at a gorgeous 1956 Packard and other classic beauties that used to be built in South Bend.

Indiana Amish Country

East of South Bend, around **Shipshewana** and **Middlebury**, is the USA's third-largest Amish community. Horses and buggies clip-clop by, and long-bearded men hand-plow the tidy fields. Get situated with maps from the **Elkhart County CVB** (☎800-262-8161; www.amishcountry.org). Better yet, pick a back oad between the two towns and head down it. Often you'll see families selling beeswax candles, quilts and fresh produce on their porch, which beats the often-touristy shops and restaurants on the main roads. Note that most places close on Sunday.

Village Inn (☎574-825-2043; 105 S Main St; mains $3-9; ⏰5am-8pm Mon-Fri, 6am-2pm Sat; 📶), in Middlebury, sells sublime pies, like the best-selling rhubarb custard. Bonneted women in pastel dresses come in at 4:30am to bake the flaky wares. Arrive before noon, or you'll be looking at crumbs. Across the street, **41 Degrees North** (104 S Main St; ⏰11am-10:30pm Tue-Thu, to midnight Fri, 1pm-midnight Sat) pours a terrific regional beer selection. **Der Ruhe Blatz Motel** (☎260-758-0670; www.therestplace.com; 1195 S Van Buren St; r $68-105; ❄📶) is no-frills, but has a perfect location on Shipshewana's main road to see morning buggy traffic.

Auburn

Just before reaching the Ohio border, classic car connoisseurs should dip south on I-69 to the town of Auburn, where the Cord Company produced the USA's favorite cars in the 1920s and '30s The **Auburn Cord Duesenberg Museum** (☎260-925-1444; www.automobilemuseum.org; 1600 S Wayne St; adult/child $12.50/7.50; ⏰10am-7pm Mon-Fri, to 5pm Sat & Sun) has a wonderful display of early roadsters in a beautiful art-deco setting. Next door are the vintage rigs of the **National Automotive and Truck Museum** (☎260-925-9100; www.natmus.org; 1000 Gordon Buehrig Pl; adult/child $8/4; ⏰9am-5pm).

OHIO

All right, time for your Ohio quiz. In the Buckeye State you can 1) buggy-ride through the nation's largest Amish community; 2) lose your stomach on one of the world's fastest roller coasters; 3) suck down a dreamy creamy milkshake fresh from a working dairy; or 4) examine a massive, mysterious snake sculpture built into the earth. And the answer is... all of these. It hurts locals' feelings when visitors think the only thing to do here is tip over cows, so c'mon, give Ohio a chance. Besides these activities, you can partake in a five-way in Cincinnati and rock out in Cleveland.

Information

Ohio Division of Travel and Tourism (☎800-282-5393; www.discoverohio.com)

Ohio Highway Conditions (www.ohgo.com)

Ohio State Park Information (☎614-265-6561; http://parks.ohiodnr.gov) State parks are free to visit; some have free wi-fi. Tent and RV sites cost $19 to $39; reservations accepted (☎866-644-6727; http://ohiostateparks.reserveamerica.com; fee $8).

Cleveland

Does it or does it not rock? That is the question. Drawing from its roots as a working man's town, Cleveland has toiled hard in recent years to prove it does. Step one was to control the urban decay/river-on-fire thing – the Cuyahoga River was once so polluted that it actually burned. Step two was to bring a worthy attraction to town, say the Rock and Roll Hall of Fame. Step three was to clean up downtown's public spaces and add hip hotels and eateries. The gritty city has come a long way. Even LeBron James has deemed it happenin' enough to return to.

Sights & Activities

Cleveland's center is Public Sq, dominated by the conspicuous Terminal Tower and a ka-chinging casino. Most attractions are downtown on the lakefront or at University Circle (the area around Case Western Reserve University, Cleveland Clinic and other institutions).

Downtown

Rock and Roll Hall of Fame & Museum MUSEUM

(☎216-781-7625; www.rockhall.com; 1100 E 9th St; adult/child $22/13; ⏰10am-5:30pm, to 9pm Wed year-round, to 9pm Sat Jun-Aug) Cleveland's top attraction is like an overstuffed attic bursting with groovy finds: Jimi Hendrix' Stratocaster, Keith Moon's platform shoes, John Lennon's Sgt Pepper suit and a 1966 piece of hate mail to the Rolling Stones from a cursive-writing Fijian. It's more than memorabilia, though. Multimedia exhibits trace the history and social context of rock music and the performers who created it.

Why is the museum in Cleveland? Because this is the hometown of Alan Freed, the disk jockey who popularized the term 'rock and roll' in the early 1950s, and because the city lobbied hard and paid big. Be prepared for crowds (especially thick until 1pm or so).

Great Lakes Science Center MUSEUM

(☎216-694-2000; www.greatscience.com; 601 Erieside Ave; adult/child $15/12; ⏰10am-5pm Mon-Sat, from noon Sun; 👪) One of 10 museums in the country with a NASA affiliation, Great Lakes goes deep in space with rockets, moon stones and the 1973 Apollo capsule, as well as exhibits on the lakes' environmental problems.

William G Mather MUSEUM

(☎216-694-2000; www.greatscience.com; 601 Erieside Ave; adult/child $8/6; ⏰11am-5pm Tue-Sat, from noon Sun Jun-Aug, Sat & Sun only May, Sep & Oct, closed Nov-Apr) Take a self-guided walk on this huge freighter incarnated as a steamship museum. It's docked beside the Great Lakes Science Center, which manages it.

The Flats WATERFRONT

(www.flatseast.com) The Flats, an old industrial zone turned nightlife hub on the Cuyahoga River, has had a checkered life. After years of neglect, it's on the upswing once again. The East Bank has a waterfront boardwalk, stylish restaurants, bars and outdoor concert pavilion. The West Bank is a bit grittier and further flung, with an old garage turned brewery-winery, a skateboard park and some vintage dive bars among its assets.

OHIO FACTS

Nickname Buckeye State

Population 11.6 million

Area 44,825 sq miles

Capital city Columbus (population 822,500)

Other cities Cleveland (population 390,100), Cincinnati (population 297,500)

Sales tax 5.75%

Birthplace of Inventor Thomas Edison (1847–1931), author Toni Morrison (b 1931), entrepreneur Ted Turner (b 1938), filmmaker Steven Spielberg (b 1947)

Home of Cows, roller coasters, aviation pioneers the Wright Brothers

Politics Swing state

Famous for First airplane, first pro baseball team, birthplace of seven US presidents

State rock song 'Hang On Sloopy'

Driving distances Cleveland to Columbus 142 miles, Columbus to Cincinnati 108 miles

Ohio City & Tremont

West Side Market MARKET

(www.westsidemarket.org; cnr W 25th St & Lorain Ave; ⏰7am-4pm Mon & Wed, to 6pm Fri & Sat) The European-style market overflows with greengrocers and their fruit and vegetable pyramids, as well as purveyors of Hungarian sausage, Italian cannoli and Polish pierogi.

Christmas Story House & Museum MUSEUM

(☎216-298-4919; www.achristmasstoryhouse.com; 3159 W 11th St; adult/child $10/6; ⏰10am-5pm Mon-Sat, from noon Sun) Remember the beloved 1983 film *A Christmas Story,* in which Ralphie yearns for a Red Ryder BB gun? The original house sits in Tremont, complete with leg lamp. It's for true fans only.

University Circle

Several museums and attractions are within walking distance of each other at University Circle, 5 miles east of downtown. Carless? Take the HealthLine bus to Adelbert. The neighborhood's northern stretch is known as Uptown, with student-filled cafes.

★ **Cleveland Museum of Art** MUSEUM

(☎216-421-7340; www.clevelandart.org; 11150 East Blvd; ⏰10am-5pm Tue-Sun, to 9pm Wed & Fri) FREE Fresh off a whopping expansion, the art museum houses an excellent collection of European paintings, as well as African, Asian and American art. Head to the 2nd floor for rock-star works from Impressionists, Picasso and surrealists. Interactive touchscreens are stationed throughout the galleries and provide fun ways to learn more. Gallery One, near the entrance, holds a cool quick hit of museum highlights.

Museum of Contemporary Art Cleveland MUSEUM
(MOCA; ☑ audio tours 216-453-3960; www.moca-cleveland.org; 11400 Euclid Ave; adult/child $8/5; ⊙ 11am-5pm Tue-Sun, to 9pm Thu) The shiny building impresses, with four stories of geometric black steel, though there's not a lot to see inside. Floors 2 and 4 have the galleries; exhibits focus on an artist or two and change often. Call for an audio tour of the architecture and installations.

Lake View Cemetery CEMETERY
(☑ 216-421-2665; www.lakeviewcemetery.com; 12316 Euclid Ave; ⊙ 7:30am-7:30pm) Beyond the circle further east, don't forget this eclectic 'outdoor museum' where President James Garfield rests in an eye-poppingly enormous tower (it's especially grand for a guy who was president for only six months!). Other notables include local comic-book hero Harvey Pekar and crimefighter Eliot Ness (who happen to be side by side).

🛌 Sleeping

Prices listed are for summer, which is high season, and do not include the 16.5% tax. Several new boutique and business hotels are opening downtown as more conventions come to the city. Modest motels are southwest of Cleveland's center, near the airport. The W 150th exit off I-71 (exit 240) has several options for less than $100.

★**Cleveland Hostel** HOSTEL $
(☑ 216-394-0616; www.theclevelandhostel.com; 2090 W 25th St; dm/r from $28/71; ❄ 🛜) This newish hostel in Ohio City, steps from an RTA stop and the West Side Market, is fantastic. There are 15 rooms, a mix of dorms and private chambers. All have fluffy beds, fresh paint in soothing hues and nifty antique decor. Add in the sociable rooftop deck and free parking lot, and no wonder it's packed.

Holiday Inn Express HOTEL $$
(☑ 216-443-1000; www.hiexpress.com; 629 Euclid Ave; r $130-190; P ❄ @ 🛜) This goes way beyond the usual chain offering and is more like a true boutique hotel with large, nattily

WORLD'S LARGEST CHANDELIER & STAMP

Hokey but true: Cleveland recently installed the **World's Largest Outdoor Chandelier** (cnr Euclid & E 14th St). The 20ft sparkler, with 4200 faux crystals, dangles over Playhouse Sq and has become a popular photo op. It joins the **World's Largest Rubber Stamp** (Willard Park, near 9th St & Lakeside Ave), a kitschy sculpture downtown by Claes Oldenburg, where food trucks congregate and live music lets loose Friday afternoons May to October.

decorated rooms and lofty views. It's set in an old bank building that's conveniently located near the E 4th St entertainment strip. Do-it-yourself hot breakfast and evening drinks included. Parking costs $15.

Glidden House BOUTIQUE HOTEL $$
(☑ 216-231-8900; www.gliddenhouse.com; 1901 Ford Dr; r $160-180; P ❄ 🛜) The French-Gothic-Eclectic former mansion of the Glidden family (who got rich making paint) has been carved into a graceful, 60-room hotel. The common areas are lush, while the rooms are more understated. Continental breakfast is included. Located in University Circle and walkable to the museums.

Hilton Garden Inn HOTEL $$
(☑ 216-658-6400; www.hiltongardeninn.com; 1100 Carnegie Ave; r $110-169; P ❄ @ 🛜 ❄) While it's nothing fancy, the Hilton's rooms are decent value with comfy beds, wi-fi-rigged workstations and mini refrigerators. It's right by the baseball park. Parking costs $16.

🍴 Eating

🍴 Downtown

E 4th St, set under twinkling lights, rolls out several great options. Off the beaten path and east of the city center, Asiatown (bounded by Payne and St Clair Aves, and E 30th and 40ths Sts) has several Chinese, Vietnamese and Korean eateries.

Noodlecat NOODLES $
(☑ 216-589-0007; www.noodlecat.com; 234 Euclid Ave; mains $11-14; ⊙ 11am-10pm Sun-Thu, to 11pm Fri & Sat) Hep-cat noodles fill bowls at this Japanese-American mash-up. Slurp mushroom

udon, spicy octopus udon, beef short rib ramen and fried chicken ramen dishes. Lots of sake and craft beer help wash it down.

Lola MODERN AMERICAN $$$
(☎216-621-5652; www.lolabistro.com; 2058 E 4th St; mains $29-34; ⏰11:30am-2:30pm Mon-Fri, 5-10pm Mon-Thu, to 11pm Fri & Sat) Famous for his piercings, Food Channel TV appearances and multiple national awards, local boy Michael Symon put Cleveland on the foodie map with Lola. The lower-priced lunch dishes are the most fun, such as the egg-and-cheese-topped fried bologna sandwich. The glowy bar and open kitchen add a swank vibe for dinner.

Ohio City & Tremont

Ohio City (especially along W 25th St) and Tremont, which straddle I-90 south of downtown, are areas with hip new establishments popping up all the time.

Barrio MEXICAN $
(☎216-999-7714; www.barrio-tacos.com; 806 Literary St; tacos $3-4; ⏰4pm-2am Mon-Thu, from 11am Fri-Sun) The Tremont outpost of this small chain is abuzz with young locals smitten with the build-your-own tacos concept. Fillings include everything from Thai chili tofu to housemade chorizo. Pear, jalapeño and other unusually flavored margaritas add to the fun.

Mitchell's Ice Cream ICE CREAM $
(☎216-861-2799; www.mitchellshomemade.com; 1867 W 25th St; scoops $3.50-5; ⏰11am-10pm Sun-Thu, to midnight fri & Sat; 🖉) Mitchell's revamped an old movie theater into an ice-cream-making facility. Watch staff blend the rich flavors through big glass windows. The goods are super creamy, and the vegan options are brilliant. Staff are generous with samples.

Little Italy & Coventry

These two neighborhoods make prime stops for refueling after hanging out in University Circle. Little Italy is closest: it's along Mayfield Rd, near Lake View Cemetery (look out for the Rte 322 sign). Alternatively, relaxed Coventry Village is a bit further east off Mayfield Rd.

Presti's Bakery BAKERY $
(☎216-421-3060; www.prestisbakery.com; 12101 Mayfield Rd; items $2-6; ⏰6am-9pm Mon-Thu, to 10pm Fri & Sat, to 6pm Sun) Try Presti's for its popular sandwiches, stromboli and divine pastries.

Tommy's INTERNATIONAL $
(☎216-321-7757; www.tommyscoventry.com; 1823 Coventry Rd; mains $8-13; ⏰9am-9pm Sun-Thu, to 10pm Fri, 7:30am-10pm Sat; 📶🖉) Tofu, seitan and other old-school veggie dishes emerge from the kitchen, though carnivores have multiple options, too.

Drinking & Nightlife

Tremont is chockablock with chic bars, Ohio City with breweries. Downtown has the young, testosterone-fueled Warehouse District (around W 6th St) and the resurgent Flats. Most places stay open until 2am.

Great Lakes Brewing Company BREWERY
(www.greatlakesbrewing.com; 2516 Market Ave; ⏰11:30am-midnight Mon-Thu, to 1am Fri & Sat) Great Lakes wins numerous prizes for its brewed-on-the-premises beers. Added historical bonus: Eliot Ness got into a shoot-out with criminals here; ask the bartender to show you the bullet holes.

Platform Beer Co BREWERY
(www.platformbeerco.com; 4125 Lorain Ave; ⏰3pm-midnight Mon-Thu, to 2am Fri & Sat) An all-ages, cool-cat crowd gathers around the silvery tanks in Platform's tasting room for $5 pints of innovative saisons, pale ales and more. The location is a bit far flung, at Ohio City's southern edge, but the brewmaster has launched a private bike-share program from the site; ask the bartender for details.

Merwin's Wharf BAR
(www.merwinswharf.com; 1785 Merwin Ave; ⏰3-10pm Tue & Wed, 11am-11pm Thu-Sat, to 9pm Sun) It's a lovely spot to sip on the riverfront patio with views of the skyline, bridges and boats gliding by; located on the Flats' West Bank.

Entertainment

Gordon Square Arts District (www.gordonsquare.org) has a fun pocket of theaters, live-music venues and cafes along Detroit Ave between W 56th and W 69th Sts, a few miles west of downtown.

Live Music

Check *Scene* (www.clevescene.com) and Friday's *Plain Dealer* (www.cleveland.com) for listings.

★ **Happy Dog** LIVE MUSIC
(www.happydogcleveland.com; 5801 Detroit Ave; ⏰4pm-12:30am Mon-Wed, 11am-2:30am Thu-Sat, to 12:30am Sun) Listen to scrappy bands while munching on a weenie, for which you can

choose from among 50 toppings, from gourmet (black truffle) to, er, less gourmet (peanut butter and jelly); in the Gordon Sq district.

Grog Shop LIVE MUSIC
(☎216-321-5588; www.grogshop.gs; 2785 Euclid Heights Blvd) Up-and-coming rockers thrash at Coventry's long-established music house.

Beachland Ballroom LIVE MUSIC
(www.beachlandballroom.com; 15711 Waterloo Rd) Hip young bands play at this venue east of downtown.

Sports

Cleveland is a serious jock town with three modern downtown venues.

Progressive Field BASEBALL
(www.indians.com; 2401 Ontario St) The Indians (aka 'the Tribe') hit here; great sightlines make it a good park to see a game.

Quicken Loans Arena BASKETBALL
(www.nba.com/cavaliers; 1 Center Ct) The Cavaliers play basketball at 'the Q,' which doubles as an entertainment venue. All is well here now that LeBron James has come home.

First Energy Stadium FOOTBALL
(www.clevelandbrowns.com; 1085 W 3rd St) The NFL's Browns pass the football and score touchdowns on the lakefront.

Performing Arts

Severance Hall CLASSICAL MUSIC
(☎216-231-1111; www.clevelandorchestra.com; 11001 Euclid Ave) The acclaimed Cleveland Symphony Orchestra holds its season (August to May) at Severance Hall, located by the University Circle museums.

Playhouse Square THEATER
(☎216-771-4444; www.playhousesquare.org; 1501 Euclid Ave) Several stages comprise the elegant center, which hosts theater, opera and ballet. Check the website for $10 to $20 'Smart Seats.'

ℹ Information

INTERNET ACCESS

Many of Cleveland's public places have free wi-fi, such as Tower City and University Circle.

MEDIA

Gay People's Chronicle (www.gaypeopleschronicle.com) Free weekly publication with entertainment listings.
Plain Dealer (www.cleveland.com) The city's main newspaper.
Scene (www.clevescene.com) A weekly entertainment paper.

MEDICAL SERVICES

MetroHealth Medical Center (☎216-778-7800; 2500 MetroHealth Dr)

TOURIST INFORMATION

Cleveland Convention & Visitors Bureau (www.thisiscleveland.com) Official website, chock-full for planning.
Visitor Center (☎216-875-6680; 334 Euclid Ave; ⏰9am-6pm Mon-Sat) Staff provide maps and reservation assistance; there's a sweet, arty souvenir shop attached.

USEFUL WEBSITES

Cool Cleveland (www.coolcleveland.com) Hip arts and cultural happenings.
Ohio City (www.ohiocity.org) Eats and drinks in the neighborhood.
Tremont (www.tremontwest.org) Eats, drinks and gallery hops.

ℹ Getting There & Around

Eleven miles southwest of downtown, **Cleveland Hopkins International Airport** (CLE; www.clevelandairport.com; 5300 Riverside Dr) is linked by the Red Line train ($2.25). A cab to downtown costs about $35.

From downtown, **Greyhound** (☎216-781-0520; 1465 Chester Ave) offers frequent departures to Chicago (7½ hours) and New York City (13 hours). **Megabus** (www.megabus.com/us) also goes to Chicago, often for lower fares; check the website for the departure point.

Amtrak (☎216-696-5115; 200 Cleveland Memorial Shoreway) runs once daily to Chicago (seven hours) and New York City (13 hours).

The **Regional Transit Authority** (RTA; www.riderta.com; fares $2.25) operates the Red Line train that goes to both the airport and Ohio City. It also runs the HealthLine bus that motors along Euclid Ave from downtown to University Circle's museums. Day passes are $5. Free trolleys also loop around downtown's core business and entertainment zones.

For taxis, try **Americab** (☎216-881-1111).

Around Cleveland

Sixty miles south of Cleveland, **Canton** is the birthplace of the NFL and home to the **Pro Football Hall of Fame** (☎330-456-8207; www.profootballhof.com; 2121 George Halas Dr; adult/child $24/17; ⏰9am-8pm, to 5pm Sep-May). The shrine for the gridiron-obsessed has new interactive exhibits and videos even casual fans will appreciate; a hotel and entertainment complex are also being built. Look for the football-shaped tower off I-77.

West of Cleveland, attractive **Oberlin** is an old-fashioned college town, with noteworthy architecture by Cass Gilbert, Frank Lloyd Wright and Robert Venturi. Further west, just south of I-90, the tiny town of **Milan** is the birthplace of Thomas Edison. His home, restored to its 1847 likeness, is now a small **museum** (☎419-499-2135; www.tomedison.org; 9 Edison Dr; adult/child $7/5; ⌚10am-5pm Tue-Sat, from 1pm Sun, reduced hours winter, closed Jan) outlining his inventions, like the light bulb and phonograph.

Erie Lakeshore & Islands

In summer this good-time resort area is one of the busiest – and most expensive – places in Ohio. The season lasts from mid-May to mid-September, and then just about everything shuts down. Make sure you prebook your accommodations.

Sandusky, long a port, now serves as the jump-off point to the Erie Islands and a mighty group of roller coasters. The **visitor center** (☎419-625-2984; www.shoresandislands.com; 4424 Milan Rd; ⌚8am-7pm Mon-Fri, 9am-6pm Sat, 9am-4pm Sun) provides lodging and ferry information. Loads of chain motels line the highways heading into town.

DON'T MISS

CEDAR POINT'S RAGING ROLLER COASTERS

Cedar Point Amusement Park (☎419-627-2350; www.cedarpoint.com; adult/child $62/40; ⌚hours vary, closed Nov–mid-May) regularly wins the 'world's best amusement park' award, chosen each year by the public, which goes wild for the venue's 16 adrenaline-pumping roller coasters. Stomach-droppers include the Top Thrill Dragster, one of the globe's tallest and fastest rides. It climbs 420ft into the air before plunging and whipping around at 120mph. Meanwhile, the wing-like GateKeeper loops, corkscrews and dangles riders from the world's highest inversion (meaning you're upside down a *lot*). If those and the 14 other coasters aren't enough to keep you occupied, the surrounding area has a nice beach, a water park and a slew of old-fashioned, cotton-candy-fueled attractions. It's about 6 miles from Sandusky. Buying tickets in advance online saves money. Parking costs $15.

Bass Islands

In 1812's Battle of Lake Erie, Admiral Perry met the enemy English fleet near **South Bass Island**. His victory ensured that all the lands south of the Great Lakes became US, not Canadian, territory. But history is all but forgotten on a summer weekend in packed **Put In Bay**, the island's main town and a party place full of boaters, restaurants and shops. Move beyond it, and you'll find a winery and opportunities for camping, fishing, kayaking and swimming.

A singular attraction is the 352ft Doric column known as **Perry's Victory and International Peace Memorial** (www.nps.gov/pevi; admission $3; ⌚10am-6pm, closed mid-Oct–mid-May). Climb to the observation deck for views of the battle site and, on a good day, Canada.

The **Chamber of Commerce** (☎419-285-2832; www.visitputinbay.com; 148 Delaware Ave; ⌚10am-4pm Mon-Fri, to 5pm Sat & Sun) has information on activities and lodging. **Ashley's Island House** (☎419-285-2844; www.ashleysislandhouse.com; 557 Catawba Ave; r $110-195; ❄📶) is a 12-room B&B, where naval officers stayed in the late 1800s. The **Beer Barrel Saloon** (www.beerbarrelpib.com; Delaware Ave; ⌚11am-1am) has plenty of space for imbibing – its bar is 406ft long. Live bands and Jello shots are part of the package.

Cabs and tour buses serve the island, though cycling is a fine way to get around. Two ferry companies make the trip regularly from the mainland. **Jet Express** (☎800-245-1538; www.jet-express.com) runs passenger-only boats direct to Put In Bay from Port Clinton (one-way adult/child $18/3, 30 minutes) almost hourly. Leave your car in the lot (per day $12) at the dock. **Miller Ferries** (☎800-500-2421; www.millerferry.com) operates a vehicle ferry that is the cheapest option, departing from further-flung Catawba (one-way adult/child $7/1.50, car $15) every 30 minutes; the crossing takes 20 minutes. It also cruises to **Middle Bass Island**, a good day trip from South Bass, offering nature and quiet.

Kelleys Island

Peaceful and green, Kelleys Island is a popular weekend escape, especially for families. It has pretty 19th-century buildings, Native American pictographs, a good beach and glacial grooves raked through its landscape. Even its old limestone quarries are scenic.

The **Chamber of Commerce** (www.kelleysislandchamber.com; 240 E Lakeshore Dr; ⌚9:30am-4pm), by the ferry dock, has information on accommodations and activities – hiking, camping, kayaking and fishing are popular. **The Village**, the island's small commercial center, has places to eat, drink, shop and rent bicycles – the recommended way to sightsee.

Kelleys Island Ferry (☎419-798-9763; www.kelleysislandferry.com) departs from the wee village of Marblehead (one-way adult/child $10/6.25, car $16). The crossing takes about 20 minutes and leaves hourly (more frequently in summer). **Jet Express** (☎800-245-1538; www.jet-express.com) departs from Sandusky (one-way adult/child $18/4.75, no cars); the trip takes 25 minutes. It also goes onward to Put In Bay on South Bass Island (one-way adult/child $13/3, no cars).

Pelee Island

Pelee, the largest Erie island, is a ridiculously green, quiet wine-producing and bird-watching destination that belongs to Canada. **Pelee Island Transportation** (☎800-661-2220; www.ontarioferries.com) runs a ferry (one-way adult/child $13.75/6.75, car $30) from Sandusky to Pelee, and then onward to Ontario's mainland. Check www.pelee.com for lodging and trip-planning information.

Amish Country

Rural Wayne and Holmes counties are home to the USA's largest Amish community. They're only 80 miles south of Cleveland, but visiting here is like entering a pre-industrial time warp.

Descendants of conservative Dutch-Swiss religious factions who migrated to the USA during the 18th century, the Amish continue to follow the *ordnung* (way of life), in varying degrees. Many adhere to rules prohibiting the use of electricity, telephones and motorized vehicles. They wear traditional clothing, farm the land with plow and mule, and go to church in horse-drawn buggies. Others are not so strict.

Unfortunately, what would surely be a peaceful country scene is often disturbed by behemoth tour buses. Many Amish are happy to profit from this influx of outside dollars, but don't equate this with free photographic access – the Amish typically view photographs as taboo. Drive carefully as roads are narrow and curvy. Many places are closed Sunday.

Sights & Activities

Kidron, on Rte 52, makes a good starting point. A short distance south, **Berlin** is the area's tchotchke-shop-filled core, while **Millersburg** is the region's largest town, more antique-y than Amish; US 62 connects these two 'busy' spots.

To get further off the beaten path, take Rte 557 or County Rd 70, both of which twist through the countryside to wee **Charm**, about 5 miles south of Berlin.

Lehman's DEPARTMENT STORE
(www.lehmans.com; 4779 Kidron Rd, Kidron; ⌚8am-6pm Mon-Sat) Lehman's is an absolute must-see. It is the Amish community's main purveyor of modern-looking products that use no electricity, housed in a 32,000-sq-ft barn. Stroll through to ogle wind-up flashlights, wood-burning stoves and hand-cranked meat grinders.

Kidron Auction MARKET
(www.kidronauction.com; 4885 Kidron Rd, Kidron; ⌚from 10am Thu) FREE If it's Thursday, follow the buggy lineup down the road from Lehman's store to the livestock barn. Hay gets auctioned at 10:15am, cows at 11am and pigs at 1pm. A flea market rings the barn for folks seeking non-mooing merchandise.

Hershberger's Farm & Bakery FARM
(☎330-674-6096; 5452 Hwy 557, Millersburg; ⌚bakery 8am-5pm Mon-Sat year-round, farm from 10am mid-Apr–Oct; 👪) Gorge on 25 kinds of pie, homemade ice-cream cones and seasonal produce from the market inside. Pet the farmyard animals (free) and take pony rides ($3) outside.

Heini's Cheese Chalet TOUR
(☎800-253-6636; www.heinis.com; 6005 Hwy 77, Berlin; ⌚8am-6pm Mon-Sat) Heini's whips up more than 70 cheeses. Learn how Amish farmers hand-milk their cows and spring-cool (versus machine-refrigerate) the output before delivering it each day. Then grab abundant samples and peruse the kitschy *History of Cheesemaking* mural. To see the curd-cutting in action, come before 11am weekdays (except on Wednesday and Saturday).

Yoder's Amish Home FARM
(☎330-893-2541; www.yodersamishhome.com; 6050 Rte 515, Walnut Creek; tours adult/child

$12/8; 10am-5pm Mon-Sat late Apr-late Oct;) Peek into a local home and one-room schoolhouse, and take a buggy ride through a field at this Amish farm that's open to visitors.

Sleeping & Eating

Hotel Millersburg HISTORIC HOTEL **$$**
(330-674-1457; www.hotelmillersburg.com; 35 W Jackson St, Millersburg; r $79-149;) Built in 1847 as a stagecoach inn, the property still provides lodging in its 26 casual rooms, which sit above a modern dining room and tavern (one of the few places to get a beer in Amish Country).

Guggisberg Swiss Inn HOTEL **$$**
(330-893-3600; www.guggisbergswissinn.com; 5025 Rte 557, Charm; r $120-150;) The 24 tidy, bright and compact rooms have quilts and light-wood furnishings. A cheesemaking facility and horseback riding stable are on the grounds, too.

Boyd & Wurthmann Restaurant AMERICAN **$**
(330-893-3287; www.boydandwurthmann.com; Main St, Berlin; mains $6-12; 5:30am-8pm Mon-Sat) Hubcap-sized pancakes, 23 pie flavors, fat sandwiches and Amish specialties such as country-fried steak draw locals and tourists alike. Cash only.

Information

Holmes County Chamber of Commerce
(www.visitamishcountry.com)

Columbus

Ohio's capital city is like the blind date your mom arranges – average looking, restrained personality, but solid and affable. Better yet, this city's easy on the wallet, an influence from Ohio State University's 57,000-plus students (the campus is the nation's second largest). A substantial gay population has taken up residence in Columbus in recent years.

Sights & Activities

German Village AREA
(www.germanvillage.com) The remarkably large, all-brick German Village, a half-mile south of downtown, is a restored 19th-century neighborhood with beer halls, cobbled streets, arts-filled parks and Italianate and Queen Anne architecture.

Short North AREA
(www.shortnorth.org) Just north of downtown, the browseworthy Short North is a redeveloped strip of High St that holds contemporary art galleries, restaurants and jazz bars.

Wexner Center for the Arts ARTS CENTER
(614-292-3535; www.wexarts.org; 1871 N High St; admission $8; 11am-6pm Tue & Wed, to 8pm Thu & Fri, noon-7pm Sat, to 4pm Sun) The campus arts center offers cutting-edge art exhibits, films and performances.

Columbus Food Tours TOUR
(www.columbusfoodadventures.com; tours $50-60) Foodie guides lead tours by neighborhood or theme (ie taco trucks, desserts, coffee), some by foot and others by van.

Sleeping & Eating

German Village and the Short North provide fertile grazing and guzzling grounds. The **Arena District** (www.arenadistrict.com) bursts with midrange chains and brewpubs. Around the university and along N High St from 15th Ave onward, you'll find everything from Mexican to Ethiopian to sushi.

Marriott Residence Inn HOTEL **$$**
(614-222-2610; www.marriott.com; 36 E Gay St; r $149-229; P@) A great location downtown, close to everything. All rooms are suites with a full kitchen. The cute free breakfast buffet is served in the old bank vault each morning. Wi-fi is free; parking is $20.

50 Lincoln-Short North B&B B&B **$$**
(614-299-5050; www.columbus-bed-breakfast.com; 50 E Lincoln St; r $139-159; P) The seven well-maintained rooms are steps away from the Short North's scene.

Schmidt's GERMAN **$**
(614-444-6808; www.schmidthaus.com; 240 E Kossuth St; mains $10-16; 11am-10pm Sun-Thu, to 11pm Fri & Sat) In German Village, shovel in Old Country staples like sausage and schnitzel, but save room for the whopping half-pound cream puffs. Oompah bands play Wednesday to Saturday.

North Market MARKET **$**
(www.northmarket.com; 59 Spruce St; 10am-5pm Sun-Mon, 9am-7pm Tue-Sat) Local farmers' produce and prepared foods; seek out the renowned Jeni's Ice Cream.

Skillet AMERICAN **$**
(614-443-2266; www.skilletruf.com; 410 E Whittier St; mains $12-16; 8am-2pm Wed-Sun) This teeny restaurant in German Village serves rustic, locally sourced fare.

Entertainment

Spectator sports rule the city.

Ohio Stadium FOOTBALL
(☎800-462-8257; www.ohiostatebuckeyes.com; 411 Woody Hayes Dr) The Ohio State Buckeyes pack a rabid crowd into legendary, horseshoe-shaped Ohio Stadium for their games, held on Saturdays in the fall. Expect 102,000 extra partiers in town.

Nationwide Arena HOCKEY
(☎614-246-2000; www.bluejackets.com; 200 W Nationwide Blvd) The pro Columbus Blue Jackets slap the puck at downtown's big arena.

Huntington Park BASEBALL
(www.clippersbaseball.com; 330 Huntington Park Lane) The Columbus Clippers (minor league team of the Cleveland Indians) bats at this stadium. Games are inexpensive and a blast.

Information

Alive (www.columbusalive.com) Free weekly entertainment newspaper.

Columbus Convention & Visitors Bureau (☎866-397-2657; www.experiencecolumbus.com)

Columbus Dispatch (www.dispatch.com) The daily newspaper.

Getting There & Around

The **Port Columbus Airport** (CMH; www.flycolumbus.com) is 10 miles east of town. A cab to downtown costs about $25.

Greyhound (☎614-221-4642; www.greyhound.com; 111 E Town St) buses run at least six times daily to Cincinnati (two hours) and Cleveland (2½ hours). Often cheaper, **Megabus** (www.megabus.com/us) runs a couple times daily to Cincinnati and Chicago. Check the website for locations.

Athens & Southeastern Ohio

Ohio's southeastern corner cradles most of its forested areas, as well as the rolling foothills of the Appalachian Mountains and scattered farms.

Around Lancaster, southeast of Columbus, the hills lead gently into **Hocking County**, a region of streams and waterfalls, sandstone cliffs and cavelike formations. It's splendid to explore in any season, with miles of trails for hiking and rivers for canoeing, as well as abundant campgrounds and cabins at **Hocking Hills State Park** (☎740-385-6165; www.thehockinghills.org; 20160 Hwy 664; campsites/cottages from $24/130). **Old Man's Cave** is a scenic winner for hiking. **Hocking Hills Adventures** (☎740-385-8685; www.hockinghillscanoeing.com; 31251 Chieftain Dr; 2hr tours $45; ⏲Apr-Oct) lets you paddle by moonlight and tiki torch from nearby Logan. The town also is home to the **Columbus Washboard Company** (☎740-380-3828; www.columbuswashboard.com; 14 Gallagher Ave; adult/child $4/2; ⏲tours 10am, noon & 2pm Mon-Fri year-round, plus 11:30am & 1pm Sat May-Oct); channel your jug band fantasies on a factory tour and in the tiny museum. Continue the hillbilly theme 12 miles east in New Straitsville, where a hissing, coil-laden **moonshine distillery** (☎740-394-2622; www.facebook.com/straitsvillespecialmoonshine; 105 W Main St; ⏲noon-7pm Mon-Thu, to 8pm Fri, 10am-8pm Sat) operates. A few sips in the tasting room will put hair on your chest.

Athens (www.athensohio.com) makes a lovely base for seeing the region. Situated where US 50 crosses US 33, it's set among wooded hills and built around the Ohio University campus (which comprises half the town). Student cafes and pubs line Court St, Athens' main road. The **Village Bakery & Cafe** (www.dellazona.com; 268 E State St; mains $4-8; ⏲7:30am-8pm Tue-Fri, to 6pm Sat, 9am-2pm Sun) uses organic veggies, grass-fed meat and farmstead cheeses in its pizzas, soups and sandwiches.

The area south of Columbus was a center for the fascinating ancient Hopewell people, who left behind huge geometric earthworks and burial mounds from around 200 BC to AD 600. For a fine introduction visit the

WORTH A TRIP

MALABAR FARM

What do Bogie, Bacall and Johnny Appleseed have in common? They've all spent time at **Malabar Farm State Park** (www.malabarfarm.org). There's a lot going on here: hiking and horse trails; pond fishing (ask for a free rod at the visitor center); tours of Pulitzer-winner Louis Bromfield's home (where Humphrey Bogart and Lauren Bacall got married); monthly barn dances; a farmhouse hostel (www.hiusa.org/lucas); and a fine restaurant (open 11am to 8pm Tuesday through Sunday) that uses ingredients from the grounds. Malabar is 30 miles west of Millersburg via Hwy 39.

Hopewell Culture National Historical Park (☎740-774-1126; www.nps.gov/hocu; Hwy 104 north of I-35; ⏲8:30am-5pm) FREE, 3 miles north of Chillicothe. Stop in at the visitor center, and then wander about the variously shaped ceremonial mounds spread over 13-acre **Mound City**, a mysterious town of the dead. **Serpent Mound** (☎937-587-2796; www.ohiohistory.org; 3850 Hwy 73; per vehicle $8; ⏲10am-4pm Mon-Thu, 9am-6pm Fri-Sun, reduced hours in winter), southwest of Chillicothe and 4 miles northwest of Locust Grove, is perhaps the most captivating site of all. The giant, uncoiling snake stretches over a quarter of a mile and is the largest effigy mound in the USA.

Dayton & Yellow Springs

Dayton has the aviation sights, but little Yellow Springs (18 miles northeast on US 68) has much more to offer in terms of accommodations and places to eat.

Sights

★National Museum of the US Air Force MUSEUM
(☎937-255-3286; www.nationalmuseum.af.mil; 1100 Spaatz St, Dayton; ⏲9am-5pm) FREE Located at the Wright-Patterson Air Force Base, 6 miles northeast of Dayton, the huuuuge museum has everything from a Wright Brothers 1909 Flyer to a Sopwith Camel (WWI biplane) and the 'Little Boy' type atomic bomb (decommissioned and rendered safe for display) dropped on Hiroshima. The hangars hold miles of planes, rockets and aviation machines. A spiffy new building adds space craft and presidential planes starting in summer 2016. Download the audio tour from the website before arriving. Plan on three or more hours here.

Wright Cycle Company HISTORIC SITE
(☎937-225-7705; www.nps.gov/daav; 16 S Williams St, Dayton; ⏲9am-5pm) FREE Browse exhibits in the original building where Wilbur and Orville developed bikes and aviation ideas.

Huffman Prairie Flying Field HISTORIC SITE
(Gate 16A off Rte 444, Dayton; ⏲8am-6pm) FREE This peaceful patch of grass looks much as it did in 1904 when the Wright Brothers tested aircraft here. A 1-mile walking trail loops around, marked with history-explaining placards. It's a 15-minute drive from the Air Force museum.

Carillon Historical Park HISTORIC SITE
(☎937-293-2841; www.daytonhistory.org; 1000 Carillon Blvd, Dayton; adult/child $8/5; ⏲9:30am-5pm Mon-Sat, from noon Sun) The many heritage attractions include the 1905 Wright Flyer III biplane, a replica of the Wright workshop and an 1850s-style brewery where you can drink the wares.

Sleeping & Eating

The following are located in artsy, beatnik Yellow Springs.

Morgan House B&B $$
(☎937-767-1761; www.arthurmorganhouse.com; 120 W Limestone St, Yellow Springs; r $125-145; ❄📶) The six comfy rooms have super-soft linens and private baths. Breakfasts are organic. It's walkable to the main business district.

★Young's Jersey Dairy AMERICAN $
(☎937-325-0629; www.youngsdairy.com; 6880 Springfield-Xenia Rd, Yellow Springs; 📶) Young's is a working dairy farm with two restaurants: the **Golden Jersey Inn** (mains $10-17; ⏲11am-8pm Mon-Thu, to 9pm Fri, 8am-9pm Sat, to 8pm Sun), serving dishes like buttermilk chicken; and the **Dairy Store** (sandwiches $3.50-6.50; ⏲7am-10pm Sun-Thu, to 11pm Fri & Sat), serving sandwiches, dreamy ice cream and Ohio's best milkshakes. There's also mini-golf, batting cages, cheesemaking tours and opportunities to watch the cows get milked.

Winds Cafe AMERICAN $$$
(☎937-767-1144; www.windscafe.com; 215 Xenia Ave, Yellow Springs; mains $23-28; ⏲11:30am-2pm & 5-9:30pm Tue-Sat, 10am-3pm Sun) A hippie co-op 30-plus years ago, the Winds has grown up to become a sophisticated foodie favorite plating seasonal dishes such as fig-sauced asparagus crepes and rhubarb halibut.

Cincinnati

Cincinnati splashes up the Ohio River's banks. Its prettiness surprises, as do its neon troves, its European-style neighborhoods, and the locals' unashamed ardor for a five-way. Amid all that action, don't forget to catch a baseball game, stroll the bridge-striped riverfront and visit the dummy museum.

Sights & Activities

Many attractions are closed on Monday.

Downtown & Over-the-Rhine

At downtown's northern edge, the historic Over-the-Rhine (OTR) neighborhood holds a whopping spread of 19th-century Italianate and Queen Anne buildings that are morphing into trendy eateries and shops. Parts of the area are edgy, but the Gateway District around 12th and Vine Sts is well trod.

National Underground Railroad Freedom Center MUSEUM

(☎513-333-7500; www.freedomcenter.org; 50 E Freedom Way; adult/child $14/10; ⏰11am-5pm Tue-Sun Jun-Aug, closed Sun Sep-May) Cincinnati was a prominent stop on the Underground Railroad and a center for abolitionist activities led by residents such as Harriet Beecher Stowe. The Freedom Center tells their stories. Exhibits show how slaves escaped to the north, and the ways in which slavery still exists today. Download the free iPhone app for extra insight while touring.

Findlay Market MARKET

(www.findlaymarket.org; 1801 Race St; ⏰9am-6pm Tue-Fri, 8am-6pm Sat, 10am-4pm Sun) Indoor-outdoor Findlay Market lies deep in Over-the-Rhine, in a somewhat blighted section. The funky, wrought-iron-framed structure has been a public market since 1855. It's a good stop for fresh produce, meats, cheeses and baked goods. The Belgian waffle guy will wow your taste buds.

Contemporary Arts Center MUSEUM

(☎513-345-8400; www.contemporaryartscenter.org; 44 E 6th St; adult/child $7.50/5.50, free Wed evening; ⏰10am-4pm Mon, to 9pm Wed-Fri, to 4pm Sat & Sun) This center displays modern art in an avant-garde building designed by Iraqi architect Zaha Hadid. The structure and artworks are a pretty big deal for traditionalist Cincy. The focus is on 'art of the last five minutes.'

Fountain Square PLAZA

(www.myfountainsquare.com; cnr 5th & Vine Sts) Fountain Sq is the city's centerpiece, a public space with a seasonal ice rink, free wi-fi, concerts (7pm Tuesday to Saturday in summer), a Reds ticket kiosk and the fancy old 'Genius of Water' fountain.

Roebling Suspension Bridge BRIDGE

(www.roeblingbridge.org) The elegant 1876 spanner was a forerunner of John Roebling's famous Brooklyn Bridge in New York. It's cool to walk across while passing cars make it 'sing' around you. It links to Covington, KY.

Purple People Bridge BRIDGE

(www.purplepeoplebridge.com) This pedestrian-only bridge provides a unique crossing from Sawyer Point (a nifty park dotted by whimsical monuments and flying pigs) to Newport, KY.

DON'T MISS

BEST OFFBEAT SIGHTS

Columbus Washboard Company (p569) Tour the quirky factory and museum.

Spam Museum (p615) Fun with canned meat.

World's Largest Ball of Twine (p613) View the 17,400lb behemoth.

Concrete Park (p602) A lumberjack's extraordinary folk art.

National Mustard Museum (p600) More than 5000 wacky condiments.

Covington & Newport

Covington and Newport, KY, are sort of suburbs of Cincinnati, just over the river from downtown. Newport is to the east and known for its massive **Newport on the Levee** (www.newportonthelevee.com) restaurant and shopping complex. Covington lies to the west and has the **MainStrasse** (www.mainstrasse.org) quarter, filled with funky restaurants and bars in the neighborhood's 19th-century brick row houses. Antebellum mansions fringe Riverside Dr, and old paddle-wheel boats tie up along the water's edge.

Newport Aquarium AQUARIUM

(☎859-491-3467; www.newportaquarium.com; 1 Aquarium Way; adult/child $23/15; ⏰9am-7pm Jun-Aug, 10am-6pm Sep-May; 👪) Meet parading penguins, Sweet Pea the shark ray and lots of other razor-toothed fish at Newport's large, well-regarded facility.

Mt Adams

It might be a bit of a stretch to compare Mt Adams, immediately east of downtown, to Paris' Montmartre, but this hilly 19th-century enclave of narrow, twisting streets, Victorian town houses, galleries, bars and restaurants is certainly a pleasurable surprise. Most visitors ascend for a quick look around and a drink.

To get here, follow 7th St east of downtown to Gilbert Ave, then turn right on Eden Park Dr and head up the hill to reach the lakes, paths and cultural offerings in Eden Park.

Cincinnati Art Museum MUSEUM
(513-721-2787; www.cincinnatiartmuseum.org; 953 Eden Park Dr; 11am-5pm Tue-Sun) FREE The collection spans 6000 years, with an emphasis on ancient Middle Eastern art and European old masters, plus a wing devoted to local works. Parking costs $4, or get here via bus 1.

West End

Cincinnati Museum Center MUSEUM
(513-287-7000; www.cincymuseum.org; 1301 Western Ave; adult/child $18/13; 10am-5pm Mon-Sat, 11am-6pm Sun;) Two miles northwest of downtown, this museum complex occupies the 1933 Union Terminal, an art-deco jewel still used by Amtrak. The interior has fantastic murals made of local Rookwood tiles. The **Museum of Natural History** is mostly geared to kids, but it does have a limestone cave with real bats inside. A history museum, children's museum and Omnimax theater round out the offerings; the admission fee provides entry to all. Parking costs $6.

OFF THE BEATEN TRACK

VENT HAVEN VENTRILOQUIST MUSEUM

Jeepers creepers! When you first glimpse the roomful of goggle-eyed wooden heads staring mutely into space, try not to run screaming for the door. (If you've seen the film *Magic*, you know what dummies are capable of.) Local William Shakespeare Berger started the **Vent Haven Museum** (859-341-0461; www.venthavenmuseum.com; 33 W Maple Ave; adult/child $10/5; by appt May-Sep) after amassing a collection of some 700 dolls. Today Jacko the red-fezzed monkey, turtleneck-clad Woody DeForest and the rest of the crew sit silently throughout three buildings. A curator gives guided tours. The museum is located in Fort Mitchell, KY, about 4 miles southwest of Covington off I-71/75.

American Sign Museum MUSEUM
(513-541-6366; www.americansignmuseum.org; 1330 Monmouth Ave; adult/child $15/free; 10am-4pm Wed-Sat, from noon Sun) This museum stocks an awesome cache of flashing, lightbulb-studded beacons in an old parachute factory. You'll burn your retinas staring at vintage neon drive-in signs, hulking genies and the Frisch's Big Boy, among other nostalgic novelties. Guides lead tours at 11am and 2pm that also visit the on-site neon-sign-making shop. It's located in the Camp Washington neighborhood (near Northside); take exit 3 off I-75.

Tours

American Legacy Tours WALKING TOUR
(www.americanlegacytours.com; 1332 Vine St; 90min tours $20; Fri-Sun) Offers a variety of historical jaunts. Best is the Queen City Underground Tour, which delves into old lagering cellars deep beneath the Over-the-Rhine district.

Festivals & Events

Bockfest BEER
(www.bockfest.com; early Mar) Traditional bock beers flow in Over-the-Rhine.

Bunbury Music Festival MUSIC
(www.bunburyfestival.com; early Jun) Big-name indie bands rock the riverfront for three days; a day pass costs $79.

Oktoberfest FOOD
(www.oktoberfestzinzinnati.com; mid-Sep) German beer, brats and mania.

Sleeping

Hotel tax adds 17.25% in Cincinnati. It's only 11.3% across the river in Kentucky, where several midrange chain options line up along the water. You'll save money (less tax, free parking), but be prepared either to walk a few miles or take a short bus ride to reach downtown Cincy.

Gateway B&B B&B $$
(859-581-6447; www.gatewaybb.com; 326 E 6th St; r $129-169; P) For something different, check in to this 1878 Italianate town house in a historic neighborhood on the Kentucky side of the river. Exquisite antique oak and walnut furnishings fill the three rooms, and intriguing baseball memorabilia decorates the common area. It's a half-mile walk to Newport on the Levee's restaurants and onward over the Purple People Bridge to downtown Cincy.

Hotel 21c HOTEL $$$

(☎513-578-6600; www.21cmuseumhotels.com/cincinnati; 609 Walnut St; r $289-379; P ❄ @) The second outpost of Louisville's popular art hotel opened in 2013, next door to the Center for Contemporary Arts. The mod rooms have accoutrements such as a Nespresso machine, free wi-fi, plush bedding and, of course, original art. The lobby is a public gallery, so feel free to ogle the trippy videos and nude sculptures. The on-site restaurant and rooftop bar draw crowds. Parking costs $35.

Residence Inn Cincinnati Downtown HOTEL $$$

(☎513-651-1234; www.residenceinncincinnatidowntown.com; 506 E 4th St; r $209-299; P ❄ @) All of the big, glistening rooms are suites with full kitchens. Continental breakfast is included. Parking costs $24.

Eating

Over-the-Rhine holds several hip new eateries, especially on Vine St between 12th and 14th Sts. Restaurants also concentrate along the riverfront and in the Northside neighborhood (north of where I-74 and I-75 intersect, 5 miles north of downtown).

★Tucker's DINER $

(☎513-721-7123; 1637 Vine St; mains $4-9; ⏲9am-3pm Tue-Sat, 10am-2pm Sun;) Located in a tough zone a few blocks from Findlay Market, family-run Tucker's has been feeding locals – African American, white, foodies, penniless – since 1946. It's an archetypal diner, serving shrimp and grits, biscuits and gravy, and other hulking breakfast dishes, along with wildly inventive vegetarian fare (like beet sliders) using ingredients sourced from the market.

Son Joe Tucker does the cookin'. Try the goetta (pronounced *get-uh*), a herb-spiced, pork-and-oats breakfast sausage that's found only in Cincinnati.

The Eagle OTR AMERICAN $

(☎513-802-5007; www.theeagleotr.com; 1342 Vine St; mains $7-10; ⏲11am-midnight Mon-Sat, to 10pm Sun) A hipster magnet serving modern soul food amid reclaimed wood decor, the Eagle rustles up fantastic fried chicken (dipped in spicy honey), white cheddar grits and spoonbread (like a sweet cornbread). Expect a queue, though the doughnut shop two doors down helps take the edge off (it's open until 9pm most nights).

LOCAL KNOWLEDGE

CHILI FIVE-WAY

Don't worry – you can keep your clothes on for this experience, though you may want to loosen your belt. A 'five-way' in Cincinnati has to do with chili, which is a local specialty. It comprises meat sauce (spiced with chocolate and cinnamon) ladled over spaghetti and beans, then garnished with cheese and onions. Although you can get it three-way (minus onions and beans) or four-way (minus onions *or* beans), you should go the whole way – after all, life's an adventure. **Skyline Chili** (www.skylinechili.com; 643 Vine St; items $4-7.50; ⏲10:30am-8pm Mon-Fri, 11am-4pm Sat) has a cultlike following devoted to its version. There are outlets throughout town; this one is downtown near Fountain Sq.

Graeter's Ice Cream ICE CREAM $

(☎513-381-4191; www.graeters.com; 511 Walnut St; scoops $2.50-5; ⏲6:30am-11pm, reduced hours in winter) A local delicacy, with scoop shops around the city. The flavors that mix in the gargantuan, chunky chocolate chips top the list.

Terry's Turf Club BURGERS $

(☎513-533-4222; 4618 Eastern Ave; mains $10-15; ⏲11am-11pm Wed & Thu, to midnight Fri & Sat, to 9pm Sun) This 15-table beer-and-burger joint glows inside and out with owner Terry Carter's neon stash. A giant, waving Aunt Jemima beckons you in, where so many fluorescent beer and doughnut signs shine that no other interior lighting is needed. Located 7 miles east of downtown via Columbia Pkwy.

Drinking & Nightlife

Over-the-Rhine, Mt Adams and Northside are busy nightspots. The Banks, the riverfront area between the baseball and football stadiums, has several new hot spots.

★Rhinegeist Brewery BREWERY

(www.rhinegeist.com; 1910 Elm St, 2nd fl; ⏲4-11pm Mon-Thu, to midnight Fri, noon-midnight Sat, to 7pm Sun) Beer buffs pile in to Rhinegeist's hoppy clubhouse to knock back Truth IPA and 13 other brews on tap. Swig at picnic tables while watching bottles roll off the production line, or play ping-pong or foosball in the sprawling open warehouse. It sits in a forlorn patch of OTR.

Moerlein Lager House BREWERY
(www.moerleinlagerhouse.com; 115 Joe Nuxall Way; ⏲11am-midnight Mon-Thu, to 1am Fri & Sat, to 11pm Sun) Copper kettles cook up the house beers, while the patio unfurls awesome views of the riverfront and Roebling bridge. It's a busy spot pre or post Reds game, as it sits across the street from the stadium.

Blind Lemon BAR
(www.theblindlemon.com; 936 Hatch St; ⏲5:30pm-2:30am Mon-Fri, from 3pm Sat & Sun) Head down the passageway to enter this atmospheric old speakeasy in Mt Adams. It has an outdoor courtyard in summer, with a fire pit added in winter, and there's live music nightly.

☆ Entertainment

Scope for free publications like *CityBeat* for current listings.

Sports

Great American Ballpark BASEBALL
(☎513-765-7000; www.reds.com; 100 Main St) Home to the Reds – pro baseball's first team – Cincy is a great place to catch a game thanks to its bells-and-whistles riverside ballpark. The Brewery Bar near section 117 pours loads of local beers.

Paul Brown Stadium FOOTBALL
(☎513-621-3550; www.bengals.com; 1 Paul Brown Stadium) The Bengals pro football team scrimmages a few blocks west of the ballpark.

Performing Arts

Music Hall CLASSICAL MUSIC
(☎513-721-8222; www.cincinnatiarts.org; 1241 Elm St) The acoustically pristine Music Hall is where the symphony orchestra, pops orchestra, opera and ballet hold their seasons.

Aronoff Center THEATER
(☎513-621-2787; www.cincinnatiarts.org; 650 Walnut St) The mod Aronoff hosts touring shows.

ℹ Information

Cincinnati Enquirer (www.cincinnati.com) Daily newspaper.

Cincinnati USA Regional Tourism Network (☎800-543-2613; www.cincinnatiusa.com) There's a visitor center on Fountain Sq.

CityBeat (www.citybeat.com) Free alternative weekly paper with good entertainment listings.

ℹ Getting There & Around

The **Cincinnati/Northern Kentucky International Airport** (CVG; www.cvgairport.com) is actually in Kentucky, 13 miles south. To get downtown, take the TANK bus ($2) from near Terminal 3; a cab costs about $35.

Greyhound (☎513-352-6012; www.greyhound.com; 1005 Gilbert Ave) buses travel daily to Columbus (two hours), Indianapolis (2½ hours) and Chicago (seven hours). Often cheaper and quicker, **Megabus** (www.megabus.com/us) travels the same routes from downtown and the University of Cincinnati; check the website for curbside locations.

Amtrak (☎513-651-3337; www.amtrak.com) choo-choos into **Union Terminal** (1301 Western Ave) thrice weekly en route to Chicago (9½ hours) and Washington, DC (14½ hours), departing in the middle of the night.

Metro (www.go-metro.com; fares $1.75) runs the local buses and links with the **Transit Authority of Northern Kentucky** (TANK; www.tankbus.org; fares $1-2). Bus 1 is useful, looping from the museum center to downtown to Mt Adams.

Red Bike (www.cincyredbike.org; 24hr pass $8) has 260 bicycles at 30 stations, mostly in downtown and Over-the-Rhine; additional charges apply for trips over 60 minutes.

MICHIGAN

More, more, more – Michigan is the Midwest state that cranks it up. It sports more beaches than the Atlantic seaboard. More than half the state is covered by forests. And more cherries and berries get shoveled into pies here than anywhere else in the USA. Plus Michigan's gritty city Detroit is the Midwest's rawest of all – and we mean that in a good way.

Michigan occupies prime real estate, surrounded by four of the five Great Lakes – Superior, Michigan, Huron and Erie. Islands – Mackinac, Manitou and Isle Royale – freckle its coast and make top touring destinations. Surfing beaches, colored sandstone cliffs and trekkable sand dunes also woo visitors.

The state consists of two parts split by water: the larger Lower Peninsula, shaped like a mitten; and the smaller, lightly populated Upper Peninsula, shaped like a slipper. They are linked by the gasp-worthy Mackinac Bridge, which spans the Straits of Mackinac (pronounced *mac*-in-aw).

Information

Michigan Highway Conditions (800-381-8477; www.michigan.gov/mdot)

Michigan State Park Information (800-447-2757; www.michigan.gov/stateparks) Park entry requires a vehicle permit (per day/year $9/31). Campsites cost $13 to $37; reservations accepted (www.midnrreservations.com; fee $8). Some parks have wi-fi.

Travel Michigan (800-644-2489; www.michigan.org)

Detroit

Tell any American that you're planning to visit Detroit, and then watch their eyebrows shoot up quizzically. They'll ask 'Why?' and warn you that the city is broke, with off-the-chart homicide rates, nearly 80,000 abandoned buildings and forsaken homes that sell for $1. 'Detroit's a crap-hole. You'll get killed there.'

While the city does have a bombed-out, apocalyptic vibe, it's these same qualities that fuel a raw urban energy you won't find anywhere else. Artists, entrepreneurs and young people are moving in, and a DIY spirit pervades. They're converting vacant lots into urban farms and abandoned buildings into cafes and museums. But there's a long way to go, and skeptics point out that Detroit's long-term African-American residents are not sharing equally in these new developments. How the city navigates the tricky path to recovery remains to be seen.

History

French explorer Antoine de La Mothe Cadillac founded Detroit in 1701. Sweet fortune arrived in the 1920s, when Henry Ford began churning out cars. He didn't invent the automobile, as so many mistakenly believe, but he did perfect assembly-line manufacturing and mass-production techniques. The result was the Model T, the first car the USA's middle class could afford to own.

Detroit quickly became the motor capital of the world. General Motors (GM), Chrysler and Ford were all headquartered in or near Detroit (and still are). The 1950s were the city's heyday, when the population exceeded two million and Motown music hit the airwaves. But racial tensions in 1967 and Japanese car competitors in the 1970s shook the city and its industry. Detroit entered an era of deep decline, losing about two-thirds of its population.

MICHIGAN FACTS

Nicknames Great Lakes State, Wolverine State

Population 9.9 million

Area 96,720 sq miles

Capital city Lansing (population 114,000)

Other cities Detroit (population 689,000)

Sales tax 6%

Birthplace of Industrialist Henry Ford (1863–1947), filmmaker Francis Ford Coppola (b 1939), musician Stevie Wonder (b 1950), singer Madonna (b 1958), Google co-founder Larry Page (b 1973)

Home of Auto assembly plants, freshwater beaches

Politics Leans Democratic

Famous for Cars, Cornflakes, tart cherries, Motown music

State reptile Painted turtle

Driving distances Detroit to Traverse City 255 miles, Detroit to Cleveland 168 miles

In July 2013 Detroit filed the largest municipal bankruptcy claim in US history: $18 billion. After extreme belt-tightening, it emerged from bankruptcy in December 2014.

Sights & Activities

Sights are commonly closed on Monday and Tuesday. And that's Canada across the Detroit River (Windsor, Canada, to be exact).

Midtown & Cultural Center

★**Detroit Institute of Arts** MUSEUM
(313-833-7900; www.dia.org; 5200 Woodward Ave; adult/child $8/4; 9am-4pm Tue-Thu, to 10pm Fri, 10am-5pm Sat & Sun) The cream of the museum crop. The centerpiece is Diego Rivera's mural *Detroit Industry,* which fills an entire room and reflects the city's blue-collar labor history. Beyond it are Picassos, suits of armor, mod African American paintings and troves more.

Museum of Contemporary Art Detroit MUSEUM
(MOCAD; 313-832-6622; www.mocadetroit.org; 4454 Woodward Ave; suggested donation $5; 11am-5pm Wed, Sat & Sun, to 8pm Thu & Fri)

Detroit

0 500 m
0 0.25 miles

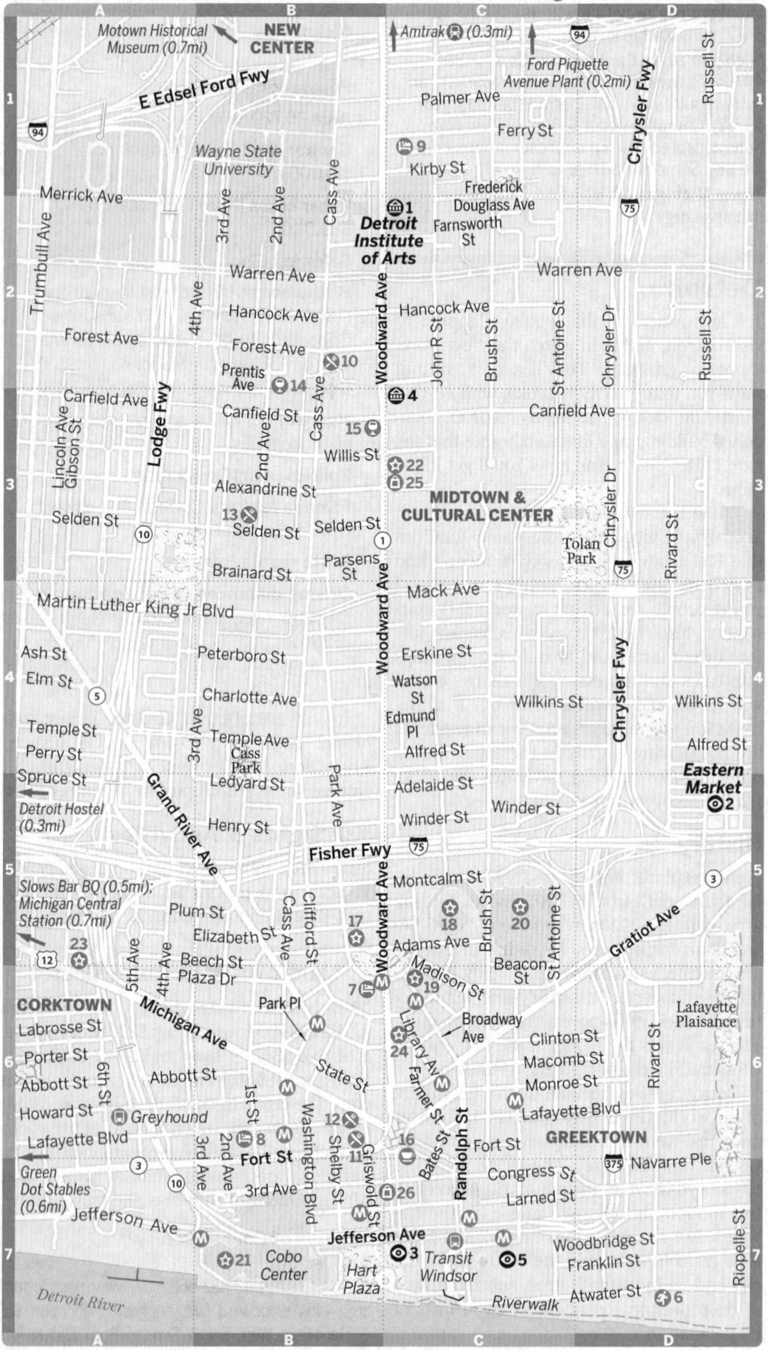

Detroit

Top Sights
1 Detroit Institute of Arts C2
2 Eastern Market D5

Sights
3 Hart Plaza C7
4 Museum of Contemporary Art Detroit C3
People Mover .... (see 5)
5 Renaissance Center C7

Activities, Courses & Tours
6 Wheelhouse Bikes D7

Sleeping
7 Aloft B6
8 Ft Shelby Doubletree Hotel B6
9 Inn on Ferry Street C1

Eating
10 Cass Cafe B2
11 Dime Store B6
12 Lafayette Coney Island B6
13 Selden Standard B3

Drinking & Nightlife
14 Bronx B2
15 HopCat B3
16 Roasting Plant C6

Entertainment
17 Cliff Bell's B5
18 Comerica Park C5
19 Detroit Opera House C6
20 Ford Field C5
21 Joe Louis Arena B7
22 Majestic Theater & Populux C3
23 PJ's Lager House A5
24 Puppet ART/Detroit Puppet Theater C6

Shopping
25 People's Records C3
26 Pure Detroit C7

MOCAD is set in an abandoned, graffiti-slathered auto dealership. Heat lamps hang from the ceiling over peculiar exhibits that change every few months. Music and literary events take place regularly. The on-site cafe/cocktail bar is uber popular.

New Center

Motown Historical Museum MUSEUM
(313-875-2264; www.motownmuseum.org; 2648 W Grand Blvd; adult $12-15, child $8; 10am-6pm Tue-Fri, to 8pm Sat, noon-6pm Sun Jul & Aug, to 6pm Tue-Sat Sep-Jun) In this row of modest houses Berry Gordy launched Motown Records – and the careers of Stevie Wonder, Diana Ross, Marvin Gaye and Michael Jackson – with an $800 loan in 1959. Gordy and Motown split for Los Angeles in 1972, but you can still step into humble Studio A and see where the famed names recorded their first hits.

A tour takes about 1½ hours, and consists mostly of looking at old photos and listening to guides' stories. The museum is 2 miles northwest of Midtown.

Ford Piquette Avenue Plant MUSEUM
(313-872-8759; www.fordpiquetteavenueplant.org; 461 Piquette Ave; adult/child $10/free; 10am-4pm Wed-Sun Apr-Oct) Henry Ford cranked out the first Model T in this landmark factory. Admission includes a detailed tour by enthusiastic docents, plus loads of shiny vehicles from 1904 onward. It's about 1 mile northeast of the Detroit Institute of Arts.

Downtown & Around

Greektown (centred on Monroe St) has a stretch of restaurants, bakeries and a casino.

★ **Eastern Market** MARKET
(www.easternmarket.com; Adelaide & Russell Sts) Produce, cheese, spice and flower vendors fill the large halls on Saturday, but you also can turn up Monday through Friday to browse the specialty shops (props to the peanut roaster) and cafes that flank the halls on Russell and Market Sts. In addition, from June through October there's a scaled-down market on Tuesdays and a Sunday craft market with food trucks.

Renaissance Center BUILDING
(RenCen; www.gmrencen.com; 330 E Jefferson Ave) GM's glossy, cloud-poking headquarters is a fine place to mooch off the free wi-fi, take a free hour-long tour (Monday through Friday at noon and 2pm) or embark on the riverfront walkway.

Hart Plaza PLAZA
(cnr Jefferson & Woodward Aves) This is the site of many free summer weekend festivals and concerts. While there, check out the sculpture of Joe Louis' mighty fist.

People Mover MONORAIL
(www.thepeoplemover.com; fares $0.75) As mass transit, the monorail's 3-mile loop on elevated tracks around downtown won't get you

very far. As a tourist attraction, it's a sweet ride providing great views of the city and riverfront. There are 13 stations, including one in the RenCen.

Heidelberg Project PUBLIC ART
(www.heidelberg.org; 3600 Heidelberg St; ⏲ sunrise-sunset) FREE Polka-dotted streets, houses covered in Technicolor paint blobs, strange sculptures in yards – this is no acid trip, but rather a block-spanning art installation. It's the brainchild of street artist Tyree Guyton, who wanted to beautify his run-down community. Arsonists have burned much of the project, but Guyton vows he'll keep it open and turn what remains into art once again.

It's located about 1.5 miles from Eastern Market. Take Gratiot Ave northeast to Heidelberg St. The project spans from Ellery to Mt Elliott Sts in a rough neighborhood.

Riverwalk & Dequindre Cut WALKING, CYCLING
(www.detroitriverfront.org) The city's swell riverfront path runs for 3 miles along the churning Detroit River from Hart Plaza east to Mt Elliott St, passing several parks, outdoor theaters, riverboats and fishing spots en route. Eventually it will extend all the way to beachy **Belle Isle** (detour onto Jefferson Ave to get there now). About halfway along the Riverwalk, near Orleans St, the 1.5-mile Dequindre Cut Greenway path juts north, offering a convenient passageway to Eastern Market.

Wheelhouse Bikes BICYCLE RENTAL
(☎313-656-2453; www.wheelhousedetroit.com; 1340 E Atwater St; per 2hr $15; ⏲10am-8pm Mon-Sat, 11am-5pm Sun Jun-Aug, reduced hours Sep-May) Cycling is a great way to explore the city. Wheelhouse rents sturdy two-wheelers (helmet and lock included) on the Riverwalk at Rivard Plaza. Themed tours ($40 including bike rental) roll by various neighborhoods, architectural sites and urban farms.

Tours

Preservation Detroit WALKING TOUR
(☎313-577-7674; www.preservationdetroit.org; 2hr tours $15; ⏲10am Sat May-Sep) Offers architectural walking tours through downtown, Midtown and other neighborhoods; departure points vary.

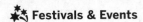

Festivals & Events

North American International Auto Show CULTURAL
(www.naias.com; tickets $13; ⏲mid-Jan) It's autos galore for two weeks at the Cobo Center.

Movement Electronic Music Festival MUSIC
(www.movement.us; day pass $75; ⏲late May) The world's largest electronic music festival congregates in Hart Plaza over Memorial Day weekend.

Sleeping

Add 9% to 15% tax (it varies by lodging size and location) to the rates listed here, unless stated otherwise.

Affordable motels abound in Detroit's suburbs. If you're arriving from Metro Airport, follow the signs for Merriman Rd when leaving the airport and take your pick.

Detroit Hostel HOSTEL $
(☎313-451-0333; www.hosteldetroit.com; 2700 Vermont St; dm $30-37, r $46-65; P@🛜) Volunteers rehabbed this old building, gathered up recycled materials and donations for the patchwork furnishings, and opened it to the public in 2011. There's a 10-bed dorm, a four-bed dorm and a handful of private rooms; everyone shares the four bathrooms and three kitchens. Bookings are taken online only (and must be done at least 24 hours in advance).

Bike rentals costs $20 per day. The hostel is located in Corktown on a desolate street, but near several good bars and restaurants.

★ **Inn on Ferry Street** INN $$
(☎313-871-6000; www.innonferrystreet.com; 84 E Ferry St; r $169-259; P❄@🛜) Forty guest rooms fill a row of Victorian mansions right by the art museum. The lower-cost rooms are small but have deliciously soft bedding; the larger rooms feature plenty of antique wood furnishings. The healthy hot breakfast and shuttle to downtown are nice touches.

Aloft HOTEL $$
(☎313-237-1700; www.aloftdetroit.com; 1 Park Ave; r $159-199; P❄@🛜🐾) The chain's new Detroit property took an exquisite 1915 neo-Renaissance skyscraper and converted it to its familiar hipster style. Mod rooms have bright pops of color and groovy city views. It's well-located near the sports venues and theaters. Parking costs $30.

Ft Shelby Doubletree Hotel HOTEL **$$**
(☎313-963-5600; http://doubletree1.hilton.com; 525 W Lafayette Blvd; r $123-189; P ❄ @ wi-fi) This hotel fills a historic beaux-arts building downtown. All rooms are suites, with both the sitting area and bedroom equipped with HDTV and free wi-fi. Parking costs $27, and there's free shuttle service around downtown.

Eating

Two nearby suburbs also have caches of hip restaurants and bars: walkable, gay-oriented Ferndale at 9 Mile Rd and Woodward Ave, and Royal Oak just north of Ferndale between 12 and 13 Mile Rds.

Midtown & Cultural Center

Cass Cafe CAFE **$**
(☎313-831-1400; www.casscafe.com; 4620 Cass Ave; mains $8-15; ⏰11am-11pm Mon-Thu, to 1am Fri & Sat, 5-10pm Sun; wi-fi V) The Cass is a bohemian art gallery fused with a bar and restaurant that serves soups, sandwiches and veggie beauties, such as the lentil-walnut burger. Service can be fickle.

Selden Standard MODERN AMERICAN **$$$**
(☎313-438-5055; www.seldenstandard.com; 3921 2nd Ave; small plates $14-20; ⏰11am-2:30pm & 5-10pm Mon-Fri, from 10am Sat & Sun) The city has its first upscale farm-to-table restaurant, the kind of place that cares enough to churn its own butter and hand-mold its own pasta. The menu changes, but you'll see dishes such as fresh-caught trout and celery root ravioli, plus creative cocktails.

Downtown

Lafayette Coney Island AMERICAN **$**
(☎313-964-8198; 118 Lafayette Blvd; items $2.50-5; ⏰9am-3am Sun-Thu, 8am-4am Fri & Sat) The 'coney' – a hot dog smothered with chili and onions – is a Detroit specialty. When the craving strikes (and it will), take care of business at Lafayette. The minimalist menu consists of burgers, fries and beer, in addition to the signature item. Cash only.

Dime Store AMERICAN **$**
(☎313-962-9106; www.eatdimestore.com; 719 Griswold St; mains $8-13; ⏰8am-3pm Mon, to 10pm Tue-Fri, 10am-3pm Sat & Sun) Take a seat in a chunky wood swivel chair in this cozy, diner-esque eatery and chow down on a duck Reuben and truffle-mayo-dipped fries, alongside a cold beer. Eggy brunch dishes are a big hit and served all day.

LOCAL KNOWLEDGE

DETROIT'S RUINS

More than 78,000 abandoned buildings blight Detroit's landscape. The city would like to demolish them, but it doesn't have the money. Many have become well-known, often-photographed sights. Top of the list is **Michigan Central Station** (2405 W Vernor Hwy), the once-grand beaux-arts rail terminal now crumbling into oblivion within eyeshot of Corktown's main drag. The **Packard Auto Plant** (E Grand Blvd at Concord St) is another. Renowned architect Albert Kahn designed the 3.5-million-sq-ft factory, and it was a thing of beauty when it opened in 1903. Now it looks like something from a zombie movie. Stay tuned though, as a developer bought the plant and has vowed to renovate it. **Detroiturbex** (www.detroiturbex.com) provides good historical information on these and other derelict structures around town.

Note that viewing the buildings has become a hot topic: some call it 'ruin porn,' as in people getting excited by urban decay. Others see it as a way to examine and take in the complex history of the city. It is illegal to enter any abandoned building.

Corktown & Mexicantown

Corktown, a bit west of downtown, shows the city's DIY spirit. Hipster joints slinging burgers, cocktails and artisanal coffee drinks line Michigan Ave. Mexicantown, along Bagley St 3 miles west of downtown, offers several inexpensive Mexican restaurants.

Green Dot Stables BURGERS **$**
(☎313-962-5588; www.greendotstables.com; 2200 W Lafayette Blvd; mains $2-3; ⏰11am-midnight Mon-Wed, to 1am Thu-Sat, noon-10pm Sun) It's a bit inconveniently located between downtown, Corktown and Mexicantown, but that doesn't deter young urbanites from flocking in to munch on 20 types of gourmet mini-burgers (say, wasabi-mayo tempeh or peanut-butter kimchi) with a side of poutine.

★**Slows Bar BQ** BARBECUE **$$**
(☎313-962-9828; www.slowsbarbq.com; 2138 Michigan Ave; mains $10-19; ⏰11am-10pm Sun & Mon, to 11pm Tue-Thu, to midnight Fri & Sat; wi-fi) Mmm, slow-cooked Southern-style barbecue

FROM MOTOWN TO ROCK CITY

Motown Records and soul music put Detroit on the map in the 1960s, while the thrashing punk rock of the Stooges and MC5 was the 1970s response to that smooth sound. By 1976, Detroit was dubbed 'Rock City' by a Kiss song (though – just Detroit's luck – the tune was eclipsed by its B-side, 'Beth'). In recent years it has been hard-edged rock – aka whiplash rock and roll – that has pushed the city to the music-scene forefront. Homegrown stars include the White Stripes, Von Bondies and Dirtbombs. Rap (thank you, Eminem) and techno are Detroit's other renowned genres. Many music aficionados say the city's blight is what produces such a beautifully angry explosion of sound, and who's to argue? Scope free publications like the *Metro Times* (www.metrotimes.com) and blogs such as Motor City Rocks (http://motorcityrocks.com) for current show and club listings.

in Corktown. Carnivores can carve into the three-meat combo plate (brisket, pulled pork and chicken). Vegetarians even have a couple of options. The taps yield 55 quality beers.

Drinking & Nightlife

★Bronx BAR
(4476 2nd Ave; noon-2am;) There's not much inside Detroit's best boozer besides a pool table, dim lighting and a couple of jukeboxes filled with ballsy rock and soul. But that's the way the hipsters, slackers and rockers (the White Stripes used to hang here) like their dive bars. They're also fond of the beefy burgers served late at night and the cheap beer selection.

HopCat PUB
(www.hopcat.com/detroit; 4265 Woodward Ave; 11am-2am Mon-Sat, from 10am Sun;) Detroit's outpost of the regional pub chain rocks: paintings of local musicians adorn the walls, and the Stooges and old Motown bang on the speakers. Around 130 beers flow from the taps, with 30 devoted to Michigan brewers. Smaller pours (5oz and 8oz glasses) are available for those who want to sample widely.

Roasting Plant COFFEE
(www.roastingplant.com; 660 Woodward Ave; 6am-7pm Mon-Fri, from 7am Sat & Sun) This slick, high-tech and super-friendly spot grinds beans fresh for each heavy-duty cup of coffee. The free gallery across the lobby usually has something cool showing. Food trucks waft their wares a few steps outside the door.

☆ Entertainment

Live Music

Cover charges hover between $5 and $15.

Majestic Theater & Populux LIVE MUSIC
(www.majesticdetroit.com; 4120-4140 Woodward Ave) The Majestic Theater and smaller Majestic Cafe host beer-splattered rock shows, while next door club Populux brings on the electronic dance music. The entertainment complex also holds a bowling alley and pizza joint. Something cool rocks here nightly.

PJ's Lager House LIVE MUSIC
(www.pjslagerhouse.com; 1254 Michigan Ave; 11am-2am) Scrappy bands or DJs play most nights at this small Corktown club. By day it serves surprisingly good grub with a New Orleans/vegan twist (like the tempeh po'boy on gluten-free bread).

Cliff Bell's JAZZ
(www.cliffbells.com; 2030 Park Ave; from 4pm Tue-Fri, 5pm Sat, 11am Sun) With its dark wood, candlelight and art-deco decor, Bell's evokes 1930s elegance. Local jazz bands and poetry readings attract a diverse young audience.

Performing Arts

Puppet ART/Detroit Puppet Theater THEATER
(313-961-7777; www.puppetart.org; 25 E Grand River Ave; adult/child $10/5;) Soviet-trained puppeteers perform beautiful shows in this 70-person theater; a small museum displays puppets from different cultures. Shows are typically held on Saturday afternoon.

Detroit Opera House OPERA
(313-237-7464; www.michiganopera.org; 1526 Broadway Ave) Gorgeous interior, top-tier company and nurturer of many renowned African American performers.

Sports

Comerica Park BASEBALL
(www.detroittigers.com; 2100 Woodward Ave;) The Detroit Tigers play pro baseball at Comerica, one of the league's most decked-out stadiums. The park is particularly kid

friendly, with a small Ferris wheel and carousel inside (both $2 per ride).

Joe Louis Arena HOCKEY
(www.detroitredwings.com; 600 Civic Center Dr) The much-loved Red Wings play pro ice hockey at this arena where, if you can wrangle tickets, you might witness the strange octopus-throwing custom (yes, a real octopus). A new stadium is slated to open at downtown's northern edge in late 2017.

Ford Field FOOTBALL
(www.detroitlions.com; 2000 Brush St) The Lions toss the pigskin at this indoor stadium next to Comerica Park.

Palace of Auburn Hills BASKETBALL
(www.nba.com/pistons; 5 Championship Dr) The Palace hosts the Pistons pro basketball team. It's about 30 miles northwest of downtown; take I-75 to exit 81.

Shopping

Pure Detroit SOUVENIRS
(www.puredetroit.com; 500 Griswold St; ⌚10:30am-5:30pm Mon-Sat) Local artists create stylish products for Pure Detroit that celebrate the city's fast-cars-and-rock-music culture. Pick up handbags made from recycled seatbelts, groovy T-shirts and local Pewabic pottery. Located in the landmark, mosaic-strewn Guardian Building (worth a peek in its own right).

People's Records MUSIC
(www.peoplesdetroit.com; 4100 Woodward Ave; ⌚11am-7pm Mon-Sat) Calling all crate-diggers: DJ-owned People's Records is your vinyl Valhalla. Used 45s are the specialty, with more than 80,000 jazz, soul and R&B titles filling bins. The front table is loaded with flyers that tell you where the latest, greatest music events are happening.

Information

The area between the sports arenas north to around Willis Rd is pretty deserted and best avoided on foot come nighttime.

EMERGENCY & MEDICAL SERVICES

Detroit Receiving Hospital (☎313-745-3000; 4201 St Antoine St)

INTERNET ACCESS

You'll find free wi-fi in many cafes and bars, as well as the Renaissance Center lobby.

MEDIA

Between the Lines (www.pridesource.com) Free, weekly gay and lesbian paper.

Detroit Free Press (www.freep.com) Daily newspaper.

Detroit News (www.detroitnews.com) Daily newspaper.

Metro Times (www.metrotimes.com) Free alternative weekly that is the best guide to the entertainment scene.

Model D (www.modeldmedia.com) Weekly e-zine about local developments and food/entertainment options, broken down by neighborhood.

TOURIST INFORMATION

Detroit Convention & Visitors Bureau (☎800-338-7648; www.visitdetroit.com)

Getting There & Around

Detroit Metro Airport (DTW; www.metroairport.com), a Delta Airlines hub, is about 20 miles southwest of Detroit. Transportation options to the city are few. Taxis cost $55 or so. The shared shuttle van **Skoot** (www.rideskoot.com) costs $20. The 125 SMART bus ($2.50) is inconvenient, unreliable and takes 1½ hours to get downtown.

Greyhound (☎313-961-8005; 1001 Howard St) runs to various cities in Michigan and beyond. **Megabus** (www.megabus.com/us) runs to/from Chicago (5½ hours) daily; departures are from downtown and Wayne State University. Check the website for exact locations.

Amtrak (☎313-873-3442; 11 W Baltimore Ave) trains go three times daily to Chicago (5½ hours). You can also head east – to New York (16½ hours) or destinations en route – but you'll first be bused to Toledo.

Transit Windsor (☎519-944-4111; www.citywindsor.ca/transitwindsor) operates the Tunnel Bus to Windsor, Canada. It costs $4.50 (American or Canadian) and departs by Mariner's Church (corner of Randolph St and Jefferson Ave) near the Detroit-Windsor Tunnel entrance, as well as other spots downtown. Bring your passport.

The **M-1 streetcar** is scheduled to start running in late 2016, providing handy transportation along Woodward Ave from Congress St downtown, past the sports venues and museums, to the Amtrak station and W Grand Blvd at the northern end. See http://m-1rail.com for updates.

For taxi service, call **Checker Cab** (☎313-963-7000).

CLASSIC CARS IN MICHIGAN

More than sand dunes, beaches and Mackinac Island fudge, Michigan is synonymous with cars. While the connection hasn't been so positive in recent years, the state commemorates its glory days via several auto museums. The following fleets are within a few hours' drive of the Motor City.

Henry Ford Museum (see below) This Dearborn museum is loaded with vintage cars, including the first one Henry Ford ever built. In adjacent Greenfield Village you can ride in a Model T that rolled off the assembly line in 1923.

Automotive Hall of Fame (313-240-4000; www.automotivehalloffame.org; 21400 Oakwood Blvd; adult/child $10/4; 9am-5pm Wed-Sun) Next door to the Henry Ford Museum, the interactive Auto Hall focuses on the people behind famed cars, such as Mr Ferdinand Porsche and Mr Soichiro Honda.

Gilmore Car Museum (269-671-5089; www.gilmorecarmuseum.org; 6865 Hickory Rd; adult/child $13/10; 9am-5pm Mon-Fri, to 6pm Sat & Sun) North of Kalamazoo along Hwy 43, this museum complex offers 22 barns filled with 120 vintage autos, including 15 Rolls-Royces dating back to a 1910 Silver Ghost.

RE Olds Transportation Museum (p584) It's a whopping garage full of shiny vintage cars that date back more than 130 years.

Around Detroit

Stunning Americana and good eatin' lie just down the road from Detroit.

Dearborn

Dearborn is 10 miles west of downtown Detroit and home to two of the USA's finest museums. The indoor **Henry Ford Museum** (313-982-6001; www.thehenryford.org; 20900 Oakwood Blvd; adult/child $20/15; 9:30am-5pm) contains a fascinating wealth of American culture, such as the chair Lincoln was sitting in when he was assassinated, the presidential limo in which Kennedy was killed, the hot-dog-shaped Oscar Mayer Wienermobile (photo op!) and the bus on which Rosa Parks refused to give up her seat. Don't worry: you'll get your vintage car fix here too. Parking is $6. The adjacent, outdoor **Greenfield Village** (adult/child $25/18.75; 9:30am-5pm daily mid-Apr–Oct, Fri-Sun Nov & Dec) features historic buildings shipped in from all over the country, reconstructed and restored, such as Thomas Edison's laboratory from Menlo Park and the Wright Brothers' airplane workshop. Plus you can add on the **Rouge Factory Tour** (adult/child $16/12; 9:30am-3pm Mon-Sat) and see F-150 trucks roll off the assembly line where Ford first perfected his self-sufficient, mass-production techniques.

The three attractions are separate, but you can get a combination ticket (adult/child $35/26.25) for Henry Ford and Greenfield Village. Plan on at least one very full day at the complex.

Dearborn has the nation's greatest concentration of people of Arab descent, so it's no surprise that the **Arab American National Museum** (313-582-2266; www.arabamerican-museum.org; 13624 Michigan Ave; adult/child $8/4; 10am-6pm Wed-Sat, noon-5pm Sun) popped up here. It's a noble concept, located in a pretty, bright-tiled building, but it's not terribly exciting unless actor Jamie Farr's *M*A*S*H* TV-show script wows you. The Arabian eateries lining nearby Warren Ave provide a more engaging feel for the culture. Turquoise-roofed **Hamido** (www.hamidorestaurant.com; 13251 W Warren Ave; mains $6-12; 11am-midnight) serves hummus, chicken shwarma and other staples. The number of birds roasting on the spit show its popularity.

Ann Arbor

Forty-odd miles west of Detroit, liberal and bookish Ann Arbor is home to the University of Michigan. The walkable downtown, which abuts the campus, is loaded with free-trade coffee shops, bookstores and brewpubs. It's a mecca for chowhounds; follow the drool trail toward anything named 'Zingerman's.'

Sights & Activities

University of Michigan Museum of Art MUSEUM
(734-764-0395; www.umma.umich.edu; 525 S State St; 11am-5pm Tue-Sat, from noon Sun) FREE The campus' bold art museum impresses with its collections of Asian ceramics, Tiffany glass and modern abstract works.

Ann Arbor Farmers Market MARKET
(www.facebook.com/a2market; 315 Detroit St; 7am-3pm Wed & Sat May-Dec, Sat only Jan-Apr) Given the surrounding bounty of orchards and farms, it's no surprise this place is stuffed to the rafters with everything from spicy pickles to cider to mushroom-growing kits; located downtown near Zingerman's Deli. On Sunday an artisan market with jewelry, ceramics and textiles takes over.

Zingerman's Bakehouse COOKING COURSE
(www.bakewithzing.com; 3723 Plaza Dr) Offers popular 'bake-cations,' making bread or pastries in Ann Arbor.

Eating & Drinking

Frita Batidos CUBAN $
(734-761-2882; www.fritabatidos.com; 117 W Washington St; mains $8-13; 11am-11pm Sun-Wed, to midnight Thu-Sat) This mod take on Cuban street food is all the rage, offering burgers with tropical, citrusy toppings and booze-spiked milkshakes.

Zingerman's Delicatessen DELI $$
(734-663-3354; www.zingermansdeli.com; 422 Detroit St; sandwiches $13-17; 7am-10pm;) The shop that launched the foodie frenzy, Z's piles local, organic and specialty ingredients onto towering sandwiches in a sprawling downtown complex that also includes a coffee shop and bakery.

★**Zingerman's Roadhouse** AMERICAN $$$
(734-663-3663; www.zingermansroadhouse.com; 2501 Jackson Ave; mains $19-33; 7am-10pm Mon-Thu, to 11pm Fri, 9am-11pm Sat, to 9pm Sun) Two words: doughnut sundae. The bourbon-caramel-sauced dessert is pure genius, as are the traditional American dishes like Carolina grits, Iowa pork chops and Maryland crab cakes, all using sustainably produced ingredients. It's 2 miles west of downtown.

Jolly Pumpkin BREWERY
(www.jollypumpkin.com; 311 S Main St; from 11am Mon-Fri, from 10am Sat & Sun) Ann Arborites young and old come here for the housemade sour beers (try the Bam Biere), pizzas and truffle fries. Eat in the cozy, antique-filled downstairs, or head to the rooftop patio.

Entertainment

If you happen to arrive on a fall weekend and wonder why 110,000 people – the size of Ann Arbor's entire population, more or less – are crowding into the school's stadium, the answer is football. Tickets are nearly impossible to purchase, especially when nemesis Ohio State is in town. You can try by contacting the **U of M Ticket Office** (734-764-0247; www.mgoblue.com/ticketoffice).

Blind Pig LIVE MUSIC
(www.blindpigmusic.com; 208 S 1st St) Everyone from John Lennon to Nirvana to the Circle Jerks has rocked the storied stage.

Ark LIVE MUSIC
(www.a2ark.org; 316 S Main St) The Ark hosts acoustic and folk-oriented tunesmiths.

Information

There are several B&Bs within walking distance of downtown. Hotels tend to be about 5 miles out, with several clustered south on State St.

Ann Arbor Convention & Visitors Bureau (www.visitannarbor.org) Accommodation information and more.

Lansing & Central Michigan

Michigan's heartland, plunked in the center of the Lower Peninsula, alternates between fertile farms and highway-crossed urban areas.

Lansing

Smallish Lansing is the state capital. A few miles east lies East Lansing, home of Michigan State University. They're worth a stop to peek into a couple of impressive museums.

Sights & Activities

Broad Museum of Art MUSEUM
(www.broadmuseum.msu.edu; 547 E Circle Dr; 10am-5pm Tue-Thu & Sat-Sun, noon-9pm Fri) FREE Renowned architect Zaha Hadid designed the wild-looking parallelogram of stainless steel and glass. It holds everything from Greek ceramics to Salvador Dalí paintings. Much of the space is devoted to avant-garde exhibitions.

RE Olds Transportation Museum MUSEUM
(517-372-0529; www.reoldsmuseum.org; 240 Museum Dr; adult/child $7/5; 10am-5pm Tue-Sat year-round, noon-5pm Sun Apr-Oct) The museum has a sweet collection of some 65 vintage cars that sit in the old Lansing City Bus Garage, including the first Oldsmobile, which was built in 1897. Note they're not all on display at once, but rotate regularly.

River Trail WALKING
(www.lansingrivertrail.org) Between Lansing's downtown and the university is the 8-mile River Trail. The paved path is popular with cyclists and joggers, and links a number of attractions, including a children's museum, zoo and fish ladder.

Sleeping

Wild Goose Inn B&B **$$**
(517-333-3334; www.wildgooseinn.com; 512 Albert St; r $139-159;) Lansing's downtown hotels feed off politicians and lobbyists, so they're fairly expensive. It's best to head to East Lansing's Wild Goose Inn, a six-room B&B one block from Michigan State's campus. All rooms have fireplaces and most have Jacuzzis.

Eating & Drinking

Golden Harvest DINER **$**
(517-485-3663; 1625 Turner St; mains $7-9; 7am-2:30pm Mon-Fri, from 8am Sat & Sun) Golden Harvest is a loud, punk-rock-meets-hippie diner serving the sausage-and-French-toast Bubba Sandwich and hearty omelets; cash only.

HopCat PUB
(www.hopcat.com/east-lansing; 300 Grove St; 11am-midnight Mon-Wed, to 2am Thu-Sat, 10am-midnight Sun) This East Lansing outpost of the regional pub chain has a bottle-cap-studded bar made from old gym bleachers, lights repurposed from a shuttered church and groovy rock-and-roll folk art. It's a treat to look at, but the 100 beers on tap (of which 20 are from Michigan) are the real draw. Beyond-the-norm burgers and sandwiches help you stay upright.

Information

Greater Lansing CVB (www.lansing.org) Has information on East Lansing, home of Michigan State University.

Grand Rapids

The second-largest city in Michigan, Grand Rapids is known for office-furniture manufacturing and, more recently, beer tourism. Twenty craft breweries operate in the area, and that's why you're here (though some non-beer sights intrigue, as well).

Sights & Activities

Gerald R Ford Museum MUSEUM
(616-254-0400; www.fordlibrarymuseum.gov; 303 Pearl St NW; adult/child $7/3; 9am-5pm Mon-Sat, from noon Sun) The downtown museum is dedicated to Michigan's only president. Ford stepped into the Oval Office after Richard Nixon and his vice president, Spiro Agnew, resigned in disgrace. It's a bizarre period in US history, and the museum does an excellent job of covering it, down to displaying the burglary tools used in the Watergate break-in. Ford and wife Betty are buried on the museum's grounds.

Frederik Meijer Gardens GARDENS
(616-957-1580; www.meijergardens.org; 1000 E Beltline NE; adult/child $12/6; 9am-5pm Mon & Wed-Sat, to 9pm Tue, 11am-5pm Sun) The 118-acre gardens feature impressive blooms, and sculptures by Auguste Rodin, Henry Moore and others. It is 5 miles east of downtown via I-196. For more on the visual theme, there's a good art museum downtown, too.

Sleeping

CityFlats Hotel HOTEL **$$**
(866-609-2489; www.cityflatshotel.com; 83 Monroe Center St NW; r $165-235;) At night, tuck in under the bamboo sheets at the CityFlats Hotel downtown. The building is gold-certified by the LEED (Leadership in Energy and Environmental Design) program.

Eating & Drinking

Founders Brewing Company BREWERY
(www.foundersbrewing.com; 235 Grandville Ave SW; 11am-2am Mon-Sat, noon-midnight Sun;) If you've only got time for one stop in Grand Rapids, make it rock-and-roll Founders Brewing Company. The ruby-tinged Dirty Bastard Ale is good swillin', and there's meaty (or vegetable-y, for vegetarians) deli sandwiches to soak it up.

Brewery Vivant BREWERY
(www.breweryvivant.com; 925 Cherry St SE; ⏲3-11pm Mon-Thu, to midnight Fri, 11am-midnight Sat, noon-10pm Sun) Set in an old chapel with stained glass and a vaulted ceiling, this atmospheric brewpub specializes in Belgian-style beers. It also serves locally sourced cheese plates and burgers at farmhouse-style communal tables.

Information

Grand Rapids CVB (www.experiencegr.com) Has maps and self-guided brewery tour information online.

Lake Michigan Shore

They don't call it the Gold Coast for nothing. Michigan's 300-mile western shoreline features seemingly endless stretches of beaches, dunes, wineries, orchards and B&B-filled towns that boom during the summer – and shiver during the snow-packed winter. Note all state parks listed here take **campsite reservations** (☎800-447-2757; www.midnrreservations.com; fee $8) and require a vehicle permit ($9/31 per day/year), unless specified otherwise.

Harbor Country

Harbor Country refers to a group of eight small, lake-hugging towns just over the Michigan border (an easy day trip from Chicago). Yep, they've got your requisite beaches, wineries and antique shops; they've got a couple of big surprises too. The **Harbor Country Chamber of Commerce** (www.harborcountry.org) has the basics.

First up, surfing. Believe it, people: you can surf Lake Michigan, and the VW-bus-driving dudes at **Third Coast Surf Shop** (☎269-932-4575; www.thirdcoastsurfshop.com; 110 N Whittaker St; ⏲10am-6pm Sun-Thu, to 7pm Fri & Sat, closed Nov-Apr) will show you how. They provide wetsuits and boards for surfing and paddleboarding (rentals $20 to $35 per day). For novices, they offer two-hour private lessons ($75, including equipment) at the local beach. The shop is in New Buffalo, Harbor Country's biggest town.

Three Oaks is the only Harbor community that's inland (6 miles in, via US 12). Here Green Acres meets Greenwich Village in a funky farm-and-arts blend. By day, rent bikes at **Dewey Cannon Trading Company** (☎269-756-3361; www.applecidercentury.com/dctc; 3 Dewey Cannon Ave; bike per day $20; ⏲9am-5pm Sun-Fri, to 8pm Sat, reduced hours Oct-Apr) and cycle lightly used rural roads past orchards and wineries. By eve, catch a provocative play or arthouse flick at Three Oaks' theaters.

Hungry? Get a wax-paper-wrapped cheeseburger, spicy curly fries and cold beer at **Redamak's** (www.redamaks.com; 616 E Buffalo St; burgers $6-12; ⏲noon-10:30pm Mar–mid-Nov) in New Buffalo. Or kick it up a notch with an organic whiskey flight at rustic **Journeyman Distillery** (www.journeymandistillery.com; 109 Generations Dr; ⏲noon-10pm Sun-Thu, to 11pm Fri & Sat) in Three Oaks.

> **WINE TRAIL**
>
> A dozen wineries cluster between New Buffalo and Saugatuck. The **Lake Michigan Shore Wine Trail** (www.lakemichiganshorewinetrail.com) provides a downloadable map of vineyards and tasting rooms. Most are signposted off the highway.

Saugatuck & Douglas

Saugatuck is one of the Gold Coast's most popular resort areas, known for its strong arts community, numerous B&Bs and gay-friendly vibe. Douglas is its twin city a mile or so south, and they've pretty much sprawled into one.

Sights & Activities

Galleries and shops proliferate downtown on Water and Butler Sts. Antiquing prevails on the Blue Star Hwy running south for 20 miles. Blueberry U-pick farms share this stretch of road and make a juicy stop, too.

Saugatuck Chain Ferry BOAT TOUR
(end of Mary St; one way $1; ⏲9am-9pm late May-early Sep) The best thing to do in Saugatuck is also the most affordable. Jump aboard the clackety chain ferry, and the operator will pull you across the Kalamazoo River.

Mt Baldhead WALKING
Huff up the stairs of this 200ft-high sand dune for a stellar view. Then race down the other side to Oval Beach. Get here via the chain ferry; walk right (north) from the dock.

Oval Beach BEACH

(Oval Beach Rd; ⌚9am-10pm) Lifeguards patrol the long expanse of fine sand. There are bathrooms and concession stands, though not enough to spoil the peaceful, dune-laden scene. It costs $8 to park. Or arrive the adventurous way, via chain ferry and a trek over Mt Baldhead.

Sleeping

Several frilly B&Bs are tucked into Saugatuck's century-old Victorian homes, with most ranging from $150 to $300 per night and two-night minimum stays.

Pines Motorlodge MOTEL $$

(☎269-857-5211; www.thepinesmotorlodge.com; 56 Blue Star Hwy; r $139-249;) Retro-cool tiki lamps, pinewood furniture and communal lawn chairs add up to a fun, social ambience amid the firs in Douglas.

Bayside Inn INN $$

(☎269-857-4321; www.baysideinn.net; 618 Water St; r $160-260;) This former boathouse has 10 rooms on Saugatuck's waterfront.

Eating & Drinking

Crane's Pie Pantry BAKERY $

(☎269-561-2297; www.cranespiepantry.com; 6054 124th Ave; pie slices $4.50; ⌚8am-8pm Mon-Sat, from 11am Sun May-Oct, reduced hours Nov-Apr) Buy a bulging slice, or pick apples and peaches in the surrounding orchards. Crane's is in Fennville, 3 miles south on the Blue Star Hwy, then 4 miles inland on Hwy 89.

Phil's Bar & Grille AMERICAN $$

(☎269-857-1555; www.philsbarandgrille.com; 215 Butler St; mains $14-26; ⌚11:30am-9:30pm Sun-Thu, to 10:30pm Fri & Sat) This humming pub turns out terrific broasted (combining broiling and roasting) chicken, fish tacos, lamb lollipops and gumbo in a cozy, wood-floored room.

Saugatuck Brewing Company BREWERY

(www.saugatuckbrewing.com; 2948 Blue Star Hwy; ⌚11am-9pm Sun-Thu, to 10pm Fri, to 11pm Sat) Locals like to hang out and sip the house-made suds.

Information

Saugatuck/Douglas CVB (www.saugatuck.com) The Saugatuck/Douglas CVB provides maps and more.

Muskegon & Ludington

These towns are jump-off points for two ferries that sail across the lake, providing a substantial shortcut over driving the Michigan-to-Wisconsin route. The **Lake Express** (☎866-914-1010; www.lake-express.com; ⌚May-Oct) crosses between Muskegon and Milwaukee (one-way adult/child/car from $86.50/30/91, 2½ hours); it's modern, faster and costs about 50% more. The **SS Badger** (☎800-841-4243; www.ssbadger.com; ⌚mid-May–mid-Oct) crosses between Ludington and Manitowoc (one-way adult/child/car from $59/24/59, four hours). The historic, coal-fired vessel is more atmospheric and cheaper, but also slower. For years it also was a polluter, though it has cleaned up its act and now meets environmental standards.

In Muskegon the **Winter Sports Complex** (☎231-744-9629; www.msports.org; 442 Scenic Dr) kicks butt with its full-on luge track (usable during summer, too) and cross-country ski trails. To the north, lakeside **Ludington State Park** (☎231-843-8671; tent & RV sites $13-33, cabins $49) is one of Michigan's largest and most popular playlots. It has a top-notch trail system, a renovated lighthouse to visit (or live in, as a volunteer lighthouse keeper) and miles of beach.

Sleeping Bear Dunes National Lakeshore

This national park stretches from north of Frankfort to just before Leland, on the Leelanau Peninsula. Stop at the park's **visitor center** (☎231-326-4700; www.nps.gov/slbe; 9922 Front St; ⌚8am-6pm Jun-Aug, 8:30am-4pm Sep-May) in Empire for information, trail maps and vehicle entry permits (week/annual $10/20).

Attractions include the famous **Dune Climb** along Hwy 109, where you trudge up the 200ft-high dune and then run or roll down. Gluttons for leg-muscle punishment can keep slogging all the way to Lake Michigan, a strenuous 1½-hour trek one way; bring water. The **Sleeping Bear Heritage Trail** (www.sleepingbeartrail.org) paves 13 pretty miles from Empire to Port Oneida, passing the Dune Climb along the way; walkers and cyclists are all over it. Short on time or stamina? Take the 7-mile, one-lane, picnic-grove-studded **Pierce Stocking Scenic Drive**, perhaps the best way to absorb the stunning lake vistas.

After you leave the park, swing into little **Leland** (www.lelandmi.com). Grab a bite at a waterfront restaurant downtown, and poke around atmospheric Fishtown with its weatherbeaten shacks-cum-shops. Boats depart from here for the Manitou Islands.

Onward near Suttons Bay, **Tandem Ciders** (www.tandemciders.com; 2055 Setterbo Rd; ⌚noon-6pm Mon-Sat, to 5pm Sun) pours delicious hard ciders in its small tasting room on the family farm.

Traverse City

Michigan's 'cherry capital' is the largest city in the northern half of the Lower Peninsula. It's got a bit of urban sprawl, but it's still a happenin' base from which to see the Sleeping Bear Dunes, Mission Peninsula wineries, U-pick orchards and other area attractions.

Road tripping out to the wineries is a must. Head north from Traverse City on Hwy 37 for 20 miles to the end of the grape- and cherry-planted Old Mission Peninsula. You'll be spoiled for choice: **Chateau Grand Traverse** (www.cgtwines.com; 6-wine tasting $3; ⌚10am-7pm Mon-Sat, to 6pm Sun) and **Chateau Chantal** (www.chateauchantal.com; ⌚11am-8pm Mon-Sat, to 6pm Sun) pour crowd-pleasing Chardonnay and Pinot Noir. **Peninsula Cellars** (www.peninsulacellars.com; 5-wine tasting $3; ⌚10am-6pm), in an old schoolhouse, makes fine whites and is often less crowded. Whatever bottle you buy, take it out to Lighthouse Park beach, at the peninsula's tip, and enjoy it with the waves chilling your toes. The wineries stay open year-round, with reduced hours in winter.

The town goes Hollywood during the **Traverse City Film Festival** (www.traversecityfilmfest.org; ⌚late Jul), when founder (and native Michigander) Michael Moore comes in and unspools a six-day slate of documentaries, international flicks and 'just great movies.'

Dozens of beaches, resorts, motels and water-sports operators line US 31 around Traverse City. Lodgings are often full – and more expensive – during weekends; check www.traversecity.com for listings. Most resorts overlooking the bay cost $175 to $275 per night. The Chantal and Grand Traverse wineries also double as B&Bs and fit into this price range.

Sugar Beach Resort (☎800-509-1995; www.tcbeaches.com; 1773 US 31 N; r $150-250; ❄📶🏊) has decent-value rooms right on the water. The motels on the other side of US 31 (away from the water) are more moderately priced, such as family-owned **Mitchell Creek Inn** (☎231-947-9330; www.mitchellcreek.com; 894 Munson Ave; r/cottages from $60/125; 📶), which is near the state park beach.

After a day of fun in the sun, refresh with sandwiches at gastronome favorite **Folgarelli's** (☎231-941-7651; www.folgarellis.net; 424 W Front St; sandwiches $8-11; ⌚9:30am-6:30pm Mon-Fri, to 5:30pm Sat, 11am-4pm Sun) and Belgian and Michigan craft beers at **7 Monks Taproom** (www.7monkstap.com; 128 S Union St; ⌚noon-midnight), which also shakes cocktails in its basement bar.

WORTH A TRIP

MANITOU ISLANDS

If you're looking for a wilderness adventure, the Manitou Islands – part of Sleeping Bear Dunes National Lakeshore – deliver. **Manitou Island Transit** (☎231-256-9061; www.manitoutransit.com) can help plan overnight camping trips on North Manitou, or day trips to South Manitou. Kayaking and hiking are popular activities, especially the 7-mile trek to the Valley of the Giants, a mystical stand of cedar trees on South Manitou. Ferries (round-trip adult/child $35/20, 1½ hours) sail from Leland two to seven times per week from mid-May to early October.

Charlevoix & Petoskey

These two towns hold several Hemingway sights. They're also where Michigan's uppercrusters maintain summer homes. The downtown areas of both places have gourmet restaurants and high-class shops, and the marinas are filled with yachts.

In Petoskey, **Stafford's Perry Hotel** (☎231-347-4000; www.staffords.com; Bay at Lewis St; r $149-269; ❄@📶) is a grand historic place in which to stay. **Petoskey State Park** (☎231-347-2311; 2475 Hwy 119; tent & RV sites $31-33) is north along Hwy 119 and has a beautiful beach. Look for indigenous Petoskey stones, which are honeycomb-patterned fragments of ancient coral. From here, Hwy 119 – aka the **Tunnel of Trees scenic route** – dips and curves through thick forest as it rolls north along a sublime bluff, en route to the Straits of Mackinac.

> ### ⓘ HIKING-TRAIL MAPS
>
> Plot out your walk in the woods with **Michigan Trail Maps** (www.michigan-trailmaps.com), a free resource with more than 200 trail guides. Search by city, county or activity (birding, day hikes, backpacking etc), then download and print the high-quality maps as PDFs. It covers trails statewide.

Straits of Mackinac

This region, between the Upper and Lower Peninsulas, features a long history of forts and fudge shops. Car-free Mackinac Island is Michigan's premier tourist draw.

One of the most spectacular sights in the area is the 5-mile-long **Mackinac Bridge** (known locally as 'Big Mac'), which spans the Straits of Mackinac. The $4 toll is worth it as the views from the bridge, which include two Great Lakes, two peninsulas and hundreds of islands, are second to none in Michigan.

And remember: despite the spelling, it's pronounced *mac*-in-aw.

Mackinaw City

At the south end of Mackinac Bridge, bordering I-75, is touristy Mackinaw City. It serves mainly as a jump-off point to Mackinac Island, but it does have a couple of interesting sights.

Next to the bridge (its visitor center is actually beneath the bridge) is **Colonial Michilimackinac** (☑231-436-5564; www.mackinacparks.com; adult/child $11/6.50; ☉9am-7pm Jun-Aug, to 5pm May & Sep–mid-Oct), a National Historic Landmark that features a reconstructed stockade first built in 1715 by the French. Some 3 miles southeast of the city on US 23 is **Historic Mill Creek** (☑231-436-4226; www.mackinacparks.com; adult/child $8/5; ☉9am-6pm Jun-Aug, to 5pm May & Sep–mid-Oct), which has an 18th-century sawmill, historic displays and nature trails. A combination ticket for both sights, along with the nearby Old Mackinac Point Lighthouse, is available at a discount.

If you can't find lodging on Mackinac Island – which should be your first choice – motels line I-75 and US 23 in Mackinaw City. Most cost $100-plus per night. Try the **Clarion Hotel Beachfront** (☑231-436-5539; 905 S Huron Ave; r $110-170; P❄@🖀🐾).

St Ignace

At the north end of Mackinac Bridge is St Ignace, the other departure point for Mackinac Island and the second-oldest settlement in Michigan – Père Jacques Marquette founded a mission here in 1671. As soon as you've paid your bridge toll, you'll pass a huge **visitor center** (☑906-643-6979; I-75N; ☉9am-5:30pm daily Jun-Aug, Thu-Mon rest of year) which has racks of statewide information.

Mackinac Island

From either Mackinaw City or St Ignace you can catch a ferry to Mackinac Island. The island's location in the straits between Lake Michigan and Lake Huron made it a prized port in the North American fur trade, and a site the British and Americans battled over many times.

The most important date on this 3.8-sq-mile island was 1898 – the year cars were banned in order to encourage tourism. Today all travel is by horse or bicycle; even the police use bikes to patrol the town. The crowds of tourists – called Fudgies by the islanders – can be crushing at times, particularly during summer weekends. But when the last ferry leaves in the evening and clears out the day-trippers, Mackinac's real charm emerges and you drift back into another, slower era.

The **visitor center** (☑800-454-5227; www.mackinacisland.org; Main St; ☉9am-5pm May-Oct, reduced hours Nov-Apr), by the Arnold Line ferry dock, has maps for hiking and cycling. Eighty percent of the island is state parkland. Not much stays open between November and April.

◉ Sights & Activities

Edging the island's shoreline is Hwy 185, the only Michigan highway that doesn't permit cars. The best way to view the incredible scenery along this 8-mile road is by bicycle; bring your own or rent one in town for $8 per hour at one of the many businesses. You can loop around the flat road in about an hour.

The two best attractions – **Arch Rock** (a huge limestone arch that sits 150ft above Lake Huron) and **Fort Holmes** (the island's other fort) – are both free. You can also ride past the **Grand Hotel**, which boasts a porch stretching halfway to Detroit. Unfortunately, if you're not staying at the Grand (minimum

$280 per night per person), it costs $10 to stroll its long porch. Best to admire from afar.

Fort Mackinac HISTORIC SITE
(906-847-3328; www.mackinacparks.com; adult/child $12/7; 9:30am-6pm Jun-Aug, to 5pm May & Sep–mid-Oct;) Fort Mackinac sits atop limestone cliffs near downtown. Built by the British in 1780, it's one of the best-preserved military forts in the country. Costumed interpreters and cannon and rifle firings (every half-hour) entertain the kids. Stop into the tearoom for a bite and million-dollar view of downtown and the Straits of Mackinac from the outdoor tables.

The fort admission price also allows you entry to five other museums in town along Market St, including the Dr Beaumont Museum (where the doctor performed his famous digestive tract experiments) and Benjamin Blacksmith Shop.

Mackinac Art Museum MUSEUM
(7070 Main St; adult/child $5.50/4; 10am-5:30pm Jun-Aug, to 4pm May & Sep–mid-Oct) It houses Native American and other arts. Admission is free with a Fort Mackinac ticket.

Sleeping

Rooms are booked far in advance during summer weekends; July to mid-August is peak season. The visitor center website has lodging contacts. Camping is not permitted anywhere on the island.

Most hotels and B&Bs charge at least $210 for two people. Exceptions (all are walkable from downtown) include the following.

Bogan Lane Inn B&B $$
(906-847-3439; www.boganlaneinn.com; Bogan Lane; r $95-135) Four rooms, shared bath.

Cloghaun B&B B&B $$
(906-847-3885; www.cloghaun.com; Market St; r $114-199; mid-May–late Oct;) Eleven rooms, some with shared bath.

Hart's B&B B&B $$
(906-847-3854; www.hartsmackinac.com; Market St; r $150-205; mid-May–late Oct;) Nine rooms, all with private bath.

Eating & Drinking

Fudge shops are the island's best-known eateries; resistance is futile when they use fans to blow the aroma out onto Huron St. Hamburger and sandwich shops abound downtown.

JL Beanery Coffeehouse CAFE $
(906-847-6533; Main St; mains $6-13; 7am-4pm;) Read the newspaper, sip a steaming cup of joe and gaze at the lake at this waterside cafe. It serves dandy breakfasts, sandwiches and soups.

HEMINGWAY'S HAUNTS

A number of writers have ties to northwest Michigan, but none are as famous as Ernest Hemingway, who spent the summers of his youth at his family's cottage on Walloon Lake. Hemingway buffs often tour the area to view the places that made their way into his writing. Key sites:

Horton Bay General Store (231-582-7827; www.hortonbaygeneralstore.com; 05115 Boyne City Rd; 8am-2pm Sun-Thu, to 2pm & 5-9pm Fri & Sat, closed mid-Oct–mid-May) As you head north on US 31, past yacht-filled Charlevoix, look for Boyne City Rd veering off to the east. It skirts Lake Charlevoix and eventually arrives at Horton Bay. Hemingway fans will recognize the store, with its 'high false front,' from his short story 'Up in Michigan.' The old-time shop now sells groceries, souvenirs, sandwiches and ice cream, plus wine and tapas on weekend nights (make reservations for the latter).

Little Traverse History Museum (231-347-2620; www.petoskeymuseum.org; 100 Depot Ct; admission $3; 10am-4pm Mon-Sat late May–mid-Oct) Further up Hwy 31 in Petoskey, stop in to see the museum's Hemingway collection, including rare first-edition books that the author autographed for a friend when he visited in 1947.

City Park Grill (231-347-0101; www.cityparkgrill.com; 432 E Lake St; 11:30am-10pm Sun-Thu, to 1:30am Fri & Sat) A few blocks from the museum, toss back a drink at this bar where Hemingway was a regular.

Tour Hemingway's Michigan (www.mihemingwaytour.org) Provides further information for self-guided jaunts.

Horn's Bar BURGERS, MEXICAN $$
(906-847-6154; www.hornsbar.com; Main St; mains $11-19; 10am-2am) Horn's saloon serves American burgers and south-of-the-border fare, and there's live entertainment nightly.

Cawthorne's Village Inn AMERICAN $$
(906-847-3542; www.grandhotel.com; Hoban St; mains $19-24; 11am-10pm) Planked whitefish, pan-fried perch and other fresh-from-the-lake fish, meat and pasta dishes stuff diners at this year-round local hangout with a bar and outdoor seating. Operated by the Grand Hotel.

Pink Pony BAR
(www.pinkponybar.com; Main St; 11am-2pm Mon-Sat, from noon Sun) Prepare for gloriously weird decor, as if Barbie designed an English pub in shades of her favorite color. Yes it's touristy, but it's also heaps of fun with rock bands and patio views that'll wallop your eyeballs. Operated by the Chippewa Hotel.

Getting There & Around

Three ferry companies – **Arnold Line** (800-542-8528; www.arnoldline.com), **Shepler's** (800-828-6157; www.sheplersferry.com) and **Star Line** (800-638-9892; www.mackinac-ferry.com) – operate out of Mackinaw City and St Ignace, and charge roughly the same rates: round-trip adult/child/bicycle $25/13/9. Book online and you'll save a few bucks. The ferries run several times daily from May through October. The trip takes about 20 minutes. (Arnold Line is a bit slower and consequently, a bit cheaper.) All of the companies have free parking lots to leave your car. Once on the island, horse-drawn cabs will take you anywhere, or rent a bicycle.

Upper Peninsula

Rugged and isolated, with hardwood forests blanketing 90% of its land, the Upper Peninsula (UP) is a Midwest highlight. Only 45 miles of interstate highway slice through the trees, punctuated by a handful of cities, of which Marquette (population 21,000) is the largest. Between the small towns lie miles of undeveloped shoreline on Lakes Huron, Michigan and Superior; scenic two-lane roads; and pasties, the local meat-and-vegetable pot pies brought over by Cornish miners 150 years ago.

You'll find it's a different world up north. Residents of the UP, aka 'Yoopers,' consider themselves distinct from the rest of the state – they've even threatened to secede in the past.

Sault Ste Marie & Tahquamenon Falls

Founded in 1668, Sault Ste Marie (Sault is pronounced 'soo') is Michigan's oldest city and the third oldest in the USA. The town is best known for its locks that raise and lower 1000ft-long freighters between the different lake levels. **Soo Locks Park & Visitor Center** (312 W Portage Ave; 9am-9pm mid-May–mid-Oct) FREE is on Portage Ave downtown (take exit 394 off I-75 and go left). It features displays, videos and observation decks from which you can watch the boats leap 21ft from Lake Superior to Lake Huron. Pubs and cafes line Portage Ave. The **Sault CVB** (www.saultstemarie.com) has the lowdown.

An hour's drive west of Sault Ste Marie, via Hwy 28 and Hwy 123, is eastern UP's top attraction: lovely **Tahquamenon Falls**, with tea-colored waters tinted by upstream hemlock leaves. The Upper Falls in **Tahquamenon Falls State Park** (906-492-3415; per vehicle $9), 200ft across with a 50ft drop, wow onlookers – including Henry Wadsworth Longfellow, who mentioned them in his *Song of Hiawatha*. The Lower Falls are a series of small cascades that swirl around an island; many visitors rent a rowboat and paddle out to it. The large state park also has camping (tent and RV sites $17 to $25), great hiking and – bonus – a brewpub near the park entrance.

North of the park, beyond the little town of Paradise, is the fascinating **Great Lakes Shipwreck Museum** (888-492-3747; www.shipwreckmuseum.com; 18335 N Whitefish Point Rd; adult/child $13/9; 10am-6pm May–late Oct), where the intriguing displays include items trawled up from sunken ships. Dozens of vessels – including the *Edmund Fitzgerald* that Gordon Lightfoot crooned about – have sunk in the area's congested sea lanes and storm-tossed weather, earning it such nicknames as the 'Shipwreck Coast' and 'Graveyard of the Great Lakes.' The grounds also include a lighthouse President Lincoln commissioned and a bird observatory that 300 species fly by. To have the foggy place to yourself, spend the night at **Whitefish Point Light Station B&B** (888-492-3747; r $150; late Apr–early Nov), which offers five rooms in the old Coast Guard crew quarters on-site.

Pictured Rocks National Lakeshore

Stretching along prime Lake Superior real estate, **Pictured Rocks National Lakeshore** (www.nps.gov/piro) is a series of wild cliffs and caves where blue and green minerals have streaked the red and yellow sandstone into a kaleidoscope of color. Rte 58 (Alger County Rd) spans the park for 52 slow miles from **Grand Marais** in the east to **Munising** in the west. Top sights (from east to west) include **Au Sable Point Lighthouse** (reached via a 3-mile round-trip walk beside shipwreck skeletons), agate-strewn **Twelvemile Beach**, hike-rich **Chapel Falls** and view-worthy **Miners Castle Overlook**.

Several boat tours launch from Munising. **Pictured Rock Cruises** (906-387-2379; www.picturedrocks.com; 100 W City Park Dr; 2½hr tours adult/child $37/10; mid-May–mid-Oct) departs from the city pier downtown and glides along the shore to Miners Castle. **Shipwreck Tours** (906-387-4477; www.shipwrecktours.com; 1204 Commercial St; 2hr tours adult/child $32/12; late May–mid-Oct) sails in glass-bottom boats to see sunken schooners.

Grand Island (www.grandislandup.com), part of Hiawatha National Forest, is also a quick jaunt from Munising. Hop aboard the **Grand Island Ferry** (906-387-3503; round-trip adult/child $15/10; late May–mid-Oct) to get there and rent a mountain bike ($30 per day) to zip around. There's also a three-hour bus tour (adult/child $15/5). The ferry dock is on Hwy 28, which is about 4 miles west of Munising.

Munising has lots of motels, such as tidy **Alger Falls Motel** (906-387-3536; www.algerfallsmotel.com; E9427 Hwy 28; r $70-105;). **Falling Rock Cafe & Bookstore** (906-387-3008; www.fallingrockcafe.com; 104 E Munising Ave; mains $5-10; 9am-8pm Sun-Fri, to 10pm Sat;) provides sandwiches and live music.

Staying in wee Grand Marais, on the park's east side, is also recommended. Turn in at **Hilltop Cabins and Motel** (906-494-2331; www.hilltopcabins.net; N14176 Ellen St; r & cabins $85-185;) after a meal of whitefish sandwiches and brewskis at woodsy **Lake Superior Brewing Company** (906-494-2337; N14283 Lake Ave; mains $9-19; noon-11pm).

Marquette

From Munising, Hwy 28 heads west and hugs Lake Superior. This beautiful stretch of highway has lots of beaches, roadside parks and rest areas where you can pull over and enjoy the scenery. Within 45 miles you'll reach outdoorsy, oft-snowy Marquette.

Stop at the log-lodge **visitor center** (2201 US 41; 9am-5:30pm) as you enter the city for brochures on local hiking trails and waterfalls.

The easy **Sugarloaf Mountain Trail** and the harder, wilderness-like **Hogsback Mountain Trail** offer panoramic views. Both are reached from County Rd 550, just north of Marquette. In the city, the high bluffs of **Presque Isle Park** make a great place to catch the sunset. The **Noquemanon Trail Network** (www.noquetrails.org) is highly recommended for mountain biking and cross-country skiing. Kayaking is awesome in the area; **Down Wind Sports** (www.downwindsports.com; 514 N Third St; 10am-7pm Mon-Fri, to 5pm Sat, 11am-3pm Sun) has the lowdown on it, as well as fly fishing, surfing, ice climbing and other adventures.

Marquette is the perfect place to stay put for a few days to explore the central UP. Budgeteers can bunk at **Value Host Motor Inn** (906-225-5000; 1101 US 41 W; r $65-75;) a few miles west of town. Downtown's **Landmark Inn** (906-228-2580; www.thelandmarkinn.com; 230 N Front St; r $179-229;) fills a historic lakefront building and has a couple of resident ghosts. Check www.travelmarquettemichigan.com for more lodgings.

Sample the local meat-and-veggie pie specialty at **Jean Kay's Pasties & Subs** (www.jeankayspasties.com; 1635 Presque Isle Ave; items $5-7.50; 11am-9pm Mon-Fri, to 8pm Sat & Sun). In a Quonset hut at Main St's foot, **Thill's Fish House** (906-226-9851; 250 E Main St; items $4-9; 8am-5:30pm Mon-Fri, 9am-4pm Sat) is Marquette's last commercial fishing operation, and it hauls in fat catches daily; try the

> DON'T MISS
>
> **DA YOOPERS TOURIST TRAP**
>
> Behold Big Gus, the world's largest chainsaw. And Big Ernie, the world's largest rifle. Kitsch runs rampant at **Da Yoopers Tourist Trap and Museum** (906-485-5595; www.dayoopers.com; 9am-8pm Mon-Sat, to 6pm Sun) FREE, 15 miles west of Marquette on Hwy 28/41, past Ishpeming. Browse the store for only-in-the-UP gifts like a polyester moose tie or beer-can wind chimes.

smoked whitefish sausage. Hop-heads and mountain bikers hang out at **Blackrocks Brewery** (www.blackrocksbrewery.com; 424 N Third St; ⌚4-11pm Mon-Thu, from noon Fri & Sun), set in a cool refurbished house downtown.

Isle Royale National Park

Totally free of vehicles and roads, **Isle Royale National Park** (www.nps.gov/isro; fee per day $4; ⌚mid-May–Oct), a 210-sq-mile island in Lake Superior, is certainly the place to go for peace and quiet. It gets fewer visitors in a year than Yellowstone National Park gets in a day, which means the 1200 moose creeping through the forest are all yours.

The island is laced with 165 miles of hiking trails that connect dozens of campgrounds along Superior and inland lakes. You must be totally prepared for this wilderness adventure, with a tent, camping stove, sleeping bags, food and water filter. Otherwise, be a softie and bunk at the **Rock Harbor Lodge** (☎906-337-4993; www.isleroyaleresort.com; r & cottages $224-256; ⌚late May-early Sep).

From the dock outside the **park headquarters** (800 E Lakeshore Dr) in Houghton, the **Ranger III** (☎906-482-0984) departs at 9am on Tuesday and Friday for the six-hour boat trip (round-trip adult/child $126/46) to Rock Harbor, at the east end of the island. **Isle Royale Seaplanes** (☎877-359-4753; www.isleroyaleseaplanes.com) offer a quicker trip, flying from Houghton County Airport to Rock Harbor in 30 minutes (round-trip $310). Or head 50 miles up the Keweenaw Peninsula to Copper Harbor (a beautiful drive) and jump on the **Isle Royale Queen** (☎906-289-4437; www.isleroyale.com) for the 8am three-hour crossing (round-trip adult/child $130/65). It usually runs daily during peak season from late July to mid-August. Bringing a kayak or canoe on the ferries costs an additional $50 round-trip; ensure you make reservations well in advance. You can also access Isle Royale from Grand Portage, MN; see p617.

Porcupine Mountains Wilderness State Park

Michigan's largest state park, with 90 miles of trails, is another UP winner, and it's a heck of a lot easier to reach than Isle Royale. 'The Porkies,' as they're called, are so rugged that loggers bypassed most of the range in the early 19th century, leaving the park with the largest tract of virgin forest between the Rocky Mountains and Adirondacks.

From Silver City, head west on Hwy 107 to reach the **Porcupine Mountains Visitor Center** (☎906-885-5275; www.michigan.gov/porkiesvc; 412 S Boundary Rd; ⌚10am-6pm mid-May–mid-Oct), where you buy vehicle entry permits ($9/31 per day/year) and backcountry permits (one to four people per night $15). Continue to the end of Hwy 107 and climb 300ft for the stunning view of **Lake of the Clouds**.

Winter is also a busy time at the Porkies, with downhill skiing (a 787ft vertical drop) and 26 miles of cross-country trails on offer; check with the **ski area** (☎906-885-5209; www.porkiesfun.com) for conditions and costs.

The park rents **rustic cabins** (☎906-885-5275; www.mi.gov/porkies; cabins $65) perfect for wilderness adventurers, as you have to hike in 1 to 4 miles, boil your own water and use a privy. **Sunshine Motel & Cabins** (☎906-884-2187; www.ontonagonmi.com; 24077 Hwy 64; r $60, cabins $68-120; 📶🐾), 3 miles west of Ontonagon, provides another good base.

WISCONSIN

Wisconsin is cheesy and proud of it. The state pumps out 2.5 billion pounds of cheddar, Gouda and other smelly goodness – a quarter of America's hunks – from its cow-speckled farmland per year. Local license plates read 'The Dairy State' with udder dignity. Folks here even refer to themselves as 'cheeseheads' and emphasize it by wearing novelty foam rubber cheese-wedge hats for special occasions (most notably during Green Bay Packers football games).

So embrace the cheese thing, because there's a good chance you'll be here for a while. Wisconsin has heaps to offer: exploring the craggy cliffs and lighthouses of Door County, kayaking through sea caves at Apostle Islands National Lakeshore, cow chip throwing along US 12 and soaking up beer, art and festivals in Milwaukee and Madison.

ℹ Information

Travel Green Wisconsin (www.travelgreenwisconsin.com) Certifies businesses as ecofriendly by grading them on waste reduction, energy efficiency and seven other categories.

Wisconsin B&B Association (www.wbba.org)

Wisconsin Department of Tourism (☎800-432-8747; www.travelwisconsin.com) Produces loads of free guides on subjects like bird-watching, biking, golf and rustic roads; also a free app.

Wisconsin Highway Conditions (☎511; www.511wi.gov)

Wisconsin Milk Marketing Board (www.eatwisconsincheese.com) Provides a free statewide map of cheesemakers titled *A Traveler's Guide to America's Dairyland.*

Wisconsin State Park Information (☎608-266-2181; www.wiparks.net) Park entry requires a vehicle permit (per day/year $10/35). Campsites cost from $14 to $25; reservations (☎888-947-2757; www.wisconsinstateparks.reserveamerica.com; fee $10) accepted.

WISCONSIN FACTS

Nicknames Badger State, America's Dairyland

Population 5.8 million

Area 65,500 sq miles

Capital city Madison (population 243,000)

Other cities Milwaukee (population 599,000)

Sales tax 5%

Birthplace of Author Laura Ingalls Wilder (1867–1957), architect Frank Lloyd Wright (1867–1959), painter Georgia O'Keeffe (1887–1986), actor Orson Welles (1915–85), guitar maker Les Paul (1915–2009)

Home of 'Cheesehead' Packer fans, dairy farms, water parks

Politics Leans Democratic

Famous for Breweries, artisanal cheese, first state to legislate gay rights

Official dance Polka

Driving distances Milwaukee to Minneapolis 336 miles, Milwaukee to Madison 80 miles

Milwaukee

Here's the thing about Milwaukee: it's cool, but for some reason everyone refuses to admit it. Yes, the reputation lingers as a working man's town of brewskis, bowling alleys and polka halls. But attractions like the Calatrava-designed art museum, badass Harley-Davidson Museum and stylish eating and shopping 'hoods have turned Wisconsin's largest city into a surprisingly groovy place. In summertime, festivals let loose with revelry by the lake almost every weekend. And where else on the planet will you see racing sausages?

History

Milwaukee was first settled by Germans in the 1840s. Many started small breweries, but a few decades later the introduction of bulk brewing technology turned beer production into a major industry here. Milwaukee earned its 'Brew City' and 'Nation's Watering Hole' nicknames in the 1880s when Pabst, Schlitz, Blatz, Miller and 80 other breweries made suds here. Today, only Miller remains of the big brewers, though microbreweries are making a comeback.

Sights & Activities

Lake Michigan sits to the east of the city, and is rimmed by parkland. The Riverwalk path runs along both sides of the Milwaukee River downtown.

★**Harley-Davidson Museum** MUSEUM

(☎877-436-8738; www.h-dmuseum.com; 400 W Canal St; adult/child $20/10; ⏰9am-6pm Fri-Wed, to 8pm Thu May-Sep, from 10am Oct-Apr) Hundreds of motorcycles show the styles through the decades, including the flashy rides of Elvis and Evel Knievel. You can sit in the saddle of various bikes (on the bottom floor, in the Experience Gallery) and take badass photos. Even nonbikers will enjoy the interactive exhibits and tough, leather-clad crowds.

It all started in 1903, when Milwaukee schoolmates William Harley and Arthur Davidson built and sold their first motorcycle. A century later the big bikes are a symbol of American manufacturing pride. The museum is located in a sprawling industrial building just south of downtown.

Harley-Davidson Plant TOUR

(☎877-883-1450; www.harley-davidson.com/experience; W156 N9000 Pilgrim Rd; 30min tours free; ⏰9am-2pm Mon) Hog-heads can get a fix at the plant where engines are built, in suburban Menomonee Falls. In addition to Monday's free tour, longer tours take place on Wednesday, Thursday and Friday in summer, but only as part of a package deal you buy from the museum (per person $46, including tour, museum admission, and transport between the two venues).

Milwaukee Art Museum MUSEUM
(☎414-224-3200; www.mam.org; 700 N Art Museum Dr; adult/child $15/12; ⏰10am-5pm, to 8pm Thu, closed Mon Sep-May) You have to see this lakeside institution, which features a stunning winglike addition by Santiago Calatrava. It soars open and closed every day at 10am, noon and 5pm (8pm on Thursday), which is wild to watch (head to the suspension bridge outside for the best view). There are fabulous folk and outsider art galleries, and a sizeable collection of Georgia O'Keeffe paintings. A 2015 renovation added photography and new-media galleries to the trove.

Miller Brewing Company BREWERY
(☎414-931-2337; www.millercoors.com/milwaukee-brewery-tour; 4251 W State St; ⏰10:30am-4:30pm Mon-Sat, to 3:30pm Sun Jun-Aug, to 3:30pm Mon-Sat only Sep-May) FREE Pabst and Schlitz have moved on, but Miller preserves Milwaukee's beer legacy. Join the legions lined up for the free tours. Though the mass-produced beer may not be your favorite, the factory impresses with its sheer scale: you'll visit the packaging plant where 2000 cans are filled each minute, and the warehouse where a half-million cases await shipment. And then there's the generous tasting session at the tour's end, where you can down three full-size samples. Don't forget your ID.

Lakefront Brewery BREWERY
(☎414-372-8800; www.lakefrontbrewery.com; 1872 N Commerce St; 1hr tours $8; ⏰11am-8pm Mon-Thu, to 9pm Fri, 9am-9pm Sat, 10am-5pm Sun) Well-loved Lakefront Brewery, across the river from Brady St, has afternoon tours, but the swellest time to visit is on Friday nights when there's a fish fry, 16 beers to try and a polka band letting loose. Tour times vary throughout the week, but there's usually at least a 2pm and 3pm walk-through.

AMERICA'S BOWLING CAPITAL

You're in Milwaukee, so you probably should just do it: bowl. The city once had more than 200 bowling alleys, and many retro lanes still hide in timeworn dives. To get your game on try **Landmark Lanes** (www.landmarklanes.com; 2220 N Farwell Ave; per game $3.50-4; ⏰5pm-midnight Mon-Thu, noon-1am Fri & Sat, to midnight Sun; 📶), offering 16 beat-up alleys in the historic 1927 Oriental Theater. An arcade, three bars and butt-cheap beer round out the atmosphere.

Discovery World at Pier Wisconsin MUSEUM
(☎414-765-9966; www.discoveryworld.org; 500 N Harbor Dr; adult/child $18/14; ⏰9am-4pm Mon-Fri, 10am-5pm Sat & Sun, closed Mon Sep-Mar; 👪) The city's lakefront science and technology museum is primarily a kid-pleaser, with freshwater and saltwater aquariums (where you can touch sharks and sturgeon) and a dockside, triple-masted Great Lakes schooner to ogle (two-hour sailing tours per person $40). Adults will appreciate the Les Paul exhibit, showcasing the Wisconsin native's pioneering guitars and sound equipment.

Lakefront Park PARK
The parkland edging Lake Michigan is prime for walking, cycling and inline skating. Also here is Bradford Beach, which is good for swimming and lounging.

Festivals & Events

Summerfest MUSIC
(www.summerfest.com; day pass $19; ⏰late Jun-early Jul) It's dubbed 'the world's largest music festival,' and indeed hundreds of rock, blues, jazz, country and alternative bands swarm its 10 stages over 11 days. The scene totally rocks; it is held at downtown's lakefront festival grounds. The headline concerts cost extra.

Other popular parties, held downtown on various summer weekends, include **PrideFest** (www.pridefest.com; ⏰mid-Jun), **Polish Fest** (www.polishfest.org; ⏰mid-Jun), **German Fest** (www.germanfest.com; ⏰late Jul) and **Irish Fest** (www.irishfest.com; ⏰mid-Aug).

Sleeping

Rates in this section are for summer, the peak season, when you should book in advance. Tax (15.1%) is not included. For cheap chain lodging, try Howell Ave, south near the airport.

County Clare Irish Inn INN $$
(☎414-272-5273; www.countyclare-inn.com; 1234 N Astor St; r $129-159; P❄📶) A winner near the lakefront. Rooms have that snug Irish-cottage feel, with four-post beds, white wainscot walls and whirlpool baths. There's free parking, free breakfast and an on-site Guinness-pouring pub, of course.

★Brewhouse Inn & Suites HOTEL $$
(☎414-810-3350; www.brewhousesuites.com; 1215 N 10th St; r $199-249; P❄@📶) This 90-room hotel opened in 2013 in the exquisitely renovated old Pabst Brewery complex. Each of the large chambers has steampunk decor, a kitchenette and free wi-fi. Continental breakfast is included. It's at downtown's far west edge, about a half-mile walk from sausagey Old World 3rd St and a good 2 miles from the festival grounds. Parking costs $26.

Iron Horse Hotel HOTEL $$$
(☎888-543-4766; www.theironhorsehotel.com; 500 W Florida St; r $220-320; P❄📶) This boutique hotel near the Harley museum is geared toward motorcycle enthusiasts, with covered parking for bikes. Most of the loft-style rooms retain the post-and-beam, exposed-brick interior of what was once a bedding factory. Parking costs $30.

Eating

Good places to scope for eats include Germanic Old World 3rd St downtown; hip, multiethnic Brady St by its intersection with N Farwell Ave; and the gastropub-filled Third Ward, anchored along N Milwaukee St south of I-94.

★Comet Cafe AMERICAN $
(☎414-273-7677; www.thecometcafe.com; 1947 N Farwell Ave; mains $8-13; ⏰10am-10pm Mon-Fri, from 9am Sat & Sun; 🌱) Students, young families, older couples and bearded, tattooed types pile in to the rock-and-roll Comet for gravy-smothered meatloaf, mac 'n' cheese, vegan gyros and hangover brunch dishes. It's a craft-beer-pouring bar on one side, and retro-boothed diner on the other. Be sure to try one of the giant cupcakes for dessert.

Milwaukee Public Market MARKET $
(☎414-336-1111; www.milwaukeepublicmarket.org; 400 N Water St; ⏰10am-8pm Mon-Fri, 8am-7pm Sat, 10am-6pm Sun; 📶) Located in the Third Ward, it stocks mostly prepared foods – cheese, chocolate, beer, tacos, frozen custard. Take them upstairs where there are tables, free wi-fi and $1 used books.

Leon's ICE CREAM $
(☎414-383-1784; www.leonsfrozencustard.us; 3131 S 27th St; items $1.50-4; ⏰11am-midnight) This 1950s-era, neon-lit drive-in specializes in frozen custard, a local concoction that's like ice cream but smoother and richer. Cash only.

DON'T MISS

THE BRONZE FONZ

Rumor has it the **Bronze Fonz** (east side of Riverwalk), just south of Wells St downtown, is the most photographed sight in Milwaukee. The Fonz, aka Arthur Fonzarelli, was a character from the 1970s TV show *Happy Days*, which was set in the city. What do you think – do the blue pants get an 'Aaay' or 'Whoa!'?

Ardent MODERN AMERICAN $$$
(☎414-897-7022; www.ardentmke.com; 1751 N Farwell St; small plates $11-16; ⏰6-10pm Wed-Sat) Milwaukee's foodies get weak-kneed when they sniff the Beard-nominated chef's ever-changing, farm-to-table dishes. It takes at least a couple of the smallish plates to make a meal, and dinner becomes a lingering affair in the tiny glowing room. Make reservations. After 11:30pm on Friday and Saturday, the restaurant reopens as a ramen noodle purveyor, with lines around the block.

Drinking & Entertainment

Bars

Milwaukee has the second most bars per capita in the country (a hair behind New Orleans). Several pour around N Water and E State Sts downtown and in the Third Ward. Drinkeries stay open to 2am.

Best Place BAR
(www.bestplacemilwaukee.com; 901 W Junau Ave; ⏰noon-6pm Mon & Wed, to 10pm Thu, 10:30am-10pm Fri & Sat, to 6pm Sun) Join the locals knocking back beers and massive whiskey pours at this small tavern in the former Pabst Brewery headquarters. A fireplace warms the cozy, dark-wood room; original murals depicting Pabst's history adorn the walls. Staff give daily tours ($8, including a 16oz Pabst or Schlitz tap brew) that explore the building.

Uber Tap Room BAR
(www.ubertaproom.com; 1048 N Old 3rd St; ⏰11am-8pm Sun-Wed, to 10pm Thu, to 11pm Fri & Sat) It's touristy, in the thick of Old World 3rd St and attached to the Wisconsin Cheese Mart, but it's a great place to sample local fare. Thirty Wisconsin beers flow from the taps, and cheese from the state's dairy bounty accompanies. Themed plates (spicy cheeses, stinky cheeses etc) cost $11 to $14.

Palm Tavern BAR
(2989 S Kinnickinnic Ave; 5pm-2am Mon-Sat, from 7pm Sun) Located in the fresh southside neighborhood of Bay View, this warm, jazzy little bar has a mammoth selection of beer (heavy on the Belgians) and single-malt Scotches.

Kochanski's Concertina Beer Hall BAR
(www.beer-hall.com; 1920 S 37th St; 6pm-2am Wed-Sat, from 1pm Sun;) Live polka and rockabilly music rules at kitschy Kochanski's, with beers from Schlitz to Polish drafts to Wisconsin craft labels. It's 5 miles southwest of downtown.

Sports

Miller Park BASEBALL
(www.brewers.com; 1 Brewers Way) The Brewers play baseball at fab Miller Park, which has a retractable roof, real grass and racing sausages. It's located near S 46th St.

Bradley Center BASKETBALL
(www.nba.com/bucks; 1001 N 4th St) The NBA's Milwaukee Bucks dunk here.

Information

The East Side neighborhood near the University of Wisconsin-Milwaukee has several coffee shops with free wi-fi.

Froedtert Hospital (414-805-3000; 9200 W Wisconsin Ave)

Milwaukee Convention & Visitors Bureau (800-554-1448; www.visitmilwaukee.org) Tourist information.

Milwaukee Journal Sentinel (www.jsonline.com) The city's daily newspaper.

On Milwaukee (www.onmilwaukee.com) Online source for restaurant and entertainment news.

Quest (www.quest-online.com) GLBT entertainment magazine.

DON'T MISS

RACING SAUSAGES

It's common to see strange things after too many stadium beers. But a group of giant sausages sprinting around the perimeter of Milwaukee's Miller Park – is that for *real*? It is if it's the middle of the 6th inning. That's when the famous 'Racing Sausages' (actually five people in costumes) waddle onto the field to give the fans a thrill. If you don't know your encased meats, that's Brat, Polish, Italian, Hot Dog and Chorizo vying for supremacy.

Shepherd Express (www.expressmilwaukee.com) Free alternative weekly paper.

Getting There & Around

General Mitchell International Airport (MKE; www.mitchellairport.com) is 8 miles south of downtown. Take public bus 80 ($2.25) or a cab ($33).

The **Lake Express ferry** (866-914-1010; www.lake-express.com; one way per adult/child/car from $86.50/30/91; May-Oct) sails from downtown (the terminal is located a few miles south of the city center) to Muskegon, MI, providing easy access to Michigan's beach-lined Gold Coast.

Badger Bus (414-276-7490; www.badgerbus.com; 635 N James Lovell St) goes to Madison ($20, two hours). **Greyhound** (414-272-2156; 433 W St Paul Ave) and **Megabus** (www.megabus.com/us; 433 St Paul Ave) run frequent buses to Chicago (two hours) and Minneapolis (6½ to seven hours). Both use the same location; Megabus is often cheaper.

Amtrak (414-271-0840; www.amtrakhiawatha.com; 433 W St Paul Ave) runs the *Hiawatha* train seven times a day to/from Chicago ($24, 1½ hours); catch it downtown (where it shares the station with Greyhound/Megabus) or at the airport.

The **Milwaukee County Transit System** (www.ridemcts.com; fares $2.25) provides the local bus service. Bus 31 goes to Miller Brewery; bus 90 goes to Miller Park.

Bublr Bikes (www.bublrbikes.com; per 30min ride $3) is Milwaukee's fledgling bike-share program, with 11 or so stations downtown (including at the train/bus depot and Public Market).

For taxi service, try phoning **Yellow Cab** (414-271-1800).

Madison

Madison reaps a lot of kudos – most walkable city, best road-biking city, most vegetarian-friendly, gay-friendly, environmentally friendly and just plain all-round friendliest city in the USA. Ensconced on a narrow isthmus between Mendota and Monona Lakes, it's a pretty combination of small, grassy state capital and liberal, bookish college town. An impressive foodie/locavore scene has been cooking here for years.

Sights & Activities

State St runs from the capitol west to the University of Wisconsin. The pedestrian-only avenue is lined with free-trade coffee shops, parked bicycles and incense-wafting stores selling hacky sacks and flowy Indian skirts.

Chazen Museum of Art MUSEUM
(www.chazen.wisc.edu; 750 University Ave; 9am-5pm Tue, Wed & Fri, to 9pm Thu, 11am-5pm Sat & Sun) FREE The university's art museum is huge and fabulous, fresh off an expansion and way beyond the norm for a campus collection. The 3rd floor holds most of the genre-spanning trove: everything from the old Dutch masters to Qing Dynasty porcelain vases, Picasso sculptures and Andy Warhol pop art. Free chamber-music concerts and art-house films take place on Sundays from September to mid-May.

Monona Terrace ARCHITECTURE
(www.mononaterrace.com; 1 John Nolen Dr; 8am-5pm) Frank Lloyd Wright designed the cool, white semicircular structure in 1938, though it wasn't completed until 1997. The one-hour tours ($5) explain why; they're offered daily at 1pm May through October (Friday through Monday only the rest of the year). The building serves as a community center, offering free lunchtime yoga classes and evening concerts; check the program schedule online. The rooftop garden and cafe offer sweeping lake views.

Dane County Farmers Market MARKET
(www.dcfm.org; Capitol Sq; 6am-2pm Sat late Apr-early Nov) On Saturdays, a food bazaar takes over Capitol Sq. It's one of the nation's most expansive markets, famed for its artisanal cheeses and breads. In winter it moves indoors to varying locations.

State Capitol BUILDING
(608-266-0382; 2 E Main St; 8am-6pm Mon-Fri, to 4pm Sat & Sun) FREE The X-shaped capitol is the largest outside Washington, DC, and marks the heart of downtown. Tours are available on the hour most days, or you can go up to the observation deck on your own for a view (summer only).

Museum of Contemporary Art MUSEUM
(608-257-0158; www.mmoca.org; 227 State St; noon-5pm Tue-Thu, to 8pm Fri, 10am-8pm Sat, noon-5pm Sun) FREE It's worth popping into the angular glass building to see what's showing. Diego Rivera? Claes Oldenburg? Exhibits change every three months or so. The museum connects to the **Overture Center for the Arts** (www.overturecenter.org; 201 State St), home to jazz, opera, dance and other performing arts.

TWO-WHEELING WISCONSIN

Wisconsin has converted an impressive number of abandoned railroad lines into paved, bike-only paths. They go up hills, through old tunnels, over bridges and alongside pastures. Wherever you are in the state, there's likely a sweet ride nearby; check the **Wisconsin Biking Guide** (downloadable at www.travelwisconsin.com, under Travel Resources, then Order Guides). The **400 State Trail** (www.400statetrail.org) and **Elroy-Sparta Trail** (www.elroy-sparta-trail.com) top the list.

Bike rentals are available in gateway towns, and you can buy trail passes ($4/20 per day/year) at area businesses or trailhead drop-boxes.

Arboretum GARDENS
(608-263-7888; http://uwarboretum.org; 1207 Seminole Hwy; 7am-10pm) FREE The campus' 1260-acre arboretum is dense with lilac and 20 miles of trails.

Machinery Row CYCLING
(608-442-5974; www.machineryrowbicycles.com; 601 Williamson St; rental per day $30; 10am-8pm Mon-Fri, 9am-7pm Sat, 10am-6pm Sun) It'd be a shame to leave town without taking advantage of the city's 120 miles of bike trails. Get wheels and maps at this shop, located by various trailheads. Rentals are per 24 hours only.

Festivals & Events

World's Largest Brat Fest FOOD
(www.bratfest.com; late May) FREE More than 209,000 bratwursts go down the hatch; carnival rides and bands provide the backdrop.

Great Taste of the Midwest Beer Festival BEER
(www.greattaste.org; tickets $60; early Aug) Tickets sell out fast for this festival where more than 100 craft brewers pour their elixirs.

Sleeping

Moderately priced motels can be found off I-90/I-94 (about 6 miles from the town center), off Hwy 12/18 and also along Washington Ave.

HI Madison Hostel HOSTEL $
(608-441-0144; www.hiusa.org/madison; 141 S Butler St; dm $25-30, r from $60; P @) The

brightly painted, 33-bed brick house is located on a quiet street a short walk from the State Capitol. The dorms are gender segregated; linens are free. There's a kitchen and common room with DVDs. Parking is $7.

★Arbor House B&B $$
(☎608-238-2981; www.arbor-house.com; 3402 Monroe St; r $140-230; 📶) 🍃 Arbor House was an old tavern back in the mid-1800s. Now it's a wind-powered, vegetarian-breakfast-serving B&B equipped with energy-efficient appliances. It's located about 3 miles southwest of the State Capitol but it's accessible to public transportation. The owners will lend you mountain bikes, too.

Graduate Madison BOUTIQUE HOTEL $$
(☎608-257-4391; www.graduatemadison.com; 601 Langdon St; r $149-209; P ❄ 📶 🐾) A block from campus and right off State St's action, this 72-room newbie (opened in spring 2015) wafts a hip academic vibe with its mod-meets-plaid decor and book-themed artwork. Rooms are on the small side and can be a bit noisy, but the location rocks.

Eating & Drinking

A global smorgasbord of restaurants peppers State St amid the pizza, sandwich and cheap-beer joints; many places have inviting patios. Cruising Williamson ('Willy') St turns up cafes, dumpling bars and Lao and Thai joints. Bars stay open to 2am. **Isthmus** (www.thedailypage.com) is the free entertainment paper.

Short Stack Eats BREAKFAST $
(www.shortstackeats.com; 301 W Johnson St; mains $7-13; ⏲24hr Thu-Sun) 🍃 It's all breakfast all day and all night at Short Stack. Order at the counter, then hopefully find a free table amid the cutesy, mismatched decor. Staff use old license plates as table markers to bring your locally sourced sweet potato pancakes, egg-and-bacon-filled breakfast sandwiches and enormous, spicy Bloody Marys.

Himal Chuli ASIAN $
(☎608-251-9225; 318 State St; mains $8-15; ⏲11am-9pm Mon-Sat, noon-8pm Sun; 🌿) Cheerful and cozy Himal Chuli serves up homemade Nepalese fare, including lots of vegetarian dishes.

Food Trucks INTERNATIONAL $
(mains $2-8; 🌿) Madison's fleet impresses. The more traditional ones, serving barbecue, burritos, Southwestern-style fare and Chinese food, ring the Capitol. Trucks ladling out more adventurous dishes – East African, Jamaican, Indonesian, vegan – huddle at the Library Mall (aka at foot of State St on campus).

★The Old Fashioned AMERICAN $$
(☎608-310-4545; www.theoldfashioned.com; 23 N Pinckney St; mains $9-19; ⏲7:30am-10:30pm Mon & Tue, to 2am Wed-Fri, 9am-2am Sat, to 10pm Sun) With its dark, woodsy decor, the Old Fashioned evokes a supper club, a type of retro eatery common in Wisconsin. The menu is all local specialties, including walleye, cheese soup and sausages. It's hard to choose among the 150 types of state-brewed suds in bottles, so opt for a sampler (four or eight little glasses) from the 30 Wisconsin tap beers.

Graze AMERICAN $$
(☎608-251-2700; www.grazemadison.com; 1 S Pinckney St; mains $14-22; ⏲11am-10pm Mon-Thu, to 11pm Fri, 9:30am-11pm Sat, to 3pm Sun) 🍃 Set in a glassy building with floor-to-ceiling windows and Capitol views, this green, cool-cat gastropub dishes up comfort foods such as fried chicken and waffles, mussels and *frites*, and burgers. Lunch piles up fat sandwiches with vodka-battered cheese curds.

L'Etoile MODERN AMERICAN $$$
(☎608-251-0500; www.letoile-restaurant.com; 1 S Pinckney St; mains $36-44; ⏲5:30-11pm Mon-Fri, from 5pm Sat) 🍃 L'Etoile started doing the farm-to-table thing more than three decades ago. It's still the best in the biz, offering creative meat, fish and vegetable dishes, all sourced locally and served in a casually elegant room. Reserve in advance. The gastropub Graze shares the glimmering building.

Memorial Union PUB
(www.union.wisc.edu/venue-muterrace.htm; 800 Langdon St; ⏲7am-midnight Mon-Fri, 8am-1am Sat, to midnight Sun; 📶) The campus Union is Madison's gathering spot. The festive lakeside terrace pours microbrews and hosts free live music and free Monday-night films, while the indoor ice-cream shop scoops hulking cones from the university dairy.

LOCAL KNOWLEDGE

FISH FRIES & SUPPER CLUBS

Wisconsin has two dining traditions that you'll likely encounter when visiting the state:

➡ **Fish Fry** Friday is the hallowed day of the 'fish fry.' This communal meal of beer-battered cod, French fries and coleslaw came about years ago, providing locals with a cheap meal to socialize around and celebrate the workweek's end. The convention is still going strong at many bars and restaurants, including Lakefront Brewery (p594) in Milwaukee.

➡ **Supper Club** This is a type of time-warped restaurant common in the upper Midwest. Supper clubs started in the 1930s, and most retain a retro vibe. Hallmarks include a woodsy location, a radish-and-carrot-laden relish tray on the table, a surf-and-turf menu and a mile-long, unironic cocktail list. See www.wisconsinsupperclubs.net for more information. The Old Fashioned (p598) in Madison is a modern take on the venue (it's named after the quintessential, brandy-laced supper-club drink).

Shopping

Fromagination FOOD
(☎608-255-2430; www.fromagination.com; 12 S Carroll St; ⏲10am-6pm Mon-Fri, 8am-5pm Sat, 11am-4pm Sun) The state's best cheese shop specializes in small-batch and hard-to-find local hunks. Browse the basket of 'orphans' by the cash register, where you can buy small quantities for $2 to $5. The shop also sells sandwiches, beer and wine.

Information

Madison Convention & Visitors Bureau (www.visitmadison.com)

Getting There & Around

Badger Bus (www.badgerbus.com) uses the Chazen Museum as its pick-up/drop-off point for trips to Milwaukee ($20, two hours), as does **Megabus** (www.megabus.com/us) for trips to Chicago (four hours) and Minneapolis (five hours).

Taliesin & Southern Wisconsin

This part of Wisconsin has some of the prettiest landscapes in the state, particularly the hilly southwest. Architecture fans can be unleashed at Taliesin, the Frank Lloyd Wright ubersight, and Racine, where a handful of his other works stand. Dairies around here cut a lot of cheese.

Racine

Racine is an unremarkable industrial town 30 miles south of Milwaukee, but it has some key Frank Lloyd Wright sights. First is the **SC Johnson Administration Building & Research Tower** (☎262-260-2154; www.scjohnson.com/visit; 1525 Howe St; ⏲1-3:30pm Wed-Fri, 9am-2:30pm Sat, 11:30am-3pm Sun) FREE. Free 75- to 90-minute tours take in the magnificent, curvy, Wright-designed structures. Six miles north is **Wingspread** (☎262-681-3353; www.scjohnson.com/visit; 33 E Four Mile Rd; ⏲9:30am-3:30pm Wed-Fri, 11:30am-3:30pm Sat, noon-2:30pm Sun) FREE, the last and largest of Wright's Prairie houses; free tours through the lakeside abode take one hour. All tours must be prebooked.

Green County

This pastoral area holds the nation's greatest concentration of cheesemakers, and **Green County Tourism** (www.greencounty.org) will introduce you to them. Monroe is a fine place to start sniffing. Follow your nose to **Roth Käse** (657 2nd St; ⏲9am-6pm Mon-Fri, 10am-5pm Sat & Sun), a store and factory where you can watch cheesemakers in action from the observation deck (weekday mornings only) and delve into the 'bargain bin' for hunks. Bite into a fresh limburger-and-raw-onion sandwich at **Baumgartner's** (www.baumgartnercheese.com; 1023 16th Ave; sandwiches $4-7; ⏲8am-11pm Sun-Thu, to midnight Fri & Sat), an old Swiss tavern on the town square. At night, catch a flick at the local drive-in movie theater, and then climb into bed at **Inn Serendipity** (☎608-329-7056; www.innserendipity.com; 7843 County Rd P; r $110-125), a two-room, wind-and-solar-powered B&B on a 5-acre organic farm in Browntown, about 10 miles west of Monroe.

For more on local dairy producers and plant tours, pick up, or download, **A Traveler's Guide to America's Dairyland** (www.eatwisconsincheese.com) map.

WORTH A TRIP

ODDBALL US 12

Unusual sights huddle around US 12, all easy to experience on a northerly day trip from Madison.

National Mustard Museum (☎800-438-6878; www.mustardmuseum.com; 7477 Hubbard Ave; ⏰10am-5pm) FREE Heading west out of Madison (take University Ave), stop first in suburban Middleton. Born of one man's ridiculously intense passion, the museum houses 5200 mustards and kooky condiment memorabilia. Tongue-in-cheek humor abounds, especially if CMO (chief mustard officer) Barry Levenson is there to give you the shtick.

Cow Chip Throw (www.wiscowchip.com; ⏰1st weekend Sep) FREE About 20 miles further on US 12 is the town of Prairie du Sac. It hosts the annual Cow Chip Throw, where 800 competitors fling dried manure patties as far as the eye can see; the record is 248ft.

Dr Evermor's Sculpture Park (☎608-219-7830; www.worldofdrevermor.com; ⏰11am-5pm Mon & Thu-Sat, from noon Sun) FREE Seven miles onward, the doc has welded old pipes, carburetors and other salvaged metal into a hallucinatory world of futuristic birds, dragons and other bizarre structures. The crowning glory is the giant, egg-domed Forevertron, once cited by Guinness World Records as the globe's largest scrap-metal sculpture. Finding the park entrance is tricky. Look for the old Badger Army Ammunition Plant, and then a small sign leading you into a driveway across the street. The doc is in poor health and isn't around much now, but his wife Lady Eleanor usually is.

Circus World (☎608-356-8341; www.circusworldbaraboo.org; 550 Water St; adult/child summer $20/10, winter $10/5; ⏰9am-5pm summer, reduced hours in winter; 👪) Baraboo, about 45 miles northwest of Madison, was once the winter home of the Ringling Brothers Circus. The museum preserves a nostalgic collection of wagons, posters and equipment from the touring big-top heyday. In summer, admission includes clowns, animals and acrobats doing the three-ring thing in live performances.

Wisconsin Dells (☎800-223-3557; www.wisdells.com; 👪) Continue north another 12 miles and you'll come to the Dells, a megacenter of kitschy diversions, including 21 water parks, water-skiing thrill shows and mini-golf courses. It's a jolting contrast to the natural appeal of the area, with its scenic limestone formations carved by the Wisconsin River. To appreciate the original attraction, take a boat tour or walk the trails at nearby Mirror Lake or Devil's Lake state parks.

Spring Green

Forty miles west of Madison and 3 miles south of the small town of Spring Green, **Taliesin** was the home of Frank Lloyd Wright for most of his life and is the site of his architectural school. It's now a major pilgrimage destination for fans and followers. The house was built in 1903, the Hillside Home School in 1932, and the **visitor center** (☎608-588-7900; www.taliesinpreservation.org; Hwy 23; ⏰9am-5:30pm May-Oct) in 1953. A wide range of guided tours ($20 to $85) cover various parts of the complex; reserve in advance for the lengthier ones. The one-hour Hillside Tour ($20) provides a nice introduction to Wright's work.

A few miles south of Taliesin is the **House on the Rock** (☎608-935-3639; www.thehouseontherock.com; 5754 Hwy 23; adult/child $15/9; ⏰9am-6pm May-Aug, to 5pm rest of year, closed mid-Nov–mid-Mar), one of Wisconsin's busiest attractions. Alex Jordan built the structure atop a rock column in 1959 (some say as an 'up yours' to neighbor Frank Lloyd Wright). He then stuffed the house to mind-blowing proportions with wonderments, including the world's largest carousel, whirring music machines, freaky dolls and crazed folk art. The house is broken into three parts, each with its own tour. Visitors with stamina (and about four hours to kill) can experience the whole shebang for adult/child $30/16.

Spring Green has a B&B in town and six motels strung along Hwy 14, north of town. Small **Usonian Inn** (☎877-876-6426; www.usonianinn.com; E 5116 Hwy 14; r $100-135; ❄📶) was designed by a Wright student.

Chomp sandwiches or inventive specials like sweet-potato stew at **Spring Green General Store** (www.springgreengeneralstore.

com; 137 S Albany St; mains $5-9; ⏲8:30am-5pm Mon-Fri, 7:30am-5pm Sat, to 4pm Sun).

The **American Players Theatre** (☎608-588-2361; www.americanplayers.org) stages classical productions at an outdoor amphitheater by the Wisconsin River.

Along the Mississippi River

The Mississippi River forms most of Wisconsin's western border, and alongside it run some of the most scenic sections of the **Great River Road** (www.wigreatriverroad.org) – the designated route that follows Old Man River from Minnesota to the Gulf of Mexico.

From Madison, head west on US 18. You'll hit the River Road (aka Hwy 35) at **Prairie du Chien**. North of town, the hilly riverside wends through the scene of the final battle in the bloody Black Hawk War. Historic markers tell part of the story, which finished at the Battle of Bad Ax when Native American men, women and children were massacred trying to flee across the Mississippi.

At Genoa, Hwy 56 leads inland for 20 miles to the trout-fishing mecca of **Viroqua** (www.viroqua-wisconsin.com), a pretty little town surrounded by organic farms and distinctive round barns. Pop into **Viroqua Food Cooperative** (www.viroquafood.coop; 609 Main St; ⏲7am-9pm) to meet farmers and munch their wares.

Back riverside and 18 miles upstream, **La Crosse** (www.explorelacrosse.com) has a historic center with restaurants and pubs. Grandad Bluff offers grand views of the river. It's east of town along Main St (which becomes Bliss Rd); follow Bliss Rd up the hill and then turn right on Grandad Bluff Rd. The **World's Largest Six-Pack** (cnr 3rd St S & Mississippi St) is also in town. The 'cans' are actually storage tanks for City Brewery and hold enough beer to provide one person with a six-pack a day for 3351 years (or so the sign says).

Door County & Eastern Wisconsin

Rocky, lighthouse-dotted Door County draws crowds in summer, while Green Bay draws crazed football fans in the freakin' freezing winter.

Green Bay

Green Bay is a modest industrial town best known as the fabled 'frozen tundra' where the Green Bay Packers win Super Bowls. The franchise is unique as the only community-owned nonprofit team in the NFL; perhaps pride in ownership is what makes the fans so die-hard (and also makes them wear foam-rubber cheese wedges on their heads).

While tickets are nearly impossible to obtain, you can always get into the spirit by joining a pregame tailgate party. The generous flow of alcohol has led to Green Bay's reputation as a 'drinking town with a football problem.' On nongame days, visit the **Green Bay Packer Hall of Fame** (☎920-569-7512; www.lambeaufield.com; adult/child $11/8; ⏲9am-6pm Mon-Sat, 10am-5pm Sun) at Lambeau Field, which is indeed packed with memorabilia and movies that'll intrigue any pigskin fan. Stadium tours are also available.

The **National Railroad Museum** (☎920-437-7623; www.nationalrrmuseum.org; 2285 S Broadway; adult/child $10/7.50; ⏲9am-5pm Mon-Sat, 11am-5pm Sun, closed Mon Jan-Mar) features some of the biggest locomotives ever to haul freight into Green Bay's vast yards; train rides ($2) are offered in summer.

Tidy, bare-bones **Bay Motel** (☎920-494-3441; www.baymotelgreenbay.com; 1301 S Military Ave; r $59-77; 📶) is a mile from Lambeau Field. **Hinterland** (☎920-438-8050; www.hinterlandbeer.com; 313 Dousman St; ⏲4pm-midnight Mon-Sat) gastropub brings a touch of rustic swankiness to the beer-drinking scene.

Door County

With its rocky coastline, picturesque lighthouses, cherry orchards and small 19th-century villages, you have to admit Door County is pretty damn lovely. The area spreads across a narrow peninsula jutting 75 miles into Lake Michigan, and visitors usually loop around on the county's two highways. Hwy 57 runs beside Lake Michigan and goes through Jacksonport and Baileys Harbor; this is known as the more scenic 'quiet side.' Hwy 42 borders Green Bay and passes through (from south to north) Egg Harbor, Fish Creek, Ephraim and Sister Bay; this side is more action oriented. Only about half the businesses stay open from November to April.

WORTH A TRIP

WASHINGTON ISLAND & ROCK ISLAND

From Door County's tip near Gills Rock, daily **ferries** (☎920-847-2546; www.wisferry.com; Northport Pier) go every half-hour to **Washington Island** (round-trip adult/child/bike/car $13.50/7/4/26), which has 700 Scandinavian descendants, a couple of museums, beaches, bike rentals and carefree roads for cycling. Accommodations and camping are available. More remote is lovely **Rock Island**, a state park with no cars or bikes at all. It's a wonderful place for hiking, swimming and camping. Get there via the **Karfi ferry** (www.wisferry.com), which departs Jackson Harbor on Washington Island (round-trip adult/child $11/5) every hour in summer.

Sights & Activities

Parkland blankets the county. Bayside **Peninsula State Park** is the largest, with bluffside hiking and biking trails and Nicolet Beach for swimming, kayaking and sailing (equipment rentals available on-site). In winter, cross-country skiers and snowshoers take over the trails. On the lake side, secluded **Newport State Park** offers trails, backcountry camping and solitude. **Whitefish Dunes State Park** has sandscapes and a wide beach (beware of riptides). Adjacent **Cave Point Park** is known for its sea caves and kayaking.

Bay Shore Outfitters OUTDOORS
(☎920-854-9220; www.kayakdoorcounty.com; Sister Bay) Rents kayaks, stand-up paddleboards and winter gear, and offers tours.

Nor Door Sport & Cyclery OUTDOORS
(☎920-868-2275; www.nordoorsports.com; Fish Creek) Nor Door rents out bikes and snow shoes near the entrance to Peninsula State Park.

Sleeping & Eating

The bay side has the most lodging. Prices listed are for July and August, the peak season; many places have minimum-stay requirements. Local restaurants often host a 'fish boil,' a regional specialty started by Scandinavian lumberjacks, in which whitefish, potatoes and onions are cooked in a fiery cauldron. Finish with Door's famous cherry pie.

Julie's Park Cafe and Motel MOTEL $
(☎920-868-2999; www.juliesmotel.com; Fish Creek; r $85-109; ❄📶) A great low-cost option located beside Peninsula State Park.

Peninsula State Park CAMPGROUND $
(☎920-868-3258; Fish Creek; tent & RV sites $17-25) Holds nearly 500 amenity-laden campsites.

Egg Harbor Lodge INN $$
(☎920-868-3115; www.eggharborlodge.com; Egg Harbor; r $165-205; ❄📶🏊) All rooms have a water view and free bike use.

Wild Tomato PIZZA $
(☎920-868-3095; www.wildtomatopizza.com; Fish Creek; mains $9-17; ⌚11am-10pm Jun-Aug, reduced hours Sep-May) Join the crowds indoors and out munching pizzas from the stone, wood-fired ovens. A lengthy list of craft beers help wash it down. It's extremely gluten-free friendly.

Village Cafe AMERICAN $
(☎920-868-3342; www.villagecafe-doorcounty.com; Egg Harbor; mains $7-10; ⌚8am-2pm, to 8pm Jul & Aug; 👪) Delicious all-day breakfast dishes, plus sandwiches and burgers.

Information

Door County Visitors Bureau (☎800-527-3529; www.doorcounty.com) Special-interest brochures on art galleries, biking and lighthouses.

Apostle Islands & Northern Wisconsin

The north is a thinly populated region of forests and lakes, where folks paddle and fish in summer, and ski and snowmobile in winter. The windswept Apostle Islands steal the show.

Northwoods & Lakelands

Nicolet National Forest is a vast, wooded district ideal for outdoor activities. The simple crossroads of **Langlade** is a center for white-water river adventures. **Bear Paw Resort** (☎715-882-3502; www.bearpawoutdoors.com; cabins $75-95; 🐾) rents kayaks and provides full-day paddling lessons that include a trip on the river ($150 per person). It also provides cozy cabins where you can dry off, get warm and celebrate your accomplishments in the on-site pub.

North on Hwy 13, folk artist and retired lumberjack Fred Smith's **Concrete Park** (www.friendsoffredsmith.org; N8236 S Hwy 13;

sunrise-sunset) FREE in Phillips is extraordinary, with 200-plus whimsical, life-size sculptures.

West on Hwy 70, **Chequamegon National Forest** offers exceptional mountain biking with 300 miles of off-road trails. The **Chequamegon Area Mountain Bike Association** (www.cambatrails.org) has trail maps and bike rental information. The season culminates in mid-September with the **Chequamegon Fat Tire Festival** (www.cheqfattire.com), when 1700 strong-legged men and women peddle 40 grueling miles through the woods. The town of **Hayward** (www.haywardareachamber.com) makes a good base.

SCENIC DRIVE: HIGHWAY 13

After departing Bayfield, head north on Hwy 13. It takes a fine route around the Lake Superior shore, past the Chippewa community of **Red Cliff** and the Apostle Islands' mainland segment, which has a beach. Tiny **Cornucopia**, looking every bit like a seaside village, has great sunsets. The road runs on through a timeless countryside of forest and farm, reaching US 2 for the final miles back to civilization at Superior. See www.lakesuperiorbyway.org for more.

Apostle Islands

The 21 rugged Apostle Islands, floating in Lake Superior and freckling Wisconsin's northern tip, are a state highlight. Forested and windblown, trimmed with cliffs and caves, the national park gems have no facilities. Various companies offer seasonal boat trips around the islands, and kayaking and hiking are very popular. Jump off from Bayfield, a humming resort town with hilly streets, Victorian-era buildings, apple orchards and nary a fast-food restaurant in sight.

Sights & Activities

Madeline Island ISLAND

(www.madelineisland.com) Inhabited Madeline Island makes a fine day trip and is reached by a 25-minute **ferry** (715-747-2051; www.madferry.com; round-trip adult/child/bicycle/car $13.50/7/7/24.50) from Bayfield. The isle's walkable village of La Pointe has a couple of mid-priced places to stay, a smattering of eateries and a groovy 'burned down' bar (made from junk and tarps). Bike and moped rentals are available – everything is near the ferry dock.

And FYI: while Madeline is an Apostle Island, it's not part of the national park group, hence its development.

Big Bay State Park STATE PARK

(715-747-6425; per car $10, tent sites $17-22) Big Bay is at Madeline Island's far edge, with a pretty beach and hiking trails. The well-maintained campsites are awesome and book up fast.

Apostle Islands Cruises BOAT TOUR

(715-779-3925; www.apostleisland.com; Bayfield City Dock; mid-May–mid-Oct) The easiest way to view the Apostles is aboard these 150-person sightseeing vessels. The 'grand tour' departs at 10am for a three-hour narrated trip past sea caves and lighthouses (adult/child $40/24). A glass-bottom boat goes out to view shipwrecks at 2pm. Other trips call at islands to drop off/pick up campers and kayakers; it's possible to arrange day trips via these shuttles.

Living Adventure KAYAKING

(715-779-9503; www.livingadventure.com; Hwy 13; half-/full-day tours $59/99; Jun-Sep) It offers guided paddling trips to sea caves and shipwrecks; beginners are welcome.

Sleeping & Eating

Seagull Bay Motel MOTEL $

(715-779-5558; www.seagullbay.com; 325 S 7th St; r $80-110;) Most rooms at no-frills Seagull Bay Motel have decks; ask for a lake view.

Fat Radish AMERICAN $

(715-779-9700; http://thefatradish.weebly.com; 200 Rittenhouse Ave; sandwiches $7-9; 11am-3pm Tue & Wed, to 3pm & 5-8pm Thu-Sat) The Radish uses quality, sustainable ingredients in its deli wares. It's located by the docks and handy for amassing snacks to take with you on the boat tours. At night the chef serves tasty pizzas and seafood dishes.

Maggie's AMERICAN $$

(715-779-5641; www.maggies-bayfield.com; 257 Manypenny Ave; mains $11-22; 11:30am-9pm) Kitschy, flamingo-themed Maggie's is the place to sample good local lake trout and whitefish; there are pizza and burgers, too.

☆ Entertainment

Big Top Chautauqua LIVE MUSIC
(☎888-244-8368; www.bigtop.org; ⏲Jun-Sep) The Chautauqua is a major regional summer event with big-name concerts and musical theater.

Information

Apostle Islands National Lakeshore Visitors Center (☎715-779-3397; www.nps.gov/apis; 410 Washington Ave; ⏲8am-4:30pm late May-Sep, closed Sat & Sun rest of year) Has camping permits ($10 per night) and paddling and hiking information.

Bayfield Chamber of Commerce (www.bayfield.org) Good listings of lodgings and things to do in the area.

MINNESOTA

Is Minnesota really the land of 10,000 lakes, as it's so often advertised? You betcha. Actually, in typically modest style, the state has undermarketed itself – there are 11,842 lakes. Which is great news for travelers. Intrepid outdoorsfolk can wet their paddles in the Boundary Waters, where nighttime brings a blanket of stars and the lullaby of wolf howls. Those wanting to get further off the beaten path can journey to Voyageurs National Park, where there's more water than roadway. If that all seems too far-flung, stick to the Twin Cities of Minneapolis and St Paul, where you can't swing a moose without hitting something cool or cultural. And for those looking for middle ground – a cross between the big city and big woods – the dramatic, freighter-filled port of Duluth beckons.

Information

Minnesota Highway Conditions (☎511; www.511mn.org)

Minnesota Office of Tourism (☎888-847-4866; www.exploreminnesota.com)

Minnesota State Park Information (☎888-646-6367; www.dnr.state.mn.us) Park entry requires a vehicle permit ($5/25 per day/year). Campsites cost $15 to $31; reservations (☎866-857-2757; www.stayatmnparks.com; fee $8.50) accepted.

Minneapolis

Minneapolis is the biggest and artiest town on the prairie, with all the trimmings of progressive prosperity – swank art museums, rowdy rock clubs, organic and ethnic eateries and edgy theaters. It's always happenin', even in winter. And here's the bonus: folks are attitude-free and the embodiment of 'Minnesota Nice.' Count how many times they tell you to 'Have a great day,' come rain or shine or snow.

History

Timber was the city's first boom industry, and water-powered sawmills rose along the Mississippi River in the mid-1800s. Wheat from the prairies also needed to be processed, so flour mills churned into the next big business. The population boomed in the late 19th century with mass immigration, especially from Scandinavia and Germany. Today Minneapolis' Nordic heritage is evident, whereas twin city St Paul is more German and Irish-Catholic.

Sights & Activities

Most attractions are closed Monday; many stay open late on Thursday.

Downtown & Loring Park

★**Walker Art Center** MUSEUM
(☎612-375-7622; www.walkerart.org; 1750 Hennepin Ave; adult/child $14/free, admission free Thu evening & 1st Sat of month; ⏲11am-5pm Tue, Wed & Fri-Sun, to 9pm Thu) The first-class center has a strong permanent collection of 20th-century art and photography, including big-name US painters and great US pop art. On Monday evenings from late July to late August, the museum hosts free movies and music across the pedestrian bridge in Loring Park that are quite the to-do.

★**Minneapolis Sculpture Garden** GARDENS
(725 Vineland Pl; ⏲6am-midnight) FREE The 11-acre garden, studded with contemporary works such as the oft-photographed *Spoonbridge & Cherry* by Claes Oldenburg, sits beside the Walker Art Center. The Cowles Conservatory, abloom with exotic hothouse flowers, is also on the grounds. In summer a trippy mini-golf course amid the sculptures adds to the fun ($12 for adults, $9 for kids). Note the garden will be closed through 2016 as it gets an ecofriendly facelift.

Mary Tyler Moore statue STATUE
(7th St S & Nicollet Mall) Mary Tyler Moore (of '70s TV fame) put Minneapolis on the

pop-culture map. The spot where she threw her hat in the air during the show's opening sequence is now marked by a great, cheesy statue depicting our girl doing just that.

Riverfront District

★Endless Bridge OBSERVATORY
(818 2nd St S; ⌚8am-8pm, to 11pm on performance days) FREE Head inside the cobalt-blue Guthrie Theater and make your way up the escalator to the Endless Bridge, a far-out cantilevered walkway overlooking the Mississippi River. You don't need a theater ticket, as it's intended as a public space. The theater's 9th floor Amber Box provides another knockout view.

Mill City Museum MUSEUM
(☎612-341-7555; www.millcitymuseum.org; 704 2nd St S; adult/child $11/6; ⌚10am-5pm Tue-Sat, noon-5pm Sun, open daily Jul & Aug) The building is indeed a former mill, and highlights include a ride inside an eight-story grain elevator (the 'Flour Tower'), Betty Crocker exhibits and a baking lab. It's not terribly exciting unless you're really into milling history, though the mill ruins in back are an atmospheric sight. A foodie-favorite farmers market takes place in the attached train shed on Saturday mornings May through September.

St Anthony Falls Heritage Trail WALKING
The 1.8-mile path provides both interesting history (placards dot the route) and the city's best access to the banks of the Mississippi River. It starts at the foot of Portland Ave and goes over the car-free Stone Arch Bridge, from which you can view cascading St Anthony Falls.

On the other side of the river, the trail goes along Main St SE, which has a stretch of redeveloped buildings housing restaurants and bars. From here you can walk down to Water Power Park and feel the river's frothy spray. Free trail maps are available at the Mill City Museum.

Northeast

Once a working-class Eastern European neighborhood, Northeast (so named because of its position to the river) is where urbanites and artists now work and play. They appreciate the dive bars pouring microbrews along with Pabst, and boutiques selling ecogifts next to companies grinding sausage. Hundreds of craftsfolk and galleries fill historic industrial buildings. They fling open their doors the first Thursday of each month when the **Northeast Minneapolis Arts Association** (www.nemaa.org) sponsors a gallery walk. Heady streets include 4th St NE and 13th Ave NE.

University Area

The **University of Minnesota**, by the river southeast of Minneapolis' center, is one of the USA's largest campuses, with some 50,000 students. Most of the campus is in the East Bank neighborhood.

Dinkytown, based at 14th Ave SE and 4th St SE, is dense with student cafes and bookshops. A small part of the university is on the West Bank of the Mississippi River, near the intersection of 4th St S and Riverside Ave. This area has a few restaurants, some student hangouts and a big Somali community.

★Weisman Art Museum MUSEUM
(☎612-625-9494; www.wam.umn.edu; 333 E River Rd; ⌚10am-5pm Tue, Thu & Fri, to 8pm Wed, 11am-5pm Sat & Sun) FREE The Weisman, which occupies a swooping silver structure by

MINNESOTA FACTS

Nicknames North Star State, Gopher State

Population 5.5 million

Area 86,940 sq miles

Capital city St Paul (population 295,000)

Other cities Minneapolis (population 400,100)

Sales tax 6.88%

Birthplace of Author F Scott Fitzgerald (1896–1940), songwriter Bob Dylan (b 1941), filmmakers Joel Coen (b 1954) and Ethan Coen (b 1957)

Home of Lumberjack legend Paul Bunyan, Spam, walleye fish, Hmong and Somali immigrants

Politics Leans Democratic

Famous for Niceness, funny accents, snowy weather, 10,000 lakes

Official muffin Blueberry

Driving distances Minneapolis to Duluth 153 miles, Minneapolis to Boundary Waters 245 miles

Minneapolis

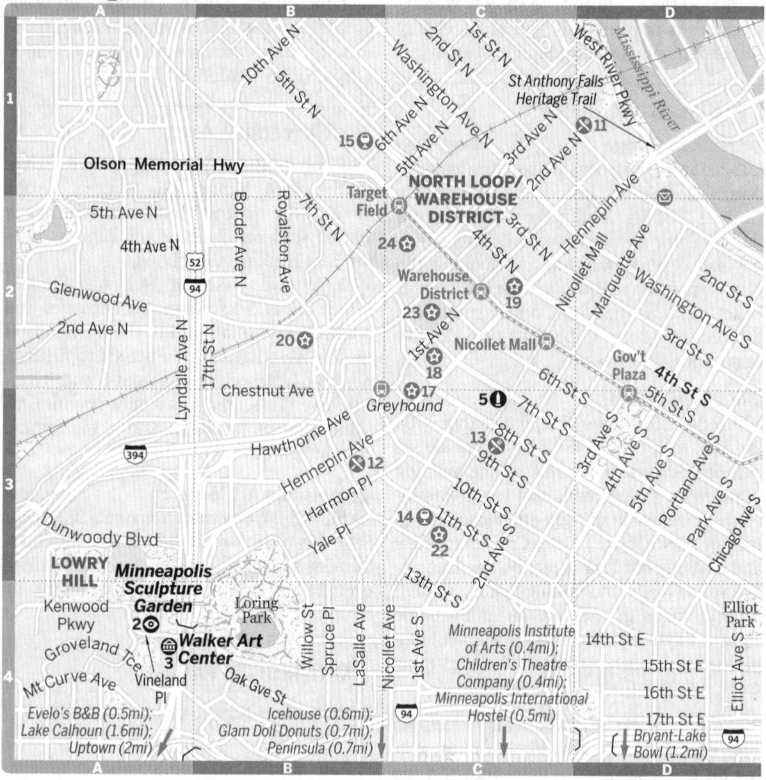

architect Frank Gehry, is a uni (and city) highlight. The airy main galleries hold cool collections of 20th-century American art, ceramics, Korean furniture and works on paper.

Uptown, Lyn-Lake & Whittier

These three neighborhoods are south of downtown.

Uptown, based around the intersection of Hennepin Ave and Lake St, is a punk-yuppie collision of shops and restaurants that stays lively until late. Lyn-Lake abuts Uptown to the east and sports a similar urban-cool vibe; it's centered on Lyndale and Lake Sts. (Get the name?)

Uptown is a convenient jump-off point to the 'Chain of Lakes' – Lake Calhoun, Lake of the Isles, Lake Harriet, Cedar Lake and Brownie Lake. Paved cycling paths (which double as cross-country ski trails in winter) meander around the five lakes, where you can go boating in summer or ice skating in winter.

Lake Calhoun sits at the foot of Lake St, where there are amenities galore. Further around Lake Calhoun, Thomas Beach is popular for swimming. Lake Harriet's castle-like band shell is always abuzz with free concerts.

★ Minneapolis Institute of Arts MUSEUM
(612-870-3131; www.artsmia.org; 2400 3rd Ave S; 10am-5pm Tue-Sat, to 9pm Thu, 11am-5pm Sun) **FREE** This museum is a huge trove housing a veritable history of art. The modern and contemporary collections astonish, while the Asian galleries (2nd floor) and Decorative Arts rooms (3rd floor) are also highlights. Allot at least a few hours to visit. The museum is a mile south of downtown via 3rd Ave S.

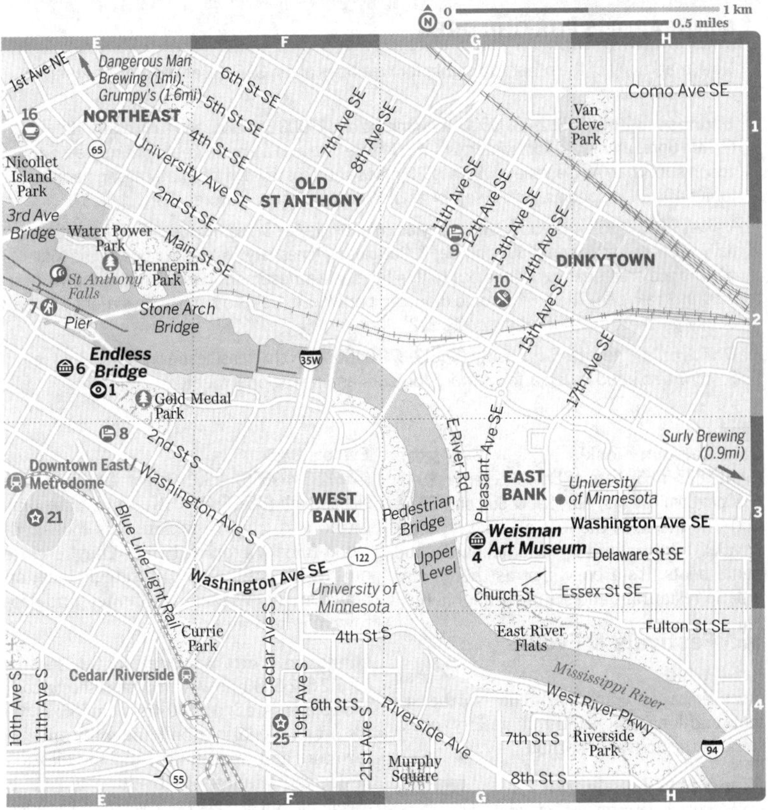

Minneapolis

Top Sights
1 Endless Bridge E2
2 Minneapolis Sculpture Garden A4
3 Walker Art Center A4
4 Weisman Art Museum G3

Sights
5 Mary Tyler Moore statue C3
6 Mill City Museum E2

Activities, Courses & Tours
7 St Anthony Falls Heritage Trail E2

Sleeping
8 Aloft E3
9 Wales House G2

Eating
10 Al's Breakfast G2
11 Bachelor Farmer D1
12 Butcher & the Boar B3
13 Hell's Kitchen C3

Drinking & Nightlife
14 Brit's Pub C3
15 Fulton Beer B1
16 Wilde Roast Cafe E1

Entertainment
17 Brave New Workshop Theatre C3
18 First Avenue & 7th St Entry....................C2
19 Gay Nineties C2
Guthrie Theater ....(see 1)
20 Lee's Liquor Lounge....................B2
21 New Minnesota Stadium E3
22 Orchestra Hall C3
23 Target Center C2
24 Target Field C2
25 Triple Rock Social Club F4

MINNEAPOLIS FOR CHILDREN

Note that many of the other top sights for wee ones are in St Paul, at the Mall of America and Fort Snelling.

Minnesota Zoo (☑ 952-431-9500; www.mnzoo.org; 13000 Zoo Blvd; adult/child $18/12; ☺ 9am-6pm summer, to 4pm winter; ⚑) You'll have to travel a way to get to the respected zoo in suburban Apple Valley, which is 20 miles south of town. It has naturalistic habitats for its 400-plus species, with an emphasis on cold-climate creatures. Parking is $7.

Valleyfair (☑ 952-445-7600; www.valleyfair.com; 1 Valleyfair Dr; admission $47; ☺ from 10am daily late May–early Sep, Fri-Sun only Sep & Oct, closing times vary; ⚑) If the rides at the Mall of America aren't enough, drive out to this full-scale amusement park 25 miles southwest in Shakopee. The animatronic dinosaur park ($5 extra) is a big hit. Save money by booking tickets online. Parking costs $12.

Children's Theatre Company (☑ 612-874-0400; www.childrenstheatre.org; 2400 3rd Ave S; ⚑) It's so good it won a Tony award for 'outstanding regional theater.'

Lake Calhoun Kiosk WATER SPORTS
(☑ 612-823-5765; base of Lake St; per hr $9-19; ☺ 10am-8pm late May-Aug, Sat & Sun only Sep & Oct) The kiosk, at the foot of Lake St, rents kayaks, bikes, stand-up paddleboards and pedal boats. It's a busy spot as there's also a patio restaurant and sailing school here.

⭐ Festivals & Events

Art-A-Whirl MUSIC
(www.nemaa.org; ☺ mid-May) The Northeast's weekend-long, rock-and-roll gallery crawl heralds the arrival of spring.

Minneapolis Aquatennial CULTURAL
(www.aquatennial.com; ☺ 3rd week Jul) Celebrates the ubiquitous lakes via parades, beach bashes and fireworks.

Holidazzle CULTURAL
(www.holidazzle.com; ☺ Dec) A German-style Christmas market, lights and lots of good cheer downtown throughout December.

🛏 Sleeping

B&Bs offer the best value – they've got budget prices but are solidly midrange in quality. Tax adds 13.4% to prices.

Wales House B&B $
(☑ 612-331-3931; www.waleshouse.com; 1115 5th St SE; r with/without shared bath $75/85; P ❋ 🛜) This cheery 10-bedroom B&B often houses scholars from the nearby University of Minnesota. Curl up with a book on the porch, or lounge by the fireplace. A two-night minimum stay is required.

Evelo's B&B B&B $
(☑ 612-374-9656; 2301 Bryant Ave S; r with shared bath $75-95; 🛜) Evelo's four rooms creak and charm within this polished-wood-filled Victorian home. They're close quartered, but the B&B's strategic location between the Walker Art Center and Uptown compensates.

Minneapolis International Hostel HOSTEL $
(☑ 612-522-5000; www.minneapolishostel.com; 2400 Stevens Ave S; dm $40-45, r from $55; ❋ 🛜) It's set in a cool old building with antique furniture and wood floors, and the location beside the Minneapolis Institute of Arts is excellent. But it's also not very well tended to. The rooms come in a variety of configurations, from a 15-bed male dorm to private rooms with en suite bath.

Aloft HOTEL $$
(☑ 612-455-8400; www.aloftminneapolis.com; 900 Washington Ave S; r $159-209; P ❋ @ 🛜 ❋) Aloft's efficiently designed, industrial-toned rooms draw a younger clientele. The clubby lobby has board games, a cocktail lounge and 24-hour snacks. There's a tiny pool, a decent fitness room and a bike-share station outside the front door. Parking costs $15.

🍴 Eating

Culinary magazine *Saveur* recently dubbed Minneapolis as 'America's next great food city' for its creative, sustainable, approachable and distinctively Midwestern fare.

Downtown

Hell's Kitchen AMERICAN $$
(☎612-332-4700; www.hellskitcheninc.com; 80 9th St S; mains $12-24; ⏰6:30am-11pm Mon-Fri, from 7:30am Sat & Sun; 📶) Descend the stairs to Hell's devilish lair, where spirited waitstaff bring you uniquely Minnesotan foods, like the walleye BLT sandwich, bison burger, Juicy Lucy (melted cheese in the middle of a burger) and lemon-ricotta hotcakes. Upstairs there's a delicious bakery and coffee shop.

Butcher & the Boar AMERICAN $$$
(☎612-238-8888; www.butcherandtheboar.com; 1121 Hennepin Ave; mains $25-36; ⏰5-10:30pm Mon-Thu, to 11pm Fri & Sat, to 10pm Sun; 📶) The coppery, candlelit room is carnivore nirvana. Get your carving knife ready for wild boar ham with country butter, chicken-fried veal sausage and many more house-crafted meats. Sampler plates are the way to go. The 30 taps flow with regional brews, backed up by a lengthy bourbon list (flights available). Make reservations, or opt for meaty small plates in the rockin' beer garden.

Bachelor Farmer MODERN AMERICAN $$$
(☎612-206-3920; www.thebachelorfarmer.com; 50 2nd Ave N; mains $19-33; ⏰5:30-9:30pm Mon-Thu, to 10:30pm Fri & Sat, 10am-2pm & 5-9:30pm Sun) 🍃 The dishes at this fun restaurant play on the region's Scandinavian heritage: smoked fish, meatballs and cheese-and-pickled-mushroom-topped toast making frequent appearances on the ever-changing menu. The chef grows all the herbs and veggies in a rooftop garden. Marvel Bar, the restaurant's sibling, hides in the basement behind an unmarked door and is primo for cocktails. Reserve ahead.

University Area

Low-priced eateries cluster in the campus area by Washington Ave and Oak St.

Al's Breakfast BREAKFAST $
(☎612-331-9991; 413 14th Ave SE; mains $5-9; ⏰6am-1pm Mon-Sat, 9am-1pm Sun) The ultimate hole in the wall: 14 stools at a tiny counter. Whenever a customer comes in, everyone picks up their plates and scoots down to make room for the newcomer. Fruitfull pancakes are the big crowd-pleaser. Cash only.

Uptown, Lyn-Lake & Whittier

Near the Minneapolis Institute of Arts, hipster eateries mingle among Vietnamese, Greek and other ethnic restaurants along Nicollet Ave S – a road known as 'Eat Street.' Lake St in Uptown is a rich vein for stylish bars and cafes.

★**Bryant-Lake Bowl** AMERICAN $
(☎612-825-3737; www.bryantlakebowl.com; 810 W Lake St; mains $10-15; ⏰8am-12:30am; 📶🍸) A workingman's bowling alley meets epicurean food at the BLB. Biscuit-and-gravy breakfasts, artisanal cheese plates, mock duck pad thai and smoked whitefish melt in the mouth. A long list of local beers washes

TAPROOM BOOM

Minneapolis is all in on the local brewing trend, and most makers have taprooms. Excellent ones to try for beer fresh from the tank:

Fulton Beer (www.fultonbeer.com; 414 6th Ave N; ⏰3-10pm Wed & Thu, to 11pm Fri, noon-11pm Sat, noon-6pm Sun) There's usually a fab pale ale and blonde ale among the selection that you sip at communal picnic tables in the warehouse. It's a few blocks from the baseball stadium and fills up on game days. Food trucks hang out in front.

Dangerous Man Brewing (www.dangerousmanbrewing.com; 1300 2nd St NE; ⏰4-10pm Tue-Thu, 3pm-midnight Fri, noon-midnight Sat) Pours strong, European-style beers in hip-happenin' Northeast. You're welcome to bring in your own food (there's a choice fish-and-chips place a block east).

Surly Brewing (www.surlybrewing.com; 520 Malcolm Ave SE; ⏰11am-11pm Sun-Thu, to midnight Fri & Sat; 👪) Designed by the same architects who built the Guthrie Theater, Surly's sprawling, mod-industrial, family-friendly beer hall is mobbed by locals who come for the 12 rotating taps and abundant meaty snacks. It's in the Prospect Park neighborhood, next to the university and a short walk from the Prospect Park Green Line rail station.

GAY & LESBIAN MINNEAPOLIS

Minneapolis has one of the country's highest percentages of gay, lesbian, bisexual and transgender (GLBT) residents, and the city enjoys strong GLBT rights. Pick up the free, biweekly magazine *Lavender* (www.lavendermagazine.com) at coffee shops around town for info on the scene. Top picks:

Wilde Roast Cafe (www.wilderoastcafe.com; 65 Main St SE; ⌚7am-11pm) It features amazing baked goods, riverfront digs and a Victorian ambience worthy of its namesake, Oscar Wilde; it was ranked 'best cafe' by *Lavender*.

Gay Nineties (www.gay90s.com; 408 Hennepin Ave) This longstanding club has dancing, dining and drag shows that attract both a gay and straight clientele.

Pride Festival (www.tcpride.org; ⌚late Jun) It's one of the USA's largest, drawing more than 300,000 revelers.

it all down. The on-site theater always has something intriguing and odd going on too.

Glam Doll Donuts BAKERY $
(www.glamdolldonuts.com; 2605 Nicollet Ave S; doughnuts $1.25-3; ⌚7am-9pm Mon-Thu, to 1am Fri & Sat, to 3pm Sun; 📶✎) These tattooed ladies with bright-hued hair make seriously badass doughnuts (including many vegan ones) in their punk pink shop. Blissful kudos to the Calendar Girl (salted caramel and chocolate) and Chart Topper (peanut butter and Sriracha hot sauce). Afterward, pop into the rock and roll fashion resale shop next door.

Peninsula ASIAN $
(☎612-871-8282; www.peninsulamalaysiancuisine.com; 2608 Nicollet Ave S; mains $9-15; ⌚11am-10pm Sun-Thu, to 11pm Fri & Sat; ✎) Malaysian dishes – including red curry hot pot, spicy crab and fish in banana leaves – rock the palate in this contemporary restaurant.

Drinking & Nightlife

Bars stay open until 2am. Happy hour typically lasts from 3pm to 6pm.

Brit's Pub PUB
(www.britspub.com; 1110 Nicollet Mall; ⌚11am-2am) A lawn bowling green on the roof, plus Brit's sweeping selection of Scotch, port and beer, is sure to unleash skills you never knew you had.

Grumpy's BAR
(www.grumpys-bar.com; 2200 4th St NE; ⌚2pm-2am Mon-Fri, from 11am Sat & Sun) Grumpy's is the Northeast's classic dive, with cheap (but good local) beer and an outdoor patio. Sample the specialty 'hot dish' on Tuesdays for $1.

☆ Entertainment

With its large student population and thriving performing-arts scene, Minneapolis has an active nightlife. Check *Vita.mn* and *City Pages* for current goings on.

Live Music

Minneapolis rocks; everyone's in a band, it seems. Acts such as Prince and post-punkers Hüsker Dü and the Replacements cut their teeth here.

First Avenue & 7th St Entry LIVE MUSIC
(www.first-avenue.com; 701 1st Ave N) This is the longstanding bedrock of Minneapolis' music scene. First Avenue is the main room featuring national acts; smaller 7th St Entry is for up-and-comers. Check out the exterior stars on the building: they're all bands that have graced the stage.

Triple Rock Social Club LIVE MUSIC
(www.triplerocksocialclub.com; 629 Cedar Ave) Triple Rock is a popular punk-alternative club.

Lee's Liquor Lounge LIVE MUSIC
(www.leesliquorlounge.com; 101 Glenwood Ave) Rockabilly and country-tinged alt bands twang here.

Icehouse LIVE MUSIC
(www.icehousempls.com; 2528 Nicollet Ave S) It's a gorgeous, great-sounding venue for jazz, folk and progressive hip-hop acts. Oh, and swank cocktails, too.

Theater & Performing Arts

The city hosts a vibrant theater scene. The neon-lit **Hennepin Theater District** (www.hennepintheatretrust.org) consists of several historic venues on Hennepin Ave between 6th and 10th Sts that host big touring shows.

Guthrie Theater THEATER
(☎612-377-2224; www.guthrietheater.org; 818 2nd St S) This is Minneapolis' top-gun theater troupe, with the jumbo facility to prove it. Unsold 'rush' tickets go on sale 30 minutes before showtime for around $25 (cash only). Download free audio tours from the website for self-guided jaunts around the funky building.

Brave New Workshop Theatre THEATER
(☎612-332-6620; www.bravenewworkshop.com; 824 Hennepin Ave) An established venue for musical comedy, revue and satire.

Orchestra Hall CLASSICAL MUSIC
(☎612-371-5656; www.minnesotaorchestra.org; 1111 Nicollet Mall) Superb acoustics for concerts by the acclaimed Minnesota Orchestra.

Sports

Minnesotans love their sports teams. Note that ice hockey happens in St Paul.

Target Field BASEBALL
(www.minnesotatwins.com; 353 N 5th St) The Twins' baseball stadium is notable for beyond-the-norm, locally focused food and drink.

New Minnesota Stadium FOOTBALL
(www.vikings.com; 900 5th St S) The NFL's Vikings begin playing in their shiny new indoor arena in fall 2016.

Target Center BASKETBALL
(www.nba.com/timberwolves; 600 1st Ave N) This is where the Timberwolves pro basketball team plays.

Information

City Pages (www.citypages.com) Weekly entertainment freebie.

Minneapolis Convention & Visitors Association (www.minneapolis.org) Coupons, maps, guides and bike-route info online.

Minneapolis Public Library (www.hclib.org; 300 Nicollet Mall; ⏲9am-9pm Mon-Thu, to 5pm Fri & Sat, noon-5pm Sun) Mod facility with free internet and wi-fi (plus a great used bookstore).

Pioneer Press (www.twincities.com) St Paul's daily newspaper.

Star Tribune (www.startribune.com) Minneapolis' daily newspaper.

University of Minnesota Medical Center (☎612-672-6000; 2450 Riverside Ave) Well-regarded hospital near downtown.

Vita.mn (www.vita.mn) The *Star Tribune*'s weekly entertainment freebie.

Getting There & Around

AIR

The **Minneapolis-St Paul International Airport** (MSP; www.mspairport.com; wi-fi) is between the two cities to the south. It's a hub for Delta Airlines, which operates several direct flights to/from Europe.

The Blue Line light-rail service (regular/rush-hour fares $1.75/2.25, 25 minutes) is the cheapest way into Minneapolis. Bus 54 (regular/rush-hour fares $1.75/2.25, 25 minutes) goes to St Paul. Taxis cost around $45.

BICYCLE

Minneapolis hovers near the top of rankings for best bike city in the US. The bicycle-share program **Nice Ride** (www.niceridemn.org; ⏲Apr-Nov) has 1500 lime-green bikes in 170 self-serve kiosks around the Twin Cities. Users pay a subscription fee ($6/65 per day/year) online or at the kiosk, plus a small fee per half-hour of use (with the first half-hour free). Bikes can be returned to any kiosk. Traditional rentals work better if you're riding for recreation versus transportation purposes. See the **Minneapolis Bicycle Program** (www.ci.minneapolis.mn.us/bicycles) for rental shops and trail maps.

BUS

Greyhound (☎612-371-3325; www.greyhound.com; 950 Hawthorne Ave; wi-fi) runs frequent buses to Milwaukee (seven hours), Chicago (nine hours) and Duluth (three hours).

Megabus (www.megabus.com/us; wi-fi) runs express to Milwaukee (6½ hours) and Chicago (8½ hours), often for lower fares than Greyhound. It departs from both downtown and the university; check the website for exact locations.

PUBLIC TRANSPORTATION

Metro Transit (www.metrotransit.org; regular/rush-hour fares $1.75/2.25) runs the handy Blue Line light-rail service between downtown and the Mall of America (stopping at the airport en route). The Green Line connects downtown Minneapolis to downtown St Paul. Machines at each station sell fare cards, including a day pass ($6) that also can be used on public buses.

TAXI

Call **Yellow Cab.** (☎612-888-8800; www.yellowcabmn.com)

TRAIN

Amtrak chugs in to the newly restored **Union Depot** (www.uniondepot.org; 214 E 4th St; wi-fi) in St Paul. Trains go daily to Chicago (eight hours) and Seattle (38 hours).

St Paul

Smaller and quieter than its twin city Minneapolis, St Paul has retained more of a historic character. Walk through F Scott Fitzgerald's old stomping grounds, trek the trails along the mighty Mississippi River, or slurp some Lao soup.

Sights & Activities

Downtown and Cathedral Hill hold most of the action. The latter features eccentric shops, Gilded Age Victorian mansions and, of course, the hulking church that gives the area its name. Downtown has the museums. An insider's tip: there's a shortcut between the two areas, a footpath that starts on the Hill House's west side and drops into downtown.

F Scott Fitzgerald Sights & Summit Ave BUILDING
The Great Gatsby author F Scott Fitzgerald is St Paul's most celebrated literary son. The Pullman-style apartment at **481 Laurel Ave** is his birthplace. Five blocks away, Fitzgerald lived in the brownstone at **599 Summit Ave** when he published *This Side of Paradise*. Both are private residences. From here stroll along Summit Ave toward the cathedral and gape at the Victorian homes rising from the street.

Literature buffs should grab the *Fitzgerald Homes and Haunts* map at the visitor center to see other footprints.

Landmark Center MUSEUM
(www.landmarkcenter.org; 75 W 5th St; 8am-5pm Mon-Fri, to 8pm Thu, 10am-5pm Sat, noon-5pm Sun) Downtown's turreted 1902 Landmark Center used to be the federal courthouse, where gangsters such as Alvin 'Creepy' Karpis were tried; plaques by the various rooms show who was brought to justice here. In addition to the city's visitor center, the building also contains a couple of small museums.

On the 2nd floor the **Schubert Club Museum** (651-292-3267; www.schubert.org; noon-4pm Sun-Fri) FREE has a brilliant collection of old pianos and harpsichords – some tickled by Brahms, Mendelssohn and the like – as well as old manuscripts and letters from famous composers. The club stages free chamber-music concerts Thursday at noon from October through April. A free wood-turning museum (it's a decorative form of woodworking) is also on the 2nd floor.

Science Museum of Minnesota MUSEUM
(651-221-9444; www.smm.org; 120 W Kellogg Blvd; adult/child $13/10; 9:30am-5pm Sun, Tue & Wed, to 9pm Thu-Sat) Has the usual hands-on kids' exhibits and Omnimax theater ($8 extra). Adults will be entertained by the wacky quackery of the 4th floor's 'questionable medical devices.'

Cathedral of St Paul CHURCH
(www.cathedralsaintpaul.org; 239 Selby Ave; 7am-6pm Sun-Fri, to 8pm Sat) Modeled on St Peter's Basilica in Rome, the cathedral presides over the city from its hilltop perch. Free tours are available at 1pm weekdays.

James J Hill House HISTORIC BUILDING
(651-297-2555; www.mnhs.org/hillhouse; 240 Summit Ave; adult/child $9/6; 10am-3:30pm Wed-Sat, from 1pm Sun) Tour the palatial stone mansion of railroad magnate Hill. It's a Gilded Age beauty, with five floors and 22 fireplaces.

Harriet Island PARK
Floating south of downtown and connected via Wabasha St, Harriet Island is a lovely place to meander. It has a river walk, paddlewheel boat cruises, concert stages and fishing docks.

★ **St Paul Curling Club** SNOW SPORTS
(www.stpaulcurlingclub.org; 470 Selby Ave; 5-11pm mid-Oct–late May) For those uninitiated in northern ways, curling is a winter sport that involves sliding a hubcap-sized 'puck' down the ice toward a bull's-eye. The friendly folks here don't mind if you stop in to watch the action. Heck, they might invite you to share a ridiculously cheap microbrew from the upstairs bar.

Mississippi River Visitor Center OUTDOORS
(651-293-0200; www.nps.gov/miss; 120 W Kellogg Blvd; 9:30am-5pm Sun & Tue-Thu, to 9pm Fri & Sat) FREE The National Park Service visitor center occupies an alcove in the science museum's lobby. Stop by to pick up trail maps and see what sort of free ranger-guided activities are going on. In summer these include short hikes to the river and bicycle rides. In winter, there are ice-fishing and snowshoeing jaunts.

Tours

Down In History Tours WALKING TOUR
(651-292-1220; www.wabashastreetcaves.com; 215 S Wabasha St; 45min tours $6; 4pm Mon, 5pm Thu, 11am Sat & Sun) Explore St Paul's underground caves, which gangsters once

used as a speakeasy. The fun ratchets up on Thursday nights, when a swing band plays in the caverns (admission $8).

Festivals & Events

St Paul Winter Carnival CULTURAL
(www.wintercarnival.com; late Jan) Ten days of ice sculptures, ice skating and ice fishing.

Sleeping

You'll find a bigger selection of accommodations in Minneapolis.

★**Hotel 340** BOUTIQUE HOTEL $$
(651-280-4120; www.hotel340.com; 340 Cedar St; r $109-189; P ❄ @) Hotel 340 delivers old-world ambience aplenty, and it's usually a great deal to boot. The 56 rooms in the stately old building have hardwood floors and plush linens. The two-story lobby stokes a grand fireplace and nifty little bar (the desk staff double as bartenders). Continental breakfast is included. Parking costs $17 per night.

Covington Inn B&B $$
(651-292-1411; www.covingtoninn.com; 100 Harriet Island Rd; r $160-250; P ❄) This four-room, Harriet Island B&B is on a tugboat floating in the Mississippi River; watch the river traffic glide by while sipping your morning coffee.

Eating & Drinking

Grand Ave between Dale St and Lexington Pkwy is a worthy browse, with cafes, foodie shops and ethnic eats in close proximity. Selby Ave by the intersection of Western Ave N also holds a quirky lineup.

Mickey's Diner DINER $
(651-222-5633; www.mickeysdiningcar.com; 36 W 7th St; mains $4-9; 24hr) Mickey's is a downtown classic, the kind of place where the friendly waitress calls you 'honey' and satisfied regulars line the bar with their coffee cups and newspapers. The food has timeless appeal, too: burgers, malts and apple pie.

Cook AMERICAN $
(651-756-1787; www.cookstp.com; 1124 Payne Ave; mains $7-12; 6:30am-2pm Mon-Fri, 7am-3pm Sat & Sun) This cute, sunny spot serves creative diner dishes (gingerbread pancakes, Asiago cheeseburgers, braised short rib sandwiches), including some with a spicy Korean twist. Cook also hosts pop-up dinners on Wednesday nights. It's located in the burgeoning East Side neighborhood, where several other foodie hot spots are sprouting on Payne Ave.

OFF THE BEATEN TRACK

BIG BALL O' TWINE

Behold the **World's Largest Ball of Twine** (1st St; 24hr) FREE in Darwin, 60 miles west of Minneapolis on US 12. OK, so there are three other Midwest twine balls also claiming to be the largest. But Darwin maintains it has the 'Largest Built by One Person' – Francis A Johnson wrapped the 17,400lb whopper on his farm over the course of 29 years. Gawk at it in the town gazebo. Better yet, visit the **museum** (320-693-7544; by appointment) FREE beside it and buy your own twine-ball starter kit in the gift shop.

Hmongtown Marketplace ASIAN $
(www.hmongtownmarketplace.com; 217 Como Ave; mains $5-8; 8am-6:30pm) The nation's largest enclave of Hmong immigrants lives in the Twin Cities, and this market delivers their favorite Vietnamese, Lao and Thai dishes at its humble food court. Find the West Building and head to the back where vendors ladle hot-spiced papaya salad, beef ribs and curry noodle soup. Then stroll the market to buy embroidered dresses, a brass gong or lemongrass.

Happy Gnome PUB
(www.thehappygnome.com; 498 Selby Ave; 11am-midnight Mon-Wed, to 1am Thu & Fri, 10am-1am Sat, to midnight Sun;) Seventy craft beers flow from the taps, best sipped on the fireplace-warmed outdoor patio. The pub sits across the parking lot from the St Paul Curling Club.

Entertainment

Fitzgerald Theater THEATER
(651-290-1221; http://fitzgeraldtheater.publicradio.org; 10 E Exchange St) Where Garrison Keillor tapes his radio show *A Prairie Home Companion*.

Ordway Center for Performing Arts CLASSICAL MUSIC
(651-224-4222; www.ordway.org; 345 Washington St) Chamber music and the Minnesota Opera fill the hall here.

Xcel Energy Center HOCKEY
(www.wild.com; 199 Kellogg Blvd) The Wild pro hockey team skates at Xcel.

Shopping

Common Good Books BOOKS
(www.commongoodbooks.com; 38 S Snelling Ave; 9am-9pm Mon-Sat, 10am-7pm Sun) Garrison Keillor owns this bright bookstore where statues of literary heroes stand guard over long shelves of tomes. It's west of downtown on the Macalester College campus.

Information

Visitor Center (651-292-3225; www.visitsaintpaul.com; 75 W 5th St; 10am-4pm Mon-Sat, from noon Sun) In the Landmark Center; makes a good first stop for maps and DIY walking tour info.

Getting There & Around

St Paul is served by the same transit systems as Minneapolis. Union Depot (p611) is the hub for everything: Greyhound buses, city buses, the Green Line light-rail service and Amtrak trains.

Around Minneapolis - St Paul

Mall of America AMUSEMENT PARK
(www.mallofamerica.com; off I-494 at 24th Ave; 10am-9:30pm Mon-Sat, 11am-7pm Sun;) Welcome to the USA's largest shopping center. Yes, it's just a mall, filled with the usual stores, movie theaters and eateries. But there's also a wedding chapel inside. And an 18-hole **mini-golf course** (952-883-8777; 3rd fl; admission $9). And a zip line. And an amusement park, aka **Nickelodeon Universe** (952-883-8600; www.nickelodeonuniverse.com), with 25 rides, including a couple of scream-inducing roller coasters. To walk through will cost you nothing; a one-day, unlimited-ride wristband is $33; or you can pay for rides individually ($3.50 to $7).

What's more, the state's largest aquarium, **Minnesota Sea Life** (952-883-0202; www.visitsealife.com/minnesota; adult/child $25/18) – where children can touch sharks (safe ones!) and stingrays – is in the mall too. Combination passes are available to save dough. The Blue Line light-rail runs to/from downtown Minneapolis. The mall is in suburban Bloomington, a 10-minute ride from the airport.

Fort Snelling HISTORIC SITE
(612-726-1171; www.historicfortsnelling.org; cnr Hwys 5 & 55; adult/child $11/6; 10am-5pm Tue-Sat & noon-5pm Sun Jun-Aug, Sat only Sep & Oct;) East of the mall, Fort Snelling is the state's oldest structure, established in 1820 as a frontier outpost in the remote Northwest Territory. Guides in period dress show restored buildings and reenact pioneer life.

Southern Minnesota

Some of the scenic southeast can be seen on short drives from the Twin Cities. Better is a loop of a few days' duration, following the rivers and stopping in some of the historic towns and state parks.

Due east of St Paul, on Hwy 36, touristy **Stillwater**, on the lower St Croix River, is an old logging town with restored 19th-century buildings, river cruises and antique stores. It's also an official 'booktown,' an honor bestowed upon a few small towns worldwide that possess an extraordinary number of antiquarian bookshops. Several classy B&Bs add to the scene. **Discover Stillwater** (www.discoverstillwater.com) has details.

Larger **Red Wing**, to the south on US 61, is a similar but less-interesting restored town, though it does offer its famous Red Wing Shoes – actually more like sturdy boots – and salt glaze pottery.

The prettiest part of the **Mississippi Valley** area begins south of here. To drive it and see the best bits, you'll need to flip-flop back and forth between Minnesota and Wisconsin on the Great River Road.

From Red Wing, cross the river on US 63. Before heading south along the water though, make a cheesy detour. Go north on US 63 in Wisconsin for 12 miles until you hit US 10. Turn right, and within a few miles you're in Ellsworth, the 'Cheese Curd Capital.' Pull into **Ellsworth Cooperative Creamery** (715-273-4311; www.ellsworthcheese.com; 232 N Wallace St; 9am-5pm) – curd-maker for A&W and Dairy Queen – and savor squeaky goodness hot off the press (11am is prime time).

Back along the river on Wisconsin Hwy 35, a great stretch of road edges the bluffs beside **Maiden Rock**, **Stockholm** and **Pepin**. Follow your nose to local bakeries and cafes in the area.

Continuing south, cross back over the river to **Wabasha** in Minnesota, which has a historic downtown and large population of bald eagles that congregate in winter. To learn more, visit the **National Eagle Center** (☎651-565-4989; www.nationaleaglecenter.org; 50 Pembroke Ave; adult/child $8/5; ⏰10am-5pm, reduced hours Nov-Feb).

Inland and south, Bluff Country is dotted with limestone bluffs, southeast Minnesota's main geological feature. **Lanesboro** (www.lanesboro.com) is a gem for rails-to-trails cycling and canoeing. Seven miles westward on County Rd 8 (call for directions) is **Old Barn Resort** (☎507-467-2512; www.barnresort.com; dm/r/campsite/RV site $25/50/34/46; ⏰Apr–early Nov;), a pastoral hostel, campground, restaurant and outfitter. **Harmony**, south of Lanesboro, is the center of an Amish community and another welcoming town.

OFF THE BEATEN TRACK

SPAM MUSEUM

Sitting by its lonesome in Austin, near where I-35 and I-90 intersect in southern Minnesota, lies the **Spam Museum** (☎800-588-7726; www.spam.com; 400 N Main St; admission free; ⏰10am-5pm Mon-Sat, from noon Sun;), an entire institution devoted to the peculiar meat. It educates on how the blue tins have fed armies, become a Hawaiian food staple and inspired legions of haiku writers. What's more, you can chat up the staff (aka 'spambassadors'), indulge in free samples, and try your hand at canning the sweet pork magic. Alas, the museum is closed until mid-2016, when it opens a shiny new facility downtown.

Duluth & Northern Minnesota

Northern Minnesota is where you come to 'do some fishing, do some drinking,' as one resident summed it up.

Duluth

At the Great Lakes' westernmost end, Duluth (with its neighbor, Superior, WI) is one of the busiest ports in the country. The town's dramatic location spliced into a cliff makes it a fab place to see changeable Lake Superior in action. The water, along with the area's trails and natural splendor, has earned Duluth a reputation as a hot spot for outdoors junkies.

Sights & Activities

The waterfront area is distinctive. Mosey along the Lakewalk trail and around Canal Park, where most of the sights cluster.

Aerial Lift Bridge BRIDGE

Duluth's main landmark raises its mighty arm to let horn-bellowing ships into port. About 1000 vessels per year glide through.

Maritime Visitor Center MUSEUM

(☎218-720-5260; www.lsmma.com; 600 S Lake Ave; ⏰10am-9pm Jun-Aug, reduced hours Sep-May) FREE Located next to the Aerial Lift Bridge, the center has computer screens inside that tell what time the big ships will be sailing through. Cool model boats and exhibits on Great Lakes shipwrecks also make it a top stop in town.

William A Irvin MUSEUM

(☎218-722-7876; www.williamairvin.com; 350 Harbor Dr; adult/child $12/8; ⏰9am-6pm Jun-Aug, 10am-4pm May & Sep) To continue the nautical theme, tour this mighty 610ft Great Lakes freighter.

Leif Erikson Park PARK

(cnr London Rd & 14th Ave E) This is a lakefront sweet spot with a rose garden, a replica of Leif's Viking ship and free outdoor movies each Friday night in summer. Take the Lakewalk from Canal Park (about 1½ miles) and you can say you hiked the Superior Trail, which traverses this stretch.

Duluth Experience ADVENTURE TOUR

(☎218-464-6337; www.theduluthexperience.com; tours from $55) It offers a range of kayaking, cycling and brewery tours; gear and transportation provided.

Vista Fleet BOAT TOUR

(☎218-722-6218; www.vistafleet.com; 323 Harbor Dr; adult/child $20/10; ⏰mid-May–Oct) Ah, everyone loves a boat ride. Vista's 75-minute waterfront cruise is a favorite, departing from the dock beside the *William A Irvin* in Canal Park.

Spirit Mountain SKIING

(☎218-628-2891; www.spiritmt.com; 9500 Spirit Mountain Pl; per day adult/child $40/30; ⏰hours vary) Skiing and snowboarding are big pastimes come winter; in summer there's a zip line, alpine slide and mini-golf. The mountain is 10 miles south of Duluth.

LOCAL KNOWLEDGE

DYLAN IN DULUTH

While Hibbing and the Iron Range are most often associated with Bob Dylan, he was born in Duluth. You'll see brown-and-white signs on Superior St and London Rd for **Bob Dylan Way** (www.bobdylanway.com), pointing out places associated with the legend (like the armory where he saw Buddy Holly in concert, and decided to become a musician). But you're on your own to find **Dylan's birthplace** (519 N 3rd Ave E), up a hill a few blocks northeast of downtown. Dylan lived on the top floor until age six, when his family moved inland to Hibbing. It's a private residence (and unmarked), so all you can do is stare from the street.

Sleeping

Duluth has several B&Bs; rooms cost at least $140 in the summer. Check **Duluth Historic Inns** (www.duluthbandb.com) for listings.

The town's accommodations fill up fast in summer, which may mean you'll have to try your luck across the border in Superior, WI (where it's cheaper too).

Fitger's Inn HOTEL $$
(☎218-722-8826; www.fitgers.com; 600 E Superior St; r $169-279; @) Fitger's created its 62 large rooms, each with slightly varied decor, from an old brewery. Located on the Lakewalk, the pricier rooms have great water views. Continental breakfast is included. The free shuttle to local sights is handy.

Willard Munger Inn INN $$
(☎218-624-4814; www.mungerinn.com; 7408 Grand Ave; r incl breakfast $70-140; @) Family-owned Munger Inn offers a fine variety of rooms (budget to Jacuzzi suites), along with perks for outdoor enthusiasts, such as hiking and biking trails right outside the door, free use of bikes and canoes, and a fire pit. It's near Spirit Mountain.

Eating

Most restaurants and bars reduce their hours in winter. The Canal Park waterfront area has eateries in all price ranges.

Duluth Grill AMERICAN $
(☎218-726-1150; www.duluthgrill.com; 118 S 27th Ave W; mains $10-16; 7am-9pm;) The garden in the parking lot is the tip-off that the Duluth Grill is a sustainable, hippie-vibed place. The diner-esque menu ranges from eggy breakfast skillets to curried polenta stew to bison burgers, with plenty of vegan and gluten-free options. It's a couple miles southwest of Canal Park, near the bridge to Superior, WI.

Northern Waters Smokehaus SANDWICHES $
(☎218-724-7307; www.northernwaterssmokehaus.com; 394 S Lake Ave, DeWitt-Seitz Marketplace; sandwiches $7-10; 10am-8pm Mon-Sat, to 6pm Sun) This little spot smokes sustainably harvested salmon and whitefish; primo for picnics.

★**New Scenic Cafe** MODERN AMERICAN $$
(☎218-525-6274; www.sceniccafe.com; 5461 North Shore Dr; sandwiches $10-15, mains $18-28; 11am-9pm Sun-Thu, to 10pm Fri & Sat) Foodies travel from far and near to New Scenic Cafe, 8 miles beyond Duluth on Old Hwy 61. There, in a humble wood-paneled room, they fork into rustic salmon with creamed leeks or a slice of triple berry pie, served with a generous helping of lake views. Make reservations.

Pizza Luce PIZZA $$
(☎218-727-7400; www.pizzaluce.com; 11 E Superior St; mains $10-20; 10:30am-2am Mon-Fri, from 8am Sat & Sun;) Cooks great brunches and gourmet pizzas (vegan and gluten-free versions too). It's also plugged into the local music scene and hosts bands. Fully licensed.

Drinking & Nightlife

★**Thirsty Pagan** BREWERY
(www.thirstypaganbrewing.com; 1623 Broadway St; 11am-10pm Mon-Thu, to 11pm Fri-Sun) This one's a bit of a trek, over the bridge in Superior, WI (a 10-minute drive), but worth it for the aggressive, spicy beers to wash down hand-tossed pizzas.

Fitger's Brewhouse BREWERY
(www.brewhouse.net; 600 E Superior St; 11am-midnight Sun & Mon, to 1am Tue-Thu, to 2am Fri & Sat) In the hotel complex, the Brewhouse rocks with live music and fresh brews. Try them via the seven-beer sampler (3oz glasses $9).

Vikre Distillery COCKTAIL BAR
(www.vikredistillery.com; 525 S Lake Ave; 5-10pm Mon, Wed & Thu, noon-10pm Fri & Sat, noon-5pm Sun) Vikre creates gin with Northwoods-foraged botanicals, as well as aquavit, a Scandinavian spirit infused with caraway and cardamom. Sample them swirled in cocktails in the Canal Park tasting room.

Information

Duluth Visitors Center (800-438-5884; www.visitduluth.com; Harbor Dr; 9:30am-7:30pm summer) Seasonal center, opposite the Vista dock.

Getting There & Away

Greyhound (218-722-5591; 4602 Grand Ave) has a couple of buses daily to Minneapolis (three hours).

North Shore

Hwy 61 is the main vein through the North Shore. It edges Lake Superior and passes numerous state parks, waterfalls, hiking trails and mom-and-pop towns en route to Canada. Lots of weekend, summer and fall traffic makes reservations essential.

Stop in **Two Harbors** (www.twoharborschamber.com) to gawk at iron-ore freighters at the town's huge docks. **Lighthouse B&B** (888-832-5606; www.lighthousebb.org; r incl breakfast $135-175) is a unique place to spend the night; the four rooms in the 1892 fog-buster have sweet lake views. Two miles north of town, **Betty's Pies** (218-834-3367; www.bettyspies.com; 1633 Hwy 61; pie slices $4; 7:30am-8pm, reduced hours Oct-May) wafts racks of flaky goodness; try a fruit-filled, crunch-topping slice.

Route highlights north of Two Harbors are Gooseberry Falls, Split Rock Lighthouse and Palisade Head. About 110 miles from Duluth, artsy little **Grand Marais** (www.grandmarais.com) makes an excellent base for exploring the Boundary Waters and environs. For Boundary permits and information, visit the **Gunflint Ranger Station** (218-387-1750; 2020 Hwy 61; 8am-4:30pm May-Sep), just south of town.

Do-it-yourself enthusiasts can learn to build boats, tie flies or butcher pigs at the **North House Folk School** (218-387-9762; www.northhouse.org; 500 Hwy 61). The course list is phenomenal – as is the school's two-hour sailing trip aboard the Viking schooner *Hjordis* ($35 to $45 per person). Reserve in advance.

Grand Marais' lodging options include camping, resorts and motels, like the well-placed **Harbor Inn** (218-387-1191; www.harborinnhotel.com; 207 Wisconsin St; r $110-145; wi-fi) in town or rustic, trail-encircled **Naniboujou Lodge** (218-387-2688; www.naniboujou.com; 20 Naniboujou Trail; r $110-150; late May-late Oct), which is 14 miles northeast of town. **Sven and Ole's** (218-387-1713; www.svenandoles.com; 9 Wisconsin St; pizzas $10-20; 11am-8pm, to 9pm Thu-Sat) is a classic for sandwiches and pizza; beer flows in the attached pub. At **Dockside Fish Market** (www.docksidefishmarket.com; 418 Hwy 61; mains $7-11; 9am-7:30pm), the boat heads out in the morning, and by noon the freshly caught herring and whitefish have been fried into fish-and-chips at the deli counter.

Hwy 61 continues to **Grand Portage National Monument** (218-475-0123; www.nps.gov/grpo; 9am-5pm Jun–mid-Oct) FREE, beside Canada, where the early voyageurs had to carry their canoes around the Pigeon River rapids. This was the center of a far-flung trading empire, and the reconstructed 1788 trading post and Ojibwe village is well worth seeing. **Isle Royale National Park** in Lake Superior is reached by **ferries** (218-475-0024; www.isleroyaleboats.com; day trip adult/child $67/37) three to five times per week from June to September. (The park is also accessible from Houghton, MI).

SCENIC DRIVE: HIGHWAY 61

Hwy 61 conjures a headful of images. Local boy Bob Dylan mythologized it in his angry 1965 album *Highway 61 Revisited*. It's the fabled 'Blues Highway' clasping the Mississippi River en route to New Orleans. And in northern Minnesota, it evokes red-tinged cliffs and forested beaches as it follows Lake Superior's shoreline.

But let's back up and get a few things straight. The Blues Highway is actually US 61, and it starts just north of the Twin Cities. Hwy 61 is a state scenic road, and it starts in Duluth. To confuse matters more, there are two 61s between Duluth and Two Harbors: a four-lane expressway and a two-lane 'Old Hwy 61' (also called North Shore Scenic Drive). Take the latter; it morphs from London Rd in Duluth and veers off to the right just past the entrance to Brighton Beach. After Two Harbors, Hwy 61 returns to one strip of pavement – a gorgeous drive that goes all the way to the Canadian border. For more information, check the North Shore Scenic Drive at www.superiorbyways.com.

SUPERIOR HIKING TRAIL

The 300-mile **Superior Hiking Trail** (www.shta.org) follows the lake-hugging ridgeline between Duluth and the Canadian border. Along the way it passes dramatic red-rock overlooks and the occasional moose and black bear. Trailheads with parking lots pop up every 5 to 10 miles, making it ideal for day hikes. The **Superior Shuttle** (☎218-834-5511; www.superiorhikingshuttle.com; from $15; ⊙Fri-Sun mid-May–mid-Oct) makes life even easier, picking up trekkers from 17 stops along the route. Overnight hikers will find 86 backcountry campsites and several lodges to cushion the body come nightfall; the trail website has details. The whole footpath is free, with no reservations or permits required. The **trail office** (☎218-834-2700; cnr Hwy 61 & 8th St; ⊙9am-5pm Mon-Fri, 10am-4pm Sat, noon-4pm Sun mid-May–mid-Oct, closed Sat & Sun mid-Oct–mid-May) in Two Harbors provides maps and planning assistance.

Boundary Waters

From Two Harbors, Hwy 2 runs inland to the legendary **Boundary Waters Canoe Area Wilderness (BWCAW)**. This pristine region has more than 1000 lakes and streams in which to dip a paddle. It's possible to go just for the day, but most people opt for at least one night of camping. If you're willing to dig in and canoe for a while, you'll lose the crowds. Camping then becomes a wonderfully remote experience where it will be you, the howling wolves, the moose who's nuzzling the tent and the aurora borealis' greenish light filling the night sky. Beginners are welcome, and everyone can get set up with gear from local lodges and outfitters. Permits for **camping** (☎877-550-6777; www.recreation.gov; adult/child $16/8, plus $6 reservation fee) are required for overnight stays. Day permits, though free, are also required; get them at BWCAW entry-point kiosks or ranger stations. Call **Superior National Forest** (☎218-626-4300; www.fs.usda.gov/attmain/superior/specialplaces) for details; the website has a useful trip planning guide. Plan ahead, as permits are quota restricted and often run out.

Many argue the best BWCAW access is via the engaging town of **Ely** (www.ely.org), northeast of the Iron Range area, which has accommodations, restaurants and scores of outfitters. The **International Wolf Center** (☎218-365-4695; www.wolf.org; 1369 Hwy 169; adult/child $10.50/6.50; ⊙10am-5pm mid-May–mid-Oct, Fri-Sun only mid-Oct–mid-May) offers intriguing exhibits and wolf-viewing trips. Across the highway from the center, **Kawishiwi Ranger Station** (☎218-365-7600; 1393 Hwy 169; ⊙8am-4:30pm May-Sep) provides expert BWCAW camping and canoeing details, trip suggestions and required permits.

In winter, Ely gets mushy – it's a renowned dogsledding town. Outfitters such as **Wintergreen Dogsled Lodge** (☎218-365-6022; www.dogsledding.com; 4hr tours adult/child $150/100) offer numerous packages.

Iron Range District

An area of red-tinged scrubby hills rather than mountains, Minnesota's Iron Range District consists of the Mesabi and Vermilion Ranges, running north and south of Hwy 169 from roughly Grand Rapids northeast to Ely. Iron was discovered here in the 1850s, and at one time more than three-quarters of the nation's iron ore was extracted from these vast open-pit mines. Visitors can see working mines and the terrain's raw, sparse beauty all along Hwy 169.

In **Calumet**, a perfect introduction is the **Hill Annex Mine State Park** (☎218-247-7215; www.dnr.state.mn.us/hill_annex; 880 Gary St; tours adult/child $10/6; ⊙12:30pm & 3pm Fri & Sat late-May-early Sep), with its open-pit tours and exhibit center. Tours are held in summertime only, on Friday and Saturday; there's also a fossil tour both days at 10am.

An even bigger pit sprawls in **Hibbing**, where a must-see **viewpoint** (401 Penobscot Rd; ⊙9am-5pm mid-May–Sep) north of town overlooks the 3-mile Hull Rust Mahoning Mine. Bob Dylan lived at 2425 E 7th Ave as a boy and teenager; the **Hibbing Public Library** (☎218-362-5959; www.hibbing.lib.mn.us; 2020 E 5th Ave; ⊙10am-7pm Mon-Thu, to 5pm Fri) has well-done Dylan displays and a free walking-tour map (available online, too) that takes you past various sites, like the place where Bobby had his bar mitzvah. To snooze try the **Mitchell-Tappan House** (☎218-262-3862; www.mitchell-tappanhouse.com; 2125 4th Avenue E; r with shared bath $90, r with private bath $100-110; ❄📶), a mining honcho's semi-frilly Victorian abode that's the best lodging around for the price.

Up in the range's northeast corner, the Soudan Underground Mine (www.mndnr.gov/ soudan; 1379 Stuntz Bay Rd; tours adult/child $12/7; ⊙10am-4pm late May-late Sep) is the state's oldest and deepest pit. Wear warm clothes for the half-mile descent below ground.

Voyageurs National Park

In the 17th century, French-Canadian fur traders, or voyageurs, began exploring the Great Lakes and northern rivers by canoe. Voyageurs National Park (www.nps.gov/ voya) FREE covers part of their customary waterway, which became the border between the USA and Canada.

It's all about water up here. Most of the park is accessible only by hiking or motorboat – the waters are mostly too wide and too rough for canoeing, though kayaks are becoming popular. A few access roads lead to campgrounds and lodges on or near Lake Superior, but these are mostly used by people putting in their own boats.

The visitor centers are car accessible and good places to begin your visit. Twelve miles east of International Falls on Hwy 11 is Rainy Lake Visitors Center (☑218-286-5258; ⊙9:30am-5pm late May–mid-Oct, reduced hours rest of year), the main park office. Ranger-guided walks and boat tours are available here. Seasonal visitor centers are at Ash River (☑218-374-3221; ⊙9:30am-5pm late May-late Sep) and Kabetogama Lake (☑218-875-2111; ⊙9:30am-5pm late May-late Sep). These areas have outfitters, rentals and services, plus some smaller bays for canoeing.

Houseboating is all the rage in the region. Outfitters such as Ebel's (☑888-883-2357; www.ebels.com; 10326 Ash River Trail) and Voyagaire Houseboats (☑800-882-6287; www.voyagaire.com; 7576 Gold Coast Rd) can set you up. Rentals range from $275 to $700 per day, depending on boat size. Novice boaters are welcome and receive instruction on how to operate the vessels.

Otherwise, for sleeping, your choices are pretty much camping or resorts. The 12-room, shared-bath Kettle Falls Hotel (☑218-240-1724; www.kettlefallshotel.com; r/cottage $80/180; ⊙May-late Oct) is an exception, located inside the park and accessible only by boat; make arrangements with the owners for pick-up ($45 per person round-trip). Nelson's Resort (☑800-433-0743; www. nelsonsresort.com; 7632 Nelson Rd; cabins from $205) at Crane Lake is a winner for hiking, fishing and relaxing under blue skies.

While this is certainly a remote and wild area, those seeking wildlife, canoeing and forest camping in all their glory are best off in the Boundary Waters.

Bemidji & Chippewa National Forest

This area is synonymous with outdoor activities and summer fun. Campsites and cottages abound; almost everybody is fishing-crazy.

Itasca State Park (☑218-266-2100; www. dnr.state.mn.us/itasca; off Hwy 71 N; per vehicle $5, tent & RV sites $17-31) is an area highlight. You can walk across the tiny headwaters of the mighty Mississippi River, rent canoes or bikes, hike the trails and camp. The log HI Mississippi Headwaters Hostel (☑218-266-3415; www.hiusa.org/parkrapids; 27910 Forest Lane; dm $26-28, r $90-145; ⊙closed Apr, Nov & Dec; ✻⊛) is in the park; winter hours vary, so call ahead. Or if you want a little rustic luxury, try the venerable Douglas Lodge (☑866-857-2757; r $99-145; ⊛), run by the park, which also has cabins and a good restaurant.

On the western edge of the forest, about 30 miles from Itasca, tidy Bemidji is an old lumber town with a well-preserved downtown and a giant statue of logger Paul Bunyan and his faithful blue ox, Babe. The visitor center (www.visitbemidji.com; 300 Bemidji Ave N; ⊙8am-5pm Mon-Fri, 10am-4pm Sat, 11am-2pm Sun Jun-Aug, closed Sat & Sun Sep-May) displays Paul's toothbrush.

USA's National Parks

Evolution of the Parks

Many parks look much the same as they did centuries ago, when this nation was just starting out. From craggy islands off the Atlantic Coast, to prairie grasslands and buffalo herds across the Great Plains, to the Rocky Mountains raising their jagged teeth along the Continental Divide, and onward to the tallest trees on earth – coast redwoods – standing sentinel on Pacific shores, you'll be amazed by the USA's natural bounty.

Go West!

Historically speaking, the nation's voracious appetite for land and material riches drove not only the false doctrine of Manifest Destiny, but also a bonanza of building – pioneer homesteads, farms, livestock fences, great dams, roadways and train tracks from sea to shining sea. This artificial infrastructure quickly swallowed up vast wilderness tracts from the Appalachian Mountains to the mighty Mississippi River and far into the West. That is, until the creation of a web of federally protected public lands, starting with the national parks.

Voices in the Wilderness

During a trip to the Dakotas in 1831, artist George Catlin had a dream. As he watched the USA's rapid westward expansion harm both the wilderness and Native American tribes, Catlin penned a call to action for 'a nation's park, containing man and beast, in all the wild and freshness of their nature's beauty!' Four decades later, Congress created Yellowstone National Park, the nation's first.

DAVE SOLDANO IMAGES / GETTY IMAGES ©

JEFF MAURITZEN / GETTY IMAGES ©

1. Canyonlands National Park (p874) **2.** Old Rag Mountain (p324), Shenandoah National Park **3.** Olympic National Park (p1038)

MARK NEWMAN / DESIGN PICS / GETTY IMAGES ©

The late 19th century saw a rush of new parks – including Yosemite, Sequoia and Mount Rainier – as a nascent conservation movement fired up public enthusiasm. The poetic herald of the Sierra Nevada, naturalist John Muir, galvanized the public while campaigning for a national park system, delivering open-air lectures and writing about the spiritual value of wilderness above its economic opportunities.

Growing the Parks

Inspired by a visit to Yosemite with Muir in 1903, President Theodore Roosevelt, a big-game hunter and rancher, worked to establish more wildlife preserves, national forests, national parks and monuments. The Antiquities Act of 1906 preserved a priceless trove of archaeological sites from Native American cultures, including Mesa Verde, and two years later the Grand Canyon itself.

The National Park Service (NPS) was created in 1916, with self-made millionaire and tireless parks promoter Stephen Mather as its first director. In the 1930s, President Franklin D Roosevelt added 50 more historic sites and monuments to the NPS portfolio and hired Depression-era Civilian Conservation Corps (CCC) workers to build scenic byways and create recreational opportunities in the parks.

After WWII, the NPS kept growing. First lady during the 1960s, 'Lady Bird' Johnson contributed to the groundbreaking report *With Heritage So Rich*, which led to the National Historic Preservation Act of 1966 expanding the NPS system. Her parks advocacy also influenced her husband, President Lyndon Johnson, who enacted more environmental-protection legislation than any administration since FDR.

The Parks Today

Today the NPS protects over 400 parklands and more than 80 million acres of land from coast to coast. Recent additions designated by President Barack Obama include noteworthy historical sites: Ohio's Charles Young Buffalo Soldiers National Monument, Maryland's Harriet Tubman Underground Railroad National Monument and First State National Monument in Delaware and Pennsylvania. Thousands more natural areas are overseen by other federal land-management agencies, including the US Forest Service (USFS; www.fs.fed.us), US Fish & Wildlife Service (USFWS; www.fws.gov) and Bureau of Land Management (BLM; www.blm.gov).

Not all national parks growth has been free of controversy – for example, when local residents protest restrictions on public land use, or when agency goals conflict with the self-determination rights of Native Americans. Federal budget cuts and the enormous pressures of 290 million visitors every year have also taken huge tolls on the parks, as has global warming, leading to habitat loss and species extinction. Recent media spotlights that have helped sway public opinion about the vital importance of parks include Ken Burns' documentary film *The National Parks: America's Best Idea* (www.pbs.org/nationalparks).

Practical Tips for Park Visitors

Park entrance fees vary from nothing at all to $25 per vehicle. The **'America the Beautiful' annual pass** ($80; http://store.usgs.gov/pass), which admits four adults and all children under 16 years old free to all federal recreational lands for 12 calendar months, is sold at park entrances

1. Glacier National Park (p801) **2.** Hiking in Zion National Park (p878) **3.** Monument Valley (p854)

and visitor centers. Lifetime senior-citizen passes ($10) and access passes for those with disabilities and current members of the US military (free) are also available. ATMs are scarce in parks, so bring cash for campsites, permits, tours and activities.

Park lodges and campgrounds book up far in advance; for summer vacations, reserve six months to one year ahead. Some parks offer first-come, first-served campgrounds – if so, try to arrive between 10am and noon, when other campers may be checking out. For overnight backpacking and some day hikes, you'll need a wilderness permit; the number of permits is often subject to quotas, so apply far in advance (up to six months before your trip). Some park stores sell basic camping and outdoor supplies, but prices are usually inflated and some items may be out of stock – try to bring your own gear if you can.

ECO-TRAVEL IN THE PARKS

Do your utmost to preserve the parks' wild and beautiful natural environments. Follow the principles of the Leave No Trace (www.lnt.org) outdoor ethics. To help kids learn about conservation and how they can help protect the parks, inquire at visitor centers about free (or low-cost) junior ranger activity programs (www.nps.gov/learn/juniorranger.cfm).

Park policies and regulations may seem restrictive, but they're intended to keep you safe and to protect both natural and cultural resources. Pets are not allowed outside of the parks' developed areas, where they must be leashed and attended to at all times.

Flora & Fauna

Along winding scenic drives and forested hiking trails, from mountain wildflower meadows to arid deserts and deep river-cut canyons, the USA's national parks present prime-time opportunities for wildlife watching. They're also biodiverse havens for endangered and threatened species that you may not be able to spot anywhere else.

1. Grizzly bear
Prowling from the Rocky Mountains up into Alaska, these fierce, omnivorous predators can grow up to 8ft tall and weigh 800lb.

2. Black bear
Smaller than their grizzly cousins, these skilled tree climbers range almost continent-wide. Their fur shows a variety of colors, even cinnamon and blond.

3. Moose
The biggest of all deer species, this forest-dwelling grazer's giant antlers spread up to 6ft across. Although sedentary, moose can surprisingly sprint up to 35mph.

4. Gray wolf
These howling pack hunters were nearly extirpated from the lower 48 states, but controversial conservation projects have reintroduced them to the Rocky Mountains.

5. Bison
Few animals evoke the spirit of the West more than the American bison, also known as the buffalo, which 19th-century hunters drove almost to extinction.

6. Beaver
Busy builders of river dams, canals and lodges with underwater entrances, North America's largest rodent has soft fur historically prized for hat-making.

7. Alligator
Native only to the US and China, these prehistoric lizard-like amphibians inhabit freshwater swamps, marshlands, ponds, rivers and lakes in southeastern USA.

8. Bighorn sheep
Identified by their curved horns, these sure-footed mountain climbers range from the Sierra Nevada and Rocky Mountains to lowland deserts in California and the Southwest.

9. Desert tortoise
Long-lived natives of the Mojave and Sonoran Deserts, slow-moving tortoises can go long periods without food or water. Habitat loss now threatens the species.

10. Bald eagle
The white-headed national bird has soared off the endangered species list. Feeding mostly on fish, these birds of prey build the world's largest tree nests.

11. Coast redwood
Holding the world's record for the tallest tree, coast redwoods thrive in forests along the foggy Pacific shores of Northern California and southern Oregon.

12. Saguaro
Symbols of the desert Southwest, these tree-sized cacti can grow over 60ft tall and live for up to 150 years.

KONRAD WOTHE / LOOK-FOTO / GETTY IMAGES ©

ZACK SCHNEPF / GETTY IMAGES ©

EASTCOTT MOMATIUK / GETTY IMAGES ©

BOB BENNETT / GETTY IMAGES ©

SCHNITZERPHOTO.COM / GETTY IMAGES ©

WAYNE LYNCH / GETTY IMAGES ©

NOPPAWAT TOM CHAROENSINPHON / GETTY IMAGES ©

MARK NEWMAN / GETTY IMAGES ©

Eastern USA

Roam from New England's rocky, wild and weather-beaten shores to Florida's sugar-sand beaches shaded by palm trees. Or immerse yourself in the USA's wealth of historic sites starting in the nation's capital, Washington, DC, then roll through the pastoral hills of old-timey Appalachia on the scenic Blue Ridge Parkway.

Great Smoky Mountains National Park

Receiving more visitors than any other US national park, this southern Appalachian woodland pocket protects thickly forested ridges where black bears, white-tailed deer, antlered elk, wild turkeys and more than 1500 kinds of flowering plants find sanctuary.

Acadia National Park

Catch the first sunrise of the new year atop Cadillac Mountain, the highest point on the USA's eastern seaboard. Or come in summer to play on end-of-the-world islands tossed along this craggy, wind-whipped North Atlantic coastline.

Shenandoah National Park

Drive from the Great Smoky Mountains north along the historic Blue Ridge Parkway past Appalachian hillside hamlets to Shenandoah, a pastoral preserve where waterfall and woodland paths await, just 75 miles from the nation's capital.

Everglades National Park

Home to snaggle-toothed crocodiles, stealthy panthers, pink flamingos and mellow manatees, South Florida's Caribbean bays and 'rivers of grass' attract wildlife watchers, especially to unique flood-plain islands called hammocks.

Mammoth Cave National Park

With hidden underground rivers and more than 400 miles of explored terrain, the world's longest cave system shows off sci-fi-looking stalactites and stalagmites up close.

1

1. Appalachian Trail, North Carolina **2.** Everglades National Park (p486) **3.** Great Smoky Mountains National Park (p356)

3

CHRIS MURRAY / GETTY IMAGES ©

Great Plains & Rocky Mountains

Wildflower-strewn meadows, saw-toothed peaks and placid lakes along the spine of the Continental Divide are among America's most prized national parks. Equally rich in wildlife, Native American culture and Old West history, the Rocky Mountains and Great Plains embody the American frontier.

Yellowstone National Park

The country's oldest national park is full of geysers, hot springs and a wealth of megafauna – grizzly bears, bison, elk and more – that range across North America's largest intact natural ecosystem.

Rocky Mountain National Park

Atop the Continental Divide, jagged mountain peaks are only the start of adventures at this park, speckled with more than 150 lakes and 450 miles of streams running through aromatic pine forests.

Glacier National Park

Fly along the high-altitude Going-to-the-Sun Rd, which appears to defy gravity as it winds for 50 miles through the mountainous landscape that some Native Americans call 'The Backbone of the World.'

Badlands National Park

Amid native prairie grasslands, where bison and bighorn sheep roam, this alarmingly named park is a captivating outdoor museum of geology, with fossil beds revealing traces of North America's prehistoric past.

Mesa Verde National Park

Clamber onto the edge of the Colorado Plateau to visit the well-preserved Native American cliff dwellings of Ancestral Puebloans who inhabited the remote Four Corners area for many generations.

1

1. Bighorn sheep, Badlands National Park (p667)
2. Grand Prismatic Spring (p786), Yellowstone National Park
3. Longs Peak, Rocky Mountain National Park (p757)

3

2

Southwest

It takes time to explore the Southwest's meandering canyon country, arid deserts and Native American archaeological ruins. An ancient, colorful chasm carved by one of the USA's most powerful rivers is just the beginning. Meander down backcountry byways to discover ancient sand dunes, twisting slot canyons and giant cacti.

Grand Canyon National Park

Arguably the USA's best-known natural attraction, the Grand Canyon is an incredible spectacle of colored rock strata, carved by the irresistible flow of the Colorado River. Its buttes and peaks spire into a landscape that's always changing with the weather.

Zion National Park

Pioneers almost believed they'd reached the promised land at this desert oasis, run through by a life-giving river. Get a thrill by rappelling down a slot canyon or pulling yourself up the cables to aerial Angels Landing viewpoint.

Bryce Canyon National Park

On the same geological 'Grand Staircase' as the Grand Canyon, Bryce Canyon shows off a whimsical landscape of totem-shaped hoodoo rock formations, some rising as tall as a 10-story building.

Arches National Park

Just outside the four-seasons base camp of Moab, Utah, this iconic landscape of more than 2000 naturally formed sandstone arches is most mesmerizing at sunrise and sunset, when the gorgeously eroded desert rocks seem to glow.

Saguaro National Park

An icon of the American West, spiky saguaro cacti stretch toward the sky in this Arizona desert park, where coyotes howl, spotted owls hoot and desert tortoises slowly crawl through the sere landscape.

1. Arches National Park (p873) **2.** Angels Landing Trail, Zion National Park (p878) **3.** Grand Canyon National Park (p845)

DEREK VON BRIESEN / GETTY IMAGES ©

West Coast

Thunderous waterfalls, the sirens' call of glacier-carved peaks and the world's tallest, biggest *and* oldest trees are just some of the natural wonders that California offers. Meet smoking volcanic mountains, misty rainforests and untamed beaches in the Pacific Northwest.

Yosemite National Park

Visit glaciated valleys, alpine wildflower meadows, groves of giant sequoia trees and earth-shaking waterfalls that tumble over sheer granite cliffs in the USA's second-oldest national park.

Olympic National Park

Lose yourself in the primeval rainforests, mist-clouded mountains carved by glaciers and lonely, wild Pacific Coast beaches. Watch salmon swim free in the restored Elwha River, site of the world's largest dam removal project.

Death Valley & Joshua Tree National Parks

Slide down sand dunes and stroll across salt flats at Badwater, the USA's lowest elevation spot, in hellishly hot Death Valley. Or hop between boulders, native fan-palm oases and forests of crooked Joshua trees, all in Southern California's deserts.

Mt Rainier National Park

Meet a glacier-covered, rumbling giant that may have last erupted only 120 years ago and still reigns over the Pacific Northwest's volcanic Cascades Range. Day hike among wildflower meadows or tramp across snow fields even in midsummer.

Redwood National Park

Be awed by towering ancient stands of coast redwoods, the tallest trees on earth, along the often foggy Northern California coast. Spot shaggy Roosevelt elk foraging in woodland prairies, then go tide-pooling along rugged beaches.

1

1. Mt Rainier National Park (p1048) **2.** Redwood National Park (p1001) **3.** Yosemite National Park (p1009)

3

2

Above: Bear Glacier Lake, Kenai Fjords National Park (p1083); Right: Green turtle, Hawa

Final Frontiers

Officially US states for little more than 50 years, far-flung Alaska and Hawaii offer some unforgettable wilderness experiences you just can't get in the 'Lower 48' or on 'da mainland'. Active volcanoes, icy glaciers, rare and endangered wildlife and a rich vein of historic sites make these parks worth a detour.

Alaska

In 1980, the Alaska National Interest Lands Conservation Act turned more than 47 million acres of wilderness over to the NPS, more than doubling the federal agency's holdings with a single stroke of President Jimmy Carter's pen.

Today Alaska's national parks give visitors a chance to see glacial icebergs calve at Kenai Fjords and Glacier Bay, watch brown bears catch salmon at Katmai or summit the USA's highest peak, Denali (Mt McKinley). Along the aquatic Inside Passage, admire Native Alaskan totem poles in Sitka and retrace the hardy steps of 19th-century Klondike gold-rush pioneers at Skagway.

Hawaii

The USA's remotest archipelago is tailor-made for tropical escapades. On Hawai'i, the Big Island, witness the world's longest continuous volcanic eruption or possibly see lava flow at Hawai'i Volcanoes National Park, then snorkel with sea turtles beside an ancient Hawaiian place of refuge on the Kona coast. On Maui, trek deep inside a volcano and swim in stream-fed pools at mind-bogglingly diverse Haleakalā National Park. Last, pay your respects to O'ahu's WWII-era USS Arizona Memorial.

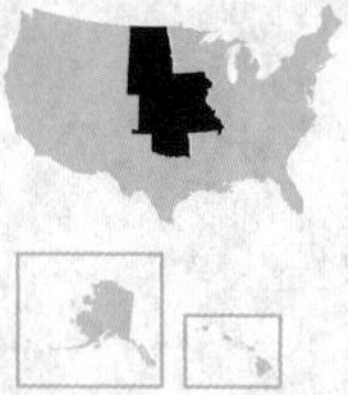

Great Plains

Includes ➜

Best Places to Eat

- ➜ Q39 (p654)
- ➜ Alba (p658)
- ➜ Ted Drewes (p646)
- ➜ MB Haskett Delicatessen (p665)

Best Wide-Open Spaces

- ➜ Tallgrass Prairie National Preserve (p684)
- ➜ South Dakota's Hwy 14 (p667)
- ➜ Nebraska's Hwy 2 (p678)
- ➜ Nebraska's Panhandle (p679)

Why Go?

To best comprehend this vast and underappreciated region in the heart of the US, you need to split the name. The first word, 'great,' is easy. Great scenery, great tornadoes, great eats, great people: all apply. The problem is with 'plains.' 'Humdrum' and 'flat' are two words that come to mind. Neither applies. Amid the endless horizons and raw natural drama are surprises such as St Louis and Kansas City, the Alpine beauty of the Black Hills and the legacy of Route 66.

Great distances across the beguiling wide-open spaces are the biggest impediment to enjoying this enormous region, which includes the states of Missouri, Iowa, North Dakota, South Dakota, Nebraska, Kansas and Oklahoma. Many sights lie near the interstates, but many more are found along the ever-intriguing small roads (the 'blue highways' of lore). Your inner great explorer, à la Lewis and Clark, will thrill to every new delight.

When to Go

St Louis

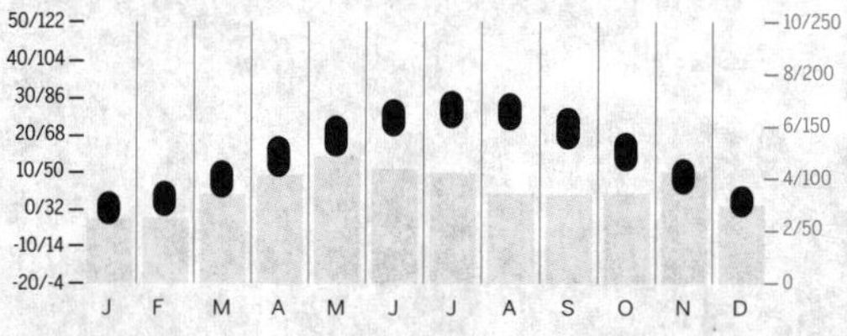

Nov–Mar Attractions cut back hours, or close. Blizzards shut down roads for days.

Apr–May, Sep–Oct Average highs of 55°F (13°C) in the north, warmer in the south; fewer visitors.

Jun–Aug Thunderstorms and even tornadoes; sultry days with blooming wildflowers.

History

Spear-toting nomads hunted mammoths here 11,000 years ago, long before cannon-toting Spaniards introduced the horse (accidentally) around 1630. Fur-frenzied French explorers, following the Mississippi and Missouri Rivers, claimed most of the land between the Mississippi and the Rocky Mountains for France. The territory passed to Spain in 1763, the French got it back in 1800 and then sold it to the USA in the 1803 Louisiana Purchase.

Settlers' hunger for land pushed resident Native American tribes westward, often forcibly, as in the notorious relocation of the Five Civilized Tribes – Cherokee, Chickasaw, Choctaw, Creek and Seminole – along the 1838–39 Trail of Tears, which led to Oklahoma from back east. Pioneers blazed west on trails such as the Santa Fe across Kansas.

Earlier occupants, including the Osage and Sioux, had different, but often tragic, fates. Many resettled in pockets across the region, while others fought for lands once promised.

Railroads, barbed wire and oil all brought change as the 20th century hovered. The 1930s Dust Bowl ruined farms and spurred many residents to say: 'I've had enough of this crap – I'm heading west.' Even today, many regions remain eerily empty.

Local Culture

The people who settled the Great Plains usually faced difficult lives of scarcity, uncertainty and isolation; and it literally drove many of them crazy. Others gave up and got out (failed homesteads dot the region). Only fiercely independent people could thrive in those conditions and that born-and-bred rugged individualism is the core of Plains culture today. Quiet restraint is considered an important and polite trait here.

Getting There & Around

The main airport is Lambert-St Louis International (p648), but visitors from abroad will be better off flying to Chicago, Denver or Dallas and connecting to one of the region's myriad airports or hitting the open roads.

Greyhound (www.greyhound.com) buses only cover some interstates, but **Jefferson Lines** (www.jeffersonlines.com) and **Burlington Trailways** (www.burlingtontrailways.com) take up some of the slack. They both honor Greyhound's Discovery Pass.

Amtrak (www.amtrak.com) routes across the Plains make getting here by train easy, but getting around impractical.

MISSOURI

The most populated state in the Plains, Missouri likes to mix things up, serving visitors ample portions of both sophisticated city life and down-home country sights. St Louis and Kansas City are the region's most interesting cities and each is a destination in its own right. But, with more forest and less farm field than neighboring states, Missouri also cradles plenty of wild places and wide-open spaces, most notably the rolling Ozark Mountains, where the winding valleys invite adventurous exploration or just some laid-back meandering behind the steering wheel. Maybe you'll find an adventure worthy of Hannibal native Mark Twain as you wander the state.

History

Claimed by France as part of the Louisiana Territory in 1682, Missouri had only a few small river towns by the start of the 19th century when the land passed to American hands and Lewis and Clark pushed up the Missouri River. Missouri was admitted to the Union as a slave state in 1821, per the Missouri Compromise (which permitted

MISSOURI FACTS

Nickname Show-Me State

Population 6.1 million

Area 69,710 sq miles

Capital city Jefferson City (population 43,300)

Other cities St Louis (population 319,000), Kansas City (population 467,000)

Sales tax 4.23% to 9.6%

Birthplace of Author Samuel Clemens (Mark Twain; 1835–1910), gunslinger Calamity Jane (1852–1903), scientist George Washington Carver (1864–1943), author William S Burroughs (1914–97), author Maya Angelou (1928–2014)

Home of Budweiser, Chuck Berry

Politics Leans Republican

Famous for Gateway Arch, Branson, BBQ

Official dance Square dance

Driving distances St Louis to Kansas City 250 miles, St Louis to Chicago 300 miles

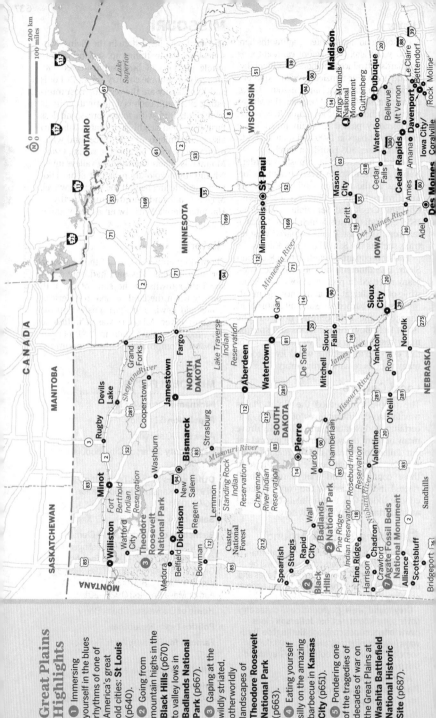

Great Plains Highlights

1. Immersing yourself in the blues rhythms of one of America's great old cities: **St Louis** (p640).
2. Going from mountain highs in the **Black Hills** (p670) to valley lows in **Badlands National Park** (p667).
3. Gaping at the wildly striated, otherworldly landscapes of **Theodore Roosevelt National Park** (p663).
4. Eating yourself silly on the amazing barbecue in **Kansas City** (p651).
5. Pondering one of the tragedies of decades of war on the Great Plains at **Washita Battlefield National Historic Site** (p687).

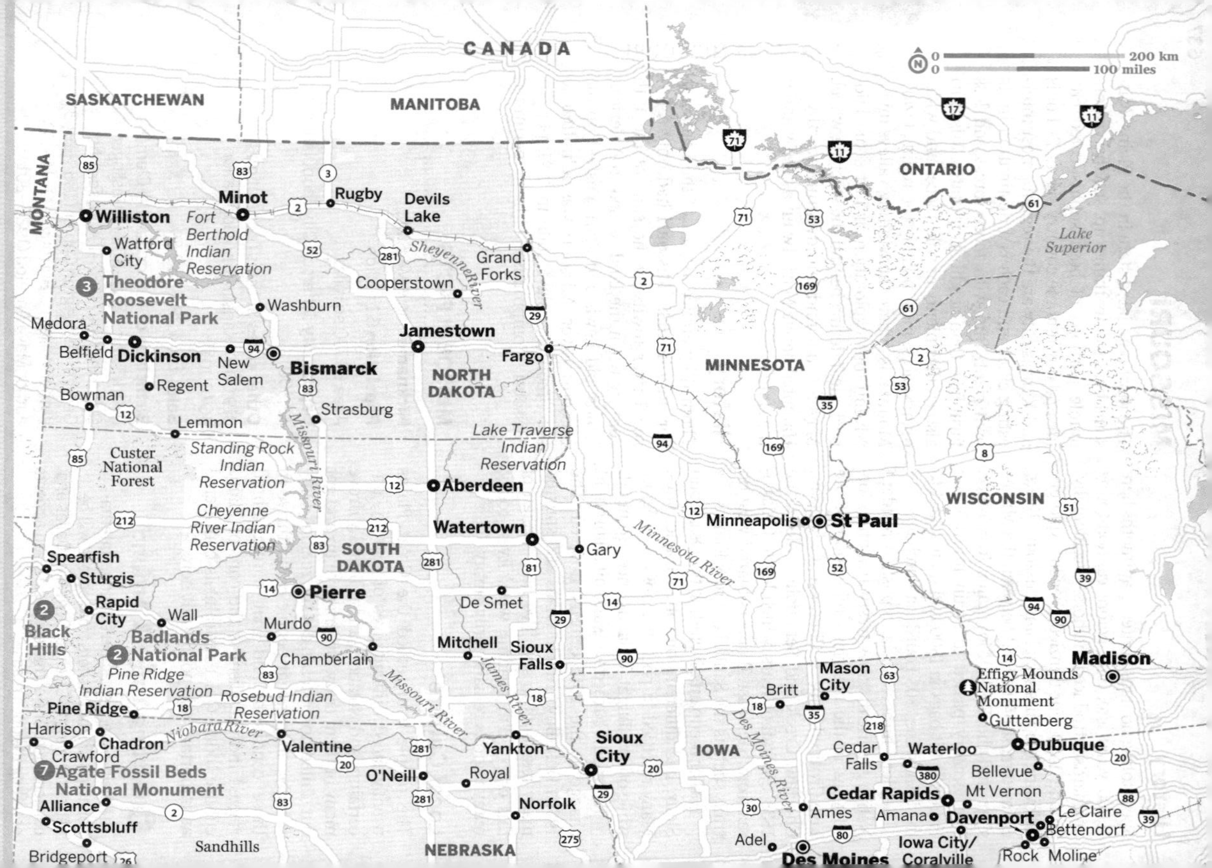

6 Veering off the interstates for beguiling alternate routes such as the old **Route 66** through **Missouri** (p650), **Kansas** (p683) and **Oklahoma** (p156).

7 Losing yourself in the wide open wilds and the great fossil finds of **Agate Fossil Beds National Monument** (p679).

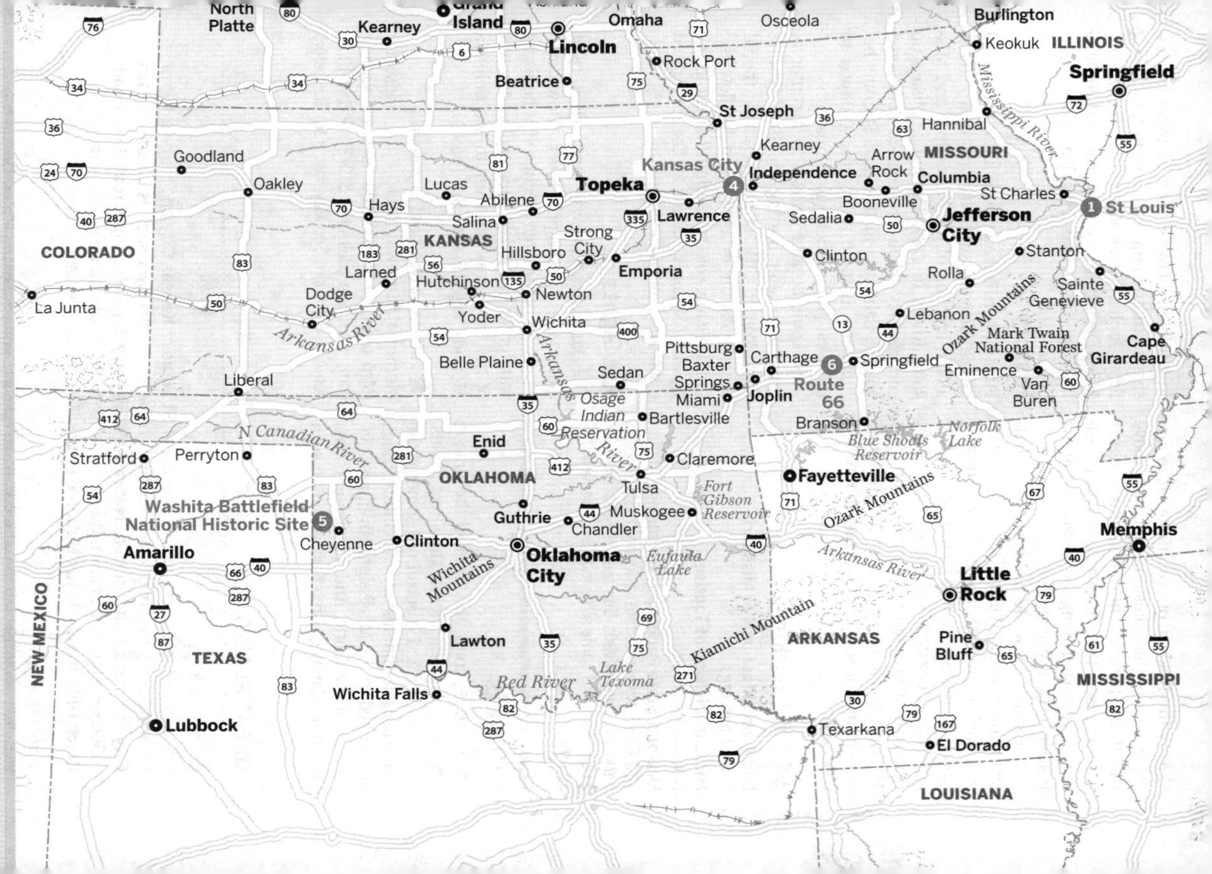

slavery in Missouri, but prohibited it in any other part of the Louisiana Territory above the 36°30´ parallel), but abolitionists never compromised their ideals, and bitter feelings were stoked along the Missouri–Kansas border by Civil War time.

The state's 'Show-Me' nickname is attributed to Congressman Willard Duncan Vandiver, who said in an 1899 speech, 'I come from a state that raises corn and cotton and cockleburs and Democrats, and frothy eloquence neither convinces nor satisfies me. I am from Missouri. You have got to show me.' The name now implies a stalwart, not-easily-impressed character.

Information

Bed & Breakfast Inns of Missouri (www.bbim.org)

Missouri Division of Tourism (www.visitmo.com)

Missouri State Parks (☎ reservations 877-422-6766; www.mostateparks.com) State parks are free to visit. Site fees range from $12 to $56 and some sites may be reserved in advance.

St Louis

Slide into St Louis and revel in the unique vibe of the largest city in the Great Plains. Beer, bowling and baseball are some of the top attractions, but history and culture, much of it linked to the Mississippi River, are a vital part of the fabric. And, of course, there's the iconic Gateway Arch that you have seen in a million pictures; it's even more impressive in reality. Many music legends, including Scott Joplin, Chuck Berry, Tina Turner and Miles Davis, got their start here and jammin' live-music venues keep the flame burning.

History

Fur-trapper Pierre Laclede knew prime real estate when he saw it, so he put down stakes at the junction of the Mississippi and Missouri Rivers in 1764. The hustle picked up considerably when prospectors discovered gold in California in 1848 and St Louis became the jump-off point (aka 'Gateway to the West') for get-rich-quick dreamers.

St Louis became known as a center of innovation after hosting the 1904 World's Fair. Aviator Charles Lindbergh furthered the reputation in 1927 when he flew the first nonstop, solo transatlantic flight in the 'Spirit of St Louis,' named for the far-sighted town that funded the aircraft.

Sights

The landmark Gateway Arch rises right along the Mississippi River. Downtown runs west of the Arch. Begin a visit here and wander for half a day. Then explore the rest of the city; cross the river to see Cahokia Mounds State Historic Site (p553).

★ Jefferson National Expansion Memorial/Gateway Arch MONUMENT
(Map p644; ☎ 314-655-1700; www.gatewayarch.com; tram ride adult/child $10/5; ⏰ 8am-10pm Jun-Aug, 9am-6pm Sep-May, last tram 1hr before

GREAT PLAINS IN...

One Week

Spend your first two or three days in either **St Louis** or **Kansas City** and the next two or three exploring the small-town standouts of Nebraska and Iowa, such as **Lincoln** or **Iowa City**. Try scenic routes such as **Nebraska's Highway 2** (p678) or the **Great River Road** (p660) at either end of Iowa. Then head north to South Dakota where the gorgeous **Black Hills** and **Badlands National Park** will vie for your remaining time.

Two Weeks

With two weeks behind the wheel, you can take a big bite out of the Plains. Do the trip as above, then head south from South Dakota along eastern Nebraska, stopping at fascinating, isolated sites such as the **Agate Fossil Beds National Monument** (p679), **Carhenge** (p679) and **Scotts Bluff National Monument** (p679).

Meander into Kansas and pick up **US 50** (p684) heading east. Stop at the amazing, astonishing **Cosmosphere & Space Center** (p684) in Hutchinson. Head south to Oklahoma and join historic **Route 66** going northeast for sights such as the **Will Rogers Memorial Museum** (p156). Follow the road into Missouri and finish your trip at either of the major cities you skipped on the way out.

closing; 👪) As a symbol for St Louis, the Arch has soared above any expectations its backers could have had in 1965 when it opened. The centerpiece of this National Park Service (NPS) property, the silvery, shimmering Gateway Arch is the Great Plains' own Eiffel Tower. It stands 630ft high and symbolizes St Louis' historical role as 'Gateway to the West.' The **tram ride** takes you to the tight confines at the top. Book tickets in advance on the NPS website (www.nps.gov/jeff).

A massive project transformed the area around the Arch in time for its 50th birthday. A large plaza now covers I-70 and connects the Arch and its park directly to the Old Courthouse and the rest of downtown. It's a huge and welcome improvement. Note that some portions of the upgrade, which includes all of the parks, won't be complete until 2017. Find out more at www.cityarchriver.org.

➡ Museum of Westward Expansion
(Map p644; www.nps.gov/jeff; Gateway Arch) FREE The museum located below the Arch is being expanded and will reopen in 2017.

➡ Old Courthouse & Museum
(Map p644; ☎314-655-1700; www.nps.gov/jeff; 11 N 4th St; ⏰7:30am-8pm Jun-Aug, 8am-5pm Sep-May) FREE Facing the Gateway Arch across the new plaza, this 1845 courthouse is where the famed Dred Scott slavery case was first tried. Galleries depict the trial's history, as well as that of the city. It also has displays on the westward expansion of the US.

★City Museum MUSEUM
(Map p644; www.citymuseum.org; 701 N 15th St; admission $12, Ferris wheel $5; ⏰9am-5pm Mon-Thu, to midnight Fri & Sat, 11am-5pm Sun; 👪) Possibly the wildest highlight to any visit to St Louis is this frivolous, frilly fun house in a vast old shoe factory. The Museum of Mirth, Mystery and Mayhem sets the tone. Run, jump and explore all manner of exhibits, including a seven-story slide. The summer-only rooftop **Ferris wheel** offers grand views of the city.

Grant's Farm AMUSEMENT PARK
(☎314-843-1700; www.grantsfarm.com; 10501 Gravois Rd; admission free, parking $12; ⏰9am-3:30pm Tue-Sun May-Aug, reduced hours mid-Apr–late Apr, Sep & Oct, closed Nov–mid-Apr; 👪) A small-time theme park on the beer-brewing Busch family's rural retreat, Grant's Farm thrills kids with its Clydesdale horses and 1000 other animals from six continents; a tram takes you through the preserve where the beasts roam uncaged. It's southeast of the centre, off Hwy 30.

ST LOUIS AT A GLANCE

The St Louis neighborhoods of most interest radiate out from the Downtown core:

Central West End Just east of Forest Park, a posh center for nightlife and shopping.

The Hill An Italian American neighborhood with good delis and eateries.

Lafayette Square Historic, upscale and trendy.

The Loop Northwest of Forest Park, funky shops and nightlife line Delmar Blvd.

Soulard The city's oldest quarter, with good cafes, bars and blues.

Grand Center Located in Midtown and rich with cultural and historic sites.

South Grand Bohemian and gentrifying, surrounds beautiful Tower Grove Park and has a slew of ethnic restaurants.

Missouri Botanical Garden GARDENS
(Map p642; ☎314-577-5100; www.mobot.org; 4344 Shaw Blvd; adult/child $8/free; ⏰9am-5pm daily Jun-Aug, to 4pm Tue-Sun Sep-May) Dating to 1859, these gardens hold a 14-acre Japanese garden, a carnivorous plant bog and a Victorian-style hedge maze. It's at the north end of Tower Grove Park, near I-44 exit 287B.

Museum of Transportation MUSEUM
(☎314-965-6885; www.transportmuseumassociation.org; 3015 Barrett Station Rd; adult/child $8/5; ⏰9am-4pm Mon-Sat, 11am-4pm Sun Jun-Aug, reduced hours Sep-May) Huge railroad locomotives (including a Union Pacific Big Boy), historic cars cooler than your rental, and more that moves. Take I-270 west to exit 8.

Pulitzer Foundation for the Arts MUSEUM
(Map p642; ☎314-754-1850; www.pulitzerarts.org; 3716 Washington Blvd; ⏰10am-5pm Wed & Sat, to 8pm Thu & Fri) FREE A Grand Center (Midtown) landmark, with programs and exhibits across disciplines, including architecture.

Columbia Bottom Conservation Area NATURE RESERVE
(☎314-877-6014; www.mdc.mo.gov; 801 Strodtman Rd; ⏰dawn-dusk) FREE Marvel at the place where two of the world's great rivers, the

Greater St Louis

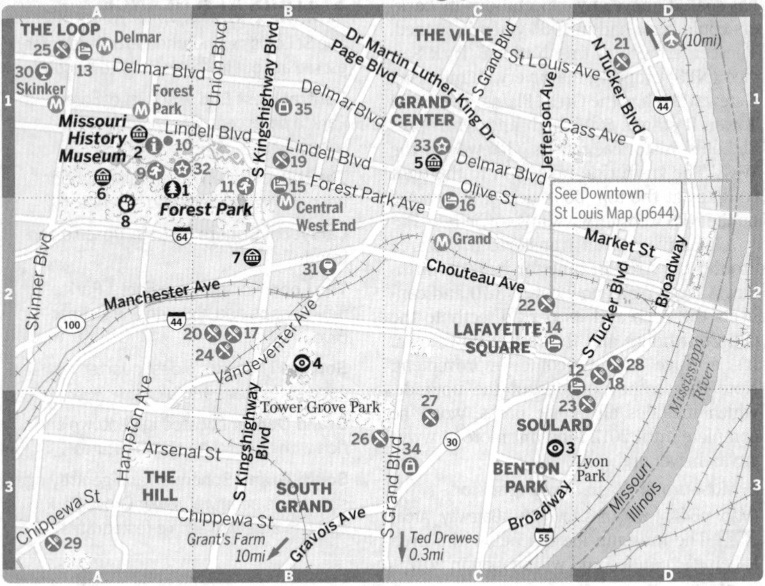

Missouri and the Mississippi, meet. View the waters once paddled by Lewis and Clark and explore the natural beauty of this 4318-acre preserve. It's 2.5 miles north of I-270 exit 34. You can see the Lewis & Clark State Historic Site (p554) on the Illinois side.

Forest Park

New York City may have Central Park, but St Louis has the bigger (by 528 acres) **Forest Park** (Map p642; 314-289-5300; bounded by Lindell Blvd, Kingshighway Blvd & I-64; 6am-10pm). The superb, 1371-acre spread was the setting of the 1904 World's Fair. It's a beautiful place to escape to and is dotted with attractions, many free.

The **Visitor and Education Center** (Map p642; 314-367-7275; www.forestparkforever.org; 5595 Grand Dr; 6am-8pm Mon-Fri, to 6pm Sat & Sun) is in an old streetcar pavilion and has a cafe. Free walking tours leave from here, or you can borrow an iPod audio tour.

★Missouri History Museum MUSEUM
(Map p642; 314-746-4599; www.mohistory.org; 5700 Lindell Blvd; 10am-5pm Wed-Mon, to 8pm Tue) FREE Presents the story of St Louis, starring such worthies as the World's Fair, Charles Lindbergh (look for the sales receipt for his first plane – he bought it at a variety store!) and a host of bluesmen. Oral histories from those who fought segregation are moving.

St Louis Art Museum MUSEUM
(Map p642; www.slam.org; 1 Fine Arts Dr; 10am-5pm Tue-Thu, Sat & Sun, to 9pm Fri) FREE A grand beaux-arts palace (with striking modern wing) originally built for the World's Fair. Now housing this storied institution, its collections span time and styles. The Grace Taylor Broughton Sculpture Garden opened in 2015.

St Louis Zoo ZOO
(Map p642; 314-781-0900; www.stlzoo.org; 1 Government Dr; 9am-5pm daily, to 7pm Fri-Sun Jun-Aug;) Divided into themed zones, this vast zoo includes a fascinating River's Edge area with African critters. There's a fee for some exhibits.

St Louis Science Center MUSEUM
(Map p642; 314-289-4400; www.slsc.org; 5050 Oakland Ave; 9:30am-5:30pm Mon-Sat, 11am-5:30pm Sun;) FREE Live demonstrations, dinosaurs, a planetarium and an IMAX theater (additional fee).

Activities

Forest Park has many activities you can enjoy amid its beauty.

Greater St Louis

Boathouse BOATING
(Map p642; ☎314-367-2224; www.boathouseforestpark.com; 6101 Government Dr; boat rental per hr $17; 11am-approx 1hr before sunset) In warm weather, rent a rowboat to paddle over Post-Dispatch Lake.

Steinberg Ice-Skating Rink SKATING
(Map p642; ☎314-361-0613; www.steinbergskatingrink.com; off N Kingshighway Blvd; admission $7, skates rental $5; 10am-9pm Sun-Thu, to midnight Fri & Sat mid-Nov–Feb) The balm for cold weather: fun on the ice.

Tours

Gateway Arch Riverboats BOAT TOUR
(Map p644; ☎877-982-1410; www.gatewayarch.com; 50 S Leonor K Sullivan Blvd; 1hr tour adult/child $18/8; various times Mar-Nov) Churn up the Big Muddy on replica 19th-century steamboats. A park ranger narrates the midday cruises, and those after 3pm sail subject to availability. There are also numerous dinner and drinking cruises.

City Cycling Tours BICYCLE TOUR
(Map p642; www.citycyclingtours.com; 5595 Grand Dr, Forest Park Visitor & Education Center; rental per hour/half-day $10/25, 3hr tour $30; rental 10am-5pm, tours daily year-round, times vary) Besides bike rentals, there are narrated rides (bikes supplied) through Forest Park starting at the visitor center.

Festivals & Events

Big Muddy Blues Festival MUSIC
(Map p644; www.bigmuddybluesfestival.com; Laclede's Landing; early Sep) Five stages of riverfront blues at Laclede's Landing on the Labor Day weekend.

Sleeping

Most midrange and upscale chains have a hotel near the Gateway Arch in Downtown. Indie cheapies are thin on the ground in interesting areas, but you'll find plenty near the airport and you can ride the MetroLink light rail into the city. Upscale Clayton on I-170 (exit 1F) also has rail access and a cluster of chains.

Huckleberry Finn Hostel HOSTEL $
(Map p642; ☎314-374-8696; www.huckfinnhostel.com; 1908 S 12th St; dm from $30; office 6-10pm; P ❄) In two old town houses, this independent hostel is basic, but it's a friendly gathering spot with a piano in the lounge/kitchen, and free lockers. Its Soulard location is ideal. Be sure to reserve ahead.

Downtown St Louis

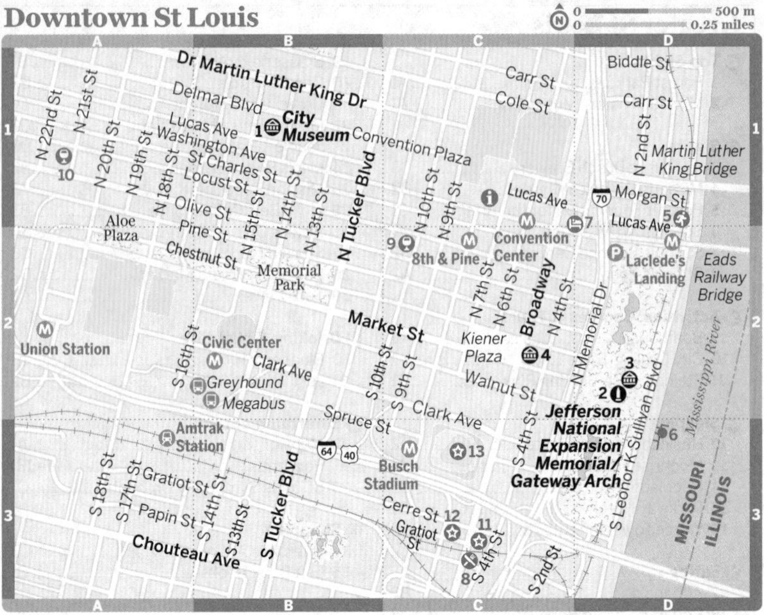

Downtown St Louis

Top Sights
1 City Museum B1
2 Jefferson National Expansion Memorial/Gateway Arch D2

Sights
3 Museum of Westward Expansion D2
4 Old Courthouse & Museum C2

Activities, Courses & Tours
5 Big Muddy Blues Festival D1
6 Gateway Arch Riverboats D3

Sleeping
7 Missouri Athletic Club D1

Eating
8 Broadway Oyster Bar C3

Drinking & Nightlife
9 Bridge Tap House & Wine Bar C2
10 Schlafly Tap Room A1

Entertainment
11 BB's C3
12 Beale C3
13 Busch Stadium C3

Water Tower Inn HOTEL $
(Map p642; ☎314-977-7500; www.watertowerinn-stl.com; 3545 Lafayette Ave, St Louis University; r $80-130; P ❄ ☜) Right in the middle of St Louis University and near the interesting Central West End, the 62 rooms over six floors here have corporate decor; some have views to the Arch. There's a laundry and free continental breakfast.

★ **Missouri Athletic Club** HOTEL $$
(Map p644; ☎314-231-7220; www.mac-stl.org; 405 Washington Ave; r $120-160; P ❄ ☜ ≋) Stay in style Downtown close to the Arch. The Missouri Athletic Club is a grand old facility with 73 nice and traditional hotel rooms. Guests can use the club's facilities, which include a 25m indoor pool ($12).

Parkway Hotel HOTEL $$
(Map p642; ☎314-256-7777; www.theparkway-hotel.com; 4550 Forest Park Ave; r $145-250; P ❄ @ ☜ 🐾) Right in the midst of Central West End's upscale fun, this indie eight-story hotel contains 217 modern rooms (with fridges and microwaves) inside a grand limestone building. A hot buffet breakfast is included, and you can't beat the location right across from Forest Park.

Napoleon's Retreat B&B $$
(Map p642; ☎314-772-6979; www.napoleonsretreat.com; 1815 Lafayette Ave; r $140-230; ❄@📶) A lovely Second French Empire–style home in historic and leafy Lafayette Sq, this B&B has five bold and beautiful rooms, each with fridges and antique furnishings.

Moonrise Hotel BOUTIQUE HOTEL $$
(Map p642; ☎314-721-1111; www.moonrisehotel.com; 6177 Delmar Blvd; r $135-260; P❄@📶🐾) Stylish eight-story Moonrise has a high profile amid the high energy of the Loop neighborhood. Its 125 rooms sport a lunar motif, but are grounded enough to be comfy.

Eating & Drinking

St Louis boasts the region's most diverse selection of food. Magazine and website *Sauce* (www.saucemagazine.com) is full of reviews.

Schlafly, Civil Life, Earthbound Brewing and Urban Chestnut are excellent local microbrews that will let you forget that you're in the home of Bud. The website **StL Hops** (www.stlhops.com) is an excellent guide to local beers and where to drink them.

Soulard and the Loop are loaded with pubs and bars, many with live music. Most bars close at 1:30am, though some have 3am licenses.

The Grove, a strip of Manchester Ave between Kingshighway Blvd and S Vandeventer Ave, is the hub of St Louis' gay and lesbian community. Peruse *Vital Voice* (www.thevitalvoice.com) for info.

Downtown & Midtown

Laclede's Landing, along the riverfront next to the historic Eads Railway Bridge, has several restaurants, though generally people pop down here for the atmosphere – cobblestoned streets, converted brick buildings and free-flowing beer – rather than the food.

★**Crown Candy Kitchen** CAFE $
(Map p642; ☎314-621-9650; www.crowncandykitchen.net; 1401 St Louis Ave; mains $5-10; ⏲10:30am-9pm Mon-Sat; 👪) An authentic family-run soda fountain that's been making families smile since 1913. Malts (hot fudge, yum!) come with spoons, the floats, well, float, and you can try the famous BLT. Homemade candies top it off. It's an oasis in the struggling North St Louis neighborhood.

Broadway Oyster Bar CAJUN $$
(Map p644; ☎314-621-8811; www.broadwayoysterbar.com; 736 S Broadway; mains $10-20; ⏲11am-3am) Part bar, part live-music venue, but all restaurant, this joint jumps year-round. When the sun shines, people flock outside where they suck down crawfish and other Cajun treats. It's nuts before and after Cardinals games.

★**Bridge Tap House & Wine Bar** BAR
(Map p644; ☎314-241-8141; www.thebridgestl.com; 1004 Locust St; ⏲11am-1am Mon-Sat, to midnight Sun) Slip onto a sofa or rest your elbows on a table at this romantic bar where you can savor fine wine or the best local beer (55 on tap) and nibble a variety of exquisite little bites from a seasonal menu.

Schlafly Tap Room BREWERY
(Map p644; ☎314-241-2337; www.schlafly.com; 2100 Locust St; ⏲11am-10pm Mon & Tue, to midnight Wed & Thu, to 1am Fri & Sat, noon-10pm Sun) The most famous local craft brewer runs this excellent pub just west of downtown. The menu has lots of pub classics (mains $8 to $20), while the beer list comprises many of the 50 brews produced during the year. Nab a seat in the beer garden.

Soulard & Lafayette Square

Restaurants and pubs occupy most corners in Soulard, with plenty of live blues and Irish music, so just wander. Historic Lafayette Sq, 1 mile northwest, has some stylish spots.

★**Soulard Farmers Market** MARKET $
(Map p642; ☎314-622-4180; www.soulardmarket.com; 730 Carroll St; ⏲8am-5pm Wed & Thu, 7am-5pm Fri & Sat) A local treasure with a range of vendors selling regional produce, baked goods and prepared foods. Picnic or snack yourself silly. Dating to 1779, it's pretension free.

Joanie's Pizzeria PIZZA $
(Map p642; www.joanies.com; 2101 Menard St; mains $10-15; ⏲11am-11pm) This unassuming neighborhood bar and grill turns out excellent local-style pizza (ask for Provel, the locally beloved cheese concoction). The sauce wins kudos. Grab a table in the hidden courtyard. Live music some nights.

Bogart's Smoke House BARBECUE $$
(Map p642; ☎314-621-3107; www.bogartssmokehouse.com; 1627 S 9th St; mains $9-27; ⏲10:30am-4pm Mon-Thu, to 8pm Fri & Sat) The soul of Soulard? The smoky meats here draw lines of people who tear into all the standards plus specialties such as prime rib. Extras, includ-

LOCAL ST LOUIS SPECIALTIES

Toasted ravioli They're filled with meat, coated in breadcrumbs, then deep-fried. Practically every restaurant on the Hill serves them, most notably Charlie Gitto's.

St Louis pizza Its thin-crusted, square-cut pizzas are really addictive. They're made with Provel cheese, a locally beloved gooey concoction of processed cheddar, Swiss and provolone. Local chain **Imo's** (www.imospizza.com; large from $16), with over 70 locations across the metro area, bakes 'the square beyond compare,' or get your pizza with Provel at the popular Joanie's Pizzeria (p645).

Frozen custard Don't dare leave town without licking yourself silly on this supercreamy ice-cream-like treat at historic **Ted Drewes** (Map p642; 314-481-4241; www.teddrewes.com; 6726 Chippewa St; cones $1-3; 11am-11pm Feb-Dec), southwest of the city center. There's a smaller summer-only branch south of the city center at 4224 S Grand Blvd. Rich and poor rub elbows enjoying a 'concrete,' a delectable stirred-up combination of flavors.

ing the searingly hot voodoo sauce and the 'fire and ice pickles,' have creative flair.

Eleven Eleven Mississippi MODERN AMERICAN $$
(Map p642; 314-241-9999; www.1111-m.com; 1111 Mississippi Ave; mains $9-25; 11am-10pm Mon-Thu, to midnight Fri, 5pm-midnight Sat;) This popular bistro and wine bar fills an old shoe factory. Dinner mains draw on regional specialties with a farm-to-table vibe. Other options on the seasonal menu include sandwiches, pizzas, steaks and veggie dishes. Excellent wine selection.

South Grand

Running along South Grand Blvd, this young, bohemian area near beautiful Tower Grove Park has a slew of excellent ethnic restaurants, many with outside terraces.

MoKaBe's Coffeehouse CAFE $
(Map p642; 314-865-2009; www.mokabes.com; 3606 Arsenal St; mains $5-7; 8am-midnight;) Overlooking Tower Grove Park, this hangout for neighborhood activists, hipsters and generally cool folk buzzes day and night. Grab a coffee, a baked treat, breakfast or a sandwich. There are seats outside.

Shaved Duck AMERICAN $$
(Map p642; 314-776-1407; www.theshavedduck.com; 2900 Virginia Ave; mains $10-20; 5-9pm Mon, 11am-10pm Tue-Fri, 4-10pm Sat) A South Grand stalwart, the Shaved Duck fires up its grills early in the day and turns out excellent BBQ, including the signature smoked duck. Options include fab sandwiches and veggie sides. Live music weeknights.

The Hill

This Italian neighborhood crammed with tortellini-sized houses has innumerable pasta joints. Stroll the tidy streets and stop for a coffee at an Italian cafe.

★ **Adriana's** ITALIAN $
(Map p642; 314-773-3833; www.adrianasonthehill.com; 5101 Shaw Ave; mains $5-10; 10:30am-3pm Mon-Sat) Redolent of herbs, this Italian deli serves up fresh salads and sandwiches (get the meaty Hill Boy) to ravenous lunching crowds.

Milo's Bocce Garden ITALIAN $
(Map p642; 314-776-0468; www.milosboccegarden.com; 5201 Wilson Ave; mains $8-14; 11am-1am Mon-Sat, kitchen to 11pm) Enjoy sandwiches, pizzas and pastas in the vast outdoor courtyard or inside the old-world bar. Watch and join the regulars on the busy bocce courts.

Charlie Gitto's ITALIAN $$$
(Map p642; 314-772-8898; www.charliegittos.com; 5226 Shaw Ave; mains $16-40; 5-10pm Mon-Thu, to 11pm Fri & Sat, 4-9pm Sun; P) Legendary Charlie Gitto's makes a strong claim to having invented St Louis' famous toasted ravioli. On any night the weather allows, dine under the huge tree on the patio. Classy but casual.

Central West End

Sidewalk cafes rule Euclid Ave in posh and trendy Central West End.

Pickles Deli DELI $
(Map p642; 314-361-3354; www.picklesdelistl.com; 22 N Euclid Ave; mains $5-10; 9am-7pm Mon-Fri, 10am-3pm Sat;) Top ingredients

separate this slick deli from humdrum sandwich chains; for example, the French dip is laden with house-roasted beef. Get your Forest Park picnic here.

Brasserie by Niche BISTRO $$$
(Map p642; ☎314-454-0600; www.brasseriebyniche.com; 4580 Laclede Ave; mains $15-30; ⏰5-10pm Mon-Fri, 10am-2pm & 5-10pm Sat & Sun; 📶) This *tres bon* French-style brasserie has an alluring lineup of specialties including garlic soup, *steak frites,* coq au vin and all the desserts you'd expect. Watch for seasonal specials, and try for a table outside.

Just John's Club GAY
(Map p642; www.justjohnsclub.com; 4112 Manchester Ave; ⏰3pm-3am) A Grove anchor, John's has bars inside and out, regular performances and an ever-welcoming vibe.

The Loop

The Loop is near Washington University and runs along Delmar Blvd (embedded with the St Louis Walk of Fame); it has many bars and ethnic restaurants catering to a hipster crowd.

Mission Taco Joint MEXICAN $
(Map p642; ☎314-932-5430; www.missiontacostl.com; 6235 Delmar Blvd; mains $4-12; ⏰11am-1am Tue-Sun) Fresh, upscale Mexican fare in a postindustrial setting. There's a full bar with cool cocktails and a long list of microbrews.

★**Blueberry Hill** BAR
(Map p642; ☎314-727-4444; www.blueberryhill.com; 6504 Delmar Blvd; ⏰11am-late) St Louis native Chuck Berry still sometimes rocks the small basement bar here. Tickets sell out very quickly. The venue hosts smaller-tier bands on the other nights. It has good pub food (mains $8 to $15), games, darts and more.

☆ Entertainment

Check the *Riverfront Times* (www.riverfronttimes.com) for updates on entertainment around town. Purchase tickets for most venues through MetroTix (www.metrotix.com).

Pageant LIVE MUSIC
(Map p642; ☎314-726-6161; www.thepageant.com; 6161 Delmar Blvd) A big venue for touring bands.

BB's BLUES
(Map p644; ☎314-436-5222; www.bbsjazzbluessoups.com; 700 S Broadway; ⏰6pm-3am) Part blues club, part blues museum, this glossy two-level joint has good music most nights. Bar food includes legendary sweet-potato fries.

Beale BLUES
(Map p644; ☎314-621-7880; www.bealeonbroadway.com; 701 S Broadway; ⏰7pm-3am) A major venue for blues, matched in stature by BB's across the street.

St Louis Symphony Orchestra CLASSICAL MUSIC
(Map p642; ☎314-534-1700; www.stlsymphony.org; 718 N Grand Blvd) Located in Grand Center, west of downtown, the symphony offers 50 free tickets for most performances (available online).

Muny PERFORMING ARTS
(Map p642; ☎314-361-1900; www.muny.com; free-$90; ⏰mid-Jun–mid-Aug) The Muny, an outdoor theater, hosts nightly summer Broadway musicals in Forest Park; 1500 of the 12,000 seats are free (lines start forming as early as 4pm).

Busch Stadium BASEBALL
(Map p644; ☎512-434-1542; www.stlcardinals.com; 700 Clark Ave; tickets $11-200) The Cardinals play in this fun, retro stadium, opened in 2006. Second only to the New York Yankees in World Series wins, the Cardinals last won the series in 2011.

Shopping

The Loop and Euclid Ave in Central West End have the best mix of local shops.

★**Left Bank Books** BOOKS
(Map p642; ☎314-367-6731; www.left-bank.com; 399 N Euclid Ave; ⏰10am-10pm Mon-Sat, 11am-6pm Sun) A great indie bookstore stocking

YOUR BELGIAN BUD

Anheuser-Busch Brewery (Map p642; ☎314-577-2626; www.budweisertours.com; cnr 12th & Lynch Sts; ⏰9am-5pm Mon-Thu, to 7pm Fri & Sat, 11:30am-5pm Sun Jun-Aug, 10am-4pm Mon-Sat, 11:30am-4pm Sun Sep-May) The world's largest beer plant, the historic Anheuser-Busch Brewery, gives marketing-driven tours. View the bottling plant and Clydesdale horses. One thing to note: the purchase of this St Louis (and American) icon by Belgium's InBev in 2008 is still a sore spot locally. And don't ask: 'How do you remove all the flavor?'

ST LOUIS MEDIA

KDHX FM 88.1 (www.kdhx.org) Community-run radio playing folk, blues, odd rock and local arts reports.

Riverfront Times (www.riverfronttimes.com) The city's alternative weekly.

St Louis Post-Dispatch (www.stltoday.com) St Louis' daily newspaper.

new and used titles. There are recommendations of books by local authors and frequent author readings.

Cherokee Antique Row ANTIQUES
(Map p642; www.cherokeeantiquerow.com; Cherokee St) Six blocks of Cherokee St, east of Jefferson Ave to Indiana Ave,are lined with antique-filled stores in the appropriately historic Cherokee-Lemp neighborhood.

Information

Explore St Louis (Map p644; ☎314-421-1023; www.explorestlouis.com; cnr 7th St & Washington Ave, America's Center; ⏲8am-5pm Mon-Sat) An excellent resource, with other branches in Kiener Plaza (corner of 6th and Chestnut) and at the airport.

Missouri Welcome Center (☎314-869-7100; www.visitmo.com; Riverview Dr, I-270 exit 34; ⏲8am-5pm)

Getting There & Away

Amtrak (www.amtrak.com; 430 S 15th St, Gateway Transportation Center) *Lincoln Service* travels five times daily to Chicago (from $27, 5½ hours). Two daily *Missouri River Runner* trains go to/from Kansas City (from $30, 5½ hours). The daily *Texas Eagle* goes to Dallas (16 hours); check the website for prices as the fare range for this route is vast.

Greyhound (Map p644; 430 S 15th St, Gateway Transportation Center) Buses depart several times daily to Chicago ($24, six to seven hours), Memphis ($67, six hours), Kansas City ($28, 4½ hours) and many more cities.

Lambert-St Louis International Airport (STL; www.flystl.com; I-70 exit 238A) The largest Great Plains airport; located 12 miles northwest of Downtown.

Megabus (Map p644; www.megabus.com; 430 S 15th St, Gateway Transportation Center) Runs services to Chicago and Kansas City from as little as $5 one way.

Getting Around

Lambert-St Louis International Airport Connected by the light-rail MetroLink ($4), taxi (about $40), and **Go Best Express** (☎314-222-5300; www.gobestexpress.com; one-way from $22) shuttles, which can drop you off in the main areas of town.

Metro (www.metrostlouis.org; single/day pass $2.25/7.50) Runs local buses and the MetroLink light-rail system (which connects the airport, the Loop, Central West End, the Gateway Transportation Center/Union Station and downtown). Buses 30 and 40 serve Soulard from downtown.

St Louis County Cabs (☎314-993-8294, text 314-971-8294; www.countycab.com) Call, text or book online.

Around St Louis

Several appealing and historic river towns north and south of St Louis on the Mississippi and just west on the Missouri make popular weekend trips for St Louisans, including the historic pair of St Charles and Hannibal.

St Charles

This Missouri River town, founded in 1769 by the French, is just 20 miles northwest of St Louis. The cobblestoned Main St anchors a well-preserved downtown.

Sights & Activities

Ask at the **visitor center** (☎800-366-2427; www.historicstcharles.com; 230 S Main St; ⏲8am-5pm Mon-Fri, 10am-5pm Sat, noon-5pm Sun) about tours, which pass some rare French colonial architecture in the Frenchtown neighborhood just north.

First State Capitol HISTORIC BUILDING
(☎636-334-6946; 200 S Main St; admission free, tours adult/child $4.50/3; ⏲10am-4pm Mon-Sat, noon-4pm Sun, closed Mon Nov-Mar) This modest brick complex was the Missouri's capitol from 1821 to 1826. The interior has been restored.

Lewis & Clark Boathouse & Nature Center MUSEUM
(www.lewisandclarkcenter.org; 1050 Riverside Dr; adult/child $5/2; ⏲10am-5pm Mon-Sat, noon-5pm Sun) Lewis and Clark began their epic journey in St Charles on May 21, 1804, and their encampment is reenacted annually on that date. This museum has displays about the duo and replicas of their boats.

Sleeping

Hotels are spread along St Charles' four I-70 exits. St Charles also has several historic B&Bs.

Boone's Colonial Inn B&B $$
(☎888-377-0003; www.boonescolonialinn.com; 322 S Main St; r $165-355; ❄📶) The three suites in these 1820 stone row houses are posh escapes.

Hannibal

When the air is sultry in this old river town, you almost expect to hear the whistle of a paddle steamer. Mark Twain's boyhood home, 100 miles northwest of St Louis, has some authentically vintage sections and plenty of sites (including caves) where you can get a sense of the muse and his creations Tom Sawyer and Huck Finn.

Sights & Activities

The **Hannibal Visitors Bureau** (☎573-221-2477; www.visithannibal.com; 505 N 3rd St; ⏲9am-5pm) has touring routes. **National Tom Sawyer Days** (www.hannibaljaycees.org; ⏲around Jul 4 weekend) features frog-jumping and fence-painting contests and much more.

Mark Twain Boyhood Home & Museum MUSEUM
(☎573-221-9010; www.marktwainmuseum.org; 415 N Main St; adult/child $11/6; ⏲9am-5pm) This museum presents eight buildings, including two homes Twain lived in and that of Laura Hawkins, the real-life inspiration for Becky Thatcher.

Mark Twain Riverboat BOAT TOUR
(☎573-221-3222; www.marktwainriverboat.com; Center St; 1hr sightseeing cruise adult/child $18/11; ⏲Apr-Nov, schedule varies) Sail the Mississippi on this replica riverboat.

Sleeping

Many of Hannibal's historic homes are now B&Bs.

Garden House B&B B&B $$
(☎573-221-7800; www.gardenhousebedandbreakfast.com; 301 N 5th St; r $90-140, ste 240; ❄📶) This Victorian house lives up to its name. Some rooms share bathrooms, others have river views.

Along I-70

The main highway artery between St Louis and Kansas City, I-70 is a congested dud (with a surprising number of porn and sex shops); whenever possible, leave the interstate.

You'll find much to engage with on **US 50**, which meanders on a parallel path south of I-70. From Jefferson City, **Highway 94** follows the Missouri River east toward St Louis and passes through a beautiful region of wineries and forests.

There are a couple of good excuses to exit if you are on I-70. **Columbia** is home to the much-lauded University of Missouri. The downtown is an attractive collection of old brick buildings that feature thriving cafes, bars, bookstores and more.

Some 30 miles west of Columbia and 10 miles north of I-70, **Arrow Rock State Historic Site** (www.mostateparks.com; ⏲visitor center 10am-4pm daily Mar-Nov, Fri-Sun Dec-Feb) is a small preserved town that feels little changed since the 1830s when it was on the main stagecoach route west.

The Ozarks

Ozark hill country spreads across southern Missouri and extends into northern Arkansas and eastern Oklahoma.

At lush and sprawling **Johnson's Shut-Ins State Park** (☎573-546-2450; www.mostateparks.com; Hwy N, Middlebrook; ⏲8am-7pm

MISSOURI: DETOURS & EXTRAS

Sainte Genevieve Sixty-five miles south of St Louis, this petite, French-founded Mississippi River town oozes history. Many of the restored 18th- and 19th-century buildings are now B&Bs or gift shops.

George Washington Carver National Monument (www.nps.gov/gwca; ⏲9am-5pm) FREE Visit the birthplace of the African American scientist. Carver's experiments with peanuts have been taught to generations of American schoolkids but, as the park makes clear, he was truly a renaissance man, with a vast range of interests and accomplishments. The museum is near Joplin. Take exit 11A off I-44, then follow US 71 4.5 miles south to Hwy V, then go east.

ROUTE 66: GET YOUR KICKS IN MISSOURI

The Show-Me State will show you a long swath of the Mother Road. Meet the route in **St Louis**, where Ted Drewes (p646) has been serving frozen custard to generations of roadies from its Route 66 location on Chippewa St. There are a couple of well-signed historic routes through the city.

Follow I-44 (the interstate is built over most of Route 66 in Missouri) west to **Route 66 State Park** (636-938-7198; www.mostateparks.com; I-44 exit 266; 7am-30min after sunset, museum 9am-4:30pm Mar-Nov) FREE, with its visitor center and museum inside a 1935 roadhouse. Although the displays show vintage scenes from around St Louis, the real intrigue here concerns the town of Times Beach, which once stood on this very site. It was contaminated with dioxin and in the 1980s the government had to raze the entire area.

Head southwest on I-44 to **Stanton**, then follow the signs to family-mobbed **Meramec Caverns** (573-468-2283; www.americascave.com; I-44 exit 230, Stanton; adult/child $21/11; 8:30am-7:30pm Jun-Aug, reduced hours Sep-May), as interesting for the Civil War history and hokey charm as for the stalactites; and the conspiracy-crazy **Jesse James Wax Museum** (573-927-5233; www.jessejameswaxmuseum.com; I-44 exit 230, Stanton; adult/child $7/3; 9am-6pm daily Jun-Aug, 9am-5pm Sat & Sun Apr, May, Sep & Oct), which posits that James faked his death and lived until 1951.

The **Route 66 Museum & Research Center** (417-532-2148; www.lebanon-laclede.lib.mo.us; 915 S Jefferson St, Lebanon; 8am-8pm Mon-Thu, to 5pm Fri & Sat) FREE at the library in **Lebanon** has memorabilia past and present. Ready for a snooze? Head to the 1940s **Munger Moss Motel** (417-532-3111; www.mungermoss.com; 1336 E Rte 66, Lebanon; r from $60;). It's got a monster of a neon sign and Mother Road–loving owners.

Ditch the interstate west of **Springfield**, taking Hwy 96 to Civil War–era **Carthage** with its historic town square and **66 Drive-In Theatre** (www.66drivein.com; 17231 Old 66 Blvd, Carthage; adult/child $7/3; after dusk Fri-Sun Apr-Oct). In **Joplin**, which is still recovering from its horrible 2011 tornado, get on State Hwy 66, turning onto old Route 66 (the pre-1940s route), before the Kansas state line.

The **Route 66 Association of Missouri** (www.missouri66.org) has loads of info. And don't miss the **Conway Welcome Center** (I-44 Mile 110, near Conway; 8am-5pm), which has an over-the-top Route 66 theme and scads of info on the historic road.

Jun-Aug, reduced hours Sep-May) FREE, the swift Black River swirls through canyon-like gorges (shut-ins). The swimming is some of the most exciting you'll find outside a water park.

North of US 60, in the state's south-central region, the **Ozark National Scenic Riverways** (www.nps.gov/ozar) – the Current and Jack's Fork Rivers – boast 134 miles of splendid canoeing and inner-tubing (rental agencies abound). Weekends often get busy and boisterous. The park headquarters, outfitters and motels are in **Van Buren**. **Eminence** also makes a good base. There are many campgrounds along the rivers. Sinuous Hwy E is a scenic gem.

Branson

Hokey Branson is a cheerfully shameless tourist resort. The main attractions are the more than 50 theaters hosting 100-plus country-music, magic and comedy shows. The neon-lit '76 Strip' (Hwy 76) packs in miles of motels, restaurants, wax museums, shopping malls, fun parks and theaters. A campaign to beautify the strip began in 2015; despite what some say, it won't involve mass demolition.

Sights & Activities

While fudge is available in copious quantities, irony is not: when we drove by a much-hyped *Titanic* attraction, the sign implored people to come in and 'renew your wedding vows.' Expect every kind of mawkish attraction along the main strips – yes, there's even a giant ball of twine.

However, there is an actual **old town** of Branson, which has an authentic charm and a nice setting down by the White River (stroll the pretty walks).

Silver Dollar City AMUSEMENT PARK
(800-888-7277; www.silverdollarcity.com; Hwy 76; adult/child $60/49; hours vary) A Branson

original, this huge amusement park west of town has thrilling roller coasters, water rides and a new firefighter-themed area.

Sleeping & Eating

There are dozens of indie and chain motels (starting at around $40) along Hwy 76 on the strip. Nicer places are in quieter locales. **Table Rock Lake**, snaking through the hills southwest of town, is a deservedly popular destination for boating, fishing, camping and other outdoor activities, and it also has good-value lodging.

Branson cuisine consists mostly of fast food, junk food and all-you-can-eat buffets (most priced from $5 to $15).

★ Branson Hotel B&B **$$**
(☎417-544-9814; www.thebransonhotel.com; 214 W Main St; r $130-170; ❄📶) Dating to 1903, this plush nine-room B&B is right in the old town. It's away from the frenetic commercialism of the strips.

Indian Trails Resort RESORT **$$**
(☎417-338-2327; www.indiantrailsresort.com; 175 Harbor Lane; cabins $100-200; ❄🏊) On Table Rock Lake, 9 miles south of Branson, this low-key resort has cozy cabins.

Grandma Ruth's BAKERY **$**
(☎417-231-5900; 625 Hwy 165; treats from $2; ⏰7am-1pm) There really is a Grandma Ruth at this bakery in the heart of the strip and she's one shrewd cookie. She'll give you her picture when you buy six of her luscious cinnamon rolls.

☆ Entertainment

Popular theater shows feature performers you may have thought were dead. However, Branson has been the salvation for scores of entertainers young and old whose careers were otherwise fading. Patriotic themes are a stock part of every show. Fundamentalist Christian themes are also common – 'daring' can mean a bared ankle.

Showtimes are geared for older travelers – you can catch a 'Red Skelton Tribute' at 10am (other tribute shows include the Eagles, Neil Diamond, Journey et al), but most performances are in the afternoon and early evening. Prices range from about $25 to $50 a head; save with a coupon book or stop by the myriad ticket outlets offering 'deals.'

Baldknobbers Jamboree LIVE PERFORMANCE
(www.baldknobbers.com; 2835 W Hwy 76; adult/child $32/16) From the fake buck teeth in the comedy acts to the cornball country music, this show helped put Branson on the map back in 1959 and it hasn't let up since. Other acts here include the Sons of the Pioneers, who were inducted into the Country Music Hall of Fame in 2014.

ℹ Information

The scores of 'visitor information' centers around town (even the 'official' ones) are fronts for time-share sales outfits. Sit through a pitch, however, and you can get free tickets to a show.

Branson/Lakes Area Convention & Visitors Bureau (☎417-334-4084; www.explorebranson.com; junction Hwy 248 & US 65; ⏰8am-5pm Mon-Sat, 10am-4pm Sun) Just west of the US 65 junction, the CVB has town and lodging information.

ℹ Getting There & Around

Tucked into the scenic southern corner of the state, Branson is surprisingly hard to reach, although this means you may end up driving some rural and lovely two-lane Ozark roads. **Branson Airport** (www.flybranson.com) has limited service.

Jefferson Lines (www.jeffersonlines.com) has buses to Kansas City ($50, five hours, one daily).

During the summer, the SUV-laden traffic often crawls. It's often faster to walk than drive, although few others have this idea.

Kansas City

Famed for its barbecues (100-plus joints smoke it up), fountains (more than 200; on par with Rome) and jazz, Kansas City is a don't-miss Great Plains highlight. Attractive neighborhoods jostle for your attention, and you can easily run aground for several days as you enjoy the local vibe.

History

Kansas City began life in 1821 as a trading post, but really came into its own once westward expansion began. The Oregon, California and Santa Fe trails all met steamboats loaded with pioneers here.

Jazz exploded in the early 1930s under Mayor Tom Pendergast's Prohibition-era tenure, when he allowed alcohol to flow freely. At its peak, KC had more than 100 nightclubs, dance halls and vaudeville houses swinging to the beat (and booze). The roaring good times ended with Pendergast's indictment on tax evasion (the same way they got Capone), and the scene had largely faded by the mid-1940s.

Sights & Activities

State Line Rd divides KC Missouri and KC Kansas (a conservative suburban sprawl with little to offer travelers). KC Missouri has some distinct areas, including the art-deco-filled downtown.

★National WWI Museum MUSEUM
(☎816-888-8100; www.theworldwar.org; 100 W 26th St; adult/child $14/8; ⏰10am-5pm, closed Mon Sep-May; P) Enter this impressive modern museum on a glass walkway over a field of red poppies, the symbol of the trench fighting. Through detailed and engaging displays, learn about a war that is almost forgotten by many Americans. The only quibble is that military hardware and uniforms take precedence over the horrible toll. The museum is crowned by the historic **Liberty Memorial**, which has sweeping views over the city.

★Negro Leagues Baseball Museum MUSEUM
(☎816-221-1920; www.nlbm.com; 1616 E 18th St; adult/child $10/6; ⏰9am-6pm Tue-Sat, noon-6pm Sun) This museum covers African American teams, such as the KC Monarchs and New York Black Yankees, that flourished until baseball became fully integrated. It's part of the Museums at 18th & Vine complex.

American Jazz Museum MUSEUM
(☎816-474-8463; www.americanjazzmuseum.org; 1616 E 18th St; adult/child $10/6; ⏰9am-6pm Tue-Sat, noon-6pm Sun) At the heart of KC's 1920s African American neighborhood, learn about different jazz styles, rhythms, instruments and musicians – including KC native Charlie Parker – at this interactive museum. It's part of the Museums at 18th & Vine complex.

Country Club Plaza AREA
(www.countryclubplaza.com) Built in the 1920s, this posh commercial district (centered on Broadway and 47th St) boasts finely detailed, sumptuous Spanish architecture. It's rich with public art and sculptures; look for the walking-tour brochure and check out, at the very least, the **Spanish Bullfight Mural** (Central St) and the **Fountain of Neptune** (47th St and Wornall Rd).

Nelson-Atkins Museum of Art MUSEUM
(☎816-751-1278; www.nelson-atkins.org; 4525 Oak St; ⏰10am-5pm Wed & Sat, to 9pm Thu & Fri, noon-5pm Sun; P) FREE Giant badminton shuttlecocks (the building represents the net) surround this encyclopedic museum, which has standout European painting, photography and Asian-art collections.

Arabia Steamboat Museum MUSEUM
(☎816-471-1856; www.1856.com; 400 Grand Blvd; adult/child $14.50/5.50; ⏰10am-5pm Mon-Sat,

KANSAS CITY AT A GLANCE

Kansas City has a number of unique and interesting neighborhoods to explore. Get ready to spend an hour or two (or a day or two):

Quality Hill Around W 10th St and Broadway, this historic area has grand, restored buildings from the 1920s.

39th St West KC's funkiest area is a strip of boutiques alongside lots of ethnic eateries and lively bars.

Country Club Plaza Often shortened to 'the Plaza,' this stunning 1920s shopping district is an attraction in itself.

Crossroads Arts District Around Baltimore and 20th Sts, it lives up to its name.

Crown Plaza South of downtown, this 1970s development is anchored by several major hotels and Hallmark (yes, the greeting-card company is located right here).

Historic Jazz District On the upswing, this old African American neighborhood is at 18th and Vine Sts.

River Market Historic and still home to a large farmers market; immediately north of downtown.

Westport On Westport Rd just west of Main St; filled with appealing restaurants and bars.

noon-5pm Sun, last tour 90min before closing) In River Market, this museum displays 200 tons of salvaged 'treasure' from a riverboat that sank in 1856 (one of hundreds claimed by the river).

Kemper Museum of Contemporary Art MUSEUM
(816-753-5784; www.kemperart.org; 4420 Warwick Blvd; 10am-4pm Tue-Thu, to 9pm Fri & Sat, 11am-5pm Sun; P) FREE Near the Nelson-Atkins Museum of Art and Country Club Plaza, this museum is small and edgy. The cafe is excellent.

College Basketball Experience MUSEUM
(816-949-7500; www.collegebasketballexperience.com; 1401 Grand Blvd; adult/child $14/11; 10am-6pm Wed-Sun; P) Really a gussied-up basketball hall of fame, this fun memorabilia-filled exhibition lets you try free throws or pretend you're an announcer calling them. It's connected to the glitzy **Sprint Center**, a vast arena in search of a major pro-sports franchise.

National Museum of Toys and Miniatures MUSEUM
(www.toyandminiaturemuseum.org; 5235 Oak St, University of Missouri-Kansas City; admission $5; 10am-4pm Wed-Mon;) More than 100 years of toys spread over 38 rooms, including the world's largest fine-scale miniature collection.

Festivals & Events

American Royal World Series of Barbecue FOOD
(www.americanroyal.com; Arrowhead Stadium at the Truman Sports Complex; Oct) On the first weekend in October, this is the world's largest barbecue contest, with over 500 teams.

Sleeping

Downtown and the Plaza offer good lodging options (mostly chains) near the action. For something cheap, you'll need to head out on the interstate: there are scores of chains north on I-35 and I-29, and east on I-70.

America's Best Value Inn MOTEL $
(816-531-9250; www.americasbestvalueinn.com; 3240 Broadway St; r $60-80; P) Convenient to everything, this basic 52-room motel has inside corridors and a pool big enough for a small family.

Oak Tree Inn MOTEL $
(913-677-3060; www.oaktreeinn.com; 501 Southwest Blvd; $70-130; P) This comfy yet unassuming motel is the value leader for KC. Rooms are standard, yet have fridges and microwaves. Just off I-35 (exit 234), it's a short walk to the pleasures of 39th St West.

★ **Southmoreland on the Plaza** B&B $$
(816-531-7979; www.southmoreland.com; 116 E 46th St, Country Club Plaza; r $150-210; P) The 12 rooms at this posh B&B are furnished like the home of your rich country-club friends. It's a big old mansion between the art museums and the Plaza. Extras include jacuzzis, decks, sherry, a fireplace and more.

AC Hotel HOTEL $$
(816-931-0001; www.achotelskansascity.com; 560 Westport Rd; r $120-240; P) This Marriott in disguise is centrally located in Westport. All 123 rooms have a clean-lined modern style. Extras include free local shuttles.

Aladdin BOUTIQUE HOTEL $$
(816-421-8888; www.hialaddin.com; 1215 Wyandotte St; r $90-220;) Affiliated with Holiday Inn, this 16-story hotel dates from 1925. It has been restored to its Italian Romanesque splendor and has 193 compact yet stylish rooms. It was a legendary haunt of mobsters and Greta Garbo. Not your ordinary chain hotel.

Eating

City Market MARKET $
(816-842-1271; www.thecitymarket.org; cnr W 5th St & Grand Blvd; hours vary, farmers market 7am-3pm Sat & Sun) City Market is a haven for small local businesses selling an idiosyncratic range of foods and other items. Ethnic groceries abound and there is a **farmers market** for regional producers on weekends. Little cafes and greasy spoons do big business from breakfast through to dinner.

TOURING THE FOUNTAINS

Spraying their streams large and small, Kansas City's over 200 fountains are beautiful amenities and many are truly spectacular works of art. The website for the **City of Fountains Foundation** (www.kcfountains.com) is a great resource, with maps, info and downloadable self-guided tours.

DON'T MISS

GREAT BARBECUE IN KANSAS CITY

Savoring hickory-smoked brisket, pork, chicken or ribs at one of the barbecue joints around town is a must for any visitor. The local style is pit-smoked and slathered with heavily seasoned vinegar-based sauces. You may well swoon for 'burnt ends,' the crispy ends of smoked pork or beef brisket. Amazing.

Q39 (816-255-3753; www.q39kc.com; 1000 W 39th St; mains $8-28; 11am-10pm Mon-Thu, to 11pm Fri & Sat, to 9pm Sun; P) KC has a new top dog in BBQ. This slick joint has fab service, great microbrews and easily the best meats to come off a grill in the region. The spare ribs are the best we've had and the burnt ends are so good, they often run out.

Arthur Bryant's (816-231-1123; www.arthurbryantsbbq.com; 1727 Brooklyn Ave; mains $8-15; 10am-9:30pm Mon-Thu, to 10pm Fri & Sat, 11am-8pm Sun; P) Not far from the Jazz District, this famous institution serves up piles of superb BBQ. The sauce is silky and fiery, the staff charming and witty. Get the burnt ends.

Joe's Kansas City Bar-B-Que (913-722-3366; www.joeskc.com; 3002 W 47th Ave; mains $6-20; 11am-9pm Mon-Thu, to 10pm Fri & Sat; P) The best reason to cross the state border (it's actually not far from the Plaza), this legendary joint is housed in a brightly lit old gas station. The pulled pork is pleasure on a plate; expect lines.

LC's Bar-B-Q (816-923-4484; 5800 Blue Pkwy; mains $6-12; 11am-9pm Mon-Sat; P) Just 4 miles east of the Plaza, this unadorned eatery does nothing to distract from KC's best burnt ends.

Winstead's Steakburger BURGERS $
(816-753-2244; www.winsteadssteakburger.com; 101 Emanuel Cleaver III Blvd; mains $4-6; 6am-midnight) Cheery servers sling plates of top-notch burgers to families, hungover hipsters and more at this Country Club Plaza institution. Don't miss the onion rings and chili.

★ **Bluestem** MODERN AMERICAN $$$
(816-561-1101; www.bluestemkc.com; 900 Westport Rd; 3-/5-/10-course meals $65/75/110, bar snacks $5-18; kitchen 5-10pm Tue-Sat, 10:30am-2:30pm Sun, bar to 1:30am; P) Multiple-award-winning Bluestem has a casual elegance that extends from the bar to the dining room. Many stop into this Westport star just for a fine cocktail and some of the small plates of exquisite snacks (the cheeses, oh!). Dinner features an array of seasonal small courses (go for the wine pairings).

Drinking & Nightlife

Westport and 39th St W are your best bets for clusters of atmospheric local bars.

The heavily hyped **Power & Light District** (www.powerandlightdistrict.com) is a vast urban development centered on Grand Blvd and W 12th St. It has dozens of chain restaurants, formula bars and live-performance venues. When there's no sporting event or convention in town it can seem rather bleak.

Be sure to try a locally brewed Boulevard Beer. Bars close between 1:30am and 3am.

★ **Up-Down** BAR
(816-982-9455; www.updownkc.com; 101 Southwest Blvd; 3pm-1am Mon-Sat, to midnight Sun) A wildly popular new bar-cum-playground just south of downtown, Up-Down caters to the kid in everyone with an array of games from pinball to video. There are huge decks and great music. The superb tap-beer line-up includes all the Boulevards (brewed just up the hill).

Westport Coffeehouse CAFE
(816-756-3222; www.westportcoffeehouse.com; 4010 Pennsylvania St; 7:30am-11pm Mon-Thu, to midnight Fri & Sat, 10am-10pm Sun;) This laid-back place off the main drag has good coffee and specialty teas. Look for comedy, jazz and blues at night.

McCoy's Public House BREWERY
(816-960-0866; www.beerkc.com; 4057 Pennsylvania Ave; 11am-3am Mon-Sat, to midnight Sun) The patio at this Westport brewpub is the place to be on a balmy day. The house-brewed beers are excellent and vary through the year. The food is strictly comfort and quite good.

Entertainment

The free weekly *Pitch* (www.pitch.com) has the best cultural calendar.

★Mutual Musicians Foundation JAZZ
(☎816-471-5212; www.mutualmusiciansfoundation.org; 1823 Highland Ave; ⏲midnight-6am Fri & Sat) Near 18th and Vine in the Historic Jazz District, this former union hall for African American musicians has hosted after-hours jam sessions since 1930. Famous veteran musicians gig with young hotshots. It's friendly and pretension free. A little bar serves cheap drinks in plastic cups. No cover charge.

Blue Room BLUES, JAZZ
(www.americanjazzmuseum.org; 1616 E 18th St; cover Mon & Thu free, Fri & Sat varies; ⏲5-11pm Mon & Thu, to 1am Fri & Sat) This slick club, part of the American Jazz Museum, hosts local talent for free on Monday and Thursday. Touring acts perform weekends. Major shows are held at the adjoining **Gem Theater**.

Riot Room LIVE MUSIC
(☎816-442-8179; www.theriotroom.com; 4048 Broadway; cover varies; ⏲5pm-3am) Part dive, part cutting-edge live-music venue, Westport's Riot Room always rocks – and has many good beers.

Kauffman Center for the Performing Arts PERFORMING ARTS
(☎816-994-7222; www.kauffmancenter.org; 1601 Broadway) Twin venues headline this stunning complex. There's a varied schedule of theater, opera, ballet, music and more.

Truman Sports Complex STADIUM
(I-70 exit 9) Locals are passionate about major-league baseball's **Royals** (www.kcroyals.com; Kauffman Stadium; tickets $12-160), who reached the World Series in 2014, and the NFL's ever-disappointing **Chiefs** (www.kcchiefs.com; Arrowhead Stadium; tickets $80-400). Both play at gleaming side-by-side stadiums east of the city near Independence.

Shopping

Historic Country Club Plaza is KC's most appealing shopping destination (its lavish architecture is modeled on Seville, Spain, and dates to 1923), though sadly it's mostly upscale national chains. Westport has more eclectic shops, as does 39th St.

★Prospero's Books BOOKS
(www.prosperosbookstore.com; 1800 W 39th St; ⏲10:30am-10pm) Funky used bookstore in a cool part of town. Great recommendations, live poetry and even a few bands.

Halls DEPARTMENT STORE
(☎816-274-3222; www.halls.com; 2450 Grand Blvd, Crown Center; ⏲10am-7pm Mon-Sat, noon-6pm Sun) Founded in 1913 by the same family behind, you guessed it, Hallmark, this high-end store is so gracious, you may wish you were wearing gloves.

Information

Greater Kansas City Visitor Center (☎800-767-7700; www.visitkc.com; 30 W Pershing Rd, Union Station; ⏲9:30am-4pm Tue-Sun) Other locations include the National WWI Museum.

Missouri Welcome Center (☎816-889-3330; www.visitmo.com; 4010 Blue Ridge Cutoff, Truman Sports Complex; ⏲8am-5pm) Statewide maps and information at I-70 exit 9.

Getting There & Away

Amtrak (www.amtrak.com; 30 W Pershing Rd, Union Station) In majestic **Union Station**; has two daily *Missouri River Runner* trains to St Louis (from $30, 5½ hours). The *Southwest Chief* stops here on its daily runs between Chicago and LA.

Greyhound (☎816-221-2835; www.greyhound.com; 1101 Troost St) Sends buses daily to St Louis ($28, 4½ hours) and Denver ($106, 11½ hours) from the station poorly located east of downtown.

Jefferson Lines (☎816-221-2885; www.jeffersonlines.com; 1101 Troost St, Greyhound Terminal) Heads to Omaha ($45, three to five hours), Des Moines ($50, 3½ hours), and Oklahoma City ($77, eight hours) via Tulsa.

Kansas City International Airport (MCI; www.flykci.com; off Hwy 70, exit 13) A confusing array of circular terminals 16 miles northwest of downtown.

Getting Around

Kansas City International Airport A taxi to downtown/Plaza costs about $40/45, or take the **Super Shuttle** (☎800-258-3826; www.supershuttle.com; from $18).

Megabus (www.megabus.com; cnr 3rd St & Grand Blvd) Serves St Louis and Chicago for as low as $5.

Metro (www.kcata.org) A one-day unlimited bus pass costs $3 on the bus. Bus 47 runs regularly between downtown, Westport and Country Club Plaza. Sometime in 2016 the KC Streetcar will debut, running for 2 miles downtown largely on Main St from River Market to Union Station.

Yellow Cab (☎888-471-6050; www.kansas-city-taxi.com)

Around Kansas City

Independence

Just east of Kansas City, picture-perfect Independence is the perfect stereotype for an old Midwestern small town. It was the home of Harry S Truman, US president from 1945 to 1953, and has some unmissable museums.

Sights & Activities

Independence's attractions easily fill a day.

★Truman Home HISTORIC BUILDING
(www.nps.gov/hstr; 219 N Delaware St; tours adult/child $5/free; 9am-4:30pm, closed Mon Nov-May) See the simple life Harry and Bess lived in this basic but charming wood house. It is furnished with their original belongings and you fully expect the couple to wander out and say hello.

Tour tickets are sold at the **visitor center** (816-254-9929; 223 N Main St; 8:30am-5pm). Ask for directions to the **Truman Family Farm**, where the future president 'got his common sense.'

Truman lived here from 1919 to 1972 and in retirement entertained visiting dignitaries in his strictly pedestrian front room – he's said to have hoped none of the callers would linger more than 30 minutes.

★National Frontier Trails Museum MUSEUM
(816-325-7575; www.frontiertrailsmuseum.org; 318 W Pacific St; adult/child $6/3; 9am-4:30pm Mon-Sat, 12:30-4:30pm Sun) Gives a compelling look at the tough life for the pioneers along the Santa Fe, California and Oregon Trails; many began their journey in Independence. You'll learn that a pioneer 'met his elephant' when he realized that the challenges of the journey were simply too big.

Truman Presidential Museum & Library MUSEUM
(800-833-1225; www.trumanlibrary.org; 500 W US 24; adult/child $8/3; 9am-5pm Mon-Sat, noon-5pm Sun) Thousands of objects, including the famous 'The BUCK STOPS here!' sign, from the man who led the US through one of its most tumultuous eras, are displayed here.

Truman Historic Walking Trail WALKING TOUR
Starting at the Truman Home visitor center, this 2.7-mile self-guided route leads to 43 Truman-related sites, including the courthouse where he began his political career. Get a copy at the NPS visitor center.

Eating

Clinton's Soda Fountain ICE CREAM $
(816-833-2046; www.clintonssodafountain.com; 100 W Maple Ave; mains $5-8; 11am-6pm Mon-Sat) Little changed from when Truman got his first job working the soda counter.

St Joseph

A major departure point for pioneers, this scruffy riverside town has several compelling museums.

Sights

★Patee House Museum MUSEUM
(816-232-8206; www.ponyexpressjessejames.com; cnr 12th & Penn Sts; adult/child $6/4; 9am-4pm Mon-Sat, 1-4pm Sun) Still imposing, the 1858 Patee House has had a long and historic life. Next door, the outlaw Jesse James was killed at what is now the **Jesse James Home Museum** (adult/child $4/2). The fateful bullet hole is still in the wall.

Pony Express National Museum MUSEUM
(816-279-5059; www.ponyexpress.org; 914 Penn St; adult/child $6/3; 9am-5pm Mon-Sat, 11am-4pm Sun) The first Pony Express set out, carrying mail from 'St Jo' 2000 miles west to California, in 1860. The service, making the trip in as little as eight days, lasted just 18 months before telegraph lines made it redundant. It's just a few brick-paved streets over from Patee House.

Glore Psychiatric Museum MUSEUM
(816-232-8471; www.stjosephmuseum.org; 3406 Frederick Ave; adult/child $6/4; 10am-5pm Mon-Sat, 1-5pm Sun) Housed in the former 'State Lunatic Asylum No 2,' this museum gives a frightening and fascinating look at lobotomies, the 'bath of surprise' and other discredited treatments. Price includes admission to two other museums on-site.

Information

Visitor center (800-785-0360; www.stjomo.com; 109 S 4th St; hours vary) Downtown.

IOWA

Instead of two girls for every boy, Iowa has eight pigs for every person. But there's more to do here than roll in the mud. The towering bluffs on the Mississippi River and the soaring Loess Hills lining the Missouri River bookend the state; in between you'll find the writers' town of Iowa City, the commune-dwellers of the Amana Colonies, and many little towns speckled with highlights.

In fact, Iowa surprises in many ways. It makes or breaks presidential hopefuls: the Iowa Caucus opens the national election battle, and wins by George W Bush in 2000 and Barack Obama in 2008 stunned many pundits and launched their victorious campaigns.

History

After the 1832 Black Hawk War pushed local Native Americans westward, immigrants flooded into Iowa from all parts of the world and hit the ground farming. Some established experimental communities such as the Germans of the Amana Colonies. Others spread out and kept coaxing the soil (95% of the land is fertile) until Iowa attained its current status as the US leader in hogs and corn (much of the latter ends up as syrup in junk food).

IOWA FACTS

Nickname Hawkeye State

Population 3.1 million

Area 56,275 sq miles

Capital city Des Moines (population 207,500)

Sales tax 6% to 7%

Birthplace of Painter Grant Wood (1891–1942), actor John Wayne (1907–79), author Bill Bryson (b 1951)

Home of Madison County's bridges

Politics Center-right with flashes of liberalism

Famous for Iowa Caucus that opens the presidential election season

Official flower Wild rose

Driving distances Dubuque to Chicago 180 miles, Des Moines to Rapid City 625 miles

Information

Iowa Bed & Breakfast Guild (800-743-4692; www.ia-bednbreakfast-inns.com)

Iowa State Parks (www.iowadnr.gov) State parks are free to visit. Some 50% to 75% of the park campsites are reservable (www.iowastateparks.reserveamerica.com); fees range from $6 to $16 per night.

Iowa Tourism Office (515-725-3084; www.traveliowa.com)

Iowa Wine & Beer (www.iowawineandbeer.com) Craft brewing and, yes, winemaking are booming in Iowa. Get the handy app.

Des Moines

Des Moines, meaning 'of the monks' not 'in the corn' as the surrounding fields might suggest, is Iowa's sleepy capital. The town does have a wowser of a state capitol and one of the nation's best state fairs. Pause, but then get out and see the rest of Iowa.

Sights

The Des Moines River slices through downtown. The Court Ave Entertainment District sits just west, while East Village, at the foot of the capitol, and east of the river, is home to galleries, eateries, clubs and a few gay bars.

State Capitol HISTORIC BUILDING

(cnr E 9th St & Grand Ave; 8am-4:30pm Mon-Fri, 9am-4pm Sat) FREE From the sparkling gold dome to the spiral staircases and stained glass in the law library, every detail at this bling-heavy capitol (1886) seems to try to outdo the next. Join a free tour and you can climb halfway up the dome.

Festivals & Events

★**Iowa State Fair** FAIR

(800-545-3247; www.iowastatefair.org; cnr E 30th St & E University Ave; adult/child $11/5; 7am-midnight mid-Aug;) Much more than just country music and butter sculpture, this festival draws a million visitors over its 10-day run. They enjoy the award-winning farm critters and just about every food that can be shoved on a stick imaginable. It's the setting for the Rodgers and Hammerstein musical *State Fair* and the 1945 film version.

Sleeping

Chains of all flavors congregate on I-80 at exits 121, 124, 131 and 136.

1900 Inn B&B $$

(515-330-5546; www.the1900inn.com; 1033 26th St; r $120-150;) Set in the historic and walkable Drake neighborhood, this B&B has three comfy rooms that will make you feel at home. There's a huge front porch for having a relaxing sit after a long day touring.

Eating & Drinking

Des Moines has a growing food scene as chefs take advantage of the state's bounty.

WORTH A TRIP

GRANT WOOD'S ELDON

Grab a 'tool' out of your trunk and make your very own parody of Grant Wood's iconic *American Gothic* (1930) – the pitchfork painting – in tiny Eldon, about 90 miles southeast of Des Moines. The original house is across from the **American Gothic House Center** (641-652-3352; www.americangothichouse.net; American Gothic St; 10am-5pm Tue-Sat, 1-4pm Sun & Mon May-Sep, 10am-4pm Tue-Fri, 1-4pm Sat-Mon Oct-Apr) FREE, which interprets the artwork that sparked a million parodies (it even has loaner costumes so you can make your own parody selfie). The actual painting is in the Art Institute of Chicago.

Wood spent much of his time in tiny **Stone City**, a cute little burg 14 miles north of Mt Vernon, off Hwy 1. It's on the 68-mile-long **Grant Wood Scenic Byway** (www.byways.org).

B & B Grocery, Meat & Deli AMERICAN $
(515-243-7607; www.bbgrocerymeatdeli.com; 2001 SE 6th St; mains $4-9; 8:30am-6pm Tue-Fri, to 3pm Sat) 'Keeping Iowans on top of the food chain since 1922!' is the slogan at this hole-in-the-wall store just south of downtown. Enjoy Iowa comfort food such as meaty sandwiches that include the 'killer pork tenderloin,' a bun-smothering creation.

★**Alba** MODERN AMERICAN $$
(515-244-0261; www.albadsm.com; 524 E 6th St; mains lunch $10-15, dinner $17-31; 11am-2pm Tue-Fri & 5-9:30pm Mon-Sat) One of Iowa's farm-to-table pioneers, Alba has a great spot in the buzzy East Village neighborhood. Dine inside or out on inventive seasonal fare that's casual yet complex.

House of Bricks BAR
(515-727-4370; www.thehouseofbricks.com; 525 E Grand Ave; 11am-late;) A gritty live-music legend in the East Village, it serves up tasty, beer-absorbent chow (meals $10 to $15) and has a rooftop bar.

Madison County

This scenic county, about 30 miles southwest of Des Moines, slumbered for half a century until Robert James Waller's blockbuster, tear-jerking novel *The Bridges of Madison County* and its 1995 Clint Eastwood/Meryl Streep movie version brought in scores of fans to check out the covered bridges where Robert and Francesca fueled their affair.

The farms and open land in this region are pleasantly bucolic, and the towns postcard perfect. **Adel**, for example, has its own beautiful courthouse square surrounded by shops and cafes, while tourism-hub **Winterset** has a silver-domed courthouse.

Sights

★**Covered Bridges** HISTORIC SITE
Six covered bridges survive in the county. Pick up a map (or download one) from the **Winterset Chamber of Commerce** (800-298-6119; www.madisoncounty.com; 73 Jefferson St, Winterset; 9am-4pm Mon-Sat, noon-3pm Sun May-Oct, 10am-3pm Mon-Fri Nov-Apr).

John Wayne Birthplace & Museum MUSEUM
(www.johnwaynebirthplace.museum; 205 S John Wayne Dr, Winterset; adult/child $15/8; 10am-5pm) This glitzy new museum is devoted to the life and career of John Wayne, aka Marion Robert Morrison. The house where he was born in 1907 is included and is just around the corner.

Along I-80

Many of Iowa's attractions are within an easy drive of bland I-80, which runs east-west across the state's center. Much more interesting alternatives are US 20 and US 30 (which is an official scenic drive for the length of Iowa).

Quad Cities

Four cities straddle the Mississippi River by I-80: **Davenport** and **Bettendorf** in Iowa and **Moline** and **Rock Island** in Illinois. The **visitor center** (563-322-3911; www.visitquadcities.com; 102 S Harrison St, Davenport; 9am-5pm Mon-Fri, to 4pm Sat Jun-Aug, 9am-5pm Mon-Fri Sep-May) is on the river in downtown Davenport and has bike rentals ($10 per hour) for a ride along the Big Muddy.

Iowa City

The youthful, artsy vibe here is courtesy of the **University of Iowa** (www.uiowa.edu) campus, home to good art and natural-history museums. It spills across both sides of the Iowa River (which has good walks on the banks); to the east it mingles with the charming downtown. In summer (when the student-to-townie ratio evens out) the city mellows somewhat. The school's writing programs are renowned, and Iowa City was named a Unesco City of Literature in 2008.

Sights

Old Capitol Museum MUSEUM
(☎319-335-0548; www.uiowa.edu/oldcap; cnr Clinton St & Iowa Ave; ⏰10am-5pm Tue, Wed, Fri & Sat, to 8pm Thu, 1-5pm Sun) FREE The cute gold-domed building at the heart of the University of Iowa campus is the Old Capitol. Built in 1840, it was the seat of government until 1857 when Des Moines grabbed the reins. It's now a museum with galleries and furnishings from back in its heyday.

Sleeping

Chain motels line 1st Ave in Coralville (I-80 exit 242) like hogs at the trough.

★**Brown Street Inn** B&B $$
(☎319-338-0435; www.brownstreetinn.com; 430 Brown St; r $100-165; ❄@📶) Four-poster beds and other antiques adorn this six-room 1913 Dutch Colonial place that's an easy walk from downtown.

Eating & Drinking

This is a college town, which means lots of cheap ethnic eateries (and beer!).

★**Shorts Burger & Shine** BURGERS $
(☎319-337-4678; 18 S Clinton St; mains $7-10; ⏰kitchen 11am-10pm, bar to 2am; 🌶) A local legend, Shorts serves up all manner of gourmet burgers, including a fine selection of veggie burgers. Great regional beer list.

Dave's Foxhead Tavern BAR
(☎319-351-9824; 402 E Market St; ⏰6pm-2am Mon-Sat) Popular with the writers' workshop crowd, who debate gerunds while slouched in booths. Pool is also big in this tiny boozer. Is that TC Boyle by the door?

Shopping

Prairie Lights BOOKS
(☎319-337-2681; www.prairielights.com; 15 S Dubuque St; ⏰10am-9pm Mon-Sat, to 6pm Sun) A bookstore worthy of the fabled Iowa Writers' Workshop.

Information

Visitor Center (☎800-283-6592; www.iowacitycoralville.org; 900 1st Ave, I-80 exit 242; ⏰8am-5pm Mon-Fri) In neighboring Coralville, an unfortunate town with all the chains and urban sprawl missing from Iowa City.

Amana Colonies

These seven villages, just northwest of Iowa City, are stretched along a 17-mile loop. All were established as German religious communes between 1855 and 1861 by inspirationists who, until the Great Depression, lived a utopian life with no wages paid and all assets communally owned. Unlike the Amish and Mennonite religions, inspirationists embrace modern technology (and tourism).

Today the seven well-preserved (and discreetly tasteful) villages offer a glimpse of this unique culture, and there are lots of arts, crafts, cheeses, baked goods and wines to buy. However they are not immune to commercial pressures as evidenced by establishments such as a 'Man Cave' amid gift shops selling the sorts of gewgaws that perplex heirs.

Sights

★**Amana Heritage Museum** MUSEUM
(☎319-622-3567; www.amanaheritage.org; 4310 220th Trail, Amana; adult/child $7/free; ⏰10am-5pm Mon-Sat, noon-4pm Sun Apr-Oct, 10am-5pm Sat Mar, Nov & Dec) Offers a good overview of the colonies. Ask about the cell-phone tours.

Sleeping & Eating

The villages have several good-value B&Bs and historic inns. A top draw is the hefty-portioned, home-cooked German cuisine dished out at various humble dining spots.

Zuber's Homestead Hotel INN $$
(☎319-622-3911; www.zubershomesteadhotel.com; 2206 44 Ave, Amana; r $100-150; ❄📶) This frilly inn has 15 individually decorated rooms in an 1890s brick building.

Amana Meat Shop & Smokehouse DELI $
(☎800-373-6328; www.amanameatshop.com; 4513 F St, Amana; snacks from $3; ⏰9am-5pm Mon-Sat, 10am-4pm Sun) A kingdom of locally produced cheeses and smoked meats. Get your picnic supplies here.

Information

Amana Colonies Visitors Center (☎319-622-7622; www.amanacolonies.com; 622 46th Ave,

DON'T MISS

SILOS & SMOKESTACKS NATIONAL HERITAGE AREA

Comprising 37 counties in Northeast Iowa, this National Park Service–designated region comprises more than 100 sites and attractions that honor the region's industrial past and storybook farm beauty. Backroad drives abound. Look for the very helpful annual guide and visit www.silosandsmokestacks.org.

Amana; ⌚9am-5pm Mon-Sat, 10am-5pm Sun May-Oct, 10am-3pm daily Nov-Apr) Stop at the grain-elevator-shaped visitor center for the essential guide-map. It also has bike rental (the best way to tour the area; $15 per day) and sells a ticket good for all the museums (adults $8).

Along US 30

Like a clichéd needlepoint come to life, US 30 passes through fertile fields dotted with whitewashed farmhouses and red-hued barns. It parallels I-80 an average of 20 to 30 miles to the north before dropping down to Nebraska near Omaha. The real attraction here is just enjoying the succession of small towns.

In a state blessed with pretty places, **Mt Vernon** is one of the loveliest. Have a great meal, just 9 miles south on Hwy 1, in Solon, where **Big Grove Brewery** (☎319-624-2337; www.biggrovebrewery.com; 101 W Main St, Solon; mains $9-30; ⌚kitchen 11am-9pm Tue-Sun) hits home runs with cliché-busting takes on Iowa comfort food. It's all seasonal and very local.

Ames, 25 miles north of Des Moines, is home to Iowa State University and has lots of good motels and undergrad dives.

Along US 20

Stretching from Dubuque on the Mississippi River to Sioux City on the Missouri River, US 20 has offered up charms similar to those on US 30 to generations of travelers seeking new lives, adventure or just a new farm implement.

Waterloo

Home to five John Deere tractor factories, Waterloo is the place to get one of those prized green-and-yellow caps you've seen across middle America. Fun **Tractor Assembly Tours** (☎319-292-7668; www.deere.com; 3500 E Donald St; ⌚tours 8am, 10am & 1pm Mon-Fri) FREE show how these vehicles are made. The minimum age is 13 years and reservations are required.

Iowa Great River Road

Iowa's Great River Road mostly hugs the Mississippi along the state's eastern edge. It combines numerous roads and passes through some beautifully isolated riverfront towns such as **Guttenberg**. Along an especially scenic stretch of US 56, **Bellevue** is a gem and lives up to its name with good river views and some verdant, rural scenery. **Burlington** has an excellent visitor center and is good for a break.

At **Effigy Mounds National Monument** (☎563-873-3491; www.nps.gov/efmo; Hwy 76, Marquette; ⌚8am-6pm Jun-Aug, to 4:30pm Sep-May) FREE hundreds of mysterious Native American burial mounds sit in the bluffs above the Mississippi River in this gorgeous corner of far northeast Iowa. Listen to songbirds as you hike the lush trails.

Get info at www.byways.org and www.iowagreatriverroad.com.

Dubuque

Dubuque makes a great entry to Iowa from Illinois; 19th-century Victorian homes line its narrow and lively streets between the Mississippi River and its seven steep limestone hills.

Sights & Activities

4th Street Elevator HISTORIC SITE
(www.dbq.com/fenplco; cnr 4th St & Fenelon; round-trip $3; ⌚8am-10pm Apr-Nov) Built in 1882, this funicular railway climbs a steep hill from downtown for huge views.

National Mississippi River Museum & Aquarium MUSEUM, AQUARIUM
(☎563-557-9545; www.rivermuseum.com; 350 E 3rd St; adult/child $15/10; ⌚9am-6pm Jun-Aug, 10am-5pm Sep-May) Learn about life (of all sorts) on the Mississippi at this impressive museum, part of a vast riverfront development.

Dubuque River Rides BOAT TOUR
(☎563-583-8093; www.dubuqueriverrides.com; 3rd St, Ice Harbor; adult/child from $34/23;

May-Oct;) The replica riverboat *Spirit of Dubuque* offers a variety of Mississippi sightseeing and dining cruises.

Sleeping & Eating

Main St has eateries both semigrand and humble.

Hotel Julien HISTORIC HOTEL **$$**
(563-556-4200; www.hoteljuliendubuque.com; 200 Main St; r $120-250;) The historic eight-story Hotel Julien was built in 1914 and was once a refuge for Al Capone. It's quite spiffy after a lavish renovation and is a real antidote for chains.

Information

Visitor Center (800-798-4748; www.traveldubuque.com; 280 Main St; 10am-4pm Mon-Thu & Sat, to 5pm Fri, to 2pm Sun) Downtown, it has information for the entire region and state.

NORTH DAKOTA

'Magnificent desolation' – Buzz Aldrin used it to describe the moon, and it applies just as well in North Dakota. Fields of grain – green in the spring and summer, bronze in the fall, and white in winter – stretch beyond every horizon. Except for the rugged 'badlands' of the far west, geographic relief is subtle; more often it is the collapsing remains of a failed homestead that breaks up the vista.

Isolated in the far north, this is one of the least visited states in the US. But that just means that there's less traffic as you whiz along. This is a place to get lost on remote two-lane routes and to appreciate the beauty of raw land. And don't forget to pause to marvel at the songs of meadowlarks.

Note that despite those seemingly endless summer fields of grain, the state's economy is tied to large oil deposits in the west. Soaring energy prices turned once-moribund towns such as Williston and Watford City into boomtowns, with vast trailer encampments for oil-field workers, roads clogged – and battered – by huge trucks, and constant parades of tanker trains filled with flammable petroleum. However, with recent downturns in prices, the boom may turn to bust.

History

During their epic journey, Lewis and Clark spent more time in what is now North Dakota than any other state, meeting up with Shoshone guide Sacagawea on their way west. In the mid-19th century, smallpox epidemics came up the Missouri River, decimating the Arikara, Mandan and Hidatsa tribes, who affiliated and established the Like-a-Fishhook Village around 1845. When the railroad arrived in North Dakota in the 1870s, thousands of settlers flocked in to take up allotments under the Homestead Act. By 1889 the state population was more than 250,000, half foreign-born (one in eight was from Norway).

Young Theodore Roosevelt came here to ditch his city-slicker image. As president, inspired by his time in North Dakota, he earned the title 'The Father of Conservation' for his work creating national forests and parks.

MOUNTAIN TIME IN NORTH DAKOTA

The southwest quarter of North Dakota, including Medora, uses Mountain Time, which is one hour earlier than the rest of the state's Central Time.

Information

North Dakota Bed & Breakfast Association (www.ndbba.com)

NORTH DAKOTA FACTS

Nickname Peace Garden State

Population 730,000

Area 70,705 sq miles

Capital city Bismarck (population 67,000)

Sales tax 5% to 8%

Birthplace of Legendary Shoshone woman Sacagawea (1788–1812), cream of wheat (1893), bandleader Lawrence Welk (1903–92), singer and writer of Westerns Louis L'Amour (1908–88)

Home of World's largest bison, turtle and Holstein statues

Politics Conservative Republican

Famous for The movie *Fargo*

Official fish Northern pike

Driving distances Fargo to Bismarck 193 miles

North Dakota State Parks (☎800-807-4723; www.parkrec.nd.gov) Vehicle permits cost $5/25 per day/year. Nearly half of the park campsites are reservable; fees range from $12 to $30 per night.

North Dakota Tourism (☎800-435-5663; www.ndtourism.com)

Along I-94

Arrowing across North Dakota, I-94 provides easy access to most of the state's top attractions, although it would not be the road of scenic choice (US 2 is more atmospheric).

Fargo

Named for the Fargo of Wells Fargo Bank, North Dakota's biggest city has been a fur-trading post, a frontier town, a quick-divorce capital and a haven for folks in the Federal Witness Protection Program; not to mention the namesake of the Coen Brothers' film *Fargo* – though the movie was set across the Red River in Minnesota. Still, expect to hear a lot of accents similar to Frances McDormand's unforgettable version in the movie. Film fame aside, there's not a lot in Fargo worth more than a quick stop off the highway.

Sights

★Fargo Woodchipper FILM LOCATION
(☎800-235-7654; www.fargomoorhead.org; 2001 44th St, I-94 exit 348; ⏲7:30am-8pm Mon-Fri, 10am-6pm Sat & Sun Jun-Aug, 8am-5pm Mon-Fri, 10am-4pm Sat Sep-May) FREE Fargo's embrace of its namesake film is on full display at the town's **visitor center**, which houses the actual woodchipper used for the scene where Gaear feeds the last of Carl's body into its maw and is discovered by Marge. You can reenact the scene – although not the results – while wearing Fargo-style hats and jamming in a fake leg (both provided!).

Plains Art Museum MUSEUM
(☎701-551-6100; www.plainsart.org; 704 1st Ave N; adult/child $7.50/free; ⏲11am-5pm Tue, Wed, Fri & Sat, to 9pm Thu, noon-5pm Sun) This ambitious museum features sophisticated programming in a renovated warehouse. The permanent collection includes contemporary work by Native American artists.

Sleeping

Chain motels cluster at exits 64 on I-29 and 348 on I-94.

★Hotel Donaldson HOTEL $$
(☎701-478-1000; www.hoteldonaldson.com; 101 Broadway; r from $180; ❄@🛜) A stylish and swank revamp of a flophouse, the 17 luxurious suites here are each decorated by a local artist. Fargo's most chic restaurant and rooftop bar (and hot tub!) await.

Bismarck

Like the surrounding plains of wheat, Bismarck, North Dakota's capital, has a quick and bountiful summer. Otherwise, it's a compact place that hunkers down for the long winters, where temperature lows average -4°F (-20°C).

In Bismarck, chain motels congregate around I-94 exit 159. Get info at the **Bismarck-Mandan Visitor Center** (☎701-222-4308; www.discoverbismarckmandan.com; 1600 Burnt Boat Dr, I-94 exit 157; ⏲8am-7pm Mon-Fri, to 5pm Sat, 10am-4pm Sun Jun-Aug, 8am-5pm Mon-Fri Sep-May).

Sights

★North Dakota Heritage Center MUSEUM
(☎701-328-2666; www.history.nd.gov; 612 East Boulevard Ave, Capitol Hill; ⏲8am-5pm Mon-Fri, 10am-5pm Sat & Sun) FREE Behind the Sacagawea statue, the North Dakota Heritage Center has details on everything from Norwegian bachelor farmers to the scores of nuclear bombs perched on missiles in silos across the state. Four new galleries have doubled its size.

State Capitol HISTORIC BUILDING
(☎701-328-2480; N 7th St, Capitol Hill; ⏲8am-4pm Mon-Fri, 9am-4pm Sat, 1-4pm Sun Jun-Aug, 9am-4pm Mon-Fri Sep-May, tours hourly except noon) FREE The stark 1930s State Capitol is often referred to as the 'skyscraper of the prairie,' and looks something like a Stalinist school of dentistry from the outside, but has some art-deco flourishes inside. There's an observation deck on the 18th floor.

Fort Abraham Lincoln State Park HISTORIC SITE
(www.parkrec.nd.gov; off Hwy 1806; per vehicle $5, tours adult/child $6/4; ⏲park 9am-5pm, tours May-Sep) The highlight at this park on the west bank of the Missouri is **On-a-Slant Indian Village**, which has five re-created Mandan earth lodges. The fort, with several replica buildings, was Custer's last stop before the Battle of Little Bighorn. It's 7 miles south of Mandan.

NORTH DAKOTA: DETOURS & EXTRAS

Ronald Reagan Minuteman Missile State Historic Site (☎701-797-3691; www.history.nd.gov; NE Hwy 45, Cooperstown; adult/child $10/3; ⏱10am-6:30pm Jun-Sep, reduced hours Oct-May) This site includes a deactivated **underground command center** from where missiles would have been launched. Visits are by tour. A nearby deactivated **missile silo** is actually more eerie. Often unattended, you can ponder the doors that hid a rocket with over 500 kilotons of nuclear explosive power (the Hiroshima bomb had 15 kilotons). It's surrounded by mundane farmland and a few distant farmhouses. Note that North Dakota still has underground nuclear missiles waiting for launch orders.

International Peace Garden (☎701-263-4390; www.peacegarden.com; off US 281; per vehicle $15; ⏱10am-5pm) With some 150,000 flowers and several monuments, the garden sits symbolically on the North Dakota–Manitoba border.

Enchanted Highway Boasting huge whimsical metal sculptures of local folks and critters by artist Gary Greff, the Enchanted Hwy runs for 32 miles straight south to Regent from I-94 exit 72. Once there, you can stay in Greff's fun motel, the **Enchanted Castle** (☎701-563-4858; www.enchantedcastlend.com; 607 Main St, Regent; r $90-125; ❄📶), which is an elementary school remodeled with crenelations.

West of Bismark

West on I-94, stop and see **Sue, the World's Largest Holstein Cow** at New Salem (exit 127). At exit 72, there's a unique detour south along the Enchanted Hwy. An hour west of Sue, the **Dakota Dinosaur Museum** (☎701-225-3466; www.dakotadino.com; 200 E Museum Dr, I-94 exit 61, Dickinson; adult/child $8/5; ⏱9am-5pm May-Aug) has oodles of dinosaur fossils and statues.

Theodore Roosevelt National Park

Theodore Roosevelt National Park PARK
(☎701-623-4466; www.nps.gov/thro; 7-day pass per vehicle $20) A tortured region known as the 'badlands' whose colors seem to change with the moods of nature, Theodore Roosevelt National Park is the state's natural highlight. Bizarre rock formations, streaked with a rainbow of red, yellow, brown, black and silver minerals, are framed by green prairie. The park is vast, with only the rush of rivers and the distant hoofbeat of animals to interrupt the silence.

Wildlife abounds: mule deer, wild horses, bighorn sheep, elk, bison, around 200 bird species and, of course, sprawling subterranean prairie-dog towns.

The park is divided into two sections. Most visitors to the **South Unit** opt for the 36-mile scenic drive that begins in **Medora**, an enjoyable town with motels just off I-94; prairie dogs are a highlight. The **North Unit** gets few visitors, but is well worth the journey for the 14-mile drive to the **Oxbow Overlook**, with its wide views into the vast and colorfully striated river canyon. The verdant surrounds are protected as the **Little Missouri National Grassland**, and bison are everywhere. It is 68 miles north of I-94 on US 85.

Hikers can explore 85 miles of backcountry trails. For a good adventure, hike or cycle the 96-mile **Maah Daah Hey Trail** between the park units. Driving, continue north on US 85 to Fort Buford.

The park has three visitor centers, including the **South Unit Visitor Center** (off I-94 exits 24 & 27, Medora; ⏱8am-6pm Jun-Aug, to 4:30pm Sep-May), with Theodore Roosevelt's old cabin out back. The park has two simple campgrounds (sites $7 to $14) and free backcountry camping (permit required).

Along US 2

US 2 is the more interesting alternative to I-94. The endless-sky vistas stretch even further than the seas of golden grain. **Grand Forks** is a stolid city, while **Devils Lake** is one of the top waterfowl-hunting destinations in the country. The entire area is subject to the flood-prone Red River.

Rugby

Rugby is about halfway down the highway, but its more notable location identity is as the geographical center of North America. The **Prairie Village Museum** (☎701-776-

WORTH A TRIP

LEWIS & CLARK IN NORTH DAKOTA

Northwest of Bismarck are several worthwhile attractions near the spot where Lewis and Clark wintered with the Mandan in 1804–05. They offer an evocative look at the lives of the Native Americans and the explorers amid lands that even today seem little changed.

Lewis & Clark Interpretive Center (☎701-462-8535; www.fortmandan.com; junction US 83 & ND Hwy 200A, Washburn; adult/child $7.50/3; ⊙9am-5pm daily Jun-Aug, 9am-5pm Mon-Sat, noon-5pm Sun Sep-May) At this impressive center you can learn about the duo's epic expedition and the Native Americans who helped them. Check out the beautiful drawings from George Catlin's portfolio.

The same ticket gets you into **Fort Mandan**, a replica of the fort built by Lewis and Clark, 2.5 miles west (10 miles downstream from the flooded original site). It sits on a lonely stretch of the Missouri River marked by a monument to Seaman, the expedition's dog.

Inside the small but worthwhile information building, look for the display on period medicine, including Dr Rush's 'Thunderclappers.'

Knife River Indian Villages National Historical Site (☎701-745-3300; www.nps.gov/knri; off Hwy 200; ⊙buildings 8am-5pm Jun-Aug, to 4:30pm Sep-May, trails 6am-10pm) Here you can still see the mounds left by three earthen villages of the Hidastas, who lived on the Knife River, a narrow tributary of the Missouri, for more than 900 years. The National Park Service has re-created one of the earthen lodges.

It's just north of Stanton (22 miles west of Washburn) on Hwy 200, which runs through verdant rolling prairie for 110 miles between US 83 and US 85.

Stroll through the mostly wide-open and wild site to the village site where Lewis and Clark met Sacagawea.

6414; www.prairievillagemuseum.com; 102 US 2 SE; adult/child $7/3; ⊙8:30am-5pm Mon-Sat, noon-5pm Sun mid-May–mid-Sep) re-creates Great Plains life through the decades.

West to Montana

Minot is nearly as bleak as the landscape. West, the land is dotted with forlorn little settlements slipping back into the prairie soil. However, the skyline is enlivened by the flames and bright lights of hundreds of oil rigs. While the peak of the boom seems past, it's still an area that's been radically changed by the need for oil.

Twenty-two miles southwest of Williston, **Fort Buford** (www.history.nd.gov; SR 1804; adult/child $5/2.50; ⊙10am-5:30pm Jun-Aug) is the bleak army outpost where Sitting Bull surrendered. The adjacent **Missouri-Yellowstone Confluence Interpretive Center** includes the fort's visitor center.

About 2 miles west, on the Montana–North Dakota border, the more evocative **Fort Union Trading Post** (☎701-572-9083; www.nps.gov/fous; SR 1804; ⊙8am-6:30pm central time Jun-Aug, 9am-5:30pm Sep-May) FREE is a reconstruction of the American Fur Company post built in 1828.

SOUTH DAKOTA

Gently rolling prairies and shallow fertile valleys mark much of this endlessly attractive state. But head southwest and all hell breaks loose – in the best possible way. The Badlands National Park is the geologic equivalent of fireworks. The Black Hills are like opera: majestic, challenging, intriguing and even frustrating. Mt Rushmore matches the Statue of Liberty for five-star icon status.

ℹ Information

Bed & Breakfast Innkeepers of South Dakota (www.southdakotabb.com)

South Dakota Department of Tourism (☎800-732-5682; www.travelsd.com)

South Dakota State Parks (☎800-710-2267; www.gfp.sd.gov) Vehicle permits cost $6/30 per day/year. Many park campsites are reservable (www.campsd.com); fees range from $8 to $25 per night. Cabins start at $35.

Sioux Falls

South Dakota's largest city lives up to its name at **Falls Park** just north of downtown where the Big Sioux River plunges through a long series of rock faces. The park has the city's excellent **visitor center** (☎605-275-6060; www.visitsiouxfalls.com; 900 N Phillips Ave; ⏰10am-9pm daily Apr–mid-Oct, reduced hours mid-Oct-Apr) with an observation tower.

Sights

Old Courthouse Museum MUSEUM
(☎605-367-4210; www.siouxlandmuseums.com; 200 W 6th St; ⏰8am-5pm Mon-Wed & Fri, to 9pm Thu, 9am-5pm Sat, noon-5pm Sun) FREE This huge and restored pink quartzite 1890s building has three floors of changing exhibits on the region.

Sleeping & Eating

Chain motels lurk at I-29 exits 77 to 83. Downtown you'll find a lot of great eats.

Queen City Bakery BAKERY $
(☎605-274-6060; www.queencitybakery.com; 324 E 8th St; items from $2; ⏰7am-5pm Mon & Wed-Fri, to 3pm Sat & Sun) The red velvet cake, goodness! The best bakery for many states around turns out amazing baked goods and coffee.

★**MB Haskett Delicatessen** MODERN AMERICAN $$
(☎605-367-1100; www.mbhaskett.com; 324 S Phillips Ave; mains $7-21; ⏰7am-8pm Sun-Thu, to 11pm Fri & Sat) Michael Haskett's retro cafe serves brilliant food throughout the day, from breakfast through dinner. The ever-changing menu draws inspiration from the seasons and from around the globe.

Along I-90 & Around

Easily one of the most mind-numbing stretches of interstate highway, I-90 across South Dakota fortunately has some worthy stops along the way.

Mitchell

Every year, half a million people pull off I-90 (exit 332) to see the Taj Mahal of agriculture, the all-time-ultimate roadside attraction, the **Corn Palace** (☎605-995-8430; www.cornpalace.org; 604 N Main St; ⏰8am-9pm Jun-Aug, reduced hours Sep-May) FREE. Close to 300,000 ears of corn are used each year to create a tableaux of murals on the outside of the building. Ponder the scenes and you may find a kernel of truth or just say, 'aw, shucks.'

SOUTH DAKOTA FACTS

Nickname Mt Rushmore State

Population 854,000

Area 77,125 sq miles

Capital city Pierre (population 14,000)

Other cities Sioux Falls (population 165,000), Rapid City (population 71,000)

Sales tax 4% to 6%

Birthplace of Sitting Bull (c 1831–90), Crazy Horse (c 1840–77) and Black Elk (c 1863–1950), all of Little Bighorn fame, and genial broadcaster Tom Brokaw (b 1940)

Home of Mt Rushmore, the Sioux

Politics Republican

Famous for HBO TV show *Deadwood*, Wounded Knee Massacre

Official animal Coyote

Driving distances Sioux Falls to Rapid City 341 miles, Sioux Falls to Des Moines 283 miles

Chamberlain

In a picturesque site where I-90 crosses the Missouri River, Chamberlain (exit 263) is home to the excellent **Akta Lakota Museum & Cultural Center** (☎800-798-3452; www.aktalakota.org; 1301 N Main St; suggested donation $5; ⏰8am-6pm Mon-Sat, 9am-5pm Sun May-Oct, 8am-5pm Mon-Fri Nov-Apr) at St Joseph's Indian School. It has Lakota cultural displays and art from numerous tribes.

History buffs should pop into the hilltop rest stop where the **Lewis & Clark Information Center** (☎605-734-4562; exit 264 I-90; ⏰8:30am-4:30pm mid-May–Sep) FREE has exhibits on the intrepid duo.

Pierre

The best reason to detour off I-90 immerses you in large swaths of South Dakota that haven't changed since the 19th century, when the Native Americans and US Army clashed. The **Native American Scenic Byway** (www.byways.org) begins in Chamberlain on Hwy 50 and meanders 100 crooked miles northwest to Pierre along Hwy 1806, following

WORTH A TRIP

LITTLE HOUSE(S) ON THE PRAIRIE

Fans of *Little House on the Prairie* should head to Laura Ingalls Wilder's former hometown, **De Smet**. The pint-sized author lived here from age 12 when her peripatetic Pa finally settled down (much of her famous book was based on her time in Independence, KS). The town is 40 miles west of I-29 (exit 133) on US 14.

For more info on the plethora of LHOTP–related sites across middle America, see www.liwfrontiergirl.com.

Laura Ingalls Wilder Memorial Society (www.discoverlaura.org; 105 Olivet Ave, De Smet; adult/child $12/6; 9am-5pm Mon-Sat, 11am-5pm Sun Jun-Aug, reduced hours Sep-May;) Right in town, the fussy and frilly complex that's home to the society has tours that include **two original Wilder homes** – the one where the Wilders spent the first winter in 1879 and the home Michael Landon, er, 'Pa,' later built.

Ingalls Homestead (605-854-3984; www.ingallshomestead.com; 20812 Homestead Rd; admission $12; 9am-7pm Jun-Aug, reduced hours Sep-May;) Just outside De Smet and down a dirt road, the actual Ingalls Homestead has been much gussied up and includes all manner of attractions about 19th-century farm life and Laura herself.

Laura Ingalls Wilder Pageant (www.desmetpageant.org; Homestead Rd; adult/child $12/8; 8pm Fri-Sun Jul) Near the Ingalls Homestead, this long-running pageant reenacts melodramatic scenes from Laura's books. Townfolk fill the roles, including one very lucky young girl.

the Missouri River through rolling, rugged countryside.

Pierre (pronounced 'peer') is just too small and ordinary to feel like a seat of power.

Sights

State Capitol HISTORIC BUILDING
(605-773-3688; 500 E Capitol Ave; 8am-7pm Mon-Fri, to 5pm Sat & Sun) FREE Small-town Victorian homes overlook the imposing 1910 State Capitol with its black copper dome.

South Dakota Cultural Heritage Center MUSEUM
(605-773-3458; www.history.sd.gov; 900 Governor's Dr; adult/child $4/free; 9am-6:30pm Mon-Sat, 1-4:30pm Sun Jun-Aug, to 4:30pm rest of year) Exhibits at this ecologically groundbreaking museum include a bloody Ghost Dance shirt from Wounded Knee.

Framboise Island ISLAND
At a bend on the Missouri River, Framboise Island has several hiking trails and plentiful wildlife. It's across from where the Lewis and Clark expedition spent four days and was nearly derailed when they inadvertently offended members of the local Brule tribe.

Minuteman Missile National Historic Site

Minuteman Missile National Historic Site HISTORIC SITE
(www.nps.gov/mimi; I-90 exit 131; 8am-4:30pm daily Jun-Sep, Mon-Fri Oct-May) In the 1960s and '70s, 450 Minutemen II intercontinental ballistic missiles, always at the ready in underground silos, were just 30 minutes from their targets in the Soviet Union. The missiles have since been retired (more modern ones still lurk underground across the northern Great Plains). The first national park dedicated to the Cold War preserves one silo and its underground launch facility. At the time of writing, tour fees were being planned for 2016.

An impressive new **visitor center** opened in 2015. It has displays and films about the missiles and the Cold War. Here you get tickets for the tours of the nearby underground **Launch Control Facility Delta-01** where two people stood ready around the clock to turn keys to launch missiles from this part of South Dakota. Tours are given daily and are first-come, first-served. Arrive early.

The **Delta-09 Missile Silo** (I-90 exit 116; 9am-4pm) can be viewed without a tour through a glass cover.

Wall

Hyped for hundreds of miles, thanks to Wall Drug. There's no reason not to succumb.

Sights

★ **Wall Drug** LANDMARK
(605-279-2175; www.walldrug.com; 510 Main St; 6:30am-8pm May-Sep, to 6pm Oct-Apr;) Hyped for hundreds of miles, Wall Drug is a surprisingly enjoyable stop. It really does have 5¢ coffee, free ice water, good donuts and enough diversions and come-ons to warm the heart of schlock-lovers everywhere. But amid the fudge in this faux frontier complex is a superb **bookstore** with a great selection of regional titles. Out back, ride the mythical **jackalope** and check out the historical photos.

Story of Wounded Knee MUSEUM
(605-279-2573; www.woundedkneemuseum.org; cnr Main St & 6th Ave; adult/child $6/free; 9am-5pm mid-May–Sep) This important small museum tells the story of the massacre from the Lakota perspective using photos and narratives. It's more insightful than anything at the actual site.

Sleeping & Eating

Wall is a good place for an overnight pause. It's compact and walkable, there are tasty and cheap cafes and bars, and several good non-chain motels.

Sunshine Inn MOTEL $
(605-279-2178; www.wallsunshineinn.weebly.com; 608 Main St; r $60-80; Apr-Oct;) An indie outpost, with a genial owner and 22 basic and sparkling rooms.

Badlands National Park

This otherworldly landscape, oddly softened by its fantastic rainbow hues, is a spectacle of sheer walls and spikes stabbing the dry air. It was understandably named *mako sica* (badland) by Native Americans. Looking over the bizarre formations from the corrugated walls surrounding Badlands is like seeing an ocean someone boiled dry.

Take **Hwy 44** for a scenic alternative between the Badlands and Rapid City as well as down to Pine Ridge Indian Reservation.

SOUTH DAKOTA: DETOURS & EXTRAS

Highway 14 This historic road runs across the middle of the state, crossing I-29 at Brookings (exit 133), then traveling west through De Smet to Pierre and on to Wall. It meanders through a sea of grassland under big skies colored by sunsets stretching across the broad horizon.

Petrified Wood Park (500 Main St, Lemmon; park 24hr, museum 9am-5pm Jun-Aug) This 1930s collection of geologic oddities covers an entire city block in the center of little **Lemmon**, way off in the northwest corner of the state.

Sights

★ **Hwy 240 Badlands Loop Rd** NATIONAL PARK
The park's **north unit** gets the most visitors; this stunning road is easily reached from I-90 (exits 110 and 131) and you can drive it in an hour if you're in a hurry (and not stuck behind an RV). Lookouts and vistas abound.

Sage Creek Rim Rd NATIONAL PARK
The portion of the Badlands west of Hwy 240 along this gravel road is much less visited. There are stops at prairie-dog towns; this is where most backcountry hikers and campers go. As there is almost no water or shade here, don't strike out into the wilderness unprepared. The even less-accessible **south units** are in the Pine Ridge Indian Reservation and see few visitors.

Buffalo Gap National Grassland NATURE RESERVE
The Badlands, along with the surrounding Buffalo Gap National Grassland, protects the country's largest prairie grasslands, several species of Great Plains mammal (including bison and black-footed ferret), prairie falcons and lots of snakes. The **National Grasslands Visitors Center** (605-279-2125; www.fs.fed.us/grasslands; 798 Main St, Wall; 8am-4:30pm Mon-Fri) has good displays on the wealth of life in this complex ecosystem, which the uninformed may dismiss as 'boring.'

Rangers can map out back-road routes that will let you do looping tours of Badlands National Park and the grasslands without ever touching I-90.

Black Hills & Badlands National Park

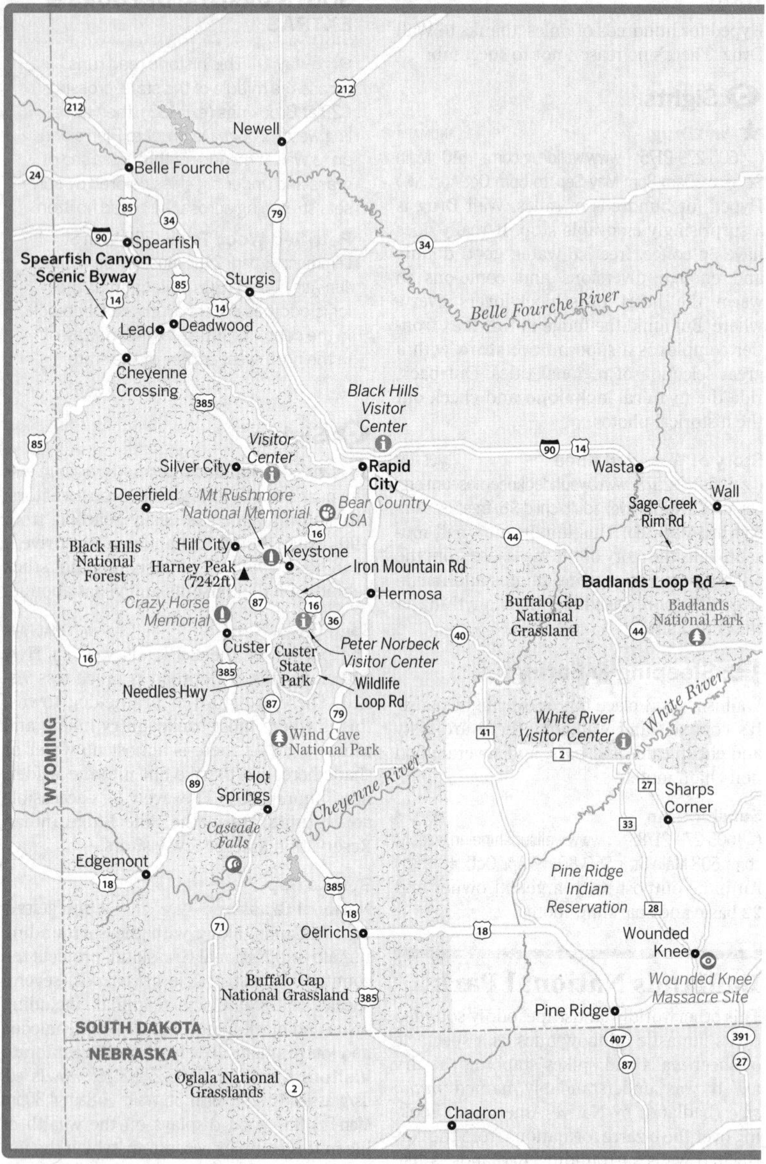

Sleeping

Neither the developed **Cedar Pass Campground** (off Hwy 240; campsites $18-30) or primitive **Sage Creek Campground** (Sage Creek Rim Rd; campsites free) take reservations. Hotels can be found on I-90 in Kadoka and Wall, or stay at a cozy cabin inside the park at the renovated **Cedar Pass Lodge** (☎605-433-5460; www.cedarpasslodge.com; Hwy 240; cabins $160; ⏱mid-Apr–mid-Oct; ❄@), which has a restaurant and shops.

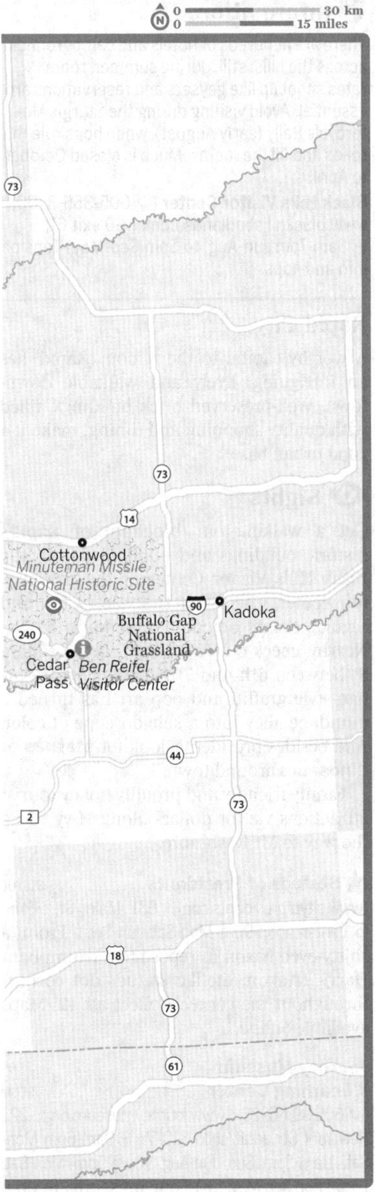

Information

Ben Reifel Visitor Center (605-433-5361; www.nps.gov/badl; Hwy 240; 7-day park pass bicycle/car $7/15; 8am-7pm Jun-Aug, to 5pm Apr, May, Sep & Oct, to 4pm Nov-Mar) The main visitor center for the park; has good exhibits and advice for ways to ditch your car to appreciate the geologic wonders.

White River Visitor Center (Hwy 27; 10am-3pm Jun-Aug) Small information outlet.

Pine Ridge Indian Reservation

Home to the Lakota Oglala Sioux, the Pine Ridge reservation south of Badlands National Park is one of the nation's poorest 'counties,' with over half the population living below the poverty line. Despite being at times a jarring dose of reality, it is also a place welcoming to visitors. Tune in to KILI (90.1 FM), which often plays traditional music.

History

In 1890 the new Ghost Dance religion, which the Lakota followers believed would bring back their ancestors and eliminate the white man, became popular. This struck fear into the area's soldiers and settlers and the frenetic circle dances were outlawed. The 7th US Cavalry rounded up a band of Lakota under Chief Big Foot and brought them to the small village of Wounded Knee.

On December 29, as the soldiers began to search for weapons, a shot was fired (nobody knows by who), leading to the massacre of more than 250 men, women and children, most of them unarmed. It's one of the most infamous atrocities in US history. Twenty-five soldiers also died.

Sights

★ Wounded Knee Massacre Site HISTORIC SITE

(Hwy 27) The massacre site, 16 miles northeast of Pine Ridge town, is marked by a faded sign. It helps to read up on the events before you arrive. The mass grave, often frequented by people looking for donations, sits atop the hill near a **church**. Small memorials appear daily amid the stones listing dozens of names such as Horn Cloud. It's a desolate place, with sweeping views. An ad hoc timeline on a pillar lists acts of genocide against Native Americans.

Red Cloud Heritage Center MUSEUM

(www.redcloudschool.org; 100 Mission Dr, Pine Ridge; 8am-6pm Mon-Sat, 10am-5pm Sun Jun-Aug, 9am-6pm Tue-Sat Sep-May) FREE This well-curated art museum has traditional and contemporary works and a craft shop. Look for photos taken after the massacre

DON'T MISS

TOP GREAT PLAINS PARKS

Theodore Roosevelt National Park (p663) Buffalo roam amid stunning canyons carved by rivers after the ice age.

Badlands National Park (p667) Bizarrely eroded rocks and canyons offer an unforgettable spectacle.

Fort Larned National Historic Site (p684) You can almost hear the creak of wheels on passing covered wagons on the Santa Fe Trail at this preserved Kansas fort.

Homestead National Monument (p677) Farmland with hikes amid rivers and wildflowers.

Brown v Board of Education National Historic Site (p683) The school that sparked the court decision ordering the desegregation of American public schools.

showing the frozen bodies of the dead with their expressions of shock locked in place. It's four miles north of Pine Ridge on Hwy 18 at the Red Cloud Indian School.

Black Hills

One of the best places in the US for a holiday, this stunning region on the Wyoming–South Dakota border lures scores of visitors with its winding canyons and wildly eroded 7000ft peaks. The region's name – the 'Black' comes from the dark ponderosa-pine-covered slopes – was conferred by the Lakota Sioux. In the 1868 Fort Laramie Treaty, they were assured that the hills would be theirs for eternity, but the discovery of gold changed that, and the Sioux were shoved out to low-value flatlands only six years later. The 1990 film *Dances with Wolves* covers some of this period.

You'll need several days to explore the bucolic back-road drives, caves, bison herds, forests, Mt Rushmore and Crazy Horse monuments, and outdoor activities (ballooning, cycling, rock climbing, boating, fishing, hiking, downhill skiing, gold-panning etc). Like fool's gold, gaudy tourist traps lurk in corners.

Information

There are hundreds of hotels and campgrounds across the hills; still, during summer, room rates shoot up like geysers and reservations are essential. Avoid visiting during the Sturgis Motorcycle Rally (early August), when hogs rule the roads and fill the rooms. Much is closed October to April.

Black Hills Visitor Center (☎605-355-3700; www.blackhillsbadlands.com; I-90 exit 61; ⏲8am-7pm Jun-Aug, to 5pm Sep-May) Tons of info and apps.

Rapid City

A worthy capital to the region, 'Rapid' has an intriguing, lively and walkable downtown. Well-preserved brick buildings, filled with quality shopping and dining, make it a good urban base.

Sights

Get a walking-tour brochure of Rapid's historic buildings and public art from the Black Hills Visitor Center or the city's visitor center. Check out the watery fun and regular events downtown on **Main St Sq**. Nearby, check out **Art Alley** (north of Main St between 6th and 7th streets), where urban-style graffiti and pop art has turned a mundane alley into a kaleidoscope of color. And besides presidents, look for **statues of dinosaurs** around town.

Family friendly and proudly hokey tourist attractions vie for dollars along Hwy 16 on the way to Mt Rushmore.

★ **Statues of Presidents** STATUE
(www.cityofpresidents.com; 631 Main St; ⏲info center noon-9pm Mon-Sat Jun-Sep) From a shifty-eyed Nixon in repose to a triumphant Harry Truman, lifelike statues dot corners throughout the center. Collect all 42. Maps available online.

Journey Museum & Learning Center MUSEUM
(☎605-394-6923; www.journeymuseum.org; 222 New York St; adult/child $10/7; ⏲9am-6pm Mon-Sat, 11am-5pm Sun Jun-Aug, 10am-5pm Mon-Sat, 1-5pm Sun Sep-May; ♿) Four museums in one! This impressive downtown facility looks at the history of the region from prehistoric times until today. Collections come from the vaunted **Museum of Geology** (☎605-394-2467; http://museum.sdsmt.edu; 501 E St Joseph St, O'Harra Bldg; ⏲9am-5pm Mon-Fri, to 6pm Sat, noon-5pm Sun Jun-Aug, 9am-4pm Mon-Fri, 10am-4pm Sat

Sep-May) FREE, the Sioux Indian Museum, the Minnilusa Pioneer Museum and the South Dakota Archaeological Research Center.

Bear Country USA WILDLIFE RESERVE
(605-343-2290; www.bearcountryusa.com; Hwy 16; adult/child $16/10; 8am-6pm May-Aug, reduced hours Sep-Nov;) Oodles of bears big and small in this drive-through park live off the land and hope you'll do something forbidden like offering them a Big Mac, or your hand. The attraction is eight miles south of Rapid City.

Sleeping

Motels cluster at I-90 exits 57 and 60, downtown and US 16 south of town.

★ **Hotel Alex Johnson** HOTEL $$
(605-342-1210; www.alexjohnson.com; 523 6th St; r $70-200;) The design of this 1927 classic magically blends Germanic Tudor architecture and traditional Lakota Sioux symbols – note the lobby's painted ceiling and the chandelier made of war lances. The 127 rooms are modernized retro and slightly posh, no two are alike, and some have fabulous views.

The hotel's timeless qualities include a portrait of guest Al Capone near the front desk. The rooftop bar is a delight.

Adoba Eco Hotel HOTEL $$
(605-348-8300; www.adobahotelrapidcity.com; 445 Mt Rushmore Rd; r $100-200; P) This highrise hotel has been transformed into a high-concept downtown gem with green accents. Furniture is made from recycled materials yet there's no skimping on comfort. The marble floor in the lobby is a stunner.

Eating & Drinking

Downtown has scores of eateries and bars and is a great place to stroll.

Tally's Silver Spoon AMERICAN $$
(605-342-7621; www.tallyssilverspoon.com; 530 6th St; mains $6-30; 7am-9pm Mon-Thu, to 10pm Fri & Sat) Carter or Reagan? Both statues are out front and you can ponder your preference while you savor the upscale diner fare at this stylish downtown cafe and bar. Breakfasts are as good as ever; more creative regional fare is on offer at night.

Delmonico Grill MODERN AMERICAN $$$
(605-791-1664; www.delmonicogrill.biz; 609 Main St; mains lunch $6-15, dinner $24-38; 11am-2pm & 5-9pm Mon-Sat) Fine burgers, sandwiches and salads star at lunch at this casually elegant downtown dining spot. At dinner, choose from superb steaks and other meaty mains from the Plains. Lots of specials by season.

★ **Independent Ale House** PUB
(605-718-9492; www.independentalehouse.com; 625 St Joseph St; 3pm-late) Enjoy a fabulous (and changing) line-up of the best microbrews from the region in this vintage-style bar. The wine list is equally good. Pizzas are excellent: the pesto offering will have you humming with pleasure (mains $8 to $15).

Information

Visitor Center (866-727-4324; www.visitrapidcity.com; 444 Mt Rushmore Rd; 8am-5pm Mon-Fri) A super-helpful resource.

Sturgis

Fast food, Christian iconography and billboards for ribald biker bars featuring dolled-up models are just some of the cacophony of images of this tacky small town on I-90 (exits 30 and 32).

Things get even louder for the annual **Sturgis Motorcycle Rally** (605-720-0800; www.sturgismotorcyclerally.com) in early August, when around 500,000 riders, fans and curious onlookers take over the town. Temporary campsites are set up and motels across the region unmuffle their rates. Check the rally website for vacancies.

Spearfish

Spearfish Canyon Scenic Byway (www.byways.org) is a waterfall-lined, curvaceous 20-mile road (US 14A) that cleaves into the heart of the hills from Spearfish. There's a sight worth stopping for around every bend; pause for longer than a minute and you'll hear beavers hard at work. It's a good alternative route to Lead and Deadwood from I-90.

Deadwood

Once the very definition of lawless, today Deadwood is very much changed, although the 80 gambling halls big and small would no doubt put a sly grin on the faces of the hard characters who founded the town. Then again, loser's largesse is paying for Deadwood's restoration.

Settled illegally by eager gold rushers in the 1870s, Deadwood is now a National Historic Landmark. Its atmospheric streets are lined with gold-rush-era buildings lavishly restored with gambling dollars. Its storied past is easy to find. There's eternal devotion to Wild Bill Hickok, who was shot in the back of the head here in 1876 while gambling.

Sights

Actors reenact famous **shootouts** (Main St; 2pm, 4pm & 6pm Jun-Aug) on Main St during summer. **Hickok's murder** (657 Main St; 1pm, 3pm, 5pm & 7pm Jun–mid-Sep) is acted out in Saloon No 10. A **trial** (cnr Main & Pine Sts, Masonic Temple; 8pm) of the killer takes place in the evening.

Downtown is walkable, but the fake **trolley** ($1 per ride) can be handy for getting between attractions, hotels and parking lots.

★Mount Moriah Cemetery HISTORIC SITE
(Mt Moriah Dr; adult/child $1/50¢, tours $9/5; 8am-8pm Jun-Aug, to 5pm Sep-May) Calamity Jane (born Martha Canary; 1850–1903) and Wild Bill Hickok (1847–76) rest side by side up on Boot Hill at the very steep cemetery. Entertaining bus tours leave hourly from Main St.

Deadwood History & Information Center MUSEUM
(800-999-1876; www.deadwood.org; Pine St; 8am-7pm Jun-Aug, 9am-5pm Sep-May) This splendid center in the restored train depot has tons of local tourist info, plus exhibits and photos of the town's history. Pick up the walking tour brochure.

Adams Museum MUSEUM
(605-578-1714; www.deadwoodhistory.com; 54 Sherman St; admission by donation; 9am-5pm daily Jun-Aug, 10am-4pm Tue-Sun Sep-May) Does an excellent job of capturing the town's colorful past; also has a great bookstore.

Days of '76 Museum MUSEUM
(www.daysof76museum.com; 18 76 Dr; adult/child $5.50/2.50; 9am-5pm daily May-Aug, Mon-Sat Sep-Apr) Focusing on 1876, this good-sized museum documents life in the region at that time.

Sleeping & Eating

Casinos offer up buffets with plenty of cheap chow. There are scores of motels to stay at right in the center; steer clear of new ones that are far removed from the heart of town. Rates plummet off-season.

Deadwood Dick's HOTEL $$
(605-578-3224; www.deadwooddicks.com; 51 Sherman St; r $60-200;) These home-style and idiosyncratic rooms feature furniture from the owner's antique shop, and range in size from small doubles to large suites with kitchens. The idiosyncratic bar lives up to the town's past.

Bullock Hotel HISTORIC HOTEL $$
(605-578-1745; www.historicbullock.com; 633 Main St; r $70-200;) Fans of the TV show will recall the conflicted but upstanding sheriff Seth Bullock. This hotel was opened by the real Bullock in 1895. The 28 rooms are modern and comfortable while retaining the building's period charm.

Drinking & Nightlife

Saloon No 10 BAR
(800-952-9398; www.saloon10.com; 657 Main St; kitchen noon-10pm, bar 8am-2am) Dark paneled walls and sawdust on the floor are features of this storied bar. The original, where Hickok literally lost big time, stood across the street, but the building burned to the ground and the owners relocated here. There's a rooftop bar, and decent pub grub and Italian-accented dinners (mains $8 to $25).

Lead

Just uphill from Deadwood, Lead (pronounced *leed*) has an unpolished charm and still bears plenty of scars from the mining era. Gape at the 1250ft-deep **Homestake Gold Mine** from the new **Sanford Lab Homestake Visitor Center** (605-584-3110; www.sanfordlabhomestake.com; 160 W Main St; viewing area free, tours adult/child $7.50/6.75; 8am-6pm, tours 10am-4pm Jun-Sep). Nearby are the same mine's shafts, which plunge more than 1.5 miles below the surface and are now being used for physics research.

The **Main Street Manor Hostel** (605-717-2044; www.mainstreetmanorhostel.com; 515 W Main St; dm/d $25/50; Feb-Nov;) is a gem in its own right. Guests can use the kitchen, garden and laundry at this friendly three-room place.

US 385

The scenic spine of the Black Hills, US 385 runs 90 miles from Deadwood to Hot Springs and beyond. Beautiful meadows and dark stands of conifers are interspersed with roadside attractions that include kangaroos, mistletoe and, of course, Elvis.

Black Hills National Forest

The majority of the Black Hills lie within this 1875-sq-mile mixture of protected and logged forest, perforated by pockets of private land on most roads. The scenery is fantastic, whether you get deep into it on the 450 miles of hiking trails or drive the byways and gravel fire roads.

The 109-mile **George S Mickelson Trail** (www.mickelsontrail.com; daily/annual pass $3/15) cuts through much of the forest, running from Deadwood through Hill City and Custer to Edgemont on an abandoned railway line. There are bike rentals at various trailside towns.

Information

Good camping abounds in the forest. There are 30 basic (no showers or electricity) **campgrounds** (☎877-444-6777; www.recreation.gov; campsites free-$25); reserve in summer. Free backcountry camping is allowed just about anywhere (no open fires).

Visitor Center (☎605-673-9200; www.fs.usda.gov/blackhills; US 385, near Hwy 44; 🕒8:30am-5pm mid-May–mid-Sep) A modern visitor center overlooks the Pactola Reservoir between Hill City and Rapid City.

Hill City

One of the most appealing towns up in the hills, Hill City (www.hillcitysd.com) is less frenzied than places such as Keystone. Its main drag has cafes and galleries.

Sights & Activities

Crazy Horse Memorial MONUMENT
(www.crazyhorsememorial.org; off US 385; per person/car $11/28; 🕒9am-dusk Jun-Aug, reduced hours Sep-May) The world's largest monument is this 563ft-tall work-in-progress (with a lot of work to go). When finished it will depict the Sioux leader astride his horse, pointing to the horizon saying, 'My lands are where my dead lie buried.'

No one is predicting when the sculpture will be complete (the face was dedicated in 1998). Although you can see the mountain in the distance, you need to pay another $4 for a van ride to get close.

Never photographed or persuaded to sign a meaningless treaty, Crazy Horse was chosen for a monument that Lakota Sioux elders hoped would balance the presidential focus of Mt Rushmore. In 1948 a Boston-born sculptor, the indefatigable Korczak Ziolkowski, started blasting granite. His family have continued the work since his death in 1982. (It should be noted that many Native Americans oppose the monument as a desecration of sacred land.)

The **visitor center** complex includes a small Native American museum, gift shops, cafes of limited merit, and a fragment of Ziolkowski's studio. A laser-light show plays off the monument on summer evenings.

★1880 Train TOUR
(☎605-574-2222; www.1880train.com; 222 Railroad Ave; adult/child round-trip $28/12; 🕒early May–mid-Oct) This classic steam train runs 10 miles through rugged country to and from Keystone. A train museum is next door.

Sleeping

Alpine Inn HISTORIC HOTEL $$
(☎605-574-2749; www.alpineinnhillcity.com; 133 Main St; r $80-180) Right in the center, the Alpine Inn dates to 1886 and has comfy rooms in bright red, and filling German fare (mains $10 to $25; 11am to 2:30pm and 5pm to 10pm).

Drinking & Nightlife

Black Hills Miner Brewing Co BREWERY
(☎605-574-2886; www.minerbrewing.com; 23845 Hwy 385; 🕒11am-8pm) Enjoy excellent beer at this brewpub 3.5 miles northeast of Hill City. You can sit outside and there are hot snacks to help absorb the brews.

> **MOUNTAIN TIME**
>
> Roughly the western one-third of South Dakota – including the Black Hills and everything west of I-90 exit 177 – uses Mountain Time, which is one hour earlier than Central Time in the rest of the state.

Mount Rushmore

Glimpses of Washington's nose from the roads leading to this hugely popular monument never cease to surprise and are but harbingers of the full impact of this mountainside sculpture once you're up close (and past the less impressive parking area and entrance walk). George Washington, Thomas Jefferson, Abraham Lincoln and Theodore Roosevelt each iconically stare into the distance in 60ft-tall granite glory.

MOUNT RUSHMORE'S FIFTH PRESIDENT

Only four presidents on Mt Rushmore right? Well, maybe not. Nature may have provided a fifth. Drive 1.3 miles northwest from the Mt Rushmore parking entrance (away from Keystone) on Hwy 244 and look for a sheer rock face that's the backside of Mt Rushmore. Pull over safely and then decide just which president might be honored by the rather lurid shape on the rock face. Which head of state it represents may depend on your politics.

Hugely popular, you can easily escape the crowds and fully appreciate the **Mount Rushmore National Memorial** (☎605-574-2523; www.nps.gov/moru; off Hwy 244; parking $11; ⏲8am-10pm Jun-Aug, to 9pm Sep, to 5pm Oct-May) while marveling at the artistry of sculptor Gutzon Borglum and the immense labor of the workers who created the memorial between 1927 and 1941.

The **Presidential Trail** loop passes right below the monument for some fine nostril views and accesses the worthwhile **Sculptor's Studio**, which conveys the drama of how the monument came to be. Start clockwise and you're right under Washington's nose in under five minutes. The **nature trail** to the right as you face the entrance connects the viewing and parking areas, passing through a pine forest and avoiding the crowds and commercialism.

The official Park Service **information centers** have excellent bookstores with proceeds going to the park. Avoid the schlocky Xanterra gift shop and the ho-hum Carvers Cafe, which looked much better in the scene where Cary Grant gets plugged in *North by Northwest*. The main **museum** is underwhelming.

The nearest lodging and restaurants to Mt Rushmore are in Hill City or Keystone, a one-time mining town now devoted to milking the monument.

Custer State Park

The only reason 111-sq-mile **Custer State Park** (☎605-255-4515; www.custerstatepark.info; 7-day pass per car $15; ⏲24hr; 👪) isn't a national park is that the state grabbed it first. It boasts one of the largest free-roaming bison herds in the world (about 1500), the famous 'begging burros' (donkeys seeking handouts) and more than 200 bird species. Other wildlife include elk, pronghorns, mountain goats, bighorn sheep, coyotes, prairie dogs, mountain lions and bobcats.

Sights & Activities

Meandering over awesome stone bridges and across sublime Alpine meadows, the 18-mile **Wildlife Loop Rd** is a sure way to see buffalo, elk, prairie dogs and more. The incredible 14-mile **Needles Hwy** (SD 87) is another superb drive. The latter links with US 385 at either end.

The real road star, however, is **Iron Mountain Rd** (US 16A). It's a 16-mile roller coaster of wooden bridges, virtual loop-the-loops, narrow tunnels and stunning vistas on the section between the park's west entrance and Keystone.

Hiking through the pine-covered hills and prairie grassland (keep an eye out for rattlesnakes) is a great way to see wildlife and rock formations. Trails through Sylvan Lake Shore, Sunday Gulch, Cathedral Spires and French Creek Natural Area are all highly recommended.

Sleeping

The town of Custer, the main gateway into the park, has plenty of hotels.

Camping CAMPGROUND $
(☎800-710-2267; www.campsd.com; tent sites $19-30, cabins $50) You can pitch a tent in eight campgrounds around the park. At four, you can rent a well-equipped camping cabin. Reservations are vital in summer. Backcountry camping ($7 per person per night) is allowed in the French Creek Natural Area.

Custer State Park Resorts RESORT $$
(☎888-875-0001; www.custerresorts.com) The park has five impressive resorts with a mix of lodge rooms and cabins starting at $100 and going much higher. Book well ahead.

Information

Peter Norbeck Visitor Center (☎605-255-4464; www.custerstatepark.info; US 16A; ⏲8am-8pm Jun-Aug, 9am-5pm Sep-May) Located on the east side of the Custer State Park, this facility has good exhibits and offers activities like guided nature walks.

Wind Cave National Park

Wind Cave National Park NATIONAL PARK
(☎605-745-4600; www.nps.gov/wica; off US 385; tours adult $10-30, child $5-6; ⊙visitor center 9am-6pm Jun-Aug, reduced hours Sep-May) This park, protecting 44 sq miles of grassland and forest, sits just south of Custer State Park. The central draw is, of course, the cave, which contains 132 miles of mapped passages. The strong wind gusts, which are felt at the entrance, but not inside, give the cave its name. The **visitor center** has details on the variety of **tours** that are offered. The four-hour Wild Cave Tour offers an orgy of spelunking.

The cave's foremost feature is its 'boxwork' calcite formations (95% of all that are known exist here), which look like honeycomb and date back 60 to 100 million years. **Hiking** is a popular activity in the park, where you'll find the southern end of the 111-mile **Centennial Trail** to Sturgis. The campground usually has space ($18 per site); backcountry camping (free with permit) is allowed in limited areas.

Jewel Cave National Monument

Jewel Cave National Monument CAVE
(☎605-673-8300; www.nps.gov/jeca; off US 16; tours adult $4-31, child free-$8; ⊙visitor center 8am-6pm Jun-Aug, reduced hours Sep-May) If you'll only visit one Black Hills cave, this would be a good choice. It's 13 miles west of Custer and is so named because calcite crystals line nearly all of its walls. Currently 145 miles have been surveyed, making it the second-longest known cave in the world, although it is presumed to be the longest.

The **visitor center** has useful exhibits. **Tours** vary in length and difficulty and are offered on a first-come basis.

Hot Springs

This surprisingly attractive town, south of the main Black Hills circuit, boasts ornate 1890s red sandstone buildings and warm mineral springs feeding the Fall River.

Sights & Activities

You can fill your water bottles at **Kidney Springs**, just south of the **visitor center** (☎800-325-6991; www.hotsprings-sd.com; 801 S 6th St; ⊙9am-7pm Jun-Aug, reduced hours Sep-May), or swim at **Cascade Falls**, which is 71°F (22°C) all year, 11 miles south on US 71.

Mammoth Site HISTORIC SITE
(☎605-745-6017; www.mammothsite.com; 1800 US 18 bypass; adult/child $10/8; ⊙8am-8pm mid-May–mid-Aug, reduced hours mid-Aug–mid-May) This is the country's largest left-as-found mammoth fossil display. Hundreds of animals perished in a sinkhole here about 26,000 years ago.

Evans Plunge SWIMMING
(☎605-745-5165; www.evansplunge.com; 1145 N River St; adult/child $12/10; ⊙10am-9pm Jun-Aug, reduced hours Sep-May) The water at this indoor geothermal springs waterpark is always 87°F (30.5°C).

Sleeping

★**Red Rock River Resort** HOTEL $$
(☎605-745-4400; www.redrockriverresort.com; 603 N River St; r $85-135; ❄📶) This resort has cozy and stylish rooms in a beautiful 1891 downtown building, plus spa facilities (day passes for nonguests $25).

NEBRASKA

Those who just see Nebraska as 480 miles of blandness along I-80 are missing out on a lot. The Cornhusker State (they do grow a lot of ears) has beautiful river valleys and an often stark bleakness that is entrancing. Its links to the past – from vast fields of dinosaur remains to Native American culture to the toils of hardy settlers – provides a dramatic storyline. Alongside the state's sprinkling of cute little towns, Nebraska's two main cities, Omaha and Lincoln, are vibrant and artful.

The key to enjoying this long stoic stretch of country is to take the smaller roads, whether it's US 30 instead of I-80, US 20 to the Black Hills, or the lonely and magnificent US 2.

Information

Nebraska Association of Bed & Breakfasts (☎877-223-6222; www.nebraskabb.com)

Nebraska State Parks (☎reservations 402-471-1414; www.outdoornebraska.ne.gov) Vehicle permits cost $5/26 per day/year. Some campsites at popular parks are reservable; fees are $8 to $28 per night.

Nebraska Tourism Commission (☎402-471-3796; www.visitnebraska.com)

Omaha

Be careful if you're planning a quick pit stop in Omaha. Home to the brick-and-cobblestoned Old Market neighborhood, a booming riverfront, a lively music scene and several good museums, this town can turn a few hours into a few days.

Omaha grew to prominence as a transport hub. Its location on the Missouri River and proximity to the Platte River made it an important stop on the Oregon, California and Mormon Trails, and later the Union Pacific Railroad stretched west from here. These days Omaha is in the nation's top 10 for billionaires and Fortune 500 companies per capita.

Sights

It's easy to spend much of your Omaha visit in Old Market on the river edge of downtown. This revitalized warehouse district, full of restaurants bars and funky shops, exudes energy and sophistication. Nearby parks boast fountains and waterside walks.

★Durham Museum MUSEUM
(☎402-444-5071; www.durhammuseum.org; 801 S 10th St; adult/child $9/6; ⏲10am-8pm Tue, to 5pm Wed-Sat, 1-5pm Sun) The soaring art-deco Union Station train depot houses a remarkable museum. Covering local history from the Lewis and Clark expedition to the Omaha stockyards to the trains that once called here, the Durham makes the most of its beautiful surrounds. The soda fountain still serves hot dogs and phosphate sodas. The museum offers themed **historic tours** ($25) of Omaha several days a week in summer.

Riverfront WATERFRONT
(8th St & Riverfront Dr) The riverfront along the Missouri River, downtown, has been massively spiffed up. Highlights include the architecturally stunning **Bob Kerry Pedestrian Bridge**, which soars over to Iowa; the **Heartland of America Park**, with fountains and lush botanical gardens; and **Lewis & Clark Landing**, where the explorers did just that in 1804. The riverfront is also home to the **Lewis & Clark National Historical Trail Visitors Center** (☎402-661-1804; www.nps.gov/lecl; 601 Riverfront Dr; ⏲9am-5pm daily May-Oct, Mon-Fri Nov-Apr), which has exhibits and a bookstore.

Joslyn Art Museum MUSEUM
(☎402-342-3300; www.joslyn.org; 2200 Dodge St; ⏲10am-4pm Tue, Wed & Fri-Sun, to 8pm Thu) FREE This admired and architecturally imposing museum has a great collection of 19th- and 20th-century European and American art. There's also a good selection of Western-themed works, plus a cool sculpture garden.

★Union Pacific Railroad Museum MUSEUM
(www.uprrmuseum.org; 200 Pearl St; ⏲10am-4pm Tue-Sat) FREE Just across the river in the cute little downtown area of Council Bluffs, IA, this grand museum tells the story of the world's most profitable railroad and the company that rammed the transcontinental line west from here in the 1860s. Look for the pictures of Ronald Reagan and his chimp-pal Bonzo aboard a train.

NEBRASKA FACTS

Nickname Cornhusker State

Population 1.9 million

Area 77,360 sq miles

Capital city Lincoln (population 269,000)

Other cities Omaha (population 435,000)

Sales tax 5.5% to 7%

Birthplace of Dancer Fred Astaire (1899–1987), civil rights leader Malcolm X (1925–65), billionaire Warren Buffett (b 1930), actor Hilary Swank (b 1974)

Home of Air Force generals

Politics Solid Republican

Famous for Johnny Carson, corn

Official beverage Milk

Driving distances Omaha to the Wyoming border on I-80 480 miles, Omaha to Kansas City 186 miles

Sleeping

There is a good mix of midrange and budget hotels along US 275 near 60th St, at I-80 exits 445 and 449, and across the river in Council Bluffs, IA, at I-29 exit 51. Old Market and downtown have several midrange chains.

Magnolia Hotel HISTORIC HOTEL **$$**
(☎402-341-2500; www.magnoliahotelomaha.com; 1615 Howard St; r $130-200; ❄@🛜🐾) Not far from Old Market, the Magnolia is a boutique hotel housed in a restored 1923 Italianate high-rise. The 145 rooms have a vibrant, modern style. Rates include a full buffet breakfast and bedtime milk and cookies.

Eating & Drinking

You can just wander Old Market and see what you find, especially on a balmy night when you want a drink. Or you can seek out some of Omaha's attention-getting restaurants.

Ted & Wally's Ice Cream ICE CREAM $
(☎402-341-5827; www.tedandwallys.com; 1120 Jackson St; ice cream from $3; ⊙11am-11pm Jun-Aug, to 10pm Sep-May) Ultra-creamy ice cream in myriad flavors made fresh daily.

★**Grey Plume** MODERN AMERICAN $$$
(☎402-763-4447; www.thegreyplume.com; 220 S 31st Ave; mains bar $9-18, restaurant $24-36; ⊙5-10pm Mon-Sat) West of downtown in Midtown Crossing, chef Clayton Chapman has upturned perceptions of Great Plains cuisine with his fiercely local and seasonal dishes. Winners: the bar burger, the duck-fat fries, the steaks, and anything with trout.

★**Boiler Room** MODERN AMERICAN $$$
(☎402-916-9274; www.boilerroomomaha.com; 1110 Jones St; mains $28-30; ⊙5:30-9pm Mon-Thu, to 10pm Fri & Sat) Global influences and French techniques shape the locally sourced foods that comprise the seasonal dishes at this trendsetting Old Market bistro. It's got an open kitchen and a cocktail bar. Want an Omaha steak? Get the Wagyu beef.

Mister Toad's PUB
(☎402-345-4488; 1002 Howard St; ⊙noon-1am) Sit out front on benches under big trees or nab a corner table inside. It's woodsy, worn and flirting with dive-bar status. There's live jazz Sunday nights.

Information

Reader (www.thereader.com) Good entertainment listings.

Visitor Center (☎866-937-6624; www.visitomaha.com; 1001 Farnam St; ⊙10am-4pm; 📶) Near Old Market.

Getting There & Away

Amtrak's *California Zephyr* stops in Omaha on its run between northern California and Chicago.

Around Omaha

If you see large military planes drifting slowly across the sky, they're likely headed for one of Omaha's large air-force bases.

After WWII Omaha's Offutt Air Force Base was home to the US Air Force Strategic Air Command, the nuclear force detailed in *Dr Strangelove*. This legacy is documented at the cavernous **Strategic Air & Space Museum** (☎402-944-3100; www.strategic-airandspace.com; 28210 West Park Hwy, I-80 exit 426; adult/child $12/6; ⊙9am-5pm), which bulges with bombers, from the B-17 to the B-52. Don't expect exhibits looking at the wider implications of bombing. It's 30 miles southwest of Omaha.

WORTH A TRIP

AMERICA'S FIRST HOMESTEAD

The **Homestead National Monument** (☎402-223-3514; www.nps.gov/home; off Hwy 4; ⊙heritage center 9am-5pm, trails dawn-dusk) is the site of the very first homestead granted under the landmark Homestead Act of 1862. It opened much of the western US to settlers who were given land if they made it productive. The pioneering Freeman family is buried here and you can see their reconstructed log house. The heritage center is a striking building with good displays. The site is 4 miles west of Beatrice, and 35 miles south of Lincoln via US 77.

Lincoln

Home to the historic Haymarket District and a lively bar scene thanks to the huge downtown campus of the University of Nebraska, Lincoln makes a good overnight stop.

Sights

University of Nebraska UNIVERSITY
(☎402-472-7211; www.unl.edu) The university has its main campus in the middle of town. The complex is as practical as a farmer and lacks highlights, but is an interesting stroll. You will, however, score plenty of excitement on one of the seven fall Saturdays when the Cornhuskers football team plays at home; on these days passions run high and games are sold out.

State Capitol LANDMARK
(☎402-471-0448; www.capitol.org; 1445 K St; ⊙8am-5pm Mon-Fri, 10am-5pm Sat, 1-5pm Sun, tours hourly) FREE From the outside, Nebraska's remarkable 1932 400ft-high state capitol represents the apex of phallic architecture (like many tall buildings in the Plains, it's

SCENIC DRIVE: NEBRASKA'S SANDHILLS

Nebraska's **Hwy 2** branches northwest from I-80 and Grand Island through Broken Bow 272 miles to Alliance in the panhandle. It crosses the lonely and lovely Sandhills – 19,000 sq miles of sand dunes covered in grass – one of the country's most isolated areas. With the wind whistling in your ears, the distant call of a hawk and the biggest skies imaginable, this is pure Great Plains travel.

often called 'the penis on the prairie'), while the symbolically rich interior curiously combines classical and art-deco motifs. Enjoy views from the 14th-floor observation decks.

Sleeping

Most hotels are near I-80. Those around exit 403 are mostly midrange, while there are budget motels aplenty at exit 399. There are also some midrange chains downtown.

Rogers House B&B $$
(402-476-6961; www.rogershouseinn.com; 2145 B St; r $90-180;) Close to downtown, the 11 rooms here are spread out over two adjoining 100-year-old houses. Refreshingly, the decor eschews the froufrou silliness of many B&Bs.

Eating

Lincoln's Haymarket District, a strolling-friendly six-block warehouse area dating from the early 20th century, has cafes, restaurants, coffeehouses and bars. If you're after wings followed by beer and body shots, follow the undergrads down O St to 14th St.

★**Indigo Bridge** CAFE $
(402-477-7770; www.indigobridgebooks.com; 701 P St; mains $5; 8am-10pm Mon-Sat, noon-6pm Sun;) This fine Haymarket cafe in a fantastic bookstore serves excellent coffee, snacks and sandwiches throughout the day.

Yia Yia's Pizza PIZZA $
(402-477-9166; www.yiayiaspizza.com; 1423 O St; mains $8-15; 11am-1pm Mon-Sat, noon-9pm Sun) Many a hangover has been chased away by the cheesy, gooey goodness at this Lincoln legend. The pizzas are cracker-thin, the regional tap-beer list thick.

★**Bread & Cup** CAFE $$
(402-438-2255; www.breadandcup.com; 440 N 8th St; mains $8-28; 7am-9pm Mon-Wed, to 10pm Thu-Sat, 10am-2pm Sun;) Boxes of beautiful Nebraska produce line the entry at this trendsetting Haymarket cafe where even common dishes (such as a pulled pork sandwich) are elevated to something special.

Information

Visitor Center (800-423-8212; www.lincoln.org; 201 N 7th St; 9am-6pm Mon-Thu, to 8pm Fri, 8am-2pm Sat & Sun Jun-Aug, reduced hours Sep-May) Inside Haymarket's Lincoln Station, where Amtrak's *California Zephyr* stops.

Along I-80

Shortly after Lincoln, I-80 runs an almost razor-straight 83 miles before following the Platte River. Several towns along its route to Wyoming make up for its often monotonous stretches. Whenever possible, use parallel US 30, which bounces from one interesting burg to the next (**Gothenburg**, exit 211, is especially attractive) and gets you closer to the river. It follows the busy Union Pacific (UP) mainline the entire way.

Grand Island & Around

A classic mid-sized Nebraska town along the Platte River Valley, Grand Island is a good place to stop and learn about the region.

Sights

★**Stuhr Museum of the Prairie Pioneer** MUSEUM
(308-385-5316; www.stuhrmuseum.org; 3133 W Hwy 34, I-80 exit 312; adult/child $8/6; 9am-5pm Mon-Sat, noon-5pm Sun;) A remarkable combination of museum exhibits with a vast outdoor living museum. Note how conditions dramatically improved from the homes in 1860 to 1890 thanks to riches made possible by the railroad.

Nebraska Nature & Visitor Center NATURE RESERVE
(308-382-1820; www.nebraskanature.org; 9325 S Alda Rd, I-80 exit 305; admission free, tours $25; 8am-6pm daily Mar, 9am-5pm Mon-Sat Apr-Feb) Upstream of Grand Island, the Platte hosts 500,000 sandhill cranes (80% of the world population) and 15 million waterfowl during the spring migration (mid-February to early

April). This nature center is a good place for viewing and has worthwhile hikes year-round.

Kearney

Like the larger towns along I-80, Kearny has all the usual chains at the exits and a more interesting old brick downtown by the UP tracks and US 30.

Arching unexpectedly over I-80 east of Kearney, the multimedia exhibits at the **Great Platte River Road Archway Monument** (☎308-237-1000; www.archway.org; 3060 East 1st St, near exit 272; adult/child $12/6; ⏲9am-6pm Mon-Sat, noon-6pm Sun May-Sep, reduced hours Oct-Apr; 👪) tell colorful tales about the people who've passed this way, from those riding wagon trains to those zipping down the interstate.

North Platte

North Platte, a rail-fan mecca, is home to the **Golden Spike Tower** (☎308-532-9920; www.goldenspiketower.com; 1249 N Homestead Rd; adult/child $7/5; ⏲9am-7pm May-Sep, to 5pm Oct-Apr); enjoy sweeping views of Union Pacific's Bailey Yard, the world's largest railroad yard, from this eight-story observation tower with indoor and outdoor decks. From I-80, take exit 177 and follow the signs.

Along US 20

The further west you go on US 20, the more space – and sandhills – you'll see between towns, trees and pickup trucks. The western end of the road, known as the **Bridges to Buttes Byway** (www.bridgestobuttes.com), traverses a Nebraska barely touched by time.

Valentine

Fortunately, 'America's Heart City' doesn't milk the schtick. It sits on the edge of the Sandhills and is a great base for canoeing, kayaking and inner-tubing the winding canyons of the federally protected **Niobrara National Scenic River** (www.nps.gov/niob). The river crosses the **Fort Niobrara National Wildlife Refuge** (☎402-376-3789; www.fws.gov/fortniobrara; Hwy 12; ⏲visitor center 8am-4:30pm daily Jun-Aug, Mon-Fri Sep-May). Driving tours here take you past bison, elk and more.

Floating down the river draws scores of people through the summer. Sheer limestone bluffs, lush forests and over 200 spring-fed waterfalls along the banks shatter any 'flat Nebraska' stereotypes. Most float tours are based in Valentine (www.visitvalentine.com).

> **WORTH A TRIP**
>
> **CARHENGE**
>
> **Carhenge** (www.carhenge.com; Hwy 87; ⏲24hr) Pay homage to the auto at this Stonehenge replica assembled from 38 discarded cars. The faithful reproduction, along with other car-part art, rises out of a field 3 miles north of Alliance and US 385, the road to the Black Hills. It will be in the path of a direct solar eclipse on August 21, 2017.

Northern Panhandle

The remote and little visited part of Nebraska panhandle is for many the most evocative part of the state. Stark vistas stretch to the horizon in lands little changed in millennia. **Scottsbluff** makes a good base. Heading north, **Hwy 29** (aka the 'Fossil Freeway') is a great drive and it segues right onto equally scenic US 20.

Sights

★Scotts Bluff National Monument PARK

(☎308-436-9700; www.nps.gov/scbl; Hwy 92, Gering; per car $5; ⏲visitor center 8am-7pm Jun-Aug, to 5pm Sep-May; 👪) Scotts Bluff has been a beacon to travelers for centuries. Rising 800ft above the flat plains of western Nebraska, it was an important waypoint on the Oregon Trail in the mid-19th century. You can still see wagon ruts today. The **visitor center** has displays and can guide you to walks and drives. It's south of Scottsbluff town.

★Agate Fossil Beds National Monument MONUMENT

(☎308-668-2211; www.nps.gov/agfo; River Rd, off Hwy 29; ⏲9am-5pm Jun-Aug, 8am-4pm Sep-May) FREE Some 20 million years ago, this part of Nebraska was like the Serengeti in Africa today: a gathering place for a rich variety of creatures. Today the bones of thousands of these ancient dinosaurs are found at this isolated site. Displays and walks detail the amazing – and ongoing – finds. Don't miss the Bone Cabin and the burrowing beaver plus the Native American exhibits.

Fort Robinson State Park HISTORIC SITE

(☎308-665-2900; www.outdoornebraska.ne.gov; Hwy 20, Crawford; museum adult/child $2/free;

CHASING TORNADOES

Much of the Great Plains is prone to severe weather, including violent thunderstorms, hail the size of softballs, spectacular lightning storms and more. Tornadoes, however, are the real stars of these meteorological nightmares. Far less benign than the cyclones that carried Dorothy off to Oz, every year tornadoes cause death and destruction from the Great Plains east across the central US.

With winds of 300mph or more, tornadoes are both awesome and terrifying. Still, each year many people visit the region hoping to spot a funnel cloud, drawn by the sheer spectacle and elemental drama.

Tour companies use gadget-filled vans to chase storms across multiple states, with no guarantee that you'll actually see a storm. Costs average $200 to $400 a day; April to July offer the best spotting. Operators include the following:

➡ **Cloud 9 Tours** (☎405-323-1145; www.cloud9tours.com)

➡ **Silver Lining Tours** (☎720-273-3948; www.silverliningtours.com)

➡ **Tempest Tours** (☎817-274-9313; www.tempesttours.com)

The book *Storm Kings: The Untold History of America's First Tornado Chasers* by Lee Sandlin, is an excellent and surprise-filled account of early tornado research. Read the recollections of veteran tornado chaser Roger Hill in *Hunting Nature's Fury.*

park dawn-dusk, museum 8:30am-5pm daily May-Aug, reduced hours Sep-Apr) This old military fort's turbulent past belies its stately appearance today: Crazy Horse was killed here in 1877, 'buffalo soldier' African American brigades were formed, it was a POW camp for Germans, and more.

Museum of the Fur Trade MUSEUM
(☎308-432-3843; www.furtrade.org; US 20; adult/child $5/free; 8am-5pm May-Oct;) Get a feel for the tough lives led by early settlers at this idiosyncratic museum. The best part is the reconstructed sod-roofed trading post where pelts were swapped for guns, blankets and whiskey from 1837 to 1876. It's 4 miles east of Chadron.

KANSAS

Wicked witches and yellow-brick roads, pitched battles over slavery and tornadoes powerful enough to pulverize entire towns are some of the more lurid images of Kansas. But the common image – amber waves of grain from north to south and east to west is closer to reality.

There's a simple beauty to the green rolling hills (six states are flatter) and limitless horizons. Places such as Chase County beguile those who value understatement. Gems abound, from the superb space museum in Hutchinson to the indie music clubs of Lawrence. Most importantly, follow the Great Plains credo of ditching the interstate for the two-laners and make your own discoveries. The website www.kansassampler.org is a brilliant resource.

Information

Kansas Bed & Breakfast Association (☎888-572-2632; www.kbba.com)

Kansas State Parks (www.ksoutdoors.com) Per vehicle per day/year $5/25. Campsites cost $8 to $20.

Kansas Travel & Tourism (☎785-296-2009; www.travelks.com)

Wichita

From its early cow-town days at the head of the Chisholm Trail in the 1870s to its current claim as Air Capital of the World (thanks to about half the world's general aviation aircraft being built here by the likes of Cessna and others), Kansas' largest city is a worthwhile stopover, but not at the expense of the rest of the state.

Sights

Wichita's historic, all-brick **Old Town**, good for shopping, eating and drinking, is on the east side of downtown.

The **Museums on the River** district includes a number of museums, plus botanical gardens and a science center aimed at kids. It fills a triangle of green space between the

Big and Little Arkansas Rivers to the west of downtown.

★ Old Cowtown Museum MUSEUM
(☎316-219-1871; www.oldcowtown.org; 1865 Museum Blvd; adult/child $8/5.50; ⏲10am-5pm Tue-Sat, noon-5pm Sun May-Oct, 10am-5pm Tue-Sat Nov-Apr; 👪) An open-air museum that re-creates the Wild West (as seen on TV...). Pioneer-era buildings, staged gunfights and guides in cowboy costumes thrill kids. Enjoy the river walks.

Mid-America All-Indian Center MUSEUM
(☎316-350-3340; www.theindiancenter.org; 650 N Seneca St; adult/child $7/3; ⏲10am-4pm Tue-Sat) Guarded by Wichita artist Blackbear Bosin's 44ft statue 'Keeper of the Plains,' this museum has exhibits of Native American art and artifacts, as well as a traditional Wichita-style grass lodge.

Exploration Place MUSEUM
(☎316-660-0600; www.exploration.org; 300 N McLean Blvd; adult/child from $10/6; ⏲10am-5pm Mon-Sat, noon-5pm Sun; 👪) Right on the river confluence, this architecturally striking museum has no end of cool exhibits, including a tornado chamber where you can feel 75mph winds and a sublime erosion model where you can see water create a new little Kansas.

Sleeping

Hotbeds for chains include I-135 exit 1AB, I-35 exit 50 and the Hwy 96 Rock Rd and Webb Rd exits. Broadway north of the center offers a mixed bag of indie cheapies.

Hotel at Old Town HOTEL $$
(☎316-267-4800; www.hotelatoldtown.com; 830 1st St; r $100-200; P❄@📶) In the midst of Old Town nightlife, this restored hotel is housed in the 1906 factory of the Keen Kutter Corp, a maker of household goods. Rooms have high ceilings, fridges and microwaves, and there's a good breakfast buffet.

Eating

Wichita is the home of Pizza Hut, but that's far from the pinnacle of the city's dining options. For some real-deal Mexican or Vietnamese, drive north on Broadway and take your pick.

★ Doo-Dah Diner DINER $
(☎316-265-7011; www.doodahdiner.com; 206 E Kellogg Dr; mains $5-9; ⏲7am-2pm Wed-Sun) The model for diners everywhere. This bustling local downtown fave has fabulous chow, including corned-beef hash, banana-bread French toast and eggs Benedict.

Anchor AMERICAN $
(☎316-260-8989; www.anchorwichita.com; 1109 E Douglas Ave; mains $7-12; ⏲11am-late) On the edge of Old Town, this vintage pub has high ceilings, a tiled floor, a great beer selection and tasty food. The good burgers and specials totally outclass the nearby chain and theme bars.

Along I-70

What it lacks in glamor, Kansas' 420-mile 'Main Street' makes up for in efficiency, quickly shuttling you from Kansas City to the Colorado border. West of Salina, the landscape around I-70 stretches into rolling, wide-open plains, with small wind-blown towns like **Hays**, which did a desolate turn in many scenes in the 1973 film *Paper Moon*. US 50 and US 56 are intriguing alternatives.

Lawrence

Forty miles west of Kansas City, Lawrence has been an island of progressive politics from

KANSAS FACTS

Nickname Sunflower State

Population 2.9 million

Area 82,282 sq miles

Capital city Topeka (population 128,000)

Other cities Wichita (population 386,000)

Sales tax 6.15% to 9.8%

Birthplace of Temperance crusader Carrie Nation (1846–1911), Aviator Amelia Earhart (1897–1937), Pizza Hut (established 1958), singer-songwriter Melissa Etheridge (b 1961)

Home of Dorothy and Toto (of *Wizard of Oz* fame)

Politics Very conservative

Famous for Wheat

Official state song 'Home on the Range'

Driving distances Wichita to Kansas City 200 miles, Dodge City to Abilene 188 miles

the start. Founded by abolitionists in 1854 and an important stop on the Underground Railroad, it became a battlefield in the clash between pro- and antislavery factions. In 1863 the Missouri 'Bushwhackers' of William Clarke Quantrill raided Lawrence, killing nearly 200 people and burning much of it to the ground. The city survived, however, and so did its free-thinking spirit, which is fitting for the home of the University of Kansas.

Sights

The appealing downtown, where townies and students merge, centers on Massachusetts St, one of the most pleasant streets in this part of the country for a stroll.

Spencer Museum of Art GALLERY
(785-864-4710; www.spencerart.ku.edu; 1301 Mississippi St; 10am-4pm Tue, Fri & Sat, to 8pm Wed & Thu, noon-4pm Sun) FREE Encompassing work by Western artist Frederic Remington and many European masters, the museum is scheduled to reopen in mid-2016 after a massive revamp.

Sleeping & Eating

Lawrence's motels cluster at the junction of US 40 and US 59 south of I-70. The nightlife along five blocks of Massachusetts St makes Lawrence the state's best stop for the night.

Halcyon House B&B B&B $$
(888-441-0314; www.thehalcyonhouse.com; 1000 Ohio St; r $70-120;) The nine colorful bedrooms here (some share bathrooms) have lots of natural light, and there's a landscaped garden, and homemade baked goods for breakfast. Downtown is just a short walk away.

Eldridge Hotel HISTORIC HOTEL $$
(785-749-5011; www.eldridgehotel.com; 701 Massachusetts St; r $140-160;) The 56 modern two-room suites at this historic 1926 downtown hotel have antique-style furnishings. The bar and restaurant are stylish, the ghost misunderstood (rumors abound).

★**Free State Brewing** PUB FOOD $
(626-414-3210; www.freestatebrewing.com; 636 Massachusetts St; mains $8-20; 11am-midnight) One of many good places on Mass downtown, this is the first brewery in Kansas since Carrie Nation got one closed in 1880. The beers are excellent, and the food creative, with daily specials.

Ladybird Diner AMERICAN $
(785-856-5239; www.ladybirddiner.com; 721 Massachusetts St; mains $4-10; 7am-10pm) A retro diner made good, everything is better at this throwback, which has a fresh and tasty ethos. Seasonal fruit pies are the bomb.

Entertainment

Bottleneck LIVE MUSIC
(785-841-5483; www.bottlenecklive.com; 737 New Hampshire St; 3pm-2am) The music scene in town is up to college-town standards, and this joint usually has the best of the newest.

Information

Visitor Information Center (785-865-4499; www.visitlawrence.com; 402 N 2nd St; 9am-5pm Mon-Sat, 1-5pm Sun) In the restored old Union Pacific depot.

KANSAS: DETOURS & EXTRAS

Nicodemus This is the only surviving town in the west built by emancipated slaves from the south after the Civil War. A national park **visitor center** (785-839-4233; www.nps.gov/nico; 304 Washington Ave; 9am-4:30pm) FREE recounts the tiny town's history and the experience of African Americans in the west. The town is 12 miles east of Hill City on US 24 and about 35 miles north of I-70.

Fort Scott (620-223-0310; www.nps.gov/fosc; Old Fort Blvd; 8am-5pm) FREE This restored fort near the Missouri border dates to 1842. While the parade grounds and buildings in the heart of its namesake city are interesting, the real draw here is the story of the battles between pro- and antislavery forces that were fought here before the Civil War.

Home on the Range Cabin (www.thehomeontherange.com; Hwy 8; 24hr) The iconic song of the American west, 'Home on the Range,' was written by Brewster M Higley in 1871 at a remote cabin in northern Kansas. Today you can visit the lovely and evocative site of the original cabin where even if you don't see any deer and antelope at play, you'll easily feel the magic that inspired Higley. It's eight sing-posted miles north of a turn off US 36, which is one mile west of Athol.

ROUTE 66: GET YOUR KICKS IN KANSAS

Only 13 miles of Route 66 pass through the southeast corner of Kansas, but it's a good drive along Hwy 66 and US 69.

Three miles down the road is **Riverton**, where you might consider a detour 20 miles north to Crawford County where legendary fried chicken is a hallmark of six famous restaurants around **Pittsburg**. Try **Chicken Mary's** (☎620-231-9460; 1133 E 600th Ave, Pittsburg; meals from $7; ⏲4-8:30pm Tue-Sat, 11am-8pm Sun), one of the best.

Cross US 400 and stay on old Route 66 to the 1923 **Marsh Rainbow Arch Bridge**, the last of its kind.

From the bridge, it's less than 3 miles south to **Baxter Springs**, the site of a Civil War massacre and numerous bank robberies. A restored 1939 Phillips 66 gas station is the **Kansas Route 66 Visitor Center** (☎620-856-2385; www.baxterspringsmuseum.org; cnr 10th St & Military Ave; ⏲10am-4:30pm Mon-Sat, 1-4pm Sun). Military Ave (US 69A) takes you into Oklahoma.

Topeka

Kansas and its vital role in America's race relations is symbolized in the otherwise humdrum state capital of Topeka.

Sights

★Brown v Board of Education National Historic Site MUSEUM
(☎785-354-4273; www.nps.gov/brvb; 1515 SE Monroe St; ⏲9am-5pm) FREE It took real guts to challenge the segregationist laws common in the US in the 1950s and the stories of these courageous men and women are here. Set in Monroe Elementary School, one of Topeka's African American schools at the time of the landmark 1954 Supreme Court decision that banned segregation in US schools, the displays cover the entire Civil Rights movement.

State Capitol LANDMARK
(☎785-296-3966; www.kshs.org/capitol; 300 SW 10th St; ⏲8am-5pm daily, tours 9am-3pm Mon-Fri) FREE Under the huge copper dome, don't miss the fiery John Steuart Curry mural of abolitionist John Brown. Climb 296 steps for great views outside.

Kansas Museum of History MUSEUM
(☎785-272-8681; www.kshs.org; 6425 SW 6th Ave; adult/child $8/6; ⏲9am-5pm Tue-Sat, 1-5pm Sun) From a Cheyenne war lance to Carrie Nation's hammer, this engaging center is packed with Kansas stories.

Eating

Porubsky's Grocery DELI $
(☎785-234-5788; 508 NE Sardou Ave; mains $4-7; ⏲10am-5pm Mon-Fri, to 3pm Sat) Hard by the old Santa Fe mainline close to downtown, this old Russian deli has been serving up simple sandwiches since 1947. The chili (only Monday to Thursday, September to April) is best with piles of crackers. Try the housemade horseradishy pickles.

Abilene

In the late 19th century, Abilene was a rowdy cow town at the end of the Chisholm Trail. Today its compact core of historic brick buildings and well-preserved neighborhoods seems perfectly appropriate for the birthplace of Dwight D Eisenhower (1890–1969), president and general.

Sights

Eisenhower Presidential Center MUSEUM
(☎785-263-6700; www.eisenhower.archives.gov; 200 SE 4th St; museum adult/child $12/3; ⏲8am-5:45pm Jun-Aug, 9am-4:45pm Sep-May) Fittingly set against a backdrop of grain elevators, the rather regal Eisenhower Center includes Ike's boyhood home, a museum and library, and his and Mamie's graves. Displays cover the Eisenhower presidential era (1953–61) and his role as allied commander in WWII. A highlight is the original text of his speech warning about the military-industrial complex.

Eating

Brookville Hotel AMERICAN $$
(www.brookvillehotel.com; 105 E Lafayette St; meals $16; ⏲11am-2pm & 4-7:30pm Wed-Sun) The Brookville Hotel has been serving fried chicken since Ike graduated from West Point (1915). Cream-style corn, fresh biscuits and much more come with every meal.

WORTH A TRIP

AMERICA'S BEST SPACE MUSEUM

Kansas Cosmosphere & Space Center (☎800-397-0330; www.cosmo.org; 1100 N Plum St, Hutchinson; all-attraction pass adult/child $23/21, museum only $12.50/10.50; ⏲9am-7pm Mon-Sat, noon-7pm Sun; 👪) Possibly the most surprising sight in Kansas, this amazing museum captures the race to the moon better than any museum on the planet. Absorbing displays and artifacts such as the Apollo 13 command module will enthrall you for hours. The museum is regularly called in to build props for Hollywood movies portraying the space race, including *Apollo 13*.

The museum's isolated location in Hutchinson is an easy day trip from Wichita or diversion off I-70.

Lucas

'Outsider art,' meaning works created outside the bounds of traditional culture, has blossomed in tiny Lucas. It's best reached via the **Post Rock Scenic Byway,** a picturesque 18-mile jaunt past Wilson Lake starting at I-70 exit 206.

Sights

★Garden of Eden GALLERY

(☎785-525-6395; www.garden-of-eden-lucas-kansas.com; 301 2nd St; adult/child $7/2; ⏲10am-5pm May-Oct, 1-4pm Mar & Apr, 1-4pm Sat & Sun Nov-Feb) In 1907 Samuel Dinsmoor began filling his yard with enormous concrete sculptures reflecting his eccentric philosophies. On a tour you hear some wonderful stories and see his remains in a glass-topped coffin (!).

Grassroots Art Center GALLERY

(☎785-525-6118; www.grassrootsart.net; 213 S Main St; adult/child $7/3; ⏲10am-5pm Mon-Sat, 1-5pm Sun May-Sep, 1-4pm Thu-Mon Oct & Apr, 1-4pm Thu-Sat Nov-Mar) A phenomenal collection of works made of buttons, barbed wire, pull-tabs and more.

Along US 50

Fabled US 50 splits off from I-35 at Emporia and follows the old Santa Fe mainline west through classic Kansas vistas.

Chase County

Nearly a perfect square, this is the county William Least Heat-Moon examined mile by mile in his best-selling *PrairyErth*. The beautiful Flint Hills roll through here and are home to two-thirds of the nation's remaining tallgrass prairie. Don't miss the showstopping **County Courthouse** in **Cottonwood Falls**, 2 miles south of Strong City. Completed in 1873, it is a fantasy of French Renaissance style.

Sights

Tallgrass Prairie National Preserve NATURE RESERVE

(☎620-273-8494; www.nps.gov/tapr; Hwy 177; ⏲buildings 8:30am-4:30pm, trails 24hr) FREE The 11,000-acre Tallgrass Prairie National Preserve, 2 miles northwest of Strong City and US 50, is a perfect place to hike the prairie and revel in its ever-changing colorful flowers. Rangers give tours of the preserved ranch and bus tours of the prairie from a beautiful visitor center. Rangers also have maps for evocative drives in the county, as well as a tour of sights from *PrairyErth*.

Along US 56

US 56 follows the old Santa Fe Trail to Dodge City through the heart of the heartland. Most sights along here are also easily reached from US 50.

The large Mennonite communities around **Hillsboro** are descendants of Russian immigrants who brought the 'Turkey Red' strain of wheat to the Plains, where it thrived despite harsh conditions.

Larned

In Larned, the grain starts to end and the evocative plains of the west begin.

Sights

★Fort Larned National Historic Site HISTORIC SITE

(☎620-285-6911; www.nps.gov/fols; Hwy 156; ⏲8:30am-4:30pm) FREE Six miles west of town, Fort Larned National Historic Site is a remarkably well-preserved fort in a lovely setting that's well worth the trip. The Santa Fe Trail passed right out front.

Santa Fe Trail Center Museum MUSEUM
(☎620-285-2054; www.santafetrailcenter.org; Hwy 156; adult/child $4/1.50; ⏲9am-5pm Tue-Sat) Two miles west of town, this open-air musuem details the vital route linking the US and Mexico for much of the 19th century.

Dodge City

Dodge City – where famous lawmen Bat Masterson and Wyatt Earp tried, sometimes successfully, to keep law and order – had a notorious reputation during the 1870s and 1880s. The long-running TV series *Gunsmoke* (1955–75) spurred interest. Geared towards mass tourism, historical authenticity here plays a distant third fiddle to fun and frolic.

Today the town milks its heritage while it slaughters over 10,000 head of cattle daily at huge factories. You may be inspired to get the hell out of Dodge.

The **visitor center** (☎800-653-9378; www.visitdodgecity.org; 400 W Wyatt Earp Blvd; ⏲8:30am-6:30pm daily Jun-Aug, to 5pm Mon-Fri Sep-May) has free walking and driving tours of historic sights. Chain motels and modest restaurants line Business US 50, aka Wyatt Earp Blvd.

Sights

The historic downtown, away from the attractions, is good for a wander. View surviving **Santa Fe Trail wagon-wheel ruts** about 9 miles west of town on US 50. The site is well marked.

Boot Hill Museum MUSEUM
(☎620-227-8188; www.boothill.org; 500 W Wyatt Earp Blvd; adult/child from $10/8; ⏲8am-8pm Jun-Aug, 9am-5pm Sep-May; 👪) This studio-backlot-like attraction includes a cemetery, jail and saloon, where (unrealistically clean) gunslingers reenact (unrealistically blood-free) shootouts while Miss Kitty and her (unrealistically wholesome) dancing gals do the cancan. It's next to an Applebee's.

OKLAHOMA

Oklahoma gets its name from the Choctaw name for 'Red People.' One look at the state's vividly red earth and you'll wonder if the name is more of a sartorial than an ethnic comment. Still, with 39 tribes located here, it is a place with deep Native American significance. Museums, cultural displays and more abound.

The other side of the Old West coin, cowboys, also figure prominently in the Sooner State. Although pickups have replaced horses, there's still a great sense of the open range, interrupted only by urban Oklahoma City and Tulsa. Oklahoma's share of Route 66 links some of the Mother Road's iconic highlights and there are myriad atmospheric old towns.

Information

Oklahoma Bed & Breakfast Association (www.okbba.com)

Oklahoma Tourism & Recreation Department (☎800-652-6552; www.travelok.com)

Oklahoma State Parks (www.travelok.com/state_parks) Most parks are free for day use; campsites cost $12 to $30 per night, and some are reservable. The website is a labyrinth.

Oklahoma City

Often abbreviated to OKC, Oklahoma City is nearly dead-center in the state and is the cultural and political capital. It has worked hard over the years to become more than just a cow town, all without turning its back on its cowboy heritage. It makes a good pause on your Route 66 travels.

The city is forever linked to the 1995 bombing of the Alfred P Murrah Federal Building; the memorials to this tragedy are moving.

Sights

You'll brush up against real cowboys in **Stockyards City** (www.stockyardscity.org; Agnew Ave & Exchange Ave), southwest of downtown, either in the shops and restaurants that cater to them or at the **Oklahoma National Stockyards** (www.onsy.com; 2501 Exchange Ave; ⏲auctions 8am Mon & Tue), the world's largest stocker and feeder cattle market.

★**Oklahoma City National Memorial Museum** MUSEUM
(www.oklahomacitynationalmemorial.org; 620 N Harvey Ave; adult/student $15/12; ⏲9am-6pm Mon-Sat, noon-6pm Sun) The story of America's worst incident of domestic terrorism is told at this poignant museum, which avoids becoming mawkish and lets the horrible events speak for themselves. The outdoor **Symbolic Memorial** has 168 empty chair sculptures for each of the people killed in the attack (the 19 small ones are for the children who perished in the day-care center).

OKLAHOMA FACTS

Nickname Sooner State

Population 3.9 million

Area 69,900 sq miles

Capital city Oklahoma City (population 611,000)

Other cities Tulsa (population 398,000)

Sales tax 4.5% to 11%

Birthplace of Humorist Will Rogers (1879–1935), athlete Jim Thorpe (1888–1953), folk musician Woody Guthrie (1912–67), actor James Garner (1928-2014), parking meters (invented 1935), country music singer Reba McEntire (b 1955)

Home of World Cow Chip Throwing Championship

Politics Deeply conservative

Famous for 1930s Dust Bowl, Carrie Underwood

Official state meal Okra, chicken fried steak and 10 more dishes

Driving distances Oklahoma City to Tulsa 104 miles, Kansas to Texas following historic Route 66 426 miles

National Cowboy & Western Heritage Museum MUSEUM
(☎405-478-2250; www.nationalcowboymuseum.org; 1700 NE 63rd St; adult/child $12.50/6; ⊙10am-5pm) Only the smells are missing. Vibrant historic displays are complemented by an excellent collection of Western painting and sculpture featuring many works by Charles M Russell and Frederic Remington.

Oklahoma History Center MUSEUM
(www.okhistory.org/historycenter; 800 Nazih Zuhdi Dr; adult/child $7/4; ⊙10am-5pm Mon-Sat) Near the capitol, this museum makes people the focus as it tells the story of the Sooner State.

State Capitol LANDMARK
(☎405-521-3356; 2300 N Lincoln Blvd; ⊙7am-7pm Mon-Fri, 9am-4pm Sat & Sun, tours 9am-3pm Mon-Fri) FREE Built in 1917, but only got its dome in 2002. Note the oil wells outside.

American Indian Cultural Center & Museum MUSEUM
(www.theamericanindiancenter.org; junction I-40 & I-35) This landmark center with its arresting design will be one of the premier Native American institutions in the world whenever it's completed (possibly 2017). In the meantime, however, budget wrangles have slowed construction.

Sleeping

Many older motels line I-35 south of town; newer chain properties stack up along I-44, the NW Expwy/Hwy 3 and at Bricktown (which puts you near nightlife action).

Grandison Inn at Maney Park B&B $$
(☎405-232-8778; www.grandisoninn.com; 1200 N Shartel St; r $110-190; P❄☜) In a genteel quarter of OKC just northwest of downtown, this gracious 1904-vintage B&B welcomes guests to eight rooms with period charm and modern amenities. The house has amazing woodwork, including a showstopping staircase.

Colcord Hotel BOUTIQUE HOTEL $$
(☎405-601-4300; www.colcordhotel.com; 15 N Robinson Ave; r $160-240; P❄@☜) OKC's first skyscraper, built in 1910, is now a luxurious 12-story hotel. Many original flourishes, such as the marble-clad lobby, survive, while the 108 rooms have a stylish, contemporary touch. It's near Bricktown.

Eating & Drinking

For listings, check out the weekly *Oklahoma Gazette* (www.okgazette.com) or just head to the renovated warehouses in the Bricktown District, which contain a vast array of bars and restaurants, some good, some purely chain.

Ann's Chicken Fry House SOUTHERN $
(☎405-943-8915; 4106 NW 39th St; mains $5-12; ⊙11am-8:30pm Tue-Sat) Part real diner, part tourist attraction, Ann's is a Route 66 veteran renowned for its – you guessed it – chicken fried steak. Okra and cream gravy also star, and the fried chicken lives up to the rep. Get the black-eyed peas.

★ **Cheever's Cafe** MODERN AMERICAN $$
(☎405-525-7007; www.cheeverscafe.com; 2409 N Hudson Ave; mains $10-25; ⊙11am-9pm Sun-Thu, to 10:30pm Fri, 5-10:30pm Sat) This former art-deco flower shop is now an upscale cafe with excellent Southern- and Mexican-influenced fare. The menu changes seasonally and is locally sourced. The ice-cream-ball dessert fills many a dream.

Cattlemen's Steakhouse STEAK $$
(☎405-236-0416; www.cattlemensrestaurant.com; 1309 S Agnew Ave; mains $7-30; ⏰6am-10pm Sun-Thu, to midnight Fri & Sat) OKC's most storied restaurant, this Stockyards City institution has been feeding cowpokes and city slickers slabs of beef since 1910. Deals are still cut at the counter (where you can jump the wait for tables) and back in the luxe booths.

Picasso's Cafe MODERN AMERICAN $$
(☎405-602-2002; www.picassosonpaseo.com; 3009 Paseo; mains $10-20; ⏰11am-late; ✍) A hip fusion of bistro, bar and venue, Picasso has a full bar and is renowned for its Bloody Mary's at noon. It also has an artistic sensibility, with works by local artists on display. Grab a table outside.

☆ Entertainment

Oklahoma City Dodgers BASEBALL
(www.okcdodgers.com; 2 Mickey Mantle Dr; tickets $10-30) The Triple A Dodgers play at Chickasaw Bricktown Ballpark.

Oklahoma City Thunder BASKETBALL
(www.nba.com/thunder; 100 W Reno Ave; tickets from $40) The NBA's Thunder play downtown at Chesapeake Energy Arena.

Shopping

Langston's CLOTHING
(☎405-235-9536; www.langstons.com; 2224 Exchange Ave; ⏰10am-8pm Mon-Sat, 1-6pm Sun) You can buy all forms of Western wear and gear in Stockyards City. Langston's has a vast selection.

ℹ Information

Oklahoma Welcome Center (☎405-478-4637; www.travelok.com; 1-35 exit 137; ⏰8am-5:30pm) Near the junction with I-44. Also has city info.

ℹ Getting There & Around

Amtrak (www.amtrak.com; 100 S EK Gaylord Blvd) The *Heartland Flyer* goes from OKC to Fort Worth ($29, 4¼ hours). Buy your ticket on the train.

Go Metro (www.gometro.org; single fare/day pass $1.75/4) Runs city buses.

Greyhound (☎405-606-4382; 1948 E Reno Ave) Daily buses to Dallas ($53, four to five hours), Wichita ($44, 2¾ hours) and Tulsa ($18, two hours, five daily), among other destinations.

Will Rogers World Airport (OKC; www.flyokc.com) Will Rogers World Airport is 5 miles southwest of downtown; a cab costs about $25 to downtown.

Western Oklahoma

West of Oklahoma City toward Texas the land opens into expansive prairie fields, nowhere as beautifully as in the Wichita Mountains, which, along with some Route 66 attractions and Native American sites, make this prime road-trip country.

US 281 also passes through beautiful landscapes.

Washita Battlefield National Historic Site

★Washita Battlefield National Historic Site HISTORIC SITE
(☎580-497-2742; www.nps.gov/waba; Hwy 47A; ⏰site dawn-dusk, visitor center 9am-5pm) FREE On November 27, 1868, George Custer's troops launched a dawn attack on the peaceful village of Chief Black Kettle. It was a slaughter of men, women, children and domestic animals, an act some would say led to karmic revenge on Custer eight years later.

Trails traverse the site of the killings, which is remarkably unchanged. An excellent visitor center 0.7 miles away contains a good **museum**; seasonal tours and talks are worthwhile. The site is 2 miles west of Cheyenne, 30 miles north of I-40 via US 283.

Tulsa

Self-billed as the 'Oil Capital of the World,' Tulsa has never dirtied its hands much on the black gold that oozes out elsewhere in the state. Rather, it is home to scores of energy companies that make their living drilling for oil, selling it or supplying those who do. The steady wealth this provides once helped create Tulsa's richly detailed art-deco downtown.

Today Tulsa suffers more than most from suburban sprawl, although the Brady Arts District downtown is a bright spot.

The website (www.visittulsa.com) is useful.

⊙ Sights

Downtown Tulsa has so much art-deco architecture it was once known as the 'Terra-Cotta City.' The **Philcade Building** (511 S Boston St), with its glorious T-shaped lobby, and the **Boston Avenue United Methodist Church** (1301 S Boston St) rising at the end of downtown, are two exceptional examples. Download a walking guide at www.visittulsa.com

by searching for 'downtown tulsa self-guided walking tour.'

The developing **Brady Arts District** is centered on Brady and Main Sts immediately north of downtown. It has galleries, venues and good restaurants.

★Woody Guthrie Center MUSEUM
(☎918-574-2710; www.woodyguthriecenter.org; 102 E Brady St; adult/child $8/6; ⏰10am-6pm Tue-Sun) Woody Guthrie gained fame for his 1930s folk ballads that told stories of the Dust Bowl and the depression. His life and music are recalled in this impressive new museum, where you can listen to his music and explore his legacy via the works of Dylan and more.

★Oklahoma Jazz Hall of Fame MUSEUM
(☎918-928-5299; www.okjazz.org; 111 E 1st St; Sun jazz concerts adult/child $15/5; ⏰9am-5pm Mon & Wed-Fri, to 9pm Tue, noon-7pm Sun, live music 5:30-8pm Tue) FREE Tulsa's beautiful Union Station is filled with sound again, but now it's melodious as opposed to cacophonous. During the first half of the 20th century, Tulsa was literally at the crossroads of American music with performers both homegrown and from afar. Learn about greats like Charlie Christian, Ernie Fields Senior and Wallace Willis in detailed exhibits. Sunday jazz concerts are played in the once-segregated grand concourse. On Tuesday nights there are free jam sessions.

OKLAHOMA: DETOURS & EXTRAS

Guthrie Oklahoma's first capital, 25 miles north of Oklahoma City, boasts streets lined with brick-and-stone Victorian buildings. The well-preserved downtown contains shops, museums, B&Bs and eateries.

Bartlesville This town still shows the riches that flowed from the ground during the first oil boom in 1905. The Phillips petroleum empire has left behind museums and a huge mansion. Soaring over it all is the 1956 221ft-tall **Price Tower** (☎918-336-4949; www.pricetower.org; 510 Dewey Ave; ⏰gallery hours vary, call for tour times), the only Frank Lloyd Wright–designed skyscraper ever built. It combines galleries, a hotel (rooms from $140) and a top-floor bar. Tours are offered.

Philbrook Museum of Art MUSEUM
(☎918-749-7941; www.philbrook.org; 2727 S Rockford Rd; adult/child $9/free; ⏰10am-5pm Tue, Wed & Fri-Sun, to 8pm Thu) South of town, this oil magnate's converted Italianate villa, ringed by fabulous foliage, houses fine Native American works and other classic art. There is a new second location, **Philbrook Downtown** (116 EMB Brady St; adult/child $7/free; ⏰11am-6pm Wed-Sat, noon-5pm Sun), in the Brady Arts District. It shows contemporary art.

Gilcrease Museum MUSEUM
(☎918-596-2700; www.gilcrease.org; 1400 Gilcrease Museum Rd; adult/child $8/free; ⏰10am-5pm Tue-Sun) Northwest of downtown, off Hwy 64, this superb American art museum sits on the manicured estate of a Native American who discovered oil on his allotment.

Sleeping

Chain motels aplenty line Hwy 244 and I-44, especially at the latter's exits 229 and 232. You can also recapture some of the adventure of Route 66 at several vintage motels on East 11th St, although quality varies widely.

Hotel Campbell HOTEL $$
(☎918-744-5500; www.thecampbellhotel.com; 2636 E 11th St; r $140-210; ❄📶) Restored to its 1927-era Route 66 splendor, this historic hotel east of downtown has 26 luxurious rooms with hardwood floors and plush period furniture. Ask for a tour.

Eating

Look for dining options in the Brookside neighborhood, on Peoria Ave between 31st and 51st Sts; on Historic Cherry St (now 15th St) just east of Peoria Ave; and in the Brady Arts District.

Ike's Chili House DINER $
(☎918-838-9410; www.ikeschilius.com; 1503 E 11th St; mains under $4-7; ⏰10am-7pm Mon-Fri, to 3pm Sat) Ike's has been serving chili for over 100 years and its classic version is much-loved. You can get it straight or over Fritos, a hot dog, beans or spaghetti. Top with red peppers, onions, jalapeños, saltines and cheddar cheese for pure joy.

Tally's Good Food Cafe AMERICAN $
(☎918-835-8039; 1102 S Yale Ave; mains $5-12; ⏰6am-11pm) Let the neon signs lure you into this diner at the corner with old Route 66, aka E 11th St. Huge omelets for breakfast segue to Tulsa's best chicken fried steaks and more classics.

★Tavern AMERICAN **$$**

(☎918-949-9801; www.taverntulsa.com; 201 N Main St; mains $10-30; ⏲11am-11pm Sun-Thu, to 1am Fri & Sat) This beautiful pub is a top choice in the Brady Arts District and serves excellent fare. The hamburgers are legendary or you can opt for steaks, salads or seasonal specials. The bartenders are true mixologists and there's a good wine list.

☆ Entertainment

Open-air **Guthrie Green** (www.guthriegreen.com; Boston Ave & Brady St), near the namesake cultural center in the Brady Arts District, often hosts events.

The *Urban Tulsa Weekly* (www.urbantulsa.com) has the scoop of what's going on.

★Cain's Ballroom LIVE MUSIC

(☎918-584-2306; www.cainsballroom.com; 423 N Main St) Rising rockers grace the boards where Bob Wills played Western swing in the '30s and the Sex Pistols caused confusion in 1978 (check out the hole Sid Vicious punched in a wall).

ℹ Getting There & Around

Greyhound (317 S Detroit Ave) Destinations include Oklahoma City ($18, two hours, five daily).

Tulsa Transit (www.tulsatransit.org; 2hr/1-day pass $1.75/3.25) The transit hub is downtown at 319 S Denver Ave.

Green Country

Subtle forested hills interspersed with iconic red dirt and lakes cover Oklahoma's northeast corner, aka Green Country (www.greencountryok.com), which includes Tulsa. The area has a strong Native American influence, as it is where several of the Five Civilized Tribes (Cherokee, Chickasaw, Choctaw, Creek and Seminole) were relocated in the 1820s and '30s.

LEGACY OF A RIOT

On Memorial Day, May 30, 1921 an African American man and a white woman were alone on an elevator in downtown Tulsa and the woman screamed. The how and why have never been answered, but it sparked three days of race riots in which 35 blocks of Tulsa's main African American neighborhood were destroyed by roving gangs and even by bombs lobbed from airplanes. Thousands were left homeless, hundreds injured and scores killed.

Near the center of the violence, the **John Hope Franklin Reconciliation Park** (www.jhfcenter.org; 415 N Detroit Ave; ⏲8am-8pm) tells the story of the riot.

Trail of Tears Country

The area southeast of present-day Tulsa was, and to some degree still is, Creek and Cherokee land. This is an excellent place to learn about Native American culture, especially before the 1800s.

Namesake of Merle Haggard's 1969 hit 'Okie from Muskogee?', **Muskogee**, 49 miles southeast of Tulsa, is home to the **Five Civilized Tribes Museum** (☎918-683-1701; www.fivetribes.org; 1101 Honor Heights Dr, Agency Hill; adult/student $3/2; ⏲10am-5pm Mon-Fri, to 2pm Sat). It's inside an 1875 Union Indian Agency house and recalls the cultures of the Native Americans forcibly moved here from America's southeast.

Twenty miles east on Hwy 62 is **Tahlequah** (tal-*ah*-quaw), the Cherokee capital since 1839. The excellent **Cherokee Heritage Center** (☎918-456-6007; www.cherokeeheritage.org; 21192 S Keeler Rd; adult/child $8.50/5; ⏲9am-5pm Mon-Sat Jun-Aug, Tue-Sat Sep-May) features Native American–led tours through a re-creation of a pre-European-contact woodland village. The museum focuses on the Trail of Tears.

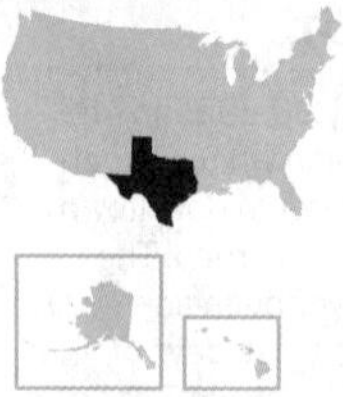

Texas

Includes ➡

Best Places to Eat

- ➡ Franklin Barbecue (p698)
- ➡ Southerleigh (p707)
- ➡ Cochineal (p736)
- ➡ Meddlesome Moth (p725)
- ➡ Hugo's (p714)

Best Places to Stay

- ➡ Hotel San José (p697)
- ➡ El Cosmico (p736)
- ➡ La Posada Milagro (p733)
- ➡ Stockyards Hotel (p729)
- ➡ Gage Hotel (p737)

Why Go?

Cue the theme music, and make it something epic: Texas is as big and sweeping a state as can be imagined. If it were a country, it would be the world's 40th largest. And as big as it is geographically, it is equally as large in people's imaginations.

Cattle ranches, pickup trucks, cowboy boots and thick Texas drawls – all of those are part of the culture, to be sure. But an Old West theme park it is not. With a state this big, there's room for Texas to be whatever you want it to be.

You can find beaches, sprawling national parks, historic towns, citified shopping and nightlife, and a vibrant music scene. And the nearly year-round warm weather makes it ideal for outdoor activities like hiking, cycling, rock climbing and kayaking. So saddle up for whatever adventure suits you best: the Lone Star state is ready to ride.

When to Go

Austin

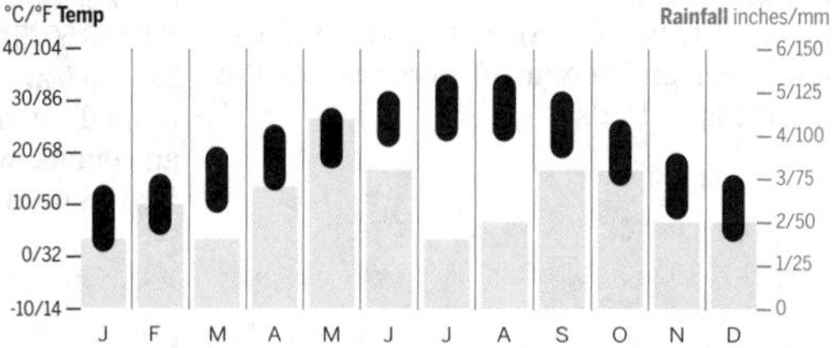

Mar Warm weather during spring break attracts college students and families with kids.

Apr–May Wildflowers line roadsides, festivals are in full swing and summer is yet to swelter.

Oct Crowds have thinned, the heat has broken, but it's still warm enough for shorts.

History

Texas hasn't always been Texas. Or Mexico, for that matter. Or the United States, or Spain, or France...or any of the six flags that once flew over this epic state in its eight changes of sovereignty.

Given that the conquerors' diseases wiped out much of the indigenous population, it seems a bit ironic that the Spaniards named the territory Tejas (*tay*-has) – a corruption of the Caddo word for 'friend.' Caddo, Apache and Karankawa were among the tribes that Spanish explorers encountered when they arrived to map the Gulf Coast in 1519.

Spain's rule of the territory continued until Mexico won its independence in 1821. That same year, Mexican general Antonio López de Santa Anna eliminated the state federation system, outlawed slavery and curtailed immigration. None of this sat well with independent-minded 'Texians' (US- and Mexico-born Texans) who had been given cheap land grants and Mexican citizenship. Clashes escalated into the Texas War for Independence (1835–6). A month after Santa Anna's forces massacred survivors of the siege in San Antonio, Sam Houston's rebels routed the Mexican troops at San Jacinto with the cry 'Remember the Alamo!' And thus the Republic of Texas was born. The nation's short life ended nine years later when, by treaty, Texas opted to become the 28th state of the Union.

The last battle of the Civil War (Texas was on the Confederate side) was reputedly fought near Brownsville in May of 1865 – one month after the war had ended. Cattle-ranching formed the core of Texas' postwar economy, but it was the black gold that spewed up from Spindletop in 1910 that really changed everything. From then on, for better or worse, the state's economy has run on oil.

Local Culture

Trying to typify Texas culture is like tryin' to wrestle a pig in mud – it's awful slippery. In vast generalization, Austin is alternative Texas, where environmental integrity and quality of life are avidly discussed. Dallasites are the shoppers and society trendsetters. In conservative, casual Houston, oil-and-gas industrialists dine at clubby steakhouses, though it's also home to great ethnic diversity (foodies take note). And San Antonio is the most Tex-Mexican of the bunch – a showplace of Hispanic culture.

SOUTH-CENTRAL TEXAS

So what if the hills are more mole-size than mountainous? They – and the rivers that flow through them – are what define south-central Texas. To the north is the state capital of Austin, where music, music and more music are on the schedule, day and night. Eighty miles south, the major metropolitan center of San Antonio is home to the Alamo and the festive Riverwalk. Between and to the west of the two towns is the Hill Country. Here you can eat great barbecue, dance across an old wooden floor or spend a lazy day floating on the river in small Texas-y towns. If you want to get to the heart of Texas in a short time, this is the way to go.

Austin

You'll see it on bumper stickers and T-shirts throughout the city: 'Keep Austin Weird.' And while old-timers grumble that Austin has lost its funky charm, the city has still managed to hang on to its incredibly laid-back vibe. Though this former college town with a hippie soul has seen an influx of tech types and movie stars, it's still a town of artists with day jobs, where people try to focus on their music or write their novel or annoy their neighbors with crazy yard art.

Along the freeway and in the 'burbs, big-box stores and chain restaurants have proliferated at an alarming rate. But the neighborhoods still have an authentically Austin feel, with all sorts of interesting, locally owned businesses, including a flock of food trailers – a symbol of the low-key entrepreneurial spirit that represents Austin at its best.

The one thing everyone seems to know about Austin, whether they've been there or not, is that it's a music town, even if they don't actually use the words 'Live Music Capital of the World' (though that's a claim no one's disputing). The city now hosts two major music festivals, South by Southwest and the Austin City Limits festival, but you don't have to endure the crowds and exorbitant hotel prices to experience the scene, because Austin has live music all over town every night of the week.

Sights

Don't limit yourself to the sights; Austin is about the experience. Bars, restaurants, even grocery stores and the airport have live music. And there are outdoor activities galore. A

Texas Highlights

1 Scooting across a well-worn wooden floor at Texas' oldest dance hall in **Gruene** (p702).

2 Strolling scenic San Antonio's **Riverwalk** (p705), stopping at cafes and waterside restaurants along the way.

3 Getting your fill of live music, backyard bars and wildly creative food trucks in **Austin** (p691).

4 Pondering JFK conspiracy theories at Dallas' one-of-a-kind **Sixth Floor Museum** (p721).

5 Watching longhorn cattle being driven through the dusty streets of cowboy-loving **Fort Worth** (p728).

6 Discovering the rugged natural beauty of **Big Bend National Park** (p732).

7 Getting a stellar view of the night sky at the **McDonald Observatory** (p734) star party.

8 Peeking at surrealist art at Houston's **Menil Collection** (p710).

9 Frolicking in the waves and taking long walks on the shimmering sands of **South Padre Island** (p720).

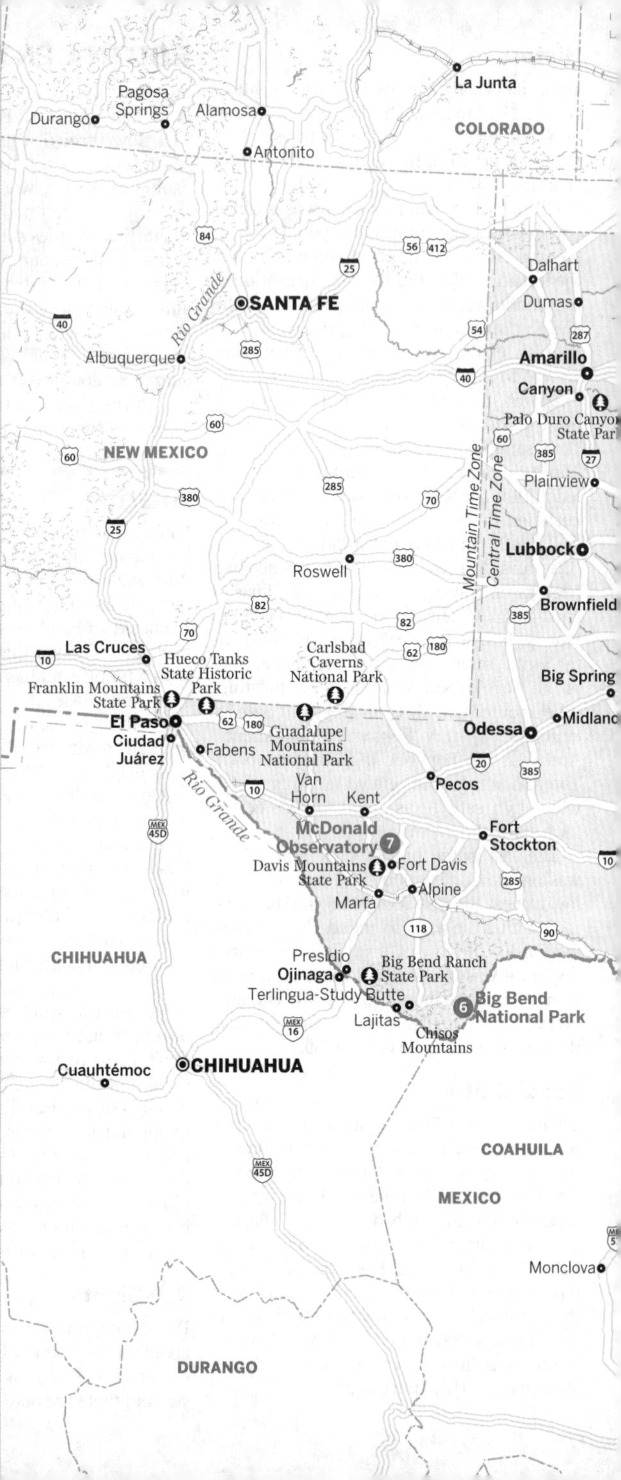

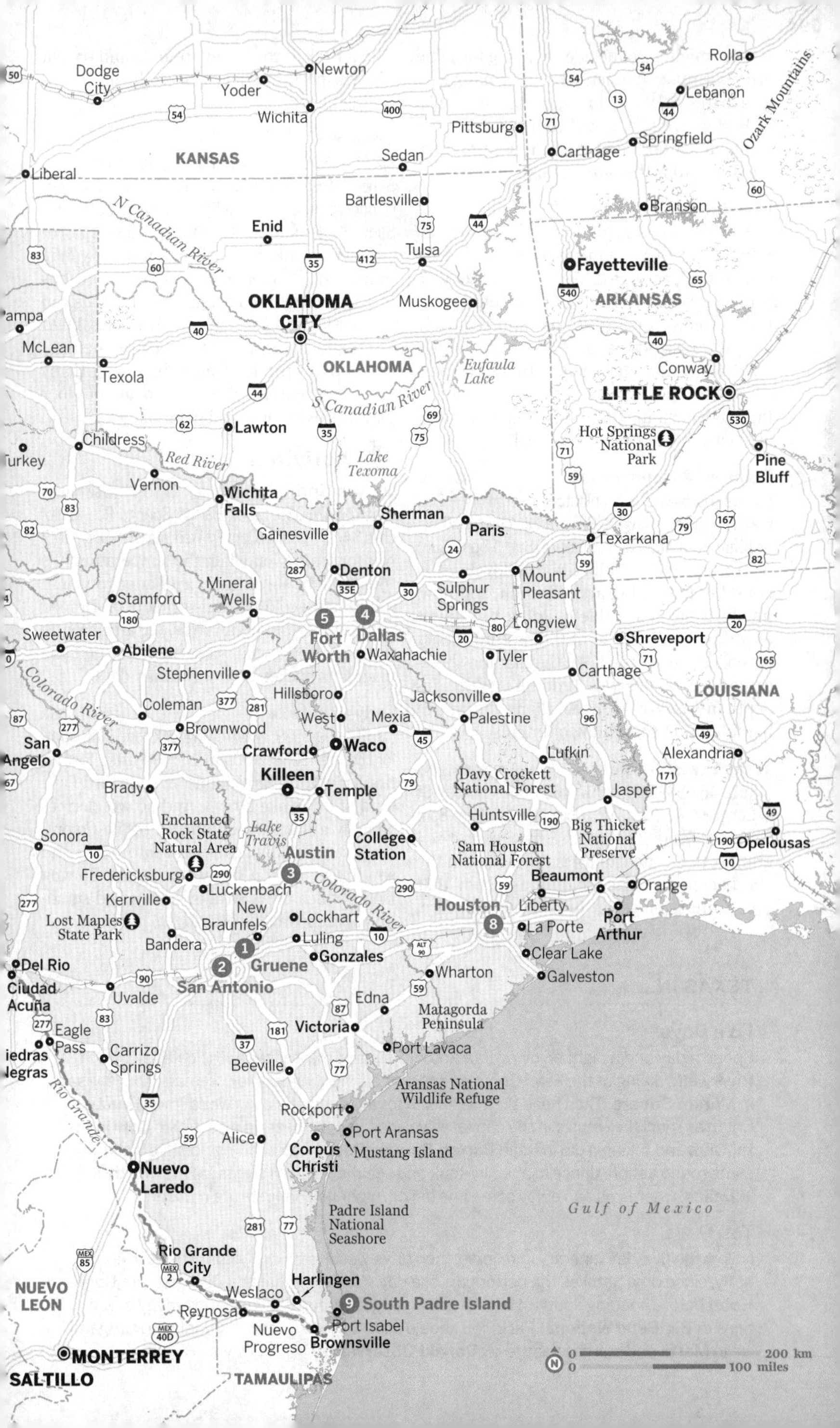
Dodge City
Yoder
Newton
Wichita
Rolla
Lebanon
Ozark Mountains
Pittsburg
Springfield
Carthage
KANSAS
Sedan
Liberal
Bartlesville
Branson
N Canadian River
Enid
Tulsa
Fayetteville
ARKANSAS
Muskogee
OKLAHOMA CITY
Pampa
McLean
Texola
OKLAHOMA
Eufaula Lake
Conway
LITTLE ROCK
S Canadian River
Lawton
Hot Springs National Park
Childress
Turkey
Red River
Lake Texoma
Pine Bluff
Vernon
Wichita Falls
Sherman
Paris
Gainesville
Texarkana
Denton
Mineral Wells
Sulphur Springs
Mount Pleasant
Stamford
Fort Worth
Dallas
Longview
Sweetwater
Abilene
Shreveport
Waxahachie
Tyler
Stephenville
Carthage
Colorado River
Hillsboro
Jacksonville
LOUISIANA
Coleman
West
Mexia
Palestine
Brownwood
San Angelo
Crawford
Waco
Lufkin
Alexandria
Killeen
Davy Crockett National Forest
Brady
Temple
Jasper
Enchanted Rock State Natural Area
Lake Travis
Huntsville
Big Thicket National Preserve
Sonora
Austin
College Station
Sam Houston National Forest
Opelousas
Fredericksburg
Luckenbach
Beaumont
Orange
Kerrville
New Braunfels
Colorado River
Houston
Liberty
Port Arthur
Lost Maples State Park
Lockhart
La Porte
Bandera
Luling
Gruene
Gonzales
Clear Lake
Del Rio
San Antonio
Wharton
Galveston
Ciudad Acuña
Uvalde
Edna
Matagorda Peninsula
Eagle Pass
Victoria
Piedras Negras
Carrizo Springs
Port Lavaca
Beeville
Rio Grande
Aransas National Wildlife Refuge
Rockport
Alice
Port Aransas
Corpus Christi
Mustang Island
Nuevo Laredo
Gulf of Mexico
Padre Island National Seashore
Rio Grande City
NUEVO LEÓN
Harlingen
Weslaco
South Padre Island
Reynosa
Nuevo Progreso
Port Isabel
Brownsville
MONTERREY
SALTILLO
TAMAULIPAS
200 km
100 miles

full day might also include shopping for some groovy vintage clothes, sipping a margarita at a patio cafe and lounging on the banks of Barton Springs. But if your vacation isn't complete without a visit to a museum, there are some stops that are worth your while.

Bob Bullock Texas State History Museum MUSEUM
(☎512-936-8746; www.thestoryoftexas.com; 1800 Congress Ave; adult/child $9/6; ⊙9am-5pm Mon-Sat, noon-5pm Sun) This is no dusty old historical museum. Big, glitzy and still relatively new, it shows off the Lone Star State's history, all the way from when it used to be part of Mexico up to the present, with high-tech interactive exhibits and fun theatrics. Allow at least a few hours for your visit.

Blanton Museum of Art MUSEUM
(☎512-471-5482; www.blantonmuseum.org; 200 E Martin Luther King Jr Blvd; adult/child $9/free; ⊙10am-5pm Tue-Fri, 11am-5pm Sat, 1-5pm Sun) A big university with a big endowment is bound to have a big art collection, and now, finally, it has a suitable building to show it off properly. With one of the best university art collections in the USA, the Blanton showcases a variety of styles. It doesn't go very in-depth into any of them, but then again you're bound to find something of interest.

Texas State Capitol HISTORIC BUILDING
(☎512-463-5495, tours 512-463-0063; cnr 11th St & Congress Ave; ⊙7am-10pm Mon-Fri, 9am-8pm Sat & Sun) FREE Built in 1888 from sunset-red granite, this state capitol is the largest in the US, backing up the ubiquitous claim that everything is bigger in Texas. If nothing else, take a peek at the lovely rotunda and try out the whispering gallery created by its curved ceiling.

Thinkery MUSEUM
(☎512-469-6200; www.thinkeryaustin.org; 1830 Simond Ave; admission $9, child under 2yr free; ⊙noon-5pm Mon, 10am-5pm Tue-Fri, to 6pm Sat & Sun;) This huge 40,000-sq-ft space north of downtown is an inspiring place for young minds, with hands-on activities in the realms of science, technology and the arts. Kids can get wet learning about fluid dynamics, build LED light structures and explore chemical reactions in the Kitchen Lab, among many other attractions. There's also an outdoor play area with nets and climbing toys.

Activities

Barton Springs Pool SWIMMING
(☎512-867-3080; 2201 Barton Springs Rd; adult/child $4/2; ⊙8am-10pm Fri-Wed late-Apr–Oct) Hot? Not for long. Even when the temperature hits 100, you'll be shivering in a jiff after you jump into this icy-cold natural-spring pool. Draped with century-old pecan trees, the area around the pool is a social scene in itself, and the place gets packed on hot summer days.

Lady Bird Lake CANOEING
(☎512-459-0999; www.rowingdock.com; 2418 Stratford Dr; ⊙7:30am-8:30pm) Named after former first lady 'Lady Bird' Johnson, Lady Bird Lake kind of looks like a river. And no wonder: it's actually a dammed-off section of the Colorado River that divides Austin into north and south. Get out on the water at the Rowing Dock, which rents kayaks, canoes and stand-up paddleboards for $10 to $25 per hour.

TEXAS IN...

Five Days

Spend a day and a night enjoying San Antonio, sipping margaritas in the cafes along the **Riverwalk**, dining at the Pearl Complex and bargain-hunting for Mexico-made souvenirs in **Market Square**. Then head 80 miles north for a two-night stay in weird-loving **Austin**. Catch as much live music in the capital as you can, maybe hearing a set at the **Continental Club** and taking a dip in frigid **Barton Springs Pool**. Keep heading north to watch some rodeo action, dance in a honky-tonk and see the Western sights in **Fort Worth**. End in **Dallas**, where you can enjoy some fine dining, nightlife and first-rate museums.

Ten Days

Follow the five-day itinerary in reverse, then drive west from San Antonio to west Texas – or fly, since driving takes the better part of a day. Stay a night at the Old West–era **Gage Hotel** before heading south to hike or raft among the deep canyons and craggy mountains of **Big Bend National Park**. You should also stop to see some stunning avant-garde art in **Marfa** and stargaze at the **McDonald Observatory** in Fort Davis.

Zilker Park PARK

(☎512-974-6700; www.austintexas.gov/department/zilker-metropolitan-park; 2100 Barton Springs Rd) This 350-acre park is a slice of green heaven, lined with hiking and biking trails. The park also provides access to the famed Barton Springs natural swimming pool and Barton Creek Greenbelt. Find boat rentals, a miniature train and a botanical garden, too. On weekends from April to early September, admission is $5 per car.

Bicycle Sport Shop BICYCLE RENTAL

(☎512-477-3472; www.bicyclesportshop.com; 517 S Lamar Blvd; per 2hr from $16; ⏲10am-7pm Mon-Fri, 9am-6pm Sat, 11am-5pm Sun) The great thing about Bicycle Sport Shop is its proximity to Zilker Park, Barton Springs and the Lady Bird Lake bike paths, all of which are within a few blocks. Rentals range from $16 for a two-hour cruise on a standard bike, to $62 for a full day on a top-end full-suspension model. On weekends and holidays, advance reservations are advised.

Festivals & Events

South by Southwest MUSIC, FILM

(SXSW; www.sxsw.com; single festival $650-1300, combo pass $1025-1745) One of the American music industry's biggest gatherings has now expanded to include film and interactive. Austin is absolutely besieged with visitors during this two-week window in mid-March, and many a new resident first came to the city to hear a little live music.

Austin City Limits Music Festival MUSIC

(www.aclfestival.com; 1-/3-day pass $100/250) What do music lovers do in autumn? The Austin City Limits Festival, which is not as big as SXSW but has been swiftly gaining on it in terms of popularity. The three-day festival held on eight stages in Zilker Park during October books more than 100 pretty impressive acts and sells out months in advance.

Formula 1 Grand Prix SPORTS

(www.formula1.com; ⏲late Oct or Nov) In Travis County, just outside of Austin, a high-speed racetrack draws legions of F1 fans during a high-octane weekend in autumn.

Sleeping

South Congress (SoCo) has the coolest and quirkiest digs, and downtown has more high-rent options. Check the Austin Visitor Information Center (p701).

Hotel rates soar and locals flee during SXSW and F1, so plan accordingly.

TEXAS FACTS

Nickname The Lone Star State

Population 27 million

Area 262,000 sq miles

Capital city Austin (population 886,000)

Other cities Houston (population 2.2 million), San Antonio (1.4 million), Dallas (1.3 million), El Paso (830,000)

Sales tax 6.25% to 8.25%

Birthplace of Singer Buddy Holly (1936–59), entrepreneur Howard Hughes (1905–76), rocker Janis Joplin (1943–70), country singer George Strait (b 1952), actor Matthew McConaughey (b 1969)

Home of Shiner Bock beer, Dr Pepper, two presidents Bush

Politics Leans Republican (but don't tell the Austinites)

Famous for Barbecue, cowboys

Best souvenir 'Don't Mess with Texas' items, from T-shirts to toilet paper

Driving distances Austin to San Antonio 78 miles, Austin to Dallas 196 miles, Dallas to Houston 242 miles, Houston to El Paso 745 miles, El Paso to Big Bend 291 miles

★**Firehouse Hostel** HOSTEL $

(☎512-201-2522; www.firehousehostel.com; 605 Brazos St; dm $32-40, r $110-170, ste $130-170; 🚭❄📶) A hostel in downtown Austin? Finally! And a pretty darned spiffy one, at that. Opened in January of 2013 in a former firehouse, it's still fresh and new, and the downtown location right across from the historic Driskill Hotel is as perfect as you can get.

Drifter Jack's HOSTEL $

(☎512-243-8410; www.drifterjackshostel.com; 2602 Guadalupe St; dm $28-35, d $75-85; ❄@📶) Across from the UT campus, Drifter Jack's is a friendly, laid-back place, with mural-covered rooms and a small lounge. The hostel draws mostly a young crowd (though all are welcome) and organizes pub crawls and other outings.

Goodall Wooten HOSTEL $

(☎512-472-1343; 2112 Guadalupe St; r $35; ❄@) A private dorm near the University of Texas,

Austin

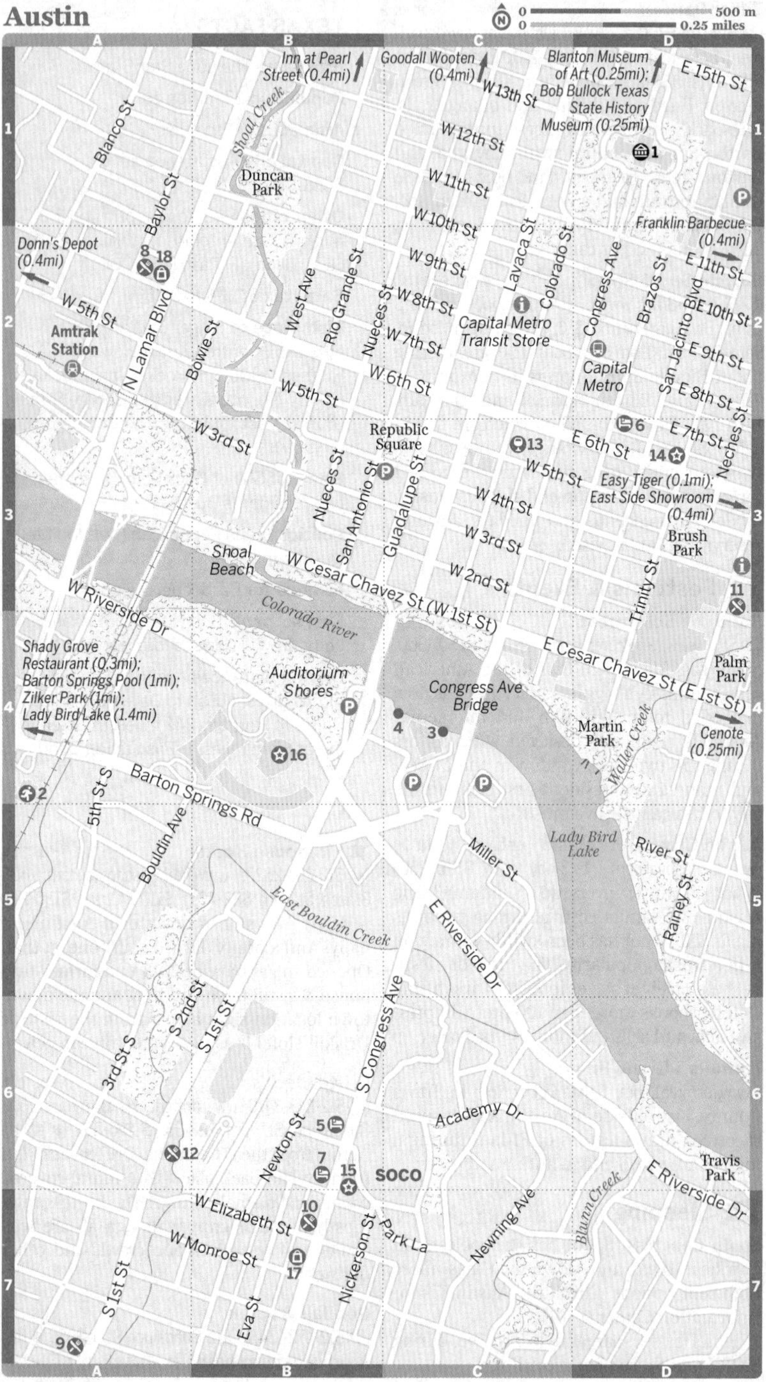
Inn at Pearl Street (0.4mi)
Goodall Wooten (0.4mi)
Blanton Museum of Art (0.25mi); Bob Bullock Texas State History Museum (0.25mi)
Franklin Barbecue (0.4mi)
Donn's Depot (0.4mi)
Amtrak Station
Duncan Park
Shoal Creek
Capital Metro Transit Store
Capital Metro
Republic Square
Easy Tiger (0.1mi); East Side Showroom (0.4mi)
Brush Park
Shoal Beach
Colorado River
Shady Grove Restaurant (0.3mi); Barton Springs Pool (1mi); Zilker Park (1mi); Lady Bird Lake (1.4mi)
Auditorium Shores
Congress Ave Bridge
Palm Park
Martin Park
Waller Creek
Cenote (0.25mi)
Lady Bird Lake
East Bouldin Creek
SOCO
Travis Park
Blunn Creek
Blanco St
Baylor St
N Lamar Blvd
Bowie St
West Ave
Rio Grande St
Nueces St
San Antonio St
Guadalupe St
Lavaca St
Colorado St
Congress Ave
Brazos St
San Jacinto Blvd
Neches St
Trinity St
W 13th St
W 12th St
W 11th St
W 10th St
W 9th St
W 8th St
W 7th St
W 6th St
W 5th St
W 4th St
W 3rd St
W 2nd St
W Cesar Chavez St (W 1st St)
E Cesar Chavez St (E 1st St)
E 15th St
E 11th St
E 10th St
E 9th St
E 8th St
E 7th St
E 6th St
W Riverside Dr
Barton Springs Rd
5th St S
Bouldin Ave
Miller St
River St
Rainey St
E Riverside Dr
S 2nd St
S 1st St
3rd St S
S Congress Ave
Academy Dr
Newton St
W Elizabeth St
W Monroe St
Nickerson St
Park La
Newning Ave
Eva St
500 m
0.25 miles

Austin

Sights
1 Texas State Capitol D1

Activities, Courses & Tours
2 Bicycle Sport Shop A4
3 Capital Cruises C4
4 Lone Star Riverboat C4

Sleeping
5 Austin Motel B6
6 Firehouse Hostel D3
7 Hotel San José B6

Eating
8 Amy's Ice Cream A2
9 Bouldin Creek Coffee House A7
10 Güero's Taco Bar B7
11 Moonshine Patio Bar & Grill D3
12 South Austin Trailer Park & Eatery A6

Drinking & Nightlife
13 Garage C3

Entertainment
14 Alamo Drafthouse Cinema D3
15 Continental Club B6
16 Long Center for the Performing Arts B4

Shopping
17 Uncommon Objects B7
18 Waterloo Records A2

'the Woo' generally has rooms available mid-May to mid-August, and sometimes has space for travelers at other times of the year. Just the basics – expect sheets, toilet paper and a small refrigerator – but no decor. Cash only.

★ Hotel San José BOUTIQUE HOTEL **$$**
(512-852-2360; www.sanjosehotel.com; 1316 S Congress Ave; r $215-360, r without bath $150, ste $335-500; P) Local hotelier Liz Lambert revamped a 1930s-vintage motel into a chic SoCo retreat with minimalist rooms in stucco bungalows, a lovely bamboo-fringe pool and a very Austin-esque hotel bar in the courtyard that's known for its celebrity-spotting potential. South Congress has become quite the scene, and this hotel's location puts you right in the thick of it.

★ Austin Motel MOTEL **$$**
(512-441-1157; www.austinmotel.com; 1220 S Congress Ave; r $95-180, ste $207-225; P) 'Garage-sale chic' is the unifying factor at this wonderfully funky motel that embodies the spirit of the 'Keep Austin Weird' movement. Each room is individually decorated with whatever happened to be lying around at the time, and with varying degrees of success. The excellent location, friendly staff and enticing pool make this a great choice.

Habitat Suites HOTEL **$$**
(512-467-6000; www.habitatsuites.com; 500 E Highland Mall Blvd; ste $100-160; P@) Locally owned and ecofriendly, this quiet place is tucked away just north of downtown, away from the hustle and bustle. The furnishings may be slightly past their prime, but practical travelers will get a lot for their money here.

Inn at Pearl Street B&B **$$**
(512-478-0051; www.innpearl.com; 809 W Martin Luther King Jr Blvd; d $195-245, ste $265-365; P) This is a preservationist's dream come true. The owners picked up this rundown property, and completely restored it, decorating the whole place in a plush European style. The rooms come in a variety of flavors and are located in two separate buildings – Victoria House or Burton House – so check the website to find one that suits.

Eating

It's easy to find good, affordable food in Austin. South Congress provides a slew of options, but you'll be competing with lots of other hungry diners for a table. Those in the know go instead to S 1st St (1400 to 2100 blocks), where Mexican herbalists and tattoo parlors alternate with trailer-park food courts and organic cafes. Barton Springs Rd (east of Lamar Blvd) also has a number of interesting eateries, and Guadalupe St, by UT, is the place to look for cheap eats. Some great meat-market barbecue is available in nearby central Texas.

Downtown

Amy's Ice Cream ICE CREAM **$**
(512-480-0673; www.amysicecreams.com; 1012 W 6th St; ice cream $3-6; 11:30am-midnight) It's not just the ice cream we love; it's the toppings that get pounded and blended in, violently but lovingly, by the staff wielding a metal scoop in each hand. Look for other locations on Guadalupe St north of the UT

DON'T MISS

MEALS ON WHEELS

Food trailers are here to stay – even if they can move around at whim. We haven't listed any of these rolling restaurants because of their transient nature, but instead invite you to explore some of the areas where they congregate. Wander from trailer to trailer till one strikes your fancy, or make a progressive dinner out of it. Look for clusters of Airstreams and taco trucks in some of these likely spots:

➡ **South Austin Trailer Park & Eatery** (1311 S 1st St) seems to be a rather settled trailer community, with a fence, an official name, a sign and picnic tables. Look for Torchy's Tacos, which whips up some of Austin's best tacos.

➡ **1503 S 1st St** has a cluster of food trailers, including Gourdough's, which serves gourmet doughnut combos, including a doughnut burger.

➡ **South Congress**, between Elizabeth and Monroe, yields lots of options, including the decadent Hey Cupcake!

➡ **East Austin** has its own little enclave, conveniently located right among all the bars on the corner of E 6th and Waller Sts. Five blocks further east you'll find East Side King, serving some of Austin's best (and spiciest!) Thai dishes (open nights only).

campus, on South Congress near all the shops, or at the airport for a last-ditch fix.

Moonshine Patio Bar & Grill AMERICAN **$$**
(☎512-236-9599; www.moonshinegrill.com; 303 Red River St; dinner mains $14-24; ⏲11am-10pm Mon-Thu, to 11pm Fri & Sat, 9am-2pm & 5-10pm Sun) Dating from the mid-1850s, this historic building is a remarkably well preserved homage to Austin's early days. Within its exposed limestone walls, you can enjoy upscale comfort food, half-price appetizers at happy hour or a lavish Sunday brunch buffet ($18). Or, chill on the patio under the shade of pecan trees.

South Austin

Bouldin Creek Coffee House VEGETARIAN **$**
(☎512-416-1601; 1900 S 1st St; mains $6-10; ⏲7am-midnight Mon-Fri, 8am-midnight Sat & Sun; 📶🌿) You can get your veggie chorizo tacos or a potato leek omelet all day long at this buzzing vegan-vegetarian eatery. It's got an eclectic South Austin vibe and is a great place for people-watching, finishing your novel or joining a band.

Shady Grove Restaurant AMERICAN **$**
(☎512-474-9991; www.theshadygrove.com; 1624 Barton Springs Rd; mains $9-15; ⏲11am-10:30pm) The large patio with its tall shady pecan trees is a huge draw at this friendly, festive spot near Barton Springs. There's plenty of satisfying American and Tex-Mex dishes on hand, including chili cheese fries, a Hippie Sandwich (grilled veggies with mozzarella) and steak tacos.

★ **Güero's Taco Bar** TEX-MEX **$$**
(☎512-447-7688; 1412 S Congress Ave; mains $6-15; ⏲11am-10pm) Set in a former feed-and-seed store from the late 1800s, Güero's is an Austin classic and always draws a crowd. Come for homemade corn tortillas (the tacos al pastor are excellent), chicken tortilla soup and refreshing margaritas. Head to the oak-shaded garden for live music (Wednesday through Sunday).

East Austin

★ **Franklin Barbecue** BARBECUE **$**
(☎512-653-1187; www.franklinbarbecue.com; 900 E 11th St; mains $6-15; ⏲11am-2pm Tue-Sun) America's most famous barbecue spot only serves lunch, and only till it runs out – usually well before 2pm. In fact, to avoid missing out, you should join the line by 10am (9am on weekends). Just treat it as a tailgating party: bring beer or mimosas to share and make friends.

Cenote CAFE **$**
(1010 E Cesar Chavez St; mains $8-15; ⏲7am-11pm Mon-Fri, from 8am Sat, 8am-4pm Sun; 📶) One of our favorite cafes in Austin, Cenote uses seasonal, largely organic ingredients in its simple but delicious anytime fare. Come for housemade granola and yogurt with fruit, banh mi sandwiches and couscous curry. The cleverly shaded patio is a fine retreat for a rich coffee or a craft beer (or perhaps a handmade popsicle from Juju).

Laundrette MODERN AMERICAN **$$**
(☎512-382-1599; 2115 Holly St; mains $18-24; ⏲5pm-10pm daily & 11am-2:30pm Sat & Sun) A brilliant repurposing of a former washateria, Laundrette boasts a stylish, streamlined design that provides a fine backdrop to the delicious Mediterranean-inspired cooking. Among the many hits: crab toast, wood-grilled octopus, brussels sprouts with apple-bacon marmalade, a perfectly rendered brick chicken and whole grilled branzino.

Justine's FRENCH **$$$**
(☎512-385-2900; www.justines1937.com; 4710 E 5th St; mains $20-28; ⏲6pm-1am Wed-Mon) With a lovely garden setting festooned with fairy lights, Justine's is a top spot for wowing a date. French onion soup, seared scallops and grilled pork chop are standouts on the small, classic brasserie menu. There are also a few more creative changing daily specials like pan-seared quail with parsnip casserole or grilled swordfish with artichokes and cauliflower puree.

Around Town

Trudy's Texas Star TEX-MEX **$**
(☎512-477-2935; www.trudys.com; 409 W 30th St; mains $9-14; ⏲2pm-2am Mon-Thu, from 11am Fri, from 9am Sat & Sun) Get your Tex-Mex fix here; the menu is consistently good, with several healthier-than-usual options. But we'll let you in on a little secret: this place could serve nothing but beans and dirt and people would still line up for the margaritas, which might very well be the best in Austin.

Stiles Switch BARBECUE **$**
(☎512-380-9199; 6610 N Lamar Blvd; mains $7-18; ⏲11am-9pm Tue-Sun) It has manageable lines, you won't have to suffer to enjoy outstanding brisket, fired up to tender, smoky perfection, at this popular eatery 6 miles north of downtown. Top it off with some ribs, a side of corn casserole and a local microbrew.

★**The Salt Lick** BARBECUE **$$**
(☎512-858-4959; www.saltlickbbq.com; 18300 FM 1826, Driftwood; mains $10-17; ⏲11am-10pm; 👪) It's worth the 20-mile drive out of town just to see the massive outdoor barbecue pits at this park-like place off US 290. It's a bit of a tourist fave, but the crowd-filled experience still gets our nod. BYOB. Hungry? Choose the family-style all-you-can-eat option (adult/child $25/9).

🍷 Drinking & Nightlife

There are bejillions of bars in Austin, so what follows is only a very short list. The legendary 6th St bar scene spills onto nearby thoroughfares, especially on Red River St.

Many places on 6th St (west of Red River St) are shot bars aimed at party-hardy college students and tourists, while the Red River establishments draw a more local crowd. The lounges around the Warehouse District (near the intersection of W 4th and Colorado Sts) are a bit more upscale. SoCo and East 6th (from Medina to Chicon Sts) caters to the more offbeat in eclectic Austin.

Easy Tiger BEER GARDEN
(easytigeraustin.com; 709 E 6th St; ⏲11am-2am) A short stroll to the nightlife mayhem of 6th St, Easy Tiger feels like a secret hideaway, with a back patio overlooking peaceful Waller Creek. You'll also find good microbrews and snacks, plus an excellent bakery (open at 7am) in the entrance.

Garage LOUNGE
(503 Colorado St; ⏲5pm-2am Mon-Sat) Hidden inside a parking garage, this cozy, dimly lit lounge draws a hip but not overly precious Austin crowd who give high marks to the first-rate cocktails, handsomely designed space and novel location.

★**East Side Showroom** BAR
(☎512-467-4280; 1100 E 6th St; ⏲5pm-2am) With an ambience that would feel right at home in Brooklyn (in the late 1800s), this bar anchoring the lively east-side scene is full of hipsters soaking up the craft cocktails and bohemian atmosphere.

GAY & LESBIAN AUSTIN

With a thriving gay population – not to mention pretty mellow straight people – Austin is arguably the most gay-friendly city in Texas. The Austin Gay & Lesbian Chamber of Commerce (www.aglcc.org) sponsors the Pride Parade in June, as well as smaller events throughout the year. The **Austin Chronicle** (www.austinchronicle.com) runs a gay event column among the weekly listings, and glossy magazine **L Style/G Style** (www.lstylegstyle.com) has a dual gal/guy focus.

★Ginny's Little Longhorn Saloon BAR
(☎512-524-1291; 5434 Burnet Rd; ⏲5pm-midnight Tue & Wed, to 1am Thu-Sat, 2-10pm Sun) This funky little cinder-block building is one of those dive bars that Austinites love so very much – and did even before it became nationally famous for chicken-shit bingo on Sunday night.

☆ Entertainment

Live Music

On any given Friday night there are several hundred acts playing in the town's 200 or so venues, and even on an off night (Monday and Tuesday are usually the slowest) you'll typically have your pick of more than two dozen performances.

To plan your attack, check out the free weekly *Austin Chronicle* or the Thursday edition of the *Austin American-Statesman*.

★Continental Club LIVE MUSIC
(☎512-441-2444; www.continentalclub.com; 1315 S Congress Ave; ⏲4pm-2am Tue-Sun, from 6pm Mon) No passive toe-tapping here; this 1950s-era lounge has a dance floor that's always swinging with some of the city's best local acts.

Donn's Depot LIVE MUSIC
(☎512-478-3142; donnsdepot.com; 1600 W 5th St; ⏲2pm-2am Mon-Fri, from 6pm Sat) Austin loves a dive bar, and Donn's combines a retro atmosphere inside an old railway car with live music six nights a week, including Donn himself performing alongside the Station Masters. A mix of young and old come to Donn's, and the dance floor sees plenty of action.

Broken Spoke LIVE MUSIC
(www.brokenspokeaustintx.com; 3201 S Lamar Blvd; ⏲11am-midnight Tue-Thu, to 1am Fri & Sat) With old wood floors and wagon-wheel chandeliers that George Strait once hung from, Broken Spoke is a true Texas honky-tonk.

Skylark Lounge BLUES
(☎512-730-0759; www.skylarkaustin.com; 2039 Airport Blvd; ⏲5pm-midnight Mon-Sat, to 10pm Sun) It's a bit of a drive (2.5 miles northeast of downtown), but well worth the effort to reach this friendly dive bar that serves up live blues – along with fairly priced drinks, free popcorn and a shaded patio.

Theater & Cinema

Long Center for the Performing Arts PERFORMING ARTS
(☎512-457-5100; www.thelongcenter.org; 701 W Riverside Dr) This state-of-the-art theater opened in late 2008 as part of a waterfront redevelopment along Lady Bird Lake. The multistage venue hosts drama, dance, concerts and comedians.

Alamo Drafthouse Cinema CINEMA
(☎512-861-7020; www.drafthouse.com; 320 E 6th St; admission $11) Easily the most fun you can have at the movies: sing along with *Grease*, quote along with *Princess Bride*, or just enjoy food and drink delivered right to your seat during first-run films. Check the website for other locations.

Sports

TXRD Lonestar Rollergirls SPECTATOR SPORT
(www.txrd.com) Get ready to rumble – it's roller-derby night and the Hellcat women skaters are expected to kick some Cherry Bomb ass. No matter who wins, the TXRD Lonestar Rollergirls league always puts on a good show, usually at the Palmer Events Center.

Shopping

Vintage is a lifestyle, and the city's best hunting grounds for retro fashions and furnishings are South Austin and Guadalupe St near UT. You can download a map at www.vintagearoundtownguide.com.

MUSIC FESTIVALS

In mid-March tens of thousands of record-label reps, musicians, journalists and rabid fans descend on Austin for **South by Southwest** (p695), a musical extravaganza that attracts a couple of thousand groups and solo artists from around the world to 90 different Austin venues.

Though SXSW started out as an opportunity for little-known bands and singers to catch the ear of a record-label rep, it has since become a wildly popular industry showcase for already signed bands. Add to that a hugely popular interactive festival, as well as a more subdued but still well-attended film festival, and you've got a major international draw that takes over the city and sends most of the locals into hiding for two weeks every spring.

Too much hoopla? Come in October for a slightly more mellow experience at the **Austin City Limits Music Festival** (p695), an outdoor event at Zilker Park.

THE SWARM: AUSTIN'S BATS

Looking very much like a special effect from a B movie, a funnel cloud of up to 1.5 million Mexican free-tailed bats swarms from under the Congress Avenue Bridge nightly from late March to early November. Turns out, Austin isn't just the live-music capital of the world; it's also home to the largest urban bat population in North America.

Austinites have embraced the winged mammals – figuratively speaking of course – and gather to watch the bats' nightly exodus right around dusk as they leave for their evening meal. (Not to worry: they're looking for insects, and they mostly stay out of your hair.)

There's lots of standing around parking lots and on the bridge itself, but if you want a more leisurely bat-watching experience, try the TGI Friday's restaurant by the Radisson Hotel on Lady Bird Lake, or the **Lone Star Riverboat** (512-327-1388; www.lonestarriverboat.com; adult/child $10/7) or **Capital Cruises** (512-480-9264; www.capitalcruises.com; adult/child $10/5) for bat-watching tours.

On the first Thursday of the month, S Congress Ave is definitely the place to be, when stores stay open until 10pm and there's live entertainment.

★Uncommon Objects VINTAGE
(512-442-4000; 1512 S Congress Ave; 11am-7pm Sun-Thu, to 8pm Fri & Sat) 'Curious oddities' is what they advertise at this quirky antique store that sells all manner of fabulous knick-knacks, all displayed with an artful eye. More than 20 different vendors scour the state to stock their stalls, so there's plenty to look at.

Waterloo Records MUSIC
(512-474-2500; www.waterloorecords.com; 600 N Lamar Blvd; 10am-11pm Mon-Sat, from 11am Sun) If you want to stock up on music, this is the record store. There are sections reserved just for local bands, and listening stations featuring Texas, indie and alt-country acts.

University Co-op SOUVENIRS
(512-476-7211; 2246 Guadalupe St; 8:30am-7:30pm Mon-Fri, 9:30am-6pm Sat, 11am-5pm Sun) Stock up on souvenirs sporting the Longhorn logo at this store brimming with school spirit. It's amazing the sheer quantity of objects that come in burnt orange and white.

Information

Austin indoors is nonsmoking, period (bars, too). A vast wi-fi network blankets downtown. City of Austin libraries have free internet.

Austin Visitor Information Center (512-478-0098; www.austintexas.org; 602 E 4th St; 9am-5pm Mon-Sat, from 10am Sun) Helpful staff, free maps, extensive racks of information brochures and a sample of local souvenirs for sale.

FedEx Office (327 Congress Ave; 7am-11pm Mon-Fri, 9am-9pm Sat & Sun) Internet access 30¢ a minute.

MEDIA

Austin American-Statesman (www.statesman.com) Daily newspaper.

Austin Chronicle (www.austinchronicle.com) Weekly newspaper, lots of entertainment info.

KLRU TV (www.klru.org) PBS affiliate with local programming that includes the popular music show *Austin City Limits*.

Getting There & Around

Austin-Bergstrom International Airport (AUS; www.austintexas.gov/airport) is off Hwy 71, southeast of downtown. The Airport Flyer (bus 100, $1.75) runs to downtown (7th St and Congress Ave) and UT (Congress Ave and 18th St) every 40 minutes or so. **SuperShuttle** (512-258-3826; www.supershuttle.com) charges around $16 from the airport to downtown. A taxi between the airport and downtown costs from $26 to $32. Most of the national rental-car companies are represented at the airport.

The downtown **Amtrak Station** (512-476-5684; www.amtrak.com; 250 N Lamar Blvd) is served by the *Texas Eagle* that extends from Chicago to Los Angeles. The **Greyhound Bus Station** (512-458-4463; www.greyhound.com; 916 E Koenig Lane) is on the north side of town off I-35; take bus 7-Duval ($1.25) to downtown.

Austin's handy public transit system is run by **Capital Metro** (CapMetro; 512-474-1200; www.capmetro.org). Call for directions to anywhere or stop into the downtown **Capital Metro Transit Store** (209 W 9th St; 7:30am-5:30pm Mon-Fri) for information.

Austinites are big bike fans. Join them by taking advantage of the shared biking scheme offered by **Austin B-cycle** (austin.bcycle.com), with self-checkout kiosks scattered around town.

Around Austin

Northwest of Austin along the Colorado River are the six Highland Lakes. One of the most popular lakes for recreation is the 19,000-sq-acre **Lake Travis** off Hwy 71. Rent boats and jet skis at the associated marina, or overnight in the posh digs at **Lakeway Resort and Spa** (☎512-261-6600; www.lakewayresortandspa.com; 101 Lakeway Dr; r from $180; ❄@📶🏊). **Lake Austin Spa Resort** (☎512-372-7300; www.lakeaustin.com; 1705 S Quinlan Park Rd, off FM 2222; 3-night packages from $1850; ❄@🏊) is the premier place to be pampered in the state. And Lake Travis has Texas' only official nude beach, **Hippie Hollow** (www.hippiehollow.com; 7000 Comanche Trail; day pass car/bicycle $15/8; ⏱9am-dusk Sep-May, 8am-dusk Jun-Aug). To get to Hippie Hollow from FM 2222, take Rte 620 south 1.5 miles to Comanche Trail and turn right. The entrance is 2 miles ahead on the left.

Hill Country

New York has the Hamptons, California has the wine country, and Texas has the Hill Country, whose natural beauty paired with its easygoing nature has inspired more than a few early retirements. Detour down dirt roads in search of fields of wildflowers, check into a dude ranch, float along the Guadalupe River or twirl around the floor of an old dance hall. Most of the small towns in the rolling hills and valleys west of Austin and San Antonio are easy day trips from either city.

Gruene

False-front wood buildings and old German homes make this the quintessential rustic Texas town. All of Gruene (pronounced 'green') is on the National Historic Register – and boy, do day-trippers know it. You won't be alone wandering among the antiques, arts-and-crafts and knickknack shops.

Sights & Activities

Gruene Hall DANCE HALL
(www.gruenehall.com; 1280 Gruene Rd; ⏱11am-midnight Mon-Fri, 10am-1am Sat, 10am-10pm Sun) Folks have been congregating here since 1878, making it one of Texas' oldest dance halls and the oldest continually operating one. Toss back a longneck, two-step to live music on the well-worn wooden dance floor, or play horseshoes out in the yard.

Rockin' R River Rides WATER SPORTS
(☎830-629-9999; www.rockinr.com; 1405 Gruene Rd; tubes $20) This popular outfit offers inner tube rides for a scenic float along the Guadalupe River.

Sleeping & Eating

Gruene Mansion Inn INN $$$
(☎830-629-2641; www.gruenemansioninn.com; 1275 Gruene Rd; d $190-260) This cluster of buildings is practically its own village, with rooms in the mansion, a former carriage house and the old barns. Richly decorated in a style the owners call 'rustic Victorian elegance,' the rooms feature lots of wood, floral prints and pressed-tin ceiling tiles. Two-night minimum.

Gristmill Restaurant AMERICAN $$
(www.gristmillrestaurant.com; 1287 Gruene Rd; mains $10-24; ⏱11am-9pm Sun-Thu, to 10pm Fri & Sat) Behind Gruene Hall and right under the water tower, this restaurant is located within the brick remnants of a long-gone gristmill. Indoor seating affords a rustic ambience, and outdoor tables get a view of the river.

Getting There & Away

Gruene is just off I-10 and Rte 46, 45 miles south of Austin and 25 miles northeast of San Antonio.

Fredericksburg

With fields full of wildflowers, shops full of antiques and streets full of historic buildings and B&Bs, Fredericksburg is the poster child for 'quaint,' serving as the region's largest old German-settled town (c 1870) and unofficial capital of the Hill Country.

It's more cute than cool, but it's not a bad place to linger a bit – especially during wildflower season. It also makes a good base of operations for exploring the surrounding areas. Stop by the **Fredericksburg Visitor Information Center** (☎830-997-6523, 888-997-3600; www.visitfredericksburgtx.com; 302 E Austin St; ⏱9am-5pm Mon-Sat, 11am-3pm Sun; 📶) to get your bearings.

Sights & Activities

Spend an hour or two wandering Fredericksburg's historic district; despite having more than its share of touristy shops, it's retained the look (if not the feel) of 125 years ago.

Mid-May through June is peach-pickin' season around town. You can get them straight from the farm, and some farms

WORTH A TRIP

LOCKHART BARBECUE

In 1999 the Texas Legislature adopted a resolution naming Lockhart – 33 miles south of Austin – the barbecue capital of Texas. Of course, that means it's the barbecue capital of the world. You can eat very well for under $12 at these places:

Black's Barbecue (215 N Main St; sandwiches $6-11, brisket per pound $16; ⏲10am-8pm) A longtime Lockhart favorite since 1932, with sausage so good Lyndon Johnson had Black's cater a party at the nation's capital.

Kreuz Market (☎512-398-2361; 619 N Colorado St; brisket per pound $17, sides extra; ⏲10:30am-8pm) Serving Lockhart since 1900, the barnlike Kreuz Market uses a dry rub. This means you shouldn't insult it by asking for barbecue sauce – Kreuz doesn't serve it, and the meat doesn't need it.

Chisholm Trail Bar-B-Q (☎512-398-6027; 1323 S Colorado St; lunch plates $7, brisket per pound $10; ⏲8am-8:30pm) Like Black's and Kreuz Market, Chisholm Trail has been named one of the top 10 barbecue restaurants in the state by *Texas Monthly* magazine.

Smitty's Market (208 S Commerce St; lunch plates $7, brisket per pound $12; ⏲7am-6pm Mon-Sat, 9am-6:30pm Sun) The blackened pit room and homely dining room are all original (knives used to be chained to the tables). Ask to have the fat trimmed off the brisket if you're particular about that.

will let you pick your own. Visit www.texaspeaches.com for a list of more than 20 local **peach farms**.

Thanks to its conducive *terroir*, the area is also becoming known for its prolific wineries. If winery-hopping is on the agenda, print a map from www.texaswinetrail.com or www.wineroad290.com.

National Museum of the Pacific War MUSEUM
(www.pacificwarmuseum.org; 340 E Main St; adult/child $14/7; ⏲9am-5pm) This museum complex consists of three war-centric galleries: the **Admiral Nimitz Museum**, chronicling the life and career of Fredericksburg's most famous son; the **George HW Bush Gallery of the Pacific War**, a large, impressive building housing big planes, big boats and big artillery; and the **Pacific Combat Zone**, a 3-acre site that's been transformed into a South Pacific battle zone.

Enchanted Rock State Natural Area PARK
(☎830-685-3636; www.tpwd.state.tx.us; 16710 Ranch Rd 965; adult/child $7/free; ⏲8am-10pm) North of town about 18 miles, you'll find a dome of pink granite dating from the Proterozoic era rising 425ft above ground – one of the largest batholiths in the US. If you want to climb it, go early; gates close when the daily attendance quota is reached.

Sleeping & Eating

Fredericksburg is a popular weekend getaway, especially during the spring, when room rates are at their highest.

Gastehaus Schmidt ACCOMMODATION SERVICES
(☎866-427-8374, 830-997-5612; www.fbglodging.com; 231 W Main St) Nearly 300 B&Bs do business in this county; this reservation service helps sort them out.

Fredericksburg Inn & Suites MOTEL **$$**
(☎830-997-0202; www.fredericksburg-inn.com; 201 S Washington St; d $110-180, ste $150-220; P ❄ ☎ ≋ 🐾) Tops in the midpriced-motel category, this place was built to look like the historic house it sits behind, and it succeeds. A fabulously inviting pool with a waterslide, a spacious hot tub and clean, updated rooms make it good value for the price.

Fredericksburg Herb Farm COTTAGE **$$$**
(☎844-596-2302; www.fredericksburgherbfarm.com; 405 Whitney St; r from $180; P ❄ ☎) In a lushly landscaped setting on the west side of town, these comfy flower-trimmed cottages make for a peaceful getaway – particularly if you add in a spa treatment. The restaurant on-site serves excellent, seasonally inspired cuisine (mains $20-$28); reserve well ahead.

Tubby's Ice House CARIBBEAN **$**
(318 E Austin St; mains $6-10; ⏲11am-9pm Sun-Thu, to midnight Fri & Sat) One block from tourist-lined Main St, Tubby's draws a laid-back,

SCENIC DRIVE: WILDFLOWER TRAILS

You know spring has arrived in Texas when you see cars pulling up roadside and families climbing out to take the requisite picture of their kids surrounded by bluebonnets – the state flower. From March to April in Hill Country, orange Indian paintbrushes, deep-purple winecups and white-to-blue bluebonnets are at their peak.

To see vast cultivated fields of color, there's **Wildseed Farms** (www.wildseedfarms.com; 100 Legacy Dr; ⏲9:30am-5pm) FREE, which is 7 miles east of Fredericksburg on US 290. Or for a more do-it-yourself experience, check with TXDOT's **Wildflower Hotline** (800-452-9292) to find out what's blooming where. Taking Rte 16 and FM 1323, north from Fredericksburg and east to Willow City, is usually a good route. Then again you might just set to wandering – most backroads host their own shows daily.

mostly local crowd, who come for plates of pulled pork, jerk chicken, chili-glazed wings, cod fritters and other snacks, plus a fine selection of microbrews. The setting: colorful outdoor picnic tables; and there's a bocce court.

Hill Top Café AMERICAN **$$**
(☎830-997-8922; 10661 N Hwy 87; mains lunch $9-18, dinner $19-30; ⏲11am-2pm & 5-9pm Tue-Sun) Located 10 miles north of town inside a renovated 1950s gas station, this cozy roadhouse serves up satisfying meals and Hill Country ambience at its best. Reservations recommended. On weekends it has live blues from the owner, Johnny Nicholas, a former member of the West Coast swing band Asleep at the Wheel. Reservations are recommended.

ℹ Getting There & Away

You can get a shuttle service from the San Antonio Airport through **Stagecoach Taxi and Shuttle** (☎830-385-7722; www.stagecoachtaxiandshuttle.com); the cost is $95 each way for up to four people. However, since driving around the Hill Country is half the fun, your best bet is to drive yourself.

Luckenbach

As small as Luckenbach is – three permanent residents, not counting the cat – it's big on Texas charm. You won't find a more laid-back place, where the main activity is sitting under an old oak tree with a bottle of Shiner Bock and listening to guitar pickers, who are often accompanied by roosters.

The heart of the, er, action is the old trading post established back in 1849 – now the **Luckenbach General Store** (☎830-997-3224; www.luckenbachtexas.com; ⏲10am-9pm Mon-Sat, noon-9pm Sun), which also serves as the local post office, saloon and community center.

Check www.luckenbachtexas.com for the **music schedule**. Sometimes the guitar picking starts at 1pm, sometimes 5pm, and weekends usually see live-music events in the old **dance hall** – a Texas classic. The 4th of July and Labor Day weekends are deluged with visitors going to the concerts.

We'd be remiss if we didn't mention that Luckenbach was made famous in a country song by Waylon Jennings – but we figured you either already knew that, or wouldn't really care.

From Fredericksburg, take US 290 east then take FM 1376 south for about 3 miles.

Bandera

It's not always easy finding real, live cowboys in Texas, but it is in Bandera, which has branded itself the Cowboy Capital of Texas. During the summer, there are usually rodeos every weekend, and on Saturday afternoons, gunslingers and cowboys roam the streets and entertain the crowds during **Cowboys on Main**. Check the **Bandera County Convention & Visitors Bureau** (CVB; ☎800-364-3833; www.banderacowboycapital.com; 126 Hwy 16; ⏲9am-5pm Mon-Fri, 10am-3pm Sat) website for the exact schedules and locations.

Ready to saddle up? The friendly folks at the visitors bureau also know nearly a dozen places in and around town where you can go **horseback riding**. For overnights, they can direct you to **dude ranch accommodations**, with packages that include lodging, meals and an equine excursion; plan on spending about $130 to $160 per adult per night ($45 to $90 for the young'uns).

Another great reason to come to Bandera? Drinking beer and dancing in one of the many hole-in-the-wall cowboy bars and honky-tonks, where you'll find friendly locals, good live music and a rich atmosphere. Mosey over to the patio at **11th Street Cowboy Bar** (www.11thstreetcowboybar.com; 307 11th St; ⏲10am-2am Tue-Sat, from noon Sun) or **Arky Blue's Silver Dollar Saloon** (308 Main St; ⏲10am-2am). Both bars have live country crooners from Friday to Sunday.

San Antonio

In most large cities, downtown is bustling with businesspeople dressed for office work hurrying to their meetings and luncheons. Not so in San Antonio. Instead, downtown is filled with tourists in shorts consulting their maps. In fact, many people are surprised to find that two of the state's most popular destinations – the Riverwalk and the Alamo – are right smack dab in the middle of downtown, surrounded by historic hotels, tourist attractions and souvenir shops. The volume of visitors is daunting, but the lively Tex-Mex culture is worth experiencing.

Sights & Activities

The intersection of Commerce and Losoya Sts is the very heart of downtown and the Riverwalk, which runs in a U-shape below street level. Signs point out access stairways, but a 3D map bought at the info center is the best way to get oriented. The artsy **Southtown** neighborhood and **King William Historic District** lie south along the river.

Downtown

★The Alamo HISTORIC BUILDING
(☎210-225-1391; www.thealamo.org; 300 Alamo Plaza; ⏲9am-5:30pm Sep-May, to 7pm Jun-Aug) FREE Find out why the story of the Alamo can rouse a Texan's sense of state pride like few other things. For many, it's not so much a tourist attraction as a pilgrimage and you might notice some of the visitors getting downright dewy-eyed at the description of how a few hundred revolutionaries died defending the fort against thousands of Mexican troops.

★Riverwalk WATERFRONT
(www.thesanantonioriverwalk.com) A little slice of Europe in the heart of downtown San Antonio, the Riverwalk is an essential part of the San Antonio experience. This is no ordinary riverfront, but a charming canal and pedestrian street that is the main artery at the heart of San Antonio's tourism efforts. For the best overview, hop on a Rio San Antonio river cruise.

Rio San Antonio Cruises BOAT TOUR
(☎210-244-5700; www.riosanantonio.com; tour $8.25, taxi one-way/24hr pass from $5/10; ⏲9am-9pm) These 40-minute narrated cruises give you a good visual overview of the river and a light history lesson. You can buy your tickets online, or get them on the waterfront at any of the stops. No reservations are necessary and tours leave every 15 to 20 minutes.

Around Town

Brackenridge Park PARK
(www.brackeridgepark.org; 3910 N St Mary's St; miniature train $3.50, carousel $2.50; ⏲5am-11pm) North of downtown near Trinity University, this 343-acre park is a great place to spend the day with your family. In addition to the **San Antonio Zoo** (☎210-734-7184; www.sazoo.org; 3903 N St Mary's St; adult/child $14.25/11.25; ⏲9am-5pm), you'll find the Brackenridge Eagle **miniature train**, an old-fashioned **carousel** and the **Japanese Tea Gardens**.

San Antonio Museum of Art MUSEUM
(SAMA; www.samuseum.org; 200 W Jones Ave; adult/child $10/free, free admission 4-9pm Tue & 10am-noon Sun; ⏲10am-5pm Wed-Sun, to 9pm Tue & Fri) Housed in the original 1880s Lone Star Brewery, which is a piece of art itself, the San Antonio Museum of Art is off Broadway St just north of downtown. San Antonio's strong Latino influence is reflected in an impressive trove of Latin American art, including Spanish colonial, Mexican and pre-Columbian – one of the most comprehensive collections in the US.

McNay Art Museum MUSEUM
(☎210-824-5368; www.mcnayart.org; 6000 N New Braunfels Ave; adult/child $10/free, extra for special exhibits; ⏲10am-4pm Tue, Wed & Fri, to 9pm Thu, to 5pm Sat, noon-5pm Sun, grounds 7am-6pm daily) In addition to seeing paintings by household names such as Van Gogh, Picasso, Matisse, Renoir, O'Keeffe and Cézanne, half the fun is wandering the spectacular Spanish Colonial revival-style mansion that was the private residence of Marion Koogler McNay.

San Antonio Missions National Historical Park HISTORIC BUILDING
(www.nps.gov/saan; ⏲9am-5pm) Spain's missionary presence can best be felt at the ruins of the four missions south of town: Missions Concepción (1731), San José (1720), San Juan (1731) and Espada (1745–56). Religious

San Antonio

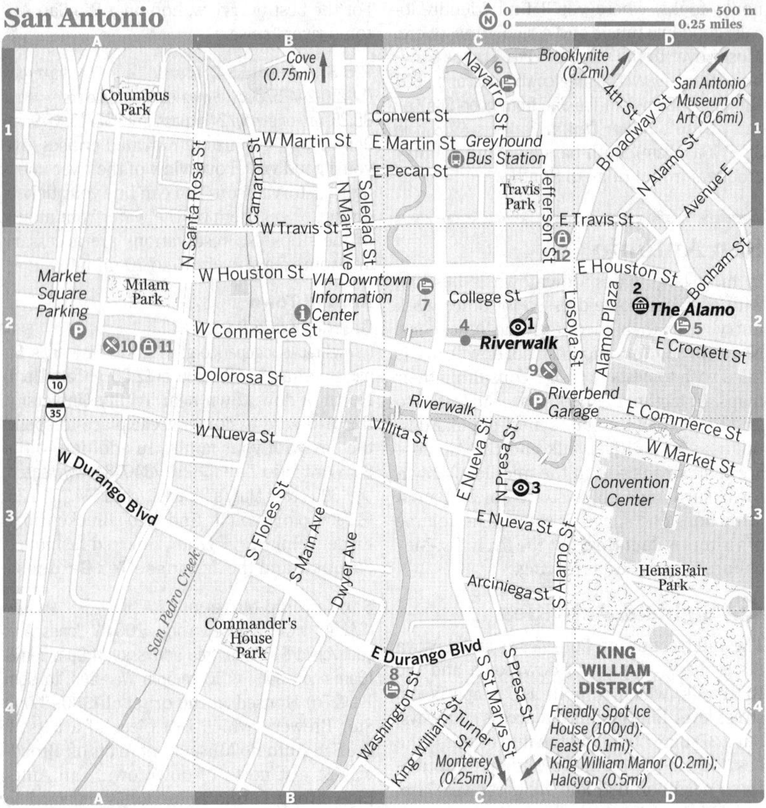

San Antonio

Top Sights
1 Riverwalk.........C2
2 The Alamo.........D2

Sights
3 La Villita Historic Arts Village.........C3

Activities, Courses & Tours
4 Rio San Antonio Cruises.........C2

Sleeping
5 Crockett Hotel.........D2
6 Hotel Havana.........C1
7 Hotel Valencia.........C2
8 Ogé House.........C4

Eating
9 Boudro's.........C2
10 Mi Tierra Cafe & Bakery.........A2

Shopping
11 Market Square.........A2
12 Paris Hatters.........C2

services are still held in the mission churches of San José, San Juan and Espada, and the mariachi Mass at 12:30pm on Sunday at San José church is a San Antonio tradition.

Festivals & Events

San Antonio Stock Show & Rodeo RODEO
(www.sarodeo.com) Big-name concerts follow each night's rodeo; 16 days in mid-February.

Fiesta San Antonio CULTURAL
(www.fiesta-sa.org) For over 10 days in mid-April there are river parades, carnivals, Tejano music, dancing and tons of food in a mammoth, citywide party.

Sleeping

San Antonio has a plethora of hotel rooms, so you have plenty of choices right in the downtown area.

★King William Manor B&B $$
(210-222-0144; www.kingwilliammanor.com; 1037 S Alamo St; d $140-190; P) In a neighborhood known for beautiful old houses and B&Bs, this grand, Greek Revival mansion occupying a large corner lot still manages to stand out. Maybe it's the columns, maybe it's the sprawling lawn or perhaps the wraparound porches. The inside lives up to the exterior, with understatedly elegant rooms, some of which are enormous.

★Hotel Havana HOTEL $$
(210-222-2008; www.havanasanantonio.com; 1015 Navarro St; r $115-280; P@) Texas design guru and hotelier Liz Lambert could make a radish look cool. Luckily she's turned her sights on fixing up a few lucky properties such as this one, judiciously adding eclectic touches – a retro pink refrigerator, for example – to her clean, elegant designs.

Crockett Hotel HOTEL $$
(210-225-6500; www.crocketthotel.com; 320 Bonham St; r $130-180; P) No wonder pictures of the Alamo are always tightly cropped. Pull back and you can see the Crockett's sign hovering just behind the fort. (In Texas, they call that 'spittin' distance.') Rooms are basic but pleasant enough, and there's an outdoor pool and Jacuzzi, plus a good breakfast buffet.

Noble Inns B&B $$
(210-223-2353; www.nobleinns.com; r from $150; P) This collection of three inns has something for everyone – at least everyone who likes antiques and Victorian style. **Ogé House** (www.nobleinns.com; 209 Washington St; d $150-250, ste $290-370; ; blue line) is the most elegant of the three, with lushly appointed rooms and a prime location on the residential end of the Riverwalk.

Hotel Valencia BOUTIQUE HOTEL $$$
(210-227-9700; www.hotelvalencia-riverwalk.com; 150 E Houston St; d $170-320; P) Faux-mink throws, molded concrete, light shining through perforated metal – this place is all about texture. It could have been transported from New York City, both in its minimalist-chic style and in the size of some of the smaller rooms, but it's a hip option for those who eschew chains and historic hotels.

Eating

The Riverwalk offers easy pickings for dinner and drinks, but they're there for the tourists, so don't be surprised if there are busloads of them. South St Marys and S Alamo Sts in the Southtown and King William districts also host a good number of eateries as does the Pearl Complex, 2 miles north of downtown. Look for hole-in-the-wall Mexican joints scattered the length of N Flores St.

★Cove AMERICAN $
(210-227-2683; www.thecove.us; 606 W Cypress St; mains $8-12; 11am-10pm Tue-Thu, to 11pm Fri & Sat, noon-8pm Sun;) This weird, wonderful place is a restaurant, bar, laundromat and car wash. As casual as the restaurant is, the food is top-notch, made from organic, sustainable meat and produce. Sure, it's just tacos, burgers, salads and appetizers but the food is made with love.

Monterey AMERICAN $$
(210-745-2581; www.themontereysa.com; 1127 S St Marys St; mains $9-19; 6-10pm Tue-Thu, to 2am Fri & Sat, 10am-2pm Sun) Extra style points to this King William gastropub located in a former gas station with a big old patio. Despite the small number of options, the menu will please most foodies and you'll be dazzled by the choices available when it comes to its extensive selection of microbrews and wine. A great all-around place to hang out.

★Southerleigh MODERN AMERICAN $$
(210-455-5701; www.southerleigh.com; 136 E Grayson St; mains lunch $12-18, dinner $18-36; 11am-midnight Mon-Fri, 2pm-1am Sat;) In the restaurant-packed Pearl Complex,

WORTH A TRIP

FLOORE'S COUNTRY STORE

This terrific old bar and dance hall first opened in 1942 as a store run by a friend of Willie Nelson. (Willie used to play here nightly; the sign still says so.) Visit **John T Floore's Country Store** (210-695-8827; www.liveatfloores.com; 14492 Old Bandera Rd, Helotes; 11am-midnight Fri & Sat, to 10pm Sun) today and you'll discover the true way to hear Texas country music, whether in the outdoor yard or by the fire in the rustic building. There are performances on Friday and Saturday nights; Sunday night is family dance night and there's no cover. Bandera Rd is off Hwy 16.

WORTH A TRIP

THE HOME OF SHINER BOCK

The highlight of any trip to Shiner, Texas, the self-proclaimed 'cleanest little city in Texas,' is a tour of the **Spoetzl Brewery** (☎361-594-3852; www.shiner.com; 603 E Brewery St; tours free; ⏲tours 11am & 1:30pm Mon-Fri year-round, plus 10am & 2:30pm Jun-Aug) FREE where Shiner Bock beer is brewed. Czech and German settlers who began making beer under brewmaster Kosmos Spoetzl founded the brewery 100 years ago. Today the brewery still produces several types using the same methods, including bock, blonde, honey wheat, summer stock and winter ale. You can sample the beers for free after the tour in the little bar.

Shiner is about an hour and a half (92 miles) east of San Antonio by car; to get there, take I-10 east 57 miles, head south on US-183, then east on US-90 at Gonzales. It's about the same distance from Austin; just take US-183 south and follow the same directions starting at Gonzales.

Southerleigh stands out for its farm-to-table comfort fare. Mac and cheese with crab, cornmeal-crusted catfish, stewed oxtail pie and an enormous gourmet chili dog are recent favorites. The setting is vintage industrial chic: this was once the historical Pearl Brewery, and the excellent and varied house brews (21 on tap) are once again flowing through the 19th-century complex.

Kids get to shape their own pretzels, which are then baked and served as appetizers (free of charge).

Paloma Blanca MEXICAN $$
(☎210-822-6151; 5800 Broadway St, Alamo Heights; mains lunch $8-11, dinner $10-25; ⏲11am-9pm Mon-Wed, to 10pm Thu & Fri, 10am-10pm Sat, 10am-9pm Sun) There are oodles of great Mexican choices around, but this place sets itself apart with a sleek and stylish ambience – think dim lighting, exposed brick walls and oversize artwork – and outstanding traditional cooking (enchiladas, chiles rellenos, quesadillas).

Mi Tierra Cafe & Bakery TEX-MEX $$
(☎210-225-1262; www.mitierracafe.com; 218 Produce Row; mains $12-18; ⏲24hr) Dishing out traditional Mexican food since 1941, this 500-seat behemoth in Market Square sprawls across several festively decorated dining areas, giving the busy waitstaff and strolling mariachis quite a workout. It's also open 24 hours, making it ideal for 3am enchilada cravings.

Feast TAPAS $$
(☎210-354-1024; www.feastsa.com; 1024 S Alamo St; small plates $7-22, brunch $10-16; ⏲5-10pm Tue-Thu, to 11pm Fri & Sat, 10:30am-2:30pm Sun) The seasonally inspired tapas dishes are solid, but the atmosphere alone is worth the trip to King William district. Clear Lucite chairs, sparkly pendant lights and faux taxidermy come together to provide a whimsically modern feel. The front patio is even more enticing, with twinkling lights beneath a big, shady tree and a garden-like backdrop.

Boudro's TEX-MEX $$$
(☎210-224-8484; 421 E Commerce St, Riverwalk; mains lunch $11-16, dinner $24-38; ⏲11am-11pm Sun-Thu, to midnight Fri & Sat) This brightly colored waterside restaurant is hugely popular with locals. Fresh guacamole is made right at your table. The upscale Tex-Mex menu reveals some gourmet surprises, such as jumbo shrimp and gulf crab enchiladas, mesquite-grilled quail stuffed with wild mushrooms, and achiote-spiced lamb chops.

Drinking & Nightlife

The Riverwalk's many chain clubs blur together even before you've started drinking. Resist their glossy allure and opt for one of these San Antonio originals.

★ **Friendly Spot Ice House** BAR
(☎210-224-2337; 943 S Alamo St; ⏲3pm-midnight Mon-Fri, from 11am Sat & Sun; 👪🐾) What could be friendlier than a big, pecan-tree-shaded yard filled with colorful metal lawn chairs? Friends (and their dogs) gather to knock back some longnecks while the kids amuse themselves in the playground area.

Brooklynite COCKTAIL BAR
(☎212-444-0707; www.thebrooklynitesa.com; 516 Brooklyn Ave; ⏲5pm-2am) Beer and wine are easy to come by in San Antonio, but this is where you head for a creative, handcrafted cocktail. Vintage wallpaper and wingback chairs give the place a dark, Victorian-esque decor, where you can sip a mezcal-topped Doxycycline or the bourbon-forward Lion's Tail in a fittingly dignified atmosphere.

Cove BEER HALL
(☎210-227-2683; www.thecove.us; 606 W Cypress St; ⊙11am-10pm Tue-Thu, to 11pm Fri & Sat, noon-8pm Sun;) Live music is just part of the reason to hang out at this chill beer hall. The Cove is a unique combo of food stand, cafe, laundromat, car wash. It even has a kiddie playground.

Halcyon CAFE
(www.halcyoncoffeebar.com; 1414 S Alamo St; ⊙7am-2am Mon-Fri, from 8am Sat & Sun;) With excellent coffees, creative cocktails and an inviting coffeehouse vibe (with outdoor seating as well), Halcyon makes a fine destination after a bike ride along the river. There's plenty of good snacking and dining choices, and even make-your-own smores for the pyrotechnically inclined. Occasional live music.

☆ Entertainment

For listings of local music and cultural events, pick up the free weekly *San Antonio Current* (www.sacurrent.com).

Four-time NBA champions the **San Antonio Spurs** (www.nba.com/spurs) shoot hoops at the **AT&T Center** (☎tickets 800-745-3000; www.attcenter.com; 1 AT&T Center Pkwy) off I-35. Purchase tickets through **Ticketmaster** (www.ticketmaster.com).

Shopping

A few artisan craft shops exist among the tourist-T-shirt-filled Riverwalk. The old buildings of the city's first neighborhood, **La Villita Historic Arts Village** (☎210-207-8614; www.lavillita.com; 418 Villita St; ⊙most shops 10am-6pm), house the largest concentration of galleries and boutiques.

Pearl Complex MALL
(www.atpearl.com; 200 E Grayson St) The old Pearl Brewery has received a massive face-lift as part of the new Pearl development north of downtown, including shops, cafes and restaurants.

Market Square MARKET
(☎210-207-8600; www.marketsquaresa.com; 514 W Commerce St; ⊙10am-8pm Jun-Aug, to 6pm Sep-May) A little bit of Mexico in downtown San Antonio, Market Square is a fair approximation of a trip south of the border, with Mexican food, mariachi bands and store after store filled with Mexican wares. A big chunk of the square is taken up by El Mercado, the largest Mexican marketplace outside of Mexico.

Paris Hatters ACCESSORIES
(☎210-223-3453; www.parishatters.com; 119 Broadway St; ⊙10:30am-6:30pm Mon-Sat, noon-5pm Sun) Despite the name, this is no Parisian haberdashery, but a purveyor of fine cowboy hats since 1917. You'll walk out looking like a real cowboy with a hat that's been shaped and fitted to your very own noggin. It's one of the best places in the state to get a Stetson (or whatever brand of hat is mutually agreed to suit you).

Information

Visitor center 'amigos' (in turquoise shirts and straw hats) roam the downtown core offering directions.

Convention & Visitors Bureau (☎800-447-3372; www.visitsanantonio.com; 317 Alamo Plaza; ⊙9am-5pm, to 6pm Jun-Aug) Stop by the well-stocked Convention & Visitors Bureau, opposite the Alamo, for maps and brochures; their website also has loads of information useful for pre-planning. The staff can answer any questions you have and can also sell you passes for tours or for VIA buses and streetcars.

San Antonio Public Library (www.mysapl.org; 600 Soledad St; ⊙9am-9pm Mon-Thu, to 5pm Fri & Sat, 11am-5pm Sun) Branch locations provide free internet access across the city.

Getting There & Away

San Antonio is served by the **San Antonio International Airport** (SAT; ☎210-207-3433; www.sanantonio.gov/sat; 9800 Airport Blvd), about 9 miles north of downtown. **VIA Metropolitan Transit** (☎210-362-2020; www.viainfo.net; ride/day pass $1.20/4) city bus 2 runs from the airport to downtown. A taxicab ride will cost about $26. Major car-rental agencies all have offices at the airport.

From the **Greyhound Bus Station** (☎210-270-5868; www.greyhound.com; 500 N St Marys St), you can get to all the big cities in the state (and lots of the small ones). The *Sunset Limited* (Florida–California) and *Texas Eagle* (San Antonio–Chicago) trains stop a few days a week (usually late at night) at the **Amtrak Station** (www.amtrak.com; 350 Hoefgen Ave).

DITCH THE CAR

Parking-garage fees in San Antonio really add up, but you can park free at the **VIA Ellis Alley Park & Ride** (btwn E Crockett & Center Sts), a quick two stops from the Alamo. Ask for a parking transfer on the bus and put it in the slot to 'pay' when you exit the garage.

The free tourist-friendly E trolleybus runs a circular route around downtown. Loads of buses go further afield. Buy a day pass ($4) at the **VIA Downtown Information Center** (210-362-2020; www.viainfo.net; 211 W Commerce St; 7am-6pm Mon-Fri, 9am-2pm Sat).

You can also get around town by checking out a bike from one of the many kiosks of **San Antonio B-cycle** (sanantonio.bcycle.com).

Houston

Concrete superhighways may blind you to Houston's good points when you first zoom into this sprawling city. You'll miss out if you limit yourself to downtown: diverse residential neighborhoods and enclaves of restaurants and shops are spread far and wide.

The leafy Museum District is the city's cultural center; Upper Kirby and River Oaks have upscale shopping and dining; Montrose contains cute bungalows, quirky shops and eateries; Midtown has up-and-coming condos and some good restaurants; Washington Ave is nightlife central; and the Heights has historic homes and boutiques.

Sights & Activities

Museum lovers will find plenty to love in the area north of Hermann Park. To get a full list of options or to plot your route, check out the map on the **Houston Museum District** (www.houstonmuseumdistrict.org) website.

A couple of the city's main attractions – NASA's Space Center Houston in Clear Lake and Galveston Island – are outside the city limits, requiring a 45-minute drive down I-45.

★ Menil Collection MUSEUM
(www.menil.org; 1515 Sul Ross St; 11am-7pm Wed-Sun) FREE The late local philanthropists John and Dominique de Menil collected more than 17,000 works of painting, drawing, sculpture, archaeological artifacts and more during their lives. The modernist building, designed by Renzo Piano, houses rotating highlights from the collection – everything from 5000-year-old antiquities to works by Kara Walker and today's art stars – plus rotating exhibitions. Don't forget to also saunter over to the Cy Twombly Gallery and the highly meditative Rothko Chapel, annexes of the collection.

Museum of Fine Arts Houston MUSEUM
(www.mfah.org; 1001 Bissonnet St; adult/teen/child $15/7.50/free; 10am-5pm Tue & Wed, to 9pm Thu, to 7pm Fri & Sat, 12:15-7pm Sun; Metro Rail-Museum District) French impressionism and post-1945 European and American painting really shine in this nationally renowned palace of art, which includes major works by Picasso and Rembrandt. Across the street, admire the talents of luminaries such as Rodin and Matisse in the associated **Cullen Sculpture Garden** (cnr Montrose Blvd & Bissonnet St; dawn to dusk) FREE.

Art Car Museum MUSEUM
(www.artcarmuseum.com; 140 Heights Blvd; 11am-6pm Wed-Sun) FREE The handful of art cars represented here are something to behold; some of them are straight out of *Mad Max*. But they're really just bait to lure you in to check out the quirky-cool rotating art exhibits, which have included subjects such as road refuse and bone art.

Houston Museum of Natural Science MUSEUM
(713-639-4629; www.hmns.org; 5555 Hermann Park Dr; adult/child $20/15, free admission 3-6pm Thu; 9am-6pm; ; Metro RailHermann Park/Rice) World-class traveling exhibits – on everything from prehistoric cave paintings to Mayan civilization – have always been a big part of the attraction at this stellar museum. The permanent collection is no less impressive, with massive dinosaur skeletons, mummies from ancient Egypt, rare gems (like a 2000-carat blue topaz) and interactive exhibits on earth's biosphere.

Festivals & Events

★ Houston Livestock Show & Rodeo RODEO
(www.rodeohouston.com) For three weeks beginning in late February or early March, rodeo fever takes over Houston. The barbecue cook-off is a hot seller, but so are the nightly rodeos followed by big-name concerts – starring Bruno Mars to Blake Shelton. Buy tickets way in advance. Fairgrounds-only admission gets you access to midway rides, livestock shows, shopping and nightly dances.

Art Car Parade & Festival PARADE
(www.thehoustonartcarparade.com) Wacky, arted-out vehicles (think *Mad Max* or giant rabbits) hit the streets en masse on the second Saturday of April. The parade itself is complemented by weekend-long festivities, including concerts.

Sleeping

Chain motels line all the major freeways. If you are visiting the Space Center and Galveston, consider staying on I-45 south.

Morty Rich Hostel HOSTEL $
(713-636-9776; www.hiusa.org/houston; 501 Lovett Blvd; dm $26-32, d $80; P ❄ @ 🛜 ≋) A beautiful Montrose mansion (a previous mayor's residence) hosts this plush Hosteling International member. The rooms are bright and clean, with four to eight rickety beds per dorm, many with ensuite. There's also one private double (book well ahead). Hang out in the billiard room or cool off in the backyard pool after a hard day's sightseeing. Accessible via public transport.

Modern B&B B&B $$
(832-279-6367; http://modernbb.com; 4003 Hazard St; r incl breakfast $100-225; P ❄ @ 🛜) An architect's dream, this mod, 11-room inn is rife with airy decks, spiral staircases and sunlight. Think organic mattresses, in-room Jacuzzi tubs, private decks and iPod docking stations. Owners also rent out several nearby apartments.

Sara's Inn on the Boulevard INN $$
(713-868-1130; www.saras.com; 941 Heights Blvd; r incl breakfast $130-200; P ❄ @ 🛜) A Queen Anne Victorian feels right at home among the historic houses of the Heights. Eleven airy rooms say 'boutique hotel' more than 'frilly B&B.' But the the inn still has the kind of sprawling Southern porch that makes you want to gossip over mint juleps.

★ **Hotel ZaZa** BOUTIQUE HOTEL $$$
(713-526-1991; www.hotelzaza.com; 5701 Main St; r $250-295; P ❄ @ 🛜 ≋; Metro RailHermann Park/Rice) Hip, flamboyant and fabulous. From the bordello-esque colors to zebra accent chairs, everything about Hotel ZaZa is good fun – and surprisingly unpretentious. Our favorite rooms are the concept suites such as the eccentric Geisha House, or the space age 'Houston We Have a Problem.' You can't beat the location overlooking the Museum district's Hermann Park, near the light rail.

La Colombe d'Or Hotel LUXURY HOTEL $$$
(713-524-7999; www.lacolombedor.com; 3410 Montrose Blvd; ste $295-395; P ❄ 🛜) Not unlike the famed Colombe d'Or in Provence (no relation), this guesthouse offers beautifully designed rooms and an excellent French restaurant. Each of the five exquisite, one-bedroom suites were inspired by the colors and styles of a great artist – Cezanne, Van Gogh, Renoir. Suitably so, as the rare oil paintings and antiques decorating this 1923 Montrose mansion are museum quality.

> DON'T MISS
>
> **HOUSTON, WE HAVE AN ATTRACTION...**
>
> Dream of a landing on the moon? You can't get any closer (without years of training) than at **Space Center Houston** (281-244-2100; http://spacecenter.org; 1601 NASA Pkwy 1; with audio guide adult/child $24/19; 10am-5pm Mon-Fri, to 7pm Sat & Sun) off I-45 S, the official visitor center and museum of NASA's Johnson Space Center. Interactive exhibits let you try your hand at picking up an object in space or landing the shuttle. Be sure to enter the theater that shows short films, because you exit past *Apollo* capsules and history exhibits. The free tram tour covers the center at work – shuttle training facilities, zero-gravity labs and the original mission control, from which was uttered the famous words, 'Houston, we have a problem.'

Eating

Houston's restaurant scene is smokin' hot – and we don't just mean the salsa. In fact, Houstonians eat out more than residents of any other US city. To keep abreast of what's in and what isn't, we recommend the razor-tongued **Fearless Critic** (www.fearlesscritic.com). Twitterites can follow @eatdrinkhouston.

Downtown

Treebeards SOUTHERN $
(http://treebeards.com; 315 Travis St; mains $8-12; 11am-2:30pm Mon-Fri) Locals flock here at lunchtime to chow down on savory Cajun gumbos and crawfish étoufée, but don't discount the appeal of daily changing specials like jerk chicken and blackened catfish.

Original Ninfas MEXICAN $$
(www.ninfas.com; 2704 Navigation Blvd; mains $11-24; 11am-10pm Mon-Fri, 10am-10pm Sat & Sun) Generations of Houstonians have come here since the 1970s for shrimp diablo, *tacos al carbon* (tacos cooked over charcoal) and handmade tamales crafted with pride.

Central Houston

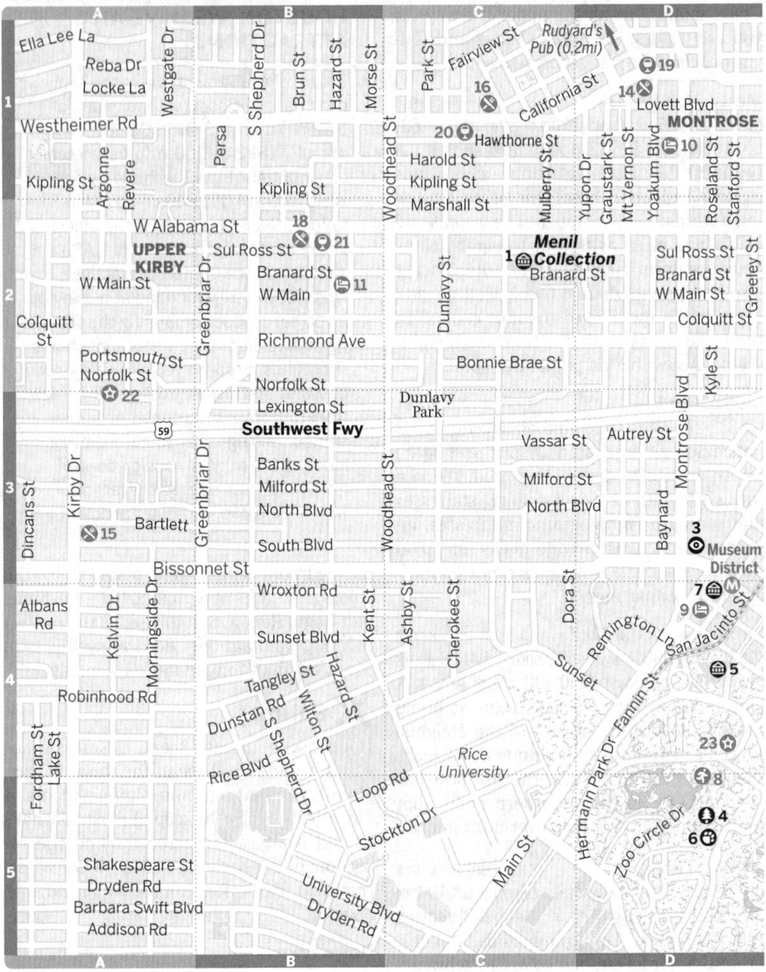

Midtown

Breakfast Klub SOUTHERN $
(www.thebreakfastklub.com; 3711 Travis St; mains $9-16; ⏲7am-2pm Mon-Fri, 8am-2pm Sat & Sun; P 📶) Come early; devotees line up around the block for down-home breakfast faves like fried wings 'n' waffles. Lunch hours are only slightly less crazy at this coffeehouse-like eatery favored by local girl Beyonce, and her boy, Jay-Z. Coffee is great and there's wi-fi.

Reef SEAFOOD $$
(☎713-526-8282; www.reefhouston.com; 2600 Travis St; lunch mains $10-30, dinner $22-36; ⏲11am-10pm Mon-Fri, 5-11pm Sat; Metro Rail McGowen) Gulf Coast seafood is creatively prepared and served in a sleek and sophisticated dining room. Chef Bryan Caswell has won oodles of national awards for himself and his restaurant.

Sparrow Bar & Cookshop MODERN AMERICAN $$$
(☎713-524-6922; http://sparrowhouston.com; 3701 Travis St; mains $16-32; ⏲10am-3pm & 5-11pm Tue-Sat; 🖊) Nationally renowned chef Monica Pope brings top-quality local and organic ingredients to life in her new American cuisine. Share plates might include

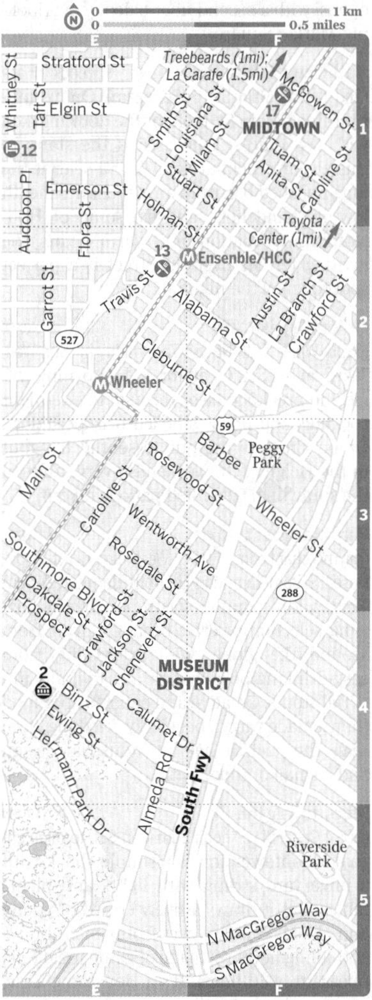

Central Houston

Top Sights
1 Menil Collection.....C2

Sights
2 Children's Museum of Houston.....E4
3 Cullen Sculpture Garden.....D3
4 Hermann Park.....D5
5 Houston Museum of Natural Science.....D4
6 Houston Zoo.....D5
7 Museum of Fine Arts Houston.....D4

Activities, Courses & Tours
8 Hermann Park Miniature Train.....D5

Sleeping
9 Hotel ZaZa.....D4
10 La Colombe d'Or Hotel.....D1
11 Modern B&B.....B2
12 Morty Rich Hostel.....E1

Eating
13 Breakfast Klub.....E2
14 El Real.....D1
15 Goode Co BBQ.....A3
16 Hugo's.....C1
17 Reef.....F1
Sparrow Bar & Cookshop.....(see 13)
18 Tacos Tierra Caliente.....B2

Drinking & Nightlife
19 Hay Merchant.....D1
20 Poison Girl.....C1
21 West Alabama Ice House.....B2

Entertainment
22 McGonigel's Mucky Duck.....A3
23 Miller Outdoor Theatre.....D4

bacon-wrapped dates stuffed with chorizo, mushroom dumplings with a blue cheese sauce or vegetable dal. Start off with a refreshing cocktail (like the grapefruit ginger spritzer). On a nice night, patio dining is a must.

Montrose & the Museum District

Tacos Tierra Caliente MEXICAN $

(1919 W Alabama St; tacos around $2; 9am-11pm) By our reckoning, these are the best tacos in the city, and thousands of Houstonians agree. They're served piled high from a battered food truck, and although there's nowhere to sit, just across the road is the **West Alabama Ice House** (713-528-6874; 1919 W Alabama St; 10am-midnight Mon-Fri, to 1am Sat, noon-midnight Sun). A fine spot for a taco feast while nursing a few cold ones.

Goode Co BBQ BARBECUE $$

(www.goodecompany.com; 5109 Kirby Dr; plates $11-17; 11am-10pm) Belly up to the beef brisket, smoked sausage and gallon ice teas in a big ol' barn or out back on picnic tables.

El Real TEX-MEX $$

(1201 Westheimer Rd; mains $10-24; 11am-10pm Sun-Thu, to midnight Fri & Sat) Set in a former movie theater, El Real serves up first-rate Tex-Mex, with sizzling fajitas, steaming enchiladas and fluffy soft-shelled tacos among many standout choices. Warm salsa and chips precede every order, which you can

AND NOW FOR SOMETHING COMPLETELY DIFFERENT

Conservative Houston has a wacky creative streak, especially when it comes to its quirkiest museums. Follow up a visit to the Art Car Museum with a pilgrimage to the **Orange Show Center for Visionary Art** (☎713-926-6368; www.orangeshow.org; 2402 Munger St; adult/child $5/2; ⊙10am-2pm Wed-Sun), a mazelike junk-art tribute to one man's favorite citrus fruit. The center fosters the folk-art vision by offering children's art education and keeping up the 50,000-strong **Beer Can House** (www.beercanhouse.org; 222 Malone St, off Memorial Dr; adult/child $5/2; ⊙noon-5pm Sat & Sun).

nibble while watching old Westerns (no sound) projected onto the back wall.

★Hugo's MEXICAN $$$
(☎713-524-7744; http://hugosrestaurant.net; 1600 Westheimer Rd; lunch mains $15-22, dinner $23-30; ⊙11am-10pm Mon-Thu, 11am-11pm Fri & Sat, 10am-9pm Sun) Chef Hugo Ortega elevates regional Mexican cooking and street food to high art in this much celebrated Montrose gem. You can sample Oaxacan-style *tlayuda* (huge corn tortilla with cheese and skirt steak), *tikin xic* (achiote-rubbed grouper with jicama salad), or nibble on sauteed *chapulines* (grasshoppers). Brunch is outstanding. Book ahead for any meal.

Drinking & Nightlife

To the youngish set, the stretch of Washington Ave bars and clubs defines all that is hip and happening in Houston nightlife (although lately downtown is none too shabby in that department). The corner of White Oak Dr and Studemont St in the Heights has a few funky little bars, including a roadhouse, a tiki bar and a live-music club in an old house.

★La Carafe BAR
(813 Congress St; ⊙1pm-2am) Set in Houston's oldest building, La Carafe is the most atmospheric bar in the city. It's a warmly lit drinking den, with exposed brick, sepia photos on the walls and flickering candles. You'll also find a great jukebox and a friendly eclectic crowd. On weekends the upstairs bar room opens, with a second floor balcony overlooking Market Square.

Bad News Bar COCKTAIL BAR
(2nd fl, 308 Main St; ⊙5pm-2am) On restaurant-lined Main St, look for the door marked with law offices, then ascend the stairs to this elegant cocktail den. Take a seat at the long polished bar, or in an armchair beneath low-lit chandeliers, and sip some of Houston's finest libations. On warm nights, the inviting terrace over the street is a perfect spot to enjoy the night air.

Onion Creek Cafe CAFE
(3106 White Oak Dr; ⊙7am-midnight Sun-Wed, 7am-2am Thu-Sat) Open for early-morning coffee and breakfast tacos through to late-night cocktails and house-smoked brisket sliders, Onion Creek is the quintessential hangout in the Heights. On weekends every table on the sprawling, tree-filled patio is taken.

Hay Merchant BAR
(haymerchant.com; 1100 Westheimer Rd, Montrose; ⊙3pm-2am Mon-Fri, from 11am Sat & Sun) This wildly popular gastropub has a dazzling selection of craft beers on draft from around the globe, with everything from easy-drinking Belgian-style ales to malty imperial stouts. Creative and delicious bar food (housemade wagyu beef jerky, fried pig ears) seals the deal. It has an industrial design and a small outdoor patio.

Moontower Inn BEER GARDEN
(3004 Canal St; ⊙noon-2am Mon-Sat, to midnight Sun) Moontower Inn is a simple shack with a huge yard strung with lights and picnic tables. But it draws a lively crowd of young and old who hunker over frothy microbrews and filling hot dogs made of game meat (elk, pheasant, wild boar). It's a Houston classic, located about 2 miles east of downtown. Wednesday is movie night.

Poison Girl LOUNGE
(1641 Westheimer Rd; ⊙4pm-2am) Add a festive back patio with a Kool Aid man statue to an arty interior with vintage pinball games and you get one very cool, dive-y bar. Nice eclectic crowd, too.

☆ Entertainment

There's a fair bit of nightlife around the Preston and Main St Sq Metro Rail stops downtown. Montrose and Midtown have clubs, but they're spread around. Look for listings in the independent weekly *Houston Press* (www.houstonpress.com) and in the Thursday edition of the *Houston Chronicle* (www.chron.com).

Live Music

Rudyard's Pub LIVE MUSIC
(713-521-0521; www.rudyards.com; 2010 Waugh Dr; 11:30am-2am) Host to unusual fare (grown-up storytime, punk comedy), plus a mix of experimental and indie bands, Rudyard's is a reliable spot for a fun night out. A great selection of microbrews and good pub grub (especially the burgers).

McGonigel's Mucky Duck LIVE MUSIC
(713-528-5999; www.mcgonigels.com; 2425 Norfolk St; 11am-11pm Mon-Thu, 11am-2am Fri & Sat, 5:30-9pm Sun) Acoustic, Irish, folk and country performers play nightly in pubby surrounds. Concert prices vary – typically running $22 to $30 – but Mondays (open-mic) and Wednesdays (Irish folk) are free. It's a great space with a classy supper-club look, and nicely prepared pub food.

Last Concert Cafe LIVE MUSIC
(713-226-8563; www.lastconcert.com; 1403 Nance St; 11am-2am Tue-Sat, 10:30am-10pm Sun) For a real local original, find your way to the warehouse district northeast of downtown. After you knock on the red door (there's no sign), you can hang out drinking frothy suds at the bar or dig into cheap Tex-Mex and listen to live music in the grassy, palm-filled backyard.

Theater & Performing Arts

The Houston Grand Opera, the Society of the Performing Arts, Houston Ballet, Da Camera chamber orchestra and the Houston Symphony all perform downtown in the **Theater District** (www.houstontheaterdistrict.org). From the district's website, you can purchase tickets and view all schedules.

Miller Outdoor Theatre THEATER
(281-373-3386; www.milleroutdoortheatre.com; 6000 Hermann Park Dr) Hermann Park's outdoor theater is a great place to lay out a blanket on a summer night and enjoy a free concert, play or ballet.

Alley Theatre THEATER
(713-220-5700; www.alleytheatre.org; 615 Texas Ave) Houston's heavy-hitter theater is one of the last in the nation to keep a resident company of actors. From classics to modern plays, the magic of this ensemble is palpable.

Sports

While Houston teams don't get quite the rabid following as, say, the UT Longhorns or the San Antonio Spurs, there's plenty of sports action to be found.

Reliant Stadium FOOTBALL
(www.reliantpark.com; 1 Reliant Park) The **Houston Texans** (www.houstontexans.com) play at this high-tech retractable roof stadium. They draw plenty of raucous crowds.

Minute Maid Park BASEBALL
(713-259-8000; 501 Crawford St) The **Houston Astros** (http://houston.astros.mlb.com) play pro baseball right downtown. The first retractable roof in town still attracts attention, or maybe it's the real steam train that chugs along every home run. See the website for ballpark tour times.

HOUSTON FOR CHILDREN

Kids in tow? Don't miss downtown's **Discovery Green** (www.discoverygreen.com; 1500 McKinney St; 6am-11pm; ; Metro Rail Main St Sq). This 12-acre park has a lake, a playground, fountains to splash in, outdoor art, restaurants and a performance space. The Green has become a hub for fun festivals and activities such as movies on the green, nighttime flea markets – even a Christmas-time ice rink. Check the online calendar for more.

Another great open space for kids is **Hermann Park** (www.hermannpark.org; Fannin St & Hermann Park Dr; 6am-11pm). This 445-acre park is home to playgrounds, a lake with paddleboats, the **Hermann Park Miniature Train** (713-526-2183; www.hermannpark.org; 6104 Hermann Park Dr, Kinder Station, Lake Plaza; rides $3.25; 10am-5:30pm;) and the **Houston Zoo** (www.houstonzoo.org; 6200 Hermann Park Dr; adult/child $16/12; 9am-7pm).

Within walking distance of Hermann Park is the activity-filled **Children's Museum of Houston** (www.cmhouston.org; 1500 Binz St; admission $10, free 5-8pm Thu; 10am-6pm Tue-Sat, to 8pm Thu, noon-6pm Sun), where little ones can make tortillas in a Mexican village or draw in an open-air art studio.

Toyota Center BASKETBALL
(www.houstontoyotacenter.com; 1510 Polk St) Basketball fans can follow the NBA's **Houston Rockets** (www.nba.com/rockets) here.

Shopping

For browsing in more eclectic and locally owned stores, hit the neighborhoods. Along 19th St (between Yale St and Shepherd Dr) in the **Heights** (www.houstonheights.org) you'll find unique antiques, clever crafts and cafes. On the first Saturday of every month, the street takes on a carnival-like air with outdoor booths and entertainment.

In Montrose, **Westheimer St** is a dream for crafty fashionistas and antique-hunters alike. Start on Dunlavy Rd and work your way down the street, where you'll find a mix of used- and new-clothing stores running the gamut from vintage to punk rock to Tokyo mod, plus lots of funky old furniture.

For slightly less rebellious fashion terrain, stroll around **Rice Village** and let the window displays lure you in.

Information

Chase Bank (www.chase.com; 712 Main St) Currency exchange and ATM.

Greater Houston Convention & Visitors Bureau (713-437-5200; www.visithoustontexas.com; City Hall, 901 Bagby St; 9am-4pm Mon-Sat) As much a giant souvenir shop as an info center.

Houston Public Library (www.hpl.lib.tx.us; 500 McKinney St; 10am-6pm Mon, Tue & Thu, to 8pm Wed, to 5pm Sat;) Free internet computers and wi-fi.

Main Post Office (401 Franklin St; 7am-7pm Mon-Fri, 8am-noon Sat) Plenty of parking, at the north edge of downtown.

Getting There & Away

Houston Airport System (www.fly2houston.com) has two airports. Twenty-two miles north of the city center, **George Bush Intercontinental** (IAH; www.fly2houston.com/iah; Will Clayton Parkway or JFK Blvd, off I-59, Beltway 8 or I-45;) serves cities worldwide and is home base for Continental Airlines. Twelve miles southeast of town, **William P Hobby Airport** (HOU; www.fly2houston.com/hobby; Airport Blvd, off Broadway or Monroe Sts;) is a major hub for Southwest Airlines and domestic travel. Read your ticket closely: some airlines, such as Delta, fly out of both airports. You can find every major car-rental agency at either airport.

If you're not renting a car, a shuttle is the most convenient and cost effective way to get downtown. **SuperShuttle** (800-258-3826; www.supershuttle.com) provides regular services from both Bush ($25) and Hobby ($24) airports to hotels and addresses around town.

Cabs are readily available at both airports. Airport rates are determined by zone, and you'll pay either the flat zone rate or the meter rate, whatever's less. You'll shell out $50 to get from George Bush Intercontinental to downtown; from Hobby it's about $25.

The **Metropolitan Transit Authority** (METRO; 713-635-4000; www.ridemetro.org; one-way $1.25) runs bus 102 between George Bush Intercontinental and downtown from 5:30am to 10:50pm. Bus 88 operates between Hobby and downtown 6am to 11pm every day except Sunday.

Long-distance buses arrive at the **Greyhound Bus Terminal** (www.greyhound.com; 2121 Main St), which is located between downtown and the Museum District, and the *Sunset Limited* train stops at the **Amtrak Station** (800-872-7245; www.amtrak.com; 902 Washington Ave) three times a week.

Getting Around

Houston's public transportation is run by the **Metropolitan Transit Authority**. Bus transit is geared toward weekday, downtown commuters. The light-rail train, Metro Rail, however, is exceptionally useful for travelers – particularly the red line. This line links most sights – and some restaurants – along its Downtown–Museum District–Reliant Park corridor. Look online for maps, including downloadable smartphone ones. The Metro Rail operates from 5am until midnight Sunday through Thursday, and until 2:20am on Friday and Saturday.

For quick jaunts about town, you can take advantage of Houston's bike sharing network, the **Houston B-Cycle** (www.houston.bcycle.com; 6am-11pm).

Around Houston

Galveston

Don't think of Galveston as just another beach town. What makes it irresistible is that it's actually a historic town that happens to have some beaches. An easy day trip from Houston, it's also a very popular cruise-ship port, which has been a vital boost to the economy.

WORTH A TRIP

SAN JACINTO MONUMENT

In the late afternoon on April 21, 1836, General Sam Houston and his ragtag Texan army caught up with the Mexican forces of General Antonio López de Santa Anna that were resting on the banks of the San Jacinto River. Fighting was fierce, as Houston's men 'remembered the Alamo,' and the massacre at Goliad. Santa Anna's surrender came relatively quickly. The final tally: 630 Mexicans dead and hundreds more wounded, but only nine Texan casualties. Victory was total. The Mexican army retreated; Texas had won its independence.

More than 1100 acres of the battleground are now preserved as the **San Jacinto Battleground State Historical Site** (www.sanjacinto-museum.org; 3523 Hwy 134; park admission free, attractions vary; ⏲9am-6pm). Tour the museum, watch the movie, then ride up to the observation deck to look over the field. Also part of the historic site is the docked 1912 battleship, USS *Texas*, one of the first steel-plated ships of its era.

The park lies 22 miles east of downtown Houston, via I-10 E. Exit at Crosby-Lynchberg Rd, turn south and take the small car ferry across to the site.

Sights & Activities

Nothing more than a sandy barrier island, Galveston stretches 30 miles in length and is no more than 3 miles wide. The center of activity on the island, the historic 'Strand' district (around the intersection of 22nd and Mechanic Sts) is best covered on foot so you can check out the many attractions, shops, restaurants and bars. Find loads more dining and activity info at **Galveston Island Visitors Center** (☎409-797-5144; www.galveston.com; Ashton Villa, 2328 Broadway; ⏲9am-5pm).

For quick and easy beach access, park anywhere along the seawall. Or, if you want more sand to spread out on, head to **East Beach** (1923 Boddecker Dr, off Seawall Blvd; per vehicle $8; ⏲dawn-dusk Mar-Oct) at the eastern end of the island.

Pier 21 Theater THEATER
(☎409-763-8808; www.galvestonhistory.org; Pier 21; adult/child per film from $6/5; ⏲10am-6pm) Pirate Jean Lafitte and Galveston itself are the subject of two of the interestingly informative films shown here. The third, the *Great Storm*, is the best of the bunch. This 30-minute multimedia documentary recounts the notorious 1900 hurricane through photos, eyewitness accounts and various special effects.

Texas Seaport Museum & Tallship Elissa MUSEUM
(www.galvestonhistory.org; cnr Harborside Dr & 21st St; adult/child $12/9; ⏲9am-6pm) This vast museum explains every facet of life around Galveston's port during its heyday in the 19th century. Outside, clamber aboard to tour the *Elissa,* a beautiful 1877 Scottish tall ship that is still seaworthy.

Moody Gardens AMUSEMENT PARK
(www.moodygardens.com; 1 Hope Blvd; rainforest/aquarium/all-attraction day pass $22/22/60; ⏲10am-6pm Sep-May, to 8pm Jun-Aug; 👪) Three colorful glass pyramids form the focus of one entertainment complex. The Aquarium Pyramid showcases king penguins, fur seals and the largest array of sea horses in the world. The 10-story Rainforest Pyramid is a lush tropical jungle full of plants, birds, butterflies and a wonderful creepy-crawly bug exhibit. The Discovery Pyramid hosts traveling exhibits and some so-so space-related stuff.

Sleeping & Eating

It's no surprise that the sea is the primary food source in Galveston; fish restaurants (mostly chains) line the bayside piers near the Strand.

Beachcomber Inn MOTEL $
(☎409-744-7133; www.galvestoninn.com; 2825 61st St; r $80-130; P❄📶🏊) A block removed from the beach, this basic two-story motel provides a neat-and-clean budget break. Minifridges and microwaves in every room.

★**Harbor House** BOUTIQUE HOTEL $$
(☎409-763-3321; www.harborhousepier21.com; Pier 21, off Harborside Dr; r $130-180; ❄📶🏊) Stay among the shops and museums of the Pier 21 complex in the heart of the historic Strand district. Rustic touches accent the 42 large, comfy rooms occupying a re-created, wharfside warehouse. You have good views of the harbor through smallish windows.

There's no pool, but guests can use the lovely facilities at the Hotel Galvez.

Oasis VEGETARIAN $
(409 25th St; mains $5-10; ⏰10am-4pm Tue-Sat, 9am-2pm Sun; ✎) An oasis in a deep-fried landscape, this inviting juice bar and cafe serves up delicious quinoa and beet salads, vegetable panini, veggie burgers and other light bites. Breakfast (served till 2pm) is also good. It's near the historic Strand district.

★**Farley Girls** AMERICAN $
(801 Post Office St; mains $8-14; ⏰10:30am-9pm Mon-Fri, from 8:30am Sat & Sun) The historic building may be elegant, with fern-studded colonnades and high wood ceilings, but the tasty comfort food and counter service are down-home casual. Eclectic offerings include both warm goat cheese and pecan salad, BBQ pulled pork and prosciutto pizza. At weekend brunch they serve tasty eggs Benedict, breakfast pizza, and eggs with their saucy Gouda-and-mushroom grits.

Gaido's SEAFOOD $$$
(☎409-762-9625; www.gaidos.com; 3800 Seawall Blvd; mains $20-35; ⏰noon-9pm) Run by the same family since 1911, Gaido's is easily the best-known and best-loved restaurant in Galveston. Expect vast platters of no-compromise seafood (oh, the oysters…) served on white tablecloths and with hushed tones. They have a more casual sister restaurant, **Nick's Kitchen & Beach Bar** (☎409-762-9625; http://nicksgalveston.com; 3800 Seawall Blvd; mains $11-24; ⏰11am-10pm), next door.

Galveston Island Brewing MICROBREWERY
(☎409-740-7000; www.galvestonislandbrewing.com; 8423 Stewart Rd; ⏰4-10pm Mon-Thu, 3pm-midnight Fri, noon-midnight Sat, noon-10pm Sun) This local icon brews up some excellent quaffs, including a refreshing half-wheat, half-barley beer (the Tiki Wheat). There's a grassy yard where you can relax (while kids clamber about on the playground), watch the sunset (note the stadium seating) and mingle with a friendly Galveston crowd.

ℹ Getting There & Away

From Houston, follow I-45 southeast for 51 miles.

Hurricane Ike knocked the Galveston Island Trolley off the rails. Until it's restored – by 2017 at current estimates – you really need a car to get around. The island's bus service caters to local commuters, not tourists.

Piney Woods

In Piney Woods, northeast Texas, 100ft-plus-tall trees outnumber people. Nature is the attraction, but don't expect breathtaking vistas; here you'll find quiet trails and varied ecosystems. At **Big Thicket National Preserve** (☎visitor center 409-951-6700; www.nps.gov/bith; 6102 FM 420) FREE, coastal plains meet desert sand dunes, and cypress swamps stand next to pine and hardwood forests. If you're lucky, you may run across one of 20 species of small wild orchids while hiking the 45 miles of trail. The eight disparate park units are 100 miles northwest of Houston.

SOUTHERN GULF COAST

Images of rowdy spring breakers aside, the Gulf Coast is known for its sparkling bays, small harbors filled with shrimp boats and more than 60 miles of protected beaches. Some parts of the Gulf Coast – like Port Arthur or Brazosport – have shunned the tourist trade and embraced the steady income that refineries and oil rigs can provide. But tiny coastal communities and wandering coastal back roads are reason enough to visit.

Aransas National Wildlife Refuge

For bird-watchers, the premier site on the Texas coast is the 115,000-acre **Aransas National Wildlife Refuge** (www.fws.gov/refuge/aransas; FM 2040; per person/carload $3/5; ⏰sunrise-sunset, visitor center 8:30am-4:30pm). The scenery alone is spectacular, and close to 400 bird species have been documented here.

None are more famous than the extremely rare whooping cranes that summer in Canada and spend their winters in the refuge. These endangered white birds – the tallest in North America – can stand 5ft tall with a 7ft wingspan.

From the observation tower you can usually spot one or two, but boats tour the estuaries from November to March, and this is easily the best way to get a good view of rare birds. Captain Tommy with **Rockport Birding & Kayak Adventures** (☎877-892-4737; www.whoopingcranetours.com; 202 N Fulton Beach Rd, Fulton Habor; 3hr tours per person from $55; ⏰7:30am & 1pm) has a relatively small, shallow-drafting boat, and so can get you into back bays that larger charters can't reach.

Corpus Christi & Around

The salt breezes and palm-tree-lined bay are quite pleasant in this 'city by the sea', whose population numbers just over 300,000. Downtown has a waterfront promenade and a few museums, but there's not too much in town to entice visitors. Trip out to Padre Island and the National Seashore for a beachy break, though don't expect the windblown surf to be azure. To the north, Port Aransas is a bustling little fishing town with tons of restaurants and boat charters.

Shoreline Dr, in downtown Corpus, has a small beach; the street continues south as Ocean Dr, which has bayfront playgrounds and parks, as well as some serious mansions lining it. **Corpus Christi Convention & Visitors Bureau** (☎800-678-6232; www.visitcorpuschristitx.org; 1590 N Shoreline Blvd; ⏲9am-5pm Mon-Thu, to 6pm Fri-Sun) has helpful coupons online.

Sights & Activities

★USS Lexington Museum MUSEUM
(www.usslexington.com; 2914 N Shoreline Blvd; adult/child $15/10; ⏲9am-5pm, to 6pm Jun-Aug) Dominating the bay is this 900ft-long aircraft carrier moored just north of the ship channel. The ship served in the Pacific during WWII and was finally retired in 1991. High-tech exhibits give visitors a chance to relive some wartime experiences, without actually dying in a kamikaze attack.

Museum of Science & History MUSEUM
(www.ccmuseum.com; 1900 N Chaparral St; adult/child $9/7; ⏲10am-5pm Tue-Sat, noon-5pm Sun & Mon; 👪) Explore shipwrecks at this fun museum, right on the south side of the ship channel. See how Texas proved to be the doom for the French explorer La Salle and see the moldering remains of reproductions of two of Columbus' ships.

Sleeping & Eating

Bars and restaurants are clustered on the streets surrounding Chaparral and Water Sts downtown – there are few restaurants on the island.

Seashell Inn MOTEL $
(☎361-888-5391; www.seashellinnmotel.com; 202 Kleberg Pl; r weekday/weekend around $75/150; P ❄ 🛜 🏊) In North Beach, the Seashell Inn has an unrivaled location overlooking the sandy shores. The remodeled rooms are in better shape than the aging facade, with comfy beds, a clean look and nice views.

V Boutique Hotel BOUTIQUE HOTEL $$
(☎361-883-9200; www.vhotelcc.com; 701 N Water St; r $170-240, ste $320; P ❄ 🛜) Adored by its guests, this small hotel in the heart of downtown offers a high level of service, and you can order room service from the excellent Vietnamese restaurant downstairs. It has eight comfy, well-equipped rooms, all with carpeting and a subdued modern design scheme; they range in size from studios to one-bedroom loft suites.

Cafe Hesters CAFE $
(☎361-885-0151; www.hesterscafe.com; 1902 N Shoreline Blvd; mains $8-12; ⏲11am-3pm Tue-Fri, from 10am Sat) Nestled artfully in the Art Museum of South Texas, Hesters is much loved for its creative salads, delicious sandwiches and quiches and beautiful desserts (key lime pie, brownies, raspberry cheesecake). Good cafes and a great outdoor setting overlooking the bridge. The original **cafe** (www.hesterscafe.com; 1714 S Alameda St; mains $7-10; ⏲7am-3pm Mon-Sat) in Six Points serves excellent breakfasts.

WORTH A TRIP

PORT ARANSAS

Driving north, Padre Island morphs imperceptibly into Mustang Island, at the tip of which (20 miles along) is Port Aransas. This bustling little fishing and vacation village is worth a stop. There are lots of places, from divey to divine, to eat seafood. Gulf fishing charters depart from here; **Fisherman's Wharf** (www.wharfcat.com; 900 N Tarpon St; 5hr trip adult/child $70/35) has regular deep-sea excursions and runs jetty boats to outer islands. Bunk for the night at the charmingly old-fashioned **Tarpon Inn** (☎361-749-5555; www.thetarponinn.com; 200 E Cotter Ave; r $110-160, ste $220-275; ❄ 🛜), which also has the island's best restaurant. For fresh crawfish, shrimp and crab legs, head to the lively eatery **Crazy Cajun** (mains $8-20; ⏲5-10pm Mon-Fri, from noon Sat & Sun). For a drink, stop at **Shorty's** (☎361-749-8077; 821 Tarpon St; ⏲10am-2am Mon-Sat, from noon Sun), the town's 'oldest and friendliest' watering hole. It's by the docks, with a handful of other bars nearby.

Executive Surf Club SOUTHERN $
(309 N Water St; mains $6-10; ⌚11am-11pm Sun-Thu, to midnight Fri & Sat) Eat a fried-shrimp po'boy from a surfboard table and sip a craft brew from local Lazy Beach Brewing at this longtime fave. It has tables inside and out plus live music, and it's just divey enough for you to forget you're downtown.

Brewster Street Icehouse BURGERS, SEAFOOD $$
(1724 N Tancahua St; mains $8-16; ⌚11am-2am; 👪) What feels like a big, open-sided roadhouse serves up good times via cold brews, live music (Thursday to Saturday night), hearty pub grub and a huge deck. This place really rocks after baseball games at nearby Whataburger Field. Kids love the playground.

Harrison's Landing SEAFOOD $$
(108 People's St, T-dock; mains $8-17; ⌚11am-9pm Sun-Thu, to 11pm Fri & Sat) Perched over the water, Harrison's Landing serves up blackened red snapper tacos, fish and chips and juicy blue-cheese burgers in a casual, open-sided setting facing the marina. Those with sea legs can sit on the floating dock. There's live music Wednesday to Sunday nights.

Padre Island National Seashore

The 60 southern miles of 'North' Padre Island that lie outside Corpus Christi city limits are all a protected part of the **Padre Island National Seashore** (www.nps.gov/pais; Park Rd 22; 7-day pass per car $10; ⌚visitor center 9am-5pm). Four-wheel drive is necessary to see the extent of the park, but if you hike even a short distance from the visitor center, you'll be free of the crowds. The constant wind not only creates and moves dunes, it also attracts kitesurfers and windsurfers to the inland-side Bird Island Basin area.

True to its name, **Horses on the Beach** (☎361-949-4944; www.horsesonthebeachcorpus.com; SPID Park Rd 22; one-hour group ride $40-45; ⌚tour times vary; 👪) offers group horseback rides along the sands. Reserve ahead.

Camping is available at the park's semi-developed, paved **Malaquite Campground** (campsites $8). Or go primitive: beach camping is free with the Padre Island National Seashore entrance permit.

Watch for the endangered Kemp Ridley sea turtles that nest in the park and are closely protected. If you're visiting in late summer, you might be able to take part in a turtle release; call the **Hatchling Hotline** (☎361-949-7163) for information.

South Padre Island

South Padre Island has discovered gold in spring break, the period in March when hordes of college students congregate at beaches for a week or more of completely pleasurable excess that's limited only by the capacity of their livers, loins and billfolds. To welcome this annual bacchanal, this condo-crammed island has beach activities and bars galore.

The website of the **South Padre Island Convention & Visitors Bureau** (☎956-761-4412; www.spichamber.com; 610 Padre Blvd; ⌚9am-5pm) has a comprehensive list of mini-golf courses, rowdy restaurants, condo rentals and beachfront hotels. The **Palms Resort** (☎956-761-1316; www.palmsresortcafe.com; 3616 Gulf Blvd; r $120-230; 📶🏊) is a friendly two-story motel with a great seaside location (though rooms themselves don't have ocean views). The fun beachfront restaurant-bar serves some of the best food in South Padre.

Stop in for a drink or a meal at the **Padre Island Brewing Company** (☎956-761-9585; www.pibrewingcompany.com; 3400 Padre Blvd; mains from $10; ⌚11am-late), where you can wash down your burgers and seafood with a microbrew, or have a seafood feast at the ramshackle **Pier 19** (1 Padre Blvd; mains $11-25; ⌚7am-11pm) jutting far over the water facing the bay (near the bridge).

For some refreshingly educational entertainment, try the tours and feeding presentations every 30 minutes at **Sea Turtle Inc** (☎956-761-4511; www.seaturtleinc.com; 6617 Padre Blvd; suggested donation adult/child $3/2; ⌚10am-4pm Tue-Sun, till 5pm Jun-Aug) rescue facility.

The Valley

Way down here in the Rio Grande Valley (known simply as 'the Valley'), you're spittin' distance from Mexico. Citrus tree plantations are gradually giving way to new subdivisions, but there are enough remaining to supply the roadside stands at which you can pick up fresh local grapefruits and oranges (harvested November through May).

Birders flock to the Valley's parks associated with the **World Birding Center** (www.worldbirdingcenter.org). Migrating avian masses, including thousands of hawks, pass through this natural corridor along the main north–south American fly route from March to April and September to October. Twenty miles or so west of Weslaco, the visitor and educational center at **Bentsen-Rio Grande Valley State Park** (www.tpwd.state.tx.us; 2800 S Bentsen Palm Dr; adult/child $5/free; ⏲park 7am-10pm, center 8am-5pm) is a model of sustainable, green-driven architecture, including rainwater collection. Rent a bike (from $5 a day) or take the tram the two miles into the park. There, alligators and birds roam the wetlands, and you may spot a javelina (wild pig) or a horny toad on your way to the hawk-observation tower.

Twenty-seven miles southwest of South Padre is **Brownsville** (www.brownsville.org), the southernmost town in Texas, with an authentic and slightly gritty culture that makes it an excellent day trip. During the 19th century, the fast-growing town was filled with ornate brick structures that drew architectural inspiration from Mexico and New Orleans. Many survive today and help make Brownsville an atmospheric stop.

DALLAS-FORT WORTH

Dallas and Fort Worth are as different as a Beemer-driving yuppie and a rancher in a Dodge pickup truck – the proverbial city slicker and his country cousin. Just 30 miles apart, the two towns anchor a giant megalopolis of six million people known as the Metroplex. Go see the excesses of the Big D and then day-trip to Fort Worth – the cowboy and Western sights and museums there might be the state's best-kept secret.

Dallas

Bright lights, big hair, shiny cars... In many ways, upscale Dallas is the belle of the Texas ball. From JR Ewing and the TV show *Dallas* to the Dallas Cowboys and their cheerleaders, Dallas has made a deep imprint on American popular culture, which seems fitting for a city whose ethos is image consciousness and conspicuous consumption.

With all that money, it's no surprise that there's an amazing dining scene. The museums are not only excellent, but unique – history buffs should not miss the memorials to former president John F Kennedy. The most impressive addition to Dallas' cultural landscape in recent years is the 68-acre Arts District, now the largest in the country.

North of downtown, uptown has smart, trendy bars, restaurants and hotels; follow Harwood St (or St Paul St, if you're taking the trolley) to McKinney Ave. Bars also line Greenville Ave, northeast of downtown off Ross Ave. Deep Ellum, at the eastern end of Elm St, is a bit gritty, but it's the nucleus of Dallas' small live-music scene.

Sights

★Sixth Floor Museum MUSEUM
(Map p724; www.jfk.org; Book Depository, 411 Elm St; adult/child $16/13; ⏲10am-6pm Tue-Sun, noon-6pm Mon; light railWest End) No city wants the distinction of being the site of an assassination – especially if the victim happens to be President John F Kennedy. But rather than downplay the events that sent the city reeling in 1963, Dallas gives visitors a unique opportunity to delve into the world-altering events unleashed by an assassin in the former Texas School Book Depository. Fascinating multimedia exhibits (plus the included audioguide) give an excellent historical context of JFK's time, as well as his life and legacy.

Dealey Plaza & the Grassy Knoll PARK
(Map p724; light railWest End) Now a National Historic Landmark, this rectangular park is south of the former Book Depository. Dealey Plaza was named in 1935 for George Bannerman Dealey, a longtime Dallas journalist, historian and philanthropist. Just steps from here, John Kennedy was assassinated in September 1963.

Dallas Museum of Art MUSEUM
(Map p724; www.dallasmuseumofart.org; 1717 N Harwood St; ⏲11am-5pm Tue-Sun, to 9pm Thu; 👪; light railSt Paul) FREE This museum is a high-caliber world tour of decorative and fine art. Among the many treasures are Edward Hopper's enigmatic *Lighthouse Hill*, Frederic Church's lush masterpiece *The Icebergs* and Rodin's *Sculptor and his Muse*. Other highlights include exquisite pre-Colombian pottery, carvings and tapestries from Oceania, and a villa modeled on Coco Chanel's Mediterranean mansion (and where you can see paintings by statesman Winston Churchill).

Nasher Sculpture Center MUSEUM
(Map p724; www.nashersculpturecenter.org; 2001 Flora St; adult/child $10/free; ⏲11am-5pm Tue-Sun; light railSt Paul) Modern-art installations shine at the fabulous glass-and-steel Nasher Sculpture Center. The Nashers accumulated what might be one of the greatest privately held sculpture collections in the world, with works by Calder, de Kooning, Rodin, Serra

Dallas-Fort Worth Metroplex

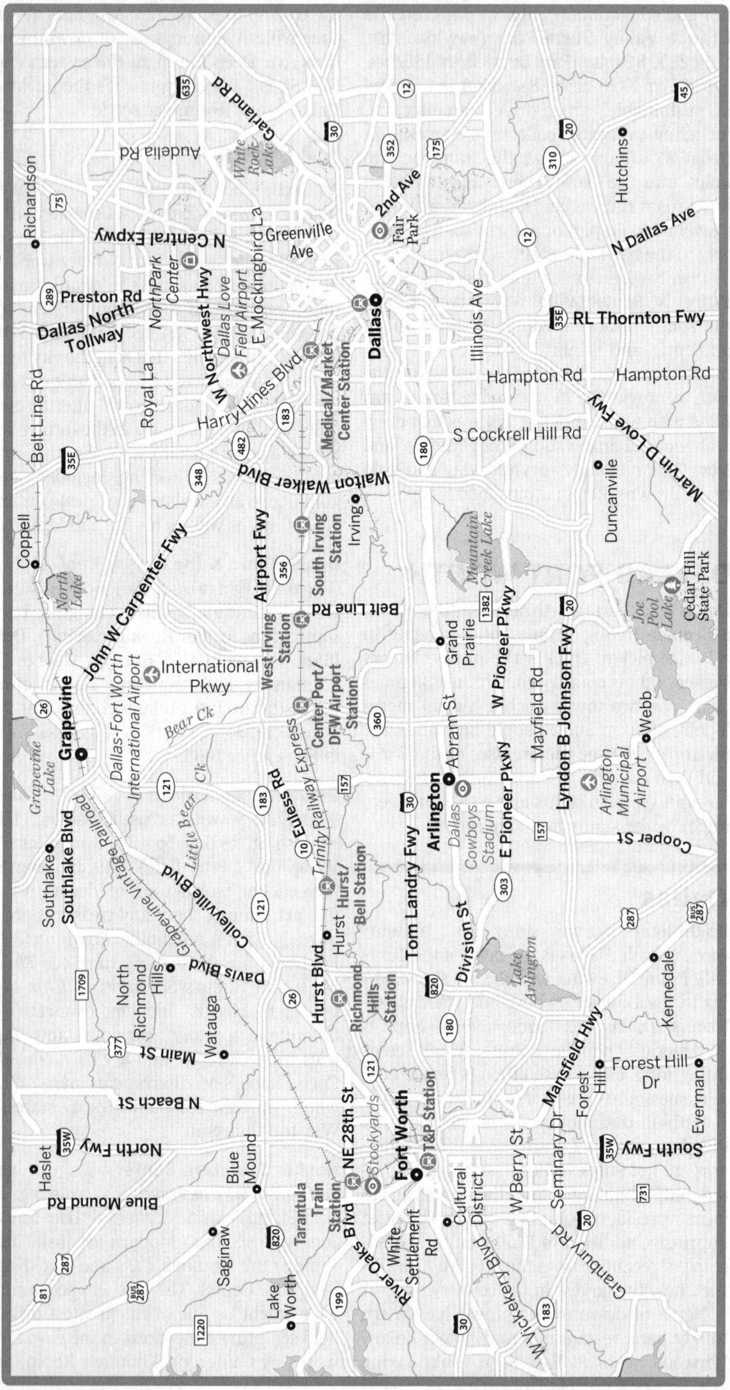

and Miró, and the divine sculpture garden is one of the best in the country.

Dallas World Aquarium AQUARIUM
(Map p724; www.dwazoo.com; 1801 N Griffin St; adult/child $21/15; 9am-5pm;) The flora and fauna of 14 countries come alive here with rich animal life (including birds, reptiles and mammals) from both the rainforest and the reef.

Festivals & Events

State Fair of Texas FAIR
(www.bigtex.com; Fair Park, 1300 Cullum Blvd; adult/child $18/14; late Sep–mid-Oct) This massive fair is the fall highlight for many a Texan. Come ride one of the tallest Ferris wheels in North America, eat corn dogs (it's claimed that this is where they were invented), and browse among the prize-winning cows, sheep and quilts.

Sleeping

Staying uptown, you're closest to restaurants and nightlife, but hotels there can get pricey. The further you get from the center, the cheaper the highway chain motels get.

Abby Guest House GUESTHOUSE $
(214-264-4804; 5417 Goodwin Ave; cottage from $85;) This bright and cheerful garden cottage is within walking distance of great cafes and bars on Upper Greenville Ave (about 5 miles northeast of downtown). With a full kitchen and sunny private patio, it's a great deal although often booked. Two-night minimum.

Days Inn Market Center Dallas MOTEL $
(214-748-2243; www.daysinn.com; 2026 Market Center Blvd; r $67;) Sure it's a generic chain hotel, but you won't find a better deal this close – it's about 2.5 miles northeast of downtown. Rooms are clean and simply furnished, and the design district is right around the corner.

Corinthian B&B GUESTHOUSE $$
(214-818-0400; www.corinthianbandb.com; 4125 Junius St; r $130-220;) Once a boarding house for young ladies, this beautifully restored 1905 mansion has attractive rooms, set with antique furnishings and original details. A lovely backyard, a stately parlor and kind hosts (not to mention the tasty cooked breakfasts), make the Corinthian good value. It's about 1.5 miles northeast of downtown.

★ **Hotel Belmont** BOUTIQUE HOTEL $$
(866-870-8010; www.belmontdallas.com; 901 Fort Worth Ave; r $115-140;) Just 2 miles west of downtown, this stylish 1940s bungalow hotel is a fabulously low-key antidote to Dallas' flashier digs, with a touch of mid-century modern design and more than its share of soul. The garden rooms – with soaking tubs, Moroccan-blue tile work, kilim rugs and some city views – are tops.

Eating

Deep Ellum, just east of downtown, is your choice for eclectic eats. Otherwise, head uptown for myriad choices. Bishop Ave, dotted with interesting places to eat and drink, merges hipster and funky – walk off your vittles by window-shopping the idiosyncratic boutiques.

Uptown & Knox-Henderson

Highland Park Soda Shop AMERICAN $
(214-521-2126; 3229 Knox St; mains $4-8; 7am-6pm Mon-Fri, from 8am Sat, 10am-5pm Sun;) Since 1912 this classic soda fountain has been serving up vanilla malts and comfort fare, such as grilled-cheese sandwiches, to

TASTES BORN IN TEXAS

- **Corn dogs** Cornbread-batter-dipped hot dogs on a stick were created in 1948 by Neil Fletcher for the State Fair of Texas; Fletcher's still sells 'em there. Now available with jalapeño cornbread, too.
- **Shiner Bock** The state's favorite amber ale came to be when Kosmos Spoetzl brought Bavarian brewing to Shiner, Texas, in 1914. Available countrywide, Shiner Bock is still brewed at Spoetzl Brewery (p708).
- **Chicken-fried bacon** You may have heard of steak coated and deep-fried like chicken, but the taste (and heart-attack factor) was taken to new heights when Sodolak's, in Somerville, started cooking bacon the same way in the early 1990s.
- **Dr Pepper** A pharmacist in a Waco drugstore-soda shop invented this aromatic cola in the 1880s.

Downtown Dallas

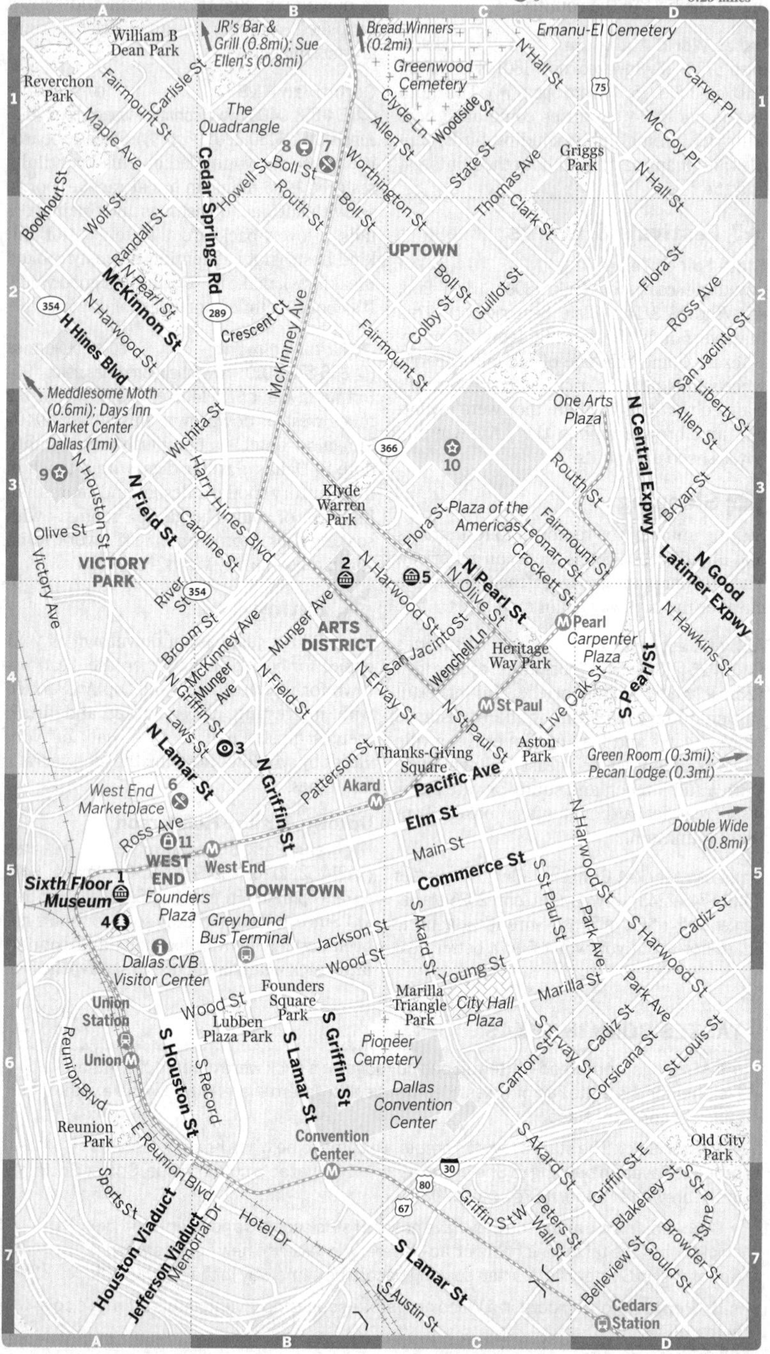
0 500 m
0 0.25 miles
A
B
C
D
1
2
3
4
5
6
7
William B Dean Park
JR's Bar & Grill (0.8mi); Sue Ellen's (0.8mi)
Bread Winners (0.2mi)
Emanu-El Cemetery
Greenwood Cemetery
Reverchon Park
Fairmount St
Carlisle St
The Quadrangle
Maple Ave
Cedar Springs Rd
Howell St
Boll St
Routh St
Worthington St
Allen St
Clyde Ln
Woodside St
State St
Thomas Ave
Clark St
N Hall St
Carver Pl
Mc Coy Pl
Griggs Park
Bookhout St
Wolf St
Randall St
N Pearl St
McKinnon St
N Harwood St
H Hines Blvd
Crescent Ct
McKinney Ave
UPTOWN
Boll St
Colby St
Guillot St
Fairmount St
Flora St
Ross Ave
San Jacinto St
Liberty St
Allen St
Meddlesome Moth (0.6mi); Days Inn Market Center Dallas (1mi)
Wichita St
One Arts Plaza
N Central Expwy
10
9
N Houston St
N Field St
Harry Hines Blvd
Klyde Warren Park
Routh St
Bryan St
Caroline St
Flora St
Plaza of the Americas
Fairmount St
Leonard St
Crockett St
Olive St
Victory Ave
VICTORY PARK
River St
2
5
N Harwood St
N Olive St
N Pearl St
Pearl
N Good Latimer Expwy
N Hawkins St
Broom St
McKinney Ave
Munger Ave
ARTS DISTRICT
San Jacinto St
Wenchell Ln
Heritage Way Park
Carpenter Plaza
S Pearl St
N Griffin St
Munger Ave
N Field St
N Ervay St
St Paul
Live Oak St
Laws St
N Lamar St
3
N St Paul St
Aston Park
Green Room (0.3mi); Pecan Lodge (0.3mi)
Patterson St
Thanks-Giving Square
Pacific Ave
West End Marketplace
6
N Griffin St
Akard
Elm St
N Harwood St
Double Wide (0.8mi)
Ross Ave
11
WEST END
West End
Main St
Sixth Floor Museum
1
Founders Plaza
DOWNTOWN
Commerce St
S St Paul St
4
Greyhound Bus Terminal
Jackson St
S Akard St
Park Ave
S Harwood St
Cadiz St
Dallas CVB Visitor Center
Wood St
Young St
Union Station
Wood St
Founders Square Park
Lubben Plaza Park
Marilla Triangle Park
City Hall Plaza
Marilla St
Park Ave
Reunion Blvd
Union
S Houston St
S Record
S Lamar St
S Griffin St
Pioneer Cemetery
Canton St
S Ervay St
Cadiz St
Corsicana St
St Louis St
Dallas Convention Center
Reunion Park
E Reunion Blvd
Convention Center
S Akard St
Griffin St E
Old City Park
Sports St
Houston Viaduct
Jefferson Viaduct
Memorial Dr
Hotel Dr
Griffin St W
Peters St
Wall St
Blakeney St
S St Paul St
Browder St
S Lamar St
Belleview St
Gould St
S Austin St
Cedars Station
354
289
366
75
30
80
67

Downtown Dallas

generations of diners. When in doubt, get the root-beer float. It's in Highland Park, about 4 miles north of downtown.

Kalachandji's VEGETARIAN $
(www.kalachandjis.com; 5430 Gurley Ave; buffet lunch/dinner $11/14; noon-2pm & 5:30-9pm Tue-Sun) Inside a lavishly decorated Hare Krishna temple, you'll find a small but varied buffet serving basmati rice, curries, mustard greens, pappadam and chutneys, pakora, tamarind tea and other changing daily specials. It's fine counterpoint to Texas' many meaty temptations. You can dine in the peaceful, plant-filled courtyard. It's located about 4 miles east of downtown.

★**Bread Winners** AMERICAN $$
(www.breadwinnerscafe.com; 3301 McKinney Ave; mains $11-19; 7am-4pm Mon, to 9pm Tue-Sun;) If sipping a mimosa in a lush courtyard atrium is the reward for the agony of choosing what to order for brunch, then bring on the pain. Lunch and dinner offer similar, though less tortuous, conundrums. In a pinch, at least stop in for something decadent from the bakery. It's in Uptown, 2 miles north of downtown.

S&D Oyster Company SEAFOOD $$
(Map p724; www.sdoyster.com; 2701 McKinney Ave; mains $13-24; 11am-10pm Mon-Sat) An uptown staple for years – complete with red-and-white checked tablecloths and old-time jazz playing overhead – S&D has earned many fans for its fresh oysters, broiled flounder, barbecue shrimp and other Gulf Coast hits. Start off with a drink on the airy back bar and deck.

Downtown & Deep Ellum

Pecan Lodge BARBECUE $
(214-748-8900; www.pecanlodge.com; 2702 Main St; mains from $9-11; 11am-3pm Sun & Tue-Thu, to 10pm Fri & Sat) An icon in Deep Ellum, Pecan Lodge fires up mouthwatering brisket, ribs and pulled pork. Add the requisite sides (mac 'n' cheese, collard greens, plus peach cobbler for dessert), local craft brews and you have one of Dallas' best BBQ joints. The downside: the lines are long, and you'll have to arrive early to score a shaded table on the patio.

Ellen's Southern Kitchen AMERICAN $
(Map p724; 469-206-3339; ellenssouthernkitchen.com; 1718 N. Market St; mains $9-15; 7am-9pm; ; light rail West End) In the center of historic West End, Ellen's serves up American comfort fare in a slightly upscale diner setting (think wild wallpaper, elegant light fixtures, dark wood furniture). Fluffy pancakes, Cajun shrimp and grits, blackened catfish and pulled pork tacos are among the many temptations. Breakfast served all day.

Around Dallas

★**Meddlesome Moth** MODERN AMERICAN $$
(214-628-7900; mothinthe.net; 1621 Oak Lawn Ave; lunch mains $10-13, dinner sharing plates $10-16; 11am-midnight Mon-Sat, 10am-10pm Sun) In the design district, this buzzing gastropub draws small groups of friends who linger over Belgian-style mussels, shrimp and homestead grits, sesame duck wings and other beautifully turned out sharing plates. You'll find good cocktails and a staggering selection of craft brews (including 40 on draught). It's in the Design district, around 2 miles northwest of downtown.

Oddfellows CAFE $$
(214-944-5958; www.oddfellowsdallas.com; 316 West 7th St; mains $10-16; 7am-3pm;) In the Bishop Arts district (around 3 miles southwest of downtown), Oddfellows is a charming spot, with first-rate espresso, outdoor seating and an airy, rustically designed interior that draws a mix of hipsters and preppsters. Breakfast is tops with eggs Benedict, fried chicken and waffles, and short rib hash.

Weekends are packed. Come early, or plan to browse the nearby shops and galleries before your table is ready.

Drinking & Nightlife

Numerous pubs with outdoor patios are to be found in uptown along not only McKinney Ave (in the 2500 to 2800 blocks especially), but also Knox St near Willis Ave. Note that bars and clubs in Dallas (at least mostly) have succumbed to the indoor smoking ban.

Green Room BAR
(☎214-748-7666; 2715 Elm St; ⏰4pm-2am Tue-Sun) In bar-lined Deep Ellum, the Green Room is a go-to spot for rooftop cocktails, a fun crowd and excellent pub grub (tacos, burgers, poutine). There's also live music – currently Wednesday nights.

★**Ginger Man** PUB
(Map p724; ☎214-754-8771; www.dallas.gingermanpub.com; 2718 Boll St; ⏰1pm-2am) An appropriately spice-colored house is home to this always-busy neighborhood pub. It has multilevel patios and porches, out front and back, plus one of the best beer menus in the city.

Double Wide BAR
(☎214-887-6510; www.double-wide.com; 3510 Commerce St; ⏰5pm-2am Mon-Fri, from 7pm Sat & Sun) Are these rednecks pretending to be hipsters or hipsters pretending to be rednecks? Live music (Friday and Saturday nights) keeps the irony from killing the fun. True to name, the bar is set up like a double-wide trailer, complete with Astroturf, wood-paneled walls and deliciously bad artwork. Catch your breath on the patio out back. It's in Deep Ellum.

GAY & LESBIAN DALLAS

You've got to love that the top gay and lesbian bars in Dallas are named JR's and Sue Ellen's, respectively, after the two lead (and presumably straight) characters in TV show *Dallas*.

JR's Bar & Grill (www.jrsdallas.com; 3923 Cedar Springs Rd; ⏰noon-2am Tue-Sun, from 1pm Mon) One of the busiest bars in Texas, JR's serves lunch daily and boasts a variety of fun entertainment at night.

Sue Ellen's (www.sueellensdallas.com; 3014 Throckmorton St; ⏰4pm-2am) Chill out in the 'lipstick lounge' or on the dance floor at Dallas' favorite lesbian bar.

Cosmo's BAR
(1212 Skillman; ⏰5pm-2am) If you long for that cool 1970s rec room you never had, Cosmo's is the place to be. A mishmash of colorful vintage lamps, worn thriftstore-esque furniture and a faux fireplace set the scene for a fun evening of drinking (martinis, cosmos), while listening to old-school hits on the jukebox. It's in Lakewood, about 4 miles northeast of downtown.

☆ Entertainment

For entertainment listings, check the weekly alternative newspaper *Dallas Observer* (www.dallasobserver.com) or *Guide Live* (www.guidelive.com), which appears in Friday's *Dallas Morning News*.

Live Music & Nightclubs

During lunch hour, office workers crowd into the bars and restaurants of downtown's **Deep Ellum** (www.deepellumtexas). The scene at night is definitely grittier, but this is still live-music central. Most of the clubs are hard-core, but you'll occasionally find country or jazz. The bars and clubs of Lower Greenville Ave (1500 to 2200 blocks) cater to a crowd temperament somewhere between the uptown yuppies and downtown grunge set.

Sports

Mesquite ProRodeo RODEO
(☎972-285-8777; www.mesquiterodeo.com; 1818 Rodeo Dr, Mesquite; ⏰rodeos at 7:30pm Fri & Sat Jun–late-Aug) The very best cowboys compete in the vaunted Mesquite Rodeo. For almost three months, the competition is fierce in classic rodeo events including bareback, steer wrestling and bull riding. The prize money attracts top talent to this series. Mesquite is 14 miles straight east of Dallas.

Dallas Cowboys FOOTBALL
(☎817-892-4467; http://stadium.dallascowboys.com; AT&T Stadium, 1 Legends Way, off I-30 exits 28 & 29; tours adult/child from $18/15; ⏰tours 10am-4:30pm Sat, 11:30am-3:30pm Sun) The Dallas Cowboys gave themselves the nickname 'America's Team' after they had great success (with cheerleaders and otherwise) in the 1970s. Although the team's fortunes have been modest of late, they still have swagger, as shown in their enormous, retractable-roof home – the AT&T Stadium, located 18 miles west of Dallas in Arlington. Tours of the stadium depart from Entry A.

WORTH A TRIP

DENTON

A bastion of college cool and indie cred, Denton has a great music scene. Home to the University of North Texas and its renowned arts programs, the fast-growing city rightfully claims the title as the most musical city in the region. The downtown, centered on **Courthouse Square**, boasts a plethora of music venues, music shops and instrument stores.

By day, pop into the **Courthouse on the Square Museum** (940-349-2850; 110 W Hickory St; 10am-4:30pm Mon-Fri, 11am-3pm Sat) FREE for local lore and an amazing display of art created with pecans. Outside, check out the 1918 **Confederate War Memorial**, which has been modified with apologetic disclaimers. Nearby, **Recycled Books Records CDs** (940-566-5688; www.recycledbooks.com; 200 N Locust St; 9am-9pm) has hard-to-find tunes.

For music, the top venue is **Dan's Silver Leaf** (940-320-2000; www.danssilverleaf.com; 103 Industrial St; 4pm-2am), with a revered owner who books top bands but doesn't gouge on drink prices. Other clubs and bars are nearby.

Every March the city hosts **35 Denton** (www.35denton.com), a music festival featuring everything from rock to blues to jazz.

American Airlines Center STADIUM
(Map p724; www.americanairlinescenter.com; 2500 Victory Ave) Located in Victory Park this stadium hosts mega-concerts and is home to the Dallas Stars ice-hockey team and the Dallas Mavericks pro-basketball team.

Theater & Culture

AT&T Performing Arts Center THEATER
(Map p724; www.attpac.org; 2403 Flora St) Four architecturally noteworthy performance venues are located here, including the 2000-seat **Winspear Opera House**, home to the **Dallas Opera** (214-443-1000; www.dallasopera.org); the 1500-seat **Wyly Theatre**; and **Strauss Sq**, an open-air stage.

Shopping

You can find some interesting gifts of arty homewares, like vintage Fiestaware plates, in the quirky, but small, **Bishop Arts District** (www.bishopartsdistrict.com). On the northern end of uptown (at Lemmon and McKinney Aves), the **West Village** (www.westvil.com) neighborhood has a collection of chain stores and individual boutiques, like 'Cowboy Cool.'

Wild Bill's Western Store CLOTHING
(Map p724; 214-954-1050; www.wildbillswestern.com; 311 N Market, West End; 10am-9pm Mon-Sat, noon-6pm Sun; light rail West End) Wild Bill's is a treasure chest of Western wear. You'll find Stetsons, snakeskin boots, oilskin jackets, oversize belt buckles, rhinestone-covered T-shirts, fun kitschy souvenirs, popguns and other toys, country music CDs and much more. Enjoy a cold beer while you shop.

Information

Dallas CVB Visitor Center (Map p724; 214-571-1316; www.visitdallas.com; Old Red Courthouse, 100 S Houston St; 9am-5pm;) Has vast amounts of material.

Police Station (214-670-4413; 334 S Hall St) In Deep Ellum.

Travelex (214-559-3564; www.travelex.com; 2911 Turtle Creek Blvd; 9am-5pm Mon-Fri) Foreign-currency exchange.

Getting There & Away

American Airlines' main hub is **Dallas-Fort Worth International Airport** (DFW; www.dfwairport.com), 16 miles northwest of the city via I-35 E.

Southwest Airlines uses the smaller **Dallas Love Field** (DAL; www.dallas-lovefield.com), just northwest of downtown.

Greyhound buses make runs all over the country from the **Greyhound Bus Terminal** (Map p724; 205 S Lamar St).

The **Amtrak** (www.amtrak.com) San Antonio–Chicago *Texas Eagle* train stops at downtown's **Union Station** (400 S Houston St).

Getting Around

TO/FROM THE AIRPORT

From Dallas-Fort Worth International Airport, you can take the new Dallas Area Rapid Transit (p728) orange line directly downtown.

From Dallas Love Field take DART's Love Link 524 that connects to Inwood/Love Field Station, where you can pick up the orange or green line.

SuperShuttle (817-329-2000; www.supershuttle.com; fare from $18) runs from DFW or Dallas Love Field to downtown and major hotels in the region. A taxi between either airport and central Dallas should cost about $40 to $60.

BUS & LIGHT RAIL

Dallas Area Rapid Transit (DART; ☎214-979-1111; www.dart.org; 2hr ticket $2.50) operates buses and an extensive light-rail system that connects downtown with outlying areas. Day passes ($5) are available from machines at all rail stations.

Travel from downtown to uptown on the historic and free **M-Line Trolley** (☎214-855-0006; www.mata.org; ⏰7am-10pm Mon-Thu, to 11pm Fri, 10am-midnight Sat, to 10pm Sun), which runs from the corner of Ross Ave and St Paul St, near the Dallas Museum of Art, and up McKinney Ave to Blackburn St.

CAR & MOTORCYCLE

If you do rent a car, be warned that rush-hour freeway traffic is bad and there's little free parking downtown. Public garages cost from $14 per day.

Fort Worth

Often called 'Where the West Begins', and more often referred to as 'Cowtown', Fort Worth is one town that still has its twang.

The place first became famous during the great open-range cattle drives of the late 19th century, when more than 10 million head of cattle tramped through the city on the Chisholm Trail. Today you can see a mini cattle drive twice a day and a rodeo on weekend nights.

Down in the Cultural District, tour the Cowgirl Museum and other major galleries, including three amazing art collections. Afterwards, Sundance Sq's restaurants and bars call you to the kick-up-your-heels downtown.

Whatever you do, don't mistake Fort Worth for being Dallas' sidekick. This city's got a headstrong spirit of its own, and it's more user-friendly than Dallas (and greener and cleaner). Bottom line? There's a lot to do here – without a lot of pretense.

Sights

The area around the Stockyards is cowboy central. There are five major museums and the Will Rogers Memorial Center in the leafy **Cultural District** (www.fwculture.com).

Stockyards HISTORIC SITE
(www.fortworthstockyards.org; Exchange Ave) Sure, you'll spot cowboys on horseback roaming around, but wander the dusty streets of the Stockyards and you'll be soon mingling with a mix of families, bikers, curious European tourists and novelty-seeking college kids. This place puts fun first, with equal parts authentic history and camera-ready tourism thrown into the pot. Western-wear stores and knickknack shops, saloons and steakhouses occupy the Old West–era buildings of the Stockyards. Don't miss the twice daily cattle drive (at 11:30am and 4pm) when cowboys drive a small herd of longhorn up Exchange Ave.

Kimbell Art Museum MUSEUM
(☎817-332-8451; www.kimbellart.org; 3333 Camp Bowie Blvd; ⏰10am-5pm Tue-Thu & Sat, noon-8pm Fri, noon-5pm Sun) FREE Welcome to one of America's best small museums, with European masterpieces by Caravaggio, El Greco and Cézanne, as well as Michelangelo's first painting, *The Torment of St Anthony*. The architecture is no less stunning. Galleries are spread between an original Louis Kahn building and a more recent edition, designed by celebrated architect Renzo Piano.

National Cowgirl Museum MUSEUM
(☎817-336-4475; www.cowgirl.net; 1720 Gendy St; adult/child $10/8; ⏰10am-5pm Tue-Sat, noon-5pm Sun) This airy, impressive museum explores the myth and the reality of cowgirls in American culture. From rhinestone costumes to rare film footage, this is a fun and educational ride: by the time you walk out, you'll have a whole new appreciation for these tough workers.

Amon Carter Museum of American Art MUSEUM
(www.cartermuseum.org; 3501 Camp Bowie Blvd; ⏰10am-5pm Tue-Sat, noon-5pm Sun) FREE Pre-1945 American art shines at this museum, including iconic works by John Singer Sargent, Winslow Homer and Alexander Calder, as well as an impressive collection of works depicting the American West by artists Frederic Remington and Charles M Russell.

Modern Art Museum of Fort Worth MUSEUM
(www.themodern.org; 3200 Darnell St; adult/child $10/free; ⏰10am-5pm Tue-Sun, to 8pm Thu) In a stunning, soaring space, this museum houses an incredible number of provocative and mind-expanding works by luminaries such as Mark Rothko and Picasso.

DON'T MISS

THE WORLD'S LARGEST HONKY-TONK

Scoot on in to **Billy Bob's Texas** (☑817-624-7117; www.billybobstexas.com; 2520 Rodeo Plaza; cover $2-5 Sun-Thu, varies Fri & Sat; ◷11am-2am Mon-Sat, noon-2am Sun), the world's largest honky-tonk. The 100,000-sq-ft building was once a barn that housed prize cattle during the Fort Worth Stock Show. After the stock show moved to the Will Rogers Memorial Center, the barn became a department store so big that the stock keepers wore roller skates.

Now Billy Bob's can hold more than 6000 people and has 40 bars to serve the thirsty masses. The most bottled beer sold in one night was 16,000 bottles, during a 1985 Hank Williams Jr concert. Top country-and-western stars, house bands and country DJs play on two stages. On Friday and Saturday nights a live bull-riding competition takes place at an indoor arena. Pool tables and games help make this a family place; under 18s are welcome with a parent.

Sundance Square   NEIGHBORHOOD
(www.sundancesquare.com; Downtown) You can stroll yourself happy in the 14-block Sundance Sq, near Main and 3rd Sts. Colorful architecture, art galleries and a host of bars and restaurants make this one 'hood not to miss. The big, spurting fountain and cafe tables are fine spots to cool off.

**Sid Richardson
Collection of Western Art**   MUSEUM
(www.sidrichardsonmuseum.org; 309 Main St, Downtown; ◷9am-5pm Mon-Thu, to 8pm Fri & Sat, noon-5pm Sun) **FREE** If the Stockyards didn't sate your hunger for all things Western, pop in here for some art. It's known for its striking paintings by Frederic Remington and Charles Russel.

★ Festivals & Events

Fort Worth Stock Show & Rodeo   RODEO
(www.fwssr.com) Catch the rodeo craze with nearly a million other people. Held in January for several weeks each year at **Will Rogers Memorial Center** (1 Amon Carter Sq) in the Cultural District.

🛏 Sleeping

Fort Worth is an easy day trip from Dallas, but if you're staying over, here are a few good options.

Hotel Texas   INN $
(☑817-624-2224; 2415 Ellis Ave; r $80-100; ☺❄🛜) This 1939 'cattleman's home away from home' is a good deal, smack in the center of the Stockyards action. Although the service isn't very friendly, it's hard to fault the simple, clean rooms decorated with framed Western art. Cash only.

Miss Molly's Hotel   B&B $$
(☑817-626-1522; www.missmollyshotel.com; 109 W Exchange Ave; r incl breakfast $100-175; ❄🛜) Set in the heart of the Stockyards, eight-room Miss Molly's occupies a former bordello. Its heavily atmospheric vibe will feel authentic to some (Miss Josie's room still looks like madame's boudoir, eerie to others (they say it's haunted...), but probably at least a little charming either way. Look for cheap deals during the week.

Etta's Place   INN $$
(☑817-255-5760; www.ettas-place.com; 200 W 3rd St; r $162-193, ste $212-245; ❄🛜) A grand piano, a comfy library and quilts galore are among the cozy pleasures at this Sundance Square inn. Breakfast can be taken on the airy patio. The 10 rooms are large; suites have kitchenettes.

Texas White House   B&B $$
(☑817-923-3597; www.texaswhitehouse.com; 1417 Eighth Ave; r $150-250; ❄🛜) A large historic home with contemporary Texas style near downtown. The five rooms are well equipped and uniquely designed. Top picks include the Tejas room (with Mexican pottery and folk art), the Lonestar (with antique furniture and cowboy gear), and the Treehouse suite (with private balcony, dry sauna and Jacuzzi tub).

★ Stockyards Hotel   HISTORIC HOTEL $$$
(☑817-625-6427; www.stockyardshotel.com; 109 E Exchange Ave; r $200-270, ste $270-390; ❄🛜) First opened in 1907, this 52-room place clings to its cowboy past with Western-themed art, cowboy-inspired rooms and a grand Old West lobby with lots of leather. Hide out in the Bonnie and Clyde room, where the outlaw pair actually stayed back

in 1933 (the faux bullet holes and Bonnie's .38 revolver only add to the mystique).

✖ Eating

Put on the feed bag and grab some Texas-style fixins' in Sundance Sq and in the Stockyards. About 2 miles south of Sundance Sq, W Magnolia Ave is lined with hip eateries and gastropubs. Many of the museums, such as the Kimbell, also have excellent cafes.

Spiral Diner & Bakery   CAFE $
(☑ 817-332-8834; 1314 W Magnolia Ave; mains $8-12; ⊙ 11am-10pm Tue-Sat, 9am-5pm Sun; 🖉🖬) One of the most inventive organic vegan restaurants in the South, this retro-feel diner serves up fresh juices, smoothies, salads and a whole bevy of delicious dishes (veggie burgers, BBQ seitan sandwiches, quesadillas). Breakfast is served all day. Craft brews and organic wines round out the menu.

★ Kincaid's   BURGERS $
(☑ 817-732-2881; www.kincaidshamburgers.com; 4901 Camp Bowie Blvd; mains $5-8; ⊙ 11am-8pm Mon-Sat, 11am-3pm Sun) Sit on picnic tables amid disused grocery shelves at this local institution (never mind the sickly green walls) and wolf down some of the best burgers in the region. They are thick, juicy and come covered in condiments.

Love Shack   BURGERS $
(www.loveburgershack.com; 110 E Exchange Ave; mains $5-9; ⊙ 11am-7pm Sun-Thu, to midnight Fri & Sat) Enjoy a gourmet burger (the signature Dirty Love has bacon, cheese and a fried quail egg) at this joint owned by Texas-born TV chef Tim Love. Don't miss the home-cut fries or Parmesan chips. Local singers take the stage from Wednesday through Sunday.

★ Joe T Garcia's   MEXICAN $$
(www.joets.com; 2201 N Commerce St; mains $8-15; ⊙ 11am-2:30pm & 5-10pm Mon-Thu, 11am-11pm Fri & Sat, to 10pm Sun) The most famous restaurant in Fort Worth, this fourth-generation place takes up a city block. Dining in the walled courtyard is a magical experience, as Mexican-tile fountains bubble among the acres of tropical foliage. On weekends the line (no reservations!) often stretches around the block.

Brewed   MODERN AMERICAN $$
(www.brewedfw.com; 801 W Magnolia Ave; breakfast mains $5-9, lunch & dinner $11-19; ⊙ 8am-10pm Tue & Wed, to 11pm Thu-Sat, 9:30am-2:30pm Sun; 🖘) Brewed is an easygoing spot with exposed brick walls, mismatched tables and chairs, taxidermy and friendly wait staff. With great coffee, craft brews and an appealing food menu, it's a good anytime spot. Start the day with chicken and waffles or housemade granola. Later, feast on a luscious 'super food' salad, pot roast, or a burger with duck-fat fries.

Shinjuku Station   JAPANESE $$
(☑ 817-923-2695; 711 W Magnolia St; lunch mains $9-15, dinner sharing plates $8-20; ⊙ 5-9pm Mon & Sat, 11am-9pm Tue-Fri; 🖉) Shinjuku is a hip little Japanese izakaya that whips up creative dishes that are ideal for sharing. Beer-braised pork buns, seared baby octopus, yellowtail ceviche and king crab corn fritters are among the hits – along with an extensive sushi menu.

★ Lonesome Dove
Western Bistro   SOUTHERN $$$
(☑ 817-740-8810; www.lonesomedovebistro.com; 2406 N Main St; lunch mains $10-14, dinner $20-42; ⊙ 11:30am-2:30pm & 5-10pm Tue-Sat, 5-10pm Mon) At Tim Love's mod-Western dining experience, even the chefs wear cowboy hats. It's Southern fusion, with the traditional flavors of the region enlivened by all manner of influences. The wine list is superb and the $10 lunch special is truly the best deal in town.

🍷 Drinking & Nightlife

All the restaurants in and around Sundance Sq have popular bars attached.

Booger Red's   BAR
(109 E Exchange Ave) At this old-fashioned Western bar in the heart of the Stockyards, you can straddle a saddle at the bar, while sipping housemade Buffalo Butt beer and contemplating one herbivorous rear-end overhead – head around to the restaurant to see the buffalo's better half.

Usual Bar   COCKTAIL BAR
(☑ 817-810-0114; www.theusualbar.com; 1408 W Magnolia Ave; ⊙ 4pm-2am Mon-Fri, from 6pm Sat & Sun) Craft-cocktail lust packs hipsters in nightly at this bar that serves up debonair drinks such as the 'Maximillian-aire' and 'the Parlor.' Of course you can be ironic and just have a well-poured Old Fashioned. Great terrace.

Flying Saucer Draught Emporium BAR
(☎817-336-7470; 111 E 3rd St; ⏲11am-1am Mon-Wed, 11am-2am Thu-Sat, noon-midnight Sun) Although it's a chain, it's hard not to like the Flying Sauce. With 80 beers on tap and a delightful tree-shaded patio, this is a much-loved destination just a short stroll from Sundance Sq.

Lola's Saloon BAR
(☎817-877-0666; www.lolasfortworth.com; 2736 W 6th St; ⏲noon-2am) Dive into this dive bar for a fairly intimate music experience. Bands (rock, honky-tonk, bluegrass) play many nights to a fun, eclectic crowd. Catch your breath on the small outside patio. On non-show nights, there's a jukebox worthy of attention.

☆ Entertainment

On weekend evenings, country music becomes common in the Stockyards district, and a variety of live bands play in and around Sundance Sq. Look for listings in *Fort Worth Weekly* (www.fwweekly.com).

Cowtown Coliseum Rodeo RODEO
(www.stockyardsrodeo.com; 121 E Exchange Ave; adult/child rodeo from $18/10, Wild West Show $15/8; ⏲8pm Fri & Sat) See a real live rodeo at 8pm on Friday and Saturday nights year-round. From June to August, horses and riders show off at Pawnee Bill's Wild West Show (at 2:30pm and 4:30pm on Saturday and Sunday).

★ **Pearls Dance Hall** LIVE MUSIC
(www.pearlsdancehall.com; 302 W Exchange Ave; ⏲6pm-2am Wed, from 7pm Fri & Sat) On the edge of the Stockyards, this raucous old brothel, once owned by Buffalo Bill Cody, is an atmospheric place to hear traditional country music with an edge. Texas luminaries such as Dale Watson are known to rock out here.

White Elephant Saloon LIVE MUSIC
(www.whiteelephantsaloon.com; 106 E Exchange Ave; ⏲noon-midnight Sun-Thu, to 2am Fri & Sat) Stockyards cowboys have been bellying up to this bar since 1887 (now owned by Tim Love). Local singers and songwriters are regularly showcased.

ℹ Information

Central Library (500 W 3rd St; ⏲10am-6pm Mon, Wed, Fri & Sat, noon-8pm Tue & Thu, 1-5pm Sun; wi-fi) Free internet access.

FREE RIDE

Fort Worth's coolest transportation option is the **Molly the Trolley** (☎817-204-0302; www.mollythetrolley.com; ⏲10am-10pm) FREE, a vintage trolley system that serves passengers traveling around downtown.

Fort Worth Convention & Visitors Bureau (☎817-882-8588; 3401 W Lancaster Ave; ⏲9am-5pm Mon-Sat) The most together tourist board in the state, with two other branches downtown (☎817-698-3300; 508 Main St; ⏲10am-6pm Mon-Sat) and at Stockyards (☎817-625-9715; www.stockyardsstation.com/information; 130 E Exchange Ave; ⏲9am-6pm Mon-Sat, 11am-5pm Sun). Ask for the spiffy free 3D maps.

ℹ Getting There & Away

Dallas-Fort Worth International Airport (p727) is 17 miles east of Fort Worth.

The **Amtrak** (www.amtrak.com; 1001 Jones St) *Texas Eagle* stops in Fort Worth en route to San Antonio and Chicago. The *Heartland Flyer* serves Oklahoma City.

Monday to Saturday the **Trinity Railway Express** (TRE; ☎817-215-8600; www.trinityrailwayexpress.org; 1001 Jones St) connects downtown Fort Worth with downtown Dallas ($5, 1¼ hours, roughly every 30 minutes).

Several **Greyhound** (www.greyhound.com; 1001 Jones St) buses a day make the one-hour trip from downtown Fort Worth to Dallas ($9). There's also service to other major Texas cities.

ℹ Getting Around

Fort Worth is fairly compact and easy to drive around: I-30 runs east–west through downtown, and I-35 W runs to the south.

The **Fort Worth Transit Authority** (The T; ☎817-215-8600; www.the-t.com; single ride/day pass $1.75/3.50) runs bus 1N to the Stockyards and bus 2 to the Cultural District. Stops include the Intermodal Transportation Center. Both of these lines run well into the evening.

You can zip around town by using the bike-sharing scheme, **Fort Worth B-Cycle** (www.fortworthbcycle.com; pass 24hr/3 days/7 days $8/15/20; ⏲24hr).

WEST TEXAS

Welcome to the land of wide open spaces. Along I-10 there's not much to look at – just scrub brush and lots of sky – but dip below the interstate and you'll find vistas that are as captivating as they are endless. Sometimes the rugged terrain looks like the backdrop in an old Western movie; other times it looks like an alien landscape, with huge rock formations suddenly jutting out of the desert.

But what is there to do? Plenty. Exploring an enormous national park that's nearly the size of Rhode Island. Stopping in small towns that surprise you with minimalist art, planet-watching parties or fascinating ghost-town ruins. Chatting with friendly locals whenever the mood strikes you. And letting the slowness of west Texas get thoroughly under your skin.

Big Bend National Park

Everyone knows Texas is huge. But you can't really appreciate just how big it is until you visit this **national park** (www.nps.gov/bibe; 7-day pass per vehicle $25) that's almost the size of Rhode Island. Despite its sprawl, Big Bend is laced with enough well-placed roads and trails to permit short-term visitors to see a lot in two to three days.

Like many popular US parks, Big Bend has one area – the Chisos Basin – that absorbs the overwhelming crunch of traffic. But any visit should also include time in the **Chihuahuan Desert**, home to curious creatures and adaptable plants, and the **Rio Grande**, providing a watery border between the US and Mexico.

With over 200 miles of trails to explore, it's no wonder hiking is big in Big Bend. Get the scoop on the most popular hikes at the **Panther Junction Visitors Center** (☎432-477-2251; ⏲9am-5pm) on the main park road, 29 miles south of the northern Persimmon Gap entrance and 26 miles east of the Maverick entrance at Study Butte. Or find a plethora of options in the park's booklet, *Hiker's Guide to Trails of Big Bend National Park* ($1.95 at park visitor centers).

In the heart of the park, **Chisos Mountain Lodge** (☎432-477-2291; www.chisosmountainslodge.com; lodge & motel r $156, cottages $174; 📶🐾) offers lodging in the sought-after Roosevelt Stone Cottages or in one of two motel-style lodges. There's also a **dining room** (Lodge Dining Room; Chisos Mountain Lodge; mains $10-24; ⏲7-10am, 11am-4pm & 5-8pm) within the complex, as well as a **camp store** (☎432-477-2291; ⏲8am-9pm) with basic supplies.

For tent campers or smaller RVs that don't require hookups, there are three main campgrounds, some of which can be reserved, some of which are first-come, first-served. When everything's full, rangers direct tent campers to primitive sites throughout the Big Bend backcountry. Most popular – thanks to its mountain climate – is the **Chisos Basin Campground** (☎877-444-6777; www.recreation.gov; campsites $14).

ROUTE 66: GET YOUR KICKS IN TEXAS

The Texas Panhandle isn't exactly a hub of tourism, but it does get plenty of folks passing through as they pay homage to the Mother Road. If you find yourself up thataway, here are the top Texas stops on a Route 66 road trip, going from west to east:

Cadillac Ranch (I-40, btwn exits 60 & 62) This iconic roadside attraction features 10 Cadillacs buried headlights down and tailfins up.

Downtown Amarillo The San Jacinto district still has original Route 66 businesses, and W 6th St is a short, but entirely original, Mother Road segment.

Big Texan Steak Ranch (www.bigtexan.com; 7701 I-40 E, exit 75; mains $10-40; ⏲7am-10:30pm; 👪) A giant waving cowboy welcomes you to this roadside attraction and steakhouse that'll serve you a 72oz steak – free if you can eat it in under an hour.

Bug Ranch (Hwy 207 access road) In response to Cadillac Ranch, five stripped-down VW bugs have sprouted 18 miles east of Amarillo.

Devil's Rope Museum (www.barbwiremuseum.com; 100 Kingsley St, McLean; ⏲9am-5pm Mon-Fri, 10am-4pm Sat Mar-Nov) FREE Learn more about barbed wire than you ever thought possible.

West of Big Bend National Park

Small towns. Ghost towns. Towns that aren't even really towns. Throw in lots of dust and a scorching summer heat that dries out the stream of visitors until it's just a trickle. This isn't everyone's idea of a dream vacation. But if you can't relax out here, then you just plain can't relax. Whatever concerns you in your everyday life is likely to melt away along with anything you leave in your car. Speaking of cars, this is the land that public transportation forgot. You'll need a car out 'round these parts.

Terlingua

A former mining boomtown in the late 19th and early 20th centuries, Terlingua went bust when the mines were closed down in the 1940s. The town dried up and blew away like a tumbleweed, leaving buildings that fell into ruins and earning Terlingua a place in Texas folklore as a ghost town. But slowly the area has become repopulated, thanks in large part to the fact that it's only a few miles outside of Big Bend National Park.

By the way, you'll hear people talk about Terlingua, Study Butte and Terlingua ghost town as if they're three different towns, but the only real town here is Terlingua; the other two are just areas of the town.

Sleeping & Eating

Chisos Mining Co Motel MOTEL $
(☎432-371-2254; www.cmcm.cc; 23280 FM 170; s/d $60/79, cabins from $101; ❄) You'll recognize this quirky little place less than a mile west of Hwy 118 when you spot the oversize Easter eggs on the roof. The rooms are minimalist but as cheap as you'll find.

★**La Posada Milagro** INN $$
(☎432-371-3044; www.laposadamilagro.net; 100 Milagro Rd; d $185-210; ❄📶) Built on top of and even incorporating some of the adobe ruins in the historic ghost town, this guesthouse pulls off the amazing feat of providing stylish rooms that blend in perfectly with the surroundings. The decor is west-Texas chic, and there's a nice patio for enjoying the cool evenings.

Espresso...Y Poco Mas CAFE $
(☎432-371-3044; 100 Milagro Rd; snacks $3-7; ⌚8am-2pm; 📶) We love this friendly little walk-up counter at La Posada Milagro, where you can find pastries, breakfast burritos, lunches and what might just be the best iced coffee in all of west Texas.

★**Starlight Theater** AMERICAN $$
(☎432-371-3400; www.thestarlighttheatre.com; 631 Ivey St; mains $10-21; ⌚5pm-midnight) You'd think a ghost town would be dead at night (pardon the pun), but the Starlight Theater keeps things lively. This former movie theater had fallen into roofless disrepair (thus the 'starlight' name) before being converted into a restaurant. There's live music nearly every night in spring and fall.

> **BOQUILLAS: CROSSING THE RIO GRANDE INTO MEXICO**
>
> For years, one of the added draws of Big Bend was crossing the Rio Grande into the quaint Mexican village of Boquillas. After more than a decade of closure, the border has again opened to visitors. A boatman will row you across ($5 return), once on the other side you can hire a burro ($8 return), walk or take a truck for the 1 mile to Boquillas village. There you need to get stamped in at the Mexican immigration office. You can have lunch, peruse local handicrafts and wander around the town before heading back to the river (leave by 5pm to avoid getting stranded). The border opens from 9am to 6pm Wednesday to Sunday. You'll need your passport. Check discoverboquillas.wordpress.com for more info.

Shopping

Terlingua Trading Co GIFTS
(☎432-371-2234; 100 Ivey St; ⌚10am-8pm) This store in the ghost town has great gifts, from hot sauces and wines to an impressive selection of books. Pick up a brochure on the walking tour of historic Terlingua, or buy a beer inside the store and hang out on the porch with locals at sunset.

Lajitas to Presidio

About half an hour west from the junction in Terlingua, you can trade funky and dusty for trendy and upscale (but still dusty) at **Lajitas Golf Resort & Spa** (☎432-424-5000; www.lajitasgolfresort.com; d from $180; 🚭❄📶🏊🐾). What used to be small-town

Texas got bought up and revamped into a swanky destination. The old Trading Post is gone and in its place is a new general store. (The former Trading Post was the stuff of folk legend, as it was the home of a beer-drinking goat who got elected mayor of the town. Alas, no more.)

The nine-hole golf course that included a shot over the river into Mexico has moved to drier ground to escape flooding, and now it's the 18-hole **Black Jack's Crossing**. **Lajitas Stables** (☎432-371-2212; www.lajitasstables.com; Rte 170; 2hr rides $75) offers short horseback trail rides as well as full-day rides to the Buena Suerte Mine and Ghost Town.

Lajitas is the eastern gateway of the massive **Big Bend Ranch State Park** (☎432-358-4444; www.tpwd.state.tx.us; off Rte 170; adult peak/nonpeak $5/3, child under 12yr free). At 433 sq miles, it's more than 11 times larger than Texas' next biggest state park (Franklin Mountains in El Paso). Taking up almost all the desert between Lajitas and Presidio, Big Bend Ranch reaches north from the Rio Grande into some of the wildest country in North America. It is full of notable features, most prominently the **Solitario**, formed 36 million years ago in a volcanic explosion. The resulting caldera measures 8 miles east to west and 9 miles north to south. As massive as it is, this former ranch is one of the best-kept secrets in Big Bend country.

Access to the park is limited and a permit is required, even if you're just passing through. Coming from Lajitas, stop at the **Barton Warnock Visitor Center** (☎432-424-3327; www.tpwd.state.tx.us; FM 170; ⏰8am-4:30pm daily) for your day-use and camping permits (primitive campsites $8, backcountry $5). This education center is staffed by some of the most knowledgeable folks in the region. On the western edge of the park, you can pick up a permit at the **Fort Leaton State Historic Site** (☎432-229-3613; FM 170; ⏰8am-4:30pm), a restored adobe fortress.

SCENIC DRIVE: RIVER ROAD

West of Lajitas, **Rte 170** (also known as River Rd, or *El Camino Del Rio* in Spanish) hugs the Rio Grande through some of the most spectacular and remote scenery in Big Bend country. Relatively few Big Bend visitors experience this driving adventure, even though it can be navigated in any vehicle with good brakes. Strap in and hold on: you have the Rio Grande on one side and fanciful geological formations all around, and at one point there's a 15% grade – the maximum allowable. When you reach Presidio, head north on US 67 to get to Marfa. Or, if you plan to go back the way you came, at least travel as far as Colorado Canyon (20 miles from Lajitas) for the best scenery.

Central West Texas

The small towns of west Texas have become more than just the gateway to Big Bend National Park. Fort Davis, Marfa, Alpine and Marathon have a sprawling, easygoing charm and plenty of ways to keep a road-tripper entertained.

Fort Davis

False-front wooden buildings, an old fort and a stellar observatory make Texas' tallest town (elevation 5000ft) a Big Bend must-see. Its altitudinal advantage makes it a popular oasis during the summer, when west Texans head towards the mountains to escape the searing desert heat.

Sights & Activities

★**McDonald Observatory** OBSERVATORY
(☎432-426-3640; www.mcdonaldobservatory.org; 3640 Dark Sky Dr; daytime pass adult/child 6-12yr/under 12yr $8/7/free, star parties adult/child $12/8; ⏰visitor center 10am-5pm; 👪) Away from all the light pollution of the big cities, the middle of west Texas has some of the clearest and darkest skies in North America, making it the perfect spot for an observatory. They have some of the biggest telescopes in the world here, perched on the peak of 6791ft Mt Locke and so enormous you can spot them from miles away.

Fort Davis National Historic Site HISTORIC SITE
(☎432-426-3224; www.nps.gov/foda; Hwy 17; adult/child $3/free; ⏰8am-5pm; 🐾) A remarkably well-preserved frontier military post with an impressive backdrop at the foot of Sleeping Lion Mountain, Fort Davis was established in 1854 and abandoned in 1891. More than 20 buildings remain – five of them restored with period furnishings – as well as 100 or so ruins.

Davis Mountains State Park PARK
(☎432-426-3337; www.tpwd.state.tx.us; Hwy 118; adult/child under 12yr $6/free) Just a few miles northwest of Fort Davis on Hwy 118, set amid the most extensive mountain range in Texas, is Davis Mountains State Park. Hiking, mountain biking, horseback riding (BYO horse) and stargazing are all big attractions here, as is bird-watching. Pick up a bird checklist from park headquarters so you know what you're looking at, or, if you already know what you're looking at, use it to impress your bird-watching friends.

Sleeping & Eating

Veranda Historic Inn B&B $$
(☎888-383-2847; www.theveranda.com; 210 Court Ave; r $115-145;) A short stroll to the town center, this charming B&B has 10 antique-filled rooms and suites set in an 1883 adobe building. The oldest hotel in west Texas (hence the 'historic' namesake) has a shaded porch and pretty gardens – fine spots for a sundowner.

★**Indian Lodge** INN $$
(☎lodge 432-426-3254, reservations 512-389-8982; Hwy 118; d $95-125, ste $150;) Located in the Davis Mountains State Park, this historic 39-room inn has 18in-thick adobe walls, hand-carved cedar furniture and ceilings of pine *viga* and *latilla* that give it the look of a Southwestern pueblo – that is, one with swimming pool, gift shop and restaurant. The comfortable and surprisingly spacious guest rooms are a good value, so reserve early.

Fort Davis Drug Store AMERICAN $$
(☎432-426-3118; www.fortdavisdrugstore.net; 113 N State St; mains $8-23; ⏱7am-9pm;) Part diner, part old-fashioned soda fountain – but no 1950s nostalgia here. The theme is pure cowboy, with corrugated metal, big wooden chairs and lots of saddles providing the backdrop. Dine on country-style breakfasts, diner-style lunches and full entrees at dinner. But whatever you do, save room for a banana split (or at least a milkshake).

Marfa

Founded in the 1880s Marfa got its first taste of fame when Rock Hudson, Elizabeth Taylor and James Dean came to town to film the 1956 Warner Brothers film *Giant*. It's also become a pilgrimage for art lovers, thanks to one of the world's largest installations of minimalist art. This, in turn, has attracted a disproportionate number of art galleries, quirky lodging options and interesting restaurants.

Marfa is on its own schedule, which is pretty much made up according to whim. Plan on coming late in the week or on a weekend; half the town is closed early in the week.

DON'T MISS

A STAR-STUDDED EVENT

On Tuesday, Friday and Saturday nights, about half an hour after sunset, **McDonald Observatory** shows off its favorite planets, galaxies and globular clusters at its popular **Star Parties**, where professional astronomers guide you in some heavy-duty stargazing. Using ridiculously powerful laser pointers, they give you a tour of the night sky, and you'll get to use some of the telescopes to play planetary Peeping Tom. (It gets surprisingly brisk up there at night, so dress warm and bring blankets.)

Sights & Activities

Marfa has all sorts of art to explore, and you can pick up a list of galleries at the **Marfa Visitors Center** (☎432-729-4772; www.visitmarfa.com; 302 S Highland Ave; ⏱9am-5pm Mon-Fri & event weekends).

Chinati Foundation Museum MUSEUM
(☎432-729-4362; www.chinati.org; 1 Calvary Row; adult/student $25/10; ⏱by guided tour 10am & 2pm Wed-Sun) This is it. This is what all the fuss is about. Minimalist artist Donald Judd single-handedly put Marfa on the art-world map when he created the Chinati Foundation on the site of a former army post, using the abandoned buildings to create and display one of the world's largest permanent installations of minimalist art.

Marfa Mystery Lights PHENOMENON
Ghost lights, mystery lights…call them what you want, but the Marfa Lights that flicker beneath the Chinati Mountains have captured the imagination of many a traveler over the decades. On many nights, the mystery seems to be whether you're actually just seeing car headlights in the distance. Try your luck at the Marfa Lights Viewing Area about 9 miles east of Marfa on Hwy 90/67.

ART IN THE MIDDLE OF NOWHERE

So you're driving along a two-lane highway in dusty west Texas, out in the middle of nowhere, when suddenly a small building appears up in the distance like a mirage. As you zip past it you glance over and see...a Prada store? Known as the **Marfa Prada** (although it's really closer to Valentine), this art installation doesn't sell $1700 handbags, but it does get your attention as a tongue-in-cheek commentary on consumerism.

Sleeping & Eating

★El Cosmico CAMPGROUND $

(☎432-729-1950; www.elcosmico.com; 802 S Highland Ave; tent sites per person $15, safari tents $85-100, teepees $90-150, trailers $120-185, yurt $150;) One of the funkiest choices in all of Texas, El Cosmico lets you sleep in a stylishly converted travel trailer, a teepee, a safari tent – or even a yurt. It's not for everyone: the grounds are dry and dusty, you might have to shower outdoors, and there's no AC (luckily, it's cool at night). But, hey, how often do you get to sleep in a Kozy Coach?

Thunderbird BOUTIQUE HOTEL $$

(☎877-729-1984; www.thunderbirdmarfa.com; 601 W San Antonio St; d $140-190;) This classic 1950s motel was reopened in 2005 as a small boutique with a spiffy new look. The rooms are hip and minimalist, and the grounds and common areas are as cool as the desert air at night.

Hotel Paisano HOTEL $$

(☎432-729-3669; www.hotelpaisano.com; 207 N Highland Ave; d $100-150, ste $160-260;) Marfa's historic hotel has a unique claim to fame: it's where the cast of the movie *Giant* stayed. The comfy rooms are nicely designed, and the whole place does have a dignified charm. The best rooms have a fireplace and a private terrace. There's a first-rate restaurant (Jett's), a snazzy covered pool and a touch of taxidermy for good measure.

Food Shark FOOD TRAILER $

(www.foodsharkmarfa.com; 222 W San Antonio St; mains $5-8; noon-3pm Fri-Sun) See that battered old food trailer near the main road through town? If you do, that means Food Shark is open for business. If you're lucky enough to catch them, you'll find incredibly fresh Greek salad and their specialty, the Marfalafel. Daily specials are excellent, and sell out early.

Squeeze Marfa CAFE $

(☎432-729-4500; www.squeezemarfa.com; 215 N Highland Ave; mains $5-10; 8am-3pm Tue-Sun;) This cute little cafe across from the courthouse serves fresh and healthy breakfasts, lunches and smoothies, all the better to enjoy on the narrow, shady patio. The address is on Highland, but the entrance is on Lincoln.

★Cochineal AMERICAN $$$

(☎432-729-3300; cochinealmarfa.com; 107 W San Antonio St; small plates $8-14, mains around $26; 9am-1pm Sun, 5:30-10pm Thu-Tue) Foodies flock to this stylish but minimalist eatery (with outdoor courtyard) for a changing menu that showcases high-quality organic ingredients. Portions are generous, so don't be afraid to share a few small plates (along the lines of brisket tacos, oyster mushroom risotto and housemade ramen with duck breast) in lieu of a full dinner. Reservations are recommended.

Drinking & Nightlife

★Planet Marfa BAR

(☎432-386-5099; 200 S Abbott St; 2pm-midnight Fri & Sat, to 7pm Sun) Nightlife, Marfa style, is epitomized in this wonderfully funky open-air bar. There's usually live music at night, and shelters are scattered about to protect you from the elements. If you're lucky, someone will save you a spot inside the teepee.

Lost Horse BAR

(www.losthorsesaloon.com; 306 E San Antonio St; 4pm-midnight) Follow the crack of pool balls and the crooning of a solitary country-and-western crooner to this atmospheric cowboy bar on the main strip. It has saddles and skulls, taxidermy and an eye-patch-wearing owner named Ty Mitchell. Thirsty folk shouldn't miss this Texas classic writ large.

Alpine

Primarily a pit stop, this university town has no real attractions of note. But it is the most sizable population (5700) in Big Bend – and the only place with big-name chain motels, numerous restaurants, grocery stores and more than one gas station. You can get region-wide information at the **Alpine Chamber of Commerce** (☎432-837-2326; www.alpinetexas.com; 106 N 3rd St; 9am-5pm Mon-Fri, to 4pm Sat).

Museum of the Big Bend MUSEUM
(☎432-837-8143; www.museumofthebigbend.com; 400 N Harrison St; donations accepted; ⏲9am-5pm Tue-Sat, 1-5pm Sun) FREE On the campus of Sul Ross State University, this little museum is a great place to delve into the past, with exhibits on marine fossils (a warm shallow sea covered Big Bend 135 million years ago), Native American pictographs, Spanish missionaries, Mexican pioneers, buffalo soldiers (nickname for the African American soldiers who fought in the Civil War) and of course cowboys (with a full-scale chuck wagon on display).

Hancock Hill VIEWPOINT
(E Ave B) Behind Sul Ross State University, a trail leads up the dusty slopes of Hancock Hill. There are fine views of the area and some curious artifacts here – including a battered desk that some uni students dragged here back in 1981. To reach the desk, head uphill to the first rock pile and follow the trail to the right. It's about a 20-minute walk.

Sleeping & Eating

Antelope Lodge CABIN $
(☎432-837-2451; www.antelopelodge.com; 2310 W Hwy 90; s $53-75, d $58-80, ste $105-120;) You'd think from the name you were getting a hunting lodge, but it's nothing like that. Rustic stucco cottages with Spanish-tile roofs – each one holding two guest rooms – sit sprinkled about a shady lawn. There's a casual, pleasant vibe, and the rooms have kitchenettes. Ask the geologically minded owner about guided rock hunts.

★**Holland Hotel** HISTORIC HOTEL $$
(☎432-837-3844; www.thehollandhoteltexas.com; 209 W Holland Ave; d $105-125, ste $140-220;) Built in 1928, this beautifully renovated Spanish Colonial building has elegantly furnished rooms set with carved wood furniture, Western-style artwork and sleek modern bathrooms. The lobby, with its stuffed leather chairs and wood-beamed ceiling is a classy setting in which to unwind. There's a good high-end restaurant attached.

Maverick Inn MOTEL $$
(☎432-837-0628; www.themaverickinn.com; 1200 E Holland Ave; r $106-125;) The maverick road-tripper will feel right at home at this retro motor court that's been smartly renovated to include luxury bedding and flat-screen TVs. Rooms have Texas-style furnishings and terracotta floors, and the pool looks mighty nice after a hot, dusty day. You can also borrow a guitar or peruse the Texas coffee-table books in the lobby.

Magoo's AMERICAN $
(905 E Ave East; mains $4-10; ⏲6am-2pm Mon-Fri, 7am-noon Sat & Sun) A no-fuss diner that's always packed, Magoo's is the go-to spot for breakfast burritos, huevos rancheros, pancakes and other breakfast fare.

★**Reata** STEAK $$
(☎432-837-9232; www.reata.net; 203 N 5th St; lunch mains $9-17, dinner $16-25; ⏲11:30am-2pm & 5-10pm Mon-Sat) Named after the ranch in the movie *Giant,* Reata does turn on the upscale ranch-style charm – at least in the front dining room, where the serious diners go. Step back into the lively bar area or onto the shady patio and it's a completely different vibe, where you can feel free to nibble your way around the menu and enjoy a margarita.

Marathon

The tiny town of Marathon (population 455) isn't much more than a main street with a few cafes and a historic hotel, but it does have two claims to fame: it's the closest town to Big Bend's north entrance, providing a last chance to fill up your car and your stomach before immersing yourself in the park; and it's got the **Gage Hotel** (☎432-386-4205; www.gagehotel.com; 102 NW 1st St/Hwy 90; r $185-243;), a true Texas treasure.

Built in 1927, the Gage has a fabulous Old West style that's matched only by its love of taxidermy. Each room at this property is individually (though similarly) decorated with Native American blankets, cowboy gear and leather accents. The associated **12 Gage** (☎432-386-4205; 101 US 90 W; mains $20-45; ⏲6-9pm Sun-Thu, to 10pm Fri & Sat) whips up gourmet renditions of Texas faves, and the **White Buffalo Bar** (☎432-386-4205; 101 US 90 W; ⏲4pm-midnight Sun-Thu, 3pm-2am Fri & Sat) invites you to enjoy a margarita while trying to ignore its namesake's glassy stare.

Before heading to Big Bend, stock up on picnic supplies at **French Co. Grocer** (☎432-386-4522; www.frenchcogrocer.com; 206 N Ave D; ⏲7:30am-9pm Mon-Fri, from 8am Sat, from 9am Sun), or enjoy them at the tables outside at this charming little grocery – formerly the WM French General Merchandise store, established in 1900.

El Paso

Well, you've made it. You're just about as far west in Texas as you can go. Surrounded mostly by New Mexico and Mexico, El Paso seems to have more in common with its non-Texas neighbors than it does with Texas itself.

Sadly, El Paso and its sister city – Ciudad Juárez, Mexico, which is right across the river – have had a bit of a falling out. At one time, the two cities were inextricably linked, with tourists streaming back and forth across the Good Neighbor International Bridge all day long. But with the rise in gang- and drug-related violence, Juárez has become so dangerous that there is now little traffic between the two sides.

Sights & Activities

★El Paso Museum of Art MUSEUM

(915-532-1707; www.elpasoartmuseum.org; 1 Arts Festival Plaza; admission charge for special exhibits; 9am-5pm Tue-Sat, to 9pm Thu, noon-5pm Sun) FREE This thoroughly enjoyable museum is in a former Greyhound station. They'd want us to brag about their *Madonna and Child* (c 1200), but the Southwestern art is terrific, and the engaging modern pieces round out the collection nicely. All this, and it's free?! Well done, El Paso, well done.

El Paso Holocaust Museum MUSEUM

(www.elpasoholocaustmuseum.org; 715 N Oregon St; 9am-4pm Tue-Fri, 1-5pm Sat & Sun) FREE It may seem a little anachronistic in a predominately Hispanic town, but the Holocaust Museum is as much a surprise inside as out for its thoughtful and moving exhibits that are imaginatively presented for maximum impact.

Franklin Mountains State Park PARK

(www.tpwd.state.tx.us; Transmountain Rd; adult/child $5/free; 8am-5pm Mon-Fri, 6:30am-8pm Sat & Sun) At over 24,000 acres, this is the largest urban park in the US. It's a quick escape from the city to the home of ringtail cats, coyotes and countless other smaller animals and reptiles. There's excellent mountain biking and hiking here, with 7192ft North Franklin Peak looming overhead.

Wyler Aerial Tramway CABLE CAR

(915-566-6622; 1700 McKinley Ave; adult/child under 12yr $8/4; noon-7pm Fri & Sat, 10am-5pm Sun) Sure, you'd feel a sense of accomplishment if you hiked to the top of the Franklin Mountains. We're not suggesting you take the easy way out (or are we?), but it only takes about four minutes to take a gondola to the top. After gliding 2600ft and gaining 940ft in elevation, you'll reach the viewing platform on top of Ranger Peak, where you'll enjoy spectacular views of Texas, New Mexico and Mexico.

WHAT TIME IS IT?

When it comes to time zones, El Paso sides with New Mexico, conforming to Mountain Time rather than Central Time like the rest of Texas. Confusing? Occasionally. If you're telling someone in neighboring Van Horn or Fort Stockton what time you'll meet them, be sure to add on the extra hour you'll lose just by leaving El Paso.

Sleeping

In addition to the following exceptions, there are scads of characterless chain motels found along I-10.

Gardner Hotel HOSTEL $

(915-532-3661; www.gardnerhotel.com; 311 E Franklin Ave; r $60-70;) El Paso's oldest continually operating hotel is also the only real downtown bargain. It probably hasn't changed a whole lot since John Dillinger stayed here in the 1930s (hint: room 221 is where the outlaw slept), but it has a certain ragtag charm.

Coral Motel MOTEL $

(915-772-3263; www.coralmotel.net; 6420 Montana Ave; r $45-60; P) Anyone who loves 1950s roadside nostalgia will feel right at home at this friendly little motel with its Spanish-style barrel-tile roof and Jetsons-esque sign. Rooms are simple with white cinder-block walls, floral bedspreads and dated bathrooms, but you can't beat the price.

Camino Real Hotel HOTEL $$

(915-534-3000; www.caminorealelpaso.com; 101 S El Paso St; r weekday/weekend from $92/81; P @) The only US location of an upscale Mexican hotel chain, the historic Camino Real – in operation for over 100 years – has a prime location steps from downtown museums; a gorgeous bar with a Tiffany art glass dome; large, comfortable rooms; and friendly service, even when it's packed with conventioneers.

Eating

Mexican is the food of choice in El Paso; the town's known for a special bright-red chili-and-tomato sauce used on enchiladas. Tex-Mex in El Paso is cheap and abundant.

Craft & Social AMERICAN $

(www.craftandsocial.com; 305 E Franklin St; mains $7-11; 11am-11pm Mon-Wed, to 2am Thu & Fri, 3pm-2am Sat, 4pm-midnight Sun) A welcome addition to El Paso, Craft & Social whips up high-end sandwiches (featuring ingredients such as oven-roasted chicken, brie, roasted red peppers), artisanal cheese and smoked-meat platters and zesty salads. All go nicely with the craft brews from Belgium, Germany and the USA.

It's an appealing, anytime sort of place, with bar stools, communal tables, a few armchairs and sidewalk seating.

L&J Cafe MEXICAN $

(915-566-8418; http://landjcafe.com; 3622 E Missouri Ave; mains $5-13; 9am-9pm) One of El Paso's best-loved Mexican joints, L&J serves up delicious tacos, fajitas and famous green-chile chicken enchiladas – plus a legendary menudo on weekends. It's next to the historic Concordia Cemetery, and at first glance looks a bit divey. Don't be deterred: it's been open since 1927, and the inside is much more inviting.

★ Tabla TAPAS $$

(115 Durango St; small plates $7-16; 11am-10pm Mon-Thu, to 11pm Fri & Sat) Get ready to share all sorts of awesomeness. The small plates here fuse Spanish classics with the flavors of the Southwest in mouthwatering combos like short rib and blue-cheese croquettes, grilled octopus with chimichurri, and pork confit sliders. Tabla is set in a beautifully converted brick warehouse with tall ceilings and an open kitchen.

Crave AMERICAN $$

(915-351-3677; www.cravekitchenandbar.com; 300 Cincinnati Ave; mains $11-28; 7am-11pm Mon-Sat, to 6pm Sun) Winning extra points for style – from the cool sign to the cutlery hanging from the ceiling – this hip little eatery serves up creative comfort food: green chile mac-and-cheese, juicy burgers with sweet potato waffle fries, and decadent breakfasts. There's also a newer location on the **east side** (915-594-7971; 11990 Rojas Dr; 7am-11pm Mon-Sat, to 6pm Sun).

★ Cattleman's Steakhouse STEAK $$$

(915-544-3200; www.cattlemansranch.com; Indian Cliffs Ranch; mains $17-48; 5-10pm Mon-Fri, 12:30-10pm Sat, 12:30-9pm Sun;) This place is 20 miles east of the city, but local folks would probably drive 200 miles to eat here. The food is good, and the scenery is even better. Portions are huge, and for just $6 extra you can share an entree and gain full access to the family-style sides.

Entertainment

Bars come and go quickly in El Paso. Your best bet is to head to El Paso's mini-entertainment district near the University of Texas El Paso (around Cincinnati St between Mesa and Stanton) to see what's happening in the bars and restaurants that are clustered there. Pick up the free weekly *El Paso Scene* (www.epscene.com) or the Friday 'Tiempo' supplement to the *El Paso Times* (www.elpasotimes.com) for cultural and music listings.

Shopping

On I-10 east of town, several warehouselike shops sell all the goodies you can find in Mexico – pottery, blankets, silver – at similar prices.

El Paso Saddleblanket SOUVENIRS

(915-544-1000; www.saddleblanket.com; 6926 Gateway Blvd E; 9am-5pm Mon-Sat) 'Incredible 2-acre shopping adventure!' the billboards scream. This place is indeed huge, and it's chock-full of all things Southwestern. Stuff your suitcases with pottery, blankets, turquoise jewelry, even a sombrero if you must. They've got mounted steer horns, but we can tell you right now you're not going to be able to carry them onto the plane.

Information

El Paso Public Library (915-543-5433; www.elpasolibrary.org; 501 N Oregon St; 10am-7pm Mon-Thu, 11am-6pm Fri, 10am-6pm Sat, noon-6pm Sun;) Free internet access. Check the website for additional branches.

El Paso Visitors Center (915-534-0600; www.visitelpaso.com; 400 W San Antonio St; 8am-5pm Mon-Fri, 9am-1pm Sat) Stocks racks and racks of brochures, and the staff is quite helpful. It also has a well-populated website for planning.

HOT TOPIC: MEXICO BORDERLANDS

Tex has always mixed well with Mex. But the flow of Texans casually crossing from El Paso into Mexican border towns has slowed to a trickle due to drug-cartel-related violence. The state department urges caution when visiting all border towns in Mexico – as do we.

Getting There & Around

El Paso International Airport (ELP; www.elpasointernationalairport.com), 8 miles northeast of downtown off I-10, serves 16 US and two Mexican cities. Numerous chain rental-car companies are on site (you really need a car here).

Amtrak's Florida–California *Sunset Limited* stops at **Union Depot** (www.amtrak.com; 700 W San Francisco Ave). The terminal for **Greyhound** (www.greyhound.com; 200 W San Antonio Ave) is four blocks from the center of downtown.

Hueco Tanks State Historical Park

About 32 miles east of El Paso is the 860-acre **Hueco Tanks State Historical Park** (☎park 915-857-1135, reservations 512-389-8911; www.tpwd.state.tx.us; 6900 Hueco Tanks Rd/FM 2775; adult/child $7/free; ⏲8am-6pm). Popular today among rock climbers, the area has attracted humans for as many as 10,000 years, and park staff estimate there are more than 2000 pictographs at the site, some dating back 5000 years.

To minimize human impact, a daily visitor quota is enforced; make reservations 24 hours in advance to gain entry. You can explore the North Mountain area by yourself, but to hike deeper into the park – where the more interesting pictographs are – you have to reserve and join one of the pictograph, birding or hiking **tours** (☎915-849-6684; tours per person $2; ⏲call for schedule).

Guadalupe Mountains National Park

We won't go so far as to call it Texas' best-kept secret, but the fact is that a lot of Texans aren't even aware of the **Guadalupe Mountains National Park** (☎915-828-3251; www.nps.gov/gumo; US Hwy 62/180; 7-day pass adult/child under 16yr $5/free). It's just this side of the Texas–New Mexico state line and a long drive from practically everywhere in the state. Despite its low profile, it is a Texas high spot, both literally and figuratively. At 8749ft, Guadalupe Peak is the highest point in the Lone Star State.

The fall foliage in **McKittrick Canyon** is the best in west Texas, and more than half the park is a federally designated wilderness area.

The National Park Service has deliberately curbed development to keep the park wild. There are no restaurants or indoor accommodations and only a smattering of services and programs. But if you're looking for some of the best hiking and high-country splendor Texas can muster, you should put this park on your itinerary.

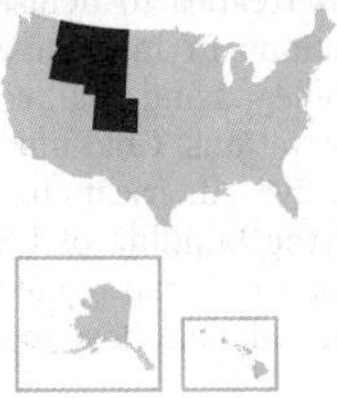

Rocky Mountains

Includes ➡

Best Places to Eat

- Root Down (p749)
- Salt (p756)
- Rickshaw (p806)
- Sweet Melissa's (p781)
- Silk Road (p799)

Best Places to Sleep

- Curtis (p747)
- Boise Guest House (p804)
- Chautauqua Lodge (p754)
- Alpine House (p783)
- Old Faithful Inn (p790)

Why Go?

The high backbone of the lower 48, the Rockies are nature on steroids, with rows of snowcapped peaks, rugged canyons and wild rivers running buckshot over the western states. With its beauty and vitality, it's no wonder that 100 years ago, this region beckoned ailing patients with last-ditch hopes for cures.

The healing power of the Rocky Mountains persists. You can choose between tranquillity (try Wyoming, the USA's least-populated state) and adrenaline (measured in vertical drop). Locals love a good frozen, wet or mud-spattered adventure and, with plenty of climbing, skiing and white-water paddling, it's easy to join in. Afterwards, relax by soaking in hot springs under a roof of stars, sipping cold microbrews or feasting farm-to-table style.

Lastly, don't miss the super-sized charms of Yellowstone, Rocky Mountain, Grand Teton and Glacier National Parks, where the big five (grizzly bears, moose, bison, mountain lions and wolves) still roam wild.

When to Go

Denver

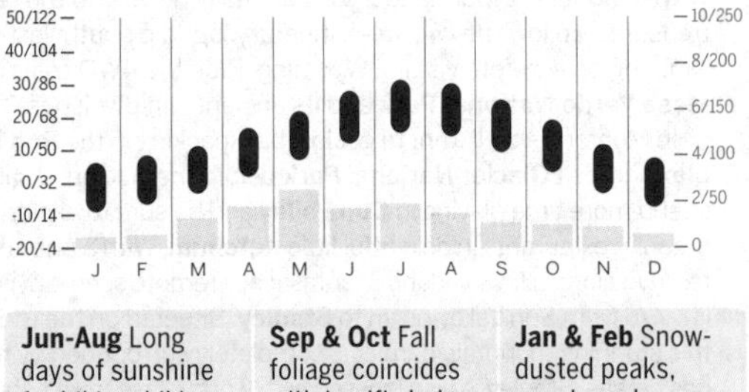

Jun-Aug Long days of sunshine for biking, hiking, farmers markets and summer festivals.

Sep & Oct Fall foliage coincides with terrific lodging deals.

Jan & Feb Snow-dusted peaks, powdery slopes and deluxe après-ski parties.

History

Before the late 18th century, when French trappers and Spaniards stepped in, the Rocky Mountain area was a land of many tribes, including the Nez Percé, the Shoshone, the Crow, the Lakota and the Ute.

Meriwether Lewis and William Clark claimed enduring fame after the USA bought almost all of present-day Montana, Wyoming and eastern Colorado in the 1803 Louisiana Purchase. Their epic survey covered 8000 miles in three years. Their success urged on other adventurers, setting migration in motion. Wagon trains voyaged to the Rockies right into the 20th century, only temporarily slowed by the completion of the Transcontinental Railroad across southern Wyoming in the late 1860s.

To accommodate settlers, the US purged the western frontier of the Spanish, the British and, in a truly shameful era, most of the Native American population. The government signed endless treaties to defuse Native American objections to increasing settlement but always reneged and shunted tribes onto smaller reservations. Gold-miners' incursions into Native American territory in Montana and the building of US Army forts along the Bozeman Trail ignited a series of wars with the Lakota, Cheyenne, Arapaho and others.

Gold and silver mania preceded Colorado's entry to statehood in 1876. Statehood soon followed for Montana (1889), Wyoming (1890) and Idaho (1890). Miners, white farmers and ranchers were the people with power in the late 19th century.

Mining, grazing and timber played major roles in regional economic development, sparking growth in financial and industrial support. They also subjected the region to boom-and-bust cycles by unsustainable resource management.

ROCKY MOUNTAINS IN...

Two Weeks

Start your Rocky Mountain odyssey in the **Denver** area. Go tubing, vintage-clothes shopping or biking in outdoor-mad, boho **Boulder**, then soak up the liberal rays eavesdropping at a sidewalk cafe. Enjoy the vistas of the **Rocky Mountain National Park** before heading west on I-70 to play in the mountains around **Breckenridge**, which also has some of the best beginner slopes in Colorado. Go to ski and mountain-bike mecca **Steamboat Springs** before crossing the border into Wyoming.

Get a taste of prairie-town life in **Laramie**, then stop in **Lander**, rock-climbing destination extraordinaire. Continue north to chic **Jackson** and the majestic **Grand Teton National Park** before hitting iconic **Yellowstone National Park**. Save at least three days for exploring this geyser-packed wonderland.

Cross the state line into 'big sky country' and slowly make your way northwest through Montana, stopping in funky **Bozeman** and lively **Missoula** before visiting **Flathead Lake**. Wrap up your trip in Idaho, exploring Basque culture in up-and-coming **Boise**.

One Month

With a month on your hands, you can really delve into the region's off-the-beaten-path treasures. Follow the two-week itinerary, but dip southwest in Colorado – a developing wine region – before visiting Wyoming. Ride the 4WD trails around **Ouray**. Be sure to visit **Mesa Verde National Park** and its ancient cliff dwellings.

In Montana, you'll want to get lost backpacking in the **Bob Marshall Wilderness Complex** and visit **Glacier National Park** before the glaciers disappear altogether. In Idaho, spend more time playing in **Sun Valley** and be sure to explore the shops, pubs and yummy organic restaurants in delightful little **Ketchum**. With a one-month trip, you also have time to drive along a few of Idaho's fantastically remote scenic byways. Make sure you cruise Hwy 75 from Sun Valley north to **Stanley**. Situated on the wide banks of the Salmon River, this stunning mountain hamlet is completely surrounded by national forestland and wilderness areas. Stanley is also blessed with world-class trout fishing and mild to wild rafting.

Take **Hwy 21** (the Ponderosa Pine Scenic Byway) from Stanley to Boise. This scenic drive takes you through miles of dense ponderosa forests and past some excellent, solitary riverside camping spots – some of which come with their own natural hot-springs pools.

After the economy boomed post-WWII, national parks started attracting vacationers. Tourism is now a leading industry in all four states, with the military trailing close behind, particularly in Colorado.

Land & Climate

Extending from Alaska's Brooks Range and Canada's Yukon Territory all the way to Mexico, the Rockies sprawl northwest to southeast, from the steep escarpment of Colorado's Front Range westward to Nevada's Great Basin. Their towering peaks and ridges form the Continental Divide: to the west, waters flow to the Pacific, and to the east, toward the Atlantic and the Gulf of Mexico.

For many travelers, the Rockies are a summer destination. It starts to feel summery around June, and the warm weather generally lasts until about mid-September (though warm outerwear is recommended). The winter, which brings in packs of powder hounds, doesn't usually hit until late November, though snowstorms can start in the mountains as early as September. Winter usually lasts until March or early April. In the mountains, the weather is constantly changing (snow in summer is not uncommon), so always be prepared. Fall, when the aspens flaunt their autumn gold, and early summer, when wildflowers bloom, are wonderful times to visit.

ℹ Getting There & Around

Travel here takes time. The Rockies are sparsely developed, with attractions spread across long distances and linked by roads that meander between mountains and canyons. With limited public transportation, touring in a private vehicle is best. After all, road-tripping is one of *the* reasons to explore this scenic region.

In rural areas services are few and far between – the I-80 across Wyoming is a notorious offender. It's not unusual to go more than 100 miles between gas stations. When in doubt, fill up.

The main travel hub is Denver International Airport (p753), although if you are coming on a domestic flight, check out **Colorado Springs Airport** (☎719-550-1900; www.springsgov.com; 7770 Milton E Proby Pkwy; 📶) as well: fares are often lower, it's quicker to navigate than DIA and it's nearly as convenient. Both Denver and Colorado Springs offer flights on smaller planes to cities and resort towns around the region – Jackson, WY, Boise, ID, Bozeman, MT, and Aspen, CO, are just a few options. Salt Lake City, UT, also has connections with destinations in all four states.

Greyhound (☎800-231-2222; www.greyhound.com) has fixed routes throughout the Rockies, and offers the most comprehensive bus service. Two **Amtrak** (☎toll-free 800-872-7245; www.amtrak.com) routes serve the region:

California Zephyr Daily between Emeryville, CA (in the Bay Area), and Chicago, IL, with six stops in Colorado, including Denver, Fraser–Winter Park, Glenwood Springs and Grand Junction.

Empire Builder Daily from Seattle, WA, or Portland, OR, to Chicago, IL, with 12 stops in Montana (including Whitefish and East and West Glacier) and one in Idaho (Sandpoint).

COLORADO

From double-diamond runs to stiff espressos, Colorado is all about vigor. This is also the state graced with the greatest concentration of high peaks – dubbed 14ers for their height over 14,000ft.

But it isn't all about the great outdoors. Universities and high-tech hubs show the state's industrious side, though even workaholics might call in sick when snow starts falling.

ℹ Information

Colorado Road Conditions (☎877-315-7623; www.state.co.us) Highway advisories.

Colorado State Parks (☎303-470-1144; www.parks.state.co.us) Tent sites cost from $10 to $20 per night, depending on facilities, while RV hook-ups are $24 per night. Advance reservations for specific campsites are taken, and are subject to an $10 nonrefundable booking fee.

Colorado Travel & Tourism Authority (☎800-265-6723; www.colorado.com) State-wide tourism information.

Denver

Denver's mile-high gravity is growing, pulling all objects in the Rocky Mountain West toward the glistening downtown towers, hopped-up brewpubs, hemped-out cannabis dispensaries, mountain trails, and growing western cosmopolitanism that's fostered a burgeoning arts scene and brought great restaurants and hip bars to a cow town gone worldwide crazy.

While most of the tourist action centers on the Downtown and Lower Downtown (LoDo) Districts, travelers in the know will also explore outlying neighborhoods like Highlands, Washington Park, Cherry Creek, Five Points, South Santa Fe and the River North (RiNo).

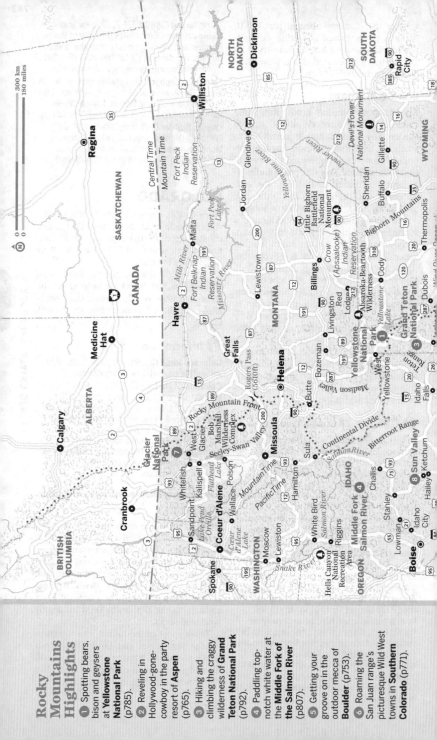

Rocky Mountains Highlights

1. Spotting bears, bison and geysers at **Yellowstone National Park** (p785).
2. Reveling in Hollywood-gone-cowboy in the party resort of **Aspen** (p765).
3. Hiking and climbing the craggy wilderness of **Grand Teton National Park** (p792).
4. Paddling top-notch white water at the **Middle Fork of the Salmon River** (p807).
5. Getting your groove on in the outdoor mecca of **Boulder** (p753).
6. Roaming the San Juan range's picturesque Wild West towns in **Southern Colorado** (p771).

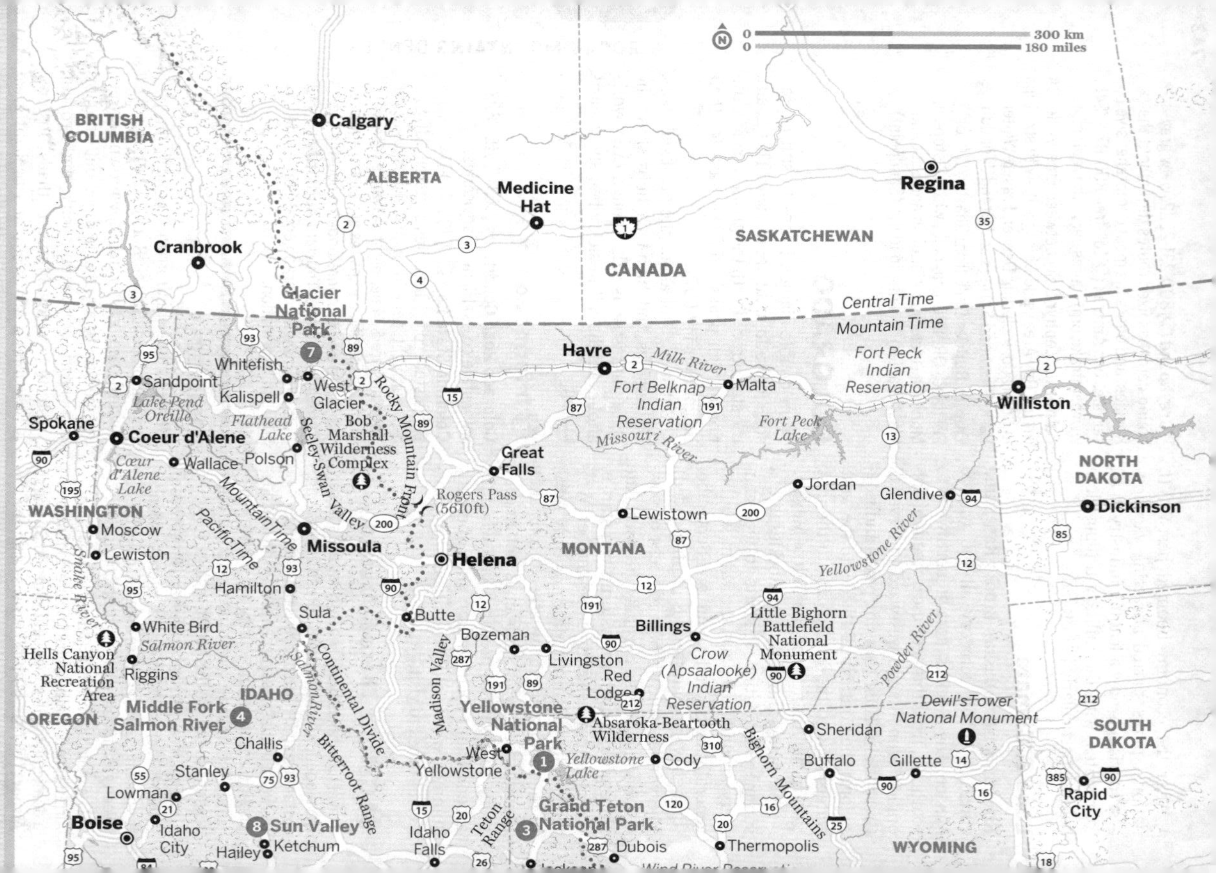

7 Enjoying the untamed splendor of **Glacier National Park** (p801).

8 Powder skiing at classic ski resort **Sun Valley** (p806).

9 Scaling the heights of majestic **Rocky Mountain National Park** (p757).

10 Roaming the high desertscapes of **Great Sand Dunes National Park** (p778).

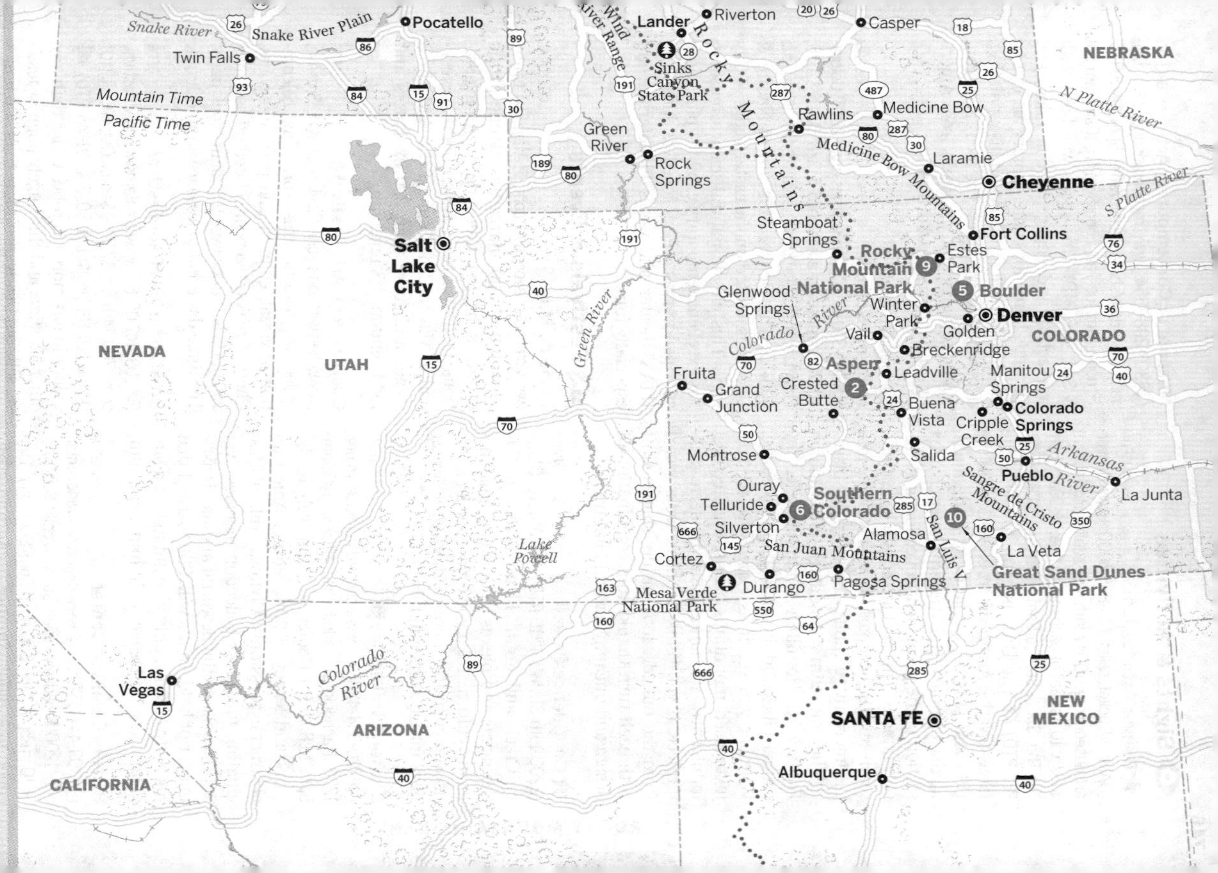

⊙ Sights & Activities

★ Denver Art Museum   MUSEUM
(DAM; ☑ ticket sales 720-865-5000; www.denver-
artmuseum.org; 100 W 14th Ave; adult/child/student
$13/5/10, 1st Sat of each month free; ⊙10am-5pm
Tue-Thu, Sat & Sun, to 8pm Fri; ℗👶; 🚌9, 16, 52,
83L RTD) ✈ The DAM is home to one of the
largest Native American art collections in the
USA and puts on special avant-garde multimedia exhibits. The Western American Art
section of the permanent collection is justifiably famous. This isn't an old, stodgy art museum, and the best part of a visit is diving into
the interactive exhibits – kids love this place.

The museum's landmark $110-million
Frederic C Hamilton wing, designed by
Daniel Libeskind, is quite simply awesome.
Whether you see it as expanding crystals,
juxtaposed mountains or just architectural
indulgence, it's an angular modern masterpiece. If you think the place looks weird
from the outside, look inside: shapes shift
with each turn thanks to a combination of
design and uncanny natural-light tricks.

★ Confluence Park   PARK
(2200 15th St; 👶; 🚌10 RTD) ✈ Where Cherry Creek and South Platte River meet is
the nexus and plexus of Denver's sunshine-
loving culture. It's a good place for an afternoon picnic, and there's a short white-water
park for kayakers and tubers.

Clyfford Still Museum   MUSEUM
(☑720-354-4880;   www.clyffordstillmuseum.org;
1250 Bannock St; adult/child $10/3; ⊙10am-
5pm, to 8pm Fri) Dedicated exclusively to the
work and legacy of 20th-century American
abstract expressionist Clyfford Still, this fascinating museum's collection includes over
2400 works by the powerful and narcissistic
master of bold. In his will, Still insisted that
his body of work only be exhibited in a singular space, so Denver built him a museum.

History Colorado Center   MUSEUM
(☑303-447-8679;   www.historycoloradocenter.
org; 1200 Broadway; adult/student/child $10/8/8;
⊙10am-5pm Mon-Sat, noon-5pm Sun; ℗) Discover Colorado's frontier roots and high-
tech modern triumphs at this sharp, smart
and charming museum. There are plenty of
interactive exhibits, including a Jules Verne–
esque 'Time Machine' that you push across
a giant map of Colorado to explore seminal
moments in the Centennial State's history.

Museum of Contemporary Art   GALLERY
(☑303-298-7554; www.mcadenver.org; 1485 Del-
gany St; adult/student/child/after 5pm $8/5/1/5;
⊙noon-7pm Tue-Thu, noon-8pm Fri, 10am-7pm Sat
& Sun; 🚌6 RTD) This space was built with
interaction and engagement in mind, and
Denver's home for contemporary art can be
provocative, delightful or a bit disappointing,
depending on the show. The focus is on contemporary mixed-media works from American and international artists.

Denver Museum of
Nature & Science   MUSEUM
(☑303-370-6000; www.dmns.org; 2001 Colorado Blvd; museum adult/child $13/8, IMAX $10/8,
Planetarium $5/4; ⊙9am-5pm; ℗👶; 🚌20, 32,
40 RTD) The Denver Museum of Nature &
Science is located on the eastern edge of City
Park. This classic natural-science museum
has excellent temporary exhibits, plus those
cool panoramas we all loved as kids. The
IMAX theater and Gates Planetarium are
especially fun.

✦✦ Festivals & Events

Cinco de Mayo   CULTURAL
(www.cincodemayodenver.com; ⊙May; 👶) Enjoy
salsa music and margaritas at one of the
country's biggest Cinco de Mayo celebrations, held over two days on the first weekend in May in Civic Center Park. With three
stages and more than 350 exhibitors and
food vendors, it's huge fun.

Cherry Creek Arts Festival   ARTS
(www.cherryarts.org; cnr Clayton St & E 3rd Ave;
⊙Jul; 👶) During this sprawling celebration of visual, culinary and performing arts,
Cherry Creek's streets are closed off and over
250,000 visitors browse the giant block party.
The three-day event takes place around July 4.

Great American Beer Festival   BEER
(☑303-447-0816; www.greatamericanbeerfestival.
com; 700 14th St; $75; ⊙Sep or Oct; 👶; 🚌101
D-Line, 101 H-Line, 🚌1, 8, 30, 30L, 31, 48 RTD) ✈
Colorado has more microbreweries than any
other US state, and this hugely popular festival sells out in advance. More than 500 breweries are represented, from the big players to
the home-brew enthusiasts. Only the Colorado Convention Center is big enough for these
big brewers and their fat brews.

Sleeping

11th Avenue Hotel HOTEL $
(303-894-0529; www.11thavenuehotel.com; 1112 Broadway; dm $19-22, r with/without bath $45/39;) This budget hotel has a good location for art lovers in the Golden Triangle district. The lobby looks vaguely like something from a Jim Jarmusch movie. The upstairs rooms, some with attached bathrooms, are bare but clean. It's safe, secure and a decent place for budget travelers.

Denver International Youth Hostel HOSTEL $
(303-832-9996; www.youthhostels.com/denver; 630 E 16th Ave; dm $19; P@; 15, 15L, 20 RTD) If cheap really matters, then the Denver International Youth Hostel might be the place for you. It's basic and vaguely chaotic, but it has a ramshackle charm and a great downtown location. All dorms have attached bathroom facilities and the common area in the basement has a large-screen TV, library and computers for guests to use.

★**Curtis** BOUTIQUE HOTEL $$
(303-571-0300; www.thecurtis.com; 1405 Curtis St; d $159-279; @; 15 RTD) It's like stepping into a doo-wop Warhol wonderworld at this temple to postmodern pop culture. Attention to detail – be it through the service or the decor in the rooms – is paramount at the Curtis, a one-of-a-kind hotel in Denver.

There are 13 themed floors and each is devoted to a different genre of American pop culture. Rooms are spacious and very mod without being too out there to sleep. The hotel's refreshingly different take on sleeping may seem too kitschy for some – you can get a wake-up call from Elvis – but if you're tired of the same old international brands, this joint in the heart of downtown might be your tonic.

★**Queen Anne Bed & Breakfast Inn** B&B $$
(303-296-6666; www.queenannebnb.com; 2147 Tremont Pl; r $135-215; P) Soft chamber music wafting through public areas, fresh flowers, manicured gardens and evening wine tastings create a romantic ambience at this ecoconscious B&B in two late-1800s Victorian homes. Featuring period antiques, private hot tubs and exquisite hand-painted murals, each room has its own personality.

Patterson Historic Inn HISTORIC HOTEL $$
(303-955-5142; www.pattersoninn.com; 420 E 11th Ave; r from $169; @) This 1891 grande dame was once a senator's home. It's now one of the best historic bed-and-breakfasts in town. The gardens are limited, but the Victorian charm, sumptuous breakfast and well-appointed chambers in the nine-room château will delight. Rooms come with modern touches such as silk robes, down comforters and flat-screen TVs.

Brown Palace Hotel HISTORIC HOTEL $$$
(303-297-3111; www.brownpalace.com; 321 17th St; r from $299; P@) Standing agape under the stained-glass crowned atrium, it's clear why this palace is shortlisted among the country's elite historic hotels. There's deco artwork, a four-star spa, imported marble and staff who discreetly float down the halls.

COLORADO FACTS

Nickname Centennial State

Population 5 million

Area 104,247 sq miles

Capital city Denver (population 649,495)

Other cities Boulder (population 103,000), Colorado Springs (population 439,800)

Sales tax 2.9% state tax, plus individual city taxes

Birthplace of Ute tribal leader Chief Ouray (1833–80); *South Park* creator Trey Parker (b 1969); actor Amy Adams (b 1974); climber Tommy Caldwell (b 1978)

Home of Naropa University (made famous by Beat poets), powder slopes, boutique beers

Politics Swing state

Famous for Sunny days (300 per year), the highest-altitude vineyards and longest ski run in the continental USA

Kitschiest souvenir Deer-hoof bottle opener

Driving distances Denver to Vail 100 miles, Boulder to Rocky Mountain National Park 38 miles

Eating

While the downtown restaurants offer the greatest depth and variety in Denver, it's also worth heading out to strollable neighborhoods like Highlands, Cherry Creek,

Denver

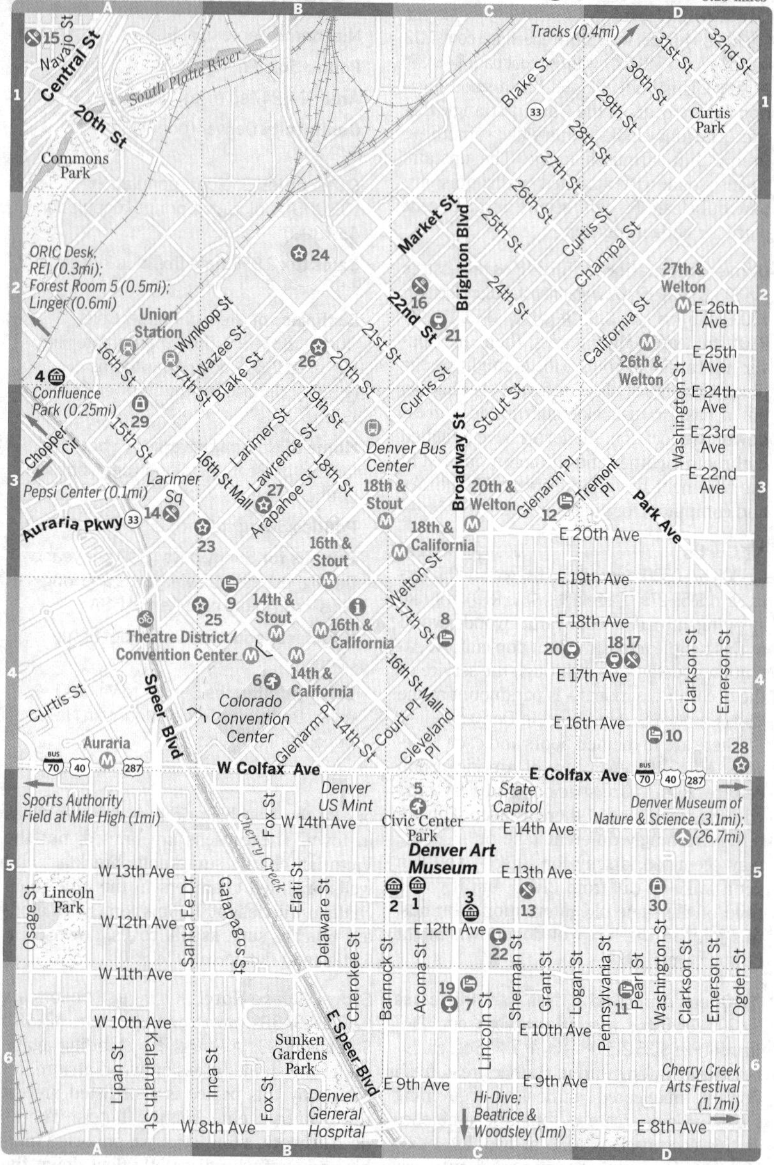

Uptown, Five Points and Washington Park, where little five-block commercial strips hold some of Denver's best eateries. Check out www.5280.com or www.diningout.com/denver for new eats.

Snooze BREAKFAST $

(☎303-297-0700; www.snoozeeatery.com; 2262 Larimer St; mains $6-12; ⊙6:30am-2:30pm Mon-Fri, 7am-2:30pm Sat & Sun;) This retro-styled cheery breakfast-and-brunch spot is one of the hottest post-party breakfast

Denver

Top Sights
1 Denver Art Museum C5

Sights
2 Clyfford Still Museum C5
3 History Colorado Center C5
4 Museum of Contemporary Art A2

Activities, Courses & Tours
5 Cinco de Mayo C5
6 Great American Beer Festival B4

Sleeping
7 11th Avenue Hotel C6
8 Brown Palace Hotel C4
9 Curtis B4
10 Denver International Youth Hostel D4
11 Patterson Historic Inn D6
12 Queen Anne Bed & Breakfast Inn C3

Eating
13 City O' City C5
14 Rioja A3
15 Root Down A1
16 Snooze C2
17 Steuben's Food Service D4

Drinking & Nightlife
18 Ace D4
19 Bar Standard C6
20 Denver Wrangler C4
21 Great Divide Brewing Company C2
22 The Church C5

Entertainment
23 Comedy Works B3
24 Coors Field B2
25 Denver Performing Arts Complex B4
26 El Chapultepec B2
27 Lannie's Clocktower Cabaret B3
28 Ogden Theatre D4

Shopping
29 Tattered Cover Bookstore A3
30 Wax Trax Records D5

joints in town. It dishes up spectacularly crafted breakfast burritos and a smokin' salmon benedict. The coffee's always good, but you have the option of an early-morning Bloody Mary. The wait can be up to an hour on weekends!

City O' City VEGETARIAN **$**
(☎303-831-6443; www.cityocitydenver.com; 206 E 13th Ave; mains $8-15; ⌚7am-2am Mon-Fri, 8am-2am Sat, 8am-midnight Sun; ☑ 👪; 🚌2, 9, 52 RTD) 🍃 This popular vegan/vegetarian restaurant mixes stylish decor with an innovative spin on greens, grains, faux meat and granola. The menu offers tapas boards, big salads, some good transnational noodle dishes and the best vegan pizza pie in D-Town…the bar has drinks for accompaniment. The comfy dining room also features shifting artworks by local artists.

★ **Beatrice & Woodsley** TAPAS **$$**
(☎303-777-3505; www.beatriceandwoodsley.com; 38 S Broadway; small plates $9-13; ⌚5-11pm Mon-Fri, 10am-2pm & 5-10pm Sat & Sun; 🚌0 RTD) Beatrice and Woodsley is the most artfully designed dining room in Denver. Chainsaws are buried into the wall to support shelves, there's an aspen growing through the back of the dining room and the feel is that of a mountain cabin being elegantly reclaimed by nature. The menu of small plates is whimsical and European inspired.

★ **Steuben's Food Service** AMERICAN **$$**
(☎303-803-1001; www.steubens.com; 523 E 17th Ave; mains $8-21; ⌚11am-11pm Sun-Thu, to midnight Fri & Sat; 👪) 🍃 Although styled as a midcentury drive-in, the upscale treatment of comfort food (mac and cheese, fried chicken, lobster rolls) and the solar-powered kitchen demonstrate Steubens' contemporary smarts. In summer, open garage doors lining the street create a breezy atmosphere and after 10pm it has the most unbeatable deal around: a burger, hand-cut fries and beer for $7.

★ **Root Down** MODERN AMERICAN **$$$**
(☎303-993-4200; www.rootdowndenver.com; 1600 W 33rd Ave; small plates $7-17, mains $18-28; ⌚5-10pm Sun-Thu, 5-11pm Fri & Sat, 10am-2:30pm Sat & Sun; ☑) 🍃 In a converted gas station, chef Justin Cucci has undertaken one of the city's most ambitious culinary concepts, marrying sustainable 'field-to-fork' practices, high-concept culinary fusions and a low-impact, energy-efficient ethos. The menu changes seasonally, but consider yourself lucky if it includes the sweet-potato falafel or hoisin-duck confit sliders.

★ **Rioja** MODERN AMERICAN **$$$**
(☎303-820-2282; www.riojadenver.com; 1431 Larimer St; mains $18-29; ⌚11:30am-2:30pm Wed-Fri, 10am-2:30pm Sat & Sun, 5-10pm daily; ❄☑; 🚌2, 12, 15, 16th St Shuttle) This is one of Denver's

most innovative restaurants. Smart, busy and upscale, yet relaxed and casual – just like Colorado – Rioja features modern cuisine inspired by Italian and Spanish traditions and powered by modern culinary flavors.

Drinking & Nightlife

Top nightlife districts include Uptown for gay bars and a young professional crowd, LoDo for loud sports bars, heavy drinking and dancing, River North for hipsters, Lower Highlands for an eclectic mix and sweet decks, and Broadway and Colfax for old school wannabees.

★Forest Room 5 BAR

(☎303-433-7001; www.forestroom5.com; 2532 15th St; ⏰4pm-2am) One of the best damn bars in Denver, this LoHi (that's Lower Highlands) juggernaut has an outdoor patio with fire circles (where you can smoke!), streams and a funked-out Airstream. It plays kitsch movies nightly and has art openings in the upstairs area. It's an odd mix of Grizzly Adams meets Andy Warhol – and it works.

Linger LOUNGE

(☎303-993-3120; www.lingerdenver.com; 2030 W 30th Ave; mains $8-14; ⏰11:30am-2:30pm & 4pm-2am Tue-Sat, 10am-2:30pm Sun) This rambling LoHi complex sits in the former Olinger mortuary. Come nighttime, they black out the 'O' and it just becomes Linger. There's an interesting international menu, but most people come for the tony feel and light-up-the-night rooftop bar, which even has a replica of the RV made famous by the Bill Murray smash *Stripes*.

Bar Standard CLUB

(☎303-534-0222; www.coclubs.com; 1037 Broadway; ⏰8pm-2am Fri & Sat; 🚌0 RTD) From the sleek deco interior to the DJ roster that spins *way* outside the typically mindless thump, Bar Standard is an inimitable gem in Denver's nightclub scene. It's ice cold without the attitude, and when the right DJ is on the tables it can be some of the best dancing in town.

Tracks GAY

(☎303-863-7326; www.tracksdenver.com; 3500 Walnut St; ⏰9pm-2am Fri & Sat, hours vary Sun-Thu) Denver's best gay dance club has an 18-and-up night on Thursdays, Friday drag shows and lesbian nights (just once a month). There's a definite pretty-boy focus, with good music and a scene to match. Saturday is the biggest dance night.

Denver Wrangler GAY

(☎303-837-1075; www.denverwrangler.com; 1700 Logan St; ⏰11am-2am; 🚌101 RTD) Denver Wrangler attracts an amiable crowd of gay male professionals after work, and its central location endows Denver's premier bear bar with a flirty pick-up scene on the weekend. The sidewalk seating is a plus.

Great Divide Brewing Company BREWERY

(www.greatdivide.com; 2201 Arapahoe St; ⏰2-8pm Mon & Tue, to 10pm Wed-Sat) This excellent local brewery does well to skip the same old burger menu and the fancy digs to keep its focus on what it does best: crafting exquisite beer. Bellying up to the bar, looking onto the copper kettles and sipping Great Divide's spectrum of seasonal brews is an experience that will make a beer drinker's eyes light up.

Ace BAR

(☎303-800-7705; www.acedenver.com; 501 E 17th Ave; ⏰11am-midnight Mon-Fri, 2pm-midnight Sat & Sun) The best ping-pong bar in Denver. Come here for fun tournaments, hipster sightings, great food and a raucous indoor-outdoor party that takes you deep into the pong underground – street rules apply.

The Church CLUB

(www.coclubs.com; 1160 Lincoln St; ⏰9pm-2am Thu-Sun) There's nothing like ordering a stiff drink inside a cathedral built in 1865. Yes, this club, which draws a large and diverse crowd, is in a former house of the Lord. Lit by hundreds of altar candles and flashing blue strobe lights, the Church has three dance floors, acrobats, a couple of lounges and even a sushi bar!

Entertainment

To find out what's happening with music, theater and other performing arts, pick up a free copy of **Westword** (www.westword.com).

★Denver Performing Arts Complex PERFORMING ARTS

(☎720-865-4220; www.artscomplex.com; cnr 14th & Champa Sts) This massive complex – one of the largest of its kind – occupies four city blocks and houses several major theaters, including the historic Ellie Caulkins Opera House and the Seawell Grand Ballroom. It's also home to the Colorado Ballet, Denver Center for the Performing Arts, Opera Colorado and the Colorado Symphony Orchestra.

WORTH A TRIP

BEST MILE-HIGH DAY HIKES

There are hundreds of day hikes within an hour of Denver. Here are a few we like:

Jefferson County Open Space Parks (www.jeffco.us/openspace;) Top picks include Matthews Winters, Mount Falcon, Elk Meadow and Lair o' the Bear.

Golden Gate Canyon State Park (303-582-3707; www.parks.state.us/parks; 92 Crawford Gulch Rd, Golden; entrance/camping $7/24; 5am-10pm) Halfway between Denver and Nederland, this 12,000-acre state park can be reached in about 45 minutes.

Staunton State Park (303-816-0912; www.parks.state.co.us/parks) Colorado's newest state park sits on a historic ranch site 40 miles west of Denver, on Hwy 285 between Conifer and Bailey.

Waterton Canyon (303-634-3745; www.denverwater.org/recreation/watertoncanyon; Kassler Center) South of the city, just west of Chatfield Reservoir, this pretty canyon has an easy 6.5-mile trail to the Strontia Springs Dam. From there, the **Colorado Trail** (CTF; 303-384-3729; www.coloradotrail.org; PO Box 260876; 9am-5pm Mon-Fri) will take you all the way to Durango!

★El Chapultepec JAZZ
(303-295-9126; www.thepeclodo.com; 1962 Market St; 11am-2am, music from 9pm) This smoky, old-school jazz joint attracts a diverse mix of people. Since it opened in 1951, Frank Sinatra, Tony Bennett and Ella Fitzgerald have played here, as have Jagger and Richards. Local jazz bands take the tiny stage nightly, but you never know who might drop by.

Hi-Dive LIVE MUSIC
(303-733-0230; www.hi-dive.com; 7 S Broadway) Local rock heroes and touring indie bands light up the stage at the Hi-Dive, a venue at the heart of Denver's local music scene. During big shows it gets deafeningly loud, cheek-to-jowl with hipsters and humid as an armpit. In other words, it's perfect.

Grizzly Rose LIVE MUSIC
(303-295-1330; www.grizzlyrose.com; 5450 N Valley Hwy; from 6pm Tue-Sun;) This is one kick-ass honky-tonk – 40,000 sq ft of hot live music – attracting real cowboys from as far as Cheyenne. The Country Music Association called it the best country bar in America. If you've never experienced line dancing, then put on the boots, grab the Stetson and let loose.

Ogden Theatre LIVE MUSIC
(303-832-1874; www.ogdentheatre.net; 935 E Colfax Ave; ; 15 RTD) One of Denver's best live-music venues, the Ogden Theatre has a checkered past. Built in 1917, it was derelict for many years and might have been dozed in the early 1990s, but it's now listed on the National Register of Historic Places. Bands such as Edward Sharpe & the Magnetic Zeros and Lady Gaga have played here.

Comedy Works COMEDY
(303-595-3637; www.comedyworks.com; 1226 15th St; 6, 9, 10, 15L, 20, 28, 32, 44, 44L RTD) Denver's best comedy club occupies a basement space in Larimer Sq (enter down a set of stairs at the corner of Larimer and 15th) and routinely brings in up-and-coming yucksters from around the country. It can be a bit cramped if you're claustrophobic, but the seats are comfortable and the quality of acts is excellent.

Lannie's Clocktower Cabaret CABARET
(303-293-0075; www.lannies.com; 1601 Arapahoe St; tickets $25-40; 1-5pm Tue, to 11pm Wed & Thu, to 1:30am Fri & Sat; Arapahoe) Bawdy, naughty and strangely romantic, Lannie's Clocktower Cabaret is a wild-child standout among LoDo's rather straight-laced (or at least straight) night spots. A table right up near the front will get you in the sparkling heart of the action, and if you parse the schedule, you might get a glance at the sexiest drag queens in Denver.

Coors Field BASEBALL
(800-388-7625; www.mlb.com/col/ballpark/; 2001 Blake St;) Denver is a city known for manic sports fans, and it boasts five pro teams. The Colorado Rockies play baseball at the highly rated Coors Field. Tickets for the outfield – the Rockpile – cost $4. Not a bad deal.

OFF THE BEATEN TRACK

LIVE AT RED ROCKS!

Red Rocks Amphitheatre (303-640-2637; www.redrocksonline.com; 18300 W Alameda Pkwy; 5am-11pm;) is set between 400ft-high red sandstone rocks 15 miles southwest of Denver. Acoustics are so good many artists record live albums here. The 9000-seat theater offers stunning views and draws big-name bands all summer.

When the setting sun brings out a rich, orange glow from the rock formations and the band on stage launches into the right tune, Red Rocks Amphitheatre is a captivating experience, wholly befitting the park's 19th-century name, 'Garden of Angels.'

The natural amphitheater, once a Ute camping spot, has been used for performances for decades, but it wasn't until 1936 that members of the Civilian Conservation Corps built a formal outdoor venue with seats and a stage. Though it originally hosted classical performances and military bands, it debuted as a rock venue with style; the first rock quartet on this stage was John, Paul, George and Ringo.

You scored tickets? Great. Now for the nitty gritty. Eat beforehand, as the food vendors are predictably expensive. You can bring a small cooler into the show, as long as there's no booze and it'll fit under your seat. Climbing on the stunning formations is prohibited; however, 250-plus steps lead to the top of the theater, offering views of both the park and Denver, miles off to the east.

Amazingly, Red Rocks Park can be almost as entertaining when it's silent. The amphitheater is only a tiny part of the 600-acre space. There are miles of hiking trails, opportunities to lose the crowds and take in lovely rock formations. There's information about the entire area on the website.

Sports Authority Field at Mile High STADIUM
(720-258-3000; www.sportsauthorityfieldatmilehigh.com; 1701 S Bryant St;) The much-lauded Denver Broncos football team and the Denver Outlaws lacrosse team play at Mile High Stadium, 1 mile west of downtown. This stadium also has an eclectic schedule of events, including major rock concerts for superstars such as U2. Stadium tours are organized through the **Colorado Sports Hall of Fame** (720-258-3888; www.coloradosports.org; 1701 Bryant St; 10am-3pm Thu-Sun Sep-May, 10am-3pm Tue-Sat Jun-Aug; P ; 16, 16L, 28, 30, 30L, 31, 36L RTD) FREE.

Pepsi Center STADIUM
(303-405-1111; www.pepsicenter.com; 1000 Chopper Circle) The mammoth Pepsi Center hosts the Denver Nuggets basketball team, the Colorado Mammoth of the National Lacrosse League and the Colorado Avalanche hockey team. Off season it's a mega concert venue.

Shopping

Head to the pedestrian mall on 16th St or LoDo for downtown shopping. Cherry Creek, Highlands Square and South Broadway are other top shopping districts.

★ **Tattered Cover Bookstore** BOOKS
(www.tatteredcover.com; 1628 16th St; 6:30am-9pm Mon-Fri, 9am-9pm Sat, 10am-6pm Sun) There are plenty of places to curl up with a book in Denver's beloved independent bookstore, which has two locations in the Denver area. Bursting with new and used books, it has a good stock of regional travel guides and nonfiction titles dedicated to the Western states and Western folklore.

★ **REI** OUTDOOR EQUIPMENT
(Recreational Equipment Incorporated; 303-756-3100; www.rei.com; 1416 Platte St;) The flagship store of this outdoor-equipment super supplier is an essential stop if you are heading to the mountains or just cruising through Confluence Park. In addition to top gear for camping, cycling, climbing and skiing, it has a rental department, maps and the Pinnacle, a 47ft-high indoor structure of simulated red sandstone for climbing and rappelling.

Wax Trax Records MUSIC
(303-831-7246; www.waxtraxrecords.com; 638 E 13th Ave; 2, 10, 15, 15L RTD) For more than 30 years, Wax Trax Records has been trading at this Denver location, stocking a huge quantity of CDs, DVDs, vinyl and music paraphernalia. Indie, alternative, punk, goth, folk, rock, hip-hop, jazz, reggae – anything that's a bit edgy you'll either find in store or it'll order for you.

Information

Visitors & Convention Bureau Information Center (☎303-892-1112; www.denver.org; 1600 California St; 📶; 🚌California) When you get to town, make for the largest and most centrally located information center, located on the 16th St Mall. You can load up on brochures and get information about local transportation. There's also a tourist info desk in the Colorado Convention Center.

ORIC Desk (Outdoor Recreation Information Center; ☎REI main line 303-756-3100; www.oriconline.org; 1416 Platte St; 📶) Inside REI, this information desk is a must for those looking to get out of town. It has maps and expert information on trip planning and safety information. The desk is staffed by volunteers, so hours vary wildly, but arriving on a weekend afternoon is a good bet.

Getting There & Away

Denver International Airport (DIA; ☎303-342-2000; www.flydenver.com; 8500 Peña Blvd; 📶) is served by around 20 airlines and offers flights to nearly every major US city. Located 24 miles east of downtown, DIA is connected with I-70 exit 238 by 12-mile-long Peña Blvd. Tourist and airport information is available at a **booth** (☎303-342-2000) in the terminal's central hall.

Greyhound buses stop at **Denver Bus Center** (☎303-293-6555; 1055 19th St), which runs services to Boise (19 hours), Los Angeles (22 hours) and other destinations.

The **Colorado Mountain Express** (CME; ☎800-525-6363; www.coloradomountainexpress.com; DIA; 📶) has shuttle service from DIA, downtown Denver or Morrison to Summit County, including Breckenridge and Keystone (2½ hours) and Vail (three hours).

Amtrak's *California Zephyr* runs daily between Chicago and San Francisco via Denver's **Union Station** (☎Amtrak 800-872-7245; www.denverunionstation.org; cnr 17th & Wynkoop Sts; 🚌31X, 40X, 80X, 86X, 120X RTD).

Getting Around

TO/FROM THE AIRPORT

Several transportation companies have booths near the baggage-claim area. Public **Regional Transit District** (RTD; ☎303-299-6000; www.rtd-denver.com) runs a SkyRide service to the airport from downtown Denver hourly ($9–13, about one hour) and Boulder (1½ hours). **SuperShuttle** (☎303-370-1300; www.supershuttle.com) offers shared van services between the Denver area and the airport.

In early 2016 a transit center will open at DIA, linking the airport with downtown Denver via a 35-minute commuter rail trip.

BICYCLE

BikeDenver.org (www.bikedenver.org) or **City of Denver** (www.denvergov.org) have downloadable bike maps for the city.

Denver B-Cycle (http://denver.bcycle.com) is the first citywide bicycle-share program in the US, with more than 80 stations throughout the city. Helmets are not included, and are not required by law in Denver.

CAR & MOTORCYCLE

Street parking can be a pain, but there are slews of pay garages in downtown and LoDo. Nearly all the major car-rental agencies have counters at DIA; a few have offices in downtown Denver.

PUBLIC TRANSPORTATION

RTD provides public transportation throughout the Denver and Boulder area. Free shuttle buses operate along the 16th St Mall. RTD's light rail line currently has six lines servicing 46 stations. Fares are $2.25 for one to two stops, $4 for three fare zones and $5 for all zones.

TAXI

Companies offering 24-hour cab service:

Metro Taxi (☎303-333-3333; www.metrotaxidenver.com)

Yellow Cab (☎303-777-7777; www.denveryellowcab.com)

Boulder

Tucked against the Flatirons' cragged and near-vertical rock face, this idyllic town has a sweet location and a palpable idealism that's a magnet to entrepreneurs, athletes, hippies and hard-bodies. It's also home to the University of Colorado and the Buddhist-founded, Beat-inspired Naropa University.

Boulder's love of the outdoors was officially legislated in 1967, when it became the first US city to tax itself specifically to preserve open space. Thanks to such vision, packs of cyclists whip up and down the Boulder Creek corridor, which links city and county parks those taxpayer dollars have purchased. The pedestrian-only Pearl St Mall is lively and perfect for strolling, especially at night, when residents promenade until the wee hours.

In fact, for outdoorsy types, Boulder, not Denver, is the region's tourist hub. The city is about the same distance from Denver International Airport, and staying here puts you closer to trails, ski resorts and Rocky Mountain National Park.

◉ Sights & Activities

Boulder's two areas to see and be seen are the downtown Pearl St Mall and the University Hill district (next to campus), both off Broadway, though the Hill is rarely the haunt of anyone over 25. Overlooking the city from the west are the Flatirons, an eye-catching rock formation.

★ Chautauqua Park   PARK

(www.chautauqua.com; 900 Baseline Rd; 🚌 HOP 2) This historic landmark park is not just the gateway to Boulder's most magnificent slab of open space adjoining the iconic Flatirons, the wide, lush lawn attracts picnicking families, sunbathers, Frisbee folk and students from nearby CU. It also gets copious hikers, climbers and trail runners.

Boulder Creek Bike Path   CYCLING

(⊙24hr; 👥) The most utilized commuter bike path in town, this smooth and mostly straight creekside concrete path follows Boulder Creek from Foothills Parkway all the way uphill to the split of Boulder Canyon and Four Mile Canyon Rd west of downtown – a total distance of over 5 miles one-way. It also feeds urban bike lanes that lead all over town.

Eldorado Canyon State Park   OUTDOORS

(☑303-494-3943; ⊙visitor center 9am-5pm) Among the country's best rock-climbing areas, Eldorado has class 5.5 to 5.12 climbs. Suitable to all visitors, a dozen miles of hiking trails also link up to Chautauqua Park. A public pool (summer only) offers chilly swims in the canyon's famous spring water.

THE THOUSAND-YEAR FLOOD

It came after a drought that followed the worst wildfire in Colorado history. On September 12, 2013, the Front Range woke up to flooding canyons and inundations that isolated mountain communities. Eight people died and thousands lost their homes. A disaster of this magnitude is considered a thousand-year flood, with a 0.1% probability in any given year. The month's 17in of rainfall blasted September's usual 1.7in average. Now cited as the second-largest natural disaster in US history, after Hurricane Katrina, it will take years to recover. The affected area was roughly the size of Connecticut. Losses were estimated at $2 billion.

University Bicycles   CYCLING

(www.ubikes.com; 839 Pearl St; 4hr rental $15; ⊙10am-6pm Mon-Sat, 10am-5pm Sun) There are plenty of rental shops, but this has the widest range of rides and the most helpful staff. For $18 you can get a townie bike for the day.

Boulder Rock Club   ROCK CLIMBING

(☑303-447-2804; http://boulderrockclub.com; 2829 Mapleton Ave; day pass adult/child $17/10; ⊙8am-10pm Mon, 6am-11pm Tue-Thu, 8am-11pm Fri, 10am-8pm Sat & Sun; 👥) An incredible indoor climbing gym popular with local rock rats. This massive warehouse is full of artificial rock faces cragged with ledges and routes, and the auto-belay system allows solo climbers an anchor. Lessons and courses available, with a special kids' program. Staff are a great resource for local climbing routes.

✷ Festivals & Events

Boulder Creek Festival   MUSIC, FOOD

(☑303-449-3137; www.bceproductions.com; Canyon Blvd, Central Park; ⊙May; 👥; 🚌206, JUMP) FREE Billed as the kick-off to summer and capped with the Bolder Boulder, this summer festival is massive. Over 10 event areas feature more than 30 live entertainers and 500 vendors. There will be food and drink, music and sunshine. What's not to love?

Bolder Boulder   ATHLETICS

(☑303-444-7223; www.bolderboulder.com; adult from $59; ⊙May; 👥) With 54,000 runners and pros mingling with costumed racers, live bands and sideline merrymakers, this may be the most fun 10k in America, ending at the CU Stadium.

🛏 Sleeping

Boulder has dozens of options – drive down Broadway or Hwy 36 to take your pick.

★ Chautauqua Lodge   HISTORIC HOTEL $$

(☑303-442-3282; www.chautauqua.com; 900 Baseline Rd; r from $73, cottages $125-183; 🅿❄🐾🛜🐕; 🚌HOP 2) Adjoining beautiful hiking trails to the Flatirons, these cottages, in a leafy neighborhood inside Chautauqua Park, are our top pick. It has contemporary rooms and one- to three-bedroom cottages with porches, and beds with patchwork quilts. It's perfect for families and pets. All cottages have full kitchens, though the wraparound porch of the Chautauqua Dining Hall is a local favorite for breakfast.

Hotel Boulderado
BOUTIQUE HOTEL $$$

(☑303-442-4344; www.boulderado.com; 2115 13th St; r from $264; P❋☎; HOP, SKIP) With a century of service, the charming Boulderado, full of Victorian elegance and wonderful public spaces, is a National Register landmark and a romantic getaway. Each antique-filled room is uniquely decorated. The stained-glass atrium and glacial water fountain accent the jazz-washed lobby. Guesthouse rooms across the street are slightly bigger and cheaper, but lack the historical gravitas.

St Julien Hotel & Spa
HOTEL $$$

(☑720-406-9696, reservations 877-303-0900; www.stjulien.com; 900 Walnut St; r from $309; P❋@☎⛱) In the heart of downtown, Boulder's finest four-star option is modern and refined, with photographs of local scenery and cork walls that warm the ambience. With fabulous Flatiron views, the back patio hosts live world music, jazz concerts and wild salsa parties. Rooms are plush, and so are the robes.

✖ Eating

Boulder's dining scene has dozens of great options. Most are centered on the Pearl St Mall, while bargains are more likely to be found on the Hill. Between 3:30pm and 6:30pm nearly every restaurant in the city features a happy hour with some kind of amazing food and drink special. It's a great way to try fine dining on a budget – check websites for details.

Spruce Confections
BAKERY $

(☑303-449-6773; 767 Pearl St; cookies from $3.25; ⊙6:30am-6pm Mon-Fri, 7am-6pm Sat & Sun; ⓘ; 206) Boulder's go-to bakehouse, where the favorites are the Ol' B Cookie (chocolate, oats, cinnamon and coconut) and the Black Bottom Cupcake (chocolate with cheesecake filling). Pair either with the Spruce Juice, possibly the world's greatest iced vanilla latte. It has sinful scones, good homemade soups and salads too. There's another branch at 4684 Broadway.

Dish
SANDWICHES $

(☑720-565-5933; www.dishgourmet.com; 1918 Pearl St; mains $10; ⊙9am-6pm Mon-Fri, 11am-4pm Sat; ⓘ; 204, HOP) Bank-length lines flank this gourmet deli at lunchtime. At $10 the sandwiches are hardly cheap but they are satisfying. Think roasted turkey carved in chunks, pâté, natural beef, slow-cooked

brisket and baguettes smothered with butter and top-tier cheeses. Side salads are alluring too.

Zoe Ma Ma
CHINESE $

(2010 10th St; mains $5-13; ⊙11am-10pm Sun-Thu, 11am-11pm Fri & Sat; 206, SKIP, HOP) ✹ At Boulder's hippest noodle bar you can find fresh street food at a long outdoor counter. Mama, the Taiwanese matriarch, is on hand, cooking and chatting up customers in her Crocs. Organic noodles are made from scratch, as are the garlicky melt-in-your-mouth pot stickers.

Sink
PUB FOOD $

(www.thesink.com; 1165 13th St; mains $5-12; ⊙11am-2am, kitchen to 10pm; ❸; 203, 204, 225, DASH, SKIP) A Hill landmark since 1923, the low-slung, graffiti-scrawled Sink even employed Robert Redford during his CU years. While he dropped out, it hasn't. The dimly lit, cavernous space still churns out legendary Sink burgers and slugs of local microbrews to the latest generation of students.

Alfalfa's
SUPERMARKET $

(www.alfalfas.com; 1651 Broadway St; ⊙7:30am-10pm; AB, B, JUMP, SKIP) A small, community-oriented natural market with a wonderful selection of prepared food and an inviting indoor-outdoor dining area to enjoy it in.

Cafe Aion
SPANISH $$

(☑303-993-8131; www.cafeaion.com; 1235 Pennsylvania Ave; tapas $5-13; ⊙11am-10pm Tue-Fri, 9am-3pm Sat & Sun; 203, 204, 225, DASH, SKIP) Though fancy fare on the Hill sounds odd, don't skip this one. Original and unpretentious, this side-street cafe captures the relaxed rhythms of Spain with fresh tapas and delectable housemade sangria. Papas bravas wedges have the perfect crisp, and the grilled spring onions and dolmas are light and flavorful. Happy hour goes all night on Tuesdays.

Lucile's
CAJUN $

(☑303-442-4743; www.luciles.com; 2142 14th St; mains $8-14; ⊙7am-2pm Mon-Fri, from 8am Sat & Sun; ⓘ; 205, 206, HOP) ✹ This New Orleans–style diner has perfected breakfast, and the Creole egg dishes (served over creamy spinach alongside cheesy grits or perfectly blackened trout) are the thing to order. Start with a steaming mug of chai or chicory coffee and an order of beignets drenched in powdered sugar which are the house specialty. Go early or be prepared to wait.

★ Salt MODERN AMERICAN **$$$**
(☎303-444-7258; www.saltboulderbistro.com; 1047 Pearl St; mains $14-28; ⏰11am-10pm Mon-Wed, to 11pm Thu-Sat, 10am-10pm Sun; 👪; 🚌208, HOP, SKIP) While farm-to-table is ubiquitous in Boulder, this is one spot that delivers and surpasses expectations. The sweet pea ravioli with lemon beurre blanc and shaved radishes is a feverish delight. But Salt also knows meat: local and grass-fed, basted, braised and slow roasted to utter perfection. When in doubt, ask – the servers really know their stuff.

Kitchen MODERN AMERICAN **$$$**
(☎303-544-5973; http://thekitchen.com; 1039 Pearl St; mains $18-32; 📶; 🚌206, HOP) 🍃 The pioneer of farm-to-table cuisine in Boulder, Kitchen features clean lines, stacks of crusty bread and a daily menu. Super-fresh ingredients are crafted into rustic tapas: think roasted root vegetables, shaved prosciutto and steamed mussels in cream. The pulled-pork sandwich rocks, but save room for the sticky toffee pudding. Visitors shouldn't miss the community hour, with sips and nibbles at a communal table 3pm to 5pm weekdays.

Upstairs there's a more casual atmosphere and menu.

🍷 Drinking & Entertainment

Playboy didn't vote CU the best party school for nothing – the blocks around the Pearl St Mall and the Hill churn out fun, with many restaurants doubling as bars or turning into all-out dance clubs come 10pm.

★ Mountain Sun Pub & Brewery BREWERY
(www.mountainsunpub.com; 1535 Pearl St; ⏰11am-1am; 👪; 🚌HOP, 205, 206) Boulder's favorite brewery cheerfully serves a rainbow of fine brews and packs in all from yuppies to hippies. But best of all is its community atmosphere. The pub grub, especially the burgers and chili, is delicious and its fully family-friendly, with board games and kids' meals. It often has live bluegrass, reggae and jam-bands on Sunday and Monday nights.

Bitter Bar COCKTAIL BAR
(☎303-442-3050; www.thebitterbar.com; 835 Walnut St; cocktails $9-15; ⏰5pm-midnight Mon-Thu, 5pm-2am Fri & Sat; 🚌HOP) A chic Boulder speakeasy where killer cocktails, such as the scrumptious lavender-infused Blue Velvet, make the evening slip happily out of focus. The patio is great for conversation and Thursdays at 9pm there's live music.

Boulder Dushanbe Teahouse TEAHOUSE
(☎303-442-4993; 1770 13th St; mains $8-19; ⏰8am-10pm; 🚌203, 204, 205, 206, 208, 225, DASH, JUMP, SKIP) It's impossible to find better ambience than this incredible Tajik teahouse, a gift from Dushanbe, Boulder's sister city. The elaborate carvings and paintings were reassembled over a decade on Central Park's edge. It's too bad the fusion fare is surprisingly dull, but it's very worth coming for a pot of tea.

Boulder Theater CINEMA, LIVE MUSIC
(☎303-786-7030; www.bouldertheatre.com; 2032 14th St) This old movie-theater-turned-historic-venue brings in slightly under-the-radar acts like jazz great Charlie Hunter, the madmen rockers of Gogol Bordello and West Afro–French divas, Les Nubians. But it also screens classic films like *The Big Lebowski* and hosts short-film festivals that can and should be enjoyed with a glass of beer.

🛍 Shopping

★ Pearl Street Mall MALL
The main feature of downtown Boulder is the Pearl St Mall, a vibrant pedestrian zone filled with kids' climbing boulders and splash fountains, bars, galleries and restaurants.

Momentum HANDICRAFTS
(www.ourmomentum.com; 1625 Pearl St; ⏰10am-7pm Tue-Sat, 11am-6pm Sun) 🍃 Committed to socially responsible and environmentally friendly business practices, Momentum makes you feel good about shopping. It sells the kitchen sink of unique global gifts – Zulu wire baskets, fabulous scarves from India, Nepal and Ecuador – all handcrafted and purchased at fair value from disadvantaged artisans. Every item purchased provides a direct economic lifeline to the artists.

Common Threads CLOTHING
(www.commonthreadsboulder.com; 2707 Spruce St; ⏰10am-6pm Mon-Sat, noon-5pm Sun) Vintage shopping at its most haute couture, this fun place is where to go for secondhand Choos and Prada purses. Prices are higher than at your run-of-the-mill vintage shop, but clothes, shoes and bags are always in good condition, and the authenticity of the designer clothing is guaranteed. Offers fun classes on altering and innovating clothes.

Boulder Bookstore BOOKS
(www.boulderbookstore.indiebound.com; 1107 Pearl St;) Boulder's favorite indie bookstore has a huge travel section downstairs, along with all the hottest new fiction and nonfiction. Check the visiting-authors lineup posted at the entry.

Information

Boulder Visitor Center (303-442-2911; www.bouldercoloradousa.com; 2440 Pearl St; 8:30am-5pm Mon-Thu, 8:30am-4pm Fri) Set in the Boulder Chamber of Commerce, this visitor center offers basic information, maps and tips on nearby hiking trails and other activities. There's a more accessible tourist info kiosk on the Pearl St Mall in front of the courthouse.

Getting There & Around

Boulder has fabulous public transportation, with services extending to Denver and its airport. Ecofriendly buses are run by **RTD** (303-299-6000; www.rtd-denver.com; per ride $2-4.50;). Maps are available at **Boulder Station** (cnr 14th & Walnut Sts). RTD buses (route B) operate between Boulder Station and Denver's Market St Bus Station ($5, 55 minutes). RTD's SkyRide bus (route AB) heads to Denver International Airport ($9–13, one hour, hourly). **SuperShuttle** (303-444-0808; www.supershuttle.com) provides hotel ($27) and door-to-door ($33) shuttle service from the airport.

For two-wheel transportation, **Boulder B-Cycle** (http://boulder.bcycle.com; 24hr rental $7) is a new citywide program with townie bikes available at strategic locations, but riders must sign up online first.

Northern Mountains

With one foot on either side of the continental divide and behemoths of granite in every direction, Colorado's Northern Mountains offer out-of-this-world alpine adventures, laid-back skiing, kick-butt hiking and biking, and plenty of rivers to raft, fish and float.

Rocky Mountain National Park

Rocky Mountain National Park showcases classic alpine scenery, with wildflower meadows and serene mountain lakes set under snowcapped peaks. There are over four million visitors annually, but many stay on the beaten path. Hike an extra mile and enjoy the incredible solitude. Elk are the park's signature mammal – you will even see them grazing hotel lawns – but also keep an eye out for bighorn sheep, moose, marmots and black bears.

Sights & Activities

With over 300 miles of trail, traversing all aspects of its diverse terrain, the park is suited to every hiking ability.

Those with kids in tow might consider the easy hikes to **Calypso Falls** in the Wild Basin, **Gem Lakes** in the Lumpy Ridge area or the trail to **Twin Sisters Peak** south of Estes Park, while those with unlimited ambition, strong legs and enough trail mix will be lured by the challenge of **Longs Peak's** summit.

Regardless, it's best to spend at least one night at 7000ft to 8000ft prior to setting out to allow your body to adjust to the elevation. Before July, many trails are snowbound and high water runoff makes passage difficult. In the winter, avalanches are a hazard.

★ **Moraine Park Museum** MUSEUM
(970-586-1206; Bear Lake Rd; 9am-4:30pm Jun-Oct) Built by the Civilian Conservation Corps in 1923 and once the park's proud visitors lodge, this building has been renovated in recent years to host exhibits on geology, glaciers and wildlife.

Sleeping

The only overnight accommodations in the park are at campgrounds. Dining options and the majority of motel or hotel accommodations are around Estes Park or Grand Lake, located on the other side of the Trail Ridge Road Pass (open late May to October).

You will need a backcountry permit to stay outside developed park campgrounds. None of the campgrounds have showers, but they do have flush toilets in summer and outhouse facilities in winter. Sites include fire rings, picnic tables and one parking spot.

Olive Ridge Campground CAMPGROUND $
(303-541-2500; State Hwy 7; tent sites $19; mid-May–Nov) This well-kept USFS campground has access to four trailheads: St Vrain Mountain, Wild Basin, Longs Peak and Twin Sisters. In the summer it can get full, though sites are mostly first-come, first-served.

Longs Peak Campground CAMPGROUND $
(970-586-1206; Longs Peak Rd, off State Hwy 7; tent sites $20; P) This is the base camp of choice for the early morning ascent of Longs Peak, one of Colorado's most easily accessible 14ers. The scenery is striking and its 26

spaces are for tents only, but don't expect much solitude in the peak of the summer.

Moraine Park Campground CAMPGROUND $
(☎877-444-6777; www.recreation.gov; off Bear Lake Rd; summer tent & RV sites $20) In the middle of a stand of ponderosa pine forest off Bear Lake Road, this is the biggest of the park's campgrounds, approximately 2.5 miles south of the Beaver Meadows Visitor Center, and with 245 sites. The walk-in, tent-only sites in the D Loop are recommended if you want quiet. Make reservations through the website.

Reservations are accepted and recommended from the end of May through to the end of September; other times of the year the campground is first-come, first-served. At night in the summer, there are numerous ranger-led programs in the amphitheater.

The campground is served by the shuttle buses on Bear Lake Rd through the summer.

Aspenglen Campground CAMPGROUND $
(☎877-444-6777; www.recreation.gov; State Hwy 34; summer tent & RV sites $20) With only 54 sites, this is the smallest of the park's reservable camping. There are many tent-only sites, including some walk-ins, and a limited number of trailers are allowed. This is the quietest campground in the park while still being highly accessible (5 miles west of Estes Park on US 34). Make reservations through the website.

Timber Creek Campground CAMPGROUND $
(Trail Ridge Rd, US Hwy 34; tent & RV sites $20) This campground has 100 sites and remains open through the winter. No reservations accepted. The only established campground on the west side of the park, it's 7 miles north of Grand Lake.

Information

For private vehicles, the park entrance fee is $20, valid for seven days. Individuals entering the park on foot, bicycle, motorcycle or bus pay $10 each. All visitors receive a free copy of the park's information brochure, which contains a good orientation map and is available in English, German, French, Spanish and Japanese.

Backcountry permits ($26 for a group of up to 12 people for seven days) are required for overnight stays in the 260 designated backcountry camping sites in the park. They are free between November 1 and April 30. Phone reservations can be made only from March 1 to May 15. Reservations by snail mail or in person are accepted via the **Backcountry Office**. (☎970-586-1242; www.nps.gov/romo; 1000 W Hwy 36 Estes Park CO 80517)

A bear box to store your food is required if you are staying overnight in the backcountry (established campsites already have them). These can be rented for around $3 to $5 per day from REI (p752) or the **Estes Park Mountain Shop** (☎970-586-6548; www.estesparkmountainshop.com; 2050 Big Thompson Ave; 2-person tent $10, bear box per night $3; 8am-9pm).

Alpine Visitor Center (www.nps.gov/romo; Fall River Pass; 10:30am-4:30pm late May–mid-Jun, 9am-5pm late Jun-early Sep, 10:30am-4:30pm early Sep–mid-Oct;) The views from this popular visitor center and souvenir store at 11,796ft, and right in the middle of the park, are extraordinary. You can see elk, deer and sometimes moose grazing on the hillside on the drive up Old Fall River Rd.

Much of the traffic that clogs Trail Ridge Road all summer pulls into Alpine Visitor Center, so the place is a zoo. Rangers here give programs and advice about trails. You can also shop for knickknacks or eat in the cafeteria-style dining room.

Beaver Meadows Visitor Center (☎970-586-1206; www.nps.gov/romo; US Hwy 36; 8am-9pm late Jun-late Aug, to 4:30pm or 5pm rest of yr;) The primary visitor center and best stop for park information if you're approaching from Estes Park. You can see a film about the park, browse a small gift shop and reserve backcountry camping sites.

Kawuneeche Visitor Center (☎970-627-3471; 16018 US Hwy 34; 8am-6pm last week May-Labor Day, 8am-4:30pm Oct-May;) This visitor center is on the west side of the park, and offers a film about the park ranger-led walks and discussions, backcountry permits and family activities.

Getting There & Away

Trail Ridge Rd (US 34) is the only east–west route through the park and is closed in winter. The most direct route from Boulder follows US 36 through Lyons to the east entrances.

There are two entrance stations on the east side, **Fall River** (US 34) and **Beaver Meadows** (US 36). The **Grand Lake Station** (also US 34) is the only entry on the west side. Year-round access is available through **Kawuneeche Valley** along the Colorado River headwaters to Timber Creek Campground.

The main centers of visitor activity on the park's east side are the Alpine Visitor Center, high on Trail Ridge Rd and Bear Lake Rd, which leads to campgrounds, trailheads and the Moraine Park Museum.

North of Estes Park, Devils Gulch Rd leads to several hiking trails. Further out on Devils Gulch Rd, you pass through the village of Glen Haven to reach the trailhead entry to the park along the North Fork of the Big Thompson River.

Getting Around

In summer a free shuttle bus operates from the Estes Park Visitor Center multiple times daily, bringing hikers to a park-and-ride location where you can pick up other shuttles. The year-round option leaves the Glacier Basin parking area toward Bear Lake, in the park's lower elevations. During the summer peak, a second shuttle operates between Moraine Park Campground and the Glacier Basin parking area. Shuttles run on weekends only from mid-August through September.

Estes Park

It's no small irony that becoming a nature-lovers hub has turned the gateway of one of the most pristine outdoor escapes in the US into a kind of Great Outdoors Disney. And while there are plenty of t-shirt shops and mountain kitsch, a nice river runs through town, and there are cool parks, decent restaurants and a haunted hotel.

Activities

★Colorado Mountain School ROCK CLIMBING
(☎800-836-4008; www.totalclimbing.com; 341 Moraine Ave; half-day guided climbs per person from $125) Simply put, there's no better resource for climbers in Colorado – this outfit is the largest climbing operator in the region, has the most expert guides and is the only organization allowed to operate within Rocky Mountain National Park. It has a clutch of classes taught by world-class instructors.

Sleeping

Estes Park's dozens of hotels fill up fast in summer. There are some passable budget options but the many lovely area campgrounds are the best value.

Try the **Estes Park Visitor Center** (☎970-577-9900; www.estesparkresortcvb.com; 500 Big Thompson Ave; ⏰9am-8pm Jun-Aug, 8am-5pm Mon-Fri, 9am-5pm Sat, 10am-4pm Sun Sep-May), just east of the US 36 junction, for help with lodging; note that many places close in winter.

Estes Park Hostel HOSTEL $
(☎970-237-0152; www.estesparkhostel.com; 211 Cleave St; dm/s/d $26/38/52; 📶) This hostel, with a handful of shared rooms and simple privates, isn't going into history books as the plushest digs ever, but there's a kitchen on site, and Terri, the owner, is helpful. The price is right too.

★YMCA of the Rockies – Estes Park Center RESORT $$
(☎970-586-3341; www.ymcarockies.org; 2515 Tunnel Rd; r from $109, cabins from $129; P 🚭 ❄ 📶 🐾) Estes Park Center is not your typical YMCA boarding house. Instead it's a favorite vacation spot with families, boasting upmarket motel-style accommodations and cabins set on hundreds of acres of high alpine terrain. Choose from roomy cabins that sleep up to 10 or motel-style rooms for singles or doubles. Both are simple and practical.

This very kid-friendly resort sits in a serene and ultrapristine location in the mountains just outside town. The 860-acre plot is home to cabins and motel rooms along with lots of wide open spaces dotted with forests and fields of wildflowers. Just a few minutes outside Estes Park (but definitely away from the hustle of town), it offers a range of activities for adults, kids or the whole family, throughout the year. It also runs special themed weekends and longer summer camps where environmental education is taught in a fun and engaging manner. This YMCA is unapologetically outdoorsy, and most guests come to participate in the activities.

Riversong BOUTIQUE HOTEL $$
(☎970 586 4666; www.romanticriversong.com; 1766 Lower Broadview Dr; d from $165; P 🚭) Tucked down a dead-end dirt road overlooking the Big Thompson River, Riversong offers nine romantic rooms with private bath in a Craftsman-style mansion. The minimum stay is two nights, and prices vary by amenities. West of town take Moraine Ave, turn onto Mary's Lake Rd and take the first right.

Stanley Hotel HOTEL $$
(☎970-577-4000; www.stanleyhotel.com; 333 Wonderview Ave; r from $199; P 📶 🏊) The white Georgian Colonial Revival hotel stands in brilliant contrast to the towering peaks of Rocky Mountain National Park that frame the skyline. A favorite local retreat, this best-in-class hotel served as the inspiration for Stephen King's famous cult novel *The Shining*. Rooms are decorated to retain some of the Old West feel while still ensuring all the creature comforts.

Eating

Ed's Cantina & Grill MEXICAN $

(☎970-586-2919; www.edscantina.com; 390 E Elkhorn Ave; mains $9-13; ⏰11am-late Mon-Fri, 8am-10pm Sat & Sun; 👪) With an outdoor patio right on the river, Ed's is a great place to kick back with a margarita. Serving Mexican and American staples, the restaurant is in a retro woodsy space with leather booth seating and bold primary colors.

Estes Park Brewery PUB FOOD $$

(www.epbrewery.com; 470 Prospect Village Dr; ⏰11am-2am Mon-Sun) The town's brewpub serves pizza, burgers and wings, and at least eight different house beers, in a big, boxy room resembling a cross between a classroom and a country kitchen. Pool tables and outdoor seating keep the place rocking late into the night.

Getting There & Away

From Denver International Airport, **Estes Park Shuttle** (☎970-586-5151; www.estespark-shuttle.com) runs four times daily to Estes Park (one-way/return $45/85).

Steamboat Springs

With tree-skiing in luxuriant areas, top-notch trails for mountain-biking and a laid-back Western feel, Steamboat beats other ski towns in both ambience and offerings. Its historic center is cool for rambling, the hot springs top off a hard day of play and locals couldn't be friendlier.

Activities

Steamboat Mountain Resort SNOW SPORTS

(☎ticket office 970-871-5252; www.steamboat.com; lift ticket adult/child $94/59; ⏰ticket office 8am-5pm) The stats of the Steamboat Ski Area speak volumes for the town's claim as 'Ski Town, USA' – 165 trails, 3668ft vertical and nearly 3000 acres. With excellent powder and trails for all levels, this is the main draw for winter visitors and some of the best skiing in the US. In the ski area there are (overpriced) food and equipment vendors galore.

★**Strawberry Park Hot Springs** HOT SPRING

(☎970-870-1517; www.strawberryhotsprings.com; 44200 County Rd; per day adult/child $10/5; ⏰10am-10:30pm Sun-Thu, to midnight Fri & Sat; 👪) 🍃 Steamboat's favorite hot springs are actually outside the city limits but offer great back-to-basics relaxation. There are very rustic cabins ($60 to $70) and camping ($55) here, too – though you are probably better off back in Steamboat. It has no electricity (you get gas lanterns) and you'll need your own linens. Be sure to reserve. Weekend reservations require a two-night stay.

Note that the thermal pools are clothing optional after dark. Check website for directions.

Orange Peel Bikes BICYCLE RENTAL

(☎970-879-2957; www.orangepeelbikes.com; 1136 Yampa St; bike rental per day $20-65; ⏰10am-6pm Mon-Fri, to 5pm Sat; 👪) In a funky old building at the end of Yampa, this is perfectly situated for renting a bike to ride the trails criss-crossing Howelsen Hill. A staff of serious riders and mechanics can offer tons of information about local trails, including maps. This is the coolest bike shop in town, hands down.

Bucking Rainbow Outfitters RAFTING, FLY-FISHING

(☎970-879-8747; www.buckingrainbow.com; 730 Lincoln Ave; inner tubes $17, rafting $43-100, fishing $150-340; ⏰daily) This excellent outfitter has fly-fishing, rafting, and outdoor apparel and the area's best fly shop, but it's renowned for its rafting trips on the Yampa and beyond. Rafting half-days start at $71. Two-hour in-town fly-fishing trips start at $155 per person. It has a tube shack that runs shuttles from Sunpies Bistro on Yampa St.

Old Town Hot Springs HOT SPRING

(☎970-879-1828; www.oldtownhotsprings.org; 136 Lincoln Ave; adult/child $16/9, waterslide $6; ⏰5:30am-10pm Mon-Fri, 7am-9pm Sat, 8am-9pm Sun; 👪) Smack dab in the center of town, the water here is warmer than most other springs in the area. Known by the Utes as the 'medicine springs,' the mineral waters here are said to have special healing powers.

Sleeping & Eating

Hotel Bristol HOTEL $$

(☎970-879-3083; www.steamboathotelbristol.com; 917 Lincoln Ave; d $129-149; 🚭📶) The elegant Hotel Bristol has small-but-sophisticated Western digs, with dark-wood and brass furnishings and Pendleton wool blankets on the beds. It has a ski shuttle, a six-person indoor Jacuzzi and a cozy restaurant.

The Boathouse MODERN AMERICAN $$

(☎970-879-4797; 609 Yampa; $12-20; ⏰restaurant 11am-10pm, bar to 1am) You can't beat the view from the riverfront deck and the creative menu takes you on a cruise of the continents with innovative dishes like 'When Pigs Fly' (wasabi-kissed pork chops). Great for evening stargazing, it gets moving as a favorite pub after dinner.

Carl's Tavern AMERICAN **$$**
(☎970-761-2060; www.carlstavern.com; 700 Yampa St; mains $14-31) This local's favorite has great pub grub, a happening patio, live music, hot wait staff, and a raucous spirit that will get your heart thumping.

Information

Steamboat Springs Visitor Center (☎970-879-0880; www.steamboat-chamber.com; 125 Anglers Drive; ⊙8am-5pm Mon-Fri, 10am-3pm Sat) This visitor center, facing Sundance Plaza, has a wealth of local information, and its website is also excellent for planning.

Getting There & Away

Buses between Denver and Salt Lake City stop at the **Greyhound Terminal** (☎800-231-2222; www.greyhound.com; 1505 Lincoln Ave), about half a mile west of town. **Steamboat Springs Transit** (☎970-879-3717, for pick-up in Mountain Area 970-846-1279; http://steamboat-springs.net) runs free buses between Old Town and the ski resort year-round. Steamboat is 166 miles northwest of Denver via US 40.

Central Colorado

Colorado's central mountains are well known for their plethora of world-class ski resorts, sky-high hikes and snow-melt rivers. To the southeast are Colorado Springs and Pikes Peak, which anchor the southern Front Range.

Winter Park

Less than two hours from Denver, unpretentious Winter Park is a favorite ski resort with Front Rangers, who flock here from as far away as Colorado Springs to ski fresh tracks each weekend. Beginners can frolic on miles of powdery groomers while experts test their skills on Mary Jane's world-class bumps. Most services are along US 40 (the main drag), including the **visitor center** (☎970-726-4118; www.winterpark-info.com; 78841 Hwy 40; ⊙9am-5pm daily).

South of town, **Winter Park Resort** (☎970-726-1564; www.winterparkresort.com; Hwy 40; lift ticket adult/child $104/62; 👪) covers five mountains and has a vertical drop of more than 2600ft. Experts love it here because more than half of the runs are geared solely for highly skilled skiers. It also has 45 miles of lift-accessible **mountain-biking trails** (www.trestlebikepark.com; day pass adult/child $39/29; ⊙mid-Jun–mid-Sep) connecting to a 600-mile trail system running through the valley.

Devil's Thumb Ranch (☎800-933-4339; www.devilsthumbranch.com; 3530 County Rd 83; bunkhouse $100-180, lodge $240-425, cabins from $365; ❄📶🏊🐾) 🍃, with a cowboy-chic lodge and cabins alongside a 65-mile network of trails, makes an ultra-romantic getaway for the active-minded. Geothermal heat, reclaimed wood and low-emission fireplaces make it green. It's ideal for **cross-country skiing and horseback rides** (☎970-726-5632; trail passes adult/child $20/8, horseback riding $95-175; 👪) in the high country.

The best deal around is the friendly **Rocky Mountain Chalet** (☎970-726-8256; www.therockymountainchalet.com; 15 County Rd 72; dm $30, r summer/winter $89/149; P❄📶), with plush, comfortable doubles, dorm rooms and a sparkling kitchen.

For inspired dining, **Tabernash Tavern** (☎970-726-4430; www.tabernashtavern.com; 72287 US Hwy 40; mains $20-34; ⊙5-9pm Tue-Sat) 🍃 whets the appetite with buffalo rib ragu or venison burgers. Reserve ahead. It's north of town.

Breckenridge & Around

Set at 9600ft, at the foot of a marvelous range of treeless peaks, Breck is a sweetly surviving gold-mining town with a lovely national historic district. With down-to-earth grace, the town boasts family-friendly ski runs that don't disappoint and always draw a giddy crowd. If you should happen to grow restless, there are five great ski resorts and outlet shopping less than an hour away.

Sights & Activities

Peak 8 Fun Park AMUSEMENT PARK
(☎800-789-7669; www.breckenridge.com; Peak 8; day pass 3-7yr/8yr & up $34/68; ⊙9:30am-5:30pm mid-Jun–mid-Sep; 👪) This park has a laundry list of made-for-thrills activities, including a big-air trampoline, climbing wall, mountain-bike park and the celebrated SuperSlide – a luge-like course taken on a sled at exhilarating speeds. Get the day pass, do activities à la carte ($10 to $18) or simply take a scenic ride up the chair lift (without/

with bike $10/17). This will eventually morph into the impressive eco-playground Epic Discovery (www.epicdiscovery.com), though not until 2016 at the earliest.

Breckenridge Ski Area SNOW SPORTS
(☎800-789-7669; www.breckenridge.com; lift ticket adult/child $115/68; ⏱8:30am-4pm Nov–mid-Apr; 👪) Breckenridge spans five mountains (Peaks 6 to 10), covering 2900 acres and featuring some of the best beginner and intermediate terrain in the state, as well as plenty of exhilarating high-alpine runs and hike-to bowls. There are also five terrain parks and two half-pipes here.

Arapahoe Basin Ski Area SNOW SPORTS
(☎970-468-0718; www.arapahoebasin.com; Hwy 6; lift adult/child 6-14yr $79/40; ⏱9am-4pm Mon-Fri, from 8:30am Sat & Sun) Near the Continental Divide where US 6 crosses 11,992-foot Loveland Pass, 6 miles east of Keystone Resort and 90 miles west of Denver, Arapahoe Basin, aka A-Basin, is Colorado's second-oldest, and North America's highest ski area. Locals dig it because the lack of lodging and dining options (it's a day-use ski area only) keeps the package tourists away.

Festivals & Events

Ullr Fest CULTURAL
(www.gobreck.com; ⏱early to mid Jan) The Ullr Fest celebrates the Norse god of winter, with a wild parade and four-day festival featuring a twisted version of the Dating Game, an ice-skating party and a bonfire.

International Snow Sculpture Championship ARTS
(www.gobreck.com; ⏱mid-Jan; 👪) The International Snow Sculpture Championship begins in mid-January and lasts for three weeks. It starts with 'Stomping Week,' when the snow blocks are made, proceeds with Sculpting Week, when the sculptures are created, and concludes with Viewing Week, when the sculptures decorate the River Walk and are enjoyed and judged by the public.

Sleeping

For upscale slope-side rentals, contact **Great Western Lodging** (☎888-453-1001; www.gwlodging.com; 322 N Main St; condos summer/winter from $125/275; P❄📶). Campers can look for **USFS campgrounds** (☎877-444-6777; www.recreation.gov) outside of town.

Fireside Inn B&B, HOSTEL $
(☎970-453-6456; www.firesideinn.com; 114 N French St; summer/winter dm $30/41, d $101/140; P❄@📶) The best deal for budget travelers in Summit County, this chummy hostel and B&B is a find. All guests can enjoy the chlorine-free barrel hot tub, fridge and microwave, movie nights with fellow ski bums and the resident snuggly dog. The English hosts are a delight and all but dorm dwellers get breakfast in the morning. It's a 10-minute walk to the gondola in ski boots.

★**Abbett Placer Inn** B&B $$
(☎970-453-6489; www.abbettplacer.com; 205 S French St; r summer $99-179, winter $119-229; P❄@📶) This violet house has five large rooms decked-out with wood furnishings, iPod docks and fluffy robes. It's very low key. The warm and welcoming hosts cook big breakfasts, and guests can enjoy a lovely outdoor Jacuzzi deck and use of a common kitchenette. The top-floor room has massive views of the peaks from a private terrace. Check-in is from 4pm to 7pm.

Eating & Drinking

Clint's Bakery & Coffee House CAFE $
(131 S Main St; sandwiches $4.95-7.25; ⏱7am-8pm; 📶👪) The coolest coffee shop in town, where brainy baristas will steam up a chalkboard full of latte and mocha flavors and dozens of loose-leaf teas. If you're hungry, the downstairs bagelry stacks burly sandwiches and tasty breakfast bagels with egg and ham, lox, sausage and cheese. Good pastries too. The bagelry closes at 3pm.

Hearthstone MODERN AMERICAN $$$
(☎970-453-1148; http://hearthstonerestaurant.biz; 130 S Ridge St; mains $26-44; ⏱4pm-late; 🍷) 🌿 One of Breck's favorites, this restored 1886 Victorian churns out creative mountain fare such as blackberry elk and braised buffalo ribs with tomatillos, roasted chilies and polenta. Fresh and delicious, it's definitely worth a splurge, or hit happy hour (4pm to 6pm) for $5 plates paired with wine.

Downstairs at Eric's BAR
(www.downstairsaterics.com; 111 S Main St; ⏱11am-midnight; 👪) Downstairs at Eric's is a Breckenridge institution. Locals flock to this game-room-style basement joint for the brews, burgers and delicious mashed potatoes. There are over 100 beers (20 on tap) to choose from and plenty of sports bar–arcade action.

DON'T MISS

CLIMBING YOUR FIRST FOURTEENER

Known as Colorado's easiest fourteener, **Quandary Peak** (www.14ers.com; County Rd 851), near Breckenridge, is the state's 15th-highest at 14,265ft. Though you will see plenty of dogs and children, 'easiest' may be misleading – the summit remains three grueling miles from the trailhead.

The trail ascends to the west; after about 10 minutes of moderate climbing, follow the right fork to a trail junction. Head left, avoiding the road, and almost immediately you will snatch some views of Mt Helen and Quandary (although the real summit is still hidden).

Just below the timberline you'll meet the trail from Monte Cristo Gulch – note it so you don't take the wrong fork on your way back down. From here it's a steep haul to the top.

Go between June and September. Start early and aim to turn around by noon, as afternoon lightning is typical during summer. It's a 6-mile round-trip, taking roughly seven to eight hours. To get here, take Colorado 9 to County Rd 850. Make a right and turn right again onto 851. Drive 1.1 miles to the unmarked trailhead. Park parallel on the fire road.

Information

Visitor Center (877-864-0868; www.gobreck.com; 203 S Main St; 9am-9pm) Along with a host of maps and brochures, this center has a fantastic riverside museum that delves into Breck's gold-mining past.

Getting There & Around

Breckenridge is about 80 miles from Denver, 9 miles south of I-70 on Hwy 9.

Colorado Mountain Express (800-525-6363; www.coloradomountainexpress.com; adult/child $70/36) runs shuttles between Breckenridge and Denver International Airport.

Free buses (www.townofbreckenridge.com; 150 Watson Ave; 8am-11:45pm) run along four routes throughout town.

To get between Breckenridge, Keystone and Frisco, hop on free **Summit Stages buses** (970-668-0999; www.summitstage.com; 150 Watson Ave). To get to Vail, take the **Fresh Tracks shuttle** (970-453-4052; www.freshtrackstransportation.com; $20 1-way).

Vail

Darling of the rich and sometime famous, Vail resembles an elaborate adult amusement park, with everything man-made from the golf greens down to the indoor waterfalls. It's compact and highly walkable, but the location (I-70 runs alongside) lacks the natural drama of other Rocky Mountain destinations. That said, no serious skier would dispute its status as the best ski resort in Colorado, with its powdery back bowls, chutes and wickedly fun terrain.

Sights & Activities

Colorado Ski Museum MUSEUM
(www.skimuseum.net; 3rd fl, Vail Village parking lot exit; 10am-5pm) FREE Humble but informative, this museum takes you from the invention of skiing to the trials of the Tenth Mountain Division, a decorated WWII alpine unit that trained in these mountains. There are also hilarious fashions from the past, as well as the fledgling Colorado Ski and Snowboard Hall of Fame.

★**Vail Mountain** SNOW SPORTS
(970-754-8245; www.vail.com; lift ticket adult/child $129/89; 9am-4pm Dec–mid-Apr) Vail Mountain is our favorite in the state, with 5289 skiable acres, 193 trails, three terrain parks and (ahem) the highest lift-ticket prices on the continent. If you're a Colorado ski virgin, it's worth paying the extra bucks to pop your cherry here – especially on a blue-sky fresh-powder day. Multiday tickets are good at four other resorts (Beaver Creek, Breck, Keystone and Arapahoe Basin).

Vail to Breckenridge Bike Path CYCLING
(www.fs.usda.gov) This paved car-free bike path stretches 8.7 miles from East Vail to the top of Vail Pass (elevation gain 1831ft), before descending 14 miles into Frisco (nine more if you go all the way to Breckenridge). If you're only interested in the downhill, hop on a shuttle from a **Bike Valet** (970-476-5385; www.bikevalet.net; 520 E Lionshead Cir; bike rental per day from $30; 10am-5pm) and enjoy the ride back to Vail.

THE ROCKIES FOR POWDER HOUNDS

Well worth the five-hour road trip from Denver, **Crested Butte** promises deep powder and lovely open terrain, next to a mining outpost re-tooled to be one of Colorado's coolest small towns. If you're short on travel time, go directly to Summit County. Use lively **Breckenridge** as your base and conquer five areas on one combo lift ticket, including the mastodon resort of **Vail**, our favorite for remote back bowl terrain, and the ultra-local and laid-back Arapahoe Basin Ski Area. A-Basin stays open into June, when spring skiing means tailgating with beer and barbecue in between slush runs.

From Crested Butte, you can head a little further south and ski the slopes at **Telluride**; from Summit County and Vail, **Aspen** is nearby. Both are true old gold towns. Be sure to devote at least a few hours to exploring Aspen's glitzy shops and Telluride's down-to-earth bars for a local vibe in a historic Wild West setting.

From Aspen, catch a local flight up to **Jackson Hole Mountain Resort** to do some vertical powder riding in the Grand Tetons.

🛌 Sleeping

Vail is as expensive as Colorado gets, and lodging – generally private condo rentals – is very hit or miss.

Gore Creek Campground   CAMPGROUND $

(☑ 877-444-6777; www.recreation.gov; Bighorn Rd; tent sites $18; ☺ mid-May–Sep; 🐾) This campground at the end of Bighorn Rd has 25 tent sites with picnic tables and fire grates nestled in the woods by Gore Creek. There is excellent fishing near here. Try the Slate Creek or Deluge Lake trails; the latter leads to a fish-packed lake. The campground is 6 miles east of Vail Village via exit 180 (East Vail) off I-70.

★ Minturn Inn   B&B $$

(☑ 970-827-9647; www.minturninn.com; 442 Main St; r summer/winter from $100/150; 🅿🛜) If you don't need to be at the heart of the action in Vail, the rustic Minturn Inn should be your pick. Set in a 1915 log-hewn building in Minturn, this cozy B&B turns on the mountain charm with handcrafted log beds, river rock fireplaces and antlered decor. Reserve one of the newer River Lodge rooms for private Jacuzzi access.

★ The Sebastian   HOTEL $$$

(☑ 800-354-6908; www.thesebastianvail.com; 16 Vail Rd; r summer/winter from $230/500; 🅿❄🛜🏊🐾) Deluxe and modern, this sophisticated hotel showcases tasteful contemporary art and an impressive list of amenities, including a mountainside ski valet, luxury spa and adventure concierge. Room rates dip to reasonable in the summer, the perfect time to enjoy the tapas bar and spectacular pool area with hot tubs frothing and spilling over like champagne.

🍴 Eating & Drinking

★ Yellowbelly   SOUTHERN $

(www.yellowbellychicken.com; unit 14, 2161 N Frontage Rd; plates $10; ☺ 11am-8:30pm; 🅿🛜🐾) It may be hidden in West Vail, but man is this fried chicken good. Although we could tout the healthy side of things (non-GMO, free-range, veggie-fed birds), it's the dynamite gluten-free batter that earns this place its stars. Spicy, tender pieces of chicken come with two sides (brussel slaw, citrus quinoa, mac and cheese) and a drink; alternatively, order an entire rotisserie bird for the whole gang.

★ bōl   MODERN AMERICAN $$

(☑ 970-476-5300; www.bolvail.com; 141 E Meadow Dr; mains $14-28; ☺ 5pm-1am, from 2pm in winter; 🛜🍴🐾) Half hip eatery, half space-age bowling alley, bōl is hands down the funkiest hangout in Vail. You can take the kids bowling in the back ($50 per hour), but it's the surprisingly eclectic menu that's the real draw: creations range from a filling chicken paillard salad with gnocchi to shrimp and grits with grapefruit. Prices are relatively affordable by Vail standards. Reserve.

Matsuhisa   JAPANESE $$$

(☑ 970-476-6628; www.matsuhisavail.com; 141 E Meadow Dr; mains $29-39, 2 pieces sushi $8-12; ☺ 6-10pm) Legendary chef Nobu Matsuhisa has upped Vail's culinary standards with this modern, airy space, set at the heart of the Solaris complex. Expect traditional sushi and tempura alongside his signature 'new-style' sashimi – Matsuhisa opened his first restaurant in Peru, and continues to incorporate South American influences into his cuisine. Star dishes include black cod with miso and scallops with jalapeño salsa. Reserve.

Los Amigos BAR
(400 Bridge St; 11:30am-9pm) If you want views, tequila, and rock and roll with your après-ski ritual, come to Los Amigos. The Mexican food is decent at best, but the happy-hour prices and slope-side seating more than make up for any culinary shortcomings.

Information

Vail Visitor Center (970-479-1385; www.visitvailvalley.com; 241 S Frontage Rd; 8:30am-5:30pm winter, to 8pm summer;)

Getting There & Around

Eagle County Airport (970-328-2680; www.flyvail.com; 219 Eldon Wilson Dr), 35 miles west of Vail, has services to destinations across the country (many of which fly through Denver) and rental-car counters.

Colorado Mountain Express (800-525-6363; www.coloradomountainexpress.com;) shuttles run between Denver International Airport and Eagle County Airport ($84–99). Greyhound buses stop at the **Vail Transportation Center** (970-476-5137; 241 S Frontage Rd) en route to Denver ($37, 2½ hours) or Grand Junction ($33, three hours).

Vail's **free buses** (www.vailgov.com; 6:30am-1:50am) shuttle between West Vail, Lionshead and Vail Village; most have ski/bike racks. **ECO egional buses (ECO)** (www.eaglecounty.us; per ride $4, to Leadville $7) also run to Beaver Creek, Minturn and Leadville. To get to Breckenridge and other Summit County resorts, take the Fresh Tracks shuttle (p763).

Compact Vail Village, filled with upscale restaurants, bars and boutiques, is traffic free. Motorists must park in the public parking garage ($25 per day in winter, free in summer) before entering the pedestrian mall area near the chairlifts. Lionshead is a secondary base area about half a mile to the west; it also has a parking garage (same rates). It has direct lift access and is usually less crowded.

Aspen

Immodestly posh Aspen is Colorado's glitziest high-octane resort, playing host to some of the wealthiest skiers in the world. The handsome, historic red-brick downtown is as alluring as the glistening slopes, but Aspen's greatest asset is its magnificent scenery. The stunning alpine environment – especially during late September and October, when the aspen trees put on a spectacular display – just adds extra sugar to an already sweet cake.

Sights & Activities

★Aspen Center for Environmental Studies WILDLIFE SANCTUARY
(ACES; 970-925-5756; www.aspennature.org; 100 Puppy Smith St, Hallam Lake; 9am-5pm Mon-Fri; P) FREE The Aspen Center for Environmental Studies is a 22-acre wildlife sanctuary that hugs the Roaring Fork River. With a mission to advance 'the ethic that the earth must be respected and nurtured,' the center's naturalists provide summertime guided walks, raptor demonstrations and special programs for youngsters.

Aspen Art Museum MUSEUM
(970-925-8050; www.aspenartmuseum.org; 637 East Hyman Ave; Tue- Sun, 10am-8pm) FREE No permanent collection here, just edgy, innovative contemporary exhibitions featuring paintings, mixed media, sculpture, video installations and photography by artists such as Mamma Andersson, Mark Manders and Susan Phiipsz. Art lovers will not leave disappointed. Visit in August and you can experience its annual artCRUSH event, an art auction and wine-tasting extravaganza.

★Aspen Mountain SNOW SPORTS
(800-525-6200; www.aspensnowmass.com; lift ticket adult/child $117/82; 9am-4pm Dec–mid-Apr;) The Aspen Skiing Company operates the area's four resorts – Snowmass (best all-around choice with the longest vertical drop in the US), Aspen (intermediate/expert), the Highlands (expert) and Buttermilk (beginner/terrain parks) – which are spread out through the valley and connected by free shuttles. Both Aspen and Snowmass are open in summer (lift ticket adult/child $28/11; mid-June to September) for hiking, mountain biking and kids' activities.

Maroon Bells WILDERNESS AREA
If you have but one day to enjoy a slice of the pristine, you'd be wise to spend it in the shadow of Colorado's most iconic mountain peaks. Hikes range from a mile-long excursion (Crater Lake) to more serious challenges like Buckskin Pass (12,462ft). To get here, you'll need to catch a **shuttle** (Aspen Highlands; adult/child $6/4; 9am-4:30pm daily Jun 15-Aug, Fri-Sun Sep-Oct 6) from the Highlands.

The access road is only open to vehicle traffic ($10) from 5pm to 9am in summer.

DON'T MISS

CYCLING TO MAROON BELLS

According to the Aspen cycling gurus, the most iconic road-bike ride in Aspen is the one to the stunning **Maroon Bells** (p765). The climb is 11 lung-wrenching miles to the foot of one of the most picturesque wilderness areas in the Rockies. If you crave sweet, beautiful pain, rent two-wheelers at **Aspen Bike Tours** (☑970-925-9169; www.aspenbikerentals.com; 430 S Spring St; half/full day adult from $33/40, child $22/29; ☺9am-6pm; ⛄).

🛏 Sleeping

Aspen is popular year-round. Reserve well in advance.

The **Aspen Ranger District** (☑970-925-3445; www.fs.usda.gov/whiteriver; 806 W Hallam St; ☺8am-4:30pm Mon-Fri) operates some 20 campgrounds (☑877-444-6777; www.recreation.gov; campsites $15-21) in the Maroon Bells, Independence Pass and Hunter–Fryingpan wilderness areas.

St Moritz Lodge   HOSTEL $
(☑970-925-3220; www.stmoritzlodge.com; 334 W Hyman Ave; dm summer/winter $60/66, d summer $130-269, d winter $155-299; P✳@🛜🏊) St Moritz is the best no-frills deal in town. Perks include a heated outdoor pool and grill overlooking Aspen Mountain, and a lobby with games, books and a piano. The European-style lodge offers a wide variety of options, from quiet dorms to two-bedroom condos; the cheapest options share bathrooms. There's a kitchen downstairs.

Annabelle Inn   HOTEL $$
(☑877-266-2466; www.annabelleinn.com; 232 W Main St; r summer/winter from $169/199; P✳@🛜) Personable and unpretentious, the cute and quirky Annabelle Inn resembles an old-school European-style ski lodge in a central location. Rooms are cozy without being too cute, and come with flat-screen TVs and warm duvets. We enjoyed the after-dark ski video screenings from the upper-deck hot tub (one of two on the property).

★ Limelight Hotel   HOTEL $$$
(☑800-433-0832; www.limelighthotel.com; 355 S Monarch St; r summer/winter from $245/395; P✳🛜🏊🏊) Sleek and trendy, the Limelight's brick-and-glass modernism reflects Aspen's vibe. Rooms are spacious and have

their perks: granite washbasins, leather headboards and mountain views from the balconies and rooftop terraces. In addition to the ski valet and transportation services, you can also catch live music most winter nights in the lobby's Italian restaurant. Breakfast is included.

🍴 Eating & Drinking

★ Justice Snow's   MODERN AMERICAN $$
(☑970-429-8192; www.justicesnows.com; 328 E Hyman Ave; mains $10-22; ☺11am-2am; 🛜🍴) 🌿 Located in the historic Wheeler Opera House, Justice Snow's is a retro-fitted old saloon that marries antique wooden furnishings with a deft modern touch. Although nominally a bar – the speakeasy cocktails are the soul of the place – the affordable and locally sourced menu ($10 gourmet burger! in Aspen!) is what keeps the locals coming back.

★ Pine Creek Cookhouse   AMERICAN $$$
(☑970-925-1044; www.pinecreekcookhouse.com; 12700 Castle Creek Rd; lunch & summer dinner mains $13-41, winter dinner with ski tour/sleigh $90/110; ☺11:30am-2:30pm daily, 2:30-8:30pm Wed-Sun Jun-Sep, seatings at noon & 1:30pm daily, plus 7pm Wed-Sun Dec-Mar; 🍴⛄) 🌿 This log-cabin restaurant, located 1.5 miles past the Ashcroft ghost town at the end of Castle Creek Rd (about 30min from Aspen), boasts the best setting around. In summer you can hike here; in winter it's cross-country skis or horse-drawn sleigh in the shadow of glorious white-capped peaks. Sample alpine delicacies like house-smoked trout, buffalo tenderloin and grilled elk brats.

Meatball Shack   ITALIAN $$$
(☑970-925-1349; www.themeatballshack.com; 312 S Mill St; lunch $13, dinner $21-28; ☺11:30am-11:30pm; ⛄) 🌿 Helmed by Florentine chef Eddie Baida and NYC transplant Michael Gurtman, the shack specializes in – you guessed it – fettuccine and meatballs (*nonna*'s, chicken or veal). It's quite the happening place come evening, but forget about the scene for a minute and concentrate on what's on your plate: those locally sourced ingredients definitely make a difference.

★ Aspen Brewing Co   BREWERY
(www.aspenbrewingcompany.com; 304 E Hopkins Ave; ☺noon-late; 🛜) With six signature flavors and a sun-soaked balcony facing the mountain, this is definitely the place to unwind after a hard day's play. Brews range from the flavorful This Year's Blonde and

high-altitude Independence Pass Ale (its IPA) to the mellower Conundrum Red Ale and the chocolaty Pyramid Peak Porter.

Woody Creek Tavern PUB
(☎970-923-4585; www.woodycreektavern.com; 2 Woody Creek Plaza, 2858 Upper River Rd; ⏰11am-10pm) Enjoying a 100% agave tequila and fresh-lime margarita at the late, great gonzo journalist Hunter S Thompson's favorite watering hole is well worth the 8-mile trek from Aspen. Here since 1980, this rustic funky tavern, a local haunt for decades now, has walls that are plastered with newspaper clippings and paraphernalia (mostly dedicated to Thompson).

Information

Aspen Visitor Center (☎970-925-1940; www.aspenchamber.org; 425 Rio Grande Pl; ⏰8:30am-5pm Mon-Fri) Located across from Rio Grande Park.

Getting There & Around

Four miles north of Aspen on Hwy 82, **Aspen-Pitkin County Airport** (☎970-920-5380; www.aspenairport.com; 233 E Airport Rd; 📶) has direct flights from Denver, Los Angeles, Dallas and Chicago. **Colorado Mountain Express** (☎800-525-6363; www.coloradomountainexpress.com; adult/child to DIA $118/61; 📶) runs frequent shuttles to/from Denver International Airport (three hours).

Roaring Fork Transit Agency (www.rfta.com) buses connect Aspen with all four ski areas (free) and runs free trips to and from Aspen-Pitkin County Airport.

If you're driving, it's easiest to park in the public garage ($15 per day) next to the Aspen Visitor Center on Rio Grande Pl.

Salida

Blessed with one of the state's largest historic downtowns, Salida is not only a charming spot to explore, it also has an unbeatable location, with the Arkansas River on one side and the intersection of two mighty mountain ranges on the other. The plan of attack here is to raft, bike or hike during the day, then come back to town to refuel with grilled buffalo ribs and a cold IPA at night.

Activities

Most rafting companies are based just south of Buena Vista (25 miles north of Salida), near where Hwys 24 and 285 diverge.

Buffalo Joe's Whitewater Rafting RAFTING
(☎866-283-3563; www.buffalojoe.com; 113 N Railroad St; half/full day adult $64/98, child $54/78; ⏰May-Sep; 👪) One of the top river outfitters in the Buena Vista–Salida swirl, offering a range of trips that run every bit of the 99 miles of the Arkansas River.

River Runners RAFTING
(☎800-723-8987; www.riverrunnersltd.com; 24070 County Rd 301; half/full day adult $60/98, child $50/88; ⏰May-Sep; 👪) Recommended river outfitter based in both Buena Vista and Cañon City, and in the business of guiding trips since 1972. It does everything from placid float trips to thrilling outings on class V rapids.

Absolute Bikes BICYCLE RENTAL
(☎719-539-9295; www.absolutebikes.com; 330 W Sackett Rd; bike rental $40-80, tours from $90; ⏰9am-7pm; 👪) The place to go for bike enthusiasts, offering maps, gear, advice and rentals. Check out the selection of guided rides, ranging from St Elmo ghost town to the Monarch Crest.

Sleeping

The Arkansas Headwaters Recreation Area operates six campgrounds (bring your own water) along the river. The nicest one is **Hecla Junction** (☎800-678-2267; http://coloradostateparks.reserveamerica.com; Hwy 285, Mile 135; tent/RV sites $16/24 ; 🐾), located north of Salida. Reserve in summer.

★**Simple Lodge & Hostel** HOSTEL $
(☎719-650-7381; www.simplelodge.com; 224 E 1st St; dm/d/q $24/55/76; P📶🐾) If only Colorado had more spots like this. Run by a super-friendly husband-wife team (Jon and Julia), this hostel is simple but stylish, with a fully stocked kitchen and a comfy communal area that feels just like home. It's a popular stopover for touring cyclists following the coast-to-coast Rte 50 – you're likely to meet some interesting folks here.

Eating

★**Amícas** PIZZA $
(www.amicassalida.com; 136 E 2nd St; pizzas & paninis $8-12; ⏰11:30am-9pm; 🌿👪) Thin-crust wood-fired pizzas and six microbrews on tap? Amícas can do no wrong. This laid-back, high-ceilinged hangout (formerly a funeral parlor) is the perfect spot to replenish all those calories you burned off during the day. Savor a Michelangelo (pesto, sausage and

WORTH A TRIP

RAFTING THE ARKANSAS RIVER

The headwaters of the Arkansas form Colorado's most popular stretch of river for rafters and kayakers, with everything from extreme rapids to mellow flat water. Although most rafting companies cover the river from Leadville to the Royal Gorge, the most popular trips descend **Brown's Canyon**, a 22-mile stretch that includes class III/IV rapids. If you're with young kids or just looking for something mellower, **Bighorn Sheep Canyon** is a good bet. Those after more of an adrenaline rush can head upstream to the **Numbers** or downstream to the **Royal Gorge**, both of which are class IV/V.

Water flow varies by season, so time your visit for early June for a wilder ride – by the time August rolls around, the water level is usually pretty low. If you're rafting with kids, note that they need to be six or older and weigh at least 50lb.

goat cheese) or Vesuvio (artichoke hearts, sun-dried tomatoes, roasted peppers) alongside a cool glass of Headwaters IPA.

Fritz TAPAS $

(719-539-0364; http://thefritzdowntown.com; 113 East Sackett St; tapas $4-8, mains $9-14; 11am-2am;) This fun and funky riverside watering hole serves up clever American-style tapas. Think three-cheese mac with bacon, fries and truffle aioli, shrimp curry, and even bone marrow with red-onion jam. It also does a mean grass-fed beef burger and other sandwiches at lunch. Good selection of local beers on tap.

Information

USFS Ranger Office (719-539-3591; www.fs.usda.gov; 5575 Cleora Rd; 8am-4:30pm Mon-Fri) Located east of town off Hwy 50, with camping and trail info for the Sawatch and northern Sangre de Cristo Ranges.

Getting There & Away

Salida is located at the intersection of Hwys 285 and 50, west of Cañon City and south of Leadville. You'll need your own car to get here.

Colorado Springs

The site of one of the country's first destination resorts, Colorado Springs sits at the foot of majestic Pikes Peak. Pinned down with four military bases and recently beset by a series of devastating summer wildfires, the city has evolved into a strange and sprawling quilt of neighborhoods – visitors can best come to grips with the layout by dividing it in three.

From east to west along Hwy 24 is the downtown district, an odd mix of fine art, Olympic dreams and downbeat desperation; Old Colorado City, whose Old West brothels and saloons now host restaurants and shops; and new-agey Manitou Springs, whose mountainside location makes it the most visitor-friendly part of town.

Sights & Activities

★**Pikes Peak** MOUNTAIN

(719-385-7325; www.springsgov.com; highway per adult/child $12/5; 7:30am-8pm Jun-Aug, 7:30am-5pm Sep, 9am-3pm Oct-May;) Pikes Peak (14,110ft) may not be the tallest of Colorado's 54 14ers, but it's certainly the most famous. The Ute originally called it the Mountain of the Sun, an apt description for this majestic peak, which crowns the southern Front Range. Rising 7400ft straight up from the plains, the mountain is climbed by over half a million visitors every year.

Its location as the easternmost 14er has contributed heavily to its place in American myth. Zebulon Pike first made note of it in 1806 (he called it 'Grand Peak' but never made it to the top) when exploring the Louisiana Purchase. Katherine Bates, a guest lecturer at Colorado College in 1893, wrote the original draft of *America the Beautiful* after reaching the summit.

Today there are three ways to ascend the peak: the Pikes Peak Hwy (about a five hour round-trip), which was built in 1915 by Spencer Penrose and winds 19 miles to the top from Hwy 24 west of town; the **cog railway** (719-685-5401; www.cograilway.com; 515 Ruxton Ave; round-trip adult/child $35/19; 8am-5:20pm May-Oct, reduced hours Nov-Apr;); and on foot via the Barr Trail.

Garden of the Gods PARK

(www.gardenofgods.com; 1805 N 30th St; 5am-11pm May-Oct, 5am-9pm Nov-Apr; P) FREE This gorgeous vein of red sandstone (about

290 million years old) appears elsewhere along Colorado's Front Range, but the exquisitely thin cathedral spires and mountain backdrop of the Garden of the Gods are particularly striking. Explore the network of paved and unpaved trails, enjoy a picnic and watch climbers test their nerve on the sometimes flaky rock.

★Colorado Springs Fine Arts Center

MUSEUM

(FAC; ☎719-634-5583; www.csfineartscenter.org; 30 W Dale St; adult/student $10/8.50; ⊙10am-5pm Tue-Sun; P) Fully renovated in 2007, this expansive museum and 400-seat theater originally opened in 1936. The museum's collection is surprisingly sophisticated, with some terrific Latin American art and photography, and great rotating exhibits that draw from the 23,000 pieces in its permanent collection.

US Air Force Academy

MILITARY ACADEMY

(☎719-333-2025; www.usafa.af.mil; I-25 exit 156B; ⊙visitor center 9am-5pm; P) FREE It is one of the highest-profile military academies in the country, and a visit to this campus offers a limited but nonetheless fascinating look into the lives of an elite group of cadets. The visitor center provides general background on the academy; from here you can walk over to the dramatic chapel (1963) or embark on a driving tour of the expansive grounds.

Barr Trail

HIKING

(www.barrcamp.com; Hydro St) The tough 12.5-mile Barr Trail ascends Pikes Peak with a substantial 7400ft of elevation gain. Most hikers split the trip into two days, stopping to overnight at Barr Camp, the halfway point at 10,200ft. The trailhead is near the Manitou Springs cog railway depot; parking is $5.

Sleeping

Barr Camp

CAMPGROUND $

(www.barrcamp.com; tent sites $12, lean-tos $17, cabin dm $28; 🐾) At the halfway point on the Barr Trail, about 6.5 miles from the Pikes Peak summit, you can pitch a tent, shelter in a lean-to or reserve a bare-bones cabin. It has drinking water and showers; dinner ($8) is available Wednesday to Sunday. Reservations are essential and must be made online in advance. It's open year-round.

Mining Exchange

HOTEL $$

(☎719-323-2000; www.wyndham.com; 8 S Nevada Ave; r $135-200; P ❄ 📶) Opened in 2012 and set in the former turn-of-the-century bank where Cripple Creek prospectors traded in their gold for cash (check out the vault door in the lobby), the Mining Exchange takes the prize for Colorado Spring's most stylish hotel. Twelve-foot-high ceilings, exposed brick walls and leather furnishings make for an inviting, contemporary feel, though its downtown location is better suited to businesspeople than tourists. Excellent-value rates.

Two Sisters Inn

B&B $$

(☎719-685-9684; www.twosisinn.com; 10 Otoe Pl, Manitou Springs; r without bath $79-94, with bath $135-155; P ❄ 📶) A longtime favorite among B&B aficionados, this place has five rooms (including the honeymoon cottage out back) set in a rose-colored Victorian home, built in 1919 by two sisters. It was originally a boarding house for school teachers, and has been an inn since 1990. It has a magnificent stained-glass front door and an 1896 piano in the parlor. The inn has won awards for its breakfast recipes.

Broadmoor

RESORT $$$

(☎855-634-7711; www.broadmoor.com; 1 Lake Ave; r from $280-500; P ❄ 📶 🏊 🐾) One of the top five-star resorts in the US, the 744-room Broadmoor sits in a picture-perfect location against the blue-green slopes of Cheyenne Mountain. Everything here is exquisite: acres of lush grounds and a lake, a glimmering pool, world-class golf, myriad bars and restaurants, an incredible spa and ubercomfortable guest rooms (which, it must be said, are of the 'grandmother' school of design).

Eating & Drinking

Shuga's

CAFE $

(www.shugas.com; 702 S Cascade St; dishes $8-9; ⊙11am-midnight; 📶 👪) If you thought Colorado Springs couldn't be hip, stroll to Shuga's, a Southern-style cafe with a knack for knockout espresso drinks and hot cocktails. Cuter than buttons, this little white house is decked out in paper cranes and red vinyl chairs. There's also patio seating. The food – brie BLT on rosemary toast, Brazilian coconut shrimp soup – comforts and delights. Don't miss vintage-movie Saturdays.

★Marigold

FRENCH $$

(☎719-599-4776; www.marigoldcafeandbakery.com; 4605 Centennial Blvd; lunch $8.25-11, dinner $9-19; ⊙11am-2:30pm & 5-9pm Mon-Sat, bakery 8am-9pm) Way out by the Garden of the Gods is this buzzy French bistro and bakery that's easy on the both the palate and the wallet. Feast

WORTH A TRIP

CRIPPLE CREEK CASINOS

Just an hour from Colorado Springs yet worlds away, Cripple Creek hurls you back into the Wild West. This once lucky lady had produced a staggering $413 million in gold by 1952.

The booze still flows and gambling still thrives, but yesteryear's saloons and brothels are now modern casinos. If you're more interested in regional history or simply need a break from the slots, check out the **Heritage Center** (www.visitcripplecreek.com; 9283 Hwy 67; 8am-7pm;), the popular **gold mine tour** (www.goldminetours.com; 9388 Hwy 67; adult/child $18/10; 8:45am-6pm mid-May–Oct;) and the **narrow gauge railroad** (http://cripplecreekrailroad.com; Bennet Ave; adult/child $13/8; 10am-5pm mid-May–mid-Oct;) to historic Victor.

Cripple Creek is 50 miles southwest of Colorado Springs on scenic Hwy 67. For an even more impressive drive, check out the old Gold Camp Rd (Hwy 336) out of Victor on the way home. It's unpaved and narrow, but provides spectacular views. It takes about 90 minutes down to the Springs. Alternatively, catch the **Ramblin' Express** (719-590-8687; www.ramblinexpress.com; round-trip tickets $25; departures 7am-midnight Wed-Sun) from Colorado Springs' 8th St Depot.

on delicacies such as snapper Marseillaise, garlic and rosemary rotisserie chicken, and gourmet salads and pizzas, and be sure to leave room for the double (and triple!) chocolate mousse cake and lemon tarts.

Adam's Mountain Cafe MODERN AMERICAN $$
(719-685-1430; www.adamsmountain.com; 934 Manitou Ave; mains $9-19; 8am-3pm daily, 5-9pm Tue-Sat;) In Manitou Springs, this slow-food cafe makes a lovely stop. Breakfast includes orange-almond French toast and huevos rancheros (eggs and beans on a tortilla). Lunch and dinner are more eclectic with offerings such as Moroccan chicken, pasta *gremolata* and grilled watermelon salad. The interior is airy and attractive with marble floors and exposed rafters, and it has patio dining and occasional live music too.

Jake & Telly's GREEK $$
(719-633-0406; www.greekdining.com; 2616 W Colorado Ave; lunch $9-12, dinner $16-25; 11:30am-9pm;) One of the best choices in Old Colorado City, this Greek eatery looks and sounds slightly touristy – lots of Greek monument murals on the walls and themed music on the stereo – but the food is absolutely delicious. It does a nice Greek-dip sandwich as well as traditional dishes such as souvlaki, dolmades and spanakopita. It's set on a 2nd-story terrace above a magic wand shop.

★ **Swirl** WINE BAR
(www.swirlwineemporium.com; 717 Manitou Ave; noon-10pm Sun-Thu, to midnight Fri & Sat) Behind a stylish bottle shop in Manitou Springs, this nook bar is intimate and cool. The garden patio has dangling lights and vines while inside are antique armchairs and a fireplace. If you're feeling peckish, sample the tapas and homemade pasta.

Bristol Brewing Co BREWERY
(www.bristolbrewing.com; 1604 S Cascade Ave; 11am-10pm;) Although a bit out of the way in south Colorado Springs, this brewery – which in 2013 spearheaded a community market center in the shuttered Ivywild Elementary School – is worth seeking out for its Laughing Lab ale and pub grub from the owner of the gourmet **Blue Star** (719-632-1086; www.thebluestar.net; 1645 S Tejon St; mains $21-35; from 3pm;). Other back-to-school tenants include a bakery, deli, cafe, art gallery and movie theater in the old gym.

Information

Colorado Springs Convention & Visitors Bureau (719-635-7506; www.visitcos.com; 515 S Cascade Ave; 8:30am-5pm;) All the usual tourist pamphlets.

Getting There & Around

Colorado Springs Municipal Airport (p743) is a smaller and much more easily navigable alternative to Denver. The **Yellow Cab** (719-777-7777) fare from the airport to the city center is around $30.

Buses between Cheyenne, WY, and Pueblo, CO, stop daily at **Greyhound** (719-635-1505; 120 S Weber St). **Mountain Metropolitan Transit** (www.springsgov.com; per trip $1.75, day pass $4) offers local bus information online.

Southern Colorado

Home to the dramatic San Juan and Sangre de Cristo mountain ranges, Colorado's bottom half is just as pretty as its top.

Crested Butte

Remote and ringed by three wilderness areas, this former mining village is counted among Colorado's best ski resorts (some say it's *the* best). The old town center features beautifully preserved Victorian-era buildings refitted with shops and businesses. Strolling two-wheel traffic matches its laid-back, happy attitude.

Most everything in town is on Elk Ave, including the **visitor center** (970-349-6438; www.crestedbuttechamber.com; 601 Elk Ave; 9am-5pm).

Two miles north of the town at the base of the impressive mountain of the same name, **Crested Butte Mountain Resort** (970-349-2222; www.skicb.com; 12 Snowmass Rd; lift ticket adult/child $98/54;) is surrounded by forests, rugged mountain peaks and the West Elk, Raggeds and Maroon Bells-Snowmass Wilderness Areas. The scenery is breathtakingly beautiful. It caters mostly to intermediate and expert riders.

Crested Butte International Hostel (970-349-0588, toll-free 888-389-0588; www.crestedbuttehostel.com; 615 Teocalli Ave; dm/d shared bath $36/89, r $104-109;) is one of Colorado's nicest hostels. The best private rooms have their own baths. Dorm bunks come with reading lamps and lockable drawers. The communal area is mountain rustic with a stone fireplace and comfortable couches. Rates vary dramatically by season, with fall being cheapest.

With phenomenal food, the funky-casual **Secret Stash** (970-349-6245; www.thesecretstash.com; 303 Elk Ave; mains $8-24; 8am-late;) is adored by locals, who also dig the original cocktails. The house specialty is pizza; its Notorious Fig (with prosciutto, fresh figs and truffle oil) won the World Pizza Championship.

Crested Butte's air link to the outside world is **Gunnison County Airport** (970-641-2304), 28 miles south of the town. Shuttle **Alpine Express** (970-641-5074; www.alpineexpressshuttle.com; per person $34) goes to Crested Butte; reserve ahead in summer. The free **Mountain Express** (970-349-7318; www.mtnexp.org) connects Crested Butte with Mt Crested Butte every 15 minutes in winter, less often in other seasons; check times at bus stops.

Ouray

With gorgeous ice falls draping the box canyon and soothing hot springs that dot the valley floor, Ouray is a privileged place for nature, even for Colorado. For ice-climbers it's a world-class destination, but hikers and 4WD fans can also appreciate its rugged charms. The town is a well-preserved quarter-mile mining village sandwiched between imposing peaks.

Between Silverton and Ouray, US 550 is one of the state's most memorable drives and is paved, but the road is scary in rain or snow, so take extra care.

Activities

The visitor center is at the hot-springs pool. Check out their leaflet on an excellent walking tour that takes in two-dozen houses and other buildings constructed between 1880 and 1904.

Ouray Ice Park ICE CLIMBING
(970-325-4061; www.ourayicepark.com; Hwy 361; 7am-5pm mid-Dec–Mar;) FREE Enthusiasts from around the globe come to ice climb at the world's first public ice park, spanning a 2-mile stretch of the Uncompahgre Gorge. The sublime (if chilly) experience offers something for all skill levels. Get instruction through a local guide service.

Ouray Hot Springs HOT SPRING
(970-325-7073; www.ourayhotsprings.com; 1200 Main St; adult/child $12/8; 10am-10pm Jun-Aug, noon-9pm Mon-Fri & 11am-9pm Sat & Sun Sep-May;) For a healing soak, try the historic Ouray Hot Springs. The natural springwater is crystal-clear and free of the sulphur smells plaguing other hot springs around here, and the giant pool features a variety of soaking areas at temperatures from 96°F to 106°F (36°C to 41°C). The complex also offers a gym and massage service.

San Juan Mountain Guides CLIMBING, SKIING
(800-642-5389, 970-325-4925; www.ouray-climbing.com; 725 Main St;) Ouray's own professional guiding and climbing group is certified with the International Federation of Mountain Guides Association (IFMGA). It specializes in ice and rock climbing and wilderness backcountry skiing.

Festivals & Events

Ouray Ice Festival ICE CLIMBING
(☎970-325-4288; www.ourayicefestival.com; donation for evening events; ⏱Jan; 👪) The Ouray Ice Festival features four days of climbing competitions, dinners, slide shows and clinics. There's even a climbing wall set up for kids. You can watch the competitions for free, but various evening events require a donation to the ice park. Once inside, you'll get free brews from popular Colorado brewer New Belgium.

Sleeping & Eating

Amphitheater Forest Service Campground CAMPGROUND $
(☎877-444-6777; www.recreation.gov; US Hwy 550; tent sites $20; ⏱Jun-Aug) With great tent sites under the trees, this high-altitude campground is a score. On holiday weekends a three-night minimum applies. South of town on Hwy 550, take a signposted left-hand turn.

★**Wiesbaden** HOTEL $$
(☎970-325-4347; www.wiesbadenhotsprings.com; 625 5th St; r $132-347; ⊖📶≋) Quirky, quaint and new age, Wiesbaden even boasts a natural indoor vapor cave, which, in another era, was frequented by Chief Ouray. Rooms with quilted bedcovers are cozy and romantic, but the sunlit suite with a natural rock wall tops all. In the morning, guests roam in thick robes, drinking the free organic coffee or tea, post-soak or awaiting massages.

Box Canyon Lodge & Hot Springs LODGE $$
(☎800-327-5080, 970-325-4981; www.boxcanyonouray.com; 45 3rd Ave; r $120-218; 📶) 🍃 It's not every hotel that offers geothermal heated rooms, and pine-board rooms prove spacious and fresh. Spring-fed barrel hot tubs are perfect for a romantic stargazing soak. With good hospitality that includes free apples and bottled water, it's popular, so book ahead.

Buen Tiempo Mexican Restaurant & Cantina MEXICAN $$
(☎970-325-4544; 515 Main St; mains $7-20; ⏱6-10pm; 🍸) This good-time spot bursts with bar-stool squatters and booths of families. From the chili-rubbed sirloin to the posole with warm tortillas, Buen Tiempo delivers. Start with a signature margarita with chips and spicy homemade salsa. End with a satisfying scoop of deep-fried ice cream. But to find out how the dollars got on the ceiling, it will cost you.

Information

Ouray Visitors Center (☎800-228-1876, 970-325-4746; www.ouraycolorado.com; 1230 Main St; ⏱10am-5pm Mon-Sat, 10am-3pm Sun; 📶👪) Staffed by volunteers, this useful visitor center has brochures and the usual information. It's near the Ouray hot-springs pool.

Getting There & Away

Ouray is 24 miles north of Silverton along US 550 and best reached by private vehicle.

DON'T MISS

SCENIC DRIVE: SAN JUAN MOUNTAIN PASSES

With rugged peaks and deep canyon drops, the scenery of the San Juan mountain range is hard to beat. Suitable for all vehicles, the **Million Dollar Highway** (US 550) takes its name from the valuable ore in the roadbed. But the scenery is also golden – the paved road clings to crumbly mountains, passing old mine-head frames and big alpine scenery.

A demanding but fantastic drive, the 65-mile **Alpine Loop Backcountry Byway** (www.alpineloop.com) begins in **Ouray** and travels east to **Lake City** – a wonderful mountain hamlet worth a visit – before looping back to its starting point. Along the way you'll cross two 12,000ft mountain passes and swap pavement and people for solitude, spectacular views and abandoned mining haunts. You'll need a high-clearance 4WD vehicle and some off-road driving skills to conquer this drive; allow six hours.

Spectacular during autumn for the splendor of its yellow aspens, **Ophir Pass** connects Ouray to Telluride via a former wagon road. The moderate 4WD route passes former mines, with a gradual ascent to 11,789ft. To get there, drive south of Ouray on Hwy 550 for 18.1 miles to the right-hand turnoff for National Forest Access, Ophir Pass.

As with all 4WD routes and mountain passes, check for road closures before going. The road can be dangerous in wet or frozen conditions, so drive carefully.

Telluride

Surrounded on three sides by mastodon peaks, exclusive Telluride feels cut off from the hubbub of the outside world, and it often is. Once a rough mining town, today it's dirtbag-meets-diva – mixing the few who can afford the real estate with those scratching out a slope-side living for the sport of it. The town center still has palpable old-time charm and the surroundings are simply gorgeous.

Colorado Ave, also known as Main St, is where you'll find most businesses. From downtown you can reach the ski mountain via two lifts and the gondola. The latter also links Telluride with Mountain Village, the true base for the Telluride Ski Area. Located 7 miles from town along Hwy 145, Mountain Village is a 20-minute drive east, but is only 12 minutes away by gondola (free for foot passengers).

Activities

Telluride Ski Resort SNOW SPORTS
(☎970-728-7533, 888-288-7360; www.tellurideskiresort.com; 565 Mountain Village Blvd; adult/child full-day lift ticket $112/67) Covering three distinct areas, Telluride Ski Resort is served by 16 lifts. Much of the terrain is for advanced and intermediate skiers, but there's still ample choice for beginners.

Festivals & Events

★ **Mountainfilm** FILM
(www.mountainfilm.org; May) A four-day screening of outdoor adventure and environmental films.

Telluride Bluegrass Festival MUSIC
(☎800-624-2422; www.planetbluegrass.com; 4-day pass $205; late Jun) This festival attracts thousands for a weekend of top-notch rollicking alfresco bluegrass. Stalls sell all sorts of food and local microbrews to keep you happy, and acts continue well into the night. Camping out for the four-day festival is very popular. Check the website for info on sites, shuttle services and combo ticket-and-camping packages – it's all very organized!

Telluride Film Festival FILM
(☎603-433-9202; www.telluridefilmfestival.com; early Sep) National and international films are premiered throughout town, and the event attracts big-name stars. For more information on the relatively complicated pricing scheme, visit the film-festival website.

WORTH A TRIP

COLORADO HUT-TO-HUT

An exceptional way to enjoy hundreds of miles of single-track in summer or virgin powder slopes in winter, **San Juan Hut Systems** (☎970-626-3033; www.sanjuanhuts.com; per person $30) continues the European tradition of hut-to-hut adventures with five backcountry mountain huts. Bring just your food, flashlight and sleeping bag: amenities include padded bunks, propane stoves, wood stoves for heating and firewood.

The website has helpful tips and information on rental skis, bikes and (optional) guides based in Ridgway or Ouray.

Sleeping

Telluride's lodgings can fill quickly, and for the best rates it's best to book online. Unless you're planning to camp, however, don't expect budget deals.

Telluride Town Park Campground CAMPGROUND $
(☎970-728-2173; 500 E Colorado Ave; campsite with/without vehicle space $23/17; mid-May–mid-Oct;) Right in the center of town, it has 20 sites with shower access ($1.50 for a hot shower). It fills up quickly in the high season. There are many other campgrounds within 10 miles of town; check with the visitor center (p774) for more info.

Victorian Inn LODGE $$
(☎970-728-6601; www.victorianinntelluride.com; 401 W Pacific Ave; r from $124;) The smell of fresh cinnamon rolls greets visitors at one of Telluride's better deals, offering comfortable rooms (some with kitchenettes) and a hot tub and dry sauna. Best off all, there are fantastic lift-ticket deals for guests. Kids aged 12 years and under stay free, and you can't beat the downtown location.

Hotel Columbia HOTEL $$$
(☎970-728-0660, toll-free 800-201-9505; www.columbiatelluride.com; 300 W San Juan Ave; d/ste from $265/365; P) Since pricey digs are a given, skiers might as well stay right across the street from the gondola. Locally owned and operated, this stylish and swank hotel pampers. Store your gear in the ski and boot storage and head directly to a room with espresso maker, fireplace and heated tile floors. With shampoo dispensers and recycling, it's also pretty eco-friendly.

DON'T MISS

TELLURIDE'S GREAT OUTDOORS

Sure, the festivals are great, but there's much more to a Telluride summer.

Mountain Biking

Follow the River Trail from Town Park to Hwy 145 for 2 miles. Join **Mill Creek Trail** west of the Texaco gas station, it climbs and follows the contour of the mountain and ends at the Jud Wiebe Trail (hikers only).

Hiking

Just over 2 miles, **Bear Creek Trail** ascends 1040ft to a beautiful cascading waterfall. From here you can access the strenuous **Wasatch Trail**, a 12-mile loop that heads west across the mountains to **Bridal Veil Falls** – Telluride's most impressive waterfalls. The Bear Creek trailhead is at the south end of Pine St, across the San Miguel River.

Cycling

A 31-mile (one-way) trip, **Lizard Head Pass** features amazing mountain panoramas.

Eating & Drinking

For the best deals, look for food carts serving Mediterranean food, hot dogs, tacos and coffee on Colorado Ave.

The Butcher & The Baker CAFE $

(970-728-3334; 217 E Colorado Ave; mains $10; 7am-7pm Mon-Sat, 8am-2pm Sun;) Two veterans of upscale local catering started this heartbreakingly cute cafe, and no one beats it for breakfast. Hearty sandwiches with local meats are the perfect takeout for the trail and there are heaps of baked goods and fresh sides.

★There TAPAS, COCKTAIL BAR $$

(970-728-1213; http://therebars.com; 627 W Pacific Ave; mains $6-28; 5pm-midnight Mon-Fri, 10am-3pm Sat & Sun) A hip social alcove for cocktails and nibbling, plus weekend brunch. Bigger appetites can dine on shareable mains such as whole Colorado trout. On a comic-book-style menu, East meets West in yummy lettuce wraps, duck ramen and sashimi tostadas, paired with original hand-shaken drinks. We liked the jalapeño kiss.

La Cocina de Luz MEXICAN, ORGANIC $$

(www.lacocinatelluride.com; 123 E Colorado Ave; mains $9-19; 9am-9pm;) As they lovingly serve two Colorado favorites (organic and Mexican), it's no wonder that the lunch line runs deep at this healthy taqueria. Order the achiote pulled pork and you might be full until tomorrow. Delicious details include a salsa and chip bar, handmade tortillas and margaritas with organic lime and agave nectar. With vegan and gluten-free options too.

New Sheridan Bar BAR

(970-728-3911; www.newsheridan.com; 231 W Colorado Ave; 5pm-2am) Well worth a visit in low season for some real local flavor and opinions. At other times, it's a rush hour of beautiful people. But old bullet holes in the wall testify to the plucky survival of the bar itself, even as the adjoining hotel sold off chandeliers and antiques to pay the heating bills when mining fortunes waned.

Entertainment

Fly Me to the Moon Saloon LIVE MUSIC

(970-728-6666; 132 E Colorado Ave; 3pm-2am) Let your hair down and kick up your heels to the tunes of live bands at this saloon, the best place in Telluride to party hard.

Sheridan Opera House THEATER

(970-728-4539; www.sheridanoperahouse.com; 110 N Oak St;) This historic venue has a burlesque charm and is always the center of Telluride's cultural life. It hosts the Telluride Repertory Theater and frequently has special performances for children.

Information

Visitor Center (888-353-5473, 970-728-3041; www.telluride.com; 398 W Colorado Ave; 9am-5pm)

Getting There & Around

Commuter aircraft serve the mesa-top **Telluride Airport** (970-778-5051; www.tellurideairport.com; Last Dollar Rd), 5 miles east of town on Hwy 145. If the weather is poor, flights may be diverted to Montrose, 65 miles north. For car rental, National and Budget both have airport locations.

In ski season Montrose has direct flights to and from Denver (on United), Houston, Phoenix and limited cities on the East Coast.

Shared shuttles by **Telluride Express** (☎970-728-6000; www.tellurideexpress.com) go from the Telluride Airport to town or Mountain Village for $15. Shuttles between the Montrose Airport and Telluride cost $50.

Silverton

Ringed by snowy peaks and steeped in sooty tales of a tawdry mining town, Silverton seems like it would be more at home in Alaska than the lower 48. But here it is. Whether you're into snowmobiling, powder skiing, fly-fishing, beer on tap or just basking in some very high-altitude sunshine, Silverton delivers.

It's a two-street town, but only one is paved. The main drag, Greene St, is where you'll find most businesses. Notorious Blair St, still unpaved, runs parallel to Greene and is a blast from the past. During the silver rush, Blair St was home to thriving brothels and boozing establishments.

Activities

In summer, Silverton has some of the West's best 4WD trails. Traveling in modified Chevy Suburbans without the top, **San Juan Backcountry** (☎970-387-5565, toll-free 800-494-8687; www.sanjuanbackcountry.com; 1119 Greene St; 2hr tour adult/child $60/40; May-Oct) offers both tours and rental jeeps.

Sleeping & Eating

Red Mountain Motel & RV Park MOTEL, CAMPGROUND $$
(☎970-382-5512, toll-free 800-970-5512; www.redmtmotelrvpk.com; 664 Greene St; motel r from $80, cabins from $70, RV/tent sites $38/22; year-round; P) The tiny log cabins stay warm and make good use of their limited space with a double bed, a bunk, a tiny TV and a fully outfitted kitchenette. The managers are friendly and keen to make sure guests and customers have a good time. It's a pet-friendly place that stays open year-round.

Inn of the Rockies at the Historic Alma House B&B $$
(☎970-387-5336, toll-free 800-267-5336; www.innoftherockies.com; 220 E 10th St; r incl breakfast $109-173; P) Opened by a local named Alma in 1898, this inn has nine unique rooms furnished with Victorian antiques. The hospitality is first-rate and its New Orleans–inspired breakfasts, served in a chandelier-lit dining room, merit special mention. Cheaper rates are available without breakfast. There's also a garden hot tub for soaking after a long day.

Stellar ITALIAN $$
(☎970-387-9940; 1260 Blair St; mains $8-20; 4-9:30pm;) This friendly place is a good choice for dinner. Locals come here for the stellar pizzas, friendly service and easy atmosphere. There's a full bar with beers on tap, and the lasagna and freshly made salads are always good.

Drinking & Nightlife

★**Montanya Distillers** BAR
(www.montanyadistillers.com; 1309 Greene St; mains $6-14; noon-10pm) Under new management, this regional favorite still delivers, now in a spacious minimalist bar on Greene St. On a summer day, score a seat on the rooftop deck. Bartenders here can talk you into anything, crafting exotic cocktails with homemade syrups and their very own award-winning rum. It's worth it just for the fun atmosphere. Note: low season hours change.

Getting There & Away

Silverton is 50 miles north of Durango and 24 miles south of Ouray off US 550.

Mesa Verde National Park

Shrouded in mystery, **Mesa Verde**, with its cliff dwellings and verdant valley walls, is a fascinating, if slightly eerie, national park to explore. It is here that a civilization of Ancestral Puebloans appears to have vanished in AD 1300, leaving behind a complex civilization of cliff dwellings, some accessed by sheer climbs. Mesa Verde is unique among parks for its focus on preserving this civilization's cultural relics so that future generations may continue to interpret the puzzling settlement, and subsequent abandonment, of the area.

Mesa Verde rewards travelers who set aside a day or more to take the ranger-led tours of Cliff Palace and Balcony House, explore Wetherill Mesa or participate in one of the campfire programs. But if you only have time for a short visit, check out the Chapin Mesa Museum and walk through the Spruce Tree House, where you can climb down a wooden ladder into the cool chamber of a *kiva* (ceremonial structure, usually partly underground).

Sights & Activities

Chapin Mesa Museum MUSEUM
(☎970-529-4475; www.nps.gov/meve; Chapin Mesa Rd; admission incl with park entry; ⊙8am-6:30pm Apr–mid-Oct, 8am-5pm mid-Oct–Apr; P ♿) The Chapin Mesa Museum has exhibits pertaining to the Mesa Verde National Park. It's a good first stop. Staff at the museum provide information on weekends when the park headquarters is closed.

Chapin Mesa ARCHAEOLOGICAL SITE
The largest concentration of Ancestral Puebloan sites is at Chapin Mesa, where you'll see the densely clustered **Far View Site** and the large **Spruce Tree House**, the most accessible of sites, with a paved half-mile round-trip path.

If you want to see **Cliff Palace** or **Balcony House**, the only way is through an hour-long ranger-led tour booked in advance at the visitor center ($4). These tours are extremely popular; go early in the morning or a day in advance to book. Balcony House requires climbing a 32ft and 60ft ladder.

Wetherill Mesa ARCHAEOLOGICAL SITE
This is the second-largest concentration of Ancestral Puebloan sites. Visitors may enter stabilized surface sites and two cliff dwellings, including the **Long House**, open from late May through August. South from Park Headquarters, the 6-mile **Mesa Top Road** connects excavated mesa-top sites, accessible cliff dwellings and vantage points to view inaccessible dwellings from the mesa rim.

★**Aramark Mesa Verde** HIKING
(☎970-529-4421; www.visitmesaverde.com; adult $42-48) The park concessionaire, Aramark Mesa Verde, offers guided tours to excavated pit homes, cliff dwellings and the Spruce Tree House daily from May to mid-October.

Sleeping & Eating

The nearby towns of Cortez and Mancos have plenty of midrange places to stay; inside the park there's camping and a lodge.

Morefield Campground CAMPGROUND $
(☎970-529-4465; www.visitmesaverde.com; North Rim Rd; tent/RV sites $30/40; ⊙May-early Oct; 🐾) The park's camping option, located 4 miles from the entrance gate, also has 445 regular tent sites on grassy grounds conveniently located near Morefield Village. The village has a general store, gas station, restaurant, showers and laundry. It's managed by Aramark. Dry RV campsites (without hookup) cost the same as tent sites.

Far View Lodge LODGE $$
(☎970-529-4421, toll-free 800-449-2288; www.visitmesaverde.com; North Rim Rd; r $117-177; ⊙mid-Apr–Oct; P 🚭 ❄ 📶 🐾) Perched on a mesa top 15 miles inside the park entrance, this tasteful Pueblo-style lodge has 150 Southwestern-style rooms, some with *kiva* fireplaces. Don't miss sunset over the mesa from your private balcony. Standard rooms don't have air con (or TV) and summer daytimes can be hot. You can even bring your dog for an extra $10 per night.

Far View Terrace Café CAFE $
(☎970-529-4421, toll-free 800-449-2288; www.visitmesaverde.com; North Rim Rd; dishes from $6; ⊙7-10am, 11am-3pm & 5-8pm May–mid-Oct; 🌿 ♿) Housed in Far View Lodge immediately south of the visitor center, this self-service place offers reasonably priced meals and a convenient espresso bar. Don't miss the house special: the Navajo Taco.

Metate Room MODERN AMERICAN $$$
(☎800-449-2288; www.visitmesaverde.com; North Rim Rd; mains $18-29; ⊙7-10am & 5-7:30pm Apr–mid-Oct, 5-7:30pm mid-Oct–Mar; 🌿 ♿) With an award in culinary excellence, this upscale restaurant in the Far View Lodge offers an innovative menu inspired by Native American food and flavors. Interesting dishes include stuffed poblano chilies, cinnamon chili pork tenderloin and grilled quail with prickly pear jam.

Information

The park entrance is off US 160, midway between Cortez and Mancos. The 2012 **Mesa Verde Visitor and Research Center** (☎800-305-6053, 970-529-5034; www.nps.gov/meve; North Rim Rd; ⊙8am-7pm Jun-early Sep, 8am-5pm early Sep–mid-Oct, closed mid-Oct–May; ♿), located near the entrance, has information and news on park closures (many areas are closed in winter). It also sells tickets for **tours** ($3) of the magnificent Cliff Palace or Balcony House.

Durango

An archetypal old Colorado mining town, Durango is a regional darling that is nothing short of delightful. Its graceful hotels, Victorian-era saloons and tree-lined streets of sleepy bungalows invite you to pedal around soaking up all the good vibes. There is plenty to do outdoors. Style-wise, Durango is torn between its ragtime past and a cool, cutting-edge future where townie bikes, caffeine and farmers markets rule.

The town's historic central precinct is home to boutiques, bars, restaurants and theater halls. Foodies will revel in the innovative organic and locavore fare that is making it the best place to eat in the state. But the interesting galleries and live music, combined with a relaxed and congenial local populace, also make it a great place to visit.

Activities

Mountain Biking CYCLING

From steep single-track to scenic road rides, Durango is a national hub for mountain biking. The easy **Old Railroad Grade Trail** is a 12.2-mile loop that uses both US Hwy 160 and a dirt road following the old railway tracks. From Durango take Hwy 160 west through the town of Hesperus. Turn right into the Cherry Creek Picnic Area, where the trail starts.

For something a bit more technical, try **Dry Fork Loop**, accessible from Lightner Creek just west of town. It has some great drops, blind corners and vegetation. Cycling shops on Main or Second Ave rent out mountain bikes.

★Durango & Silverton Narrow Gauge Railroad RAILWAY

(970-247-2733; www.durangotrain.com; 479 Main Ave; return adult/child 4-11yr from $85/51; May-Oct;) Riding the Durango & Silverton Narrow Gauge Railroad is a Durango must. These vintage steam locomotives have been making the scenic 45-mile trip north to Silverton (3½ hours each way) for more than 125 years. The dazzling journey allows two hours for exploring Silverton. This trip operates only from May through October. Check online for winter options.

Durango Mountain Resort SNOW SPORTS

(970-247-9000; www.durangomountainresort.com; 1 Skier Pl; lift tickets adult/child from $77/45; mid-Nov–Mar;) Durango Mountain Resort, 25 miles north of Durango on US 550, is Durango's winter highlight. The resort, also known as Purgatory, offers 1200 skiable acres of varying difficulty and boasts 260in of snow per year. Two terrain parks offer plenty of opportunities for snowboarders to catch big air.

Check local grocery stores and newspapers for promotions and 2-for-1 lift tickets and other ski season specials before purchasing directly from the ticket window.

Sleeping

Adobe Inn MOTEL $

(970-247-2743; www.durangohotels.com; 2178 Main Ave; d $84;) Locally voted the best lodging value, this friendly motel gets the job done with clean, decent rooms and friendly service. You might even be able to talk staff into giving their best rate if you arrive late at night. Check out the Durango tip sheet.

★Rochester House HOTEL $$

(970-385-1920, toll-free 800-664-1920; www.rochesterhotel.com; 721 E 2nd Ave; d $169-229;) Influenced by old Westerns (movie posters and marquee lights adorn the hallways), the Rochester is a little bit of old Hollywood in the new West. Rooms are spacious, with high ceilings. Two formal sitting rooms, where you're served cookies, and a breakfast room in an old train car are other perks at this pet-friendly establishment.

Strater Hotel HOTEL $$$

(970-247-4431; www.strater.com; 699 Main Ave; d $197-257;) The past lives large in this historical Durango hotel with walnut antiques, hand-stenciled wallpapers and relics ranging from a Stradivarius violin to a gold-plated Winchester. Rooms lean toward the romantic, with comfortable beds amid antiques, crystal and lace. The boast-worthy staff goes out of its way to assist with inquiries.

Eating & Drinking

Durango Diner DINER $$

(970-247-9889; www.durangodiner.com; 957 Main Ave; mains $7-18; 6am-2pm Mon-Sat, 6am-1pm Sun;) To watch Gary work the grill in this lovable greasy spoon is to be in the presence of greatness. Backed by button-cute waitstaff, Gary's fluid, graceful wielding of a Samurai spatula turns out downright monstrous plates of eggs, smothered potatoes and French toast. The best diner in the state? No doubt.

Jean Pierre Bakery FRENCH, BAKERY $$

(970-247-7700; www.jeanpierrebakery.com; 601 Main Ave; mains $9-22; 8am-9pm;) A charming patisserie serving mouthwatering delicacies made from scratch. Breakfasts are all-out while dinner is a much more formal affair. Prices are dear, but the soup-and-sandwich lunch special with a sumptuous

French pastry (we recommend the sticky pecan roll) is a deal.

East by Southwest FUSION, SUSHI $$
(☎970-247-5533; http://eastbysouthwest.com; 160 E College Dr; sushi $4-13, mains $12-24; ⏲11:30am-3pm & 5-10pm Mon-Sat, 5-10pm Sun;) Low-lit but vibrant, it's packed with locals on date night. Skip the standards for goose-bump-good sashimi with jalapeño or rolls with mango and wasabi honey. Fish is fresh and endangered species are off the menu. Fusion plates include Thai, Vietnamese and Indonesian, well matched with creative martinis or sake cocktails. The best deals are the happy-hour food specials (5pm to 6:30pm).

Steamworks Brewing BREWERY
(☎970-259-9200; www.steamworksbrewing.com; 801 E 2nd Ave; ⏲11am-midnight Mon-Thu, 11am-2am Fri-Sun) Industrial meets ski lodge at this popular microbrewery, with high sloping rafters and metal pipes. It has a large bar area, as well as a separate dining room with a Cajun-influenced menu. At night there are DJs and live music.

Information

Visitor Center (☎800-525-8855; www.durango.org; 111 S Camino del Rio) South of town at the Santa Rita exit from US 550.

Getting There & Around

Durango-La Plata County Airport (DRO; ☎970-247-8143; www.flydurango.com; 1000 Airport Rd) is 18 miles southwest of Durango via US 160 and Hwy 172. Greyhound buses run daily from the **Durango Bus Center** (☎970 259 2755; 275 E 8th Ave), north to Grand Junction and south to Albuquerque, NM.

Check **Durango Transit** (☎970-259-5438; www.getarounddurango.com; 250 W 8th St) for local travel information. Durango buses are fitted with bicycle racks. It's free to ride the red T shuttle bus that circulates Main St.

Durango is at the junction of US 160 and US 550, 42 miles east of Cortez, 49 miles west of Pagosa Springs and 190 miles north of Albuquerque.

Great Sand Dunes National Park

Landscapes collide in a shifting sea of sand at **Great Sand Dunes National Park** (☎719-378-6399; www.nps.gov/grsa; 11999 Hwy 150; adult/child $3/free; ⏲visitor center 8:30am-6:30pm summer, shorter hr rest of yr), making you wonder whether a spaceship has whisked you to another planet. The 55-sq-mile dune park – the tallest sand peak rises 700ft above the valley floor – is squeezed between the jagged 14,000ft peaks of the Sangre de Cristo and San Juan Mountains and flat, arid scrub brush of the San Luis Valley.

Plan a visit to this excellent-value national park (at just $3, admission is a steal) around a full moon. Stock up on supplies, stop by the visitor center for your free backcountry camping permit and hike into the surreal landscape to set up camp in the middle of nowhere (bring plenty of water). You won't be disappointed.

There are numerous **hiking trails**, like the half-mile **Zapata Falls** (BLM Road 5415), reached through a fun slot canyon (wear grippy shoes, you may be in standing water). And there's always **sandboarding**, where you ride a snowboard down the dunes, though it's best left to those who already snowboard.

The most popular month to visit is June, when Medano Creek is flowing and kids get a natural refreshment from wading in. Be sure to bring lots of water. Walking in loose sand is difficult, and summer temperatures on the dunes can exceed 130°F (54°C).

Sleeping

Pinyon Flats Campground CAMPGROUND $
(☎888-448-1474; www.recreation.gov; Great Sand Dunes National Park; tent & RV sites $20;) This is the official park campground, with a great location not far from the dune field. There are 88 sites here, but be warned: it is very popular and regularly fills up from mid-May through August. Half are available on a first-come, first-served basis (open year round); the other 44 (open May to November 15) can be reserved online.

Zapata Falls Campground CAMPGROUND $
(www.fs.usda.gov; BLM Rd 5415; tent & RV sites $11; ⏲yr round;) Seven miles south of the national park, this campground offers glorious panoramas of the San Luis Valley from its 9000ft perch in the Sangre de Cristos. There are 23 first-come, first-served sites, but note that there is no water and that the 3.6-mile access road is steep and fairly washed out, making for slow going.

Zapata Ranch RANCH $$$
(☎719-378-2356; www.zranch.org; 5303 Hwy 150; d $300) Ideal for horseback-riding enthusiasts, this exclusive preserve is a working cattle and bison ranch set amid groves of

cottonwood trees. Owned and operated by the Nature Conservancy, the main inn is a refurbished 19th-century log structure, with distant views of the sand dunes.

ⓘ Getting There & Away

The national park is about 35 miles northeast of Alamosa and 250 miles south of Denver. From Denver, take I-25 south to Hwy 160 west and turn onto Hwy 150 north. There is no public transportation.

WYOMING

With wind, restless grasses and wide blue skies, the most sparsely populated state offers solitude to spare. Wyoming may be nuzzled in the bosom of America, but emptiness defines it.

Though steeped in ranching culture – just see the line of Stetsons at the local credit union – Wyoming is the number-one coal producer in the US and is also big in natural gas, crude oil and diamonds. Deeply conservative, its propensity toward industry has sometimes made it an uneasy steward of the land.

But wilderness may be Wyoming's greatest bounty. Its northwestern corner is home to the magnificent national parks of Yellowstone and Grand Teton. Chic Jackson and sporty Lander make great bases for epic hiking, climbing and skiing. For a truer taste of Western life, check out the plain prairie towns of Laramie and Cheyenne.

ⓘ Information

Even on highways, distances are long, with gas stations few and far between. Driving hazards include frequent high gusty winds and fast-moving snow squalls that can create whiteout blizzard conditions. If the weather gets too rough, the highway patrol will shut the entire interstate until it clears.

Wyoming Road Conditions (☑ 888-996-7623; www.wyoroad.info) Up-to-date info on road conditions and closures.

Wyoming State Parks & Historic Sites (☑ 307-777-6323; www.wyo-park.com; admission $6, historic site $4, campsite per person $17) Wyoming has 12 state parks. Camping reservations are taken online or over the phone.

Wyoming Travel & Tourism (☑ 800-225-5996; www.wyomingtourism.org; 5611 High Plains Rd, Cheyenne) At a rest area just south of Cheyenne on I-25, this info center has tons of information and kid-friendly displays about local wildlife, activities and the environment. Worth a stop!

Cheyenne

Many a country tune has been penned about Wyoming's state capital and largest city, though Cheyenne is more like the Hollywood Western *before* the shooting begins. That is, until Frontier Days festival, a raucous July celebration of cowboy fun. At the junction of I-25 and I-80, the city is a useful pit stop.

ⓞ Sights

Frontier Days Old West Museum MUSEUM
(☑ 307-778-7290; www.oldwestmuseum.org; 4610 N Carey Ave; adult/child $10/free; ⊙ 9am-5pm Mon-Fri, from 10am Sat & Sun) For a peek into the pioneer past, visit the lively Frontier Days Old West Museum at I-25 exit 12. It is chock-full of rodeo memorabilia – from saddles to trophies. For the audio tour, call ☑ 307-316-0079.

Big Boy Steam Engine PARK
(Holliday Park; ⊙ 24hr) Inside pretty Holliday Park you'll find the world's largest steam engine – Old Number 4004, now retired. The locomotive made its name pulling 3600-ton trains across about a million miles of steep mountain terrain.

⚝ Festivals & Events

★ **Cheyenne Frontier Days** RODEO
(☑ 1-800-227-6336; www.cfdrodeo.com; 4501 N Carey Ave; free-$39; ⊙ Jul; ☗) If you've never seen a steer wrestler leap into action, this very Western event is bound to brand an impression. Beginning in late July, Wyoming's largest celebration features 10 days of rodeos, concerts, dances, air shows and chili cook-offs. Free events include morning 'slack' rodeos, pancake breakfasts and parades. There's also an art sale and 'Indian village.'

🛏 Sleeping & Eating

Reservations are a must during Frontier Days, when rates double and everything within 50 miles is booked; see www.cheyenne.org/availability for bookings. The cheapest motels line noisy Lincolnway (I-25 exit 9).

Nagle Warren Mansion Bed & Breakfast B&B $$
(☑ 307-637-3333; www.naglewarrenmansion.com; 222 E 17th St; r from $163; ❇ 🖧 🐾) This lavish spread is a fabulous find. The historic 1888 house is decked out with late-19th-century regional antiques. Spacious and elegant, it boasts a hot tub, a reading room tucked into

WYOMING FACTS

Nickname Equality State

Population 584,000

Area 97,100 sq miles

Capital city Cheyenne (population 62,400)

Other cities Laramie (population 31,800), Cody (population 9,800), Jackson (population 10,100)

Sales tax 4%

Birthplace of Artist Jackson Pollock (1912–56)

Home of Women's suffrage, coal mining, geysers, wolves

Politics Conservative to the core

Famous for Rodeo, ranches, former vice-president Dick Cheney

Kitschiest souvenir Fur bikini from a Jackson boutique

Driving distances Cheyenne to Jackson 432 miles

a turret and classic 1954 Schwinn bikes for cruising. There are six individually decorated rooms in the mansion and another six in the carriage house, all with private bath.

Tortilla Factory MEXICAN $
(2706 S Greeley Hwy; mains $2-11; 7am-8pm Mon-Sat, 8am-5pm Sun) A delicious Mexican fast-food joint serving homemade tamales for $2 and authentic classics such as *menudo* (Mexican soup) and green chili.

Drinking & Entertainment

Cheyenne Brewing Company BREWERY
(Depot Station; 11am-11pm) The name and ownership have changed, but the ambience is still cool at this brewpub inside the 1860s Union Pacific depot. There are good craft brews on tap, and three seating areas – a bar, an all-ages dining room and an outdoor terrace.

Cheyenne Gunslingers WILD WEST SHOW
(800-426-5009; www.cheyennegunslingers.com; cnr Lincolnway & Carey Ave; noon Sat & 6pm Mon-Fri Jun-Jul;) FREE A nonprofit group of actors puts on a lively, if not exactly accurate, Old West show in Gunslinger Sq – from near hangings to slippery jailbreaks. Stars include corrupt judges, smiling good guys and, of course, the bad-ass villains.

Information

Cheyenne Visitor Center (307-778-3133; www.cheyenne.org; 1 Depot Sq; 8am-5pm Mon-Sat, 11am-5pm Sun, closed Sat & Sun winter)

Getting There & Around

Cheyenne Airport (CYS; 307-634-7071; www.cheyenneairport.com; 200 E 8th Ave) Daily flights to Denver.

Black Hills Stage Lines (307-635-1327; www.blackhillsstagelines.com; 5401 Walker Rd) Greyhound buses depart from the Black Hills Stage Lines daily for Billings, MT ($96, 8½ hours), and Denver, CO ($34, 2¾ hours), among other destinations.

Cheyenne Street Railway Trolley (800-426-5009; 121 W 15th St; adult/child $10/5; 10am, 11:30am, 1pm, 2:30pm and 4pm May-Sep) Takes visitors on tours through downtown, leaving from Depot Plaza.

Laramie

Home to the state's only four-year university, Laramie can be both hip and boisterous, a vibe which is missing from most Wyoming prairie towns. Well worth exploring is the small historic downtown, a lively five-block grid of attractive two-story brick buildings with hand-painted signs and murals pushed up against the railroad tracks.

Sights

Wyoming Territorial Prison MUSEUM
(www.wyomingterritorialprison.com; 975 Snowy Range Rd; adult/child $5/2.50; 8am-7pm May-Oct;) The only prison ever to hold Butch Cassidy – he was in for grand larceny from 1894 to '96 and emerged to become one of history's greatest robbers – the Wyoming Territorial Prison operated until 1903, holding about a thousand 'malicious and desperate outlaws.' While inside, convicts produced over 700 brooms a day. The restored prison is surrounded by other historical buildings of the era; guided tours at 11am and 2pm are included in admission.

Geological Museum MUSEUM
(307-766-2646; www.uwyo.edu/geomuseum; UW, Hwy 287 at I-80; 10am-4pm Mon-Sat) FREE This University of Wyoming museum features an impressive collection of dinosaur remains, including a 75ft Apatosaurus skeleton.

Sleeping

Gas Lite Motel MOTEL $

(☎ 307-742-6616; www.facebook.com/GasLiteMotel; 960 N 3rd St; s/d $50/55;) The Gas Lite Motel stands out, even on a street lined with eye-catching, neon-signed retro motels. A plastic horse and rooster perch on the roof, and tattered plywood cowboys lean here and there. The swimming pool is in a greenhouse, surrounded by fake deer and grizzlies. Rooms are pet-friendly and dressed with playful Wild West touches.

Mad Carpenter Inn B&B $$

(☎ 307-742-0870; http://madcarpenter.com; 353 N 8th St; r $95-125;) With landscaped gardens, homemade granola and two comfy, snug rooms plus a backyard cottage, the homey Mad Carpenter Inn has warmth to spare. A serious game room features billiards and ping-pong.

Eating & Drinking

★ **Sweet Melissa's** VEGETARIAN $

(213 S 1st St; mains $7-11, cocktails $5-7; 11am-9pm Mon-Sat;) Doubtless the healthiest food for miles, Sweet Melissa's makes delicious vegetarian food, like portabella fajitas or black bean and sweet potato sliders. Tip: grab a seat at the adjoining Front Street Tavern and watch the trains roll by – it's usually less crowded, and the two places share a kitchen.

Coal Creek Coffee Co CAFE $

(110 E Grand Ave; panini $9-10; 6am-11pm;) With superlative brews, Coal Creek Coffee Co is modern and stylish, even borderline hipster – but not in a bad way. That just means you'll get a really good latte, made with fair-trade beans by people who know what they're doing. Sandwiches and quiches are tasty, too.

Old Buckhorn Bar BAR

(☎ 307-742-3554; 114 Ivinson St; 9am-midnight Sun-Wed, to 2am Thu-Sat) For live country music and beers, you'll want to head to the Old Buckhorn Bar. Established in 1900, it's Laramie's oldest standing bar and a fantastic example of what a good Wild West saloon should look like in this century – check out the hand-scratched graffiti and half-century-old condom dispenser in the bathroom.

Getting There & Away

Laramie Regional Airport (LAR; ☎ 307-742-4164; www.laramieairport.com) Located 4 miles west of town via I-80 exit 311, Laramie Regional Airport has daily flights to Denver (40 minutes).

Lander

Lander is a cheerful example of the many cool little one-street towns across Wyoming. Just a stone's throw from the Wind River Reservation, it's a rock-climbing and mountaineering mecca in a friendly foothills setting.

Sights & Activities

Sinks Canyon State Park PARK

(☎ 307-332-3077; 3079 Sinks Canyon Rd; admission $6; visitor center 9am-6pm Jun-Sep) The beautiful Sinks Canyon State Park, 6 miles south of Lander, features a curious underground river. Flowing through a narrow

IF YOU HAVE A FEW MORE DAYS IN WYOMING

Wyoming is full of great places to get lost – here's a taster.

With vast grassy meadows, seas of wildflowers and peaceful conifer forests, the **Bighorn Mountains** in north-central Wyoming are truly awe-inspiring. Factor in gushing waterfalls and abundant wildlife and you've got a stupendous natural playground with hundreds of miles of marked trails.

Nestled in the shadow of the Bighorn Mountains, the town of **Sheridan** boasts century-old buildings once home to Wyoming cattle barons. It's popular with adventure fanatics who come to play in the Bighorns.

Rising a dramatic 1267ft above the Belle Fourche River, the nearly vertical monolith of **Devil's Tower National Monument** is an awesome sight. Known as Bears Lodge by some of the 20-plus Native American tribes who consider it sacred, it's a must-see if you are traveling between the Black Hills (on the Wyoming–South Dakota border) and the Tetons or Yellowstone.

West of Laramie, the lofty national forest stretching across **Medicine Bow Mountains** and **Snowy Range** is a wild and rugged place, perfect for multi-day hiking and camping trips.

canyon, the Middle Fork of the Popo Agie River disappears into the soluble Madison limestone called the Sinks and returns warmer a quarter-mile downstream in a pool called the Rise.

National Outdoor Leadership School ADVENTURE TOUR
(NOLS; www.nols.edu; 284 Lincoln St) The renowned NOLS leads trips around the world and locally into the Wind River Range.

Gannett Peak Sports MOUNTAIN BIKING
(351b Main St; ⌚10am-6pm Mon-Fri, 9am-5pm Sat, 10am-2pm Sun) If you want to check out the single-track trails outside town, head to Gannett Peak Sports for advice, gear and equipment rentals.

Wild Iris Mountain Sports OUTDOOR EQUIPMENT
(☎307-332-4541; 166 Main St; ⌚9:30am-6:30pm Mon-Sat, 10am-5pm Sun) If you've come to hike, camp or climb, pop into this gear shop for good advice and climbing rental or snowshoes. Pick up their cheat sheet with local tips.

Sleeping

Sinks Canyon State Park Campgrounds CAMPGROUND $
(☎877-444-6777; htttp://recreation.gov; campsites $15; ⌚May-Sep) This scenic campground, run by Shoshone National Forest, is highly recommended.

Holiday Lodge MOTEL $
(☎307-332-2511; www.holidaylodgelander.com; 210 McFarlane Dr; tent sites per person $10, RV sites $38, s/d from $85/90; ❄📶) It's under new ownership, but this funky motor lodge still offers a great alternative to the standard chains lining Main St. The look says 1961, but it's scrubbed shiny and friendly, with thoughtful extras like an iron, makeup remover and sewing kits. Riverside camping includes breakfast and showers.

Eating & Drinking

Gannett Grill AMERICAN $
(☎307-332-8227; 128 Main St; mains $8-11; ⌚11am-9pm) Decompress from long hours of travel or adventure at the backyard patio of Gannett Grill, an institution serving local beef burgers, crisp waffle fries and stone-oven pizzas. If you're feeling fancy, try the adjoining **Cowfish**, a more upscale dinner offering (mains $17–33) from the same folks.

Lander Bar BAR
(☎307-332-8228; 126 Main St; ⌚11am-late) Adjoining the Gannett Grill, this big, wooden, barn-like place is the place to go for climbing and mountain-biking gossip. There's live music many nights.

Information

Lander Visitor Center (☎307-332-3892; www.landerchamber.org; 160 N 1st St; ⌚9am-5pm Mon-Fri)

Getting There & Away

Wind River Transportation Authority (☎307-856-7118; www.wrtabuslines.com; fare one-way $1, airport shuttle $30) Wind River Transportation Authority provides scheduled Monday-to-Friday services between Lander, Riverton, Dubois, Rock Springs and Riverton Regional Airport, plus bus service to Jackson ($160) and other destinations; check the website for schedules.

Jackson

Technically this is Wyoming, but you may have a hard time believing it. With a median age of 32, this Western town has evolved into a mecca for mountain lovers, hard-core climbers and skiers, easily recognizable as sunburned baristas.

The upside of being posh and popular? Jackson is abuzz with life: trails and outdoor opportunities abound. Fresh sushi is flown in daily and generous purse-strings support a vigorous cultural life. Skip the souvenirs and remember why you came to Jackson in the first place: to visit its glorious backyard, Grand Teton National Park.

Sights & Activities

★**National Museum of Wildlife Art** MUSEUM
(☎307-733-5771; www.wildlifeart.org; 2820 Rungius Rd; adult/child $14/6; ⌚9am-5pm, from 11am Sun spring & fall) If you visit one area museum, make it this one, with major works by Bierstadt, Rungius, Remington and Russell. It's worth driving up just for the outdoor sculptures and the building itself (inspired by a ruined Scottish castle). The **discovery gallery** has a kids' studio for drawing and print rubbing that adults plainly envy. Check the website for summer film-series and art-class schedules.

National Elk Refuge WILDLIFE RESERVE
(☎307-733-9212; www.fws.gov/refuge/national_elk_refuge; Hwy 89; ⊙8am-5pm Sep-May, to 7pm Jun-Aug) FREE This refuge protects Jackson's herd of several thousand elk, offering them a winter habitat from November to March. During summer, ask at the Jackson visitor center for the best places to see elk. An hour-long horse-drawn sleigh ride is the highlight of a winter visit; buy tickets at the visitor center.

★ **Jackson Hole Mountain Resort** SNOW SPORTS
(☎307-733-2292; www.jacksonhole.com; day pass adult/child $121/75; ⊙late Nov-early Apr) 'The Hole' is all about vertical, boasting a continuous vertical rise of 4139ft – beaten only by Big Sky, by 41ft (we're sure that some front loader is poised to adjust this injustice). Among the world's top ski destinations, the resort has 2500 acres of ski terrain blessed by an average of 380in of snow annually.

The runs (10% beginner, 40% intermediate and 50% advanced) are served by six lifts, an aerial tram, two high-speed quads and the Bridger gondola. Depending on snowfall, the ski season may start early or end late.

Festivals & Events

Town Square Shoot-out WILD WEST SHOW
(Jackson Town Sq; ⊙6:15pm Mon-Sat Memorial Day-Labor Day;) FREE This hokey tourist draw takes place in summer.

Sleeping

Jackson has plenty of lodging, both in town and around the ski hill. There are also great camping options scattered outside of town. Reservations are essential in summer and winter.

Hostel HOSTEL $
(☎307-733-3415; www.thehostel.us; 3315 Village Dr, Teton Village; dm $34-40, r $79-119; @) The area's only budget option, this old ski lodge in Teton Village offers private doubles and bunk-bed rooms with renovated showers for up to four. The spacious lounge with fireplace is ideal for movies or Scrabble tournaments and there's a playroom for tots. There's a microwave and outdoor grill, coin laundry and ski-waxing area. Rates drop in fall and spring.

Antler Inn HOTEL $$
(☎307-733-2535; www.townsquareinns.com/antler-inn; 43 W Pearl; s/d from $110/115) The 'cedar log' rooms at this comfy motor inn give the place an appreciably Western feel, and it's right in the midst of the Jackson action. Rates drop sharply in winter.

★ **Alpine House** B&B $$$
(☎307-739-1570; www.alpinehouse.com; 285 N Glenwood St; r $240-330, cottage $330-515; @) Two former Olympic skiers have infused this downtown home with sunny Scandinavian style and personal touches, like great service and a cozy mountaineering library. Amenities include plush robes, down comforters, a shared Finnish sauna and an outdoor Jacuzzi. Save your appetite for the creative breakfast options, like lemon-ricotta blueberry pancakes or eggs Benedict.

Eating

Jackson Whole Grocer HEALTH FOOD $
(☎307-733-0450; http://jacksonwholegrocer.com; 1155 S Hwy 89; ⊙7am-10pm;) A health-food market and deli, this is a good place to load up for a day's hiking or skiing adventure. There's even wine and beer by the glass, so you can sip while you shop.

Lotus Cafe VEGETARIAN $$
(☎307-734-0882; http://tetonlotuscafe.com; 145 N Glenwood; mains $7-24; ⊙8am-10pm;) You can hardly swing a cat in this town without hitting a primo steak, but good veggie fare is harder to find. The Lotus solves that with things like kale-avocado salad, veggie lasagna and giant grain-and-veg bowls. (There is some meat on the menu too, all organic.)

Bubba's Bar-B-Que BARBECUE $$
(☎307-733-2288; 100 Flat Creek Dr; mains $7-23; ⊙7am-10pm;) Get the biggest, fluffiest breakfast biscuits for miles at this friendly and energetic diner. Later on, bring your own bottle (BYOB) and settle in for some BBQ ribs and racks.

Snake River Grill MODERN AMERICAN $$$
(☎307-733-0557; 84 E Broadway; mains $23-51; ⊙from 5:30pm) With a roaring stone fireplace, an extensive wine list and snappy white linens, this grill creates notable American haute cuisine. Try the wild game Korean hot bowl, with venison and spring veggies in spicy black-bean sauce. Or munch on a cast-iron bucket of truffle fries. Splurge-desserts like buttermilk *panna cotta* or homemade ice cream easily satisfy two.

Drinking & Nightlife

Stagecoach Bar BAR
(☎307-733-4407; http://stagecoachbar.net; 5800 W Hwy 22, Wilson; ⏰11am-late) Wyoming has no better place to shake your booty. Thursday is disco night plus Ladies' Night, and most Sundays the long-standing house band croons country-and-western favorites until 10pm. Worth the 6-mile drive to Wilson (just past the Teton Village turnoff).

The Rose COCKTAIL BAR
(http://therosejh.com; 50 W Broadway; cocktails $9-14; ⏰5:30pm-2am) A swank little lounge upstairs inside the Pink Garter theater, with red-leather booths, low lighting and chandeliers, the Rose is the place for craft cocktails in Jackson.

Snake River Brewing Co MICROBREWERY
(☎307-739-2337; www.snakeriverbrewing.com; 265 S Millward St; pints $4-5, mains $11-14; ⏰11:30am-midnight) With an arsenal of more than 20 microbrews crafted on the spot, some award-winning, it's no wonder this is a local favorite. Food includes wood-fired pizzas, bison burgers and wild-game stew.

Million Dollar Cowboy Bar BAR
(☎307-733-4790; 25 N Cache Dr; ⏰from 11am) Touristy to the gills, but you kind of have to give it a whirl. Plunk your hindquarters on a saddle stool and order a shot of Wyoming whiskey or a pint of the bar's namesake beer. Most nights there's Western swing dancing, and there's an upscale steakhouse downstairs (reservations recommended).

Information

Jackson Hole & Greater Yellowstone Visitor Center (☎307-733-3316; www.jacksonhole-chamber.com; 532 N Cache Dr; ⏰9am-5pm) Provides information, books, restrooms, an ATM and a courtesy phone for free local calls.

Getting There & Around

Jackson Hole Airport (JAC; ☎307-733-7682; www.jacksonholeairport.com) Jackson Hole Airport is 7 miles north of Jackson off US 26/89/189/191 within Grand Teton National Park. Daily flights serve Denver, Salt Lake City, LA, San Francisco, Chicago, Dallas and Houston.

START Bus (www.startbus.com; Teton Village one-way $3) This Teton County commuter bus system runs free shuttles within Jackson as well as approximately hourly trips to and from Teton Village; check current schedules online.

Alltrans' Jackson Hole Express (☎307-733-3135; www.jacksonholebus.com; ⏰park shuttle mid-May–Oct) Alltrans' Jackson Hole Express buses provide a shuttle to Grand Teton National Park ($14 per day) and the airport ($16). Buses also depart at 6:30am daily from Maverik County Store (on the corner of Hwy 89 S and S Park Loop Rd) for Salt Lake City ($75, 5½ hours).

Cody

Raucous Cody revels in its Wild West image (the town is named after legendary showman William 'Buffalo Bill' Cody, who founded it). Summer is high season, and Cody puts on quite an Old West show for the throngs of visitors making their way to Yellowstone National Park, 52 miles to the west.

From Cody, the approach to geyserland through the Wapiti Valley is dramatic to say the least. The **visitor center** (☎307-587-2777; www.codychamber.org; 836 Sheridan Ave; ⏰8am-7pm Jun-Aug, to 5pm Mon-Fri Sep-May) is the logical starting point.

Sights

★**Buffalo Bill Center of the West** MUSEUM
(www.centerofthewest.org; 720 Sheridan Ave; adult/child $19/11; ⏰8am-6pm May–mid-Sep, 8am-5pm mid-Sep–Oct, 10am-5pm Nov, Mar & Apr, 10am-5pm Thu-Sun Dec-Feb) Cody's major tourist attraction is the superb Buffalo Bill Historical Center of the West. A sprawling complex of five museums, it showcases everything Western: from posters, grainy films and artifacts pertaining to Buffalo Bill's world-famous Wild West shows, to galleries showcasing frontier-oriented artwork, to museums dedicated to Native Americans. Its **Draper Museum of Natural History** explores the Yellowstone region's ecosystem with excellent results. The galleries are given regular overhauls to keep presentations fresh. There's also a daily (1pm) **raptor presentation**.

Entry is valid for two consecutive days. Save a couple of bucks by booking online.

Sleeping

Irma Hotel HISTORIC HOTEL $$
(☎800-745-4762; www.irmahotel.com; 1192 Sheridan Ave; r $132-152, ste $162-197) Built in 1902 by Buffalo Bill himself, and named for his daughter, this old-fashioned saloon has charming original historical suites named after past guests (Annie Oakley, Calamity Jane), plus

less-inspiring modern rooms in an annex. The creaky hallways, dining room and lobby drip with atmosphere – the ornate cherrywood bar was a gift from Queen Victoria.

It's well worth stopping in for dinner or drinks. Gunfights break out nightly at 6pm in front of the hotel from June through September.

Chamberlin Inn INN $$
(307-587-0202; http://chamberlininn.com; 1032 12th St; d/ste from $175/255) An elegant downtown retreat, this historic boutique hotel (built in 1903) has a library and a pretty inner courtyard. The registry claims Hemingway crashed in room 18 ($275) on a 1932 fishing trip.

Drinking & Entertainment

Silver Dollar Bar BAR
(1313 Sheridan Ave; mains $9-11; 11am-late) The Silver Dollar Bar is a historic watering hole with lots of TV screens and live music or DJs nightly. The tap list is strong, with lots of great regional craft beers, and the burgers are tasty (the signature half-pounder goes for $15). In nice weather, an outdoor bar offers excellent views of street life.

Cody Nite Rodeo SPECTATOR SPORT
(www.codystampederodeo.com; 519 W Yellowstone Ave; adult/child $20/10; 8pm Jun-Aug) If you're wondering why Cody is known as the 'rodeo capital of the world,' check out this nightly event, where you'll see future (and some current) pro-rodeo superstars putting in the hours all summer. It's rain or shine, with fireworks at dusk.

Getting There & Away

Yellowstone Regional Airport (COD; www.flyyra.com) Yellowstone Regional Airport is 1 mile east of Cody and runs daily flights to Salt Lake City and Denver.

Yellowstone National Park

They grow their critters and geysers big up in Yellowstone, America's first national park and Wyoming's flagship attraction. From shaggy grizzlies to oversized bison and magnificent packs of wolves, this park boasts the lower 48's most enigmatic concentration of wildlife. Throw in half the world's geysers, the country's largest high-altitude lake and a plethora of blue-ribbon rivers and waterfalls, all sitting pretty atop a giant supervolcano, and you'll quickly realize you've stumbled across one of Mother Nature's most fabulous creations.

When John Colter became the first white man to visit the area in 1807, the inhabitants were Tukadikas (aka Sheepeaters), a Shoshone Bannock people who hunted bighorn sheep. Colter's reports of exploding geysers and boiling mud holes (at first dismissed as tall tales) brought in expeditions and tourism interest eagerly funded by the railroads. The park was established in 1872 (as the world's first) to preserve Yellowstone's spectacular geography: the geothermal phenomena, the fossil forests and Yellowstone Lake.

Of the park's five entrance stations, only the North Entrance, near Gardiner, MT, is open year-round. The others, typically open mid-May to October, offer access from the

NATIONAL PARKS

The Rocky Mountains region is home to some of the USA's biggest national parks. The heavy-hitters include the following:

Rocky Mountain National Park (Colorado) Awesome hiking through alpine forests and tundra.

Great Sand Dunes National Park (Colorado) Sahara-like wonder.

Mesa Verde National Park (Colorado) An archaeological preserve with elaborate cliff-side dwellings.

Grand Teton National Park (Wyoming) Dramatic craggy peaks.

Yellowstone National Park (Wyoming) The country's first, a true wonderland of volcanic geysers, hot springs and forested mountains.

Glacier National Park (Montana) High sedimentary peaks, glaciers and lots of wildlife.

Hells Canyon National Recreation Area (Idaho) The Snake River carves the deepest canyon in North America. The **National Park Service** (NPS; www.nps.gov) also manages over two dozen other historic sites, monuments, nature preserves and recreational areas in Idaho.

northeast (Cooke City, MT), east (Cody, WY), south (Grand Teton National Park) and west (West Yellowstone, MT). The park's main road is the 142-mile Grand Loop Rd scenic drive.

Sights

Just sitting on the porch of the Old Faithful Inn with a cocktail in hand waiting for Old Faithful geyser to erupt could be considered enough activity by itself but there's plenty else to keep you busy here, from hiking and backpacking to kayaking and fly-fishing. Most park trails are not groomed, but unplowed roads and trails are open for cross-country skiing.

Yellowstone is split into five distinct regions, each with unique attractions. Upon entering the national park you'll be given a basic map and a park newspaper detailing the excellent ranger-led talks and walks (well worth attending). All the visitor centers have information desks staffed by park rangers who can help you tailor a hike to your tastes, from great photo spots to best chance of spotting a bear.

Geyser Country

With the densest collection of geothermal features in the park, **Upper Geyser Basin** contains 180 of the park's 250-odd geysers. For an easy walk, check out the predicted eruption times at the brand-new visitor center and then follow the easy boardwalk trail around the **Upper Geyser Loop**. The Firehole and Madison Rivers offer superb fly-fishing and wildlife viewing.

Old Faithful GEYSER

(Old Faithful Rd, Upper Geyser Basin) FREE You can feel the tension build as you wait for an eruption of Old Faithful - not the biggest, not the most frequent, but easily the most iconic geyser in the park. Erupting every 90 minutes, Old Faithful spouts some 30,000L (8000 gallons) of water up to 55m (180ft) in the air. Tip: the first thing to do when you arrive is to check the predicted geyser eruption times at the visitor center and then plan your explorations around these.

Old Faithful Visitor Center VISITOR CENTER

(307-545-2750; 8am-8pm mid-Apr–early Nov & mid-Dec–mid-Mar;) The new, improved and environmentally friendly center offers a bookstore and information booth and shows films 30 minutes before and 15 minutes after an eruption of Old Faithful. Kids will enjoy the Young Scientist displays, which include a working laboratory geyser and experiments involving elk jaw bones. The center closes at 5pm or 6pm outside of summer.

Grand Prismatic Spring SPRING

(Midway Geyser Basin) The park's most beautiful thermal feature is Grand Prismatic Spring.

Mammoth Country

Known for the geothermal terraces and elk herds of historic **Mammoth** and the hot springs of **Norris Geyser Basin**, Mammoth Country is North America's most volatile and oldest-known continuously active thermal area. The peaks of the Gallatin Range rise to the northwest, towering above the area's lakes, creeks and numerous hiking trails.

Mammoth Hot Springs HOT SPRINGS

The imposing **Lower** and **Upper Terraces** of Mammoth Hot Springs are the product of dissolved subterranean limestone (itself originally deposited by ancient seas), which is continuously deposited as the spring waters cool on contact with air. The mountain is in effect turning itself inside out, depositing over a ton of travertine (limestone deposits) here every year. The colored runoff from the naturally white terraces is due to the bacteria and algae that flourish in the warm waters.

An hour's worth of boardwalks wend their way around the Lower Terraces and connect to the **Upper Terraces Loop**. The rutting Rocky Mountain elk that sometimes lounge on **Opal Terrace** in fall are a favorite photo opportunity.

Surreal **Palette Springs** (accessed from the bottom parking lot) and sulfur-yellow **Canary Springs** (accessed from the top loop) are the most beautiful sites, but thermal activity is constantly in flux, so check the current state of play at the visitor center.

Roosevelt Country

Fossil forests, the commanding **Lamar River Valley** and its tributary trout streams, Tower Fall and the Absaroka Mountains' craggy peaks are the highlights of Roosevelt Country, the park's most remote, scenic and undeveloped region. Several good hikes begin near **Tower Junction**.

Tower Fall WATERFALL

Two-and-a-half miles south of Tower-Roosevelt Junction, Tower Creek plunges over 132ft Tower Fall before joining the Yellowstone River. The fall gets its name from the volcanic breccia towers around it, which are like a demonic fortress and earn it the nickname the Devil's Den. Local storytellers claim that prominent Minaret Peak gets its name from one Minnie Rhett, the girlfriend of an early park visitor, but that sounds to us like one of Jim Bridger's tall tales. Iconic landscape painter Thomas Moran created one of his most famous paintings here.

Canyon Country

A series of scenic overlooks linked by hiking trails highlight the colorful beauty and grandeur of the Grand Canyon of the Yellowstone and its impressive Lower Falls. South Rim Dr leads to the canyon's most spectacular overlook, at **Artist Point**. **Mud Volcano** is Canyon Country's primary geothermal area.

★Grand Canyon of the Yellowstone CANYON

(☎307 242 2550; ⏲Canyon Visitor Education Center late May–mid-Oct) This is one of the park's true blockbuster sights. After its placid meanderings north from Yellowstone Lake, the Yellowstone River suddenly plummets over **Upper Falls** and then the much larger **Lower Falls**, before raging through the 300m-deep (1000ft) canyon.

Lake Country

Yellowstone Lake, the centerpiece of Lake Country and one of the world's largest alpine lakes, is a watery wilderness lined with volcanic beaches and best explored by boat or sea kayak. Rising east and southeast of the lakes, the wild and snowcapped Absaroka Range hides the wildest lands in the lower 48, perfect for epic backpacking or horseback trips.

BEAT THE CROWDS

Yellowstone's wonderland attracts up to 30,000 visitors daily in July and August and over three million gatecrashers annually. Avoid the worst of the crowds with the following advice:

- Visit in May, September or October for decent weather and few people; or even in winter.
- Ditch 95% of the crowds by hiking a backcountry trail. Lose 99% by camping in a backcountry site (permit required).
- Mimic the wildlife and be most active in the golden hours after dawn and before dusk.
- Pack lunch for one of the park's many scenic picnic areas.
- Make reservations for park lodging months in advance and book concession campgrounds *at least* the day before.

Activities

Hiking

Hikers can explore Yellowstone's backcountry from more than 92 trailheads that give access to 1100 miles of hiking trails. A free backcountry-use permit, which is available at visitor centers and ranger stations, is required for overnight trips. Backcountry camping is allowed in 300 designated sites, 60% of which can be reserved in advance by mail; a $25 fee applies to all bookings that are more than three days in advance.

After much debate and a narrowly avoided fistfight, we have settled on the following as our five favorite day hikes in the park.

Lone Star Geyser Trail HIKING

This paved and pine-lined hike is an easy stroll along a former service road to one of the park's largest backcountry geysers. It's popular with both day hikers and cyclists, yet is quite a contrast to the chaotic scene around Old Faithful. Isolated Lone Star erupts every three hours for between two and 30 minutes and reaches 30ft to 45ft in height, and it's definitely worth timing your visit with an eruption – check with Old Faithful Visitor Center for predicted times.

The hike begins at the Lone Star Trailhead, above **Kepler Cascades** (where the Firehole River speeds through a spectacular gorge). The 4.8-mile round-trip walk takes 2½ hours at most.

South Rim Trail & Ribbon Lake HIKING

Southeast of the canyon's South Rim, a network of trails meanders through meadows and forests and past several small lakes. This loop links several trails and makes a nice antidote to seeing canyon views from your car. It's an incredibly varied hike, with awesome views of the Grand Canyon of the

Yellowstone & Grand Teton National Parks

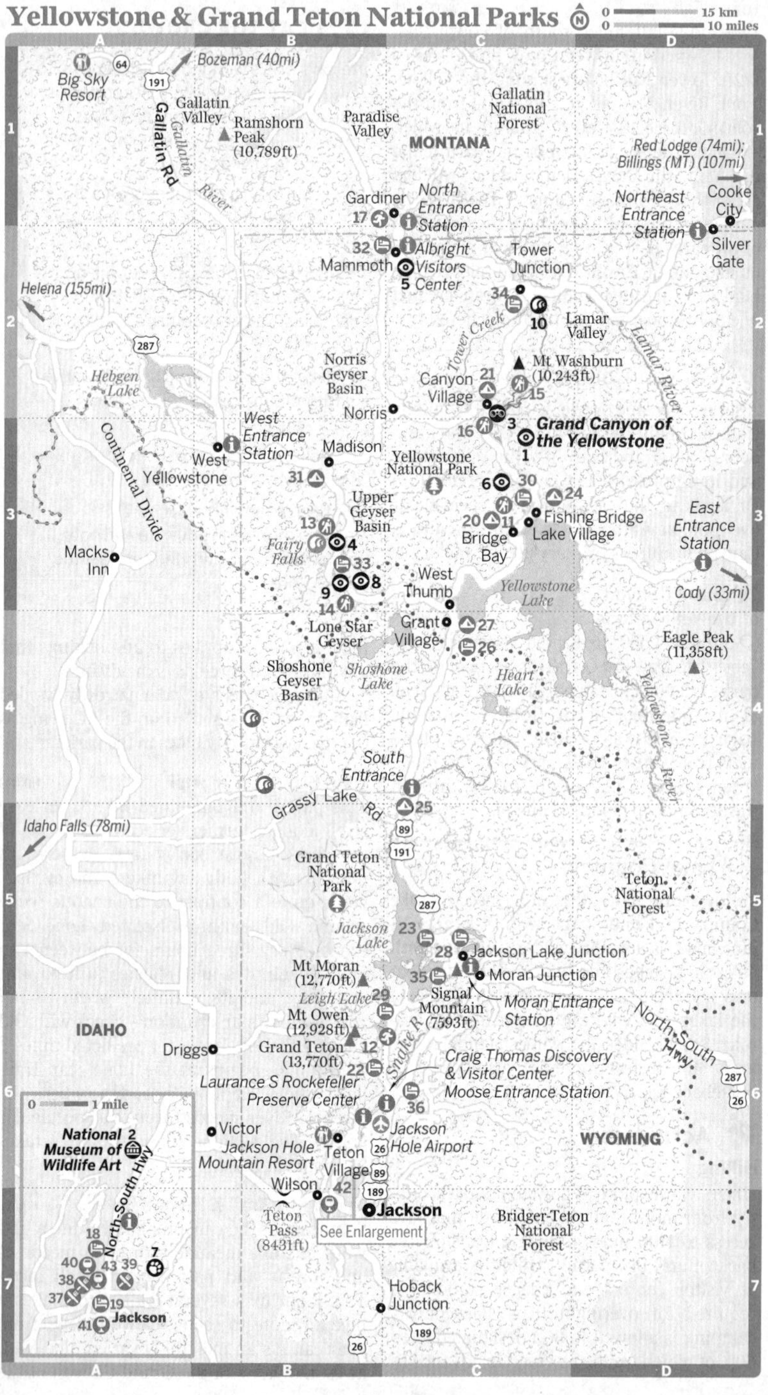
0 15 km
0 10 miles
Bozeman (40mi)
Big Sky Resort
Gallatin Valley
Gallatin Rd
Gallatin River
Ramshorn Peak (10,789ft)
Paradise Valley
Gallatin National Forest
MONTANA
Red Lodge (74mi); Billings (MT) (107mi)
Gardiner
North Entrance Station
Northeast Entrance Station
Cooke City
Silver Gate
Mammoth
Albright Visitors Center
Tower Junction
Helena (155mi)
Lamar Valley
Tower Creek
Lamar River
Mt Washburn (10,243ft)
Norris Geyser Basin
Canyon Village
Norris
Grand Canyon of the Yellowstone
Hebgen Lake
West Entrance Station
West Yellowstone
Madison
Yellowstone National Park
Continental Divide
Upper Geyser Basin
Fishing Bridge
Lake Village
Bridge Bay
East Entrance Station
Macks Inn
Fairy Falls
West Thumb
Yellowstone Lake
Cody (33mi)
Lone Star Geyser
Grant Village
Eagle Peak (11,358ft)
Shoshone Geyser Basin
Shoshone Lake
Heart Lake
Yellowstone River
South Entrance
Grassy Lake Rd
Idaho Falls (78mi)
Grand Teton National Park
Teton National Forest
Jackson Lake
Jackson Lake Junction
Moran Junction
Mt Moran (12,770ft)
Signal Mountain (7593ft)
Moran Entrance Station
Leigh Lake
Mt Owen (12,928ft)
IDAHO
Driggs
Grand Teton (13,770ft)
Snake R
North-South Hwy
Craig Thomas Discovery & Visitor Center
Moose Entrance Station
Laurance S Rockefeller Preserve Center
Jackson Hole Airport
Victor
WYOMING
Jackson Hole Mountain Resort
Teton Village
Wilson
Jackson
Teton Pass (8431ft)
See Enlargement
Bridger-Teton National Forest
Hoback Junction
0 1 mile
National Museum of Wildlife Art
North-South Hwy
Jackson

Yellowstone & Grand Teton National Parks

Top Sights

1	Grand Canyon of the Yellowstone	C3
2	National Museum of Wildlife Art	A6

Sights

3	Artist Point	C2
4	Grand Prismatic Spring	B3
5	Mammoth Hot Springs	C2
6	Mud Volcano	C3
7	National Elk Refuge	A7
8	Old Faithful	B3
9	Old Faithful Visitor Center	B3
10	Tower Falls	C2

Activities, Courses & Tours

11	Elephant Back Mountain Trail	C3
12	Exum Mountain Guides	C6
13	Fairy Falls Trail & Twin Buttes	B3
14	Lone Star Geyser Trailhead	B3
15	Mt Washburn Trail	C2
16	South Rim Trailhead	C3
17	Yellowstone Raft Company	B1

Sleeping

18	Alpine House	A7
19	Antler Inn	A7
20	Bridge Bay Campground	C3
21	Canyon Campground	C2
	Canyon Lodge	(see 21)
22	Climbers' Ranch	B6
23	Colter Bay Village	C5
24	Fishing Bridge RV Park	C3
25	Flagg Ranch Campground	C5
26	Grant Village	C4
27	Grant Village Campground	C4
28	Jackson Lake Lodge	C5
29	Jenny Lake Lodge	C6
	Lake Lodge	(see 30)
30	Lake Yellowstone Hotel	C3
31	Madison Campground	B3
32	Mammoth Hot Springs Hotel	B2
33	Old Faithful Inn	B3
	Old Faithful Lodge Cabins	(see 33)
	Old Faithful Snow Lodge	(see 33)
34	Roosevelt Lodge Cabins	C2
35	Signal Mountain Lodge	C5
36	Spur Ranch Log Cabins	C6

Eating

37	Bubba's Bar-B-Que	A7
	Jenny Lake Lodge Dining Room	(see 29)
	Lake Yellowstone Hotel Dining Room	(see 30)
38	Lotus Cafe	A7
	Mural Room	(see 28)
	Old Faithful Inn Dining Room	(see 33)
	Peaks	(see 35)
	Pioneer Grill	(see 28)
39	Snake River Grill	A7

Drinking & Nightlife

40	Million Dollar Cowboy Bar	A7
41	Snake River Brewing Co	A7
42	Stagecoach Bar	B7
43	The Rose	A7

Yellowstone (p787) and even a backcountry thermal area.

Park at Uncle Tom's parking area on the canyon's South Rim Dr and, after checking out the views of the Upper and Lower Falls from Uncle Tom's Trail, take the South Rim Trail east along the rim of the canyon to Artist Point for some of the finest canyon views available.

From Artist Point take the trail east toward Point Sublime, then branch right past Lily Pad Lake for 0.3 miles to another junction. Branch left here and descend to Ribbon Lake, actually two conjoined ponds, with a good chance of spotting moose. Allow about four hours.

Mt Washburn Trail HIKING

Opt for this fairly strenuous uphill hike from Dunraven Pass trailhead to a mountaintop fire tower for 360-degree views over the park and likely sightings of bighorn sheep (6.4 miles).

Elephant Back Mountain Trail HIKING

This popular ascent is a great short-but-sweet picnic option, suitable for families with teenagers. The stunning views from the panoramic overlook (8600ft) include Yellowstone Lake and Stevenson Island, Pelican Valley and the Absaroka Range.

The trailhead is 1 mile south of Fishing Bridge Junction and 0.5 miles north of the Lake Village turnoff on the Grand Loop Rd. From Lake Hotel it is 0.25 miles one way through the woods past Section J of the hotel's cabins. Allow about 2½ hours for the 3.5-mile loop.

Fairy Falls Trail & Twin Buttes HIKING

Tucked away in the northwest corner of the Midway Geyser Basin, 197ft Fairy Falls is a popular hike, largely because it's only a short jaunt from Old Faithful. Beyond Fairy Falls the lollipop-loop trail continues to a hidden thermal area at the base of the Twin Buttes, two conspicuous bald hills severely charred in the 1988 fires.

The geysers are undeveloped, and you're likely to have them to yourself – in stark contrast to the throngs around Grand Prismatic Spring.

The Fairy Falls (Steel Bridge) Trailhead is just west of the Grand Loop Rd, 1 mile south of the Midway Geyser Basin turnoff and 4.5 miles north of the Old Faithful overpass.

Cycling

Cyclists can ride on public roads and a few designated service roads, but not on the backcountry trails. The best season is May to October, when the roads are usually snow-free. From mid-March to mid-April the Mammoth–West Yellowstone park road is closed to cars but open to cyclists, offering a long but stress-free ride.

White-Water Rafting

Yellowstone Raft Company RAFTING
(800-858-7781; www.yellowstoneraft.com; half-day adult/child $42/32) There is exhilarating white water through Yankee Jim Canyon on the Yellowstone River just north of the park boundary in Montana. This company offers a range of guided adventures out of Gardiner starting in late May.

Sleeping

NPS and private campgrounds, along with cabins, lodges and hotels, are all available in the park. Reservations are essential in summer. Contact the park concessionaire **Xanterra** (866-439-7375, 307-344-7311; www.yellowstonenationalparklodges.com) to reserve a spot at its campsites, cabins or lodges, including all those reviewed here.

Plentiful accommodations can also be found in the gateway towns of Cody, Gardiner and West Yellowstone.

The best budget options are the seven NPS-run campgrounds (campsites from $15 to $20) in Mammoth, Tower Falls, Indian Creek, Pebble Creek, Slough Creek, Norris and Lewis Lake, which are first-come, first-served. Xanterra runs five more campgrounds (listed here; reservations accepted, $20 to $45 per night), all with cold-water bathrooms, flush toilets and drinking water. RV sites with hookups are available at Fishing Bridge.

Xanterra-run cabins, hotels and lodges are spread around the park and are open from May or June to October. Mammoth Hot Springs Hotel and Old Faithful Snow Lodge are the exceptions; these are also open mid-December through March. All places are nonsmoking and none have aircon or TV. Where wi-fi is available, it costs extra.

Bridge Bay Campground CAMPGROUND $
(sites $22.50; late May–mid-Sep) Near the west shore of Yellowstone Lake, popular with boaters, and with 430-plus sites for tents and RVs.

Canyon Campground CAMPGROUND $
(sites $27; late May-early Sep) Centrally located, with pay showers and coin laundry nearby. There are 273 sites for tents and RVs.

Fishing Bridge RV Park CAMPGROUND $
(RV site $47.75; early May-late Sep) Full hookups for hard-shell RVs only ($37). Pay showers and coin laundry. There are 325 sites.

Grant Village Campground CAMPGROUND $
(sites $27; mid-Jun–mid-Sep) On Yellowstone Lake's southwest shore, it has 430 sites for tents and RVs. Pay showers and coin laundry nearby.

Madison Campground CAMPGROUND $
(307-344-7311; www.yellowstonenationalparklodges.com; sites $22.50; early May–mid-Oct) The closest campground to Old Faithful, with 278 sites for tents and RVs.

★ **Old Faithful Inn** HOTEL $$
(866-439-7375; www.yellowstonenationalparklodges.com; old house d with shared/private bath from $108/162, standard $199-260; early May-early Oct) Next to the signature geyser, this grand inn is the most requested lodging in the park. A national historic landmark, it features an immense timber lobby, with its huge stone fireplaces and sky-high knotted-pine ceilings. Rooms come in all price ranges, and many of the most interesting historic rooms share baths. Public areas offer plenty of allure.

It's worth staying two nights to soak up the atmosphere.

Old Faithful Lodge Cabins CABIN $$
(cabins with/without bath $140/83; mid-May–early Oct) Views of Old Faithful; simple, rustic cabins.

Roosevelt Lodge CABIN $$
(866-439-7375; www.yellowstonenationalparklodges.com; cabins with/without bath $135/80; Jun-early Sep;) These cabins are good for families. With a cowboy vibe, the place offers nightly 'Old West dinner cookouts,' during which guests travel by horse or wagon to

a large meadow 3 miles from the lodge for open-air buffets (book ahead).

Lake Lodge CABIN $$
(cabins $83-194) The main lodge boasts a large porch with lakeside mountain views and a cozy room with two fireplaces. Choose from rustic 1920s wooden cabins or more modern motel-style modules.

Old Faithful Snow Lodge HOTEL $$
(cabins $109-155, r from $240-259; ⏲ May–mid-Oct & late Dec-Feb; 📶) A stylish modern option that combines timber lodge style with modern fittings and park motifs.

Lake Yellowstone Hotel HOTEL $$
(☎ 866-439-7375; www.yellowstonenationalparklodges.com; cabins $149, annex r $160, hotel r $363-405; ⏲ mid-May–early Oct; @📶) Oozing grand 1920s Western ambience, this romantic, historic hotel is a classy option. It has Yellowstone's most divine lounge, which was made for daydreaming, with big picture windows overlooking the lake, ample natural light and a live string quartet playing in the background. Rooms are well appointed, cabins more rustic.

Canyon Lodge LODGE $$
(cabins $194, r $122-222; ⏲ Jun-Sep) Centrally located, the Canyon area has the largest number of accommodations options in Yellowstone and is adding more: several new lodges were under construction at press time.

Mammoth Hot Springs Hotel HOTEL $$
(cabins $93-250, r with/without bath $140/90; ⏲ May–mid-Oct) Wide variety of sleeping options, including cabins with hot tubs; elk are often seen grazing on the front lawn.

Grant Village HOTEL $$
(Grant Village; r $160-201; ⏲ late May-Sep; 📶) Near the southern edge of the park with comfortable but uninspiring motel-style rooms. Two nearby restaurants have fabulous lake views.

Eating

Snack bars, delis, burger counters and grocery stores are scattered around the park. In addition, most of the lodges offer breakfast buffets, salad bars, and serves lunch and dinner in formal dining rooms. Food, while not always exceptional, is quite good, considering how many people the chef is cooking for, and not too overpriced for the exceptional views.

WORTH A TRIP

SCENIC DRIVE: THE ROOF OF THE ROCKIES

The most scenic route into Yellowstone Park, **Beartooth Highway** (www.beartoothhighway.com; US 212; ⏲ Jun–mid-Oct) connects Red Lodge to Cooke City and Yellowstone's north entrance by an incredible 68-mile journey alongside 11,000ft peaks and wildflower-sprinkled alpine tundra. It's been called both America's most scenic drive and its premier motorcycle ride. There are a dozen USFS campgrounds (reservations for some accepted at www.recreation.gov) along the highway, four within 12 miles of Red Lodge. Open late May or early June through early October.

★ Lake Yellowstone Hotel Dining Room AMERICAN $$$
(☎ 307-344-7311; mains $14-40; ⏲ 6:30-10am, 11:30am-2:30pm & 5-10pm mid-May–Oct; ✎) Keep one unwrinkled outfit to dine in style at the dining room of the Lake Yellowstone Hotel, the best in the park. Lunch options include Montana lamb sliders, lovely salads and bison burgers. There's a focus on local and sustainable ingredients as well as gluten-free options. Dinner reservations are strongly suggested.

Old Faithful Inn Dining Room AMERICAN $$$
(☎ 307-545-4999; dinner mains $13-29, breakfast/lunch/dinner buffet $13/16/30; ⏲ 6:30-10:30am, 11:30am-2:30pm & 5-10pm early May-Oct; ✎) The buffets here will maximize your time spent geyser gazing but the à la carte options are more innovative, with things like bison and pheasant sausages, red trout hash and the ever-popular pork osso bucco. With gluten-free options. Reservations strongly encouraged.

Information

The park is open year-round, but most roads close in winter. Park entrance permits (hiker/vehicle $12/25) are valid for seven days for entry into both Yellowstone and Grand Teton National Parks. Summer-only visitor centers are evenly spaced every 20 to 30 miles along Grand Loop Rd.

Albright Visitor Center (☎ 307-344-2263; www.nps.gov/yell; ⏲ 8am-7pm Jun-Sep, 9am-5pm Oct-May) This newly renovated visitor center in Mammoth Hot Springs serves as park headquarters. The park website is a fantastic resource.

Getting There & Away

The closest year-round airports are Yellowstone Regional Airport (p785) in Cody (52 miles); Jackson Hole Airport (p784) in Jackson (56 miles); Gallatin Field Airport (p795) in Bozeman, MT, (65 miles); and Idaho Falls Regional Airport (IDA) in Idaho Falls, ID, (107 miles). The airport (WYS) in West Yellowstone, MT, is usually open June to September. It's often more affordable to fly into Billings, MT, 170 miles away, Salt Lake City, UT, (390 miles) or Denver, CO, 563 miles away, and rent a car. There is no public transportation to or within Yellowstone National Park.

Grand Teton National Park

With its jagged, rocky peaks, cool alpine lakes and fragrant forests, the Tetons rank among the finest scenery in America. Directly south of Yellowstone, Grand Teton National Park has 12 glacier-carved summits, which frame the singular Grand Teton (13,770ft). For mountain enthusiasts, this sublime and crazy terrain is thrilling. Less crowded than Yellowstone, the Tetons also have plenty of tranquillity, along with wildlife such as bear, moose, grouse and marmot.

The park has two entrance stations: Moose (south), on Teton Park Rd west of Moose Junction; and Moran (east), on US 89/191/287 north of Moran Junction. The park is open year-round, although some roads and entrances close from around November to May 1, including part of Moose-Wilson Rd, restricting access to the park from Teton Village.

Activities

With 200 miles of **hiking trails** you can't really go wrong. Consult at the visitor center where you can grab a hiking map. A free backcountry-use permit, also available at the visitor center, is required for overnight trips. The Tetons are also known for excellent short-route **rock climbs** as well as classic longer routes to summits like Grant Teton, Mt Moran and Mt Owen; Jenny Lake Ranger Station has information.

Fishing is another draw, with several species of whitefish and cutthroat, lake and brown trout thriving in local rivers and lakes. Get a license at the Moose Village store, Signal Mountain Lodge or Colter Bay Marina.

Cross-country skiing and **snowshoeing** are the best ways to take advantage of park winters. Pick up a brochure detailing routes at Craig Thomas Discovery & Visitor Center in Moose.

Exum Mountain Guides ROCK CLIMBING
(☎307-733-2297; www.exumguides.com) For instruction and guided climbs.

Sleeping

Three different concessionaires run the park's six campgrounds. Demand is high from early July to Labor Day. Most campgrounds fill by 11am (Jenny Lake fills much earlier; Gros Ventre rarely fills up). Colter Bay and Jenny Lake have tent-only sites reserved for backpackers and cyclists.

Climbers' Ranch CABIN $
(☎307-733-7271; www.americanalpineclub.org; Teton Park Rd; dm $25; ⌚Jun-Sep) Started as a refuge for serious climbers, these rustic log cabins run by the American Alpine Club are now available to hikers who can take advantage of the spectacular in-park location. There is a bathhouse with showers and sheltered cook station with locking bins for coolers. Bring your own sleeping bag and pad (bunks are bare, but still a steal).

Flagg Ranch Campground CAMPGROUND $
(www.flaggranch.com; 2-person campsites $35, RV sites $69) Flagg Ranch campground, which also has cabins, is run by Flagg Ranch Resorts.

Grand Teton Lodge Company ACCOMMODATION SERVICES $
(☎307-543-2811; www.gtlc.com; campsites $24) This company runs most of the park's private lodges, cabins and the campgrounds of Colter Bay, Jenny Lake and Gros Ventre. It's best to reserve ahead, as nearly everything is completely booked by early June.

Colter Bay Village CABIN $$
(☎307-543-2811; www.gtlc.com; tent cabins $66, cabins with bath $155-290, without bath $85; ⌚Jun-Sep) Half a mile west of Colter Bay Junction, the village has two types of accommodations. Tent cabins (June to early September) are very basic structures with bare bunks and shared bathrooms in a separate building. At these prices, you're better off camping. The log cabins, some original, are much more comfortable and a better deal; they're available late May to late September.

Signal Mountain Lodge LODGE $$
(☎307-543-2831; www.signalmtnlodge.com; r $221-326, cabins $173-233, ste $350, tent/RV sites

$22/45; May–mid-Oct) This spectacularly located place at the edge of Jackson Lake offers cozy, well-appointed cabins and rather posh rooms with stunning lake and mountain views.

Spur Ranch Log Cabins CABIN $$
(307-733-2522; www.dornans.com; cabins $195-285; year-round) Gravel paths running through a broad wildflower meadow link these tranquil duplex cabins on the Snake River in Moose. Lodgepole pine furniture, Western styling and down bedding create a homey feel, but the views are what make it.

★ **Jenny Lake Lodge** LODGE $$$
(307-733-4647; www.gtlc.com; Jenny Lake; cabins from $699; Jun-Sep) Worn timbers, down comforters and colorful quilts imbue this elegant lodging off Teton Park Rd with a cozy atmosphere. It doesn't come cheap, but includes breakfast, a five-course dinner, bicycle use and guided horseback riding. Rainy days are for hunkering down at the fireplace in the main lodge with a game or book from the stacks.

The log cabins sport a deck but no TVs or radios (phones on request).

Jackson Lake Lodge LODGE $$$
(307-543-2811; www.gtlc.com; r & cottages $289-385; mid-May–Sep;) Aim for the main lodge, with its enormous, breathtaking picture window in the lobby framing views of the peaks. The cottages are more modern than cozy; if you go this route, ask for one with a view of Moose Pond. There's a heated pool and pets are OK in designated cottages.

Eating

Colter Bay Village, Jackson Lake Lodge, Signal Mountain and Moose Junction have several reasonably priced cafes for breakfast and fast meals.

Pioneer Grill DINER $$
(307-543-1911; Jackson Lake Lodge; mains $9-25; 6am-10:30pm;) A casual classic lunch counter with leatherette stools lined up in a maze, the Pioneer serves solid diner fare – wraps, burgers and salads. Kids adore the hot-fudge sundaes. A takeout window serves boxed lunches (order a day ahead) and room-service pizza for pooped hikers (5pm to 9pm).

Mural Room MODERN AMERICAN $$$
(307-543-1911; Jackson Lake Lodge; mains $22-44, lunch mains $12-20; 7am-9pm) With stirring views of the Tetons, gourmet selections at this classy dining room include game dishes and imaginative takes on trout. Breakfasts are very good; dinner reservations are required.

Peaks AMERICAN $$$
(307-543-2831; Signal Mountain Lodge; mains $18-38; 5:30-10pm) Dine on selections of cheese and fruit, local free-range beef and organic polenta cakes. Small plates, like wild game sliders, are also available. The indoor ambience is rather drab; hit the patio for sunsets over Jackson Lake and top-notch huckleberry margaritas. If you're here at lunchtime, try the more casual Trapper Grill (mains $11 to $14) or Deadman's Bar (all adjoining).

Jenny Lake Lodge Dining Room MODERN AMERICAN $$$
(307-543-3352; Jenny Lake Lodge; breakfast $26, lunch mains $11-15, dinner prix-fixe $88; 7am-9pm) A real splurge, this may be the only five-course wilderness meal of your life, but it's well worth it. For breakfast, try Rocky Mountain trout with eggs. Rotating five-course dinner menus include things like wild-game crepes and buffalo carpaccio. And you can't beat the atmosphere, snuggled in the Tetons. Reservations are required. Dress up in the evening.

Information

Park permits (hiker/vehicle $12/25) are valid for seven days for entry into both Yellowstone and Grand Teton National Parks. It's easy to stay in one park and explore the other in the same day.

Park Headquarters (307-739-3600; www.nps.gov/grte; 8am-7pm Jun-Aug, to 5pm Sep-May) Shares a building with the Craig Thomas Discovery & Visitor Center (307-739-3399, backcountry permits 307-739-3309; Teton Park Rd; 8am-7pm Jun-Aug, to 5pm Sep-May;) at Moose Junction.

Jenny Lake Ranger Station (307-739-3343; 8am-6pm Jun-Aug) Offers backcountry permits and climbing information.

Laurance S Rockefeller Preserve Center (307-739-3654; Moose-Wilson Rd; 8am-6pm Jun-Aug, 9am-5pm Sep-May) Learn about the new and highly recommended Rockefeller Preserve, a less crowded option for hiking. The center is 4 miles south of Moose (road is closed in winter).

MONTANA

Maybe it's the independent frontier spirit, wild and free and oh-so-American, that earned Montana its 'live and let live' state motto. The sky seems bigger and bluer. The air is crisp and pine-scented. From mountains that drop into undulating ranchlands to brick brewhouses and the shaggy grizzly found lapping at an ice-blue glacier lake, Montana brings you to that euphoric place, naturally. And then it remains with you long after you've left its beautiful spaces behind.

Information

Montana Fish, Wildlife & Parks (406-444-2535; http://fwp.mt.gov) Reservations for camping in Montana's 24 state parks can be made at 1-855-922-6768 or http://montanastateparks.reserveamerica.com.

Montana Road Conditions (800-226-7623, within Montana 511; www.mdt.mt.gov/travinfo)

Travel Montana (800-847-4868; www.visitmt.com)

Bozeman

In a gorgeous locale, surrounded by rolling green hills, pine forests and snowcapped peaks, Bozeman is the defending title holder of Coolest Town in Montana. Brick buildings with brewpubs and boutiques line historic Main St, mashing bohemian style up against cowboy cool and triathlete verve. A prime location up against the Bridger and Gallatin mountains makes it one of the best towns in the West for outdoor activities.

Sights & Activities

★Museum of the Rockies MUSEUM
(406-994-2251; www.museumoftherockies.org; 600 W Kagy Blvd; adult/child $14.50/9.50; 8am-8pm Jun-Aug, 9am-5pm Mon-Sat, noon-5pm Sun Sep-May;) Montana State University's museum is the most entertaining in Montana and shouldn't be missed, with stellar dinosaur exhibits, early Native American art and laser planetarium shows, as well as a living-history outdoors section (closed in winter) and various temporary exhibits. Guided tours happen more or less constantly and are recommended for families with young children, as they let kids get more interactive with some of the displays.

Bridger Bowl Ski Area SNOW SPORTS
(406-587-2111; www.bridgerbowl.com; 15795 Bridger Canyon Rd; day lift ticket adult/child $54/19; mid-Dec–Apr) Only in Bozeman would you find a nonprofit ski resort. But this excellent community-owned facility, 16 miles north of Bozeman, is just that. It's known for its fluffy, light powder and unbeatable prices – especially for children under 12. (Kids under six ski free.)

Sleeping

The full gamut of chain motels lies north of downtown on 7th Ave, near I-90. There are more budget motels east of downtown on Main St.

Bear Canyon Campground CAMPGROUND $
(800-438-1575; www.bearcanyoncampground.com; I-90 exit 313; tent sites $20, RV sites $30-40; May–mid-Oct;) Bear Canyon Campground is on top of a hill 3 miles east of Bozeman, with great views of the surrounding valley. There's even a pool.

Lewis & Clark Motel MOTEL $
(800-332-7666; www.lewisandclarkmotelbozeman.com; 824 W Main St; r $94-179;) For a drop of Vegas in your Montana, stay at this flashy, locally owned motel. The large rooms have floor-to-ceiling front windows and the piped 1950s music adds to the retro Rat Pack vibe. With hot tub and steam room. Prices go up on weekends in summer.

Howlers Inn B&B $$
(406-587-5229; www.howlersinn.com; 3185 Jackson Creek Rd; r $145-160, 2-person cabin $205;) Wolf-watchers will love this beautiful sanctuary 15 minutes outside of Bozeman. Rescued captive-born wolves live in enclosed natural areas on 4 acres, supported by the profits of the B&B. There are three spacious Western-style rooms in the main lodge and a two-bedroom carriage house. With luck, you will drift off to sleep serenaded by howls. Take exit 319 off I-90.

Eating & Drinking

As a college town, Bozeman has no shortage of student-oriented cheap eats and enough watering holes to quench a college football team's thirst. Most are on Main St.

Community Co-Op SUPERMARKET $
(www.bozo.coop; 908 W Main St; mains $7-12; 7am-10pm Mon-Sat, 8am-10pm Sun;) This beloved local market and deli is the best place to stock up on organic and bulk foods, as well as hot meals, salads and soups to eat in or take away. There's another branch at 44 E Main St.

★ **John Bozeman's Bistro** AMERICAN $$
(☎406-587-4100; www.johnbozemansbistro.com; 125 W Main St; mains $12-28; ⏲11:30am-2:30pm, 5-9:30pm Tue-Sat) Bozeman's best restaurant, this pretty blonde-and-gold space offers Thai, Creole and pan-Asian slants on the cowboy dinner steak, plus globally influenced soups and starters and a weekly 'superfood' special ($14.95). Service is classy, friendly and unpretentious. Lunchtime offers an $8 menu of healthy salads and sandwiches. The beer taps are all local; sample five for $8.75.

Plonk BISTRO $$$
(www.plonkwine.com; 29 E Main St; small plates $5-12, mains $15-30; ⏲11:30am-midnight Tue-Sat, from 4pm Sun & Mon Oct-Apr) Where to go for a drawn-out three-martini, gossipy lunch? Plonk serves a wide-ranging menu from light snacks to full meals, mostly made from local organic products. In summer the entire front opens up and cool breezes enter the long building, which also has a shotgun bar and pressed-tin ceilings.

Zebra Cocktail Lounge LOUNGE
(☎406-585-8851; 321 E Main St; ⏲9pm-2am) This basement-level nightclub is the epicenter of the local live-music scene, strong on club and hip-hop.

ℹ Information

Visitor Center (☎406-586-5421; www.bozemancvb.com; 2000 Commerce Way; ⏲8am-5pm Mon-Fri)

ℹ Getting There & Away

Gallatin Field Airport (BZN; ☎406-388-8321; www.bozemanairport.com) Gallatin Field Airport is 8 miles northwest of downtown.

Karst Stage (☎406-556-3540; www.karststage.com) Runs buses daily, December to April, from the airport to Big Sky ($103, one hour) and West Yellowstone ($310, two hours); summer service is by reservation only.

Gallatin & Paradise Valleys

Outdoor enthusiasts could explore the expansive beauty around the Gallatin and Paradise Valleys for days. **Big Sky Resort** (☎800-548-4486; www.bigskyresort.com; Big Sky; lift tickets adult $103, child over/under 10 $83/53), with multiple mountains, 400in of annual powder and Montana's longest vertical drop (4350ft), is one of the nation's premier downhill and cross-country ski destinations, especially now it has merged with neighboring Moonlight Basin. Lift lines are the shortest in the Rockies, and if you are traveling with kids then Big Sky is too good a deal to pass up – children under 10 ski free if you book lodging through the resort's central reservations system. In summer it offers gondola-served hiking and mountain-biking.

For backpacking and backcountry skiing, head to the Spanish Peaks section of the **Lee Metcalf Wilderness**. It covers 389 sq miles of Gallatin and Beaverhead National Forest land west of US 191. Numerous scenic USFS campgrounds snuggle up to the Gallatin Range on the east side of US 191.

Twenty miles south of Livingston, off US 89 en route to Yellowstone, unpretentious **Chico Hot Springs** (☎406-333-4933; www.chicohotsprings.com; 1 Old Chico Rd, Pray; 2-person cabin $237, main lodge r $61-98; ⏲7am-11pm; 👪)

MONTANA FACTS

Nickname Treasure State, Big Sky Country

Population 1,024,000

Area 145,552 sq miles

Capital city Helena (population 29,500)

Other cities Billings (population 109,000), Missoula (population 69,000), Bozeman (population 39,800)

Sales tax No state sales tax

Birthplace of Movie star Gary Cooper (1901–61), motorcycle daredevil Evel Knievel (1938–2007), actress Michelle Williams (1980)

Home of Crow, Blackfeet and Salish Native Americans

Politics Republican ranchers and oil-execs generally edge out the Democratic students and progressives of left-leaning Bozeman and Missoula

Famous for Fly-fishing, cowboys and grizzly bears

Random fact Some Montana highways didn't have a speed limit until the 1990s!

Driving distances Bozeman to Denver 695 miles, Missoula to Whitefish 133 miles

DON'T MISS

FLY-FISHING IN BIG SKY

Ever since Robert Redford and Brad Pitt made it look sexy in the 1992 classic *A River Runs Through It*, Montana has been closely tied to fly-fishing cool. Whether you are just learning or you're a world-class trout wrangler, the wide, fast rivers are always spectacularly beautiful and filled with fish. Although the film – and the book it is based on – is set in Missoula and the nearby Blackfoot River, the movie was actually shot around Livingston and the Yellowstone and Gallatin Rivers.

For DIY trout fishing, the Gallatin River, 8 miles southwest of Bozeman along Hwy 191, has the most accessible, consistent angling spots, closely followed by the beautiful Yellowstone River, 25 miles east of Bozeman in the Paradise Valley.

For the scoop on differences between rainbow, brown and cutthroat trout – as well as flies, rods and a Montana fishing license – visit **Bozeman Angler** (406-587-9111; www.bozemanangler.com; 23 E Main St; one-day class adult/child $125/75; 9am-5:30pm Mon-Sat, to 4pm Sun). Owned by a local couple for nearly two decades, the downtown shop runs a great introduction-to-fly-fishing class ($125 per person, casting lessons $40 per hour) on the second Saturday of the month between May and September.

has garnered quite a following in the last few years, even attracting celebrity residents from Hollywood. Some come to soak in the swimming-pool-sized, open-air hot pools (admission for nonguests is $8.50), others for the lively bar hosting swinging country-and-western dance bands on weekends. The on-site restaurant (mains $20 to $32) is known for fine steak and seafood. You can stay here overnight, too. It's not called Paradise for nothing.

Absaroka Beartooth Wilderness

The fabulous, vista-packed Absaroka Beartooth Wilderness covers more than 943,377 acres and is perfect for a solitary adventure. Thick forests, jagged peaks and marvelous, empty stretches of alpine tundra are all found in this wilderness, saddled between Paradise Valley in the west and Yellowstone National Park in the south. The thickly forested Absaroka Range dominates the area's west half and is most easily reached from Paradise Valley or the Boulder River Corridor. The Beartooth Range's high plateau and alpine lakes are best reached from the Beartooth Hwy south of Red Lodge (closed October to May). Because of its proximity to Yellowstone, the Beartooth portion gets two-thirds of the area's traffic.

A picturesque old mining town with fun bars and restaurants and a good range of places to stay, **Red Lodge** offers great day hikes, backpacking and, in winter, skiing right near town. The **Red Lodge Visitor Center** (406-446-1718; www.redlodge.com; 601 N Broadway Ave; 10am-4pm Mon-Fri) has information on accommodations; hikers should seek out the **Yodeler** (406-446-1435; www.yodelermotel.com; 601 S Broadway Ave; basement r from $60, upper level from $90;), whose owners have great intel on local trails. For fancier digs, try the **Pollard** (406-446-0001; www.thepollard.net; 2 N Broadway Ave; r $150-195, ste $185-265;).

Billings

It's hard to believe laid-back little Billings is Montana's largest city. The friendly oil and ranching center is not a must-see but makes for a decent overnight pit stop. The historic downtown has its own unpolished charm.

Sleeping

Dude Rancher Lodge MOTEL $
(800-221-3302; www.duderancherlodge.com; 415 N 29th St; d from $89;) Road-weary travelers will appreciate this downtown motor lodge, a fine and friendly motel with groovy oak furniture dating back to the 1940s, Western touches like split-log paneling and cattle-brand carpet, plus flat-screen TVs and in-room coffee. The attached diner is a local breakfast favorite.

Eating & Drinking

Harper & Madison CAFE $
(406-281-8550; 3115 10th Ave N; mains $7-9; 7am-4pm Mon-Fri, to 1pm Sat) With a hefty dose of Martha Stewart, this sweet cafe does some brisk business. It's no wonder with the

excellent coffee, homemade quiches, and gourmet salads and sandwiches. If you're rushing to hit the road, grab some French pastries to go.

Walkers Grill MODERN AMERICAN $$
(www.walkersgrill.com; 2700 1st Ave N; tapas $5-12, mains $15-36; ⏲5-10pm) Upscale Walkers offers good grill items and fine tapas at the bar (open from 4pm), in a large-windowed, elegant space.

Doc Harper's BAR
(116 N Broadway; cocktails $7-9; ⏲4pm-midnight Mon-Sat) This long, narrow, pretty martini bar is run by a lawyer who won a (hard-to-get) liquor license in a state lottery and named the place after his dad, a physician who delivered hundreds of babies in the area. Slink up to the mezzanine or sit at the bar and watch the cocktail magic happen.

Getting There & Away

Logan International Airport (BIL; www.flybillings.com) Logan International Airport, 2 miles north of downtown, has direct flights to Salt Lake City, Denver, Minneapolis, Seattle, Phoenix and destinations within Montana.

Bus Depot (☎406-245-5116; 2502 1st Ave N; ⏲24hr) The bus depot has services to Bozeman ($37, three hours) and Missoula ($77, seven hours) twice daily.

WORTH A TRIP

CUSTER'S LAST STAND

The best detour from Billings is to the **Little Bighorn Battlefield National Monument** (☎406-638-3224; www.nps.gov/libi; US 212; per car $10; ⏲8am-9pm), 65 miles outside town in the arid plains of the Crow (Apsaalooke) Indian Reservation. Home to one of the USA's best-known Native American battlefields, this is where General George Custer made his famous 'last stand.'

Custer, and 272 soldiers, messed one too many times with Native Americans (including Crazy Horse of the Lakota Sioux), who overwhelmed the force in a frequently painted massacre. A visitor center tells the tale or, better, take one of the five daily tours with a Crow guide through **Apsaalooke Tours** (☎406-638-3897; adult/child $10/5; ⏲hourly 10am-3pm Memorial Day-Labor Day). The entrance is a mile east of I-90 on US 212. If you're here for the last weekend of June, the **Custer's Last Stand Re-enactment** (www.littlebighornreenactment.com; adult/child $20/10) is an annual hoot, 6 miles west of Hardin.

Helena

With one foot in cowboy legend (Gary Cooper was born here) and the other in the more hip, less stereotypical lotus land of present-day Montana, diminutive Helena is one of the nation's smallest state capitals (population 29,500), a place where white-collared politicians draft legislation, while white-knuckle adventurers race into the foothills to indulge in that other Montana passion.

Back in town, half hidden among the Gore-Tex and outdoor outfitters, you will find an unexpected Gallic-inspired, neo-Gothic cathedral. Another pleasant surprise is the artsy pedestrian-only shopping quarter along Last Chance Gulch.

Sights & Activities

State Capitol LANDMARK
(cnr Montana Ave & 6th St; ⏲7am-6pm Mon-Fri, 9am-3pm Sat & Sun) FREE This grand neoclassical building was completed in 1902 and is known for its beacon-like dome, richly decorated with gold-rimmed paintings inside.

Cathedral of St Helena CHURCH
(530 N Ewing St; ⏲tours 1pm Tue-Thu) Rising like an apparition from old Europe over the town is this neo-Gothic cathedral completed in 1914. Highlights include the baptistery, organ and intricate stained-glass windows.

Holter Museum of Art MUSEUM
(www.holtermuseum.org; 12 E Lawrence St; ⏲10am-5:30pm Tue-Sat, noon-4pm Sun) FREE This museum in downtown Helena exhibits contemporary art by Montana artists in a variety of mediums.

Mt Helena City Park HIKING, CYCLING
Nine hiking and mountain-biking trails wind through Mt Helena City Park, including one that takes you to the 5460ft-high summit of Mt Helena.

Sleeping & Eating

East of downtown near I-15 is the usual string of chain motels.

Sanders B&B $$
(406-442-3309; www.sandersbb.com; 328 N Ewing St; r $130-145;) A historic B&B with seven elegant guest rooms, a wonderful old parlor and a breezy front porch. Each bedroom is unique and thoughtfully decorated, and it's run by a relative of the Ringling Brothers Circus family, with appropriate memorabilia.

Fire Tower Coffee House CAFE, BREAKFAST $
(www.firetowercoffee.com; 422 Last Chance Gulch; breakfast $4-9; 6am-6pm Mon-Fri, 7am-3pm Sat;) This eclectic space toward the lower end of Last Chance Gulch is a hub for coffee, light meals and live music on Friday evenings. The menu features pastries, granola, breakfast burritos and a wholesome sandwich selection.

Information

Helena Visitor Center (406-442-4120; www.helenachamber.com; 225 Cruse Ave; 8am-5pm Mon-Fri)

Getting There & Away

Helena Regional Airport (HNL; www.helenaairport.com) Two miles north of downtown, Helena Regional Airport operates flights to most other airports in Montana, as well as to Salt Lake City, Denver and Minneapolis.

Missoula

Outsiders in Missoula usually spend the first 30 minutes wondering where they took a wrong turn: Austin, Texas? Portland, Oregon? Canada, perhaps? The confusion is understandable given the city's lack of standard Montana stereotypes. There's no Wild West saloons here and even fewer errant cowboys. Instead, Missoula is a refined university city with ample green space and abundant home pride.

Not surprisingly, its metro-west bounty is contagious. Though it's among the fastest-growing cities in the US, sensible planning means that Missoula rarely feels clamorous. The small traffic-calmed downtown core, with its interesting array of historic buildings, invites exploration by foot or bicycle.

Sights

Missoula is a great city for walking, especially in the spring and summer, when enough people emerge onto its broad streets to give it a definable metro personality.

Missoula Art Museum MUSEUM
(www.missoulaartmuseum.org; 335 North Pattee; 10am-5pm Tue-Sat) FREE All hail a city that encourages free-thinking art and then displays it free of charge in a sleek building that seamlessly grafts a contemporary addition onto a 100-year-old library.

Smokejumper Visitor Center MUSEUM
(W Broadway; 10am-4pm Jun-Aug) FREE Located 7 miles west of downtown, near the airport, is this active base for the heroic men and women who parachute into forests to combat raging wildfires. Its visitor center has thought-provoking displays that do a great job illustrating the life of the Western firefighter.

Activities

Clark Fork River Trail System CYCLING, HIKING
Taking advantage of its location astride the Clark Fork River, Missoula has built an attractive riverside trail system punctuated by numerous parks. **Caras Park** is the most central and active green space, with over a dozen annual festivals and a unique hand-carved carousel.

Mount Sentinel HIKING
A steep switchback trail from behind the football stadium leads up to a concrete whitewashed 'M' (visible for miles around) on 5158ft Mt Sentinel. Tackle it on a warm summer's evening for glistening views of this much-loved city and its spectacular environs.

Adventure Cycling HQ CYCLING
(www.adventurecycling.org; 150 E Pine St; 8am-5pm Mon-Fri year-round, also 9am-1pm Sat Jun-Aug) The HQ for America's premier nonprofit bicycle travel organization is something of a pilgrimage site for cross-continental cyclists, many of whom plan their route to pass through Missoula. Staff offer a warm welcome and plenty of cycling information.

Sleeping & Eating

All the usual chain hotels are represented, many along W Broadway within an easy walk of the city center.

Goldsmith's Bed & Breakfast B&B $$
(406-728-1585; www.missoulabedandbreakfast.com; 809 E Front St; r $129-164;) This delightful riverside B&B was once a frat house,

and before that, home to the university's president. The wraparound deck is the perfect place to kick back with other guests or a good novel. Comfy Victorian-style rooms are simply lovely. Some have private decks, river views, fireplaces and reading nooks.

★Silk Road INTERNATIONAL **$$**
(www.silkroadcatering.com; 515 S Higgins; tapas $6-11; ⏲5-10pm Wed-Sat) Spanning global dishes from the Ivory Coast to Piedmont, Silk Road takes on lesser-known world cuisine and, more often than not, nails it. Dishes are tapas-sized, allowing you to mix and match. A warm welcome and an ambience of cushions and candlelit tapestries set the scene.

Caffe Dolce MODERN AMERICAN **$$**
(☎406-830-3055; www.caffedolcemissoula.com; 500 Brooks St; breakfast $6-11, lunch & dinner mains $7-36; ⏲7am-9pm Mon-Thu, 7am-10pm Fri, 8am-9pm Sat, 9am-2pm Sun) In a stately stone building, this chic local favorite is abuzz with well-clad Missoulians getting their fix of gelato, pastries, wine and gorgeous salads. Dinner can be pricey, but exotic pizzas offer a lighter, cheaper option. Coffee is a serious business here; this is your best bet for a good breakfast. Patio seating.

Dolce is located south of the town center on route 12.

Drinking & Nightlife

★Liquid Planet COFFEE
(www.liquidplanet.com; 223 N Higgins; ⏲7:30am-9pm) Considering how much Missoula loves its beverages, it's no surprise Liquid Planet was born here. Opened by a university professor in 2003, it's a sustainable coffeehouse, cafe and bottle shop selling carefully curated wines and craft beers, loose-leaf tea, coffee beans (with handwritten pedigrees) and sports drinks.

Draught Works BREWERY
(915 Toole Ave; pints $4; ⏲noon-9pm) This cool brewery in a rehabbed industrial-chic building serves great pints with saucy names (try a 'That's What She Said' cream ale) and free pretzel snacks. There's no menu, but most days you can order from food carts in the parking lot.

The Old Post BAR
(103 W Spruce St; mains $8-12; ⏲11am-2:30am Mon-Fri, from 9am Sat & Sun) This comfortable, unpretentious Western bar has a lived-in feel, with well-worn booths and bar stools and a cozy little patio out back. Great beer on tap, friendly servers and decent pub food – what's not to love?

Information

Visitor Center (☎406-532-3250; http://destinationmissoula.org; 101 E Main St; ⏲8am-5pm Mon-Fri) Destination Missoula has a useful website as well as a walk-in space downtown.

Getting There & Around

Missoula International Airport (MSO; www.flymissoula.com; 5225 Hwy 10 W) Missoula International Airport is 5 miles west of Missoula on US 10 W (which becomes W Broadway in town).

Depot (1660 W Broadway) Greyhound buses serve most of the state and stop at the depot, 1 mile west of town.

Flathead Lake

The largest natural freshwater lake west of the Mississippi, sitting not an hour's drive from Glacier National Park, completes western Montana's embarrassment of natural lures. The lake's north shore is dominated by the nothing-to-write-home-about city of **Kalispell**; far more interesting is the southern end embellished by the small polished settlement of **Polson**, which sits on the Flathead Indian Reservation.

Sights & Activities

Flathead Lake's eastern shore is kissed by the mysterious Mission Mountains and dotted with apple orchards, cottages and fruit stands, while the west offers patches of evergreen, small farms and grassy hills. To get the best all-round view, hit the water. Soloists can kayak or canoe the conceptual **Flathead Lake Marine Trail** (fwp.mt.gov/recreation/activities/boating) which links various state parks and campsites around the lake.

Miracle of America Museum MUSEUM
(www.miracleofamericamuseum.org; 58176 Hwy 93, Polson; adult/child $6/3; ⏲8am-8pm Mon-Sat, to 3pm Sun) For a concentrated dose of Americana, visit this museum 2 miles south of Polson on Hwy 93. At turns baffling and fascinating, it consists of 5 acres cluttered with the leftovers of American history. Wander past old motorcycles, a reconstructed soda fountain, chainsaws, old quilts and countless other weird artifacts, including the biggest buffalo (now stuffed) ever recorded in Montana.

Lake Cruises BOATING
(406-883-3636; www.kwataqnuk.com; Polson; family/adult/child $40/15/free, dinner cruise $30) Lake cruises are run out of the Kwataqnuk Resort in Polson. Departure times vary by season; most cruises are one to two hours. Dinner cruises leave at 7pm Thursdays and Sundays.

Sleeping & Eating

Flathead Lake Marine Trail Campsites CAMPGROUND $
(855-922-6768, 406-751-4577; http://montanastateparks.reserveamerica.com; tent sites from $10) Montana Fish & Wildlife maintains camp sites along the Flathead Lake Marine Trail. The nearest site to Polson is Finley Point, 5.5 miles away by water.

Kwataqnuk Resort HOTEL $$
(406-883-3636; www.kwataqnuk.com; 49708 US 93, Polson; r from $115; P) The lakeside Kwataqnuk Resort, run by the Salish and Kootenai tribes, has a boat dock, indoor pool and a mellow casino-lounge. The spacious rooms have balconies, Keurig coffeemakers, mini-fridges and microwaves; even-numbered rooms have impressive lake views.

Betty's Diner DINER $
(49779 US 93, Polson; mains $8-15; 7am-8pm Mon-Sat, to 3pm Sun) This lurid-pink diner delivers salt-of-the-earth American food – burgers, steaks and omelets – with customary Montana charm.

Information

Visitor Center (www.polsonchamber.com; 418 Main St; 9am-5pm Mon-Fri) The chamber of commerce has visitor information.

Bob Marshall Wilderness Complex

Away from the Pacific coast, America's northwest harbors some of the most lightly populated areas in the lower 48. Case in point: the Bob Marshall Wilderness Complex, an astounding 2344 sq miles of land strafed with 3200 miles of trails including sections that are a 40-mile slog from the nearest road. And you thought the US was car-obsessed.

Running roughly from the southern boundary of Glacier National Park in the north to Rogers Pass (on Hwy 200) in the south, there are actually three designated wilderness areas within the complex: Great Bear, Bob Marshall and Scapegoat. On the periphery the complex is buffered with national-forest lands offering campgrounds, road access to trailheads and quieter country when 'the Bob' (as locals and park rangers call it) hosts hunters in fall.

The main access point to the Bob from the south is from Hwy 200 via the **Monture Guard Station Cabin** (406-677-2233; www.recreation.gov; cabins $60; Dec-Apr), on the wilderness perimeter. To reach it you'll need to drive 7 miles north of Ovando and snowshoe or hike the last mile to your private abode at the edge of the gorgeous Lewis and Clark Range. Contact the forest service about reservations.

Other Bob access points include the Seeley-Swan Valley in the west, Hungry Horse Reservoir in the north and the Rocky Mountain Front in the east. The easiest (and busiest) access routes are from the Benchmark and Gibson Reservoir trailheads in the Rocky Mountain Front.

Trails generally start steep, reaching the wilderness boundary after around 7 miles. It takes another 10 miles or so to really get into the Bob's heart. Good day-hikes run from all sides. Two USFS districts tend to the Bob, **Flathead National Forest Headquarters** (406-758-5208; www.fs.fed.us/r1/flathead; 650 Wolfpack Way; 8am-4:30pm Mon-Fri) and **Lewis & Clark National Forest Supervisors** (406-791-7700; www.fs.fed.us/r1/lewis-clark; 1101 15th St N, Great Falls; 8am-4:30pm Mon-Fri).

Whitefish

One square mile of rustic Western chic, tiny Whitefish (population 8000) easily charms. Once sold as the main gateway to Glacier National Park, this charismatic and caffeinated New West town merits a visit on its own. Aside from grandiose Glacier (an easy day's cycling distance), Whitefish is home to an attractive stash of restaurants, a historic railway station and an underrated ski resort.

Sights & Activities

Stumptown Historical Society Museum MUSEUM
(www.stumptownhistoricalsociety.org; 500 Depot St; 10am-4pm Mon-Sat;) FREE Whitefish's fine old Tudor Revival Great Northern Railway Depot, built in the 1920s, doubles as a history museum displaying train memorabilia and fascinating photos of early Whitefish.

Whitefish Mountain Resort SNOW SPORTS
(☎406-862-2900; www.bigmtn.com; adult/child $71/37) Whitefish Mountain Resort, known as Big Mountain until 2008, guards 3000 acres of varied ski terrain and offers night skiing on weekends. In the summer there's lift-assisted mountain biking and ziplines.

Sleeping

Whitefish Lake State Park Campground CAMPGROUND $
(☎406-862-3991; State Park Rd; camp sites $20; ⏲late May-early Oct) On the southwest edge of Whitefish Lake, shady forested grounds hold 25 first-come, first-served sites, including one that is wheelchair-friendly.

Downtowner Inn MOTEL $$
(☎406-862-2535; www.downtownermotel.cc; 224 Spokane Ave; r from $130; ❄@📶) Cozier than the chain motels that line US 93 south of Whitefish, the cheerful Downtowner has spacious rooms, friendly staff and a morning bagel bar. (There's no longer a Jacuzzi and fitness center, though, despite the signs.)

Eating & Drinking

★**Buffalo Café** CAFE $
(www.buffalocafewhitefish.com; 514 3rd St E; breakfast mains $8-10; ⏲7am-2pm & 5-9pm Mon-Sat, from 8am Sun) Hopping with neighborly locals, the Buffalo serves hearty meals a step above standard cafe fare. Try the 'Buffalo pie,' a mountain of poached eggs and various add-ins (cheese, veggies, bacon) piled atop a wedge of hash browns. You won't leave hungry.

Great Northern Brewing Co BREWPUB
(☎406-863-1000; www.greatnorthernbrewing.com; 2 Central Ave; ⏲tours 1pm & 3pm Mon-Thu) Stop in to this high-ceilinged brewpub and tasting room for a pint or sampler anytime, or join a tour to up your beer-nerd game.

Information

Whitefish Visitor Center (www.whitefishvisit.com; 307 Spokane Ave; ⏲9am-5pm Mon-Fri) Check with the Whitefish Visitor Center for info on activities.

Getting There & Away

Railroad Depot (☎406-862-2268; 500 Depot St; ⏲6am-1:30pm, 4:30pm-midnight) Amtrak stops daily at Whitefish's railroad depot en route to West Glacier ($7, 30 minutes) and East Glacier ($15, two hours).

Glacier National Park

Few national parks are as magnificent and pristine as Glacier. Created in 1910 during the first flowering of the American conservationist movement, Glacier easily ranks with Yellowstone, Yosemite and the Grand Canyon.

Apart from stunning mountain scenery, it is renowned for its historic 'parkitecture' lodges, the spectacular Going-to-the-Sun Road, and an intact pre-Columbian ecosystem. This is the only place in the lower 48 states where grizzly bears still roam in abundance. Smart park management has kept the place accessible, yet authentically wild (there is no populated town site à la Banff or Jasper). Among a slew of outdoor attractions, the park is particularly noted for its hiking, wildlife-spotting and sparkling lakes, ideal for boating and fishing.

Although Glacier's tourist numbers are relatively high (two million a year), few visitors stray far from the Going-to-the-Sun Road and almost all visit between June and September. Choose your moment and splendid isolation is yours for the taking. The park remains open year-round; however, most services and parts of the Going-to-the-Sun Road are open only from mid-May to September.

Glacier's 1562 sq miles are divided into five regions, each centered on a ranger station: Polebridge (northwest); Lake McDonald (southwest), including the West Entrance and Apgar village; Two Medicine (southeast); St Mary (east); and Many Glacier (northeast). The approximate 50-mile Going-to-the-Sun Road is the only paved road that traverses the park.

Sights & Activities

Going-to-the-Sun Road OUTDOORS
(⏲mid-Jun–late Sep) A strong contender for the most spectacular road in America, the approximate 50-mile Going-to-the-Sun Road is a national historic landmark, flanked by hiking trails and a mountain pass and served by a free shuttle.

The road skirts near shimmering Lake McDonald before angling sharply to the **Garden Wall** – the main dividing line between the west and east sides of the park. At Logan Pass you can – and should – stroll 1.5 miles to **Hidden Lake Overlook**; heartier hikers can try the one-way, 7.6-mile **Highline Trail**. The shuttle stops on the western side of the road at the trailhead for **Avalanche Lake**, an easy 4-mile return hike to a stunning alpine lake in a cirque beautified with numerous weeping waterfalls.

Many Glacier HIKING

Anchored by the historic 1915 Many Glacier Lodge and sprinkled with more lakes than glaciers, this picturesque valley on the park's east side has some tremendous hikes, some of which link to the Going-to-the-Sun Road. A favorite is the 9.4-mile (return) **Iceberg Lake Trail**, a steep but rewarding jaunt through flower meadows and pine forest to an iceberg-infested lake.

Glacier Park Boat Co BOAT TOUR

(☎406-257-2426; www.glacierparkboats.com; St Mary Lake cruise adult/child $25.50/12.50) Rents out kayaks and canoes, and runs popular lake cruises, some with guided hikes included in the price, from five locations in Glacier National Park.

Sleeping

There are 13 **NPS campgrounds** (☎406-888-7800; www.recreation.gov; tent & RV sites $10-23) and seven historic lodges in the park, dating from the early 1900s, which operate between mid-May and the end of September. Of the camp sites, only Fish Creek and St Mary can be reserved in advance (up to five months). Sites fill by mid-morning, particularly in July and August.

★**Many Glacier Hotel** HISTORIC HOTEL $$

(☎855-733-4522; www.glaciernationalparklodges.com; r US$165-225, ste US$330; ⏰mid-Jun–mid-Sep; 📶) Modeled after a Swiss chalet, this national historic landmark on Swiftcurrent Lake is the park's largest hotel, with 215 rooms, many with panoramic views. Evening entertainment, a lounge and fine-dining restaurant specializing in fondue all add to the appeal.

Lake McDonald Lodge HISTORIC HOTEL $$

(☎855-733-4522; www.glaciernationalparklodges.com; r US$85-190, cabins US$140-205, ste US$329; ⏰mid-May–Sep; 📶) 🍃 Built in 1913, this old hunting lodge is adorned with stuffed-animal trophies and exudes relaxation. The 100 rooms are lodge, cabin or motel style. Nightly park-ranger talks and lake cruises add a rustic ambience. There's a restaurant and pizzeria.

Glacier Park Lodge HISTORIC HOTEL $$

(☎406-226-5600; www.glacierparkinc.com; r $169-256; ⏰Jun-Sep; 📶🏊) 🍃 The park's flagship lodge is a graceful, elegant place featuring interior balconies supported by Douglas fir timbers and a massive stone fireplace in the lobby. It's an aesthetically appealing, historically charming and very comfortable place to stay. Pluses include nine holes of golf and cozy reading nooks.

Rising Sun Motor Inn MOTEL $$

(☎855-733-4522; www.glaciernationalparklodges.com; r US$135, cabin US$140; ⏰Jun–mid-Sep; 📶) One of two classic 1940s-era wooden motels, the Rising Sun lies on the north shore of St Mary Lake in a small complex that includes a store, restaurant and boat launch. The rustic rooms and cabins offer everything an exhausted hiker could hope for.

Eating

In summer there are grocery stores with limited camping supplies in Apgar, Lake McDonald Lodge, Rising Sun and at the Swiftcurrent Motor Inn. Most lodges have on-site restaurants. Dining options in West Glacier and St Mary offer mainly hearty hiking fare.

Polebridge Mercantile BAKERY, GROCERY $

(☎406-888-5105; www.polebridgemerc.com; Polebridge Loop Rd, North Fork Valley; pastries from $4; ⏰8am-6pm mid-May–Nov; 📶) An odd little grocery store reached via the scenic dirt road to Bowman Lake, Polebridge Mercantile has all the odds and ends you forgot you needed, plus huge cinnamon buns, known to pump a good couple of hours into tired hiking legs.

Park Café AMERICAN $$

(☎406-732-9979; www.parkcafe.us; US 89; mains US$12-25; ⏰7:30am-9pm Jun-Sep) Offers hearty breakfasts until noon, and comes recommended for the homemade pies topped in whipped cream or ice cream.

Ptarmigan Dining Room INTERNATIONAL $$$

(Many Glacier Hotel; mains $15-35; ⏰6:30am-9:30pm, mid-Jun–mid-Sep) With its lakeside views, this is the most refined of the lodge restaurants, also serving wine and microbrews.

Information

Visitor centers and ranger stations in the park sell field guides and hand out hiking maps. Those at Apgar and St Mary are open daily May to October; the visitor center at Logan Pass is open when the Going-to-the-Sun Road is open. The Many Glacier, Two Medicine and Polebridge Ranger Stations close at the end of September. **Park headquarters** (☎406-888-7800; www.nps.gov/glac; ⏰8am-4:30pm Mon-Fri year-round) is in West Glacier between US 2 and Apgar.

Entry to the park (hiker/vehicle $12/25) is valid for seven days. Day-hikers don't need permits, but overnight backpackers do (May to October only). Half of the permits are available on a first-come, first-served basis from the **Apgar Backcountry Permit Center** (Apgar Village; permit per person per day $4; ⌚ May-Oct), St Mary Visitor Center, and the Many Glacier, Two Medicine and Polebridge ranger stations.

The other half can be reserved at the Apgar Backcountry Permit Center, St Mary and Many Glacier visitor centers and Two Medicine and Polebridge ranger stations.

Getting There & Around

Amtrak's *Empire Builder* train stops daily at West Glacier (year round) and East Glacier Park (April to October) on its route between Seattle and Chicago. **Glacier National Park** (www.nps.gov/glac) runs free shuttles from Apgar Village to St Mary over Going-to-the-Sun Road from July 1 to Labor Day. **Glacier Park, Inc** (www.glacierparkinc.com) offers the East Side Shuttle ($15 to $45 depending on route) on the eastern side of the park with daily links to Waterton (Canada), Many Glacier, St Mary, Two Medicine and East Glacier; reserve in advance.

IDAHO

Famous for not being particularly famous, the nation's 43rd state is a pristine wilderness of Alaskan proportions, rudely ignored by passing traffic heading west to Seattle or east to Montana. In truth, much of this lightly trodden land is little changed since the days of Lewis and Clark, including a vast 15,000-sq-km 'hole' in the middle of the state and bereft of roads, settlements, or any other form of human interference.

Flatter, dryer southern Idaho is largely dominated by the Snake River, deployed as a transportation artery by early settlers on the Oregon Trail and tracked today by busy Hwy 84. But, outside of this narrow populated strip, the Idaho landscape is refreshingly free of the soulless strip-mall, fast-food infestations so ubiquitous elsewhere in the US.

Boise

Understated, underrated and under-appreciated, Idaho's state capital (and largest city) gets little name recognition from people outside the northwest. The affable downtown impresses unsuspecting visitors with the modest spirit of an underdog. Cool surprises include Basque culture, a grandiose Idaho capitol building and a fair number of well-heeled bars and Parisian-style bistros. There's also a university campus and enough greenery to make its 'city of trees' moniker more than just a marketing ploy. Boise leaves a lasting impression – primarily because it's not supposed to.

Sights & Activities

Idaho State Capitol LANDMARK
(700 W Jefferson St; ⌚ 6am-10pm Mon-Fri, 9am-5pm Sat & Sun) FREE The joy of US state capitol buildings is that visitors can admire some of the nation's best architecture for free. The Boise building, constructed from native sandstone, celebrates the neoclassical style in vogue when it was built in 1920. It was extensively refurbished in 2010 and is now heated with geothermal hot water.

Ridge to Rivers Trail System HIKING
(www.ridgetorivers.org) More rugged than Boise's greenbelt are the scrub- and brush-covered foothills above town, offering 75 miles of scenic, sometimes strenuous hiking and mountain-biking routes. The most immediate access from downtown is via Fort Boise Park on E Fort St, five blocks southeast of the state capitol building.

Basque Block

Unbeknownst to many, Boise harbors one of the largest Basque populations outside Spain. European émigrés first arrived in the 1910s to work as Idaho shepherds. Elements of their distinct culture can be glimpsed along Grove St between 6th St and Capitol Blvd.

Basque Museum & Cultural Center MUSEUM
(www.basquemuseum.com; 611 Grove St; adult/child $5/3; ⌚ 10am-4pm Tue-Fri, 11am-3pm Sat) Sandwiched between the ethnic taverns, restaurants and bars is the Basque Museum & Cultural Center, a commendable effort to unveil the intricacies of Basque culture and how it was transposed 6000 miles west to Idaho. Language lessons in Euskara, one of Europe's oldest languages, are held here.

Anduiza Fronton Building LANDMARK
(619 Grove St) Originally a boarding house from 1912, this building is home to Boise's popular indoor *pala* (Basque racquetball) court – check at the Basque Museum for a schedule of games.

⊙ Boise River & Greenbelt

Laid out in the 1960s, the tree-lined river-banks of the Boise River protect 30 miles of vehicle-free trails. It personifies Boise's 'city of trees' credentials, with parks, museums and river fun.

Boise Art Museum   MUSEUM

(www.boiseartmuseum.org; 670 N Julia Davis Dr; adult/child $6/3; ⊙10am-5pm Tue-Sat, noon-5pm Sun) Inside 90-acre Julia Davis Park, this art museum displays contemporary art in all media, including touring exhibitions by some big names (Kara Walker, Nick Cave). On First Thursdays each month, admission is by donation and the museum stays open until 8pm.

Barber Park   PARK

(barber-park.com; Eckert Rd; tube rentals $12) In summer everyone loves to float down the Boise River. Rent tubes or rafts from Epley's Adventures in Barber Park and float 5 or 6 miles downstream. A shuttle bus ($3) runs hourly 1pm to 8pm, to 9pm Friday, from June to August from the take-out point.

IDAHO FACTS

Nickname Gem State

Population 1,596,000

Area 83,570 sq miles

Capital city Boise (population 210,100)

Other cities Idaho Falls (population 57,600)

Sales tax 6%

Birthplace of Lewis and Clark guide Sacagawea (1788–1812); politician Sarah Palin (b 1964); poet Ezra Pound (1885–1972)

Home of Star garnet, Sun Valley ski resort

Politics Reliably Republican with small pockets of Democrats, eg Sun Valley

Famous for Potatoes, wilderness, the world's first chairlift

North America's deepest river gorge Idaho's Hells Canyon (7900ft deep)

Driving distances Boise to Idaho Falls 280 miles, Lewiston to Coeur d'Alene 116 miles

---

🛏 Sleeping

★ Boise Guest House   GUESTHOUSE $$

(☑208-761-6798; http://boiseguesthouse.com; 614 North 5th St; ste $99-189; 🛜🐾) As close as you can get to a home away from home, this artist-owned guesthouse has a handful of suites with kitchenettes and living areas. Whimsical and well thought-out, it has lovely decor with good books on the shelf and appealing local art. The beach-cruiser bike rentals ($10) encourage further exploration.

Modern Hotel   BOUTIQUE MOTEL $$

(☑208-424-8244; www.themodernhotel.com; 1314 W Grove St; d from $120, brunch mains $7-12; 🅿✳🛜) Making an oxymoron (a boutique motel!?) into a fashion statement, the Modern Hotel offers retro-trendy minimalist rooms and a slavishly hip bar in the middle of downtown. The power showers are huge and the service is five-star. On weekends, a fancy brunch menu includes things like truffled eggs and chilled asparagus vichyssoise.

🍴 Eating

Restaurants and nightspots are found downtown in the brick-lined pedestrian plaza of the Grove, and the gentrified former warehouse district between 8th St and Idaho Ave. Seek out some Basque specialties.

Goldy's Breakfast Bistro   BREAKFAST $

(http://goldysbreakfastbistro.com; 108 S Capitol Blvd; mains $6-12; ⊙6:30am-2pm Mon-Fri, 7:30am-2pm Sat & Sun) This breakfast joint is a long-standing local favorite – to the point that you want to get here right when it opens or expect a wait. It's cozy and cheerful, with good coffee and a menu built around the many variations of eggs Benedict. Whatever you order, don't skip the Goldy's special potatoes.

Vietnam Pho Nouveau   VIETNAMESE $$

(☑208-367-1111; www.phonouveau.com; 780 W Idaho St; mains $9-16; ⊙11am-9:30pm Mon-Thu, 11am-10:30pm Fri & Sat, noon-8:30pm Sun) A small, smart cafe oozing understated cool, it's Boise's happy destination for Asian comfort food. Dig into *bun*, a big bowl of noodles with grilled meat and plenty of greens, lily-blossom salad with tender shredded pork, or Saigon crepes.

★ Fork   MODERN AMERICAN $$

(☑207-287-1700; www.boisefork.com; 199 North 8th St; mains $14-28; ⊙11am-10pm; ✐) ❧

Twenty years ago, this kind of upscale green-boosted menu would have been Idaho heresy. No more. Down-home starts with cast-iron fried chicken with waffles and balsamic maple syrup. But there's also creative salads, braised greens, locally and regionally sourced meat and – of course – Idaho potatoes. (Don't even think of skipping the rosemary Parmesan fries.)

Bittercreek Ale House & Red Feather Lounge INTERNATIONAL **$$**
(www.justeatlocal.com; 246 N 8th St; mains $10-20; ⌚11am-late) These adjoining restaurants offer lively, intimate environs and lots of personality. They also serve wholesome, usually locally produced food with an emphasis on sustainable growth. The nouveau-American menu features a good selection of vegetarian options. The more polished Red Feather does delicious wood-oven pizza. Order one of the whiskey cocktails made with an old-fashioned pre-Prohibition-era recipe.

Drinking & Nightlife

★**Bar Gernika** PUB
(www.bargernika.com; 202 S Capitol Blvd; mains $8-11; ⌚11am-midnight Mon-Thu, to 1am Fri & Sat) *Ongi etorri* (welcome) to the Basque block's most accessible pub-tavern, with a menu that leans heavily on old-country favorites such as lamb kabob, chorizo and beef tongue (Saturdays only). Pair your meal with a 20oz Guinness or a *kalimotxo* (red wine and cola). It's a true only-in-Boise kind of place.

Leku Ona BAR
(☎208-345-6665; www.lekuonaid.com; 117 S 6th St; ⌚11am-late Mon-Sat; 📶) Run by a Basque-born immigrant, this bar and restaurant in the heart of the downtown Basque block is always hopping. Don't miss the chance to try some delicious *pintxos* (Basque tapas). You can also stay at the well-worn little five-room boarding house next-door (singles/doubles $65/85).

Bardenay PUB
(www.bardenay.com; 610 Grove St; cocktails from $7; ⌚11am-late) Bardenay was the USA's very first 'distillery-pub,' and remains a one-of-a-kind watering hole. Today it serves its own home-brewed vodka, rum and gin in casual, airy environs.

Information

Visitor Center (☎208-344-7777; www.boise.org; 250 S 5th St, Ste 300; ⌚10am-5pm Mon-Fri, 10am-2pm Sat Jun-Aug, 9am-4pm Mon-Fri Sep-May) The website has a useful events calendar.

Getting There & Around

Boise Municipal Airport (BOI; I-84 exit 53) Daily flights to Denver, Las Vegas, Phoenix, Portland, Salt Lake City, Seattle and Spokane.

Bus Station (1212 W Bannock St) Greyhound services depart from the bus station with routes fanning out to Spokane, Pendleton and Portland, Twin Falls and Salt Lake City.

Ketchum & Sun Valley

In one of Idaho's most stunning natural locations sits a piece of ski history. Sun Valley was the first purpose-built ski resort in the US, handpicked by Union Pacific Railroad scion William Averell Harriman (after an exhaustive search) in the 1930s and publicized by glitterati Ernest Hemingway, Clark Gable and Gary Cooper. When Sun Valley opened in 1936 it sported the world's first chairlift and a showcase 'parkitecture' lodge that remains its premier resort.

Sun Valley has kept its swanky Hollywood clientele and extended its facilities to include the legendary Bald Mountain, yet it remains a refined and pretty place (no fast-food joints or condo sprawl here). Highly rated nationwide, the resort is revered for its reliably good snow, big elevation drop and almost windless weather. The adjacent village of Ketchum, 1 mile away, holds a rustic beauty despite the skiing deluge. Hemingway made it prime territory for fishing and hunting, though these days fat tires are the summer rage.

Activities

Main St between 1st and 5th Sts is Ketchum's main drag. Sun Valley is 1 mile north and easily walkable. Twelve miles south of Ketchum, also on Hwy 75, is **Hailey**, another delightful small town with a bar scene.

Wood River Trail HIKING, CYCLING
There are numerous hiking and mountain-biking trails around Ketchum and Sun Valley, as well as excellent fishing spots. The Wood River Trail is the all-connecting artery linking Sun Valley with Ketchum and continuing 32 bucolic miles south down to Bellevue via Hailey. Rent bikes from **Pete Lane's** (☎208-622-2276; petelanes@sunvalley.com; 1 Sun Valley Rd; bike rentals from $35; ⌚9am-6pm).

Sun Valley Resort
SNOW SPORTS

(www.sunvalley.com; adult/child Bald Mountain $115/69, Dollar Mountain $79/56) Famous for its light, fluffy powder and celebrity guests, this dual-sited resort comprises advanced-terrain **Bald Mountain** and easier-on-the-nerves **Dollar Mountain**, which also has a **tubing hill**. In summer, take the chairlift to the top of either mountain (adult/child $23/19), and hike or cycle down. Facilities are predictably plush.

🛌 Sleeping

In summer, there is free camping on Bureau of Land Management (BLM) land very close to town; see the visitor center for details.

Tamarack Lodge
HOTEL $$

(☑208-726-3344; www.tamaracksunvalley.com; 500 E Sun Valley Rd; r $129-169; ❄ 🛜 ⛲) Tasteful rooms complete with fireplace, balcony and many amenities are offered at this well-maintained lodge, along with sterling service, a Jacuzzi and an indoor pool. Discounts are often available midweek and off-season.

Sun Valley Lodge
HOTEL $$$

(☑208-622-2001; www.sunvalley.com; 1 Sun Valley Rd; r from $289; ❄ @ 🛜 ⛲) Reopened in June 2015 after a massive renovation that cut the number of rooms in half, this swank 1930s-era beauty – the country's first destination ski resort – is cranking up the luxury and toning down the old woodsy charm. Rooms now feel more like spacious modern apartments, and a new wing contains a 20,000-sq-ft spa.

There's also a pool and poolside cafe, Jacuzzi and downstairs bowling alley (also redone), plus a winter ski-shuttle service and children's program.

🍴 Eating & Drinking

Despo's
MEXICAN $

(☑208-726-3068; 211 4th St; mains $6-12; ⏱11:30am-10pm Mon-Sat) Locals dig this healthy Mexican joint. Everything is fresh (if not entirely authentic), salads are huge and homemade salsas (warm, hot and smokin') are worthy.

Glow
VEGAN $

(380 Washington #105; mains $6-12; ⏱10am-5pm Mon-Sat; 🌿) An oasis of raw and vegan dining. Sample from its laundry list of smoothies, chia puddings, organic salads, blended soups and (thank god) handmade raw chocolates, and you too might glow.

★ Rickshaw
ASIAN $$

(www.eat-at-rickshaw.com; 460 N Washington Ave; lunch mains $11-15, dinner small plates $7-15; ⏱from 5:30pm Tue-Sat, lunch 11:30am-2pm Fri) Small and crooked as an actual rickshaw, welcoming and with the vitality of a busy thoroughfare, this restaurant turns out A+ street food from Vietnam, Thailand, Korea and Indonesia. Tender short ribs served with a jalapeno-cilantro glaze are maddeningly wonderful. From green curry to cashew stir fry, the default here is spicy. A must. Opening hours vary; check website for latest.

Pioneer Saloon
STEAK $$$

(www.pioneersaloon.com; 320 N Main St; mains $15-35; ⏱5-10pm, bar from 4pm) Around since the 1950s and originally an illicit gambling hall, the Pio is an unashamed Western den decorated with deer heads, antique guns (one being Hemingway's) and bullet boards, and – oh yes – some good food too, as long as you like beef and trout.

Casino Club
BAR

(220 N Main St) This dive bar is the oldest thing still standing from days of yore. It has witnessed everything from gambling fistfights, to psychedelic hippies, to the rise and fall of Ernest Hemingway, to tattooed men on Harleys riding through the front door.

ℹ Information

Sun Valley/Ketchum Visitors Center (☑208-726-3423; www.visitsunvalley.com; 491 Sun Valley Rd; ⏱6am-7pm) Staffed only from 9am to 6pm, but you can still come in and get maps and brochures before and after hours.

ℹ Getting There & Around

Friedman Memorial Airport (SUN; http://iflysun.com) The region's airport is in Hailey, 12 miles south of Ketchum.

Sun Valley Express (www.sunvalleyexpress.com) Operates a daily shuttle between Sun Valley and Boise Airport in both directions ($69 one-way).

Stanley

Backed by the ragged Sawtooths, Stanley (population 100), with its gravel roads, log homes and rusted iron sheds, might be the most scenic small town in America. Surrounded by protected wilderness and national-forest land, the remote outpost sits in the crook of the Salmon River, miles from anywhere. Here the high summer twilight stretches past 10pm and the roaring creek lulls you to sleep.

DON'T MISS

CENTRAL IDAHO'S SCENIC BYWAYS

Goodbye suburban strip malls, hello unblemished wilderness. All three roads into the remote Idahoan outpost of Stanley are designated National Scenic Byways (it's the only place in the US where this happens). Considering there are only 125 such roads in the country, it means 2.4% of America's prettiest pavement runs through bucolic Stanley.

Sawtooth Scenic Byway

Following the Salmon River along Hwy 75 north from Ketchum to Stanley, this 60-mile drive is gorgeous, winding through a misty, thick ponderosa pine forest – where the air is crisp and fresh and smells like rain and nuts – before ascending the 8701ft **Galena Summit**. From the overlook at the top, there are views of the glacially carved Sawtooth Mountains.

Ponderosa Pine Scenic Byway

Hwy 21, between Stanley and Boise, is so beautiful it will be hard to reach your destination because you'll want to stop so much. From Stanley the trees increase in density, until you find yourself cloaked in pine – more Pacific Northwest than classic Rockies. With frequent bursts of rain, the roadway can feel dangerous. Even in late May the snowfields stretch right down to the highway. Two of the road's many highlights are **Kikham Creek Hot Springs** (208-373-4100; parking per car $5; 6am-10pm), 4 miles east of Lowman, a primitive campground and natural hot spring boiling out of the creek; and the old restored gold rush town of **Idaho City**.

Salmon River Scenic Byway

Northeast of Stanley, Hwy 75 and US 93 make up another scenic road that runs beside the Salmon River for 161 miles to historic **Lost Trail Pass** on the Montana border, the point where Lewis and Clark first crossed the continental divide in 1805. The surrounding scenery has changed little in over 200 years.

Activities

Middle Fork of the Salmon River RAFTING
(877-444-6777; http://recreation.gov) Stanley is the jumping-off point for rafting the legendary Middle Fork of the Salmon. Billed as the 'last wild river,' it's part of the longest undammed river system in the US, outside Alaska. Permits are required; visit or call the National Recreation Reservation Service for details.

Full trips last six days and allow you to float for 106 miles through 300 or so rapids (class I to IV) in the 2.4-million-acre Frank Church–River of No Return Wilderness, miles from any form of civilization.

Main Fork of the Salmon River RAFTING
(877-444-6777; http://recreation.gov;) For more affordable, albeit slightly less dramatic, white-water action than Middle Fork, do a DIY float trip down the Main Fork of the Salmon in a raft or inflatable kayak. There are 8 miles of quiet water, starting in Stanley, with views of the Sawtooth Mountains you can't see from the road. Bring fishing gear. Permits are required for certain sections.

Fly Fishing FISHING
(http://stanleycc.org/do/fishing; Mar-Nov) The Salmon River and surrounding mountain lakes have epic trout fishing from March until November, with late June to early October best for dry fly-fishing. The eight species of local trout include the mythical steelhead, which measure up to 40in. These fish travel 900 miles from the Pacific Ocean at winter's end, arriving near Stanley in March and April.

Tours

White Otter RAFTING
(208-788-5005; www.whiteotter.com; 100 Yankee Fork Road & Hwy 75, Sunbeam; full-day float trips per person $300, half-day river rafting adult/child $75/55) The sole rafting outfit that's locally run, White Otter is recommended for fun class III day trips. It also arranges float trips in inflatable kayaks.

Solitude River Trips RAFTING
(800-396-1776; www.rivertrips.com; 6-day trip per person $3140; Jun-Aug) Offers top-notch, multiday trips on the famed Middle Fork of the Salmon. Camping is riverside and guides cook excellent food.

Silver Creek Outfitters FISHING
(☎207-622-5282; www.silver-creek.com; 1 Sun Valley Rd; full-day drift boat trip $525) Based in Sun Valley, Silver Creek does custom trips to the Salmon and remote river spots, only accessible via drift boat or float tube.

Sleeping & Eating

There are about half a dozen hotels in Stanley, all done in traditional pioneer log-cabin style. During the short summer season a couple of restaurants open up.

Sawtooth Hotel HOTEL $
(☎208-721-2459; www.sawtoothhotel.com; 755 Ace of Diamonds St; d with/without bath $100/70; ⏲mid-May–mid-Oct; 📶) Set in a nostalgic 1931 log motel, the Sawtooth updates the slim comforts of yesteryear, but keeps the hospitality effusively Stanley-esque. Six rooms are furnished old-country style, two with private bathrooms. Room No 9 is the fave. Don't expect TVs or room phones, but count on homespun dining that is exquisite.

On weekends in peak summer season, a two-night minimum stay is required.

★ **Stanley Baking Co** BAKERY, BREAKFAST $
(www.stanleybakingco.com; 250 Wall St; mains $9-12; ⏲7am-2pm May-Oct) This middle-of-nowhere bakery and brunch spot, from the same couple that runs the Sawtooth Hotel, is a godsend. Operating for five months of the year out of a small log cabin, Stanley Baking Co is the only place in town where you're likely to see a queue. The reason: off-the-ratings-scale homemade baked goods and oatmeal pancakes.

Idaho Panhandle

Idaho grabbed the long skinny spoon-handle that brushes up against Canada in an 1880s land dispute with Montana. Yet in both looks and attitude, the area has more in common with the Pacific Northwest than the Rockies. Spokane, a few miles west in Washington, acts as the regional hub and most of the panhandle observes Pacific Standard Time (one hour behind the rest of Idaho on mountain time).

Near the Washington border, fast-growing **Coeur d'Alene** (population 46,000) is an extension of the Spokane metro area and the panhandle's largest town. There's a small boardwalk and a manicured park in front of the landmark resort, itself rather anonymous until the gorgeous evening sunlight makes it shimmer. The adjacent **lake** is ideal for water-based activities like standup paddleboarding. Most of the dining-and-drinking action takes place along a stretch of Sherman leading uphill from the lake.

Sandpoint, on Lake Pend Oreille, is the nicest panhandle town, with a cute, walkable core of historic buildings housing cafes, shops and Pilates studios. Set in a gorgeous wilderness locale surrounded by mountains, it also sports Idaho's only serviceable Amtrak **train station**, an attractive brick structure dating from 1916. The *Empire Builder*, running daily between Seattle/Portland and Chicago, stops here.

You can soak up Idaho's largest lake from the **Pend Oreille Scenic Byway** (US 200), which hugs the north shore.

Sights & Activities

Schweitzer Mountain Resort SNOW SPORTS
(www.schweitzer.com; adult/child $72/50) Eleven miles northwest of Sandpoint is highly rated Schweitzer Mountain Resort, lauded for its tree-skiing, with mountain biking in summer.

Sleeping & Eating

Country Inn MOTEL $
(☎208-263-3333; www.countryinnsandpoint.com; 470700 Hwy 95; s/d $80/90; 📶🐾) The best accommodation bargain for miles around is the clean, friendly, mom-and-pop-run Country Inn, 3 miles south of Sandpoint.

Flamingo Motel MOTEL $$
(☎208-664-2159; www.flamingomotelidaho.com; 718 Sherman Ave, Coeur d'Alene; r $102; ❄📶) This fun, friendly place, a retro '50s throwback, has rooms elaborately decked out in various themes – from over-the-top 'Flamingo' to 'Irish' – plus updates like flat-screen TVs and mini-fridges. For the fanciest digs, book the Victorian Room.

Java on Sherman CAFE $
(819 Sherman Ave, Coeur d'Alene; mains $7-13, coffee $2-5; ⏲6am-7pm) In a new, roomier location a little further up the hill, this local favorite serves good coffee and breakfast along with beer, wine and excellent people-watching.

Information

Coeur d'alene Visitors Center (☎208-665-2350; www.coeurdalene.org; 115 Northwest Blvd, Coeur d'Alene; ⏲10am-3pm Tue-Sat, to 5pm Jun-Aug) The Coeur d'Alene Visitors Center is a good regional-info starting point.

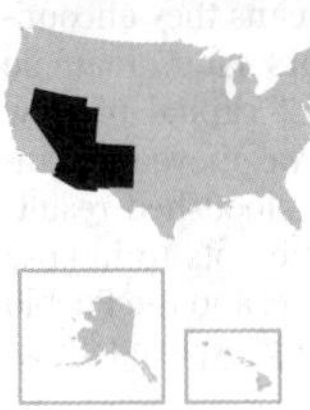

Southwest

Includes ➡

Why Go?

The Southwest is America's untamed backyard, where life plays out before a stunning backdrop of red rocks, lofty peaks, shimmering lakes and deserts dotted with saguaro cacti. Reminders of the region's Native American heritage and hardscrabble Wild West heyday dot the landscape, from enigmatic pictographs and abandoned cliff dwellings to crumbling Hispanic missions and rusty mining towns. Today, history making continues, with astronomers and rocket builders peering into star-filled skies while artists and entrepreneurs flock to urban centers and quirky mountain towns.

The best part for travelers? A splendid network of scenic drives linking the most beautiful and iconic sites. But remember: it's not just iconic, larger-than-life landscapes that make a trip through the Southwest memorable. Study that saguaro up close; ask a Hopi artist about their craft; savor some green-chile stew. You may just cherish those moments the most.

Best Places to Eat

- Elote Cafe (p842)
- Hell's Backbone (p876)
- Love Apple (p897)
- Cafe Roka (p861)
- The Curious Kumquat (p901)

Best Places to Stay

- Ellis Store Country Inn (p903)
- El Tovar Hotel (p849)
- La Posada (p854)
- Motor Lodge (p839)
- Los Poblanos (p883)

When to Go

Las Vegas

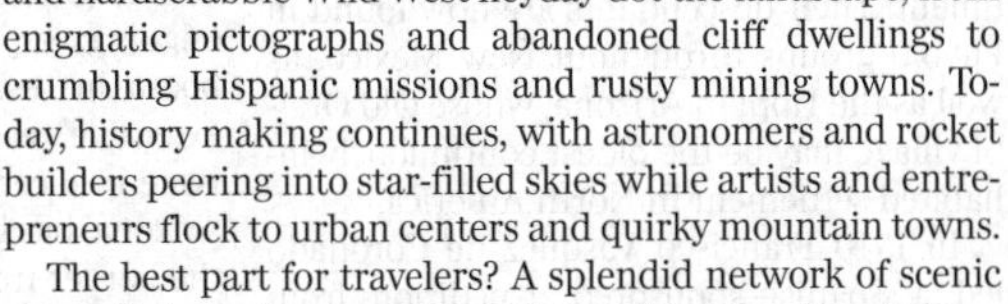

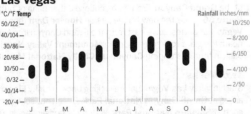

Jan Ski near Taos and Flagstaff. In Park City, hit the slopes and the Sundance Film Festival.

Jun–Aug High season for exploring national parks in New Mexico, Utah and northern Arizona.

Sep–Nov Hike to the bottom of the Grand Canyon or gaze at bright leaves in northern New Mexico.

History

By about AD 100, three dominant cultures had emerged in the Southwest: the Hohokam, the Mogollon and the Ancestral Puebloans (previously known as the Anasazi).

The Hohokam lived in the Arizona deserts from 300 BC to AD 1450, and created an incredible canal irrigation system, earthen pyramids and a rich heritage of pottery. A cataclysmic event in the mid-15th century caused a dramatic decrease in the Hohokam population; it's not entirely clear what became of them, but the oral traditions suggest that certain local tribes are their direct descendants.

From 200 BC to AD 1450 the Mogollon lived in the central mountains and valleys of the Southwest; they left behind what are now called the Gila Cliff Dwellings, and many beautifully decorated bowls.

The Ancestral Puebloans left the richest heritage of archaeological sites, such as those at Chaco Culture National Historic Park and Canyon de Chelly National Monument. Their descendants are now found in Pueblo groups throughout New Mexico, as well as the Hopi in Arizona, whose Old Oraibi village may be the oldest continuously inhabited settlement in North America.

In 1540 Francisco Vásquez de Coronado led a Spanish-sponsored expedition from Mexico City to the Southwest. Searching in vain for riches, his party killed or displaced many of the Native Americans they encountered. More than 50 years later, Juan de Oñate established the first capital of New Mexico at San Gabriel; it was moved to Santa Fe around 1610. Great bloodshed resulted from the Spaniards' attempts to impose their religion and way of life, and the Pueblo Revolt of 1680 even briefly expelled them altogether.

Development in the Southwest expanded rapidly during the 19th century, mainly due to railroad and geological surveys. As the US pushed west, the army forcibly removed entire tribes of Native Americans in horrifyingly brutal Indian Wars. Gold and silver mines drew fortune seekers, and the lawless mining towns of the Wild West mushroomed practically overnight. Soon the Santa Fe Railroad was luring a flood of tourists to the West.

Modern settlement is closely linked to water use. Following the Reclamation Act of 1902, huge federally funded dams were built to control rivers and irrigate the desert. Rancorous disagreements over water rights are ongoing, especially with the phenomenal boom in residential development and the extensive recent drought. The other major issue in recent years, especially in southern Arizona, has been illegal immigration across the border from Mexico.

SOUTHWEST IN...

One Week

Museums and a burgeoning arts scene set an inspirational tone in **Phoenix**. In the morning, follow Camelback Rd into **Scottsdale** for top-notch shopping and gallery-hopping in Old Town. Drive north to **Sedona** for spiritual recharging before pondering the immensity of the **Grand Canyon**. From here, choose either bling or buttes. For bling, detour onto **Route 66**, cross the new bridge beside **Hoover Dam** then indulge your fantasies in **Las Vegas**. For buttes, drive east from the Grand Canyon into Navajo country, cruising beneath the giant rock formations in **Monument Valley Navajo Tribal Park** then stepping back in time at stunning **Canyon de Chelly National Monument**.

Two Weeks

Start in glitzy **Las Vegas** before kicking back in funky **Flagstaff** and peering into the abyss at **Grand Canyon National Park**. Check out collegiate **Tucson** or frolic among cacti at **Saguaro National Park**. Watch the gunslingers in **Tombstone** before settling into Victorian **Bisbee**.

Secure your sunglasses for the blinding dunes of **White Sands National Monument** in New Mexico then sink into **Santa Fe**, a magnet for art-lovers. Explore the pueblo in **Taos** and watch the sunrise at awesome **Monument Valley Navajo Tribal Park**. Head into Utah for the red-rock national parks, **Canyonlands** and **Arches**. Do the hoodoos at **Bryce Canyon** then pay your respects at glorious **Zion**.

Local Culture

The peoples of the Southwest encompass a rich mix of Native American, Hispanic and Anglo populations. All have influenced the region's cuisine, architecture and arts, and the Southwest's vast Native American reservations offer exceptional opportunities to learn about Native American culture and history. Visual arts are a strong force as well, from the art colonies dotting New Mexico to the roadside kitsch on view everywhere.

Getting There & Around

Las Vegas' McCarran International Airport and Phoenix' Sky Harbor International Airport are the region's busiest airports, followed by those at Salt Lake City and Albuquerque.

Greyhound stops at major cities, but barely serves national parks or off-the-beaten-path towns such as Moab. Amtrak train service is even more limited, although it too links several Southwestern cities and offers bus connections to others (including Santa Fe and Phoenix). The California Zephyr crosses Utah and Nevada; the Southwest Chief stops in Arizona and New Mexico; and the Sunset Limited traverses southern Arizona and New Mexico.

That means private vehicles are often the only means to reach out-of-the-way towns, trailheads and swimming spots, and to explore the region in any depth.

NEVADA FACTS

Nickname Silver State

Population 2.84 million

Area 109,800 sq miles

Capital city Carson City (population 54,080)

Other cities Las Vegas (population 606,762), Reno (population 233,300)

Sales tax 6.85%

Birthplace of Andre Agassi (b 1970), Greg LeMond (b 1961)

Home of The slot machine, Burning Man

Politics Nevada has six electoral votes – the state went for Obama in the 2012 presidential election, but it is split evenly in sending elected officials to Washington

Famous for The 1859 Comstock Lode (the country's richest known silver deposit), legalized gambling and prostitution (outlawed in certain counties), and liberal alcohol laws allowing 24-hour bars

Best Las Vegas T-Shirt 'I saw nothing at the Mob Museum.'

Driving distances Las Vegas to Reno 452 miles, Great Basin National Park to Las Vegas 313 miles

NEVADA

Nevada has a devil-may-care exuberance that's dangerously intoxicating – and sometimes a little bit wacky. Here, dazzling replicas of the Eiffel Tower, the Statue of Liberty and an Egyptian pyramid rise from the desert. Cowboys gather to recite poetry. Artists build a temporary city on a windswept playa. An Air Force base inspires alien conspiracies. And smack in the middle of it all is a lonely tree, its branches draped in sneakers tossed by mischievous road-trippers.

On the map, the state is a vast and mostly empty stretch of desert, dotted with former mining towns that have traded pickaxes for slot machines. The mother lode is Las Vegas, an over-the-top extravaganza where people still catch gold fever. In the west, adventure outfitters are staking their claims on new treasures: gorgeous scenery and outdoor fun, which beckon from the Sierra Nevada mountains.

The first state to legalize gambling, Nevada is loud with the chime of slot machines singing out from gas stations, supermarkets and hotel lobbies. There's no legally mandated closing time for bars, and in rural areas, legalized brothels and hole-in-the-wall casinos sit side by side with Mormon and cowboy culture.

Our advice? Never ask 'Why?' Just embrace the state's go-for-broke joie de vivre.

Information

Prostitution is illegal in Clark County (which includes Las Vegas) and Washoe County (which includes Reno), although there are legal brothels in many of the smaller counties.

Nevada is on Pacific Standard Time.

Nevada Commission on Tourism (☎800-638-2328; www.travelnevada.com) Sends free books, maps and information on accommodations, campgrounds and events.

Nevada Division of State Parks (☎775-684-2770; www.parks.nv.gov; 901 S Stewart St, 5th fl, Carson City; ⊙8am-5pm Mon-Fri) Camping in state parks ($10 to $15 per night) is first-come, first-served.

Southwest Highlights

❶ Strolling the Rim Trail at **Grand Canyon National Park** (p845).

❷ Living your own John Wayne Western in northeastern Arizona's **Monument Valley** (p854).

❸ Practicing your fast draw in dusty **Tombstone** (p860).

❹ Gallery-hopping and jewelry-shopping on the stylish streets of **Santa Fe** (p886).

❺ Sledding down a shimmering sand dune at **White Sands National Monument** (p902).

❻ Wandering a wonderland of stalactites at **Carlsbad Caverns National Park** (p904).

❼ Cruising the casinos on the legendary Las Vegas **Strip** (p815).

❽ Hiking to flaming-red sandstone formations in **Arches National Park** (p873).

❾ Skiing incredible terrain and enjoying chichi nightlife in **Park City** (p867).

❿ Exploring a majestic canyon and climbing Angels Landing at **Zion National Park** (p878).

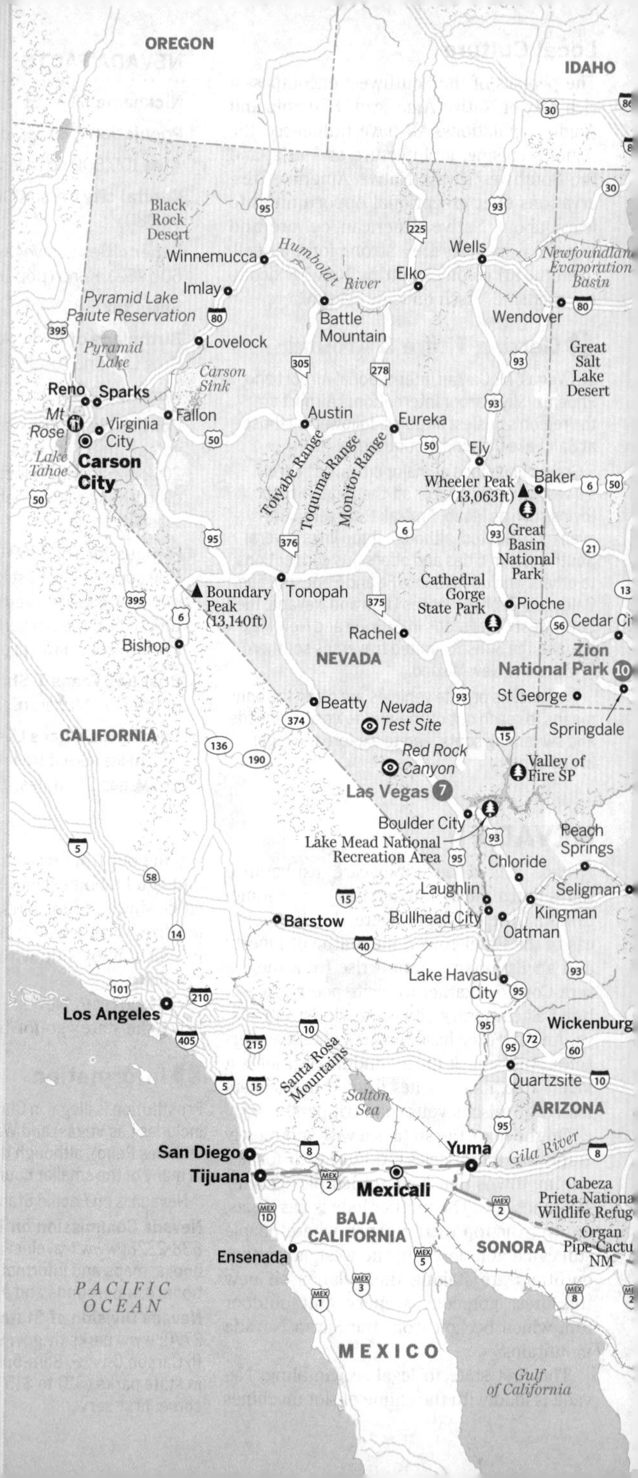

0 200 km
0 100 miles
NEBRASKA
WYOMING
UTAH
COLORADO
NEW MEXICO
TEXAS
CHIHUAHUA
Cheyenne
Fort Collins
Boulder
Denver
Colorado Springs
Granada
Logan
Brigham City
Great Salt Lake
Ogden
Salt Lake City
Wasatch-Cache NF
9 Park City
Kamas
Provo
Utah Lake
Wasatch-Cache NF
Roosevelt
Vernal
Dutch John
Flaming Gorge Reservoir
Flaming Gorge National Recreation Area
Dinosaur NM
Price
Green River
Glen Canyon National Recreation Area
Grand Junction
8 Arches National Park
Moab
Dead Horse Point SP
Canyonlands National Park
Richfield
Capitol Reef NP
Torrey
Circleville
Bryce Canyon NP
Boulder
Escalante
Manti-La Sal NF
Monticello
Colorado River
Blanding
Natural Bridges NM
Hovenweep NM
Mesa Verde NP
Bluff
Grand Staircase-Escalante NM
Lake Powell
Kanab
Lees Ferry
Page
Mexican Hat
2 Monument Valley Navajo Tribal Park
Four Corners Navajo Tribal Park
Chama
Wheeler Peak (13,161ft)
Raton
Capulin Volcano NM
Clayton
Kayenta
Jacob Lake
Grand Canyon National Park
1
Hopi Reservation
Chinle
Shiprock
Farmington
Bloomfield
Santa Fe NF
Taos Box
Taos
Cimarron
Ojo Caliente
Abiquiú
Española
Bandelier NM
Los Alamos
Cuba
Chaco Culture NHP
Canyon de Chelly NM
Third Mesa
Grand Canyon Village
Kaibab NF
Oraibi
First Mesa
Second Mesa
Old Oraibi
Window Rock
Gallup
San Ysidro
4 Santa Fe
Las Vegas
Tucumcari
Santa Rosa
Williams
Flagstaff
Petrified Forest NP
El Morro NM
Grants
Albuquerque
Acoma Pueblo
Zuni Pueblo
El Malpais NM
Winslow
Coconino NF
Holbrook
Jerome
Sedona
Prescott
Fort Sumner
Clovis
Cibola NF
Payson
Magdalena
Socorro
San Antonio
Springerville
Gila Cliff Dwellings National Monument
Mogollon Mountains
Cibola NF
Bosque del Apache National Wildlife Refuge
Lincoln NF
Capitan
Lincoln
Roswell
Phoenix
Scottsdale
Roosevelt Dam
Tempe
Mesa
Globe
Gila NF
Truth or Consequences
Ruidoso
Cloudcroft
Alamogordo
Lovington
Artesia
Hobbs
Safford
Silver City
City of Rocks SP
Hatch
5 White Sands National Monument
Carlsbad
Lincoln NF
6 Carlsbad Caverns National Park
Tohono O'odham Indian Reservation
Biosphere 2
Saguaro NP
Tucson
Willcox
Lordsburg
Deming
Las Cruces
Mesilla
Benson
Kartchner Caverns SP
Chiricahua NM
El Paso
Guadalupe Mountains NP
Sells
Tubac
3 Tombstone
Patagonia
Bisbee
Nogales
Douglas

NATIONAL PARKS & MONUMENTS

Holding well more than 60 national parks and monuments, and many stunning state parks, the Southwest is a scenic and cultural jackpot. Arizona's Grand Canyon National Park (p845) surely heads any list, while Arizona's other stupendous parks include Monument Valley (p854), with its towering sandstone pillars and buttes, and Canyon de Chelly (p853), home to magnificent ancient cliff dwellings.

The red-rock Canyon Country of southern Utah holds five national parks – Arches (p873), Canyonlands (p874), Zion (p878), Bryce Canyon (p877) and Capitol Reef (p876) – while New Mexico boasts Carlsbad Caverns (p904) and the mysterious Chaco Culture National Historic Park (p898), and Nevada has Great Basin National Park (p829), a rugged, remote mountain oasis.

Las Vegas

Las Vegas remains the ultimate escape. Where else can you party in ancient Rome, get hitched at midnight, wake up in Egypt and brunch beneath the Eiffel Tower? Double down with the high rollers, browse couture or tacky souvenirs, sip a neon 3ft-high margarita or a frozen vodka martini from a bar made of ice – it's all here for the taking.

Ever notice that there are no clocks inside casinos? Vegas exists outside time, a sequence of never-ending buffets, ever-flowing drinks and adrenaline-fueled gaming tables. In this never-ending desert dreamscape of boom and bust, once-famous signs collect dust in a neon boneyard while the clang of construction echoes over the Strip. After the alarming hiccup of the 2008 recession, the city is once more back on track, attracting well over 40 million visitors per year and bursting with schemes to lure in even more in future.

Las Vegas' largest casinos – each one a gigantic and baffling mélange of theme park, gambling den, shopping and dining destination, hotel and theater district – line up along the legendary Strip. Once you've explored those, head to the city's compact downtown to encounter Vegas' nostalgic beginnings, peppered with indie shops and cocktail bars where local culture thrives. Then detour further afield to find intriguing museums that investigate Vegas' gangster, atomic-fueled past.

History

Contrary to popular legend, there was much more at the dusty crossroads than a gambling parlor and a few tumbleweeds when mobster Ben 'Bugsy' Siegel rolled in in 1946 and erected a glamorous tropical-themed casino, the Flamingo, under the searing sun.

Spawned by the completion of the railroad that linked Salt Lake City to Los Angeles in 1902, Las Vegas boomed in the 1930s thanks to federal construction projects. The legalization of gambling in 1931 carried Vegas through the Depression, WWII brought a huge air-force base and aerospace bucks, plus a paved highway to Los Angeles. During the Cold War, the Nevada Test Site proved to be a textbook case of 'any publicity is good publicity': monthly above-ground atomic blasts shattered casino windows downtown while the city's official Miss Mushroom Cloud mascot promoted atomic everything in tourism campaigns.

Meanwhile, the Flamingo sparked a building spree in which mob-backed tycoons upped the glitz ante at every turn. Big-name entertainers such as Frank Sinatra, Liberace and Sammy Davis Jr arrived at the same time as topless French showgirls.

The high-profile purchase of the Desert Inn in 1966 by eccentric billionaire Howard Hughes gave the gambling industry a much-needed patina of legitimacy, while the debut of the MGM Grand in 1993 signaled the dawn of the corporate megaresort era. These days almost all the major casinos are owned by two rival empires, Caesars Entertainment and Mirage Resorts.

Sights

Roughly 4 miles long, the Strip, aka Las Vegas Blvd South, is the center of gravity in Sin City, running from around a mile south of downtown to Mandalay Bay near the airport. Whether you're walking or driving, Strip distances are deceiving: a walk to what looks like a nearby casino always takes longer than expected.

Downtown Las Vegas is home to the city's oldest hotels and casinos: expect a retro feel, cheaper drinks and lower table limits. Its main drag is fun-loving Fremont St, a four-block stretch of casinos and restaurants covered by a dazzling canopy that runs a groovy light show every evening. Schemes to 'revitalize' downtown have come and gone with monotonous regularity over the years; the latest, the Downtown Project, spearheaded by Zappo's CEO Tony Hsieh, has yet to make a significant impact on Las Vegas visitors.

Major tourist areas are safe. However, Las Vegas Blvd between downtown and the Strip is shabby, and Fremont St east of downtown can be rather unsavory.

The Strip

★CityCenter LANDMARK

(www.citycenter.com; 3780 Las Vegas Blvd S) We've seen this symbiotic relationship before (think giant hotel anchored by a mall 'concept') but the way that this futuristic-feeling complex places a small galaxy of hypermodern, chichi hotels in orbit around the glitzy Crystals (p824) shopping center is a first. The uber-upscale spread includes the subdued, stylish **Vdara** (☎702-590-2111, 866-745-7767; www.vdara.com; 2600 W Harmon Ave; weekday/weekend ste from $119/179; P ⊖ ❄ @ ≋ ≈), the hush-hush opulent **Mandarin Oriental** (www.mandarinoriental.com; 3752 Las Vegas Blvd S) and the dramatic architectural showpiece **Aria** (☎702-590-7111; www.aria.com; 3730 Las Vegas Blvd S; ⏲24hr), the sophisticated casino of which provides a fitting backdrop to its many drop-dead-gorgeous restaurants.

Cosmopolitan CASINO

(☎702-698-7000; www.cosmopolitanlasvegas.com; 3708 Las Vegas Blvd S; ⏲24hr) Hipsters who thought they were too cool for Vegas finally have a place to go where they don't need irony to endure – or enjoy – the aesthetics of the Strip. Like the new Hollywood 'It' girl, the Cosmopolitan casino looks absolutely fabulous at all times. A steady stream of ingenues and entourages parade through the lobby, along with anyone else who adores contemporary art and design.

Fountains of Bellagio FOUNTAIN

(www.bellagio.com; Bellagio; ⏲shows every 30min 3-7pm Mon-Fri, noon-7pm Sat & Sun, every 15min 7pm-midnight daily; 👪) FREE With a backdrop of Tuscan architecture, the Bellagio's faux Lake Como and dancing fountains are the antithesis of the Mojave Desert – although the resort does use reclaimed water. The fountain show's recorded soundtrack varies, so cross your fingers that it will be Italian opera or Ol' Blue Eyes crooning 'Luck Be a Lady,' instead of country-and-western twang.

Paris Las Vegas CASINO

(☎702-946-7000; www.parislasvegas.com; 3655 Las Vegas Blvd S; ⏲24hr) Welcome to the City of Light, Vegas-style. This mini-version of the French capital may not exude the true charm of Paris – it feels like a themed section of Disney World's Epcot – but efforts to emulate the city's great landmarks, including a 34-story Hotel de Ville replica and famous facades from the Paris Opera House and the Louvre, make it a fun stop for families and Francophiles who've yet to see the real thing.

LINQ & High Roller LANDMARK

(☎800-223-7277; www.thelinq.com; 3545 Las Vegas Blvd S; High Roller ride before/after 5:50pm $25/35; ⏲High Roller noon-2am daily; monorail Flamingo or Harrah's/Quad) A mammoth open-air dining, entertainment and retail complex, the $550-million LINQ project has transformed what was once a lackluster stretch of the center Strip between the Flamingo and Quad casino hotels. Eclectic shops, buzzing bars, trendy restaurants, live-music venues and even a bowling alley line the pedestrian promenade, where you'll also find the High Roller, a 550ft-tall observation wheel.

Caesars Palace CASINO

(☎702-731-7110; www.caesarspalace.com; 3570 Las Vegas Blvd S; ⏲24hr) Despite recent upgrades that have lent the once-gaudy Palace a more sophisticated air, some of the resort's original features from the swinging '60s have survived. Out front are the same spritzing fountains that daredevil Evil Knievel made famous when he jumped them on a motorcycle on December 31, 1967 (and ended up with a shattered pelvis and a fractured skull.; more than two decades later, his son Robby repeated the attempt – more successfully).

Wynn CASINO

(☎702-770-7000; www.wynnlasvegas.com; 3131 Las Vegas Blvd S; ⏲24hr) Steve Wynn's signature (literally, his name is written in script across the top, punctuated by a period) casino hotel stands on the site of the imploded 1950s-era Desert Inn. The curvaceous, copper-toned 50-story tower exudes secrecy – the entrance is obscured from the Strip by an artificial mountain of greenery. Inside, the resort comes alive with vibrant colors, inlaid flower mosaics, natural-light windows, lush foliage and waterfalls. The sprawling casino is always crowded, especially the cutthroat poker room.

Las Vegas

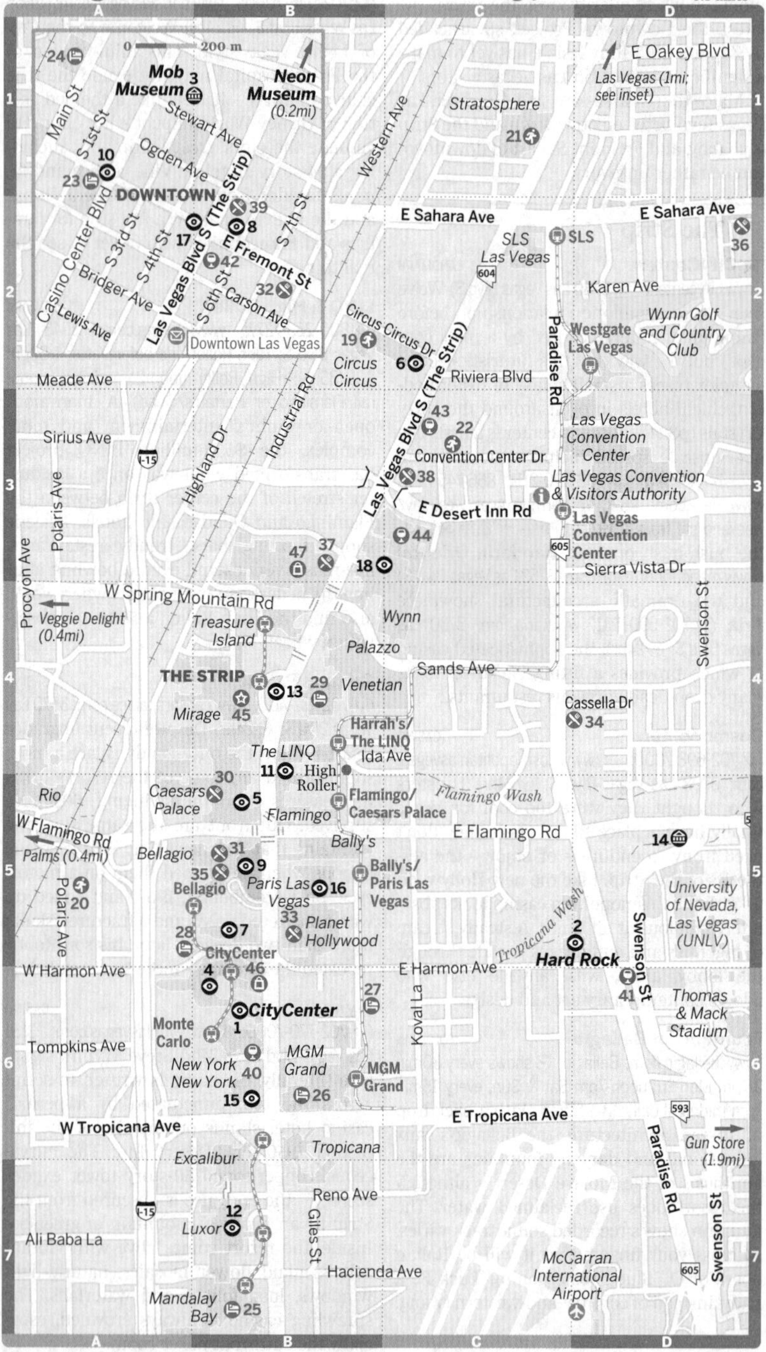

0 1 km
0 0.5 miles
Mob Museum 3
Neon Museum (0.2mi)
DOWNTOWN
Main St
S 1st St
Stewart Ave
Ogden Ave
Casino Center Blvd
S 3rd St
S 4th St
Las Vegas Blvd S (The Strip)
E Fremont St
S 6th St
S 7th St
Bridger Ave
Carson Ave
Lewis Ave
Downtown Las Vegas
E Oakey Blvd
Las Vegas (1mi; see inset)
Stratosphere
Western Ave
E Sahara Ave
SLS
SLS Las Vegas
Karen Ave
Wynn Golf and Country Club
Westgate Las Vegas
Paradise Rd
Circus Circus Dr
Circus Circus
Riviera Blvd
Meade Ave
Sirius Ave
Industrial Rd
Highland Dr
Las Vegas Convention Center
Convention Center Dr
Las Vegas Convention & Visitors Authority
E Desert Inn Rd
Sierra Vista Dr
Polaris Ave
Procyon Ave
W Spring Mountain Rd
Veggie Delight (0.4mi)
Treasure Island
Wynn
Palazzo
Sands Ave
Swenson St
THE STRIP
Venetian
Mirage
Cassella Dr
Harrah's/The LINQ
The LINQ
Ida Ave
High Roller
Rio
Caesars Palace
Flamingo/Caesars Palace
Flamingo Wash
Flamingo
W Flamingo Rd
E Flamingo Rd
Palms (0.4mi)
Bellagio
Bally's
Bally's/Paris Las Vegas
Paris Las Vegas
University of Nevada, Las Vegas (UNLV)
Planet Hollywood
Tropicana Wash
Hard Rock
CityCenter
W Harmon Ave
E Harmon Ave
Koval La
Thomas & Mack Stadium
Monte Carlo
Tompkins Ave
New York New York
MGM Grand
W Tropicana Ave
E Tropicana Ave
Excalibur
Tropicana
Gun Store (1.9mi)
Reno Ave
Giles St
Luxor
Ali Baba La
Hacienda Ave
McCarran International Airport
Mandalay Bay
SOUTHWEST LAS VEGAS

Las Vegas

Top Sights
- 1 CityCenter B6
- 2 Hard Rock D5
- 3 Mob Museum B1

Sights
- 4 Aria B6
- Big Apple Roller Coaster .... (see 15)
- 5 Caesars Palace B5
- 6 Circus Circus C2
- 7 Cosmopolitan B5
- 8 Emergency Arts B2
- 9 Fountains of Bellagio B5
- 10 Fremont Street Experience A1
- 11 LINQ & High Roller B4
- 12 Luxor B7
- Madame Tussauds .... (see 29)
- Mandarin Oriental .... (see 1)
- 13 Mirage Volcano B4
- 14 National Atomic Testing Museum D5
- 15 New York–New York B6
- 16 Paris Las Vegas B5
- Shark Reef Aquarium .... (see 25)
- 17 Slotzilla A2
- 18 Wynn B3

Activities, Courses & Tours
- 19 Adventuredome B2
- 20 Fast Lap A5
- Qua Baths & Spa .... (see 5)
- 21 Stratosphere Tower C1
- 22 Vegas Indoor Skydiving C3

Sleeping
- Caesars Palace .... (see 5)
- Cosmopolitan .... (see 7)
- Four Seasons Hotel .... (see 25)
- 23 Golden Nugget A1
- Hard Rock .... (see 2)
- 24 Main Street Station A1
- 25 Mandalay Bay B7
- 26 MGM Grand B6
- New York–New York .... (see 15)
- Paris Las Vegas .... (see 16)
- 27 Signature at MGM Grand B6
- Skylofts .... (see 26)
- 28 Vdara A5
- 29 Venetian B4

Eating
- 30 Bacchanal B5
- Bouchon .... (see 29)
- 31 Buffet at Bellagio B5
- 32 Container Park B2
- 33 Earl of Sandwich B5
- 34 Firefly D4
- Gordon Ramsay Steak .... (see 16)
- 35 Jean Philippe Patisserie B5
- Joël Robuchon .... (see 26)
- 36 Lotus of Siam D2
- Sage .... (see 4)
- Social House .... (see 46)
- 37 Stripburger B3
- 38 Tacos El Gordo C3
- Wicked Spoon Buffet .... (see 7)
- 39 Wild B2

Drinking & Nightlife
- Beat .... (see 8)
- Chandelier Bar .... (see 7)
- 40 Double Barrel Roadhouse B6
- 41 Double Down Saloon D6
- 42 Downtown Cocktail Room B2
- 43 Fireside Lounge C3
- Marquee .... (see 7)
- Tao .... (see 29)
- 44 XS C3

Entertainment
- 45 Beatles LOVE B4
- House of Blues .... (see 25)
- Le Rêve The Dream .... (see 18)
- Michael Jackson ONE .... (see 25)
- Midway .... (see 6)

Shopping
- 46 Crystals B6
- 47 Fashion Show B3
- Forum Shops .... (see 5)
- Grand Canal Shoppes at the Venetian .... (see 29)

New York–New York CASINO

(702-740-6969; www.newyorknewyork.com; 3790 Las Vegas Blvd S; 24hr) Opened in 1997, the mini-megalopolis of New York–New York features scaled-down replicas of the Big Apple's landmarks, such as the **Statue of Liberty** and a miniature **Brooklyn Bridge**, out front. Rising above are perspective-warping replicas of the Chrysler, Empire State and Ziggurat buildings. Wrapped around the hotel's flashy facade is the pièce de résistance: the **Big Apple roller coaster** (1 ride/day pass $14/25; 11am-11pm Sun-Thu, 10:30am-midnight Fri & Sat;), with cars resembling NYC taxicabs.

Luxor CASINO

(702-262-4000; www.luxor.com; 3900 Las Vegas Blvd S; 24hr) Named after Egypt's splendid ancient city on the east bank of the Nile, the landmark Luxor once had the biggest wow factor on the south Strip. While the theme easily could have produced a pyramid of gaudiness, instead it resulted in a relatively refined shrine to Egyptian art, architecture and antiquities. Some of the more outrageous kitsch has gone the way of the pharaohs, though – in efforts to modernize, the Luxor was 'de-themed' some years ago.

Mirage Volcano LANDMARK
(Mirage; shows 8pm-midnight;) FREE When the Mirage's trademark artificial volcano erupts with a roar out of a 3-acre lagoon, it inevitably brings traffic on the Strip to a screeching halt. Be on the lookout for wisps of smoke escaping from the top, signaling that the fiery Polynesian-style inferno, with a soundtrack by a Grateful Dead drummer and an Indian tabla musician, is about to begin.

Shark Reef Aquarium AQUARIUM
(702-632-4555; www.sharkreef.com; 3950 Las Vegas Blvd S, Mandalay Bay; adult/child 5-12yr $18/12; 10am-10pm daily late May-early Sep, 10am-8pm Sun-Thu, to 10pm Fri & Sat early Sep-late May, last admission 1hr before closing;) M-Bay's unusual walk-through aquarium is home to 2000 submarine beasties, including jellyfish, moray eels, stingrays and, yes, some sharks. Other rare and endangered toothy reptiles on display include some of the world's last remaining golden crocodiles. A staff of scuba-diver caretakers and naturalists are available to chat as you wander around. Better yet, go scuba diving yourself (from $650).

Madame Tussauds MUSEUM
(866-841-3739, 702-862-7800; www.madametussauds.com/lasvegas; 3355 Las Vegas Blvd S, Venetian; adult/child 4-12yr $30/20; usually 10am-9pm;) Outside the Venetian next to the mock Rialto Bridge is this interactive version of the wax museum many love to loathe. Strike a pose with Elvis, pretend to marry George Clooney, go '4D' with Marvel Super Heroes or don Playboy Bunny ears and sit on Hugh Hefner's lap (be sure to touch him, because Hef's made of silicone – how appropriate!)

Downtown & Off the Strip

★Mob Museum MUSEUM
(702-229-2734; www.themobmuseum.org; 300 Stewart Ave; adult/child 11-17yr $20/14; 10am-7pm Sun-Thu, to 8pm Fri & Sat; Deuce) It's hard to say what's more impressive: the museum's physical location in a historic federal courthouse where mobsters sat for federal hearings in 1950–51, the fact that the board of directors is headed up by a former FBI special agent, or the thoughtfully curated exhibits telling the story of organized crime in America. In addition to hands-on FBI equipment and mob-related artifacts, the museum boasts a series of multimedia exhibits featuring interviews with real-life Tony Sopranos.

★Neon Museum – Neon Boneyard MUSEUM
(702-387-6366; www.neonmuseum.org; 770 Las Vegas Blvd N; 1hr tour adult/child 7-17yr daytime $18/12, after dark $25/22; tours daily, schedules vary; 113) This nonprofit project is doing what almost no one else does: saving Las Vegas' history. Book ahead for a fascinating guided walking tour of the 'neon boneyard,' where irreplaceable vintage neon signs – Las Vegas' original art form – spend their retirement. Start exploring at the visitor center inside the salvaged La Concha Motel lobby, a mid-Century Modern icon designed by African American architect Paul Revere Williams. Tours are usually given throughout the day, special events and weather permitting.

★Hard Rock CASINO
(702-693-5000; www.hardrockhotel.com; 4455 Paradise Rd; 24hr; 108) The world's original rock 'n' roll casino houses what may be

LAS VEGAS FOR CHILDREN

With its current focus on adult-oriented fun – 'What happens in Vegas stays in Vegas' – the city isn't a great choice for families. Visitors under 21 can walk through casinos to reach shops, shows and restaurants but they cannot stop, and younger children should always be with an adult for safety reasons. Some casinos prohibit strollers.

If you do land in Sin City with the kids, don't abandon hope. The **Circus Circus** (702-734-0410; www.circuscircus.com; 2880 Las Vegas Blvd S; 24hr;) hotel complex is all about kiddie fun, and its **Adventuredome** (www.adventuredome.com; Circus Circus; per ride $5-8, day pass over/under 48in tall $30/17; 10am-6pm daily, later on weekends & May-Sep;) is a 5-acre indoor theme park with rock climbing, bumper cars and, above all (literally) roller coasters. The **Midway** (Circus Circus; 11am-midnight;) features animals, acrobats and magicians performing on center stage.

the most impressive collection of rock-star memorabilia ever assembled under one roof. Priceless items being watched over by security guards suited up like bouncers are concert attire worn by Elvis, Britney Spears and Prince; a display case filled with Beatles mementos; Jim Morrison's handwritten lyrics to one of The Doors' greatest hits; and dozens of leather jackets and guitars formerly owned by everyone from the Ramones to U2.

Fremont Street Experience LIGHT SHOW
(www.vegasexperience.com; Fremont St, btwn Main St & Las Vegas Blvd; hourly dusk-midnight; Deuce, SDX) FREE A five-block pedestrian mall topped by an arched steel canopy and filled with computer-controlled lights, the Fremont Street Experience, between Main St and Las Vegas Blvd, has brought life back to downtown. Every evening, the canopy is transformed by hokey six-minute light-and-sound shows enhanced by 550,000 watts of wraparound sound and a larger-than-life screen lit up by 12.5 million synchronized LEDs. Soar through the air on zip-lines strung underneath the canopy from Slotzilla (p820), a 12-story, slot-machine-themed platform.

National Atomic Testing Museum MUSEUM
(702-794-5151; www.nationalatomictestingmuseum.org; 755 E Flamingo Rd, Desert Research Institute; adult/child 7-17yr $14/12; 10am-5pm Mon-Sat, noon-5pm Sun; 202) Fascinating multimedia exhibits focus on science, technology and the social history of the 'Atomic Age', which lasted from WWII until atmospheric bomb testing was driven underground in 1961 and a worldwide ban on nuclear testing was declared in 1992. View historical footage of atomic testing and examine southern Nevada's past, present and future, from Native American ways of life to the environmental legacy of atomic testing. Don't miss the cool museum shop near the ticket booth, a replica of a wNevada Test Site guard station replica.

Activities

★**Desert Adventures** KAYAKING
(702-293-5026; www.kayaklasvegas.com; 1647a Nevada Hwy, Boulder City; full-day Colorado River kayak $169; 9am-6pm Apr-Oct, 10am-4pm Nov-Mar) With Lake Mead and the Black Canyon of the Colorado River just a short drive away, would-be river rats should check in here for guided kayaking and stand up paddling (SUP) tours. Experienced paddlers can rent canoes and kayaks for DIY trips.

Escape Adventures MOUNTAIN BIKING
(800-596-2953; www.escapeadventures.com; 10575 Discovery Dr; trips incl bike from $129) The source for guided mountain-bike tours of Red Rock Canyon State Park.

Qua Baths & Spa SPA
(866-782-0655; 3570 Las Vegas Blvd, Caesars Palace; fitness center day pass $25, incl spa facilities $45; 6am-8pm) Qua evokes the ancient Roman rituals of indulgent bathing. Try a signature 'bath liqueur,' a personalized potion of herbs and oils poured into your own private tub. The women's side includes a tea lounge, an herbal steam room and an arctic ice room where artificial snow falls. On the men's side, there's a barber spa and big-screen sports TVs.

Sleeping

Room rates in Las Vegas rise and fall dramatically each and every day; visiting on weekdays is almost always cheaper than weekends. Note that almost every Strip hotel also charges an additional 'resort fee' of up to $25 per day.

The Strip

New York–New York CASINO HOTEL $
(702-740-6969, 866-815-4365; www.newyorknewyork.com; 3790 Las Vegas Blvd S; weekday/weekend r from $50/110; P ❄ @ ≈) A favorite of college students, these decent digs are rather tiny (just what one would expect in NYC).

MGM Grand CASINO HOTEL $$
(877-880-0880, 702-891-1111; www.mgmgrand.com; 3799 Las Vegas Blvd S; weekday/weekend r from $70/140; P ❄ @ ≈) Vegas' biggest hotel, with high-end **Skylofts** (877-646-5638, 702-891-3832; www.skyloftsmgmgrand.com; ste from $1000; P ❄ @ ≈), apartment-style **Signature** (877-727-0007, 702-797-6000; www.signaturemgmgrand.com; 145 E Harmon Ave; weekday/weekend ste from $95/170; P ❄ @ ≈) suites and the Strip's most mammoth pool complex.

Caesars Palace CASINO HOTEL $$
(702-731-7110, 866-227-5938; www.caesarspalace.com; 3570 Las Vegas Blvd S; weekday/weekend r from $90/125; P ❄ @ ≈) Expect towers of oversized rooms with marble bathrooms, Nobu boutique hotel and the Garden of the Gods pool complex.

LAS VEGAS: HIGH-OCTANE THRILLS

- **Driving** Hop into a race car at **Richard Petty Driving Experience** (800-237-3889; www.drivepetty.com; 6975 Speedway Blvd, Las Vegas Motor Speedway, off I-15 exit 54; ride-alongs from $99; drives from $449; hours vary) or careen around the track in a souped-up go-kart at **Fast Lap** (702-736-8113; www.fastlaplv.com; 4288 S Polaris; per race $25; Mon-Sat 10am-11pm, Sun 10am-10pm).
- **Indoor Skydiving** No time to jump from a plane? Enjoy the thrill without the altitude at **Vegas Indoor Skydiving** (702-731-4768; www.vegasindoorskydiving; 200 Convention Center Dr; single flight $85; 9.45am-8pm).
- **Shooting** If you're dying to fire a sub-machine gun or feel the heft of a Glock in your hot little hands, visit the high-powered **Gun Store** (702-454-1110; http://thegunstorelasvegas.com; 2900 E Tropicana Ave; packages from $90; 9am-6:30pm; 201), with an indoor video training range.
- **Stratosphere** Atop this 110-story **casino** (702-380-7777; www.stratospherehotel.com; Stratosphere, 2000 Las Vegas Blvd S; elevator adult/concession $18/15, incl 3 thrill rides $33, all-day pass $34, SkyJump from $110; monorail Sahara) you can ride a roller coaster, drop 16 stories on the Big Shot, spin above thin air, or plummet 108ft over the edge.
- **Ziplining** Swoop above Fremont St's throngs from the world's largest slot machine, the 12-story **Slotzilla** (844-947-8342; www.vegasexperience.com; Fremont Street Experience; rides from $20; noon-midnight Sun-Thu, to 2am Fri & Sat).

Paris Las Vegas CASINO HOTEL $$
(702-946-7000, 877-796-2096; www.parislasvegas.com; 3655 Las Vegas Blvd S; weekday/weekend r from $60/135; P ❄ @ ⓦ ≋ 🐾) Standard rooms are far from Parisian, but upgraded Red Luxury Rooms, some with lipstick-shaped sofas, evoke Moulin Rouge.

Mandalay Bay CASINO HOTEL $$
(877-632-7800, 702-632-7777; www.mandalaybay.com; 3950 Las Vegas Blvd S; weekday/weekend r from $105/130; P ❄ @ ⓦ ≋; Deuce) The upscale Mandalay Bay casino hotel, exclusive **Four Seasons** (702-632-5000; www.fourseasons.com/lasvegas; weekday/weekend r from $229/289; P ❄ @ ⓦ ≋) hotel and boutique **Delano** (www.delanolasvegas.com; P ❄ @ ⓦ ≋) hotel offer variety at the Strip's southernmost resort.

Venetian CASINO HOTEL $$
(866-659-9643, 702-414-1000; www.venetian.com; 3355 Las Vegas Blvd S; weekday/weekend ste from $149/289; P ❄ @ ⓦ ≋) Vegas' own 'Most Serene Republic' features huge suites with sunken living rooms and countless luxuries from deep soaking tubs to pillow menus.

Cosmopolitan CASINO HOTEL $$$
(855-435-0005, 702-698-7000; www.cosmopolitanlasvegas.com; 3708 Las Vegas Blvd S; r/ste from $160/220; P ❄ @ ⓦ ≋ 🐾; Deuce) Frequented by style-conscious clientele, the arty, cool Cosmo wins the contest for the Strip's hippest hotel rooms.

Downtown & Off the Strip

Main Street Station CASINO HOTEL $
(702-387-1896, 800-713-8933; www.mainstreetcasino.com; 200 N Main St; weekday/weekend r from $35/70; P ❄ @ ⓦ) With tiled foyers, Victorian sconces and marble-trimmed hallways, the hotel has turn-of-the-century charm; bright, cheerful rooms have plantation shutters.

Golden Nugget CASINO HOTEL $
(702-385-7111, 800-634-3454; www.goldennugget.com; 129 E Fremont St; weekday/weekend r from $49/89; P ❄ @ ⓦ ≋) Pretend to relive the fabulous heyday of Vegas in the 1950s at this swank Fremont St address. Upgrade to a Rush Tower room.

Hard Rock CASINO HOTEL $
(702-693-5000, 800-473-7625; www.hardrockhotel.com; 4455 Paradise Rd; weekday/weekend r from $45/89; P ❄ @ ⓦ ≋) Sexy, oversized rooms and HRH suites at this shrine to rock 'n' roll pull in the SoCal party crowd. Free Strip shuttles for guests.

Eating

Sin City is an unmatched eating adventure. Reservations are a must for fancier restaurants.

The Strip

On the Strip itself, cheap eats beyond fast-food joints are hard to find.

Earl of Sandwich DELI $
(www.earlofsandwichusa.com; Planet Hollywood; menu $2-7; 24hr;) Pennypinchers sing the praises of this super-popular deli next to the casino, which pops out sandwiches on toasted artisan bread, tossed salads, wraps and a kids' menu, all with quick service, unbeatable opening hours and some of the lowest prices on the Strip.

Stripburger BURGERS $
(702-737-8747; www.stripburger.com; 3200 Las Vegas Blvd S, Fashion Show; menu $4-14; 11am-11pm Sun-Thu, to midnight Fri & Sat;) This shiny silver, open-air diner in the round serves up all-natural (hormone free etc) beef, chicken, tuna and veggie burgers, atomic cheese fries, thick milkshakes, buckets of beer and fruity cocktails, with elevated patio tables overlooking the Strip.

Tacos El Gordo MEXICAN $
(702-641-8228; http://tacoselgordobc.com; 3049 Las Vegas Blvd S; menu items $2-10; 9pm-3am Sun-Thu, to 5am Fri & Sat; Deuce, SDX) This Tijuana-style taco shop from SoCal is just the ticket when it's way late, you've got almost no money left and you're desperately craving *carne asada* (beef) or *adobada* (chili-marinated pork) tacos in hot, handmade tortillas. Adventurous eaters order the authentic *sesos* (beef brains), *cabeza* (roasted cow's head) or tripe (intestines) variations.

Jean Philippe Patisserie BAKERY, DESSERTS $
(www.jpchocolates.com; Bellagio; snacks & drinks $4-11; 7am-11pm Mon-Thu, to midnight Fri-Sun;) As certified by the *Guinness Book of World Records*, the world's largest chocolate fountain cascades inside the front windows of this champion pastry-maker's shop, known for its fantastic sorbets, gelati, pastries and chocolate confections. Coffee and espresso are above the Strip's low-bar average.

Social House ASIAN, SUSHI $$$
(702-736-1122; www.angelmg.com; 3720 Las Vegas Blvd S, Crystals, CityCenter; prix-fixe lunch $20-25, shared plates $5-50, dinner mains $25-50; noon-5pm & 6-10pm daily) You won't find a sexier sushi bar and pan-Asian grill anywhere on the Strip. Low-slung tatami cushions, faded Japanese woodblock prints and a sky terrace inside Crystals mall add up to a seductively date-worthy atmosphere. Be thrilled by the imported sake list. Dinner reservations recommended.

Bouchon FRENCH $$$
(702-414-6200; www.bouchonbistro.com; Venezia Tower, 3355 Las Vegas Blvd S, Venetian; mains breakfast & brunch $12-26, dinner $19-51; 7-10:30am & 5-10pm Mon-Fri, 8am-2pm & 5-10pm Sat & Sun) Napa Valley wunderkind Thomas Keller's rendition of a Lyonnaise bistro features a seasonal menu of French classics. The poolside setting complements the oyster bar (open 3pm to 10:30pm daily) and an extensive raw seafood selection. Decadent breakfasts and brunches, imported cheeses, caviar, foie gras and a superb French and Californian wine list all make appearances. Reservations essential.

Joël Robuchon FRENCH $$$
(702-891-7925; www.joel-robuchon.com/en; 3799 Las Vegas Blvd S, MGM Grand; tasting menus $120-425; 5:30-10pm Sun-Thu, to 10:30pm Fri & Sat) The acclaimed 'Chef of the Century' leads the pack in the French culinary invasion of the Strip. Adjacent to the high-rollers' gaming area, Robuchon's plush dining rooms, done up in leather and velvet, feel like a dinner party at a 1930s Paris mansion. Complex seasonal tasting menus promise the meal of a lifetime – and they often deliver.

Gordon Ramsay Steak STEAK $$$
(877-346-4642, 702-946-4663; www.gordonramsay.com; 3655 Las Vegas Blvd S, Paris Las Vegas; mains $32-105, tasting menu without/with wine pairings $145/220; 4:30-10:30pm daily, bar to midnight Fri & Sat) Carnivores, leave Paris behind and stroll through a miniaturized Chunnel into British chef Gordon Ramsay's

WORTHY INDULGENCES: BEST BUFFETS

Extravagant all-you-can-eat buffets are a Sin City tradition. Three of the best:

Bacchanal Buffet (3570 Las Vegas Blvd S, Caesars Palace; buffet per adult $26-54, child 4-10yr $15-27; ; Deuce)

Wicked Spoon Buffet (3708 Las Vegas Blvd S, Cosmopolitan; per person $26-40; 8am-2pm & 5-9pm Mon-Fri, 8am-9pm Sat & Sun;)

Buffet at Bellagio (www.bellagio.com; Bellagio; per person $19-40; 7am-10pm)

steakhouse. Ribboned in red and domed by a jaunty Union Jack, this is one of the top tables in town. Fish, chops and signature beef Wellington round out a menu of Himalayan salt room-aged steaks. No reservation? Sit at the bar instead.

Sage AMERICAN **$$$**
(☎702-590-8690; Aria, CityCenter; mains $35-54, tastings menus $59-150; ⏲5-11pm Mon-Sat) Chef Shawn McClain brings seasonal Midwestern farm-to-table cuisine to the Strip. The backlit mural over the bar almost steals the scene, but creative twists on meat-and-potatoes classics – imagine pork terrine with blue corn succotash and salsa verde – and seafood and pasta also shine. After dinner, sip absinthe poured from a rolling cart. Reservations essential; business casual dress.

Downtown & Off the Strip

As a rule, downtown's restaurants offer better value than those on the Strip.

Container Park FAST FOOD **$**
(☎702-637-4244; http://downtowncontainerpark.com; 707 E Fremont St; menu $3-9; ⏲11am-11pm Sun-Thu, to 1am Fri & Sat; 🚌Deuce) With food-truck-style menus, outdoor patio seating and late-night hours, food vendors inside the cutting-edge Container Park sell something to satisfy everyone's appetite. When we last stopped by, the ever-changing line-up included Pinche's Tacos for Mexican flavors, Pork & Beans for piggy goodness, Southern-style Big Ern's BBQ, raw-food and healthy vegan cuisine from Simply Pure and Bin 702 wine bar. After 9pm only over-21s are allowed.

Veggie Delight VEGETARIAN **$**
(☎702-310-6565; www.veggiedelight.biz; 3504 Wynn Rd; menu $3-10; ⏲11am-9pm; 🖉) This Buddhist-owned, Vietnamese-flavored vegetarian and vegan kitchen mixes up chakra color-coded Chinese herbal tonics and makes *banh mi*-style sandwiches, hot pots and noodle soups.

Wild PIZZA, AMERICAN **$$**
(☎702-778-8800; http://eatdrinkwild.com; 150 Las Vegas Blvd N, Ogden; pizzas $9-26, brunch prix-fixe menu $18; ⏲7am-7pm Mon-Sat; 🖉; 🚌Deuce) At sidewalk level in a high-rise condo complex, this gluten-free pizzeria sources farm-fresh ingredients that are sustainably harvested. Up the feel-good factor with a fruit smoothie from the juice bar or with a side salad of kale and smoked tofu. Pizza flavors are rule-breaking, from white-truffle ricotta to chicken tikka masala. The unique beer and wine list encourages socializing.

Firefly TAPAS **$$**
(☎702-369-3971; www.fireflylv.com; 3824 Paradise Rd; shared plates $5-12, mains $15-20; ⏲11:30am-midnight; 🚌108) Firefly is always packed with a fashionable local crowd, who come for well-prepared Spanish and Latin American tapas, such as *patatas bravas* (potatoes in spicy tomato sauce), chorizo-stuffed empanadas and vegetarian bites like garbanzo beans seasoned with chili, lime and sea salt. A backlit bar dispenses the house specialty sangria – red, white or sparkling – and fruity mojitos. Reservations recommended.

Lotus of Siam THAI **$$**
(☎702-735-3033; www.saipinchutima.com; 953 E Sahara Ave; mains $9-30; ⏲11:30am-2:30pm Mon-Fri, 5:30-10pm daily; 🖉; 🚌SDX) Saipin Chutima's authentic northern Thai cooking has won almost as many awards as her distinguished European and New World wine cellar. Renowned food critic Jonathan Gold once called it 'the single best Thai restaurant in North America.' Although the strip-mall hole-in-the-wall may not look like much, foodies flock here. Reservations essential.

Drinking & Nightlife

The Strip

Chandelier Bar COCKTAIL BAR
(3708 Las Vegas Blvd S, Cosmopolitan; ⏲24hr; 🚌Deuce) Towering high in the center of Cosmopolitan, this ethereally designed cocktail bar is inventive yet beautifully simple, with three levels connected by romantic curved staircases, all draped with glowing strands of glass beads. The second level is headquarters for molecular mixology (order a martini made with liquid nitrogen), while the third specializes in floral and fruit infusions.

Double Barrel Roadhouse BAR
(www.sbe.com/doublebarrel; 3770 Las Vegas Blvd S, Monte Carlo; ⏲11am-2am) With a Strip-view patio, this double-decker bar and grill anchors the new pedestrian district between the Monte Carlo and New York–New York casino hotels. Staff pour stiff housemade wine coolers into mason jars, cook up Southern comfort food and cheer the live rock bands on stage.

Fireside Lounge LOUNGE
(www.peppermilllasvegas.com; 2985 Las Vegas Blvd S, Peppermill; 24hr; Deuce) Don't be blinded by the outlandishly bright neon outside. The Strip's most spellbinding retro hideaway awaits at the pint-sized Peppermill casino. Courting couples adore the sunken fire pit, fake tropical foliage and 64oz goblet-sized 'Scorpion' cocktails served by waiters in black evening gowns.

Downtown & Off the Strip

Want to chill out with the locals? Loads of new and interesting bars and cafes are opening along E Fremont St, making it the number-one alternative to the Strip.

Downtown Cocktail Room LOUNGE
(702-880-3696; www.thedowntownlv.com; 111 Las Vegas Blvd S; 4pm-2am Mon-Fri, 7pm-2am Sat; Deuce) With a serious list of classic cocktails and housemade inventions, this low-lit speakeasy is undeniably romantic, and it feels decades ahead of downtown's old-school casinos. The entrance is ingeniously disguised: the door looks like just another part of the wall until you discover the sweet spot you have to push to get in. Happy hour runs 4pm to 8pm weekdays.

Double Down Saloon BAR
(www.doubledownsaloon.com; 4640 Paradise Rd; 24hr; 108) This dark, psychedelic gin joint appeals to the lunatic fringe. It never closes, there's never a cover charge, the house drink is called 'ass juice' and it claims to be the birthplace of the bacon martini. When live bands aren't terrorizing the crowd, the jukebox vibrates with New Orleans jazz, British punk, Chicago blues and surf-guitar king Dick Dale.

EMERGENCY ARTS

A coffee shop, an art gallery, studios and a de facto community center of sorts, all under one roof and right smack downtown? The **Emergency Arts** (www.emergencyartslv.com; 520 E Fremont St; Deuce) FREE building, also home to **Beat Coffeehouse** (702-385-2328; www.thebeatlv.com; 7am-midnight Mon-Fri, from 9am Sat, 9am-5pm Sun; ; Deuce) is a friendly bastion of laid-back cool and strong coffee where vintage vinyl spins on old turntables. If you're aching to meet some savvy locals who know their way around town, this is your hangout spot.

Entertainment

There's always plenty going on in Las Vegas, and **Ticketmaster** (www.ticketmaster.com) sells tickets for pretty much everything. **Tix 4 Tonight** (877-849-4868; www.tix4tonight.com; 3200 Las Vegas Blvd S, Fashion Show; 10am-8pm) offers half-price tickets for a limited lineup of same-day shows, plus smaller discounts on 'always sold-out' shows.

Nightclubs & Live Music

In 2015 seven of the 10 highest-earning nightclubs in the US were in Vegas; a couple earned more than $100 million each. Admission prices vary wildly, according to the mood of door staff, male-to-female ratio, and how crowded the club may be. Avoid waiting in line by booking ahead with the club VIP host. Most bigger clubs have someone working the door in the late afternoon and early evening. Hotel concierges often have free passes for clubs, or can at least make reservations. Bottle service usually waives cover charges and waiting in line, but is hugely expensive.

XS CLUB
(702-770-0097; www.xslasvegas.com; Encore; cover $20-50; 9:30pm-4am Fri & Sat, from 10:30pm Sun & Mon) XS is *the* hottest nightclub in Vegas – at least for now. Its extravagantly gold-drenched decor and over-the-top design mean you'll be waiting in line for cocktails at a bar towered over by ultra-curvaceous, larger-than-life golden statues of female torsos. Famous-name electronica DJs make the dance floor writhe, while high rollers opt for VIP bottle service at private poolside cabanas.

Marquee CLUB
(702-333-9000; www.marqueelasvegas.com; 3708 Las Vegas Blvd S, Cosmopolitan; 10pm-5am Thu-Sat & Mon) The Cosmopolitan's glam nightclub cashes in on its multi-million-dollar sound system and a happening dance floor surrounded by towering LED screens displaying light projections that complement EDM tracks handpicked by famous-name DJs. From late spring through early fall, Marquee's mega-popular daytime pool club heads outside to a lively party deck overlooking the Strip, with VIP cabanas and bungalows.

Tao CLUB
(☎702-388-8588; www.taolasvegas.com; 3355 Las Vegas Blvd S, Grand Canal Shoppes at the Venetian; cover $20-50; ⏲nightclub 10pm-5am Thu-Sat, lounge 5pm-1am daily) Like a Top 40 hit that's maxed out on radio play, Tao has reached a been-there, done-that saturation point. Newbies still gush at the decadent details and libidinous vibe, from a giant golden Buddha to nearly naked go-go dancers languidly caressing themselves in rose petal-strewn bathtubs. On the crowded dance floor, Paris Hilton look-alikes bump and grind to hip-hop remixes.

Production Shows

There are hundreds of shows to choose from in Vegas. Any Cirque du Soleil offering tends to be an unforgettable experience.

Beatles LOVE THEATER
(☎702-792-7777, 800-963-9634; www.cirquedusoleil.com; Mirage; tickets $79-180; ⏲7pm & 9:30pm Thu-Mon; 👪) Another smash hit from Cirque du Soleil, *Beatles LOVE* started as the brainchild of the late George Harrison. Using *Abbey Road* master tapes, the show psychedelically fuses the musical legacy of the Beatles with Cirque's high-energy dancers and signature aerial acrobatics. Come early to photograph the trippy, rainbow-colored entryway and grab drinks at Abbey Road bar, next to Revolution Lounge.

Michael Jackson ONE THEATER
(☎800-745-3000, 877-632-7400; www.cirquedusoleil.com; 3950 Las Vegas Blvd S, Mandalay Bay; tickets from $69; ⏲7pm & 9:30pm Sat-Wed) Cirque du Soleil's musical tribute to the King of Pop blasts onto M-Bay's stage with show-stopping dancers and lissome acrobats and aerialists all moving to a soundtrack of MJ's hits, moon-walking all the way back to his break-out platinum album *Thriller*. No children under five years old allowed.

Le Rêve The Dream THEATER
(☎888-320-7110, 702-770-9966; http://boxoffice.wynnlasvegas.com; 3131 Las Vegas Blvd S, Wynn; tickets $105-195; ⏲7pm & 9:30pm Fri-Tue) Underwater acrobatic feats by scuba-certified performers are the centerpiece of this intimate 'aqua-in-the-round' theater, which holds a 1-million-gallon swimming pool. Critics call it a less-inspiring version of Cirque's *O*, while devoted fans find the romantic underwater tango, thrilling high dives and visually spectacular adventures to be superior. Beware: the cheapest seats are in the 'splash zone.'

House of Blues LIVE MUSIC
(☎702-632-7600; www.houseofblues.com; 3950 Las Vegas Blvd S, Mandalay Bay; ⏲box office 9am-9pm) Live blues is definitely not the only game at this imitation Mississippi Delta juke joint. Big-name touring acts entertain the standing room-only audiences with soul, pop, rock, metal, country, jazz and even burlesque. For some shows, you can skip the long lines to get in by eating dinner in the restaurant beforehand, then showing your same-day receipt.

Shopping

Fashion Show MALL
(www.thefashionshow.com; 3200 Las Vegas Blvd S; ⏲10am-9pm Mon-Sat, 11am-7pm Sun; 👪) Nevada's largest shopping mall is an eye-catcher: topped off by 'the Cloud,' a silver multimedia canopy resembling a flamenco hat, Fashion Show harbors more than 250 chain shops and department stores. Hot European additions to the mainstream lineup include British clothier Topshop (and Topman for men). Live runway shows happen hourly from noon to 5pm on Friday, Saturday and Sunday.

Forum Shops MALL
(www.simon.com; Caesars Palace; ⏲10am-11pm Sun-Thu, to midnight Fri & Sat) Caesars' fanciful nod to ancient Roman marketplaces houses 160 designer emporiums, including catwalk wonders Armani, DKNY, Jimmy Choo, John Varvatos and Versace; trendsetting jewelry and accessory stores; and one-of-a-kind specialty boutiques such as Agent Provocateur lingerie, Bettie Page pin-up fashions, MAC cosmetics and Kiehl's bath-and-body shop. Don't miss the spiral escalator, a grand entrance for divas strutting off the Strip.

Crystals MALL
(www.crystalsatcitycenter.com; 3720 Las Vegas Blvd S; ⏲10am-11pm Sun-Thu, to midnight Fri & Sat) Design-conscious Crystals is the most striking shopping center on the Strip. Win big at blackjack? Waltz inside Christian Dior, Dolce & Gabbana, Prada, Hermès, Harry Winston, Paul Smith or Stella McCartney showrooms at CityCenter's shrine to haute couture. For sexy couples with unlimited cash to burn, Kiki de Montparnasse is a one-stop shop for lingerie and bedroom toys.

Grand Canal Shoppes at the Venetian MALL
(www.grandcanalshoppes.com; 3355 Las Vegas Blvd S, Venetian; ⏲10am-11pm Sun-Thu, to midnight Fri & Sat) Wandering painted minstrels, jugglers and laughable living statues perform in Piazza San Marco, while gondolas float past in the canals and mezzo-sopranos serenade shoppers. In this airy Italianate mall adorned with frescoes, cobblestone walkways strut past Burberry, Godiva, Sephora and 85 more luxury shops.

Information

EMERGENCY & MEDICAL SERVICES

Police (☎702-828-3111; www.lvmpd.com)

Sunrise Hospital & Medical Center (☎702-731-8000; http://sunrisehospital.com; 3186 S Maryland Pkwy; ⏲24hr) Specialized children's trauma services available at a 24-hour emergency room.

University Medical Center (UMC; ☎702-383-2000; www.umcsn.com; 1800 W Charleston Blvd; ⏲24hr) Southern Nevada's most advanced trauma center has a 24-hour ER.

INTERNET ACCESS & MEDIA

Wi-fi is available in every hotel room (usually costing $10 to $25 per day, included in the 'resort fee' wherever there is one). The Venetian and the Tropicana on the Strip, and Main Street Station downtown, offer free wi-fi throughout the property. Useful websites include:

Eater Vegas (www.vegas.eater.com) The latest news about Sin City's chefs and new restaurants. Posts a regularly updated list of the city's top 38 eateries.

Las Vegas Review-Journal (www.lvrj.com) Daily paper with a weekend guide, *Neon*, on Friday.

Las Vegas Weekly (http://lasvegasweekly.com) Free weekly with good entertainment and restaurant listings.

POST

Post Office (www.usps.com; 201 Las Vegas Blvd S; ⏲9am-5pm Mon-Fri) Downtown.

TOURIST INFORMATION

Websites offering travel information and booking services include www.lasvegas.com and www.vegas.com.

Las Vegas Convention & Visitors Authority (LVCVA; ☎702-892-7575, 877-847-4858; www.lasvegas.com; 3150 Paradise Rd; ⏲8am-5:30pm Mon-Fri; monorail Las Vegas Convention Center)

Getting There & Around

Just southeast of the major Strip casinos and easily accessible from I-15, **McCarran International Airport** (LAS; ☎702-261-5211; www.mccarran.com; 5757 Wayne Newton Blvd; 📶) has direct flights from all over the world. Most domestic flights arrive in Terminal 1, and international flights in Terminal 3. **Bell Trans** (☎800-274-7433; www.bell-trans.com) offers a shuttle service ($8 to $15) to the Strip and downtown; exit at door 9 near baggage claim to find the Bell Trans booth.

Most of the attractions in Vegas have free self-parking and valet parking available (tip $2). Fast, fun and fully wheelchair accessible, the **Las Vegas Monorail** (☎702-699-8299; www.lvmonorail.com; single-ride $5, 72hr pass $40; ⏲7am-midnight Mon, to 2am Tue-Thu, to 3am Fri-Sun) connects the SLS Station to the MGM Grand, stopping at major Strip mega-resorts along the way, but does not go to the airport or downtown. The **Deuce** (☎702-228-7433; www.rtcsnv.com; 2hr/24hr/3-day pass $6/8/20), a double-decker bus, runs 24 hours daily between the Strip and downtown.

Around Las Vegas

Sights

Red Rock Canyon National Conservation Area CANYON
(☎702-515-5350; www.redrockcanyonlv.org; entry per car/bicycle $7/3; ⏲scenic loop 6am-8pm Apr-Sep, to 7pm Mar & Oct, to 5pm Nov-Feb; visitor center 8am-4:30pm; 👪) The startling contrast between Las Vegas' artificial neon glow and the awesome natural forces found here can't be exaggerated. Created about 65 million years ago, the canyon is more like a valley, with a steep, rugged red-rock escarpment rising 3000ft on its western edge, dramatic evidence of tectonic-plate collisions. A 13-mile, one-way scenic drive passes some of the canyon's most striking features, where you can access hiking trails and rock-climbing routes, or simply be mesmerized by the vistas.

Lake Mead & Hoover Dam LAKE, HISTORIC SITE
Lake Mead and Hoover Dam are the most visited sites within the **Lake Mead National Recreation Area** (☎info desk 702-293-8906, visitor center 702-293-8990; www.nps.gov/lake; 7-day entry per vehicle $10; ⏲24hr; visitor center 9am-4:30pm Wed-Sun; 👪), which encompasses 110-mile-long Lake Mead, 67-mile-long Lake Mohave and many miles of desert around the lakes. The excellent **Alan Bible Visitors Center** (☎702-293-8990; www.nps.gov/lake; Lakeshore Scenic Dr, off US Hwy 93; ⏲9am-4.30pm), on Hwy 93 halfway between Boulder City and Hoover Dam, has information

VALLEY OF FIRE STATE PARK

A masterpiece of desert scenery filled with psychedelically shaped sandstone outcroppings, **Valley of Fire State Park** (☑ 702-397-2088; www.parks.nv.gov; per vehicle $10 ; ☉ visitor center 8:30am-4:30pm) is a great escape 55 miles northeast of Vegas. Hwy 169 runs past the visitor center, which has hiking and camping (tent/RV sites $20/30) information and excellent desert-life exhibits.

on recreation and desert life. From there, North Shore Rd winds around the lake and makes a great scenic drive.

Straddling the Arizona–Nevada border, the graceful curve and art-deco style of the 726ft **Hoover Dam** (☑ 702-494-2517, 866-730-9097; www.usbr.gov/lc/hooverdam; off Hwy 93; admission & 30min tour adult/child 4-16yr $15/12; with 1hr tour $30; ☉ 9am-6pm Apr-Oct, to 5pm Nov-Mar; ♿) contrasts superbly with the stark landscape. Don't miss a stroll over the new **Mike O'Callaghan-Pat Tillman Memorial Bridge** (Hwy 93) which features a pedestrian walkway with perfect views upstream of Hoover Dam. (Not recommended for anyone with vertigo.) Visitors can either take the 30-minute **power plant tour** or the more in-depth, one-hour Hoover Dam tour.

Tickets for both tours are sold at the visitor center. Tickets for the power plant tour only can be purchased online.

For a relaxing lunch or dinner break, head to nearby downtown Boulder City, where **Milo's** (☑ 702-293-9540; www.miloswinebar.com; 534 Nevada Hwy, Boulder City; mains $9-14; ☉ 11am-10pm Sun-Thu, to 11pm Fri & Sat) serves fresh sandwiches, salads and gourmet cheese plates at sidewalk tables outside the wine bar.

Western Nevada

A vast and mostly undeveloped sagebrush steppe, Nevada's western corner is carved by mountain ranges and parched valleys. Modern Nevada began here, with the discovery of Virginia City's famous Comstock silver lode. Modern visitors flock here for hiking, biking and skiing adventures on its many mountains. Contrasts are as extreme as the weather: one moment you're driving through a quaint historic town full of grand homes built by silver barons, and the next you spot a tumbleweed blowing past a homely little bar that turns out to be the local (and legal) brothel.

Reno

In downtown Reno you can gamble at one of two-dozen casinos in the morning then walk down the street and shoot rapids at the Truckee River Whitewater Park. That's what makes 'The Biggest Little City in the World' so interesting – it's holding tight to its gambling roots but also earning kudos as a top-notch base camp for outdoor adventure. The Sierra Nevada Mountains and Lake Tahoe are less than an hour's drive away, and the region teems with lakes, trails and ski resorts. Wedged between the I-80 and the Truckee River, downtown's N Virginia St is casino central; south of the river it continues as S Virginia St.

◉ Sights

National Automobile Museum MUSEUM
(☑ 775-333-9300; www.automuseum.org; 10 S Lake St; adult/child 6-18yr $10/4; ☉ 9:30am-5:30pm Mon-Sat, 10am-4pm Sun; ♿) Stylized street scenes illustrate a century's worth of automobile history at this engaging car museum. The collection is enormous and impressive, with one-of-a-kind vehicles – including James Dean's 1949 Mercury from *Rebel Without a Cause*, a 1938 Phantom Corsair and a 24-karat-gold-plated DeLorean – and rotating exhibits bringing in all kinds of souped-up or fabulously retro rides.

Nevada Museum of Art MUSEUM
(☑ 775-329-3333; www.nevadaart.org; 160 W Liberty St; adult/child 6-12yr $10/1; ☉ 10am-5pm Wed & Fri-Sun, to 8pm Thu) In a sparkling building inspired by the geological formations of the Black Rock Desert north of town, a floating staircase leads to galleries showcasing temporary exhibits and eclectic collections on the American West, labor and contemporary landscape photography.

Circus Circus CASINO
(www.circusreno.com; 500 N Sierra St; ☉ 24hr; ♿) The most family friendly of the bunch, Circus Circus has free circus acts to entertain kids beneath a giant, candy-striped big top, which also harbors a gazillion carnival and video games that look awfully similar to slot machines.

Silver Legacy CASINO
(www.silverlegacyreno.com; 407 N Virginia St; ⏲24hr) A Victorian-themed place, the Silver Legacy is easily recognized by its white landmark dome, where a giant mock mining rig periodically erupts into a fairly tame sound-and-light spectacle.

Eldorado CASINO
(www.eldoradoreno.com; 345 N Virginia St; ⏲24hr) The Eldorado has a kitschy Fountain of Fortune that probably has Italian sculptor Bernini spinning in his grave.

Harrah's CASINO
(www.harrahsreno.com; 219 N Center St; ⏲24hr) Founded by Nevada gambling pioneer William Harrah in 1946, it's still one of the biggest and most popular casinos in town.

Activities

Reno is a 30- to 60-minute drive from Tahoe ski resorts, and many hotels and casinos offer special stay-and-ski packages.

Mere steps from the casinos, the Class II and III rapids at the city-run **Truckee River Whitewater Park** (www.reno.gov) are gentle enough for kids riding inner tubes, yet also sufficiently challenging for professional freestyle kayakers. Two courses wrap around Wingfield Park, a small river island that hosts free concerts in summertime. **Tahoe Whitewater Tours** (☎775-787-5000; www.truckeewhitewaterrafting.com; 400 Island Ave; rafting adult/child $68/58) and **Wild Sierra Adventures** (☎866-323-8928; www.wildsierra.com; 11 N Sierra St; tubing $29) offer kayak trips and lessons.

Sleeping

Lodging rates vary widely, day by day. Sunday through Thursday are generally the best; Friday is more expensive and Saturday can be as much as triple the midweek rate.

In summer there's gorgeous high-altitude camping at **Mt Rose** (☎877-444-6777; www.recreation.gov; Hwy 431; RV & tent sites $17-50; ⏲mid-Jun–Sep).

Sands Regency HOTEL $
(☎775-348-2200; www.sandsregency.com; 345 N Arlington Ave; r Sun-Thu from $39, Fri & Sat from $85; P ❄ 🛜 ≈ 🐾) With some of the largest standard digs in town, rooms here are decked out in a cheerful tropical palette of upbeat blues, reds and greens – a visual relief from standard-issue motel decor. The 17th-floor gym and Jacuzzi are perfectly positioned to capture your eyes with drop-dead panoramic mountain views. An outdoor pool opens in summer. Empress Tower rooms are best.

RENO AREA TRAIL INFORMATION

For extensive information on regional hiking and biking trails, including the Mt Rose summit trail and the Tahoe-Pyramid Bikeway, download the Truckee Meadows Trails Guide (www.washoecounty.us), or pick up a copy at the **visitor center** (www.galenacreekvisitorcenter.org; 18250 Mt Rose Hwy; ⏲9am-6pm Tue-Sun) at Galena Creek Regional Park, where you'll find three of the trails it describes.

Wildflower Village MOTEL, B&B $
(☎775-747-8848; www.wildflowervillage.com; 4395 W 4th St; dm $34, motel $63, B&B $142; P ❄ @ 🛜) Perhaps more of a state of mind than a motel, this artists colony on the west edge of town has a tumbledown yet creative vibe. Individual murals decorate the facade of each room, and you can hear the freight trains rumble on by. Frequent live music and poetry readings at its cafe and pub, and bike rentals available.

Peppermill CASINO HOTEL $$
(☎866-821-9996, 775-826-2121; www.peppermillreno.com; 2707 S Virginia St; r Sun-Thu $59-129, Fri & Sat $79-209, resort fee $16; P ❄ @ 🛜 ≈) 🍃 With a dash of Vegas-style opulence, the ever-popular Peppermill boasts Tuscan-themed suites in its newest 600-room tower, and plush remodeled rooms throughout the rest of the property. The three sparkling pools (one indoor) are dreamy, with a full spa on hand. Geothermal energy powers the resort's hot water and heat.

Eating

Reno's dining scene goes far beyond the casino buffets.

Peg's Glorified Ham & Eggs DINER $
(www.eatatpegs.com; 420 S Sierra St; mains $7-14; ⏲6:30am-2pm; 👪) Locally regarded as the best breakfast in town, Peg's offers tasty grill food that's not too greasy.

★ **Old Granite Street Eatery** NEW AMERICAN $$
(☎775-622-3222; www.oldgranitestreeteatery.com; 243 S Sierra St; dinner mains $12-26; ⏲11am-10pm Mon-Thu, to 11pm Fri, 10am-11pm Sat, to 3pm Sun)

WORTH A TRIP

BURNING MAN

For one week at the end of August, **Burning Man** (www.burningman.com; admission $380) explodes onto the sunbaked Black Rock Desert, and Nevada sprouts a third major population center – Black Rock City. An experiential art party (and alternate universe) that climaxes in the immolation of a towering stick figure, Burning Man is a whirlwind of outlandish theme camps, dust-caked bicycles, bizarre bartering, costume-enhanced nudity and a general relinquishment of inhibitions.

A lovely well-lit place for organic and local comfort food, old-school artisanal cocktails and seasonal craft beers, this antique-strewn hotspot enchants diners with its stately wooden bar, water served in old liquor bottles and lengthy seasonal menu. Forgot to make a reservation? Check out the iconic rooster and pig murals and wait at a communal table fashioned from a barn door.

Silver Peak Restaurant & Brewery BREWPUB $$
(www.silverpeakrestaurant.com; 124 Wonder St; lunch $8.50-11, dinner $10-23; ⌚restaurant 11am-10pm Sun-Thu, to 11pm Sat & Sun, pub open 1hr later) Casual and pretense free, this place hums with the chatter of happy locals settling in for a night of microbrews and great eats, from pizza with barbecue chicken to shrimp curry and filet mignon.

Drinking

Jungle CAFE, WINE BAR
(www.thejunglereno.com; 246 W 1st St; ⌚coffee 6am-midnight, wine 3pm-midnight Mon-Thu, 3pm-2am Fri, noon-2am Sat, noon-midnight Sun; wi-fi) A side-by-side coffee shop and wine bar with a cool mosaic floor and riverside patio all rolled into one. The wine bar has weekly tastings, while the cafe serves breakfast bagels and lunchtime sandwiches ($6 to $8) and puts on diverse music shows.

Entertainment

The free weekly *Reno News & Review* (www.newsreview.com) is your best source for listings.

Edge CLUB
(www.edgeofreno.com; 2707 S Virginia St, Peppermill; admission $20; ⌚Thu & Sat from 10pm, Fri from 7pm) The Peppermill reels in the nighthounds with a big glitzy dance club, where go-go dancers, smoke machines and laser lights may cause sensory overload. If so, step outside to the lounge patio and relax in front of cozy fire pits.

Knitting Factory LIVE MUSIC
(☎775-323-5648; http://re.knittingfactory.com; 211 N Virginia St) This midsized music venue books mainstream and indie favorites.

Information

Reno-Sparks Convention & Visitors Authority Visitor Center (☎775-682-3800; www.visitrenotahoe.com; 135 N Sierra St; ⌚9am-6pm) Also has an airport desk.

Getting There & Away

About 5 miles southeast of downtown, **Reno-Tahoe International Airport** (RNO; www.renoairport.com; wi-fi) is served by most major airlines.

The **North Lake Tahoe Express** (☎866-216-5222; www.northlaketahoeexpress.com) operates a shuttle ($45 one-way, about six to eight daily, 3:30am to midnight) to and from the airport to North Shore Lake Tahoe locations, including Truckee, Squaw Valley and Incline Village. Reserve in advance.

Greyhound (☎775-322-2970; www.greyhound.com; 155 Stevenson St) buses run daily services to Truckee, Sacramento and San Francisco ($12 to $45, five to seven hours), as does the once-daily westbound California Zephyr train route operated by **Amtrak** (☎800-872-7245, 775-329-8638; www.amtrak.com; 280 N Center St). The train is more scenic and comfortable, with a bus connection from Emeryville to San Francisco ($45, seven hours).

Getting Around

The casino hotels offer frequent free airport shuttles for their guests.

Local **RTC Ride buses** (☎775-348-7433; www.rtcwashoe.com; per ride $2) blanket the city. Most routes converge at the RTC 4th St Station downtown; useful options include the RTC Rapid line for Center St and S Virginia St, 11 for Sparks and 19 for the airport. The free Sierra Spirit bus, which has wi-fi, loops around downtown landmarks every 15 minutes from 7am to 7pm.

Carson City

An easy drive from Reno or Lake Tahoe, this underrated town is a perfect stop for lunch and a stroll around the quiet, old-fashioned downtown.

The **Kit Carson Blue Line Trail** passes pretty historic buildings on pleasant tree-lined streets. Pick up a trail map at the **visitor center** (800-638-2321, 775-687-7410; www.visitcarsoncity.com; 1900 S Carson St; 9am-4pm), a mile south of downtown.

The **1870 Nevada State Capitol** (cnr Musser & Carson; 8am-5pm Mon-Fri) FREE anchors downtown; you might spot the governor himself chatting with a constituent. Train buffs shouldn't miss the **Nevada State Railroad Museum** (775-687-6953; www.museuems.nevadaculture.org; 2180 S Carson St; adult/child under 18yr $6/free; 9am-5pm Thu-Mon), which displays train cars and locomotives from the 1800s to the early 1900s.

Grab lunch at fetching **Comma Coffee** (www.commacoffee.com; 312 S Carson St; breakfast $6-8, lunch $8-10; 7am-8pm Mon & Wed-Sat to 10pm Tue;) and eavesdrop on the politicians, or spend the evening in an English-style pub, the **Firkin and Fox** (www.thefirkinandfox.com; 310 S Carson St; mains $10-15; 11am-midnight Sun-Thu, to 2am Fri & Sat).

Hwy 395/Carson St is the main drag. For hiking and camping information, stop by the United States Forest Service (USFS) **Carson Ranger District Office** (775-882-2766; 1536 S Carson St; 8am-4:30pm Mon-Fri).

Virginia City

The discovery of the legendary Comstock Lode in 1859 sparked a silver bonanza in the mountains 25 miles south of Reno. During the 1860s gold rush, Virginia City was a high-flying, rip-roaring Wild West boomtown. Newspaperman Samuel Clemens, alias Mark Twain, spent time here during its heyday, and described the mining life in his book *Roughing It*.

The high-elevation town is a National Historic Landmark, with a main street of Victorian buildings, wooden sidewalks and some hokey but fun museums. To see how the mining elite lived, stop by the **Mackay Mansion** (775-847-0173; 129 South D St; adult/child $5/free; 10am-5pm Tue-Sun summer, hours vary winter) and the **Castle** (B St).

Locals agree that **Cafe del Rio** (www.cafedelriovc.com; 394 S C St; mains $11-16; 11am-8pm Wed-Sat, 10am-7pm Sun) serves the town's best food – a nice blend of *nuevo* Mexican and good cafe meals, including breakfast. Wet your whistle at the longtime family-run **Bucket of Blood Saloon** (www.bucketofbloodsaloonvc.com; 1 S C St; 10am-7pm), which serves up beer and 'bar rules' at its antique wooden bar ('If the bartender doesn't laugh, you are not funny').

The **visitor center** (800-718-7587, 775-847-7500; www.visitvirginiacitynv.com; 86 S C St; 9am-5pm Mon-Sat, 10am-4pm Sun) is on the main drag, C St.

The Great Basin

A trip across Nevada's Great Basin is a serene, almost haunting experience. Anyone seeking the 'Great American Road Trip' will relish the fascinating historic towns and quirky diversions tucked away along lonely desert highways.

Along I-80

The culture of the American West is diligently cultivated in **Elko**, almost 300 miles along I-80 northeast of Reno. Aspiring cowboys and cowgirls should visit the **Western Folklife Center** (www.westernfolklife.org; 501 Railroad St; adult/child 6-18yr $5/1; 10am-5:30pm Mon-Fri, to 5pm Sat), which offers art and history exhibits, musical jams, and dance nights, and hosts the **Cowboy Poetry Gathering** each January. Elko also holds a **National Basque Festival** every July 4, with games, traditional dancing and a 'Running of the Bulls'. If you've never sampled Basque food, the best place for your inaugural experience is the **Star Hotel** (www.elkostarhotel.com; 246 Silver St; lunch $6-12, dinner $15-32; 11am-2pm & 5-9pm Mon-Fri, 4:30-9:30pm Sat), a family-style supper club located in a circa-1910 boarding house for Basque sheepherders.

Along Highway 50

The transcontinental Hwy 50 cuts across the heart of Nevada, connecting Carson City in the west to Great Basin National Park in the east. Better known here by its nickname, 'The Loneliest Road in America,' it once formed part of the Lincoln Hwy, and follows the route of the Overland Stagecoach, the Pony Express and the first transcontinental telegraph line. Towns are few, and the only sounds are the hum of the engine or the whisper of wind.

CATHEDRAL GORGE STATE PARK

A hundred miles south of Great Basin National Park, at **Cathedral Gorge State Park** (☎775-728-4460; http://parks.nv.gov; Hwy 93; entry $7; ⏰visitor center 9am-4:30pm), it really does feel like you've stepped into a magnificent, many-spired cathedral, albeit one whose dome is a view of the sky. Sleep under the stars at its first-come, first-served tent & RV sites ($17), set amid badlands-style cliffs.

About 25 miles southeast of Fallon, the **Sand Mountain Recreation Area** (☎775-885-6000; www.blm.gov/nv; 7-day permit $40, admission free Tue-Wed; ⏰24hr) is worth a stop for a look at its 600ft sand dune and the ruins of a Pony Express station. Just east, enjoy a juicy burger at an old stagecoach stop, **Middlegate Station** (42500 Austin Hwy) then toss your sneakers onto the new **Shoe Tree** on the north side of Hwy 50 just ahead (the old one was cut down).

A fitting reward for surviving Hwy 50 is the awesome, uncrowded **Great Basin National Park**. Near the Nevada–Utah border, it's home to 13,063ft Wheeler Peak, which rises abruptly from the desert. Hiking trails near the summit take in superb country with glacial lakes, ancient bristlecone pines and even a permanent ice field. Admission is free; in summer, you can get oriented at the **Great Basin Visitor Center** (☎775-234-7331; www.nps.gov/grba; ⏰8am-4:30pm year-round Jun-Aug), just north of Baker.

Along Highway 95

Hwy 95 runs roughly north–south through western Nevada; its starkly scenic southern section passes the Nevada Test Site, where more than 720 nuclear weapons were exploded in the 1950s.

Along Highways 375 & 93

Hwy 375 is dubbed the 'Extraterrestrial Hwy', both for its huge number of UFO sightings and because it intersects Hwy 93 near top-secret **Area 51**, part of Nellis Air Force Base that's a supposed holding area for captured UFOs. Some people may find Hwy 375 more unnerving than the Loneliest Road; it's a desolate stretch of pavement where cars are few and far between. In the tiny town of **Rachel**, on Hwy 375, **Little A'Le' Inn** (☎775-729-2515; www.littlealeinn.com; 1 Old Mill Rd, Alamo; RV sites with hookups $15, r $45-150; ⏰restaurant 8am-9pm; ❄📶🐾) accommodates earthlings and aliens alike, and sells extraterrestrial souvenirs. Probings not included.

ARIZONA

The nation's sixth-largest state is dotted with stunning works of nature: the Grand Canyon, Monument Valley, the Chiricahua Mountains and the red rocks of Sedona, to name a few. In the shadows of these icons, a compelling cast of Native Americans, Wild West pioneers and intrepid explorers set out to tame Arizona's wilds, building prehistoric irrigation canals through desert scrub, mapping the labyrinth of canyons and mining the underground riches. Gorgeous back roads link these natural and historic sites, making Arizona a prime destination for road trippers.

Greater Phoenix, ringed by mountains, is a huge metro area with all the sights, restaurants and spas you'd expect in a spot that stakes its claim on rest and renewal. Tucson is the funky, artsy gateway to southern Arizona. Only 60 miles from the Mexican border, it embraces its cross-border heritage.

Up north is Flagstaff, a cool mountain town where locals seek relief from the searing summer heat and people come to play on the nearby San Francisco Peaks all year long. Arizona's star attraction is on its northern edge – the Grand Canyon, carved over aeons by the mighty Colorado River.

History

Native American tribes inhabited Arizona for centuries before Spanish explorer Francisco Vásquez de Coronado led an expedition from Mexico City in 1540. Settlers and missionaries followed in his wake, and by the mid-19th century the US controlled Arizona. The Indian Wars, in which the US Army battled Native Americans to protect settlers and claim land for the government, officially ended in 1886 with the surrender of Apache warrior Geronimo.

Railroad and mining expansion followed, and people arrived in ever larger numbers. After President Theodore Roosevelt visited Arizona in 1903 he supported the damming of its rivers to provide year-round water for irrigation and drinking, thus paving the way to statehood: in 1912 Arizona became the last of the 48 contiguous US states to be admitted to the Union.

The hot-button topic in Arizona these days is immigration. As many as 250,000 illegal immigrants are estimated to cross the state's 250-mile border with Mexico each year, and Arizona's legislature has responded with a wide range of controversial measures.

Information

Although Arizona is on Mountain Standard Time, it's the only western state that does not observe daylight saving time from spring to early fall – except for on the Navajo Reservation.

Generally speaking, lodging rates in southern Arizona (including Phoenix, Tucson and Yuma) are much higher in winter and spring, considered to be the 'high season', so great deals can be found in the hotter areas in summer.

Arizona Office of Tourism (602-364-3700; www.arizonaguide.com) Free state information.

Arizona Public Lands Information Center (602-417-9200; www.publiclands.org) Information about USFS, NPS, Bureau of Land Management (BLM) and state lands and parks.

Phoenix

There's much more to Phoenix than initially meets the eye. Just when you've dismissed the Southwest's largest and most populous urban area as a scorching faux-dobe wasteland of cookie-cutter subdivisions, bland malls and golf courses, you're pulled up short by a golden sunset setting the urban peaks aglow. Or a stubborn desert bloom determined to make a go of it in the dry, scrubby heat, or a busy mom-and-pop breakfast joint thumbing its nose at the ubiquitous chains.

Also known as the Valley of the Sun, Greater Phoenix includes not only Phoenix itself but also the separate communities of Scottsdale, Tempe and Mesa. The whole ensemble is ringed by mountains that range from 2500ft to more than 7000ft high. Central Ave runs north–south through Phoenix, dividing west addresses from east addresses; Washington St runs west–east, dividing north addresses from south addresses.

Above all else, Phoenix is *hot*. In summer when temperatures reach above 110°F (43°C), resort rates drop dramatically. That's great for travelers on a budget, but the most popular seasons to visit are winter and spring, when pleasant days prevail.

Sights

Greater Phoenix consists of several distinct cities. Phoenix, the largest, combines a businesslike demeanor with top-notch museums, a burgeoning cultural scene and great sports facilities. Southeast of here, lively, student-flavored Tempe (tem-pee), hugs two-mile-long Tempe Town Lake, while ho-hum Mesa, further east, holds a couple of interesting museums. Two ritzy enclaves lie northeast of Phoenix – Scottsdale, known for its cutesy old town, galleries and lavish resorts, and the largely residential Paradise Valley.

Phoenix

★**Heard Museum** MUSEUM
(602-252-8848; www.heard.org; 2301 N Central Ave; adult/child 6-12yr & student/senior $18/7.50/13.50; 9:30am-5pm Mon-Sat, 11am-5pm Sun;) This extraordinary museum spotlights the history, life, arts and culture of Native American tribes in the Southwest. Visitors will find art galleries, ethnographic displays, a get-creative kids exhibit and an unrivaled Hopi kachina gallery (many of the pieces were a gift from Barry Goldwater).

ARIZONA FACTS

Nickname Grand Canyon State

Population 6.7 million

Area 113,637 sq miles

Capital city Phoenix (population 1.51 million)

Other cities Tucson (population 526,100), Flagstaff (population 68,700), Sedona (population 10,100)

Sales tax 7.6%

Birthplace of Cesar Chavez (1927–93), singer Linda Ronstadt (b 1946)

Home of The OK Corral, mining towns turned art colonies

Politics Majority vote Republican

Famous for Grand Canyon, saguaro cacti

Best souvenir Pink cactus-shaped neon lamp from roadside stall

Driving distances Phoenix to Grand Canyon Village 235 miles, Tucson to Sedona 230 miles

Phoenix

The Heard emphasizes quality over quantity and is one of the best museums of its kind in America.

★ **Musical Instrument Museum** MUSEUM
(☎480-478-6000; www.themim.org; 4725 E Mayo Blvd; adult/child 13-19yr/under 13yr $18/14/10; ⏰9am-5pm Mon-Sat, 10am-5pm Sun, to 9pm first Fri of the month) From Uganda thumb pianos to Hawaiian ukuleles to Indonesian boat lutes, the ears have it at this lively museum that celebrates the world's musical instruments. More than 200 countries and territories are represented within five regional galleries, where music and video performances begin as you stop beside individual displays. You can also bang a drum in the Experiences Gallery and listen to Taylor Swift rock out in the Artist Gallery.

★ **Desert Botanical Garden** GARDENS
(☎480-941-1225; www.dbg.org; 1201 N Galvin Pkwy; adult/child 3-12yr/student/senior $22/10/12/20; ⏰8am-8pm Oct-Apr, 7am-8pm May-Sep) Blue bells and Mexican gold poppies are just two of the colorful showstoppers blooming from March to May along the Desert Wildflower Loop Trail at this well-nurtured botanical garden, a lovely place to reconnect with nature while learning about desert plant life. Looping trails lead past an astonishing variety of desert denizens, arranged by theme (including a Sonoran Desert nature loop and an edible desert garden).

Phoenix Art Museum MUSEUM
(☎602-257-1222; www.phxart.org; 1625 N Central Ave; adult/child 6-17yr/student/senior $15/6/10/12, Wed 3-9pm & 1st Fri of the month 6-10pm free; ⏰10am-9pm Wed, 10am-5pm Thu, Fri & Sat, noon-5pm Sun; 👪) Arizona's premier repository of fine art includes works by Claude Monet, Diego Rivera and Georgia O'Keeffe. The striking landscapes in the Western American gallery will get you in the mind-set for adventure. Got kids? Pick up a

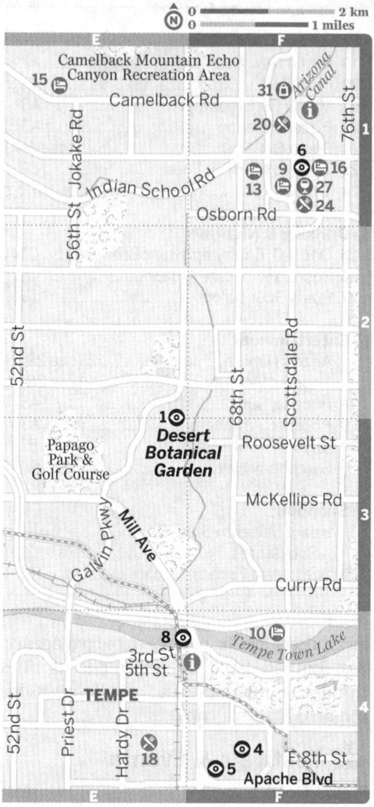

Kidpack at visitor services, examine the ingeniously crafted miniature period Thorne Rooms or visit the PhxArtKids Gallery.

Scottsdale

Scottsdale is best known for its shopping districts, which include Old Town, packed with century-old buildings (amid others built to look old), and the adjacent Arts District. Both are stuffed with art galleries, clothing stores for the modern cowgirl, and some fabulous eating and drinking.

Taliesin West ARCHITECTURE

(☎480-860-2700; www.franklloydwright.org; 12621 Frank Lloyd Wright Blvd; Insights Tour adult/child 4-12yr $36/17; ⏲tours 9am-4pm, closed Tue & Wed Jun-Aug) Frank Lloyd Wright was one of the seminal American architects of the 20th century. Taliesin West was his desert home and studio, built between 1938 and 1940. Still home to an architecture school and open to the public for guided tours, it's a prime example of organic architecture with buildings incorporating elements and structures found in surrounding nature.

Tempe

Founded in 1885 and home to around 50,000 students, **Arizona State University** (ASU; www.asu.edu) is the heart and soul of Tempe. The **Gammage Auditorium** (☎box office 480-965-3434, tours 480-965-6912; www.asugammage.com; 1200 S Forest Ave, cnr Mill Ave & Apache Blvd; admission free, performances from $20; ⏲1-4pm Mon-Fri Oct-May) was Frank Lloyd Wright's last major building.

Easily accessible by light-rail from downtown Phoenix, **Mill Avenue**, Tempe's main drag, is packed with chain restaurants, themed bars and other collegiate hangouts. It's also worth checking out **Tempe Town Lake** (www.tempe.gov/lake), an artificial lake with boat rides and hiking paths.

Mesa

Founded by Mormons in 1877, low-key Mesa is one of the fastest-growing cities in the nation and is the third-largest city in Arizona, with a population of 458,000.

★**Arizona Museum of Natural History** MUSEUM

(☎480-644-2230; www.azmnh.org; 53 N MacDonald St; adult/child 3-12yr/student/senior $10/6/8/9; ⏲10am-5pm Tue-Fri, 11am-5pm Sat, 1-5pm Sun; 👪) Even if you're not staying in Mesa, this museum is worth a trip, especially if your kids are into dinosaurs (and aren't they all?). In addition to the multi-level Dinosaur Mountain, there are loads of life-size casts of the giant beasts plus a touchable apatosaurus thighbone. Be warned: we saw one small child shrieking in abject terror at it all. Other exhibits highlight Arizona's colorful past, from a prehistoric Hohokam village to an eight-cell territorial jail.

Activities

Camelback Mountain HIKING

(☎602-261-8318; www.phoenix.gov; ⏲sunrise-sunset) This 2704ft mountain sits smack in the center of the Phoenix action. Two trails, the Cholla Trail (6131 E Cholla Ln) and the Echo Canyon Trail (4925 E McDonald Dr) climb about 1,200ft to the summit. The newly

Phoenix

Top Sights
1 Desert Botanical Garden E2
2 Heard Museum A2

Sights
3 Arizona Science Center A3
4 Arizona State University F4
5 Gammage Auditorium F4
6 Old Town Scottsdale F1
7 Phoenix Art Museum A2
8 Tempe Town Lake E4

Sleeping
9 Bespoke Inn, Cafe & Bicycles F1
10 Best Western Inn of Tempe F4
11 Budget Lodge Downtown A3
12 HI Phoenix Hostel B3
13 Hotel Valley Ho F1
14 Palomar Phoenix A3
15 Royal Palms Resort & Spa E1
16 The Saguaro F1

Eating
17 Durant's A2
18 Essence E4
19 Green New American Vegetarian A2
20 Herb Box F1
21 Matt's Big Breakfast A3
22 Pizzeria Bianco A3
Sugar Bowl .... (see 6)
23 Tee Pee Mexican Food D1
24 The Mission F1

Drinking & Nightlife
25 O.H.S.O. Eatery and nanoBrewery D1
26 Postino Winecafé Arcadia D1
27 Rusty Spur Saloon F1

Entertainment
Arizona Opera .... (see 29)
Phoenix Mercury .... (see 28)
28 Phoenix Suns A3
29 Phoenix Symphony A3
30 Rhythm Room B1
Symphony Hall .... (see 29)

Shopping
Heard Museum Shop & Bookstore .... (see 2)
31 Scottsdale Fashion Square F1

renovated Echo Canyon Trail is extremely popular and fills very early, even with 135 parking spots.

Piestewa Peak/ Dreamy Draw Recreation Area HIKING
(602-261-8318; www.phoenix.gov; Squaw Peak Dr, Phoenix; trails 5am-11pm, last entry 6:59pm) Dotted with saguaros, ocotillos and other local cacti, this convenient summit was previously known as Squaw Peak. It was renamed for local Native American soldier Lori Piestewa who was killed in Iraq in 2003. Be forewarned: the trek to the 2608ft summit is hugely popular and the park can get jammed on winter weekends. Parking lots northeast of Lincoln Dr between 22nd and 24th Sts fill early. Dogs are allowed on some park trails but not the Summit Trail.

Cactus Adventures MOUNTAIN BIKING
(480-688-4743; www.cactusadventures.com; half-day rental from $55; hours vary) Cactus Adventures rents bikes for use at South Mountain and offers guided hiking and biking tours at various parks. For rentals, they will meet you at the trailhead.

Ponderosa Stables HORSEBACK RIDING
(602-268-1261; www.arizona-horses.com; 10215 S Central Ave, Phoenix; 1/2/3hr rides $33/55/75, min 2 riders for 3hr rides; 7am-6pm Apr-Aug, 8am-6pm Sep-Mar) This outfitter leads rides through South Mountain Park. Reservations required for most trips.

Festivals & Events

Fiesta Bowl SPORT
(480-350-0911; www.fiestabowl.org; 1 Cardinals Dr, Glendale) The most popular event in Phoenix is the Fiesta Bowl football game held in early January at the University of Phoenix Stadium. It's preceded by one of the largest parades in the Southwest.

Arizona State Fair FAIR
(www.azstatefair.com; 1826 W McDowell Rd; adult/child 5-13yr $10/5) This fair lures folks to the Arizona State Fairgrounds the last two weeks of October and first week of November with a rodeo, livestock displays, a pie-eating contest and concerts.

Sleeping

Greater Phoenix is well stocked with hotels and resorts, but you won't find many B&Bs or cozy inns. When prices plummet in the scorching summer, Valley residents take advantage of super-low prices at their favorite resorts.

Phoenix

HI Phoenix Hostel HOSTEL $
(602-254-9803; www.phxhostel.org; 1026 N 9th St; dm from $23, s/d $35/45;) Fall back in love with backpacking at this small hostel with fun owners who know Phoenix and want to enjoy it with you. The 22-bed hostel sits in a working-class residential neighborhood and has relaxing garden nooks. Check-in is from 8am to 10am and 5pm to 10pm. Cash or travelers check only.

Budget Lodge Downtown MOTEL $
(602-254-7247; www.blphx.com; 402 W Van Buren St; r incl breakfast $63-70;) The Budget Lodge doesn't have time for sassiness or charisma. It's got a job to do, and it does it well: providing a clean, low-cost place to sleep. Rooms have a microwave and fridge.

La Quinta Inn & Suites Phoenix I-10 West HOTEL $
(602-595-6451; www.lq.com; 4929 W McDowell Rd; r $79-89, ste $119-129;) If you want a no-hassle, low-cost hotel that's easily accessible from the airport and the I-10, try this welcoming La Quinta. For tasty fast food, El Pollo Loco is next door. No pet fee.

Palomar Phoenix HOTEL $$$
(877-488-1908, 602-253-6633; www.hotelpalomar-phoenix.com; 2 E Jefferson St; r $309-429, studios & ste $359-369;) Shaggy pillows, antler-shaped lamps and portraits of blue cows. Yep, whimsy takes a stand at the 242-room Palomar, and we like it. Rooms are larger than average and pop with fresh, modern style. All come with yoga mats, animal-print robes and pillowtop beds with Italian Frette linens. And did we mention the nightly wine reception?

Royal Palms Resort & Spa RESORT $$$
(602-840-3610; www.royalpalmshotel.com; 5200 E Camelback Rd; r/stes/casitas from $519/529/559 ste;) Camelback Mountain is the photogenic backdrop for this posh and intimate resort, which was once the winter retreat of New York industrialist Delos Cook. Today, it's a hushed and elegant place, dotted with Spanish Colonial villas, flower-lined walkways and palms imported from Egypt. Pets can go Pavlovian for soft beds, personalized biscuits and walking services.

Scottsdale

Sleep Inn HOTEL $$
(480-998-9211; www.sleepinnscottsdale.com; 16630 N Scottsdale Rd; r incl breakfast $129-134;) It's part of a national chain, but this Sleep Inn wins points for its extensive complimentary breakfast, afternoon cookies, friendly staff and proximity to Taliesin West. There's also a laundry and free 24hr hotel shuttle that runs within 5 miles of the hotel.

★**Hotel Valley Ho** BOUTIQUE HOTEL $$$
(480-248-2000; www.hotelvalleyho.com; 6850 E Main St; r $249-299, ste $439-609;) Everything's swell at the Valley Ho, where mid-Century Modern gets a 21st-century twist. This jazzy joint once bedded Bing Crosby, Natalie Wood and Janet Leigh, and today it's a top pick for movie stars filming on location in Phoenix. Bebop music, upbeat staff and eye-magnets like the 'ice fireplace' recapture the Rat Pack vibe, and the theme travels well to the balconied rooms.

★**Bespoke Inn, Cafe & Bicycles** B&B $$$
(480-664-0730; www.bespokeinn.com; 3701 N Marshall Way; r incl brunch from $319;) Ooh la la. Are we in the English countryside

PHOENIX FOR CHILDREN

Wet 'n' Wild Phoenix (623-201-2000; www.wetnwildphoenix.com; 4243 W Pinnacle Peak Rd, Glendale; over/under 42in tall $40/30, senior $30; 10am-6pm Sun-Wed, 10am-10pm Thu-Sat Jun & Jul, varies May, Aug & Sep;) This water park has pools, tube slides, wave pools, waterfalls and floating rivers. It's in Glendale, 2 miles west of I-17 at exit 217.

Rawhide Western Town & Steakhouse (480-502-5600; www.rawhide.com; 5700 W N Loop Rd, Chandler; admission free, per attraction or show $5, unlimited day pass $15; 5-10pm Thu-Sun Jun & Jul, hr vary rest of year;) At this re-created 1880s frontier town ,about 20 miles south of Mesa, kids can enjoy all sorts of hokey-but-fun shenanigans. The steakhouse has rattlesnake for adventurous eaters.

Arizona Science Center (602-716-2000; www.azscience.org; 600 E Washington St; adult/3-17yr/senior $17/12/15; 10am-5pm;) A high-tech temple of discovery; there are more than 300 hands-on exhibits and a planetarium.

or downtown Scottsdale? At this breezy B&B guests can nibble chocolate scones in the chic cafe, loll in the infinity edge pool or pedal the neighborhood on Pashley city bikes. Rooms are plush with handsome touches like handcrafted furniture and nickel bath fixtures. Gourmet brunch served at the onsite restaurant Virtu. Book early.

The Saguaro
HOTEL **$$$**

(☑ 480-308-1100; www.jdvhotels.com; 4000 N Drinkwater Blvd; r $169-229, ste 249-669; P❋◈☎☀) Embrace your inner hipster at this candy-bright hideaway beside Old Town Scottsdale. When compared to more established Scottsdale properties there may be less attention to detail here, and the vibe skews young, but the location is great, there's a palm-dotted pool and the Saguaro's rates are lower than its neighborhood competitors.

🛏 Tempe

Best Western Inn of Tempe
HOTEL **$$**

(☑ 480-784-2233; www.innoftempe.com; 670 N Scottsdale Rd; r incl breakfast from $117; P❋@☎☀☀) This well-kept contender sits right next to the busy 202 freeway but is within walking distance of Tempe Town Lake. ASU and Mill Ave are within staggering distance. The hotel also offers a free airport shuttle. Pets are $10 each per day.

Sheraton Wild Horse Pass Resort & Spa
RESORT **$$$**

(☑ 602-225-0100; www.wildhorsepassresort.com; 5594 W Wild Horse Pass Blvd, Chandler; r $259, ste from $334; P❋@☎☀) At sunset, scan the lonely horizon for the eponymous wild horses silhouetted against the South Mountains. Owned by the Gila River tribe and nestled on their sweeping reservation south of Tempe, this 500-room resort is a stunning alchemy of luxury and Native American traditions. The domed lobby is a mural-festooned roundhouse, and rooms reflect the traditions of local tribes.

✗ Eating

Between them, Phoenix and Scottsdale hold the largest selection of restaurants in the Southwest.

✗ Phoenix

★ Matt's Big Breakfast
BREAKFAST **$**

(☑ 602-254-1074; www.mattsbigbreakfast.com; 825 N 1st St, at Garfield St; breakfast $5-10, lunch $7-10; ⊙6:30am-2:30pm) First, a warning: even on weekdays lines are often out the door. There are no reservations, so sign your name on the clipboard and expect a 20-minute wait (and bring quarters for the meter). The upside? Best. Breakfast. Ever.

★ Green New American Vegetarian
VEGAN, VEGETARIAN **$**

(☑ 602-258-1870; www.greenvegetarian.com; 2022 N 7th St; mains $6-9; ◈) Whoa, whoa, whoa. Vegan food isn't supposed to taste this good. Or is it? Your expectations will be forever raised after dining at this hip cafe where vegan chef Damon Brasch stirs up savory vegan and vegetarian dishes. The burgers, po-boys and Asian-style bowls taste as good, if not better, than their carnivorous counterparts. Order at the counter then take a seat in the garage-style digs.

Tee Pee Mexican Food
MEXICAN **$**

(☑ 602-956-0178; www.teepeemexicanfood.com; 4144 E Indian School Rd; mains $5-14; ⊙11am-10pm Mon-Sat, to 9pm Sun) If you're snobby about Mexican food, you will not be happy at Tee Pee. If, however, you like piping-hot plates piled high with cheesy, messy, American-style Mexican food, then grab a booth at this 40-year-old Phoenix fave. George W Bush ate here in 2004 and ordered two enchiladas, rice and beans – now called the Presidential Special. Dig in!

★ Dick's Hideaway
NEW MEXICAN **$$**

(☑ 602-241-1881; http://richardsonsnm.com; 6008 N 16th St; breakfast $5-20, lunch $12-16, dinner $12-35; ⊙7am-midnight Sun-Wed, to 1am Thu-Sat) At this pocket-sized ode to New Mexican cuisine, grab a small table beside the bar or settle in at the communal table in the side room and prepare for hearty servings of savory, chili-slathered New Mexican fare, from enchiladas to tamales to *rellenos*. We especially like the Hideaway for breakfast, when the Bloody Marys arrive with a shot of beer.

Pizzeria Bianco
PIZZA **$$**

(☑ 602-258-8300; www.pizzeriabianco.com; 623 E Adams St; pizzas $13-18; ⊙11am-9pm Mon, 11am-10pm Tue-Sat) James Beard–winner Chris Bianco is back in the kitchen at his famous downtown pizza joint after stepping back in 2010 due to allergies. But thanks to new medicine and his love of pizza crafting, Bianco has returned in full force, and his thin-crust gourmet pies are as popular as ever. The tiny restaurant is a convenient stop for travelers exploring the adjacent Heritage Square.

Durant's STEAK $$$
(☎602-264-5967; www.durantsaz.com; 2611 N Central Ave; lunch $12-26, dinner $22-61; ⏰11am-10pm Mon-Fri, 5-11pm Sat, 4:30-10pm Sun) This dark and manly place is a gloriously old-school steak house. You will get steak. It will be big and juicy. There will be a potato. The ambience is awesome too: red velvet cozy booths and the sense that the Rat Pack is going to waltz in at any minute.

Scottsdale

Sugar Bowl ICE CREAM $
(☎480-946-0051; www.sugarbowlscottsdale.com; 4005 N Scottsdale Rd; ice cream $2.25-9, mains $6-12; ⏰11am-10pm Sun-Thu, to midnight Fri & Sat; 👪) Get your ice-cream fix at this pink-and-white Valley institution. Also serves a full menu of sandwiches and salads.

The Mission MEXICAN $$
(☎480-636-5005; www.themissionaz.com; 3815 N Brown Ave; lunch $9-23, dinner $12-36; ⏰11am-10pm Sun-Thu, to 11pm Fri & Sat) With its dark interior and glowing votives, we'll call this *nuevo* Latin spot sexy – although our exclamations about the food's deliciousness may ruin the sultry vibe. The *tecate*-marinated steak taco with lime and avocado is superb and makes for a satisfying light lunch. The guacamole is made tableside, and wins raves. Margaritas and mojitos round out the fun.

Herb Box AMERICAN $$
(☎480-289-6160; www.theherbbox.com; 7134 E Stetson Dr; lunch $10-16, dinner $15-28, brunch $7-16; ⏰11am-3pm Mon, 11am-9pm Tue-Fri, 9am-10pm Sat, 9am-3pm Sun) It's not just about sparkle and air kisses at this chichi bistro in the heart of Old Town's Southbridge. It's also about fresh regional ingredients, artful presentation and attentive service. For a light, healthy, ever-so-stylish lunch (steak salad, turkey avocado wrap, kale and *capicola* flatbread), settle in on the patio and toast your good fortune with a blackberry mojito.

Tempe

Essence CAFE $
(☎480-966-2745; www.essencebakery.com; 825 W University Dr; breakfast $6-9.25, lunch $8-9; ⏰7am-3pm Tue-Sat; 📶) Look for French toast and egg dishes at breakfast, and salads, gourmet sandwiches and a few Mediterranean specialties at lunch. The eco-minded cafe strives to serve organic, locally grown fare. The popular macaroons are mighty fine.

★**Kai Restaurant** NATIVE AMERICAN $$$
(☎602-225-0100; www.wildhorsepassresort.com; 5594 W Wild Horse Pass Blvd, Chandler; mains $42-54, tasting menus $135-$225; ⏰5:30-9pm Tue-Sat) Native American cuisine soars to new heights at Kai, enhanced and transformed by traditional crops grown along the Gila River. Dinners strike just the right balance between adventure and comfort. Dress nicely (no shorts or hats). It's at the Sheraton Wild Horse Pass Resort & Spa on the Gila River Indian Reservation.

Drinking

Scottsdale has the greatest concentration of trendy bars and clubs; Tempe attracts the student crowd.

★**Postino Winecafé Arcadia** WINE BAR
(http://postinowinecafe.com; 3939 E Campbell Ave, at 40th St, Arcadia; ⏰11am-11pm Mon-Thu, 11am-midnight Fri, 9am-midnight Sat, 9am-10pm Sun) Your mood will improve the moment you step into this convivial, indoor-outdoor wine bar. It's a perfect gathering spot for friends ready to enjoy the good life – but solos will do fine too. Highlights include the misting patio, rave-worthy bruschetta, and more than 20 wines by the glass for $5 between 11am and 5pm.

Edge Bar BAR
(5700 E McDonald Dr, Sanctuary on Camelback Mountain, Paradise Valley) This stylish cocktail bar, perched narrowly on the side of Camelback Mountain, is an inviting place to watch the sunset. If it's full, the equally posh, big-windowed Jade Bar next door should do just fine. Both are within the plush confines of Sanctuary on Camelback Mountain. Free valet, but they'll accept a gratuity and a smile.

O.H.S.O. Eatery and nanoBrewery BREWERY
(www.ohsobrewery.com; 4900 E Indian School Rd, Phoenix) Small-batch brews and Arizona beers are the stars at this bustling nanobrewery in Arcadia. Dog-lovers can bring Fido with them to the patio. Parking is tight, so be prepared to valet (free) when it's busy. And the name? We hear it stands for Outrageous Homebrewers Social Outpost.

Rusty Spur Saloon BAR
(☎480-425-7787; www.rustyspursaloon.com; 7245 E Main St, Scottsdale; ⏲10am-1am Sun-Thu, to 2am Fri & Sat) Nobody's putting on airs at this fun-lovin', pack-'em-in-tight country bar where the grizzled Budweiser crowd gathers for cheap drinks and twangy bands. It's in an old bank building that closed during the Depression; the vault now holds liquor instead of greenbacks – except for the dollar bills hanging from the ceiling. Pardner, we kinda like this place.

Entertainment

The **Phoenix Symphony** (☎administration 602-495-1117, box office 602-495-1999; www.phoenixsymphony.org; 75 N 2nd St, box offices 1 N 1st St, 75 N 2nd St) performs at **Symphony Hall** (75 N 2nd St) and other local venues, while the **Arizona Opera** (☎602-266-7464; www.azopera.com; 75 N 2nd St) is now based at a new opera hall across the street from the Phoenix Art Museum.

The Arizona Diamondbacks play baseball at downtown's air-conditioned Chase Field, while the men's basketball team, the **Phoenix Suns** (☎602-379-7867; www.nba.com/suns; 201 E Jefferson St), and the women's team, the **Phoenix Mercury** (☎602-252-9622; www.wnba.com/mercury; 201 E Jefferson St), are also downtown, at the US Airways Center. The **Arizona Cardinals** (☎602-379-0101; www.azcardinals.com; 1 Cardinals Dr, Glendale) play football in Glendale at the new University of Phoenix Stadium, which hosted the Super Bowl in 2015.

Rhythm Room LIVE MUSIC
(☎602-265-4842; www.rhythmroom.com; 1019 E Indian School Rd, Phoenix; ⏲doors usually open 7:30pm) Some of the Valley's best live acts take the stage at this small venue, where you feel like you're in the front row of every gig. It tends to attract more local and regional talent than big names, which suits us just fine. Check the calendar for show times.

Shopping

For upscale shopping, visit the **Scottsdale Fashion Square** (www.fashionsquare.com; 7014 E Camelback, at Scottsdale Rd; ⏲10am-9pm Mon-Sat, 11am-6pm Sun) and the even more exclusive **Biltmore Fashion Park** (www.shopbiltmore.com; 2502 E Camelback Rd, at N 24th St, Phoenix; ⏲10am-8pm Mon-Sat, noon-6pm Sun). In northern Scottsdale, the outdoor **Kierland Commons** (www.kierlandcommons.com; 15205 N Kierland Blvd; ⏲10am-9pm Mon-Sat, noon-6pm Sun) pulls in the crowds.

Heard Museum Shop & Bookstore ARTS & CRAFTS
(www.heardmuseumshop.com; 2301 N Central Ave; ⏲shop 9:30am-5pm, from 11am Sun, bookstore 9:30am-5:30pm Mon-Sat, to 5pm Sun) This museum store has a top-notch collection of Native American original arts and crafts. The kachina collection alone is mind-boggling. Jewelry, pottery, Native American books and a broad selection of fine arts are also on offer. The bookstore sells a wide array of books about the Southwest.

Information

EMERGENCY & MEDICAL SERVICES

Banner Good Samaritan Medical Center (☎602-839-2000; www.bannerhealth.com; 1111 E McDowell Rd, Phoenix)

Police (☎emergency 911, non-emergency 602-262-6151; http://phoenix.gov/police; 620 W Washington St, Phoenix)

INTERNET RESOURCES & MEDIA

Arizona Republic (www.azcentral.com) Arizona's largest newspaper; publishes a free entertainment guide, *Calendar*, every Thursday.

KJZZ 91.5 FM (http://kjzz.org) National Public Radio (NPR).

Phoenix New Times (www.phoenixnewtimes.com) The major free weekly; lots of event and restaurant listings.

POST

Downtown Post Office (☎602-253-9648; 522 N Central Ave, Phoenix; ⏲9am-5pm Mon-Fri)

TOURIST INFORMATION

Downtown Phoenix Visitor Information Center (☎877-225-5749; www.visitphoenix.com; 125 N 2nd St; ⏲8am-5pm Mon-Fri) The Valley's most complete source of tourist information. Located across from the Hyatt Regency.

Mesa Convention & Visitors Bureau (☎480-827-4700, 800-283-6372; www.visitmesa.com; 120 N Center St; ⏲8am-5pm Mon-Fri)

Scottsdale Convention & Visitors Bureau (☎800-782-1117, 480-421-1004; www.experiencescottsdale.com; 4343 N Scottsdale Rd, Suite 170; ⏲8am-5pm Mon-Fri) Inside the Galleria Corporate Center.

Tempe Convention & Visitors Bureau (☎866-914-1052, 480-894-8158; www.tempetourism.com; 51 W 3rd St, Suite 105; ⏲8:30am-5pm Mon-Fri)

Getting There & Around

Sky Harbor International Airport (☎602-273-3300; http://skyharbor.com; 3400 E Sky Harbor Blvd;), 3 miles southeast of downtown Phoenix, is served by all major airlines. Its three terminals (Terminals 2, 3 and 4; there's no 1!) and the parking lots are linked by the free 24-hour Airport Shuttle Bus. The free Phoenix Sky Train runs between the economy parking lot, Terminals 3 and 4 and the METRO light-rail station at 44th St and E Washington St.

Greyhound (☎602-389-4200; www.greyhound.com; 2115 E Buckeye Rd) runs buses to Tucson ($18, two hours, six daily), Flagstaff ($25, three hours, five daily), Albuquerque ($70 to $87, 9½ hours, three daily) and Los Angeles ($46, 7½ hours, eight daily). Valley Metro's No 13 buses link the airport and the Greyhound station.

Valley Metro (☎602-253-5000; www.valleymetro.org) operates daily buses all over the Valley, and a 20-mile light-rail line linking north Phoenix with downtown Phoenix, Tempe/ASU and downtown Mesa. Fares for light-rail and bus are $2 per ride (no transfers) or $4 for a day pass. **Flash buses** (www.tempe.gov) run daily around ASU and downtown Tempe, while the **Scottsdale Trolley** (www.scottsdaleaz.gov/trolley; 11am-6pm Fri-Wed, to 9pm Thu during Artwalk) loops around downtown Scottsdale, both at no charge.

SCENIC DRIVES: ARIZONA'S BEST

Oak Creek Canyon A thrilling plunge past swimming holes, rockslides and crimson canyon walls on Hwy 89A between Flagstaff and Sedona.

Hwy 89/89A Wickenburg to Sedona The Old West meets the New West on this lazy drive past dude ranches, mining towns, art galleries and stylish wineries.

Patagonia–Sonoita Scenic Road This one's for the birds, and those who like to track them, in Arizona's southern wine country on Hwys 82 and 83.

Kayenta–Monument Valley Star in your own Western on an iconic loop past cinematic red rocks in Navajo country.

Vermilion Cliffs Scenic Road A solitary drive on Hwy 89A through the Arizona Strip linking condor country, the North Rim and Mormon hideaways.

Central Arizona

North of Phoenix, the wooded, mountainous and much cooler Colorado Plateau is draped with scenic sites and attractions. You can channel your inner goddess on a vortex, hike through sweet-smelling canyons, admire ancient Native American dwellings and delve into Old West history. The main hub, Flagstaff, is a lively and delightful college town that's the gateway to the Grand Canyon South Rim. Summer, spring and fall are the best times to visit.

On I-17, you can drive the 145 miles between Phoenix and Flagstaff in just over two hours. Opt for the more leisurely Hwy 89, though, and you'll be rewarded with beautiful landscapes and intriguing diversions.

Prescott

With its historic Victorian-era downtown and colorful Wild West heritage, Prescott feels like the Midwest meets cowboy country. Boasting more than 500 buildings on the National Register of Historic Places, it's the home of the world's oldest rodeo, while the infamous strip of old saloons on Whiskey Row, along the plaza, still ply their patrons with booze.

Just south of downtown, the fun-loving **Motor Lodge** (☎928-717-0157; www.themotorlodge.com; 503 S Montezuma St; r $119-139, ste $149, apt $159;) welcomes guests with 12 snazzy bungalows arranged around a central driveway – it's indie lodging at its best.

For breakfast, mosey into the friendly **Lone Spur Café** (☎928-445-8202; www.thelonespur.com; 106 W Gurley St; breakfast $8-18, lunch $8-11, dinner $9-24; 8am-2pm daily, 4:30-8pm Fri), where you always order your breakfast with a biscuit and a side of sausage gravy. Cajun and Southwest specialties spice up the menu at welcoming **Iron Springs Cafe** (☎928-443-8848; www.ironspringscafe.com; 1501 Iron Springs Rd; brunch $9-13, lunch $9-12, dinner $9-21; 8am-8pm Wed-Sat, 9am-2pm Sun), which sits inside an old train station 3 miles northwest of downtown.

On Whiskey Row, the **Palace** (☎928-541-1996; www.historicpalace.com; 120 S Montezuma St; 11am-9pm Sun-Thu, to 10pm Fri & Sat) is an atmospheric place to drink; you enter through swinging saloon doors into a big room anchored by a Brunswick bar.

The **chamber of commerce** (☎800-266-7534, 928-445-2000; www.visit-prescott.com; 117 W Goodwin St; ⏲9am-5pm Mon-Fri, 10am-2pm Sat & Sun) has tourist information, while **Arizona Shuttle** (☎928-776-7433; www.prescotttransit.com; 820 E Sheldon St) runs buses to/from Phoenix airport (one-way adult $32–35, child $25, 2¼ hours, up to 22 daily).

Jerome

The childhood game Chutes and Ladders comes to mind as you stroll up and down the stairways of Jerome, which clings – not always successfully, if the crumbling Sliding Jail is anything to go by – to the side of Cleopatra Hill, between Prescott and Sedona. This resurrected ghost town was known as the 'Wickedest Town in the West' during its late-1800s mining heyday, but its historic buildings have now been restored to hold galleries, restaurants, B&Bs and wine-tasting rooms.

Feeling brave? Stand on the glass platform covering the 1910ft mining shaft at **Audrey Headframe Park** (www.jeromehistoricalsociety.com; 55 Douglas Rd; ⏲8am-5pm) FREE – it's longer than the Empire State Building by 650ft! Just ahead, the excellent **Jerome State Historic Park** (☎928-634-5381; www.azstateparks.com; 100 Douglas Rd; adult/child 7-13yr $5/2; ⏲8:30am-5pm) preserves the 1916 mansion of mining mogul Jimmy 'Rawhide' Douglas.

A community hospital in the mining era, the **Jerome Grand Hotel** (☎928-634-8200; www.jeromegrandhotel.com; 200 Hill St; r $130-190, ste $275-460; ❄📶) plays up its past with medical relics in the hallways and an entertaining ghost tour kids will enjoy. The adjoining **Asylum Restaurant** (☎928-639-3197; www.asylumrestaurant.com; 200 Hill St; lunch $11-18, dinner $23-35; ⏲11am-9pm), with its red-rock valley views, is a breathtaking spot for a fine meal and glass of wine. Downtown, the **Spirit Room Bar** (☎928-634-8809; www.spiritroom.com; 166 Main St; ⏲11am-midnight Sun-Thu, until 1am Fri & Sat) is a lively watering hole.

Step into the **Flatiron Café** (☎928-634-2733; www.theflatironjerome.com; 416 Main St; breakfast $3-11, lunch $8-10; ⏲7am-4pm Wed-Mon) at the Y intersection for a savory gourmet breakfast or lunch; the specialty coffees are delicious.

For information, call in at the **chamber of commerce** (☎928-634-2900; www.jeromechamber.com; Hull Ave, Hwy 89A north after the Flatiron Café split; ⏲10am-3pm).

Sedona

Nestled amid majestic red sandstone formations at the southern end of Oak Creek Canyon, Sedona attracts artists, spiritual seekers, hikers and cyclists, and day-trippers from Phoenix fleeing the oppressive heat. Its combination of scenic beauty and mysticism draws throngs of tourists year-round. New Age businesses, fueled by the claim that this

VERDE VALLEY WINE TRAIL

Vineyards, wineries and tasting rooms have opened their doors along Hwy 89A and I-17, bringing a dash of style and energy to Cottonwood, Jerome and Cornville.

In Cottonwood, you can float to Verde River–adjacent **Alcantara Vineyards** (www.alcantaravineyard.com; 3445 S Grapevine Way; wine tasting $10-15; ⏲11am-5pm daily) then stroll through Old Town where two tasting rooms, **Arizona Stronghold** (www.azstronghold.com; 1023 N Main St; wine tasting $9; ⏲noon-7pm Sun-Thu, to 9pm Fri & Sat) and **Pillsbury Wine Company** (www.pillsburywine.com; 1012 N Main St; wine tasting $10; ⏲11am-5pm Mon-Thu, 11am-9pm Fri-Sun), sit across from each other on Main St.

Art, views and wine-sipping converge in Jerome, where there's a tasting room on every level of town. Start with **Cellar 433** (www.cellar433.com; 240 Hull Ave; wine tasting $10-12; ⏲11am-6pm Thu-Sun, 11am-5pm Mon-Wed) near the visitor center, then stroll up to **Caduceus Cellars** (www.caduceus.org; 158 Main St; wine tasting $9-13; ⏲11am-6pm Sun-Thu, to 8pm Sun).

Three wineries with tasting rooms hug a short stretch of Page Springs Rd east of Cornville: bistro-housing **Page Springs Cellars** (www.pagespringscellars.com; 1500 N Page Springs Rd; wine tasting $10; ⏲11am-7pm Mon-Wed, to 9pm Thu-Sun), welcoming **Oak Creek Vineyards** (www.oakcreekvineyards.net; 1555 N Page Springs Rd; wine tasting $10; ⏲10am-6pm) and mellow-rock-playing **Javelina Leap Vineyard** (www.javelinaleapwinery.com; 1565 Page Springs Rd; wine tasting $8; ⏲11am-5pm).

RED ROCK PASS

To park anywhere in the forest surrounding Sedona, buy a Red Rock Pass, available from ranger stations, visitor centers and vending machines at trailheads and picnic areas. Costing $5 per day or $15 per week, passes must be displayed within your car; for details, see www.redrockcountry.org. You don't need a pass if you stop briefly to take a photo or enjoy a viewpoint, or if you have a Federal Interagency Pass. Passes are not valid at the day-use areas of Crescent Moon, Call of the Canyon (West Fork Trail) and Grasshopper Point.

area stands at the center of vortexes that tap into the earth's power, dot downtown, as do galleries and gourmet restaurants, while the surrounding canyons offer excellent hiking and mountain biking.

In the middle of town, the 'Y' is the landmark junction of Hwys 89A and 179.

Sights & Activities

New Agers believe Sedona's rocks, cliffs and rivers radiate Mother Earth's mojo. The four best-known vortexes are **Bell Rock** near Village of Oak Creek east of Hwy 179; **Cathedral Rock** near Red Rock Crossing; **Airport Mesa** along Airport Rd; and **Boynton Canyon**. Airport Rd is also a great location for watching the Technicolor sunsets.

Red Rock State Park PARK
(928-282-6907; www.azstateparks.com/parks/rero; 4050 Red Rock Loop Rd; adult/child 7-13yr/6yr & under $5/3/free; 8am-5pm, visitor center 9am-4.30pm;) Not to be confused with Slide Rock State Park, this low-key 286-acre park includes an environmental education center, a visitor center, picnic areas and 5 miles of well-marked, interconnecting trails in a riparian habitat amid gorgeous scenery. Ranger-led activities include nature walks and bird walks. Popular moonlight hikes are offered April though October; reservations required ($5 reservation fee).

Slide Rock State Park SWIMMING
(928-282-3034; www.azstateparks.com/parks/slro; 6871 N Hwy 89A, Oak Creek Canyon; per car Jun-Sep $20, Sep-May $10; 8am-7pm Jun-Aug, shorter hours rest of year;) Swoosh down big rocks into cool creek water at Oak Creek Canyon's star attraction, or walk the hiking trails. No entry one hour before closing time.

★**Pink Jeep Tours** DRIVING TOUR
(928-282-5000; www.pinkjeeptours.com; 204 N Hwy 89A;) At first glance, Pink Jeep may annoy you. It seems like the 50-year-old company's jeeps are everywhere, buzzing around like pink flies. But once you join a tour, well, you just might find yourself laughing, bumping around and having a blast in spite of initial peevishness. We concede to your domination, Pink Jeep!

Bike & Bean BICYCLE RENTAL
(928-284-0210; www.bike-bean.com; 75 Bell Rock Plaza; bike rental 2hr/day from $30/$50)

Sleeping

Sedona hosts many beautiful B&Bs, creekside cabins, motels and full-service resorts.

Dispersed camping is not permitted in Red Rock Canyon. The **USFS** (877-444-6777; http://www.fs.usda.gov/coconino; Hwy 89A; campsites $16-20) runs campgrounds, without hookups, in the woods of Oak Creek Canyon, just off Hwy Alt 89. It costs $18 to camp, and you don't need a Red Rock Pass. All campgrounds except Pine Flat East accept reservations. Six miles north of town, **Manzanita** has 19 sites, showers and is open year-round; 11.5 miles north, **Cave Springs** has 82 sites, and showers; **Pine Flat East** and **Pine Flat West**, 12.5 miles north, together have 58 sites, 18 of which can be reserved.

Star Motel MOTEL $
(928-282-3641; www.starmotelsedona.com; 295 Jordan Rd; r $80-126, ste $176;) This ten-room motel in Uptown is one of Sedona's best deals. Rooms are simple, with a few artsy touches, but what we like most is the hospitality. And hey, the beds in this 1950s-era motel are clean, the shower strong and the refrigerators handy for chilling those sunset beers. Shops, eateries and the visitor center are just a hop, skip and jump away.

Cozy Cactus B&B $$$
(928-284-0082; www.cozycactus.com; 80 Canyon Circle Dr; r incl breakfast $190-340;) This five-room B&B, run by Carrie and Mark, works well for adventure-loving types ready to enjoy the great outdoors. The Southwest-style house bumps up against a

National Forest trail and is just around the bend from cyclist-friendly Bell Rock Pathway. Post-adventuring, get comfy beside the firepit on the back patio for wildlife-watching and stargazing.

Eating & Drinking

Coffee Pot Restaurant BREAKFAST $
(☎928-282-6626; www.coffeepotsedona.com; 2050 W Hwy 89A; breakfast $5-10, lunch $5-14; ⌚6am-2pm; 👪) This has been the go-to breakfast and lunch joint for decades. It's always busy and service can be slow, but it's friendly, the meals are reasonably priced and the selection is huge: 101 types of omelet for starters (peanut butter, jelly and banana perhaps?)

Sedona Memories DELI $
(☎928-282-0032; 321 Jordan Rd; sandwiches under $10; ⌚10am-2pm Mon-Fri) This tiny local spot assembles gigantic sandwiches on slabs of homemade bread. A great choice for a picnic, they're packed tight to-go, so less mess. You can also nosh on the quiet porch. If you call in your order, they'll toss in a free cookie. Cash only.

Oak Creek Brewery & Grill AMERICAN $$
(☎928-282-3300; www.oakcreekpub.com; 336 Hwy 179; mains $10-23; ⌚11.30am-8.30pm; 📶) Fortunately, this spacious brewery at Tlaquepaque Village will satisfy your post-hike drinking needs (although it closes ridiculously early). The menu includes upmarket pub-style dishes like a grilled mahimahi salad and 'fire-kissed' pizza. Oak Creek also runs a low-frills **brewery** (☎928-204-1300; www.oakcreekbrew.com; 2050 Yavapai Dr; ⌚4pm-close Mon-Thu, noon-close Fri-Sun) in West Sedona.

★ **Elote Cafe** MEXICAN $$$
(☎928-203-0105; www.elotecafe.com; Arabella Hotel, 771 Hwy 179; mains $19-26; ⌚5pm-late Tue-Sat) Some of the best, most authentic Mexican food in the region. Serves unusual traditional dishes you won't find elsewhere, like the namesake *elote* (fire-roasted corn with spicy mayo, lime and *cotija* cheese) or the tender, smoky pork cheeks.

Information

Sedona Chamber of Commerce Visitor Center (☎928-282-7722, 800-288-7336; www.visitsedona.com; 331 Forest Rd; ⌚8:30am-5pm) Located in Uptown Sedona, pick up free maps and brochures and buy a Red Rock Pass.

Getting There & Around

Ace Xpress (☎800-336-2239, 928-649-2720; www.acexshuttle.com; one way/round-trip adult $68/109, child $60/40; ⌚office hours 7am-8pm Mon-Fri, 8am-8pm Sat & Sun) runs door-to-door shuttles between Phoenix Sky Harbor International Airport and Sedona For Jeep rentals, try **Barlow Jeep Rentals** (☎928-282-8700, 800-928-5337; www.barlows.us; 3009 W Hwy 89A; half-/full-/3-day rental $195/295/589; ⌚8am-6pm).

Flagstaff

Flagstaff's laid-back charms are myriad, from its pedestrian-friendly historic downtown crammed with eclectic vernacular architecture and vintage neon to its high-altitude pursuits such as skiing and hiking. Locals are generally a happy, athletic bunch, skewing more toward granola than gunslinger. Northern Arizona University (NAU) gives Flagstaff its college-town flavor, while railroad history still figures firmly in its identity. Throw in a healthy appreciation for craft beer, freshly roasted coffee beans and an all-round good time, and you have the makings of a town you want to slow down and savor.

Flagstaff also makes an ideal gateway for visitors to the Grand Canyon. Hwy 180 is the most direct route northwest to Tusayan and the South Rim (80 miles), while Hwy 89 beelines north to Cameron (59 miles), from where Hwy 64 heads west to the canyon's East Entrance.

Sights

Museum of Northern Arizona MUSEUM
(☎928-774-5213; www.musnaz.org; 3101 N Fort Valley Rd; adult/senior/child 10-17y $10/9/6; ⌚10am-5pm Mon-Sat, noon-5pm Sun; 👪) Before venturing across the Colorado Plateau, introduce yourself to the region at this small but excellent museum that spotlights local Native American archaeology, history and culture, as well as geology, biology and the arts. Don't miss the extensive collection of Hopi kachina (also spelled katsina) dolls and a wonderful variety of Native American basketry and ceramics.

Lowell Observatory OBSERVATORY
(☎main phone 928-774-3358, recorded information 928-233-3211; www.lowell.edu; 1400 W Mars Hill Rd; adult/child 5-17yr $12/6; ⌚9am-10pm Jun-Aug, shorter hours Sep-May; 👪) Sitting atop a hill just west of downtown, this National Historic Landmark was built by Percival Lowell in

1894. The first sighting of Pluto occurred here in 1930. Weather permitting, visitors can stargaze through on-site telescopes, including the famed Clark Telescope. This 1896 telescope was the impetus behind the now-accepted theory of an expanding universe.

Walnut Canyon RUIN
(☎928-526-3367; www.nps.gov/waca; I-40 exit 204, 8 miles east of Flagstaff; adult/child under 17 $5/free; ⏲8am-5pm May-Oct, from 9am Oct-May; entry to trails close 1hr before park closing;) The Sinagua cliff dwellings here are set in the nearly vertical limestone walls of a small piñon-studded canyon. The mile-long Island Trail steeply descends 185ft (more than 200 stairs), passing 25 rooms built under the natural overhangs and a shorter, wheelchair-accessible Rim Trail affords views of the cliff dwelling from across the canyon.

Activities

Absolute Bikes BICYCLE RENTAL
(☎928-779-5969; www.absolutebikes.net; 202 E Route 66; bike rentals per day from $39; ⏲9am-7pm Mon-Fri, 9am-6pm Sat, 10am-4pm Sun Apr-Dec, shorter hr Jan-Mar) Visit the super-friendly gearheads for an inside track on the local mountain-biking scene.

Arizona Snowbowl SKIING
(☎928-779-1951; www.arizonasnowbowl.com; 9300 N Snowbowl Rd, Hwy 180 & Snowbowl Rd; lift ticket adult/youth 13-18yr/child 8-12yr $59/55/35; ⏲9am-4pm mid-Dec–mid-Apr) About 14 miles north of downtown, Arizona Snowbowl is small but lofty, with four lifts that service 32 ski runs between 9200ft and 11,500ft.

Sleeping

Flagstaff provides the widest range of lodging choices you'll find this close to the Grand Canyon. Unlike in southern Arizona, summer is high season.

Dubeau Hostel HOSTEL $
(☎928-774-6731; www.grandcanyonhostel.com; 19 W Phoenix Ave; dm $27, r $50-130; P❄@📶) This independent hostel offers the same friendly service and clean, well-run accommodations as its sister property, Grand Canyon International Hostel. The basic rooms are like basic hotel rooms, with refrigerators and bathroom with showers, but at half the price. The quieter of the two hostels. Breakfast is included.

ARIZONA'S QUIRKIEST SLEEPS

- **Wigwam Motel** (p844) Concrete tipi.
- **Bisbee Grand Hotel** (p861) Covered wagon.
- **Red Garter Inn** (p845) An 1897 bordello.
- **Jerome Grand Hotel** (p840) Former mining hospital.
- **Shady Dell RV Park** (p861) Retro Airstream.
- **Canyon Motel & RV Park** (p845) Santa Fe train caboose.

Grand Canyon International Hostel HOSTEL $
(☎928-779-9421; www.grandcanyonhostel.com; 19½ S San Francisco St; dm $25, r with shared bath $52-60; ❄@📶) Housed in a historic building with hardwood floors and Southwestern decor, this bright, homey hostel offers private rooms or dorms with a four-person maximum. Dorms are small but clean. There's also a kitchen and laundry. This hotel gets more traffic than sister property Dubeau Hostel. Breakfast is included.

★**Inn at 410** B&B $$
(☎928-774-0088; www.inn410.com; 410 N Leroux St; r $170-220; P❄@📶) This elegant and fully renovated 1894 house offers nine spacious, beautifully decorated and themed bedrooms, each with a refrigerator and private bathroom. Many rooms have four-poster beds and views of the garden or the San Francisco Peaks. A short stroll from downtown, the inn has a shady garden with fruit trees and a cozy dining room, where the full gourmet breakfast and afternoon snacks are served.

Hotel Monte Vista HISTORIC HOTEL $$
(☎928-779-6971; www.hotelmontevista.com; 100 N San Francisco St; r $85-160, ste $145-180; ❄📶) A huge, old-fashioned neon sign towers over this allegedly haunted 1926 hotel, hinting at what's inside: feather lampshades, vintage furniture, bold colors and eclectic decor. Rooms are named for the movie stars who slept in them, such as the Humphrey Bogart room, with dramatic black walls, yellow ceiling and gold satin bedding. Several resident ghosts supposedly make regular appearances.

Eating

Macy's CAFE $

(www.macyscoffee.net; 14 S Beaver St; mains under $8; 6am-8pm;) The delicious house-roasted coffee at this Flagstaff institution has kept the city buzzing for more than 30 years now. The vegetarian menu includes many vegan choices, along with traditional cafe grub like pastries, steamed eggs, waffles, yogurt and granola, salads and veggie sandwiches.

Diablo Burger BURGERS $

(928-774-3274; www.diabloburger.com; 120 N Leroux St; mains $11-14; 11am-9pm Sun-Wed, to 10pm Thu-Sat) The beef maestros at this gourmet burger joint are so proud of their locally sourced creations that they sear the DB brand onto the English-muffin bun. The cheddar-topped Blake gives a nod to New Mexico with Hatch chile mayo and roasted green chiles. The place is tiny, so come early or plan to sit outside. Beer and wine are also served.

Beaver Street Brewery BREWPUB $$

(www.beaverstreetbrewery.com; 11 S Beaver St; lunch $8-23, dinner $13-23; 11am-11pm Sun-Thu, to midnight Fri & Sat;) Families, river guides, ski bums and businesspeople – everybody is here or on the way. The menu is typical brewpub fare, with delicious pizzas, burgers and salads, and there's usually eight handcrafted beers on tap, like its Railhead Red Ale or R&R Oatmeal Stout, plus some seasonal brews. Serious drinkers can walk next door to play pool at the 21-and-over Brews & Cues.

★**Brix Restaurant & Wine Bar** MODERN AMERICAN $$$

(928-213-1021; www.brixflagstaff.com; 413 N San Francisco St; mains $23-34; from 5pm Tue-Sat) Are you settled in at the bar? Inhale, look around, relax. This is your vacation reward. Brix brings a breath of fresh, unpretentious sophistication to Flagstaff's dining scene as well as easygoing but polished hospitality. The menu varies seasonally, regularly using what is fresh, ripe, local and organic for dishes like wild mushroom risotto with truffles and grilled rib-eye with red onion jam.

Drinking & Entertainment

Follow the 1-mile **Flagstaff Ale Trail** (www.flagstaffaletrail.com) to sample craft beer at downtown breweries and a pub or two.

★**Museum Club** BAR

(928-526-9434; www.themuseumclub.com; 3404 E Route 66; 11am-2am) This honky-tonk roadhouse on Route 66 has been kicking up its heels since 1936. Inside what looks like a huge log cabin, you'll find a large wooden dance floor, animal mounts and a sumptuous elixir-filled mahogany bar. The origins of the name? In 1931 it housed a taxidermy museum.

ROADSIDE ATTRACTIONS ON ROUTE 66

Route 66 enthusiasts will find 400 miles of pavement stretching across Arizona, including the longest uninterrupted portion of old road left in the country, between Seligman and Topock. The **Mother Road** (www.azrt66.com) connects the dots between gun-slinging Oatman, Kingman's mining settlements, Williams' 1940s-vintage downtown and Winslow's windblown streets, with plenty of kitschy sights, listed here from west to east, along the way.

Wild burros of Oatman Mules beg for treats in the middle of the road.

Grand Canyon Caverns & Inn (928-422-3223; www.gccaverns.com; Rte 66, mile 115; 45min tour adult/child $20/13; 9am-5pm Jun-Sep, 10am-5pm Oct-May;) A guided tour 21 stories underground loops past mummified bobcats, civil-defense supplies and an $800 motel room.

Burma Shave signs Red-and-white ads from a bygone era between Grand Canyon Caverns and Seligman.

Seligman's Snow-Cap Drive In Prankish burger and ice-cream joint open since 1953.

Meteor Crater (928-289-5898; www.meteorcrater.com; adult/child 6-17yr/senior $18/9/16; 7am-7pm Jun–mid-Sep, 8am-5pm mid-Sep–May) A 550ft-deep pockmark that's nearly 1 mile across, 38 miles east of Flagstaff.

Wigwam Motel (928-524-3048; www.galerie-kokopelli.com/wigwam; 811 W Hopi Dr; r $56-62;) Concrete wigwams with hickory logpole furniture in Holbrook.

Charly's Pub & Grill LIVE MUSIC
(☎928-779-1919; www.weatherfordhotel.com; 23 N Leroux St; ⏲8am-2am) This restaurant at the Weatherford Hotel has regular live music. Its fireplace and brick walls provide a cozy setting for the blues, jazz and folk played here. Head upstairs to stroll the wraparound veranda outside the popular third-floor Zane Grey Ballroom, which overlooks the historic district.

ℹ Information

Visitor Center (☎928-774-9541, 800-842-7293; www.flagstaffarizona.org; 1 E Route 66; ⏲8am-5pm Mon-Sat, 9am-4pm Sun) Inside the Amtrak station, the visitor center has a great Flagstaff Discovery map and tons of information on things to do.

ℹ Getting There & Away

Flagstaff Pulliam Airport is 4 miles south of town off I-17. **US Airways** (☎800-428-4322; www.usairways.com) offers several daily flights between Pulliam Airport and Phoenix Sky Harbor International Airport. **Greyhound** (☎800-231-2222, 928-774-4573; www.greyhound.com; 880 E Butler Ave; ⏲midnight-6.30am, 10am-midnight Mon-Sun) stops in Flagstaff en route to/from Albuquerque, Las Vegas, Los Angeles and Phoenix. **Arizona Shuttle** (☎928-226-8060, 800-888-2749; www.arizonashuttle.com; ⏲year-round) has shuttles that run to the park ($30 one-way), Sedona ($39 one-way) and Phoenix Sky Harbor Airport ($45 one-way).

Operated by **Amtrak** (☎928-774-8679, 800-872-7245; www.amtrak.com; 1 E Route 66; ⏲3am-10.45pm), the Southwest Chief stops at Flagstaff on its daily run between Chicago and Los Angeles.

Williams

Affable Williams, 60 miles south of Grand Canyon Village and 35 miles west of Flagstaff, is a gateway town with character. Classic motels and diners line Route 66, and the old-school homes and train station give a nod to simpler times.

Most tourists visit to ride the turn-of-the-19th-century **Grand Canyon Railway** (☎reservations 800-843-8724; www.thetrain.com; Railway Depot, 233 N Grand Canyon Blvd; round-trip adult/child from $65/25; 👪) to the South Rim, which departs Williams 9:30am and returns at 5:45pm. Even if you're not a train buff, a trip is a scenic stress-free way to visit the Grand Canyon. Characters in period costumes provide historical and regional narration, and banjo folk music sets the tone.

The **Red Garter Inn** (☎928-635-1484; www.redgarter.com; 137 W Railroad Ave; d $150-175; ❄📶) is an 1897 bordello turned B&B where the ladies used to hang out the windows to flag down customers. The four rooms have nice period touches and the downstairs bakery has good coffee. The funky little **Grand Canyon Hotel** (☎928-635-1419; www.thegrandcanyonhotel.com; 145 W Route 66; hostel dm/r $28/32, r with shared bath $70, r with private bath $75-125; ⏲Mar-Nov; ❄@📶) has small themed rooms and a six-bed dorm room; no TVs. You can sleep inside a 1929 Santa Fe train caboose or a Pullman railcar at the **Canyon Motel & RV Park** (☎928-635-9371; www.thecanyonmotel.com; 1900 E Rodeo Rd; tent/RV sites $31/43, r $88-94, train cars $94-192; ❄📶🏊🐾), just east of downtown.

Grand Canyon National Park

No matter how much you read about the Grand Canyon, or how many photographs you've seen, nothing really prepares you for the sight of it. The sheer immensity of the canyon grabs you first, followed by the dramatic layers of rock, which pull you in for a closer look. Next up are the artistic details – rugged plateaus, crumbly spires, maroon ridges – that flirt and catch your eye as shadows flicker across the rock.

Snaking along its floor are 277 miles of the Colorado River, which has carved the canyon over the past six million years and exposed rocks up to two billion years old – half the age of the earth.

The two rims of the Grand Canyon offer quite different experiences; they lie more than 200 miles apart by road and are rarely visited on the same trip. Most visitors choose the South Rim with its easy access, wealth of services and vistas that don't disappoint. The quieter North Rim has its own charms; at 8200ft elevation (1000ft higher than the South Rim), its cooler temperatures support wildflower meadows and tall, thick stands of aspen and spruce.

June is the driest month, July and August the wettest. January has average overnight lows of 13°F (-11°C) to 20°F (-7°C) and daytime highs around 40°F (4°C). Summer temperatures inside the canyon regularly soar above 100°F (38°C). While the South Rim is open year-round, most visitors come between late May and early September.

Grand Canyon National Park

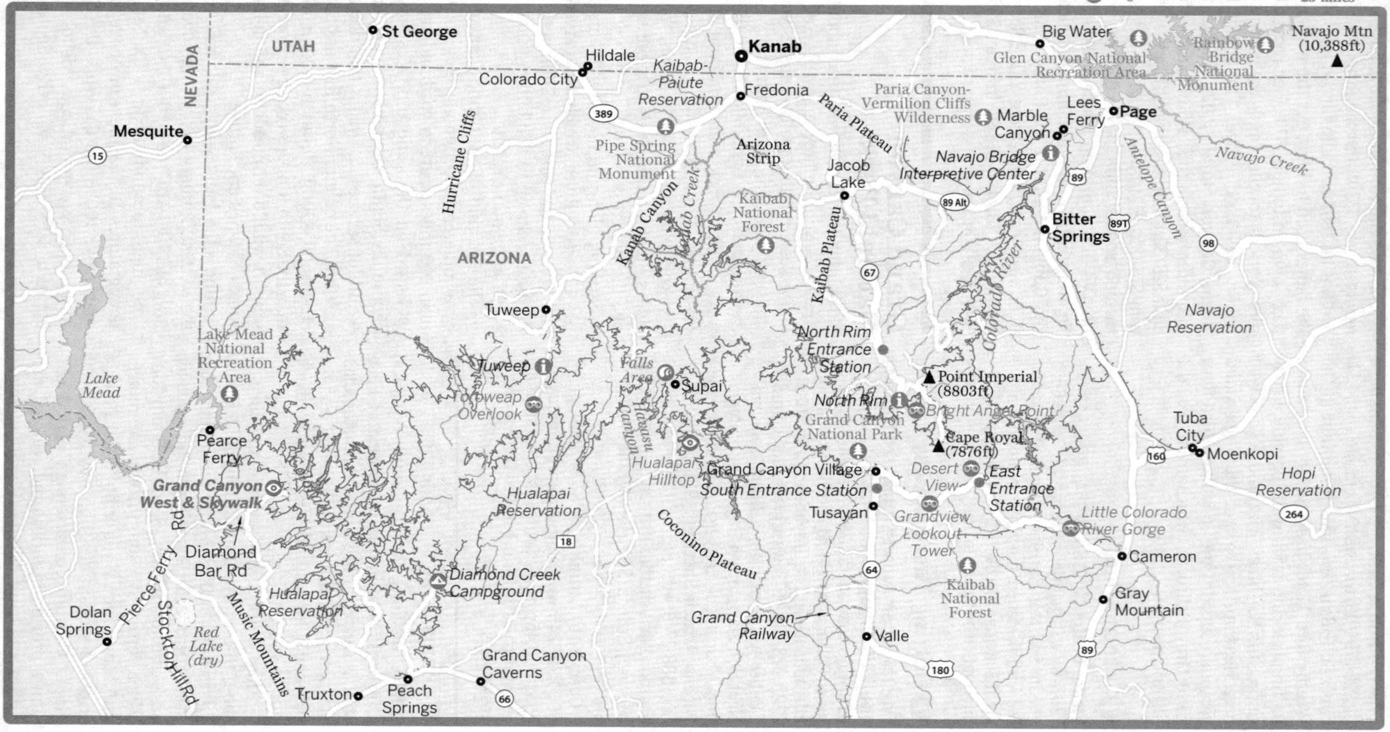

The North Rim is open from mid-May to mid-October.

Information

The most developed area in the **Grand Canyon National Park** (928-638-7888; www.nps.gov/grca; vehicles/cyclists & pedestrians $25/12) is Grand Canyon Village, 6 miles north of the South Rim Entrance Station. The North Rim has one entrance, which is 30 miles south of Jacob Lake on Hwy 67; continue another 14 miles south to the actual rim. The North and South Rims are 215 miles apart by car, 21 miles on foot through the canyon, or 10 miles as the condor flies.

The park entrance ticket is valid for seven days and can be used at both rims.

All overnight hikes and backcountry camping in the park require a permit. The **Backcountry Information Center** (928-638-7875; www.nps.gov/grca; Grand Canyon Village; 8am-noon & 1-5pm, phone staffed 1-5pm Mon-Fri; Village) accepts applications for backpacking permits ($10, plus $5 per person per night) starting four months before the proposed month. Your chances are decent if you apply early and provide alternative hiking itineraries. Reservations are accepted in person or by mail or fax, *not* by phone or email. For more information see www.nps.gov/grca/planyourvisit/backcountry-permit.htm.

If you arrive at the South Rim without a permit, head to the backcountry office, by Maswik Lodge, to join the waiting list.

As a conservation measure, the park no longer sells bottled water. Fill your flask at water filling stations along the rim or at Canyon View Marketplace.

SOUTH RIM VISITOR CENTERS

Grand Canyon Visitor Center (928-638-7888; www.nps.gov/grca; Visitor Center Plaza, Grand Canyon Village; 8am-5pm Mar-Nov, 9am-5pm Dec-Feb; Village, Kaibab/Rim) Three hundred yards behind Mather Point, a large plaza holds the visitor center and the Books & More Store. Outdoor bulletin boards display information about trails, tours, ranger programs and the weather.

National Geographic Visitor Center (928-638-2468; www.explorethecanyon.com; 450 Hwy 64, Tusayan; adult/child $14/11; 8am-10pm Mar-Oct, 10am-8pm Nov-Feb) In Tusayan, 7 miles south of Grand Canyon Village; pay your $25 vehicle entrance fee here to spare yourself a potentially long wait at the park entrance. The IMAX theater screens the terrific film *Grand Canyon – The Hidden Secrets*.

In addition to the visitor centers listed above, information is available inside the park at:

Yavapai Museum of Geology (www.nps.gov/grca; Grand Canyon Village; 8am-7pm Mar-May & Sep-Nov, to 6pm Dec-Feb, to 8pm Jun-Aug; ; Kaibab/Rim), **Verkamp's Visitor Center** (www.nps.gov/grca; National Historic Landmark District, Grand Canyon Village; 8am-7pm; ; Village), **Kolb Studio** (928-638-2771; www.nps.gov/grca; National Historic Landmark District, Grand Canyon Village; 8am-7pm Mar-May & Sep-Nov, to 6pm Dec-Feb, to 8pm Jun-Aug; ; Village), **Tusayan Ruin & Museum** (www.nps.gov/grca; Desert View Dr; 9am-5pm;) and **Desert View Information Center** (928-638-7893; 8am-5pm Jun-Aug, from 9am rest of year).

South Rim

If you don't mind bumping elbows with other travelers, you'll be fine on the South Rim, where you'll find an entire village worth of lodging, restaurants, bookstores, libraries, a supermarket and a deli. Museums and historic stone buildings illuminate the park's human history, and rangers lead daily programs on subjects from geology to resurgent condors.

In summer, when day-trippers converge en masse, escaping the crowds can be as easy as taking a day hike below the rim or merely tramping a hundred yards away from a scenic overlook.

Activities

Driving & Hiking

A **scenic route** follows the rim on the west side of Grand Canyon Village along Hermit Rd. Closed to private vehicles March through November, the 7-mile road is serviced by free park shuttle buses; cycling is encouraged because of the relatively light traffic. Stops offer spectacular views and interpretive signs explain canyon features.

Desert View Drive starts east of Grand Canyon Village and follows the canyon rim for 26 miles to Desert View, the east entrance of the park. Pullouts offer tremendous views.

Hiking trails along the South Rim include options for every skill level. The **Rim Trail** is the most popular, and easiest, walk in the park. It dips in and out of the scrubby pines of Kaibab National Forest to connect scenic points and historical sights over 13 miles. Portions are paved, and every viewpoint is accessed by one of the three shuttle routes. Along the **Trail of Time**, bordering the Rim Trail just west of Yavapai Museum of Geology, every meter represents one million years of geologic history.

Hiking down into the canyon itself is a serious undertaking; most visitors content themselves with short day hikes. Bear in mind that the climb back out of the canyon is much harder than the descent into it, and do not attempt to hike all the way to the Colorado River and back in a single day. On the most popular route, the beautiful **Bright Angel Trail**, the scenic 8-mile drop to the river is punctuated with four logical turnaround spots. Summer heat can be crippling; day hikers should either turn around at one of the two resthouses (a 3- or 6-mile round-trip) or hit the trail at dawn to safely make the longer hikes to Indian Garden and Plateau Point (9.2 and 12.2 miles round-trip respectively).

The steeper and much more exposed **South Kaibab Trail** is one of the park's prettiest routes, combining stunning scenery and unobstructed 360-degree views with every step. Hikers overnighting at Phantom Ranch generally descend this way, and return the next day via the Bright Angel. Summer ascents can be dangerous, and during this season rangers advise day hikers to turn around at **Cedar Ridge**, (about 3 miles round-trip), for the park's finest short day hike.

Cycling

Bright Angel Bicycles & Cafe at Mather Point BICYCLE RENTAL

(☎928-814-8704, 928-638-3055; www.bikegrandcanyon.com; Visitor Center Plaza, Grand Canyon Village; 24hr rental adult/child 16yr & under $40/30, 5hr rental $30/20; wheelchair $10; single/double stroller up to 8hrs $18/27; ⏲Apr-Nov; 🚌Village, 🚌Kaibab/Rim) Renting 'comfort cruiser' bikes on the South Rim, the friendly folks here custom-fit each bike to the individual. Rates include helmet; child trailers, strollers and wheelchairs also available. Roads bikes are $45 per day. Three-hour interpretative tours are also offered, with trips on on either Hermit Rd or Yaki Rd (adult/child 15years and under from $48/38).

Tours

Grand Canyon Mule Rides GUIDED TOUR

(☎888-297-2757, same-/next-day reservation 928-638-3283; www.grandcanyonlodges.com; Bright Angel Lodge; 3hr mule ride $120, 1-/2-night mule ride $533/758 incl meals & accommodation; ⏲rides available year-round, hours vary; 👪) Due to erosion concerns, the NPS has limited inner-canyon mule rides to those traveling all the way to Phantom Ranch. Rather than going below the rim, three-hour day trips now take riders along the rim, through the ponderosa, piñon and juniper forest to the Abyss overlook. Overnight trips and two-night trips follow the Bright Angel Trail to the river, travel east on the River Trail and cross the river on the Kaibab Suspension Bridge. Riders spend the night at Phantom Ranch. If you arrive at the park and want to join a mule trip the following day, ask about availability at the transportation desk at Bright Angel Lodge.

Sleeping

The South Rim's six lodges are operated by **Xanterra** (☎888-297-2757, 303-297-2757, 928-638-3283; www.grandcanyonlodges.com). Contact them to make advance reservations (essential in summer), although it's best to call Phantom Ranch, down beside the Colorado River, directly. For same-day reservations or to reach a guest, call the South Rim switchboard (☎928-638-2631). If you can't find accommodations in the national park, try Tusayan (at South Rim Entrance Station), Valle (31 miles south), Cameron (53 miles east), Williams (about 60 miles south) or Flagstaff (80 miles southeast).

All campgrounds and lodges are open year-round except Desert View.

Phantom Ranch CABIN $

(☎888-297-2757, same-/next-day reservation 928-638-3283; www.grandcanyonlodges.com; Grand Canyon National Park, canyon bottom; dm/d cabin $48/135; ❄) Bunks at this camplike complex are spread across cozy private cabins sleeping up to four people and single-sex dorms outfitted for 10 people. Rates include bedding, liquid soap and towels, but meals are extra and must be reserved when booking your bunk. You're free to bring your own food and stove.

Desert View Campground CAMPGROUND $

(www.nps.gov/grca; Desert View, East Entrance; campsites $12; reservations not accepted; ⏲mid-April–mid-Oct; 🐾) In a piñon-juniper forest near the East Entrance, this first-come, first-served campground with 50 sites is quieter than Mather Campground in the Village, with a nicely spread-out design that ensures a bit of privacy. The best time to secure a spot is mid-morning, when people are breaking camp; usually fills by mid-afternoon. Facilities include toilets and drinking water, but no showers or hookups.

Mather Campground
CAMPGROUND $

(☑877-444-6777, late arrival 928-638-7851; www.
recreation.gov; Market Plaza, Grand Canyon Village;
sites $18; ⊘year-round; 🛜🚻; 🚌Village) Sites are
shaded and fairly well dispersed, and the flat
ground offers a comfy platform for your tent.
You'll find pay showers, laundry facilities,
drinking water, toilets, grills and a small general store; a full grocery store is a short walk
away. Reservations are accepted from March
through November; the rest of the year it's
first-come, first-served. No hookups.

Trailer Village
CAMPGROUND $

(☑877-404-4611, same-day reservation 928-638-
3047; www.visitgrandcanyon.com; Market Plaza,
Grand Canyon Village; hook-ups $36; ⊘year-round;
🚻; 🚌Village) This Xanterra-run campground
is basically a trailer park, with RVs lined
up tightly at paved pull-through sites amid
a rather barren patch of ground. Check for
spots with trees on the far north side. You'll
find picnic tables, barbecue grills and full
hook-ups, but showers are a quarter-mile
away at Mather Campground.

Bright Angel Lodge
LODGE $$

(☑888-297-2757, front desk & reservations within
48hr 928-638-2631 ext 6285; www.grandcanyon-
lodges.com; National Historic Landmark District,
Grand Canyon Village; r with bath $100, r without
bath $77-89, ste $426, cabins $128-197; 🅿🛜; 🚌Vil-
lage) This 1935 log-and-stone lodge on the
ledge delivers historic charm by the bucket-
load as well as nicely appointed rooms. Pub-
lic spaces, though, are busy and less elegant.
If you're economizing, get a basic double (no
TV – just a bed, desk and sink) with shared
bathrooms down the hall. Cabins are bright-
er, airier and have tasteful Western charac-
ter; the most expensive have rim views.

Maswik Lodge
MOTEL $$

(☑888-297-2757, front desk & reservations within
48hrs 928-638-2631 ext 6784; www.grandcanyon-
lodges.com; Grand Canyon Village; r south/north
$107/205; 🅿✳@🛜; 🚌Village) The Maswik
Lodge complex includes 18 modern two-story buildings set in the woods; rooms are of
the standard motel variety. Rooms at Maswik North feature private patios, air-con,
cable TV, high ceilings and forest views,
while those at Maswik South are smaller,
with fewer amenities, no air-con and more
forgettable views.

Kachina & Thunderbird Lodges
LODGE $$

(☑888-297-2757, reservations within 48hr 928-
638-2631; www.grandcanyonlodges.com; National
Historic Landmark District, Grand Canyon Village; r
streetside/rimside $216/232; 🅿✳🛜; 🚌Village)
Beside the Rim Trail between El Tovar and
Bright Angel, these institutional-looking
lodges, built in the late 1960s, offer standard
motel-style rooms with two queen beds, full
bath, flat-screen TV, Keurig coffeemaker and
a refrigerator. It's worth spending up a lit-
tle for the rimside rooms, some with partial
canyon views.

Yavapai Lodge
MOTEL $$

(☑877-404-4611, reservations within 48hr 928-
638-6421; www.visitgrandcanyon.com; Market
Plaza, Grand Canyon Village; r West/East $140/174;
⊘year-round; 🅿✳@🛜🚻; 🚌Village) The motel-style lodgings are stretched out amid a
peaceful piñon and juniper forest. Rooms
in Yavapai East are in six two-story buildings with air-conditioning, while rooms
in Yavapai West are spread out in 10 sin-
gle-story buildings, with vault ceilings but
no air-conditioning. These are basic, clean
motel rooms with tubs, showers and TVs.

★ El Tovar
LODGE $$$

(☑888-297-2757, front desk & res within 48hrs 928-
638-2631 ext 6380; www.grandcanyonlodges.com;
National Historic Landmark District, Grand Canyon
Village; r $187-305, ste $381-465; ⊘year-round;
🅿✳🛜; 🚌Village) Stuffed mounts. Thick pine
walls. Sturdy fireplaces. Is this the fanciest
hotel on the South Rim or a backcountry
hunting lodge? We'd say it's a charismatic
mix of both. Despite renovations, this ram-
bling 1905 wooden lodge hasn't lost a lick of
its genteel historic patina, or its charm.

🍴 Eating & Drinking

Maswik Food Court
CAFETERIA $

(☑928-638-2631; www.grandcanyonlodges.com;
Maswik Lodge, Grand Canyon Village; mains $7-
13; ⊘6am-10pm May-Aug, varies rest of year; 🔸;
🚌Village) Though fairly predictable, the food
encompasses a nice variety and isn't too
greasy. The various food stations serve burg-
ers, pasta, Mexican food, chili bowls and hot
turkey sandwiches. Deli and grab-and-go
sandwiches also available. The adjoining
Maswik Pizza Pub serves beer and shows
sporting events on TV.

Yavapai Lodge Restaurant AMERICAN $
(☎928-638-6421; www.visitgrandcanyon.com; Yavapai Lodge, Market Plaza, Grand Canyon Village; breakfast $7-12, lunch & dinner $8-22; ⏰6.30am-9pm May-Aug, varies rest of year; 👪; 🚌Village) Next to Yavapai Lodge, this cafe has burgers, salads, hot dogs and pizzas. Closed November through February, except for holidays.

Canyon Village Deli CAFETERIA $
(☎928-638-2262; Canyon Village Market, Market Plaza, Grand Canyon Village; mains $3-9; ⏰8am-6pm May-Aug, varies rest of year; 👪; 🚌Village) Fresh-made sandwiches, hot dogs and grab-and-go meals inside the grocery store.

★ **El Tovar Dining Room & Lounge** AMERICAN $$$
(☎928-638-2631; www.grandcanyonlodges.com; El Tovar, National Historic Landmark District, Grand Canyon Village; mains $17-35; ⏰restaurant 6.30-10.45am & 11.15am-2pm & 4.30-10pm, lounge 11am-11pm; 👪; 🚌Village) The setting and the food are equally superb. Dark-wood tables are set with china and white linen, eye-catching murals spotlight Native American tribes and huge windows frame views of the rim and canyon. The service is generally excellent, the menu creative, and the portions big.

Arizona Room AMERICAN $$$
(www.grandcanyonlodges.com; Bright Angel Lodge, National Historic Landmark District, Grand Canyon Village; mains $12-29; ⏰11.30am-3pm Jan-Oct & 4.30-10pm; 👪; 🚌Village) Antler chandeliers hang from the ceiling and picture windows overlook a small lawn, the rim walk and the canyon. Try to get on the waitlist when doors open at 4:30pm, because by 4:40pm you may have an hour's wait – reservations are not accepted. Mains include steak, chicken and fish dishes, while appetizers include such creative options as pulled-pork quesadillas.

ℹ Getting There & Around

Most people arrive at the canyon in private vehicles or on a tour. Parking can be a chore in Grand Canyon Village. Once inside the park, free park shuttles operate along three routes: around Grand Canyon Village, west along Hermits Rest Route and east along Kaibab Trail Route. Buses typically run every 15 minutes, from one hour before sunset to one hour afterward.

In summer a free shuttle from Bright Angel Lodge, the Hiker's Express, has early-morning pickups at the Backcountry Information Center and Grand Canyon Visitor Center, and then heads to the South Kaibab trailhead.

North Rim

Solitude reigns supreme on the North Rim. There are no shuttles or bus tours, no museums, shopping centers, schools or garages. In fact, there isn't much of anything here beyond a classic rimside national park lodge, a campground, a motel, a general store and miles of trails carving through sunny meadows thick with wildflowers, willowy aspen and towering ponderosa pines.

The entrance to the North Rim is 24 miles south of Jacob Lake on Hwy 67; Grand Canyon Lodge lies another 20 miles beyond.

RAFTING THE COLORADO RIVER

A boat trip down the Colorado is an epic, adrenaline-pumping adventure, which will take you beyond contact with civilization for several nights. The biggest single drop at Lava Falls plummets 37ft in just 300yd. But the true highlight is experiencing the Grand Canyon by looking up, not down from the rim. Its human history comes alive in ruins, wrecks and rock art. Commercial trips run from three days to three weeks and vary in the type of watercraft used. At night you camp under stars on sandy beaches (gear provided). It takes about two or three weeks to run the entire 279 miles of river through the canyon. Shorter sections of around 100 miles take four to nine days. Space is limited and the trips are popular, so book well in advance.

Arizona Raft Adventures (☎800-786-7238, 928-526-8200; www.azraft.com; 6-day Upper Canyon hybrid/paddle trips $2050/2150, 10-day Full Canyon motor trips $3000) This multigenerational family-run outfit offers paddle, oar, hybrid (with opportunities for both paddling and floating) and motor trips. Music fans can join one of the folk and bluegrass trips, with professional pickers and banjo players providing background music.

Arizona River Runners (☎602-867-4866, 800-477-7238; www.raftarizona.com; 6-day Upper Canyon oar trip $1984, 8-day Full Canyon motor trip $2745) Has been at its game since 1970, offering oar-powered and motorized trips.

At 8000ft, it's about 10°F (6°C) cooler here than the South Rim – even on summer evenings you'll need a sweater. All facilities on the North Rim are closed from mid-October to mid-May, although you can drive into the park and stay at the campground until snow closes the road from Jacob Lake.

Activities

The short and easy paved trail (0.5 miles) to **Bright Angel Point** is a canyon must. Beginning from the back porch of Grand Canyon Lodge, it goes to a narrow finger of an overlook with fabulous views.

The **North Kaibab Trail**, the North Rim's only maintained rim-to-river trail, connects with trails to the South Rim in the Phantom Ranch area. The first 4.7 miles are the steepest, dropping 3050ft to **Roaring Springs** – a popular all-day hike. If you prefer a shorter day hike below the rim, walk just 0.75 miles down to **Coconino Overlook**, or 2 miles to the **Supai Tunnel** to get a taste of steep inner-canyon hiking. The 28-mile round-trip to the Colorado River is a multiday affair.

For a short hike up on the rim, which works well for families, try the 4-mile round-trip **Cape Final** trail, on the Walhalla Plateau east of Grand Canyon Lodge, which leads through ponderosa pines to sweeping views of the eastern Grand Canyon area.

Canyon Trail Rides (435-679-8665; www.canyonrides.com; North Rim; 1hr/half-day mule ride $40/80; schedules vary mid-May–mid-Oct) offers mule trips. Of the half-day trips (minimum age 10 years), one is along the rim and the other drops into the Canyon on the North Kaibab Trail.

Sleeping

Accommodations are limited to one lodge and one campground. If these are booked, try your luck 80 miles north in Kanab, UT, or 84 miles northeast in Lees Ferry. There are also campgrounds in the Kaibab National Forest north of the park.

North Rim Campground CAMPGROUND $
(928-638-7814, 877-444-6777; www.recreation.gov; tent sites $18, RV sites $18-25; mid-May–mid-Oct by reservation, first-come, first-served Oct 16-31;) This campground, 1.5 miles north of the lodge, offers shaded sites on level ground blanketed in pine needles. Sites 11, 14, 15, 16 and 18 overlook the Transept (a side canyon) and cost $25. There's water, a store, a snack bar, coin-op showers and laundry facilities, but no hookups. Reservations are accepted up to six months in advance.

Grand Canyon Lodge HISTORIC HOTEL $$
(advance reservations 877-386-4383, reservations outside USA 480-337-1320, same-day reservations 928-638-2611; www.grandcanyonlodgenorth.com; r $130, cabins per 2 people $138-191; mid-May–mid-Oct) Walk through the front door of Grand Canyon Lodge into the lofty sunroom and there, framed by picture windows, is the canyon in all its glory. Rooms are not in the lodge itself, but in rustic cabins sleeping up to five people. The nicest are the bright and spacious Western cabins, made of logs and buffered by trees and grass.

Eating & Drinking

The lodge will prepare sack lunches ($15), ready for pickup as early as 5:30am, for those wanting to picnic on the trail. Place your order the day before. For sandwiches, pizza and breakfast burritos, try **Deli in the Pines** (Grand Canyon Lodge; lunch & dinner $7-15; 10.30am-9pm mid-May–mid-Oct), also at the Lodge.

★ **Grand Canyon Lodge Dining Room** AMERICAN $$
(928-638-2611, off-season 928-645-6865; www.grandcanyonlodgenorth.com; mains breakfast $6-13, lunch $10-15, dinner $13-33; 6.30-10am, 11.30am-2.30pm & 4.45-9.45pm mid-May–mid-Oct;) Although seats beside the window are wonderful, views from the dining room are so huge it really doesn't matter where you sit. While the solid dinner menu includes buffalo steak, western trout and several vegetarian options, don't expect culinary memories – the view is the thing. Make reservations in advance of your arrival to guarantee a spot for dinner (reservations are not accepted for breakfast or lunch).

Grand Canyon Cookout Experience AMERICAN $$$
(928-638-2611; Grand Canyon Lodge; adult/child 6-15yr $30/$15; 5.45pm Jun 1-Sep 30;) Chow down on barbecued meat, roasted chicken, skillet cornbread and beans served buffet-style with a side of Western songs and cheesy jokes. A cute steam train will take you there.

Information

North Rim Visitor Center (928-638-7864; www.nps.gov/grca; North Rim; 8am-6pm) Beside Grand Canyon Lodge, this is the place to get information on the park, and the starting point for ranger-led nature walks.

Getting There & Around

The **Transcanyon Shuttle** (☎877-638-2820, 928-638-2820; www.trans-canyonshuttle.com; one way rim-to-rim $85, one-way South Rim to Marble Canyon $70; ⏲mid-May–mid-Oct) departs daily from Grand Canyon Lodge for the South Rim (five hours) and is perfect for rim-to-rim hikers. Reserve at least one or two weeks in advance. A complimentary hikers' shuttle to the North Kaibab Trail departs at both 5:45am and 7:10am from Grand Canyon Lodge. You must sign up for it at the front desk 24 hours ahead; if no one signs up, it will not run.

Around the Grand Canyon

Havasu Canyon

In a hidden side canyon off the Colorado River, complete with stunning, spring-fed waterfalls and azure swimming holes, this beautiful spot is hard to reach, but the hike down and back up makes the trip unique – and an amazing adventure.

Located on the Havasupai Indian Reservation, Havasu Canyon is just 35 miles directly west of the South Rim, but it's more like 195 miles by road. The four falls lie 10 miles below the rim, accessed via a moderately challenging hiking trail that starts from Hualapai Hilltop, and is reached by following a 62-mile road that leaves Route 66 7 miles east of Peach Springs.

All trips require an overnight stay, which must be reserved in advance, and there's a $35 entrance fee for all guests. The village of Supai, 8 miles along the trail, is home to the **Havasupai Lodge** (☎928-448-2201, 928-448-2111; www.havasuwaterfalls.net; Supai; r for up to 4 people $145; ❄), where the motel-style rooms have canyon views but no phones or TVs. Check in by 5pm, when the lobby closes. A village cafe serves meals and accepts credit cards. The Havasupai Campground, 2 miles beyond, has primitive campsites along a creek; every camper must pay an additional $5 environmental fee. Continue deeper into Havasu Canyon to reach the waterfalls and blue-green swimming holes.

If you don't want to hike to Supai, call the lodge or campground to arrange for a mule or horse (round-trip to lodge/campground $135/197) to carry you there.

Hualapai Nation

Run by the Hualapai Nation, around 215 driving miles west of the South Rim 70 miles northeast of Kingman, the remote site known as Grand Canyon West is not part of Grand Canyon National Park. The rough road out here is partly unpaved, and unsuitable for RVs.

Grand Canyon West (West Rim) SCENIC OVERLOOK

(☎888-868-9378, 928-769-2636; www.grandcanyonwest.com; Hualapai Reservation; per person $44-81; ⏲7am-7pm Apr-Sep, 8am-5pm Oct-Mar) Nowadays, the only way to visit Grand Canyon West, the section of the west rim overseen by the Hualapai Nation, is to purchase a package tour. These include a hop-on, hop-off shuttle ride which loops to scenic points along the rim. Tours can include lunch, cowboy activities at an ersatz Western town and informal Native American performances.

All but the cheapest package include admission to the Grand Canyon Skywalk, the horseshoe-shaped glass bridge cantilevered 4000ft above the canyon floor. Jutting out almost 70ft over the canyon, the Skywalk allows visitors to see the canyon through the glass walkway. Another stop, the unfortunately named Guano Point, is good for lunch, shopping and a bit of exploring, with fantastic canyon and river views.

Since would-be visitors to the Skywalk are required to purchase a package tour – and the extra-cost Skywalk is the primary draw – the experience can be a pricey prospect.

Northeastern Arizona

Between the brooding buttes of Monument Valley, the blue waters of Lake Powell and the fossilized logs of the Petrified Forest National Park are photogenic lands locked in ancient history. Inhabited by Native Americans for centuries, this region is dominated by the Navajo reservation – widely known as the Navajo Nation – which spills into surrounding states. The Hopi reservation is here as well, completely surrounded by Navajo land.

Lake Powell

The country's second-largest artificial reservoir, Lake Powell, stretches north from Arizona into Utah. Set amid striking red-rock formations, sharply cut canyon and dramatic desert scenery, and part of the **Glen Canyon National Recreation Area** (928-608-6200; www.nps.gov/glca; 7-day pass per vehicle $15, per pedestrian or cyclist $7), it's water-sports heaven.

The lake was created by the construction of Glen Canyon Dam, 2.5 miles north of what's now the region's central town, Page. The Carl Hayden Visitor Center is located beside the dam.

To visit photogenic **Antelope Canyon**, a stunning sandstone slot canyon, you must join a tour. Several tour companies offer trips into **Upper Antelope Canyon**, which is easier to navigate. Expect a bumpy ride and a bit of a cattle call; try **Roger Ekis' Antelope Canyon Tours** (928-645-9102; www.antelopecanyon.com; 22 S Lake Powell Blvd; adult/child 5-12yr from $37/27). The more strenuous **Lower Antelope Canyon** sees much smaller crowds.

A deservedly popular hike is the 1.5 mile round-trip trek to **Horseshoe Bend**, where the river wraps around a dramatic stone outcropping to form a perfect U. The trailhead is south of Page off Hwy 89, across from mile marker 541.

Chain hotels line Page's main strip, Hwy 89, with independent alternatives along 8th Ave. The revamped **Lake Powell Motel** (928-645-3919; www.powellmotel.com; 750 S Navajo Dr; $69-159; Apr-Oct;) was originally built to house Glen Canyon Dam builders; four of its units have kitchens, and book up quickly, while a fifth, smaller room is usually held for walk-ins.

For breakfast in Page, the **Ranch House Grille** (www.ranchhousegrille.com; 819 N Navajo Dr; mains $7-16; 6am-3pm) has good food, huge portions and fast service. The murals of local landcapes are impressive inside **Bonkers** (928-645-2706; www.bonkerspageaz.com; 810 N Navajo Dr; mains $9-23; 4pm-close Mar-Oct), which serves satisfying steaks, seafood, pasta and a few burgers and sandwiches.

Navajo Nation

Arizona's Navajo lands hold some of North America's most spectacular scenery, including Monument Valley and Canyon de Chelly. Cultural pride remains strong and many speak Navajo as their first language. The Navajo rely heavily on tourism; visitors can help keep Navajo heritage alive by staying on reservation land or purchasing crafts. Stopping at roadside stalls offers a great opportunity for personal interaction and helps to ensure that money goes straight into the artisan's pocket.

HOPI INDIAN RESERVATION

Direct descendants of the Ancestral Puebloans, the Hopi have arguably changed less in the last five centuries than any other Native American group. Their village of Old Oraibi may be the oldest continuously inhabited settlement in North America.

Hopi land is surrounded by the Navajo Nation. Hwy 264 runs past the three mesas (First, Second and Third Mesa) that form the heart of the reservation. On Second Mesa, 8 miles west of First Mesa, the **Hopi Cultural Center Restaurant & Inn** (928-734-2401; www.hopiculturalcenter.com; Hwy 264; r $95-105, meals $7-16; restaurant 7am-9pm summer, to 8pm winter) is as visitor-oriented as things get on the Hopi reservation. It provides food and lodging, and holds the small **Hopi Museum** (928-734-6650; adult/child 12yr & under $3/1; 8am-5pm Mon-Fri, 9am-3pm Sat), filled with historic photographs and cultural exhibits.

Photographs, sketching and recording are not allowed.

Unlike the rest of Arizona, the Navajo Nation observes mountain daylight saving time. During summer, the reservation is one hour ahead of Arizona.

For details about hiking and camping, and required permits, visit www.navajonationparks.org.

CAMERON

Cameron, a historic settlement that serves as the gateway to the east entrance of the Grand Canyon's South Rim, is one of the few worthwhile stops on Hwy 89 between Flagstaff and Page. The **Cameron Trading Post** (gift shop 928-679-2231, motel 800-338-7385; www.camerontradingpost.com; Hwy 89; r $109, ste $179; 6am-9.30pm summer, 7am-9pm winter;), just north of the Hwy 64 turnoff to the Grand Canyon, offers food, lodging, a gift shop and a post office.

CANYON DE CHELLY NATIONAL MONUMENT

The many-fingered Canyon De Chelly (pronounced *duh-shay*) contains several beautiful Ancestral Puebloan sites, including ancient cliff dwellings. For centuries, though, it has been home to Navajo farmers, who winter on the rims then move to hogans on the canyon floor in spring and summer. The canyon is private Navajo property administered by the NPS. Enter hogans only with a guide and don't photograph people without their permission.

The only lodging in the park is **Sacred Canyon Lodge** (☎800-679-2473; www.sacredcanyonlodge.com; r $99-109, ste $169;), formerly Thunderbird Lodge, which is just outside the canyon itself. It has comfortable rooms and an inexpensive cafeteria serving Navajo and American meals. The nearby Navajo-run campground has about 90 sites on a first-come, first-served basis ($10), with water but no showers.

The Canyon de Chelly **visitor center** (☎928-674-5500; www.nps.gov/cach; 8am-5pm) is 3 miles off Rte 191, beyond the small village of Chinle, near the mouth of the canyon. Two scenic drives follow the canyon's rim, but you can only explore the canyon floor on a guided tour. Stop by the visitor center, or check the park website, for a list of tour companies. The only unguided hiking trail you can follow in the park is a short but very spectacular round-trip route that descends to the amazing **White House Ruin**.

FOUR CORNERS NAVAJO TRIBAL PARK

Don't be shy: do a spread eagle at the **four corners marker** (☎928-871-6647; www.navajonationparks.org; admission $3; 8am-7pm May-Sep, 8am-5pm Oct-Apr), the middle-of-nowhere landmark that's the only spot in the US where you can straddle four states – Arizona, New Mexico, Colorado, Utah. It makes a good photograph, even if it's not 100% accurate; according to government surveyors, the marker is almost 2000ft east of where it should be, even if it is the legally recognized border point.

MONUMENT VALLEY NAVAJO TRIBAL PARK

With flaming-red buttes and impossibly slender spires bursting to the heavens, the Monument Valley landscape off Hwy 163 has starred in countless Hollywood Westerns and looms large in many a road-trip daydream.

For up-close views of the towering formations, visit the **Monument Valley Navajo Tribal Park** (☎435-727-5874; www.navajonationparks.org; per 4-person vehicle $20; drive 6am-8:30pm May-Sep, 8am-4:30pm Oct-Apr; visitor center 6am-8pm May-Sep, 8am-5pm Oct-Apr), where a rough and unpaved scenic driving loop covers 17 miles of stunning valley views. You can drive it in your own vehicle, or arrange a tour through one of the kiosks in the parking lot, which will take you to areas where private vehicles can't go (1½ hours $75, 2½ hours $95) .

Inside the tribal park, the sandstone-colored **View Hotel at Monument Valley** (☎435-727-5555; www.monumentvalleyview.com; Hwy 163; r/ste from $209/$299;) blends naturally with its surroundings, and most of the 96 rooms have private balconies facing the monuments. The Navajo-based specialties at the adjoining restaurant (mains $10 to $30, no alcohol) are mediocre, but the red-rock panorama is stunning. The revamped **Monument Valley Campground** (☎435-727-5802; www.monumentvalley.com/campground; tent/RV sites $20/40) is located at the other end of the parking lot.

The historic **Goulding's Lodge** (☎435-727-3231; www.gouldings.com; r $205-242;), just across the border in Utah, offers lodge rooms, camping and small cabins. Book early for summer. Kayenta, 20 miles south, holds a handful of okay hotels; try the **Wetherill Inn** (☎928-697-3231; www.wetherill-inn.com; 1000 Main St/Hwy 163; r incl breakfast $140;) if everything in Monument Valley is booked.

Winslow

'Standing on a corner in Winslow, Arizona, such a fine sight to see...' Sound familiar? Thanks to the Eagles' twangy 1970s tune 'Take It Easy,' otherwise nondescript Winslow has earned its wings in pop-culture heaven. A small **park** (www.standinonthecorner.com; 2nd St & Kinsley Ave) on Route 66 at Kinsley Ave pays homage to the band.

Just 50 miles east of Petrified Forest National Park, Winslow is a good regional base. Old motels border Route 66, and diners sprinkle downtown. The real showpiece here is the irresistible 1929 **La Posada** (☎928-289-4366; www.laposada.org; 303 E 2nd St; r $139-169;), a restored hacienda designed by star architect Mary Jane Colter. Elaborate tilework, glass-and-tin chandeliers, Navajo rugs and other details accent its palatial Western-style elegance. The on-site restaurant, the much-lauded **Turquoise Room** (www.theturquoiseroom.net; La Posada; breakfast $8-12, lunch $10-13, dinner $19-42; 7am-4pm, 5-9pm), serves the best meals between Flagstaff and Albuquerque; dishes have a neo-Southwestern flair.

Petrified Forest National Park

Home not only to an extraordinary array of fossilized ancient logs that predate the dinosaurs but also the multicolored sandscape of the Painted Desert, this **national park** (☎928-524-6228; www.nps.gov/pefo; vehicle/walk-in, bicycle & motorcycle $10/5; ⏲scenic drive 7am-8pm Jun & Jul, shorter hr Aug-May) is an unmissable spectacle.

The park straddles I-40 at exit 311, 25 miles east of Holbrook. Its visitor center, just half a mile north of I-40, holds maps and information on guided tours, while the 28-mile paved park road beyond offers a splendid scenic drive. There are no campsites, but a number of short trails, ranging from less than a mile to 2 miles, pass through the stands of petrified rock and ancient Native American dwellings. Those prepared for rugged backcountry camping need to pick up a free permit at the visitor center.

Western Arizona

The Colorado River is alive with sun worshippers at Lake Havasu City, while Route 66 offers well-preserved stretches of classic highway near Kingman. Much further south, beyond I-10 towards Mexico, the wild, empty landscape is among the most barren in the West. If you're already here, there are some worthwhile sites, but there's nothing worth planning an itinerary around unless you're a Route 66 or boating fanatic.

Kingman & Around

Faded motels and gas stations galore grace Kingman's main drag, but several century-old buildings remain. If you're following the Route 66 trail (aka Andy Devine Ave here) or looking for cheap lodging, it's worth a stroll.

Pick up maps and brochures at the historic **Powerhouse Visitor Center** (☎866-427-7866, 928-753-6106; www.gokingman.com; 120 W Andy Devine Ave; ⏲8am-5pm), which has a small but engaging **Route 66 museum** (☎928-753-9889; www.gokingman.com; 120 W Andy Devine Ave; adult/senior/child 12yr & under $4/3/free; ⏲9am-5pm).

A cool neon sign draws road-trippers to the **Hilltop Motel** (☎928-753-2198; www.hilltopmotelaz.com; 1901 E Andy Devine Ave; r from $44; ❄@📶🏊🐾) on Route 66. Rooms are a bit of a throwback, but are well kept, and the views are superb. Pets (dogs only) stay for $5. There's tasty Southern-style pork at **Redneck's Southern Pit BBQ** (www.redneckssouthernpitbbq.com; 420 E Beale St; mains $5.25-24; ⏲11am-8pm Tue-Sat; 👪).

Lake Havasu City

When the city of London auctioned off its 1831 bridge in the late 1960s, developer Robert McCulloch bought it, took it apart, shipped it, and then reassembled it at Lake Havasu City, which sits along a dammed-up portion of the Colorado River. The place now attracts hordes of young spring-breakers and weekend warriors who come to play in the water and party hard. An 'English Village' of pseudo-British pubs and tourist gift shops surrounds the bridge and houses the **visitor center** (☎928-855-5655; www.golakehavasu.com; 422 English Village; ⏲9am-5pm).

The hippest hotel in town is **Heat** (☎928-854-2833; www.heathotel.com; 1420 N McCulloch Blvd; r $209-299, ste $249-439; ❄📶), a slick boutique property where the front desk doubles as a bar, and most of the contemporary-styled rooms have private patios with views of London Bridge. For a hearty, open-air breakfast, rise and shine at the **Red Onion** (☎928-505-0302; www.redonionhavasu.com; 2013 N McCulloch Blvd; breakfast & lunch $6.25-12, dinner $10-15; ⏲7am-8pm Mon-Thu, 7am-9pm Fri & Sat, 7am-2pm Sun), where the menu is loaded with omelets and diet-busting fare. For microbrews and good pub grub, try the **Barley Brothers** (☎928-505-7837; www.barleybrothers.com; 1425 N McCulloch Blvd; mains $9-24; ⏲11am-9pm Sun-Thu, to 10pm Fri & Sat), which has great views of the lake.

Tucson

Arizona's second-largest city is set in the Sonoran Desert, full of rolling, sandy hills and crowds of cacti. The vibe here is ramshackle-cool and cozy compared with the shiny vastness of Phoenix. A college town, Tucson (the 'c' is silent) is home turf to the 40,000-strong University of Arizona (U of A), and was an artsy, dress-down kind of place before that was the cool thing to be. Eclectic shops and scores of funky restaurants and bars flourish in this arid ground. Tucsonans are proud of the city's geographic and cultural proximity to Mexico (65 highway miles south); more than 40% of the population is of Hispanic descent.

Sights & Activities

Downtown Tucson and the historic district lie east of I-10 exit 258. The U of A campus is a mile northeast of downtown; 4th Ave, the main drag here, is packed with cafes, bars and interesting shops.

★Arizona-Sonora Desert Museum MUSEUM
(☎520-883-2702; www.desertmuseum.org; 2021 N Kinney Rd; adult/child 13-17yr $19.50/15.50; ⏱8:30am-5pm Oct-Feb, 7:30am-5pm Mar-Sep, to 10pm Sat Jun-Aug) Home to cacti, coyotes and palm-sized hummingbirds, this ode to the Sonoran desert is one part zoo, one part botanical garden and one part museum – a trifecta that'll entertain young and old for easily half a day. Desert denizens, from precocious coatis to playful prairie dogs, inhabit natural enclosures. The grounds are thick with desert plants, and docents give demonstrations.

Old Tucson Studios FILM LOCATION
(☎520-883-0100; www.oldtucson.com; 201 S Kinney Rd; adult/child 4-11yr $18/11; ⏱Oct–late May, hr vary; 👪) Nicknamed 'Hollywood in the Desert,' this old movie set of Tucson in the 1860s was built in 1939 for the filming of *Arizona*. Hundreds of flicks followed, bringing in movie stars from Clint Eastwood to Leonardo DiCaprio. Now a Wild West theme park, it's all about shootouts, stagecoach rides, stunt shows and dancing saloon girls.

Pima Air & Space Museum MUSEUM
(☎520-574-0462; www.pimaair.org; 6000 E Valencia Rd; adult/child 7-12yr/senior & military $16/9/13 Nov-May, $14/8/12 Jun-Oct; ⏱9am-5pm, last admission 4pm; 🐾) An SR-71 Blackbird spy plane and a massive B-52 bomber are among the stars of this extraordinary private aircraft museum. Allow at least two hours to wander through hangars and around the airfield where more than 300 'birds' trace the evolution of civilian and military aviation. A free 50-minute walking tour is offered at 10:30am and 11:30am daily (plus 1:30pm & 2:30pm December through April).

> **DON'T MISS**
>
> **MINI TIME MACHINE MUSEUM OF MINIATURES**
>
> 'Meddle ye not in the affairs of Dragons, for ye are crunchy and tasteth good with condiments,' reads the sign beside the Pocket Dragons, one of several species of magical creatures that inhabit the Enchanted Realm gallery at this gob-smackingly entertaining **museum** (www.theminitimemachine.org; 4455 E Camp Lowell Dr; adult/child 4-17yr $9/6; ⏱9am-4pm Tue-Sat, noon-4pm Sun; 👪). Here you can walk over a snowglobe-y Christmas village, peer into intricate mini-homes built in the 1700s and 1800s, and search for the tiny inhabitants of a magical tree. It's great for families and for adults who still have a sense of fun.
>
> To get here from downtown, follow E Broadway Blvd east 3.5 miles. Turn left onto N Alvernon Way and drive 3 miles to E Fort Lowell Rd, which turns into Camp Lowell. Turn right and continue almost 1 mile.

Festivals & Events

Fiesta de los Vaqueros RODEO
(Rodeo Week; ☎520-741-2233; www.tucsonrodeo.com; ⏱Feb) Held the last week of February for 90 years, the Fiesta brings world-famous cowboys to town and features a spectacular parade with Western-themed floats and buggies, historic horse-drawn coaches, folk dancers and marching bands.

Sleeping

Lodging prices vary considerably, with lower rates in summer and fall. To sleep under stars and saguaros, try **Gilbert Ray Campground** (☎520-883-4200; www.pima.gov; Kinney Rd; tent/RV sites $10/20; 🐾) near the western district of Saguaro National Park.

Roadrunner Hostel & Inn HOSTEL $
(☎520-940-7280; www.roadrunnerhostelinn.com; 346 E 12th St; dm/r incl breakfast $22/45; ❄@📶🐾) Cultural and language barriers melt faster than snow in the desert at this small and friendly hostel within walking distance of 4th Ave. The guest kitchen and TV lounge are convivial spaces and freebies include coffee, tea and a waffle breakfast. The 1900 adobe building once belonged to the sheriff involved in capturing the Dillinger gang at the Hotel Congress in 1934.

Quality Inn Flamingo Downtown MOTEL $
(☎520-770-1910; www.flamingohoteltucson.com; 1300 N Stone Ave; r incl breakfast $65-80; ❄@📶🏊🐾) Though recently purchased by the Quality Inn chain, the former Flamingo Hotel retains a bit of its great 1950s Rat Pack vibe, and the fact that Elvis slept here doesn't hurt (although the rooms were

renumbered and now no one is sure which room he slept in). Rooms come with chic striped bedding, flat-screen plasma TVs, a good-sized desk and comfy beds.

★Catalina Park Inn B&B $$
(☎520-792-4541; www.catalinaparkinn.com; 309 E 1st St; r $145-189; ⊙closed Jul & Aug;) Style, hospitality and comfort merge seamlessly at this inviting B&B just west of the University of Arizona and 4th Ave. Hosts Mark Hall and Paul Richard have poured their hearts into restoring this 1927 Mediterranean-style villa, and their efforts are on display in each of the six rooms, which vary in style.

Hotel Congress HISTORIC HOTEL $$
(☎520-622-8848; www.hotelcongress.com; 311 E Congress St; r $89-149;) Charming, confident and occasionally a pain in the ass? Yes. But rest assured, downtown Tucson's most famous lodging is never, ever boring. Beautifully restored, this 1919 hotel feels very modern, mostly because of its popular cafe, bar and club. Many rooms have period furnishings, rotary phones and wooden radios – but no TVs.

Aloft Tucson HOTEL $$
(☎520-908-6800; www.starwoodhotels.com; 1900 E Speedway Blvd; r $169;) Tucson is surprisingly light on trendy boutique hotels. The new Aloft, near the university, isn't an indie property, but it does project a cool, modern vibe that caters to tech-minded, style-conscious travelers. Rooms and common areas pop with bright but spare decor that manages to feel inviting. Beer and cocktails are served at the on-site bar, and there's 24hr grab-n-go food beside the lobby.

Arizona Inn RESORT $$$
(☎800-933-1093, 520-325-1541; www.arizonainn.com; 2200 E Elm St; r $199-259, ste $299-379;) Our favorite part? High tea in the library, complete with scones and finger sandwiches. Croquet might be a highlight too, if only we could find a teammate. Historic and aristocratic touches such as these provide a definite sense of privilege – and we like it. Mature gardens and old Arizona grace also provide a respite from city life and the 21st century.

Eating

Mi Nidito MEXICAN $
(☎520-622-5081; www.minidito.net; 1813 S 4th Ave; mains $6-13; ⊙from 11am Wed-Sun) Former president Bill Clinton's order (pre-quadruple bypass) at 'My Little Nest' has become the signature president's plate, a heaping mound of Mexican favorites – tacos, tostadas, burritos, enchiladas and more – groaning under melted cheese. Give the prickly pear cactus chili or the *birria* (spicy, shredded beef) a whirl.

HOT DIGGETY DOG

Tucson's signature 'dish' is the Sonoran hot dog, a tasty example of what happens when Mexican ingredients meet America's processed meat and penchant for excess. The ingredients? A bacon-wrapped hot dog layered with tomatillo salsa, pinto beans, shredded cheese, mayo, ketchup or mustard or both, chopped tomatoes and onions. We like 'em at **El Guero Canelo** (www.elguerocanelo.com; 5201 S 12th Ave; mains $3-8.29; ⊙10am-11pm Mon-Thu, 8am-midnight Fri & Sat, 9am-11pm Sun).

Lovin' Spoonfuls VEGAN $
(☎520-325-7766; 2990 N Campbell Ave; breakfast $6-9, lunch $5.25-8, dinner $7.25-11.25; ⊙9:30am-9pm Mon-Sat, 10am-3pm Sun;) Burgers, country-fried chicken and club sandwiches – the menu reads like those at your typical diner but there's one big difference: no animal products will ever find their way into this vegan haven. Outstandingly creative choices include the cashew-mushroom pâté and the adzuki-bean burger.

★Cafe Poca Cosa SOUTH AMERICAN $$
(☎520-622-6400; www.cafepocacosatucson.com; 110 E Pennington St; lunch $12-15, dinner $18-26; ⊙11am-9pm Tue-Thu, to 10pm Fri & Sat) At this award-winning *nuevo*-Mexican bistro, a Spanish-English blackboard menu circulates between tables because dishes change twice daily. It's all freshly prepared, innovative and beautifully presented. The undecided can't go wrong by ordering the Plato Poca Cosa and letting chef Suzana Davila decide. Great margaritas, too.

Cup Cafe AMERICAN, GLOBAL $$
(☎520-798-1618; www.hotelcongress.com/food; 311 E Congress St; breakfast $7-12, lunch $10-12, dinner $13-25; ⊙7am-10pm Sun-Thu, to 11pm Fri & Sat;) Cup Cafe, we like your style. Wine-bottle chandeliers. A penny-tiled floor. And 'Up on Cripple Creek' on the speakers. In the morning, choices include a Creole

dish with andouille sausage, eggs, potatoes, buttermilk biscuits and sausage gravy, and cast-iron baked eggs with Gruyère cheese. And the coffee is excellent. There's a global mix of dishes, with a decent selection of vegetarian options.

Hub Restaurant & Creamery AMERICAN $$
(☎520-207-8201; www.hubdowntown.com; 266 E Congress Ave; lunch $10-16, dinner $10-24; ⏰11am-2am; 👪) Exposed-brick walls, a lofty ceiling, sleek booths and, surprisingly, a walk-up ice-cream stand beside the hostess desk – industrial chic takes a Mayberry spin. Upscale comfort food is the name of the game here, from lobster mac & cheese to chicken pot pie, plus a few sandwiches and salads.

Drinking & Entertainment

Downtown 4th Ave, near 6th St, is the happening bar-hop spot, and there are a number of nightclubs on downtown Congress St.

Che's Lounge BAR
(☎520-623-2088; 350 N 4th Ave; ⏰noon-2am) Drinkers unite! If everyone's favorite revolutionary heartthrob was still in our midst, he wouldn't have charged a cover either. A slightly skanky but hugely popular watering hole with $1.50 drafts, a huge wraparound bar and local art gracing the walls, this college hangout rocks with live music most Saturday nights and on the patio on Sunday afternoons (4-7pm) in the summer.

Thunder Canyon Brewery MICROBREWERY
(www.thundercanyonbrewery.com; 220 E Broadway Blvd; ⏰11am-11pm Sun-Thu, to 2am Fri & Sat) This cavernous microbrewery, within walking distance of Hotel Congress, has more than 40 beers on tap, serving up its own creations as well as handcrafted beers from across the US.

Chocolate Iguana COFFEE SHOP
(www.chocolateiguanaon4th.com; 500 N 4th Ave; ⏰7am-8pm Mon-Thu, 7am-10pm Fri, 8am-10pm Sat, 9am-6pm Sun) Chocoholics have their pick of sweets and pastries inside this green-and-purple cottage, while coffee-lovers can choose from numerous coffee brews and a long list of specialty drinks. Watching your diet? The delicious Frozen Explosion is a fat-free mocha. Also sells sandwiches ($6-7) and gifts.

Club Congress LIVE MUSIC
(☎520-622-8848; www.hotelcongress.com; 311 E Congress St) Skinny jeansters, tousled hipsters, aging folkies, dressed-up hotties – the crowd at Tucson's most-happening club inside the grandly aging Hotel Congress defines the word eclectic. And so does the musical line-up, which usually features the finest local and regional talent. Wanna sit and just drink at a no-fuss bar? Step inside the adjacent Tap Room, open since 1919.

Information

EMERGENCY & MEDICAL SERVICES

Police (☎520-791-4444; www.police.tucsonaz.gov/police; 270 S Stone Ave)

Tucson Medical Center (☎520-327-5461; www.tmcaz.com/TucsonMedicalCenter; 5301 E Grant Rd) 24-hour emergency services.

MEDIA

Arizona Daily Star (http://azstarnet.com) The Tucson region's daily newspaper.

Tucson Weekly (www.tucsonweekly.com) A free weekly full of entertainment and restaurant listings.

POST

Post Office (☎520-903-1958; 141 S 6th Ave; ⏰9am-5pm)

TOURIST INFORMATION

Tucson Convention & Visitors Bureau (☎800-638-8350, 520-624-1817; www.visittucson.org; 100 S Church Ave; ⏰9am-5pm Mon-Fri, to 4pm Sat & Sun) Ask for its free Tucson travel guide.

Getting There & Around

Tucson International Airport (☎520-573-8100; www.flytucson.com; 7250 S Tucson Blvd; 📶) is 15 miles south of downtown. **Arizona Stagecoach** (☎520-889-1000; www.azstagecoach.com) runs a shared van service with fares for about $25 between downtown and the airport. **Greyhound** (☎520-792-3475; www.greyhound.com; 471 W Congress St) runs buses to Phoenix ($21 to $23, two hours, daily) and other destinations. The station is on the western end of Congress St, on the western edge of downtown. **Amtrak** (☎800-872-7245, 520-623-4442; www.amtrak.com; 400 E Toole Ave), across from Hotel Congress, is connected to Los Angeles by the Sunset Limited service (from $56, 10 hours, three weekly).

From the **Ronstadt Transit Center** (215 E Congress St, cnr Congress St & 6th Ave), the major downtown transit hub, Sun Tran buses (www.suntran.com) serve metropolitan Tucson (day pass $3.50).

Around Tucson

All the places listed here are less than 1½ hours' drive from Tucson, and make great day trips.

Saguaro National Park

Saguaros are the most iconic symbol of the American Southwest, and an entire army of these majestic ribbed sentinels is protected in this two-part desert playground. **Saguaro National Park** (☎Rincon 520-733-5153, Tucson 520-733-5158, park information 520-733-5100; www.nps.gov/sagu; 7-day pass per vehicle/bicycle $10/5; ⊙sunrise to sunset) is divided into two units, 30 miles apart to either side of the city of Tucson, and each filled with trails and desert flora.

The larger section is the **Rincon Mountain District**, about 15 miles east of downtown. The **visitor center** (☎520-733-5153; 3693 S Old Spanish Trail; ⊙9am-5pm) has information on day hikes, horseback riding and backcountry camping. The latter requires a permit ($6 per site per day), which must be obtained by noon on the day of your hike. The meandering 8-mile Cactus Forest Scenic Loop Drive, a paved road open to cars and bicycles, provides access to picnic areas, trailheads and viewpoints. Hikers pressed for time should follow the 1-mile round-trip Freeman Homestead Trail to a grove of massive saguaro.

West of town, the **Tucson Mountain District** has its own **visitor center** (☎520-733-5158; 2700 N Kinney Rd; ⊙9am-5pm). The Scenic Bajada Loop Drive is a 6-mile graded dirt road through cactus forest that begins 1.5 miles north of the visitor center. Two quick, easy and rewarding hikes are the 0.8-mile Valley View Overlook (awesome at sunset) and the half-mile Signal Hill Trail to scores of ancient petroglyphs.

Trailers longer than 35ft and vehicles wider than 8ft are not permitted on the park's narrow scenic loop roads.

West of Tucson

You want wide solitude? Follow Hwy 86 west from Tuscon into some of the emptiest parts of the Sonoran Desert – except for the ubiquitous green-and-white border-patrol trucks.

The lofty **Kitt Peak National Observatory** (☎520-318-8726; www.noao.edu/kpno; Hwy 86; by donation; ⊙9am-4pm), west of Sells and about a 75-minute drive from Tucson, features the largest collection of optical telescopes in the world. Guided tours (adult/child $10/3.25, at 10am, 11:30am and 1:30pm) last about an hour. Book two to four weeks in advance for the worthwhile nightly observing program (adult/child $49/45; no programs from mid-July through August). Clear, dry skies equal an awe-inspiring glimpse of the cosmos. Dress warmly, buy gas in Tucson (the nearest gas station is 30 miles from the observatory) and note that children under eight years of age are not allowed at the evening program. The picnic area draws amateur astronomers at night.

If you truly want to get away from it all, you can't get much further off the grid than the huge and exotic **Organ Pipe Cactus National Monument** (☎520-387-6849; www.nps.gov/orpi; Hwy 85; per vehicle $8; ⊙visitor center 8:30am-4:30pm) along the Mexican border. It's a gorgeous, forbidding land that supports an astonishing number of animals and plants, including 28 species of cacti, first and foremost its namesake organ-pipe. A giant columnar cactus, it differs from the more prevalent saguaro in that its branches radiate from the base. The 21-mile **Ajo Mountain Drive** takes you through a spectacular landscape of steep-sided, jagged cliffs and rock tinged a faintly hellish red. There are 208 first-come, first-served sites at **Twin Peaks Campground** (www.nps.gov/orpi; tent & RV sites $12) by the visitor center.

South of Tucson

South of Tucson, I-19 is the main route to Nogales and Mexico. Along the way are several interesting stops.

The magnificent **Mission San Xavier del Bac** (☎520-294-2624; www.patronatosanxavier.org; 1950 W San Xavier Rd; donations appreciated; ⊙museum 8:30am-5pm, church 7am-5pm), on the San Xavier reservation 9 miles south of downtown Tucson, is Arizona's oldest Hispanic-era building still in use. Complete in 1797, it's a graceful blend of Moorish, Byzantine and late Mexican Renaissance architecture with an unexpectedly ornate interior.

At exit 69, 16 miles south of the mission, the **Titan Missile Museum** (☎520-625-7736; www.titanmissilemuseum.org; 1580 W

Duval Mine Rd, Sahuarita; adult/child 7-12yr/senior $9.50/6/8.50; ⌚8:45am-5pm, last tour at 4pm) features an underground launch site for Cold War–era intercontinental ballistic missiles. Tours are chilling and informative.

If history or shopping for crafts interest you, head 48 miles south of Tucson to the small village of **Tubac** (www.tubacaz.com), with more than 100 galleries, studios and shops.

Patagonia & the Mountain Empire

This lovely riparian region, sandwiched between the Mexican border and the Santa Rita and Patagonia Mountains, is one of the shiniest gems in Arizona's jewel box. It's a tranquil destination for bird-watching and wine tasting.

Bird-watchers and nature-lovers wander the gentle trails at the **Patagonia-Sonoita Creek Preserve** (☎520-394-2400; www.nature.org/arizona; 150 Blue Heaven Rd; admission $6; ⌚6:30am-4pm Wed-Sun Apr-Sep, 7:30am-4pm Wed-Sun Oct-Mar), an enchanting creekside willow and cottonwood forest managed by the Nature Conservancy. The peak migratory seasons are April through May, and late August to September. For a leisurely afternoon of wine tasting, head to the villages of **Sonoita** and **Elgin** north of Patagonia.

If you stick around for dinner, try the fantastic gourmet pizzas at **Velvet Elvis** (☎520-394-2102; www.velvetelvispizza.com; 292 Naugle Ave, Patagonia; mains $8-24; ⌚11:30am-8:30pm Thu-Sat, to 7:30pm Sun). Salute the Old West and its simple charms at the **Stage Stop Inn** (☎520-394-2211; www.stagestophotelpatagonia.com; 303 McKeown, Patagonia; s $79, d $89-109, ste $139; 📶🏊🐾), where rooms surround a central courtyard and pool. The stage coach did indeed stop here on the Butterfield Trail, and a small **visitor center** (☎888-794-0060; www.patagoniaaz.com; 307 McKeown Ave, Patagonia; ⌚10am-4pm Mon-Sat) now provides information.

Southeastern Arizona

Chockablock with places that loom large in Wild West history, southern Arizona is home to the wonderfully preserved mining town of Bisbee, the OK Corral in Tombstone, and a wonderland of stone spires at Chiricahua National Monument.

Kartchner Caverns State Park

The emphasis is on education at **Kartchner Caverns State Park** (☎information 520-586-4100, reservations 520-586-2283; http://azstateparks.com; Hwy 90; park entrance per vehicle/bicycle $6/3, Rotunda Tour adult/child 7-13yr $23/13, Big Room Tour mid-Oct–mid-Apr $23/13; ⌚park 7am-6pm, visitor center 8am-6pm Nov-May, shorter hours rest of year), a 2.5-mile wet limestone fantasia of rocks. Two guided tours explore different areas of the caverns, which were discovered in 1974. The Rotunda/Throne Room Tour is open year-round; the Big Room Tour closes in mid-April for five months to protect the migratory bats that roost here. The park is 9 miles south of Benson, off I-10 at exit 302. The $6 entrance fee is waived if you already have a reserved tour ticket.

Tombstone

In Tombstone's 19th-century heyday as a booming mining town, the whiskey flowed and six-shooters blazed over disputes large and small, most famously at the OK Corral. Now a National Historic Landmark, it attracts hordes of tourists to its old Western buildings, stagecoach rides and gunfight reenactments.

And yes, you must visit the **OK Corral** (☎520-457-3456; www.ok-corral.com; Allen St btwn 3rd & 4th Sts; admission $10, without gunfight $6; ⌚9am-5pm), site of the legendary gunfight where the Earps and Doc Holliday took on the McLaurys and Billy Clanton on October 26, 1881. The McClaurys and Clanton now rest at the **Boot Hill Graveyard** on Hwy 80 north of town. Also make time for the dusty **Bird Cage Theater** (☎520-457-3421; www.tombstonebirdcage.com; 517 E Allen St; adult/child 8-18yr/senior $10/8/9; ⌚8am-6pm), a one-time dance hall and saloon crammed with historic odds and ends. And a merman.

The **Visitor & Information Center** (☎520-457-3929, 888-457-3929; www.tombstonechamber.com; 395 E Allen St, at cnr of 4th St; ⌚9am-4pm Mon-Thu, to 5pm Fri-Sun) has walking maps.

Bisbee

Oozing old-fashioned ambience, Bisbee is a former copper-mining town that's now a delightful mix of aging bohemians, elegant buildings, sumptuous restaurants and charming hotels. Most businesses are in the

Historic District (Old Bisbee), along Subway and Main Sts.

To burrow under the earth in a tour led by the retired miners who worked here, take the **Queen Mine Tour** (☎520-432-2071; www.queenminetour.com; 478 Dart Rd, off Hwy 80; adult/child 4-12yr $13/5.50;). The Queen Mine Tour Building, just south of downtown, also holds the local **visitor center** (☎866-224-7233, 520-432-3554; www.discoverbisbee.com; 478 Dart Rd; 8am-5pm Mon-Fri, 10am-4pm Sat & Sun), and makes the obvious place to start exploring. Right outside of town, check out the **Lavender Pit**, an ugly yet impressive testament to strip mining.

Rest your head at **Shady Dell RV Park** (☎520-432-3567; www.theshadydell.com; 1 Douglas Rd; rates $87-145, closed early Jul–mid-Sep;), a deliciously retro trailer park extraordinaire where meticulously restored Airstream trailers are neatly fenced off and kitted out with fun furnishings. Swamp coolers provide cold air. You can sleep in a covered wagon at the quirky but fun **Bisbee Grand Hotel** (☎520-432-5900; www.bisbeegrandhotel.com; 61 Main St; r incl breakfast $79-179;), which brings the Old West to life (maybe it never died?) with Victorian-era decor and a kick-up-your-spurs saloon.

For good food, stroll up Main St and pick a restaurant – you can't go wrong. For fine American food, try stylish **Cafe Roka** (☎520-432-5153; www.caferoka.com; 35 Main St; dinner $17-24; 5-9pm Wed-Sat), where four-course dinners include salad, soup, sorbet and a rotating choice of crowd-pleasing mains. Continue up Main St for wood-fired pizzas and punk-rock style at **Screaming Banshee** (☎520-432-1300; www.screamingbansheepizza.net; 200 Tombstone Canyon Rd; mains $7-15; 4-9pm Tue & Wed, 11am-10pm Thu-Sat, 11am-9pm Sun). Bars cluster in Brewery Gulch, at the south end of Main St.

Chiricahua National Monument

The towering rock spires at remote but mesmerizing **Chiricahua National Monument** (☎520-824-3560; www.nps.gov/chir; Hwy 181; adult/child $5/free) in the Chiricahua Mountains sometimes rise hundreds of feet high and often look like they're on the verge of tipping over. The **Bonita Canyon Scenic Drive** takes you 8 miles to Massai Point (6870ft) where you'll see thousands of spires positioned on the slopes like some petrified army. There are numerous hiking trails, but if you're short on time, hike the **Echo Canyon Trail** at least half a mile to the Grottoes, an amazing 'cathedral' of giant boulders where you can lie still and enjoy the wind-caressed silence. The monument is 36 miles southeast of Willcox off Hwy 186/181.

UTAH

Shhhhh, don't tell. This oft-overlooked state is really one of nature's most perfect playgrounds. Utah's rugged terrain comes ready-made for hiking, biking, rafting, rappelling, rock climbing, skiing, snowboarding, snow riding, horseback riding, four-wheel driving… Need we go on?

More than 65% of the state's lands are public, including 12 national parks and monuments – a dazzling display of geology that leaves visitors awestruck. Southern Utah is a seemingly endless expanse of sculpted sandstone desert, its red-rock country defined by soaring Technicolor cliffs, spindles and spires. The 11,000ft-high forest- and snow-covered peaks of the Wasatch and other mountains and valleys dominate northeastern Utah.

Across the state you'll find well-organized towns with pioneer-era buildings dating to when the first Mormon settlers arrived; church members still make up more than half the impeccably polite population. Rural towns may be quiet and conservative, but the rugged beauty attracts outdoorsy, independent thinkers as well. Salt Lake and Park cities especially have vibrant nightlife and foodie scenes.

So come wonder at the roadside geologic kaleidoscope, hike out into the vast expanses or enjoy a great microbrew. Just don't tell your friends: we'd like to keep this secret to ourselves.

History

Traces of the Ancestral Puebloan and Fremont peoples, this land's earliest human inhabitants, remain in in the rock art and ruins they left behind. But the modern Ute, Paiute and Navajo tribes were living here when settlers of European heritage arrived in large numbers. Led by Brigham Young (second president of the Mormon church), Mormons fled to this territory to escape religious persecution starting in the late 1840s. They set out to settle every inch of their new land, no matter how inhospitable, which resulted

UTAH FACTS

Nickname Beehive State

Population 2.94 million

Area 82,169 sq miles

Capital city Salt Lake City (population 186,440), metro area (1.2 million)

Other cities St George (population 76,917)

Sales tax 6.85%

Birthplace of Entertainers Donny (b 1957) and Marie (b 1959) Osmond, beloved bandit Butch Cassidy (1866–1908)

Home of 2002 Winter Olympic Games

Politics Mostly conservative

Famous for Mormons, red-rock canyons, polygamy

Best souvenir Wasatch Brewery T-shirt: 'Polygamy Porter – Why Have Just One?'

in skirmishes with Native Americans – and more than one abandoned ghost town.

For nearly 50 years after the United States acquired the Utah Territory from Mexico, petitions for statehood were rejected due to the Mormon practice of polygamy (taking multiple wives). Tension and prosecutions grew until 1890, when Mormon leader Wilford Woodruff had a divine revelation and the church officially discontinued the practice. Utah became the 45th state in 1896. The modern Mormon church, now called the Church of Jesus Christ of Latter-Day Saints (LDS), continues to exert a strong influence.

Information

Utah Office of Tourism (☎800-200-1160; www.utah.com) Publishes the free *Utah Travel Guide* and runs several visitor centers statewide. Website has links in six languages.

Utah State Parks & Recreation Department (☎801-538-7220; www.stateparks.utah.gov) Produces comprehensive guide to the 40-plus state parks; available online and at visitor centers.

Getting There & Away

Salt Lake City (SLC) has Utah's only international airport. It may be cheaper to fly into Las Vegas (425 miles south) and rent a car.

Getting Around

You will need a private vehicle to get around anywhere besides SLC and Park City. Most Utah towns are laid out in a grid with streets aligned north–south or east–west. Addresses and numerical street names radiate out from a zero point at the central intersection (typically Main St and Center St), rising by 100 with each city block. Thus, 500 South 400 East will be five blocks south and four blocks east of the zero point. It sounds complicated, but it's surprisingly easy to use.

Salt Lake City

Snuggled up against the soaring peaks of the Wasatch Mountains, Salt Lake City is a small town with just enough edge to satisfy city slickers. Yes, it is the Mormon equivalent of the Vatican, but Utah's capital city is surprisingly modern. A redeveloped downtown and local foodie scene balance out the city's charming anachronisms.

Sights & Activities

Top church-related sights cluster near downtown's zero point: the corner of S Temple (east–west) and Main St (north–south). See those 132ft-wide streets? They were originally built so that four oxen pulling a wagon could turn around.

Don't forget that just 45 minutes away, world-class hiking, climbing and snow sports await in the Wasatch Mountains.

Temple Square Area

Temple Square PLAZA

(www.visittemplesquare.com; cnr S Temple & N State Sts; ⏲grounds 24hr; visitor centers 9am-9pm) FREE The city's most famous sight occupies a 10-acre block surrounded by 15ft-high walls. LDS docents give free, 30-minute tours continually, leaving from the visitor centers at the two entrances on South and North Temple Sts. Sisters, brothers and elders are stationed every 20ft or so to answer questions. (Don't worry, no one is going to try to convert you – unless you express interest.) In addition to the noteworthy sights, there are administrative buildings and two theater venues.

Salt Lake Temple RELIGIOUS SITE

(Temple Sq; ⏲closed to the public) Lording over Temple Sq is the impressive 210ft-tall Salt Lake Temple. Atop the tallest spire stands a statue of the angel Moroni, who appeared to LDS founder Joseph Smith. Rumor has it that when the place was renovated, cleaners found old bullet marks in one of the gold-plated surfaces. The temple and ceremonies are private, open only to LDS members in good standing.

Tabernacle RELIGIOUS SITE
(www.mormontabernaclechoir.org; Temple Sq; admission free; ⏲9am-9pm) FREE The domed, 1867 auditorium – with a massive 11,000-pipe organ – has incredible acoustics. A pin dropped in the front can be heard in the back, almost 200ft away. Free daily organ recitals are held at noon Monday through Saturday, and at 2pm Sunday.

Beehive House HISTORIC SITE
(☎801-240-2671; www.visittemplesquare.com; 67 E South Temple St; admission free; ⏲9am-8:30pm Mon-Sat) FREE Brigham Young lived with one of his wives and families in the Beehive House during much of his tenure as governor and church president in Utah. The required tours vary in the amount of historic house detail provided versus religious education offered, depending on the particular LDS docent. The attached 1855 **Lion House**, which was home to a number of Young's other wives, has a self-service restaurant (p865) in the basement. Feel free to look around the dining rooms during mealtimes.

Greater Downtown

Utah State Capitol HISTORIC BUILDING
(www.utahstatecapitol.utah.gov; 350 N State St; ⏲7am-8pm Mon-Fri, 8am-6pm Sat & Sun; visitor center 8:30am-5pm Mon-Fri) FREE The grand 1916 State Capitol is set among 500 cherry trees on a hill north of Temple Sq. Inside, colorful Works Progress Administration (WPA) murals of pioneers, trappers and missionaries adorn part of the building's dome. Free guided tours (hourly, 9am to 5pm, Monday to Friday) start at the 1st-floor visitor center; self-guided tours are available from the visitor center.

City Creek Center MALL
(www.shopcitycreekcenter.com; Social Hall Ave, btwn Regent & Richards Sts) Inaugurated in 2012, this LDS-funded, 20-acre pedestrian plaza has fountains, restaurants, a creek stocked with trout and retail area with a retractable roof.

University-Foothill District & Beyond

★**Natural History Museum of Utah** MUSEUM
(http://nhmu.utah.edu; 301 Wakara Way; adult/child $11/9; ⏲10am-5pm Thu-Tue, to 9pm Wed) The stunning architecture of the Rio Tinto Center forms a multistory indoor 'canyon' that showcases exhibits to great effect. Walk up through the layers as you explore both indigenous peoples' cultures and natural history. Past Worlds paleontological displays are the most impressive – an incredible perspective from beneath, next to and above a vast collection of dinosaur fossils offers the full breadth of pre-history.

This is the Place Heritage Park HISTORIC SITE
(www.thisistheplace.org; 2601 E Sunnyside Ave; adult/child $11/8; ⏲9am-5pm Mon-Sat, 10am-5pm Sun; 👪) Dedicated to the 1847 arrival of the Mormons, the heritage park covers 450 acres. The centerpiece is a living-history village where, June through August, costumed docents depict mid-19th-century life. Admission includes a tourist-train ride and activities. The rest of the year, access is limited to varying degrees at varyingly reduced prices; you'll at least be able to wander around the exterior of the 41 buildings. Some are replicas, but some are originals, such as Brigham Young's farmhouse.

Red Butte Garden GARDENS
(www.redbuttegarden.org; 300 Wakara Way; adult/child $10/6; ⏲9am-7:30pm) Both landscaped and natural gardens cover a lovely 150 acres,

POLYGAMY TODAY

Though the Mormon church eschewed plural marriage in 1890, some unaffiliated offshoot sects still believe it is a divinely decreed practice. Most of the roughly 7000 residents in Hilldale-Colorado City on the Utah–Arizona border are polygamy-practicing members of the Fundamentalist Church of Jesus Christ of Latter-Day Saints (FLDS). Walk into a Walmart in Washington or Hurricane and the shoppers you see in pastel-colored, prairie-style dresses – with lengthy braids or elaborate up-dos – are likely sister wives. Other, less-conspicuous polygamy-practicing sects are active in the southern parts of the state as well.

with access to trails in the Wasatch foothills. Check online to see who's playing at the popular, outdoor summer concert series also held here.

Church Fork Trail
HIKING

(Mill Creek Canyon Rd, off Wasatch Blvd; day-use $3) Looking for the nearest workout with big views? Hike the 6-mile round-trip, pet-friendly trail up to Grandeur Peak (8299ft). Mill Creek Canyon is 13.5 miles southwest of downtown.

🛏 Sleeping

Downtown, rates vary greatly depending on local events and occupancy. Cheaper chain motels cluster off I-80 near the airport and south in suburban Midvale. Outside ski season, prices plunge at Wasatch Mountain resorts, 45 minutes from downtown.

Avenues Hostel
HOSTEL $

(☑ 801-539-8888, 801-359-3855; www.saltlake-hostel.com; 107 F St; dm $19-23, s/d with shared bath $40/47, with private bath $50/57; ❋@🛜) Well-worn hostel; a bit halfway-house-like with long-term residents, but a convenient location.

★ Inn on the Hill
INN $$

(☑ 801-328-1466; www.inn-on-the-hill.com; 225 N State St; r incl breakfast $150-189; P❋@🛜) Exquisite woodwork and Maxfield Parrish Tiffany glass adorn this sprawling, 1906 Renaissance Revival mansion-turned-inn. Guest rooms are classically comfortable, not stuffy, with Jacuzzi tubs and some fireplaces and balconies. Great shared spaces include patios, billiard room, library and a dining room where chef-cooked breakfasts are served. The location is high above Temple Sq; expect great views and an uphill hike back from town.

Peery Hotel
HOTEL $$

(☑ 801-521-4300, 800-331-0073; www.peeryhotel.com; 110 W 300 South; r $99-130; P❋@🛜) Egyptian-cotton robes and sheets, carved dark-wood furnishings, individually decorated rooms – prepare to be charmed by the 1910 Peery. Small but impeccable bathrooms have pedestal sinks and aromatherapy bath products. This throwback hotel stands smack in the center of the Broadway Ave entertainment district – walking distance to restaurants, bars and theaters. Parking is $12 per day.

Crystal Inn & Suites
MOTEL $$

(☑ 800-366-4466, 801-328-4466; www.crystalinnsaltlake.com; 230 W 500 South; r incl breakfast $94-179; P❋@🛜🏊) Restaurants and Temple Sq are within walking distance of the downtown, multistory branch of Crystal Inns, a Utah-owned chain. Smiling staff here are genuinely helpful and there are lots of amenities for this price point (including a huge, hot breakfast).

Grand America
HOTEL $$$

(☑ 800-621-4505; www.grandamerica.com; 555 S Main St; r from $260; P❋@🛜🏊) Rooms in SLC's only true luxury hotel are decked out with Italian marble bathrooms, English wool carpeting, tasseled damask draperies and other cushy details. If that's not enough to spoil you, there's always afternoon high tea or the lavish Sunday brunch. Overnight parking is $13.

🍴 Eating

Many of Salt Lake City's bountiful assortment of ethnic and organically minded restaurants are within the downtown core. There's also a good collection (Middle Eastern, a noodle house, upscale new American, a cafe...) at 9th and 9th.

SALT LAKE CITY FOR CHILDREN

Young and old alike appreciate the attractions in the University-Foothill District, but there are also a couple of kid-specific sights to see.

Discovery Gateway (www.childmuseum.org; 444 W 100 South; admission $8.50; ⊘10am-6pm Mon-Thu, to 8pm Fri & Sat, noon-6pm Sun; 🚸) An enthusiastic, hands-on children's museum. The mock network-news desk in the media zone is particularly cool for budding journos.

Hogle Zoo (www.hoglezoo.org; 2600 E Sunnyside Ave; adult/child $15/11; ⊘9am-5pm; 🚸). More than 800 animals inhabit zones like the Asian Highlands on the landscaped 42-acre grounds of this zoo. Daily animal-encounter programs help kids learn more about their favorite species.

Lion House Pantry Restaurant AMERICAN $
(www.templesquarehospitality.com; 63 E South Temple St; meals $8-14; ⏲11am-8pm Mon-Sat) Down-home, carb-rich cookin' just like your Mormon grandmother used to make – only it's served cafeteria-style in the basement of an historic house. Several of Brigham Young's wives used to live here (including a previous author's great-great-great grandmother).

★**Red Iguana** MEXICAN $$
(www.rediguana.com; 736 W North Temple; mains $10-16; ⏲11am-10pm) Mexico at its most authentic, aromatic and delicious – no wonder the line is usually snaking out the door at this family-run restaurant. Ask for samples of the mole to decide on one of seven chile- and chocolate-based sauces. The incredibly tender *conchinita pibil* (shredded roast pork) tastes like it's been roasting for days.

Squatters Pub Brewery AMERICAN $$
(www.squatters.com; 147 W Broadway; dishes $10-22; ⏲11am-midnight Sun-Thu, to 1am Fri & Sat) Come for an Emigration Pale Ale, stay for the blackened tilapia salad. In addition to great microbrews, Squatters does a wide range of American casual dishes as well. The lively pub atmosphere is always fun.

Wild Grape MODERN AMERICAN $$
(www.wildgrapebistro.com; 481 E South Temple; breakfast & lunch $7-15, dinner $13-28; ⏲8am-10pm Mon-Fri, 9am-10pm Sat & Sun) Billing itself as a 'new West' bistro, Wild Grape creates modern versions of country classics. We like the weekend brunch dishes best.

Mazza MIDDLE EASTERN $$
(www.mazzacafe.com; 1515 S 1500 East; sandwiches $8-10, dinner $15-25; ⏲11am-3pm & 5-10pm Mon-Sat; 🖉) In an inviting ambience with warm tones and copper highlights, this local favorite consistently delivers well-known fare like kebabs, shawarma and hummus plus wonderful regional specialties, many from Lebanon. We love what they do with lamb and eggplant.

★**Copper Onion** INTERNATIONAL $$$
(☎801-355-3282; www.thecopperonion.com; 111 E Broadway Ave; brunch & small plates $7-15, dinner mains $22-29; ⏲11am-3pm & 5-10pm) Locals keep the Copper Onion bustling at lunch (for $10 specials), at dinner, at weekend brunch, at Happy Hour in the bar... And for good reason: small plates like wagyu beef tartare and pasta carbonara call out to be shared. Design-driven rustic decor provides a convivial place to enjoy it all.

CAN I GET A DRINK IN UTAH?

Absolutely. In recent years, laws have relaxed and private club membership bars are no more. Some rules to remember:

➡ Few restaurants have full liquor licenses: most serve beer and wine only. You have to order food to drink.

➡ Minors aren't allowed in bars.

➡ Mixed drinks and wine are available only after midday; 3.2% alcohol beer can be served starting at 10am.

➡ Mixed drinks cannot contain more than 1.5 ounces of a primary liquor, or 2.5 ounces total including secondary alcohol. Sorry, no Long Island Iced Teas or double shots.

➡ Packaged liquor can only be sold at state-run liquor stores; grocery and convenience stores can sell 3.2% alcohol beer and malt beverages. Sales are made from Monday through Saturday only.

Drinking & Nightlife

★**Beer Bar** PUB
(161 E 200 South; ⏲11am-2am Mon-Sat, 10am-2am Sun) With shared wooden tables and over 140 beers and 13 sausage styles, Beer Bar is a little slice of Bavaria in Salt Lake City. The crowd is diverse and far more casual than at Bar X next door (a linked venue). A great place to meet friends and make friends, but it gets pretty loud.

Gracie's BAR
(326 S West Temple; ⏲11am-2am) Even with two levels and four bars, Gracie's trendy bar-restaurant still gets crowded. The two sprawling patios are the best place to kick back. Live music or DJs most nights.

Beerhive Pub PUB
(128 S Main St; ⏲noon-1am) More than 200 beer choices, including many Utah-local microbrews, are wedged into this downtown storefront bar. Good for drinking and conversation.

Coffee Garden CAFE
(895 E 900 South; ⏲6am-11pm Sun-Thu, to midnight Fri & Sat; 📶) Perfection in a coffee shop,

with substance and style, good treats, desserts and ample seating. At the heart of the eclectic 9th and 9th neighborhood.

☆ Entertainment

Music

For a complete list of local music, visit www.cityweekly.net. Orchestra, organ, choir and other LDS-linked performances are listed at www.mormontabernaclechoir.org.

Mormon Tabernacle Choir LIVE MUSIC
(801-570-0080; www.mormontabernaclechoir.org) FREE Hearing the world-renowned Mormon Tabernacle Choir is a must-do on any SLC bucket list. A live choir broadcast goes out every Sunday at 9:30am. September through November, and January through May, attend in person at the Tabernacle (p863). Free public rehearsals are held here from 8pm to 9pm Thursday.

From June to August and in December – to accommodate larger crowds – choir broadcasts and rehearsals are held at the 21,000-seat LDS Conference Center. Performance times stay the same, except that an extra organ recital takes place at 2pm, Monday through Saturday.

Theater

The Salt Lake City Arts Council provides a complete cultural events calendar on its website (www.slcgov.com/city-life/ec). Local venues include the **Gallivan Center** (www.thegallivancenter.com; 200 South, btwn State & Main Sts), **Depot** (801-355-5522; www.smithstix.com; 400 W South Temple), and the **Rose Wagner Performing Arts Center** (www.slccfa.org; 138 W 300 South); you can reserve through **ArtTix** (888-451-2787, 801-355-2787; www.arttix.org).

Sports

Utah Jazz BASKETBALL
(801-325-2500; www.nba.com/jazz) Utah Jazz, the men's professional basketball team, plays at the **Energy Solutions Arena** (801-355-7328; www.energysolutionsarena.com; 301 W South Temple St), where concerts are also held.

Utah Grizzlies ICE HOCKEY
(801-988-7825; www.utahgrizzlies.com) The International Hockey League's Utah Grizzlies plays at the **Maverik Center** (tickets 800-745-3000; www.maverikcenter.com; 3200 S Decker Lake Dr, West Valley City), which hosted most of the men's ice-hockey competitions during the 2002 Winter Olympics.

> **THE BOOK OF MORMON, THE MUSICAL**
>
> Singing and dancing Mormon missionaries? You betcha...the musical *The Book of Mormon* opened to critical acclaim at the Eugene O'Neill Theatre in New York in 2011. The light-hearted satire about Latter-Day Saints (LDS) missionaries in Uganda came out of the comic minds that also created the musical *Avenue Q* and the animated TV series *South Park*. No wonder people laughed them all the way to nine Tony Awards.
>
> The LDS church's official response? Actually quite measured, avoiding any direct criticism – though it was made clear that their belief is that while 'the Book, the musical' can entertain you, the scriptures of the actual Book of Mormon can change your life. The show has even been staged in Salt Lake City, at the Capitol Theatre in 2015.

Shopping

City Creek (p863) is the indoor-outdoor mall of choice for big-name-brand shopping downtown. A small but interesting array of boutiques line up along Broadway Ave (300 South), between 100 and 300 East. A few crafty shops can be found on the 300 block of W Pierpont Ave.

Information

EMERGENCY & MEDICAL SERVICES

University Hospital (801-581-2121; 50 N Medical Dr) For emergencies, 24/7.

MEDIA

City Weekly (www.cityweekly.net) Free alternative weekly with good restaurant and entertainment listings; twice annually it publishes the free City Guide.

Salt Lake Tribune (www.sltrib.com) Utah's largest-circulation daily paper.

TOURIST INFORMATION

Public Lands Information Center (801-466-6411; www.publiclands.org; REI Store, 3285 E 3300 South; 10:30am-5:30pm Mon-Fri, 9am-1pm Sat) Recreation information for nearby public lands (state parks, BLM, USFS), including the Wasatch-Cache National Forest.

Visit Salt Lake (801-534-4900; www.visitsaltlake.com; 90 S West Temple, Salt Palace Convention Center; 9am-6pm Mon-Fri, to 5pm Sat & Sun) Publishes free visitor-guide booklet; large gift shop on site at the visitor center.

WORTH A TRIP

GREAT SALT LAKE

Once part of prehistoric Lake Bonneville, Great Salt Lake today covers 2000 sq miles and is far saltier than the ocean; you can easily float on its surface. The pretty, 15-mile-long **Antelope Island State Park** (☎801-773-2941; http://stateparks.utah.gov; Antelope Dr; day-use per vehicle $10; tent & RV sites without hookups $15; ⏰7am-10pm Jul-Sep, to 7pm Oct-Jun), 40 miles northwest of SLC, has nice hiking and the best beaches for lake swimming (though at low levels they're occasionally smelly). It's also home to one of the largest bison herds in the country. The basic **Bridger Bay Campground** (☎reservations 800-322-3770; http://utahstateparks.reserveamerica.com; tent & RV sites $15) operates year-round.

ℹ Getting There & Away

AIR

Five miles northwest of downtown, **Salt Lake City International Airport** (SLC; www.slcairport.com; 776 N Terminal Dr; 📶) has mostly domestic flights, though you can fly direct to Canada and Mexico. Delta (www.delta.com) is the main SLC carrier.

BUS

Greyhound (☎800-231-2222; www.greyhound.com; 300 S 600 West) connects SLC with Southwestern towns such as Las Vegas, NV ($62, eight hours), and Denver, CO ($86, 10 hours).

TRAIN

Traveling between Chicago and Oakland/Emeryville, the California Zephyr from **Amtrak** (☎800-872-7245; www.amtrak.com) stops daily at **Union Pacific Rail Depot** (340 S 600 West). Schedule delays can be substantial, and trains depart at odd hours, but you can connect with destinations such as Denver (from $79, 15 hours) and Reno, NV (from $70, 10 hours).

ℹ Getting Around

TO/FROM THE AIRPORT

Utah Transit Authority (UTA; www.rideuta.com; one-way $2.50; 📶) With light-rail service to the international airport and free rides within the downtown area. Bus 550 travels downtown from the parking structure between terminals 1 and 2.

Express Shuttle (☎800-397-0773; www.xpressshuttleutah.com) Shared van service; $17 to downtown.

Yellow Cab (☎801-521-2100) Private taxi to Salt Lake, Park City and area destinations.

PUBLIC TRANSPORTATION

UTA (www.rideuta.com) Trax, UTA's light-rail system, runs from Central Station (600 W 250 South) west to the University of Utah and south past Sandy. The center of downtown SLC is a free-fare zone. During ski season UTA buses serve the local ski resorts ($4.50 one-way).

Park City & the Wasatch Mountains

Utah offers some of North America's most awesome skiing, with fabulous low-density, low-moisture snow – between 300in and 500in annually – and thousands of acres of high-altitude terrain. The Wasatch Mountain Range, which towers over SLC, holds numerous ski resorts, abundant hiking, camping and mountain biking – not to mention chichi Park City, with its upscale amenities and famous film festival.

Salt Lake City Resorts

On the western side of the Wasatch mountain range, the four impressive snow-sport resorts in Little Cottonwood and Big Cottonwood Canyons lie within 40 minutes' drive of downtown SLC. All have lodging and dining facilities.

Activities

Solitude SNOW SPORTS
(☎801-534-1400; www.skisolitude.com; 12000 Big Cottonwood Canyon Rd; day lift-ticket adult/child $74/46) Exclusive, European-style village surrounded by excellent terrain. The Nordic Center has cross-country skiing in winter and nature trails in summer.

Brighton SNOW SPORTS
(☎801-532-4731, 800-873-5512; www.brightonresort.com; Big Cottonwood Canyon Rd; day lift-ticket adult/child $68/35) Slackers, truants and badass boarders rule at Brighton. But don't be intimidated: the low-key resort where many Salt Lake residents first learned to ski remains a good first-timers' spot, especially if you want to snowboard. Thick stands of pines line sweeping groomed trails and wide boulevards, and from the top, the views are gorgeous.

SCENIC DRIVE: MIRROR LAKE HIGHWAY

This alpine route, also known as Hwy 150, begins about 12 miles east of Park City in Kamas and climbs to elevations of more than 10,000ft as it winds the 65 miles into Wyoming. The highway provides breathtaking mountain vistas, passing scores of lakes, campgrounds and trailheads in the **Uinta-Wasatch-Cache National Forest** (www.fs.usda.gov/uwcnf). Sections may be closed to traffic into late spring due to heavy snowfall; check online.

Snowbird SNOW SPORTS
(☎800-232-9542; www.snowbird.com; Hwy 210, Little Cottonwood Canyon; day lift-ticket adult/child $95/45) The biggest and the busiest of them all, with all-round great snow riding – think steep and deep. Numerous lift-assist summer hiking trails; aerial tramway runs year-round.

Alta SNOW SPORTS
(☎801-359-1078, 888-782-9258; www.alta.com; Little Cottonwood Canyon; day lift-pass adult/child $79/42) Dyed-in-the-wool skiers make a pilgrimage to Alta, at the top of the valley. No snowboarders are allowed here, which keeps the snow cover from deteriorating, especially on groomers. Locals have grown up with Alta, a resort filled not with see-and-be-seen types, but rather the see-and-say-hello crowd. Wide-open powder fields, gullies, chutes and glades, such as East Greeley, Devil's Castle and High Rustler, have helped make Alta famous. Warning: you may never want to ski anywhere else.

Park City

A mere 35 miles east of SLC via I-80, Park City (elevation 6900ft) boasts two claims to international fame – hosting the downhill, jumping and sledding events at the 2002 Winter Olympics, and being the primary venue for the prestigious annual Sundance Film Festival. The Southwest's most popular ski destination is still home to the US ski team. Come summer, residents (pop 7873) gear up for hiking and mountain biking among the nearby peaks.

The town itself – a silver-mining community during the 19th century – has an attractive main street lined with galleries, shops, hotels, restaurants and bars. Despite the spread of prefab condos, the setting remains relatively charming. Winter is high season.

Sights

Utah Olympic Park ADVENTURE SPORTS
(☎435-658-4200; www.utaholympiclegacy.com; 3419 Olympic Pkwy; museum admission free, tours adult/child $10/7; ⊙10am-6pm, tours 11am-4pm) Visit the site of the 2002 Olympic ski jumping, bobsledding, skeleton, Nordic combined and luge events, which continues to host national competitions. There are 10m, 20m, 40m, 64m, 90m and 120m Nordic ski-jumping hills as well as a bobsled-luge run. The US Ski Team practices here year-round – in summer, the freestyle jumpers land in a bubble-filled jetted pool, and the Nordic jumpers on a hillside covered in plastic. Call for a schedule; it's free to observe.

Activities

In addition to snow sports, each area resort has posh lodging close to the slopes, abundant dining and summer activities including mountain-bike rental and lift-assist hiking. More than 300 miles of interconnecting hiking/biking trails crisscross area mountains; maps are available from the visitor center or online at http://mountaintrails.org. Two trails, **Armstrong** (4 miles; Park City Mountain Resort trailhead) and **Pinecone Ridge** (4 miles), combine for excellent mountain biking.

Park City Mountain Resort ADVENTURE SPORTS
(☎435-649-8111; www.parkcitymountainresort.com; 1310 Lowell Ave; alpine pass adult/child $70/35) We love the **Town Lift**–served hiking and mountain biking (day pass $21 to $23). The alpine pass is priced by size: those over 54" in height pay the adult fare, which includes access to the alpine slide, lifts and base-area activities. Or you can go á la carte: a 3000ft-long **alpine slide** ($12), where a wheeled sled flies down 550ft along a cement track, as well as a super-long **zipline ride** (2300ft long, 550ft vertical; $20).

Deer Valley ADVENTURE SPORTS
(☎800-424-3337; www.deervalley.com; Deer Valley Dr; scenic chairlift all-day adult/child $23/18) In summer Deer Valley has more than 50 miles of hiking and mountain-biking trails served by its three operating lifts. Horseback riding and free guided hikes are available by request.

Canyons ADVENTURE SPORTS
(☎888-226-9667; www.thecanyons.com; 4000 Canyons Resort Dr; adventure pass adult/child $69/59) Adventure passes cover a range of activities. A scenic ride on the **gondola** (round-trip adult/junior $18/13) is great for sightseers, but hiking trails also lead off from here. Mountain bikers should head over to the **Gravity Bike Park** (day pass adult/junior $32/27), which has varied trails accessed by the High Meadow Lift. Other activities include disc golf, miniature golf, lake pedal-boats and hot-air balloon rides. On weekends in summer and winter live-music concerts rock the base area.

Festivals & Events

Sundance Film Festival FILM
(☎888-285-7790; www.sundance.org/festival) Independent films and their makers and movie stars and their fans fill the town to bursting for 10 days in late January. Passes, ticket packages and the few individual tickets sell out well in advance – plan ahead.

Sleeping

More than 100 condos, hotels and resorts rent rooms in Park City; none are dirt cheap. For complete listings, check www.visitparkcity.com. High-season winter rates are quoted below (some require minimum stays); prices drop by half or more out of peak season. Chain motels at the intersection of I-40 and Hwy 248, and in SLC, offer better deals.

Chateau Apres Lodge HOSTEL $
(☎800-357-3556, 435-649-9372; www.chateauapres.com; 1299 Norfolk Ave; dm $45, r $130; wi-fi) The only budget-oriented accommodation in town is this basic, 1963 lodge – with a 1st-floor dorm – near the town ski lift. Reserve ahead, as it's very popular with groups and seniors.

Park City Peaks HOTEL $$
(☎800-333-3333, 435-649-5000; www.parkcitypeaks.com; 2121 Park Ave; r $139-189; air-con, internet, wi-fi, pool) Comfortable, contemporary rooms include access to heated outdoor pool, hot tub, restaurant and bar. Great deals off season. December through April, breakfast is included.

★**Old Town Guest House** B&B $$$
(☎800-290-6423, 435-649-2642; www.oldtownguesthouse.com; 1011 Empire Ave; r incl breakfast $219-269; air-con, internet, wi-fi) Grab the flannel robe, pick a paperback off the shelf and snuggle under a quilt on your lodgepole bed or kick back on the large deck at this comfy in-town B&B. The host will gladly give you the lowdown on the great outdoors, guided ski tours, mountain biking, and the rest.

★**Torchlight Inn** B&B $$$
(www.torchlightinn.com; r $225-300; parking, air-con, wi-fi) Right off the traffic circle, this new six-room inn charms with elegant and inviting contemporary spaces, gas fireplaces and flatscreen TVs. There's also a rooftop hot tub, Jeep rentals on-site and two friendly bulldogs to keep you company. With friendly, helpful service, family suites and wheelchair access (including an elevator).

Eating

While not known for cheap eats, Park City has exceptional upscale dining. Pick up Park City Magazine's menu guide (www.parkcitymagazine.com) for more. Between April and November, restaurants reduce hours and may take extended breaks. Reservations are required for all top-end ($$$) establishments.

Uptown Fare CAFE $
(227 Main St; sandwiches $8-11; ⏲11am-3pm) Comforting, house-roasted turkey sandwiches and homemade soups at the hole-in-the-wall hidden below the Treasure Mountain Inn.

DON'T MISS

ROBERT REDFORD'S SUNDANCE RESORT

Wind your way up narrow and twisting Hwy 92, for a truly special experience at Robert Redford's **Sundance Resort** (☎800-892-1600, 801-225-4107; www.sundanceresort.com; 9521 Alpine Loop Rd, Provo; r $209-500; wi-fi). Even if a night's stay at this elegantly rustic, ecoconscious wilderness getaway is out of reach, you can have a stellar meal at the Treehouse Restaurant or deli, attend an outdoor performance at the amphitheater or watch pottery being made (and sold) at the art shack. Skiing, hiking and spa services are also on site. Just walking the grounds is an experience. The resort is 30 miles south of Park City and 50 miles southeast of SLC.

Good Karma INDIAN, FUSION $$
(www.goodkarmarestaurants.com; 1782 Prospector Ave; breakfast $7-12, mains $12-22; ⏲7am-10pm;) Whenever possible, local and organic ingredients are used in the Indo-Persian meals at Good Karma. You'll recognize the place by the Tibetan prayer flags flapping out front.

★**Riverhorse on Main** NEW AMERICAN $$$
(☎435-649-3536; www.riverhorseparkcity.com; 540 Main St; dinner mains $34-49; ⏲5-10pm Mon-Thu, to 11pm Fri & Sat, 11am-2:30pm & 5-10pm Sun;) A fine mix of the earthy and exotic, with cucumber quinoa salad, polenta fries and Rocky Mountain rack of lamb. There's a separate menu for vegetarians. A wall-sized window and the sleek modern design creates a stylish atmosphere. Reserve ahead: this is a longtime, award-winning restaurant.

★**J&G Grill** AMERICAN $$$
(☎435-940-5760; www.jggrilldeercrest.com; 2300 Deer Valley Drive E, Deer Valley Resort; breakfast & lunch mains $14-22, dinner mains $26-55; ⏲7am-9pm) A favorite of locals, who love the tempura onion rings and seared scallops with sweet chili sauce. The bold flavors of meat and fish star here at one of celebrity chef Jean-Georges Vongerichten's collaborative projects. The mid-mountain St Regis setting is spectacular.

Wahso ASIAN $$$
(☎435-615-0300; www.wahso.com; 577 Main St; mains $30-50; ⏲5:30-10pm Wed-Sun, closed mid-Apr–mid-Jun) Park City's cognoscenti flock to this modern pan-Asian phenomenon, where fine-dining dishes may include lamb vindaloo or Malaysian snapper. Expect to see and be seen.

Drinking & Nightlife

Main St is where it's at, with half a dozen or more bars, clubs and pubs. In winter, there's action nightly – even restaurants have music. Outside peak season, the scene is weekends-only. For listings, see www.thisweekinparkcity.com.

High West Distillery & Saloon BAR
(703 Park St; ⏲11am-10pm, tours 3pm & 4pm) A former livery and Model A–era garage is now home to Park City's most happenin' nightspot. You can ski in for homemade rye whiskey at this micro distillery. What could be cooler?

No Name Saloon & Grill BAR
(447 Main St; ⏲11am-1am) There's a motorcycle hanging from the ceiling and Johnny Cash's 'Jackson' playing on the stereo at this memorabilia-filled bar.

Information

Visitor Information Center (☎435-658-9616, 800-453-1360; www.visitparkcity.com; 1794 Olympic Pkwy; ⏲9am-6pm;) Vast visitor center with a coffee bar, terrace and incredible views of the mountains at Olympic Park. Visitor guides available online.

Getting There & Around

Park City Transportation (☎800-637-3803, 435-649-8567; www.parkcitytransportation.com) and **Powder For The People** (☎888-482-7547, 435-649-6648) run shared-van service ($44 one-way) and private-charter vans (from $220 for one to three people) to/from Salt Lake City airport. The latter also has ski shuttles between Park City and Salt Lake City resorts.

PC-SLC Connect (bus 902) takes you from central Salt Lake to the **Park City Transit Center** (www.parkcity.org; 558 Swede Alley). No need for a car once you get to Park City. The excellent transit system covers the town: accessing the historic district, Kimbell Junction and all three ski resorts. The free buses run one to six times an hour from 8am to 11pm (reduced frequency in summer).

Northeastern Utah

Most visitors head northeast to explore Dinosaur National Monument, but this rural, oil-rich area also has some captivating wilderness terrain. All towns are a mile above sea level.

Vernal

As the closest town to Dinosaur National Monument, it's not surprising that Vernal welcomes you with a large pink dino-buddy. The informative film, interactive exhibits, video clips and giant fossils at the **Utah Field House of Natural History State Park Museum** (☎435-789-3799; http://stateparks.utah.gov; 496 E Main St; adult/child $6/3; ⏲9am-5pm;) make a great all-round introduction to Utah's dinosaurs.

Don Hatch River Expeditions (☎435-789-4316, 800-342-8243; www.donhatchrivertrips.com; 221 N 400 East; one-day adult/child $99/76) offers rapid-riding and gentler float trips on the nearby Green and Yampa Rivers.

Chain motels are numerous along Main St, but they book up with local workers – so don't expect a price break. **Holiday Inn Express & Suites** (☎800-315-2621, 435-789-4654; www.holidayinn.com/vernal; 1515 W Hwy 40; r incl breakfast $199-222;) has the most amenities, and **Econo Lodge** (☎435-789-2000; www.econolodge.com; 311 E Main St; r $79-119) will do in a bargain pinch.

Backdoor Grille (87 W Main St; mains $5-8; 11am-6pm Mon-Sat) makes fresh sandwiches and cookies, which are great to take on a picnic; you can also pick up a hiking guide at the associated bookshop. For dinner, the **Porch** (www.facebook.com/theporchvernal; 251 E Main St; lunches $8-12, dinner mains $14-23; 11am-2pm & 5-9pm Mon-Fri, 5-9pm Sat) is the place to go for Southern US favorites.

Dinosaur National Monument

Straddling the Utah-Colorado state line, **Dinosaur National Monument** (www.nps.gov/dino; off Hwy 40, Vernal; 7-day pass per vehicle $10; 24hr) protects a huge dinosaur fossil bed, discovered in 1909. Both states' sections are beautiful, but Utah has the bones. Don't miss the **Quarry Exhibit** (9am-4pm), an enclosed, partially excavated wall of rock with more than 1600 bones protruding.

In summer, shuttles run to the Quarry itself, 15 miles northeast of Vernal, UT, on Hwy 149, from the **Quarry Visitor Center** (8am-6pm mid-May–late Sep, 9am-5pm late Sep–mid-May); out of season you drive there in a ranger-led caravan. Follow the Fossil Discovery Trail from below the parking lot (2.2 miles round-trip) to see a few more giant femurs sticking out of the rock. The rangers' interpretive hikes are highly recommended.

In Colorado, the **Canyon Area** – 30 miles further east, outside Dinosaur, CO, and home to the monument's main **visitor center** (☎970-374-3000; 4545 E Hwy 40; 8am-4:30pm daily Jun-Aug, Mon-Fri only Dec-Feb) – holds some stunning overlooks, but thanks to its higher elevation is closed by snow until late spring.

Both sections have numerous hiking trails, interpretive driving tours, Green or Yampa river access and campgrounds ($8 to $15 per tent and RV site).

Flaming Gorge National Recreation Area

Named for its fiery red sandstone formations, this gorge-ous park has 375 miles of reservoir shoreline, part of the Green River system. Resort activities at **Red Canyon Lodge** (☎435-889-3759; www.redcanyonlodge.com; 790 Red Canyon Rd, Dutch John; cabins $115-155) include fly-fishing, rowing, rafting and horseback riding; its pleasantly rustic cabins have no TVs. **Flaming Gorge Resort** (☎435-889-3773; www.flaminggorgeresort.com; 155 Greendale/Hwy 191, Dutch John; r/ste $125/165, RV site $35;) has similar water-based offerings and rents motel rooms and suites. Both have decent restaurants.

Contact the **USFS Flaming Gorge Headquarters** (☎435-784-3445; www.fs.usda.gov/ashley; 25 W Hwy 43, Manila; 8am-5pm Mon-Fri) for the public camping lowdown. The area's 6040ft elevation ensures pleasant summers.

Moab & Southeastern Utah

Snow-blanketed peaks in the distance provide stark contrast to the red-rock canyons that define this rugged corner of the Colorado Plateau. For 65 million years water has carved serpentine, sheer-walled gorges along the course of the Colorado and Green Rivers. Today these define the borders of expansive Canyonlands National Park (p874). At nearby Arches National Park (p873), erosion sculpted thousands of arches and fin rock formations. Base yourself between the parks in Moab, aka activity central – a town built for mountain biking, river running and four-wheel driving. In Utah's far southeastern corner, Ancestral Puebloan sites are scattered among remote and rocky wilderness areas and parks. Most notable is Monument Valley, which extends into Arizona.

Green River

The 'World's Watermelon Capital,' the town of Green River offers a good base for river running on the Green and Colorado Rivers. The legendary one-armed Civil War veteran, geologist and ethnologist John Wesley Powell first explored these rivers in 1869 and 1871. Learn about his amazing travels at the **John Wesley Powell River History Museum** (☎435-564-3427; www.jwprhm.com; 885 E Main St; adult/child $6/2; 8am-7pm Apr-Oct, to 4pm Nov-Mar), which doubles as the local visitor center.

Holiday River Expeditions (☎800-624-6323, 435-564-3273; www.holidayexpeditions.com; 10 Holiday River St; day trip $165) run one-day rafting trips in Westwater Canyon, as well as multiday excursions.

Family-owned, clean and cheerful, **Robbers Roost Motel** (☑ 435-564-3452; www.rr-motel.com; 325 W Main St; r from $38; ❋ 🐾 🛜 🐾) is a motorcourt budget-motel gem. Otherwise, there are numerous chain motels where W Main St (Business 70) connects with I-70. Residents and rafters alike flock to **Ray's Tavern** (25 S Broadway; dishes $8-27; ⊙ 11am-9:30pm), the local beer joint, for hamburgers and fresh-cut French fries.

Green River is 182 miles southeast of Salt Lake City and 52 miles northwest of Moab, and is a stop on the daily California Zephyr train, run by **Amtrak** (☑ 800-872-7245; www.amtrak.com; 250 S Broadway) to Denver, CO (from $59, 10¾ hours).

Moab

Southeastern Utah's largest community (population 5130) bills itself as the state's recreation capital, and... oh man, does it deliver. Scads of rafting and riding (mountain bike, horse, 4WD...) outfitters here make forays into surrounding public lands. Make this your base, and you can hike Arches or Canyonlands National Parks during the day, then come back to a comfy bed, a hot tub and your selection of surprisingly good restaurants at night. Note, though, that this alfresco adventure gateway is not a secret: Moab is mobbed, especially during spring and fall events. If the traffic irritates you, you can disappear into the vast surrounding desert in no time.

🏃 Activities

Moab's information center carries brochures on near-town rock art, hiking trails, driving tours, etc, and keeps a list of the many outfitters that offer half-day to multiday adventures (from $80 for a sunset 4WD tour to around $175 for a white-water day on the river). Book ahead.

★ Moab Desert Adventures   ROCK CLIMBING
(☑ 804-814-3872; www.moabdesertadventures.com; 415 N Main St; half/full day from $165/265) Top-notch climbing tours scale area towers and walls; the 140ft arch rappel is especially exciting. Canyoneering and multisport packages available.

Sheri Griffith Expeditions   RAFTING
(☑ 800-332-2439; www.griffithexp.com; 2231 S Hwy 191) Operating since 1971, this rafting specialist has a great selection of river trips on the Colorado, Green and San Juan Rivers – from family floats to Cataract Canyon rapids, from a couple hours to a couple weeks.

Poison Spider Bicycles   MOUNTAIN BIKING
(☑ 435-259-7882, 800-635-1792; www.poisonspiderbicycles.com; 497 N Main St; rental per day $45-75) Friendly staff are always busy helping wheel jockeys map out their routes. Well-maintained road and suspension rigs for rent; private guided trips organized in conjunction with Magpie Adventures.

Farabee's Outlaw Jeep Tours   DRIVING TOUR
(☑ 435-259-7494; www.farabeesjeeprentals.com; 35 Grand St) Customized Jeep rental and off-road ride-along or guide-led tours.

🛏 Sleeping

Most lodgings have bike-storage facilities and hot tubs. Despite having an incredible number of motels, Moab does fill up; reservations are highly recommended March through October.

Individual **BLM campsites** (☑ 435-259-2100; www.blm.gov/utah/moab; Hwy 128; tent sites $15; ⊙ year-round) in the area are first-come, first-served. In peak season, check with the Moab Information Center to see which sites are full.

Adventure Inn   MOTEL $
(☑ 435-259-6122; www.adventureinnmoab.com; 512 N Main St; r $69-105; ⊙ Mar-Oct; ❋ 🛜) A great little indie motel, the Adventure Inn has spotless rooms (some with refrigerators) and decent linens, as well as laundry facilities. There's a picnic area on-site and the owners prove helpful.

Lazy Lizard Hostel   HOSTEL $
(☑ 435-259-6057; www.lazylizardhostel.com; 1213 S Hwy 191; dm/s/d $11/30/34, cabins $35-41; 🅿 ❋ @ 🛜) Hippie hangout with frayed couches, worn bunks and small kitchen.

★ Cali Cochitta   B&B $$
(☑ 435-259-4961, 888-429-8112; www.moabdreaminn.com; 110 S 200 East; cottages $140-180; ❋ 🛜) Charming and central, these adjoining brick cottages offer snug rooms fitted with smart decor. A long wooden table on the patio makes a welcome setting for community breakfasts. You can also take advantage of the porch chairs, hammock or backyard hot

tub. The vibe is warm but the innkeepers live off-site, leaving you alone to enjoy the house.

Sunflower Hill Inn INN $$
(☎435-259-2974; www.sunflowerhill.com; 185 N 300 East; r $175-250; ❄📶🏊) A top-shelf B&B, Sunflower Hill offers rooms in two inviting buildings –a cedar-sided early-20th-century home and a 100-year-old farmhouse amid manicured gardens and cottonwoods. Rooms have an elegant country style, with quilt-piled beds and antiques. The staff are eager to please and the hot tub works magic.

Sorrel River Ranch LODGE $$$
(☎877-317-8244; www.sorrelriver.com; Mile 17, Hwy 128; r $429-779; ❄@🏊) Southeast Utah's only full-service luxury resort and gourmet restaurant was originally an 1803 homestead. The lodge and log cabins sit on 240 lush acres, with riding areas and alfalfa fields along the Colorado River. Details strive for rustic perfection, with bedroom fireplaces, handmade log beds, copper-top tables and Jacuzzi tubs.

Eating

Moab holds everything from backpacker coffeehouses to gourmet dining rooms; pick up the *Moab Menu Guide* (www.moabmenuguide.com) at area lodgings.

★**Milt's** BURGERS $
(356 Mill Creek Dr; dishes $4-9; ⏰11am-8pm Mon-Sat) Meet greasy goodness. A triathlete couple bought this classic 1954 burger stand and smartly changed nothing. Heaven is one of their honest burgers, jammed with pickles, fresh lettuce, a side of fresh-cut fries and creamy milkshake. Be patient: the line can get long. It's near the Slickrock Bike Trail.

★**Pantele's Deli** DELI $
(☎435-259-0200; 98 E Center St; sandwiches $8-10; ⏰11am-4pm Mon-Sat) Doing a brisk business, this deli makes everything fresh and it shows. Salads come in heaping bowls and high-piled sandwiches are stuffed with fresh roasted turkey or roast beef cooked in-house. The wait is worth it.

Sabaku Sushi SUSHI $$
(☎435-259-4455; www.sabakusushi.com; 90 E Center St; rolls $6-9, mains $13-17; ⏰5pm-midnight Tue-Sun) The ocean is about a million miles away, but you still get a creative selection of fresh rolls, catches of the day and a few Utah originals at this small hole-in-the-wall sushi joint.

Stick with the status quo with traditional sashimi and *nigiri* offerings or get adventurous with the lip-smacking Elk Tataki and Devil's Garden Roll (topped with a pineapple habanero sauce).

★**Desert Bistro** SOUTHWESTERN $$$
(☎435-259-0756; www.desertbistro.com; 36 S 100 West; mains $22-42; ⏰5:30-11pm Wed-Sun) Stylized preparations of game and fresh, flown-in seafood are the specialty at this welcoming white-tablecloth restaurant inside an old house. Think smoked elk in a huckleberry glaze, pepper-seared scallops and jicama salad with crisp pears. Everything is made on-site, from freshly baked bread to delicious pastries. Great wine list, too.

Information

Moab Information Center (www.discovermoab.com; cnr Main & Center Sts; ⏰8am-7pm; 📶) Excellent source of information on area parks, trails, activities, camping and weather. Extensive bookstore and knowledgeable staff. Walk-in only.

Getting There & Around

Delta has regularly scheduled flights from **Canyonlands Airport** (CNY; www.moabairport.com; off Hwy 191), 16 miles north of town via Hwy 191, to Salt Lake City.

Moab Luxury Coach (☎435-940-4212; www.moabluxurycoach.com) operates a van service to and from SLC ($159 one-way, 4¾ hours) and Grand Junction ($95 one-way, 2 hours). **Roadrunner Shuttle** (☎435-259-9402; www.roadrunnershuttle.com) and **Coyote Shuttle** (☎435-260-2097; www.coyoteshuttle.com) offer on-demand Canyonlands Airport, hiker-biker and river shuttles.

Moab is 235 miles southeast of Salt Lake City, and 150 miles northeast of Capital Reef National Park.

Arches National Park

Stark, exposed, and unforgettably spectacular, **Arches National Park** (☎435-719-2299; www.nps.gov/arch; Hwy 191; 7-day pass per vehicle $10; ⏰24hr; visitor center 7:30am-6:30pm Mar-Oct, 9am-4pm Nov-Feb) boasts the world's greatest concentration of sandstone arches – more than 2000, ranging from 3ft to 300ft wide at last count. Nearly one-million visitors make the pilgrimage here each year; it's just 5 miles north of Moab, and small enough for you to see most of it within a day. Many noteworthy arches are easily reached by paved roads and relatively short hiking trails. To avoid crowds, consider a moonlight exploration, when it's cooler and the rocks feel ghostly.

Highlights along the park's main scenic drive include **Balanced Rock**, precariously perched beside the main park road, and, for hikers, the moderate-to-strenuous, 3-mile round-trip trail that ascends the slickrock to reach the unofficial state symbol, **Delicate Arch** (best captured in the late afternoon).

Further along the road, the spectacularly narrow canyons and maze-like fins of the **Fiery Furnace** are most safely explored on the three-hour, ranger-led hikes, for which advance reservation is usually necessary. This is no walk in the park. (Well, it is, but...) Be prepared to scramble up and over boulders, chimney down between rocks and navigate narrow ledges.

The scenic drive ends 19 miles from the visitor center at **Devils Garden**. The trailhead marks the start of a 2- to 7.7-mile round-trip hike that passes at least eight arches, though most hikers only go the relatively easy 1.3 miles to Landscape Arch, a gravity-defying, 290ft-long behemoth. For stays between March and October, advance reservations are a must for the **Devils Garden Campground** (☎877-444-6777; www.recreation.gov; tent & RV sites $20). No showers, no hookups.

Because of water scarcity and heat, few visitors backpack, though it is allowed with free permits (available from the visitor center).

Canyonlands National Park

Red-rock fins, bridges, needles, spires, craters, mesas, buttes – **Canyonlands National Park** (www.nps.gov/cany; per vehicle 7 days $10; tent & RV sites without hookups $10-15; ⏲24hr) is a crumbling, decaying beauty, a vision of ancient earth. Roads and rivers make inroads into this high-desert wilderness stretching 527 sq miles, but much of it is still untamed. You can hike, raft and 4WD here but be sure that you have plenty of gas, food and water.

The canyons of the Colorado and Green Rivers divide the park into several entirely separate areas. The appropriately named **Island in the Sky** district, just over 30 miles northwest of Moab, consists of a 6000ft-high flat-topped mesa that provides astonishing long-range vistas. Starting from the **visitor center** (☎435-259-4712; www.nps.gov/cany; Hwy 313, 1 mile after park entrance; ⏲8am-6pm Mar-Oct, 9am-4:30pm Nov-Feb), a scenic drive leads past numerous overlooks and trailheads, ending after 12 miles at **Grand View Point**, where a sinuous trail runs for a mile along the very lip of the mesa. Our favorite short hike en route is the half-mile loop to oft-photographed **Mesa Arch**, a slender, cliff-hugging span that frames a magnficent view of Washer Woman Arch. Seven miles from the visitor center, the first-come, first-served, 12-site **Willow Flat Campground** (www.nps.gov/cany/planyourvisit/islandinthesky.htm; tent & RV sites $10) has vault toilets but no water, and no hookups.

Named for the spires of orange-and-white sandstone jutting skyward from the desert floor, the wild and remote **Needles** district is ideal for backpacking and off-roading. To reach the **visitor center** (☎435-259-4711; Hwy 211; ⏲8am-6pm Mar-Oct, 9am-4:30pm Nov-Feb), follow Hwy 191 south for 40 miles from Moab, then take Hwy 211 west. This area is much more about long, challenging hikes than roadside overlooks. The awesome **Chesler Park/Joint Trail Loop** is an 11-mile route across desert grasslands, past towering red-and-white-striped pinnacles, and through deep, narrow slot canyons, at times just 2ft across. Elevation changes are mild, but the distance makes it an advanced day hike. The first-come, first-served, 27-site **Squaw Flat Campground** (www.nps.gov/cany; tent & RV sites $15), 3 miles west of the visitor center, fills up every day, spring to fall. It has flush toilets and running water, but no showers or hookups.

In addition to normal entrance fees, advance-reservation permits ($10 to $30) are required for backcountry camping, 4WD trips and river trips. Remoter areas west of the rivers, only accessible southwest of the town of Green River, include **Horseshoe Canyon**, where determined hikers are rewarded with extraordinary ancient rock art, and the **Maze**.

Dead Horse Point State Park

Tiny but stunning **Dead Horse Point State Park** (www.stateparks.utah.gov; Hwy 313; park day use per vehicle $10; tent & RV sites $25; ⏲park 6am-10pm, visitor center 8am-6pm Mar-Oct, 9am-4pm Nov-Feb) has been the setting for numerous movies, including the climactic scenes of *Thelma & Louise*. It's not a hiking destination, but mesmerizing views merit the short detour off Hwy 313 en route to the Island in the Sky in Canyonlands National Park: look out at red-rock canyons rimmed with white cliffs, the Colorado River, Canyonlands and the distant La Sal Mountains. The 21-site campground has limited water (bring your own if possible); no showers, no hookups. Reserve ahead.

Bluff

One hundred miles south of Moab, this little community (population 258) makes a comfortable, laid-back base for exploring Utah's desolately beautiful southeastern corner. Founded by Mormon pioneers in 1880, Bluff sits surrounded by red rock and public lands near the junction of Hwys 191 and 162, along the San Juan River. Other than a trading post and a couple of places to eat or sleep, there's not much town.

For backcountry tours that access rock art and ruins, join **Far Out Expeditions** (☎435-672-2294; www.faroutexpeditions.com; day tours $195) on a day or multiday hike into the remote region. A rafting trip along the San Juan with **Wild Rivers Expeditions** (☎800-422-7654; www.riversandruins.com; 101 Main St; day trip adult/child $175/133), a history and geology-minded outfitter, also includes ancient site visits.

The hospitable **Recapture Lodge** (☎435-672-2281; www.recapturelodge.com; Hwy 191; r incl breakfast $85;) is a rustic, cozy place to stay. Owners sell maps and know the region inside and out. Also nice are the spacious log rooms at the **Desert Rose Inn** (☎435-672-2303, 888-475-7673; www.desertroseinn.com; 701 West Main Street; r $140-189, cabins $179-289;).

Artsy **Comb Ridge Coffee** (www.combridgecoffee.com; 680 S Hwy 191; dishes $3-10; 7am-9pm Tue-Sat, to 5pm Sun, varies Nov-Feb;) serves espresso, muffins and sandwiches inside a timber and adobe cafe, while the Western-themed **Cottonwood Steakhouse** (☎435-672-2282; www.cottonwoodsteakhouse.com; Hwy 191, cnr Main & 4th East Sts; mains $18-25; 5:30-9:30pm Mar-Nov) serves substantial portions of barbecued steak and beans.

Hovenweep National Monument

Beautiful, little-visited **Hovenweep** (www.nps.gov/hove; Hwy 262; park 7-day per vehicle $6; tent & RV sites $10; park dusk-dawn, visitor center 8am-6pm Jun-Sep, 9am-5pm Oct-May), meaning 'deserted valley' in the Ute language, showcases several neighboring Ancestral Puebloan sites, where impressive towers and granaries stand in shallow desert canyons. The Square Tower Group is accessed near the visitor center; other sites require long hikes. The campground has 31 basic, first-come, first-served sites (no showers, no hookups). The main access is east of Hwy 191 on Hwy 262 via Hatch Trading Post, more than 40 miles northeast of Bluff.

DON'T MISS

NEWSPAPER ROCK RECREATION AREA

This tiny, free recreation area is really just a parking lot beside a single large sandstone rock panel that's packed with more than 300 **petroglyphs** attributed to Ute and Ancestral Puebloan peoples during a 2000-year period. It's about 12 miles along Hwy 211 from Hwy 191, en route to the Needles section of Canyonlands National Park (8 miles further).

Monument Valley

Twenty-five miles southwest from Bluff, after the village of **Mexican Hat** (named for an easy-to-spot sombrero-shaped rock), Hwy 163 winds southwest and enters the Navajo Indian reservation. Another 25 miles southwest, the incredible mesas and buttes of Monument Valley rise up. Most of the area, including the tribal park with a 17-mile unpaved driving loop circling the massive formations, is in Arizona (p854).

Natural Bridges National Monument

Fifty-five miles northwest of Bluff, the ultra-remote **Natural Bridges National Monument** (www.nps.gov/nabr; Hwy 275; 7-day pass per vehicle $6; tent & RV sites $10; 24hr, visitor center 8am-6pm May-Sep, 9am-5pm Oct-Apr) protects a white sandstone canyon (it's not red!) containing three impressive and easily accessible natural bridges. The oldest, Owachomo Bridge, spans 180ft but is only 9ft thick. The flat 9-mile Scenic Drive loop is ideal for overlooking. The campground offers 13 basic sites on a first-come, first-served basis; no showers, no hookups. There is some primitive overflow camping space, but be aware that the nearest services are in Blanding, 40 miles east.

Zion & Southwestern Utah

Local tourist boards call it 'color country,' but the cutesy label hardly does justice to the eye-popping hues that saturate the landscape. The deep-crimson canyons of Zion, the delicate pink-and-orange minarets at Bryce Canyon, the swirling yellow-white domes of Capitol Reef – the region is so spectacular that it holds three national parks and the gigantic Grand Staircase-Escalante National Monument (GSENM).

Capitol Reef National Park

Not as crowded as its fellow parks but equally scenic, **Capitol Reef** (☎435-425-3791, ext 4111; www.nps.gov/care; cnr Hwy 24 & Scenic Dr; admission free, 7-day scenic drive per vehicle $5; tent & RV sites $10; ⏱24hr, visitor center & scenic drive 8am-6pm Apr-Oct, to 4:30pm Nov-Mar) contains much of the 100-mile Waterpocket Fold, created 65 million years ago when the earth's surface buckled up and folded, exposing a cross-section of geologic history that is downright painterly in its colorful intensity.

Hwy 24 cuts grandly through the park, but make sure to take the **scenic drive** south, a paved, dead-end 9-mile road that passes through orchards – a legacy of Mormon settlement. In season you can freely pick cherries, peaches and apples, as well as stop by the historic **Gifford Farmhouse** to see an old homestead and buy fruit-filled mini-pies. Great walks en route include the **Grand Wash** and **Capitol Gorge** trails, each following the level floor of a separate slender canyon; if you're in the mood for a more demanding hike, climb the **Golden Throne Trail** instead. The shady, green campground (no showers, no hookups) is first-come, first-served; it fills early spring through fall.

Torrey

Just 15 miles west of Capital Reef, the small pioneer town of Torrey serves as the base for most national-park visitors. In addition to a few Old West–era buildings, there are a dozen or so restaurants and motels.

Western-themed on the outside, **Austin's Chuckwagon Motel** (☎435-425-3335; www.austinschuckwagonmotel.com; 12 W Main St, Torrey; r $61-91, cabins $147; ⏱Mar-Oct; ❄📶🏊🐾) has nice, clean, slightly characterless guest rooms on the inside. Note that budget digs are over the general store, where you can grab supplies or sandwiches.

Dressed with country elegance, each airy room at the 1914 **Torrey Schoolhouse B&B** (☎435-633-4643; www.torreyschoolhouse.com; 150 N Center St, Torrey; r incl breakfast $115-145; ⏱Apr-Oct; ❄📶) has a story to tell. (Butch Cassidy may have attended a town dance here.) After consuming the gourmet breakfast, laze in the garden or the huge 1st-floor lounge.

Thanks to its outstanding, highly stylized Southwestern cooking, **Cafe Diablo** (☎435-425-3070; www.cafediablo.net; 599 W Main St, Torrey; lunch $10-14, dinner mains $22-40; ⏱11:30am-10pm mid-Apr–Oct; 🖉) ranks high among the finest restaurants in southern Utah.

Boulder

Though the tiny outpost of **Boulder** (www.boulderutah.com; population 227), is just 32 miles south of Torrey on Hwy 12, you have to cross Boulder Mountain to reach it. From here, the attractive **Burr Trail Rd** heads east across the northeastern corner of the Grand Staircase-Escalante National Monument, eventually winding up on a gravel road that leads either up to Capital Reef or down to Bullfrog Marina on Lake Powell.

The small **Anasazi State Park Museum** (www.stateparks.utah.gov; Main St/Hwy 12; admission $5; ⏱8am-6pm Mar-Oct, 9am-5pm Nov-Apr) curates artifacts and a Native American site inhabited from AD 1130 to 1175.

Rooms at **Boulder Mountain Lodge** (☎435-335-7460; www.boulder-utah.com; 20 N Hwy 12; r $135-184, ste $310, apt $220; ❄@📶🐾) are plush, but it's the 15-acre wildlife sanctuary setting that's unsurpassed. An outdoor hot tub with mountain views is a soothing spot to bird-watch. The lodge's destination restaurant, **Hell's Backbone Grill** (☎435-335-7464; www.hellsbackbonegrill.com; 20 N Hwy 12, Boulder Mountain Lodge; breakfast $8-12, lunch $12-18, dinner $18-27; ⏱7:30-11:30am & 5-9:30pm Mar-Nov) serves soulful, earthy preparations of regionally inspired and sourced cuisine – book ahead – while the nearby **Burr Trail Grill & Outpost** (www.burrtrailgrill.com; cnr Hwy 12 & Burr Trail Rd; dishes $8-18; ⏱grill 11:30am-9:30pm, outpost 8:30am-6pm Mar-Oct; 📶) offers organic vegetable tarts, eclectic burgers and scrumptious homemade desserts.

Grand Staircase-Escalante National Monument

The 2656-sq-mile **Grand Staircase-Escalante National Monument** (GSENM; ☎435-826-5499; www.ut.blm.gov/monument; admission free; ⏲24hr) FREE, a waterless region so inhospitable that it was the last to be mapped in the continental US, covers more territory than Delaware and Rhode Island combined. The nearest services, and GSENM visitor centers, are in Boulder and Escalante on Hwy 12 in the north, and Kanab on US 89 in the south. Otherwise, infrastructure is minimal, leaving a vast, uninhabited canyon land full of 4WD roads that call to adventurous travelers who have the time, equipment and knowledge to explore.

The most accessible and most used trail in the monument is the 6-mile round-trip hike to the magnificent multicolored waterfall on **Lower Calf Creek** (Mile 75, Hwy 12; day use $5; ⏲day use dawn-dusk), between Boulder and Escalante. The 13 creekside campsites, just off Hwy 12, fill fast; no showers, no hookups, and no reservations taken.

Escalante

This national-monument gateway town of 779 people is the closest thing to a metropolis for many a lonely desert mile. Thirty slow and winding miles from Boulder, and 65 from Torrey, it's a good place to base yourself before venturing into the adjacent GSENM. The **Escalante Interagency Office** (☎435-826-5499; www.ut.blm.gov/monument; 775 W Main St; ⏲8am-4:30pm daily Apr-Sep, Mon-Fri Oct-Mar) is a superb resource center with complete information on nearby monument and forest-service lands.

Escalante Outfitters & Cafe (☎435-826-4266; www.escalanteoutfitters.com; 310 W Main St; natural history tours $45; ⏲7am-9pm) is a traveler's oasis: the bookstore sells maps, guides, camping supplies – and liquor(!) – while the pleasant cafe serves homemade breakfast, pizzas and salads. It also rents out tiny, rustic cabins ($45) and mountain bikes (from $35 per day). Long-time area outfitter **Excursions of Escalante** (☎800-839-7567; www.excursionsofescalante.com; 125 E Main St; full-day from $150; ⏲8am-6pm) leads canyoneering, climbing and photo hikes.

Other decent lodgings in town include **Canyons Bed & Breakfast** (☎435-826-4747, 866-526-9667; www.canyonsbnb.com; 120 E Main St; d incl breakfast $140; ⏲Mar-Oct; ❄📶) with upscale cabin-rooms that surround a shady courtyard, and the **Circle D Motel** (☎435-826-4297; www.escalantecircledmotel.com; 475 W Main St; r $74-99, cottage $125; ❄📶🐾), an older-but-updated budget motel with a friendly proprietor and a full-service restaurant.

> **ELEVATION MATTERS**
>
> Southern Utah is generally warmer than northern Utah. But before you go making any assumptions about weather, check the elevation of your destination. Places less than an hour apart may have several thousand feet of elevation – and 20°F (10°C) temperature – difference.
>
> - St George (3000ft)
> - Zion National Park – Springdale entrance (3900ft)
> - Cedar Breaks National Monument (10,000ft)
> - Bryce National Park Lodge (8100ft)
> - Moab (4026ft)
> - Salt Lake City (4226ft)
> - Park City (7100ft)

Bryce Canyon National Park

The Grand Staircase, a series of uplifted rock layers that climb in clearly defined 'steps' north from the Grand Canyon, culminates in the Pink Cliffs formation at this deservedly popular **national park** (☎435-834-5322; www.nps.gov/brca; Hwy 63; 7-day pass per vehicle $25; ⏲24hr; visitor center 8am-8pm May-Sep, to 4:30pm Oct-Apr). Not actually a 'canyon', but an amphitheater eroded from the cliffs, it's filled with wondrous sorbet-colored pinnacles and points, steeples and spires, and totem-pole-shaped 'hoodoos'. The park is 50 miles southwest of Escalante; from Hwy 12, turn south on Hwy 63.

Rim Road Scenic Drive (8000ft) travels 18 miles, roughly following the canyon rim past the visitor center, the lodge, incredible overlooks (don't miss **Inspiration Point**) and trailheads, ending at **Rainbow Point** (9115ft). From early May through early October, a free shuttle bus runs (8am until at least 5:30pm) from a staging area just north of the park to as far south as **Bryce Amphitheater**.

The park has two camping areas, both of which accept some reservations through the park website. Sunset Campground is bit more wooded, but is not open year-round. Coin-op laundry and showers are available at the general store near North Campground. During summer, remaining first-come sites fill before noon.

The 1920s **Bryce Canyon Lodge** (☎435-834-8700, 877-386-4383; www.brycecanyonforever.com; Hwy 63, Bryce Canyon National Park; r & cabins $208-256; ⊙Apr-Oct; @☎) exudes rustic mountain charm. Rooms are in modern hotel-style units, with up-to-date furnishings, and thin-walled duplex cabins with gas fireplaces and front porches. No TVs. The lodge **restaurant** (☎435-834-8700; breakfasts $6-12, lunch & dinner mains $18-40; ⊙7-10am, 11:30am-3pm & 5:30-10pm Apr-Oct) is excellent, if expensive.

Just north of the park boundaries, **Ruby's Inn** (☎866-866-6616, 435-834-5341; www.rubysinn.com; 1000 S Hwy 63; r $135-180; ❄@☎≋) is a resort complex with multiple motel lodging options, plus a campground. You can also dine at several restaurants, admire Western art, wash laundry, shop for groceries, fill up with gas, and take a helicopter ride.

Eleven miles east on Hwy 12, the small town of **Tropic** (www.brycecanyoncountry.com) has additional food and lodging.

Kanab

At the southern edge of Grand Staircase-Escalante National Monument, vast expanses of rugged desert surround remote Kanab (population 4468). Western filmmakers made dozens of movies here from the 1920s to the 1970s, and the town still has an Old West feel.

John Wayne and Gregory Peck are among Hollywood notables who slumbered at the somewhat dated **Parry Lodge** (☎888-289-1722, 435-644-2601; www.parrylodge.com; 89 E Center St; r $109-139; ❄☎≋🐾).

SCENIC DRIVE: HIGHWAY 12

Arguably Utah's most diverse and stunning route, **Highway 12 Scenic Byway** (www.scenicbyway12.com) winds through rugged canyonland on a 124-mile journey northeast of Bryce Canyon to near Capitol Reef. The section between Escalante and Torrey traverses a moonscape of sculpted slickrock, crosses narrow ridgebacks and climbs over the 11,000ft Boulder Mountain.

The renovated **Canyons Lodge** (☎435-644-3069, 800-644-5094; www.canyonslodge.com; 236 N 300 West; r incl breakfast $89-179; ❄@☎≋🐾) 🍃 motel has an art-house Western feel; rooms feature original artwork. Stay there, then eat downtown at **Rocking V Cafe** (www.rockingvcafe.com; 97 W Center St; lunch $8-18, dinner $15-34; ⊙11:30am-10pm; 🌿), where fresh ingredients star in dishes such as buffalo tenderloin and curried quinoa.

The **Kanab GSENM Visitor Center** (☎435-644-1300; www.ut.blm.gov/monument; 745 E Hwy 89; ⊙8am-4:30pm) provides monument information; **Kane County Office of Tourism** (☎435-644-5033, 800-733-5263; www.visitsouthernutah.com; 78 S 100 East; ⊙8:30am-6pm Mon-Fri, to 4pm Sat) focuses on town and movie sites.

Zion National Park

Get ready for an overdose of awesome. **Zion National Park** (www.nps.gov/zion; Hwy 9; 7-day pass per vehicle $25; ⊙24hr; visitor center Jun-Aug 8am-7:30pm, closes earlier Sep-May) abounds in amazing experiences: gazing up at the red-and-white cliffs of Zion Canyon, soaring high over the Virgin River; peering beyond Angels Landing after a 1400ft ascent; or hiking downriver through the notorious Narrows. But it also holds more delicate beauties: weeping rocks, tiny grottoes, hanging gardens and meadows of mesa-top wildflowers. Lush vegetation and low elevation give the magnificent rock formations a far lusher feel than the barren parks in the east.

Most visitors enter the park along Zion Canyon floor; even the most challenging hikes become congested May through September (shuttle required). If you've time for only one activity, the 6-mile **Scenic Drive**, which pierces the heart of Zion Canyon, is the one. From April through October, you have to take a free shuttle from the visitor center, but you can hop off and on at any of the scenic stops and trailheads along the way.

Of the easy-to-moderate trails, the paved, mile-long **Riverside Walk** at the end of the road is a good place to start. The **Angels Landing Trail** is a much more strenuous, 5.4-mile vertigo-inducer (1400ft elevation gain, with sheer drop-offs), but the canyon views are phenomenal. Allow four hours round-trip.

The most famous backcountry route is the unforgettable **Narrows**, a 16-mile journey into skinny canyons along the Virgin

River's north fork (June through October). Plan on getting wet: at least 50% of the 12-hour hike is in the river. Split the hike into two days, reserving an overnight camping spot in advance, or finish it in time to catch the last park shuttle. A trailhead shuttle is necessary for this one-way trip.

Heading eastwards, Hwy 9 climbs out of Zion Canyon in a series of six tight switchbacks to reach the 1.1-mile Zion-Mt Carmel Tunnel, a 1920s engineering marvel. It then leads quickly into dramatically different terrain – a landscape of etched multicolor slickrock, culminating at the mountainous **Checkerboard Mesa**.

Reserve far ahead and request a riverside site in the canyon's cottonwood-shaded **Watchman Campground** (reservations 877-444-6777; www.recreation.gov; Hwy 9; tent sites $20, RV sites with hookups $30; year-round;). Adjacent **South Campground** (435-772-3256; Hwy 9; tent & RV sites $20; year-round;) is first-come, first-served only.

Smack in the middle of the scenic drive, rustic **Zion Lodge** (888-297-2757, 435-772-7700; www.zionlodge.com; Zion Canyon Scenic Dr; cabin/r/ste $204/210/270;) has 81 well-appointed motel rooms and 40 cabins with gas fireplaces. All have wooden porches with stellar red-rock cliff views, but no TVs. The lodge's full-service dining room, **Red Rock Grill** (435-772-7760; Zion Canyon Scenic Dr, Zion Lodge; breakfast & sandwiches $5.85-14.75, dinner $15.75-29.50; 6:30-10am, 11:30am-2:30pm & 5-9pm Mar-Oct, hours vary Nov-Feb), has similarly amazing views. Just outside the park, the town of Springdale offers many more services.

Note that you must pay the park-entrance fee to drive on public Hwy 9 through the park, even if you are just passing through.

Springdale

Positioned at the main, south entrance to Zion National Park, Springdale is a perfect little park town. Stunning red cliffs form the backdrop to eclectic cafes, restaurants are big on organic ingredients, and artist galleries are interspersed with indie motels and B&Bs.

In addition to hiking trails in the national park, you can take outfitter-led climbing, canyoneering, mountain biking and 4WD trips (from $140 per person, per half-day) on adjacent BLM lands. **Zion Adventure Company** (435-772-1001; www.zionadventures.com; 36 Lion Blvd; canyoneering day from $177; 8am-8pm Mar-Oct, 9am-noon & 4-7pm Nov-Feb) offer excellent excursions, Narrows outfitting, hiker/biker shuttles and river tubing.

The updated rooms at **Canyon Ranch Motel** (435-772-3357, 866-946-6276; www.canyonranchmotel.com; 668 Zion Park Blvd; r $109-169;) ring a shady lawn with picnic tables and swings, while five flower-filled acres spill down to the Virgin River bank at **Cliffrose Lodge** (435-772-3234, 800-243-8824; www.cliffroselodge.com; 281 Zion Park Blvd; r $200-219, ste from $269;).

Zion Canyon B&B (435-772-9466; www.zioncanyonbandb.com; 101 Kokopelli Circle; r incl breakfast $115-190;) is the most traditional local B&B, serving a full, sit-down repast. The owners' creative collections of art and artifacts enliven the 1930s bungalow that is **Under the Eaves Inn** (435-772-3457; www.undertheeaves.com; 980 Zion Park Blvd; r incl breakfast $95-185;); the morning meal is a gift certificate to a local restaurant.

For a coffee and *trés bonnes* crepes – both sweet and savory – make **MeMe's Cafe** (www.memescafezion.com; 975 Zion Park Blvd; breakfast & lunch $8-13, dinner $11-17; 7am-9pm) your first stop of the day. It also serves paninis and waffles, and in season has live music and barbecues on the patio. In the evening, the Mexican-tiled patio with twinkly lights at **Oscar's Cafe** (www.cafeoscars.com; 948 Zion Park Blvd; mains $12-18, breakfast $6-12; 8am-9pm) and the rustic **Bit & Spur Restaurant & Saloon** (www.bitandspur.com; 1212 Zion Park Blvd; mains $13-28; 5-11pm daily Mar-Oct, 5-10pm Thu-Sat Nov-Feb;) are local-favored places to hang out, eat and drink.

St George

Nicknamed 'Utah's Dixie' for its warm weather and southern location, St George (population 76,917) is popular with retirees. This spacious, ever-growing Mormon town, with an eye-catching temple and pioneer buildings, is a potential stop between Las Vegas (120 miles) and Salt Lake City (304 miles) – or en route to Zion National Park. The 15,000-sq-ft collection of in-situ dino tracks and exhibits at **Dinosaur Discovery Site** (www.dinosite.org; 2180 E Riverside Dr; adult/child under 12yr $6/3; 10am-6pm Mon-Sat, 11am-5pm Sun, shorter hours Oct-Feb) are worth a detour.

Nearly every chain motel is represented somewhere in St George, at cheaper rates than you'll find 40 miles (one hour) east in Springdale. **Best Western Coral Hills** (435-673-4844, 800-542-7733; www.coralhills.com;

125 E St George Blvd; r incl breakfast from $130; ❄@📶🏊) is walking distance from downtown restaurants and historic buildings. Two lovely, late-1800 houses contain **Seven Wives Inn** (☎435-628-3737, 800-600-3737; www.sevenwivesinn.com; 217 N 100 West; r incl breakfast $99-199; ❄@📶🏊), a B&B with a small, central swimming pool.

The **Utah Welcome Center** (☎435-673-4542; http://travel.utah.gov; 1835 S Convention Center Dr, Dixie Convention Center; ⏰8:30am-5:30pm), off I-15, addresses statewide queries.

NEW MEXICO

They call this the 'Land Of Enchantment' for a reason. Maybe it's the drama of sunlight and shadow playing out across juniper-speckled hills; or the Hispanic mountain villages of horse pastures and adobe homes; or the centuries-old towns like soulful Santa Fe and arty Taos on the northern plateaus, overlooked by the magnificent Sangre de Cristos; or the volcanoes, canyons and vast desert plains spread beneath an even vaster sky. The beauty casts a powerful spell. Mud-brick churches filled with sacred art; ancient Indian pueblos; rippling dunes of sheer white sand; real-life cowboys and legendary Wild West characters such as Billy the Kid and Geronimo; chile-smothered enchiladas – all add to the pervasive sense of otherness that often makes New Mexico feel like a foreign country.

Perhaps the state's all-but-indescribable charm is best expressed in the iconic paintings of Georgia O'Keeffe. The artist herself exclaimed, on her very first visit: 'Well! Well! Well!...This is wonderful! No one told me it was like this.'

But seriously, how could they?

History

People have roamed this land for at least 12,000 years. By the time Francisco Vasquez de Coronado got here in the 16th century, Pueblo Indians were the dominant presence. After Santa Fe was established as the Spanish colonial capital, around 1610, Hispanic farmers settled across northern New Mexico, and Catholic missionaries set about converting the Puebloans. Following the Pueblo Revolt of 1680, Native Americans occupied Santa Fe until 1692, when Don Diego de Vargas recaptured the city.

New Mexico became a US Territory in 1850. Native American wars, settlement by cowboys and miners, and trade along the Santa Fe Trail further transformed the region, and the arrival of the railroad in the 1870s prompted an economic boom.

Painters and writers set up art colonies in Santa Fe and Taos in the early 20th century, while a top-secret scientific community developed the atomic bomb in Los Alamos in 1943. Some say aliens crashed outside of Roswell four years later. Maybe that's why New Mexico is now a pioneer in space tourism and commercial space flights.

ℹ Information

For information on the New Mexico stretch of Route 66, visit www.rt66nm.org.

New Mexico State Parks Division (☎888-667-2757; www.emnrd.state.nm.us/SPD) Info on state parks, with a link to camping reservations.

Public Lands Information Center (☎877-851-8946; www.publiclands.org) Camping and recreation information.

Albuquerque

This bustling desert crossroads has an understated charm, one based more on its locals than on any urban sparkle. In New Mexico's largest city, just west of the Sandia mountains where the east–west Route 66 bridges the north–south Rio Grande, folks are more than happy to share history, highlights and must-try restaurants.

Centuries-old adobes pepper the lively Old Town area, and the shops, restaurants and bars in the hip Nob Hill zone are all within easy walking distance. Good hiking trails abound just outside of town, through evergreen forests or among panels of ancient petroglyphs, while modern museums explore space and nuclear energy. There's a vibrant mix of university students, Native Americans, Hispanics, and gays and lesbians. Flyers for square dances and yoga classes are distributed with equal enthusiasm, while ranch hands and real-estate brokers chow down beside each other at hole-in-the-wall taquerias and retro cafes.

Albuquerque's major boundaries are Paseo del Norte Dr to the north, Central Ave to the south, Rio Grande Blvd to the west and Tramway Blvd to the east. Central Ave, aka old Route 66, is the main artery, passing through Old Town, Downtown, the university and Nob

Hill. The city is divided into four quadrants (NW, NE, SW and SE), with the intersection of Central Ave and the railroad tracks just east of Downtown as the central point.

Sights

Old Town

From its foundation in 1706 until the arrival of the railroad in 1880, the plaza, centering on the diminutive 1793 **San Felipe de Neri Church** (www.sanfelipedeneri.org; Old Town Plaza; 7am-5:30pm daily, museum 9:30am-5pm Mon-Sat), was the hub of Albuquerque. Today Old Town is the city's most popular tourist area.

★American International Rattlesnake Museum MUSEUM

(www.rattlesnakes.com; 202 San Felipe St NW; adult/child $5/3; 10am-6pm Mon-Sat, 1-5pm Sun Jun-Aug; 11:30am-5:30pm Mon-Fri, 10am-6pm Sat, 1-5pm Sun, Sep-May) Anyone charmed by snakes and all things slithery will find this museum fascinating; for ophidiaphobes, it's a complete nightmare, filled with the world's largest collection of different rattlesnake species. You'll also find snake-themed beer bottles and postmarks from every town named 'Rattlesnake' in the US.

Albuquerque Museum of Art & History MUSEUM

(505-242-4600; www.cabq.gov/museum; 2000 Mountain Rd NW; adult/child $4/1; 9am-5pm Tue-Sun, Old Town walking tours 11am Tue-Sun, Mar–mid-Dec) With revamped history galleries exploring the city's past from Spanish days onward, and a permanent art collection that extends to outsider and vernacular work as well as 20th-century masterpieces from the Taos School, this showpiece museum should not be missed. There's free admission on the first Wednesday of the month and on Sunday until 1pm, and free guided walking tours of Old Town.

Around Town

The University of New Mexico (UNM) area has loads of good restaurants, casual bars, offbeat shops and hip college hangouts. The main drag is Central Ave between University and Carlisle Blvds. Just east is trendy Nob Hill, a pedestrian-friendly neighborhood lined with indie coffee shops, stylish boutiques and patio-wrapped restaurants.

NEW MEXICO FACTS

Nickname Land of Enchantment

Population 2.1 million

Area 121,599 sq miles

Capital city Santa Fe (population 69,00)

Other cities Albuquerque (population 550,000), Las Cruces (population 94,000)

Sales tax 5% to 9%

Birthplace of John Denver (1943–97), Smokey Bear (1950–76)

Home of International UFO Museum & Research Center (Roswell), Julia Roberts

Politics A 'purple' state, with a more liberal north and conservative south

Famous for Ancient pueblos, the first atomic bomb (1945), where Bugs Bunny should have turned left

State question 'Red or green?' (chili sauce, that is)

Highest/Lowest points Wheeler Peak (13,161ft) / Red Bluff Reservoir (2842ft)

Driving distances Albuquerque to Santa Fe 50 miles, Santa Fe to Taos 71 miles

★Indian Pueblo Cultural Center MUSEUM

(IPCC; 505-843-7270; www.indianpueblo.org; 2401 12th St NW; adult/child $6/3; 9am-5pm) Collectively run by New Mexico's 19 Pueblos, this cultural center makes an essential stop-off during even the shortest Albuquerque visit. The museum downstairs holds fascinating displays on the Pueblos' collective history and individual artistic traditions, while the galleries above offer changing temporary exhibitions. They're arrayed in a crescent around a plaza that's regularly used for dances and crafts demonstrations, and as well as the recommended **Pueblo Harvest Cafe** (505-724-3510; www.indianpueblo.org; 2401 12th St NW; lunch $9-11, dinner $9-28; 8am-8:30pm Mon-Sat, 8am-4pm Sun;) there's also a large gift shop and retail gallery.

National Museum of Nuclear Science & History MUSEUM

(505-245-2137; www.nuclearmuseum.org; 601 Eubank Blvd SE; adult/child & senior $8/7; 9am-5pm;) Located at the edge of the massive

Kirtland Air Force Base in Albuquerque's southeast corner, and surrounded by an outdoor Heritage Park holding discarded missiles and fighter planes, this lively museum explores the history of nuclear energy in war and peace, from the Manhattan Project and the Cold War up to today. Retired military personnel serve as docents.

Petroglyph National Monument ARCHAEOLOGICAL SITE
(☎505-899-0205; www.nps.gov/petr; 6001 Unser Blvd NW; ⊙visitor center 8am-5pm) The lava field preserved in this large desert park, west of the Rio Grande, is adorned with more than 20,000 ancient petroglyphs. Take exit 154 off I-40 to reach the visitor center, 5.5 miles northwest of Old Town, and choose a hiking trail. Boca Negra Canyon is the busiest; Rinconada Canyon – the longest at 2.2 miles round-trip – offers the most solitude; and Piedras Marcadas holds 300 petroglyphs. Smash-and-grab thefts have been reported, so don't leave valuables in your vehicle.

Sandia Peak Tramway CABLE CAR
(☎505-856-7325; www.sandiapeak.com; 30 Tramway Rd NE; parking $1, adult/youth 13-20/child $20/17/12; ⊙9am-9pm Jun-Aug, 9am-8pm Wed-Mon Sep-May, from 5pm Tue) The world's longest aerial tram climbs 2.7 miles from the desert floor in the northeast corner of the city to the summit of 10,378ft Sandia Crest. The views are spectacular at any time, though sunsets are particularly brilliant. The complex at the top holds gift shops and restaurants, while hiking trails lead off through the woods, and there's also a small ski area.

Activities

The omnipresent Sandia Mountains and the less-crowded Manzano Mountains offer outdoor activities, including hiking, skiing (downhill and cross-country), mountain biking, rock climbing and camping.

Elena Gallegos Open Space HIKING
(www.cabq.gov; Simms Park Rd; weekday/weekend parking $1/2; ⊙7am- 9pm Apr–Oct, closes 7pm Nov-Mar) Sandia Crest is Albuquerque's outdoor playground, popular for skiing and hiking. As well as several picnic areas, this foothills park holds trailheads for hiking, running and mountain biking; some routes are wheelchair accessible. Come early, before the sun gets too hot, or late, to enjoy the panoramic views at sunset, as the city lights start to twinkle below. Time evening walks carefully, though; darkness falls quickly and howling coyotes ring the park. They won't bother you, but it can be unnerving.

Tours

Story of New Mexico Program TOUR
(☎505-277-0077; www.dcereg.com) The UNM Department of Continuing Education offers excellent lectures on all things New Mexico, as well as tours to Santa Fe, Taos and sites throughout the state, including visits to Pueblo feast days and trips to the otherwise inaccessible Lawrence Ranch, home to the ashes of novelist DH Lawrence. Advance registration is required.

Festivals & Events

Gathering of Nations Powwow CULTURAL
(www.gatheringofnations.com; ⊙Apr) Dance competitions, displays of Native American arts and crafts, and the 'Miss Indian World' contest. Held in late April.

International Balloon Fiesta BALLOON
(www.balloonfiesta.com; ⊙early Oct) The largest balloon festival in the world. You simply haven't lived until you've seen a three-story-tall Tony the Tiger land in your hotel courtyard, and that's exactly the sort of thing that

ALBUQUERQUE FOR CHILDREN

¡Explora! (www.explora.us; 1701 Mountain Rd NW; adult/child $8/4; ⊙10am-6pm Mon-Sat, noon-6pm Sun;) This gung-ho place will captivate kiddies for hours. From the lofty high-wire bike to the mind-boggling Light, Shadow, Color area, there's a hands-on exhibit for every type of child (don't miss the elevator).

New Mexico Museum of Natural History & Science (www.nmnaturalhistory.org; 1801 Mountain Rd NW; adult/child $7/4; ⊙9am-5pm;) Across the street, this huge, dinosaur-crazy museum is crammed with ferocious ancient beasts, from the T Rex in the main atrium onwards. The emphasis throughout is on New Mexico, with dramatic displays on the state's geological origins and details of the impact of climate change – and did you know this is where Microsoft first started out?

happens during the festival, which features mass dawn take-offs on each of its nine days, overlapping the first and second weekends in October.

Sleeping

Route 66 Hostel HOSTEL $
(☎505-247-1813; www.rt66hostel.com; 1012 Central Ave SW; dm $20, r from $25; P@?) This pastel-lemon hostel, in a former residence a few blocks west of Downtown, holds male and female dorms plus simple private rooms, some of which share bathrooms. The beds are aging, but there's a welcoming atmosphere, with common facilities including a library and a kitchen offering free self-serve breakfasts. Voluntary chores; no check-ins between 1:30pm and 4:30pm.

Econo Lodge Old Town MOTEL $
(☎505-243-8475; www.econolodge.com; 2321 Central Ave NW; r incl breakfast $69; P❄@?≋) Just five minutes' walk west of the plaza, this bright, clean motel makes a great deal for anyone planning to explore the Old Town or the BioPark, with spacious and well-equipped modern rooms, an indoor pool and free hot breakfasts.

★ **Andaluz** BOUTIQUE HOTEL $$
(☎505-242-9090; www.hotelandaluz.com; 125 2nd St NW; r $112-279; P❄@?) Albuquerque's finest historic hotel, built in the heart of Downtown in 1939, has been comprehensively modernized while retaining period details like its stunning central atrium, where cozy arched nooks hold tables and couches. Rooms feature hypoallergenic bedding and carpets, the **Más Tapas Y Vino** (☎505-923-9080; www.hotelandaluz.com; 125 2nd St NW; ⏲7am-2pm & 5-9:30pm) restaurant is excellent, and there's a rooftop bar. Reserve 30 days in advance for the best rates.

Böttger Mansion B&B $$
(☎505-243-3639; www.bottger.com; 110 San Felipe St NW; r incl breakfast $104-179; P❄@?🐾) The friendly proprietor gives this well-appointed B&B, built in 1912 and one minute's walk from the plaza, an edge over tough competition. Three of its seven themed, antique-furnished rooms have pressed-tin ceilings, one has a Jacuzzi tub, and sumptuous breakfasts are served in a honeysuckle-lined courtyard loved by bird-watchers. Past guests include Elvis, Janis Joplin and Machine Gun Kelly.

★ **Los Poblanos** B&B $$$
(☎505-344-9297; www.lospoblanos.com; 4803 Rio Grande Blvd NW; r $180-330; P❄@?) This amazing 20-room B&B, on a 1930s rural ranch that's a National Historic Place, is five minutes' drive north of Old Town. Close to the Rio Grande, it's set amid 25 acres of gardens, lavender fields (blooming mid-June through July) and an organic farm. The gorgeous rooms feature kiva fireplaces, while produce from the farm is served for breakfast.

Eating

★ **Frontier** NEW MEXICAN $
(☎505-266-0550; www.frontierrestaurant.com; 2400 Central Ave SE; mains $3-12; ⏲5am-1am; ✎👪) Get in line for enormous cinnamon rolls (made with something approaching a stick of butter each) and some of the best huevos rancheros in town. The food, people-watching and Western art are all outstanding.

★ **Golden Crown Panaderia** BAKERY $
(☎505-243-2424; www.goldencrown.biz; 1103 Mountain Rd NW; mains $7-20; ⏲7am-8pm Tue-Sat, 10am-8pm Sun) Who doesn't love a friendly neighborhood cafe/bakery? Especially one in a cozy old adobe, with gracious staff, oven-fresh bread and pizza, fruity empanadas, smooth espresso coffees and free cookies all round? Call ahead to reserve a loaf of quick-selling green chili bread – then eat it hot, out on the patio.

Annapurna's World Vegetarian Cafe INDIAN $
(☎505-262-2424; www.chaishoppe.com; 2201 Silver Ave SE; mains $7-11; ⏲7am-9pm Mon-Fri, 8am-9pm Sat, 10am-8pm Sun) This awesome vegetarian and vegan cafe, one block south of Route 66 and part of a small local chain, serves fresh, tasty Indian specialties, including delicately spiced Ayurvedic delights that even carnivores love. Dishes are complemented by authentic chai.

Flying Star Cafe AMERICAN $$
(☎505-255-6633; www.flyingstarcafe.com; 3416 Central Ave SE; mains $8-13; ⏲6am-11pm, to midnight Fri & Sat; ?✎👪) For visitors, the Nob Hill location of this deservedly popular local chain is the most convenient of outlets throughout Albuquerque and beyond. Locals flock here from early morning onwards, to enjoy an extensive breakfast menu and innovative main courses later on, amid creative, colorful decor. The whole experience is enhanced by the

use of organic, free-range and antibiotic-free ingredients.

Artichoke Cafe MODERN AMERICAN $$$
(☎505-243-0200; www.artichokecafe.com; 424 Central Ave SE; lunch mains $10-16, dinner mains $19-39; ⏰11am-2:30pm & 5-9pm Mon-Fri, 5-10pm Sat) Elegant and unpretentious, this popular bistro prepares creative gourmet cuisine with panache and is always high on foodies' lists of Albuquerque's best. It's on the eastern edge of Downtown, between the bus station and I-40.

Drinking & Entertainment

Popejoy Hall (www.popejoypresents.com; Central Ave, at Cornell St SE) and the historic **KiMo Theatre** (☎505-768-3544; www.cabq.gov/kimo; 423 Central Ave NW) are the primary venues for big-name national acts, local opera, symphony and theater. To find out what's happening in town, pick up the free weekly *Alibi* (www.alibi.com). Most of Albuquerque's trendy cafes and bars are found in the Nob Hill/UNM Districts.

Satellite Coffee CAFE
(www.satellitecoffee.com; 2300 Central Ave SE; ⏰6am-11pm Mon-Fri, from 7am Sat & Sun; 📶) Albuquerque's answer to Starbucks lies in these hip coffee shops – look for the other eight locations around town – luring lots of laptop-toting regulars. Set up and still owned by the same brilliant folks responsible for the Flying Star chain.

Anodyne BAR
(☎505-244-1820; www.theanodyne.com; 409 Central Ave NW; ⏰4pm-1:30am Mon-Sat, 7-11:30pm Sun) An excellent spot for a game of pool, Anodyne is a huge space with book-lined walls, wood ceilings, plenty of overstuffed chairs, more than 100 bottled beers and great people-watching on Central Ave.

Launch Pad LIVE MUSIC
(☎505-764-8887; www.launchpadrocks.com; 618 Central Ave SW) This retro-modern place is the hottest stage for local live music.

Shopping

For eclectic gifts, head to Nob Hill, east of the university, and take a stroll past the inviting boutiques and specialty stores.

Palms Trading Post ARTS & CRAFTS
(www.palmstrading.com; 1504 Lomas Blvd NW; ⏰9am-5:30pm Mon-Fri, 10am-5:30pm Sat) Large gallery where knowledgeable salespeople sell Native American pottery, jewelery, rugs and crafts.

Silver Sun JEWELRY
(☎505-246-9692; www.silversunalbuquerque.com; 116 San Felipe St NW; ⏰9am-4pm) A reputable Old Town store specializing in natural American turquoise, as stones as well as finished jewelry.

Mariposa Gallery ARTS & CRAFTS
(☎505-268-6828; www.mariposa-gallery.com; 3500 Central Ave SE) Beautiful and funky arts, crafts and jewelry, mostly by regional artists.

Information

EMERGENCY & MEDICAL SERVICES

Police (☎505-242-2677; 400 Roma Ave NW)

Presbyterian Hospital (☎505-841-1234; www.phs.org; 1100 Central Ave SE; ⏰24hr emergency)

UNM Hospital (☎505-272-2411; 2211 Lomas Blvd NE; ⏰24hr emergency) Head here if you don't have insurance.

POST

Post Office (201 5th St SW; ⏰9am-4:30pm Mon-Fri)

TOURIST INFORMATION

Old Town Information Center (☎505-243-3215; www.itsatrip.org; 303 Romero Ave NW; ⏰10am-5pm Oct-May, to 6pm Jun-Sep)

Albuquerque Convention & Visitors Bureau (☎505-842-9918; www.itsatrip.org; 20 First Plaza NW, cnr 2nd St & Copper Ave; ⏰9am-4pm Mon-Fri) At the corner of 2nd St and Copper Ave.

USEFUL WEBSITE

City of Albuquerque (www.cabq.gov) Public transportation, area attractions and more.

Getting There & Around

AIR

Albuquerque International Sunport (ABQ; ☎505-244-7700; www.cabq.gov/airport; 📶) is New Mexico's main airport and most major US airlines fly here. Cabs to Downtown cost $20 to $25; try **Albuquerque Cab** (☎505-883-4888; www.albuquerquecab.com).

BUS

The **Alvarado Transportation Center** (100 1st St SW, cnr Central Ave) houses **ABQ RIDE** (☎505-243-7433; www.cabq.gov/transit; 100 1st St SW; adult/child $1/0.35; day pass $2), the public bus system. It covers most of Albuquerque from Monday to Friday and hits the major tourist spots daily. Most lines run until 6pm. ABQ

RIDE Route 50 connects the airport with downtown (last bus at 8pm Monday to Friday; limited service Saturday). Route 36 stops near Old Town and the Indian Pueblo Cultural Center.

Greyhound (800-231-2222, 505-243-4435; www.greyhound.com; 320 1st St SW) serves destinations throughout New Mexico. **Sandia Shuttle** (888-775-5696; www.sandiashuttle.com; 1-way/round-trip $28/48; 8:45am-11:45pm) runs daily shuttles from the airport to many Santa Fe hotels, while **Twin Hearts Express** (575-751-1201; www.twinheartsexpresstransportation.com) runs a shuttle service from the airport to northern New Mexico destinations, including Taos and surrounding communities.

TRAIN

The Southwest Chief stops daily at Albuquerque's **Amtrak station** (800-872-7245, 505-842-9650; www.amtrak.com; 320 1st St SW; 9:45am-5pm), heading east to Chicago (from $140, 26 hours) or west through Flagstaff, AZ ($91, five hours), to Los Angeles, CA (from $100, 16½ hours).

A commuter line, the **New Mexico Rail Runner Express** (www.nmrailrunner.com), shares the station, with eight departures for Santa Fe weekdays plus four on Saturday and three on Sunday (one-way/day pass $9/10, 1½ hours).

Along I-40

Although you can zip between Albuquerque and Flagstaff, AZ, in less than five hours, the national monuments and pueblos along the way are well worth a visit. For a scenic loop, take Hwy 53 southwest from Grants, which leads to all the following sights except Acoma. Hwy 602 brings you north to Gallup.

Acoma Pueblo

The dramatic mesa-top 'Sky City' sits 7000ft above sea level and 367ft above the surrounding plateau. One of the oldest continuously inhabited settlements in North America, this place has been home to pottery-making Pueblo peoples since the 11th century. Guided tours leave from the **visitor center** (800-747-0181; www.acomaskycity.org; adult/child/camera $23/15/13; tours 9:30am-3:30pm Mar-Nov) at the foot of the mesa and take two hours, or one hour just to tour the historic mission. From I-40, take exit 102, which is about 60 miles west of Albuquerque, then drive 12 miles south. Check ahead to make sure it's not closed for ceremonial or other reasons.

El Morro National Monument

The 200ft sandstone outcropping at the **El Morro National Monument** (505-783-4226; www.nps.gov/elmo; 9am-6pm Jun-Aug, to 5pm Sep-May) FREE, also known as 'Inscription Rock,' has been a travelers' oasis for millennia. Thousands of carvings – from petroglyphs in the pueblo at the top (c 1275) to elaborate inscriptions by Spanish conquistadors and Anglo pioneers – offer a unique historical record. It's about 38 miles southwest of Grants via Hwy 53.

Zuni Pueblo

The Zuni are known for their delicately inlaid silverwork, which is sold in stores lining Hwy 53. Check in at the **visitor center** (505-782-7238; www.zunitourism.com; 1239 Hwy 53; tours $10; 8:30am-5:30pm Mon-Fri, 10:30am-

SCENIC DRIVES: NEW MEXICO'S BEST

Billy the Kid National Scenic Byway (www.billybyway.com) This mountain-and-valley loop in southeastern New Mexico swoops past Billy the Kid's stomping grounds, Smokey Bear's gravesite and the orchard-lined Hondo Valley. From Roswell, take Hwy 380 west.

High Road to Taos The back road between Santa Fe and Taos passes through sculpted sandstone desert, fresh pine forests and rural villages with historic adobe churches and horse-filled pastures. The 13,000ft Truchas Peaks soar above. From Santa Fe, take Hwy 84/285 to Hwy 513 then follow the signs.

NM Highway 96 From Abiquiu to Cuba, this little road wends through the heart of Georgia O'Keeffe country, beneath the distinctive profile of Cerro Pedernal, then passing Martian-red buttes and sandstone cliffs striped purple, yellow and ivory.

NM Highway 52 Head west from Truth or Consequences into the dramatic foothills of the Black Range, through the old mining towns of Winston and Chloride. Continue north, passing the Monticello Box – where Geronimo finally surrendered – and emerging onto the sweeping Plains of San Augustin before reaching the bizarre Very Large Array.

4pm Sat, noon-4pm Sun) for information, photo permits and tours of the pueblo, which lead you among stone houses and beehive-shaped adobe ovens to the massive **Our Lady of Guadalupe Mission**, featuring impressive kachina murals. The **Ashiwi Awan Museum & Heritage Center** (505-782-4403; www.ashiwi-museum.org; Ojo Caliente Rd; admission by donation; 9am-5pm Mon-Fri) displays early photos and other tribal artifacts.

The friendly, eight-room **Inn at Halona** (505-782-4547; www.halona.com; 23b Pia Mesa Rd; r from $75; P), decorated with local Zuni arts and crafts, is the only place to stay on the pueblo. Its breakfasts rank with the best in the state.

Gallup

Not just a classic Route 66 town, Gallup also serves as the Navajo and Zuni peoples' major trading center, making it a great place to buy top-quality Native American art and crafts at fair prices. The historic district is filled with trading posts, pawnshops, jewelry stores and crafts galleries.

The town's lodging jewel is **El Rancho** (505-863-9311; www.elranchohotel.com; 1000 E Hwy 66; r from $102; P). It features a superb Southwestern lobby, a restaurant, a bar and an eclectic selection of simple rooms, in which many of Hollywood's greatest actors once slept. Chain hotels line Route 66, west of the town center.

Santa Fe

Welcome to 'the city different,' a place that makes its own rules without ever forgetting its long and storied past. Walking around the busy Plaza that remains its core, or through its historic neighborhoods, there's no denying that Santa Fe has a timeless, earthy soul. Founded around 1610, this is the second-oldest city and the oldest state capital in the US, its seductive original adobe buildings now standing alongside modern counterparts built in the same style. And yet Santa Fe is also synonymous with contemporary chic, thanks to its thriving art market, gourmet restaurants, great museums, upscale spas and world-class opera.

Santa Fe is also the nation's highest state capital, set over 7000ft above sea level at the foot of the glowing Sangre de Cristo range. A fantastic base for hiking, mountain biking, backpacking and skiing, it's home to a mind-boggling array of characters, taking in artists, New Agers, long-established Hispanic families and recent Mexican immigrants, and more than a few big Hollywood names.

Cerrillos Rd (I-25 exit 278), a 6-mile strip of hotels and fast-food restaurants, enters town from the south; Paseo de Peralta circles the center; and to the west St Francis Dr (I-25 exit 282) turns into Hwy 285 and heads north toward Los Alamos and Taos.

Sights

★Georgia O'Keeffe Museum MUSEUM

(505-946-1000; www.okeeffemuseum.org; 217 Johnson St; adult/child $12/free; 10am-5pm, to 7pm Fri) With 10 beautifully lit galleries in a rambling 20th-century adobe, this museum boasts the world's largest collection of O'Keeffe's work. She's best known for her luminous New Mexican landscapes, but the changing exhibitions here range through her entire career, focusing for example on her years in New York. Major museums worldwide own her most famous canvases, so you may not see familiar paintings, but you're sure to be bowled over by the thick brushwork and transcendent colors on show.

Canyon Road GALLERY

(www.canyonroadarts.com) The epicenter of the city's upscale art scene. More than 100 galleries, studios, shops and restaurants line the narrow historic road. Look for Santa Fe School masterpieces, rare Native American antiquities and wild contemporary work. The area positively buzzes with activity during the early-evening art openings on Fridays, and especially on Christmas Eve.

Wheelwright Museum of the American Indian MUSEUM

(505-982-4636; www.wheelwright.org; 704 Camino Lejo; 10am-5pm) FREE Mary Cabot established this museum in 1937 to showcase Navajo ceremonial art, and its major strength continues to be exquisite Navajo textiles, displayed under dim lighting to protect the natural dyes. Recent expansion work has added extra space for contemporary Native American art and historical artifacts. The gift store, known as the Case Trading Post, sells museum-quality rugs, vintage jewelry, kachinas and crafts.

St Francis Cathedral CHURCH

(www.cbsfa.org; 131 Cathedral Pl; 8:30am-4:30pm) Santa Fe's French-born bishop

DON'T MISS

THE MUSEUM OF NEW MEXICO

The Museum of New Mexico administers four excellent museums in Santa Fe. Two are at the Plaza, two are on Museum Hill, 2 miles southwest. A four-day pass gives adults entry to all four for $20; under-16s get in free.

Palace of the Governors (505-476-5100; www.palaceofthegovernors.org; 105 W Palace Ave; adult/child $9/free; 10am-5pm, closed Mon Oct-May) The oldest public building in the US, this low-slung adobe complex started out as home to New Mexico's first Spanish governor in 1610; was occupied by Pueblo Indians following their Revolt in 1680; and after 1846 became the seat of the US Territory's earliest governors. It now holds fascinating displays on Santa Fe's multi-faceted past, and some superb Hispanic religious artworks, while its modern adjunct alongside, the **New Mexico History Museum**, tells the story of the state as a whole.

New Mexico Museum of Art (505-476-5072; www.museumofnewmexico.org; 107 W Palace Ave; adult/child $9/free; 10am-5pm Tue-Sun, tours 1:30pm) Built in 1917, and a prime early example of Santa Fe's Pueblo Revival architecture, the New Mexico Museum of Art has spent a century collecting and displaying works by regional artists. A treasure trove of works by the great names who put New Mexico on the cultural map, from Georgia O'Keeffe to printmaker Gustave Baumann, it's also a lovely building in which to stroll around, with a cool garden courtyard. Constantly changing temporary exhibitions ensure its continuing relevance.

Museum of International Folk Art (505-827-6344; www.internationalfolkart.org; 706 Camino Lejo; adult/child $9/free; 10am-5pm, closed Mon Sep-May) Santa Fe's most unusual and exhilarating museum centers on the world's largest collection of folk art. Its huge main gallery displays whimsical and mind-blowing objects from more than 100 different countries. Tiny human figures go about their business in fully realized village and city scenes, while dolls, masks, toys and garments spill across the walls. Changing exhibitions in other wings explore vernacular art and culture worldwide.

Try to hit the incredible **International Folk Art Market**, held here in mid-July.

Museum of Indian Arts & Culture (www.indianartsandculture.org; 710 Camino Lejo; adult/child $9/free; 10am-5pm, closed Mon Sep-May) This top-quality museum sets out to trace the origins and history of the various Native American peoples of the entire desert Southwest, and explain and illuminate their widely differing cultural traditions. Pueblo, Navajo and Apache interviewees describe the contemporary realities each group now faces, while a truly superb collection of ceramics, modern and ancient, is complemented by stimulating temporary displays.

Jean-Baptiste Lamy – hero of Willa Cather's *Death Comes for the Archbishop* – set about building this cathedral in 1869. Its Romanesque exterior might seem more suited to Europe than the Wild West, but the Hispanic altarpiece inside lends a real New Mexican flavor. A side chapel holds a diminutive Madonna statue that was taken into exile following the Pueblo Revolt, and has been known since the Spaniards' triumphant return in 1692 as *La Conquistadora*.

Loretto Chapel HISTORIC BUILDING
(505-982-0092; www.lorettochapel.com; 207 Old Santa Fe Trail; adult/child $3/2.50; 9am-5pm Mon-Sat, 10:30am-5pm Sun) Built in 1878 for the Sisters of Loretto, this tiny Gothic chapel is famous as the site of St Joseph's Miraculous Staircase, a spiraling and apparently unsupported wooden staircase added by a mysterious young carpenter who vanished without giving the astonished nuns his name. The chapel is no longer consecrated, and can be rented for (nondenominational) weddings.

Activities

The **Pecos Wilderness** and **Santa Fe National Forest**, east of town, have more than 1000 miles of hiking and biking trails, several of which lead to 12,000ft peaks. Contact the Public Lands Information Center for maps and details, and check weather reports for advance warnings of frequent summer storms. **Mellow Velo** (505-995-8356; www.mellowvelo.com; 132 E Marcy St; rentals per day

Santa Fe

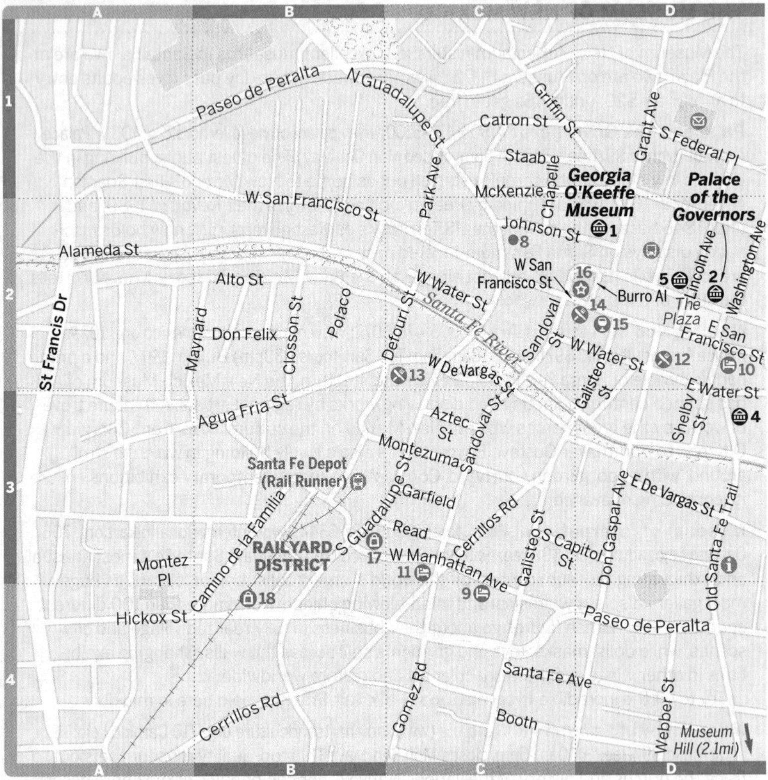

from $35; ⏲10am-6pm Mon-Sat) rents mountain bikes and provides trail information.

Operators including **New Wave Rafting Co** (☎800-984-1444; www.newwaverafting.com) offer white-water rafting adventures through the Rio Grande Gorge (half-day $55), the wild Taos Box (full day $110) and the Rio Chama Wilderness (three days $400).

Dale Ball Trails MOUNTAIN BIKING

(www.santafenm.gov/trails_1) Over 20 miles of paved and unpaved bike and hiking trails, with fabulous desert and mountain views. The challenging **South Dale Ball Trails** start with a super-long, hard and rocky single-track climb, followed by harrowing switchbacks, while the intermediate **Winsor Trail** (No 254) leads through breathtaking scenery in Hyde State Park and Santa Fe National Forest.

Ski Santa Fe SKIING

(☎505-982-4429, snow report 505-983-9155; www.skisantafe.com; lift ticket adult/child $69/49; ⏲9am-4pm late Nov-early Apr) Often overlooked for its more famous cousin outside Taos, the Santa Fe ski area boasts the same fluffy powder (though usually a little less), with a higher base elevation (10,350ft) and higher chairlift service (12,075ft). It caters to families and expert skiers, who fly down powder glade shoots, steep bump runs or long groomers, though the length and quality of the season varies wildly from year to year.

Courses

Santa Fe School of Cooking COOKING

(☎505-983-4511; www.santafeschoolofcooking.com; 125 N Guadalupe St; 2/3hr class $75/98; ⏲9:30am-5pm Mon-Sat, noon-4pm Sun) If your love for New Mexican cuisine knows no bounds, take a lesson at this Southwestern-style cooking school, where the cost includes the meal at the end.

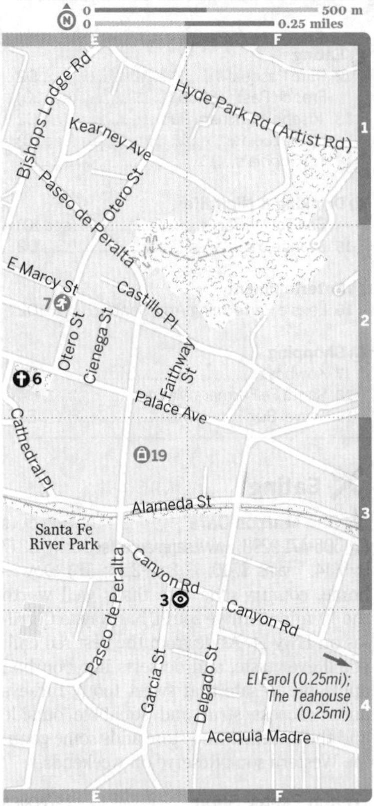

✨ Festivals & Events

★ **Spanish Market**   CULTURAL
(www.spanishcolonial.org; ⊘late Jul) Traditional Spanish Colonial arts, from *retablos* and *bultos* (carved wooden religious statues) to handcrafted furniture and metalwork, make this juried show in late July an artistic extravaganza, second only to Indian Market.

★ **Santa Fe Indian Market**   CULTURAL
(☑505-983-5220; www.swaia.org; ⊘Aug) Over a thousand artists from 100 tribes and Pueblos show work at this world-famous juried show, held the weekend after the third Thursday in August. One hundred thousand visitors converge on the Plaza, at open studios, gallery shows and the Native Cinema Showcase. Come Friday or Saturday to see pieces competing for the top prizes; wait until Sunday before trying to bargain.

★ **Santa Fe Fiesta**   CULTURAL
(☑505-913-1517; www.santafefiesta.org; ⊘early Sep) This two-week celebration of the September 4, 1692, resettlement of Santa Fe after the Pueblo Revolt, from Labor Day through early September, includes concerts, a candlelit procession and the much-loved Pet Parade. Everything kicks off with the bizarrely pagan Friday-night torching of Zozobra – a 50-foot-tall effigy of 'Old Man Gloom' – before a baying mob in Fort Marcy Park.

🛏 Sleeping

Cerrillos Rd is lined with chains and independent motels. There's camping in developed sites in Santa Fe National Forest and Hyde State Park on Hwy 475, the road to the ski basin; for more information, go to the Public Lands Information Center.

★ **Silver Saddle Motel**   MOTEL $
(☑505-471-7663; www.santafesilversaddlemotel.com; 2810 Cerrillos Rd; r from $62; P❋@🐾🖥) This old-fashioned, even kitschy Route 66 motel compound, 3 miles southwest of the Plaza, offers the best budget value in town. Some rooms have pleasant tiled kitchenettes, while all have shady wooden arcades outside and comfortable cowboy-inspired decor inside – get the Kenny Rogers or Wyatt Earp rooms if you can. Rates include continental breakfast.

Rancheros de Santa Fe Campground   CAMPGROUND $
(☑505-466-3482; www.rancheros.com; 736 Old Las Vegas Hwy; tent/RV sites/cabins $25/42/49; ⊘mid-Mar–Oct; 🐾🖥) Eight miles southeast of the Plaza, off I-25 exit 290, Rancheros has shady, spacious sites for tents and RVs, plus simple forest cabins, nice views, a convenience store and free wi-fi. Enjoy hot showers, cheap morning coffee and evening movies.

★ **El Paradero**   B&B $$
(☑505-988-1177; www.elparadero.com; 220 W Manhattan Ave; r from $130; P❋@🖥) Each room in this 200-year-old adobe B&B, south of the river, is unique and loaded with character. Two have their own bathrooms across the hall, the rest are en-suite; our favorites are rooms 6 and 12. The full breakfasts satisfy, and rates also include afternoon tea. A separate casita holds two kitchenette suites that can be combined into one ($350).

Santa Fe

Top Sights

1 Georgia O'Keeffe Museum D2
2 Palace of the Governors D2

Sights

3 Canyon Road E3
4 Loretto Chapel D3
5 New Mexico Museum of Art D2
6 St Francis Cathedral E2

Activities, Courses & Tours

7 Mellow Velo E2
8 Santa Fe School of Cooking C2

Sleeping

9 El Paradero C4
10 La Fonda D2
11 Santa Fe Motel & Inn C3

Eating

12 Cafe Pasqual's D2
French Pastry Shop .... (see 10)
13 Joseph's Culinary Pub C2
La Plazuela .... (see 10)
14 Tia Sophia's D2

Drinking & Nightlife

Bell Tower Bar .... (see 10)
15 Evangelo's D2

Entertainment

16 Lensic Performing Arts Center D2

Shopping

17 Kowboyz B3
18 Santa Fe Farmers Market B4
19 Travel Bug E3

Santa Fe Motel & Inn HOTEL $$
(505-982-1039; www.santafemotel.com; 510 Cerrillos Rd; r from $149, casitas from $169;) Even the motel rooms in this downtown option, close to the Railyard and a real bargain in low season, have the flavor of a Southwestern B&B, with colorful tiles, clay sunbursts and tin mirrors. The courtyard casitas cost a little more and come with kiva fireplaces and little patios. Rates include a full hot breakfast, served outdoors in summer.

El Rey Inn HOTEL $$
(505-982-1931; www.elreyinnsantafe.com; 1862 Cerrillos Rd; r from $105;) This classic courtyard hotel is highly recommended, thanks to its super, Southwestern-themed rooms and suites, scattered through 5 acres of landscaped gardens. Some rooms have kitchenettes, and the sizable outdoor pool has a hot tub alongside.

★ **La Fonda** HISTORIC HOTEL $$$
(800-523-5002; www.lafondasantafe.com; 100 E San Francisco St; r/ste from $219/309;) Long renowned as the 'Inn at the end of the Santa Fe Trail,' Santa Fe's loveliest historic hotel sprawls through an old adobe just off the Plaza. Recently upgraded while retaining its beautiful folk-art windows and murals, it's both classy and cozy, with some wonderful top-floor luxury suites, and superb sunset views from the rooftop Bell Tower Bar.

Eating

★ **San Marcos Cafe** NEW MEXICAN $
(505-471-9298; www.sanmarcosfeed.com; 3877 Hwy 14; mains $7-10; 8am-2pm;) Down-home, country-style cafe that's well worth the 10-minute drive south, halfway to Cerrillos on Hwy 14. Aside from the best red chili you'll ever taste, and desserts like bourbon apple pie to sate that sweet tooth, turkeys and peacocks strut and squabble outside and the attached feed store adds some genuine Western soul. Reserve on weekends.

French Pastry Shop CREPERIE $
(505-983-6697; www.thefrenchpastryshop.com; 100 E San Francisco St; mains $6-10; 6:30am-5pm) Charming cafe serving delicious French bistro food inside La Fonda Hotel, including crepes filled with everything from ham and cheese to strawberries and cream – along with a host of quiches, sandwiches, cappuccinos and, of course, pastries.

Tia Sophia's NEW MEXICAN $
(505-983-9880; 210 W San Francisco St; mains $7-10; 7am-2pm Mon-Sat, 8am-1pm Sun;) Local artists and visiting celebrities outnumber tourists at this long-standing and always-packed Santa Fe favorite. Breakfast is the meal of choice, with fantastic burritos and other Southwestern dishes, but lunch is pretty damn tasty too; try the perfectly prepared *chile rellenos* (stuffed chile peppers), or the rota of daily specials. The shelf of kids' books helps little ones pass the time.

★ Jambo Cafe AFRICAN $$

(☎505-473-1269; www.jambocafe.net; 2010 Cerrillos Rd; mains $9-16; ⊙11am-9pm Mon-Sat) Despite expanding year on year, this African-flavored cafe is hard to spot from the highway; once inside, though, it's a lovely spot, always busy with locals who love its distinctive goat, chicken and lentil curries, veggie sandwiches and roti flatbreads, not to mention the reggae soundtrack.

★ Cafe Pasqual's INTERNATIONAL $$$

(☎505-983-9340; www.pasquals.com; 121 Don Gaspar Ave; breakfast & lunch $9-16, dinner $24-43; ⊙8am-3pm & 5:30-9:30pm Sun-Thu, to 10pm Fri & Sat;) Whatever time you visit this exuberantly colorful, utterly unpretentious place, the food, most of which has a definite south-of-the-border flavor, is worth every penny of the high prices. The breakfast menu is famous for dishes like *huevos motuleños,* made with sautéed bananas, feta cheese and more; later on, the meat and fish mains are superb. Reservations taken for dinner only.

★ Joseph's Culinary Pub MEDITERRANEAN $$$

(☎505-982-1272; www.josephsofsantafe.com; 428 Agua Fria St; ⊙5:30-10pm Sun-Thu, to 11pm Fri & Sat) This romantic old adobe, open for dinner only, is best seen as a fine-dining restaurant rather than a pub. Order from the shorter, cheaper bar menu if you'd rather, but it's worth lingering in the warm-hued dining room to savor rich, modern Mediterranean dishes like crispy duck with French lentils, or rabbit lasagna with mascarpone cheese.

★ La Plazuela NEW MEXICAN $$$

(☎505-982-5511; www.lafondasantafe.com; 100 E San Francisco St, La Fonda de Santa Fe; lunch $11-18, dinner $14-32; ⊙7am-2pm & 5-10pm Mon-Fri, 7am-3pm & 5-10pm Sat & Sun) One of Santa Fe's greatest pleasures is a meal in the Fonda's irresistible see-and-be-seen central atrium, with its excited bustle, colorful decor and high-class New Mexican food, with contemporary dishes sharing menu space with standards like fajitas and tamales.

Drinking & Entertainment

★ The Teahouse CAFE

(☎505-992-0972; www.teahousesantafe.com; 821 Canyon Rd; ⊙9am-9pm;) This spacious, relaxed indoor/outdoor cafe at the eastern end of Canyon Rd makes the perfect break while gallery-hopping. There are 160 teas from all over the world – with scones – plus a full menu (mains $11 to $16) of eggy brunch items, panini and salads.

Evangelo's BAR

(200 W San Francisco St; ⊙noon-1:30am Mon-Sat, to midnight Sun) Everyone is welcome in this casual, rowdy, cash-only joint, owned by the Klonis family since 1971 (ask owner/bartender Nick about his father's unusual fame). Drop in, put on some Patsy Cline and grab a draft beer – it's the perfect escape from Plaza culture. Live Goth and alternative bands perform downstairs in the appropriately named Underground.

Bell Tower Bar BAR

(100 E San Francisco St; ⊙3pm-sunset Mon-Thu, 2pm-sunset Fri-Sun May-Oct, closed Nov-Apr) In summer this bar atop La Fonda hotel is the premier spot to catch one of those patented New Mexican sunsets while sipping a killer margarita. After dark, retire to the hotel's lobby Fiesta Bar for live country or folk music.

★ El Farol DINNER SHOW

(☎505-983-9912; www.elfarolsf.com; 808 Canyon Rd; dinner shows $25; ⊙11am-midnight Mon-Sat, 11am-11pm Sun) Aside from its weekly flamenco dinner shows, this popular restaurant-bar programs live entertainment every night, including regular Latin soul shows.

★ Santa Fe Opera OPERA

(☎505-986-5900; www.santafeopera.org; Hwy 84/285, Tesuque; tickets $32-254; backstage tours adult/child $5/free; ⊙Jun-Aug, backstage tours 9am Mon-Fri Jun-Aug) Many visitors flock to Santa Fe for the opera alone: the theater is a marvel, with 360-degree views of sandstone wilderness crowned with sunsets and moonrises, while at center stage the world's finest talent performs magnificent masterworks. It's still the Wild West, though; you can even wear jeans. Shuttles run to and from Santa Fe and Albuquerque; reserve online.

Lensic Performing Arts Center PERFORMING ARTS

(☎505-988-7050; www.lensic.com; 211 W San Francisco St) A beautifully renovated 1930 movie house, the theater hosts touring productions and classic films as well as seven different performance groups, including the Santa Fe Symphony Orchestra & Chorus.

Shopping

Offering carved howling coyotes, turquoise jewelry and fine art, Santa Fe attracts shoppers of all budgets. Head to the sidewalk outside the Palace of the Governors to buy Indian jewelry direct from the craftspeople who make it.

★ Santa Fe Farmers Market MARKET

(☎505-983-4098; www.santafefarmersmarket.com; Paseo de Peralta & Guadalupe St, Railyard; ⊙8am-1pm Sat, plus Tue May-Nov;) Local produce, much of it heirloom and organic, is on sale at this spacious indoor/outdoor market, alongside homemade goodies, inexpensive food, natural body products, and arts and crafts.

Pueblo of Tesuque Flea Market MARKET

(☎505-670-2599; www.pueblooftesuquefleamarket.com; 15 Flea Market Rd; ⊙8am-4pm Fri-Sun Mar-Dec) Vendors at this outdoor market, beside the Santa Fe Opera 7 miles north of Santa Fe, sell everything from high-quality rugs, turquoise rings and clothing to the best used (read: broken-in) cowboy boots in the state. Nowadays, most booths are like small shops; a few individuals still turn up to sell funky junk.

Kowboyz CLOTHING

(☎505-984-1256; www.kowboyz.com; 345 W Manhattan Ave; ⊙10am-5:30pm) Secondhand shop selling everything you need to cowboy up. Shirts are a great deal at $12 each; the amazing selection of boots, however, demands top dollar. Movie costumers in search of authentic Western wear often come here.

Travel Bug BOOKS

(☎505-992-0418; www.mapsofnewmexico.com; 839 Paseo de Peralta; ⊙7:30am-5:30pm Mon-Sat, 11am-4pm Sun;) One of the largest selections of travel books and maps you'll ever find; you can even print topo maps on demand, on waterproof paper. Local travelers, authors and photographers give free talks about their adventures Saturday at 5pm. There's also a coffee bar with wi-fi.

Information

EMERGENCY & MEDICAL SERVICES

Police (☎505-428-3710; 2515 Camino Entrada)

St Vincent's Hospital (☎505-983-3361; www.stvin.org; 455 St Michael's Dr; ⊙24hr emergency)

POST

Post Office (120 S Federal Pl; ⊙8am-5:30pm Mon-Fri, 9am-4pm Sat)

TOURIST INFORMATION

New Mexico Visitor Information Center (☎505-827-7336; www.newmexico.org; 491 Old Santa Fe Trail; ⊙8am-5pm Mon-Fri, 8am-4pm Sat & Sun) Housed in the historic 1878 Lamy Building, this friendly place offers helpful advice – and free coffee.

Public Lands Information Center (☎505-954-2002; www.publiclands.org; 301 Dinosaur Trail; ⊙8:30am-4pm Mon-Fri) Staff at this hugely helpful office have maps and information on public lands throughout New Mexico, and can talk you through all the hiking options.

Getting There & Around

A few commercial airlines fly daily between **Santa Fe Municipal Airport** (SAF; ☎505-955-2900; www.santafenm.gov/airport; 121 Aviation Dr) and Dallas, Denver, and Los Angeles, though these routes are added and cut with surprising frequency. Many more flights arrive at and depart from Albuquerque (one-hour drive south of Santa Fe).

Sandia Shuttle Express (☎888-775-5696; www.sandiashuttle.com) runs between Santa Fe and the Albuquerque Sunport ($28). **North Central Regional Transit** (☎505-629-4725; www.ncrtd.org) provides a free shuttle bus service to Espanola on weekdays, where you can transfer to shuttles to Taos, Los Alamos, Ojo Caliente and other northern destinations. Downtown pickup/drop-off is on Sheridan St, northwest of the plaza.

The **Rail Runner** (www.nmrailrunner.com) commuter train has multiple daily departures for Albuquerque, with connections to the airport. The trip takes about 1½ hours. **Amtrak** (☎800-872-7245; www.amtrak.com) stops at Lamy; buses continue 17 miles to Santa Fe.

Santa Fe Trails (☎505-955-2001; www.santafenm.gov; 1-way adult/child $1/free, day pass $2) provides local bus services. If you need a taxi, call **Capital City Cab** (☎505-438-0000; www.capitalcitycab.com).

If driving between Santa Fe and Albuquerque, try to take Hwy 14 – the Turquoise Trail – which passes through the old mining town (now arts colony) of Madrid, 28 miles south of Santa Fe.

DON'T MISS

CHIMAYÓ

The so-called 'Lourdes of America' – the extraordinarily beautiful two-towered adobe chapel of **El Santuario de Chimayó** (☎505-351-9961; www.elsantuariodechimayo.us; ⏲9am-5pm Oct-Apr, to 6pm May-Sep) – nestles amid the hills of the so-called High Road, east of Hwy 84 28 miles north of Santa Fe. It was built in 1826, on a site where the earth was said to have miraculous healing properties. Even today, the faithful come to rub the *tierra bendita* – holy dirt – from a small pit inside the church on whatever hurts. During Holy Week, about 30,000 pilgrims walk to Chimayó from Santa Fe, Albuquerque and beyond, in the largest Catholic pilgrimage in the USA. The artwork in the *santuario* is worth a trip on its own. Stop at **Rancho de Chimayó** (☎505-984-2100; www.ranchodechimayo.com; County Rd 98; mains $8-21; ⏲11:30am-9pm, closed Mon Nov-Apr) afterward for lunch or dinner.

Around Santa Fe

Pueblos

The region north of Santa Fe remains the heartland of New Mexico's Pueblo Indian peoples. Eight miles west of Pojoaque along Hwy 502, the ancient **San Ildefonso Pueblo** (☎505-455-2273; www.sanipueblo.org; per vehicle $10, camera/video/sketching permits $10/20/25; ⏲8am-5pm) was the home of Maria Martinez, who in 1919 revived a distinctive traditional black-on-black pottery style. Stop at the **Maria Poveka Martinez Museum** (⏲8am-4pm Mon-Fri) FREE and browse the shops of the exceptional potters (including Maria's direct descendants) who work in the pueblo today.

Just north of San Ildefonso, on Hwy 30, **Santa Clara Pueblo** is home to the **Puyé Cliff Dwellings** (☎888-320-5008; www.puyecliffs.com; 300 Hwy 30; tour adult/child $20/18; 2 tours $35/33; ⏲hourly tours 9am-5pm May-Sep, 10am-2pm Oct-Apr), where you can visit Ancestral Puebloan cliffside and mesa-top ruins.

Las Vegas

Not to be confused with Nevada's glittery gambling megalopolis, this Las Vegas is one of the loveliest towns in New Mexico, and the largest and oldest community east of the Sangre de Cristo Mountains. Its eminently strollable downtown has a pretty Old Town Plaza and holds some 900 Southwestern and Victorian buildings listed in the National Register of Historic Places.

Built in 1882 and carefully remodeled a century later, the elegant **Plaza Hotel** (☎505-425-3591; www.plazahotel-nm.com; 230 Old Town Plaza; r incl breakfast from $54; P❄@🛜🐾) is Las Vegas' most celebrated lodging, as seen in the movie *No Country For Old Men*. Choose between Victorian-style, antique-filled rooms in the original building or bright, modern rooms in a newer adjoining wing.

You can get your caffeine fix at **World Treasures Traveler's Cafe** (☎505-426-8638; 1814 Plaza St; snacks $3-6; ⏲7am-7pm Mon-Sat; 🛜), right on the plaza, and substantial Mexican meals at **El Rialto** (☎505-454-0037; 141 Bridge St; mains $7-11; ⏲10:30am-8:30pm Tue-Thu, to 9pm Fri & Sat, closed Sun & Mon) nearby.

Los Alamos

When the top-secret Manhattan Project sprang to life in 1943, it turned the sleepy mesa-top village of Los Alamos into a busy laboratory of secluded brainiacs. Here, in the 'town that didn't exist,' the first atomic bomb was developed in almost total secrecy. Today you'll encounter a fascinating dynamic in which souvenir T-shirts emblazoned with atomic explosions and 'La Bomba' wine are sold next to books on pueblo history and wilderness hiking.

While you can't visit the **Los Alamos National Laboratory**, where classified cutting-edge research still takes place, the interactive **Bradbury Science Museum** (☎505-667-4444; www.lanl.gov/museum; 1350 Central Ave; ⏲10am-5pm Tue-Sat, 1-5pm Sun & Mon) FREE covers atomic history in fascinating detail. The small but interesting **Los Alamos Historical Museum** (☎505-662-6272; www.losalamoshistory.org; 1050 Bathtub Row; ⏲9:30am-4:30pm Mon-Fri, 11am-4pm Sat & Sun) FREE is on the nearby grounds of the former Los Alamos Ranch School – an outdoorsy school for boys that closed when the scientists arrived.

Grab a bite with a boffin at the **Blue Window Bistro** (☑505-662-6305; www.labluewindowbistro.com; 813 Central Ave; lunch $10-12, dinner $10-27; ⊘11am-2:30pm & 5-8:30pm Mon-Fri, 5-9pm Sat).

Bandelier National Monument

Ancestral Puebloans dwelt in the cliffsides of beautiful Frijoles Canyon, now preserved within **Bandelier** (www.nps.gov/band; per vehicle $12; ⊘dawn-dusk; 🖐). The adventurous can climb ladders to reach ancient caves and kivas used until the mid-1500s. Backpacking trails within the park sustained severe damage during recent floods, but there's still camping at **Juniper Campground** (☑877-444-6777; www.recreation.gov; campsites $12), set among the pines near the monument entrance. Note that between 9am and 3pm, from the end of May to late October, you have to take a shuttle bus to Bandelier from the **White Rock Visitor Center** (⊘8am-6pm May-Sep, 10am-2pm Oct-Apr), 11 miles north on Hwy 4.

Abiquiu

The Hispanic village of Abiquiu (sounds like 'barbecue'), on Hwy 84 about 45 minutes' drive northwest of Santa Fe, is famous because artist Georgia O'Keeffe lived and painted here from 1949 until her death in 1986. With the Chama River flowing through farmland and spectacular rock landscape, this ethereal setting continues to attract artists. O'Keeffe's adobe house is open for limited visits, with one-hour **tours** (☑505-685-4539; www.okeeffemuseum.org; tours $35-65; ⊘Tue-Sat Jun-Oct, Tue, Thu & Fri mid-Mar–May & Nov, by private arrangement any other time) offered at least three days per week, but often booked months in advance.

Set amid 21,000 Technicolor acres 15 miles northwest, **Ghost Ranch** (☑505-685-1000; www.ghostranch.org; US Hwy 84; suggested donation $3; Day Pass adult/child $29/14.50; 🖐) is a retreat center where O'Keeffe stayed many times. Besides fabulous hiking trails, it holds a **dinosaur museum** (suggested donation $2; ⊘9am-5pm Mon-Sat, 1-5pm Sun) and offers basic **lodging** (☑505-685-4333; www.ghostranch.org; US Hwy 84; tent/RV sites $23/27, dm incl board $53, r with shared/private bath incl breakfast $118/131; 🅿) plus horseback rides (from $50).

The lovely **Abiquiú Inn** (☑505-685-4378; www.abiquiuinn.com; US Hwy 84; r from $120, casitas from $220; 🅿🛜) is a sprawling collection of shaded faux-adobes. Its spacious casitas have kitchenettes, and the menu at the on-site restaurant, **Cafe Abiquiú** (☑505-685-4378; www.abiquiuinn.com; Abiquiú Inn; breakfast $11, lunch & dinner $12-28; ⊘7am-9pm), includes numerous fish dishes, from chipotle honey-glazed salmon to trout tacos.

Ojo Caliente

At 140 years old, **Ojo Caliente Mineral Springs Resort & Spa** (☑505-583-2233; www.ojospa.com; 50 Los Baños Rd; r $139-169, cottages $179-209, ste $229-349; 🌡🛜) is one of the country's oldest health resorts – and Pueblo Indians have used the springs for centuries! Fifty miles north of Santa Fe on Hwy 285, it offers 10 soaking pools with several combinations of minerals (shared/private pools from $12/30). In addition to the pleasant, if nothing special, historic hotel rooms, the resort has several plush, boldly colored suites with kiva fireplaces and private soaking tubs, and New Mexican–style cottages. Its **Artesian Restaurant** (www.ojospa.com; breakfast $7-10, lunch $9-13, dinner $16-29; ⊘7:30am-11am, 11:30am-2:30pm & 5-9pm) prepares organic and local ingredients with aplomb.

Taos

A magical spot even by the standards of this land of enchantment, Taos remains forever under the spell of its elemental surroundings: 12,300ft snowcapped peaks soar behind town, while a sage-speckled plateau unrolls to the west before plunging 800ft into the Rio Grande Gorge.

Taos Pueblo, a marvel of adobe architecture, ranks among the oldest continuously inhabited communities in the US, and stands at the root of a long history that extends from conquistadors to cowboys.

During the 20th century, this little town also became a magnet for artists, writers and creative thinkers, from DH Lawrence to Dennis Hopper. It remains a relaxed and eccentric place, with classic mud-brick buildings, fabulous museums, quirky cafes and excellent restaurants, that's home to 5700 residents including bohemians and hippies, alternative-energy aficionados and old-time Hispanic families.

Sights

The Museum Association of Taos sells a $25 pass, valid for a year, that covers admission to five museums: the Millicent Rogers, Harwood Foundation and Taos Art museums, plus the Blumenschein Home and Martínez Hacienda.

★Millicent Rogers Museum MUSEUM

(☎575-758-2462; www.millicentrogers.org; 1504 Millicent Rogers Rd; adult/child $10/2; ⏲10:10am-5pm Apr-Oct, closed Mon Nov-Mar) Rooted in the private collection of model and oil heiress Millicent Rogers, who moved to Taos in 1947, this superb museum, 4 miles northwest of the Plaza, ranges from Hispanic folk art to Navajo weaving, and even modernist jewelry designed by Rogers herself. The principal focus, however, is on Native American ceramics, and especially the beautiful black-on-black pottery created during the 20th century by Maria Martínez from San Ildefonso Pueblo.

Martínez Hacienda MUSEUM

(☎575-758-1000; www.taoshistoricmuseums.org; 708 Hacienda Way, off Lower Ranchitos Rd; adult/child $8/4; ⏲10am-5pm Mon-Sat, noon-5pm Sun Apr-Oct, Mon-Tue & Thu-Sat 10am-4pm Nov-Mar) Set amid the fields 2 miles southwest of the Plaza, this fortified adobe homestead was built in 1804. It served as a trading post, first for merchants venturing north from Mexico City along the Camino Real, and then west along the Santa Fe Trail. Its 21 rooms, arranged around a double courtyard, are furnished with the few possessions that even a wealthy family of the era would have been able to afford. Cultural events are held here regularly.

Harwood Foundation Museum MUSEUM

(☎575-758-9826; www.harwoodmuseum.org; 238 Ledoux St; adult/child $10/free; ⏲10am-5pm Mon-Sat, noon-5pm Sun Apr-Oct, closed Mon Nov-Mar) Attractively displayed in a gorgeous and very spacious mid-19th-century adobe compound, the paintings, drawings, prints, sculpture and photographs here are predominantly the work of northern New Mexican artists, both historical and contemporary. Founded in 1923, the Harwood is the second-oldest museum in New Mexico, and is as strong on local Hispanic traditions as it is on Taos' 20th-century school.

Taos Art Museum & Fechin Institute MUSEUM

(☎575-758-2690; www.taosartmuseum.org; 227 Paseo del Pueblo Norte; adult/child $8/free; ⏲10am-5pm Tue-Sun May-Oct, to 4pm Nov-Apr) Russian artist Nicolai Fechin moved to Taos in 1926, aged 46, and adorned the interior of this adobe home with his own distinctly Russian woodcarvings between 1928 and 1933. Now a museum, it displays Fechin's paintings and sketches along with his private collection and choice works by members of the Taos Society of Artists, and also hosts occasional chamber music performances in summer.

Blumenschein Home & Museum MUSEUM

(☎575-758-0505; www.taoshistoricmuseums.org; 222 Ledoux St; adult/child $8/4; ⏲10am-5pm Mon-Sat, noon-5pm Sun Apr-Oct, Mon-Tue & Thu-Sat 10am-4pm Nov-Mar) Wonderfully preserved adobe residence, dating originally from 1797, which provides a vivid glimpse of life in Taos' artistic community during the 1920s. Ernest L Blumenschein, founder member of the Taos Society of Artists, lived here with his wife and daughter, Mary and Helen Greene Blumenschein, both also artists, and every room remains alive with their artworks and personal possessions.

San Francisco de Asís Church CHURCH

(☎575-751-0518; St Francis Plaza, Ranchos de Taos; ⏲9am-4pm Mon-Fri) Just off Hwy 68 in Ranchos de Taos, 4 miles south of Taos Plaza, this iconic church was completed in 1815. Famed for the rounded curves and stark angles of its sturdy adobe walls, it was repeatedly memorialized by Georgia O'Keeffe in paint, and Ansel Adams with his camera. Mass is celebrated at 6pm the first Saturday of the month, and usually at 7am, 9am and 11:30am every Sunday.

Rio Grande Gorge Bridge BRIDGE, CANYON

Constructed in 1965, this vertigo-inducing steel bridge carries Hwy 64 across the Rio Grande about 12 miles northwest of Taos. It's the seventh-highest bridge in the US, 565ft above the river and measuring 600ft long. The views from the pedestrian walkway, west over the empty Taos Plateau as well as down the jagged walls of the gorge, will surely make you gulp as you gape. Vendors selling jewelry, sage sticks and other souvenirs congregate on the eastern side.

DON'T MISS

TAOS PUEBLO

New Mexico's most extraordinary – and most beautiful – Native American site, **Taos Pueblo** (575-758-1028; www.taospueblo.com; Taos Pueblo Rd; adult/child $16/free; 8am-4pm Mon-Sat, 8:30am-4pm Sun; closed mid-Feb–mid-Apr), stands 3 miles northeast of Taos Plaza. Continuously inhabited for almost a thousand years, Taos Pueblo focuses on twin five-story adobe complexes, thought to have been completed by around 1450 AD. Modern visitors are thus confronted by the same staggering spectacle as New Mexico's earliest Spanish explorers. Guided walking tours explain the Pueblo's history and provide a chance to buy fine jewelry, pottery and other arts and crafts.

The Pueblo closes for 10 weeks around February to April, and at other times for ceremonies and events; check the website for dates.

Earthships ARCHITECTURE
(575-613-4409; www.earthship.com; US Hwy 64; self-guided tours $7; 9am-6pm Apr-Oct; 10am-4pm Nov-Mar) Numbering 70 Earthships, with capacity for 60 more, Taos' pioneering community was the brainchild of architect Michael Reynolds. Built with recycled materials like used automobile tires and cans, and buried on three sides, Earthships heat and cool themselves, make their own electricity and catch their own water; dwellers grow their own food. Stay overnight (p896) if possible; the 'tour' is a little disappointing. The visitor center is 1.5 miles west of the Rio Grande Gorge Bridge on US Hwy 64.

Activities

During summer, **white-water rafting** is popular in the **Taos Box**, the steep-sided cliffs that frame the Rio Grande. There are also plenty of excellent **hiking** and **mountain-biking** trails.

Taos Ski Valley SKIING
(www.skitaos.org; half-/full-day lift ticket $64/77; 9am-4pm) With a peak elevation of 11,819ft and a 2612ft vertical drop, Taos Ski Valley offers some of the most challenging skiing in the US and yet remains low-key and relaxed. The resort now allows snowboarders on its slopes.

Los Rios River Runners RAFTING
(575-776-8854; www.losriosriverrunners.com; 1033 Paseo Del Pueblo Sur; Box trips $105-125, Racecourse trips adult/child $54/44, 3-day Chama trips adult/child $495/375; 8am-6pm) Half-day trips on the Racecourse (in one- and two-person kayaks if you prefer), full-day trips on the Box (minimum age 12), and multinight expeditions on the scenic Chama. On the 'Native Cultures Feast and Float' ($85) you're accompanied by a Native American guide and have lunch homemade by a local Pueblo family. Rates rise slightly at weekends.

Sleeping

★ **Doña Luz Inn** B&B $
(575-758-9000; www.stayintaos.com; 114 Kit Carson Rd; r $94-229;) Funky and fun, this central B&B is a labor of love by owner Paul Castillo. Rooms are decorated in colorful themes from Spanish colonial to Native American, with abundant art, murals and artifacts plus adobe fireplaces, kitchenettes and hot tubs. The cozy La Luz room is the best deal in town, and there are also sumptuous larger suites.

Abominable Snowmansion HOSTEL $
(575-776-8298; www.snowmansion.com; 476 Hwy 150; tent sites/dm/tipi $22/27/55, r without/with bath $50/55;) Popular and affordable hostel in the heart of Arroyo Seco, which makes a cozy high-country alternative to paying Taos prices. A big round fireplace in the central lodge warms guests in winter, there's a shared kitchen, and you can choose between clean (if a tad threadbare) private rooms, simple dorms, a wonderful campground, and even, in summer, a tipi.

★ **Earthship Rentals** BOUTIQUE HOTEL $$
(575-751-0462; www.earthship.com; US Hwy 64; Earthship $145-350;) How about an off-grid night in a boutique-chic, solar-powered dwelling? Part Gaudí-esque visions, part space-age fantasy, these futuristic structures are built using recycled tires and aluminum cans, not that those components are visible. Set on a beautiful mesa across the river 14 miles northwest, they offer a unique experience, albeit rather different to staying in Taos itself. Drop-ins welcome.

★ **Historic Taos Inn** HISTORIC HOTEL $$
(575-758-2233; www.taosinn.com; 125 Paseo del Pueblo Norte; r from $105;) Lovely and

always lively old inn, where the 45 characterful rooms have Southwest trimmings like heavy-duty wooden furnishings and adobe fireplaces (some functioning, some for show). The famed Adobe Bar spills into the cozy central atrium, and features live music every night – for a quieter stay, opt for one of the detached separate wings – and there's also a good restaurant.

✖ Eating

Michael's Kitchen   NEW MEXICAN $
(☑575-758-4178; www.michaelskitchen.com; 304c Paseo del Pueblo Norte; mains $7-16; ☺7am-2:30pm Mon-Thu, to 8pm Fri-Sun; 🚼) Locals and tourists alike converge on this old favorite because the menu is long, the food's reliably good, it's an easy place for kids, and the in-house bakery produces goodies that fly out the door. Plus, it serves the best damn breakfast in town. You just may spot a Hollywood celebrity or two digging into a chile-smothered breakfast burrito.

El Gamal   MIDDLE EASTERN $
(☑575-613-0311; 12 Doña Luz St; mains $7-12; ☺9am-5pm Mon-Wed, 9am-9pm Thu-Sat, 11am-3pm Sun; 🛜🚻🚼) Vegetarians rejoice – at this casual Middle Eastern place, there's no meat anywhere. Even if the falafel doesn't quite achieve the stated aim to promote peace through 'evolving people's consciousness and taste buds,' it certainly tastes good. There's a kids playroom in the back with tons of toys, plus a pool table and free wi-fi.

★Love Apple   NEW MEXICAN $$
(☑575-751-0050; www.theloveapple.net; 803 Paseo del Pueblo Norte; mains $14-25; ☺5-9pm Tue-Sun) A real 'only in New Mexico' find, from the setting in the converted 19th-century adobe Placitas Chapel, to the delicious, locally sourced and largely organic food. Everything – from the local beefburger with red chile and blue cheese, via the tamales with mole sauce, to the wild boar tenderloin – is imbued with regional flavors, and the understated rustic-sacred atmosphere enhances the experience. Make reservations.

★Lambert's   MODERN AMERICAN $$$
(☑505-758-1009; www.lambertsoftaos.com; 123 Bent St; lunch $9-19, dinner $18-39; ☺noon-2pm & 5:30-9pm mid-May–mid-Sep, 5:30-9pm Mon-Sat, 10am-2pm Sun mid-Sep–mid-May; 🚻🚼) Consistently hailed as the 'Best of Taos,' and

now relocated into a charming old adobe just north of the Plaza, Lambert's remains what it's always been – a cozy, romantic local hangout where patrons relax and enjoy sumptuous contemporary cuisine, with mains ranging from lunchtime's barbecue-pork sliders to dinner dishes like chicken mango enchiladas or Colorado rack of lamb.

♀ Drinking & Entertainment

Adobe Bar   BAR
(☑575-758-2233; Historic Taos Inn, 125 Paseo del Pueblo Norte; ☺11am-11pm; music 7-10pm) There's something about the Adobe Bar. All Taos seems to turn up at some point each evening, to kick back in the comfy covered atrium, enjoying no-cover live music from bluegrass to jazz, and drinking the famed 'Cowboy Buddha' margaritas. If you decide to stick around, you can always order food off the well-priced bar menu.

Coffee Spot   CAFE
(☑575-758-8556; 900 Paseo del Pueblo Norte; ☺7am-5pm) Large, ramshackle and very popular coffeehouse and bakery, serving all-day breakfasts – try the chile-smothered Taos Benedict – plus espresso, juices, smoothies and salads, and plentiful gluten-free options. Locals lured by the free wi-fi spread out through the copious indoor space and sunny patio.

KTAO Solar Center   LIVE MUSIC
(☑575-758-5826; www.ktao.com; 9 Ski Valley Rd; ☺bar 4-9pm Sun-Thu, to 11pm Fri & Sat) Taos' best live-music venue, at the start of Ski Valley Rd, shares its space with much-loved radio station KTAO 101.9FM. Local and touring acts stop by to rock the house; when there's no show, watch the DJs in the booth at the 'world's most powerful solar radio station' while hitting happy hour at the bar.

🛍 Shopping

Taos has historically been a mecca for artists, demonstrated by the huge number of galleries and studios in and around town. Indie stores and galleries line the **John Dunn Shops** (www.johndunnshops.com) pedestrian walkway linking Bent St to Taos Plaza, which is home to the well-stocked **Moby Dickens Bookshop** (☑575-758-3050; www.mobydickens.com; 124a Bent Street; ☺10am-5pm Mon-Wed, 10am-6pm Thu-Sat, noon-5pm Sun).

Just east of the Plaza, pop into **El Rincón Trading Post** (575-758-9188; 114 Kit Carson Rd; 10am-5pm) for classic Western memorabilia.

Information

Taos Visitor Center (575-758-3873; http://taos.org; 1139 Paseo del Pueblo Sur; 9am-5pm;) This excellent visitor center stocks information of all kinds on northern New Mexico and doles out free coffee; everything, including the comprehensive *Taos Vacation Guide*, is also available online.

Getting There & Away

From Santa Fe, take either the scenic 'High Road' along Hwys 76 and 518, with galleries, villages and sites worth exploring, or follow the lovely unfolding Rio Grande landscape on Hwy 68.

North Central Regional Transit (866-206-0754; www.ncrtd.org) provides a free shuttle-bus service to Espanola on weekdays, where you can transfer to Santa Fe and other destinations, while **Taos Express** (575-751-4459; www.taosexpress.com) can get you to Santa Fe at weekends ($10).

Northwestern New Mexico

Dubbed 'Indian Country' for good reason (huge swaths of land fall under the aegis of the Navajo, Pueblo, Zuni, Apache and Laguna tribes), New Mexico's northwestern quadrant showcases remarkable ancient sites alongside solitary Native American settlements and colorful badlands.

Farmington & Around

The largest town in northwest New Mexico, Farmington makes a convenient base from which to explore the Four Corners area. The **visitors bureau** (505-326-7602; www.farmingtonnm.org; 3041 E Main St; 8am-5pm Mon-Sat) has more information.

Shiprock, a 1700ft-high volcanic plug that rises eerily over the landscape to the west, was a landmark for the Anglo pioneers and is a sacred site to the Navajo.

Fourteen miles northeast of Farmington, the 27-acre **Aztec Ruins National Monument** (505-334-6174; www.nps.gov/azru; 84 Ruins Rd; adult/child $5/free; 8am-5pm Sep-May, to 6pm Jun-Aug) features the largest reconstructed kiva in the country, with an internal diameter of almost 50ft. A few steps away, let your imagination wander as you stoop through low doorways and dark rooms inside the West Ruin.

About 35 miles south of Farmington along Hwy 371, the undeveloped **Bisti Badlands & De-Na-Zin Wilderness** is a trippy, surreal landscape of strange, colorful rock formations, especially spectacular in the hours before sunset; desert enthusiasts shouldn't miss it. The Farmington **BLM office** (505-564-7600; www.nm.blm.gov; 6251 College Blvd; 7:45am-4:30pm Mon-Fri) has information.

The lovely, three-room **Silver River Adobe Inn B&B** (575-325-8219; www.silveradobe.com; 3151 W Main St; r $115-175;) offers a peaceful respite among the trees along the San Juan River.

Managing to be both trendy *and* kid-friendly, the hippish **Three Rivers Eatery & Brewhouse** (505-324-2187; www.threeriversbrewery.com; 101 E Main St; mains $9-32; 11am-9pm;) has good steaks, pub grub and its own microbrews. It's the best restaurant in town by a mile.

Chaco Culture National Historic Park

Featuring massive Ancestral Puebloan buildings set in an isolated high-desert environment, intriguing **Chaco** (www.nps.gov/chcu; per vehicle $8; 7am-sunset) contains evidence of 5000 years of human occupation. In its prime, the community at Chaco Canyon was a major trading and ceremonial hub for the region – and the city the Puebloan people created here was masterly in its layout and design. Pueblo Bonito is four stories tall and may have had 600 to 800 rooms and kivas. As well as driving the self-guided loop tour, you can hike various **backcountry trails**. For stargazers, there are evening astronomy presentations in summer.

The park is in a remote area approximately 80 miles south of Farmington, far beyond the reach of any public transport. **Gallo Campground** (877-444-6777; www.recreation.gov; sites $15) is 1 mile east of the visitor center. No RV hookups.

Chama

Nine miles south of the Colorado border, Chama's **Cumbres & Toltec Scenic Railway** (888-286-2737; www.cumbrestoltec.com; adult/child 2-12 yr from $95/49; late May–mid-

Oct) is the longest (64 miles) and highest (over the 10,015ft-high Cumbres Pass) authentic narrow-gauge steam railroad in the US. It's a beautiful trip (particularly in September and October during the fall foliage) through mountains, canyons and high desert. Lunch is included and on many trips kids ride free. See the website for details.

Northeastern New Mexico

East of Santa Fe, the lush Sangre de Cristo Mountains give way to vast rolling plains. Dusty grasslands stretch to infinity and beyond (well, to Texas, anyway). Cattle and dinosaur prints dot a landscape punctuated with volcanic cones. Ranching is an economic mainstay, and on many roads you'll see more cows than cars.

The Santa Fe Trail, along which pioneer settlers rolled in wagon trains, ran from New Mexico to Missouri. You can still see the wagon ruts in places, off I-25 between Santa Fe and Raton.

Cimarron

Cimarron once ranked among the rowdiest of Wild West towns; its name even means 'wild' in Spanish. According to local lore, murder was such an everyday occurrence in the 1870s that peace and quiet was newsworthy, one paper going so far as to report: 'Everything is quiet in Cimarron. Nobody has been killed in three days.'

Today, the town is quiet, luring nature-minded travelers who want to enjoy the great outdoors. Driving to or from Taos, you'll pass through gorgeous **Cimarron Canyon State Park**, a steep-walled canyon with several hiking trails, excellent trout fishing and camping.

You can stay or dine at what's reputed to be one of the most haunted hotels in the USA, the 1872 **St James** (575-376-2664; www.exstjames.com; 617 Collison St; r $85-135;) – one room is so spook-filled that it's never rented out! Many legends of the West stayed here, including Buffalo Bill, Annie Oakley, Wyatt Earp and Jesse James, and the front desk has a long list of who shot whom in the hotel bar.

Capulin Volcano National Monument

Rising 1300ft above the surrounding plains, **Capulin** (575-278-2201; www.nps.gov/cavo; vehicle $5; 8am-5pm Jun-Aug, to 4:30pm Sep-May) is the most accessible of several volcanoes hereabouts. A 2-mile road spirals up the mountain to a parking lot at the rim (8182ft), where trails lead around and into the crater. The entrance is 3 miles north of Capulin village, which itself is 30 miles east of Raton on Hwy 87.

Southwestern New Mexico

The Rio Grande Valley unfurls from Albuquerque down to the bubbling hot springs of funky Truth or Consequences and beyond. Before the river hits the Texas line, it feeds one of New Mexico's agricultural treasures: Hatch, the so-called 'chili capital of the world.' The first atomic device was detonated at the Trinity Site, in the bone-dry desert east of the Rio Grande.

To the west, the rugged Gila National Forest is wild with backpacking and fishing adventures. The mountains' southern slopes descend into the Chihuahuan Desert that surrounds Las Cruces, the state's second-largest city.

Truth or Consequences & Around

An offbeat joie de vivre permeates the funky little town of Truth or Consequences ('T or C'), which was built on the site of natural hot springs in the 1880s. Originally, sensibly enough, called Hot Springs, it changed its name in 1950, after a then-popular radio game show called, you guessed it, Truth or Consequences. Publicity these days comes courtesy of Virgin Galactic CEO Richard Branson and other space-travel visionaries driving the development of nearby **Spaceport America**, where wealthy tourists are expected to launch into orbit sometime soon.

About 60 miles north, sandhill cranes and Arctic geese winter in the 90 sq miles of fields and marshes at **Bosque del Apache National Wildlife Refuge** (www.fws.gov/refuge/bosque_del_apache; per vehicle $5; dawn-dusk).

Sleeping & Eating

★ **Riverbend Hot Springs** BOUTIQUE HOTEL $
(575-894-7625; www.riverbendhotsprings.com; 100 Austin St; r/ste from $70/105;) This delightful place, occupying a fantastic perch beside the Rio Grande, is the only T or C hotel to feature outdoor, riverside hot tubs – tiled, decked and totally irresistible. Accommodations, colorfully decorated by local artists,

WORTH A TRIP

EAVESDROPPING ON OUTER SPACE

Beyond the town of Magdalena on Hwy 60, 130 miles southwest of Albuquerque, the amazing **Very Large Array** (VLA; ☎505-835-7243; www.nrao.edu; off Hwy 52; ⊙8:30am-sunset) FREE radio telescope consists of 27 huge antenna dishes sprouting like giant mushrooms in the high plains. Watch a short film at the visitor center, then take a self-guided walking tour with a window peek into the control building.

ranges from motel-style rooms to a three-bedroom suite. Guests can use the public pools for free, and private tubs for $10.

Blackstone Hotsprings BOUTIQUE HOTEL $

(☎575-894-0894; www.blackstonehotsprings.com; 410 Austin St; r $75-135; P ❄ 📶) Blackstone embraces the T or C spirit with an upscale wink, decorating each of its seven rooms in the style of a classic TV show, from *The Jetsons* to *The Golden Girls* to *I Love Lucy*. Best part? Each room comes with its own over-sized tub or waterfall fed from the hot springs.

Passion Pie Cafe CAFE $

(☎575-894-0008; http://deepwaterfarm.com; 406 Main St; breakfast & lunch mains $5-10, pizzas $13-18; ⊙7am-3pm daily, plus 4-9:30pm Fri & Sat) Watch T or C get its morning groove on through the windows of this espresso cafe, and set yourself up with a breakfast waffle; the Elvis (with peanut butter) or the Fat Elvis (with bacon too) should do the job. Later on there are plenty of healthy salads and sandwiches, plus pizza on Friday and Saturday nights.

Latitude 33 FUSION $$

(☎575-740-7804; 334 S Pershing St; mains $8-16; ⊙11am-8pm Mon-Sat) Relaxed, friendly bistro, tucked away downtown between the two main drags, which serves excellent pan-Asian dishes at good prices. Spicy peanut noodles cost $8 at lunch, $10 for dinner.

Las Cruces & Around

The second-largest city in New Mexico, Las Cruces is home to New Mexico State University (NMSU), but there's surprisingly little of real interest for visitors.

Sights

For many, a visit to neighboring **Mesilla** (aka Old Mesilla) is the highlight of their time in Las Cruces. Wander a few blocks off Old Mesilla's plaza to gather the essence of a mid-19th-century Southwestern town of Hispanic heritage.

★New Mexico Farm & Ranch Heritage Museum MUSEUM

(☎575-522-4100; www.nmfarmandranchmuseum.org; 4100 Dripping Springs Rd; adult/child $5/2; ⊙9am-5pm Mon-Sat, noon-5pm Sun; 👪) This terrific museum doesn't just hold engaging exhibits on the state's agricultural history – it's got livestock too. Enclosures on the working farm alongside hold assorted breeds of cattle, along with horses, donkeys, sheep and goats. The taciturn cowboys who tend the animals proffer little extra information, but they add color, and you can even buy a pony if you have $450 to spare. There are daily milking demonstrations plus weekly displays of blacksmithing, spinning and weaving, and heritage cooking.

White Sands Missile Test Center Museum MUSEUM

(☎575-678-8800; www.wsmr-history.org; ⊙8am-4pm Mon-Fri, 10am-3pm Sat) FREE Explore New Mexico's military technology history with a visit to this museum, 25 miles east of Las Cruces along Hwy 70. It represents the heart of the White Sands Missile Range, a major testing site since 1945. There's a missile garden, a real V-2 rocket and a museum with lots of defense-related artifacts. Visitors have to park outside the Test Center gate and check in at the office before walking in.

Sleeping

★Best Western Mission Inn MOTEL $

(☎575-524-8591; www.bwmissioninn.com; 1765 S Main St; r from $69) A truly out-of-the-ordinary accommodation option; yes it's a roadside chain motel, but the rooms are beautifully kitted out with attractive tiling, stonework and colorful stenciled designs; they're sizeable and comfortable; and the rates are great.

★Lundeen Inn of the Arts B&B $$

(☎505-526-3326; www.innofthearts.com; 618 S Alameda Blvd, Las Cruces; r incl breakfast $82, ste from $99; P ❄ 📶 🐾) Each of the 20 guest rooms in this large and very lovely century-old Mexican Territorial-style inn is unique and named for – and decorated in the style of – a New Mexico artist. Check out the soaring pressed-tin ceilings in the great room. Owners Linda and Jerry offer the kind of genteel hospitality you seldom find these days.

Eating

Nellie's Cafe MEXICAN $
(575-524-9982; 1226 W Hadley Ave; mains $5-9; 8am-2pm Tue-Sat) Cherished by locals, Nellie's has been serving homemade burritos, *chile rellenos* and tamales for decades now, under the slogan 'Chile with an Attitude.' It's small and humble in decor but big in taste, with deliciously spicy food.

★**Double Eagle Restaurant** STEAK $$$
(575-523-6700; www.double-eagle-mesilla.com; 308 Calle de Guadalupe; mains $23-49; 11am-10pm Mon-Sat, noon-9pm Sun) A glorious mélange of Wild West opulence, all dark wood and velvet hangings, and featuring a fabulous old bar, this Plaza restaurant is on the National Register of Historic Places. The main dining room offers delicious continental and Southwestern cuisine, especially steaks, while the less formal Peppers in the courtyard claims to serve the world's largest green chili cheeseburger ($25).

Information

Las Cruces CVB (575-541-2444; www.lascrucescvb.org; 211 N Water St) Helpful office with all sorts of visitor information.

Getting There & Away

Greyhound (575-524-8518; www.greyhound.com; 800 E Thorpe Rd, Chucky's Convenience Store) buses traverse the two interstate corridors (I-10 and I-25). Daily destinations include Albuquerque ($14, 3½ hours), Roswell ($38, four hours) and El Paso ($10, one hour).

Silver City & Around

The spirit of the Wild West still hangs in the air in Silver City, 113 miles northwest of Las Cruces, as if Billy the Kid himself – who grew up here – might amble past at any moment. But things are changing, as the mountain-man/cowboy vibe succumbs to the charms of art galleries, coffeehouses and gelato.

Silver City is also the gateway to outdoor activities in the **Gila National Forest**, which is rugged country suitable for remote cross-country skiing, backpacking, camping, and fishing. Two hours north of town, up a winding 42-mile road, is **Gila Cliff Dwellings National Monument** (www.nps.gov/gicl; admission $3; trail 9am-4pm, visitor center to 4:30pm), occupied in the 13th century by the Mogollon people. Mysterious and relatively isolated, these remarkable cliff dwellings are easily accessed from a 1-mile loop trail and look very much as they would have at the turn of the first millennium. For **pictographs**, stop by the Lower Scorpion Campground and walk a short distance along the marked trail.

Weird rounded monoliths make the **City of Rocks State Park** (575-536-2800; www.nmparks.com; Hwy 61; day-use $5, tent/RV sites $8/14) an intriguing playground, with great camping among the formations; there are tables and fire pits. For a rock-lined gem of a spot, check out campsite 43, the Lynx. Head 33 miles southeast of Silver City along Hwy 180 and Hwy 61.

For a smattering of Silver City's architectural history, overnight in the 22-room **Palace Hotel** (575-388-1811; www.silvercitypalacehotel.com; 106 W Broadway; r from $51;). Exuding a low-key, turn-of-the-19th-century charm (no air-con, older fixtures), the Palace is a great choice for those tired of cookie-cutter chains.

Downtown eating options range from the comfy, come-as-you-are **Javalina** (575-388-1350; 201 N Bullard St; pastries from $2; 6am-6pm Sun-Thu, to 9pm Fri & Sat;) coffee shop to the **Curious Kumquat** (575-534-0337; http://curiouskumquat.com; 111 E College Ave; lunch mains $7-8, dinner mains $17-23; 11am-4:30pm & 5:30-8:30pm Tue-Sat), an acclaimed gourmet hotspot where many dishes use locally foraged ingredients. For a taste of local culture, head 7 miles north to Pinos Altos and the **Buckhorn Saloon** (575-538-9911; www.buckhornsaloonandoperahouse.com; 32 Main St, Pinos Altos; mains $10-39; 3-11pm Mon-Sat), where the specialty is steak and there's live music most nights. Call for reservations.

Information

The **visitor center** (575-538-5555; www.silvercitytourism.org; 201 N Hudson St; 9am-5pm Mon-Sat, 10am-4pm Sun) and the **Gila National Forest Ranger Station** (575-388-8201; www.fs.fed.us/r3/gila; 3005 E Camino Del Bosque; 8am-4:30pm Mon-Fri) have area information.

Southeastern New Mexico

Two of New Mexico's greatest natural wonders are tucked down in the state's arid southeast – mesmerizing White Sands National Monument and magnificent Carlsbad Caverns National Park. This region is also home to some enduring legends: aliens in Roswell, Billy the Kid in Lincoln and Smokey Bear in Capitan. Most of the lowlands are covered by hot, rugged Chihuahuan Desert, but you can escape to cooler climes by driving up to higher altitudes around forested resort towns such as Cloudcroft and Ruidoso.

White Sands National Monument

Slide, roll and slither through brilliant, towering sand hills. Sixteen miles southwest of Alamogordo (15 miles southwest of Hwy 82/70), gypsum covers 275 sq miles to create a dazzling white landscape at this crisp, stark **monument** (575-479-6124; www.nps.gov/whsa; adult/under 16yr $3/free; 7am-9pm Jun-Aug, to sunset Sep-May). These captivating windswept dunes, which doubled as space-alien David Bowie's home planet in *The Man Who Fell To Earth*, are a highlight of any trip to New Mexico. Don't forget your sunglasses – the sand is as bright as snow!

Spring for a $15 plastic saucer at the visitor center gift store then sled one of the back dunes. It's fun, and you can sell the disc back for $5 at day's end. Backcountry campsites, with no water or toilet facilities, are a mile from the scenic drive. Pick up a permit ($3, issued first-come, first-served) in person at the visitor center at least one hour before sunset.

Alamogordo & Around

In Alamogordo, a desert outpost famous for its space- and atomic-research programs, the four-story **New Mexico Museum of Space History** (575-437-2840; www.nmspacemuseum.org; 3198 Hwy 2001; adult/child $6/4; 9am-5pm;) has excellent exhibits on space research and flight, and shows outstanding science-themed films in its **Tombaugh IMAX Theater & Planetarium** (adult/child $6/4.50;).

Motels stretch along White Sands Blvd, including **Best Western Desert Aire Hotel** (575-437-2110; www.bestwestern.com; 1021 S White Sands Blvd; r from $79;), with standard-issue rooms and suites (some with kitchenettes), along with a sauna. If you'd rather camp, hit **Oliver Lee State Park** (575-437-8284; www.nmparks.com; 409 Dog Canyon Rd; day-use $5; tent/RV sites $8/14), 12 miles south of Alamogordo. Grab some grub at the friendly **Pizza Patio & Pub** (575-434-9633; 2203 E 1st St; mains $7-16; 11am-8pm Mon-Thu & Sat, to 9pm Fri;), which serves pizzas, pastas, big salads and pitchers or pints of beer on tap.

Cloudcroft

Situated high in the mountains, little Cloudcroft provides welcome relief from the lowlands heat. With turn-of-the-19th-century buildings, it offers lots of outdoor recreation, is a good base for exploration and has a low-key feel. **High Altitude** (575-682-1229; www.highaltitude.org; 310 Burro Ave; rentals from $30 per day; 10am-5:30pm Mon-Thu, to 6pm Fri & Sat, to 5pm Sun) rents mountain bikes and has maps of local fat-tire routes.

The **Lodge Resort & Spa** (800-395-6343; www.thelodgeresort.com; 601 Corona Pl; r from $141;) is one of the Southwest's finest historic hotels. Rooms in the main Bavarian-style hotel are furnished with period and Victorian pieces, while **Rebecca's** (575-682-3131; Lodge Resort, 601 Corona Pl; mains $8-38; 7-10am, 11:30am-2pm & 5:30-9pm), named after the resident ghost, offers by far the best food in town.

Ruidoso

Downright bustling in summer and big with racetrack bettors, resorty Ruidoso (it means 'noisy' in Spanish) has an utterly pleasant climate thanks to its lofty and forested perch near Sierra Blanca (12,000ft). It's spread out along Hwy 48 (known as Mechem Dr or Sudderth Dr), the main drag.

Sights & Activities

To stretch your legs, try the easily accessible **forest trails** on Cedar Creek Rd just west of **Smokey Bear Ranger Station** (575-257-4095; www.fs.usda.gov/lincoln; 901 Mechem Dr; 7:30am-4:30pm Mon-Fri, plus Sat in summer). Choose from the USFS Fitness Trail or the meandering paths at the Cedar Creek Picnic Area. Longer day hikes and backpacking routes abound in the White Mountain Wilderness, north of town. Always check fire restrictions around here – the forest closes during dry spells.

Hubbard Museum of the American West MUSEUM
(☎575-378-4142; www.hubbardmuseum.org; 26301 Hwy 70; adult/child $7/2; ⏲9am-5pm; 🚸) This town-run museum focuses on local history, with a wonderful gallery of old photos, and also displays Native American kachinas, war bonnets, weapons and pottery. Traces of its original incarnation as the Museum of the Horse linger in various horse-related exhibits – and be sure to check out the fascinating, if completely irrelevant, history of toilets in the restrooms.

Ski Apache SKIING
(www.skiapache.com; lift ticket adult/child $51/33) Unlikely as it sounds, Ski Apache, 18 miles northwest of Ruidoso on the slopes of Sierra Blanca Peak, really is owned by the Apache. Potentially it's the finest ski area south of Albuquerque, a good choice for affordability and fun – and it's also home to New Mexico's only gondola. Recent seasons, however, have seen poor snowfall – check ahead.

Sleeping & Eating

Motels, hotels and cute little cabin complexes line the streets. There's plenty of primitive camping along forest roads on the way to the ski area.

Sitzmark Chalet HOTEL $
(☎575-257-4140; www.sitzmark-chalet.com; 627 Sudderth Dr; r from $59; ❄📶) This ski-themed chalet offers 17 simple but nice rooms. Picnic tables, grills and an eight-person hot tub are welcome perks.

Upper Canyon Inn LODGE $$
(☎575-257-3005; www.uppercanyoninn.com; 215 Main Rd; r/cabins from $89/129; 📶) Rooms and cabins here range from simple good value to rustic-chic luxury. Bigger doesn't necessarily mean more expensive, so look at a few options. The pricier cabins have some fine interior woodwork and Jacuzzi tubs.

★ **Cornerstone Bakery** CAFE $
(☎575-257-1842; www.cornerstonebakerycafe.com; 359 Sudderth Dr; mains under $10; ⏲7am-2pm; 🌱) Totally irresistible, hugely popular local bakery-cafe, where everything, from the breads, pastries and espresso to the omelets and croissant sandwiches, is just the way it should be. Stick around long enough and the Cornerstone may become your morning touchstone.

Entertainment

Ruidoso Downs Racetrack HORSE RACING
(☎575-378-4431; www.raceruidoso.com; Hwy 70; grandstand seats free; ⏲Fri-Mon late May-early Sep) National attention focuses on the Ruidoso Downs racetrack on Labor Day for the world's richest quarter-horse race, the All American Futurity, which has a purse of $2.4 million. The course is also home to the Racehorse Hall of Fame, and the small Billy the Kid Casino.

Flying J Ranch MUSIC
(☎575-336-4330; www.flyingjranch.com; 1028 Hwy 48; adult/child $27/15; ⏲from 5:30pm Mon-Sat late May-early Sep, Sat only early Sep–mid-Oct; 🚸) Families with little ones will love this 'Western village,' 1.5 miles north of Alto, as it delivers a full night of entertainment, with gunfights, pony rides and Western music, to go with its cowboy-style chuckwagon dinner.

Information

Chamber of commerce (☎575-257-7395; www.ruidosonow.com; 720 Sudderth Dr; ⏲8am-5pm Mon-Fri, 9am-3pm Sat) Has visitor information.

Lincoln & Capitan

Fans of Western history won't want to miss little Lincoln. Twelve miles east of Capitan along the Billy the Kid National Scenic Byway (www.billybyway.com), this is where the gun battle known as the Lincoln County War turned Billy the Kid into a legend. The whole town is beautifully preserved in close to original form, with its unspoiled main street designated as the **Lincoln Historic Site** (☎575-653-4372; www.nmmonuments.org/lincoln; adult/child $5/free; ⏲hours vary for individual sites).

Buy tickets to the historic town buildings at the **Anderson-Freeman Visitors Center**, where you'll also find exhibits on Buffalo soldiers, Apaches and the Lincoln County War. Make the fascinating **Courthouse Museum**, the well-marked site of Billy's most daring – and violent – escape, your last stop. A plaque marks where one of his bullets slammed into the wall.

For overnighters, the **Ellis Store Country Inn** (☎800-653-6460; www.ellisstore.com; Hwy 380; r incl breakfast $89-129) offers three antique-filled rooms (complete with wood stove) in the main house. Five additional rooms are located in a historic mill on the property, and an amazing six-course dinner

DON'T MISS

CARLSBAD CAVERNS NATIONAL PARK

Scores of wondrous caves hide under the hills at this unique **national park** (575-785-2232, bat info 505-785-3012; www.nps.gov/cave; adult/child $10/free; caves 8:30am-5pm late May-early Sep, to 3:30pm early Sep-late May;), which covers 73 sq miles. The cavern formations are an ethereal wonderland of stalactites and fantastical geological features. From the **visitor center** (8am-5pm, to 7pm late May-early Sep) you can ride an elevator, which descends the equivalent of the length of the Empire State Building in under a minute, or take a 2-mile subterranean walk from the cave mouth to the Big Room, an underground chamber 1800ft long, 255ft high and more than 800ft below the surface. If you've got kids (or are just feeling goofy), plastic caving helmets with headlamps are sold in the gift shop.

Guided tours (877-444-6777; www.recreation.gov; adult $7-20, child $3.50-10) of additional caves are available, and should be reserved well in advance. Wear long sleeves and closed shoes; it gets chilly.

The cave's other claim to fame is the 300,000-plus Mexican free-tailed bat colony that roosts here from mid-May to mid-October. Be here by sunset, when they cyclone out for an all-evening insect feast.

is served in the lovely dining room ($75 per person; not Sundays). Perfect for special occasions; reservations recommended.

Like Lincoln, cozy Capitan is surrounded by the beautiful mountains of **Lincoln National Forest**. The main reason to come is so the kids can visit **Smokey Bear Historical State Park** (575-354-2748; 118 W Smokey Bear Blvd; adult/child $2/1; 9am-5pm), where Smokey (yes, there actually was a real Smokey Bear) is buried.

Roswell

If you believe 'The Truth Is Out There', then the Roswell Incident is already filed away in your memory banks. In 1947 a mysterious object crashed at a nearby ranch. No one would have skipped any sleep over it, but the military made a big to-do of hushing it up, and for a lot of folks, that sealed it: the aliens had landed! International curiosity and local ingenuity have transformed the city into a quirky extraterrestrial-wannabe zone. Bulbous white heads glow atop the downtown streetlamps and busloads of tourists come to find good souvenirs.

Believers and kitsch-seekers must check out the **International UFO Museum & Research Center** (575-625-9495; www.roswellufomuseum.com; 114 N Main St; adult/child $5/$2; 9am-5pm), displaying documents supporting the cover-up as well as lots of far-out art and exhibitions. The annual **Roswell UFO Festival** (www.roswellufofestival.com) beams down in early July, with an otherworldly costume parade, workshops and concerts.

Ho-hum chain motels line N Main St. About 36 miles south of Roswell, the **Heritage Inn** (575-748-2552; www.artesiaheritageinn.com; 209 W Main St, Artesia; r incl breakfast from $119;) in Artesia offers 11 Old West–style rooms and is the nicest lodging in the area.

For simple, dependable New Mexican fare, try **Martin's Capitol Cafe** (575-624-2111; 110 W 4th St; mains $7-15; 6am-8:30pm Mon-Sat); for American eats, **Big D's Downtown Dive** (www.bigdsdowntowndive.com; 505 N Main St; $7-10; 11am-9pm) has the best salads, sandwiches and burgers in town.

Pick up local information at the **visitors bureau** (575-624-6860; www.seeroswell.com; 912 N Main St; 8:30am-5:30pm Mon-Fri, 10am-3pm Sat & Sun;).

The **Greyhound Bus Depot** (575-622-2510; www.greyhound.com; 1100 N Virginia Ave) has buses to Las Cruces ($42, four hours).

Carlsbad

Carlsbad is the closest town to Carlsbad Caverns National Park and the Guadalupe Mountains. The **Park Service office** (575-785-2232; 3225 National Parks Hwy; 8am-4:30pm Mon-Fri) on its southern edge has information on both.

On the northwestern outskirts, off Hwy 285, **Living Desert State Park** (575-887-5516; www.nmparks.com; 1504 Miehls Dr N, off Hwy 285; adult/child $5/3; 8am-5pm Jun-Aug, 9am-5pm Sep-May, last zoo entry 3:30pm) is a great place to see and learn about desert plants and wildlife. There's a good 1.3-mile trail that showcases different habitats of the Chihuahuan Desert, with live antelopes, wolves, roadrunners and more.

However, a recent boom in the oil industry means that even the most ordinary motel room in Carlsbad is liable to cost well over $200 per night, so it makes much more sense to visit on a *long* day-trip from, say, Roswell or Alamogordo. The best room rates, oddly enough, tend to be at the appealing **Trinity Hotel** (575-234-9891; www.thetrinityhotel.com; 201 S Canal St; r from $189;), a historic building that was originally the First National Bank. The sitting room of one suite is inside the old vault, and the restaurant is Carlsbad's classiest.

The perky **Blue House Bakery & Cafe** (575-628-0555; 609 N Canyon St; mains $4-10; 6am-noon Mon-Sat) brews the best coffee in these parts, while the lip-smackin' **Red Chimney Pit Barbecue** (575-885-8744; 817 N Canal St; mains $7-15; 11am-2pm & 4:30-8:30pm Mon-Fri) serves succulent Southern-style meats.

For other in-the-know advice, visit the **chamber of commerce** (575-887-6516; www.carlsbadchamber.com; 302 S Canal St; 9am-5pm Mon, 8am-5pm Tue-Fri).

Greyhound (575-628-0768; www.greyhound.com; 3102 National Parks Hwy) buses depart from the Allsup's gas station a few miles south of town on Hwy 180, heading to El Paso ($57, three hours).

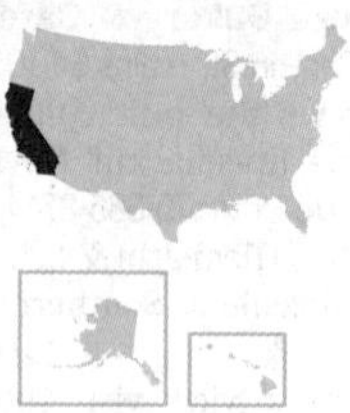

California

Includes ➡

Best Places to Eat

- ➡ Chez Panisse (p992)
- ➡ Oxbow Public Market (p994)
- ➡ State Bird Provisions (p985)
- ➡ George's at the Cove (p944)
- ➡ Bestia (p926)

Best Places to Hike

- ➡ Yosemite National Park (p1009)
- ➡ Sequoia & Kings Canyon National Parks (p1013)
- ➡ Marin County (p990)
- ➡ Redwood National & State Parks (p1001)
- ➡ Death Valley National Park (p952)

Why Go?

With bohemian spirit and high-tech savvy, not to mention a die-hard passion for the good life – whether that means cracking open a bottle of old-vine Zinfandel, climbing a 14,000ft peak or surfing the Pacific – California soars beyond any expectations sold on Hollywood's silver screens.

More than anything, California is iconic. It was here that the hurly-burly gold rush kicked off in the mid-19th century, where poet-naturalist John Muir rhapsodized about the Sierra Nevada's 'range of light,' and where Jack Kerouac and the Beat Generation defined what it really means to hit the road.

California's multicultural melting pot has been cookin' since this bountiful promised land was staked out by Spain and Mexico. Today, waves of immigrants from around the world still look to find their own American dream on these palm-studded Pacific shores.

Come see the future in the making here in the Golden State.

When to Go

Los Angeles

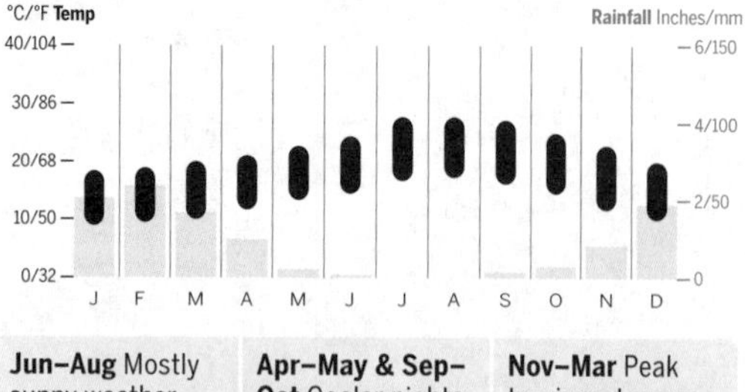

Jun–Aug Mostly sunny weather, occasional coastal fog; summer vacation crowds.

Apr–May & Sep–Oct Cooler nights, many cloudless days; travel bargains galore.

Nov–Mar Peak tourism at mountain ski resorts and in SoCal's warm deserts.

History

By the time European explorers arrived in the 16th century, more than 100,000 indigenous people called this land we now call California home. Spanish conquistadors combed through what they named Alta (Upper) California in search of a fabled 'city of gold,' but they left the territory virtually alone after failing to find it. Not until the Mission Period (1769–1833) did Spain make a serious attempt to settle the land, establishing 21 Catholic missions – many founded by Franciscan priest Junípero Serra – and presidios (military forts) to deter the British and Russians.

After winning independence from Spain in 1821, Mexico briefly ruled California, but got trounced by the fledgling United States in the Mexican-American War (1846–48). The discovery of gold just weeks before the Treaty of Guadalupe Hidalgo was signed saw the territory's nonindigenous population quintuple to 93,000 by 1850, when California became the 31st US state. Thousands of imported Chinese laborers helped complete the transcontinental railroad in 1869, which opened up markets and further spurred migration to the Golden State.

The 1906 San Francisco earthquake was barely a hiccup as California continued to grow exponentially in size, diversity and importance. Mexican immigrants streamed in during the 1910–20 Mexican Revolution, and again during WWII, to fill labor shortages. Military-driven industries developed during wartime, while anti-Asian sentiments led to the unjust internment of many Japanese Americans, including at Manzanar in the Eastern Sierra.

California has long been a social pioneer thanks to its size, confluence of wealth, diversity of immigration and technological innovation. Since the early 20th century, Hollywood has mesmerized the world with its cinematic dreams. Meanwhile, San Francisco reacted against the banal complacency of post-WWII suburbia with Beat poetry in the 1950s, hippie free love in the '60s and gay pride in the '70s.

California is not a finished work. Today's issues revolve around growth. In a state that has an economy bigger than Canada's and is the headquarters for cutting-edge industries, from space probes to biotechnology to Silicon Valley, the question of how to manage a burgeoning human population – with accompanying traffic gridlock, scarce affordable housing and the sky-high cost of living – is challenging.

Meanwhile, prisons are overflowing, state parks are underfunded and the conundrum of illegal immigration from Mexico, which fills a critical cheap labor shortage (especially in agriculture), vexes the state. Most worrying is California's extreme, years-long drought that shows no signs of abating, affecting farmers and urban dwellers alike with water shortages. In response, Governor Jerry Brown officially declared a state of emergency and instituted strict water-conservation measures statewide.

CALIFORNIA IN...

One Week

California in a nutshell: start in beachy **Los Angeles**, detouring to **Disneyland**. Head up the breezy Central Coast, stopping in **Santa Barbara** and **Big Sur**, before getting a dose of big-city culture in **San Francisco**. Head inland to nature's temple, **Yosemite National Park**, then zip back to LA.

Two Weeks

Follow the one-week itinerary above, but at a saner pace. Add jaunts to NorCal's **Wine Country**; **Lake Tahoe**, perched high in the Sierra Nevada; the bodacious beaches of **Orange County** and laid-back **San Diego**; or **Joshua Tree National Park**, near the chic desert resort of **Palm Springs**.

One Month

Do everything described above, and more. From San Francisco, head up the foggy North Coast, starting in Marin County at **Point Reyes National Seashore**. Stroll Victorian-era **Mendocino** and **Eureka**, find yourself on the **Lost Coast** and ramble through fern-filled **Redwood National & State Parks**. Inland, snap a postcard-perfect photo of **Mt Shasta**, drive through **Lassen Volcanic National Park** and ramble in California's historic **Gold Country**. Trace the backbone of the **Eastern Sierra** before winding down into otherworldly **Death Valley National Park**.

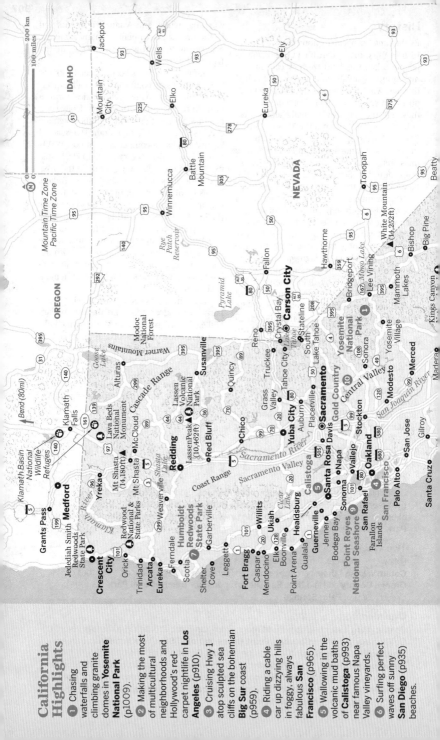

California Highlights

1. Chasing waterfalls and climbing granite domes in **Yosemite National Park** (p1009).
2. Making the most of multicultural neighborhoods and Hollywood's red-carpet nightlife in **Los Angeles** (p910).
3. Cruising Hwy 1 atop sculpted sea cliffs on the bohemian **Big Sur** coast (p959).
4. Riding a cable car up dizzying hills in foggy, always fabulous **San Francisco** (p965).
5. Wallowing in the volcanic mud baths of **Calistoga** (p993) near famous Napa Valley vineyards.
6. Surfing perfect waves off sunny **San Diego** (p935) beaches.

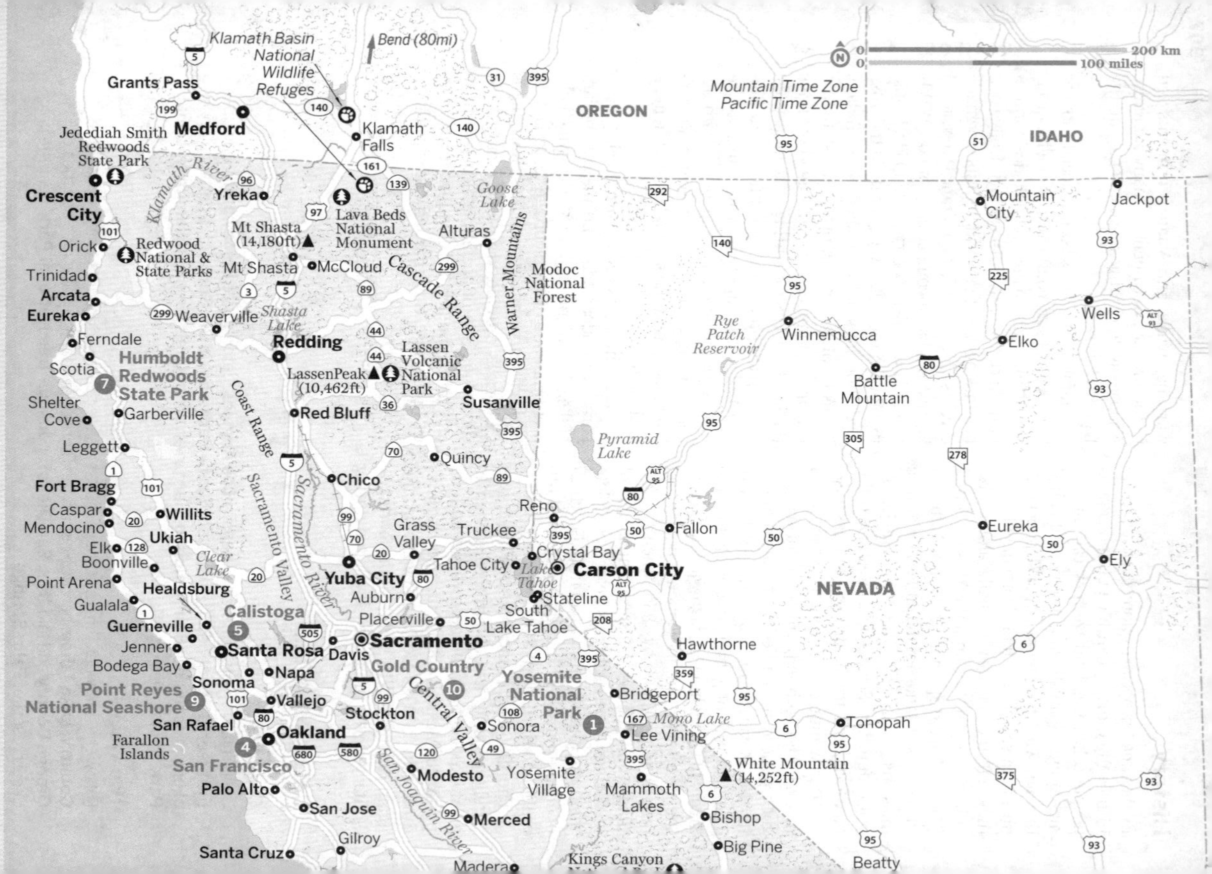

7 Craning your neck at the world's tallest trees along the Avenue of the Giants in **Humboldt Redwoods State Park** (p1000).

8 Trekking across sand dunes and uncovering Old West ghost towns in **Death Valley National Park** (p952).

9 Spotting whales, elephant seals and tule elk at wind-blown **Point Reyes National Seashore** (p991).

10 Dipping into swimming holes and panning like a forty-niner prospector in **Gold Country** (p1004).

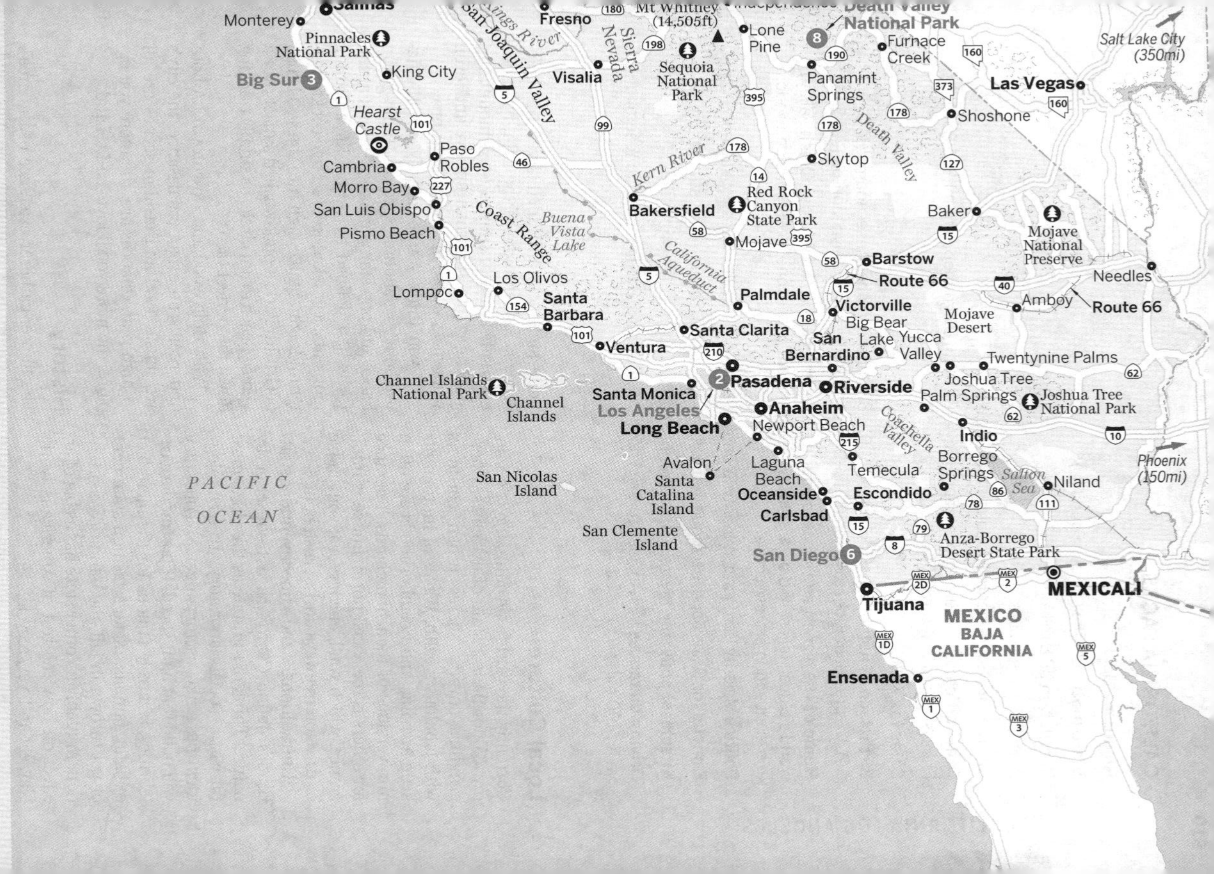

CALIFORNIA FACTS

Nickname Golden State

State motto Eureka ('I Have Found It')

Population 38.8 million

Area 155,779 sq miles

Capital city Sacramento (population 479,686)

Other cities Los Angeles (population 3,884,307), San Diego (population 1,355,896), San Francisco (population 837,442)

Sales tax 7.5%

Birthplace of Author John Steinbeck (1902–68), photographer Ansel Adams (1902–84), US president Richard Nixon (1913–94), pop-culture icon Marilyn Monroe (1926–62)

Home of The highest and lowest points in the contiguous US (Mt Whitney, Death Valley), world's oldest, tallest and biggest living trees (ancient bristlecone pines, coast redwoods and giant sequoias, respectively)

Politics Majority Democrat, minority Republican, one in five Californians vote independent

Famous for Disneyland, earthquakes, Hollywood, hippies, Silicon Valley, surfing

Kitschiest souvenir 'Mystery Spot' bumper sticker

Driving distances Los Angeles to San Francisco 380 miles, San Francisco to Yosemite Valley 190 miles

Local Culture

Currently the world's seventh-largest economy, California is a state of extremes, where grinding poverty shares urban corridors with fabulous wealth. Waves of immigrants keep arriving, and neighborhoods are often miniversions of their homelands. Tolerance for others is the social norm, but so is intolerance, which you'll encounter if you smoke or drive on freeways during rush hour.

Untraditional and unconventional attitudes define California, a trendsetter by nature. Think of the state as the USA's most futuristic social laboratory. If technology identifies a new useful gadget, Silicon Valley will build it at light speed. If postmodern celebrities, bizarrely famous for the mere fact of being famous, make a fashion statement or get thrown in jail, the nation pays attention. Arguably no other state has as big of an effect on how the rest of Americans work, play, eat and, yes, recycle.

LOS ANGELES

LA County represents the nation in extremes. Its people are among America's richest and poorest, most established and newest arrivals, most refined and roughest, most beautiful and most botoxed, most erudite and most airheaded. Even the landscape is a microcosm of the USA, from cinematic beaches to snow-dusted mountains, skyscrapers to suburban sprawl and even wilderness where mountain lions prowl.

If you think you've already got LA figured out – celebutantes, smog, traffic, bikini babes and pop-star wannabes – think again. LA is best defined by simple life-affirming moments: a cracked-ice, jazz-age cocktail after midnight, a hike high into the sagebrush of Griffith Park, a pink-washed sunset over a Venice Beach drum circle, or simply tracking down the perfect taco.

With Hollywood and Downtown LA both undergoing an urban renaissance, the city's art, music, food and fashion scenes are all in high gear. Chances are, the more you explore, the more you'll love 'La-La Land.'

History

The hunter-gatherer existence of the area's Gabrieleño and Chumash peoples ended with the arrival of Spanish missionaries and colonists in the late 18th century. Spain's first civilian settlement, El Pueblo de Nuestra Señora la Reina de Los Ángeles del Río de Porciúncula, remained an isolated farming outpost for decades after its founding in 1781. The city wasn't officially incorporated until 1850.

LA's population repeatedly swelled after the collapse of the California gold rush, the arrival of the transcontinental railroad, the growth of the citrus industry, the discovery of oil, the launch of the port of LA, the birth of the movie industry and the opening of the California Aqueduct. After WWII, the city's population doubled from nearly two million in 1950 to almost four million today.

Sights

A dozen miles inland from the Pacific, Downtown LA combines history and highbrow arts and culture. Hip-again Hollywood awaits northwest of Downtown, while urban-designer chic and gay pride rule West Hollywood. South of WeHo, Museum Row is Mid-City's main draw. Further west are ritzy Beverly Hills, Westwood near the University of California, Los Angeles (UCLA) campus and West LA. Beach towns include kid-friendly Santa Monica, boho Venice, star-powered Malibu and busy Long Beach. Leafy Pasadena lies northeast of Downtown.

Downtown

For decades, LA's historic core and main business and government district emptied out on nights and weekends. No more. Crowds fill fine-arts performance and pop-entertainment venues, and young professionals and artists have moved into lofts, bringing bars, restaurants and art galleries. Downtown is most easily explored on foot, combined with short Metro Rail and DASH minibus rides. Parking lots are cheapest around Little Tokyo and Chinatown.

El Pueblo de Los Angeles & Around

Compact, colorful and car free, this historic district immerses you in LA's Spanish-Mexican roots. Its spine is festive **Olvera St** (Map p914; www.calleolvera.com; 👪), where you can snap up handmade folkloric trinkets, then chomp on tacos and sugar-sprinkled churros.

'New' **Chinatown** (Map p914; www.chinatownla.com) is about a half mile north along Broadway and Hill St, crammed with dim-sum parlors, herbal apothecaries, curio shops and Chung King Rd's edgy art galleries.

La Plaza de Cultura y Artes MUSEUM
(Map p914; ☎213-542-6200; www.lapca.org; 501 N Main St; ⏰noon-5pm Mon, Wed & Thu, to 6pm Fri-Sun) FREE This museum chronicles the Mexican-American experience in Los Angeles, from the Mexican-American War when the border crossed the original pueblo, to the Zoot Suit Riots to Cesar Chavez and the Chicana movement.

Avila Adobe MUSEUM
(Map p914; ☎213-628-1274; http://elpueblo.lacity.org; Olvera St; ⏰9am-4pm) FREE The oldest surviving house in LA was built in 1818 by a wealthy ranchero and one-time LA mayor, and later became a boarding house and (restaurant. Restored and furnished in heavy

LOS ANGELES IN...

Distances are ginormous in LA, so allow extra time for traffic and don't try to pack too much into a day.

One Day

Fuel up for the day at the **Original Farmers Market**, then go star-searching on the **Hollywood Walk of Fame** along Hollywood Blvd. Up your chances of spotting actual celebs by hitting the fashion-forward boutiques on paparazzi-infested **Robertson Boulevard**, or get a dose of nature at **Griffith Park**. Then drive west to the lofty **Getty Center** or head out to the **Venice Boardwalk** to see the seaside sideshow. Catch a Pacific sunset in **Santa Monica**.

Two Days

Explore rapidly evolving Downtown LA. Dig up the city's roots at **El Pueblo de Los Angeles**, then catapult to the future at dramatic **Walt Disney Concert Hall** topping Grand Ave's **Cultural Corridor**. Walk off lunch ambling between Downtown's historic buildings, **Arts District** galleries and **Little Tokyo**. At South Park's glitzy **LA Live** entertainment center, romp through the multimedia **Grammy Museum**, then join real-life celebs cheering on the LA Lakers next door at the **Staples Center**. After dark, hit the dance floor at clubs in **Hollywood**.

Greater Los Angeles

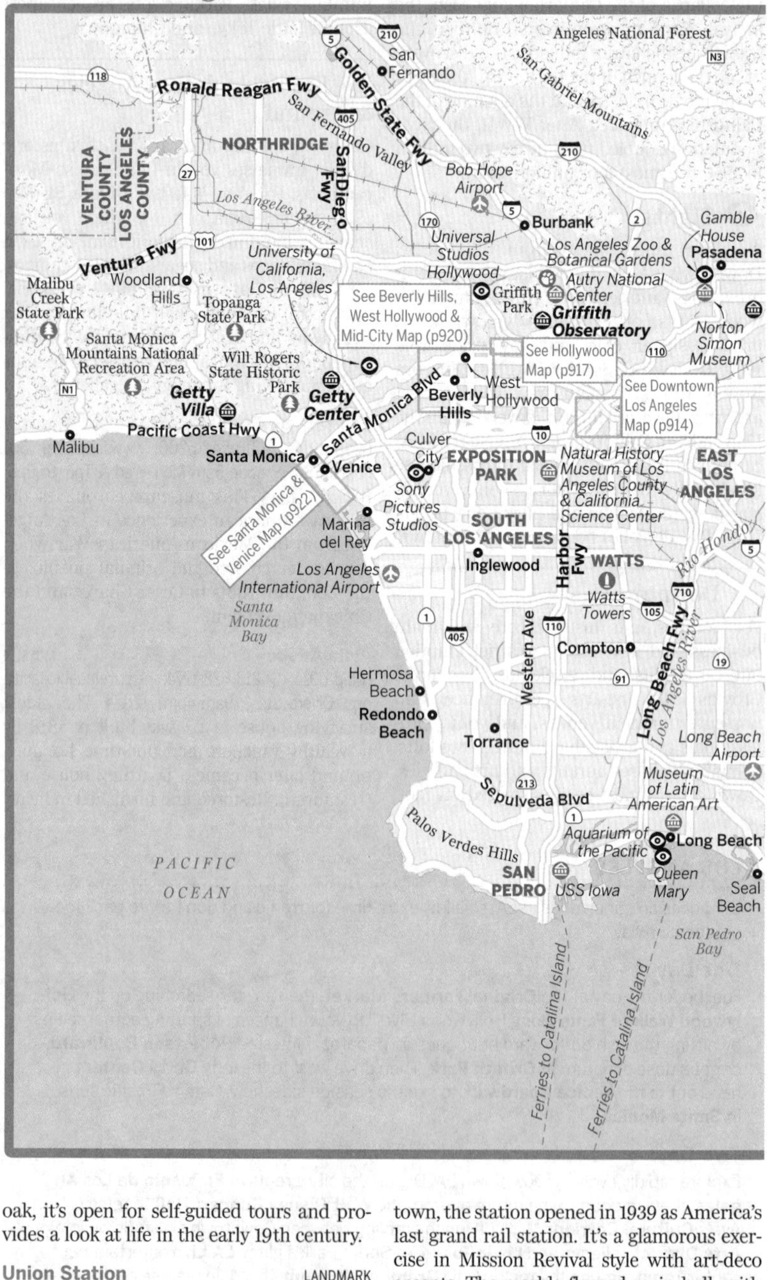

oak, it's open for self-guided tours and provides a look at life in the early 19th century.

Union Station LANDMARK

(Map p914; www.amtrak.com; 800 N Alameda St; P) Built on the site of LA's original Chinatown, the station opened in 1939 as America's last grand rail station. It's a glamorous exercise in Mission Revival style with art-deco accents. The marble-floored main hall, with cathedral ceilings, original leather chairs and grand chandeliers, is breathtaking.

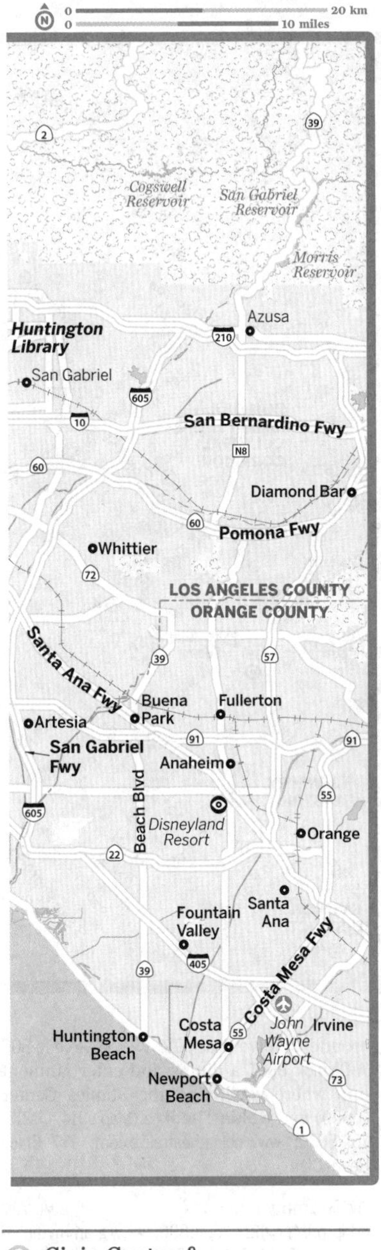

Civic Center & Cultural Corridor

★**Walt Disney Concert Hall** BUILDING
(Map p914; info 213-972-7211, tickets 323-850-2000; www.laphil.org; 111 S Grand Ave; guided tours usually noon & 1pm Tue-Sat; P) FREE A molten blend of steel, music and psychedelic architecture, this iconic concert venue is the home base of the Los Angeles Philharmonic, but has also hosted contemporary bands such as Phoenix and classic jazz men like Sonny Rollins. Frank Gehry pulled out all the stops: the building is a gravity-defying sculpture of heaving and billowing stainless steel.

Museum of Contemporary Art MUSEUM
(MOCA; Map p914; 213-626-6222; www.moca.org; 250 S Grand Ave; adult/child $12/free, 5-8pm Thu free; 11am-5pm Mon & Fri, to 8pm Thu, to 6pm Sat & Sun) A collection that arcs from the 1940s to the present and includes works by Mark Rothko, Dan Flavin, Joseph Cornell and other big-shot contemporary artists is housed in a postmodern building by Arata Isozaki. Galleries are below ground, yet sky-lit bright.

Cathedral of Our Lady of the Angels CHURCH
(Map p914; 213-680-5200; www.olacathedral.org; 555 W Temple St; 6:30am-6pm Mon-Fri, from 9am Sat, from 7am Sun; P) FREE José Rafael Moneo mixed Gothic proportions with contemporary design for his 2002 Cathedral of Our Lady of the Angels, which exudes a calming serenity achieved by soft light filtering through its alabaster panes. Wall-sized tapestries as detailed as a Michelangelo fresco festoon the main nave.

City Hall LANDMARK
(Map p914; 213-978-1995; www.lacity.org; 200 N Spring St; 9am-5pm Mon-Fri) FREE Until 1966 no LA building stood taller than the 1928 City Hall, which appeared in the *Superman* TV series and 1953 sci-fi thriller *War of the Worlds*. On clear days you'll have views of the city, the mountains and several decades of Downtown growth from the observation deck.

Little Tokyo

Little Tokyo swirls with shopping arcades, Buddhist temples, traditional gardens, authentic sushi bars and noodle shops, and a provocative branch of **MOCA** (Map p914; 213-626-6222; www.moca.org; 152 N Central Ave; adult/child/student 12yr & under $12/free/7; 11am-5pm Mon & Fri, to 8pm Thu, to 6pm Sat & Sun).

Japanese American National Museum MUSEUM
(Map p914; 213-625-0414; www.janm.org; 100 N Central Ave; adult/child $9/5; 11am-5pm Tue-Wed & Fri-Sun, noon-8pm Thu) A great first

Downtown Los Angeles

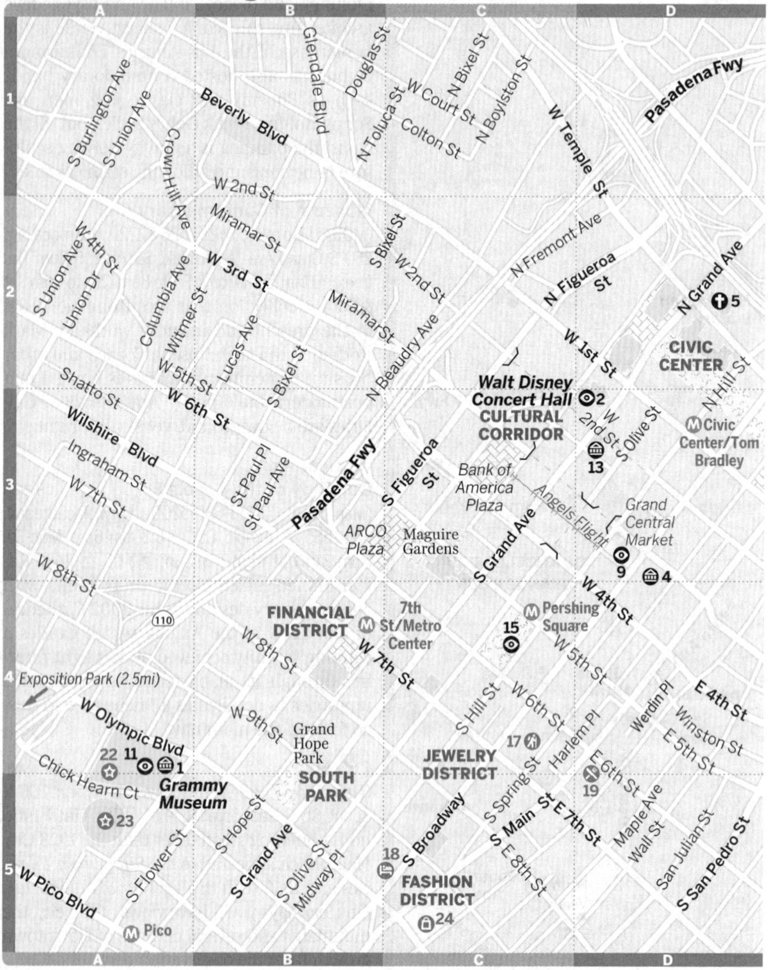

stop in Little Tokyo, this is the country's first museum dedicated to the Japanese immigrant experience. You'll be moved by galleries dealing with the painful chapter of the WWII internment camps. Afterward relax in the tranquil garden, and browse the well-stocked gift shop. Admission is free on Thursdays from 5pm to 8pm, and all day on the third Thursday of each month.

South Park

South Park isn't actually a park but an emerging Downtown LA neighborhood around **LA Live** (Map p914; www.lalive.com; 800 W Olympic Blvd), a dining and entertainment hub where you'll find the Staples Center (p929) and **Nokia Theatre** (Map p914; ☎213-763-6030; www.nokiatheatrelive.com; 777 Chick Hearn Ct).

★Grammy Museum MUSEUM

(Map p914; ☎213-765-6800; www.grammymuseum.org; 800 W Olympic Blvd; adult/child $13/11, after 6pm $8; ⏰11:30am-7:30pm Mon-Fri, from 10am Sat & Sun; 👪) It's the highlight of LA Live. Music lovers will get lost in interactive exhibits, which define, differentiate and link

Downtown Los Angeles

Top Sights
1 Grammy Museum....A4
2 Walt Disney Concert Hall....D3

Sights
3 Avila Adobe....E2
4 Bradbury Building....D3
5 Cathedral of Our Lady of the Angels....D2
6 Chinatown....E2
7 City Hall....E3
8 Geffen Contemporary at MOCA....E3
9 Grand Central Market....D3
10 Japanese American National Museum....E4
11 LA Live....A4
12 La Plaza de Cultura y Artes....E2
13 Museum of Contemporary Art....D3
14 Olvera Street....E2
15 Pershing Square....C4
16 Union Station....F3

Activities, Courses & Tours
17 Downtown Art Walk....C4

Sleeping
18 Ace Hotel....C5

Eating
19 Cole's....D4
20 Sushi Gen....E4

Drinking & Nightlife
21 Angel City Brewery....E4

Entertainment
22 Nokia Theatre....A4
23 Staples Center....A5
United Artists Theatre....(see 18)

Shopping
24 Fashion District....C5
25 Raggedy Threads....E4

musical genres, while live footage strobes. You can glimpse such things as Guns N' Roses' bass drum, Lester Young's tenor sax, Yo Yo Ma's cello and Michael's glove (though exhibits and collections do rotate).

Exposition Park & Around

Just south of the University of Southern California (USC) campus, this park has a full day's worth of kid-friendly museums. Outdoor landmarks include the **Rose Garden** (www.laparks.org; 701 State Dr; 9am-sunset Mar 16–Dec 31) FREE and the **Los Angeles Memorial Coliseum**, site of the 1932 and 1984 Summer Olympic Games.

Parking costs around $10. From Downtown, take the Metro Expo Line or DASH minibus F.

Natural History Museum of Los Angeles MUSEUM
(213-763-3466; www.nhm.org; 900 Exposition Blvd; adult/child/student & senior $12/5/9; 9:30am-5pm;) Dinos to diamonds, bears to beetles, hissing roaches to African elephants – this museum will take you around the world and back, across millions of years in time. It's all housed in a beautiful 1913 Spanish Renaissance–style building that

stood in for Columbia University in the first Toby McGuire *Spider-Man* movie – yup, this was where Peter Parker was bitten by the radioactive arachnid.

California Science Center MUSEUM
(film schedule 213-744-2109, info 323-724-3623; www.californiasciencecenter.org; 700 Exposition Park Dr; IMAX movie adult/child $8.25/5; 10am-5pm;) FREE A simulated earthquake, baby chicks hatching and a giant techno-doll named Tess bring out the kid in all of us at this multimedia museum with plenty of buttons to push, lights to switch on and knobs to pull. Don't miss seeing the space shuttle *Endeavour*, which requires a timed-ticket reservation (fee $2)

Watts Towers LANDMARK
(213-847-4646; www.wattstowers.us; 1761-1765 E 107th St; adult/child under 13yr/child 13-17yr & senior $7/free/$3; 11am-3pm Fri, 10:30am-3pm Sat, 12:30-3pm Sun; P) The fabulous Watts Towers rank among the world's greatest monuments of folk art. In 1921 Italian immigrant Simon Rodia set out 'to make something big' and then spent 33 years cobbling together this whimsical free-form sculpture from a motley assortment of found objects, from green 7-Up bottles to sea shells, and rocks to pottery.

Hollywood

Just as aging movie stars get the occasional face-lift, so has Hollywood. While it still hasn't recaptured its mid-20th-century 'Golden Age' glamour, its contemporary seediness is disappearing. The **Hollywood Walk of Fame** (Map p917; www.walkoffame.com; Hollywood Blvd) honors more than 2400 celebrities with stars embedded in the sidewalk.

The Metro Red Line stops beneath **Hollywood & Highland** (Map p917; www.hollywoodandhighland.com; 6801 Hollywood Blvd; 10am-10pm Mon-Sat, to 7pm Sun) FREE, a multistory mall with nicely framed views of the hillside **Hollywood Sign**, erected in 1923 as an advertisement for a land development called Hollywoodland. Two-hour validated mall parking costs $2 (daily maximum $15).

TCL Chinese Theatre LANDMARK
(Map p917; 323-463-9576; www.tclchinesetheatres.com; 6925 Hollywood Blvd; tours & movie tickets adult/child/senior $13.50/6.50/11.50) Ever wondered what it's like to be in George Clooney's shoes? Just find his footprints in the forecourt of this world-famous movie palace. The exotic pagoda theater – complete with temple bells and stone heaven dogs from China – has shown movies since 1927 when Cecil B DeMille's *The King of Kings* first flickered across the screen.

Hollywood Museum MUSEUM
(Map p917; 323-464-7776; www.thehollywoodmuseum.com; 1660 N Highland Ave; adult/child $15/5; 10am-5pm Wed-Sun) We quite like this musty temple to the stars, crammed with kitsch posters, costumes and rotating props. The museum is housed inside the handsome 1914 art-deco Max Factor Building, where the make-up pioneer once worked his magic on Marilyn Monroe and Judy Garland.

Dolby Theatre THEATER
(Map p917; www.dolbytheatre.com; 6801 Hollywood Blvd; tours adult/child, senior & student $19/15; 10:30am-4pm) The Academy Awards are handed out at the Dolby Theatre, which has

HISTORIC DOWNTOWN LOS ANGELES

At the center of Downtown's historic district, **Pershing Square** (Map p914; www.laparks.org; 532 S Olive St) was LA's first public park (1866). Now encircled by high-rises, the park exhibits public art and hosts summer concerts and outdoor movie nights.

Nearby, some of LA's turn-of-the-last century architecture remains as it once was. Pop into the 1893 **Bradbury Building** (Map p914; www.laconservancy.org; 304 S Broadway; lobby usually 9am-5pm), the dazzling galleried atrium of which has had a cameo in several hit movies, including *Blade Runner*, *(500) Days of Summer* and *The Artist*.

In the early 20th century, Broadway was a glamorous shopping and theater strip, where megastars like Charlie Chaplin leapt from limos to attend premieres at lavish movie palaces. Some – such as the 1927 **United Artists Theatre** (Map p914; 213-623-3233; www.acehotel.com/losangeles/theatre; 929 S Broadway) – have been restored and once again host film screenings and live shows. Otherwise, take a weekend walking tour (reservations advised) with the **Los Angeles Conservancy** (info 213-430-4219, reservations 213-623-2489; www.laconservancy.org; adult/child $10/5).

Hollywood

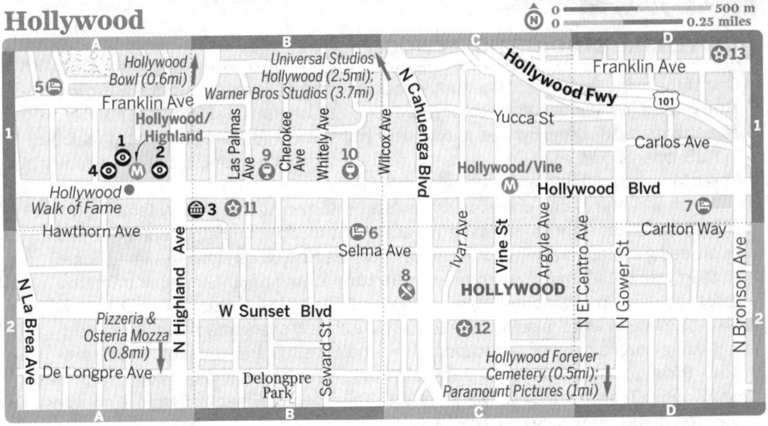

also hosted the American Idol finale, the ESPY awards, the Miss USA pageant and a recent Neil Young residency. On the tour you get to sniff around the auditorium, admire a VIP room and see an Oscar statuette up close.

Hollywood Forever Cemetery CEMETERY
(323-469-1181; www.hollywoodforever.com; 6000 Santa Monica Blvd; 8am-5pm; P) Next to Paramount, Hollywood Forever boasts lavish landscaping, over-the-top tombstones, epic mausoleums and a roll call of departed superstars. Residents include Cecil B DeMille, Rudolph Valentino, femme fatale Jayne Mansfield and punk-rock icons Johnny and Dee Dee Ramone. For a full list of residents, pick up a map ($5) at the flower shop (open from 9am to 5pm).

Griffith Park

America's largest urban **park** (323-913-4688; www.laparks.org/dos/parks/griffithpk; 4730 Crystal Springs Dr; 5am-10:30pm, trails sunrise-sunset; P) FREE is five times the size of New York's Central Park, with an outdoor theater, zoo, observatory, museum, merry-go-round, antique and miniature trains, children's playgrounds, golf, tennis and over 50 miles of hiking paths, including to the original *Batman* TV series cave.

★ **Griffith Observatory** MUSEUM
(213-473-0800; www.griffithobservatory.org; 2800 E Observatory Rd; planetarium shows adult/child $7/3; noon-10pm Tue-Fri, from 10am Sat & Sun; P) FREE This landmark 1935 observatory opens a window onto the universe from its perch on the southern slopes of Mt Hollywood. Its planetarium boasts the world's most advanced star projector. Astronomical touch displays cover the evolution of the telescope and the ultraviolet x-rays used to map our solar system. We loved the camera obscura on the main floor.

Hollywood

Sights

1 Dolby Theatre A1
Egyptian Theatre .... (see 11)
2 Hollywood & Highland A1
3 Hollywood Museum B1
4 TCL Chinese Theatre A1

Activities, Courses & Tours

TMZ Tours .... (see 4)

Sleeping

5 Magic Castle Hotel A1
6 USA Hostels Hollywood B2
7 Vibe Hotel D1

Eating

8 Life Food Organic C2

Drinking & Nightlife

9 Musso & Frank Grill B1
10 No Vacancy B1

Entertainment

11 American Cinematheque B1
12 Arclight Cinemas C2
13 Upright Citizens Brigade Theatre D1

Information

Hollywood Visitor Information Center .... (see 2)

DON'T MISS

UNIVERSAL STUDIOS HOLLYWOOD

One of the world's oldest continuously operating movie studios, **Universal Studios Hollywood** (www.universalstudioshollywood.com; 100 Universal City Plaza, Universal City; admission from $87, under 3yr free; ⌚ open daily, hours vary; P 🚸) first opened to the public in 1915, when studio head Carl Laemmle invited visitors at a quaint 25¢ each (including a boxed lunch) to watch silent films being made.

Nearly a century later, Universal presents an entertaining mix of fairly tame – and sometimes dated – thrills, including live-action shows, rides and attractions. The chances of seeing any action, however, let alone a real-life Hollywood star, are slim to none.

Start with the 45-minute narrated **studio tour** aboard a giant, multicar tram that takes you past working soundstages, outdoor sets and **King Kong 360 3-D**, the world's biggest 3D experience. Also prepare to survive a cheesy shark attack à la *Jaws*.

Among dozens of other attractions, take a motion-simulated romp on **The Simpsons Ride**, splash down among **Jurassic Park – The Ride** dinosaurs or fight off Decepticons in **Transformers: The Ride 3-D**. The **Special Effects Stage** illuminates the craft of movie-making up close.

Self-parking costs from $17 (after 3pm from $10). Free park shuttle buses connect with the Metro Red Line.

Los Angeles Zoo & Botanical Gardens ZOO
(☎323-644-4200; www.lazoo.org; 5333 Zoo Dr; adult/child/senior $18/13/15; ⌚10am-5pm, closed Christmas; P 🚸) The Los Angeles Zoo, with its 1100 finned, feathered and furry friends from over 250 species, rarely fails to enthrall the little ones. What began in 1912 as a refuge for retired circus animals now brings in over a million visitors each year.

Autry National Center MUSEUM
(☎323-667-2000; www.autrynationalcenter.org; 4700 Western Heritage Way; adult/child/senior & student $10/4/6, 2nd Tue each month free; ⌚10am-4pm Tue-Fri, to 5pm Sat & Sun; P) Want to know how the West was really won? Then mosey over to this excellent museum – its exhibits on the good, the bad and the ugly of America's westward expansion rope in even the most reluctant cowpokes. Kids can pan for gold and explore a stagecoach. Year-round gallery talks, symposia, film screenings and other cultural events spur the intellect.

West Hollywood & Mid-City

In WeHo, rainbow flags fly proudly over Santa Monica Blvd, while celebs keep gossip rags happy by misbehaving at clubs on the fabled **Sunset Strip**. Boutiques along Robertson Blvd and Melrose Ave purvey sassy and ultrachic fashions for Hollywood royalty and celebutantes. WeHo's also a hotbed of cutting-edge interior design, fashion and art, particularly in the **West Hollywood Design District** (http://westhollywooddesigndistrict.com). Further south, some of LA's best museums line Mid-City's **Museum Row** along Wilshire Blvd east of Fairfax Ave.

★**Los Angeles County Museum of Art** MUSEUM
(LACMA; Map p920; ☎323-857-6000; www.lacma.org; 5905 Wilshire Blvd; adult/child $15/free; ⌚11am-5pm Mon, Tue & Thu, to 9pm Fri, 10am-7pm Sat & Sun; P) LA's premier art museum, LACMA's galleries are stuffed with all the major players – Rembrandt, Cézanne, Magritte, Mary Cassat, Ansel Adams, to name a few – plus several millennia worth of ceramics from China, woodblock prints from Japan, pre-Columbian art, and ancient sculpture from Greece, Rome and Egypt.

Page Museum & La Brea Tar Pits MUSEUM
(Map p920; www.tarpits.org; 5801 Wilshire Blvd; adult/child/student & senior $12/5/9, 1st Tue of month Sep-Jun free; ⌚9:30am-5pm; P 🚸) Mammoths and saber-toothed cats used to roam LA's savannah in prehistoric times. We know this because of an archaeological trove of skulls and bones unearthed at La Brea Tar Pits, one of the world's most fecund and famous fossil sites.

Beverly Hills & the Westside

The mere mention of Beverly Hills conjures images of Maseratis, manicured mansions and megarich moguls. Take a saunter along pricey, pretentious **Rodeo Drive**, a three-block ribbon where sample-size fembots browse for fashions from international houses of couture. **Via Rodeo** is a cobbled lane lined with outdoor cafes for primo people-watching.

Several municipal lots and garages in downtown Beverly Hills offer two hours of free parking.

★Getty Center MUSEUM
(☎310-440-7300; www.getty.edu; 1200 Getty Center Dr, off I-405 Fwy; ⏲10am-5:30pm Tue-Fri & Sun, to 9pm Sat; P) FREE In its billion-dollar, in-the-clouds perch, high above the city grit and grime, the Getty Center presents triple delights: a stellar art collection (everything from Renaissance artists to David Hockney), Richard Meier's cutting-edge architecture, and the visual splendor of seasonally changing gardens. Admission is free, but parking is $15 ($10 after 5pm).

Paley Center for Media MUSEUM
(Map p920; ☎310-786-1000; www.paleycenter.org; 465 N Beverly Dr; suggested donation adult/child $10/5; ⏲noon-5pm Wed-Sun; P) The main lure here is the mind-boggling archive of TV and radio broadcasts dating to 1918. The Beatles' US debut on the *Ed Sullivan Show*? The moon landing? The *All In The Family* pilot? All here. Plus, two theaters for screenings and discussions with the casts of shows such as the great *Key & Peele* and *How I Met Your Mother*.

Hammer Museum MUSEUM
(http://hammer.ucla.edu; 10899 Wilshire Blvd; ⏲11am-8pm Tue-Fri, to 5pm Sat & Sun) FREE Once a vanity project of the late oil tycoon Armand Hammer, his eponymous museum has become a widely respected art space. Selections from Hammer's personal collection include relatively minor works by Monet, Van Gogh and Mary Cassat, but the museum really shines when it comes to cutting-edge contemporary exhibits featuring local, under-represented and controversial artists. Best of all, it's free.

Malibu

Hugging 27 spectacular miles of the Pacific Coast Hwy, Malibu has long been synonymous with surfing and Hollywood stars, but it actually looks far less posh than glossy tabloids make it sound. Still, it has been celebrity central since the 1930s. Many A-listers have homes here, and can sometimes be spotted shopping at the villagelike **Malibu Country Mart** (www.malibucountrymart.com; 3835 Cross Creek Rd).

One of Malibu's natural treasures is mountainous **Malibu Creek State Park** (www.parks.ca.gov; Las Virgenes/Malibu Canyon Rd), a popular movie and TV filming location with hiking trails galore (parking $12). A string of famous beaches include aptly named **Surfrider** near Malibu Pier, secretive **El Matador**, family fave **Zuma Beach** and wilder **Point Dume** (beach parking $3 to $12.50).

★Getty Villa MUSEUM
(☎310-430-7300; www.getty.edu; 17985 Pacific Coast Hwy; ⏲10am-5pm Wed-Mon; P) FREE Although self-described as the Getty Villa Malibu, this famous museum in a replica 1st-century Roman villa is actually in Pacific Palisades. It's a stunning 64-acre showcase for exquisite Greek, Roman and Etruscan antiquities amassed by oil tycoon J Paul Getty. Admission requires a timed ticket, reservable online; parking costs $15.

Santa Monica

The belle by the beach mixes urban cool with a laid-back vibe. Tourists, teens and street performers throng car-free, chain-store-lined **Third Street Promenade**. For more local flavor, shop posh **Montana Avenue** or eclectic **Main Street**, backbone of the neighborhood once nicknamed 'Dogtown,' the birthplace of skateboard culture.

There's free 90-minute parking in most public garages downtown.

Santa Monica Pier LANDMARK
(Map p922; ☎310-458-8900; www.santamonicapier.org; 👪) Once the very end of the mythical Route 66, and still the object of a tourist love affair, the Santa Monica Pier dates back to 1908, and is the city's most compelling landmark. There are arcades, carnival games, a vintage carousel, a Ferris wheel, a roller coaster and an aquarium, and the pier comes alive with free concerts (Twilight Dance Series) and outdoor movies in the summertime.

Venice

The **Venice Boardwalk** (Ocean Front Walk) is a freak show, a human zoo, a wacky carnival and an essential LA experience. This cauldron of counterculture is the place to get your hair braided and a qigong back massage, or pick up a Rastafarian-colored knit beret. Encounters with bodybuilders, a Speedo-clad snake charmer or a roller-

Beverly Hills, West Hollywood & Mid-City

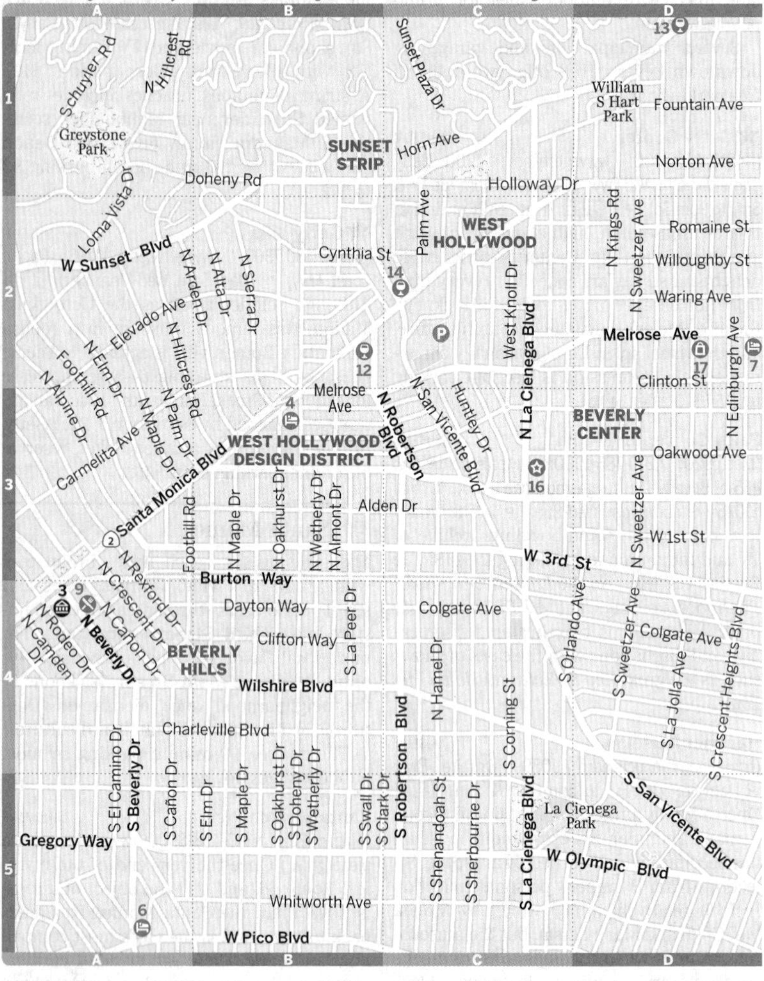

skating Sikh minstrel are possible, especially on sunny afternoons.

To escape the hubbub, meander inland to the **Venice Canals**, a vestige of Venice's early days when Italian gondoliers poled tourists along artificial waterways. Funky, hipper-than-ever **Abbot Kinney Blvd** is a palm-lined mile of restaurants, cafes, art galleries and eclectic shops selling vintage furniture and handmade fashions.

There's street parking near Abbot Kinney Blvd. Beach parking lots cost $4 to $18.

Long Beach

Long Beach stretches along LA County's southern flank, harboring the world's third-busiest container port after Singapore and Hong Kong. Its industrial edge has been worn smooth downtown – **Pine Ave** is chockablock with restaurants and bars – and along the restyled waterfront.

The Metro Blue Line connects Downtown LA with Long Beach in under an hour. **Passport** (www.lbtransit.com) minibuses shuttle around major tourist sights for free.

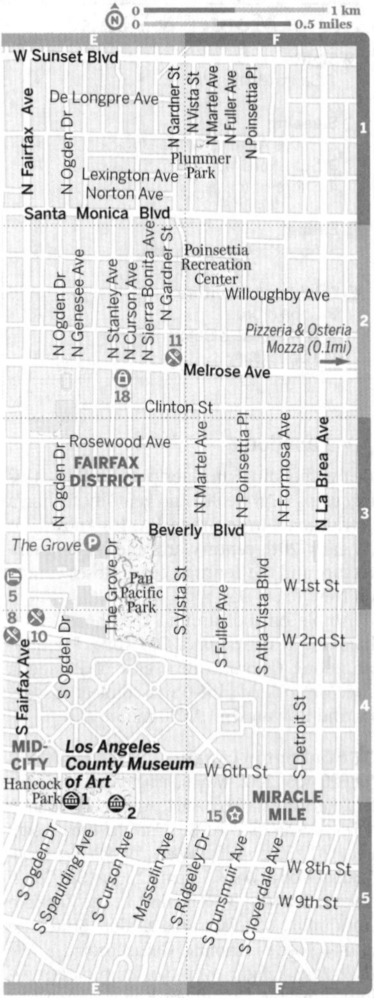

Beverly Hills, West Hollywood & Mid-City

Top Sights
1 Los Angeles County Museum of Art .. E4

Sights
2 Page Museum & La Brea Tar Pits E5
3 Paley Center for Media A4

Sleeping
4 Beverly Terrace Hotel B3
5 Farmer's Daughter Hotel E3
6 Mr C A5
7 Pali Hotel D2

Eating
8 Mercado E4
9 Nate'n Al A4
10 Original Farmers Market E4
11 Pingtung E2

Drinking & Nightlife
12 Abbey B2
13 Bar Marmont D1
14 Micky's C2

Entertainment
15 El Rey F5
16 Largo at the Coronet C3

Shopping
17 Fred Segal D2
18 Melrose Avenue E2

Aquarium of the Pacific AQUARIUM
(tickets 562-590-3100; www.aquariumofpacific.org; 100 Aquarium Way; adult/child/senior $29/15/26; 9am-6pm;) Long Beach's most mesmerizing experience, the Aquarium of the Pacific is a vast, high-tech indoor ocean where sharks dart, jellyfish dance and sea lions frolic. More than 12,000 creatures inhabit four re-created habitats: the bays and lagoons of Baja California, the frigid northern Pacific, the coral reefs of the tropics, and local kelp forests. Parking costs $8.

Queen Mary BOAT
(www.queenmary.com; 1126 Queens Hwy; tours adult/child from $26/15; 10am-6:30pm; P) Long Beach's 'flagship' attraction is this grand and supposedly haunted British luxury liner. Larger and more luxurious than even the *Titanic,* she transported royals, dignitaries, immigrants, WWII troops and vacationers between 1936 and 1966. Sure, it's a tourist trap, but study the memorabilia, and you may envision dapper gents escorting ladies in gowns to the art-deco lounge for cocktails or to the sumptuous Grand Salon for dinner.

USS Iowa MUSEUM, MEMORIAL
(877-446-9261; www.pacificbattleship.com; 250 S Harbor Blvd, Berth 87; adult/child $18/10; 10am-5pm, from 9am Jun-Aug; P) Step onto the gangway and take a self-guided audio tour of this retired Pacific battleship, which transported Franklin D Roosevelt (FDR) and General Douglas MacArthur during WWII and saw action in the Cold War and beyond. Hourly parking is $1.

Santa Monica & Venice

Santa Monica & Venice

Sights
1 Santa Monica Pier...A2

Sleeping
2 HI Los Angeles-Santa Monica...A2
3 Sea Shore Motel...A3
4 Shore Hotel...A2

Eating
5 Abbot's Pizza Company...B5

Drinking & Nightlife
6 Copa d'Oro...A2
7 Townhouse & Delmonte Speakeasy...A5

Museum of Latin American Art MUSEUM
(www.molaa.org; 628 Alamitos Ave; adult/child/senior & student $9/free/6, Sun free; 11am-5pm Wed, Thu, Sat & Sun, to 9pm Fri; P) This gem of a museum presents a rare survey of Latin American art created since 1945. Cecilia Míguez' whimsical bronze statuettes, Eduardo Kingman's wrenching portraits of indigenous people and Arnaldo Roche Rabel's intensely spiritual abstracts are among the many outstanding pieces in the permanent collection.

Pasadena

Below the lofty San Gabriel Mountains, this city drips with wealth and gentility, feeling a world apart from urban LA. It's known for its early 20th-century arts-and-crafts architecture and the Tournament of Roses Parade on New Year's Day.

Amble on foot around the shops, cafes, bars and restaurants of **Old Town Pasadena**, along Colorado Blvd east of Pasadena Ave. Metro Gold Line trains connect Pasadena and Downtown LA (20 minutes).

★**Huntington Library** MUSEUM, GARDENS
(626-405-2100; www.huntington.org; 1151 Oxford Rd, San Marino; adult weekday/weekend & holidays $23/25, child $10, 1st Thu each month free; 10:30am-4:30pm Wed-Mon Jun-Aug, noon-4:30pm Mon & Wed-Fri, from 10:30am Sat, Sun & holidays Sep-May; P) Unwind in the Zen-like tranquillity of a Japanese garden. Study the jaunty pose of Thomas Gainsborough's *The Blue Boy*. Linger over the illuminated vellum of a 1455 Gutenberg Bible. It's hard to know where to start exploring this genteel country estate, the legacy of railroad tycoon Henry Huntington, and one of the most delightful and inspirational spots in LA.

Advance tickets are required for free day admission.

Gamble House ARCHITECTURE
(info 626-793-3334, tickets 800-979-3370; www.gamblehouse.org; 4 Westmoreland Pl, Pasadena; tours adult/child $15/free; tours noon-3pm Thu-Sun, gift shop 10am-5pm Tue-Sat, 11:30am-5pm Sun; P) It's the exquisite attention to detail that impresses most at the Gamble House,

a 1908 masterpiece of arts-and-crafts architecture built by Charles and Henry Greene for Procter & Gamble–heir David Gamble. The entire home is a work of art, its foundation, furniture and fixtures all united by a common design and theme inspired by its Southern California environs.

Norton Simon Museum MUSEUM
(www.nortonsimon.org; 411 W Colorado Blvd, Pasadena; adult/child $10/free; noon-5pm Mon, Wed & Thu, 11am-8pm Fri-Sat; P) Rodin's *The Thinker* is only a mind-teasing overture to the full symphony of art in store at this exquisite museum. Norton Simon (1907–93) was an entrepreneur with a Midas touch and a passion for art who parlayed his millions into a respectable collection of Western art and Asian sculpture.

Activities

Cycling & In-line Skating

Get scenic exercise pedaling or skating along the paved **South Bay Bicycle Trail**, which parallels the beach for most of the 22 miles between Santa Monica and Pacific Palisades. Rental shops are plentiful in busy beach towns. Warning: it's crowded on weekends.

Hiking

Turn on your celeb radar while strutting it with the hot bods along **Runyon Canyon Park** above Hollywood. **Griffith Park** is also laced with trails. For longer rambles, head to the Santa Monica Mountains, where **Will Rogers State Historic Park**, **Topanga State Park** and **Malibu Creek State Park** are all excellent gateways to beautiful terrain (parking $8 to $12).

Swimming & Surfing

Top beaches for swimming are Malibu's **Leo Carrillo State Park**, **Santa Monica State Beach** and the South Bay's **Hermosa Beach**. Malibu's **Surfrider Beach** is a legendary surfing spot. Parking rates vary seasonally.

'Endless summer' is, sorry to report, a myth; much of the year you'll want a wet suit in the Pacific. Water temperatures become tolerable by June and peak just under 70°F (21°C) in August. Water quality varies; check the 'Beach Report Card' at http://brc.healthebay.org.

Tours

★Esotouric BUS TOUR
(323-223-2767; www.esotouric.com; tours $58) Discover LA's lurid and fascinating underbelly on these offbeat, insightful and entertaining walking and bus tours themed around famous crime sites (Black Dahlia anyone?), literary lions (Chandler to Bukowski) and more.

Dearly Departed BUS TOUR
(855-600-3323; www.dearlydepartedtours.com; tours $48-75) This long-running, occasionally creepy, frequently hilarious tour will clue you in on where celebs kicked the bucket, George Michael dropped his trousers, Hugh Grant received certain services and the Charles Manson gang murdered Sharon Tate. Not for kids.

TMZ Tours BUS TOUR
(Map p917; 855-486-9868; www.tmz.com/tour; 6925 Hollywood Blvd; adult/child $55/45; approx 10 tours daily) Cut the shame, do you really want to spot celebrities, glimpse their homes, and gawk and laugh at their dirt? Join this

WORTH A TRIP

TOURING MOVIE & TV STUDIOS

Half the fun of visiting Hollywood is hoping you'll see stars. Up the odds by joining the studio audience of a sitcom or game show, which usually tape between August and March. For free tickets, check with **Audiences Unlimited** (818-260-0041; www.tvtickets.com).

For an authentic behind-the-scenes look, take a shuttle tour of **Warner Bros Studios** (877-492-8687, 818-972-8687; www.wbstudiotour.com; 3400 W Riverside Dr, Burbank; tours from $54; 8:15am-4pm Mon-Sat, hours vary Sun) or **Paramount Pictures** (323-956-1777; www.paramountstudiotour.com; 5555 Melrose Ave; tours from $53; tours 9:30am-2pm Mon-Fri, hours vary Sat & Sun), or a walking tour of **Sony Pictures Studios** (310-244-8687; www.sonypicturesstudiostours.com; 10202 W Washington Blvd; tour $38; tours usually 9:30am, 10:30am, 1:30pm & 2:30pm Mon-Fri). All of these tours show you around soundstages and backlots (outdoor sets), and inside wardrobe and make-up departments. Reservations are required (minimum-age requirements apply); bring photo ID.

LOS ANGELES FOR CHILDREN

Keeping kids happy is child's play in LA. The sprawling Los Angeles Zoo (p918) in family-friendly Griffith Park (p917) is a sure bet. Dino-fans will dig the La Brea Tar Pits (p918) and the Natural History Museum (p915), while budding scientists crowd the Griffith Observatory (p917) and California Science Center (p916). For under-the-sea creatures, head to the Aquarium of the Pacific (p921) in Long Beach. The amusement park at Santa Monica Pier (p919) is fun for all ages. Activities for younger kids are more limited at tween/teen-oriented Universal Studios Hollywood (p918). In neighboring Orange County, Disneyland (p932) and Knott's Berry Farm (p933) are ever-popular theme parks.

branded tour imagined by the papparazzi made famous. Tours are two hours long, and you will likely meet some of the TMZ stars and perhaps even celebrity guests on the bus!

Festivals & Events

Monthly street fairs for art-gallery-hopping, shopping and food truck meet-ups include **Downtown Art Walk** (Map p914; www.downtownartwalk.org; noon-9pm 2nd Thu of month) FREE and Venice's **First Friday** (www.abbotkinney1stfridays.com) events.

Rose Parade PARADE
(www.tournamentofroses.com; Jan) This cavalcade of flower-festooned floats snakes through Pasadena on New Year's Day. Get close-ups during postparade viewing at Victory Park. Avoid traffic and take the Metro Rail Gold Line to Memorial Park.

Academy Awards FILM
(www.oscars.org; Feb-Mar) Ogle your favorite film stars from the Dolby Theatre's red-carpet-adjacent bleachers. Apply in September for one of 600 lucky spots. Held in late February or early March.

West Hollywood Halloween Carnaval CARNIVAL
(www.visitwesthollywood.com; Oct) This rambunctious street fair brings 350,000 revelers – many in over-the-top and/or X-rated costumes – out for a day of dancing, dishing and dating on Halloween.

Sleeping

For seaside life, base yourself in Santa Monica, Venice or Long Beach. Cool-hunters and party people will be happiest in Hollywood or WeHo; culture-vultures, in Downtown LA. Prices do not include lodging taxes (12% to 14%).

Downtown

Ace Hotel HOTEL $$$
(Map p914; 213-623-3233; www.acehotel.com/losangeles; 929 S Broadway Ave; r/ste from $250/400) Either lovingly cool, a bit too hip or a touch self-conscious depending upon your purview, there is no denying that Downtown's newest hotel opened to universal acclaim. And the minds behind it care deeply about their product. Some rooms are cubby-box small, but the 'medium' rooms are doable.

Hollywood

USA Hostels Hollywood HOSTEL $
(Map p917; 323-462-3777; www.usahostels.com; 1624 Schrader Blvd; dm $30-40, r without bath $81-104;) This sociable hostel puts you within steps of the Hollywood party circuit. Private rooms are a bit cramped, but making new friends is easy during staff-organized barbecues, comedy nights and $25 all-you-can-drink limo tours. Freebies include a cook-your-own-pancake breakfast. It has cushy lounge seating on the front porch and free beach shuttles too.

Vibe Hotel HOSTEL $
(Map p917; 323-469-8600; www.vibehotel.com; 5920 Hollywood Blvd; dm $22-25, r $85-95; P@) A funky motel turned hostel with both coed and female-only dorms, each with a flat-screen TV and kitchenette, and several recently redone private rooms that sleep three. You'll share space with a happening international crowd.

Magic Castle Hotel HOTEL $$
(Map p917; 323-851-0800; http://magiccastlehotel.com; 7025 Franklin Ave; r from $174; P@) Walls at this perennial pleaser are a bit thin, but otherwise it's a charming base of operations with large, modern rooms, exceptional staff and a petite courtyard pool where days start with fresh pastries and gourmet coffee. Enquire about access to the Magic Castle, a fabled members-only magic club in an adjacent Victorian mansion. Parking costs $11.

West Hollywood & Mid-City

Pali Hotel
BOUTIQUE HOTEL **$$**

(Map p920; ☑ 323-272-4588; www.pali-hotel. com; 7950 Melrose Ave; r from $179; P@🖛) We love the rustic wood-panelled exterior, the polished-concrete floor in the lobby, the Thai massage spa (just $35 for 30 minutes), and the 32 contemporary rooms with two-tone paint jobs, wall-mounted, flat-screen TV, and enough room for a sofa. Some have terraces. Terrific all-around value.

Farmer's Daughter Hotel
MOTEL **$$**

(Map p920; ☑ 323-937-3930; www.farmersdaughter-hotel.com; 115 S Fairfax Ave; r from $209; P✳@🖛🖳) Denim bedspreads and rocking chairs lend this flirty motel a farmhouse vibe. Long before the renovation, a young Charlize Theron stayed here with mom when they were hunting for a Hollywood career. Adventurous lovers should ask about the No Tell Room, which has mirrored headboards and another mirror on the ceiling.

Beverly Hills

Beverly Terrace Hotel
HOTEL **$$**

(Map p920; ☑ 310-274-8141; www.hotelbeverly-terrace.com; 469 N Doheny Dr; r from $199; P🖛) This older, but high-value, Euro-style property dances on the border with West Hollywood and puts you close to the Santa Monica Blvd fun zone. Rooms aren't huge but are decorated in Mid-Century Modern style with soothing greens, crisp blues and bright reds. The rooftop sundeck is blessed with beautiful views of the Hollywood Hills. Parking is $12.

★ Mr C
HOTEL **$$$**

(Map p920; ☑ 877-334-5623; www.mrchotels. com; 1224 Beverwil Dr; r from $320) This long-standing tower hotel has been redesigned by the Cipriani brothers, who have been so involved in their passion project, they've designed everything down to the furniture in the rooms. Rooms on even floors offer white decor, odd floors are brown, and both varieties include marble baths, leather sofas and lounges. North-facing rooms have spectacular views.

Santa Monica

HI Los Angeles-Santa Monica
HOSTEL **$**

(Map p922; ☑ 310-393-9913; www.hilosangeles. org; 1436 2nd St; dm $38-49, r without bath $99-159; ✳@🖛) Near the beach and Promenade, this hostel has an enviable location on the cheap. Its 200 beds in single-sex dorms and bed-in-a-box doubles with shared bathrooms are clean and safe, and there are plenty of public spaces to lounge and surf, but those looking to party are better off in Venice or Hollywood.

Sea Shore Motel
MOTEL **$$**

(Map p922; ☑ 310-392-2787; www.seashoremotel. com; 2637 Main St; r from $140; P✳🖛) These friendly, family-run lodgings put you just a Frisbee toss from the beach on happening Main St (expect some street noise). The tiled rooms are basic, but families can stretch out comfortably in the modern suites with kitchen and balcony in a nearby building.

Shore Hotel
HOTEL **$$$**

(Map p922; ☑ 310-458-1515; www.shorehotel.com; 1515 Ocean Ave; r from $309) 🖉 Massive and modern with clean lines, this is one of the newest hotels on Ocean Ave, and the only gold LEED-certified hotel in Santa Monica, which means it has a reasonably light footprint. Case in point: the lovely back garden is seeded with drought-tolerant plants. The wood-and-glass rooms each have private terraces.

Long Beach

Dockside Boat & Bed
B&B **$$**

(☑ 562-436-3111; www.boatandbed.com; Rainbow Harbor, Dock 5, 330 S Pine Ave; r from $175; P🖛) Get rocked to sleep by the waves aboard your own private yacht with retro '70s charm, galley kitchen and high-tech entertainment center. Boats are moored right along the newly expanded waterfront fun zone in downtown Long Beach, so expect some noise. Breakfast is delivered to your vessel.

Pasadena

★ Bissell House B&B
B&B **$$**

(☑ 626-441-3535; www.bissellhouse.com; 201 S Orange Grove Ave, South Pasadena; r $159-259; P🖛🖳) Antiques, hardwood floors and a crackling fireplace make this secluded Victorian B&B on 'Millionaire's Row' a bastion of warmth and romance. The hedge-framed garden feels like a sanctuary, and there's a pool for cooling off on hot summer days. The Prince Albert room has gorgeous wallpaper and a claw-foot tub. All seven rooms have private baths.

Eating

With some 140 nationalities living in LA, ethnic neighborhoods for foodies to explore abound, including Downtown LA's Little Tokyo and Chinatown; Mid-City's Koreatown; Thai Town, east of Hollywood; East LA's Boyle Heights for Mexican flavors; and the Westside's Little Osaka for Japanese kitchens.

Downtown

For cheap, fast meals-on-the-go, graze the international food stalls of the historic **Grand Central Market** (Map p914; www.grandcentralmarket.com; 317 S Broadway; ⏲8am-6pm Sun-Wed, to 9pm Thu-Sat).

Cole's SANDWICHES **$**
(Map p914; www.213nightlife.com/colesfrenchdip; 118 E 6th St; sandwiches $6-9; ⏲11am-10pm Sun-Wed, to midnight Thu, to 1am Fri & Sat) A funky old basement tavern known for originating the French Dip sandwich way back in 1908, when those things cost a nickel. You know the drill: French bread piled with sliced lamb, beef, turkey, pork or pastrami, dipped once or twice in au jus.

Sushi Gen JAPANESE **$$**
(Map p914; ☎213-617-0552; www.sushigen.org; 422 E 2nd St; sushi $11-21; ⏲11:15am-2pm & 5:30-9:45pm) Come early to grab a table, and know that it doesn't do the ubercreative 'look at me' kind of rolls. In this Japanese classic sushi spot, seven chefs stand behind the blonde wood bar, carving thick slabs of melt-in-your-mouth salmon, buttery toro and a wonderful Japanese snapper, among other staples. Their sashimi special at lunch ($18) is a steal.

★**Bestia** ITALIAN **$$$**
(☎213-514-5724; http://bestiala.com; 2121 7th Pl; dishes $10-29; ⏲5-11pm Sun-Thu, to midnight Fri & Sat) The most sought-after reservation in town can be found at this new and splashy Italian kitchen in the Arts District. The antipasti ranges from crispy lamb pancetta to sea urchin crudo to veal tartare crostino. Did we mention the lamb's heart? Yeah, you may have to leave the vegan at home.

Hollywood & Griffith Park

★**Yuca's** MEXICAN **$**
(☎323-662-1214; www.yucasla.com; 2056 Hillhurst Ave; items $4-10; ⏲11am-6pm Mon-Sat) Location, location, location…is definitely not what lures people to this parking-lot snack shack. It's the tacos! And the *tortas,* burritos and other Mexican faves that earned the Herrera family the coveted James Beard Award in 2005.

Life Food Organic RAW **$**
(Map p917; www.lifefoodorganic.com; 1507 N Cahuenga Ave; dishes $4-14; ⏲7:30am-9pm) This place serves the healthiest fast food around. Have a chocolate shake made with almond milk, a veggie chili burger with a sesame seaweed salad on the side and a chocolate cream pie for dessert. None of it cooked! You can dine in, but most take it away.

Pizzeria & Osteria Mozza ITALIAN **$$$**
(☎323-297-0100; www.mozza-la.com; 6602 Melrose Ave; pizzas $11-19, dinner mains $27-38; ⏲pizzeria noon-midnight daily, osteria 5:30-11pm Mon-Fri, 5-11pm Sat, 5-10pm Sun) Osteria Mozza is all about fine cuisine crafted from market-fresh, seasonal ingredients; but being a Mario Batali joint, you can expect adventure (squid-ink *chitarra freddi* with Dungeness crab, sea urchin and jalapeno) and consistent excellence. Reservations are recommended.

West Hollywood & Mid-City

Original Farmers Market MARKET **$**
(Map p920; www.farmersmarketla.com; 6333 W 3rd St; mains $6-12; ⏲9am-9pm Mon-Fri, to 8pm Sat, 10am-7pm Sun; P) The Farmers Market is a great spot for a casual meal any time of day, especially if the rug rats are tagging along. There are lots of options here, from gumbo to Singapore-style noodles to tacos.

Pingtung ASIAN **$**
(Map p920; ☎323-866-1866; www.pingtungla.com; 7455 Melrose Ave; dishes $6-12; ⏲11:30am-10pm Sun-Thu, to 11pm Fri & Sat;) Our new favorite place to eat on Melrose is this Pan-Asian market cafe where the dim sum (wild crab dumplings), seaweed and green papaya salads, and rice bowls piled with curried chicken and BBQ beef are all worthy of praise. It has an inviting back patio with ample seating, wi-fi and good beer on tap.

★**Mercado** MEXICAN **$$**
(Map p920; ☎323-944-0947; www.mercadorestaurant.com; 7910 W 3rd St; dishes $9-26; ⏲5-10pm Mon-Wed, to 11pm Thu & Fri, 11am-3pm & 4-11pm Sat, 11am-3pm & 4-10pm Sun) Terrific

nuovo-Mexican food served in white-washed brick environs, with dangling bird-cage chandeliers and a terrific marble tequila bar. The slow-cooked *carnitas* (braised pork) melt in your mouth. It also spit-roasts beef, grills sweet corn, and folds tasty tacos and enchiladas. The *hora feliz* (happy hour) is among the best in the city.

Nate 'n Al DELI $$
(Map p920; ☎310-274-0101; www.natenal.com; 414 N Beverly Dr; dishes $7-13; ⏰7am-9pm; 👪) Dapper seniors, chatty girlfriends, busy execs and even Larry King have kept this New York–style nosh spot busy since 1945. The huge menu brims with corned beef, lox and other old-school favorites, but we're partial to the pastrami, made fresh on-site.

Santa Monica & Venice

Lemonade CALIFORNIAN $
(http://lemonadela.com; 1661 Abbot Kinney Blvd; meals $8-13; ⏰11am-9pm) The first incarnation of an imaginative, local market cafe with a lineup of tasty salads (watermelon radish and chili or tamarind pork and spicy carrots), and stockpots bubbling with lamb and stewed figs or miso-braised short ribs. It has six kinds of lemonade augmented with blueberries and mint or watermelon and rosemary. Yummy sweets too.

Abbot's Pizza Company PIZZA $
(Map p922; ☎310-396-7334; www.abbotspizzaco.com; 1407 Abbot Kinney Blvd; slices $3-5, pizzas $12-29; ⏰11am-11pm Sun-Thu, to midnight Fri & Sat; 👪) Join the flip-flop crowd at this shoebox-sized pizza kitchen for habit-forming bagel-crust pies tastily decorated with tequila-lime chicken, portobello mushrooms, goat's cheese and other gourmet morsels served up at tummy-grumbling speed.

Father's Office PUB FOOD $$
(☎310-736-2224; www.fathersoffice.com; 1018 Montana Ave; dishes $5-15; ⏰5-10pm Mon-Wed, 5-11pm Thu, 4-11pm Fri, noon-11pm Sat, noon-10pm Sun) This elbow-to-elbow gastropub is famous for its burger: a dry-aged-beef number dressed in smoky bacon, sweet caramelized onion and an ingenious combo of Gruyère and blue cheese. Pair it with fries served in a mini shopping cart and a mug of handcrafted brew chosen from the three dozen on tap. No substitutions tolerated.

Long Beach

Pier 76 SEAFOOD $$
(☎562-983-1776; www.pier76fishgrill.com; 95 Pine Ave; mains $8-19; ⏰11am-9pm) A terrific, affordable seafood house in downtown Long Beach. Step to the counter and order yellowtail, salmon, trout, mahimahi or halibut glazed and grilled, and served with two sides. The fries and kale salad are both good. It has fish tacos, sandwiches, poke and ceviche, too. It even has a $19 lobster.

Pasadena

Ración SPANISH $$$
(☎626-396-3090; www.racionrestaurant.com; 119 W Green St; dishes $5-45; ⏰6-10pm Mon, 11:30am-3pm & 6-10pm Tue-Thu, to 11pm Fri & Sat, 5:30-10pm Sun) This Basque-inspired restaurant offers tapas such as duck sausage, stuffed squid, beer-braised octopus and seared prawns in salsa verde. It house-cures yellowfin tuna in anchovy vinegrette, and offers *raciones* (larger plates) ranging from a wild market fish with heirloom beans to slow-braised lamb belly.

Drinking & Nightlife

Hollywood has been legendary sipping territory since before the Rat Pack days. Creative cocktails are the order of the day at reinvented watering holes in Downtown LA and edgier neighborhoods. Beachside bars run the gamut from surfer dives to candlelit cocktail lounges.

To confirm all your preconceived prejudices about LA, look no further than a velvet-roped nightclub in Hollywood. Come armed with a hot bod or a fat wallet to impress the bouncers.

★**No Vacancy** BAR
(Map p917; ☎323-465-1902; www.novacancyla.com; 1727 N Hudson Ave; ⏰8pm-2am) An old, shingled Victorian has been converted into LA's hottest night out. Even the entrance is theatrical: you'll follow a rickety staircase into a narrow hall and enter the room of a would-be madame, dressed in fishnet and brimming with hospitality, who will soon press a button to reveal another staircase down into the living room and out into a courtyard.

Bar Marmont BAR

(Map p920; ☎323-650-0575; www.chateaumarmont.com/barmarmont.php; 8171 Sunset Blvd; ⏲6pm-2am) Elegant, but not stuck up; been around, yet still cherished. With high ceilings, molded walls and terrific martinis, the famous, and wish-they-weres, still flock here. If you time it right you might see Tom Yorke, or perhaps Lindsay Lohan? Come midweek. Weekends are for amateurs.

Angel City Brewery BREWERY

(Map p914; ☎213-622-1261; www.angelcitybrewery.com; 216 S Alameda St; ⏲4-10pm Mon-Wed, to midnight Thu & Fri, noon-midnight Sat, noon-10pm Sun) This wonderful microbrewer of fine beers and ales is the only one of its kind in Downtown LA. Located on the edge of the Arts District, it runs tours on weekends, but you can always stop by its Public House to drink beer, listen to occasional live music and patronize the food trucks that descend with welcome flavor.

Copa d'Oro BAR

(Map p922; www.copadoro.com; 217 Broadway; ⏲5:30pm-midnight Mon-Wed, to 2am Thu-Sat) The cocktail menu was created by the talented Vincenzo Marianella – a man who knows his spirits, and has trained his team to concoct addictive cocktails from a well of top-end spirits and a produce bin of fresh herbs, fruits, juices and a few veggies too. The rock tunes and the smooth, dark ambience don't hurt.

Tiki-Ti BAR

(☎323-669-9381; www.tiki-ti.com; 4427 W Sunset Blvd; ⏲4pm-2am Wed-Sat) This garage-sized tropical tavern packs in grizzled old-timers and young cuties for sweet and wickedly strong drinks (try a Rae's Mistake, named for the bar's founder). The under-the-sea decor is surreal. Cash only.

Townhouse & Delmonte Speakeasy BAR

(Map p922; www.townhousevenice.com; 52 Windward Ave; ⏲5pm-2am Mon-Thu, noon-2am Fri-Sun) Upstairs is a cool, dark and perfectly dingy bar with pool tables, booths and good booze. Downstairs is the speakeasy, where DJs spin pop, funk and electronic music, comics take the mic, and jazz players set up and jam. It's a reliably good time almost any night.

Musso & Frank Grill BAR

(Map p917; www.mussoandfrankgrill.com; 6667 Hollywood Blvd) Hollywood history hangs in the thick air at Musso & Frank Grill, Tinseltown's oldest eatery (since 1919). Charlie Chaplin used to knock back vodka gimlets at the bar and Raymond Chandler penned scripts in the high-backed booths.

☆ Entertainment

For discounted and half-price tickets, check **Goldstar** (www.goldstar.com) or **LA Stage Tix** (www.lastagetix.com), the latter strictly for theater.

GAY & LESBIAN LA

'Boystown,' along Santa Monica Blvd in West Hollywood (WeHo), is gay ground zero, where dozens of high-energy bars, cafes, restaurants, gyms and clubs are found. The diverse crowd in Silver Lake is all-inclusive, from leather-and-Levi's bars to hipster haunts. Venice and Long Beach have neighborly scenes.

Out & About (www.outandabout-tours.com) Leads weekend walking tours of the city's lesbi-gay cultural landmarks. The festival season kicks off in May with **Long Beach Pride** (http://longbeachpride.com) and continues with WeHo's **LA Pride** (http://lapride.org) in June.

Abbey (Map p920; www.abbeyfoodandbar.com; 692 N Robertson Blvd; mains $9-13; ⏲11am-2am Mon-Thu, from 10am Fri, from 9am Sat & Sun) At WeHo's definitive gay bar and restaurant, take your pick of preening on an outdoor patio, in a chill lounge or on the dance floor, and enjoy flavored martinis. A dozen other bars and nightclubs are a short stumble away.

Micky's (Map p920; www.mickys.com; 8857 Santa Monica Blvd; ⏲5pm-2am Sun-Thu, to 4am Fri & Sat) A two-story, quintessential WeHo dance club, with go-go boys, expensive drinks, attitude and plenty of eye candy. Check online for special events.

Akbar (www.akbarsilverlake.com; 4356 W Sunset Blvd; ⏲4pm-2am) Killer jukebox, casbah-style atmosphere and a Silver Lake crowd that's been known to change from hour to hour – gay, straight or just hip, but not too-hip-for-you.

★Hollywood Bowl CONCERT VENUE
(☎323-850-2000; www.hollywoodbowl.com; 2301 N Highland Ave; rehearsals free, performance costs vary; ⏲Jun-Sep) Summers in LA just wouldn't be the same without this chill spot for music under the stars, from symphonies to big-name acts such as Baaba Maal, Sigur Ros, Radiohead and Paul McCartney. A huge natural amphitheater, the Hollywood Bowl has been around since 1922 and has great sound.

★Upright Citizens Brigade Theatre COMEDY
(Map p917; ☎323-908-8702; http://franklin.ucbtheatre.com; 5919 Franklin Ave; tickets $5-10) Founded in New York by *Saturday Night Life* alums Amy Poehler and Ian Roberts along with Matt Besser and Matt Walsh, this sketch-comedy group cloned itself in Hollywood in 2005 and is arguably the best improv theater in town.

Dodger Stadium BASEBALL
(☎866-363-4377; www.dodgers.com; 1000 Elysian Park Ave; ⏲Apr-Sep) Few clubs can match the Dodgers when it comes to history (Jackie Robinson, Sandy Koufax, Kirk Gibson, and Vin Scully), success and fan loyalty. The club's newest owners bought the organization for roughly two billion dollars, an American team-sports record.

Staples Center BASKETBALL
(Map p914; ☎213-742-7340; www.staplescenter.com; 1111 S Figueroa St; 👪) The **LA Lakers** (☎213-742-7340; www.nba.com/lakers; tickets $50-250) were down on their luck as of this writing, but the NBA's most successful organization still packs all 19,000 seats on a regular basis. Floor seats, like those filled by the ubiquitous Jack Nicholson, cost in excess of $5000 per game.

Largo at the Coronet LIVE MUSIC, PERFORMING ARTS
(Map p920; ☎310-855-0530; www.largo-la.com; 366 N La Cienega Blvd) Ever since its early days on Fairfax Ave, Largo has been progenitor of high-minded pop culture (it nurtured Zach Galifinakis to stardom). Now part of the Coronet Theatre complex, it features edgy comedy, such as Sarah Silverman and Jon Hodgman, and nourishing night music from Brad Meldau and his jazz piano to Andrew Bird's acoustic ballads.

Arclight Cinemas CINEMA
(Map p917; ☎323-464-1478; www.arclightcinemas.com; 6360 W Sunset Blvd; tickets $14-16) Assigned seats and exceptional celeb-sighting potential make this 14-screen multiplex the best around. If your taste dovetails with its schedule, the awesome 1963 geodesic Cinerama Dome is a must. Bonuses: age 21-plus screenings where you can booze it up, and Q&As with directors, writers and actors. Parking is $3 for four hours.

El Rey LIVE MUSIC
(Map p920; www.theelrey.com; 5515 Wilshire Blvd; cover varies) An old art-deco dance hall decked out in red velvet and chandeliers and flaunting an awesome sound system and excellent sightlines. Although it can hold 800 people, it feels quite small. Performance-wise, it's popular with indie acts such as Black Joe Lewis and the Honeybears, and the rockers who love them.

American Cinematheque CINEMA
(Map p917; www.americancinematheque.com; 6712 Hollywood Blvd; adult/senior & student $11/9) A nonprofit screening tributes, retrospectives and foreign films in the **Egyptian Theatre** (Map p917; www.egyptiantheatre.com; 6712 Hollywood Blvd). Directors, screenwriters and actors often swing by for postshow Q&As.

Kirk Douglas Theatre THEATER
(www.centertheatergroup.org; 9820 Washington Blvd) An old-timey movie house has been recast as a 300-seat theater, thanks to a major cash infusion from the Douglas family. Since its opening in 2004, it has become an integral part of Culver City's growing arts scene. It's primarily a showcase for terrific new plays by local playwrights.

★Echo LIVE MUSIC
(www.attheecho.com; 1822 W Sunset Blvd; cover varies) Eastsiders hungry for an eclectic alchemy of sounds pack this funky-town dive that's basically a sweaty bar with a stage and a smoking patio. It books indie bands, and also has regular club nights. Its Funky Sole party every Saturday is always a blast.

Shopping

Although Beverly Hills' Rodeo Drive is the most iconic shopping strip in LA, the city abounds with other options for retail therapy. Fashionistas and their paparazzi piranhas flock to Mid-City's Robertson Blvd. You also might spot celebs shopping on nearby 3rd St. Unusual and unique local boutiques line Main St in Santa Monica, Venice's Abbot Kinney Blvd and Sunset Blvd in Silver Lake.

Fashion District FASHION
(Map p914; www.fashiondistrict.org) Fashion Institute of Design & Merchandising (FIDM) graduates often go on to launch their own brands or work for established labels in this 90-block nirvana for shopaholics. Bounded by Main and Wall Sts and 7th St and Pico Blvd, the district's prices are lowest in bazaar-like Santee Alley, but the styles are grooviest in the Gerry Building and Cooper Design Space.

Melrose Avenue FASHION
(Map p920; Melrose Ave) A popular shopping strip as famous for its epic people-watching as it is for its consumer fruits. You'll see hair (and people) of all shades and styles, and everything from gothic jewels to custom sneakers to medical marijuana to stuffed porcupines available for a price. The strip is located between Fairfax and La Brea Aves.

Fred Segal FASHION
(Map p920; ☎323-651-4129; www.fredsegal.com; 8100 Melrose Ave; ⏰10am-7pm Mon-Sat, noon-6pm Sun) Celebs and beautiful people circle for the very latest from Babakul, Aviator Nation and Robbi & Nikki at this warren of high-end boutiques under one impossibly chic but slightly snooty roof. The only time you'll see bargains (sort of) is during the two-week blowout sale in September.

It's a Wrap! VINTAGE
(www.itsawraphollywood.com; 3315 W Magnolia Blvd, Burbank; ⏰10am-8pm Mon-Fri, 11am-6pm Sat & Sun) Here are fashionable, postproduction wares worn by TV and film stars. What that means to you is great prices on mainstream designer labels, including racks of casual and formal gear worn on such shows as *Nurse Jackie* and *Scandal*. The suits are a steal, and so is the denim. New arrivals are racked by show affiliation.

Raggedy Threads VINTAGE
(Map p914; ☎213-620-1188; www.raggedythreads.com; 330 E 2nd St; ⏰noon-8pm Mon-Sat, to 6pm Sun) A tremendous vintage Americana store just off the main Little Tokyo strip. There's plenty of beautifully raggedy denim and overalls, soft T-shirts, a few Victorian dresses, and a wonderful turquoise collection at great prices. She also collects sensational glasses frames and watches.

Rose Bowl Flea Market MARKET
(www.rgcshows.com; 1001 Rose Bowl Dr, Pasadena; admission from $8; ⏰9am-4:30pm 2nd Sun each month, last entry 3pm) California's Marketplace of Unusual Items descends upon the Rose Bowl football field bringing forth the rummaging hordes. There are over 2500 vendors and 15,000 buyers here every month, and it's always a great time.

ℹ Information

DANGERS & ANNOYANCES

Crime rates are lowest in West LA, Beverly Hills, beach towns (except Venice and Long Beach) and Pasadena. Avoid walking alone and after dark around Downtown's 'Skid Row,' roughly bounded by 3rd, Alameda, 7th and Main Sts.

MEDIA

KCRW 89.9 FM (www.kcrw.org) Santa Monica–based National Public Radio (NPR) station for eclectic and indie music and intelligent talk.

LA Weekly (www.laweekly.com) Free alternative news, live music and entertainment listings newspaper.

Los Angeles Magazine (www.lamag.com) Glossy lifestyle monthly with a useful restaurant and bar guide.

Los Angeles Times (www.latimes.com) California's leading daily newspaper, winner of dozens of Pulitzer Prizes.

MEDICAL SERVICES

Cedars-Sinai Medical Center (☎310-423-3277; http://cedars-sinai.edu; 8700 Beverly Blvd, West Hollywood; ⏰24hr) 24-hour emergency room.

MONEY

Travelex (☎310-659-6093; www.travelex.com; US Bank, 8901 Santa Monica Blvd, West Hollywood; ⏰9:30am-5pm Mon-Thu, 9am-6pm Fri, to 1pm Sat)

Travelex (☎310-260-9219; www.travelex.com; 201 Santa Monica Blvd, Suite 101, Santa Monica; ⏰9am-5pm Mon-Thu, to 6pm Fri)

TELEPHONE

LA County is covered by multiple area codes. Dial ☎1+(area code) before all local seven-digit numbers.

TOURIST INFORMATION

Downtown LA Visitor Center (Map p914; www.discoverlosangeles.com; 800 N Alameda St, Downtown; ⏰8:30am-5pm Mon-Fri)

Hollywood Visitor Information Center (Map p917; ☎323-467-6412; http://discoverlosangeles.com; Hollywood & Highland complex, 6801 Hollywood Blvd, Hollywood; ⏰10am-10pm Mon-Sat, to 7pm Sun) In the Dolby Theatre walkway.

Santa Monica Visitor Information Center (Map p922; ☎800-544-5319; www.santamonica.com; 2427 Main St, Santa Monica) Roving information officers patrol the promenade on Segways.

USEFUL WEBSITES

Discover Los Angeles (http://discoverlosangeles.com) Official tourism site.

Experience LA (www.experiencela.com) Comprehensive cultural events calendar.

LAist (http://laist.com) Arts, entertainment, food and pop-culture gossip.

Getting There & Away

AIR

LA's gateway hub is Los Angeles International Airport (www.lawa.org/lax; 1 World Way), the USA's second-busiest airport. Its nine terminals are linked on the lower (arrivals) level by free shuttle bus A. Hotel and car-rental shuttles stop there as well.

Smaller **Long Beach Airport** (www.lgb.org; 4100 Donald Douglas Dr, Long Beach) and Burbank's **Bob Hope Airport** (www.burbankairport.com; 2627 N Hollywood Way, Burbank) handle mostly domestic flights.

BUS

Greyhound's main **bus terminal** (☎213-629-8401; www.greyhound.com; 1716 E 7th St) is in an unsavory part of Downtown LA, so avoid arriving after dark.

CAR

The usual international car-rental agencies have branches at LAX airport and throughout LA.

TRAIN

Long-distance Amtrak trains roll into Downtown LA's historic **Union Station** (☎800-872-7245; www.amtrak.com; 800 N Alameda St). Pacific Surfliner regional trains run south to San Diego ($37, 2¾ hours) and north to Santa Barbara ($31, 2¾ hours) and San Luis Obispo ($41, 5½ hours).

Getting Around

TO/FROM THE AIRPORT

Door-to-door shuttles, such as those operated by **Prime Time** (☎800-733-8267; www.primetimeshuttle.com) and **Super Shuttle** (☎800-258-3826; www.supershuttle.com), leave from the lower level of LAX terminals. Destinations include Santa Monica ($21), Hollywood ($27) and Downtown LA ($16).

Curbside dispatchers summon taxis at LAX. A flat fare applies to Downtown LA ($46.50). Otherwise, metered fares (including $4 airport surcharge) average $30 to $35 to Santa Monica or $50 to Hollywood, excluding tip.

LAX FlyAway Buses (☎866-435-9529; www.lawa.org/FlyAway; one-way $8) depart hourly for Santa Monica ($8, 40 minutes) or Hollywood ($8, 60 to 90 minutes) from early morning until late night, and every 30 minutes around the clock to Downtown LA's Union Station ($8, 35 minutes).

Other public transportation is slower and less convenient but cheaper. From the lower level outside any LAX terminal, catch free shuttle bus C to the Metro Bus Center, a hub for buses serving all of LA; or take free shuttle bus G to light-rail Aviation Station on the Metro Green Line.

CAR & MOTORCYCLE

Driving in LA doesn't need to be a hassle, but be prepared for some of the worst traffic in the country during weekday rush hours (roughly 7am to 10am and 3pm to 7pm).

Self-parking at motels is usually free; most hotels charge from $10 to $40. Valet parking at restaurants, hotels and nightspots is common, with average rates of $5 to $10.

PUBLIC TRANSPORTATION

If you're not in a hurry, public transportation suffices around – but not necessarily between – LA's most touristed neighborhoods.

Online trip-planning help is available from LA's **Metro** (☎323-466-3876; www.metro.net), which operates 200 bus lines and the following six subway and light-rail lines:

Blue Line Downtown (7th St/Metro Center) to Long Beach.

Expo Line Downtown (7th St/Metro Center) to Culver City (and Santa Monica from early 2016), via Exposition Park.

Gold Line East LA to Pasadena via Little Tokyo, Union Station and Chinatown.

Green Line Norwalk to Redondo Beach via Aviation Station.

Purple Line Downtown LA (Union Station) to Koreatown.

Red Line Downtown LA (Union Station) to North Hollywood, via Hollywood and Universal City.

Metro train or bus fares are $1.75 upon boarding; for buses, bring cash (exact change). Metro 'TAP card' unlimited-ride passes cost $7/25 per day/week. Purchase TAP cards at ticket-vending machines inside Metro Rail stations. Day passes are also sold on board buses.

Local **DASH minbuses** (☎213-808-2273, 323-808-2273; www.ladottransit.com; per ride 50¢; ⊙info line 6:30am-7pm) run around Downtown LA, Hollywood and other neighborhoods; schedules vary, with reduced weekend services.

Big Blue Bus (☎310-451-5444; www.bigbluebus.com; fares from $1) covers much of West LA, including Santa Monica, Venice, Westwood, Culver City and LAX; Rapid 10 Express connects Santa Monica with Downtown LA ($2, 45 minutes to 1¾ hours).

TAXI

Because of LA's size and heavy traffic, getting around by cab will cost you. Metered taxis charge $2.85 at flagfall, then $2.70 per mile. Except for taxis lined up outside airports, train stations and major hotels, it's best to phone for a cab.

SOUTHERN CALIFORNIA COAST

Disneyland & Anaheim

The mother of all West Coast theme parks, aka the 'Happiest Place on Earth,' Disneyland is a parallel world that's squeaky-clean, enchanting and wacky all at once. It's an 'imagineered' hyper-reality where the employees – called 'cast members' – are always upbeat and there are parades every day of the year. More than 16 million kids, grandparents, honeymooners and international tourists stream through the front gates annually.

Disneyland opened to great fanfare in 1955 and the workaday city of Anaheim grew up around it. Today the Disneyland Resort comprises the original Disneyland Park and newer Disney California Adventure theme park. Anaheim itself doesn't have much in the way of attractions outside the Disney juggernaut.

Sights & Activities

Going on all the rides at both theme parks requires at least two days, as queues for top attractions can be an hour or more. To minimize wait times, arrive midweek (especially during summer) before the gates open, buy print-at-home tickets online and take advantage of the parks' Fastpass system, which preassigns boarding times at select rides and attractions. For seasonal park hours and schedules of parades, shows and fireworks, check the official website.

Disneyland Park THEME PARK

(☎714-781-4565; http://disneyland.disney.go.com; 1313 Disneyland Dr; adult/child $99/93, 1-day pass to both parks $155/149;) Spotless, wholesome Disneyland is still laid out according to Walt's original plans. It's here you'll find plenty of rides and some of the attractions most asscociated with the Disney name: Main Street USA, Sleeping Beauty Castle, Tomorrowland.

Disney California Adventure THEME PARK

(DCA; ☎714-781-4400, 714-781-4565; www.disneyland.com; 1313 Harbor Blvd, Anaheim; adult/child $99/93, 1-day pass to both parks $155/149;) Disneyland resort's larger but less crowded park, California Adventure celebrates the natural and cultural glories of the Golden State but lacks the density of attractions and depth of imagination. The best rides are Soarin' Over California, a virtual hang glide, and the famous Twilight Zone Tower of Terror that drops you 183ft down an elevator chute.

Sleeping

Chain motels and hotels are a dime a dozen in Anaheim.

HI Fullerton HOSTEL $

(☎714-738-3721; www.hihostels.com; 1700 N Harbor Blvd, Fullerton; dm $26-29, r per person $52-56; mid-Jun–mid-Sep; P) On a former dairy farm in Brea Dam State Park, 6 miles north of Disneyland, this two-story hacienda houses 20 beds in three dorm types (male, female, mixed), and the usual youth-hostel amenities. Rates include continental breakfast and parking. By bus from Disneyland, walk to Harbor Blvd and Ball Rd to catch OCTA bus 43 ($2, 30 minutes).

★**Anabella** HOTEL $$

(☎714-905-1050; www.anabellahotel.com; 1030 W Katella Ave; r $89-199, ste $109-199; P@) Formerly three separate motels, this 7-acre complex has the feel of a laid-back country club, complete with trams that carry guests effortlessly from the lobby to their buildings. Large rooms have wooden floors and a whisper of Spanish Colonial style, with extras like minifridges and TV entertainment systems. Bunk-bedded kids' suites have Disney-inspired decor.

Alpine Inn MOTEL $$

(☎714-535-2186; www.alpineinnanaheim.com; 715 W Katella Ave; r $60-190; P@) Connoisseurs of kitsch will hug their Hummels over this 42-room, snow-covered chalet sporting an A-frame exterior and icicle-covered roofs – framed by palm trees, of course. Right on the border of DCA, the inn also has Ferris-wheel views. It's circa 1958, and air-con rooms are aging but clean. Simple continental breakfast (included) served in the lobby.

Paradise Pier Hotel HOTEL $$$
(info 714-999-0990, reservations 714-956-6425; http://disneyland.disney.go.com/paradise-pier-hotel; 1717 S Disneyland Dr; d from $240;) Sunbursts, surfboards and a giant superslide are all on deck at the Paradise Pier Hotel, the smallest (472 rooms), cheapest and maybe the most fun of the Disney hotel trio. Kids will love the beachy decor and game arcade, not to mention the roof deck pool and the tiny-tot video room filled with mini Adirondack chairs.

Eating & Drinking

There are dozens of dining options inside the theme parks. Hit the walk-up food stands for carnival treats like giant turkey legs and sugar-dusted churros. For table reservations and meals with Disney characters, call **Disney Dining** (714-781-3463; http://disneyland.disney.go.com/dining).

No alcohol is allowed inside Disneyland Park; it's sold at DCA and Downtown Disney. Budget-conscious visitors and families with kids can store their own food and drinks (no glass) in the lockers (per day $7 to $15) along Disneyland's Main Street, USA, DCA's Buena Vista Street and outside both parks' main entrance.

An open-air pedestrian mall adjacent to the parks, Downtown Disney has mostly generic, yet family-friendly chain restaurants. The same is true of Anaheim GardenWalk (www.anaheimgardenwalk.com; 400 W Disney Way; h11am-9pm), an outdoor mall just east of the parks. If you want to steer clear of Mickey Mouse food, drive to the Anaheim Packing District (3 miles northeast), Old Towne Orange (7 miles southeast), Little Arabia (3 miles west) or Little Saigon (8 miles southwest).

Earl of Sandwich SANDWICHES $
(714-817-7476; Downtown Disney; mains $4-7; 8am-11pm Sun-Thu, to midnight Fri & Sat) This counter-service spot near the Disneyland Hotel serves grilled sandwiches that are both kid- and adult-friendly. The 'original 1762' is roast beef, cheddar and horseradish, or look for chipotle chicken with avocado or holiday turkey. There are also pizza, salad and breakfast options.

Café Orleans CAJUN, CREOLE $$
(New Orleans Sq; mains $16-20; seasonal hours vary;) This Southern-flavored restaurant is famous for its Monte Cristo sandwiches at lunch. Breakfast is served seasonally.

WORTH A TRIP

KNOTT'S BERRY FARM

What, Disney's not enough for you? Find even more thrill rides and cotton candy at **Knott's Berry Farm** (714-220-5200; www.knotts.com; 8039 Beach Blvd, Buena Park; adult/child $67/37; from 10am, closing time varies 6-11pm;). This Old West–themed amusement park teems with packs of speed-crazed adolescents testing their mettle on a line-up of rides. Gut-wrenchers include the Boomerang 'scream machine,' wooden GhostRider and 1950s-themed Xcelerator, while younger kids will enjoy tamer action at Camp Snoopy. From late September through October, the park transforms at night into Halloween-themed 'Knott's Scary Farm.'

When summer heat waves hit, jump next door to **Soak City Orange County** (714-220-5200; www.soakcityoc.com; 8039 Beach Blvd, Buena Park; adult/child 3-11yr $38/27; 10am-5pm, 6pm or 7pm mid-May–mid-Sep) water park. Save time and money by buying print-at-home tickets for either park online. Parking is $15.

★ **Carthay Circle** AMERICAN $$$
(Buena Vista St; mains lunch $24-32, dinner $34-47; lunch & dinner) Decked out like a Hollywood country club, new Carthay Circle is the best dining in either park, with steaks, seafood, pasta, smart service and a good wine list. Your table needs at least one order of fried biscuits, stuffed with white cheddar, bacon and jalapeño and served with apricot honey butter. Inquire about special packages including dinner and the World of Color show.

Napa Rose CALIFORNIAN $$$
(714-300-7170; Grand Californian Hotel & Spa; mains $39-45, 4-course prix-fixe dinner from $90; 5:30-10pm;) Soaring windows, high-back Arts and Crafts–style chairs, leaded-glass windows and towering ceilings befit the Disneyland Resort's top-drawer restaurant. On the plate, seasonal 'California Wine Country' (read: NorCal) cuisine is as impeccably crafted as Sleeping Beauty Castle. Kids' menu available. Reservations essential. Enter the hotel from DCA or Downtown Disney.

Information

ATMs, foreign-currency exchange and medical services are available inside both parks.

Disneyland Resort (☎ live assistance 714-781-7290, recorded info 714-781-4565; www.disneyland.com)

MousePlanet (www.mouseplanet.com) A one-stop fan site for all things Disney, with weekly park updates and discussion boards.

MouseWait (www.mousewait.com) This free mobile app reports up-to-the-minute ride wait times and park news.

ℹ Getting There & Around

Disneyland Resort is just off I-5 (Santa Ana Fwy), about 30 miles southeast of Downtown LA.

Disneyland Resort Express (☎ 800-828-6699; www.graylineanaheim.com; ⊙ 8am-8pm) buses travel between LAX (one way/round-trip $30/48) and Disneyland-area hotels; one child rides free with each paying adult.

The Anaheim Regional Transportation Intermodal Center (ARTIC), next to Angel Stadium, is a quick bus or taxi ride east of Disneyland. **Amtrak** (☎ 800-872-7245; www.amtrak.com; 2626 E Katella Ave) trains between LA's Union Station ($15, 40 minutes) and San Diego ($28, 2¼ hours) arrive almost hourly. **Metrolink** (☎ 800-371-5465; www.metrolinktrains.com; 2626 E Katella Ave) commuter trains from LA's Union Station ($8.75, 50 minutes) stop at the same station.

Anaheim Resort Transit (ART; ☎ 888-364-2787; www.rideart.org; adult/child fare $3/1, day pass $5/2) provides frequent bus service between Disneyland Resort and many area hotels and motels. Shuttles start running an hour before Disneyland opens, operating from 7am to midnight daily in summer.

A free tram connects Disneyland Resort's main parking structures (per day from $17) and Downtown Disney, a short walk from the parks.

Orange County Beaches

If you've seen *The OC* or *Real Housewives*, you might imagine you already know what to expect from this giant quilt of suburbia connecting LA and San Diego, lolling beside 42 miles of glorious coastline. In reality, Hummer-driving hunks and Botoxed beauties mix it up with hang-loose surfers and beatnik artists to give each of Orange County's beach towns a distinct vibe.

Just across the LA–OC county line, old-fashioned **Seal Beach** is refreshingly noncommercial, with a quaint walkable downtown. Less than 10 miles further south along the Pacific Coast Hwy (Hwy 1), **Huntington Beach** – aka 'Surf City, USA' – epitomizes SoCal's surfing lifestyle. Fish tacos and happy-hour specials abound at bars and cafes along downtown HB's Main St, not far from a shortboard-sized **surfing museum** (www.surfingmuseum.org; 411 Olive Ave; donations welcome; ⊙ noon-5pm Wed-Fri & Sun, to 8pm Tue, to 7pm Sat).

Next up is the ritziest of the OC's beach communities: yacht-filled **Newport Beach**. Families and teens steer toward Balboa Peninsula for its beaches, vintage wooden pier and quaint amusement center. From near the 1906 Balboa Pavilion, **Balboa Island Ferry** (www.balboaislandferry.com; 410 S Bay Front; adult/child $1/50¢, car incl driver $2; ⊙ 6:30am-midnight Sun-Thu, to 2am Fri & Sat) shuttles across the bay to Balboa Island for strolls past historic beach cottages and boutiques along Marine Ave.

Continuing south, Hwy 1 zooms past the wild beaches of **Crystal Cove State Park** (☎ 949-494-3539; www.parks.ca.gov; 8471 N Coast Hwy; per car $15, campsites $25-75; ⊙ 6am-sunset) before winding downhill into **Laguna Beach**, the OC's most cultured seaside community. Secluded beaches, glassy waves and eucalyptus-covered hillsides create a Riviera-like feel. Art galleries dot the narrow streets of the 'village' and the coastal highway, where the **Laguna Art Museum** (☎ 949-494-8971; www.lagunaartmuseum.org; 307 Cliff Dr; adult/child/student & senior $7/free/5, 5-9pm 1st Thu of month free; ⊙ 11am-5pm Fri-Tue, to 9pm Thu) exhibits modern and contemporary Californian works. Soak up the natural beauty right in the center of town at **Main Beach**.

Another 10 miles south, detour inland to **Mission San Juan Capistrano** (☎ 949-234-1300; www.missionsjc.com; 26801 Ortega Hwy, San Juan Capistrano; adult/child $9/6; ⊙ 9am-5pm), one of California's most beautifully restored Spanish Colonial missions, with flowering gardens, a fountain courtyard and the charming 1778 Serra Chapel.

Sleeping & Eating

Oceanside motels and hotels along Pacific Coast Hwy (Hwy 1) charge surprisingly steep rates, especially on summer weekends. Dive inland near the freeways for better bargains.

★ **Crystal Cove Beach Cottages** CABIN $$
(☎ reservations 800-444-7275; www.crystalcovebeachcottages.com; 35 Crystal Cove, Newport

Beach; r without bath $42-127, cottages $162-249; ⏲check-in 4-9pm; 👪) To snag these historic oceanfront cottages, book on the first day of the month six months before your intended stay – or pray for last-minute cancellations.

Shorebreak Hotel BOUTIQUE HOTEL **$$$**
(☎714-861-4470; www.shorebreakhotel.com; 500 Pacific Coast Hwy, Huntington Beach; r $189-495; P❄@🛜🐾) Stow your surfboard (lockers provided) as you head inside HB's hippest hotel, a stone's throw from the pier. The Shorebreak has a surf concierge, a fitness center and yoga studio, bean-bag chairs in the lobby and rattan and hardwood furniture in geometric-patterned air-con rooms (some pet-friendly). Have sunset cocktails on the upstairs deck at Zimzala restaurant. Parking is $27.

Sugar Shack CAFE **$**
(www.hbsugarshack.com; 213½ Main St, Huntington Beach; mains $4-10; ⏲6am-2pm Mon-Tue & Thu-Fri, to 8pm Wed, to 3pm Sat & Sun; 👪) Expect a wait at this HB institution, or get here early to see surfer dudes don their wet suits. Breakfast is served all day on the bustling Main St patio and inside, where you can grab a spot at the counter or a two-top. Photos of surf legends plastering the walls raise this place almost to shrine status.

★ **Bear Flag Fish Company** SEAFOOD **$$**
(☎949-673-3434; www.bearflagfishco.com; 3421 Via Lido, Newport Beach; mains $8-15; ⏲11am-9pm Tue-Sat, to 8pm Sun & Mon; 👪) This is *the* place for generously sized, grilled and panko-breaded fish tacos, ahi burritos, spankin' fresh ceviche and oysters. Pick out what you want from the ice-cold display cases, then grab a picnic-table seat. About the only way this seafood could be any fresher is if you caught and hauled it off the boat yourself!

242 Cafe Fusion Sushi JAPANESE **$$$**
(www.fusionart.us; 242 N Coast Hwy, Laguna Beach; mains $18-45; ⏲4:30-10pm Sun-Thu, to 10:30pm Fri & Sat) One of the only female sushi chefs in Orange County, Miki Izumisawa slices and rolls organic rice into Laguna's best sushi, artfully presented. The place seats maybe two dozen people at a time, so expect a wait or come early. The 'sexy' handroll – spicy ahi and scallops with mint, cilantro, avocado and crispy potato – is date-enhancing.

DON'T MISS

LAGUNA'S FESTIVAL OF ARTS

Hey, did that painting just move? Welcome to the **Pageant of the Masters** (☎800-487-3378; www.foapom.com; 650 Laguna Canyon Rd; tickets from $15; ⏲8:30pm daily mid-Jul–Aug), in which elaborately costumed humans step into painstaking re-creations of famous paintings on an outdoor stage. The pageant began in 1933 as a sideshow to Laguna Beach's **Festival of Arts** (www.foapom.com; 650 Laguna Canyon Rd; admission $7-10; ⏲usually 10am-11:30pm Jul & Aug) and has been a prime attraction ever since. Our favorite part: watching the paintings deconstruct.

San Diego

San Diegans shamelessly promote their hometown as 'America's Finest City.' It's easy to see where that breezy confidence comes from: the sunny weather is practically perfect, and beaches are rarely more than a quick drive away. San Diego's population (1.38 million) makes it the USA's eighth-largest city and California's second largest (after LA), yet we're hard-pressed to think of a more laid-back metropolis anywhere.

The city grew by leaps and bounds during WWII, when the Japanese attack on Pearl Harbor prompted the US Navy to relocate the US Pacific Fleet from Hawaii to San Diego's natural harbor. The military, tourism, education and scientific-research industries (especially medicine and oceanography), as well as high-tech ventures cropping up in inland valleys, have helped shape this city set against the Mexico borderlands.

Sights

San Diego's compact downtown hinges on the historic Gaslamp Quarter, a beehive after dark. Coronado is reached via a stunning bridge, while museum-rich Balboa Park (home of the San Diego Zoo) is north of downtown. Heading west is touristy Old Town and Mission Bay's aquatic playground. Cruising up the coast, Ocean Beach, Mission Beach and Pacific Beach live the laid-back SoCal dream, while La Jolla sits pretty and privileged. The I-5 Fwy cuts through the region north–south.

Greater San Diego

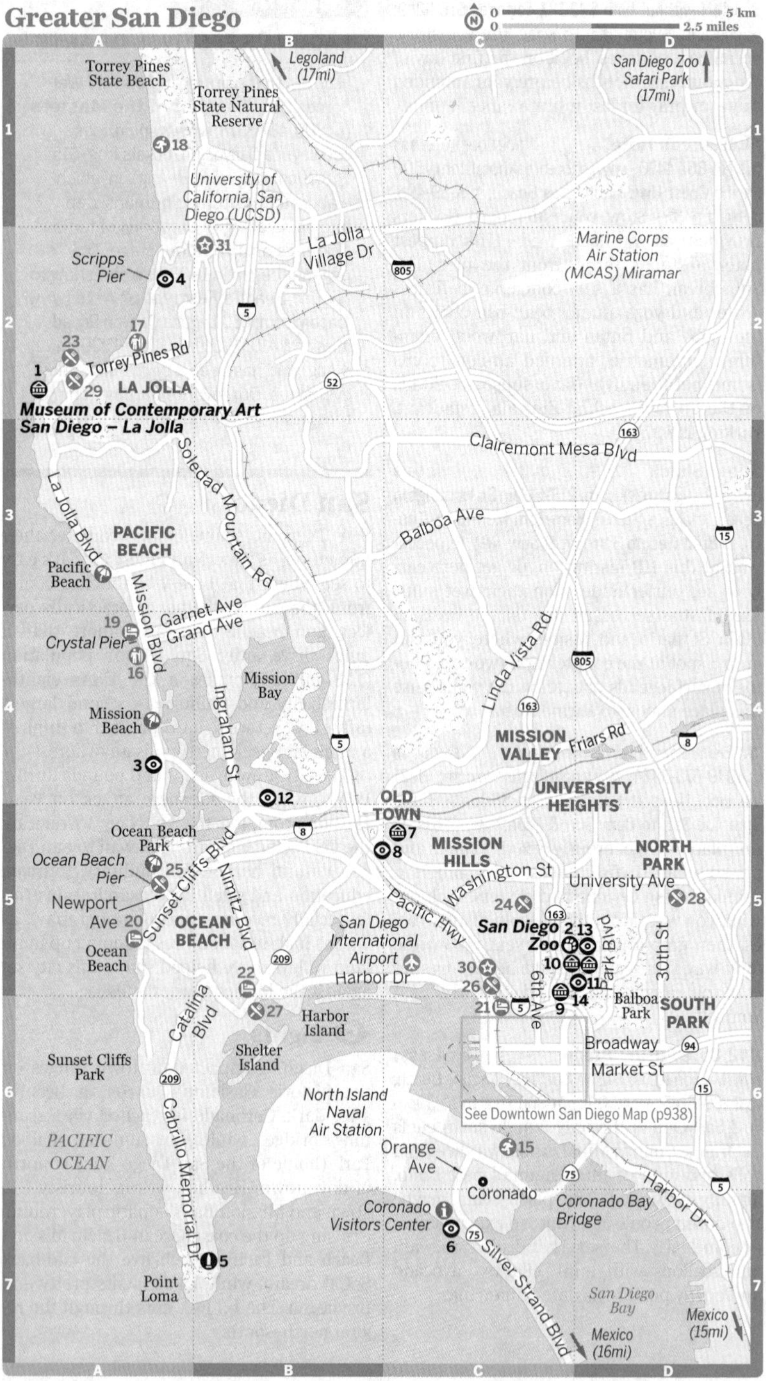

Greater San Diego

Top Sights

1	Museum of Contemporary Art San Diego – La Jolla	A2
2	San Diego Zoo	C5

Sights

3	Belmont Park	A4
4	Birch Aquarium at Scripps	A2
5	Cabrillo National Monument	B7
6	Hotel del Coronado	C7
7	Junípero Serra Museum	C5
	Mingei International Museum	(see 10)
	Museum of Man	(see 10)
8	Old Town State Historic Park	B5
	Reuben H Fleet Science Center	(see 11)
9	San Diego Air & Space Museum	C5
10	San Diego Museum of Art	C5
11	San Diego Natural History Museum	D5
12	SeaWorld San Diego	B4
13	Spanish Village Art Center	D5
14	Spreckels Organ Pavilion	D5
	Timken Museum of Art	(see 10)

Activities, Courses & Tours

15	Bikes & Beyond	C6
16	Pacific Beach Surf Shop	A4
17	Surf Diva	A2
18	Torrey Pines Gliderport	A1

Sleeping

19	Crystal Pier Hotel & Cottages	A4
	Hotel del Coronado	(see 6)
20	Inn at Sunset Cliffs	A5
21	La Pensione Hotel	C6
22	Pearl	B5

Eating

	Bencotto	(see 21)
23	George's at the Cove	A2
24	Hash House a Go Go	C5
25	Hodad's	A5
26	Juniper & Ivy	C5
27	Point Loma Seafoods	B6
	Prado	(see 10)
28	Urban Solace	D5
29	Whisknladle	A2

Drinking & Nightlife

	Ballast Point Tasting Room & Kitchen	(see 26)

Entertainment

30	Casbah	C5
31	La Jolla Playhouse	B2

Information

	Balboa Park Visitors Center	(see 10)

Downtown & Embarcadero

Downtown once harbored a notorious strip of saloons, gambling joints and bordellos known as Stingaree. These days, Stingaree has been beautifully restored and rechristened the **Gaslamp Quarter**, a heart-thumping playground of restaurants, bars, clubs, boutiques and galleries.

At downtown's northern edge, **Little Italy** has evolved into one of the city's hippest neighborhoods to live, eat and shop.

★USS Midway Museum — MUSEUM

(Map p938; ☎619-544-9600; www.midway.org; 910 N Harbor Dr; adult/child $20/10; ⏰10am-5pm, last entry 4pm; 👪) The giant aircraft carrier USS *Midway* was one of the navy's flagships from 1945 to 1991, last playing a combat role in the first Gulf War. On the flight deck of the hulking vessel, walk right up to some 25 restored aircraft including an F-14 Tomcat and F-4 Phantom jet fighter. Admission includes an audio tour, along the narrow confines of the upper decks to the bridge, admiral's war room, brig and 'pri-fly' (primary flight control; the carrier's equivalent of a control tower).

Maritime Museum — MUSEUM

(Map p938; ☎619-234-9153; www.sdmaritime.org; 1492 N Harbor Dr; adult/child $16/8; ⏰9am-9pm late May-early Sep, to 8pm early Sep-late May; 👪) This museum is easy to find: look for the 100ft-high masts of the iron-hulled square-rigger *Star of India*. Built on the Isle of Man and launched in 1863, the tall ship plied the England–India trade route, carried immigrants to New Zealand, became a trading ship based in Hawaii and, finally, ferried cargo in Alaska. It's a handsome vessel, but don't expect anything romantic or glamorous on board.

Museum of Contemporary Art — MUSEUM

(MCASD Downtown; Map p938; ☎858-454-3541; www.mcasd.org; 1001 Kettner Blvd; adult/child under 25yr/senior $10/free/$5, 5-7pm 3rd Thu each month free; ⏰11am-5pm Thu-Tue, to 7pm 3rd Thu each month) This Financial District museum has brought an ever-changing variety of innovative artwork to San Diegans since the 1960s here in the downtown location and **La Jolla branch** (MCASD; Map p936; ☎858-454-3541; www.mcasd.org; 700 Prospect St, La Jolla; adult/child $10/free, 5-7pm 3rd Thu each month free; ⏰11am-5pm Thu-Tue, to 7pm 3rd Thu each month); check the website for exhibits.

Downtown San Diego

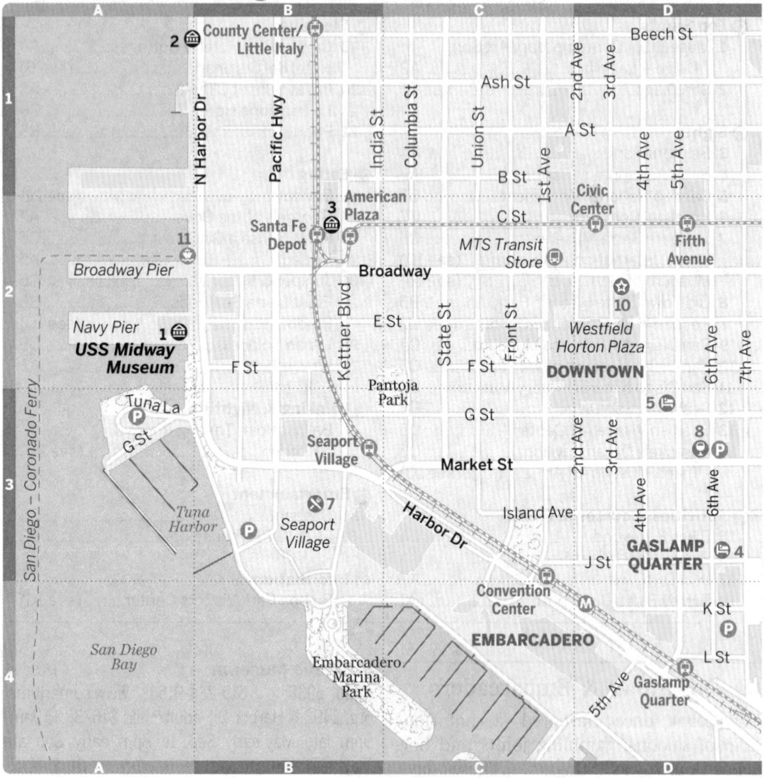

Across from the main building, a slickly renovated section of San Diego's train station houses permanent works by Jenny Holzer and Richard Serra. Tickets are valid for seven days in all locations.

Coronado

Technically a peninsula, Coronado Island is joined to the mainland by a 2.2-mile-long bridge. The peninsula's main draw is the Hotel del Coronado (p942), known for its seaside Victorian architecture and illustrious guest book, which includes Thomas Edison, Babe Ruth and Marilyn Monroe (its exterior stood in for a Miami hotel in the classic flick *Some Like it Hot*).

The hourly **Coronado Ferry** (Map p938; ☎619-234-4111; www.flagshipsd.com; tickets $4.75; ⊙9am-10pm) departs from the Embarcadero's Broadway Pier (990 N Harbor Dr) and from downtown's convention center. All ferries arrive on Coronado at the foot of 1st St, where **Bikes & Beyond** (Map p936; ☎619-435-7180; www.bikes-and-beyond.com; 1201 1st St, Coronado; per hr/day from $8/30; ⊙9am-sunset) rents cruisers and tandems, perfect for pedaling past Coronado's white-sand beaches sprawling south along the **Silver Strand**.

Balboa Park

Balboa Park is an urban oasis brimming with more than a dozen museums, gorgeous gardens and architecture, performance spaces and a zoo. Early 20th-century beaux-arts and Spanish Colonial Revival–style buildings (the legacy of world's fairs) are grouped around plazas along east–west El Prado promenade.

A free tram shuttles visitors around the park, but it's more enjoyable to stroll around the botanical gardens, past the 1915 **Spreckels Organ Pavilion** (Map p936; http://

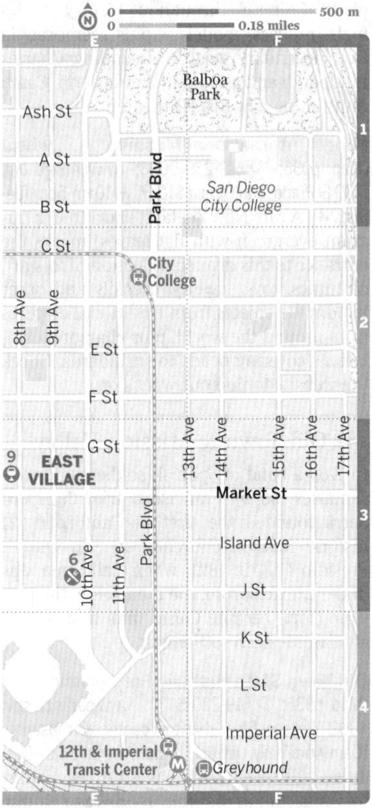

Downtown San Diego

Top Sights
1 USS Midway Museum A2

Sights
2 Maritime Museum A1
3 Museum of Contemporary Art B2

Activities, Courses & Tours
Flagship Cruises .... (see 11)

Sleeping
4 Hotel Solamar D3
5 USA Hostels San Diego D3

Eating
6 Basic E3
7 Puesto at the Headquarters B3

Drinking & Nightlife
8 Bang Bang D3
9 Noble Experiment E3

Entertainment
10 Arts Tix D2

Transport
11 Coronado Ferry A2

spreckelsorgan.org), the shops and galleries of the **Spanish Village Art Center** (Map p936; 11am-4pm) FREE and the international-themed exhibition cottages by the **United Nations Building**.

Stop by the Balboa Park Visitors Center (p945) for maps, events information and discount attraction passes. Free parking lots off Park Blvd fill quickly on weekends. From downtown, take MTS bus 7 ($2.25, 20 minutes).

★San Diego Zoo ZOO
(Map p936; 619-231-1515; http://zoo.sandiego.org; 2920 Zoo Dr; 1-day pass adult/child from $48/38, 2-visit pass to zoo and/or safari park adult/child $86/66; 9am-9pm mid-Jun–early Sep, to 5pm or 6pm early Sep–mid-Jun; P) This justifiably famous zoo is one of SoCal's biggest attractions, showing more than 3000 animals representing over 800 species in a beautifully landscaped setting, typically in enclosures that replicate their natural habitats. Its sister park is San Diego Zoo Safari Park (p945) in northern San Diego County.

Arrive early, as many of the animals are most active in the morning – though many perk up again in the afternoon. Pick up a map at the entrance to the zoo to find your own favorite exhibits.

Reuben H Fleet Science Center MUSEUM
(Map p936; 619-238-1233; www.rhfleet.org; 1875 El Prado; adult/child incl IMAX $20/17; 10am-5pm Mon-Thu, to 6pm Fri-Sun;) One of Balboa Park's most popular venues, this hands-on science museum features interactive displays and a toddler room. Look out for opportunities to build gigantic structures with Keva planks and visit the **Gallery of Illusions and Perceptions**. The biggest draw-card is the **Giant Dome Theater**, which screens several different films each day. The hemispherical, wraparound screen and 152-speaker state-of-the-art sound system create sensations ranging from pretty cool to mind-blowing.

San Diego Natural History Museum MUSEUM
(Map p936; 619-232-3821; www.sdnhm.org; 1788 El Prado; adult/child $19/11; 10am-5pm;) The 'Nat' houses 7.5 million specimens,

including rocks, fossils and taxidermied animals, as well as an impressive dinosaur skeleton and a California fault-line exhibit, all in beautiful spaces. Kids love the movies about the natural world in the giant-screen cinema; the selections change frequently. Children's programs are held most weekends. Special exhibits (some with an extra charge) span pirates to King Tut. The museum also arranges field trips and nature walks in Balboa Park and further afield.

Museum of Man MUSEUM

(Map p936; ☎619-239-2001; www.museumofman.org; Plaza de California, 1350 El Prado; adult/child/student/child $12.50/5/8; ⏰10am-5pm Sun-Wed, to 8:30pm Thu-Sat) This is the county's only anthropological museum, with exhibits spanning ancient Egypt, the Mayans and local native Kumeyaay people, human evolution and the human life cycle. Recent temporary exhibits have covered everything from women's empowerment to beer. The basket and pottery collections are especially fine. The museum shop sells handicrafts from Central America and elsewhere.

Timken Museum of Art MUSEUM

(Map p936; ☎619-239-5548; www.timkenmuseum.org; 1500 El Prado; ⏰10am-4:30pm Tue-Sat, from noon Sun) FREE Don't skip the Timken, home of the Putnam collection, a small but impressive group of paintings, including works by Rembrandt, Rubens, El Greco, Cézanne and Pissarro, plus a wonderful selection of Russian icons. Built in 1965, the building stands out for *not* being in imitation Spanish style.

San Diego Museum of Art MUSEUM

(SDMA; Map p936; ☎619-232-7931; www.sdmart.org; 1450 El Prado; adult/child $12/4.50; ⏰10am-5pm Mon-Tue & Thu-Sat, from noon Sun, also 5-8pm Fri mid-Jul–mid-Sep) The SDMA is the city's largest art museum. The permanent collection has works by a number of European masters from the renaissance to the modernist eras (though no renowned pieces), American landscape paintings, and several fantastic pieces in the Asian galleries, and there are often important traveling exhibits. The **Sculpture Garden** has works by Alexander Calder and Henry Moore.

San Diego Air & Space Museum MUSEUM

(Map p936; ☎619-234-8291; www.sandiegoairandspace.org; 2001 Pan American Plaza; adult/child $18/9; ⏰10am-4:30pm; 👪) The round building at the southern end of the plaza houses an excellent museum with extensive displays of aircraft throughout history – originals, replicas, models – plus memorabilia from legendary aviators including Charles Lindbergh and astronaut John Glenn. Catch films in the new 3D/4D theater.

Mingei International Museum MUSEUM

(Map p936; ☎619-239-0003; www.mingei.org; 1439 El Prado; adult/child $10/7; ⏰10am-5pm Tue-Sun; 👪) A rare New Zealand kauri tree (a fragrant evergreen with flat leaves) marks the entrance to this diverse collection of folk art, costumes, toys, jewelry, utensils and other handmade objects from traditional cultures from around the world, plus changing exhibitions covering beads to surfboards. Check the website to find out what's on.

Old Town & Mission Valley

In 1769 a band of Spanish soldiers and missionaries led by Franciscan friar Junípero Serra founded the first of California's 21 historic mission churches on San Diego's Presidio Hill. In 1821, when California was under Mexican rule, the area below the presidio (fort) became California's first official civilian Mexican settlement.

Old Town State Historic Park HISTORIC SITE

(Map p936; ☎619-220-5422; www.parks.ca.gov; 4002 Wallace St; ⏰visitor center & museums 10am-4pm daily Oct-Apr, to 5pm Fri-Sun May-Sep; P 👪) FREE This park has an excellent history museum in the **Robinson-Rose House** at the southern end of the plaza. You'll also find a diorama depicting the original pueblo and the park's **visitors center**, where you can pick up a copy of the *Old Town San Diego State Historic Park Tour Guide & Brief History* ($3), or take a guided tour (free) at 11am and 2pm daily.

Mission Basilica San Diego de Alcalá CHURCH

(☎619-281-8449; www.missionsandiego.com; 10818 San Diego Mission Rd; adult/child $3/1; ⏰9am-4:30pm; P) Although the site of the first California mission (1769) was on Presidio Hill by present-day Old Town, in 1774 Padre Junípero Serra moved it about 7 miles upriver, closer to water and more arable land, now the Mission Basilica San Diego de Alcalá. In 1784 missionaries built a solid adobe-and-timber church, which was destroyed by an earthquake in 1803. The church was promptly rebuilt, and at least some of it still stands on a slope overlooking Mission Valley.

Junípero Serra Museum MUSEUM
(Map p936; ☎619-232-6203; www.sandiegohistory.org; 2727 Presidio Dr; adult/child $6/3; ⏲10am-5pm Sat & Sun year-round, also 10am-5pm Fri early Jun-early Sep; P 👪) Located in one of the most important historical buildings in the city, this small but interesting collection of artifacts and pictures is from the Mission and rancho periods, and it gives a good sense of the earliest days of European settlement up to 1929 when the museum was founded.

Point Loma

Cabrillo National Monument MONUMENT
(Map p936; ☎619-557-5450; www.nps.gov/cabr; 1800 Cabrillo Memorial Dr; per car $5; ⏲9am-5pm; P) Atop a steep hill at the tip of the peninsula, this is San Diego's finest locale for history, views and nature walks. It's also the best place in town to see the gray-whale migration (January to March) from land. You may forget you're in a major metropolitan area.

The **visitor center** has a comprehensive, old-school presentation on Portuguese explorer Juan Rodríguez Cabrillo's 1542 voyage up the California coast, plus good exhibits on early Native Californian inhabitants and the area's natural history.

Mission Bay & Beaches

San Diego's big three beach towns all have ribbons of hedonism where armies of tanned, taut bodies frolic in the sand.

West of amoeba-shaped Mission Bay, surf-friendly **Mission Beach** and its northern neighbor, **Pacific Beach** (aka 'PB'), are connected by car-free **Ocean Front Walk**, which swarms with skaters, joggers and cyclists year-round. South of Mission Bay, bohemian **Ocean Beach** (OB) has a fishing pier, beach volleyball and good surf. Its main drag, **Newport Avenue**, is chockablock with scruffy bars, flip-flop eateries and shops selling surf gear, tattoos, vintage clothing and antiques.

Belmont Park AMUSEMENT PARK
(Map p936; ☎858-458-1549; www.belmontpark.com; 3146 Mission Blvd; per ride $3-6, all-day pass adult/child $29/18; ⏲from 11am daily, closing time varies; P) Pint-sized Belmont Park beckons with a historic wooden roller coaster, wave simulator and indoor pool.

SeaWorld San Diego THEME PARK
(Map p936; ☎800-257-4268; www.seaworldsandiego.com; 500 SeaWorld Dr; adult/child 3-9yr $89/83; ⏲daily; P 👪) SeaWorld opened in San Diego in 1964 and for years has been one of California's most popular theme parks. Many visitors spend the whole day here, shuttling between aquatic-themed rides, animal encounters and exhibits. However, the park's best-known attraction is also its most controversial: live shows featuring trained dolphins, sea lions and killer whales. Since the release of the 2013 documentary *Blackfish*, SeaWorld's treatment of its captive orcas has come under intense scrutiny and the company has been hit by falling visitor numbers and a catalogue of negative PR.

La Jolla

Facing one of SoCal's loveliest sweeps of coastline, wealthy La Jolla (Spanish for 'the jewel,' pronounced la-*hoy*-ah) possesses shimmering beaches and an upscale downtown filled with boutiques and cafes. Oceanfront diversions include the **Children's Pool** (no longer for swimming, it's now home to barking sea lions), kayaking and exploring sea caves at **La Jolla Cove** and snorkeling at **San Diego-La Jolla Underwater Park**.

Torrey Pines State Natural Reserve PARK
(☎858-755-2063; www.torreypine.org; 12600 N Torrey Pines Park Rd; ⏲7:15am-dusk, visitor center 10am-4pm Oct-Apr, 9am-6pm May-Sep; P) Between N Torrey Pines Rd and the ocean, and from the **Torrey Pines Gliderport** (Map p936; ☎858-452-9858; www.flytorrey.com; 2800 Torrey Pines Scenic Dr; 20min paragliding $175, hang gliding tandem flight per person $225) to Del Mar, this reserve preserves the last mainland stands of the Torrey pine *(Pinus torreyana)*, a species adapted to sparse rainfall and sandy, stony soils. Steep sandstone gullies have eroded into wonderfully textured surfaces, and the views over the ocean and north, including whale-watching, are superb. Rangers lead nature walks on weekends and holidays. Several walking trails wind through the reserve and down to the beach. Parking fees per car vary from $4 per hour to $15 per day.

Birch Aquarium at Scripps AQUARIUM
(Map p936; ☎858-534-3474; www.aquarium.ucsd.edu; 2300 Expedition Way; adult/child $17/12.50; ⏲9am-5pm; P 👪) Marine scientists were working at the Birch Aquarium at Scripps Institution of Oceanography (SIO) as early as 1910 and, helped by donations from the ever-generous Scripps family, the institute has grown to be one of the world's largest

marine research institutions. It is now a part of University of California, San Diego (UCSD). Off N Torrey Pines Rd, the aquarium has brilliant displays. The **Hall of Fishes** has more than 30 fish tanks, simulating marine environments from the Pacific Northwest to tropical seas.

Activities

Surfing and windsurfing are both excellent, although beware of territorial locals in some places. Call ☎619-221-8824 for surf reports.

Pacific Beach Surf Shop SURFING
(Map p936; ☎858-373-1138; www.pbsurfshop.com; 4150 Mission Blvd; ⏰store 9am-7pm, lessons hourly until 4pm) This shop provides instruction through its Pacific Beach Surf School. It has friendly service, and also rents wetsuits and both soft (foam) and hard (fiberglass) boards. Call ahead for lessons.

Surf Diva SURFING
(Map p936; ☎858-454-8273; www.surfdiva.com; 2160 Avenida de la Playa; ⏰store 8:30am-6pm, varies seasonally) The wonderful women here offer surf classes from $75 and rent boards and wetsuits.

Flagship Cruises BOAT TOUR
(Map p938; ☎619-234-4111; www.flagshipsd.com; 990 N Harbor Dr; tours adult/child from $23/11.50; 👪) Harbor tours and seasonal whale-watching cruises from the Embarcadero, from one to several hours long.

Sleeping

Rates skyrocket in summer, especially by the beaches. Chain hotels and motels cluster inland off major freeways and in Mission Valley. Rates quoted here do not include lodging tax (10.5%).

Downtown & Around

★**USA Hostels San Diego** HOSTEL $
(Map p938; ☎619-232-3100; www.usahostels.com; 726 5th Ave; dm/r without bath from $33/79; @📶) Lots of charm and color at this convivial hostel in a former Victorian-era hotel. Look for cheerful rooms, a full kitchen, a communal lounge for chilling and in-house parties and beach barbecues. Rates include linens, lockers and pancakes for breakfast. It's smack-dab in the middle of Gaslamp nightlife. No air-con.

La Pensione Hotel BOUTIQUE HOTEL $$
(Map p936; ☎619-236-8000; www.lapensionehotel.com; 606 W Date St; r from $150; P❄📶) Despite the name, Little Italy's La Pensione isn't a pension but an intimate, friendly, recently renovated hotel of 68 rooms with queen-size beds and private bathrooms. It's set around a frescoed courtyard and it's just steps to the neighborhood's dining, cafes and galleries, and walking distance to most downtown attractions. There's an attractive cafe downstairs. Parking is $15.

Hotel Solamar BOUTIQUE HOTEL $$
(Map p938; ☎877-230-0300, 619-819-9500; www.hotelsolamar.com; 435 6th Ave; r $169-299; P❄@📶🏊) A great compromise in the Gaslamp: hip style that needn't break the bank. Lounge beats animate your view of skyscrapers from the pool deck and bar, and rooms have sleek lines and nautical blue and neorococo accents for a touch of fun. There's a fitness center, in-room yoga kit, loaner bikes and a nightly complimentary wine hour. Parking costs $45.

Beaches

Pearl MOTEL $$
(Map p936; ☎619-226-6100, 877-732-7574; www.thepearlsd.com; 1410 Rosecrans St; r $129-169; P❄📶🏊) The midcentury modern Pearl feels more Palm Springs than San Diego. The 23 rooms in its 1959 shell have soothing blue hues, trippy surf motifs and bettas in fishbowls. There's a lively pool scene (including 'dive-in' movies on Wednesday nights), or play Jenga or Parcheesi in the groovy, shag-carpeted lobby. Light sleepers: request a room away from busy street traffic.

Inn at Sunset Cliffs INN $$
(Map p936; ☎866-786-2453, 619-222-7901; www.innatsunsetcliffs.com; 1370 Sunset Cliffs Blvd; r/ste from $175/289; P❄@📶🏊) At the south end of Ocean Beach, wake up to the sound of surf crashing onto the rocky shore. This low-key 1965 charmer wraps around a flower-bedecked courtyard with small heated pool. Its 24 breezy rooms are compact, but most have attractive stone-and-tile bathrooms, and some suites have full kitchens. Even if the ocean air occasionally takes its toll on exterior surfaces, it's hard not to love this place. Free parking.

★**Hotel del Coronado** LUXURY HOTEL $$$
(Hotel Del; Map p936; ☎619-435-6611; www.hoteldel.com; 1500 Orange Ave; r from $289; P🚭❄@📶🏊👪🐾) San Diego's iconic hotel provides the essential Coronado experience: over a century of history, a pool, full-service

spa, shops, restaurants, manicured grounds, a white-sand beach and an ice-skating rink in winter. Even the basic rooms have luxurious marbled bathrooms. Note: half the accommodations are not in the main Victorian-era hotel (368 rooms) but in an adjacent seven-story building constructed in the 1970s. For a sense of place, book a room in the original hotel. Parking is $37.

★Crystal Pier Hotel & Cottages COTTAGE $$$
(Map p936; ☎858-483-6983, 800-748-5894; www.crystalpier.com; 4500 Ocean Blvd; d $185-525; P 📶 👪) Charming, wonderful and unlike anyplace else in San Diego, Crystal Pier has cottages built right on the pier above the water. Almost all 29 cottages have full ocean views and kitchens; most date from 1936. Newer, larger cottages sleep up to six. Book eight to 11 months in advance for summer reservations. Minimum-stay requirements vary by season. No air-con. Rates include parking.

Eating

Generally speaking, you'll find steakhouses and seafood institutions near downtown's waterfront, boisterous gastropubs in the Gaslamp Quarter, casual seafood and burgers by the beach, hip kitchens in neighborhoods around Balboa Park, and tacos and margaritas, well, everywhere.

Downtown & Around

Basic PIZZA $
(Map p938; ☎619-531-8869; www.barbasic.com; 410 10th Ave; small/large pizzas from $9/14; ⏲11:30am-2am) East Village hipsters feast on fragrant thin-crust, brick-oven-baked pizzas under Basic's high-ceilinged roof (it's in a former warehouse). Small pizzas have a large footprint but are pretty light. Toppings span the usual to the newfangled, like the mashed pie with mozzarella, mashed potatoes and bacon. Wash them down with beers (craft, naturally) or one of several mule cocktails.

★Puesto at the Headquarters MEXICAN $$
(Map p938; ☎610-233-8800; www.eatpuesto.com; 789 W Harbor Dr, The Headquarters; mains $11-19; ⏲11am-10pm) This upscale eatery serves Mexican street food that knocked our *zapatos* off: innovative takes on traditional tacos such as chicken (with hibiscus, chipotle, pineapple and avocado) and some out-there fillings such as potato-soy chorizo. Other highlights: crab guacamole, *barbacoa* short ribs (braised in chili sauce) and a Mexican street bowl (tropical fruits with chili, sea salt and lime).

Bencotto ITALIAN $$
(Map p936; ☎619-450-4786; www.lovebencotto.com; 750 W Fir St; mains $14-26; ⏲11:30am-9:30pm Sun-Thu, to 10:30pm Fri & Sat; P) Bencotto melds the old with the new of Little Italy – contemporary, angular, multistory, architect-designed, arty and green – and the food is great too, from fresh-sliced prosciutto to pasta *a modo tuo* (your way), with more than 100 potential combos of fresh pasta and sauce.

Juniper & Ivy MODERN AMERICAN $$$
(Map p936; ☎619-269-9036; www.juniperandivy.com; 2228 Kettner Blvd; small plates $9-17, mains $19-36; ⏲4-10pm Sun-Thu, to 11pm Fri & Sat) Chef Richard Blais has opened San Diego's restaurant of the moment. The menu changes daily, but if we mention molecular gastronomic takes on prawn and pork rigatoni; artisan-farmed strip steak with smoked potato, porcini onion rings and kimchi ketchup; and homemade Yodels snack cakes for dessert, do you get the idea? It's in a rockin' refurbished warehouse.

Balboa Park & Around

Hash House a Go Go AMERICAN $$
(Map p936; ☎619-298-4646; www.hashhouseagogo.com; 3628 5th Ave, Hillcrest; mains breakfast $9-18, dinner $15-29; ⏲7.30am-2pm Mon-Fri, to 2:30pm Sat & Sun, plus 5:30-9pm Tue-Thu, to 9:30pm Fri-Sun; 👪) This buzzing bungalow makes biscuits and gravy straight outta Indiana, towering Benedicts, large-as-your-head pancakes and – wait for it – hash seven different ways. Eat your whole breakfast, and you won't need to eat the rest of the day. It's worth coming back for the equally massive burgers, sage fried chicken and award-winning meatloaf sandwich. No wonder it's called 'twisted farm food.'

Urban Solace CALIFORNIAN $$
(Map p936; ☎619-295-6464; www.urbansolace.net; 3823 30th St, North Park; mains lunch $10-23, dinner $17-27; ⏲11am-10pm Mon-Thu, 11am-11pm Fri, 10:30am-11pm Sat, 9:30am-2:30pm & 4-9pm Sun) North Park's young hip gourmets revel in creative comfort food here: bluegrass burger; 'not your mama's' meatloaf of ground lamb, fig, pine nuts and feta;

'duckaroni' (mac 'n' cheese with duck confit); and chicken and dumplings. The setting's surprisingly chilled out for such great eats; maybe it's the creative cocktails.

Prado CALIFORNIAN $$$
(Map p936; ☎619-557-9441; www.pradobalboa.com; House of Hospitality, 1549 El Prado; mains lunch $12-21, dinner $22-35; ⏱11:30am-3pm Mon-Fri, from 11am Sat & Sun, 5-9pm Sun & Tue-Thu, to 10pm Fri & Sat) In one of San Diego's most beautiful dining rooms, feast on Cal-eclectic cooking by one of San Diego's most renowned chefs: bakery sandwiches, chicken and orecchiette pasta, and pork prime rib. Go for a civilized lunch on the verandah or for afternoon cocktails and appetizers in the bar.

Beaches

Hodad's BURGERS $
(Map p936; ☎619-224-4623; www.hodadies.com; 5010 Newport Ave, Ocean Beach; dishes $4-13; ⏱11am-9pm Sun-Thu, to 10pm Fri & Sat) Since the flower-power days of 1969, OB's legendary burger joint has served great shakes, massive baskets of onion rings and succulent hamburgers wrapped in paper. The walls are covered in license plates, grunge/surf-rock plays (loud!) and your bearded, tattooed server might sidle in to your booth to take your order. No shirt, no shoes, no problem, dude.

Point Loma Seafoods SEAFOOD $
(Map p936; www.pointlomaseafoods.com; 2805 Emerson St; mains $7-16; ⏱9am-7pm Mon-Sat, 10am-7pm Sun; P ♿) For off-the-boat-fresh seafood sandwiches, salads, fried dishes and icy-cold beer, order at the counter at this fish-market-cum-deli and grab a seat at a picnic table on the upstairs, harbor-view deck. In the Shelter Island Marina, it's a San Diego institution dating back to Portuguese fisherman days. It also does great sushi and takeout dishes from ceviche to clam chowder.

Whisknladle CALIFORNIAN $$
(Map p936; ☎858-551-7575; www.wnlhosp.com; 1044 Wall St; mains lunch $14-21, dinner $15-36; ⏱11:30am-9pm Mon-Thu, to 10pm Fri, 10am-10pm Sat, 10am-9:30pm Sun) Gourmets and gourmands alike love Whisknladle's 'slow food' preparations of local, farm-fresh ingredients, served on a breezy covered patio and meant for sharing. Every minute preparation, from curing to pickling and macerating, is done in-house. The menu changes daily, but it's always clever. So are the cocktails (the London's Burning mixes gin and jalapeño water).

★George's at the Cove CALIFORNIAN $$$
(Map p936; ☎858-454-4244; www.georgesatthecove.com; 1250 Prospect St, La Jolla; mains $13-50; ⏱11am-10pm Mon-Thu, to 11pm Fri-Sun) If you've got the urge to splurge, the Euro-Cal cooking is as dramatic as the oceanfront location thanks to the bottomless imagination of chef Trey Foshée. George's has graced just about every list of top restaurants in California, and indeed the USA. Three venues allow you to enjoy it at different price points: Ocean Terrace, George's Bar and George's California Modern.

Drinking & Nightlife

Downtown's Gaslamp Quarter has the rowdiest bars and hottest nightclubs. Lesbigay nightlife hits up Hillcrest and North Park.

Bang Bang BAR
(Map p938; www.bangbangsd.com; 526 Market St; ⏱closed Mon & Tue) Beneath lantern-light, the Gaslamp's hottest new spot has local and world-known DJs and serves sushi and Asian small plates like dumplings and panko-crusted shrimp to nurse the imaginative cocktails (some in giant goblets meant for sharing with your posse). Plus, the bathrooms are shrines to Ryan Gosling and Hello Kitty: in a word, awesome.

Noble Experiment BAR
(Map p938; ☎619-888-4713; http://nobleexperimentsd.com; 777 G St; ⏱7pm-2am Tue-Sun) This place is literally a find. Open a secret door and enter a contemporary speakeasy with miniature gold skulls on the walls, classical paintings on the ceilings and some 400 cocktails on the list (from $12). The hard part: getting in. Text for a reservation, and staff will tell you if your requested time is available and how to find the place.

Ballast Point Tasting Room & Kitchen PUB
(Map p936; ☎619-255-7213; www.ballastpoint.com; 2215 India St; ⏱11am-11pm) Opened in 2013, this is the newest and funnest location from this San Diego–based brewery, and it does a lot of R&D for the rest of the company. Three 4oz tasters of beer for just $5 is the best deal in town. Enjoy them with a full menu including housemade pretzels, beer-steamed mussels, salads and grilled dishes.

☆ Entertainment

Arts Tix (Map p938; ☎858-381-5595; www.sdartstix.com; 28 Horton Plaza) sells half-price and discounted tickets to plays, comedy shows and more.

Casbah LIVE MUSIC

(Map p936; ☎619-232-4355; www.casbahmusic.com; 2501 Kettner Blvd; tickets $5-45) Bands from Smashing Pumpkins to Death Cab for Cutie all rocked the Casbah on their way up the charts and it's still a good place to catch tomorrow's headliners.

La Jolla Playhouse THEATER

(Map p936; ☎858-550-1010; www.lajollaplayhouse.org; 2910 La Jolla Village Dr; tickets $20-75) Inside the Mandell Weiss Center for the Performing Arts, this theater has sent dozens of productions to Broadway including *Jersey Boys*, *Peter and the Starcatcher* and 2010 Tony winner *Memphis*.

ℹ Information

MEDIA

San Diego Magazine (www.sandiegomagazine.com) Glossy monthly.

San Diego Reader (www.sandiegoreader.com) Free tabloid covers entertainment, food, beer and more.

U-T San Diego (www.utsandiego.com) The city's major daily newspaper.

MEDICAL SERVICES

Scripps Mercy Hospital (☎619-294-8111; www.scripps.org; 4077 5th Ave) Has a 24-hour emergency room.

MONEY

TravelEx (☎858-457-2412; www.travelex.com; Westfield UTC, 4417 La Jolla Village Dr; ⏰10am-7pm Mon-Fri, to 6pm Sat, 11am-4pm Sun) For foreign-currency exchange.

TOURIST INFORMATION

Balboa Park Visitors Center (Map p936; ☎619-239-0512; www.balboapark.org; House of Hospitality, 1549 El Prado; ⏰9:30am-4:30pm) In the House of Hospitality, the visitor center sells park maps and discount passports to museums and the zoo.

Coronado Visitors Center (Map p936; ☎866-599-7242, 619-437-8788; www.coronadovisitorcenter.com; 1100 Orange Ave; ⏰9am-5pm Mon-Fri, 10am-5pm Sat & Sun)

USEFUL WEBSITES

Gaslamp Quarter Association (http://gaslamp.org) Everything you need to know about the bustling Gaslamp Quarter, including parking secrets.

San Diego Tourism (www.sandiego.org) Search sights, activities, neighborhoods and more, and make hotel reservations.

ℹ Getting There & Away

Served mainly by domestic US and Mexico flights, **San Diego International Airport** (SAN; Map p936; www.san.org; 3325 N Harbor Dr; 📶) sits 3 miles northwest of downtown.

Greyhound (Map p938; ☎800-231-2222, 619-515-1100; www.greyhound.com; 1313 National Ave) has hourly direct buses to Los Angeles ($19, two hours).

Amtrak (☎800-872-7245; www.amtrak.com) runs the Pacific Surfliner several times daily to Los Angeles ($37, 2¾ hours) and Santa Barbara ($42, 5¾ hours) from downtown's historic **Union Station** (Santa Fe Depot; 1050 Kettner Blvd).

Major international car-rental companies have desks at the airport. Smaller, independent **West Coast Rent a Car** (☎619-544-0606; www.sandiegoautos.org; 834 W Grape St; ⏰9am-6pm Mon-Sat) rents to under-25s, with free airport pickups.

ℹ Getting Around

MTS bus 992 'The Flyer' ($2.25) runs every 15 to 30 minutes between the airport and Downtown from 5am until 11pm daily. Airport shuttles like **Super Shuttle** (☎800-258-3826; www.supershuttle.com) charge around $8 to $13 to downtown; book in advance. An airport taxi to downtown averages $10 to $16, plus tip.

City buses ($2.25 to $2.50) and trolleys ($2.50), including south to the Mexico border, are operated by **Metropolitan Transit System** (MTS; ☎619-233-3004; www.sdmts.com). MTS's **Transit Store** (Map p938; 102 Broadway; ⏰9am-5pm Mon-Fri) sells regional passes (one/two/three/four days $5/9/12/15); purchase one-day passes on board buses (surcharge $2).

Metered taxis charge $2.80 at flag fall, then $3 per mile.

Around San Diego

San Diego Zoo Safari Park ZOO

(☎760-747-8702; www.sdzsafaripark.org; 15500 San Pasqual Valley Rd, Escondido; admission adult/child $48/38, 2-visit pass to zoo and/or safari park $86/66; ⏰9am-5pm late Aug–mid-Jun, to 7pm late Jun–mid-Aug; 👪). At this 1800-acre open-range zoo, giraffes graze, lions lounge and rhinos roam more or less freely on the valley floor.

For that instant safari feel, board the Africa Tram, which tours the second-largest continent in just 25 minutes.

The park is in Escondido, about 35 miles northeast of Downtown San Diego. Take the I-15 Fwy to the E Via Rancho Pkwy exit, then follow the signs. Parking is $12.

Legoland

Legoland THEME PARK
(☎760-918-5346; http://california.legoland.com; 1 Legoland Dr, Carlsbad; adult/child from $87/81; ⏲open almost daily year-round, hours vary; P) This fun fantasy theme park of rides, shows and attractions is mostly suited to the elementary-school set. Tots can dig for dinosaur bones, pilot helicopters and earn their driver's license. Families with young children can overnight in the brand-new, colorful Lego-themed **hotel** (☎760-918-5346, 877-534-6526; http://california.legoland.com/legoland-hotel; 5885 The Crossings Dr; r incl breakfast from $369; P @).

From Downtown San Diego (about 33 miles), take the I-5 Fwy north to Carlsbad's Cannon Rd exit. Parking is $15.

PALM SPRINGS & THE DESERTS

From swanky Palm Springs to desolate Death Valley, Southern California's desert region swallows up 25% of the entire state. At first what seems harrowingly barren may eventually be transformed in your mind's eye to perfect beauty: weathered volcanic peaks, booming sand dunes, purple-tinged mountains, cactus gardens, tiny wildflowers pushing up from hard-baked soil in spring, lizards scurrying beside colossal boulders, and in the night sky, uncountable stars. California's deserts are serenely spiritual, surprisingly chic and ultimately irresistible, whether you're a bohemian artist, movie star, rock climber or 4WD adventurer.

Palm Springs

The Rat Pack is back, baby – or, at least, its hangout is. In the 1950 and '60s, Palm Springs (population 45,000), some 100 miles east of LA, was the swinging getaway of Sinatra, Elvis and other stars. Once the Rat Pack packed it in, Palm Springs surrendered to retirees in golf clothing. Recently a new generation has rediscovered the city's retro-chic charms: kidney-shaped pools, 'starchitect' bungalows, Mid-Century Modern boutique hotels and bars serving perfect martinis. Today retirees mix comfortably with hipsters, hikers and an out-and-proud LGBTIQ community.

Sights & Activities

Palm Springs is the hub of the Coachella Valley, a string of desert towns along Hwy 111. In PS' compact downtown, one-way southbound Palm Canyon Dr is paralleled by northbound Indian Canyon Dr.

★ **Palm Springs Aerial Tramway** CABLE CAR
(☎888-515-8726; www.pstramway.com; 1 Tram Way; adult/child $24/17; ⏲from 10am Mon-Fri, 8am Sat & Sun, last tram up 8pm Sun-Thu, 9pm Fri & Sat, last tram down 9:45pm Sun-Thu, 10:30pm Fri & Sat) North of downtown, this rotating cable car is a highlight of any Palm Springs trip. It climbs nearly 6000 vertical feet through five different vegetation zones, from the Sonoran desert floor to the San Jacinto Mountains, in less than 15 minutes. The 2.5-mile ascent is said to be the temperature equivalent of driving from Mexico to Canada. It's 30°F to 40°F (up to 22°C) cooler as you step out into pine forests at the top, so bring warm clothing.

Sunnylands NOTABLE BUILDING
(☎760-202-2222; www.sunnylands.org; 37977 Bob Hope Dr, Rancho Mirage; admission free, tours $20-40; ⏲9am-4pm Thu-Sun, closed Jul & Aug) Sunnylands is the Mid-Century Modern estate of Walter and Leonore Annenberg, one of America's 'first families.' At their winter estate in Rancho Mirage, the Annenbergs entertained seven US presidents, royalty, Hollywood celebrities and international heads of state.

A new visitor center and museum screen a film and show changing exhibits about the estate. Just beyond is a magnificent desert garden. Reserve as early as possible for tours of the stunning house with its art collection, architecture and furniture.

Palm Springs Art Museum MUSEUM
(☎760-322-4800; www.psmuseum.org; 101 Museum Dr; adult/child $12.50/free, 4-8pm Thu free; ⏲10am-5pm Tue-Wed & Fri-Sun, noon-8pm Thu) See the evolution of American painting, sculpture, photography and glass art over the past century. Alongside well-curated

temporary exhibitions, the permanent collection is especially strong in modern painting and sculpture, with works by Henry Moore, Ed Ruscha, Mark di Suvero and other heavy hitters. There's also stunning glass art by Dale Chihuly and William Morris and a collection of pre-Columbian figurines.

Living Desert Zoo & Gardens ZOO
(☎760-346-5694; www.livingdesert.org; 47900 Portola Ave, Palm Desert, off Hwy 111; adult/child $20/10; ⊙9am-5pm Oct-May, 8am-1:30pm Jun-Sep;) This amazing zoo exhibits a variety of desert plants and animals, alongside exhibits on desert geology and Native American culture. Highlights include a walk-through wildlife hospital and an African-themed village with a fair-trade market and storytelling grove. Camel rides, a spin on the endangered-species carousel, and a hop-on, hop-off shuttle cost extra. It's educational fun and worth the 30-minute (15-mile) drive down-valley.

Indian Canyons HIKING
(☎760-323-6018; www.indian-canyons.com; 38520 S Palm Canyon Dr; adult/child $9/5, 90min guided hike $3/2; ⊙8am-5pm Oct-Jun, Fri-Sun only Jul-Sep) Streams flowing from the San Jacinto Mountains sustain a rich variety of plants in oases around Palm Springs. Home to Native American communities for hundreds of years and now part of the Agua Caliente Indian Reservation, these canyons, shaded by fan palms and surrounded by towering cliffs, are a delight for hikers.

Smoke Tree Stables HORSEBACK RIDING
(☎760-327-1372; www.smoketreestables.com; 2500 S Toledo Ave; 1/2hr guided ride $50/100) Near the Indian Canyons, this outfit arranges trail rides ranging from one-hour outings to all-day treks, for both novice and experienced riders. Reservations required.

Sleeping

High-season winter rates are quoted below; rates drop midweek and during summer. Motels hug Hwy 111 southeast of downtown. Book ahead, especially for weekends.

Caliente Tropics MOTEL $
(☎760-327-1391; www.calientetropics.com; 411 E Palm Canyon Dr; r weekday/weekend from $54/109;) Elvis once frolicked poolside at this premier budget pick, a nicely kept 1964 tiki-style motor lodge. Drift off to dreamland on quality mattresses in rooms that are spacious and dressed in warm colors.

★Orbit In BOUTIQUE HOTEL $$
(☎877-966-7248, 760-323-3585; www.orbitin.com; 562 W Arenas Rd; r from $149;) Swing back to the '50s – pinkie raised and all – during the 'Orbitini' happy hour at this fabulously retro property, with high-end Mid-Century Modern furniture (Eames, Noguchi et al) in rooms set around a quiet saline pool with a Jacuzzi and fire pit. The long list of freebies includes bike rentals and daytime sodas and snacks.

Ace Hotel & Swim Club HOTEL $$
(☎760-325-9900; www.acehotel.com/palmsprings; 701 E Palm Canyon Dr; r from $200; @) Palm Springs goes Hollywood – with all the sass, but sans the attitude – at this former Howard Johnson motel turned hipster hangout. Rooms (many with patio) sport a glorified tent-cabin look and are crammed with lifestyle essentials (big flat-screen TVs, MP3 plugs). Happening pool scene and there's the **Feel Good Spa** (☎760-866-6188; www.acehotel.com/palmsprings/spa; 701 E Palm Canyon Dr), on-site restaurant and a bar to boot.

Del Marcos Hotel BOUTIQUE HOTEL $$
(☎760-325-6902; www.delmarcoshotel.com; 225 W Baristo Rd; r incl breakfast $139-269;) At this 1947 gem, designed by William F Cody, groovy lobby tunes usher you to a saltwater pool and ineffably chic rooms. And it's steps from the shops and eats of downtown Palm Springs' village.

WORLD'S BIGGEST DINOSAURS

World's Biggest Dinosaurs (☎951-922-0076; www.cabazondinosaurs.com; 50770 Seminole Dr, Cabazon; adult/child $9/8; ⊙10am-8pm, off-season hours vary). You may do a double-take when you see this place, west of Palm Springs, near Cabazon's outlet malls. Claude K Bell, a sculptor for Knott's Berry Farm (p933), spent over a decade crafting these concrete behemoths, now owned by Christian creationists. In the gift shop, alongside the sort of dino-swag you might find at science museums, you can read about the alleged hoaxes and fallacies of evolution and Darwinism. To get here, exit the I-10 Fwy W at Main St in Cabazon.

El Morocco Inn & Spa BOUTIQUE HOTEL $$
(☎760-288-2527, 888-288-9905; www.elmoroccoinn.com; 66810 4th St, Desert Hot Springs; $179-219;) Heed the call of the casbah at this drop-dead-gorgeous hideaway where the scene is set for romance. Twelve exotically furnished rooms wrap around a pool deck where your enthusiastic host serves free 'Moroccotinis' during happy hour. Other perks: on-site spa, huge DVD library and delicious homemade mint iced tea.

Eating

Some restaurants keep shorter hours or even close for a few weeks during the hot, hot summer.

Tyler's Burgers BURGERS $
(www.tylersburgers.com; 149 S Indian Canyon Dr; dishes $3-9; 11am-4pm Mon-Sat;) This tiny shack in the center of downtown Palm Springs serves the best burgers in town, bar none. Waits are practically inevitable, which is presumably why there's an amazingly well-stocked magazine rack. Cash only.

★**Cheeky's** CALIFORNIAN $$
(☎760-327-7595; www.cheekysps.com; 622 N Palm Canyon Dr; mains $8-13; 8am-2pm Wed-Mon, last seating 1:30pm) Waits can be long and service only so-so, but the farm-to-table menu dazzles with witty inventiveness. Dishes change weekly, but custardy scrambled eggs, arugula pesto frittata and bacon bar 'flights' keep making appearances.

Sherman's DELI, BAKERY $$
(☎760-325-1199; www.shermansdeli.com; 401 E Tahquitz Canyon Way; mains $9-19; 7am-9pm;) Every community with a sizable retired contingent needs a good Jewish deli. Sherman's is it. With a breezy sidewalk patio, it pulls in an all-ages crowd with its 40 sandwich varieties (great hot pastrami!), finger-lickin' rotisserie chicken, lox and bagels and to-die-for pies. Walls are festooned with head shots of celebrity regulars, including Don Rickles.

Trio CALIFORNIAN $$$
(☎760-864-8746; www.triopalmsprings.com; 707 N Palm Canyon Dr; mains lunch $11-26, dinner $14-29; 11am-10pm Sun-Thu, to 11pm Fri & Sat) The winning formula in this '60s modernist space: updated American comfort food (awesome Yankee pot roast!), eye-catching artwork and picture windows. The $19 prix-fixe three-course dinner (served until 6pm) is a steal.

Drinking & Nightlife

Arenas Rd, east of Indian Canyon Dr, is gay and lesbian nightlife central.

Birba BAR
(www.birbaps.com; 622 N Palm Canyon Dr; 5-11pm Sun & Wed-Thu, to midnight Fri & Sat) It's cocktails and pizza at this fabulous indoor-outdoor space where floor-to-ceiling sliding glass doors separate the long marble bar from a hedge-fringed patio with sunken fire pits.

Koffi COFFEE
(www.kofficoffee.com; 515 N Palm Canyon Dr; snacks & drinks $3-6; 5:30am-7pm;) Tucked among the art galleries on N Palm Canyon Dr, this coolly minimalist, indie java bar serves strong organic coffee. There's a second Palm Springs location at 1700 S Camino Real, near the Ace Hotel.

Shopping

For art galleries, modern design stores and fashion boutiques, including fabulous **Trina Turk** (☎760-416-2856; www.trinaturk.com; 891 N Palm Canyon Dr; 10am-5pm Mon-Fri, to 6pm Sat, 11am-5pm Sun), head 'Uptown' to North Palm Canyon Dr. If you're riding the retro wave, uncover treasures in thrift, vintage and consignment shops scattered around downtown and along Hwy 111. For a local version of Rodeo Dr, drive down-valley to Palm Desert's El Paseo.

Information

Palm Springs Library (www.palmspringsca.gov; 300 S Sunrise Way; 10am-6pm Mon & Thu, to 8pm Tue & Wed, to 5pm Fri & Sat;) Free wi-fi and internet terminals.

Palm Springs Official Visitors Center (☎760-778-8418; www.visitpalmsprings.com; 2901 N Palm Canyon Dr; 9am-5pm) Well-stocked and well-staffed visitors center 3 miles north of downtown, in a 1965 Albert Frey–designed gas station at the tramway turnoff.

Getting There & Around

About 3 miles east of downtown, **Palm Springs International Airport** (PSP; ☎760-318-3800; www.palmspringsairport.com; 3400 E Tahquitz Canyon Way) is served by US and Canadian airlines; major car-rental agencies are on-site.

Thrice-weekly **Amtrak** trains to/from LA ($41, 2¾ hours) stop at the unstaffed, kinda-creepy North Palm Springs station, 5 miles north of downtown, as do a few daily **Greyhound** buses to/from LA ($27, 2½ to 3½ hours).

SunLine (☎800-347-8628; www.sunline.org; one way/day pass $1/3) runs slow-moving local buses throughout the valley.

Joshua Tree National Park

Like figments from a Dr Seuss book, whimsical-looking Joshua trees (actually tree-sized yuccas) welcome visitors to this wilderness park where the Sonora and Mojave Deserts converge. You'll find most of the main attractions, including all of the Joshua trees, in the park's northern half. 'J-Tree' is perennially popular with rock climbers and day hikers, especially in spring when the trees bloom with cream-colored flowers. The mystical quality of this stark, boulder-strewn landscape has inspired countless artists, most famously the rock band U2.

Sights & Activities

Dominating the north side of the **park** (☎760-367-5500; www.nps.gov/jotr; 7-day entry per car $20), the epic **Wonderland of Rocks** calls to climbers, as does **Hidden Valley**. Sunset-worthy **Keys View** overlooks the San Andreas Fault and on clear days, you can see as far as Mexico. For pioneer history, tour **Keys Ranch** (☎reservations 760-367-5522; tour adult/child $10/5; ⏰tour schedules vary, reservations required). Hikers seek out native desert fan-palm oases like **49 Palms Oasis** (3-mile round-trip) and **Lost Palms Oasis** (7.2-mile round-trip). Kid-friendly nature trails include **Barker Dam** (1.1-mile loop), which passes Native American petroglyphs; **Skull Rock** (1.7-mile loop); and **Cholla Cactus Garden** (0.25-mile loop). For a scenic 4WD route, tackle bumpy 18-mile **Geology Tour Road**, also open to mountain bikers.

Sleeping

The park itself only has camping. Budget and midrange motels line Hwy 62.

Joshua Tree National Park Campgrounds CAMPGROUND $
(www.nps.gov/jotr; tent & RV sites $10-15; 👪🐾) Of the park's eight campgrounds, only Cottonwood and Black Rock have potable water, flush toilets and dump stations. Indian Cove and Black Rock accept reservations (p1167); the others are first-come, first-served. None have showers. Backcountry camping (no campfires) is allowed 1 mile from any trailhead or road and 100ft from water sources; free self-registration is required at the park's 12 backcountry boards at trailheads. **Joshua Tree Outfitters** (☎760-366-1848; www.joshuatreeoutfitters.com; 61707 Hwy 62) rents quality camping gear.

> **WORTH A TRIP**
>
> **PIONEERTOWN**
>
> Less than 5 miles northwest of Hwy 62 in Yucca Valley, **Pioneertown** was built as a Hollywood movie set in 1946, and it hasn't changed much since. Witness mock gunfights at 2:30pm on Sundays from April to October. Enjoy BBQ, cheap beer and live music at honky-tonk **Pappy & Harriet's Pioneertown Palace** (☎760-365-5956; www.pappyandharriets.com; 53688 Pioneertown Rd; mains $8-29; ⏰11am-2am Thu-Sun, from 5pm Mon). Snooze at the **Pioneertown Motel** (☎760-365-7001; www.pioneertown-motel.com; 5040 Curtis Rd; r $70-120; ❄📶🐾), where old-timey movie stars once slept and simple rooms are crammed with Western-themed memorabilia.

Harmony Motel MOTEL $
(☎760-367-3351; www.harmonymotel.com; 71161 Twentynine Palms Hwy, Twentynine Palms; r $75-85; P❄@📶🏊) This 1950s motel, where U2 stayed while working on the *Joshua Tree* album, has a small pool and large, cheerfully painted rooms; some have kitchenettes.

★**Spin & Margie's Desert Hide-a-Way** INN $$
(☎760-366-9124; www.deserthideaway.com; 64491 Hwy 62; ste $145-175; ❄📶) This handsome hacienda-style inn is perfect for restoring calm after a long day on the road. The five boldly colored suites are an eccentric symphony of corrugated tin, old license plates and cartoon art. Each has its own kitchen and flat-screen TV with DVD and CD player. Knowledgeable, gregarious owners ensure a relaxed visit. It's down the dirt Sunkist Rd, about 3 miles east of downtown Joshua Tree.

Joshua Tree Inn MOTEL $$
(☎760-366-1188; www.joshuatreeinn.com; 61259 Twentynine Palms Hwy, Joshua Tree; r/ste incl breakfast from $89/159; ⏰reception 3pm to 8pm; ❄📶🏊) This funky-cool, rock-and-roll–infused, wisteria-strewn motel has 11 spacious rooms behind turquoise doors leading off from a desert-garden courtyard with great views. It gained notoriety in 1973

when rock legend Gram Parsons overdosed in room 8, now decorated in tribute. Other famous guests have included John Wayne, Donovan and Emmylou Harris.

Eating

Crossroads Cafe AMERICAN $
(☎760-366-5414; 61715 Twentynine Palms Hwy, Joshua Tree; mains $5-12; ⏰7am-9pm Mon-Sat, to 8pm Sun;) The much-loved Crossroads is the go-to place for carbo-loaded breakfasts, fresh sandwiches and dragged-through-the-garden salads that make both omnivores (burgers, Reuben sandwich) and vegans (spinach salad) happy.

Pie for the People PIZZA $$
(☎760-366-0400; www.pieforthepeople.com; 61740 Hwy 62, Joshua Tree; pizzas $11-25; ⏰11am-9pm Mon-Thu, to 10pm Fri & Sat, to 8pm Sun;) Thin-crust pizzas for takeout and delivery. Flavors span standards to the David Bowie: white pizza with mozzarella, Guinness caramelized onions, jalapenos, pineapple, bacon, and sweet plum sauce. Enjoy yours under the exposed rafters in the wood-and-corrugated-metal dining room, or under the tree on the back patio.

Information

Pick up park information at NPS visitor centers at **Joshua Tree** (6554 Park Blvd, Joshua Tree; ⏰8am-5pm), **Oasis** (74485 National Park Dr, Twentynine Palms; ⏰8:30am-5pm) and **Cottonwood** (Cottonwood Springs, 8 miles north of I-10 Fwy; ⏰8:30am-4pm), and at **Black Rock Nature Center** (9800 Black Rock Canyon Rd; ⏰8am-4pm Sat-Thu, noon-8pm Fri Oct-May;). There are no park facilities aside from restrooms, so bring all the drinking water and food you'll need. Get gas and stock up in the three towns linked by the Twentynine Palms Hwy (Hwy 62) along the park's northern boundary: Yucca Valley, with the most services (banks, supermarkets etc); beatnik Joshua Tree, where outdoor outfitters and shops offering internet access cluster; and Twentynine Palms, home of the USA's largest marine base.

Anza-Borrego Desert State Park

Shaped by an ancient sea and tectonic forces, Anza-Borrego is the USA's largest state park outside Alaska. Cradling the park's only commercial hub – tiny Borrego Springs (pop 3429) – are more than 600,000 acres of mountains, canyons and badlands; a fabulous variety of plants and wildlife; and intriguing historical relics of Native American tribes, Spanish explorers and gold-rush pioneers. Early spring wildflower blooms bring the biggest crowds. In summer Hades-like heat makes daytime exploring dangerous.

Sights & Activities

Two miles west of Borrego Springs, the park **visitor center** (☎760-767-4205; www.parks.ca.gov; 200 Palm Canyon Dr, Borrego Springs; ⏰9am-5pm daily Oct 15-May 15, Sat & Sun only May 16-Sep 14) has natural-history exhibits, information handouts and updates on road conditions. Driving through the park is free, but if you camp, hike or picnic, a day-use parking fee ($5 per car) applies. You'll need a 4WD to tackle the 500 miles of backcountry dirt roads. If you're hiking, always bring extra water.

Park highlights include **Fonts Point** desert lookout, **Clark Dry Lake** for birding, the **Elephant Tree Discovery Trail** near Split Mountain's wind caves, and **Blair Valley**, with its Native American pictographs and pioneer traces. Further south, soak in concrete hot-springs pools at **Agua Caliente Regional Park** (☎760-765-1188; www.sdcounty.ca.gov/parks/; 39555 Rte S2; entry per car $5; ⏰9:30am-5pm Sep-May).

Sleeping & Eating

Free backcountry camping without a permit is permitted anywhere in the park at least 100ft from water or roads (no campfires).

For country-style B&Bs and famous apple pie, the gold-mining town of **Julian** (www.julianca.com) is a 30-mile drive southwest of Borrego Springs.

Borrego Palm Canyon Campground CAMPGROUND $
(☎800-444-7275; www.reserveamerica.com; tent/RV sites $25/35; P) Near the visitor center, this campground has award-winning toilets, close-together campsites and an amphitheater with ranger programs.

Palm Canyon Hotel & RV Resort MOTEL $$
(☎760-767-5341; www.palmcanyonrvresort.com; 221 Palm Canyon Dr, Borrego Springs; d $65-310; P) For that Old West flair, check into this welcoming motel, but don't be fooled: the place was only built in the '80s! It's about a mile from the park's visitor center and has two pools for unwinding, and a restaurant and saloon for sustenance.

★**Borrego Valley Inn** INN $$$
(☎760-767-0311; www.borregovalleyinn.com; 405 Palm Canyon Dr; r $180-320;) This petite, immaculately kept inn, filled with Southwestern knickknacks and Native American weavings, is an intimate spa-resort, perfect for adults. There are 15 rooms on 10 acres. One pool is clothing-optional. Most rooms have kitchenettes. The grounds are entirely nonsmoking.

Carlee's Place AMERICAN $$
(☎760-767-3262; 660 Palm Canyon Dr; mains lunch $8-14, dinner $12-27; ⊙11am-9pm) Even though the decor feels like it hasn't been updated since the 1970s, locals pick Carlee's for its burgers, pastas and steak dinners. The pool table, live music and karaoke are big draws, too.

Information

Borrego Springs has banks with ATMs, gas stations, a supermarket, a post office and a public library with free wi-fi and internet terminals, all on Palm Canyon Dr.

Mojave National Preserve

If you're on a quest for the 'middle of nowhere,' you may find it in **Mojave National Preserve** (☎760-252-6100; www.nps.gov/moja) FREE, a 1.6-million-acre jumble of sand dunes, Joshua trees, volcanic cinder cones and habitat for endangered desert tortoises. Warning: no gas is available here.

Southeast of Baker and the I-15 Fwy, Kelbaker Rd crosses a ghostly landscape of cinder cones before arriving at **Kelso Depot**, a 1920s Mission Revival–style railroad station. It now houses the park's main **visitor center** (☎760-252-6108; ⊙9am-5pm), which has excellent natural-and-cultural history exhibits, and an old-fashioned lunch counter. It's another 11 miles southwest to 'singing' **Kelso Dunes**. When wind conditions are right, they emanate low-pitched vibrations caused by shifting sands – running downhill can jump-start the effect.

From Kelso Depot, Kelso–Cima Rd takes off northeast. After 19 miles, Cima Rd slingshots northwest toward I-15 around **Cima Dome**, a 1500ft-high hunk of granite with lava outcroppings, the slopes of which are home to the world's largest **Joshua tree forest**. For close-ups, summit **Teutonia Peak** (3 miles round-trip); the trailhead is 6 miles northwest of Cima.

OFF THE BEATEN TRACK

SALTON SEA & SALVATION MOUNTAIN

East of Anza-Borrego and south of Joshua Tree awaits a most unexpected sight: the **Salton Sea** (☎760-393-3810; www.parks.ca.gov; per car $5; ⊙visitor center 10am-4pm Oct-May, Fri-Sun only Jun-Sep), California's largest lake in the middle of its biggest desert. After the Colorado River flooded in 1905, it took 1500 workers and half a million tons of rock to put it back on course. With no natural outlet, the artificial lake's surface is 220ft below sea level and its waters 50% saltier than the Pacific – an environmental nightmare that's yet to be cleaned up.

An even stranger sight near the lake's eastern shore is **Salvation Mountain** (www.salvationmountain.us), a 100ft-high hill of hand-mixed clay slathered in colorful acrylic paint and found objects, and inscribed with Christian messages. It was the vision of folk artist Leonard Knight (1931–2014). It's in Niland, about 3 miles east of Hwy 111, via Main St/Beal Rd.

Further east, partly paved Mojave Rd is a scenic backdoor route to first-come, first-served campgrounds (campsites $12) with potable water at Mid Hills (no RVs) and Hole-in-the-Wall. The campgrounds bookend a rugged 12-mile scenic drive along dirt **Wild Horse Canyon Road**, ending near Hole-in-the-Wall's **visitor center** (☎760-252-6104; ⊙9am-4pm Wed-Sun Oct-Apr, 10am-4pm Sat May-Sep) and the slot-canyon **Rings Loop Trail**. Both roads usually don't require 4WD.

Sleeping & Eating

Free backcountry and roadside camping is permitted in already impacted areas; ask at the visitor center for details or consult the free park newspaper.

For historical ambience, **Hotel Nipton** (☎760-856-2335; http://nipton.com; 107355 Nipton Rd; cabins/r without bath from $65/80; ⊙reception 8am-6pm;) encompasses a century-old adobe villa with rustic rooms and tent cabins in a remote railway outpost, northeast of the preserve. Check in at the trading post next to a simple Mexican-American cafe.

Off I-15, Baker (35 miles northwest of Kelso) is the nearest town with bare-bones motels and fast food.

Death Valley National Park

The name itself evokes all that is harsh and hellish – a punishing, barren and lifeless place of Old Testament severity. Yet closer inspection reveals nature puts on a spectacular show of water-sculpted canyons, windswept sand dunes, palm-shaded oases, jagged mountains and wildlife aplenty here. It's also a land of superlatives, holding the US records for hottest temperature (134°F, or 57°C), lowest point (Badwater, 282ft below sea level) and largest national park outside Alaska (more than 5000 sq miles). Peak tourist season is when spring wildflowers bloom.

◉ Sights & Activities

In summer, stick to paved roads, limit your exertions outdoors to early morning hours and at night, and visit higher-elevation areas of the park.

From **Furnace Creek**, the central hub of the **park** (☑ 760-786-3200; www.nps.gov/deva; 7-day entry per car $20), drive southeast up to **Zabriskie Point** for spectacular sunset views across the valley and golden badlands eroded into waves, pleats and gullies. Twenty miles southeast at **Dante's View**, you can simultaneously spot the highest (Mt Whitney, 14,505ft) and lowest (Badwater) points in the contiguous USA.

Badwater itself, a timeless landscape of crinkly salt flats, is 17 miles south of Furnace Creek. Along the way, **Golden Canyon** and **Natural Bridge** are easily explored on short hikes. A 9-mile detour along **Artists Drive** through a narrow canyon is best in late afternoon when the eroded hillsides erupt in fireworks of color.

Northwest of Furnace Creek, near Stovepipe Wells Village, trek across Saharanesque **Mesquite Flat sand dunes** – magical under a full moon – and scramble along the smooth marble walls of **Mosaic Canyon**.

About 55 miles northwest of Furnace Creek at whimsical **Scotty's Castle** (☑ 877-444-6777; www.recreation.gov; tours adult/child from $15/7.50; ⊙ grounds 8:30am-4:15pm, tour schedules vary, closed Tue-Thu mid-May–mid-Aug), tour guides in historical character dress bring to life the Old West tales of con man 'Death Valley Scotty' (reservations advised). Five miles west of Grapevine junction, circumambulate volcanic **Ubehebe Crater** and its younger sibling.

A scenic drive up **Emigrant Canyon**, starting 8 miles west of Stovepipe Wells, passes turnoffs to ghost towns and ends with a 3-mile unpaved stretch up to the historic beehive-shaped **Charcoal Kilns**. Nearby is the trailhead for the 8.4-mile round-trip hike up **Wildrose Peak** (9064ft). At the park's western edge, utterly remote **Panamint Springs** offers panoramic vistas and a 2-mile round-trip hike to tiny Darwin Falls.

Activities offered at the Ranch at Furnace Creek Ranch resort include horseback riding, golf, mountain biking and hot-springs pool swimming. For 4WD adventures, talk to **Farabee's Jeep Rentals** (☑ 760-786-9872; http://farabeesjeeprentals.com; 2-/4-door Jeep incl 200 miles $195/235; ⊙ mid-Sep–late May) near the Inn at Furnace Creek.

🛏 Sleeping & Eating

In-park lodging is often booked solid, especially on weekends and during the spring wildflower bloom.

The closest town with a few roadside motels is Beatty, NV (40 miles northeast of Furnace Creek); many more accommodations are found in Las Vegas, NV (125 miles southeast) and Ridgecrest, CA (125 miles southwest).

Ranch at Furnace Creek   RESORT $$
(☑ 760-786-2345; www.furnacecreekresort.com; Hwy 190, Furnace Creek; cabins $130-162, r $162-213; P ⊕ ❄ 🛜 ≋ 🐾) Tailor-made for families, this rambling resort with multiple motel-style buildings has received a vigorous face-lift, resulting in spiffy rooms swathed in desert colors, updated bathrooms and French doors leading to porches with comfortable patio furniture. The grounds encompass a playground, spring-fed swimming pool, tennis courts, restaurants, shops and the **Borax Museum** (☑ 760-786-2345; ⊙ 9am-9pm Oct-May, variable in summer) FREE.

Stovepipe Wells Village   MOTEL $$
(☑ 760-786-2387; www.escapetodeathvalley.com; Hwy 190, Stovepipe Wells; RV sites $33, r $117-176; P ❄ @ 🛜 ≋ 🐾) The 83 rooms at this sea-level tourist village are newly spruced-up and have quality linens beneath Death Valley–themed artwork, cheerful Native American–patterned bedspreads, coffee-makers and TVs. The small pool is cool and the cowboy-style **Toll Road Restaurant** (dinner mains $13-26; ⊙ 7-10am & 6-10pm; 🛜🐾) serves breakfast and lunch daily.

Cynthia's HOSTEL, INN $$

(760-852-4580; www.discovercynthias.com; 2001 Old Spanish Trail Hwy, Tecopa; dm $22-25, r $75-118, tipis $165-225; check-in 3-8pm; P) Match your budget to the bed at this congenial inn helmed by the friendly Cynthia, about 3 miles from central Tecopa. Your choices: a colorful and eclectically decorated private room in a vintage trailer, a bed in a dorm, or a Native American–style tipi (a short drive away) with thick rugs, fire pits and comfy king-size beds.

Inn at Furnace Creek HOTEL $$$

(760-786-2345; www.furnacecreekresort.com; Hwy 190; r/ste from $345/450; mid-Oct–mid-May; P@) Roll out of bed and count the colors of the desert as you pull back the curtains in your room at this elegant 1927 Mission-style hotel. After a day of sweaty touring, enjoy languid valley views while lounging by the spring-fed swimming pool, cocktail in hand. The lobby has a 1930s retro look.

Information

Purchase a seven-day entry pass (per car $20) at self-service pay stations throughout the park. For a free map and newspaper, show your receipt at the **visitor center** (760-786-3200; www.nps.gov/deva; 8am-5pm mid-Oct–mid-Jun, 9am-6pm mid-Jun–mid-Oct) in Furnace Creek, where you'll also find a general store, expensive gas station, post office, ATM, coin-op laundromat and pay showers. Stovepipe Wells Village, a 30-minute drive northwest, has a general store, expensive gas station, ATM and pay showers. Cell-phone reception is spotty to nonexistent in the park.

CENTRAL COAST

No trip to California would be worth its salt without a jaunt along the surreally scenic Central Coast. Among California's most iconic roads, Hwy 1 skirts past posh Santa Barbara, retro Pismo Beach, collegiate San Luis Obispo, fantastical Hearst Castle, soul-stirring Big Sur, cutesy Carmel, down-to-earth Monterey and hippie Santa Cruz, often within view of the Pacific. Slow down – this idyllic coast deserves to be savored, not gulped. (That same advice goes for the award-winning locally grown wines too.)

WORTH A TRIP

RHYOLITE

Four miles west of Beatty, NV, look for the turnoff to the ghost town of **Rhyolite** (www.rhyolitesite.com; off Hwy 374; sunrise-sunset) FREE, which epitomizes the hurly-burly, boom-and-bust story of so many Western gold-rush mining towns. Don't miss the 1906 'bottle house' or the skeletal remains of a three-story bank. Next door is the bizarre **Goldwell Open Air Museum** (www.goldwellmuseum.org; off Hwy 374; 24hr) FREE of trippy art installations begun by Belgian artist Albert Szukalski in 1984.

Santa Barbara

Life is sweet in Santa Barbara, a coastal Shangri-La where the air is redolent of citrus and jasmine, flowery bougainvillea drapes whitewashed buildings with Spanish red-tiled roofs, and it's all cradled by pearly beaches – just ignore those pesky oil derricks out to sea. Downtown's main drag, State St, and the Funk Zone, south of the railroad tracks, abound with restaurants, bars, art galleries and boutiques.

Sights

★ **Mission Santa Barbara** CHURCH

(www.santabarbaramission.org; 2201 Laguna St; adult/child 5-15yr $7/2; 10am-5pm, last entry 4:15pm; P) California's 'Queen of the Missions' reigns above the city on a hilltop perch over a mile northwest of downtown. Its imposing Doric facade, an architectural homage to an ancient Roman chapel, is topped by an unusual twin bell tower. Inside the mission's 1820 stone church, notice the striking Chumash artwork. Outside is an eerie cemetery – skull carvings hang over the door leading outside – with 4000 Chumash graves and the elaborate mausoleums of early California settlers.

Santa Barbara County Courthouse HISTORIC SITE

(805-962-6464; www.santabarbaracourthouse.org; 1100 Anacapa St; 8am-4:45pm Mon-Fri, 10am-4:15pm Sat & Sun) FREE Built in Spanish-Moorish Revival style in 1929, the courthouse features hand-painted ceilings, wrought-iron chandeliers, and tiles from Tunisia and Spain. Step inside the hushed mural room depicting

Spanish-colonial history on the 2nd floor, then climb El Mirador, the 85ft clock tower, for arch-framed panoramas of the city, ocean and mountains. You're free to explore on your own, but you'll get a lot more out of a free docent-guided tour, usually at 2pm daily and 10:30am on weekdays.

Santa Barbara Museum of Art MUSEUM
(☎805-963-4364; www.sbmuseart.org; 1130 State St; adult/child 6-17yr $10/6, 5-8pm Thu free; ⏰11am-5pm Tue-Wed & Fri-Sun, to 8pm Thu) This thoughtfully curated, bite-sized art museum displays European and American masters – think Matisse and Diego Rivera – along with contemporary photography, classical antiquities and thought-provoking temporary exhibits. Traipse up to the 2nd floor, where impressive Asian art collections include an intricate, colorful Tibetan sand mandala and the iron-and-leather armor of a Japanese warrior. Guided tours usually start at 1pm daily. There's also an interactive children's space, a museum shop and a cafe.

Santa Barbara Maritime Museum MUSEUM
(☎805-962-8404; www.sbmm.org; 113 Harbor Way; adult/child 6-17yr $7/4, 3rd Thu of month free; ⏰10am-5pm, to 6pm late May-early Sep; P 👪) On the harborfront, this jam-packed, two-story exhibition hall celebrates the town's briny history with nautical artifacts, memorabilia and hands-on exhibits, including a big-game fishing chair from which you can 'reel in' a trophy marlin. Take a virtual trip through the Santa Barbara Channel, stand on a surfboard or watch deep-sea diving documentaries in the theater. There's 90 minutes of free parking in the public lot or take the Lil' Toot water taxi from Stearns Wharf.

Activities

Overlooking busy municipal beaches, 1872 **Stearns Wharf** is the West's oldest continuously operating wooden pier, strung with touristy shops and restaurants. Outside town off Hwy 101, bigger palm-fringed **state beaches** await at Carpinteria, 12 miles east, and El Capitan and Refugio, more than 20 miles west.

Wheel Fun Rentals CYCLING
(www.wheelfunrentals.com; 23 E Cabrillo Blvd; ⏰8am-8pm Mar-Oct, to 6pm Nov-Feb; 👪) Hourly rentals of beach cruisers ($10), mountain bikes ($11) and two-/four-person surreys ($29/39), with discounted half-day and full-day rates.

Santa Barbara Sailing Center KAYAKING
(☎805-962-2826; www.sbsail.com; off Harbor Way; single/double kayak rental per hr $10/15, 2hr kayak tour $50; 👪) Just about the cheapest kayak rental and guided tours around, with paddling instruction available by prior arrangement. Call for seasonal hours.

Condor Express CRUISE
(☎805-882-0088, 888-779-4253; www.condorcruises.com; 301 W Cabrillo Blvd; adult/child 5-12yr 2½hr cruise $50/30, 4½hr cruise from $99/50; 👪) Take a whale-watching excursion aboard the high-speed catamaran *Condor Express*. Whale sightings are guaranteed, so if you miss out the first time, you'll get a free voucher for another cruise.

Sleeping

Hello, sticker shock: even basic motel rooms can command over $200 in summer. Less expensive motels line upper State St, north of downtown, and Hwy 101.

Santa Barbara Auto Camp CAMPGROUND $$
(☎888-405-7553; http://autocamp.com/sb; 2717 De La Vina St; d $175-215; P ❄ 📶 👪 🐾) Bed down with vintage style in one of five shiny metal Airstream trailers parked near upper State St, north of downtown. All five architect-designed trailers have unique perks, such as a clawfoot tub or extra twin-size beds for kiddos, as well as a full kitchen and complimentary cruiser bikes to borrow. Book ahead; two-night minimum may apply. Pet fee $25.

Agave Inn MOTEL $$
(☎805-687-6009; http://agaveinnsb.com; 3222 State St; r incl breakfast from $119; P ❄ 📶) While it's still just a motel at heart, this boutique-on-a-budget property's 'Mexican pop meets modern' motif livens things up with a color palette from a Frieda Kahlo painting. Flat-screen TVs, microwaves, minifridges and air-con make it a standout option. Family-sized rooms have kitchenettes and pull-out sofa beds. Continental breakfast included.

Harbor House Inn MOTEL $$
(☎888-474-6789, 805-962-9745; www.harborhouseinn.com; 104 Bath St; r from $180; P 📶 🐾) Down by the harbor, this converted motel offers brightly lit studios with hardwood floors and a beachy design scheme. A few have full kitchens and fireplaces, but there's no air-con. Rates include a welcome basket of breakfast goodies (with a two-night minimum stay), and beach towels, chairs and

OFF THE BEATEN TRACK

CHANNEL ISLANDS NATIONAL PARK

Remote, rugged **Channel Islands National Park** (www.nps.gov/chis) earns the nickname 'California's Galápagos' for its unique wildlife. These islands offer superb snorkeling, scuba diving and sea kayaking. Spring, when wildflowers bloom, is a gorgeous time to visit; summer and fall are bone-dry, but the latter brings the calmest water and winds; winter can be stormy.

Anacapa, an hour's boat ride from the mainland, is the best island for day-tripping, with easy hikes and unforgettable views. Santa Cruz, the biggest island, is for overnight camping excursions, kayaking and hiking. Other islands require longer channel crossings and multiday trips. San Miguel is often shrouded in fog. Tiny Santa Barbara supports seabird and seal colonies. So does Santa Rosa, which also protects Torrey pine trees.

Boats leave from Ventura Harbor, off Hwy 101, where the park's **visitor center** (805-658-5730; www.nps.gov/chis; 1901 Spinnaker Dr, Ventura; 8:30am-5pm;) has info and maps. The main tour-boat operator is **Island Packers** (805-642-1393; www.islandpackers.com; 1691 Spinnaker Dr, Ventura; 3hr cruise adult/child 3-12yr from $36/26); book ahead. Primitive island campgrounds require reservations; book through Recreation.gov (p1167) and bring food and water.

umbrellas and three-speed bicycles to borrow. Pet fee $20.

★ **Inn of the Spanish Garden** BOUTIQUE HOTEL $$$
(866-564-4700, 805-564-4700; www.spanishgardeninn.com; 915 Garden St; d incl breakfast from $309;) At this Spanish Colonial-style inn, casual elegance, top-notch service and an impossibly romantic central courtyard will have you lording about like the don of your own private villa. Beds have luxurious linens, bathrooms have oversized bathtubs and concierge service is top-notch. Palms surround a small outdoor pool, or unwind with a massage in your room.

Eating

Lilly's Taquería MEXICAN $
(http://lillystacos.com; 310 Chapala St; items from $1.60; 10:30am-9pm Sun-Mon & Wed-Thu, to 10pm Fri & Sat) There's almost always a line roping around this downtown taco shack at lunchtime. But it goes fast, so you'd best be snappy with your order – the *adobada* (marinated pork) and *lengua* (beef tongue) are standout choices. Second location in Goleta west of the airport, off Hwy 101.

Santa Barbara Shellfish Company SEAFOOD $$
(www.sbfishhouse.com; 230 Stearns Wharf; dishes $4-19; 11am-9pm;) 'From sea to skillet to plate' sums up this end-of-the-wharf seafood shack that's more of a buzzing counter joint than a sit-down restaurant. Chase away the seagulls as you chow down on garlic-baked clams, crab cakes and coconut-fried shrimp at wooden picnic tables outside. Awesome lobster bisque, ocean views and the same location for over 25 years.

★ **Lark** CALIFORNIAN $$$
(805-284-0370; www.thelarksb.com; 131 Anacapa St; shared plates $5-32, mains $24-38; 5-10pm Tue-Sun, bar till midnight) There's no better place in Santa Barbara County to taste the bountiful farm and fishing goodness of this stretch of SoCal coast. Named after an antique Pullman railway car, this chef-run restaurant in the Funk Zone morphs its menu with the seasons, presenting unique flavor combinations like fried olives with chorizo aioli and chili-spiced mussels in lemongrass-lime broth. Make reservations.

Drinking & Nightlife

Nightlife orbits lower State St and the Funk Zone. You can ramble between a dozen wine-tasting rooms along the city's **Urban Wine Trail** (www.urbanwinetrailsb.com). Check the free alt-weekly *Santa Barbara Independent* (www.independent.com) for an entertainment calendar.

Figueroa Mountain Brewing Co BAR
(www.figmtnbrew.com; 137 Anacapa St; 11am-11pm) Father and son brewers have brought their gold-medal-winning hoppy IPA, Danish red lager and double IPA from Santa Barbara's Wine Country to the Funk Zone. Clink pint glasses on the taproom's open-air patio while acoustic acts play. Enter on Yanonali St.

ℹ Information

Santa Barbara Car Free (www.santabarbara-carfree.org) is a helpful website for ecotravel tips and discounts.

Santa Barbara Visitors Center (☑ 805-965-3021, 805-568-1811; www.santabarbaraca.com; 1 Garden St; ☺ 9am-5pm Mon-Sat, 10am-5pm Sun, closing 1hr earlier Nov-Jan) Pick up maps and brochures while consulting with the helpful, but busy staff. The website offers free downloadable DIY touring maps and itineraries, from famous movie locations to wine trails, art galleries and outdoors fun. Self-pay metered parking lot nearby.

ℹ Getting There & Around

From a downtown **bus station** (☑ 805-965-7551; www.greyhound.com; 224 Chapala St), Greyhound has a few daily buses to LA ($17, two to three hours) and via San Luis Obispo ($31, two hours) to Santa Cruz ($59, six hours) and San Francisco ($63, nine hours).

From the **train station** (☑ 800-872-7245; www.amtrak.com; 209 State St) south of downtown, Amtrak trains roll toward LA ($31, 2¾ hours) and San Luis Obispo ($35, 2¾ hours).

Metropolitan Transit District (MTD; ☑ 805-963-3366; www.sbmtd.gov) runs citywide buses ($1.75). Its electric shuttles (50¢) loop between downtown's State St and Stearns Wharf and along beachfront Cabrillo Blvd.

Santa Barbara to San Luis Obispo

You can speed up to San Luis Obispo in less than two hours along Hwy 101, or take all day detouring to wineries, historical missions and hidden beaches.

A scenic backcountry drive north of Santa Barbara follows Hwy 154, where you can go for the grape in the **wine country** (www.sbcountywines.com) of the Santa Ynez and Santa Maria Valleys. Ride along with **Sustainable Vine** (☑ 805-698-3911; www.sustainablevine.com) 🖉 for ecoconscious winery tours ($150), or just follow the pastoral **Foxen Canyon Wine Trail** (www.foxencanyonwinetrail.com) north to discover cult winemakers' vineyards. In the town of **Los Olivos**, where two dozen more wine-tasting rooms await, **Los Olivos Wine Merchant & Café** (☑ 805-688-7265; www.losolivoscafe.com; 2879 Grand Ave; mains breakfast $9-12, lunch & dinner $12-29; ☺ 11:30am-8:30pm daily, also 8-10:30am Sat & Sun) is a charming Cal-Mediterranean bistro with a wine bar.

Further south, the Danish-immigrant village of **Solvang** (www.solvangusa.com) abounds with windmills and fairy-tale-esque bakeries. Fuel up on breakfast biscuits, buttermilk fried-chicken sandwiches and farm-fresh salads at **Succulent Café** (☑ 805-691-9444; www.succulentcafe.com; 1555 Mission Dr; mains breakfast & lunch $9-13, dinner $19-29; ☺ breakfast 8:30am-noon Sat & Sun, lunch 11am-3pm Mon & Wed-Fri, noon-3pm Sat & Sun, dinner 5-9pm Wed-Mon) 🖉. For a picnic lunch or BBQ takeout, swing into **El Rancho Market** (http://elranchomarket.com; 2886 Mission Dr; ☺ 6am-11pm), east of Solvang's 19th-century Spanish colonial **mission** (☑ 805-688-4815; www.missionsantaines.org; 1760 Mission Dr; adult/child under 12yr $5/free; ☺ 9am-4:30pm).

Follow Hwy 246 about 15 miles west of Hwy 101 to **La Purísima Mission State Historic Park** (☑ 805-733-3713; www.lapurisimamission.org; 2295 Purísima Rd, Lompoc; per car $6; ☺ 9am-5pm; 🖈) 🖉. Exquisitely restored, it's one of California's most evocative Spanish Colonial missions, with flowering gardens, livestock pens and adobe buildings. South of Lompoc off Hwy 1, Jalama Rd travels 14 twisting miles to windswept **Jalama Beach County Park** (🖉 recorded info 805-736-3616; http://cosb.countyofsb.org/parks/; 9999 Jalama Rd, Lompoc; per car $10). Book ahead for its crazy-popular **campground** (www.sbparks.org/reservations; tent/RV sites from $23/38, cabins $110-210), where simple cabins have kitchenettes.

Where Hwy 1 rejoins Hwy 101, **Pismo Beach** has a long, lazy stretch of sand and a **butterfly grove** (www.monarchbutterfly.org; ☺ sunrise-sunset; 🖈) **FREE**, where migratory monarchs perch in eucalyptus trees from late October until February. Adjacent **North Beach Campground** (🖉 reservations 800-444-7275; www.reserveamerica.com; 399 S Dolliver St; tent & RV sites $35; 🖈 🐾) offers beach access and hot showers. Dozens of motels and hotels stand by the ocean and along Hwy 101, but rooms fill quickly, especially on weekends. **Pismo Lighthouse Suites** (☑ 805-773-2411; www.pismolighthousesuites.com; 2411 Price St; ste incl breakfast from $275; @ 🛜 🏊 🖈 🐾) has everything vacationing families need, even a life-sized outdoor chessboard; ask about off-season discounts. Near Pismo's seaside pier, **Old West Cinnamon Rolls** (861 Dolliver St; snacks $2-5; ☺ 6:30am-5:30pm) offers gooey goodness. Uphill at the **Cracked Crab** (☑ 805-773-2722; www.crackedcrab.com; 751 Price St; mains $12-45; ☺ 11am-9pm Sun-Thu, to 10pm Fri & Sat; 🖈), make sure you don a plastic bib before a fresh bucket o' seafood gets dumped on your butcher-paper-covered table.

The nearby town of **Avila Beach** has a sunny waterfront promenade, an atmospherically creaky wooden fishing pier and a historical **lighthouse** (guided hike reservations 805-541-8735, trolley tour reservations 855-533-7843; www.sanluislighthouse.org; lighthouse admission adult/child under 12yr $5/free, trolley tour incl admission per adult/child 3-12yr $20/15; guided hikes usually 8:45am-1pm Wed & Sat, trolley tours usually noon, 1pm & 2pm Wed & Sat). Back toward Hwy 101, pick juicy fruit and feed the goats at **Avila Valley Barn farmstand** (www.avilavalleybarn.com; 560 Avila Beach Dr; usually 9am-6pm mid-Mar–late-Dec;), then do some stargazing from a private redwood hot tub at **Sycamore Mineral Springs** (805-595-7302; www.sycamoresprings.com; 1215 Avila Beach Dr; 1hr per person $13.50-17.50; 8am-midnight, last reservation 10:45pm).

San Luis Obispo

Halfway between LA and San Francisco, San Luis Obispo is a low-key place. But CalPoly university students inject a healthy dose of hubbub into the streets, bars and cafes, especially during the weekly **farmers market** (www.downtownslo.com; 6-9pm Thu;) , which turns downtown's Higuera St into a party with live music and sidewalk BBQs.

Like several other California towns, SLO grew up around a Spanish Catholic **mission** (805-543-6850; www.missionsanluisobispo.org; 751 Palm St; donation $2; 9am-5pm late Mar-Oct, to 4pm Nov–mid-Mar), founded in 1772 by Junípero Serra. These days, SLO is just a grape's throw from thriving **Edna Valley wineries** (www.slowine.com), known for crisp Chardonnay and subtle Pinot Noir.

Sleeping

SLO's motel row is north of downtown along Monterey St. Budget and midrange motels and hotels line Hwy 101.

HI Hostel Obispo HOSTEL $
(805-544-4678; www.hostelobispo.com; 1617 Santa Rosa St; dm $27-31, r from $60, all without bath; check-in 4:30-10pm;) On a tree-lined street near the train station, this solar-powered, avocado-colored hostel inhabits a converted Victorian, which gives it a bit of a B&B feel. Amenities include a kitchen, bike rentals (from $10 per day) and complimentary sourdough pancakes and coffee for breakfast. BYOT (bring your own towel).

Madonna Inn HOTEL $$
(805-543-3000; www.madonnainn.com; 100 Madonna Rd; r $189-309;) The fantastically campy Madonna Inn is a garish confection visible from Hwy 101. Japanese tourists, vacationing Midwesterners and irony-loving hipsters adore the 110 themed rooms – including Yosemite Rock, Caveman and hot-pink Floral Fantasy (check out photos online). The urinal in the men's room is a bizarre waterfall. But the best reason to stop here? Old-fashioned cookies from the storybook bakery.

Eating & Drinking

Downtown abounds with cafes, restaurants, wine bars, brewpubs and the solar-powered **Palm Theatre** (805-541-5161; www.thepalmtheatre.com; 817 Palm St; tickets $5-8) , screening indie films.

Firestone Grill BARBECUE $
(www.firestonegrill.com; 1001 Higuera St; dishes $4-10; 11am-10pm Sun-Wed, to 11pm Thu-Sat;) If you can stomach huge lines, long waits for a table, and sports-bar-style service, you'll get to sink your teeth into an authentic Santa Maria–style tri-tip steak sandwich on a toasted garlic roll and a basket of super-crispy fries.

Big Sky Café CALIFORNIAN $$
(www.bigskycafe.com; 1121 Broad St; dinner mains $11-22; 7am-9pm Mon-Thu, to 10pm Fri, 8am-10pm Sat, to 9pm Sun;) Big Sky is a big room, and still the wait can be long – its tagline is 'analog food for a digital world.' Vegetarians have almost as many options as carnivores, and many of the ingredients are sourced locally. Big-plate dinners can be a bit bland, but breakfast (served until 1pm daily) gets top marks.

Luna Red FUSION $$$
(805-540-5243; www.lunaredslo.com; 1023 Chorro St; shared plates $6-20, mains $20-39; 11am-9pm Mon-Wed, to 11:30pm Thu & Fri, 9am-11:30pm Sat, 9am-9pm Sun;) Local bounty from the land and sea, artisan cheeses and farmers-market produce pervade the chef's Californian, Asian and Mediterranean small-plates menu. Cocktails and glowing lanterns enhance a sophisticated ambience indoors, or linger over brunch on the mission-view garden patio. Reservations recommended.

❶ Information

San Luis Obispo Car Free (http://slocarfree.org) A helpful website for ecotravel tips and discounts.

San Luis Obispo Visitor Center (☑ 805-781-2777; www.visitslo.com; 895 Monterey St; ☉10am-5pm Sun-Wed, to 7pm Thu-Sat) Free maps and tourist brochures.

❶ Getting There & Around

Amtrak trains from Santa Barbara ($28 to $35, 2¾ hours) and LA ($41, 5½ hours) arrive at SLO's **train station** (☑ 800-872-7245; www.amtrak.com; 1011 Railroad Ave), a 10-minute walk from downtown. Inconveniently stopping 3.5 miles southwest of downtown off Hwy 101, **Greyhound** (☑ 800-231-2222; www.greyhound.com; 1460 Calle Joaquin) has a few daily buses to Santa Barbara ($31, two hours), LA ($33, 5¼ hours), Santa Cruz ($46, 3¾ hours) and San Francisco ($59, 6¾ hours). You'll have to call for a taxi to connect to downtown.

Operated by **SLO RTA** (RTA; ☑ 805-541-2228; www.slorta.org; single-ride fares $1.50-3, day pass $5), countywide buses with limited weekend services converge on downtown's **transit center** (cnr Palm & Osos Sts).

Morro Bay to Hearst Castle

A dozen miles northwest of San Luis Obispo via Hwy 1, Morro Bay is a sea-sprayed fishing town where **Morro Rock**, a volcanic peak jutting up from the ocean floor, is your first hint of the coast's upcoming drama. (Never mind those powerplant smokestacks obscuring the views.) Hop aboard boat cruises or rent kayaks along the **Embarcadero**, which is packed with touristy shops. A classic seafood shack, **Giovanni's** (www.giovannisfishmarket.com; 1001 Front St; mains $6-15; ☉9am-6pm; 🖶) cooks killer garlic fries and fish-and-chips. Midrange motels cluster uphill off Harbor and Main Sts and along Hwy 1.

Nearby are fantastic state parks for coastal hikes and **camping** (☑ reservations 800-444-7275; www.reserveamerica.com; tent & RV sites $20-50; 🖶🖷). South of the Embarcadero, **Morro Bay State Park** (☑ 805-772-2694; www.parks.ca.gov; park entry free, museum admission adult/child under 17yr $3/free; ☉museum 10am-5pm) has a natural-history museum for kids. Further south in Los Osos, west of Hwy 1, wilder **Montaña de Oro State Park** (☑ 805-772-7434; www.parks.ca.gov; 3550 Pecho Valley Rd, Los Osos; ☉6am-10pm) **FREE** features

coastal bluffs, tide pools, sand dunes, peak hiking and mountain-biking trails. Its Spanish name (which means 'mountain of gold') comes from native California poppies that blanket the hillsides in spring.

Heading north of downtown Morro Bay along Hwy 1, surfers love the Cal-Mexican **Taco Temple** (2680 Main St; mains $8-20; ☉11am-9pm Wed-Mon; 🖶), a cash-only joint, and **Ruddell's Smokehouse** (www.smokerjim.com; 101 D St; dishes $4-13; ☉11am-6pm; 🖶🖷), serving smoked-fish tacos by the beach in Cayucos. Vintage motels on Cayucos' Ocean Ave include the cute, family-run **Seaside Motel** (☑ 805-995-3809; www.seasidemotel.com; 42 S Ocean Ave; d $80-160; 🛜). You can fall asleep to the sound of the surf at the ocean-view **Shoreline Inn on the Beach** (☑ 805-995-3681; www.cayucosshorelineinn.com; 1 N Ocean Ave; r $139-199; 🖶🖷).

North of Harmony (population: just 18 souls), Hwy 46 leads east into the vineyards of **Paso Robles wine country** (www.pasowine.com). Tired of wine? Off Hwy 101 in Paso Robles, **Firestone Walker Brewing Company** (☑ 805-225-5911; www.firestonebeer.com; 1400 Ramada Dr; ☉tasting room 10am-5pm Mon-Thu, to 6pm Fri-Sun, tours 10:30am-3:30pm) offers brewery tours ($3; reservations recommended), or just stop by the taproom for samples.

Further north along Hwy 1, quaint **Cambria** has lodgings along unearthly pretty Moonstone Beach, where the **Blue Dolphin Inn** (☑ 805-927-3300; www.cambriainns.com; 6470 Moonstone Beach Dr; r from $199; 🛜🖷) embraces modern rooms with romantic fireplaces. Inland, **HI Cambria Bridge Street Inn** (☑ 805-927-7653; www.bridgestreetinncambria.com; 4314 Bridge St; dm from $32, r $57-95, all without bath; ☉check-in 5-9pm; 🛜) sleeps like a hostel but feels like a grandmotherly B&B, while the retro **Cambria Palms Motel** (☑ 805-927-4485; www.cambriapalmsmotel.com; 2662 Main St; r $109-149; ☉check-in 3-9pm; 🛜) has clean-lined rooms and cruiser bicycles to borrow. An artisan cheese and wine shop, **Indigo Moon** (☑ 805-927-2911; www.indigomooncafe.com; 1980 Main St; lunch $9-14, dinner $14-33; ☉10am-9pm) has breezy bistro tables and market-fresh salads and sandwiches at lunch. With a sunny patio and takeout counter, **Linn's Easy as Pie Cafe** (www.linnsfruitbin.com; 4251 Bridge St; dishes $6-11; ☉10am-6pm Oct-Apr, to 7pm May-Sep; 🖶) is famous for its olallieberry pie.

About 10 miles north of Cambria, hilltop **Hearst Castle** (☑ info 805-927-2020, reservations 800-444-4445; www.hearstcastle.org; 750 Hearst Castle Rd, San Simeon; tours adult/child 5-12yr from $25/12; ⏲ from 9am daily except Thanksgiving, Christmas & New Year's Day, closing time varies) is California's most famous monument to wealth and ambition. William Randolph Hearst, the newspaper magnate, entertained Hollywood stars and royalty at this fantasy estate dripping with European antiques, accented by shimmering pools and surrounded by flowering gardens. Try to make tour reservations in advance or show up early in the day.

Across Hwy 1, overlooking a historic whaling pier, **Sebastian's Store** (442 SLO-San Simeon Rd; mains $7-12; ⏲ 11am-5pm, kitchen closes at 4pm) sells Hearst Ranch beef burgers and giant sandwiches for impromptu beach picnics. Five miles back south along Hwy 1, past a forgettable row of budget and mid-range motels in San Simeon, **Hearst San Simeon State Park** (☎ reservations 800-444-7275; www.reserveamerica.com; Hwy 1; tent & RV sites $20-25) offers primitive and developed creekside campsites.

Heading north, Point Piedras Blancas is home to an enormous **elephant seal colony** that breeds, molts, sleeps, frolics and, occasionally, goes aggro on the beach. Keep your distance from these wild animals who move faster on the sand than you can. The signposted vista point, about 4.5 miles north of Hearst Castle, has interpretive panels. Seals haul out year-round, but the frenzied birthing and mating season runs from January through March. Nearby, the 1875 **Piedras Blancas Light Station** (☎ 805-927-7361; www.piedrasblancas.gov; tours adult/child 6-17yr $10/5; ⏲ tours usually 9:45am Mon-Sat mid-Jun–Aug, 9:45am Tue, Thu & Sat Sep–mid-Jun) is an outstandingly scenic spot; call ahead to confirm tour schedules (no reservations) and directions to the meet-up point.

WORTH A TRIP

PINNACLES NATIONAL PARK

Named for the towering spires that rise abruptly out of the chapparal-covered hills, **Pinnacles National Park** (☎ 831-389-4486; www.nps.gov/pinn; per car $10) is a study in geologic drama, with craggy monoliths, sheer-walled canyons and ancient volcanic remnants. Besides hiking and rock climbing, the park's biggest attractions are talus caves and endangered California condors. Visit during spring or fall – summer heat and humidity are extreme. A **campground** (☎ 877-444-6777; www.recreation.gov; tent/RV sites $23/36;) with a seasonal swimming pool lies near the park's east entrance, off Hwy 25 about 30 miles northwest of King City on Hwy 101.

Big Sur

Much ink has been spilled extolling the raw beauty and energy of this 100-mile stretch of craggy coastline sprawling south of Monterey Bay. More a state of mind than a place you can pinpoint on a map, Big Sur has no traffic lights, banks or strip malls. When the sun goes down, the moon and stars are the only illumination – if summer fog hasn't extinguished them, that is.

Lodging, food and gas are all scarce and pricey in Big Sur. Demand for rooms is high year-round, especially on weekends, so book ahead. The free *Big Sur Guide* (www.bigsurcalifornia.org), an info-packed newspaper, is available at roadside businesses. The day-use parking fee (per car $10) charged at Big Sur's state parks is valid for same-day entry to all except Limekiln.

It's about 25 miles from Hearst Castle to blink-and-you-miss-it Gorda, home of **Treebones Resort** (☎ 877-424-4787, 805-927-2390; www.treebonesresort.com; 71895 Hwy 1; d without bath from $265;), which offers back-to-nature clifftop yurts. Basic United States Forest Service (USFS) campgrounds are just off Hwy 1 at shady **Plaskett Creek** (☎ reservations 877-477-6777; www.recreation.gov; Hwy 1; tent & RV sites $25) and oceanside **Kirk Creek** (☎ reservations 877-444-6777; www.recreation.gov; Hwy 1; tent & RV sites $25).

Ten miles north of Lucia is new-agey **Esalen Institute** (☎ 888-837-2536; www.esalen.org; 55000 Hwy 1), famous for its esoteric workshops and ocean-view hot springs. By reservation only (call ☎ 831-667-3047 between 9am and noon daily), you can frolic nekkid in the baths from 1am to 3am nightly ($30, credit cards only). It's surreal.

Another 3 miles north, **Julia Pfeiffer Burns State Park** (☎ 831-667-2315; www.parks.ca.gov; Hwy 1; per car $10; ⏲ 30min before sunrise-30min after sunset;) hides 80ft-high McWay Falls, one of California's only coastal waterfalls. From the viewpoint, you can photograph it tumbling over granite cliffs into the ocean – or onto the beach, depending on the tide.

DRIVING HIGHWAY 1

Navigating the narrow two-lane highway through Big Sur can be slow going. Allow at least 2½ hours to drive nonstop between Hearst Castle and Monterey Bay, much more if you stop to explore. Driving after dark can be risky and, more to the point, it's futile because you'll miss all the scenery. Watch out for cyclists and please use signposted roadside pullouts to let faster-moving traffic pass. For current road conditions and temporary closures, call ☎800-427-7623.

Over 7 miles further north, the beatnik **Henry Miller Memorial Library** (☎831-667-2574; www.henrymiller.org; 48603 Hwy 1; 🕒11am-6pm) is the art and soul of Big Sur bohemia, with a jam-packed bookstore, live-music concerts, open-mic nights and outdoor film screenings. Opposite, food takes a backseat to dramatic panoramic views at clifftop **Nepenthe** (☎831-667-2345; www.nepenthebigsur.com; 48510 Hwy 1; mains $15-42; 🕒11:30am-4:30pm & 5-10pm), meaning 'island of no sorrow.'

Heading north, rangers at **Big Sur Station** (☎831-667-2315; www.fs.usda.gov/lpnf; 47555 Hwy 1; 🕒8am-4pm, closed Mon & Tue Nov-Mar) have information on area camping and hiking, including the popular 10-mile one-way hike to **Sykes Hot Springs**. On the opposite side of Hwy 1 just south, turn onto Sycamore Canyon Rd, which drops two narrow, twisting miles to crescent-shaped **Pfeiffer Beach** (www.fs.usda.gov/lpnf; end of Sycamore Canyon Rd; per car $10; 🕒9am-8pm; 🐾), with a towering offshore sea arch. Strong currents make it too dangerous for swimming. Dig down into the sand – it's purple!

Next up, **Pfeiffer Big Sur State Park** (☎831-667-2315; www.parks.ca.gov; 47225 Hwy 1; per car $10; 🕒30min before sunrise-30min after sunset; 👪) is crisscrossed by sun-dappled trails through redwood forests. Make **campground** (☎reservations 800-444-7275; www.reserveamerica.com; 47225 Hwy 1; tent & RV sites $35-50; 👪🐾) reservations or stay at the rambling, old-fashioned **Big Sur Lodge** (☎831-667-3100; www.bigsurlodge.com; 47225 Hwy 1; d $205-395; 🏊👪), which has rustic duplex cottages (some with kitchenettes and wood-burning fireplaces), a simple restaurant and a well-stocked general store.

Most of Big Sur's commercial activity is concentrated just north along Hwy 1, including private campgrounds with rustic cabins, motels, restaurants, gas stations and shops. **Glen Oaks Motel** (☎831-667-2105; www.glenoaksbigsur.com; 47080 Hwy 1; d $225-390; 📶) 🌿 is a redesigned 1950s redwood-and-adobe motor lodge with romantic, woodsy cabins and cottages. Nearby, the Big Sur River Inn's **general store** (www.bigsurriverinn.com; 46840 Hwy 1; mains $8-10; 🕒11am-7pm; 👪) hides a burrito and fruit-smoothie bar at the back, while **Maiden Publick House** (☎831-667-2355; Village Center Shops, Hwy 1; 🕒noon-2am) pulls off an encyclopedic beer menu and live-music jams. Back south by the post office, put together a picnic at **Big Sur Deli** (www.bigsurdeli.com; 47520 Hwy 1; dishes $2-7; 🕒7am-8pm), attached to the laid-back **Big Sur Taphouse** (www.bigsurtaphouse.com; 47520 Hwy 1; 🕒noon-10pm Mon-Thu, to midnight Fri & Sat, 10am-10pm Sun; 📶), a beer-centric bar with board games and pub grub.

Heading north again, don't skip **Andrew Molera State Park** (☎831-667-2315; www.parks.ca.gov; Hwy 1; per car $10; 🕒30min before sunrise-30min after sunset; 👪), a gorgeous trail-laced pastiche of grassy meadows, waterfalls, ocean bluffs and rugged beaches. Learn all about endangered California condors at the park's **Discovery Center** (☎831-624-1202; www.ventanaws.org/discovery_center/; 🕒10am-4pm Sat & Sun late May-early Sep; 👪) 🌿 FREE. From the dirt parking lot, a 0.3-mile trail leads to a primitive, no-reservations **campground** (www.parks.ca.gov; Hwy 1; tent sites $25).

Six miles before the landmark **Bixby Creek Bridge**, you can tour 1889 **Point Sur Lightstation** (☎831-625-4419; www.pointsur.org; off Hwy 1; adult/child 6-17yr from $12/5; 🕒tours usually at 1pm Wed, 10am Sat & Sun Nov-Mar, 10am & 2pm Wed & Sat, 10am Sun Apr-Oct, also 10am Thu Jul & Aug). Check online or call for tour schedules, including seasonal moonlight walks, and directions to the meeting point. Arrive early since space is limited (no reservations).

Carmel

Once a bohemian artists' seaside resort, quaint Carmel-by-the-Sea now has the well-manicured feel of a country club. Simply plop down in any cafe and watch the parade of behatted ladies toting fancy-label shopping bags and dapper gents driving top-down convertibles along Ocean Ave, the village's slow-mo main drag.

Sights & Activities

Often foggy, municipal **Carmel Beach** is a gorgeous white-sand crescent, where pampered pups excitedly run off-leash.

San Carlos Borroméo de Carmelo Mission CHURCH
(www.carmelmission.org; 3080 Rio Rd; adult/child 7-17yr $6.50/2; 9:30am-7pm) Monterey's original mission was established by Franciscan friar Junípero Serra in 1770, but poor soil and the corrupting influence of Spanish soldiers forced the move to Carmel two years later. Today this is one of California's most strikingly beautiful missions, an oasis of solemnity bathed in flowering gardens. The mission's adobe chapel was later replaced with an arched basilica made of stone quarried in the Santa Lucia Mountains. Museum exhibits are scattered throughout the meditative complex.

Point Lobos State Natural Reserve PARK
(831-624-4909; www.pointlobos.org; Hwy 1; per car $10; 8am-7pm, closes 30min after sunset early Nov–mid-Mar;) They bark, they bathe and they're fun to watch – sea lions are the stars here at Punta de los Lobos Marinos (Point of the Sea Wolves), almost 4 miles south of Carmel, where a dramatically rocky coastline offers excellent tide-pooling. The full perimeter hike is 6 miles, but shorter walks take in wild scenery too, including Bird Island, shady cypress groves, the historical Whaler's Cabin and Devil's Cauldron, a whirlpool that gets splashy at high tide.

Eating & Drinking

Bruno's Market & Deli DELI, MARKET $
(www.brunosmarket.com; cnr 6th & Junípero Aves; sandwiches $6-9; 7am-8pm) This small supermarket deli counter makes a saucy sandwich of oakwood-grilled tri-tip beef and stocks all the accoutrements for a beach picnic, including Sparkys root beer from Pacific Grove.

Mundaka SPANISH, TAPAS $$
(831-624-7400; www.mundakacarmel.com; San Carlos St, btwn Ocean & 7th Aves; small plates $6-25; 5:30-10pm Sun-Wed, to 11pm Thu-Sat) This stone courtyard hideaway is a svelte escape from Carmel's stuffy 'newly wed and nearly dead' crowd. Taste Spanish tapas and house-made sangria while world beats spin.

Monterey

Working-class Monterey is all about the sea. It lures visitors with a top-notch aquarium that's a veritable temple to Monterey Bay's underwater universe. A National Marine Sanctuary since 1992, the bay begs for exploration by kayak, boat, scuba or snorkel. Meanwhile, downtown's historic quarter preserves California's Spanish and Mexican roots. Don't waste too much time on touristy Fisherman's Wharf or Cannery Row, the latter immortalized by novelist John Steinbeck back when it was the hectic, smelly epicenter of the sardine-canning industry, Monterey's lifeblood until the 1950s.

Sights

★ **Monterey Bay Aquarium** AQUARIUM
(info 831-648-4800, tickets 866-963-9645; www.montereybayaquarium.org; 886 Cannery Row; adult/child 3-12yr/youth 13-17yr $40/25/30; 9:30am-6pm daily Jun, 9:30am-6pm Mon-Fri, to 8pm Sat & Sun Jul-Aug, 10am-5pm or 6pm daily Sep-May;) Monterey's most mesmerizing experience is its enormous aquarium, built on the former site of the city's largest sardine cannery. All kinds of aquatic creatures are featured, from kid-tolerant sea stars and slimy sea slugs to animated sea otters and surprisingly nimble 800lb tuna. The aquarium is much more than an impressive collection of glass tanks – thoughtful placards underscore the bay's cultural and historical contexts.

Monterey State Historic Park HISTORIC SITE
(audio tour 831-998-9458, info 831-649-7118; www.parks.ca.gov) FREE Old Monterey is home to an extraordinary assemblage of 19th-century brick and adobe buildings, administered as Monterey State Historic Park, all found along a 2-mile self-guided walking tour portentously called the 'Path of History.' You can inspect dozens of buildings, many with charming gardens; expect some to be open while others aren't, according to a capricious schedule dictated by unfortunate state-park budget cutbacks.

Point Pinos Lighthouse LIGHTHOUSE
(831-648-3176; www.pointpinoslighthouse.org; 90 Asilomar Ave; suggested donation adult/child 6-17yr $2/1; 1-4pm Thu-Mon) The West Coast's oldest continuously operating lighthouse has been warning ships off the hazardous tip of the Monterey Peninsula since 1855. Inside

are modest exhibits on the lighthouse's history and alas, its failures – local shipwrecks.

Monarch Grove Sanctuary PARK
(www.ci.pg.ca.us; off Ridge Rd, btwn Lighthouse Ave & Short St; dawn-dusk;) FREE Between October and February, over 25,000 migratory monarch butterflies cluster in this thicket of tall eucalyptus trees, secreted inland. During peak season, volunteer guides answer all of your questions.

Activities

Year-round, whale-watching boats depart from Fisherman's Wharf. Cycle or walk the paved **Monterey Peninsula Recreation Trail**, which edges the coast past Cannery Row, ending at Lovers Point in Pacific Grove. The overhyped **17-Mile Drive** (www.pebblebeach.com; per car/bicycle $10/free) toll road connects Monterey and Pacific Grove with Carmel-by-the-Sea.

Adventures by the Sea CYCLING, KAYAKING
(831-372-1807; www.adventuresbythesea.com; 299 Cannery Row; rental per day kayak or bicycle $30, SUP set $50, tours from $60;) Beach cruisers, electric bikes and water-sports gear rentals and tours available at multiple locations on Cannery Row and **downtown** (831-372-1807; www.adventuresbythesea.com; 210 Alvarado St;).

Aquarius Dive Shop DIVING
(831-375-1933; www.aquariusdivers.com; 2040 Del Monte Ave; snorkel/scuba-gear rental $35/65, dive tours from $65) Talk to this five-star PADI operation for gear rentals, classes and guided dives into Monterey Bay.

Sanctuary Cruises WHALE-WATCHING
(831-917-1042; www.sanctuarycruises.com; 7881 Sandholdt Rd; adult/child 12yr & under $50/40;) Departing from Moss Landing, 20 miles north of Monterey, this biodiesel boat runs recommended whale-watching and dolphin-spotting tours (reservations essential).

Sleeping

No-frills motels (which are exorbitantly priced in summer) are found on Munras Ave south of downtown and N Fremont St east of Hwy 1.

HI Monterey Hostel HOSTEL $
(831-649-0375; www.montereyhostel.org; 778 Hawthorne St; dm $27-37, d $79-199, all without bath; check-in 4-10pm;) Four blocks from Cannery Row and the aquarium, this simple, clean hostel houses single-sex and mixed dorms, as well as private rooms (call for rates). Budget backpackers stuff themselves silly with make-your-own pancake breakfasts. Reservations strongly recommended. Take MST bus 1 from downtown's Transit Plaza.

Monterey Hotel HISTORIC HOTEL $$
(831-375-3184; www.montereyhotel.com; 406 Alvarado St; r $80-220;) In the heart of downtown and a short walk from Fisherman's Wharf, this 1904 edifice harbors five-dozen small, somewhat noisy, but freshly renovated rooms with Victorian-styled furniture and plantation shutters. No elevator. Parking is $17.

★**InterContinental–Clement** HOTEL $$$
(831-375-4500, 866-781-2406; www.icthe-clementmonterey.com; 750 Cannery Row; r from $250;) Like an upscale version of a New England millionaire's seaside mansion, this all-encompassing resort presides over Cannery Row. For the utmost luxury and romance, book an ocean-view suite with a balcony and private fireplace, then breakfast in bayfront C Restaurant downstairs. Parking is $23.

Eating

Restaurants, bars and live-music venues line Cannery Row and downtown's Alvarado St.

LouLou's Griddle in the Middle AMERICAN $$
(www.loulousgriddle.com; Municipal Wharf 2; mains $8-16; usually 7:30am-3pm & 5-8:30pm Wed-Mon;) Stroll down the municipal wharf to this zany diner, best for breakfasts of ginormous pancakes and omelets with Mexican *pico de gallo* salsa or fresh seafood for lunch. Breezy outdoor tables are dog friendly.

Red House Cafe CAFE $$
(831-643-1060; www.redhousecafe.com; 662 Lighthouse Ave; mains breakfast & lunch $8-14, dinner $12-23; 8am-2:30pm daily, 5-9pm Tue-Sun;) Crowded with locals, this shingled late-19th-century house dishes up comfort food with haute touches, like cinnamon-brioche French toast, grilled eggplant-fontina sandwiches or spinach-cheese ravioli in lemon beurre blanc sauce. Oatmeal-apricot-pecan cookies are what's for dessert. Reservations helpful.

★**Passionfish** SEAFOOD $$$
(831-655-3311; www.passionfish.net; 701 Lighthouse Ave, Pacific Grove; mains $16-32; 5-9pm Sun-Thu, to 10pm Fri & Sat) Fresh, sustain-

able seafood is artfully presented in any number of inventive ways, and a seasonally inspired menu also carries slow-cooked meats and vegetarian dishes spotlighting local farms. The earth-tone decor is spare, with tables squeezed conversationally close together. An ambitious world-ranging wine list is priced near retail, and there are twice as many Chinese teas as wines by the glass.

Reservations strongly recommended.

Information

Monterey Visitors Center (☎831-657-6400, 888-221-1010; www.seemonterey.com; 401 Camino El Estero; 9am-6pm Mon-Sat, to 5pm Sun, closing 1hr earlier Nov-Mar) Free tourist brochures; ask for a *Monterey County Literary & Film Map*.

Getting There & Around

Regional and local **Monterey-Salinas Transit** (MST; ☎888-678-2871; www.mst.org; single-ride fares $1.50-3.50, day pass $10) buses converge on downtown's **Transit Plaza** (cnr Pearl & Alvarado Sts), including routes to Pacific Grove, Carmel, Big Sur (daily in summer, otherwise weekends only) and Salinas (for Greyhound bus and Amtrak train connections). During summer, free trolleys shuttle between downtown Monterey and Cannery Row.

Santa Cruz

SoCal beach culture meets NorCal counterculture here. The university student population makes this old-school radical town youthful, hip and lefty-liberal. Some worry that Santa Cruz' weirdness quotient is dropping, but you'll disagree when you witness the freak show (and we say that with love, man) along Pacific Ave downtown.

Sights & Activities

You'll find the most action at **Main Beach**, about a mile south of downtown. Locals favor less-trampled beaches off E Cliff Dr.

★Santa Cruz Beach Boardwalk AMUSEMENT PARK
(☎831-423-5590; www.beachboardwalk.com; 400 Beach St; per ride $3-6, all-day pass $32-40; daily Apr-early Sep, seasonal hours vary;) The West Coast's oldest beachfront amusement park, this 1907 boardwalk has a glorious old-school Americana vibe. The smell of cotton candy mixes with the salt air, punctuated by the squeals of kids hanging upside down on carnival rides. Famous thrills include the Giant Dipper, a 1924 wooden roller coaster, and the 1911 Looff carousel, both National Historic Landmarks. During summer, catch free midweek movies and Friday-night concerts by rock veterans you may have thought were already dead.

Santa Cruz Surfing Museum MUSEUM
(www.santacruzsurfingmuseum.org; 701 W Cliff Dr; admission by donation; 10am-5pm Wed-Mon Jul 4-early Sep, noon-4pm Thu-Mon early Sep-Jul 3) A mile southwest of the wharf along the coast, this tiny museum inside an old lighthouse is packed with memorabilia, including vintage redwood surfboards. Fittingly, Lighthouse Point overlooks two popular surf breaks.

Natural Bridges State Beach BEACH
(www.parks.ca.gov; 2531 W Cliff Dr; per car $10; 8am-sunset;) Best for sunsets, this family favorite has lots of sand, tide pools and monarch butterflies from mid-October through mid-February. It's at the far end of W Cliff Dr.

Seymour Marine Discovery Center MUSEUM
(☎831-459-3800; http://seymourcenter.ucsc.edu; 100 Shaffer Rd; adult/child 3-16yr $8/6; 10am-5pm Tue-Sun year-round, also 10am-5pm Mon Jul & Aug;) By Natural Bridges State Beach, this kids' educational center is part of UCSC's Long Marine Laboratory. Interactive natural-science exhibits include tidal touch pools and aquariums, while outside you can gawk at the world's largest blue-whale skeleton. Guided one-hour tours happen at 1pm, 2pm and 3pm daily, with a special half-hour tour for families with younger children at 11am; sign up for tours in person an hour in advance (no reservations).

Venture Quest KAYAKING
(☎831-425-8445, 831-427-2267; www.kayaksantacruz.com; Municipal Wharf; kayak rental/tour from $30/55; 10am-7pm Mon-Fri, from 9am Sat & Sun late May-late Sep, hours vary late Sep–mid-May) Convenient rentals on the wharf, plus whale-watching and coastal sea-cave tours, moonlight paddles and kayak-sailing trips. Book ahead for kayak-surfing lessons.

O'Neill Surf Shop SURFING
(☎831-475-4151; www.oneill.com; 1115 41st Ave; wetsuit/surfboard rental from $10/20; 9am-8pm Mon-Fri, from 8am Sat & Sun) Head east toward Pleasure Point to worship at this internationally renowned surfboard maker's flagship store, with branches on the beach boardwalk and downtown.

Richard Schmidt Surf School SURFING
(☎831-423-0928; www.richardschmidt.com; 849 Almar Ave; 2hr group/1hr private lesson $90/120) Award-winning, time-tested surf school can get you out there, all equipment included. Summer surf camps hook adults and kids alike.

Sleeping

Motels border Ocean St near downtown, Mission St by the university campus and Hwy 1 heading south. Make reservations for state-park **campgrounds** (☎reservations 800-444-7275; www.reserveamerica.com; tent & RV sites $35-65;) by beaches off Hwy 1 and in redwood forests off Hwy 9.

HI Santa Cruz Hostel HOSTEL $
(☎831-423-8304; www.hi-santacruz.org; 321 Main St; dm $26-29, r $60-110, all without bath; check-in 5-10pm; @) Budget overnighters dig this cute hostel at the century-old Carmelita Cottages surrounded by flowering gardens, just two blocks from the beach. Cons: midnight curfew, daytime lockout (11am to 5pm) and three-night maximum stay. Reservations are essential. Street parking costs $2.

★**Adobe on Green B&B** B&B $$
(☎831-469-9866; www.adobeongreen.com; 103 Green St; r incl breakfast $169-219;) Peace and quiet are the mantras at this place, a short walk from Pacific Ave. The hosts are practically invisible, but their thoughtful touches are everywhere, from boutique-hotel amenities in spacious, stylish and solar-powered rooms to breakfast spreads from their organic gardens.

Pelican Point Inn INN $$
(☎831-475-3381; www.pelicanpointinn-santacruz.com; 21345 E Cliff Dr; ste $139-219;) Ideal for families, these roomy apartments near a kid-friendly beach come with everything you'll need for a lazy vacation, including kitchenettes. Weekly rates available. Pet fee $20.

Dream Inn HOTEL $$$
(☎866-774-7735, 831-426-4330; www.dreaminnsantacruz.com; 175 W Cliff Dr; r $249-479; @) Overlooking the wharf from a spectacular hillside perch, this chic boutique hotel is as stylish as Santa Cruz gets. Rooms have all mod cons, while the beach is just steps away. Don't miss happy hour at Aquarius restaurant's ocean-view bar. Parking is $25.

Eating

Downtown is chockablock with so-so cafes. Mission St near the university campus and 41st Ave in neighboring Capitola offer cheaper takeout and international flavors.

Picnic Basket DELI $
(http://thepicnicbasketsc.com; 125 Beach St; dishes $3-10; 7am-9pm, shorter off-season hours;) Across the street from the beach boardwalk, this locavarian kitchen puts together creative sandwiches such as beet with lemony couscous or 'fancy pants' grilled cheese with fruit chutney, plus homemade soups, breakfast burritos and baked goods. Staff can be sour, but ice-cream treats are sweet.

Pono Hawaiian Grill FUSION $$
(www.ponohawaiiangrill.com; 120 Union St; mains $7-15; 11am-10pm Sun-Wed, to 11pm Thu-Sat) Inside the Reef bar, this kitchen runs on 'island time' as it mixes up your fresh ahi tuna, salmon, shellfish or veggie *poke* (cubed raw salad) in a bowl or ladled on a plate with two-scoop rice and creamy macaroni or tossed green salad. The loco moco burrito with spicy gravy is a huge hit.

Soif BISTRO $$$
(☎831-423-2020; www.soifwine.com; 105 Walnut Ave; small plates $5-17, mains $19-25; 5-9pm Sun-Thu, to 10pm Fri & Sat) Bon vivants swoon over a heady selection of three dozen international wines by the glass, paired with a sophisticated, seasonally driven Euro-Cal menu. Expect tastebud-ticklers like roasted beet salad with fava beans and maple vinaigrette or squid-ink linguini with spicy chorizo.

Drinking & Nightlife

Downtown is jam-packed with bars, live-music lounges, low-key nightclubs and coffeehouses. Check the free *Good Times Santa Cruz* (www.gtweekly.com) tabloid for more venues and current events.

★**Verve Coffee Roasters** CAFE
(www.vervecoffeeroasters.com; 1540 Pacific Ave; 6:30am-9pm;) To sip finely roasted artisan espresso or a cup of rich pour-over coffee, join the surfers and hipsters at this industrial-zen cafe. Single-origin brews and house blends rule.

Caffe Pergolesi CAFE
(www.theperg.com; 418 Cedar St; 7am-11pm;) Discuss conspiracy theories over stalwart coffee, tea or beer at this landmark Victori-

an house with a big ol' tree-shaded veranda. There's live music some evenings.

Discretion Brewing BREWERY (www.discretionbrewing.com; 2703 41st Ave, Soquel; ⏲11:30am-9pm) Rye IPA, English ales and traditional Belgian and German brews are always on tap, off Hwy 1.

Information

KPIG 107.5 FM (www.kpig.com) Streams the classic Santa Cruz soundtrack – think Bob Marley, Janis Joplin and Willie Nelson.

Santa Cruz Visitor Center (☎831-425-1234; www.santacruzca.org; 303 Water St; ⏲9am-noon & 1-4pm Mon-Fri, 11am-3pm Sat & Sun; @) Free public internet terminal, maps and brochures.

Getting There & Around

Local and regional **Santa Cruz Metro** (☎831-425-8600; www.scmtd.com; single ride/day pass $2/6) buses converge on downtown's **Metro Center** (920 Pacific Ave). From there, Greyhound operates a few daily buses to San Francisco ($20, three hours), San Luis Obispo ($46, 3¾ hours), Santa Barbara ($59, six hours) and LA ($65, 8¾ hours). During summer, a trolley (25¢) shuttles between downtown and Main Beach and the wharf.

Santa Cruz to San Francisco

Far more scenic than any freeway, this curvaceous, 70-mile stretch of coastal Hwy 1 is bordered by wild beaches, organic farms and sea-salted villages, all scattered like loose diamonds in the rough.

About 20 miles northwest of Santa Cruz, **Año Nuevo State Reserve** (☎information 650-879-0227, tour reservations 800-444-4445; www.parks.ca.gov; off Hwy 1; entry per car $10, 2½hr tour per person $7; ⏲8:30am-5pm, last entry 3:30pm Apr-Nov, tours only mid-Dec–Mar) is the seasonal home of a gigantic colony of elephant seals. Book well in advance for a guided walking tour, given during the cacophonous winter birthing and mating season.

On a windswept coastal perch further north, **HI Pigeon Point Lighthouse Hostel** (☎650-879-0633; www.norcalhostels.org/pigeon; 210 Pigeon Point Rd; dm $26-31, d/tr from $76/104, all without bath; @ 📶 👪) 🌿 inhabits historic lightkeepers' quarters; it's popular, so reserve ahead. For more creature comforts, backtrack 4 miles south to bed down in a tent bungalow or a fireplace cabin at **Costanoa** (☎877-262-7848, 650-879-1100; www.costanoa.com; 2001 Rossi Rd; tents/cabins without bath from $89/179, lodge r $203-291; 📶 👪).

Five miles north of Pigeon Point, turn off at **Pescadero State Beach** (www.parks.ca.gov; off Hwy 1; per car $8; ⏲8am-sunset) and drive a few miles inland to Pescadero village. Pick up picnic supplies at the bakery-deli inside **Arcangeli Grocery Co** (Norm's Market; www.normsmarket.com; 287 Stage Rd; ⏲10am-6pm). Nearby, family-owned **Harley Farms Cheese Shop** (☎650-879-0480; http://harleyfarms.com; 250 North St; 2hr tour adult/child $20/10; ⏲10am-5pm; 👪) offers goat-dairy farm tours by reservation.

Another 15 miles north, busy Half Moon Bay is bordered by 4-mile-long **Half Moon Bay State Beach** (www.parks.ca.gov; off Hwy 1; per car $10; ⏲8am-sunset; 👪), which has scenic campgrounds. Get out on the water with **Half Moon Bay Kayak** (☎650-773-6101; www.hmbkayak.com; 2 Johnson Pier; kayak/SUP rental per hour from $25; ⏲9am-5pm Wed-Mon, last rental 3:30pm). Offshore from Pillar Point Harbor, which has a decent brewpub with a sunset-view patio, dangerous **Mavericks** surf break attracts the world's top big-wave riders in winter. In Half Moon Bay's quaint downtown, eclectic shops, cafes and restaurants line Main St, just inland from Hwy 1.

North of Moss Beach off Hwy 1, **Fitzgerald Marine Reserve** (☎650-728-3584; www.fitzgeraldreserve.org; 200 Nevada Ave; ⏲8am-sunset; 👪) 🌿 FREE protects tide pools teeming with colorful sea life; time your visit for low tide. Another mile north, **HI Point Montara Lighthouse Hostel** (☎650-728-7177; www.norcalhostels.org/montara; cnr Hwy 1 & 16th St; dm $27-30, r $78-107, all without bath; @ 📶) 🌿 perches on an ocean bluff (reservations essential). From there, it's less than 20 miles to San Francisco via beachy Pacifica and the Devil's Slide Tunnels.

SAN FRANCISCO & THE BAY AREA

San Francisco

If you've ever wondered where the envelope goes when it's pushed, here's your answer. Good times and social revolutions have often started here, from manic gold rushes to blissful hippie be-ins. Psychedelic drugs, newfangled technology, gay liberation, green ventures, free speech and culinary experimentation all became mainstream long ago in San Francisco.

Consider permission permanently granted to be outlandish: other towns may surprise you, but in San Francisco you may surprise yourself. Grab your coat and a handful of glitter, and enter the land of fog and fabulousness. So long, inhibitions; hello, San Francisco.

History

Before gold changed everything, San Francisco was a Spanish colonial mission built by conscripts from the indigenous Ohlone and Miwok communities. In 1849 the gold rush turned an 800-person village into a port city of 100,000 prospectors, con artists, prostitutes and honest folk.

Frustrated miners rioted against San Francisco's Chinese community, who from 1877 to 1943 were restricted to living and working in Chinatown by anti-Chinese laws. In the late 19th century, Chinese laborers had few options besides dangerous work building railroads for the city's robber barons, who dynamited, mined and clear-cut across the West, and built grand Nob Hill mansions. When the 1906 earthquake and fire reduced the city to rubble, San Franciscans rebuilt an astounding 15 buildings per day. By 1915, the rebuilt city hosted the Panama-Pacific International Exposition in grand style.

During WWII, soldiers accused of homosexuality and insubordination were dismissed in San Francisco, cementing the city's counterculture reputation. The 1967 'Summer of Love' brought free food, sex and music to the hippie Haight, while enterprising gay activists founded an out-and-proud community in the Castro. San Francisco's unconventional thinking is behind today's boom in social media, mobile apps and biotech.

Sights

Let San Francisco's 43 hills stretch your legs and your imagination as they deliver breathtaking views.

Embarcadero

★Ferry Building LANDMARK

(Map p974; ☎415-983-8030; www.ferrybuildingmarketplace.com; Market St & the Embarcadero; ⏰10am-6pm Mon-Fri, 9am-6pm Sat, 11am-5pm Sun; P 👪; 🚌2, 6, 9, 14, 21, 31, M Embarcadero, B Embarcadero) Hedonism is alive and well at this transit hub turned gourmet emporium, where foodies happily miss their ferries slurping local oysters and bubbly. Star chefs are frequently spotted at the farmers market (p982) that wraps around the building year-round.

★Exploratorium MUSEUM

(Map p974; ☎415-528-4444; www.exploratorium.edu; Pier 15; adult/child $29/19, 6-10pm Thu $15; ⏰10am-5pm Tue-Sun, over 18yr only Thu 6-10pm; P 👪; M F) Is there a science to skateboarding? Do toilets really flush counterclockwise in Australia? Find answers to questions you wished you'd learned in school, at San Francisco's thrilling hands-on science museum. Combining science with art, and investigating human perception, the Exploratorium nudges you to question how you perceive the world around you. The setting is thrilling – a 9-acre, glass-walled pier jutting straight into San Francisco Bay, with large outdoor portions you can explore free of charge, 24 hours a day.

Union Square & Civic Center

Bordered by high-end department stores, **Union Square** (Map p974; intersection of Geary, Powell, Post & Stockton Sts; 🚋Powell-Mason, Powell-Hyde, M Powell, B Powell) was named for pro-Union Civil War rallies held here 150 years ago. People-watch with espresso from **Emporio Rulli** (Map p974; ☎415-433-1122; www.rulli.com; Union Sq; ⏰7am-7pm; M Powell, B Powell) cafe.

★Asian Art Museum MUSEUM

(Map p974; ☎415-581-3500; www.asianart.org; 200 Larkin St; adult/child/student $15/free/10, 1st Sun of month free; ⏰10am-5pm Tue-Sun, to 9pm Thu; 👪; M Civic Center, B Civic Center) Imaginations race from ancient Persian miniatures to cutting-edge Japanese fashion through three floors spanning 6000 years of Asian arts. Besides the largest collection outside Asia – 18,000 works – the museum offers excellent programs for all ages, from shadow-puppet shows and yoga for kids to mixers with cross-cultural DJ mash-ups.

Powell St Cable Car Turnaround LANDMARK

(Map p974; cnr Powell & Market Sts; 🚋Powell-Mason, Mason-Hyde, M Powell, B Powell) Stand awhile at Powell and Market Sts and spot arriving cable-car operators leaping out, gripping the trolley's chassis and slooowly turning the car atop a revolving wooden

SAN FRANCISCO IN...

One Day

Since the Gold Rush, San Francisco adventures have started in **Chinatown**, where you can still find hidden fortunes – in cookies, that is. After dining on dim sum, beat it to **City Lights Bookstore** to revel in Beat poetry. Stroll past the Italian streetside cafes of **North Beach** to climb **Coit Tower** for 360-degree city and bay views. Then head to Civic Center's **Asian Art Museum**, where art transports you across centuries and oceans within an hour. Have an early dinner at the **Ferry Building** before taking a spooky night tour of **Alcatraz**. Make your escape from the island prison in time to hit the dance floor in **SoMa** clubs.

Two Days

Start your day in the **Mission** amid mural-covered garage doors lining **Balmy Alley**, then step inside meditative **Mission Dolores**. Break for burritos before hoofing it to the **Haight** for flashbacks at vintage boutiques and the Summer of Love site: **Golden Gate Park**. Glimpse bay views atop the **de Young Museum**, take a walk on the wild side at the **California Academy of Sciences** and brave howling winds on the **Golden Gate Bridge**.

platform. Cable cars can't go in reverse, so they need to be turned around by hand here at the terminus of Powell St lines. Riders queue up midmorning to early evening here to secure a seat, with raucous street performers and doomsday preachers on the sidelines as entertainment.

Chinatown

Since 1848, this community has survived riots, bootlegging gangsters and earthquakes.

Chinese Historical Society of America MUSEUM

(CHSA; Map p974; ☎415-391-1188; www.chsa.org; 965 Clay St; ⊙noon-5pm Tue-Fri, 11am-4pm Sat; 🚌1, 8, 30, 45, 🚋California St, Powell-Mason, Mason-Hyde) FREE Picture what it was like to be Chinese in America during the Gold Rush, transcontinental railroad construction or Beat heyday in this 1932 landmark, built as Chinatown's YWCA by Julia Morgan (chief architect of Hearst Castle). CHSA historians unearth fascinating artifacts, such as 1920s silk *qipao* dresses worn by socialites from Shanghai to San Francisco. Exhibits reveal once-popular views of Chinatown, including the sensationalist opium-den exhibit at San Francisco's 1915 Panama-Pacific International Expo, inviting fairgoers to 'Go Slumming' in Chinatown.

North Beach

City Lights CULTURAL CENTER, LANDMARK

(Map p974; ☎415-362-8193; www.citylights.com; 261 Columbus Ave; ⊙10am-midnight; 👪; 🚌8, 10, 12, 30, 41, 45, 🚋Powell-Mason, Powell-Hyde) Free speech and free spirits have flourished at City Lights since 1957, when founder and poet Lawrence Ferlinghetti and manager Shigeyoshi Murao won a landmark ruling defending their right to publish Allen Ginsberg's magnificent epic poem 'Howl.' Celebrate your right to read freely in the sunny upstairs Poetry Room, with its piles of freshly published verse and designated Poet's Chair.

Beat Museum MUSEUM

(Map p974; ☎800-537-6822; www.kerouac.com; 540 Broadway; adult/student $8/5, walking tours $25; ⊙museum 10am-7pm, walking tours 2-4pm Mon, Wed & Sat; 🚌8, 10, 12, 30, 41, 45, 🚋Powell-Mason) The closest you can get to the complete Beat experience without breaking a law. The 1000-plus artifacts in this museum's literary ephemera collection include the sublime (the banned edition of Ginsberg's *Howl*) and the ridiculous (those Kerouac bobble-head dolls are definite head-shakers). Downstairs, watch Beat-era films in ramshackle theater seats redolent with the odors of literary giants, pets and pot. Upstairs, pay respects at shrines to individual Beat writers. Guided two-hour walking tours cover the museum, Beat history and literary alleys.

San Francisco & the Bay Area

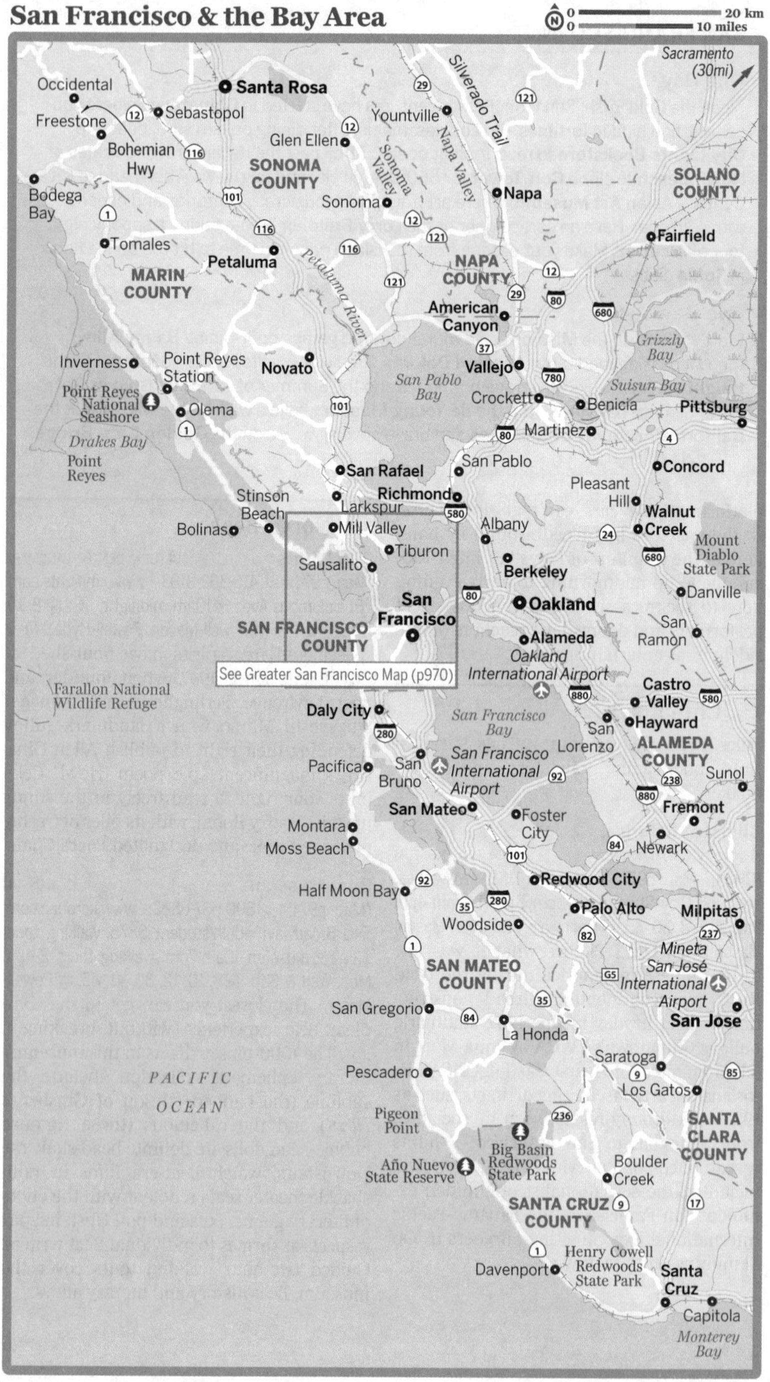

Russian Hill & Nob Hill

Lombard Street AREA

(Map p974; 900 block of Lombard St; Powell-Hyde) You've seen its eight switchbacks in a thousand photographs. The tourist board has dubbed this 'the world's crookedest street,' which is factually incorrect. Vermont St in Potrero Hill deserves that award, but Lombard is much more scenic, with its red-brick pavement and lovingly tended flowerbeds. It wasn't always so bent; before the arrival of the automobile it lunged straight down the hill.

Cable Car Museum HISTORIC SITE

(Map p974; 415-474-1887; www.cablecarmuseum.org; 1201 Mason St; donations appreciated; 10am-6pm Apr-Sep, to 5pm Oct-Mar; ; Powell-Mason, Powell-Hyde) FREE Hear that whirring beneath the cable-car tracks? That's the sound of the cables that pull the cars, and they all connect inside the city's long-functioning cable-car barn. Grips, engines, braking mechanisms…if these warm your gearhead heart, you'll be besotted by the Cable Car Museum. See three original 1870s cable cars and watch cables whir over massive bull wheels – as awesome a feat of physics now as when Andrew Hallidie invented it in 1873.

Fisherman's Wharf

Maritime National Historical Park HISTORIC SITE

(Map p974; www.nps.gov/safr; 499 Jefferson St, Hyde St Pier; 7-day ticket adult/child $5/free; 9:30am-5pm Oct-May, to 5:30pm Jun-Sep; ; 19, 30, 47, Powell-Hyde, M F) Four historic ships are floating museums at this national park, Fisherman's Wharf's most authentic attraction. Moored along Hyde St Pier, standouts include the 1891 schooner *Alma*, 1890 steamboat *Eureka*, paddle-wheel tugboat *Eppleton Hall* and iron-hulled *Balclutha*, which brought coal to San Francisco. It's free to walk the pier; pay only to board ships.

Maritime Museum MUSEUM

(Aquatic Park Bathhouse; Map p974; www.maritime.org; 900 Beach St; 10am-4pm; ; 19, 30, 47, Powell-Hyde) FREE A monumental hint to sailors in need of a scrub, this restored, shipshape 1939 streamline-moderne landmark is decked out with Works Progress Administration (WPA) art treasures: playful seal and frog sculptures by Beniamino Bufano, Hilaire Hiler's surreal underwater dreamscape murals and recently uncovered wood reliefs by Richard Ayer. Acclaimed African American artist Sargent Johnson created the stunning carved green slate marquee doorway and the verandah's mesmerizing aquatic mosaics.

> **DON'T MISS**
>
> **ALCATRAZ**
>
> **Alcatraz** (Map p970; Alcatraz Cruises 415-981-7625; www.alcatrazcruises.com; day tours adult/child/family $30/18/90, night tours adult/child $37/22; call center 8am-7pm, ferries depart Pier 33 half-hourly 8:45am-3:50pm, night tours 5:55pm & 6:30pm) For more than 150 years, Alcatraz has given the innocent chills and the guilty cold sweats. It served as the nation's first military prison, a maximum-security penitentiary housing A-list criminals including Al Capone, and disputed territory between Native American activists and the FBI. No prisoners ever escaped Alcatraz alive, but since importing guards and supplies cost more than putting up prisoners at the Ritz, the prison was shuttered in 1963.
>
> Day visits include the cruise to and from the island and captivating audio tours, with past prisoners and guards recalling life on 'the Rock.' Eerie night tours are led by a park ranger. Reserve tickets at least a month ahead.

The Marina & Presidio

Crissy Field PARK

(Map p970; www.crissyfield.org; 1199 East Beach; P; 30, PresidiGo Shuttle) War is for the birds at Crissy Field, a military airstrip turned waterfront nature preserve with knockout Golden Gate views. Where military aircraft once zoomed in for landings, bird-watchers now huddle in the silent rushes of a reclaimed tidal marsh. Joggers pound beachside trails and the only security alerts are raised by puppies suspiciously sniffing surfers. On foggy days, stop by the certified-green Warming Hut to browse regional-nature books and warm up with fair-trade coffee.

Presidio Officers' Club HISTORIC BUILDING

(Map p970; 415-561-4165; www.presidioofficersclub.com; 50 Moraga Ave; 10am-6pm Tue-Sun;

Greater San Francisco

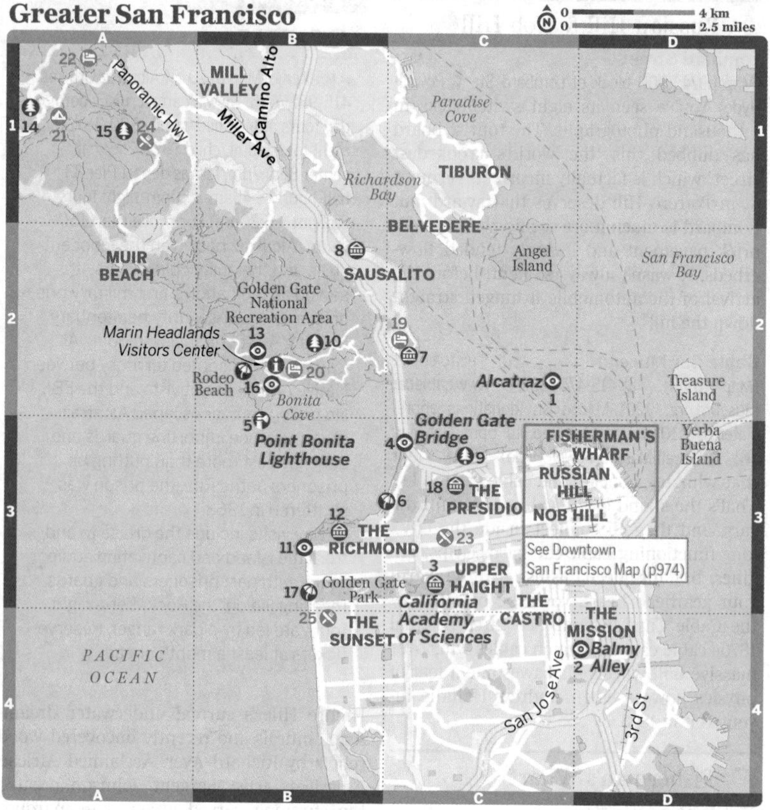

(🚌 PresidiGo Shuttle) **FREE** The Presidio's oldest building dates to the late 1700s, and got a total renovation in 2015, revealing gorgeous Spanish-Moorish adobe architecture. The free Heritage Gallery shows the history of the Presidio, from Native American days to present. Moraga Hall – the former officers' club lounge – is a lovely spot to sit fireside and also has free wi-fi. Thursday and Friday evenings, the Club hosts a dynamic lineup of events and lectures; check the website.

Baker Beach BEACH

(Map p970; ⏲ sunrise-sunset; P; 🚌 29, PresidiGo Shuttle) Picnic amid wind-sculpted pines, fish from craggy rocks or frolic nude at mile-long Baker Beach, with spectacular views of the bridge. Crowds come weekends, especially on fog-free days; arrive early. For nude sunbathing (mostly straight girls and gay boys), head to the north end. Families in clothing stick to the south end, nearer the parking lot. Mind the currents and the c-c-cold water.

The Mission & the Castro

★ Balmy Alley PUBLIC ART

(Map p970; ☎ 415-285-2287; www.precitaeyes.org; btwn 24th & 25th Sts; 🚌 10, 12, 14, 27, 48, B 24th St Mission) Inspired by Diego Rivera's 1930s San Francisco murals and outraged by US foreign policy in Central America, 1970s Mission *muralistas* (muralists) set out to transform the political landscape, one mural-covered garage door at a time. Today, Balmy Alley murals span three decades, from an early memorial for El Salvador activist Archbishop Óscar Romero to a homage to Frida Kahlo, Georgia O'Keefe and other trailblazing modern women artists.

Mission Dolores CHURCH

(Misión San Francisco de Asís; ☎ 415-621-8203; www.missiondolores.org; 3321 16th St; adult/child

Greater San Francisco

Top Sights

1 Alcatraz C2
2 Balmy Alley D4
3 California Academy of Sciences C3
4 Golden Gate Bridge C3
5 Point Bonita Lighthouse B3

Sights

6 Baker Beach C3
7 Bay Area Discovery Museum C2
8 Bay Model Visitors Center B2
Cliff House .... (see 11)
9 Crissy Field C3
10 Golden Gate National Recreation Area B2
11 Lands End B3
12 Legion of Honor B3
13 Marine Mammal Center B2
14 Mt Tamalpais State Park A1
15 Muir Woods National Monument A1
16 Nike Missile Site SF-88 .... B2
17 Ocean Beach B3
18 Presidio Officers' Club C3
Sutro Baths .... (see 11)

Sleeping

19 Cavallo Point C2
20 HI Marin Headlands Hostel B2
21 Pantoll Campground A1
22 West Point Inn A1

Eating

23 Burma Superstar C3
24 Muir Woods Trading Company A1
25 Outerlands B4

$5/3; 9am-4pm Nov-Apr, to 4:30pm May-Oct; 22, 33, B 16th St Mission, M J) The city's oldest building and its namesake, whitewashed adobe Misión San Francisco de Asís was founded in 1776 and rebuilt in 1782 with conscripted Ohlone and Miwok labor – a graveyard memorial hut commemorates 5000 Ohlone and Miwok laborers who died in mission measles epidemics in 1814 and 1826. Today the modest adobe mission is overshadowed by the ornate adjoining 1913 basilica, featuring stained-glass windows of California's 21 missions.

GLBT History Museum MUSEUM
(415-621-1107; www.glbthistory.org/museum; 4127 18th St; admission $5, 1st Wed of month free; 11am-7pm Mon-Sat, noon-5pm Sun; closed Tue fall-spring; M Castro) America's first gay-history museum cobbles ephemera from the community – Harvey Milk's campaign literature, matchbooks from long-gone bathhouses, photographs of early activists – together with harder-hitting installations that focus on various aspects of queer history, incorporating electronic media to tell personal stories that illuminate the evolution of the struggle to gain rights and acceptance into the larger culture.

Dolores Park PARK
(http://sfrecpark.org/destination/mission-dolores-park/; Dolores St, btwn 18th & 20th Sts; ; 14, 33, 49, B 16th St Mission, M J) Semiprofessional tanning, taco picnics and a Hunky Jesus Contest at Easter: welcome to San Francisco's sunny side. Dolores Park has something for everyone, from street ball and tennis to the Mayan-pyramid playground (sorry kids: no blood sacrifice allowed). Political protests and other favorite local sports happen year-round, and there are free movie nights and Mime Troupe performances in summer. Climb to the upper southwest corner for the best views of downtown, framed by palm trees.

The Haight & Around

Haight & Ashbury LANDMARK
(6, 7, 33, 37, 43) This legendary intersection was the epicenter of the psychedelic '60s and remains a counterculture magnet. On average Saturdays here you can sign Green Party petitions, commission a poem, hear Hare Krishna on keyboards and Bob Dylan on banjo. The clock overhead always reads 4:20 – better known in herbal circles as International Bong-Hit Time. A local clockmaker recently fixed it; within a week it was stuck at 4:20.

Alamo Square Park PARK
(www.sfparksalliance.org/our-parks/parks/alamo-square; Hayes & Scott Sts; sunrise-sunset; ; 5, 21, 22, 24) The pastel Painted Ladies of famed Postcard Row along the east side pale in comparison with the colorful characters along the northwest end of this 1857 Victorian hilltop park. Alamo Square's north side features Barbary Coast baroque mansions at their most bombastic, bedecked with fish-scale shingles and gingerbread trim dripping from peaked roofs.

Alcatraz

Book a ferry from Pier 33 and ride 1.5 miles across the bay to explore America's most notorious former prison. The trip itself is worth the money, providing stunning views of the city skyline. Once you've landed at the **Ferry Dock & Pier** 1, you begin the 580-yard walk to the top of the island and prison; if you're out of shape, there's a twice-hourly tram.

As you climb toward the **Guardhouse** 2, notice the island's steep slope; before it was a prison, Alcatraz was a fort. In the 1850s, the military quarried the rocky shores into near-vertical cliffs. Ships could then only dock at a single port, separated from the main buildings by a sally port (a drawbridge and moat in what became the guardhouse). Inside, peer through floor grates to see Alcatraz' original prison.

Volunteers tend the brilliant **Officer's Row Gardens** 3 – an orderly counterpoint to the overgrown rose bushes surrounding the burned-out shell of the **Warden's House** 4. At the top of the hill, by the front door of the **Main Cellhouse** 5, beautiful shots unfurl all around, including a **view of the Golden Gate Bridge** 6. Above the main door of the administration building, notice the **historic signs & graffiti** 7, before you step inside the dank, cold prison to find the **Frank Morris cell** 8, former home to Alcatraz' most notorious jail-breaker.

TOP TIPS

- Book at least one month prior for self-guided daytime visits, longer for ranger-led night tours. For info on garden tours, see www.alcatrazgardens.org.
- Be prepared to hike; a steep path ascends from the ferry landing to the cell block. Most people spend two to three hours on the island. You need only reserve for the outbound ferry; take any ferry back.
- There's no food (just water) but you can bring your own; picnicking is allowed at the ferry dock only. Dress in layers as weather changes fast and it's usually windy.

EMMA DURNFORD / GETTY IMAGES ©

Historic Signs & Graffiti

During their 1969–71 occupation, Native Americans graffitied the water tower: 'Home of the Free Indian Land.' Above the cellhouse door, examine the eagle-and-flag crest to see how the red-and-white stripes were changed to spell 'Free.'

Warden's House

Fires destroyed the warden's house and other structures during the Indian Occupation. The government blamed the Native Americans; the Native Americans blamed agents provocateurs acting on behalf of the Nixon Administration to undermine public sympathy.

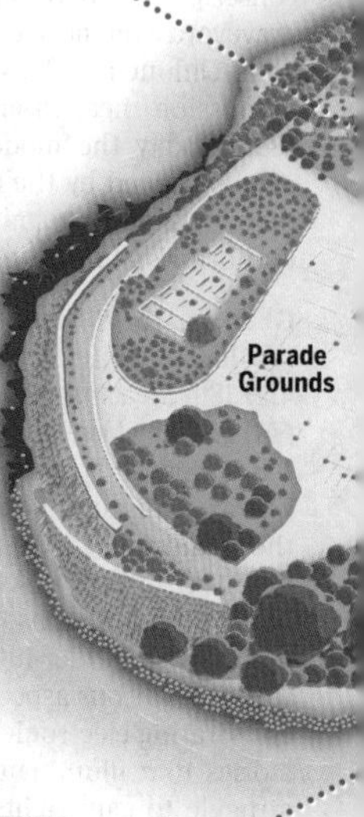

DAVID CLAPP / GETTY IMAGES ©

Ferry Dock & Pier

A giant wall map helps you get your bearings. Inside nearby Bldg 64, short films and exhibits provide historical perspective on the prison and details about the Indian Occupation.

FRANK VAN DEN BERGH / GETTY IMAGES ©

FRANCKREPORTER / GETTY IMAGES ©

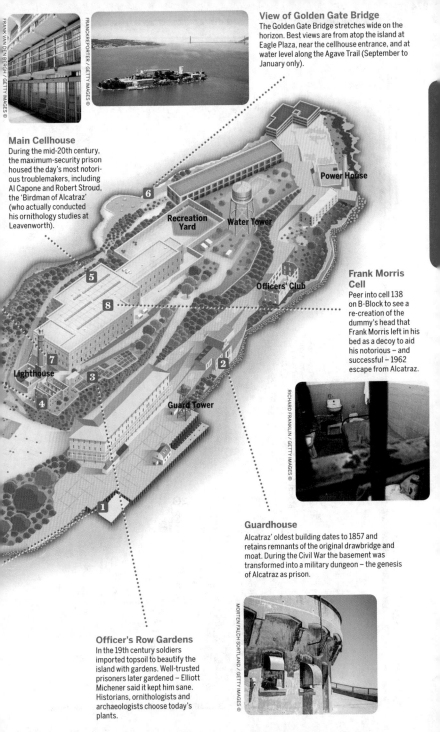

View of Golden Gate Bridge
The Golden Gate Bridge stretches wide on the horizon. Best views are from atop the island at Eagle Plaza, near the cellhouse entrance, and at water level along the Agave Trail (September to January only).

Main Cellhouse
During the mid-20th century, the maximum-security prison housed the day's most notorious troublemakers, including Al Capone and Robert Stroud, the 'Birdman of Alcatraz' (who actually conducted his ornithology studies at Leavenworth).

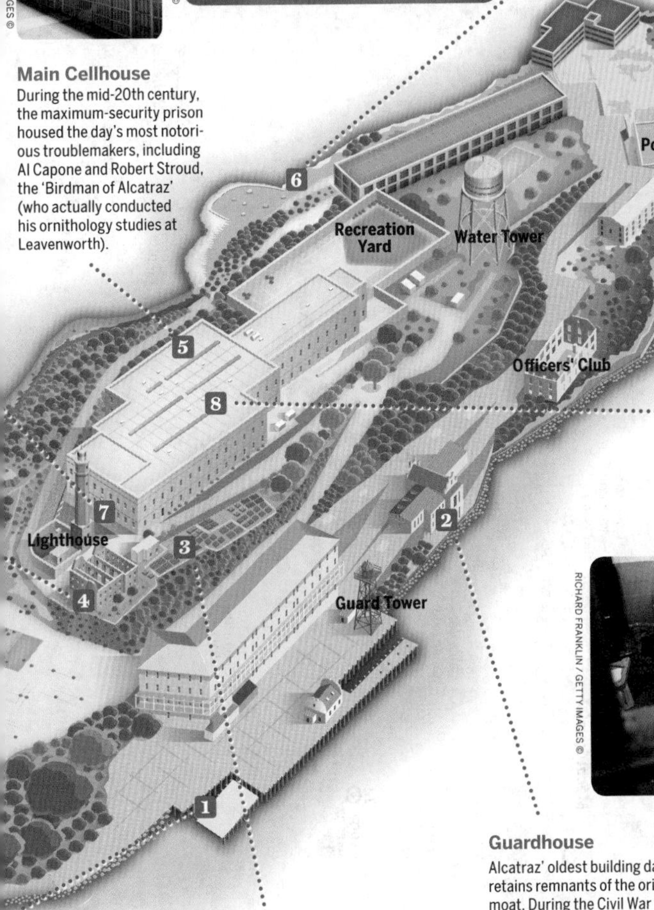

Frank Morris Cell
Peer into cell 138 on B-Block to see a re-creation of the dummy's head that Frank Morris left in his bed as a decoy to aid his notorious – and successful – 1962 escape from Alcatraz.

RICHARD FRANKLIN / GETTY IMAGES ©

Guardhouse
Alcatraz' oldest building dates to 1857 and retains remnants of the original drawbridge and moat. During the Civil War the basement was transformed into a military dungeon – the genesis of Alcatraz as prison.

Officer's Row Gardens
In the 19th century soldiers imported topsoil to beautify the island with gardens. Well-trusted prisoners later gardened – Elliott Michener said it kept him sane. Historians, ornithologists and archaeologists choose today's plants.

MORTEN FALCH SORTLAND / GETTY IMAGES ©

Downtown San Francisco

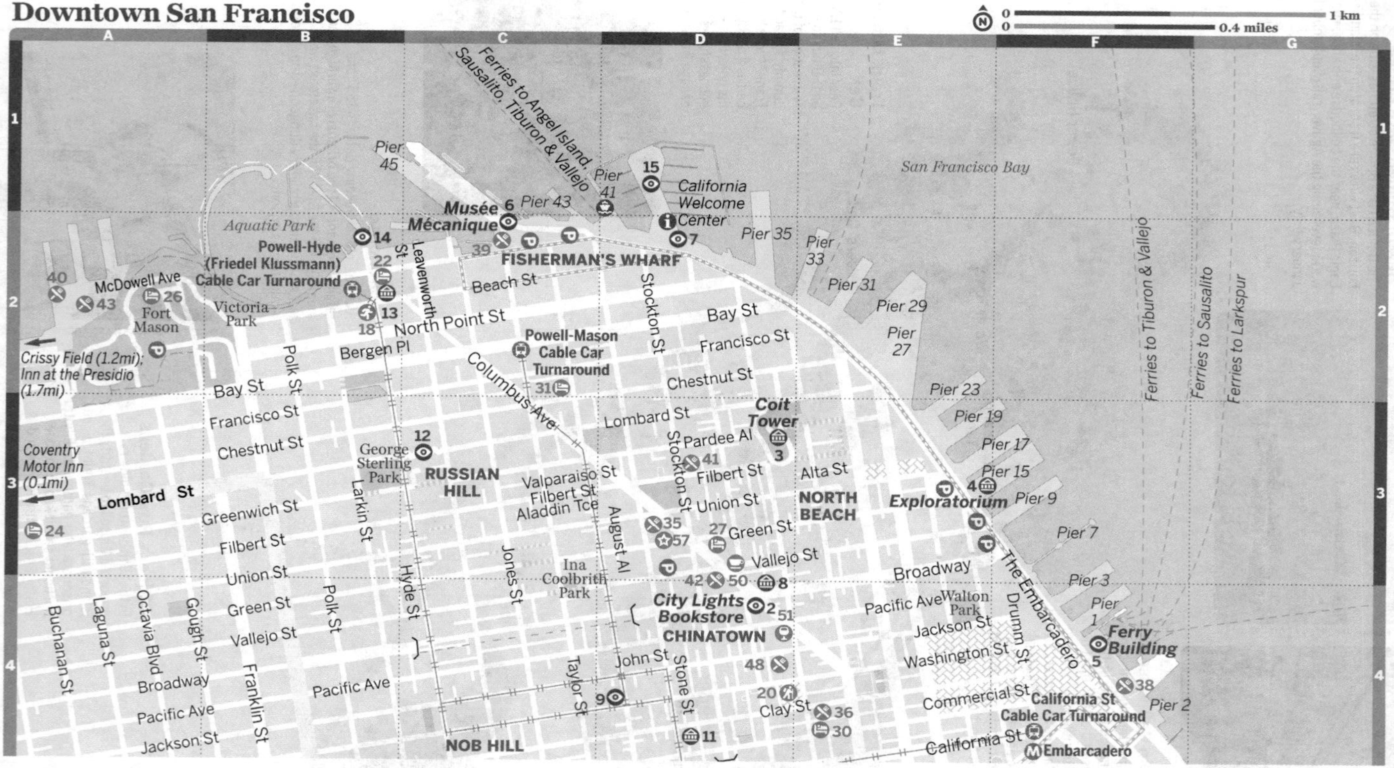
0 1 km
0 0.4 miles
A B C D E F G
1 2 3 4
San Francisco Bay
Aquatic Park
Ferries to Angel Island, Sausalito, Tiburon & Vallejo
Ferries to Tiburon & Vallejo
Ferries to Sausalito
Ferries to Larkspur
Pier 45
Pier 43
Pier 41
Pier 35
Pier 33
Pier 31
Pier 29
Pier 27
Pier 23
Pier 19
Pier 17
Pier 15
Pier 9
Pier 7
Pier 3
Pier 1
Pier 2
Musée Mécanique
California Welcome Center
FISHERMAN'S WHARF
Powell-Hyde (Friedel Klussmann) Cable Car Turnaround
Powell-Mason Cable Car Turnaround
McDowell Ave
Fort Mason
Victoria Park
Crissy Field (1.2mi); Inn at the Presidio (1.7mi)
Coventry Motor Inn (0.1mi)
Lombard St
Bay St
Francisco St
Chestnut St
Greenwich St
Filbert St
Union St
Green St
Vallejo St
Broadway
Pacific Ave
Jackson St
Buchanan St
Laguna St
Octavia Blvd
Gough St
Franklin St
Polk St
Larkin St
Hyde St
Leavenworth St
North Point St
Bergen Pl
Beach St
Columbus Ave
George Sterling Park
RUSSIAN HILL
Valparaiso St
Filbert St
Aladdin Tce
Jones St
Ina Coolbrith Park
August Al
Taylor St
John St
Stone St
NOB HILL
Stockton St
Coit Tower
Pardee Al
Alta St
NORTH BEACH
City Lights Bookstore
CHINATOWN
Clay St
Exploratorium
The Embarcadero
Walton Park
Washington St
Drumm St
Commercial St
California St
California St Cable Car Turnaround
Embarcadero
Ferry Building

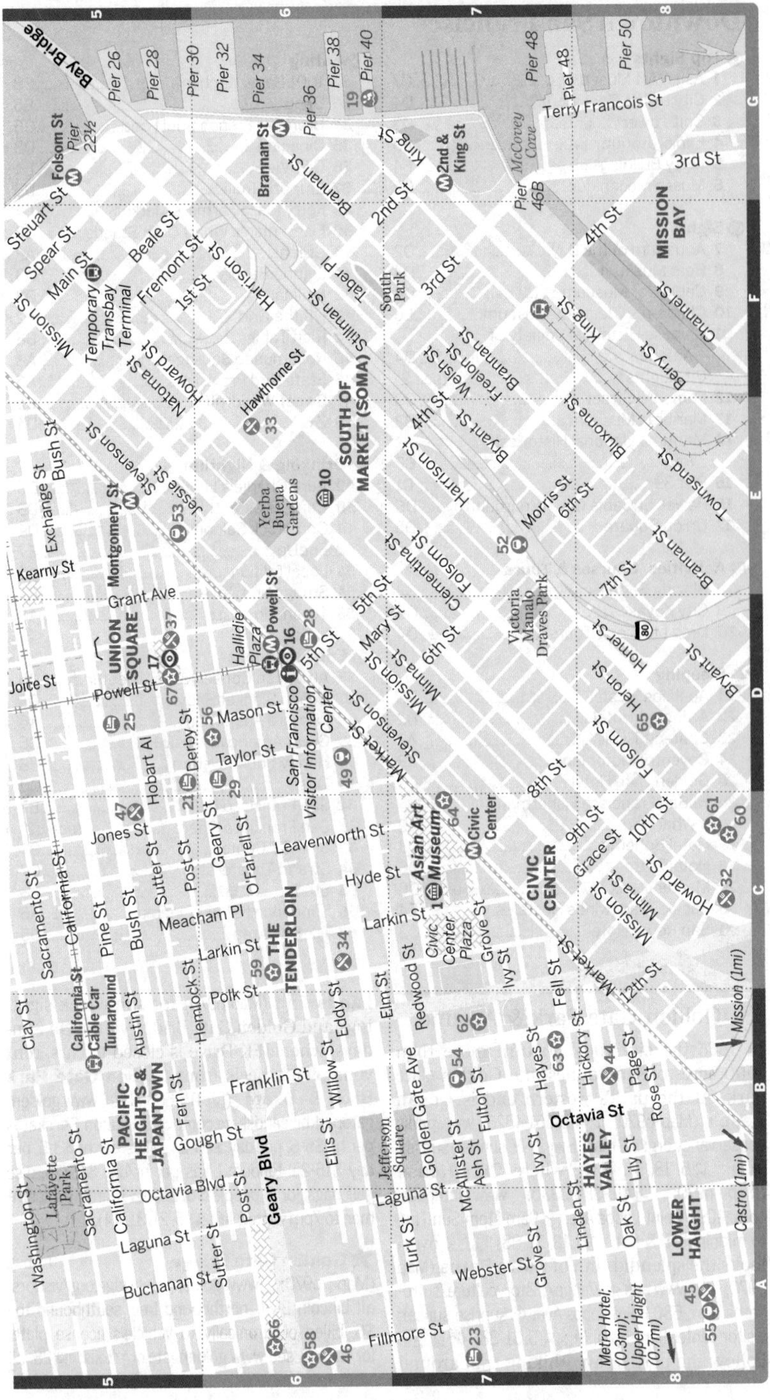

Bay Bridge
Pier 26
Pier 28
Pier 30
Pier 32
Pier 34
Pier 36
Pier 38
Pier 40
Pier 48
Pier 50
Pier 22½
Pier 46B
Folsom St
Brannan St
2nd & King St
McCovey Cove
Terry Francois St
3rd St
King St
Brannan St
2nd St
MISSION BAY
4th St
Channel St
Berry St
Steuart St
Spear St
Main St
Beale St
Fremont St
1st St
Harrison St
Mission St
Temporary Transbay Terminal
Howard St
Natoma St
Taber Pl
Stillman St
South Park
3rd St
Welsh St
Freelon St
Hawthorne St
SOUTH OF MARKET (SOMA)
Bryant St
Bluxome St
Townsend St
Bush St
Exchange St
Stevenson St
Jessie St
Montgomery St
Yerba Buena Gardens
Morris St
6th St
Kearny St
Grant Ave
Powell St
Clementina St
5th St
7th St
Victoria Manalo Draves Park
UNION SQUARE
Hallidie Plaza
Mary St
6th St
Homer St
Joice St
Minna St
Heron St
San Francisco Visitor Information Center
Mason St
Derby St
Taylor St
Hobart Al
Market St
8th St
Jones St
Sutter St
Post St
Geary St
O'Farrell St
Leavenworth St
Asian Art Museum
Civic Center
9th St
10th St
Grace St
CIVIC CENTER
Sacramento St
California St
Pine St
Bush St
Meacham Pl
Hyde St
Larkin St
Civic Center Plaza
Grove St
Clay St
California St Cable Car Turnaround
Austin St
Hemlock St
Polk St
THE TENDERLOIN
Eddy St
Elm St
Redwood St
Ivy St
Fell St
12th St
PACIFIC HEIGHTS & JAPANTOWN
Fern St
Franklin St
Willow St
Golden Gate Ave
Fulton St
Hayes St
Hickory St
Page St
Rose St
Mission (1mi)
Lafayette Park
Washington St
Sacramento St
California St
Gough St
Octavia Blvd
Post St
Geary Blvd
Ellis St
Jefferson Square
McAllister St
Ash St
Ivy St
Octavia St
HAYES VALLEY
Lily St
Castro (1mi)
Laguna St
Buchanan St
Sutter St
Turk St
Webster St
Grove St
Linden St
Oak St
LOWER HAIGHT
Fillmore St
Metro Hotel; (0.3mi); Upper Haight (0.7mi)

CALIFORNIA

Downtown San Francisco

Top Sights
1 Asian Art Museum ... C7
2 City Lights Bookstore ... D4
3 Coit Tower ... D3
4 Exploratorium ... E3
5 Ferry Building ... F4
6 Musée Mécanique ... C2

Sights
7 Aquarium of the Bay ... D2
8 Beat Museum ... D4
9 Cable Car Museum ... D4
10 Children's Creativity Museum ... E6
11 Chinese Historical Society of America ... D4
City Lights ... (see 2)
12 Lombard Street ... C3
13 Maritime Museum ... B2
14 Maritime National Historical Park ... B2
15 Pier 39 ... D1
16 Powell St Cable Car Turnaround ... D6
17 Union Square ... D5

Activities, Courses & Tours
18 Blazing Saddles ... B2
19 City Kayak ... G6
20 Drag Me Along Tours ... D4

Sleeping
21 Adelaide Hostel ... D5
22 Argonaut Hotel ... B2
23 Chateau Tivoli ... A7
24 Coventry Motor Inn ... A3
25 Golden Gate Hotel ... D5
26 HI San Francisco Fisherman's Wharf ... A2
27 Hotel Bohème ... D3
28 Hotel Zetta ... D6
29 Marker ... D6
30 Pacific Tradewinds Hostel ... E4
31 San Remo Hotel ... C2

Eating
32 1601 Bar & Kitchen ... C8
33 Benu ... E6
34 Brenda's French Soul Food ... C6
35 Cinecittà ... D3
36 City View ... E4
37 Emporio Rulli ... D5
38 Ferry Plaza Farmers Market ... F4
39 Fisherman's Wharf Crab Stands ... C2
40 Greens ... A2
41 Liguria Bakery ... D3
42 Molinari ... D3
43 Off the Grid ... A2
44 Rich Table ... B8
45 Rosamunde Sausage Grill ... A8
46 State Bird Provisions ... A6
47 Sweet Woodruff ... C5
48 Z & Y ... D4

Drinking & Nightlife
49 Aunt Charlie's Lounge ... D6
50 Caffe Trieste ... D3
51 Comstock Saloon ... D4
52 EndUp ... E7
53 Local Edition ... E5
54 Smuggler's Cove ... B7
55 Toronado ... A8

Entertainment
56 American Conservatory Theater ... D6
57 Beach Blanket Babylon ... D3
58 Fillmore Auditorium ... A6
59 Great American Music Hall ... C6
60 Honey Soundsystem ... C8
61 Oasis ... C8
62 San Francisco Ballet ... B7
San Francisco Opera ... (see 62)
63 SFJAZZ Center ... B7
64 Strand Theater ... C7
65 Stud ... D8
66 Sundance Kabuki Cinema ... A6
67 TIX Bay Area ... D5

Golden Gate Park & Around

In 1865 the city voted to turn more than 1000 acres of sand dunes into Golden Gate Park. At the park's western end is **Ocean Beach** (Map p970; ☎415-561-4323; www.parksconservancy.org; Great Hwy; ⏰sunrise-sunset; P 🚻; 🚌5, 18, 31, Ⓜ N), where **Cliff House** (Map p970; ☎415-386-3330; www.cliffhouse.com; 1090 Point Lobos Ave; ⏰9am-11pm Sun-Thu, to midnight Fri & Sat; 🚌5, 18, 31, 38) FREE overlooks the splendid ruin of **Sutro Baths** (Map p970; www.nps.gov/goga/historyculture/sutro-baths.htm; 680 Point Lobos Ave; ⏰sunrise-sunset; visitor center 9am-5pm; P; 🚌5, 31, 38) FREE. Follow the partly paved hiking trail around **Lands End** (Map p970) for shipwreck sightings and Golden Gate Bridge views. On Sundays, when JFK Drive is closed to cars, rent your own wheels from **Golden Gate Park Bike & Skate** (☎415-668-1117; www.goldengateparkbikeandskate.com; 3038 Fulton St; skates per hr $5-6, per day $20-24, bikes per hr $3-5, per day $15-25, tandem bikes per hr/day $15/75, disc golf bags for 2 people $6/25; ⏰10am-6pm summer, to 7pm winter; 🚻; 🚌5, 21, 31, 44).

★ **Golden Gate Bridge** BRIDGE
(Map p970; www.goldengatebridge.org/visitors; off Lincoln Blvd; northbound free, southbound toll $6, billed electronically to vehicle's license plate, for details, see www.goldengate.org/tolls; 🚌28, all

Golden Gate Transit buses) San Franciscans have passionate perspectives on every subject, especially their signature landmark, though everyone agrees that it's a good thing that the navy didn't get its way over the bridge's design – naval officials preferred a hulking concrete span, painted with caution-yellow stripes, over the soaring art-deco design of architects Gertrude and Irving Murrow and engineer Joseph B Strauss, which, luckily, won the day.

★ California Academy of Sciences MUSEUM
(Map p970; ☎415-379-8000; www.calacademy.org; 55 Music Concourse Dr; adult/child $34.95/24.95; ⏲9:30am-5pm Mon-Sat, 11am-5pm Sun; P 👪; 🚌5, 6, 7, 21, 31, 33, 44, Ⓜ N) Architect Renzo Piano's 2008 landmark LEED-certified green building houses 40,000 weird and wonderful animals in a four-story rainforest and split-level aquarium under a 'living roof' of California wildflowers. After the penguins nod off to sleep, the wild rumpus starts at kids-only Academy Sleepovers ($109; ages five to 17, plus adult chaperones; 6pm to 8am including snack and breakfast) and over-21 NightLife Thursdays ($12), when rainforest-themed cocktails encourage strange mating rituals among shy internet daters.

de Young Museum MUSEUM
(☎415-750-3600; http://deyoung.famsf.org/; 50 Hagiwara Tea Garden Dr; adult/child $10/6, discount with Muni ticket $2, 1st Tue of month free, online booking fee per ticket $1; ⏲9:30am-5:15pm Tue-Sun, to 8:45pm Fri Apr-Nov; 🚌5, 7, 44, Ⓜ N) Follow sculptor Andy Goldsworthy's artificial fault line in the sidewalk into Herzog & de Meuron's sleek, copper-clad building that's oxidizing green to blend into the park. Don't be fooled by the de Young's camouflaged exterior: shows here boldly broaden artistic horizons, from Oceanic ceremonial masks and Oscar de la Renta gowns to James Turrell's domed 'Skyspace' installation, built into a hill in the sculpture garden.

Legion of Honor MUSEUM
(Map p970; ☎415-750-3600; http://legionofhonor.famsf.org; 100 34th Ave; adult/child $10/6, discount with Muni ticket $2, 1st Tue of month free; ⏲9:30am-5:15pm Tue-Sun; 👪; 🚌1, 2, 18, 38) A museum as eccentric and illuminating as San Francisco itself, the Legion showcases a wildly eclectic collection ranging from Monet water lilies to John Cage soundscapes, ancient Iraqi ivories to R Crumb comics. Upstairs are blockbuster shows of Old Masters and Impressionists, but don't miss selections from the Legion's Achenbach Foundation of Graphic Arts collection of 90,0000 works on paper, ranging from Rembrandt to Ed Ruscha.

Japanese Tea Garden GARDENS
(☎tea ceremony reservations 415-752-1171; www.japaneseteagardensf.com; 75 Hagiwara Tea Garden Dr; adult/child $8/2, before 10am Mon, Wed & Fri free; ⏲9am-6pm Mar-Oct, to 4:45pm Nov-Feb; P 👪; 🚌5, 7, 44, Ⓜ N) Since 1894, this picturesque 5-acre garden and bonsai grove has blushed with cherry blossoms in spring, turned flaming red with maple leaves in fall, and lost all track of time in the meditative Zen Garden.

Activities

Blazing Saddles CYCLING
(Map p974; ☎415-202-8888; www.blazingsaddles.com/san-francisco; 2715 Hyde St; bicycle rental per hour $8-15, per day $32-88, electric bikes per day $48-88; ⏲8am-8pm; 👪; 🚋Powell-Hyde) Blazing Saddles is tailored to visitors, with a main shop on Hyde St and six rental stands around Fisherman's Wharf, convenient for biking the Embarcadero or to the Golden Gate Bridge. It also rents electric bikes and offers 24-hour return service – a big plus. Reserve online for a 10% discount; rental includes all extras (bungee cords, packs etc).

DON'T MISS

COIT TOWER

Adding an exclamation mark to San Francisco's skyline, **Coit Tower** (Map p974; ☎415-249-0995; http://sfrecpark.org/destination/telegraph-hill-pioneer-park/coit-tower; Telegraph Hill Blvd; elevator entry (nonresident) adult/child $8/5; ⏲10am-6pm May-Oct, 9am-5pm Nov-Apr; 🚌39) offers views worth shouting about – especially after you climb the steep wooden **Filbert Street steps** up Telegraph Hill to get here. Check out 360-degree panoramas from the open-air viewing platform, and the wraparound 1930s lobby murals glorifying workers – once denounced as communist but now a landmark. To glimpse more murals hidden inside a stairwell, join a free docent-led tour at 11am on Wednesday or Saturday.

City Kayak KAYAKING
(Map p974; ☎415-294-1050; www.citykayak.com; Pier 40, South Beach Harbor; kayak rentals per hour $35-65, 3hr lesson & rental $59, tours $58-98; ⊙rentals 11am-3pm, return by 5pm Thu-Mon; 🚌30, 45, Ⓜ N, T) You haven't seen San Francisco until you've seen it from the water. Newbies to kayaking can take lessons and paddle calm waters near the Bay Bridge, alone or escorted; experienced paddlers can brave choppy Bay currents near the Golden Gate (conditions permitting; get advice first). Sporty romantics take note: calm-water moonlight tours are ideal for proposals. Check website for details.

Tours

★Precita Eyes Mission Mural Tours WALKING TOUR
(☎415-285-2287; www.precitaeyes.org; adult $15-20, child $3; ⊙see website calendar for tour dates; 👪; 🚌12, 14, 48, 49, Ⓑ24th St Mission) Muralists lead weekend walking tours covering 60 to 70 Mission murals in a six- to 10-block radius of mural-bedecked Balmy Alley. Tours last from 90 minutes and up to 2½ hours for the more in-depth Classic Mural Walk. Proceeds fund mural upkeep at this community arts nonprofit.

Drag Me Along Tours WALKING TOUR
(Map p974; http://www.dragmealongtours.com; tour begins in Portsmouth Square; tours $20; ⊙tours usually 11am-1pm Sun; 🚌1, 8, 10, 12, 30, 41, 45, 🚋California, Powell-Mason, Powell-Hyde) Explore San Francisco's bawdy Barbary Coast with a bona-fide legend: Gold Rush burlesque star Countess Lola Montez, reincarnated in drag by San Francisco historian Rick Shelton. Her Highness leads you through Chinatown alleyways where Victorian ladies made and lost reputations to Jackson Square saloons where sailors were shanghaied, introducing Barbary Coast characters who gambled big, loved hard and lived large.

Adult content; reservations required; cash only.

Haight-Ashbury Flower Power Walking Tour WALKING TOUR
(☎415-863-1621; www.haightashburytour.com; adult/under 10yr $20/free; ⊙10:30am Tue & Sat, 2pm Fri; 🚌6, 71, Ⓜ N) Take a long, strange trip through 12 blocks of hippie history, following in the steps of Jimi, Jerry and Janis – if you have to ask for last names, you really need this tour, man. Tours meet at the corner of Stanyan and Waller Sts and last about two hours; reservations required.

Public Library City Guides TOUR
(☎415-557-4266; www.sfcityguides.org; donations/tips welcome) FREE Volunteer local historians lead nonprofit tours organized by neighborhood and theme: Art Deco Marina, Gold Rush Downtown, Secrets of Fisherman's Wharf, Telegraph Hill Stairway Hike and more.

Festivals & Events

Lunar New Year CULTURAL
(www.chineseparade.com; ⊙Feb) Chase the 200ft dragon, lion dancers and frozen-smile runners-up for the Miss Chinatown title during Lunar New Year celebrations. Firecrackers and fierce legions of tiny-tot martial artists make this parade at the end of February the highlight of San Francisco winters.

Bay to Breakers SPORTS
(www.baytobreakers.com; race registration from $64; ⊙May) Run in costume or wearing not much at all from Embarcadero to Ocean Beach the third Sunday in May, while joggers dressed as salmon run upstream.

SF Pride Celebration CULTURAL
(⊙Jun) A day isn't enough to do SF proud: June begins with the **International LGBT Film Festival** (www.frameline.org; ⊙mid-Jun), and goes out in style the last weekend with Saturday's **Dyke March** (www.dykemarch.org) to the Castro's Pink Party and the joyous, million-strong Pride Parade.

Hardly Strictly Bluegrass MUSIC
(http://www.hardlystrictlybluegrass.com; ⊙Oct) The West goes wild for free bluegrass at Golden Gate Park, with three days of concerts and three stages of headliners; held early October.

Sleeping

Boutique and luxury hotels abound around Union Square, Nob Hill and SoMa, while Fisherman's Wharf and the Marina accommodations are mostly motels and chain hotels. Offbeat inns, small hotels and cozy B&Bs await in less-touristed neighbourhoods.

Expect to pay $35 to $55 for overnight parking.

Quoted rates do not include hotel tax (15.5%), from which hostels are exempt.

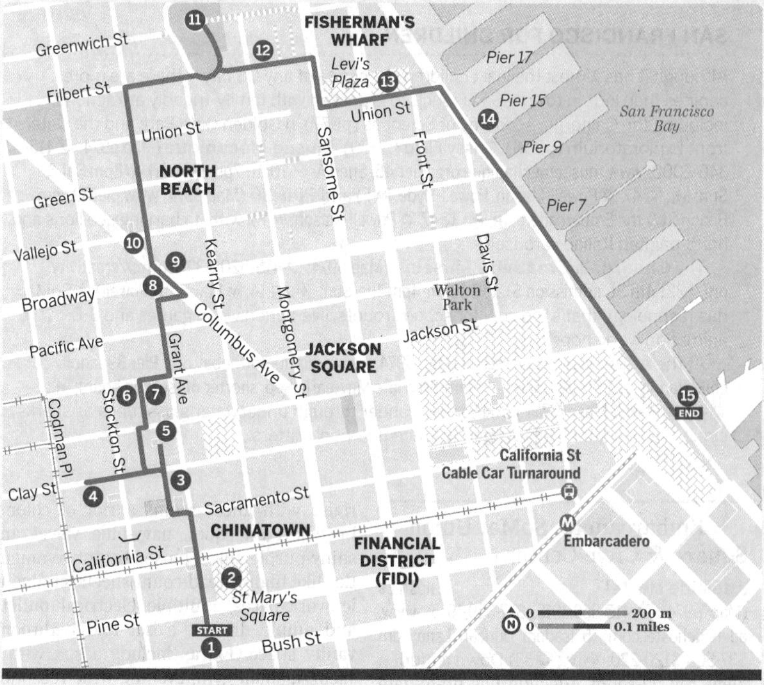

City Walk
Chinatown to the Waterfront

START CHINATOWN'S DRAGON GATE
END FERRY BUILDING
LENGTH 2.5 MILES; FIVE HOURS

Starting at Chinatown's 1 **Dragon Gate**, head past Grant St's gilded dragon lamps to 2 **Old St Mary's Square**, site of a brothel leveled in the 1906 fire. Today, renegade skateboarders turn different kinds of tricks under the watchful eye of Beniamino Bufano's 1929 statue of Chinese revolutionary Sun Yat-Sen. Pass flag-festooned temple balconies along 3 **Waverly Place**, then head to the 4 **Chinese Historical Society of America** (p967) museum, in the majestic Chinatown YWCA designed by Julia Morgan.

Enter 5 **Spofford Alley**, where mah-jongg tiles click, Chinese orchestras play and beauticians gossip over blow-dryers – hard to believe this is where Prohibition bootleggers fought turf wars, and Sun Yat-Sen plotted the 1911 overthrow of China's last dynasty at No 36. Once packed with brothels, 6 **Ross Alley** turned movie star as a location for *Karate Kid II* and *Indiana Jones and the Temple of Doom*. At No 56, make a fortune and watch it get folded into a warm cookie at the 7 **Golden Gate Fortune Cookie Factory**.

Back on Grant Ave, take a shortcut through Jack Kerouac Alley, where the binge-prone author often wound up 'on the road'. Stop by 8 **City Lights Bookstore** (p967) on Columbus Ave, champion of Beat poetry and free speech, then hop down Broadway into the 9 **Beat Museum** (p967). Savor espresso at 10 **Caffe Trieste**, under the Sardinian fishing mural where Francis Ford Coppola wrote *The Godfather* script.

Climb waaaay up to 11 **Coit Tower** (p977) for glorious bay-view panoramas and historic murals. Take the head-spinning 12 **Filbert Street Steps** downhill past wild parrots and hidden cottages to 13 **Levi's Plaza**, named for the coinventor of denim pants with rivets – aka American blue jeans. Head right on Embarcadero to the fun-for-all-ages 14 **Exploratorium** (p966) before having lunch bayside at the landmark 15 **Ferry Building** (p966), with its thrice-weekly outdoor farmers market.

SAN FRANCISCO FOR CHILDREN

Although it has almost the least children per capita of any US city – there are more canines than kids in town – San Francisco is packed with family-friendly attractions, including the California Academy of Sciences (p977) in Golden Gate Park and the waterfront Exploratorium (p966), Crissy Field (p969), **Musée Mécanique** (Map p974; ☎415-346-2000; www.museemechanique.org; Pier 45, Shed A; ⏲10am-7pm Mon-Fri, to 8pm Sat & Sun; 👪; 🚌47, 🚋Powell-Mason, Powell-Hyde, Ⓜ F) and **Pier 39** (Map p974; www.pier39.com; Beach St & the Embarcadero; Ⓟ👪; 🚌47, 🚋Powell-Mason, Ⓜ F), with its barking sea lions and hand-painted Italian carousel.

The **Children's Creativity Museum** (Map p974; ☎415-820-3320; http://creativity.org/; 221 4th St; admission $12; ⏲10am-4pm Tue-Sun; 👪; 🚌14, Ⓜ Powell, Ⓑ Powell) in SoMa has technology that's too cool for school: robots, live-action video games and 3-D animation workshops.

At the **Aquarium of the Bay** (Map p974; www.aquariumofthebay.org; Pier 39; adult/child/family $21.95/12.95/64; ⏲9am-8pm late May-early Sep, shorter off-season hours; 👪; 🚌49, 🚋Powell-Mason, Ⓜ F) on Pier 39, wander through underwater glass tubes as sharks circle overhead, then let tots gently touch tide-pool critters.

Embarcadero, SoMa, Union Square & Civic Center

Adelaide Hostel HOSTEL $

(Map p974; ☎415-359-1915, 877-359-1915; www.adelaidehostel.com; 5 Isadora Duncan Lane; dm $37-50, r $120-220; @📶; 🚌38) Down a hidden alley, the 22-room Adelaide has up-to-date furnishings and marble-tiled baths – also the occasional rust stain and dust bunny. Extras include breakfast, group activities and two common areas (one quiet). Good service; friendly crowd. Note: your private room may wind up being in the nearby Dakota or Fitzgerald Hotels; of the two, Fitzgerald is the better.

Golden Gate Hotel HOTEL $$

(Map p974; ☎415-392-3702; www.goldengatehotel.com; 775 Bush St; r $215, without bathroom $145; @📶; 🚌2, 3, 🚋Powell-Hyde, Powell-Mason) Like an old-fashioned pension, the Golden Gate has kindly owners and simple rooms with mismatched furniture, inside a 1913 Edwardian hotel safely up the hill from the Tenderloin. Rooms are small, clean and comfortable and most have private bathrooms (some with antique claw-foot bathtubs). Enormous croissants, homemade cookies and a resident cat provide TLC after long days of sightseeing.

★**Marker** BOUTIQUE HOTEL $$

(Map p974; ☎844-736-2753, 415-292-0100; http://themarkersanfrancisco.com; 501 Geary St; r from $209; ❄@📶🐾; 🚌38, 🚋Powell-Hyde, Powell-Mason) 🍃 Snazzy Marker gets details right, with guest rooms a riot of color – lipstick-red lacquer, navy-blue velvet and shiny-purple silk – plus substantive amenities like high-thread-count sheets, ergonomic workspaces, multiple electrical outlets, and ample drawer, closet and bathroom-vanity space. Extras include a spa with a Jacuzzi, small gym, evening wine reception and bragging rights to a stylin' address.

Hotel Zetta HOTEL $$$

(Map p974; ☎415-543-8555, 855-212-4187; www.hotelzetta.com; 55 5th St; r from $324; ❄@📶👪🐾; Ⓑ Powell St, Ⓜ Powell St) 🍃 Opened 2013, this snappy eco-conscious downtowner by the Viceroy group plays to techies who work too much, with a mezzanine-level 'play room' with billiards, shuffleboard and two-story-high Plinko wall rising above the art-filled lobby. Upstairs, bigger-than-average rooms look sharp with padded black-leather headboards and low-slung platform beds; web-enabled flat-screen TVs link with your devices.

North Beach

Pacific Tradewinds Hostel HOSTEL $

(Map p974; ☎415-433-7970, 888-734-6783; http://san-francisco-hostel.com; 680 Sacramento St; dm $38; ⏲front desk 8am to midnight; @📶; 🚌1, 🚋California St, Ⓑ Montgomery) San Francisco's smartest-looking all-dorm hostel has a blue-and-white nautical theme, fully equipped kitchen, spotless glass-brick showers and no lockout time. Bunks are bolted to the wall so there's no bed-shaking when your bunkmate shifts. Alas, no elevator means hauling bags up three flights but it's worth it. Great service, fun staff.

San Remo Hotel HOTEL $

(Map p974; 415-776-8688; www.sanremohotel.com; 2237 Mason St; r without bathroom $119-159; ; 30, 47, Powell-Mason) One of the city's best-value stays, the San Remo dates to 1906 and is long on old-fashioned charm. Rooms are simply done with mismatched turn-of-the-century furnishings and all rooms share bathrooms. Think reputable, vintage boarding house. Note: least expensive rooms have windows onto the corridor, not the outdoors. Family suites accommodate up to five. No elevator.

Hotel Bohème BOUTIQUE HOTEL $$

(Map p974; 415-433-9111; www.hotelboheme.com; 444 Columbus Ave; r $225-295; ; 10, 12, 30, 41, 45) Our favorite boutique hotel is a love letter to the Beat era, with moody color schemes, Chinese umbrellas as light fixtures and photos from the Beat years on the walls. Rooms are smallish, some front on noisy Columbus Ave (quieter rooms are in back) and bathrooms are teensy, but it's smack in North Beach's vibrant scene. No elevator.

Fisherman's Wharf, the Marina & Presidio

★ **HI San Francisco Fisherman's Wharf** HOSTEL $

(Map p974; 415-771-7277; www.sfhostels.com; Bldg 240, Fort Mason; dm incl breakfast $30-42, r $75-109; ; 28, 30, 47, 49) Trading downtown convenience for a glorious parklike setting with million-dollar waterfront views, this hostel occupies a former army hospital building, with bargain-priced private rooms and dorms (some coed) with four to 22 beds (avoid bunks one and two – they're by doorways). Huge kitchen. No curfew but no heat during daytime: bring warm clothes. Limited free parking.

Coventry Motor Inn MOTEL $$

(Map p974; 415-567-1200; www.coventrymotorinn.com; 1901 Lombard St; r $160-225; ; 22, 28, 30, 43) Of the many motels lining Lombard St (Hwy 101), the generic Coventry has the highest quality-to-value ratio with spacious, well-maintained (if plain) rooms and extras like air-con (good for quiet sleeps) and covered parking. Parents: there's plenty of floor space to unpack kids' toys, but no pool.

★ **Inn at the Presidio** HOTEL $$$

(415-800-7356; www.innatthepresidio.com; 42 Moraga Ave; r $270-360; ; 43, PresidiGo Shuttle) Built in 1903 as bachelor quarters for army officers, this three-story red-brick building in the Presidio was transformed in 2012 into a spiffy national-park lodge, styled with leather, linen and wood. Oversized rooms are plush, including feather beds with Egyptian-cotton sheets. Suites have fireplaces. Nature surrounds you, with hiking trailheads out back, but taxis downtown cost $25.

Argonaut Hotel BOUTIQUE HOTEL $$$

(Map p974; 415-563-0800; www.argonauthotel.com; 495 Jefferson St; r from $439, with view from $489; ; 19, 47, 49, Powell-Hyde) Fisherman's Wharf's top hotel was built as a cannery in 1908 and has century-old wooden beams and exposed-brick walls. Rooms sport an over-the-top nautical theme, with porthole-shaped mirrors and plush, deep-blue carpets. Though all have the amenities of an upper-end hotel – ultracomfy beds, iPod docks – some rooms are tiny with limited sunlight.

The Mission & the Castro

Inn San Francisco B&B $$

(415-641-0188; www.innsf.com; 943 S Van Ness Ave; r $215-255, without bathroom $165-225, cottages $385-475; ; 14, 49) This stately Mission-district inn occupies an elegant 1872 Italianate-Victorian mansion, impeccably maintained, packed with antiques. All rooms have fresh-cut flowers and sumptuous mattresses with featherbeds; some have a Jacuzzi. There's also a freestanding garden cottage that sleeps up to six. Outside there's an English garden and redwood hot tub open 24 hours (a rarity). Limited parking: reserve ahead. No elevator.

Inn on Castro B&B $$

(415-861-0321; www.innoncastro.com; 321 Castro St; r incl breakfast $235-275, without bathroom $165-185, self-catering apt $235-290; ; M Castro) A portal to the Castro's disco heyday, this Edwardian townhouse is decked out with top-end '70s-mod furnishings. Rooms are retro-cool and spotlessly kept. Exceptional breakfasts – the owner is a chef. Several nearby, great-value apartments are also available for rental. No elevator. LGBT friendly.

The Haight

Metro Hotel HOTEL $
(415-861-5364; www.metrohotelsf.com; 319 Divisadero St; r $88-100; ; 6, 24, 71) On a thoroughfare bisecting the Upper and Lower Haight districts, this straightforward, zero-frills hotel provides cheap, clean rooms with private bathroom, an outdoor garden patio and 24-hour reception. Some rooms have two double beds; one room sleeps six ($150). The location is largely residential but you can walk to the Haight's bars and restaurants. No elevator.

Chateau Tivoli B&B $$
(Map p974; 415-776-5462; www.chateautivoli.com; 1057 Steiner St; r $175-300, without bathroom $130-200; ; 5, 22) This imposing, glorious chateau on a secondary thoroughfare near Alamo Square once hosted Isadora Duncan and Mark Twain, and though its two-toned gabled roofs have faded, its grand domed turrets, cornices and gorgeous carved woodwork retain their luster. Guest rooms are full of soul, character and, rumor has it, the ghost of a Victorian opera diva. No elevator, no TVs.

Eating

Hope you're hungry – there are more restaurants per capita in San Francisco than in any other US city. Most of the top-ranked restaurants are quite small, so reserve ahead. For bargain eats, hit Mission taquerias, Chinatown dim sum joints, North Beach delis and food trucks all around town.

Embarcadero & SoMa

Ferry Plaza Farmers Market MARKET $
(Map p974; 415-291-3276; www.cuesa.org; Market St & the Embarcadero; 10am-2pm Tue & Thu, 8am-2pm Sat; Embarcadero) The Ferry Building market showcases California-grown, organic produce, artisan meats and gourmet-prepared foods at moderate-to-premium prices – plus an excellent selection of food trucks on weekends.

1601 Bar & Kitchen CALIFORNIAN, FUSION $$
(Map p974; 415-552-1601; http://1601sf.com/; 1601 Howard St; mains $12-22; 6-10pm Tue-Thu, to 11pm Fri & Sat; 9, 12, 47, Van Ness) Rising star-chef alert: Brian Fernando is turning Sri Lankan inspirations into Californian cravings. Velvety halibut ceviche in coconut milk is an instant obsession, Marin Sun Farms goat stew with red basmati rice for two is date worthy, and you'll want the pork belly and fenugreek-vinegar home fries again for breakfast. Ingenuity without pretension, at half the cost of most downtown tasting menus ($76 here).

★ **Benu** CALIFORNIAN, FUSION $$$
(Map p974; 415-685-4860; www.benusf.com; 22 Hawthorne St; tasting menu $228; 5:30-8:30pm seatings Tue-Sat; 10, 12, 14, 30, 45) SF has set fusion-cuisine standards for 150 years, but chef-owner Corey Lee remixes California ingredients and Pacific Rim inspiration with a superstar DJ's finesse. Dungeness crab and truffle custard bring such outsize flavor to Lee's faux-shark's fin soup, you'll swear there's Jaws in there. The prix-fixe menu is pricey (plus 20% service), but don't miss star-sommelier Yoon Ha's ingenious pairings ($160).

Union Square, Civic Center & Hayes Valley

Sweet Woodruff CALIFORNIAN $
(Map p974; 415-292-9090; www.sweetwoodruffsf.com; 798 Sutter St; mains $8-14; 8am-9:30pm Mon-Fri, 9:30am-9:30pm Sat & Sun; ; 2, 3, California) Little sister to ground-breaking, Michelin-starred Sons & Daughters, this storefront gourmet hot spot uses ingredients grown on the restaurant's own farm in its abbreviated, affordable small-plates menu. There's limited service and a tiny kitchen, yet somehow it turns out sourdough pancakes, homemade soups, impeccable bone-marrow deviled eggs and inspired vegetarian options like beet burgers.

Brenda's French Soul Food CREOLE, SOUTHERN $$
(Map p974; 415-345-8100; www.frenchsoulfood.com; 652 Polk St; mains lunch $9-13, dinner $12-17; 8am-3pm Mon & Tue, to 10pm Wed-Sat, to 8pm Sun; 19, 31, 38, 47, 49) Chef-owner Brenda Buenviaje blends New Orleans–style Creole cooking with French technique into 'French soul food.' Expect updated classics like beignets, serious biscuits and grits, impeccable Hangtown Fry (eggs with bacon and fried oysters), and fried chicken with collard greens and hot-pepper jelly. Long waits on sketchy sidewalks are unavoidable – but Brenda serves takeout sandwiches two doors down.

Rich Table CALIFORNIAN $$$

(Map p974; ☎415-355-9085; http://richtablesf.com; 199 Gough St; mains $12-30; ⏱5:30-10pm Sun-Thu, to 10:30pm Fri & Sat; 🚌5, 6, 7, 21, 47, 49, Ⓜ Van Ness) Satisfy cravings for taste adventures at Rich Table, home of dried porcini doughnuts, octopus confit and totally trippy beet marshmallows. Married co-chefs/owners Sarah and Evan Rich riff on seasonal California fare like jazz masters, hitting their groove with exquisitely playful amuse-bouches like the Dirty Hippie: silky goat-buttermilk *panna cotta* with hemp – a dish as offbeat and entrancing as Hippie Hill drum circles.

Chinatown & North Beach

Liguria Bakery BAKERY $

(Map p974; ☎415-421-3786; 1700 Stockton St; focaccia $4-5; ⏱8am-1pm Tue-Fri, from 7am Sat; 🚌8, 30, 39, 41, 45, Powell-Mason) Bleary-eyed art students and Italian grandmothers are in line by 8am for cinnamon-raisin focaccia hot out of the 100-year-old oven, leaving 9am dawdlers a choice of tomato or classic rosemary/garlic and 11am stragglers out of luck. Take yours in wax paper or boxed for picnics – but don't kid yourself that you're going to save some for later. Cash only.

Molinari DELI $

(Map p974; ☎415-421-2337; www.molinarisalame.com; 373 Columbus Ave; sandwiches $10-12.50; ⏱9am-6pm Mon-Fri, to 5:30pm Sat, 10am-4pm Sun; 🚌8, 10, 12, 30, 39, 41, 45, Powell-Mason) Grab a number and a crusty roll, and when your number rolls around, wise-cracking deli staff in paper hats will stuff it with translucent sheets of *prosciutto di Parma,* milky buffalo mozzarella, tender marinated artichokes or slabs of the legendary house-cured salami. Enjoy yours hot from the panini press at sidewalk tables or in Washington Sq.

City View CHINESE $

(Map p974; ☎415-398-2838; http://cityviewdimsum.com; 662 Commercial St; dishes $3-8; ⏱11am-2:30pm Mon-Fri, from 10am Sat & Sun; 🚌1, 8, 10, 12, 30, 45, California St) Take your seat in the sunny dining room and your pick from carts loaded with delicate shrimp and leek dumplings, garlicky Chinese broccoli, tangy spare ribs, coconut-dusted custard tarts and other tantalizing dim sum. Arrive before the midday lunch rush, so you can nab seats in the sunny upstairs room and get first dibs from passing carts.

Cinecittà PIZZA $$

(Map p974; ☎415-291-8830; www.cinecittarestaurant.com; 663 Union St; pizzas $12-15; ⏱noon-10pm Sun-Thu, to 11pm Fri & Sat; 🚌8X, 30, 39, 41, 45, Powell-Mason) Follow tantalizing aromas into this tiny hot spot for thin-crust Roman pizza, made from scratch and served with sass by Roman owner Romina. Local loyalties are divided between the Roman Travestere (fresh mozzarella, arugula and prosciutto) and Neapolitan O Sole Mio (capers, olives, mozzarella and anchovies). Local brews are on tap, house wine is $5 from 4pm to 7pm, and Romina's tiramisu is San Francisco's best.

Z & Y CHINESE $$

(Map p974; ☎415-981-8988; www.zandyrestaurant.com; 655 Jackson St; mains $9-20; ⏱11am-10pm Mon-Thu, to 11pm Fri-Sun; 🚌8, 10, 12, 30, 45, Powell-Mason, Powell-Hyde) Graduate from ho-hum sweet-and-sour and middling *mushu* to sensational Szechuan dishes that go down in a blaze of glory. Warm up with spicy pork dumplings and heat-blistered string beans, take on the housemade *tantan* noodles with peanut-chili sauce, and leave lips buzzing with fish poached in flaming chili oil and buried under red Szechuan chili peppers. Go early; it's worth the wait.

Fisherman's Wharf, the Marina & Presidio

Off the Grid FOOD TRUCK $

(Map p974; www.offthegridsf.com; items $5-12; ⏱Fort Mason Center 5-10pm Fri Apr-Oct, Presidio 5-9pm Thu Apr-Oct, 11am-4pm Sun Apr-Nov; 🚌22, 28) Some 30 food trucks circle their wagons at SF's largest mobile-gourmet hootenannys on Friday night at Fort Mason Center (2 Marina Blvd), and Sunday midday for Picnic at the Presidio and Thursday evenings for Twilight at the Presidio (both on the Main Post Lawn). Arrive early for best selection and to minimize waits. Cash only.

Fisherman's Wharf Crab Stands SEAFOOD $

(Map p974; Taylor St; mains $5-15; Ⓜ F) Brawny-armed men stir steaming cauldrons of Dungeness crab at several side-by-side takeout stands at the foot of Taylor St, the epicenter of Fisherman's Wharf. Crab season typically runs winter through spring, but you'll find shrimp and other seafood year-round.

★Greens VEGETARIAN, CALIFORNIAN $$

(Map p974; ☎415-771-6222; www.greensrestaurant.com; Bldg A, Fort Mason Center, cnr Marina

Blvd & Laguna St; lunch $15-18, dinner $18-25; ⌚11:45am-2:30pm & 5:30-9pm Tue-Fri, from 11am Sat, 10:30am-2pm & 5:30-9pm Sun, 5:30-9pm Mon; ; 28) Career carnivores won't realize there's zero meat in the hearty black-bean chili, or in the other flavor-packed vegetarian dishes, made using ingredients from a Zen farm in Marin. And oh!, what views – the Golden Gate rises just outside the window-lined dining room. The on-site cafe serves to-go lunches. For sit-down meals, including Sunday brunch, reservations are essential.

The Mission & the Castro

★La Taqueria MEXICAN $

(415-285-7117; 2889 Mission St; burritos $6-8; ⌚11am-9pm Mon-Sat, to 8pm Sun; ; 12, 14, 48, 49, B 24th St Mission) SF's definitive burrito has no debatable saffron rice, spinach tortilla or mango salsa – just perfectly grilled meats, slow-cooked beans and classic tomatillo or mesquite salsa wrapped in a flour tortilla. You'll pay extra without beans, because they pack in more meat. Spicy pickles and *crema* (Mexican sour cream) bring complete burrito bliss.

Craftsman & Wolves BAKERY, CALIFORNIAN $

(415-913-7713; http://craftsman-wolves.com; 746 Valencia St; pastries $3-7; ⌚7am-7pm Mon-Thu, to 8pm Fri, 8am-8pm Sat, to 7pm Sun; 14, 22, 33, 49, B 16th St Mission, M J) Conventional breakfasts can't compare to the Rebel Within: savory sausage-spiked Asiago cheese muffin with a silken soft-boiled egg baked inside. SF's surest pick-me-up is Highwire macchiato and *matcha* (green tea) snickerdoodle cookies; Thai coconut curry scone, chilled pea soup and Provence rosé make a sublime lunch. Exquisite hazelnut and *horchata* (cinnamon-rice) cube cakes are ideal for celebrating SF half-birthdays, foggy days and imaginary holidays.

Mission Chinese FUSION $$

(Lung Shan; 415-863-2800; www.missionchinesefood.com; 2234 Mission St; mains $12-20; ⌚11:30am-3pm & 5-10:30pm Thu-Mon, 5-10:30pm Tue & Wed; 14, 33, 49, B 16th St Mission) Extreme gourmets and Chinese takeout fans converge on Danny Bowien's cult-food dive. Tiki pork belly with pickled pineapple and spicy lamb-face (sheep's cheek) noodles are big enough for two – though not for the salt-shy – and satisfy your conscience: 75¢ from each main is donated to San Francisco Food Bank. Wine corkage is $10; parties of eight or less.

★Frances CALIFORNIAN $$$

(415-621-3870; www.frances-sf.com; 3870 17th St; mains $22-30; ⌚5-10pm Sun-Thu, to 10:30pm Fri & Sat; M Castro) Chef/owner Melissa Perello earned a Michelin star for fine dining, then ditched downtown to start this market-inspired neighborhood bistro. Daily menus showcase bright, seasonal flavors and luxurious textures: cloudlike sheep's-milk ricotta gnocchi with crunchy breadcrumbs and broccolini, grilled calamari with preserved Meyer lemon, and artisan wine served by the ounce, directly from Wine Country.

Commonwealth CALIFORNIAN $$$

(415-355-1500; www.commonwealthsf.com; 2224 Mission St; small plates $13-18; ⌚5:30-10pm Sun-Thu, to 11pm Fri & Sat; ; 14, 22, 33, 49, B 16th St Mission) Wildly imaginative farm-to-table dining where you'd least expect it: in a converted cinderblock Mission dive. Chef Jason Fox serves adventurous, exquisitely Instagrammable compositions like *uni* (sea urchin) and popcorn atop cauliflower pudding, and foie gras in an oatmeal crust with tangy rhubarb. Dishes are dainty but pack wallops of earthy flavors. Savor the $75 prix fixe, knowing $10 is donated to charity.

The Haight & Fillmore

Rosamunde Sausage Grill FAST FOOD $

(Map p974; 415-437-6851; http://rosamunde-sausagegrill.com; 545 Haight St; sausages $7-7.50; ⌚11:30am-10pm Sun-Wed, to 11pm Thu-Sat; 6, 7, 22, M N) Impress a dinner date on the cheap: load up classic Brats or duck-fig links with complimentary roasted peppers, grilled onions, whole-grain mustard and mango chutney, and enjoy with your choice of 45 seasonal draft brews at Toronado (p985) next door. To impress a local lunch date, call ahead or line up by 11:30 Tuesdays for massive $6 burgers.

Magnolia Brewpub CALIFORNIAN, AMERICAN $$

(415-864-7468; www.magnoliapub.com; 1398 Haight St; mains $14-26; ⌚11am-midnight Mon-Thu, to 1am Fri, 10am-1am Sat, 10am-midnight Sun; 6, 7, 33, 43) Organic pub grub and home-brew samplers keep conversation flowing at communal tables, while grass-fed Prather Ranch burgers satisfy stoner appetites in booths – it's like the Summer of Love all over again, only with better food. Morning-after brunches of quinoa hash with brewer's yeast are plenty curative, but Cole Porter pints are powerful enough to revive the Grateful Dead.

★ State Bird Provisions CALIFORNIAN **$$$**
(Map p974; ☎415-795-1272; http://statebirdsf.com; 1529 Fillmore St; dishes $9-26; ⊙5:30-10pm Sun-Thu, to 11pm Fri & Sat; 🚌22, 38) Even before winning back-to-back James Beard Awards, State Bird attracted lines for 5:30pm seatings not seen since the Dead played neighbouring Fillmore Auditorium. The draw is a thrilling play on dim sum, wildly inventive with seasonal-regional ingredients and esoteric flavors, like fennel pollen or garum. Plan to order multiple dishes. Book exactly 60 days ahead.

Golden Gate Park & Around

Outerlands CALIFORNIAN **$$**
(Map p970; ☎415-661-6140; www.outerlandssf.com; 4001 Judah St; sandwiches & small plates $7-14, mains $18-22; ⊙10am-3pm Tue-Fri, from 9am Sat & Sun, 5:30-10pm Tue-Sun; ; 🚌18, Ⓜ N) When windy Ocean Beach leaves you feeling shipwrecked, drift into this beach-shack bistro for organic, California-coastal comfort food. Brunch demands Dutch pancakes in iron skillets with housemade ricotta, lunch brings $12 grilled artisan cheese combos with surfer-warming soup, and dinner means light, creative coastal fare like clam stew with mezcal broth (hungry surfers: order house-baked levain bread). Reserve ahead.

Burma Superstar BURMESE **$$**
(Map p970; ☎415-387-2147; www.burmasuperstar.com; 309 Clement St; mains $11-28; ⊙11:30am-3:30pm & 5-9:30pm Sun-Thu, to 10pm Fri & Sat; 🚌1, 2, 33, 38, 44) Yes, there's a wait, but do you see anyone walking away? Blame it on fragrant *moh hinga* (catfish curry) and traditional Burmese green-tea salads tarted up with lime and dried shrimp. Reservations aren't accepted; ask the host to call you so you can browse Burmese cookbooks at Green Apple Books while you wait.

Drinking & Nightlife

For a pub crawl, start with North Beach saloons or Mission bars around Valencia and 16th Sts. The Castro has historic gay bars; SoMa adds dance clubs. Downtown and around Union Square mix dives with speakeasies. Haight bars draw mixed alterna-crowds.

★ Smuggler's Cove BAR
(Map p974; ☎415-869-1900; www.smugglerscovesf.com; 650 Gough St; ⊙5pm-1:15am; 🚌5, 21, 47, 49, Ⓜ Civic Center) Yo-ho-ho and a bottle of rum…or maybe a Dead Reckoning with Angostura bitters, Nicaraguan rum, tawny port and vanilla liqueur, unless someone will share the flaming Scorpion Bowl? Pirates are bedeviled by choice at this Barbary Coast shipwreck tiki bar, hidden behind a tinted-glass door. With 400-plus rums and 70 cocktails gleaned from rum-running around the world, you won't be dry-docked long.

Comstock Saloon BAR
(Map p974; ☎415-617-0071; www.comstocksaloon.com; 155 Columbus Ave; ⊙noon-2am Mon-Fri, 4pm-2am Sat, 4pm-midnight Sun; 🚌8, 10, 12, 30, 45, 🚋Powell-Mason) Relieving yourself in the marble trough below the bar is no longer advisable, but otherwise this 1907 Victorian saloon revives the Barbary Coast's glory days. Get the authentic Pisco Punch or martini-precursor Martinez (gin, vermouth, bitters, maraschino liqueur). Reserve booths or back-parlor seating, so you can hear dates when ragtime-jazz bands play. Call it dinner with pot pie and buckets of shrimp.

Ritual Coffee Roasters CAFE
(☎415-641-1011; www.ritualroasters.com; 1026 Valencia St; ⊙6am-8pm Mon-Thu, to 10pm Fri, 7am-10pm Sat, to 8pm Sun; 🚌14, 49, Ⓑ 24th St Mission) Cults wish they inspired the same devotion as Ritual, where regulars solemnly queue for house-roasted cappuccino with ferns drawn in foam and specialty drip coffees with highly distinctive flavor profiles – descriptions comparing roasts to grapefruit peel or hazelnut aren't exaggerating. Electrical outlets are limited to encourage conversation, so you can eavesdrop on dates, art debates and political-protest plans.

Local Edition BAR
(Map p974; ☎415-795-1375; www.localeditionsf.com; 691 Market St; ⊙5pm-2am Mon-Fri, from 7pm Sat; Ⓜ Montgomery, Ⓑ Montgomery) Get the scoop on the SF cocktail scene at this new speakeasy in the basement of the historic Hearst newspaper building. Lighting is so dim you might bump into typewriters, but all is forgiven when you get The Pulitzer – a scotch-sherry cocktail that goes straight to your head.

Toronado PUB
(Map p974; ☎415-863-2276; www.toronado.com; 547 Haight St; ⊙11:30am-2am; 🚌6, 7, 22, Ⓜ N)

Glory hallelujah, beer lovers: your prayers have been answered. Be humbled before the chalkboard altar that lists 45-plus beers on tap and hundreds more bottled, including spectacular seasonal microbrews. Bring cash and order sausages from Rosamunde (p984) next door to accompany ale made by Trappist monks. It may get too loud to hear your date talk, but you'll hear angels sing.

Elixir BAR

(☎415-522-1633; www.elixirsf.com; 3200 16th St; ⏰3pm-2am Mon-Fri, from noon Sat, from 10am Sun; 🚌14, 22, 33, 49, B 16th St Mission, M J) Do the planet a favor and have another drink at SF's first certified-green bar, in an actual 1858 Wild West saloon. Elixir expertly blends farm-fresh seasonal mixers with small-batch, organic, even biodynamic spirits – dastardly tasty organic basil Negronis and kumquat caipirinhas will get you air-guitar-rocking to the killer jukebox. Drink-for-a-cause Wednesdays encourage imbibing, with proceeds supporting local charities.

Trick Dog BAR

(☎415-471-2999; www.trickdogbar.com; 3010 20th St; ⏰3pm-2am; 🚌12, 14, 49) Drink adventurously with ingenious cocktails inspired by local obsessions: SF landmarks, Chinese diners, '70s hits, horoscope signs. Every six months, Trick Dog adopts a new theme, and the entire menu changes – proof that you can teach an old dog new tricks, and improve on classics like the Manhattan. Arrive early for bar stools or hit the mood-lit loft for high-concept bar bites.

El Rio CLUB

(☎415-282-3325; www.elriosf.com; 3158 Mission St; cover free-$8; ⏰1pm-2am; 🚌12, 14, 27, 49, B 24th St Mission) Work it all out on the dance floor with SF's most down and funky crowd – SF's full rainbow spectrum of colorful characters is here to party. Calendar highlights include Wednesday's aptly named Mayhem Karaoke, Thursday ping-pong marathons, free oysters Fridays at 5:30pm, and monthly drag-star Daytime Realness. Expect knockout margaritas and shameless flirting in the back garden. Cash only.

☆ Entertainment

At Union Square, **TIX Bay Area** (Map p974; www.tixbayarea.org; 350 Powell St) sells last-minute theater tickets for half-price.

★ SFJAZZ Center JAZZ

(Map p974; ☎866-920-5299; www.sfjazz.org; 201 Franklin St; tickets $25-120; ⏰showtimes vary; 🚌5, 6, 7, 21, 47, 49, M Van Ness) Jazz greats coast-to-coast and legends from Argentina to Yemen are showcased at America's newest, largest jazz center. Hear fresh takes on classic jazz albums like *Ah Um* and *Getz/Gilberto* downstairs in the Lab, or book ahead for extraordinary main-stage collaborations like Laurie Anderson with David Coulter playing the saw, or pianist Jason Moran's performance with skateboarders improvising moves on indoor ramps.

★ American Conservatory Theater THEATER

(ACT; Map p974; ☎415-749-2228; www.act-sf.org; 415 Geary St; ⏰box office noon-6pm Mon, to curtain Tue-Sun; 🚌8, 30, 38, 45, 🚋Powell-Mason, Powell-Hyde, B Powell, M Powell) Breakthrough shows launch at this turn-of-the-century landmark, which has hosted ACT's landmark productions of Tony Kushner's *Angels in America* and Robert Wilson's *Black Rider*, with William S Burroughs' libretto and music by Tom Waits. Major playwrights like Tom Stoppard, David Mamet and Sam Shepard premiere work here, while experimental works are staged at ACT's new **Strand Theater** (Map p974; 1127 Market St).

San Francisco Opera OPERA

(Map p974; ☎415-864-3330; www.sfopera.com; War Memorial Opera House, 301 Van Ness Ave; tickets $10-350; 🚌21, 45, 47, B Civic Center, M Van Ness) Opera was SF's Gold Rush soundtrack – and today, SF rivals NYC's the Met with world premieres of original works covering WWII Italy *(Two Women,* or *La Ciociara),* Stephen King thrillers *(Dolores Claiborne),* and Qing-dynasty Chinese courtesans *(Dream of the Red Chamber).* Don't miss Tuscany-born musical director Nicola Luisotti's signature Verdi operas. Score $10 same-day standing-room tickets at 10am and two hours before curtain.

San Francisco Ballet DANCE

(Map p974; ☎tickets 415-865-2000; www.sfballet.org; War Memorial Opera House, 301 Van Ness Ave; tickets $15-160; ⏰ticket sales 10am-4pm Mon-Fri; 🚌5, 21, 47, 49, M Van Ness, B Civic Center) America's oldest ballet company is looking sharp in more than 100 shows annually, from the *Nutcracker* (the US premiere was here) to modern Mark Morris originals. It performs mostly at War Memorial Opera House January to May, with occasional performances at Yerba Buena Center for the Arts. Score $15 to $20 same-day standing-room tickets at the box office (noon Tuesday to Friday, 10am weekends).

Fillmore Auditorium LIVE MUSIC

(Map p974; ☎415-346-6000; http://thefillmore.com; 1805 Geary Blvd; admission $20-50; ⏲box office 10am-3pm Sun, plus 30min before doors open on show nights until 10pm; 🚌22, 38) Jimi Hendrix, Janis Joplin, the Doors – they all played the Fillmore. Now you might catch the Indigo Girls, Duran Duran or Tracy Chapman in the historic 1250-capacity, standing-room theater (if you're polite and lead with the hip, you might squeeze up to the stage). Don't miss the priceless collection of psychedelic posters in the upstairs gallery.

Great American Music Hall LIVE MUSIC

(Map p974; ☎415-885-0750; www.gamh.com; 859 O'Farrell St; shows $16-26; ⏲box office 10:30am-6pm Mon-Fri & on show nights; 🚌19, 38, 47, 49) Everyone busts out their best sets at this opulent 1907 former bordello – the Dead occasionally show up, Tuvan throat-singing supergroup Huun Huur Tu throws down and John Waters throws Christmas extravaganzas here. Pay $25 extra for dinner with priority admission and prime balcony seating where you can watch shows comfortably, or enter the standing-room scrum downstairs and rock out on the floor.

LGBTIQ SAN FRANCISCO

Doesn't matter where you're from, who you love or who your daddy is: if you're here, and queer, welcome home. The Castro is the heart of the gay cruising scene, but South of Market (SoMa) has leather bars and thump-thump clubs. The Mission is the preferred 'hood for many women and a diverse transgender community.

Bay Area Reporter (aka BAR; www.ebar.com) covers community news and listings. *San Francisco Bay Times* (www.sfbaytimes.com) focuses on LGBTIQ perspectives and events. Free *Gloss Magazine* (www.glossmagazine.net) locks down nightlife.

Over 1.5 million people come out for SF Pride (p978) parades and parties in late June. For weekly roving dance parties, check **Honey Soundsystem** (Map p974; http://hnysndsystm.tumblr.com/).

Blackbird (☎415-503-0630; www.blackbirdbar.com; 2124 Market St; ⏲3pm-2am Mon-Fri, from 2pm Sat & Sun; Ⓜ Church) Castro's first-choice lounge offers craft cocktails, billiards and everyone's favorite: a photo booth.

Hi Tops (http://hitopssf.com; 2247 Market St; ⏲4pm-midnight Mon-Wed, 4pm-2am Thu & Fri, 11am-2am Sat, noon-2am Sun; Ⓜ Castro) Castro's prime-time sports bar for friendly guys, big-screen TVs, shuffleboard and pub grub.

Cafe Flore (☎415-621-8579; www.cafeflore.com; 2298 Market St; ⏲7am-1am Sun-Thu, to 2am Fri & Sat; 📶; Ⓜ Castro) You haven't done the Castro till you've lollygagged on the sun-drenched patio here.

Stud (Map p974; www.studsf.com; 399 9th St; admission $5-8; ⏲noon-2am Tue, 5pm-3am Thu-Sat, 5pm-midnight Sun; 🚌12, 19, 27, 47) Rocking SoMa's gay scene since 1966. Anything goes here, especially on 'Club Some Thing' Fridays.

Oasis (Map p974; ☎415-795-3180; www.sfoasis.com/; 298 11th St; tickets $10-30; 🚌9, 12, 14, 47, Ⓜ Van Ness) SoMa drag shows so fearless and funny, you'll laugh till it hurts. Afterwards, shake it on the dance floor.

EndUp (Map p974; ☎415-646-0999; www.theendup.com; 401 6th St; admission $5-20; ⏲10pm Thu-4am Fri, 11pm Fri-11am Sat, 10pm Sat-4am Mon, 10pm Mon-4am Tue; 🚌12, 19, 27, 47) A mixed gay/straight crowd and marathon dance parties that don't end with sunrise over the 101 freeway ramp.

Aunt Charlie's Lounge (Map p974; ☎415-441-2922; www.auntcharlieslounge.com; 133 Turk St; admission free-$5; ⏲noon-2am Mon-Fri, from 10am Sat, 10am-midnight Sun; 🚌27, 31, Ⓜ Powell, Ⓑ Powell) Tenderloin drag dive bar for fabulously seedy glamour and a vintage pulp fiction vibe.

Beach Blanket Babylon CABARET
(BBB; Map p974; ☎415-421-4222; www.beachblanketbabylon.com; 678 Green St; admission $25-100; ⊙shows 8pm Wed, Thu & Fri, 6:30pm & 9:30pm Sat, 2pm & 5pm Sun; 🚌8, 30, 39, 41, 45, 🚋Powell-Mason) Snow White searches for Prince Charming in San Francisco: what could possibly go wrong? The Disney-spoof musical-comedy cabaret has been running since 1974, but topical jokes keep it outrageous and wigs big as parade floats are gasp-worthy. Spectators must be over 21 to handle racy humor, except at cleverly sanitized Sunday matinees. Reservations essential; arrive one hour early for best seats.

Independent LIVE MUSIC
(☎415-771-1421; www.theindependentsf.com; 628 Divisadero St; tickets $12-45; ⊙box office 11am-6pm Mon-Fri, to 9:30pm show nights; 🚌5, 6, 7, 21, 24) Shows earn street cred at the intimate Independent, featuring indie dreamers (Magnetic Fields, Death Cab for Cutie), rock legends (Meat Puppets, Luscious Jackson), alterna-pop (The Killers, Imagine Dragons) and comedians (Dave Chapelle, Comedians of Comedy). Ventilation is poor, but drinks are cheap – and movie nights offer free shows with a two-drink minimum.

SAN FRANCISCO'S BEST SHOPPING AREAS

All those rustic-chic dens, well-stocked cupboards and fabulous outfits don't just pull themselves together – San Franciscans scoured their city for it all. Here's where to find what:

Ferry Building Local food, wine and kitchenware.

Hayes Valley Independent fashion designers, housewares, gifts.

Valencia Street Bookstores, local design collectives, art galleries, vintage whatever.

Haight Street Head shops, music, vintage, skate and surf gear.

Union Square Department stores, megabrands, discount retail, Apple store.

Russian Hill and the Marina Date outfits, urban accessories, housewares, gifts.

Grant Avenue From Chinatown souvenirs to funky North Beach boutiques.

Castro Theatre CINEMA
(☎415-621-6120; www.castrotheatre.com; 429 Castro St; adult/child $11/8.50; ⊙showtimes vary; Ⓜ Castro) The Mighty Wurlitzer organ rises from the orchestra pit before evening performances and the audience cheer for the Great American Songbook, ending with: 'San Francisco open your Golden Gate/You let no stranger wait outside your door...' If there's a cult classic on the bill, say, *Whatever Happened to Baby Jane?*, expect participation. Otherwise, crowds are well behaved and rapt.

Roxie Cinema CINEMA
(☎415-863-1087; www.roxie.com; 3117 16th St; regular screening/matinee $10/7.50; ⊙showtimes vary; 🚌14, 22, 33, 49, Ⓑ16th St Mission) This little neighborhood nonprofit cinema earns international clout for distributing documentaries and showing controversial films banned elsewhere. Tickets to film-festival premieres, rare revivals and raucous annual Oscars telecasts sell out – reserve tickets online – but if the main show is packed, check out documentaries in teensy next-door Little Roxy instead. No ads, plus personal introductions to every film.

Sundance Kabuki Cinema CINEMA
(Map p974; ☎415-346-3243; www.sundancecinemas.com; 1881 Post St; adult $10.50-15, child $9.75-13; 🚌2, 3, 22, 38) 🍃 Cinema-going at its best. Reserve a stadium seat, belly up to the bar, and order wine and surprisingly good food to enjoy during the film. A multiplex initiative by Robert Redford's Sundance Institute, Kabuki features big-name flicks and festivals – and it's green, with recycled-fiber seating, reclaimed-wood decor and local chocolates and booze. Validated parking available.

🛍 Shopping

Aggregate Supply CLOTHING, GIFTS
(☎415-474-3190; www.aggregatesupplysf.com; 806 Valencia St; ⊙11am-7pm Mon-Sat, noon-6pm Sun; 🚌14, 33, 49, Ⓑ16th St Mission) Wild West modern is the look at Aggregate Supply, purveyors of West Coast cool fashion and home decor. Local designers and indie makers get pride of place, including vintage Heath stoneware mugs, Turk+Taylor's ombre plaid shirt-jackets, and ingeniously repurposed rodeo-saddle tassel necklaces. Souvenirs don't get more authentically local than Aggregate Supply's own op-art California graphic tee and NorCal-forest-scented organic soaps.

Betabrand CLOTHING
(800-694-9491; www.betabrand.com; 780 Valencia St; 11am-7pm Mon-Fri, to 8pm Sat, noon-6pm Sun; 14, 22, 33, 49, 16th St Mission) Crowdsource your fashion choices at Betabrand, where experimental designs are put to an online vote and winners are produced in limited editions. Recent approved designs include office-ready dress yoga pants, disco-ball windbreakers and sundresses with a smiling-poo-emoji print. Some styles are clunkers – including the 'suitsy,' a business-suit onesie – but at these prices you can afford to take fashion risks.

Local Take GIFTS
(www.localtakesf.com; 3979 B 17th St; 11am-7pm; Castro) This marvelous little shop, next to the F-Market terminus, carries the perfect gifts to take home: SF-specific merchandise, all made locally. Our favorite items include a miniature scale model of Sutro Tower; T-shirts emblazoned with iconic SF locales; cable-car and Golden Gate Bridge jewelry; woodcut city maps; knit caps; and snappy one-of-a-kind belt buckles.

Information

DANGERS & ANNOYANCES

Keep your city smarts and wits about you in the Tenderloin and SoMa.

MEDIA

KPFA 94.1 FM (www.kpfa.org) Alternative news, music and culture.

KPOO 89.5 FM (www.kpoo.com) Community radio plays jazz, blues, soul and world beats.

KQED 88.5 FM (www.kqed.org) NPR affiliate for news, talk, arts and educational programming.

San Francisco Chronicle (www.sfgate.com) The city's main daily newspaper.

SF Weekly (www.sfweekly.com) Free weekly tabloid covering food, arts, entertainment and events.

MEDICAL SERVICES

San Francisco General Hospital (emergency 415-206-8111, main hospital 415-206-8000; www.sfdph.org; 1001 Potrero Ave; 24hr; 9, 10, 33, 48) Best for serious trauma. Provides care to uninsured patients, including psychiatric care; no documentation required beyond ID.

MONEY

Currency Exchange International (415-974-6600; www.sanfranciscocurrencyexchange.com; Westfield Center, 865 Market St, Level 1; 10am-8:30pm Mon-Sat, 11am-7pm Sun; Powell St, Powell St) Good rates on exchange; centrally located near Union Square.

TOURIST INFORMATION

San Francisco Visitor Information Center (Map p974; 415-391-2000; www.sanfrancisco.travel; Hallidie Plaza, Market & Powell Sts, lower level; 9am-5pm Mon-Fri, to 3pm Sat & Sun; Powell-Mason, Powell-Hyde, Powell St, Powell St) Provides practical multilingual information, sells transportation passes, publishes glossy maps and booklets, and provides interactive touch screens.

USEFUL WEBSITES

7x7 (www.7x7.com) Trend spotting SF restaurants, bars, style and tech.

SFGate (www.sfgate.com) News and arts, entertainment and events listings.

Getting There & Away

AIR

San Francisco International Airport (SFO; www.flysfo.com; S McDonnell Rd) is 14 miles south of downtown, off Hwy 101 and accessible by Bay Area Rapid Transit (BART). Serving primarily domestic destinations, **Oakland International Airport** (OAK; www.oaklandairport.com; 1 Airport Dr;) is a 40-minute BART ride across the Bay, while **Mineta San José International Airport** (www.flysanjose.com; 1701 Airport Blvd, San Jose) is 45 miles south via Hwy 101.

BUS

Until 2017, San Francisco's intercity hub remains the **Temporary Transbay Terminal** (Map p974; Howard & Main Sts), where you can catch buses on **AC Transit** (511; www.actransit.org) to the East Bay, **Golden Gate Transit** (415-455-2000, 511; www.goldengatetransit.org) north to Marin and Sonoma Counties, and **SamTrans** (800-660-4287; www.samtrans.com) south to Palo Alto and along coastal Hwy 1. **Greyhound** (800-231-2222; www.greyhound.com) buses leave several times daily for Los Angeles ($59, eight to 12 hours) and many other destinations.

TRAIN

Two long-distance **Amtrak** (800-872-7245; www.amtrakcalifornia.com) trains, the Coast Starlight (Los Angeles–Seattle) and California Zephyr from Chicago, stop at Oakland's Jack London Sq. So do the Capitol Corridor and San Joaquin intra-California trains to/from Sacramento; the latter has connecting bus services to Yosemite Valley from Merced. Amtrak runs free shuttle buses for its passengers to San Francisco's Ferry Building and CalTrain station.

CalTrain (www.caltrain.com; cnr 4th & King Sts) connects San Francisco with Silicon Valley hubs and San Jose.

Getting Around

For Bay Area transit options, call ☎511 or check http://511.org.

TO/FROM SAN FRANCISCO INTERNATIONAL AIRPORT

From SFO's **BART** (Bay Area Rapid Transit; www.bart.gov; one way $8.65) station, connected to the International Terminal, it's a 30-minute ride to downtown SF. A taxi to downtown SF from SFO costs $40 to $55, plus tip.

SuperShuttle (☎800-258-3826; www.supershuttle.com) offers shared van rides for $17 per person.

BOAT

Blue & Gold Fleet (☎415-705-8200; www.blueandgoldfleet.com) operates ferries to Sausalito ($11.50), Angel Island ($9) and Oakland's Jack London Sq ($6.40) from SF's Ferry Building and/or Pier 41.

Golden Gate Ferry (☎415-455-2000, 511; http://goldengateferry.org) runs from SF's Ferry Building to Sausalito ($11.25) in Marin County.

CAR & MOTORCYCLE

Street parking can be harder to find than true love, and meter readers are ruthless. Municipal parking garages charge $1 to $5.50 per hour, or around $16 to $36 per day; for more info, check www.sfmta.com.

PUBLIC TRANSPORTATION

Muni (Municipal Transit Agency; ☎511; www.sfmta.com) operates bus, streetcar and cable-car lines. Standard fare for buses or streetcars is $2.25; cable-car rides are $7. Ask for a free transfer (not valid on cable cars) when boarding.

A **Visitor Passport** (one/three/seven days $17/26/35) allows unlimited travel on all Muni transport, including cable cars; it's sold at the Powell St cable car turnaround (p966), San Francisco Visitor Information Center (p989) and Union Square's TIX Bay Area (p986) kiosk.

A nine-day **City Pass** (www.citypass.com; adult/child $94/69) covers Muni, a bay cruise and admission to three attractions.

BART links San Francisco with the East Bay and runs beneath Market St, down Mission St and south to SFO and Millbrae, where it connects with CalTrain.

TAXI

Fares run about $2.75 per mile; meters start at $3.50. Hailing a cab in the street can be difficult. Download the mobile app **Flywheel** (http://flywheel.com) for prompt service.

Marin County

Majestic redwoods cling to tawny coastal headlands just across the Golden Gate Bridge in laid-back Marin. The southernmost town, **Sausalito** (www.sausalito.org), is a tiny bayfront destination for cycling trips over the bridge (take the ferry back to San Francisco). Near the harbor, where picturesque bohemian houseboats are docked, the **Bay Model Visitors Center** (Map p970; ☎415-332-3871; www.spn.usace.army.mil/Missions/Recreation/BayModelVisitorCenter.aspx; 2100 Bridgeway Blvd; ⏲9am-4pm Tue-Sat, plus 10am-5pm Sat & Sun in summer; 👪) FREE houses a giant hydraulic re-creation of the entire bay and delta.

Marin Headlands

These windswept, rugged headlands are laced with hiking trails, providing panoramic bay and city views. To find the **visitor center** (Map p970; ☎415-331-1540; www.nps.gov/goga/marin-headlands.htm; Fort Barry; ⏲9:30am-4:30pm), take the Alexander Ave exit after crossing north over the Golden Gate Bridge, turn left under the freeway and follow the signs.

Attractions west of Hwy 101 include **Point Bonita Lighthouse** (Map p970; www.nps.gov/goga/pobo.htm; off Field Rd; ⏲12:30-3:30pm Sat-Mon) FREE, Cold War–era **Nike Missle Site SF-88** (Map p970; ☎415-331-1453; www.nps.gov/goga/nike-missile-site.htm; off Field Rd; ⏲12:30pm-3:30pm Thu-Sat) FREE and the educational **Marine Mammal Center** (Map p970; ☎415-289-7325; www.marinemammalcenter.org; 2000 Bunker Rd; ⏲10am-5pm; 👪) 🍃 FREE uphill from **Rodeo Beach** (Map p970). East of Hwy 101 at Fort Baker, the interactive **Bay Area Discovery Museum** (Map p970; ☎415-339-3900; www.baykidsmuseum.org; 557 McReynolds Rd; admission $14, 1st Wed each month free; ⏲9am-5pm Tue-Sun; 👪) is awesome for kids.

Near the visitor center, **HI Marin Headlands Hostel** (Map p970; ☎415-331-2777; www.norcalhostels.org/marin; Fort Barry, Bldg 941; dm $26-30, r $72-92, all without bath; @) 🍃 occupies two 1907 military buildings on a forested hill. For historical luxury, book a fireplace room with bay views at Fort Baker's LEED-certified **Cavallo Point** (Map p970; ☎888-651-2003, 415-339-4700; www.cavallopoint.com; 601 Murray Circle; r from $359; ❄@📶🏊👪🐾) 🍃 lodge.

Muir Woods National Monument

Wander among an ancient stand of the world's tallest trees at 550-acre **Muir Woods National Monument** (Map p970; ☎415-388-2595; www.nps.gov/muwo; 1 Muir Woods Rd, Mill Valley; adult/child $10/free; ⏲8am-sunset), 10 miles northwest of the Golden Gate Bridge. Easy hiking trails loop past thousand-year-old coast redwoods at Cathedral Grove. By the entrance, **Muir Woods Trading Company** (Map p970; ☎415-388-7059; www.muirwoodstradingcompany.com; 1 Muir Woods Rd, Mill Valley; items $3-11; ⏲from 9am daily, closing varies 4pm to 7pm; 👪) serves light lunches, snacks and drinks in the cafe. Come midweek to avoid crowds, or arrive early morning or before sunset. Take Hwy 101 to the Hwy 1 exit, then follow the signs.

The **Muir Woods Shuttle** (Route 66F; www.marintransit.org; round-trip adult/child $5/free; ⏲weekends & holidays Apr-Oct) operates weekends and holidays from April through October (daily in peak summer season), connecting with Hwy 101 and Sausalito's ferry terminal.

Mt Tamalpais State Park

Majestic Mt Tam (2572ft) is a woodsy playground for hikers and mountain bikers. **Mt Tamalpais State Park** (Map p970; ☎415-388-2070; www.parks.ca.gov/mttamalpais; parking $8) encompasses 6300 acres of parklands and over 200 miles of trails. Don't miss driving up to East Peak Summit lookout. Panoramic Hwy passes through the park, connecting Muir Woods with **Stinson Beach**, a coastal town with a sandy crescent-shaped beach on Hwy 1.

Park headquarters are **Pantoll Station** (☎415-388-2070; www.parks.ca.gov/?page_id=471; 801 Panoramic Hwy; ⏲variable hours; 📶), the nexus of many trails, with a first-come, first-served **campground** (Map p970; Panoramic Hwy; tent sites $25). Book far ahead for a rustic cabin (no electricity or running water) or walk-in campsite at **Steep Ravine** (☎800-444-7275; www.reserveamerica.com; Nov-Sep; tent sites $25, cabins $100), off Hwy 1 south of Stinson Beach. Or hike in with a sleeping bag, towel and food to off-the-grid **West Point Inn** (Map p970; ☎info 415-388-9955, reservations 415-646-0702; www.westpointinn.com; 100 Old Railroad Grade Fire Rd, Mill Valley; r per adult/child $50/25); reservations required.

Point Reyes National Seashore

The windswept peninsula of **Point Reyes National Seashore** (www.nps.gov/pore) FREE juts 10 miles out to sea on an entirely different tectonic plate, protecting over 100 sq miles of beaches, lagoons and forested hills. A mile west of Olema, **Bear Valley Visitor Center** (☎415-464-5100; www.nps.gov/pore; ⏲10am-5pm Mon-Fri, from 9am Sat & Sun) has maps, information and natural-history displays. The 0.6-mile **Earthquake Trail**, which crosses the San Andreas Fault zone, starts nearby.

Crowning the peninsula's westernmost tip, **Point Reyes Lighthouse** (☎415-669-1534; ⏲lighthouse 10am-4:30pm Fri-Mon, lens room 2:30-4pm Fri-Mon) FREE is ideal for winter whale-watching. Off Pierce Point Rd, the 10-mile round-trip **Tomales Point Trail** rolls atop blustery bluffs past herds of tule elk to the peninsula's northern tip. To paddle out into Tomales Bay, **Blue Waters Kayaking** (☎415-669-2600; www.bluewaterskayaking.com; rentals/tours from $50/68; 👪) launches from Inverness and Marshall.

Nature-lovers bunk at the only in-park lodging, **HI Point Reyes Hostel** (☎415-663-8811; www.norcalhostels.org/reyes; 1390 Limantour Spit Rd; dm $26-29, r $87-130, all without bath; @👪), 8 miles inland from the visitor center. In the coastal town of Inverness, the **Cottages at Point Reyes Seashore** (☎415-669-7250; www.cottagespointreyes.com; 13275 Sir Francis Drake Blvd; r $129-239; 📶🏊👪🐾) is a family-friendly place tucked away in the woods. The **West Marin Chamber of Commerce** (☎415-663-9232; www.pointreyes.org) checks availability at more cozy inns, cottages and B&Bs.

Two miles north of Olema, the tiny town of **Point Reyes Station** has heart-warming bakeries, cafes and restaurants. Gather a picnic lunch at **Tomales Bay Foods & Cowgirl Creamery** (www.cowgirlcreamery.com; 80 4th St; sandwiches $6-12; ⏲10am-6pm Wed-Sun; 🖉) or 2 miles west of town at **Perry's Deli** (http://perrysinvernessparkgrocery.com; 12301 Sir Francis Drake Blvd, Inverness Park; sandwiches $5-11; ⏲7am-8pm Mon-Thu, to 9pm Fri & Sat, 8am-8pm Sun).

Berkeley

As the birthplace of the 1960s Free Speech Movement, and the home of the hallowed halls of the University of California,

Berkeley is no bashful wallflower. You can't legally walk around nude anymore, but 'Berserkeley' remains the Bay Area's radical hub, crawling with university students, punk skaters and aging Birckenstock-shod hippies. 'Nuclear Free Zone' signs mark the city limits.

Sights & Activities

Leading to the campus's south gate, **Telegraph Avenue** is a youthful street carnival, packed with cheap cafes, music stores, street hawkers and buskers.

University of California, Berkeley UNIVERSITY
(www.berkeley.edu) 'Cal' is one of the country's top universities and home to 35,000 diverse, politically conscious students. The **Visitor Services Center** (☎510-642-5215; http://visitors.berkeley.edu; 101 Sproul Hall; ⊙tours usually 10am Mon-Sat & 1pm Sun) has info and leads free campus tours (reservations required). Cal's landmark is the 1914 **Campanile** (Sather Tower; http://visitors.berkeley.edu/camp/; adult/child $3/2; ⊙10am-3:45pm Mon-Fri, to 4:45pm Sat, 10am-1:30pm & 3-4:45pm Sun; 👪), with elevator rides ($3) to the top. The **Bancroft Library** (☎510-642-3781; www.bancroft.berkeley.edu; ⊙10am-5pm Mon-Fri) displays the small gold nugget that started the California gold rush in 1848.

Sleeping

Midrange motels line University Ave west of downtown.

Downtown Berkeley Inn MOTEL $$
(☎510-843-4043; www.downtownberkeleyinn.com; 2001 Bancroft Way; r $79-129; ❄📶) A 27-room budget boutique-style motel with good-sized rooms and correspondingly ample flat-screen TVs.

Hotel Shattuck Plaza HOTEL $$$
(☎510-845-7300; www.hotelshattuckplaza.com; 2086 Allston Way; r from $195; ❄@📶) Peace is quite posh following a $15-million renovation and greening of this 100-year-old downtown jewel. A foyer of red Italian glass lighting, flocked Victorian-style wallpaper – and yes, a peace sign tiled into the floor – leads to comfortable rooms with down comforters, and an airy, columned restaurant serving all meals. Accommodations off Shattuck are quietest; cityscape rooms boast bay views.

Eating & Drinking

Ippuku JAPANESE $$
(☎510-665-1969; www.ippukuberkeley.com; 2130 Center St; shared plates $5-20; ⊙5-10pm Sun-Thu, to 11pm Fri & Sat) Specializing in *shōchū*, a distilled alcohol often made from rice or barley, Ippuku is similar to a Tokyo *izakaya* (Japanese pubs serving food) and beloved by its Japanese expat patrons. Choose from a menu of skewered meats and vegetables and handmade noodles as you settle in at one of the traditional tatami tables (no shoes, please) or cozy booth perches. Reservations essential.

★**Chez Panisse** CALIFORNIAN $$$
(☎cafe 510-548-5049, restaurant 510-548-5525; www.chezpanisse.com; 1517 Shattuck Ave; cafe dinner mains $19-32, restaurant prix-fixe dinner $75-125; ⊙cafe 11:30am-2:45pm & 5-10:30pm Mon-Thu, 11:30am-3pm & 5-11:30pm Fri & Sat, restaurant seatings 5:30pm & 8pm Mon-Sat) 🍃 Foodies come to worship here at the church of Alice Waters, the inventor of California cuisine. It's in a lovely arts-and-crafts house in the Gourmet Ghetto, and you can choose to pull all the stops with a prix-fixe meal downstairs, or go less expensive and a tad less formal in the cafe upstairs. Reservations accepted one month ahead.

Jupiter PUB
(www.jupiterbeer.com; 2181 Shattuck Ave; ⊙11:30am-1am Mon-Thu, to 1:30am Fri, noon-1:30am Sat, to midnight Sun) This downtown pub has loads of regional microbrews, a beer garden, good pizza and live bands most nights. Sit upstairs for a bird's-eye view of bustling Shattuck Ave.

Entertainment

Freight & Salvage Coffeehouse LIVE MUSIC
(☎510-644-2020; www.thefreight.org; 2020 Addison St; 👪) This legendary club has almost 50 years of history and is conveniently located in the downtown arts district. It features great traditional folk and world music and welcomes all ages, with half-price tickets for patrons under 21.

Berkeley Repertory Theatre THEATER
(☎510-647-2949; www.berkeleyrep.org; 2025 Addison St; tickets $40-100) This highly respected company has produced bold versions of classical and modern plays since 1968. Most shows have half-price tickets for patrons under 30.

ℹ Getting There & Around

BART (☎ 511, 510-465-2278; www.bart.gov) trains connect downtown Berkeley, a short walk from campus, with San Francisco ($3.90, 25 minutes). AC Transit (p989) runs local buses around Berkeley ($2.10) and to San Francisco ($4.20, 40 minutes).

NORTHERN CALIFORNIA

The Golden State goes wild in Northern California, with coast redwoods swirled in fog, Wine Country vineyards and hidden hot springs. Befitting this dramatic meeting of land and water is an unlikely mélange of local residents: timber barons and hippie tree huggers, dreadlocked Rastafarians and biodynamic ranchers, pot farmers and political radicals of every stripe. Come for the scenery, but stay for the top-notch wine and farm-to-fork restaurants, misty hikes among the world's tallest trees and rambling conversations that begin with 'Hey, dude!' and end hours later.

Wine Country

America's premier viticulture region has earned its reputation among the world's best. Century-old oaks and swaths of vineyards carpet rolling hillsides as far as the eye can see. Where they end, lush redwood forests follow serpentine rivers to the sea. Napa has art-filled tasting rooms by big-name architects, with prices to match. In down-to-earth Sonoma, you may drink in a tin-roofed shed and meet the vintner's dog.

ℹ Getting There & Around

Either Napa or Sonoma is at least an hour's drive north of San Francisco via Hwy 101 or I-80.

Getting to and around the valleys by public transportation (mainly buses, perhaps in combination with BART trains or ferries) is slow and complicated, but just possible; consult http://511.org for trip planning and schedules.

Rent bicycles from **Wine Country Cyclery** (☎ 707-966-6800; www.winecountrycyclery.com; 262 W Napa St, Sonoma; bicycle rental per day $30-65; ⏰10am-6pm), **Napa Valley Bike Tours** (☎ 707-251-8687; www.napavalleybiketours.com; 6500 Washington St, Yountville; bicycle rental per day $45-90, tours from $109; ⏰8:30am-5pm), **Calistoga Bike Shop** (☎ 707-942-9687; www.calistogabikeshop.com; 1318 Lincoln Ave, Calistoga; bicycle rental from $12/39 per hour/day; ⏰10am-6pm) or **Spoke Folk Cyclery** (☎ 707-433-7171; www.spokefolk.com; 201 Center St, Healdsburg; bicycle rental per hour/day from $15/40; ⏰10am-6pm Mon-Fri, to 5pm Sat & Sun).

Napa Valley

More than 200 wineries crowd 30-mile-long Napa Valley along three main routes. Traffic-jammed on weekends, **Highway 29** is lined with blockbuster wineries. Running parallel, **Silverado Trail** moves faster, passing boutique winemakers, bizarre architecture and cult-hit Cabernet Sauvignon. Heading west toward Sonoma, **Carneros Highway** (Hwy 121) winds by landmark vineyards specializing in sparkling wines and Pinot Noir.

At the southern end of the valley, **Napa** – the valley's workaday hub – lacks rusticity, but has trendy restaurants and tasting rooms downtown. Stop by the **Napa Valley Welcome Center** (☎ 855-847-6272, 707-251-5895; www.visitnapavalley.com; 600 Main St; ⏰9am-5pm; 👪) for wine-tasting passes and winery maps.

Heading north on Hwy 29, the former stagecoach stop of tiny **Yountville** has more Michelin-starred eateries per capita than San Francisco. Another 10 miles north, traffic snarls in charming **St Helena**, where there's genteel strolling and shopping – if you can find parking. At the valley's northern end, folksy **Calistoga** is home to hot-springs spas and mud-bath emporiums using volcanic ash from nearby Mt St Helena.

👁 Sights & Activities

Many Napa wineries require reservations. Plan to visit no more than a few tasting rooms each day.

★**Hess Collection** WINERY, GALLERY

(☎ 707-255-1144; www.hesscollection.com; 4411 Redwood Rd, Napa; museum entry free, tasting $20, tours free-$65; ⏰10am-5:30pm, last tasting 5pm, tours 10:30am-3pm) 🌿 Art-lovers: don't miss Hess Collection, the galleries of which display mixed-media and large-canvas works, including pieces by Francis Bacon and Robert Motherwell. In the cave-like tasting room, find well-known Cabernet Sauvignon and Chardonnay, but also try the Viognier. Hess overlooks the valley: be prepared to drive a winding road. Reservations recommended. Bottles: $20 to $100. (NB: don't confuse Hess Collection with Hess Select, the grocery-store brand.)

★ **Frog's Leap** WINERY
(707-963-4704; www.frogsleap.com; 8815 Conn Creek Rd, Rutherford; tasting $20, incl tour $25; 10am-4pm by appointment only;) Meandering paths wind through magical gardens and fruit-bearing orchards surrounding an 1884 barn and farmstead with cats and chickens. The vibe is casual and down-to-earth, with a major emphasis on *fun*. Sauvignon Blanc is its best-known wine, but the Merlot merits attention. There's also a dry, restrained Cabernet, atypical of Napa.

All wines are organic. Appointments required. Bottles cost $22 to $42.

Castello di Amorosa WINERY, CASTLE
(707-967-6272; www.castellodiamorosa.com; 4045 Hwy 29, Calistoga; admission & tasting $20-45, incl guided tour $35-75; 9:30am-6pm Mar-Oct, to 5pm Nov-Feb) It took 14 years to build this perfectly replicated, 13th-century Italian castle, complete with moat, hand-cut stone walls, ceiling frescoes by Italian artisans, Roman-style cross-vault brick catacombs, and a torture chamber with period equipment. You can taste without an appointment, but this is one tour worth taking. Oh, the wine? Some respectable Italian varietals, including a velvety Tuscan blend, and a Merlot blend that goes great with pizza. Bottles are $29 to $95.

Casa Nuestra WINERY
(707-963-5783, 866-844-9463; www.casanuestra.com; 3451 Silverado Trail N, St Helena; tasting $10; 10am-4:30pm by appointment only;) A peace flag and portrait of Elvis greet you at this old-school, mom-and-pop winery, which produces unusual blends and interesting varietals (including good Chenin Blanc). Vineyards are all-organic; the sun provides power. Picnic free (call ahead and buy a bottle) beneath weeping willows shading happy goats. Bottles are $20 to $60.

di Rosa Art + Nature Preserve GALLERY, GARDENS
(707-226-5991; www.dirosaart.org; 5200 Hwy 121, Napa; admission $5, tours $12-15; 10am-4pm Wed-Sun) West of downtown, scrap-metal sheep graze Carneros vineyards at 217-acre di Rosa Preserve, a stunning collection of Northern California art, displayed indoors in galleries and outdoors in sculpture gardens. Reservations recommended for tours.

Indian Springs Spa SPA
(707-942-4913; www.indianspringscalistoga.com; 1712 Lincoln Ave; by appointment 9am-8pm) California's longest continually operating spa, and original Calistoga resort, has concrete mud tubs and mines its own ash. Treatments include use of the huge, hot-spring-fed pool. Great cucumber body lotion.

Culinary Institute of America at Greystone COOKING COURSE
(707-967-2320; www.ciachef.edu/california; 2555 Main St; mains $25-29, cooking demonstration $20; cooking demonstrations 1:30pm Sat & Sun) Inside an 1889 stone chateau, now a cooking school, there's a gadget- and cookbook-filled culinary shop; fine restaurant; weekend cooking demonstrations; and wine-tasting classes by luminaries including Karen MacNeil, author of *The Wine Bible*.

Sleeping

The valley's best-value deals are midweek at Napa's less-than-exciting motels.

Maison Fleurie INN $$
(707-944-2056; www.maisonfleurienapa.com; 6529 Yount St, Yountville; r $170-395;) Rooms at this ivy-covered country inn are in a century-old home and carriage house, decorated in French-provincial style. Big breakfasts (included), afternoon wine and *hors d'oeuvres*, hot tub.

El Bonita MOTEL $$
(707-963-3216; www.elbonita.com; 195 Main St, St Helena; r $169-239;) Book in advance to secure this sought-after motel, with up-to-date rooms (quietest are in back), attractive grounds, hot tub and sauna.

Indian Springs Resort RESORT $$
(707-942-4913; www.indianspringscalistoga.com; 1712 Lincoln Ave, Calistoga; r/cottages from $239/359;) The definitive old-school Calistoga resort, Indian Springs has cottages facing a central lawn with palm trees, shuffleboard, bocce, hammocks and Weber grills – not unlike a vintage Florida resort. Some sleep six. There are also top-end, motel-style lodge rooms (adults only). Huge hot-springs-fed swimming pool.

Eating

Many wine-country restaurants keep shorter hours in winter; book ahead for lunch and dinner.

★ **Oxbow Public Market** MARKET $
(707-226-6529; http://oxbowpublicmarket.com; 610 & 644 1st St, Napa; items from $3; 9am-7pm

Wed-Mon, to 8pm Tue, some restaurants open later) Graze this gourmet market and plug into the Northern California food scene. Standouts: Hog Island Oyster Co; comfort cooking at celeb-chef Todd Humphries' Kitchen Door; Venezuelan arepa (corn-cake sandwiches) at Pica Pica; great Cal-Mexican tacos at C Casa; Italian pastries at Ca' Momi; espresso from Ritual Coffee; and Three Twins certified-organic ice cream.

Bouchon Bakery BAKERY $
(707-944-2253; www.thomaskeller.com; 6528 Washington St, Yountville; items from $3; 7am-7pm) Bouchon makes as-good-as-in-Paris French pastries and strong coffee. There's always a line and rarely a seat: get it to go.

Gott's Roadside AMERICAN $$
(707-963-3486; http://gotts.com; 933 Main St, St Helena; mains $8-16; 10am-10pm May-Sep, 8am-9pm Oct-Apr;) Wiggle your toes in the grass and feast on quality burgers – of beef or ahi tuna – plus Cobb salads and fish tacos at this classic roadside drive-in, whose original name, 'Taylor's Auto Refresher,' remains on the sign. Avoid weekend waits by phoning ahead or ordering online. There's another at Oxbow Public Market.

★ **French Laundry** CALIFORNIAN $$$
(707-944-2380; www.frenchlaundry.com; 6640 Washington St, Yountville; prix-fixe dinner $295; seatings 11am-1pm Fri-Sun, 5:30-9:15pm daily) The pinnacle of California dining, Thomas Keller's French Laundry is epic, a high-wattage culinary experience on par with the world's best. Book two months ahead at 10am sharp, or log onto OpenTable.com precisely at midnight. Avoid tables before 7pm; first-service seating moves a touch quickly. This is the meal you can brag about the rest of your life.

Sonoma Valley

More laid-back and less commercial than Napa, Sonoma Valley shelters more than 40 wineries off Hwy 12 – and unlike in Napa, most don't require tasting appointments. Note there are actually three Sonomas: the town, the valley and the county.

Sights & Activities

Downtown Sonoma was once the capital of the short-lived Bear Flag Republic. Today **Sonoma Plaza** – the state's largest town square – is bordered by historic hotels, busy restaurants, chic shops and a **visitor center** (866-966-1090, 707-996-1090; www.sonomavalley.com; 453 1st St E; 9am-5pm Mon-Sat, 10am-5pm Sun).

Bartholomew Park Winery WINERY
(707-939-3026; www.bartpark.com; 1000 Vineyard Lane, Sonoma; tasting $10-30; 11am-4:30pm) A great bike-to winery, Bartholomew Park occupies a 400-acre nature preserve, with oak-shaded picnicking and valley-view hiking. The vineyards were originally cultivated in 1857 and now yield certified-organic, citrusy Sauvignon Blanc, Cabernet Sauvignon softer in style than Napa and lush Zinfandel. Bottles are $21 to $48.

Gundlach-Bundschu Winery WINERY
(707-939-3015; www.gunbun.com; 2000 Denmark St, Sonoma; tasting $10-25, incl tour $30-50; 11am-4:30pm, to 5:30pm Jun–mid-Oct) California's oldest family-run winery looks like a castle, but has a down-to-earth vibe. Founded in 1858 by a Bavarian immigrant, its signatures are Gewürztraminer and Pinot Noir, but 'Gun-Bun' was the first American winery to produce 100% Merlot. Down a winding lane, it's a terrific bike-to winery, with picnicking, hiking and a lake. Tour the 1800-barrel cave by reservation only. Bottles are $21 to $90.

Benziger WINERY
(707-935-3000, 888-490-2739; www.benziger.com; 1883 London Ranch Rd, Glen Ellen; tasting $15-40, tours $25-50; 10am-5pm, tram tours 11am-3:30pm;) If you're new to wine, make Benziger your first stop for Sonoma's best crash course in winemaking. The worthwhile, nonreservable tour includes an open-air tram ride (weather permitting) through biodynamic vineyards, and a five-wine tasting. Great picnicking, plus a playground, make it tops for families. The large-production wine is OK (head for the reserves); the tour's the thing. Bottles are $15 to $80.

Jack London State Historic Park STATE PARK
(707-938-5216; www.jacklondonpark.com; 2400 London Ranch Rd, Glen Ellen; per car $10, cottage entry adult/child $4/2; park 9:30am-5pm, museum 10am-5pm, cottage noon-4pm) Napa has Robert Louis Stevenson, but Sonoma's got Jack London. This 1400-acre park frames that author's last years; don't miss the excellent on-site museum. Miles of hiking trails (some open to mountain bikes) weave through oak-dotted woodlands, between

600ft and 2300ft elevations; an easy 2-mile loop meanders to a lake, great for picnicking. Watch for poison oak.

Cline Cellars WINERY
(707-940-4030; www.clinecellars.com; 24737 Arnold Dr, Sonoma; tasting free-$20; tasting room 10am-6pm, museum 10am-4pm) Balmy days are for pond-side picnics, and rainy ones for fireside tastings of old-vine Zinfandel and Mouvedre inside an 1850s farmhouse. Stroll out back to the California Mission Museum, housing 1930s miniature replicas of California's original 21 Spanish Colonial missions.

Kunde WINERY
(707-833-5501; www.kunde.com; 9825 Hwy 12, Kenwood; tasting $10-25, incl tour $30-40; 10:30am-5pm) It's worth making reservations in advance for sustainable vineyard tours, mountain-top tastings and monthly guided hikes.

Sleeping

At the valley's north end, Santa Rosa has budget-saving motels and hotels.

Sonoma Hotel HISTORIC HOTEL $$
(707-996-2996; www.sonomahotel.com; 110 W Spain St; r from $160;) Long on charm, this good-value, vintage-1880s hotel, decorated with country-style willow-wood furnishings, sits right on the plaza. Double-pane glass blocks the noise, but there's no elevator or parking lot.

★ **Beltane Ranch** B&B $$
(707-833-4233; www.beltaneranch.com; 11775 Hwy 12, Glen Ellen; d $205-295;) Surrounded by horse pastures and vineyards, Beltane is a throwback to 19th-century Sonoma. The cheerful, lemon-yellow, 1890s ranch house has double porches, lined with swinging chairs and white wicker. Though it's technically a B&B, each country-Americana-style room has a private entrance – nobody will make you pet the cat. No phones or TVs mean zero distraction from pastoral bliss.

Eating & Drinking

Fremont Diner AMERICAN, SOUTHERN $$
(707-938-7370; www.thefremontdiner.com; 2698 Fremont Dr, Sonoma; mains $9-22; 8am-3pm Mon-Wed, to 9pm Thu-Sun;) Lines snake out the door peak times at this farm-to-table roadside diner. We prefer the indoor tables, but will happily accept a picnic table in the big outdoor tent to feast on ricotta pancakes with real maple syrup, chicken and waffles, oyster po'boys, finger-licking barbecue and skillet-baked cornbread. Arrive early, or late, to beat queues.

fig cafe & winebar FRENCH, CALIFORNIAN $$
(707-938-2130; www.thefigcafe.com; 13690 Arnold Dr, Glen Ellen; mains $14-26, 3-course prix-fixe dinner $36; brunch 10am-2:30pm Sat & Sun, dinner 5-9pm Sun-Thu, to 9:30pm Fri & Sat) The fig's earthy California-Provençal comfort food includes flash-fried calamari with spicy-lemon aioli, duck confit and *moules-frites* (mussels and french fries). Good wine prices and weekend brunch give reason to return.

Hopmonk Tavern PUB FOOD $$
(707-935-9100; www.hopmonk.com; 691 Broadway, Sonoma; mains $11-23; 11:30am-9pm Sun-Thu, to 9:30pm Fri & Sat) This happening gastropub and beer garden takes its brews seriously, with more than a dozen of its own and guest beers on tap, served in type-appropriate glassware. Live music Friday through Sunday.

★ **Cafe La Haye** CALIFORNIAN $$$
(707-935-5994; www.cafelahaye.com; 140 E Napa St, Sonoma; mains $18-30; 5:30-9pm Tue-Sat;) One of Sonoma's top tables for earthy New American cooking, La Haye only uses produce sourced from within 60 miles. Its dining room gets packed cheek-by-jowl and service can border on perfunctory, but the clean simplicity and flavor-packed cooking make it many foodies' first choice. Reserve well ahead.

Russian River Valley

Redwoods tower over small wineries in the Russian River Valley, about 75 miles northwest of San Francisco (via Hwys 101 and 116), in western Sonoma County.

Famous for its apple orchards and farm-tour trails, **Sebastopol** has a new-age spiritual aura, with downtown bookshops, art galleries and boutiques, and antiques stores further south. Wander around the **Barlow** (707-824-5600; thebarlow.net; 6770 McKinley St; 8:30am-9:30pm;), an indoor market of food producers, winemakers, coffee roasters, spirit distillers and indie chefs. Or go straight to the source by driving or cycling local farm trails (www.farmtrails.org).

Guerneville is the main river beach town, buzzing with Harleys and gay-friendly honky-tonks. Explore old-growth redwoods at **Armstrong Redwoods State Reserve** (info 707-869-2015, visitor center 707-869-2958; www.parks.ca.gov; 17000 Armstrong Woods Rd; per car $8; 8am-sunset;), next to no-reservations **Bullfrog Pond Campground** (707-869-2015; www.stewardscr.org; sites reserved/nonreserved $35/25;). Paddle downriver with **Burke's Canoe Trips** (707-887-1222; www.burkescanoetrips.com; 8600 River Rd, Forestville; canoe/kayak rental incl shuttle $65/45, cash only; 10am-6pm Mon-Fri, 9am-6pm Sat & Sun). Head southeast to sip sparkling wines at hilltop **Iron Horse Vineyards** (707-887-1507; www.ironhorsevineyards.com; 9786 Ross Station Rd, Sebastopol; tasting $20, incl tour $25-50; 10am-4:30pm); reserve tours in advance. Other excellent wineries, many known for award-winning Pinot Noir, scatter along rural **Westside Road**, which follows the river toward Healdsburg. Guerneville's **visitor center** (877-644-9001, 707-869-9000; www.russianriver.com; 16209 1st St, Guerneville; 10am-4:45pm Mon-Sat, plus 10am-3pm Sun May-Oct) offers winery maps and lodging info. It's worth the wait for a table at California-smart **Boon Eat + Drink** (707-869-0780; http://eatatboon.com; 16248 Main St; lunch mains $14-18, dinner $15-26; lunch 11am-3pm Mon, Tue, Thu & Fri, brunch 10am-3pm Sat & Sun, dinner 5-9pm Sun-Thu, to 10pm Fri & Sat), which also manages boutique **Boon Hotel + Spa** (707-869-2721; www.boonhotels.com; 14711 Armstrong Woods Rd; r $165-275;) , a minimalist oasis with a saline pool.

The aptly named Bohemian Hwy winds 10 miles south of the river to tiny **Occidental**, where **Howard Station Cafe** (707-874-2838; www.howardstationcafe.com; 3611 Bohemian Hwy; mains $6-13; 7am-2:30pm Mon-Fri, to 3pm Sat & Sun;) serves hearty breakfasts like blueberry cornmeal pancakes (cash only), and **Barley & Hops Tavern** (707-874-9037; www.barleynhops.com; 3688 Bohemian Hwy; mains $10-15; 4-9:30pm Mon-Thu, 11am-10pm Fri & Sat, 11am-9:30pm Sun) pours craft beers. It's another few miles south to **Freestone**, home of the phenomenal bakery **Wild Flour Bread** (www.wildflourbread.com; 140 Bohemian Hwy, Freestone; items from $3; 8:30am-6:30pm Fri-Mon) and invigorating cedar-enzyme baths at **Osmosis** (707-823-8231; www.osmosis.com; 209 Bohemian Hwy, Freestone; by appointment) spa.

Healdsburg & Around

More than 100 wineries dot the valleys within a 20-mile radius of Healdsburg, where upscale eateries, wine-tasting rooms and stylish hotels surround a leafy plaza. For tasting passes and maps, drop by the **visitor center** (07-433-6935; www.healdsburg.com; 217 Healdsburg Ave, Healdsburg; 10am-4pm Mon-Fri, to 3pm Sat & Sun). Dine with California-chic locavores at the **Shed** (707-431-7433; healdsburgshed.com; 25 North St; dishes $3-15; 8am-7pm Wed-Mon;) gourmet marketplace and culinary center, or grab lunch near the vineyards at country-style **Dry Creek General Store** (707-433-4171; www.drycreekgeneralstore1881.com; 3495 Dry Creek Rd; sandwiches $8-10; 6:30am-6pm Mon-Thu, to 6:30pm Fri & Sat, 7am-6pm Sun). Afterward bed down at old-fashioned **L&M Motel** (707-433-6528; www.landmmotel.com; 70 Healdsburg Ave; r $150-180;) or romantic **Healdsburg Modern Cottages** (707-395-4684; www.healdsburgcottages.com; 425 Foss St; d $250-500;).

Picture-perfect farmstead wineries await discovery in Dry Creek Valley, west of Hwy 101 and Healdsburg. Pedal a bicycle out to taste citrusy Sauvignon Blanc and peppery Zinfandel at biodynamic **Preston Vineyards** (www.prestonvineyards.com; 9282 W Dry Creek Rd; tasting $10; 11am-4:30pm;) and **Quivira Vineyards** (707-431-8333; www.quivirawine.com; 4900 W Dry Creek Rd; tasting $15, incl tour $25; 11am-5pm;) . Motor toward the Russian River and **Porter Creek Vineyards** (707-433-6321; www.portercreekvineyards.com; 8735 Westside Rd, Healdsburg; tasting $10; 10:30am-4:30pm;) for forest-floor Pinot Noir and fruity Viognier poured at a bar made from a bowling-alley lane.

Northwest of Healdsburg off Hwy 101, follow Hwy 128 through the **Anderson Valley**, known for its fruit orchards and family-owned wineries like **Navarro** (707-895-3686; www.navarrowine.com; 5601 Hwy 128, Philo; 9am-6pm, to 5pm Nov-Mar) FREE and **Husch** (www.huschvineyards.com; 4400 Hwy 128, Philo; 10am-6pm, to 5pm Nov-Mar) FREE. Outside **Boonville**, which has roadside cafes, bakeries and delis, brake for disc-golf and beer at solar-powered **Anderson Valley Brewing Company** (707-895-2337; www.avbc.com; 17700 Hwy 253, Boonville; tasting from $2, tours & disc-golf course free; tasting room 11am-6pm Sat-Thu, to 7pm Fri, tours 1:30pm & 3pm daily) .

North Coast

Metropolitan San Francisco, only a few hours behind in the rearview mirror, feels eons away from the frothing, frigid crash of Pacific tide and two-stoplight towns on this jagged edge of the continent. Forested valleys brush up against moody ocean waves and rural farms here on California's weirdest coast, home to hippies, hoppy microbrews, marijuana farms and, most famously, the tallest trees on earth. The winding coastal drive gets more rewarding with every gorgeous, white-knuckled mile of narrow highway.

Coastal Highway 1 to Mendocino

Often winding precariously atop ocean cliffs, this serpentine slice of Hwy 1 passes salty fishing harbors and hidden beaches. Use roadside pullouts to scan the Pacific horizon for migrating whales or to amble coves bounded by startling rock formations and relentlessly pounded by the surf. The 110-mile stretch from Bodega Bay to Fort Bragg takes at least three hours of nonstop driving; at night or in the fog, it takes steely nerves and much, much longer.

Bodega Bay, the first pearl in a string of sleepy fishing villages, was the setting for Hitchcock's terrifying 1963 psycho-horror flick *The Birds*. Today the skies are free from bloodthirsty gulls, but you'd best keep an eye on that picnic basket as you explore the arched rocks, blustery coves and wildflower-covered bluffs of **Sonoma Coast State Park** (www.parks.ca.gov; per car $8), with beaches rolling beyond Jenner, 10 miles north. **Bodega Bay Sportfishing Center** (☎707-875-3495; www.bodegacharters.com; 1410 Bay Flat Rd) runs winter whale-watching trips (adult/child $50/35). Landlubbers hike Bodega Head or saddle up at **Chanslor Riding Stables** (☎707-875-2721, 707-875-3333; www.horsenaroundtrailrides.com; 2660 N Hwy 1; rides from $40).

Where the wide, lazy Russian River meets the Pacific, there isn't much to **Jenner**, a cluster of shops and restaurants dotting coastal hills. Informative volunteers protect the resident colony of harbor seals at the river's mouth during pupping season, between March and August. **Water Treks Ecotours** (☎707-865-2249; http://watertreks.com; kayak rental from $30; ⏲10am-3pm Mon-Thu, 9am-5pm Fri-Sun) rents kayaks on Hwy 1; reservations recommended.

Twelve miles north of Jenner, the salt-weathered structures of **Fort Ross State Historic Park** (☎707-847-3437; www.fortross.org; 19005 Hwy 1; per car $8; ⏲10am-4:30pm Fri-Mon) preserve an 1812 trading post and Russian Orthodox church. It's a quiet place, but the history is riveting: this was once the southernmost reach of Tsarist Russia's North American trading expeditions. The small, wood-scented museum offers historical exhibits and respite from the windswept cliffs.

Several miles further north, **Salt Point State Park** (☎707-847-3221; www.parks.ca.gov; per car $8; ⏲park sunrise-sunset, visitor center 10am-3pm Sat & Sun Apr-Oct) abounds with hiking trails and tide pools and has two **campgrounds** (☎800-444-7275; www.reserveamerica.com; tent & RV sites $25-35; 👪). At neighboring **Kruse Rhododendron State Natural Reserve**, pink blooms spot the misty green woods between April and June. Cows graze the fields on the bluffs heading north to **Sea Ranch** (www.tsra.org), where public-access hiking trails lead downhill from roadside parking lots (per car $7) to pocket beaches.

Two miles north of Point Arena town, detour to wind-battered **Point Arena Lighthouse** (☎877-725-4448, 707-882-2809; www.pointarenalighthouse.com; 45500 Lighthouse Rd; adult/child $7.50/1; ⏲10am-3:30pm, to 4:30pm late May-early Sep), built in 1908. Ascend 145 steps to inspect the flashing Fresnel lens and get jaw-dropping coastal views. Eight miles north of the Little River crossing at Hwy 128 is **Van Damme State Park** (☎707-937-5804; www.parks.ca.gov; 8001 N Hwy 1, Little River; per car $8; ⏲8am-9pm), where the popular 5-mile round-trip **Fern Canyon Trail** passes through a lush river canyon with young redwoods, continuing another mile each way to a pygmy forest. The park's **campground** (☎800-444-7275; www.reserveamerica.com; tent & RV sites $25-35; 📶👪) has coin-op hot showers.

In **Mendocino**, a historical village perched on a gorgeous headland, baby boomers stroll around New England saltbox and water-tower B&Bs, quaint shops and art galleries. Wilder paths pass berry brambles, wildflowers and cypress trees standing guard over rocky cliffs and raging surf at **Mendocino Headlands State Park** (www.parks.ca.gov) FREE. The **Ford House Museum & Visitor Center** (☎707-537-5397;

http://mendoparks.org; 45035 Main St; ⊘11am-4pm) is nearby. Just south of town, paddle your way up the Big River with **Catch a Canoe & Bicycles, Too!** (☑707-937-0273; www.catchacanoe.com; Stanford Inn by the Sea, 44850 Comptche-Ukiah Rd; kayak & canoe rental adult/child from $28/14; ⊘9am-5pm). North of town, 1909 **Point Cabrillo Light Station** (☑707-937-6123; www.pointcabrillo.org; 45300 Lighthouse Rd; ⊘park sunrise-sunset, lighthouse 11am-4pm) **FREE** is a perfect winter whale-watching perch.

🛏 Sleeping

Every other building in Mendocino seems to be a pricey B&B; book ahead. Fort Bragg, just 10 miles north, has cheaper motels.

Gualala Point Regional Park   CAMPGROUND $
(☑707-567-2267; http://parks.sonomacounty.ca.gov; 42401 Hwy 1, Gualala; tent & RV sites $35; ⊡) Shaded by a stand of redwoods and fragrant California bay laurel trees, a short trail connects this creekside campground to the windswept beach. The quality of sites, including several secluded hike-in spots, makes it the best drive-in camping on this part of the coast.

Andiron   CABIN $$
(☑707-937-1543; http://theandiron.com; 6051 N Hwy 1, Little River; most r $109-199; 🛜⊡🖥) 🎣 Styled with hip vintage decor, this cluster of 1950s roadside cottages is a refreshingly playful option amid the cabbage-rose and lace aesthetic of Mendocino. Each cabin houses two rooms with complementing themes: 'Read' has old books, comfy vintage chairs and hip retro eyeglasses, while the adjoining 'Write' features a huge chalkboard and a ribbon typewriter.

Alegria   B&B $$$
(☑707-937-5150; www.oceanfrontmagic.com; 44781 Main St, Mendocino; r $239-299; 🛜) A perfect romantic hideaway, beds have views over the coast, decks have ocean view and all rooms have wood-burning fireplaces; outside a gorgeous path leads to a big, amber-grey beach. Ever-so-friendly innkeepers whip up amazing breakfasts served in the sea-view dining area. Less expensive rooms are available across the street at bright and simple **Raku House** (www.rakuhouse.com; r $159-189).

Mar Vista Cottages   CABIN $$$
(☑707-884-3522, 877-855-3522; www.marvista-mendocino.com; 35101 S Hwy 1, Gualala; cottages $185-305; 🛜⊡🖥) 🎣 The elegantly renovated 1930s fishing cabins offer a simple, stylish seaside escape with a vanguard commitment to sustainability. The harmonious environment is the result of pitch-perfect details: linens are line-dried over lavender, guests browse the organic vegetable garden to harvest their own dinner and chickens cluck around the grounds laying the next morning's breakfast. It often requires two-night stays.

🍴 Eating & Drinking

Even tiny coastal towns usually have a bakery, deli, natural-foods market and a couple of roadside cafes and restaurants.

★Franny's Cup & Saucer   BAKERY $
(www.frannyscupandsaucer.com; 213 Main St, Point Arena; items from $2; ⊘8am-4pm Wed-Sat) The cutest patisserie on this stretch of coast is run by Franny and her mother, Barbara (a veteran of Chez Panisse). The fresh berry tarts and creative housemade chocolates seem too beautiful to eat, until you take the first bite and immediately want to order another. Several times a year they pull out all the stops for a Sunday garden brunch ($25).

Spud Point Crab Company   SEAFOOD $
(www.spudpointcrab.com; 1910 Westshore Rd, Bodega Bay; dishes $4-12; ⊘9am-5pm; ⊡) In the classic tradition of dockside crab shacks, Spud Point serves salty-sweet crab cocktails and *real* clam chowder. Eat at picnic tables overlooking the marina. Take Bay Flat Rd to get here.

Café Aquatica   CAFE $
(☑707-865-2251; 10439 Hwy 1, Jenner; items $3-10; ⊘8am-5pm; 🛜) This is the kind of North Coast coffee shop you've been dreaming of: fresh pastries, fog-lifting organic coffee and chatty locals. The expansive view of the Russian River from the patio and gypsy sea-hut decor make it hard to leave.

Piaci Pub & Pizzeria   ITALIAN $$
(www.piacipizza.com; 120 W Redwood Ave, Fort Bragg; mains $8-18; ⊘11am-9:30pm Mon-Thu, to 10pm Fri & Sat, 4-9:30pm Sun) Fort Bragg's must-visit pizzeria is known for its sophisticated wood-fired, brick-oven pies as much as for its long list of microbrews. Try the 'Gustoso' – with chèvre, pesto and seasonal pears – all carefully orchestrated on a thin crust. It's tiny, loud and fun, with much more of a bar atmosphere than a restaurant. Expect to wait at peak times.

North Coast Brewing Company BREWERY $$
(☎707-964-2739; www.northcoastbrewing.com; 455 N Main St, Fort Bragg; mains $16-25; ⊙restaurant 4-10pm Sun-Thu, to 11pm Fri & Sat, bar from 2pm daily) Though thick, rare slabs of steak and a list of specials demonstrate that this brewery takes the food as seriously as the bevvies, it's burgers and garlic fries that soak up the fantastic selection of handcrafted brews. A great stop for serious beer-lovers.

Café Beaujolais CALIFORNIAN $$$
(☎707-937-5614; www.cafebeaujolais.com; 961 Ukiah St, Mendocino; mains lunch $10-18, dinner $23-38; ⊙11:30am-2:30pm Wed-Sun, dinner from 5:30pm daily) Mendocino's iconic, beloved country-Cal–French restaurant occupies an 1893 house restyled into a monochromatic urban-chic dining room, perfect for holding hands by candlelight. The refined, inspired cooking draws diners from San Francisco, who make this the centerpiece of their trip. The locally sourced menu changes with the seasons, but the Petaluma duck breast served with crispy skin is a gourmand's delight.

Getting There & Around

Mendocino Transit Authority (MTA; ☎707-462-1422; http://mendocinotransit.org; most one-way fares $1.50-6) bus 95 travels daily between Fort Bragg and Santa Rosa ($23, 2½ hours), while MTA bus 65 travels once or twice daily between Santa Rosa and Point Arena ($8.25, three hours) via Hwy 1. From Santa Rosa, catch Golden Gate Transit (p989) bus 101 to San Francisco ($12.50, 2½ hours, every 30 to 60 minutes). On weekdays, MTA bus 60 shuttles four times between Fort Bragg and Mendocino ($1.50, one hour), with two onward connections daily except Sunday to Point Arena ($4.50, 2¼ hours).

Along Highway 101 to Avenue of the Giants

To get into the most remote and wild parts of the North Coast behind the 'Redwood Curtain' on the quick, eschew winding Hwy 1 for inland Hwy 101, which occasionally pauses under the traffic lights of small towns. Diversions along the way include bountiful redwood forests past Leggett and the abandoned wilds of the Lost Coast.

Although **Ukiah** is mostly a place to gas up or grab a bite downtown, it's worth a 30-minute meandering mountain drive west to soak at clothing-optional **Orr Hot Springs** (☎707-462-6277; www.orrhotsprings.org; 13201 Orr Springs Rd; day-use fee adult/child $30/20; ⊙10am-10pm by appointment only).

Just north of tiny **Leggett** on Hwy 101, take a dip in the Eel River at **Standish-Hickey State Recreation Area** (☎707-925-6482; www.parks.ca.gov; 69350 Hwy 101; per car $8;), where hiking trails traipse through virgin and second-growth redwoods. South of **Garberville** on Hwy 101, **Richardson Grove State Park** (☎707-247-3318; www.parks.ca.gov; 1600 Hwy 101, Garberville; per car $8) also protects old-growth redwood forest beside the river. Both parks have developed **campgrounds** (☎800-444-7275; www.reserveamerica.com; tent & RV sites $35-45;).

The **Lost Coast** tempts hikers with the most rugged coastal backpacking in California. It became 'lost' when the state's highway bypassed the mountains of the King Range, which rises over 4000ft within a few miles of the ocean. From Garberville, it's 23 steep, twisting miles along a paved road to **Shelter Cove**, the main supply point but little more than a seaside subdivision with a general store, cafes and none-too-cheap ocean-view lodgings.

Along Hwy 101, 82-sq-mile **Humboldt Redwoods State Park** (☎707-946-2409; www.parks.ca.gov) FREE protects some of California's oldest redwoods, including more than half of the world's tallest 100 trees. Magnificent groves rival those in Redwood National Park, a long drive further north. If you don't have time to hike, at least drive the awe-inspiring **Avenue of the Giants**, a 31-mile, two-lane road parallel to Hwy 101. Book ahead for **campsites** (☎800-444-7275; www.reserveamerica.com; tent & RV sites $20-35;). Get hiking info and maps at the **visitor center** (☎707-946-2263; www.humboldtredwoods.org; ⊙9am-5pm Apr-Oct, 10am-4pm Nov-Mar).

Sleeping & Eating

Campgrounds and RV parks are plentiful along Hwy 101, where every one-horse town guarantees at least a natural-foods store with a deli, a drive-thru espresso stand, a hippie-owned cafe and a handful of motels. Woodsy cabin resorts and aging motels along Avenue of the Giants are mediocre.

Inn of the Lost Coast INN $$
(☎707-986-7521, 888-570-9676; www.innofthelostcoast.com; 205 Wave Dr, Shelter Cove; r $180-300;) Shelter Cove's most family-friendly hotel has clean rooms, some with basic cooking facilities, breathtaking ocean views

and fireplaces. Downstairs there's a serviceable takeout pizza place and coffee shop as well as ping-pong and a hot tub.

Benbow Inn HISTORIC HOTEL **$$$**
(☎707-923-2124; www.benbowinn.com; 445 Lake Benbow Dr, Garberville; d $150-395;) This inn is a monument to 1920s rustic elegance; the Redwood Empire's first luxury resort is a National Historic Landmark. Hollywood's elite once frolicked in the Tudor-style resort's lobby, where you can play chess by the crackling fire, and enjoy complimentary afternoon tea and scones.

Saucy PIZZA **$$**
(☎707-462-7007; http://saucyukiah.com; 108 W Standley St, Ukiah; mains $11-19; 11:30am-9pm Mon-Thu, to 10pm Fri, noon-10pm Sat) Yes there are arty pizzas with toppings like Calabrian love sausage (really), fennel pollen and almond basil pesto but there are also amazing soups, salads, pastas and starters – Nana's meatballs are to die for and the 'kicking' minestrone lives up to its name. The small-town ambience is slightly chic but boistrous at the same time.

Woodrose Café BREAKFAST, AMERICAN **$$**
(www.woodrosecafe.com; 911 Redwood Dr, Garberville; meals $10-18; 8am-2pm;) Garberville's beloved cafe serves organic omelets, veggie scrambles and buckwheat pancakes with *real* maple syrup in a cozy room. Lunch brings crunchy salads, sandwiches with all-natural meats and good burritos. Plenty of gluten-free options.

Getting There & Around

Daily Greyhound buses connect San Francisco with Ukiah ($39, three hours) and Garberville ($53, 5½ hours). **Redwood Transit System** (☎707-443-0826; www.redwoodtransit.org) operates infrequent weekday buses between Garberville and Eureka ($5.50, 1¾ hours), making a few stops along the Avenue of the Giants.

Highwayy 101 from Eureka to Crescent City

Past the strip malls sprawling around its edges, the heart of Eureka is Old Town, abounding with fine Victorians buildings, antique shops and restaurants. Cruise the harbor aboard the blue-and-white 1910 **Madaket** (☎707-445-1910; www.humboldtbaymaritimemuseum.com; narrated cruise adult/child $18/10), departing from the foot of C St; sunset cocktail cruises serve from the state's smallest licensed bar. The **visitor center** (☎707-442-3738; www.eurekachamber.com; 2112 Broadway; 8:30am-5pm Mon-Fri;) is on Hwy 101, south of downtown.

On the north side of Humboldt Bay, **Arcata** is a patchouli-dipped hippie haven of radical politics. Biodiesel-fueled trucks drive in for the weekly **farmers market** (www.humfarm.org; 9am-2pm Sat Apr-Nov) on the central plaza, surrounded by art galleries, shops, cafes and bars. Make reservations to soak at **Finnish Country Sauna & Tubs** (☎707-822-2228; http://cafemokkaarcata.com; 495 J St; 30min per adult/child $9.75/2; noon-11pm Sun-Thu, to 1am Fri & Sat). Northeast of downtown stands eco-conscious, socially responsible **Humboldt State University** (HSU; www.humboldt.edu; 1 Harpst St).

Sixteen miles north of Arcata, **Trinidad** sits on a bluff overlooking a breathtakingly beautiful fishing harbor. Stroll sandy beaches or take short hikes around Trinidad Head after meeting tide-pool critters at the **HSU Telonicher Marine Laboratory** (☎707-826-3671; www.humboldt.edu/marinelab; 570 Ewing St; self-guided tour $1; 9am-4:30pm Mon-Fri, 10am-5pm Sat & Sun mid-Sep–mid-May;). Heading north of town, Patrick's Point Dr is dotted with forested campgrounds, cabins and lodges. **Patrick's Point State Park** (☎707-677-3570; www.parks.ca.gov; 4150 Patrick's Point Dr; per car $8) has stunning rocky headlands, beachcombing, an authentic reproduction of a Yurok village and a **campground** (☎reservations 800-444-7275; www.reserveamerica.com; tent & RV sites $35-45) with coin-op hot showers.

Heading north, Hwy 101 passes Redwood National Park's **Thomas H Kuchel Visitor Center** (☎707-464-6101; www.nps.gov/redw; Hwy 101; 9am-6pm Jun-Aug, to 5pm Sep-Oct & Mar-May, to 4pm Nov-Feb). Together, the national park and three state parks – Prairie Creek, Del Norte and Jedediah Smith – are a World Heritage site containing more than 40% of the world's remaining old-growth redwood forests. The national park is free, while state parks have an $8 day-use parking fee and developed **campgrounds** (☎reservations 800-444-7275; www.reserveamerica.com; tent & RV sites $35).

This patchwork of state and federally managed land stretches all the way north to the Oregon border, interspersed with several towns. Furthest south, you'll encounter **Redwood National Park** (www.nps.gov/redw;) FREE, where a 1-mile nature trail winds through Lady Bird Johnson Grove.

Six miles north of Orick, the 10-mile Newton B Drury Scenic Parkway runs parallel to Hwy 101 through **Prairie Creek Redwoods State Park**. Roosevelt elk graze in the meadow outside the **visitor center** (707-488-2039; www.parks.ca.gov; 9am-5pm May-Sep, off-season hours vary;), where sunlight-dappled hiking trails begin. Three miles back south, mostly unpaved Davison Rd heads northwest to Gold Bluffs Beach, dead-ending at the trailhead for unbelievably lush **Fern Canyon**.

North of tiny Klamath, Hwy 101 passes the **Trees of Mystery** (707-482-2251; www.treesofmystery.net; 15500 Hwy 101, Klamath; adult/child $15/8; 8:30am-6:30pm Jun-Aug, 9:30am-4:30pm Sep-May;), a kitschy roadside attraction. Next up, **Del Norte Coast Redwoods State Park** preserves virgin redwood groves and unspoiled coastline. The 4.5-mile round-trip **Damnation Creek Trail** careens over 1000ft downhill past redwoods to a hidden rocky beach, best visited at low tide. Find the trailhead at a parking turn-out near mile-marker 16 on Hwy 101.

Backed by a fishing harbor and bay, Crescent City is drab because, after more than half the town was destroyed by a tidal wave in 1964, it was rebuilt with utilitarian architecture. When the tide's out, you can walk across to the 1856 **Battery Point Lighthouse** (707-467-3089; www.delnortehistory.org; adult/child $3/1; 10am-4pm daily Apr-Sep, Sat & Sun only Oct-Mar) from the south end of A St.

Beyond Crescent City, **Jedediah Smith Redwoods State Park** is the northernmost park in the system. The redwood stands here are so dense that there are few trails, but a couple of easy hikes start near riverside swimming holes along Hwy 199 and rough, unpaved Howland Hill Rd, a 10-mile scenic drive. The Redwood National & State Parks' **Crescent City Information Center** (707-465-7335; www.nps.gov/redw; 1111 2nd St; 9am-5pm Apr-Oct, to 4pm Nov-Mar) has maps and info.

Sleeping

A mixed bag of budget and midrange motels are scattered along Hwy 101, including in Eureka, Arcata and Crescent City.

Curly Redwood Lodge MOTEL $
(707-464-2137; www.curlyredwoodlodge.com; 701 Hwy 101 S, Crescent City; r $69-100;) The Redwood Lodge is a marvel: it's entirely built and paneled from a single curly redwood tree which measured over 18ft thick in diameter. Progressively restored and polished into a gem of mid-20th-century kitsch, the inn is a delight for retro junkies. Rooms are clean, large and comfortable (request one away from the road). For truly modern accommodations, look elsewhere.

★**Historic Requa Inn** HISTORIC HOTEL $$
(707-482-1425; www.requainn.com; 451 Requa Rd, Klamath; r $119-199;) A woodsy country lodge on bluffs overlooking the mouth of the Klamath, the creaky and bright 1914 Requa Inn is a North Coast favorite and – even better – it's a carbon-neutral facility. Many of the charming old-timey Americana rooms have mesmerizing views over the misty river, as does the dining room, which serves locally sourced, organic New American cuisine.

Carter House Inns B&B $$$
(707-444-8062; http://carterhouse.com; 301 L St, Eureka; r $179-385;) Recently constructed in period style, this hotel is a Victorian lookalike, holding rooms with top-quality linens and modern amenities; suites have in-room Jacuzzis and marble fireplaces. The same owners operate four other sumptuously decorated lodgings: a single-level house, two honeymoon hideaway cottages and a replica of an 1880s San Francisco mansion, which the owner built himself, entirely by hand.

Eating & Drinking

Arcata has the biggest variety of dining options, from organic juice bars and vegan cafes to Californian and world-fusion bistros.

Wildberries Marketplace MARKET, DELI $
(www.wildberries.com; 747 13th St, Arcata; sandwiches $4-10; 7am-midnight;) Wildberries Marketplace is Arcata's best grocery, with natural foods, a good deli, bakery and juice bar.

★**Brick & Fire** CALIFORNIAN $$
(707-268-8959; www.brickandfirebistro.com; 1630 F St, Eureka; dinner mains $14-23; 11:30am-9pm Mon & Wed-Fri, 5-9pm Sat & Sun) Eureka's best restaurant is in an intimate, warm-hued, bohemian-tinged setting that is almost always busy. Choose from thin-crust pizzas, delicious salads (try the pear and blue cheese) and an ever-changing selection of appetizers and mains that highlight local produce and wild mushrooms. There's a weighty wine list and servers are well-versed in pairings.

Lost Coast Brewery BREWERY
(☎707-445-4480; www.lostcoast.com; 617 4th St, Eureka; 11am-10pm Sun-Thu, to 11pm Fri & Sat;) The roster of the regular brews at Eureka's colorful brewery might not knock the socks off a serious beer snob (and can't hold a candle to some of the others on the coast), but highlights include the Downtown Brown Ale, Great White and Lost Coast Pale Ale. After downing a few pints, the fried pub grub starts to look pretty tasty.

Redwood Curtain Brewing Company BREWERY
(www.redwoodcurtainbrewing.com; 550 S G St, Arcata; noon-11pm Sun-Tue, to midnight Wed-Sat) A newer brewery (started in 2010), this tiny gem has a varied collection of rave-worthy craft ales and live music most Thursdays and Saturdays. Plus it offers free wheat thins and goldfish crackers to munch on.

Getting There & Around

Arcata's **Greyhound depot** (☎707-825-8934; 925 E St at 9th St) has daily buses to San Francisco ($57, seven hours) via Eureka, Garberville, Ukiah and Santa Rosa. Several daily Redwood Transit System (p1001) buses stop in Eureka and Arcata on the Hwy 101 (Trinidad–Scotia) route ($3, 2½ hours).

Sacramento

In California's capital city, politicians in SUVs go bumper-to-bumper with farmers driving muddy, half-ton pickups at rush hour. 'Sac' got its start when eccentric Swiss immigrant John Sutter built a fort here in 1839. Once gold was discovered in the nearby Sierra foothills in 1848, the town's population boomed. After much legislative waffling, it became California's state capital in 1854.

Old Sacramento remains a visitor's magnet – a riverside area with raised wooden sidewalks that can feel like a ye olde tourist trap. More interesting food and culture are hidden on the grid of streets downtown and in Midtown, where an arts scene quietly defies the city's reputation as a cow town.

Sights

California State Railroad Museum MUSEUM
(☎916-323-9280; www.csrmf.org; 125 I St; adult/child $10/5; 10am-5pm Fri-Wed, to 8pm Thu;) At Old Sac's north end is this impressive collection of railcars and locomotives from miniature to true scale. While the candy-coated recounting of the struggles of those who laid the track is unsettling, the fully outfitted Pullman sleeper and vintage diner cars will thrill rail fans. Board a restored passenger train (adult/child $12/6) from the Sacramento Southern Railroad ticket office, across the plaza on Front St, for a 40-minute jaunt along the river.

Weather permitting, train rides run hourly from 11am to 4pm on weekends from April to September.

California State Capitol HISTORIC BUILDING
(☎916-324-0333; http://capitolmuseum.ca.gov; 1315 10th St; 8am-5pm Mon-Fri, from 9am Sat & Sun) FREE The gleaming dome of the California State Capitol is Sacramento's most recognizable structure. A painting of Arnold Schwarzenegger in a suit hangs in the West Wing with the other governors' portraits. Some will find **Capitol Park**, the 40 acres of gardens and memorials surrounding the building, more interesting than what's inside. Tours run hourly until 4pm.

California Museum MUSEUM
(☎916-653-0650; www.californiamuseum.org; 1020 O St; adult/child $9/6.50; 10am-5pm Tue-Sat, from noon Sun;) This modern museum is home to the California Hall of Fame and so the only place to simultaneously encounter César Chávez, Mark Zuckerberg and Amelia Earhart. The *California Indians* exhibit is a highlight, with artifacts and oral histories of more than 100 distinct tribes.

Crocker Art Museum MUSEUM
(☎916-808-7000; https://crockerartmuseum.org; 216 O St; adult/child $10/5; 10am-5pm Tue, Wed & Fri-Sun, to 9pm Thu) Housed in the Crocker family's ornate Victorian mansion (and sprawling additions), this museum is stunning as much for its striking architecture (old and new) as its collections. There are some very fine works by both California painters and European masters. The contemporary collection is most enthusiastically presented.

Sleeping

Hotels cater to business travelers, so look for weekend bargains. The freeways and suburbs around the city are glutted with budget and midrange chain lodgings.

HI Sacramento Hostel HOSTEL $
(☎916-443-1691; http://norcalhostels.org/sac; 925 H St; dm $30-33, r with/without bath from $86/58;

check-in 2-10:30pm;) In a grand Victorian mansion, this hostel offers impressive trimmings at rock-bottom prices. It's within walking distance of the capitol, Old Sac and the train station and has a piano in the parlor and large dining room. It attracts an international crowd often open to sharing a ride to San Francisco or Lake Tahoe. Limited parking $5.

★Citizen Hotel BOUTIQUE HOTEL **$$**
(info 916-447-2700, reservations 916-492-4460; www.jdvhotels.com; 926 J St; r from $159;) With an elegant, ultrahip upgrade by the Joie de Vivre group, the long-vacant Citizen has suddenly become one of the coolest stays in these parts. Rooms are sleek, with luxe linen and bold-patterned decor. There's an upscale farm-to-fork restaurant, **Grange Sacramento** (916-492-4450; www.grangesacramento.com; 926 J St; dinner mains $19-39; 6:30-10:30am & 11:30am-2pm Mon-Fri, 8am-2pm Sat & Sun, 5:30pm-10pm Mon-Thu, to 11pm Fri & Sat, to 10pm Sun;), on the ground floor.

Delta King B&B **$$**
(916-444-5464; www.deltaking.com; 1000 Front St; d incl breakfast from $145;) It's a treat to sleep aboard the *Delta King*, a 1927 paddle wheeler docked in Old Sac that lights up like a Christmas tree at night.

Eating & Drinking

For more restaurants and bars, make for Midtown, especially J St east of 16th St.

La Bonne Soupe Cafe DELI **$**
(916-492-9506; 920 8th St; items $5-8; 11am-3pm Mon-Sat) Divine soup and sandwiches assembled with such care that the line of downtown lunchers snakes out the door. If you're in a hurry, skip it. This humble lunch counter is focused on quality that predates drive-through haste.

Mulvaney's B&L MODERN AMERICAN **$$$**
(916-441-6022; www.mulvaneysbl.com; 1215 19th St; mains $32-40; 11:30am-2:30pm Tue-Fri, 5-10pm Tue-Sat) With an obsessive commitment to seasonality, the menu at this swank converted firehouse includes delicate pastas and grilled meats that change every day.

Rubicon Brewing Company BREWERY
(www.rubiconbrewing.com; 2004 Capitol Ave; 11am-11:30pm Mon-Thu, to 12:30am Fri & Sat, to 10pm Sun) These people take their hops *seriously*. Their heady selection is brewed on-site. Monkey Knife Fight Pale Ale is ideal for washing back platters of hot wings.

Getting There & Around

About 11 miles northwest of downtown off I-5, **Sacramento International Airport** (SMF; www.sacramento.aero/smf; 6900 Airport Blvd) is served mainly by domestic flights.

Inconveniently stopping 2 miles northwest of downtown, **Greyhound** (800-231-2222; www.greyhound.com; 420 Richards Blvd) has several daily buses to San Francisco ($20, two to 2½ hours).

From downtown's **train station** (877-974-3322; www.capitolcorridor.org; 401 I St), Amtrak runs frequent Capitol Corridor trains to/from the San Francisco Bay Area ($29, two hours); thrice-daily San Joaquin trains, with onward bus connections to Yosemite Valley ($38, five hours); and daily long-distance Coast Starlight and California Zephyr trains.

Sacramento Regional Transit (RT; 916-321-2877; www.sacrt.com; fare/day pass $2.50/6) runs a bus and light-rail system around town.

Gold Country

Hard to believe, but this is where it all began – these quaint hill towns and drowsy oak-lined byways belie the wild, chaotic, often violent founding of California. After a glint caught James Marshall's eye in Sutter's Creek in 1848, the gold rush brought a 300,000-stong stampede of forty-niners to these Sierra foothills. The frenzy paid little heed to the starched moral decorum of Victorian society, populating lawless boom towns and wreaking environmental havoc.

Traveling here might be a thrill for history buffs – the fading historical markers tell tales of bloodlust and banditry – but more tactile pleasures await anyone willing to plunge into a swimming hole, rattle down a mountain-biking trail or go white-water rafting in the icy currents of local rivers.

Hwy 50 divides the Northern and Southern Mines. Winding Hwy 49, which connects everything, provides plenty of vistas of the famous hills. The **Gold Country Visitors Association** (www.calgold.org) has many more touring ideas.

Getting There & Around

A patchwork of public buses sporadically serves some towns.

For the Northern Mines, several daily **Gold Country Stage** (888-660-7433, 530-477-

0103; www.goldcountrystage.com; fares $1.50-3) buses link Nevada City via Grass Valley with Auburn, an **Amtrak** (800-872-7245; www.amtrak.com; 277 Nevada St) train stop. **Placer County Transit** (530-885-2877; www.placer.ca.gov/transit; fare $1.25) buses connect Auburn with Sacramento hourly.

Among the Southern Mines, weekday-only **Amador Transit** (209-267-9395; http://amadortransit.com; fares $1-3; Mon-Fri) runs twice-daily buses between Sutter Creek and Sacramento, Amador City, Plymouth and Jackson. A few daily **Calaveras Transit** (209-754-4450; http://transit.calaverasgov.us; fare $2) buses serve Jackson, Mokelumne Hill, Angels Camp and Murphys. Weekday-only **Tuolumne County Transit** (209-532-0404; www.tuolumnecountytransit.com; fare $1.50; Mon-Fri) buses and trolleys loop between Sonora, Columbia and Jamestown.

Northern Mines

Known as the 'Queen of the Northern Mines,' the narrow streets of Nevada City gleam with lovingly restored buildings, tiny theaters, art galleries, cafes and shops. The **visitor center** (530-265-2692; www.nevadacitychamber.com; 132 Main St; 9am-5pm Mon-Fri, 11am-4pm Sat, 11am-3pm Sun) dispenses information and self-guided walking-tour maps. On Hwy 49, the **Tahoe National Forest Headquarters** (530-265-4531; www.fs.usda.gov/tahoe; 631 Coyote St; 8am-4:30pm Mon-Fri) provides camping and hiking information and wilderness permits.

Just over a mile east of utilitarian **Grass Valley** and Hwy 49, **Empire Mine State Historic Park** (530-273-8522; www.empiremine.org; 10791 E Empire St; adult/child $7/3; 10am-5pm) marks the site of one of the richest mines in California. From 1850 to 1956 it produced almost 6 million ounces of gold – over $6 billion in today's market.

When it's swelteringly hot outside during summer, if you see a line of cars parked roadside along Hwy 49, that's your signal to discover a swimming hole. One of the best is where the North and Middle Forks of the American River join up at **Auburn State Recreation Area** (530-885-4527; www.parks.ca.gov; per car $10; 7am-sunset). It's just east of **Auburn**, an I-80 pit stop about 25 miles south of Grass Valley.

Coloma is where California's gold rush started. Riverside **Marshall Gold Discovery State Historic Park** (530-622-3470; http://marshallgold.org; per car $8; 8am-5pm, to 7pm late May-early Sep, museum 10am-5pm, to 4pm Nov-Mar;) pays tribute to James Marshall's riot-inducing discovery, with restored buildings and gold-panning opportunities. There's a hilltop monument to Marshall himself, who ironically died a penniless ward of the state.

Sleeping & Eating

Nevada City has the biggest spread of restaurants and historical B&Bs. Motels speckle Hwy 49 in Grass Valley and I-80 in Auburn.

★Outside Inn MOTEL, CABIN $$
(530-265-2233; www.outsideinn.com; 575 E Broad St, Nevada City; d $79-210;) The best option for active explorers, this is an unusually friendly and fun motel, with 12 rooms and three cottages maintained by staff that loves the outdoors and has excellent information about area hiking. Some rooms have a patio overlooking a small creek; all have nice quilts and access to BBQ grills. It's a 10-minute walk from downtown.

Broad Street Inn INN $$
(530-265-2239; www.broadstreetinn.com; 517 W Broad St, Nevada City; r $115-125;) This six-room inn is a favorite because it keeps things simple. (No weird old dolls, no yellowing lace doilies.) The good-value rooms are modern, brightly furnished and elegant.

Ikedas MARKET $
(www.ikedas.com; 13500 Lincoln Way; sandwiches $6-9; 11am-7pm Mon-Thu, 10am-8pm Fri-Sun;) If you're cruising this part of the state without time to explore, the best pit stop is this expanded farm stand off I-80 a few miles north of downtown. Thick, grass-fed beef or tofu burgers, homemade pies and the seasonal fresh peach shake are deliriously good.

★New Moon Café CALIFORNIAN $$$
(530-265-6399; www.thenewmooncafe.com; 203 York St; dinner mains $23-38; 11:30am-2pm Tue-Fri, 5-8:30pm Tue-Sun) Pure elegance, Peter Selaya's organic and local-ingredient menu changes with the seasons. If you visit during spring or summer, go for the line-caught fish or the housemade, moon-shaped fresh ravioli.

Southern Mines

The towns of the Southern Mines – from Placerville to Sonora – receive less traffic and their dusty streets have a whiff of Wild West, today evident in the motley crew of

Harley riders and gold prospectors (still!) who populate them. Some, like **Plymouth** (ol' Pokerville), **Volcano** and **Mokelumne Hill**, are virtual ghost towns, slowly crumbling into photogenic oblivion. Others, like **Sutter Creek**, **Murphys** and **Angels Camp**, are gussied-up showpieces of Victorian Americana. Get off the beaten path at family-run vineyards and subterranean caverns, where geological wonders reward those who first navigate the touristy gift shops above ground.

A short detour off Hwy 49, **Columbia State Historic Park** (☎209-588-9128; www.parks.ca.gov; 11255 Jackson St, Columbia; ⌚museum 10am-5pm Apr-Sep, to 4pm Oct-Mar;) FREE preserves blocks of authentic 1850s buildings complete with shopkeepers and street musicians in period costumes. Also near Sonora, **Railtown 1897 State Historic Park** (☎209-984-3953; www.railtown1897.org; 18115 5th Ave, Jamestown; adult/child $5/3, incl train ride $15/10; ⌚9:30am-4:30pm Apr-Oct, 10am-3pm Nov-Mar, train rides 10:30am-3pm Sat & Sun Apr-Oct;) offers excursion trains through the surrounding hills where Hollywood Westerns including *High Noon* have been filmed.

Sleeping & Eating

Lacy B&Bs, cafes and ice-cream parlors are found in nearly every town. Sonora, about an hour's drive from Yosemite National Park, and Placerville have the most motels.

Indian Grinding Rock State Historic Park CAMPGROUND $

(☎reservations 800-444-7275; www.reserveamerica.com; 148881 Pine Grove-Volcano Rd, Pine Grove; tent & RV sites $30) The beautiful campground at Indian Grinding Rock State Historic Park has fresh water, plumbing and 22 nonreservable sites set among the trees, with tent sites and hookups for RVs.

City Hotel HOTEL $$

(☎info 209-532-1479, reservations 800-444-7275; www.reserveamerica.com; 22768 Main St, Columbia; r $85-115;) Among the handful of restored Victorian hotels in the area, the City Hotel is the most elegant, with rooms that overlook a shady stretch of Main St and that open on lovely sitting rooms. The acclaimed restaurant (mains $15 to $30) is frequented by a Twain impersonator and the adjoining **What Cheer Saloon** is an atmospheric Gold Country joint with oil paintings of lusty ladies and striped wallpaper.

Imperial Hotel B&B $$

(☎209-267-9172; www.imperialamador.com; 14202 Hwy 49, Amador City; r $105-155, ste $125-195;) Built in 1879, it's one of the area's most inventive updates to the typical antique-cluttered hotels, with sleek deco touches accenting the usual gingerbread flourish, a genteel bar and a very good, seasonally minded restaurant (dinner mains $14 to $30). On weekends and holidays, expect a two-night minimum.

Volcano Union Inn HISTORIC HOTEL $$

(☎209-296-7711; www.volcanounion.com; 21375 Consolation St, Volcano; r incl breakfast $119-139;) The preferred of two historic hotels in Volcano, this one has four lovingly updated rooms with crooked floors: two have street-facing balconies. Flat-screen TVs and modern touches are a bit incongruous with the old building, but it's a comfortable place to stay. The on-site **Union Pub** (dinner mains $12 to $28) has a superb menu and will host the occasional fiddler.

Cozmic Café & Pub HEALTH FOOD $

(www.ourcoz.com; 594 Main St; items $4-10; ⌚7am-8pm;) In the historic Placerville Soda Works building, the menu is organic and boasts vegetarian and healthy fare backed by fresh smoothies. There's a good selection of microbrews and live music on weekends, when it stays open late.

Northern Mountains

Remote, empty and eerily beautiful, these are some of California's least visited wild lands, an endless show of geological wonders, clear lakes, rushing rivers and high desert. The major peaks – Lassen, Shasta and the Trinity Alps – have few geological features in common, but all offer backcountry camping under starry skies. Small towns dotting the region aren't attractions themselves, but are handy resupply points for further wilderness adventures.

Redding to Mt Shasta

Much of the drive north of Redding is dominated by **Mt Shasta**, a 14,180ft snowcapped goliath at the southern end of the volcanic Cascades Range. It arises dramatically, fueling the anticipation felt by mountaineers who seek to climb its slopes.

Don't believe the tourist brochures: Redding, the region's largest city, is a snooze. The best reason to detour off I-5 is the **Sundial Bridge**, a glass-bottomed pedestrian marvel designed by Spanish neofuturist architect Santiago Calatrava. It spans the Sacramento River at **Turtle Bay Exploration Park** (800-887-8532; www.turtlebay.org; 844 Sundial Bridge Dr; adult/child $16/12, after 3:30pm $11/7; 9am-5pm Mon-Sat, 10am-5pm Sun, closing 1hr earlier Nov–mid-Mar;), a kid-friendly science and nature center with botanical gardens.

Six miles west of Redding along Hwy 299, explore a genuine gold-rush town at **Shasta State Historic Park** (520-243-8194; www.parks.ca.gov; museum entry adult/child $3/2; 10am-5pm Thu-Sun). Two miles further west, **Whiskeytown National Recreation Area** (530-246-1225; Hwy 299 at JFK Memorial Dr, Whiskeytown; 10am-4pm) harbors **Whiskeytown Lake**, with sandy beaches, waterfall hikes and water-sports and camping opportunities. In sleepy **Weaverville**, another 35 miles further west, **Joss House State Historic Park** (530-623-5284; www.parks.ca.gov; 630 Main St; tour adult/child $4/2; tours hourly 10am-4pm Thu-Sun) preserves an ornate 1874 Chinese immigrant temple.

North of Redding, I-5 crosses deep-blue **Shasta Lake**, California's biggest reservoir, formed by colossal **Shasta Dam** (530-275-4463; www.usbr.gov/mp/ncao/shasta/; 16349 Shasta Dam Blvd; visitor center 8am-5pm, tours 9am-3:30pm) FREE and ringed by houseboat marinas and RV campgrounds. High in the limestone megaliths on the lake's northern side are prehistoric **Lake Shasta Caverns** (530-238-2341; http://lakeshastacaverns.com; 20359 Shasta Caverns Rd, Lakehead; 2hr tour adult/child $24/14; tours every 30min 9am-4pm late May-early Sep, hourly 9am-3pm Apr-late May & early-late Sep, 10am, noon & 2pm Oct-Mar;), where tours include a catamaran ride.

Another 35 miles north on I-5, **Dunsmuir** is a teeny historic railroad town with vibrant art galleries inhabiting a quaint downtown district. Six miles south off I-5, **Castle Crags State Park** (530-235-2684; www.parks.ca.gov; per car $8; sunrise-sunset) shelters forested **campsites** (reservations 800-444-7275; www.reserveamerica.com; tent & RV sites $15-30). Be awed by stunning views of Mt Shasta from the top of the park's hardy 5.6-mile round-trip **Crags Trail**.

Nine miles north of Dunsmuir, **Mt Shasta city** lures climbers, new-age hippies and back-to-nature types, all of whom revere the majestic mountain looming overhead. Usually open and snow free beyond Bunny Flat from June until October, **Everitt Memorial Hwy** ascends the mountain to a perfect sunset-watching perch at almost 8000ft – simply head east from town on Lake St and keep going. For experienced mountaineers, climbing the peak above 10,000ft requires a Summit Pass ($20), available from **Mt Shasta Ranger Station** (530-926-4511; www.fs.usda.gov/stnf; 204 W Alma St; 8am-4:30pm Mon-Fri), which has weather reports and sells topgraphic maps. Stop by downtown's **Fifth Season** (530-926-3606; http://thefifthseason.com; 300 N Mt Shasta Blvd; 9am-6pm Mon-Fri, from 8am Sat, 10am-5pm Sun) outdoor-gear shop for equipment rentals. **Shasta Mountain Guides** (530-926-3117; http://shastaguides.com) offers mountaineering trips (from $550).

Sleeping

Roadside motels are abundant, including in Mt Shasta city. Redding has the most chain lodgings, clustered near major highways. Campgrounds are abundant, especially on public lands.

★ McCloud River Mercantile Hotel INN $$
(530-964-2330; www.mccloudmercantile.com; 241 Main St, McCloud; r $129-250;) Stoll upstairs to the 2nd floor of McCloud's central Mercantile and try not to fall in love; it's all high ceilings, exposed brick and a perfect marriage of preservationist class and modern panache. The rooms with antique furnishings are situated within open floor plans.

Shasta MountInn B&B $$
(530-926-1810; www.shastamountinn.com; 203 Birch St, Mt Shasta city; r $150-175;) Only antique on the outside, this bright Victorian 1904 farmhouse is all relaxed minimalism, bold colors and graceful decor on the inside. Each airy room has a great bed and exquisite views of the luminous mountain. Enjoy the expansive garden, wraparound deck, outdoor hot tub and sauna. Not relaxed enough yet? Chill on the perfectly placed porch swings.

Railroad Park Resort INN, CAMPGROUND $$
(530-235-4440; www.rrpark.com; 100 Railroad Park Rd, Dunsmuir; tent/RV sites from $29/37, d $135-165;) About 2 miles south

of town, off I-5, visitors can spend the night inside refitted vintage railroad cars and cabooses. The grounds are fun for kids, who can run around the engines and plunge in a centrally situated pool. The deluxe boxcars are furnished with antiques and claw-foot tubs, although the cabooses are simpler and a bit less expensive.

Eating & Drinking

Dunsmuir Brewery Works PUB FOOD $

(530-235-1900; www.dunsmuirbreweryworks.com; 5701 Dunsmuir Ave, Dunsmuir; mains $10-15; 11am-9pm Tue-Sun;) It's hard to describe this little microbrew pub without veering into hyperbole. Start with the beer: the crisp ales and porter are perfectly balanced and the IPA is apparently pretty good too, because patrons are always drinking it dry. Soak it up with awesome bar food; a warm potato salad, bratwurst or a thick Angus burger.

Yaks AMERICAN $

(www.yaks.com; 4917 Dunsmuir Ave, Dunsmuir; mains $8-18; 11am-9pm Mon-Sat, to 8pm Sun;) Hiding under the Hitching Post sign just off I-5, this is where you come to blow your diet. Breakfast means Cuban peppersteak hash or perhaps home-baked cinnamon roll French toast with choice of house syrups like Baileys-and-bourbon. Lunch offers a huge range of burgers (try the one with the house-roasted coffee rub). There's also a takeout counter.

Berryvale Grocery MARKET, DELI $

(www.berryvale.com; 305 S Mt Shasta Blvd, Mt Shasta city; items $4-11; store 8am-8pm, cafe to 7pm;) This market sells groceries and organic produce to health-conscious eaters. The excellent cafe serves good coffee and an array of tasty – mostly veggie – salads, sandwiches and wraps.

★ **Café Maddalena** EUROPEAN, NORTH AFRICAN $$$

(530-235-2725; www.cafemaddalena.com; 5801 Sacramento Ave, Dunsmuir; mains $15-26; 5-9pm Thu-Sun Feb-Dec) Simple and elegant, this cafe put Dunsmuir on the foodie map. The menu was designed by chef Bret LaMott (of Trinity Cafe fame) and changes weekly to feature dishes from southern Europe and northern Africa. Some highlights include pan-roasted king salmon with basil cream, or sauteed rabbit with carrots and morel sauce.

Getting There & Around

Amtrak's Coast Starlight trains inconveniently stop in Redding and Dunsmuir in the dead of night. Thrice-daily **Greyhound** (800-231-2222; www.greyhound.com) buses connect Weed, 10 miles north of Mt Shasta via I-5, with Redding ($27, 80 minutes) and Sacramento ($63, 4½ to 5½ hours). **STAGE** (530-842-8295; www.co.siskiyou.ca.us; fares $1.75-6) buses travel the I-5 corridor a few times daily, linking Weed, Mt Shasta city, McCloud and Dunsmuir.

Northeast Corner

Site of California's last major Native American conflict and a half-million years of volcanic destruction, **Lava Beds National Monument** (530-667-8113; www.nps.gov/labe; 7-day entry per car $15) is a peaceful monument to centuries of turmoil. This park's got it all: lava flows, cinder and spatter cones, volcanic craters and amazing lava tubes. It was the site of the Modoc War, and ancient Native American petroglyphs are etched into rocks and pictographs painted on cave walls. Pick up info and maps at the **visitor center** (530-667-8113; www.nps.gov/labe; Tulelake; 8am-6pm late May-early Sep, to 5pm mid-Sep–mid-May), which sells basic spelunking gear (borrow flashlights for free). Nearby is the park's basic **campground** (tent & RV sites $10;), where drinking water is available. Over 20 miles northeast of the park, the dusty town of Tulelake off Hwy 139 has basic motels, roadside diners and gas.

Comprising six separate refuges in California and Oregon, **Klamath Basin National Wildlife Refuge Complex** is a prime stopover on the Pacific Flyway and an important wintering site for bald eagles. When the spring and fall migrations peak, more than a million birds can fill the sky. The **visitor center** (530-667-2231; http://klamathbasinrefuges.fws.gov; 4009 Hill Rd, Tulelake; 8am-4:30pm Mon-Fri, 9am-4pm Sat & Sun) FREE is off Hwy 161, about 4 miles south of the Oregon border. Self-guided 10-mile auto tours of the Lower Klamath and Tule Lake refuges provide excellent birding opportunities. Paddle the Upper Klamath refuge's 9.5-mile canoe trail by launching from **Rocky Point Resort** (541-356-2287; www.rockypointoregon.com; 28121 Rocky Point Rd, Klamath Falls, OR; canoe & kayak rental per hr/half-day/day $20/45/60). For gas, food and lodging, drive into Klamath Falls, OR, off Hwy 97.

Quietly impressive **Lassen Volcanic National Park** (☎530-595-4480; www.nps.gov/lavo; 7-day entry per car $20) has hydrothermal sulfur pools, boiling mud pots and steaming pools, as glimpsed from the **Bumpass Hell** boardwalk. Tackle **Lassen Peak** (10,457ft), the world's largest plug-dome volcano, on a strenuous, but nontechnical 5-mile round-trip trail. The park has two entrances: an hour's drive east of Redding off Hwy 44, near popular **Manzanita Lake Campground** (☎reservations 877-444-6777; www.recreation.gov; tent & RV sites $15-24, cabins $69-95;); and a 40-minute drive northwest of Lake Almanor off Hwy 89, by the **Kohm Yah-ma-nee Visitor Center** (☎530-595-4480; www.nps.gov/lavo; 9am-5pm, closed Mon & Tue Nov-Mar;) . Hwy 89 through the park is typically snow free and open to cars from June though October.

SIERRA NEVADA

The mighty Sierra Nevada – baptized the 'Range of Light' by poet-naturalist John Muir – is California's backbone. This 400-mile phalanx of craggy peaks, chiseled and gouged by glaciers and erosion, both welcomes and challenges outdoor-sports enthusiasts. Cradling three national parks (Yosemite, Sequoia and Kings Canyon), the Sierra is a spellbinding wonderland of superlative wilderness, boasting the contiguous USA's highest peak (Mt Whitney), North America's tallest waterfall (Yosemite Falls) and the world's oldest and biggest trees (ancient bristlecone pines and giant sequoias, respectively).

Yosemite National Park

There's a reason why everybody's heard of it: the granite-peak heights are dizzying, the mist from thunderous waterfalls drenching, the Technicolor wildflower meadows amazing and the majestic silhouettes of El Capitan and Half Dome almost shocking against a crisp blue sky. It's a landscape of dreams, surrounding oh-so-small people on all sides.

Then, alas, the hiss and belch of another tour bus, disgorging dozens, rudely breaks the spell. While staggering crowds can't be ignored, these rules will shake most of 'em:

- Avoid summer in the valley. Spring's best, especially when waterfalls gush in May. Autumn is blissfully peaceful, and snowy winter days can be magical too.
- Park your car and leave it – by hiking a short distance up almost any trail, you'll lose car-dependent hordes.
- Forget jet lag. Get up for sunrise, or go for moonlit hikes with stargazing.

Sights

The main entrances to the **park** (☎209-372-0200; www.nps.gov/yose; 7-day entry per car $30) are at Arch Rock (Hwy 140), Wawona (Hwy 41) and Big Oak Flat (Hwy 120 west). Tioga Pass (Hwy 120 east) is open only seasonally.

Yosemite Valley

From the ground up, this dramatic valley cut by the meandering Merced River is song-inspiring: rippling green meadow-grass; stately pines; cool, impassive pools reflecting looming granite monoliths; and cascading ribbons of glacially cold white water. Often overrun and traffic-choked, **Yosemite Village** is home to the park's main visitor center (p1012), **museum** (9am-5pm summer, 10am-4pm winter, often closed noon-1pm) FREE, photography gallery, movie theater, general store and many more services. **Curry Village** is another valley hub, offering public showers and outdoor-equipment rental and sales, including camping gear.

Spring snowmelt turns the valley's famous waterfalls into thunderous cataracts; most are reduced to a mere trickle by late summer. **Yosemite Falls** is North America's tallest, dropping 2425ft in three tiers. A wheelchair-accessible trail leads to the bottom of this cascade or, for solitude and different perspectives, you can trek the grueling trail to the top (6.8 miles round-trip). No less impressive are other waterfalls around the valley. A strenuous granite staircase beside **Vernal Fall** leads you, gasping, right to the waterfall's edge for a vertical view – look for rainbows in the clouds of mist.

You can't ignore the valley's monumental **El Capitan** (7569ft), an El Dorado for rock climbers. Toothed **Half Dome** (8842ft) soars above the valley as Yosemite's spiritual centerpiece. The classic panoramic photo op is at **Tunnel View** on Hwy 41 as you drive into the valley.

Glacier Point

Rising over 3000ft above the valley floor, dramatic Glacier Point (7214ft) practically puts you at eye level with Half Dome. It's at least an hour's drive from Yosemite Valley up Glacier Point Rd (usually open from May into November) off Hwy 41, or a strenuous hike along the **Four Mile Trail** (actually, 4.6 miles one way) or the less-crowded, waterfall-strewn **Panorama Trail** (8.5 miles one way). To hike one way downhill from Glacier Point, reserve a seat on the hikers' shuttle bus (adult/child $25/15).

Wawona

At Wawona, an hour's drive south of Yosemite Valley, drop by the **Pioneer Yosemite History Center** (rides adult/child $5/4; 24hr, rides Wed-Sun Jun-Sep;) FREE, with its covered bridge, historic buildings and horse-drawn stagecoach rides. Further south stands towering **Mariposa Grove**, home of the Grizzly Giant and other giant sequoia trees. Free shuttle buses usually run to the grove from spring through fall. Note that the grove is closed to visitors for restoration until spring 2017.

Tuolumne Meadows

A 90-minute drive from Yosemite Valley, high-altitude Tuolumne Meadows (pronounced *twol*-uh-mee) draws hikers, backpackers and climbers to the park's northern wilderness. The Sierra Nevada's largest subalpine meadow (8600ft), it's a vivid contrast to the valley, with wildflower fields, azure lakes, ragged granite peaks, polished domes and cooler temperatures. Hikers and climbers have a paradise of options; lake swimming and picnicking are also popular. Access is via scenic Tioga Rd (Hwy 120), which is only open seasonally. West of Tuolumne Meadows and **Tenaya Lake**, stop at **Olmsted Point** for epic vistas of Half Dome.

Hetch Hetchy

A 40-mile drive northwest of Yosemite Valley, it's the site of perhaps the most controversial dam in US history. Despite not existing in its natural state, Hetch Hetchy Valley remains pretty and mostly crowd free. A 5.4-mile round-trip hike across the dam and through a tunnel to the base of **Wapama Falls** lets you get thrillingly close to an avalanche of water crashing down into the sparkling reservoir.

Activities

With more than 800 miles of varied hiking trails, you're spoiled for choice. Easy valley-floor routes can get jammed; escape the teeming masses by heading up. The ultimate hike summits **Half Dome** (14 to 16 miles round-trip), but be warned: it's very strenuous, and advance lottery permits (from $12.50) are required even for day hikes. Without a permit, it's rewarding to hike as far as the top of Vernal Fall (2.4 miles round-trip) or Nevada Fall (5.4 miles round-trip) via the **Mist Trail**.

CAMPING IN YOSEMITE

From mid-March through mid-October or November, many park campgrounds accept or require **reservations** (518-885-3639, 877-444-6777; www.recreation.gov), which are available starting five months in advance. Campsites routinely sell out online within *minutes*. All campgrounds have bear-proof lockers and campfire rings; most have potable water.

In summer most campgrounds are noisy and booked to bulging, especially **North Pines** (tent & RV sites $26; Apr-Oct;), **Lower Pines** (tent & RV sites $26; Apr-Oct;) and **Upper Pines** (tent & RV sites $26; year-round;) in Yosemite Valley; **Tuolumne Meadows** (tent & RV sites $26; Jul-Sep;) off Tioga Rd; and riverside **Wawona** (tent & RV sites $18-26; year-round;).

Year-round the following are all first-come, first served: **Camp 4** (shared tent sites per person $6; year-round), a rock climber's hangout in the valley; **Bridalveil Creek** (tent & RV sites $18; Jul-early Sep;), off Glacier Point Rd; and **White Wolf** (tent & RV sites $18; Jul-early Sep;), off Tioga Rd. They often fill before noon, especially on weekends.

Looking for a quieter, more rugged experience? Try the primitive campgrounds (no potable water) off Tioga Rd at **Tamarack Flat** (tent sites $12; late Jun-Sep;), **Yosemite Creek** (tent sites $12; Jul-early Sep;) and **Porcupine Flat** (tent & RV sites $12; Jul–mid-Oct;), all first-come, first-served.

For overnight backpacking trips, wilderness permits (from $10) are required year-round. A quota system limits the number of hikers leaving daily from each trailhead. Make reservations up to 26 weeks in advance, or try your luck at the **Yosemite Valley Wilderness Center** (☑209-372-0745; Yosemite Village; ⊙8am-5pm May-Sep) or another permit-issuing station, starting at 11am on the day before you aim to hike.

Yosemite
Mountaineering School　　　ROCK CLIMBING
(☑209-372-8344; Curry Village; ⊙Apr-Oct) Offers topflight instruction for novice to advanced climbers, plus guided climbs and equipment rental.

🛏 Sleeping & Eating

Concessionaire **DNC** (☑801-559-4884; www.yosemitepark.com) has a monopoly on park lodging and eating establishments, including fast-food courts and snack bars. Lodging reservations (up to 366 days in advance) are essential for peak season (May to September). During summer, DNC sets up simple canvas-tent cabins at riverside **Housekeeping Camp** (q $106; ⊙Apr-Oct) in Yosemite Valley and at busy **Tuolumne Meadows Lodge** (tent cabins $123; ⊙mid-Jun–mid-Sep) and quieter **White Wolf Lodge** (tent cabins $126, cabins with bath $158; ⊙Jul–mid-Sep) off Tioga Rd.

Curry Village　　　CABIN $$
(tent cabins $121-126, cabins $193, without bath $146; 🛜🏊) Founded in 1899 as a summer camp, Curry has hundreds of units squished tightly together beneath towering evergreens. The canvas cabins are basically glorified tents, so for more comfort, quiet and privacy get one of the cozy wood cabins, which have bedspreads, drapes and vintage posters. There are also 18 attractive motel-style rooms in the **Stoneman House** (r $202), including a loft suite sleeping up to six.

Wawona Hotel　　　HISTORIC HOTEL $$
(r $226, without bath $155; ⊙mid-Mar–Dec; 🛜🏊) This National Historic Landmark, dating from 1879, is a collection of six graceful, whitewashed New England–style buildings flanked by wide porches. The 104 rooms – with no phone or TV – come with Victorian-style furniture and other period items, and about half the rooms share bathrooms, with nice robes provided for the walk there.

ⓘ IMPASSABLE TIOGA PASS

Hwy 120 is the only road connecting Yosemite National Park with the Eastern Sierra, climbing through Tioga Pass (9945ft). Most maps mark this road 'closed in winter,' which, while literally true, is also misleading. Tioga Rd is usually closed from the first heavy snowfall in October or November, not reopening until May or June. Call ☑209-372-0200 or check www.nps.gov/yose/planyourvisit/conditions.htm for current road conditions.

⭐**Ahwahnee Hotel**　　　HISTORIC HOTEL $$$
(r from $458; @🛜🏊) The crème de la crème of Yosemite's lodging, this sumptuous historic property dazzles with soaring ceilings, Turkish kilims lining the hallways and atmospheric lounges with mammoth stone fireplaces. It's the gold standard for upscale lodges, though if you're not blessed with bullion, you can still soak up the ambience during afternoon tea, a drink in the bar or a gourmet meal.

Yosemite Lodge at the Falls　　　MOTEL $$$
(r from $235; @🛜🏊) 🅿 Situated a short walk from Yosemite Falls, this multibuilding complex contains a wide range of eateries, a lively bar, big pool and other handy amenities. Delightful rooms, thanks to a recent eco-conscious renovation, now feel properly lodge-like, with rustic wooden furniture and striking nature photography. All have cable TV, telephone, fridge and coffeemaker, and great patio or balcony panoramas.

Degnan's Loft　　　PIZZA $
(Yosemite Village; mains $8-12.50; ⊙11am-9pm late May-Sep; 🖉🍴) Head upstairs to this convivial place with high-beamed ceilings and a many-sided fireplace, and kick back under the dangling lift chair for decent salads, lasagna and pizza.

⭐**Mountain Room Restaurant** AMERICAN $$$
(☑209-372-1403; Yosemite Lodge; mains $17-36; ⊙5:30-9:30pm; 🖉🍴) 🅿 With killer views of Yosemite Falls, the window tables at this casual and elegant contemporary steakhouse are a hot commodity. The chefs whip up the best meals in the park, with flat-iron steak and locally caught mountain trout wooing diners under a rotating display of nature photographs. Reservations are

DON'T MISS

SUPERSIZED FORESTS

In California you can stand under the world's oldest trees (ancient bristlecone pines) and its tallest (coast redwoods), but the record for biggest in terms of volume belongs to giant sequoias *(Sequoiadendron giganteum)*. They grow only on the western slope of the Sierra Nevada range and are most abundant in Sequoia, Kings Canyon and Yosemite National Parks. John Muir called them 'Nature's forest masterpiece,' and anyone who's ever craned their neck to take in their soaring vastness has probably done so with the same awe. These trees can grow to almost 275ft tall and 100ft in circumference, protected by bark up to 2ft thick. The Giant Forest Museum in Sequoia National Park has exhibits about the trees' unusual ecology.

accepted only for groups larger than eight; casual dress OK.

Outside Yosemite National Park

Gateway towns that have a mixed bag of motels, hotels, lodges and B&Bs include Fish Camp, Oakhurst, El Portal, Midpines, Mariposa, Groveland and, in the Eastern Sierra, Lee Vining.

★**Yosemite Bug Rustic Mountain Resort** HOSTEL, CABIN $
(209-966-6666, 866-826-7108; www.yosemitebug.com; 6979 Hwy 140, Midpines; dm $30, tent cabins $45-75, r with/without bath from $150/75;) The highlight of the almost nonexistent town of Midpines is this folksy oasis, tucked away on a forested hillside about 25 miles from Yosemite. It's more like a convivial mountain retreat than a hostel: at night, friendly folks of all ages and backgrounds share stories, music and delicious freshly prepared meals and beer and wine in the woodsy cafe before retreating to their beds.

★**Evergreen Lodge** CABIN, CAMPGROUND $$$
(209-379-2606; www.evergreenlodge.com; 33160 Evergreen Rd; tents $90-125, cabins $180-415;) Outside the park near the entrance to Hetch Hetchy, this classic 90-year-old resort consists of a series of lovingly decorated and comfy cabins (each with its own cache of board games) spread out among the trees. Accommodations run from rustic to deluxe, and all cabins have private porches without distracting phone or TV. Roughing-it guests can cheat with comfy, prefurnished tents.

The place has just about everything you could ask for, including a tavern (complete with pool table), a general store, a fantastic restaurant serving all meals, live music, horseshoes, ping-pong, a giant outdoor chess set, a kids' zip line and all sorts of guided hikes and outdoor activities – many of them family-oriented. Seasonal equipment rentals are also available.

Information

Yosemite Village, Curry Village and Wawona stores all have ATMs. Drivers should fill up before entering the park. High-priced gas is sold at Wawona and Crane Flat year-round and at Tuolumne Meadows in summer. Cell-phone service is spotty throughout the park. Check the free park newspaper for wi-fi hot spots and pay-as-you-go internet terminals.

Yosemite Medical Clinic (209-372-4637; 9000 Ahwahnee Dr, Yosemite Village; 9am-7pm daily late May-late Sep, 9am-5pm Mon-Fri late Sep-late May) Twenty-four-hour emergency service available.

Yosemite Valley Visitor Center (209-372-0200; Yosemite Village; 9am-5pm) The main office, with exhibits and free film screenings in the theater.

Getting There & Around

From the Greyhound and Amtrak stations in Merced, **Yosemite Area Regional Transportation System** (YARTS; 877-989-2787; www.yarts.com) buses travel year-round to Yosemite Valley via Hwy 140, stopping at towns along the way. In summer YARTS buses run from Yosemite Valley to Mammoth Lakes via Tuolumne Meadows along Hwys 120 and 395. One-way fares (including park entry fee) are $13 from Merced, $18 from Mammoth Lakes.

Free shuttle buses loop around Yosemite Valley year-round and, in summer, the Tuolumne Meadows/Tioga Rd area. Bicycle rentals (per hour/day $12/34) are available seasonally at Curry Village and Yosemite Lodge at the Falls, both in the valley.

In winter highways to the park are kept open (except Tioga Rd/Hwy 120), although snow chains may be required at any time; Glacier Point Rd remains open only as far as Badger Pass ski area, with free shuttle service from the valley.

Sequoia & Kings Canyon National Parks

In these neighboring parks, giant sequoia trees are bigger – up to 27 stories high! – and more numerous than anywhere else in the Sierra Nevada. Tough and fire-charred, they'd easily swallow two freeway lanes each. Giant, too, are the mountains – including Mt Whitney (14,505ft), the tallest peak in the lower 48 states. Finally, there is the deep Kings Canyon, carved out of granite by ancient glaciers and a powerful river. For quiet, solitude and close-up sightings of wildlife, including black bears, hit the trails and lose yourself in wilderness.

Sights

Sequoia was designated a national park in 1890; Kings Canyon, in 1940. Though distinct, these **parks** (☎559-565-3341; www.nps.gov/seki; 7-day entry per car $20) operate as one unit with a single admission fee. From the south, Hwy 198 enters Sequoia National Park beyond the town of Three Rivers at Ash Mountain, then ascends the zigzagging Generals Hwy to Giant Forest. From the west, Hwy 180 enters Kings Canyon National Park near Grant Grove, then plunges down into the canyon all the way to Cedar Grove.

Sequoia National Park

We dare you to try hugging the trees in **Giant Forest**, a 3-sq-mile grove protecting gargantuan specimens – the world's largest is the **General Sherman Tree**. With sore arms and sticky sap fingers, lose the crowds on a network of forested hiking trails (bring a map).

Worth a detour is **Mineral King Valley**, a late-19th-century mining and logging camp ringed by craggy peaks and alpine lakes. The 25-mile one-way scenic drive – navigating almost 700 hair-raising hairpin turns – is usually open from late May until late October.

Giant Forest Museum MUSEUM
(☎559-565-4480; Generals Hwy, at Crescent Meadow Rd; 9am-4:30pm;) FREE For a primer on the intriguing ecology and history of giant sequoias, this pint-sized modern museum will entertain both kids and adults. Hands-on exhibits teach about the life stages of these big trees, which can live for over 3000 years, and the fire cycle that releases their seeds and allows them to sprout on bare soil. The museum itself is housed in a 1920s historic building designed by Gilbert Stanley Underwood, famed architect of Yosemite's Ahwahnee Hotel.

Crystal Cave CAVE
(☎559-565-3759; www.explorecrystalcave.com; Crystal Cave Rd, off Generals Hwy; tours adult/child/youth from $16/5/8; May-Nov;) Discovered in 1918, the cave has marble formations estimated to be 10,000 years old. First-come, first-served tickets for the 50-minute introductory tour are only available in person at the Lodgepole and Foothills visitor centers, *not* at the cave. Bring a jacket.

Kings Canyon National Park & Scenic Byway

Just north of Grant Grove Village, **General Grant Grove** brims with majestic giants. Beyond, Hwy 180 begins its 30-mile descent into **Kings Canyon**, serpentining past chiseled rock walls laced with waterfalls. The road meets the Kings River, its roar ricocheting off granite cliffs soaring over 8000ft high, making this one of North America's deepest canyons.

At the bottom of the canyon, **Cedar Grove** is the last outpost before the rugged grandeur of the Sierra Nevada backcountry begins. A popular day hike climbs 4.6 miles one way to gushing **Mist Falls** from Roads End. A favorite of birders, an easy 1.5-mile nature trail loops around **Zumwalt Meadow**, just west of Roads End. Watch for lumbering black bears and springy mule deer.

The scenic byway past Hume Lake to Cedar Grove Village is usually closed from mid-November to late April.

Boyden Cavern CAVE
(☎888-956-8243; www.caverntours.com/BoydenRt.htm; Hwy 180; tours adult/child from $14.50/8.75; late Apr-Sep;) While the rooms are smaller and the interiors less eye-popping than Crystal Cave in Sequoia National Park, touring the beautiful and fantastical formations here requires no advance tickets. Just show up for the basic 45-minute tour, which departs hourly from 10am to 5pm during peak summer season. Reaching the cave entrance requires a short walk up a steep, paved grade.

Activities

Hiking is why people come here – with over 800 miles of marked trails to prove it. Cedar Grove and Mineral King offer the best backcountry access. Trails at higher elevations usually start opening by early summer. Overnight backcountry trips require wilderness permits (per trip $15), subject to a quota system from late May to late September; reserve well in advance for popular routes.

In summer cool off by swimming in **Hume Lake**, on national forest land off Hwy 180, and at riverside swimming holes in both parks. In winter you can cross-country ski or snowshoe among giant sequoias; equipment rental is available at Grant Grove Village and Wuksachi Lodge.

Sleeping & Eating

Camping reservations (p1167) are accepted only from late spring through early fall at Lodgepole, Potwisha and Buckeye Flat Campgrounds (tent and RV sites $22) in Sequoia National Park. The parks' 10 other developed campgrounds (tent and RV sites $10 to $20) are first-come, first-served. Potwisha, Azalea and remote South Fork are open year-round. Overflow camping is available on surrounding national-forest land.

The markets at Lodgepole, Grant Grove and Cedar Grove have limited groceries. Lodgepole and Cedar Grove snack bars serve basic, budget-friendly meals. Grant Grove has a simple restaurant and espresso cart.

Outside Sequoia's southern entrance, mostly well-worn cabins and chain motels, as well as down-home eateries, line Hwy 198 through Three Rivers town.

Wuksachi Lodge LODGE $$
(☎559-565-4070, 866-807-3598; www.visitsequoia.com; 64740 Wuksachi Way, off Generals Hwy; r $185-290;) Built in 1999, Wuksachi Lodge is the park's most upscale lodging and dining option. But don't get too excited – the wood-paneled atrium lobby has an inviting stone fireplace and forest views, but charmless motel-style rooms with coffee makers, minifridges, oak furniture and thin walls have an institutional feel. The lodge's location near Lodgepole Village, however, can't be beat.

John Muir Lodge LODGE $$
(☎559-335-5500, 866-807-3598; www.visitsequoia.com; off Hwy 180, Grant Grove Village; r from $170;) An atmospheric wooden building hung with historical black-and-white photographs, this year-round hotel is a place to lay your head and still feel like you're in the forest. Wide porches have wooden rocking chairs, and homespun rooms contain rough-hewn wood furniture and patchwork bedspreads. Cozy up to the big stone fireplace on chilly nights with a board game.

Cedar Grove Lodge LODGE $$
(☎559-565-3096, 866-807-3598; www.visitsequoia.com; Hwy 180, Cedar Grove Village; r from $130; ⊙early May–mid-Oct;) The only indoor sleeping option in the canyon, the riverside lodge offers 21 unexciting motel-style rooms. A recent remodel has dispelled some of the frumpy decor. Three ground-floor rooms with shady furnished patios have spiffy river views and kitchenettes. All rooms have phones and TVs.

Information

Lodgepole Village and Grant Grove Village are the parks' main commerical hubs. Both have visitor centers, post offices, markets, ATMs, a coin-op laundry and public showers (summer only).

The following visitor centres are open year-round:

Foothills Visitor Center (☎559-565-4212; 47050 Generals Hwy; ⊙8am-4:30pm) At Ash Mountain.

Lodgepole Visitor Center (☎559-565-4436; off Generals Hwy, Lodgepole Village; ⊙8am-5pm early May-early Oct, 7am-7pm peak season) Near Giant Forest.

Kings Canyon Visitor Center (☎559-565-4307; Hwy 180, Grant Grove Village; ⊙8am-noon & 1-5pm late May-early Sep, shorter off-season hours) In Grant Grove.

The following open seasonally:

Cedar Grove Visitor Center (☎559-565-3793; Hwy 180, Cedar Grove Village; ⊙9am-5pm late May-late Sep) In Kings Canyon.

Mineral King Ranger Station (☎559-565-3768; Mineral King Rd; ⊙8am-4pm late May-late Sep)

Check the free park newspaper for other visitor services, including wi-fi hot spots.

Expensive gas is available at Hume Lake (year-round) and Stony Creek (closed in winter) outside the parks on national-forest land.

Getting There & Around

From late May to early September, free shuttle buses loop around the Giant Forest, Lodgepole/Wuksachi and Foothills areas of Sequoia and also Grant Grove in Kings Canyon. **Sequoia**

Shuttle (☎877-287-4453; www.sequoiashuttle.com; round-trip incl park entry $15; ⌚late May-late Sep) links the Giant Forest to Three Rivers and Visalia (for onward connections to Amtrak), while Big Trees Transit (☎800-325-7433; www.bigtreestransit.com; round-trip incl park entry fee $15; ⌚late May-early Sep) connects Grant Grove with Fresno's airport and Amtrak and Greyhound stations; round-trip fares include the park entry fee (reservations required).

Eastern Sierra

Vast, empty and majestic, here jagged peaks plummet down into the desert, a dramatic juxtaposition that creates a potent scenery cocktail. Hwy 395 runs the entire length of the eastern side of the Sierra Nevada, with turnoffs leading to pine forests, wildflower-strewn meadows, placid lakes, hot springs and glacier-gouged canyons. Hikers, backpackers, mountain bikers, fishers and skiers all find escapes here.

At Bodie State Historic Park (☎760-647-6445; www.parks.ca.gov/bodie; Rte 270; adult/child $5/3; ⌚9am-6pm mid-May–Oct, to 4pm Nov–mid-May), the weathered buildings of a gold-rush boomtown sit frozen in time on a dusty, windswept plain. To get there, head east for 13 miles (the last three unpaved) on Hwy 270, about 7 miles south of Bridgeport. Snow usually closes the access road in winter and early spring.

Further south at Mono Lake (www.monolake.org), unearthly tufa towers rise from the alkaline water like drip sand castles. Off Hwy 395, Mono Basin Scenic Area Visitor Center (☎760-647-3044; www.fs.usda.gov/inyo; ⌚8am-5pm, shorter spring & fall hours, closed Dec-Mar) has excellent views and educational exhibits, but the best photo ops are from the mile-long nature trail at the South Tufa Area (adult/child $3/free). From the nearby town of Lee Vining, Hwy 120 heads west into Yosemite National Park via seasonal Tioga Pass.

Continuing south on Hwy 395, detour along the scenic 16-mile June Lake Loop or push on to Mammoth Lakes, a popular four-seasons resort guarded by 11,053ft Mammoth Mountain (☎760-934-2571, 24hr snow report 888-766-9778; www.mammothmountain.com; lift tickets adult/child 7-12yr/youth/senior 13-18yr/$105/35/82/89), a top-notch skiing area. The slopes morph into a mountain-bike park in summer, when scenic gondola rides run. There's also camping and day hiking around Mammoth Lakes Basin and Reds Meadow, the latter near the 60ft-high basalt columns of Devils Postpile National Monument (☎760-934-2289; www.nps.gov/depo; shuttle day pass adult/child $7/4; ⌚late May-Oct), formed by volcanic activity. Hot-springs fans can soak in primitive pools off Benton Crossing Rd or view the geysering water at Hot Creek Geological Site, both off Hwy 395 southeast of town. The in-town Mammoth Lakes Welcome Center & Ranger Station (☎760-924-5500, 888-466-2666; www.visitmammoth.com; ⌚8am-5pm) has helpful maps and information.

Further south, Hwy 395 descends into the Owens Valley. In frontier-flavored Bishop, Mountain Light Gallery (☎760-873-7700; www.mountainlight.com; 106 S Main St; ⌚10am-5pm Mon-Sat, 11am-4pm Sun) FREE and the historical Laws Railroad Museum (☎760-873-5950; www.lawsmuseum.org; Silver Canyon Rd, off Hwy 6; donation $5; ⌚10am-4pm early Sep-late May, 9:30am-4pm late May-early Sep; 👪) are minor attractions. A gateway for packhorse trips, Bishop accesses the Eastern Sierra's best fishing and rock climbing.

Budget a half-day for the thrilling drive up to the Ancient Bristlecone Pine Forest. These gnarled, otherworldly looking trees – the world's oldest – are found above 10,000ft on the slopes of the White Mountains. The road (closed by snow in winter and early spring) is paved to the visitor center (☎760-873-2500; www.fs.usda.gov/inyo; per person/car $3/6; ⌚10am-4pm Fri-Mon late May-early Nov) at Schulman Grove, where hiking trails await. From Hwy 395 in Big Pine, take Hwy 168 east for 12 miles, then follow White Mountain Rd uphill for 10 miles.

Hwy 395 barrels south to Manzanar National Historic Site (☎760-878-2194; www.nps.gov/manz; 5001 Hwy 395, Independence; ⌚dawn-dusk, visitor center 9am-4:30pm, to 5:30pm Apr-Oct; 👪) FREE, which memorializes the camp where some 10,000 Japanese Americans were unjustly interned during WWII following the attack on Pearl Harbor. Interpretive exhibits and a short film vividly chronicle life at the camp, which today is marked by a short self-guided auto-tour route.

Further south in Lone Pine, you'll finally glimpse Mt Whitney (14,505ft), the highest mountain in the lower 48 states. The heart-stopping, 12-mile scenic drive up **Whitney Portal Road** (closed in winter and early spring) is spectacular. Climbing the peak is hugely popular, but requires a permit (per person $15) awarded via annual lottery. Just south of town, the **Eastern Sierra Interagency Visitor Center** (☑760-876-6222; www.fs.fed.us/r5/inyo; cnr Hwys 395 & 136; ☺8am-5pm) issues wilderness permits, dispenses outdoor-recreation info and sells books and maps.

West of Lone Pine, the bizarrely shaped boulders of the **Alabama Hills** have enchanted filmmakers of Hollywood Westerns. Peruse vintage memorabilia and movie posters back in town at the **Museum of Western Film History** (☑760-876-9909; www.museumofwesternfilmhistory.org; 701 S Main St; adult/child $5/free; ☺10am-5pm Mon-Sat, to 4pm Sun, longer summer hours).

🛏 Sleeping

The Eastern Sierra is freckled with campgrounds; backcountry camping requires a wilderness permit, available at ranger stations. Bishop, Lone Pine and Bridgeport have the most motels. Mammoth Lakes has a few motels and hotels and dozens of inns, B&Bs, condos and vacation rentals. Reservations are essential everywhere in summer.

El Mono Motel
MOTEL **$**

(☑760-647-6310; www.elmonomotel.com; 51 Hwy 395, Lee Vining; r $69-99; ☺mid-May–Oct; ☎) Grab a board game or soak up some mountain sunshine in this friendly flower-ringed place attached to an excellent cafe. In operation since 1927, and often booked solid, each of its 11 simple rooms (a few share bathrooms) is unique, decorated with vibrant and colorful art and fabrics.

Whitney Portal Hostel & Hotel
HOSTEL, MOTEL **$**

(☑760-876-0030; www.whitneyportalstore.com; 238 S Main St; dm/d $25/85; ❄☎☎) A popular launching pad for Whitney trips and for posthike wash-ups (public showers available), its hostel rooms are the cheapest beds in town – reserve them months ahead for July and August. There's no common space for the carpeted single-sex bunk-bed rooms, though amenities include towels, TVs, in-room kitchenettes and stocked coffeemakers. The majority of the establishment consists of plush and modern motel rooms, and many look out towards Whitney and its neighbors.

Dow Hotel & Dow Villa Motel
HOTEL, MOTEL **$$**

(☑760-876-5521; www.dowvillamotel.com; 310 S Main St; hotel r with/without bath $87/69, motel r $115-173; ❄@☎☎☎) John Wayne and Errol Flynn are among the stars who have stayed at this venerable hotel. Built in 1922, the place has been restored but retains much of its rustic charm. The rooms in the newer motel section have air-con and are more comfortable and bright, but also more generic.

Tamarack Lodge
LODGE, CABIN **$$$**

(☑760-934-2442; www.tamaracklodge.com; 163 Twin Lakes Rd; r with/without bath $219/169, cabins from $299; @☎☎) 🍃 In business since 1924, this charming year-round resort on Lower Twin Lake has a cozy fireplace lodge, a bar and excellent restaurant, 11 rustic-style rooms and 35 cabins. The cabins range from very simple to simply deluxe, and come with full kitchen, private bathroom, porch and wood-burning stove. Some can sleep up to 10 people. Daily resort fee $20.

🍴 Eating & Drinking

Alabama Hills Cafe
DINER **$**

(111 W Post St; mains $8-14; ☺7am-2pm; 🍴) Everyone's favorite breakfast joint, the portions here are big, the bread fresh-baked, and the hearty soups and scratch-made fruit pies make lunch an attractive option too.

Mammoth Tavern
PUB FOOD **$$**

(www.mammothtavern.com; 587 Old Mammoth Rd; mains $12-35; ☺3:30-11pm Tue-Sun) Warm lighting, wood-paneled walls rising to a circular ceiling and drop-dead gorgeous views of the snowcapped Sherwin Range mean the big screen TVs here are an unnecessary distraction. A newcomer to the local dining scene, Mammoth Tavern hits the spot with comfort food like shepherd's pie, oysters, gorgeous salads and fondue garlic turkey meatballs. Worthy libations include tasty house cocktails, local drafts, interesting whiskeys and over two-dozen wines by the glass.

Whoa Nellie Deli
CALIFORNIAN **$$**

(☑760-647-1088; www.whoanelliedeli.com; Tioga Gas Mart, Hwys 120 & 395, Lee Vining; mains $10-22; ☺6:30am-9pm late Apr-Oct; 🍴) After putting this unexpected gas-station restaurant on the map, its famed chef has moved on to Mammoth, but locals think the food is still damn good. Stop in for delicious fish tacos, wild-buffalo meatloaf and other tasty morsels, and live bands two nights a week.

Mammoth Brewing Company Tasting Room BREWERY
(www.mammothbrewingco.com; 18 Lake Mary Rd; ⌚10am-9:30pm Sun-Thu, to 10:30pm Fri & Sat) In a large and central location, this place has a dozen brews on tap (flights $5 to $7) – including special seasonal varieties not found elsewhere. Pick up some IPA 395 or Double Nut Brown to go. Tasty bar food available.

June Lake Brewing MICROBREWERY
(www.junelakebrewing.com; 131 S Crawford Ave, June Lake; ⌚11am-8pm Wed-Mon, to 9pm Fri & Sat; 🐾) A top new regional draw, June Lake Brewing's open tasting room serves 10 drafts, including a 'SmoKin' Porter, Deer Beer Brown Ale and some awesome IPAs. Brewers swear the June Lake water makes all the difference. Flights $4 to $6.

Lake Tahoe

Shimmering in myriad blues and greens, Lake Tahoe is the USA's second-deepest lake. Driving around its spellbinding 72-mile scenic shoreline gives you quite a workout behind the wheel. The north shore is quiet and upscale; the west shore, rugged and old-timey; the east shore, largely undeveloped; and the south shore, busy with families and flashy casinos. Horned peaks surrounding the lake (elevation 6255ft), which straddles the California–Nevada state line, are four-seasons outdoor playgrounds.

Tahoe gets packed in summer, on winter weekends and during holidays, when camping and lodging reservations are essential.

Information

Lake Tahoe Visitors Authority (☎530-541-5255; www.tahoesouth.com; 3066 Lake Tahoe Blvd, South Lake Tahoe; ⌚9am-5pm) and **North Lake Tahoe Visitors' Bureaus** (☎800-468-2463; www.gotahoenorth.com) run multiple visitor information centers.

Getting There & Around

South Tahoe Airporter (☎775-325-8944, 866-898-2463; www.southtahoeexpress.com; adult/child 4-12yr $30/17) runs several daily shuttles from Nevada's Reno-Tahoe International Airport to Stateline. **North Lake Tahoe Express** (☎866-216-5222; www.northlaketahoeexpress.com; per person $49) connects Reno's airport with Truckee, Northstar, Squaw Valley and north-shore towns.

Truckee's **Amtrak depot** (☎800-872-7245; www.amtrak.com; 10065 Donner Pass Rd) has daily trains to Reno ($13, 1¼ hours) and Sacramento ($41, 4½ hours), and twice-daily **Greyhound** (☎800-231-2222; www.greyhound.com) buses to Reno ($16, one hour), Sacramento ($40, 2½ hours) and San Francisco ($41, 5¾ hours). Daily Amtrak buses connect South Lake Tahoe with Sacramento ($34, 2¾ hours).

Tahoe Area Rapid Transit (TART; ☎530-550-1212; www.laketahoetransit.com; single/day pass $1.75/3.50) operates local buses from Truckee around the north and west shores. South Lake Tahoe is served by **BlueGO** (☎530-541-7149; www.tahoetransportation.org/transit; fare/day pass $2/5) buses. Making limited runs during summer, **Emerald Bay Trolley** (fare $2) connects BlueGo with TART.

If you're driving, tire chains are often required in winter on I-80, US 50 and other mountain highways, which may close temporarily due to heavy snow. Call ☎800-427-7623 to check current road condtions and closures.

South Lake Tahoe & West Shore

With retro motels and eateries lining busy Hwy 50, South Lake Tahoe gets crowded. Gambling at Stateline's casino hotels, just across the Nevada border, attracts thousands, as does the world-class ski resort of **Heavenly** (☎775-586-7000; www.skiheavenly.com; 4080 Lake Tahoe Blvd, South Lake Tahoe; adult/child 5-12yr/youth 13-18yr $99/59/89; ⌚9am-4pm Mon-Fri, 8:30am-4pm Sat, Sun & holidays; 👪). In summer a trip up Heavenly's **gondola** (adult/child $42/20) guarantees fabulous views of the lake and the **Desolation Wilderness**, with its raw granite peaks, glacier-carved valleys and alpine lakes favored by hikers. Get maps, information and wilderness permits (per adult $5 to $10) from the **USFS Taylor Creek Visitor Center** (☎530-543-2674; www.fs.usda.gov/ltbmu; Visitor Center Rd, off Hwy 89; ⌚8am-5pm late May-Sep, to 4pm Oct). It's 3 miles north of the 'Y' intersection of Hwys 50/89, at **Tallac Historic Site** (www.tahoeheritage.org; Tallac Rd; optional tour adult/child $10/5; ⌚10am-4pm daily mid-Jun–Sep, Fri & Sat late May–mid-Jun; 🐾) FREE, preserving swish early-20th-century vacation estates.

From sandy, swimmable **Zephyr Cove** (www.zephyrcove.com; 760 Hwy 50; per car $10; 👪) across the Nevada border or the in-town Ski Run Marina, **Lake Tahoe Cruises** (☎800-238-2463; www.zephyrcove.com; adult/child from $51/15) plies the 'Big Blue' year-round. Paddle under your own power with

Kayak Tahoe (☎530-544-2011; www.kayak-tahoe.com; 3411 Lake Tahoe Blvd; kayak single/double 1hr $25/35, 1 day $65/85, lessons & tours from $40; ⊙9am-5pm Jun-Sep). Back on shore, boutique-chic motels include the **Alder Inn** (☎530-544-4485; www.thealderinn.com; 1072 Ski Run Blvd; r $99-150;) and the hip **Basecamp Hotel** (☎530-208-0180; www.basecamphotels.com; 4143 Cedar Ave; d $109-229, 8-person bunkroom $209-299;) , which has a rooftop hot tub, or pitch a tent at lakeside **Fallen Leaf Campground** (☎info 530-544-0426, reservations 877-444-6777; www.recreation.gov; 2165 Fallen Leaf Lake Rd; tent & RV sites $33-35, yurts $84; ⊙mid-May–mid-Oct;). Fuel up at vegetarian-friendly **Sprouts** (www.sprouts-cafetahoe.com; 3123 Harrison Ave; mains $7-10; ⊙8am-9pm;) natural-foods cafe, or with a peanut-butter-topped burger and garlic fries at the **Burger Lounge** (☎530-542-2010; www.burgerloungeintahoe.com; 717 Emerald Bay Rd; dishes $4-10; ⊙10am-8pm daily Jun-Sep, 11am-7pm Wed-Sun Oct-May;).

Hwy 89 threads northwest along the thickly forested west shore to **Emerald Bay State Park** (☎530-541-6498; www.parks.ca.gov; per car $10; ⊙late May-Sep), where granite cliffs and pine trees frame a sparkling fjordlike inlet. A 1-mile trail leads steeply downhill to **Vikingsholm Castle** (tour adult/child $10/8; ⊙11am-4pm late May-Sep), a 1920s Scandinavian-style mansion. From there, the **Rubicon Trail** ribbons 4.5 miles north along the lakeshore past petite coves to **DL Bliss State Park** (☎530-525-7277; www.parks.ca.gov; per car $10; ⊙late May-Sep;), offering sandy beaches. Further north, **Tahoma Meadows B&B Cottages** (☎866-525-1553, 530-525-1553; www.tahomameadows.com; 6821 W Lake Blvd, Tahoma; cottages $99-389;) rents darling country cabins.

North & East Shores

A busy commercial hub, **Tahoe City** is great for grabbing food and supplies and renting outdoor-sports gear. It's not far from **Squaw Valley USA** (☎530-452-4331; www.squaw.com; 1960 Squaw Valley Rd, off Hwy 89, Olympic Valley; adult/child under 13yr/youth 13-22yr $114/66/94;), a megasized ski resort that hosted the 1960 Winter Olympics. Après-ski crowds gather at woodsy **Bridgetender Tavern & Grill** (www.tahoebridgetender.com; 65 W Lake Blvd; ⊙11am-11pm, to midnight Fri & Sat) back in town. In the morning, gobble eggs Benedict with house-smoked salmon at down-home **Fire Sign Cafe** (www.firesigncafe.com; 1785 W Lake Blvd; mains $7-13; ⊙7am-3pm;), 2 miles further south.

In summer, swim or kayak at **Tahoe Vista** or **Kings Beach**. Overnight at **Cedar Glen Lodge** (☎530-546-4281; www.tahoecedarglen.com; 6589 N Lake Blvd; r/ste/cottages $139-350; @), where rustic-themed cottages and rooms have kitchenettes, or well-kept, compact **Hostel Tahoe** (☎530-546-3266; www.hosteltahoe.com; 8931 N Lake Blvd; dm $35, d/q $70/85, all incl tax; @) . East of Kings Beach's casual lakeside eateries, Hwy 28 barrels into Nevada. Catch a live-music show at **Crystal Bay Club Casino** (☎775-833-6333; www.crystalbaycasino.com; 14 Hwy 28), but for more happening bars and bistros, drive further to **Incline Village**.

With pristine beaches, lakes and miles of multiuse trails, **Lake Tahoe-Nevada State Park** (www.parks.nv.gov; per car $7-12) is the east shore's biggest draw. Summer crowds splash in the turquoise waters of **Sand Harbor**. The 13-mile **Flume Trail**, a mountain biker's holy grail, ends further south at **Spooner Lake**. Back in Incline Village, **Flume Trail Bikes** (☎775-298-2501; http://flumetrailtahoe.com; 1115 Tunnel Creek Rd, Incline Village; mountain-bike rental per day $35-85, shuttle $15) offers bicycle rentals and shuttles.

Truckee & Around

North of Lake Tahoe off I-80, Truckee is not in fact a truck stop but a thriving mountain town, with coffee shops, trendy boutiques and dining in downtown's historical district. Ski bums have several resorts to pick from, including glam **Northstar California** (☎530-562-1010; www.northstarcalifornia.com; 5001 Northstar Dr, off Hwy 267, Truckee; adult/child 5-12yr/youth 13-22yr $116/69/96; ⊙8:30am-4pm;); kid-friendly **Sugar Bowl** (☎530-426-9000; www.sugarbowl.com; 629 Sugar Bowl Rd, off Donner Pass Rd, Norden; adult/child 6-12yr/youth 13-22yr $82/30/70; ⊙9am-4pm;), cofounded by Walt Disney; and **Royal Gorge** (☎530-426-3871; www.royalgorge.com; 9411 Pahatsi Rd, off I-80 exit Soda Springs/Norden, Soda Springs; adult/youth 13-22yr $29/22; ⊙9am-5pm during snow season;), paradise for cross-country skiers.

West of Hwy 89, Donner Summit is where the infamous Donner Party became trapped during the fierce winter of 1846–47. Fewer than half survived – some by cannibalizing their dead friends. The grisly tale is chronicled at the museum inside **Donner Memorial State Park** (☎530-582-7892; www.parks.ca.gov; Donner Pass Rd; per car $8; ⏲museum 10am-5pm, closed Tue & Wed Sep-May; 👪), which offers **camping** (☎530-582-7894, reservations 800-444-7275; www.reserveamerica.com; tent & RV sites $35; ⏲late May-late Sep; 👪). Nearby **Donner Lake** is popular with swimmers and paddlers.

On the outskirts of Truckee, green-certified **Cedar House Sport Hotel** (☎866-582-5655, 530-582-5655; www.cedarhousesporthotel.com; 10918 Brockway Rd; r $180-295; @📶🐾) 🍃 offers stylish boutique rooms and an outstanding restaurant. Down pints of Donner Party Porter at **Fifty Fifty Brewing Co** (www.fiftyfiftybrewing.com; 11197 Brockway Rd; ⏲11:30am-9am Sun-Thu, to 9:30pm Fri & Sat).

Pacific Northwest

Includes ➡

Best Places to Eat

- Sitka & Spruce (p1033)
- Toulouse Petit (p1033)
- Saffron Mediterranean Kitchen (p1050)
- Andina (p1058)
- Chow (p1069)

Best Places to Stay

- Ace Hotel (p1031)
- Davenport Hotel (p1047)
- Kennedy School (p1056)
- Timberline Lodge (p1066)
- Moore Hotel (p1031)

Why Go?

As much a state of mind as a geographical region, the northwest corner of the US is a land of subcultures and new trends, where evergreen trees frame snow-dusted volcanoes, and inspired ideas scribbled on the back of napkins become tomorrow's start-ups. You can't peel off the history in layers here, but you *can* gaze wistfully into the future in fast-moving, innovative cities such as Seattle and Portland, which are sprinkled with food carts, streetcars, microbreweries, green belts, coffee connoisseurs and weird urban sculpture.

Ever since the days of the Oregon Trail, the Northwest has had a hypnotic lure for risk takers and dreamers, and the metaphoric carrot still dangles. There's the air, so clean they ought to bottle it; the trees, older than many of Rome's Renaissance palaces; and the end-of-the-continent coastline, holding back the force of the world's largest ocean. Cowboys take note: it doesn't get much more 'wild' or 'west' than this.

When to Go

Seattle

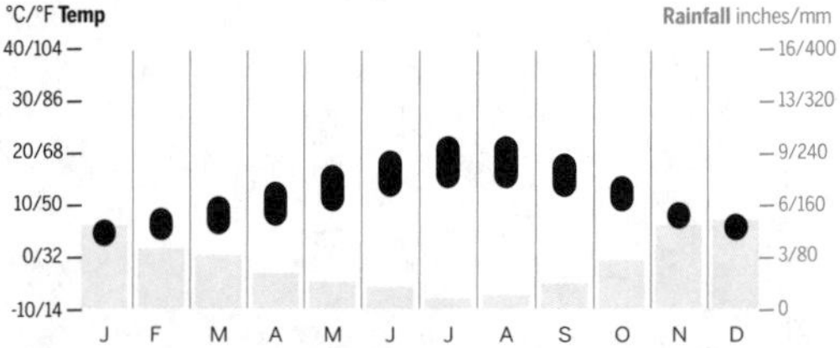

Jan–Mar Most reliable snow cover for skiing in the Cascades and beyond.

May Festival season: Portland Rose, International Film Festival and Oregon Shakespeare Festival.

Jul–Sep The best hiking months: between the spring snowmelt and the first fall flurries.

History

Native American societies, including the Chinook and the Salish, had long-established coastal communities by the time Europeans arrived in the Pacific Northwest in the 18th century. Inland, on the arid plateaus between the Cascades and the Rocky Mountains, the Spokane, Nez Percé and other tribes thrived on seasonal migration between river valleys and temperate uplands.

Three hundred years after Columbus landed in the New World, Spanish and British explorers began probing the northern Pacific coast, seeking the fabled Northwest Passage. In 1792 Captain George Vancouver was the first explorer to sail the waters of Puget Sound, claiming British sovereignty over the entire region. At the same time, an American, Captain Robert Gray, found the mouth of the Columbia River. In 1805 the explorers Lewis and Clark crossed the Rockies and made their way down the Columbia to the Pacific Ocean, extending the US claim on the territory.

In 1824 the British Hudson's Bay Company established Fort Vancouver in Washington as headquarters for the Columbia region. This opened the door to waves of settlers, but had a devastating impact on the indigenous cultures, which were assailed by European diseases and alcohol.

In 1843 settlers at Champoeg, on the Willamette River south of Portland, voted to organize a provisional government independent of the Hudson's Bay Company, thereby casting their lot with the US, which formally acquired the territory from the British by treaty in 1846. Over the next decade, some 53,000 settlers came to the Northwest via the 2000-mile Oregon Trail.

Arrival of the railroads set the region's future. Agriculture and lumber became the pillars of the economy until 1914, when WWI and the opening of the Panama Canal brought increased trade to Pacific ports. Shipyards opened along Puget Sound, and the Boeing aircraft company set up shop near Seattle.

Big dam projects in the 1930s and '40s provided cheap hydroelectricity and irrigation. WWII offered another boost for aircraft manufacturing and shipbuilding, and agriculture continued to thrive. In the postwar period, Washington's population, especially around Puget Sound, grew to twice that of Oregon.

In the 1980s and '90s, the economic emphasis shifted with the rise of the high-tech industry, embodied by Microsoft in Seattle and Intel in Portland.

Hydroelectricity production and massive irrigation projects along the Columbia have threatened the river's ecosystem in the past few decades, and logging has also left its scars. But the region has reinvigorated its eco-credentials by attracting some of the country's most environmentally conscious companies, and its major cities are among the greenest in the US. It stands at the forefront of US efforts to tackle climate issues.

Local Culture

The stereotypical image of a Pacific Northwesterner is a casually dressed latte-sipping urbanite who drives a Prius, votes Democrat and walks around with an unwavering diet of Nirvana-derived indie rock programmed into their iPod. But, as with most fleeting

THE PACIFIC NORTHWEST IN...

Four Days

Hit the ground running in **Seattle** to see the main sights, including Pike Place Market and the Seattle Center. On day three, head down to **Portland**, where you can do like the locals do and cycle to bars, cafes, food carts and shops.

One Week

Add a couple highlights such as **Mt Rainier, Olympic National Park**, the **Columbia River Gorge** or **Mt Hood**. Or explore the spectacular Oregon Coast (try the **Cannon Beach** area) or the historic seaport of **Port Townsend** on the Olympic Peninsula.

Two Weeks

Crater Lake is unforgettable, and can be combined with a trip to **Ashland** and its Shakespeare Festival. Don't miss the ethereal **San Juan Islands** up near the watery border with Canada, or **Bend**, the region's biggest outdoor draw. If you like wine, Washington's **Walla Walla** is your mecca, while the **Willamette Valley** is Oregon's Pinot Noir paradise.

Pacific Northwest Highlights

1. Cycling and kayaking around the quieter corners of the **San Juan Islands** (p1042).
2. Exploring the gorgeous **Oregon Coast** (p1070), from scenic Astoria to balmy Port Orford.
3. Admiring trees older than Europe's Renaissance castles in Washington's **Olympic National Park** (p1038).
4. Watching the greatest outdoor show in the Pacific Northwest in Seattle's theatrical **Pike Place Market** (p1025).
5. Walking the green and serene neighborhoods of **Portland** (p1051), energized by beer, coffee and food-cart treats.
6. Witnessing the impossibly deep-blue waters and scenic panoramas of **Crater Lake National Park** (p1069).
7. Going mountain biking, rock climbing or skiing in the outdoor mecca of **Bend** (p1067).
8. Tasting sumptuous reds and whites in the wine regions around **Walla Walla** (p1050).

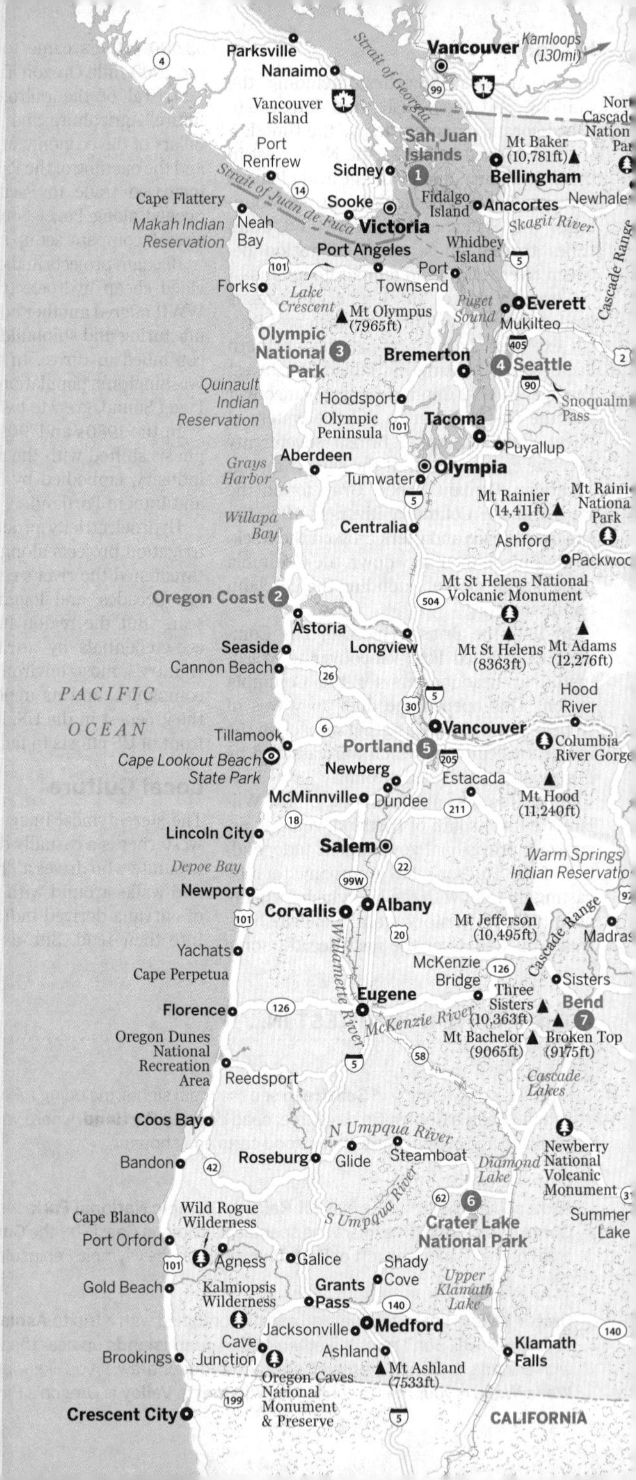

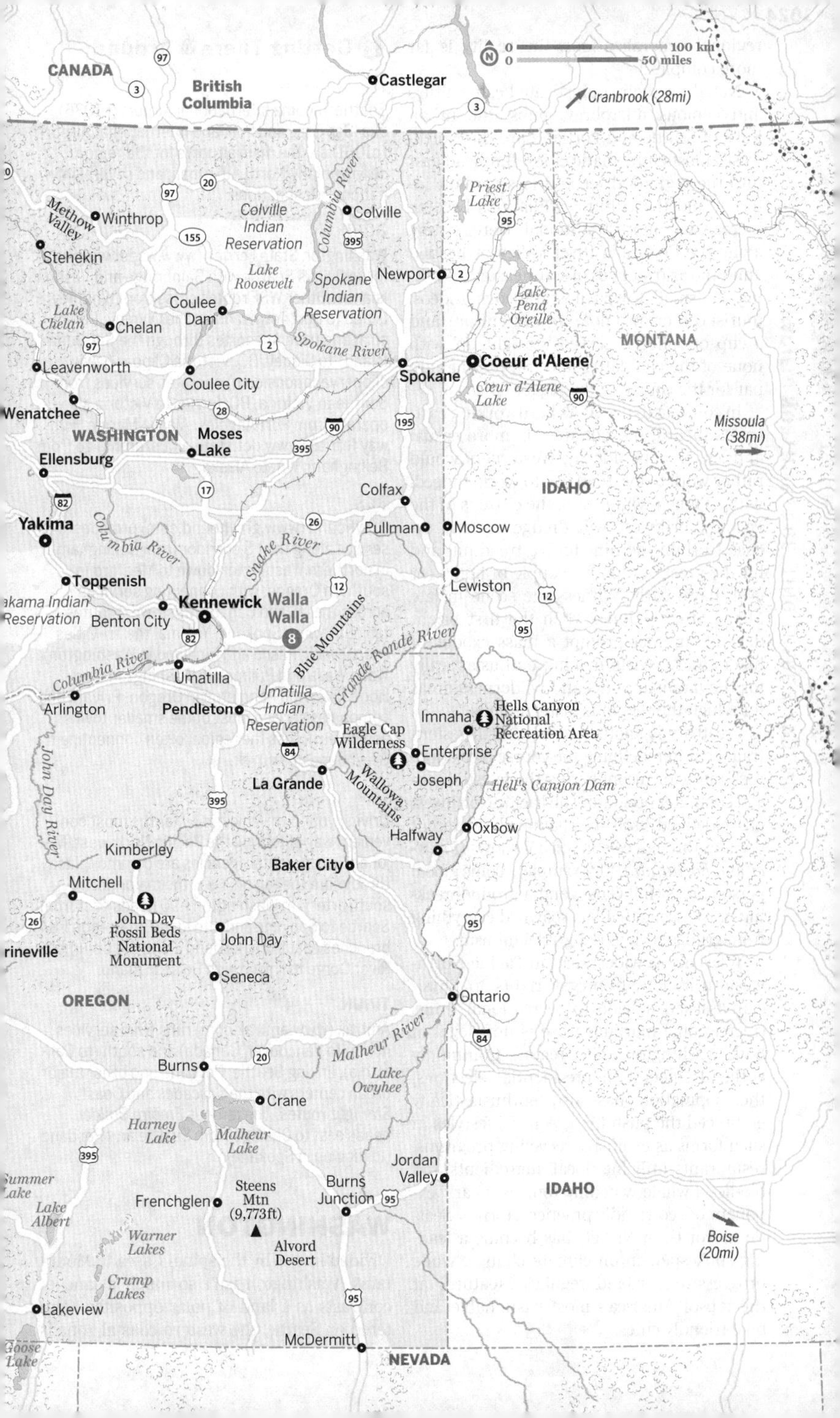

0 100 km
0 50 miles
CANADA
British Columbia
Castlegar
Cranbrook (28mi)
Priest Lake
Methow Valley
Winthrop
Stehekin
Colville Indian Reservation
Columbia River
Colville
Lake Roosevelt
Spokane Indian Reservation
Newport
Lake Pend Oreille
MONTANA
Coulee Dam
Lake Chelan
Chelan
Spokane River
Leavenworth
Coulee City
Spokane
Coeur d'Alene
Cœur d'Alene Lake
Wenatchee
WASHINGTON
Moses Lake
Missoula (38mi)
Ellensburg
Colfax
IDAHO
Yakima
Columbia River
Snake River
Pullman
Moscow
Toppenish
Lewiston
Yakama Indian Reservation
Benton City
Kennewick
Walla Walla
8
Blue Mountains
Grande Ronde River
Columbia River
Umatilla
Arlington
Pendleton
Umatilla Indian Reservation
Imnaha
Hells Canyon National Recreation Area
Eagle Cap Wilderness
Enterprise
Joseph
John Day River
La Grande
Wallowa Mountains
Hell's Canyon Dam
Oxbow
Halfway
Kimberley
Baker City
Mitchell
John Day Fossil Beds National Monument
John Day
Prineville
Seneca
OREGON
Ontario
Malheur River
Burns
Lake Owyhee
Crane
Harney Lake
Malheur Lake
Jordan Valley
IDAHO
Summer Lake
Steens Mtn (9,773ft)
Burns Junction
Lake Albert
Frenchglen
Boise (20mi)
Warner Lakes
Alvord Desert
Crump Lakes
Lakeview
Goose Lake
McDermitt
NEVADA

regional generalizations, the reality is far more complex.

Noted for their sophisticated cafe culture and copious microbrew pubs, the urban hubs of Seattle and Portland are the Northwest's most emblematic cities. But head east into the region's drier and less verdant interior, and the cultural affiliations become increasingly more traditional. Here, strung along the Columbia River Valley or nestled amid the arid steppes of southeastern Washington, small towns host raucous rodeos, tourist centers promote cowboy culture, and a cup of coffee is served 'straight up' with none of the chai lattes and frappés that are par for the course in the bigger cities.

In contrast to the USA's hardworking eastern seaboard, life out west is more casual and less frenetic. Ideally, Westerners would rather work to live than live to work. Indeed, with so much winter rain, the citizens of the Pacific Northwest will dredge up any excuse to shun the nine-to-five treadmill and hit the great outdoors a couple of hours (or even days) early. Witness the scene in late May and early June, when the first bright days of summer prompt a mass exodus of hikers and cyclists making enthusiastically for the national parks and wilderness areas for which the region is justly famous.

Creativity is another strong Northwestern trait, be it in redefining the course of modern rock music or reconfiguring the latest Microsoft computer program. The Pacific Northwest has redefined itself internationally in recent decades through celebrated TV shows (*Frasier* and *Portlandia*, for example), iconic global personalities (Bill Gates) and a groundbreaking music scene that has spawned everything from grunge rock to riot grrrl feminism.

Tolerance is widespread in Pacific Northwestern society, from gay rights to physician-assisted suicide to recreational drugs (recreational marijuana use is now legal in both Washington and Oregon). Commonly voting Democrat in presidential elections, the population has also enthusiastically embraced the push for 'greener' lifestyles in such forms as extensive recycling programs, restaurants utilizing 'local' ingredients and biodiesel whale-watching tours. An early exponent of ecofriendly practices, former Seattle mayor Greg Nickels has become a leading spokesperson on climate change, while progressive Portland regularly features at the top of America's most sustainable and bike-friendly cities.

Getting There & Around

AIR

Seattle-Tacoma International Airport (p1036), aka 'Sea-Tac,' and Portland International Airport (p1061) are the main airports for the region, serving many North American, and several international, destinations.

BOAT

Washington State Ferries (www.wsdot.wa.gov/ferries) links Seattle with Bainbridge and Vashon Islands. Other WSF routes cross from Whidbey Island to Port Townsend on the Olympic Peninsula, and from Anacortes through the San Juan Islands to Sidney, BC. Victoria Clipper (www.clippervacations.com) operates services from Seattle to Victoria, BC; ferries to Victoria also operate from Port Angeles. Alaska Marine Highway ferries (www.dot.state.ak.us/amhs) go from Bellingham, WA, to Alaska.

BUS

Greyhound (www.greyhound.com) provides service along the I-5 corridor from Bellingham in northern Washington down to Medford in southern Oregon, with connecting services across the US and Canada. East–west routes fan out toward Spokane, Yakima, the Tri-Cities (Kennewick, Pasco and Richland in Washington), Walla Walla and Pullman in Washington, and Hood River and Pendleton in Oregon. Private bus companies service most of the smaller towns and cities across the region, often connecting to Greyhound or Amtrak.

CAR

Driving your own vehicle is by far the most convenient way of touring the Pacific Northwest. Major and minor rental agencies are commonplace throughout the region. I-5 is the major north–south artery. In Washington I-90 heads east from Seattle to Spokane and into Idaho. In Oregon I-84 branches east from Portland along the Columbia River Gorge to link up with Boise in Idaho.

TRAIN

Amtrak (www.amtrak.com) runs train services north (to Vancouver, Canada) and south (to California), linking Seattle, Portland and other major urban centers with the *Cascades* and *Coast Starlight* routes. The famous *Empire Builder* heads east to Chicago from Seattle and Portland (joining up in Spokane).

WASHINGTON

Divided in two by the spinal Cascade Mountains, Washington isn't so much a land of contrasts as a land of polar opposites. Centered on Seattle, the western coastal zone is wet, urban, liberal and famous for its fecund evergreen forests; splayed to the east between the less celebrated cities of Spokane and Yakima, the inland plains are arid, rural, conservative and covered by mile after mile of scrublike steppe.

Of the two halves it's the west that harbors most of the quintessential Washington sights, while the more remote, less heralded east is understated and full of surprises.

WASHINGTON FACTS

Nickname Evergreen State

Population 7 million

Area 71,362 sq miles

Capital city Olympia (population 48,340)

Other cities Seattle (population 653,000), Spokane (population 210,800), Yakima (population 93,300), Bellingham (population 83,000), Walla Walla (population 32,000)

Sales tax 6.5%

Birthplace of Singer and actor Bing Crosby (1903–77), guitarist Jimi Hendrix (1942–70), computer geek Bill Gates (b 1955), political commentator Glen Beck (b 1964), musical icon Kurt Cobain (1967–94)

Home of Mt St Helens, Microsoft, Starbucks, Amazon.com, Evergreen State College

Politics Democrat governors since 1985

Famous for Grunge rock, coffee, *Grey's Anatomy, Twilight,* volcanoes, apples, wine, precipitation

State vegetable Walla Walla sweet onion

Driving distances Seattle to Portland, 174 miles; Spokane to Port Angeles, 365 miles

Seattle

Combine the brains of Portland, OR, with the beauty of Vancouver, BC, and you'll get something approximating Seattle. It's hard to believe that the Pacific Northwest's largest metropolis was considered a 'secondary' US city until the 1980s, when a combination of bold innovation and unabashed individualism turned it into one of the dot-com era's biggest trendsetters, spearheaded by an unlikely alliance of coffee-sipping computer geeks and navel-gazing musicians.

Reinvention is the buzzword these days in a city where grunge belongs to the history books and Starbucks is just one in a cavalcade of precocious indie coffee providers eking out their market position.

Surprisingly elegant in places and coolly edgy in others, Seattle is notable for its strong neighborhoods, top-rated university, monstrous traffic jams and proactive city mayors who harbor green credentials. Although it has fermented its own pop culture in recent times, it has yet to create an urban mythology befitting Paris or New York, but it does have 'the Mountain.' Better known as Rainier to its friends, Seattle's unifying symbol is a 14,411ft mass of rock and ice, which acts as a perennial reminder to the city's huddled masses that raw wilderness, and potential volcanic catastrophe, are never far away.

Sights

Downtown

★Pike Place Market MARKET

(www.pikeplacemarket.org; 85 Pike St; 9am-6pm Mon-Sat, to 5pm Sun; Westlake) Take a bunch of small-time businesses and sprinkle them liberally around a waterside strip amid crowds of old-school bohemians, new-wave restaurateurs, tree-huggers, students, artists, buskers and tourists, and the result: Pike Place Market, a cavalcade of noise, smells, personalities, banter and urban theater. You'll find produce stalls, vintage shops, handmade crafts, souvenir kitsch and funky eateries. In operation since 1907, Pike Place is a wonderfully 'local' experience that highlights the city for what it really is: all-embracing, eclectic and proudly singular.

Seattle Art Museum MUSEUM

(SAM; 206-654-3210; www.seattleartmuseum.org; 1300 1st Ave; adult/student $19.50/12.50; 10am-5pm Wed & Fri-Sun, to 9pm Thu; University St) Over the last decade, SAM has added over 100,000 sq ft to its gallery space and acquired about $1 billion worth of new art, including works by Zurbarán and Murillo. The museum is known for its extensive Native American artifacts and work from the local Northwest School, in particular by

Seattle

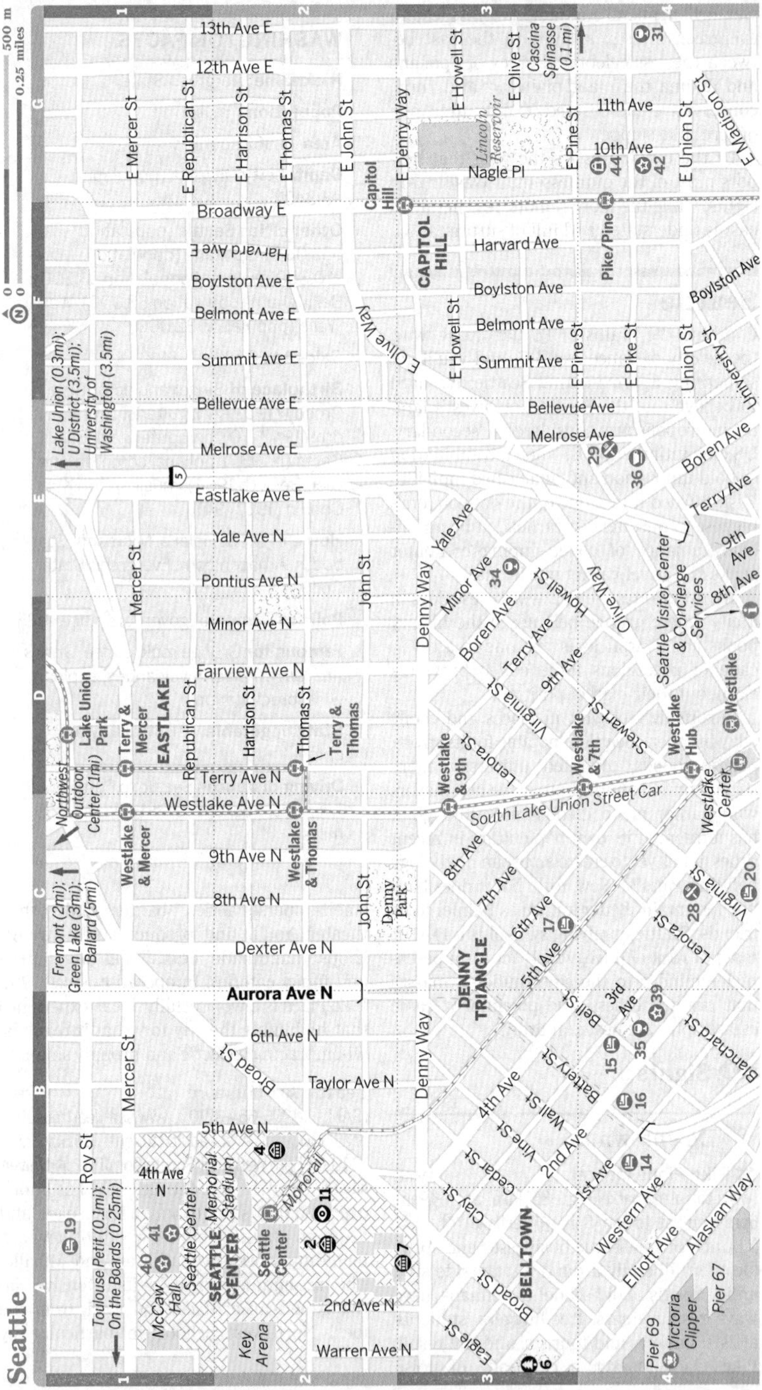
0 500 m
0 0.25 miles
Lake Union (0.3mi); U District (3.5mi); University of Washington (3.5mi)
Fremont (2mi); Green Lake (3mi); Ballard (5mi)
Northwest Outdoor Center (1mi)
Toulouse Petit (0.1mi); On the Boards (0.25mi)
Cascina Spinasse (0.1 mi)
CAPITOL HILL
EASTLAKE
DENNY TRIANGLE
SEATTLE CENTER
BELLTOWN
Lake Union Park
Denny Park
Lincoln Reservoir
Capitol Hill
Pike/Pine
Westlake & Mercer
Terry & Mercer
Westlake & Thomas
Terry & Thomas
Westlake & 9th
Westlake & 7th
Westlake Hub
Westlake
Westlake Center
South Lake Union Street Car
Monorail
Seattle Center
Seattle Visitor Center & Concierge Services
McCaw Hall
Key Arena
Memorial Stadium
Pier 69
Pier 67
Victoria Clipper
13th Ave E
12th Ave E
Broadway E
Harvard Ave E
Boylston Ave E
Belmont Ave E
Summit Ave E
Bellevue Ave E
Melrose Ave E
Eastlake Ave E
Yale Ave N
Pontius Ave N
Minor Ave N
Fairview Ave N
Terry Ave N
Westlake Ave N
9th Ave N
8th Ave N
Dexter Ave N
Aurora Ave N
6th Ave N
Taylor Ave N
5th Ave N
4th Ave N
2nd Ave N
Warren Ave N
E Mercer St
E Republican St
E Harrison St
E Thomas St
E John St
E Denny Way
E Howell St
E Olive St
E Pine St
E Pike St
E Union St
E Madison St
Nagle Pl
11th Ave
10th Ave
Harvard Ave
Boylston Ave
Belmont Ave
Summit Ave
Bellevue Ave
Melrose Ave
E Olive Way
Union St
University St
Boren Ave
Terry Ave
9th Ave
8th Ave
Mercer St
Republican St
Harrison St
Thomas St
John St
Denny Way
Yale Ave
Minor Ave
Howell St
Olive Way
Virginia St
Stewart St
Lenora St
7th Ave
6th Ave
5th Ave
4th Ave
3rd Ave
2nd Ave
1st Ave
Bell St
Battery St
Wall St
Vine St
Cedar St
Clay St
Broad St
Eagle St
Blanchard St
Western Ave
Elliott Ave
Alaskan Way
Roy St
1
2
4
6
7
11
14
15
16
17
19
20
28
29
31
34
35
36
39
40
41
42
44
A
B
C
D
E
F
G
1
2
3
4

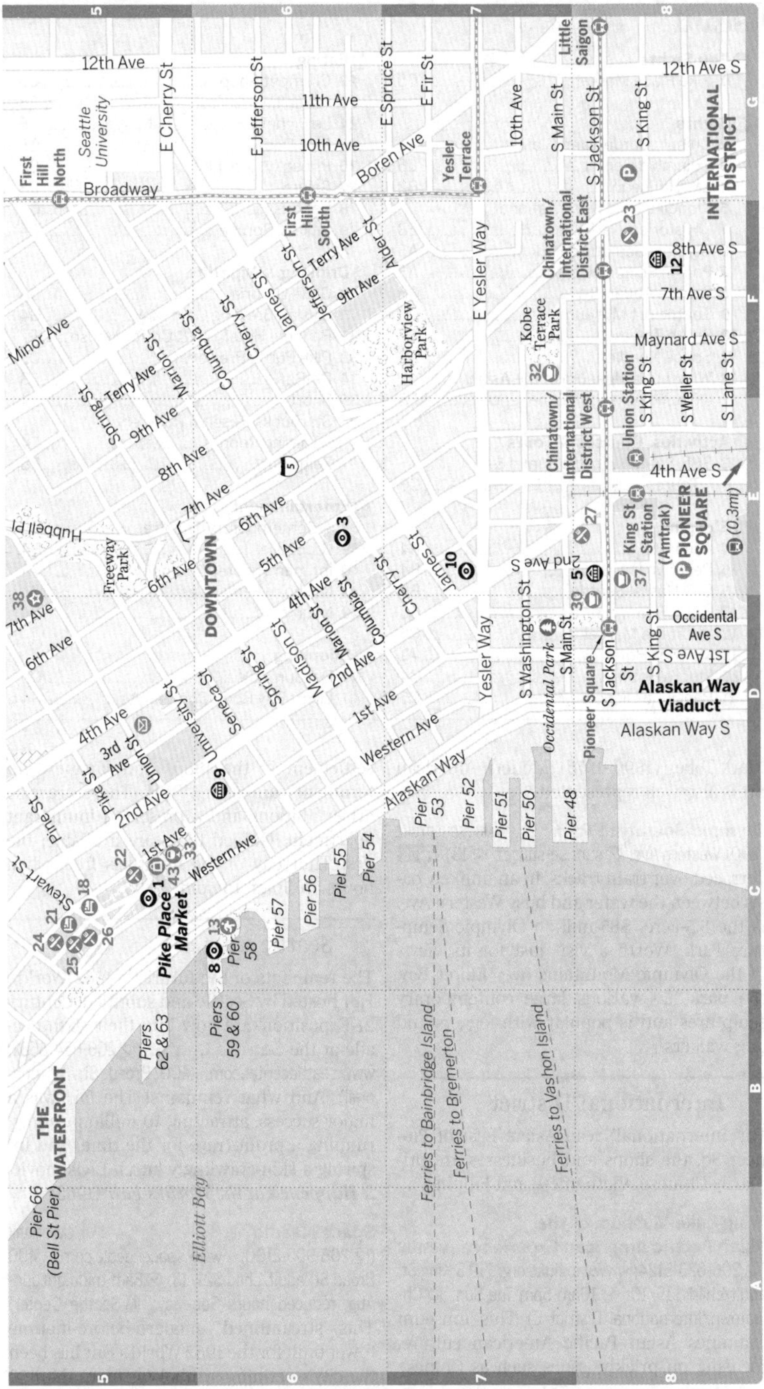

PACIFIC NORTHWEST

Seattle

Top Sights
1 Pike Place Market C5

Sights
2 Chihuly Garden and Glass A2
3 Columbia Center E6
4 EMP Museum B2
5 Klondike Gold Rush National Historical Park E8
6 Olympic Sculpture Park A3
7 Pacific Science Center A3
8 Seattle Aquarium C6
9 Seattle Art Museum D6
10 Smith Tower E7
11 Space Needle A2
12 Wing Luke Museum of the Asian Pacific American Experience F8

Activities, Courses & Tours
13 SBR Seattle Bicycle Rental & Tours C6

Sleeping
14 Ace Hotel B4
15 Belltown Inn B4
16 City Hostel Seattle B4
17 Hotel Five C3
18 Inn at the Market C5
19 Maxwell Hotel A1
20 Moore Hotel C4
21 Pensione Nichols C5

Eating
22 Crumpet Shop C5
23 Green Leaf F8
24 Le Pichet C5
25 Pink Door C5
26 Piroshky Piroshky C5
27 Salumi E8
28 Serious Pie C4
29 Sitka & Spruce E4

Drinking & Nightlife
30 Caffè Umbria D8
31 Elysian Brewing Company G4
32 Panama Hotel Tea & Coffee House F7
33 Pike Pub & Brewery C5
34 Re-Bar E3
35 Shorty's B4
36 Starbucks Reserve Roastery & Tasting Room E4
37 Zeitgeist E8

Entertainment
38 A Contemporary Theatre D5
39 Crocodile B4
40 Intiman Theater Company A1
41 Nesholm Family Lecture Hall A1
42 Neumo's G4

Shopping
43 DeLaurenti's C5
44 Elliott Bay Book Company G4

Mark Tobey (1890–1976). Modern American art is also well represented.

Olympic Sculpture Park PARK, SCULPTURE
(2901 Western Ave; sunrise-sunset; 13) FREE Terraced over train tracks, in an unlikely oasis between the water and busy Western Ave, is the 8.5-acre, $85-million Olympic Sculpture Park. Worth a visit just for its views of the Olympic Mountains over Elliott Bay, the park has various large contemporary sculptures and is popular with joggers and dog-walkers.

International District

For 'international', read Asian. East of Pioneer Sq, the shops and businesses are primarily Chinese, Vietnamese and Filipino.

Wing Luke Museum of the Asian Pacific American Experience MUSEUM
(206-623-5124; www.wingluke.org; 719 S King St; adult/child $15/10; 10am-5pm Tue-Sun; Chinatown/International District E) This museum examines Asian Pacific American culture, focusing on prickly issues such as Chinese settlement in the 1880s and Japanese internment camps in WWII. There are also art exhibitions and a preserved immigrant apartment. Guided tours are available; the first Thursday of the month is free, when hours are 10am to 8pm.

Seattle Center

The remnants of the futuristic 1962 World's Fair hosted by Seattle and subtitled 'Century 21 Exposition' are now into their sixth decade at the **Seattle Center** (206-684-8582; www.seattlecenter.com; 400 Broad St; monorail). And what remnants! The fair was a major success, attracting 10 million visitors, running a profit (rare for the time) and inspiring a skin-crawlingly kitsch Elvis movie, *It Happened at the World's Fair* (1963).

Space Needle LANDMARK
(206-905-2100; www.spaceneedle.com; 400 Broad St; adult/child $21/13; 8am-midnight Jun-Aug, reduced hours Sep-May; Seattle Center) This streamlined, modern-before-its-time tower built for the 1962 World's Fair has been the city's defining symbol for more than 50

years. The needle anchors the complex now called Seattle Center and draws over one million annual visitors to its flying-saucer-like observation deck and pricey rotating restaurant. Purchase a combination ticket with Chihuly Garden and Glass for $36.

EMP Museum MUSEUM
(☎206-770-2700; www.empmuseum.org; 325 5th Ave N; adult/child $25/16; ⏰10am-7pm Jun-Aug, to 5pm Sep-May; Ⓜ Seattle Center) This museum, a marriage of super modern architecture and rock-and-roll history, was founded by Microsoft co-creator Paul Allen. It was inspired by the music of Seattle-born guitar icon, Jimi Hendrix, though today its collection has morphed to include pop-culture and science-fiction history. Buy discounted tickets online.

Chihuly Garden and Glass MUSEUM
(☎206-753-4940; www.chihulygardenandglass.com; 305 Harrison St; adult/child $25/16; ⏰8am-9pm Sun-Thu, to 10pm Fri & Sat; Ⓜ Seattle Center) Opened in 2012 and reinforcing Seattle's position as the Venice of North America, this exquisite exposition of the life and work of dynamic local glass sculptor Dale Chihuly might just take your breath away. It shows off Chihuly's colorfully creative designs within an airy glass atrium and landscaped gardens. Hours vary throughout the year; check the website.

Capitol Hill

Millionaires mingle with goth musicians in Capitol Hill, a well-heeled but liberal neighborhood rightly renowned for its fringe theater, alternative music scene, indie coffee bars, and vital gay and lesbian culture. You can take your dog for a herbal bath here, go shopping for ethnic crafts on Broadway, or blend in (or not) with the young punks and old hippies on the eclectic Pike–Pine corridor. The junction of Broadway and E John St is the nexus from which to navigate the quarter's various restaurants, brewpubs, boutiques and dingy, but not dirty, dive bars.

Fremont

Fremont pitches young hipsters among old hippies in an unlikely urban alliance, and vies with Capitol Hill as Seattle's most irreverent neighborhood. It's full of junk shops, urban sculpture, and a healthy sense of its own ludicrousness.

LOCAL KNOWLEDGE

HIGHER THAN THE SPACE NEEDLE

Columbia Center (☎206-386-5564; www.skyviewobservatory.com; 701 5th Ave; adult/student $15/9; ⏰9am-10pm) Everyone makes a rush for the iconic Space Needle, but it's not the tallest of Seattle's glittering viewpoints. That honor goes to the sleek, tinted-windowed Columbia Center (1985); at 943ft high, it's the loftiest building in the Pacific Northwest. From the plush observation deck on the 73rd floor you can look down on ferries, cars, islands – even the Space Needle!

Waiting for the Interurban MONUMENT
(cnr N 34th St & Fremont Ave N) Seattle's most popular piece of public art, *Waiting for the Interurban,* is cast in recycled aluminum and depicts six people waiting for a train that never comes. Occasionally locals will lovingly decorate the people in outfits corresponding to a special event, the weather, someone's birthday, a Mariners win – whatever. Check out the human face on the dog; it's Armen Stepanian, once Fremont's honorary mayor, who made the mistake of objecting to the sculpture.

Fremont Troll SCULPTURE
(cnr N 36th St & Troll Ave) The Fremont Troll lurks beneath the north end of the Aurora Bridge at N 36th St. The troll's creators – artists Steve Badanes, Will Martin, Donna Walter and Ross Whitehead – won a competition sponsored by the Fremont Arts Council in 1990. The 18ft-high cement figure snacking on a Volkswagen Beetle is now a favorite place for late-night beer drinking.

The U District

U-dub, a neighborhood of young, studious out-of-towners, places the beautiful, leafy University of Washington campus next to the shabbier 'Ave,' an eclectic strip of cheap boutiques, dive bars and ethnic restaurants.

Burke Museum MUSEUM
(☎206-543-5590; www.burkemuseum.org; cnr 17th Ave NE & NE 45th St; admission $10; ⏰10am-5pm; 🚌70) One of the Northwest's best natural history museums, the Burke boasts an impressive stash of fossils, including a 20,000-year-old sabre-toothed cat. Equally compelling is the focus on over a dozen different Native

DON'T MISS

PIONEER SQUARE

Pioneer Sq is Seattle's oldest quarter, which isn't saying much if you're visiting from Rome or London. Most of the buildings here date from just after the 1889 fire (a devastating inferno that destroyed 25 city blocks, including the entire central business district), and are referred to architecturally as Richardsonian Romanesque, a redbrick revivalist style in vogue at the time. In the early years, the neighborhood's boom-bust fortunes turned its arterial road, Yesler Way, into the original 'skid row' – an allusion to the skidding logs that were pulled downhill to Henry Yesler's pier-side mill. When the timber industry fell on hard times, the road became a haven for the homeless, and its name subsequently became a byword for poverty-stricken urban enclaves countrywide.

Thanks to a concerted public effort, the neighborhood avoided being laid to waste by the demolition squads in the 1960s and is now protected in the Pioneer Sq–Skid Rd Historic District.

The quarter today mixes the historic with the seedy while harboring art galleries, cafes and nightlife. Its most iconic building is the 42-story **Smith Tower** (206-622-4004; www.smithtower.com; 506 2nd Ave), completed in 1914 and, until 1931, the tallest building west of the Mississippi. Other highlights include the 1909 **Pergola** (cnr Yesler Way & James St), a decorative iron shelter reminiscent of a Parisian Metro station, and **Occidental Park** (btwn S Washington & S Main Sts; Pioneer Sq), containing totem poles carved by Chinook artist Duane Pasco.

The **Klondike Gold Rush National Historical Park** (206-553-3000; www.nps.gov/klse; 319 2nd Ave S; 9am-5pm; International District/Chinatown) FREE is a city-based visitor-center outpost. It shows off exhibits, photos and news clippings from the 1897 Klondike gold rush, when a Seattle-on-steroids acted as a fueling depot for prospectors bound for the Yukon in Canada

American cultures. There's free admission on the first Thursday of the month, when the museum stays open until 8pm.

Ballard

A former seafaring community with a strong Scandinavian heritage, Ballard still feels like a small town engulfed by a bigger city. Traditionally gritty, no-nonsense and uncommercial, it's slowly being condo-ized, but remains a good place to down a microbrew or see a live band.

Hiram M Chittenden Locks CANAL
(3015 NW 54th St; locks 24hr, ladder & gardens 7am-9pm, visitor center 10am-6pm May-Sep; 62) Seattle shimmers like an impressionist painting on sunny days at the Hiram M Chittenden Locks. Here, the fresh waters of Lake Washington and Lake Union drop 22ft into salt-water Puget Sound. Construction of the canal and locks began in 1911; today 100,000 boats pass through them annually. You can view fish-ladder activity through underwater glass panels, stroll through botanical gardens and visit a small museum.

Activities

Cycling

A cycling favorite, the 16.5-mile **Burke-Gilman Trail** winds from Ballard to Log Boom Park in Kenmore on Seattle's Eastside. There, it connects with the 11-mile **Sammamish River Trail**, which winds past the Chateau Ste Michelle winery in Woodinville before terminating at Redmond's Marymoor Park.

More cyclists pedal the popular loop around **Green Lake**, situated just north of Fremont and 5 miles north of the downtown core. From Belltown, the 2.5-mile **Elliott Bay Trail** runs along the Waterfront to Smith Cove.

Get a copy of the *Seattle Bicycling Guide Map,* published by the City of Seattle's Transportation Bicycle & Pedestrian Program online (www.seattle.gov/transportation/bikemaps.htm) or at bike shops.

For bicycle rentals and tours, try **Recycled Cycles** (206-547-4491; www.recycledcycles.com; 1007 NE Boat St; rental per day $40-50; 10am-8pm Mon-Fri, to 6pm Sat & Sun; 66), a friendly U District shop that also rents out chariots and trail-a-bike attachments for kids, or **SBR Seattle Bicycle Rental & Tours** (800-349-0343; www.seattlebicyclerentals.com; Pier 58; rental per hour $10-15, per day $45-65; 11am-7pm Wed-

Mon; University St), which offers reasonable rates and daily tours (book online).

Water Sports

Seattle is not just on a network of cycling trails. With Venice-like proportions of downtown water, it is also strafed with kayak-friendly marine trails. The **Lakes to Locks Water Trail** links Lake Sammamish with Lake Washington, Lake Union and – via the Hiram M Chittenden Locks – Puget Sound. For launching sites and maps, check the website of the Washington Water Trails Association (www.wwta.org).

Northwest Outdoor Center KAYAKING
(206-281-9694; www.nwoc.com; 2100 Westlake Ave N; rental per hour from $15; 62) On Lake Union, rents kayaks and offers tours and instruction in sea and white-water kayaking.

Tours

Seattle Free Walking Tours WALKING TOUR
(www.seattlefreewalkingtours.org) A nonprofit set up in 2012 by two world travelers. Choose from a general downtown tour or a Pike Place Market option. Suggested $15 donation.

Seattle by Foot WALKING TOUR
(206-508-7017; www.seattlebyfoot.com; tours $25-35) Offers different tours focusing on the city's coffeehouses, pubs, downtown areas or the Fremont neighborhood. Book online for a $5 discount.

Festivals & Events

Seattle International Film Festival FILM
(SIFF; www.siff.net) Held in mid-May, the city's biggest film festival uses a half dozen cinemas, but also has its own dedicated cinema, in McCaw Hall's **Nesholm Family Lecture Hall** (321 Mercer St).

Seafair FAIR
(www.seafair.com) Huge crowds attend this festival held on the water in late July/August, with hydroplane races, a torchlight parade, an air show, music and even a Milk Carton Derby (look it up!).

Bumbershoot MUSIC, PERFORMING ARTS
(www.bumbershoot.com) A major arts and cultural event at Seattle Center on the Labor Day weekend in September, with live music, comedy, theater, visual arts and dance.

Sleeping

Reserve ahead in summer, when hotels book up and prices tend to skyrocket.

> **SEATTLE CITY PASS**
>
> If you're planning on visiting the Space Needle, Seattle Aquarium, Woodland Park Zoo and Chihuly Garden and Glass (among other sights), consider buying the Seattle City Pass (www.citypass.com/seattle), which will save you nearly 50% on admission costs.

Moore Hotel HOTEL $
(206-448-4851; www.moorehotel.com; 1926 2nd Ave; r with private/shared bath from $112/87; ; Westlake) Old-world and allegedly haunted, the central, hip and whimsical Moore offers 119 good-size budget rooms at bargain rates. Two rooms sleep up to eight, and the suites have kitchenettes. The cute cafe serves up great coffee. Reserve in summer.

Hotel Hotel HOSTEL $
(206-257-4543; www.hotelhotel.co; 3515 Fremont Ave N; dm $29-35, r $79-99; @; 26) This slick hostel almost feels like a boutique hotel – walls are painted dark earth colors and there are cool retro touches. Dorms are wonderful and spacious, while private rooms have trendy sliding bathroom doors. All boast hardwood floors. A kitchen is available, or eat downstairs in the wood-fired-pizza restaurant-bar.

City Hostel Seattle HOSTEL $
(206-706-3255; www.hostelseattle.com; 2327 2nd Ave; dm/d from $29/79; @; Westlake) Every awesome room in this well-located, boutique 'art hostel' has colorful murals on its walls painted by local artists. There's also a common room, hot tub, in-house movie theater and all-you-can-eat breakfast.

★ **Ace Hotel** HOTEL $$
(206-448-4721; www.acehotel.com; 2423 1st Ave; r with private/shared bath from $219/119; P; 13) The original locale of the trendy Ace Hotel chain, sports minimal decor, sliding barn-door bathrooms and Pendleton wool blankets. Some rooms even come with record players. Continental breakfast is free, but parking costs $26.

Pensione Nichols GUESTHOUSE $$
(206-441-7125; www.pensionenichols.com; 1923 1st Ave; r from $180;) For a homey stay right near Pike Place, this cozy guesthouse is hard to beat. Interior rooms are quiet, but still bright with skylights, while deluxe rooms offer street views. Apartment suites

DON'T MISS

DISCOVERY PARK

A former military installation that has been transformed into a wild coastal park, **Discovery Park** (www.seattle.gov/parks/environment/discovery.htm; 33) is a relatively recent addition to the city landscape – it wasn't officially inaugurated until 1973, and the American military finally left in 2012. Comprising the largest green space in the city, the park's 534 acres are laced with cliffs, meadows, sand dunes, forest and beaches, all of which provide a welcome breathing space for hemmed-in Seattleites and a vital corridor for wildlife.

For a map of the park's trail and road system, stop by the **Discovery Park Environmental Learning Center** (206-386-4236; 3801 W Government Way; 8:30am-5pm) near the Government Way entrance. The park is five miles northwest of downtown Seattle in the neighborhood of Magnolia. To get there, catch bus 33 from 3rd Ave & Union St downtown.

sleep four to six and boast full kitchens. There are great water views from the common room, where continental breakfast is served.

Maxwell Hotel BOUTIQUE HOTEL $$
(206-286-0629; www.themaxwellhotel.com; 300 Roy St; r from $240; ; Rapid Ride D-Line) Located in Lower Queen Anne, the Maxwell's huge designer-chic lobby welcomes you, while the 139 gorgeously modern rooms offer up hardwood floors and Scandinavian bedding. There's a small pool, a gym and free bike rentals.

★**Inn at the Market** BOUTIQUE HOTEL $$$
(206-443-3600; www.innatthemarket.com; 86 Pine St; r with/without water view from $385/325; ; Westlake) Just a block from Pike Place Market, this 71-room boutique hotel has elegant, good-size rooms, many with large windows or small balconies. There's an awesome communal terrace offering views of market activity and Puget Sound. A swimming pool is available at a nearby gym; parking costs $32.

Hotel Five BOUTIQUE HOTEL $$$
(206-448-0924; www.hotelfiveseattle.com; 2200 5th Ave; r from $285; ; 13) This trendy hotel mixes retro-'70s furniture with sharp color accents to produce something dazzlingly modern. The ultra comfortable beds are a valid cure for insomnia, while the large reception area invites lingering, especially when they lay out the complimentary cupcakes and coffee in the late afternoon. Day-of or online rates can be a good deal.

Belltown Inn HOTEL $$$
(206-529-3700; www.belltown-inn.com; 2301 3rd Ave; r from $239; ; Westlake) Rooms at this modern, centrally located hotel are modestly sized but very comfortable, and offer good amenities (some have kitchenettes). There's a roof terrace and free bike rentals. It's popular with cruises, so reserve in summer.

Eating

The best budget meals are to be found in Pike Place Market. Take your pick from fresh produce, baked goods, deli items and take-out ethnic foods.

★**Salumi** SANDWICHES $
(206-621-8772; www.salumicuredmeats.com; 309 3rd Ave S; sandwiches $8.50-11; 11am-1:30pm Mon, to 3:30pm Tue-Fri; International District/Chinatown) Be ready for a queue outside Salumi, well known and loved for its delicious salami and cured-meat sandwiches (grilled lamb, pork shoulder, meatball...). Vegetarians can go for the seasonal veggie offering or eggplant balsamico. Meats and cheeses are also sold by the pound.

Green Leaf VIETNAMESE $
(206-340-1388; www.greenleaftaste.com; 418 8th Ave S; pho $9, specials $10-12; 11am-10pm; Chinatown/International District E) Popular Green Leaf, located in Chinatown, shoots out rapid-fire dishes from its tiny kitchen to its small, crowded dining room. Choose the traditional *pho* (beef noodle soup) or go for the excellent rice- or vermicelli-noodle dishes. Also located in Belltown at 2800 1st Ave.

Piroshky Piroshky BAKERY $
(www.piroshkybakery.com; 1908 Pike Pl; snacks $3-6; 8am-6pm; Westlake) Piroshky knocks out its delectable sweet and savory Russian pies and pastries in a space about the size of a walk-in closet. Get the savory smoked-salmon pâté or the sauerkraut with cabbage and onion, and follow it with the chocolate-cream hazelnut roll or a fresh rhubarb piroshki.

Crumpet Shop BAKERY $
(☎ 206-682-1598; www.thecrumpetshop.com; 1503 1st Ave; crumpets $3-6; ⏰ 7am-3pm Mon-Thu, to 4pm Fri-Sun; Ⓡ Westlake) The treasured British crumpet has been given a distinct American twist with lavish toppings such as pesto, wild salmon or lemon curd at this casual Pike Place Market eatery, family-owned and operated for almost 40 years. Organic ingredients make it very Pacific Northwest, though there's marmite for homesick Brits.

★ Toulouse Petit CAJUN, CREOLE $$
(☎ 206-432-9069; www.toulousepetit.com; 601 Queen Anne Ave N; mains $13-17; ⏰ 8am-2am; 🚌 13) Hailed for its generous happy hours, cheap brunches and rollicking atmosphere, this perennially busy Queen Anne eatery has something for everyone. The menu is large and varied, offering choices such as blackened rib-eye steak, freshwater gulf prawns and house-made gnocchi with artichoke hearts.

Revel ASIAN $$
(☎ 206-547-2040; www.revelseattle.com; 403 N 36th St; small plates $12-16; ⏰ 11am-2pm & 5-10pm Mon-Fri, 10am-2pm & 5-10pm Sat & Sun) Walk into this slick, modern restaurant and you'll notice this isn't your typical Asian eatery. The menu is small but delicious, from the short-rib dumplings to the lemongrass beef with cilantro noodles. Dishes are small-ish and meant to be shared; down them with a creative cocktail or two.

Serious Pie PIZZA $$
(☎ 206-838-7388; www.tomdouglas.com; 316 Virginia St; pizzas $16-18; ⏰ 11am-11pm; Ⓡ Westlake) In the crowded confines of Serious Pie you can enjoy beautifully blistered pizza bases topped with such unconventional ingredients as clams, potatoes, nettles, soft eggs, truffle cheese and more. Other locations around town.

Jack's BBQ BARBECUE $$
(☎ 206-467-4038; www.jacksbbq.com; 3924 Airport Way S; mains $12-23; ⏰ 11am-9pm Tue-Sat) Some of Seattle's best BBQ can be had at this casual, family-friendly joint, located south towards the airport. Meats are smoked slowly over hardwoods and come out tender and delicious – the ribs are a mainstay, and on Tuesdays they serve up a giant beef rib (reserve ahead).

Pink Door ITALIAN $$
(☎ 206-443-3241; www.thepinkdoor.net; 1919 Post Alley; mains $18-27; ⏰ 11:30am-4pm & 5-11pm Mon-Thu, 11.30am-midnight Fri & Sat, 4-10pm Sun) Finding this upscale Italian restaurant is an adventure in itself – look for the unsigned pink door down a busy alleyway near Pike Place Market. Pastas are the specialty here, with a few seafood and meat options, and there's an emphasis on organic, seasonal ingredients.

Le Pichet FRENCH $$
(☎ 206-256-1499; www.lepichetseattle.com; 1933 1st Ave; mains $11-25; ⏰ 8am-midnight; Ⓡ Westlake) Say *bonjour* to Le Pichet, just up from Pike Place Market, a cute and very French bistro with pâtés, cheeses, wine, *chocolat* and a refined Parisian feel. Dinner means delicacies such as wild boar shoulder or grilled rabbit sausage.

Sitka & Spruce MODERN AMERICAN $$$
(☎ 206-324-0662; www.sitkaandspruce.com; 1531 Melrose Ave; small plates $8-33; ⏰ 11:30am-2pm & 5-10pm Mon-Fri, 10am-2pm & 5-11pm Sat, 10am-2pm & 5-9pm Sun; 🚌 10) Located in a

SEATTLE FOR CHILDREN

Make a beeline for the Seattle Center, preferably on the monorail, where food carts, street entertainers, fountains and green spaces will make the day fly by. One essential stop is the **Pacific Science Center** (☎ 206-443-2001; www.pacificsciencecenter.org; 200 2nd Ave N; adult/child exhibits only $19.50/14.50, with Imax $23.50/18.50; ⏰ 10am-5pm Mon-Fri, to 6pm Sat & Sun; 👪; Ⓜ Seattle Center), which entertains and educates with virtual-reality exhibits, laser shows, holograms, an Imax theater and a planetarium. Parents won't be bored either.

Downtown on Pier 59, **Seattle Aquarium** (☎ 206-386-4300; www.seattleaquarium.org; 1483 Alaskan Way, at Pier 59; adult/child 4-12yr $23/16; ⏰ 9:30am-5pm; 👪; Ⓡ University St) is a fun way to learn about the natural world of the Pacific Northwest. Even better is **Woodland Park Zoo** (☎ 206-548-2500; www.zoo.org; 5500 Phinney Ave N; adult/child 3-12yr May-Sep $20/12.25, Oct-Apr $13.75/9.25; ⏰ 9:30am-6pm May-Sep, to 4pm Oct-Apr; 👪; 🚌 5) in the Green Lake neighborhood, one of Seattle's greatest tourist attractions and consistently rated as one of the top 10 zoos in the country.

marketplace-like building on trendy Capitol Hill, this small-plates fine diner has won acclaim for its casual vibe, constantly changing menu and good wine selection. Sample items such as the house-made charcuterie, conica morels or king-trumpet escabeche. All the ingredients are obtained from local producers. Reserve ahead.

Cascina Spinasse ITALIAN $$$
(☎ 206-251-7673; www.spinasse.com; 1531 14th Ave; mains $28-31; ⊙ 5-10pm Sun-Thu, to 11pm Fri & Sat; 🚌 11) Spinasse specializes in cuisine of the Piedmont region of northern Italy. This means seasonally inspired dishes such as roasted morels stuffed with pork, or milk-braised chicken with roasted baby artichokes. The finely curated wine list includes a number of impressive Piedmontese reds.

Drinking & Nightlife

Starbucks is the tip of the iceberg when it comes to coffee culture in Seattle; the city has spawned plenty of smaller indie chains, many with their own roasting rooms. Look out for Uptown Espresso, Caffe Ladro and Espresso Vivace.

You'll find cocktail bars, dance clubs and live music on Capitol Hill. The main drag in Ballard has brick taverns both old and new, filled with the hard-drinking older set in daylight hours and indie rockers at night. Belltown has gone from grungy to shabby chic, and has the advantage of many drinking holes neatly lined up in rows.

★ Starbucks Reserve Roastery & Tasting Room COFFEE
(www.starbucks.com/roastery; 1124 Pike St; coffees $3-12; ⊙ 7am-11pm) Often likened to Willy Wonka's Chocolate Factory, this roastery – Starbucks' largest venue to date – is a multi-leveled mecca of over-caffeinated proportions. Up front a greeter welcomes you with a map, while in back gigantic roasters spin beans. It's a Scandinavian-inspired arena of glass, wood, copper and concrete – a perfect place to sip your cup of siphoned West Java Preanger ($12). Coffee flights available.

★ Fremont Brewing BREWERY
(☎ 206-420-2407; www.fremontbrewing.com; 3409 Woodland Park Ave N; ⊙ 11am-9pm; 🚌 26) Hipsters and cyclists frequent this trendy brewery for its award-winning beers and sustainable practices. On sunny days, sitting at the communal tables out back in the beer garden is mandatory. Free pretzels and apples to snack on, but no real food.

Noble Fir BAR
(☎ 206-420-7425; www.thenoblefir.com; 5316 Ballard Ave NW; ⊙ 4pm-midnight Tue-Thu, to 1am Fri & Sat, 1-9pm Sun; 🚌 17) Possibly the first bar devoted to the theme of wilderness-hiking, the upscale Noble Fir is a bright, shiny spot in the Ballard neighborhood with an epic beer list that might just make you want to abandon all your plans for outdoor adventure. Fine wine and hard ciders, too, along with meat and cheese plates.

Zeitgeist CAFE
(☎ 206-583-0497; www.zeitgeistcoffee.com; 171 S Jackson St; ⊙ 6am-7pm Mon-Fri, 7am-7pm Sat, 8am-6pm Sun; 📶; 🚊 Pioneer Sq) Possibly Seattle's best indie coffee bar, Zeitgeist brews up smooth *doppio macchiatos* to go along with the sweet almond croissants (and other luscious baked goods). The atmosphere is airy industrial, with brick walls and large windows for people-watching. Soups, salads and sandwiches on offer.

Pike Pub & Brewery BREWERY
(☎ 206-622-6044; www.pikebrewing.com; 1415 1st Ave; ⊙ 11am-midnight; 🚊 University St) Leading the way in the microbrewery revolution, this brewpub was an early starter, opening in 1989 underneath Pike Place Market. Today it continues to serve good pub food (mains $11 to $20) and hop-heavy beers in a busily decorated but fun multilevel space. Free tours available.

Elysian Brewing Company BREWERY
(☎ 206-860-1920; www.elysianbrewing.com; 1221 E Pike St; ⊙ 11:30am-2am Mon-Fri, noon-2am Sat & Sun; 🚊 Pike-Pine) Located on hip Capitol Hill, the Elysian's huge windows are great for people-watching. This is one of Seattle's best brewpubs, loved in particular for its spicy pumpkin beers on draft, available in the fall. The Elysian has other locations around town.

Panama Hotel Tea & Coffee House CAFE
(☎ 206-515-4000; www.panamahotel.net; 607 S Main St; ⊙ 8am-9pm; 🚊 Chinatown/International District W) The Panama, a historic 1910 building containing the only remaining Japanese bathhouse in the US, doubles as a memorial to the neighborhood's Japanese residents forced into internment camps during WWII. The beautifully relaxed cafe has a wide selection of teas, serves Lavazza Italian coffee, and boasts a National Treasure designation.

Caffè Umbria CAFE

(☎206-624-5847; www.caffeumbria.com; 320 Occidental Ave S; ⏲6am-7pm Mon-Fri, 7am-6pm Sat, 8am-5pm Sun; 🚋Pioneer Sq) Umbria has a European flavor with its 8oz cappuccinos, chatty clientele, pretty Italianate tiles and baguettes so fresh they must have been teleported over from Milan. Beautiful pastry and gelato case, too. Ideal for Italophiles and Starbucks-phobes.

Shorty's DIVE BAR

(☎206-441-5449; www.shortydog.com; 2222 2nd Ave; ⏲noon-2am; 🚌13) Shorty's is all about beer, arcade games and music, which is mostly punk and metal. A remnant of Belltown's grungier days that refuses to become an anachronism, it keeps the lights low and the music loud. Pinball machines are built into every table, and basic snacks (hot dogs, nachos) soak up the booze.

Blue Moon DIVE BAR

(☎206-675-9116; www.bluemoonseattle.wordpress.com; 712 NE 45th St; ⏲2pm-late Mon-Fri, noon-late Sat, 1pm-late Sun; 🚌66) A legendary counterculture dive near the university that first opened in 1934 to celebrate the repeal of the prohibition laws, the Blue Moon makes much of its former literary patrons – doyens Dylan Thomas, Allen Ginsberg and Tom Robbins get mentioned a lot. These days you're more likely to run into its comedy, open-mic and vinyl-revival nights.

Re-Bar GAY

(☎206-233-9873; www.rebarseattle.com; 1114 Howell St; 🚌70) This storied indie dance club, where many of Seattle's defining cultural events happened (such as Nirvana album releases), welcomes gay, straight, bi or undecided revelers to its lively dance floor. Also come for its offbeat theater, burlesque shows and poetry slams – among other wacky offerings.

☆ Entertainment

Consult *The Stranger, Seattle Weekly* or the daily papers for listings. Tickets for big events are available at TicketMaster (www.ticketmaster.com).

Live Music

Crocodile LIVE MUSIC

(☎206-441-4618; www.thecrocodile.com; 2200 2nd Ave; 🚌13) Nearly old enough to be called a Seattle institution, the Crocodile is a clamorous 560-capacity music venue that first opened in 1991, just in time to grab the coattails of the grunge explosion. Everyone who's anyone in Seattle's alt-music scene has since played here, including a famous occasion in 1992 when Nirvana appeared unannounced supporting Mudhoney.

Tractor Tavern LIVE MUSIC

(☎206-789-3599; www.tractortavern.com; 5213 Ballard Ave NW; 🚌17) The premier venue for folk and acoustic music, Tractor Tavern books local songwriters and regional bands, plus quality touring acts. Music runs towards country, rockabilly, folk, blues and old-time. It's an intimate place with a small stage and great sound; occasional square dancing is frosting on the cake.

Neumo's LIVE MUSIC

(☎206-709-9442; www.neumos.com; 925 E Pike St; 🚋Pike-Pine) This punk, hip-hop and alternative-music Capitol Hill venue counts Radiohead and Bill Clinton (not together) among its former guests. It can get hot and sweaty, and even smelly, but that's rock and roll.

GRUNGE & OTHER MUSICAL SUBCULTURES

Synthesizing Gen X angst with a questionable approach to personal hygiene, grunge first dive-bombed onto Seattle's music scene in the early 1990s like a clap of thunder on an otherwise dry and sunny afternoon. The anger had been fermenting for years. Hardcore punk originated in Portland in the late 1970s, led by resident contrarians the Wipers, whose antifashion followers congregated in legendary dive bars such as Satyricon. Another musical blossoming occurred in Olympia, where DIY–merchants Beat Happening invented 'lo-fi' and coyly mocked the corporate establishment. Scooping up the fallout of a disparate youth culture, Seattle quickly became grunge's pulpit, spawning bands such as Pearl Jam, Soundgarden and Alice in Chains. The genre went global in 1991 when Nirvana's *Nevermind* album knocked Michael Jackson off the number-one spot, but the movement was never meant to be successful, and the kudos quickly killed it. Since the mid-1990s the Pacific Northwest has kept its subcultures largely to itself, though the music's no less potent or relevant.

Performing Arts

A Contemporary Theatre THEATER
(ACT; ☎206-292-7676; www.acttheatre.org; 700 Union St; University St) One of the three big companies in the city, this theater fills its $30-million home at Kreielsheimer Place with performances by Seattle's best thespians and occasional big-name actors. Terraced seating surrounds a central stage, and the interior has gorgeous architectural embellishments.

Intiman Theater Company THEATER
(☎206-441-7178; www.intiman.org; 201 Mercer St; Ⓜ Seattle Center) Artistic director Andrew Russell curates magnificent stagings of Shakespeare and Ibsen, among others.

On the Boards DANCE, THEATER
(☎206-217-9888; www.ontheboards.org; 100 W Roy St; 13) *The* place for avant-garde performance art, the nonprofit On the Boards makes its home at the intimate Behnke Center for Contemporary Performance, and showcases some innovative and occasionally weird dance and music.

Shopping

The main big-name shopping area is downtown between 3rd and 6th Aves and University and Stewart Sts. Pike Place Market is a maze of arts-and-crafts stalls, galleries and small shops. Pioneer Sq and Capitol Hill have locally owned gift and thrift shops. There are many only-in-Seattle shops worth seeking out.

DeLaurenti's FOOD
(☎206-622-0141; 1435 1st Ave; ⏲9am-6pm Mon-Sat, 10am-5pm Sun; University St) Offers a stunning selection of wine, cheese, sausages, hams and pasta, along with a large range of capers, olive oils and anchovies. The sandwich counter is a great place to order panini, salads and pizza slices.

Elliott Bay Book Company BOOKS
(☎206-624-6600; www.elliottbaybook.com; 1521 10th Ave; ⏲10am-10pm Mon-Fri, to 11pm Sat, 11am-9pm Sun; Pike-Pine) This beloved local bookstore offers over 150,000 titles in a large, airy, wood-beamed space with cozy nooks that can inspire hours of serendipitous browsing.

Information

EMERGENCY

Seattle Police (☎206-625-5011; www.seattle.gov/police)

MEDICAL SERVICES

Harborview Medical Center (☎206-744-3000; www.uwmedicine.org/harborview; 325 9th Ave) Full medical care, with emergency room.

MEDIA

KEXP 90.3 FM (www.kexp.org) Legendary independent music and community station.

Seattle Times (www.seattletimes.com) The state's largest daily paper.

Stranger (www.thestranger.com) Irreverent and intelligent free weekly, edited by Dan Savage of 'Savage Love' fame.

POST

Post Office (☎206-748-5417; www.usps.com; 301 Union St; ⏲8:30am-5:30pm Mon-Fri)

TOURIST INFORMATION

Seattle Visitor Center & Concierge Services (☎206-461-5840; www.visitseattle.org; cnr Pike St & 7th Ave, Washington State Convention Center; ⏲9am-5pm daily Jun-Sep, Mon-Fri Oct-May) Also look for an information kiosk at the entrance to Pike Place Market.

Getting There & Away

AIR

Seattle-Tacoma International Airport (SEA; ☎206-787-5388; www.portseattle.org/Sea-Tac; 17801 International Blvd;), 13 miles south of Seattle on I-5, has daily services to Europe, Asia, Mexico and points throughout the USA and Canada, with frequent flights to and from Portland, OR, and Vancouver, BC.

BOAT

Victoria Clipper (☎206-448-5000; www.clippervacations.com; 2701 Alaskan Way, Pier 69) Operates several high-speed passenger ferries to the San Juan Islands and Victoria, BC, as well as offering package tours.

Washington State Ferries (WSF; ☎888-808-7977; www.wsdot.wa.gov/ferries) Routes, prices and schedules available on the website; fares depend on the destination, vehicle size and trip duration, and are collected either for round-trip or one-way travel depending on the departure terminal. Reserve ahead, as bookings are becoming almost mandatory to some destinations (ie San Juan Islands).

BUS

Various intercity coaches serve Seattle at different drop-off points.

Bellair Airporter Shuttle (☎866-235-5247; www.airporter.com) Buses connect downtown Seattle and Sea-Tac airport with Anacortes (for the San Juan Island ferries) and Bellingham.

Greyhound (☎206-628-5526; www.greyhound.com; 503 S Royal Brougham Way) Greyhound connects Seattle with cities all over the country, including Chicago, Spokane, San Francisco and Vancouver, BC.

Quick Shuttle (☎800-665-2122; www.quickcoach.com;) Fast and efficient Quick Shuttle has several daily buses to Vancouver, BC.

TRAIN

King Street Station (☎206-296-0100; www.amtrak.com; 303 S Jackson St) Amtrak serves Seattle's King Street Station. Three main routes run through town: the *Amtrak Cascades* (connecting Vancouver, Seattle, Portland and Eugene); the very scenic *Coast Starlight* (connecting Seattle, Oakland and Los Angeles) and the *Empire Builder* (a cross-continental to Chicago).

Getting Around

TO/FROM THE AIRPORT

There are a number of options for making the 13-mile trek from the airport to downtown Seattle. The most efficient is via the new light-rail service run by Sound Transit (www.soundtransit.org).

Seattle's Link Light Rail operates between Sea-Tac Airport and downtown (Westlake Center). It runs every 10 to 15 minutes between 5am and midnight; the ride takes 36 minutes. There are additional stops in Pioneer Sq and the International District.

Shuttle Express (☎425-981-7000; www.shuttleexpress.com) has a pickup and drop-off point on the 3rd floor of the airport garage; it charges approximately $18 and is handy if you have a lot of luggage.

Taxis are available at the parking garage on the 3rd floor. The average fare to downtown is $46 (not including tip).

CAR & MOTORCYCLE

Trapped in a narrow corridor between mountains and sea, Seattle is a horrendous traffic bottleneck and its nightmarish jams are famous. I-5 has a high-occupancy vehicle lane for vehicles carrying two or more people. Otherwise, try to work around the elongated 'rush hours.'

PUBLIC TRANSPORTATION

Buses are operated by Metro Transit (www.metro.kingcounty.gov), part of the King County Department of Transportation.

Seattle has a bike share system (www.prontocycleshare.com) with 50 stations around the city.

Monorail (☎206-905-2620; www.seattlemonorail.com; adult/child 5-12yr $2.25/1) Travels only between two stops: Seattle Center and Westlake Center.

Seattle Streetcar (www.seattlestreetcar.org) Runs about every 15 minutes from downtown Seattle (Westlake) to South Lake Union; stops allow connections with numerous bus routes. Expansion lines are planned.

TAXI

All Seattle taxi cabs operate at the same rate, set by King County; $2.60 at meter drop, then $2.70 per mile.

Seattle Orange Cab (☎206-522-8800; www.orangecab.net)

Seattle Yellow Cab (☎206-622-6500; www.seattleyellowcab.com)

Around Seattle

Olympia

Small in size, but big in clout, state capital Olympia is a musical, political and outdoor powerhouse. Look no further than the street-side buskers on 4th Ave belting out acoustic grunge, the smartly attired bureaucrats marching across the lawns of the state legislature, or the Goretex-clad outdoor fiends overnighting before sorties into the Olympic Mountains. Progressive Evergreen State College has long lent the place an artsy turn (Matt Groening, creator of the *Simpsons,* studied here), while the dive bars and secondhand guitar shops of downtown provided an original pulpit for riot grrrl music and grunge.

Sights & Activities

Washington State Capitol LANDMARK

(☎360-902-8880; 416 Sid Snyder Ave SW; 7am-5:30pm Mon-Fri, 11am-4pm Sat & Sun) FREE Olympia's capitol complex is set in a 30-acre park overlooking Capitol Lake with the Olympic Mountains glistening in the background. The campus' crowning glory is the magnificent **Legislative Building**. Completed in 1927, it's a dazzling display of craning columns and polished marble, topped by a 287ft dome that is only slightly smaller than its namesake in Washington, DC. Tours available.

Olympia Farmers Market MARKET

(☎360-352-9096; www.olympiafarmersmarket.com; 700 N Capitol Way; 10am-3pm Thu-Sun Apr-Oct, Sat & Sun Nov & Dec) Second only to Seattle's Pike Place in size and character, Olympia's local market is a great place to shop for organic herbs, vegetables, flowers, baked goods and the famous specialty oysters.

Sleeping & Eating

Fertile Ground Guesthouse GUESTHOUSE $$
(360-352-2428; www.fertileground.org; 311 9th Ave SE; s/d from $110/120;) Surrounded by a lush and leafy organic garden, this comfortable and homey guesthouse offers three lovely rooms, one en suite and two with shared bath. Breakfast is made mostly from organic and locally sourced ingredients. Sauna on premises. More rooms (including a dorm) are available at other locations; check the website for details.

Traditions Cafe & World Folk Art AMERICAN $
(360-705-2819; www.traditionsfairtrade.com; 300 5th Ave SW; sandwiches $9-10; 9am-6pm Mon-Fri, 10am-6pm Sat, 11am-5pm Sun;) Fair Trade hippy enclave of fresh salads (lemon-tahini, smoked salmon etc), sandwiches (meat, veggie and vegan), a few Mexican and Italian plates, coffee drinks, herbal teas and local ice cream. Attached is an eclectic folk-art store. Check the website for music, poetry nights and more.

Information

State Capitol Visitor Center (360-704-7544; www.visitolympia.com; 103 Sid Snyder Ave SW; 10am-3pm Mon-Fri, 11am-3pm Sat & Sun) Offers information on the capitol campus, the Olympia area and Washington state. Note the limited opening hours.

Olympic Peninsula

Surrounded on three sides by sea and exhibiting many of the characteristics of a full-blown island, the remote Olympic Peninsula is about as 'wild' and 'west' as America gets. What it lacks in cowboys it makes up for in rare, endangered wildlife and dense primeval forest. The peninsula's roadless interior is largely given over to the notoriously wet Olympic National Park, while the margins are the preserve of loggers, Native American reservations and a smattering of small but interesting settlements, most notably Port Townsend. Equally untamed is the western coastline, America's isolated end point, where tempestuous ocean and misty old-growth Pacific rainforest meet in aqueous harmony.

Olympic National Park

Declared a national monument in 1909 and a national park in 1938, the 1406-sq-mile **Olympic National Park** (www.nps.gov/olym) shelters one of the world's only temperate rainforests and a 57-mile strip of Pacific coastal wilderness that was added in 1953. Opportunities for independent exploration abound, with activities from hiking and fishing to kayaking and skiing.

EASTERN ENTRANCES

The graveled Dosewallips River Rd follows the river from US 101 (turnoff approximately 1km north of Dosewallips State Park) for 15 miles to **Dosewallips Ranger Station**, where hiking trails begin; call 360-565-3130 for road conditions. Even hiking smaller portions of the two long-distance paths, including the 14.9 mile Dosewallips River Trail, with views of glaciated **Mt Anderson**, is reason enough to visit the valley. Another eastern entry for hikers is the **Staircase Ranger Station** (360-877-5569), just inside the national-park boundary, 15 miles from Hoodsport on US 101. Two state parks along the eastern edge of the national park are popular with campers: **Dosewallips State Park** (888-226-7688; www.parks.wa.gov/499/Dosewallips; 306996 Hwy 101; tent sites $12-35, RV sites $30-45) and **Lake Cushman State Park** (888-226-7688; campsites $15-66). Both have running water, flush toilets and some RV hookups. Reservations are accepted.

NORTHERN ENTRANCES

The park's easiest – and hence most popular – entry point is at **Hurricane Ridge**, 18 miles south of Port Angeles. At the road's end, an interpretive center gives a stupendous view of Mt Olympus (7965ft) and dozens of other peaks. The 5200ft altitude can mean you'll hit inclement weather, and the winds here (as the name suggests) can be ferocious. Aside from various summer trekking opportunities, the area maintains the small, family-friendly **Hurricane Ridge Ski & Snowboard Area** (www.hurricaneridge.com;).

Popular for boating and fishing is **Lake Crescent**, the site of the park's oldest and most reasonably priced **lodge** (888-896-3818; www.olympicnationalparks.com; 416 Lake Crescent Rd; lodge r from $120, cabins from $260;). Delicious sustainable food is served in the lodge's ecofriendly restaurant. From **Storm King Information Station** (360-928-3380; 343 Barnes Point Rd; May-Sep) on the lake's south shore, a 1-mile hike climbs through old-growth forest to Marymere Falls.

Along the Sol Duc River, the **Sol Duc Hot Springs Resort** (☎360-327-3583; www.olympicnationalparks.com; 12076 Sol Duc Hot Springs Rd, Port Angeles; day use $12.25, RV sites $43, cabins from $196; ⊙Apr-Oct;) has lodging, dining, massage and, of course, hot-spring pools, as well as great day hikes.

WESTERN ENTRANCES

Isolated by distance and home of one of the country's rainiest microclimates, the Pacific side of the Olympics remains the wildest. Only US 101 offers access to its noted temperate rainforests and untamed coastline. The **Hoh River Rainforest**, at the end of the 19-mile Hoh River Rd, is a Tolkienesque maze of dripping ferns and moss-draped trees. The **Hoh Visitor Center and Campground** (☎360-374-6925; ⊙9am-5pm) has information on guided walks and longer backcountry hikes. There are no hookups or showers, and it's first-come, first-served.

A little to the south lies **Lake Quinault**, a beautiful glacial lake surrounded by forested peaks. It's popular for fishing, boating and swimming, and is surrounded by some of the nation's oldest trees. **Lake Quinault Lodge** (☎360-288-2900; www.olympicnationalparks.com; 345 S Shore Rd; r from $269;), a luxury classic of 1920s 'parkitecture,' has a heated pool and sauna, a crackling fireplace and a memorable dining room. For a cheaper sleep nearby, try the ultrafriendly **Quinault River Inn** (☎360-288-2237; www.quinaultriverinn.com; 8 River Dr; r from $139;) in Amanda Park, a favorite with anglers.

A number of short hikes begin just outside the Lake Quinault Lodge, or you can try the longer **Enchanted Valley Trail**, a medium-grade 13-miler that begins from the Graves Creek Ranger station at the end of South Shore Rd and climbs up to a large meadow resplendent with wildflowers and copses of alder trees.

Information

The park entry fee is $5/15 per person/vehicle, valid for one week and payable at park entrances. Many park visitor centers double as United States Forestry Service (USFS) ranger stations, where you can pick up permits for wilderness camping (per group $5, valid up to 14 days, plus $2 per person per night).

Forks Visitor Information Center (☎360-374-2531; www.forkswa.com; 1411 S Forks Ave; ⊙10am-5pm Mon-Sat, 11am-4pm Sun)

Olympic National Park Visitor Center (☎360-565-3130; www.nps.gov/olym; 3002 Mt Angeles Rd, Port Angeles; ⊙9am-5pm) The best overall center is situated at the Hurricane Ridge gateway, a mile off Hwy 101 in Port Angeles. Hours vary according to the season.

Wilderness Information Center (☎360-565-3100; www.nps.gov/olym; 3002 Mt Angeles Rd, Port Angeles; ⊙8am-6pm Jul & Aug, to 4pm Sep-Jun) Provides backcountry permits and backpacking information.

Port Townsend

Historic relics are rare in the Pacific Northwest, which makes time-warped Port Townsend all the more fascinating. Small, nostalgic and culturally vibrant, this showcase of 1890s Victorian architecture is the 'New York of the West that never was,' a onetime boomtown that went bust at the turn of the 20th century, only to be rescued 70 years later by a group of far-sighted locals. Port Townsend today is a buoyant blend of inventive eateries, historic hotels and quirky annual festivals.

Sights

Jefferson Art & History Museum MUSEUM
(www.jchsmuseum.org; 540 Water St; adult/child $6/1; ⊙11am-4pm daily Mar-Dec, Sat & Sun Jan & Feb) The local historic society runs this well-maintained exhibition area that includes mock-ups of an 1892 jail, maritime artifacts and an art-gallery room. You can also learn about the history of prostitution in innocent-seeming Port Townsend.

Fort Worden State Park PARK
(☎360-344-4431; www.parks.wa.gov/511/Fort-Worden; 200 Battery Way; ⊙6:30am-dusk Apr-Oct, 8am-dusk Nov-Mar) This attractive park located within Port Townsend's city limits is the remains of a large fortification system constructed in the 1890s to protect the strategically important Puget Sound area from outside attack – supposedly from the Spanish during the 1898 war. Sharp-eyed film buffs might recognize the area as the backdrop for the movie *An Officer and a Gentleman.*

The Commanding Officer's Quarters, a 12-bedroom mansion, is open for tours, and part of one of the barracks is now the Puget Sound Coast Artillery Museum, which tells the story of early Pacific coastal fortifications.

Hikes lead along the headland to **Point Wilson Lighthouse Station** and some wonderful windswept beaches. On the park's fishing pier is the **Port Townsend**

Marine Science Center (www.ptmsc.org; 532 Battery Way; adult/child $5/3; ⏲11am-5pm Wed-Mon Jun-Aug, reduced hours Sep-May) featuring four touch tanks and daily interpretive programs. There are also several camping and lodging possibilities.

Sleeping & Eating

Waterstreet Hotel HOTEL $
(☎360-385-5467; www.watersthotel.com; 635 Water St; r $60-175; ❄📶) Homey and friendly, the Waterstreet offers great-value rooms, some with shared bathrooms. If you're a family or group go for suite 5 – it's essentially an apartment with a loft, full kitchen and charming back porch with views of Puget Sound. Reception is in the gift shop next door to the hotel.

Palace Hotel HISTORIC HOTEL $$
(☎360-385-0773; www.palacehotelpt.com; 1004 Water St; r $109-229; 📶🐾) Built in 1889, this beautiful Victorian building is a former brothel that was once run by the locally notorious Madame Marie, who did business out of the 2nd-floor corner suite. It's been reincarnated as an attractive period hotel with antique furnishings. Pleasant common spaces; kitchenettes available.

Doc's Marina Grill AMERICAN $$
(☎360-344-3627; www.docsgrill.com; 141 Hudson St; mains $13-24; ⏲11am-11pm) With a great location by Port Townsend's marina, Doc's offers up something for everyone. There are burgers, sandwiches, fish and chips, various salads, pastas, steaks, seafood and a few vegetarian selections. It is housed in a historic building that was a nurses' barracks back in the 1940s.

Waterfront Pizza PIZZA $$
(☎360-379-9110; 951 Water St; large pizzas $16-28; ⏲11am-8pm Sun-Thu, to 9pm Fri & Sat) If you're craving a quick snack, grab a slice downstairs – just be prepared for lines in the closet-size dining room. For more relaxed, sit-down service, climb the stairs and sample the pies topped with treats such as Cajun sausage, feta cheese, artichoke hearts and pesto.

Information

Visitor Center (☎360-385-2722; www.ptchamber.org; 2409 Jefferson; ⏲9am-5pm)

Getting There & Away

Washington State Ferries (☎206-464-6400; www.wsdot.wa.gov/ferries) Goes to/from Coupeville on Whidbey Island (35 minutes); reserve ahead.

Port Angeles

Despite the name, there's nothing Spanish or particularly angelic about Port Angeles, propped up by the lumber industry and backed by the steep-sided Olympic Mountains. Rather than visiting to see the town per se, people come here to catch a ferry for Victoria, BC, or to plot an outdoor excursion into the nearby Olympic National Park.

Activities

The **Olympic Discovery Trail** (www.olympicdiscoverytrail.com) is a 30-mile off-road hiking and cycling trail between Port Angeles and Sequim, starting at the end of **Ediz Hook**, the sand spit that loops around the bay. Bikes can be rented at **Sound Bikes & Kayaks** (www.soundbikekayaks.com; 120 Front St; bike rental per hour/day $10/45).

Sleeping & Eating

Toadlily House HOSTEL $
(☎360-797-3797; www.toadlilyhouse.com; 105 E 5th St; dm $25-30; 📶) This bright and clean hostel in a lime-green heritage home has several bunk rooms and one private room ($40) off the back garden. The bathroom and kitchen are shared, the layout is perfect for socializing, and the owner is hip and friendly.

Olympic Lodge HOTEL $$
(☎360-452-2993; www.olympiclodge.com; 140 Del Guzzi Dr; r from $190; ❄@📶🏊) This is the most comfortable place in town, offering gorgeous rooms, on-site bistro, swimming pool with hot tub, and complimentary cookies and soup in the afternoon. Prices vary widely depending on the day and month.

Bella Italia ITALIAN $$
(☎360-457-5442; www.bellaitaliapa.com; 118 E 1st St; mains $14-24; ⏲4pm-late) Bella Italia has been around a lot longer than Bella, the heroine of the *Twilight* saga, but its mention in the book as the place where Bella and Edward Cullen go for their first date has turned what was already a popular restaurant into an icon. Try the clam linguine, chicken marsala or smoked duck breast, washed down with an outstanding wine from a list featuring 500 selections.

Information

Port Angeles Visitor Center (☎360-452-2363; www.portangeles.org; 121 E Railroad Ave; ⏲8am-5pm Mon-Sat, noon-3pm Sun) Adjacent to the ferry terminal. Open later in summer if volunteers are available.

Getting There & Away

Clallam Transit (☎360-452-4511; www.clallamtransit.com) Buses go to Forks and Sequim, where they link up with other transit buses that circumnavigate the Olympic Peninsula.

Coho Vehicle Ferry (☎888-993-3779; www.cohoferry.com) Runs to/from Victoria, BC (1½ hours).

Dungeness Line (www.olympicbuslines.com; 123 East Front St, Gateway Transit Center) Runs twice daily to Seattle.

Northwest Peninsula

Several Native American reservations cling to the extreme northwest corner of the continent, and are welcoming to visitors. The small weather-beaten settlement of **Neah Bay** on Hwy 112 is home to the Makah Indian Reservation, whose **Makah Museum** (☎360-645-2711; www.makahmuseum.com; 1880 Bayview Ave; admission $5; ⊙10am-5pm) displays artifacts from one of North America's most significant archaeological finds, the 500-year-old Makah village of Ozette. Several miles beyond the museum, a short boardwalk trail leads to stunning **Cape Flattery**, a 300ft promontory that marks the most northwesterly point in the lower 48 states.

Convenient to the Hoh River Rainforest and the Olympic coastline is **Forks**, a one-horse lumber town that's now more famous for its *Twilight* paraphernalia. It's a central town for exploring Olympic National Park; a good accommodation choice is the **Miller Tree Inn** (☎360-374-6806; www.millertreeinn.com; 654 E Division St; r $135-235; 📶🐾).

Northwest Washington

Wedged between Seattle, the Cascades and Canada, northwest Washington draws influences from three sides. Its urban hub is collegiate Bellingham, while its outdoor highlight is the pastoral San Juan Islands, an extensive archipelago that glimmers like a sepia-toned snapshot from another era. Anacortes is the main hub for ferries to the San Juan Islands and Victoria, BC.

Whidbey Island

While not as detached (there's a bridge connecting it to adjacent Fidalgo Island at its northernmost point) or nonconformist as the San Juans, life is almost as slow, quiet and pastoral on Whidbey Island. Having six state parks is a bonus, along with a plethora of B&Bs, two historic fishing villages (Langley and Coupeville), famously good clams and a thriving artist's community.

Deception Pass State Park (☎360-675-2417; 41229 N State Hwy 20) straddles the eponymous steep-sided water chasm that flows between Whidbey and Fidalgo Islands, and incorporates lakes, islands, campsites and 38 miles of hiking trails.

Ebey's Landing National Historical Reserve (☎360-678-6084; www.nps.gov/ebla; 162 Cemetery Rd) comprises 17,400 acres encompassing working farms, sheltered beaches, two state parks and the town of **Coupeville**. This small settlement is one of Washington's oldest towns and has an attractive seafront, antique stores and a number of old inns, including the **Coupeville Inn** (☎800-247-6162; www.thecoupevilleinn.com; 200 NW Coveland St; r $110-170, condos $175-300; ❄@📶🐾), which bills itself as a French-style motel (if that's not an oxymoron), with fancy furnishings and a substantial breakfast. For the famous fresh local clams, head to **Christopher's** (☎360-678-5480; www.christophersonwhidbey.com; 103 NW Coveland St; mains $18-23; ⊙11:30am-2pm & 5pm-close).

Getting There & Around

Washington State Ferries (www.wsdot.wa.gov/ferries) link Clinton to Mukilteo (20 minutes, every 30 minutes). They also ply the waters between Coupeville and Port Townsend (35 minutes, every 45 minutes). Free **Island Transit** (☎360-678-7771; www.islandtransit.org) buses run the length of Whidbey every hour daily, except Sundays, from the Clinton ferry dock.

Bellingham

Welcome to a green, liberal and famously livable settlement that has taken the libertine, nothing-is-too-weird ethos of Oregon's 'City of Roses' and given it a peculiarly Washingtonian twist. Mild in both manners and weather, the 'city of subdued excitement,' as a local mayor once dubbed it, is an unlikely alliance of espresso-sipping students, venerable retirees, all-weather triathletes and placard-waving peaceniks. Publications such as *Outside Magazine* have consistently lauded it for its abundant outdoor opportunities.

Sights & Activities

Bellingham offers outdoor sights and activities by the truckload. **Whatcom Falls Park** is a natural wild region that bisects Bellingham's eastern suburbs. The change in elevation is marked by four sets of waterfalls, including **Whirlpool Falls**, a popular summer swimming hole.

Fairhaven Bike & Mountain Sports CYCLING
(☎360-733-4433; www.fairhavenbike.com; 1103 11th St; rental per 4hr $25-37.50) Bellingham is one of the most bike-friendly cities in the Northwest, with a well-maintained intra-urban trail going as far south as Larrabee State Park. This outfit rents bikes and has maps on local routes.

San Juan Cruises CRUISE
(☎360-738-8099; www.whales.com; 355 Harris Ave; cruises $35-99) Runs cruises around Bellingham Bay with beer- or wine-tasting, plus whale-watching around the San Juan Islands and more.

Sleeping & Eating

GuestHouse Inn MOTEL $
(☎360-671-9600; www.guesthouseintl.com; 805 Lakeway Dr; r from $90;) This clean, comfortable and friendly motel is just off I-5 and about a 20-minute walk from downtown Bellingham. Rooms come with modern amenities such as flat-screen TV, fridge and microwave. Continental breakfast and hot-tub use included.

★**Hotel Bellwether** BOUTIQUE HOTEL $$$
(☎360-392-3100; www.hotelbellwether.com; 1 Bellwether Way; r from $250;) Bellingham's finest and most charismatic hotel lies on the waterfront and offers views of Lummi Island. Standard rooms come with Italian furnishings and Hungarian-down duvets, but the finest stay is the 900-sq-ft lighthouse suite (from $500), an old converted three-story lighthouse with a wonderful private lookout. Spa and restaurant on premises.

Old Town Cafe CAFE $
(☎360-671-4431; www.theoldtowncafe.com; 316 W Holly St; mains $7-10; ⏰6:30am-3pm Mon-Sat, 8am-2pm Sun) Very popular for its casual, artsy atmosphere, this bohemian breakfast joint cooks up tasty dishes such as custom omelets, egg tortillas and whole wheat French toast. There's also homemade granola, gluten-free hot cakes, organic tofu scrambles, garden salads and 10 different kinds of sandwiches.

★**Pepper Sisters** MODERN AMERICAN $$
(☎360-671-3414; www.peppersisters.com; 1055 N State St; mains $10-18; ⏰4:30-9pm Tue-Sun;) This cheerful, colorful restaurant serves innovative food that is hard to categorize – let's call it Mexican cuisine with a Northwestern twist. Try the grilled eggplant tostada, chipotle-and-pink-peppercorn enchilada or Southwest pizza; there's even a chicken-strip-free kids' menu.

Information

Downtown Info Center (☎360-671-3990; www.bellingham.org; 1306 Commercial St; ⏰9am-5pm)

Getting There & Away

Alaska Marine Highway (AMHS; ☎800-642-0066; www.dot.state.ak.us/amhs; 355 Harris Ave) ferries go to Juneau (60 hours) and other southeast Alaskan ports (from $326 without car). The Bellair Airporter Shuttle (www.airporter.com) runs to Sea-Tac Airport, with connections en route to Anacortes and Whidbey Island.

San Juan Islands

Take the ferry west out of Anacortes and you'll feel like you've dropped off the edge of the continent. A thousand metaphoric miles from the urban inquietude of Puget Sound, the nebulous San Juan archipelago conjures up Proustian flashbacks from another era and often feels about as American as – er – Canada (which surrounds it on two sides).

There are 172 landfalls in this expansive archipelago, but unless you're rich enough to charter your own yacht or seaplane, you'll be restricted to seeing the big four – San Juan, Orcas, Shaw and Lopez Islands – all served daily by Washington State Ferries. Communally, the islands are famous for their tranquillity, whale-watching opportunities, sea kayaking and seditious nonconformity.

A great way to explore the San Juans is by sea kayak or bicycle. Expect a guided half-day trip to cost from $45 to $65. Cycling-wise, Lopez is flat and pastoral and San Juan is worthy of an easy day loop, while Orcas offers the challenge of undulating terrain and a steep 5-mile ride to the top of Mt Constitution.

Getting There & Around

Airlines serving the San Juan Islands include **San Juan Airlines** (☎800-874-4434; www.

sanjuanairlines.com) and **Kenmore Air** (☎866-435-9524; www.kenmoreair.com).

Washington State Ferries (www.wsdot.wa.gov/ferries) leave Anacortes for the San Juans; some continue to Sidney, BC, near Victoria. Ferries run to Lopez Island (45 minutes), Orcas Landing (60 minutes) and Friday Harbor on San Juan Island (75 minutes). Fares vary by season; the cost of the entire round-trip is collected on westbound journeys only (except those returning from Sidney, BC). To visit all the islands, it's cheapest to go to Friday Harbor first and work your way back through the other islands.

Shuttle buses ply Orcas and San Juan Island in the summer months.

San Juan Island

San Juan Island is the archipelago's unofficial capital, a harmonious mix of low forested hills and small rural farms that resonate with a dramatic and unusual 19th-century history. The only real settlement is Friday Harbor, home to the **visitor center** and **Chamber of Commerce** (www.sanjuanisland.org; 135 Spring St, Friday Harbor; ⏲10am-5pm) located inside a small mall off the main street.

Sights

San Juan Island National Historical Park HISTORIC SITE
(☎360-378-2240; www.nps.gov/sajh; ⏲visitor center 8:30am-5pm Jun-Aug, to 4:30pm Sep-May) FREE More known for their scenery than their history, the San Juans nonetheless hide one of the 19th century's oddest political confrontations, the so-called 'Pig War' between the USA and Britain. This curious stand-off is showcased in two separate historical parks on either end of the island that once housed opposing American and English military encampments.

Lime Kiln Point State Park PARK
(☎360-902-8844; www.parks.wa.gov/540/Lime-Kiln-Point; 1567 Westside Rd, Friday Harbor; ⏲8am-dusk) Clinging to the island's rocky west coast, this beautiful park overlooks the deep Haro Strait and is, reputedly, one of the best places in the world to view whales from the shoreline. Word is out, however, so the view areas are often packed with hopeful picnickers. There is a small **interpretive center** (☎360-378-2044; ⏲Jun-Aug) in the park, along with trails, a restored lime kiln and the landmark Lime Kiln Lighthouse, built in 1919.

Sleeping & Eating

There are hotels, B&Bs and resorts scattered around the island, but Friday Harbor has the highest concentration.

Wayfarer's Rest HOSTEL $
(☎360-378-6428; www.hostelssanjuan.com; 35 Malcolm St, Friday Harbor; dm $40, r from $85;) A short walk from the ferry terminal, this pleasant hostel is located in a homey house with comfortable dorms and affordable private rooms. The main kitchen overlooks the grassy backyard, and there's also a suite that sleeps six ($245). Reserve two months ahead in summer.

Juniper Lane Guest House INN $$
(☎360-378-7761; www.juniperlaneguesthouse.com; 1312 Beaverton Valley Rd, Friday Harbor; r $85-135, cabins $219;) The five great rooms at this cozy, hip inn are decorated with an eclectic assortment of furnishings, much of it refurbished. In summer, there are hammocks in the backyard and views over the surrounding countryside. Communal kitchen and two-bedroom cabin available. It's 1.3 miles from the ferry dock.

Market Chef DELI $
(☎360-378-4546; 225 A St, Friday Harbor; sandwiches $9; ⏲10am-4pm Mon-Fri) Super popular and famous for its delicious sandwiches, such as roast beef and rocket or (their signature) curried egg salad with roasted peanuts and chutney. Salads are also available; local ingredients used. If you're in town on a Saturday in summer, visit Market Chef at the San Juan Island Farmer's Market (10am to 1pm).

Backdoor Kitchen FUSION $$$
(☎360-378-9540; www.backdoorkitchen.com; 400 A St, Friday Harbor; mains $30-37; ⏲11:30am-2:30pm Mon, 5-9pm Wed-Sun) One of San Juan Island's finest restaurants, Backdoor Kitchen uses fresh local ingredients to serve up creative multi-ethnic dishes such as Spanish-style pork with wild prawn stew and east Indian spiced lentils with spinach cake. Dine in the pretty garden in summer. Reserve ahead.

Orcas Island

Precipitous, unspoiled and ruggedly beautiful, Orcas Island is the San Juans' emerald icon, excellent for hiking and, more recently, gourmet food. The ferry terminal is at Orcas Landing, 8 miles south of the main village, Eastsound.

On the island's eastern lobe is **Moran State Park** (☎360-376-6173; 3572 Olga Rd; Discover Pass required at some parking lots, $10; ⏱6:30am-dusk Apr-Sep, 8am-dusk Oct-Mar), dominated by Mt Constitution (2409ft), with 40 miles of trails and an amazing 360-degree mountaintop view.

Sleeping

Doe Bay Village Resort & Retreat HOSTEL $
(☎360-376-2291; www.doebay.com; campsites from $60, cabins from $100, yurts from $125;) By far the least expensive resort in the San Juans, Doe Bay has the atmosphere of an artists' commune combined with a hippie retreat. Accommodations include sea-view campsites and various cabins and yurts, some with views of the water.

Golden Tree Hostel HOSTEL $$
(☎360-317-8693; www.goldentreehostel.com; 1159 North Beach Rd, Eastsound; dm/d with shared bath $45/115;) Located in an 1890s-era heritage house, this hip hostel offers cozy rooms and pleasant common spaces, along with a hot tub and sauna in the grassy garden. There's even a separate recreation building with pool, foosball, shuffleboard and darts. Friday pizza nights. Reserve in summer.

Outlook Inn HOTEL $$
(☎360-376-2200; www.outlookinn.com; 171 Main St, Eastsound; r with shared/private bath from $79/99;) Eastsound's oldest and most eye-catching building, the Outlook Inn (1888) is an island institution. Budget rooms are cozy and neat (try for room 30), while the luxurious suites have fireplaces, Jacuzzi tubs and stunning water views from their balconies. Excellent attached cafe.

Eating & Drinking

Kitchen ASIAN $
(☎360-376-6958; www.thekitchenorcas.com; 249 Prune Alley, Eastsound; mains $10-15; ⏱11am-8pm Mon-Fri, to 4pm Sat) By using mostly local, organic and sustainably produced ingredients, Kitchen serves up some of the island's freshest and tastiest 'fast' food. Choose from various wraps, all made with sprouted-wheat tortillas, or go for a noodle or fried rice bowl with creative sauces.

Mijita's MEXICAN $$
(☎360-376-6722; 310 A St, Eastsound; mains $14-22; ⏱4-9pm Mon-Sat) It's difficult to go wrong in this creative, indoor-outdoor restaurant with its rustic Mexican furnishings and fairy-lit garden. The Mexican native chef's family recipes include delicacies such as slow-braised short ribs with blackberry mole or vegetarian quinoa cakes with mushrooms, chèvre, almonds and *pipian* – but there are also the basics such as fish tacos and enchiladas. Reserve ahead.

Island Hoppin' Brewery BREWERY
(www.islandhoppinbrewery.com; 33 Hope Lane, Eastsound; ⏱noon-9pm Tue-Sun) The location, just off Mt Baker Rd near the airport, makes this tiny brewery hard to find, but the locals sure know it's there – this is *the* place to go to enjoy seven changeable brews on tap. Don't come hungry – only snacks are served. Happy hour runs from 7pm to 9pm Sunday to Thursday, while a ping-pong table adds some action.

Lopez Island

If you're going to Lopez – or 'Slow-pez,' as locals prefer to call it – take a bike. With its undulating terrain and salutation-offering residents (who are famous for their three-fingered 'Lopezian wave'), this is the ideal cycling isle. A leisurely pastoral spin can be tackled in a day, with good overnight digs available next to the marina in the **Lopez Islander Resort** (☎360-468-2233; www.lopezfun.com; 2864 Fisherman Bay Rd; r from $119;), which has a restaurant, gym and pool and offers free parking in Anacortes (another incentive to dump the car). If you arrive cycleless, call up **Village Cycles** (☎360-468-4013; www.villagecycles.net; 214 Lopez Rd; rental per hour $7-16), which can deliver a bicycle to the ferry terminal for you.

North Cascades

Geologically different from their southern counterparts, the North Cascade Mountains are peppered with sharp, jagged peaks, copious glaciers and a preponderance of complex metamorphic rock. Thanks to their virtual impregnability, the North Cascades were an unsolved mystery to humans until relatively recently. The first road was built across the region in 1972 and, even today, it remains one of the Northwest's most isolated outposts.

Mt Baker

Rising like a ghostly sentinel above the sparkling waters of upper Puget Sound, Mt Baker has been mesmerizing visitors to the

Northwest for centuries. A dormant volcano that last belched smoke in the 1850s, this haunting 10,781ft peak shelters 12 glaciers, and in 1999 registered a record-breaking 95ft of snow in one season.

Well-paved Hwy 542, known as the Mt Baker Scenic Byway, climbs 5100ft to **Artist Point**, 56 miles from Bellingham. Near here you'll find the **Heather Meadows Visitor Center** (Mt Baker Hwy, Mile 56; ⌚8am-4:30pm May-Sep) and a plethora of varied hikes, including the 7.5-mile **Chain Lakes Loop** that leads you around a half-dozen lakes surrounded by huckleberry meadows.

Receiving more annual snow than any ski area in North America, the **Mt Baker Ski Area** (☎360-734-6771; www.mtbakerskiarea.com) has 38 runs, eight lifts and a vertical rise of 1500ft. The resort has gained something of a cult status among snowboarders, who have been coming here for the Legendary Baker Banked Slalom every January since 1985.

On your way up the mountain, stop for a bite at authentic honky-tonk bar and restaurant **Graham's** (☎360-599-9883; 9989 Mt Baker Hwy; mains $6-14; ⌚noon-9pm Mon-Fri, 8-11am & noon-9pm Sat & Sun) and grab trail munchies at **Wake & Bakery** (☎360-599-1658; www.getsconed.com; 6903 Bourne St, Glacier; snacks from $4; ⌚7:30am-5pm), both in the town of **Glacier**.

Leavenworth

Blink hard and rub your eyes. This isn't some strange Germanic hallucination. This is Leavenworth, a former lumber town that underwent a Bavarian makeover back in the 1960s after the rerouting of the cross-continental railway threatened to put it permanently out of business. Swapping wood for tourists, Leavenworth today has successfully reinvented itself as a traditional Romantische Strasse village, right down to the beer, sausages and lederhosen-loving locals (25% of whom are German). The classic *Sound of Music* mountain setting helps, as does the fact that Leavenworth serves as the main activity center for sorties into the nearby Alpine Lakes Wilderness.

The **Leavenworth Ranger Station** (☎509-548-2550; 600 Sherbourne St; ⌚8am-4:30pm Mon-Sat) can advise on the local outdoor activities. Highlights include the best climbing in the state at **Castle Rock** in Tumwater Canyon, about 3 miles northwest of town off US 2.

The **Devil's Gulch** is a popular off-road mountain bike trail (25 miles, four to six hours). Local outfitters **Der Sportsmann** (☎509-548-5623; www.dersportsmann.com; 837 Front St; ⌚9am-6pm) rents mountain bikes.

Sleeping & Eating

Hotel Pension Anna HOTEL $$

(☎509-548-6273; www.pensionanna.com; 926 Commercial St; r from $155) The most authentic Bavarian hotel in town is also spotless and incredibly friendly. Each room is decorated in imported Austrian decor, and the European-inspired breakfasts (included) may induce joyful yodels. Our favorite room is the double with hand-painted furniture, but the spacious suite in the adjacent St Joseph's chapel is perfect for families.

Enzian Inn HOTEL $$

(☎509-548-5269; www.enzianinn.com; 590 Hwy 2; d from $125;) At this Leavenworth classic, long-term owner Bob Johnson starts the day with a blast on his famous alpenhorn before breakfast. If this doesn't send you running for your lederhosen, cast an eye over the free putting green (with resident grass-trimming goats), the indoor and outdoor swimming pools, or the nightly pianist pounding out requests in the Bavarian lobby.

München Haus GERMAN $

(☎509-548-1158; www.munchenhaus.com; 709 Front St; snacks from $6; ⌚11am-9pm Mon-Wed, to 10pm Thu & Sun, to 11pm Fri & Sat;) The Haus is 100% alfresco, meaning that the hot German sausages and pretzels are essential stomach-warmers in winter, while the Bavarian brews will cool you down in summer. The casual beer-garden atmosphere is complemented by vibrant flower baskets, laid-back staff and a stash of top-quality relishes, including cider kraut and mustard. Hours vary outside summer.

Lake Chelan

Long, slender Lake Chelan is central Washington's water playground. The town of **Chelan**, at the lake's southeastern tip, is the primary base for accommodations and services, and has a **USFS ranger station** (☎509-682-4900; 428 W Woodin Ave).

Lake Chelan State Park (☎509-687-3710; 7544 S Lakeshore Rd; primitive/standard tent sites from $12/25) has 144 campsites; a number of lakeshore campgrounds are accessible only by boat. If you'd rather sleep in a real bed, try the great-value **Midtowner Motel** (800-572-0943; www.midtowner.com; 721 E Woodin Ave; r $92-129;) in town.

Several wineries have also opened in the area and many have excellent restaurants. Try **Tsillan Cellars** (509-682-9463; www.tsillancellars.com; 3875 Hwy 97A; noon-5pm).

Link Transit (509-662-1155; www.linktransit.com) buses connect Chelan with Wenatchee and Leavenworth ($1).

Beautiful **Stehekin**, on the northern tip of Lake Chelan, is accessible only by **boat** (509-682-4584; www.ladyofthelake.com), **seaplane** (509-682-5555; www.chelanairways.com) or a long hike across Cascade Pass, 28 miles from the lake. You'll find lots of information about hiking, campgrounds and cabin rentals at www.stehekin.com. Most facilities are open from mid-June to mid-September.

Methow Valley

The Methow's combination of powdery winter snow and abundant summer sunshine has transformed this valley into one of Washington's primary recreation areas. You can bike, hike and fish in summer, and cross-country ski on the second-biggest snow trail network in the US in winter.

The 200km of trails are maintained by the nonprofit **Methow Valley Sport Trails Association** (MVSTA; 509-996-3287; www.mvsta.com; 309 Riverside Ave, Winthrop), which in winter provides the most comprehensive network of hut-to-hut (and hotel-to-hotel) skiing in North America. An extra blessing is that few people seem to know about it. For classic accommodations and easy access to the skiing, hiking and cycling trails, decamp at the exquisite **Sun Mountain Lodge** (509-996-2211; www.sunmountainlodge.com; 604 Patterson Lake Rd, Winthrop; r from $300, cabins from $405; Dec-late Oct;), 10 miles west of the town of Winthrop. While the rooms and facilities are cosy cabin-style (including a lot of taxidermy), it's the views from up here, and the endless choice of hiking and cross-country skiing trails surrounding the resort, that make it so special.

North Cascades National Park

Even the names of the lightly trodden dramatic mountains in **North Cascades National Park** (www.nps.gov/noca) sound wild and untamed: Desolation Peak, Jagged Ridge, Mt Despair and Mt Terror. Not surprisingly, the region offers some of the best backcountry adventures outside of Alaska.

The **North Cascades Visitor Center** (206-386-4495, ext 11; 502 Newhalem St, Newhalem; 9am-6pm Jun-Sep, reduced hours Oct-May), in the small settlement of Newhalem on Hwy 20, is the best orientation point for visitors and is staffed by expert rangers who can enlighten you on the park's highlights.

Built in the 1930s for loggers working in the valley which was soon to be flooded by Ross Dam, the floating cabins at the **Ross Lake Resort** (206-386-4437; www.rosslakeresort.com; 503 Diablo St, Rockport; cabins $175-350; mid-Jun–late Oct) on the eponymous lake's west side are the state's most unique accommodations. There's no road in – guests can either hike the 2-mile trail from Hwy 20 or take the resort's tugboat-taxi-and-truck shuttle from the parking area near Diablo Dam.

Northeastern Washington

Spokane

Washington's second-biggest population center is one of the state's latent surprises and a welcome break after the treeless monotony of the eastern scablands. Situated at the nexus of the Pacific Northwest's so-called 'Inland Empire,' this understated yet confident city sits on the banks of the Spokane River, close to where British fur traders founded a short-lived trading post in 1810. Though rarely touted in national tourist blurbs, Spokane hosts one of the world's largest mass-participation running events (May's annual Bloomsday).

Sights

Riverfront Park PARK

(www.spokaneriverfrontpark.com;) The former site of the 1974 World's Fair and Exposition, this park's highlights include a 17-point **sculpture walk** and **Spokane Falls**, a gushing combination of scenic waterfalls and foaming rapids. A short **gondola ride** (adult/child under 12yr $7.50/5; 10am-8pm Sun-Thu, to 9pm Fri & Sat Jul & Aug, reduced hours Sep-Jun) takes you directly above the falls, as does the cheaper and equally spectacular **Monroe St Bridge**, built in 1911 and one of the largest concrete arches in the USA.

Northwest Museum of Arts & Culture MUSEUM
(MAC; ☎509-456-3931; www.northwestmuseum.org; 2316 W 1st Ave; adult/child $10/5; ⏰10am-5pm Wed-Sun) In a striking state-of-the-art building in the historic Browne's Addition neighborhood, this museum has – arguably – one of the finest collections of indigenous artifacts in the Northwest. Leading off a plush glass foyer overlooking the Spokane River are four galleries showcasing Spokane's history, as well as a number of rotating exhibitions that change every three to four months. Your ticket also earns you the right to visit the adjacent English Tudor–revival **Campbell House**.

Sleeping & Eating

Hotel Ruby MOTEL $
(☎509-747-1041; www.hotelrubyspokane.com; 901 W 1st Ave; r from $90;) This basic motel, retrofitted in hip, artistic decor, retains its '70s feel. Diagonally opposite the Davenport Hotel, it's walking distance to dining and drinking establishments.

★ **Davenport Hotel** HISTORIC HOTEL $$
(☎509-455-8888; www.thedavenporthotel.com; 10 S Post St; r from $220;) This historical landmark (opened in 1914) is considered one of the best hotels in the country. Even if you're not staying here, linger in the gorgeous lobby or have a drink in the Peacock Lounge. The adjacent modern Davenport Tower sports a safari-themed lobby and bar.

Mizuna FUSION $$$
(☎509-747-2004; www.mizuna.com; 214 N Howard St; mains lunch $12-14, dinner $27-32; ⏰11am-10pm Mon-Sat, 4-10pm Sun;) This fine restaurant is located in an antique brick building with simple furnishings, and is well-known for its specialties such as seed-crushed quinoa croquettes and pan-seared pork tenderloin. Wash dinner down with an exquisite wine for a memorable experience.

Drinking & Entertainment

With a vibrant student population based at Gonzaga University, Spokane has a happening nighttime scene.

NoLi Brewhouse BREWERY
(☎509-242-2739; www.nolibrewhouse.com; 1003 E Trent Ave; ⏰11am-9pm Sun & Mon, to 10pm Tue-Sat) A student hangout situated near Gonzaga University, Spokane's best microbrewery serves some weird and wonderful flavors, including a tart cherry ale and an imperial stout with coffee, chocolate and brown-sugar tones. Food-wise, check out the cod and chips cooked in batter made with the brewery's own pale ale.

Mootsy's BAR
(☎509-838-1570; 406 W Sprague Ave) This popular bar is the hub for the nightlife and alternative-music scene that hops all along this block between Stevens and Washington Sts. Its cheap Pabst Blue Ribbon (PBR) during happy hour keeps its customer base loyal.

Bing Crosby Theater THEATER
(☎509-227-7638; www.bingcrosbytheater.com; 901 W Sprague Ave) Yes, Bing Crosby hailed from Spokane, and now the 'Bing' presents concerts, plays and festivals in a fairly intimate setting.

WORTH A TRIP

GRAND COULEE DAM

While the more famous Hoover Dam (conveniently located between Las Vegas and the Grand Canyon) gets over a million visitors per year, the much larger (four times) and arguably more significant **Grand Coulee Dam** (inconveniently located far from everything) gets only a trickle of tourism. It's the largest concrete structure in the US and also the largest producer of electricity in the US.

The **Grand Coulee Visitor Arrival Center** (☎509-633-9265; www.usbr.gov/pn/grandcoulee/visit; ⏰8:30am-10:30pm Jun-Aug, to 9:30pm Sep, 9am-5pm Oct-May) details the history of the dam and surrounding area with movies, photos and interactive exhibits, while free guided tours of the facility run on the hour from 10am to 5pm (from May to September); there are fewer tours outside summer.

Similarly spectacular is the nightly **laser show** (www.usbr.gov/pn/grandcoulee/visit; ⏰10pm Jun & Jul, 9:30pm Aug, 8:30pm Sep) – purportedly the world's largest – which illustrates the history of the Columbia River and its various dams against a gloriously vivid backdrop.

Information

Spokane Area Visitor Information Center (☎888-776-5263; www.visitspokane.com; 808 W Main Ave; ⏰8am-5pm Mon-Sat, 11am-6pm Sun)

Getting There & Away

Spokane Intermodal Transportation Station (221 W 1st Ave) Buses and trains depart from this station.

South Cascades

The South Cascades are taller but less clustered than their northern counterparts, extending from Snoqualmie Pass east of Seattle down to the mighty Columbia River on the border with Oregon. The highpoint in more ways than one is 14,411ft Mt Rainier. Equally compelling for different reasons is Mt St Helens (8363ft), still recovering from a devastating 1980 volcanic eruption. Lesser-known Mt Adams (12,276ft) is notable for the huckleberries and wildflowers that fill its grassy alpine meadows during the short but intense summer season.

Mt Rainier National Park

The USA's fourth-highest peak (outside Alaska), majestic Mt Rainier is also one of its most beguiling. Encased in a 368-sq-mile national park (the world's fifth national park when it was inaugurated in 1899), the mountain's snowcapped summit and forest-covered foothills boast numerous hiking trails, huge swaths of flower-carpeted meadows, and an alluring conical peak that presents a formidable challenge for aspiring climbers.

Mt Rainier National Park (www.nps.gov/mora; entry per car $25) has four entrances. Call ☎800-695-7623 for road conditions. The National Park Service (NPS) website includes downloadable maps and descriptions of dozens of park trails. The most famous trail is the hardcore, 93-mile-long Wonderland Trail that completely circumnavigates Mt Rainier and takes around 10 to 12 days to tackle.

Campgrounds in the park have running water and toilets, but no showers or RV hookups. Reservations at **park campsites** (☎800-365-2267; www.nps.gov/mora; campsites $20) are strongly advised during summer months and can be made up to two months in advance by phone or online. For overnight backcountry trips, you'll need a wilderness permit; check the NPS website for details.

NISQUALLY ENTRANCE

The busiest and most convenient gate to Mt Rainier National Park, Nisqually lies on Hwy 706 via Ashford, near the park's southwest corner. It's open year-round. **Longmire**, 7 miles inside the Nisqually entrance, has a **museum and information center** (☎360-569-6575; ⏰9am-4:30pm), a number of important trailheads, and the rustic **National Park Inn** (☎360-569-2275; www.mtrainierguestservices.com; r with shared/private bath from $119/169, units $252; P ❄), complete with an excellent restaurant. More hikes and interpretive walks can be found 12 miles further east at loftier **Paradise**, which is served by the informative **Henry M Jackson Visitor Center** (☎360-569-6571; Paradise; ⏰10am-7pm daily Jun-Sep, 10am-5pm Sat & Sun Oct-May), and the vintage **Paradise Inn** (☎360-569-2275; www.mtrainierguestservices.com; r with shared/private bath from $117/174; ⏰May-Oct), a historical 'parkitecture' inn constructed in 1916 and long part of the national park's fabric. Climbs to the top of Rainier leave from the inn; excellent four-day guided ascents are led by **Rainier Mountaineering Inc** (☎888-892-5462; www.rmiguides.com; 30027 SR 706 E, Ashford).

OTHER ENTRANCES

The three other entrances to Mt Rainier National Park are **Ohanapecosh**, via Hwy 123 and accessed via the town of **Packwood**, where lodging is available; **White River**, off Hwy 410, which literally takes the high road (6400ft) to the beautiful viewpoint at the **Sunrise Lodge Cafeteria** (snacks $6-9; ⏰10am-7pm Jul & Aug); and remote **Carbon River** in the northwest corner, which gives access to the park's inland rainforest.

Mt St Helens National Volcanic Monument

What it lacks in height, Mt St Helens makes up for in fiery infamy – 57 people perished on the mountain when it erupted with a force of 1500 atomic bombs on May 18, 1980. The cataclysm began with an earthquake measuring 5.1 on the Richter scale, which sparked the biggest landslide in human history and buried 230 sq miles of forest under millions of tons of volcanic rock and ash. Today it's a fascinating landscape of recovering forests, new river valleys and ash-covered slopes. There's an $8 per person fee to use the services at Coldwater Lake Recreation Area and Johnston Ridge Observatory.

NORTHEASTERN ENTRANCE

From the main northeast entrance on Hwy 504, your first stop should be the **Silver Lake Visitor Center** (www.parks.wa.gov/245/Mount-St-Helens; 3029 Spirit Lake Hwy; adult/child $5/2.50; 9am-5pm mid-May–mid-Sep, reduced hours mid-Sep–mid-May;) , which has films, exhibits and free information about the mountain (including trail maps). For a closer view of the destructive power of nature, venture to the **Johnston Ridge Observatory** (360-274-2140; 24000 Spirit Lake Hwy; admission $8; 10am-6pm mid-May–Oct), situated at the end of Hwy 504, which looks directly into the mouth of the crater.

A welcome stop in an accommodations-light area, the **Eco Park Resort** (360-274-7007; www.ecoparkresort.com; 14000 Spirit Lake Hwy, Toutle; campsites $22, yurts $75-150, cabins $125-130) offers seven rooms in a large house opposite the Silver Lake Visitor Center.

SOUTHEASTERN & EASTSIDE ENTRANCES

The southeastern entrance via the town of **Cougar** on Hwy 503 holds some serious lava terrain, including the 2-mile-long **Ape Cave** lava tube, which you can explore year-round; be prepared for the chill as it remains a constant 41°F (5°C). Bring two light sources per adult or rent lanterns at **Apes' Headquarters** (360-449-7800; 10am-5pm Jun-Sep) for $5 each.

The eastside entrance is the most remote, but the harder-to-reach **Windy Ridge** viewpoint on this side gives you a palpable, if eerie, sense of the destruction from the blast. It's often closed until June. A few miles down the road you can descend 600ft on the 1-mile-long **Harmony Trail** (hike 224) to Spirit Lake.

Central & Southeastern Washington

The sunny, dry near-California-looking central and southeastern parts of Washington harbor one not-so-secret weapon: wine. The fertile land that borders the Nile-like Yakima and Columbia River Valleys is awash with enterprising new wineries producing quality grapes that now vie with the Napa and Sonoma Valleys for national recognition. Yakima and its more attractive cousin Ellensburg once held the edge, but nowadays the real star is Walla Walla, where talented restaurateurs and a proactive local council are crafting a wine destination par excellence.

Yakima & Ellensburg

Situated in its eponymous river valley, the city of Yakima is a rather bleak trading center that doesn't really live up to its 'Palm Springs of Washington' tourist label. The main reason to stop here is to visit one of the numerous wineries that lie between Yakima and Benton City; pick up a map at the **Yakima Valley Visitors & Convention Bureau** (800-221-0751; www.visityakima.com; 101 N Fair Ave; 9am-5pm Mon-Sat, 10am-4pm Sun Jun-Aug, reduced hours Sep-May).

A better layover is Ellensburg, a diminutive settlement 36 miles to the northwest that juxtaposes the state's largest rodeo (each Labor Day) with a town center that has more coffee bars per head than anywhere else in the world (allegedly). Grab your latte at local roaster **D&M Coffee** (509-962-9333; www.dmcoffee.com; 301 N Pine St; 7am-5pm) and overnight at centrally located and charming Victorian **Guesthouse Ellensburg** (509-962-3706; www.guesthouseellensburg.com; 606 Main St; r from $145), which also runs the excellent **Yellow Church Cafe** (509-933-2233; www.theyellowchurchcafe.com; 111 S Pearl St; mains brunch $9-13, dinner $13-20; 11am-9pm Tue-Thu, 8am-9pm Fri-Mon).

Greyhound services both cities, with buses to Seattle, Spokane and points in between.

Walla Walla

Over the last decade, Walla Walla has converted itself from an obscure agricultural backwater, famous for its sweet onions and large state penitentiary, into the hottest wine-growing region outside of California. While venerable Marcus Whitman College is the town's most obvious cultural attribute, you'll also find zany coffee bars, cool wine-tasting rooms, fine Queen Anne architecture, and one of the state's freshest and most vibrant farmers markets.

Sights & Activities

You don't need to be sloshed on wine to appreciate Walla Walla's historical and cultural heritage. Its Main St has won countless historical awards, and to bring the settlement to life, the local **chamber of commerce** (509-525-0850; www.wallawalla.org; 29 E Sumach St;

DON'T MISS

YAKIMA VALLEY WINE TOUR

If you find yourself driving between Ellensburg and Walla Walla, why not go wine-tasting? The Yakima Valley AVA (American Viticultural Area) is the oldest, largest and most diverse in the state. You'll find www.wineyakimavalley.org is a good resource for finding wineries.

Bonair Winery (509-829-6027; www.bonairwine.com; 500 S Bonair Rd, Zillah; 10am-5pm) In the Rattlesnake Hills near Zillah, this winery has lovely gardens and is a laid-back place to sample luscious reds.

Terra Blanca (509-588-6082; www.terrablanca.com; 34715 N DeMoss Rd, Benton City; 10am-6pm Apr-Oct, 11am-6pm Nov-Mar) Majestically located up on Red Mountain with views over the valley, this is one of the fanciest vineyards in the region, and perfect for sipping sweet dessert wines on the patio. There is a restaurant on-site.

Maison Bleue (509-525-9084; www.mbwinery.com; 20 N 2nd Ave, Walla Walla; 11am-5pm Thu-Sun Apr-Dec) Family-owned winery producing lauded Rhône-style wines.

8:30am-5pm Mon-Fri) has concocted some interesting walking tours, complete with leaflets and maps.

Fort Walla Walla Museum MUSEUM
(509-525-7703; www.fwwm.org; 755 Myra Rd; adult/child 6-12yr $8/3; 10am-5pm Mar-Oct, to 4pm Nov-Feb;) This is a pioneer village of 17 historical buildings, with the museum housed in the old cavalry stables. There are collections of farm implements, ranching tools and what could be the world's largest plastic replica of a mule team.

Waterbrook Wine WINERY
(509-522-1262; www.waterbrook.com; 10518 W US 12; 11am-6pm Sun-Thu, to 7pm Fri & Sat) About 10 miles west of town, the pond-side patio of this large winery is a great place to imbibe a long selection of wines on a sunny day. Food served Thursday to Sunday; hours vary outside summer.

Amavi Cellars WINERY
(509-525-3541; www.amavicellars.com; 3796 Peppers Bridge Rd; 10am-4pm) South of Walla Walla, amid a scenic spread of grape and apple orchards, you can sample some of the most talked-about wines in the valley (try the Syrah and Cabernet Sauvignon). The classy yet comfortable outdoor patio has views of the Blue Mountains.

Sleeping & Eating

Colonial Motel MOTEL $
(509-529-1220; www.colonial-motel.com; 2279 Isaacs Ave; r $68-129;) A simple family-run motel halfway to the airport, the Colonial is welcoming and bike-friendly with safe bike storage and plenty of local maps.

Marcus Whitman Hotel HOTEL $$
(509-525-2200; www.marcuswhitmanhotel.com; 6 W Rose St; r from $144;) Walla Walla's best-known landmark is also the town's only tall building, impossible to miss with its distinctive rooftop turret. In keeping with the settlement's well-preserved image, the red-brick 1928 beauty has been elegantly renovated and decorated, with ample rooms in rusts and browns, embellished with Italian-crafted furniture, huge beds and great views over the nearby Blue Mountains.

Graze CAFE $
(509-522-9991; 5 S Colville St; sandwiches from $8; 10am-7:30pm Mon-Sat, to 3:30pm Sun;) Amazing sandwiches are packed for your picnic, or (if you can get a table) eaten in at this simple cafe. Try the turkey pear panini with provolone and blue cheese, or the flank-steak torta with pickled jalapeños, avocado, tomato, cilantro and chipotle dressing. Plenty of vegetarian and non-vegetarian options.

Saffron Mediterranean Kitchen MEDITERRANEAN $$$
(509-525-2112; www.saffronmediterraneankitchen.com; 125 W Alder St; mains $17-30; 2-10pm Tue-Sat, to 9pm Sun May-Oct, 2-9pm Tue-Sun Nov-Apr) This place isn't about cooking, it's about alchemy: Saffron takes seasonal, local ingredients and turns them into pure gold. The Med-inspired menu lists dishes such as bison rib eye, nettle pappardelle with duck ragù, and wild Burgundy snail flatbread. Then there are the intelligently paired wines – and beers. Reserve ahead.

Getting There & Away

Greyhound buses run once daily to Seattle via Yakima and Ellensburg; change buses in Pasco for buses east to Spokane and beyond.

Walla Walla Regional Airport (www.wallawallaairport.com) Alaska Airlines services Walla Walla Regional Airport with several daily flights to Seattle.

OREGON

It's hard to slap a single characterization onto Oregon's geography and people. Its landscape ranges from rugged coastline and thick evergreen forests to barren, fossil-strewn deserts, volcanoes and glaciers. As for its denizens, you name it – Oregonians run the gamut from pro-logging conservatives to tree-hugging liberals to beer-making, sideburn-wearing hipsters. What they all have in common is an independent spirit, a love of the outdoors and a fierce devotion to where they live.

Portland

Call it what you want – PDX, Stumptown, City of Roses, Bridge City, Beervana or Portlandia – Portland positively rocks. It's a city with a vibrant downtown, pretty residential neighborhoods, ultragreen ambitions and zany characters. Here, liberal idealists outnumber conservative stogies, Gortex jackets are acceptable in fine restaurants and everyone supports countless brewpubs, coffeehouses, knitting circles, lesbian potlucks and eclectic book clubs. Portland is an up-and-coming destination that has finally arrived, and makes for an appealing, can't-miss stop on your adventures in the Pacific Northwest.

Sights

Downtown

★Tom McCall Waterfront Park PARK
This popular riverside park, which lines the west bank of the Willamette River, was finished in 1978 after four years of construction. It replaced an old freeway with 1.5 miles of paved sidewalks and grassy spaces, and attracts heaps of joggers, in-line skaters, strollers and cyclists. During summer the park is perfect for hosting large outdoor events such as the Oregon Brewers Festival. Walk over the Steel and Hawthorne bridges to the **Eastbank Esplanade**, making a 2.6-mile loop.

★Pioneer Courthouse Square LANDMARK
(www.thesquarepdx.org) The heart of downtown Portland, this brick plaza is nicknamed 'Portland's living room' and is the most-visited public space in the city. When it isn't full of Hacky Sack players, sunbathers or office workers lunching, the square hosts concerts, festivals, rallies, farmers markets, and even summer Friday-night movies (aka 'Flicks on the Bricks').

Portland Building LANDMARK
(cnr SW 5th Ave & SW Main St) This controversial 15-story building (1982) was designed by Michael Graves and catapulted the postmodern architect to celebrity status. The people working inside the blocky, pastel-colored edifice, however, have had to deal with tiny windows, cramped spaces and general user-unfriendliness. The building suffered from major design flaws that later proved very costly to fix – not a great start for what was considered to be the world's first major postmodern structure. At least it's been made somewhat green: an ecofriendly roof was installed in 2006.

Oregon Historical Society MUSEUM
(503-222-1741; www.ohs.org; 1200 SW Park Ave; adult/child $11/5; 10am-5pm Mon-Sat, noon-5pm Sun) Along the tree-shaded South Park Blocks sits the state's primary history museum, which dedicates most of its space to the story of Oregon and the pioneers who made it. There are interesting sections on Native American tribes and the travails of the Oregon Trail. Temporary exhibitions furnish the downstairs space. Check their website for free admission days.

Portland Art Museum MUSEUM
(503-226-2811; www.portlandartmuseum.org; 1219 SW Park Ave; adult/child $15/free; 10am-5pm Tue, Wed, Sat & Sun, to 8pm Thu & Fri) Just across the South Park Blocks, the art museum's excellent exhibits include Native American carvings, Asian and American art, and English silver. The museum also houses the Whitsell Auditorium, a first-rate theater that frequently screens rare or international films.

Aerial Tram CABLE CAR
(www.gobytram.com; 3303 SW Bond Ave; round trip $4.50; 5:30am-9:30pm Mon-Fri, 9am-5pm Sat, 1-5pm Sun Oct–mid-May, 1-5pm Sun mid-May–Sep) Portland's aerial tram runs from the

OREGON FACTS

Nickname Beaver State

Population 4 million

Area 98,466 sq miles

Capital city Salem (population 160,000)

Other cities Portland (population 610,000), Eugene (population 160,000), Bend (population 82,000)

Sales tax Oregon has no sales tax

Birthplace of Former US president Herbert Hoover (1874–1964), actor and dancer Ginger Rogers (1911–95), writer and merry prankster Ken Kesey (1935–2001), filmmaker Gus Van Sant (b 1952), *The Simpsons* creator Matt Groening (b 1954)

Home of Oregon Shakespeare Festival, Nike, Crater Lake

Politics Democrat governors since 1987

Famous for Forests, rain, microbrews, coffee, Death with Dignity Act

State beverage Milk (dairy's big here)

Driving You can't pump your own gas in Oregon; Portland to Eugene, 110 miles; Portland to Astoria, 96 miles

south Waterfront (there's a streetcar stop) to Marquam Hill. The tram runs along a 3300ft line up a vertical ascent of 500ft and the ride takes four minutes. The tram opened in 2007, far exceeding its budget predictions and causing much public controversy.

Old Town & Chinatown

The core of rambunctious 1890s Portland, the once-notorious Old Town used to be the lurking grounds of unsavory characters, but today disco queens outnumber drug dealers. It's one of the livelier places in town after dark, when nightclubs and bars open their doors and hipsters start showing up.

Saturday Market MARKET

(☎503-222-6072; www.portlandsaturdaymarket.com; 2 SW Naito Pkwy; ⏲10am-5pm Sat, 11am-4:30pm Sun Mar-Dec) The best time to hit the river walk is on a weekend to catch this famous market, which showcases handicrafts, street entertainers and food booths.

Lan Su Chinese Garden GARDENS

(☎503-228-8131; www.lansugarden.org; 239 NW Everett St; adult/child $9.50/7; ⏲10am-6pm mid-Apr–mid-Oct, to 5pm mid-Oct–mid-Apr) This classical Chinese garden is a one-block haven of tranquillity, reflecting ponds and manicured greenery. Guided tours are available.

Shanghai Tunnels HISTORIC SITE

(☎503-622-4798; www.shanghaitunnels.info; 120 NW 3rd Ave; adult/child under 12yr $13/8) Downtown Portland's basements were once connected by tunnels running beneath the streets and down to riverside docks. While built for shipping and flood control, rumors persist they were also used to transport unconscious men to be sold to unscrupulous ship's captains. Though long sealed, remnants can be visited on tour; book at www.portlandwalkingtours.com.

Chinatown Gates GATE

(cnr W Burnside St & NW 4th Ave) Don't expect flashbacks of Shanghai in Portland's lackluster Chinese quarter, which begins (and largely ends) at the deceptively impressive pagoda-style Chinatown Gates.

The Pearl District & Northwest

Pearl District NEIGHBORHOOD

(www.explorethepearl.com) Slightly to the northwest of downtown, the Pearl District is an old industrial quarter that has transformed its once grotty warehouses into expensive lofts, upscale boutiques and creative restaurants. On the first Thursday of every month, the zone's abundant art galleries extend their evening hours and the area turns into a fancy street party of sorts. The **Jamison Square Fountain** (810 NW 11th Ave) is one of its prettier urban spaces.

Northwest 23rd Avenue NEIGHBORHOOD

Nob Hill – or 'Snob Hill' to its detractors – has its hub on NW 23rd Ave, a trendy thoroughfare that brims with clothing boutiques, home-decor shops and cafes. The restaurants – including some of Portland's finest – lie mostly along NW 21st Ave. This is a perfect neighborhood for strolling, window-shopping and looking at houses that most of us will never be able to afford.

West Hills

Behind downtown Portland is the West Hills area, known for its exclusive homes, huge parks and – if you're lucky – peek-a-boo views of up to five Cascade volcanoes.

Forest Park PARK
(☎503-223-5449; www.forestparkconservancy.org) Abutting the more manicured Washington Park to the south (to which it is linked by various trails) is the far wilder 5100-acre Forest Park, a temperate rainforest that harbors plants, animals and an avid hiking fraternity. The **Portland Audubon Society** (☎503-292-6855; www.audubonportland.org; 5151 NW Cornell Rd; ⏲9am-5pm, nature store 10am-6pm Mon-Sat, to 5pm Sun) maintains a bookstore, wildlife rehabilitation center and 4.5 miles of trails within its Forest Park sanctuary.

Washington Park PARK
(www.washingtonparkpdx.org) Tame and well-tended Washington Park contains several key attractions within its 400 acres of greenery. The **International Rose Test Garden** (www.rosegardenstore.org; 400 SW Kingston Ave; ⏲7:30am-9pm) FREE is the centerpiece of Portland's famous rose blooms; there are 400 types on show here, plus great city views. Further uphill is the **Japanese Garden** (☎503-223-1321; www.japanesegarden.com; 611 SW Kingston Ave; adult/child $9.50/6.75; ⏲noon-7pm Mon, 10am-7pm Tue-Sun mid-Mar–Sep, noon-4pm Mon, 10am-4pm Tue-Sun Oct–mid-Mar), another oasis of tranquillity. If you have kids, the Oregon Zoo and Portland Children's Museum should be on your docket.

Northeast & Southeast

Across the Willamette River from downtown is the **Lloyd Center** (www.lloydcenter.com; 2201 Lloyd Center), Oregon's largest shopping mall and where notorious ice-queen Tonya Harding first learned to skate in the rink here. A few blocks to the southwest are the unmissable glass towers of the **Oregon Convention Center** (www.oregoncc.org; 777 NE Martin Luther King Jr Blvd), and nearby is the **Moda Center** (☎503-235-8771; www.center-or.com; 1 N Center Court St) (previously called the Rose Quarter), home of professional basketball team the Trailblazers.

Further up the Willamette, **N Mississippi Ave** used to be full of run-down buildings, but is now a hot spot of trendy shops and eateries. Northeast is artsy **NE Alberta St**, a long ribbon of art galleries, boutiques and cafes (don't miss the Last Thursday street-art event here, taking place the last Thursday of each month). **SE Hawthorne Blvd** (near SE 39th Ave) is affluent hippy territory, with gift stores, cafes, coffeeshops and two branches of Powell's bookstores. One leafy mile to the south, **SE Division St** has become a foodie destination, with plenty of excellent restaurants, bars and pubs. The same is true of **E Burnside at NE 28th Ave**, though it has a more concentrated and upscale feel.

Activities

Hiking

The best hiking is found in Forest Park (p1053), which harbors an unbelievable 80 miles of trails and often feels more like Mt Hood's foothills than Portland's city limits.

PORTLAND FOR CHILDREN

Washington Park has the most to offer families with young kids. Here you'll find the world-class **Oregon Zoo** (☎503-226-1561; www.oregonzoo.org; 4001 SW Canyon Rd; adult/child 3-11yr $11.50/8.50; ⏲9am-6pm Jun-Aug, reduced hours Sep-May; 👪), which is set in a beautiful natural environment even parents will enjoy. Next door is the **Portland Children's Museum** (☎503-233-6500; www.portlandcm.org; 4015 SW Canyon Rd; admission $10.75; ⏲9am-5pm; 👪) and **World Forestry Center** (☎503-228-1367; www.worldforestry.org; 4033 SW Canyon Rd; adult/child $9/6; ⏲10am-5pm; 👪), both offering fun learning activities and exhibits.

On the other side of the Willamette River, the **Oregon Museum of Science and Industry** (OMSI; ☎503-797-4000; www.omsi.edu; 1945 SE Water Ave; adult/child 3-13yr $13.50/9.75; ⏲9.30am-7pm Jun-Aug, reduced hours Sep-May; 👪) is a top-notch destination with a theater, planetarium and even a submarine to explore. And finally, further south is **Oaks Amusement Park** (☎503-233-5777; www.oakspark.com; 7805 SE Oaks Park Way; ride bracelets $13-26, individual rides $2.75; ⏲hours vary; 👪), home to pint-size roller coasters, miniature golf and carnival games.

Portland

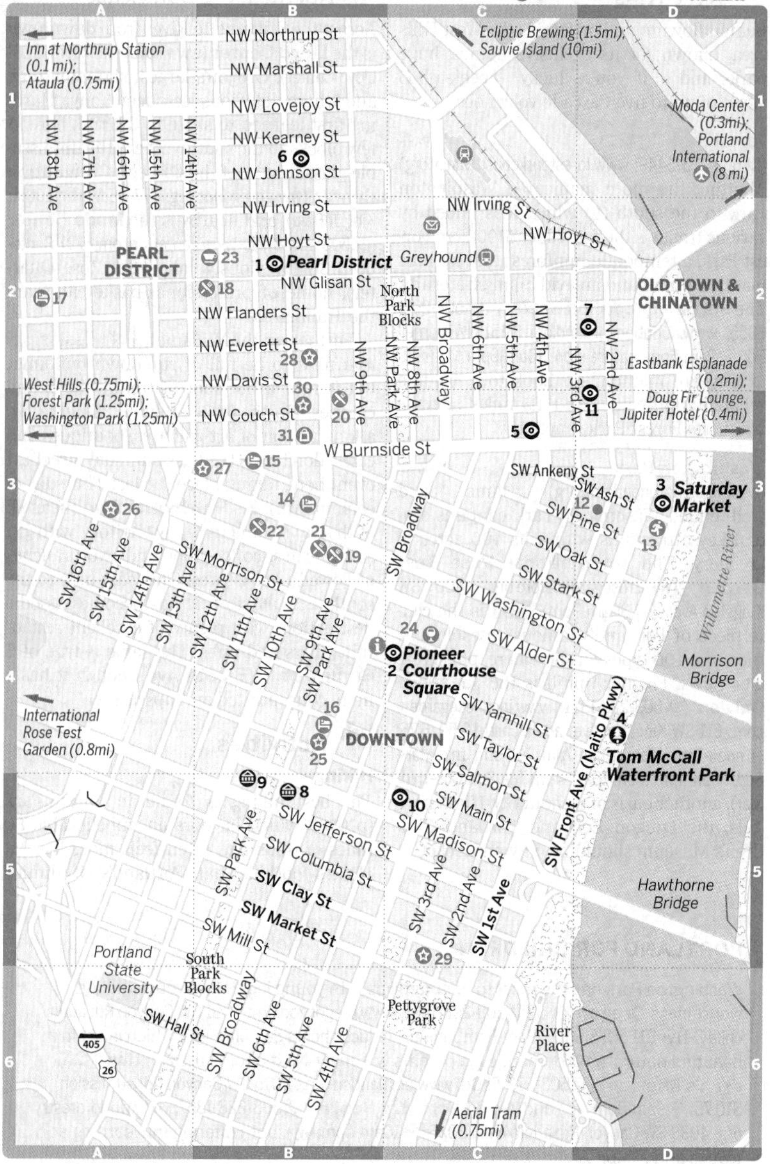

The park's **Wildwood Trail** starts at the Hoyt Arboretum and winds through 30 miles of forest, with many spur trails that allow for loop hikes. Other trailheads into Forest Park are located at the western ends of NW Thurman and NW Upshur Sts.

Cycling

Portland has been voted the 'most bike-friendly city in the US' several times in the media by the likes of CNN Travel, NBC News and *Bicycling Magazine*. There are many streets that cater to bicycles, and

Portland

Top Sights
1 Pearl District....B2
2 Pioneer Courthouse Square....C4
3 Saturday Market....D3
4 Tom McCall Waterfront Park....D4

Sights
5 Chinatown Gates....C3
6 Jamison Square Fountain....B1
7 Lan Su Chinese Garden....D2
8 Oregon Historical Society....B5
9 Portland Art Museum....B5
10 Portland Building....C5
11 Shanghai Tunnels....D3

Activities, Courses & Tours
12 Pedal Bike Tours....D3
13 Waterfront Bicycle Rentals....D3

Sleeping
14 Ace Hotel....B3
15 Crystal Hotel....B3
16 Heathman Hotel....B4
17 Northwest Portland Hostel....A2

Eating
18 Andina....B2
19 Bing Mi!....B3
20 Little Big Burger....B3
21 Nong's Khao Man Gai....B3
22 Tasty n Alder....B3

Drinking & Nightlife
23 Barista....B2
24 Departure Lounge....C4

Entertainment
25 Arlene Schnitzer Concert Hall....B4
26 Artists Repertory Theatre....A3
27 Crystal Ballroom....B3
28 Jimmy Mak's....B2
29 Keller Auditorium....C5
30 Portland Center Stage....B3

Shopping
31 Powell's City of Books....B3

drivers are used to watching out for cyclists. Riding along downtown riverside paths is a great way to see the city.

To the east of downtown the **Springwater Corridor** starts near the Oregon Museum of Science & Industry (as an extension of the Eastbank Esplanade) and goes all the way to the suburb of Boring – 21 miles away. In the northwest, **Leif Erikson Dr** is an old logging road leading 11 miles into Forest Park and offering occasional peeks over the city.

For scenic farm country, head to **Sauvie Island**, 10 miles northwest of downtown Portland. This island is prime cycling land – it's flat, has relatively little traffic and much of it is wildlife refuge.

Good cycling maps can be found at the tourist office and any bike store.

Waterfront Bicycle Rentals BICYCLE RENTAL
(503-227-1719; www.waterfrontbikes.com; 10 SW Ash St; rental per hour from $9; 10am-6pm Mon-Fri, to 4pm Sat & Sun) Bike rentals near the waterfront bike trails.

Kayaking

Situated close to the confluence of the Columbia and Willamette Rivers, Portland has miles of navigable waterways.

Portland Kayak Company KAYAKING
(503-459-4050; www.portlandkayak.com; 6600 SW Macadam Ave; rental per hour from $12) Kayaking rentals (minimum two hours), instruction and tours, including a three-hour circumnavigation of Ross Island on the Willamette River ($45).

Tours

Pedal Bike Tours BICYCLE TOUR
(503-243-2453; www.pedalbiketours.com; 133 SW 2nd Ave; tours $49-199; 10am-6pm) Bike tours with all sorts of themes – history, food carts, beer – plus trip to the coast or gorge.

Portland Walking Tours WALKING TOUR
(503-774-4522; www.portlandwalkingtours.com; tours $20-59) Food, chocolate, underground and even ghost-oriented tours.

Festivals & Events

Portland Rose Festival CULTURAL
(www.rosefestival.org; late May–mid-Jun) Rose-covered floats, dragon-boat races, a riverfront carnival, fireworks, roaming packs of sailors and the crowning of a Rose Queen all make this Portland's biggest celebration.

Oregon Brewers Festival BEER
(www.oregonbrewfest.com) In the last full weekend in July you can quaff microbrews from near and far in Waterfront Park – everyone's happy and even nondrinkers have fun. Plenty of food stalls.

Bite of Oregon FOOD
(www.biteoforegon.com; early Aug) All the food (and beer) you could think of consuming, much of it from great local restaurants – and some of it from Portland's famous food carts. Good microbrews too. The festival benefits Special Olympics Oregon.

Sleeping

Reserve ahead in summer, when many Portland hotels book up solid. Prices noted here don't include lodging taxes, which can range up to 14.5%.

Northwest Portland Hostel HOSTEL $
(503-241-2783; www.nwportlandhostel.com; 425 NW 18th Ave; dm $29-34, d with shared bath $63-114;) Perfectly located between the Pearl District and NW 21st and 23rd Aves, this friendly and clean hostel takes up four old buildings and features plenty of common areas (including a small deck) and discounted bike rentals. Dorms are spacious and private rooms can be as nice as in hotels, though all share outside bathrooms. Non-HI members pay $3 extra.

Hawthorne Portland Hostel HOSTEL $
(503-236-3380; www.portlandhostel.org; 3031 SE Hawthorne Blvd; dm $29-34, d with shared bath $80;) This ecofriendly hostel has a great Hawthorne location. The two private rooms are good and the dorms are spacious; all share outside bathrooms. There are summertime open-mic nights in the grassy backyard, and bike rentals (and a fix-it station) are available. The hostel composts and recycles, uses rainwater to flush toilets, and has a nice eco-roof. Discounts offered to those bike-touring.

★**Kennedy School** HOTEL $$
(503-249-3983; www.mcmenamins.com/KennedySchool; 5736 NE 33rd Ave; d from $145;) Portland's most unusual institution, this former elementary school is now home to a hotel (sleep in old classrooms!), a restaurant with a great garden courtyard, several bars, a microbrewery and a movie theater. Guests can use the soaking pool for free, and the whole school is decorated in funky art style – mosaics, fantasy paintings and historical photographs. It's a unique stay and very Portland.

★**Ace Hotel** BOUTIQUE HOTEL $$
(503-228-2277; www.acehotel.com; 1022 SW Stark St; d with shared/private bath from $185/285;) One of Portland's trendiest places to sleep is this hipster hotel fusing industrial, minimalist and retro styles. From the photo booth and sofa lounge in its lobby to the recycled fabrics and furniture in its rooms, the Ace makes the warehouse feel work. A Stumptown coffee shop and underground bar are on the premises, and the fancy Clyde Common restaurant is next door. Parking costs $25.

McMenamins Edgefield HOTEL $$
(503-669-8610; www.mcmenamins.com/54-edgefield-home; 2126 SW Halsey St, Troutdale; dm $30, d with shared/private bath from $130/165;) This former county poor farm, restored by the McMenamin brothers, is now a one-of-a-kind, 38-acre hotel complex with a dizzying variety of services. Taste wine and homemade beer, play golf, watch movies, shop at the gift store, listen to live music, walk the extensive gardens and eat at one of its restaurants. It's about a 20-minute drive east from downtown.

Jupiter Hotel BOUTIQUE MOTEL $$
(503-230-9200; www.jupiterhotel.com; 800 E Burnside St; d from $179;) This slick, remodeled motel is within walking distance of downtown and right next to Doug Fir, a top-notch live-music venue. Standard rooms are tiny – go for the Metro rooms instead – and ask for a pad away from the bar patio if you're more into sleeping than staying up late. Bike rentals are available; walk-ins after midnight get a discount if there are vacancies.

Caravan BOUTIQUE HOTEL $$
(503-288-5225; www.tinyhousehotel.com; 5009 NE 11th Ave; r from $145;) Only in Portland: stay in a tiny-house (84 to 170 sq ft – smaller than most hotel rooms!), complete with kitchen and bathroom, in the artsy Alberta neighborhood. It's the first and, currently, only tiny house hotel in the country. Free s'mores nightly and Wednesday night live music from 7pm to 10pm. Book way ahead in summer.

Crystal Hotel HOTEL $$
(503-972-2670; www.mcmenamins.com/CrystalHotel; 303 SW 12th Ave; r with shared/private bath from $145/175;) Each room here is dedicated to a different artist, musician or poet at this funky McMenamins hotel. It's located smack-dab in the middle of town, and on the premises are Zeus Café (a good restaurant) and Al's Den (a speakeasy bar). An original, creaky wood elevator and basement saltwater soaking pool complete the picture.

Clinton Street Guesthouse
GUESTHOUSE **$$**

(☑ 503-234-8752; www.clintonstreetguesthouse. com; 4220 SE Clinton St; d $150; ❄ 🛜) Just two simple but beautiful rooms are on offer in this lovely Craftsman house in a residential neighborhood near trendy Division St. Furnishings are elegant, the linens luxurious, and your hosts hands-off. Simple continental breakfast included. There are also two small houses available to rent less than a mile away.

Inn at Northrup Station
BOUTIQUE HOTEL **$$$**

(☑ 503-224-0543; www.northrupstation.com; 2025 NW Northrup St; d from $225; 🅿 ❄ @ 🛜) Almost over the top with its bright color scheme and funky decor, this super-trendy hotel boasts huge artsy suites, many with patio or balcony, and all with kitchenettes or full kitchens. There's a cool rooftop patio with plants, and complimentary streetcar tickets are included (the streetcar runs just outside).

Heathman Hotel
LUXURY HOTEL **$$$**

(☑ 503-241-4100; www.heathmanhotel.com; 1001 SW Broadway; d from $300; 🅿 ❄ @ 🛜 🐾) A Portland institution, the Heathman has top-notch services and one of the best restaurants in the city. Rooms are elegant, stylish and luxurious, and the location is very central. It also hosts high tea in the afternoons, jazz from Wednesday to Saturday evenings and has a library stocked with 1700 signed books by authors who have stayed here. Parking costs $39.

✖ Eating

Portland's rapidly evolving food scene tore up the rule book years ago and has branched out into countless genres and subgenres. Vegetarianism is well represented, as is brunch, Asian fusion and the rather loose concept known as 'Pacific Northwest.' Then there are the city's famous food carts, representing dozens of cuisines and quirky food niches.

Little Big Burger
BURGERS **$**

(☑ 503-274-9008; www.littlebigburger.com; 122 NW 10th Ave; burgers $4; ⊙ 11am-10pm) A simple six-item menu takes fast food to the next level with mini burgers made from prime ingredients. Try a beef burger topped with cheddar, Swiss, chèvre or blue cheese, with a side of truffled fries – then wash it down with a gourmet root-beer float. Several locations; check the website.

Paadee
THAI **$$**

(☑ 503-360-1453; www.paadeepdx.com; 6 SE 28th Ave; mains $11-17; ⊙ 11:30am-3pm & 5-10pm) Located on a strip of 28th Ave dubbed 'Restaurant Row' is this beautiful dining room with bird cages as lampshades. Bright, fresh flavors come alive in plates such as the steak salad or *gra prao muu grob* (crispy pork belly with basil and chili). Tasty cocktails are available, too, and the lauded restaurant **Langbaan** is secreted away behind a wall – though it's booked out months in advance.

Tasty n Sons
AMERICAN **$$**

(☑ 503-621-1400; www.tastynsons.com; 3808 N Williams Ave; ⊙ 9am-2:30pm & 5:30-10pm Sun-Thu, to 11pm Fri & Sat) Superb small plates in a trendy, high-ceilinged, industrial-feel dining room. Share delicacies such as bacon-wrapped dates, grilled quail with couscous, and lamb souvlaki. Especially popular for brunch, when a wait is guaranteed. There is a more extensive menu at their other location, **Tasty n Alder** (☑ 503-621-9251; www.tastynalder.com; 580 SW 12th Ave; mains $15-20; ⊙ 9am-2pm & 5:30-10pm Sun-Thu, to 11pm Fri & Sat).

Olympia Provisions
FRENCH **$$**

(☑ 503-894-8136; www.olympiaprovisions.com; 1632 NW Thuman St; mains lunch $9-15, dinner $19-28; ⊙ 11am-10pm Mon-Fri, 10am-10pm Sat, to 9pm Sun) This French-inspired rotisserie bistro serves up charcuterie and cheese boards, gourmet sandwiches, salads and deli items, and main plates such as rotisserie chicken and confit duck leg. Delicious Benedicts for brunch. Also at 107 SE Washington St.

Ken's Artisan Pizza
PIZZA **$$**

(☑ 503-517-9951; www.kensartisan.com; 304 SE 28th Ave; pizza for one $11-13; ⊙ 5-10pm Mon-Sat, 4-9pm Sun) Glorious wood-fired, thin-crust pizzas with toppings such as prosciutto, fennel sausage and green garlic. Super-trendy atmosphere, with huge sliding windows that open to the street on warm nights. Expect a long wait – no reservations taken.

Pambiche
CUBAN **$$**

(☑ 503-233-0511; www.pambiche.com; 2811 NE Glisan St; mains $12-20; ⊙ 11am-10pm Mon-Thu, to midnight Fri, 9am-midnight Sat, to 10pm Sun) Portland's best Cuban food, with a trendy and riotously colorful atmosphere. All your regular favorites are available, but leave room for dessert. Lunch is a good deal, but happy hour is even better (2pm to 6pm Monday to Friday, 10pm to midnight Friday and Saturday). Be prepared to wait for dinner.

PORTLAND'S FOOD CARTS

One of the most fun ways to explore Portland's cuisine is to eat at a food cart. These semipermanent kitchens-on-wheels inhabit parking lots around town and are usually clustered together in 'pods,' often with their own communal tables, ATMs and portaloos. As many of the owners are immigrants (who can't afford a hefty restaurant start-up), the carts are akin to an international potluck.

Food-cart locations vary, but the most significant cluster is at SW Alder St and SW 9th Ave. For a current list and some background information, see www.foodcartsportland.com. Highlights in a highly competitive field:

Nong's Khao Man Gai (971-255-3480; www.khaomangai.com; cnr SW 10th Ave & SW Alder St; mains $8; 10am-4pm Mon-Fri) Tender poached chicken with rice. That's it – and enough. Also at 411 SW College St (another food cart) and 609 SE Ankeny St (a brick-and-mortar restaurant), both of which have a more extensive menu.

Holy Mole (503-347-4270; www.facebook.com/holymoleportlandor; 1419 SE 33rd Ave; mains $7-11) Not your typical taco cart (though Fernando Otero does have one taco choice on his menu). Try the *pozole* (a hearty corn soup) or his trademark mole dishes. Hours change daily; check the website.

Viking Soul Food (971-506-5579; www.vikingsoulfood.com; 4262 SE Belmont St; mains $7-9; noon-8pm Tue-Thu & Sun, to 9pm Fri & Sat) Delicious Norwegian wraps. Savory stuffings include meatballs, chicken sausage, house-smoked salmon and mushroom-hazelnut patties. Sweet stuffings include rhubarb chèvre, lemon curd and lingonberry preserves. Several pickled sides available, too.

Bing Mi! (www.bingmiportland.com; cnr SW 9th Ave & SW Alder St; savory crepes $6; 7:30am-3pm Mon-Fri, 11am-4pm Sat) Savory grilled crepes in Northern Chinese style, stuffed with scrambled egg, pickled vegetables, fried crackers, black-bean paste and chili sauce. That's all you get, and that's all you'll need.

Bollywood Theater INDIAN $$

(971-200-4711; www.bollywoodtheaterpdx.com; 2039 NE Alberta St; small plates $9-12, thalis $15-17; 11am-10pm;) This popular Indian restaurant serves up 'street food' such as lamb samosas and *kati* rolls (meat and chutney rolled up in flatbread), along with small plates (chicken curry, pork vindaloo) and *thalis* (platters with several dishes). Plenty of vegetable and side dishes as well; wash it all down with a chai, yogurt *lassi*.

Podnah's Pit BARBECUE $$

(503-281-3700; www.podnahspit.com; 1625 NE Killingsworth St; mains $12-30; 11am-10pm Mon-Fri, 9am-10pm Sat & Sun) Possibly Portland's best barbecue joint, serving amazingly tender and tasty pork ribs that have been smoked for four hours. There's also brisket, chicken and pulled-pork sandwiches, along with typical sides such as coleslaw, potato salad and collard greens.

★ **Andina** PERUVIAN $$$

(503-228-9535; www.andinarestaurant.com; 1314 NW Glisan St; mains $23-35; 11:30am-2:30pm & 5-9:30pm Sun-Thu, to 10:30pm Fri & Sat) A modern take on traditional Peruvian food produces delicious mains such as slow-cooked lamb shank in cilantro-and-black-beer sauce or wok-fried wild mushrooms served with garlic rice. For lighter fare, hit the bar for tapas, great cocktails and Latin-inspired live music.

★ **Ned Ludd** AMERICAN $$$

(503-288-6900; www.nedluddpdx.com; 3925 NE Martin Luther King Jr Blvd; small plates $9-25; 5pm-late Wed-Sat, 9am-2pm & 5pm-close Sun) Too quintessentially Portland, this offbeat, upscale joint exudes artisan vibes, from its rustic-peasant decor to the prominent brick wood-fired oven where all dishes are cooked. The beautifully presented small plates are rotated daily. Not a place to simply fill your tummy, but rather to sample eclectic 'American craft' delicacies. Also does a good brunch.

★ **Ox** STEAK $$$

(503-284-3366; www.oxpdx.com; 2225 Martin Luther King Jr Blvd; mains $23-42; 5-10pm Tue-Thu & Sun, to 11pm Fri & Sat) One of Portland's most popular restaurants is this upscale, Argentine-inspired steakhouse. Start with the smoked bone-marrow clam chowder, then go for the gusto: the grass-fed beef rib eye. Or, if there's two of you, the *asado* ($60) is a good choice for trying several different cuts. Reserve ahead.

Ataula SPANISH **$$$**
(☎503-894-8904; www.ataulapdx.com; 1818 NW 23rd Pl; tapas $7-12, paella dishes $32-37; ⏰4:30-10pm Tue-Sat) This critically acclaimed Spanish tapas restaurant offers outstanding cuisine. If they're on the menu, try the *nuestras bravas* (sliced, fried potatoes in milk alioli), *croquetas* (salt-cod fritters), *xupa-xup* (chorizo lollipop) or *ataula montadito* (salmon with marscapone yogurt and black-truffle honey). Great cocktails, too. Reserve ahead.

Ava Gene's ITALIAN **$$$**
(☎971-229-0571; www.avagenes.com; 3377 SE Division St; mains $20-32; ⏰5-11pm) Renowned trattoria-inspired eatery owned by Duane Sorenson, who founded Stumptown Coffee. Rustic Italian cuisine rules the menu, with exquisite pasta and vegetable dishes as highlights. Exceptional ingredients, great wine list and cocktails, and outstanding service. Reserve ahead.

Drinking & Nightlife

Portland is world famous for its coffee, and boasts more than 70 breweries within its metro area – more than any other city on earth. It also offers a wide range of excellent bars, from dive bars to hipster joints to pubs and ultra-modern lounges. You'll never get thirsty in these parts.

★**Barista** COFFEE
(☎503-274-1211; www.baristapdx.com; 539 NW 13th Ave; ⏰6am-6pm Mon-Fri, 7am-6pm Sat & Sun) One of Portland's best coffeeshops, owned by award-winning barista Billy Wilson and known for its lattes. Beans are sourced from specialty roasters. Three other locations in town.

Breakside Brewery BREWERY
(☎503-719-6475; www.breakside.com; 820 NE Dekum St; ⏰3-10pm Mon-Thu, noon-11pm Fri & Sat, to 10pm Sun) Over 20 taps of some of the most experimental, tastiest beer you'll ever drink, laced through with fruits, vegetables and spices (try the hoppy Breakside IPA). Past beers have included a Meyer lemon kolsch, a mango IPA and a beet beer with ginger. For dessert, pray they have the salted-caramel stout. Good food and nice outdoor seating, too.

Departure Lounge BAR
(☎503-802-5370; www.departureportland.com; 525 SW Morrison St; ⏰4pm-midnight Sun-Thu, to 1am Fri & Sat) This rooftop restaurant-bar, atop the 15th floor of the Nines Hotel, fills a deep downtown void: a cool bar with unforgettable views of Portland. The vibe is distinctly spaceship-LA, with mod couches and sleek lighting. Hit happy hour from 4pm to 6pm Tuesday to Thursday (or late night) for select drinks and appetizers.

Stumptown Coffee Roasters COFFEE
(☎503-230-7702; www.stumptowncoffee.com; 4525 SE Division St; ⏰6am-7pm Mon-Fri, 7am-7pm Sat & Sun) The microroaster who put Portland on the coffee map, and still its most famous coffeeshop – though some bemoan the fact that it has 'gone corporate.' See the website for other Portland (and US) locations.

Coava Coffee COFFEE
(☎503-894-8134; www.coavacoffee.com; 1300 SE Grand Ave; ⏰6am-6pm Mon-Fri, 7am-6pm Sat, 8am-6pm Sun) The decor takes the concept of 'neo-industrial' to extremes, but most people love that – and Coava delivers where it matters. The pour-over makes for a fantastic cup of java, and the espressos are exceptional, too. Also at 2631 SE Hawthorne Blvd.

Heart COFFEE
(☎503-206-6602; www.heartroasters.com; 2211 E Burnside St; ⏰7am-6pm) Artsy-industrial atmosphere on busy E Burnside; check out its large visible roaster. A bit too hipster-y for some, but most of the beans are well (and lightly) roasted. Also at 537 SW 12th Ave.

Ecliptic Brewing BREWERY
(☎503-265-8002; www.eclipticbrewing.com; 825 N Cook St; ⏰11am-10pm Sun-Thu, to 11pm Fri & Sat) Founded by John Harris, who previously brewed for the McMenamins, Deschutes and Full Sail before starting Ecliptic, his own brewery-restaurant. Instantly popular, it now puts out interesting creations such as Spica Pilsner (an unfiltered ale) and Mintaka Stout (a dry beer with caramel and coffee notes).

Migration BREWERY
(☎503-206-5221; www.migrationbrewing.com; 2828 NE Glisan St; ⏰11am-midnight Mon-Sat, to 10pm Sun) Popular neighborhood brewpub with great casual-industrial atmosphere. Wood picnic tables outside make it easy to see and be seen, and are especially wonderful

A BRIEF HISTORY OF MICROBREWING IN THE PACIFIC NORTHWEST

Beer connoisseurship is a nationwide phenomenon these days, but the campaign to put a dash of flavor into commercially brewed beer was first ignited in the Pacific Northwest in the 1980s.

One of America's first microbreweries was the mercurial Cartwright Brewing Company, set up in Portland in 1980. The nation's first official brewpub was the now defunct Grant's, which opened in the Washington city of Yakima in 1982. The trend went viral in 1984 with the inauguration of Bridgeport Brewing Company in Portland, followed a year later by Beervana's old-school brewing brothers Mike and Brian McMenamin, whose quirky beer empire still acts as a kind of personification of the craft-brewing business in the region.

Today, Washington and Oregon operate over 450 microbreweries (the Portland metro area alone has over 70). These take classic, natural ingredients – malt, hops and yeast – to produce high-quality beer in small batches.

on a warm day. There's great food, too – the gringo bowl and steak salad are favorites – while sports fans will appreciate a Blazers or Timbers game on the screens inside.

Hair of the Dog Brewing BREWERY
(☎503-232-6585; www.hairofthedog.com; 61 SE Yamhill St; ⏲11:30am-10pm Tue-Sat, to 8pm Sun) HOTD brews unusual beer styles, some of which are 'bottle-conditioned,' whereby the brewing cycle is finished inside the bottle. This results in complex flavors and high alcohol content, and the beer ages like a fine wine. Food is served to complement the beer's flavors.

Rontoms BAR
(☎503-236-4536; 600 E Burnside St; ⏲11am-2:30am Mon-Fri, 2pm-2:30am Sat & Sun) First the downside – the food's just OK, the service is mediocre and if you're not a hipster you'll feel out of place. But if it's a nice day, the large patio in back is *the* place to be. It's at the corner of E Burnside and 6th (too cool for a sign).

☆ Entertainment

The best guide to local entertainment is the free *Willamette Week* (www.wweek.com), which comes out on Wednesday and lists theater, music, clubs, cinema and events in the metro area. Also, try the *Portland Mercury* (www.portlandmercury.com).

For summer outdoor concerts, check what's happening at the Oregon Zoo (www.oregonzoo.org) or at McMenamins Edgefield (p1056).

Live Music

Doug Fir Lounge LIVE MUSIC
(☎503-231-9663; www.dougfirlounge.com; 830 E Burnside St) Combining futuristic elements with a rustic log-cabin aesthetic, this ultra-trendy venue has helped transform the LoBu (lower Burnside) neighborhood from seedy to slick. Doug Fir books edgy, hard-to-get talent, drawing crowds from tattooed youth to suburban yuppies. Its decent restaurant has long hours. Find it next door to the rock-star-quality Jupiter Hotel.

Crystal Ballroom LIVE MUSIC
(☎503-225-0047; www.mcmenamins.com; 1332 W Burnside St) This large, historic ballroom has hosted some major acts, including the Grateful Dead, James Brown and Jimi Hendrix. The 'floating' dance floor makes dancing a balancing act. If you like '80s music, come on a Friday night.

Mississippi Studios LIVE MUSIC
(☎503-288-3895; www.mississippistudios.com; 3939 N Mississippi Ave) Good for checking out budding acoustic talent, along with more established musical acts. Excellent sound system and good restaurant-bar with patio next door. Located right on trendy N Mississippi Ave.

Jimmy Mak's LIVE MUSIC
(☎503-295-6542; www.jimmymaks.com; 221 NW 10th Ave) Stumptown's premier jazz venue, serving excellent Mediterranean food in its dining room.

Performing Arts

Portland Center Stage THEATER
(☎503-445-3700; www.pcs.org; 128 NW 11th Ave) The city's main theater company now performs in the Portland Armory – a renovated Pearl District landmark with state-of-the-art features.

Arlene Schnitzer Concert Hall CLASSICAL MUSIC
(☎503-248-4335; www.portland5.com; 1037 SW Broadway) The Oregon Symphony performs in this beautiful, if not acoustically brilliant, downtown venue.

Artists Repertory Theatre THEATER
(☎503-241-1278; www.artistsrep.org; 1515 SW Morrison St) Some of Portland's best plays, including regional premieres, are performed in two intimate theaters.

Keller Auditorium PERFORMING ARTS
(☎503-248-4335; www.portland5.com; 222 SW Clay St) The Portland Opera and Oregon Ballet Theatre stage performances here, along with some Broadway productions.

Shopping

Portland's downtown shopping district extends in a two-block radius from Pioneer Courthouse Sq and hosts all of the usual suspects. The Pearl District is dotted with high-end galleries, boutiques and home-decor shops. On weekends, you can visit the quintessential Saturday Market (p1052) by the Skidmore Fountain. For a pleasant, upscale shopping street, head to NW 23rd Ave.

Eastside has lots of trendy shopping streets that also host restaurants and cafes. SE Hawthorne Blvd is the biggest, N Mississippi Ave is the newest and NE Alberta St is the most artsy and funkiest. Down south, Sellwood is known for its antique shops.

DON'T MISS

POWELL'S CITY OF BOOKS

You remember bookstores, don't you? Well they haven't all disappeared. **Powell's City of Books** (☎800-878-7323; www.powells.com; 1005 W Burnside St; ⏲9am-11pm), an empire of reading that takes up a whole city block on multiple stories, once claimed to be 'the largest independent bookstore in the world.' Don't miss it during your Portland tenure; it's a local institution, tourist attraction and a worthy place to hang out for a few hours (it'll take you that long to get through it). There are other branches around town and at the airport, but none as large.

Information

EMERGENCY

Portland Police Bureau (☎503-823-0000; www.portlandoregon.gov/police; 1111 SW 2nd Ave)

INTERNET ACCESS

Central Library (☎503-988-5123; www.multcolib.org; 801 SW 10th Ave; ⏲10am-8pm Mon, noon-8pm Tue & Wed, 10am-6pm Thu-Sat, to 5pm Sun) Downtown; for other branches check the website.

MEDIA

KBOO 90.7 FM (www.kboo.fm) Progressive local station run by volunteers; alternative news and views.

Portland Mercury (www.portlandmercury.com) Free local sibling of Seattle's *The Stranger*.

Willamette Week (www.wweek.com) Free weekly covering local news and culture.

MEDICAL SERVICES

Legacy Good Samaritan Medical Center (☎503-413-7711; www.legacyhealth.org; 1015 NW 22nd Ave) Convenient to downtown.

POST

Post Office (☎503-525-5398; www.usps.com; 715 NW Hoyt St; ⏲8am-6:30pm Mon-Fri, 8:30am-5pm Sat)

TOURIST INFORMATION

Portland Oregon Visitors Association (☎503-275-8355; www.travelportland.com; 701 SW 6th Ave; ⏲8:30am-5:30pm Mon-Fri, 10am-4pm Sat, to 2pm Sun May-Oct, 8:30am-5:30pm Mon-Fri, 10am-4pm Sat Nov-Apr) Super-friendly volunteers staff this office in Pioneer Courthouse Sq. There's a small theater with a 12-minute film about the city, and Tri-Met bus and light-rail offices inside.

Getting There & Away

AIR

Portland International Airport (PDX; ☎503-460-4234; www.flypdx.com; 7000 NE Airport Way; 📶) Award-winning Portland International Airport has daily flights all over the US, as well as to several international destinations. It's situated just east of I-5 on the banks of the Columbia River (20 minutes' drive from downtown).

BUS

Greyhound (☎503-243-2361; www.greyhound.com; 550 NW 6th Ave) Greyhound connects Portland with cities along I-5 and I-84. Destinations include Chicago, Denver, San Francisco, Seattle and Vancouver, BC.

Bolt Bus (☎877-265-8287; www.boltbus.com) Connects Portland with Seattle, Bellingham, Eugene and San Francisco, among other cities.

TRAIN

Amtrak (☎800-872-7245; www.amtrak.com; 800 NW 6th Ave) Amtrak serves Chicago, Oakland, Seattle and Vancouver, BC.

Getting Around

TO/FROM THE AIRPORT

Portland International Airport (PDX) is about 10 miles northeast of downtown, next to the Columbia River. Tri-Met's light-rail MAX line takes about 40 minutes to get from downtown to the airport. **Blue Star** (☎503-249-1837; www.bluestarbus.com) offers shuttle services between PDX and several downtown stops.

Taxis charge around $40 from the airport to downtown (not including tip).

BICYCLE

It's easy riding a bicycle around Portland, often voted 'the most bike-friendly city in America.'

Rental companies include **Clever Cycles** (☎503-334-1560; www.clevercycles.com/rentals; 900 SE Hawthorne Blvd; rentals per day from $30; ⊙11am-6pm Mon-Fri, to 5pm Sat & Sun) and Waterfront Bicycle Rentals (p1055).

PUBLIC TRANSPORTATION

Portland has a good public-transportation system, which consists of local buses, streetcars and the MAX light-rail. All are run by **TriMet** (☎503-238-7433; www.trimet.org; 701 SW 6th Ave; ⊙8:30am-5:30pm Mon-Fri), which has an information center at Pioneer Courthouse Sq.

Tickets for the transportation systems are completely transferable within 2½ hours of the time of purchase. Buy tickets for local buses from the fare machines as you enter; for streetcars, you can buy tickets either at streetcar stations or on the streetcar itself. Tickets for the MAX must be bought from ticket machines at MAX stations (before you board); there is no conductor or ticket seller on board (but there are enforcers).

Be aware that there are fewer services at night, and only a few run past 1am; check the website for details on a specific line.

CAR

Most major car-rental agencies have outlets both downtown and at Portland International Airport. Many of these agencies have added hybrid vehicles to their fleets. **Zipcar** (www.zipcar.com) is a popular car-sharing option, but there are many. For cheap parking downtown, see www.portlandoregon.gov/transportation/35272.

CHARTER SERVICE

EcoShuttle (☎503-548-4480; www.ecoshuttle.net) For custom bus or van charters and tours, try EcoShuttle. Vehicles are run on 100% biodiesel.

PEDICAB

PDX Pedicab (☎503-828-9888; www.pdxpedicab.com) For an ecofriendly option, there are several pedicab operators in town, including PDX Pedicab. Bicycle pedicabs come with 'drivers' that pedal you around downtown.

TAXI

Cabs are available 24 hours by phone. Downtown, you can sometimes just flag them down.

Broadway Cab (☎503-333-3333; www.broadwaycab.com)

Radio Cab (☎503-227-1212; www.radiocab.net)

Willamette Valley

The Willamette Valley, a fertile 60-mile-wide agricultural basin, was the Holy Grail for Oregon Trail pioneers who headed west more than 170 years ago. Today it's the state's breadbasket, producing more than 100 kinds of crops – including renowned Pinot Noir grapes. Salem, Oregon's capital, is about an hour's drive from Portland at the northern end of the valley, and most of the other attractions in the area make easy day trips as well. Toward the south is Eugene, a dynamic college town worth a day or two of exploration.

Salem

Oregon's legislative center (not the Salem associated with witches, which is in Massachusetts) is renowned for its cherry trees, art-deco capitol building and Willamette University.

Willamette University's **Hallie Ford Museum of Art** (☎503-370-6855; www.willamette.edu/arts/hfma; 900 State St; adult/child $6/free; ⊙10am-5pm Tue-Sat, 1-5pm Sun) showcases the state's best collection of Pacific Northwest art, including an impressive Native American gallery.

The **Oregon State Capitol** (☎503-986-1388; www.oregonlegislature.gov; 900 Court St NE; ⊙8am-5pm Mon-Fri) FREE, built in 1938, looks like a background prop from a lavish Cecil B DeMille movie; free tours are offered. Rambling 19th-century **Bush House** (☎503-363-4714; www.salemart.org; 600 Mission St SE; adult/child $6/3; ⊙1-4pm Wed-Sun Mar-Dec) is an Italianate mansion now preserved as a museum with historical accents, including original wallpapers and marble fireplaces.

You can get oriented at the **Visitors Information Center** (☎503-581-4325; www.travelsalem.com; 181 High St NE; ⊙9am-5pm Mon-Fri, 10am-4pm Sat).

Salem is served daily by **Greyhound** (☎503-362-2428; www.greyhound.com; 500 13th St SE) buses and **Amtrak** (☎503-588-1551; www.amtrak.com; 500 13th St SE) trains.

Eugene

Eclectic Eugene – also known as 'Track-town' – is full of youthful energy and liberal politics, and famous for its track-and-field champions (Nike was born here, after all). And while the city maintains a working-class base in timber and manufacturing, some unconventional citizens live here as well, from ex-hippie activists to eco-green anarchists to upscale entrepreneurs to high-tech heads.

Eugene offers a great arts scene, exceptionally fine restaurants, boisterous festivals, miles of riverside paths and several lovely parks. It's an awesome place to be, both for energetic visitors and those lucky enough to settle here.

Sights

Alton Baker Park PARK
(100 Day Island Rd) This popular, 400-acre riverside park, which provides access to the **Ruth Bascom Riverbank Trail System**, a 12-mile bikeway that flanks both sides of the Willamette, is heaven for cyclists and joggers. There's good downtown access via the DeFazio Bike Bridge.

University of Oregon UNIVERSITY
(☎541-346-1000; www.uoregon.edu; 1585 E 13th Ave) Established in 1872, the University of Oregon is the state's foremost institution of higher learning, with a focus on the arts, sciences and law. The campus is filled with historical ivy-covered buildings and includes a **Pioneer Cemetery**, with tombstones that give vivid insight into life and death in the early settlement. Campus tours are held in the summer.

Sleeping

Eugene has all the regular chain hotels and motels. Prices rise sharply during key football games and graduation.

Campus Inn MOTEL $
(☎541-343-3376; www.campus-inn.com; 390 E Broadway; d $70-80;) This very pleasant motel near the university offers spacious business-style rooms in simple, stylish decor. Go for the $10 upgrade: it's worth it for a bigger bed and more space. Small gym, communal Jacuzzi and upstairs outside patio available.

WORTH A TRIP

WILLAMETTE VALLEY WINE COUNTRY

Just a hour's drive from Portland is the Willamette Valley, home to hundreds of wineries producing world-class tipples, especially Pinot Noir. McMinnville, Newberg and Dundee provide many of this region's services, which include some very fine restaurants, shops, B&Bs and wine-tasting rooms. Check out www.willamettewines.com for more information on the region's wineries.

Meandering through plush green hills on winding country roads from one wine-tasting room to another is a delightful way to spend an afternoon (just make sure you designate a driver). If you'd rather go on a tour, **Grape Escape** (☎503-283-3380; www.grapeescapetours.com) offers some good ones. If you like to bicycle, Portland-based **Pedal Bike Tours** (p1055) runs five-hour bike tours ($89).

For something more cerebral, head to McMinnville's **Evergreen Aviation & Space Museum** (☎503-434-4185; www.evergreenmuseum.org; 500 NE Captain Michael King Smith Way; adult/child incl 3-D movie $25/23; ⏱9am-5pm) and check out Howard Hughes' **Spruce Goose**, the world's largest wood-framed airplane. There's also a replica of the Wright brothers' *Flyer*, along with a 3-D theater and – oddly enough – an excellent water park.

For an interesting place to stay, head to **McMenamins Hotel Oregon** (☎503-472-8427; www.mcmenamins.com; 310 NE Evans St; d $83-138;), an older building renovated into a charming hotel. It has a wonderful rooftop bar. And for a spectacular restaurant experience, consider **Joel Palmer House** (☎503-864-2995; www.joelpalmerhouse.com; 600 Ferry St, Dayton; prix fixe menus from $55; ⏱4:30-9:30pm Tue-Sat) Its dishes are peppered with wild mushrooms collected locally by the chefs.

Eugene Whiteaker International Hostel HOSTEL $
(541-343-3335; www.eugenehostels.com; 970 W 3rd Ave; dm $30-35, r $40-75;) This casual hostel in an old rambling house has an artsy vibe, nice front and back patios to hang out in, and a free simple breakfast. Campsites are available ($25 per person), and there's a second location (the Emerald Garden Hostel) nearby.

C'est La Vie Inn B&B $$
(541-302-3014; www.cestlavieinn.com; 1006 Taylor St; d $150-170, ste $260;) This gorgeous Victorian house, run by a friendly French/American couple, is a neighborhood showstopper. Beautiful antique furniture fills the living and dining areas, while the three tastefully appointed rooms offer comfort and luxury. Also available is an amazing suite with kitchenette.

Eating & Drinking

Papa's Soul Food Kitchen SOUTHERN $
(541-342-7500; www.papassoulfoodkitchen.com; 400 Blair Blvd; mains $8-12; noon-2pm & 5-10pm Tue-Fri, 2-10pm Sat) This popular Southern-food spot grills up awesome jerk chicken, pulled-pork sandwiches, crawfish jambalaya and fried okra. The best part is the live blues music that keeps the joint open late on Friday and Saturday nights. Nice back patio, too.

Sweet Life Patisserie BAKERY $
(541-683-5676; www.sweetlifedesserts.com; 755 Monroe St; pastries $2.50-5; 7am-11pm Mon-Fri, 8am-11pm Sat & Sun) Eugene's best dessert shop: think pecan sticky buns, savory croissants and *pain au chocolat*. Even the day-old pastries are delicious (and half-price). Organic coffee, too.

★ **Beppe & Gianni's Trattoria** ITALIAN $$
(541-683-6661; www.beppeandgiannis.net; 1646 E 19th Ave; mains $15-20; 5-9pm Sun-Thu, to 10pm Fri & Sat) One of Eugene's most beloved restaurants and its favorite Italian food. Homemade pastas are the real deal here, and the desserts are excellent. Expect a wait, especially on weekends.

Pizza Research Institute PIZZA $$
(PRI; 541-343-1307; www.pizzaresearchinstitute.com; 325 Blair Blvd; pizzas $16-24; 4-9:30pm;) Located in a cute bungalow house, PRI bakes up some of Eugene's best (vegetarian, vegan, gluten-free) pies. Try the pear with vegan pesto, apple and smoked gouda, or chèvre with marinated eggplant. You can build your own pizza, too, adding toppings such as artichoke hearts, asparagus or roasted zucchini.

Ninkasi Brewing Company BREWERY
(541-344-2739; www.ninkasibrewing.com; 272 Van Buren St; noon-9pm Sun-Wed, to 10pm Thu-Sat) Head to this tasting room to sample some of Oregon's best microbrews. There's a sweet outdoor patio with snacks to purchase, and there's usually a food cart or two nearby. Brewery tours available.

Information

Visitor Center (541-484-5307; www.eugenecascadescoast.org; 754 Olive St; 8am-5pm Mon-Fri) On weekends, stop by the visitor center at 3312 Gateway St in Springfield for information.

WORTH A TRIP

HOT SPRINGS

Oregon has an abundance of hot springs and there are some not far from Salem:

Bagby Hot Springs (www.bagbyhotsprings.org; admission $5) A couple of hours' drive east of Salem is this rustic hot spring with various wood tubs in semiprivate bathhouses. It's accessible via a lovely 1.5-mile hiking trail.

Terwilliger Hot Springs (admission $6) About 40 miles east of Eugene, Terwilliger Hot Springs (aka Cougar Hot Springs) is a beautiful cluster of terraced outdoor pools framed by large rocks. They're rustic, but well-maintained, with the hottest on top. Clothing is optional, no alcohol is allowed and it's day-use only. From the parking lot, you'll have to walk a quarter-mile to the springs. To get here, turn south onto Aufderheide Scenic Byway from Hwy 126 and drive 7.5 miles.

Breitenbush Hot Springs (503-854-3320; www.breitenbush.com) Enjoy salubrious climes at Breitenbush Hot Springs, a fancy spa with massages, yoga and the like. Day-use prices are $16 to $30, but you can also stay in the dorm, cabins or lodge.

ℹ Getting There & Around

Eugene's **Amtrak station** (☑ 541-687-1383; www.amtrak.com; 433 Willamette St) runs daily trains to Vancouver, BC, and LA, and everywhere in between on its *Cascade* and *Coast Starlight* lines. **Greyhound** (☑ 541-344-6265; www.greyhound.com; 987 Pearl St) runs north to Salem and Portland, and south to Grants Pass and Medford. **Porter Stage Lines** (www.kokkola-bus.com) runs a daily bus from outside the train station to the coast.

Local bus service is provided by **Lane Transit District** (☑ 541-687-5555; www.ltd.org). For bike rentals, try **Paul's Bicycle Way of Life** (☑ 541-344-4105; www.bicycleway.com; 566 Charnelton St; rentals per day $24-48; ☉ 9am-7pm Mon-Fri, 10am-5pm Sat & Sun).

Columbia River Gorge

The fourth-largest river in the US by volume, the mighty Columbia runs 1243 miles from Alberta, Canada, into the Pacific Ocean just west of Astoria. For the final 309 miles of its course, the heavily dammed waterway delineates the border between Washington and Oregon and cuts though the Cascade Mountains via the spectacular Columbia River Gorge. Showcasing numerous ecosystems, waterfalls and magnificent vistas, the land bordering the river is protected as a National Scenic Area and is a popular sporting nexus for windsurfers, cyclists, anglers and hikers.

Not far from Portland, **Multnomah Falls** is a huge tourist draw, while **Vista House** offers stupendous gorge views. And if you want to stretch your legs, the **Eagle Creek Trail** is the area's premier tromping ground – provided you don't get vertigo!

Hood River & Around

Famous for its surrounding fruit orchards and wineries, the small town of Hood River – 63 miles east of Portland on I-84 – is also a huge mecca for windsurfing and kiteboarding. Strong river currents, prevailing westerly winds and the vast Columbia River provide the perfect conditions for these wind sports.

◉ Sights & Activities

Mt Hood Railroad   HISTORIC SITE
(☑ 800-872-4661; www.mthoodrr.com; 110 Railroad Ave) Built in 1906, the railroad once transported fruit and lumber from the upper Hood River Valley to the main railhead in Hood River. The vintage trains now transport tourists beneath Mt Hood's snowy peak and past fragrant orchards, on various excursions. See the website for schedules and fares. Reserve in advance.

Cathedral Ridge Winery   WINERY
(☑ 800-516-8710; www.cathedralridgewinery.com; 4200 Post Canyon Dr) Attractive winery with signature red blends and an award-winning Barbera.

Hood River Waterplay   WATER SPORTS
(☑ 541-386-9463; www.hoodriverwaterplay.com; Port of Hood River Marina) To partake in Hood River's wind sports, such as catamaran sailing and windsurfing, contact this outfitter for rentals and classes.

Discover Bicycles   CYCLING
(☑ 541-386-4820; www.discoverbicycles.com; 210 State St; rentals per day $30-80; ☉ 10am-6pm Mon-Sat, to 5pm Sun) Rents road, hybrid and mountain bikes and can give advice on area trails.

🛏 Sleeping & Eating

Inn of the White Salmon   INN $$
(☑ 509-493-2335; www.innofthewhitesalmon.com; 172 West Jewett Blvd; d $129-189; ❋🔊) Over in White Salmon, WA, is this very pleasant and contemporary 18-room inn with comfortable accommodations and a lovely patio-garden out back. There's also a very nice four-bed dorm (single bunk $25, queen bunk for two $40), along with a common-use kitchenette area.

Hood River Hotel   HISTORIC HOTEL $$
(☑ 541-386-1900; www.hoodriverhotel.com; 102 Oak St; d $109-209; ❋🔊❋) Located right in the heart of downtown, this fine 1913 hotel offers comfortable old-fashioned rooms with four-poster or sleigh beds, some with tiny baths. The suites have the best amenities and views. Kitchenettes are also available, and there's a restaurant and sauna on the premises.

Double Mountain Brewery   PUB $$
(☑ 541-387-0042; www.doublemountainbrewery.com; 8 4th St; sandwiches $7.50-10, pizzas $16-22; ☉ 11am-11pm Sun-Thu, to midnight Fri & Sat) For a casual bite, step into this popular brewpub-restaurant for a tasty sandwich or excellent brick-oven pizza. The menu is limited, but the food is great and the beer even better. Live music on weekends.

Information

Chamber of Commerce (541-386-2000; www.hoodriver.org; 720 E Port Marina Dr; 9am-5pm Mon-Fri, 10am-5pm Sat & Sun Apr-Oct, 9am-5pm Mon-Fri Nov-Mar)

Getting There & Away

Hood River is connected to Portland by daily **Greyhound** (541-386-1212; www.greyhound.com; 110 Railroad Ave) buses. Amtrak runs on the Washington side.

Oregon Cascades

The Oregon Cascades offer plenty of dramatic volcanoes that dominate the skyline for miles around. Mt Hood, overlooking the Columbia River Gorge, is the state's highest peak, and has year-round skiing plus a relatively straightforward summit ascent. Tracking south you'll pass Mt Jefferson and the Three Sisters before reaching Crater Lake, the ghost of erstwhile Mt Mazama that collapsed in on itself after blowing its top approximately 7000 years ago.

Mt Hood

The state's highest peak, Mt Hood (11,240ft) pops into view over much of northern Oregon whenever there's a sunny day, exerting an almost magnetic tug on skiers, hikers and sightseers. In summer, wildflowers bloom on the mountainsides and hidden ponds shimmer blue, making for some unforgettable hikes; in winter, downhill and cross-country skiing dominates people's minds and bodies.

Mt Hood is accessible year-round from Portland on US 26 and from Hood River on Hwy 35. Together with the Columbia River Hwy, these routes comprise the **Mt Hood Loop**, a popular scenic drive. **Government Camp** is at the pass over Mt Hood and is the center of business on the mountain.

Activities

Skiing

Hood is rightly revered for its skiing. There are six ski areas on the mountain, including **Timberline** (503-272-3158; www.timberlinelodge.com), which lures snow-lovers with the only year-round skiing in the US. Closer to Portland, **Mt Hood SkiBowl** (503-272-3206; www.skibowl.com) is no slacker either. It's the nation's largest night-ski area and popular with city slickers who ride up for an evening of powder play from the metro zone. The largest ski area on the mountain is **Mt Hood Meadows** (503-337-2222; www.skihood.com), and the best conditions usually prevail here.

Hiking

The Mt Hood National Forest protects an astounding 1200 miles of trails. A Northwest Forest Pass ($5) is required at most trailheads.

One popular trail loops 7 miles from near the village of Zigzag to beautiful **Ramona Falls**, which tumbles down mossy columnar basalt. Another heads 1.5 miles up from US 26 to **Mirror Lake**, continues 0.5 miles around the lake, then tracks 2 miles beyond to a ridge.

The 41-mile **Timberline Trail** circumnavigates Mt Hood through scenic wilderness. Noteworthy portions include the hike to McNeil Point and the short climb to Bald Mountain. From Timberline Lodge, Zigzag Canyon Overlook is a 4.5-mile round-trip. At the time of writing, however, part of the trail was washed out, with no timetable for when it would be repaired.

Climbing Mt Hood should be taken seriously, as deaths do occur, though dogs have made it to the summit and the climb can be done in a long day. Contact **Timberline Mountain Guides** (541-312-9242; www.timberlinemtguides.com) for guided climbs.

Sleeping & Eating

Reserve **campsites** (877-444-6777; www.recreation.gov) in summer. On US 26 are streamside campgrounds **Tollgate** and **Camp Creek**. Large and popular **Trillium Lake** has great views of Mt Hood.

★**Timberline Lodge** — LODGE $$
(800-547-1406; www.timberlinelodge.com; 27500 Timberline Rd; d from $135;) More a community treasure than a hotel, this gorgeous historical lodge offers a variety of rooms, from bunk rooms that sleep up to 10 to deluxe fireplace rooms. Huge wooden beams tower over multiple fireplaces, there's a year-round heated outdoor pool, and the ski lifts are close by. Enjoy awesome views of Mt Hood, nearby hiking trails, two bars and a good dining room. Rates can vary widely, so check ahead.

Huckleberry Inn — INN $$
(503-272-3325; www.huckleberry-inn.com; 88611 E Government Camp Loop; r $90-160;) Simple and comfortably rustic rooms are

available here, and there are bunk rooms that sleep up to 14. It's in a great central location in Government Camp, and has a casual restaurant (which doubles as the hotel's reception). Peak holiday rates go up 20%.

Mt Hood Brewing Co PUB $
(☎503-272-3172; www.mthoodbrewing.com; 87304 E Government Camp Loop, Government Camp; mains $12-18; ⏲11am-10pm) Government Camp's only brewery-restaurant offers a friendly, family-style atmosphere and pub fare including hand-tossed pizzas, sandwiches and short ribs.

Rendezvous Grill & Tap Room AMERICAN $$
(☎503-622-6837; www.rendezvousgrill.net; 67149 E US 26, Welches; mains lunch $10-17, dinner $18-23; ⏲11:30am-9pm) In a league of its own is this excellent restaurant with outstanding dishes such as wild salmon with caramelized shallots and artichoke hash or chargrilled pork chop in rhubarb chutney. Lunch means gourmet sandwiches, burgers and salads on the outdoor patio.

ℹ Information

If you're approaching from Hood River, visit the **Hood River Ranger Station** (☎541-352-6002; 6780 Hwy 35, Parkdale; ⏲8am-4:30pm Mon-Fri). The **Zigzag Ranger Station** (☎503-622-3191; 70220 E Hwy 26; ⏲7:45am-4:30pm Mon-Sat) is more handy for Portland arrivals. **Mt Hood Information Center** (☎503-272-3301; 88900 E US 26; ⏲9am-5pm) is in Government Camp. The weather changes quickly here; carry chains in winter.

ℹ Getting There & Away

From Portland, Mt Hood is one hour (56 miles) by car along Hwy 26. Alternatively, you can take the prettier and longer approach via Hwy 84 to Hood River, then Hwy 35 south (1¾ hours, 95 miles). The **Central Oregon Breeze** (☎800-847-0157; www.cobreeze.com) shuttle between Bend and Portland stops briefly at Government Camp, 6 miles from the Timberline Lodge. There are regular **shuttles** (☎503-286-9333; www.seatosummit.net) from Portland to the ski areas during the winter.

Sisters

Straddling the Cascades and high desert, where mountain pine forests mingle with desert sage and juniper, is the darling town of Sisters. Once a stagecoach stop and a trade town for loggers and ranchers, today Sisters is a bustling tourist destination whose main street is lined with boutiques, art galleries and eateries housed in Western-facade buildings. Visitors come for the mountain scenery, spectacular hiking, fine cultural events and awesome climate – there's plenty of sun and little precipitation here. And while the town's atmosphere is a bit upscale, people are still friendly and the back streets are still undeveloped enough that deer are often seen nibbling in neighborhood garden plots.

At the southern end of Sisters, the city park has **camp sites** ($15), but no showers. For ultracomfort, bag a room in the luxurious **Five Pine Lodge** (☎866-974-5900; www.fivepinelodge.com; 1021 Desperado Trail; d $170-293, cabins $179-329; ❄@📶🏊🐾). On the quieter and cheaper side is **Sisters Motor Lodge** (☎541-549-2551; www.sistersmotorlodge.com; 511 W Cascade St; r $129-229; ❄📶🐾), offering 11 cozy rooms with homey decor (and some with kitchenettes).

For great gourmet treats head to **Porch** (☎541-549-3287; www.theporch-sisters.com; 243 N Elm St; small plates $8-17, mains $24-29; ⏲5-9pm Fri-Tue), which offers morsels such as truffle fries and creamy butternut-squash risotto. **Three Creeks Brewing** (☎541-549-1963; www.threecreeksbrewing.com; 721 Desperado Ct; ⏲11:30am-9pm Sun-Thu, till 10pm Fri & Sat) is the place to go for home brew and pub grub.

ℹ Information

Chamber of Commerce (☎541-549-0251; www.sisterscountry.com; 291 Main St; ⏲10am-4pm Mon-Sat)

ℹ Getting There & Away

Valley Retriever (☎541-265-2253; www.kokkola-bus.com/VRBSchedule; cnr Cascade & Spruce Sts) Buses connect Sisters with Bend, Newport, Corvallis, Salem, McMinnville and Portland.

Bend

Bend is where all outdoor-lovers should live – it's an absolute paradise. You can ski fine powder in the morning, paddle a kayak in the afternoon and take in a game of golf into the evening. Or would you rather go mountain biking, hiking, mountaineering, stand-up paddleboarding, fly-fishing or rock climbing? It's all close by, and top-drawer. Plus, you'll probably be enjoying it all in great weather, as the area gets nearly 300 days of sunshine each year.

With the lovely Deschutes River carving its way through the heart of the city, Bend also offers a vibrant and attractive downtown area full of shops, galleries and upscale dining. South of downtown, the Old Mill District has been renovated into a large shopping area full of brand-name stores, fancy eateries and modern movie theaters. Bend has also become a beer-lover's dream; it has more than a dozen breweries per capita more than any other city in Oregon.

Sights

★High Desert Museum MUSEUM

(☎541-382-4754; www.highdesertmuseum.org; 59800 S US 97; adult/child 5-12yr $15/9; ⏲9am-5pm May-Oct, 10am-4pm Nov-Apr) Don't miss this excellent museum about 3 miles south of Bend on US 97. It charts the exploration and settlement of the West, using reenactments of a Native American camp, a hard-rock mine and an old Western town. The region's natural history is also explored; kids love the live snake, tortoise and trout exhibits, and watching the birds of prey and otters is always fun.

Activities

Cycling

Bend is a mountain biking paradise, with hundreds of miles of awesome bike trails to explore. For a good bike-trails map, get the *Bend Oregon Adventure Map* ($12), available at the Visit Bend tourist office and elsewhere.

The king of Bend's mountain biking trails is **Phil's Trail** network, which offers a variety of excellent fast single-track forest trails just minutes from town. If you want to catch air, don't miss the **Whoops Trail**.

Cog Wild BICYCLE TOUR

(☎541-385-7002; www.cogwild.com; 255 SW Century Dr, ste 201; half-day tours from $60) Offers organized tours and shuttles to the best trailheads. Separate rental shop downstairs.

Rock Climbing

Smith Rock State Park ROCK CLIMBING

(☎800-551-6949; www.oregonstateparks.org; 9241 NE Crooked River Dr; day use $5) About 25 miles northeast of Bend lies Smith Rock State Park, where 800ft cliffs over the Crooked River offer gorgeous lead and trad climbing. The park's 1800-plus routes are among the best in the nation.

Smith Rock Climbing Guides Inc ROCK CLIMBING

(☎541-788-6225; www.smithrockclimbingguides.com) Offers a variety of climbing instruction (basic, lead, trad, multi-pitch, aid and self-rescue), along with guided climbs to famous routes at Smith Rock State Park.

Skiing

Mount Bachelor Ski Resort SKIING

(☎800-829-2442; www.mtbachelor.com) Bend hosts Oregon's best skiing, 22 miles southwest of town, at the glorious Mount Bachelor Ski Resort, famous for its 'dry' powdery snow, long season and ample terrain (it's the largest ski area in the Pacific Northwest). The mountain has long advocated cross-country skiing in tandem with downhill, and maintains 35 miles of groomed trails.

Sleeping & Eating

Mill Inn INN $$

(☎541-389-9198; www.millinn.com; 642 NW Colorado Ave; d incl breakfast $95-165; ⊖ 📶) A 10-room boutique hotel with small, classy rooms decked out with velvet drapes and comforters; four share outside bathrooms. Full breakfast and hot-tub use is included, and there are nice small patios on which to hang out.

★McMenamins Old St Francis School HOTEL $$

(☎541-382-5174; www.mcmenamins.com; 700 NW Bond St; d $135-185, 5-bedroom cottage from $350; ❄ 📶) One of McMenamins' best venues, this old schoolhouse has been remodeled into a classy 19-room hotel – two rooms even have side-by-side clawfoot tubs. The fabulous tiled saltwater Turkish bath is worth the stay alone, though nonguests can soak for $5. A restaurant-pub, three bars, a movie theater and creative artwork complete the picture.

★Oxford Hotel BOUTIQUE HOTEL $$$

(☎541-382-8436; www.oxfordhotelbend.com; 10 NW Minnesota Ave; d $389-599; ❄ 📶 🐾) 🍃 Bend's premier boutique hotel is deservedly popular. The smallest rooms are still huge (470 sq ft) and are decked out with eco-friendly features such as soy-foam mattresses and cork flooring. High-tech aficionados will love the smart-panel desks. Suites (with kitchen and steam-shower) are available, and the basement restaurant is slick.

★Chow AMERICAN $

(☎541-728-0256; www.chowbend.com; 1110 NW Newport Ave; mains $8-15; ⏱7am-2pm) The signature poached-egg dishes here are spectacular and beautifully presented, coming with sides such as crab cakes, house-cured ham and corn-meal-crusted tomatoes (don't miss their housemade hot sauces). Gourmet sandwiches and salads are served for lunch, some with an Asian influence. Much of the produce is grown in the garden, and there are good cocktails, too.

Jackson's Corner AMERICAN $

(☎541-647-2198; www.jacksonscornerbend.com; 845 NW Delaware Ave; mains $10-16; ⏱7am-9pm;) This homey corner restaurant, very popular with families, has a market-like feel and boasts seasonal ingredients. Homemade pizzas and pastas are always good, as are the organic salads (add on chicken, steak or prawns). There's a kids' menu and outside seating for sunny days; just remember to order at the counter first. Also at 1500 NE Cushing Dr.

10 Barrel Brewing Co AMERICAN $

(☎541-678-5228; www.10barrel.com; 1135 NW Galveston; mains $10-14; ⏱11am-11pm Mon-Thu, to midnight Fri-Sun) Located in a charming house, this popular brewery-restaurant has a great patio for warm nights. The tasty pub-food menu includes starters such as fried brussels sprouts and steak and gorgonzola nachos, while mains run the gamut from gourmet burgers to fish tacos with chipotle slaw. Sports-lovers should head to the bar in back.

Zydeco AMERICAN $$$

(☎541-312-2899; www.zydecokitchen.com; 919 NW Bond St; mains $16-30; ⏱11:30am-2:30pm & 5-9pm Mon-Fri, 5-9pm Sat & Sun) One of Bend's most acclaimed restaurants, and with good reason. Start with the duck fries (french fries fried in duck fat) or tri-colored beet salad with goat's cheese, then move onto your main course: pan-roasted steelhead, crawfish jambalaya or roasted wild mushroom pork tenderloin. Reserve ahead.

ℹ Information

Visit Bend (☎800-949-6086; www.visitbend.com; 750 NW Lava Rd; ⏱9am-5pm Mon-Fri, 10am-4pm Sat & Sun) Great information, plus maps and recreation passes.

ℹ Getting There & Around

Central Oregon Breeze (www.cobreeze.com) offers transport to Portland two or more times daily. Connect to Sisters, Willamette Valley destinations and the coast with Valley Retriever (www.kokkola-bus.com/VRBSchedule) and Porter Stage Lines (www.pslporterstageline.com).

Cascades East Transit (☎541-385-8680; www.cascadeseasttransit.com) The regional bus company in Bend, covering La Pine, Mt Bachelor, Sisters, Prineville and Madras. It also provides bus transport within Bend.

High Desert Point (☎541-923-1732; www.highdesert-point.com) Buses link Bend with Chemult, where the nearest train station is located (65 miles south). High Desert Point also has bus services to Eugene, Ontario and Burns.

Newberry National Volcanic Monument

Newberry National Volcanic Monument (day use $5) showcases 400,000 years of dramatic seismic activity. Start your visit at the **Lava Lands Visitor Center** (☎541-593-2421; 58201 S Hwy 97; ⏱9am-5pm late May-Sep, reduced hours Oct-late May), 13 miles south of Bend. Nearby attractions include **Lava Butte**, a perfect cone rising 500ft, and **Lava River Cave**, Oregon's longest lava tube. Four miles west of the visitor center is **Benham Falls**, a good picnic spot on the Deschutes River.

Newberry Crater was once one of the most active volcanoes in North America, but after a large eruption a caldera was born. Close by are **Paulina Lake** and **East Lake**, deep bodies of water rich with trout, while looming above is 7985ft **Paulina Peak**.

Crater Lake National Park

It's no exaggeration: Crater Lake is so blue, you'll catch your breath. And if you get to see it on a calm day, the surrounding cliffs are reflected in those deep waters like a mirror. It's a stunningly beautiful sight. Crater Lake is Oregon's only **national park** (☎541-594-3000; www.nps.gov/crla; 7-day vehicle pass $15).

The secret lies in the water's purity. No rivers or streams feed the lake, meaning its content is made up entirely of rain and melted snow. It is also exceptionally deep – at 1949ft, it's the deepest lake in the US. The classic tour is the 33-mile rim drive (open from approximately June to mid-October), but there are also exceptional hiking and cross-country skiing opportunities. Note that because the area receives some of the highest snowfalls in North America, the rim drive and north entrance are sometimes closed up until early July.

You can stay from late May to mid-October at the **Cabins at Mazama Village** (888-774-2728; www.craterlakelodges.com; d $144; late May–mid-Oct) or the majestic and historic **Crater Lake Lodge** (888-774-2728; www.craterlakelodges.com; d $169-295; late May–mid-Oct;), opened in 1915. Campers head to **Mazama Campground** (888-774-2728; www.craterlakelodges.com; tent/RV sites from $22/31;).

For more information, head to **Steel Visitors Center** (541-594-3000; 9am-5pm May-Oct, 10am-4pm Nov-Apr).

Oregon Coast

Thanks to a far-sighted government in the 1910s, Oregon's 363-mile Pacific Coast was set aside as public land. This magnificent littoral is paralleled by US 101, a scenic highway that winds its way through towns, resorts, state parks (more than 70 of them) and wilderness areas. Everyone from campers to gourmet-lovers will find a plethora of ways to enjoy this exceptional region, which is especially popular in summer (reserve accommodations in advance).

Astoria

Astoria sits at the 5-mile-wide mouth of the Columbia River and was the first US settlement west of the Mississippi. The city has a long seafaring history and has seen its old harbor, once home to poor artists and writers, attract fancy hotels and restaurants in recent years. Inland are many historical houses, including lovingly restored Victorians – a few converted into romantic B&Bs.

Sights

Adding to the city's scenery is the 4.1-mile **Astoria-Megler Bridge**, the longest continuous truss bridge in North America, which crosses the Columbia River into Washington state. See it from the **Astoria Riverwalk**, which follows the trolley route. **Pier 39** is an interesting covered wharf with informal cannery museum and a couple of places to eat.

Columbia River Maritime Museum MUSEUM
(503-325-2323; www.crmm.org; 1792 Marine Dr; adult/child $12/5; 9:30am-5pm) Astoria's seafaring heritage is well interpreted at this wave-shaped museum. It's hard to miss the Coast Guard boat, frozen in action, through a huge outside window. Other exhibits highlight the salmon-packing industry, local lighthouses and the river's commercial history; also check out the Columbia River Bar exhibit and 3-D theater.

Flavel House HISTORIC BUILDING
(503-325-2203; www.cumtux.org; 441 8th St; adult/child $6/2; 10am-5pm) The extravagant Flavel House was built by Captain George Flavel, one of Astoria's leading citizens during the 1880s. This Queen Anne house has been repainted in its original colors and the grounds have been returned to Victorian-era landscaping; it has great views of the Columbia River, too.

Astoria Column LANDMARK
(503-325-2963; www.astoriacolumn.org; 1 Coxcomb Dr; parking $2; 9am-5:30pm Mon-Fri, to 5pm Sat & Sun) Rising high on Coxcomb Hill, the Astoria Column (built in 1926) is a 125ft tower painted with scenes from the westward sweep of US exploration and settlement. The top of the column (up 164 steps) offers excellent views over the area.

Fort Stevens State Park PARK
(503-861-3170 ext 21; www.oregonstateparks.org; 100 Peter Iredale Rd, Hammond; day use $5) Ten miles west of Astoria, this park holds the historical military installation that once guarded the mouth of the Columbia River. Near the **Military Museum** (503-861-2000; 10am-6pm May-Sep, to 4pm Oct-Apr) FREE are gun batteries dug into sand dunes – interesting remnants of the fort's mostly demolished military stations (truck and walking tours available). There's a popular beach at the small *Peter Iredale* 1906 shipwreck, and good ocean views from parking lot C. There's also camping and 12 miles of paved bike trails.

Sleeping & Eating

Norblad Hotel & Hostel HOSTEL $
(503-325-6989; www.norbladhotel.com; 443 14th St; dm $29, d $59-99;) This central hostel-hotel offers six simple but elegant, private rooms, most with shared bathroom (just one is en suite). There are also several dorm rooms and a communal kitchen. Some rooms have flat-screen TVs and views of the river.

LEWIS & CLARK: JOURNEY'S END

In November 1805 William Clark and his fellow explorer Meriwether Lewis of the Corps of Discovery staggered, with three dozen others, into a sheltered cove on the Columbia River, 2 miles west of the present-day Astoria-Megler Bridge, completing what was indisputably the greatest overland trek in American history.

After the first truly democratic ballot in US history (in which a woman and a black slave both voted), the party elected to make their bivouac 5 miles south of Astoria at Fort Clatsop, where the Corps spent a miserable winter in 1805–06. Today this site is called the **Lewis and Clark National Historical Park** (503-861-2471; www.nps.gov/lewi; 92343 Fort Clatsop Rd; adult/child $3/free; 9am-6pm mid-Jun–Aug, to 5pm Sep–mid-Jun), where you'll find a reconstructed Fort Clatsop, along with a visitors center and historical reenactments in summer.

Commodore Hotel BOUTIQUE HOTEL $$
(503-325-4747; www.commodoreastoria.com; 258 14th St; d with shared/private bath from $89/199;) Hip travelers should beeline to this slick and trendy hotel, which offers small, chic, minimalist rooms. Choose either private bathrooms or go Euro-style (sinks in rooms, but baths down the hall; 'deluxe' rooms have better views). There's a great living-room-style lobby with attached cafe. Room 309 has the best river view.

Blue Scorcher Bakery Café CAFE $
(503-338-7473; www.bluescorcher.com; 1493 Duane St; mains $7-13; 7am-4pm;) This artsy, organic co-op coffeehouse and bakery with free wi-fi boasts tasty salads, sandwiches, pizza, and egg dishes for breakfast. Vegetarian/vegan friendly; doughnut-free.

Fort George Brewery PUB $
(503-325-7468; www.fortgeorgebrewery.com; 1483 Duane St; mains $9-14; 11am-11pm Mon-Thu, to midnight Fri & Sat, noon-11pm Sun) Atmospheric brewery-restaurant in a historical building – this was the original settlement site of Astoria. Today you can get gourmet burgers, house-made sausages, organic salads and a few eclectic dishes. Afternoon brewery tours on weekends.

Information

Visitors Center (503-325-6311; www.oldoregon.com; 111 W Marine Dr; 9am-5pm Mon-Fri, 10am-4pm Sat) Sells permits such as the Oregon Pacific Coast Passport and State Park Recreation Pass.

Getting There & Away

Northwest Point (503-484-4100; www.northwest-point.com) Daily buses head to Seaside, Cannon Beach and Portland; check the website for schedules.

Sunset Empire Transit (503-861-7433; www.ridethebus.org; 900 Marine Dr) Local transport; buses also head to Warrenton, Cannon Beach and Seaside.

Cannon Beach

Charming Cannon Beach is one of the most popular and upscale beach resorts on the Oregon coast. The streets are full of boutiques and art galleries, and lined with colorful flowers. Lodging is expensive, and the streets are jammed; on a warm sunny Saturday, you'll spend a good chunk of time just finding a parking spot.

Sights & Activities

Photogenic **Haystack Rock**, a 295ft sea stack, is the most spectacular landmark on the Oregon coast and is accessible from the beach at low tide. Birds cling to its ballast cliffs and tide pools ring its base.

The coast to the north, protected inside **Ecola State Park** (503-436-2844; www.oregonstateparks.org; day use $5), is the Oregon you may have already visited in your dreams: sea stacks, crashing surf, hidden beaches and gorgeous pristine forest. The park is 1.5 miles from town and is crisscrossed by paths, including part of the **Oregon Coast Trail**, which leads over Tillamook Head to the town of Seaside.

The Cannon Beach area is good for surfing, though not the beach itself. The best spots are **Indian Beach** in Ecola State Park, 3 miles to the north, and **Oswald West State Park**, 10 miles south. **Cleanline Surf Shop** (503-738-2061; www.cleanlinesurf.com; 171 Sunset Blvd) is a friendly local shop that rents out boards and mandatory wetsuits.

WORTH A TRIP

SCENIC DRIVE: THREE CAPES

Cape Meares, Cape Lookout and Cape Kiwanda, about halfway between Cannon Beach and Newport, are some of the coast's most stunning headlands, strung together on a slow, winding and sometimes bumpy 40-mile alternative to US 101. It's a worthwhile drive, though in March 2013 a section of road north of Cape Meares began sinking and was closed. Repairs are ongoing, so you might have to drive to Cape Meares via Netarts and Oceanside, then backtrack.

The forested headland at **Cape Meares** offers good views from its 38ft-tall lighthouse (Oregon's shortest). Short trails lead to Oregon's largest Sitka spruce and the 'Octopus Tree,' another Sitka shaped like a candelabra.

A panoramic vista atop sheer cliffs that rise 800ft above the Pacific makes **Cape Lookout State Park** a highlight. In winter, the end of the cape, which juts out nearly a mile, is thronged with whale-watchers. There are wide sandy beaches, hiking trails and a popular campground near the water.

Finally there's **Cape Kiwanda**, a sandstone bluff that rises just north of the little town of Pacific City. You can hike up tall dunes, or drive your truck onto the beach. It's the most developed of the three capes, with plenty of services nearby (don't miss **Pelican Pub & Brewery** (☑503-965-7007; www.yourlittlebeachtown.com/pelican; 33180 Cape Kiwanda Dr, Pacific City; mains $12-32; ⊘8am-10pm Sun-Thu, to 11pm Fri & Sat) if you like beer). Watch the dory fleet launch their craft or, after a day's fishing, land as far up the beach as possible.

🛏 Sleeping & Eating

Cannon Beach Hotel   HISTORIC HOTEL **$$**
(☑503-436-1392; www.cannonbeachhotel.com; 1116 S Hemlock St; d from $139; 🕾) If you don't need much space, check out this classy, centrally located hotel with just 10 rooms. Standard rooms are lovely, but very small; even the regular suites are tight. A good breakfast at the cafe on the premises is included.

Blue Gull Inn Motel   MOTEL **$$**
(☑800-507-2714; www.haystacklodgings.com; 487 S Hemlock St; d $119-219; 🕾🐾) These are some of the more affordable rooms in town, with comfortable atmosphere and toned-down decor, except for the colorful Mexican headboards and serapes on the beds. Kitchenette and Jacuzzi units are available. It's run by Haystack Lodgings, which also manages six other properties in town and does vacation rentals.

Sleepy Monk Coffee   CAFE **$**
(☑503-436-2796; www.sleepymonkcoffee. com; 1235 S Hemlock St; ⊘8am-3pm Mon, Tue & Thu, to 4pm Fri-Sun) 🌱 For organic, certi-fied-fair-trade coffee, try this little coffee shop on the main street. Sit on an Adirondack chair in the tiny front yard and enjoy the rich brews, all tasty and roasted on the premises. Good homemade pastries, too.

Newman's at 988   FRENCH, ITALIAN **$$$**
(☑503-436-1151; www.newmansat988.com; 988 Hemlock St; mains $21-35; ⊘5:30-9pm daily Jul–mid-Oct, Tue-Sun mid-Oct–Jun) Expect a fine dining experience at this small, quality restaurant on the main drag. Award-winning chef John Newman comes up with a fusion of French and Italian dishes such as marinated rack of lamb and char-grilled portabello mushrooms with spinach and Gorgonzola. Desserts are sublime; reserve ahead.

ℹ Information

Chamber of Commerce (☑503-436-2623; www.cannonbeach.org; 207 N Spruce St; ⊘10am-5pm) Has good local information, including tide tables.

ℹ Getting There & Away

Northwest Point (☑541-484-4100; www.north-west-point.com) buses head from Astoria to Portland (and vice versa) every morning, stopping at Cannon Beach; buy tickets at the Beach Store, next to Cannon Beach Surf.

The **Cannon Beach Shuttle** (☑503-861-7433; www.ridethebus.org), also known as 'the Bus', runs the length of Hemlock St to the end of Tolovana Beach; the schedule varies seasonally. Both buses go to Seaside and Astoria, too.

Wave (www.tillamookbus.com) buses go south towards Manzanita and Lincoln City several times daily.

Newport

Home to Oregon's largest commercial fishing fleet, Newport is a lively tourist city with several fine beaches and a world-class aquarium. In 2011 it became the host of NOAA, the National Oceanic and Atmospheric Administration. Good restaurants – along with some tacky attractions, gift shops and barking sea lions – abound in the historic bay-front area, while bohemian Nye Beach offers art galleries and a friendly village atmosphere. The area was first explored in the 1860s by fishing crews who found oyster beds at the upper end of Yaquina Bay.

Sights

The world-class **Oregon Coast Aquarium** (☎541-867-3474; www.aquarium.org; 2820 SE Ferry Slip Rd; adult/child 3-12yr/child 13-17yr $19.95/12.95/17.95; ⊙9am-6pm May-Aug, to 5pm Sep-Apr; 👪) is an unmissable attraction, featuring a sea-otter pool, surreal jellyfish tanks and Plexiglas tunnels through a shark tank. Nearby, the **Hatfield Marine Science Center** (☎541-867-0100; www.hmsc.oregonstate.edu; 2030 SE Marine Science Dr; ⊙10am-5pm daily Jun-Aug, 10am-4pm Thu-Mon Sep-May) FREE is much smaller, but still worthwhile. For awesome tide-pooling and views, don't miss the **Yaquina Head Outstanding Area** (☎541-574-3100; 750 NW Lighthouse Dr; vehicle fee $7; ⊙8am-sunset, interpretive center 10am-6pm), site of the coast's tallest lighthouse and an interesting interpretive center.

Sleeping & Eating

Campers can head to large and popular **South Beach State Park** (☎541-867-4715; www.oregonstateparks.org; tent sites/RV sites/yurts $21/29/44; 🐾), two miles south on US 101. Book-lovers can stay at the **Sylvia Beach Hotel** (☎541-265-5428; www.sylviabeachhotel.com; 267 NW Cliff St; d $165-230), which has simple but comfy rooms, each named after a famous author; reservations are mandatory.

For tasty seafood, head to **Local Ocean Seafoods** (☎541-574-7959; www.localocean.net; 213 SE Bay Blvd; mains $10-28; ⊙11am-9pm) 🌿 – it's especially great for lunch, when the glass walls open to the port area.

Information

Visitors Center (☎541-265-8801; www.newportchamber.org; 555 SW Coast Hwy; ⊙8:30am-5pm Mon-Fri, 10am-2pm Sat)

Yachats & Around

One of the Oregon coast's best-kept secrets is the neat and friendly little town of Yachats (ya-hots). People come here and to the small remote inns and B&Bs just south of town to get away from it all, which isn't hard to do along this relatively undeveloped coast.

Three miles to the south, lofty **Cape Perpetua** was first sighted by Captain Cook in 1778. Volcanic intrusions have formed a beautifully rugged shoreline, with dramatic features such as the **Devil's Churn**, where powerful waves crash through a 30ft inlet. For an easy hike, take the paved **Captain Cook Trail** (a 1.2-mile round trip) down to tide pools near **Cooks Chasm**, where at high tide the geyser-like spouting horn blasts water out of a sea cave. For information head to the **Cape Perpetua Visitor Center** (☎541-547-3289; www.fs.usda.gov/siuslaw; 2400 US 101; vehicle fee $5; ⊙10am-5pm Jun-Aug, reduced hours Sep-May).

Fifteen miles to the south on US 101 is the almost-tourist-trap, but fun, **Sea Lion Caves** (☎541-547-3111; www.sealioncaves.com; 91560 US 101; adult/child 5-12yr $14/8; ⊙9am-5pm), a noisy grotto filled with groaning sea lions accessed via an elevator.

Camp at **Beachside State Park** (☎541-563-3220; www.oregonstateparks.org; tent sites/RV sites/yurts $21/29/44; 🐾), five miles north of Yachats on US 101. The **Ya'Tel Motel** (☎541-547-3225; www.yatelmotel.com; cnr US 101 & 6th St; d $64-84; ⊖@📶🐾) is a good, inexpensive place to sleep, and for snacks there's the **Green Salmon Coffee House** (☎541-547-3077; www.thegreensalmon.com; 220 US 101; mains $7-11; ⊙7:30am-2:30pm; 🖉) 🌿.

Oregon Dunes National Recreation Area

Stretching for 50 miles between Florence and Coos Bay, the Oregon Dunes form the largest expanse of coastal dunes in the USA. They tower up to 500ft and undulate inland as far as three miles to meet coastal forests, harboring curious ecosystems that sustain an abundance of wildlife. Hiking trails, bridle paths, and boating and swimming areas are available, but avoid the stretch south of Reedsport as noisy dune buggies dominate. Find out more at the Oregon Dunes National Recreation Area's **headquarters** (☎541-271-6000; www.fs.usda.gov/siuslaw; 855 Highway

Ave; 8am-4:30pm Mon-Sat Jun-Aug, Mon-Fri Sep-May) in Reedsport.

State parks with camping include popular **Jessie M Honeyman** (541-997-3641, 800-452-5687; www.oregonstateparks.org; 84505 US 101 S; tent sites/RV sites/yurts $21/28/44;), 3 miles south of Florence, and pleasant **Umpqua Lighthouse** (541-271-4118; www.oregonstateparks.org; 460 Lighthouse Rd; tent sites/RV sites/yurts/deluxe yurts from $19/26/40/80;), 4 miles south of Reedsport. There's plenty of other camping in the area, too.

Port Orford

Occupying a rare natural harbor and guarding plenty of spectacular views, the scenic hamlet of Port Orford sits on a headland wedged between two magnificent state parks. **Cape Blanco State Park** (541-332-2973; www.oregonstateparks.org; US 101), nine miles to the north, is the second-most-westerly point in the continental US, and the promontory is often lashed by fierce 100mph winds. As well as hiking, visitors can tour the **Cape Blanco Lighthouse** (541-332-2207; www.oregonstateparks.org; US 101; tour $2; 10am-3:30pm Wed-Mon Apr-Oct) built in 1870; it's the oldest and highest operational lighthouse in Oregon.

Six miles south of Port Orford, in **Humbug Mountain State Park** (541-332-6774), mountains and sea meet in aqueous disharmony with plenty of angry surf. You can climb the 1750ft peak on a 3-mile trail through old-growth cedar groves.

For an affordable stay try **Castaway-by-the-Sea Motel** (541-332-4502; www.castawaybythesea.com; 545 W 5th St; d $75-165;). Food in this fishing village means a visit to slick **Redfish** (541-336-2200; www.redfishportorford.com; 517 Jefferson St; mains lunch $12-14, dinner $22-25; 11am-3pm & 5-9pm Mon-Fri, 9am-3pm & 5-9pm Sat & Sun) for the freshest seafood in town.

Southern Oregon

With a warm and sunny climate that belongs in nearby California, southern Oregon is the state's banana belt. Rugged landscapes, scenic rivers and a couple of attractive towns top the highlights list.

Ashland

Oregon was unknown territory to the Elizabethan explorers of William Shakespeare's day, so it might seem a little strange to find that the pretty settlement of Ashland in southern Oregon has established itself as the English playwright's second home. The irony probably wouldn't have been lost on Shakespeare himself. 'All the world's a stage,' the great Bard once opined, and fittingly people come from all over to see Ashland's famous Shakespeare Festival, which has been held here under various guises since the 1930s. The 'festival' moniker is misleading; the shows here are a semipermanent fixture occupying nine months of the annual town calendar and attracting up to 400,000 theater-goers per season.

Even without the shows, Ashland is an attractive town, propped up by various wineries, upscale B&Bs and fine restaurants.

Sights & Activities

Lithia Park PARK

(59 Winburn Way) Adjacent to Ashland's three splendid theaters (one of which is outdoors) lies what is arguably the loveliest city park in Oregon, and its 93 acres wind along Ashland Creek above the center of town. Unusually, the park is in the National Register of Historic Places. It is embellished with fountains, flowers, gazebos and an ice-skating rink (winter only).

Schneider Museum of Art MUSEUM

(541-552-6245; www.sou.edu/sma; 1250 Siskiyou Blvd; suggested donation $5; 10am-4pm Mon-Sat) Ashland's culture extends beyond the OSF; if you like contemporary art, check out this Southern Oregon University museum. The university also puts on theater performances of its own, along with classical concerts and opera performances.

Jackson Wellsprings SPA

(541-482-3776; www.jacksonwellsprings.com; 2253 Hwy 99; 8am-midnight mid-Apr–mid-Oct, noon-midnight mid-Oct–mid-Apr) For a good soak check out this casual, New Age–style place, which boasts a mineral-fed swimming pool, private soaking tubs, saunas and steam rooms. There's also yoga, massages and spa services, and you can camp or stay in tipis in summer. It's 1 mile north of town. Note that Monday night is women only.

DON'T MISS

OREGON SHAKESPEARE FESTIVAL

One of Southern Oregon's highlights is Ashland's wildly popular Oregon Shakespeare Festival (OSF). Despite being deeply rooted in Shakespearean and Elizabethan drama, the festival also features plenty of revivals and contemporary theater from around the world.

Productions run from February to October in three theaters near Main and Pioneer Sts: the outdoor **Elizabethan Theatre** (⊙ Jun-Oct), the **Angus Bowmer Theatre** and the intimate **Thomas Theatre**. Children under six are not allowed. There are no performances on Mondays.

Performances sell out quickly; obtain tickets at www.osfashland.org. The **box office** (☑ 541-482-4331; 15 S Pioneer St; tickets $30-96) also has last-minute tickets. Be sure to book backstage **tours** well in advance.

Check the **OSF Welcome Center** (76 N Main St; ⊙ 10am-6pm Tue-Sun) for other events, which may include scholarly lectures, play readings, concerts and preshow talks.

Mt Ashland Ski Resort   SKIING
(☑ 541-482-2897; www.mtashland.com) Powdery snow is abundant at this resort, 16 miles southwest of town on 7533ft Mt Ashland.

Siskiyou Cyclery   CYCLING
(☑ 541-482-1997; www.siskiyoucyclery.com; 1729 Siskiyou Blvd; rental per hour $10-15; ⊙ 10am-6pm Mon-Sat) Rent a bike and explore the countryside on Bear Creek Greenway, a 21-mile bike path between Ashland and the town of Central Point.

🛌 Sleeping

Reserve ahead in summer when the thespians descend in droves. There are many B&Bs in town.

Ashland Hostel   HOSTEL $
(☑ 541-482-9217; www.theashlandhostel.com; 150 N Main St; dm $28, d $45-64; ✳ @ 🖥) Central and somewhat upscale hostel (shoes off inside!). Most private rooms share bathrooms; some are connected to dorms. Hangout spaces include the cozy basement living room and the shady front porch. No alcohol or smoking on the premises. Call ahead, as reception times are limited.

Ashland Commons   HOSTEL $
(☑ 541-482-6753; www.ashlandcommons.com; 437 Williamson Way; dm from $26, s $45-65, d $60-80; ✳ 🖥) These unconventional dorm or private room accommodations are provided within three large apartments. All vary in atmosphere, and are either two- or four-bedroom, with kitchen and living areas. Great for large groups, as entire apartments can be rented. Located in a mixed industrial-residential area just outside the center.

Palm   BOUTIQUE HOTEL $$
(☑ 541-482-2636; www.palmcottages.com; 1065 Siskiyou Blvd; d $98-239; ✳ 🖥 🖥 ✳) Fabulous small motel remodeled into 16 charming garden cottage rooms and suites (some with kitchens). It's an oasis of green on a busy avenue, complete with grassy lawns and a saltwater pool. A house nearby harbors three large suites ($299).

Columbia Hotel   HOTEL $$
(☑ 541-482-3726; www.columbiahotel.com; 262 1/2 E Main St; d $89-179; ✳ 🖥) Awesomely located 'European-style' hotel – which means most rooms share outside bathrooms. It's the best deal in downtown Ashland, with 24 quaint vintage rooms (no TVs), a nice lobby and a historical feel. Park in back for fewer stairs to climb.

🍴 Eating & Drinking

There are plenty of great eating choices in Ashland, which levies a 5% restaurant tax. Dinner reservations in summer are a good idea at the fancier spots.

Morning Glory   CAFE $
(☑ 541-488-8636; 1149 Siskiyou Blvd; mains $11-14; ⊙ 8am-1:30pm) This colorful, casual cafe is one of Ashland's best breakfast joints. Creative dishes include the Alaskan crab omelet, vegetarian hash with roasted chilis, and shrimp cakes with poached eggs. For lunch there's gourmet salad and sandwiches. Go early or late to avoid a long wait.

Agave   MEXICAN $
(☑ 541-488-1770; www.agavetaco.net; 92 N Main St; tacos $3-4.25; ⊙ 11am-10pm Sun-Thu, to 11pm Fri & Sat) Tasty and creative tacos are cooked

up at this popular restaurant. There's the regular stuff such as *carnitas* and grilled chicken, but for something more exotic go for the shredded duck or sautéed main lobster ($8.25). A few salads and tamales, too.

Standing Stone Brewery   AMERICAN $
(☑541-482-2448; www.standingstonebrewing. com; 101 Oak St; mains $9-15; ⊙11am-midnight) Popular and hip brewery-restaurant with gourmet burgers, salads, sandwiches and wood-fired pizzas, along with a few seafood dishes. Wash it all down with some microbrews or a cocktail. Great back patio.

Caldera Tap House   BREWERY
(☑541-482-4677; www.calderabrewing.com; 590 Clover Lane; ⊙11am-11pm) This bright and airy brewery-restaurant just off I-5 has pleasant outdoor seating and views of the countryside. It serves dishes such as pizza, housemade gnocchi, flat-iron steak and white truffle mac 'n' cheese (mains $10 to $21). Wash it all down with one of 40 beers on tap. Also located at 31 Water St in downtown Ashland, but the vibe is more local and the atmosphere darker.

🛈 Information

Ashland Chamber of Commerce (☑541-482-3486; www.ashlandchamber.com; 110 E Main St; ⊙9am-5pm Mon-Fri) There is also an information booth at the Plaza (open summer weekends only).

Jacksonville

This small but endearing ex-gold-prospecting town is the oldest settlement in southern Oregon and a National Historic Landmark. The main drag is lined with well-preserved buildings dating from the 1880s, now converted into boutiques and galleries. Music-lovers shouldn't miss the September **Britt Festival** (www.brittfest.org; ⊙Jun-Sep), a world-class musical experience with top-name performers. Seek more enlightenment at the **Chamber of Commerce** (☑541-899-8118; www.jacksonvilleoregon.org; 185 N Oregon St; ⊙10am-3pm daily May-Oct, Mon-Sat Nov-Apr).

Jacksonville is full of fancy B&Bs; for budget motels head 6 miles east to Medford. The **Jacksonville Inn** (☑541-899-1900; www. jacksonvilleinn.com; 175 E California St; d from $159; ❋🌀🐾) is the most pleasant abode, shoehorned downtown in an 1863 building

with regal antique-stuffed rooms. There's a fine restaurant on-site.

Wild Rogue Wilderness

Situated between the town of Grants Pass on I-5 and Gold Beach on the Oregon coast, the aptly named Wild Rogue Wilderness is anchored by the turbulent Rogue River, which cuts through 40 miles of untamed, roadless canyon. The area is known for challenging white-water rafting (classes III and IV) and long-distance hikes.

The humble city of **Grants Pass** is the gateway to adventures along the Rogue. For information, the **Chamber of Commerce** (☑541-450-6180; www.visitgrantspass.org; 1995 NW Vine St; ⊙8am-5pm Mon-Fri) is right off I-5, exit 58. For raft permits and backpacking advice, contact the Bureau of Land Management's **Smullin Visitors Center** (☑541-479-3735; www.blm.gov/or/resources/recreation/rogue; 14335 Galice Rd, Galice; ⊙7am-3pm mid-May–mid-Oct) in Galice, 16 miles northwest of Grants Pass.

Rafting the Rogue is legendary, but not for the faint of heart. A typical trip takes three days and costs around $1000. A good outfitter is **Rogue Wilderness Adventures** (☑800-336-1647; www.wildrogue.com; 325 Galice Rd, Merlin). Kayaking the river is equally exhilarating; for instruction and guidance, contact **Sundance Kayak.** (☑541-708-3601; www.sundancekayak.com; day trips from $95).

Another highlight of the region is the 42-mile **Rogue River Trail**, once a supply route from Gold Beach. The full trek takes four to five days; day hikers might aim for Whiskey Creek Cabin, a 6-mile round-trip from the Grave Creek trailhead. The trail is dotted with rustic lodges ($130 to $165 per person including meals; reservations required) – try **Black Bar** (☑541-479-6507; www.blackbarlodge. com; Merlin; s/d from $230/260). There are also primitive campgrounds along the way.

North Umpqua River

This 'Wild and Scenic' river boasts world-class fly-fishing, fine hiking and serene camping. The 79-mile **North Umpqua Trail** begins near Idleyld Park, 3 miles east of Glide, and passes through Steamboat en route to the Pacific Crest Trail. A popular sideline is pretty **Umpqua Hot Springs**, east of Steamboat near Toketee Lake. Not far away, stunning, two-tiered **Toketee Falls**

(113ft) flows over columnar basalt, while **Watson Falls** (272ft) is one of the highest waterfalls in Oregon. For information, stop by Glide's **Colliding Rivers Information Center** (☎541-496-0157; 18782 N Umpqua Hwy, Glide; ⏰9am-5pm May-Sep). Adjacent is the **North Umpqua Ranger District** (☎541-496-3532; 18782 N Umpqua Hwy, Glide; ⏰8am-4:30pm Mon-Fri).

Between Idleyld Park and Diamond Lake are dozens of riverside campgrounds; these include lovely **Susan Creek** and primitive **Boulder Flat** (no water). Area accommodations fill up quickly in summer; try the log-cabin-like rooms at **Dogwood Motel** (☎541-496-3403; www.dogwoodmotel.com; 28866 N Umpqua Hwy; d $70-75; ❄📶🐾).

Oregon Caves National Monument & Preserve

This very popular cave (there's only one) lies 19 miles east of Cave Junction on Hwy 46. Three miles of passages are explored via 90-minute cave tours that include 520 rocky steps and dripping chambers running along the River Styx. Dress warmly, wear shoes with good traction and be prepared to get dripped on.

Cave Junction, 28 miles south of Grants Pass on US 199 (Redwood Hwy), provides the region's services – though the best area sleeps are at the **Holiday Motel** (☎541-592-3003; www.holidaymotelkerby.com; 24810 Redwood Hwy; d $75-85; ❄📶), two miles north in Kerby. For fancy lodgings right at the cave there's the impressive **Oregon Caves Chateau** (☎541-592-3400; www.oregoncaveschateau.com; 20000 Caves Hwy; r $109-199; ⏰May-Oct); grab a milkshake at the old-fashioned soda fountain here. Campers should head to **Cave Creek Campground** (☎541-592-4000; campsites $10), 14 miles up Hwy 46, about 4 miles from the cave.

Eastern Oregon

Oregon east of the Cascades bears little resemblance to its wetter western cohort, either physically or culturally. Few people live here – the biggest town, Pendleton, numbers only 20,000 – and the region hoards high plateaus, painted hills, alkali lakebeds and the country's deepest river gorge.

John Day Fossil Beds National Monument

Within the soft rocks and crumbly soils of John Day country lies one of the world's greatest fossil collections, laid down between six and 50 million years ago. Roaming the forests at the time were saber-toothed nimravids, pint-sized horses, bear-dogs and other early mammals.

The national monument includes 22 sq miles at three different units: Sheep Rock Unit, Painted Hills Unit and Clarno Unit. Each has hiking trails and interpretive displays. To visit all of the units in one day requires quite a bit of driving, as more than 100 slow miles of curvy roads separate the fossil beds – it's best to take it easy and spend the night somewhere.

Visit the excellent **Thomas Condon Paleontology Center** (☎541-987-2333; www.nps.gov/joda; 32651 Hwy 19, Kimberly; ⏰10am-5pm), 2 miles north of US 26 at the **Sheep Rock Unit**. Displays include a three-toed horse and petrified dung-beetle balls, along with many other fossils and geologic history exhibits. If you feel like walking, take the short hike up the Blue Basin Trail.

The **Painted Hills Unit**, near the town of Mitchell, consists of low-slung, colorfully banded hills formed about 30 million years ago. Ten million years older is the **Clarno Unit**, which exposes mud flows that washed over an Eocene-era forest and eroded into distinctive, sheer white cliffs topped with spires and turrets of stone.

Rafting is popular on the John Day River, the longest free-flowing river in the state. **Oregon River Experiences** (☎800-827-1358; www.oregonriver.com) offers trips of up to five days. There's also good fishing for smallmouth bass and rainbow trout; find out more at the Oregon Department of Fish & Wildlife (www.dfw.state.or.us).

Most towns in the area have at least one hotel; these include the atmospheric **Historic Oregon Hotel** (☎541-462-3027; www.theoregonhotel.net; 104 E Main St; dm $20, d $49-69; 📶) in Mitchell and the economical **Dreamers Lodge** (☎800-654-2849; www.dreamerslodge.com; 144 N Canyon Blvd; d from $70; ❄📶🐾) in the town of John Day (which has most of the area's services). There are several public campgrounds in the area (sites $5), including **Lone Pine** and **Big Bend** on Hwy 402.

Wallowa Mountains Area

The Wallowa Mountains, with their glacier-hewn peaks and crystalline lakes, are among the most beautiful natural areas in Oregon. The only drawback is the large number of visitors who flock here in summer, especially to the pretty Wallowa Lake area. Escape them all on one of several long hikes into the nearby **Eagle Cap Wilderness**, such as the 6-mile one-way jaunt to **Aneroid Lake** or the 8-mile trek on the **Ice Lake Trail**.

Just north of the mountains, in the Wallowa Valley, **Enterprise** is a homely backcountry town with several motels; try the **Ponderosa** (541-426-3186; 102 E Greenwood St; d from $82;). If you like beer and good food, don't miss the town's microbrewery, **Terminal Gravity Brewing** (541-426-0158; www.terminalgravitybrewing.com; 803 SE School St; mains $9-12; 11am-9pm Sun-Tue, to 10pm Wed-Sat). Just 6 miles south is Enterprise's fancy cousin, the upscale town of **Joseph**. Expensive bronze galleries and artsy boutiques line the main strip, along with some good eateries.

Hells Canyon

North America's deepest river gorge (yes, even deeper than the Grand Canyon when measured from the highest mountain peak) provides visitors with some wild and scenic vistas. The mighty Snake River has taken 13 million years to carve its path through the high plateaus of eastern Oregon to its present depth of 8000ft. The canyon itself is a true wilderness bereft of roads, but open to the curious and the brave.

For perspective, drive 30 miles northeast from Joseph to Imnaha, where a slow-going 24-mile gravel road leads up to the excellent lookout at **Hat Point**. From here you can see the Wallowa Mountains, Idaho's Seven Devils, the Imnaha River and the wilds of the canyon itself. This road is open from late May until snowfall; give yourself two hours each way for the drive.

For white-water action and spectacular scenery, head down to **Hells Canyon Dam**, 25 miles north of the small community of Oxbow. A few miles past the dam, the road ends at the **Hells Canyon Visitor Center** (8am-4pm May-Sep), which has good advice on the area's campgrounds and hiking trails. Beyond here, the Snake River drops 1300ft in elevation through wild rapids accessible only by jet boat or raft. **Hells Canyon Adventures** (800-422-3568; www.hellscanyonadventures.com; jet-boat tours from $60; May-Sep) is the main operator running raft trips and jet-boat tours (reservations required).

The area has many campgrounds. Just outside Imnaha is the beautiful **Imnaha River Inn** (541-577-6002; www.imnahariver-inn.com; 73946 Rimrock Rd; s/d from $70/130), a B&B replete with Hemingway-esque animal trophies, while Oxbow has the good-value **Hells Canyon B&B** (541-785-3373; www.hcbb.us; 49922 Homestead Rd; s/d $80/90;). For more services, head to the towns of Enterprise, Joseph and Halfway.

Steens Mountain & Alvord Desert

The highest peak in southeastern Oregon, Steens Mountain (9773ft) is part of a massive, 30-mile-long fault-block range that was formed about 15 million years ago. On the western slope of the range, Ice Age glaciers bulldozed trenches that formed massive U-shaped gorges and hanging valleys. To the east, 'the Steens' – as the range is usually referred to – drop off to the Alvord Desert, 5000ft below.

Beginning in Frenchglen, the gravel 59-mile **Steens Mountain Loop Rd** is Oregon's highest road and offers the range's best sights with its awesome overlooks, and also has access to camping and hiking trails. You'll see sagebrush, bands of junipers and aspen forests, and finally fragile rocky tundra at the top. **Kiger Gorge Viewpoint** is especially stunning; it's 25 miles up from Frenchglen. It takes about three hours all the way around if you're just driving through, but you'll want to see the sights, so give yourself much more time. You can also see the eastern side of the Steens via the **Fields-Denio Rd**, which goes through the Alvord Desert between Hwys 205 and 78. Take a full tank of gas and plenty of water, and be prepared for weather changes at any time of year.

Frenchglen (population 12) has the charming **Frenchglen Hotel** (541-493-2825; www.frenchglenhotel.com; 39184 Hwy 205; d from $75; mid-Mar–Oct;) with its small dining room (reserve for dinners), a small store with seasonal gas pump and not much else. There are camping options on the Steens Mountain Loop Rd, such as the BLM's pretty **Page Springs**, open year-round. A few other campgrounds (sites $6 to $8), further into the loop, are very pleasant, but accessible in summer only. Water is available at all of these campgrounds. Free backcountry camping is also allowed in the Steens. For more accommodation information in the region, check www.steensmountain.net/lodging.htm.

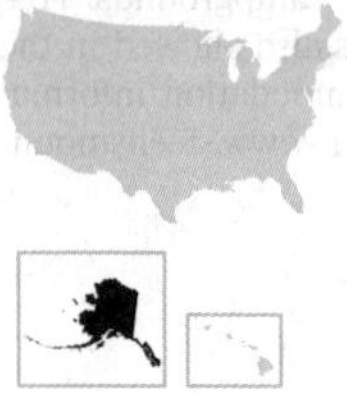

Alaska

Includes ➡

Best Places to Eat

- ➡ Snow City Café (p1086)
- ➡ Rookery (p1091)
- ➡ Homeport Eatery (p1089)
- ➡ Fireweed Restaurant (p1093)

Best Places to Stay

- ➡ Copper Whale Inn (p1085)
- ➡ Beach Roadhouse (p1092)
- ➡ Juneau International Hostel (p1091)
- ➡ Sitka International Hostel (p1089)

Why Go?

Pure, raw, unforgiving and humongous in scale, Alaska is a place that arouses basic instincts and ignites what Jack London termed the 'call of the wild.' Yet, unlike London and his gutsy, gold-rush companions, visitors today will have a far easier time penetrating the region's vast, feral wilderness. Indeed, one of the beauties of the 49th state is its accessibility. Nowhere else in North America is it realistically possible to climb an unclimbed mountain, walk where – quite conceivably – no human foot has trodden before, or sally forth into a national park that gets fewer annual visitors than the International Space Station.

With scant phone coverage and a dearth of hipster-friendly coffee bars to plug in your iPad, Alaska is a region for 'doing' rather than observing. Whether you go it alone with bear spray and a backpack, or place yourself in the hands of an experienced 'sourdough' (Alaskan old-timer), the rewards are immeasurable.

When to Go

Anchorage

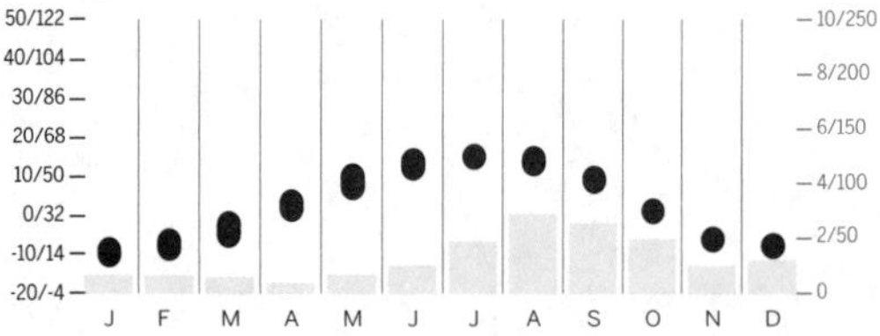

Jun Enjoy summer solstice festivals and 20-hour days. Stay up and play outdoors.

Jul Salmon runs, with millions of spawning fish choking streams, hit their peaks.

Late Sep The mystical northern lights begin to appear in the night skies.

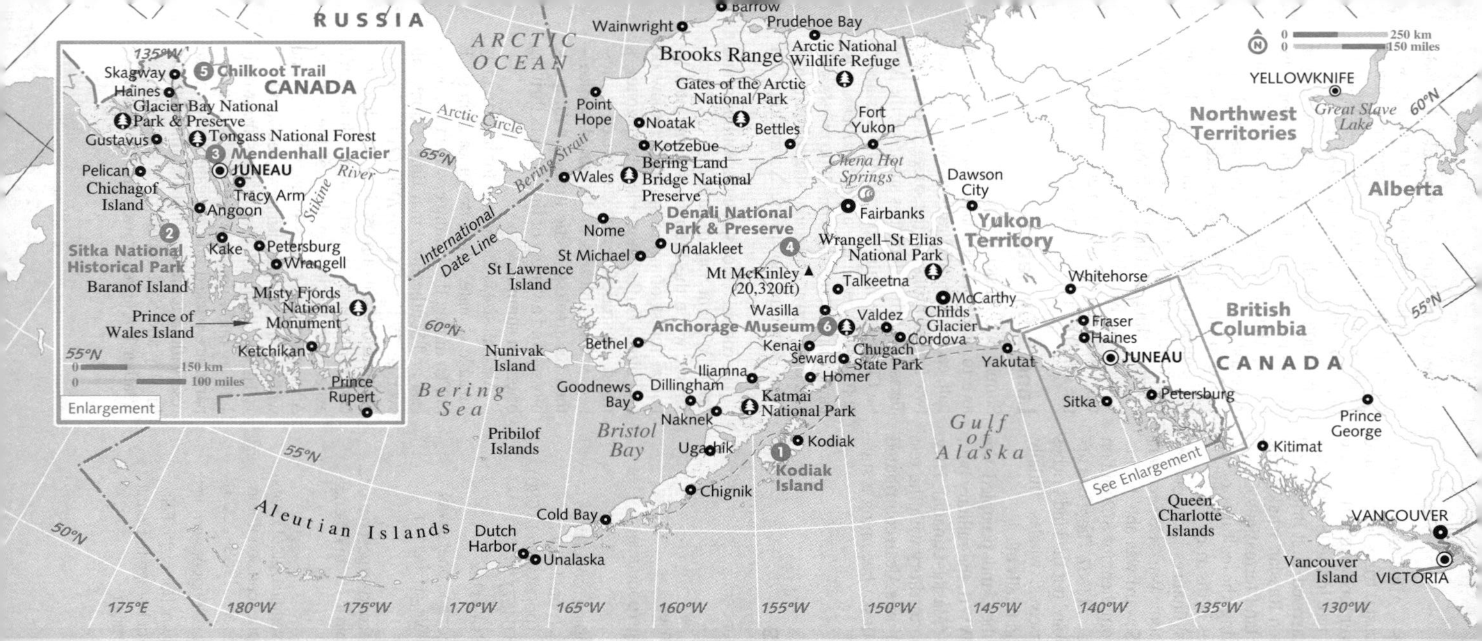

Alaska Highlights

1. Viewing the world's largest bears feasting on salmon on emerald green **Kodiak Island** (p1093).
2. Uncovering Russia's history in Alaska at **Sitka National Historical Park** (p1088).
3. Hiking alongside Alaska's most popular river of ice, **Mendenhall Glacier** (p1090).
4. Seeing the huge, hulking, icy mass of Mt McKinley (Denali) during a bus tour in **Denali National Park** (p1096).
5. Following the Klondike stampeders of 1898, hiking the **Chilkoot Trail** (p1095).
6. Exploring Alaska's history and culture at the **Anchorage Museum** (p1084).

History

Indigenous Alaskans – Athabascans, Aleuts and Inuit, and the coastal tribes Tlingits and Haidas – migrated over the Bering Strait land bridge 20,000 years ago. In the 18th century waves of Europeans arrived: first British and French explorers, then Russian whalers and fur traders, naming land formations, taking otter pelts and leaving the cultures of the Alaska Native peoples in disarray.

With the Russians' finances badly overextended by the Napoleonic Wars, US Secretary of State William H Seward was able to purchase the territory from them for $7.2 million – less than 2¢ an acre – in 1867. There was uproar over 'Seward's Folly,' but the land's riches soon revealed themselves: whales initially, then salmon, gold and finally oil.

After Japan bombed and occupied the Aleutian Islands in WWII, the military built the famous Alcan (Alaska-Canada) Hwy, which connected the territory with the rest of the USA. The 1520-mile Alcan contributed greatly to postwar Alaska becoming a state in 1959.

ALASKA FACTS

Nickname Final Frontier

Population 735,132

Area 586,400 sq miles

Capital City Juneau (population 33,060)

Other cites Anchorage (population 298,610), Fairbanks (population 32,204), Ketchikan (population 13,680), Kodiak (population 6457)

Sales tax No state sales tax

Birthplace of Singer and poet Jewel (b 1974), cartoonist Virgil F Partch (1916–84)

Home of World's second-largest national park, tallest mountain in North America

Politics Red state

Famous for Giant veggies, giant bears, longest serving Republican senator in US history (Ted Stevens: 1968–2009)

Best souvenir Moose nugget earrings

Driving distances Anchorage to Fairbanks 586 miles, Anchorage to Denali National Park 425 miles

The Good Friday earthquake in 1964 left Alaska in a shambles, but recovery was boosted when oil was discovered under Prudhoe Bay, resulting in the construction of a 789-mile pipeline to Valdez.

In 2006 Sarah Palin, a former mayor of Wasilla, stunned the political world by beating the incumbent governor to become Alaska's first female governor as well as its youngest at 42. Two years later presidential candidate John McCain named her as his running mate on the Republican ticket. Commanding a little less international attention was Republican Senator Ted Stevens who, when he left office in 2009, had served the state for a record 41 years.

Land & Climate

Simply put, Alaska is huge. Or, as residents love to point out: if Alaska were divided in half, each half would rank as one of the top two largest states in the country, dropping Texas to third. At latitudes spanning the Arctic Circle, the main body of Alaska is about 800 sq miles, with the arc of the Aleutian Islands chain stretching some 1600 miles south and west, and a 'panhandle' strip running 600 miles southeast down the North American coast.

The coastal regions, such as Southeast and Prince William Sound, have lush coniferous forests, while the Interior is dominated by boreal forest of white spruce, cottonwood and birch. Further north is a taiga zone – a moist, subarctic forest characterized by muskeg, willow thickets and stunted spruce – then the treeless Arctic tundra, with grass, mosses and a variety of tiny flowers thriving briefly in summer.

Alaska's size is the reason for its extremely variable climate. The Interior can top 90°F (32°C) during the summer, while the Southeast and Southcentral maritime regions will average 55°F (13°C) to 70°F (21°C). In the Southeast it rains almost daily from late September through October, while in June you'll experience the longest days of the year. In Anchorage that means 19 hours of sunshine while in Barrow the sun never sets at all.

The peak tourist season runs from early July to mid-August, when the best-known parks are packed and it's essential to make reservations for ferries and accommodations. In May and September you'll still find mild weather, but fewer crowds and lower prices.

Parks & Activities

Alaska has room to play outdoors and plenty of parks to do it in. Travelers come here for the mountains, the trails, the wildlife, the camping – the adventure. Hiking trails are boundless and are the best way to escape the summer crowds in places like Juneau and the Kenai Peninsula. Mountain biking is allowed on many trails, and bikes can be rented throughout the state. You can also rent kayaks throughout the Southeast, where paddlers enjoy sea kayaking in protective fjords, often within view of glaciers. Other popular outdoor activities are rafting, bear- and whale-watching, fishing, zip-lining and just pulling over on the road and admiring the scenery.

The best places to play and see wildlife are Alaska's many parks and preserves. Within the state the National Park Service administers 54 million acres as national parks, preserves and monuments. The most popular national parks are Klondike Gold Rush National Historical Park (p1094) in Skagway, Denali National Park & Preserve (p1096) in the Interior and **Kenai Fjords National Park** (907-224-2125; www.nps.gov/kefj) near Seward. **Wrangell-St Elias National Park** (907-822-7250; www.nps.gov/wrst; Mile 106.8, Richardson Hwy; 8am-4:30pm) is the second-largest park in the world, covering an area bigger than Switzerland. Access is via the former mining communities of McCarthy and Kennicott, seven hours' drive from Anchorage.

Getting There & Around

AIR

The vast majority of visitors to Alaska fly into **Ted Stevens Anchorage International Airport** (ANC; www.dot.state.ak.us/anc;). Low-cost airline **JetBlue** (800-538-2583; www.jetblue.com) offers some of the better deals flying direct to Seattle and Portland, OR.

Alaska Airlines (800-252-7522; www.alaskaair.com) Has direct flights to Anchorage from Seattle, Chicago, Los Angeles and Denver. It also flies between many towns within Alaska, including daily north-bound and south-bound flights year-round through Southeast Alaska, with stops at all main towns including Ketchikan and Juneau.

Delta (800-221-1212; www.delta.com) Direct flights from Minneapolis, Phoenix and Salt Lake City.

United Airlines (800-863-8331; www.united.com) Flies nonstop from Houston, Chicago, Denver and San Francisco.

BOAT

The **Alaska Marine Highway** (AMHS; 800-642-0066; www.dot.state.ak.us/amhs) ferries connect Bellingham, WA, with 14 towns in Southeast Alaska. The complete trip (Bellingham–Haines, $369, 3½ days) stops at ports along the way and should be scheduled in advance. Trips within the Inside Passage, weaving through the islands of Alaska's panhandle, include Ketchikan–Petersburg ($63, 11 hours), Sitka–Juneau ($48, five hours) and Juneau–Haines ($39, two hours). The ferries are equipped to handle cars (Bellingham–Haines $483), but space must be reserved months ahead.

Cruise ships are another convenient way to tour Alaska, especially Southeast. A smaller boat will afford more flexibility and intimacy, while the larger companies will be more affordable. You can expect to have all meals included and a menu of tour and learning options. Larger cruise companies include **Princess** (800-774-6237; www.princess.com) and family-friendly **Celebrity** (877-202-4345; www.celebritycruises.com;). For smaller boats consider **AdventureSmith Explorations** (800-344-2875; www.adventuresmithexplorations.com), which has charters for 12 people or a larger boat that carries 100, and **Discovery Voyages** (800-324-7602; www.discoveryvoyages.com). Both offer excellent excursions and are learning-focused.

BUS

From Anchorage bus services are available to many areas of the state.

Alaska/Yukon Trails (907-888-5659, 907-479-2277; www.alaskashuttle.com) Runs a bus up the George Parks Hwy to Denali ($75, six hours) and Fairbanks ($99, nine hours).

Seward Bus Line (907-563-0800; www.sewardbuslines.net) Runs between Anchorage and Seward ($40, three hours) twice daily in summer. For an extra $5, you can arrange an airport pickup/drop-off.

TRAIN

The **Alaska Railroad** (907-265-2494; www.akrr.com) offers service between Seward and Anchorage and between Anchorage and Denali, before ending in Fairbanks. It's a fantastic journey, but book seats in advance.

ANCHORAGE

Anchorage offers the comforts of a large US city but is only a 30-minute drive from the Alaskan wilderness. Founded in 1914 as a work camp for the Alaska Railroad, the city was devastated by the 1964 Good Friday earthquake but quickly rebounded as the industry headquarters for the Prudhoe Bay oil boom. Today almost half the state's residents live in or around the city, as Anchorage serves as the economic and political heart of Alaska.

Sights & Activities

★Anchorage Museum MUSEUM
(www.anchoragemuseum.org; 625 C Street; adult/child $15/7; summer 9am-6pm;) What was once simply Alaska's best museum is now a world-class facility thanks to the 2010, $106-million expansion of Anchorage's cultural jewel. The West Wing, a four-story, shimmering, mirrored facade, added 80,000 sq ft to what was already the largest museum in the state. Its flagship exhibit is the **Smithsonian Arctic Studies Center**, which has more than 600 Alaska Native objects – art, tools, masks and household implements – which was previously housed in Washington DC.

★Alaska Native Heritage Center CULTURAL CENTER
(097-330-8000; www.alaskanative.net; 8800 Heritage Center Dr; adult/child $25/17; 9am-5pm) To experience Alaska Native culture firsthand, you can travel to the Bush or come to this 26-acre center and see how humans survived – and thrived – before central heating. This is much more than just a museum: it represents a knowledge bank of language, art and culture that will survive no matter how many sitcoms are crackling through the Alaskan stratosphere. It's a labor of love, and of incalculable value.

Alaska Aviation Heritage Museum MUSEUM
(www.alaskaairmuseum.org; 4721 Aircraft Dr; adult/child $15/8; 9am-5pm) On the south shore of Lake Hood, the world's busiest floatplane lake, this museum is a tribute to Alaska's colorful Bush pilots and their faithful planes. Housed within are 25 planes along with historic photos and displays of pilots' achievements, from the first flight to Fairbanks (1913) to the early history of Alaska Airlines.

Flattop Mountain Trail HIKING
This very popular 3-mile round-trip hike to the 3550ft peak is easy to follow, though you'll scramble at the summit. It begins at Glen Alps and climbs steeply from there. Another trail continues 3 miles more along the ridgeline to Flaketop Peak, and the 2-mile Blueberry Loop at the base is great for kids.

For transportation there's **Flattop Mountain Shuttle** (907-279-3334; www.hike-anchorage-alaska.com; round-trip $23), which leaves Downtown Bicycle Rental at 1pm daily, returning at 4.30pm.

Tony Knowles Coastal Trail CYCLING
Anchorage's favorite trail is the scenic 11-mile Tony Knowles Coastal Trail. It begins at the west end of 2nd Ave downtown and reaches Elderberry Park a mile away, before winding through Earthquake Park, around Point Woronzof and finally to Point Campbell in Kincaid Park. There are good views of Knik Arm and the Alaska Range along the way, and the Anchorage Lightspeed Planet Walk.

Downtown Bicycle Rental BICYCLE RENTAL
(www.alaska-bike-rentals.com; 333 W 4th Ave; 3/24hr rental $16/32; 8am-10pm) Has road, hybrid and mountain bikes as well as tandems, trailers and even clip-in pedals and shoes. Locks, helmets and bike maps are free, and the staff is a wealth of information on where to ride.

Tours

Rust's Flying Service SCENIC FLIGHTS
(907-243-1595; www.flyrusts.com; 4525 Enstrom Circle) Offers a three-hour Mt McKinley flight that includes flying the length of Ruth Glacier ($415) and a three-hour Prince William Sound tour ($355 to $395). All flights have a 3% transportation fee.

Anchorage City Trolley Tours BUS TOUR
(907-775-5603; www.alaskatrolley.com; 546 W 4th Ave; adult/child $20/10; tours 9am-7pm) One-hour rides in a bright-red trolley past Lake Hood, Earthquake Park and Cook Inlet, among other sights. Tours depart on the hour.

Sleeping

Alaska Backpackers Inn HOSTEL $
(907-277-2770; www.alaskabackpackers.com; 409 Eagle St; dm/s/d $30/70/80;) Taking up two city blocks, this hostel is roomy but

showing some wear. Most rooms have four or two beds and the dayroom has a 50in TV, a Foosball table and a massive clean kitchen. A bit east of central downtown, it's still within walking distance of restaurants and bars. There's a large annex with one-bedroom suites.

Wildflower Inn B&B $$
(907-274-1239; www.alaska-wildflower-inn.com; 1239 I St; r $149-159; @ wi-fi) Housed in a historic home, a duplex built in 1945 for Federal Aviation Administration (FAA) families, this B&B offers three large rooms, pleasant sitting areas and a full breakfast in the morning featuring treats such as caramelized French toast. For anybody who packed their walking shoes, the location is ideal, just three blocks south of Delaney Park.

Long House Alaskan Hotel HOTEL $$
(907-243-2133; www.longhousehotel.com; 4335 Wisconsin St; s/d $163/173; wi-fi) Near Spenard Rd, this log hotel has large rooms that have been recently updated. It offers continental breakfast, guest laundry facilities, in-room fridges, microwaves, TV, coffee service and 24-hour shuttle to the airport. And to top it off, the staff is really friendly.

Puffin Inn MOTEL $$
(907-243-4044; www.puffininn.net; 4400 Spenard Rd; r $125-229; wi-fi) Anchorage's best late-night-airport-arrival motel. It has four tiers of fine rooms, from 26 sardine-can economy rooms ($119) to full suites with hot tubs and hideaway kitchens, all recently updated and accessible via free 24-hour airport shuttle.

City Garden B&B B&B $$
(907-276-8686; www.citygarden.biz; 1352 W 10th Ave; r $125-175; wi-fi) One of several B&Bs located on a two-block stretch of 10th Ave, this is an open, sunny, gay- and lesbian-friendly place with more cutting-edge art than antiques. The nicest of the three rooms has a private bath, which has recently been remodeled. Catch bus 7A.

Anchorage Downtown Hotel BOUTIQUE HOTEL $$
(907-258-7669; www.theanchoragedowntownhotel.com; 826 K St; r $179-199; wi-fi) Recently remodeled with fun murals on the walls, this not-so-downtown hotel is a very pleasant place to stay, with 16 colorful and comfortable rooms that feature private baths, coffeemakers and small refrigerators. It offers a light continental breakfast, parking and a free shuttle.

★**Copper Whale Inn** INN $$$
(907-258-7999; www.copperwhale.com; cnr W 5th Ave & L St; r $199-229, ste $269; @ wi-fi) An ideal downtown location and a bright and elegant interior make this inn one of the best top-end places in Anchorage. The suite has a full kitchen. Two relaxing waterfall courtyards make it easy to consume that novel, while many rooms and the breakfast lounge give way to views of Cook Inlet. Are those beluga whales out there?

Lakefront Anchorage Hotel HOTEL $$$
(907-243-2300; www.millenniumhotels.com/usa/destinations/anchorage; 4800 Spenard Rd; r $239-340; wi-fi) A large, 248-room resort with a woodsy lodge feel overlooking Lake Spenard. Take note: there are stuffed animals, trophy mounts and large fish everywhere. All rooms are large with king or full beds and scheduled for renovation at the time of writing. There's a decent pub with a great deck for imbibing on sunny evenings.

Eating

In Anchorage you'll enjoy great menus, from Polynesian and Mexican to good old burgers, and clean air. All restaurants and bars are smoke free.

Yak & Yeti Cafe ASIAN $
(www.yakandyetialaska.com; 1360 W Northern Lights Blvd; mains $8-13; 10am-8pm Mon-Thu, to 9pm Fri & Sat, 11am-7pm Sun; vegetarian) A small cafe serving 'Himalayan' food: Tibeten, Nepalese and Indian. Excellent bowls (choose one, two or three curry options over rice), homemade chai tea and baked goods.

Arctic Roadrunner BURGERS $
(5300 Old Seward Hwy; burgers $5-7; 10am-9:30pm Mon-Sat) Since 1964 this place has been turning out beefy burgers and great onion pieces and rings. If your timing is right, you can eat outdoors while watching salmon spawn up Campbell Creek.

Ray's Place VIETNAMESE $
(907-279-2932; www.raysplaceak.com; 32412 Spenard Rd; mains $8-15; 10am-3pm & 5-9pm Mon-Fri; vegetarian) This Vietnamese restaurant does great cold noodle salads and stir-fries, huge bowls of pho, and stocks Vietnamese beer.

★ Snow City Café CAFE $$

(907-272-2489; www.snowcitycafe.com; 1034 W 4th Ave; breakfast $8-15, lunch $10-15; 7am-3pm Mon-Fri, to 4pm Sat & Sun;) Consistently voted best breakfast by *Anchorage Press* readers, this busy cafe serves healthy grub to a clientele that ranges from the tattooed to the up-and-coming. For breakfast, skip the usual eggs and toast and try a bowl of Snow City granola with dried fruit, honey and nuts.

Moose's Tooth Brewpub PIZZA $$

(www.moosestooth.net; 3300 Old Seward Hwy; large pizzas $16-25; 10:30am-midnight Mon-Fri, from 11am Sat & Sun;) An Anchorage institution serving two dozen custom-brewed beers, including monthly specials. This is *the* place to refuel after climbing Flattop, with 40 gourmet pizzas on the menu, including 10 veggie pies.

Bear Tooth Grill TEX-MEX $$

(www.beartoothgrill.net; 1230 W 27th St; burgers $10-16, mains $12-20; 11am-11:30pm Mon-Fri, 9:30am-11:30pm Sat & Sun) A popular hangout with an adjacent theater. It serves excellent burgers and seafood as well as Mexican and Asian fusion dishes. The microbrews are fresh and the cocktails are the best in town – if you're up for a splurge, lash out on *el Cielo* (the Sky) margarita. There's an excellent Mexican-leaning brunch menu (with matching cocktails).

Middle Way Cafe CAFE $$

(www.middlewaycafe.com; 1200 W Northern Lights Blvd, Suite G; lunch & brunch $8-13; 7am-6pm Mon-Fri, from 8am Sat & Sun;) This veggie-friendly cafe serves healthy breakfasts and organic salads, soups and sandwiches in a cozy, artsy atmosphere. Many vegan and gluten-free options, and really, it's one of the best brunch spots in town.

Glacier Brewhouse BREWERY $$

(www.glacierbrewhouse.com; 737 W 5th Ave; lunch $12-19, dinner $18-30; 11am-11pm Mon-Fri, 10am-11pm Sat & Sun) Grab a table overlooking the three giant copper brewing tanks and enjoy wood-fired pizzas and rotisserie-grilled ribs and chops with a pint of oatmeal stout. But be prepared to wait for that table, as this place is unbelievably (and deservedly) popular.

Sack's Café FUSION $$$

(907-274-4022; www.sackscafe.com; 328 G St; lunch mains $12-16, dinner $19-36; 11am-2:30pm & 5:30-9pm Mon-Fri, from 10am Sat & Sun) An upscale, chic restaurant serving elegant fare that is consistently creative. It is always bustling (reservations recommended) and has the best weekend brunch in town.

Drinking & Nightlife

Bernie's Bungalow Lounge LOUNGE

(www.berniesak.com; 626 D St; 2:30pm-2am) Pretty people, pretty drinks: this is the place to see and be seen. Its outdoor patio, complete with a water-spewing serpent, is the best in Anchorage and on summer weekends it rocks late into the night with DJs up in the VIP room.

Crush WINE BAR

(www.crushak.com; 343 W 6th Ave; 11:30am-10pm Mon-Thu, to midnight Fri & Sat) This swanky wine bar serves 'bistro bites,' a menu of appetizers, salads and small plates, as well as more than 40 wines by the glass. Nibble and sip.

SubZero COCKTAIL BAR

(www.subzerolounge.com; 612 F St; 11am-2am;) Cool and jazzy, this hot spot has two pages of cocktails, including almost a dozen martinis and affordable 'Microlounge Micro-plates,' nibbles that range from crab-cake sliders to macadamia seared goat cheese. Good discounts on food during happy hour.

☆ Entertainment

Check the *Anchorage Press* for the latest entertainment listings.

Chilkoot Charlie's LIVE MUSIC

(www.koots.com; 2435 Spenard Rd; 11:30am-2am) More than just Anchorage's favorite meat market, 'Koots,' as the locals call it, is a landmark. The sprawling, wooden edifice has 22 beers on tap, 10 bars, four dance floors and a couple of stages where almost every band touring Alaska ends up.

Cyrano's Theatre Company THEATER

(907-274-2599; www.cyranos.org; 413 D St) This off-center playhouse is the best live theater in town, staging everything from *Hamlet* to *Archy and Mehitabel* (comic characters of a cockroach and a cat), Mel Brooks' jazz musical based on the poetry of Don Marquis and an ever-changing lineup of original shows. Only in Anchorage. Shows typically run Thursday to Sunday.

Shopping

Oomingmak Musk Ox Producers Co-op CLOTHING
(www.qiviut.com; 604 H St; 8am-8pm Mon-Fri, 10am-6pm Sat & Sun) Handles a variety of very soft, very warm and very expensive garments made of arctic musk-ox wool, hand-knitted in isolated Inupiaq villages.

REI OUTDOOR EQUIPMENT
(1200 W Northern Lights Blvd; 10am-9pm Mon-Fri, 9am-7pm Sat, 10am-7pm Sun) Anchorage's largest outdoor store has everything you might ever need, from wool socks to backpacks to kayaks to camp chairs. Besides being able to repair your camp stove or bicycle tire, it will also rent canoes, bear containers, tents and bicycles.

Information

MEDICAL SERVICES

Alaska Regional Hospital (907-276-1131; www.alaskaregional.com; 2801 DeBarr Rd; 24hr; 13, 15) Near Merrill Field.

First Care Medical Center (907-248-1122; 3710 Woodland Dr, Suite 1100; 7am-11pm; 7) Walk-in clinic just off Spenard Rd in midtown.

Providence Alaska Medical Center (907-562-2211; www.alaska.providence.org; 3200 Providence Dr; 24hr; 1, 3, 13, 36, 45, 102) The largest medical center in the state.

MONEY

Wells Fargo (907-265-2805; 301 W Northern Lights Blvd; 10am-6pm Mon-Sat) The main bank is in midtown.

POST

Post office (320 W 5th Ave; 10am-2pm & 3-6pm Mon-Fri) This one's downtown in the 5th Ave Mall, but there are nearly a dozen more in town.

TOURIST INFORMATION

Alaska Public Lands Information Center (907-644-3661; www.alaskacenters.gov; 605 W 4th Ave, Suite 105; 9am-5pm) In the Federal Building (you'll need photo ID). The center has handouts for hikers, mountain bikers, kayakers, fossil-hunters and just about everyone else, on almost every wilderness area in the state. There are also excellent wildlife displays, free movies, fun dioramas, and guided walks including ones about Captain Cook (11am and 4pm) and the 1964 earthquake (2:45pm).

Log Cabin Visitor Center (907-257-2363; www.anchorage.net; 524 W 4th Ave; 8am-7pm) Has pamphlets, maps, bus schedules, city guides in several languages and a lawn growing on its roof.

Getting There & Around

TO/FROM THE AIRPORT

Alaska Shuttle (907-338-8888, 907-694-8888; www.alaskashuttle.net) offers door-to-door transportation between the airport and downtown and South Anchorage (one to three people $50) and Eagle River ($60). The city's bus service (People Mover) picks up from the South Terminal (bus 7) on a route that heads back downtown.

AIR

Ted Stevens Anchorage International Airport (p1083) has frequent inter- and intrastate flights. Terminals are off International Airport Rd. Alaska Airlines (p1083) flies to 19 Alaskan towns, including Fairbanks, Juneau, Nome and Barrow.

Pen Air (800-448-4226; www.penair.com) Flies smaller planes to 27 difficult-to-pronounce destinations in Southwest Alaska, including Unalakleet, Aniak and Igiugig.

Ravn Alaska (www.flyravn.com) Fairbanks, Nome, Barrow, Deadhorse, Valdez and Kodiak.

BUS

People Mover (907-343-6543; muni.org/Departments/transit/PeopleMover; adult/child $2/1; 6am-11:30pm Mon-Fri, 8am-9pm Sat, 10am-7pm Sun) Anchorage's excellent bus system. Its main terminal is located at the **Downtown Transit Center** (cnr W 6th Ave & G St); pick up a schedule ($1) there or call for specific route information.

CAR

Midnight Sun Car & Van Rental (907-243-8806; www.ineedacarrental.com; 4211 Spenard Rd) rents compacts ($70/420 per day/week).

TRAIN

Alaska Railroad (907-265-2494; www.akrr.com) chugs its way south to Whittier (adult/child $77/39, 2½ hours) and Seward ($89/45, four hours), and north to Denali ($163/82, eight hours) and then Fairbanks ($233/117, 12 hours).

SOUTHEAST ALASKA

The Southeast is as close as Alaska comes to the continental USA, but most of it is inaccessible by road. It's possible to fly to the panhandle for a quick visit, but a better option, if you can spare a week, is to cruise the Inside Passage, a waterway made up of thousands of islands, glacier-filled fjords and a mountainous coastline. You can jump on a state ferry and stop at a handful of ports for hiking, kayaking and whale-watching. Cruises are also popular, as they offer easy transport and lodging, with meals included.

Wrangell

Strategically located near the mouth of the Stikine River, Wrangell is the only town to have been ruled by four nations: Tlingit, Russia, Britain and the USA. Today it is one of the few ports in which the state ferries dock downtown, so at the very least jump off the boat for a quick look around town.

Sights

For its size, Wrangell has an impressive collection of totems. Pick up the free *Wrangell Guide* at the visitor center and spend an afternoon locating them all. Make sure you stop at **Chief Shakes Island**, near the boat harbor downtown.

★Wrangell Museum MUSEUM
(296 Campbell Dr; adult/child/family $5/2/12; ⏲10am-5pm Mon-Sat) This impressive museum is what the colorful history and characters of Wrangell deserve. As you stroll through the many rooms, an audio narration automatically comes on and explains that chapter of Wrangell's history, from Tlingit culture and the gold-rush era to the time Hollywood arrived in 1972 to film the movie *Timber Tramps*. You can marvel at a collection of Alaskan art that includes a Sidney Laurence painting or be amused that this rugged little town has had two presidential visits.

Sleeping & Eating

Wrangell Hostel HOSTEL $
(☎907-874-3534; 220 Church St; dm $20) In the First Presbyterian Church, this basic place has separate-sex dorm rooms with inflatable mattresses, showers and a large kitchen and dining room. It has no curfew and will graciously let you hang out there during an all-day rain.

Stikine Inn MOTEL $$
(☎907-874-3388; www.stikineinn.com; 107 Stikine Ave; s $150-196, d $168-189; 📶) Wrangell's swankiest lodging is on the waterfront near the ferry dock and comes with a bar, coffee shop, restaurant and 34 clean rooms. The water-view rooms cost more, but they are among the best in town.

Alaskan Sourdough Lodge LODGE $$
(☎907-874-3613; www.akgetaway.com; 1104 Peninsula St; s/d $119/129; @📶) This family-owned lodge is showing some signs of wear; it was hosting visitors when there were still lumber mills in Wrangell. But the 16 rooms are large, there's free transportation to/from the ferry or airport and outdoor decks full of flowers and wicker furniture, some with a view of the harbor. Family-style meals are served in a large eating area.

Diamond C Café CAFE $$
(223 Front St; breakfast $6-12, lunch $8-17; ⏲6am-2pm) Eat what the locals eat – eggs and hash browns, biscuits and gravy, deep-fried fish-and-chips – and listen to the conservative pulse of the community from the tables around you.

Information

Wrangell Visitor Center (☎907-874-3901; www.wrangell.com; 293 Campbell Dr; ⏲10am-5pm Mon-Sat) In the Nolan Center, it stocks the free *Wrangell Guide* and shows a 10-minute film on the area in a small theater.

Sitka

Russians established Southeast Alaska's first nonindigenous settlement here in 1799, and the town flourished on fur. Today Sitka sees itself as both the cultural center of the Southeast and, because it's the only one facing the Pacific Ocean, the region's most beautiful city.

Sights & Activities

Sitka has superb hiking, and the **Gaven Hill Trail** into the mountains is accessible from the downtown area. There are also many kayaking trips around **Baranof** and **Chichagof Islands**.

Thanks to Sitka's ocean location, marine-wildlife boat tours have mushroomed in the town.

Centennial Building LANDMARK
(☎907-747-3225; 330 Harbor Drive; admission by donation; ⏲9am-5pm Mon-Fri, 10am-4pm Sat)Also known as Harrigan Centennial Hall, this is one of Sitka's main landmarks and hosts a museum, convention facilities, an auditorium and some Native Alaskan carvings. Built in 1967, in 2015 a major renovation began to significantly increase its floor space.

Sitka National Historical Park HISTORIC SITE
(www.nps.gov/sitk/index.htm; Lincoln St; ⏲6am-10pm) FREE Lincoln St ends at this 113-acre park, Alaska's smallest national park, at the site where the Tlingits were finally defeated by the Russians in 1804.

Totem Trail leads you one mile past 18 totems that were first displayed at the 1904 Louisiana Exposition in St Louis and then moved to the park. It is these intriguing totems, standing in a beautiful rainforest setting by the sea and often enveloped in mist, that have become synonymous with the national park and even the city itself.

Alaska Raptor Center WILDLIFE RESERVE
(☎907-747-8662; www.alaskaraptor.org; 101 Sawmill Creek Rd; adult/child $12/6; ⌚8am-4pm; 👪) The raptor center is reached by turning left on the first gravel road after crossing Indian River. The 17-acre center treats 200 injured birds a year, with its most impressive facility being a 20,000-sq-ft flight-training center that helps injured eagles, owls, falcons and hawks regain their ability to fly. In the center eagles literally fly past you, only 2ft or 3ft away, at eye level; it's so close you can feel the wind from their beating wings – amazing.

St Michael's Cathedral CHURCH
(240 Lincoln St; suggested donation $10; ⌚9am-4pm Mon-Fri or by appt) Built between 1844 and 1848, the church stood for more than 100 years as Alaska's finest Russian Orthodox cathedral. When a fire destroyed it in 1966, the church had been the oldest religious structure from the Russian era in Alaska. Luckily the priceless treasures and icons inside were saved by Sitka's residents, who immediately built a replica of their beloved church. There's a cathedral-run bookstore across the street.

Russian Bishop's House HISTORIC BUILDING
(☎907-747-0135; Lincoln St; adult/child $4/free; ⌚9am-5pm) East of downtown along Lincoln St, the Russian Bishop's House is the oldest intact Russian building in Sitka. Built in 1843 out of Sitka spruce, the two-story log house is one of the few surviving examples of Russian colonial architecture in North America. The National Park Service (NPS) has restored the building to its condition in 1853, when it served as a school, bishop's residence and chapel.

Sitka Sound Ocean Adventures KAYAKING
(☎907-752-0660; www.kayaksitka.com) Rents kayaks and runs guided trips; its office is a blue bus at the Centennial Building.

Allen Marine Tours CRUISE
(☎907-747-8100; www.allenmarinetours.com; adult/child $99/69; ⌚1:30-4:30pm Sat) Offers wildlife cruises whenever cruise ships are in. On Saturday the three-hour tour (adult/child $99/69) departs 1:30pm from the Crescent Harbor dock to view whales, sea otters, puffins and other wildlife. Reservations are not needed for the Saturday special.

Sleeping

★ Sitka International Hostel HOSTEL $
(☎907-747-8661; http://sitkahostel.org; 109 Jeff Davis St; dm/d $24/60; 📶) Sitka's top-notch hostel is downtown in the historic Tillie Paul Manor, which once served as the town's hospital. The building has been totally renovated and now features a men's room with its own kitchen and several women's rooms, along with a family room, another small kitchen and a lovely sun porch with a mountain view.

Totem Square Inn HOTEL $$$
(☎907-747-3693; www.totemsquarehotel.com; 201 Katlian St; r $225-245; @📶) This is Sitka's largest hotel, with 68 comfortable rooms featuring the traditional (Alaska Native art and prints on the walls) and the modern (flat-screen TVs, hair dryers and wi-fi). There's a workout facility, laundry, business center and free airport shuttle. The rooms overlook either the historic square or a harbor bustling with boats bringing in the day's catch.

Eating & Drinking

★ Homeport Eatery CAFE $
(www.homeporteatery.com; 209 Lincoln St; panini & crepes $6-10; ⌚7:30am-5pm Mon-Sat) 🌿 A gourmet, indoor food court with stalls that serve crepes, panini and espresso – and there's even a little tavern serving wine and a beer bar in the back. Mix and match and then sit at a big wood table and watch the rain outside.

Highliner Coffee CAFE $
(www.highlinercoffee.com; 327 Seward St, Seward Sq Mall; light fare under $5; ⌚6am-5pm Mon-Sat, 7am-4pm Sun; 📶) At the Highliner they like their coffee black and their salmon wild, which explains why the walls are covered with photos of local fishing boats or political stickers like 'Invest in Wild Salmon's Future: Eat One!' Sip a warming latte and indulge in a bagel sandwich.

Ludvig's Bistro MEDITERRANEAN $$$
(☎907-966-3663; www.ludvigsbistro.com; 256 Katlian St; tapas $14-18, mains $28-40; ⌚4:30-9:30pm Mon-Sat) Sitka's boldest restaurant has only seven tables and a few stools at its

brass-and-blue-tile bar. Described as 'rustic Mediterranean fare,' almost every dish is local, even the sea salt. If seafood paella is on the menu, order it. The traditional Spanish rice dish comes loaded with scallops, king crab, salmon, calamari, prawns and whatever else the local boats netted that day.

Baranof Island Brewing Co BREWERY
(www.baranofislandbrewing.com; 215 Smith St; ⊙noon-8pm) Off Sawmill Creek Rd, past the main post office, is Sitka's microbrewery and taproom, producing such beers as Halibut Point Hefeweisen and Redoubt Red Ale. Order a sampler of its beers to wash down a slice of pizza or salmon dip.

Information

Sitka Convention & Visitors Bureau (☎907-747-5940; www.sitka.org; 303 Lincoln St, Suite 4; ⊙8am-5pm Mon-Fri) Across the street from St Michael's Cathedral.

Getting There & Away

Alaska Marine Highway (☎907-747-8737; www.ferryalaska.com) ferries stop almost daily at the terminal, which is 7 miles north of town.

Ferry Transit Bus (☎907-747-5800) will take you into town for $8 (round-trip $12).

Northstar Rental (☎907-966-2552; www.northstarrentacar.com) has midsize cars from $69 per day.

Sitka Airport (SIT; ☎907-966-2960), on Japonski Island, is served by Alaska Airlines (p1083).

Juneau

The first town to be founded after Alaska's purchase from the Russians, Juneau became the territorial capital in 1906 and today is the most scenic capital in the country. Its historic downtown clings to the gap between snowcapped mountains and a bustling waterfront. The rest of the city spreads north into the Mendenhall Valley. Juneau is also Alaska's cruise-ship capital and the gateway to many attractions, including Tracy Arm and Glacier Bay National Park.

Sights

Mendenhall Glacier GLACIER
The most famous of Juneau's ice floes, and the city's most popular attraction, is Mendenhall Glacier, Alaska's famous drive-in glacier. The glacier flows 13 miles from its source, the Juneau Ice Field, and has a half-mile-wide face. It ends at Mendenhall Lake, the reason for all the icebergs, but naturalists estimate that within a few years it will retreat onto land and within 25 years retreat out of view entirely from the observation area.

Last Chance Mining Museum HISTORIC SITE
(☎907-586-5338; 1001 Basin Rd; adult/child $5/free; ⊙9:30am-12:30pm & 3:30-6:30pm) Amble out to the end of Basin Rd, a beautiful half-mile walk from the north end of Gastineau Ave, to the intriguing Last Chance Mining Museum. The former Alaska-Juneau Gold Mining Company complex is now a museum where you can view the remains of the compressor house and examine the tools of what was once the world's largest hard-rock gold mine.

Juneau-Douglas City Museum MUSEUM
(www.juneau.org/parkrec/museum; 114 W 4th St; adult/child $6/free; ⊙9am-6pm Mon-Fri, 10am-4:30pm Sat & Sun) This museum focuses on gold with interesting mining displays and the video *Juneau: City Built on Gold*. If you love to hike in the mountains, the museum's 7ft-long relief map is the best overview of the area's rugged terrain. Tuesday to Thursday the staff leads a historical walking tour (adult/child $25/20) of the downtown area beginning 1:30pm at the museum.

Activities

Hiking is the most popular activity in the area, and some trails access United States Forest Service (USFS) cabins. **Juneau Parks & Recreation** (☎907-586-0428; www.juneau.org/parksrec; 155 South Seward St) organizes free hikes. **West Glacier Trail**, which sidles along Mendenhall Glacier, has the most stunning scenery. The **Mt Roberts Trail** is the most popular hike to the alpine country above Juneau.

Taku Glacier Lodge SCENIC FLIGHTS
(☎907-586-6275; www.wingsairways.com; adult/child $299/260) The most popular tours in Juneau are flightseeing, glacier-viewing and salmon bakes, and a trip to this historic camp combines all three. You reach it via a floatplane that includes flying across a half-dozen glaciers. At the log lodge you enjoy an incredible meal of wild salmon to the view of Taku Glacier.

Mt Roberts Tram TRAMWAY
(www.goldbelttours.com; 490 S Franklin St; adult/child $33/16; ⊙11am-9pm Mon, 8am-9pm Tue-

Sun;) As far as trams go, this tramway is rather expensive for a five-minute ride. But from a marketing point of view its location couldn't be better. It whisks you right from the cruise-ship dock up 1800ft to the timberline of Mt Roberts, where you'll find a restaurant, gift shops and a small theater with a film on Tlingit culture.

Alaska Boat & Kayak Center KAYAKING
(907-364-2333; www.juneaukayak.com; 11521 Glacier Hwy; single/double kayak $50/70; 9am-5pm) Kayak rentals are available from this place, which is based in the Auke Bay Harbor and offers transportation services and multiday discounts. The company also offers half-day and full-day guided paddles.

Orca Enterprises WHALE WATCHING
(907-789-6801; www.alaskawhalewatching.com; adult/child $124.95/93.45) Uses jet boats that are fully wheelchair accessible to look at sea lions, orcas and harbor seals as well as humpback whales. Lower prices for infants and kids under six years.

Sleeping

★ Juneau International Hostel HOSTEL $
(907-586-9559; www.juneauhostel.net; 614 Harris St; dm adult/child $12/5;) Alaska's best hostel and certainly its most affordable. One of the eight bunk rooms is a family room, while amenities include laundry, storage and free internet access and wi-fi. In the lounge area, the overstuffed sofas are strategically placed around a large bay window with a view of snowy peaks and Douglas Island.

Driftwood Hotel MOTEL $$
(907-586-2280; www.driftwoodalaska.com; 435 Willoughby Ave; r $115-125, ste $145-165;) Near the Alaska State Museum, this lodge is the best value in accommodations downtown. The 63 rooms are clean and updated regularly, the motel offers 24-hour courtesy transportation to the airport and the ferry, and it's hard to top the location unless you're willing to spend twice as much.

Silverbow Inn BOUTIQUE HOTEL $$$
(907-586-4146; www.silverbowinn.com; 120 2nd St; r $89-249;) A swanky (for Alaska) boutique inn with 11 rooms. The 100-year-old building is filled with antiques and rooms come with private bath, king and queen beds and flat-screen TVs. A 2nd-floor deck features a hot tub with a view of Douglas Island's mountains. Breakfast is served in the morning, wine and cheese in the new wine bar in the evening.

Eating & Drinking

S Franklin St is Juneau's historic, and at times colorful, drinking sector.

Pel'Meni DUMPLING $
(Merchant's Wharf, Marine Way; dumplings $7; 11:30am-1:30am Sun-Thu, 11:30am-3:30am Fri & Sat) There's no menu here, just authentic, homemade Russian dumplings, filled with either potato or beef, spiced with hot sauce, curry and cilantro. The perfect end to a night of drinking – Pel'Meni is open until the wee hours. Record buffs will be amazed by the wall full of LPs and the turntable that provides the proper late-night atmosphere.

★ Saffron INDIAN $$
(907-586-1036; www.saffronalaska.com; 112 N Franklin St; lunch $14, dinner $8-19; 11:30am-9pm Mon-Fri, 5-9pm Sat & Sun;) Saffron serves up hot, chewy naan bread and complex yet delicate curries for dinner, and *thalis* (plates with a little bit of everything) for lunch. All dishes are made from scratch and the dinner menu is à la carte so you can sample many items. Curries are just spicy enough that you'll leave feeling warm on the inside.

★ Rookery CAFE $$
(907-463-3013; www.therookerycafe.com; 111 Seward St; lunch $9-14, dinner mains $15-24; 7am-9pm Mon-Fri, 9am-9pm Sat;) Laid-back coffee shop by day, hip bistro by night. The Rookery serves Portland, OR's Stumptown coffee and original breakfasts, lunches and dinners. Buttermilk corncakes, sandwiches on homemade foccacia, and breakfast rice bowls are just some of the daytime offerings. At 4pm, the wi-fi is turned off and a daily-changing menu that includes charcuterie, house-ground burgers and salads is served.

Red Dog Saloon BAR
(www.reddogsaloon.com; 278 S Franklin St; 11am-10pm) A sign at the door says it all: 'Booze, Antiques, Sawdust Floor, Community Singing' – and the cruise-ship passengers love it! Most don't realize, much less care, that this Red Dog is but a replica of the original, a famous Alaskan drinking hole that was across the street until 1987. Now *that* was a bar.

Information

Juneau Visitor Center (907-586-2201; www.traveljuneau.com; 470 S Franklin St;

8am-5pm) The new visitor center is in the cruise-ship terminal right next to the Mt Roberts Tram, and has all the information you need to explore Juneau, find a trail or book a room. The center also maintains smaller information booths at the airport, the marine ferry terminal and downtown near the library.

Getting There & Away

AIR

The main airline serving Juneau is Alaska Airlines (p1083). Smaller companies such as **Wings of Alaska** (907-789-0790; www.wingsofalaska.com) provide services to isolated communities.

BOAT

Ferries dock at Auke Bay Ferry Terminal, 14 miles northwest of downtown. In summer the main-line ferries traversing the Inside Passage depart daily south-bound for Sitka ($45, nine hours), Petersburg ($66, eight hours) and Ketchikan ($107, 18 hours).

Getting Around

Juneau's public bus system, **Capital Transit** (907-789-6901; www.juneau.org/capitaltransit; adult/child $2/1), stops way short of the ferry terminal and a mile short of the Mendenhall Glacier Visitor Center. Even getting to/from the airport can be problematic: only the 'express' route goes right to the terminal, and it only runs during business hours on weekdays

Juneau Car Rental (907-957-7530, 907-789-0951; www.juneaucarrentals.com) is a mile from the airport but provides pickups and has a designated airport parking spot for when you drop the car off.

Haines

Haines is Southeast Alaska's most scenic departure point and a crucial link to the Alcan Hwy for thousands of recreational vehicle drivers (RVers) every summer on their way to Interior Alaska. The Northwest Trading Company arrived here in 1878, followed by gold prospectors and the US Army, which built its first permanent post in Alaska, Fort Seward, in 1903. The perceived threat of a Japanese invasion in WWII resulted in the construction of the Haines and Alcan Hwys, connecting Haines to the rest of the USA. If mammoth cruise ships depress you, Haines is a much better destination choice than nearby Skagway.

Sights & Activities

Haines offers two major hiking-trail systems – Mt Riley and Mt Ripinsky – as well as afternoon walking tours of **Fort Seward** (the visitor center has details).

Sheldon Museum MUSEUM
(www.sheldonmuseum.org; 11 Main St; adult/child $5/free; 10am-5pm Mon-Fri, 1-4pm Sat) The Sheldon Museum houses a collection of indigenous artifacts upstairs, including a particularly interesting display on rare Chilkat blankets. Downstairs is devoted to Haines' pioneer and gold-rush days and even includes the sawed-off shotgun that Jack Dalton used to convince travelers to pay his toll.

American Bald Eagle Foundation MUSEUM
(www.baldeagles.org; 113 Haines Hwy; adult/child $10/5; 9am-5pm Mon-Fri, from 1pm Sat;) An impressive wildlife diorama is featured at the American Bald Eagle Foundation – it displays more than 180 specimens and almost two dozen eagles. Two live raptors are always on display, with handlers giving demonstrations.

Chilkat Guides RAFTING
(907-766-2491; www.raftalaska.com; floats $128) Runs a four-hour Chilkat River raft float.

Sleeping

Bear Creek Cabins & Hostel HOSTEL $
(907-766-2259; www.bearcreekcabinsalaska.com; Small Tract Rd; dm/cabins $20/68;) A 20-minute walk outside town (follow Mud Bay Rd and when it veers right, continue straight onto Small Tract Rd for 1½ miles) this hostel is comprised of a number of cabins around a grassy common area. A restroom/shower building also has laundry facilities, and there is a common, fully equipped kitchen reminiscent of a mess hall.

★ **Beach Roadhouse** B&B $$
(907-766-3060; www.beachroadhouse.com; 717 Beach Rd; r/cabins $115/145;) This B&B is what Alaska is all about. The large cedar home is perched above Lynn Canal and surrounded by impressive pines for a tranquil, woodsy setting. Four rooms are large and include kitchenettes. The three cabins are even larger with full kitchens and lofts that sleep three to four persons.

WORTH A TRIP

KODIAK ISLAND

Kodiak, immediately southeast of the elongated Alaska peninsula, is the island of plenty. Consider its famous brown bears, the largest ursine creatures in the world. Thanks to an unblemished ecosystem and an unlimited diet of rich salmon that spawn in Kodiak's lakes and rivers, adult male bears can weigh up to 1400lb. Part of the wider Kodiak archipelago and the second-largest island in the US after Hawaii's Big Island, Kodiak acts as a kind of ecological halfway house between the forested Alaskan panhandle and the treeless Aleutian Islands. Its velvety green mountains and sheltered ice-free bays were the site of the earliest Russian settlement in Alaska and are still home to one of the US's most important fishing fleets.

For bear-watching opportunities call into the **Kodiak National Wildlife Refuge Visitor Center** (907-487-2626; www.fws.gov/refuge/kodiak; 402 Center St; 9am-5pm;) in the town of Kodiak.

Elsewhere, Kodiak harbors one of the largest coastguard stations in the US, hides smatterings of abandoned WWII defenses in **Fort Abercrombie State Historical Park** (www.dnr.alaska.gov/parks; Abercrombie Dr) and retains some genuine Russian colonial heritage.

It's also a good embarkation point for the *MV Tustamena* ferryboat that plies the **Alaska Marine Highway** (800-642-0066; www.ferryalaska.com) on an epic three-day voyage west to Dutch Harbor in the remote Aleutian Islands (mid-May to early October). Book tickets well in advance.

Alaska Guardhouse Lodging B&B $$

(907-766-2566; www.alaskaguardhouse.com; 15 Seward Dr; r $125-155;) What used to jail misbehaved soldiers is now housing visitors in comfort and luxury. Four large bedrooms, a pleasant living room and sunporch with rocking chairs all give way to views of mountains and water. When we visited they were restoring the old Fort Seward fire hall next door; you'll recognize it by the giant tower.

Captain's Choice Motel MOTEL $$

(907-766-3111; www.capchoice.com; 108 2nd Ave N; s/d $127/137) Haines' largest motel has the best view of the Chilkat Mountains and Lynn Canal and a huge sundeck to enjoy it on. The wood-paneled rooms are simple but spacious enough to include a microwave, small refrigerator, coffeemaker and TV. A light breakfast is offered in the morning, and courtesy transportation to the ferries and airport is available.

Eating & Drinking

★**Fireweed Restaurant** BISTRO $$

(37 Blacksmith St; pizzas $14-30, salads $10-19; 11:30am-3pm Wed-Sat & 4:30-9pm Tue-Sat;) This clean, bright and laid-back bistro is in an old Fort Seward building and its salads are an antidote to Southeast's penchant for fried food. On its menu are words like 'organic,' 'veggie' and 'grilled' as opposed to 'deep fried' and 'captain's special.'

Mosey's Cantina MEXICAN $$

(www.moseyscantina.com; 1 Soap Suds Alley; lunch $8-14, dinner $16-24; 11:30am-2:30pm & 5:30-8:30pm Wed-Sat) This may be Haines, but Mosey's offers some of the best Mexican fare outside of Anchorage. The mole sauce is outstanding, the salsa is fire roasted and the tacos are filled with everything from applewood-grilled chicken and carne asada to locally caught rockfish. There is a delightful deck and garden seating as well as nine tables inside.

Haines Brewing Company BREWERY

(www.hainesbrewing.com; Dalton City; 1-6pm Mon-Sat) It's well worth the walk to the town's delightful one-room brewery. It's the maker of such beer as Dalton Trail Ale, Elder Rock Red and the potent Black Fang (9% alcohol content). Tours are short – hey this is a one-room brewery – but pints are available and you can have a half-gallon growler ($10 to $13) filled for later.

Information

Haines Convention & Visitors Bureau (907-766-2234; www.haines.ak.us; 122 2nd Ave; 8am-5pm Mon-Fri, 9am-4pm Sat & Sun) Has restrooms, free coffee and racks of free information for tourists. There is also a lot of information on Canada's Yukon for those heading up the Alcan.

Getting There & Around

Several air-charter companies service Haines, the cheapest being **Wings of Alaska** (907-983-2442; www.wingsofalaska.com).

The **Haines–Skagway Fast Ferry** (907-766-2100; www.hainesskagwayfastferry.com; round-trip adult/child $73/36.50; Jun-Sep) will get you to and from Skagway.

Any Time Taxi (907-303-8984, 907-303-9246) offers rides from the airport into town for $6, or from the ferry terminal for $12.

Skagway

The northern terminus of the Alaska Marine Highway (p1083), Skagway was a gold-rush town infamous for its lawlessness. In 1887 the population was two; 10 years later it was Alaska's largest city, with 20,000 residents. Today Skagway survives entirely on tourism and gets packed when a handful of cruise ships pull in and thousands of passengers converge on the town as if the Klondike gold rush were still on.

Sights & Activities

Klondike Gold Rush National Historical Park HISTORIC SITE

(907-983-9200; www.nps.gov/klgo; Visitor Center, Broadway St, at 2nd Ave; 8am-6pm, to 7pm Fri) FREE The **NPS center** is in the original 1898 White Pass & Yukon Route depot. The center features displays – the most impressive being a replica of the ton of supplies every miner had to carry over the Chilkoot Pass – ranger programs and a small bookstore. The 25-minute film *Gold Fever: Race to the Klondike*, an excellent introduction to the gold rush, is shown on the hour.

Skagway Museum MUSEUM

(907-983-2420; cnr 7th Ave & Spring St; adult/child $2/1; 9am-5pm Mon-Fri, 10am-5pm Sat, noon-4pm Sun) Skagway Museum is not only one of the finest in a town filled with museums but one of the finest in the Southeast. It occupies the entire 1st floor of the venerable century-old McCabe Building, a former college, and is devoted to various aspects of local history, including Alaska Native baskets, beadwork and carvings, and, of course, the Klondike Gold Rush. The display that draws the most looks is the small pistol Soapy Smith (Skagway's most notorious gold-rush-era gangster) kept up his sleeve.

Mascot Saloon Museum MUSEUM

(Broadway St, at 3rd Ave; 8am-6pm) FREE The only saloon in Alaska that doesn't serve booze – but it did during the gold rush, and plenty of it. Built in 1898, the Mascot was one of Skagway's 80 to 100 saloons in its heyday as 'the roughest place in the world.' The NPS has turned it into a museum that looks into the vices – gambling, drinking, prostitution – that followed the stampeders to the goldfields, encouraging visitors to belly up to the bar for a shot of sinful history.

★**White Pass & Yukon Route Railroad** TOUR

(800-343-7373; www.wpyr.com; 231 2nd Ave; Jun-Aug) Without a doubt the most spectacular tour from Skagway is a ride aboard the historic railway of the White Pass & Yukon Route (WPYR). Two different narrated sightseeing tours are available; reservations are recommended for both. Remember your passport, as some of the tours cross into Canada and back.

Sleeping

Mile Zero B&B B&B $$

(907-983-3045; www.mile-zero.com; 901 Main St; r $135-145; @) This B&B is more like a motel with the comforts of home, as the six large rooms have their own private entrance on the wraparound porch. If you hook the fish of your dreams, there's a BBQ area where you can grill it for dinner.

Skagway Inn INN $$

(907-983-2289; www.skagwayinn.com; Broadway St, at 7th Ave; r $129-229; @) In a restored 1897 Victorian building that was originally one of the town's brothels, this beautiful inn is downtown and features 10 rooms, four with shared baths. All are small but filled with antique dressers, iron beds and chests. Breakfast is included, as is ferry/airport/train connections.

Sgt Preston's Lodge MOTEL $$

(907-983-2521; www.sgtprestonslodge.com; 370 6th Ave; s $90-115, d $100-151; @) This motel is the best bargain in Skagway and its 38 rooms are nicer than outside appearances indicate. It's just far enough from Broadway St to escape most of the cruise-ship crush. Courtesy transportation and complimentary coffee provided.

Eating & Drinking

Skagway has more than 20 restaurants operating during the summer, and there's a higher per capita rate of excellent ones than elsewhere in Southeast.

DON'T MISS

CHILKOOT TRAIL

The Chilkoot is the ultimate Alaska trek, combining great scenery, a historical site and an incredible sense of adventure. It was the route used by the Klondike gold miners in the 1898 gold rush, and walking it is not so much a wilderness adventure as a history lesson. The 33-mile trek takes four days and includes the **Chilkoot Pass** – a steep climb up to 3525ft that has hikers scrambling on all fours. The highlight for many is riding the historic White Pass & Yukon Route Railroad back to Skagway.

Interested? Stop at the **Trail Center** (907-983-9234; www.nps.gov/klgo; Broadway St, at 2nd Ave; 8am-5pm) to obtain backpacking permits and set up the hike.

★ **Olivia's Bistro** SEAFOOD $$
(Broadway St, at 7th Ave; breakfast & lunch mains $9-15, dinner mains $14-27; 10am-9pm;) A charming bistro in the Skagway Inn. The menu features wild game and seafood and whatever is growing in the lovely garden outside. How can you top that? With a serving of homegrown rhubarb crisp for dessert.

★ **Skagway Brewing Company** BREWERY
(www.skagwaybrewing.com; cnr 7th Ave & Broadway; burgers $15; 10am-10pm Mon-Fri, 11am-10pm Sat & Sun) Skagway's microbrewery offers stampeders such choices as Prospector Pale Ale, Boomtown Brown and Chilkoot Trail IPA. There's a full menu with nightly dinner specials and a quiet outdoor deck in the back to escape the rowdiness at the front. It's the best place in town to relax after a long hike.

Red Onion Saloon BAR
(www.redonion1898.com; Broadway St, at 2nd Ave; 4pm-10pm Mon-Fri, noon-10pm Sat & Sun Apr-Oct) Skagway's most beloved brothel at the turn of the century is now its most famous saloon. The 'RO' is done up as a gold-rush saloon, complete with mannequins leering down at you from the 2nd story to depict pioneer-era working girls. When bands are playing here, it'll be packed, noisy and rowdy. It also has the best pizza in town.

Information

Klondike Gold Rush National Historical Park Visitors Center (907-983-9200; www.nps.gov/klgo; 154 Broadway St; 8am-6pm) Info on everything outdoors – local trails, public campgrounds, NPS programs.

Getting There & Away

Wings of Alaska (p1094) has regularly scheduled flights from Skagway to Juneau, Haines and Glacier Bay. Alaska Marine Highway (p1083) has ferries departing every day in summer, and Haines–Skagway Fast Ferry (p1094) runs daily to Haines.

Sourdough Car Rentals (907-983-2523; 6th Ave, at Broadway St) has compacts for $80 a day.

White Pass & Yukon Route Railroad (p1094) goes to Fraser, British Columbia, where there's a bus connection to Whitehorse (adult/child $129/64.50).

THE INTERIOR

Compared to most places in the developed world, the Interior is a trackless hinterland. For Alaska, however, it's got roads galore. Drawcard Denali National Park is blessed with the continent's mightiest mountain, abundant megafauna and easy access.

Fairbanks

The only thing that constitutes a 'city' in Interior Alaska, Fairbanks often feels more like a crossroads than a metropolis. But at the nexus of some truly epic routes (north to the Arctic, east to Canada and south to Denali), the mix of people in this once-rough-and-ready gold-rush town is rarely boring.

The city itself isn't particularly pretty – its 'downtown' is soporific and, elsewhere, the local businesses lie clustered around dull strung-out strip malls. However, there are saving graces. The modern university campus gives the city a young, forward-thinking demographic, while caught in the right light on a long summer's evening, the Chena River is a pleasant place to float or have a picnic (or both). If you come during the frigid winter, Fairbanks is the start or end point of the Yukon Quest 1000-mile dog-sled race and ground zero for viewing the aurora borealis.

Sights

The **University of Alaska Museum of the North** (907-474-7505; www.uaf.edu/museum; 907 Yukon Dr; admission $12; 9am-7pm) has

WORTH A TRIP

DENALI NATIONAL PARK & PRESERVE

For many travelers, **Denali National Park & Preserve** (907-683-2294; www.nps.gov/dena) is the beginning and end of their Alaskan adventure. And why shouldn't it be? Here is probably your best chance in the Interior (if not in the entire state) of seeing a grizzly bear, moose or caribou, and maybe even a fox or wolf. And unlike most wilderness areas in the country, you don't have to be a hiker to view this wildlife. The window of the park bus will do just fine for a close look at these magnificent creatures roaming free in their natural habitat.

For those with a bit more time and the desire to get further into the wild, there are vast expanses of untracked country to explore – more than six million acres of it, to be exact. That's more landmass than the US state of Massachusetts. At the center of it all is the icy behemoth of Mt McKinley, known to most Alaskans as Denali and to native Athabascans as the Great One. This is North America's highest peak and rightly celebrated as an icon of all that is awesome and wild in the state.

There's only one road through the park: the 92-mile unpaved Park Rd, which is closed to private vehicles after Mile 14. The park entrance area, where most visitors congregate, extends a scant 4 miles up Park Rd. It's here you'll find the park headquarters, **visitor center** (907-683-2294; www.nps.gov/dena; Mile 1.5, Park Rd; 8am-6pm) and main campground, as well as the **Wilderness Access Center** (WAC; 907-683-9274; Mile 0.5, Park Rd; 5am-7pm), where you pay your park entrance fee and arrange campground and shuttle-bus bookings to take you further into the park. In a trailer across the lot from the WAC sits the **Backcountry Information Center** (BIC; 907-683-9510; Mile 0.5, Park Rd; 9am-6pm), where backpackers get backcountry permits and bear-proof food containers.

There are few places to stay within the park, excluding campgrounds, and only one restaurant. The majority of visitors base themselves in the nearby communities of Canyon, McKinley Village, Carlo Creek and Healy. A decent budget option in Canyon is **Denali Park Salmon Bake Restaurant & Cabins** (907-683-7283; www.thebakerocks.com; Mile 238.5, George Parks Hwy; cabins with/without bath $149/69;), which offers no-frills cabins as well as a restaurant, shuttle service to the park and bar with live music. Directly opposite across the George Parks Hwy is the more luxurious **Denali Princess Wilderness Lodge** (907-683-2282; www.princesslodges.com; Mile 238.5 George Parks Hwy; r from $269;), a miniresort run by the famous cruise company.

artifact-rich exhibits on the geology, history, culture and trivia of each region of the state.

Morris Thompson Cultural & Visitors Center (www.morristhompsoncenter.org; 101 Dunkel St; 8am-9pm) is an invaluable and ingenious mix of museum, info point and cultural center.

Sleeping & Eating

Bridgewater Hotel HOTEL $$
(907-456-3642; www.fountainheadhotels.com; 723 1st Ave; r $130; P@) Your best affordable option in what passes for downtown in Fairbanks, the Bridgewater is on the Chena River and abuts a pretty riverside walking path. Rooms are unlikely to blow your mind but will keep you comfortable, and there's a decent buffet breakfast and a handy free 'around town' shuttle.

Silver Gulch Brewery BURGERS $$
(907-452-2739; www.silvergulch.com; Mile 11, Old Steese Hwy; mains $15-34; 4-10pm Mon-Fri, 11am-10pm Sat & Sun) Cavernous and slightly overdone, this northernmost microbrewery in the US makes jolly good beer, but plenty of people come just for the pub grub. There are free brewery tours at 3pm Wednesdays and Fridays.

Getting There & Away

Fairbanks International Airport (www.dot.state.ak.us/faiiap) has regular flights to Anchorage. Delta flies direct to Seattle, and Condor flies seasonally to Frankfurt in Germany.

Several bus companies including **Alaska/Yukon Trails** (800-770-7275; www.alaskashuttle.com) travel up and down the George Parks Hwy, stopping at Denali ($55, three hours), Talkeetna ($92, seven hours) and Anchorage ($99, 10 hours). The company also has a service to Dawson City ($265, nine hours), and Whitehorse in Canada.

Alaska Railroad (907-458-6025; www.alaskarailroad.com) runs daily trains to Denali National Park and Anchorage from mid-May to mid-September.

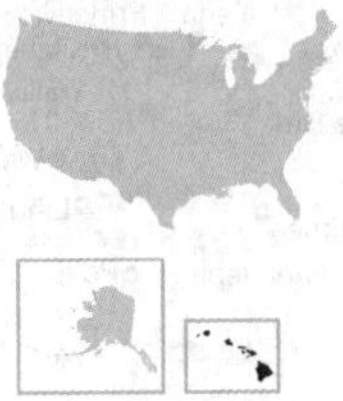

Hawaii

Includes ➡

Best Beaches

- Pupukea Beach (p1105)
- Kapalua Beach (p1110)
- Hapuna Beach (p1107)
- Hanalei Bay (p1115)
- Kailua Beach (p1104)

Best Local Food

- Ted's Bakery (p1105)
- Koloa Fish Market (p1116)
- Umeke (p1106)
- Da Kitchen (p1113)
- Super J's (p1107)

Why Go?

Truth: this string of emerald islands in the cobalt blue Pacific, more than 2000 miles from any continent, takes work to get to. And besides, aren't the beaches totally crushed by sunbaked tourists and cooing honeymooners? Cue the galloping *Hawaii Five-0* theme music and lei-draped beauties dancing hula beneath wind-rustled palms.

Hawaii, as tourist bureaus and Hollywood constantly remind us, is 'paradise.' Push past the hype and you may find they're not far wrong. Hawaii is diving into coral-reef cities in the morning and listening to slack key guitar at sunset. It's biting into juicy *liliko'i* (passion fruit) with hibiscus flowers in your hair. These Polynesian islands show off nature's diversity at its most divine, from fiery volcanoes to lacy rainforest waterfalls to crystal-clear aquamarine bays.

Locals know Hawaii isn't always paradise, but on any given day it can sure feel like it.

When to Go

Honolulu

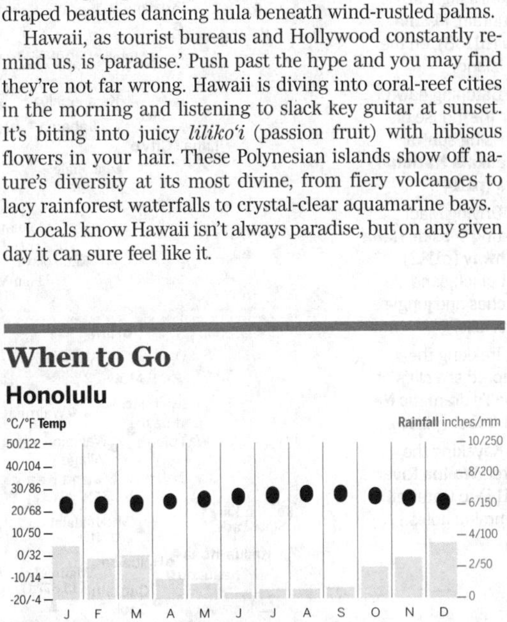

Dec–Apr Slightly cooler, wetter weather; peak season for tourism, surfing and whale-watching.

May–Sep Mostly sunny, cloudless days; summer vacation keeps beaches and resorts busy.

Oct–Nov Hotter, humid weather; fewer visitors mean cheaper accommodations.

Hawaii Highlights

1. Exploring multicultural **Honolulu** (p1100), with its eye-popping museums and ethnic eats.
2. Snorkeling with tropical fish and sea turtles in sparkling **Hanauma Bay** (p1104).
3. Watching pros surf monster winter waves on O'ahu's **North Shore** (p1104).
4. Witnessing a living volcano erupt inside **Hawai'i Volcanoes National Park** (p1109).
5. Stargazing atop Hawaii's highest mountain, **Mauna Kea** (p1108), on the Big Island.
6. Catching dawn over the 'house of the rising sun' at **Haleakalā National Park** (p1114).
7. Driving Maui's twisting seaside **Hana Highway** (p1113) past black-sand beaches and jungle waterfalls.
8. Trekking the sculpted sea cliffs of Kaua'i's dramatic **Na Pali Coast** (p1115).
9. Kayaking the sacred **Wailua River** (p1114) to waterfall swimming holes.

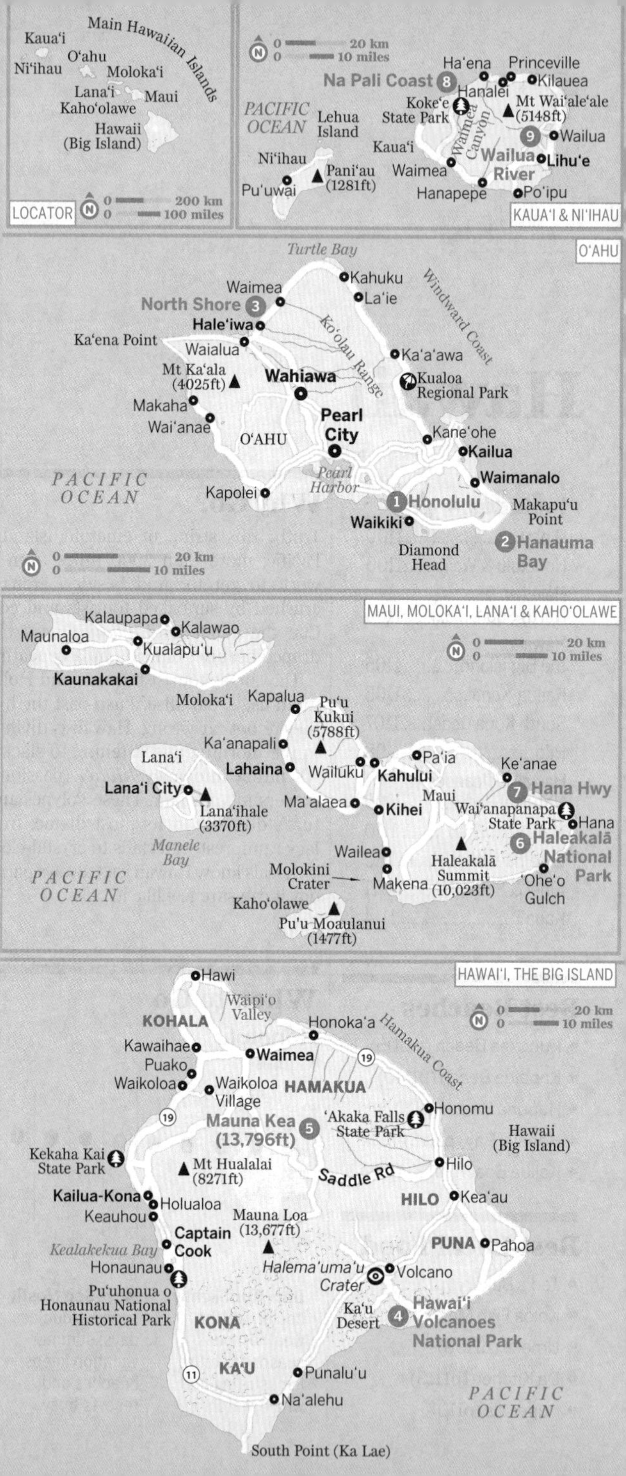

History

Little is known about Hawai'i's first Polynesian settlers, who arrived between AD 300 and 600. Tahitians landed by AD 1000 and, for the next three centuries, navigated thousands of miles back and forth across the Pacific Ocean in double-hulled canoes. Ruled by chiefs, ancient Hawaiian society and its religion followed strict laws called *kapu*.

Beginning in the 1790s, a Big Island chief named Kamehameha conquered and united the main Hawaiian Islands. He is credited with bringing peace and stability to a society that was often in flux due to wars and ruling-class power struggles. After Kamehameha's death in 1819, his son Liholiho inherited the throne, while Kamehameha's favored wife, Ka'ahumanu, became co-regent. In a stunning repudiation of traditional Hawaiian religion, they deliberately violated *kapu*, an act followed up by the destruction of many temples.

Christian missionaries arrived soon after and, amid Hawai'i's social and spiritual chaos, began to 'save souls.' New England whalers also weighed anchor, and by the 1840s Lahaina and Honolulu were the busiest whaling towns in the Pacific. Foreign residents made a grab for Hawai'i's fertile land, turning vast tracts into sugarcane plantations; needing field workers, they encouraged a flood of immigrants from Asia and Europe. This gave rise to Hawai'i's multiethnic culture, but also displaced Native Hawaiians, who mostly became landless.

In 1893 a group of American businessmen overthrew the Hawaiian monarchy. The US government was initially reluctant to support the coup, but soon rationalized colonialism by citing the islands' strategic economic, political and military importance, annexing Hawaii in 1898. Hawaii played another pivotal role in history when a surprise attack on Pearl Harbor in 1941 catapulted the US into WWII. Hawaii became the 50th state in 1959.

Local Culture

Compared to 'the mainland' – a blanket term for the rest of the USA – Hawaii may as well be another country. (Not coincidentally, some Native Hawaiian activists would like to restore its status as an independent nation.) Both geographically and culturally speaking, Hawaii developed in isolation and, like its flora and fauna, lifestyles here are unique.

No ethnicity can claim a majority, but Hawaii's racial diversity is distinct from typical US multiculturalism: it has large Asian populations and tiny African American and Latino communities. About 10% of residents identify themselves as Native Hawaiian.

As befits a tropical paradise, Hawaii is relaxingly casual. Except in big-city Honolulu, aloha shirts and sandals or 'rubbah slippahs' (flip-flops) are acceptable attire for almost any occasion. Socializing revolves around food and family, and fun means outdoor sports. Caring for the land and the community are intertwined.

Then there's aloha. It's a greeting, meaning 'hello' or 'goodbye'. Beyond that, it describes a gentle, everyday practice of openness, hospitality and loving welcome that's extended by and to pretty much everyone.

Language

Hawaii has two official state languages, English and Hawaiian, and one unofficial language, pidgin. The Hawaiian language has experienced a renaissance but, outside a formal setting (eg classroom, performance), you are unlikely to hear it spoken. All residents speak English, but when locals 'talk story' with each other they may reach for the relaxed, fun-loving cadences of pidgin. Pidgin developed on sugar plantations as a common tongue for immigrant workers.

HAWAII FACTS

Nickname Aloha State

Population 1.4 million

Area 6423 sq miles

Capital city Honolulu (population 337,250)

Sales tax 4% (4.5% on O'ahu)

Birthplace of Olympian Duke Kahanamoku (1890–1968), entertainer Don Ho (1930–2007), President Barack Obama (b 1961), actor Nicole Kidman (b 1967)

Home of The ukulele and the USA's only royal palace

Politics Majority vote Democrat, minority Native Hawaiian separatists

Famous for Surfing, hula, lei, aloha shirts, mai tais

State fish *Humuhumunukunukuapua'a* (reef triggerfish, literally 'fish with a nose like a pig')

O'AHU

O'ahu is the *ali'i* (chief) of Hawaii's main islands – so much so that others are referred to as 'Neighbor Islands.' Honolulu is the center of state government, commerce and culture, while nearby Waikiki's beaches gave birth to the whole tiki-craze fantasia. If you want to take the measure of Hawaii's diversity, O'ahu offers the full buffet in one tidy package: in the blink of an eye you can go from crowded metropolis to turquoise bays teeming with sea life – and surfers.

Getting There & Around

Honolulu International Airport (HNL; ☎808-836-6411; http://hawaii.gov/hnl; 300 Rodgers Blvd, Honolulu;) is Hawaii's major air hub. **Roberts Hawaii** (☎808-441-7800; www.airportwaikikishuttle.com) runs 24-hour airport shuttles to/from Waikiki (one way/round-trip $16/30).

Hawaiian Airlines (☎800-367-5320; www.hawaiianairlines.com), **Mokulele Airlines** (☎866-260-7070; www.mokuleleairlines.com) and **Island Air** (☎800-652-6541; www.islandair.com) are the main carriers flying between islands. Service is frequent and flight times are short; one-way fares vary wildly from $50 to $190 (book ahead).

O'ahu's public transit, **TheBus** (☎808-848-5555; www.thebus.org; adult fare $2.50, 4-day visitor pass $35; infoline 5:30am-10pm), covers the entire island, excluding most hiking trailheads and scenic lookouts.

Honolulu & Waikiki

Besides its many museums, historical sites and cultural offerings, Honolulu is also a foodie haven dishing up everything from cheap noodles to gourmet Hawaii Regional cuisine. Saunter over to Waikiki Beach to lounge on the sand, play in the ocean, hear Hawaiian music and watch hula dancers sway after sunset.

Sights

Neighboring downtown Honolulu, **Chinatown** lends itself to exploring on foot. Bring an appetite for grazing pan-Asian marketplaces and cafes between the antiques and lei shops, temples and art galleries.

★**Bishop Museum** MUSEUM
(☎808-847-3511; www.bishopmuseum.org; 1525 Bernice St; adult/child $20/15; 9am-5pm Wed-Mon;) Like Hawaii's version of the Smithsonian Institute in Washington, DC, the Bishop Museum showcases a remarkable array of cultural and natural-history exhibits. It is often ranked as the finest Polynesian anthropological museum in the world. Founded in 1889 in honor of Princess Bernice Pauahi Bishop, a descendant of the Kamehameha dynasty, it originally housed only Hawaiian and royal artifacts. These days it honors all of Polynesia.

HAWAII IN...

Four Days

Anyone on a trans-Pacific stopover will land at **Honolulu**, so spend the few days you have on **O'ahu**. In between surfing and sunning on **Waikiki Beach**, check out Honolulu's museums and wander **Chinatown**, summit **Diamond Head** and snorkel **Hanauma Bay**. In winter admire gargantuan waves on the **North Shore**.

One Week

With a week, fit in another island – say, **Maui**. Explore the old whaling town of **Lahaina**, head to **Haleakalā National Park** to see sunrise at the volcano's summit, take a whale-watching cruise, snorkel or dive **Molokini** crater, drive the serpentine **Hana Highway** and swim in waterfall pools at **Ohe'o Gulch**.

Two Weeks

With two weeks, tack on a third island. On **Hawai'i, the Big Island**, lounge on golden beaches in **North Kona** and **South Kohala**; visit coffee farms in **South Kona**; summit Hawaii's highest peak, **Mauna Kea**; and say aloha to the goddess Pele at **Hawai'i Volcanoes National Park**. If you choose **Kaua'i**, kayak the **Wailua River** to take a dip in a jungle waterfall, hike in spectacular **Waimea Canyon** and **Koke'e State Park**, hang 10 at **Hanalei Bay**, and trek or paddle past towering sea cliffs on the **Na Pali Coast**.

★**'Iolani Palace**   PALACE
(☑808-522-0832; www.iolanipalace.org; 364 S King St; grounds admission free, adult/child basement galleries $7/3, self-guided audiotour $15/6, guided tour $22/6; ⊙9am-5pm Mon-Sat, last entry 4pm) No other place evokes a more poignant sense of Hawaii's history. The palace was built under King David Kalakaua in 1882. At that time, the Hawaiian monarchy observed many of the diplomatic protocols of the Victorian world. The king traveled abroad meeting with leaders around the globe and received foreign emissaries here. Although the palace was modern and opulent for its time, it did little to assert Hawaii's sovereignty over powerful US-influenced business interests who overthrew the kingdom in 1893.

★**Honolulu Museum of Art**   MUSEUM
(☑808-532-8700; www.honolulumuseum.org; 900 S Beretania St; adult/child $10/free, 1st Wed & 3rd Sun each month free; ⊙10am-4:30pm Tue-Sat, 1-5pm Sun; P✪) This exceptional fine-arts museum may be the biggest surprise of your trip to O'ahu. The museum, dating to 1927, has a classical facade that's invitingly open and airy, with galleries branching off a series of garden and water-fountain courtyards. Plan on spending a couple of hours at the museum, possibly combining a visit with lunch at the Honolulu Museum of Art Cafe. Admission tickets are also valid for same-day visits to Spalding House.

Hawai'i State Art Museum   MUSEUM
(☑808-586-0900; www.hawaii.gov/sfca; 2nd fl, No 1 Capitol District Bldg, 250 S Hotel St; ⊙10am-4pm Tue-Sat, also 6-9pm 1st Fri each month) ✦ FREE With its vibrant, thought-provoking collections, this public art museum brings together traditional and contemporary art from Hawaii's multiethnic communities. The museum inhabits a grand 1928 Spanish Mission Revival–style building, formerly a YMCA and today a nationally registered historic site.

Lyon Arboretum   GARDENS
(☑info 808-988-0456, tour reservations 808-988-0461; www.hawaii.edu/lyonarboretum; 3860 Manoa Rd; donation $5, guided tour $10; ⊙8am-4pm Mon-Fri, 9am-3pm Sat, tours usually 10am Mon-Sat; P✪) ✦ Beautifully unkempt walking trails wind through this highly regarded 200-acre arboretum managed by the University of Hawai'i. It was originally founded in 1918 by a group of sugar planters growing native and exotic flora species to restore Honolulu's watershed and test their economic benefit. This is not your typical overly manicured tropical flower garden, but a mature and largely wooded arboretum, where related species cluster in a seminatural state. For a guided tour, call at least 24 hours in advance.

Waikiki Aquarium   AQUARIUM
(☑808-923-9741; www.waikikiaquarium.org; 2777 Kalakaua Ave; adult/child $12/5; ⊙9am-5pm, last entry 4:30pm; ✪) ✦ Located on Waikiki's shoreline, this university-run aquarium features dozens of tanks that re-create diverse tropical Pacific reef habitats. Check the website or call ahead to make reservations for special family-friendly events and fun educational programs for kids such as Aquarium After Dark adventures. It's about a 15-minute walk southeast of the main Waikiki beach strip.

🏃 **Activities**

It's all about loooong **Waikiki Beach**. Catamarans and outrigger canoes pull right up onto the sand, while concession stands offer surf lessons and rent boards at central **Kuhio Beach Park**.

A few of Honolulu's hiking trails in the verdant upper Manoa and Makiki Valleys are just barely accessible by TheBus, including the 1.6-mile round-trip **Manoa Falls Trail**. Consult **Na Ala Hele** (http://hawaiitrails.ehawaii.gov) for trail information and directions.

🛏 **Sleeping**

Waikiki's main beachfront strip is lined with swanky high-rise resorts; for better-value hotels, head inland. Partyin' international backpacker hostels line back-alley Lemon Rd.

Hostelling International (HI) Waikiki   HOSTEL $
(☑808-926-8313; www.hostelsaloha.com; 2417 Prince Edward St; dm/r from $28/64, all with shared bath; ⊙reception 7am-midnight; P@✦) Occupying a converted low-rise apartment building, this tidy hostel is just a few blocks from the beach. Inside are fan-cooled single-sex dormitories and simple private rooms, a self-catering kitchen, coin-op laundry and free bodyboards to borrow. No smoking or alcohol allowed, but no daytime lockout or curfew either. Reservations are strongly recommended (seven-night maximum stay). Limited self-parking ($5 per night).

Hotel Renew BOUTIQUE HOTEL $$
(☎844-485-7639; www.hotelrenew.com; 129 Pa'oakalani Ave; r from $180; P ❄ @ 📶) At this fabulous find, just a half-block from the beach, a $25 per room 'amenity fee' brings a slew of services, from chilled drinks upon arrival to daily continental breakfast to free beach mats and bodyboards to borrow. Design-savvy, ecofriendly accommodations come with mod platform beds, projection-screen TVs, spa robes, earth-toned furnishings and Japanese-style *shōji* (sliding paper-screen doors).

★Royal Hawaiian RESORT $$$
(☎866-716-8110, 808-923-7311; www.royal-hawaiian.com; 2259 Kalakaua Ave; r from $400; P ❄ @ 📶 🏊 👪) Waikiki's original luxury hotel, this pink Spanish-Moorish-style landmark is loaded with charm, especially since recent splendid, multi-million-dollar renovations. The historic section of the aristocratic 'Pink Palace' maintains its classic appeal, although you may prefer the modern high-rise tower for its ocean views.

Eating

Honolulu is a global chowhound capital, from Chinatown's street-front kitchens to locals' joints near the Ala Moana Center mall to star chef's kitchens by the beach.

★Marukame Udon JAPANESE $
(☎808-931-6000; www.facebook.com/marukameudon; 2310 Kuhio Ave; mains $2-8; ⏰7am-9am & 11am-10pm; 👪) Everybody loves this Japanese noodle shop, which is so popular there is often a line stretching down the sidewalk. Watch those thick udon noodles get rolled, cut and boiled fresh right in front of you, then stack mini plates of giant tempura and *musubi* (rice balls) stuffed with salmon or a sour plum on your cafeteria tray.

Leonard's BAKERY $
(☎808-737-5591; www.leonardshawaii.com; 933 Kapahulu Ave; snacks from $1; ⏰5:30am-10pm Sun-Thu, to 11pm Fri & Sat; 👪) It's almost impossible to drive by the Leonard's eye-catching vintage 1950s neon sign without stopping in. This bakery is famous on O'ahu for its *malasadas,* sweet fried dough rolled in sugar, Portuguese-style – like a doughnut without the hole. Order ones with *haupia* (coconut cream) or *liliko'i* (passion fruit) filling, and you'll be hooked for life.

Lucky Belly ASIAN, FUSION $
(☎808-531-1888; www.luckybelly.com; 50 N Hotel St; mains $8-14; ⏰11am-2pm & 5pm-midnight Mon-Sat) Where Japanese pop art hangs over sleek bistro tables packed elbows-to-shoulders, this arts-district noodle bar crafts hot and spicy Asian fusion bites, knockout artisanal cocktails and amazingly fresh, almost architectural salads that the whole table can share. A 'Belly Bowl' of ramen soup topped with buttery pork belly, smoked bacon and pork sausage is carnivore heaven.

Haili's Hawaiian Foods HAWAIIAN $
(☎808-735-8019; http://hailishawaiianfood.com; 760 Palani Ave; meals $11-16; ⏰10am-7pm Tue-Sat, to 2pm Sun) Haili's has been cooking up homegrown Hawaiian fare since the 1950s. Locals cheerfully shoehorn themselves into kid-friendly booths and tables, then dig into heaping plates of *kalua* pig, *lomilomi* salmon and *laulau* (meat wrapped in ti leaves and steamed) served with poi or rice.

Side Street Inn HAWAIIAN $$
(☎808-591-0253; http://sidestreetinn.com; 1225 Hopaka St; mains $7-20; ⏰2pm-midnight Sun-Thu, to 1am Fri & Sat) This late-night mecca is where you'll find Honolulu's top chefs hanging out after their own kitchens close, along with partyin' locals who come for hearty portions of *kalbi* and pan-fried pork chops. Make reservations and bring friends, or join the construction-worker crews ordering plate lunches at the takeout counter. Warning: big portions!

★Roy's Waikiki HAWAII REGIONAL $$$
(☎808-923-7697; www.royshawaii.com; 226 Lewers St; mains $30-60; ⏰11am-9:30pm Mon-Thu, to 10pm Fri-Sun) This contemporary incarnation of Roy Yamaguchi's island-born chain is perfect for a flirty date or just celebrating the good life. The ground-breaking chef doesn't actually cook in the kitchen here, but his signature *misoyaki* butterfish, blackened ahi (tuna) and macadamia-nut-encrusted mahimahi are always on the menu (vegans and vegetarians have options too). Molten-chocolate soufflé for dessert is a must.

Drinking & Entertainment

Waikiki's beach bars are bursting with Hawaiian hula and live music. Honolulu's hippest nightlife scene revolves around Hotel St in Chinatown's once-notorious red-light district.

Hula's Bar & Lei Stand GAY

(808-923-0669; www.hulas.com; 2nd fl, Castle Waikiki Grand, 134 Kapahulu Ave; 10am-2am;) This friendly, open-air bar, Waikiki's main gay venue, is a great place to make new friends, boogie and have a few drinks. Hunker down at the pool table, or gaze at the spectacular vista of Diamond Head. The breezy balcony bar also has views of Queen's Surf Beach, a prime destination for a sun-worshipping LGBTQ crowd.

★ **House Without a Key** LIVE MUSIC, HULA

(808-923-2311; www.halekulani.com; Halekulani, 2199 Kalia Rd; 7am-9pm) Named after a 1925 Charlie Chan novel set in Honolulu, this genteel open-air hotel lounge sprawled beneath a century-old kiawe tree simply has no doors to lock. A sophisticated crowd gathers here for sunset cocktails, Hawaiian music and solo hula dancing by former Miss Hawaii pageant winners. Panoramic ocean views are as intoxicating as the tropical cocktails.

★ **Kuhio Beach Torch Lighting & Hula Show** LIVE MUSIC

(808-922-5331; www.honolulu.gov/moca; Kuhio Beach Park; 6:30-7:30pm Tue, Thu & Sat Feb-Oct, 6-7pm Nov-Jan, weather permitting;) FREE It all begins at the Duke Kahanamoku statue with the sounding of a conch shell and the lighting of torches after sunset. At the nearby hula mound, lay out your beach towel and enjoy the authentic Hawaiian music and dance show. It's full of aloha!

Shopping

★ **Native Books/ Nā Mea Hawaii** BOOKS, GIFTS

(808-596-8885; www.nativebookshawaii.com; Ward Warehouse, 1050 Ala Moana Blvd; 10am-8:30pm Mon-Thu, to 9pm Fri & Sat, to 6pm Sun) So much more than just a bookstore stocking Hawaiiana tomes, CDs and DVDs, this cultural gathering spot also sells beautiful silk-screened fabrics, koa-wood bowls, Hawaiian quilts, fish-hook jewelry and hula supplies. Call or check online for special events, including author readings, live local music and cultural classes.

Bailey's Antiques & Aloha Shirts CLOTHING, ANTIQUES

(http://alohashirts.com; 517 Kapahulu Ave; 10am-6pm) Bailey's has, without a doubt, the finest aloha-shirt collection on O'ahu, possibly the world! Racks are crammed with thousands of collector-worthy vintage aloha shirts in every conceivable color and style, from 1920s kimono-silk classics to 1970s polyester specials to modern offerings. Prices dizzyingly vary from five bucks to several thousand dollars. 'Margaritaville' musician Jimmy Buffett is Bailey's biggest fan.

Kamaka Hawaii MUSIC

(808-531-3165; www.kamakahawaii.com; 550 South St; 8am-4pm Mon-Fri) Skip right by those tacky souvenir shops selling cheap plastic and wooden ukuleles. Kamaka specializes in handcrafted ukuleles made on O'ahu since 1916, with prices starting at around $500. Its signature is an oval-shaped 'pineapple' ukulele, which has a more mellow sound. Call ahead for free 30-minute factory tours, usually starting at 10:30am Tuesday through Friday.

Tin Can Mailman ANTIQUES, BOOKS

(http://tincanmailman.net; 1026 Nu'uanu Ave; 11am-5pm Mon-Thu, to 9pm Fri, to 4pm Sat) If you're a big fan of vintage tiki wares and 20th-century Hawaiiana books, you'll fall in love with this little Chinatown antiques shop. Thoughtfully collected treasures include jewelry and ukuleles, silk aloha shirts, tropical-wood furnishings, vinyl records, rare prints and tourist brochures from the post-WWII tourism boom. No photos allowed.

Information

At Waikiki and University of Hawai'i neighborhood cybercafes, internet costs about $6 to $12 per hour.

Doctors on Call (808-973-5250; www.straubhealth.org; 2nd fl, Rainbow Bazaar, Hilton Hawaiian Village, 2005 Kalia Rd; 8am-4:30pm Mon-Fri) Nonemergency walk-in clinics accept some travel health insurance policies. Also in South Waikiki (808-971-6000; www.straubhealth.org; Sheraton Waikiki, 2255 Kalakaua Ave; open 7am-11pm daily).

Queen's Medical Center (808-691-1000; www.queensmedicalcenter.net; 24hr) O'ahu's biggest, best-equipped hospital has a 24-hour emergency room downtown.

Pearl Harbor

On December 7, 1941, a Japanese attack on Pearl Harbor took 2500 military and civilian lives, destroyed more than 20 ships and fatefully pushed the US into WWII. Today about 1.6 million people a year remember 'a date which will live in infamy' by visiting the USS Arizona Memorial (808-422-3300;

www.nps.gov/valr; 1 Arizona Memorial Pl; boat-tour reservation fee $1.50; ⏲7am-5pm, boat tours 7:30am-3pm) **FREE**. The memorial sits directly over the sunken USS *Arizona*; visitors look down at the shallow wreck, still a tomb for more than 1100 sailors. Departing from the shoreline National Park Service (NPS) visitor center and museum, 75-minute guided tours include a documentary film and boat ride to the memorial. Reserve tours in advance online (www.recreation.gov); otherwise, first-come, first-served tickets may all be gone by mid-morning.

Visit the adjacent **USS Bowfin Submarine Museum & Park** (☎808-423-1341; www.bowfin.org; 11 Arizona Memorial Dr; museum adult/child $5/4, incl self-guided submarine tour $12/5; ⏲7am-5pm, last entry 4:30pm) to clamber down inside the 'Pearl Harbor Avenger' submarine. Shuttle buses head over to the hangar-sized **Pacific Aviation Museum** (☎808-441-1000; www.pacificaviationmuseum.org; 319 Lexington Blvd, Ford Island; adult/child $25/15, incl guided tour $35/25; ⏲8am-5pm, last entry 4pm) and the **Battleship Missouri Memorial** (☎808-455-1600; www.ussmissouri.com; 63 Cowpens St, Ford Island; admission incl tour adult/child from $25/13; ⏲8am-4pm, to 5pm Jun-Aug) on Ford Island. Interestingly, the 'Mighty Mo' hosted the Japanese surrender ending WWII.

From Waikiki and Honolulu, bus 42 stops at Pearl Harbor ($2.50, one hour).

Diamond Head & Southeast O'ahu

O'ahu's southeast coast abounds in dramatic scenery and outdoor activities. For windy 360-degree panoramas, make the 0.8-mile climb up **Diamond Head** (www.hawaiistateparks.org; off Diamond Head Rd btwn Makapu'u & 18th Aves; admission per pedestrian/car $1/5; ⏲6am-6pm, last trail entry 4:30pm; 👪), the 760ft extinct volcanic tuff cone visible from Waikiki.

Go eyeball-to-mask with tropical fish at **Hanauma Bay** (☎808-396-4229; www.honolulu.gov/parks/facility/hanaumabay; adult/child under 13yr $7.50/free; ⏲6am-7pm Wed-Mon Apr-Oct, to 6pm Wed-Mon Nov-Mar), a turquoise bathtub set in a rugged volcanic ring. For the best snorkeling conditions, arrive early. You can rent snorkel gear on-site. Parking costs $1, but when the lot fills, often by mid-morning, all cars are turned away. From Waikiki, take bus 22 ($2.50, 40 minutes, no service Tuesday).

Kailua & Windward Coast

The snaggletoothed Ko'olau Mountains are a scenic backdrop for the entire Windward Coast. From Honolulu, drive the Pali Hwy (Hwy 61) over the mountains, stopping at the windy lookout at **Nu'uanu Pali State Wayside** (www.hawaiistateparks.org; per car $3; ⏲sunrise-sunset).

Beneath the windswept *pali* (cliffs) sits beautiful **Kailua Beach**, O'ahu's top windsurfing spot, while offshore islands are popular with kayakers. Water-sports gear rental, lessons and tours are available from several outfitters, including **Kailua Sailboards & Kayaks** (☎808-262-2555; www.kailuasailboards.com; Kailua Beach Center, 130 Kailua Rd; ⏲8:30am-5pm) near the beach. From Honolulu, take bus 57 ($2.50, 40 minutes).

Other jewel-like Windward Coast beaches include reef-protected **Waimanalo Bay**, cinematic **Kualoa Regional Park** and **Malaekahana State Recreation Area** (www.hawaiistateparks.org; Kamehameha Hwy; ⏲7am-7:45pm Apr-early Sep, to 6:45pm early Sep-Mar) **FREE**, a dramatic stretch near La'ie for swimming, snorkeling and camping, with Moku'auia (Goat Island), a near-shore bird sanctuary. To see where Hurley built his *Lost* golf course and *Jurassic Park* dinosaurs rampaged, tour **Kualoa Ranch** (☎808-237-7321; www.kualoa.com; 49-560 Kamehameha Hwy; tours adult/child from $35/25; ⏲tours 9am-3pm; 👪); reservations advised.

Run by the Mormon church, La'ie's **Polynesian Cultural Center** (PCC; ☎808-293-3333; www.polynesia.com; 55-370 Kamehameha Hwy; adult/child from $50/40; ⏲11:45am-5pm Mon-Sat; 👪) is a tour-bus theme park with villages, performances and luau buffets – only Pearl Harbor draws more visitors. Further northwest in **Kahuku**, roadside food trucks sell plates of fried shrimp for around $13 – expect long lines around lunchtime.

From Honolulu, bus 55 trundles along the Windward Coast to Hale'iwa ($2.50, 2½ hours).

Hale'iwa & North Shore

O'ahu's North Shore is legendary for the massive 30ft winter waves that thunder against its beaches. In the 1950s surfers learned to ride these deadly waves, and today the North Shore hosts the world's premier pro contest, the annual **Triple Crown**

of Surfing (http://vanstriplecrownofsurfing.com; ⌚Nov-Dec).

The gateway to the North Shore, **Hale'iwa** is the region's only real town, along its main drag you'll spot art galleries, shops selling surf gear and bikinis, and rusty pick-up trucks with surfboards tied to the roof. When the surf's up, folks drop everything to hit the waves. They don't have to go far: in-town **Hale'iwa Ali'i Beach Park** (66-167 Hale'iwa Rd) gets towering swells.

Outside town, **Waimea Bay Beach Park** (61-031 Kamehameha Hwy) has a split personality. In summer the water can be as calm as a lake and ideal for swimming and snorkeling; in winter it rips with the island's highest waves. **Sunset Beach Park** (59-104 Kamehameha Hwy) is another classic winter surf spot with powerful breaks. At **'Ehukai Beach Park** (59-337 Ke Nui Rd), the famous Banzai Pipeline breaks over a shallow reef, creating a death-defying ride for pro surfers only. Snorkelers, divers and tide-poolers gather at **Pupukea Beach Park** (59-727 Kamehameha Hwy), a marine-life conservation district. For calmer cove swimming, hit resort-backed **Turtle Bay**.

Team Real Estate (☎808-637-3507; www.teamrealestate.com; North Shore Marketplace, 66-250 Kamehameha Hwy; studio/1/2/3/4 bedrooms from $60/95/150/165/250) rents accommodations, from studio apartments to beachfront luxury homes, along the North Shore; book in advance. Food trucks park alongside the Kamehameha Hwy and on the south side of Hale'iwa town. Opposite Sunset Beach, **Ted's Bakery** (☎808-638-8207; www.tedsbakery.com; 59-024 Kamehameha Hwy; meals $7-16; ⌚7am-8pm; 👪) is renowned for island-style plate lunches and *haupia* (coconut) cream pie. In Hale'iwa town, get your raw-fish fix at **Banzai Sushi Bar** (☎808-637-4404; http://banzaisushibarhawaii.com; 66-246 Kamehameha Hwy, North Shore Marketplace; mains $10-20; ⌚noon-9:30pm) or good-karma, healthy deli dishes at **Beet Box Cafe** (☎808-637-3000; www.thebeetboxcafe.com; Celestial Natural Foods, 66-443 Kamehameha Hwy; mains $7-10; ⌚9am-4pm daily; 🌱) 🍃. Day-trippers queue for shave ice at **Matsumoto's** (☎808-637-4827; www.matsumotoshaveice.com; 66-087 Kamehameha Hwy; snacks $3-5; ⌚9am-6pm; 👪) tin-roofed general store.

From Honolulu, bus 52 runs to Hale'iwa ($2.50, 1¾ hours), from where bus 55 continues along the North Shore and Windward Coast.

HAWAI'I, THE BIG ISLAND

Almost twice the size of all the other Hawaiian Islands combined, the Big Island contains a continent's worth of adventures. Even more thrillingly, it's still growing – Hawai'i's most active volcano, Kilauea, has been erupting here almost nonstop for over three decades. Along with red-hot lava, the Big Island offers summit stargazing, ancient places of refuge, rugged hikes into forgotten valleys and hypnotizing beaches, from bone white strands to black sands cratered with lava-rock tide pools.

Getting There & Around

Mainland and interisland flights arrive at **Kona** (KOA; ☎808-327-9520; http://hawaii.gov/koa; 73-200 Kupipi St) or **Hilo** (ITO; ☎808-961-9300; http://hawaii.gov/ito; 2450 Kekuanaoa St) airports, both of which have car-rental booths and taxis. **Hele-On** (☎808-961-8744; www.heleonbus.org; fare $2) public buses circle the island, but with mostly limited Monday-to-Saturday commuter routes.

Kailua-Kona

With gold-medal beaches heading north and south, and stacks of ocean-centric activities close at hand, this condo-rich area makes a convenient base camp. It's the sort of tourist town where you can sit in open-air cafes and bars and lose count of all the sunburnt vacationers passing by.

Sights & Activities

Near Kailua Pier, **Kamakahonu Beach** (👪) was once Kamehameha the Great's royal retreat and includes the restored **Ahu'ena Heiau** (75-5660 Palani Rd) FREE, the temple where he died in 1819. Meander southeast on Ali'i Dr to **Hulihe'e Palace** (☎808-329-1877; http://daughtersofhawaii.org; 75-5718 Ali'i Dr; adult/child $8/1; ⌚9am-4pm Mon-Sat) 🍃, another retreat for Hawaiian royalty. Its museum is packed with memorabilia and historical artifacts.

A few miles south of town via Ali'i Dr, sun yourself at sparkling **White (Magic) Sands Beach** (La'aloa Beach Park; Ali'i Dr; P), but don't swim in winter when the sand disappears. Further south, Keauhou's **Kahalu'u Beach Park** (👪) affords surfing and snorkeling with sea turtles. Myriad outfitters in Kailua-Kona rent water-sports gear and guide boat tours, including amazing nighttime snorkeling and diving with manta rays; talk to **Jack's Diving Locker** (808-329-7585; www.jacksdivinglocker.com; 75-5813 Ali'i Dr, Coconut Grove Marketplace, Bldg H; 8am-8pm Mon-Sat, to 6pm Sun;) or **Sea Paradise** (808-322-2500; www.seaparadise.com; 78-6831 Ali'i Dr; snorkel cruise adult/child 5-12yr from $72/42).

Sleeping

Koa Wood Hale Inn/Patey's Place HOSTEL $
(808-329-9663; 75-184 Ala Ona Ona St; dm/r with shared bath from $25/55; reception 8am-noon & 5-10pm;) Kailua-Kona's only hostel is a backpacker crash pad, with fan-cooled dorms and private rooms, a common kitchen and the usual crowd of backpackers, misfits and the globally road-weary. As with many hostels, it's as enjoyable as the crowd that is staying there. It's on a residential street within walking distance of Ali'i Dr. No drugs, alcohol or shoes indoors.

Kona Tiki Hotel HOTEL $$
(808-329-1425; www.konatikihotel.com; 75-5968 Ali'i Dr; r $95-179;) You can find affordable oceanfront views at this retro three-story hotel, a quirky, well-kept complex south of downtown Kailua-Kona. The motel-style rooms are forgettably basic (no TVs, phones or air-con), but all have a fridge and enchanting lanai. Book well ahead, because the hotel regularly fills with nostalgic repeat guests. No credit cards.

★ **King Kamehameha's Kona Beach Hotel** HOTEL $$
(808-329-2911, 800-367-2111; www.konabeachhotel.com; 75-5660 Palani Rd; r $140-240, ste from $340;) A prime beachfront location and spiffy renovations are watchwords for the historic 'King Kam,' anchoring the north end of Ali'i Dr. Chic decor by the Courtyard Marriott chain, Herb Kawainui Kane's artwork and Hawaiian historical artifact exhibits in the lobby, a 24-hour fitness center and free wi-fi are all draws at this favorite with both vacationers and business types.

Hale Kona Kai APARTMENT $$
(808-329-6402, 800-421-3696; www.halekonakai-hkk.com; 75-5870 Kahakai Rd; apt $190-215;) All condos overlook crashing surf at this well-managed, oceanfront complex off the busy commercial stretch of Ali'i Dr. The one-bedroom units vary in style, but each has a separate living room, full kitchen and ocean-view lanai. Poolside wi-fi only. Minimum-night stay varies, and prices drop in the low season.

Eating & Drinking

★ **Umeke** HAWAII REGIONAL CUISINE $
(808-329-3050; www.umekespoke808.com; 75-143 Hualalai Rd; mains $5-10; 10am-8pm Mon-Sat;) Umeke takes island-style food to the next level. Local ingredients such as ahi tuna, spicy crab salad and salted Waimea beef are served plate-lunch style with excellent, innovative sides such as seasoned seaweed and cucumber kimchi (along with heaping scoops of rice). It's some of the best value grinds (local food) on the island.

Jackie Rey's Ohana Grill HAWAII REGIONAL CUISINE $$
(808-327-0209; www.jackiereys.com; 75-5995 Kuakini Hwy; mains lunch $10-16, dinner $15-33; 11am-9pm Mon-Fri, 5-9pm Sat & Sun;) Jackie Rey's is a casual, family-owned grill with a delightfully retro-kitsch Hawaii vibe. Haute versions of local grinds include guava-glazed ribs, wasabi-seared ahi and *mochiko* (rice-flour battered) fish with Moloka'i purple sweet potatoes. Locals, tourists, kids, aunties – pretty much everyone loves it. Pop by between 3pm and 5pm on weekdays for half-price *pupu* (snacks or appetizers), tropical cocktails and island microbrews.

Kona Brewing Company AMERICAN $$
(808-334-2739; http://konabrewingco.com; 75-5629 Kuakini Hwy; mains $13-18; 11am-9pm Sun-Thu, to 10pm Fri & Sat;) Expect a madhouse crowd at this sprawling, eco-sustainable brewpub, with tiki-torch-lit outdoor seating and laid-back waitstaff. Everyone's here for the handcrafted 'liquid aloha' made on-site (Pipeline Porter and Castaway IPA are our faves). Pizza toppings verge on gourmet, but crusts can be soggy; BBQ sandwiches and fish tacos are better bets. Enter the parking lot off Kaiwi St.

Kanaka Kava CAFE
(75-5803 Ali'i Dr, Coconut Grove Marketplace; bar 10am-11pm, kitchen to 9:30pm) This tiny, locals' grass-shack hangout is the place to try Hawaiian-style kava (the mildly sedative juice of the *'awa* plant) or organic *noni* (Indian mulberry) juice, another herbal elixir. *Pupu* such as squid luau and ahi *poke* (cubed, marinated raw fish) are just an afterthought. Cash only.

South Kona Coast

Linger along the verdant South Kona coast, with its fragrant coffee farms, ancient Hawaiian sites and characterful small towns. For a window on local life, escape up the cool, misty slopes of Mt Hualalai to **Holualoa** village, packed with artist-owned galleries. **Kimura Lauhala Shop** (808-324-0053; www.holualoahawaii.com/member_sites/kimura.html; Hwy 180, cnr Hualalai Rd; 9am-5pm Mon-Fri, to 4pm Sat) sells traditional Hawaiian pandanus-leaf woven goods.

Off Hwy 11, Napo'opo'o Rd switchbacks down to sparkling, mile-wide **Kealakekua Bay**. Ka'awaloa Cove, where Captain Cook was killed in 1779, is a premier snorkeling destination. You can hike in via a steep 3.6-mile round-trip trail, but it's more fun to kayak – local tour and rental outfitters include **Kona Boys** (808-328-1234; www.konaboys.com; 79-7539 Mamalahoa Hwy; single/double kayak rental per day $54/74, tours $119-169; 7:30am-5pm) and **Aloha Kayak Co** (808-322-2868; www.alohakayak.com; 79-7248 Mamalahoa Hwy; single/double/triple kayak per 24hr $35/60/85, tours $50-130; usually 7:30am-5pm).

In the town of **Captain Cook**, the 1917 **Manago Hotel** (808-323-2642; www.managohotel.com; 82-6151 Mamalahoa Hwy; s/d from $61/64, with shared bath from $35/38;) is a classic experience: stay in the simple, no-frills motel rooms and order hearty island fare in the dining room. **Ka'awa Loa Plantation** (808-323-2686; www.kaawaloaplantation.com; 82-5990 Upper Napo'opo'o Rd; r $129-149, cottages/ste $159/199; @), a stylish garden estate with four-poster beds and a sunset-view lanai, is perfect for romantics. Roadside **Super J's** (808-328-9566; 83-5409 Mamalahoa Hwy; plates $8-12; 10am-6:30pm Mon-Sat) kitchen does right by Hawaiian soul food like *laulau* and *kalua* pork.

South of Kealakekua Bay, **Pu'uhonua o Honaunau National Historical Park** (808-328-2326, 808-328-2288; www.nps.gov/puho; off Hwy 160, Honaunau; 7-day entry per car $5; park 7am-sunset, visitor center 8:30am-4:30pm) is an ancient place of refuge, a sanctuary where *kapu* breakers could have their lives spared. Walk the evocative grounds and inspect a reconstructed temple. Immediately north of the park is a terrific snorkeling spot called **Two-Step**. Afterward refresh yourself with an organic smoothie from **South Kona Fruit Stand** (808-328-8547; www.southkonafruitstand.com; 84-4770 Mamalahoa Hwy; items $3-10; 9am-6pm Mon-Sat, 10am-4pm Sun;).

DON'T MISS

KONA COFFEE FARMS

Gourmet 100% Kona coffee is grown on South Kona's small family-run farms. With harvesting still done by hand, the region has a lost-in-time feel, seemingly little changed from when 19th-century immigrants established themselves here. In the town of Captain Cook, the excellent **Kona Coffee Living History Farm** (808-323-3222; www.konahistorical.org; 82-6199 Mamalahoa Hwy; 1hr tour adult/child 5-12yr $15/5; 10am-2pm Mon-Fri) re-creates Japanese immigrants' rural lifestyle. In November don't miss the 10-day **Kona Coffee Cultural Festival** (www.konacoffeefest.com;).

North Kona & South Kohala Coasts

The lava-blackened coast running north of Kailua-Kona is strung with secluded palm-lined beaches, ancient Hawaiian sites and posh resorts. Standout strands, all off Hwy 19, include dreamy sugar-colored **Kekaha Kai (Kona Coast) State Park** (www.hawaiistateparks.org; 9am-7pm) FREE; black-sand **Kiholo Bay** (www.hawaiistateparks.org; 7am-7pm Apr-1st Mon in Sep, to 6pm 1st Tue in Sep-Mar); windsurfers' **'Anaeho'omalu Beach** (Waikoloa Beach Dr; 6am-8pm;); the **Puako Tide Pools**; resort-backed **Mauna Kea Beach** on crescent-shaped Kauna'oa Bay; and powdery white **Hapuna Beach** (www.hawaiistateparks.org/parks/hawaii; gate 7am-8pm; P).

The Waikaloa resort is home to a Hawaiian **petroglyph preserve** (Waikoloa Beach Dr; 10:30am Thu-Sun) FREE and two shopping malls offering eateries and free entertainment. Nearby, the Mauna Lani resort area also has ancient Hawaiian sites – fishponds, lava tubes and over 3000 rock-art etchings inside the **Puako Petroglyph Preserve**. Nearby, the ecofriendly **Mauna Lani Bay Hotel & Bungalows** (800-367-2323, 808-885-6622; www.maunalani.com; 68-1400 Mauna Lani Dr; r from $390; P) is a full-service oceanfront resort with aloha spirit.

Mauna Kea

When measured from its base beneath the sea, this sacred mountain (13,796ft) is the planet's tallest. Its summit is clustered with world-class astronomical observatories.

Partway up the mountain, **Mauna Kea Visitor Information Station** (MKVIS; ☎808-961-2180; www.ifa.hawaii.edu/info/vis; ⏲9am-10pm) FREE offers educational displays and free stargazing programs nightly. Continuing to the summit for sunset is unforgettable, but it requires either 4WD, a challenging 6-mile (one-way) high-altitude hike (eight-hours plus, round-trip), or a guided van tour with **Hawaii Forest & Trail** (☎800-464-1993, 808-331-8505; www.hawaii-forest.com; tour $199; ⏲tours nightly, weather permitting).

To get here, drive Saddle Rd (Hwy 200), connecting the Kona and Hilo coasts; although scenic, it's accident-prone, especially when it's foggy. From the marked turn-off near mile marker 28, it's another 6 miles uphill along Mauna Kea's paved summit access road to MKVIS. Call ☎808-935-6268 for current weather and road conditions.

Hamakua Coast

The Hamakua Coast ranks among the Big Island's most spectacular scenery. It's a cinematic show of jungly ravines, steep sea cliffs and cascading waterfalls.

Most scenic of all is **Waipi'o Valley**, the largest of seven magnificent amphitheater valleys on Hawai'i's windward side. Hwy 240 dead-ends at a dramatic lookout: the road down is so steep that only 4WDs can make it. It's worth the mile-long hike down – *and* the huff-and-puff return uphill – to meditate on the thunderous black-sand beach, with ribbony waterfalls and taro patches behind.

The valley viewpoint is less than 10 miles from the sleepy ex-sugar-plantation town of **Honoka'a**, speckled with eclectic shops. **Tex Drive-In** (☎808-775-0598; www.texdrivein-hawaii.com; 45-690 Pakalana St; mains $5-10; ⏲6am-8pm) is famous for hot *malasadas*. Outside town, a handful of family-run farms (taste vanilla, coffee and tea) are open for agri-tours.

Heading southeast along Hwy 19, **'Akaka Falls State Park** (www.hawaiistateparks.org; 'Akaka Falls Rd; entry per car/pedestrian $5/1) has two stunning waterfalls easily accessed along a 0.4-mile rainforest loop trail.

Hilo

The Big Island's capital has been dubbed the 'rainiest city in the USA,' a soggy reputation that keeps some tourists away. It's their loss, however: Hilo, with its working-class waterfront and historical buildings downtown, brims with weather-beaten charm. It's a slice of 'real Hawaii.'

Sights & Activities

★'Imiloa Astronomy Center of Hawai'i MUSEUM

(☎808-969-9700; www.imiloahawaii.org; 600 'Imiloa Pl; adult/child 6-17yr $17.50/9.50; ⏲9am-5pm Tue-Sun;) 'Imiloa, which means 'exploring new knowledge,' is a $28-million museum and planetarium complex with a twist: it juxtaposes modern astronomy on Mauna Kea with ancient Polynesian ocean voyaging. Who would've thought that the mythical *kumulipo* (Hawaiian creation story) and the scientific big bang theory have parallels? It's a great family attraction and the natural complement to a summit tour. One planetarium show is included with admission.

Pacific Tsunami Museum MUSEUM

(☎808-935-0926; www.tsunami.org; 130 Kamehameha Ave; adult/child 6-17yr $8/4; ⏲10am-4pm Tue-Sat) You cannot understand Hilo without knowing its history as a two-time tsunami survivor (1946 and 1960). This seemingly modest museum is chock-full of riveting information, including a section on the Japanese tsunami of 2011, which damaged Kona. Allow enough time to experience the multimedia exhibits, including chilling computer simulations and heart-wrenching first-person accounts.

Mokupapapa Discovery Center MUSEUM

(☎808-933-8180; www.papahanaumokuakea.gov/education/center.html; 76 Kamehameha Ave; ⏲9am-4pm Tue-Sat;) FREE The Hawaiian archipelago extends far beyond the eight main islands to the Northwestern Hawaiian Islands, forming a long chain of uninhabited islets and atolls containing the healthiest coral reefs in the USA. Learn more about the islands' pristine ecosystems at this compelling museum, which integrates displays on physical science with the Hawaiian creation chant serving as a sonic backdrop, a reminder of the deep cultural folkways that derived from this unique environmental background.

🛏 Sleeping

Hilo Bay Hostel HOSTEL $

(☑808-933-2771; www.hawaiihostel.net; 101 Waianuenue Ave; dm $29, r with/without bath $79/69; 🛜) Perfectly situated downtown, this well-managed hostel occupies an airy, historic building with hardwood floors, remarkably clean restrooms and a kitchen in which you could cook Thanksgiving dinner.

Dolphin Bay Hotel HOTEL $$

(☑808-935-1466, 877-935-1466; www.dolphinbay-hotel.com; 333 Iliahi St; studio/apt from $129/$169; 🛜) This family-run hotel attracts countless loyal, repeat guests. No surprise. The 18 apartment units, each with full kitchen, are clean and conveniently located within a five-minute walk of downtown Hilo. Enjoy free coffee and locally grown fruit for breakfast amid tropical foliage. For longer stays, ask about the one-bedroom apartments in the **Annex** (per day/week/month $119/763/1600) across the street.

Shipman House B&B B&B $$$

(☑808-934-8002; www.hilo-hawaii.com; 131 Ka'iulani St; r incl breakfast $219-249; 🛜) Staying at the Shipman family's grand Victorian mansion is pricey, albeit peerless in historical significance. Queen Lili'uokalani played the grand piano, and Jack London slept in the guest cottage. Surrounded by museum-quality antiques, three rooms in the main house are sedate and finely (although not luxuriously) furnished. In a separate cottage, two rooms are more casual and private.

🍴 Eating

★Suisan Fish Market SEAFOOD $

(☑808-935-9349; 93 Lihiwai St; poke per pound $13; ⊙8am-6pm Mon-Fri, 8am-4pm Sat, 10am-4pm Sun) For a fantastic variety of *poke* (sold by the pound), you can't beat Suisan, where you know the fish is freshly caught. Honestly, a bowl of fresh takeout *poke* and rice ($5 to $7) is as good as food gets on the Big Island.

Cafe 100 FAST FOOD $

(☑808-935-8683; 969 Kilauea Ave; loco moco $3-5, plate lunches $5-7; ⊙6:15am-8:30pm Mon-Thu, to 9pm Fri, to 7:30pm Sat) Locals love this drive-in for its generous plate lunches and 20 rib-sticking varieties of *loco moco*, including fish and veggie burger options. With a clean seating area and efficient service, it's local fast food at its finest.

★Takenoko Sushi SUSHI $$$

(☑808-933-3939; 681 Manono St; nigiri $2.50-8, chef's choice $40; ⊙11:30am-1:30pm & 5-9pm Thu-Mon) Drop everything and make a reservation at this superb eight-seat sushi bar. Expect top-quality fish (mostly flown fresh from Japan), a spotlessly clean setting, expert sushi chef and gracious service. Each bite is a memorable experience. The three dinner seating times: 5pm, 7pm and 9pm.

☆ Entertainment

Palace Theater THEATER

(☑808-934-7010, box office 808-934-7777; www.hilopalace.com; 38 Haili St) This historic theater is Hilo's cultural crown jewel. Its eclectic programming includes art-house and silent films (accompanied by the house organ), music and dance concerts, Broadway musicals and cultural festivals. On Wednesday morning (11am to noon) it hosts 'Hawai'iana Live' (adult/child $5/free), a touching, small-town intro to Hawaiian culture through storytelling, film, music, *oli* (chant) and hula.

Hawai'i Volcanoes National Park

Even among Hawaii's many natural wonders, this **national park** (HAVO; ☑808-985-6000; www.nps.gov/havo; 7-day entry per car $10; 🚶) stands out: its active volcanoes testify to the ongoing birth of the islands. Mauna Loa (13,677ft) looms like a sleeping giant, while youthful Kilauea has been erupting continually since 1983. But the park contains much more to see, including sun-baked lava deserts, steaming craters, lava tubes and rainforest oases.

By the main entrance, **Kilauea Visitor Center & Museum** (☑808-985-6000; www.nps.gov/havo; Crater Rim Dr; ⊙9am-5pm, film screenings hourly 9am-4pm; 🚶) 🏞 makes a great introduction, with free movies and rangers providing updates on volcanic activity and guided walks. The nearby **Volcano Art Center** (☑808-967-7565; www.volcanoartcenter.org; Crater Rim Dr; ⊙9am-5pm) 🏞 gallery coordinates special events, including Hawaiian hula performances and craft workshops.

Volcanic activity may unexpectedly close roads and trails. When open, the 11-mile **Crater Rim Drive** circles Kilauea Caldera, offering almost nonstop views of the goddess Pele's scorched, smoldering home. At the **Jaggar Museum** (☑808-985-6051; Crater Rim Dr; ⊙10am-9pm daily; 🚶), see working seismographs and a stupendous vista of **Halema'uma'u Crater**. Don't miss **Thurston Lava Tube**, an enormous cave left by flowing lava, or the 4-mile **Kilauea Iki Trail** across a cratered moonscape. The park's equally scenic 19-mile **Chain of Craters Road** leads down to the coast, ending abruptly where modern lava flows have buried its end.

Free, drive-up **Kulanaokuaiki Campground** (www.nps.gov/havo; Hilina Pali Rd) is first-come, first-served (no water). Book ahead for a campsite or an A-frame cabin at **Namakanipaio Campground** (info 808-756-9625, reservations 866-536-7972; www.hawaiivolcanohouse.com; campsites/cabins $15/80) or a crater-view room at the historic **Volcano House** (808-756-9625, 866-536-7972; www.hawaiivolcanohouse.com; Crater Rim Dr; r $185-385;) lodge. The lodge's panoramic-view restaurant serves elegant Hawaii Regional cuisine, while the social lounge has island-style *pupu* with live music.

The nearby village of Volcano hides arty, heart-warming B&Bs and rainforest cottages. With country-cozy rooms, rambling **Chalet Kilauea** (808-937-7786; www.volcanohawaii.com; 19-4178 Wright Rd; r $110-225, r with shared bath $63-75, bungalows $265;) offers accommodations for all budgets. Lovingly restored **Volcano Country Cottages** (808-967-7960; www.volcanocottages.com; 19-3990 Old Volcano Rd; d $105-155;) are stocked with DIY breakfast fixings; the hot tub beckons after dark.

MAUI

According to some, you can't have it all. Perhaps those folks haven't been to Maui, which consistently lands atop travel-magazine reader polls as one of the world's most romantic islands. And why not? With its sandy beaches, deluxe resorts, gourmet cuisine, fantastic luau, whale-watching, surfing, snorkeling and hiking, it leaves most people more in love than when they arrived.

Getting There & Around

US mainland and interisland flights land at **Kahului** (OGG; 808-872-3830; http://hawaii.gov/ogg; 1 Kahului Airport Rd, Kahului). From the airport, bio-diesel **Speedi Shuttle** (877-242-5777; www.speedishuttle.com) charges from $35 to Kihei or $55 to Lahaina.

Maui Bus (808-871-4838; www.mauicounty.gov/bus; per boarding $2) operates several daily routes that stop at some main towns, but exclude many tourist destinations (eg Haleakalā National Park). For your own wheels, **Bio-Beetle** (808-873-6121; www.bio-beetle.com; 55 Amala Pl; per day $50-90, per week $199-399) rents ecofriendly cars and Jeeps.

Lahaina & West Maui

Go for the all-in resort experience in West Maui, with its prime sunset beaches. For historical atmosphere, dining out and entertainment, make time for oceanfront Lahaina, a 19th-century whaling port town.

Sights & Activities

Lahaina's bobbing small-boat harbor is backed by **Banyan Tree Square** (cnr Front & Hotel Sts), home to Hawaii's largest banyan tree. Seaside **Front St** is chock-a-block with art galleries, shops and restaurants. Within walking distance of the waterfront are a handful of historical sites, including a missionary home, a prison built for rowdy sailors and a Chinese temple. Downstairs from a tiny island heritage **museum** (www.lahainarestoration.org; 9am-5pm) FREE, Lahaina's **visitor center** (808-667-9193; www.visitlahaina.com; 648 Wharf St, Old Lahaina Courthouse; 9am-5pm) sells walking-tour maps.

Further north in Kaaanapali, stop by the little **Whalers Village Museum** (808-661-5992; www.whalersvillage.com/museum.htm; 2435 Ka'anapali Pkwy, Whalers Village; adult/child 6-18yr $3/1; 10am-4pm;) to inspect scrimshaw carvings and whistle sea shanties.

For those world-famous beaches, keep heading north: between Ka'anapali and Kapalua, one impossible perfect strand follows another. Three top-ranked gems are **Kahekili Beach**, **Kapalua Beach** and **DT Fleming Beach** (Honoapi'ilani Hwy).

Sleeping

Ka'anapali Beach Hotel RESORT $$
(808-661-0011, reservations 800-262-8450; www.kbhmaui.com; 2525 Ka'anapali Pkwy; r $176-299; P) This welcoming property feels like summer camp – but in the best possible way. The hotel is a little older than its neighbors and the style is more comfy than posh, but it has its own special charms: warm staff, hula shows, an outdoor tiki bar, tidy grounds framed by palm trees and an enviable location on a gorgeous stretch of beach.

Plantation Inn B&B $$
(☎808-667-9225, reservations 800-433-6815; www.theplantationinn.com; 174 Lahainaluna Rd; r/ste incl breakfast from $160/248; P❄📶🏊) Alohas are warm at this genteel oasis, which is set back from the hustle and bustle of Lahaina's waterfront. Inside the stylish lanai rooms, flat-screen TVs and DVD players blend seamlessly with plantation-era decor. Victorian-style standard rooms come with four-poster beds. The highlight? Complimentary breakfast from **Gerard's** (☎808-661-8939; www.gerardsmaui.com) served by the pool – the savory eggs Florentine are delicious.

Eating

Star Noodle ASIAN $$
(☎808-667-5400; www.starnoodle.com; 286 Kupuohi St; shared plates $3-30, mains $7-15; ⏱10:30am-10pm) This hillside hot spot is constantly busy – and rightfully so. Inside this sleek noodle shop, grazers can nibble on an eclectic array of Asian-fusion share plates. Those seeking heartier fare can dive into garlic noodles, kim chi ramen and saimin (local-style noodle soup; Spam included). A central communal table and the chatty bar keep the vibe lively.

Sansei Seafood Restaurant & Sushi Bar JAPANESE $$
(☎808-669-6286; www.sanseihawaii.com; 600 Office Rd; sushi from $3, mains from $16; ⏱dinner 5:15-10pm Sat-Wed, to 1am Thu & Fri) The innovative sushi menu is the draw, but the non-sushi house specials, which often blend Japanese and Pacific Rim flavors, shouldn't be overlooked. The spicy Dungeness crab ramen with truffle broth is a noteworthy prize. Order between 5:15pm and 6pm Tuesday to Saturday and food is discounted by 25%. No reservation? Queue up early for one of the seats at the sushi bar.

★**Mala Ocean Tavern** FUSION $$$
(☎808-667-9394; www.malaoceantavern.com; 1307 Front St; mains brunch $8-15, lunch $15-26, dinner $19-45; ⏱11am-10pm Mon-Fri, 9am-10pm Sat, 9am-9pm Sun) This smart bistro from chef Marl Ellman fuses Mediterranean and Pacific influences with sophisticated flair. Recommended tapas include the Kobe beef cheeseburger slathered with caramelized onions and smoked applewood bacon, and the 'adult' mac 'n' cheese with mushroom cream and three fancy fromages. For main meals, anything with fish is a sure pleaser. At sunset, tiki torches on the waterfront lanai add a romantic touch.

Drinking & Entertainment

★**Old Lahaina Luau** LUAU
(☎808-667-1998; www.oldlahainaluau.com; 1251 Front St; adult/child under 13yr $105/75; ⏱5:15-8:15pm Oct-Mar, 5:45-8:45pm Apr-Sep; 👪) From the warm aloha greeting to the extravagant feast and the mesmerizing hula dances, everything here is first rate. No other luau on Maui comes close to matching this one for its authenticity, presentation and all-around aloha. The feast is outstanding, with high-quality Hawaiian fare that includes *kalua* pork, ahi *poke*, *pulehu* (broiled) steak and an array of salads and sides.

Feast at Lele LUAU
(☎866-244-5353, 808-667-5353; www.feastatlele.com; 505 Front St; adult/child under 13yr $120/90; ⏱from 5:30pm Oct-Jan, 6pm Feb-Apr & Sep, 6:30pm May-Aug) 🌿 Food takes center stage at this intimate Polynesian luau held on the beach. Dance performances in Hawaiian, Maori, Tahitian and Samoan styles are each matched to a food course. With the Hawaiian music, you're served *kalua* pork and *pohole* ferns; with the Maori, duck tenderloin salad with *poha* berry dressing. A true gourmet feast.

Ma'alaea

Ma'alaea Bay runs along the low isthmus separating West Maui's mountains from Haleakalā volcano. Prevailing trade winds funnel between the mountain masses, creating strong gusts and some of Maui's top **windsurfing** conditions.

The USA's largest tropical aquarium, **Maui Ocean Center** (☎808-270-7000; www.mauioceancenter.com; 192 Ma'alaea Rd; adult/child 3-12yr $26/19; ⏱9am-5pm Sep-Jun, to 6pm Jul & Aug; 👪) is a feast for the eyes (but not your stomach!). Dedicated to Hawaii's marine life, exhibits are as close as you can get to underwater critters without donning scuba gear.

Kihei & South Maui

Sun-kissed beaches run for miles and miles south of Kihei. Vacationers frequent this more affordable coast for swimming, snorkeling, kayaking and abundant condos. **South Pacific Kayaks & Outfitters** (☎808-875-4848; www.southpacifickayaks.com; kayak

DON'T MISS

WHALE-WATCHING

Every winter from early November through mid-May, around 10,000 humpback whales crowd the shallow waters along Maui's western shores to breed, calve and nurse. These truly awesome creatures can be easily spotted from shore, particularly when they do acrobatic breaches.

To get a closer look at these majestic mammals, take a whale-watching cruise with the nonprofit **Pacific Whale Foundation** (808-249-8811; www.pacificwhale.org; 300 Ma'alaea Rd, Ma'alaea Harbor Shops; adult/child 7-12yr from $36/19; schedules vary), which sails from Ma'alaea and Lahaina harbors. Kihei's coastal **Hawaiian Islands Humpback Whale National Marine Sanctuary Headquarters** (808-879-2818; http://hawaiihumpbackwhale.noaa.gov; 726 S Kihei Rd; 10am-4pm Mon-Fri;) FREE has educational displays and telescopes for spotting whales from shore.

rental/tour from $45/69; rentals 6:45-11am, reservations 6am-8pm) leads adventurous coastal paddles and teaches surfing and stand-up paddle boarding (SUP).

South of Kihei, **Wailea** boasts million-dollar resorts and a prized stretch of coastline cradling tawny beaches of dreamy perfection. Further south, **Makena** has knockout, mostly undeveloped beaches – particularly **Malu'aka Beach** (aka 'Turtle Town'), **Big Beach** (Oneloa Beach; www.hawaiistateparks.org) and secluded **Little Beach** (Pu'u Ola'i Beach; www.hawaiistateparks.org) – as well as the **'Ahihi-Kina'u Natural Area Reserve**, which protects hidden coves for snorkeling.

To reach **Molokini**, an underwater volcanic crater favored by snorkelers and divers, climb aboard with **Blue Water Rafting** (808-879-7238; www.bluewaterrafting.com; tours $39-135) or **Maui Dreams Dive Co** (808-874-5332; www.mauidreamsdiveco.com; 1993 S Kihei Rd; shore dives $69-99, boat dives $129; 7am-6pm).

Sleeping

Pineapple Inn Maui INN $$

(877-212-6284, 808-298-4403; www.pineappleinnmaui.com; 3170 Akala Dr; r $159-169, cottages $255;) The Pineapple Inn may be the best deal going in South Maui. This inviting boutique property offers style and functionality with a personal touch, and it's less than a mile from the beach. The four rooms, which have ocean-view lanai and private entrances, are as attractive as those at the exclusive resorts, but at a fraction of the cost. Rooms have kitchenettes, and the two-bedroom cottage comes with a full kitchen.

★ **Andaz Maui** RESORT HOTEL $$$

(808-573-1234; www.maui.andaz.hyatt.com; 3550 Wailea Alanui Dr; r/ste from $569/1144;) As you glide down the portico to the chic and airy lobby – complete with lounge chairs placed artfully in the sand – it feels as if you're beginning a grand adventure. The impression continues in the uncluttered rooms: low beds, simple wooden furniture, plantation shutters. It's basecamp for your cushy tropical expedition.

Punahoa CONDO $$$

(808-879-2720; www.punahoabeach.com; 2142 Ili'ili Rd; studios $206, 1 bedroom $279-304, 2 bedrooms $309;) Sip coffee, scan for whales, savor sunsets – it's hard to leave your lanai at Punahoa, a classy boutique condo where every unit has a clear-on ocean view. Tucked on a quiet side street, this 15-unit complex offers privacy and warm alohas. It's also next to a gorgeous strand of sand, Punahoa Beach, that's a favorite of turtles and surfers. Penthouse units have air-conditioning.

Eating & Drinking

Eskimo Candy SEAFOOD $

(808-879-5686; www.eskimocandy.com; 2665 Wai Wai Pl; most mains $8-14; 10:30am-7pm Mon-Fri;) For top-notch fresh seafood served in a casual setting, come to this busy fish market with a takeout counter and a few tables. Fresh-fish fanatics should key in on the *poke* (cubed, marinated raw fish), ahi (yellowfin tuna) wraps and fish tacos. Parents will appreciate the under $8 kids' menu.

★ **Monkeypod Kitchen** PUB FOOD $$$

(808-891-2322; www.monkeypodkitchen.com; 10 Wailea Gateway Pl, Wailea Gateway Center; lunch $14-26, dinner $14-37; 11:30am-11pm, happy hour 3-5:30pm & 9-11pm) The bar scene is convivial at Chef Peter Merriman's newest venture, where the staff, your fellow drinkers and the 36 beers on tap keep the alohas real. But microbrews are not the only draw. Gourmet pub grub takes a delicious Hawaiian spin and is typically sourced from organic and local ingredients, with Maui Cattle burgers and plenty of Upcountry veggies.

Maui Brewing Co BREWERY
(☎808-213-3002; www.mauibrewingco.com; 605 Lipoa Pkwy; ⏲tasting room 11am-10pm) At Maui Brewing's new Kihei taproom, the raucous tasting room is open daily for pints and food-truck fare. Tours (per person $5) of the production facility are currently offered three times daily, with a flight of four beers included in the price. Check the website for tour times; reservations recommended.

Kahului & Wailuku

Maui's two largest communities flow together into one urban sprawl. Kahului has Maui's windsurfing shops, which often give kitesurfing lessons at gusty **Kanaha Beach** near the airport. On the outskirts of Wailuku, **'Iao Valley State Monument** (www.hawaiistateparks.org; admission per car $5; ⏲7am-7pm) centers on picturesque 'Iao Needle, a rock pinnacle jutting above the valley floor.

Step back into the 1920s at **Old Wailuku Inn** (☎808-244-5897, reservations 800-305-4899; www.mauiinn.com; 2199 Kaho'okele St; r $165-195; ❄📶), an elegant period home turned B&B. In downtown Wailuku, international backpackers of all ages bed down at the **Northshore Hostel** (☎866-946-7835, 808-986-8095; www.northshorehostel.com; 2080 W Vineyard St; dm $33, r with shared bath $79-99; ⏲reception 8am-2pm & 5-11pm; ❄@📶).

Near the airport at **Da Kitchen** (☎808-871-7782; www.da-kitchen.com; 425 Koloa St, Triangle Sq; mains $10-26; ⏲11am-9pm Mon-Sat), island-style *'ono grinds* ('good eats') fill plates big enough to feed two, and the *kalua* pork is 'so tender it falls off da bone.' Expect a crowd.

Pa'ia

A former sugar-plantation town, Pai'a is Maui's windsurfing and surfing capital. To gawk at all the action, head to **Ho'okipa Beach** (⏲5:30am-7pm). Nearby, **Mama's Fish House** (☎808-579-8488; www.mamasfishhouse.com; 799 Poho Pl; mains $36-75; ⏲11am-9pm daily) is Maui's most celebrated seafood restaurant, pairing beachside romance with impeccably prepared fish (reservations essential).

Downtown has a vibrant row of restaurants, bars and boutique shops. **Pa'ia Fish Market** (☎808-579-8030; www.paiafishmarket.com; 100 Baldwin Ave; mains $10-21; ⏲11am-9:30pm; 👪) is the go-to place for fish-and-chips. **Flatbread Company** (☎808-579-8989; www.flatbreadcompany.com; 89 Hana Hwy; pizzas $12-22; ⏲11am-10pm) 🍃 crafts wood-oven-fired pizzas topped with local, often-organic ingredients.

Hana

In Hana, many residents are Hawaiian, and they treasure the town's sleepy pace and rural isolation. Families splash and swim at **Hana Beach Park** by the bay and at gorgeous gray-sand **Hamoa Beach** (Haneo'o Rd), south of town.

Can't pull yourself away? Hana's only condo complex, **Hana Kai-Maui** (☎808-248-8426, reservations 800-346-2772; www.hanakaimaui.com; 4865 Uakea Rd; studios/1 bedroom from $210/220; 📶) sits literally a stone's throw from a black-pebble beach. Opposite the ballpark, **Pranee's & Nucharee's Thai Food** (5050 Uakea Rd; meals $10-15; ⏲10am-4pm) is an ever-popular lunch stop.

The road south from Hana is incredibly beautiful, passing organic farms and fruit stands. **'Ohe'o Gulch** is a breathtaking series of wide pools and waterfalls, each tumbling downstream into the one below. It's inside the coastal section of Haleakalā National Park,

DON'T MISS

SCENIC DRIVE: ROAD TO HANA

One of Hawaii's most spectacular scenic drives, the **Hana Highway** (Hwy 360) winds its way past jungle valleys and back out above a rugged coastline. The road is a real cliff-hugger with 54 one-lane bridges and head-spinning views. Gas up and buy snacks and drinks in Pa'ia before starting out.

Waterfall swimming holes and hikes with heart-stopping vistas call out almost nonstop along the highway. Detour for the black-sand beach and rugged coastal hikes at **Wai'anapanapa State Park** (www.hawaiistateparks.org; off Hana Hwy/Hwy 360), and to stroll ethnobotanical **Kahanu Garden** (☎808-248-8912; www.ntbg.org; 650 'Ula'ino Rd; adult/child under 13yr $10/free, guided tour $25/free; ⏲9am-4pm Mon-Fri, to 2pm Sat), surrounding a massive ancient Hawaiian temple.

where hiking trails lead through bamboo groves and there's a primitive campground (no reservations). Bring insect repellent and drinking water!

Haleakalā National Park

No trip to Maui is complete without visiting this sublime **park** (808-572-4400; www.nps.gov/hale; 3-day pass car $10, individual on foot, bicycle or motorcycle $5;). From the towering volcano's rim near the summit, there are dramatic views of a lunarlike surface and multicolored cinder cones. For an unforgettable (and chilly) experience, arrive in time for sunrise – an event Mark Twain called the 'sublimest spectacle' he'd ever seen. Check weather conditions before driving up.

With hiking boots and warm, waterproof clothing layers, you can walk down into the volcano on the Halemau'u or Sliding Sands Trails. Find free drive-up tent camping (no reservations) at Hosmer Grove, near the park entrance. For an unforgettable overnight, rent a **wilderness cabin** (808-572-4400, reservations 877-444-6777; www.recreation.gov; per cabin with 1-12 people $75) inside the volcano's belly; demand is sky-high, so book online up to 180 days in advance.

KAUA'I

Lush Kaua'i has been the darling of honeymooners ever since Elvis tied the knot here in *Blue Hawaii*. Here on Hawaii's oldest main island, nature's fingers have had time to dig deep, carving the Na Pali Coast's fluted cliffs and the tremendous depths of Waimea Canyon. Everyone comes to the 'Garden Isle' for its heavenly temple – the one you'll find outside, that is. And the price of salvation? Just a pair of boots or a paddle and a little sweat.

Getting There & Around

Limited US mainland and frequent interisland flights land at **Lihu'e** (LIH; 808-274-3800; http://hawaii.gov/lih; 3901 Mokulele Loop, Lihu'e), where taxis and major car-rental companies wait. With reduced weekend services, **Kaua'i Bus** (808-246-8110; www.kauai.gov; 3220 Ho'olako St, Lihu'e; 1-way fare adult/senior & child 7-18yr $2/1) reaches many towns, but not all tourist destinations.

Lihu'e

Kaua'i's capital and commercial center is a slow-paced ex-plantation town. The insightful **Kaua'i Museum** (808-245-6931; www.kauaimuseum.org; 4428 Rice St; adult/child $10/2; 10am-5pm Mon-Sat, tours 10:30am Mon-Fri) traces the island's fiercely independent history.

Just minutes from **Kalapaki Beach** (), the **Garden Island Inn** (800-648-0154, 808-245-7227; http://gardenislandinn.com; 3445 Wilcox Rd; r from $115;) offers cheerful rooms. Seafood and *poke* lovers grab island-style takeout plates at **Fish Express** (808-245-9918; 3343 Kuhio Hwy; mains $7-12; 10am-6pm Mon-Sat, grill until 3pm). A young crowd gravitates to **Kauai Beer Company** (808-245-2337; http://kauaibeer.com; 4265 Rice St; 3-10pm Wed-Sat) downtown and the **Feral Pig** (808-246-1100; www.theferalpigkauai.com; Harbor Mall, 3501 Rice St; mains $8-13; 7:30am-9pm Wed-Mon) pub, serving meaty burgers by the beach.

Wailua & Eastside

You wouldn't know it from the strip-mall-lined Kuhio Hwy, but the Eastside offers outdoor fun galore. Family-friendly **Lydgate Beach Park** (www.kamalani.org;) has the island's best playground and safe, protected swimming. The mountains above Wailua are networked with hiking routes, including the **Kuilau Ridge & Moalepe Trails** and **Nounou Mountain Trails**.

Most people come to kayak the **Wailua River**. It was sacred to ancient Hawaiians, who built royal temples along its banks. The easy, bucolic 5-mile paddle upriver – stopping for hikes to waterfall swimming holes – is a popular DIY trip or guided tour (daily except Sunday). Book ahead with **Kayak Wailua** (808-822-3388; www.kayakwailua.com; 4565 Haleilio Rd; 4½hr tours $50) or **Ali'i Kayaks & Water Sports** (877-246-2544, 808-241-7700; www.aliikayaks.com; 174 Wailua Rd; kayak tours $40, SUP rental per 2hr/day $30/45, SUP lessons $60).

Budgeteers will be spoiled by **Rosewood Kaua'i** (808-822-5216; www.rosewoodkauai.com; 872 Kamalu Rd; r with shared bath $75-85;), where tidy private bunkrooms have kitchenettes; the owner also rents beach homes, cottages and condos nearby. Stop by **Kilauea Fish Market** (808-822-3474; 440 Aleka Pl; mains $9-19; 11am-8pm Mon-Sat;) for *broke* *da mout* (delicious) ahi wraps and fresh *poke*, or **Tiki Tacos** (☑808-823-8226; www.facebook.com/tikitacos; Waipouli Complex, 4-961 Kuhio Hwy; mains $5-8; ☺11am-8:30pm) for a 'surfing pig' taco with *kalua* pork and mahimahi.

Hanalei & North Shore

Unspoiled and unhurried, Kaua'i's North Shore features otherworldly scenery and adventures enough for a lifetime.

Detour to **Kilauea Point National Wildlife Refuge** (☑808-828-1413; www.fws.gov/kilaueapoint; Kilauea Rd; adult/child under 16yr $5/free; ☺10am-4pm Tue-Sun, closed federal holidays) ⚑, a thriving seabird sanctuary with a century-old lighthouse. Gentle **'Anini Beach** ('Anini Rd; ♿) has reef-protected waters, easy snorkeling and Kaua'i's best windsurfing.

Known for glamorous resort living (golf, tennis, horse riding, spas etc), **Princeville** provides glorious sunset perches, like at tiny **Pali Ke Kua (Hideaways) Beach**, accessed via the posh **St Regis Princeville** (☑808-826-9644, 866-716-8140; www.stregisprinceville.com; 5520 Ka Haku Rd; d from $500; ❋@ 🛜♨♿) resort.

In Hanalei, the hippie-surfer vibe is palpable. Magnificent **Hanalei Bay** (♿) brings spectacular surfing – it really swells in winter – or take a meditative trip upriver with **Kayak Kaua'i** (☑808-826-1881; http://kayakhanalei.com; Ching Young Village, 5-5070a Kuhio Hwy; kayak/SUP set rental per day from $35/40, 2hr surfing or SUP lessons $90, kayak tours adult/child 5-12yr $105/95; ☺8am-4:30pm). Outfitter **Pedal 'n Paddle** (☑808-826-9069; www.pedalnpaddle.com; Ching Young Village, 5-5190 Kuhio Hwy; ☺9am-6pm) rents kayaks, snorkel and SUP sets, bicycles and camping gear.

Doubters become converts at **Hanalei Taro & Juice Co** (☑808-826-1059; www.hanaleitaro.com; 5-5070a Kuhio Hwy; items $1.50-6, meals $9-11; ☺11am-3pm Mon-Sat; ☑♿) ⚑, where taro-based smoothies and Hawaiian plate lunches are farm fresh. Trendy **BarAcuda Tapas & Wine** (☑808-826-7081; www.restaurantbaracuda.com; Hanalei Center, 5-5161 Kuhio Hwy; shared plates $7-26; ☺5:30-10pm, kitchen closes at 9:30pm) ⚑ features local produce like North Shore honeycomb and goat cheese. Sport your vintage aloha shirt at **Tahiti Nui** (☑808-826-6277; http://thenui.com; 5-5134 Kuhio Hwy; ☺11am-10pm Sun-Thu, to midnight Fri & Sat), a tiki dive bar with live music and a weekly luau night (make reservations).

WORTH A TRIP

NA PALI COAST

Hikers on Kaua'i shouldn't miss the challenging but oh-so-rewarding 11-mile **Kalalau Trail**, which runs along the dizzying Na Pali cliffs and through lush valleys inside **Na Pali Coast Wilderness State Park**. To hike beyond Hanakoa Valley and for backcountry camping, reserve permits ($20 per person, per night) online up to a year in advance with Hawaii's **Division of State Parks** (☑808-274-3444; www.hawaiistateparks.org; Room 306, 3060 Eiwa St, Lihu'e; ☺8am-3:30pm Mon-Fri).

Hard-core paddlers can admire the same scenery from the sea during a strenuous 17-mile Na Pali Coast kayak tour (from $225). Taking all day, it's only possible between April and October. **Na Pali Kayak** (☑808-826-6900; www.napalikayak.com; 5-5075 Kuhio Hwy, Hanalei) is an experienced outfitter.

Near the western end of Hwy 560 is **Makua (Tunnels) Beach**, where snorkelers splash in summer. Nearby, **Limahuli Garden** (☑808-826-1053; http://ntbg.org/gardens/limahuli.php; 5-8291 Kuhio Hwy; self-guided/guided tours $20/40; ☺9:30am-4pm Tue-Sat, guided tours 10am; ♿) ⚑ conserves Hawaii's native botanical wealth. At **Ha'ena Beach Park**, camping is allowed nightly (except Monday) with an advance permit from Kaua'i's **Division of Parks & Recreation** (☑808-241-4463; www.kauai.gov; Suite 105, Lihu'e Civic Center, 4444 Rice St, Lihu'e; ☺8am-4pm Mon-Fri). Time-warped **Hanalei Colony Resort** (☑808-826-6235, 800-628-3004; www.hcr.com; 5-7130 Kuhio Hwy; 2-bedroom ste from $255; @🛜♨) may have dated decor, but peaceful condos (no TVs or phones) are in an idyllic waterfront location.

Po'ipu & South Shore

Sunny, family-friendly Po'ipu fronts a fabulous run of sandy beaches. It's good for swimming and snorkeling year-round and summer surfing. Tour the stunning **Allerton Garden** (☑808-742-2623; www.ntbg.org; 4425 Lawa'i Rd; 2½hr tours adult/child 6-12yr $40/15; ☺visitor center 8:30am-5pm, tours by reservation only) or admire windswept cliffs, tide pools and pristine beaches while hiking the 4-mile

Maha'ulepu Heritage Trail (www.hikemahaulepu.org).

Po'ipu is awash with resorts, condos and vacation rentals; browse listings with **Parrish Collection Kaua'i** (808-742-2000, 800-325-5701; www.parrishkauai.com; 3176 Po'ipu Rd, Koloa) and **Po'ipu Connection Realty** (808-742-2233, 800-742-2260; www.poipuconnection.com; 5488 Koloa Rd, Koloa). Get magnificent valley views from **Marjorie's Kaua'i Inn** (800-717-8838, 808-332-8838; www.marjorieskauaiinn.com; Hailima St, Lawa'i; r $150-215;), where tropical rooms have kitchenettes.

At dinnertime, head to chef-owned **Josselin's Tapas Bar & Grill** (808-742-7117; www.josselins.com; Shops at Kukui'ula, 2829 Ala Kalanikaumaka St; shared plates $11-32; 5-9pm or 10pm) for Asian fusion cuisine and lychee sangria. Locals line up at **Koloa Fish Market** (808-742-6199; 5482 Koloa Rd; meals $7-11; 10am-6pm Mon-Fri, to 5pm Sat) for outstanding *poke,* Japanese-inspired bento boxes and island-style plate lunches to go.

Waimea & Westside

The top destinations here are **Waimea Canyon** (www.hawaiistateparks.org;) – the 'Grand Canyon of the Pacific' with cascading waterfalls – and adjacent **Koke'e State Park** (www.hawaiistateparks.org;) FREE. Both feature breathtaking views and leg-stretching clifftop hikes, like Koke'e's **Awa'awapuhi & Nu'alolo Trails**. Waimea Canyon Dr (Hwy 550) is peppered with scenic lookouts. Pick up trail information at the pint-sized **Koke'e Museum** (808-335-9975; www.kokee.org; donation $1; 9am-4:30pm;) .

Back downhill by the coast in quaint **Hanapepe** town, false-fronted historical buildings hide art galleries, boutique shops and cafes. Outside town, **Salt Pond Beach Park** () is perfect for swimming with kids; camping is allowed nightly (except Tuesday) with an advance permit from Kaua'i's Division of Parks & Recreation (p1115). Nearby **Port Allen** offers snorkeling and whale-watching cruises and Zodiac tours of the Na Pali Coast.

Understand USA

USA Today

A historic ruling by the Supreme Court heralded a new era of equality for the world's largest democracy – this on the heels of another high court ruling on health care, a pivotal legacy of President Obama. Other hot topics of the day are the hopeless regularity of mass shootings, greener lifestyles and the ever-increasing allure of city life – resulting in a lack of affordable housing, among other things.

Best in Print

On the Road (1957) Jack Kerouac on post-WWII America.

The Great Gatsby (1925) F Scott Fitzgerald's powerful Jazz Age novel.

Beloved (1987) Toni Morrison's searing Pulitzer Prize–winning novel set during the post–Civil War years.

Huckleberry Finn (1884) Mark Twain's moving tale of journey and self-discovery.

Best on Film

Singin' in the Rain (1952) Among the best in the era of musicals, with an exuberant Gene Kelly and a timeless score.

Annie Hall (1977) Woody Allen's brilliant romantic comedy, with New York City playing a starring role.

North by Northwest (1959) Alfred Hitchcock thriller with Cary Grant on the run across America.

Godfather (1972–90) Famed trilogy that looks at American society through immigrants and organized crime.

A Rainbow Nation

No one who witnessed the Stonewall Riots – which sparked the gay liberation movement in 1969 – could have imagined that he or she would live to see the day when gay marriage would become legal in the USA. Yet on June 26, 2015, that's exactly what happened when the US Supreme Court ruled that all states must recognize same-sex marriage licenses. The historic ruling was the culmination of a long, legal battle by gay rights advocates, and there was much euphoria on the streets – especially since the ruling coincided with Pride events happening across the nation. Major sites like the Empire State Building, Cinderella's Castle at Disney World – and even the White House – lit up their facades in rainbow colors, in proud support of the ruling. A Gallup poll after the verdict found that nearly 60% of Americans supported same-sex marriage, with some eight in 10 young adults favoring gay marriage – clearly a sign that the winds of change are sweeping across the US.

Health Care for All

The ruling on same-sex marriages came just days after another important ruling. This one related to the Affordable Care Act (ACA), President Obama's program to extend health care through subsidies to millions of uninsured Americans. The court upheld key provisions of the law (the second time the Supreme Court had ruled on Obamacare), though the future of the ACA remains far from certain. Since the law's implementation the House and Senate had tried (unsuccessfully) to repeal Obamacare more than 50 times.

Despite congressional obstructionism, the program has been a success, allowing over 16 million uninsured Americans to obtain coverage. Republican critics of the program claim Obamacare would kill jobs and cripple the US economy – a claim Obama refuted, saying that instead of hurting the economy, the ACA had actually provided a boost. Aside from helping the insured, the ACA has saved hospitals money. In 2015 Health and Human Services Secretary Sylvia Burwell announced that hospitals had saved $7.4 billion in uncompensated care costs during the previous year owing to patient enrolment in Obamacare health insurance exchanges and Medicaid.

Changing Cityscapes

Cities are booming in America, growing at a faster rate than the rest of the country. Far from being the burned-out hulls of decades past, American cities are safer, and have wide-ranging appeal (in the realm of culture, food, nightlife, liveability). Yet with more people moving from the suburbs and the exurbs to city centers, this has brought many challenges – particularly in the realm of housing and transportation. Creating affordable housing is one of the biggest challenges facing American cities. In many places rent and housing prices have skyrocketed. In particular, middle-class families – whose incomes aren't rising fast enough to meet the price increases – are feeling the pinch. Nationally, more than half of all renters are spending over 30% of their income on rent. And low-income families spend more than half their income on rent. To meet the growing demand, housing units are being built across the country, though often these new units cater to the luxury market, doing little to exacerbate demand. Some mayors, like Bill de Blasio of New York City and Ed Lee of San Francisco, have launched ambitious programs to create more affordable housing. De Blasio stated that unless New York acted boldly the city risked becoming a gated community of exclusivity rather than opportunity. The same could be said for many American cities.

A Divided Nation

Speaking of exclusivity, the income gap continues to widen in the US. The top 1% of the population earns 20% of the income (up from 9% in 1976). Meanwhile, the poor are getting poorer: the median wage earner took home 11% less than in 1999. Unfortunately, it isn't just the income gap that is widening. Rich people in America are living longer than poor people: the wealthy lived 2.7 years longer than the poor in the 1980s, today this has extended to 4.5 years. And their children are outpacing their peers by bigger margins (the gap in test scores between rich and poor is over 30% wider than it was two decades ago). The challenge: how to fix the problem. The obvious solution – raising taxes on the rich – is considered political suicide, and raising minimum wage, strengthening unions and creating universal pre-kindergarten programs has received little traction in the current political climate.

POPULATION: **320 MILLION**

GDP: **$17.5 TRILLION**

GDP PER CAPITA: **$55,000**

UNEMPLOYMENT: **5.5%**

POPULATION BELOW POVERTY LINE: **15.1%**

ANNUAL INFLATION: **2%**

if USA were 100 people

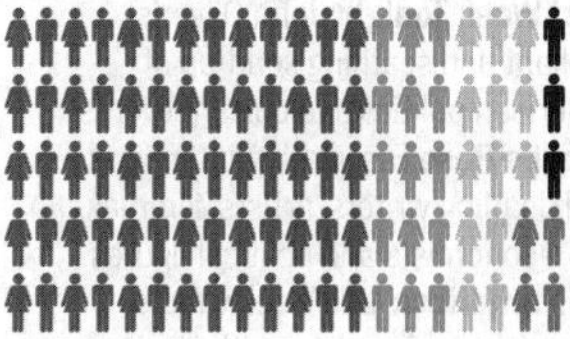

65 would be white
15 would be Hispanic
13 would be African American
4 would be Asian American
3 would be other

belief systems

(% of population)

population per sq mile

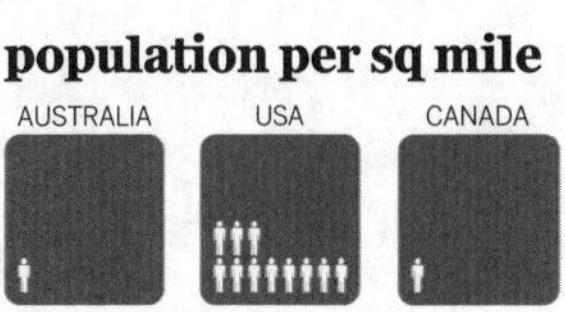

Greenest Cities

Portland, OR Huge parks, 200 miles of bike lanes, a walkable city center and an eco-mad populace.

San Francisco, CA Abundant green markets, organic restaurants and ecofriendly buildings (even the ballpark is solar-powered). Biking, walking and public transit rules.

New York City, NY Bike-sharing programs, waterfront parks and green spaces, with 100,000 trees planted each year. Plus no need for a car – ever.

Best Media

Last Week Tonight John Oliver's brilliant and scathing send-up of American politics and current events.

Charlie Rose Fascinating interviews with leading writers, artists, filmmakers, economists and political figures.

This American Life Weekly radio show (available online) with stories ranging from the humorous to the thought-provoking.

Myths Debunked

Urban residents are sophisticated and rural folk hillbillies You'll find foodies in Appalachia and rednecks in Chicago.

Americans are monolingual Spanish is commonly spoken across the United States.

Greener Futures

With more people moving to urban areas, cities have also had to grapple with transportation. Building more roads has never helped alleviate traffic congestion – as engineers have known since the 1960s. The answer has been greater investment in public transit. Cities, once deeply married to the automobile – Houston, we're looking at you – have greatly expanded public transport options, with new light rail lines, express bus lanes and dedicated bus lanes. Bike-sharing programs have also exploded across the country, with more than 50 cities offering easy rental (usually by the day and week) for residents and visitors. The benefits – fewer cars on the streets, a bit of exercise for commuters, less carbon in the atmosphere – are obvious, though critics worry about injuries (since no bike-sharing programs provide helmets), as well as the long-term financial viability of these often expensive programs.

Gun Crazy

In the USA there have been scores of mass shootings in the past 30 years. The most recent happened in 2015, when a 21-year-old man attended a bible study session at a historic African American–Baptist church in Charleston and murdered nine people, including the pastor. Other devastating incidents include the 2012 Newtown, CT, massacre, where a heavily armed 20-year-old man slaughtered 20 young children and six adults. On average, 32 Americans are murdered by guns every day and another 140 wounded. Add to this accidental shootings and suicides and some 34,000 Americans are killed each year by guns. Despite evidence (including a 2013 study published in the *American Journal of Medicine*) that more guns equals more murders, and the comparatively low rates of death by firearms in countries with strict gun laws, American legislators have been unwilling to enact even modest gun control laws. After the racially motivated mass shooting in Charleston, Obama seemed resigned to the idea that nothing would ever change. The reason in part: gun lobbies such as the National Rifle Association (NRA) wield incredible power, contributing over $35 million annually to state and national political campaigns. But Americans are also enamored of their guns. In a recent Pew Research poll 52% of Americans said it was more important to protect the right of Americans to own guns compared to 46% who said it was more important to control gun ownership (ie have stricter hand-gun laws).

History

From its early days as an English colony to its rise to number one on the world stage in the 20th century, American history has been anything but dull. War against the British, westward expansion, slavery and its abolishment, Civil War and Reconstruction, the Great Depression, the post-war boom and more recent conflicts in the 21st century – they've all played a part in shaping the nation's complicated identity.

Turtle Island

According to oral traditions and sacred myths, indigenous peoples have always lived on the North American continent, which some called Turtle Island. When Europeans arrived, approximately two to 18 million Native American people occupied the turtle's back north of present-day Mexico and spoke more than 300 languages.

Among North America's most significant prehistoric cultures were the Mound Builders, who inhabited the Ohio and Mississippi River valleys from around 3000 BC to AD 1300. In Illinois, Cahokia was once a metropolis of 20,000 people, the largest in pre-Columbian North America.

In the Southwest, Ancestral Puebloans occupied the Colorado Plateau from around AD 100 to AD 1300, until warfare, drought and scarcity of resources likely drove them out. You can still see their cliff dwellings at Colorado's Mesa Verde National Park and desert adobe pueblos at New Mexico's Chaco Culture National Historic Park.

It was the Great Plains cultures that came to epitomize 'Indians' in the popular American imagination, in part because these tribal peoples put up the longest fight against the USA's westward expansion. Oklahoma is rich in sites that interpret Native American life before Europeans arrived, including at Anadarko and along the Trail of Tears.

In 1502 Italian explorer Amerigo Vespucci used the term Mundus Novus (New World) to describe his discoveries. His reward? In 1507 new maps labeled the western hemisphere 'America.'

Enter the Europeans

In 1492 Italian explorer Christopher Columbus, backed by Spain, voyaged west – looking for the East Indies. He found the Bahamas. With visions of gold, Spanish explorers quickly followed: Cortés conquered much of today's Mexico; Pizarro conquered Peru; Ponce de León wandered through

TIMELINE

20,000–40,000 BC

The first peoples to the Americas arrive from Central Asia by migrating over a wide land bridge between Siberia and Alaska (when sea levels were lower than today).

8000 BC

Widespread extinction of ice-age mammals including the woolly mammoth, due to cooperative hunting by humans and a warming climate. Indigenous peoples begin hunting smaller game and gathering native plants.

7000 BC–AD 100

'Archaic period' marked by nomadic hunter-gatherer lifestyle. By the end of this period, corn, beans and squash (the agricultural 'three sisters') and permanent settlements are well established.

Florida looking for the fountain of youth. Not to be left out, the French explored Canada and the Midwest, while the Dutch and English cruised North America's eastern seaboard.

European explorers left in their wake diseases to which indigenous peoples had no immunity. More than any other factor – war, slavery or famine – disease epidemics devastated Native populations by between 50% and 90%. By the 17th century, indigenous North Americans numbered only about a million, and many of their once-thriving societies were in turmoil and transition.

The People: Indians of the American Southwest (1993), by Stephen Trimble, is a diverse account of indigenous history and contemporary culture as related by Native Americans themselves.

In 1607 English noblemen established North America's first permanent European settlement in Jamestown. Earlier settlements had ended badly, and Jamestown almost did too: the English chose a swamp, planted their crops late and died from disease and starvation. Some despairing colonists ran off to live with the local tribes, who provided the settlement with enough aid to survive.

For Jamestown and America, 1619 proved a pivotal year: the colony established the House of Burgesses, a representative assembly of citizens to decide local laws, and it received its first boatload of 20 African slaves.

The next year was equally momentous, as a group of radically religious Puritans pulled ashore at what would become Plymouth, MA. The Pilgrims were escaping religious persecution under the 'corrupt' Church of England, and in the New World they saw a divine opportunity to create a new society that would be a religious and moral beacon. The Pilgrims signed a 'Mayflower Compact,' one of the seminal texts of American democracy, to govern themselves by consensus.

Colonial Sights

- *Williamsburg, Virginia*
- *Jamestown, Virginia*
- *Plymouth, Massachusetts*
- *North End, Boston*
- *Philadelphia, Pennsylvania*
- *Annapolis, Maryland*
- *Charleston, South Carolina*

Capitalism & Colonialism

For the next two centuries, European powers competed for position and territory in the New World, extending European politics into the Americas. As Britain's Royal Navy came to rule Atlantic seas, England increasingly profited from its colonies and eagerly consumed the fruits of their labors – sweet tobacco from Virginia, sugar and coffee from the Caribbean.

Over the 17th and 18th centuries, slavery in America was slowly legalized into a formal institution to support this plantation economy. By 1800, one out of every five persons was a slave.

Meanwhile, Britain mostly left the American colonists to govern themselves. Town meetings and representative assemblies, in which local citizens (that is, white men with property) debated community problems and voted on laws and taxes, became common.

However, by the end of the Seven Years' War in 1763, Britain was feeling the strains of running an empire: it had been fighting France for a

1492

Italian explorer Christopher Columbus 'discovers' America, making three voyages throughout the Caribbean. He names the indigenous people 'Indians,' mistakenly thinking he had reached the Indies.

1607

The English found the first English colony, the Jamestown settlement on marshland in present-day Virginia. The first few years are hard, with many dying from sickness and starvation.

1620

The Mayflower lands at Plymouth with 102 English Pilgrims, who have come to the New World to escape religious persecution. The Wampanoag tribe saves them from starvation.

1675

For decades, the Pilgrims and local tribes live fairly cooperatively, but deadly conflict erupts in 1675. King Philip's War lasts 14 months and kills over 5000 people (mostly Native Americans).

century and had colonies scattered all over the world. It was time to clean up bureaucracies and share financial burdens.

The colonies, however, resented English taxes and policies. Public outrage soon culminated in the 1776 Declaration of Independence. With this document, the American colonists took many of the Enlightenment ideas then circulating worldwide – of individualism, equality and freedom; of John Locke's 'natural rights' of life, liberty and property – and fashioned a new type of government to put them into practice.

Frustrations came to a head with the Boston Tea Party in 1773, after which Britain clamped down hard, shutting Boston's harbor and increasing its military presence. In 1774 representatives from 12 colonies convened the First Continental Congress in Philadelphia's Independence Hall to air complaints and prepare for the inevitable war ahead.

The HBO miniseries *John Adams* (2008) is a riveting story, told from all sides, of the years when the American Revolution hung in the balance and fate could have swung either way.

Revolution & the Republic

In April 1775, British troops skirmished with armed colonists in Massachusetts, and the Revolutionary War began. George Washington, a wealthy Virginia farmer, was chosen to lead the American army. Trouble was, Washington lacked gunpowder and money (the colonists resisted taxes even for their own military), and his troops were a motley collection of poorly armed farmers, hunters and merchants, who regularly quit and returned to their farms due to lack of pay. On the other side, the British 'Redcoats' represented the world's most powerful military. The inexperienced General Washington had to improvise constantly, sometimes wisely retreating, sometimes engaging in 'ungentlemanly' sneak attacks. During the winter of 1777–78, the American army nearly starved at Valley Forge.

Meanwhile, the Second Continental Congress tried to articulate what exactly they were fighting for. In January 1776, Thomas Paine published the wildly popular *Common Sense,* which passionately argued for independence from England. Soon, independence seemed not just logical, but noble and necessary, and on July 4, 1776, the Declaration of Independence was finalized and signed. Largely written by Thomas Jefferson, it elevated the 13 colonies' particular gripes against the monarchy into a universal declaration of individual rights and republican government.

However, to succeed on the battlefield, General Washington needed help, not just patriotic sentiment. In 1778 Benjamin Franklin persuaded France (always eager to trouble England) to ally with the revolutionaries, and they provided the troops, materials and sea power that helped win the war. The British surrendered at Yorktown, VA, in 1781, and two years later the Treaty of Paris formally recognized the 'United States of America.'

The New World (2005), directed by Terrence Malick, is a brutal but passionate film that retells the tragic story of the Jamestown colony and the pivotal peacemaking role of Pocahontas, a Powhatan chief's daughter.

1756–63

In the Seven Years' War (or the 'French and Indian War'), France loses to England and withdraws from Canada. Britain now controls most territory east of the Mississippi River.

1773

To protest a British tax on tea, Bostonians dress as Mohawks, board East India Company ships and toss their tea overboard during what would be named the Boston Tea Party.

1775

Paul Revere rides from Boston to warn colonial 'Minutemen' that the British are coming. The next day, 'the shot heard round the world' is fired at Lexington, starting the Revolutionary War.

1776

On July 4, the colonies sign the Declaration of Independence. Famous figures who helped create this document include John Hancock, Samuel Adams, John Adams, Benjamin Franklin and Thomas Jefferson.

At first, the nation's loose confederation of fractious, squabbling states was hardly 'united.' So the founders gathered again in Philadelphia, and in 1787 drafted a new-and-improved Constitution: the US government was given a stronger federal center, with checks and balances between its three major branches; and to guard against the abuse of centralized power, a citizen's Bill of Rights was approved in 1791.

With the Constitution, the scope of the American Revolution solidified to a radical change in government, and the preservation of the economic and social status quos. Rich landholders kept their property, which included their slaves; Native Americans were excluded from the nation; and women were excluded from politics. These blatant discrepancies and injustices, which were widely noted, were the results of both pragmatic compromise (eg to get slave-dependent Southern states to agree) and also widespread beliefs in the essential rightness of things as they were.

According to legend, George Washington was so honest that after chopping down his father's cherry tree when he was just a child, he admitted, 'I cannot tell a lie. I did it with my little hatchet.'

Westward, Ho!

As the 19th century dawned on the young nation, optimism was the mood of the day. With the invention of the cotton gin in 1793 – followed by threshers, reapers, mowers and, later, combines – agriculture was industrialized, and US commerce surged. The 1803 Louisiana Purchase doubled US territory, and expansion west of the Appalachian Mountains began in earnest.

Relations between the US and Britain – despite lively trade – remained tense, and in 1812 the US declared war on England again. The two-year conflict ended without much gain by either side, although the British abandoned their forts, and the US vowed to avoid Europe's 'entangling alliances.'

In the 1830s and 1840s, with growing nationalist fervor and dreams of continental expansion, many Americans came to believe it was 'Manifest Destiny' that all the land should be theirs. The 1830 Indian Removal Act aimed to clear one obstacle, while the building of the railroads cleared another hurdle, linking Midwestern farmers with East Coast markets.

You can follow the Lewis and Clark expedition on its extraordinary journey west to the Pacific and back again online at www.pbs.org/lewisandclark, which features historical maps, photo albums and journal excerpts.

In 1836 a group of Texans fomented a revolution against Mexico. (Remember the Alamo?) Ten years later, the US annexed the Texas Republic, and when Mexico resisted, the US waged war for it – and while they were at it, took California too. In 1848 Mexico was soundly defeated and ceded this territory to the US. This completed the USA's continental expansion.

By a remarkable coincidence, only days after the 1848 treaty with Mexico was signed, gold was discovered in California. By 1849 surging rivers of wagon trains were creaking west filled with miners, pioneers, entrepreneurs, immigrants, outlaws and prostitutes, all seeking their fortunes. This made for exciting, legendary times, but throughout loomed a troubling question: as new states joined the USA, would they be slave states or free states? The nation's future depended on the answer.

1787

The Constitutional Convention in Philadelphia draws up the US Constitution. Power is balanced between the presidency, Congress and judiciary.

1791

Bill of Rights adopted as constitutional amendments outlining citizens' rights, including free speech, assembly, religion and the press; the right to bear arms; and prohibition of 'cruel and unusual punishments.'

1803

France's Napoleon sells the Louisiana Territory to the US for just $15 million, thereby extending the boundaries of the new nation from the Mississippi River to the Rocky Mountains.

1803–6

President Thomas Jefferson sends Meriwether Lewis and William Clark west. Guided by the Shoshone tribeswoman Sacagawea, they trailblaze from St Louis, MO, to the Pacific Ocean and back.

The Civil War

The US Constitution hadn't ended slavery, but it had given Congress the power to approve (or not) slavery in new states. Public debates raged constantly over the expansion of slavery, particularly since this shaped the balance of power between the industrial North and the agrarian South.

Since the founding, Southern politicians had dominated government and defended slavery as 'natural and normal,' which an 1856 *New York Times* editorial called 'insanity.' The Southern proslavery lobby enraged Northern abolitionists. But even many Northern politicians feared that ending slavery would be ruinous. Limit slavery, they reasoned, and in the competition with industry and free labor, slavery would wither without inciting a violent slave revolt – a constantly feared possibility. Indeed, in 1859 radical abolitionist John Brown tried unsuccessfully to spark just that at Harpers Ferry.

James McPherson is a preeminent Civil War historian, and his Pulitzer Prize–winning *Battle Cry of Freedom* (1988) somehow gets the whole heartbreaking saga between two covers.

The economics of slavery were undeniable. In 1860 there were more than four million slaves in the US, most held by Southern planters – who grew 75% of the world's cotton, accounting for more than half of US exports. Thus, the Southern economy supported the nation's economy, and it required slaves. The 1860 presidential election became a referendum on this issue, and the election was won by a young politician who favored limiting slavery: Abraham Lincoln.

In the South, even the threat of federal limits was too onerous to abide, and as President Lincoln took office, 11 states eventually seceded from the union and formed the Confederate States of America. Lincoln faced the nation's greatest moment of crisis. He had two choices: let the Southern states secede and dissolve the union or wage war to keep the union intact. He chose the latter, and war soon erupted.

It began in April 1861, when the Confederacy attacked Fort Sumter in Charleston, SC, and raged on for the next four years – in the most gruesome combat the world had ever known until that time. By the end, more than 600,000 soldiers, nearly an entire generation of young men, were dead; Southern plantations and cities (most notably Atlanta) lay

TECUMSEH'S CURSE

According to legend, a curse spanning more than 100 years hung over every president elected in a year ending in zero (every 20 years). It all began with future president William Henry Harrison, who in 1811 led a battle against the Shawnee, which devastated the hopes of Tecumseh (Native American chief of the Shawnee) for a pan-Indian alliance. After the bitter defeat, Tecumseh placed a curse, uttering something along the lines of 'Harrison will die, and after him every great chief chosen 20 years thereafter will also die. And when each dies, let everyone remember the death of my people.'

1812

The War of 1812 begins with battles against the British and Native Americans in the Great Lakes region. Even after the 1815 Treaty of Ghent, fighting continues along Gulf Coast.

1823

President Monroe articulates the Monroe Doctrine, seeking to end European military interventions in America. Roosevelt later extends it to justify US interventions in Latin America.

1849

After the 1848 discovery of gold near Sacramento, an epic cross-country gold rush sees 60,000 'forty-niners' flock to California's Mother Lode. San Francisco's population explodes from 850 to 25,000.

1861–65

American Civil War erupts between North and South (delineated by the Mason-Dixon line). The war's end on April 9, 1865, is marred by President Lincoln's assassination five days later.

sacked and burned. The North's industrial might provided an advantage, but its victory was not preordained; it unfolded, battle by bloody battle.

As fighting progressed, Lincoln recognized that if the war didn't end slavery outright, victory would be pointless. In 1863 his Emancipation Proclamation expanded the war's aims and freed all slaves. In April 1865, Confederate General Robert E Lee surrendered to Union General Ulysses S Grant in Appomattox, VA. The Union had been preserved, but at a staggering cost.

This Republic of Suffering (2008), by historian Drew Gilpin Faust, is a poignant look at the Civil War through the eyes of loved ones left behind by fallen soldiers on both sides of the Mason-Dixon line.

The Great Depression, the New Deal & World War II

In October 1929, investors, worried over a gloomy global economy, started selling stocks, and seeing the selling, everyone panicked until they had sold everything. The stock market crashed, and the US economy collapsed like a house of cards.

Thus began the Great Depression. Frightened banks called in their dodgy loans, people couldn't pay, and the banks folded. Millions lost their homes, farms, businesses and savings, and as much as 50% of the American workforce became unemployed.

In 1932 Democrat Franklin D Roosevelt was elected president on the promise of a 'New Deal' to rescue the US from its crisis, which he did with resounding success. When war once again broke out in Europe in 1939, the isolationist mood in America was as strong as ever. However, the extremely popular President Roosevelt, elected to an unprecedented third term in 1940, understood that the US couldn't sit by and allow victory for fascist, totalitarian regimes. Roosevelt sent aid to Britain and persuaded a skittish Congress to go along with it.

Then, on December 7, 1941, Japan launched a surprise attack on Hawaii's Pearl Harbor, killing more than 2000 Americans and sinking several battleships. As US isolationism transformed overnight into outrage, Roosevelt suddenly had the support he needed. Germany also declared war on the US, and America joined the Allied fight against Hitler and the Axis powers. From that moment, the US put almost its entire will and industrial prowess into the war effort.

Initially, neither the Pacific nor European theaters went well for the US. In the Pacific, fighting didn't turn around until the US unexpectedly routed the Japanese navy at Midway Island in June 1942. Afterward, the US drove Japan back with a series of brutal battles recapturing Pacific islands.

In Europe, the US dealt the fatal blow to Germany with its massive D-Day invasion of France on June 6, 1944: unable to sustain a two-front war (the Soviet Union was savagely fighting on the eastern front), Germany surrendered in May 1945.

1870

Freed black men are given the vote, but the South's segregationist 'Jim Crow' laws (which remain until the 1960s) effectively disenfranchise blacks from every meaningful sphere of daily life.

1880–1920

Millions of immigrants flood in from Europe and Asia, fueling the age of cities. New York, Chicago and Philadelphia swell in size, becoming global centers of industry and commerce.

1882

Racist sentiment, particularly in California (where over 50,000 Chinese immigrants have arrived since 1848), leads to the Chinese Exclusion Act, the only US immigration law to exclude a specific race.

1896

In *Plessy v. Ferguson*, the US Supreme Court rules that 'separate but equal' public facilities for blacks and whites are legal, arguing that the Constitution addresses only political, not social, equality.

Nevertheless, Japan continued fighting. Newly elected President Harry Truman – ostensibly worried that a US invasion of Japan would lead to unprecedented carnage – chose to drop experimental atomic bombs on Hiroshima and Nagasaki in August 1945. Created by the government's top-secret Manhattan Project, the bombs devastated both cities, killing over 200,000 people. Japan surrendered days later. The nuclear age was born.

The Red Scare, Civil Rights & the Wars in Asia

The US enjoyed unprecedented prosperity in the decades after WWII, but little peace.

Formerly wartime allies, the communist Soviet Union and the capitalist USA soon engaged in a running competition to dominate the globe. The superpowers engaged in proxy wars – notably the Korean War (1950–53) and Vietnam War (1954–75) – with only the mutual threat of nuclear annihilation preventing direct war. Founded in 1945, the UN couldn't overcome this worldwide ideological split and was largely ineffectual in preventing Cold War conflicts.

In *The Souls of Black Folk* (1903), WEB Du Bois, who helped found the National Association for the Advancement of Colored People (NAACP), eloquently describes the racial dilemmas of politics and culture facing early-20th-century America.

Meanwhile, with its continent unscarred and its industry bulked up by WWII, the American homeland entered an era of growing affluence. In the 1950s, a mass migration left the inner cities for the suburbs, where affordable single-family homes sprang up. Americans drove cheap cars using cheap gas over brand-new interstate highways. They relaxed with the comforts of modern technology, swooned over TV, and got busy, giving birth to a 'baby boom.'

Middle-class whites did, anyway. African Americans remained segregated, poor and generally unwelcome at the party. Echoing 19th-century abolitionist Frederick Douglass, the Southern Christian Leadership Coalition (SCLC), led by African American preacher Martin Luther King Jr, aimed to end segregation and 'save America's soul': to realize color-blind justice, racial equality and fairness of economic opportunity for all.

Beginning in the 1950s, King preached and organized nonviolent resistance in the form of bus boycotts, marches and sit-ins, mainly in the South. White authorities often met these protests with water hoses and batons, and demonstrations sometimes dissolved into riots, but with the 1964 Civil Rights Act, African Americans spurred a wave of legislation that swept away racist laws and laid the groundwork for a more just and equal society.

Meanwhile, the 1960s saw further social upheavals: rock and roll spawned a youth rebellion, and drugs sent Technicolor visions spinning in their heads. President John F Kennedy was assassinated in Dallas in 1963, followed by the assassinations in 1968 of his brother, Senator Robert Kennedy, and of Martin Luther King Jr. Americans' faith in their

1898
Victory in the Spanish-American War gives US control of the Philippines, Puerto Rico and Guam, and indirect control of Cuba. But the Philippines' bloody war for independence deters future US colonialism.

1906
Upton Sinclair publishes *The Jungle*, an exposé of Chicago's unsavory meatpacking industry. Many workers suffer through poverty and dangerous, even deadly, conditions in choking factories and sweatshops.

1908
The first Model T (aka 'Tin Lizzie') car is built in Detroit, MI. Assembly-line innovator Henry Ford is soon selling one million automobiles annually.

1914
Panama Canal opens, linking the Atlantic and Pacific Oceans. The US wins the right to build and run the canal by inciting a Panamanian revolt over independence from Colombia.

THE AFRICAN AMERICAN EXPERIENCE: THE STRUGGLE FOR EQUALITY

It's impossible to properly grasp American history without taking into account the great struggles and hard-won victories of African Americans who come from all spheres of life.

Slavery

From the early 17th century until the 19th century, an estimated 600,000 slaves were brought from Africa to America. Those who survived the horrific transport on crowded ships (which sometimes had 50% mortality rates) were sold in slave markets (African males cost $27 in 1638). The majority of slaves ended up in Southern plantations where conditions were usually brutal – whipping and branding were commonplace.

All (White) Men are Created Equal

Many of the founding fathers – George Washington, Thomas Jefferson and Benjamin Franklin – owned slaves, though privately expressed condemnation for the abominable practice. The abolition movement, however, wouldn't appear until the 1830s, long after the appearance of the rousing but ultimately hollow words 'all men are created equal' on the Declaration of Independence.

Free at Last

While some revisionist historians describe the Civil War as being about states' rights, most scholars agree that the war was really about slavery. Following the Union victory at Antietam, Lincoln drafted the Emancipation Proclamation, which freed all blacks in occupied territories. African Americans joined the Union effort, with more than 180,000 serving by war's end.

Jim Crow Laws

During Reconstruction (1865–77) federal laws provided civil rights protection for newly freed blacks. Southern bitterness, however, coupled with centuries of prejudice, fueled a backlash. By the 1890s, the Jim Crow laws (named after a derogatory character in a minstrel show) appeared. African Americans were effectively disenfranchised, and America became a deeply segregated society.

Civil Rights Movement

Beginning in the 1950s, a movement was underway in African American communities to fight for equality. Rosa Parks, who refused to give up her seat to a white passenger, inspired the Montgomery bus boycott. There were sit-ins at lunch counters where blacks were excluded; massive demonstrations led by Martin Luther King Jr in Washington, DC; and harrowing journeys by 'freedom riders' that aimed to end bus segregation. The work of millions paid off: in 1964 President Johnson signed the Civil Rights Act, which banned discrimination and racial segregation.

1917

President Woodrow Wilson enters US into WWI. The US mobilizes 4.7 million troops, and suffers around 110,000 of the war's nine million military deaths.

1920s

Spurred by African American migration to northern cities, the Harlem Renaissance inspires an intellectual flowering of literature, art and music. Important figures include WEB Du Bois and Langston Hughes.

1941–45

WWII: America deploys 16 million troops and suffers 400,000 deaths. Overall, civilian deaths outpace military deaths two to one, and total 50 to 70 million people from over 50 countries.

1948–51

The US-led Marshall Plan funnels $12 billion in material and financial aid to help Europe recover from WWII. The plan also aims to contain Soviet influence and reignite America's economy.

leaders and government was further shocked by the bombings and brutalities of the Vietnam War, as seen on TV, which led to widespread student protests.

Yet President Richard Nixon, elected in 1968 partly for promising an 'honorable end to the war,' instead escalated US involvement and secretly bombed Laos and Cambodia. Then, in 1972, the Watergate scandal broke: a burglary at Democratic Party offices was, through dogged journalism, tied to 'Tricky Dick,' who, in 1974, became the first US president to resign from office.

The tumultuous 1960s and '70s also witnessed the sexual revolution, women's liberation, struggles for gay rights, energy crises over the supply of crude oil from the Middle East, and, with the 1962 publication of Rachel Carson's *Silent Spring,* the realization that the USA's industries had created a polluted, diseased environmental mess.

Suspicious of political factoids? Factcheck.org is a nonpartisan, self-described 'consumer advocate' that monitors the accuracy of statements made by US politicians during debates, speeches, interviews and in campaign ads. It's a great resource for parsing truth from bombast and is particularly handy during election cycles.

Reagan, Clinton & Bush

In 1980 Republican California governor and former actor Ronald Reagan campaigned for president by promising to make Americans feel good about America again. The affable Reagan won easily, and his election marked a pronounced shift to the right in US politics.

Reagan wanted to defeat communism, restore the economy, deregulate business and cut taxes. To tackle the first two, he launched the biggest peacetime military build-up in history, and dared the Soviets to keep up. They went broke trying, and the USSR collapsed.

Military spending and tax cuts created enormous federal deficits, which hampered the presidency of Reagan's successor, George HW Bush. Despite winning the Gulf War – liberating Kuwait in 1991 after an Iraqi invasion – Bush was soundly defeated in the 1992 presidential election by Southern Democrat Bill Clinton. Clinton had the good fortune to catch the 1990s high-tech internet boom, which seemed to augur a 'new economy' based on white-collar telecommunications. The US economy erased its deficits and ran a surplus, and Clinton presided over one of America's longest economic booms.

In 2000 and 2004, George W Bush, the eldest son of George HW Bush, won the presidential elections so narrowly that the divided results seemed to epitomize an increasingly divided nation. 'Dubya' had the misfortune of being president when the high-tech bubble burst in 2000, but he nevertheless enacted tax cuts that returned federal deficits even greater than before. He also championed the right-wing conservative 'backlash' that had been building since Reagan.

On September 11, 2001, Islamic terrorists flew hijacked planes into New York's World Trade Center and the Pentagon in Washington, DC.

1963

On November 22, President John F Kennedy is publicly assassinated by Lee Harvey Oswald while riding in a motorcade through Dealey Plaza in Dallas, TX.

1964

Congress passes the Civil Rights Act, outlawing discrimination on the basis of race, color, religion, sex or national origin. First proposed by Kennedy, it was one of President Johnson's crowning achievements.

1965–75

US involvement in the Vietnam War tears the nation apart as 58,000 Americans die, along with four million Vietnamese and 1.5 million Laotians and Cambodians.

1969

American astronauts land on the moon, fulfilling President Kennedy's unlikely 1961 promise to accomplish this feat within a decade and culminatin in the 'space ra between the U

This catastrophic attack united Americans behind their president as he vowed revenge and declared a 'war on terror.' Bush soon attacked Afghanistan in an unsuccessful hunt for Al-Qaeda terrorist cells, then he attacked Iraq in 2003 and toppled its anti-US dictator, Saddam Hussein. Meanwhile, Iraq descended into civil war.

Following scandals and failures – torture photos from Abu Ghraib, the federal response in the aftermath of Hurricane Katrina and the inability to bring the Iraq War to a close – Bush's approval ratings reached historic lows in the second half of his presidency.

Obama

In 2008, hungry for change, Americans elected political newcomer, Barack Obama, America's first African American president. He certainly had his work cut out for him. These were, after all, unprecedented times economically, with the US in the largest financial crisis since the Great Depression. What started as a collapse of the US housing bubble in 2007, spread to the banking sector, with the meltdown of major financial institutions. The shock wave quickly spread across the globe, and by 2008 many industrialized nations were experiencing a recession in one form or another.

Steven Spielberg's *Lincoln* (2012) does a masterful job in conjuring up the final months of America's greatest president (Daniel Day-Lewis won an Academy Award for his portrayal).

The 21st century has certainly been a tumultuous one for the USA. As Americans looked toward the future, many found it difficult to leave the past behind. This was not surprising since wars in Afghanistan and Iraq, launched a decade prior, continued to simmer on the back burner of the ever-changing news cycle, and the 10-year anniversary of September 11 brought back memories of that day when thousands perished in terrorist attacks. Earlier in 2011, in a subterfuge operation vetted by President Obama, Navy Seals raided Osama bin Laden's Pakistan hideout, bringing an end to the mastermind behind Al-Qaeda and America's greatest public enemy.

Following his sober announcement describing the raid, President Obama saw his approval ratings jump by 11%. The president, for his part, certainly needed a boost. The economy remained in bad shape, and the ambitious $800-billion stimulus package passed by Congress in 2009 hadn't born much fruit in the eyes of many Americans – even though economists estimated that the stimulus did soften the blow of the recession, which would have been much worse without it. At the end of his first term, his approval ratings were around 49%, drawn down no doubt by the sluggish economy.

With lost jobs, overvalued mortgages and little relief in sight, millions of Americans found themselves adrift. This was not a recession they could spend their way out of, as Obama's predecessor had suggested. Nor was a little extra thrift going to make a difference. People were upset

1973

In *Roe v. Wade*, the Supreme Court legalizes abortion. Today this decision remains controversial and divisive, pitting 'right to choose' advocates against the 'right to life' anti-abortion lobby.

1980s

New Deal–era financial institutions, deregulated under President Reagan, gamble with their customers' savings and loans, and fail, leaving the government with the bill: $125 billion.

1989

The 1960s-era Berlin Wall is torn down, marking the end of the Cold War between the US and USSR (now Russia). The USA becomes the world's last remaining superpower.

1990s

The World Wide Web debuts in 1991. Silicon Valley, CA, leads a high-tech internet revolution, remaking communications and media, and overvalued tech stocks drive the massive boom (and subsequent bust).

and gathered in large numbers to voice their anger. This, in turn, gave birth to the Tea Party, a wing of politically conservative Republicans who believed that Obama was leaning too far to the left, and that government handouts would destroy the economy and, thus, America. High federal spending, government bailouts (of the banking and auto industries) and especially Obama's health-care reform (derisively named 'Obamacare') particularly roused their ire.

Although Democrats cheered his victory, Obama returned to office without quite the same hope and optimism that surrounded him the first time. Times had changed, and America, like much of the world, had struggled through tough years since the global economic crisis erupted in 2007. When Obama took the oath of office in 2013, the unemployment

FIGHTING FOR CHANGE: FIVE WHO SHAPED HISTORY

American history is littered with larger-than-life figures who brought dramatic change through bold deeds, sometimes at great personal cost. While presidents tend to garner all the attention, there are countless lesser-known visionaries who have made enormous contributions to civic life.

Rachel Carson (1907–64) An eloquent writer with a keen scientific mind, Carson helped spawn the environmental movement. Her pioneering work *Silent Spring* illustrated the ecological catastrophe unleashed by pesticides and unregulated industry. The ensuing grassroots movement spurred the creation of the Environmental Protection Agency.

Cesar Chavez (1927–93) A second-generation Mexican-American who grew up in farm labor camps (where entire families labored for $1 a day), Chavez was a charismatic and inspiring figure – Gandhi and Martin Luther King Jr were among his role models. He gave hope, dignity and a brighter future to thousands of poor migrants by creating the United Farm Workers.

Harvey Milk (1930–78) California's first openly gay public servant was a tireless advocate in the fight against discrimination, encouraging gays and lesbians to 'come out, stand up and let the world know. Only that way will we start to achieve our rights.' Milk, along with San Francisco mayor George Moscone, was assassinated in 1978.

Betty Friedan (1921–2006) Founder of the National Organization of Women (NOW), Friedan was instrumental in leading the feminist movement of the 1960s. Friedan's groundbreaking book *The Feminine Mystique* inspired millions of women to envision a life beyond mere 'homemaker.'

Ralph Nader (b 1934) The frequent presidential contender (in 2008, Nader received 738,000 votes) is one of America's staunchest consumer watchdogs. The Harvard-trained lawyer has played a major role in insuring Americans have safer cars, cheaper medicines and cleaner air and water.

2001

On September 11, Al-Qaeda terrorists hijack four commercial airplanes, flying two into NYC's twin towers, and one into the Pentagon (the fourth crashes in Pennsylvania); nearly 3000 people are killed.

2003

After citing evidence that Iraq possesses weapons of mass destruction, President George W Bush launches a preemptive war that will cost over 4000 American lives and some $3 trillion.

2005

On August 29, Hurricane Katrina hits the Mississippi and Louisiana coasts, rupturing poorly maintained levees and flooding New Orleans. Over 1800 people die, and cost estimates exceed $110 billion.

2008–9

Barack Obama becomes the first African American president. The stock market crashes due to mismanagement by major American financial institutions. The crisis spreads worldwide.

rate, hovering around 8%, was about what it had been during his first inauguration, back in 2009, though economic growth seems at last to be on a solid foundation. On other fronts, Obama has had mixed success. He ended the US involvement in Iraq, but 63,000 troops still remained in Afghanistan, and the US mission there seems increasingly obscure, particularly after the successful operation that finally brought down Osama bin Laden.

If history is a partisan affair, Howard Zinn makes his allegiance clear in *A People's History of the United States* (1980 and 2005), which tells the often-overlooked stories about laborers, minorities, immigrants, women and radicals.

Obamacare

For Democrats, however, Obama's health-care bill, which became law in 2010, was a major victory in bringing health-care coverage to more Americans, lowering the cost of health care and closing loopholes that allowed insurance companies to deny coverage to individuals. Despite challenges by Republicans who threatened to repeal it, and two close calls by the Supreme Court (which narrowly ruled the new health-care act constitutional on both occasions), the law went into effect in 2014. Whether it will be a success or failure is still hotly debated by Democrats and Republicans, though the outcome probably won't be clear for some years. As of 2015, however, the program has had some notable successes, adding coverage to millions of uninsured and helping lower costs for health-care providers. Obamacare could be the president's greatest legacy after leaving office.

2012

Hurricane Sandy devastates the East Coast, becoming the second-costliest hurricane ($65 billion) in American history. Over 80 Americans (plus 200 in other countries) die.

2013

Scandal erupts when former National Security Agency contractor Edward Snowden leaks classified information about a US intelligence program that monitors communication between American citizens and its allies.

2015

In a historic decision, the US Supreme Court legalizes same-sex marriage, giving gay couples in all 50 states the right to marry.

The Way of Life

One of the world's great melting pots, America boasts an astonishing variety of cultures and creeds. The country's diversity was shaped by its rich history of immigration, though today, regional differences (East Coast, South, West Coast and Midwest) play an equally prominent role in defining American identity. Religion, sport, politics and, of course, socio-economic backgrounds are also pivotal in creating the complicated American portrait.

Multiculturalism

From the get-go, America was called a 'melting pot,' which presumed that newcomers came and blended into the existing American fabric. The country hasn't let go of that sentiment completely. On one hand, diversity is celebrated (Cinco de Mayo, Martin Luther King Jr Day and Chinese New Year all get their due), but on the other hand, many Americans are comfortable with the status quo.

Immigration is at the crux of the matter. Immigrants currently make up around 13% of the population. Nearly half a million newcomers enter the US legally each year, with the majority from Mexico, followed by Asia and Europe. Another 11.2 million or so are in the country illegally. This is the issue that makes Americans edgy, especially because it gets politicized.

'Immigration reform' has been a Washington buzzword for nearly two decades. Some people believe the nation's current system deals with illegal immigrants too leniently – that higher walls should be built on the border, immigrants who are here unlawfully should be deported and employers who hire them should be fined. Other Americans think those rules are too harsh – that immigrants who have been here for years working, contributing to society and abiding by the law deserve amnesty. Perhaps they could pay a fine and fill out the paperwork to become citizens while continuing to live here with their families. Despite several attempts, Congress has not been able to pass a comprehensive package addressing illegal immigration, though it has put through various measures to beef up enforcement.

The US holds the world's second-largest Spanish-speaking population, behind Mexico and just ahead of Spain. Latino people are also the fastest-growing minority group in the nation.

Age has a lot to do with multicultural tolerance in America. When asked in a survey if immigration strengthens the nation, only about one-third of older Americans said yes, whereas more than half of 18- to 26-year-olds said yes, according to the Pew Research Center. In a similar survey, those aged 60 and older were asked if it's acceptable for whites and African Americans to date each other: 35% said no, but that dropped to 6% when asked of Americans aged 30 and younger.

Many people point to the election of President Barack Obama as proof of America's multicultural achievements. It's not just his personal story (white mother, black father, Muslim name, has lived among the diverse cultures of Hawaii, Indonesia and the Midwest, among others). Or that he's the first African American to hold the nation's highest office (in a country where as recently as the 1960s African Americans couldn't even vote in certain regions). It's that Americans of all races and creeds voted overwhelmingly to elect the self-described 'mutt' and embrace his message of diversity and change.

Religion

When the Pilgrims (early settlers to the US who fled their European homeland to escape religious persecution) came ashore, they were adamant that their new country would be one of religious tolerance. They valued the freedom to practice religion so highly they refused to make their Protestant faith official state policy. What's more, they forbade the government from doing anything that might sanction one religion or belief over another. Separation of church and state became the law of the land.

Americans are increasingly defining their spiritual beliefs outside of organized religion. The proportion of those who say they have 'no religion' is now around 16%. Some in this catch-all category disavow religion altogether (around 4%), but the majority sustain spiritual beliefs that simply fall outside the box.

Today Protestants are on the verge of becoming a minority in the country they founded. According to the Pew Research Center, Protestant numbers have declined steadily to just over 50%. Meanwhile, other faiths have held their own or seen their numbers increase.

The country is also in a period of exceptional religious fluidity. Forty-four percent of American adults have left the denomination of their childhood for another denomination, another faith or no faith at all, according to Pew. A unique era of 'religion shopping' has been ushered in. As for the geographic breakdown: the USA's most Catholic region is shifting from the Northeast to the Southwest; the South is the most evangelical; and the West is the most unaffiliated.

All that said, America's biggest schism isn't between religions or even between faith and skepticism. It's between fundamentalist and progressive interpretations within each faith. Most Americans don't care much if you're Catholic, Episcopalian, Buddhist or atheist. What they do care about are your views on abortion, contraception, gay rights, stem-cell research, teaching of evolution, school prayer and government displays of religious icons. The country's Religious Right (the oft-used term for evangelical Christians) has pushed these issues onto center stage, and the group has been effective at using politics to codify its conservative beliefs into law. This effort has prompted a slew of court cases, testing the nation's principles on separation of church and state. The split remains one of America's biggest culture wars, and it almost always plays a role in politics, especially during elections.

Lifestyle

The USA has one of the world's highest standards of living. The median household income is around $51,000, though it varies by region (with higher earnings in the Northeast and West followed by the Midwest and the South). Wages also vary by ethnicity, with African Americans and Latinos earning less than whites and Asians ($34,600 and $41,000 respectively, versus $58,000 and $67,000, according to the most recent census data). Likewise the wage gap between men and women continues to persist, with women earning roughly 78% of what men earn.

NPR radio host Terry Gross interviews Americans from all walks of life, from rock stars to environmental activists to nuclear scientists. Listen online at www.npr.org/freshair.

About 86% of Americans are high-school graduates, while some 29% go on to graduate from college with a four-year bachelor degree.

More often than not there are two married parents in an American household, and both of them work. Single parents head 9% of households. Twenty-eight percent of Americans work more than 40 hours per week. Divorce is common – more than 40% of first marriages go kaput – but both divorce and marriage rates have declined over the last three decades. Despite the high divorce rate, Americans spend more than $160 billion annually on weddings. The average number of children in an American family is two.

While many Americans hit the gym or walk, bike or jog regularly, over 50% don't exercise at all during their free time, according to the Centers for Disease Control (CDC). Health researchers speculate this lack of exercise and Americans' fondness for sugary and fatty foods have led to rising rates of obesity and diabetes. More than two-thirds of Americans are overweight, with one-third considered obese, the CDC says.

STATES & TRAITS

Regional US stereotypes now have solid data behind them, thanks to a study titled *The Geography of Personality*. Researchers processed more than a half-million personality assessments collected from individual US citizens, then looked at where certain traits stacked up on the map. Turns out 'Minnesota nice' is for real – the most 'agreeable' states cluster in the Midwest, Great Plains and South. These places rank highest for friendliness and cooperation. The most neurotic states? They line up in the Northeast. But New York didn't place number one, as you might expect; that honor goes to West Virginia. Many of the most 'open' states lie out West. California, Nevada, Oregon and Washington all rate high for being receptive to new ideas, although they lag behind Washington, DC, and New York. The most dutiful and self-disciplined states sit in the Great Plains and Southwest, led by New Mexico. Go figure.

About 26% of Americans volunteer their time to help others or help a cause. This is more so in the Midwest, followed by the West, South and Northeast, according to the Corporation for National and Community Service. Eco-consciousness has entered the mainstream: over 75% of Americans recycle at home, and most big-chain grocery stores, including Walmart, now sell organic foods.

Americans tend to travel close to home. Just over one-third of Americans have passports so most people take vacations within the 50 states. According to the US Department of Commerce's Office of Travel and Tourism Industries, Mexico and Canada are the top countries for international getaways, followed by the UK, Italy, France, Germany and Japan. America's reputation as the 'no-vacation nation,' with many workers having only five to 10 paid annual vacation days, contributes to this stay-at-home scenario.

Four million Americans tune in every week to Midwestern raconteur Garrison Keillor's old-timey radio show, *A Prairie Home Companion;* listen to the live music, sketches and storytelling online at http://prairiehome.org.

Sports

What really draws Americans together, sometimes slathered in blue body paint or with foam-rubber cheese wedges on their heads, is sport. It provides a social glue, so no matter whether a person is conservative or liberal, married or single, Mormon or pagan, chances are come Monday at the office they'll be chatting about the weekend performance of their favorite team.

The fun and games go on all year long. In spring and summer there's baseball nearly every day. In fall and winter, a weekend or Monday night doesn't feel right if there isn't a football game on, and through the long days and nights of winter there's plenty of basketball to keep the adrenaline going. Those are the big three sports. Car racing has revved up interest in recent years. Major League Soccer (MLS) is attracting an ever-increasing following. And ice hockey, once favored only in northern climes, is popular nationwide, with five Stanley Cup winners since 2000 hailing from either California or the South.

Baseball

Despite high salaries and its biggest stars being dogged by steroid rumors, baseball remains America's pastime. It may not command the same TV viewership (and subsequent advertising dollars) as football, but baseball has 162 games over a season versus 16 for football.

Besides, baseball isn't about seeing it on TV, it's all about the live version: being at the ballpark on a sunny day, sitting in the bleachers with a beer and hot dog, and indulging in the seventh-inning stretch, when the entire park erupts in a communal singalong of 'Take Me Out to the Ballgame.' The play-offs, held every October, still deliver excitement and unexpected champions. The New York Yankees, Boston Red Sox and Chicago Cubs continue to be America's favorite teams, even when they're abysmal (the Cubs haven't won a World Series in more than 100 years).

Tickets are relatively inexpensive – the cheap seats average about $15 at most stadiums – and are easy to get for most games. Minor-league baseball games cost half as much, and can be even more fun, with lots of audience participation, stray chickens and dogs running across the field, and wild throws from the pitcher's mound. For info, go to www.milb.com.

Even college and high-school football games enjoy an intense amount of pomp and circumstance, with cheerleaders, marching bands, mascots, songs and mandatory pre- and post-game rituals, especially the tailgate – a full-blown beer-and-barbecue feast that takes place over portable grills in parking lots where games are played.

Football

Football is big, physical and rolling in dough. With the shortest season and least number of games of any of the major sports, every match takes on the emotion of an epic battle, where the results matter and an unfortunate injury can deal a lethal blow to a team's play-off chances.

Football's also the toughest because it's played in fall and winter in all manner of rain, sleet and snow. Some of history's most memorable matches have occurred at below-freezing temperatures. Green Bay Packers fans are in a class by themselves when it comes to severe weather. Their stadium in Wisconsin, known as Lambeau Field, was the site of the infamous Ice Bowl, a 1967 championship game against the Dallas Cowboys during which the temperature plummeted to –13°F – mind you, that was with a wind-chill factor of –48°F.

The rabidly popular Super Bowl is pro football's championship match, held in late January or early February. The bowl games (such as Rose Bowl and Orange Bowl) are college football's title matches, held on and around New Year's Day.

Basketball

The teams bringing in the most fans these days include the Chicago Bulls (thanks to the lingering Michael Jordan effect), Detroit Pistons (a rowdy crowd in which riots have broken out), Cleveland Cavaliers, the San Antonio Spurs and last but not least, the Los Angeles Lakers, which won five championships between 2000 and 2010. Small-market teams like Sacramento and Portland have true-blue fans, and such cities can be great places to take in a game.

The Super Bowl costs America $800 million dollars in lost workplace productivity as employees gossip about the game, make bets and shop for new TVs online. It's still less than the $1.9 billion estimate for March Madness when many folks get caught up in the NCAA basketball tournament.

College-level basketball also draws millions of fans, especially every spring when March Madness rolls around. This series of college play-off games culminates in the Final Four, when the four remaining teams compete for a spot in the championship game. The Cinderella stories and unexpected outcomes rival the pro league for excitement. The games are widely televised – and bet on. This is when Las Vegas bookies earn their keep.

Politics

There's nothing quite like a good old-fashioned discussion of politics to throw a bucket of cold water onto a conversation. Many Americans have fairly fixed ideas when it comes to political parties and ideologies, and bridging the Republican-Democratic divide can often seem as insurmountable as leaping over the Grand Canyon. Here's a quick cheat sheet on the dominant American parties and where they stand on the major topics of the day.

Republicans

Known as the GOP (Grand Old Party), Republicans believe in a limited role of federal government. They also subscribe to fiscal conservatism: free markets and lower taxes are the path toward prosperity. Historically, Republicans were strong supporters of the environment: Theodore Roosevelt was a notable conservationist who helped create the National Parks system, and Nixon established the Environmental Protection Agency in

KNOW YOUR GENERATIONS

American culture is often stratified by age groups. Here's a quick rundown to help you tell Generation X from Z, and then some.

Baby Boomers Those born from 1946 to 1964. After American soldiers came home from WWII, they got busy with the ladies, and the birthrate exploded (hence the term 'baby boom'). Youthful experimentation, self-expression and social activism was often followed by midlife affluence.

Generation X Those born between 1965 and 1984. Characterized by their rejection of Baby Boomer values, skepticism and alienation are X's pop-culture hallmarks.

Millennials Those born from roughly the early 1980s to the late '90s. Known for being brash and self-confident, they were the first to grow up with the internet. Weaned on iPods, instant messaging and social-networking websites, they are a work in progress, and also the largest living generation in the US.

The ? Generation As of 2015, no one had come up with a catchy name to describe the generation after the millennials. The 'selfie generation,' 'generation like' and straight-up 'post-millennials' are a few suggestions that have been bandied about.

1970. More recently, however, Republicans have sided with business over environmental regulation. Climate change remains a hot topic: more than 55% of Congressional Republicans and 72% of Republican Senators deny its basic tenets. This includes James Inhofe, a veteran lawmaker from Oklahoma, who chairs the Environment and Public Works Committee – he is also the author of the book *The Greatest Hoax: How the Global Warming Conspiracy Threatens Your Future*. There's also a fundamentalist wing in the party that believes in creationism and a literal interpretation of the bible. Republicans also believe in social conservatism, promoting family and church values, and are often opposed to same-sex marriage and abortion. The Republican Party is most successful in the South and Midwest.

Democrats

The Democratic Party is liberal and progressive. The role model for most Democrats is Franklin Roosevelt, whose New Deal policies (namely creating government jobs for the unemployed and regulating Wall Street) are credited with partially ending the Great Depression. Democrats believe government should take an active role in regulating the economy to help keep inflation and unemployment low, and in a progressive tax structure to reduce economic inequality. They also have a strong social agenda, endorsing the government to take an active role in providing poverty relief, maintaining a social safety net, creating a health-care system for all and ensuring civil and political rights. By and large, Democrats support abortion rights and same-sex marriage, and believe in subsidizing alternative energy sources to help combat climate change, which most party members accept as indisputable. The Democratic Party is strongest in big cities and in the Northeast.

Native Americans

Although the population is a fraction of its pre-Columbian size, there are more than three million Native Americans from 500 tribes, speaking some 175 languages and residing in every region of the United States. Not surprisingly, North America's indigenous peoples are an extremely diverse bunch with unique customs and beliefs molded in part by the landscapes they inhabit – from the Inuit living in the frozen tundra of Alaska to the many tribes of the arid, mountainous Southwest.

The Tribes

The Cherokee, Navajo, Chippewa and Sioux are the largest tribal groupings in the lower 48 (ie barring Alaska and Hawaii). Other well-known tribes include the Choctaw (descendants of a great mound-building society originally based in the Mississippi valley), the Apache (a nomadic hunter-gatherer tribe that fiercely resisted forced relocation) and the Hopi (a Pueblo people with Southwest roots dating back 2000 years).

Culturally speaking, America's tribes today grapple with questions about how to prosper in contemporary America while protecting their traditions from erosion and their lands from further exploitation, and how to lift their people from poverty while maintaining their sense of identity and the sacred.

Cherokee

The Cherokee (www.cherokee.org) originally lived in an area of more than 80 million acres, covering a huge swath of the South (including Tennessee, Virginia, the Carolinas and Kentucky). However, in 1830 they were forcibly relocated west of the Mississippi and today reside largely in

NATIVE AMERICAN ART & CRAFTS

It would take an encyclopedia to cover the myriad artistic traditions of America's tribal peoples, from pre-Columbian rock art to the contemporary multimedia scene.

What ties such diverse traditions together is that Native American arts and crafts are not just functional for everyday life but can also serve ceremonial purposes and have social and religious significance. The patterns and symbols are woven with meanings that provide a window into the heart of Native American peoples. This is as true of Zuni fetish carvings as it is of patterned Navajo rugs, Southwestern pueblo pottery, Sioux beadwork, Inuit sculptures and Cherokee and Hawaiian woodcarvings, to name just a few examples.

In addition to preserving their culture, contemporary Native American artists have used sculpture, painting, textiles, film, literature and performance art to reflect and critique modernity since the mid-20th century, especially after the civil rights activism of the 1960s and cultural renaissance of the '70s. *Native North American Art*, by Berlo and Phillips, offers an introduction to North America's varied indigenous art.

Many tribes run craft outlets and galleries, usually in the main towns of reservations. The **Indian Arts & Crafts Board** (www.iacb.doi.gov) has a state-by-state online listing of Native American–owned galleries and shops (click on 'Source Directory of Businesses.')

Oklahoma (home to more than 200,000 Cherokee). Tahlequah has been the Cherokee capital since 1839.

Cherokee society was originally matrilineal (bloodlines traced through the mother). Like some other native tribes, the Cherokee recognize seven cardinal directions: north, south, east and west along with up, down and center (or within).

Navajo

The Navajo Reservation (www.discovernavajo.com) is by far the largest and most populous in the US. Also called the Navajo Nation and Navajoland, it covers 17.5 million acres (over 27,000 sq miles) in Arizona and parts of New Mexico and Utah.

The Navajo were feared nomads and warriors who both traded with and raided the Pueblos and who fought settlers and the US military. They also borrowed generously from other traditions: they acquired sheep and horses from the Spanish, learned pottery and weaving from the Pueblos and picked up silversmithing from Mexico. Today, the Navajo are renowned for their woven rugs, pottery and inlaid silver jewelry, as well as for their intricate sandpainting, which is used in healing ceremonies.

Chippewa

Although Chippewa or Ojibway is the commonly used term for this tribe, members prefer to be called Anishinabe. They are based in Minnesota, Wisconsin and Michigan. According to legend, the Chippewa once lived on the Atlantic coast and gradually migrated west over 500 years. They traditionally survived by fishing, hunting and farming corn and squash. They also harvested (by canoe) wild rice, which remains an essential Chippewa tradition.

Sioux

Like the Iroquois, the Sioux is not one tribe but a consortium of three major tribes (and various sub-branches) speaking different dialects but sharing a common subculture. Prior to European arrival they lived in the northeast of present-day North America but slowly migrated to the Great Plains by 1800. The Sioux were fierce defenders of their lands, and fought many battles to preserve them, although the slaughter of the buffalo (on whom they had survived) did more to remove them from their lands than anything else. Today, they live in Minnesota, Nebraska, North Dakota and South Dakota – the latter contains the 2-million-acre Pine Ridge Reservation, the nation's second-largest.

TIMELINE

700–1400

North America's largest ancient city, Cahokia, supports a population of 10,000 to 20,000 at its peak. By 1400 it is mysteriously abandoned.

750–1300

Ancestral Pueblo peoples living near Chaco Canyon flourish. This advanced desert civilization develops adobe dwellings in enormous complexes.

1831

Following the 1830 *Indian Removal Act*, Cherokee and other tribes are forced to abandon homelands and relocate to areas west of the Mississippi. Thousands die on the 1000-mile Trail of Tears.

1876

Lakota chief Sitting Bull defeats Custer at the Battle of Little Bighorn, one of the last military victories by Native Americans in the effort to protect their lands.

1968

The American Indian Movement (AIM) is founded. Through protests, marches and demonstrations, AIM brings attention to marginalized peoples.

1968

Navajo Community College becomes the first college on any reservation founded and run by Native Americans. Later, other tribal community colleges are founded, growing to 30 today.

1975

President Nixon passes the *Indian Self-Determination Act*, empowering Native Americans to control how federal money is spent on native matters.

2011

FNX, the first Native American television network, launches in California.

American Cuisine

In a country of such size and regional variation, you could spend a lifetime eating your way across America and barely scratch the surface. Owing to such scope, dining American-style could mean many things: from munching on pulled pork sandwiches at an old road-house to feasting on sustainably sourced seafood at a waterfront dining room.

Culinary Revolution

Not until the 1960s did food and wine become serious topics for American newspapers, magazines and TV, with the help of a Californian named Julia Child who taught Americans how to cook French food through black-and-white programs broadcast from Boston's public TV station. By the 1970s, everyday folks (and not just hippies) had started turning their attention to issues of organic, natural foods and sustainable agriculture. In the 1980s and '90s, the 'foodie revolution' encouraged entrepreneurs to open restaurants featuring regional American cuisine, from the South to the Pacific Northwest, that would rank with Europe's best.

Food Trucks

The hottest dining craze on wheels is food trucks. From Korean-style barbecue tacos to curry-filled Indian *dosas*, there's no telling what creative, healthy, gourmet, decadent or downright bizarre twist on 'fast food' you'll discover. To find the best trucks, visit Portland, Austin, Minneapolis, Los Angeles, New York, Las Vegas, San Francisco and Miami.

Slow, Local, Organic

The Slow Food movement, along with renewed enthusiasm for eating local, organically grown fare, is a leading trend in American restaurants. The movement, which was arguably started in 1971 by chef Alice Waters at Berkeley's Chez Panisse, continued with First Lady Michelle Obama – the First Lady of food if there ever was one – and her daughters, who even planted an organic garden on the White House lawn. All across the country, you can find farmers markets, which are great places to meet locals and take a big bite out of America's cornucopia of foods, from heritage fruit and vegetables to fresh, savory and sweet regional delicacies.

Staples & Specialties

Waves of immigrants have added great variety to American gastronomy by adapting foreign ideas to home soil, from Italian pizza and German hamburgers to Eastern European borscht, Mexican huevos rancheros and Japanese sushi.

Pizza

Pizza made its way over to New York in the 1900s through Italian immigrants, and the first pizzeria in America – Lombardi's in Manhattan's Little Italy – opened in 1905. Pizza's popularity quickly spread across the country, with different varieties taking root. While Chicago-style pizza is 'deep dish' and Californian tends to be light and doughy, New York prides itself on its thin crust which allowing for faster cooking time in a city where everyone is always in a hurry.

Mexican & Tex-Mex

No matter where you roam in the US, you probably won't be far from a restaurant serving up Mexican or Tex-Mex fare (don't bother trying to sort the two: there's much overlap between them). This is not surprising given that people of Latin American descent make up over 16% of the population. Tacos, burritos and other quick foods are favorites, with snack carts and food trucks popular with people of all walks of life. Places like Chipotle, which serve up largely organic Tex-Mex in a hurry, are among the fastest-growing chains. Casual sit-down places are also popular, with margaritas and chips and salsa a nearly essential part of every meal.

Barbecue

Barbecue is a big deal in America. Although its popularity is unrivaled in the South, you'll find that smoky, tender meat everywhere from San Francisco to New York City. Barbecue in America dates back to colonial times, and even George Washington (who had a smokehouse at his Mt Vernon estate) was a fan. The dish is simple enough: meat slow-roasted over fire pits until tender. You'll find a wide variety of cooking styles and specialties. Kansas City, MO, serves a wide range of meats, including lamb, and emphasizes thick, sweet sauces. In the Carolinas, pulled or sliced pork is most popular. Memphis, TN, favors ribs, served either 'dry' or 'wet' (ie slathered in sauce). In Texas, beef is the dish of choice – no surprise given this is cattle country. It's also home to some of the nation's best barbecue joints: Lockhart is the epicenter for all things smoked and meaty.

Comfort Foods

While food trends come and go, the American love for a simple and hearty meal never goes out of style. Comfort foods at their roots are warm, traditional dishes that evoke nostalgia for childhood staples. Classics like mac 'n' cheese, chicken noodle soup, lasagna, pot roast, grilled cheese sandwiches, biscuits and gravy, fried chicken, hamburgers and filling pastas all fall into this category. American diners serve mostly this sort of food, churning out uncomplicated, tried-and-true recipes. Comfort foods can also be found in more creative versions at gastropubs, bistros, and upmarket restaurants and bars. You might find mac 'n' cheese with fresh crabmeat, burgers topped with applewood smoked bacon and goat cheese and served with duck-fat fries, or spicy Thai chicken noodle soup with coconut milk and curry.

Habits & Customs

Outside of big cities, Americans tend to eat early at restaurants and at home, so don't be surprised to find a restaurant half full at noon or 5:30pm. In smaller towns, it may be hard to find anywhere to eat after 8:30pm or 9pm. Dinner parties for adults usually begin around 6:30pm or 7pm, with cocktails followed by a buffet or sit-down meal. If invited to dinner, it's polite to be prompt: ideally, you should plan to arrive within 15 minutes of the designated time.

Americans are informal in their dining manners, although they will usually wait until everyone is served before eating. Many foods are eaten with the fingers, and an entire piece of bread may be buttered and eaten all at once. To the surprise of some foreign visitors, the sight of beer bottles on the dinner table is not uncommon.

Breakfast

Long billed by American nutritionists as 'the most important meal of the day,' morning meals in America are big business – no matter how many folks insist on skipping them. From a giant stack of buttermilk pancakes at a vintage diner to lavish Sunday brunches, Americans love their eggs and bacon, their waffles and hash browns, and their big glasses of fresh-squeezed orange juice. Most of all, they love that seemingly inalienable

Do's & Don'ts

Do tip: 15% to 20% of the total bill (pretax) is standard.

It's customary to place your napkin on your lap, even before the meal is served.

In general, try to avoid putting your elbows on the table.

Wait until everyone is served to begin eating.

In formal situations, diners customarily wait to eat until the host has lifted their fork.

At home, some Americans say a prayer before meals; it's fine to sit quietly if you prefer not to participate.

THE AMERICAN DIET CRAZE

America is almost as well known for its fad diets as it is for its fast food. In the 1920s and 1930s, there was the Cigarette Diet, the Bananas and Skim Milk Diet and the Grapefruit Diet – also called the Hollywood Diet. The 1960s brought the Steak and Martini Diet; the 1980s ushered in the Cabbage Soup Diet. In the 1990s fat-free and high carb was all the rage – until, that is, the Atkins Diet came in with its low-carb mantra. Stars embraced the 'Master Cleanse,' aka the Lemonade Diet, and then just as quickly abandoned it. Today's most popular diet? It's called the Paleo diet, and it entails eating like a cave dweller: organic meats, broths, fresh and fermented vegetables – but no grains, refined sugar, pasteurized dairy products, peanuts or other food items unavailable to prehistoric peoples.

American right: a steaming cup of morning coffee with unlimited refills. (Try asking for a free refill in other nations, and you'll get anything from an eye-roll to a smirk to downright confusion.)

Lunch

Usually taken after a midmorning coffee break, an American worker's lunch hour typically affords only a sandwich, quick burger or hearty salad. The formal 'business lunch' is more common in big cities like New York, where the food is not necessarily as important as the conversation.

While you'll spot diners drinking a beer or a glass of wine with their lunch, long gone are the days when the 'three-martini lunch' was socially acceptable. It was a phenomenon common enough in the mid-20th century to become a kind of catchphrase for indulgent business lunches, usually written off as a corporate, tax-deductible expense. The classic noontime beverage, in fact, is a far cry from a martini: iced tea (and yes, almost always with unlimited refills).

Top Food TV Shows

- Anthony Bourdain: Parts Unknown *(Travel Channel)*
- Top Chef *(Bravo)*
- Iron Chef America *(Food Network)*
- Diners, Drive-Ins and Dives *(Food Network)*
- Bizarre Foods with Andrew Zimmern *(Travel Channel)*

Dinner

Usually early in the evening, Americans settle in to a more substantial weeknight dinner, which, given the workload of so many American families, might be takeout (eg pizza or Chinese food) or prepackaged microwave meals. Desserts tend toward ice cream, pies and cakes. Some families still cook a traditional Sunday night dinner, when relatives and friends gather for a big feast. Traditional dishes might include roast chicken with all the fixings (mashed potatoes, green beans and corn on the cob). In warmer months, many Americans like to fire up the barbecue to grill steaks, burgers and veggies, which are served alongside plenty of cold beer and wine.

Celebrations

The late historian Arthur Schlesinger Jr noted that after just a single generation, the children of American immigrants lost nearly all ties to their ethnicities – except with regard to food culture.

Thanksgiving may be the only holiday (held the last Thursday in November) where most Americans would agree on the menu – roast turkey, stuffing, mashed potatoes, cranberry sauce and, perhaps, pumpkin pie – but even then appetizers, side dishes and desserts might be Latino, African or Asian.

Food Glossary

barbecue	a technique of slow-smoking spice-rubbed and basted meat over a grill
beignet	New Orleans doughnut-like fritter dusted with powdered sugar
biscuit	flaky yeast-free roll served in the South
blintze	Jewish pancake stuffed with various fillings such as jam, cheese or potatoes
BLT	bacon, lettuce and tomato sandwich
blue plate	special of the day in a diner or luncheonette
Boston baked beans	beans cooked with molasses and bacon in a casserole
buffalo wings	deep-fried chicken wings glazed with a buttery hot sauce and served with blue cheese dressing; originated in Buffalo, NY
burrito	Mexican American flour tortilla wrapped around beans, meat, salsa and rice
California roll	fusion sushi made with avocado, crabmeat and cucumbers wrapped in vinegared rice and nori (dried seaweed)
chili	hearty meat stew spiced with ground chilies, vegetables and beans; also called chili con carne
clam chowder	potato-based soup full of clams, vegetables and sometimes bacon, thickened with milk
club sand-wich	three-layered sandwich with chicken or turkey, bacon, lettuce and tomato
corned beef	salt-cured or brined beef, traditionally served with cabbage on St Patrick's Day (March 17)
crab cake	crabmeat bound with bread crumbs and eggs then fried
eggs Benedict	poached eggs, ham and hollandaise sauce on top of English muffins
French toast	egg-dipped fried bread served with maple syrup
grits	white cornmeal porridge; a Southern breakfast or side dish
guacamole	mashed avocado dip with lime juice, onions, chilies and cilantro, served with tortilla chips
hash browns	shredded pan-fried potatoes
huevos rancheros	Mexican breakfast of corn tortillas topped with fried eggs and salsa
jambalaya	Louisiana stew of rice, ham, sausage, shrimp and seasonings
lobster roll	lobster meat mixed with mayonnaise and seasonings, and served in a toasted frankfurter bun
lox	Jewish version of brine-cured salmon
nachos	Mexican American fried tortilla chips often topped with cheese, ground beef, jalapeño peppers, salsa and sour cream
pastrami	Jewish American brined brisket beef that is smoked and steamed
pickle	cucumber brined in vinegar
Reuben sandwich	sandwich of corned beef, Swiss cheese and sauerkraut on rye bread
smoothie	cold, thick drink made with pureed fruit, ice and sometimes yogurt
stone crab	Floribbean crab whose claws are eaten with melted butter or mustard-mayonnaise sauce
surf 'n' turf	combination plate of seafood (often lobster) and steak
wrap	tortilla or pita bread stuffed with a variety of fillings

Wine, Beer & Beyond

Americans have a staggering range of choices when it comes to beverages. A booming microbrewery industry has brought finely crafted beers to every corner of the country. The US wine industry continues to produce first-rate vintages – and it's not just Californian vineyards garnering all the awards. Washington, Oregon, New York, Virginia and many other states create celebrated pinots and rosés. Meanwhile, coffee culture continues to prevail, with cafes and roasteries elevating the once humble cup of coffee to high art.

Beer

It's hard to deny that beer is about as American as Chevrolet, football and apple pie: just tune in to the Super Bowl commercials (America's most popular yearly televised event, featuring its most expensive advertisements) and you'll see how beer has become intertwined with American cultural values. Just look at the slogans, celebrating individuality ('This Bud's for You'), sociability ('It's Miller Time!'), ruggedness ('Head for the Mountains') and authenticity ('Real Men Drink Bud Light').

Despite their ubiquity, popular brands of American beer have long been the subject of ridicule abroad due to their low alcohol content and 'light' taste. Regardless of what the critics say, sales indicate that American beer is more popular than ever – and now, with the meteoric rise of microbreweries and craft beer, even beer snobs admit that American beer has reinvented itself.

In the USA, where restaurants and bars often pay the legal minimum wage (or less), servers rely on tips for their livelihood. A good rule: tip at least a dollar per drink (more for pricey cocktails), or roughly 15% to 20% of the total bill.

Craft & Local Beer

Today, beer aficionados (otherwise known as beer geeks) sip and savor beer as they would wine, and some urban restaurants even have beer 'programs,' 'sommeliers' and cellars. Many brewpubs and restaurants host beer dinners, a chance to experience just how beers pair with different foods.

Microbrewery and craft-beer production is rising meteorically, generating roughly $20 billion in retail sales in 2015. Today there are around 1900 craft breweries across the USA. Portland, Oregon, is the current capital of the industry with some 70-plus small breweries – more than any other city in the world. In recent years, it's become possible to 'drink local' all over the country as microbreweries pop up in urban centers, small towns and unexpected places.

Wine

In the seminal 1972 film *The Godfather,* Marlon Brando's Vito Corleone muses, 'I like to drink wine more than I used to.' The country soon followed suit, and nearly four decades later Americans are drinking more wine than ever. These days the US actually consumes more wine than France (though per capita, France still towers over the US, with the French drinking 46 liters per person to America's paltry 9 liters per person).

To the raised eyebrows of European winemakers, who used to regard even Californian wines as second class, many American wines are now winning prestigious international awards. In fact, the nation is the world's fourth-largest producer of wine, behind Italy, France and Spain.

Wine isn't cheap in the US, as it's considered a luxury rather than a staple – go ahead and blame the Puritans for that. But it's possible to procure a perfectly drinkable bottle of American wine at a liquor store or wine shop for under $12.

Blame it on Hollywood: Merlot is just not that cool anymore. Paul Giamatti's Academy Award–winning performance in the film *Sideways* single-handedly destroyed its sophisticated reputation through the following line: 'If anyone orders Merlot, I'm leaving. I am *not* drinking any f*&%ing Merlot!' In the film, he favors Pinot Noir.

Wine Regions

Today almost 90% of US wine comes from California, while other regions are producing wines that have achieved international status. In particular, the wines of New York's Finger Lakes, Hudson Valley and Long Island are well worth sampling, as are the wines from both Washington and Oregon, especially Pinot Noirs and Rieslings.

Without a doubt, the country's hotbed of wine tourism is in Northern California, just outside of the Bay Area in the Napa and Sonoma Valleys. As other regions, from Oregon's Willamette Valley to Texas' Hill Country, have evolved as wine regions, they have spawned an entire industry of bed-and-breakfast tourism that seems to go hand and hand with the quest to find the perfect Pinot Noir.

So, what are the best American wines? Amazingly, though it's only been a few decades since many American restaurants served either 'red,' 'white,' or sometimes 'pink' wine, there are many excellent 'New World' wines that have flourished in the rich American soil. The most popular white varietals made in the US are Chardonnay and Sauvignon Blanc; best-selling reds include Cabernet Sauvignon, Merlot, Pinot Noir and Zinfandel.

The Hard Stuff

You might know him by his first name, Jack. (Hint: Daniels is his last name.) Good ole Jack Daniels remains the most well-known brand of American whiskey around the world, and it is also the oldest continually operating US distillery, going strong since 1870.

While whiskey and bourbon are the most popular American exports, rye, gin and vodka are also crafted in the USA. Bourbon, made from corn, is the only spirit native to the US; traditionally it is made in Kentucky.

Cocktails were invented in America before the Civil War. Born in New Orleans, an appropriately festive city to launch America's contribution to booze history, the first cocktail was the Sazerac – a mix of rye whiskey or brandy, simple syrup, bitters and a dash of absinthe (before it was

LEGENDARY AMERICANS DISH ABOUT DRINKING

While these Americans are all lauded for their talents in the arts or entertainment, they were undeniably (and often infamously) associated with the boozing life. Here are a few choice words they have on the subject.

- Ernest Hemingway: 'Always do sober what you said you'd do drunk. That will teach you to keep your mouth shut.'
- Frank Sinatra: 'Alcohol may be man's worst enemy, but the Bible says "love your enemy."'
- Dorothy Parker: 'I'd rather have a bottle in front of me than a frontal lobotomy.'
- WC Fields: 'A woman drove me to drink, and I never had the courtesy to thank her.'
- William Faulkner: 'The tools I need for my work are paper, tobacco, food, and a little whiskey.'
- Homer Simpson: 'Beer – the cause of and solution to all of life's problems.'

banned in 1912, that is). American cocktails created at bars in the late 19th and early 20th centuries include such long-standing classics as the martini, the Manhattan and the old-fashioned.

Vintage Cocktail Craze

Across US cities, it's become decidedly cool to party like it's 1929 by drinking retro cocktails from the days – less than a century ago – when consuming alcohol was illegal across the entire United States. Good old Prohibition, of course, instead of spawning a nation of teetotalers, only solidified a culture in which the forbidden became appealing, and so-called respectable citizens congregated in secret 'speakeasies' to drink homemade moonshine and dance to hot jazz.

Fast forward to the 21st century: while Prohibition isn't in danger of being reinstated, you'll find plenty of bars where the spirit of the Roaring '20s and the illicit 1930s lives on. Inspired by vintage recipes featuring spirits and elixirs – remember, back in the day you couldn't just grab a bottle of scotch at the grocery store! – these cocktails, complete with ingredients like small-batch liqueurs, whipped egg whites, hand-chipped ice and fresh fruits, are lovingly concocted by nattily dressed bartenders who regard their profession as something between an art and a science.

DUI (driving under the influence) is taken very seriously in the USA. Designating a sober driver who doesn't drink has become a widespread practice among groups of friends consuming alcohol at restaurants, bars, nightclubs and parties.

Nonalcoholic Drinks

Tap water in the USA is safe to drink, though its taste varies depending on the region and city. Most nonalcoholic drinks are quite sugary and served over ice, from Southern-style iced 'sweet tea' and lemonade to quintessential American soft drinks such as Coca-Cola, Pepsi and Dr Pepper, along with retro and nouveau soft-drinks, often made with cane sugar instead of corn syrup.

Interestingly, carbonated nonalcoholic beverages have different nicknames depending on where you order them. In many parts of the South, a 'coke' means any kind of soda, so you may have to specify which kind you mean, for example, if you say 'I'll have a Coke,' the waiter might ask, 'Which kind?' In the Midwest, soda is called 'pop.' On the East Coast and elsewhere, it's called 'soda.' Go figure...

Coffee Addiction

While Americans kick back with beer and unwind with wine, the country runs on caffeine. The coffee craze has only intensified in the last 30 years, ever since cafe culture exploded in urban centers and spread throughout the country.

Blame it on Starbucks – the coffee that America loves (or loathes) above all others. The world's biggest coffee chain was born amid the Northwest's progressive coffee culture in 1971, when Starbucks opened its first location across from Pike Place Market in Seattle. The idea, to offer a variety of roasted beans from around the world in a comfortable cafe, helped start filling the American coffee mug with more refined, complicated (and expensive) drinks compared to the ubiquitous Folgers and diner cups o' joe. By the early 1990s, specialty coffeehouses began springing up across the country.

The most infamous rumor about Coca-Cola, developed in 1886 at an Atlanta pharmacy, is true: once marketed as a medicine, it did indeed contain trace amounts of cocaine. Having once contained about 9mg per glass, Coca-Cola eliminated cocaine from the product in 1903.

While many coffee chains only have room for a few chairs and a take-out counter, independent coffee shops support a coffeehouse culture that encourages lingering; think free wi-fi, comfortable indoor and outdoor seating, and good snacks and light fare. At high-level cafes, experienced baristas will happily banter about the origins of any roast (single-origin beans rather than blends are the latest in coffee snobbery) and will share their ideas about bean grinds and more.

Arts & Architecture

Geography and race together create the varied regionalism that is key to understanding America's arts. And despite a popular affinity for technology, nature and wilderness still inspire the nation's soul and, consequently, much of its art.

Film

Hollywood and American film are virtually inseparable. No less an American icon than the White House itself, Hollywood is increasingly the product of an internationalized cinema and film culture. This evolution is partly pure business: Hollywood studios are the showpieces of multinational corporations, and funding flows to talent that brings the biggest grosses, regardless of nationality.

But this shift is also creative. It's Hollywood's recognition that if the studios don't incorporate the immense filmmaking talent emerging worldwide, they will be made irrelevant by it. Co-option is an old Hollywood strategy, used most recently to subvert the challenge posed by the independent film movement of the 1990s that kicked off with daring homegrown films like *Sex, Lies, and Videotape* and *Reservoir Dogs,* and innovative European imports. That said, for the most part, mainstream American audiences remain steadfastly indifferent to foreign films.

Top US Photographers

- Ansel Adams
- Diane Arbus
- Richard Avedon
- Walker Evans
- Robert Frank
- Lee Friedlander
- Dorothea Lange
- Vivian Maier
- Man Ray
- Cindy Sherman
- Alfred Stieglitz
- Edward Weston

Television

In the 20th century, it could be argued that TV was the defining medium of the modern age. The average American still watches loads of TV a week (34 hours, if you believe the commonly touted figure), but they are watching differently, often streaming their favorite shows via providers like Netflix.

For many decades, critics sneered that TV was lowbrow, and movie stars wouldn't be caught dead on it. But well-written, thought-provoking shows have existed almost since the beginning. In the 1950s, the original *I Love Lucy* show was groundbreaking: shot on film before a live audience and edited before airing, it pioneered syndication. It established the sitcom ('situation comedy') formula, and showcased a dynamic female comedian, Lucille Ball, in an interethnic marriage.

In its brief history, TV has proved to be one of the most passionately contested cultural battlegrounds in American society, blamed for a whole host of societal ills, from skyrocketing obesity to plummeting attention spans and school test scores. On the other hand, as cable TV has emerged as the frontier for daring and innovative programming, some of the TV shows of the past decade have proved as riveting and memorable as anything Americans viewers (and the scores of people around the world who watch American TV) have ever seen.

Of course, 'good' American TV has been around for a long time, whether through artistic merit or cultural and political importance. The 1970s comedy *All in the Family* aired an unflinching examination of prejudice, as embodied by bigoted patriarch Archie Bunker, played by Carroll O'Connor. Similarly, the sketch-comedy show *Saturday Night Live,* which debuted in 1975, pushed social hot buttons with its subversive, politically charged humor.

In the 1980s videotapes brought movies into American homes, blurring the distinction between big and small screens, and the stigma Hollywood attached to TV slowly faded. The decade also saw the rise of shows like *The Golden Girls*, a humorous sitcom that explored themes like aging and mortality (as well as more taboo topics like sexuality among the elderly). It starred four retired women living in Miami and was both critically acclaimed and a commercial success.

In the 1990s TV audiences embraced the nonformulaic, no-holds-barred weird cult show *Twin Peaks*, leading to a slew of provocative idiosyncratic shows like *The X-Files*.

These days the most popular shows are a mix of edgier, long-narrative serial dramas, as well as cheap-to-produce, 'unscripted' reality TV: what *Survivor* started in 2000, the contestants and 'actors' of *American Idol, Dancing with the Stars, Project Runway* and *Keeping Up with the Kardashians* keep alive today, for better or for worse.

In the last decade networks have created some much-loved series, including *Mad Men* (which followed the antics of 1960s advertising execs in NYC), *Parks and Recreation* (a mock documentary-style comedy that revolves around midlevel bureaucrats in a fictional Indiana town), *Portlandia* (a satire of Oregonian subcultures) and *Breaking Bad* (about a terminally ill high school teacher who builds a meth lab to safeguard his family's financial future). More recent favorites include *House of Cards* (a behind-the-scenes political drama), *Game of Thrones* (a risqué series set in a mythical kingdom) and *Orange Is the New Black* (a comedy-drama set in a women's prison in upstate New York).

Literature

American Identity Through Literature

The US first articulated a vision of itself through its literature. Until the American Revolution, most of its citizens of European descent identified with England, but after independence, an immediate call went out to develop an American national voice. Not until the 1820s, however, did writers take up the two aspects of American life that had no counterpart in Europe: the untamed wilderness and the frontier experience.

James Fenimore Cooper is credited with creating the first truly American novel with *The Pioneers* (1823). In Cooper's 'everyman' humor and individualism, Americans first recognized themselves.

In his essay *Nature* (1836), Ralph Waldo Emerson articulated similar ideas, but in more philosophical and spiritual terms. Emerson claimed that nature reflected God's instructions for humankind as plainly as the Bible did, and that individuals could understand these through rational thought and self-reliance. Emerson's writings became the core of the transcendentalist movement, which Henry David Thoreau championed in *Walden; or, Life in the Woods* (1854).

Literary highlights of this era include Herman Melville's ambitious *Moby-Dick; or, The Whale* (1851) and Nathaniel Hawthorne's examination of the dark side of conservative New England in *The Scarlet Letter* (1850). Canonical poet Emily Dickinson wrote haunting, tightly structured poems, which were first published in 1890, four years after her death.

Books Once Banned in America

- Are You There, God? It's Me, Margaret. *(Judy Blume)*
- Lord of the Flies *(William Golding)*
- 1984 *(George Orwell)*
- The Catcher in the Rye *(JD Salinger)*
- Adventures of Huckleberry Finn *(Mark Twain)*
- The Color Purple *(Alice Walker)*

Civil War & Beyond

The celebration of common humanity and nature reached its apotheosis in Walt Whitman, whose poetry collection *Leaves of Grass* (1855) signaled the arrival of an American literary visionary. In Whitman's informal, intimate, rebellious free verse were songs of individualism, democracy, earthy spirituality, taboo-breaking sexuality and joyous optimism that encapsulated the heart of a throbbing new nation.

But not everything was coming up roses. Abolitionist Harriet Beecher Stowe's controversial novel *Uncle Tom's Cabin* (1852) depicted African American life under slavery with Christian romanticism but also enough realism to inflame passions on both sides of the 'great debate' over slavery, which would shortly plunge the nation into civil war.

After the Civil War (1861–65), two enduring literary trends emerged: realism and regionalism. Regionalism was especially spurred by the rapid late-19th-century settlement of the West; novelist Jack London serialized his adventures for popular magazines such as the *Saturday Evening Post*.

However, it was Samuel Clemens (aka Mark Twain) who came to define American letters. In *Adventures of Huckleberry Finn* (1884), Twain made explicit the quintessential American narrative of an individual journey of self-discovery. The image of Huck and Jim – a poor white teenager and a runaway black slave – standing outside society's norms and floating together toward an uncertain future down the Mississippi River challenges American society still. Twain wrote in the vernacular, loved 'tall tales' and reveled in satirical humor and absurdity, while his folksy, 'anti-intellectual' stance endeared him to everyday readers.

Disillusionment & Diversity

With the dramas of world wars and a newly industrialized society for artistic fodder, American literature came into its own in the 20th century.

Dubbed the 'Lost Generation,' many US writers, most famously Ernest Hemingway, became expats in Europe. His novels exemplified the era, and his spare, stylized realism has often been imitated, yet never bettered. Other notable American figures at Parisian literary salons included modernist writers Gertrude Stein and Ezra Pound, and iconoclast Henry Miller, whose semiautobiographical novels were published in Paris, only to be banned for obscenity and pornography in the USA until the 1960s.

F Scott Fitzgerald eviscerated East Coast society life with his fiction, while John Steinbeck became the great voice of rural working poor in the West, especially during the Great Depression. William Faulkner examined the South's social rifts in dense prose riddled with bullets of black humor.

Between the world wars, the Harlem Renaissance also flourished, as African American intellectuals and artists took pride in their culture and undermined racist stereotypes. Among the best-known writers were poet Langston Hughes and novelist Zora Neale Hurston.

After WWII American writers delineated ever-sharper regional and ethnic divides, pursued stylistic experimentation and often caustically repudiated conservative middle-class American values. Writers of the 1950s Beat Generation, such as Jack Kerouac, Allen Ginsburg and Lawrence Ferlinghetti, threw themselves like Molotov cocktails onto the profusion of smug suburban lawns. Meanwhile, novelists JD Salinger, Russian immigrant Vladimir Nabokov, Ken Kesey and poet Sylvia Plath darkly chronicled descents into madness by characters who struggled against stifling social norms.

The South, always ripe with paradox, inspired masterful short-story writers and novelists Flannery O'Connor and Eudora Welty and novelist Dorothy Allison. The mythical romance and modern tragedies of the West have found their champions in Chicano writer Rudolfo Anaya, Larry McMurtry and Cormac McCarthy, whose characters poignantly tackle the rugged realities of Western life.

As the 20th century ended, American literature became ever more personalized, starting with the 'me' decade of the 1980s. Narcissistic,

The Great American Novel: A Crash Course

- My Antonia *(Willa Cather)*
- The Color Purple *(Alice Walker)*
- The Sound and the Fury *(William Faulkner)*
- The Great Gatsby *(F Scott Fitzgerald)*
- Beloved *(Toni Morrison)*
- The Sun Also Rises *(Ernest Hemingway)*
- The Plague of Doves *(Louise Erdrich)*
- To Kill a Mockingbird *(Harper Lee)*
- Tropic of Cancer *(Henry Miller)*
- Go Tell It on the Mountain *(James Baldwin)*
- The Grapes of Wrath *(John Steinbeck)*
- Rabbit, Run *(John Updike)*
- Slaughterhouse-Five *(Kurt Vonnegut)*
- The Goldfinch *(Donna Tartt)*
- The Age of Innocence *(Edith Wharton)*
- Native Son *(Richard Wright)*

often nihilistic narratives by writers such as Jay McInerney and Brett Easton Ellis catapulted the 'Brat Pack' into pop culture.

Since the 1990s an increasingly diverse panoply of voices reflects the kaleidoscopic society Americans live in. Ethnic identity (especially that of immigrant cultures), regionalism and narratives of self-discovery remain at the forefront of American literature, no matter how experimental. The quarterly journal *McSweeney's,* founded by Dave Eggers (*A Heartbreaking Work of Staggering Genius,* 2000), publishes titans of contemporary literature such as prolific Joyce Carol Oates and Michael Chabon, both Pulitzer Prize winners. Watch out for the next novel by emerging novelists like Nicole Krauss, Junot Díaz, Gary Shteyngart, and Jonathan Safran-Foer. For a sweeping, almost panoramic look at American society, read Jonathan Franzen's *The Corrections* (2001) or *Freedom,* the 2010 novel that wowed critics at home and abroad, prompting London's *Guardian* to deem it 'the novel of the century.'

More recent literary hits include Phil Klay's powerful *Redeployment* (2014), a series of 12 short stories set during the US war in Iraq and Afghanistan. Anthony Doerr's Pulitzer Prize–winning *All the Light We Cannot See,* is about a blind Parisian girl who meets a German soldier in WWII. In 2013 the reclusive award-winning author Thomas Pynchon published *Bleeding Edge,* a bold and labyrinthine novel set in NYC during the terrorist attacks of September 11.

Edgar Allan Poe was the first American writer to achieve international acclaim. His gruesome stories (such as 'The Tell-Tale Heart,' 1843) helped popularize the short-story form, and he is credited with inventing the mystery story, the horror story and science fiction, all extremely popular and enduring genres in America.

Painting & Sculpture

An ocean away from Europe's aristocratic patrons, religious commissions and historic art academies, colonial America was not exactly fertile ground for the visual arts. Since then, thankfully, times have changed: once a swampy Dutch trading post, New York City is the red-hot center of the art world, and its make-or-break influence shapes tastes across the nation and around the globe.

Shaping a National Identity

Artists played a pivotal role in the USA's 19th-century expansion, disseminating images of far-flung territories and reinforcing the call to Manifest Destiny. Thomas Cole and his colleagues in the Hudson River School translated European romanticism to the luminous wild landscapes of upstate New York, while Frederic Remington offered idealized, often stereotypical portraits of the Western frontier.

After the Civil War and the advent of industrialization, realism increasingly became prominent. Eastman Johnson painted nostalgic scenes of rural life, as did Winslow Homer, who later became renowned for watercolor seascapes.

Art in Out-of-the-Way Places

- *Marfa, TX*
- *Santa Fe, NM*
- *Traverse City, MI*
- *Park City, UT*
- *Bellingham, WA*
- *Beacon, NY*
- *Provincetown, MA*

An American Avant-Garde

Polite society's objections to Thomas Eakins' realist painting had nothing on the near-riots inspired by New York's Armory Show of 1913. This exhibition introduced the nation to European modernism and changed the face of American art. It showcased impressionism, fauvism and cubism, including the notorious 1912 *Nude Descending a Staircase, No. 2* by Marcel Duchamp, a French artist who later became an American citizen.

New York's 1913 Armory Show was merely the first in a series of exhibitions evangelizing the radical aesthetic shifts of European modernism, and it was inevitable that American artists would begin to grapple with what they had seen. Alexander Calder, Joseph Cornell and Isamu Noguchi produced sculptures inspired by surrealism and constructivism; the precisionist paintings of Charles Demuth, Georgia O'Keeffe and Charles Sheeler combined realism with a touch of cubist geometry.

In the 1930s, the Works Progress Administration's (WPA) Federal Art Project, part of FDR's New Deal, commissioned murals, paintings and sculptures for public buildings nationwide. WPA artists borrowed from Soviet social realism and Mexican muralists to forge a socially engaged figurative style with regional flavor.

Abstract Expressionism

In the wake of WWII, American art underwent a sea change at the hands of New York School painters such as Franz Kline, Jackson Pollock and Mark Rothko. Moved by surrealism's celebration of spontaneity and the unconscious, these artists explored abstraction and its psychological potency through imposing scale and the gestural handling of paint. The movement's 'action painter' camp went extreme; Pollock, for example, made his drip paintings by pouring and splattering pigments over large canvases.

Having stood the test of time, abstract expressionism is widely considered to be the first truly original school of American art.

Art + Commodity = Pop

Once established in America, abstract expressionism reigned supreme. However, stylistic revolts had begun much earlier, in the 1950s. Most notably, Jasper Johns came to prominence with thickly painted renditions of ubiquitous symbols, including targets and the American flag, while Robert Rauschenberg assembled artworks from comics, ads and even – à la Duchamp – found objects (a mattress, a tire, a stuffed goat). Both artists helped break down traditional boundaries between painting and sculpture, opening the field for pop art in the 1960s.

America's postwar economic boom also influenced pop. Not only did artists embrace representation, they drew inspiration from consumer images such as billboards, product packaging and media icons. Employing mundane mass-production techniques to silkscreen paintings of movie stars and Coke bottles, Andy Warhol helped topple the myth of the solitary artist laboring heroically in the studio. Roy Lichtenstein combined newsprint's humble benday dots with the representational conventions of comics. Suddenly, so-called 'serious' art could be political, bizarre, ironic and fun – and all at once.

> Pop art icon Andy Warhol turned the art world on its head in the early 1960s with his celebrity portraits of figures such as Marilyn Monroe and Jackie Onassis. His works were both a comment on celebrity and commercial culture while also showing these legendary figures in a startling new light.

Minimalism

What became known as minimalism shared pop's interest in mass production, but all similarities ended there. Like the abstract expressionists, artists such as Donald Judd, Agnes Martin and Robert Ryman eschewed representational subject matter; many of their cool, reductive works of the 1960s and '70s were arranged in gridded compositions and were fabricated from industrial materials.

The '80s & Beyond

By the 1980s, civil rights, feminism and AIDS activism had made inroads in visual culture; artists not only voiced political dissent through their work but embraced a range of once-marginalized media, from textiles and graffiti to video, sound and performance. The decade also ushered in the so-called Culture Wars, which commenced with tumult over photographs by Robert Mapplethorpe and Andres Serrano.

To get the pulse of contemporary art in the US, check out works by artists like Jenny Holzer, Kara Walker, Chuck Close, Martin Puryear and Frank Stella.

Theater

American theater is a three-act play of sentimental entertainment, classic revivals and urgent social commentary. From the beginning Broadway musicals (www.livebroadway.com) have aspired to be 'don't-miss-this-show!' tourist attractions. And today they continue to be one of NYC's biggest draws. Broadway shows earn over a billion dollars in revenue from ticket sales each year, with top shows pulling in a cool $2 million a week. The most successful Broadway shows often go on to even greater earnings worldwide. (Gross worldwide earnings of *The Phantom of the Opera* has now topped an astounding $6 billion.) Meanwhile, long-running classics such as *The Lion King* and *Wicked* continue to play before sold-out houses. Keep an eye out for the much-loved classic, *Les Misérables*, which returned to Broadway in 2014.

Independent theater arrived in the 1920s and '30s, with the Little Theatre Movement, which emulated progressive European theater and developed into today's 'off-Broadway' scene. Always struggling and scraping, and mostly surviving, the country's 1500 nonprofit regional theaters are breeding grounds for new plays and foster new playwrights. Some also develop Broadway-bound productions, while others sponsor festivals dedicated to the Bard himself, William Shakespeare.

AMERICA DANCES

America fully embraced dance in the 20th century. New York City has always been the epicenter for dance innovation and the home of many premier dance companies, but every major city supports resident and touring troupes, both ballet and modern.

Modern ballet is said to have begun with Russian-born choreographer George Balanchine's *Apollo* (1928) and *Prodigal Son* (1929). With these, Balanchine invented the 'plotless ballet' – in which he choreographed the inner structure of music, not a pantomimed story – and thereby created a new, modern vocabulary of ballet movement. In 1934, Balanchine founded the School of American Ballet; in 1948 he founded the New York City Ballet, turning it into one of the world's foremost ballet companies. Jerome Robbins took over that company in 1983, after achieving fame choreographing huge Broadway musicals, such as *West Side Story* (1957). Broadway remains an important venue for dance today. National companies elsewhere, like San Francisco's Lines Ballet, keep evolving contemporary ballet.

The pioneer of modern dance, Isadora Duncan, didn't find success until she began performing in Europe at the turn of the 20th century. Basing her ideas on ancient Greek myths and concepts of beauty, she challenged the strictures of classical ballet and sought to make dance an intense form of self-expression.

Martha Graham founded the Martha Graham School for Contemporary Dance in 1926 after moving to New York, and many of today's major American choreographers developed under her tutelage. In her long career she choreographed more than 140 works and developed a new dance technique, now taught worldwide, aimed at expressing inner emotion and dramatic narrative. Her most famous work is *Appalachian Spring* (1944).

Merce Cunningham, Paul Taylor and Twyla Tharp succeeded Graham as leading exponents of modern dance; they all have companies that are active today. In the 1960s and '70s, Cunningham explored abstract expressionism in movement, collaborating famously with musician John Cage. Taylor experimented with everyday movements and expressions, while Tharp is known for incorporating pop music, jazz and ballet.

Another student of Martha Graham, Alvin Ailey, was part of the post-WWII flowering of African American culture. He made his name with *Revelations* (1960), two years after he founded the still-lauded Alvin Ailey American Dance Theater in New York City.

Other celebrated postmodern choreographers include Mark Morris and Bill T Jones. Beyond New York, San Francisco, Los Angeles, Chicago, Minneapolis and Philadelphia are noteworthy for modern dance.

Eugene O'Neill – the first major US playwright and still widely considered the best – put American drama on the map. After WWII American playwrights joined the nationwide artistic renaissance. Two of the most famous were Arthur Miller, who famously married Marilyn Monroe and wrote about everything from middle-class male disillusionment to the dark psychology of the mob mentality of the Salem witch trials, and the prolific Southerner Tennessee Williams.

As in Europe, absurdism and the avant-garde marked American theater in the 1960s. Few were more scathing than Edward Albee, who started provoking bourgeois sensibilities. Neil Simon arrived at around the same time; his ever-popular comedies kept Broadway humming for 40 years.

Other prominent, active American dramatists emerging in the 1970s include David Mamet, Sam Shepard and innovative 'concept musical' composer Stephen Sondheim. August Wilson created a monumental 10-play 'Pittsburgh Cycle' dissecting 20th-century African American life.

Today, American theater is evolving in its effort to remain a relevant communal experience in an age of ever-isolating media. Shows including *Breakfast with Mugabe* explore the trauma of the past, while *Avenue Q*, with its trash-talking, love-making puppets, presents a hilarious send-up of life on *Sesame Street*. More immersive experiences such as *Sleep No More* put theatergoers inside the play to wander freely among wildly decorated rooms – including a graveyard, stables, a psychiatric ward and a ballroom – as the drama (loosely based on *Macbeth*) unfolds around them.

Jhumpa Lahiri won the Pulitzer Prize for her first breathtaking collection of stories, *The Interpreter of Maladies*, about the experience of Indian immigrants in the contemporary United States.

Architecture

In the 21st century computer technology and innovations in materials and manufacturing allow for curving, asymmetrical buildings once considered impossible, if not inconceivable. Architects are being challenged to 'go green,' and the creativity unleashed is riveting, transforming skylines and changing the way Americans think about their built environments. The public's architectural taste remains conservative, but never mind: avant-garde 'starchitects' are revising urban landscapes with radical visions that the nation will catch up with – one day.

Colonial Period

Perhaps the only lasting indigenous influence on American architecture has been the adobe dwellings of the Southwest. In the 17th and 18th centuries, Spanish colonists incorporated elements of what they called the Native American *pueblo* (village). It reappeared in late-19th and early-20th-century architecture in both the Southwest's Pueblo Revival style and Southern California's Mission Revival style.

Elsewhere, until the 20th century, immigrant Americans mainly adopted English and continental European styles and followed their trends. For most early colonists in the eastern US, architecture served necessity rather than taste, while the would-be gentry aped grander English homes; the period is well preserved in Williamsburg, Virginia.

After the Revolutionary War, the nation's leaders wanted a style befitting the new republic and adopted neoclassicism. Virginia's capitol, designed by Thomas Jefferson, was modeled on an ancient Roman temple, and Jefferson's own private estate, Monticello, sports a Romanesque rotunda.

Professional architect Charles Bulfinch helped develop the more monumental Federal style, which paralleled the English Georgian style. The grandest example is the US Capitol in Washington, DC, which became a model for state legislatures nationwide. As they moved into the 19th century, Americans, mirroring English fashions, gravitated toward the Greek and Gothic Revival styles, still seen today in many churches and college campuses.

Building the Nation

Meanwhile, small-scale architecture was revolutionized by 'balloon-frame' construction: a light frame of standard-milled timber joined with cheap nails. Easy and economical, balloon-frame stores and houses made possible swift settlement of the expanding West and, later, the surreal proliferation of the suburbs. Home-ownership was suddenly within reach of average middle-class families, making real the enduring American Dream.

After the Civil War, influential American architects studied at Paris' École des Beaux-Arts, and American buildings began to show increasing refinement and confidence. Major examples of the beaux-arts style include Richard Morris Hunt's Biltmore Estate in North Carolina and New York's Public Library.

In San Francisco and other cities across America, Victorian architecture appeared as the 19th century progressed. Among well-to-do classes, larger and fancier private houses added ever more adornments: balconies, turret, towers, ornately painted trim and intricate 'gingerbread' wooden millwork.

In a reaction against Victorian opulence, the arts-and-crafts movement arose after 1900 and remained popular until the 1930s. Its modest bungalows, such as the Gamble House in Pasadena, California, featured locally handcrafted wood and glasswork, ceramic tiles and other artisan details.

Reaching for the Sky

By the 1850s, internal iron-framed buildings had appeared in Manhattan, and this freed up urban architectural designs, especially after the advent of Otis hydraulic elevators in the 1880s. The Chicago School of architecture went beyond beaux-arts style to produce the skyscraper – considered the first truly 'modern' architecture, and America's most prominent architectural contribution to the world at that time.

In the 1930s, the influence of art deco – which became instantly popular in the US after the Paris Exposition of 1925 – meant that urban high-rises soared, becoming fitting symbols of America's technical achievements, grand aspirations, commerce and affinity for modernism.

Remarkable examples of art-deco skyscrapers include New York City's Chrysler Building and Empire State Building. Art deco simultaneously appeared nationwide in the design of movie houses, train stations, and office buildings across the country, and in neighborhoods like Miami's South Beach.

Modernism & Beyond

When the Bauhaus school fled the rise of Nazism in Germany, architects such as Walter Gropius and Ludwig Mies van der Rohe brought their pioneering modern designs to American shores. Mies van der Rohe landed in Chicago, where Louis Sullivan, considered to be the inventor of the modern skyscraper, was already working on a simplified style of architecture in which 'form ever follows function.' This evolved into the International style, which favored glass 'curtain walls' over a steel frame. IM Pei, who designed Cleveland's Rock and Roll Hall of Fame, is considered the last living high-modernist architect in America.

In the mid-20th century, modernism moved into America's suburbs, especially in Southern California. Mid-Century Modern architecture was influenced not only by the organic nature of Frank Lloyd Wright homes but also the spare, geometric, clean-lined designs of Scandinavia. Post-and-beam construction allowed for walls of sheer glass that gave the illusion of merging indoor and outdoor living spaces. Today, a striking collection of Mid-century Modern homes and public buildings by Albert Frey, Richard Neutra and other luminaries can be found in Palm Springs, CA.

Rejecting modernism's 'ugly boxes' later in the 20th century, postmodernism reintroduced decoration, color, historical references and whimsy. In this, architects like Michael Graves and Philip Johnson took the lead. Another expression of postmodernism is the brash, mimetic architecture of the Las Vegas Strip, which Pritzker Prize–winning architect Robert Venturi held up as the triumphant antithesis of modernism (he sardonically described the latter as 'less is a bore').

Today, aided and abetted by digital tools, architectural design favors the bold and the unique. Leading this plunge into futurama has been Frank Gehry; his Walt Disney Concert Hall in Los Angeles is but one example. Other notable contemporary architects include Richard Meier (Los Angeles' Getty Center), Thom Mayne (San Francisco's Federal Building) and Daniel Libeskind (San Francisco's Contemporary Jewish Museum and the Denver Art Museum's Hamilton Building).

Even as the recession crippled the American economy in 2008 and stalled new construction, several phenomenal new examples of visionary architecture have burst upon the scene in American cities. Notable examples include Jeanne Gang's Acqua building in Chicago, Santiago Calatrava's soaring World Trade Center transportation hub in New York City, Renzo Piano's California Academy of Sciences in San Francisco, and David Ajaye's shimmering National Museum of African American History and Culture in Washington, DC.

Upton Sinclair's *The Jungle* (1906) shocked the public with its harrowing exposé of Chicago's meatpacking industry and instantly became a modern classic. Nearly a century later, Eric Schlosser's *Fast Food Nation* (2001) similarly alerted America to the dark underside of the fast-food industry.

The Music Scene

American popular music is the nation's heartbeat and its unbreakable soul. It's John Lee Hooker's deep growls and John Coltrane's passionate cascades. It's Hank Williams' yodel and Elvis' pout. It's Beyoncé and Bob Dylan, Duke Ellington and Patti Smith. It's a feeling as much as a form – always a foot-stomping, defiant good time, whether folks are boot scooting to bluegrass, sweating to zydeco, jumping to hip-hop or stage-diving to punk rock.

Blues

The South is the birthplace of American music, most of which has roots in the frisson and interplay of racial relations. The blues developed after the Civil War, out of the work songs, or 'shouts,' of slaves and out of black spiritual songs and their 'call-and-response' pattern, both of which were adaptations of African music.

Improvisational and intensely personal, the blues remain at heart an immediate expression of individual pain, suffering, hope, desire and pride. Nearly all subsequent American music has tapped this deep well.

At the turn of the 20th century, traveling blues musicians, and particularly female blues singers, gained fame and employment across the South. Early pioneers included Robert Johnson, WC Handy, Ma Rainey, Huddie Ledbetter (aka Lead Belly) and Bessie Smith, who some consider the best blues singer who ever lived. At the same time, African American Christian choral music evolved into gospel, whose greatest singer, Mahalia Jackson, came to prominence in the 1920s.

After WWII, blues from Memphis and the Mississippi Delta dispersed northward, in the hands of a new generation of musicians such as Muddy Waters, Buddy Guy, BB King, John Lee Hooker and Etta James.

Today's generation of blues players include the likes of Bonamassa, Warren Haynes (a longtime player for the Allman Brothers), Seasick Steve, the Tedeschi Trucks Band and the sometimes-blues players The Black Keys.

Jazz

Congo Sq, New Orleans, where slaves gathered to sing and dance from the late 18th century onward, is considered the birthplace of jazz. There ex-slaves adapted the reed, horn and string instruments used by the city's often French-speaking, multiracial Creoles – who themselves preferred formal European music – to play their own African-influenced music. This fertile cross-pollination produced a steady stream of innovative sounds.

The first variation was ragtime, so-called because of its 'ragged,' syncopated African rhythms. Beginning in the 1890s, ragtime was popularized by musicians such as Scott Joplin and was made widely accessible through sheet music and player-piano rolls.

Dixieland jazz, centered on New Orleans' infamous Storyville red-light district, soon followed. In 1917 Storyville shut down and New Orleans' jazz musicians dispersed. In 1919 bandleader King Oliver moved to Chicago, and his star trumpet player, Louis Armstrong, soon followed. Armstrong's distinctive vocals and talented improvisations led to the solo becoming an integral part of jazz throughout much of the 20th century.

The 1920s and '30s are known as the Jazz Age, but music was just part of the greater flowering of African American culture during New York's Harlem Renaissance. Swing – an urbane, big-band jazz style – swept the country, led by innovative bandleaders Duke Ellington and Count Basie. Jazz singers Ella Fitzgerald and Billie Holiday combined jazz with its Southern sibling, the blues.

After WWII, bebop (aka bop) arose, reacting against the smooth melodies and confining rhythms of big-band swing. A new crop of musicians came of age, including Charlie Parker, Dizzy Gillespie and Thelonious Monk. Critics at first derided such 1950s and '60s permutations as cool jazz, hard-bop, free or avant-garde jazz, and fusion (which combined jazz and Latin or rock music) – but there was no stopping the postmodernist tide deconstructing jazz. Pioneers of this era include Miles Davis, Dave Brubeck, Chet Baker, Charles Mingus, John Coltrane, Melba Liston and Ornette Coleman.

The country that spawned the world's most successful recording industry also popularized the technology accused of killing it. From the emergence of file sharing to Apple's iTunes and more recent music-streaming services like Spotify, it's no surprise that the American music industry is under stress – though from its ability to evolve, you'd hardly know it.

Country

Early Scottish, Irish and English immigrants brought their own instruments and folk music to America, and what emerged over time in the secluded Appalachian Mountains was fiddle-and-banjo hillbilly, or 'country,' music. In the Southwest, steel guitars and larger bands distinguished 'western' music. During the 1920s, these styles merged into 'country-and-western' music and became centered on Nashville, Tennessee, especially once the *Grand Ole Opry* began its radio broadcasts in 1925. Country musicians that are now 'classics' include Hank Williams, Johnny Cash, Willie Nelson, Patsy Cline and Loretta Lynn.

Country music influenced rock and roll in the 1950s, while rock-flavored country was dubbed 'rockabilly.' In the 1980s, country and western achieved new levels of popularity with stars like Garth Brooks. Today, country-music stations dominate other genres. Musicians with record-breaking success include Shania Twain, Dwight Yoakam, Tim McGraw and Taylor Swift. Occupying the eclectic 'alt-country' category are Lucinda Williams and Lyle Lovett.

Folk

The tradition of American folk music was crystallized by Woody Guthrie, who traveled the country during the Depression singing politically conscious songs. In the 1940s, Pete Seeger emerged as a tireless preserver of America's folk heritage. Folk music experienced a revival during 1960s protest movements, but then-folkie Bob Dylan ended it almost single-handedly when he plugged in an electric guitar to shouts of 'traitor!'

Folk has seen a resurgence in the last decade, particularly in the Pacific Northwest. Iron and Wine's mournful tunes channel pop, blues and rock, while Joanna Newsom, with her extraordinary voice and unusual instrumentation (she plays the harp) add a new level of complexity to folk. The young sister duo Lily & Madeleine sing ethereal, incredibly rich folk ballads.

One of rock music's most phenomenal success stories, Prince, was born Prince Rogers Nelson in 1950s Minneapolis. He originally tried out for the high-school basketball team, but, being too short at 5ft 2in, he was cut. His back-up hobby? He took up the guitar.

Rock & Roll

Most say rock and roll was born in 1954 the day Elvis Presley walked into Sam Phillips' Sun Studio and recorded 'That's All Right.' Initially, radio stations weren't sure why a white country boy was singing black music, or whether they should play it. Two years later Presley scored his first big breakthrough with 'Heartbreak Hotel.'

Musically, rock and roll was a hybrid of guitar-driven blues, rhythm and blues (R & B) and country-and-western music. R & B evolved in the 1940s out of swing and the blues and was then known as 'race music.' With rock and roll, white performers and some African American musicians transformed 'race music' into something that white youths could embrace freely – and oh, did they.

Rock and roll instantly abetted a social revolution even more significant than its musical one: openly sexual as it celebrated youth and dancing freely across color lines, rock scared the nation. Authorities worked diligently to control 'juvenile delinquents' and to sanitize and suppress rock and roll, which might have withered if not for the early 1960s 'British invasion,' in which the Beatles and the Rolling Stones, emulating Chuck Berry, Little Richard and others, shocked rock and roll back to life.

The 1960s witnessed a full-blown youth rebellion, epitomized by the drug-inspired psychedelic sounds of the Grateful Dead and Jefferson Airplane, and the electric wails of Janis Joplin and Jimi Hendrix. Ever since, rock has been about music *and* lifestyle, alternately torn between hedonism and seriousness, commercialism and authenticity.

Punk arrived in the late 1970s, led by the Ramones and the Dead Kennedys, as did the working-class rock of Bruce Springsteen and Tom Petty. As the counterculture became the culture in the 1980s, critics prematurely pronounced 'rock is dead.' Rock was saved (by the Talking Heads, REM, Nirvana, Sonic Youth, Pavement and Pearl Jam among others) as it always has been: by splintering and evolving, whether it's called new wave, heavy metal, grunge, indie rock, skate punk, hardcore, goth, emo or electronica.

In the early 2000s guitar groups The Killers, The Strokes, the Yeah Yeah Yeahs and The White Stripes were dubbed the saviors of rock for their stripped-back sound, which saw the genre established as the commercial mainstream.

Today, while American rock music may be waiting for its next big revival, bands such as Alabama Shakes, pop-rockers Haim and various incarnations by Jack White ensure it's not going anywhere soon.

The American Soundtrack

- *'Respect,' Aretha Franklin (1967)*
- *'America,' Simon & Garfunkel (1968)*
- *'Carolina in My Mind,' James Taylor (1968)*
- *'Jolene,' Dolly Parton (1973)*
- *'Heart of Saturday Night,' Tom Waits (1974)*
- *'Born to Run,' Bruce Springsteen (1975)*
- *'Gloria,' Patti Smith (1975)*
- *'Jack & Diane,' John Cougar Mellencamp (1982)*
- *'Push it,' Salt-N-Pepa (1987)*
- *'Fast Car,' Tracy Chapman (1988)*
- *'Like a Prayer,' Madonna (1989)*
- *'Fade into You,' Mazzy Star (1994)*
- *'I've Been Everywhere,' Johnny Cash (1996)*
- *'West Coast,' Coconut Records (2007)*
- *'Uptown Funk,' Mark Ronson & Bruno Mars (2014)*

Hip-Hop

From the ocean of sounds coming out of the early 1970s – funk, soul, Latin, reggae and rock and roll – young DJs from the Bronx in NYC began to spin a groundbreaking mixture of records together in an effort to drive dancefloors wild. And so hip-hop was born. Groups such as Grandmaster Flash and the Furious Five were soon taking the party from the streets to the trendy clubs of Manhattan and mingling with punk and new wave bands including the Clash and Blondie. Break-out artists Futura 2000, Keith Haring and Jean-Michel Basquiat moved from the subways and the streets to the galleries, and soon to the worlds of fashion and advertising.

As groups like Run-DMC, Public Enemy and the Beastie Boys sold millions, the sounds and styles of the growing hip-hop culture rapidly diversified. The daring 'gangsta rap' sound of NWA (Niggaz With Attitude) came out of Los Angeles, and the group got both accolades and bad press for its daring sounds and social commentary on racism, drugs, sex and urban poverty.

Come the turn of the millennium, what started as some raggedy gang kids playing their parents' funk records at illegal block parties had evolved into a multibillion-dollar business. Russell Simmons and P Diddy stood atop media empires, and stars Queen Latifah and Will Smith were Hollywood royalty. A white rapper from Detroit, Eminem, sold millions of records and hip-hop then overtook country as America's second-most-popular music, behind pop rock.

Today, many view hip-hop as a vapid wasteland of commercial excess – glorifying consumerism, misogyny, homophobia, drug use and a host of other social ills. But just as the hedonistic days of arena rock and roll gave birth to the rebel child of punk, the evolving offspring of hip-hop and DJ culture are constantly breaking the rules to create something new and even more energizing. Major players of the moment include Jay-Z, Kanye West, Nicki Minaj and the more experimental and feel-good hip-hop duo of Macklemore & Ryan Lewis.

The Land & Wildlife

The USA is home to creatures both great and small, from the ferocious grizzly to the industrious beaver, with colossal bison, snowy owls, soaring eagles, howling coyotes and doe-eyed manatees all part of the great American menagerie. The nation's varied geography – coastlines along two oceans, mountains, deserts, rainforests, and massive bay and river systems – harbor ecosystems where an extraordinary array of plant and animal life can flourish.

Geography

The USA is big, no question. Covering more than 3.5 million sq miles, it's the world's third-largest country, trailing only Russia and Canada, its friendly neighbor to the north. The continental USA is made up of 48 contiguous states ('the lower 48'), while Alaska, its largest state, is northwest of Canada, and the volcanic islands of Hawaii, the 50th state, are 2600 miles southwest of the mainland in the Pacific Ocean.

It's more than just size, though. America feels big because of its incredibly diverse topography, which began to take shape around 50 to 60 million years ago.

In the contiguous USA, the east is a land of temperate, deciduous forests and contains the ancient Appalachian Mountains, a low range that parallels the Atlantic Ocean. Between the mountains and the coast lies the country's most populated, urbanized region, particularly in the corridor between Washington, DC, and Boston, MA.

To the north are the Great Lakes, which the USA shares with Canada. These five lakes, part of the Canadian Shield, are the greatest expanse of freshwater on the planet, constituting nearly 20% of the world's supply.

Going south along the East Coast, things get wetter and warmer till you reach the swamps of southern Florida and make the turn into the Gulf of Mexico, which provides the USA with a southern coastline.

West of the Appalachians are the vast interior plains, which lie flat all the way to the Rocky Mountains. The eastern plains are the nation's breadbasket, roughly divided into the northern 'corn belt' and the southern 'cotton belt.' The plains, an ancient sea bottom, are drained by the mighty Mississippi River, which together with the Missouri River forms the world's fourth-longest river system, surpassed only by the Nile, Amazon and Yangtze Rivers. Going west, farmland slowly gives way to cowboys and ranches in the semiarid, big-sky Great Plains.

The young, jagged Rocky Mountains are a complex set of tall ranges that run all the way from Mexico to Canada, providing excellent skiing. West of these mountains are the Southwestern deserts, an arid region of extremes that has been cut to dramatic effect by the Colorado River system. This land of eroded canyons leads to the unforgiving Great Basin as you go across Nevada. Also an ancient sea bottom, the Great Basin is used as a training ground and a test range by the US military. It's also where the USA plans to bury its nuclear waste.

High in the White Mountains (east of California's Sierra Nevada) stand the oldest single living plant species on earth. Known as bristlecone pines, these bare and dramatically twisted trees date back more than 4000 years and have long mystified scientists for their extraordinary longevity.

Wilderness Films

Wild (*Jean-Marc Vallée*)

Winged Migration (*Jacques Perrin*)

Grizzly Man (*Werner Herzog*)

Into the Wild (*Sean Penn*)

Jeremiah Johnson (*Sydney Pollack*)

Then you reach America's third major mountain system: the southern, granite Sierra Nevada and the northern, volcanic Cascades, which both parallel the Pacific Coast. California's Central Valley is one of the most fertile places on earth, while the coastline from San Diego to Seattle is celebrated in folk songs and Native American legends – a stretch of sandy beaches and old-growth forests, including coast redwoods.

But wait, there's more. Northwest of Canada, Alaska reaches the Arctic Ocean and contains tundra, glaciers, an interior rainforest and the lion's share of federally protected wilderness. Hawaii, in the Pacific Ocean, is a string of tropical island idylls.

Land Mammals

Nineteenth-century Americans did not willingly suffer competing predators, and federal eradication programs nearly wiped out every single wolf and big cat and many of the bears in the continental US. Almost all share the same story of abundance, precipitous loss and, today, partial recovery.

The grizzly bear, a subspecies of brown bear, is one of North America's largest land mammals. Male grizzlies can stand 7ft tall, weigh up to 850lb and consider 500 sq miles home. At one time, perhaps 50,000 grizzlies

AMERICA'S WORST NATURAL DISASTERS

Earthquakes, wildfires, tornadoes, hurricanes and blizzards – the US certainly has its share of natural disasters. A few of the more infamous events that have shaped the national conscience:

Johnstown Flood In 1889 torrential rains overwhelmed the South Fork dam that stood high on the Little Conemaugh River in Central Pennsylvania. When the dam broke, some 20 million tons of water and debris quickly inundated nearby Johnstown, killing over 2200 people and destroying 1600 homes.

Galveston Hurricane In 1900 Galveston – then known as 'the jewel of Texas' – was practically obliterated by a category-4 hurricane. Fifteen-foot waves destroyed buildings, and at one point the entire island was submerged. More than 8000 perished, making it America's deadliest natural disaster.

1906 San Francisco Earthquake A powerful earthquake (estimated to be around an 8 on the Richter scale) leveled the city, followed by even more devastating fires. The quake was felt as far away as Oregon and central Nevada. An estimated 3000-plus died, while more than 200,000 people (of a population of 410,000) were left homeless.

Dust Bowl During a prolonged drought in the 1930s, the overworked topsoil of the Great Plains dried up, turned to dust and billowed eastward in massive windstorm-fueled 'black blizzards,' reaching all the way to NYC and Washington, DC. Millions of acres of crops were decimated and more than 500,000 people were left homeless. The great exodus westward by stricken farmers and migrants was immortalized in John Steinbeck's *The Grapes of Wrath*.

Hurricane Katrina August 29, 2005, is not a day easily forgotten in New Orleans. A massive category-5 hurricane swept across the Gulf of Mexico and slammed into Louisiana. As levees failed, floods inundated more than 80% of the city. The death toll reached 1836, with more than $100 billion in estimated damages – making it America's costliest natural disaster. Heartbreaking images of the destroyed city, and anger over the government's response, still linger.

Hurricane Sandy In 2012 America suffered its second-costliest hurricane in US history. It affected some 24 states, with New Jersey and New York among the hardest hit. More than 80 died in the USA, and estimated damages amounted to more than $68 billion. It was also the largest Atlantic hurricane ever recorded, with storm winds spanning over 1000 miles.

RETURN OF THE WOLF

The wolf is a potent symbol of North America's wilderness. This smart, social predator is the largest species of canine – averaging more than 100lb and reaching nearly 3ft at the shoulder. An estimated 400,000 once roamed the continent from coast to coast, from Alaska to Mexico.

Wolves were not regarded warmly by European settlers. The first wildlife legislation in the British colonies was a wolf bounty. As 19th-century Americans tamed the West, they slaughtered the once-uncountable herds of bison, elk, deer and moose, replacing them with domestic cattle and sheep, which wolves found equally tasty.

To stop wolves from devouring the livestock, the wolf's extermination soon became official government policy. Up until 1965, wolves were shot, poisoned, trapped and dragged from dens until in the lower 48 states only a few hundred gray wolves remained, in northern Minnesota and Michigan.

In 1944 naturalist Aldo Leopold called for the return of the wolf. His argument was ecology, not nostalgia. His studies showed that wild ecosystems need their top predators to maintain a healthy biodiversity; in complex interdependence, all animals and plants suffered with the wolf gone.

Despite dire predictions from ranchers and hunters, gray wolves were reintroduced to the Greater Yellowstone Region in 1995–96 and red wolves to Arizona in 1998.

Protected and encouraged, wolf populations have made a remarkable recovery, with more than 5000 now counted in the continental US, and around 8000 in Alaska.

roamed the West, but by 1975 fewer than 300 remained. Conservation efforts, particularly in the Greater Yellowstone Region, have increased the population in the lower 48 states to around 1300. By contrast, Alaska remains chock-full of grizzlies, with upwards of 30,000. Despite a decline in numbers, black bears survive nearly everywhere. Smaller than grizzlies, these opportunistic, adaptable and curious animals can survive on very small home ranges.

Another extremely adaptable creature is the coyote, which looks similar to a wolf but is about half the size, ranging from 15lb to 45lb. An icon of the Southwest, coyotes are found all over, even in cities. The USA has one primary big-cat species, which goes by several names: mountain lion, cougar, puma and panther. In the southeast, a remnant population of panthers is defended within Everglades National Park. In the West, mountain lions are common enough for human encounters to be on the increase. These powerful cats are about 150lb of pure muscle, with short tawny fur, long tails and a secretive nature.

The story of the great American buffalo is a tragic one. These massive herbivores numbered as many as 65 million in 1800 – in herds so thick they 'darkened the whole plains,' as explorers Lewis and Clark wrote. They were killed for food, hides, sport and to impoverish Native Americans, who depended on them for survival. By the 20th century, only a few hundred bison remained. Overcoming near extinction, new herds arose from these last survivors, so that one of America's noblest animals can again be admired in its gruff majesty – among other places, in Yellowstone, Grand Teton and Badlands National Parks.

Unusual Wildlife Reads

- Rats *(Robert Sullivan)*
- Pigeons *(Andrew Blechman)*
- Cod *(Mark Kurlansky)*
- Ants *(Bert Hölldobler and EO Wilson)*
- Secret Life of Lobsters *(Trevor Corson)*

Marine Mammals & Fish

Perhaps no native fish gets more attention than salmon, whose spawning runs up Pacific Coast rivers and provides famous spectacles. However, both Pacific and Atlantic salmon are considered endangered; hatcheries release millions of young every year, but there is debate about whether this practice hurts or helps wild populations.

WILDLIFE-WATCHING: USA'S ENDANGERED SPECIES

Currently, more than 1300 plants and animals are listed in the USA as either endangered or threatened. All endangered species are vital to the ecosystem, but if it's brag-worthy animals that you're keen to see (and photograph), here are places to spot them before it's too late:

Bighorn sheep Anza-Borrego Desert State Park, CA, and Zion National Park, UT

California condor Big Sur, CA, and Grand Canyon National Park, AZ

Desert tortoise Mojave National Preserve, CA

Florida panther Everglades National Park, FL

Gray wolf Yellowstone National Park, WY

Hawaiian goose Haleakalā National Park, HI

Hawaiian monk seal Waikiki Aquarium, HI

Manatee Everglades National Park, FL

Mexican long-nosed bat Big Bend National Park, TX

Whooping cranes Aransas National Wildlife Refuge, TX, and Bosque del Apache National Wildlife Refuge, NM

As for marine life, gray, humpback and blue whales migrate annually along the Pacific Coast, making whale-watching very popular. Alaska and Hawaii are important breeding grounds for whales and marine mammals, and Washington's San Juan Islands are visited by orcas. The Pacific Coast is also home to ponderous elephant seals, playful sea lions and endangered sea otters.

In California, Channel Islands National Park and Monterey Bay preserve unique, highly diverse marine worlds. For coral reefs and tropical fish, Hawaii and the Florida Keys are the prime destinations. The coast of Florida is also home to the unusual, gentle manatee, which moves between freshwater rivers and the ocean. Around 10ft long and weighing on average 1000lb, these agile, expressive creatures number around 3800 today, and may once have been mistaken for mermaids.

The Gulf of Mexico is another vital marine habitat, perhaps most famously for endangered sea turtles, which nest on coastal beaches.

Birds

Birding is the most popular wildlife-watching activity in the US, and little wonder: all the hemisphere's migratory songbirds and shorebirds rest here at some point, and the USA consequently claims some 800 native avian species.

The fastest bird in North America is believed to be the peregrine falcon, which has been clocked diving for prey at speeds of over 200mph!

The bald eagle was adopted as the nation's symbol in 1782. It's the only eagle unique to North America, and perhaps half a million once ruled the continent's skies. By 1963, habitat destruction and, in particular, poisoning from DDT had caused the population to plummet to 487 breeding pairs in the lower 48. By 2006, however, bald eagles had recovered so well, increasing to almost 9800 breeding pairs across the continent (plus 50,000 in Alaska), that they've now been removed from the endangered species list.

Another impressive bird is the endangered California condor, a prehistoric, carrion-eating bird that weighs about 20lb and has a wingspan of over 9ft. Condors were virtually extinct by the 1980s (reduced to just 22 birds), but they have been successfully bred and reintroduced in California and northern Arizona, where they can sometimes be spotted soaring above the Grand Canyon.

The Environmental Movement

The USA is well known for its political and social revolutions, but it also birthed environmentalism. The USA was the first nation to make significant efforts to preserve its wilderness, and US environmentalists often spearhead preservation efforts worldwide.

America's Protestant settlers believed that civilization's Christian mandate was to bend nature to its will. Not only was wilderness deadly and difficult, but it was a potent symbol of humanity's godless impulses, and the Pilgrims set about subduing both with gusto.

Then, in the mid-19th century, taking their cue from European Romantics, the USA's transcendentalists claimed that nature was not fallen, but holy. In *Walden; or, Life in the Woods* (1854), iconoclast Henry David Thoreau described living for two years in the woods, blissfully free of civilization's comforts. He persuasively argued that human society was harmfully distant from nature's essential truths. This view marked a profound shift toward believing that nature, the soul and God were one.

The Sierra Club (www.sierraclub.org) was the USA's first conservation group, and it remains the nation's most active, with educational programs, organized trips and tons of information.

IT'S NOT EASY BEING GREEN

The USA has long been one of the world's greatest consumers of energy, accounting for a quarter of the world's greenhouse gases. Sustainability, however, seems to be on everyone's lips these days, and interest in renewable energy is at an all-time high.

Though enormous obstacles lie ahead, the US has made marked advances in lowering its carbon footprint:

Winds of change Wind turbines generate about 4% of the nation's electricity, making the US the world's second-largest producer of wind energy (after China), and shows enormous potential for growth. The US Department of Energy envisions 20% of the nation's power supplied by this clean energy by 2030.

Solar power Interest in solar power is high – with solar power growing at a rate of over 30% per year. California leads the way, with over 5% of its overall electricity coming from large-scale solar plants. Speaking of California, its recently opened Desert Sunlight Solar Farm and the Topaz Solar Farm each produce over 550MW, making them the largest solar plants on earth. Private citizens and small businesses are also contributing, adding solar panels to help meet energy needs.

Biofuels The USA is now the world's largest producer of ethanol (fuel made from corn and other common crops). It currently accounts for roughly 10% of the nation's total domestic fuel consumption – a big jump from 2001 when it was only 1%.

Electric cars American automobile manufacturers, once wedded to gas-guzzling SUVs and trucks, have responded to consumer demand for more fuel-efficient cars. About 120,000 plug-in vehicles were sold in 2014, a 23% jump from the year before and a 128% increase from 2012. More than 9000 charging stations are scattered across the country. The US government also has pledged over $2 billion in federal grants to support the development of next-generation electric cars as well as expanding electric-vehicle charging infrastructure.

Ecofriendly architecture Green buildings have arrived and are garnering much attention at home and abroad. Energy-efficient windows, more ecofriendly building materials and water conservation features (such as greywater systems that utilize rainwater) are just a few features of LEED-certified buildings going up nationwide.

Greenways Back in the 1980s, the notion of riding a bicycle down Broadway in New York City seemed pure suicide. Today, NYC – along with Chicago, Boston, Houston, Miami, Washington, DC, and many other cities – has added hundreds of miles of bike lanes, and urbanites are finding greener (and sometimes faster) ways of getting around town.

John Muir & National Parks

The continent's natural wonders – vividly captured by America's 19th-century landscape painters – had a way of selling themselves, and rampant nationalism led to a desire to promote them. In the late 1800s, US presidents began setting aside land for state and national parks.

Scottish naturalist John Muir soon emerged to champion wilderness for its own sake. Muir considered nature superior to civilization, and he spent much of his life wandering the Sierra Nevada mountain range and passionately advocating on its behalf. Muir was the driving force behind the USA's emerging conservation movement, which had its first big victory in 1890 when Yosemite National Park was established. Muir founded the Sierra Club in 1892 and slowly gained national attention.

Reading Climate Change

- Field Notes from a Catastrophe *(Elizabeth Kolbert)*
- The Weather Makers *(Tim Flannery)*
- Eaarth *(Bill McKibben)*
- The Collapse of Western Civilization *(Naomi Oreskes)*

Environmental Laws & Climate Change

As the 19th century drew to a close and in the decades that followed, the USA passed a series of landmark environmental and wildlife laws that resulted in significant improvements in the nation's water and air quality, and the partial recovery of many near-extinct plants and animals. The movement's focus steadily broadened – to preserving entire ecosystems, not just establishing parks – as it confronted devastation wrought by pollution, overkill of species, habitat destruction through human impact and the introduction of nonnative species.

Today environmentalism is a worldwide movement, one that understands that each nation's local problems also contribute to a global threat: climate change. In the USA, the dangers of global warming are inspiring an environmental awareness as widespread as at any time in US history. Whether or not average Americans believe God speaks through nature, they're increasingly disturbed by the messages they are hearing.

Survival Guide

Directory A-Z

Accommodations

For all but the cheapest places and the slowest seasons, reservations are advised. In high-season tourist hot spots, hotels can book up months ahead. In general, many hotels offer specials on their websites, but low-end chains sometimes give a slightly better rate over the phone. Chain hotels also offer frequent-flyer mileage deals and other rewards programs; ask when booking. Online travel booking, bidding and comparison websites are another good way to find discounted hotel rates, but are usually limited to chain hotels; also check out Hotels.com, **Hotwire** (www.hotwire.com) and Booking.com. If you have a smartphone, each of these sites has a free app – which often are great for finding great last-minute deals. The Hotel Tonight is another good app for booking rooms on the fly, and includes boutique hotels and historic properties.

House & Apartment Rentals

To rent a house or apartment from locals, visit **Airbnb** (www.airbnb.com), which has thousands of listings across the country. Budget travelers can also rent a room, a great way to connect with locals if you don't mind sharing facilities.

B&Bs

In the USA, many B&Bs are high-end romantic retreats in restored historic homes that are run by personable, independent innkeepers who serve gourmet breakfasts. These B&Bs often take pains to evoke a theme – Victorian, rustic, Cape Cod and so on – and amenities range from merely comfortable to indulgent. Rates normally top $120, and the best run are $200 to $300. Some B&Bs have minimum-stay requirements, and most exclude young children.

European-style B&Bs also exist: these may be rooms in someone's home, with plainer furnishings, simpler breakfasts, shared bathrooms and cheaper rates. These often welcome families.

B&Bs can close out of season and reservations are essential, especially for top-end places. To avoid surprises, always ask about bathrooms (whether shared or private). Recommended B&B agencies:

Bed & Breakfast Inns Online (www.bbonline.com)

BedandBreakfast.com (www.bedandbreakfast.com)

BnB Finder (www.bnbfinder.com)

Select Registry (www.selectregistry.com)

Hostels

Hostels are mainly found in urban areas, in the northeast, the Pacific Northwest, California and the Southwest.

Hostelling International USA (☎240-650-2100; www.hiusa.org) runs more than 50 hostels in the US. Most have gender-segregated dorms, a few private rooms, shared bathrooms and a communal kitchen. Overnight fees for dorm beds typically cost between $25 and $45 (though in NYC, a dorm bed can cost upwards of $75). HI-USA members are entitled to small discounts. Reservations are accepted (you can book online) and advisable during high season, when there may be a three-night maximum stay.

The USA has many independent hostels not affiliated with HI-USA. For online listings, check the following:

Hostels.com

Hostelworld.com

Hostelz.com

Camping

Most federally managed public lands and many state parks offer camping. First-

BOOK YOUR STAY ONLINE

For more accommodations reviews by Lonely Planet authors, check out http://lonelyplanet.com/hotels. You'll find independent reviews, as well as recommendations on the best places to stay. Best of all, you can book online.

come, first-served 'primitive' campgrounds offer no facilities; overnight fees range from free to less than $10. 'Basic' sites usually provide toilets (flush or pit), drinking water, fire pits and picnic tables; they cost $8 to $20 a night, and some or all may be reserved in advance. 'Developed' campgrounds, usually in national or state parks, have nicer facilities and more amenities: showers, barbecue grills, RV sites with hookups etc. These are $18 to $50 a night, and many can be reserved in advance.

Camping on most federal lands – including national parks, national forests and Bureau of Land Management land – can be reserved through **Recreation.gov** (☎877-444-6777, international 518-885-3639; www.recreation.gov). Camping is limited to 14 days and can be reserved up to six months in advance. For some state park campgrounds, you can make bookings through **ReserveAmerica** (☎California State Park Reservations 800 444 7275, Colorado State Park Reservations 800 678 2267, NRRS Federal Campground Reservations 877 444 6777; www.reserveamerica.com). Both websites let you search for campground locations and amenities, check availability, reserve a site, view maps and get driving directions.

Private campgrounds tend to cater to RVs and families (tent sites may be few and lack atmosphere). Facilities may include playgrounds, convenience stores, wi-fi access, swimming pools and other activities. Some rent camping cabins, ranging from canvas-sided wooden platforms to log-frame structures with real beds, heating and private bathrooms. **Kampgrounds of America** (www.koa.com) is a national network of private campgrounds with a full range of facilities. You can browse its comprehensive campground listings and make bookings online.

Hotels

Hotels in all categories typically include in-room phones, cable TV, private bathrooms, wi-fi and a simple continental breakfast. Many midrange properties provide minibars, microwaves, hairdryers, internet access, air-con and/or heating, swimming pools and writing desks, while top-end hotels add concierge services, fitness and business centers, spas, restaurants, bars and higher-end furnishings.

Even if hotels advertise that children 'sleep free,' cots or rollaway beds may cost extra. Always ask about the hotel's policy for telephone calls; all charge an exorbitant amount for long-distance and international calls, but some also charge for dialing local and toll-free numbers.

Motels

Motels – distinguishable from hotels by having rooms that open onto a parking lot – tend to cluster around interstate exits and on main routes into town. Some remain smaller, less-expensive 'mom-and-pop' operations; breakfast is rarely included, and amenities might be a phone and TV (maybe with cable); most also have free wi-fi. Motels often have a few rooms with simple kitchenettes.

Although many motels are of the bland, cookie-cutter variety, these can be good for discount lodging or when other options fall through.

Don't judge a motel solely on looks. Facades may be faded and tired, but the proprietor may keep rooms spotlessly clean. Of course, the reverse could also be true. Try to see your room before you commit.

Customs Regulations

For a complete list of US customs regulations, visit the official portal for **US Customs & Border Protection** (www.cbp.gov).

Duty-free allowance per person:

- 1L of liquor (provided you are at least 21 years old)
- 100 cigars and 200 cigarettes (if you are at least 18 years old)
- $200 worth of gifts and purchases ($800 if you're a returning US citizen)

If you arrive with $10,000 in US or foreign currency, it must be declared.

There are heavy penalties for attempting to import illegal drugs. Forbidden items include drug paraphernalia, lottery tickets, items with fake brand names, and most goods

SLEEPING PRICE RANGES

The following price ranges refer to double occupancy in high season (generally May to September), and don't include taxes, which can add 10% to 15%. When booking, ask for the rate including taxes.

$ less than $100

$$ $100–250

$$$ more than $250

For New York City, San Francisco and Washington, DC, the following price ranges are used:

$ less than $150

$$ $150–350

$$$ more than $350

made in Iran, North Korea, Myanmar (Burma) and Sudan. Fruit, vegetables or other food or plant material must be declared or binned.

Discount Cards

The following passes can net you savings on museums, accommodations and some transport (including Amtrak):

International Student Identity Card (ISIC; www.isic.org) For international nonstudents under 26 years.

Student Advantage Card (www.studentadvantage.com) For US and foreign travelers.

American Association of Retired Persons (AARP; www.aarp.org) For US travelers aged 50 and older.

Membership in the American Automobile Association (AAA; www.aaa.com) and reciprocal clubs in the UK, Australia and elsewhere can also earn discounts.

Electricity

120V/60Hz

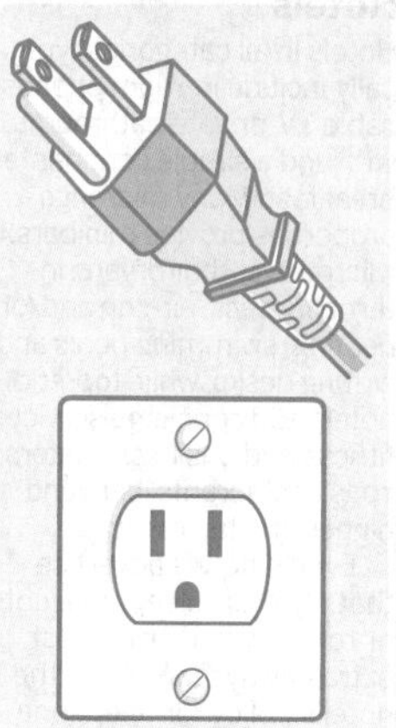

120V/60Hz

Embassies & Consulates

In addition to the following foreign embassies in Washington, DC (see www.embassy.org for a complete list), most countries have an embassy for the UN in New York City. Some countries have consulates in other large cities; go online, look under 'Consulates' in the *Yellow Pages*, or call local directory assistance.

Australian Embassy (☎20 2-797-3000; www.usa.embassy.gov.au; 1601 Massachusetts Ave NW; M Farragut North)

Canadian Embassy (☎20 2-682-1740; www.can-am.gc.ca; 501 Pennsylvania Ave NW; M Archives)

French Embassy (☎20 2-944-6000; www.info-france-usa.org; 4101 Reservoir Rd NW; D6)

German Embassy (☎20 2-298-4000; www.germany.info; 4645 Reservoir Rd NW; D6)

Irish Embassy (☎20 2-462-3939; www.dfa.ie/irish-embassy/USA; 2234 Massachusetts Ave NW; M Dupont Circle)

Mexican Embassy (☎20 2-728-1600; http://embamex.sre.gob.mx/eua; 1911 Pennsylvania Ave NW; M Farragut West)

Netherlands Embassy (☎877-388-2443; http://dc.the-netherlands.org; 4200 Linnean Ave NW; M Van Ness-UDC)

New Zealand Embassy (☎202-328-4800; www.nzembassy.com/usa; 37 Observatory Circle NW; M Dupont Circle, then bus N2 or N4)

UK Embassy (☎20 2-588-6500; www.gov.uk/government/world/usa; 3100 Massachusetts Ave NW; M Dupont Circle, then bus N2 or N4)

Gay & Lesbian Travelers

It's never been a better time to be gay in the USA. GLBT travelers will find lots of places where they can be themselves without thinking twice. Beaches and big cities typically are the most gay-friendly destinations.

Hot Spots

Manhattan has loads of great gay bars and clubs, especially in Hells Kitchen, Chelsea and the West Village. A few hours away (by train and ferry) is Fire Island, the sandy gay mecca on Long Island. Other East Coast cities that flaunt it are Boston, Philadelphia, Washington, DC, Massachusetts' Provincetown on Cape Cod and Delaware's Rehoboth Beach. Even Maine brags a gay beach destination: Ogunquit.

In the South, there's always steamy 'Hotlanta' and Texas gets darn-right gay-friendly in Austin and parts of Houston and Dallas. In Florida, Miami and the 'Conch Republic' of Key West support thriving gay communities, though Fort Lauderdale attracts bronzed boys and girls too. New Orleans has a lively gay scene.

In the Midwest, seek out Chicago and Minneapolis. Further west, you'll find

San Francisco, probably the happiest gay city in America. There's also Los Angeles and Las Vegas, where pretty much anything goes. When LA or Vegas gets to be too much, flee to the desert resorts of Palm Springs.

Lastly, for an island idyll, Hawaii is generally gay-friendly, especially in Waikiki.

Attitudes

Most major US cities have a visible and open GLBT community that is easy to connect with.

The level of acceptance varies nationwide. In some places, there is absolutely no tolerance whatsoever, and in others acceptance is predicated on GLBT people not 'flaunting' their sexual preference or identity. Bigotry still exists. In rural areas and conservative enclaves, it's unwise to be openly out, as violence and verbal abuse can sometimes occur. When in doubt, assume locals follow a 'don't ask, don't tell' policy. Same-sex marriage is now legally recognized by the federal government, and 37 states plus the District of Columbia have same-sex marriages.

Resources

The Queerest Places: A Guide to Gay and Lesbian Historic Sites, by Paula Martinac, is full of juicy details and history, and covers the country. Visit her blog at www.queerestplaces.com.

Advocate (www.advocate.com) Gay-oriented news website reports on business, politics, arts, entertainment and travel.

Damron (www.damron.com) Publishes the classic gay travel guides, but they're advertiser-driven and sometimes outdated.

Gay & Lesbian National Help Center (☎888-843-4564; www.glnh.org; ⊙1-9pm PST Mon-Fri, 9am-2pm PST Sat) A national hotline for counseling, information and referrals.

Gay Travel (www.gaytravel.com) Online guides to dozens of US destinations.

National Gay & Lesbian Task Force (www.thetaskforce.org) National activist group's website covers news, politics and current issues.

Out Traveler (www.outtraveler.com) Gay-oriented travel articles.

Purple Roofs (www.purpleroofs.com) Lists gay-owned and gay-friendly B&Bs and hotels.

Health

The USA offers excellent health care. The problem is that, unless you have good insurance, it can be prohibitively expensive. It's essential to purchase travel health insurance if your regular policy doesn't cover you when you're abroad.

Bring any medications you may need in their original containers, clearly labeled. A signed, dated letter from your physician that describes all medical conditions and medications, including generic names, is also a good idea.

If your health insurance does not cover you for medical expenses abroad, consider supplemental insurance. Find out in advance if your insurance plan will make payments directly to providers or reimburse you later for overseas health expenditures.

Medical Checklist

Recommended items for a medical kit:

- acetaminophen (Tylenol) or aspirin
- antibacterial ointment (eg Bactroban) for cuts and abrasions
- antihistamines (for hay fever and allergic reactions)
- anti-inflammatory drugs (eg ibuprofen)
- bandages, gauze, gauze rolls
- sunblock
- insect repellent for the skin

EATING PRICE RANGES

The following price ranges refer to a main course. Tax (5% to 10%) and tip (generally 15% to 20%) are not included in price listings unless otherwise indicated.

$ less than $15

$$ $15–25

$$$ more than $25

Resources

The World Health Organization publishes a superb book, called *International Travel and Health*, which is revised annually and is available free online at www.who.int/ith/en. **MD Travel Health** (www.mdtravelhealth.com) provides travel health recommendations for every country, updated regularly.

It's usually a good idea to consult your government's travel health website before departure:

Australia (www.smartraveller.gov.au)

Canada (www.hc-sc.gc.ca/index-eng.php)

UK (www.nhs.uk/nhsengland/Healthcareabroad)

Availability & Cost Of Health Care

In general, if you have a medical emergency the best bet is for you to find the nearest hospital and go to its emergency room. If the problem isn't urgent, you can call a nearby hospital and ask for a referral to a local physician, which is usually cheaper than a trip to the emergency room. Stand-alone, for-profit urgent-care centers can be convenient, but may perform large numbers of expensive tests, even for minor illnesses.

Pharmacies are abundantly supplied, but you may find

that some medications that are available over the counter in your home country (such as Ventolin, for asthma) require a prescription in the USA and, as always, if you don't have insurance to cover the cost of prescriptions, they can be shockingly expensive.

Insurance

No matter how long or short your trip, make sure you have adequate travel insurance, purchased before departure. At a minimum, you need coverage for medical emergencies and treatment, including hospital stays and an emergency flight home if necessary. Medical treatment in the USA is of the highest caliber, but the expense could bankrupt you.

You should also consider getting coverage for luggage theft or loss and trip cancellation. If you already have a home-owner's or renter's policy, see what it will cover and consider getting supplemental insurance to cover the rest. If you have prepaid a large portion of your trip, cancellation insurance is a worthwhile expense. A comprehensive travel insurance policy that covers all these things can cost up to 10% of the total cost of your trip.

If you will be driving, it's essential that you have liability insurance. Car-rental agencies offer insurance that covers damage to the rental vehicle and separate liability insurance, which covers damage to people and other vehicles.

Worldwide travel insurance is available at www.lonelyplanet.com/travel-insurance. You can buy, extend and claim online anytime – even if you're already on the road.

Internet Access

Travelers will have few problems staying connected in tech-savvy USA. Most hotels, guesthouses, hostels and motels have wi-fi (usually free, though luxury hotels are more likely to charge for access); ask when reserving.

Across the US, most cafes offer free wi-fi. Some cities have wi-fi-connected parks and plazas; and the public library is always a good standby. If you're not packing a laptop or other web-accessible device, try the library – most have public terminals (though they have time limits) in addition to wi-fi. Occasionally out-of-state residents are charged a small fee.

If you're not from the US, remember that you will need an AC adapter for your laptop, plus a plug adapter for US sockets; both are available at larger electronics shops, such as Best Buy.

Legal Matters

In everyday matters, if you are stopped by the police, bear in mind that there is no system of paying traffic or other fines on the spot. Attempting to pay a fine to an officer is frowned upon at best and may result in a charge of bribery. For traffic offenses, the police officer or highway patroller will explain the options to you. There is usually a 30-day period to pay a fine. Most matters can be handled by mail.

If you are arrested, you have a legal right to an attorney, and you are allowed to remain silent. There is no legal reason to speak to a police officer if you don't wish to, but never walk away from an officer until given permission to do so. Anyone who is arrested is legally allowed to make one phone call. If you can't afford a lawyer, a public defender will be appointed to you free of charge. Foreign visitors who don't have a lawyer, friend or family member to help should call their embassy; the police will provide the number upon request.

As a matter of principle, the US legal system presumes a person innocent until proven guilty. Each state has its own civil and criminal laws, and what is legal in one state may be illegal in others.

PRACTICALITIES

- **Electricity** AC 120V is standard; buy adapters to run most non-US electronics.
- **Newspapers & Magazines** The *New York Times*, *Wall Street Journal* and *USA Today* are the national newspapers; *Time* and *Newsweek* are the mainstream news magazines.
- **Radio & TV** National Public Radio (NPR) can be found at the lower end of the FM dial. The main TV broadcasting channels are ABC, CBS, NBC, FOX and PBS (public broadcasting); the major cable channels are CNN (news), ESPN (sports), HBO (movies), Weather Channel.
- **Video Systems** NTSC standard (incompatible with PAL or SECAM); DVDs are coded for Region 1 (US and Canada only).
- **Weights & Measures** Weights are measured in ounces (oz), pounds (lb) and tons; liquids in fluid ounces (fl oz), pints, quarts and gallons (gal); and distance in feet (ft), yards (yd) and miles (mi).

Drinking

Bars and stores often ask for photo ID to prove you are of legal drinking age (ie 21 years or over). Being 'carded' is standard practice; don't take it personally. The sale of liquor is subject to local government regulations; some counties prohibit liquor sales on Sunday, after midnight or before breakfast. In 'dry' counties, liquor sales are banned altogether.

Driving

In all states, driving under the influence of alcohol or drugs is a serious offense, and subject to stiff fines and even imprisonment.

Marijuana & Other Substances

The states have quite different laws regarding the use of marijuana, and what's legal in Colorado (and Washington, Oregon, Alaska and DC) may be illegal in other states (like Texas). Aside from Colorado and the other aforementioned states, 23 other states have either legalized medical marijuana or treat possession of small amounts of marijuana as a misdemeanor (generally punishable with a fine of around $100 or $200 for the first offense) rather than a felony. In 23 other states, marijuana use is illegal. Thus, it's essential to know the local laws before lighting up.

Aside from marijuana, recreational drugs are prohibited by federal and state laws. Possession of any illicit drug, including cocaine, ecstasy, LSD, heroin and hashish, is a felony potentially punishable by a lengthy jail sentence. For foreigners, conviction of any drug offense is grounds for deportation.

Money

The currency is the US dollar. Most locals do not carry large amounts of cash for everyday use, relying instead on credit cards, ATMs and debit cards. Smaller businesses may refuse to accept bills larger than $20. Prices in our listings exclude taxes, unless otherwise noted.

ATMs

ATMs are available 24/7 at most banks, and in shopping centers, airports, grocery stores and convenience shops. Most ATMs charge a service fee of $2.50 or more per transaction and your home bank may impose additional charges. Withdrawing cash from an ATM using a credit card usually incurs a hefty fee; check with your credit-card company first.

For foreign visitors, ask your bank or credit-card company for exact information about using its cards in stateside ATMs. If you will be relying on ATMs (not a bad strategy), bring more than one card and carry them separately. The exchange rate on ATM transactions is usually as good as you'll get anywhere. Before leaving home, notify your bank and credit-card providers of your upcoming travel plans. Otherwise, you may trigger fraud alerts with atypical spending patterns, which may result in your accounts being temporarily frozen.

Credit Cards

Major credit cards are almost universally accepted. In fact, it's almost impossible to rent a car or make phone reservations without one (some airlines require your credit-card billing address to be in the USA – a hassle if you're booking domestic flights once there). It's highly recommended that you carry at least one credit card, if only for emergencies. Visa and MasterCard are the most widely accepted.

If your credit cards are lost or stolen, contact the issuing company immediately:

American Express (☎800-528-4800; www.americanexpress.com)

Diners Club (☎800-234-6377; www.dinersclub.com)

Discover (☎800-347-2683; www.discover.com)

MasterCard (☎800-627-8372; www.mastercard.com)

Visa (☎800-847-2911; www.visa.com)

Money Changers

Banks are usually the best places to exchange foreign currencies. Most large city banks offer currency exchange, but banks in rural areas may not. Currency-exchange counters at the airport and in tourist centers typically have the worst rates; ask about fees and surcharges first. **Travelex** (☎516-300-1622; www.travelex.com) is a major currency-exchange company, but **American Express** (☎800-528-4800; www.americanexpress.com) travel offices may offer better rates.

Taxes

Sales tax varies by state and county, and ranges from 5% to 10%. Hotel taxes vary by city from about 10% to over 18% (in NYC).

Tipping

Tipping is *not* optional; only withhold tips in cases of outrageously bad service.

SMOKING

As of 2015, 30 states, the District of Columbia and many municipalities across the US were entirely smoke-free in restaurants, bars and workplaces. You may still encounter smoky lobbies in chain hotels and budget-minded inns, but most other accommodations are smoke-free. For more on smoking laws, see www.cdc.gov.

Airport & hotel porters $2 per bag, minimum per cart $5

Bartenders 15% to 20% per round, minimum per drink $1

Hotel maids $2 to $4 per night, left under the card provided

Restaurant servers 15% to 20%, unless a gratuity is already charged on the bill

Taxi drivers 10% to 15%, rounded up to the next dollar

Valet parking attendants At least $2 when handed back the keys

Traveler's Checks

Since the advent of ATMs, traveler's checks are becoming obsolete, except as a trustworthy backup. If you carry them, buy them in US dollars; local businesses may not cash them in a foreign currency. Keep a separate record of their numbers in case they are lost or stolen. American Express and Visa traveler's checks are the most widely accepted.

Opening Hours

Typical normal opening times are as follows:

Bars 5pm to midnight Sunday to Thursday, to 2am Friday and Saturday

Banks 8:30am to 4:30pm Monday to Thursday, to 5:30pm Friday (and possibly 9am to noon Saturday)

Nightclubs 10pm to 4am Thursday to Saturday

Post offices 9am to 5pm Monday to Friday

Shopping malls 9am to 9pm

Stores 9am to 6pm Mon-Sat, noon to 5pm Sunday

Supermarkets 8am to 8pm, some open 24 hours

Photography

Digital camera memory cards are widely available at chain retailers such as Best Buy and Target.

Some Native American tribal lands prohibit photography and video completely; when it's allowed, you may be required to purchase a permit. Always ask permission if you want to photograph someone close up; anyone who then agrees to be photographed may expect a small tip.

For more advice on photography, consult Lonely Planet's *Travel Photography* book.

Post

For 24-hour postal information, including post office locations and hours, contact the **US Postal Service** (USPS; ☎800-275-8777; www.usps.com), which is reliable and inexpensive.

For sending urgent or important letters and packages either domestically or internationally, **Federal Express** (☎800-463-3339; www.fedex.com) and **United Parcel Service** (UPS; ☎800-742-5877; www.ups.com) offer more-expensive door-to-door delivery services.

Sending & Receiving Mail

If you have the correct postage, you can drop mail weighing less than 13oz into any blue mailbox. To send a package weighing 13oz or more, you must go to a post office.

Public Holidays

On the following national public holidays, banks, schools and government offices (including post offices) are closed, and transportation, museums and other services operate on a Sunday schedule. Holidays falling on a weekend are usually observed the following Monday.

New Year's Day January 1

Martin Luther King Jr Day Third Monday in January

Presidents' Day Third Monday in February

Memorial Day Last Monday in May

Independence Day July 4

Labor Day First Monday in September

Columbus Day Second Monday in October

Veterans' Day November 11

Thanksgiving Fourth Thursday in November

Christmas Day December 25

During spring break, high school and college students get a week off from school so they can overrun beach towns and resorts. This occurs throughout March and April. For students of all ages, summer vacation runs from June to August.

Safe Travel

Despite its seemingly apocalyptic list of dangers – violent crime, riots, earthquakes, tornadoes – the USA is actually a pretty safe country to visit. The greatest danger for travelers is posed by car accidents (buckle up – it's the law).

Crime

For the traveler it's not violent crime but petty theft that is the biggest concern. When possible, withdraw money from ATMs during the day, or at night in well-lit, busy areas. When driving, don't pick up hitchhikers, and lock valuables in the trunk of your car before arriving at your destination. In hotels, you can secure valuables in room or hotel safes.

Scams

Pack your street smarts. In big cities, don't forget that three-card-monte card games are always rigged, and that expensive electronics, watches and designer items sold on the cheap from sidewalk tables are either fakes or stolen.

Natural Disasters

Most areas with predictable natural disturbances – tornadoes in the Midwest, tsunamis in Hawaii, hurricanes in the South, earthquakes in California – have an emergency siren system to alert communities to imminent danger. These sirens are tested periodically at noon, but if you hear one and suspect trouble, turn on a local TV or radio station, which will be broadcasting safety warnings and advice. Incidentally, hurricane season runs from June to November.

The **US Department of Health & Human Services** (www.phe.gov) has preparedness advice, news and information on all the ways your vacation could go horribly, horribly wrong. But relax: it probably won't.

Telephone

The US phone system comprises regional service providers, competing long-distance carriers and several cell-phone and payphone companies. Overall, the system is very efficient, but it can be expensive. Avoid making long-distance calls on a hotel phone or on a pay phone. It's usually cheaper to use a regular landline or cell phone. Most hotels allow guests to make free local calls.

Telephone books can be handy resources: some list community services, public transportation and things to see and do as well as phone and business listings. The main online phone directories include www.411.com and www.yellowpages.com.

Cell Phones

In the USA cell phones use GSM 1900 or CDMA 800, operating on different frequencies from other systems around the world. The only foreign phones that will work in the USA are GSM tri- or quad-band models. If you have one of these phones, check with your service provider about using it in the USA. Ask if roaming charges apply, as these will turn even local US calls into pricey international calls.

It might be cheaper to buy a compatible prepaid SIM card for the USA, like those sold by AT&T, which you can insert into your international cell phone to get a local phone number and voicemail. **Telestial** (www.telestial.com) offers these services, as well as cell-phone rentals.

If you don't have a compatible phone, you can buy inexpensive, no-contract (prepaid) phones with a local number and a set number of minutes, which can be topped up at will. Virgin Mobile, T-Mobile, AT&T and other providers offer phones starting at US$10, with a package of minutes starting around $40 for 400 minutes. Electronics stores such as Radio Shack and Best Buy sell these phones.

Huge swathes of rural America, including many national parks and recreation areas, don't pick up a signal. Check your provider's coverage map.

Dialing Codes

All phone numbers within the USA consist of a three-digit area code followed by a seven-digit local number. In most places, you will need to dial the entire 10-digit number even for a local call.

If you are calling long distance, dial ☎1 plus the area code plus the phone number. If you're not sure whether the number is local or long distance (new area codes are added all the time, confusing even residents), try one way, and if it's the wrong one, usually a recorded voice will correct you.

Toll-free numbers begin with ☎800, ☎888, ☎877 and ☎866, and when dialing are preceded by ☎1. Most can only be used within the USA, some only within the state, and some only from outside the state. You won't know until you try dialing. The 900-series of area codes and a few other prefixes are for calls charged at a premium per-minute rate – phone sex, horoscopes, jokes etc.

- The international country code for the USA is ☎1 if calling from abroad (the same as Canada, but international rates apply between the two countries).
- Dial ☎011 to make an international call from the USA (followed by country code, area code and phone number).
- Dial ☎00 for assistance making international calls.
- Dial ☎411 for directory assistance nationwide.
- Call ☎800-555-1212 if you need directory assistance for toll-free numbers.

Pay Phones

Pay phones are an endangered species in an ever-expanding cell-phone world. Local calls at pay phones that work (listen for a dial tone before inserting coins) cost 35¢ to 50¢ for the first few minutes; talking longer costs more. Only put in the exact amount because pay phones don't give change. Some pay phones (eg in national parks) only accept credit cards or prepaid phone cards. Local calls from pay phones get expensive quickly, while long-distance calls can be prohibitive, especially if you use the operator (☎0) to facilitate long-distance or collect (reverse-charge) calls. It's usually cheaper to use a prepaid phone card or the access line of a major carrier like AT&T (☎800-321-0288).

Phonecards

A prepaid phonecard is a good solution for travelers on a budget. Phonecards are easy to find in larger towns and cities, where they are sold at newsstands, convenience stores, supermarkets and major retailers. Be sure to read the fine print, as many cards contain hidden charges such as 'activation fees' or per-call 'connection fees' in addition to the rates. AT&T sells a reliable phonecard that is widely available in the USA.

Time

The USA uses Daylight Saving Time (DST). On the second Sunday in March, clocks are set one hour ahead ('spring forward'). Then, on the first Sunday of November, clocks are turned back one hour ('fall back'). Just to keep you on your toes, Arizona (except the Navajo Nation), Hawaii and much of Indiana don't follow DST.

The US date system is written as month/day/year. Thus, 8 June 2015 becomes 6/8/15.

Time Zones

The Continental USA has four time zones:

- **EST Eastern** (GMT -5 hours): NYC, New England and Atlanta
- **CST Central** (GMT -6 hours): Chicago, New Orleans and Houston
- **MST Mountain** (GMT -7 hours): Denver, Santa Fe, Phoenix
- **PST Pacific** (GMT -8 hours): Seattle, San Francisco, Las Vegas

Most of Alaska is one hour behind Pacific time (GMT -9), while Hawaii is two hours behind Pacific time.

So if it's 9pm in New York, it's 8pm in Chicago, 7pm in Denver, 6pm in Los Angeles, 4pm in Anchorage and 3pm in Honolulu.

Tourist Information

The official tourism website of the USA is www.discoveramerica.com. It has links to every US state and territory tourism office and website, plus loads of ideas for itinerary planning.

Any tourist office worth contacting has a website, where you can download free travel e-guides. They also field phone calls; some local offices maintain daily lists of hotel room availability, but few offer reservation services. All tourist offices have self-service racks of brochures and discount coupons; some also sell maps and books.

State-run 'welcome centers,' usually placed along interstate highways, tend to have materials that cover wider territories, and offices are usually open longer hours, including weekends and holidays.

Many cities have an official convention and visitors bureau (CVB); these sometimes double as tourist bureaus, but since their main focus is drawing the business trade, CVBs can be less useful for independent travelers.

Keep in mind that in smaller towns, when the local chamber of commerce runs the tourist bureau, its lists of hotels, restaurants and services usually mention only chamber members; the town's cheapest options may be missing.

Similarly, in prime tourist destinations, some private 'tourist bureaus' are really agents who book hotel rooms and tours on commission. They may offer excellent service and deals, but you'll get what they're selling and nothing else.

Travelers with Disabilities

If you have a physical disability, the USA can be an accommodating place. The Americans with Disabilities Act (ADA) requires that all public buildings, private buildings built after 1993 (including hotels, restaurants, theaters and museums) and public transit be wheelchair accessible. However, call ahead to confirm what is available. Some local tourist offices publish detailed accessibility guides.

Telephone companies offer relay operators, available via teletypewriter (TTY) numbers, for the hearing impaired. Most banks provide ATM instructions in Braille and via earphone jacks for hearing-impaired customers. All major airlines, Greyhound buses and Amtrak trains will assist travelers with disabilities; just describe your needs when making reservations at least 48 hours in advance. Service animals (guide dogs) are allowed to accompany passengers, but make sure you bring documentation.

Some car-rental agencies, such as Budget and Hertz, offer hand-controlled vehicles and vans with wheelchair lifts at no extra charge, but you must reserve them well in advance. **Wheelchair Getaways** (☎800-642-2042; www.wheelchairgetaways.com) rents accessible vans throughout the USA. In many cities and towns, public buses are accessible to wheelchair riders and will 'kneel' if you are unable to use the steps; just let the driver know that you need the lift or ramp.

Most cities have taxi companies with at least one accessible van, though you'll have to call ahead. Cities with underground transport have elevators for passengers needing assistance; DC has the best network (every station has an elevator); NYC's elevators are few and far between.

Many national and some state parks and recreation areas have wheelchair-accessible paved, graded dirt or boardwalk trails. US citizens and permanent residents with permanent disabilities are entitled to a free 'America the Beautiful' Access Pass. Go online (www.nps.gov/findapark/passes.htm) for details.

For tips on travel and thoughtful insight on traveling with a disability, check out online posts by Martin Heng, Lonely Planet's Accessible Travel Manager: twitter.com/martin_heng.

Some helpful resources for travelers with disabilities:

Disabled Sports USA (☎301-217-0960; www.disabledsportsusa.org) Offers sport, adventure and recreation programs for those with disabilities. Also publishes *Challenge* magazine.

Flying Wheels Travel (☎612-381-1622; www.flyingwheelstravel.com) A full-service travel agency, highly recommended for those with mobility issues or chronic illness.

Mobility International USA (☎541-343-1284; www.miusa.org) Advises disabled travelers on mobility issues and runs educational international exchange programs.

Visas

Be warned that all of the following information is highly subject to change. US entry requirements keep evolving as national security regulations change. All travelers should double-check current visa and passport regulations *before* coming to the USA.

The **US State Department** (www.travel.state.gov) maintains the most comprehensive visa information, providing downloadable forms, lists of US consulates abroad and even visa wait times calculated by country.

Visa Applications

Apart from most Canadian citizens and those entering under the Visa Waiver Program, all foreign visitors will need to obtain a visa from a US consulate or embassy abroad. Most applicants must schedule a personal interview, to which you must bring all your documentation and proof of fee payment. Wait times for interviews vary, but afterward, barring problems, visa issuance takes from a few days to a few weeks.

➡ Your passport must be valid for at least six months after the end of your intended stay in the USA. You'll need a recent photo (2in by 2in), and you must pay a nonrefundable $160 processing fee, plus in a few cases an additional visa issuance reciprocity fee. You'll also need to fill out the online DS-160 nonimmigrant visa electronic application.

➡ Visa applicants are required to show documents of financial stability (or evidence that a US resident will provide financial support), a round-trip or onward ticket and 'binding obligations' that will ensure their return home, such as family ties, a home or a job. Because of these requirements, those planning to travel through other countries before arriving in the USA are generally better off applying for a US visa while they are still in their home country, rather than while on the road.

➡ The most common visa is a nonimmigrant visitor's visa, type B-1 for business purposes, B-2 for tourism or visiting friends and relatives. A visitor's visa is good for multiple entries over one or five years, and specifically prohibits the visitor from taking paid employment in the USA. The validity period depends on what country you are from. The actual length of time you'll be allowed to stay in the USA is determined by US immigration at the port of entry.

VISA WAIVER PROGRAM

Currently under the Visa Waiver Program (VWP), citizens of the following countries may enter the USA without a visa for stays of 90 days or fewer: Andorra, Australia, Austria, Belgium, Brunei, Chile, Czech Republic, Denmark, Estonia, Finland, France, Germany, Greece, Hungary, Iceland, Ireland, Italy, Japan, Latvia, Liechtenstein, Lithuania, Luxembourg, Malta, Monaco, the Netherlands, New Zealand, Norway, Portugal, San Marino, Singapore, Slovakia, Slovenia, South Korea, Spain, Sweden, Switzerland, Taiwan and the UK.

If you are a citizen of a VWP country, you do not need a visa only *if* you have a passport that meets current US standards *and* you have gotten approval from the Electronic System for Travel Authorization (ESTA) in advance. Register online with the Department of Homeland Security at https://esta.cbp.dhs.gov/esta at least 72 hours before arrival; once travel authorization is approved, your registration is valid for two years. The fee, payable online, is $14.

Visitors from VWP countries must still produce at the port of entry all the same evidence as for a nonimmigrant visa application. They must demonstrate that their trip is for 90 days or less, and that they have a round-trip or onward ticket, adequate funds to cover the trip and binding obligations abroad.

In addition, the same 'grounds for exclusion and deportation' apply, except that you will have no opportunity to appeal or apply for an exemption. If you are denied under the Visa Waiver Program at a US point of entry, you will have to use your onward or return ticket on the next available flight.

- If you're coming to the USA to work or study, you will need a different type of visa, and the company or institution to which you are going should make the arrangements.
- Other categories of nonimmigrant visas include an F-1 visa for students attending a course at a recognized institution; an H-1, H-2 or H-3 visa for temporary employment; and a J-1 visa for exchange visitors in approved programs.

Grounds for Exclusion & Deportation

If on your visa application form you admit to being a subversive, a smuggler, a prostitute, a drug addict, a terrorist or an ex-Nazi, you may be excluded. You can also be refused a visa or entry to the USA if you have a 'communicable disease of public health significance' or a criminal record, or if you've ever made a false statement in connection with a US visa application. However, if these last three apply, you are still able to request an exemption; many people are granted them and then given visas.

Communicable diseases include tuberculosis, the Ebola virus, SARS and most particularly HIV. US immigration doesn't test people for disease, but officials at the point of entry may question anyone about his or her health. They can exclude anyone whom they believe has a communicable disease, perhaps because they are carrying medical documents, prescriptions or AIDS/HIV medicine. Being gay is not grounds for exclusion; being an IV drug user is. Visitors may be deported if US immigration finds out they have HIV but did not declare it. Being HIV-positive is not grounds for deportation, but failing to provide accurate information on the visa application is.

The US immigration department has a very broad definition of a criminal record. If you've ever been arrested or charged with an offense, that's a criminal record, even if you were acquitted or discharged without conviction. Don't attempt to enter through the VWP if you have a criminal record of any kind; assume US authorities will find out about it.

Often United States Citizenship & Immigration Services (USCIS) will grant an exemption (a 'waiver of ineligibility') to a person who would normally be subject to exclusion, but this requires referral to a regional immigration office and can take some time (allow at least two months). If you're tempted to conceal something, remember that US immigration is strictest of all about false statements. It will often view favorably an applicant who admits to an old criminal charge or a communicable disease, but it is extremely harsh on anyone who has ever attempted to mislead it, even on minor points. After you're admitted to the USA, any evidence of a false statement to US immigration is grounds for deportation.

Prospective visitors to whom grounds of exclusion may apply should consider their options before applying for a visa.

Entering the USA

- All those arriving in the US need to fill out the US customs declaration, which is usually handed out on the plane. Have it completed before you approach the immigration desk. For the question, 'US Street Address,' give the address where you will spend the first night (a hotel address is fine).
- No matter what your visa says, US immigration officers have an absolute authority to refuse admission to the USA or to impose conditions on admission. They may ask about your plans and whether you have sufficient funds; it's a good idea to list an itinerary, produce an onward or round-trip ticket and have at least one major credit card.
- The Department of Homeland Security's registration program, called Office of Biometric Identity Management, includes every port of entry and nearly every foreign visitor to the USA. For most visitors (excluding, for now, most Canadian and some Mexican citizens), registration consists of having a digital photo and electronic (inkless) fingerprints taken; the process takes less than a minute.

Visa Extensions

To stay in the USA longer than the date stamped on your passport, go to a local **USCIS** (www.uscis.gov) office to apply for an extension well *before* the stamped date. If the date has passed, your best chance will be to bring a US citizen with you to vouch for your character, and to produce lots of other verification that you are not trying to work illegally and have enough money to support yourself. However, if you've overstayed, the most likely scenario is that you will be deported. Travelers who enter the USA under the VWP are ineligible for visa extensions.

Short-Term Departures & Re-entry

- It's temptingly easy to make trips across the border to Canada or Mexico, but upon return to the USA, non-Americans will be subject to the full immigration procedure.
- Always take your passport when you cross the border.
- If your immigration card still has plenty of time on it, you will probably be able to re-enter using the same one, but if it has nearly expired,

you will have to apply for a new card, and border control may want to see your onward air ticket, sufficient funds and so on.

- Traditionally, a quick trip across the border has been a way to extend your stay in the USA without applying for an extension at a USCIS office. Don't assume this still works. First, make sure you hand in your old immigration card to the immigration authorities when you leave the USA, and when you return make sure you have all the necessary application documentation from when you first entered the country. US immigration will be very suspicious of anyone who leaves for a few days and returns immediately hoping for a new six-month stay; expect to be questioned closely.
- Citizens of most Western countries will not need a visa to visit Canada, so it's really not a problem at all to cross to the Canadian side of Niagara Falls, detour up to Québec or pass through on the way to Alaska.
- Travelers entering the USA by bus from Canada may be closely scrutinized. A round-trip ticket that takes you back to Canada will most likely make US immigration feel less suspicious.
- Mexico has a visa-free zone along most of its border with the USA, including the Baja Peninsula and most of the border towns, such as Tijuana and Ciudad Juárez; note that the latter, with a staggering murder rate, is not a safe place to visit – though things have improved in recent years. You'll need a Mexican visa or tourist card if you want to go beyond the border zone.

Volunteering

Volunteer opportunities abound in the USA, and they can be a great way to break up a long trip. They can also provide truly memorable experiences: you'll get to interact with people, society and the land in ways you never would by just passing through.

Casual, drop-in volunteer opportunities are plentiful in big cities, where you can socialize with locals while helping out nonprofit organizations. Check weekly alternative newspapers for calendar listings, or browse the free classified ads online at **Craigslist** (www.craigslist.org). The public website Serve.gov and private websites Idealist.org and **VolunteerMatch** (www.volunteermatch.org) offer free searchable databases of short- and long-term volunteer opportunities nationwide.

More-formal volunteer programs, especially those designed for international travelers, typically charge a hefty fee of $250 to $1000, depending on the length of the program and what amenities are included (eg housing, meals). None cover travel to the USA.

Recommended volunteer organizations:

Green Project (☎504-945-0240; www.thegreenproject.org) Working to improve battered communities in New Orleans in sustainable, green ways.

Habitat for Humanity (☎800-422-4828; www.habitat.org) Focuses on building affordable housing for those in need.

Sierra Club (☎415-977-5500; www.sierraclub.org) 'Volunteer vacations' restore wilderness areas and maintain trails, including in national parks and nature preserves.

Volunteers for Peace (☎802-540-3060; www.vfp.org) Grassroots, multiweek volunteer projects emphasize manual labor and international exchange.

Wilderness Volunteers (☎928-255-1128; www.wildernessvolunteers.org) Week-long trips helping maintain national parklands and outdoor recreation areas.

World Wide Opportunities on Organic Farms USA (☎415-621-3276; www.wwoofusa.org) Represents more than 2000 organic farms in all 50 states that host volunteer workers in exchange for meals and accommodations, with opportunities for both short- and long-term stays.

Women Travelers

Women traveling alone or in groups should not expect to encounter any particular problems in the USA. The community website www.journeywoman.com facilitates women exchanging travel tips, and has links to other helpful resources. The booklet *Her Own Way*, published by the Canadian government, is filled with general travel advice, useful for any woman; click to http://travel.gc.ca/travelling/publications to download the PDF or read it online.

When first meeting someone, don't advertise where you are staying, or even that you are traveling alone. Americans can be eager to help and even take in solo travelers, but don't take all offers of help at face value. If someone who seems trustworthy invites you to his or her home, let someone (eg hostel or hotel manager) know where you're going. This advice also applies if you go for a hike by yourself. If something happens and you don't return as expected, you want to know that someone will notice and know where to begin looking for you.

Some women carry a whistle, mace or cayenne-pepper spray in case of assault. If you purchase a spray, contact a police station to find out about local regulations. Laws regarding sprays vary from state to state; federal law prohibits them being carried on planes.

If you are assaulted, consider calling a rape-crisis hotline before calling the police, unless you are in immediate danger, in which case you should call ☎911. But be aware that not all police have as much sensitivity training or experience assisting sexual assault survivors, whereas staff at rape crisis centers will tirelessly advocate on your behalf and act as a link to other community services, including hospitals and the police. Telephone books have listings of local rape-crisis centers, or contact the 24-hour **National Sexual Assault Hotline** (☎800-656-4673; www.rainn.org). Alternatively, go straight to a hospital emergency room.

National advocacy groups that may be useful:

National Organization for Women (NOW;☎202-628-8669; www.now.org) A grassroots movement fighting for women's rights.

Planned Parenthood (☎800-230-7526; www.plannedparenthood.org) Offers referrals to women's health clinics throughout the country.

Work

If you are a foreigner in the USA with a standard nonimmigrant visitor's visa, you are expressly forbidden to partake in paid work in the USA and will be deported if you're caught working illegally. Employers are required to establish the bona fides of their employees or face fines, making it much tougher for a foreigner to get work than it once was.

To work legally, foreigners need to apply for a work visa before leaving home. A J-1 visa, for exchange visitors, is issued to young people (age limits vary) for study, student vacation employment, work in summer camps, and short-term traineeships with a specific employer. One organization that can help arrange international student exchanges, work placements and J-1 visas is International Exchange Programs (IEP), which operates in **Australia** (IEP; ☎03-9329-3866; www.iep.com.au) and **New Zealand.** (IEP; ☎0800-443-769; www.iep.org.nz).

For nonstudent jobs, temporary or permanent, you need to be sponsored by a US employer who will have to arrange an H-category visa. These are not easy to obtain, since the employer has to prove that no US citizen or permanent resident is available to do the job.

Seasonal work is possible in national parks and at tourist attractions and ski resorts. Contact park concessionaire businesses, local chambers of commerce and ski-resort management. Lonely Planet's *Gap Year Book* has more ideas on how best to combine work and travel.

American Institute for Foreign Study (☎866-906-2437; www.aifs.com) Good resource for tracking down study-abroad programs.

Au Pair in America (☎800-928-7247; www.aupairinamerica.com) Find a job as an au pair in the USA.

BUNAC (☎866-220-7771; www.bunac.org) Organization with links to volunteer and study-abroad programs.

Camp America (☎in the UK 020-7581-7373; www.campamerica.co.uk) Offers opportunities to work in a youth summer camp.

Council on International Educational Exchange (☎207-553-4000; www.ciee.org) CIEE has a wide range of programs including internships, study-abroad programs, work-travel combos and work-exchange programs.

InterExchange (☎212-924-0446; www.interexchange.org) Camp and au-pair programs.

Driving in the USA

For maximum flexibility and convenience, and to explore rural America and its wide-open spaces, a car is essential. Although gas prices are high, you can often score fairly inexpensive rentals (NYC excluded), with rates as low as $20 per day.

Automobile Associations

The **American Automobile Association** (AAA; www.aaa.com) has reciprocal membership agreements with several international auto clubs (check with AAA and bring your membership card from home). For its members, AAA offers travel insurance, tour books, diagnostic centers for used-car buyers and a wide-ranging network of regional offices. AAA advocates politically for the auto industry.

A more ecofriendly alternative, the **Better World Club** (☎866-238-1137; www.betterworldclub.com) donates 1% of revenue to assist environmental cleanup, offers ecologically sensitive choices for every service it provides and advocates politically for environmental causes.

With organizations, the primary member benefit is 24-hour emergency roadside assistance anywhere in the USA. Both also offer trip planning, free travel maps, travel-agency services, car insurance and a range of travel discounts (eg on hotels, car rentals, attractions).

Bringing Your Own Vehicle

It's possible to drive your own car over the border from Canada or from Mexico (p1184). Unless you're moving to the USA, don't even think about freighting your car.

Drive-Away Cars

'Drive-away cars' refers to the business of driving cars across the country for people who are moving or otherwise can't transport their cars themselves. For flexible travelers, they can be a dream come true: you can cover the long distances between A and B for the price of gas. Timing and availability are key.

To be a driver you must be at least 23 years old with a valid driver's license (non-US citizens should have an International Driving Permit). you'll also need to provide a $350 deposit – sometimes requested in cash – which is refunded upon safe delivery of the car, a printout of your 'clean' driving record from home, a major credit card and/or three forms of identification (or a passport).

The drive-away company provides insurance; you pay for gas. The stipulation is that you must deliver the car to its destination within a specified time and mileage, which usually requires that you drive no more than eight hours and about 400 miles a day along the shortest route (ie no sightseeing). Availability depends on demand.

One major company is **Auto Driveaway** (☎800-346-2277; www.autodriveaway.com/driver), which has more than 40 offices nationwide.

Driver's License

Foreign visitors can legally drive a car in the USA for up to 12 months using their home driver's license. However, an International Driving Permit (IDP) will have more credibility with US traffic police, especially if your home license doesn't have a photo or isn't in English. Your automobile association at home can issue an IDP, valid for one year, for a small fee. Always carry your home license together with the IDP.

To ride a motorcycle in the USA, you will need either a valid US state motorcycle license or an IDP specially endorsed for motorcycles.

Insurance

Don't put the key into the ignition if you don't have insurance, which is legally required. You risk financial ruin and legal consequences if there's an accident. If you

Driving Distances & Times

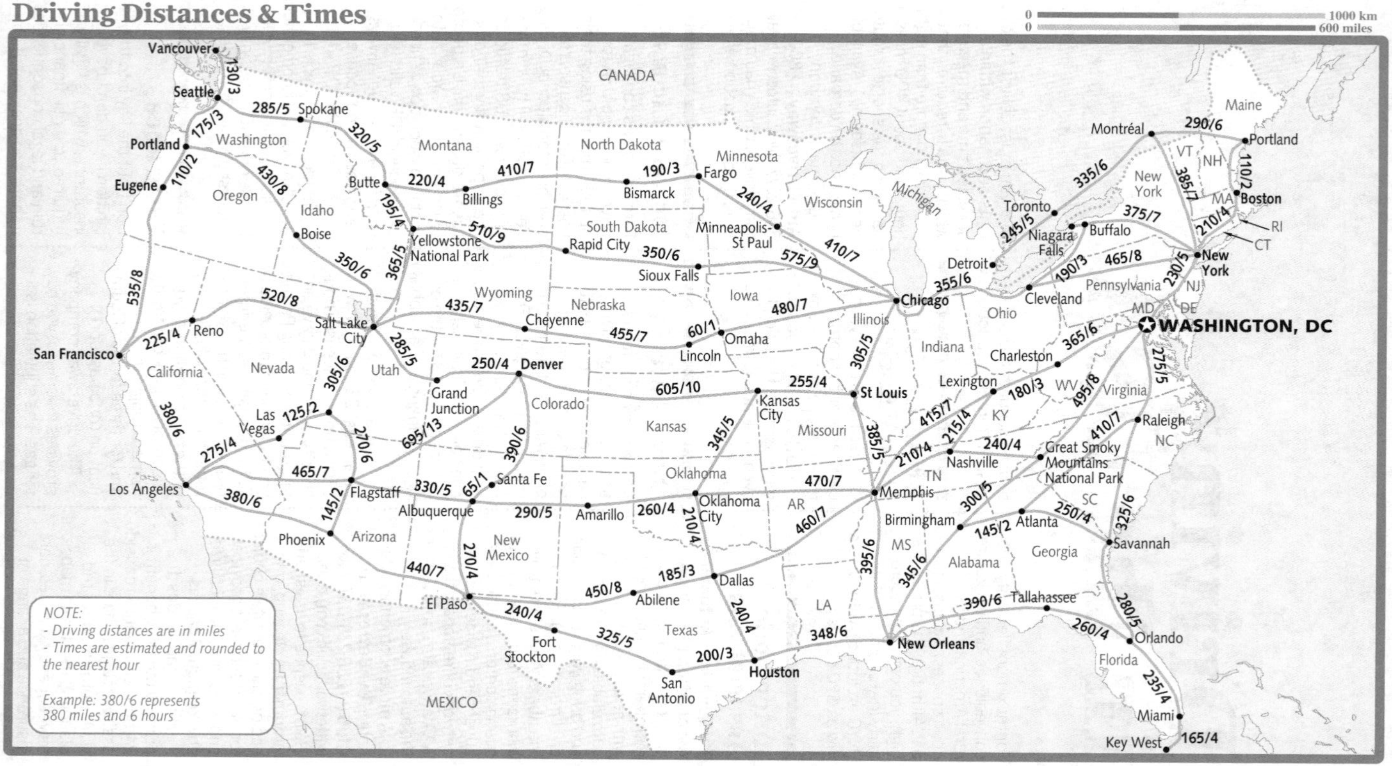

NOTE:
- Driving distances are in miles
- Times are estimated and rounded to the nearest hour

Example: 380/6 represents 380 miles and 6 hours

already have auto insurance, or if you buy travel insurance that covers car rentals, make sure your policy has adequate liability coverage for where you will be driving; it probably does, but beware that states specify different minimum levels of coverage.

Car-rental companies will provide liability insurance, but most charge extra. Rental companies almost never include collision-damage insurance for the vehicle. Instead, they offer an optional Collision Damage Waiver (CDW) or Loss Damage Waiver (LDW), usually with an initial deductible cost of between $100 and $500. For an extra premium, you can usually get this deductible covered as well. Paying extra for some or all of this insurance increases the cost of a rental car by as much as $30 a day.

Many credit cards offer free collision-damage coverage for rental cars, if you rent for 15 days or less and charge the total rental to your card. This is a good way to avoid paying extra fees to the rental company, but note that if there's an accident, sometimes you must pay the car-rental company first and then seek reimbursement from the credit-card company. There may be exceptions that are not covered, too, such as 'exotic' rentals (eg 4WD Jeeps, convertibles). Check your credit-card policy.

Purchase

Buying a car is usually much more hassle than it's worth, particularly for foreign visitors and for trips of less than four months. Foreigners will have the easiest time arranging this if they have stateside friends or relatives who can provide a fixed address for registration, licensing and insurance.

Once purchased, the car's transfer-of-ownership papers must be registered with the state's Department of Motor Vehicles (DMV) within 10 days; you'll need the bill of sale, the title (or 'pink slip') and proof of insurance. Some states also require a 'smog certificate.' This is the seller's responsibility, so don't buy a car without a current certificate. A dealer will submit all necessary paperwork to the DMV for you.

For foreigners, independent liability insurance is difficult to virtually impossible to arrange without a US driver's license. A car dealer or AAA may be able to suggest an insurer who will do this. Even with a local license, insurance can be expensive and difficult to obtain if you don't have evidence of a good driving record. Bring copies of your home auto-insurance policy if it helps establish that you are a good risk. All drivers under 25 years will have problems getting insurance.

Finally, selling a car can become a desperate business. Selling to dealers gets you the worst price but involves a minimum of paperwork. Otherwise, fellow travelers and college students are the best bets – but be sure the DMV is properly notified about the sale, or you may be on the hook for someone else's traffic tickets later on.

Rental

Car

Car rental is a competitive business in the USA. Most rental companies require that you have a major credit card, be at least 25 years old and have a valid driver's license. Some major national companies may rent to drivers between the ages of 21 and 24 for an additional charge of around $25 per day. Those under 21 years are usually not permitted to rent at all.

Car-rental prices vary wildly so shop around. The average daily rate for a small car ranges from around $30 to $75, or $200 to $500 per week. If you belong to an auto club or frequent-flier program, you may get a discount (or earn rewards points or miles).

Some other things to keep in mind: most national agencies make 'unlimited mileage' standard on all cars, but independents might charge extra for this. Tax on car rental varies by state and agency location; always ask for the total cost *including* all taxes and fees. Most agencies charge more if you pick the car up in one place and drop it off in another; usually only national agencies even offer this option. Be careful about adding extra days or turning in a car early; extra days may be charged at a premium rate, or an early return may jeopardize any weekly or monthly discounts you originally arranged.

Some major national companies, including Avis, Budget and Hertz, offer 'green' fleets of hybrid rental cars (eg Toyota Priuses, Honda Civics), although you'll usually have to pay quite a bit more to rent a hybrid. Some

FUELING UP

Many gas stations in the USA have fuel pumps with automated credit-card pay screens. Most machines ask for your ZIP code after you swipe your card. For foreign travelers – or those with cards issued outside the US – you'll have to pay inside before fueling up. Just indicate how much you'd like to put on the card. If there's still credit left over after you fuel up, just pop back inside, and the attendant will put the difference back on your card.

independent local agencies, especially on the West Coast, also offer hybrid-vehicle rentals. Try Southern California's **Simply RAC** (☎323-653-0022; www.simplyrac.com) and Hawaii's **Bio-Beetle** (www.bio-beetle.com).

Motorcycle

If you dream of cruising across America on a Harley, **EagleRider** (☎310-321-3180; www.eaglerider.com) has offices in major cities nationwide and rents other kinds of adventure vehicles too. Beware that motorcycle rental and insurance are expensive.

Road Conditions & Hazards

America's highways are thought of as legendary ribbons of unblemished asphalt, but not always. Road hazards include potholes, city commuter traffic, wandering wildlife and, of course, cell-phone-wielding, kid-distracted and enraged drivers. Caution, foresight, courtesy and luck usually gets you past them. For nationwide traffic and road-closure information, click to www.fhwa.dot.gov/trafficinfo/index.htm.

In places where winter driving is an issue, many cars are fitted with steel-studded snow tires; snow chains can sometimes be required in mountain areas. Driving off-road, or on dirt roads, is often forbidden by car-rental companies, and it can be very dangerous in wet weather.

In deserts and range country, livestock sometimes graze next to unfenced roads. These areas are signed as 'Open Range' or with the silhouette of a steer. Where deer and other wild animals frequently appear roadside, you'll see signs with the silhouette of a leaping deer. Take these signs seriously, particularly at dusk and dawn.

Road Rules

In the USA, cars drive on the right-hand side of the road. The use of seat belts and child safety seats is required in every state. Most car-rental agencies rent child safety seats for around $13 per day, but you must reserve them when booking. In some states, motorcyclists are required to wear helmets.

On interstate highways, the speed limit is sometimes raised to 75mph. Unless otherwise posted, the speed limit is generally 55mph or 65mph on highways, 25mph to 35mph in cities and towns, and as low as 15mph in school zones (strictly enforced during school hours). It's forbidden to pass a school bus when its lights are flashing.

Unless signs prohibit it, you may turn right at a red light after first coming to a full stop – note that turning right on red is illegal in NYC. At four-way stop signs, cars should proceed in order of arrival; when two cars arrive simultaneously, the one on the right has the right of way. When in doubt, just politely wave the other driver ahead. When emergency vehicles (ie police, fire or ambulance) approach from either direction, pull over safely and get out of the way.

In many states, it is illegal to talk on a handheld cell phone while driving; use a hands-free device instead.

The maximum legal blood-alcohol concentration for drivers is 0.08%. Penalties are very severe for driving under the influence of alcohol and/or drugs (DUI). Police can give roadside sobriety checks to assess if you've been drinking or using drugs. If you fail, they'll require you to take a breath test, urine test or blood test to determine the level of alcohol or drugs in your body. Refusing to be tested is treated the same as if you'd taken the test and failed.

In some states it is illegal to carry 'open containers' of alcohol in a vehicle, even if they are empty.

Transportation

GETTING THERE & AWAY

Flights and tours can be booked online at www.lonelyplanet.com/bookings.

Entering the USA

If you are flying to the US, the first airport that you land in is where you must go through immigration and customs, even if you are continuing on the flight to another destination. Upon arrival, all international visitors must register with the Department of Homeland Security's Office of Biometric Identity Management program, which entails having your fingerprints scanned and a digital photo taken.

Once you go through immigration, you collect your baggage and pass through customs. If you have nothing to declare, you'll probably clear customs without a baggage search, but don't assume this. If you are continuing on the same plane or connecting to another one, it is your responsibility to get your bags to the right place. There are usually airline representatives just outside the customs area who can help you.

If you are a single parent, grandparent or guardian traveling with anyone under 18 years, carry proof of legal custody or a notarized letter from the nonaccompanying parent(s) authorizing the trip. This isn't required, but the USA is concerned with thwarting child abduction, and not having authorizing papers could cause delays or even result in being denied admittance to the country.

Passports

Every visitor entering the USA from abroad needs a passport. Your passport must be valid for at least six months longer than your intended stay in the USA. Also, if your passport does not meet current US standards, you'll be turned back at the border. If it was issued on or after October 26, 2006, it must be an e-Passport with a digital photo and an integrated RFID chip containing biometric data.

Air

Airports

The USA has more than 375 domestic airports, but only a baker's dozen are the main international gateways. Many other airports are called 'international' but may have only a few flights from other countries – typically Mexico or Canada. Even travel to an international gateway sometimes requires a connection in another gateway city (eg London–Los Angeles flights may involve transferring in Houston).

International gateway airports in the USA:

Dallas-Fort Worth International Airport (www.dfwairport.com)

Hartsfield-Jackson International Airport (Atlanta; www.atlanta-airport.com)

Honolulu International Airport (☎808-836-6411; http://hawaii.gov/hnl; 300 Rodgers Blvd, Honolulu; 📶)

Houston George Bush Intercontinental Airport (www.fly2houston.com/iah; Will Clayton Parkway or JFK Blvd, off I-59, Beltway 8 or I-45; 📶)

John F Kennedy (New York; www.panynj.gov)

Logan International Airport (Boston; www.massport.com/logan-airport)

Los Angeles International Airport (www.lawa.org/lax; 1 World Way)

Miami International Airport (Map p470; ☎305-876-7000; www.miami-airport.com; 2100 NW 42nd Ave)

Newark Liberty International (Newark; www.panynj.gov)

O'Hare International Airport (Chicago; www.ohare.com)

San Francisco International Airport (www.flysfo.com; S McDonnell Rd)

Seattle-Tacoma International Airport (☎206-787-5388; www.portseattle.org/

Sea-Tac; 17801 International Blvd; 📶)

Washington Dulles International Airport (www.metwashairports.com)

Land

Border Crossings

The USA has more than 20 official border crossings with Canada in the north and almost 40 with Mexico in the south. It is relatively easy crossing from the USA into either country; it's crossing *into* the USA that can pose problems if you haven't brought all your documents. Some borders are open 24 hours, but most are not.

Busy entry points with Canada include those at Detroit, MI; Windsor, Buffalo, NY; Niagara Falls and Blaine, WA; and British Columbia.

The main USA–Mexico posts are San Diego, CA; Tijuana, Nogales West, AZ; Nogales East, El Paso, TX; Ciudad Juárez and Brownsville, TX; and Matamoros. As always, have your papers in order, be polite and don't make jokes or casual conversation with US border officials.

Cartel violence and crime still pose risks along the US–Mexico border. Before heading out, check the latest warnings of the **US State Department** (www.travel.state.gov).

Canada

BUS

Greyhound has direct connections between main cities in Canada and the northern USA, but you may have to transfer to a different bus at the border. Book through **Greyhound USA** (☎800-231-2222, international customer service 214-849-8100; www.greyhound.com) or **Greyhound Canada** (☎800-661-8747; www.greyhound.ca). Greyhound's Discovery Pass allows unlimited travel in both the USA and Canada.

CAR & MOTORCYCLE

If you're driving into the USA from Canada, bring the vehicle's registration papers, proof of liability insurance and your home driver's license. Canadian auto insurance is typically valid in the USA, and vice versa. Canadian driver's licenses are also valid, but an International Driving Permit (IDP) is a good supplement.

If your papers are in order, taking your own car across the US–Canadian border is usually fast and easy, but occasionally the authorities of either country decide to search a car *thoroughly*. On weekends and holidays, especially in summer, traffic at the main border crossings can be heavy and waits long.

TRAIN

Amtrak (☎800-872-7245; www.amtrak.com) and **VIA Rail Canada** (☎888-842-7245; www.viarail.ca) operate daily services between Montreal and New York, Toronto and New York via Niagara Falls, Toronto and Chicago via Detroit, and Vancouver and Seattle. Customs inspections occur at the border.

Mexico

BUS

Greyhound USA (☎800-231-2222, international customer service 214-849-8100; www.greyhound.com) and **Greyhound México** (☎in Mexico 800-710-8819; www.greyhound.com.mx) operate direct bus routes between main towns in Mexico and the USA. For connections to smaller destinations south of the border, there are numerous domestic Mexican bus companies; **Ticketbus** (☎800-009-9090, in Mexico 5133-5133; www.ticketbus.com.mx) is an alliance of several.

CAR & MOTORCYCLE

As with Canada, if you're driving into the USA from Mexico, bring the vehicle's registration papers, proof of liability insurance and your driver's license. Mexican driver's licenses are valid, but it's worth having an IDP.

Very few car-rental companies will let you take a car from the US into Mexico. US auto insurance is not valid in Mexico, so even a short trip into Mexico's border region requires you to buy Mexican car insurance, available for around $25 per day at most border crossings, as well as from the **American Automobile Association** (AAA; ☎877-288-4546; www.aaa.com).

For a longer driving trip into Mexico beyond the border zone or Baja California, you'll need a Mexican *permiso de importación temporal de vehículos* (temporary vehicle import permit). You can call Mexico's tourist-information number in the USA on ☎800-446-3942.

Sea

If you're interested in taking a cruise ship to America – as well as to other interesting ports of call – a good specialized travel agency is **Cruise Web** (☎800-377-9383; www.cruiseweb.com).

You can also travel to and from the USA on a freighter, though it will be much slower and less cushy than a cruise. Nevertheless, freighters aren't spartan (some advertise cruise-ship-level amenities), and they are much cheaper (sometimes by half). Trips range from a week to two months; stops at interim ports are usually quick.

The **Cruise & Freighter Travel Association** (☎800-872-8584; www.travltips.com) has listings for freighter cruises and other boat travel.

Tours

Group travel can be an enjoyable way to get to and tour the USA.

Reputable tour companies:

American Holidays (☎in Ireland 01-960-9279; www.americanholidays.com) Ireland-based company that specializes in tours to North America.

Contiki (☎866-266-8454; www.contiki.com) Party-hardy sightseeing tour-bus vacations for 18- to 35-year-olds.

North America Travel Service (☎in the UK 020-7499 7299; www.northamericatravelservice.co.uk) UK-based tour operator that arranges luxury US trips.

Trek America (☎in North America 800-873-5872, in the UK 0333-999 7951; www.trekamerica.com) For active outdoor adventures; group sizes are kept small.

GETTING AROUND

Air

When time is tight, book a flight. The domestic air system is extensive and reliable, with dozens of competing airlines, hundreds of airports and thousands of flights daily. Flying is usually more expensive than traveling by bus, train or car, but it's the way to go when you're in a hurry.

Main 'hub' airports in the USA include all international gateways plus many other large cities. Most cities and towns have a local or county airport, but you usually have to travel via a hub airport to reach them.

Airlines in the USA

Overall, air travel in the USA is very safe (much safer than driving out on the nation's highways); for comprehensive details by carrier, check out AirSafe.com.

The main domestic carriers:

Alaska Airlines (☎800-252-7522; www.alaskaair.com) Has direct flights to Anchorage from Seattle, Chicago, Los Angeles and Denver. It also flies between many towns within Alaska, including daily north-bound and south-bound flights year-round through Southeast Alaska, with stops at all main towns including Ketchikan and Juneau.

American Airlines (☎800-433-7300; www.aa.com) Nationwide service.

Delta Air Lines (☎800-221-1212; www.delta.com) Nationwide service.

Frontier Airlines (☎801-401-9000; www.flyfrontier.com) Denver-based airline with service across the continental US.

Hawaiian Airlines (☎800-367-5320; www.hawaiianairlines.com) Nonstop flights between the Hawaiian Islands and the West Coast as well as New York City.

JetBlue Airways (☎800-538-2583; www.jetblue.com) Nonstop connections between eastern and western US cities, plus Florida, New Orleans and Texas.

Southwest Airlines (☎800-435-9792; www.southwest.com) Service across the continental USA.

Spirit Airlines (☎801-401-2200; www.spiritair.com) Florida-based budget airline; serves many US gateway cities.

United Airlines (☎800-864-8331; www.united.com) Nationwide service.

US Airways (☎800-428-4322; www.usairways.com) Nationwide service with hubs in Charlotte and Philadelphia.

Virgin America (☎877-359-8474; www.virginamerica.com) Flights between east- and west-coast cities plus Las Vegas, Austin and Dallas.

Air Passes

International travelers who plan on doing a lot of flying might consider buying a North American air pass. Passes are normally available only to non-North American citizens, and they must be purchased in conjunction with an international ticket. Conditions and cost structures can be complicated, but all passes include a certain number of domestic flights (from two to 10) that typically must be used within a 60-day period. Often you must plan your itinerary in advance, but sometimes dates (and even destinations) can be left open. Talk with a travel agent to determine if an air pass will save you money. Two of the biggest airline networks offering air passes are **Star Alliance** (www.staralliance.com) and **One World** (www.oneworld.com).

Bicycle

Regional bicycle touring is popular. It means coasting winding back roads (because

CLIMATE CHANGE & TRAVEL

Every form of transport that relies on carbon-based fuel generates CO_2, the main cause of human-induced climate change. Modern travel is dependent on airplanes, which might use less fuel per kilometer per person than most cars but travel much greater distances. The altitude at which aircraft emit gases (including CO_2) and particles also contributes to their climate change impact. Many websites offer 'carbon calculators' that allow people to estimate the carbon emissions generated by their journey and, for those who wish to do so, to offset the impact of the greenhouse gases emitted with contributions to portfolios of climate-friendly initiatives throughout the world. Lonely Planet offsets the carbon footprint of all staff and author travel.

bicycles are often not permitted on freeways), and calculating progress in miles per day, not miles per hour. Cyclists must follow the same rules of the road as drivers, but don't expect drivers to respect your right of way. **Better World Club** (www.betterworldclub.com) offers a bicycle roadside-assistance program.

For epic cross-country journeys, get the support of a tour operator; it's about two months of dedicated pedaling coast to coast.

For advice, and lists of local bike clubs and repair shops, browse the website of the **League of American Bicyclists** (www.bikeleague.org). If you're bringing your own bike to the USA, be sure to call around to check oversize-luggage prices and restrictions. Amtrak trains and Greyhound buses will transport bikes within the USA, sometimes charging extra.

It's not hard to buy a bike once you're here and resell it before you leave. Every city and town has bike shops; if you prefer a cheaper, used bicycle, try garage sales, bulletin boards at hostels and colleges, or the free classified ads at **Craigslist** (http://craigslist.org). These are also the best places to sell your bike, though stores selling used bikes may also buy from you.

Long-term bike rentals are also easy to find. Rates run from $100 per week and up, and a credit-card authorization for several hundred dollars is usually necessary as a security deposit.

Boat

There is no river or canal public-transportation system in the USA, but there are many smaller, often state-run, coastal ferry services, which provide efficient, scenic links to the many islands off both coasts. Most larger ferries will transport private cars, motorcycles and bicycles.

The most spectacular coastal ferry runs are on the southeastern coast of Alaska and along the Inside Passage. The Great Lakes have several islands that can be visited only by boat, such as Mackinac Island, MI; the Apostle Islands, off Wisconsin; and remote Isle Royale National Park, MN. Off the coast of Washington, ferries reach the scenic San Juan Islands.

Bus

To save money, travel by bus, particularly between major towns and cities. Middle-class Americans prefer to fly or drive, but buses let you see the countryside and meet folks along the way. As a rule, buses are reliable, cleanish and comfortable, with air-conditioning, barely reclining seats, lavatories and no smoking.

Greyhound (☎800-231-2222, international customer service 214-849-8100; www.greyhound.com) is the major long-distance bus company, with routes throughout the USA and Canada. To improve efficiency and profitability, Greyhound has recently stopped service to many small towns; routes generally trace major highways and stop at larger population centers. To reach country towns on rural roads, you may need to transfer to local or county bus systems; Greyhound can usually provide their contact information. Greyhound often has excellent online fares – web-only deals will net you substantial discounts over buying at a ticket counter.

Competing with Greyhound are the 75-plus franchises of **Trailways** (☎703-691-3052; www.trailways.com). Trailways may not be as useful as Greyhound for long trips, but fares can be competitive. Long-distance bus lines that offer decent fares and free wi-fi (that doesn't always work) include **Megabus** (☎877-462-6342; www.megabus.com) and **BoltBus** (www.boltbus.com); both operate routes primarily in the Northeast and Midwest.

Most baggage has to be checked in; label it loudly and clearly to avoid it getting lost. Larger items, including skis, surfboards and bicycles, can be transported, but there may be an extra charge. Call to check.

The frequency of bus services varies widely, depending on the route. Despite the elimination of many tiny destinations, nonexpress Greyhound buses still stop every 50 to 100 miles to pick up passengers, and long-distance buses will stop for meal breaks and driver changes.

Many bus stations are clean and safe, but some are in dodgy areas; if you arrive in the evening, it's worth spending the money on a taxi. Some towns have just a flag stop. If you are boarding at one of these, pay the driver with exact change.

Costs

For lower fares on Greyhound, purchase tickets at least seven days in advance (purchasing 14 days in advance will save even more). Round-trips are also cheaper than two one-way fares. Special promotional fares are regularly offered on Greyhound's website, especially for online bookings. If you're traveling with family or friends, Greyhound's companion fares let up to two additional travelers get 50% off with a minimum three-day advance purchase.

As for other Greyhound discounts: tickets for children aged two to 11 get 25% off; seniors over 62 years get a whopping 5% off; and students get 20% off if they have purchased the $23 **Student Advantage Discount Card** (www.studentadvantage.com).

Reservations

Tickets for some Trailways and other buses can only be

purchased immediately prior to departure. Greyhound, Megabus and BoltBus tickets can be bought online. You can print all tickets at home or in the case of Megabus or BoltBus, simply show ticket receipts through an email on a smartphone. Greyhound also allows customers to pick up tickets at the terminal using 'Will Call' service.

Seating is normally first-come, first-served. Greyhound recommends arriving an hour before departure to get a seat.

Car & Motorcycle

For information about driving, see the Driving in the USA chapter (p1179) and the Road Trips & Scenic Drives chapter (p41).

Local Transportation

Except in large US cities, public transportation is rarely the most convenient option for travelers, and coverage can be sparse to outlying towns and suburbs. However, it is usually cheap, safe and reliable. In addition, more than half the states in the nation have adopted ☎511 as an all-purpose local-transportation help line.

Airport Shuttles

Shuttle buses provide inexpensive and convenient transport to/from airports in most cities. Most are 12-seat vans; some have regular routes and stops (which include the main hotels) and some pick up and deliver passengers 'door to door' in their service area. Costs range from $15 to $30 per person.

Bicycle

Some cities are more amenable to bicycles than others, but most have at least a few dedicated bike lanes and paths, and bikes can usually be carried on public transportation.

Bus

Most cities and larger towns have dependable local bus systems, though they are often designed for commuters and provide limited service in the evening and on weekends. Costs range from free to between $1 and $3 per ride.

Subway & Train

The largest systems are in New York, Chicago, Boston, Philadelphia, Washington, DC, Chicago, Los Angeles and the San Francisco Bay Area. Other cities may have small, one- or two-line rail systems that mainly serve downtown.

Taxi

Taxis are metered, with flagfall charges of around $2.50 to start, plus $2 to $3 per mile. They charge extra for waiting and handling baggage, and drivers expect a 10% to 15% tip. Taxis cruise the busiest areas in large cities; otherwise, it's easiest to phone and order one.

BUS FARES

Here are some sample standard one-way adult fares and trip times on Greyhound:

Service	Price ($)	Duration (hr)
Boston–Philadelphia	45-61	7
Chicago–New Orleans	96-164	24
Los Angeles–San Francisco	35-71	8
New York–Chicago	70-138	18
New York–San Francisco	250-330	72
Washington, DC–Miami	87-170	25

Tours

Hundreds of companies offer all kinds of organized tours of the USA; most focus on either cities or regions.

Backroads (☎800-462-2848, 510-527-1555; www.backroads.com) Designs a range of active, multisport and outdoor-oriented trips for all abilities and budgets.

Gray Line (☎800-472-9546; www.grayline.com) For those short on time, Gray Line offers a comprehensive range of standard sightseeing tours across the country.

Green Tortoise (☎415-956-7500; www.greentortoise.com) Offering budget adventures for independent travelers, Green Tortoise is famous for its sleeping-bunk buses. Most trips leave from San Francisco, traipsing through the West and nationwide.

Road Scholar (☎800-454-5768; www.roadscholar.org) For those aged 50 and older, this venerable nonprofit offers 'learning adventures' in all 50 states.

Train

Amtrak (☎800-872-7245; www.amtrak.com) has an extensive rail system throughout the USA, with Amtrak's Thruway buses providing connections to and from the rail network to some smaller centers and national parks. Compared with other modes of travel, trains are rarely the quickest, cheapest, timeliest or most convenient option, but they turn the journey into a relaxing, social and scenic all-American experience.

Amtrak has several long-distance lines traversing the nation east to west, and even more running north to south. These connect all of America's biggest cities and many of its smaller ones.

ALL ABOARD!

Who doesn't enjoy the steamy puff and whistle of a mighty locomotive as glorious scenery streams by? Dozens of historic narrow-gauge railroads still operate today as attractions, rather than as transportation. Most trains only run in the warmer months, and they can be extremely popular – so book ahead.

Here are some of the best:

1880 Train (☎605-574-2222; www.1880train.com; 103 Winter St; round-trip adult/child US$21/12) Classic steam train running through rugged Black Hills country.

Cass Scenic Railroad (www.cassrailroad.com) Nestled in the Appalachian Mountains in West Virginia.

Cumbres & Toltec Scenic Railroad Depot (☎888-286-2737; www.cumbrestoltec.com; 5234 Hwy 285, Antonito; adult/child from $89/49;) Living, moving museum from Chama, NM, into Colorado's Rocky Mountains.

Durango & Silverton Narrow Gauge Railroad (☎970-247-2733; www.durangotrain.com; 479 Main Ave; return adult/child 4-11yr from $85/51; May-Oct;) Ends at historic mining town Silverton in Colorado's Rocky Mountains.

Great Smoky Mountain Railroad (☎800-872-4681; www.gsmr.com; 226 Everett St, Bryson City; Nantahala Gorge trip adult/child 2-12yr from $55/31) Rides from Bryson City, NC, through the Great Smoky Mountains.

Mount Hood Railroad (☎800-872-4661; www.mthoodrr.com; 110 Railroad Ave) Winds through the scenic Columbia River Gorge outside Portland, OR.

Skunk Train (☎707-964-6371; www.skunktrain.com; foot of Laurel St; adult/child 2-12yr $60/34;) Runs between Fort Bragg, CA, on the coast and Willits further inland, passing through redwoods.

White Pass & Yukon Route Railroad (☎800-343-7373; www.wpyr.com; 231 2nd Ave; May-Sep) Klondike gold-rush-era railroad has departures from Skagway, AK, and Fraser (British Columbia), and Carcross and Whitehorse (Yukon) in Canada.

Also worth riding are the vintage steam and diesel locomotives of Arizona's **Grand Canyon Railway** (☎reservations 800-843-8724; www.thetrain.com; Railway Depot, 233 N Grand Canyon Blvd; round-trip adult/child from $65/25;), New York State's **Delaware & Ulster Rail Line** (☎845-586-3877; www.durr.org; 43510 Hwy 28, Arkville; adult/child $18/12; Sat & Sun Jun-Nov, additional trips Thu & Fri Jul-Sep;) and Colorado's **Pikes Peak Cog Railway** (p768).

Long-distance services (on named trains) mostly operate daily on these routes, but some run only three to five days per week. See Amtrak's website for detailed route maps.

Amtrak Vacations (☎800-268-7252; www.amtrakvacations.com) offers vacation packages that include car rental, hotels, tours and attractions. Air-Rail packages let you travel by train in one direction, then return by plane the other way.

Commuter trains provide faster, more frequent services on shorter routes, especially the northeast corridor from Boston, MA, to Washington, DC. Amtrak's high-speed Acela Express trains are the most expensive, and rail passes are not valid on these trains. Other commuter rail lines include those serving the Lake Michigan shoreline near Chicago, IL, major cities on the West Coast and the Miami, FL, area.

Classes & Costs

Amtrak fares vary according to the type of train and seating; on long-distance lines, you can travel in coach seats (reserved or unreserved), business class, or 1st class, which includes all sleeping compartments. Sleeping cars include simple bunks (called 'roomettes'), bedrooms with en-suite facilities and suites sleeping four with two bathrooms. Sleeping-car rates include meals in the dining car, which offers everyone sit-down meal service (pricey if not included). Food service on commuter lines, when it exists, consists of sandwich and snack bars. Bringing your own food and drink is recommended on all trains.

Various one-way, round-trip and touring fares are available from Amtrak, with discounts of 15% for seniors aged 62 and over and for students with a 'Student Advantage' card ($23) or an International Student Identity Card (ISIC), and 50% discounts for children aged two to 15 when accompanied by a paying adult. AAA members get 10% off. Web-only 'Weekly Specials' offer deep discounts on certain undersold routes.

Generally, the earlier you book, the lower the price. To get many of the standard discounts, you need to reserve at least three days in advance. If you want to take an Acela Express or Metroliner train, avoid peak commute times and aim for weekends.

Reservations

Reservations can be made any time from 11 months in advance up to the day of departure. Space on most trains is limited, and certain routes can be crowded, especially during summer and holiday periods, so it's a good idea to book as far in advance as you can; this also gives you the best chance of fare discounts.

Train Passes

Amtrak's USA Rail Pass offers coach-class travel for 15 ($460), 30 ($690) or 45 ($900) days, with travel limited to eight, 12 or 18 one-way 'segments,' respectively. A segment is *not* the same as a one-way trip. If reaching your destination requires riding more than one train (for example, getting from New York to Miami with a transfer in Washington, DC), that one-way trip will actually use two segments of your pass.

Present your pass at an Amtrak office to pick up your ticket(s) for each trip. Reservations should be made by phone (call ☎800-872-7245, or ☎215-856-7953 from outside the USA) as far in advance as possible. Each segment of the journey must be booked. At some rural stations, trains will only stop if there's a reservation.

Tickets are not for specific seats, but a conductor on board may allocate you a seat. Business-class, 1st-class and sleeper accommodations cost extra and must be reserved separately.

All travel must be completed within 180 days of purchasing your pass. Passes are not valid on the Acela Express, Auto Train, Thruway motorcoach connections or the Canadian portion of Amtrak routes operated jointly with Via Rail Canada. Fares can double if you don't buy them at least three or four days in advance.

TRAIN FARES

Sample standard, one-way, adult coach-class fares and trip times on Amtrak's long-distance routes:

Service	Price ($)	Duration (hr)
Chicago–New Orleans	127	20
Los Angeles–San Antonio	182	29
New York–Chicago	104	19
New York–Los Angeles	357	68
Seattle–Oakland	163	23
Washington, DC–Miami	140	23

Behind the Scenes

SEND US YOUR FEEDBACK

We love to hear from travelers – your comments keep us on our toes and help make our books better. Our well-traveled team reads every word on what you loved or loathed about this book. Although we cannot reply individually to postal submissions, we always guarantee that your feedback goes straight to the appropriate authors, in time for the next edition. Each person who sends us information is thanked in the next edition – the most useful submissions are rewarded with a selection of digital PDF chapters.

Visit **lonelyplanet.com/contact** to submit your updates and suggestions or to ask for help. Our award-winning website also features inspirational travel stories, news and discussions.

Note: We may edit, reproduce and incorporate your comments in Lonely Planet products such as guidebooks, websites and digital products, so let us know if you don't want your comments reproduced or your name acknowledged. For a copy of our privacy policy visit lonelyplanet.com/privacy.

OUR READERS

Many thanks to the travelers who used the last edition and wrote to us with helpful hints, useful advice and interesting anecdotes:

Anne Mickler, Ariane Courtemanche, Barry Burlingham, Christina Stauffer, Hans Bevers, Hector Carrillo, Itzhak Goldberg, James Ramsden, Jane Vincent, Jodie Barlow, Jules Feiler, Mhairi Harris, Rosa Le Mains, Sain Alizada, Shaan Frazer, Stefano Pasero, Susan Desousa, Trevor Payne, Willis Harte

AUTHOR THANKS

Regis St Louis

I'm grateful to the many kind friends and locals who provided insight into their cities and neighborhoods. In particular, thanks to Jason and Beth Blair for fun times in Dallas and Galveston, Julien Devereux and Erik Rune in Austin, and co-author Amy Balfour in Virginia. Big hugs to Kristie and David (and the girls) for hosting me in NY. A *grand merci* to my family: Cassandra, Magdalena and Genevieve for joining me on the road in Texas.

Amy Balfour

Many thanks to old friends and new friends for introducing me to the best spots in their communities. In the South, thank you Ben and Alison Kimball, Jeff Otto, Anna Schleunes, Jennifer Troch, Lavan Green, Blaire Postman, Gary Haymes, John Park, Sarah Ray Bunn and AT co-warriors Ames Shea and Lynn Neumann. In New England, thank you Mt Monadnock madman Whit Andrews, Peaches and Genienne Hockensmith, John Shea, Amy Smereck and Amy Stone Scannell.

Sandra Bao

A big shout-out to those who've made my life much happier while researching the Pacific Northwest: Carolyn Hubbard and Mike Hainsworth in Seattle, Adrienne Robineau in Port Townsend and Celeste Brash in Portland. Special thanks also to my husband Ben Greensfelder, who has supported my research trips over the years (whether he joins me on my travels or not), and to my parents and brother, who have always been there for me throughout my peripatetic life.

Adam Karlin

Thank you: the folks who put me up in many an American town, from Fort Lauderdale to Birmingham and Lafayette to Little Rock. To the waiters, waitresses, bartenders, politicians, park rangers, musicians and mad folks who all gave me (and by extension, you) a tip on what to find. Thank you Regis and Dora for helming this beast, and thank you co-authors, especially my regional chapter homies, Kevin and Amy. Thanks mom and dad, who always liked to rub my itchy feet. Thanks Gizmo, for keeping me company on late-night writing jags. Thank you

Rachel, my best friend and love and traveling companion extraordinaire, for pushing me to climb the next hill. And thank you Sanda, for the first of many joint explorations.

Becky Ohlsen

Thanks to Ryan McCluskey, Joëlle Jones, Mike Russell, Leila del Duca, Michael Byrne, the Admiral 589, Joel and Christina and Karl and Natalie Ohlsen for all the help!

Zora O'Neill

Many thanks to: Christina Stone-Millan, Meredith Stone, Rich Tyson, Beth Kracklauer, Gabriela Gonzalez, Waverly Duck, Katie Trainor, Brandon del Pozo, Michael LoBianco, Robbi Kearns and Michael Grosberg. Also thanks to generous and kind Filona Ryan, Matt the tow-truck guy, and Bill and Melissa of Bird's Towing. And sort of thanks to the inhospitable residents of Tabernacle-Chatsworth Road: I guess that 5-mile walk was good for me.

Kevin Raub

Thanks to my wife, Adriana Schmidt Raub, who sure does get jealous of all that mac and cheese! Thanks Dora Whitaker and all my partners-in-crime. On the road thanks also to Jason and Jennifer Hatfield, David and Anysley Corbett, Katherine Roberts, Matti Bek Pauli, Ari Glantz, Cindy and Tim Moore, Erica Backus, Carey Dye Ferrara, Katherine Williams, Enma and Andrew Weber, Juliana Mesanelli, Cory O-Born and Luiza and Michael Wettrau.

Ryan Ver Berkmoes

Serious thanks to my parents who believed in the value of road trips and my sister who always sided with demanding the motel pool have a slide. Big thanks to all the fine Great Plains folk who tipped me off to secrets and treasures – the Home on the Range Cabin was a major score. Also thanks to John Holden for giving me a good excuse to add more road to my road trip. Finally thanks to Alexis Averbuck for proving that it's always Plum season no matter where I am.

Mara Vorhees

What a great opportunity to explore some new parts of New England. I'm grateful for the guys at Goodyear for keeping me moving! Thanks to J, V and S for joining me on some fun outings – and for holding down the fort at the pink house when I had to go it alone.

Greg Ward

Thanks to everyone at Lonely Planet, especially Alex Howard and my co-authors on Lonely Planet *Southwest USA*; to the many people who helped me on the road, including Steve Lewis and Steve Horak; and, above all, to my wife Sam.

Karla Zimmerman

Many thanks to Kate Armstrong, Ted Bonar, Bill Brockschmidt, Joe Cimperman, Lisa DiChiera, Lea Dooley, Jim DuFresne, Ruggero Fatica, Julie Lange, Alex Leviton, Kari Lydersen, Zora O'Neill, Keith Pandolfi, Betsy Riley, Neil Anderson, Tamara Robinson, Amy Schwenkmeyer, Susan Hayes, Stephan, Andrea and Greg Thomson, and Karen and Don Zimmerman. Thanks most to Eric Markowitz, the world's best partner-for-life, who indulges all my harebrained, pie-filled road trips.

ACKNOWLEDGEMENTS

Climate map data adapted from Peel MC, Finlayson BL & McMahon TA (2007) 'Updated World Map of the Koppen-Geiger Climate Classification', *Hydrology and Earth System Sciences*, 11, 1633-44

Illustrations pp90-1, pp270-1 by Javier Martinez Zarracina; pp972-3 by Michael Weldon.

Cover photograph: Toroweap Point at the North Rim of the Grand Canyon, Arizona; Maurizio Rellini/4Corners

THIS BOOK

This 9th edition of Lonely Planet's *USA* guidebook was researched and written by Regis St Louis, Amy Balfour, Sandra Bao, Sara Benson, Adam Karlin, Becky Ohlsen, Zora O'Neill, Kevin Raub, Brendan Sainsbury, Ryan Ver Berkmoes, Mara Vorhees, Greg Ward and Karla Zimmerman. This guidebook was produced by the following:

Destination Editors Alexander Howard, Dora Whitaker, Clifton Wilkinson

Product Editors Anne Mason, Luna Soo

Senior Cartographer Alison Lyall

Book Designer Cam Ashley

Assisting Editors Judith Bamber, Janice Bird, Samantha Forge, Gabrielle Green, Carly Hall, Paul Harding, Victoria Harrison, Amy Karafin, Ali Lemer, Kristin Odijk, Charlotte Orr, Susan Paterson, Monique Perrin, Kirsten Rawlings, Vicky Smith, Gabrielle Stefanos, Ross Taylor, Saralinda Turner, Jeanette Wall, Tracy Whitmey

Cartographers Hunor Csutoros, Julie Sheridan

Cover Researcher Naomi Parker

Thanks to Shahara Ahmed, Anita Banh, Jane Grisman, Andi Jones, Claire Naylor, Karyn Noble, Lauren Wellicome, Tony Wheeler

Index

Map Pages **000**
Photo Pages **000**

B

Map Pages **000**
Photo Pages **000**

Map Pages **000**
Photo Pages **000**

Map Pages **000**
Photo Pages **000**

Map Pages **000**
Photo Pages **000**

O

P

Map Pages **000**
Photo Pages **000**

Q

R

Map Pages **000**
Photo Pages **000**

S

T

Map Pages **000**
Photo Pages **000**

Map Legend

Sights
- Beach
- Bird Sanctuary
- Buddhist
- Castle/Palace
- Christian
- Confucian
- Hindu
- Islamic
- Jain
- Jewish
- Monument
- Museum/Gallery/Historic Building
- Ruin
- Shinto
- Sikh
- Taoist
- Winery/Vineyard
- Zoo/Wildlife Sanctuary
- Other Sight

Activities, Courses & Tours
- Bodysurfing
- Diving
- Canoeing/Kayaking
- Course/Tour
- Sento Hot Baths/Onsen
- Skiing
- Snorkeling
- Surfing
- Swimming/Pool
- Walking
- Windsurfing
- Other Activity

Sleeping
- Sleeping
- Camping

Eating
- Eating

Drinking & Nightlife
- Drinking & Nightlife
- Cafe

Entertainment
- Entertainment

Shopping
- Shopping

Information
- Bank
- Embassy/Consulate
- Hospital/Medical
- Internet
- Police
- Post Office
- Telephone
- Toilet
- Tourist Information
- Other Information

Geographic
- Beach
- Gate
- Hut/Shelter
- Lighthouse
- Lookout
- Mountain/Volcano
- Oasis
- Park
- Pass
- Picnic Area
- Waterfall

Population
- Capital (National)
- Capital (State/Province)
- City/Large Town
- Town/Village

Transport
- Airport
- BART station
- Border crossing
- Boston T station
- Bus
- Cable car/Funicular
- Cycling
- Ferry
- Metro/Muni station
- Monorail
- Parking
- Petrol station
- Subway/SkyTrain station
- Taxi
- Train station/Railway
- Tram
- Underground station
- Other Transport

Note: Not all symbols displayed above appear on the maps in this book

Routes
- Tollway
- Freeway
- Primary
- Secondary
- Tertiary
- Lane
- Unsealed road
- Road under construction
- Plaza/Mall
- Steps
- Tunnel
- Pedestrian overpass
- Walking Tour
- Walking Tour detour
- Path/Walking Trail

Boundaries
- International
- State/Province
- Disputed
- Regional/Suburb
- Marine Park
- Cliff
- Wall

Hydrography
- River, Creek
- Intermittent River
- Canal
- Water
- Dry/Salt/Intermittent Lake
- Reef

Areas
- Airport/Runway
- Beach/Desert
- Cemetery (Christian)
- Cemetery (Other)
- Glacier
- Mudflat
- Park/Forest
- Sight (Building)
- Sportsground
- Swamp/Mangrove

Mara Vorhees

New England Born and raised in St Clair Shores, Michigan, Mara traveled the world (if not the universe) before finally settling in the Hub. She spent several years pushing papers and tapping keys at Harvard University, but she has since embraced the life of a full-time travel writer, covering destinations as diverse as Russia and Belize. She lives in a pink house in Somerville, Massachusetts with her husband, two kiddies and two kitties. She is often seen eating doughnuts in Union Square and pedaling her bike along the Charles River. Mara is the author of Lonely Planet's guides to New England and *New England's Best Trips*, among other titles. Follow her adventures online at www.havetwinswilltravel.com.

Read more about Mara at:
http://auth.lonelyplanet.com/profiles/mvorhees

Greg Ward

Southwest Greg Ward has been exploring the deserts of the Southwest for more than twenty years and has written several guidebooks to the region. He also writes extensively about history, music and European destinations. He lives in London, and his website is gregward.info.

Karla Zimmerman

Washington, DC & the Capital Region, Great Lakes As a life-long Midwesterner, Karla is well versed in the region's beaches, ballparks, breweries and pie shops. When she's not home in Chicago watching the Cubs, and writing for magazines, websites and books, she's out exploring. For this gig, she curled in Minnesota, caught a wave in Michigan, heard the curds squeak in Wisconsin and drank an embarrassing number of milkshakes in Ohio. She also covers DC, where she never fails to shake hands with Racing Abe Lincoln at Nationals Park. Karla has written for several Lonely Planet guides to the USA, Canada, Caribbean and Europe.

Adam Karlin
The South, Florida Adam has written around 50 guidebooks for Lonely Planet and he always enjoys exploring his native stomping grounds: the US. On this trip, he stumbled into Key West secret gardens, discovered Miami speakeasies, took shots with Birmingham bartenders, weathered tornado watches in Mississippi cotton shacks, found pizza on Arkansas mountain tops, listened to music in dozens of Louisiana bars, paddled through clear Florida mangrove channels and ate a lot of barbeque. He wants you to know that there is a lot of good light in the world, but the way it attaches to a late spring day in the South is something else.

Becky Ohlsen
Rocky Mountains Becky Ohlsen grew up in the Rockies and seizes every chance she gets to explore the region. She has a huge crush on the Tetons, believes that jackalopes are real and likes to watch a storm roll in across a far-away horizon.

Zora O'Neill
New York, New Jersey & Pennsylvania Zora O'Neill has lived in New York City since 1998 – far from her home state of New Mexico, but very close to where, as a kid and the daughter of a New Jersey native, she spent a week nearly every summer 'down the shore,' eating pizza and fried scallops. Zora has written guidebooks since 2002; for Lonely Planet, she has covered Amsterdam, southern Spain and Egypt. She is online at www.rovinggastronome.com.

Read more about Zora at:
http://auth.lonelyplanet.com/profiles/zora_oneill

Kevin Raub
The South, Florida Kevin Raub grew up in Atlanta and started his career as a music journalist in New York, working for *Men's Journal* and *Rolling Stone* magazines. He ditched the rock 'n' roll lifestyle for travel writing and moved to Brazil. Living outside the country, it's fair to say he immensely enjoyed gorging on Nashville hot chicken, Memphis BBQ, craft beer out the wazoo and various other unmentionables on his voyage through the Southern US. This is Kevin's 34th Lonely Planet guide. Follow him on Twitter (@RaubOnTheRoad).

Read more about Kevin at:
http://auth.lonelyplanet.com/profiles/kraub

Brendan Sainsbury
Alaska An expat Brit from Hampshire, England, now living near Vancouver, Canada; Brendan has long relished the 'thrill' of masochistic endurance events in remote wilderness areas and thus jumped at the chance to cover Alaska for Lonely Planet. He particularly relished getting his hands numb in Nome, re-reading Jack London, and bussing it along the Top of the World Highway from Chicken to the Yukon. When not scribbling research notes for Lonely Planet in countries such as Cuba, Peru, Spain and Canada, Brendan likes refining his cross-country skiing technique, strumming old Clash songs on the guitar and experiencing the pain and occasional pleasures of following Southampton Football Club.

Ryan Ver Berkmoes
Great Plains Ryan first drove across the Great Plains with his family in the 1960s. Among the treasured memories are marveling at the Jackalope at Wall Drugs in South Dakota and which he relived when he tried riding the big one out back this year. Through the years he never passes up a chance to wander the backroads of America's heartland finding beauty and intrigue where you least expect it. Find more at www.ryanverberkmoes.com; @ryanvb

OUR STORY

A beat-up old car, a few dollars in the pocket and a sense of adventure. In 1972 that's all Tony and Maureen Wheeler needed for the trip of a lifetime – across Europe and Asia overland to Australia. It took several months, and at the end – broke but inspired – they sat at their kitchen table writing and stapling together their first travel guide, *Across Asia on the Cheap*. Within a week they'd sold 1500 copies. Lonely Planet was born.

Today, Lonely Planet has offices in Franklin, London, Melbourne, Oakland, Beijing and Delhi, with more than 600 staff and writers. We share Tony's belief that 'a great guidebook should do three things: inform, educate and amuse'.

OUR WRITERS

Regis St Louis

Coordinating Author; New York, New Jersey & Pennsylvania; Washington, DC & the Capital Region; Texas A Hoosier by birth, Regis grew up in a sleepy riverside town where he dreamed of big-city intrigue. He's lived all over the US (including New York City, San Francisco, Los Angeles and New Orleans), and has crossed the country by train, bus and car while visiting remote corners of America. Favorite memories from his most recent trip include crab feasting on Maryland's eastern shore, hiking through striking state parks in west Texas, catching music jams in the Blue Ridge Mountains of Virginia and going eye-to-eye with wild horses on Assateague Island. Regis has contributed to more than 50 Lonely Planet titles, including *New York City* and *Washington, DC*. Regis also wrote the Plan Your Trip, Understand and Survival Guide sections of this guide.

Amy Balfour

New England, The South Amy has hiked, biked and paddled her way across the US. Raised in the South, she's been visiting the Outer Banks since childhood and for this trip she backpacked along the Appalachian Trail in the Great Smokies. In New Hampshire she explored the White Mountains and tackled Mt Monadnock for the first time. She has authored 26 guidebooks for Lonely Planet and has written for *Backpacker*, *Redbook*, *Southern Living* and the *Washington Post*.

Sandra Bao

Pacific Northwest Sandra has lived in Buenos Aires, New York and California, but the glorious Pacific Northwest has become her final stop. Researching this region has been a highlight of Sandra's 15-year-long authoring career with Lonely Planet, which has covered four continents and dozens of guidebooks. She's come to appreciate the beauty of this region, how much it has to offer and how friendly people can be in those tiny towns in the middle of nowhere.

Sara Benson

California, Hawaii After graduating from college, Sara jumped on a plane to California with just one suitcase and $100 in her pocket. After driving tens of thousands of miles to every corner of the state, she settled on the sunny side of San Francisco Bay in Oakland. The author of more than 65 travel and nonfiction books, Sara's latest adventures are online at www.indietraveler.blogspot.com, www.indietraveler.net, @indie_traveler on Twitter and indietraveler on Instagram.

Read more about Sara at:
http://auth.lonelyplanet.com/profiles/sara_benson

OVER PAGE MORE WRITERS

Published by Lonely Planet Publications Pty Ltd
ABN 36 005 607 983
9th edition – Mar 2016
ISBN 978 1 74321 861 7

10 9 8 7 6 5 4 3 2 1
Printed in Singapore